C000319021

REV

The game's oracular masterpiece for 139 years.
Ian Wooldridge, *Daily Mail*

The 139th edition of *Wisden Cricketers' Almanack* is an extraordinary achievement... It remains the gospel of cricket.
Christopher Ondaatje, *Literary Review*

***Wisden* remains the most comprehensive guide available in any sport... as fresh as ever despite its long and distinguished history.**
Sunday Express

The sport's most easily recognised and influential publication.
David Lloyd, London *Evening Standard*

A far better read than anyone could expect.
Simon Briggs, *Daily Telegraph*

This annual delectable doorstop.
Frank Keating, *The Guardian*

As ever, the articles live up to the highest standards... The 2002 version will surely prove as popular as its 138 predecessors.
Trevor Crowe, Amazon.co.uk

***Wisden*... has often moved quicker than the game itself.**
Ralph Dellor, CricInfo

To dear Thomas
with much love,
Grannie & Grandpa.

December 2003.   uchy.

WISDEN
2003

JOHN WISDEN & CO LTD
13 Old Aylesfield, Golden Pot, Alton, Hampshire GU34 4BY
enquiries@johnwisden.co.uk
www.wisden.com

Deputy editors **Harriet Monkhouse** and **Hugh Chevallier**
Editorial assistant **Paul Coupar**
Contributing editor **Lawrence Booth**
Production co-ordinator **Peter Bather**
Chief typesetter **Mike Smith**
Proofreader **Gordon Burling**
Advertisement sales **Colin Ackehurst** (020 7565 3150)
Publisher **Christopher Lane**

Typeset in Times New Roman and Univers
by LazerType, Colchester
Printed and bound in Great Britain by Clays Ltd, St Ives plc

"Wisden" and its woodcut device are registered trademarks of John Wisden & Co Ltd

EDITIONS
Cased ISBN 0-947766-77-4 **£35**
Soft cover ISBN 0-947766-78-2 **£35**
Leatherbound ISBN 0-947766-79-0 **£225**

Distributed by The Penguin Group
Distributed in Australia by Hardie Grant Books, Melbourne

140TH EDITION

WISDEN
CRICKETERS' ALMANACK
2003

Edited by
Tim de Lisle

Published by John Wisden & Co Ltd
13 Old Aylesfield, Golden Pot,
Alton, Hampshire GU34 4BY

4

CONTRIBUTORS

Kamran Abbasi
Nabila Ahmed
Tanya Aldred
Andy Arlidge
Chris Aspin
Charlie Austin
Philip Bailey
Vaneisa Baksh
Sambit Bal
Simon Barnes
Greg Baum
Scyld Berry
Edward Bevan
Rahul Bhattacharya
Martin Blake
Paul Bolton
Richard Boock
Lawrence Booth
Simon Briggs
Rohit Brijnath
Robert Brooke
Colin Bryden
Don Cameron
Tony Cozier
John Curtis

Gareth Davies
Geoffrey Dean
Ralph Dellor
Norman de
　Mesquita
Philip Eden
Peter English
Colin Evans
Stephen Fay
Paul Fearn
David Foot
Neville Foulger
Nigel Fuller
Pat Gibson
Andrew Gidley
Gideon Haigh
David Hallett
David Hardy
Norman Harris
Shahid A. Hashmi
Les Hatton
Murray Hedgcock
Grenville Holland
David Hopps
Martin Johnson

Abid Ali Kazi
Frank Keating
Neil Leitch
David Llewellyn
Steven Lynch
John MacKinnon
Alastair McLellan
Neil Manthorp
Christopher Martin-
　Jenkins
Mohandas Menon
Andrew Miller
R. Mohan
Gerald Mortimer
Francis Payne
Gordon Phillips
Dileep
　Premachandran
Derek Pringle
Qamar Ahmed
Andrew Radd
Camilla Rossiter
Graham Russell
Dicky Rutnagur
Chris Ryan

Carol Salmon
Samiul Hasan
Andrew Samson
Derek Scott
Utpal Shuvro
Jasmer Singh
Anirban Sircar
Rob Smyth
Rob Steen
Duncan Steer
John Stern
Pat Symes
Bruce Talbot
Sa'adi Thawfeeq
Huw Turbervill
Gerry Vaidyasekera
Gordon Vince
John Ward
David Warner
Tim Wellock
Simon Wilde
Graeme Wright

Photographers: Joe Alexander, Jack Atley, Martin Bennet, Hamish Blair, Shaun Botterill, Sam Bowles, Gordon Brooks, Philip Brown, Howard Burditt, Andy Clark, Andrew Cornaga, Arko Datta, John Dawson, Ian Dobson, Patrick Eagar, Mike Finn-Kelcey, Stu Forster, John Gichigi, John Grainger, Laurence Griffiths, Mike Hutchings, Huw John, Ross Kinnaird, Anuruddha Lokuhapuarachchi, Terry Mahoney, Pradeep Mandhani, Clive Mason, Chris McGrath, Graham Morris, Adrian Murrell, Rebecca Naden, Pete Norton, Roger Ockenden, Darren Pateman, Mike Pollard, Mohsin Raza, Alan Roach, Mohammad Shahidullah, Tom Shaw, Bill Smith, Michael Steele, Mark Thompson, January Traylen, Philip Walters, Steve Waugh, Colin Whelan, Nick Wilson, Roger Wootton.

Round the World: Anthony Adams, Andy Armitage, Norman Baldwin, Musaji Bhana, Saleh Bhana, A. M. Banks, Alum Bati, Fatima Boujoual, Tony Brennan, Simon Cottrell, John Cribbin, Grant Dugmore, Peter D. Eckersley, Geoff Edwards, Brian Fell, T. J. Finlayson, Simone Gambino, Bob Gibb, Peter S. Hargreaves, Ewa Henshaw, Simon Hewitt, T. Richard Illingworth, Damian Johnson, Umair Khan, Peter Knight, John McKillop, Arfat Malik, Taj Malik, Naoya Miyaji, Tony Munro, Pierre Naudi, Guy Parker, Stanley Perlman, Laurie Pieters, John Rich, Bryan Rouse, Ken Sainsbury, Amarchande Samgi, Jack Sands, Juggoo Sawhney, Jai Kumar Shah, Narinder Pal Singh, Mark Stafford, Derek Thursby, Mike Tsesmelis, Colin Wolfe.

Thanks are accorded to the following for checking the scorecards of county and tourist matches: Keith Booth, John Brown, Wally Clarke, Jack Foley, Keith Gerrish, Neil Harris, John Hartridge, Brian Hunt, Vic Isaacs, David Kendix, Tony Kingston, Gordon Lewis, Ray Markham, David Norris, John Potter, Mike Smith, Gerry Stickley, Gordon Stringfellow, David Wainwright, Alan West, Roy Wilkinson, Graham York.

The editor also thanks the following: Neville Birch, Michael Bushby, Gerry Byrne, Marion Collin, Mike Coward, Brian Cowley, Brian Croudy, Frank Duckworth, Robert Eastaway, Matthew Engel, M. L. Fernando, Ric Finlay, Bill Frindall, Ghulam Mustafa Khan, Ray Goble, Peter Griffiths, Col. Malcolm Havergal, Keith Hayhurst, Brian Heald, Andrew Hignell, Robin Isherwood, Guy Jackson, Mohammad Ali Jafri, Emma John, Rajesh Kumar, Stephanie Lawrence, Nirav Malavi, Mahendra Mapagunaratne, Eric Midwinter, S. Pervez Qaiser, Major R. W. K. Ross-Hurst, Adrian Thomas, Charlie Wat, Wendy Wimbush, Danny Window, Robert Wood, John Woodcock, Peter Wynne-Thomas.

The production of *Wisden* would not be possible without the support and co-operation of many other cricket officials, writers and lovers of the game. To them all, many thanks.

PREFACE

Welcome to the 140th edition of *Wisden* – the biggest yet, with a page for every yard in a mile. Some readers may relish this more than others. To those who are unsure, I can only paraphrase an old line: sorry to be sending you such a long book – there wasn't time to do a short one. The main factor is cricket itself, forever expanding. This year we report 55 Tests in full and 23 more in brief. The number of one-day internationals doesn't bear thinking about. It is also the most up-to-date Almanack yet. We held back publication by four weeks to include the 2003 World Cup, which appears in potted form starting on page 1724. Full coverage will be in next year's *Wisden*.

There are several new elements. The World View section gives an overview of each Test team. Arrivals and Departures sketches those taking or leaving the big stage. International Coaches logs the managers and their results. Two staple ingredients, Births and Deaths, and Records, come with commentaries. These new things will doubtless evolve; Five Cricketers of the Year, *Wisden's* best idea ever, took a decade to crystallise.

Wisden has been a great book since time immemorial, but sometimes a closed book. This year, we have tried to make it a more open one. We have given the features some air, added a Guide for New Readers, given each county a headline, introduced keys to individual sections and planted pull-quotes through the book, to encourage the process whereby you dart in to check something and end up somewhere quite different. All *Wisden's* regular features are here except the Laws, left out as in 1987, owing to pressure of space. The current code appears on page 1452 of *Wisden 2002*.

Two contributors sadly died in February. Gordon Phillips had written the Cricketana column in five editions, including this one, after retiring as an archivist at *The Times*. Les Hatton, the Worcestershire statistician, had been a contributor for 20 years. "He specialised in areas others found unglamorous," Matthew Engel said, "and was perhaps the jolliest of statisticians." Obituaries of both will appear next year.

Editing is a team game and many thanks are in order. The book has benefited from the enduring strengths of its regulars: Gordon Burling, our near-invisible proof-reader; Stephen Mitchell at the printers, Clays; Philip Bailey, our unflappable statistician; Peter Bather and Mike Smith at LazerType, models of quiet efficiency; Sir Paul Getty, the Wisden management committee and Christopher Lane, *Wisden's* managing director, a creative guiding hand. Lawrence Booth, contributing editor, and Nigel Davies, consulting designer, added skill and vision; Tanya Aldred, Chris Ryan and John Woodcock sparked ideas; Steven Lynch was an editor without portfolio but with an endless desire to help. My family, Amanda, Daniel and Laura, put up with the whole thing without losing their cool or their warmth.

The staff worked phenomenally hard and well. Paul Coupar, our new editorial assistant, stayed cool through a baptism of fire. Harriet Monkhouse, the deputy editor, introduced me to new heights of rigour; should you come across an error, you can be sure it had nothing to do with her. Hugh Chevallier, the other deputy, was the pilot who landed the plane on time while coping with an editor who was something between a passenger and a patch of turbulence.

Next year, Matthew Engel returns as editor. Graeme Wright becomes the first editor to step down twice. He has been a pillar of *Wisden* since the days of Norman Preston, and a genial force for good. He had enough enthusiasm left this year to take charge of the obituaries, which are highly recommended. I am here for one year only, the most fleeting of *Wisden* editors. I hope to avoid the fate of the previous record-holder, Sydney Southerton, who, after finishing his second edition, proposed a toast to cricket at a Ferrets Club dinner, sat down and died.

Tim de Lisle, Islington, London, March 26, 2003

WISDEN
A GUIDE FOR NEW READERS

Welcome to *Wisden's* 140th edition, and its first reader's guide. We hope you find what you need here and throughout the book. If not, please write to enquiries@johnwisden.co.uk or Wisden, 13 Old Aylesfield, Golden Pot, Alton, Hampshire GU34 4BY.

How the book works

- **Wisden is really four books in one:** a set of essays, a work of reference, an annual and a miscellany, in that order. Some of these are subdivided, so there are eight parts in all, listed in Contents (page 8) and divided by full-page pictures (e.g. page 13). Throughout the Almanack, the name of the part you're in is given at the top of the left-hand page.
- **The eight parts:** part one is Comment, embracing features and profiles. Next come World View, the Players and Records. The middle is devoted to English Cricket, followed by Overseas Cricket. Part seven is Administration, and the Miscellany, including Chronicle, Obituaries and reviews, is at the back.
- **The Wisden year** runs from September to September. Test matches after September 9, 2002, including the Ashes, are reported in brief at the back and will be covered in full next year. Likewise the 2003 World Cup (page 1724).

Where to start

Five ways in, other than the obvious one:

- **Nasser Hussain:** profile by Scyld Berry, page 72
- **Richie Benaud's** favourite Tests, page 45
- **colour section:** some of the year's best images, after page 48
- **Chronicle of 2002,** page 1600: the main stories of the year, and the quirky ones
- **The 2003 World Cup:** pages 14 and 1724

Richie Benaud, p45

New items this year

- **World View,** page 85: results and comment on each Test team
- **Arrivals and Departures,** page 106: players taking or leaving the big stage

Lisa Keightley, p106

- **International coaches** and their results, page 177
- **Help** – look out for the key symbol at the start of a section to see how it works
- **Signpost quotes** – a line to entice you to another part of the book

Where to find ...

Five famous numbers

Six Almanack traditions

- **Notes by the Editor**: page 14
- **Five Cricketers of the Year**: the game's oldest honour, established in 1889, page 64; full list of winners, page 252
- **Births and Deaths**: the ultimate directory, now introduced by its own Notes, page 181
- **Obituaries**, page 1612: the lives of cricket people who died in 2002, among them Hansie Cronje, Ben Hollioake, Winston Place and Geoffrey Howard

Hansie Cronje, p1649

- **Books**, page 1667: a guest writer reviews the year's major titles. This year it's Frank Keating
- **Index of Unusual Occurrences**, page 1705: a tradition begun in 1996. Entries include "Galloping elk stops play"

Two famous names

- **The Ashes**: what they are, page 304; who won them last winter, page 1712
- **Lord's**: what, where and who founded it, page 457

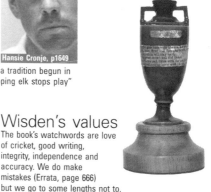

Wisden on the web

Every major article and Test report published in the Almanack can be found on our website, **www.wisden.com**, along with minute-to-minute comment on the latest news and scores.

Wisden's values

The book's watchwords are love of cricket, good writing, integrity, independence and accuracy. We do make mistakes (Errata, page 666) but we go to some lengths not to.

Launched in 1864 by the diminutive fast bowler John Wisden, the Almanack has had 14 editors, including John Woodcock of *The Times* (1982–87) and Matthew Engel of *The Guardian* (1993–2000), who returns in 2004.

CONTENTS

Colour section

Page 86

Page 105

Page 708

Page 903

Page 1284

Page 1200

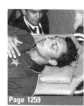

Page 1259

Page 1406

Page 1575

Administration and Regulations

Page 1630

Miscellany

Page 1665

1

COMMENT

Shades of Bradman: Sachin Tendulkar gives catching practice, Nagpur, February 2002. A portrait of Tendulkar at 30, page 48. *Picture by Arko Datta, Popperfoto/Reuters*

NOTES BY THE EDITOR
THE AGE OF SPEED

If you had to choose one word to sum up cricket in the early 21st century, what would it be? Some might say Australia, others Tendulkar or Murali. The cynical observer would be tempted to go for match-fixing or chucking; a South African might just say aaaarrrghh. A more persuasive contender might be something else altogether. In 2003, the name of the game is speed. The concentrated verve of Steve Waugh's Australians has galvanised international cricket as a whole.

For most of the past 126 years, Test cricket was conducted at a leisurely pace. The occasional burst of frenzied activity only emphasised that the standard tempo was sedate. Nowadays, the longest form of the game – of any game – rattles along like a good television drama (which it is).

It helps that two of the fastest bowlers ever, Brett Lee and Shoaib Akhtar, are in their prime, turning every ball into theatre. But they are only a fraction of a second faster than their predecessors, if that: Shoaib's 100mph delivery to Nick Knight at Cape Town, while pressing useful buttons in the minds of small boys and journalists, had the benefit of a wind roaring in from the Antarctic, and still, like Lee's 100mph ball a week later, gave Knight no trouble. The more meaningful acceleration has come at the other end. The great dramatic art of fast bowling has been joined by that of fast batting.

Two of the fastest-scoring calendar years in Test history have been 2001 and 2002 (table, page 27). Four of the five fastest Test double-centuries of all time in terms of balls were made in the year to January 2003. In 2001-02, two marauding Australian left-handers, Matthew Hayden and Justin Langer, reinvented the business of opening the innings, seeing it as their job to blaze a trail rather than lay a foundation. As Simon Barnes shows on page 24, fast scoring is no longer the province of the occasional showman, a Botham or Jessop, but a stratagem used by whole teams, all day long. Beyond the turnstiles, life in general is moving faster, and for once the game is keeping up. Always a dance to the music of time, Test cricket is no longer a quadrille: it is a quickstep, maybe even a jive.

Far from being undermined or overshadowed by the growth of one-day internationals, Test cricket has sharpened up its act. One-day cricket, often regarded as a little trollop lowering her older sister's standards, has actually enabled her to let her hair down. When you consider the electricity of the fielding and the exuberance of the fans, the immaculate virtuosity of Tendulkar, the flawed genius of Lara and Warne, the mysteries of the new-model off-spinners, the spread of express bowling to New Zealand and India, the classical craftsmanship of McGrath and Dravid, the rampaging audacity of Adam Gilchrist, the wiles of Stephen Fleming and Nasser Hussain, the Greek tragedy of South Africa and the Ealing comedy of Pakistan, Test cricket may be more entertaining now than it has ever been.

Promises, promises

But if it is the best of times, it is also the worst. Speed is not just the name of the game, but of the man who runs it: in July 2001, Malcolm Speed, boss of the Australian Cricket Board, moved to London to take on one of the world's trickier jobs as chief executive of the International Cricket Council. His credentials were strong, his intentions were good and his urgency was striking. Within three months, the time once taken to organise an executive board meeting, Speed was standing on a designer podium at Lord's, giving a glossy presentation of the ICC's new strategy to an invited audience of the great, the good and the media.

He made all the right noises, and the air grew thick with abstract nouns: "transparency... accountability... relevance... progress... innovation... decisiveness... inclusiveness... vision... tradition... spirit of cricket... major culture shift... high impact..." Speed didn't just promise us the world, he promised to act on his promises. The game's governing body was acquiring a face, and leading us to expect some teeth.

Eighteen months later, we can begin exercising that accountability. It does not look good. Just when cricket has become more fun to watch, its bosses have made it harder to follow. For much of the past year, the ICC were at their worst, which is saying something. Their Champions Trophy did not produce a champion. Their Test Championship produced the wrong one. Their new One-Day Championship was so arcane that it went virtually unnoticed. Their World Cup consisted of more than 50 matches but hardly any real contests. And they adopted a stance on Zimbabwe that shamed the game.

When sport meets tyranny

The cricket administrator's favourite charge down the years, the catch-all phrase deployed to deal with naughty boys, has been "bringing the game into disrepute". More often than not, it is hogwash. But early in 2003, the game really was brought into disrepute – by its own rulers.

Months before the World Cup began on February 9, it was clear that Zimbabwe was in a desperate state. Robert Mugabe's government, returned to power in a flagrantly fixed election, was running a vicious, thuggish police state, apparently indifferent at best to the famine afflicting millions of its people. Those in Zimbabwe who raised the alarm risked imprisonment or worse: in 2002, the local human-rights forum reported 1,061 cases of torture. As the banners on marches say, if you weren't outraged, you weren't paying attention. This was no place to stage a major sports event.

The 2003 World Cup had not been awarded to Zimbabwe. It had been awarded to South Africa, which decided to make it more African, and more helpful to their World Cup football bid, by handing six matches to Zimbabwe and a couple to Kenya. Irrespective of whether you approved, it was an unmistakably political decision, taken, as the World Cup organiser Dr Ali Bacher was careful to point out, by the government. There was no sporting reason to stage matches in Zimbabwe or Kenya: it meant worse pitches, smaller crowds, longer flights. Companies wishing to be World Cup sponsors had to show they were furthering the cause of black employment: again, this was a fine thing, but clearly political. The South African team was selected on political lines, with pressure from above to make sure it wasn't all-white, even though the success of Herschelle Gibbs and Makhaya Ntini all but guaranteed that anyway. The Zimbabwean selectors were under similar orders to pick Dion Ebrahim, who was palpably not in the strongest XI; one of those selectors, Andy Pycroft, resigned in protest. The notion that politics should be kept out of sport, still trotted out by the more blinkered inhabitants of planet cricket, was never an option. Politics ran through this World Cup like the zebra-skin logo that bedecked the stands.

One poll after another suggested that three-quarters of UK sports followers thought visiting teams should be allowed to switch their Zimbabwe games to South African venues (which were already on stand-by in case of security problems). Malcolm Speed reacted to this idea like a new father who hears someone criticising his baby. He took umbrage and insisted, to the open-mouthed disbelief of those who had observed their machinations over the years, that the ICC were non-political. It hadn't stopped them stomaching plenty of political activity from the South Africans. It hadn't stopped them letting matches go ahead in Zimbabwe under a repugnant regime. And it didn't stop them standing by in silence as Mugabe's police arrested dozens of people for making polite protests at Australia's game in Bulawayo.

Before the tournament, Nasser Hussain grasped three crucial points: that England and Zimbabwe had a singularly complex relationship, the legacy of colonialism; that the England players could hardly represent their country if their country didn't want them to go; and that they would be making a political statement whether they went to Zimbabwe or not. Speed couldn't see it. Vision? Decisiveness? Spirit? None of the above. The ICC ended up doing something that ought to have been impossible: washing their hands at the same time as burying their heads in the sand.

The gravest threat

Before becoming an administrator, initially with Basketball Australia, Speed was a barrister, then a businessman with his own sports-management company. His time at the top of world cricket already bears this double stamp. It has been the most grimly legalistic period in the game's history, and the most dismally corporate.

Not content with being a body, the ICC decided in 2001 that they should also be a brand. It was a need that possibly only a sports-management executive would have felt. The 2003 World Cup became the ICC Cricket World Cup. In South Africa in February, the ICC's name was everywhere: on bats, balls, hats, shirts, stickers, badges, postcards, and every player's chest. Supporters could go to the game in an ICC T-shirt and smear themselves in ICC sun-block, which perfectly encapsulated the ICC's sudden desire to go from behind the scenes to in your face.

What the fans couldn't do was drink Coke, because Pepsi was a sponsor; or express opinions, because they might offend Mugabe. The back of each ticket was a thicket of rules and regulations. The organisers were so anxious to quash ambush marketing, they even persuaded the South African government to pass a law banning spectators from carrying the wrong brand of mineral water. At the gate, fans found themselves being frisked by the soft-drink police. As if cricket didn't have enough fussy rules, here were a load more. Sport ought to have at least some connection with freedom and self-expression, and a game famous for its spirit should tread very softly in this area. Instead, cricket is marching to the beat of big business. A couple of years ago, the gravest threat to the game's fabric was corruption; now, it is corporatisation.

Armband protest: Andy Flower and Henry Olonga wore black armbands for Zimbabwe's first match in the World Cup. *Pictures by Howard Burditt, Popperfoto/Reuters and Joe Alexander, AFP.*

Two black armbands

When the ICC failed to give a lead over Zimbabwe, the England and Wales Cricket Board had the chance to fill the void. Instead, Tim Lamb said: why us? Cricket, he argued, was part of the international leisure and entertainment industry. About 300 British companies were continuing to do business with Zimbabwe; why should cricket alone be expected to take a stand? The answer hardly needs spelling out. A national team has a symbolic dimension that a firm importing mangetouts does not. A cricket board is not a company: it may be businesslike, but it does not exist to make money. It exists to stage cricket, to promote it and protect its good name. Lamb's stance, like Speed's, brought the game into disrepute. How can they govern cricket, who only cricket know?

Not that the administrators were alone in ducking the issue. Ricky Ponting played a great captain's innings in the final, but he hadn't shown much leadership in Bulawayo, where he went with a shrug of the shoulders. The Australians were reportedly asked to wear black armbands and refused. (The reporter who disclosed this was Peter Oborne, the political correspondent and presenter of a Channel 4 documentary on Zimbabwe which influenced Hussain's thinking. Oborne reappears on page 579, making a fifty for the Lords and Commons.) The only visible flickers of conscience in the Australian camp came from Matthew Hayden and Adam Gilchrist, who was so deeply affected that three weeks later, he walked when given not out. Bulawayo was the one moment where Australia missed Steve Waugh: a man who had founded a ward for the daughters of lepers in Calcutta would have been able to see beyond the boundary.

Hussain and his players did better than most. They at least managed to raise the moral issue, before allowing tactical considerations to tilt the argument towards security grounds: that got the ECB on board, and could have given the ICC a way out. The price to be paid for that pragmatism was the loss of the high ground. It looked as if nobody else would come along to claim it, and cricket would have to file for moral bankruptcy. But then, out of nowhere, came two black armbands.

England had got stuck thinking there were only two options: go or don't go, kowtow or boycott. Henry Olonga and Andy Flower, in a far tighter corner, found a more agile solution. The statement they issued at Zimbabwe's first game was calm, dignified and lethally clear. Their stand was not just brave but shrewd: there were two of them, one black, one white, they were both senior players, and they had not even been friends until this episode made them, in Olonga's words, "blood brothers". Together they were responsible for a shining moment in the game's history, which is already on the way to entering its mythology (armbands and the men I sing…). The Zimbabwe Cricket Union dropped Olonga, and would have dumped Flower too had it not been for a players' mutiny, thus neatly proving that it was a politicised organisation. Two strips of black tape, more potent than any logo, breathed life back into the game's battered spirit. And the ICC were so blind to this that they asked for the armbands to be taken off.

Aussies and Kenyans

If the governors are going to see the world in narrow terms, the cricket they stage had better be good. This World Cup was one-third party, two-thirds flop. The good things were the balance between bat and ball, the renewed power of attacking bowling, the romance of the Kenyans, and the sustained excellence, against all teams and in mixed conditions, of the Australians. They rode the loss of Warne and Jason Gillespie and found fringe players who not only filled in for absent stars but got the remaining ones out of any scrape. If Tendulkar was rightly named man of the tournament, he only just outshone Andy Bichel, who sparked fire from slow pitches, made crucial runs and even pulled off a direct-hit run-out. His desire was so great, you could see it throbbing in his veins.

The Kenyans were a big bonus. The ICC shrewdly signed up Bob Woolmer two years ago to fly around as a consultant to all four non-Test teams, and it showed in their fielding, bowling and pacing of an innings: like Brad Hogg, Australia's postman-spinner, they proved that part-timers can be highly professional. The Kenyans' story is a film waiting to happen, with its lyrical start (boys learning the game with a maize cob for a ball – corny, but true) and its heart-warming climax as a forgotten old-timer returns from his job in insurance to torment the mighty Aussies with his left-arm slows. Kenya's celebrations were irresistible: their shimmying huddle made its English equivalent look like Stonehenge.

The Super... how many?

So much for the good news. The bad things were the politics, the legal battles, the corporate bullying, the fact that there were only two good teams, and above all, the way that there were seven or eight non-events for every close contest.

The decision to punish England and New Zealand for their no-shows distorted the whole tournament. The four points the ICC insisted on awarding to Zimbabwe and Kenya stayed in the system like a virus thanks to the quirky business of carrying points through to the Super Six, which should have been dumped after 1999. The Kenyans, for all their romance, were not quite the giant-killers they were made out to be: their three wins over Test opposition came against the wretched Bangladeshis, the downtrodden Zimbabweans and a Sri Lankan side with food poisoning.

Of the 14 teams, only four enhanced their standing: Australia, India, Kenya and Canada. The pool stage had just enough interesting games, and some of the mismatches were redeemed by splashes of colour from John Davison and others. But the Super Six was dire. Australia and India each went through to the semi-finals in their first match. The carrying-through of points baffled the public and wrecked any sense of suspense, and the semi-finals, once Sri Lanka's top order rolled over, fell horribly flat. The World Cup was six days of great entertainment spread over six weeks. It dragged, which is just what one-day cricket was designed not to do. It was run in the interests not of the supporters, the players and the game itself, but the sponsors, broadcasters, politicians and lawyers.

Not simple, not effective

When it comes to putting on tournaments, everything the ICC touch turns to maths. The World Cup, like the Test Championship and especially the new One-Day Championship, was hard to follow: dangerous for any sport, and for cricket more than most. The intricacies of the game are part of its strange magic, but they are all the more reason for its surface to be straightforward. It should not try to shed its historic appeal to solemn 12-year-olds (of all ages) with a weakness for neat columns of numbers. But it must be attractive to other constituencies, more representative of an age in which the word anorak no longer signifies a waterproof jacket.

In some eyes, the Duckworth/Lewis system for resolving rain-affected one-day matches is a charming eccentricity. In rather more, it is a turn-off. It allows crucial matches, and the fates of captains and coaches, to hinge on pieces of paper covered in figures which not even the players always understand. Stats are one of the joys of cricket, but there is a place for them and it is not on the field. Duckworth/Lewis may be the fairest system imaginable, but it is out of tune with the game. It bewilders, where sport is supposed to bewitch. Before the next World Cup, Dave Richardson, the ICC's wicket-keeper turned gamekeeper, must find a system that is radically different and a great deal simpler.

The wrong champions

At least the World Cup produced the right winner. In January, the ICC Test Championship mace passed from Australia, one of the best teams ever, to South Africa, who were not even the best South African team ever. By no stretch of the imagination were they the best team in the world. They went top partly on the strength of fine victories in India and the West Indies, but largely because they had had the political will to play the minnows.

This didn't make the Test Championship (table, page 104) a bad idea, but it did show up severe flaws in its execution. Something had to be done. The ICC agreed on a new format, to begin in June 2003, at their meeting the day before the World Cup final, but did not say what it was (transparency? accountability?). The only clue was that it would take account of every match. In other words, it would get more complicated.

The best thing about the original idea, floated in these pages by Matthew Engel in 1995 and known as the Wisden World Championship until 2001, was its simplicity. You could explain it on the back of a bus ticket. Two points for a series win, one for a draw, none for a defeat; count only the latest meeting between each pair of teams, home and away; take an average until such time as all play all. Engel's championship began with South Africa top, but that was then – Hansie Cronje wasn't yet a crook, and Australia, under Mark Taylor, were only three-quarters of the way to becoming the victory machine of today (table, page 27).

Once Australia went top, only a dud system could dislodge them. The ICC made an elementary error in counting South Africa's two one-off Tests against Zimbabwe in 1999-2000, home and away, as a two-Test home series for South Africa: it wasn't. They made a more general blunder in not allowing one-off Tests to count. A single Test is enough for a series between the strong and the weak; Bangladesh would surely have learned more and suffered less if they didn't have to keep playing two-Test series. Better still, Bangladesh's results could be discounted for their opponents as well as for them. We can only hope the ICC get it right second time.

It's all too much
There is a deeper problem which the Test Championship has only exacerbated. The international game, as Christopher Martin-Jenkins argues on page 34, is bloated. Test matches now come along at a rate of more than one a week. In the 18 months covered by this book, England played in seven countries: Zimbabwe, India, New Zealand, England, Sri Lanka, Australia and South Africa. A generation ago, there weren't that many countries in Test cricket. By the World Cup, there had been 157 Tests this century; in the last century, the same number took 32 years, up to the middle of Bodyline.

If you divide the whole of Test history into two halves, Ian Botham's debut is now in the first half. The Test at Cape Town in January 2003 which sent South Africa to the top was the 1,637th ever. Botham's first hurrah, in July 1977 in the days when young Englishmen could waltz in and knock over Australians, was the 806th. In one-day cricket, the imbalance is even more pronounced. The 2003 World Cup final was the 1,993rd one-day international; the half-way point, like someone playing Grandmother's Footsteps, had sneaked up to April 1995. So Allan Border's entire one-day career now lies in the first half of history. It's ridiculous.

Overload drains the players, risks boring the fans, and makes for one-sided Tests and series. Of the 78 Tests freshly recorded in this book, 24 were innings victories, and only ten finished in definite results that were remotely close – five wickets or 100 runs, or fewer. Quite a few Test series are settled in seven playing days, as touring teams arrive undercooked and leave overtired; whitewashes no longer happen once in a blue moon. The whole programme needs a drastic rethink.

The art of un-intimidation
Given all this quantity, the quality is amazing. There may be only one great team in the world, but there are six or seven very decent ones. England are in the middle, a solid Test side capable of competing with anyone except Australia. Against South Africa this summer, thanks to the UCBSA's panic-stricken gamble on a 22-year-old captain, England should start favourites.

At the toss on that hopeless first morning of the Ashes, Nasser Hussain looked, for once in his life, intimidated. It made little difference to the result: two weeks later, when he called right again and batted, England still lost by an innings. But it was a symbolic moment that took a lot out of England. In the end, they did pull themselves up off the floor, once their injury epidemic spread to the Australian dressing-room. Hussain's achievement, through December, was to un-intimidate his team. After that, they pushed Australia harder than anyone else at the World Cup.

His dubious reward was to be exhausted even before England reached South Africa. The next World Cup, in the West Indies, is also at the end of an Ashes winter. That's in 2007, which happens to be the date the ECB have set for England becoming world-beaters. If the players are given a reasonable break after the Ashes, we will know that the board are serious.

Domestic harmony (almost)

Like the national team, the county game is getting there, slowly. The County Championship had a reasonable year in 2002, as Pat Gibson argues on page 554. Lord MacLaurin, the outgoing chairman of the ECB, did much more good than harm, even if he bears some of the blame for the board's over-corporate culture. But there are still big problems. The step up to the international game has yet to shrink: the typical English batsman, making his Test debut, goes out to bat like a lamb to the slaughter. Last summer Robert Key, a character with a mind of his own, was amazed at the size of the crowd and the intensity of the media.

He duly joined the ranks of those who make no runs to speak of in their first match. It is nearly 15 years since a right-handed English specialist batsman made even 50 on Test debut (the last was Kim Barnett, father of the county circuit in 2002). The best since Barnett's 66 is 65, by Darren Gough of all people. Only Graham Thorpe and Marcus Trescothick, two left-handers carefully nurtured through the A team, have bucked the trend.

There are still too many domestic competitions, even as the Benson and Hedges Cup drifts into history. The new knockabout Twenty20 Cup is a valid experiment in itself, which shows cricket noticing at last that some of its followers have other commitments. But the circuit is still overloaded. It's practically impossible to do well in four competitions. Somerset and Yorkshire, the 2002 C&G finalists, were both relegated in the Championship. Glamorgan, the one-day league champions, finished 14th in the four-day game. Only Surrey, Warwickshire and Essex achieved any consistency, and of those only Warwickshire were in both first divisions. The elite that the divisional system was designed to create is barely visible on the horizon.

The Championship tables are a bad joke. You cannot have decimal points on a league table and expect to broaden your appeal, a vital consideration when total county membership stands at a perilous 128,000. Like a fingernail with its DNA, the Championship tables carry the imprint of cricket's fudges and fussings. Relegating three counties out of nine is recognised as too many everywhere but the First-Class Forum. The column some of the media list as "ded" is ugly and puzzling (it stands for deduction, or points docked for slow over-rates). And bonus points are one of the worst ideas ever to last 35 years, even in cricket.

Imagine a world in which the only points on offer were three for a win and one for a draw (it's easy if you try). How would the Championship look? We applied it to the last two years' tables, and it made no significant difference. The champions were the same, and the relegations, and the promotions. A couple of teams swapped places, but in mid-table. And each line contained seven or eight digits, rather than as many as 18. Being easily understood, it'll never catch on.

A star is Vaughan

In *Roget's Thesaurus*, cricket appears in the same section as dancing. Sport and dance aspire to the same beautiful aimlessness – light-footed, swivel-hipped, free-spirited. But you wouldn't know it from the recent history of English batsmanship.

For a decade the dominant influence has been Graham Gooch, a batsman admirable in almost every way but not noted for twinkling toes. Gooch's method disregarded the feet in favour of shifting his weight, and that of the boulder he used for a bat. It worked for him and seeped into the technique of a couple of his opening partners, Alec Stewart and Mike Atherton, who had a spring in their heels but edited it out as the arteries hardened. Stewart and Atherton in turn opened with Marcus Trescothick, who was Gooch in a mirror: tall, strong, and stiff as a toy soldier.

Now Trescothick's partner is Michael Vaughan, who became, in 2002, both a top-class player and a one-man reversal of this trend. He pirouetted to pull respectable deliveries; he went right forward, with a high elbow and a mean look in his eye, to send the ball skimming past cover; he went back to late-cut as if in a sepia newsreel. He reminded John Woodcock of Len Hutton. Best of all, he went down the wicket to loft world-renowned spinners over mid-wicket. With his quick feet, hands and wits, he could not have been nimbler if he had been wearing white tie and tails.

Vaughan's hundreds at home came on flat pitches, against modest seam attacks, but then he did it all over again on his first Ashes tour, in cricket's hottest kitchen. Asked to name the best moment of his career, he said the Ashes – scoring his three centuries. Asked for the worst moment, he said the Ashes again – losing them 4–1. So he has balance as well as talent. He is, with all respect to the two durable gentlemen in top hats, a worthy cover star for *Wisden*.

Vaughan was as automatic a choice for Five Cricketers of the Year as Bradman was for Five Cricketers of the Century. So was Matthew Hayden, another who has come in from the fringe to make huge runs at high speed. There were seven strong contenders for the last three places, which went in the end to Nasser Hussain, England's most influential figure in a generation; Shaun Pollock, one of the world's top two seamers, as well as a stylish batsman (and a now ex-captain, who won 14 Tests and lost only five); and Adam Hollioake, the outstanding county captain of the past few years. The choice of Hussain and Pollock may raise eyebrows, as both led national teams to heavy defeats in Australia, but if we ruled out players who get hammered by the Australians, we wouldn't have many left.

Steve Waugh and the art of fast batting

THE MAN WHO CHANGED THE GAME

By SIMON BARNES

Never has a cricketer had so appropriate a surname. But let us understand that aright. Steve Waugh's cricketing warfare has never been a matter of hatred, jingoism and senseless aggression, any more than a matter of chivalry, romance and the search for personal glory.

No. Waugh's wars have been about the most efficient possible means of despatching the enemy. They are about a clear understanding of the opposition's strengths and weaknesses, and an equally uncluttered understanding of the strengths and weaknesses of his own side. Sometimes the results are spectacular, but that is by the way. Spectacle is a by-product of a hard head, clear vision, an analytical mind and an impersonal lust for victory.

Waugh wants to defeat you personally – but nothing personal, if you see what I mean. He has that air possessed by very few, even at the highest level of sport: that sense of vocation, that urge to beat not the opposition but the limitations of your self, your game, your world. There was something of that unearthly quality in Ayrton Senna, the Brazilian racing driver. Ellen MacArthur, the British sailor, has it too.

Waugh has the gift of reducing complex matters to simple ones: he sees without prejudice how best to exploit the opposition's weakness, how best to deploy his own strengths. The approach, cold-blooded, scientific, is that of a general, rather than a character in Sir Thomas Malory.

Waugh has conducted his cricketing campaigns in a mood of dispassionate ferocity. He famously remarked that sledging was "mental disintegration"; but that is not so much the aim of Waugh's sledging as of Waugh's cricket. The batting, bowling and fielding of his teams have all had the aim of causing mental disintegration: a moment of uncertainty that leads to self-doubt that leads to defeat. Waugh always wants defeat to be personal and complete, the better to prey on the opposition mind.

And in the process, he has transformed Test cricket. Over the past four years, his Australians played in a manner that was once unthinkable.

A captain is usually assessed on the way he operates his bowlers and sets his field, for it is supposed to be the fielding captain who controls the tempo of a match. Waugh is, of course, spectacularly good at all that. But it is the way he manages his batting line-up that is revolutionary.

In 1990, when there had been a long-running debate about intimidatory bowling, runs suddenly flowed in county cricket through a combination of flat pitches and a different type of ball. Simon Hughes, still operating as a bowler, asked the plaintive question: "What about intimidatory batting?" Under Waugh, Australia's batting has become the most intimidating aspect of modern cricket. The Australian batsmen seek to frighten opponents every bit as much as the fast-bowling quartet of the 1980s West Indians. They all act the same way, and they're all coming to get you.

Waugh's Australia bat with Waugh's dispassionate ferocity. They bat as a team, with personal glory very much a secondary matter. And above all, they bat fast. In 2001, Australia scored at 3.77 runs an over: breathtakingly fast by traditional standards. In 2002, Australia scored their Test runs at a rate of 3.99 an over. Only once in history has a team scored faster through a whole year – in 1910, Australia scored their runs at 4.47 every six balls, and there were far fewer Tests then. By comparison, England's run-rate in 2002 was 3.37 – and that was England's fastest rate in almost a century. Other nations are following the Australian lead, but they're not as good at it yet.

Speed is not an accident. It is a tactic

South Africa, once dour, now bat at a significantly faster tempo: the first thing they did in 2003 was to score 445 in a day against Pakistan. The sea-change in Michael Vaughan of England over the past year was in tempo. Speed is not an accident. It is a tactic. It can't be done without very good players, but it is not the direct result of having good players. It is the result of astute, logical, cold-blooded thought on the subject of how best to win a cricket match.

We traditionally think of fast scoring as something dashing and devil-may-care: Jessop, Milburn, Botham. It was merry and jaunty and beery, the way you batted if you were a bit of a lad. Fast scoring was not altogether serious – it came in the drive-for-show category. Waugh's Australians have put it into the putt-for-dough department. For them, fast scoring is not a bonnets-over-the-windmill slogfest: it is deadly serious. It is done first to undermine the opposing bowlers, and with them the rest of the fielding side. And then it gives Australia extra time in the quest for 20 wickets: a free session for your bowlers every innings. No wonder it took them only 11 playing days to win each of the last two Ashes series.

Most non-Australian cricket followers would admit when pressed that they can't always tell one Australian batsman from another. They all wear green helmets with the Australian coat of arms above the grille, they are all good, they are all vindictively aggressive towards anything loose, they

Fastest-scoring calendar years

Qualification: 10 Tests

		RPO† (all teams)	Tests	Runs (all teams)	Highest		Lowest	
1	2002	3.18	54	54,133	**Australia**	3.99	**Zimbabwe**	2.58
2	1921	3.13	11	11,147	Australia	3.48	South Africa	2.47
3	2001	3.03	55	55,310	Australia	3.77	West Indies	2.68
4	1982	3.00	28	27,935	West Indies	3.46	New Zealand	2.65
5	1983	2.99	30	28,821	Australia	3.17	Sri Lanka	2.63
6	1991	2.97	21	20,774	West Indies	3.21	India	2.65

Australia's run-rate of 3.99 during 2002 was the second highest by any team in history – behind only the 1910 Australians, who scored 4.47 runs every six balls (but played only four Tests). England's rate of 3.37 runs an over in 2002 was their fifth-best in a calendar year. *Research: Chris Ryan.* † *Runs per six balls in 1921, when there were some eight-ball overs.*

Who dares wins

Under Allan Border, Australia's scoring-rate was nothing special, and they drew more games than they won. When Mark Taylor took over, the draws fell away, mostly turning into wins – the losses remained about the same – and the scoring-rate nudged up but remained within the bounds of tradition at three an over. Under Steve Waugh, the change has been much more marked: the ratio of wins to losses has more than doubled, the draw has become an endangered species, and the scoring-rate has leapt by an extra half a run an over or 50 runs a day. The only column here that hasn't been transformed is the average runs per wicket – although there is a slight rise, showing that scoring faster doesn't mean playing less safely. Above all, it means winning matches: by the end of the Ashes series, Waugh had more victories as captain than Border from half as many Tests.

		Results					Scoring-rate	
	P	W	L	T	D	W/L	RPW	RPO
Under Border	93	32	22	1	38	1.45	36.19	**2.79**
Under Taylor	50	26	13	0	11	2.00	35.07	**3.02**
Under Waugh	45	33	7	0	5	4.71	39.86	**3.55**

To March 2003.

Who dares twins

Steve Waugh has finished on the winning side more than anyone else in Test history. His nearest rival is also his nearest relative: his twin brother, who retired with 72 wins under his belt. Steve Waugh could yet be caught by the men who took most of the wickets for him, Shane Warne and Glenn McGrath. This is a club open only to members of the two great winning machines of the modern era: the West Indies team of the 1970s and 80s, or the Australians of the last decade.

		P	W
1	**S. R. Waugh (A)**	156	78
2	**M. E. Waugh (A)**	128	72
3	I. V. A. Richards (WI)	121	63
4	**S. K. Warne (A)**	107	62
5	D. L. Haynes (WI)	116	60
6	**G. D. McGrath (A)**	91	59
7	C. G. Greenidge (WI)	108	57
8	I. A. Healy (A)	119	55
9	M. A. Taylor (A)	104	52
	C. A. Walsh (WI)	132	52

To March 2003.

are all hugely confident. They bat as a unit and there's always another one waiting to destroy you. A bit like the film *Zulu*.

The wicket-keeper scores even faster than the top six and the tail bat seriously, always an aspect of a consistently victorious side. And just as the West Indian bowling ground the opposition down, softened them up and destroyed their confidence, so the Australian batting does the same thing.

The influence of one-day cricket is obvious, but it is not that the Australians bat in Test matches as if they were in a one-dayer. It is rather that the thought processes of one-day cricket – the need to capitalise on every error of the opposition, the presumption that you look to make runs off every ball – have been adapted to the Test context.

Hit-and-giggle? Far from it. There is no suggestion that a wicket is any less valuable to an Australian than it was before: Sydney 2003 was the first time since England's previous visit four years earlier that they had been bowled out twice in a home Test. But wickets are seen more as team than as individual possessions. Every batting tactic, including that of speed, must be adapted to the conditions. In knuckling-down conditions, Australian batsmen will knuckle down. But send them a bad ball at any time in any context and hear it thwack into the boundary board: first over of the day, last over of the day, just after a wicket, just before tea, 50 for three or 200 for nought – bam. And don't even think about a night-watchman. When Andy Bichel was moved up to No. 3 at Sydney in January 2003, night-watchman was the word that sprang to some commentators' lips, but what he was actually doing was the opposite – softening the new ball.

It is not so much a tactic as an emphasis: when in doubt, attack. Not for fun – as a thought-out ploy. As a team policy. Speed is not self-indulgence but duty. The idea is to win every session of every Test match, and mostly that is what Australia have been doing. If things go amiss, there is always the captain to come in later in the order. The only disappointment in Waugh's later career is that there have been so few occasions when he has been required to do his one-man rescue act.

The tactic of speed has been enthralling, but Waugh did not do it to enthral. He did it to enslave. There was an awful lot of guff talked about "brighter cricket" in the 1960s: if that was brighter cricket, what would audiences of 40 years back have made of the Australian speed machine? Waugh doesn't employ the tactic to make cricket brighter. But – and it is an aspect of his greatness – he didn't allow his prejudice against mere entertainment to muddle his thinking. In its intention, the Australian stroke-making is as flamboyant as an atom bomb.

The definitive treatise on warfare as a science of destruction rather than a chivalric art was written by Karl von Clausewitz in Napoleonic times. It is called *On War*. If a similarly hard-nosed book were to be written on cricket, the same title could be used. With a small adjustment to the spelling.

Simon Barnes is chief sportswriter on The Times.

Different strokes for different times

THE 21st-CENTURY COACHING BOOK

By SIMON BRIGGS

According to the *MCC Coaching Manual* of 1952, the art of batting is a very simple one. This central text, which acquired an almost religious status within the game, has at its core the argument that every shot is really an adaptation of either the forward or back defence. It proceeds to list five major species – drives, cuts, pulls, hooks and leg glances – with all the fussiness of a lepidopterist.

Out on the field, even in 1952, things were a little more flexible. Denis Compton, the book's principal model, was a master of the sweep – a shot MCC appeared not to recognise. Yet the dominance of Test cricket, with the draw common and timeless Tests not consigned to history, fostered an essential conservatism among batsmen. For most of them, the first concern was to minimise risk; run-scoring came a long way down the agenda.

Fifty years on, the world's bowlers find themselves facing a quite different challenge. One-day cricket, with its improvised twists and pre-emptive strikes, is the paymaster now, and its values have spread. Two of the three most prolific Test batsmen of 2002, Michael Vaughan and Matthew Hayden, were both openers, but not the eggshell-treaders of old. This pair would rather put dents in the new ball than see it off.

Something has happened to the players' inbuilt coaching manuals since 1952, something that Charles Darwin might have recognised. And even as this addendum to the batting handbook was being compiled, the pace of change kept rising, driven on by the sheer volume of top-level cricket.

Whether he is bowling or batting, the modern player needs to be quick-witted and adaptable. Predictability is soon overtaken. Even Sachin Tendulkar, probably the world's leading exponent of classical technique, has found that artistry is not enough. Harried by opposition strategists armed with video evidence, he has proved his greatness by developing new weapons of his own. In contrast to the reliably orthodox Brian Lara, Tendulkar is often first to try an unfamiliar stroke. And thanks to his insatiable work ethic, he usually ends up playing it better than anyone else.

The uppercut

We start with one of Tendulkar's specialities, a stroke that has kept evolving since South Africa's Eddie Barlow first copyrighted it in the early 1960s. Despite the enthusiastic patronage of Tony Greig and Alan Knott, who used it against the bounce of Lillee and Thomson in 1974-75, the uppercut remained something of an oddity until the 1996 World Cup, where Sanath Jayasuriya audaciously attacked the new ball inside the first 15 overs.

With the fast bowlers finding lift, and the field up inside the circle, the diminutive Jayasuriya reversed the advice of the coaching manual, which sermonises in bold type on the "importance of coming down on the ball from above". Instead, he leant back and whirled his bat like a hammer-thrower beginning his first revolution. To the astonishment of several fielding sides, the ball kept disappearing over wide third man for six.

Left-handed batsmen are always going to have an advantage playing this stroke, as most balls they face are already slanting across them in the right general direction. Though much taller, Hayden and Adam Gilchrist have both made plenty of capital from their own versions of the Jayasuriya slash. But Gilchrist has also mastered an alternative form, in which the ball is simply cuffed over the slips with the gentle but precise assistance that a football goalkeeper uses to tip a high shot over the bar.

This variant is likely to be seen more and more now that bouncers have been brought back into the one-day game. For Tendulkar, it functions as the perfect riposte to the bouncer aimed at the point of the right shoulder – a tactic designed to make the batsman hook in the air. Instead of stepping in behind the ball, he leans back far enough to get his body out of the way, then flips his bat up like a cook on pancake day. The ball sails over the cordon into the acres of space beyond third man's left hand. This shot is bad news for captains who put their fast bowlers out to pasture.

Adam Gilchrist plays his version of the uppercut (*left*); Damien Martyn reverse-sweeps (*above*); Ryan Campbell's ramp (*right*) Pictures by Patrick Eagar; Jack Atley; Hamish Blair, Getty Images

The reverse sweep

There is evidence that the reverse sweep dates back at least to the 1920s, when K. S. Duleepsinhji played a wide off-side ball "backwards towards third man with his bat turned and facing the wicket-keeper". This contemporary account, written by the non-striker L. P. Jai, adds that "there was an appeal for unfair play but the umpire ruled it out".

Duleepsinhji's opponents may never have seen the shot before, but they instinctively knew it was a transgressive stroke. In its most common form, it combines a right-hander's body position – left foot forward, right knee on ground, right hand below left on the handle – with a left-hander's horizontal swing of the bat, which moves clockwise from three o'clock to nine, sweeping the ball to third man: cricket's equivalent of cross-dressing.

This flagrant disregard for the first rule of Fred Trueman – cricket is a sideways-on game – explains why the reverse sweep has been treated with suspicion. The stroke's most famous moment came when the England captain Mike Gatting bungled it catastrophically during the 1987 World Cup final. But it was rehabilitated in the early 1990s thanks to Warwickshire's captain–coach team, Dermot Reeve and Bob Woolmer.

Their tactics were a response to the challenges thrown up by off-spinners in one-day cricket. If a bowler could sustain a good length, he could wheel away to a 3–6 on-side field with no one behind square on the off side. Woolmer and Reeve reckoned the reverse sweep could be more than just a run-getter in itself. By forcing the fielding side to cover third man, it would open up gaps for more orthodox strokeplay to exploit.

With respect to Duleepsinhji, the reverse sweep is basically a creature of the last two decades. Having successfully percolated down to club level, it can now claim to be the most important batting innovation since the arrival of helmets. Among the professionals, though, the stroke is undergoing further development. Virender Sehwag, Damien Martyn and

Andy Blignaut tries the scoop (*above*); Matthew Hayden's cross-court flick (*right*) Pictures Hamish Blair, Getty Images

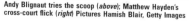

Andy Flower have all played it in Tests. Jonty Rhodes has pioneered the reverse pull, for use against shorter balls and quicker bowlers.

Most controversially, New Zealand's Craig McMillan has started switching his hands as well as his intended scoring area, so transforming himself from right-hander to left-hander as the ball comes down. This has implications for the lbw law, among other things. The ploy has already forced an amendment to the Laws, defining off and leg stumps according to the batsman's stance "at the moment the ball comes into play for that delivery". The reverse-sweep taboo has been well and truly broken.

The scoop

This is another new twist on an old standard. In the early 20th century, an Australian undertaker-cum-wicket-keeper by the name of Hanson Carter developed a novel alternative to the leg glance. As Christopher Martin-Jenkins writes in his biographical dictionary of Test cricketers, Carter's "chief delight was a stroke by which he lifted the ball over his left shoulder just as a labourer shovels the dirt out of a drain he is digging".

We could call it the shovel, in Carter's honour, but that term has become associated with a subspecies of on-side deflections, so let's settle for the scoop. Pakistan's Moin Khan was a prime exponent of the stroke, using it to fine effect against Glenn McGrath in the 1999 World Cup. But while Moin's scoop was usually played off a good-length ball, with the aim of lofting it over the fine-leg boundary, the shot can also be a useful counter to the yorkers and low full tosses that dominate the final overs. To make this play, the batsman attenuates the stroke, bending his front knee and cocking his wrists like a tennis player punching a low forehand volley.

The scoop has produced two memorable moments. The first was in a one-day international at Perth in 2000-01 when Zimbabwe, chasing 303, needed 15 off the last over to beat Australia and Doug Marillier had just come in. Marillier had told his team-mates he would "probably sweep" McGrath. He did so first ball, moving over to the off and helping the ball past fine leg. After taking a two into the off side, he did it again third ball. The target was down to five off three. McGrath put his fine leg back and Zimbabwe managed only three singles to lose by one run, but the scoop became famous in southern Africa – as the Marillier.

A happier ending came in last summer's Benson and Hedges semi-final at Old Trafford. Warwickshire were the visitors, and after a seesawing match their No. 11, Neil Carter (what is it about men named Carter?), found himself walking to the wicket with one ball left and two runs needed. Most tailenders would have opted for a cow-shot, but when Glen Chapple fired in the usual full, straight ball, Carter, a left-hander, reached forward and flicked it over short fine leg's head for four.

The scoop relies on the bowler's pace, simply using an angled blade to deflect the ball past the infield. It is therefore rarely played against a spinner, and requires some courage. The body position tends to be low to the ground, as in a conventional sweep, with the eyes behind the line of the ball. If the bat fails to make contact, the result could be painful.

The ramp

A few more radical improvisers – notably Ryan Campbell, another Australian wicket-keeper – have taken the shovel to its logical extension. Instead of sending the ball over the left shoulder like a man throwing salt for good luck, they manage to hoist it almost directly over their own heads into the unguarded territory behind the wicket-keeper. This is the ramp.

When Campbell plays it, he ducks into a bizarre posture, with both knees on the ground and his chest facing down the pitch. He positions the bat with its toe pointing at the umpire, then brings it up towards his face like a drawbridge. Though he needs a moment to scramble to his feet, this hardly matters: the ball has usually scooted away for four.

There is a certain irony in the fact that the bat remains virtually straight, in partial accordance with the textbook. Yet instead of taming the ball's bounce, it is used to amplify it. If the ramp catches on, it could yet bring the Under-10s' fielding position of long-stop into the professional game. For now, though, it has to rate as the most exotic trick shot in the book.

The cross-court flick

How do you score off a straight ball that is what the professionals call "back of a length"? A full-blooded pull is too risky unless the pitch is a belter or your name is Aravinda de Silva. But Tendulkar and Hayden have worked out a higher-percentage option: you offer a straight bat, as if to force down the ground, then turn the wrists at the last second. The ball tends to be heading just over the top of off stump, so the result looks like a waist-high tennis forehand, whipped cross-court with top-spin.

It is hard to imagine this stroke being coached; it is best left to the elite, and even the world's top players have spent years developing their own takes on it. Tendulkar and his disciple, Sehwag, like to hang right back in the crease. Hayden, with his extra height, tends to step into the ball slightly. And then there is Vaughan, who has a technique all his own.

Less wristy than the others, Vaughan uses a kind of straight-batted pull to hit back-of-a-length balls wide of mid-on. Because he shuffles across the stumps as the bowler releases, he can get his back foot outside off stump and swivel his hips to face mid-wicket. The bat comes down like a straight forcing shot, with Vaughan's body position providing the angle.

When a batsman can work the ball so aggressively off the back foot, or drive it on the up, the bowler has virtually nowhere left to go. And that is good news for run-hungry spectators. Anyone who saw much Test cricket in 2002 will know that the one-day bug has infected the whole game. Cricket is the richer for it.

Simon Briggs, formerly assistant editor of Wisden Cricketers' Almanack, *is deputy cricket correspondent of the* Daily Telegraph.

The crisis of international overload
CRYING OUT FOR LESS
By CHRISTOPHER MARTIN-JENKINS

"They are as sick that surfeit with too much, as they that starve with nothing." – *The Merchant of Venice*

As usual Shakespeare hit the nail bang in the middle, and as usual we do well to listen to his wisdom. There is too much cricket. There has been too much cricket for far too long and if we do not act now to stop the rot, we will all be driven to distraction: players, media, spectators; umpires, groundsmen, administrators; everyone with a stake in the game.

The media have to take it on the chin: we make a lifelong living from the game and there are ways of sharing the load. But for players there is sometimes no way off the treadmill. In January 2003, the nucleus of England's team made a vain attempt to spend three precious nights at home between the end of the VB Series in Australia and the start of their preparations for the World Cup in South Africa. They were away from October to March, an acceptable absence, perhaps, in the days of sea travel, infrequent tours and mothers who expected to change every nappy; hardly so today, if there is to be any balance in their lives.

No wonder Graham Thorpe opted out altogether for a time and others such as Jonty Rhodes have chosen to retire from one form of the game. No wonder India's team made the same plea for a break at home in the midst of a remorseless programme last year when, hard on the heels of the contentious series in South Africa late in 2001, they played host to England and Zimbabwe, toured the West Indies and England, went hot-foot to the Champions Trophy in September, then began a series of three Tests and seven one-day internationals against West Indies – and fitted in a Test series and seven more one-dayers in New Zealand by mid-January.

When Nasser Hussain made his plea for a break in the *Sunday Telegraph* towards the end of England's tour of Australia, he was echoing the *cri de coeur* made by a number of Test captains over the years, among them the Australians Kim Hughes and Allan Border. In 1989-90 Border resigned the captaincy of Queensland, publicly asking the Australian Cricket Board what point there was in leading his state team when he was able to play for them only twice a season.

It is a reminder that this is not a new problem, only one that becomes a little more exacerbated with every year that passes, like creeping rheumatism in an ageing body. Each year cricket boards round the world agree to just a little more to feed the insatiable appetites of the television companies. The leading players do not want to play more, and they risk injury by doing so, but they are sucked in, knowing that someone else will take their place should they desist, and feeling that they might as well take the money on offer while they can. The result is shorter careers and shorter tempers; more wearisome travel, more soulless hotels; more tired players playing to preserve their batteries as well as to win; less time with loved ones and less enjoyment.

In 1972, 14 Tests started around the world and only three one-day internationals, all between England and Australia, the pioneers. By 1982, the totals had risen gently to 33 one-dayers and 28 Tests. In 1992, it was 89 one-dayers and only 26 Tests, but that had something to do with it being a World Cup year; in 1993, there were 36 Tests. By 2002, the total was 145 one-day internationals and 54 Tests. Last year, the ICC permitted, no, encouraged, a bigger Champions Trophy. And this year they let the World Cup expand again, to 14 countries playing what was intended to be 54 matches in 43 days.

For 20 years after the Packer Revolution – the event that started this rapid proliferation – the ICC did nothing to prevent the steady rise in the amount of cricket. Then came their plan for a ten-year programme of Tests, already disrupted by political disputes. It was a laudable attempt to bring some order to the whole programme, but it was designed less to put a sensible limit on the number of matches than to give a framework for a rolling world championship table.

Domestic professional cricket in every country is completely dependent for its viability on income generated by internationals. But it has to be an interdependent system. Without first-class cricket, players of the necessary quality to make Tests and one-day internationals attractive would be very hard to find, if not impossible. They would have to learn their advanced skills on the big stage, and there are few players good enough to do that. That is why it is vitally important for the county game in England, and for domestic cricket elsewhere, to find a sensible balance in the programme.

Cricket was looked forward to more eagerly by all involved in the days when there were clearly defined seasons. Once upon a time, only England staged cricket between May and September: these days West Indies have Tests in June, Sri Lanka and Zimbabwe in July, Pakistan in August. Australia have taken to playing indoors in Melbourne at the height of the British summer and now they are to have outdoor Tests in the tropical north as well. England's response has been to organise even more incoming tours. Since 1997, they have gone from three one-day internationals and six Tests to 13 one-dayers and seven Tests in 2003. Every extra international event makes enthusiasm for the major occasions of county cricket that much less. Every quarter-final of the Cheltenham & Gloucester Trophy that does not fill all the seats and marquees means a greater dependence on the international profits. So the vicious circle turns.

It all revolves around money: that is inevitable for any professional sport. Therefore, what used to be called the $64,000 question (probably about $550 million by now) is this: has the surfeit become counter-productive not just for players, media and others closely involved, but also for paying spectators and subscribing television viewers?

There is much evidence to suggest that it has. Swathes of empty seats could be seen last year at Tests from Christchurch to Old Trafford. Channel 4's coverage, good as it is, tends to attract smaller audiences than the BBC did. On the phone to me in the later stages of England's tour of Australia, one of the keenest followers of sport I have ever known said: "I'm afraid I stopped reading, watching and listening after we lost in Perth." So he had taken no close interest in Michael Vaughan's hundreds at Melbourne and Sydney, two of the most attractive innings anyone could hope to see.

Surely heed has to be taken of the implications. The aim should be a happy medium – providing enough cricket for the game to remain solvent, but not so much that when the keen follower sees in his morning paper that there is another match to watch today he feels complete indifference or, worse, a heart-sinking revulsion.

The answer, as the Test captains have argued, is for the ICC to impose limits on each nation, for the good of all involved. Home and away, 12 Tests and 20 one-day internationals a year seems now to be a reasonable and realistic maximum for any country. Within the bounds it would be possible for each nation to suit its programme to its particular needs. Perhaps India, with its uniquely large market, apparently unquenchable enthusiasm for the one-day game and no need to compete with anything so formidable as the market for football in Britain, might be treated as a special case, adding, if politics will permit, an Asian tournament to its commitments in the ICC's Test and one-day championships.

Long before Shakespeare had his say, Solomon had put it equally succinctly: "To everything there is a season and a time to every purpose under the heaven."

Christopher Martin-Jenkins is chief cricket correspondent of The Times. *He is a former cricket correspondent of the* Daily Telegraph *and the BBC.*

Can a leading player also be a family man?

DON'T MARRY
A CRICKETER

By DEREK PRINGLE

Cricket and family life have never been easy bedfellows. A relationship which was at odds long before women were given the vote appears to have reached a crisis of late. Within the game, there has been a spate of well-publicised marital break-ups; outside it, the world is adapting to new rules of engagement between the sexes. The leading players are finding that cricket is making greater demands on them than ever before – and so are their wives.

Even though a successful Test career is now shorter than it used to be, at six to ten years, wives and girlfriends are no longer tolerating their lot as cricket widows and virtual single parents. A high-profile husband may have his allure but, once the cachet fades, many are swapping them for men who spend their weekends at home washing the car and mowing the lawn – or even cooking the lunch and bathing the kids.

The sheer time taken by the game, especially at weekends, has rarely been popular with families: up to ten hours a day, often seven days a week, if you include journeys and preparation time. Normal folk who receive an invitation to a christening from a professional cricketer have to look at it twice because it tends to be during the week. Add lengthy tours of three or four months to the load and it amounts to a huge strain, particularly on those who have come to expect more of husbands and fathers than previous generations.

The problems appear both generational and cultural, with the majority of divorces occurring in England, though a quick check reveals that nowhere is immune. India, to pick a country with different social mores, has its marital casualties: before he was ever accused of match-fixing, Mohammad Azharuddin caused a scandal by walking out of an arranged marriage and settling down with a Bollywood actress. Javagal Srinath's marriage broke up and Sourav Ganguly's touched breaking point when he was photographed at a temple with another film star. Other cricketers caught in the full glare of Indian celebrity have been tempted, though many feel it is a honey-trap used by underworld figures hoping to blackmail players into fixing matches.

The absenteeism is felt far more in England, where little more than a few weeks separate the hectic six-month home season and the moment wives wave their husbands off on tour in October. It would not be sanctioned now, but on the 1982-83 tour of Australia and New Zealand, Chris Tavaré, who had recently married, brought his wife Vanessa along for the entire 148-day trip. What none of the team knew at the time was that Vanessa had phobias about flying and heights, both of which required heavy sedation. With 23 flights and most of the hotels set in downtown skyscrapers, a lot of sedative was needed. If Tavaré was unhappy he never showed it. It wasn't until the Fourth Test in Melbourne that he played his first shot in anger.

Once a relationship becomes strained, cricket rarely seems able to offer a compromise. Recently, Darren Gough, Graham Thorpe, Mark Butcher and Dominic Cork have all seen their marriages break up while on England duty. In Thorpe's case, the public saw it too: he flew home from India at the beginning of a Test match in an attempt to save his marriage, appeared on his doorstep in Surrey to talk frankly about it, and later played for England at Lord's when clearly not himself during a custody battle over his two small children. He retired from one-day internationals with the World Cup looming to spend more time with the children, giving up a sizeable income as a result.

Others are doing the sums, and players who spent last winter with both the Test and one-day sides in Australia and the World Cup in South Africa did not see their own beds for 140 nights. Missing the kids growing up is a regret many cricketers cite as a downside of their job, but it is one that most do little about. On the same 1982-83 tour as the Tavarés, the England team were sponsored by JVC. Getting some of their product was part of the deal; while most of the players chose hi-fi, Derek Randall picked a fussy-looking video camera. He said it was "for the missus", so she could film the kids growing up for him.

Keith Fletcher's playing career with Essex and England lasted more than 20 years from tentative newcomer to wise old guru. He was married throughout, and still is, to Sue, and they have two grown-up daughters, Sarah and Tara. Sue doesn't feel she or the children suffered unduly as a result of his absence. "I certainly don't look back with resentment, and the girls grew up thinking it was the norm," she says. "I don't feel it has affected them in any way and they both have a great relationship with their father."

An itinerant father can confuse young children. In his diary of the 1997-98 West Indies tour, Phil Tufnell's last entry tells of arriving back at Heathrow to be greeted by his three-year-old daughter Poppy waving and shouting: "Bye-bye, Daddy."

Being away for long periods does not just affect wives and children. Players spending half their year in hotel rooms become lonely and

Ashes captaincy, 2002-style: Nasser Hussain (*left*) goes for a walk in Perth with Jacob and newborn Joel, while his opposite number, Steve Waugh, takes his three-year-old, Austin, to nets at the Gabba. *Pictures by Tom Shaw and Nick Wilson, Getty Images*. It was all very different in 1929 when Frank Woolley (*below*) said goodbye to his family for a full six months before sailing for New Zealand. *Picture by Getty Images*.

frustrated. When that happens, temptation to stray can be hard to resist and public disclosures of affairs have, in some cases, precipitated the split. Fame has always been a potent aphrodisiac.

In England, marital break-up among cricketers has increased steadily, a trend in step with a wider society that has seen the divorce rate treble in a generation. Research recently commissioned by the Lord Chancellor's department found many of today's generation "selfishly pursue careers and other interests at the expense of marriage or long-term relationships". Cricketers, like most professional sportsmen, have probably just been selfish for longer. Before the 1990s, the situation was largely tolerated, though not by Phillip DeFreitas's first wife, who made it clear she considered her own career far more important – thanks to its relative longevity – then her spouse's. These days, wives with children expect husbands to contribute more than a pay packet. Many cricketers struggle to deliver, and not only because of their absence. Cricket dressing-rooms act as quasi-family units, though ones where responsibility, beyond the immediate task of scoring runs or taking wickets, is often lacking.

> "We rallied round and got on with it," says Sue Fletcher, "because that's how it was"

The laddish bonhomie and sporting drama that come with the job do not prepare players for the raw emotions of life. But while an upset on the pitch can be sorted in the nets or by having a chat with the coach, a failing relationship with a loved one is not so easily remedied, especially when the player is a few time zones away.

The fact that players now move county more frequently than in the past means that traditional support networks for wives, such as aunts and grandmothers, may no longer be within easy reach. Where children are settled at school, many simply refuse to move, leaving players to live like the blokes in *Men Behaving Badly* for virtually the whole season. Part of the problem stems, as one wife of a well-known player confirms, from the women not thinking the whole deal through before they settle down with a professional cricketer. Often they meet their man before he has been picked for international duty. Only when the merry-go-round of touring meets the treadmill of county cricket does the antisocial nature of the whole business hit them.

There is a distinct generation gap. Sue Fletcher, a stoic by nature, recalls the England wives of the late 1960s and early 70s being a close-knit group that was more like a self-help collective than a bunch of disillusioned housewives. "We knew what the form was about looking after the kids; our husbands made that clear from day one," she says. "When they were on tour, and they were long tours in those days, the wives used to visit each other back in England. It helped that we all got on well and had children roughly the same age. But we rallied round and got on with it because that's how it was."

In those days, families were allowed to tour but were not encouraged. As at the gentlemen's clubs of the time, women were seen as a distraction and rather too civilising for cricketers sent to win important battles on foreign soil. The Test and County Cricket Board used to control visits, which players had to pay for, including flights and hotel rooms.

"I remember going to visit Keith on tour and being allowed to spend 21 nights with him," Sue Fletcher says. "We had to pay every penny and often it took up the entire tour fee so you'd make nothing. Because of those financial constraints, wives on tour, especially with kids in tow, were the exception rather than the rule."

These days, there are still limits, but they are less strict. Providing a player is abroad for more than 60 days, the England and Wales Cricket Board allow 30 days' family provision for players who are in both the Test and one-day sides and 16 for those in one or the other. The board also pay for return flights (in economy) for wives and children under 18, all accommodation, some internal travel and a modest daily meal allowance.

The timing of visits is still controlled and has to be agreed in advance by the captain and coach. Usually the period falls around Christmas and New Year, just as the Test series is coming to a climax, a situation that can add to the tension, especially when families come to realise that Daddy is not on holiday too.

Occasionally, special cases are allowed. Not wanting to miss the birth of his second child, Nasser Hussain settled his wife Karen and toddler Jacob in Perth just before the start of the 2002-03 tour of Australia, a first for an England captain. He flew out ahead of the team and was given a few days off after the First Test so he could be there for the birth, which was even timed to fit into his schedule: as he chivalrously put it in his newspaper column, "we had her induced". This prompted much huffing and puffing from the old guard, led by Ray Illingworth, who accused Hussain of leaving a sinking ship. Put it down to the David Beckham effect if you like, but such instances are likely to rise, along with the costs, as the board try to keep players and their wives happy.

Family visits, even when the cost to players is minimal, are often fraught. Denise Fraser, wife of Angus, was one of the generation of England wives after Sue Fletcher. They have been together since before Fraser became an England regular, fitness permitting, in 1989. They had a son, Alexander, in 1993, a daughter, Bethan, in 1995, and got married in 1996. Denise had mixed feelings about her times on tour. "Before the children were born, trips to the West Indies were great fun, especially when players like David Gower and Allan Lamb were about. But in my experience, we were not always made to feel welcome and, although the wives and kids often lifted morale when we arrived, we also added to the stress."

Denise Fraser remembers the 1995-96 tour of South Africa as particularly blighted. England's tour party grew from 20 to over 70 as families arrived for Christmas in Port Elizabeth and Cape Town. The team manager, Illingworth, was so incensed by the chaos that he blamed it for

England's defeat in the series – the Fifth Test, at Newlands, was the only one with a result.

"It was disastrous," Denise Fraser says. "We stayed in a city-centre hotel that had no facilities for the kids, and players had to give up their seats for us on the team bus. We felt unwelcome, especially when Illingworth blamed us for the defeat, which was unfair. I remember England winning in both Barbados and Melbourne just after the wives had come out."

According to Denise Fraser, the situation could have been avoided with a bit of foresight and planning. The board tacitly acknowledged as much after that tour, when they began to send Medha Laud, the international teams administrator and one of their most senior women employees, ahead of the team, to vet hotels for their suitability.

Families on tour need to be looked after. South Africa make their team bus available to ferry them to and from the game, though at different times from the players, or to the shops or sights. Bob Woolmer, South Africa's coach from 1994 to 1999, got the idea from Kerry Packer's World Series in the 1970s, where the wives were given a manager who organised shopping trips and sightseeing for them. "Players didn't have to worry about whether the wife was being looked after or not and could get on with playing cricket," Woolmer says. "You'd then meet up in the evening for supper like couples leading normal lives. It's simple and effective, but few teams bother."

> "We felt unwelcome," says Denise Fraser, "especially when Illingworth blamed us for the defeat"

South Africa's enlightened approach extends further, and players have been allowed to miss tours to spend time with their families. Jonty Rhodes skipped the tour of India in 2000, with the board's blessing, to be present at the birth of his first child – the first recorded case of a cricketer being given more than a day or two's paternity leave. In the past, leading England players would pick and choose, as Graham Gooch did when he missed the 1986-87 Ashes tour and half the next winter, but that is almost unheard-of now; after Alec Stewart, who chose not to tour India in 2001-02, mentioned that it would be nice to be around for the Christmas shopping, he faced criticism from the England management. Competition for places is keener and, Bangladesh apart, there are no longer opponents who allow you to get away with fielding a sub-strength side.

Australia's home series are much like a succession of tours, with every game bar one a flight – and maybe a time zone or two – away. And so the Australian board are proactive in getting the families involved. Wives and kids are always invited to the Melbourne and Sydney Tests, where they are put up in apartment-style suites with the players. When the men go overseas, there is usually a dedicated period of two weeks when their other halves can visit, but if a wife wants to come away for the entire trip, she can. On the 2001 Ashes tour, Steve Waugh rented a flat in London

CRICKET AND MARRIAGE: A FEW GLIMPSES

"Playing for England can seriously damage your wedlock." – Mike Walters, *Daily Mirror*, 2002

The record for the Test cricketer with the most marriages is believed to be shared by two players: Bill Edrich, the England batsman of the 1940s, and Hugh Tayfield, the South African off-spinner of the 1950s, with five each.

Dr Roy Park played his only Test for Australia at Melbourne in 1920-21, as a replacement for the injured Charles Macartney. Legend has it that Park's wife dropped her knitting as she faced his first ball, bent down to pick it up, and missed his entire Test career – he was bowled by Harry Howell, and never played again.

Leslie Hylton, a Jamaican fast bowler who played six Tests for West Indies in the 1930s, shot his wife Lurline dead in 1954 after she admitted to adultery. Hylton was sentenced to death and hanged in Jamaica in May 1955. Australia were touring the West Indies, and when the Jamaican opener J. K. Holt followed a run of low scores by dropping two catches in the Test at Bridgetown, a placard urged "Save Hylton, hang Holt."

Contrasting views from the mid-1970s on whether wives should go on tour are recorded in *A Century of Cricket Quotations*, by David Hopps. "It is no more the place for them than a trench on the Somme," wrote John Woodcock in *The Times*. "Wives and families must never tour again," said Keith Miller, the former Australian star (referring to England in 1974-75). But Alan Knott, one of England's greatest wicket-keepers, said in 1977: "I have played my best cricket when I have been with my wife."

In 1986, the lid was lifted on life in the England camp by a bestselling book – *Another Bloody Tour* by Frances Edmonds, wife of the slow left-armer Phil. As Frances's fame grew, the Australian wicket-keeper Tim Zoehrer reputedly said to Phil as he batted in a Test: "At least I have an identity. You're only Frances Edmonds' husband."

In November 1999, Steve Waugh's wife Lynette showed signs of going into labour in Sydney as Australia were rounding off a Test win over Pakistan in Brisbane. Quizzed about it, Waugh replied: "Once you guys stop asking questions, I'm in with a chance of getting home." His son Austin was born two days later. Back at Brisbane in November 2002, ahead of the Ashes, Steve was joined in the nets by Austin, now three. In between, while playing for Kent in 2002, Waugh broke off from an interview to sing "Happy Birthday" down the phone to his one-year-old daughter Lilian.

The first cricketer to be given proper paternity leave is thought to be Jonty Rhodes, who was allowed to miss South Africa's tour of India in 2000 (the one on which his friend Hansie Cronje was overheard by the police) for the birth of his first child. "Jonty has always kept his priorities straight," said his wife Kate. "God and myself before cricket."

In 2002, Australia's one-day captain Ricky Ponting, 27, married Rianna Cantor, a 23-year-old law student, in Sydney. His father, Graeme, said Rianna was "a very special woman" who had helped give Ricky the maturity to lead the national team. A hundred guests dined on oysters and Tasmanian champagne at a reception paid for by a women's magazine in exchange for exclusive access. The couple had met at a Melbourne restaurant on Boxing Day 2000. "I had no idea who he was," Rianna said. "I hate cricket with a passion."

for the summer as a base for his wife Lynette, then pregnant, and their two children. Waugh warmed up for the First Test by taking them all over to Disneyland Paris for a few days.

The paradox of all the time away from home is that the problems can start when it finishes. A player comes off an arduous tour, expecting to be greeted like a conquering king (or a defeated one), and may find that he no longer fits into the rhythms of home life. "You become so used to

Storming the barricades: Australia's players are joined by their families in the SCG pavilion as they celebrate a 3–0 series win over South Africa in January 2002. *Picture by Nick Wilson, Getty Images.*

their absence," Denise Fraser says, "that Angus would upset my routines when he got back. Suddenly there is another body in the equation and you have to get used to living together again.

"Let's face it, most players are a selfish breed who, if not too tired to help out around the house, bring their problems home with them. They are used to getting everything put on a plate and there were times when I couldn't wait to get him on his way again." Angus is now doing it all over again as cricket correspondent of *The Independent*. "He seems to be away more than ever."

Top-level sport is accompanied by self-analysis and narcissism, which do not lend themselves to the give-and-take required in most long-term relationships. The endless insecurity tends to propel most cricketers up the aisle by their early twenties, before life skills have been acquired. Some, like Imran Khan, David Gower and Mike Atherton, wait until their careers are all but over before starting a family, but they are unusual.

Darren Gough, who moved out of the family home last year into a bachelor pad in Milton Keynes, said he felt playing cricket for England was becoming a single man's game. Given that the international programme has doubled in the last decade, he may be right, but it would be sad if the game's player-power were further compromised. The hike in matches has come at the behest of television, which bankrolls the modern game. Until that is addressed, something the ICC has yet to do despite the pleas of senior Test captains like Nasser Hussain and Steve Waugh, cricket's biggest battle will be on the home front.

Derek Pringle, now with the Daily Telegraph, *played for England between 1982 and 1992. He is unmarried.*

Who has seen the most Test cricket?

BEING THERE

By TIM DE LISLE

If you want to know who has played the most Tests, the answer is easily found, whether on page 340 of this book or elsewhere. As we went to press, Steve Waugh was poised to pass Allan Border at the top. But what if you were wondering who has *seen* the most Tests?

We decided to work it out. Given the inflation in the international game, it was probably someone involved in a professional capacity over the past 30 years. We decided not to count watching on television, nor any Tests but official ones between male teams. During the winter, while professional cricket-watchers were scattered around the world, we fired off e-mails to a few likely suspects. Some didn't fancy the idea; others were too busy – watching cricket. But enough were intrigued for answers to trickle in.

Tony Cozier, voice of the Caribbean since time immemorial, came in at 266 Tests. Patrick Eagar, doyen of cricket photography, worked out the figure from his computer reference system ("what a dweeb"): he had watched, more closely than most, 265 Tests. Bill Frindall, *Test Match Special*'s Bearded Wonder since 1966, could be relied upon to keep his own score: 252 ("I have also watched an entire Women's Test in Adelaide").

D. J. Rutnagur, who specialises in India, knew he had started in 1951-52, but could only guess at his tally – "over 300". Graham Morris, the photographer, thought he was in the 300s too: "Sorry to be so vague, only I have never been a bedpost notcher. This is like being asked to do one's expenses for the last 20 years – without the obvious advantages."

The first definite 300 came from Qamar Ahmed, the Pakistan expert: he had just reached his triple-century, with a wave of the pen, at Cape Town. Christopher Martin-Jenkins did some sums ("1972–2002: all Tests in England") and came up with 302. It was the highest exact figure so far, but if even CMJ wasn't much above 300, who would be?

The same three names kept coming up: Richie Benaud, 72, a fine player who has been commentating ever since, in England and Australia, in one never-ending summer; E. W. (Jim) Swanton, whose cricket-writing career ran from the 1930s to his death, aged 92, in 2000; and John Woodcock, 76, today's elder statesman of cricket writing, who was the *Times* correspondent 1954–87 and still pops up there, radiating genial authority.

I rang Woodcock at home in Longparish. How many Tests had he been to? "About 400 for *The Times*, so it would be over 400 now. There was a time I think when I had watched half the Test matches ever played, or very nearly. It came and went very quickly, can't remember when."

His most recent Test had been at Lord's last summer, against India. The first had also been against India – 66 years earlier, in 1936. "I went up from my prep school."

What about Swanton, his old friend? "Oh, Jim's way behind. We discussed it once and he was on about 270. He never went to Pakistan, and I think he only saw two Tests in India – on Tony Lewis's tour [1972-73], when England won on Christmas Day. He did it in style of course: he was met by the Maharajah of Baroda's driver."

Who might be ahead? "Richie. I'd have thought he would be way ahead."

Richie Benaud, naturally, was in the commentary box, in Melbourne, for the Australia–England one-day finals. We sent a message via Ian Healy. For a couple of weeks, there was silence: Richie's signature tune.

One morning, an e-mail landed – "From: Richie Benaud". It was like getting a postcard from the Pope. "Sorry to be so long coming back to you, but it has all been slightly hectic out here." He had a figure, but needed to check it when he was back home in Sydney. "Cheers, Richie."

Next morning, another e-mail. "I hope the following might fit in with what you want, and I hope I've got the figures right…"

He had totted them all up, scrupulously: 63 Tests as a player, three as twelfth man, one on tour that he didn't play in (Lord's, 1961), one at the MCG in 1963-64, when he had broken a finger and covered it for the *Sydney Sun…* "68 in my playing time, 11 covered in the West Indies, 8 in South Africa, 5 in New Zealand, 223 in England, 171 in Australia, 0 in India, 0 in Pakistan, 0 in Sri Lanka, 0 in Zimbabwe, 0 in Bangladesh". He listed all the ducks as if he planned on breaking them.

In Australia and England together, he had seen 394 Tests, out of 733: more than half. His grand total was 486, a phenomenal figure. There had been 1,636 Tests in history, and Richie had been there for nearly a third of them, weighing his silences, composing his understatements, keeping his cool, distilling all that experience. Within a year, he should reach 500.

It made you wonder how he had sprung so swiftly from the top of one tree to the top of the next. Anticipating this, he had added an informal CV. "Did a three-week BBC television course devised for me by Tom Sloan at the end of the 1956 tour of England, then joined the team in Rome to fly to Pakistan and India for four Tests. On return to Australia, started as a journalist on Police Rounds and Sports at the *Sydney Sun*.

"Covered the five 1960 Tests E v SA for BBC Radio whilst still an Australian player. Captained the side to England in 1961, and BBC TV asked me back to cover E v WI 1963. Retired from cricket after the 1963-64 series A v SA. Didn't cover E v P and I in 1971. Didn't cover Tests during World Series Cricket [which he helped set up]. I watched Tests at the SCG 1946-47 to 1951-52, but haven't counted them as I was playing club cricket on the Saturdays and then was in the NSW team on tour."

"I thought Johnny Woodcock would have considerably more than the figure he has given you." A nice touch, deflecting the spotlight.

We had asked Benaud to name a favourite Test. "Three of them from different points of view." His reasons are in the panel below.

One last question. When was his first glimpse of Test cricket? "1946-47, Sydney, Second [Ashes] Test. Great disappointment, Lindwall had chicken-pox, but Ian Johnson and Colin McCool were there, taking nine of the ten wickets. Australia were 159 for four when Bradman, injured and ill, came out at No. 6 and put on 400 with Barnes. McCool took another five wickets to reinforce the thought that leg-spinners were great. I had just turned 16. Over 40,000 spectators the first three days." Australia won by an innings, but Benaud's recollection skips that to focus on the fans. He always was on our side.

Richie Benaud's favourite Tests...

From a personal point of view: England v Australia, Old Trafford, 1961. "Otherwise life might have been very different." Bowling his leg-breaks round the wicket into the rough, he took five for 12 off 25 balls on the last afternoon, to turn the match and help regain the Ashes.

As a game: Australia v West Indies, Brisbane, 1960-61 – the Tied Test. "Frank Worrell was at Sydney airport on his way to Perth to join his team. He had been delayed by a seafood allergy and Alan Barnes, the board secretary, phoned me at the *Sun* to say his plane was about to land and perhaps I might want to interview him. We had a good chat and as he was turning to walk to the plane I said, 'I hope it's a great series.' He came back, smiled and replied, 'Well, we'll have a lot of fun anyway.'

"Then there was the matter of Bradman asking permission to speak at our team meeting the night before the game. I checked with the players and told him that was fine. His was a very short address, but of extreme importance and unique in Australian cricket. It was a personal message to the effect that we had the chance to make this one of the greatest summers in Australian history, after some ordinary ones. He and his co-selectors, Jack Ryder and Dudley Seddon, would look in kindly fashion on players who had as their priority the entertainment of the people paying at the turnstiles. And in less kindly fashion on those who didn't.

"This fitted in with our pre-series planning, but it was comforting to know that the selectors were thinking that way and by the time the motorcade farewell had taken place in Melbourne after the final Test, the face of cricket had been changed for ever in Australia."

From the commentary box: England v Australia, Headingley, 1981. "The sheer drama of it all. Botham sacked, Brearley recalled, England following on and then winning, booking out of their hotel a day early, Ladbrokes' 500–1, England 221 for their last three wickets, Botham's 149, Willis eight for 43. A commentator's dream match for Jim Laker and me."

For a multimedia feature on the Tied Test, go to www.wisden.com/tiedtest/.

... and his tips for aspiring commentators

"Everyone should develop a distinctive style, but a few pieces of advice might be:
Put your brain into gear before opening your mouth.
Never say "we" if referring to a team.
Discipline is essential; fierce concentration is needed at all times.

"Then try to avoid allowing past your lips: *"Of course"*... *"As you can see on the screen"*... *"You know..."* or *" I tell you what"*, *"That's a tragedy..."* or *"a disaster..."*. (The *Titanic* was a tragedy, the Ethiopian drought a disaster, but neither bears any relation to a dropped catch.)

"Above all: when commentating, don't take yourself too seriously, and have fun."

Tyrant and technician, thug and sculptor, India's deliverance... Tendulkar at 30

BATTING FOR A BILLION

By ROHIT BRIJNATH

Sachin Ramesh Tendulkar is now 30, he has a wife and two children, his face is wreathed in a goatee and faintly lined by time and travel, but to the world, and to India in particular, he is still a boy wonder. Thirteen years and 105 Tests have passed since he first took guard at Karachi in November 1989, but the poet's son with the almost-falsetto voice and the supremely dignified manner continues to write an elegant, belligerent and unprecedented history. When he walks to the crease – one eye occasionally turning to the sun, one hand hitching up his box – it is cricket's equivalent of Michelangelo ascending a ladder towards the ceiling of the Sistine Chapel. He is short, 5ft 4in, and his stance is a study in stillness, his body finely balanced, his muscles relaxed. His mind has already mapped the geography of the field: as the ball is bowled, rarely does tension or indecision impede the instructions from brain to body. Only sometimes, so it seems, will he silently struggle within, caught between the responsibility he carries for his team and the force of his natural attacking instincts.

Then he plays. He is both tyrant and technician, batting with a thug's ferocity and a sculptor's finesse, though sometimes he fails to strike the necessary balance between the two. In his room, he occasionally takes one last look at his technique in front of the mirror; on the field, most days, we see that genius reflected.

He will uppercut the ball gleefully for six with muscle, and next ball, in a perfect marriage of feet and bat and judgment of length, slide it softly past the bowler for four. He will generously shoulder arms and allow the ball to pass him as if it is not worthy of being struck, then explode into a flurry of shot-making that has the scoreboard ticking over like a slot machine. In full cry, his bat looks wider than the laws allow, though he hardly needs its full extent: as Greg Chappell once put it, he would do well batting with a single stump, like Bradman in the backyard.

The crowd is a blur, the roar a hum, for he is too busy, as he said years ago, "reading the bowler's mind", or, better still, manufacturing shots that "compel the bowlers" to bowl where he wants them to. It is not so much

By a street: the Australian captain Ricky Ponting lifts the World Cup, Johannesburg, March 23.
Picture by Patrick Eagar.

Man of the tournament: Sachin Tendulkar at the World Cup. *Picture by Tom Shaw, Getty Images.*

Surprise packet of the tournament: Andy Bichel. *Picture by Stu Forster, Getty Images.*

Rainbow nations: the 14 World Cup squads gather in Cape Town harbour. *Picture by Touchline Photo, Getty Images.*

Fallen star: Shane Warne after testing positive for a banned substance. *Picture by Getty Images.*

Transport of delight: England's game against Otago at Queenstown beside the Remarkables mountain range, March 2002. *Picture by Tom Shaw, Getty Images.*

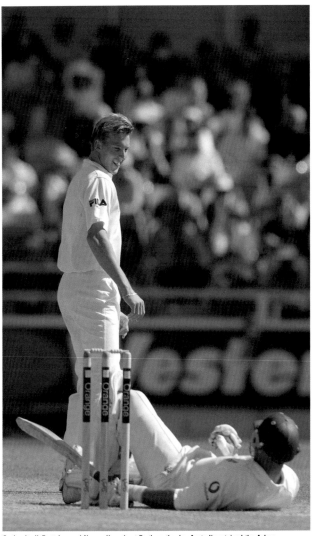

Saying it all: Brett Lee and Nasser Hussain at Perth on the day Australia retained the Ashes.
Picture by Patrick Eagar.

If you can stand the heat: club cricketers in Cessnock, north of Sydney, play on as a bushfire rages. *Picture by Darren Pateman, Newcastle Herald.*

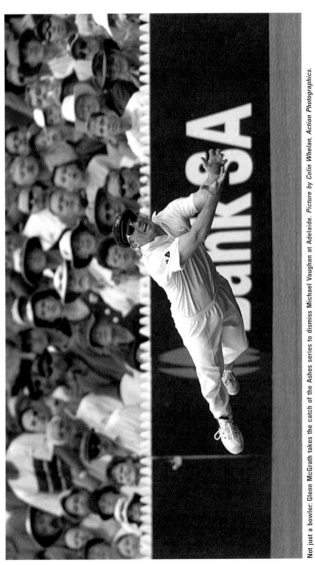

Not just a bowler: Glenn McGrath takes the catch of the Ashes series to dismiss Michael Vaughan at Adelaide. *Picture by Colin Whelan, Action Photographics.*

Instant whip: Ally Brown of Surrey after making 268 against Glamorgan – in a one-day match. *Picture by Phil Walters. EMPICS.*

Five Cricketers of the Year: Michael Vaughan drives Kumble at Lord's. *Picture by Patrick Eagar.*

Five Cricketers of the Year: Matthew Hayden. *Picture by Philip Brown.*

Five Cricketers of the Year: Adam Hollioake reaches a 52-ball century at Hove. *Picture by Graham Morris*.

Five Cricketers of the Year: Nasser Hussain, England's engine. *Picture by Graham Morris.*

Five Cricketers of the Year: Shaun Pollock – seven years of excellence. *Picture by Graham Morris.*

that there are shots he does not have; it is merely that he has chosen not to play them.

Many things are unique to Tendulkar, and most of all the fact that the man has stayed faithful to the gifts he was given as a boy. Once, according to a possibly apocryphal story, a junior Indian team on tour was awakened by a thumping on the roof. On investigation, it was Tendulkar lost in some midnight practice.

Later, too, he took little for granted. When Shane Warne toured India, Tendulkar went into the nets, scuffed the pitch on the leg side and had a spinner pitch it there; before India toured Australia, Tendulkar had the seamers deliver the ball from closer to his end, artificially manufacturing the pace and bounce he expected to face. The net has remained his temple. Asked about this once, he was gently annoyed that people felt it all came so naturally to him, thus discounting how disciplined his journey had been: his gifts, he explained, were oiled with sweat.

He will never be the greatest batsman in history: that seat is taken. But as much as Donald Bradman's Test average (99.94) outstrips Tendulkar's (57.58), the gap diminishes substantially when other factors are taken into account. Tendulkar travels more in a year than Bradman did in a decade; he has had to manage the varying conditions of 49 Test grounds, to

Most international centuries

Sachin Tendulkar holds a number of records, but there is one list he dominates in a Bradman-like way: of those with most international hundreds – lumping both forms of the game together – Tendulkar comes top by a mile. He has 65, while no one else has 40. The closest rival currently playing international cricket is Brian Lara with 34. To be very high on this table you have to open in one-day cricket, but you still have to do it well: for comparison, look at Sunil Gavaskar. No Englishman appears on the list; Graham Gooch is highest, with 28 international hundreds.

One-day master: Tendulkar as England first saw him, aged 17, in 1990

		100s in Tests	100s in ODIs
65	S. R. Tendulkar (I)	31 in 105	34 in 314
38	M. E. Waugh (A)	20 in 128	18 in 244
35	S. M. Gavaskar (I)	34 in 125	1 in 108
35	I. V. A. Richards (WI)	24 in 121	11 in 187
35	D. L. Haynes (WI)	18 in 116	17 in 238
34	B. C. Lara (WI)	18 in 90	16 in 209
32	S. R. Waugh (A)	29 in 156	3 in 325
31	Javed Miandad (P)	23 in 124	8 in 233
31	P. A. de Silva (SL)	20 in 93	11 in 308
31	Saeed Anwar (P)	11 in 55	20 in 247
31	S. C. Ganguly (I)	9 in 67	22 in 229
30	C. G. Greenidge (WI)	19 in 108	11 in 128
30	A. R. Border (A)	27 in 156	3 in 273
29	D. G. Bradman (A)	29 in 52	–
29	M. Azharuddin (I)	22 in 99	7 in 334
29	G. Kirsten (SA)	16 in 89	13 in 185

To March 23, 2003.

Bradman's ten; he has already played twice as many Tests as Bradman, and over 300 one-day games, nearly all of them under the unrelenting scrutiny of television. And whereas Bradman had to cope with the expectations of a small populace, not given to idolatry, in an age of restraint, Tendulkar must play god to one billion expectant worshippers.

Steve Waugh has said, "You take Bradman away and he is next up, I reckon," though those who swear by Vivian Richards are not completely convinced. Still, his peers – Brian Lara in particular – have been pushed aside by sheer weight of consistent numbers. Tendulkar has 32 Test centuries to Lara's 18; by the end of the World Cup, he had 34 one-day centuries, with his nearest rival his captain, Sourav Ganguly, on 22. But one statistic will please more than most. Starting when he was 20, in 1993, his Test averages for each calendar year read like this: 91.42 (8 Tests), 70 (7), 29 (3), 41.53 (8), 62.50 (12), 80.87 (5), 68 (10), 63.88 (6), 62.69 (10), 55.68 (16). The year when he averaged 29, he had only two completed innings. Otherwise, in the worst of years, his average is 41 – the usual benchmark of a very good player. This, better than anything, reflects the unwavering purity of his purpose.

When Tendulkar plays, India stills. He is deliverance

He has not really known bad years, has never woken to a slump, though in the West Indies in 2002 he had successive Test scores of 0, 0, 8, 0, which – as if to prove the point – was enough to make eyebrows rise in astonishment. So true has his form been that it is easy to overlook the distinctive burdens he has carried. Wasim Akram once suggested that when Tendulkar is out, heads droop in the Indian dressing-room. Rarely has Tendulkar had the comfort of knowing that the men who follow him are as certain in rising to a challenge.

More demanding is his nation, for when Tendulkar plays, India stills, it quietens, till it is almost possible to hear a collective exhalation with every shot. In a land where governments stutter, the economy stagnates and life itself is an enduring struggle against failure, he is deliverance. For most of a billion people, unmoved by any other sport, he is escape as much as he is hope, standing like some solitary national advertisement of success. Tendulkar is not allowed to fail.

His genius has caged him, for he cannot walk any street without sparking a riot, nor sit unmolested in any restaurant. That he must indulge his passion for cars by driving through Mumbai's deserted streets in the hours before dawn points to the absurdity of his existence. It is easier written than lived. But he finds no refuge in rages or sulks; his serenity is startling for a man surrounded by an audience prostrated in hysterical worship. It points to a gift of temperament but also to his balance as a man. When a spectator invaded the field and escorted him off the ground at Lord's in 2002, he did not flinch or fuss, brandish his bat or bellow, but coolly walked on, the very picture of a warrior monk. Later, he said the fellow meant no harm.

It may well be that the sight of Glenn McGrath at the other end does not offer so much a threat as relief. If Tendulkar is India's escape, it may well be that the crease is his escape, the place where he finds his full expression. Only once, under persistent interrogation, did he admit: "People expect too much of me, a hundred every innings. They call and say, 'you scored a hundred in Kanpur, so why not in Delhi?'. They must accept my failures."

And there have been a few. His career has been marked by two curious blemishes. In 105 Tests, he has won only nine match awards, and although there are mitigating factors – India have mostly been abysmal abroad, as tradition dictates, and their spinners have claimed most of the honours at home – it is still an incongruously low number. It is linked to a more damning charge, that his batting, in contrast to Lara's, has wrought too few victories. It suggests that his beauty is often ineffectual, painting

His hundredth Test: Tendulkar at The Oval, September 2002. *Picture by Patrick Eagar*

masterpieces in isolation, and that he is apt to leave more of a memory than an impact. Two matches are repeatedly cited as evidence: Barbados, March 1997, when he made four on a dicey wicket as India failed to chase 120 for a historic win; and Chennai, January 1999, when he made a stirring 136 against Pakistan, chasing 271, but then played a shot of poor discipline and fell with just 17 needed.

He has said, "I have been disappointed with myself... I have to learn to finish Tests," and it must eat at his stomach like an acid. This is the boy who, on his first tour of Pakistan, lost a set of tennis to Sanjay Manjrekar and then pleaded with him to play on to salvage his honour. He is a proud man, but too graceful also to state the obvious. Many of his 31 Test centuries have either set up wins or fended off defeat.

In March 1998, in Chennai, Australia were 71 ahead of India on first innings, and as Tendulkar explained then: "They had a lead and I said this will be the innings of a player's life. Because 75-plus by any player would be a big score in the second innings and would help us win the game."

In a quiet moment, the Indian coach, Anshuman Gaekwad, corralled Tendulkar and told him, "I want you to score." Tendulkar, who was still only 24, replied: "I will get it for you, don't worry." He scored 155 and India won the Test.

Still, if we are intent on nailing Tendulkar, then we must crucify his team as well. If he has failed us, they have failed him, specifically in their willingness to turn an ensemble piece into a one-man show. Perhaps we should acknowledge too that our own expectations distort the picture. To indict him for getting out for 136 against Pakistan is to disregard the fact that the rest of the team contributed 86 runs between them, and 52 of those came from Nayan Mongia. Similarly, if we are quick to remember Tendulkar's cheap dismissal in Barbados in the second innings, we are quicker to forget that, in a low-scoring match, he had already made a valiant 92.

He stands now, closer to the end of his career than the beginning, with 8,811 Test runs, sixth on the all-time list. The only current player ahead of him is Steve Waugh, who is nearing retirement. Barring catastrophe, Tendulkar will surpass Allan Border's 11,174 with some ease; Sunil Gavaskar's record 34 centuries will be outstripped as well. In the one-day game, Tendulkar already stands alone and untouchable at the summit – Border and Gavaskar rolled into one, with more than 12,000 runs, while nobody else has 10,000, and 34 centuries. He even has a hundred wickets.

In the Test arena, Bradman will never be equalled. In Tests and one-dayers together, the reality of international cricket today, Sachin Ramesh Tendulkar will take some catching, too.

Rohit Brijnath, former sports editor of India Today *magazine, is now a freelance writer in Melbourne. He has interviewed Tendulkar several times.*

**Fifty years ago, television reached the people,
and England won back the Ashes with perhaps
their best XI ever**

ON TOP OF THE WORLD

By STEVEN LYNCH

There was something special about 1953. In England, things were finally looking up after the grim war years and the struggle to put matters on an even keel afterwards. Rationing was on the way out, it was no longer obligatory to wear a hat in public at all times, and pop charts and flighty fashions were tiptoeing their way in. The mood was epitomised by a youthful new sovereign – the youngest since Victoria in 1837. Queen Elizabeth II, aged 25 on her accession, was crowned at Westminster Abbey on June 2, 1953. Within a month she was meeting 22 of her subjects, English and Australian, in front of the Lord's pavilion.

In an age of uncomplicated national pride, there were plenty of reasons to be proud of Britain. The day before the Coronation it was announced that a British-led expedition had become the first to climb Everest. At Epsom, Gordon Richards, the master jockey, won the Derby at his 27th attempt. At Wembley, Stanley Matthews jinked his way to an FA Cup-winner's medal at last, in a classic final. At Cambridge, Francis Crick and James Watson were breaking the code of human life with their paper on DNA.

Some things don't change, though. An American won Wimbledon – Vic Seixas, whose movie-star looks won him almost as many fans as his cross-court volleys won rallies. Then, as now, England hadn't held the Ashes for a dismally long time – 19 years – and as usual these days the only Test they won against Australia in 1953 was the fifth and final one. But since England had taken the precaution of drawing the previous four games, this was cause for celebration rather than consolation. The Ashes, surrendered in 1934 in the series after Bodyline, were back home at last. England would remain on top of the Test tree for most of the 1950s.

And for the first time ever, large numbers of their supporters would be able to see them in action. The 1953 Ashes were the first Test series watched by a significant number of people on television. The first TVs were very expensive and largely confined to rich homes, but many British households splashed out on their first set in 1953 to watch the Coronation

"My signature tune": Trevor Bailey's forward defensive. *Right:* A pair of legends – Len Hutton and Alec Bedser lead England out for the decisive Oval Test. *Pictures by Getty Images.*

(in Australia, the explosion had to wait a little longer, for the 1956 Olympics in Melbourne). In the nation's great love affair with the television, 1953 was the first date. Apparently my aunts and uncles, and most of the neighbours too, sat down to watch the Queen being crowned on the sparkling new set with its giant wooden cabinet and tiny grey screen. My grandfather had bought it at a knockdown price from the Ideal Home Exhibition, where he was working at the time.

And after all the pageantry and panoply, and in between potter's-wheel interludes and playful-kitten intermissions, ordinary people sat spellbound at the exploits of Hutton and Bedser, Lindwall and Miller, Bailey and Watson. It was such early days in the relationship between the game and the screen that players barely noticed. "I wasn't conscious of that," says Trevor Bailey, England's key all-rounder in that series and many more in the 1950s. "To a degree there was more recognition, yes, but I put it down to everyone being so interested in the series. This was England not long after the war, remember – there weren't many other distractions, and cricket was very popular. On the last day at The Oval there was a big and enthusiastic crowd."

Fred Trueman, called up for the first of many jousts with the Aussies for the decider at The Oval, also has vivid memories of that far-off finale. He told *Wisden Cricket Monthly* in 2003: "On the fourth morning we

"It's the Ashes, England have won the Ashes!": the famous image of the crowd swarming round Denis Compton and Bill Edrich at The Oval. *Picture by Getty Images.*

needed 94 to win. I came down to the ground from the Great Western at Paddington with Leonard [Hutton, the England captain]. Outside there was already an excited throng, and I remember like it was yesterday seeing across the road a newspaper placard with a picture of the urn and in great big type the simple three words, 'LEN – THEY'RE OURS!'"

"It was the most satisfactory game I'd ever played in," says Bailey, who turns 80 at the end of 2003 but retains the snappy, decisive bark that characterised his radio summaries for *Test Match Special*. "But it was a very close series, an intriguing battle. We had the better of two draws, and they had the better of the other two. We should probably have won the First Test and the Third, and they looked likely to win the Second and the Fourth. But there was a lot of rain about."

Indeed there was. England were well placed in the First Test at Trent Bridge, after Alec Bedser's 14 wickets had set up a modest target of 229. Hutton, England's anchor since 1938, was still there, but rain washed out all the fourth day and most of the fifth – and when play did resume, after tea on the final day, there was insufficient time for a result. Peter West wrote of Bedser's display of medium-fast bowling: "This was the sublime performance in all his glowing career... I can recall his bowling only one bad ball in the whole match."

At Lord's, Australia held the upper hand after centuries from their puckish captain, Lindsay Hassett – his second of the series – and Keith Miller, whose flickback of a skein of unruly hair predated Shoaib Akhtar's by half a century. By the close on the fourth day, England were floundering at 20 for three, chasing 343, and it might have been worse if Ray Lindwall at short leg had clung on to either of two sharp chances from Willie Watson in the last over of the day. Watson survived, and combined with Bailey in an epic final-day stand which lasted more than four hours to deny Australia victory. Bailey, whose previous-best against Australia was only 15, made 71 in 257 minutes. "I enjoyed that," he says with relish. *Wisden* noted that he played "a deadbat pendulum stroke to every ball on his wicket". It defined Bailey's career. A few years earlier, *Wisden* had called him an attractive strokemaker, but now… "I became known as The Barnacle, with the forward-defensive my signature tune."

That partnership remained Watson's finest hour. A slight left-hander from Yorkshire, he would be acclaimed these days as a sporting superstar – he also played football for England, and had been in the squad for the 1950 World Cup, when England famously lost to the United States, but didn't actually play. Long after, he would remember going up to Bailey during their stand and asking whether they should go for the runs; 343, in those days, was unthinkable unless you had Bradman in your team. "Trevor just turned his back on me and walked away." Watson seemed set for a long run in the side, but England's selectors, then as now, could be capricious: he fell from favour before the end of the series, and was not at The Oval to see the victory he had made possible.

England were back on top in the Third Test at Old Trafford, and this time it was the Australians' turn to be saved by the rain. When Neil Harvey was bothered by water on the knee, Brian Johnston observed that it was hardly surprising. The total playing time was restricted to a shade under 14 hours, but the last part was action-packed. Johnny Wardle, bowling the left-arm chinamen that his county, Yorkshire, frowned upon as too frivolous for Championship cricket, reduced Australia to 35 for eight before time ran out.

England managed only 142 off 96 overs on the first day of the Fourth Test at Headingley, watched by those Bodyline rivals Don Bradman and Douglas Jardine, sitting "cheek by jowl" in the press box, according to Jack Fingleton in his excellent book *The Ashes Crown the Year*. Australia grabbed the upper hand with a lead of 99, but again ran into a stone wall named Bailey. This time he made 38 in 262 minutes. "We were fighting hard to save the game again," Bailey remembers. "I was in with Jim Laker, and two minutes before lunch I called him over and said I was going to appeal against the light. He said 'But the sun's out,' and that's what the umpires said too – but by the time they'd talked about it, there wasn't time for another over and we all trooped off for lunch."

As if his innings wasn't enough, Bailey deliberately bowled down the leg side as Australia vainly chased a target of 177 in 115 minutes. This ensured it was all square going into the final Test, which was extended to six days to maximise the chances of a result.

At The Oval, Bedser pounded in for three more wickets, to take his series tally to an amazing 39, most of them greeted by a handshake, a hitch of his heavy flannels, and a hike back to the mark to prepare for the next victim. That walk was child's play for a man used to a twice-daily trudge of over a mile between his home and Woking station for the train-ride to The Oval.

Hutton and Bailey ground out a narrow lead before Jim Laker and Tony Lock, on their home turf, bowled Australia out for 162. It wouldn't have been as many but for a robust 49 from Ron Archer, one of a trio of young all-rounders in the Australian party. Richie Benaud and Alan Davidson were the others, and are better remembered now, but Archer was equally promising. Tall and strong, he was only 19 in 1953, but the glittering career that beckoned was restricted to 19 Tests by back trouble and a serious knee injury.

England were left needing 132 to regain the Ashes – just enough to enable a hiccough or two. There was about an hour's play remaining on the third day, and England lost Hutton to an unnecessary run-out – John Arlott recalled that it was "an added anxiety" for a tense crowd. "The prospect of winning the Ashes after 19 years has been so distant," he said, "that we have become like some small boy who has looked forward to a special treat for so long that he fears something will happen to stop it – or is himself sick with excitement so that he cannot enjoy it." But next day England made light of the target, eventually reaching it at 2.55. The last couple of balls became some of the most-screened film in cricket – for years the BBC used the footage of Denis Compton pulling Arthur Morris to the boundary for its trade-test transmissions, complete with an ecstatic Brian Johnston yelling "It's the Ashes!"

The crowds were huge, and expectant – and they went away happy in the end. But, as Bailey argues, "I've always thought that if Hassett had gambled and put us in at The Oval then they might have won. But he batted instead, and the ball moved about a bit on the first day, then it turned later on. They had left both of their spinners out, but we had Laker and Lock. Actually I always had my doubts about Hassett as a tactician. His players adored him – he was one of the boys, whereas his predecessor Don Bradman was of a different generation – but tactically he wasn't as strong or as sharp as Bradman. Bradman was especially good after the war, I think. He was still scoring an awful lot of runs, and he was like a god to the younger players. In 1948, England were short of fast bowlers and I thought I had a chance. I was at Cambridge University at the time but I went down specially to play for Essex against the Australians in May. That was the day they made 721 at Southend – and it was then I realised that I was never going to be an out-and-out fast bowler, not once I'd seen people like Lindwall and Miller. I did get Bradman out once, though. It was a long-hop, as I recall."

England's XI from The Oval in 1953 has a good claim to being their best ever. Stuffed with all-time greats, the side was Len Hutton, Bill Edrich, Tom Graveney, Denis Compton, Peter May, Trevor Bailey, Godfrey

The team that won back the Ashes at The Oval in 1953 – England's best-ever? *Standing:* Trevor Bailey, Peter May, Tom Graveney, Jim Laker, Tony Lock, Johnny Wardle (twelfth man), Fred Trueman. *Seated:* Bill Edrich, Alec Bedser, Len Hutton (*captain*), Denis Compton, Godfrey Evans. *Picture by Getty Images.*

Evans, Jim Laker, Alec Bedser, Tony Lock and Fred Trueman, with Johnny Wardle huffing and puffing about the indignity of being made twelfth man.

They not only had formidable Test careers but remained closely involved with cricket long after retiring. There were no forgotten men as there are in most teams, such as their opponents (remember Graeme Hole, or Jim de Courcy?) and the Ray Wilsons and Roger Hunts of England's 1966 football World Cup winners. Bedser and May both became chairman of the Test selectors, and Hutton was a selector too for a time. Compton juggled a chaotic life of commentaries, endorsements and missed engagements – often with his lifelong soulmate Edrich. Laker added northern nous to the television commentary box, along with an inability to pronounce the "g" in words like "batting" and "innings" that drove retired schoolmasters in Eastbourne to distraction. Graveney also had a longish career at the microphone with his catchphrase "really speaking". Bailey and Trueman were trenchant radio summarisers for years, stressing the need for line and length to generations of cricket-lovers. Lock moved to Australia to prolong his playing career, led Western Australia to the Sheffield Shield title, and became a coach there. Evans, complete with improbably large sideburns, set the cricket odds for bookmakers in the days before that assumed sinister overtones.

John Woodcock, the veteran *Times* correspondent and former *Wisden* editor, is better placed than most to comment on just how exceptional this team was. "It was certainly as good a side as England have fielded in my time," he says. "It's a better team than those that won the Ashes in Australia in 1970-71 and 1986-87, and as well balanced as the one that won in 1954-55. The side that won easily in Australia in 1928-29 was obviously a very good one, and there's always talk of the team from 1902 that had 11 century-makers in it – but even I'm not old enough to have seen them. Comparisons between different eras are awfully difficult, but you have to go by how many great players there are in each team, and there were plenty in that 1953 side."

Bailey is inclined to agree. "By 1953 Bradman had retired, and although Australia still had probably the better team, there wasn't much in it. We had Hutton and Compton, who were world-class batsmen, a world-class medium-pacer in Bedser, and Evans was the best wicket-keeper around. We had Laker and Lock, who were a real handful on a dodgy pitch, and young batsmen like May and Graveney. For the final Test of 1953 we also had a genuine fast bowler in Fred, who was certainly a lot quicker than Alec and myself. We had a good side, we were just coming to the top – and we stayed there until the end of the 1950s."

It wasn't all praise, though. Hutton's reign as captain is remembered now for slow scoring, and over-rates that were considered funereal for the time. England may have achieved world domination for the rest of the decade, but they were often unappetising to watch. Freddie Brown, chairman of selectors in 1953, took the unusual step of attacking his own team: in the following year's *Wisden*, he wrote that he had found "an almost unanimous disquiet about the lack of attack in the England batting."

Brown pointed out that England had scored at 33 runs per 100 balls in the series, as against Australia's 44. The difference was most marked in the Fourth Test at Headingley, where England, trying to save the game, pottered about at a strike-rate of 24 to Australia's 56. However, Woodcock isn't sure about the near-unanimity: "I don't remember too much fuss being made at the time. If England batted slowly, which I dare say they did at times, it was because it was important that they did so in order to win, and I think they can be forgiven for that."

The slow batting, and all the rain, mean that 1953 cannot be ranked as the best Ashes series of them all. That remains a toss-up between 1894-95, 1902 and 1981. But this one did signal a shift in power, from Australia to England, and defined the style of the decade. There were more soggy draws than rumbustious run-chases.

Bailey is unequivocal. "Nobody seemed terribly bothered about it at the time. We were winning. We got the result, that's what it was all about."

Steven Lynch is editor of Wisden Online. *He is working on a book of interviews with Wimbledon champions of the 1950s.*

How interactive statistics have changed cricket fandom

NO ANORAK REQUIRED

By CHRIS RYAN

When Romeo laid eyes on Juliet he gushed: "I ne'er saw true beauty till this night." A million cricket nuts felt much the same way the first time they logged on to StatsGuru on CricInfo. Hearts skipped. Pulses danced. Minds boggled. An arcane world – a world of averages, aggregates and algorithms – suddenly became accessible. The impossible was possible.

The love affair between cricket and statistics dates back almost as far as the Capulets and Montagues. Nowhere else are stats so expressive. A batting average tells you a batsman's mean score, but it hints at so much more – his flourishes and frailties, likes and dislikes, willpower, greed and a thousand other qualities. That's why old men's bookshelves sag under the weight of dusty volumes. It's why boys – and girls – study them, like learner drivers poring over the *Highway Code*.

Mostly, though, it is a one-way relationship. Like thunder and rain, statistics are something that come down from on high. Something the average fan has no control over. We recite and rejoice in them but, unless you are Bill Frindall or Gordon Vince, you do not actually create them.

Until now. The advent in the past three years of interactive statistical search engines is the biggest revolution in cricket fandom since colour television. Just as TV transported cricket into people's living-rooms, StatsGuru and the Wisden Wizard have brought cricket statistics into people's bedrooms and kitchens. When the late B. J. Wakley compiled the statistical masterwork *Bradman the Great* (1959), it took him the best part of ten years. Now he could do it in three days.

The only limit is your imagination. Ever wondered which Test batsman scored the highest percentage of his team's runs over a career? Once, you would have had to pick a player, sift through a trolley-load of books, and log his team's total in every innings of every Test he played, then add all those totals together (Tally A) before totalling what he scored off his own bat (Tally B). Then you would divide Tally B by Tally A and multiply by 100. You would do that for every likely suspect in Test history and, to double-check, you would do it again. Estimated time? Three months.

Now you can do it in three afternoons. Pick a player – let's say Brian Lara – go to the Wisden Wizard and click on "team records, Tests". Then type: *Team* West Indies; *Where match involves* B. C. Lara; *Sort by* runs total. Click on "submit query". Seconds later, you have Tally A. Simply repeat the process for the likely suspects, and hey presto…

HIGHEST PERCENTAGE OF TEAM'S RUNS IN TESTS

%		Tests	Runs
24.28	D. G. Bradman (A)	52	6,996
21.39	G. A. Headley (WI)	22	2,190
18.41	**B. C. Lara (WI)**	**90**	**7,572**
18.13	L. Hutton (E)	79	6,971
18.08	**M. W. Goodwin (Z)**	**19**	**1,414**
17.91	J. B. Hobbs (E)	61	5,410
17.77	A. D. Nourse (SA)	34	2,960
17.36	E. D. Weekes (WI)	48	4,455
17.20	B. Mitchell (SA)	42	3,471
17.12	H. Sutcliffe (E)	54	4,555
16.88	**S. R. Tendulkar (I)**	**105**	**8,811**
16.87	B. Sutcliffe (NZ)	42	2,727
16.82	**Habibul Bashar (B)**	**17**	**1,039**

Qualification: 15 Tests to March 2003.

Or perhaps you noticed that Matthew Hayden often lets Justin Langer take the business end first-up. And it set you wondering: is Hayden a pushover when he faces the first ball? Log on to the Wizard, enter the player analysis section, and moments later you could come up with this:

TEST OPENERS WITH A FONDNESS FOR THE NON-STRIKER'S END…

	Batting at No. 1		Batting at No. 2		Difference
	Avge	Innings	Avge	Innings	
M. C. Cowdrey (E)	7.25	4	46.81	34	39.56
S. M. Gavaskar (I)	48.08	186	78.28	17	30.20
E. J. Barlow (SA)	23.22	9	50.75	43	27.53
A. C. MacLaren (E)	32.22	32	59.71	8	27.49
M. L. Hayden (A)	**30.84**	**15**	**57.34**	**49**	**26.50**
G. T. Dowling (NZ)	25.69	53	50.93	18	25.24
C. P. S. Chauhan (I)	10.71	7	34.37	60	23.66
N. J. Contractor (I)	15.00	9	36.41	39	21.41
C. J. Tavaré (E)	18.09	12	38.35	21	20.26
G. W. Flower (Z)	**22.05**	**52**	**41.60**	**32**	**19.55**

… AND THOSE WHO WOULD RATHER FACE

	Batting at No. 1		Batting at No. 2		Difference
	Avge	Innings	Avge	Innings	
W. H. Ponsford (A)	136.00	4	44.36	27	91.64
J. B. Stollmeyer (WI)	80.20	6	37.78	49	42.42
Saeed Anwar (P)	**50.17**	**78**	**18.00**	**8**	**32.17**
K. C. Wessels (A/SA)	46.51	29	15.87	8	30.64
W. Rhodes (E)	63.75	4	33.72	39	30.03
C. C. Hunte (WI)	47.69	71	20.71	7	26.98
B. C. Broad (E)	53.84	21	27.73	23	26.11
A. R. Morris (A)	65.00	12	42.31	64	22.69
Sadiq Mohammad (P)	46.23	31	26.65	41	19.58
J. B. Hobbs (E)	58.03	88	39.12	9	18.91

Qualification: opened in 30 innings, at least four in each position, to March 2003.

The man we have to thank for all this is a 27-year-old from Geelong, Victoria. He always had a head for numbers and fell for cricket during the summer of 1983-84 when, bedridden with the measles, he had little choice but to lie back and watch Kim Hughes's Australian side beat Imran Khan's Pakistanis. It was a landmark summer that witnessed the departure of three iconic Australians – Dennis Lillee, Greg Chappell and Rod Marsh – and the arrival of another, far less famous but no less significant.

Travis Basevi was 19 when he started volunteering at CricInfo, then a fledgling, amateurish operation destined to become the world's biggest single-sport website. Four years on, he was a paid employee. In March 2000, he moved from Sydney to CricInfo's UK headquarters – and StatsGuru went from pipe dream to work in progress.

"CricInfo had always wanted something like it," Basevi explains, "but everyone was flat out just trying to tread water." StatsGuru took six months to develop before hitting computer screens in mid-2000. The ideas were largely his own. "It just came from being a cricket fan and knowing what kind of things I'd like to see."

By that time CricInfo already had plenty going for it: a bulging database of seemingly endless scorecards, plus live ball-by-ball coverage of every game everywhere. But StatsGuru was something else. Its powers seemed frightening, almost voyeuristic. In an instant it could scan its database and dredge up stats you had never contemplated, let alone computed. Had you, in the past, wanted to calculate the number of match awards a player had, you had to plough through old Almanacks until your thumbs were blacker than the MCG sightscreen. With StatsGuru it became a doddle: type a player's name and tick the box marked "match awards list".

MOST INTERNATIONAL MATCH AWARDS

		Tests	ODIs
56	S. R. Tendulkar (I)	9	47
42	P. A. de Silva (SL)	11	31
41	I. V. A. Richards (WI)	10	31
39	Wasim Akram (P)	17	22
37	S. T. Jayasuriya (SL)	3	34
36	B. C. Lara (WI)	8	28
33	S. R. Waugh (A)	13	20
31	S. C. Ganguly (I)	3	28
30	Saeed Anwar (P)	2	28
	D. L. Haynes (WI)	5	25
29	J. H. Kallis (SA)	10	19
	A. Ranatunga (SL)	5	24

To March 23, 2003 (the end of the World Cup).

Six months after leaving CricInfo, Basevi was asked by Wisden Online to build something similar – "but better". Four months later, in August 2002, the Wisden Wizard was born. Where StatsGuru's strength is its ability to crunch an individual player's vital statistics, the Wizard specialises in multiple-player comparisons. Together they are as formidable a pair as Hobbs and Sutcliffe, Greenidge and Haynes, Langer and Hayden.

Say you were having a conversation with a friend about captaincy and how it affects batsmen – which Test cricketers have been invigorated by it and which enfeebled. In the past, your mate would have forgotten all about the conversation by the time you had looked it up. With StatsGuru and the Wizard, it became a breeze…

CAPTAINS WHO BUCKLED UNDER THE STRAIN…

	As captain	In ranks	Difference
I. T. Botham (E).	276 @ 13.14	4,924 @ 36.74	**−23.60**
J. Darling (A)	750 @ 21.42	907 @ 39.43	**−18.01**
V. S. Hazare (I)	874 @ 39.72	1,318 @ 54.91	**−15.19**
J. C. Adams (WI).	686 @ 31.18	2,326 @ 45.60	**−14.42**
R. B. Richardson (WI)	1,302 @ 35.18	4,647 @ 47.90	**−12.72**
F. M. M. Worrell (WI)	849 @ 40.42	3,011 @ 52.82	**−12.40**

… AND THOSE WHO THRIVED

	As captain	In ranks	Difference
Imran Khan (P)	2,408 @ 52.34	1,399 @ 25.43	**26.91**
G. A. Gooch (E)	3,582 @ 58.72	5,318 @ 35.93	**22.79**
T. L. Goddard (SA)	1,092 @ 49.63	1,424 @ 27.92	**21.71**
R. B. Simpson (A)	3,623 @ 54.07	1,246 @ 33.67	**20.40**
P. B. H. May (E)	3,080 @ 54.03	1,457 @ 36.42	**17.61**
H. H. Streak (Z)	**629 @ 33.10**	**801 @ 16.34**	**16.76**

Qualification: 12 Tests as captain, 12 in ranks. To March 2003.

Which is not to say these toys are perfect. If you want to know Michael Vaughan and Marcus Trescothick's average opening stand, you have to ferret it out the old-fashioned way. First-class cricket, too, remains statistical no man's land; the Guru and the Wizard, like the top players most of the time, don't venture below international level. But there is no doubting the impact of the new breed of statistics. They have accelerated the trend towards coaches, epitomised by Australia's John Buchanan, whose prowess lies in dabbling with databases rather than wielding the willow. They have changed the way the game is analysed and reported, to the point where numbers are usurping narrative. By March 2003, Wisden Online and CricInfo were about to merge, and for the Wizard and the Guru, the immediate future looked uncertain. Their legacy looks everlasting.

Chris Ryan, former managing editor of Wisden Cricket Monthly*, is now a Sydney-based cricket writer. He wrote Wisden Online's Australian View column from 2000 to 2003.*

FIVE CRICKETERS OF THE YEAR
MICHAEL VAUGHAN
By DAVID HOPPS

Michael Vaughan began 2002 keenly aware of the impatience for him to prove his worth as a Test batsman. If it emanated less from the England management than from the media, none the less the time was nigh for Vaughan to establish himself as a senior player and a worthy opening partner for Marcus Trescothick. Such was his response that, by the year's end, he was not just established, but had become England's most accomplished performer since the heydays of Gooch and Gower.

The transformation was striking enough in the scorebook. In 13 Tests up to the end of 2001, he had scored 679 runs at 33.95, respectable enough without being particularly eye-catching; in 2002, in one Test more, he stacked up 1,481 runs at 61.70, with six centuries – and another in 2003, in the final Ashes Test at Sydney, for good measure. He was Test cricket's leading run-getter in 2002, an impressive feat, if not the most meaningful one in England, where the cricketing year, like the financial, traditionally begins in April. Even more impressive was the style in which he made his runs. He had always been technically sound, but a reflective, somewhat pottering, even stressful air in his formative years encouraged some to harbour suspicions that he would be overpowered by attacks of the highest class. He answered that in wonderfully emphatic style. In 2002, cricket grounds in England and Australia resounded to a new Michael Vaughan, a batsman more confident in his method and much more forceful in his strokeplay. Deliveries that were once sneaked into the covers now pummelled the boundary boards. Short balls, and some not very short, were pulled and hooked in a manner that must have surprised even Vaughan himself. By the end of the year, his habit of touching the peak of his helmet, like a classical batsman of old respectfully touching the peak of his cap, had become a familiar sight. Throughout, he played with a dignity that signalled him a player of true worth.

Earlier in the year, Trescothick had been the England batsman attracting the plaudits. Vaughan remained on the fringe of the team after a lengthy apprenticeship in which he had always been thereabouts but not always there. Although he had made one Test century, against Pakistan in 2001, and had contributed crucial runs to two low-scoring victories over the

West Indies in 2000, he had also attracted more than his share of injuries and other mishaps, culminating in being given out handled-the-ball in a Test match in India. Yet by the end of the English summer, Vaughan's four Test hundreds against Sri Lanka and India invited hopes that his opening partnership with Trescothick could be the springboard of a serious Ashes challenge. When an injury-ravaged England lost the Ashes series 4–1, Trescothick, who performed moderately, had been eclipsed; Vaughan was looking like the batsman around whom England could build for the next decade.

Yorkshiremen were quick to hail Vaughan as one of their own, although had the ancient tradition of fielding only players born within the county boundary been maintained a few years longer, he might easily have been representing the old foe, Lancashire. MICHAEL PAUL VAUGHAN was born at Salford's Hope Hospital on October 29, 1974, and lived in Manchester to the age of nine, when the family moved to Sheffield. Encouraged by his elder brother, he began netting at the Yorkshire League club Sheffield Collegiate, under the guidance of their junior coach, Jack Bethel, and Yorkshire age-group cricket quickly followed. It was while he was hitting a ball on the outfield at Abbeydale Park, during the interval of a county match, that Yorkshire's coach, the taciturn, gentle Doug Padgett, was stirred to put down his cup of tea on the pavilion balcony and wander on to the field to jot down his name. When

> Even Australians were speaking of him with undiluted respect

Padgett heard that Vaughan had been born in Lancashire, he could barely conceal his dismay, but Yorkshire's junior ranks were relatively enlightened and Vaughan was repeatedly assured that the home-grown-only policy would soon be relaxed to encompass players raised within the county. So it did, although not before he had been invited to nets at both Lancashire and Northamptonshire (a perpetual scavenger of unwanted Yorkshire talent).

Vaughan's presence in the Yorkshire side was never likely to bring protests. Polite and eager to learn, he won over even the crabbiest defenders of a faith that seemed even more outdated once Headingley's doors had been flung open to overseas players. He proved adept, as he remains to this day, at filtering advice from many sources. From Martyn Moxon he understood something of the opening batsman's art. From David Byas came the value of discipline. He watched Michael Bevan, who had two seasons with Yorkshire, and wondered at his ability to pace an innings with such calm.

An upbringing on Headingley's inconsistent pitches is not easy even for a batsman of high pedigree. Vaughan does not cavil at suggestions that it slowed his entry into the England side. But equally he credits life at Headingley with toughening him mentally, teaching him with every rogue ball and waspish comment from the crowd that cricket did not bestow its favours easily.

That only made him work harder. He takes his profession seriously, if not himself. He respects the game, but he is a level-headed young man who keeps life in perspective and does not overreact to reward or failure. His head was not turned by winning the *Daily Telegraph* Under-15 Cricketer of the Year award in 1990, nor by becoming England Under-19 captain four years later, in preference to Trescothick. When he faced his first ball in Tests, at Johannesburg in 1999-2000, England were two for four; Vaughan kept his cool and stayed in for two hours to make a composed 33.

He has always regarded his batting as a matter of trial and error, trying things to see if they work, discarding them quietly, without fuss, if they do not. By the end of the Ashes series even the Australians, not given to over-praising English cricketers, were speaking of him with undiluted respect. As the runs finally flowed, Vaughan kept telling the media, and himself, that the real test would come when they dried up. He will survive all this adulation without too much bother.

His early England innings were introspective affairs. Another Yorkshire Australian, Darren Lehmann, advised him to quicken his running between the wickets, to run in Tests as he would in one-day cricket. Vaughan credits something so simple with perking up his entire game. He felt more confident, his feet moved faster, his mind was more aware of run-scoring possibilities.

Going into the England side at No. 4, and moving down the order before he went up it, he regards as beneficial, rather than adding to his uncertainty. He believes it made him a more adaptable player, as did his increasing opportunities in the one-day game. To Duncan Fletcher, whose stint as coach began with that same torrid Test in Johannesburg, he gives the warmest praise of all. "He does not just grab your technique and try to change it. He will watch and watch and eventually volunteer something for you to consider. He might even spot a blemish in your game when you are about 120 not out. Not many coaches do that." Not many batsmen give the coach five opportunities to do it in eight Tests.

Early in 2002, in New Zealand, Vaughan opened for England for the first time and unveiled his new liberated persona, twice racing into the twenties in as many balls. He felt he was playing well, but the ball zipped around on seaming pitches and the runs did not quite come. By the time Sri Lanka arrived at Lord's in May, Vaughan was not in great form. He was out hooking for a dogged 64 and guiltily apologised to his team-mates as England followed on. But his first-innings graft had got him back into form and a hundred in the second saved the match, turned the series and began the sequence that changed his life.

Lord's seemed to inspire him: another hundred followed against India. A duck in the first innings, when he was defeated by a big nip-backer from the left-armer Zaheer Khan, nudged him into a subtle shift in technique, to prevent his front foot getting too far across, and the rewards were gratifying. His 197 at Trent Bridge was celebratory: warm summer's day, flat pitch, large Saturday crowd and "one of those days when everything was coming down like a beach ball". He was in such command that he scored 99 between lunch and tea.

The final Test of the summer, at The Oval, brought more sober satisfaction. England were weakening as the series went on and needed a draw to share the spoils. Vaughan steadied them by batting with great deliberation throughout a day's play – another ambition achieved, another hundred to add to the list. And the sobriety was relative: he made 182 in the day, scoring at a rate that only Trescothick could match, and dealt so commandingly with Anil Kumble's top-spinners and leg-breaks that Rahul Dravid, of all people, asked his advice on how to play spin.

A knee operation and a rest while England went to Sri Lanka for the ICC Champions Trophy ensured he was fitter than most for the start of the Ashes. He needed to be, as Glenn McGrath paid him the compliment of making him his No. 1 target. The first impression Vaughan made on the series was to drop two catches at Brisbane, a persistent and puzzling frailty, but a breezy 33 off only 36 balls announced that he was not cowed by facing an Australian attack for the first time in Tests. Two weeks later at Adelaide, a resplendent hundred proved that unlike many good batsmen, including his predecessor Mike Atherton, Vaughan had it in him to see off McGrath and flourish against the rest of Australia's arsenal. To get out in the last over of the day frustrated him as much as it did England's travelling band of supporters, who knew in their hearts, as they applauded him into the pavilion, that another defeat was on the cards.

His run of injuries continued with a broken bone in his shoulder to go with the still-mending knee, but by now he was in good enough form to shrug them off. Back-to-back hundreds over Christmas and New Year, in Melbourne and Sydney, completed a wonderful series – 633 runs in five Tests, joining Brian Lara (546 in four) and V. V. S. Laxman (503 in three) as the only men to have taken 500 in a series off Australia in Steve Waugh's time as captain. To Vaughan, not one of the victors, went the spoils of the Player of the Series award, which prompted an Anglo-Aussie debate over whether he or Matthew Hayden should rightly be regarded as the No. 1 opener in the world.

By the World Cup, he had joined England's management committee, alongside Hussain, Alec Stewart and Trescothick. He will probably captain England, although one hopes not too soon, because England's main requirement of Michael Vaughan at the moment is a mountain of runs. The responsibility is an onerous one, but he is equipped for the task.

David Hopps writes on cricket for The Guardian.

FIVE CRICKETERS OF THE YEAR
MATTHEW HAYDEN
By GREG BAUM

Sometimes in their worthy search for the perfect alignment of talent, technique and temperament, selectors outsmart themselves by overlooking the most fundamental and blindingly obvious virtue a batsman can have: the faculty for making runs. Matthew Hayden was passed over for all manner of training institutions, squads and teams in his cricketing youth, up to and including the Australian Test team, because of a universal suspicion about flawed technique. "It always baffled me a bit, because I always, always had scores on the board," he said. "It was like I had to win the perception." When he finally established himself in the Australian team, and was asked by one of his press-box critics what had changed, he was tempted to reply: "Only your mind."

Just one man never, ever wavered in his faith: Hayden himself. By January 2003, when he was ranked the No. 1 batsman in the world, he was well placed to thumb his nose at the doubters. But he would not, because he thinks of this peak as a staging-post, not a destination. Although he has never been more content, he is as possessed now as when he was a schoolboy thumping the ball all around outback Queensland. He realised it last Australian summer when given four days off to refresh himself. He went to Stradbroke Island, a favourite haunt, with his wife, infant daughter, surfboard and fishing rod, which along with his bat and his Catholic faith constitute all that is dear to him. When he returned, he was itching for a net. "I just love the feeling of hitting the cricket ball," he said. "That's what stimulates me. That won't ever wane."

MATTHEW LAWRENCE HAYDEN was born on October 29, 1971, in Kingaroy, land of wide skies, beef cattle and peanuts, home also to Carl Rackemann and the former Queensland premier Joh Bjelke Petersen, who because of an infamous gerrymander ran the state for two decades and so could be said to be another who was intent on never getting out. The teenage Hayden's boon companion was his elder brother Gary, who was also his first coach. "He was always amazed at the way I just went out to hit the ball," Hayden said. "He was all about leaving it. I just wanted to bludgeon the ball everywhere." In the off-seasons, they did triathlons together.

Hayden went to school and university in Brisbane, and all the while made runs, breaking his club's scoring record in his first full season and also breaking Greenmount's record in the Bolton League as soon as he spent a winter in England. He was not picked for a youth tour of England, nor invited to the vaunted academy, but regarded that as a lucky break because he was by then on the threshold of state selection. The day before his Sheffield Shield debut against South Australia in November 1991, when another man might have been worrying about whether he belonged in this company, Hayden asked if anyone had made a double-century on debut. The next day, standing a metre outside his crease and hammering the ball back down the ground as if with a rivet gun, he made 149. "I was thinking that I wanted to be successful," he said. "That was my mindset."

At 21, Hayden toured England and made 1,000 runs without playing a Test. It was 1993 and Michael Slater was just establishing himself as Mark Taylor's opening partner. The next year, Hayden made his Test debut when Taylor was ill on the morning of the Johannesburg match. Early in the second innings, Allan Donald broke his thumb. In the next six years, he played only six Tests, all in the southern summer of 1996-97. So it was that all his first seven Tests were played against the powerful seam attacks of either South Africa or West Indies. It was hardly surprising that his performances were uneven and he could not make a permanent place for himself. He saw this period not as exile, but preparation. "The thing is,

> An opponent said it was like bowling to a sightscreen

you'd have it no other way. Within myself, I knew I was gathering momentum," he said. "I knew I was good enough, but I couldn't get the opportunity." He said he felt frustration, but never despair.

He admitted to quirks in his technique, but no more than any other left-hander. "Even today, if a guy is swinging the ball into your pads, and you're trying to play straight, it's really hard to make the adjustment." Three seasons of county cricket, batting day in day out for Hampshire and Northants, helped refine his method. "The guys were bowling straight at my pads. It's the way the English bowl: at the pads and stumps and look for the LBs," he said. "Gradually, it became a strength, to the point now where, if I was to say what was my favourite shot, it would be through mid-wicket, forcing off the back foot. To get anywhere, you have to face your weaknesses."

His style still was not classical, but it worked. Tall, broad-shouldered and immensely powerful, he did not just occupy the crease, but filled it. He knew from a young age that if he remained patient and played with the full face of the bat, he had the strength to hit boundaries for days at a time. He continued to make runs in epic numbers – an opponent at this time said it was like bowling to a sightscreen – and never lost his inner conviction. "I never thought about what I could or should have been doing, but what it is that I have to do to become a better player," he said. "Even now, with one-day cricket, it doesn't stop. I want to become a better player."

Hayden regained his Test place and his vocation in New Zealand in March 2000. The next year in India, the country of reincarnation, the explosion came. In a series memorable for prodigious feats on both sides, but also for the failure of most of Australia's batting, Hayden made 549 runs in six innings. An astonishing number came from the sweep, a shot he said he always possessed, but rarely got to play on Australian pitches against Australian bowlers. "I've got a big advantage with the sweep because I've got a big stride. I can get to the length and sweep on the length," he said. "Unless it's a genuinely short ball, you can almost sweep anything."

MADE IN INDIA

The slow, dusty surfaces of the subcontinent have not been to the taste of many Australian batsmen, but they were the making of Matthew Hayden. When Australia toured India early in 2001, Hayden arrived a fringe player and left a star. Shortly before that, Steve Waugh had said Hayden had it in him to double his Test average, and so he did. In one-day internationals, he made fewer hundreds, but still took another giant leap.

Tests	*M*	*I*	*NO*	*R*	*100s*	*50s*	*Avge*
March 1994–January 2001	13	22	0	536	1	2	**24.36**
February 2001–January 2003 . . .	25	42	4	2,560	11	8	**67.36**
Total	38	64	4	3,096	12	10	51.60
One-day internationals	*M*	*I*	*NO*	*R*	*100s*	*50s*	*Avge*
May 1993–April 2000	19	18	2	477	0	5	**29.81**
March 2001–January 2003	35	33	6	1,481	2	10	**54.85**
Total	54	51	8	1,958	2	15	45.53

The runs have not abated since. Hayden's tally of 1,391 in 2001 was then third only to Viv Richards and Sunil Gavaskar in a calendar year. Starting with that Indian series, Hayden made 2,560 runs in 25 Tests, with 11 centuries, including a run of eight in 13 Tests, prompting Steve Waugh to compare him with the incomparable – Donald Bradman. At the end of the 2001 Ashes tour, he and Justin Langer came together serendipitously to form an opening partnership that was instantly world-beating, yielding four double-century stands in their first seven Tests together and reducing South Africa to a quivering wreck. They set out deliberately to revolutionise the opening business; rather than simply absorb the early buffeting and dull the shine, they made up their minds to attack the puny bowlers and their piddling ball. They set out to intimidate the bowling team. "We're about really asserting ourselves. We're about making sure the opposition feel how close we are, not in a false way, but because that's the way we play cricket," Hayden said. "It starts with us."

Hayden has also emerged as a brilliant fieldsman, either in the gully or suffocatingly close to the batsman when the spinners are on. He had looked unsuited to one-day cricket – a statutory limitation on his time at the crease was anathema to him – and did not establish himself in Australia's one-day side until Mark Waugh's axing in March 2002. Yet within ten months, he was rated No. 1 in the world in both forms of the game. His temperament was such that he could thrash and dash, but also bat through the innings, as circumstances demanded. The VB Series finals against England in January 2003 illustrated this. In the first at Sydney, Hayden belted 45 not out from 37 balls as he and Adam Gilchrist demolished a 118-run target in just 74 scintillating balls. Two days later at Melbourne, when Gilchrist was out early, Hayden made a measured 69 from 91 to found what ultimately proved a winning score.

Hayden had one other salutary experience on his way to the top. While he was fishing before dawn one morning off his beloved Stradbroke Island with an Australian team-mate, Andrew Symonds, and another friend, his boat hit a sandbar and sank. They had to swim for an hour to safety through waters where, the previous day, they had seen a school of sharks run amok among pilchards. Hayden said he had been scared. "But I controlled it. It was a good life lesson. There were three of us, and we had to support each other through it." Shaun Pollock and the new ball would never be so threatening again.

Otherwise, Hayden said the last two years had passed in something of a haze. "People look at the overall picture; that's how we all are," he said. "When I look at the footy, I look at the results and who scored the tries. When you're involved, it's different. To me, it's not really about results. I know they will come. The important thing for me is hitting the cricket ball." He said he cherished individual awards only on behalf of all who had remained true to him over the years. The spoils he enjoyed were the freedom to surf and fish at his leisure. Fishing and surfing are occupations that demand infinite patience, which enthusiasts want to do for days at a time: much like batting.

Hayden's life is like his mind – uncluttered. He and his wife Kellie have an infant daughter, Gracie, upon whom he dotes, and they are hoping for more children. He is a devout Catholic who tries to go to church every Sunday wherever he is in the world and says his faith is the cornerstone of his life. In a fiercely secular country and team, this staunchness is unusual. "It's everything to me, without being over the top about it," he said.

He easily reconciles his Christianity with a reputation for remorseless sledging. "I am who I am. I'm someone who plays the game with great passion," he said. "That's how you become the best player in the world. That's how you become the best team in the world. We're a competitive nation. We love to beat people. At some stage, we all go over the line. Hopefully, it's a lot less often than we could."

It was the same competitive strain that led to him breaking a dressing-room window when he was given out on the fourth day of the last Ashes Test, for not even in a dead rubber was failure against England acceptable. It cost him a portion of his match fee, but he did not complain. The window of opportunity had proved much harder to budge than this mere pane of glass, and he had paid plenty in sweat and blood over the years trying to crash through it. He never doubted that it would be worth every drop.

Greg Baum is senior sports writer on The Age, *Melbourne.*

FIVE CRICKETERS OF THE YEAR
NASSER HUSSAIN
By SCYLD BERRY

Nasser Hussain has always been too intense to inspire mass affection. Like Nick Faldo, or Steve Redgrave, or other English sportsmen suspected of being obsessive, he has inspired respect instead. In his four years as England's captain, Hussain should have inspired gratitude too. Last winter, in the first three Ashes Tests, England were a rowing-boat overwhelmed by the mountainous waves of Australian cricket. Almost every touring side had capsized against Steve Waugh's team in Australia; but Hussain, a beleaguered skipper if ever there was, kept England afloat. If one image could sum up the tour, it came in the one-day matches before Christmas when England – 3-0 down in the Test series – had to play four one-day internationals in eight days at venues as widespread as Melbourne, Brisbane and Perth. Any other England captain might have let his exhaustion, physical or mental, show. But there was Hussain in the field, hectoring, urging, berating, then exploding in celebration at the fall of each wicket. England have not had such an ardent captain since Douglas Jardine, another cricketer whose obsessiveness was not to English taste. Spurred on by this zeal, and blessed when injuries at last struck Australia instead, England won the Fifth Test in Sydney.

It has not been zeal alone which has fuelled the England team since 1999, but a sharp intellect blended with a diplomat's skill. Hussain has helped to educate the cricket public, and media, as Mark Taylor did in Australia a few years earlier. With his honest insights into the state of English cricket (and occasional propaganda), Hussain has raised the level of debate above the platitudes which used to prevail. Using a mind that won a Maths scholarship to Forest School and achieved a 2.2 in Geology and Chemistry at Durham University when cricket allowed, Hussain also advanced the moral argument for England not to play in Zimbabwe: it was believed to be the first time in England that team sportsmen at national level, and certainly the whole cricket team, had exercised their consciences. Above all, Hussain's legacy is that he has raised standards inside and outside the England team.

NASSER HUSSAIN was born on March 28, 1968 in Madras (now Chennai). His father Javaid, or Joe, represented Madras in the Ranji Trophy before emigrating to England, where he married an Englishwoman, Shireen. He then returned to India to set up an electronic-components factory in Madras, where the youngest of his three sons was born. Nasser's first experiences of cricket were family visits to Chepauk, where his father was a member of the Madras Cricket Club. His elder brothers Mel and Abbas used to bat on the outfield while he chased after the ball. When Joe returned with his family to England, and took charge of the indoor cricket school in Ilford, Nasser used to bowl for hours on end at his elder brothers, and not just because he was the youngest: he found leg-spin interesting. He was keener on football at first – supporting Leeds United, as he still does, and playing for school teams – but Sunday mornings were always dedicated to cricket, and his father kept pushing him in this direction. At eight, he was bowling leg-breaks for Essex Schools Under-11s, and at 12 for their Under-15s.

Born five days apart, Hussain and Mike Atherton soon found their careers progressing in parallel as they captained, batted and bowled leg-spin for England age-group teams, while also passing enough exams to go to a leading university. In his mid-teens however, Hussain "grew a foot in a winter" and the trajectory of his bowling was altered: "I went from bowling out Graham Gooch in the indoor school with everyone watching to hitting the roof or bowling triple bouncers in deadly silence."

His father remembers him crying in bed at the loss of his leg-break; the son felt he was letting his father down. He was also anxious not to be left behind by his peers, boys like Atherton, Trevor Ward, Martin Bicknell and Chris Lewis. So he made himself into a batsman, moving up the order from tail-end to opening or No. 3, and becoming the first boy at Forest to score 1,000 runs in a season since 1901. Vestiges of this manufacturing process remain in his technique: he bats with little left elbow and plenty of bottom hand, and backs up with the bat in his right hand (not that Duncan Fletcher minds). In general, his runs seem to be scored as much by an exceptional effort of will as through natural talent. These characteristics have been most apparent in one-day cricket, or when Michael Vaughan at the other end has been stroking the ball around with classical orthodoxy.

He also developed a reputation. The fieriest of three brothers who had all inherited their father's short temper, he vented his frustration at being dismissed – and at being unable to bowl leg-spin? – on his equipment or anything else in sight. He came to be bracketed with Graham Thorpe and Mark Ramprakash as a brat pack. By the time he became captain, Hussain was as unpopular as any cricketer in England. The perception, though, was worse than the reality. Self-obsessed as he may have been, driven to succeed as many migrants are, and seldom the one to depart after a run-out, he confined his tantrums to the dressing-room (including altercations with his Essex team-mates Neil Foster and Mark Ilott). He describes himself as "a fairly shy sort of bloke". According to his father, he inherited "good sense" from his mother, together with a sturdy sense of right and wrong.

The frustrations built up through his early twenties. Taken under the wing of Gooch, his Essex and England captain, who urged him to play straighter and less behind point with an open face, Hussain made his Test debut on the 1989-90 tour of the West Indies but was mostly out of the side thereafter. His Essex record was good without being outstanding. He spent the 1994-95 winter playing in South Africa, where he was prescribed a contact lens (he has since had laser treatment on his left eye). The England A-team captaincy in Pakistan the following winter was a lifeline: it took him out of himself, encouraged him to think he might be fulfilled, and proved that he was not as bad or moody as his reputation suggested. When he was recalled to the Test team at the start of the 1996 season in the problem position of No. 3, he survived a big appeal off Javagal Srinath, and went on to his maiden Test hundred. A year later, he made 207 as England for once went ahead in a modern Ashes series. Only injury has kept him out of the team since.

When Atherton resigned as England captain in 1998, Hussain had to wait while Alec Stewart had his turn. But when Stewart was sacked after the 1999 World Cup, he was matured and ready for the responsibility. His first Test in charge ended in victory as England dismantled a modest New Zealand side; his first series in failure when Hussain broke a finger in the Second Test and England fell apart. But help was on its way with Duncan Fletcher joining as coach for that winter's tour of South Africa. They had not met before but it was a fine partnership from the first. Hussain generated heat, Fletcher light.

Fletcher planned and prepared the players – identifying those with the right character and refining their technique, especially when batting against spin – while Hussain led them zealously on the field. Once a new system of squad players contracted to the ECB was put in place, English cricket was set for its finest achievements – four successive Test series won – since the Ian Botham era ended in the mid-1980s.

But for Hussain himself, 2000 was also an *annus horribilis*. He did not make a first-class fifty until his final match, the Karachi Test. His place in the side was never questioned as his players and the media appreciated his captaincy, but he still couldn't make a run. Looking back, Hussain can see that he gave too little attention to his own game, that he took his own form for granted after a hugely productive tour of South Africa. It didn't matter if he didn't make runs against Zimbabwe, while against West Indies he became consumed by the prospect of England beating them in a series for the first time since 1969. By the Oval Test, completely out of form, he went out to bat in the second innings unaware that he was on a pair, and duly bagged one. Once he learned to compartmentalise, he worked out that 60 per cent of his attention had to go on the team, 40 on his own game. And the effect on his own game may be judged by the fact that he has been England's one consistent batsman in their last five Test series. Every time, his first innings of the series has yielded at least a half-century: the captain stamping his mark.

England's series victories in 2000-01, by 1–0 in Pakistan and 2–1 in Sri Lanka, were the apogee of Hussain's captaincy – and of a generation of England cricketers, including Atherton, Stewart, Thorpe, Darren Gough and Andy Caddick. In Pakistan, England held on doggedly until the pressure told on the home team, who had never lost at Karachi before. In Sri Lanka, England overcame the stifling heat and the stifling spin of Muttiah Muralitharan. If one session marked the climax, it was when England dismissed Sri Lanka in the Third Test in Colombo in only 28.1 overs. Hussain went into the match injured and could barely walk by the end of it, but his zeal – his passion – won the day.

The hope was that England could go on to win the Ashes series of 2001. Instead, they went from apogee to nadir with a 4–1 defeat. England began a run of injuries which lasted into the following Ashes series and raised numerous questions about their medical team. Hussain himself broke a finger in the First Test against Australia at Edgbaston and missed the next two. If any good came of it, it was the plastic coating which he adopted as extra protection on his gloves. Since then, he has not missed a Test.

A mark of his captaincy has been his refusal to accept mediocrity, however often his batsmen have failed to follow his example and given their wickets away, however inaccurate his seamers have been, however little his spinners have turned the ball. Atherton in the end became resigned to his bowlers' and fielders' fallibility; Hussain has barked at every foible and thought up new ways to dismiss batsmen. His imaginative use of 8–1 fields paid off in India when the home batsmen, after their First Test win, were content to be tied down; and again at times last summer when Sri Lanka were beaten 2–0, the one win to set against three recent losses and three drawn series; but in Australia the batsmen refused to be tied down and it was widely reckoned that Hussain asked his bowlers to experiment too much. He thought his seamers had matured to the extent that he could send Australia in at Brisbane and give his bowlers best use of the pitch; he admitted his mistake long before the match ended in massive defeat. By the Third Test in Perth he was considering his position, not for the first or last time, but in the darkest hour he pushed himself as hard as ever. While England were lucky that Glenn McGrath and Shane Warne were both injured, they still had to be in good enough shape to take advantage. After the Sydney Test, Hussain received "a really nice e-mail" from Gough, which meant a lot as an expression of esteem from his peers.

After the World Cup he retired as England's one-day captain, sensibly deciding to concentrate on Test cricket. By then his wish to be remembered as "a decent leader of men" had already been fulfilled. The only dispute is whether he has been the equal of Mike Brearley as the best England captain since World Series Cricket; or, as their fellow-captain David Gower believes, even better, in more troubled times. To have been captain of England for four years, the most stressful job in cricket, is an achievement in itself. To leave the team better off than when he started, doubly so.

Scyld Berry is cricket correspondent of the Sunday Telegraph.

FIVE CRICKETERS OF THE YEAR
SHAUN POLLOCK
By NEIL MANTHORP

Shaun Pollock has not had an outstanding year. He has had seven. Sport's holy grail is consistency, and Pollock found it as soon as he entered international cricket. Whatever happens in his thirties, he will go down as one of the game's great all-rounders. His bowling is as straight, tight and incisive as Glenn McGrath's, and he is also an elegant, sometimes explosive batsman who averages 59 at No. 9. And all this consistency was sustained through the daunting business of succeeding Hansie Cronje as South Africa's captain.

Few players in history had as much to live up to as SHAUN MACLEAN POLLOCK, born in Port Elizabeth on July 16, 1973. Father–son combinations at first-class and even Test level are not uncommon, but in most cases one or other is a fringe player. Shaun's family was already among cricket's two or three richest gene pools. His uncle Graeme was one of the greatest batsmen ever, and his father Peter was one of South Africa's finest fast bowlers. The young Shaun shouldn't have had a chance, especially with a shock of red hair making him stand out even further.

His childhood memories are understandably mixed. "It wasn't easy being a Pollock at school. I remember a lot of suspicion every time I was selected – people would say 'it's only because of his name' and then I'd have to play twice as well as everyone else just to justify my place."

But selected he was, year after year through the ranks of junior school, high school, university and then his province, KwaZulu-Natal. In South Africa the annual Schools Week has always been seen as an avenue to the national side and when Shaun was chosen for that too, in 1991, people finally sat up and took serious notice.

Graeme had two sons of his own, Anthony and Andrew, and all three boys embarked on careers together. Was there really room for three Pollocks in South African first-class cricket? The answer was no, and as Shaun's career quickly took off with a Natal B debut as a schoolboy, followed by a First XI call-up the next year, his cousins battled to make a lasting impact with Transvaal and Easterns.

A medium-pacer with an upright action that earned him bags of wickets on Kingsmead's green, grassy pitches, as well as an uncanny ability to find the meat of the bat immediately in the middle order, Shaun was regarded as very, very useful. The truth is, however, that while he was being taken seriously, no one spoke of him as an international prospect.

The season after his debut, in 1992-93, Natal signed Malcolm Marshall as overseas professional. It was to be the making of Pollock. "He was my mentor," Pollock says with deep affection. "Everything I've learned about bowling since then has just been a refinement of something he taught me."

Perhaps Pollock's finest achievement as captain of South Africa was to secure a 2–1 series victory on their first full tour of the West Indies in 2000-01. Although Marshall died before the tour, his influence was crucial. "I was desperately keen to see his resting place in Barbados. I wanted to bowl on the wickets he bowled on, to meet the people he spent time with and to see where he grew up. Sadly I had to pay tribute to his grave rather than have dinner with him."

During Marshall's fourth and final year at Natal, Jonty Rhodes came of age, Lance Klusener was set on his way to becoming an international all-rounder and Pollock was ready for international cricket. There was just one problem; his father, Peter, was convenor of the national selectors.

"The team for the first Test against England…" Peter announced on November 14, 1995, "is: Andrew Hudson, Gary Kirsten, Hansie Cronje… Craig Matthews, Allan Donald and Shaun Pollock." He did not look up until he had finished.

"Shaun still has a lot to learn," he added a little later, a touch awkwardly. "But he is having a useful season and we think he can do a job for us…" Finally, he was asked how he felt as a father: "Umm… yes. As a father I feel proud." Peter always played it pretty straight.

So, as usual, Shaun had had to produce ten per cent more than anyone else to prove himself, and even then the plaudits from Dad were grudging. At least in public. "He always supported me," Shaun says now. "He was always there if I wanted a chat or some advice. But generally he believed it was better for me to find my own path, to do things my way."

TOP OF THE TAIL

Shaun Pollock is the most successful tailender in Test history, with an average of 35.75 when batting at No. 8 or lower. Several players have achieved an average in the high twenties, including Mark Boucher, who often precedes Pollock in the South African order, but only Pollock and Kapil Dev are above 30. The top nine tailenders have played in the past 20 years.

	Tests	Runs	100s	50s	Avge
S. M. Pollock (SA).	**35**	**1,287**	2	3	**35.75**
Kapil Dev (I).	57	1,967	2	13	32.78
P. A. Strang (Z)	21	737	1	2	29.48
M. V. Boucher (SA).	**31**	**922**	1	6	28.81
Imran Khan (P)	27	839	1	1	27.96
I. D. S. Smith (NZ)	53	1,667	2	6	27.78
S. M. H. Kirmani (I)	57	1,594	1	6	27.55
P. R. Reiffel (A).	33	936	0	6	27.52
C. L. Cairns (NZ).	**24**	**760**	**0**	**6**	**27.14**
R. Benaud (A).	23	782	1	4	26.96

Qualification: 20 Tests. To March 2003.

For most of that rainy first series, Shaun was, as his father predicted, useful. Then, at 0–0 going into the final match, Allan Donald took five wickets in the first innings and Pollock five for 32 in the second as England were crushed by ten wickets. It was the beginning of a fast-bowling partnership that would go down among the best of all time, and not just in South Africa.

One of Pollock's assets is the position from which he delivers the ball – tall and upright, and so close to the stumps that he often dislodges a bail. The height exacerbates any bounce in the pitch while the gun-barrel straight, wicket-to-wicket approach means that even the slightest seam movement can be fatal. His pace has undoubtedly dropped in recent years. But his economy-rate has become even more parsimonious and his career average remains phenomenal, at under 21.

There have been three other magical spells since that one against England. His five for 37 helped dismiss Pakistan for 92 when they were chasing just 146 in the deciding Test at Faisalabad in October 1997, still among South Africa's greatest triumphs. Three months later, with Donald injured, Pollock bowled 41 overs in the brutal heat of the Adelaide sun and finished with a Test-best seven for 87. Finally, against India at Bloemfontein in 2001-02, he took four for 91 and six for 56 in a comfortable victory, and was told he had become the first South African captain to bag a ten-for. "Thank you," he whimsied. "And how many other captains have been bowlers?"

He does tend to be referred to as a bowler, because he is so good at it, but the figures are unmistakably those of an all-rounder. By January 2003, he had a batting average of 33.45 with two Test centuries and 278 wickets at an average of 20.71. Ian Botham averaged 33 with the bat and 28 with the ball. Pollock had also worked hard to earn a coveted place in the slip cordon, a precious prize for the man more often than not bowling the most overs in the innings.

One job no one thought of giving him was the captaincy. (In 1991 his SA Schools captain was Nicky Boje. The vice-captain was Pollock – Anthony Pollock, Shaun's cousin.) Then, in 1998, Gary Kirsten suddenly quit as Cronje's deputy. It was an odd decision that cost him kudos as well as cash, and he never explained it, leaving others to wonder if it might have had anything to do with Cronje. Pollock was named as the new vice-captain, not because he was being groomed for the job, but because he was cheerful, presentable and clean-living. His first taste of captaincy came in October 1998, when South Africa beat Australia to win gold at the Commonwealth Games in Kuala Lumpur. But everyone knew that Cronje was impregnable, brilliant and fit: he missed only two matches out of 185 in his crowded reign. Some even thought Pollock's career would end before that of Cronje, who was four years older but a batsman-who-bowled rather than one of the hardest-working men in the game.

Then the world fell in on South Africa.

When Cronje was exposed, Pollock not only had to take charge of the team, but – with all due respect to the country's political, religious and

MASTER AND PUPIL

Shaun Pollock's mentor, Malcolm Marshall, used to have the lowest bowling average of those with 100 Test wickets since Alan Davidson played his last Test in 1963. Now the lead has passed to Pollock. Eight bowlers from the past 40 years, all seamers, average under 23:

	Tests	Wickets	Avge	SR
S. M. Pollock (SA)	**68**	**278**	**20.71**	**54.34**
M. D. Marshall (WI)	81	376	20.94	46.76
J. Garner (WI)	58	259	20.97	50.84
C. E. L. Ambrose (WI)	98	405	20.99	54.57
G. D. McGrath (A)	**91**	**422**	**21.45**	**51.12**
A. A. Donald (SA)	**72**	**330**	**22.25**	**47.02**
R. J. Hadlee (NZ)	86	431	22.29	50.85
Imran Khan (P)	88	362	22.81	53.75

Qualification: 100 wickets. To March 2003.

"moral" leaders – of the sporting nation. Every time a plaintive call of "say it ain't so" was made, he was the man who had to answer. And answer he did, time and time again, proving himself over and over as a man with sensitivity, feeling and respect for others.

He made a mistake in dedicating the team's first victory to Cronje because he sowed the seed for what was to become an insidious weed of selective judgment among many South Africans in the years to come. But again, it showed the sympathetic side of Pollock's character, both a strength and a weakness in his captaincy.

Before his elevation Pollock was always among the jokers on the team bus, in the changing-room, on planes and in hotels. He would squirt drinks, throw bread rolls, pour salt in Bob Woolmer's third bowl of ice cream – anything for a laugh. Then, on April 11, 2000, he was suddenly in charge of a shattered, confused squad of players in desperate need of comfort. "There were tears," Kirsten remembers. "We were stunned. The last thing we wanted to do was play cricket."

Despite being a practising Christian and the son of a lay-preacher, Pollock's approach was down-to-earth and practical. This was a mess the Lord wasn't going to clean up. The players had to, and they had to do it by playing winning cricket. "There was definitely a point where things could have gone badly wrong for the team," Pollock said early in 2003. "But we were also lucky in some ways because people didn't expect too much from us, given what had happened. People expected us to fall apart – it was almost like a honeymoon period in which we could just get on with the game."

Faced with a three-match one-day series against Australia beginning the day after Cronje's confession, South Africa won. Then the scandal began to sink in. The King inquiry into match-fixing revealed nothing except that Herschelle Gibbs and Henry Williams had accepted offers to underperform. A week later, Pollock was leading the national team – minus Gibbs – on a three-Test tour of Sri Lanka. On the field, he was a disaster. He could handle an intimidating press conference with nearly 200 scandal-seeking, bloodthirsty journalists on arrival in Colombo, but he could not handle Sanath Jayasuriya on the first morning of the series in Galle. Jayasuriya raced to 96 not out at lunch while Pollock played a game of chicken, maintaining rigidly attacking fields and just hoping. Nothing happened, and his team were hammered by an innings inside four days.

"When a guy starts out as captain, he probably feels like he has to make something happen – that he has to score runs, take wickets, take charge of everything," Pollock says. "That was the case with me. But you quickly learn… Basically it comes down to one word: patience. And I learned it the hard way."

South Africa fought back to draw that first series and went on to win every other Test series under Pollock except the one they wanted most – in Australia in 2001-02, when they were annihilated 3–0. Those defeats brought heavy criticism of Pollock's captaincy, but there are several points to remember. His own form never suffered, he was let down by his normally reliable match-winners and no one ever suggested a better man for the job. He handled every trial and tribulation with dignity and never once turned on his players, even when they turned on him. The formulaic approach he adopted in one-day matches was a direct inheritance from his predecessor, something the critics somehow forgot. Finally, he was the first to admit he wasn't perfect and was never shy to ask advice.

There were many high points too, none greater than the series victory in the West Indies. "No question," he says. "A highlight of any cricketer's career." With his team teetering in no man's land at 315 for eight on a perfect batting wicket in Barbados, Pollock played an innings that not only protected a 1–0 lead but ultimately set up the series win. His previous century, reached in 95 balls against Sri Lanka at Centurion in January 2001, had been a kaleidoscope of tall drives and swatted hooks. His second showed meaner, tougher qualities. Pollock and his partner, Donald, changed from poachers to gamekeepers, adding 132 for the ninth wicket.

He went into a World Cup that South Africa's fans expected to win, looking as if he would be captain as long as he wanted. Instead he was "relieved of his duties" because South Africans needed someone to blame for their collective misery at missing half their own party. Unlike his predecessor, he left with honour.

Personally and professionally, Pollock is one of the most balanced cricketers to represent South Africa in the modern era. He is approachable, honest and thoughtful. He also has a temper and can be a sulker, although captaincy curbed both tendencies. He has grown up in other ways too. The jokes about him being the only member of the squad to use his UCB travel allowance to bring his mum and dad on tour are over: Shaun married Trish in July 2001, so Peter and Inez now pay for themselves. During the World Cup, it was announced that Trish was expecting their first child in September. And if it's a boy? Shaun smiles. "He won't come under any pressure from me to play cricket."

Neil Manthorp heads the MWP sports news agency in South Africa.

FIVE CRICKETERS OF THE YEAR
ADAM HOLLIOAKE
By SIMON WILDE

In 1995, Surrey epitomised all that was wrong with English cricket. They had plenty of talent but were habitual underachievers whose glory days were receding into the distance: after winning the Championship seven seasons in a row in the 1950s, they had won it only once more, and that was back in 1971. The team was poorly run and visibly divided – literally so, with a separate dressing-room for capped players. In July 1995, Surrey hit rock bottom, tumbling to 18th place in the table.

It was a custom at The Oval not to appoint an official vice-captain, even though the then captain, Alec Stewart, was an automatic choice for England. That July, the task of standing in for Stewart was handed to a 23-year-old all-rounder, Adam Hollioake. Stewart was the ultimate Surrey insider, son of Micky, who had led the team to the 1971 Championship and later became manager. Hollioake, raised in Australia until he was 12, was much more of an outsider, as was the new coach, the former Australian seamer David Gilbert.

Hollioake's approach was refreshingly positive and results improved almost instantly: Surrey won three first-class games and hauled themselves to 12th in the Championship and ninth in the Sunday League (divisions, in those days, existed only in dressing-rooms). But there was still deep disquiet. A special general meeting was called by disaffected members in October: the incoming chairman, Mike Soper, was "staggered" by the depth of feeling. In December, the chief executive, Glyn Woodman, resigned, to be replaced by Paul Sheldon. "Surrey," said *Wisden* in 1996, "are nothing if not consistent in their inability to win something."

Stewart remained in place but Hollioake, now officially vice-captain, played a larger role. In 1996, he led the team to four Championship victories as Surrey climbed to third, and they confounded *Wisden* and other observers by winning the Sunday League. In 1997, Hollioake was appointed captain and Surrey won the Benson and Hedges Cup. In 1999, finally, they won the Championship. Unlike 1971, this was not an isolated triumph: they retained the title in 2000, won the B&H again in 2001, and the Championship for the third time in four years in 2002. They had become the most successful team in the country.

If Hollioake changed one thing, it was to defenestrate the tired thinking prevailing in most county dressing-rooms. "It was the blame culture," he reflects. "Captains and managers pointing the finger for not winning. People covering their tracks. We would not be like that. We'd do everything to win but there'd be no aimless stuff. No five-hour fielding practice for the sake of it. If we were fielding well, we wouldn't bother. We asked ourselves what we needed to do to win and suggestions could come from anyone. No one questioned another's desire to win. Democracy's hard to get in county cricket. It comes through trust. If we have to sit around in pink underwear for half an hour beforehand, we will."

The collective realisation of what was required brought with it a need for collective maturity. Martin Bicknell, Alistair Brown, Mark Butcher and Graham Thorpe were all aged 24 to 28 when Hollioake's reign began; they have grown wiser together. Hollioake was helped by his outsider's perspective, by two key confidants – his father, John, and Alec Stewart, who could have been old-laggish but went along with the new broom. Both had experience of Australian grade cricket and espoused its virtues. "I grew up with the Australian view," Adam says. "The main thing was to win, not how. I have carried that with me."

ADAM JOHN HOLLIOAKE was born in Melbourne on September 5, 1971, into a family with roots going back five generations in the old gold-mining city of Ballarat. Helpfully, there was a cricketing seam. Adam's great-uncle Rex played against Len Hutton's touring MCC side in 1955 and his father, a talented player but better coach, represented Ballarat and Fitzroy. Adam's mother, Daria, is half Australian, half Indonesian.

At first, he was not that fussed about cricket. Like many boys in Victoria, he preferred Australian Rules football, which was the main sport at St Patrick's College in Ballarat, and even when his father's work as an engineer took the family across the world to Weybridge in 1983, he found rugby union more appealing. He first considered taking up cricket full-time when Surrey offered him a contract in 1991. He saw cricket as a way to get out of going to Durham University.

As Surrey's interest indicated, his ability with bat and ball had by now made itself apparent. He was a useful performer, good enough to have trials for England Under-15s. "A quite fast bowler, No. 11 bat and a bit rough, but Surrey thought there was something they could mould," is how he put it, looking back. "There were better players," he added. By the time of his first Championship appearance, against Derbyshire at Ilkeston in August 1993, he was considered good enough to bat at No. 7. A second-innings 123 from 178 balls suggested that was a conservative estimate. In 1994, his first full season, his haul was 722 first-class runs and 26 wickets. The following year he collected 1,099 runs, 21 wickets and a county cap. In 1996 he went up another level with 1,522 runs at 66 and five hundreds. But his aggressive batting and inventive medium-pace allsorts were among the few bright spots for a county embroiled in special meetings, management reviews and accusations of undemocratic administration.

Hollioake was not the most obvious choice to share the captaincy with Stewart. "At 21, I would have been the last person to captain a side," he says now. "I led a pretty wild lifestyle and was fairly anti-establishment. I've never been keen on the job, it's not something I've ever had a desire to do and I have no fear of losing it. I've wanted to be the best all-rounder in Surrey and England but never the best captain. I've tried to hand it in half a dozen times, thinking maybe someone else should do it, but have been talked out of it."

Whatever Hollioake's views, Surrey's opinion was shared by England, who asked him to lead the A team to his native Australia in 1996-97. The tour was an outstanding success. England had brought him into the one-day international side in August 1996 and he marked two appearances against Pakistan with four wickets in each. More glory followed against Australia early in 1997, this time with the bat: he scored 66, 53 and four, all unbeaten, and hit the winning run in each game. His 19-year-old brother and Surrey team-mate, Ben, made a princely entrance in the third game, at Lord's; Adam was man of the series. For a heady, overheated month or two, the Hollioakes were all over the media as the bright new faces of English cricket.

The Ashes series began without them and England amazed themselves by taking the lead before Australia fought back to go 2–1 up with two to play. England's last throw of the dice was to send for both Hollioakes – the first brothers to play in the same England Test team in 40 years. Adam fought gamely in their debut match at Trent Bridge, making a composed 45 and adding a hundred with Thorpe, but the sight of him misreading Shane Warne made a more lasting impression, and his front-foot technique struggled to adjust to Test cricket. Retained, unlike Ben, for the winter Test tour of the West Indies, he was soon cast into the cold, like so many England cricketers of the 1990s, without playing a full series.

In one-day cricket, he did get a decent run. When Mike Atherton opted out of a four-team tournament in Sharjah at the end of 1997, Hollioake was the adventurous, if logical, choice to captain the side. A revamped team strong on all-rounders and enthusiasm surprised India, Pakistan and West Indies (twice) and walked off with England's first tournament success for ten years. Pakistan's defeat later earned a reference in Justice Malik Qayyum's inquiry into match-fixing and Hollioake, who was himself approached for information, admits the triumph became tainted. But Matthew Fleming, who was in that squad and knew something about leadership from the Army, declared him "a natural leader".

When Atherton resigned at the end of another lost Test series in the West Indies, Hollioake kept the one-day job but soon found that harder too. He dislocated his shoulder, his form crumbled and six games were lost in succession. Within a few months the idea of having two captains was abandoned and the one-day captaincy devolved on Stewart, Atherton's successor as Test captain. Fleming felt the decision meant that "England lost the 1999 World Cup before it started".

Hollioake remained a one-day regular until the premature end of that World Cup campaign, but he was destined for the wilderness. "My game deteriorated," he said. "I stopped playing my shots. After a few low scores, I started thinking it would be best to work the ball around and that is not the way I play." The novelty of his bowling had worn off too, and the shoulder injury stopped him hurling himself into his delivery.

The self-doubt carried over into county cricket. While his captaincy work finally bore fruit in four-day cricket in 1999 and 2000 with Surrey's first Championship titles since the year of his birth, his batting average fell and bowling average rose for three successive seasons from 1998.

Liberation arrived last year by the most painful means imaginable. The death of Ben, in a car crash on the way home from a family reunion in Perth, forced Adam to reappraise his life. He stayed in Australia for the birth of his first child, Bennaya, and did not rejoin Surrey until two months into the English season, keeping in touch with the team's fortunes by phone and the internet. After some discussion, it was decided he should resume as captain – in another sign of a well-run club, both Mark Butcher and Ian Ward had led capably in his absence – and he immediately showed the old sureness of touch. But more practical skills felt different. When he picked up a bat for the first time in weeks, it felt like an axe.

He was soon wielding it like one as his batting assumed greater assurance than ever. In his Championship comeback against Somerset he struck 87 off 83 balls and he followed up with two brisk fifties against Warwickshire. Then, in the space of a few days, he hit 117 in 59 balls in a one-day quarter-final at Hove and a counter-attacking Championship century – his first for three years – at Canterbury. "That wasn't me," he observed. "I can't bat that well."

With the title in the bag, he rounded off the season with a maiden double-hundred against Leicestershire. The death of the placid Ben had taught his more aggressive brother to relax. "It made me get a perspective back on life as a whole," he said. "My job was important and I had pride in it but I realised that happiness was more important. I enjoyed hitting the ball into the crowd but to hit sixes you need to take risks. I had no fear of failure."

The year ended with Hollioake, now 31, called back to Australia as cover for England's one-day squad. He made it on to the field only once, in a warm-up game against a Bradman XI at Bowral, but took his chance with a hard-hit 53 off 38 balls. Although he could not push his way past Ronnie Irani into the World Cup squad, his name was bandied about as soon as Nasser Hussain handed in the one-day captaincy. The Hollioake story is not yet run.

Simon Wilde is cricket correspondent of The Sunday Times.

2

**WORLD
VIEW**

Ricky Ponting: bags of runs and half a captaincy. Australia, page 88. *Picture by Philip Brown.*

PART TWO: WORLD VIEW

ENGLAND
ONE STEP FORWARD...

Test: P8 W5 L7 D6
Lost to India (a) 0–1 (D2).
Drew with New Zealand (a) 1–1 (D1).
Beat Sri Lanka (h) 2–0 (D1).
Drew with India (h) 1–1 (D2).
Lost to Australia (a) 1–4.

One-day: P40 W20 L19 NR1
Beat Zimbabwe (a) 5–0.
Drew with India (a) 3–3.
Lost to New Zealand (a) 2–3.
Runners-up in NatWest Series (h) v India and Sri Lanka: W3 L3 NR1.
Group stage of ICC Champions Trophy (Sri Lanka): W1 L1.
Runners-up in VB Series (Australia) v Australia and Sri Lanka: W3 L7.
Pool stage of World Cup: W3 L2 (excluding one game forfeited).

A year that started promisingly and peaked in midsummer with three straight Test wins ended in frustration, exhaustion and resignation. England lost their eighth consecutive Ashes series, a modern record, and fell at the first meaningful hurdle in a World Cup for the third time in a row. Fed up with the political wranglings that probably cost them a place in the Super Six – they forfeited their match in Zimbabwe by staying away on security grounds – Nasser Hussain quit as the one-day captain. It was another winter of discontent, brightened only by flashes of brilliance from Andrew Flintoff and the sustained electricity of Michael Vaughan.

As so often, failure against Australia overshadowed the stop–start progress that preceded it. England travelled to India for only the second time in 17 years with a side weakened by defections, but in the end were denied a draw by the Bangalore weather. They should have beaten New Zealand in a series that was scarred by the death of Ben Hollioake, but the English summer lent a spring to their step. After following on in the First Test, England hammered

Sri Lanka, who had arrived on the back of nine straight wins, then took an early lead against India. But the hesitation that had cost them in New Zealand resurfaced and they again snatched a draw from the jaws of victory. The Ashes, surrendered after just 11 days' cricket, were as lop-sided as ever; fifth place in the Test Championship felt about right.

Their one-day fortunes petered out too after they had whitewashed Zimbabwe and drawn in style in India. But the stuffing was really knocked out of England on a heady evening at Lord's, when India successfully chased 326 to win the NatWest Series. After that, England's World Cup plans were scuppered by injury and indecision, particularly over the No. 3 position. In all, 29 players wore the pyjama blue, but just two – the dashing left-handed openers, Marcus Trescothick and Nick Knight – appeared in all 40 games.

Flying high: when he wasn't injured, Andrew Flintoff finally shone. *Picture by Philip Brown*

Of the rest, only Hussain, who never quite felt at home in the one-day game, and Paul Collingwood, who emerged as England's middle-order nudger in the self-imposed absence of Graham Thorpe, averaged 30 or more. But the individual success story of the year was Vaughan, who in the space of nine months moved from merely promising to unquestionably world-class. In a period of purest purple, he cracked seven Test hundreds – including five scores of 145 or more – and raised his Test average from 30 to 50. Vaughan's sequence was the most merciless by an England batsman since Graham Gooch's hammer blows of the early 1990s.

Hussain's captaincy remained full of narrow-eyed grit, although the inspiration that had driven England to four successive series wins from 2000 began to wear off and he fretted in the field more than ever. His efforts were clouded by a near-permanent injury crisis epitomised by Andrew Flintoff's tortuous recovery from a double hernia operation. But there was a silver lining: Jimmy Anderson, a 20-year-old swing bowler from Burnley, hurried across from the Academy in Adelaide to join the senior tour, settled in instantly and bowled England to a spanking World Cup win over Pakistan. Simon Jones and the more wayward Steve Harmison both made speedgun-rattling Test debuts, and although Matthew Hoggard faded after rushing to 50 wickets in 12 Tests, and Alex Tudor too lost the confidence of the management, Flintoff finished the winter on a high. As Darren Gough, who struggled with knee trouble, and Andy Caddick approached old age, England could at least see the future beginning to take shape. **Lawrence Booth**

AUSTRALIA
BLAZING THE TRAIL

Test: P17 W12 L2 D3
Drew with New Zealand (h) 0–0 (D3).
Beat South Africa (h) 3–0.
Beat South Africa (a) 2–1.
Beat Pakistan (Sri Lanka and Sharjah, counts as away) 3–0.
Beat England (h) 4–1.

One-day: P47 W36 L9 T1 NR1
Last in VB Series (h) v South Africa and New Zealand: W4 L4.
Beat South Africa (a) 5–1 (T1).
Lost to Pakistan (h) 1–2.
Shared PSO Trophy (Kenya) with Pakistan, also v Kenya: W4 NR1.
Reached semi-finals of ICC Champions Trophy (Sri Lanka): W2 L1.
Won VB Series (h) v England and Sri Lanka: W9 L1.
Won World Cup: W11 L0.

Australians spent an unhealthy amount of their spare time in 2002 debating what to call their overpowering cricket side. The Dominators caught on for a while but seemed too macho. The Invincibles had a sweet ring to it but had been used before. The Unbeatables? They certainly were in the World Cup, but they still muffed the occasional dead Test.

Keith Miller, an original Invincible from 1948, praised Steve Waugh's team as the best in history, a view shared by 52 per cent of the public, according to a survey in *The Australian* in October 2001. If that remained a contentious point, one thing was unarguable: they were certainly the most buccaneering. They consistently scored 350 runs a day, then uprooted their opponents with an attack that consisted of four strike bowlers. They lost only two Tests – both dead ones – and drew three, two of them rain-affected. They played the same way whether in control or crisis, a policy that finally backfired against England at Sydney, Australia's first home defeat in four years.

At the epicentre of this blazing approach stood Adam Gilchrist, who rocketed along at 87 runs per 100 balls – a strike-rate previously considered improbable in one-dayers and impertinent in Tests. The Test Championship showdown became a no-show. Gilchrist bulldozed 204 not out at Johannesburg – the speediest double-ton in history at the time – then bettered it with 138 in 108 balls at Cape Town, performances that made the late *Age* reporter Peter McFarline, watching his last series, think of Victor Trumper.

Matthew Hayden went one better: he was, gushed Steve Waugh and sundry others, the new Don Bradman. It was not just his mountains of runs but the belligerent way he scaled them that impressed. Exuding the intimidatory aura of a fast bowler in pads, he clouted over square leg balls too full to pull and clumped past the bowler balls too short to drive. Justin Langer, hitherto written off as a slowcoach, somehow managed to keep pace. Together they shared four double-century stands in the 2001-02 summer alone.

Damien Martyn's booming progress levelled out as opposition bowlers fenced him in with some old-fashioned off-theory. Ricky Ponting, stiffened by the one-day captaincy, demonstrated a new patience, rebutting the critics who reckoned his hard wrists made him a soft No. 3. Glenn McGrath was his usual miserly self, conceding just 2.37 runs an over, and the underrated Jason Gillespie stayed fit for long periods. Before he was sent home from the World Cup for testing positive for a banned substance, Shane Warne shed kilos, muscled up and revisited his golden days. Although his famed flipper made only sporadic appearances, he mastered the slider, a delivery which – like his zooter, back-spinner and top-spinner – confounded batsmen despite staying impeccably straight. If it was mostly bluster and mind games, it worked: in three Tests against Pakistan he bewitched 27 wickets, 13 of them lbw.

Only one headache persisted: what to do with the Waughs? In February 2002 Australia's one-day side missed out on the VB Series finals, which in retrospect looked like a blip but sparked panic at the time. The Waughs, who had underperformed, were jettisoned. Mark was subsequently scratched from the Test team too, immediately announcing his retirement with the same panache he always saved for the crease. Steve defiantly clung on to lead the Test side to the West Indies in April. His starts were shakier than ever but his centuries at Sharjah and Sydney were feats of immense willpower.

Meanwhile the victories kept coming, so emphatically, so predictably, that minds inevitably strayed elsewhere: to the South African batsman Graeme Smith's accusations of filthy sledging; Brett Lee's headhunting of tailenders; Darren Lehmann's racist outburst against the Sri Lankans; Warne's one-year ban for his dalliance with diuretics. The team was still without a nickname but a new contender had emerged. The Unlovables, anyone? **Chris Ryan**

SOUTH AFRICA
CHAMPIONS IN NAME ONLY

Test: P16 W9 L5 D2
Beat Zimbabwe (a) 1–0 (D1).
Beat India (h) 1–0 (D1).
Lost to Australia (a) 0–3.
Lost to Australia (h) 1–2.
Beat Bangladesh (h) 2–0.
Beat Sri Lanka (h) 2–0.
Beat Pakistan (h) 2–0.

One-day: P54 W34 L18 T2
Beat Zimbabwe (a) 3–0.
Won Standard Bank Tournament (h) v India
   and Kenya: W6, L1
Won VB Series (Australia) v NZ and
   Australia: W6, L4.
Lost to Australia (h) 1–5 (T1).
Runners-up in Morocco Cup (Tangier) v Sri
   Lanka and Pakistan: W2, L3.
Semi-finals of ICC Champions Trophy (Sri
   Lanka): W2, L1.
Beat Bangladesh (h) 3–0.
Beat Sri Lanka (h) 4–1.
Beat Pakistan (h) 4–1.
Pool stage of World Cup: W3 L2 T1.

South Africa were probably the second-best team in the world in 2002, but
it wasn't saying much. At home against subcontinental teams they were
unbeatable; against Australia, home or away, they crumbled. The much-hyped
Race for the Mace was a one-horse affair with South Africa going lame at
the first fence. Their only victory over Australia came when they were, in
effect, 5–0 down. A year later, a wretched World Cup on home soil confirmed
that this was a team in decline, and brought down the captain, Shaun Pollock.

They had warmed up for the Aussie onslaught with some boot-filling in
Zimbabwe followed by a home series against India which drowned in
controversy. What became known as the Sehwag Affair threatened the uneasy
peace of world cricket. The South African board did not distinguish itself,
replacing the ICC referee, Mike Denness, with one of their own, Denis
Lindsay, but the ICC stripped the match of Test status. For those who noticed
the cricket, Jacques Kallis maintained his commanding form with two fifties
and then a hundred in the unofficial Test at Centurion; Pollock took 16
wickets in the two Tests that counted.

In Australia, South Africa ran into opponents wounded by criticism of
their failure to beat New Zealand. After two hefty defeats, South Africa's
plight worsened with a row over the inclusion of Justin Ontong in the last
Test. The selectors wanted to play Jacques Rudolph, a young left-hander who
had been deprived of a Test debut by the unofficial status of the third match
against India. But Percy Sonn, the outspoken president of the UCBSA,
insisted on the selection of Ontong even though the quota of one player of
colour was satisfied by the presence of Herschelle Gibbs.

The trauma of the Tests was alleviated by victory in the VB Series. New
Zealand again spiked the Aussies' guns, and Jonty Rhodes (345 runs at 57.50)
and Kallis (322 at 53.66) took full advantage. But normal service resumed
in the return leg of the Test series. Pollock missed all three Tests through
injury; Daryll Cullinan was bizarrely recalled to the side as stand-in captain,
only to walk out in high dudgeon after having his request for a 13-month

contract refused by the UCBSA. The only pluses were a couple of bright debuts – Graeme Smith made 68 in the Second Test, Andrew Hall shone in the consolation victory – and the fact that the quota debate seemed to have been put to bed by the Third Test, when four non-white players were picked on merit.

Shaun Pollock with ICC Championship mace
Picture by Clive Mason, Getty Images

South Africa even got hammered in the one-day series, despite the absence of their bogeyman Steve Waugh. While their one-day form was mostly excellent, with 32 wins out of 43 against other teams, they lost eight out of 11 to Australia. This dual personality bred confusion among the selectors, who couldn't decide whether to put their veterans out to pasture. They dropped Lance Klusener but recalled him for the World Cup; Allan Donald retired from Test cricket but was asked by the board to consider a comeback and tour England in 2003. Smith, amazingly, was left out of the World Cup squad until an injury to Rhodes happened to open the door. Unsure whether to stick or twist, the selectors stuck. The defensiveness that had dogged South Africa's cricket ever since readmission had not gone away. Then, when their policy blew up in their faces at the World Cup, the board went the other way, appointing Smith as captain at the age of 22.

The death of Hansie Cronje united South African cricket in grief, but even that was complicated. Should his misdemeanours be put aside in memory of his much-missed leadership qualities, or not? White South Africa seemed to think so, and Rhodes and Donald vowed to dedicate a World Cup victory to Cronje – a tribute that was to remain hypothetical.

After the winter break, South Africa entertained Bangladesh, Sri Lanka and Pakistan, thus becoming the first nation to host all four subcontinental teams in the space of just over a year – not to mention welcoming them back again for the World Cup. Against the hopeless Bangladeshis, Gary Kirsten became the first man to take centuries off all nine other Test nations and Kallis the fifth to score 4,000 Test runs and take 100 wickets, after Garry Sobers, Ian Botham, Kapil Dev and Carl Hooper.

There was a bad-tempered rubber with Sri Lanka, who almost pulled off an unlikely victory to level the series at Centurion when they had South Africa seven down chasing only 121. Against an exhausted Pakistan, South Africa found life tediously easy. At Newlands in the new year, Smith and Gibbs put on 368 for the first wicket, the highest stand by South Africa for any wicket, at more than a run a minute. The series victory put South Africa ahead of Australia in the ICC Test Championship by one 20th of a point. Pollock accepted the mace with good grace; the rest of the cricket world looked on in disbelief. **John Stern**

WEST INDIES
LEARNING TO WALK AGAIN

Test: P7 W4 L9 D4
Lost to Sri Lanka (a) 0–3.
Lost to Pakistan (Sharjah, counts
   as away) 0–2.
Beat India (h) 2–1 (D2).
Lost to New Zealand (h) 0–1
   (D1).
Lost to India (a) 0–2 (D1).
Beat Bangladesh (a) 2–0.

One-day: P34 W17 L14 NR3
Runners-up in LG Abans Series (Sri Lanka) v
   Sri Lanka and Zimbabwe: W2 L3.
Lost to Pakistan (Sharjah) 1–2.
Lost to India (h) 1–2.
Beat New Zealand (h) 3–1 (NR1).
Group stage of ICC Champions Trophy: W1
   L1.
Beat India (a) 4–3.
Beat Bangladesh (a) 2–0 (NR1).
Pool stage of World Cup: W3 L2 NR1.

They had spent the previous few years plummeting traumatically from the top of the world, but at least West Indies levelled off in 2002. If they didn't come close to regaining their former glory, they did manage a few unsteady steps forward, like a patient learning to walk again after a stroke. They came back from 1–0 down to beat India in a five-Test series, and they had two excellent one-day victories, over New Zealand and in India. But a facile victory in Bangladesh could not disguise the fact that West Indies remained feeble in Tests overseas, and another citadel fell when, for the first time, they lost a home series to New Zealand – for whom Shane Bond bowled with more pace and hostility than any West Indian. Stuck in seventh place in the Test Championship, they could hardly complain.

Carl Hooper, who had returned as captain in 2001, found the job no easier than his predecessors, Jimmy Adams and Brian Lara. His batting continued to be more consistent than for his first 80 Tests or so, and occasionally he issued reminders of his brilliance, as when he made a Test-best 233 against India. But he seldom led with the bat at the critical moments which West Indies have a penchant for creating. Before the World Cup, the team had done enough in one-day internationals to be many observers' outside tip for a place in the final, and they started with a memorable upset over the hosts, South Africa, inspired by a beautifully paced hundred from Lara. But they couldn't sustain their challenge, and although the rain cruelly robbed them of a cheap win against Bangladesh, they never lived up to their early promise. The plight of Hooper, who managed just 99 runs in the competition, was typical.

The younger batsmen gave plenty of reasons to be hopeful. Ramnaresh Sarwan was consistent in both forms of the game, raising his one-day average to a Bevanesque 55 by the end of the World Cup, and his deft strokeplay uncannily reminded older fans of Rohan Kanhai (whom Sarwan himself had never seen play). His return to the crease after a blow on the head in the crucial World Cup match against Sri Lanka was an exhibition of guts and stamina. And he was not alone. Chris Gayle, Marlon Samuels, Wavell Hinds and Ricardo Powell all showed signs of converting promise into runs. Yet their performances were uneven; mismanagement didn't help, nor did the fact that not everyone appeared to be playing in their best position. At greatest risk was Powell, whose powerful hitting tended to pigeonhole him in the niche marked One-Day Specialist. He may be reckless, but so was Viv Richards at his age. For openers, the team still hadn't found the synergy of Haynes and Greenidge. The Gayle–Hinds combination, prolific in India, didn't work in the World Cup. With Glenn McGrath and Brett Lee due in the Caribbean, the batting order needed rethinking.

With the ball, after Walsh and Ambrose retired, it was up to Mervyn Dillon, who finally delivered during India's tour of the Caribbean. But Pedro Collins was inconsistent, and there was still no real spinner. The one youngster with the speed of a Holding was Jermaine Lawson, whose astonishing analysis of 6.5–4–3–6 may have come against Bangladesh but none the less deserved an investment of faith. The fact that he didn't play in the World Cup until the final match against Kenya, when it didn't matter anyway, was a sign of Hooper's inflexibility.

So, the team had talent, and with experienced players like Shivnarine Chanderpaul, Ridley Jacobs and the new-old Vasbert Drakes, it was at least possible to imagine them turning round their dismal record in overseas Tests. They were a little like the West Indies teams before Frank Worrell: a collection of skilled individuals, adding up to less than the sum of their parts. The problem came back to leadership and management, as Roger Harper confirmed by resigning after the World Cup; an honourable man, he seemed destined to be remembered as a great fielder rather than a great manager. He departed with a well-aimed blast at the continuing insularity of the islands.

When it came to leadership, Lara was still an essential figure. In Sri Lanka, he pulled off a stunning revival before a fractured arm sent him home. Against India, he was back to blowing hot and cold, and developed a curious weakness when facing Ashish Nehra, as if trying to match Tendulkar's blind spot against Pedro Collins. Lara sharpened up once more against New Zealand without producing the big scores that made his name. Then he went down with what was reported to be hepatitis, and didn't play again until the World Cup. Misfortune aside, it still wasn't clear whether he had decided to commit himself fully to West Indies. On a bad day, the team's biggest liability has been Hooper, and since Lara, the boy who should have been king, never stepped up to the crease with his heart in it, the team has been forced to keep a stopgap captain for too long. In 1999, the Australians' visit brought out the very best in Lara; for the good of West Indian cricket, history badly needed to repeat itself. **Vaneisa Baksh**

NEW ZEALAND
THIRD IN THE WORLD

Test: P13 W6 L2 D5
Drew with Australia (a) 0–0 (D3).
Beat Bangladesh (h) 2–0.
Drew with England (h) 1–1 (D1).
Lost to Pakistan (a) 0–1.
Beat West Indies (a) 1–0 (D1).
Beat India (h) 2–0.

One-day: P44 W20 L23 NR1
Runner-up in VB Series (Australia) v South
   Africa and Australia: W4 L6.
Beat England (h) 3–2.
Last in Sharjah Cup v Pakistan and Sri
   Lanka: W1 L3.
Lost to Pakistan (a) 0–3.
Lost to West Indies (a) 1–3 (NR1).
Group stage of ICC Champions Trophy (Sri
   Lanka): W1 L1.
Beat India (h) 5–2.
*Super Six stage of World Cup: W5 L3
   (excluding one game forfeited).*

New Zealand are often regarded as the quiet men of international cricket, but last year they began to make some noise. After holding the all-conquering Australians in their own backyard – a result that gained lustre later, when Australia made short work of South Africa and England – they dealt swiftly with Bangladesh, pulled off a last-ditch draw with England, then won their first series in the Caribbean. But there was tragedy too, when their tour of Pakistan was cut short after a bomb exploded outside the team hotel in Karachi, killing 14 people. Even so, New Zealand ended the year ranked third in the ICC Test Championship. The position flattered them, but not by much. And if their one-day form wasn't quite as persuasive – an inconsistent World Cup was typical – people were still beginning to take note.

They owed a lot to the thoughtfully aggressive captaincy of Stephen Fleming, who had become the most quietly respected leader in Test cricket and continued to get more value for money out of his squad than any other captain in the world. Helped by a streamlined board and a dedicated backroom staff, he stunned Australia with a series of superbly conceived plans and piqued their machismo by declaring behind in the rain-affected First Test at Brisbane. New Zealand were grateful for more bad weather at Hobart, but by the end of the series, Fleming could reflect on two poor umpiring decisions at Perth that had cost his side a sensational upset.

More kudos followed in the one-day VB Series, where New Zealand knocked out Australia by beating them in three group games out of four and then ruthlessly exploiting the bonus-point system. But the biggest plus was the emergence of Shane Bond, the Canterbury policeman who sounded like a secret agent and bowled like a hired assassin. Not since the early days of Richard Hadlee had New Zealand seen speed like it, and Bond finished a whirlwind first year in international cricket with 38 Test wickets at 22, including six hauls of four or more.

His record would have been even more startling if he hadn't missed the England series with an injury. He wasn't the only one to break down, and in 13 Tests New Zealand used 11 different pairs of opening bowlers. But by the time they were hammering a jaded India at home, they had settled on a new-ball attack of Bond and Daryl Tuffey, a Jekyll-and-Hyde who took 22 wickets at ten in three Tests at home, but only four wickets at nearly 57 in three Tests overseas. But he developed a priceless knack of taking an early wicket: he struck in his first over of an international 11 times. Jacob Oram's stock as a beefy all-rounder and future captain rose too.

The batting line-up rarely changed, but results were mixed. Craig McMillan's Test average dipped below 40 for the first time since December 1998, and there were doubts about Lou Vincent's technique at the top of the order: after a hundred on debut at Perth, he managed just five more fifties in 19 innings. By contrast, his partner, Mark Richardson, was a rock. But the greatest individual achievement was Nathan Astle's all-guns-blazing 222 against England at Christchurch. A once-in-a-lifetime, blink-or-you'll-miss-it innings, it was the fastest double-hundred ever in Tests, by a long way, and the most exciting single feat achieved by any New Zealander in Test history. The quiet men just couldn't stop talking about it. **Lawrence Booth**

Stephen Fleming: thoughtful but aggressive. *Picture by Andrew Cornaga, Photosport.*

INDIA
A NEW STEEL

Test: P21 W7 L6 D8
Lost to South Africa (a) 0–1 (D1).
Beat England (h) 1–0 (D2).
Beat Zimbabwe (h) 2–0.
Lost to West Indies (a) 1–2 (D2).
Drew with England (a) 1–1 (D2).
Beat West Indies (h) 2–0 (D1).
Lost to New Zealand (a) 0–2.

One-day: P58 W33 L22 NR3
Runners-up in Standard Bank Tournament (South Africa) v South Africa and Kenya: W3, L4.
Drew with England (h) 3–3.
Beat Zimbabwe (h) 3–2.
Beat West Indies (a) 2–1.
Won NatWest Series (England) v England and Sri Lanka: W5, L1, NR1.
Shared ICC Champions Trophy (Sri Lanka): W3, NR2.
Lost to West Indies (h) 3–4.
Lost to New Zealand (a) 2–5.
Runners-up in World Cup: W9 L2.

The Test year ended in despair. On seaming wickets in New Zealand, India's batsmen came unhinged like a door the carpenter was so obsessed with varnishing that he forgot to tighten the screws. But let that distract no one: by their standards, India had a good 18 months. And they were, by any measure, the second-best team in the World Cup.

Study the balance sheet and you will find a blank in the overseas series-wins column, but plenty of ticks when it came to surpassing expectations. India didn't lose 2–0 in South Africa, they won a Test in the West Indies, and they bounced back from a hopeless start to level a series in England. All told, this was a better showing outside the subcontinent than any Indian side had achieved since 1986, when Kapil Dev's team won 2–0 in England.

The real story, however, was not in the scorebook, which was still pitiable for a team that advertises itself as the best – all right, second-best – batting line-up in the world, but in the way India transformed themselves from stoic losers to chest-thumping warriors. If they lost, it was because they lacked skill and armoury in foreign conditions, not nerve and heart. The hub of this transformation was Sourav Ganguly, who despite not being able to put bat to ball for 60 per cent of this period, lifted Indian cricket from a state of factionalist torpor by the sheer force of his personality. He showed passion, vim and an unflinching commitment to talent. He won loyalty because he gave it in good measure, and to every deserving player, irrespective of his postal address. For India, it was a big step forward.

In the NatWest Series final at Lord's in July, two young Indian batsmen, Mohammad Kaif and Yuvraj Singh, forged a fightback almost as stirring as Kapil's solo against Zimbabwe in the 1983 World Cup; and India's one-day team proved throughout the year that it had, at long last, added nous and steel to the talent it had always possessed. Late in the year, against West Indies and in New Zealand, they faltered, but it turned out that they were just keeping their powder dry for the World Cup. Once there, they started with a wobble but gathered strength as the tournament went on, sweeping aside England, Pakistan and Sri Lanka with intensity in the field as well as elegance with the bat. If Sachin Tendulkar was majestic, the seamers were a revelation.

As individuals, the team had their usual mixed year. Harbhajan Singh's stature as a wicket-taking spin bowler grew even as Anil Kumble's diminished. Zaheer Khan learned the virtue of fitness and rediscovered his zest for bowling fast, while Javagal Srinath wrestled with an ageing body and an indecisive mind. Ashish Nehra finally put his foot on the gas and the ball in the right place in the World Cup.

Virender Sehwag, with three scintillating Test centuries in three continents, announced the emergence of a major talent, but V. V. S. Laxman reverted to the batsman he had been before his 281 rather than the one he had promised to be. Tendulkar, unmindful of all the whispers about his indifferent form, chalked up 1,892 runs at 59; with bad patches like that, who needs good form? Rahul Dravid was just behind in figures, with 1,581 runs at nearly 53, but his contributions proved more significant. He saved Tests at Port Elizabeth, Georgetown, Trent Bridge and The Oval, and in between played the definitive innings of his career on a difficult pitch at Headingley to set up a memorable Test win – India's biggest overseas. He was easily India's Man of the Year. And finally, a boy from Gujarat answered India's prayers for a wicket-keeper of genuine class. Parthiv Patel, only 17 years old, looked good to serve India for 17 more. **Sambit Bal**

PAKISTAN
NOT HAPPY

Test: P14 W8 L6 D0
Runners-up in Asian Test
   Championship: beat
   Bangladesh (h) 1–0, lost to Sri
   Lanka (h) 0–1.
Beat Bangladesh (a) 2–0.
Beat West Indies (Sharjah,
   counts as home) 2–0.
Beat New Zealand (h) 1–0.
*Lost to Australia (Sri Lanka and
   Sharjah, counts as home) 0–3.*
Beat Zimbabwe (a) 2–0.
Lost to South Africa (a) 0–2.

One-day: P49 W29 L18 NR2
Won Khaleej Times Trophy (Sharjah) v Sri
   Lanka and Zimbabwe, W4 L1.
Beat Bangladesh (a) 3–0.
Beat West Indies (Sharjah, counts as home)
   2–1.
Won Sharjah Cup v Sri Lanka and New
   Zealand, W3 L2.
Beat New Zealand (h) 3–0.
Beat Australia (a) 2–1.
Last in Morocco Cup (Tangier) v Sri Lanka
   and South Africa, W1 L3.
Shared PSO Tri-Nation Tournament (Kenya)
   with Australia, also v Kenya, W2 L2 NR1.
Group stage of ICC Champions Trophy (in
   Sri Lanka): W1 L1.
Beat Zimbabwe (h) 5–0.
Lost to South Africa (a) 1–4.
Pool stage of World Cup: W2 L3 NR1.

Pakistan's year fell under the twin shadows of the war against terrorism and Waqar Younis's captaincy. When the USA and its allies decided the best way to secure their lands was by bombing Afghanistan, Pakistan became destabilised – much less than it could have been, but enough to ensure that Sri Lanka and New Zealand pulled out of tours. Others played Pakistan on neutral ground, while India's stance on Kashmir kept them away.

Shoaib Akhtar *Picture by Anuruddha Lokuhapuarachchi, Popperfoto/Reuters*

None the less, the ICC's hectic Test Championship ensured that tours came and went faster than a game of street cricket. And neutral venues allowed Pakistan to make cricketing history in Sharjah. West Indies were the reluctant tourists, at such a low ebb that they were thrashed. Later, New Zealand swallowed their security fears and arrived in Pakistan. It went swimmingly for a while, particularly for Inzamam-ul-Haq who clobbered 329 in Lahore, the second-highest Test score by a Pakistani. Shoaib Akhtar thrilled too with a blistering return of six for 11. In the one-dayers he claimed a world record by delivering a ball unofficially measured at 100mph; in the World Cup he made it official. He was the first fast bowler since Waqar and Wasim Akram to rank among Pakistan's greats. But Shoaib is a man of extremes, be it hyperextensible joints or hyperactive party life, and Pakistan were only occasionally able to rely on his fitness or form.

When they could, mighty Australian and South African batsmen were humbled by his ferocity. Notoriously poor in Australia, Pakistan shocked even themselves by defeating them 2–1 in a mostly indoor series in June.

That was the apogee of Pakistan's year, when Waqar's rule was a mirage of unity and World Cup optimism. A few weeks later it was revealed that Pakistan's players were not happy with him. They found him stubborn and aloof. He was never a master tactician, but a leader of men, and when the men do not want to follow, leadership fails. A closer examination revealed that Waqar's success was largely a matter of carpet-bombing two of the weakest teams in world cricket: Bangladesh and West Indies. But a string of defeats in late 2002 called the bluff in Waqar's bravado. Pakistan only momentarily recovered their bullying form to hammer an enfeebled Zimbabwe, before South Africa administered a dose of reality. The World Cup, for a team that had won in 1992 and reached the final in 1999, was a disaster, even allowing for the misfortune of a lost toss against England and a washout in Zimbabwe.

It didn't help that Pakistan's top players cherry-picked their matches, that Saeed Anwar was stricken with grief at the death of his daughter and missed most of the year, and that Richard Pybus resumed as coach, was replaced by Mudassar Nazar, and then got the job back. As a consequence, Pakistan seemed unable to settle on a consistent approach. Batsmen were shuffled up and down, Saqlain Mushtaq was mostly in but sometimes out, and Shahid Afridi was a match-winner or a match-loser. Pakistan's brains trust made plenty of decisions but their sense of direction was paralysed. Pybus became a laughing stock when he tried to out-psych Steve Waugh, only for Pakistan to crumble for scores of 59 and 53 in Sharjah. "Pybusisms" were born and up to 145 million people humiliated. It was the batting that most troubled Pakistan, particularly the opening slot, although Taufeeq Umar emerged as a future prospect. Yousuf Youhana bolstered his world-class reputation by becoming the leading one-day run-scorer in 2002 (1,362 runs at over 54), even if it had a lot to do with his slaughter of Zimbabwe (405 for once out).

The biggest casualty of this period, apart from the batting manual, was Waqar. With his effectiveness as a bowler waning, his leadership was also exposed as ineffectual, and he was sacked after the World Cup. Pybus declined to continue, so Javed Miandad returned as coach with the wicket-keeper, Rashid Latif, assuming the captaincy. Meanwhile allegations about the social lives of several senior players drifted from the rubble of the World Cup. All in all, another typical year for Pakistan cricket. **Kamran Abbasi**

SRI LANKA
ASIA'S NUMBER ONE

Test: **P15 W10 L4 D1**
Won Asian Test Championship:
  beat Bangladesh (h) 1–0 and
  Pakistan (a) 1–0.
Beat West Indies (h) 3–0.
Beat Zimbabwe (h) 3–0.
Lost to England (a) 0–2 (D1).
Beat Bangladesh (h) 2–0.
Lost to South Africa (a) 0–2.

One-day: P57 W29 L25 T1 NR2
Runners-up in Khaleej Times Trophy (Sharjah)
  v Pakistan and Zimbabwe: W3 L2.
Won LG Abans Trophy (h) v West Indies and
  Zimbabwe: W4 L1.
Runners-up in Sharjah Cup v Pakistan and
  New Zealand: W3 L2.
Last in NatWest Series (a) v England and
  India: W1 L5.
Beat Bangladesh (h) 3–0.
Won Morocco Cup (Tangier) v Pakistan and
  South Africa: W4 L1.
Shared ICC Champions Trophy (h) with
  India: W3 NR2.
Lost to South Africa (a) 1–4.
*Last in VB Series (Australia) v Australia and
  England: W2 L6.*
Semi-finals of World Cup: W5 L4 T1.

Sri Lanka started the 2001-02 season with eight consecutive Test victories, which made them the most successful team in the subcontinent, if not necessarily the best. But their results in whites turned sour whenever they left the subcontinent. Heroes at home, they were hopeless overseas and failed to add to their record of three Test wins outside Asia. And they did rely rather too heavily on one man, the phenomenal Muttiah Muralitharan.

Clean sweeps over West Indies and Zimbabwe, and victory in the devalued, three-team Asian Test Championship – India had withdrawn – left Sri Lanka sitting comfortably in third place in the ICC Test Championship in March 2002. Three of the eight wins were by an innings; another three by eight wickets or more. However, the dominant displays, led by Muralitharan's off-spin and rampant batting from Hashan Tillekeratne (who averaged 142 in those eight wins), Kumar Sangakkara (80), Mahela Jayawardene (71) and Thilan Samaraweera (70), all came against sides in the bottom half of the Championship.

The first warning of the massive impact caused by a missing Muralitharan sounded in the Sharjah Cup final in April 2002. Murali tore ligaments in his shoulder while fielding and did not bowl; Sri Lanka were beaten by 217 runs. The injury prevented him from playing in the First Test against England and the team's unshakeable self-belief at home quickly returned to self-doubt again.

The change was particularly noticeable in the performance of the captain, Sanath Jayasuriya, who twice dropped Vaughan in the second innings at Lord's and then set defensive fields when Sri Lanka were the only side that could win. England racked up 529 for five declared and ended their opponents' streak of nine Test wins in a row, which had begun against India in September 2001.

When Murali was rushed back for the final two Tests, his spark was missing, although he did produce one amazing delivery to bowl Mark Butcher at Edgbaston. But Sri Lanka lost both games; the out-of-form Jayasuriya dropped from opener to No. 6 at Manchester, where he allowed England more than a run a ball during their final-evening run-chase; disharmony filled the dressing-room; and the bowling coach, Daryl Foster, resigned after an argument over airfares when he visited his sick grandchild in Australia.

Calm resurfaced during a Colombo stroll against Bangladesh but disappeared again when they landed in South Africa. A hiding in the First Test was followed by a competitive Second, when Marvan Atapattu replaced the injured Jayasuriya as captain and impressed with innovative fields and a willingness to rotate the bowling. But, as in England, Sri Lanka's gifted batsmen – six regulars averaged at least 50 during the 15 Tests – were overpowered by pace and bounce, and the bowlers lacked consistency. Murali totalled an amazing 97 wickets in his 13 Tests but only 15 came outside Asia. Chaminda Vaas was his main support with 53, while 18 other bowlers managed only 105 between them.

Mahela Jayawardene *Picture by Patrick Eagar*

Similar patterns emerged in the one-day internationals. With Muralitharan on the prowl, Sri Lanka triumphed in the LG Abans triangular at home and the Morocco Cup in Tangier, shared the ICC Champions Trophy with India and reached the semi-finals of the World Cup; without him they were last in the NatWest Series and lost the Sharjah Cup final. As usual their home form was excellent but in England, Australia, and – until the World Cup – South Africa their play was poor. **Peter English**

ZIMBABWE
BLIGHTED BY POLITICS

Test: P11 W1 L8 D2
Lost to South Africa (h) 0–1 (D1).
Beat Bangladesh (a) 1–0 (D1).
Lost to Sri Lanka (a) 0–3.
Lost to India (a) 0–2.
Lost to Pakistan (h) 0–2.

One-day: P42 W10 L30 NR2
Lost to South Africa (h) 0–3.
Lost to England (h) 0–5.
Last in Khaleej Times Trophy (Sharjah) v
    Pakistan and Sri Lanka: W0 L4.
Beat Bangladesh (a) 3–0.
Last in LG Abans Series (Sri Lanka), v
    Sri Lanka and West Indies: W1 L3.
Lost to India (a) 2–3.
Group stage of ICC Champions Trophy: L2.
Lost to Pakistan (h) 0–5.
Beat Kenya (h) 2–0 (NR1).
*Super Six stage of World Cup: W2 (excluding
    one forfeit counted as a win) L5 NR1.*

Although Geoff Marsh, who succeeded his compatriot Carl Rackemann as
Zimbabwe's coach in October 2001, earned praise for his professional and
thorough approach, it is difficult to escape the conclusion that Zimbabwe went
backwards in his first 18 months in charge. Against an almost impossible
background of political intrigue, their only Test win came against Bangladesh;
and from 33 completed one-day internationals against Test-playing countries
– Bangladesh apart – they won just three. Under Rackemann, one-day series
had been won both at home and away against New Zealand, and India had
been beaten in a Test match. Towards the end of his time in charge Andy
Flower proved his world-class status yet again by scoring 142 and 199 not
out in a losing cause agaisnt South Africa, which took him to the top of the
Test batting ratings. But for Marsh's team, the only highlights came when
Zimbabwe won just their second Test series away from home, and when they
reached the Super Six stage of the World Cup for the second time in a row.
But the Test win came in Bangladesh, and the Super Six place was theirs
largely by default: they collected four points from England's refusal to travel
to Harare and two more in the washout of Pakistan's match in Bulawayo.

   Seldom, however, can an international coach have faced such a daunting
set of problems, and there was no doubt that politics – both cricketing and
national – severely affected team performance. With farm and land seizure
by the Mugabe regime an ever-present and growing threat, and with the
economy and the infrastructure of the country declining by the week, the
best could hardly be expected from players who mostly came from farming
families. By the start of the World Cup, the Streak family had lost nine-
tenths of their land at Turk Mine in Matabeleland, the Whittalls half their
ranch on the low veld, and the Viljoen family had been evicted from their
farm. By the end of it, Andy Flower and Henry Olonga, who together upset
the authorities by issuing a heartfelt statement lamenting the "death of
democracy in our beloved Zimbabwe", had retired from international cricket.
Guy Whittall joined them, and Andy Pycroft, a white selector, stepped down
after alleging that he hadn't been consulted over team selection.

They hadn't been the first to leave: the Strang brothers, Paul and Bryan, quit the game prematurely, and the fast bowler Brighton Watambwa emigrated to the United States at the age of 25. Another black player, 26-year-old Everton Matambanadzo, had already made the same move. Hamilton Masakadza, who in July 2001 had become the youngest player to score a Test century on debut, stagnated in university cricket in Bloemfontein. And then there was the "imposition of goals" – a misnomer for a new quota system in which the starting eleven had to include three non-whites rather than one. The continued inclusion of the coloured Dion Ebrahim, out of his depth at the top of the order, epitomised Zimbabwe's self-imposed mess. When the Zimbabwe Cricket Union (patron: R. G. Mugabe) commissioned a "Task Force" report, which stipulated racial make-up of cricketing teams and administration at all levels, the ramifications were considerable.

Another destabilising factor was the number of captains Zimbabwe were obliged to use. Brian Murphy, the leg-spinner, was earmarked as the best candidate in the long term, but was plagued by injuries that severely restricted his availability, culminating in the World Cup when he tore a calf muscle warming up to bowl against New Zealand. In 11 Tests, Zimbabwe had four captains – Heath Streak, Murphy, Stuart Carlisle and Alistair Campbell. Carlisle was sacked for speaking out of turn to the press and Campbell, one of the so-called "Royal Family" – a group of players regarded by the ZCU as overly headstrong and influential – was sidelined. Dirk Viljoen, a good one-day performer, was also dropped for supposedly belonging to this group.

One key cricketing factor in Zimbabwe's poor performance was the lack of penetration in their attack. Streak's loss of pace converted him from a spearhead to a stock bowler; Olonga only came to life in the Tests against Pakistan in November 2002; and Murphy's leg-breaks were badly missed. Travis Friend and Andy Blignaut, two promising young pace bowlers, developed painfully slowly, although Blignaut's batting reached new levels, notably in a 25-ball fifty against Australia in the World Cup. If Zimbabwe cricket was sliding into the abyss, at least it was going down fighting. **Geoffrey Dean**

BANGLADESH
A DULL THROB

Test: P14, W0, L13, D1
Last in Asian Test
Championship: lost to
Pakistan (a) 0–1, lost to Sri
Lanka (a) 0–1.
Lost to Zimbabwe (h) 0–1 (D1).
Lost to New Zealand (a) 0–2.
Lost to Pakistan (h) 0–2.
Lost to Sri Lanka (a) 0–2.
Lost to South Africa (a) 0–2.
Lost to West Indies (h) 0–2 (NR1).

One-day: P23, W0, L21, NR 2
Lost to Zimbabwe (h) 0–3.
Lost to Pakistan (h) 0–3.
Lost to Sri Lanka (a) 0–3.
Group stage of ICC Champions Trophy (Sri
Lanka): L2.
Lost to South Africa (a) 0–3.
Lost to West Indies (h) 0–2.
Pool stage of World Cup: L5 NR1.

After two years of incessant beatings, the pain of defeat for Bangladesh had given way to a dull throb, and the desire for self-improvement had been swamped by the hopelessness of the task. Long before they bombed out of the World Cup with defeats to Canada and Kenya, their cricketers had been stripped of all dignity. Their players deserved some sympathy for being rushed into Test cricket before they were ready, but the privileged status demanded responsibility. In 14 Tests since August 2001, Bangladesh failed to pass 200 in 20 completed innings, while bowling the opposition out on four meagre occasions. The wider danger was to the reputation of Test cricket itself.

Tests involving Bangladesh were a chore, not a challenge, and by the end of 2002 the record books had been cheapened to the tune of 25 hundreds and 18 five-fors. In the Asian Test Championship in September 2001, two Sri Lankan batsmen were so sated that they retired bored, and 11 months later, a virtual Sri Lankan Second XI opted for batting practice instead of helping themselves to an innings victory.

Reputations were as short-lived as public interest. Aminul Islam, a century-maker in Bangladesh's inaugural Test, like two other former captains, Naimur Rahman and Akram Khan, dropped in and out, as a batch of teenagers were drafted into the front line. Partly influenced by Mohammad Ashraful's historic century against Sri Lanka, the chopping and changing also stemmed from a rootless domestic structure – talent had to be plucked before it ripened, or it would wither on the vine.

In time, Bangladesh's struggles could transform them into a battle-hardened team. In reality, however, they had reached saturation point. For their sakes and the good of the game, they needed to be sent for a lengthy period of reflection. **Andrew Miller**

THE ICC TEST CHAMPIONSHIP

For the first time since its official adoption in May 2001, the Test Championship was led by a side other than Australia. When South Africa beat Pakistan 2–0 at home in January 2003, they edged ahead of Australia by one 20th of a point per series, and the mace changed hands, to widespread bafflement. To regain the title, Australia needed to beat West Indies away, where they only drew last time. South Africa were likely to pick up two cheap points in Bangladesh, but Australia would still be in front by 0.004.

While the top two remained streets ahead, the congestion in the middle got worse: New Zealand rose from mid-table to the heady heights of third, but were just 0.30 ahead of seventh-placed West Indies. Sri Lanka dropped one place in the year, and so did England, who were hotly pursued by an improving India. Pakistan continued to flounder inexplicably near the bottom, ahead of only Zimbabwe and Bangladesh, who were not due a full rating until they had played nine Test series.

On March 22, 2003, the ICC said the format would change in June, but gave no details. This table, possibly the last of its kind, was based on the results of the most recent series between each pair of teams, both home and away. Two points were awarded for a win, one for a draw, and every time a new series – which must be of at least two Tests to count – was played, it replaced the previous one between the same teams. Positions were determined by average points per series.

		Series played	Won	Lost	Drawn	Points	Average
1	South Africa (2)	17	13	3	1	27	**1.59**
2	Australia (1)	13	9	2	2	20	**1.54**
3	New Zealand (5)	17	8	5	4	20	**1.18**
4	Sri Lanka (3)	16	8	6	2	18	**1.13**
5	England (4)	16	6	6	4	16	**1.00**
6	India (8)	15	5	6	4	14	**0.93**
7	West Indies (6)	17	7	9	1	15	**0.88**
8	Pakistan (7)	16	4	8	4	12	**0.75**
9	Zimbabwe (9)	16	3	11	2	8	**0.50**
–	Bangladesh (–)	7	0	7	0	0	**0.00**

*As at March 31, 2003. Last year's positions in brackets (*Wisden 2002*, page 1611).*

THE ICC ONE-DAY INTERNATIONAL CHAMPIONSHIP

In October 2002, the ICC launched an official one-day championship, based initially on all matches since August 1, 2000. The first man to lift the trophy, a shield, was Ricky Ponting, Australia's one-day captain. Straight after the World Cup, the table split into five distinct clumps: Australia at the top with South Africa in shouting distance; Pakistan and Sri Lanka scrapping for third, with India closing fast; West Indies, England and New Zealand separated by just one point in a hundred; Zimbabwe, somewhat isolated; and Kenya and Bangladesh – with Kenya now some way ahead.

The trophy changes hands every time there is a new leader, and only matches between teams on the table are included. Positions are determined by dividing total points by matches played. After every game, both teams receive a certain number of points and an updated rating. Points are awarded according to a mathematical formula which takes into account the strength of the opposition. Recent results carry greater weight: matches played in the first year of each cycle receive a weighting of one-third, so 33 games played count as 11. Matches played in the second year receive a weighting of two-thirds, and the remaining matches a weighting of one (i.e. no weighting). Every August, the first year's results are dropped from the table; all games until the start of the following August will be added. World Cup matches are included as long as they are between two of these 11 teams: curiously, the only teams to change places were New Zealand (up one) and England (down one).

		Matches	Points	Rating
1	**Australia**	45	6,115	**136**
2	**South Africa**	53	6,501	**123**
3	**Pakistan**	45	4,951	**110**
4	**Sri Lanka**	57	6,157	**108**
5	**India**	53	5,488	**104**
6	**West Indies**	35	3,463	**99**
7	**New Zealand**	45	4,431	**98**
8	**England**	34	3,337	**98**
9	**Zimbabwe**	40	2,503	**63**
10	**Kenya**	22	654	**30**
11	**Bangladesh**	19	119	**6**

As at March 31, 2003. Updated tables can be found at www.icc.org.

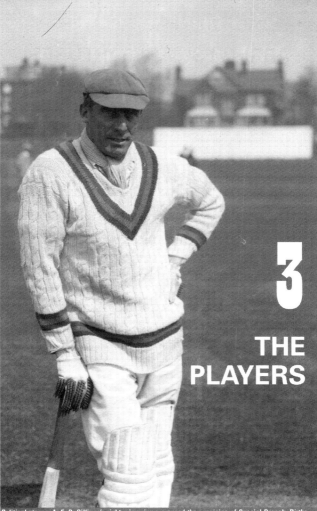

3

THE PLAYERS

Political stance: A. E. R. Gilligan's right-wing views aroused the suspicion of Special Branch. Births and Deaths page 181. *Picture from Getty Images.*

PART THREE: THE PLAYERS

ARRIVALS & DEPARTURES

A new section giving brief portraits of those taking or leaving the big stage. The line-up is not intended to be exhaustive, or even representative, but selective. The arrivals are a handful of young players who have emerged in the past year and made an unusual impact; the departures are the biggest figures to have announced their retirement from international cricket by March 16, 2003. Updated career records can be found on the player's individual page on Wisden.com

Fair cop: Shane Bond bowls Brian Lara, Barbados, June 2002. *Picture by Andy Clark, Reuters.*

ARRIVALS

Shane Bond New Zealand fast bowler

Trust a man called Bond to burst on to the scene in style. With all of Australia expecting another cakewalk to the final of their annual one-day series, Shane Bond unleashed a blizzard of 90mph in-swinging yorkers to take 21 wickets, win the Man of the Series award – and knock out the hosts. In a flash, he had become New Zealand's fastest bowler ever. He followed that by upstaging West Indies' quicks in their own backyard, but continued to save his shaking and stirring best for the Aussies: six for 23 in the World Cup Super Six match took his one-day record against them to 22 wickets at the unlikely average of ten and the unthinkable strike rate of 15. New Zealand had found their first match-winning bowler since Chris Cairns, and possibly their best since Richard Hadlee. **Lawrence Booth**

Virender Sehwag Indian batsman

To watch Virender Sehwag bat is to recall the immortal W. B. Yeats line, "a terrible beauty is born". There is an uncanny physical resemblance to his hero, Sachin Tendulkar, which extends to the fluency and flourish with which he plays the straight drive, the ferocious cut past point and the disdainful flick off the legs. But the unfettered nature and charming rusticity are all his own, the legacy of a childhood spent playing gully cricket in the village of Najafgarh on the outskirts of Delhi. A century in trying conditions on Test debut at Bloemfontein silenced the cynics who said his cavalier style, first seen in a blistering 69-ball one-day hundred against New Zealand, wouldn't suit the five-day game. Since being promoted to open, he has devastated attacks when in both white and blue, notably in a century on a seaming track in a Trent Bridge Test and a swashbuckling 77-ball hundred in the ICC Champions Trophy, also against England. He precipitated an international crisis in only his second Test, after he was banned for excessive appealing and dissent by the referee, Mike Denness, but his batting has already put all that behind him. **Dileep Premachandran**

Jimmy Anderson England fast bowler

In spring 2002, Jimmy Anderson was a 19-year-old playing, with mixed success, for Burnley in the Lancashire League; nine months later he was being thrown the new ball in the World Cup. And all it took was a handful of county games, an athletic run, a sure wrist, a hip on a well-greased axle and the nous and nerve to land the ball in the right place when it was swinging. Suddenly rival counties were whispering in his ear, he was in the Academy squad and, as older bowlers continued their domino impression, the England one-day team. His highlighted head disappears as he bowls, as if jerked behind by a rogue puppeteer, but it kept cool enough on the big stage to scare Australia and destroy Pakistan. For England, that was more than enough, even if reality bit as the World Cup went on. **Tanya Aldred**

Graeme Smith South African opener – and captain

Long-limbed and left-handed, Smith made a profound impact on the South African team in his first year, as much through attitude as results. The force of his personality – equal parts passion, determination and wit – is only just

matched by the power in his hooks, pulls and on-drives. A broad stance and equally broad shoulders have led to comparisons with Graeme Pollock, but Smith, 22, is simply too strong off his legs and not yet accomplished enough on the off side to be regarded as a complete player, let alone a great one. He has hands like coal-scoops in the slips and bowls off-breaks which have potential if he can keep them alive in the shadow of his batting. His maturity and powers of motivation made him seem a regular five minutes after making his debut, in the deep end against Australia. His maiden century, a round 200, came against Bangladesh in his third Test; a sensational 151 against Pakistan in January 2003 confirmed he was no popgun-attack bully. South Africa's

Graeme Smith. Picture by Philip Brown.

wretched World Cup, which he joined halfway through, meant that the captaincy was thrust upon him ahead of schedule as South Africa yearned for a fresh start. He was due to begin the job with only 31 first-class matches behind him – and a Test average of 55. **Neil Manthorp**

Parthiv Patel Indian wicket-keeper

In 2002, Parthiv Patel emerged as the little boy of world cricket. Younger teenagers may have played internationals – though only Tendulkar and Laxman Sivaramakrishnan from India, and no wicket-keeper from anywhere – but none has looked so obviously guilty of having skipped school to be there. Wide-eyed, Patel went to England without a first-class appearance for his state, Gujarat, and made his debut aged 17 years 152 days in the Second Test at Trent Bridge, where Nasser Hussain accused him of looking just 12 and commentators had fun pointing out that, according to ECB regulations, he shouldn't be keeping wicket without a helmet unless he had a note from his mother. Patel rose above all this by surviving 84 minutes on the last evening to help save the Test and turn the series. But it was a few months later, when he coped with Anil Kumble and Harbhajan Singh on two crumbling pitches at Mumbai and Chennai against West Indies, that India knew for sure they had found their man. Patel's one-day career struggled to take off as the team searched for balance, but it seemed to be merely a matter of adding some power to his well-grounded batting. And he has plenty of time. **Rahul Bhattacharya**

Mark of genius: an outrageous catch by Mark Waugh, fielding at second slip, set Australia on course for their crushing victory in the 1999 World Cup final. Glenn McGrath was the grateful bowler; Wajahatulla Wasti the unfortunate batsman. *Picture by Adrian Murrell, Getty Images*

DEPARTURES

Mark Waugh Australian batsman and slip fielder

Mark Waugh's talents were dual-edged. He made cricket look easy – and this extended also to getting out. He could whisk a game away from opponents in half an hour, or vanish in half an instant. He could drive bowlers to distraction, or frustrate his own admirers. None in his era timed their leg-side strokes more sweetly, or scored quickly with so little hint of haste, or made challenging conditions seem simpler – as in the best of his Test hundreds, at Port Elizabeth in 1997. He took a record number of Test catches with uncanny anticipation and economy of movement. Yet few so irked detractors, who felt he didn't make the runs that his abilities justified – though he might almost have made too many, and played for too long, cheapening his effect. His name will be stained by his misadventures during the match-fixing controversies of the mid-1990s, which he wandered into as heedlessly as one of his lazier strokes. His defence was the same ground on which he was so often criticised: carelessness. **Gideon Haigh**

Angus Fraser England bowler

Gus Fraser was a throwback, in method and morality if not – thankfully – outlook. Even his Lancastrian birthplace, Billinge, conjures up an era of steam trains and stout hearts. Alastair was the gifted Fraser sibling, but it was Angus who made the grade – twice over. Able, at 6ft 5in, to generate steep bounce, he had an almost puritanical devotion to line and length which made him England's most dependable bowler of the 1990s. There were four cheap wickets on debut against the rampant 1989 Australians, and 47 in his first 11 Tests before a hip condition threatened early retirement. Defying all predictions, he returned at the end of the 1993 Ashes series, taking eight wickets to win the Oval Test, the start of a second chapter that brought 130 more victims, global respect and the affection of a nation grateful for a symbol of constancy. In 1998, his belated *annus mirabilis*, he acted as twelfth man during a one-day international – red-faced, rueful and willing as ever – and received perhaps the warmest ovation ever given at Lord's to someone not playing in a match. The finest English seamer of his type since Bedser? Probably. **Rob Steen**

Allan Donald South African fast bowler

The fastest of all South African bowlers, Allan Donald didn't so much bowl at batsmen as hunt them. He was not exceptionally tall or broad but he was a great athlete whose spring at the crease allowed him to fire bullets, angling into the body and curving away. He grew up during isolation, representing South Africa only against rebel touring teams, but apartheid fell just in time for him to have a career to match his talent. In a nation of hunters, he was the spearhead for a decade. His battles with Tendulkar and Steve Waugh were legendary, but nothing beat the electricity of that half hour in the Nottingham gloom against Michael Atherton in 1998, when every ball sizzled with intent. A gentlemanly sort of destroyer, Donald found time that evening

to console Mark Boucher after he dropped Nasser Hussain, and to ask Atherton afterwards to hand over and sign his glove – complete with giveaway red mark. He continued to hoover the wickets, passing 300 in Tests in his home town, Bloemfontein, where he was loved as much as in Birmingham. His hamstrings began to give up before his heart, and he retired from Tests in 2002. The end, when it came, was sad: left out of South Africa's final pool match in the World Cup – in which he had played every time since 1992, and had his most infamous moment, dropping his bat hopelessly to let Australia into the final in 1999. The man with the white stripe forever smeared across his nose will be remembered for better. His only rival as South Africa's greatest bowler is his old new-ball partner, Shaun Pollock.
Tanya Aldred

Lightning strikes no more: Allan Donald. *Picture by Patrick Eagar.*

Aravinda de Silva Sri Lankan batsman

Sri Lanka's finest-ever batsman was one of the game's great entertainers, though he fell a few steps short of the batting pantheon. Despite being just 5ft-and-a-deep-breath tall, and stocky, de Silva played the cut and pull with as much elan as an Aussie brought up on bouncy tracks. He possessed the soundest of techniques, yet it took him years, and over 20 Tests, to play to anything like his true potential. A monumental 267 against New Zealand bucked the trend of underachievement, though only four of his 20 Test hundreds came outside Asia. He assured himself of immortality back home with a sensational unbeaten century against Mark Taylor's Australians in the World Cup final of 1996 and, on his day, was a peerless, cultured strokemaker. But barring a purple patch following the World Cup triumph, consistency was never his forte. In the final analysis, the man whose attitude to fitness was often as cavalier as Colin Milburn's, could best be compared to the sleek racing cars he loved to collect – easy on the eye, with reliability only an expensive option. **Dileep Premachandran**

Jonty Rhodes South Africa fielder and batsman

There will be no more bottom-patting, no more scampering between the wickets, no more exocet throws, no more blond choirboy chirrups irritating the opposition beyond composure. Jonty Rhodes' career ended in the cruellest way possible when he fractured a bone in his right hand against Kenya in South Africa's second game of the World Cup. He had been, of course, trying to save a run. Rhodes was, is, a South African icon. A devout Christian, he became as feared as the meanest bowler purely through speed of leg, arm and eye. At backward point or in the covers, he would leap skyward and pouch impossible catches – the number eight on his back the sign of a praying mantis. He hurtled into cricket's consciousness in the 1992 World Cup, South Africa's re-entry into the sporting fold, when he transformed himself into a human cannonball: smashing full length and head first into the stumps of the young Inzamam-ul-Haq. Many more unforgettable images followed. His batting was vital too: he guarded the gateway to the South African tail, sweeping the spinners and pressing the field, but more important still was his constant geeing-up of his team-mates. The only question mark against him, which came at the end of his career, was his desire to rehabilitate his friend Hansie Cronje. He retired from Tests in 2000 to concentrate on the World Cup, his last hurrah. It wasn't to be, but he left cricket as the best fielder in the world, and he had made it a better game. **Tanya Aldred**

Colin Miller Australian utility bowler

Colin Miller was a showman, but he was too successful to be merely a sideshow. A versatile support act with his two-dimensional bowling, he played in seven of Australia's record 16 successive Test victories. Miller caught the eye by dyeing his hair blue, among other colours, and his bouncing off-breaks became even more underrated than they already were. He represented three states and Holland before making his Australia debut at 34 – older than Dennis Lillee, Tim May and his captain Mark Taylor were when they retired. In his first Test against Pakistan in 1998-99 he dismissed Salim Malik with his fifth ball and after four overs switched from medium-pace to off-spin, the method he had most impact with during his 18 matches, 12 of them victories. He finished with 69 wickets at 26.15, six more than Shane Warne during the same period and almost tens runs per wicket cheaper. An accidental hero, Miller left the stage as suddenly as he had arrived when he was cut from the Victoria squad at the end of 2001-02. **Peter English**

Lisa Keightley
Australian opener

Growing up in the New South Wales country town of Mudgee, Lisa Keightley was barred from the primary school cricket team because she was a girl. How those teachers would have been shamed nearly two decades later, in 1998, when Keightley became the first woman to make a century at Lord's, as Australia completed a 5–0 rout of England in a one-day series. Ushered into the national team at the age of 23 following Australia's disastrous World Cup loss in 1993, Keightley held down a place for the next eight years, helped win the World Cup back in 1997 and formed a fine opening partnership with Belinda Clark. An elegant batsman, she loved socialising, surfing and sleeping. In December 2002, aged 31, she retired, feeling her form was waning and that touring had lost its allure. She had scored 1,827 runs in 54 one-day internationals, making her Australia's third-highest scorer behind Clark and Karen Rolton. Keightley averaged 36.2 in her seven Tests, with three fifties, and 44.56 in one-dayers, with two other hundreds apart from the famous one. **Nabila Ahmed**

First lady of Lord's: Lisa Keightley.
Picture by Laurence Griffiths, Getty Images

Andy Flower Zimbabwe wicket-keeper/batsman

Andy Flower's retirement from international cricket after the World Cup left a hole in Zimbabwe's batting that they may never be able to fill. An ever-present in his country's first 52 Tests and 172 one-day internationals, Flower was blessed with more time than lesser mortals, an excellent technique and quick footwork, and could play pace bowling off either foot with equal ease.

It is as one of the leading players of spin, however, that he will be best remembered. His zenith as a batsman came in India in November 2000 when, in a two-Test series, he amassed 540 runs. The following July, he collected the PricewaterhouseCoopers International Player of the Year Award in London, beating off the likes of Tendulkar, McGrath and Muralitharan. The cricket world's admiration for Flower was sealed by the courageous anti-Mugabe statement that he and Henry Olonga made on the morning of their first World Cup match, when they wore black armbands to mourn the death of democracy in Zimbabwe. **Geoffrey Dean**

Adam Parore New Zealand wicket-keeper

Adam Parore was New Zealand's most natural and prolific wicket-keeper and the greatest Maori ever to play the game. He was also one of Test cricket's most feisty, fidgety, mercurial characters, and his degree in law didn't stop him ruffling the establishment's feathers – particularly on the 1995-96 tour of the West Indies, when he fell out with the coach, Glenn Turner. His athletic glovework made an immediate impact when he toured England as a 19-year-old in 1990, but his restless, dogged, back-foot batting caught the eye too: as New Zealand stumbled to defeat in the final Test at Edgbaston, the debutant Parore held a rampant Devon Malcolm and Chris Lewis at bay for nearly an hour and a half. Versatility became his trademark, and he batted in every position from No. 2 to No. 9 in Tests. The big occasion brought the best out of him: in 15 Tests against Australia and West Indies he averaged 39. In his final game, against England at Auckland in April 2002, he became only the eighth wicket-keeper in Test history to pass 200 dismissals. **Lawrence Booth**

TEST CRICKETERS

This section covers
- all 2,335 players who won a cap from the first Test in March 1877 to the 1,614th on September 5–9, 2002 (pages 115–175).
- the 232 to have played one-day internationals for the Test-playing countries by September 29, 2002, without playing a Test (pages 176–177).
- the 51 full-time coaches to have been employed by the Test-playing nations, and their record (pages 177–180) – a new feature.

The sequence
- players are arranged by country, in the order that the countries entered Test cricket: first England and Australia, then South Africa, West Indies, New Zealand, India, Pakistan, Sri Lanka, Zimbabwe and Bangladesh.
- within each country, players are arranged alphabetically by surname. Muslim names are not reversed: Wasim Akram is under W, not A.

The format
- each entry begins with the player's name and his total number of Tests
- after the colon come the countries he played against, arranged first by whether the series was home or away, then in the historical order given above. So for most players, home games against England come first, followed by home games against everyone else, then away games, in the same order. Away series are given in italics.
- the southern-hemisphere season, given elsewhere in the book as 1876-77 etc, is here shortened to the first year – 1876 etc.

Abbreviations
- E – England. A – Australia. SA – South Africa. WI – West Indies. NZ – New Zealand. In – India. P – Pakistan. SL – Sri Lanka. Z – Zimbabwe. B – Bangladesh.

ENGLAND

Number of Test cricketers: 612

Abel, R. 13: v A 1888 (3) 1896 (3) 1902 (2); *v A 1891 (3); v SA 1888 (2)*
Absolom, C. A. 1: *v A 1878*
Adams, C. J. 5: *v SA 1999 (5)*
Afzaal, U. 3: v A 2001 (3)
Agnew, J. P. 3: v A 1985 (1); v WI 1984 (1); v SL 1984 (1)
Allen, D. A. 39: v A 1961 (4) 1964 (1); v WI 1963 (2) 1966 (1); v P 1962 (4); *v A 1962 (1) 1965 (4); v SA 1964 (4); v WI 1959 (5); v NZ 1965 (3); v In 1961 (5); v P 1961 (3)*
Allen, G. O. B. 25: v A 1930 (1) 1934 (2); v WI 1933 (1); v NZ 1931 (3); v In 1936 (3); *v A 1932 (5) 1936 (5); v WI 1947 (3); v NZ 1932 (2)*
Allom, M. J. C. 5: *v SA 1930 (1); v NZ 1929 (4)*
Allott, P. J. W. 13: v A 1981 (1) 1985 (4); v WI 1984 (3); v In 1982 (2); v SL 1984 (1); *v In 1981 (1); v SL 1981 (1)*
Ames, L. E. G. 47: v A 1934 (5) 1938 (2); v SA 1929 (1) 1935 (4); v WI 1933 (3); v NZ 1931 (3) 1937 (3); v In 1932 (1); *v A 1932 (5) 1936 (5); v SA 1938 (5); v WI 1929 (4) 1934 (4); v NZ 1932 (2)*
Amiss, D. L. 50: v A 1968 (1) 1975 (2) 1977 (2); v WI 1966 (1) 1973 (3) 1976 (1); v NZ 1973 (3); v In 1967 (2) 1971 (1) 1974 (3); v P 1967 (1) 1971 (1) 1974 (3); *v A 1974 (5) 1976 (1); v WI 1973 (5); v NZ 1974 (2); v In 1972 (3) 1976 (5); v P 1972 (3)*
Andrew, K. V. 2: v WI 1963 (1); *v A 1954 (1)*
Appleyard, R. 9: v A 1956 (1); v SA 1955 (1); v P 1954 (1); *v A 1954 (4); v NZ 1954 (2)*
Archer, A. G. 1: *v SA 1898*
Armitage, T. 2: *v A 1876 (2)*

Arnold, E. G. 10: v A 1905 (4); v SA 1907 (2); *v A 1903 (4)*

Arnold, G. G. 34: v A 1972 (3) 1975 (1); v WI 1973 (3); v NZ 1969 (1) 1973 (3); v In 1974 (2); v P 1967 (2) 1974 (3); *v A 1974 (4); v WI 1973 (3); v NZ 1974 (2); v In 1972 (4); v P 1972 (3)*

Arnold, J. 1: v NZ 1931

Astill, W. E. 9: *v SA 1927 (5); v WI 1929 (4)*

Atherton, M. A. 115: v A 1989 (2) 1993 (6) 1997 (6) 2001 (5); v SA 1994 (3) 1998 (5); v WI 1991 (5) 1995 (6) 2000 (5); v NZ 1990 (3) 1994 (3) 1999 (2); v In 1990 (3) 1996 (3); v P 1992 (3) 1996 (3) 2001 (2); v Z 2000 (2); *v A 1990 (5) 1994 (5) 1998 (4); v SA 1995 (5) 1999 (5); v WI 1993 (5) 1997 (6); v NZ 1996 (3); v In 1992 (1); v P 2000 (3); v SL 1992 (1) 2000 (3); v Z 1996 (2)*

Athey, C. W. J. 23: v A 1980 (1); v WI 1988 (1); v NZ 1986 (3); v In 1986 (2); v P 1987 (4); *v A 1986 (5) 1987 (1); v WI 1980 (2); v NZ 1987 (1); v P 1987 (1)*

Attewell, W. 10: v A 1890 (1); *v A 1884 (5) 1887 (1) 1891 (3)*

Bailey, R. J. 4: v WI 1988 (1); *v WI 1989 (3)*

Bailey, T. E. 61: v A 1953 (5) 1956 (4); v SA 1951 (2) 1955 (5); v WI 1950 (2) 1957 (4); v NZ 1949 (4) 1958 (4); v P 1954 (3); *v A 1950 (4) 1954 (5) 1958 (5); v SA 1956 (5); v WI 1953 (5); v NZ 1950 (2) 1954 (2)*

Bairstow, D. L. 4: v A 1980 (1); v WI 1980 (1); v In 1979 (1); *v WI 1980 (1)*

Bakewell, A. H. 6: v SA 1935 (2); v WI 1933 (1); v NZ 1931 (2); *v In 1933 (1)*

Balderstone, J. C. 2: v WI 1976 (2)

Barber, R. W. 28: v A 1964 (1) 1968 (1); v SA 1960 (1) 1965 (3); v WI 1966 (2); v NZ 1965 (3); *v A 1965 (5); v SA 1964 (4); v In 1961 (5); v P 1961 (3)*

Barber, W. 2: v SA 1935 (2)

Barlow, G. D. 3: v A 1977 (1); *v In 1976 (2)*

Barlow, R. G. 17: v A 1882 (1) 1884 (3) 1886 (3); *v A 1881 (4) 1882 (4) 1886 (2)*

Barnes, S. F. 27: v A 1902 (1) 1909 (3) 1912 (3); v SA 1912 (3); *v A 1901 (3) 1907 (5) 1911 (5); v SA 1913 (4)*

Barnes, W. 21: v A 1880 (1) 1882 (1) 1884 (2) 1886 (3) 1888 (3) 1890 (2); *v A 1882 (4) 1884 (5) 1886 (1)*

Barnett, C. J. 20: v A 1938 (3) 1948 (1); v SA 1947 (3); v WI 1933 (1); v NZ 1937 (3); v In 1936 (1); *v A 1936 (5); v In 1933 (3)*

Barnett, K. J. 4: v A 1989 (3); v SL 1988 (1)

Barratt, F. 5: v SA 1929 (1); *v NZ 1929 (4)*

Barrington, K. F. 82: v A 1961 (5) 1964 (5) 1968 (3); v SA 1955 (2) 1960 (4) 1965 (3); v WI 1963 (5) 1966 (2); v NZ 1965 (2); v In 1959 (5) 1967 (3); v P 1962 (4) 1967 (3); *v A 1962 (5) 1965 (5); v SA 1964 (5); v WI 1959 (5) 1967 (5); v NZ 1962 (3); v In 1961 (5) 1963 (1); v P 1961 (2)*

Barton, V. A. 1: *v SA 1891*

Bates, W. 15: *v A 1881 (4) 1882 (4) 1884 (5) 1886 (2)*

Bean, G. 3: *v A 1891 (3)*

Bedser, A. V. 51: v A 1948 (5) 1953 (5); v SA 1947 (2) 1951 (5) 1955 (1); v WI 1950 (3); v NZ 1949 (2); v In 1946 (3) 1952 (4); v P 1954 (2); *v A 1946 (5) 1950 (5) 1954 (1); v SA 1948 (5); v NZ 1946 (1) 1950 (2)*

Benjamin, J. E. 1: v SA 1994

Benson, M. R. 1: v In 1986

Berry, R. 2: v WI 1950 (2)

Bicknell, M. P. 2: v A 1993 (2)

Binks, J. G. 2: *v In 1963 (2)*

Bird, M. C. 10: *v SA 1909 (5) 1913 (5)*

Birkenshaw, J. 5: *v WI 1973 (2); v In 1972 (2); v P 1972 (1)*

Blakey, R. J. 2: *v In 1992 (2)*

Bligh, Hon. I. F. W. 4: *v A 1882 (4)*

Blythe, C. 19: v A 1905 (1) 1909 (2); v SA 1907 (3); *v A 1901 (5) 1907 (1); v SA 1905 (5) 1909 (2)*

Board, J. H. 6: *v SA 1898 (2) 1905 (4)*

Bolus, J. B. 7: v WI 1963 (2); *v In 1963 (5)*

Booth, M. W. 2: *v SA 1913 (2)*

Bosanquet, B. J. T. 7: v A 1905 (3); *v A 1903 (4)*

Botham, I. T. 102: v A 1977 (2) 1980 (1) 1981 (6) 1985 (6) 1989 (3); v WI 1980 (5) 1984 (5) 1991 (1); v NZ 1978 (3) 1983 (4) 1986 (1); v In 1979 (4) 1982 (3); v P 1978 (3) 1982 (3) 1987 (5) 1992 (2); v SL 1984 (1) 1991 (1); *v A 1978 (6) 1979 (3) 1982 (5) 1986 (4); v WI 1980 (4) 1985 (5); v NZ 1977 (3) 1983 (3) 1991 (1); v In 1979 (1) 1981 (6); v P 1983 (1); v SL 1981 (1)*

Bowden, M. P. 2: *v SA 1888* (2)

Bowes, W. E. 15: v A 1934 (3) 1938 (2); v SA 1935 (4); v WI 1939 (2); v In 1932 (1) 1946 (1); *v A 1932 (1); v NZ 1932 (1)*

Bowley, E. H. 5: v SA 1929 (2); *v NZ 1929 (3)*

Boycott, G. 108: v A 1964 (4) 1968 (3) 1972 (2) 1977 (3) 1980 (1) 1981 (6); v SA 1965 (2); v WI 1966 (4) 1969 (3) 1973 (3) 1980 (5); v NZ 1965 (2) 1969 (3) 1973 (3) 1978 (2); v In 1967 (2) 1971 (1) 1974 (1) 1979 (4); v P 1967 (1) 1971 (2); *v A 1965 (5) 1970 (5) 1978 (6) 1979 (3); v SA 1964 (5); v WI 1967 (5) 1973 (5) 1980 (4); v NZ 1965 (2) 1977 (3); v In 1979 (1) 1981 (4); v P 1977 (3)*

Bradley, W. M. 2: v A 1899 (2)

Braund, L. C. 23: v A 1902 (5); v SA 1907 (3); *v A 1901 (5) 1903 (5) 1907 (5)*

Brearley, J. M. 39: v A 1977 (5) 1981 (4); v WI 1976 (2); v NZ 1978 (3); v In 1979 (4); v P 1978 (2); *v A 1976 (1) 1978 (6) 1979 (3); v In 1976 (5) 1979 (1); v P 1977 (2)*

Brearley, W. 4: v A 1905 (2) 1909 (1); v SA 1912 (1)

Brennan, D. V. 2: v SA 1951 (2)

Briggs, John 33: v A 1886 (3) 1888 (3) 1893 (2) 1896 (1) 1899 (1); *v A 1884 (5) 1886 (2) 1887 (1) 1891 (3) 1894 (5) 1897 (5)*; v SA 1888 (2)

Broad, B. C. 25: v A 1989 (2); v WI 1984 (4) 1988 (2); v P 1987 (4); v SL 1984 (1); *v A 1986 (5) 1987 (1); v NZ 1987 (3); v P 1987 (3)*

Brockwell, W. 7: v A 1893 (1) 1899 (1); *v A 1894 (5)*

Bromley-Davenport, H. R. 4: *v SA 1895* (3) 1898 (1)

Brookes, D. 1: *v WI 1947*

Brown, A. 2: *v In 1961 (1); v P 1961 (1)*

Brown, D. J. 26: v A 1968 (4); v SA 1965 (2); v WI 1966 (1) 1969 (3); v NZ 1969 (1); v In 1967 (2); *v A 1965 (4); v WI 1967 (4); v NZ 1965 (2); v P 1968 (3)*

Brown, F. R. 22: v A 1953 (1); v WI 1950 (1); v NZ 1931 (2) 1937 (1) 1949 (2); v In 1932 (1); *v A 1950 (5); v NZ 1932 (2) 1950 (2)*

Brown, G. 7: v A 1921 (3); *v SA 1922* (4)

Brown, J. T. 8: v A 1896 (2) 1899 (1); *v A 1894 (5)*

Brown, S. J. E. 1: v P 1996

Buckenham, C. P. 4: *v SA 1909 (4)*

Butcher, A. R. 1: v In 1979

Butcher, M. A. 45: v A 1997 (5) 2001 (5); v SA 1998 (3); v NZ 1999 (3); v In 2002 (4); v SL 1998 (1) 2002 (3); *v A 1998 (5); v SA 1999 (5); v WI 1997 (5); v NZ 2001 (3); v In 2001 (3)*

Butcher, R. O. 3: *v WI 1980 (3)*

Butler, H. J. 2: v SA 1947 (1); *v WI 1947 (1)*

Butt, H. R. 3: *v SA 1895 (3)*

Caddick, A. R. 58: v A 1993 (4) 1997 (5) 2001 (5); v WI 2000 (5); v NZ 1999 (4); v In 2002 (2); v P 1996 (1) 2001 (2); v SL 2002 (3); v Z 2000 (2); *v SA 1999 (5); v WI 1993 (4) 1997 (5); v NZ 1996 (2) 2001 (3); v P 2000 (3); v SL 2000 (3)*

Calthorpe, Hon. F. S. G. 4: *v WI 1929 (4)*

Capel, D. J. 15: v A 1989 (1); v WI 1988 (2); v P 1987 (1); *v A 1987 (1); v WI 1989 (4); v NZ 1987 (3); v P 1987 (3)*

Carr, A. W. 11: v A 1926 (4); v SA 1929 (2); *v SA 1922 (5)*

Carr, D. B. 2: *v In 1951 (2)*

Carr, D. W. 1: v A 1909

Cartwright, T. W. 5: v A 1964 (2); v SA 1965 (1); v NZ 1965 (1); *v SA 1964 (1)*

Chapman, A. P. F. 26: v A 1926 (4) 1930 (4); v SA 1924 (2); v WI 1928 (3); *v A 1924 (4) 1928 (4); v SA 1930 (5)*

Charlwood, H. R. J. 2: *v A 1876 (2)*

Chatterton, W. 1: *v SA 1891*

Childs, J. H. 2: v WI 1988 (2)

Christopherson, S. 1: v A 1884

Clark, E. W. 8: v A 1934 (2); v SA 1929 (1); v WI 1933 (2); *v In 1933 (3)*

Clay, J. C. 1: v SA 1935

Close, D. B. 22: v A 1961 (1); v SA 1955 (1); v WI 1957 (2) 1963 (5) 1966 (1) 1976 (3); v NZ 1949 (1); v In 1959 (1) 1967 (3); v P 1967 (3); *v A 1950 (1)*

Coldwell, L. J. 7: v A 1964 (2); v P 1962 (2); *v A 1962 (2); v NZ 1962 (1)*

Compton, D. C. S. 78: v A 1938 (4) 1948 (5) 1953 (5) 1956 (1); v SA 1947 (5) 1951 (4) 1955 (5); v WI 1939 (3) 1950 (1); v NZ 1937 (1) 1949 (4); v In 1946 (3) 1952 (2); v P 1954 (4); *v A 1946 (5) 1950 (4) 1954 (4); v SA 1948 (5) 1956 (5); v WI 1953 (5); v NZ 1946 (1) 1950 (2)*

Cook, C. 1: v SA 1947

Cook, G. 7: v In 1982 (3); *v A 1982 (3); v SL 1981 (1)*

Cook, N. G. B. 15: v A 1989 (3); v WI 1984 (3); v NZ 1983 (2); *v NZ 1983 (1); v P 1983 (3) 1987 (3)*

Cope, G. A. 3: *v P 1977 (3)*

Copson, W. H. 3: v SA 1947 (1); v WI 1939 (2)

Cork, D. G. 37: v A 2001 (1); v SA 1998 (5); v WI 1995 (5) 2000 (4); v In 1996 (3) 2002 (2); v P 1996 (3) 2001 (2); v SL 1998 (1) 2002 (1); *v A 1998 (2); v SA 1995 (5); v NZ 1996 (3)*

Cornford, W. L. 4: *v NZ 1929 (4)*

Cottam, R. M. H. 4: *v In 1972 (2); v P 1968 (2)*

Coventry, Hon. C. J. 2: *v SA 1888 (2)*

Cowans, N. G. 19: v A 1985 (1); v WI 1984 (1); v NZ 1983 (4); *v A 1982 (4); v NZ 1983 (2); v In 1984 (5); v P 1983 (2)*

Cowdrey, C. S. 6: v WI 1988 (1); *v In 1984 (5)*

Cowdrey, M. C. 114: v A 1956 (5) 1961 (4) 1964 (3) 1968 (4); v SA 1955 (1) 1960 (5) 1965 (3); v WI 1957 (5) 1963 (2) 1966 (4); v NZ 1958 (4) 1965 (3); v In 1959 (5); v P 1962 (4) 1967 (2) 1971 (1); *v A 1954 (5) 1958 (5) 1962 (5) 1965 (4) 1970 (3) 1974 (5); v SA 1956 (5); v WI 1959 (5) 1967 (5); v NZ 1954 (2) 1958 (2) 1962 (3) 1965 (3) 1970 (1); v In 1963 (3); v P 1968 (3)*

Coxon, A. 1: v A 1948

Cranston, J. 1: v A 1890

Cranston, K. 8: v A 1948 (1); v SA 1947 (3); *v WI 1947 (4)*

Crapp, J. F. 7: v A 1948 (3); *v SA 1948 (4)*

Crawford, J. N. 12: v SA 1907 (2); *v A 1907 (5); v SA 1905 (5)*

Crawley, J. P. 34: v A 1997 (3); v SA 1994 (3); v WI 1995 (3); v In 2002 (4); v P 1996 (2); v SL 1998 (1) 2002 (1); *v A 1994 (3) 1998 (3); v SA 1995 (1); v WI 1997 (3); v NZ 1996 (3); v Z 1996 (2)*

Croft, R. D. B. 21: v A 1997 (5) 2001 (1); v SA 1998 (3); v WI 2000 (2); v P 1996 (1); *v A 1998 (1); v WI 1997 (3); v NZ 1996 (2); v SL 2000 (3); v Z 1996 (2)*

Curtis, T. S. 5: v A 1989 (3); v WI 1988 (2)

Cuttell, W. R. 2: *v SA 1898 (2)*

Dawson, E. W. 5: *v SA 1927 (1); v NZ 1929 (4)*

Dawson, R. K. J. 3: *v In 2001 (3)*

Dean, H. 3: v A 1912 (2); v SA 1912 (1)

DeFreitas, P. A. J. 44: v A 1989 (1) 1993 (1); v SA 1994 (3); v WI 1988 (3) 1991 (5) 1995 (3); v NZ 1990 (2) 1994 (3); v P 1987 (1) 1992 (2); v SL 1991 (1); *v A 1986 (4) 1990 (3) 1994 (4); v WI 1989 (2); v NZ 1987 (1) 1991 (3); v In 1992 (1); v P 1987 (2)*

Denness, M. H. 28: v A 1975 (1); v NZ 1969 (1); v In 1974 (3); v P 1974 (3); *v A 1974 (5); v WI 1973 (5); v NZ 1974 (2); v In 1972 (5); v P 1972 (3)*

Denton, D. 11: v A 1905 (1); *v SA 1905 (5) 1909 (5)*

Dewes, J. G. 5: v A 1948 (1); v WI 1950 (2); *v A 1950 (2)*

Dexter, E. R. 62: v A 1961 (5) 1964 (5) 1968 (2); v SA 1960 (5); v WI 1963 (5); v NZ 1958 (1) 1965 (2); v In 1959 (2); v P 1962 (5); *v A 1958 (2) 1962 (5); v SA 1964 (5); v WI 1959 (5); v NZ 1958 (2) 1962 (3); v In 1961 (5); v P 1961 (3)*

Dilley, G. R. 41: v A 1981 (3) 1989 (2); v WI 1980 (3) 1988 (4); v NZ 1983 (1) 1986 (2); v In 1986 (2); v P 1987 (4); *v A 1979 (2) 1986 (4) 1987 (1); v WI 1980 (4); v NZ 1987 (3); v In 1981 (4); v P 1983 (1) 1987 (1)*

Dipper, A. E. 1: v A 1921

Doggart, G. H. G. 2: *v WI 1950 (2)*

D'Oliveira, B. L. 44: v A 1968 (2) 1972 (5); v WI 1966 (4) 1969 (3); v NZ 1969 (3); v In 1967 (2) 1971 (3); v P 1967 (3) 1971 (3); *v A 1970 (6); v WI 1967 (5); v NZ 1970 (2); v P 1968 (3)*

Dollery, H. E. 4: v A 1948 (2); v SA 1947 (1); v WI 1950 (1)

Dolphin, A. 1: *v A 1920*

Douglas, J. W. H. T. 23: v A 1912 (1) 1921 (5); v SA 1924 (1); *v A 1911 (5) 1920 (5) 1924 (1); v SA 1913 (5)*

Downton, P. R. 30: v A 1981 (1) 1985 (6); v WI 1984 (5) 1988 (3); v In 1986 (1); v SL 1984 (1); *v WI 1980 (3) 1985 (5); v In 1984 (5)*

Druce, N. F. 5: *v A 1897 (5)*

Ducat, A. 1: v A 1921

Duckworth, G. 24: v A 1930 (5); v SA 1924 (1) 1929 (4) 1935 (1); v WI 1928 (1); v In 1936 (3); *v A 1928 (5); v SA 1930 (3); v NZ 1932 (1)*

Duleepsinhji, K. S. 12: v A 1930 (4); v SA 1929 (1); v NZ 1931 (3); *v NZ 1929 (4)*

Durston, F. J. 1: v A 1921

Ealham, M. A. 8: v A 1997 (4); v SA 1998 (2); v In 1996 (1); v P 1996 (1)

Edmonds, P. H. 51: v A 1975 (2) 1985 (5); v NZ 1978 (3) 1983 (2) 1986 (3); v In 1979 (4) 1982 (3) 1986 (2); v P 1978 (3) 1987 (5); *v A 1978 (1) 1986 (5); v WI 1985 (3); v NZ 1977 (3); v In 1984 (5); v P 1977 (2)*

Edrich, J. H. 77: v A 1964 (3) 1968 (5) 1972 (5) 1975 (4); v SA 1965 (1); v WI 1963 (3) 1966 (1) 1969 (3) 1976 (2); v NZ 1965 (1) 1969 (3); v In 1967 (2) 1971 (3) 1974 (3); v P 1971 (3) 1974 (3); *v A 1965 (5) 1970 (6) 1974 (4); v WI 1967 (5); v NZ 1965 (3) 1970 (2) 1974 (2); v In 1963 (2); v P 1968 (3)*

Edrich, W. J. 39: v A 1938 (4) 1948 (5) 1953 (3); v SA 1947 (4); v WI 1950 (2); v NZ 1949 (4); v In 1946 (1); v P 1954 (1); *v A 1946 (5) 1954 (4); v SA 1938 (5); v NZ 1946 (1)*

Elliott, H. 4: v WI 1928 (1); *v SA 1927 (1); v In 1933 (2)*

Ellison, R. M. 11: v A 1985 (2); v WI 1984 (1); v In 1986 (1); v SL 1984 (1); *v WI 1985 (3); v In 1984 (3)*

Emburey, J. E. 64: v A 1980 (1) 1981 (4) 1985 (6) 1989 (3) 1993 (1); v WI 1980 (3) 1988 (3) 1995 (1); v NZ 1978 (1) 1986 (2); v In 1986 (3); v P 1987 (4); v SL 1988 (1); *v A 1978 (4) 1986 (5) 1987 (1); v WI 1980 (4) 1985 (4); v NZ 1987 (3); v In 1979 (1) 1981 (3) 1992 (1); v P 1987 (3); v SL 1981 (1) 1992 (1)*

Emmett, G. M. 1: v A 1948

Emmett, T. 7: *v A 1876 (2) 1878 (1) 1881 (4)*

Evans, A. J. 1: v A 1921

Evans, T. G. 91: v A 1948 (5) 1953 (5) 1956 (5); v SA 1947 (5) 1951 (3) 1955 (3); v WI 1950 (3) 1957 (5); v NZ 1949 (4) 1958 (5); v In 1946 (1) 1952 (4) 1959 (2); v P 1954 (4); *v A 1946 (4) 1950 (5) 1954 (4) 1958 (3); v SA 1948 (3) 1956 (5); v WI 1947 (4) 1953 (4); v NZ 1946 (1) 1950 (2) 1954 (2)*

Fagg, A. E. 5: v WI 1939 (1); v In 1936 (2); *v A 1936 (2)*

Fairbrother, N. H. 10: v NZ 1990 (3); v P 1987 (1); *v NZ 1987 (2); v In 1992 (2); v P 1987 (1); v SL 1992 (1)*

Fane, F. L. 14: *v A 1907 (4); v SA 1905 (5) 1909 (5)*

Farnes, K. 15: v A 1934 (2) 1938 (4); v In 1936 (2); *v SA 1938 (5); v WI 1934 (2)*

Farrimond, W. 4: v SA 1935 (1); *v SA 1930 (2); v WI 1934 (1)*

Fender, P. G. H. 13: v A 1921 (2); v SA 1924 (2) 1929 (1); *v A 1920 (3); v SA 1922 (5)*

Ferris, J. J. 1: *v SA 1891*

Fielder, A. 6: *v A 1903 (2) 1907 (4)*

Fishlock, L. B. 4: v In 1936 (2) 1946 (1); *v A 1946 (1)*

Flavell, J. A. 4: v A 1961 (2) 1964 (2)

Fletcher, K. W. R. 59: v A 1968 (1) 1972 (1) 1975 (2); v WI 1973 (3); v NZ 1969 (2) 1973 (3); v In 1971 (2) 1974 (3); v P 1974 (3); *v A 1970 (5) 1974 (5) 1976 (1); v WI 1973 (4); v NZ 1970 (1) 1974 (2); v In 1972 (5) 1976 (3) 1981 (6); v P 1968 (3) 1972 (3); v SL 1981 (1)*

Flintoff, A. 21: v SA 1998 (2); v WI 2000 (1); v In 2002 (3); v SL 2002 (3); v Z 2000 (2); *v SA 1999 (4); v NZ 2001 (3); v In 2001 (3)*

Flowers, W. 8: v A 1893 (1); *v A 1884 (5) 1886 (2)*

Ford, F. G. J. 5: *v A 1894 (5)*

Foster, F. R. 11: v A 1912 (3); v SA 1912 (3); *v A 1911 (5)*

Foster, J. S. 6: *v NZ 2001 (3); v In 2001 (3)*

Foster, N. A. 29: v A 1985 (1) 1989 (3) 1993 (1); v WI 1984 (1) 1988 (2); v NZ 1983 (1) 1986 (1); v In 1986 (1); v P 1987 (5); v SL 1988 (1); *v A 1987 (1); v WI 1985 (3); v NZ 1983 (2); v In 1984 (2); v P 1983 (2) 1987 (2)*

Foster, R. E. 8: v SA 1907 (3); *v A 1903 (5)*

Fothergill, A. J. 2: *v SA 1888 (2)*

Fowler, G. 21: v WI 1984 (5); v NZ 1983 (2); v P 1982 (1); v SL 1984 (1); *v A 1982 (3); v NZ 1983 (2); v In 1984 (5); v P 1983 (2)*

Fraser, A. R. C. 46: v A 1989 (3) 1993 (1); v SA 1994 (2) 1998 (5); v WI 1995 (5); v NZ 1994 (3); v In 1990 (3); v SL 1998 (1); *v A 1990 (3) 1994 (3) 1998 (2); v SA 1995 (3); v WI 1989 (2) 1993 (4) 1997 (6)*

Freeman, A. P. 12: v SA 1929 (3); v WI 1928 (3); *v A 1924 (2); v SA 1927 (4)*

French, B. N. 16: v NZ 1986 (3); v In 1986 (2); v P 1987 (4); *v A 1987 (1); v NZ 1987 (3); v P 1987 (3)*

Fry, C. B. 26: v A 1899 (5) 1902 (3) 1905 (4) 1909 (3) 1912 (3); v SA 1907 (3) 1912 (3); *v SA 1895 (2)*

Gallian, J. E. R. 3: v WI 1995 (2); *v SA 1995 (1)*

Gatting, M. W. 79: v A 1980 (1) 1981 (6) 1985 (6) 1989 (1) 1993 (2); v WI 1980 (4) 1984 (1) 1988 (2); v NZ 1983 (2) 1986 (3); v In 1986 (3); v P 1982 (3) 1987 (5); *v A 1986 (5) 1987 (1) 1994 (5); v WI 1980 (1) 1985 (1); v NZ 1977 (1) 1983 (2) 1987 (3); v In 1981 (5) 1984 (5) 1992 (3); v P 1977 (1) 1983 (3) 1987 (3); v SL 1992 (1)*

Gay, L. H. 1: *v A 1894*

Geary, G. 14: v A 1926 (2) 1930 (1) 1934 (2); v SA 1924 (1) 1929 (2); *v A 1928 (4); v SA 1927(2)*

Gibb, P. A. 8: v In 1946 (3); *v A 1946 (1); v SA 1938 (5)*

Giddins, E. S. H. 4: v WI 2000 (1); v NZ 1999 (1); v Z 2000 (2)

Gifford, N. 15: v A 1964 (2) 1972 (3); v NZ 1973 (2); v In 1971 (2); v P 1971 (2); *v In 1972 (2); v P 1972 (2)*

Giles, A. F. 18: v A 2001 (1); v SA 1998 (1); v In 2002 (3); v SL 2002 (2); *v NZ 2001 (3); v In 2001 (2); v P 2000 (3); v SL 2000 (2)*

Gilligan, A. E. R. 11: v SA 1924 (4); *v A 1924 (5); v SA 1922 (2)*

Gilligan, A. H. H. 4: *v NZ 1929 (4)*

Gimblett, H. 3: v WI 1939 (1); v In 1936 (2)

Gladwin, C. 8: v SA 1947 (2); v NZ 1949 (1); *v SA 1948 (5)*

Goddard, T. W. 8: v A 1930 (1); v WI 1939 (2); v NZ 1937 (2); *v SA 1938 (3)*

Gooch, G. A. 118: v A 1975 (2) 1980 (1) 1981 (5) 1985 (6) 1989 (5) 1993 (6); v SA 1994 (3); v WI 1980 (5) 1988 (5) 1991 (5); v NZ 1978 (3) 1986 (3) 1990 (3) 1994 (3); v In 1979 (4) 1986 (3) 1990 (3); v P 1978 (2) 1992 (5); v SL 1988 (1) 1991 (1); *v A 1978 (6) 1979 (2) 1990 (4) 1994 (5); v WI 1980 (4) 1985 (5) 1989 (2); v NZ 1991 (3); v In 1979 (1) 1981 (6) 1992 (2); v P 1987 (3); v SL 1981 (1)*

Gough, D. 56: v A 1997 (4) 2001 (5); v SA 1994 (3) 1998 (4); v WI 1995 (3) 2000 (5); v NZ 1994 (1); v P 2001 (2); v SL 1998 (1); v Z 2000 (2); *v A 1994 (3) 1998 (5); v SA 1995 (2) 1999 (5); v NZ 1996 (3); v P 2000 (3); v SL 2000 (2); v Z 1996 (2)*

Gover, A. R. 4: v NZ 1937 (2); v In 1936 (1) 1946 (1)

Gower, D. I. 117: v A 1980 (1) 1981 (5) 1985 (6) 1989 (6); v WI 1980 (1) 1984 (5) 1988 (4); v NZ 1978 (3) 1983 (4) 1986 (3); v In 1979 (4) 1982 (3) 1986 (2) 1990 (3); v P 1978 (3) 1982 (3) 1987 (5) 1992 (3); v SL 1984 (1); *v A 1978 (6) 1979 (3) 1982 (5) 1986 (5) 1990 (5); v WI 1980 (4) 1985 (5); v NZ 1983 (3); v In 1979 (1) 1981 (6) 1984 (5); v P 1983 (3); v SL 1981 (1)*

Grace, E. M. 1: v A 1880

Grace, G. F. 1: v A 1880

Grace, W. G. 22: v A 1880 (1) 1882 (1) 1884 (3) 1886 (3) 1888 (3) 1890 (2) 1893 (2) 1896 (3) 1899 (1); *v A 1891 (3)*

Graveney, T. W. 79: v A 1953 (5) 1956 (2) 1968 (5); v SA 1951 (1) 1955 (5); v WI 1957 (4) 1966 (4) 1969 (1); v NZ 1958 (4); v In 1952 (4) 1967 (3); v P 1954 (3) 1962 (4) 1967 (3); *v A 1954 (2) 1958 (5) 1962 (3); v WI 1953 (5) 1967 (5); v NZ 1954 (2) 1958 (2); v In 1951 (4); v P 1968 (3)*

Greenhough, T. 4: v SA 1960 (1); v In 1959 (3)

Greenwood, A. 2: *v A 1876 (2)*

Greig, A. W. 58: v A 1972 (5) 1975 (4) 1977 (5); v WI 1973 (3) 1976 (5); v NZ 1973 (3); v In 1974 (3); v P 1974 (3); *v A 1974 (6) 1976 (1); v WI 1973 (5); v NZ 1974 (2); v In 1972 (5) 1976 (5); v P 1972 (3)*

Greig, I. A. 2: v P 1982 (2)

Grieve, B. A. F. 2: *v SA 1888 (2)*

Griffith, S. C. 3: *v SA 1948 (2); v WI 1947 (1)*

Gunn, G. 15: v A 1909 (1); *v A 1907 (5) 1911 (5); v WI 1929 (4)*

Gunn, J. 6: v A 1905 (1); *v A 1901 (5)*

Gunn, W. 11: v A 1888 (2) 1890 (2) 1893 (3) 1896 (1) 1899 (1); *v A 1886 (2)*

Habib, A. 2: v NZ 1999 (2)

Haig, N. E. 5: v A 1921 (1); *v WI 1929 (4)*

Haigh, S. 11: v A 1905 (2) 1909 (1) 1912 (1); *v SA 1898 (2) 1905 (5)*

Hallows, C. 2: v A 1921 (1); v WI 1928 (1)

Hamilton, G. M. 1: *v SA 1999*

Hammond, W. R. 85: v A 1930 (5) 1934 (5) 1938 (4); v SA 1929 (4) 1935 (5); v WI 1928 (3) 1933 (3) 1939 (3); v NZ 1931 (3) 1937 (3); v In 1932 (1) 1936 (2) 1946 (3); *v A 1928 (5) 1932 (5) 1936 (5) 1946 (4); v SA 1927 (5) 1930 (5) 1938 (5); v WI 1934 (4); v NZ 1932 (2) 1946 (1)*

Hampshire, J. H. 8: v A 1972 (1) 1975 (1); v WI 1969 (2); *v A 1970 (2); v NZ 1970 (2)*

Hardinge, H. T. W. 1: v A 1921

Hardstaff, J. 5: *v A 1907 (5)*

Hardstaff, J. jun. 23: v A 1938 (2) 1948 (1); v SA 1935 (1); v WI 1939 (3); v NZ 1937 (3); v In 1936 (2) 1946 (2); *v A 1936 (5) 1946 (1); v WI 1947 (3)*

Harmison, S. J. 1: v In 2002

Harris, Lord 4: v A 1880 (1) 1884 (2); *v A 1878 (1)*

Hartley, J. C. 2: *v SA 1905 (2)*

Hawke, Lord 5: *v SA 1895 (3) 1898 (2)*

Hayes, E. G. 5: v A 1909 (1); v SA 1912 (1); *v SA 1905 (3)*

Hayes, F. C. 9: v WI 1973 (3) 1976 (2); *v WI 1973 (4)*

Hayward, T. W. 35: v A 1896 (2) 1899 (5) 1902 (5) 1905 (5) 1909 (1); v SA 1907 (3); *v A 1897 (5) 1901 (5) 1903 (5); v SA 1895 (3)*

Headley, D. W. 15: v A 1997 (3); v SA 1998 (1); v NZ 1999 (2); *v A 1998 (3); v WI 1997 (6)*

Hearne, A. 1: *v SA 1891*

Hearne, F. 2: *v SA 1888 (2)*

Hearne, G. G. 1: *v SA 1891*

Hearne, J. T. 12: v A 1896 (3) 1899 (3); *v A 1897 (5); v SA 1891 (1)*

Hearne, J. W. 24: v A 1912 (3) 1921 (1) 1926 (1); v SA 1912 (2) 1924 (3); *v A 1911 (5) 1920 (2) 1924 (4); v SA 1913 (3)*

Hegg, W. K. 2: *v A 1998 (2)*

Hemmings, E. E. 16: v A 1989 (1); v NZ 1990 (3); v In 1990 (3); v P 1982 (2); *v A 1982 (3) 1987 (1) 1990 (1); v NZ 1987 (1); v P 1987 (1)*

Hendren, E. H. 51: v A 1921 (2) 1926 (5) 1930 (2) 1934 (4); v SA 1924 (5) 1929 (4); v WI 1928 (1); *v A 1920 (5) 1924 (5) 1928 (5); v SA 1930 (5); v WI 1929 (4) 1934 (4)*

Hendrick, M. 30: v A 1977 (3) 1980 (1) 1981 (2); v WI 1976 (2) 1980 (2); v NZ 1978 (2); v In 1974 (3) 1979 (4); v P 1974 (2); *v A 1974 (2) 1978 (5); v NZ 1974 (1) 1977 (1)*

Heseltine, C. 2: *v SA 1895 (2)*

Hick, G. A. 65: v A 1993 (3); v SA 1994 (3) 1998 (2); v WI 1991 (4) 1995 (5) 2000 (4); v NZ 1994 (3) 1999 (1); v In 1996 (3); v P 1992 (4) 1996 (1); v SL 1998 (3); v Z 2000 (2); *v A 1994 (3) 1998 (4); v SA 1995 (5); v WI 1993 (5); v NZ 1991 (3); v In 1992 (3); v P 2000 (3); v SL 1992 (1) 2000 (2)*

Higgs, K. 15: v A 1968 (1); v WI 1966 (5); v SA 1965 (1); v In 1967 (1); v P 1967 (3); *v A 1965 (1); v NZ 1965 (3)*

Hill, A. 2: *v A 1876 (2)*

Hill, A. J. L. 3: *v SA 1895 (3)*

Hilton, M. J. 4: v SA 1951 (1); v WI 1950 (1); *v In 1951 (2)*

Hirst, G. H. 24: v A 1899 (1) 1902 (4) 1905 (3) 1909 (4); v SA 1907 (3); *v A 1897 (4) 1903 (5)*

Hitch, J. W. 7: v A 1912 (1) 1921 (1); v SA 1912 (1); *v A 1911 (3) 1920 (1)*

Hobbs, J. B. 61: v A 1909 (3) 1912 (3) 1921 (1) 1926 (5) 1930 (5); v SA 1912 (3) 1924 (4) 1929 (1); v WI 1928 (1); *v A 1907 (4) 1911 (5) 1920 (5) 1924 (5) 1928 (5); v SA 1909 (5) 1913 (5)*

Hobbs, R. N. S. 7: v In 1967 (3); v P 1967 (1) 1971 (1); *v WI 1967 (1); v P 1968 (1)*

Hoggard, M. J. 15: v WI 2000 (1); v In 2002 (4); v P 2001 (1); v SL 2002 (3); *v NZ 2001 (3); v In 2001 (3)*

Hollies, W. E. 13: v A 1948 (1); v SA 1947 (3); v WI 1950 (2); v NZ 1949 (4); *v WI 1934 (3)*

Hollioake, A. J. 4: v A 1997 (2); *v WI 1997 (2)*

Hollioake, B. C. 2: v A 1997 (1); v SL 1998 (1)

Holmes, E. R. T. 5: v SA 1935 (1); *v WI 1934 (4)*

Holmes, P. 7: v A 1921 (1); v In 1932 (1); *v SA 1927 (5)*

Hone, L. 1: *v A 1878*

Hopwood, J. L. 2: v A 1934 (2)

Hornby, A. N. 3: v A 1882 (1) 1884 (1); *v A 1878 (1)*

Horton, M. J. 2: v In 1959 (2)

Howard, N. D. 4: *v In 1951 (4)*

Howell, H. 5: v A 1921 (1); v SA 1924 (1); *v A 1920 (3)*

Howorth, R. 5: v SA 1947 (1); *v WI 1947 (4)*

Humphries, J. 3: *v A 1907 (3)*

Hunter, J. 5: *v A 1884 (5)*

Hussain, N. 76: v A 1993 (4) 1997 (6) 2001 (3); v SA 1998 (5); v WI 2000 (4); v NZ 1999 (3); v In 1996 (3) 2002 (4); v P 1996 (2) 2001 (1); v SL 2002 (3); v Z 2000 (2); *v A 1998 (5); v SA 1999 (5); v WI 1989 (3) 1997 (6); v NZ 1996 (3) 2001 (3); v In 2001 (3); v P 2000 (3); v SL 2000 (3); v Z 1996 (3)*

Hutchings, K. L. 7: v A 1909 (2); *v A 1907 (5)*

Hutton, L. 79: v A 1938 (3) 1948 (5) 1953 (5); v SA 1947 (5) 1951 (5); v WI 1939 (5) 1950 (3); v NZ 1937 (3) 1949 (4); v In 1946 (3) 1952 (4); v P 1954 (2); *v A 1946 (5) 1950 (5) 1954 (5); v SA 1938 (4) 1948 (5); v WI 1947 (2) 1953 (5); v NZ 1950 (2) 1954 (2)*

Hutton, R. A. 5: v In 1971 (3); v P 1971 (2)

Iddon, J. 5: v SA 1935 (1); *v WI 1934 (4)*

Igglesden, A. P. 3: v A 1989 (1); *v WI 1993 (2)*

Ikin, J. T. 18: v SA 1951 (3) 1955 (1); v In 1946 (2) 1952 (2); *v A 1946 (5); v NZ 1946 (1); v WI 1947 (1)*

Illingworth, R. 61: v A 1961 (2) 1968 (3) 1972 (5); v SA 1960 (4); v WI 1966 (2) 1969 (3) 1973 (3); v NZ 1958 (1) 1965 (1) 1969 (3) 1973 (3); v In 1959 (2) 1967 (3) 1971 (3); v P 1962 (1) 1967 (1) 1971 (3); *v A 1962 (2) 1970 (6); v WI 1959 (5); v NZ 1962 (3) 1970 (2)*

Illingworth, R. K. 9: v WI 1991 (2) 1995 (4); *v SA 1995 (3)*

Ilott, M. C. 5: v A 1993 (3); *v SA 1995 (2)*

Insole, D. J. 9: v A 1956 (1); v SA 1955 (1); v WI 1950 (1) 1957 (1); *v SA 1956 (5)*

Irani, R. C. 3: v NZ 1999 (1); v In 1996 (2)

Jackman, R. D. 4: v P 1982 (2); *v WI 1980 (2)*

Jackson, F. S. 20: v A 1893 (2) 1896 (3) 1899 (5) 1902 (5) 1905 (5)

Jackson, H. L. 2: v A 1961 (1); v NZ 1949 (1)

James, S. P. 2: v SA 1998 (1); v SL 1998 (1)

Jameson, J. A. 4: v In 1971 (2); *v WI 1973 (2)*

Jardine, D. R. 22: v WI 1928 (2) 1933 (2); v NZ 1931 (3); v In 1932 (1); *v A 1928 (5) 1932 (5); v NZ 1932 (1); v In 1933 (3)*

Jarvis, P. W. 9: v A 1989 (2); v WI 1988 (2); *v NZ 1987 (2); v In 1992 (2); v SL 1992 (1)*

Jenkins, R. O. 9: v WI 1950 (2); v In 1952 (2); *v SA 1948 (5)*

Jessop, G. L. 18: v A 1899 (1) 1902 (4) 1905 (1) 1909 (2); v SA 1907 (3) 1912 (2); *v A 1901 (5)*

Jones, A. O. 12: v A 1899 (1) 1905 (2) 1909 (2); *v A 1901 (5) 1907 (2)*

Jones, I. J. 15: v WI 1966 (2); *v A 1965 (4); v WI 1967 (5); v NZ 1965 (3); v In 1963 (1)*

Jones, S. P. 1: v In 2002

Jupp, H. 2: *v A 1876 (2)*

Jupp, V. W. C. 8: v A 1921 (2); v WI 1928 (2); v SA 1922 (4)

Keeton, W. W. 2: v A 1934 (1); v WI 1939 (1)

Kennedy, A. S. 5: *v SA 1922 (5)*

Kenyon, D. 8: v A 1953 (2); v SA 1955 (3); v In 1951 (3)

Key, R. W. T. 2: v In 2002 (2)

Killick, E. T. 2: v SA 1929 (2)

Kilner, R. 9: v A 1926 (4); v SA 1924 (2); *v A 1924 (3)*

King, J. H. 1: v A 1909

Kinneir, S. P. 1: *v A 1911*

Knight, A. E. 3: *v A 1903 (3)*

Knight, B. R. 29: v A 1968 (2); v WI 1966 (1) 1969 (3); v NZ 1969 (2); v P 1962 (2); *v A 1962 (1) 1965 (2); v NZ 1962 (3) 1965 (2); v In 1961 (4) 1963 (5); v P 1961 (2)*

Knight, D. J. 2: v A 1921 (2)

Knight, N. V. 17: v SA 1998 (1); v WI 1995 (2) 2000 (2); v In 1996 (1); v P 1996 (3) 2001 (1); v Z 2000 (2); *v NZ 1996 (3); v Z 1996 (2)*

Knott, A. P. E. 95: v A 1968 (5) 1972 (5) 1975 (4) 1977 (5) 1981 (2); v WI 1969 (3) 1973 (3) 1976 (5) 1980 (4); v NZ 1969 (2) 1973 (3); v In 1971 (3) 1974 (3); v P 1967 (2) 1971 (3) 1974 (3); *v A 1970 (6) 1974 (6) 1976 (1); v WI 1967 (2) 1973 (5); v NZ 1970 (1) 1974 (2); v In 1972 (5) 1976 (5); v P 1968 (3) 1972 (3)*

Knox, N. A. 2: v SA 1907 (2)

Maddy, D. L. 3: v NZ 1999 (1); *v SA 1999 (2)*

Makepeace, J. W. H. 4: *v A 1920 (4)*

Malcolm, D. E. 40: v A 1989 (1) 1993 (1) 1997 (4); v SA 1994 (1); v WI 1991 (2) 1995 (2); v NZ 1990 (3) 1994 (1); v In 1990 (3); v P 1992 (3); *v A 1990 (5) 1994 (4); v SA 1995 (2); v WI 1989 (4) 1993 (1); v In 1992 (2); v SL 1992 (1)*

Mallender, N. A. 2: v P 1992 (2)

Mann, F. G. 7: v NZ 1949 (2); *v SA 1948 (5)*

Mann, F. T. 5: *v SA 1922 (5)*

Marks, V. J. 6: v NZ 1983 (1); v P 1982 (1); *v NZ 1983 (1); v P 1983 (3)*

Marriott, C. S. 1: v WI 1933

Martin, F. 2: v A 1890 (1); *v SA 1891 (1)*

Martin, J. W. 1: v SA 1947

Martin, P. J. 8: v A 1997 (1); v WI 1995 (3); v In 1996 (1); *v SA 1995 (3)*

Mason, J. R. 5: *v A 1897 (5)*

Matthews, A. D. G. 1: v NZ 1937

May, P. B. H. 66: v A 1953 (2) 1956 (5) 1961 (4); v SA 1951 (2) 1955 (5); v WI 1957 (5); v NZ 1958 (5); v In 1952 (4) 1959 (3); v P 1954 (4); *v A 1954 (5) 1958 (5); v SA 1956 (5); v WI 1953 (5) 1959 (3); v NZ 1954 (2) 1958 (2)*

Maynard, M. P. 4: v A 1993 (2); v WI 1988 (1); *v WI 1993 (1)*

Mead, C. P. 17: v A 1921 (2); *v A 1911 (4) 1928 (1); v SA 1913 (5) 1922 (5)*

Mead, W. 1: v A 1899

Midwinter, W. E. 4: *v A 1881 (4)*

Milburn, C. 9: v A 1968 (2); v WI 1966 (4); v In 1967 (1); v P 1967 (1); *v P 1968 (1)*

Miller, A. M. 1: *v SA 1895*

Miller, G. 34: v A 1977 (2); v WI 1976 (1) 1984 (2); v NZ 1978 (2); v In 1979 (3) 1982 (1); v P 1978 (3) 1982 (1); *v A 1978 (6) 1979 (1) 1982 (5); v WI 1980 (1); v NZ 1977 (3); v P 1977 (3)*

Milligan, F. W. 2: *v SA 1898 (2)*

Millman, G. 6: v P 1962 (2); *v In 1961 (2); v P 1961 (2)*

Milton, C. A. 6: v NZ 1958 (2); v In 1958 (2); *v A 1958 (2)*

Mitchell, A. 6: v SA 1935 (2); v In 1936 (1); *v In 1933 (3)*

Mitchell, F. 2: *v SA 1898 (2)*

Mitchell, T. B. 5: v A 1934 (2); v SA 1935 (1); *v A 1932 (1); v NZ 1932 (1)*

Mitchell-Innes, N. S. 1: v SA 1935

Mold, A. W. 3: v A 1893 (3)

Moon, L. J. 4: *v SA 1905 (4)*

Morley, F. 4: v A 1880 (1); *v A 1882 (3)*

Morris, H. 3: v WI 1991 (2); v SL 1991 (1)

Morris, J. E. 3: v In 1990 (3)

Mortimore, J. B. 9: v A 1964 (1); v In 1959 (2); *v A 1958 (1); v NZ 1958 (2); v In 1963 (3)*

Moss, A. E. 9: v A 1956 (1); v SA 1960 (2); v In 1959 (3); *v WI 1953 (1) 1959 (2)*

Moxon, M. D. 10: v A 1989 (1); v WI 1988 (2); v NZ 1986 (2); v P 1987 (1); *v A 1987 (1); v NZ 1987 (3)*

Mullally, A. D. 19: v A 2001 (1); v NZ 1999 (3); v In 1996 (3); v P 1996 (3); *v A 1998 (4); v SA 1999 (2); v NZ 1996 (1); v Z 1996 (2)*

Munton, T. A. 2: v P 1992 (2)

Murdoch, W. L. 1: *v SA 1891*

Murray, J. T. 21: v A 1961 (5); v WI 1966 (1); v In 1967 (3); v P 1962 (3) 1967 (1); *v A 1962 (1); v SA 1964 (1); v NZ 1962 (1) 1965 (1); v In 1961 (3); v P 1961 (1)*

Newham, W. 1: *v A 1887*

Newport, P. J. 3: v A 1989 (1); v SL 1988 (1); *v A 1990 (1)*

Nichols, M. S. 14: v A 1930 (1); v SA 1935 (4); v WI 1933 (1) 1939 (1); *v NZ 1929 (4); v In 1933 (3)*

Oakman, A. S. M. 2: v A 1956 (2)

O'Brien, Sir T. C. 5: v A 1884 (1) 1888 (1); *v SA 1895 (3)*

O'Connor, J. 4: v SA 1929 (1); *v WI 1929 (3)*

Old, C. M. 46: v A 1975 (3) 1977 (2) 1980 (1) 1981 (2); v WI 1973 (1) 1976 (2) 1980 (1); v NZ 1973 (2) 1978 (1); v In 1974 (3); v P 1974 (3) 1978 (3); *v A 1974 (2) 1976 (1) 1978 (1); v WI 1973 (4) 1980 (1); v NZ 1974 (1) 1977 (2); v In 1972 (4) 1976 (4); v P 1972 (1) 1977 (1)*

Oldfield, N. 1: v WI 1939

Ormond, J. 2: v A 2001 (1); *v In 2001 (1)*

Padgett, D. E. V. 2: v SA 1960 (2)
Paine, G. A. E. 4: *v WI 1934 (4)*
Palairet, L. C. H. 2: v A 1902 (2)
Palmer, C. H. 1: *v WI 1953*
Palmer, K. E. 1: *v SA 1964*
Parfitt, P. H. 37: v A 1964 (4) 1972 (3); v SA 1965 (2); v WI 1969 (1); v NZ 1965 (2); v P 1962 (5); *v A 1962 (2); v SA 1964 (5); v NZ 1962 (3) 1965 (3); v In 1961 (2) 1963 (3); v P 1961 (2)*
Parker, C. W. L. 1: v A 1921
Parker, P. W. G. 1: v A 1981
Parkhouse, W. G. A. 7: v WI 1950 (2); v In 1959 (2); *v A 1950 (2); v NZ 1950 (1)*
Parkin, C. H. 10: v A 1921 (4); v SA 1924 (1); *v A 1920 (5)*
Parks, J. H. 1: v SA 1937
Parks, J. M. 46: v A 1964 (5); v SA 1960 (5) 1965 (3); v WI 1963 (4) 1966 (4); v NZ 1965 (3); v P 1954 (1); *v A 1965 (5); v SA 1964 (5); v WI 1959 (1) 1967 (3); v NZ 1965 (2); v In 1963 (5)*
Pataudi sen., Nawab of, 3: v A 1934 (1); *v A 1932 (2)*
Paynter, E. 20: v A 1938 (4); v WI 1939 (2); v NZ 1931 (1) 1937 (2); v In 1932 (1); *v A 1932 (3); v SA 1938 (5); v NZ 1932 (2)*
Peate, E. 9: v A 1882 (1) 1884 (3) 1886 (1); *v A 1881 (4)*
Peebles, I. A. R. 13: v A 1930 (2); v NZ 1931 (3); *v SA 1927 (4) 1930 (4)*
Peel, R. 20: v A 1888 (3) 1890 (1) 1893 (1) 1896 (1); *v A 1884 (5) 1887 (1) 1891 (3) 1894 (5)*
Penn, F. 1: v A 1880
Perks, R. T. D. 2: v WI 1939 (1); *v SA 1938 (1)*
Philipson, H. 5: *v A 1891 (1) 1894 (4)*
Pigott, A. C. S. 1: *v NZ 1983*
Pilling, R. 8: v A 1884 (1) 1886 (1) 1888 (1); *v A 1881 (4) 1887 (1)*
Place, W. 3: *v WI 1947 (3)*
Pocock, P. I. 25: v A 1968 (1); v WI 1976 (2) 1984 (2); v SL 1984 (1); *v WI 1967 (2) 1973 (4); v In 1972 (1) 1984 (5); v P 1968 (1) 1972 (3)*
Pollard, R. 4: v A 1948 (2); v In 1946 (1); *v NZ 1946 (1)*
Poole, C. J. 3: *v In 1951 (3)*
Pope, G. H. 1: v SA 1947
Pougher, A. D. 1: *v SA 1891*
Price, J. S. E. 15: v A 1964 (2) 1972 (1); v In 1971 (3); v P 1971 (1); *v SA 1964 (4); v In 1963 (4)*
Price, W. F. F. 1: v A 1938
Prideaux, R. M. 3: v A 1968 (1); *v P 1968 (2)*
Pringle, D. R. 30: v A 1989 (2); v WI 1984 (3) 1988 (4) 1991 (4); v NZ 1986 (1); v In 1982 (3) 1986 (3); v P 1982 (1) 1992 (3); v SL 1988 (1); *v A 1982 (3); v NZ 1991 (2)*
Pullar, G. 28: v A 1961 (5); v SA 1960 (3); v In 1959 (3); v P 1962 (2); *v A 1962 (4); v WI 1959 (5); v In 1961 (3); v P 1961 (3)*

Quaife, W. G. 7: v A 1899 (2); *v A 1901 (5)*

Radford, N. V. 3: v NZ 1986 (1); v In 1986 (1); *v NZ 1987 (1)*
Radley, C. T. 8: v NZ 1978 (3); v P 1978 (3); *v NZ 1977 (2)*
Ramprakash, M. R. 52: v A 1993 (1) 1997 (1) 2001 (4); v SA 1998 (5); v WI 1991 (5) 1995 (2) 2000 (2); v NZ 1999 (2); v P 1992 (3); v SL 1991 (1) 1998 (1); v Z 2000 (2); *v A 1994 (1) 1998 (5); v SA 1995 (2); v WI 1993 (4) 1997 (3); v NZ 2001 (3); v In 2001 (3)*
Randall, D. W. 47: v A 1977 (5); v WI 1984 (1); v NZ 1983 (3); v In 1979 (3) 1982 (3); v P 1982 (3); *v A 1976 (1) 1978 (6) 1979 (2) 1982 (4); v NZ 1977 (3) 1983 (3); v In 1976 (4); v P 1977 (3) 1983 (3)*
Ranjitsinhji, K. S. 15: v A 1896 (2) 1899 (5) 1902 (3); *v A 1897 (5)*
Read, C. M. W. 3: v NZ 1999 (3)
Read, H. D. 1: v SA 1935
Read, J. M. 17: v A 1882 (1) 1890 (2) 1893 (1); *v A 1884 (5) 1886 (2) 1887 (1) 1891 (3); v SA 1888 (2)*
Read, W. W. 18: v A 1884 (2) 1886 (3) 1888 (3) 1890 (3) 1893 (2); *v A 1882 (4) 1887 (1); v SA 1891 (1)*
Reeve, D. A. 3: *v NZ 1991 (3)*
Relf, A. E. 13: v A 1909 (1); *v A 1903 (2); v SA 1905 (5) 1913 (5)*
Rhodes, H. J. 2: v In 1959 (2)

Rhodes, S. J. 11: v A 1994 (3); v NZ 1994 (3); *v A 1994 (5)*

Rhodes, W. 58: v A 1899 (3) 1902 (5) 1905 (4) 1909 (4) 1912 (3) 1921 (1) 1926 (1); v SA 1912 (3); *v A 1903 (5) 1907 (5) 1911 (5) 1920 (5); v SA 1909 (5) 1913 (5); v WI 1929 (4)*

Richards, C. J. 8: v WI 1988 (2); v P 1987 (1); *v A 1986 (5)*

Richardson, D. W. 1: v WI 1957

Richardson, P. E. 34: v A 1956 (5); v WI 1957 (5) 1963 (1); v NZ 1958 (4); *v A 1958 (4); v SA 1956 (5); v NZ 1958 (2); v In 1961 (5); v P 1961 (3)*

Richardson, T. 14: v A 1893 (1) 1896 (3); *v A 1894 (5) 1897 (5)*

Richmond, T. L. 1: v A 1921

Ridgway, F. 5: *v In 1951 (5)*

Robertson, J. D. 11: v SA 1947 (1); v NZ 1949 (1); *v WI 1947 (4); v In 1951 (5)*

Robins, R. W. V. 19: v A 1930 (2); v SA 1929 (1) 1935 (3); v WI 1933 (2); v NZ 1931 (1) 1937 (3); v In 1932 (1) 1936 (2); *v A 1936 (4)*

Robinson, R. T. 29: v A 1985 (6) 1989 (1); v In 1986 (1); v P 1987 (5); v SL 1988 (1); *v A 1987 (1); v WI 1985 (4); v NZ 1987 (3); v In 1984 (5); v P 1987 (2)*

Roope, G. R. J. 21: v A 1975 (1) 1977 (2); v WI 1973 (1); v NZ 1973 (3) 1978 (1); v P 1978 (3); *v NZ 1977 (3); v In 1972 (2); v P 1972 (2) 1977 (3)*

Root, C. F. 3: v A 1926 (3)

Rose, B. C. 9: v WI 1980 (3); *v WI 1980 (1); v NZ 1977 (2); v P 1977 (3)*

Royle, V. P. F. A. 1: *v A 1878*

Rumsey, F. E. 5: v A 1964 (1); v SA 1965 (1); v NZ 1965 (3)

Russell, A. C. 10: v A 1921 (2); *v A 1920 (4); v SA 1922 (4)*

Russell, R. C. 54: v A 1989 (6); v WI 1991 (4) 1995 (3); v NZ 1990 (3); v In 1990 (3) 1996 (3); v P 1992 (3) 1996 (2); v SL 1988 (1) 1991 (1); *v A 1990 (3); v SA 1995 (5); v WI 1989 (4) 1993 (5) 1997 (5); v NZ 1991 (3)*

Russell, W. E. 10: v SA 1965 (1); v WI 1966 (2); v P 1967 (1); *v A 1965 (1); v NZ 1965 (3); v In 1961 (1); v P 1961 (1)*

Salisbury, I. D. K. 15: v SA 1994 (1) 1998 (2); v P 1992 (2) 1996 (2); v SL 1998 (1); *v WI 1993 (2); v In 1992 (2); v P 2000 (3)*

Sandham, A. 14: v A 1921 (1); v SA 1924 (2); *v A 1924 (2); v SA 1922 (5); v WI 1929 (4)*

Schofield, C. P. 2: v Z 2000 (2)

Schultz, S. S. 1: *v A 1878*

Scotton, W. H. 15: v A 1884 (1) 1886 (3); *v A 1881 (4) 1884 (5) 1886 (2)*

Selby, J. 6: *v A 1876 (2) 1881 (4)*

Selvey, M. W. W. 3: v WI 1976 (2); *v In 1976 (1)*

Shackleton, D. 7: v SA 1951 (1); v WI 1950 (1) 1963 (4); *v In 1951 (1)*

Sharp, J. 3: v A 1909 (3)

Sharpe, J. W. 3: v A 1890 (1); *v A 1891 (2)*

Sharpe, P. J. 12: v A 1964 (2); v WI 1963 (3) 1969 (3); v NZ 1969 (3); *v In 1963 (1)*

Shaw, A. 7: v A 1880 (1); *v A 1876 (2) 1881 (4)*

Sheppard, Rev. D. S. 22: v A 1956 (2); v WI 1950 (1) 1957 (2); v In 1952 (1); v P 1954 (2) 1962 (2); *v A 1950 (2) 1962 (5); v NZ 1950 (1) 1962 (3)*

Sherwin, M. 3: v A 1888 (1); *v A 1886 (2)*

Shrewsbury, A. 23: v A 1884 (3) 1886 (3) 1890 (2) 1893 (3); *v A 1881 (4) 1884 (5) 1886 (2) 1887 (1)*

Shuter, J. 1: v A 1888

Shuttleworth, K. 5: v P 1971 (1); *v A 1970 (2); v NZ 1970 (2)*

Sidebottom, A. 1: v A 1985

Sidebottom, R. J. 1: v P 2001

Silverwood, C. E. W. 5: *v SA 1999 (4); v Z 1996 (1)*

Simpson, R. T. 27: v A 1953 (3); v SA 1951 (3); v WI 1950 (3); v NZ 1949 (2); v In 1952 (2); v P 1954 (3); *v A 1950 (5) 1954 (1); v SA 1948 (1); v NZ 1950 (2) 1954 (2)*

Simpson-Hayward, G. H. 5: *v SA 1909 (5)*

Sims, J. M. 4: v SA 1935 (1); v In 1936 (1); *v A 1936 (2)*

Sinfield, R. A. 1: v A 1938

Slack, W. N. 3: v In 1986 (1); *v WI 1985 (2)*

Smailes, T. F. 1: v In 1946

Small, G. C. 17: v A 1989 (1); v WI 1988 (1); v NZ 1986 (2) 1990 (3); *v A 1986 (2) 1990 (4); v WI 1989 (4)*

Smith, A. C. 6: *v A 1962 (4); v NZ 1962 (2)*

Smith, A. M. 1: v A 1997
Smith, C. A. 1: *v SA 1888*
Smith, C. I. J. 5: v NZ 1937 (1); *v WI 1934 (4)*
Smith, C. L. 8: v NZ 1983 (2); v In 1986 (1); *v NZ 1983 (2); v P 1983 (3)*
Smith, D. 2: v SA 1935 (2)
Smith, D. M. 2: *v WI 1985 (2)*
Smith, D. R. 5: *v In 1961 (5)*
Smith, D. V. 3: v WI 1957 (3)
Smith, E. J. 11: v A 1912 (3); v SA 1912 (3); *v A 1911 (4); v SA 1913 (1)*
Smith, H. 1: v WI 1928
Smith, M. J. K. 50: v A 1961 (1) 1972 (3); v SA 1960 (4) 1965 (3); v WI 1966 (1); v NZ 1958 (3) 1965 (3); v In 1959 (2); *v A 1965 (5); v SA 1964 (5); v WI 1959 (5); v NZ 1965 (3); v In 1961 (4) 1963 (5); v P 1961 (3)*
Smith, R. A. 62: v A 1989 (5) 1993 (5); v WI 1988 (2) 1991 (4) 1995 (4); v NZ 1990 (3) 1994 (3); v In 1990 (3); v P 1992 (5); v SL 1988 (1) 1991 (1); *v A 1990 (5); v SA 1995 (5); v WI 1989 (4) 1993 (5); v NZ 1991 (3); v In 1992 (3); v SL 1992 (1)*
Smith, T. P. B. 4: v In 1946 (1); *v A 1946 (2); v NZ 1946 (1)*
Smithson, G. A. 2: *v WI 1947 (2)*
Snow, J. A. 49: v A 1968 (5) 1972 (5) 1975 (4); v SA 1965 (1); v WI 1966 (3) 1969 (3) 1973 (1) 1976 (3); v NZ 1965 (1) 1969 (2) 1973 (3); v In 1967 (3) 1971 (2); v P 1967 (1); *v A 1970 (6); v WI 1967 (4); v P 1968 (2)*
Southerton, J. 2: *v A 1876 (2)*
Spooner, R. H. 10: v A 1905 (2) 1909 (2) 1912 (3); v SA 1912 (3)
Spooner, R. T. 7: v SA 1955 (1); *v In 1951 (5); v WI 1953 (1)*
Stanyforth, R. T. 4: *v SA 1927 (4)*
Staples, S. J. 3: *v SA 1927 (3)*
Statham, J. B. 70: v A 1953 (1) 1956 (3) 1961 (4); v SA 1951 (2) 1955 (4) 1960 (5) 1965 (1); v WI 1957 (3) 1963 (2); v NZ 1958 (2); v In 1959 (3); v P 1954 (4) 1962 (3); *v A 1954 (5) 1958 (4) 1962 (5); v SA 1956 (4); v WI 1953 (4) 1959 (3); v NZ 1950 (1) 1954 (2); v In 1951 (5)*
Steel, A. G. 13: v A 1880 (1) 1882 (1) 1884 (3) 1886 (3) 1888 (1); *v A 1882 (4)*
Steele, D. S. 8: v A 1975 (3); v WI 1976 (5)
Stephenson, J. P. 1: v A 1989
Stevens, G. T. S. 10: v A 1926 (2); *v SA 1922 (1) 1927 (5); v WI 1929 (2)*
Stevenson, G. B. 2: *v WI 1980 (1); v In 1979 (1)*
Stewart, A. J. 122: v A 1993 (6) 1997 (6) 2001 (5); v SA 1994 (3) 1998 (5); v WI 1991 (1) 1995 (3) 2000 (5); v NZ 1990 (3) 1994 (3) 1999 (4); v In 1996 (2) 2002 (4); v P 1992 (5) 1996 (3) 2001 (2); v SL 1991 (1) 1998 (1) 2002 (3); v Z 2000 (3); *v A 1990 (5) 1994 (2) 1998 (5); v SA 1995 (5) 1999 (5); v WI 1989 (4) 1993 (5) 1997 (6); v NZ 1991 (3) 1996 (3); v In 1992 (3); v P 2000 (3); v SL 1992 (1) 2000 (3); v Z 1996 (2)*
Stewart, M. J. 8: v WI 1963 (4); v P 1962 (2); *v In 1963 (2)*
Stoddart, A. E. 16: v A 1893 (3) 1896 (2); *v A 1887 (1) 1891 (3) 1894 (5) 1897 (2)*
Storer, W. 6: v A 1899 (1); *v A 1897 (5)*
Street, G. B. 1: *v SA 1922*
Strudwick, H. 28: v A 1921 (2) 1926 (5); v SA 1924 (1); *v A 1911 (1) 1920 (4) 1924 (5); v SA 1909 (5) 1913 (5)*
Studd, C. T. 5: v A 1882 (1); *v A 1882 (4)*
Studd, G. B. 4: *v A 1882 (4)*
Subba Row, R. 13: v A 1961 (5); v SA 1960 (4); v NZ 1958 (1); v In 1959 (1); *v WI 1959 (2)*
Such, P. M. 11: v A 1993 (5); v NZ 1994 (3) 1999 (1); *v A 1998 (2)*
Sugg, F. H. 2: v A 1888 (2)
Sutcliffe, H. 54: v A 1926 (5) 1930 (4) 1934 (4); v SA 1924 (5) 1929 (3) 1935 (2); v WI 1928 (3) 1933 (3); v NZ 1931 (2); v In 1932 (1); *v A 1924 (5) 1928 (4) 1932 (2); v SA 1927 (5); v NZ 1932 (2)*
Swetman, R. 11: v In 1959 (3); *v A 1958 (2); v WI 1959 (4); v NZ 1958 (2)*

Tate, F. W. 1: v A 1902
Tate, M. W. 39: v A 1926 (5) 1930 (5); v SA 1924 (5) 1929 (3) 1935 (1); v WI 1928 (3); v NZ 1931 (1); *v A 1924 (5) 1928 (5); v SA 1930 (5); v NZ 1932 (1)*
Tattersall, R. 16: v A 1953 (1); v SA 1951 (5); v P 1954 (1); *v A 1950 (2); v NZ 1950 (2); v In 1951 (5)*

Tavaré, C. J. 31: v A 1981 (2) 1989 (1); v WI 1980 (2) 1984 (1); v NZ 1983 (4); v In 1982 (3); v P 1982 (3); v SL 1984 (1); *v A 1982 (5); v NZ 1983 (2); v In 1981 (6); v SL 1981 (1)*

Taylor, J. P. 2: v NZ 1994 (1); *v In 1992 (1)*

Taylor, K. 3: v A 1964 (1); v In 1959 (2)

Taylor, L. B. 2: v A 1985 (2)

Taylor, R. W. 57: v A 1981 (3); v NZ 1978 (3) 1983 (4); v In 1979 (3) 1982 (3); v P 1978 (3) 1982 (3); *v A 1978 (6) 1979 (3) 1982 (5); v NZ 1970 (1) 1977 (3) 1983 (3); v In 1979 (1) 1981 (6); v P 1977 (3) 1983 (3); v SL 1981 (1)*

Tennyson, Hon. L. H. 9: v A 1921 (4); *v SA 1913 (5)*

Terry, V. P. 2: v WI 1984 (2)

Thomas, J. G. 5: v NZ 1986 (1); *v WI 1985 (4)*

Thompson, G. J. 6: v A 1909 (1); *v SA 1909 (5)*

Thomson, N. I. 5: *v SA 1964 (5)*

Thorpe, G. P. 77: v A 1993 (3) 1997 (6) 2001 (1); v SA 1994 (2) 1998 (3); v WI 1995 (6) 2000 (3); v NZ 1999 (4); v In 1996 (3) 2002 (1); v P 1996 (3) 2001 (2); v SL 2002 (3); *v A 1994 (5) 1998 (1); v SA 1995 (5); v WI 1993 (5) 1997 (6); v NZ 1996 (3) 2001 (1); v In 2001 (1); v P 2000 (3); v SL 2000 (3); v Z 1996 (2)*

Titmus, F. J. 53: v A 1964 (5); v WI 1955 (2) 1965 (3); v In 1963 (4) 1966 (3); v NZ 1965 (3); v P 1962 (2) 1967 (2); *v A 1962 (5) 1965 (5) 1974 (4); v SA 1964 (5); v WI 1967 (2); v NZ 1962 (3); v In 1963 (5)*

Tolchard, R. W. 4: *v In 1976 (4)*

Townsend, C. L. 2: v A 1899 (2)

Townsend, D. C. H. 3: *v WI 1934 (3)*

Townsend, L. F. 4: *v WI 1929 (1); v In 1933 (3)*

Tremlett, M. F. 3: *v WI 1947 (3)*

Trescothick, M. E. 26: v A 2001 (5); v WI 2000 (3); v In 2002 (1); v P 2001 (2); v SL 2002 (3); *v NZ 2001 (3); v In 2001 (3); v P 2000 (3); v SL 2000 (3)*

Trott, A. E. 2: *v SA 1898 (2)*

Trueman, F. S. 67: v A 1953 (1) 1956 (2) 1961 (4) 1964 (4); v SA 1955 (1) 1960 (5); v WI 1957 (5) 1963 (5); v NZ 1958 (5) 1965 (2); v In 1952 (4) 1959 (5); v P 1962 (4); *v A 1958 (3) 1962 (5); v WI 1953 (3) 1959 (5); v NZ 1958 (2) 1962 (2)*

Tudor, A. J. 9: v A 2001 (2); v NZ 1999 (1); v In 2002 (2); v SL 2002 (2); *v A 1998 (2)*

Tufnell, N. C. 1: *v SA 1909*

Tufnell, P. C. R. 42: v A 1993 (2) 1997 (1) 2001 (1); v SA 1994 (1); v WI 1991 (1); v NZ 1999 (4); v P 1992 (1); v SL 1991 (1); *v A 1990 (4) 1994 (4); v SA 1999 (3); v WI 1993 (2) 1997 (6); v NZ 1991 (3) 1999 (4); v In 1992 (2); v SL 1992 (1); v Z 1996 (2)*

Turnbull, M. J. 9: v WI 1933 (2); v In 1936 (1); *v SA 1930 (5); v NZ 1929 (1)*

Tyldesley, E. 14: v A 1921 (3) 1926 (1); v SA 1924 (1); v WI 1928 (3); *v A 1928 (1); v SA 1927 (5)*

Tyldesley, J. T. 31: v A 1899 (2) 1902 (5) 1905 (5) 1909 (4); v SA 1907 (3); *v A 1901 (5) 1903 (5); v SA 1898 (2)*

Tyldesley, R. K. 7: v A 1930 (2); v SA 1924 (4); *v A 1924 (1)*

Tylecote, E. F. S. 6: v A 1886 (2); *v A 1882 (4)*

Tyler, E. J. 1: *v SA 1895*

Tyson, F. H. 17: v A 1956 (1); v SA 1955 (2); v P 1954 (1); *v A 1954 (5) 1958 (2); v SA 1956 (2); v NZ 1954 (2) 1958 (2)*

Ulyett, G. 25: v A 1882 (1) 1884 (3) 1886 (3) 1888 (2) 1890 (1); *v A 1876 (2) 1878 (1) 1881 (4) 1884 (5) 1887 (1); v SA 1888 (2)*

Underwood, D. L. 86: v A 1968 (4) 1972 (2) 1975 (4) 1977 (5); v WI 1966 (2) 1969 (2) 1973 (3) 1976 (5) 1980 (1); v NZ 1969 (3) 1973 (1); v In 1971 (1) 1974 (3); v P 1967 (2) 1971 (1) 1974 (3); *v A 1970 (5) 1974 (5) 1976 (1) 1979 (3); v WI 1973 (4); v NZ 1970 (2) 1974 (2); v In 1972 (4) 1976 (5) 1979 (1) 1981 (6); v P 1968 (3) 1972 (2); v SL 1981 (1)*

Valentine, B. H. 7: *v SA 1938 (5); v In 1933 (2)*

Vaughan, M. P. 23: v WI 2000 (4); v In 2002 (4); v P 2001 (2); v SL 2002 (3); *v SA 1999 (4); v NZ 2001 (3); v In 2001 (2); v SL 2000 (1)*

Verity, H. 40: v A 1934 (5) 1938 (4); v SA 1935 (4); v WI 1933 (2) 1939 (1); v NZ 1931 (2) 1937 (1); v In 1936 (3); *v A 1932 (4) 1936 (5); v SA 1938 (5); v NZ 1932 (1); v In 1933 (3)*

Vernon, G. F. 1: *v A 1882*

Vine, J. 2: *v A 1911 (2)*

Voce, W. 27: v NZ 1931 (1) 1937 (1); v In 1932 (1) 1936 (1) 1946 (1); *v A 1932 (4) 1936 (5) 1946 (2); v SA 1930 (5); v WI 1929 (4); v NZ 1932 (2)*

Waddington, A. 2: *v A 1920 (2)*
Wainwright, E. 5: v A 1893 (1); *v A 1897 (4)*
Walker, P. M. 3: v SA 1960 (3)
Walters, C. F. 11: v A 1934 (5); v WI 1933 (3); *v In 1933 (3)*
Ward, A. 5: v WI 1976 (1); v NZ 1969 (3); v P 1971 (1)
Ward, A. 7: v A 1893 (2); *v A 1894 (5)*
Ward, I. J. 5: v A 2001 (3); v P 2001 (2)
Wardle, J. H. 28: v A 1953 (3) 1956 (1); v SA 1951 (2) 1955 (3); v WI 1950 (1) 1957 (1); v P 1954 (1); *v A 1954 (4); v SA 1956 (4); v WI 1947 (1) 1953 (2); v NZ 1954 (2)*
Warner, P. F. 15: v A 1909 (1) 1912 (1); v SA 1912 (1); *v A 1903 (5); v SA 1898 (2) 1905 (5)*
Warr, J. J. 2: *v A 1950 (2)*
Warren, A. R. 1: v A 1905
Washbrook, C. 37: v A 1948 (4) 1956 (3); v SA 1947 (5); v WI 1950 (2); v NZ 1937 (1) 1949 (2); v In 1946 (3); *v A 1946 (5) 1950 (5); v SA 1948 (5); v NZ 1946 (1) 1950 (1)*
Watkin, S. L. 3: v A 1993 (1); v WI 1991 (2)
Watkins, A. J. 15: v A 1948 (1); v NZ 1949 (1); v In 1952 (3); *v SA 1948 (5); v In 1951 (5)*
Watkinson, M. 4: v WI 1995 (3); *v SA 1995 (1)*
Watson, W. 23: v A 1953 (3) 1956 (2); v SA 1951 (5) 1955 (1); v NZ 1958 (2); v In 1952 (1); *v A 1958 (2); v WI 1953 (5); v NZ 1958 (2)*
Webbe, A. J. 1: *v A 1878*
Wellard, A. W. 2: v A 1938 (1); v NZ 1937 (1)
Wells, A. P. 1: v WI 1995
Wharton, A. 1: v NZ 1949
Whitaker, J. J. 1: *v A 1986*
White, C. 26: v A 2001 (3); v SA 1994 (1); v WI 1995 (2) 2000 (4); v NZ 1994 (3); v In 2002 (2); *v NZ 1996 (1); v In 2001 (3); v P 2000 (3); v SL 2000 (3); v Z 1996 (1)*
White, D. W. 2: v P 1961 (2)
White, J. C. 15: v A 1921 (1) 1930 (1); v SA 1929 (3); v WI 1928 (1); *v A 1928 (5); v SA 1930 (4)*
Whysall, W. W. 4: v A 1930 (1); *v A 1924 (3)*
Wilkinson, L. L. 3: *v SA 1938 (3)*
Willey, P. 26: v A 1980 (1) 1981 (4) 1985 (1); v WI 1976 (2) 1980 (5); v NZ 1986 (1); v In 1979 (1); *v A 1979 (3); v WI 1980 (4) 1985 (4)*
Williams, N. F. 1: v In 1990
Willis, R. G. D. 90: v A 1977 (5) 1981 (6); v WI 1973 (1) 1976 (2) 1980 (4) 1984 (3); v NZ 1978 (3) 1983 (4); v In 1974 (1) 1979 (3) 1982 (3); v P 1974 (1) 1978 (3) 1982 (2); *v A 1970 (4) 1974 (5) 1976 (1) 1978 (6) 1979 (3) 1982 (5); v WI 1973 (3); v NZ 1970 (1) 1977 (3) 1983 (3); v In 1976 (5) 1981 (5); v P 1977 (3) 1983 (1); v SL 1981 (1)*
Wilson, C. E. M. 2: *v SA 1898 (2)*
Wilson, D. 6: *v NZ 1970 (1); v In 1963 (5)*
Wilson, E. R. 1: *v A 1920*
Wood, A. 4: v A 1938 (1); v WI 1939 (3)
Wood, B. 12: v A 1972 (1) 1975 (3); v WI 1976 (1); v P 1978 (1); *v NZ 1974 (2); v In 1972 (3); v P 1972 (1)*
Wood, G. E. C. 3: v SA 1924 (3)
Wood, H. 4: v A 1888 (1); *v SA 1888 (2) 1891 (1)*
Wood, R. 1: *v A 1886*
Woods S. M. J. 3: *v SA 1895 (3)*
Woolley, F. E. 64: v A 1909 (1) 1912 (3) 1921 (5) 1926 (5) 1930 (2) 1934 (1); v SA 1912 (3) 1924 (5) 1929 (3); v NZ 1931 (1); v In 1932 (1); *v A 1911 (5) 1920 (5) 1924 (5); v SA 1909 (5) 1913 (5) 1922 (5); v NZ 1929 (4)*
Woolmer, R. A. 19: v A 1975 (2) 1977 (5) 1981 (2); v WI 1976 (5) 1980 (2); *v A 1976 (1); v In 1976 (2)*
Worthington, T. S. 9: v In 1936 (2); *v A 1936 (3); v NZ 1929 (4)*
Wright, C. W. 3: *v SA 1895 (3)*
Wright, D. V. P. 34: v A 1938 (3) 1948 (1); v SA 1947 (4); v WI 1939 (3) 1950 (1); v NZ 1949 (1); v In 1946 (2); *v A 1946 (5) 1950 (5); v SA 1938 (3) 1948 (3); v NZ 1946 (1) 1950 (2)*
Wyatt, R. E. S. 40: v A 1930 (1) 1934 (4); v SA 1929 (2) 1935 (5); v WI 1933 (2); v In 1936 (1); *v A 1932 (5) 1936 (2); v SA 1927 (5) 1930 (5); v WI 1929 (2) 1934 (4); v NZ 1932 (2)*

Wynyard, E. G. 3: v A 1896 (1); *v SA 1905 (2)*

Yardley, N. W. D. 20: v A 1948 (5); v SA 1947 (5); v WI 1950 (3); *v A 1946 (5); v SA 1938 (1); v NZ 1946 (1)*
Young, H. I. 2: v A 1899 (2)
Young, J. A. 8: v A 1948 (3); v SA 1947 (1); v NZ 1949 (2); *v SA 1948 (2)*
Young, R. A. 2: *v A 1907 (2)*

AUSTRALIA

Number of Test cricketers: 384

a'Beckett, E. L. 4: v E 1928 (2); v SA 1931 (1); *v E 1930 (1)*
Alderman, T. M. 41: v E 1982 (1) 1990 (4); v WI 1981 (2) 1984 (3) 1988 (2); v NZ 1989 (1); v P 1981 (3) 1989 (2); v SL 1989 (2); *v E 1981 (6) 1989 (6); v WI 1983 (3) 1990 (1); v NZ 1981 (3) 1989 (1); v P 1982 (1)*
Alexander, G. 2: v E 1884 (1); *v E 1880 (1)*
Alexander, H. H. 1: v E 1932
Allan, F. E. 1: v E 1878
Allan, P. J. 1: v E 1965
Allen, R. C. 1: v E 1886
Andrews, T. J. E. 16: v E 1924 (3); *v E 1921 (5) 1926 (5); v SA 1921 (3)*
Angel, J. 4: v E 1994 (1); v WI 1992 (1); *v P 1994 (2)*
Archer, K. A. 5: v E 1950 (3); v WI 1951 (2)
Archer, R. G. 19: v E 1954 (4); v SA 1952 (1); *v E 1953 (3) 1956 (5); v WI 1954 (5); v P 1956 (1)*
Armstrong, W. W. 50: v E 1901 (4) 1903 (3) 1907 (5) 1911 (5) 1920 (5); v SA 1910 (5); *v E 1902 (5) 1905 (5) 1909 (5) 1921 (5); v SA 1902 (3)*

Badcock, C. L. 7: v E 1936 (3); *v E 1938 (4)*
Bannerman, A. C. 28: v E 1878 (1) 1881 (3) 1882 (4) 1884 (4) 1886 (1) 1887 (1) 1891 (3); *v E 1880 (1) 1882 (1) 1884 (3) 1888 (3) 1893 (3)*
Bannerman, C. 3: v E 1876 (2) 1878 (1)
Bardsley, W. 41: v E 1911 (4) 1920 (5) 1924 (3); v SA 1910 (5); *v E 1909 (5) 1912 (3) 1921 (5) 1926 (5); v SA 1912 (3) 1921 (3)*
Barnes, S. G. 13: v E 1946 (4); v In 1947 (3); *v E 1938 (1) 1948 (4); v NZ 1945 (1)*
Barnett, B. A. 4: *v E 1938 (4)*
Barrett, J. E. 2: *v E 1890 (2)*
Beard, G. R. 3: *v P 1979 (3)*
Benaud, J. 3: *v P 1972 (2); v WI 1972 (1)*
Benaud, R. 63: v E 1954 (5) 1958 (5) 1962 (5); v SA 1952 (4) 1963 (4); v WI 1951 (1) 1960 (5); *v E 1953 (3) 1956 (5) 1961 (4); v SA 1957 (5); v WI 1954 (5); v In 1956 (3) 1959 (5); v P 1956 (1) 1959 (3)*
Bennett, M. J. 3: v WI 1984 (2); *v E 1985 (1)*
Bevan, M. G. 18: v E 1994 (3); v SA 1997 (1); v WI 1996 (4); *v E 1997 (3); v SA 1996 (3); v In 1996 (1); v P 1994 (2)*
Bichel, A. J. 6: v SA 1997 (1) 2001 (1); v WI 1996 (2) 2000 (2)
Blackham, J. McC. 35: v E 1876 (2) 1878 (1) 1881 (4) 1882 (4) 1884 (2) 1886 (1) 1887 (1) 1891 (3) 1894 (1); *v E 1880 (1) 1882 (1) 1884 (3) 1886 (3) 1888 (3) 1890 (2) 1893 (3)*
Blackie, D. D. 3: v E 1928 (3)
Blewett, G. S. 46: v E 1994 (2); v SA 1997 (3); v WI 1996 (4); v NZ 1997 (3); v In 1999 (3); v P 1995 (3) 1999 (3); *v E 1997 (6); v SA 1996 (3); v WI 1994 (4) 1998 (3); v NZ 1999 (2); v In 1997 (3); v SL 1999 (3); v Z 1999 (1)*
Bonnor, G. J. 17: v E 1882 (1) 1884 (3); *v E 1880 (1) 1882 (1) 1884 (3) 1886 (2) 1888 (3)*
Boon, D. C. 107: v E 1986 (4) 1987 (1) 1990 (5) 1994 (5); v SA 1993 (3); v WI 1984 (3) 1988 (5) 1992 (5); v NZ 1985 (3) 1987 (3) 1989 (1) 1993 (3); v In 1985 (3) 1991 (5); v P 1989 (2) 1995 (3); v SL 1987 (1) 1989 (2) 1995 (3); *v E 1985 (4) 1989 (6) 1993 (6); v SA 1993 (3); v WI 1990 (5) 1994 (4); v NZ 1985 (3) 1989 (1) 1992 (3); v In 1986 (3); v P 1988 (3) 1994 (3); v SL 1992 (3)*
Booth, B. C. 29: v E 1962 (5) 1965 (3); v SA 1963 (4); v P 1964 (1); *v E 1961 (2) 1964 (5); v WI 1964 (5); v In 1964 (3); v P 1964 (1)*

Border, A. R. 156: v E 1978 (3) 1979 (3) 1982 (5) 1986 (5) 1987 (1) 1990 (5); v SA 1993 (3); v WI 1979 (3) 1981 (3) 1984 (5) 1988 (5) 1992 (5); v NZ 1980 (3) 1985 (3) 1987 (3) 1989 (1) 1993 (3); v In 1980 (3) 1985 (3) 1991 (5); v P 1978 (2) 1981 (3) 1983 (5) 1989 (3); v SL 1987 (1) 1989 (2); *v E 1980 (1) 1981 (6) 1985 (6) 1989 (6) 1993 (6); v SA 1993 (3); v WI 1983 (5) 1990 (5); v NZ 1981 (3) 1985 (3) 1989 (1) 1992 (3); v In 1979 (6) 1986 (3); v P 1979 (3) 1982 (3) 1988 (3); v SL 1982 (1) 1992 (3)*

Boyle, H. F. 12: v E 1878 (1) 1881 (4) 1882 (1) 1884 (1); *v E 1880 (1) 1882 (1) 1884 (3)*

Bradman, D. G. 52: v E 1928 (4) 1932 (4) 1936 (5) 1946 (5); v SA 1931 (5); v WI 1930 (5); v In 1947 (5); *v E 1930 (5) 1934 (5) 1938 (4) 1948 (5)*

Bright, R. J. 25: v E 1979 (1); v WI 1979 (1); v NZ 1985 (1); v In 1985 (3); *v E 1977 (3) 1980 (1) 1981 (5); v NZ 1985 (2); v In 1986 (3); v P 1979 (3) 1982 (2)*

Bromley, E. H. 2: v E 1932 (1); *v E 1934 (1)*

Brown, W. A. 22: v E 1936 (2); v In 1947 (3); *v E 1934 (5) 1938 (4) 1948 (2); v SA 1935 (5); v NZ 1945 (1)*

Bruce, W. 14: v E 1884 (2) 1891 (3) 1894 (4); *v E 1886 (2) 1893 (3)*

Burge, P. J. 42: v E 1954 (1) 1958 (1) 1962 (3) 1965 (4); v SA 1963 (5); v WI 1960 (2); *v E 1956 (3) 1961 (5) 1964 (5); v SA 1957 (1); v WI 1954 (1); v In 1956 (3) 1959 (2) 1964 (3); v P 1959 (2) 1964 (1)*

Burke, J. W. 24: v E 1950 (2) 1954 (2) 1958 (5); v WI 1951 (1); *v E 1956 (5); v SA 1957 (5); v In 1956 (3); v P 1956 (1)*

Burn, K. E. 2: *v E 1890 (2)*

Burton, F. J. 2: v E 1886 (1) 1887 (1)

Callaway, S. T. 3: v E 1891 (2) 1894 (1)

Callen, I. W. 1: v In 1977

Campbell, G. D. 4: v P 1989 (1); v SL 1989 (1); *v E 1989 (1); v NZ 1989 (1)*

Carkeek, W. 6: *v E 1912 (3); v SA 1912 (3)*

Carlson, P. H. 2: v E 1978 (2)

Carter, H. 28: v E 1907 (5) 1911 (5) 1920 (2); v SA 1910 (5); *v E 1909 (5) 1921 (4); v SA 1921 (2)*

Chappell, G. S. 87: v E 1970 (5) 1974 (6) 1976 (1) 1979 (3) 1982 (5); v WI 1975 (6) 1979 (3) 1981 (3); v NZ 1973 (3) 1980 (3); v In 1980 (3); v P 1972 (3) 1976 (3) 1981 (3) 1983 (5); *v E 1972 (5) 1975 (4) 1977 (5) 1980 (1); v WI 1972 (5); v NZ 1973 (3) 1976 (2) 1981 (3); v P 1979 (3); v SL 1982 (1)*

Chappell, I. M. 75: v E 1965 (2) 1970 (6) 1974 (6) 1979 (2); v WI 1968 (5) 1975 (6) 1979 (1); v NZ 1973 (3); v In 1967 (4); v P 1964 (1) 1972 (3); *v E 1968 (5) 1972 (5) 1975 (4); v SA 1966 (5) 1969 (4); v WI 1972 (5); v NZ 1973 (3); v In 1969 (5)*

Chappell, T. M. 3: *v E 1981 (3)*

Charlton, P. C. 2: *v E 1890 (2)*

Chipperfield, A. G. 14: v E 1936 (3); *v E 1934 (5) 1938 (1); v SA 1935 (5)*

Clark, W. M. 10: v In 1977 (5); v P 1978 (1); *v WI 1977 (4)*

Colley, D. J. 3: *v E 1972 (3)*

Collins, H. L. 19: v E 1920 (5) 1924 (5); *v E 1921 (3) 1926 (3); v SA 1921 (3)*

Coningham, A. 1: v E 1894

Connolly, A. N. 29: v E 1965 (1) 1970 (1); v SA 1963 (3); v WI 1968 (5); v In 1967 (3); *v E 1968 (5); v SA 1969 (4); v In 1964 (2) 1969 (5)*

Cook, S. H. 2: v NZ 1997 (2)

Cooper, B. B. 1: v E 1876

Cooper, W. H. 2: v E 1881 (1) 1884 (1)

Corling, G. E. 5: *v E 1964 (5)*

Cosier, G. J. 18: v E 1976 (3) 1978 (2); v WI 1975 (3); v In 1977 (4); v P 1976 (3); *v WI 1977 (3); v NZ 1976 (2)*

Cottam, J. T. 1: v E 1886

Cotter, A. 21: v E 1903 (2) 1907 (2) 1911 (4); v SA 1910 (5); *v E 1905 (3) 1909 (5)*

Coulthard, G. 1: v E 1881

Cowper, R. M. 27: v E 1965 (4); v In 1967 (4); v P 1964 (1); *v E 1964 (1) 1968 (4); v SA 1966 (5); v WI 1964 (5); v In 1964 (2); v P 1964 (1)*

Craig, I. D. 11: v SA 1952 (1); *v E 1956 (2); v SA 1957 (5); v In 1956 (2); v P 1956 (1)*

Crawford, P. 4: *v E 1956 (1); v In 1956 (3)*

Dale, A. C. 2: *v WI 1998 (1); v In 1997 (1)*

Darling, J. 34: v E 1894 (5) 1897 (5) 1901 (3); *v E 1896 (3) 1899 (5) 1902 (5) 1905 (5); v SA 1902 (3)*

Darling, L. S. 12: v E 1932 (2) 1936 (1); *v E 1934 (4); v SA 1935 (5)*

Darling, W. M. 14: v E 1978 (4); v In 1977 (1); v P 1978 (1); *v WI 1977 (3); v In 1979 (5)*

Davidson, A. K. 44: v E 1954 (3) 1958 (5) 1962 (5); v WI 1960 (4); *v E 1953 (5) 1956 (2) 1961 (5); v SA 1957 (5); v In 1956 (1) 1959 (5); v P 1956 (1) 1959 (3)*

Davis, I. C. 15: v E 1976 (1); v NZ 1973 (3); v P 1976 (3); *v E 1977 (3); v NZ 1973 (3) 1976 (2)*

Davis, S. P. 1: *v NZ 1985*

De Courcy, J. H. 3: *v E 1953 (3)*

Dell, A. R. 2: v E 1970 (1); v NZ 1973 (1)

Dodemaide, A. I. C. 10: v E 1987 (1); v WI 1988 (2); v NZ 1987 (1); v SL 1987 (1); *v P 1988 (3); v SL 1992 (2)*

Donnan, H. 5: v E 1891 (2); *v E 1896 (3)*

Dooland, B. 3: v E 1946 (2); v In 1947 (1)

Duff, R. A. 22: v E 1901 (4) 1903 (5); *v E 1902 (5) 1905 (5); v SA 1902 (3)*

Duncan, J. R. F. 1: v E 1970

Dyer, G. C. 6: v E 1986 (1) 1987 (1); v NZ 1987 (3); v SL 1987 (1)

Dymock, G. 21: v E 1974 (1) 1978 (3) 1979 (3); v WI 1979 (2); v NZ 1973 (1); v P 1978 (1); *v NZ 1973 (2); v In 1979 (5); v P 1979 (3)*

Dyson, J. 30: v E 1982 (5); v WI 1981 (2) 1984 (3); v NZ 1980 (3); v In 1977 (3) 1980 (3); *v E 1981 (5); v NZ 1981 (3); v P 1982 (3)*

Eady, C. J. 2: v E 1901 (1); *v E 1896 (1)*

Eastwood, K. H. 1: v E 1970

Ebeling, H. I. 1: *v E 1934*

Edwards, J. D. 3: *v E 1888 (3)*

Edwards, R. 20: v E 1974 (5); v P 1972 (2); *v E 1972 (4) 1975 (4); v WI 1972 (5)*

Edwards, W. J. 3: v E 1974 (3)

Elliott, M. T. G. 20: v SA 1997 (3); v WI 1996 (2); v NZ 1997 (3); *v E 1997 (6); v SA 1996 (3); v WI 1998 (3)*

Emery, P. A. 1: *v P 1994*

Emery, S. H. 4: *v E 1912 (2); v SA 1912 (2)*

Evans, E. 6: v E 1881 (2) 1882 (1) 1884 (1); *v E 1886 (2)*

Fairfax, A. G. 10: v E 1928 (1); v WI 1930 (5); *v E 1930 (4)*

Favell, L. E. 19: v E 1954 (4) 1958 (2); v WI 1960 (4); *v WI 1954 (2); v In 1959 (4); v P 1959 (3)*

Ferris, J. J. 8: v E 1886 (2) 1887 (1); *v E 1888 (3) 1890 (2)*

Fingleton, J. H. 18: v E 1932 (3) 1936 (5); v SA 1931 (1); *v E 1938 (4); v SA 1935 (5)*

Fleetwood-Smith, L. O'B. 10: v E 1936 (3); *v E 1938 (4); v SA 1935 (3)*

Fleming, D. W. 20: v E 1994 (3) 1998 (4); v In 1999 (3); v P 1999 (3); *v In 2000 (1); v P 1994 (1) 1998 (2); v SL 1999 (2); v Z 1999 (1)*

Francis, B. C. 3: *v E 1972 (3)*

Freeman, E. W. 11: v WI 1968 (4); v In 1967 (2); *v E 1968 (2); v SA 1969 (2); v In 1969 (1)*

Freer, F. W. 1: v E 1946

Gannon, J. B. 3: v In 1977 (3)

Garrett, T. W. 19: v E 1876 (2) 1878 (1) 1881 (3) 1882 (3) 1884 (3) 1886 (2) 1887 (1); *v E 1882 (1) 1886 (3)*

Gaunt, R. A. 3: v SA 1963 (1); *v E 1961 (1); v SA 1957 (1)*

Gehrs, D. R. A. 6: v E 1903 (1); v SA 1910 (4); *v E 1905 (1)*

Giffen, G. 31: v E 1881 (3) 1882 (4) 1884 (3) 1891 (3) 1894 (5); *v E 1882 (1) 1884 (3) 1886 (2) 1893 (3) 1896 (3)*

Giffen, W. F. 3: v E 1886 (1) 1891 (2)

Gilbert, D. R. 9: v NZ 1985 (3); v In 1985 (2); *v E 1985 (1); v NZ 1985 (1); v In 1986 (2)*

Gilchrist, A. C. 31: v SA 2001 (3); v WI 2000 (5); v NZ 2001 (3); v In 1999 (3); v P 1999 (3); *v E 2001 (5); v SA 2001 (3); v NZ 1999 (3); v In 2000 (3)*

Gillespie, J. N. 33: v E 1998 (1); v SA 2001 (1); v WI 1996 (2) 2000 (4); v NZ 2001 (3); *v E 1997 (4) 2001 (5); v SA 1996 (3) 2001 (3); v WI 1998 (3); v In 2000 (3); v SL 1999 (1)*

Gilmour, G. J. 15: v E 1976 (1); v WI 1975 (5); v NZ 1973 (2); v P 1976 (3); *v E 1975 (1); v NZ 1973 (1) 1976 (2)*

Gleeson, J. W. 29: v E 1970 (5); v WI 1968 (5); v In 1967 (4); *v E 1968 (5) 1972 (3); v SA 1969 (4); v In 1969 (3)*

Graham, H. 6: v E 1894 (2); *v E 1893 (3) 1896 (1)*

Gregory, D. W. 3: v E 1876 (2) 1878 (1)

Gregory, E. J. 1: v E 1876

Gregory, J. M. 24: v E 1920 (5) 1924 (5) 1928 (1); *v E 1921 (5) 1926 (5); v SA 1921 (3)*

Gregory, R. G. 2: v E 1936 (2)

Gregory, S. E. 58: v E 1891 (1) 1894 (5) 1897 (5) 1901 (5) 1903 (4) 1907 (2) 1911 (1); *v E 1890 (2) 1893 (3) 1896 (3) 1899 (5) 1902 (5) 1905 (3) 1909 (5) 1912 (3); v SA 1902 (3) 1912 (3)*

Grimmett, C. V. 37: v E 1924 (1) 1928 (5) 1932 (3); v SA 1931 (5); v WI 1930 (5); *v E 1926 (3) 1930 (5) 1934 (5); v SA 1935 (3)*

Groube, T. U. 1: *v E 1880*

Grout, A. T. W. 51: v E 1958 (5) 1962 (2) 1965 (5); v SA 1963 (5); v WI 1960 (5); *v E 1961 (5) 1964 (5); v SA 1957 (5); v WI 1964 (5); v In 1959 (4) 1964 (1); v P 1959 (3) 1964 (1)*

Guest, C. E. J. 1: v E 1962

Hamence, R. A. 3: v E 1946 (1); v In 1947 (2)

Hammond, J. R. 5: *v WI 1972 (5)*

Harry, J. 1: v E 1894

Hartigan, R. J. 2: v E 1907 (2)

Hartkopf, A. E. V. 1: v E 1924

Harvey, M. R. 1: v E 1946

Harvey, R. N. 79: v E 1950 (5) 1954 (5) 1958 (5) 1962 (5); v SA 1952 (5); v WI 1951 (5) 1960 (4); v In 1947 (2); *v E 1948 (2) 1953 (5) 1956 (5) 1961 (5); v SA 1949 (5) 1957 (4); v WI 1954 (5); v In 1956 (3) 1959 (5); v P 1956 (1) 1959 (3)*

Hassett, A. L. 43: v E 1946 (5) 1950 (5); v SA 1952 (5); v WI 1951 (4); v In 1947 (4); *v E 1938 (4) 1948 (5) 1953 (5); v SA 1949 (5); v NZ 1945 (1)*

Hawke, N. J. N. 27: v E 1962 (1) 1965 (4); v SA 1963 (4); v In 1967 (1); v P 1964 (1); *v E 1964 (5) 1968 (3); v SA 1966 (2); v WI 1964 (5); v In 1964 (1); v P 1964 (1)*

Hayden, M. L. 30: v SA 2001 (3); v WI 1996 (3) 2000 (5); v NZ 2001 (3); *v E 2001 (5); v SA 1993 (1) 1996 (3) 2001 (3); v NZ 1999 (1); v In 2000 (3)*

Hazlitt, G. R. 9: v E 1907 (2) 1911 (1); *v E 1912 (3); v SA 1912 (3)*

Healy, I. A. 119: v E 1990 (5) 1994 (5) 1998 (5); v SA 1993 (3) 1997 (3); v WI 1988 (5) 1992 (5) 1996 (5); v NZ 1989 (1) 1993 (3) 1997 (3); v In 1991 (5); v P 1989 (3) 1995 (3); v SL 1989 (2) 1995 (3); *v E 1989 (6) 1993 (6) 1997 (6); v SA 1993 (3) 1996 (3); v WI 1990 (5) 1994 (4) 1998 (4); v NZ 1989 (1) 1992 (3); v In 1996 (1) 1997 (3); v P 1988 (3) 1994 (2) 1998 (3); v SL 1992 (3) 1999 (3); v Z 1999 (1)*

Hendry, H. L. 11: v E 1924 (1) 1928 (4); *v E 1921 (4); v SA 1921 (2)*

Hibbert, P. A. 1: v In 1977

Higgs, J. D. 22: v E 1978 (5) 1979 (1); v WI 1979 (1); v NZ 1980 (3); v In 1980 (2); *v WI 1977 (4); v In 1979 (6)*

Hilditch, A. M. J. 18: v E 1978 (1); v WI 1984 (2); v NZ 1985 (1); v P 1978 (2); *v E 1985 (6); v In 1979 (6)*

Hill, C. 49: v E 1897 (5) 1901 (5) 1903 (5) 1907 (5) 1911 (5); v SA 1910 (5); *v E 1896 (3) 1899 (3) 1902 (5) 1905 (5); v SA 1902 (3)*

Hill, J. C. 3: *v E 1953 (2); v WI 1954 (1)*

Hoare, D. E. 1: v WI 1960

Hodges, J. 2: v E 1876 (2)

Hogan, T. G. 7: v P 1983 (1); *v WI 1983 (5); v SL 1982 (1)*

Hogg, G. B. 1: *v In 1996*

Hogg, R. M. 38: v E 1978 (6) 1982 (3); v WI 1979 (2) 1984 (4); v NZ 1980 (3); v In 1980 (2); v P 1978 (2) 1983 (4); *v E 1981 (2); v WI 1983 (4); v In 1979 (6); v SL 1982 (1)*

Hohns, T. V. 7: v WI 1988 (2); *v E 1989 (5)*

Hole, G. B. 18: v E 1950 (1) 1954 (3); v SA 1952 (4); v WI 1951 (5); *v E 1953 (5)*

Holland, R. G. 11: v WI 1984 (3); v NZ 1985 (3); v In 1985 (1); *v E 1985 (4)*

Hookes, D. W. 23: v E 1976 (1) 1982 (5); v WI 1979 (1); v NZ 1985 (2); v In 1985 (2); *v E 1977 (5); v WI 1983 (5); v P 1979 (1); v SL 1982 (1)*

Hopkins, A. J. 20: v E 1901 (2) 1903 (5); *v E 1902 (5) 1905 (3) 1909 (2); v SA 1902 (3)*

Horan, T. P. 15: v E 1876 (1) 1878 (1) 1881 (4) 1882 (4) 1884 (4); *v E 1882 (1)*

Hordern, H. V. 7: v E 1911 (5); v SA 1910 (2)

Hornibrook, P. M. 6: v E 1928 (1); *v E 1930 (5)*

Howell, W. P. 18: v E 1897 (3) 1901 (4) 1903 (3); *v E 1899 (5) 1902 (1); v SA 1902 (2)*

Hughes, K. J. 70: v E 1978 (6) 1979 (3) 1982 (5); v WI 1979 (3) 1981 (3) 1984 (4); v NZ 1980 (3); v In 1977 (2) 1980 (3); v P 1978 (2) 1981 (3) 1983 (5); *v E 1977 (1) 1980 (1) 1981 (6); v WI 1983 (5); v NZ 1981 (3); v In 1979 (6); v P 1979 (3) 1982 (3)*

Hughes, M. G. 53: v E 1986 (4) 1990 (4); v WI 1988 (4) 1992 (5); v NZ 1987 (1) 1989 (1); v In 1985 (1) 1991 (5); v P 1989 (3); v SL 1987 (1) 1989 (2); *v E 1989 (6) 1993 (6); v SA 1993 (2); v WI 1990 (5); v NZ 1992 (3)*

Hunt, W. A. 1: v SA 1931

Hurst, A. G. 12: v E 1978 (6); v NZ 1973 (1); v In 1977 (1); v P 1978 (2); *v In 1979 (2)*

Hurwood, A. 2: v WI 1930 (2)

Inverarity, R. J. 6: v WI 1968 (1); *v E 1968 (2) 1972 (3)*

Iredale, F. A. 14: v E 1894 (5) 1897 (4); *v E 1896 (2) 1899 (3)*

Ironmonger, H. 14: v E 1928 (2) 1932 (4); v SA 1931 (4); v WI 1930 (4)

Iverson, J. B. 5: v E 1950 (5)

Jackson, A. A. 8: v E 1928 (2); v WI 1930 (4); *v E 1930 (2)*

Jarman, B. N. 19: v E 1962 (3); v WI 1968 (4); v In 1967 (4); v P 1964 (1); *v E 1968 (4); v In 1959 (1) 1964 (2)*

Jarvis, A. H. 11: v E 1884 (3) 1894 (4); *v E 1886 (2) 1888 (2)*

Jenner, T. J. 9: v E 1970 (2) 1974 (2); v WI 1975 (1); *v WI 1972 (4)*

Jennings, C. B. 6: *v E 1912 (3); v SA 1912 (3)*

Johnson I. W. 45: v E 1946 (4) 1950 (5) 1954 (4); v SA 1952 (1); v WI 1951 (4); v In 1947 (4); *v E 1948 (4) 1956 (5); v SA 1949 (5); v WI 1954 (5); v NZ 1945 (1); v In 1956 (2); v P 1956 (1)*

Johnson, L. J. 1: v In 1947

Johnston, W. A. 40: v E 1950 (5) 1954 (4); v SA 1952 (5); v WI 1951 (5); v In 1947 (4); *v E 1948 (5) 1953 (3); v SA 1949 (5); v WI 1954 (4)*

Jones, D. M. 52: v E 1986 (5) 1987 (1) 1990 (5); v WI 1988 (3); v NZ 1987 (3) 1989 (1); v In 1991 (5); v P 1989 (3); v SL 1987 (1) 1989 (2); *v E 1989 (6); v WI 1983 (2) 1990 (5); v NZ 1989 (1); v In 1986 (3); v P 1988 (3); v SL 1992 (3)*

Jones, E. 19: v E 1894 (1) 1897 (5) 1901 (2); *v E 1896 (3) 1899 (5) 1902 (2); v SA 1902 (1)*

Jones, S. P. 12: v E 1881 (2) 1884 (4) 1886 (1) 1887 (1); *v E 1882 (1) 1886 (3)*

Joslin, L. R. 1: v In 1967

Julian, B. P. 7: v SL 1995 (1); *v E 1993 (2); v WI 1994 (4)*

Kasprowicz, M. S. 17: v E 1998 (1); v SA 1997 (2); v WI 1996 (2); v NZ 1997 (3); v In 1999 (1); v P 1999 (1); *v E 1997 (3); v In 1997 (3) 2000 (1)*

Katich, S. M. 1: *v E 2001*

Kelleway, C. 26: v E 1911 (4) 1920 (5) 1924 (5) 1928 (1); v SA 1910 (5); *v E 1912 (3); v SA 1912 (3)*

Kelly, J. J. 36: v E 1897 (5) 1901 (5) 1903 (5); *v E 1896 (3) 1899 (5) 1902 (5) 1905 (5); v SA 1902 (3)*

Kelly, T. J. D. 2: v E 1876 (1) 1878 (1)

Kendall, T. 2: v E 1876 (2)

Kent, M. F. 3: *v E 1981 (3)*

Kerr, R. B. 2: v NZ 1985 (2)

Kippax, A. F. 22: v E 1924 (1) 1928 (5) 1932 (1); v SA 1931 (4); v WI 1930 (5); *v E 1930 (5) 1934 (1)*

Kline L. F. 13: v E 1958 (2); v WI 1960 (2); *v SA 1957 (5); v In 1959 (3); v P 1959 (1)*

Laird, B. M. 21: v E 1979 (2); v WI 1979 (3) 1981 (3); v P 1981 (3); *v E 1980 (1); v NZ 1981 (3); v P 1979 (3) 1982 (3)*

Langer, J. L. 51: v E 1998 (5); v SA 2001 (3); v WI 1992 (2) 1996 (2) 2000 (5); v NZ 2001 (3); v In 1999 (3); v P 1999 (3); *v E 2001 (1); v SA 2001 (3); v WI 1998 (4); v NZ 1992 (3) 1999 (3); v In 2000 (3); v P 1994 (1) 1998 (3); v SL 1999 (3); v Z 1999 (1)*

Langley, G. R. A. 26: v E 1954 (2); v SA 1952 (5); v WI 1951 (5); *v E 1953 (4) 1956 (3); v WI 1954 (4); v In 1956 (2); v P 1956 (1)*

Laughlin, T. J. 3: v E 1978 (1); *v WI 1977 (2)*

Laver, F. 15: v E 1901 (1) 1903 (1); *v E 1899 (4) 1905 (5) 1909 (4)*

Law, S. G. 1: v SL 1995

Lawry, W. M. 67: v E 1962 (5) 1965 (5) 1970 (5); v SA 1963 (5); v WI 1968 (5); v In 1967 (4); v P 1964 (1); *v E 1961 (5) 1964 (5) 1968 (4); v SA 1966 (5) 1969 (4); v WI 1964 (5); v In 1964 (3) 1969 (5); v P 1964 (1)*

Lawson, G. F. 46: v E 1982 (5) 1986 (1); v WI 1981 (1) 1984 (5) 1988 (1); v NZ 1980 (1) 1985 (2) 1989 (1); v P 1983 (5); v SL 1989 (1); *v E 1981 (3) 1985 (6) 1989 (6); v WI 1983 (5); v P 1982 (3)*

Lee, B. 21: v SA 2001 (3); v WI 2000 (2); v NZ 2001 (3); v In 1999 (2); *v E 2001 (5); v SA 2001 (3); v NZ 1999 (3)*

Lee, P. K. 2: v E 1932 (1); v SA 1931 (1)

Lehmann, D. S. 5: v E 1998 (2); *v In 1997 (1); v P 1998 (2)*

Lillee, D. K. 70: v E 1970 (2) 1974 (6) 1976 (1) 1979 (3) 1982 (1); v WI 1975 (5) 1979 (3) 1981 (3); v NZ 1980 (3); v In 1980 (3); v P 1972 (3) 1976 (3) 1981 (3) 1983 (5); *v E 1972 (5) 1975 (4) 1980 (1) 1981 (6); v WI 1972 (1); v NZ 1976 (2) 1981 (3); v P 1979 (3); v SL 1982 (1)*

Lindwall, R. R. 61: v E 1946 (4) 1950 (5) 1954 (4) 1958 (2); v SA 1952 (4); v WI 1951 (5); v In 1947 (5); *v E 1948 (5) 1953 (5) 1956 (4); v SA 1949 (4); v WI 1954 (5); v NZ 1945 (1); v In 1956 (3) 1959 (2); v P 1956 (1) 1959 (2)*

Love, H. S. B. 1: v E 1932

Loxton, S. J. E. 12: v E 1950 (3); v In 1947 (1); *v E 1948 (3); v SA 1949 (5)*

Lyons, J. J. 14: v E 1886 (1) 1891 (3) 1894 (3) 1897 (1); *v E 1888 (1) 1890 (2) 1893 (3)*

McAlister, P. A. 8: v E 1903 (2) 1907 (4); *v E 1909 (2)*

Macartney, C. G. 35: v E 1907 (5) 1911 (1) 1920 (2); v SA 1910 (4); *v E 1909 (5) 1912 (3) 1921 (5) 1926 (5); v SA 1912 (3) 1921 (2)*

McCabe, S. J. 39: v E 1932 (1) 1936 (5); v SA 1931 (5); v WI 1930 (5); *v E 1930 (5) 1934 (5) 1938 (4); v SA 1935 (5)*

McCool, C. L. 14: v E 1946 (5); v In 1947 (3); *v SA 1949 (5); v NZ 1945 (1)*

McCormick, E. L. 12: v E 1936 (4); *v E 1938 (3); v SA 1935 (5)*

McCosker, R. B. 25: v E 1974 (3) 1976 (1) 1979 (2); v WI 1975 (4) 1979 (1); v P 1976 (3); *v E 1975 (4) 1977 (5); v NZ 1976 (2)*

McDermott, C. J. 71: v E 1986 (1) 1987 (1) 1990 (2) 1994 (5); v SA 1993 (3); v WI 1984 (2) 1988 (2) 1992 (5); v NZ 1985 (2) 1987 (3) 1993 (3); v In 1985 (2) 1991 (5); v P 1995 (3); v SL 1987 (1) 1995 (3); *v E 1985 (6) 1993 (2); v SA 1993 (3); v WI 1990 (5); v NZ 1985 (2) 1992 (3); v In 1986 (2); v P 1994 (2); v SL 1992 (3)*

McDonald, C. C. 47: v E 1954 (2) 1958 (5); v SA 1952 (5); v WI 1951 (1) 1960 (5); *v E 1956 (5) 1961 (5); v SA 1957 (5); v WI 1954 (5); v In 1956 (2) 1959 (5); v P 1956 (1) 1959 (3)*

McDonald, E. A. 11: v E 1920 (3); *v E 1921 (5); v SA 1921 (3)*

McDonnell, P. S. 19: v E 1881 (4) 1882 (3) 1884 (2) 1886 (2) 1887 (1); *v E 1880 (1) 1884 (3) 1888 (3)*

MacGill, S. C. G. 17: v E 1998 (4); v SA 1997 (1) 2001 (1); v WI 2000 (4); *v WI 1998 (4); v P 1998 (3)*

McGrath, G. D. 84: v E 1994 (2) 1998 (5); v SA 1993 (1) 1997 (2) 2001 (3); v WI 1996 (5) 2000 (5); v NZ 1993 (2) 1997 (1) 2001 (3); v In 1999 (3); v P 1995 (3) 1999 (3); v SL 1995 (3); *v E 1997 (6) 2001 (5); v SA 1993 (2) 1996 (3) 2001 (3); v WI 1994 (4) 1998 (4); v NZ 1999 (3); v In 1996 (1) 2000 (3); v P 1994 (2) 1998 (3); v SL 1999 (3); v Z 1999 (1)*

McIlwraith, J. 1: *v E 1886*

McIntyre, P. E. 2: v E 1994 (1); *v In 1996 (1)*

Mackay, K. D. 37: v E 1958 (5) 1962 (3); v WI 1960 (5); *v E 1956 (3) 1961 (5); v SA 1957 (5); v In 1956 (3) 1959 (2); v P 1959 (3)*

McKenzie, G. D. 60: v E 1962 (5) 1965 (4) 1970 (3); v SA 1963 (5); v WI 1968 (5); v In 1967 (2); v P 1964 (1); *v E 1961 (3) 1964 (5) 1968 (5); v SA 1966 (3) 1969 (3); v WI 1964 (5); v In 1964 (3) 1969 (5); v P 1964 (1)*

McKibbin, T. R. 5: v E 1894 (1) 1897 (2); *v E 1896 (2)*

McLaren, J. W. 1: v E 1911

Maclean, J. A. 4: v E 1978 (4)

McLeod, C. E. 17: v E 1894 (1) 1897 (5) 1901 (2) 1903 (1); *v E 1899 (1) 1905 (5)*

McLeod, R. W. 6: v E 1891 (3); *v E 1893 (3)*

McShane, P. G. 3: v E 1884 (1) 1886 (1) 1887 (1)

Maddocks, L. V. 7: v E 1954 (2); *v E 1956 (2); v WI 1954 (1); v In 1956 (1)*

Maguire, J. N. 3: v P 1983 (1); *v WI 1983 (2)*

Mailey, A. A. 21: v E 1920 (5) 1924 (5); *v E 1921 (3) 1926 (5); v SA 1921 (3)*

Mallett, A. A. 38: v E 1970 (5) 1974 (5) 1979 (1); v WI 1968 (1) 1975 (6) 1979 (1); v NZ 1973 (3); v P 1972 (2); *v E 1968 (1) 1972 (2) 1975 (4) 1980 (1); v SA 1969 (1); v NZ 1973 (3); v In 1969 (5)*

Malone, M. F. 1: *v E 1977*

Mann, A. L. 4: v In 1977 (4)

Marr, A. P. 1: v E 1884

Marsh, G. R. 50: v E 1986 (5) 1987 (1) 1990 (5); v WI 1988 (5); v NZ 1987 (3); v In 1985 (3) 1991 (4); v P 1989 (2); v SL 1987 (1); *v E 1989 (6); v WI 1990 (5); v NZ 1985 (3) 1989 (1); v In 1986 (3); v P 1988 (3)*

Marsh, R. W. 96: v E 1970 (6) 1974 (6) 1976 (1) 1979 (3) 1982 (5); v WI 1975 (6) 1979 (3) 1981 (3); v NZ 1973 (3) 1980 (3); v In 1980 (3); v P 1972 (3) 1976 (3) 1981 (3) 1983 (5); *v E 1972 (5) 1975 (4) 1977 (5) 1980 (3) 1981 (6); v WI 1972 (5); v NZ 1973 (3) 1976 (2) 1981 (3); v P 1979 (3) 1982 (3)*

Martin, J. W. 8: v SA 1963 (1); v WI 1960 (3); *v SA 1966 (1); v In 1964 (2); v P 1964 (1)*

Martyn, D. R. 25: v SA 1993 (2) 2001 (3); v WI 1992 (4) 2000 (5); v NZ 2001 (3); *v E 2001 (5); v SA 2001 (3); v NZ 1992 (1) 1999 (3)*

Massie, H. H. 9: v E 1881 (4) 1882 (3) 1884 (1); *v E 1882 (1)*

Massie, R. A. L. 6: v P 1972 (2); *v E 1972 (4)*

Matthews, C. D. 3: v E 1986 (2); v WI 1988 (1)

Matthews, G. R. J. 33: v E 1986 (4) 1990 (5); v WI 1984 (1) 1992 (2); v NZ 1985 (3); v In 1985 (3); v P 1983 (2); *v E 1985 (1); v WI 1983 (1) 1990 (2); v NZ 1985 (3); v In 1986 (3); v SL 1992 (3)*

Matthews, T. J. 8: v E 1911 (1); *v E 1912 (3); v SA 1912 (3)*

May, T. B. A. 24: v E 1994 (3); v SA 1993 (3); v WI 1988 (3) 1992 (1); v NZ 1987 (1) 1993 (2); *v E 1993 (3); v SA 1993 (1); v P 1988 (3) 1994 (2)*

Mayne, E. R. 4: *v E 1912 (1); v SA 1912 (1) 1921 (2)*

Mayne, L. C. 6: *v SA 1969 (2); v WI 1964 (3); v In 1969 (1)*

Meckiff, I. 18: v E 1958 (4); v SA 1963 (1); v WI 1960 (2); *v SA 1957 (4); v In 1959 (5); v P 1959 (2)*

Meuleman, K. D. 1: *v NZ 1945*

Midwinter, W. E. 8: v E 1876 (2) 1882 (1) 1886 (2); *v E 1884 (3)*

Miller, C. R. 18: v E 1998 (3); v WI 2000 (3); *v WI 1998 (1); v NZ 1999 (3); v In 2000 (1); v P 1998 (3); v SL 1999 (3); v Z 1999 (1)*

Miller, K. R. 55: v E 1946 (5) 1950 (5) 1954 (4); v SA 1952 (4); v WI 1951 (5); v In 1947 (5); *v E 1948 (5) 1953 (5) 1956 (5); v SA 1949 (5); v WI 1954 (5); v NZ 1945 (1); v P 1956 (1)*

Minnett, R. B. 9: v E 1911 (5); *v E 1912 (1); v SA 1912 (3)*

Misson, F. M. 5: v WI 1960 (3); *v E 1961 (2)*

Moody, T. M. 8: v NZ 1989 (1); v In 1991 (1); v P 1989 (2); v SL 1989 (2); *v SL 1992 (3)*

Moroney, J. 7: v E 1950 (1); v WI 1951 (1); *v SA 1949 (5)*

Morris, A. R. 46: v E 1946 (5) 1950 (5) 1954 (4); v SA 1952 (5); v WI 1951 (4); v In 1947 (4); *v E 1948 (5) 1953 (5); v SA 1949 (5); v WI 1954 (4)*

Morris, S. 1: v E 1884

Moses, H. 6: v E 1886 (2) 1887 (1) 1891 (2) 1894 (1)

Moss, J. K. 1: v P 1978

Moule, W. H. 1: *v E 1880*

Muller, S. A. 2: v P 1999 (2)

Murdoch, W. L. 18: v E 1876 (1) 1878 (1) 1881 (4) 1882 (4) 1884 (1); *v E 1880 (1) 1882 (1) 1884 (3) 1890 (2)*

Musgrove, H. 1: v E 1884

Nagel, L. E. 1: v E 1932

Nash, L. J. 2: v E 1936 (1); v SA 1931 (1)

Nicholson, M. J. 1: v E 1998

Nitschke, H. C. 2: v SA 1931 (2)

Noble, M. A. 42: v E 1897 (4) 1901 (5) 1903 (5) 1907 (5); *v E 1899 (5) 1902 (5) 1905 (5) 1909 (5); v SA 1902 (3)*

Noblet, G. 3: v SA 1952 (1); v WI 1951 (1); *v SA 1949 (1)*

Nothling, O. E. 1: v E 1928

O'Brien, L. P. J. 5: v E 1932 (2) 1936 (1); *v SA 1935 (2)*

O'Connor, J. D. A. 4: v E 1907 (3); *v E 1909 (1)*

O'Donnell, S. P. 6: v NZ 1985 (1); *v E 1985 (5)*

Ogilvie, A. D. 5: v In 1977 (3); *v WI 1977 (2)*

O'Keeffe, K. J. 24: v E 1970 (2) 1976 (1); v NZ 1973 (3); v P 1972 (2) 1976 (3); *v E 1977 (3); v WI 1972 (5); v NZ 1973 (3) 1976 (2)*

Oldfield, W. A. 54: v E 1920 (3) 1924 (5) 1928 (5) 1932 (4) 1936 (5); v SA 1931 (5); v WI 1930 (5); *v E 1921 (5) 1926 (5) 1930 (5) 1934 (5); v SA 1921 (1) 1935 (5)*

O'Neill, N. C. 42: v E 1958 (5) 1962 (5); v SA 1963 (4); v WI 1960 (5); *v E 1961 (5) 1964 (4); v WI 1964 (4); v In 1959 (5) 1964 (2); v P 1959 (3)*

O'Reilly, W. J. 27: v E 1932 (5) 1936 (5); v SA 1931 (5); *v E 1934 (5) 1938 (4); v SA 1935 (5); v NZ 1945 (1)*

Oxenham, R. K. 7: v E 1928 (3); v SA 1931 (1); v WI 1930 (3)

Palmer, G. E. 17: v E 1881 (4) 1882 (4) 1884 (2); *v E 1880 (1) 1884 (3) 1886 (3)*

Park, R. L. 1: v E 1920

Pascoe, L. S. 14: v E 1979 (2); v WI 1979 (1) 1981 (1); v NZ 1980 (3); v In 1980 (3); *v E 1977 (3) 1980 (1)*

Pellew, C. E. 10: v E 1920 (4); *v E 1921 (5); v SA 1921 (1)*

Phillips, W. B. 27: v WI 1984 (2); v NZ 1985 (3); v In 1985 (3); v P 1983 (5); *v E 1985 (6); v WI 1983 (2); v NZ 1985 (3)*

Phillips, W. N. 1: v In 1991

Philpott, P. I. 8: v E 1965 (3); *v WI 1964 (5)*

Ponsford, W. H. 29: v E 1924 (5) 1928 (2) 1932 (3); v SA 1931 (4); v WI 1930 (5); *v E 1926 (2) 1930 (4) 1934 (4)*

Ponting, R. T. 56: v E 1998 (3); v SA 1997 (3) 2001 (3); v WI 1996 (2) 2000 (5); v NZ 1997 (3) 2001 (3); v In 1999 (3); v P 1999 (3); v SL 1995 (3); *v E 1997 (3) 2001 (5); v SA 2001 (3); v WI 1998 (2); v In 1996 (1) 1997 (3) 2000 (3); v P 1998 (1); v SL 1999 (3); v Z 1999 (1)*

Pope, R. J. 1: v E 1884

Rackemann, C. G. 12: v E 1982 (1) 1990 (1); v WI 1984 (1); v NZ 1989 (1); v P 1983 (2) 1989 (3); v SL 1989 (1); *v WI 1983 (1); v NZ 1989 (1)*

Ransford, V. S. 20: v E 1907 (5) 1911 (5); v SA 1910 (5); *v E 1909 (5)*

Redpath, I. R. 66: v E 1965 (1) 1970 (6) 1974 (6); v SA 1963 (1); v WI 1968 (5) 1975 (6); v In 1967 (3); v P 1972 (3); *v E 1964 (5) 1968 (5); v SA 1966 (5) 1969 (4); v WI 1972 (5); v NZ 1973 (3); v In 1964 (2) 1969 (5); v P 1964 (1)*

Reedman, J. C. 1: v E 1894

Reid, B. A. 27: v E 1986 (5) 1990 (4); v WI 1992 (1); v NZ 1987 (2); v In 1985 (3) 1991 (2); *v WI 1990 (2); v NZ 1985 (3); v In 1986 (2); v P 1988 (3)*

Reiffel, P. R. 35: v SA 1993 (2) 1997 (2); v WI 1996 (3); v NZ 1993 (2) 1997 (3); v In 1991 (1); v P 1995 (3); v SL 1995 (2); *v E 1993 (3) 1997 (4); v SA 1993 (1); v WI 1994 (4); v NZ 1992 (3); v In 1996 (1) 1997 (1)*

Renneberg, D. A. 8: v In 1967 (3); *v SA 1966 (5)*

Richardson, A. J. 9: v E 1924 (4); *v E 1926 (5)*

Richardson, V. Y. 19: v E 1924 (3) 1928 (2) 1932 (5); *v E 1930 (4); v SA 1935 (5)*

Rigg, K. E. 8: v E 1936 (3); v SA 1931 (4); v WI 1930 (1)

Ring, D. T. 13: v SA 1952 (5); v WI 1951 (5); v In 1947 (1); *v E 1948 (1) 1953 (1)*

Ritchie, G. M. 30: v E 1986 (4); v WI 1984 (1); v NZ 1985 (3); v In 1985 (2); *v E 1985 (6); v WI 1983 (5); v NZ 1985 (3); v In 1986 (3); v P 1982 (3)*

Rixon, S. J. 13: v WI 1984 (3); v In 1977 (5); *v WI 1977 (5)*

Robertson, G. R. 4: *v In 1997 (3); v P 1998 (1)*

Robertson, W. R. 1: v E 1884

Robinson, R. D. 3: *v E 1977 (3)*

Robinson, R. H. 1: v E 1936

Rorke, G. F. 4: v E 1958 (2); *v In 1959 (2)*

Rutherford, J. W. 1: *v In 1956*

Ryder, J. 20: v E 1920 (5) 1924 (3) 1928 (5); *v E 1926 (4); v SA 1921 (3)*

Saggers, R. A. 6: *v E 1948 (1); v SA 1949 (5)*

Saunders, J. V. 14: v E 1901 (1) 1903 (2) 1907 (5); *v E 1902 (4); v SA 1902 (2)*

Scott, H. J. H. 8: v E 1884 (2); *v E 1884 (3) 1886 (3)*

Sellers, R. H. D. 1: *v In 1964*

Serjeant, C. S. 12: v In 1977 (4); *v E 1977 (3); v WI 1977 (5)*

Sheahan, A. P. 31: v E 1970 (2); v WI 1968 (5); v NZ 1973 (2); v In 1967 (4); v P 1972 (2); *v E 1968 (5) 1972 (2); v SA 1969 (4); v In 1969 (5)*

Shepherd, B. K. 9: v E 1962 (2); v SA 1963 (4); v P 1964 (1); *v WI 1964 (2)*

Sievers, M. W. 3: v E 1936 (3)

Simpson, R. B. 62: v E 1958 (1) 1962 (5) 1965 (3); v SA 1963 (5); v WI 1960 (5); v In 1967 (3) 1977 (5); v P 1964 (1); *v E 1961 (5) 1964 (5); v SA 1957 (5) 1966 (5); v WI 1964 (5) 1977 (5); v In 1964 (3); v P 1964 (1)*

Sincock, D. J. 3: v E 1965 (1); v P 1964 (1); *v WI 1964 (1)*

Slater, K. N. 1: v E 1958

Slater, M. J. 74: v E 1994 (5) 1998 (5); v SA 1993 (3); v WI 2000 (5); v NZ 1993 (3); v In 1999 (3); v P 1995 (3) 1999 (3); v SL 1995 (3); *v E 1993 (6) 2001 (4); v SA 1993 (3); v WI 1994 (4) 1998 (4); v NZ 1999 (3); v In 1996 (1) 1997 (3) 2000 (3); v P 1994 (3) 1998 (3); SL 1999 (3); v Z 1999 (1)*

Sleep, P. R. 14: v E 1986 (3) 1987 (1); v NZ 1987 (3); v P 1978 (1) 1989 (1); v SL 1989 (1); *v In 1979 (2); v P 1982 (1) 1988 (1)*

Slight, J. 1: *v E 1880*

Smith, D. B. M. 2: *v E 1912 (2)*

Smith, S. B. 3: *v WI 1983 (3)*

Spofforth, F. R. 18: v E 1876 (1) 1878 (1) 1881 (1) 1882 (4) 1884 (3) 1886 (1); *v E 1882 (1) 1884 (3) 1886 (3)*

Stackpole, K. R. 43: v E 1965 (2) 1970 (6); v WI 1968 (5); v NZ 1973 (3); v P 1972 (1); *v E 1972 (5); v SA 1966 (5) 1969 (4); v WI 1972 (4); v NZ 1973 (3); v In 1969 (5)*

Stevens, G. B. 4: *v In 1959 (4); v P 1959 (2)*

Taber, H. B. 16: v WI 1968 (1); *v E 1968 (1); v SA 1966 (5) 1969 (4); v In 1969 (5)*

Tallon, D. 21: v E 1946 (5) 1950 (5); v In 1947 (5); *v E 1948 (4) 1953 (1); v NZ 1945 (1)*

Taylor, J. M. 20: v E 1920 (5) 1924 (5); *v E 1921 (5) 1926 (3); v SA 1921 (2)*

Taylor, M. A. 104: v E 1990 (5) 1994 (5) 1998 (5); v SA 1993 (3) 1997 (3); v WI 1988 (2) 1992 (4) 1996 (5); v NZ 1989 (1) 1993 (3) 1997 (3); v In 1991 (5); v P 1989 (3) 1995 (3); v SL 1989 (2) 1995 (3); *v E 1989 (6) 1993 (6) 1997 (6); v SA 1993 (2) 1996 (3); v WI 1990 (5) 1994 (4); v NZ 1989 (1) 1992 (3); v In 1996 (1) 1997 (3); v P 1994 (3) 1998 (3); v SL 1992 (3)*

Taylor, P. L. 13: v E 1986 (1) 1987 (1); v WI 1988 (2); v In 1991 (2); v P 1989 (2); v SL 1987 (1); *v WI 1990 (1); v NZ 1989 (1); v P 1988 (2)*

Thomas, G. 8: v E 1965 (3); *v WI 1964 (5)*

Thoms, G. R. 1: v WI 1951

Thomson, A. L. 4: v E 1970 (4)

Thomson, J. R. 51: v E 1974 (5) 1979 (1) 1982 (4); v WI 1975 (6) 1979 (1) 1981 (2); v In 1977 (5); v P 1972 (1) 1976 (1) 1981 (3); *v E 1975 (4) 1977 (5) 1985 (2); v WI 1977 (5); v NZ 1981 (3); v P 1982 (3)*

Thomson, N. F. D. 2: v E 1876 (2)

Thurlow, H. M. 1: v SA 1931

Toohey, P. M. 15: v E 1978 (5) 1979 (1); v WI 1979 (1); v In 1977 (5); *v WI 1977 (3)*

Toshack, E. R. H. 12: v E 1946 (5); v In 1947 (2); *v E 1948 (4); v NZ 1945 (1)*

Travers, J. P. F. 1: v E 1901

Tribe, G. E. 3: v E 1946 (3)

Trott, A. E. 3: v E 1894 (3)

Trott, G. H. S. 24: v E 1891 (3) 1894 (5) 1897 (5); *v E 1888 (3) 1890 (2) 1893 (3) 1896 (3)*

Trumble, H. 32: v E 1894 (1) 1897 (5) 1901 (5) 1903 (4); *v E 1890 (2) 1893 (3) 1896 (3) 1899 (5) 1902 (3); v SA 1902 (1)*

Trumble, J. W. 7: v E 1884 (4); *v E 1886 (3)*

Trumper, V. T. 48: v E 1901 (5) 1903 (5) 1907 (5) 1911 (5); v SA 1910 (5); *v E 1899 (5) 1902 (5) 1905 (5) 1909 (5); v SA 1902 (3)*

Turner, A. 14: v WI 1975 (6); v P 1976 (3); *v E 1975 (3); v NZ 1976 (2)*

Turner, C. T. B. 17: v E 1886 (1) 1887 (1) 1891 (3) 1894 (3); *v E 1888 (3) 1890 (2) 1893 (3)*

Veivers, T. R. 21: v E 1965 (4); v SA 1963 (3); v P 1964 (1); *v E 1964 (5); v SA 1966 (4); v In 1964 (3); v P 1964 (1)*

Veletta, M. R. J. 8: v E 1987 (1); v WI 1988 (2); v NZ 1987 (3); v P 1989 (1); v SL 1987 (1)

Waite, M. G. 2: *v E 1938 (2)*

Walker, M. H. N. 34: v E 1974 (6) 1976 (1); v WI 1975 (3); v NZ 1973 (1); v P 1972 (1) 1976 (2); *v E 1975 (4) 1977 (5); v WI 1972 (5); v NZ 1973 (3) 1976 (2)*

Wall, T. W. 18: v E 1928 (1) 1932 (4); v SA 1931 (3); v WI 1930 (1); *v E 1930 (5) 1934 (4)*

Walters, F. H. 1: v E 1884

Walters, K. D. 74: v E 1965 (5) 1970 (6) 1974 (6) 1976 (1); v WI 1968 (4); v NZ 1973 (3) 1980 (3); v In 1967 (2) 1980 (3); v P 1972 (1) 1976 (3); *v E 1968 (5) 1972 (4) 1975 (4) 1977 (5); v SA 1969 (4); v WI 1972 (5); v NZ 1973 (3) 1976 (2); v In 1969 (5)*

Ward, F. A. 4: v E 1936 (3); *v E 1938 (1)*

Warne, S. K. 101: v E 1994 (5) 1998 (1); v SA 1993 (3) 1997 (3) 2001 (3); v WI 1992 (4) 1996 (5); v NZ 1993 (3) 1997 (3) 2001 (3); v In 1991 (2) 1999 (3); v P 1995 (3) 1999 (3); v SL 1995 (3); *v E 1993 (6) 1997 (6) 2001 (5); v SA 1993 (3) 1996 (3) 2001 (3); v WI 1994 (4) 1998 (3); v NZ 1992 (3) 1999 (3); v In 1997 (3) 2000 (3); v P 1994 (3); v SL 1992 (2) 1999 (3); v Z 1999 (1)*

Watkins, J. R. 1: v P 1972

Watson, G. D. 5: *v E 1972 (2); v SA 1966 (3)*

Watson, W. J. 4: v E 1954 (1); *v WI 1954 (3)*

Waugh, M. E. 125: v E 1990 (2) 1994 (5) 1998 (5); v SA 1993 (3) 1997 (3) 2001 (3); v WI 1992 (5) 1996 (5) 2000 (5); v NZ 1993 (3) 1997 (3) 2001 (3); v In 1991 (4) 1999 (3); v P 1995 (3) 1999 (3); v SL 1995 (3); *v E 1993 (6) 1997 (6) 2001 (5); v SA 1993 (3) 1996 (3) 2001 (3); v WI 1990 (5) 1994 (4) 1998 (3); v NZ 1992 (2) 1999 (3); v In 1996 (1) 1997 (3) 2000 (3); v P 1994 (3) 1998 (3); v SL 1992 (3) 1999 (3); v Z 1999 (1)*

Waugh, S. R. 148: v E 1986 (5) 1987 (1) 1990 (3) 1994 (5) 1998 (5); v SA 1993 (1) 1997 (3) 2001 (3); v WI 1988 (5) 1992 (5) 1996 (4) 2000 (4); v NZ 1987 (3) 1989 (1) 1993 (3) 1997 (3) 2001 (3); v In 1985 (2) 1999 (3); v P 1989 (3) 1995 (3) 1999 (3); v SL 1987 (1) 1989 (2) 1995 (2); *v E 1989 (6) 1993 (6) 1997 (6) 2001 (4); v SA 1993 (3) 1996 (3) 2001 (3); v WI 1990 (2) 1994 (4) 1998 (4); v NZ 1985 (3) 1989 (1) 1992 (3) 1999 (3); v In 1986 (3) 1996 (1) 1997 (2) 2000 (3); v P 1988 (3) 1994 (2) 1998 (3); SL 1999 (3); v Z 1999 (1)*

Wellham, D. M. 6: v E 1986 (1); v WI 1981 (1); v P 1981 (2); *v E 1981 (1) 1985 (1)*

Wessels, K. C. 24: v E 1982 (4); v WI 1984 (5); v NZ 1985 (1); v P 1983 (5); *v E 1985 (6); v WI 1983 (2); v SL 1982 (1)*

Whatmore, D. F. 7: v P 1978 (2); *v In 1979 (5)*

Whitney, M. R. 12: v WI 1988 (1) 1992 (1); v NZ 1987 (1); v In 1991 (3); *v E 1981 (2); v WI 1990 (2); v SL 1992 (2)*

Whitty, W. J. 14: v E 1911 (2); v SA 1910 (5); *v E 1909 (1) 1912 (3); v SA 1912 (3)*

Wiener, J. M. 6: v E 1979 (2); v WI 1979 (2); *v P 1979 (2)*

Wilson, J. W. 1: *v In 1956*

Wilson, P. 1: *v In 1997*

Wood, G. M. 59: v E 1978 (6) 1982 (1); v WI 1981 (3) 1984 (5) 1988 (3); v NZ 1980 (3); v In 1977 (1) 1980 (3); v P 1978 (1) 1981 (3); *v E 1980 (1) 1981 (6) 1985 (5); v WI 1977 (5) 1983 (1); v NZ 1981 (3); v In 1979 (2); v P 1982 (3) 1988 (3); v SL 1982 (1)*

Woodcock, A. J. 1: v NZ 1973

Woodfull, W. M. 35: v E 1928 (5) 1932 (5); v SA 1931 (5); v WI 1930 (5); *v E 1926 (5) 1930 (5) 1934 (5)*

Woods, S. M. J. 3: *v E 1888 (3)*

Woolley, R. D. 2: *v WI 1983 (1); v SL 1982 (1)*

Worrall, J. 11: v E 1884 (1) 1887 (1) 1894 (1) 1897 (1); *v E 1888 (3) 1899 (4)*

Wright, K. J. 10: v E 1978 (2); v P 1978 (2); *v In 1979 (6)*

Yallop, G. N. 39: v E 1978 (6); v WI 1975 (3) 1984 (1); v In 1977 (1); v P 1978 (1) 1981 (1) 1983 (5); *v E 1980 (1) 1981 (6); v WI 1977 (4); v In 1979 (6); v P 1979 (3); v SL 1982 (1)*

Yardley, B. 33: v E 1978 (4) 1982 (5); v WI 1981 (3); v In 1977 (1) 1980 (2); v P 1978 (1) 1981 (3); *v WI 1977 (5); v NZ 1981 (3); v In 1979 (3); v P 1982 (2); v SL 1982 (1)*

Young, S. 1: *v E 1997*

Zoehrer, T. J. 10: v E 1986 (4); *v NZ 1985 (3); v In 1986 (3)*

SOUTH AFRICA

Number of Test cricketers: 286

Ackerman, H. D. 4: v P 1997 (2); v SL 1997 (2)

Adams, P. R. 36: v E 1995 (2) 1999 (4); v A 1996 (2) 2001 (2); v WI 1998 (2); v In 1996 (2); v P 1997 (1); v SL 1997 (2); v Z 1999 (1); *v E 1998 (4); v A 1997 (1); v WI 2000 (1); v NZ 1998 (3); v In 1996 (3); v P 1997 (3); v SL 2000 (3); v Z 1999 (1)*

Adcock, N. A. T. 26: v E 1956 (5); v A 1957 (5); v NZ 1953 (5) 1961 (2); *v E 1955 (4) 1960 (5)*

Anderson, J. H. 1: v A 1902
Ashley, W. H. 1: v E 1888

Bacher, A. 12: v A 1966 (5) 1969 (4); *v E 1965 (3)*
Bacher, A. M. 19: v A 1996 (2); v WI 1998 (1); v In 1996 (3); v P 1997 (3); v SL 1997 (1); v Z 1999 (1); *v E 1998 (1); v A 1997 (3); v P 1997 (3); v Z 1999 (1)*
Balaskas, X. C. 9: v E 1930 (2) 1938 (1); v A 1935 (3); *v E 1935 (1); v NZ 1931 (2)*
Barlow, E. J. 30: v E 1964 (5); v A 1966 (5) 1969 (4); v NZ 1961 (5); *v E 1965 (3); v A 1963 (5); v NZ 1963 (3)*
Baumgartner, H. V. 1: v E 1913
Beaumont, R. 5: v E 1913 (2); *v E 1912 (1); v A 1912 (2)*
Begbie, D. W. 5: v E 1948 (3); v A 1949 (2)
Bell, A. J. 16: v E 1930 (3); *v E 1929 (3) 1935 (3); v A 1931 (5); v NZ 1931 (2)*
Bisset, M. 3: v E 1898 (2) 1909 (1)
Bissett, G. F. 4: v E 1927 (4)
Blanckenberg, J. M. 18: v E 1913 (5) 1922 (5); v A 1921 (3); *v E 1924 (5)*
Bland, K. C. 21: v E 1964 (5); v A 1966 (1); v NZ 1961 (5); *v E 1965 (3); v A 1963 (4); v NZ 1963 (3)*
Bock, E. G. 1: v A 1935
Boje, N. 19: v A 2001 (1); v NZ 2000 (3); v In 2001 (2); v SL 2000 (3); *v A 2001 (1); v WI 2000 (4); v In 1999 (2); v SL 2000 (3)*
Bond, G. E. 1: v E 1938
Bosch, T. 1: *v WI 1991*
Botten, J. T. 3: *v E 1965 (3)*
Boucher, M. V. 52: v E 1999 (5); v A 2001 (3); v WI 1998 (5); v NZ 2000 (3); v In 2001 (2); v P 1997 (3); v SL 1997 (2) 2000 (3); v Z 1999 (1); *v E 1998 (5); v A 2001 (3); v WI 2000 (5); v NZ 1998 (3); v In 1999 (2); v P 1997 (1); v SL 2000 (3); v Z 1999 (1) 2001 (2)*
Brann, W. H. 3: v E 1922 (3)
Briscoe, A. W. 2: v E 1938 (1); v A 1935 (1)
Bromfield, H. D. 9: v E 1964 (3); v NZ 1961 (5); *v E 1965 (1)*
Brown, L. S. 2: *v A 1931 (1); v NZ 1931 (1)*
Burger, C. G. de V. 2: v A 1957 (2)
Burke, S. F. 2: v E 1964 (1); v NZ 1961 (1)
Buys, I. D. 1: v E 1922

Cameron, H. B. 26: v E 1927 (5) 1930 (5); *v E 1929 (4) 1935 (5); v A 1931 (5); v NZ 1931 (2)*
Campbell, T. 5: v E 1909 (4); *v E 1912 (1)*
Carlstein, P. R. 8: v A 1957 (1); *v E 1960 (5); v A 1963 (2)*
Carter, C. P. 10: v E 1913 (2); v A 1921 (3); *v E 1912 (2) 1924 (3)*
Catterall, R. H. 24: v E 1922 (5) 1927 (5) 1930 (4); *v E 1924 (5) 1929 (5)*
Chapman, H. W. 2: v E 1913 (1); v A 1921 (1)
Cheetham, J. E. 24: v E 1948 (1); v A 1949 (5); v NZ 1953 (5); *v E 1951 (5) 1955 (3); v A 1952 (5); v NZ 1952 (2)*
Chevalier, G. A. 1: v A 1969
Christy, J. A. J. 10: v E 1930 (1); *v E 1929 (2); v A 1931 (5); v NZ 1931 (2)*
Chubb, G. W. A. 5: *v E 1951 (5)*
Cochran, J. A. K. 1: v E 1930
Coen, S. K. 2: v E 1927 (2)
Commaille, J. M. M. 12: v E 1909 (5) 1927 (2); *v E 1924 (5)*
Commins, J. B. 3: v NZ 1994 (2); v P 1994 (1)
Conyngham, D. P. 1: v E 1922
Cook, F. J. 1: v E 1895
Cook, S. J. 3: v In 1992 (2); *v SL 1993 (1)*
Cooper, A. H. C. 1: v E 1913
Cox, J. L. 3: v E 1913 (3)
Cripps, G. 1: v E 1891
Crisp, R. J. 9: v A 1935 (4); *v E 1935 (5)*
Cronje, W. J. 68: v E 1995 (5) 1999 (5); v A 1993 (3) 1996 (3); v WI 1998 (5); v NZ 1994 (3); v In 1992 (3) 1996 (3); v P 1994 (1) 1997 (2); v SL 1997 (2); v Z 1999 (1); *v E 1994 (3) 1998 (5); v A 1993 (3) 1997 (3); v WI 1991 (1); v NZ 1994 (3) 1998 (3); v In 1996 (3) 1999 (2); v P 1997 (3); v SL 1993 (3); v Z 1995 (1) 1999 (1)*

Cullinan, D. J. 70: v E 1995 (5) 1999 (5); v A 1996 (3); v WI 1998 (5); v NZ 1994 (3) 2000 (3); v In 1992 (1) 1996 (3); v P 1994 (1) 1997 (1); v SL 1997 (2) 2000 (3); v Z 1999 (1); *v E 1994 (1) 1998 (5); v A 1993 (3) 1997 (1); v WI 2000 (5); v NZ 1994 (3) 1998 (3); v In 1996 (3) 1999 (1); v P 1997 (3); v SL 1993 (3) 2000 (3); v Z 1995 (1) 1999 (1)*
Curnow, S. H. 7: v E 1930 (3); *v A 1931 (4)*

Dalton, E. L. 15: v E 1930 (1) 1938 (4); v A 1935 (1); *v E 1929 (1) 1935 (4); v A 1931 (2); v NZ 1931 (2)*
Davies, E. Q. 5: v E 1938 (3); v A 1935 (2)
Dawson, O. C. 9: v E 1948 (4); *v E 1947 (5)*
Deane, H. G. 17: v E 1927 (5) 1930 (2); *v E 1924 (5) 1929 (5)*
de Villiers, P. S. 18: v A 1993 (3); v NZ 1994 (3); v P 1994 (1) 1997 (2); *v E 1994 (3); v A 1993 (3); v NZ 1994 (1); v In 1996 (2)*
Dippenaar, H. H. 15: v A 2001 (1); v NZ 2000 (3); v In 2001 (2); v SL 2000 (2); v Z 1999 (1); *v A 2001 (3); v Z 1999 (1) 2001 (2)*
Dixon, C. D. 1: v E 1913
Donald, A. A. 72: v E 1995 (5) 1999 (4); v A 1993 (3) 1996 (3) 2001 (1); v WI 1998 (5); v NZ 2000 (2); v In 1992 (4) 1996 (3); v P 1994 (1) 1997 (3); v SL 1997 (2) 2000 (1); v Z 1999 (1); *v E 1994 (3) 1998 (5); v A 1993 (3) 1997 (2) 2001 (2); v WI 1991 (1) 2000 (4); v NZ 1994 (1) 1998 (2); v In 1996 (2) 1999 (2); v P 1997 (2); v SL 1993 (3); v Z 1995 (1) 1999 (1)*
Dower, R. R. 1: v E 1898
Draper, R. G. 2: v A 1949 (2)
Duckworth, C. A. R. 2: v E 1956 (2)
Dumbrill, R. 5: v A 1966 (2); *v E 1965 (3)*
Duminy, J. P. 3: v E 1927 (2); *v E 1929 (1)*
Dunell, O. R. 2: v E 1888 (2)
Du Preez, J. H. 2: v A 1966 (2)
Du Toit, J. F. 1: v E 1891
Dyer, D. V. 3: *v E 1947 (3)*

Eksteen, C. E. 7: v E 1995 (1); v NZ 1994 (2); v P 1994 (1); *v NZ 1994 (1); v In 1999 (1); v SL 1993 (1)*
Elgie, M. K. 3: v NZ 1961 (3)
Elworthy, S. 2: *v E 1998 (1); v NZ 1998 (1)*
Endean, W. R. 28: v E 1956 (5); v A 1957 (5); v NZ 1953 (5); *v E 1951 (1) 1955 (5); v A 1952 (5); v NZ 1952 (2)*

Farrer, W. S. 6: v NZ 1961 (3); *v NZ 1963 (3)*
Faulkner, G. A. 25: v E 1905 (5) 1909 (5); *v E 1907 (3) 1912 (3) 1924 (1); v A 1910 (5) 1912 (3)*
Fellows-Smith, J. P. 4: *v E 1960 (4)*
Fichardt, C. G. 2: v E 1891 (1) 1895 (1)
Finlason, C. E. 1: v E 1888
Floquet, C. E. 1: v E 1909
Francis, H. H. 2: v E 1898 (2)
Francois, C. M. 5: v E 1922 (5)
Frank, C. N. 3: v A 1921 (3)
Frank, W. H. B. 1: v E 1895
Fuller, E. R. H. 7: v A 1957 (1); *v E 1955 (2); v A 1952 (2); v NZ 1952 (2)*
Fullerton, G. M. 7: v A 1949 (2); *v E 1947 (2) 1951 (3)*
Funston, K. J. 18: v E 1956 (3); v A 1957 (5); v NZ 1953 (3); *v A 1952 (5); v NZ 1952 (2)*

Gamsy, D. 2: v A 1969 (2)
Gibbs, H. H. 38: v E 1999 (5); v A 1996 (1) 2001 (3); v WI 1998 (4); v In 1996 (1) 2001 (2); v P 1997 (1); v SL 2000 (2); *v A 1997 (2) 2001 (3); v WI 2000 (5); v NZ 1998 (3); v In 1996 (2) 1999 (2); v Z 2001 (2)*
Gleeson, R. A. 1: v E 1895
Glover, G. K. 1: v E 1895
Goddard, T. L. 41: v E 1956 (5) 1964 (5); v A 1957 (5) 1966 (5) 1969 (3); *v E 1955 (5) 1960 (5); v A 1963 (5); v NZ 1963 (3)*
Gordon, N. 5: v E 1938 (5)
Graham, R. 2: v E 1898 (2)

Grieveson, R. E. 2: v E 1938 (2)
Griffin, G. M. 2: *v E 1960 (2)*

Hall, A. E. 7: v E 1922 (4) 1927 (2) 1930 (1)
Hall, A. J. 2: v A 2001 (2)
Hall, G. G. 1: v E 1964
Halliwell, E. A. 8: v E 1891 (1) 1895 (3) 1898 (1); v A 1902 (3)
Halse, C. G. 3: *v A 1963 (3)*
Hands, P. A. M. 7: v E 1913 (5); v A 1921 (1); *v E 1924 (1)*
Hands, R. H. M. 1: v E 1913
Hanley, M. A. 1: v E 1948
Harris, T. A. 3: v E 1948 (1); *v E 1947 (2)*
Hartigan, G. P. D. 5: v E 1913 (3); *v E 1912 (1); v A 1912 (1)*
Harvey, R. L. 2: v A 1935 (2)
Hathorn, C. M. H. 12: v E 1905 (5); v A 1902 (3); *v E 1907 (3); v A 1910 (1)*
Hayward, M. 10: v E 1999 (3); v In 2001 (2); *v A 2001 (2); v In 1999 (1); v SL 2000 (2)*
Hearne, F. 4: v E 1891 (1) 1895 (3)
Hearne, G. A. L. 3: v E 1922 (2); *v E 1924 (1)*
Heine, P. S. 14: v E 1956 (5); v A 1957 (4); v NZ 1961 (1); *v E 1955 (4)*
Henderson, C. W. 5: *v A 2001 (3); v Z 2001 (2)*
Henry, O. 3: v In 1992 (3)
Hime, C. F. W. 1: v E 1895
Hudson, A. C. 35: v E 1995 (5); v A 1993 (3) 1996 (1); v NZ 1994 (2); v In 1992 (4) 1996 (3); v P
    1997 (3); *v E 1994 (2); v A 1993 (3); v WI 1991 (1); v NZ 1994 (1); v In 1996 (3); v SL 1993 (3);
    v Z 1995 (1)*
Hutchinson, P. 2: v E 1888 (2)

Ironside, D. E. J. 3: v NZ 1953 (3)
Irvine, B. L. 4: v A 1969 (4)

Jack, S. D. 2: v NZ 1994 (2)
Johnson, C. L. 1: v E 1895

Kallis, J. H. 60: v E 1995 (2) 1999 (5); v A 1996 (3) 2001 (3); v WI 1998 (5); v NZ 2000 (3);
    v In 2001 (2); v P 1997 (3); v SL 1997 (2) 2000 (3); v Z 1999 (1); *v E 1998 (5); v A 1997 (3) 2001
    (3); v WI 2000 (5); v NZ 1998 (3); v In 1999 (2); v P 1997 (1); v SL 2000 (3); v Z 1999 (1)
    2001 (2)*
Keith, H. J. 8: v E 1956 (3); *v E 1955 (4); v A 1952 (1)*
Kemp, J. M. 3: v SL 2000 (1); *v WI 2000 (2)*
Kempis, G. A. 1: v E 1888
Kirsten, G. 83: v E 1995 (5) 1999 (5); v A 1993 (3) 1996 (3) 2001 (3); v WI 1998 (5); v NZ 1994
    (3) 2000 (3); v In 1996 (3) 2001 (2); v P 1994 (1) 1997 (3); v SL 1997 (2) 2000 (2); *v E 1994 (3)
    1998 (5); v A 1993 (3) 1997 (3) 2001 (3); v WI 2000 (5); v NZ 1994 (1) 1998 (3); v In 1996 (3)
    1999 (2); v P 1997 (3); v SL 2000 (3); v Z 1995 (1) 2001 (2)*
Kirsten, P. N. 12: v A 1993 (3); v In 1992 (4); *v E 1994 (3); v A 1993 (1); v WI 1991 (1)*
Klusener, L. 48: v E 1999 (5); v A 1996 (2); v WI 1998 (1); v NZ 2000 (3); v In 1996 (3) 2001 (2);
    v P 1997 (2); v SL 2000 (2); v Z 1999 (1); *v E 1998 (3); v A 1997 (2) 2001 (2); v WI 2000 (5);
    v NZ 1998 (3); v In 1996 (2) 1999 (2); v P 1997 (2); v SL 2000 (3); v Z 1999 (1) 2001 (2)*
Kotze, J. J. 3: v A 1902 (2); *v E 1907 (1)*
Kuiper, A. P. 1: *v WI 1991*
Kuys, F. 1: v E 1898

Lance, H. R. 13: v A 1966 (5) 1969 (3); v NZ 1961 (2); *v E 1965 (3)*
Langton, A. B. C. 15: v E 1938 (5); v A 1935 (5); *v E 1935 (5)*
Lawrence, G. B. 5: v NZ 1961 (5)
le Roux, F. L. 1: v E 1913
Lewis, P. T. 1: v E 1913
Liebenberg, G. F. J. 5: v SL 1997 (1); *v E 1998 (4)*
Lindsay, D. T. 19: v E 1964 (3); v A 1966 (5) 1969 (2); *v E 1965 (3); v A 1963 (3); v NZ 1963 (3)*
Lindsay, J. D. 3: *v E 1947 (3)*
Lindsay, N. V. 1: v A 1921

Ling, W. V. S. 6: v E 1922 (3); v A 1921 (3)
Llewellyn, C. B. 15: v E 1895 (1) 1898 (1); v A 1902 (3); *v E 1912 (3); v A 1910 (5) 1912 (2)*
Lundie, E. B. 1: v E 1913

Macaulay, M. J. 1: v E 1964
McCarthy, C. N. 15: v E 1948 (5); v A 1949 (5); *v E 1951 (5)*
McGlew, D. J. 34: v E 1956 (1); v A 1957 (5); v NZ 1953 (5) 1961 (5); *v E 1951 (2) 1955 (5) 1960 (5); v A 1952 (4); v NZ 1952 (2)*
McKenzie, N. D. 24: v A 2001 (3); v NZ 2000 (3); v In 2001 (2); v SL 2000 (3); *v A 2001 (3); v WI 2000 (5); v SL 2000 (3); v Z 2001 (2)*
McKinnon, A. H. 8: v E 1964 (2); v A 1966 (2); v NZ 1961 (1); *v E 1960 (1) 1965 (2)*
McLean, R. A. 40: v E 1956 (5) 1964 (2); v A 1957 (4); v NZ 1953 (4) 1961 (5); *v E 1951 (3) 1955 (5) 1960 (5); v A 1952 (5); v NZ 1952 (2)*
McMillan, B. M. 38: v E 1995 (5); v A 1993 (3) 1996 (2); v NZ 1994 (3); v In 1992 (4) 1996 (3); v P 1994 (1); *v E 1994 (3) 1998 (1); v A 1993 (1) 1997 (3); v In 1996 (3); v P 1997 (3); v SL 1993 (2); v Z 1995 (1)*
McMillan, Q. 13: v E 1930 (3); *v E 1929 (2); v A 1931 (4); v NZ 1931 (2)*
Mann, N. B. F. 19: v E 1948 (5); v A 1949 (5); *v E 1947 (5) 1951 (4)*
Mansell, P. N. F. 13: *v E 1951 (2) 1955 (4); v A 1952 (5); v NZ 1952 (2)*
Markham, L. A. 1: v E 1948
Marx, W. F. E. 3: v A 1921 (3)
Matthews, C. R. 18: v E 1995 (5); v A 1993 (3); v NZ 1994 (2); v In 1992 (3); *v E 1994 (3); v A 1993 (2); v NZ 1994 (1); v Z 1995 (1)*
Meintjes, D. J. 2: v E 1922 (2)
Melle, M. G. 7: v A 1949 (2); *v E 1951 (1); v A 1952 (4)*
Melville, A. 11: v E 1938 (5) 1948 (1); *v E 1947 (5)*
Middleton, J. 6: v E 1895 (2) 1898 (2); v A 1902 (2)
Mills, C. 1: v E 1891
Milton, W. H. 3: v E 1888 (2) 1891 (1)
Mitchell, B. 42: v E 1930 (5) 1938 (5) 1948 (5); v A 1935 (5); *v E 1929 (5) 1935 (5) 1947 (5); v A 1931 (5); v NZ 1931 (2)*
Mitchell, F. 3: *v E 1912 (1); v A 1912 (2)*
Morkel, D. P. B. 16: v E 1927 (5); *v E 1929 (5); v A 1931 (5); v NZ 1931 (1)*
Murray, A. R. A. 10: v NZ 1953 (4); *v A 1952 (4); v NZ 1952 (2)*

Nel, A. 3: v A 2001 (1); *v Z 2001 (2)*
Nel, J. D. 6: v A 1949 (5) 1957 (1)
Newberry, C. 4: v E 1913 (4)
Newson, E. S. 3: v E 1930 (1) 1938 (2)
Ngam, M. 3: v NZ 2000 (1); v SL 2000 (2)
Nicholson, F. 4: v A 1935 (4)
Nicolson, J. F. W. 3: v E 1927 (3)
Norton, N. O. 1: v E 1909
Nourse, A. D. 34: v E 1938 (5) 1948 (5); v A 1935 (5) 1949 (5); *v E 1935 (4) 1947 (5) 1951 (5)*
Nourse, A. W. 45: v E 1905 (5) 1909 (5) 1913 (5) 1922 (5); v A 1902 (3) 1921 (3); *v E 1907 (3) 1912 (3) 1924 (5); v A 1910 (5) 1912 (3)*
Ntini, M. 23: v A 2001 (3); v NZ 2000 (3); v In 2001 (2); v SL 1997 (2) 2000 (3); *v A 2001 (1); v E 1998 (2); v WI 2000 (4); v SL 2000 (1); v Z 2001 (2)*
Nupen, E. P. 17: v E 1922 (4) 1927 (5) 1930 (3); v A 1921 (2) 1935 (1); *v E 1924 (2)*

Ochse, A. E. 2: v E 1888 (2)
Ochse, A. L. 3: v E 1927 (1); *v E 1929 (2)*
O'Linn, S. 7: v NZ 1961 (2); *v E 1960 (5)*
Ontong, J. L. 1: *v A 2001*
Owen-Smith, H. G. 5: *v E 1929 (5)*

Palm, A. W. 1: v E 1927
Parker, G. M. 2: *v E 1924 (2)*
Parkin, D. C. 1: v E 1891
Partridge, J. T. 11: v E 1964 (3); *v A 1963 (5); v NZ 1963 (3)*
Pearse, O. C. 3: *v A 1910 (3)*

Pegler, S. J. 16: v E 1909 (1); *v E 1912 (3) 1924 (5); v A 1910 (4) 1912 (3)*
Pithey, A. J. 17: v E 1956 (3) 1964 (5); *v E 1960 (2); v A 1963 (4); v NZ 1963 (3)*
Pithey, D. B. 8: v A 1966 (2); *v A 1963 (3); v NZ 1963 (3)*
Plimsoll, J. B. 1: *v E 1947*
Pollock, P. M. 28: v E 1964 (5); v A 1966 (5) 1969 (4); v NZ 1961 (3); *v E 1965 (3); v A 1963 (5); v NZ 1963 (3)*
Pollock, R. G. 23: v E 1964 (5); v A 1966 (5) 1969 (4); *v E 1965 (3); v A 1963 (5); v NZ 1963 (1)*
Pollock, S. M. 63: v E 1995 (5) 1999 (5); v A 1996 (2); v WI 1998 (5); v NZ 2000 (3); v In 1996 (3) 2001 (2); v P 1997 (3); v SL 1997 (2) 2000 (3); v Z 1999 (1); *v E 1998 (4); v A 1997 (3) 2001 (3); v WI 2000 (5); v NZ 1998 (3); v In 1999 (2); v P 1997 (3); v SL 2000 (3); v Z 1999 (1) 2001 (2)*
Poore, R. M. 3: v E 1895 (3)
Pothecary, J. E. 3: *v E 1960 (3)*
Powell, A. W. 1: v E 1898
Pretorius, D. 1: v A 2001
Prince, A. G. 3: v A 2001 (3)
Prince, C. F. H. 1: v E 1898
Pringle, M. W. 4: v E 1995 (1); v In 1992 (2); *v WI 1991 (1)*
Procter, M. J. 7: v A 1966 (3) 1969 (4)
Promnitz, H. L. E. 2: v E 1927 (2)

Quinn, N. A. 12: v E 1930 (1); *v E 1929 (4); v A 1931 (5); v NZ 1931 (2)*

Reid, N. 1: v A 1921
Rhodes, J. N. 52: v E 1995 (5) 1999 (3); v A 1993 (3) 1996 (1); v WI 1998 (5); v NZ 1994 (3); v In 1992 (4); v P 1994 (1); v Z 1999 (1); *v E 1994 (3) 1998 (5); v A 1993 (3) 1997 (1); v NZ 1994 (1) 1998 (3); v In 1996 (1); v P 1997 (1); v SL 1993 (3) 2000 (3); v Z 1995 (1) 1999 (1)*
Richards, A. R. 1: v E 1895
Richards, B. A. 4: v A 1969 (4)
Richards, W. H. 1: v E 1888
Richardson, D. J. 42: v E 1995 (5); v A 1993 (3) 1996 (3); v NZ 1994 (3); v In 1992 (4) 1996 (3); v P 1994 (3); *v E 1994 (3); v A 1993 (3) 1997 (3); v WI 1991 (1); v NZ 1994 (1); v In 1996 (3); v P 1997 (2); v SL 1993 (3); v Z 1995 (1)*
Robertson, J. B. 3: v A 1935 (3)
Rose-Innes, A. 2: v E 1888 (2)
Routledge, T. W. 4: v E 1891 (1) 1895 (3)
Rowan, A. M. B. 15: v E 1948 (5); *v E 1947 (5) 1951 (5)*
Rowan, E. A. B. 26: v E 1938 (4) 1948 (4); v A 1935 (3) 1949 (5); *v E 1935 (5) 1951 (5)*
Rowe, G. A. 5: v E 1895 (2) 1898 (2); v A 1902 (1)
Rushmere, M. W. 1: *v WI 1991*

Samuelson, S. V. 1: v E 1909
Schultz, B. N. 9: v E 1995 (1); v A 1996 (1); v In 1992 (2); *v P 1997 (1); v SL 1993 (3); v Z 1995 (1)*
Schwarz, R. O. 20: v E 1905 (5) 1909 (4); *v E 1907 (3) 1912 (1); v A 1910 (5) 1912 (2)*
Seccull, A. W. 1: v E 1895
Seymour, M. A. 7: v E 1964 (2); v A 1969 (1); *v A 1963 (4)*
Shalders, W. A. 12: v E 1898 (1) 1905 (5); v A 1902 (3); *v E 1907 (3)*
Shepstone, G. H. 2: v E 1895 (1) 1898 (1)
Sherwell, P. W. 13: v E 1905 (5); *v E 1907 (3); v A 1910 (5)*
Siedle, I. J. 18: v E 1927 (1) 1930 (5); v A 1935 (5); *v E 1929 (3) 1935 (4)*
Sinclair, J. H. 25: v E 1895 (3) 1898 (2) 1905 (5) 1909 (4); v A 1902 (3); *v E 1907 (3); v A 1910 (5)*
Smith, C. J. E. 3: v A 1902 (3)
Smith, F. W. 3: v E 1888 (2) 1895 (1)
Smith, G. C. 2: v A 2001 (2)
Smith, V. I. 9: v A 1949 (3) 1957 (1); *v E 1947 (4) 1955 (1)*
Snell, R. P. 5: v NZ 1994 (1); *v A 1993 (1); v WI 1991 (1); v SL 1993 (2)*
Snooke, S. D. 1: *v E 1907*
Snooke, S. J. 26: v E 1905 (5) 1909 (5) 1922 (3); *v E 1907 (3) 1912 (3); v A 1910 (5) 1912 (2)*
Solomon, W. R. 1: v E 1898
Stewart, R. B. 1: v E 1888

Steyn, P. J. R. 3: v NZ 1994 (1); v P 1994 (1); *v NZ 1994 (1)*
Stricker, L. A. 13: v E 1909 (4); *v E 1912 (2); v A 1910 (5) 1912 (2)*
Strydom, P. C. 2: v E 1999 (1); *v In 1999 (1)*
Susskind, M. J. 5: *v E 1924 (5)*
Symcox, P. L. 20: v A 1996 (1); v WI 1998 (3); v P 1997 (1); *v A 1993 (2) 1997 (3); v In 1996 (3); v P 1997 (3); v SL 1993 (3); v Z 1995 (1)*

Taberer, H. M. 1: v A 1902
Tancred, A. B. 2: v E 1888 (2)
Tancred, L. J. 14: v E 1905 (5) 1913 (1); v A 1902 (3); *v E 1907 (1) 1912 (2); v A 1912 (2)*
Tancred, V. M. 1: v E 1898
Tapscott, G. L. 1: v E 1913
Tapscott, L. E. 2: v E 1922 (2)
Tayfield, H. J. 37: v E 1956 (5); v A 1949 (5) 1957 (5); v NZ 1953 (5); *v E 1955 (5) 1960 (5); v A 1952 (5); v NZ 1952 (2)*
Taylor, A. I. 1: v E 1956
Taylor, D. 2: v E 1913 (2)
Taylor, H. W. 42: v E 1913 (5) 1922 (5) 1927 (5) 1930 (4); v A 1921 (3); *v E 1912 (3) 1924 (5) 1929 (3); v A 1912 (3) 1931 (5); v NZ 1931 (1)*
Terbrugge, D. J. 5: v A 2001 (1); v WI 1998 (4)
Theunissen, N. H. 1: v E 1888
Thornton, P. G. 1: v A 1902
Tomlinson, D. S. 1: *v E 1935*
Traicos, A. J. 3: v A 1969 (3)
Trimborn, P. H. J. 4: v A 1966 (3) 1969 (1)
Tuckett, L. 9: v E 1948 (4); *v E 1947 (5)*
Tuckett, L. R. 1: v E 1913
Twentyman-Jones, P. S. 1: v A 1902

van der Bijl, P. G. V. 5: v E 1938 (5)
Van der Merwe, E. A. 2: v A 1935 (1); *v E 1929 (1)*
Van der Merwe, P. L. 15: v E 1964 (2); v A 1966 (5); *v E 1965 (3); v A 1963 (3); v NZ 1963 (2)*
Van Ryneveld, C. B. 19: v E 1956 (5); v A 1957 (4); v NZ 1953 (5); *v E 1951 (5)*
Varnals, G. D. 3: v E 1964 (3)
Viljoen, K. G. 27: v E 1930 (3) 1938 (4) 1948 (2); v A 1935 (4); *v E 1935 (4) 1947 (5); v A 1931 (4); v NZ 1931 (1)*
Vincent, C. L. 25: v E 1927 (5) 1930 (5); *v E 1929 (4) 1935 (4); v A 1931 (5); v NZ 1931 (2)*
Vintcent, C. H. 3: v E 1888 (2) 1891 (1)
Vogler, A. E. E. 15: v E 1905 (5) 1909 (5); *v E 1907 (3); v A 1910 (2)*

Wade, H. F. 10: v A 1935 (5); *v E 1935 (5)*
Wade, W. W. 11: v E 1938 (3) 1948 (5); v A 1949 (3)
Waite, J. H. B. 50: v E 1956 (5) 1964 (2); v A 1957 (5); v NZ 1953 (5) 1961 (5); *v E 1951 (4) 1955 (5) 1960 (5); v A 1952 (5) 1963 (4); v NZ 1952 (2) 1963 (3)*
Walter, K. A. 2: v NZ 1961 (2)
Ward, T. A. 23: v E 1913 (5) 1922 (5); v A 1921 (3); *v E 1912 (2) 1924 (5); v A 1912 (3)*
Watkins, J. C. 15: v E 1956 (2); v A 1949 (3); v NZ 1953 (3); *v A 1952 (5); v NZ 1952 (2)*
Wesley, C. 3: *v E 1960 (3)*
Wessels, K. C. 16: v A 1993 (3); v In 1992 (4); *v E 1994 (3); v A 1993 (2); v WI 1991 (1); SL 1993 (3)*
Westcott, R. J. 5: v A 1957 (2); v NZ 1953 (3)
White, G. C. 17: v E 1905 (5) 1909 (4); *v E 1907 (3) 1912 (2); v A 1912 (3)*
Willoughby, J. T. 2: v E 1895 (2)
Wimble, C. S. 1: v E 1891
Winslow, P. L. 5: v A 1949 (2); *v E 1955 (3)*
Wynne, O. E. 6: v E 1948 (3); v A 1949 (3)

Zulch, J. W. 16: v E 1909 (5) 1913 (3); v A 1921 (3); *v A 1910 (5)*

The Players

WEST INDIES

Number of Test cricketers: 243

Achong, E. 6: v E 1929 (1) 1934 (2); *v E 1933 (3)*

Adams, J. C. 54: v E 1993 (5) 1997 (4); v A 1994 (4) 1998 (4); v SA 1991 (1); v NZ 1995 (2); v P 1999 (3); v Z 1999 (2); *v E 1995 (4) 2000 (5); v A 1992 (3) 1996 (5) 2000 (5); v NZ 1994 (2) 1999 (2); v In 1994 (3)*

Alexander, F. C. M. 25: v E 1959 (5); v P 1957 (5); *v E 1957 (2); v A 1960 (5); v In 1958 (5); v P 1958 (3)*

Ali, Imtiaz 1: v In 1975

Ali, Inshan 12: v E 1973 (2); v A 1972 (3); v In 1970 (1); v P 1976 (1); v NZ 1971 (3); *v E 1973 (1); v A 1975 (1)*

Allan, D. W. 5: v A 1964 (1); v In 1961 (2); *v E 1966 (2)*

Allen, I. B. A. 2: *v E 1991 (2)*

Ambrose, C. E. L. 98: v E 1989 (3) 1993 (5) 1997 (6); v A 1990 (5) 1994 (4) 1998 (4); v SA 1991 (1); v NZ 1995 (2); v In 1988 (4) 1996 (5); v P 1987 (3) 1992 (3) 1999 (3); v SL 1996 (2); v Z 1999 (2); *v E 1988 (5) 1991 (5) 1995 (5) 2000 (5); v A 1988 (5) 1992 (5) 1996 (4); v SA 1998 (4); v NZ 1994 (2); v P 1990 (3) 1997 (2); v SL 1993 (1)*

Arthurton, K. L. T. 33: v E 1993 (5); v A 1994 (3); v SA 1991 (1); v In 1988 (4); v P 1992 (3); *v E 1988 (1) 1995 (5); v A 1992 (5); v NZ 1994 (2); v In 1994 (3); v SL 1993 (1)*

Asgarali, N. 2: *v E 1957 (2)*

Atkinson, D. St E. 22: v E 1953 (4); v A 1954 (4); v P 1957 (1); *v E 1957 (2); v A 1951 (2); v NZ 1951 (1) 1955 (4); v In 1948 (4)*

Atkinson, E. St E. 8: v P 1957 (3); *v In 1958 (3); v P 1958 (2)*

Austin, R. A. 2: v A 1977 (2)

Bacchus, S. F. A. F. 19: v A 1977 (2); *v E 1980 (5); v A 1981 (2); v In 1978 (6); v P 1980 (4)*

Baichan, L. 3: *v A 1975 (1); v P 1974 (2)*

Baptiste, E. A. E. 10: v E 1989 (1); v A 1983 (3); *v E 1984 (5); v In 1983 (1)*

Barrett, A. G. 6: v E 1973 (2); v In 1970 (2); *v In 1974 (2)*

Barrow, I. 11: v E 1929 (1) 1934 (1); *v E 1933 (3) 1939 (1); v A 1930 (5)*

Bartlett, E. L. 5: *v E 1928 (1); v A 1930 (4)*

Benjamin, K. C. G. 26: v E 1993 (5) 1997 (2); v A 1994 (4); v SA 1991 (1); *v E 1995 (5); v A 1992 (1) 1996 (2); v NZ 1994 (2); v In 1994 (3)*

Benjamin, W. K. M. 21: v E 1993 (5); v A 1994 (4); v In 1988 (1); v P 1987 (3) 1992 (2); *v E 1988 (3); v NZ 1994 (1); v In 1987 (1); v SL 1993 (1)*

Best, C. A. 8: v E 1985 (3) 1989 (3); *v P 1990 (2)*

Betancourt, N. 1: v E 1929

Binns, A. P. 5: v A 1954 (1); v In 1952 (1); *v NZ 1955 (3)*

Birkett, L. S. 4: *v A 1930 (4)*

Bishop, I. R. 43: v E 1989 (4) 1997 (3); v NZ 1995 (2); v In 1988 (4) 1996 (4); v P 1992 (2); v SL 1996 (2); *v E 1995 (6); v A 1992 (5) 1996 (5); v P 1990 (3) 1997 (3)*

Black, M. I. 6: v In 2001 (1); *v A 2000 (3); v SL 2001 (1); v Z 2001 (1)*

Boyce, K. D. 21: v E 1973 (4); v A 1972 (4); v In 1970 (1); *v E 1973 (3); v A 1975 (4); v In 1974 (2); v P 1974 (2)*

Browne, C. O. 14: v A 1994 (1); v NZ 1995 (2); v In 1996 (3); v SL 1996 (2); *v E 1995 (2); v A 1996 (3); v Z 2001 (1)*

Browne, C. R. 4: v E 1929 (2); *v E 1928 (2)*

Butcher, B. F. 44: v E 1959 (2) 1967 (5); v A 1964 (5); *v E 1963 (5) 1966 (5) 1969 (3); v A 1968 (5); v NZ 1968 (3); v In 1958 (5) 1966 (3); v P 1958 (3)*

Butler, L. 1: v A 1954

Butts, C. G. 7: v NZ 1984 (1); *v NZ 1986 (1); v In 1987 (3); v P 1986 (2)*

Bynoe, M. R. 4: *v In 1966 (3); v P 1958 (1)*

Camacho, G. S. 11: v E 1967 (5); v In 1970 (2); *v E 1969 (2); v A 1968 (2)*

Cameron, F. J. 5: *v In 1948 (5)*

Cameron, J. H. 2: *v E 1939 (2)*

Campbell, S. L. 52: v E 1997 (4); v A 1994 (1) 1998 (4); v NZ 1995 (2); v In 1996 (5); v P 1999 (3); v SL 1996 (2); v Z 1999 (2); *v E 1995 (6) 2000 (5); v A 1996 (5) 2000 (5); v NZ 1994 (2) 1999 (2); v P 1997 (3) 2001 (1)*

Carew, G. M. 4: v E 1934 (1) 1947 (2); *v In 1948 (1)*

Carew, M. 19: v E 1967 (1); v NZ 1971 (3); v In 1970 (3); *v E 1963 (2) 1966 (1) 1969 (1); v A 1968 (5); v NZ 1968 (3)*

Challenor, G. 3: *v E 1928 (3)*

Chanderpaul, S. 58: v E 1993 (4) 1997 (6); v SA 2000 (2); v NZ 1995 (2) 2002 (2); v In 1996 (5) 2001 (5); v P 1999 (2); v Z 1999 (2); *v E 1995 (2) 2000 (2); v A 1996 (5) 2000 (1); v SA 1998 (5); v NZ 1994 (2) 1999 (2); v In 1994 (1); v P 1997 (3) 2001 (2); v Z 2001 (2)*

Chang, H. S. 1: *v In 1978*

Christiani, C. M. 4: v E 1934 (4)

Christiani, R. J. 22: v E 1947 (4) 1953 (1); v In 1952 (2); *v E 1950 (4); v A 1951 (5); v NZ 1951 (1); v In 1948 (5)*

Clarke, C. B. 3: *v E 1939 (3)*

Clarke, S. T. 11: v A 1977 (1); *v A 1981 (1); v In 1978 (5); v P 1980 (4)*

Collins, P. T. 13: v A 1998 (3); v NZ 2002 (2); v In 2001 (3); *v P 2001 (2); SL 2001 (1); v Z 2001 (1)*

Collymore, C. D. 1: v A 1998

Constantine, L. N. 18: v E 1929 (3) 1934 (3); *v E 1928 (3) 1933 (1) 1939 (3); v A 1930 (5)*

Croft, C. E. H. 27: v E 1980 (4); v A 1977 (2); v P 1976 (5); *v E 1980 (3); v A 1979 (3) 1981 (3); v NZ 1979 (3); v P 1980 (3)*

Cuffy, C. E. 13: v SA 2000 (2); v NZ 2002 (1); v In 2001 (5); *v A 1996 (1); v In 1994 (2); v P 2001 (2)*

Cummins, A. C. 5: v P 1992 (2); *v A 1992 (1); v In 1994 (2)*

Da Costa, O. C. 5: v E 1929 (1) 1934 (1); *v E 1933 (3)*

Daniel, W. W. 10: v A 1983 (2); v In 1975 (1); *v E 1976 (4); v In 1983 (3)*

Davis, B. A. 4: v A 1964 (4)

Davis, C. A. 15: v A 1972 (2); v NZ 1971 (5); v In 1970 (4); *v E 1969 (3); v A 1968 (1)*

Davis, W. W. 15: v A 1983 (1); v NZ 1984 (2); v In 1982 (1); *v E 1984 (1); v In 1983 (6) 1987 (4)*

De Caires, F. I. 3: v E 1929 (3)

Depeiza, C. C. 5: v A 1954 (3); *v NZ 1955 (2)*

Dewdney, T. 9: v A 1954 (2); v P 1957 (3); *v E 1957 (1); v NZ 1955 (3)*

Dhanraj, R. 4: v NZ 1995 (1); *v E 1995 (1); v NZ 1994 (1); v In 1994 (1)*

Dillon, M. 27: v A 1998 (1); v SA 2000 (5); v NZ 2002 (1); v In 1996 (2) 2001 (5); *v A 2000 (4); v SA 1998 (3); v P 1997 (2) 2001 (2); v SL 2001 (2)*

Dowe, U. G. 4: v A 1972 (1); v NZ 1971 (1); v In 1970 (2)

Dujon, P. J. L. 81: v E 1985 (4) 1989 (4); v A 1983 (5) 1990 (5); v NZ 1984 (4); v In 1982 (5) 1988 (4); v P 1987 (3); *v E 1984 (5) 1988 (5) 1991 (5); v A 1981 (3) 1984 (5) 1988 (5); v NZ 1986 (2); v In 1983 (6) 1987 (4); v P 1986 (2) 1990 (3)*

Edwards, R. M. 5: *v A 1968 (2); v NZ 1968 (3)*

Ferguson, W. 8: v E 1947 (4) 1953 (1); *v In 1948 (3)*

Fernandes, M. P. 2: v E 1929 (1); *v E 1928 (1)*

Findlay, T. M. 10: v A 1972 (1); v NZ 1971 (5); v In 1970 (2); *v E 1969 (2)*

Foster, M. L. C. 14: v E 1973 (1); v A 1972 (4) 1977 (1); v NZ 1971 (3); v In 1970 (2); v P 1976 (1); *v E 1969 (1) 1973 (1)*

Francis, G. N. 10: v E 1929 (1); *v E 1928 (3) 1933 (1); v A 1930 (5)*

Frederick, M. 1: v E 1953

Fredericks, R. C. 59: v E 1973 (5); v A 1972 (5); v NZ 1971 (5); v In 1970 (4) 1975 (4); v P 1976 (5); *v E 1969 (3) 1973 (3) 1976 (5); v A 1968 (4) 1975 (6); v NZ 1968 (3); v In 1974 (5); v P 1974 (2)*

Fuller, R. L. 1: v E 1934

Furlonge, H. A. 3: v A 1954 (1); *v NZ 1955 (2)*

Ganga, D. 15: *v A 2000 (4); v SA 1998 (3); v NZ 1999 (1); v P 2001 (2); v SL 2001 (3); v Z 2001 (2)*

Ganteaume, A. G. 1: v E 1947

Garner, J. 58: v E 1980 (4) 1985 (5); v A 1977 (2) 1983 (5); v NZ 1984 (4); v In 1982 (4); v P 1976 (5); *v E 1980 (5) 1984 (5); v A 1979 (3) 1981 (3) 1984 (5); v NZ 1979 (3) 1986 (2); v P 1980 (3)*

Garrick, L. V. 1: v SA 2000

Gaskin, B. B. M. 2: v E 1947 (2)

Gayle, C. H. 23: v SA 2000 (5); v NZ 2002 (2); v In 2001 (5); v P 1999 (1); v Z 1999 (2); *v E 2000 (1); v P 2001 (2); v SL 2001 (3); v Z 2001 (2)*

Gibbs, G. L. 1: v A 1954

Gibbs, L. R. 79: v E 1967 (5) 1973 (5); v A 1964 (5) 1972 (5); v NZ 1971 (2); v In 1961 (5) 1970 (1); v P 1957 (4); *v E 1963 (5) 1966 (5) 1969 (3) 1973 (3); v A 1960 (3) 1968 (3) 1975 (6); v NZ 1968 (3); v In 1958 (1) 1966 (3) 1974 (5); v P 1958 (3) 1974 (2)*

Gibson, O. D. 2: *v E 1995 (1); v SA 1998 (1)*

Gilchrist, R. 13: v P 1957 (5); *v E 1957 (4); v In 1958 (4)*

Gladstone, G. 1: v E 1929

Goddard, J. D. C. 27: v E 1947 (4); *v E 1950 (4) 1957 (5); v A 1951 (4); v NZ 1951 (2) 1955 (3); v In 1948 (5)*

Gomes, H. A. 60: v E 1980 (4) 1985 (5); v A 1977 (3) 1983 (2); v NZ 1984 (4); v In 1982 (5); *v E 1976 (2) 1984 (5); v A 1981 (3) 1984 (5); v NZ 1986 (3); v In 1978 (6) 1983 (6); v P 1980 (4) 1986 (3)*

Gomez, G. E. 29: v E 1947 (4) 1953 (4); v In 1952 (4); *v E 1939 (2) 1950 (4); v A 1951 (5); v NZ 1951 (1); v In 1948 (5)*

Grant, G. C. 12: v E 1934 (4); *v E 1933 (3); v A 1930 (5)*

Grant, R. S. 7: v E 1934 (4); *v E 1939 (3)*

Gray, A. H. 5: *v NZ 1986 (2); v P 1986 (3)*

Greenidge, A. E. 6: v A 1977 (2); *v In 1978 (4)*

Greenidge, C. G. 108: v E 1980 (4) 1985 (5) 1989 (4); v A 1977 (2) 1983 (5) 1990 (5); v NZ 1984 (4); v In 1982 (5) 1988 (4); v P 1976 (5) 1987 (3); *v E 1976 (5) 1980 (5) 1984 (5) 1988 (4); v A 1975 (2) 1979 (3) 1981 (2) 1984 (5) 1988 (5); v NZ 1979 (3) 1986 (3); v In 1974 (5) 1983 (6) 1987 (3); v P 1986 (3) 1990 (3)*

Greenidge, G. A. 5: v A 1972 (3); v NZ 1971 (2)

Grell, M. G. 1: v E 1929

Griffith, A. F. G. 14: v A 1998 (2); v P 1999 (3); v Z 1999 (2); *v E 2000 (4); v A 1996 (1); v NZ 1999 (2)*

Griffith, C. C. 28: v E 1959 (1) 1967 (4); v A 1964 (5); *v E 1963 (5) 1966 (5); v A 1968 (3); v NZ 1968 (2); v In 1966 (3)*

Griffith, H. C. 13: v E 1929 (3); *v E 1928 (3) 1933 (2); v A 1930 (5)*

Guillen, S. C. 5: *v A 1951 (3); v NZ 1951 (2)*

Hall, W. W. 48: v E 1959 (5) 1967 (4); v A 1964 (5); v In 1961 (5); *v E 1963 (5) 1966 (5); v A 1960 (5) 1968 (2); v NZ 1968 (3); v In 1958 (5) 1966 (3); v P 1958 (3)*

Harper, R. A. 25: v E 1985 (2); v A 1983 (4); v NZ 1984 (1); *v E 1984 (5) 1988 (3); v A 1984 (2) 1988 (1); v In 1983 (2) 1987 (1); v P 1986 (3); v SL 1993 (1)*

Haynes, D. L. 116: v E 1980 (4) 1985 (5) 1989 (4) 1993 (4); v A 1977 (2) 1983 (5) 1990 (5); v SA 1991 (1); v NZ 1984 (4); v In 1982 (5) 1988 (4); v P 1987 (3) 1992 (3); *v E 1980 (5) 1984 (5) 1988 (4) 1991 (5); v A 1979 (3) 1981 (3) 1984 (5) 1988 (5) 1992 (5); v NZ 1979 (3) 1986 (3); v In 1983 (6) 1987 (4); v P 1980 (4) 1986 (3) 1990 (3); v SL 1993 (1)*

Headley, G. A. 22: v E 1929 (4) 1934 (4) 1947 (1) 1953 (1); *v E 1933 (3) 1939 (3); v A 1930 (5); v In 1948 (1)*

Headley, R. G. A. 2: *v E 1973 (2)*

Hendriks, J. L. 20: v A 1964 (4); v In 1961 (1); *v E 1966 (3) 1969 (1); v A 1968 (5); v NZ 1968 (3); v In 1966 (3)*

Hinds, R. O. 2: *v P 2001 (2)*

Hinds, W. W. 24: v SA 2000 (4); v NZ 2002 (2); v In 2001 (2); v P 1999 (3); v Z 1999 (2); *v E 2000 (5); v A 2000 (4); v P 2001 (2)*

Hoad, E. L. G. 4: v E 1929 (1); *v E 1928 (1) 1933 (2)*

Holder, R. I. C. 11: v E 1997 (2); v A 1998 (1); v In 1996 (5); v SL 1996 (2); *v P 1997 (1)*

Holder, V. A. 40: v E 1973 (1); v A 1972 (3) 1977 (3); v NZ 1971 (4); v In 1970 (3) 1975 (1); v P 1976 (1); *v E 1969 (3) 1973 (2) 1976 (4); v A 1975 (3); v In 1974 (4) 1978 (6); v P 1974 (2)*

Holding, M. A. 60: v E 1980 (4) 1985 (4); v A 1983 (3); v NZ 1984 (3); v In 1975 (4) 1982 (5); *v E 1976 (4) 1980 (5) 1984 (4); v A 1975 (3) 1979 (3) 1981 (3) 1984 (3); v NZ 1979 (3) 1986 (1); v In 1983 (6)*

Holford, D. A. J. 24: v E 1967 (4); v NZ 1971 (5); v In 1970 (1) 1975 (1); *v E 1966 (5); v A 1968 (2); v NZ 1968 (3); v In 1966 (1)*

Holt, J. K. 17: v E 1953 (5); v A 1954 (5); *v In 1958 (5); v P 1958 (2)*

Hooper, C. L. 99: v E 1989 (3) 1997 (6); v A 1990 (5) 1994 (4) 1998 (2); v SA 2000 (5); v NZ 2002 (2); v In 1996 (5) 2001 (5); v P 1987 (3) 1992 (3); v SL 1996 (2); *v E 1988 (5) 1991 (5) 1995 (5); v A 1988 (5) 1992 (4) 1996 (5); v SA 1998 (5); v In 1987 (3) 1994 (3); v P 1990 (3) 1997 (3) 2001 (2); v SL 1993 (1) 2001 (3); v Z 2001 (2)*

Howard, A. B. 1: v NZ 1971

Hunte, C. C. 44: v E 1959 (5); v A 1964 (5); v In 1961 (5); v P 1957 (5); *v E 1963 (5) 1966 (5); v A 1960 (5); v In 1958 (5) 1966 (3); v P 1958 (1)*

Hunte, E. A. C. 3: v E 1929 (3)

Hylton, L. G. 6: v E 1934 (4); *v E 1939 (2)*

Jacobs, R. D. 42: v A 1998 (4); v SA 2000 (5); v NZ 2002 (2); v In 2001 (3); v P 1999 (3); v Z 1999 (2); *v E 2000 (5); v A 2000 (5); v SA 1998 (5); v NZ 1999 (2); v P 2001 (2); v SL 2001 (3); v Z 2001 (1)*

Johnson, H. H. H. 3: v E 1947 (1); *v E 1950 (2)*

Johnson, T. F. 1: *v E 1939*

Jones, C. M. 4: v E 1929 (1) 1934 (3)

Jones, P. E. 9: v E 1947 (1); *v E 1950 (2); v A 1951 (1); v In 1948 (5)*

Joseph, D. R. E. 4: v A 1998 (4)

Julien, B. D. 24: v E 1973 (5); v In 1975 (4); v P 1976 (1); *v E 1973 (3) 1976 (2); v A 1975 (3); v In 1974 (4); v P 1974 (2)*

Jumadeen, R. R. 12: v A 1972 (1) 1977 (2); v NZ 1971 (1); v In 1975 (4); v P 1976 (1); *v E 1976 (1); v In 1978 (2)*

Kallicharran, A. I. 66: v E 1973 (5); v A 1972 (5) 1977 (2); v NZ 1971 (2); v In 1975 (4); v P 1976 (1); *v E 1973 (3) 1976 (3) 1980 (5); v A 1975 (6) 1979 (3); v NZ 1979 (3); v In 1974 (5) 1978 (6); v P 1974 (2) 1980 (4)*

Kanhai, R. B. 79: v E 1959 (5) 1967 (5) 1973 (5); v A 1964 (5) 1972 (5); v In 1961 (5) 1970 (5); v P 1957 (5); *v E 1957 (5) 1963 (5) 1966 (5) 1973 (3); v A 1960 (5) 1968 (5); v In 1958 (5) 1966 (3); v P 1958 (3)*

Kentish, E. S. M. 2: v E 1947 (1) 1953 (1)

King, C. L. 9: v P 1976 (1); *v E 1976 (3) 1980 (1); v A 1979 (1); v NZ 1979 (3)*

King, F. M. 14: v E 1953 (3); v A 1954 (4); v In 1952 (5); v NZ 1955 (2)

King, L. A. 2: v E 1967 (1); v In 1961 (1)

King, R. D. 14: v P 1999 (3); v Z 1999 (2); *v E 2000 (4); v SA 1998 (1); v NZ 1999 (2); v Z 2001 (2)*

Lambert, C. B. 5: v E 1997 (2); *v E 1991 (1); v SA 1998 (2)*

Lara, B. C. 90: v E 1993 (5) 1997 (6); v A 1994 (4) 1998 (4); v SA 1991 (1) 2000 (5); v NZ 1995 (2) 2002 (2); v In 1996 (5) 2001 (5); v P 1992 (3); v SL 1996 (2); *v E 1995 (6) 2000 (5); v A 1992 (5) 1996 (5) 2000 (5); v SA 1998 (5); v NZ 1994 (2) 1999 (2); v In 1994 (3); v P 1990 (1) 1997 (3); v SL 1993 (1) 2001 (3)*

Lashley, P. D. 4: *v E 1966 (2); v A 1960 (2)*

Legall, R. 4: v In 1952 (4)

Lewis, D. M. 3: v In 1970 (3)

Lewis, R. N. 3: *v SA 1998 (2); v P 1997 (1)*

Lloyd, C. H. 110: v E 1967 (5) 1973 (5) 1980 (4); v A 1972 (3) 1977 (2) 1983 (4); v NZ 1971 (2); v In 1970 (5) 1975 (4) 1982 (5); v P 1976 (5); *v E 1969 (3) 1973 (3) 1976 (5) 1980 (4) 1984 (5); v A 1968 (4) 1975 (6) 1979 (2) 1981 (3) 1984 (5); v NZ 1968 (3) 1979 (3); v In 1966 (3) 1974 (5) 1983 (6); v P 1974 (2) 1980 (4)*

Logie, A. L. 52: v E 1989 (3); v A 1983 (1) 1990 (5); v NZ 1984 (4); v In 1982 (5) 1988 (4); v P 1987 (3); *v E 1988 (5) 1991 (4); v A 1988 (5); v NZ 1986 (3); v In 1983 (3) 1987 (4); v P 1990 (3)*

McGarrell, N. C. 4: v SA 2000 (1); *v SL 2001 (1); v Z 2001 (2)*

McLean, N. A. M. 19: v E 1997 (4); v SA 2000 (2); v P 1999 (3); *v E 2000 (2); v A 2000 (5); v SA 1998 (4)*

McMorris, E. D. A. St J. 13: v E 1959 (4); v In 1961 (5); v P 1957 (1); *v E 1963 (2) 1966 (2)*

McWatt, C. A. 6: v E 1953 (5); v A 1954 (1)

Madray, I. S. 2: v P 1957 (2)

Marshall, M. D. 81: v E 1980 (1) 1985 (5) 1989 (2); v A 1983 (4) 1990 (5); v NZ 1984 (4); v In 1982 (5) 1988 (3); v P 1987 (2); *v E 1980 (4) 1984 (4) 1988 (5) 1991 (5); v A 1984 (5) 1988 (5); v NZ 1986 (3); v In 1978 (3) 1983 (6); v P 1980 (4) 1986 (3) 1990 (3)*

Marshall, N. E. 1: v A 1954
Marshall, R. E. 4: *v A 1951 (2); v NZ 1951 (2)*
Martin, F. R. 9: v E 1929 (1); *v E 1928 (3); v A 1930 (5)*
Martindale, E. A. 10: v E 1934 (4); *v E 1933 (3) 1939 (3)*
Mattis, E. H. 4: v E 1980 (4)
Mendonca, I. L. 2: v In 1961 (2)
Merry, C. A. 2: *v E 1933 (2)*
Miller, R. 1: v In 1952
Moodie, G. H. 1: v E 1934
Moseley, E. A. 2: v E 1989 (2)
Murray, D. A. 19: v E 1980 (4); v A 1977 (3); *v A 1981 (2); v In 1978 (6); v P 1980 (4)*
Murray, D. L. 62: v E 1967 (5) 1973 (5); v A 1972 (4) 1977 (2); v In 1975 (4); v P 1976 (5); *v E 1963 (5) 1973 (3) 1976 (5) 1980 (5); v A 1975 (6) 1979 (3); v In 1962 (5) 1970 (1) 1974 (2)*
Murray, J. R. 33: v E 1993 (5) 1997 (1); v A 1994 (3); v In 1996 (2) 2001 (2); v P 1992 (3); *v E 1995 (4); v A 1992 (3) 1996 (2); v SA 1998 (2); v NZ 1994 (2); v In 1994 (3); v SL 1993 (1)*

Nagamootoo, M. V. 4: v NZ 2002 (1); v In 2001 (1); *v E 2000 (1); v A 2000 (1)*
Nanan, R. 1: *v P 1980*
Neblett, J. M. 1: v E 1934
Noreiga, J. M. 4: v In 1970 (4)
Nunes, R. K. 4: v E 1929 (1); *v E 1928 (3)*
Nurse, S. M. 29: v E 1959 (1) 1967 (5); v A 1964 (4); v In 1961 (1); *v E 1966 (5); v A 1960 (3) 1968 (5); v NZ 1968 (3); v In 1966 (2)*

Padmore, A. L. 2: v In 1975 (1); *v E 1976 (1)*
Pairaudeau, B. H. 13: v E 1953 (2); v In 1952 (5); *v E 1957 (2); v NZ 1955 (4)*
Parry, D. R. 12: v A 1977 (5); *v NZ 1979 (3); v In 1978 (6)*
Passailaigue, C. C. 1: v E 1929
Patterson, B. P. 28: v E 1985 (5) 1989 (1); v A 1990 (5); v SA 1991 (5); v P 1987 (1); *v E 1988 (2) 1991 (5); v A 1988 (4) 1992 (1); v In 1987 (4); v P 1986 (1)*
Payne, T. R. O. 1: v E 1985
Perry, N. O. 4: v A 1998 (3); *v NZ 1999 (1)*
Phillip, N. 9: v A 1977 (3); *v In 1978 (6)*
Pierre, L. R. 1: v E 1947
Powell, D. B. 1: v NZ 2002
Powell, R. L. 1: *v NZ 1999*

Rae, A. F. 15: v In 1952 (2); *v E 1950 (4); v A 1951 (3); v NZ 1951 (1); v In 1948 (5)*
Ragoonath, S. 2: v A 1998 (2)
Ramadhin, S. 43: v E 1953 (5) 1959 (4); v A 1954 (4); v In 1952 (4); *v E 1950 (4) 1957 (5); v A 1951 (5) 1960 (2); v NZ 1951 (2) 1955 (4); v In 1958 (2); v P 1958 (2)*
Ramnarine, D. 12: v E 1997 (2); v SA 2000 (5); *v NZ 1999 (1); v P 2001 (1); v SL 2001 (3)*
Reifer, F. L. 4: v SL 1996 (2); *v SA 1998 (2)*
Richards, I. V. A. 121: v E 1980 (4) 1985 (5) 1989 (3); v A 1977 (2) 1983 (5) 1990 (5); v NZ 1984 (3); v In 1975 (4) 1982 (5) 1988 (4); v P 1976 (5) 1987 (2); *v E 1976 (4) 1980 (5) 1984 (5) 1988 (5) 1991 (5); v A 1975 (6) 1979 (3) 1981 (3) 1984 (5) 1988 (5); v NZ 1986 (3); v In 1974 (5) 1983 (6) 1987 (4); v P 1974 (2) 1980 (4) 1986 (3)*
Richardson, R. B. 86: v E 1985 (5) 1989 (4) 1993 (4); v A 1983 (5) 1990 (5) 1994 (4); v SA 1991 (1); v NZ 1984 (1); v In 1988 (4); v P 1987 (3) 1992 (3); *v E 1988 (3) 1991 (5) 1995 (6); v A 1984 (5) 1988 (4) 1992 (5); v NZ 1986 (3); v In 1983 (1) 1987 (4); v P 1986 (3) 1990 (3); v SL 1993 (1)*
Rickards, K. R. 2: v E 1947 (1); *v A 1951 (1)*
Roach, C. A. 16: v E 1929 (4) 1934 (1); *v E 1928 (3) 1933 (3); v A 1930 (5)*
Roberts, A. M. E. 47: v E 1973 (1) 1980 (3); v A 1977 (2); v In 1975 (2) 1982 (5); v P 1976 (5); *v E 1976 (4) 1980 (3); v A 1975 (5) 1979 (3) 1981 (2); v NZ 1979 (2); v In 1974 (5) 1983 (2); v P 1974 (2)*
Roberts, A. T. 1: *v NZ 1955*
Roberts, L. A. 1: v A 1998
Rodriguez, W. V. 5: v E 1967 (1); v A 1964 (1); v In 1961 (2); *v E 1963 (1)*
Rose, F. A. 19: v E 1997 (1); v In 1996 (5); v P 1999 (1); v SL 1996 (2); v Z 1999 (2); *v E 2000 (3); v SA 1998 (1); v NZ 1999 (2); v P 1997 (2)*

Rowe, L. G. 30: v E 1973 (5); v A 1972 (3); v NZ 1971 (4); v In 1975 (4); *v E 1976 (2); v A 1975 (6) 1979 (3); v NZ 1979 (3)*

St Hill, E. L. 2: v E 1929 (2)
St Hill, W. H. 3: v E 1929 (1); *v E 1928 (2)*
Samuels, M. N. 12: v SA 2000 (4); *v A 2000 (3); v SL 2001 (3); v Z 2001 (2)*
Samuels, R. G. 6: v NZ 1995 (2); *v A 1996 (4)*
Sanford, A. 7: v NZ 2002 (2); v In 2001 (5)
Sarwan, R. R. 24: v SA 2000 (4); v NZ 2002 (2); v In 2001 (5); v P 1999 (2); *v E 2000 (3); v A 2000 (3); v SL 2001 (3); v Z 2001 (2)*
Scarlett, R. O. 3: v E 1959 (3)
Scott, A. P. H. 1: v In 1952
Scott, O. C. 8: v E 1929 (1); *v E 1928 (2); v A 1930 (5)*
Sealey, B. J. 1: *v E 1933*
Sealy, J. E. D. 11: v E 1929 (2) 1934 (4); *v E 1939 (3); v A 1930 (2)*
Shepherd, J. N. 5: v In 1970 (2); *v E 1969 (3)*
Shillingford, G. C. 7: v NZ 1971 (2); v In 1970 (3); *v E 1969 (2)*
Shillingford, I. T. 4: v A 1977 (1); v P 1976 (3)
Shivnarine, S. 8: *v In 1978 (3)*
Simmons, P. V. 26: v E 1993 (2); v SA 1991 (1); v NZ 1995 (2); v P 1987 (1) 1992 (3); *v E 1991 (5); v A 1992 (5) 1996 (1); v In 1987 (1) 1994 (3); v P 1997 (1); v SL 1993 (1)*
Singh, C. K. 2: v E 1959 (2)
Small, J. A. 3: v E 1929 (1); *v E 1928 (2)*
Small, M. A. 2: v A 1983 (1); *v E 1984 (1)*
Smith, C. W. 5: v In 1961 (1); *v A 1960 (4)*
Smith, O. G. 26: v A 1954 (4); v P 1957 (5); *v E 1957 (5); v NZ 1955 (4); v In 1958 (5); v P 1958 (3)*
Sobers, G. S. 93: v E 1953 (1) 1959 (5) 1967 (5) 1973 (4); v A 1954 (4) 1964 (5); v NZ 1971 (5); v In 1961 (5) 1970 (5); v P 1957 (5); *v E 1957 (5) 1963 (5) 1966 (5) 1969 (3) 1973 (3); v A 1960 (5) 1968 (5); v NZ 1955 (4) 1968 (3); v In 1958 (5) 1966 (3); v P 1958 (3)*
Solomon, J. S. 27: v E 1959 (2); v A 1964 (4); v In 1961 (4); *v E 1963 (5); v A 1960 (5); v In 1958 (4); v P 1958 (3)*
Stayers, S. C. 4: v In 1961 (4)
Stollmeyer, J. B. 32: v E 1947 (2) 1953 (5); v A 1954 (2); v In 1952 (5); *v E 1939 (3) 1950 (4); v A 1951 (2); v NZ 1951 (2); v In 1948 (4)*
Stollmeyer, V. H. 1: *v E 1939*
Stuart, C. E. L. 6: *v A 2000 (2); v SL 2001 (2); v Z 2001 (2)*

Taylor, J. 3: v P 1957 (1); *v In 1958 (1); v P 1958 (1)*
Thompson, P. I. C. 2: v NZ 1995 (1); *v A 1996 (1)*
Trim, J. 4: v E 1947 (1); *v A 1951 (1); v In 1948 (2)*

Valentine, A. L. 36: v E 1953 (3); v A 1954 (3); v In 1952 (5) 1961 (2); v P 1957 (1); *v E 1950 (4) 1957 (2); v A 1951 (5) 1960 (5); v NZ 1951 (2) 1955 (4)*
Valentine, V. A. 2: *v E 1933 (2)*

Walcott, C. L. 44: v E 1947 (4) 1953 (5) 1959 (2); v A 1954 (5); v In 1952 (5); v P 1957 (4); *v E 1950 (4) 1957 (5); v A 1951 (3); v NZ 1951 (2); v In 1948 (5)*
Walcott, L. A. 1: v E 1929
Wallace, P. A. 7: v E 1997 (2); *v SA 1998 (4); v P 1997 (1)*
Walsh, C. A. 132: v E 1985 (1) 1989 (3) 1993 (5) 1997 (6); v A 1990 (5) 1994 (4) 1998 (4); v SA 1991 (1) 2000 (5); v NZ 1984 (1) 1995 (2); v In 1988 (4) 1996 (4); v P 1987 (3) 1992 (3) 1999 (3); v SL 1996 (2); v Z 1999 (2); *v E 1988 (5) 1991 (5) 1995 (6) 2000 (5); v A 1984 (5) 1988 (5) 1992 (5) 1996 (5) 2000 (5); v SA 1998 (4); v NZ 1986 (3) 1994 (2) 1999 (2); v In 1987 (4) 1994 (3); v P 1986 (3) 1990 (3) 1997 (3); v SL 1993 (1)*
Watson, C. 7: v E 1959 (5); v In 1961 (1); *v A 1960 (1)*
Weekes, E. D. 48: v E 1947 (4) 1953 (4); v A 1954 (5); v In 1952 (5); v P 1957 (5); *v E 1950 (4) 1957 (5); v A 1951 (5); v NZ 1951 (2) 1955 (4); v In 1948 (5)*
Weekes, K. H. 2: *v E 1939 (2)*
White, W. A. 2: v A 1964 (2)
Wight, C. V. 2: v E 1929 (1); *v E 1928 (1)*
Wight, G. L. 1: v In 1952

Wiles, C. A. 1: *v E 1933*
Willett, E. T. 5: v A 1972 (3); *v In 1974 (2)*
Williams, A. B. 7: v A 1977 (3); *v In 1978 (4)*
Williams, D. 11: v E 1997 (5); v SA 1991 (1); *v A 1992 (2); v P 1997 (3)*
Williams, E. A. V. 4: v E 1947 (3); *v E 1939 (1)*
Williams, S. C. 31: v E 1993 (1) 1997 (4); v A 1994 (4); v In 1996 (5) 2001 (3); v SL 1996 (2); *v E 1995 (2); v SA 1998 (2); v NZ 1994 (2); v In 1994 (3); v P 1997 (3)*
Wishart, K. L. 1: v E 1934
Worrell, F. M. M. 51: v E 1947 (3) 1953 (4) 1959 (4); v A 1954 (4); v In 1952 (5) 1961 (5); *v E 1950 (4) 1957 (5) 1963 (5); v A 1951 (5) 1960 (5); v NZ 1951 (2)*

NEW ZEALAND

Number of Test cricketers: 221

Adams, A. R. 1: v E 2001
Alabaster, J. C. 21: v E 1962 (2); v WI 1955 (1); v In 1967 (4); *v E 1958 (2); v SA 1961 (5); v WI 1971 (2); v In 1955 (4); v P 1955 (1)*
Allcott, C. F. W. 6: v E 1929 (2); v SA 1931 (1); *v E 1931 (3)*
Allott, G. I. 10: v E 1996 (2); v SA 1998 (2); v Z 1995 (2); *v E 1999 (2); v A 1997 (2)*
Anderson, R. W. 9: v E 1977 (3); *v E 1978 (3); v P 1976 (3)*
Anderson, W. M. 1: v A 1945
Andrews, B. 2: *v A 1973 (2)*
Astle, N. J. 55: v E 1996 (3) 2001 (3); v A 1999 (3); v SA 1998 (3); v WI 1999 (2); v In 1998 (1); v P 2000 (3); v SL 1996 (2); v Z 1995 (2) 1997 (2) 2000 (1); v B 2001 (1); *v E 1999 (4); v A 1997 (3) 2001 (3); v SA 2000 (3); v WI 1995 (2) 2002 (2); v In 1999 (3); v P 1996 (3); v SL 1997 (3); v Z 1997 (2) 2000 (2)*

Badcock, F. T. 7: v E 1929 (3) 1932 (2); v SA 1931 (2)
Barber, R. T. 1: v WI 1955
Bartlett, G. A. 10: v E 1965 (2); v In 1967 (2); v P 1964 (1); *v SA 1961 (5)*
Barton, P. T. 7: v E 1962 (3); *v SA 1961 (4)*
Beard, D. D. 4: v WI 1951 (2) 1955 (2)
Beck, J. E. F. 8: v WI 1955 (4); *v SA 1953 (4)*
Bell, M. D. 13: v SA 1998 (1); v In 1998 (2); v P 2000 (3); *v E 1999 (3); v A 2001 (2); v In 1999 (2)*
Bell, W. 2: *v SA 1953 (2)*
Bilby, G. P. 2: v E 1965 (2)
Blain, T. E. 11: v A 1992 (2); v P 1993 (3); *v E 1986 (1); v A 1993 (3); v In 1988 (2)*
Blair, R. W. 19: v E 1954 (1) 1958 (2) 1962 (2); v SA 1952 (2) 1963 (3); v WI 1955 (2); *v E 1958 (3); v SA 1953 (4)*
Blunt, R. C. 9: v E 1929 (4); v SA 1931 (2); *v E 1931 (3)*
Bolton, B. A. 2: v E 1958 (2)
Bond, S. E. 6: v B 2001 (2); *v A 2001 (2); v WI 2002 (2)*
Boock, S. L. 30: v E 1977 (3) 1983 (2) 1987 (1); v WI 1979 (3) 1986 (2); v P 1978 (3) 1984 (2) 1988 (1); *v E 1978 (3); v A 1985 (1); v WI 1984 (3); v P 1984 (3); v SL 1983 (3)*
Bracewell, B. P. 6: v P 1978 (1) 1984 (1); *v E 1978 (3); v A 1980 (1)*
Bracewell, J. G. 41: v E 1987 (3); v A 1985 (2) 1989 (1); v WI 1986 (3); v In 1980 (1) 1989 (2); v P 1988 (2); *v E 1983 (4) 1986 (3) 1990 (3); v A 1980 (3) 1985 (2) 1987 (3); v WI 1984 (1); v In 1988 (3); v P 1984 (2); v SL 1983 (2) 1986 (1)*
Bradburn, G. E. 7: v P 2000 (2); v SL 1990 (1); *v P 1990 (3); v SL 1992 (1)*
Bradburn, W. P. 2: v SA 1963 (2)
Brown, V. R. 2: *v A 1985 (2)*
Burgess, M. G. 50: v E 1970 (1) 1977 (3); v A 1973 (1) 1976 (2); v WI 1968 (2); v In 1967 (4) 1975 (3); v P 1972 (3) 1978 (3); *v E 1969 (2) 1973 (3) 1978 (3); v A 1980 (3); v WI 1971 (5); v In 1969 (3) 1976 (3); v P 1969 (3) 1976 (3)*
Burke, C. 1: v A 1945
Burtt, T. B. 10: v E 1946 (1) 1950 (2); v SA 1952 (1); v WI 1951 (2); *v E 1949 (4)*
Butler, I. G. 4: v E 2001 (2); *v WI 2002 (2)*
Butterfield, L. A. 1: v A 1945

Cairns, B. L. 43: v E 1974 (1) 1977 (1) 1983 (3); v A 1976 (1) 1981 (3); v WI 1979 (3); v In 1975 (1) 1980 (3); v P 1978 (3) 1984 (3); v SL 1982 (2); *v E 1978 (2) 1983 (4); v A 1973 (1) 1980 (3) 1985 (1); v WI 1984 (2); v In 1976 (2); v P 1976 (2); v SL 1983 (2)*

Cairns, C. L. 55: v E 1991 (3) 1996 (3) 2001 (1); v A 1992 (2) 1999 (3); v WI 1999 (2); v In 1998 (2); v P 1993 (1) 1995 (1); v SL 1990 (1) 1996 (2); v Z 1995 (2) 1997 (2); v B 2001 (2); *v E 1999 (4); v A 1989 (1) 1993 (2) 1997 (3) 2001 (3); v In 1995 (3) 1999 (3); v P 1996 (2); v SL 1997 (3); v Z 1997 (2) 2000 (2)*

Cameron, F. J. 19: v E 1962 (3); v SA 1963 (3); v P 1964 (3); *v E 1965 (2); v SA 1961 (5); v In 1964 (1); v P 1964 (2)*

Cave, H. B. 19: v E 1954 (2); v WI 1955 (3); *v E 1949 (4) 1958 (2); v In 1955 (5); v P 1955 (3)*

Chapple, M. E. 14: v E 1954 (1) 1965 (1); v SA 1952 (1) 1963 (1); v WI 1955 (1); *v SA 1953 (5) 1961 (2)*

Chatfield, E. J. 43: v E 1974 (1) 1977 (1) 1983 (3) 1987 (3); v A 1976 (2) 1981 (1) 1985 (3); v WI 1986 (3); v P 1984 (3) 1988 (2); v SL 1982 (2); *v E 1983 (3) 1986 (1); v A 1985 (2) 1987 (2); v WI 1984 (4); v In 1988 (3); v P 1984 (1); v SL 1983 (2) 1986 (1)*

Cleverley, D. C. 2: v SA 1931 (1); v A 1945 (1)

Collinge, R. O. 35: v E 1970 (2) 1974 (2) 1977 (3); v A 1973 (3) 1976 (2); v In 1967 (2) 1975 (3); v P 1964 (3) 1972 (2); *v E 1965 (3) 1969 (1) 1973 (3) 1978 (1); v In 1964 (2) 1976 (1); v P 1964 (2) 1976 (2)*

Colquhoun, I. A. 2: v E 1954 (2)

Coney, J. V. 52: v E 1983 (3); v A 1973 (2) 1981 (3) 1985 (3); v WI 1979 (3) 1986 (3); v In 1980 (3); v P 1978 (3) 1984 (3); v SL 1982 (2); *v E 1983 (4) 1986 (3); v A 1973 (2) 1980 (2) 1985 (3); v WI 1984 (4); v P 1984 (3); v SL 1983 (3)*

Congdon, B. E. 61: v E 1965 (3) 1970 (2) 1974 (2) 1977 (3); v A 1973 (3) 1976 (2); v WI 1968 (3); v In 1967 (4) 1975 (3); v P 1964 (3) 1972 (3); *v E 1965 (3) 1969 (3) 1973 (3) 1978 (3); v A 1973 (3); v WI 1971 (5); v In 1964 (3) 1969 (3); v P 1964 (1) 1969 (3)*

Cowie, J. 9: v E 1946 (1); v A 1945 (1); *v E 1937 (3) 1949 (4)*

Cresswell G. F. 3: v E 1950 (2); *v E 1949 (1)*

Cromb, I. B. 5: v SA 1931 (2); *v E 1931 (3)*

Crowe, J. J. 39: v E 1983 (3) 1987 (2); v A 1989 (1); v WI 1986 (3); v P 1984 (3) 1988 (2); v SL 1982 (2); *v E 1983 (2) 1986 (3); v A 1985 (3) 1987 (3) 1989 (1); v WI 1984 (4); v P 1984 (3); v SL 1983 (3) 1986 (1)*

Crowe, M. D. 77: v E 1983 (3) 1987 (3) 1991 (3); v A 1981 (3) 1985 (3) 1992 (3); v SA 1994 (1); v WI 1986 (3); v In 1989 (3); v P 1984 (3) 1988 (2); v SL 1990 (2); *v E 1983 (4) 1986 (3) 1990 (3) 1994 (3); v A 1985 (3) 1987 (3) 1989 (1) 1993 (1); v SA 1994 (3); v WI 1984 (4); v In 1995 (3); v P 1984 (3) 1990 (3); v SL 1983 (3) 1986 (1) 1992 (2); v Z 1992 (2)*

Cunis, R. S. 20: v E 1965 (3) 1970 (2); v SA 1963 (1); v WI 1968 (3); *v E 1969 (1); v WI 1971 (5); v In 1969 (3); v P 1969 (2)*

D'Arcy, J. W. 5: *v E 1958 (5)*

Davis, H. T. 5: v E 1996 (1); v SL 1996 (2); *v E 1994 (1); v Z 1997 (1)*

de Groen, R. P. 5: v P 1993 (2); *v A 1993 (2); v SA 1994 (1)*

Dempster, C. S. 10: v E 1929 (4) 1932 (2); v SA 1931 (2); *v E 1931 (2)*

Dempster, E. W. 5: v SA 1952 (1); *v SA 1953 (4)*

Dick, A. E. 17: v E 1962 (3); v SA 1963 (2); v P 1964 (2); *v E 1965 (2); v SA 1961 (5); v P 1964 (3)*

Dickinson, G. R. 3: v E 1929 (2); v SA 1931 (1)

Donnelly, M. P. 7: *v E 1937 (3) 1949 (4)*

Doull, S. B. 32: v E 1996 (3); v A 1999 (2); v SA 1998 (3); v WI 1994 (3); v In 1998 (2); v P 1993 (3); v SL 1996 (2); v Z 1997 (2); *v E 1999 (1); v A 1993 (2) 1997 (3); v SA 1994 (3); v P 1996 (2); v SL 1997 (1); v Z 1992 (1)*

Dowling, G. T. 39: v E 1962 (3) 1970 (2); v SA 1963 (1); v WI 1968 (3); v In 1967 (4); v P 1964 (2); *v E 1965 (3) 1969 (3); v SA 1961 (4); v WI 1971 (2); v In 1964 (4) 1969 (3); v P 1964 (2) 1969 (3)*

Drum, C. J. 5: v E 2001 (3); v P 2000 (1); v B 2001 (1)

Dunning, J. A. 4: v E 1932 (1); *v E 1937 (3)*

Edgar, B. A. 39: v E 1983 (3); v A 1981 (3) 1985 (3); v WI 1979 (3); v In 1980 (3); v P 1978 (3); v SL 1982 (2); *v E 1978 (3) 1983 (4) 1986 (3); v A 1980 (3) 1985 (3); v P 1984 (3)*

Edwards, G. N. 8: v E 1977 (1); v A 1976 (2); v In 1980 (3); *v E 1978 (2)*

Emery, R. W. G. 2: v WI 1951 (2)

Fisher, F. E. 1: v SA 1952

Fleming, S. P. 71: v E 1996 (3) 2001 (3); v A 1999 (3); v SA 1994 (1); v WI 1994 (2) 1999 (2); v In 1993 (1) 1998 (2); v P 1995 (1) 2000 (3); v SL 1994 (2) 1996 (2); v Z 1995 (2) 1997 (2) 2000 (1); v B 2001 (2); *v E 1994 (3) 1999 (4); v A 1997 (3) 2001 (3); SA 1994 (3) 2000 (3); v WI 1995 (2) 2002 (2); v In 1995 (3) 1999 (3); v P 1996 (2) 2002 (1); v SL 1997 (3); v Z 1997 (2) 2000 (2)*

Foley, H. 1: v E 1929

Franklin, J. E. C. 2: v P 2000 (2)

Franklin, T. J. 21: v E 1987 (2); v A 1985 (1) 1989 (1); v In 1989 (3); v SL 1990 (3); *v E 1983 (1) 1990 (3); v In 1988 (3); v P 1990 (3)*

Freeman, D. L. 2: v E 1932 (2)

Gallichan, N. 1: *v E 1937*

Gedye, S. G. 4: v SA 1963 (3); v P 1964 (1)

Germon, L. K. 12: v E 1996 (2); v P 1995 (1); v Z 1995 (2); *v WI 1995 (2); v In 1995 (3); v P 1996 (2)*

Gillespie, S. R. 1: v A 1985

Gray, E. J. 10: *v E 1983 (2) 1986 (3); v A 1987 (1); v In 1988 (1); v P 1984 (2); v SL 1986 (1)*

Greatbatch, M. J. 41: v E 1987 (2) 1991 (1); v A 1989 (1) 1992 (3); v In 1989 (3) 1993 (1); v P 1988 (1) 1992 (1) 1993 (3); v SL 1990 (2) 1994 (2); *v E 1990 (3) 1994 (1); v A 1989 (1) 1993 (3); v In 1988 (3) 1995 (3); v P 1990 (3) 1996 (2); v Z 1992 (2)*

Guillen, S. C. 3: v WI 1955 (3)

Guy, J. W. 12: v E 1958 (2); v WI 1955 (2); *v SA 1961 (2); v In 1955 (5); v P 1955 (1)*

Hadlee, D. R. 26: v E 1974 (2) 1977 (1); v A 1973 (3) 1976 (1); v In 1975 (3); v P 1972 (2); *v E 1969 (2) 1973 (3); v A 1973 (3); v In 1969 (3); v P 1969 (3)*

Hadlee, R. J. 86: v E 1977 (3) 1983 (3) 1987 (1); v A 1973 (3) 1976 (2) 1981 (3) 1985 (3) 1989 (1); v WI 1979 (3) 1986 (3); v In 1975 (3) 1980 (3) 1989 (3); v P 1972 (1) 1978 (3) 1984 (3) 1988 (2); v SL 1982 (2); *v E 1973 (1) 1978 (3) 1983 (4) 1986 (3) 1990 (3); v A 1973 (3) 1980 (3) 1985 (3) 1987 (3); v WI 1984 (4); v In 1976 (3) 1988 (3); v P 1976 (3); v SL 1983 (3) 1986 (1)*

Hadlee, W. A. 11: v E 1946 (1) 1950 (2); v A 1945 (1); *v E 1937 (3) 1949 (4)*

Harford, N. S. 8: *v E 1958 (4); v In 1955 (2); v P 1955 (2)*

Harford, R. I. 3: v In 1967 (3)

Harris, C. Z. 23: v E 2001 (1); v A 1992 (1); v SA 1998 (3); v P 1992 (1); *v E 1999 (1); v A 1993 (1) 1997 (1); v WI 1995 (2) 2002 (2); v In 1999 (1); v P 1996 (2) 2002 (1); v SL 1992 (2) 1997 (2); v Z 1997 (2)*

Harris, P. G. Z. 9: v P 1964 (1); *v SA 1961 (5); v In 1955 (1); v P 1955 (2)*

Harris, R. M. 2: v E 1958 (2)

Hart, M. N. 14: v SA 1994 (1); v WI 1994 (2); v In 1993 (2); v P 1993 (2); *v E 1994 (3); v SA 1994 (3); v In 1995 (2)*

Hart, R. G. 3: *v WI 2002 (2); v P 2002 (1)*

Hartland, B. R. 9: v E 1991 (3); v In 1993 (1); v P 1992 (1) 1993 (1); *v E 1994 (1); v SL 1992 (2)*

Haslam, M. J. 4: *v In 1995 (2); v Z 1992 (2)*

Hastings, B. F. 31: v E 1972 (2); v A 1973 (3); v WI 1968 (3); v In 1975 (1); v P 1972 (3); *v E 1969 (3) 1973 (3); v A 1973 (3); v WI 1971 (5); v In 1969 (2); v P 1969 (3)*

Hayes, J. A. 15: v E 1950 (2) 1954 (1); v WI 1951 (2); *v E 1958 (4); v In 1955 (5); v P 1955 (1)*

Henderson, M. 1: v E 1929

Horne, M. J. 33: v E 1996 (1) 2001 (2); v A 1999 (3); v SA 1998 (3); v WI 1999 (1); v In 1998 (2); v SL 1996 (2); v Z 1997 (2) 2000 (1); v B 2001 (2); *v E 1999 (4); v A 1997 (1); v In 1999 (3); v P 2002 (1); v SL 1997 (3); v Z 1997 (2) 2000 (1)*

Horne, P. A. 4: v WI 1986 (1); *v A 1987 (1); v P 1990 (1); v SL 1986 (1)*

Hough, K. W. 2: v E 1958 (2)

Howarth, G. P. 47: v E 1974 (2) 1977 (3) 1983 (3); v A 1976 (2) 1981 (3); v WI 1979 (3); v In 1980 (3); v P 1978 (3) 1984 (3); v SL 1982 (2); *v E 1978 (3) 1983 (4); v A 1980 (2); v WI 1984 (4); v In 1976 (2); v P 1976 (2); v SL 1983 (3)*

Howarth, H. J. 30: v E 1970 (2) 1974 (2); v A 1973 (3) 1976 (2); v In 1975 (2); v P 1972 (3); *v E 1969 (3) 1973 (2); v WI 1971 (5); v In 1969 (3); v P 1969 (3)*

James, K. C. 11: v E 1929 (4) 1932 (2); v SA 1931 (2); *v E 1931 (3)*

Jarvis, T. W. 13: v E 1965 (1); v P 1972 (3); *v WI 1971 (4); v In 1964 (2); v P 1964 (3)*

Jones, A. H. 39: v E 1987 (1) 1991 (3); v A 1989 (1) 1992 (3); v WI 1994 (2); v In 1989 (3); v P 1988 (2) 1992 (1) 1993 (3); v SL 1990 (3); *v E 1990 (3); v A 1987 (3) 1993 (3); v In 1988 (3); v SL 1986 (1) 1992 (2); v Z 1992 (2)*

Kennedy, R. J. 4: v Z 1995 (2); *v WI 1995 (2)*
Kerr, J. L. 7: v E 1932 (2); v SA 1931 (1); *v E 1931 (2) 1937 (2)*
Kuggeleijn, C. M. 2: *v In 1988 (2)*

Larsen, G. R. 8: v SA 1994 (1); v P 1995 (1); v SL 1994 (2); v Z 1995 (1); *v E 1994 (1); v WI 1995 (2)*
Latham, R. T. 4: v E 1991 (1); v P 1992 (1); *v Z 1992 (2)*
Lees, W. K. 21: v E 1977 (2); v A 1976 (1); v WI 1979 (3); v P 1978 (3); v SL 1982 (2); *v E 1983 (2); v A 1980 (2); v In 1976 (3); v P 1976 (3)*
Leggat, I. B. 1: *v SA 1953*
Leggat, J. G. 9: v E 1954 (1); v SA 1952 (1); v WI 1951 (1) 1955 (1); *v In 1955 (3); v P 1955 (2)*
Lissette, A. F. 2: v WI 1955 (2)
Loveridge, G. R. 1: v Z 1995
Lowry, T. C. 7: v E 1929 (4); *v E 1931 (3)*

McEwan, P. E. 4: v WI 1979 (1); *v A 1980 (2); v P 1984 (1)*
MacGibbon, A. R. 26: v E 1950 (2) 1954 (2); v SA 1952 (1); v WI 1955 (3); *v E 1958 (5); v SA 1953 (5); v In 1955 (5); v P 1955 (3)*
McGirr, H. M. 2: v E 1929 (2)
McGregor, S. N. 25: v E 1954 (2) 1958 (2); v SA 1963 (3); v WI 1955 (4); v P 1964 (2); *v SA 1961 (5); v In 1955 (4); v P 1955 (3)*
McLeod, E. G. 1: v E 1929
McMahon, T. G. 5: v WI 1955 (1); *v In 1955 (3); v P 1955 (1)*
McMillan, C. D. 42: v E 2001 (3); v A 1999 (3); v SA 1998 (1); v WI 1999 (2); v In 1998 (2); v P 2000 (3); v Z 1997 (2) 2000 (1); v B 2001 (2); *v E 1999 (4); v A 1997 (3) 2001 (3); v SA 2000 (3); v WI 2002 (2); v In 1999 (2); v P 2002 (1); v SL 1997 (3); v Z 2000 (2)*
McRae, D. A. N. 1: v A 1945
Marshall, H. J. H. 1: *v SA 2000*
Martin, C. S. 11: v E 2001 (1); v P 2000 (3); v Z 2000 (1); v B 2001 (1); *v A 2001 (1); v SA 2000 (3); v P 2002 (1)*
Matheson, A. M. 2: v E 1929 (1); *v E 1931 (1)*
Meale, T. 2: *v E 1958 (2)*
Merritt, W. E. 6: v E 1929 (4); *v E 1931 (2)*
Meuli, E. M. 1: v SA 1952
Milburn, B. D. 3: v WI 1968 (3)
Miller, L. S. M. 13: v SA 1952 (2); v WI 1955 (3); *v E 1958 (4); v SA 1953 (4)*
Mills, J. E. 7: v E 1929 (3) 1932 (1); *v E 1931 (3)*
Moir, A. M. 17: v E 1950 (2) 1954 (2) 1958 (2); v WI 1951 (2) 1955 (1); *v E 1958 (2); v In 1955 (2); v P 1955 (3)*
Moloney D. A. R. 3: *v E 1937 (3)*
Mooney, F. L. H. 14: v E 1950 (2); v SA 1952 (2); v WI 1951 (2); *v E 1949 (3); v SA 1953 (5)*
Morgan, R. W. 20: v E 1965 (2) 1970 (2); v WI 1968 (1); v P 1964 (2); *v E 1965 (3); v WI 1971 (3); v In 1964 (4); v P 1964 (3)*
Morrison, B. D. 1: v E 1962
Morrison, D. K. 48: v E 1987 (3) 1991 (3) 1996 (1); v A 1989 (1) 1992 (3); v SA 1994 (1); v WI 1994 (2); v In 1989 (3) 1993 (1); v P 1988 (1) 1992 (1) 1993 (2) 1995 (1); v SL 1990 (3) 1994 (1); *v E 1990 (3); v A 1987 (3) 1989 (1) 1993 (3); v SA 1994 (2); v WI 1995 (2); v In 1988 (1) 1995 (3); v P 1990 (3)*
Morrison, J. F. M. 17: v E 1974 (2); v A 1973 (3) 1981 (3); v In 1975 (3); *v A 1973 (3); v In 1976 (1); v P 1976 (2)*
Motz, R. C. 32: v E 1962 (2) 1965 (3); v SA 1963 (2); v WI 1968 (3); v In 1967 (4); v P 1964 (3); *v E 1965 (3) 1969 (3); v SA 1961 (5); v In 1964 (3); v P 1964 (1)*
Murray, B. A. G. 13: v E 1970 (1); v In 1967 (4); *v E 1969 (2); v In 1969 (3); v P 1969 (3)*
Murray, D. J. 8: v SA 1994 (1); v WI 1994 (2); v SL 1994 (2); *v SA 1994 (3)*

Nash, D. J. 32: v SA 1994 (1) 1998 (3); v WI 1994 (1) 1999 (2); v In 1993 (1) 1998 (2); v P 1995 (1); v SL 1994 (1); v Z 1997 (2); *v E 1994 (3) 1999 (4); v A 2001 (1); v SA 1994 (1); v In 1995 (3) 1999 (3); v SL 1992 (1); v Z 1992 (1) 2000 (1)*
Newman J. 3: v E 1932 (2); v SA 1931 (1)

O'Connor, S. B. 19: v A 1999 (2); v SA 1998 (1); v WI 1999 (1); v Z 1997 (1) 2000 (1); *v E 1999 (1); v A 1997 (2) 2001 (1); v SA 2000 (3); v In 1999 (1); v SL 1997 (1); v Z 1997 (2) 2000 (2)*
O'Sullivan, D. R. 11: v In 1975 (1); v P 1972 (1); *v A 1973 (3); v In 1976 (3); v P 1976 (3)*
Overton, G. W. F. 3: *v SA 1953 (3)*
Owens, M. B. 8: v A 1992 (2); v P 1992 (1) 1993 (1); *v E 1994 (2); v SL 1992 (2)*

Page, M. L. 14: v E 1929 (4) 1932 (2); v SA 1931 (2); *v E 1931 (3) 1937 (3)*
Parker, J. M. 36: v E 1974 (2) 1977 (3); v A 1973 (3) 1976 (2); v WI 1979 (3); v In 1975 (3); v P 1972 (1) 1978 (2); *v E 1973 (3) 1978 (2); v A 1973 (3) 1980 (3); v In 1976 (3); v P 1976 (3)*
Parker, N. M. 3: *v In 1976 (2); v P 1976 (1)*
Parore, A. C. 78: v E 1991 (1) 1996 (3) 2001 (3); v A 1992 (1) 1999 (3); v SA 1994 (1) 1998 (3); v WI 1994 (1) 1999 (2); v In 1993 (1) 1998 (2); v P 1992 (1) 1995 (1) 2000 (3); v SL 1994 (2) 1996 (2); v Z 1995 (2) 1997 (2) 2000 (1); v B 2001 (2); *v E 1990 (1) 1994 (3) 1999 (4); v A 1997 (3) 2001 (3); v SA 1994 (3) 2000 (3); v WI 1995 (1); v In 1995 (3) 1999 (3); v P 1996 (2); v SL 1992 (2) 1997 (3); v Z 1992 (2) 1997 (2) 2000 (2)*
Patel, D. N. 37: v E 1991 (3) 1996 (2); v A 1992 (3); v SA 1994 (1); v WI 1986 (3); v P 1988 (1) 1992 (1) 1995 (1); v SL 1990 (2) 1994 (1) 1996 (2); v Z 1995 (2); *v A 1987 (3) 1989 (1) 1993 (3); v WI 1995 (1); v In 1990 (3) 1996 (2); v Z 1992 (2)*
Petherick, P. J. 6: v A 1976 (1); *v In 1976 (3); v P 1976 (2)*
Petrie, E. C. 14: v E 1958 (2) 1965 (3); *v E 1958 (5); v In 1955 (2); v P 1955 (2)*
Playle, W. R. 8: v E 1962 (3); *v E 1958 (5)*
Pocock, B. A. 15: v E 1996 (3); v P 1993 (3); v SL 1996 (2); *v E 1994 (1); v A 1993 (3) 1997 (2); v Z 1997 (2)*
Pollard, V. 32: v E 1965 (3) 1970 (1); v WI 1968 (3); v In 1967 (4); v P 1972 (1); *v E 1965 (3) 1969 (3) 1973 (3); v In 1964 (4) 1969 (1); v P 1964 (3) 1969 (3)*
Poore, M. B. 14: v E 1954 (1); v SA 1952 (1); *v In 1955 (4); v P 1955 (4)*
Priest, M. W. 3: v Z 1997 (1); *v E 1990 (1); v SL 1997 (1)*
Pringle, C. 14: v E 1991 (1); v In 1993 (1); v P 1993 (1); v SL 1990 (2) 1994 (1); *v E 1994 (2); v SA 1994 (2); v P 1990 (3); v SL 1992 (1)*
Puna, N. 3: v E 1965 (3)

Rabone, G. O. 12: v E 1954 (2); v SA 1952 (1); v WI 1951 (2); *v E 1949 (4); v SA 1953 (3)*
Redmond, R. E. 1: v P 1972
Reid, J. F. 19: v A 1985 (3); v In 1980 (3); v P 1978 (1) 1984 (3); *v A 1985 (3); v P 1984 (3); v SL 1983 (3)*
Reid, J. R. 58: v E 1950 (2) 1954 (2) 1958 (2) 1962 (3); v SA 1952 (2) 1963 (3); v WI 1951 (2) 1955 (4); v P 1964 (3); *v E 1949 (2) 1958 (5) 1965 (3); v SA 1953 (5) 1961 (5); v In 1955 (5) 1964 (2); v P 1955 (3) 1964 (3)*
Richardson, M. H. 20: v E 2001 (3); v P 2000 (3); v Z 2000 (1); v B 2001 (2); *v A 2001 (3); v SA 2000 (3); v WI 2002 (2); v P 2002 (1); v Z 2000 (2)*
Roberts, A. D. G. 7: v In 1975 (2); *v In 1976 (3); v P 1976 (2)*
Roberts, A. W. 5: v E 1929 (1); v SA 1931 (3); *v E 1937 (2)*
Robertson, G. K. 1: v A 1985
Rowe, C. G. 1: v A 1945
Rutherford, K. R. 56: v E 1987 (2) 1991 (2); v A 1985 (3) 1989 (1) 1992 (3); v SA 1994 (1); v WI 1986 (2) 1994 (2); v In 1989 (3) 1993 (1); v P 1992 (1) 1993 (3); v SL 1990 (3) 1994 (2); *v E 1986 (1) 1990 (2) 1994 (3); v A 1987 (1) 1993 (3); v SA 1994 (3); v WI 1984 (4); v In 1988 (2); v P 1990 (3); v SL 1986 (1) 1992 (3); v Z 1992 (2)*

Scott, R. H. 1: v E 1946
Scott, V. J. 10: v E 1946 (1) 1950 (2); v A 1945 (1); v WI 1951 (2); *v E 1949 (4)*
Sewell, D. G. 1: *v Z 1997*
Shrimpton, M. J. F. 10: v E 1962 (2) 1965 (3) 1970 (2); v SA 1963 (1); *v A 1973 (2)*
Sinclair, B. W. 21: v E 1962 (3) 1965 (3); v SA 1963 (3); v In 1967 (2); v P 1964 (3); *v E 1965 (3); v In 1964 (2); v P 1964 (3)*
Sinclair, I. M. 2: v WI 1955 (2)

Sinclair, M. S. 18: v A 1999 (3); v WI 1999 (1); v P 2000 (3); v Z 2000 (1); v B 2001 (2); *v A 2001 (3); v SA 2000 (3); v Z 2000 (2)*

Smith, F. B. 4: v E 1946 (1); v WI 1951 (1); *v E 1949 (2)*

Smith, H. D. 1: v E 1932

Smith, I. D. S. 63: v E 1983 (3) 1987 (3) 1991 (2); v A 1981 (3) 1985 (3) 1989 (1); v WI 1986 (3); v In 1980 (3) 1989 (3); v P 1984 (3) 1988 (2); v SL 1990 (3); *v E 1983 (2) 1986 (2) 1990 (2); v A 1980 (1) 1985 (3) 1987 (3) 1989 (1); v WI 1984 (4); v In 1988 (3); v P 1984 (3) 1990 (3); v SL 1983 (3) 1986 (1)*

Snedden, C. A. 1: v E 1946

Snedden, M. C. 25: v E 1983 (1) 1987 (2); v A 1981 (3) 1989 (1); v WI 1986 (1); v In 1980 (3) 1989 (3); v SL 1982 (2); *v E 1983 (1) 1990 (3); v A 1985 (1) 1987 (1) 1989 (1); v In 1988 (1); v SL 1986 (1)*

Sparling, J. T. 11: v E 1958 (2) 1962 (1); v SA 1963 (2); *v E 1958 (3); v SA 1961 (3)*

Spearman, C. M. 19: v A 1999 (3); v WI 1999 (2); v P 1995 (1); v Z 1995 (2); *v SA 2000 (2); v WI 1995 (2); v In 1999 (3); v SL 1997 (1); v Z 1997 (2) 2000 (1)*

Stead, G. R. 5: v SA 1998 (3); v WI 1999 (2); *v In 1999 (1)*

Stirling, D. A. 6: *v E 1986 (2); v WI 1984 (1); v P 1984 (3)*

Styris, S. B. 1: *v WI 2002*

Su'a, M. L. 13: v E 1991 (2); v A 1992 (2); v WI 1994 (1); v P 1992 (1); v SL 1994 (1); *v A 1993 (2); v SL 1992 (2); v Z 1992 (2)*

Sutcliffe, B. 42: v E 1946 (1) 1950 (2) 1954 (2) 1958 (2); v SA 1952 (2); v WI 1951 (2) 1955 (2); *v E 1949 (4) 1958 (4) 1965 (1); v SA 1953 (5); v In 1955 (5) 1964 (4); v P 1955 (3) 1964 (3)*

Taylor, B. R. 30: v E 1965 (1); v WI 1968 (3); v In 1967 (3); v P 1972 (3); *v E 1965 (2) 1969 (2) 1973 (3); v WI 1971 (4); v In 1964 (3) 1969 (2); v P 1964 (3) 1969 (1)*

Taylor, D. D. 3: v E 1946 (1); v WI 1955 (2)

Thomson, K. 2: v In 1967 (2)

Thomson, S. A. 19: v E 1991 (1); v WI 1994 (2); v In 1989 (1) 1993 (1); v P 1993 (1); v SL 1990 (1) 1994 (1); *v E 1994 (3); v SA 1994 (3); v In 1995 (2)*

Tindill, E. W. T. 5: v E 1946 (1); v A 1945 (1); *v E 1937 (3)*

Troup, G. B. 15: v A 1981 (2) 1985 (2); v WI 1979 (3); v In 1980 (2); v P 1978 (2); *v A 1980 (2); v WI 1984 (1); v In 1976 (1)*

Truscott, P. B. 1: v P 1964

Tuffey, D. R. 10: v E 2001 (1); v A 1999 (1); v P 2000 (3); *v A 2001 (1); v SA 2000 (2); v WI 2002 (1); v P 2002 (1)*

Turner, G. M. 41: v E 1970 (2) 1974 (2); v A 1973 (3) 1976 (3); v WI 1968 (3); v In 1975 (3); v P 1972 (3); v SL 1982 (2); *v E 1969 (2) 1973 (3); v A 1973 (2); v WI 1971 (5); v In 1969 (3) 1976 (3); v P 1969 (1) 1976 (2)*

Twose, R. G. 16: v SA 1998 (3); v In 1998 (1); v P 1995 (1); v Z 1995 (2); *v E 1999 (4); v A 1997 (1); v WI 1995 (2); v In 1995 (2)*

Vance, R. H. 4: v E 1987 (1); v P 1988 (2); *v A 1989 (1)*

Vaughan, J. T. C. 6: v E 1996 (1); *v WI 1995 (2); v SA 1994 (3); v SL 1992 (1)*

Vettori, D. L. 42: v E 1996 (2) 2001 (3); v A 1999 (2); v SA 1998 (3); v WI 1999 (3); v In 1998 (2); v SL 1996 (2); v Z 1997 (2); v B 2001 (2); *v E 1999 (4); v A 1997 (3) 2001 (3); v WI 2002 (2); v In 1999 (3); v P 1997 (2); v SL 1997 (3); v Z 1997 (2) 2000 (1)*

Vincent, L. 9: v E 2001 (3); v B 2001 (2); *v A 2001 (1); v WI 2002 (2); v P 2002 (1)*

Vivian, G. E. 5: *v WI 1971 (4); v In 1964 (1)*

Vivian, H. G. 7: v E 1932 (1); v SA 1931 (1); *v E 1931 (2) 1937 (3)*

Wadsworth, K. J. 33: v E 1970 (2) 1974 (2); v A 1973 (3); v In 1975 (3); v P 1972 (3); *v E 1969 (3) 1973 (3); v A 1973 (3); v WI 1971 (5); v In 1969 (3); v P 1969 (3)*

Walker, B. G. K. 5: v Z 2000 (1); *v SA 2000 (3); v P 2002 (1)*

Wallace, W. M. 13: v E 1946 (1) 1950 (2); v A 1945 (1); v SA 1952 (2); *v E 1937 (3) 1949 (4)*

Walmsley, K. P. 3: v SL 1994 (2); *v SA 2000 (1)*

Ward, J. T. 8: v SA 1963 (1); v In 1967 (1); v P 1964 (1); *v E 1965 (1); v In 1964 (4)*

Watson, W. 15: v E 1991 (1); v A 1992 (2); v SL 1990 (3); *v E 1986 (2); v A 1989 (1) 1993 (1); v P 1990 (3); v Z 1992 (2)*

Watt, L. 1: v E 1954

Webb, M. G. 3: v E 1970 (1); v A 1973 (1); *v WI 1971 (1)*

Webb, P. N. 2: v WI 1979 (2)

Weir, G. L. 11: v E 1929 (3) 1932 (2); v SA 1931 (2); *v E 1931 (3) 1937 (1)*

White, D. J. 2: *v P 1990 (2)*

Whitelaw, P. E. 2: v E 1932 (2)

Wiseman, P. J. 14: v A 1999 (2); v WI 1999 (1); v In 1998 (2); v P 2000 (1); v Z 2000 (1); *v In 1999 (2); v SL 1997 (3); v Z 2000 (2)*

Wright, J. G. 82: v E 1977 (3) 1983 (3) 1987 (3) 1991 (3); v A 1981 (3) 1985 (2) 1989 (1) 1992 (3); v WI 1979 (3) 1986 (3); v In 1980 (3) 1989 (3); v P 1978 (3) 1984 (3)1988 (2); v SL 1982 (2) 1990 (3); *v E 1978 (2) 1983 (3) 1986 (3) 1990 (3); v A 1980 (3) 1985 (3) 1987 (3) 1989 (1); v WI 1984 (4); v In 1988 (3); v P 1984 (3); v SL 1983 (3) 1992 (2)*

Young, B. A. 35: v E 1996 (3); v SA 1994 (1) 1998 (2); v WI 1994 (2); v In 1993 (1); v P 1993 (3) 1995 (1); v SL 1994 (2) 1996 (2); v Z 1997 (2); *v E 1994 (3); v A 1993 (1) 1997 (3); v SA 1994 (3); v In 1995 (1); v P 1996 (2); v SL 1997 (3)*

Yuile, B. W. 17: v E 1962 (2); v WI 1968 (3); v In 1967 (1); v P 1964 (3); *v E 1965 (1); v In 1964 (3) 1969 (1); v P 1964 (1) 1969 (2)*

INDIA

Number of Test cricketers: 244

Abid Ali, S. 29: v E 1972 (4); v A 1969 (1); v WI 1974 (2); v NZ 1969 (3); *v E 1971 (3) 1974 (3); v A 1967 (4); v WI 1970 (5); v NZ 1967 (4)*

Adhikari, H. R. 21: v E 1951 (3); v A 1956 (3); v WI 1948 (5) 1958 (1); v P 1952 (2); *v E 1952 (3); v A 1947 (5)*

Agarkar, A. B. 15: v A 2000 (1); v SA 1999 (1); v Z 2000 (2); *v E 2002 (4); v A 1999 (3); v SA 2001 (1); v Z 1998 (1) 2001 (1); v B 2000 (1)*

Amarnath, L. 24: v E 1933 (3) 1951 (3); v WI 1948 (5); v P 1952 (5); *v E 1946 (3); v A 1947 (5)*

Amarnath, M. 69: v E 1976 (2) 1984 (5); v A 1969 (1) 1979 (1) 1986 (3); v WI 1978 (2) 1983 (3) 1987 (3); v NZ 1976 (3); v P 1983 (2) 1986 (5); v SL 1986 (2); *v E 1979 (2) 1986 (2); v A 1977 (5) 1985 (3); v WI 1975 (4) 1982 (5); v NZ 1975 (3); v P 1978 (3) 1982 (6) 1984 (2); v SL 1985 (2)*

Amarnath, S. 10: v E 1976 (2); *v WI 1975 (2); v NZ 1975 (3); v P 1978 (3)*

Amar Singh 7: v E 1933 (3); *v E 1932 (1) 1936 (3)*

Amir Elahi 1: *v A 1947*

Amre, P. K. 11: v E 1992 (3); v Z 1992 (1); *v SA 1992 (4); v SL 1993 (3)*

Ankola, S. A. 1: *v P 1989*

Apte, A. L. 1: *v E 1959*

Apte, M. L. 7: v P 1952 (2); *v WI 1952 (5)*

Arshad Ayub 13: v WI 1987 (4); v NZ 1988 (3); *v WI 1988 (4); v P 1989 (2)*

Arun, B. 2: v SL 1986 (2)

Arun Lal 16: v WI 1987 (4); v NZ 1988 (3); v P 1986 (1); v SL 1982 (1); *v WI 1988 (4); v P 1982 (3)*

Azad, K. 7: v E 1981 (3); v WI 1983 (2); v P 1983 (1); *v NZ 1980 (1)*

Azharuddin, M. 99: v E 1984 (3) 1992 (3); v A 1986 (3) 1996 (1) 1997 (3); v SA 1996 (3) 1999 (1); v WI 1987 (3) 1994 (3); v NZ 1988 (3) 1995 (3); v P 1986 (5) 1998 (3); v SL 1986 (1) 1990 (1) 1993 (3) 1997 (3); v Z 1992 (1); *v E 1986 (3) 1990 (3) 1996 (3); v A 1985 (3) 1991 (5); v SA 1992 (4) 1996 (3); v WI 1988 (3) 1996 (5); v NZ 1989 (3) 1993 (1) 1998 (2); v P 1989 (4); v SL 1985 (3) 1993 (3) 1997 (2) 1998 (1); v Z 1992 (1) 1998 (1)*

Badani, H. K. 4: *v SL 2001 (3); v Z 2001 (1)*

Bahutule, S. V. 2: v A 2000 (1); *v SL 2001 (1)*

Baig, A. A. 10: v A 1959 (3); v WI 1966 (2); v P 1960 (3); *v E 1959 (2)*

Banerjee, S. A. 1: v WI 1948

Banerjee, S. N. 1: v WI 1948

Banerjee, S. T. 1: *v A 1991*

Bangar, S. B. 7: v E 2001 (1); v Z 2001 (2); *v E 2002 (2); v WI 2001 (2)*

Baqa Jilani, M. 1: *v E 1936*

Bedi, B. S. 67: v E 1972 (5) 1976 (5); v A 1969 (5); v WI 1966 (2) 1974 (4) 1978 (3); v NZ 1969 (3) 1976 (3); *v E 1967 (3) 1971 (3) 1974 (3) 1979 (3); v A 1967 (2) 1977 (5); v WI 1970 (5) 1975 (4); v NZ 1967 (4) 1975 (2); v P 1978 (3)*

Bhandari, P. 3: v A 1956 (1); v NZ 1955 (1); *v P 1954 (1)*

Bharadwaj, R. V. 3: v NZ 1999 (2); *v A 1999 (1)*

Bhat, A. R. 2: v WI 1983 (1); v P 1983 (1)

Binny, R. M. H. 27: v E 1979 (1); v WI 1983 (6); v P 1979 (6) 1983 (2) 1986 (3); *v E 1986 (3); v A 1980 (1) 1985 (2); v NZ 1980 (1); v P 1984 (1); v SL 1985 (1)*

Borde, C. G. 55: v E 1961 (5) 1963 (5); v A 1959 (5) 1964 (5) 1969 (1); v WI 1958 (4) 1966 (3); v NZ 1964 (4); v P 1960 (5); *v E 1959 (4) 1967 (3); v A 1967 (4); v WI 1961 (5); v NZ 1967 (4)*

Chandrasekhar, B. S. 58: v E 1963 (4) 1972 (5) 1976 (5); v A 1964 (2); v WI 1966 (3) 1974 (4) 1978 (4); v NZ 1964 (2) 1976 (3); *v E 1967 (3) 1971 (3) 1974 (2) 1979 (1); v A 1967 (2) 1977(5); v WI 1975 (4); v NZ 1975 (3); v P 1978 (3)*

Chauhan, C. P. S. 40: v E 1972 (2); v A 1969 (1) 1979 (6); v WI 1978 (6); v NZ 1969 (2); v P 1979 (6); *v E 1979 (4); v A 1977 (4) 1980 (3); v NZ 1980 (3); v P 1978 (3)*

Chauhan, R. K. 21: v E 1992 (1); v A 1997 (2); v WI 1994 (2); v NZ 1995 (2); v SL 1993 (3) 1997 (3); v Z 1992 (1); *v NZ 1993 (1); v SL 1993 (3) 1997 (1)*

Chopra, N. 1: v SA 1999

Chowdhury, N. R. 2: v E 1951 (1); v WI 1948 (1)

Colah, S. H. M. 2: v E 1933 (1); *v E 1932 (1)*

Contractor, N. J. 31: v E 1961 (5); v A 1956 (1) 1959 (5); v WI 1958 (5); v NZ 1955 (4); v P 1960 (5); *v E 1959 (4); v WI 1961 (2)*

Dahiya, V. 2: v Z 2000 (2)

Dani, H. T. 1: v P 1952

Das, S. S. 23: v E 2001 (3); v A 2000 (3); v Z 2000 (3) 2001 (2); *v SA 2001 (2); v WI 2001 (5); v SL 2001 (3); v Z 2001 (2); v B 2000 (1)*

Dasgupta, D. 8: v E 2001 (3); v Z 2001 (2); *v SA 2001 (2); v WI 2001 (1)*

Desai, R. B. 28: v E 1961 (4) 1963 (2); v A 1959 (3); v WI 1958 (1); v NZ 1964 (3); v P 1960 (5); *v E 1959 (5); v A 1967 (1); v WI 1961 (3); v NZ 1967 (1)*

Dighe, S. S. 6: v A 2000 (1); *v SL 2001 (3); v Z 2001 (2)*

Dilawar Hussain 3: v E 1933 (1); *v E 1936 (1)*

Divecha, R. V. 5: v E 1951 (2); v P 1952 (1); *v E 1952 (2)*

Doshi, D. R. 33: v E 1979 (1) 1981 (6); v A 1979 (6); v P 1979 (6) 1983 (1); v SL 1982 (1); *v E 1982 (1); v A 1980 (3); v NZ 1980 (2); v P 1982 (4)*

Dravid, R. 64: v E 2001 (3); v A 1996 (1) 1997 (3) 2000 (3); v SA 1996 (3) 1999 (2); v NZ 1999 (3); v P 1998 (3); v SL 1997 (3); v Z 2000 (2) 2001 (2); *v E 1996 (2) 2002 (4); v A 1999 (3); v SA 1996 (3) 2001 (2); v WI 1996 (5) 2001 (5); v NZ 1998 (2); v SL 1997 (2) 1998 (1) 2001 (3); v Z 1998 (1) 2001 (2); v B 2000 (1)*

Durani, S. A. 29: v E 1961 (5) 1963 (5) 1972 (3); v A 1959 (1) 1964 (3); v WI 1966 (1); v NZ 1964 (3); *v WI 1961 (5) 1970 (3)*

Engineer, F. M. 46: v E 1961 (4) 1972 (5); v A 1969 (5); v WI 1966 (1) 1974 (5); v NZ 1964 (4) 1969 (2); *v E 1967 (3) 1971 (3) 1974 (3); v A 1967 (4); v WI 1961 (3); v NZ 1967 (4)*

Gadkari, C. V. 6: *v WI 1952 (3); v P 1954 (3)*

Gaekwad, A. D. 40: v E 1976 (4) 1984 (3); v WI 1974 (3) 1978 (5) 1983 (6); v NZ 1976 (3); v P 1983 (3); *v E 1979 (2); v A 1977 (1); v WI 1975 (3) 1982 (5); v P 1984 (2)*

Gaekwad, D. K. 11: v WI 1958 (1); v P 1952 (2) 1960 (1); *v E 1952 (1) 1959 (4); v WI 1952 (2)*

Gaekwad, H. G. 1: v P 1952

Gandhi, D. J. 4: v NZ 1999 (3); *v A 1999 (1)*

Gandotra, A. 2: v A 1969 (1); v NZ 1969 (1)

Ganesh, D. 4: *v SA 1996 (2); v WI 1996 (2)*

Ganguly, S. C. 62: v E 2001 (3); v A 1996 (1) 1997 (3) 2000 (3); v SA 1996 (2) 1999 (2); v NZ 1999 (3); v P 1998 (3); v SL 1997 (3); v Z 2000 (2) 2001 (2); *v E 1996 (2) 2002 (4); v A 1999 (3); v SA 1996 (3) 2001 (2); v WI 1996 (4) 2001 (5); v NZ 1998 (2); v SL 1997 (2) 1998 (1) 2001 (3); v Z 1998 (1) 2001 (2); v B 2000 (1)*

Gavaskar, S. M. 125: v E 1972 (5) 1976 (5) 1979 (1) 1981 (6) 1984 (5); v A 1979 (6) 1986 (3); v WI 1974 (2) 1978 (6) 1983 (6); v NZ 1976 (3); v P 1979 (6) 1983 (3) 1986 (4); v SL 1982 (1) 1986 (3); *v E 1971 (3) 1974 (3) 1979 (4) 1982 (3) 1986 (3); v A 1977 (5) 1980 (3) 1985 (3); v WI 1970 (4) 1975 (4) 1982 (5); v NZ 1975 (3) 1980 (3); v P 1978 (3) 1982 (6) 1984 (2); v SL 1985 (3)*

Ghavri, K. D. 39: v E 1976 (3) 1979 (1); v A 1979 (6); v WI 1974 (3) 1978 (6); v NZ 1976 (2); v P 1979 (6); *v E 1979 (4); v A 1977 (3) 1980 (3); v NZ 1980 (1); v P 1978 (1)*

Ghorpade, J. M. 8: v A 1956 (1); v WI 1958 (1); v NZ 1955 (1); *v E 1959 (3); v WI 1952 (2)*

Ghulam Ahmed 22: v E 1951 (2); v A 1956 (2); v WI 1948 (3) 1958 (2); v NZ 1955 (1); v P 1952 (4); *v E 1952 (4); v P 1954 (4)*

Gopalan, M. J. 1: v E 1933

Gopinath, C. D. 8: v E 1951 (3); v A 1959 (1); v P 1952 (1); *v E 1952 (1); v P 1954 (2)*

Guard, G. M. 2: v A 1959 (1); v WI 1958 (1)

Guha, S. 4: v A 1969 (3); *v E 1967 (1)*

Gul Mahomed 8: v P 1952 (2); *v E 1946 (1); v A 1947 (5)*

Gupte, B. P. 3: v E 1963 (1); v P 1960 (1)

Gupte, S. P. 36: v E 1951 (1) 1961 (2); v A 1956 (1); v WI 1958 (5); v NZ 1955 (5); v P 1952 (2) 1960 (3); *v E 1959 (5); v WI 1952 (5); v P 1954 (5)*

Gursharan Singh 1: *v NZ 1989*

Hafeez, A. 3: *v E 1946 (3)*

Hanumant Singh 14: v E 1963 (2); v A 1964 (3); v WI 1966 (2); v NZ 1964 (4) 1969 (1); *v E 1967 (2)*

Harbhajan Singh 28: v E 2001 (3); v A 1997 (1) 2000 (3); v NZ 1999 (2); v P 1998 (2); v Z 2001 (2); *v E 2002 (3); v SA 2001 (1); v WI 2001 (3); v NZ 1998 (1); v SL 1998 (1) 2001 (3); v Z 1998 (1) 2001 (2)*

Hardikar, M. S. 2: v WI 1958 (2)

Harvinder Singh 3: v A 1997 (2); *v SL 2001 (1)*

Hazare, V. S. 30: v E 1951 (5); v WI 1948 (5); v P 1952 (3); *v E 1946 (3) 1952 (4); v A 1947 (5); v WI 1952 (5)*

Hindlekar, D. D. 4: *v E 1936 (1) 1946 (3)*

Hirwani, N. D. 17: v SA 1996 (2); v WI 1987 (1); v NZ 1988 (3) 1995 (1); v SL 1990 (1); *v E 1990 (3); v WI 1988 (3); v NZ 1989 (3)*

Ibrahim, K. C. 4: v WI 1948 (4)

Indrajitsinhji, K. S. 4: v A 1964 (3); v NZ 1969 (1)

Iqbal Siddiqui 1: v E 2001

Irani, J. K. 2: *v A 1947 (2)*

Jadeja, A. 15: v SA 1999 (1); v NZ 1995 (3) 1999 (1); *v E 1996 (2); v SA 1992 (3); v WI 1996 (2); v NZ 1998 (2); v SL 1997 (1)*

Jahangir Khan, M. 4: *v E 1932 (1) 1936 (3)*

Jai, L. P. 1: v E 1933

Jaisimha, M. L. 39: v E 1961 (5) 1963 (5); v A 1959 (1) 1964 (3); v WI 1966 (2); v NZ 1964 (4) 1969 (1); v P 1960 (4); *v E 1959 (1); v A 1967 (2); v WI 1961 (4) 1970 (3); v NZ 1967 (4)*

Jamshedji, R. J. 1: v E 1933

Jayantilal, K. 1: *v WI 1970*

Johnson, D. J. 2: v A 1996 (1); *v SA 1996 (1)*

Joshi, P. G. 12: v E 1951 (2); v A 1959 (1); v WI 1958 (1); v P 1952 (1) 1960 (1); *v E 1959 (3); v WI 1952 (3)*

Joshi, S. B. 15: v A 1996 (1); v SA 1996 (3); v NZ 1999 (2); v P 1998 (1); v Z 2000 (2); *v E 1996 (1); v WI 1996 (4); v B 2000 (1)*

Kaif, M. 4: v SA 1999 (1); *v SL 2001 (3)*

Kambli, V. G. 17: v E 1992 (3); v WI 1994 (3); v NZ 1995 (3); v SL 1993 (3); v Z 1992 (1); *v NZ 1993 (1); v SL 1993 (3)*

Kanitkar, H. H. 2: *v A 1999 (2)*

Kanitkar, H. S. 2: v WI 1974 (2)

Kapil Dev 131: v E 1979 (1) 1981 (6) 1984 (4) 1992 (3); v A 1979 (6) 1986 (3); v WI 1978 (6)
    1983 (6) 1987 (4); v NZ 1988 (3); v P 1979 (6) 1983 (3) 1986 (5); v SL 1982 (1) 1986 (3)
    1990 (1) 1993 (3); v Z 1992 (1); *v E 1979 (4) 1982 (3) 1986 (3) 1990 (3); v A 1980 (3) 1985 (3)
    1991 (5); v SA 1992 (4); v WI 1982 (5) 1988 (4); v NZ 1980 (3) 1989 (3) 1993 (1); v P 1978 (3)
    1982 (6) 1984 (2) 1989 (4); v SL 1985 (3) 1993 (3); v Z 1992 (1)*
Kapoor, A. R. 4: v A 1996 (1); v SA 1996 (1); v WI 1994 (1); v NZ 1995 (1)
Kardar, A. H. (*see* Hafeez)
Karim, S. S. 1: *v B 2000*
Kartik, M. 4: v SA 1999 (2); v Z 2000 (1); *v B 2000 (1)*
Kenny, R. B. 5: v A 1959 (4); v WI 1958 (1)
Kirmani, S. M. H. 88: v E 1976 (5) 1979 (1) 1981 (6) 1984 (5); v A 1979 (6); v WI 1978 (6)
    1983 (6); v NZ 1976 (3); v P 1979 (6) 1983 (3); v SL 1982 (1); *v E 1982 (3); v A 1977 (5)
    1980 (3) 1985 (3); v WI 1975 (4) 1982 (5); v NZ 1975 (3) 1980 (3); v P 1978 (3) 1982 (6)
    1984 (2)*
Kischenchand, G. 5: v P 1952 (1); *v A 1947 (4)*
Kripal Singh, A. G. 14: v E 1961 (3) 1963 (2); v A 1956 (2) 1964 (1); v WI 1958 (1); v NZ 1955 (4);
    v E 1959 (1)
Krishnamurthy, P. 5: *v WI 1970 (5)*
Kulkarni, N. M. 3: v A 2000 (1); v SL 1997 (1); *v SL 1997 (1)*
Kulkarni, R. R. 3: v A 1986 (1); v P 1986 (2)
Kulkarni, U. N. 4: *v A 1967 (3); v NZ 1967 (1)*
Kumar, V. V. 2: v E 1961 (1); v P 1960 (1)
Kumble, A. 73: v E 1992 (3) 2001 (3); v A 1996 (1) 1997 (3); v SA 1996 (3) 1999 (2); v WI 1994
    (3); v NZ 1995 (3) 1999 (3); v P 1998 (3); v SL 1993 (3) 1997 (3); v Z 1992 (1) 2001 (2); *v E
    1990 (1) 1996 (3) 2002 (3); v A 1999 (3); v SA 1992 (4) 1996 (3) 2001 (2); v WI 1996 (5) 2001
    (2); v NZ 1993 (1) 1998 (2); v SL 1993 (3) 1997 (2) 1998 (1); v Z 1992 (1) 1998 (1)*
Kunderan, B. K. 18: v E 1961 (1) 1963 (5); v A 1959 (3); v WI 1966 (2); v NZ 1964 (1); v P
    1960 (2); *v E 1967 (2); v WI 1961 (2)*
Kuruvilla, A. 10: v SL 1997 (3); *v WI 1996 (5); v SL 1997 (2)*

Lall Singh 1: *v E 1932*
Lamba, R. 4: v WI 1987 (1); v SL 1986 (3)
Laxman, V. V. S. 39: v E 2001 (3); v A 1997 (2) 2000 (3); v SA 1996 (2) 1999 (1); v P 1998 (3);
    v Z 2000 (1) 2001 (1); *v E 2002 (4); v A 1999 (3); v SA 1996 (2) 2001 (2); v WI 1996 (4) 2001
    (5); v SL 1998 (2); v Z 2001 (2)*

Madan Lal 39: v E 1976 (1) 1981 (6); v WI 1974 (2) 1983 (3); v NZ 1976 (1); v P 1983 (3); v SL
    1982 (1); *v E 1974 (2) 1982 (3) 1986 (1); v A 1977 (2); v WI 1975 (4) 1982 (2); v NZ 1975 (3);
    v P 1982 (3) 1984 (1)*
Maka, E. S. 2: v P 1952 (1); *v WI 1952 (1)*
Malhotra, A. 7: v E 1981 (2) 1984 (1); v WI 1983 (3); *v E 1982 (1)*
Maninder Singh 35: v A 1986 (3); v WI 1983 (4) 1987 (3); v P 1986 (4); v SL 1986 (3); v Z
    1992 (1); *v E 1986 (3); v WI 1982 (3); v P 1982 (5) 1984 (1) 1989 (3); v SL 1985 (2)*
Manjrekar, S. V. 37: v SA 1996 (1); v WI 1987 (1) 1994 (3); v NZ 1995 (1); v SL 1990 (1) 1993 (3);
    *v E 1990 (3) 1996 (2); v A 1991 (5); v SA 1992 (4); v WI 1988 (4); v NZ 1989 (3) 1993 (1); v P
    1989 (4); v Z 1992 (1)*
Manjrekar, V. L. 55: v E 1951 (2) 1961 (5) 1963 (4); v A 1956 (3) 1964 (3); v WI 1958 (4); v NZ
    1955 (5) 1964 (1); v P 1952 (3) 1960 (5); *v E 1952 (4) 1959 (2); v WI 1952 (4) 1961 (5); v P
    1954 (5)*
Mankad, A. V. 22: v E 1976 (1); v A 1969 (5); v WI 1974 (1); v NZ 1969 (2) 1976 (3); *v E 1971 (3)
    1974 (1); v A 1977 (3); v WI 1970 (3)*
Mankad, V. 44: v E 1951 (5); v A 1956 (3); v WI 1948 (5) 1958 (5); v NZ 1955 (4); v P 1952 (4);
    v E 1946 (3) 1952 (3); v A 1947 (5); v WI 1952 (5); v P 1954 (5)
Mansur Ali Khan (*see* Pataudi)
Mantri, M. K. 4: v E 1951 (1); *v E 1952 (2); v P 1954 (1)*
Meherhomji, K. R. 1: *v E 1936*
Mehra, V. L. 8: v E 1961 (1) 1963 (2); v NZ 1955 (2); *v WI 1961 (2)*
Merchant, V. M. 10: v E 1933 (3) 1951 (1); *v E 1936 (3) 1946 (3)*
Mhambrey, P. L. 2: *v E 1996 (2)*
Milkha Singh, A. G. 4: v E 1961 (1); v A 1959 (1); v P 1960 (2)

Modi, R. S. 10: v E 1951 (1); v WI 1948 (5); v P 1952 (1); *v E 1946 (3)*
Mohanty, D. S. 2: v SL 1997 (1); *v SL 1997 (1)*
Mongia, N. R. 44: v A 1996 (1) 1997 (3) 2000 (2); v SA 1996 (3) 1999 (2); v WI 1994 (3); v NZ
    1995 (3); v P 1998 (3); v SL 1993 (3) 1997 (3); *v E 1996 (3); v SA 1996 (3); v WI 1996 (5); v NZ
    1993 (1) 1998 (2); v SL 1997 (2) 1998 (1); v Z 1998 (1)*
More, K. S. 49: v E 1992 (3); v A 1986 (2); v WI 1987 (4); v NZ 1988 (3); v P 1986 (5); v SL
    1986 (3) 1990 (1); *v E 1986 (3) 1990 (3); v A 1991 (3); v SA 1992 (4); v WI 1988 (4); v NZ
    1989 (3); v P 1989 (4); v SL 1993 (3); v Z 1992 (1)*
Muddiah, V. M. 2: v A 1959 (1); v P 1960 (1)
Mushtaq Ali, S. 11: v E 1933 (2) 1951 (1); v WI 1948 (3); *v E 1936 (3) 1946 (2)*

Nadkarni, R. G. 41: v E 1961 (1) 1963 (5); v A 1959 (5) 1964 (3); v WI 1958 (1) 1966 (1); v NZ
    1955 (1) 1964 (4); v P 1960 (4); *v E 1959 (4); v A 1967 (3); v WI 1961 (5); v NZ 1967 (4)*
Naik, S. S. 3: v WI 1974 (2); *v E 1974 (1)*
Naoomal Jeoomal 3: v E 1933 (2); *v E 1932 (1)*
Narasimha Rao, M. V. 4: v A 1979 (2); v WI 1978 (2)
Navle, J. G. 2: v E 1933 (1); *v E 1932 (1)*
Nayak, S. V. 2: *v E 1982 (2)*
Nayudu, C. K. 7: v E 1933 (3); *v E 1932 (1) 1936 (3)*
Nayudu, C. S. 11: v E 1933 (2) 1951 (1); *v E 1936 (2) 1946 (2); v A 1947 (4)*
Nazir Ali, S. 2: v E 1933 (1); *v E 1932 (1)*
Nehra, A. 10: *v E 2002 (2); v SA 2001 (1); v WI 2001 (4); v SL 1998 (1); v Z 2001 (2)*
Nissar, Mahomed 6: v E 1933 (2); *v E 1932 (1) 1936 (3)*
Nyalchand, S. 1: v P 1952

Pai, A. M. 1: v NZ 1969
Palia, P. E. 2: *v E 1932 (1) 1936 (1)*
Pandit, C. S. 5: v A 1986 (2); *v E 1986 (1); v A 1991 (2)*
Parkar, G. A. 1: *v E 1982*
Parkar, R. D. 2: v E 1972 (2)
Parsana, D. D. 2: v WI 1978 (2)
Patankar, C. T. 1: v NZ 1955
Pataudi sen., Nawab of, 3: *v E 1946 (3)*
Pataudi jun., Nawab of (now Mansur Ali Khan) 46: v E 1961 (3) 1963 (5) 1972 (3); v A 1964 (3)
    1969 (5); v WI 1966 (3) 1974 (4); v NZ 1964 (4) 1969 (3); *v E 1967 (3); v A 1967 (3); v WI
    1961 (3); v NZ 1967 (4)*
Patel, B. P. 21: v E 1976 (5); v WI 1974 (3); v NZ 1976 (3); *v E 1974 (2); v A 1977 (2); v WI
    1975 (3); v NZ 1975 (3)*
Patel, J. M. 7: v A 1956 (3) 1959 (3); v NZ 1955 (1); *v P 1954 (1)*
Patel, P. A. 2: *v E 2002 (2)*
Patel, R. 1: v NZ 1988
Patiala, Yuvraj of, 1: v E 1933
Patil, S. M. 29: v E 1979 (1) 1981 (4) 1984 (2); v WI 1983 (2); v P 1979 (2) 1983 (3); v SL
    1982 (1); *v E 1982 (2); v A 1980 (3); v NZ 1980 (3); v P 1982 (4) 1984 (2)*
Patil, S. R. 1: v NZ 1955
Phadkar, D. G. 31: v E 1951 (4); v A 1956 (1); v WI 1948 (4) 1958 (1); v NZ 1955 (4); v P
    1952 (2); *v E 1952 (4); v A 1947 (4); v WI 1952 (4); v P 1954 (3)*
Prabhakar, M. 39: v E 1984 (2) 1992 (3); v WI 1994 (3); v NZ 1995 (3); v SL 1990 (1) 1993 (3);
    v Z 1992 (1); *v E 1990 (3); v A 1991 (5); v SA 1992 (4); v NZ 1989 (3); v P 1989 (4); v SL
    1993 (3); v Z 1992 (1)*
Prasad, B. K. V. 33: v A 1996 (1) 2000 (1); v SA 1996 (3); v NZ 1999 (2); v P 1998 (3); v SL 1997
    (1); *v E 1996 (3); v A 1999 (3); v SA 1996 (3); v WI 1996 (5); v NZ 1998 (2); v SL 1997 (2) 1998
    (1) 2001 (3)*
Prasad, M. S. K. 6: v NZ 1999 (3); *v A 1999 (3)*
Prasanna, E. A. S. 49: v E 1961 (1) 1972 (3) 1976 (4); v A 1969 (5); v WI 1966 (1) 1974 (5); v NZ
    1969 (3); *v E 1967 (3) 1974 (2); v A 1967 (4) 1977 (4); v WI 1961 (1) 1970 (3) 1975 (1); v NZ
    1967 (4) 1975 (3); v P 1978 (2)*
Punjabi, P. H. 5: *v P 1954 (5)*

Rai Singh, K. 1: *v A 1947*

Rajinder Pal 1: v E 1963

Rajindernath, V. 1: v P 1952

Rajput, L. S. 2: *v SL 1985 (2)*

Raju, S. L. V. 28: v E 1992 (3); v A 1997 (3) 2000 (1); v WI 1994 (3); v NZ 1995 (2); v SL 1990 (1) 1993 (3); *v E 1996 (1); v A 1991 (4); v SA 1992 (2); v NZ 1989 (2) 1993 (1); v SL 1993 (1); v Z 1992 (1)*

Raman, W. V. 11: v E 1987 (1); v WI 1987 (1); v NZ 1988 (1); *v SA 1992 (1) 1996 (2); v WI 1988 (1); v NZ 1989 (3); v Z 1992 (1)*

Ramaswami, C. 2: *v E 1936 (2)*

Ramchand, G. S. 33: v A 1956 (3) 1959 (5); v WI 1958 (3); v NZ 1955 (5); v P 1952 (3); *v E 1952 (4); v WI 1952 (5); v P 1954 (5)*

Ramesh, S. 19: v A 2000 (3); v NZ 1999 (3); v P 1998 (3); v Z 2000 (2); *v A 1999 (2); v SL 1998 (1) 2001 (3); v Z 2001 (1); v B 2000 (1)*

Ramji, L. 1: v E 1933

Rangachari, C. R. 4: v WI 1948 (2); *v A 1947 (2)*

Rangnekar, K. M. 3: *v A 1947 (3)*

Ranjane, V. B. 7: v E 1961 (3) 1963 (1); v A 1964 (1); v WI 1958 (1); *v WI 1961 (1)*

Rathore, V. 6: v A 1996 (1); *v E 1996 (3); v SA 1996 (2)*

Ratra, A. 6: *v E 2002 (2); v WI 2001 (4)*

Razdan, V. 2: *v P 1989 (2)*

Reddy, B. 4: *v E 1979 (4)*

Rege, M. R. 1: v WI 1948

Roy, A. 4: v A 1969 (2); v NZ 1969 (2)

Roy, Pankaj 43: v E 1951 (5); v A 1956 (3) 1959 (5); v WI 1958 (5); v NZ 1955 (3); v P 1952 (3) 1960 (1); *v E 1952 (4) 1959 (5); v WI 1952 (4); v P 1954 (5)*

Roy, Pranab 2: v E 1981 (2)

Sandhu, B. S. 8: v WI 1983 (1); *v WI 1982 (4); v P 1982 (3)*

Sanghvi, R. L. 1: v A 2000

Sarandeep Singh 3: v E 2001 (1); v Z 2000 (1); *v WI 2001 (1)*

Sardesai, D. N. 30: v E 1961 (1) 1963 (5) 1972 (1); v A 1964 (3) 1969 (1); v WI 1966 (2); v NZ 1964 (3); *v E 1967 (1) 1971 (3); v A 1967 (2); v WI 1961 (3) 1970 (5)*

Sarwate, C. T. 9: v E 1951 (1); v WI 1948 (2); *v E 1946 (1); v A 1947 (5)*

Saxena, R. C. 1: *v E 1967*

Sehwag, V. 9: v E 2001 (2); v Z 2001 (1); *v E 2002 (4); v SA 2001 (2)*

Sekar, T. A. P. 2: *v P 1982 (2)*

Sen, P. 14: v E 1951 (2); v WI 1948 (5); v P 1952 (2); *v E 1952 (2); v A 1947 (3)*

Sen Gupta, A. K. 1: v WI 1958

Sharma, Ajay 1: v WI 1987

Sharma, Chetan 23: v E 1984 (3); v A 1986 (2); v WI 1987 (3); v SL 1986 (2); *v E 1986 (2); v A 1985 (2); v WI 1988 (4); v P 1984 (2); v SL 1985 (3)*

Sharma, Gopal 5: v E 1984 (1); v P 1986 (2); v SL 1990 (1); *v SL 1985 (1)*

Sharma, P. 5: v E 1976 (2); v WI 1974 (2); *v WI 1975 (1)*

Sharma, Sanjeev 2: v NZ 1988 (1); *v E 1990 (1)*

Shastri, R. J. 80: v E 1981 (6) 1984 (5); v A 1986 (3); v WI 1983 (6) 1987 (4); v NZ 1988 (3); v P 1983 (2) 1986 (5); v SL 1986 (3) 1990 (1); *v E 1982 (3) 1986 (3) 1990 (3); v A 1985 (3) 1991 (3); v SA 1992 (3); v WI 1982 (5) 1988 (4); v NZ 1980 (3); v P 1982 (2) 1984 (2) 1989 (4); v SL 1985 (3); v Z 1992 (1)*

Shinde, S. G. 7: v E 1951 (3); v WI 1948 (1); *v E 1946 (1) 1952 (2)*

Shodhan, R. H. 3: v P 1952 (1); *v WI 1952 (2)*

Shukla, R. C. 1: v SL 1982

Sidhu, N. S. 51: v E 1992 (3); v A 1997 (3); v WI 1983 (2) 1994 (3); v NZ 1988 (3) 1995 (2); v SL 1993 (3) 1997 (3); v Z 1992 (1); *v E 1990 (3); v A 1991 (3); v WI 1988 (4) 1996 (4); v NZ 1989 (1) 1993 (1) 1998 (2); v P 1989 (4); v SL 1993 (3) 1997 (2); v Z 1998 (1)*

Singh, R. 1: *v NZ 1998*

Singh, R. R. 1: *v Z 1998*

Sivaramakrishnan, L. 9: v E 1984 (5); *v A 1985 (2); v WI 1982 (1); v SL 1985 (1)*

Sohoni, S. W. 4: v E 1951 (1); *v E 1946 (2); v A 1947 (1)*

Solkar, E. D. 27: v E 1972 (5) 1976 (1); v A 1969 (4); v WI 1974 (4); v NZ 1969 (1); *v E 1971 (3) 1974 (3); v WI 1970 (5) 1975 (1)*

Sood, M. M. 1: v A 1959
Srikkanth, K. 43: v E 1981 (4) 1984 (2); v A 1986 (3); v WI 1987 (4); v NZ 1988 (3); v P 1986 (5); v SL 1986 (3); *v E 1986 (3); v A 1985 (3) 1991 (4); v P 1982 (2) 1989 (4); v SL 1985 (3)*
Srinath, J. 64: v E 2001 (2); v A 1997 (2) 2000 (1); v SA 1996 (3) 1999 (2); v WI 1994 (3); v NZ 1995 (3) 1999 (3); v P 1998 (3); v SL 1997 (3); v Z 2000 (2) 2001 (3); *v E 1996 (3); v A 1991 (5) 1999 (3); v SA 1992 (3) 1996 (3) 2001 (2); v WI 2001 (5); v NZ 1993 (1) 1998 (2); v SL 1993 (2) 2001 (1); v Z 1992 (1) 1998 (1) 2001 (2); v B 2000 (1)*
Srinivasan, T. E. 1: *v NZ 1980*
Subramanya, V. 9: v WI 1966 (2); v NZ 1964 (1); *v E 1967 (2); v A 1967 (2); v NZ 1967 (2)*
Sunderram, G. 2: v NZ 1955 (2)
Surendranath, R. 11: v A 1959 (2); v WI 1958 (2); v P 1960 (2); *v E 1959 (5)*
Surti, R. F. 26: v E 1963 (1); v A 1964 (2) 1969 (1); v WI 1966 (2); v NZ 1964 (1) 1969 (2); v P 1960 (2); *v E 1967 (2); v A 1967 (4); v WI 1961 (5); v NZ 1967 (4)*
Swamy, V. N. 1: v NZ 1955

Tamhane, N. S. 21: v A 1956 (3) 1959 (1); v WI 1958 (4); v NZ 1955 (4); v P 1960 (2); *v E 1959 (2); v P 1954 (5)*
Tarapore, K. K. 1: v WI 1948
Tendulkar, S. R. 100: v E 1992 (3) 2001 (3); v A 1996 (1) 1997 (3) 2000 (3); v SA 1996 (3) 1999 (2); v WI 1994 (3); v NZ 1995 (3) 1999 (3); v P 1998 (3); v SL 1990 (1) 1993 (3) 1997 (3); v Z 1992 (1) 2000 (2) 2001 (2); *v E 1990 (3) 1996 (3) 2002 (4); v A 1991 (5) 1999 (3); v SA 1992 (4) 1996 (3) 2001 (2); v WI 1996 (5) 2001 (5); v NZ 1989 (3) 1993 (1) 1998 (2); v P 1989 (4); v SL 1993 (3) 1997 (2) 1998 (1); v Z 1992 (1) 1998 (1) 2001 (2); v B 2000 (1)*

Umrigar, P. R. 59: v E 1951 (5) 1961 (4); v A 1956 (3) 1959 (3); v WI 1948 (1) 1958 (5); v NZ 1955 (5); v P 1952 (5) 1960 (5); *v E 1952 (4) 1959 (4); v WI 1952 (5) 1961 (5); v P 1954 (5)*

Vengsarkar, D. B. 116: v E 1976 (1) 1979 (1) 1981 (6) 1984 (5); v A 1979 (6) 1986 (2); v WI 1978 (6) 1983 (5) 1987 (3); v NZ 1988 (3); v P 1979 (5) 1983 (1) 1986 (5); v SL 1982 (1) 1986 (3) 1990 (1); *v E 1979 (4) 1982 (3) 1986 (3) 1990 (3); v A 1977 (5) 1980 (3) 1985 (3) 1991 (5); v WI 1975 (2) 1982 (5) 1988 (4); v NZ 1975 (3) 1980 (3) 1989 (2); v P 1978 (3) 1982 (6) 1984 (2); v SL 1985 (3)*
Venkataraghavan, S. 57: v E 1972 (2) 1976 (1); v A 1969 (5) 1979 (3); v WI 1966 (2) 1974 (2) 1978 (6); v NZ 1964 (4) 1969 (2) 1976 (3); v P 1983 (2); *v E 1967 (1) 1971 (3) 1974 (2) 1979 (4); v A 1977 (1); v WI 1970 (5) 1975 (3) 1982 (5); v NZ 1975 (1)*
Venkataramana, M. 1: *v WI 1988*
Viswanath, G. R. 91: v E 1972 (5) 1976 (5) 1979 (1) 1981 (6); v A 1969 (4) 1979 (6); v WI 1974 (5) 1978 (6); v NZ 1976 (3); v P 1979 (6); v SL 1982 (1); *v E 1971 (3) 1974 (3) 1979 (4) 1982 (3); v A 1977 (5) 1980 (3); v WI 1970 (3) 1975 (4); v NZ 1975 (3) 1980 (3); v P 1978 (3) 1982 (6)*
Viswanath, S. 3: *v SL 1985 (3)*
Vizianagram, Maharaj Kumar of, Sir Vijay A. 3: *v E 1936 (3)*

Wadekar, A. L. 37: v E 1972 (5); v A 1969 (5); v WI 1966 (2); v NZ 1969 (3); *v E 1967 (3) 1971 (3) 1974 (3); v A 1967 (4); v WI 1970 (5); v NZ 1967 (4)*
Wasim Jaffer 7: v SA 1999 (2); *v E 2002 (2); v WI 2001 (3)*
Wassan, A. S. 4: *v E 1990 (1); v NZ 1989 (3)*
Wazir Ali, S. 7: v E 1933 (3); *v E 1932 (1) 1936 (3)*

Yadav, N. S. 35: v E 1979 (1) 1981 (1) 1984 (4); v A 1979 (5) 1986 (3); v WI 1983 (1); v P 1979 (5) 1986 (4); v SL 1986 (2); *v A 1980 (2) 1985 (3); v NZ 1980 (1); v P 1984 (1)*
Yadav, V. S. 1: v Z 1992
Yajurvindra Singh 4: v E 1976 (2); v A 1979 (1); *v E 1979 (1)*
Yashpal Sharma 37: v E 1979 (1) 1981 (2); v A 1979 (6); v WI 1983 (1); v P 1979 (6) 1983 (3); v SL 1982 (1); *v E 1979 (3) 1982 (3); v A 1980 (3); v WI 1982 (5); v NZ 1980 (1); v P 1982 (2)*
Yograj Singh 1: *v NZ 1980*
Yohannan, T. 2: v E 2001 (2)

Zaheer Khan 20: v A 2000 (2); v Z 2000 (1) 2001 (2); *v E 2002 (4); v SA 2001 (1); v WI 2001 (5); v SL 2001 (3); v Z 2001 (1); v B 2000 (1)*

Note: Hafeez, on going later to Oxford University, took his correct name, Kardar.

PAKISTAN

Number of Test cricketers: 171

Aamer Malik 14: v E 1987 (2); v A 1988 (1) 1994 (1); v WI 1990 (1); v In 1989 (4); *v A 1989 (2); v WI 1987 (1); v NZ 1988 (2)*

Aamir Nazir 6: v SL 1995 (1); *v SA 1994 (1); v WI 1992 (1); v NZ 1993 (1); v Z 1994 (2)*

Aamir Sohail 47: v A 1994 (3) 1998 (3); v SA 1997 (1); v WI 1997 (3); v SL 1995 (3) 1999 (2); v Z 1993 (3) 1996 (2) 1998 (1); *v E 1992 (5) 1996 (2); v A 1995 (3); v SA 1994 (1) 1997 (3); v WI 1992 (2); v NZ 1992 (1) 1993 (3) 1995 (1); v SL 1994 (2); v Z 1994 (3)*

Abdul Kadir 4: v A 1964 (1); *v A 1964 (1); v NZ 1964 (2)*

Abdul Qadir 67: v E 1977 (3) 1983 (3) 1987 (3); v A 1982 (3) 1988 (3); v WI 1980 (2) 1986 (3) 1990 (2); v NZ 1984 (3) 1990 (2); v In 1982 (5) 1984 (1) 1989 (4); v SL 1985 (3); *v E 1982 (3) 1987 (4); v A 1983 (5); v WI 1987 (3); v NZ 1984 (2) 1988 (2); v In 1979 (3) 1986 (3); v SL 1985 (2)*

Abdul Razzaq 21: v E 2000 (3); v WI 2001 (2); v NZ 2002 (1); v SL 1999 (2) 2001 (1); v B 2001 (1); *v E 2001 (2); v A 1999 (1); v WI 1999 (3); v SL 2000 (3); v B 2001 (2)*

Afaq Hussain 2: v E 1961 (1); *v A 1964 (1)*

Aftab Baloch 2: v WI 1974 (1); v NZ 1969 (1)

Aftab Gul 6: v E 1968 (2); v NZ 1969 (1); *v E 1971 (3)*

Agha Saadat Ali 1: v NZ 1955

Agha Zahid 1: v WI 1974

Akram Raza 9: v A 1994 (2); v WI 1990 (1); v In 1989 (1); v SL 1991 (1); *v NZ 1993 (2); v SL 1994 (1); v Z 1994 (1)*

Ali Hussain Rizvi 1: v SA 1997

Alim-ud-Din 25: v E 1961 (2); v A 1956 (1) 1959 (1); v WI 1958 (1); v NZ 1955 (3); v In 1954 (5); *v E 1954 (3) 1962 (3); v WI 1957 (5); v In 1960 (1)*

Ali Naqvi 5: v SA 1997 (3); *v Z 1997 (2)*

Amir Elahi 5: *v In 1952 (5)*

Anil Dalpat 9: v E 1983 (3); v NZ 1984 (3); *v NZ 1984 (3)*

Anwar Hussain 4: *v In 1952 (4)*

Anwar Khan 1: *v NZ 1978*

Aqib Javed 22: v A 1994 (1); v NZ 1990 (3); v SL 1991 (3) 1995 (3); v Z 1998 (3); *v E 1992 (5); v A 1989 (1); v SA 1994 (1); v NZ 1988 (1) 1992 (1); v Z 1994 (2)*

Arif Butt 3: *v A 1964 (1); v NZ 1964 (2)*

Arshad Khan 8: v E 2000 (1); v A 1998 (1); v WI 1997 (1); v SL 1999 (1); *v SL 1998 (1) 2000 (3)*

Ashfaq Ahmed 1: v Z 1993

Ashraf Ali 8: v E 1987 (3); v In 1984 (2); v SL 1981 (2) 1985 (1)

Asif Iqbal 58: v E 1968 (3) 1972 (3); v A 1964 (1); v WI 1974 (2); v NZ 1964 (3) 1969 (3) 1976 (3); v In 1978 (3); *v E 1967 (3) 1971 (3) 1974 (3); v A 1964 (1) 1972 (3) 1976 (3) 1978 (2); v WI 1976 (5); v NZ 1964 (3) 1972 (3) 1978 (2); v In 1979 (6)*

Asif Masood 16: v E 1968 (2) 1972 (1); v WI 1974 (2); v NZ 1969 (1); *v E 1971 (3) 1974 (3); v A 1972 (3) 1976 (1)*

Asif Mujtaba 25: v E 1987 (1); v WI 1986 (2); v Z 1993 (3); *v E 1992 (5) 1996 (2); v SA 1994 (1); v WI 1992 (3); v NZ 1992 (1) 1993 (2); v SL 1994 (2) 1996 (2); v Z 1994 (1)*

Ata-ur-Rehman 13: v SL 1995 (1); v Z 1993 (3); *v E 1992 (1) 1996 (2); v WI 1992 (3); v NZ 1993 (2) 1995 (1)*

Atif Rauf 1: *v NZ 1993*

Atiq-uz-Zaman 1: v SL 1999

Azam Khan 1: v Z 1996

Azeem Hafeez 18: v E 1983 (2); v NZ 1984 (3); v In 1984 (2); *v A 1983 (5); v NZ 1984 (3); v In 1983 (3)*

Azhar Khan 1: v A 1979

Azhar Mahmood 21: v A 1998 (2); v SA 1997 (3); v WI 1997 (3); v Z 1998 (1); *v E 2001 (2); v A 1999 (3); v SA 1997 (3); v In 1998 (1); v SL 2000 (1); v Z 1997 (2)*

Azmat Rana 1: v A 1979

Basit Ali 19: v A 1994 (2); v SL 1995 (1); v Z 1993 (3); *v A 1995 (3); v WI 1992 (3); v NZ 1993 (3) 1995 (1); v SL 1994 (2); v Z 1994 (1)*

Burki, J. 25: v E 1961 (3); v A 1964 (1); v NZ 1964 (3) 1969 (1); *v E 1962 (5) 1967 (3); v A 1964 (1); v NZ 1964 (3); v In 1960 (5)*

Danish Kaneria 8: v E 2000 (2); v WI 2001 (2); v NZ 2002 (1); v B 2001 (1); *v B 2001 (2)*
D'Souza, A. 6: v E 1961 (2); v WI 1958 (1); *v E 1962 (3)*

Ehtesham-ud-Din 5: v A 1979 (1); *v E 1982 (1); v In 1979 (3)*

Faisal Iqbal 5: v B 2001 (1); *v E 2001 (1); v NZ 2000 (3)*
Farooq Hamid 1: *v A 1964*
Farrukh Zaman 1: v NZ 1976
Fazal Mahmood 34: v E 1961 (1); v A 1956 (1) 1959 (2); v WI 1958 (3); v NZ 1955 (2); v In 1954 (4); *v E 1954 (4) 1962 (2); v WI 1957 (5); v In 1952 (5) 1960 (5)*
Fazl-e-Akbar 4: v SL 1998 (1); *v SA 1997 (1); v NZ 2000 (2)*

Ghazali, M. E. Z. 2: *v E 1954 (2)*
Ghulam Abbas 1: *v E 1967*
Gul Mahomed 1: v A 1956

Hanif Mohammad 55: v E 1961 (3) 1968 (3); v A 1956 (1) 1959 (3) 1964 (1); v WI 1958 (1); v NZ 1955 (1) 1964 (3) 1969 (1); v In 1954 (5); *v E 1954 (4) 1962 (5) 1967 (3); v A 1964 (1); v WI 1957 (5); v NZ 1964 (3); v In 1952 (5) 1960 (5)*
Haroon Rashid 23: v E 1977 (3); v A 1979 (2) 1982 (3); v In 1982 (1); v SL 1981 (2); *v E 1978 (3) 1982 (1); v A 1976 (1) 1978 (1); v WI 1976 (5); v NZ 1978 (1)*
Hasan Raza 2: v Z 1996 (1) 1998 (1)
Haseeb Ahsan 12: v E 1961 (3); v A 1959 (3); v WI 1958 (1); *v WI 1957 (3); v In 1960 (5)*
Humayun Farhat 1: *v NZ 2000*

Ibadulla, K. 4: v A 1964 (1); *v E 1967 (2); v NZ 1964 (1)*
Ijaz Ahmed, sen. 60: v E 1987 (3); v A 1988 (3) 1994 (1) 1998 (2); v SA 1997 (3); v WI 1990 (3) 1997 (3); v NZ 1996 (2); v SL 1999 (1); v Z 1996 (2) 1998 (2); *v E 1987 (4) 1996 (3); v A 1989(3) 1995 (2) 1999 (3); v SA 1994 (1) 1997 (3); v WI 1987 (2); v NZ 1995 (1) 2000 (2); v In 1986 (1) 1998 (3); v SL 1996 (2) 1998 (1); v Z 1994 (3) 1997 (1)*
Ijaz Ahmed, jun. 2: v SL 1995 (2)
Ijaz Butt 8: v A 1959 (2); v WI 1958 (3); *v E 1962 (3)*
Ijaz Faqih 5: v WI 1980 (1); *v A 1981 (1); v WI 1987 (2); v In 1986 (1)*
Imran Farhat 3: *v NZ 2000 (3)*
Imran Khan 88: v A 1979 (2) 1982 (3); v WI 1980 (4) 1986 (3) 1990 (3); v NZ 1976 (3); v In 1978 (3) 1982 (6) 1989 (4); v SL 1981 (1) 1985 (3) 1991 (3); *v E 1971 (1) 1974 (3) 1982 (3) 1987 (5); v A 1976 (3) 1978 (2) 1981 (3) 1983 (2) 1989 (3); v WI 1976 (5) 1987 (3); v NZ 1978 (2) 1988 (2); v In 1979 (5) 1986 (5); v SL 1985 (3)*
Imran Nazir 6: v E 2000 (1); v NZ 2002 (1); v SL 1998 (1); *v WI 1999 (2); v SL 2000 (1)*
Imtiaz Ahmed 41: v E 1961 (3); v A 1956 (1) 1959 (3); v WI 1958 (3); v NZ 1955 (3); v In 1954 (5); *v E 1954 (4) 1962 (4); v WI 1957 (5); v In 1952 (5) 1960 (5)*
Intikhab Alam 47: v E 1961 (2) 1968 (3) 1972 (3); v A 1959 (1) 1964 (1); v WI 1974 (2); v NZ 1964 (3) 1969 (3) 1976 (3); *v E 1962 (3) 1967 (3) 1971 (3) 1974 (3); v A 1964 (1) 1972 (3); v WI 1976 (1); v NZ 1964 (3) 1972 (3); v In 1960 (3)*
Inzamam-ul-Haq 81: v E 2000 (3); v A 1994 (3) 1998 (3); v SA 1997 (3); v WI 1997 (3) 2001 (2); v NZ 1996 (2) 2002 (1); v SL 1996 (1) 1999 (3) 2001 (1); v Z 1996 (3) 1998 (1); v B 2001 (1); *v E 1992 (4) 1996 (3) 2001 (2); v A 1995 (3) 1999 (3); v SA 1994 (1) 1997 (2); v WI 1992 (3) 1999 (3); v NZ 1992 (1) 1993 (3) 1995 (1) 2000 (2); v In 1998 (2); v SL 1994 (2) 1996 (2) 1998 (1) 2000 (3); v Z 1994 (3) 1997 (2); v B 2001 (2)*
Iqbal Qasim 50: v E 1977 (3) 1987 (3); v A 1979 (1) 1982 (2) 1988 (3); v WI 1980 (4); v NZ 1984 (3); v In 1978 (3) 1982 (2); v SL 1981 (3); *v E 1978 (3); v A 1976 (3) 1981 (2); v WI 1976 (2); v NZ 1984 (1); v In 1979 (6) 1983 (1) 1986 (3)*
Irfan Fazil 1: v SL 1999
Israr Ali 4: v A 1959 (2); *v In 1952 (2)*

Jalal-ud-Din 6: v A 1982 (1); v In 1982 (1) 1984 (2); v SL 1985 (1)
Javed Akhtar 1: *v E 1962*

Javed Miandad 124: v E 1977 (3) 1987 (3); v A 1979 (3) 1982 (3) 1988 (3); v WI 1980 (4) 1986 (3) 1990 (2); v NZ 1976 (3) 1984 (3) 1990 (3); v In 1978 (3) 1982 (6) 1984 (2) 1989 (4); v SL 1981 (3) 1985 (3) 1991 (3); v Z 1993 (3); *v E 1978 (3) 1982 (3) 1987 (5) 1992 (5); v A 1976 (3) 1978 (2) 1981 (3) 1983 (5) 1989 (3); v WI 1976 (1) 1987 (3) 1992 (3); v NZ 1978 (3) 1984 (3) 1988 (2) 1992 (1); v In 1979 (6) 1983 (3) 1986 (4); v SL 1985 (3)*

Kabir Khan 4: *v SA 1994 (1); v SL 1994 (1); v Z 1994 (2)*
Kardar, A. H. 23: v A 1956 (1); v NZ 1955 (3); v In 1954 (5); v E 1954 (4); v WI 1957 (5); *v In 1952 (5)*
Khalid Hassan 1: *v E 1954*
Khalid Wazir 2: *v E 1954 (2)*
Khan Mohammad 13: v A 1956 (1); v NZ 1955 (3); v In 1954 (4); *v E 1954 (2); v WI 1957 (2); v In 1952 (1)*

Liaqat Ali 5: v E 1977 (2); v WI 1974 (1); *v E 1978 (2)*

Mahmood Hussain 27: v E 1961 (1); v WI 1958 (3); v NZ 1955 (1); v In 1954 (5); *v E 1954 (2) 1962 (3); v WI 1957 (3); v In 1952 (4) 1960 (5)*
Majid Khan 63: v E 1968 (3) 1972 (3); v A 1964 (1) 1979 (3); v WI 1974 (2) 1980 (4); v NZ 1964 (3) 1976 (3); v In 1978 (3) 1982 (1); v SL 1981 (1); *v E 1967 (3) 1971 (2) 1974 (3) 1982 (1); v A 1972 (3) 1976 (3) 1978 (2) 1981 (3); v WI 1976 (5); v NZ 1972 (3) 1978 (2); v In 1979 (6)*
Mansoor Akhtar 19: v A 1982 (3); v WI 1980 (2); v In 1982 (3); v SL 1981 (1); *v E 1982 (3) 1987 (5); v A 1981 (1) 1989 (1)*
Manzoor Elahi 6: v NZ 1984 (1); v In 1984 (1); *v In 1986 (2); v Z 1994 (2)*
Maqsood Ahmed 16: v NZ 1955 (2); v In 1954 (5); *v E 1954 (4); v In 1952 (5)*
Masood Anwar 1: v WI 1990
Mathias, Wallis 21: v E 1961 (1); v A 1956 (1) 1959 (2); v WI 1958 (3); v NZ 1955 (1); *v E 1962 (3); v WI 1957 (5); v In 1960 (5)*
Miran Bux 2: v In 1954 (2)
Misbah-ul-Haq 1: *v NZ 2000*
Mohammad Akram 9: v NZ 1996 (1); v SL 1995 (2) 1999 (1); *v E 1996 (1); v A 1995 (2) 1999 (1); v NZ 2000 (1)*
Mohammad Aslam 1: *v E 1954*
Mohammad Farooq 7: v NZ 1964 (3); *v E 1962 (2); v In 1960 (2)*
Mohammad Hussain 2: v A 1998 (1); v Z 1996 (1)
Mohammad Ilyas 10: v E 1968 (2); v NZ 1964 (3); *v E 1967 (1); v A 1964 (1); v NZ 1964 (3)*
Mohammad Munaf 4: v E 1961 (2); v A 1959 (2)
Mohammad Nazir 14: v E 1972 (1); v WI 1980 (4); v NZ 1969 (3); *v A 1983 (3); v In 1983 (3)*
Mohammad Ramzan 1: v SA 1997
Mohammad Sami 3: v SL 2001 (1); *v NZ 2000 (2)*
Mohammad Wasim 18: v A 1998 (1); v SA 1997 (2); v WI 1997 (3); v NZ 1996 (2); *v A 1999 (2); v SA 1997 (2); v WI 1999 (3); v SL 2000 (2); v Z 1997 (1)*
Mohammad Zahid 4: v A 1998 (1); v NZ 1996 (1); *v SL 1996 (2)*
Mohsin Kamal 9: v E 1983 (1); v A 1994 (3); v SL 1985 (1); *v E 1987 (4); v SL 1985 (1)*
Mohsin Khan 48: v E 1977 (1) 1983 (3); v A 1982 (3); v WI 1986 (3); v NZ 1984 (2); v In 1982 (6) 1984 (2); v SL 1981 (2) 1985 (2); *v E 1978 (3) 1982 (3); v A 1978 (1) 1981 (2) 1983 (5); v NZ 1978 (1) 1984 (3); v In 1983 (3); v SL 1985 (3)*
Moin Khan 63: v E 2000 (3); v A 1994 (1) 1998 (3); v SA 1997 (3); v WI 1990 (2) 1997 (3); v NZ 1996 (2); v SL 1991 (3) 1995 (3) 1998 (1) 1999 (1); v Z 1996 (2) 1998 (2); *v E 1992 (4) 1996 (2); v A 1995 (2) 1999 (3); v SA 1994 (1) 1997 (3); v WI 1992 (2) 1999 (2); v NZ 2000 (2); v In 1998 (3); v SL 1996 (2) 1998 (1) 2000 (3); v Z 1997 (2)*
Mudassar Nazar 76: v E 1977 (3) 1983 (1) 1987 (3); v A 1979 (3) 1982 (3) 1988 (3); v WI 1986 (2); v NZ 1984 (3); v In 1978 (2) 1982 (6) 1984 (2); v SL 1981 (1) 1985 (3) ; *v E 1978 (3) 1982 (3) 1987 (5); v A 1976 (1) 1978 (1) 1981 (1) 1983 (5); v WI 1987 (3); v NZ 1978 (1) 1984 (3) 1988 (2); v In 1979 (5) 1983 (3); v SL 1985 (3)*
Mufasir-ul-Haq 1: *v NZ 1964*
Munir Malik 3: v A 1959 (1); *v E 1962 (2)*

Mushtaq Ahmed 50: v E 2000 (1); v A 1994 (3) 1998 (2); v SA 1997 (3); v WI 1990 (2) 1997 (3); v NZ 1996 (2); v Z 1993 (2) 1998 (1); *v E 1992 (5) 1996 (3); v A 1989 (1) 1995 (2) 1999 (1); v SA 1997 (3); v WI 1992 (1) 1999 (3); v NZ 1992 (1) 1993 (1) 1995 (1) 2000 (1); v In 1998 (1); v SL 1994 (2) 1996 (2) 2000 (2); v Z 1997 (1)*
Mushtaq Mohammad 57: v E 1961 (3) 1968 (3) 1972 (3); v WI 1958 (1) 1974 (2); v NZ 1969 (2) 1976 (3); v In 1978 (3); *v E 1962 (5) 1967 (3) 1971 (3) 1974 (3); v A 1972 (3) 1976 (3) 1978 (2); v WI 1976 (5); v NZ 1972 (2) 1978 (3); v In 1960 (5)*

Nadeem Abbasi 3: v In 1989 (3)
Nadeem Ghauri 1: *v A 1989*
Nadeem Khan 2: *v WI 1992 (1); v In 1998 (1)*
Nasim-ul-Ghani 29: v E 1961 (2); v A 1959 (2) 1964 (1); v WI 1958 (3); *v E 1962 (5) 1967 (2); v A 1964 (1) 1972 (1); v WI 1957 (5); v NZ 1964 (3); v In 1960 (4)*
Naushad Ali 6: v NZ 1964 (3); *v NZ 1964 (3)*
Naved Anjum 2: v NZ 1990 (1); v In 1989 (1)
Naved Ashraf 2: v SL 1999 (1); v Z 1998 (1)
Naved Latif 1: v WI 2001
Nazar Mohammad 5: *v In 1952 (5)*
Nazir Junior (*see* Mohammad Nazir)
Niaz Ahmed 2: v E 1968 (1); *v E 1967 (1)*

Pervez Sajjad 19: v E 1968 (1) 1972 (2); v A 1964 (1); v NZ 1964 (3) 1969 (3); *v E 1971 (3); v NZ 1964 (3) 1972 (3)*

Qaiser Abbas 1: v E 2000
Qasim Omar 26: v E 1983 (3); v WI 1986 (3); v NZ 1984 (3); v In 1984 (3); v SL 1985 (3); *v A 1983 (5); v NZ 1984 (3); v In 1983 (1); v SL 1985 (3)*

Ramiz Raja 57: v E 1983 (2) 1987 (3); v A 1988 (3); v WI 1986 (3) 1990 (2); v NZ 1990 (3); v In 1989 (4); v SL 1985 (1) 1991 (3) 1995 (3); *v E 1987 (2) 1992 (5); v A 1989 (2) 1995 (3); v WI 1987 (3) 1992 (3); v NZ 1992 (1) 1995 (1); v In 1986 (5); v SL 1985 (3) 1996 (2)*
Rashid Khan 4: v SL 1981 (2); *v A 1983 (1); v NZ 1984 (1)*
Rashid Latif 31: v A 1994 (2); v WI 2001 (2); v NZ 2002 (1); v SL 2001 (1); v Z 1993 (3); v B 2001 (1); *v E 1992 (1) 1996 (1) 2001 (2); v A 1995 (1); v SA 1997 (1); v WI 1992 (1); v NZ 1992 (1) 1993 (3) 1995 (1); v SL 1994 (2); v Z 1994 (3) 1997 (2); v B 2001 (2)*
Rehman, S. F. 1: *v WI 1957*
Rizwan-uz-Zaman 11: v WI 1986 (1); v SL 1981 (2); *v A 1981 (1); v NZ 1988 (2); v In 1986 (5)*

Sadiq Mohammad 41: v E 1972 (3) 1977 (2); v WI 1974 (1) 1980 (3); v NZ 1969 (3) 1976 (3); v In 1978 (1); *v E 1971 (3) 1974 (3) 1978 (3); v A 1972 (3) 1976 (2); v WI 1976 (5); v NZ 1972 (3); v In 1979 (3)*
Saeed Ahmed 41: v E 1961 (3) 1968 (3); v A 1959 (3) 1964 (1); v WI 1958 (3); v NZ 1964 (3); *v E 1962 (5) 1967 (3) 1971 (1); v A 1964 (1) 1972 (2); v WI 1957 (5); v NZ 1964 (3); v In 1960 (5)*
Saeed Anwar 55: v E 2000 (3); v A 1994 (3) 1998 (2); v SA 1997 (3); v WI 1990 (1) 1997 (3); v NZ 1996 (2); v SL 1995 (2) 1998 (1) 1999 (2); v Z 1996 (2) 1998 (2); v B 2001 (1); *v E 1996 (3) 2001 (2); v A 1999 (3); v SA 1994 (1) 1997 (3); v NZ 1993 (3); v In 1998 (3); v SL 1994 (2) 1998 (1) 2000 (3); v Z 1994 (2) 1997 (2)*
Salah-ud-Din 5: v E 1968 (1); v NZ 1964 (3) 1969 (1)
Saleem Jaffer 14: v E 1987 (1); v A 1988 (2); v WI 1986 (1); v NZ 1990 (2); v In 1989 (1); v SL 1991 (2); *v WI 1987 (1); v NZ 1988 (2); v In 1986 (2)*
Salim Altaf 21: v E 1972 (3); v NZ 1969 (2); v In 1978 (1); *v E 1967 (2) 1971 (2); v A 1972 (3) 1976 (2); v WI 1976 (3); v NZ 1972 (3)*
Salim Elahi 9: v E 2000 (3); *v E 2001 (1); v A 1995 (2); v NZ 2000 (1); v SL 1996 (2)*
Salim Malik 103: v E 1983 (3) 1987 (3); v A 1988 (3) 1994 (3) 1998 (3); v WI 1986 (1) 1990 (3); v NZ 1984 (3) 1990 (3) 1996 (2); v In 1984 (6) 1984 (2) 1989 (4); v SL 1981 (2) 1985 (3) 1991 (3); v Z 1996 (2) 1998 (1); *v E 1987 (5) 1992 (5) 1996 (3); v A 1983 (3) 1989 (1) 1995 (2); v SA 1994 (1); v WI 1987 (3); v NZ 1984 (3) 1988 (2) 1992 (1) 1993 (3) 1995 (1); v In 1983 (2) 1986 (5) 1998 (3); v SL 1985 (3) 1994 (2) 1996 (2); v Z 1994 (3)*
Salim Yousuf 32: v A 1988 (3); v WI 1986 (3) 1990 (1); v NZ 1990 (3); v In 1989 (1); v SL 1981 (1) 1985 (2); *v E 1987 (5); v A 1989 (3); v WI 1987 (3); v NZ 1988 (2); v In 1986 (5)*

Saqlain Mushtaq 40: v E 2000 (3); v A 1998 (1); v SA 1997 (3); v WI 1997 (1) 2001 (2); v NZ 1996 (1) 2002 (1); v SL 1995 (2) 1998 (1) 1999 (1); v Z 1996 (2) 1998 (1); *v E 2000 (1); v A 1995 (2) 1999 (2); v SA 1997 (1); v WI 1999 (3); v NZ 2000 (3); v In 1998 (3); v SL 1996 (2) 1998 (1); v Z 1997 (1); v B 2001 (2)*

Sarfraz Nawaz 55: v E 1968 (1) 1972 (2) 1977 (2) 1983 (3); v A 1979 (3); v WI 1974 (2) 1980 (2); v NZ 1976 (3); v In 1978 (3) 1982 (6); *v E 1974 (3) 1978 (2) 1982 (1); v A 1972 (2) 1976 (2) 1978 (2) 1981 (3) 1983 (3); v WI 1976 (4); v NZ 1972 (3) 1978 (3)*

Shadab Kabir 5: v Z 1996 (1); *v E 1996 (2); v B 2001 (2)*

Shafiq Ahmed 6: v E 1977 (3); v WI 1980 (2); *v E 1974 (1)*

Shafqat Rana 5: v E 1968 (2); v A 1964 (1); v NZ 1969 (2)

Shahid Afridi 14: v E 2000 (3); v A 1998 (1); v WI 2001 (1); v NZ 2002 (1); v SL 1998 (1) 1999 (2) 2001 (1); *v In 1998 (3); v SL 1998 (1)*

Shahid Israr 1: v NZ 1976

Shahid Mahboob 1: v In 1989

Shahid Mahmood 1: *v E 1962*

Shahid Nazir 8: v WI 1997 (1); v NZ 1996 (2); v SL 1998 (1); v Z 1996 (2); *v SL 1996 (2)*

Shahid Saeed 1: v In 1989

Shakeel Ahmed, sen. 1: v A 1998

Shakeel Ahmed, jun. 3: *v WI 1992 (1); v Z 1994 (2)*

Sharpe, D. 3: v A 1959 (3)

Shoaib Akhtar 21: v A 1998 (2); v WI 1997 (1) 2001 (2); v NZ 2002 (1); v SL 1999 (2) 2001 (1); v Z 1998 (1); *v E 2001 (1); v A 1999 (3); v SA 1997 (3); v In 1998 (1); v SL 1998 (1); v Z 1997 (1); v B 2001 (1)*

Shoaib Malik 2: v SL 2001 (1); v B 2001 (1)

Shoaib Mohammad 45: v E 1983 (1) 1987 (1); v A 1988 (3); v WI 1990 (3); v NZ 1984 (1) 1990 (3); v In 1989 (4); v SL 1985 (1) 1991 (3) 1995 (3); v Z 1993 (3); *v E 1987 (4) 1992 (1); v A 1989 (3); v WI 1987 (3); v NZ 1984 (1) 1988 (2); v In 1983 (2) 1986 (3)*

Shuja-ud-Din 19: v E 1961 (2); v A 1959 (3); v WI 1958 (3); v NZ 1955 (3); v In 1954 (5); *v E 1954 (3)*

Sikander Bakht 26: v E 1977 (2); v WI 1980 (1); v NZ 1976 (1); v In 1978 (2) 1982 (1); *v E 1978 (3) 1982 (2); v A 1978 (2) 1981 (3); v WI 1976 (1); v NZ 1978 (3); v In 1979 (5)*

Tahir Naqqash 15: v A 1982 (3); v In 1982 (2); v SL 1981 (3); *v E 1982 (2); v A 1983 (1); v NZ 1984 (1); v In 1983 (3)*

Talat Ali 10: v E 1972 (3); *v E 1978 (2); v A 1972 (1); v NZ 1972 (1) 1978 (3)*

Taslim Arif 6: v A 1979 (3); v WI 1980 (2); *v In 1979 (1)*

Taufeeq Umar 6: v WI 2001 (2); v SL 2001 (1); v B 2001 (1); *v B 2001 (2)*

Tauseef Ahmed 34: v E 1983 (2) 1987 (2); v A 1979 (3) 1988 (3); v WI 1986 (3); v NZ 1984 (1) 1990 (2); v In 1984 (1); v SL 1981 (3) 1985 (1); v Z 1993 (3); *v E 1987 (2); v A 1989 (3); v NZ 1988 (1); v In 1986 (4); v SL 1985 (2)*

Wajahatullah Wasti 6: v SL 1998 (1) 1999 (1); *v A 1999 (1); v WI 1999 (1); v In 1998 (1); v SL 1998 (1)*

Waqar Hassan 21: v A 1956 (1) 1959 (1); v WI 1958 (1); v NZ 1955 (3); v In 1954 (5); *v E 1954 (4); v WI 1957 (1); v In 1952 (5)*

Waqar Younis 80: v E 2000 (1); v A 1994 (2); v SA 1997 (2); v WI 1990 (3) 1997 (2) 2001 (2); v NZ 1990 (3) 1996 (1) 2002 (1); v In 1989 (2); v SL 1991 (3) 1995 (1) 1999 (3) 2001 (1); v Z 1993 (3) 1996 (2) 1998 (2); v B 2001 (1); *v E 1992 (5) 1996 (3) 2001 (2); v A 1989 (3) 1995 (3) 1999 (1); v SA 1997 (3); v WI 1992 (3) 1999 (3); v NZ 1992 (1) 1993 (3) 1995 (1) 2000 (3); v In 1998 (2); v SL 1994 (2) 2000 (3); v Z 1997 (3); v B 2001 (2)*

Wasim Akram 104: v E 1987 (2) 2000 (2); v A 1994 (2) 1998 (2); v SA 1997 (2); v WI 1986 (2) 1990 (3) 1997 (3); v NZ 1990 (2); v In 1989 (4); v SL 1985 (3) 1991 (3) 1995 (2) 1998 (1) 1999 (1); v Z 1993 (2) 1996 (2) 1998 (2); v B 2001 (1); *v E 1987 (5) 1992 (4) 1996 (3) 2001 (2); v A 1989 (3) 1995 (3) 1999 (3); v SA 1994 (1) 1997 (1); v WI 1987 (3) 1992 (3) 1999 (3); v NZ 1984 (2) 1992 (1) 1993 (3) 1995 (1); v In 1986 (3) 1998 (3); v SL 1985 (3) 1994 (2) 1998 (1) 2000 (3); v Z 1994 (3) 1997 (1); v B 2001 (1)*

Wasim Bari 81: v E 1968 (3) 1972 (3) 1977 (3); v A 1982 (3); v WI 1974 (2) 1980 (2); v NZ 1969 (3) 1976 (2); v In 1978 (3) 1982 (6); *v E 1967 (3) 1971 (3) 1974 (3) 1978 (3) 1982 (3); v A 1972 (3) 1976 (3) 1978 (2) 1981 (3) 1983 (5); v WI 1976 (5); v NZ 1972 (3) 1978 (3); v In 1979 (6) 1983 (3)*

Wasim Raja 57: v E 1972 (1) 1977 (3) 1983 (3); v A 1979 (3); v WI 1974 (2) 1980 (4); v NZ 1976 (1) 1984 (1); v In 1982 (1) 1984 (1); v SL 1981 (3); *v E 1974 (2) 1978 (3) 1982 (1); v A 1978 (1) 1981 (3) 1983 (2); v WI 1976 (5); v NZ 1972 (3) 1978 (3) 1984 (2); v In 1979 (6) 1983 (3)*

Wazir Mohammad 20: v A 1956 (1) 1959 (1); v WI 1958 (3); v NZ 1955 (2); v In 1954 (5); *v E 1954 (2); v WI 1957 (5); v In 1952 (1)*

Younis Ahmed 4: v NZ 1969 (2); *v In 1986 (2)*
Younis Khan 20: v WI 2001 (3); v NZ 2002 (1); v SL 1999 (3) 2001 (3); *v E 2001 (2); v WI 1999 (3); v NZ 2000 (3); v SL 2000 (3); v B 2001 (2)*
Yousuf Youhana 39: v E 2000 (3); v A 1998 (3); v WI 2001 (2); v NZ 2002 (1); v SL 1998 (1) 1999 (3) 2001 (1); v Z 1998 (2); v B 2001 (1); *v E 2001 (2); v A 1999 (3); v SA 1997 (1); v WI 1999 (3); v NZ 2000 (3); v In 1998 (3); v SL 1998 (1) 2000 (3); v Z 1997 (2); v B 2001 (2)*

Zaheer Abbas 78: v E 1972 (2) 1983 (3); v A 1979 (2) 1982 (3); v WI 1974 (2) 1980 (3); v NZ 1969 (1) 1976 (3) 1984 (3); v In 1978 (3) 1982 (6) 1984 (2); v SL 1981 (1) 1985 (2); *v E 1971 (3) 1974 (3) 1982 (3); v A 1972 (3) 1976 (3) 1978 (2) 1981 (2) 1983 (5); v WI 1976 (3); v NZ 1972 (3) 1978 (2) 1984 (2); v In 1979 (5) 1983 (3)*
Zahid Fazal 9: v A 1994 (2); v WI 1990 (3); v SL 1991 (3) 1995 (1)
Zahoor Elahi 2: v NZ 1996 (2)
Zakir Khan 2: v In 1989 (1); *v SL 1985 (1)*
Zulfiqar Ahmed 9: v A 1956 (1); v NZ 1955 (3); *v E 1954 (2); v In 1952 (3)*
Zulqarnain 3: v SL 1985 (3)

SRI LANKA

Number of Test cricketers: 92

Ahangama, F. S. 3: v In 1985 (3)
Amalean, K. N. 2: v P 1985 (1); *v A 1987 (1)*
Amerasinghe, A. M. J. G. 2: v NZ 1983 (2)
Anurasiri, S. D. 18: v A 1992 (3); v WI 1993 (1); v NZ 1986 (1) 1992 (2); v P 1985 (2); v Z 1997 (1); *v E 1991 (1); v In 1986 (1) 1993 (3); v P 1991 (3)*
Arnold, R. P. 41: v E 2000 (3); v A 1999 (3); v SA 2000 (3); v WI 2001 (3); v In 1998 (1) 2001 (3); v P 1996 (2) 2000 (3); v Z 2001 (3); v B 2002 (1); *v E 2002 (3); v SA 2000 (3); v WI 1996 (1); v P 1998 (2) 1999 (3) 2001 (1); v Z 1999 (3)*
Atapattu, M. S. 59: v E 2000 (3); v A 1992 (1) 1999 (3); v SA 2000 (3); v WI 2001 (3); v NZ 1997 (3); v In 1997 (2) 1998 (1) 2001 (3); v P 1996 (2) 2000 (3); v Z 1997 (2) 2001 (3); v B 2001 (1) 2002 (1); *v E 1998 (1) 2002 (3); v SA 1997 (2) 2000 (3); v WI 1996 (1); v NZ 1996 (1); v In 1990 (1) 1993 (1) 1997 (3); v P 1998 (2) 1999 (3) 2001 (1); v Z 1999 (3)*

Bandara, C. M. 1: v NZ 1997
Bandaratilleke, M. R. C. N. 7: v WI 2001 (3); v NZ 1997 (3); *v P 1998 (1)*

Chandana, U. D. U. 7: v A 1999 (1); v SA 2000 (3); v Z 2001 (1); v B 2002 (1); *v P 1998 (1)*

Dassanayake, P. B. 11: v SA 1993 (3); v WI 1993 (1); v P 1994 (2); *v In 1993 (3); v Z 1994 (2)*
de Alwis, R. G. 11: v A 1982 (1); v NZ 1983 (3); v P 1985 (2); *v A 1987 (1); v NZ 1982 (1); v In 1986 (2)*
de Mel, A. L. F. 17: v E 1981 (1); v A 1982 (1); v In 1985 (3); v P 1985 (3); *v E 1984 (1); v In 1982 (1) 1986 (2); v P 1981 (3) 1985 (3)*
de Saram, S. I. 4: *v P 1999 (1); v Z 1999 (3)*
de Silva, A. M. 3: v E 1992 (1); v In 1993 (2)
de Silva, D. S. 12: v E 1981 (1); v A 1982 (1); v NZ 1983 (3); *v E 1984 (1); v NZ 1982 (2); v In 1982 (1); v P 1981 (3)*
de Silva, E. A. R. 10: v In 1985 (1); v P 1985 (1); *v A 1989 (2); v NZ 1990 (3); v In 1986 (3)*
de Silva, G. R. A. 4: v E 1981 (1); *v In 1982 (1); v P 1981 (2)*
de Silva, K. S. C. 8: v In 1997 (1); v P 1996 (1); *v WI 1996 (2); v NZ 1996 (1); v In 1997 (1); v P 1998 (2)*
de Silva, P. A. 93: v E 1992 (1) 2000 (3); v A 1992 (3) 1999 (3); v SA 1993 (3) 2000 (1); v WI 1993 (1); v NZ 1992 (2) 1997 (3); v In 1985 (3) 1993 (3) 1997 (2) 1998 (1); v P 1985 (3) 1994

(2) 1996 (2) 2000 (3); v Z 1996 (2) 1997 (2); v B 2002 (1); *v E 1984 (1) 1988 (1) 1991 (1) 1998 (1) 2002 (3); v A 1987 (1) 1989 (2) 1995 (3); v SA 1997 (2) 2000 (1); v WI 1996 (2); v NZ 1990 (3) 1994 (2) 1996 (2); v In 1986 (3) 1990 (1) 1993 (3) 1997 (3); v P 1985 (3) 1991 (3) 1995 (2) 1998 (1) 1999 (2); v Z 1994 (3)*

de Silva, S. K. L. 3: *v In 1997 (3)*
de Silva, W. R. S. 2: v B 2002 (2)
Dharmasena, H. D. P. K. 25: v E 2000 (2); v SA 1993 (2) 2000 (2); v NZ 1997 (2) v P 1994 (2) 1996 (1) 2000 (1); v Z 1996 (1); *v E 1998 (1); v A 1995 (2); v WI 1996 (2); v NZ 1996 (1); v In 1997 (2); v P 1995 (2); v Z 1994 (2)*
Dias, R. L. 20: v E 1981 (1); v A 1982 (1); v NZ 1983 (2) 1986 (1); v In 1985 (3); v P 1985 (1); *v E 1984 (1); v In 1982 (1) 1986 (3); v P 1981 (3) 1985 (3)*
Dilshan, T. M. 10: v E 2000 (2); *v SA 2000 (2); v P 1999 (2); v Z 1999 (3)*
Dunusinghe, C. I. 5: *v NZ 1994 (2); v P 1995 (3)*

Fernando, C. R. D. 11: v E 2000 (2); v In 2001 (3); v P 2000 (1); v B 2002 (1); *v E 2002 (1); v SA 2000 (3)*
Fernando, E. R. N. S. 5: v A 1982 (1); v NZ 1983 (2); *v NZ 1982 (2)*
Fernando, T. C. B. 9: v WI 2001 (1); v Z 2001 (3); v B 2002 (2); *v E 2002 (1); v P 2001 (1)*

Gallage, I. S. 1: *v Z 1999*
Goonatillake, H. M. 5: v E 1981 (1); *v In 1982 (1); v P 1981 (3)*
Gunasekera, Y. 2: *v NZ 1982 (2)*
Gunawardene, D. A. 3: *v SA 2000 (1); v P 1998 (2)*
Guneratne, R. P. W. 1: v A 1982
Gurusinha, A. P. 41: v E 1992 (1); v A 1992 (3); v SA 1993 (1); v NZ 1986 (1) 1992 (2); v In 1993 (3); v P 1985 (2) 1994 (1); v Z 1996 (2); *v E 1991 (1); v A 1989 (2) 1995 (3); v NZ 1990 (3) 1994 (2); v In 1986 (3) 1990 (1); v P 1985 (1) 1991 (3) 1995 (3); v Z 1994 (3)*

Hathurusinghe, U. C. 26: v E 1992 (1); v A 1992 (3); v SA 1993 (3); v NZ 1992 (2); v In 1993 (3) 1998 (1); *v E 1991 (1); v A 1995 (3); v NZ 1990 (2); v P 1991 (3) 1995 (3) 1998 (1)*
Herath, H. M. R. K. B. 3: v A 1999 (2); v P 2000 (1)
Hettiarachchi, D. 1: v E 2000

Jayasekera, R. S. A. 1: *v P 1981*
Jayasuriya, S. T. 75: v E 1992 (1) 2000 (3); v A 1992 (2) 1999 (3); v SA 1993 (2) 2000 (3); v WI 1993 (1) 2001 (3); v NZ 1997 (3); v In 1993 (1) 1997 (2) 2001 (3); v P 1994 (1) 1996 (2) 2000 (3); v Z 1996 (2) 1997 (2) 2001 (3); v B 2001 (1) 2002 (2); *v E 1991 (1) 1998 (1) 2002 (3); v A 1995 (1); v SA 1997 (2) 2000 (3); v WI 1996 (2); v NZ 1990 (2) 1996 (2); v In 1993 (1) 1997 (3); v P 1991 (3) 1999 (3) 2001 (1); v Z 1994 (1) 1999 (3)*
Jayawardene, D. P. M. D. 45: v E 2000 (3); v A 1999 (3); v SA 2000 (3); v WI 2001 (3); v NZ 1997 (3); v In 1997 (2) 1998 (1) 2001 (3); v P 2000 (3); v Z 2001 (3); v B 2001 (1) 2002 (1); *v E 1998 (1) 2002 (3); v SA 2000 (3); v P 1998 (2) 1999 (3) 2001 (1); v Z 1999 (3)*
Jayawardene, H. A. P. W. 3: v P 2000 (1); v B 2002 (2)
Jeganathan, S. 2: *v NZ 1982 (2)*
John, V. B. 6: v NZ 1983 (3); *v E 1984 (1); v NZ 1982 (2)*
Jurangpathy, B. R. 2: v In 1985 (1); *v In 1986 (1)*

Kalpage, R. S. 11: v SA 1993 (1); v WI 1993 (1); v NZ 1997 (1); v In 1993 (1); v P 1994 (1) 1996 (1); *v In 1993 (3); v P 1998 (1); v Z 1994 (1)*
Kaluperuma, L. W. 2: v E 1981 (1); *v P 1981 (1)*
Kaluperuma, S. M. S. 4: v NZ 1983 (2); *v A 1987 (1)*
Kaluwitharana, R. S. 40: v A 1992 (2) 1999 (3); v NZ 1997 (3); v In 1993 (1) 1997 (2) 1998 (1); v P 1996 (2) 2000 (3); v Z 1996 (2) 1997 (2); *v E 1998 (1); A 1995 (3); v SA 1997 (2) 2000 (2); v WI 1996 (2); v NZ 1996 (2); v P 1998 (2) 1999 (3); v Z 1999 (3)*
Kuruppu, D. S. B. P. 4: v NZ 1986 (1); *v E 1988 (1) 1991 (2); v A 1987 (1)*
Kuruppuarachchi, A. K. 2: v NZ 1986 (1); v P 1985 (1)

Labrooy, G. F. 9: *v E 1988 (1); v A 1987 (1) 1989 (2); v NZ 1990 (3); v In 1986 (1) 1990 (1)*
Lakshitha, M. K. G. C. P. 1: v B 2002
Liyanage, D. K. 9: v A 1992 (2); v SA 1993 (1); v NZ 1992 (2); v In 1993 (2) 2001 (1); *v In 1993 (1)*

Madugalle, R. S. 21: v E 1981 (1); v A 1982 (1); v NZ 1983 (3) 1986 (1); v In 1985 (3); *v E 1984 (1) 1988 (1); v A 1987 (1); v NZ 1982 (1); v In 1982 (1); v P 1981 (3) 1985 (3)*

Madurasinghe, A. W. R. 3: v A 1992 (1); *v E 1988 (1); v In 1990 (1)*

Mahanama, R. S. 52: v E 1992 (1); v A 1992 (3); v SA 1993 (3); v WI 1993 (1); v NZ 1986 (1) 1992 (2); v In 1993 (3) 1997 (2); v P 1985 (2) 1994 (2); v Z 1996 (2) 1997 (2); *v E 1991 (1); v A 1987 (1) 1989 (2) 1995 (2); v SA 1997 (2); v WI 1996 (2); v NZ 1990 (1) 1996 (2); v In 1990 (1) 1993 (3) 1997 (3); v P 1991 (2) 1995 (3); v Z 1994 (3)*

Mendis, L. R. D. 24: v E 1981 (1); v NZ 1983 (3) 1986 (1); v In 1985 (3); v P 1985 (3); *v E 1984 (1) 1988 (1); v In 1982 (1) 1986 (3); v P 1981 (3) 1985 (3)*

Mubarak, J. 1: v B 2002

Muralitharan, M. 76: v E 1992 (1) 2000 (3); v A 1992 (2) 1999 (3); v SA 1993 (3) 2000 (3); v WI 1993 (1) 2001 (3); v NZ 1992 (1) 1997 (3); v In 1993 (2) 1997 (2) 2001 (3); v P 1994 (1) 1996 (1) 2000 (3); v Z 1996 (2) 1997 (2) 2001 (3); v B 2001 (1) 2002 (1); *v E 1998 (1) 2002 (2); v A 1995 (2); v SA 1997 (2) 2000 (2); v WI 1996 (2); v NZ 1993 (1) 1997 (2); v P 1995 (3) 1999 (3) 2001 (1); v Z 1994 (2) 1999 (3)*

Nawaz, M. N. 1: v B 2002

Perera, A. S. A. 3: v In 2001 (2); *v E 1998 (1)*

Perera, P. D. R. L. 7: v SA 2000 (1); v In 1998 (1) 2001 (2); v B 2001 (1); *v E 2002 (1); v SA 2000 (1)*

Pushpakumara, K. R. 23: v In 1997 (2); v P 1994 (1) 2000 (1); v Z 1996 (1) 1997 (2); v B 2001 (1); *v A 1995 (1); v SA 1997 (2); v WI 1996 (1); v NZ 1994 (2); v In 1997 (2); v P 1995 (1) 1999 (2); v Z 1994 (2) 1999 (1)*

Ramanayake, C. P. H. 18: v E 1992 (1); v A 1992 (3); v SA 1993 (2); v NZ 1992 (1); v In 1993 (1); *v E 1988 (1) 1991 (1); v A 1987 (1) 1989 (2); v NZ 1990 (3); v P 1991 (2)*

Ranasinghe, A. N. 2: *v In 1982 (1); v P 1981 (1)*

Ranatunga, A. 93: v E 1981 (1) 1992 (1); v A 1982 (1) 1992 (3) 1999 (3) ; v SA 1993 (3) 2000 (3); v WI 1993 (1); v NZ 1983 (3) 1986 (1) 1992 (2) 1997 (3); v In 1985 (3) 1993 (3) 1997 (2) 1998 (1); v P 1985 (3) 1994 (2) 1996 (2) 2000 (3); v Z 1996 (2) 1997 (2); *v E 1984 (1) 1988 (1) 1998 (1); v A 1987 (1) 1989 (2) 1995 (2); v SA 1997 (2); v WI 1996 (2); v NZ 1990 (3) 1994 (2) 1996 (2); v In 1982 (1) 1986 (3) 1990 (1) 1993 (3) 1997 (3); v P 1981 (2) 1985 (3) 1991 (3) 1995 (3) 1999 (1); v Z 1994 (3)*

Ranatunga, D. 2: *v A 1989 (2)*

Ranatunga, S. 9: v P 1994 (1); *v A 1995 (1); v WI 1996 (1); v NZ 1994 (2); v P 1995 (1); v Z 1994 (3)*

Ratnayake, R. J. 23: v A 1982 (1); v NZ 1983 (1) 1986 (1); v In 1985 (3); v P 1985 (1); *v E 1991 (1); v A 1989 (1); v NZ 1982 (2) 1990 (3); v In 1986 (2) 1990 (1); v P 1985 (3) 1991 (3)*

Ratnayake, J. R. 22: v NZ 1983 (2) 1986 (1); v P 1985 (3); *v E 1984 (1) 1988 (1); v A 1987 (1) 1989 (2); v NZ 1982 (2); v In 1982 (1) 1986 (3); v P 1981 (2) 1985 (3)*

Samarasekera, M. A. R. 4: *v E 1988 (1); v A 1989 (1); v In 1990 (1); v P 1991 (1)*

Samaraweera, D. P. 7: v WI 1993 (1); v P 1994 (1); *v NZ 1994 (2); v In 1993 (3)*

Samaraweera, T. T. 10: v WI 2001 (3); v In 2001 (1); v Z 2001 (3); v B 2001 (1) 2002 (1); *v P 2001 (1)*

Sangakkara, K. C. 24: v E 2000 (3); v SA 2000 (3); v WI 2001 (3); v In 2001 (3); v Z 2001 (3); v B 2001 (1); *v E 2002 (3); v SA 2000 (3); v P 2001 (1)*

Senanayake, C. P. 3: *v NZ 1990 (3)*

Silva, K. J. 7: v In 1997 (1); v P 1996 (1); v Z 1996 (1) 1997 (1); *v A 1995 (1); v In 1997 (1)*

Silva, S. A. R. 9: v In 1985 (3); v P 1985 (1); *v E 1984 (1) 1988 (1); v NZ 1982 (1); v P 1985 (2)*

Tillekeratne, H. P. 71: v E 1992 (1); v A 1992 (1); v SA 1993 (3); v WI 1993 (1) 2001 (3); v NZ 1992 (2) 1997 (2); v In 1993 (3) 1998 (1) 2001 (3); v P 1994 (2) 1996 (2); v Z 1996 (2) 1997 (2) 2001 (3); v B 2001 (1) 2002 (1); *v E 1991 (1) 1998 (1) 2002 (3); v A 1989 (1) 1995 (3); v SA 1997 (2); v WI 1996 (1); v NZ 1990 (3) 1994 (2) 1996 (2); v In 1990 (1) 1993 (3) 1997 (3); v P 1991 (3) 1995 (3) 1998 (2) 2001 (1); v Z 1994 (3)*

Upashantha, K. E. A. 2: v In 1998 (1); *v E 2002 (1)*

Vaas, W. P. U. J. C. 62: v E 2000 (3); v A 1999 (3); v SA 2000 (3); v WI 2001 (3); v In 1997 (2) 1998 (1) 2001 (3); v P 1994 (1) 1996 (2) 2000 (3); v Z 1996 (2) 1997 (2) 2001 (3); v B 2001 (1); *v E 2002 (3); v A 1995 (3); v SA 1997 (1) 2000 (2); v NZ 1994 (2) 1996 (2); v In 1997 (3); v P 1995 (3) 1998 (1) 1999 (3) 2001 (1); v Z 1994 (3) 1999 (3)*

Vandort, M. G. 2: v B 2001 (1) 2002 (1)

Warnapura, B. 4: v E 1981 (1); *v In 1982 (1); v P 1981 (2)*

Warnaweera, K. P. J. 10: v E 1992 (1); v NZ 1992 (2); v In 1993 (3); v P 1985 (1) 1994 (1); *v NZ 1990 (1); v In 1990 (1)*

Weerasinghe, C. D. U. S. 1: v In 1985

Wettimuny, M. D. 2: *v NZ 1982 (2)*

Wettimuny, S. 23: v E 1981 (1); v A 1982 (1); v NZ 1983 (3); v In 1985 (3); v P 1985 (3); *v E 1984 (1); v NZ 1982 (2); v In 1986 (3); v P 1981 (3) 1985 (3)*

Wickremasinghe, A. G. D. 3: v NZ 1992 (2); *v A 1989 (1)*

Wickremasinghe, G. P. 40: v A 1992 (1); v SA 1993 (2); v WI 1993 (1); v NZ 1997 (3); v In 1993 (2); v P 1994 (1); *v E 1998 (1); v A 1995 (3); v SA 1997 (2) 2000 (1); v NZ 1994 (2) 1996 (1); v In 1993 (3) 1997 (1); v P 1991 (3) 1995 (3) 1998 (2) 1999 (3); v Z 1994 (2) 1999 (3)*

Wijegunawardene, K. I. W. 2: *v E 1991 (1); v P 1991 (1)*

Wijesuriya, R. G. C. E. 4: *v P 1981 (1) 1985 (3)*

Wijetunge, P. K. 1: v SA 1993

Zoysa, D. N. T. 24: v E 2000 (1); v A 1999 (3); v SA 2000 (2); v WI 2001 (2); v P 1996 (1) 2000 (2); v Z 2001 (2); *v E 2002 (2); v SA 1997 (1) 2000 (3); v NZ 1996 (2); v P 1999 (1) 2001 (1); v Z 1999 (1)*

ZIMBABWE

Number of Test cricketers: 54

Arnott, K. J. 4: v NZ 1992 (2); v In 1992 (1); *v In 1992 (1)*

Blignaut, A. M. 6: v WI 2001 (2); v In 2001 (2); v B 2000 (2)

Brain, D. H. 9: v NZ 1992 (1); v P 1994 (3); v SL 1994 (2); *v In 1992 (1); v P 1993 (2)*

Brandes, E. A. 10: v E 1996 (1); v NZ 1992 (1); v In 1992 (1); v SL 1999 (1); *v NZ 1995 (2); v In 1992 (1); v P 1993 (3)*

Brent, G. B. 4: v SL 1999 (2); *v SL 2001 (1); v B 2001 (1)*

Briant, G. A. 1: *v In 1992*

Bruk-Jackson, G. K. 2: *v P 1993 (2)*

Burmester, M. G. 3: v NZ 1992 (2); v In 1992 (1)

Butchart, I. P. 1: v P 1994

Campbell, A. D. R. 58: v E 1996 (2); v A 1999 (1); v SA 1995 (1) 1999 (1) 2001 (2); v WI 2001 (2); v NZ 1992 (2) 1997 (2) 2000 (2); v In 1992 (1) 1998 (1) 2001 (2); v P 1994 (1) 1997 (2); v SL 1994 (3) 1999 (3); v B 2000 (2); *v E 2000 (2); v SA 1999 (1); v WI 1999 (2); v NZ 1995 (2) 1997 (2) 2000 (1); v In 1992 (1) 2000 (2) 2001 (2); v P 1993 (3) 1996 (2) 1998 (2); v SL 1996 (2) 1997 (2)*

Carlisle, S. V. 27: v E 1996 (1); v SA 2001 (1); v WI 2001 (1); v NZ 2000 (2); v In 2001 (2); v P 1994 (1); v B 2000 (2); *v E 2000 (1); v WI 1999 (2); v NZ 1995 (2) 2000 (1); v In 2000 (2) 2001 (2); v SL 2001 (3); v B 2001 (2)*

Crocker, G. J. 3: v NZ 1992 (2); v In 1992 (1)

Dekker, M. H. 14: v E 1996 (1); v SA 1995 (1); v P 1994 (2); v SL 1994 (3); *v P 1993 (3) 1996 (2); v SL 1996 (2)*

Ebrahim, D. D. 12: v SA 2001 (2); v WI 2001 (2); v In 2001 (2); v B 2001 (2); *v In 2001 (1); v SL 2001 (1); v B 2001 (2)*

Evans, C. N. 2: v In 1998 (1); *v SL 1996 (1)*

Flower, A. 61: v E 1996 (2); v A 1999 (1); v SA 1995 (1) 1999 (1) 2001 (2); v NZ 1992 (2) 1997 (2) 2000 (2); v In 1992 (1) 1998 (1) 2001 (2); v P 1994 (3) 1997 (2); v SL 1994 (3) 1999 (3); v B 2000 (2); *v E 2000 (2); v SA 1999 (1); v WI 1999 (2); v NZ 1995 (2) 1997 (2) 2000 (1); v In 1992 (1) 2000 (2) 2001 (2); v P 1993 (3) 1996 (2) 1998 (2); v SL 1996 (2) 1997 (2) 2001 (3); v B 2001 (2)*

Flower, G. W. 61: v E 1996 (2); v A 1999 (1); v SA 1995 (1) 1999 (1) 2001 (2); v WI 2001 (2); v NZ 1992 (2) 1997 (2) 2000 (2); v In 1992 (1) 2001 (2); *v SA 1999 (1); v WI 1999 (2); v NZ 1995 (2) 1997 (2); v In 1992 (1) 2000 (2) 2001 (2); v P 1993 (3) 1996 (2) 1998 (2); v SL 1996 (2) 1997 (2) 2001 (3); v B 2001 (2)*
Friend, T. J. 10: v SA 2001 (2); v In 2001 (1); *v In 2001 (2); v SL 2001 (3); v B 2001 (2)*

Goodwin, M. W. 19: v A 1999 (1); v SA 1999 (1); v In 1998 (1); v P 1997 (1); v SL 1999 (3); *v E 2000 (2); v SA 1999 (1); v WI 1999 (2); v NZ 1997 (2); v P 1998 (2); v SL 1997 (2)*
Gripper, T. R. 14: v A 1999 (1); v SA 1999 (1); v SL 1999 (1); *v E 2000 (1); v SA 1999 (1); v WI 1999 (2); v In 2001 (2); v SL 2001 (3); v B 2001 (2)*

Hondo, D. T. 1: v SA 2001
Houghton, D. L. 22: v E 1996 (2); v SA 1995 (1); v NZ 1992 (2) 1997 (2); v In 1992 (1); v P 1994 (3); v SL 1994 (3); *v NZ 1995 (2); v In 1992 (1); v P 1993 (3) 1996 (2)*
Huckle, A. G. 8: v NZ 1997 (2); v In 1998 (1); v P 1997 (1); *v NZ 1997 (2); v P 1998 (1); v SL 1997 (1)*

James, W. R. 4: v SL 1994 (3); *v P 1993 (1)*
Jarvis, M. P. 5: v In 1992 (1); v SL 1994 (3)
Johnson, N. C. 13: v A 1999 (1); v SA 1999 (1); v In 1998 (1); v SL 1999 (3); *v E 2000 (2); v SA 1999 (1); v WI 1999 (2); v P 1998 (2)*

Lock, A. C. I. 1: v SA 1995

Madondo, T. N. 3: v P 1997 (2); *v NZ 2000 (1)*
Marillier, D. A. 5: *v NZ 2000 (1); v SL 2001 (2); v B 2001 (2)*
Masakadza, H. 5: v SA 2001 (2); v WI 2001 (1); *v SL 2001 (2)*
Matambanadzo, E. Z. 3: v NZ 1997 (1); v SL 1999 (1); *v P 1996 (1)*
Mbangwa, M. 15: v SA 1999 (1); v NZ 2000 (1); v In 1998 (1); v P 1997 (2); *v E 2000 (2); v SA 1999 (1); v WI 1999 (1); v NZ 1997 (2); v P 1996 (1) 1998 (2); v SL 1997 (1)*
Murphy, B. A. 11: v In 2001 (2); v B 2000 (1); *v E 2000 (2); v WI 1999 (2); v NZ 2000 (1); v In 2000 (2); v B 2001 (1)*
Mutendera, D. T. 1: v NZ 2000

Nkala, M. L. 6: v NZ 2000 (2); v B 2000 (2); *v E 2000 (1); v In 2000 (1)*

Olonga, H. K. 28: v E 1996 (2); v A 1999 (1); v SA 1999 (1); v NZ 2000 (1); v In 1998 (1) 2001 (1); v P 1994 (1); v SL 1999 (3); *v SA 1999 (1); v WI 1999 (2); v NZ 1995 (1) 2000 (1); v In 2000 (2); v P 1996 (1) 1998 (2); v SL 1996 (2) 2001 (3); v B 2001 (2)*

Peall, S. G. 4: v SL 1994 (2); *v P 1993 (2)*
Price, R. W. 8: v SA 2001 (2); v WI 2001 (2); v SL 1999 (1); v B 2000 (1); *v In 2001 (2)*
Pycroft, A. J. 3: v NZ 1992 (2); v In 1992 (1)

Ranchod, U. 1: *v In 1992*
Rennie, G. J. 23: v A 1999 (1); v SA 1999 (1); v NZ 1997 (2) 2000 (2); v In 1998 (1); v P 1997 (1); v SL 1999 (1); *v SA 1999 (1); v NZ 1997 (2) 2000 (1); v In 2000 (2) 2001 (1); v P 1998 (2); v SL 1997 (2) 2001 (3)*
Rennie, J. A. 4: v NZ 1997 (1); v SL 1994 (1); *v P 1993 (2)*

Shah, A. H. 3: v NZ 1992 (1); *v In 1992 (1); v SL 1996 (1)*
Strang, B. C. 26: v E 1996 (1); v A 1999 (1); v SA 1995 (1) 1999 (1); v WI 2001 (2); v NZ 1997 (2) 2000 (1); v P 1994 (2) 1997 (1); v SL 1999 (3); *v E 2000 (2); v SA 1999 (1); v WI 1999 (1); v NZ 1995 (2) 2000 (1); v In 2000 (2); v P 1996 (2); v SL 1996 (1) 1997 (1)*
Strang, P. A. 24: v E 1996 (2); v SA 1995 (1) 2001 (1); v NZ 1997 (2) 2000 (2); v P 1994 (3) 1997 (1); v SL 1994 (1); *v NZ 1995 (2) 1997 (2); v In 2000 (2); v P 1996 (1); v SL 1996 (2) 1997 (2)*
Streak, H. H. 51: v E 1996 (2); v A 1999 (1); v SA 1995 (1) 2001 (2); v WI 2001 (2); v NZ 1997 (2) 2000 (2); v In 1998 (1) 2001 (2); v P 1994 (3) 1997 (2); v SL 1994 (3); v B 2000 (2); *v E 2000 (2); v WI 1999 (2); v NZ 1995 (2) 1997 (2) 2000 (2); v In 2000 (2) 2001 (2); v P 1993 (3) 1998 (2); v SL 1996 (1) 1997 (2) 2001 (3); v B 2001 (2)*

Taibu, T. 4: v WI 2001 (2); *v In 2001 (2)*
Traicos, A. J. 4: v NZ 1992 (2); v In 1992 (1); *v In 1992 (1)*

Viljoen, D. P. 2: v P 1997 (1); *v In 2000 (1)*

Waller, A. C. 2: v E 1996 (2)
Watambwa, B. T. 6: v In 2001 (2); v B 2000 (2); *v In 2001 (2)*
Whittall, A. R. 10: v P 1997 (1); v SL 1999 (1); *v NZ 1997 (2); v P 1996 (1) 1998 (1); v SL 1996 (2) 1997 (2)*
Whittall, G. J. 45: v E 1996 (1); v A 1999 (1); v SA 1995 (1) 1999 (1) 2001 (2); v WI 2001 (2); v NZ 1997 (2) 2000 (1); v In 2001 (2); v P 1994 (3) 1997 (2); v SL 1994 (3) 1999 (3); v B 2000 (2); *v E 2000 (2); v SA 1999 (1); v NZ 1995 (2) 1997 (2) 2000 (1); v In 2000 (2); v P 1993 (3) 1996 (2); v SL 1996 (2) 1997 (1)*
Wishart, C. B. 21: v SA 1995 (1) 2001 (1); v WI 2001 (2); v NZ 2000 (1); v In 1998 (1); v SL 1999 (1); *v NZ 1995 (1); v P 1996 (2) 1998 (2); v SL 1996 (2) 1997 (2) 2001 (3); v B 2001 (2)*

BANGLADESH

Number of Test cricketers: 28

Akram Khan 6: v In 2000 (1); v Z 2001 (1); *v P 2001 (1); v SL 2002 (1); v Z 2000 (2)*
Al Sahariar 11: v In 2000 (1); v P 2001 (2); v Z 2001 (2); *v NZ 2001 (2); v SL 2001 (1) 2002 (2); v Z 2000 (1)*
Alamgir Kabir 1: *v SL 2002*
Alok Kapali 1: *v SL 2002*
Aminul Islam, sen. 12: v In 2000 (1); v P 2001 (2); v Z 2001 (2); *v NZ 2001 (2); v P 2001 (1); v SL 2001 (1) 2002 (1); v Z 2000 (2)*

Bikash Ranjan Das 1: v In 2000

Ehsanul Haque 1: *v SL 2002*
Enamul Haque 7: v P 2001 (2); v Z 2001 (2); *v P 2001 (1); v SL 2002 (1); v Z 2000 (1)*

Fahim Muntasir 3: v P 2001 (2); *v SL 2002 (1)*

Habibul Bashar 13: v In 2000 (1); v P 2001 (2); v Z 2001 (2); *v NZ 2001 (2); v P 2001 (1); v SL 2001 (1) 2002 (2); v Z 2000 (2)*
Hannan Sarkar 2: *v SL 2002 (2)*
Hasibul Hussain 5: v In 2000 (1); *v NZ 2001 (1); v P 2001 (1); v SL 2001 (1); v Z 2000 (1)*

Javed Omar 9: v P 2001 (1); v Z 2001 (2); *v NZ 2001 (2); v P 2001 (1); v SL 2001 (1); v Z 2000 (2)*

Khaled Mahmud 3: v Z 2001 (1); *v NZ 2001 (2)*
Khaled Masud 12: v In 2000 (1); v P 2001 (2); v Z 2001 (2); *v NZ 2001 (2); v P 2001 (1); v SL 2001 (1) 2002 (2); v Z 2000 (1)*

Manjurul Islam 11: v P 2001 (2); v Z 2001 (1); *v NZ 2001 (2); v P 2001 (1); v SL 2001 (1) 2002 (2); v Z 2000 (2)*
Mashrafe bin Mortaza 4: v Z 2001 (2); *v NZ 2001 (2)*
Mehrab Hossain 7: v In 2000 (1); v P 2001 (2); *v P 2001 (1); v SL 2001 (1); v Z 2000 (2)*
Mohammad Ashraful 7: v P 2001 (1); v Z 2001 (2); *v NZ 2001 (2); v SL 2001 (1) 2002 (1)*
Mohammad Rafiq 1: v In 2000
Mohammad Sharif 8: v P 2001 (2); v Z 2001 (1); *v NZ 2001 (1); v P 2001 (1); v SL 2001 (1); v Z 2000 (2)*
Mushfiqur Rehman 2: *v Z 2000 (2)*

Naimur Rahman 7: v In 2000 (1); v Z 2001 (2); *v P 2001 (1); v SL 2001 (1); v Z 2000 (2)*

Sanuar Hossain 4: v P 2001 (2); *v NZ 2001 (2)*
Shahriar Hossain 1: v In 2000

Talha Jubair 2: *v SL 2002 (2)*
Tapash Baisya 1: *v SL 2002*
Tushar Imran 1: *v SL 2002*

TWO COUNTRIES

Fourteen cricketers have appeared for two countries in Test matches, namely:

Amir Elahi, *India and Pakistan.*
J. J. Ferris, *Australia and England.*
S. C. Guillen, *West Indies and NZ.*
Gul Mahomed, *India and Pakistan.*
F. Hearne, *England and South Africa.*
A. H. Kardar, *India and Pakistan.*
W. E. Midwinter, *England and Australia.*

F. Mitchell, *England and South Africa.*
W. L. Murdoch, *Australia and England.*
Nawab of Pataudi, sen., *England and India.*
A. J. Traicos, *South Africa and Zimbabwe.*
A. E. Trott, *Australia and England.*
K. C. Wessels, *Australia and South Africa.*
S. M. J. Woods, *Australia and England.*

ENGLAND v REST OF THE WORLD

In 1970, owing to the cancellation of the South African tour to England, a series of matches was arranged, with the trappings of a full Test series, between England and the Rest of the World. It was played for the Guinness Trophy.

The following were awarded England caps for playing against the Rest of the World in that series, although the five matches played are now generally considered not to have rated as full Tests: D. L. Amiss (1), G. Boycott (2), D. J. Brown (2), M. C. Cowdrey (4), M. H. Denness (1), B. L. D'Oliveira (4), J. H. Edrich (2), K. W. R. Fletcher (4), A. W. Greig (3), R. Illingworth (5), A. Jones (1), A. P. E. Knott (5), P. Lever (1), B. W. Luckhurst (5), C. M. Old (2), P. J. Sharpe (1), K. Shuttleworth (1), J. A. Snow (5), D. L. Underwood (3), A. Ward (1), D. Wilson (2).

The following players represented the Rest of the World: E. J. Barlow (5), F. M. Engineer (2), L. R. Gibbs (4), Intikhab Alam (5), R. B. Kanhai (5), C. H. Lloyd (5), G. D. McKenzie (3), D. L. Murray (3), Mushtaq Mohammad (2), P. M. Pollock (1), R. G. Pollock (5), M. J. Procter (5), B. A. Richards (5), G. S. Sobers (5).

LIMITED-OVERS INTERNATIONAL CRICKETERS

The following players have appeared for Test-playing countries in limited-overs internationals but had not represented their countries in Test matches by September 30, 2002:

England M. W. Alleyne, I. D. Austin, I. D. Blackwell, A. D. Brown, D. R. Brown, M. V. Fleming, P. J. Franks, I. J. Gould, A. P. Grayson, G. W. Humpage, T. E. Jesty, R. J. Kirtley, G. D. Lloyd, J. D. Love, M. A. Lynch, M. J. Smith, N. M. K. Smith, J. N. Snape, V. S. Solanki, G. P. Swann, S. D. Udal, C. M. Wells, V. J. Wells.

Australia G. A. Bishop, N. W. Bracken, R. J. Campbell, M. J. Di Venuto, S. F. Graf, B. J. Haddin, I. J. Harvey, M. Hauritz, S. Lee, R. J. McCurdy, K. H. MacLeay, J. P. Maher, G. D. Porter, J. D. Siddons, A. M. Stuart, A. Symonds, G. S. Trimble, S. R. Watson, B. A. Williams, B. E. Young, A. K. Zesers.

South Africa S. Abrahams, D. M. Benkenstein, R. E. Bryson, D. J. Callaghan, D. N. Crookes, A. C. Dawson, J. C. Kent, L. J. Koen, C. K. Langeveldt, P. V. Mpitsang, S. J. Palframan, R. J. Peterson, N. Pothas, C. E. B. Rice, M. J. R. Rindel, D. B. Rundle, T. G. Shaw, E. O. Simons, E. L. R. Stewart, R. Telemachus, C. J. P. G. van Zyl, H. S. Williams, C. M. Willoughby, M. Yachad.

West Indies H. A. G. Anthony, D. Brown, B. St A. Browne, H. R. Bryan, V. C. Drakes, R. S. Gabriel, R. C. Haynes, K. C. B. Jeremy, S. S. Joseph, J. J. C. Lawson, R. S. Morton, M. R. Pydanna, K. F. Semple, C. M. Tuckett, L. R. Williams.

New Zealand M. D. Bailey, B. R. Blair, C. E. Bulfin, P. G. Coman, M. W. Douglas, B. G. Hadlee, R. T. Hart, R. L. Hayes, P. A. Hitchcock, L. G. Howell, B. B. McCullum, B. J. McKechnie, E. B. McSweeney, J. P. Millmow, K. D. Mills, C. J. Nevin, J. D. P. Oram, A. J. Penn, R. G. Petrie, B. R. Reid, S. J. Roberts, L. W. Stott, G. P. Sulzberger, A. R. Tait, R. J. Webb, J. W. Wilson, W. A. Wisneski.

India A. C. Bedade, A. Bhandari, Bhupinder Singh, sen., G. Bose, V. B. Chandrasekhar, U. Chatterjee, N. A. David, P. Dharmani, R. S. Ghai, S. C. Khanna, G. K. Khoda, A. R. Khurasiya, T. Kumaran, J. J. Martin, D. Mongia, S. P. Mukherjee, G. K. Pandey, J. V. Paranjpe, A. K. Patel, Randhir Singh, S. S. Raul, L. R. Shukla, R. P. Singh, R. S. Sodhi, S. Somasunder, S. Sriram, Sudhakar Rao, P. S. Vaidya, Yuvraj Singh.

Pakistan Aamer Hameed, Aamer Hanif, Akhtar Sarfraz, Arshad Pervez, Asif Mahmood, Ghulam Ali, Haafiz Shahid, Hasan Jamil, Imran Abbas, Iqbal Sikandar, Irfan Bhatti, Javed Qadir, Kashif Raza, Mahmood Hamid, Mansoor Rana, Manzoor Akhtar, Maqsood Rana, Masood Iqbal, Moin-ul-Atiq, Mujahid Jamshed, Naeem Ahmed, Naeem Ashraf, Naseer Malik, Parvez Mir, Saadat Ali, Saeed Azad, Sajid Ali, Sajjad Akbar, Salim Pervez, Shabbir Ahmed, Shahid Anwar, Shakil Khan, Sohail Fazal, Tanvir Mehdi, Wasim Haider, Yasir Arafat, Zafar Iqbal, Zahid Ahmed.

Sri Lanka J. W. H. D. Boteju, D. L. S. de Silva, G. N. de Silva, E. R. Fernando, K. H. R. K. Fernando, T. L. Fernando, U. N. K. Fernando, J. C. Gamage, W. C. A. Ganegama, F. R. M. Goonatillake, P. W. Gunaratne, A. A. W. Gunawardene, P. D. Heyn, S. A. Jayasinghe, S. H. U. Karnain, C. Mendis, A. M. N. Munasinghe, R. A. P. Nissanka, A. R. M. Opatha, S. P. Pasqual, K. G. Perera, H. S. M. Pieris, S. K. Ranasinghe, N. Ranatunga, N. L. K. Ratnayake, L. P. C. Silva, A. P. B. Tennekoon, M. H. Tissera, D. M. Vonhagt, A. P. Weerakkody, K. Weeraratne, S. R. de S. Wettimuny, R. P. A. H. Wickremaratne.

Zimbabwe R. D. Brown, K. M. Curran, S. G. Davies, K. G. Duers, S. M. Ervine, E. A. Essop-Adam, D. A. G. Fletcher, J. G. Heron, V. R. Hogg, A. J. Mackay, G. C. Martin, M. A. Meman, G. A. Paterson, G. E. Peckover, P. W. E. Rawson, M. A. Vermeulen.

Bangladesh Ahmed Kamal, Alam Talukdar, Aminul Islam, jun., Anisur Rahman, Ather Ali Khan, Azhar Hussain, Faruq Ahmed, Faruq Chowdhury, Gazi Ashraf, Ghulam Faruq, Ghulam Nausher, Hafizur Rahman, Harunur Rashid, Jahangir Alam, Jahangir Badshah, Mafizur Rahman, Mahbubur Rahman, Mazharul Haque, Minhazul Abedin, Morshed Ali Khan, Nasir Ahmed, Neeyamur Rashid, Nurul Abedin, Rafiqul Alam, Raqibul Hassan, Saiful Islam, Sajjad Ahmed, Samiur Rahman, Shafiuddin Ahmed, Shahidur Rahman, Shariful Haq, Sheikh Salahuddin, Tareq Aziz, Wahidul Gani, Zahid Razzak, Zakir Hassan.

A. C. Gilchrist appeared for Australia in 76 limited-overs internationals before making his Test debut.

INTERNATIONAL COACHES

In a world where Australia seem to be the fount of all innovation, it comes as a surprise to discover that it was New Zealand who appointed the first full-time coach (or cricket manager) to their national team. That was Glenn Turner, in 1985-86. Australia and England followed suit the following year, and eventually every country had one.

This list attempts to log the full-time coaches employed by the Test teams and the results they enjoyed or endured. It is sometimes difficult to establish exactly when the post became full-time. Ken Barrington, for example, organised practice on a succession of England tours before his untimely death in 1981 – but usually as assistant manager, and never as a fixture on the payroll. That system lived on in Sri Lanka, where a series of assistant managers were contracted until as late as 1995-96. The policy has been to leave out coaches who were assistant managers under contract for a specific tour or term, in order to home in on those engaged as full employees of the national board, responsible, alongside the captain, for all cricket matters. By this reckoning, there have been 51 coaches (as distinct from coaching stints) shared between the ten Test nations.

Australia have had fewest coaches and most success. The first, Bob Simpson, lasted longer than any other coach anywhere – nine and a half years. The second, Geoff Marsh, helped them to the double triumph of heading the Wisden World Championship (as it then was) and winning the World Cup – and later became the first man to coach two Test-playing nations, when he joined Zimbabwe. The third Australian, John Buchanan, is the most successful coach in Test history, by a long chalk: his victory percentage is 81, while nobody else who has served for ten Tests or more can manage even 50 per cent.

Buchanan is also the most successful one-day coach (among those in office for 20 or more matches), just squeezing past Bob Woolmer, whose South Africans were the one-day form team of the late 1990s: Buchanan's victory percentage is 74, Woolmer's 73. Next come Bruce Yardley (Sri Lanka) with 69, Intikhab Alam (in his second stint in charge of Pakistan) with 67, Mudassar Nazar (also on his return to Pakistan) with 66, Graham Ford (Woolmer's successor) with 65 and then Dav Whatmore (in his current spell with Sri Lanka) and Bob Simpson (Australia), both with 64. Even if the Ashes series had ended in a whitewash, Duncan Fletcher would have remained England's most successful Test coach; in one-day cricket the winner is Micky Stewart, who steered England to a World Cup final in 1992. **Steven Lynch**

- Figures in brackets after a country indicate the number of separate stints as a coach, which is not necessarily the same as the number of coaches
- %W = percentage of completed games won (this assumes a tie is equivalent to half a win)
- Letters in brackets give nationalities of non-native coaches
- WC = World Cup winner

England (5)	Starting date	P	W	Tests D	L	%W	P	W	ODIs T	L	NR	%W
M. J. Stewart	Oct 1986	58	12	26	20	21	91	52	1	35	3	60
K. W. R. Fletcher	Oct 1992	26	5	6	15	19	23	10	0	13	0	43
R. Illingworth	Mar 1995	11	2	6	3	18	16	5	0	11	0	31
D. Lloyd	Apr 1996	34	9	12	13	26	54	25	1	27	1	48
D. A. G. Fletcher (Z)	Oct 1999	41	14	12	15	34	55	25	0	28	2	47

G. A. Gooch acted as coach for the 1999 Test series against New Zealand (W1, D1, L2) after Lloyd resigned. Illingworth, already chairman of selectors, became manager as well for a year. Figures to end of Third Test in Australia 2002-03.

Australia (3)	Starting date	P	W	Tests D	L	%W	P	W	ODIs T	L	NR	%W
R. B. Simpson	Sept 1986	93	39	35*	19	42	195	123	2	68	2	64
G. R. Marsh	June 1996	39	18	9	12	46	90	49	2	39	0	56WC
J. M. Buchanan	Nov 1999	37	30	3	4	81	70	49	2	17	2	74

*A. R. Border acted as coach in Zimbabwe (one Test, three ODIs, all won) after Marsh resigned. * Includes one tie. Figures to end of Third Test v England 2002-03.*

South Africa (4)	Starting date	P	W	Tests D	L	%W	P	W	ODIs T	L	NR	%W
M. J. Procter	Sept 1991	17	5	8	4	29	56	24	0	30	2	44
R. A. Woolmer (E)	Oct 1994	44	21	14	9	48	117	83	1	30	3	73
G. X. Ford	July 1999	33	16	9	8	48	83	52	2	28	1	65
E. O. Simons	June 2002	4	4	0	0	100	11	7	0	4	0	64

Figures to 24 Nov. 2002.

West Indies (6)	Starting date	P	W	Tests D	L	%W	P	W	ODIs T	L	NR	%W
R. B. Kanhai	Oct 1992	19	9	7	3	47	54	32	1	19	2	63
A. M. E. Roberts	Feb 1995	10	3	3	4	30	27	13	0	14	0	48
C. H. Lloyd	Apr 1996	2	1	1	0	50	6	3	0	3	0	50
M. D. Marshall	Oct 1996	30	9	7	14	30	49	24	1	24	0	50
Sir Viv Richards	June 1999	2	0	0	2	0	21	7	0	13	1	35
R. A. Harper	Feb 2000	37	8	10	19	22	64	29	0	33	2	47

Lloyd continued as manager after bringing in Marshall as coach. Richards took over during the 1999 World Cup when Marshall fell ill, but those results are included in Marshall's record. Figures to end of 2002-03 tour of India (not including Bangladesh), 24 Nov. 2002.

New Zealand (9)	Starting date	Tests					ODIs					
		P	W	D	L	%W	P	W	T	L	NR	%W
G. M. Turner	Sept 1985	13	5	6	2	**38**	25	8	0	16	1	33
G. D. Alabaster	Apr 1986	6	0	5	1	**0**	22	9	0	13	0	41
R. S. Cunis	Nov 1988	16	3	6	7	**19**	19	7	0	12	0	37
W. K. Lees	Nov 1990	10	1	6	3	**10**	36	17	0	18	1	49
G. P. Howarth	Dec 1992	17	3	5	9	**18**	38	11	1	24	2	32
G. M. Turner	Oct 1995	8	0	5	3	**0**	23	11	0	12	0	48
S. J. Rixon (A)	Nov 1996	26	9	8	9	**35**	69	25	3	35	6	42
D. G. Trist	Oct 1999	17	5	5	7	**29**	47	18	0	27	2	40
D. C. Aberhart	July 2001	11	4	5	2	**36**	35	12	0	22	1	35
Coach with more than one term												
G. M. Turner	two stints	21	5	11	5	**24**	48	19	0	28	1	40

Alabaster's record includes four ODIs in Sri Lanka and Sharjah in April 1986 (W1, L3) when he deputised for Turner (unavailable). Howarth resigned in Jan 1995 and was temporarily replaced by J. R. Reid for the Third Test against Pakistan and the four-Test series in the West Indies (Tests: D2, L3; ODIs: W4, L6). Figures to 29 Nov, 2002.

India (8)	Starting date	Tests					ODIs					
		P	W	D	L	%W	P	W	T	L	NR	%W
B. S. Bedi	July 1990	4	1	2	1	**25**	8	6	0	2	0	75
A. A. Baig	Sept 1991	5	0	1	4	**0**	26	10	1	14	1	42
A. L. Wadekar	Oct 1992	22	10	10	2	**45**	70	41	1	27	1	60
S. M. Patil	Apr 1996	3	0	2	1	**0**	10	2	0	7	1	22
Madan Lal	Sept 1996	20	5	10	5	**25**	79	33	1	38	7	46
A. D. Gaekwad	Sept 1998	7	1	2	4	**14**	47	24	0	22	1	52
Kapil Dev	Aug 1999	8	1	2	5	**12**	40	16	0	23	1	41
J. G. Wright (NZ)	Nov 2000	30	13	9	8	**43**	62	35	0	24	3	59

Gaekwad returned in Sept–Oct 2000 for nine one-day games (W5, L4) after Kapil Dev resigned. Figures to end of 2002-03 series v West Indies.

Pakistan (15)	Starting date	Tests					ODIs					
		P	W	D	L	%W	P	W	T	L	NR	%W
Intikhab Alam	Oct 1991	9	4	4	1	**44**	42	19	2	20	1	49WC
Mudassar Nazar	Feb 1993	–	–	–	–	**–**	8	4	0	4	0	50
Javed Miandad	Mar 1993	6	2	2	2	**33**	13	8	1	4	0	65
Intikhab Alam	Feb 1994	12	7	2	3	**59**	33	21	2	10	0	67
Mushtaq Mohammad	Sept 1995	13	5	3	5	**38**	60	34	0	25	1	58
Haroon Rashid	May 1997	11	5	4	2	**45**	37	14	0	21	2	40
Javed Miandad	Sept 1998	10	3	4	3	**30**	23	14	0	9	0	61
Mushtaq Mohammad	May 1999	–	–	–	–	**–**	10	6	0	4	0	60
Wasim Raja	Sept 1999	–	–	–	–	**–**	8	7	1	0	0	94
R. A. Pybus (SA)	Nov 1999	3	0	0	3	**0**	–	–	–	–	–	–
Intikhab Alam	Jan 2000	2	0	0	2	**0**	13	4	0	9	0	31
Javed Miandad	Mar 2000	13	4	6	3	**31**	38	22	0	16	0	58
R. A. Pybus (SA)	May 2001	3	2	0	1	**67**	6	3	0	3	0	50
Mudassar Nazar	Sept 2001	6	5	0	1	**83**	33	21	0	11	1	66
R. A. Pybus (SA)	Oct 2002	5	2	0	3	**40**	4	4	0	0	0	100
Coaches with more than one term												
Intikhab Alam	three stints	23	11	6	6	**48**	88	44	4	39	1	53
Javed Miandad	three stints	29	9	12	8	**31**	74	44	1	29	0	60
Mushtaq Mohammad	two stints	13	5	3	5	**38**	70	40	0	29	1	58
R. A. Pybus (SA)	on 3rd stint	11	4	0	7	**36**	10	7	0	3	0	70
Mudassar Nazar	two stints	6	5	0	1	**83**	41	25	0	15	1	63

K. Ibadulla acted as coach for a Sharjah one-day tournament in April 1995 (W2, L1). Mushtaq did not tour England in 1996, when Nasim-ul-Ghani, styled assistant manager, took over (Tests: W2, D1; ODIs: W1, L2). Intikhab resigned after the Second Test against Sri Lanka in 1999-2000 and Javed took over for the Third. Figures to 30 Nov, 2002 (after fourth ODI v Zimbabwe).

Sri Lanka (4)	Starting date	Tests					ODIs					
		P	W	D	L	%W	P	W	T	L	NR	%W
D. F. Whatmore	Sept 1995	8	4	0	4	**50**	40	24	1	14	1	63WC
B. Yardley (A)	Jan 1997	15	2	8	5	**13**	37	24	0	11	2	69
R. L. Dias	May 1998	7	3	2	2	**43**	33	12	0	21	0	36
D. F. Whatmore	July 1999	39	18	8	13	**46**	94	58	1	32	3	64

Coach with more than one term

		P	W	D	L	%W	P	W	T	L	NR	%W
D. F. Whatmore	on 2nd stint	47	22	8	17	**47**	134	82	2	46	4	64

E. R. Fernando (1994) and T. B. Kehelgemuwa (1995) were the last in a long line of assistant managers-cum-coaches, none a full-time appointment. Figures to 24 Nov, 2002.

Zimbabwe (4)	Starting date	Tests					ODIs					
		P	W	D	L	%W	P	W	T	L	NR	%W
J. H. Hampshire (E)	Sept 1992	16	1	8	7	**6**	37	5	2	28	2	17
D. L. Houghton	Oct 1996	23	2	9	12	**9**	90	31	2	55	2	36
C. G. Rackemann (A)	Sept 2001	13	3	4	6	**23**	39	9	0	30	0	23
G. R. Marsh (A)	Oct 2001	9	1	1	7	**11**	20	6	0	14	0	30

Hampshire did not travel to India in 1992-93, but the results are included in his figures. D. H. Streak was assistant manager in Sri Lanka in Aug–Sept 1996 when Houghton was unavailable (two Tests, three ODIs, all lost). A. J. Pycroft filled in May–July 2000 (Tests: D1, L1; ODIs: W4, L3). Figures to 24 Nov, 2002.

Bangladesh (4)	Starting date	Tests					ODIs					
		P	W	D	L	%W	P	W	T	L	NR	%W
C. G. Greenidge (WI)	Nov 1996	–	–	–	–	–	35	3	0	32	0	9
E. J. Barlow (SA)	Oct 1999	1	0	0	1	**0**	3	0	0	3	0	0
T. M. Chappell (A)	Mar 2001	10	0	1	9	**0**	9	0	0	9	0	0
Mohsin Kamal (P)	Mar 2002	4	0	0	4	**0**	8	0	0	8	0	0

Mudassar Nazar (P) and M. Amarnath (I) both coached Bangladesh before they attained full ODI status. Sarwar Imran deputised for the three one-day matches in the Asia Cup in May 2000, all lost, after Barlow fell ill.

BIRTHS AND DEATHS OF PAST CRICKETERS

 This section includes cricketers no longer playing first-class cricket who have
- appeared in a Test
- appeared in a one-day international for a Test-playing country
- played county cricket and 200 or more first-class matches – 100 or more since the Second World War
- captained a county for three seasons or more since 1890

The section also contains
- all *Wisden* Cricketers of the Year no longer playing first-class cricket, including the schoolboys chosen in the 1918 and 1919 Almanacks
- players or personalities thought to be of special interest

Abbreviations
- a full list appears on page 183

Symbols
- * = Test player   ** = appeared for two countries in Tests   † = also played for team under its previous name

Notes
- for cricketers who played in 2001-02 or 2002, see the Register of Current Players (pages 230–251)
- *CY* = Cricketer of the Year, followed by the year of selection
- a list of Cricketers of the Year appears on pages 252–254

NOTES ON BIRTHS AND DEATHS

By ROBERT BROOKE

The births and deaths of leading cricketers were included in the very first *Wisden*, in 1864, although they originally appeared in calendar form, alongside such information as the closing dates of the British Museum, the start of the university terms, and the martyrdom of Charles I. The section switched to alphabetical order in 1867, when it contained 394 past and present cricketers, though not W. G. Grace, who was already entering his third first-class season at the age of 18. The omission was rectified in 1871, and Grace has been there ever since – accompanied, as time went on, by seven members of his immediate family.

Births and Deaths have appeared in almost every edition since and now contain more than 3,000 names. This year's new entries include two Test captains, Richie Richardson and Mike Atherton, as well as Trevor Penney, the Warwickshire batsman and cover fielder, and Steve Watkin, who was forever in charge of one end at Sophia Gardens, Cardiff; some of them are strictly speaking re-entries, as they were in the list before 1990 when the Register of Players was introduced to cover those still playing. Among non-players recognised for their contribution to the game are the new chairman of the England and Wales Cricket Board, David Morgan, the historian David Frith, and the administrator Geoffrey Howard, who died as the list was being prepared.

The oldest surviving player in this year's list is Frank Shipston, a Nottinghamshire batsman from 1925 to 1933, who was born in July 1906. The oldest surviving Test player is the New Zealand batsman Lindsay Weir, born June 1908, while the oldest surviving Wisden Cricketer of the Year is Bill Brown of Australia, born July 1912, and picked in 1939 after carrying his bat for 206 in the Lord's Test. A curiosity attaches itself to H. L. Calder, who became the youngest Cricketer of the Year as a 17-year-old schoolboy in 1918, while first-class cricket was curtailed by war; when he died, aged 94, in 1995, he was the oldest.

The oldest player for whom no death date is known is J. R. Hodges, who represented Australia in the inaugural Test in 1876-77. More recently, South Africa's J. M. Blanckenberg left no forwarding address after backing the wrong side in the Second World War. His fellow-countryman I. D. Buys, and India's Cota Ramaswami and E. S. Maka, are surely dead, but the details are unknown and the files remain open.

The earliest entry is Robert Colchin of Kent and All-England, born in 1713 and known as "Long Robin", who helped to support himself with a little smuggling, while William Lambert of Surrey (1779–1851) sought to supplement his income by selling matches – a weakness not unknown in our own time.

The letter of the alphabet with most entries is S, with 314 – helped greatly by the Smiths, of whom there are 39. The Joneses, with 17, just can't keep up. The longest single-barrelled surname belongs to L. Sivaramakrishnan, the Indian leg-spinner of the 1980s. The players with most teams to their name are Javed Burki, Imran Khan, Naushad Ali and Kepler Wessels, with seven each, excluding their Test sides – so if a winner is needed, it must be Wessels, who played international cricket for both Australia and South Africa.

The first woman to be included, as far back as 1915, was Mrs H. M. Grace, mother of three Test cricketers. The Royal Family is represented by Prince Philip, Duke of Edinburgh, twice President of MCC, while Lord Frederick Beauclerk was descended from a King, albeit through Nell Gwynn. The only prime minister on the list is Lord Home of the Hirsel, who may also hold the record for the most versions of his name – he also appeared as Lord Dunglass, the 14th Earl of Home, Sir Alec Douglas-Home, and Lord Home of the Hirschel (a *Wisden* error). Learie Constantine is the only professional to become a peer. Vijay Thackersey appears under the name of his father's trade: Merchant.

Sir C. Aubrey Smith, a renowned Hollywood actor who captained England in his only Test, is also probably the only true Cockney in Births and Deaths; he is joined this year by another Hollywood knight, Sir Tim Rice, current president of MCC and winner of three Oscars for his song lyrics. Peter Gibbs, once a Derbyshire batsman, is now a distinguished television playwright, while Maurice Allom was an amateur jazz saxophonist of some standing. "Félix" (N. Wanostrocht) – cricketer, artist, musician and inventor – excelled at everything bar making a decent living.

Roy Fredericks, the left-handed West Indies opener, was also a political left-winger and minister in Guyana. A. E. R. Gilligan, a right-hander, was also a right-wing activist whose name was forwarded to the Australian government by Special Branch. The ancestry of A. J. D. Diver and his nephew E. J. included the Irish freedom fighter Michael Dwyer. He was transported to Australia, a form of emigration used by forebears of two Test captains, D. W. Gregory (Australia) and Gubby Allen (England).

No such luck for Leslie Hylton, a West Indies fast bowler of the 1930s, who was executed for murdering his wife. Circumstantial evidence was enough to get Billy Bestwick, Derbyshire seam bowler and first-class umpire, arrested for murder, although he was later released; his long-time bowling partner, A. R. Warren, was rescued by well-wishers after taking to the road. The England all-rounder F. R. Foster, of quirky view and lifestyle, finished life as a psychiatric detainee. R. J. Crisp climbed Mount Kilimanjaro before becoming a Test fast bowler, and wrote on his exploits in the Second World War; A. J. Evans went into print about his adventures as an escaping prisoner in the First. David Sheppard became an Anglican bishop, J. H. Parsons a canon after entering Births and Deaths in 1912 as a professional. The Studds were Christian missionaries, of whom C. T. died a celebrity, G. B. in obscurity and abject poverty.

Cricketers were never just players of a game.

Abbreviations

ADBP	Agricultural Development Bank of Pakistan (P)
Ant.	Antonians (SL)
Auck.	Auckland (NZ)
B'dos	Barbados (WI)
B'pur	Bahawalpur (P)
BG	British Guiana *Guyana since 1966* (WI)
Bloom.	Bloomfield Cricket and Athletic Club (SL)
BRC	Burgher Recreation Club (SL)
C. Dist.	Central Districts (NZ)
C. Ind.	Central India *to 1939-40, Holkar to 1954-55, Madhya Bharat to 1956-57, Madhya Pradesh since 1957-58* (In)
Cant.	Canterbury (NZ)
CCC	Colombo Cricket Club (SL)
Comb. Is.	Combined Islands (WI)
CU	Cambridge University (E)
Customs	Pakistan Customs (P)
CY	Cricketer of the Year
E. Prov.	Eastern Province (SA)
E. Tvl	Eastern Transvaal *Easterns since 1995-96* (SA)
Eur.	Europeans (In)
F'bad	Faisalabad (P)
FS	Free State *Orange Free State to 1994-95* (SA)
Griq. W.	Griqualand West (SA)
Guj.	Gujarat (In)
H'bad	Hyderabad (In)
HBFC	House Building Finance Corporation (P)
HBL	Habib Bank Ltd (P)
H. Pradesh	Himachal Pradesh (In)
I'bad	Islamabad (P)
IDBP	Industrial Development Bank of Pakistan (P)
Ind. Rlwys	Indian Railways (In)
Ind. Serv.	Indian Services (In)
Jam.	Jamaica (WI)
J/K	Jammu and Kashmir (In)
Kar.	Karachi (P)
Karn.	Karnataka *Mysore to 1972-73* (In)
KRL	Khan Research Laboratories (P)
KZN	KwaZulu-Natal *Natal to 1997-98* (SA)
Mash.	Mashonaland (Z)
Mat.	Matabeleland (Z)
MCB	Muslim Commercial Bank (P)
MCC	Marylebone Cricket Club (E)
MCD	Mashonaland Country Districts (Z)
Mor.	Moratuwa Sports Club (SL)
M. Pradesh	Madhya Pradesh *Central India to 1939-40, Holkar to 1954-55, Madhya Bharat to 1956-57* (In)
M'tra	Maharashtra (In)
Naw.	Nawanagar (In)
NBP	National Bank of Pakistan (P)
NCC	Nondescripts Cricket Club (SL)
N. Dist.	Northern Districts (NZ)
NE Tvl	North-Eastern Transvaal (SA)
NSW	New South Wales (A)
N. Tvl	Northern Transvaal *Northerns since 1997-98* (SA)
NWFP	North-West Frontier Province (P)
OFS	Orange Free State *Free State since 1995-96* (SA)
OU	Oxford University (E)
PACO	Pakistan Automobile Corporation (P)
Pak. Rlwys	Pakistan Railways (P)
Pak. Us	Pakistan Universities (P)
Pan.	Panadura Sports Club (SL)
PIA	Pakistan International Airlines (P)
PNSC	Pakistan National Shipping Corporation (P)
PWD	Public Works Department (P)
Qld	Queensland (A)
R'pindi	Rawalpindi (P)
Raja.	Rajasthan (In)
Rhod.	Rhodesia (SA)
S. Aust.	South Australia (A)
Seb.	Sebastianites (SL)
SLAF	Air Force (SL)
S. Punjab	Southern Punjab *Patiala to 1958-59, Punjab since 1968-69* (In)
SSC	Sinhalese Sports Club (SL)
S'tra	Saurashtra *West India to 1945-46, Kathiawar to 1949-50* (In)
Tas.	Tasmania (A)
TC	Travancore-Cochin *Kerala since 1956-57* (In)
TN	Tamil Nadu *Madras to 1959-60* (In)
T/T	Trinidad & Tobago (WI)
TU	Tamil Union Cricket and Athletic Club (SL)
Tvl	Transvaal *Gauteng since 1997-98* (SA)
UBL	United Bank Ltd (P)
Under-23	Board Under-23 XI (SL)
Under-24	Mashonaland Under-24 (Z)
U. Pradesh	Uttar Pradesh *United Provinces to 1948-49* (In)
U. Prov.	United Provinces *to 1948-49, Uttar Pradesh since 1949-50* (In)
Vic.	Victoria (A)
Vidarbha	CP & Berar *to 1949-50, Madhya Pradesh to 1956-57* (In)
W. Aust.	Western Australia (A)
WAPDA	Water and Power Development Authority (P)
Wgtn	Wellington (NZ)
W. Ind.	West India *to 1945-46, Kathiawar to 1949-50, Saurashtra since 1950-51* (In)
WPC	Western Province (City) (SL)
WPN	Western Province (North) (SL)
W. Prov.	Western Province (SA)
WPS	Western Province (South) (SL)
W. Tvl	Western Transvaal *North West since 1996-97* (SA)
Zimb.	Zimbabwe

Aamer Hameed (Pak. Us, Lahore, Punjab & OU) b Oct. 18, 1954
*Aamer Malik (ADBP, PIA, Multan & Lahore) b Jan. 3, 1963
*Aamir Sohail (Lahore, HBL, Sargodha, Allied Bank & Som) b Sept. 14, 1966
Abberley, R. N. (Warwicks) b April 22, 1944
*a'Beckett, E. L. (Vic.) b Aug. 11, 1907, d June 2, 1989
*Abdul Kadir (Kar. & NBP) b May 10, 1944
*Abdul Qadir (HBL, Lahore & Punjab) b Sept. 15, 1955
*Abel, R. (Surrey; *CY 1890*) b Nov. 30, 1857, d Dec. 10, 1936
Aberhart, D. C. (Cant. & C. Dist; NZ coach) b March 23, 1953
*Abid Ali, S. (H'bad) b Sept. 9, 1941
Abrahams, J. (Lancs) b July 21, 1952
*Absolom, C. A. (CU & Kent) b June 7, 1846, d July 30, 1889
Acfield, D. L. (CU & Essex) b July 24, 1947
*Achong, E. (T/T) b Feb. 16, 1904, d Aug. 29, 1986
Ackerman, H. M. (Border, NE Tvl, Northants, Natal & W. Prov.) b April 28, 1947
Adams, P. W. (Cheltenham & Sussex; *CY 1919*) b Sept. 5, 1900, d Sept. 28, 1962
*Adcock, N. A. T. (Tvl & Natal; *CY 1961*) b March 8, 1931
*Adhikari, H. R. (Guj., Baroda & Ind. Serv.) b July 31, 1919
*Afaq Hussain (Kar., Pak Us, PIA & PWD) b Dec. 31, 1939
Afford, J. A. (Notts) b May 12, 1964
*Aftab Baloch (PWD, Kar., Sind, NBP & PIA) b April 1, 1953
*Aftab Gul (Punjab U., Pak. Us & Lahore) b March 31, 1946
*Agha Saadat Ali (Pak. Us, Punjab, B'pur & Lahore) b June 21, 1929, d Oct. 26, 1995
*Agha Zahid (Pak Us, Punjab, Lahore & HBL) b Jan. 7, 1953
*Agnew, J. P. (Leics; *CY 1988*; broadcaster) b April 4, 1960
*Ahangama, F. S. (SSC) b Sept. 14, 1959
Aird, R. (CU & Hants; Sec. MCC 1953–62, Pres. MCC 1968–69) b May 4, 1902, d Aug. 16, 1986
Aislabie, B. (Surrey, Hants, Kent & Sussex; Sec. MCC 1822–42) b Jan. 14, 1774, d June 2, 1842
Aitchison, Rev. J. K. (Scotland) b May 26, 1920, d Feb. 13, 1994
Alabaster, G. D. (N. Dist., Otago, Cant.; NZ coach) b Dec. 10, 1933
*Alabaster, J. C. (Otago) b July 11, 1930
Alcock, C. W. (Sec. Surrey CCC 1872–1907; Editor *Cricket* 1882–1907) b Dec. 2, 1842, d Feb. 26, 1907
Alderman, A. E. (Derbys) b Oct. 30, 1907, d June 4, 1990

*Alderman, T. M. (W. Aust., Kent & Glos; *CY 1982*) b June 12, 1956
*Alexander, F. C. M. (CU & Jam.) b Nov. 2, 1928
*Alexander, G. (Vic.) b April 22, 1851, d Nov. 6, 1930
*Alexander, H. H. (Vic.) b June 9, 1905, d April 15, 1993
Alexander, Lord (Pres. MCC 2000–01) b Sept. 5, 1936
*Ali Hussain Rizvi (Kar. & Customs) by Jan. 6, 1974
Alikhan, R. I. (Sussex, PIA, Surrey & PNSC) b Dec. 28, 1962
*Alim-ud-Din (Rajputana, Guj., Sind, B'pur, Kar. & PWD) b Dec. 15, 1930
*Allan, D. W. (B'dos) b Nov. 5, 1937
*Allan, F. E. (Vic.) b Dec. 2, 1849, d Feb. 9, 1917
Allan, J. M. (OU, Kent, Warwicks & Scotland) b April 2, 1932
*Allan, P. J. (Qld) b Dec. 31, 1935
*Allcott, C. F. W. (Auck.) b Oct. 7, 1896, d Nov. 19, 1973
Allen, B. O. (CU & Glos) b Oct. 13, 1911, d May 1, 1981
*Allen, D. A. (Glos) b Oct. 29, 1935
*Allen, Sir George O. B. (CU & Middx; Pres. MCC 1963–64) b July 31, 1902, d Nov. 29, 1989
*Allen, I. B. A. (Windwards) b Oct. 6, 1965
Allen, M. H. J. (Northants & Derbys) b Jan. 7, 1933, d Oct. 6, 1995
*Allen, R. C. (NSW) b July 2, 1858, d May 2, 1952
Alletson, E. B. (Notts) b March 6, 1884, d July 5, 1963
Alley, W. E. (NSW & Som; Test umpire; *CY 1962*) b Feb. 3, 1919
*Allom, M. J. C. (CU & Surrey; Pres. MCC 1969–70) b March 23, 1906, d April 8, 1995
*Allott, G. I. (Cant.) b Dec. 24, 1971
*Allott, P. J. W. (Lancs & Wgtn) b Sept. 14, 1956
Altham, H. S. CBE (OU, Surrey & Hants; historian; Pres. MCC 1959–60) b Nov. 30, 1888, d March 11, 1965
*Amalean, K. N. (SL) b April 7, 1965
*Amarnath, Lala (N. B.) (N. Ind., S. Punjab, Guj., Patiala, U. Pradesh & Ind. Rlwys) b Sept. 11, 1911, d Aug. 5, 2000
*Amarnath, M. (Punjab & Delhi; *CY 1984*) b Sept. 24, 1950
*Amarnath, S. (Punjab & Delhi) b Dec. 30, 1948
*Amar Singh, L. (Patiala, W. Ind. & Naw.) b Dec. 4, 1910, d May 20, 1940
*Ambrose, C. E. L. (Leewards & Northants; *CY 1992*) b Sept. 21, 1963
*Amerasinghe, A. M. J. G. (Nomads & Ant.) b Feb. 2, 1954

*Ames, L. E. G. CBE (Kent; *CY 1929*) b Dec. 3, 1905, d Feb. 26, 1990

**Amir Elahi (Baroda, N. Ind., S. Punjab & B'pur) b Sept. 1, 1908, d Dec. 28, 1980

*Amiss, D. L. MBE (Warwicks; *CY 1975*) b April 7, 1943

*Amre, P. K. (†Mumbai, Ind. Rlwys, Raja., Bengal, Boland & Goa) b Aug. 14, 1968

Anderson, I. S. (Derbys & Boland) b April 24, 1960

*Anderson, J. H. (W. Prov.) b April 26, 1874, d March 11, 1926

*Anderson, R. W. (Cant., N. Dist., Otago & C. Dist.) b Oct. 2, 1948

*Anderson, W. M. (Cant.) b Oct. 8, 1919, d Dec. 21, 1979

*Andrew, K. V. (Northants) b Dec. 15, 1929

Andrew, S. J. W. (Hants & Essex) b Jan. 27, 1966

*Andrews, B. (Cant., C. Dist. & Otago) b April 4, 1945

*Andrews, T. J. E. (NSW) b Aug. 26, 1890, d Jan. 28, 1970

Andrews, W. H. R. (Som) b April 14, 1908, d Jan. 9, 1989

Angell, F. L. (Som) b June 29, 1922

*Anil Dalpat (Kar. & PIA) b Sept. 20, 1963

Anisur Rehman (Bangladesh) b March 1, 1971

*Ankola, S. A. (M'tra & †Mumbai) b March 1, 1968

Anthony, H. A. G. (Leewards & Glam) b Jan 16, 1971

*Anurasiri, S. D. (Pan. & WPS) b Feb. 25, 1966

*Anwar Hussain (N. Ind., Bombay, Sind & Kar.) b July 16, 1920

*Anwar Khan (Kar., Sind & NBP) b Dec. 24, 1955

*Appleyard, R. (Yorks; *CY 1952*) b June 27, 1924

*Apte, A. L. (Ind. Us, Bombay & Raja.) b Oct. 24, 1934

*Apte, M. L. (Bombay & Bengal) b Oct. 5, 1932

*Archer, A. G. (Worcs) b Dec. 6, 1871, d July 15, 1935

Archer, G. F. (Notts) b Sept. 26, 1970

*Archer, K. A. (Qld) b Jan. 17, 1928

*Archer, R. G. (Qld) b Oct. 25, 1933

*Arif Butt (Lahore & Pak. Rlwys) b May 17, 1944

Arlott, John OBE (Writer & broadcaster) b Feb. 25, 1914, d Dec. 14, 1991

*Armitage, T. (Yorks) b April 25, 1848, d Sept. 21, 1922

Armstrong, N. F. (Leics) b Dec. 22, 1892, d Jan. 19, 1990

*Armstrong, W. W. (Vic.; *CY 1903*) b May 22, 1879, d July 13, 1947

Arnold, A. P. (Cant. & Northants) b Oct. 16, 1926

*Arnold, E. G. (Worcs) b Nov. 7, 1876, d Oct. 25, 1942

*Arnold, G. G. (Surrey & Sussex; *CY 1972*) b Sept. 3, 1944

*Arnold, J. (Hants) b Nov. 30, 1907, d April 4, 1984

Arnott, D. B. (Rhod.; ICC referee) b March 3, 1936

*Arnott, K. J. (MCD) b March 8, 1961

Arnott, T. (Glam) b Feb. 16, 1902, d Feb. 2, 1975

*Arshad Ayub (H'bad) b Aug. 2, 1958

Arshad Pervez (Sargodha, Lahore, Pak. Us, Servis Ind., HBL & Punjab) b Oct. 1, 1952

*Arthurton, K. L. T. MBE (Leewards) b Feb. 21, 1965

*Arun, B. (TN) b Dec. 14, 1962

*Arun Lal (Delhi & Bengal) b Aug. 1, 1955

*Asgarali, N. (T/T) b Dec. 28, 1920

Ashdown, W. H. (Kent) b Dec. 27, 1898, d Sept. 15, 1979

*Ashfaq Ahmed (PIA, PACO & Lahore) b June 6, 1973

*Ashley, W. H. (W. Prov.) b Feb. 10, 1862, d July 14, 1930

*Ashraf Ali (Lahore, Income Tax, Pak. Us, Pak. Rlwys & UBL) b April 22, 1958

Ashton, C. T. (CU & Essex) b Feb. 19, 1901, d Oct. 31, 1942

Ashton, G. (CU & Worcs) b Sept. 27, 1896, d Feb. 6, 1981

Ashton, Sir Hubert (CU & Essex; *CY 1922*; Pres. MCC 1960–61) b Feb. 13, 1898, d June 17, 1979

Asif Din, M. (Warwicks) b Sept. 21, 1960

*Asif Iqbal (H'bad, Kar., Kent, PIA & NBP; *CY 1968*) b June 6, 1943

Asif Mahmood (R'pindi & KRL) b Dec. 18, 1975

*Asif Masood (Lahore, Punjab U. & PIA) b Jan. 23, 1946

Aslett, D. G. (Kent) b Feb. 12, 1958

*Astill, W. E. (Leics; *CY 1933*) b March 1, 1888, d Feb. 10, 1948

Athar Zaidi (Test umpire) b Nov. 12, 1946

Ather Ali Khan (Bangladesh) b Feb. 10, 1962

*Atherton, M. A. OBE (CU & Lancs; *CY 1991*) b March 23, 1968

*Athey, C. W. J. (Yorks, Glos & Sussex) b Sept. 27, 1957

*Atif Rauf (Lahore, I'bad & ADBP) b March 3, 1964

Atkinson, C. R. M. CBE (Som) b July 23, 1931, d June 25, 1991

*Atkinson, D. St E. (B'dos & T/T) b Aug. 9, 1926, d Nov. 9, 2001

*Atkinson, E. St E. (B'dos) b Nov. 6, 1927, d May 29, 1998

Atkinson, G. (Som & Lancs) b March 29, 1938

*Attewell, W. (Notts; *CY 1892*) b June 12, 1861, d June 11, 1927

Austin, Sir Harold B. G. (B'dos) b July 15, 1877, d July 27, 1943

Austin, I. D. (Lancs; *CY 1999*) b May 30, 1966

*Austin, R. A. (Jam.) b Sept. 5, 1954

Avery, A. V. (Essex) b Dec. 19, 1914, d May 10, 1997

Aylward, James (Hants & All-England) b 1741, *buried* Dec. 27, 1827

*Azad, K. (Delhi) b Jan. 2, 1959

*Azam Khan (Kar. & Customs) b March 1, 1969

*Azeem Hafeez (Kar., Allied Bank & PIA) b July 29, 1963

*Azhar Khan (Lahore, Punjab, Pak. Us, PIA & HBL) b Sept. 7, 1955

*Azharuddin, M. (H'bad & Derbys; *CY 1991*) b Feb. 8, 1963

*Azmat Rana (B'pur, PIA, Punjab, Lahore & MCB) b Nov. 3, 1951

*Bacchus, S. F. A. F. (Guyana, W. Prov. & Border) b Jan. 31, 1954

*Bacher, Dr A. (Tvl; Managing Director UCBSA) b May 24, 1942

*Badcock, C. L. (Tas. & S. Aust.) b April 10, 1914, d Dec. 13, 1982

*Badcock, F. T. (Wgtn & Otago) b Aug. 9, 1897, d Sept. 19, 1982

Baggallay, R. R. C. (Derbys) b May 4, 1884, d Dec. 12, 1975

*Baichan, L. (Guyana) b May 12, 1946

*Baig, A. A. (H'bad, OU & Som; Ind. coach) b March 19, 1939

Bailey, J. (Hants) b April 6, 1908, d Feb. 9, 1988

Bailey, J. A. (Essex & OU; Sec. MCC 1974–87) b June 22, 1930

*Bailey, R. J. (Northants & Derbys) b Oct. 28, 1963

*Bailey, T. E. CBE (Essex & CU; *CY 1950*; broadcaster) b Dec. 3, 1923

Baillie, A. W. (Sec. MCC 1858–63) b June 22, 1830, d May 10, 1867

Bainbridge, H. W. (Surrey, CU & Warwicks) b Oct. 29, 1862, d March 3, 1940

Bainbridge, P. (Glos & Durham; *CY 1986*) b April 16, 1958

*Bairstow, D. L. (Yorks & Griq. W.) b Sept. 1, 1951, d Jan. 5, 1998

Baker, C. S. (Warwicks) b Jan. 5, 1883, d Dec. 16, 1976

Baker, G. R. (Yorks & Lancs) b April 18, 1862, d Dec. 6, 1938

*Bakewell, A. H. (Northants; *CY 1934*) b Nov. 2, 1908, d Jan. 23, 1983

*Balaskas, X. C. (Griq. W., Border, W. Prov., Tvl & NE Tvl) b Oct. 15, 1910, d May 12, 1994

*Balderstone, J. C. (Yorks & Leics) b Nov. 16, 1940, d March 6, 2000

Baldry, D. O. (Middx & Hants) b Dec. 26, 1931

*Banerjee, S. A. (Bengal & Bihar) b Nov. 1, 1919, d Sept. 14, 1992

*Banerjee, S. N. (Bengal, Naw., Bihar & M. Pradesh) b Oct. 3, 1911, d Oct. 14, 1980

*Banerjee, S. T. (Bihar & Bengal) b Feb. 13, 1969

*Bannerman, A. C. (NSW) b March 22, 1854, d Sept. 19, 1924

*Bannerman, Charles (NSW) b July 23, 1851, d Aug. 20, 1930

Bannister, J. D. (Warwicks) b Aug. 23, 1930

*Baptiste, E. A. E. (Kent, Leewards, Northants, E. Prov. & KZN) b March 12, 1960

*Baqa Jilani, M. (N. Ind.) b July 20, 1911, d July 2, 1941

*Barber, R. T. (Wgton & C. Dist.) b June 3, 1925

*Barber, R. W. (Lancs, CU & Warwicks; *CY 1967*) b Sept. 26, 1935

*Barber, W. (Yorks) b April 18, 1901, d Sept. 10, 1968

Barclay, J. R. T. (Sussex & OFS) b Jan. 22, 1954

*Bardsley, W. (NSW; *CY 1910*) b Dec. 6, 1882, d Jan. 20, 1954

Barker, G. (Essex) b July 6, 1931

Barling, T. H. (Surrey) b Sept. 1, 1906, d Jan. 2, 1993

*Barlow, E. J. (Tvl, E. Prov., W. Prov., Derbys & Boland; Bang. coach) b Aug. 12, 1940

*Barlow, G. D. (Middx) b March 26, 1950

*Barlow, R. G. (Lancs) b May 28, 1851, d July 31, 1919

Barnard, H. M. (Hants) b July 18, 1933

*Barnes, S. F. (Warwicks & Lancs; *CY 1910*) b April 19, 1873, d Dec. 26, 1967

*Barnes, S. G. (NSW) b June 5, 1916, d Dec. 16, 1973

*Barnes, W. (Notts; *CY 1890*) b May 27, 1852, d March 24, 1899

*Barnett, B. A. (Vic.) b March 23, 1908, d June 29, 1979

*Barnett, C. J. (Glos; *CY 1937*) b July 3, 1910, d May 28, 1993

Baroda, Maharaja of (Manager, Ind. in Eng. 1959) b April 2, 1930, d Sept. 1, 1988

*Barratt, F. (Notts) b April 12, 1894, d Jan. 29, 1947

*Barrett, A. G. (Jam.) b April 5, 1942

*Barrett, Dr J. E. (Vic.) b Oct. 15, 1866, d Feb. 6, 1916

Barrick, D. W. (Northants) b April 28, 1926

*Barrington, K. F. (Surrey; *CY 1960*) b Nov. 24, 1930, d March 14, 1981

Barron, W. (Lancs & Northants) b Oct. 26, 1917

*Barrow, I. (Jam.) b Jan. 6, 1911, d April 2, 1979

*Bartlett, E. L. (B'dos) b March 10, 1906, d Dec. 21, 1976

*Bartlett, G. A. (C. Dist. & Cant.) b Feb. 3, 1941

Bartlett, H. T. (CU, Surrey & Sussex; *CY 1939*) b Oct. 7, 1914, d June 26, 1988

Bartley, T. J. (Test umpire) b March 19, 1908, d April 2, 1964

Barton, M. R. (OU & Surrey) b Oct. 14, 1914

*Barton, P. T. (Wgtn) b Oct. 9, 1935

*Barton, V. A. (Kent & Hants) b Oct. 6, 1867, d March 23, 1906

Barwick, S. R. (Glam) b Sept. 6, 1960

Base, S. J. (W. Prov., Glam, Boland, Derbys & Border) b Jan. 2, 1960

*Basit Ali (Kar. & UBL) b Dec. 13, 1970

Bates, D. L. (Sussex) b May 10, 1933

Bates, L. A. (Warwicks) b March 20, 1895, d March 11, 1971

*Bates, W. (Yorks) b Nov. 19, 1855, d Jan. 8, 1900

Bates, W. E. (Yorks & Glam) b March 5, 1884, d Jan. 17, 1957

*Baumgartner, H. V. (OFS & Tvl) b Nov. 17, 1883, d April 8, 1938

*Bean, G. (Notts & Sussex) b March 7, 1864, d March 16, 1923

Bear, M. J. (Essex & Cant.) b Feb. 23, 1934, d April 7, 2000

*Beard, D. D. (C. Dist. & N. Dist.) b Jan. 14, 1920, d July 15, 1982

*Beard, G. R. (NSW) b Aug. 19, 1950

Beauclerk, Lord Frederick (Middx, Surrey & MCC) b May 8, 1773, d April 22, 1850

*Beaumont, R. (Tvl) b Feb. 4, 1884, d May 25, 1958

*Beck, J. E. F. (Wgtn) b Aug. 1, 1934, d April 23, 2000

*Bedi, B. S. (N. Punjab, Delhi & Northants; Ind. coach) b Sept. 25, 1946

*Bedser, Sir Alec V. (Surrey; *CY 1947;* Chairman Eng. selectors) b July 4, 1918

Bedser, E. A. (Surrey) b July 4, 1918

Beet, G. (Derbys; Test umpire) b April 24, 1886, d Dec. 13, 1946

*Begbie, D. W. (Tvl) b Dec. 12, 1914

Beldam, W. (Hambledon & Surrey) b Feb. 5, 1766, d Feb. 20, 1862

*Bell, A. J. (W. Prov. & Rhod.) b April 15, 1906, d Aug. 1, 1985

Bell, R. V. (Middx & Sussex) b Jan. 7, 1931, d Oct. 26, 1989

*Bell, W. (Cant.) b Sept. 5, 1931, d July 23, 2002

Bellamy, B. W. (Northants) b April 22, 1891, d Dec. 22, 1985

*Benaud, J. (NSW) b May 11, 1944

*Benaud, R. OBE (NSW; *CY 1962;* broadcaster) b Oct. 6, 1930

*Benjamin, J. E. (Warwicks & Surrey) b Feb. 2, 1961

*Benjamin, K. C. G. (Leewards, Worcs, Gauteng & Easterns) b April 8, 1967

*Benjamin, W. K. M. (Leewards, Leics & Hants) b Dec. 31, 1964

Bencraft, Sir H. W. Russell (Hants) b March 4, 1858, d Dec. 25, 1943

Bennett, D. (Middx) b Dec. 18, 1933

*Bennett, M. J. (NSW) b Oct. 6, 1956

*Benson, M. R. (Kent) b July 6, 1958

Berry, L. G. (Leics) b April 28, 1906, d Feb. 5, 1985

*Berry, R. (Lancs, Worcs & Derbys) b Jan. 29, 1926

Berry, Scyld (Writer) b April 28, 1954

*Best, C. A. (B'dos & W. Prov.) b May 14, 1959

Bestwick, W. (Derbys) b Feb. 24, 1875, d May 2, 1938

*Betancourt, N. (T/T) b June 4, 1887, d Oct. 12, 1947

Bhalekar, R. B. (M'tra) b Feb. 17, 1952

*Bhandari, P. (Delhi & Bengal) b Nov. 27, 1935

*Bhat, A. R. (Karn.) b April 16, 1958

Bhupinder Singh (Punjab) b April 1, 1965

Bick, D. A. (Middx) b Feb. 22, 1936, d Jan. 13, 1992

*Bilby, G. P. (Wgtn) b May 7, 1941

*Binks, J. G. (Yorks; *CY 1969*) b Oct. 5, 1935

*Binns, A. P. (Jam.) b July 24, 1929

*Binny, R. M. H. (Karn.) b July 19, 1955

Birch, J. D. (Notts) b June 18, 1955

Bird, H. D. MBE (Yorks & Leics; Test umpire) b April 19, 1933

*Bird, M. C. (Lancs & Surrey) b March 25, 1888, d Dec. 9, 1933

Bird, R. E. (Worcs) b April 4, 1915, d Feb. 20, 1985

*Birkenshaw, J. (Yorks, Leics & Worcs) b Nov. 13, 1940

Birkett, L. S. (B'dos, BG & T/T) b April 14, 1904, d Jan. 16, 1998

Bishop, G. A. (S. Aust.) b Feb. 25, 1960

*Bishop, I. R. (T/T & Derbys) b Oct. 24, 1967

*Bisset, Sir Murray (M.) (W. Prov.) b April 14, 1876, d Oct. 24, 1931

*Bissett, G. F. (Griq. W., W. Prov. & Tvl) b Nov. 5, 1905, d Nov. 14, 1965

Bissex, M. (Glos) b Sept. 28, 1944

*Blackham, J. McC. (Vic; *CY 1891*) b May 11, 1854, d Dec. 28, 1932

*Blackie, D. D. (Vic.) b April 5, 1882, d April 18, 1955

*Blain, T. E. (C. Dist.) b Feb. 17, 1962

Blair, B. R. (Otago) b Dec. 27, 1957

*Blair, R. W. (Wgtn & C. Dist.) b June 23, 1932

*Blanckenberg, J. M. (W. Prov. & Natal) b Dec. 31, 1892, dead

*Bland, K. C. (Rhod., E. Prov. & OFS; *CY 1966*) b April 5, 1938

Blenkiron, W. (Warwicks) b July 21, 1942

*Bligh, Hon. Ivo (I. F. W.) (8th Earl of Darnley) (CU & Kent; Pres. MCC 1900) b March 13, 1859, d April 10, 1927

*Blignaut, A. M. (Mash.) b Aug. 1, 1978

Blofeld, H. C. OBE (CU; writer & broadcaster) b Sept. 23, 1939

*Blunt, R. C. MBE (Cant. & Otago; *CY 1928*) b Nov. 3, 1900, d June 22, 1966

*Blythe, C. (Kent; *CY 1904*) b May 30, 1879, d Nov. 8, 1917

*Board, J. H. (Glos) b Feb. 23, 1867, d April 15, 1924

*Bock, E. G. (Griq. W., Tvl & W. Prov.) b Sept. 17, 1908, d Sept. 5, 1961

*Bolton, B. A. (Cant. & Wgtn) b May 31, 1935

*Bolus, J. B. (Yorks, Notts & Derbys) b Jan. 31, 1934

*Bond, G. E. (W. Prov.) b April 5, 1909, d Aug. 27, 1965

Bond, J. D. (Lancs & Notts; *CY 1971*) b May 6, 1932

*Bonnor, G. J. (Vic. & NSW) b Feb. 25, 1855, d June 27, 1912

Boock, S. L. (Otago & Cant.) b Sept. 20, 1951

*Boon, D. C. MBE (Tas. & Durham; *CY 1994*) b Dec. 29, 1960

Boon, T. J. (Leics) b Nov. 1, 1961

*Booth, B. C. MBE (NSW) b Oct. 19, 1933

Booth, B. J. (Lancs & Leics) b Dec. 3, 1935

Booth, C. (CU & Hants) b May 11, 1842, d July 14, 1926

*Booth, M. W. (Yorks; *CY 1914*) b Dec. 10, 1886, d July 1, 1916

Booth, R. (Yorks & Worcs) b Oct. 1, 1926

*Borde, C. G. (Baroda & M'tra) b July 21, 1933

*Border, A. R. (NSW, Glos, Qld & Essex; *CY 1982*) b July 27, 1955

Bore, M. K. (Yorks & Notts) b June 2, 1947

Borrington, A. J. (Derbys) b Dec. 8, 1948

*Bosanquet, B. J. T. (OU & Middx; *CY 1905*) b Oct. 13, 1877, d Oct. 12, 1936

*Bosch, T. (N. Tvl & Natal) b March 14, 1966, d Feb. 13, 2000

Bose, G. (Bengal) b May 20, 1947

Boshier, B. S. (Leics) b March 6, 1932

*Botham, I. T. OBE (Som, Worcs, Durham & Qld; *CY 1978*; broadcaster) b Nov. 24, 1955

*Botten, J. T. (NE Tvl & N. Tvl) b June 21, 1938

Boucher, J. C. (Ireland) b Dec. 22, 1910, d Dec. 25, 1995

Bowden, J. (Derbys) b Oct. 8, 1884, d March 1, 1958

Bowden, M. P. (Surrey & Tvl) b Nov. 1, 1865, d Feb. 19, 1892

Bowell, A. (Hants) b April 27, 1880, d Aug. 28, 1957

*Bowes, W. E. (Yorks; *CY 1932*) b July 25, 1908, d Sept. 5, 1987

*Bowley, E. H. (Sussex & Auck.; *CY 1930*) b June 6, 1890, d July 9, 1974

Bowley, F. L. (Worcs) b Nov. 9 1873, d May 31, 1943

Box, T. (Sussex) b Feb. 7, 1808, d July 12, 1876

*Boyce, K. D. (B'dos & Essex; *CY 1974*) b Oct. 11, 1943, d Oct. 11, 1996

*Boycott, G. OBE (Yorks & N. Tvl; *CY 1965*; broadcaster) b Oct. 21, 1940

Boyd-Moss, R. J. (CU & Northants) b Dec. 16, 1959

Boyes, G. S. (Hants) b March 31, 1899, d Feb. 11, 1973

*Boyle, H. F. (Vic.) b Dec. 10, 1847, d Nov. 21, 1907

*Bracewell, B. P. (C. Dist., Otago & N. Dist.) b Sept. 14, 1959

*Bracewell, J. G. (Otago & Auck.) b April 15, 1958

*Bradburn, W. P. (N. Dist.) b Nov. 24, 1938

*Bradley, W. M. (Kent) b Jan. 2, 1875, d June 19, 1944

*Bradman, Sir Donald G. (NSW & S. Aust.; *CY 1931, Cricketer of the Century 2000*) b Aug. 27, 1908, d Feb. 25, 2001

Brain, B. M. (Worcs & Glos) b Sept. 13, 1940

*Brain, D. H. (Mash.) b Oct. 4, 1964

*Brandes, E. A. (MCD & Mash.) b March 5, 1963

Brann, G. (Sussex) b April 23, 1865, d June 14, 1954

*Brann, W. H. (E. Prov.) b April 4, 1899, d Sept. 22, 1953

Brassington, A. J. (Glos) b Aug. 9, 1954

*Braund, L. C. (Surrey & Som; *CY 1902*) b Oct. 18, 1875, d Dec. 23, 1955

Bray, C. (Essex) b April 6, 1898, d Sept. 12, 1993

Brayshaw, I. J. (W. Aust.) b Jan. 14, 1942

Breakwell, D. (Northants & Som) b July 2, 1948

*Brearley, J. M. OBE (CU & Middx; *CY 1977*) b April 28, 1942

*Brearley, W. (Lancs; *CY 1909*) b March 11, 1876, d Jan. 13, 1937

*Brennan, D. V. (Yorks) b Feb. 10, 1920, d Jan. 9, 1985

*Briant, G. A. (Mash.) b April 11, 1969

Bridges, J. J. (Som) b June 28, 1887, d Sept. 26, 1966

Brierley, T. L. (Glam, Lancs & Canada) b June 15, 1910, d Jan. 7, 1989

Briers, N. E. (Leics; *CY 1993*) b Jan. 15, 1955

*Briggs, John (Lancs; *CY 1889*) b Oct. 3, 1862, d Jan. 11, 1902

*Bright, R. J. (Vic.) b July 13, 1954

*Briscoe, A. W. (Tvl) b Feb. 6, 1911, d April 22, 1941

*Broad, B. C. (Glos & Notts; ICC referee) b Sept. 29, 1957

Broadbent, R. G. (Worcs) b June 21, 1924, d April 26, 1993

*Brockwell, W. (Surrey & Kimberley; *CY 1895*) b Jan. 21, 1865, d June 30, 1935

Broderick, V. (Northants) b Aug. 17, 1920

*Bromfield, H. D. (W. Prov.) b June 26, 1932

*Bromley, E. H. (W. Aust. & Vic.) b Sept. 2, 1912, d Feb. 1, 1967

*Bromley-Davenport, H. R. (CU, Eur., & Middx) b Aug. 18, 1870, d May 23, 1954

*Brookes, D. (Northants; *CY 1957*) b Oct. 29, 1915

Brookes, Wilfrid H. (Editor of *Wisden* 1936–39) b Dec. 5, 1894, d May 28, 1955

*Brown, A. (Kent) b Oct. 17, 1935

Brown, A. S. (Glos) b June 24, 1936

*Brown, D. J. (Warwicks) b Jan. 30, 1942

*Brown, F. R. MBE (CU, Surrey & Northants; *CY 1933*; Pres. MCC 1971–72) b Dec. 16, 1910, d July 24, 1991

*Brown, G. (Hants) b Oct. 6, 1887, d Dec. 3, 1964

Brown, J. MBE (Scotland) b Sept. 24, 1931

*Brown, J. T. (Yorks; *CY 1895*) b Aug. 20, 1869, d Nov. 4, 1904

Brown, K. R. (Middx) b March 18, 1963

*Brown, L. S. (Tvl, NE Tvl & Rhod.) b Nov. 24, 1910, d Sept. 1, 1983

Brown, R. D. (Mash.) b March 11, 1951

Brown, S. M. (Middx) b Dec. 8, 1917, d Dec. 28, 1987

*Brown, V. R. (Cant. & Auck.) b Nov. 3, 1959

*Brown, W. A. (NSW & Qld; *CY 1939*; oldest and last surviving pre-war CY at end of 2002*) b July 31, 1912

Brown, W. C. (Northants) b Nov. 13, 1900, d Jan. 20, 1986

Browne, B. St A. (Guyana) b Sept. 16, 1967

*Browne, C. R. (B'dos & BG) b Oct. 8, 1890, d Jan. 12, 1964

*Bruce, W. (Vic.) b May 22, 1864, d Aug. 3, 1925

*Bruk-Jackson, G. K. (MCD & Mash.) b April 25, 1969

Bryan, G. J. CBE (Kent) b Dec. 29, 1902, d April 4, 1991

Bryan, H. R. (B'dos & Griq. W.) b March 21, 1970

Bryan, J. L. (CU & Kent; *CY 1922*) b May 26, 1896, d April 23, 1985

Bryan, R. T. (Kent) b July 30, 1898, d July 27, 1970

Buchanan, J. M. (Qld; Aust. coach) b April 5, 1953

*Buckenham, C. P. (Essex) b Jan. 16, 1876, d Feb. 23, 1937

Bucknor, S. A. (ICC umpire) b May 31, 1946

Buckston, R. H. R. (Derbys) b Oct. 10, 1908, d May 16, 1967

Budd, E. H. (Middx & All-England) b Feb. 23, 1785, d March 29, 1875

Budd, W. L. (Hants; Test umpire) b Oct. 25, 1913, d Aug. 23, 1986

Bulfin, C. E. (C. Dist. & Wgtn) b Aug. 19, 1973

Bull, F. G. (Essex; *CY 1898*) b April 2, 1875, d Sept. 16, 1910

Buller, J. S. MBE (Yorks & Worcs; Test umpire) b Aug. 23, 1909, d Aug. 7, 1970

Burden, M. D. (Hants) b Oct. 4, 1930, d Nov. 9, 1987

*Burge, P. J. (Qld; *CY 1965; ICC referee) b May 17, 1932, d Oct. 5, 2001

*Burger, C. G. de V. (Natal) b July 12, 1935

Burgess, G. I. (Som) b May 5, 1943

*Burgess, M. G. (Auck.) b July 17, 1944

*Burke, C. (Auck.) b March 22, 1914, d Aug. 4, 1997

*Burke, J. W. (NSW; *CY 1957*) b June 12, 1930, d Feb. 2, 1979

*Burke, S. F. (NE Tvl & OFS) b March 11, 1934

*Burki, Javed (Pak. Us, OU, Punjab, Lahore, Kar., R'pindi & NWFP; ICC referee) b May 8, 1938

*Burmester, M. G. (Mash. & Man.) b Jan. 24, 1968

*Burn, K. E. (Tas.) b Sept. 17, 1862, d July 20, 1956

Burns, W. B. (Worcs) b Aug. 29, 1883, d July 7, 1916

Burnup, C. J. (CU & Kent; *CY 1903*) b Nov. 21, 1875, d April 5, 1960

Burrough, H. D. (Som) b Feb. 6, 1909, d April 9, 1994

Burrows, R. D. (Worcs) b June 6, 1871, d Feb. 12, 1943

Burton, D. C. F. (Yorks) b Sept. 13, 1887, d Sept. 24, 1971

*Burton, F. J. (Vic. & NSW) b Nov. 2, 1865, d Aug. 25, 1929

*Burtt, T. B. (Cant.) b Jan. 22, 1915, d May 24, 1988

Buse, H. T. F. (Som) b Aug. 5, 1910, d Feb. 23, 1992

Buss, A. (Sussex) b Sept. 1, 1939

Buss, M. A. (Sussex & OFS) b Jan. 24, 1944

*Butchart, I. P. (MCD) b May 9, 1960

*Butcher, A. R. (Surrey & Glam; *CY 1991*) b Jan. 7, 1954

*Butcher, B. F. (Guyana; *CY 1970*) b Sept. 3, 1933

Butcher, I. P. (Leics & Glos) b July 1, 1962

*Butcher, R. O. (Middx, B'dos & Tas.) b Oct. 14, 1953

*Butler, H. J. (Notts) b March 12, 1913, d July 17, 1991

*Butler, L. (T/T) b Feb. 9, 1929

*Butt, H. R. (Sussex) b Dec. 27, 1865, d Dec. 21, 1928

*Butterfield, L. A. (Cant.) b Aug. 29, 1913, d July 7, 1999

*Butts, C. G. (Guyana) b July 8, 1957

Buxton, I. R. (Derbys) b April 17, 1938

*Buys, I. D. (W. Prov.) b Feb. 3, 1895, dead

*Bynoe, M. R. (B'dos) b Feb. 23, 1941

Byrne, J. F. (Warwicks) b June 19, 1871, d May 10, 1954

Cadman, S. (Derbys) b Jan. 29, 1877, d May 6, 1952

Caesar, Julius (Surrey & All-England) b March 25, 1830, d March 6, 1878

Caffyn, W. (Surrey & NSW) b Feb. 2, 1828, d Aug. 28, 1919

Caine, C. Stewart (Editor of *Wisden* 1926–33) b Oct. 28, 1861, d April 15, 1933

*Cairns, B. L. (C. Dist., Otago & N. Dist.) b Oct. 10, 1949

*Calder, H. L. (Cranleigh; *CY 1918*) b Jan. 24, 1901, d Sept. 15, 1995

*Callaway, S. T. (NSW & Cant.) b Feb. 6, 1868, d Nov. 25, 1923

*Callen, I. W. (Vic. & Boland) b May 2, 1955

*Calthorpe, Hon. F. S. Gough- (CU, Sussex & Warwicks) b May 27, 1892, d Nov. 19, 1935

*Camacho, G. S. (Guyana; Chief Exec. WICB) b Oct. 15, 1945

*Cameron, F. J. (Jam.) b June 22, 1923, d Feb. 1995

*Cameron, F. J. MBE (Otago) b June 1, 1932

*Cameron, H. B. (Tvl, E. Prov. & W. Prov.; *CY 1936*) b July 5, 1905, d Nov. 2, 1935

*Cameron, J. H. (CU, Jam. & Som) b April 8, 1914, d Feb. 13, 2000

*Campbell, G. D. (Tas.) b March 10, 1964

*Campbell, T. (Tvl) b Feb. 9, 1882, d Oct. 5, 1924

Cannings, V. H. D. (Warwicks & Hants) b April 3, 1919

*Capel, D. J. (Northants & E. Prov.) b Feb. 6, 1963

Cardus, Sir Neville (Writer) b April 3, 1888, d Feb. 27, 1975

*Carew, G. M. (B'dos) b June 4, 1910, d Dec. 9, 1974

*Carew, M. C. (T/T) b Sept. 15, 1937

*Carkeek, W. (Vic.) b Oct. 17, 1878, d Feb. 20, 1937

*Carlson, P. H. (Qld) b Aug. 8, 1951

*Carlstein, P. R. (OFS, Tvl, Natal & Rhod.) b Oct. 28, 1938

Carpenter, D. (Glos) b Sept. 12, 1935

Carpenter, H. A. (Essex) b July 12, 1869, d Dec. 12, 1933

Carpenter, R. (Cambs & Utd England XI) b Nov. 18, 1830, d July 13, 1901

*Carr, A. W. (Notts; *CY 1923*) b May 21, 1893, d Feb. 7, 1963

*Carr, D. B. OBE (OU & Derbys; *CY 1960*; Sec. TCCB 1974–86) b Dec. 28, 1926

*Carr, D. W. (Kent; *CY 1910*) b March 17, 1872, d March 23, 1950

Carr, J. D. (OU & Middx) b June 15, 1963

Carrick, P. (Yorks & E. Prov.) b July 16, 1952, d Jan. 11, 2000

*Carter, C. P. (Natal & Tvl) b April 23, 1881, d Nov. 8, 1952

*Carter, H. (NSW) b March 15, 1878, d June 8, 1948

Carter, R. G. M. (Worcs) b July 11, 1937

*Cartwright, T. W. MBE (Warwicks, Som & Glam) b July 22, 1935

Case, C. C. C. (Som) b Sept. 7, 1895, d Nov. 11, 1969

Cass, G. R. (Essex, Worcs & Tas.) b April 23, 1940

Catt, A. W. (Kent & W. Prov.) b Oct. 2, 1933

*Catterall, R. H. (Tvl, Rhod., Natal & OFS; *CY 1925*) b July 10, 1900, d Jan. 3, 1961

*Cave, H. B. (Wgtn & C. Dist.) b Oct. 10, 1922, d Sept. 15, 1989

Chalk, F. G. H. (OU & Kent) b Sept. 7, 1910, d Feb. 17, 1943

*Challenor, G. (B'dos) b June 28, 1888, d July 30, 1947

Chamberlain, W. R. F. (Northants; Chairman TCCB 1990–94) b April 13, 1925

*Chandrasekhar, B. S. (†Karn.; *CY 1972*) b May 17, 1945

Chandrasekhar, V. B. (Goa) b Aug. 21, 1961

*Chang, H. S. (Jam.) b July 22, 1952

Chaplin, H. P. (Sussex & Eur.) b March 1, 1883, d March 6, 1970

*Chapman, A. P. F. (Uppingham, CU & Kent; *CY 1919*) b Sept. 3, 1900, d Sept. 16, 1961

*Chapman, H. W. (Natal) b June 30, 1890, d Dec. 1, 1941

Chapman, J. (Derbys) b March 11, 1877, d Aug. 12, 1956

*Chappell, G. S. MBE (S. Aust., Som & Qld; *CY 1973*) b Aug. 7, 1948

*Chappell, I. M. (S. Aust. & Lancs; *CY 1976*; broadcaster) b Sept. 26, 1943

*Chappell, T. M. (S. Aust., W. Aust. & NSW; Bang. coach) b Oct. 21, 1952

*Chapple, M. E. (Cant. & C. Dist.) b July 25, 1930, d July 31, 1985

Charlesworth, C. (Warwicks) b Feb. 12, 1875, d June 15, 1953

*Charlton, P. C. (NSW) b April 9, 1867, d Sept. 30, 1954

*Charlwood, H. R. J. (Sussex) b Dec. 19, 1846, d June 6, 1888

*Chatfield, E. J. MBE (Wgtn) b July 3, 1950

*Chatterton, W. (Derbys) b Dec. 27, 1861, d March 19, 1913

*Chauhan, C. P. S. (M'tra & Delhi) b July 21, 1947

*Chauhan, R. K. (M. Pradesh) b Dec. 19, 1966

*Cheetham, J. E. (W. Prov.) b May 26, 1920, d Aug. 21, 1980

Chester, F. (Worcs; Test umpire) b Jan. 20, 1895, d April 8, 1957

*Chevalier, G. A. (W. Prov.) b March 9, 1937

*Childs, J. H. (Glos & Essex; *CY 1987*) b Aug. 15, 1951

*Chipperfield, A. G. (NSW) b Nov. 17, 1905, d July 29, 1987

Chisholm, R. H. E. (Scotland) b May 22, 1927

*Chowdhury, N. R. (Bihar & Bengal) b May 23, 1923, d Dec. 14, 1979

*Christiani, C. M. (BG) b Oct. 28, 1913, d April 4, 1938

*Christiani, R. J. (BG) b July 19, 1920

*Christopherson, S. (Kent; Pres. MCC 1939–45) b Nov. 11, 1861, d April 6, 1949

*Christy, J. A. J. (Tvl & Qld) b Dec. 12, 1904, d Feb. 1, 1971

*Chubb, G. W. A. (Border & Tvl) b April 12, 1911, d Aug. 28, 1982

Clark, D. G. (Kent; Pres. MCC 1977–78) b Jan. 27, 1919

Clark, E. A. (Middx) b April 15, 1937

*Clark, E. W. (Northants) b Aug. 9, 1902, d April 28, 1982

Clark, T. H. (Surrey) b Oct. 5, 1924, d June 14, 1981

*Clark, W. M. (W. Aust.) b Sept. 19, 1953

*Clarke, Dr C. B. OBE (B'dos, Northants & Essex) b April 7, 1918, d Oct. 14, 1993

Clarke, R. W. (Northants) b April 22, 1924, d Aug. 3, 1981

*Clarke, S. T. (B'dos, Surrey, Tvl, OFS & N. Tvl) b Dec. 11, 1954, d Dec. 4, 1999

Clarke, William (Notts; founded All-England XI & Trent Bridge ground) b Dec. 24, 1798, d Aug. 25, 1856

Clarkson, A. (Yorks & Som) b Sept. 5, 1939

*Clay, J. C. (Glam) b March 18, 1898, d Aug. 12, 1973

Clay, J. D. (Notts) b Oct. 15, 1924

Clayton, G. (Lancs & Som) b Feb. 3, 1938

*Cleverley, D. C. (Auck.) b Dec. 23, 1909

Clift, Patrick B. (Rhod., Leics & Natal) b July 14, 1953, d Sept. 3, 1996

Clift, Phil B. (Glam) b Sept. 3, 1918

Clinton, G. S. (Kent, Surrey & Zimb.-Rhod.) b May 5, 1953

*Close, D. B. CBE (Yorks & Som; *CY 1964*) b Feb. 24, 1931

Cobb, R. A. (Leics & N. Tvl) b May 18, 1961

Cobham, 10th Visct (Hon. C. J. Lyttelton) (Worcs; Pres. MCC 1954) b Aug. 8, 1909, d March 20, 1977

*Cochrane, J. A. K. (Tvl & Griq. W.) b July 15, 1909, d June 15, 1987

Coe, S. (Leics) b June 3, 1873, d Nov. 4, 1955

*Coen, S. K. (OFS, W. Prov., Tvl & Border) b Oct. 14, 1902, d Jan. 28, 1967

*Colah, S. M. H. (Bombay, W. Ind. & Naw.) b Sept. 22, 1902, d Sept. 11, 1950

Colchin, Robert ("Long Robin") (Kent & All-England) b Nov. 1713, d April 1750

*Coldwell, L. J. (Worcs) b Jan. 10, 1933, d Aug. 6, 1996

*Colley, D. J. (NSW) b March 15, 1947

*Collinge, R. O. (C. Dist., Wgtn & N. Dist.) b April 2, 1946

Collins, A. E. J. (Clifton Coll. & Royal Engineers) b Aug. 18, 1885, d Nov. 11, 1914

Collins, G. C. (Kent) b Sept. 21, 1889, d Jan. 23, 1949

*Collins, H. L. (NSW) b Jan. 21, 1888, d May 28, 1959

Collins, R. (Lancs) b March 10, 1934

Colquhoun, I. A. (C. Dist.) b June 8, 1924

Coman, P. G. (Cant.) b April 13, 1943

*Commaille, J. M. M. (W. Prov., Natal, OFS & Griq. W.) b Feb. 21, 1883, d July 28, 1956

*Commins, J. B. (Boland & W. Prov.) b Feb. 19, 1965

*Compton, D. C. S. CBE (Middx & Holkar; *CY 1939*) b May 23, 1918, d April 23, 1997

Compton, L. H. (Middx) b Sept. 12, 1912, d Dec. 27, 1984

*Coney, J. V. MBE (Wgtn; *CY 1984*) b June 21, 1952

*Congdon, B. E. OBE (C. Dist., Wgtn, Otago & Cant.; *CY 1974*) b Feb. 11, 1938

*Coningham, A. (NSW & Qld) b July 14, 1863, d June 13, 1939

*Connolly, A. N. (Vic. & Middx) b June 29, 1939

Connor, C. A. (Hants) b March 24, 1961

Constable, B. (Surrey) b Feb. 19, 1921, d May 15, 1997

Constant, D. J. (Kent & Leics; Test umpire) b Nov. 9, 1941

*Constantine, L. N. (later Baron Constantine of Maraval and Nelson) (T/T & B'dos; *CY 1940*) b Sept. 21, 1901, d July 1, 1971

Constantine, L. S. (T/T) b May 25, 1874, d Jan. 5, 1942

*Contractor, N. J. (Guj. & Ind. Rlwys) b March 7, 1934

*Conyngham, D. P. (Natal, Tvl & W. Prov.) b May 10, 1897, d July 7, 1979

*Cook, C. (Glos) b Aug. 23, 1921, d Sept. 4, 1996

*Cook, F. J. (E. Prov.) b 1870, d Nov. 30, 1914

*Cook, G. (Northants & E. Prov.) b Oct. 9, 1951

Cook, L. W. (Lancs) b March 28, 1885, d Dec. 2, 1933

*Cook, N. G. B. (Leics & Northants) b June 17, 1956

*Cook, S. H. (Vic. & NSW) b Jan. 29, 1972

*Cook, S. J. (Tvl & Som; *CY 1990*) b July 31, 1953

Cook, T. E. R. (Sussex) b Jan. 5, 1901, d Jan. 15, 1950

*Cooper, A. H. C. (Tvl) b Sept. 2, 1893, d July 18, 1963

*Cooper, B. B. (Middx, Kent & Vic.) b March 15, 1844, d Aug. 7, 1914

Cooper, E. (Worcs) b Nov. 30, 1915, d Oct. 29, 1968

Cooper, F. S. Ashley- (Historian) b March 2, 1877, d Jan. 31, 1932

Cooper, G. C. (Sussex) b Sept. 2, 1936

Cooper, K. E. (Notts & Glos) b Dec. 27, 1957

*Cooper, W. H. (Vic.) b Sept. 11, 1849, d April 5, 1939

Cooray, B. C. (Test umpire) b May 15, 1941

Cope, G. A. (Yorks) b Feb. 23, 1947

*Copson, W. H. (Derbys; *CY 1937*) b April 27, 1908, d Sept. 14, 1971

Cordle, A. E. (Glam) b Sept. 21, 1940

*Corling, G. E. (NSW) b July 13, 1941

Cornford, J. H. (Sussex) b Dec. 9, 1911, d June 17, 1985

*Cornford, W. L. (Sussex) b Dec. 25, 1900, d Feb. 6, 1964

Cornwallis, W. S. (later 2nd Baron) (Kent) b March 14, 1892, d Jan. 4, 1982

Corrall, P. (Leics) b July 16, 1906, d Feb. 1994

Corran, A. J. (OU & Notts) b Nov. 25, 1936

*Cosier, G. J. (Vic., S. Aust. & Qld) b April 25, 1953

*Cottam, J. T. (NSW) b Sept. 5, 1867, d Jan. 30, 1897

*Cottam, R. M. H. (Hants & Northants) b Oct. 16, 1944

*Cotter, A. (NSW) b Dec. 3, 1884, d Oct. 31, 1917

Cotton, J. (Notts & Leics) b Nov. 7, 1940

*Coulthard, G. (Vic.; Test umpire) b Aug. 1, 1856, d Oct. 22, 1883

*Coventry, Hon. C. J. (Worcs) b Feb. 26, 1867, d June 2, 1929

*Cowans, N. G. (Middx & Hants) b April 17, 1961

*Cowdrey, C. S. (Kent & Glam) b Oct. 20, 1957

Cowdrey, G. R. (Kent) b June 27, 1964

*Cowdrey, M. C. (later Baron Cowdrey of Tonbridge) (OU & Kent; *CY 1956*; Pres. MCC 1986–87) b Dec. 24, 1932, d Dec. 4, 2000

Cowie, D. B. (Test umpire) b Dec. 2, 1946

*Cowie, J. OBE (Auck.) b March 30, 1912, d June 3, 1994

Cowley, N. G. (Hants & Glam) b March 1, 1953

*Cowper, R. M. (Vic. & W. Aust.) b Oct. 5, 1940

Cox, A. L. (Northants) b July 22, 1907, d Nov. 13, 1986

Cox, G., jun. (Sussex) b Aug. 23, 1911, d March 30, 1985

Cox, G., sen. (Sussex) b Nov. 29, 1873, d March 24, 1949

*Cox, J. L. (Natal) b June 28, 1886, d July 4, 1971

*Coxon, A. (Yorks) b Jan. 18, 1916

Cozier, Tony (Writer & broadcaster) b July 10, 1940

*Craig, I. D. (NSW) b June 12, 1935

Cranfield, L. M. (Glos) b Aug. 29, 1909, d Nov. 18, 1993

Cranmer, P. (Warwicks & Eur.) b Sept. 10, 1914, d May 29, 1994

*Cranston, J. (Glos) b Jan. 9, 1859, d Dec. 10, 1904

*Cranston, K. (Lancs) b Oct. 20, 1917

*Crapp, J. F. (Glos; Test umpire) b Oct. 14, 1912, d Feb. 15, 1981

*Crawford, J. N. (Surrey, S. Aust., Wgtn & Otago; *CY 1907*) b Dec. 1, 1886, d May 2, 1963

*Crawford, P. (NSW) b Aug. 3, 1933

Crawford, V. F. S. (Surrey & Leics) b April 11, 1879, d Aug. 21, 1922

Crawley, A. M. MBE (OU & Kent; Pres. MCC 1972–73) b April 10, 1908, d Nov. 3, 1993

Cray, S. J. (Essex) b May 29, 1921

Creese, W. L. (Hants) b Dec. 27, 1907, d March 9, 1974

*Cresswell, G. F. (Wgtn & C. Dist.) b March 22, 1915, d Jan. 10, 1966

*Cripps, G. (W. Prov.) b Oct. 19, 1865, d July 27, 1943

*Crisp, R. J. (Rhod., W. Prov. & Worcs) b May 28, 1911, d March 3, 1994

*Crocker, G. J. (MCD) b May 16, 1962

*Croft, C. E. H. (Guyana & Lancs) b March 15, 1953

*Cromb, I. B. (Cant.) b June 25, 1905, d March 6, 1984

*Cronje, W. J. (†FS & Leics) b Sept. 25, 1969, d June 1, 2002

Croom, A. J. (Warwicks) b May 23, 1896, d Aug. 16, 1947

*Crowe, J. J. (S. Aust. & Auck.) b Sept. 14, 1958

*Crowe, M. D. MBE (Auck., C. Dist., Som & Wgtn; *CY 1985*) b Sept. 22, 1962

Crump, B. S. (Northants) b April 25, 1938

Cuffe, J. A. (NSW & Worcs) b June 26, 1880, d May 16, 1931

Cumbes, J. (Lancs, Surrey, Worcs & Warwicks) b May 4, 1944

*Cummins, A. C. (B'dos & Durham) b May 7, 1966

*Cunis, R. S. (Auck. & N. Dist.; NZ coach) b Jan. 5, 1941

*Curnow, S. H. (Tvl) b Dec. 16, 1907, d July 28, 1986

Curran, K. M. (Zimb., Glos, Natal, Northants, Boland) b Sept. 7, 1959

*Curtis, T. S. (Worcs & CU) b Jan. 15, 1960

Cutmore, J. A. (Essex) b Dec. 28, 1898, d Nov. 30, 1985

*Cuttell, W. R. (Lancs; *CY 1898*) b Sept. 13, 1864, d Dec. 9, 1929

*Da Costa, O. C. (Jam.) b Sept. 11, 1907, d Oct. 1, 1936

Dacre, C. C. (Auck. & Glos) b May 15, 1899, d Nov. 2, 1975

Daft, H. B. (Notts) b April 5, 1866, d Jan. 12, 1945

Daft, Richard (Notts & All-England) b Nov. 2, 1835, d July 18, 1900

Dalmeny, Lord (later 6th Earl of Rosebery) (Middx, Surrey & Scotland) b Jan. 8, 1882, d May 30, 1974

Dalmiya, J. (President ICC 1997–2000) b May 30, 1940

*Dalton, E. L. (Natal) b Dec. 2, 1906, d June 3, 1981

*Dani, H. T. (M'tra & Ind. Serv.) b May 24, 1933, d Dec. 19, 1999

*Daniel, W. W. (B'dos, Middx & W. Aust.) b Jan. 16, 1956

Daniell, J. (Som) b Dec. 12, 1878, d Jan 24, 1963

*D'Arcy, J. W. (Cant., Wgtn & Otago) b April 23, 1936

Dare, R. (Hants) b Nov. 26, 1921

*Darling, J. (S. Aust.; *CY 1900*) b Nov. 21, 1870, d Jan. 2, 1946

*Darling, L. S. (Vic.) b Aug. 14, 1909, d June 24, 1992

*Darling, W. M. (S. Aust.) b May 1, 1957

*Dassanayake, P. B. (Colts & Bloom.) b July 11, 1970

Davey, J. (Glos) b Sept. 4, 1944

David, N. A. (H'bad) b Feb. 26, 1971

*Davidson, A. K. OBE (NSW; *CY 1962*) b June 14, 1929

Davidson, G. (Derbys) b June 29, 1866, d Feb. 8, 1899

Davies, Dai (Glam; Test umpire) b Aug. 26, 1896, d July 16, 1976

Davies, Emrys (Glam; Test umpire) b June 27, 1904, d Nov. 10, 1975

*Davies, E. Q. (E. Prov., Tvl & NE Tvl) b Aug. 26, 1909, d Nov. 11, 1976

Davies, H. G. (Glam) b April 23, 1912, d Sept. 4, 1993

Davies, J. G. W. OBE (CU & Kent; Pres. MCC 1985–86) b Sept. 10, 1911, d Nov. 5, 1992

Davies, S. G. (Mat.) b May 7, 1977

Davies, T. (Glam) b Oct. 25, 1960

*Davis, B. A. (T/T & Glam) b May 2, 1940

*Davis, C. A. (T/T) b Jan. 1, 1944

Davis, E. (Northants) b March 8, 1922

Davis, H. T. (Wgtn) b Nov. 30, 1971

*Davis, I. C. (NSW & Qld) b June 25, 1953

Davis, C. P. (Northants) b May 24, 1915, d July 4, 2001

Davis, R. C. (Glam) b Jan. 15, 1946

Davis, R. P. (Kent, Warwicks, Glos & Leics) b March 18, 1966

*Davis, S. P. (Vic.) b Nov. 8, 1959

*Davis, W. W. (Windwards, Glam, Tas., Northants & Wgtn) b Sept. 18, 1958

Davison, B. F. (Rhod., Leics, Tas. & Glos) b Dec. 21, 1946

Davison, I. J. (Notts) b Oct. 4, 1937

Dawkes, G. O. (Leics & Derbys) b July 19, 1920

*Dawson, E. W. (CU & Leics) b Feb. 13, 1904, d June 4, 1979

*Dawson, O. C. (Natal & Border) b Sept. 1, 1919

Day, A. P. (Kent; *CY 1910*) b April 10, 1885, d Jan. 22, 1969

*de Alwis, R. G. (SSC) b Feb. 15, 1959

*Dean, H. (Lancs) b Aug. 13, 1884, d March 12, 1957

Dean, J., sen. (Sussex) b Jan. 4, 1816, d Dec. 25, 1881

*Deane, H. G. (Natal & Tvl) b July 21, 1895, d Oct. 21, 1939

*De Caires, F. I. (BG) b May 12, 1909, d Feb. 2, 1959

*De Courcy, J. H. (NSW) b April 18, 1927, d June 20, 2000

*de Groen, R. P. (Auck. & N. Dist.) b Aug. 5, 1962

*Dekker, M. H. (Mat.) b Dec. 5, 1969

*Dell, A. R. (Qld) b Aug. 6, 1947

*de Mel, A. L. F. (SL) b May 9, 1959

*Dempster, C. S. (Wgtn, Leics, Scotland & Warwicks; *CY 1932*) b Nov. 15, 1903, d Feb. 14, 1974

*Dempster, E. W. (Wgtn) b Jan. 25, 1925

*Denness, M. H. (Scotland, Kent & Essex; *CY 1975*; ICC referee) b Dec. 1, 1940

Dennett, G. (Glos) b April 27, 1880, d Sept. 14, 1937

Denning, P. W. (Som) b Dec. 16, 1949

Dennis, F. (Yorks) b June 11, 1907, d Dec. 21, 2000

Dennis, S. J. (Yorks, OFS & Glam) b Oct. 18, 1960

*Denton, D. (Yorks; *CY 1906*) b July 4, 1874, d Feb. 16, 1950

Deodhar, D. B. (M'tra) b Jan. 14, 1892, d Aug. 24, 1993

*Depeiza, C. C. (B'dos) b Oct. 10, 1927, d Nov. 10, 1995

Desai, R. B. (Bombay) b June 20, 1939, d April 27, 1998

*de Silva, A. M. (CCC) b Dec. 3, 1963

de Silva, D. L. S. (SL) b Nov. 17, 1956, d April 12, 1980

*de Silva, D. S. (Bloom.) b June 11, 1942

*de Silva, E. A. R. (NCC & Galle; ICC umpire) b March 28, 1956

de Silva, G. N. (SL) b March 12, 1955

*de Silva, G. R. A. (SL) b Dec. 12, 1952

de Smidt, R. W. (W. Prov.) b Nov. 24, 1883, d Aug. 3, 1986

De Trafford, C. E. (Lancs & Leics) b May 21, 1864, d Nov. 11, 1951

Devereux, L. N. (Middx, Worcs & Glam) b Oct. 20, 1931

*de Villiers, P. S. (Northerns, N. Tvl & Kent) b Oct. 13, 1964

*Dewdney, C. T. (Jam.) b Oct. 23, 1933

*Dewes, J. G. (CU & Middx) b Oct. 11, 1926

Dews, G. (Worcs) b June 5, 1921

*Dexter, E. R. CBE (CU & Sussex; *CY 1961*; Chairman Eng. selectors; Pres. MCC 2001–02) b May 15, 1935

*Dhanraj, R. (T/T) b Feb. 6, 1969

*Dias, R. L. (CCC; ICC referee; SL coach) b Oct. 18, 1952

*Dick, A. E. (Otago & Wgtn) b Oct. 10, 1936

*Dickinson, G. R. (Otago) b March 11, 1903, d March 17, 1978

*Dilawar Hussain (C. Ind. and U. Prov.) b March 19, 1907, d Aug. 26, 1967

*Dilley, G. R. (Kent, Natal & Worcs) b May 18, 1959

Dillon, E. W. (Kent & OU) b Feb. 15, 1881, d April 20, 1941

*Dipper, A. E. (Glos) b Nov. 9, 1885, d Nov. 7, 1945

*Divecha, R. V. (Bombay, OU, Northants, Vidarbha & S'tra) b Oct. 18, 1927

Diver, A. J. D. (Cambs., Middx, Notts & All-England) b June 6, 1824, d March 25, 1876

Diver, E. J. (Surrey & Warwicks) b March 20, 1861, d Dec. 27, 1924

Dixon, A. L. (Kent) b Nov. 27, 1933

*Dixon, C. D. (Tvl) b Feb. 12, 1891, d Sept. 9, 1969

Dixon, J. A. (Notts) b May 27, 1861, d June 8, 1931

Dodds, T. C. (Essex) b May 29, 1919, d Sept. 17, 2001

*Dodemaide, A. I. C. (Vic. & Sussex) b Oct. 5, 1963

*Doggart, G. H. G. OBE (CU & Sussex; Pres. MCC 1981–82) b July 18, 1925

*D'Oliveira, B. L. OBE (Worcs; *CY 1967*) b Oct. 4, 1931

D'Oliveira, D. B. (Worcs) b Oct. 19, 1960

*Dollery, H. E. (Warwicks & Wgtn; *CY 1952*) b Oct. 15, 1914, d Jan. 20, 1987

*Dolphin, A. (Yorks) b Dec. 24, 1885, d Oct. 23, 1942

*Donnan, H. (NSW) b Nov. 12, 1864, d Aug. 13, 1956

*Donnelly, M. P. (Wgtn, Cant., OU, Middx & Warwicks; *CY 1948*) b Oct. 17, 1917, d Oct. 22, 1999

*Dooland, B. (S. Aust. & Notts; *CY 1955*) b Nov. 1, 1923, d Sept. 8, 1980

Dorrinton, W. (Kent & All-England) b April 29, 1809, d Nov. 8, 1848

Dorset, 3rd Duke of (Kent) b March 24, 1745, d July 19, 1799

*Doshi, D. R. (Bengal, Notts, Warwicks & S'tra) b Dec. 22, 1947

Douglas, J. W. H. T. (Essex; *CY 1915*) b Sept. 3, 1882, d Dec. 19, 1930

Douglas, M. W. (C. Dist. & Wgtn) b Oct. 20, 1968

Dovey, R. R. (Kent) b July 18, 1920, d Dec. 27, 1974

*Dowe, U. G. (Jam.) b March 29, 1949

*Dower, R. R. (E. Prov.) b June 4, 1876, d Sept. 15, 1964

*Dowling, G. T. OBE (Cant.; ICC referee) b March 4, 1937

*Downton, P. R. (Kent & Middx) b April 4, 1957

*Draper, R. G. (E. Prov. & Griq. W.) b Dec. 24, 1926

Dredge, C. H. (Som) b Aug. 4, 1954

*Druce, N. F. (CU & Surrey; *CY 1898*) b Jan. 1, 1875, d Oct. 27, 1954

Drybrough, C. D. (OU & Middx) b Aug. 31, 1938

*D'Souza, A. (Kar., Peshawar & PIA) b Jan. 17, 1939

*Ducat, A. (Surrey; *CY 1920*) b Feb. 16, 1886, d July 23, 1942

*Duckworth, C. A. R. (Natal & Rhod.) b March 22, 1933

*Duckworth, G. (Lancs; *CY 1929*) b May 9, 1901, d Jan. 5, 1966

Dudleston, B. (Leics, Glos & Rhod.; Test umpire) b July 16, 1945

Duers, K. G. (Mash.) b June 30, 1960

*Duff, R. A. (NSW) b Aug. 17, 1878, d Dec. 13, 1911

*Dujon, P. J. L. (Jam.; *CY 1989*) b May 28, 1956

*Duleepsinhji, K. S. (CU & Sussex; *CY 1930*) b June 13, 1905, d Dec. 5, 1959

*Dumbrill, R. (Natal & Tvl) b Nov. 19, 1938

*Duminy, J. P. (OU, W. Prov. & Tvl) b Dec. 16, 1897, d Jan. 31, 1980

*Duncan, J. R. F. (Qld & Vic.) b March 25, 1944

*Dunell, O. R. (E. Prov.) b July 15, 1856, d Oct. 21, 1929

Dunne, R. S. (Otago; Test umpire) b April 22, 1943

*Dunning, J. A. (Otago & OU) b Feb. 6, 1903, d June 24, 1971

*Dunusinghe, C. I. (Ant. & NCC) b Oct. 19, 1970

*Du Preez, J. H. (Rhod. & Zimb.) b Nov. 14, 1942

*Durani, S. A. (S'tra, Guj. & Raja.) b Dec. 11, 1934

*Durston, F. J. (Middx) b July 11, 1893, d April 8, 1965

*Du Toit, J. F. (SA) b April 5, 1868, d July 10, 1909

Dye, J. C. J. (Kent, Northants & E. Prov.) b July 24, 1942

*Dyer, D. V. (Natal) b May 2, 1914, d June 18, 1990

*Dyer, G. C. (NSW) b March 16, 1959

*Dymock, G. (Qld) b July 21, 1945

Dyson, A. H. (Glam) b July 10, 1905, d June 7, 1978

Dyson, Jack (Lancs) b July 8, 1934, d Nov. 16, 2000

*Dyson, John (NSW) b June 11, 1954

*Eady, C. J. (Tas.) b Oct. 29, 1870, d Dec. 20, 1945

Eagar, E. D. R. (OU, Glos & Hants) b Dec. 8, 1917, d Sept. 13, 1977

Eagar, E. Patrick (photographer) b March 9, 1944

Ealham, A. G. E. (Kent) b Aug. 30, 1944

East, D. E. (Essex) b July 27, 1959

East, R. E. (Essex) b June 20, 1947

Eastman, L. C. (Essex & Otago) b June 3, 1897, d April 17, 1941

*Eastwood, K. H. (Vic.) b Nov. 23, 1935

*Ebeling, H. I. MBE (Vic.) b Jan. 1, 1905, d Jan. 12, 1980

Ebrahim, Ahmed (ICC referee) b Dec. 2, 1937

Eckersley, P. T. (Lancs) b July 2, 1904, d Aug. 13, 1940

*Edgar, B. A. (Wgtn) b Nov. 23, 1956

Edinburgh, HRH Duke of (Pres. MCC 1948–49, 1974–75) b June 10, 1921

Edmeades, B. E. A. (Essex) b Sept. 17, 1941

*Edmonds, P. H. (CU, Middx & E. Prov.) b March 8, 1951

Edrich, B. R. (Kent & Glam) b Aug. 18, 1922

Edrich, E. H. (Lancs) b March 27, 1914, d July 9, 1993

Edrich, G. A. (Lancs) b July 13, 1918

*Edrich, J. H. MBE (Surrey; *CY 1966*) b June 21, 1937

*Edrich, W. J. (Middx; *CY 1940*) b March 26, 1916, d April 24, 1986

*Edwards, G. N. (C. Dist.) b May 27, 1955

*Edwards, J. D. (Vic.) b June 12, 1862, d July 31, 1911

Edwards, M. J. (CU & Surrey) b March 1, 1940

*Edwards, R. (W. Aust. & NSW) b Dec. 1, 1942

*Edwards, R. M. (B'dos) b June 3, 1940

*Edwards, W. J. (W. Aust.) b Dec. 23, 1949

*Ehtesham-ud-Din (Lahore, Punjab, PIA, NBP & UBL) b Sept. 4, 1950

*Elgie, M. K. (Natal) b March 6, 1933

Elliott, C. S. MBE (Derbys; Test umpire) b April 24, 1912

Elliott, Harold (Lancs; Test umpire) b June 15, 1904, d April 15, 1969

*Elliott, Harry (Derbys) b Nov. 2, 1891, d Feb. 2, 1976

*Ellison, R. M. (Kent & Tas.; *CY 1986*) b Sept. 21, 1959

*Emburey, J. E. (Middx, W. Prov. & Northants; *CY 1984*) b Aug. 20, 1952

*Emery, P. A. (NSW) b June 25, 1964

*Emery, R. W. G. (Auck. & Cant.) b March 28, 1915, d Dec. 18, 1982

*Emery, S. H. (NSW) b Oct. 16, 1885, d Jan. 7, 1967

*Emmett, G. M. (Glos) b Dec. 2, 1912, d Dec. 18, 1976

*Emmett, T. (Yorks) b Sept. 3, 1841, d June 30, 1904

*Endean, W. R. (Tvl) b May 31, 1924

Engel, Matthew L. (Editor of *Wisden* 1993–2000) b June 11, 1951

*Engineer, F. M. (Bombay & Lancs) b Feb. 25, 1938

Enthoven, H. J. (CU & Middx) b June 4, 1903, d June 29, 1975

Essop-Adam, E. A. (Mash.) b Nov. 16, 1968

*Evans, A. J. (OU, Hants & Kent) b May 1, 1889, d Sept. 18, 1960

Evans, D. G. L. (Glam; Test umpire) b July 27, 1933, d March 25, 1990

*Evans, E. (NSW) b March 26, 1849, d July 2, 1921

Evans, K. P. (Notts) b Sept. 10, 1963

*Evans, T. G. CBE (Kent; *CY 1951*) b Aug. 18, 1920, d May 3, 1999

Evershed, Sir Sydney H. (Derbys) b Jan. 13, 1861, d March 7, 1937

Every, T. (Glam) b Dec. 19, 1909, d Jan. 20, 1990

Eyre, T. J. P. (Derbys) b Oct. 17, 1939

*Fagg, A. E. (Kent; Test umpire) b June 18, 1915, d Sept. 13, 1977

*Fairfax, A. G. (NSW) b June 16, 1906, d May 17, 1955

Fairservice, W. J. (Kent) b May 16, 1881, d June 26, 1971

*Fane, F. L. (OU & Essex) b April 27, 1875, d Nov. 27, 1960

*Farnes, K. (CU & Essex; *CY 1939*) b July 8, 1911, d Oct. 20, 1941

Farooq Hamid (Lahore & PIA) b March 3, 1945

*Farrer, W. S. (Border) b Dec. 8, 1936

*Farrimond, W. (Lancs) b May 23, 1903, d Nov. 14, 1979

*Farrukh Zaman (Peshawar, NWFP, Punjab & MCB) b April 2, 1956

Faruq Ahmed (Biman) b July 24, 1966

*Faulkner, G. A. (Tvl) b Dec. 17, 1881, d Sept. 10, 1930

*Favell, L. E. MBE (S. Aust.) b Oct. 6, 1929, d June 14, 1987

*Fazal Mahmood (N. Ind., Punjab & Lahore; *CY 1955*) b Feb. 18, 1927

Fearnley, C. D. (Worcs; bat-maker) b April 12, 1940

Featherstone, N. G. (Tvl, N. Tvl, Middx & Glam) b Aug. 20, 1949

"Felix", N. (Wanostrocht) (Kent, Surrey & All-England) b Oct. 4, 1804, d Sept. 3, 1876

*Fellows-Smith, J. P. (OU, Tvl & Northants) b Feb. 3, 1932

Feltham, M. A. (Surrey & Middx) b June 26, 1963

Felton, N. A. (Som & Northants) b Oct. 24, 1960

*Fender, P. G. H. (Sussex & Surrey; *CY 1915*) b Aug. 22, 1892, d June 15, 1985

*Ferguson, W. (T/T) b Dec. 14, 1917, d Feb. 23, 1961

Ferguson, W. H. BEM (Scorer) b June 6, 1880, d Sept. 22, 1957

*Fernandes, M. P. (BG) b Aug. 12, 1897, d May 8, 1981

Fernando, E. R. (SL; SL coach) b Feb. 22, 1944

*Fernando, E. R. N. S. (SLAF) b Dec. 19, 1955

Fernando, T. L. (Colts & BRC) b Dec. 27, 1962

Fernando, U. N. K. (SSC & BRC) b March 10, 1970

Ferreira, A. M. (N. Tvl & Warwicks) b April 13, 1955

**Ferris, J. J. (NSW, Glos & S. Aust.; *CY 1889*) b May 21, 1867, d Nov. 21, 1900

*Fichardt, C. G. (OFS) b March 20, 1870, d May 30, 1923

Fiddling, K. (Yorks & Northants) b Oct. 13, 1917, d June 19, 1992

Field, F. E. (Warwicks) b Sept. 23, 1874, d Aug. 25, 1934

*Fielder, A. (Kent; *CY 1907*) b July 19, 1877, d Aug. 30, 1949

*Findlay, T. M. MBE (Comb. Is. & Windwards) b Oct. 19, 1943

Findlay, W. (OU & Lancs; Sec. Surrey CCC 1907–19; Sec. MCC 1926–36) b June 22, 1880, d June 19, 1953

*Fingleton, J. H. OBE (NSW; writer) b April 28, 1908, d Nov. 22, 1981

*Finlason, C. E. (Tvl & Griq. W.) b Feb. 19, 1860, d July 31, 1917

Finney, R. J. (Derbys) b Aug. 2, 1960

Firth, Canon J. D'E. E. (Winchester, OU & Notts; *CY 1918*) b Jan. 21, 1900, d Sept. 21, 1957

Firth, J. (Yorks & Leics) b June 27, 1917, d Sept. 7, 1981

*Fisher, F. E. (Wgtn & C. Dist.) b July 28, 1924, d June 19, 1996

*Fishlock, L. B. (Surrey; *CY 1947*) b Jan. 2, 1907, d June 26, 1986

Fishwick, T. S. (Warwicks) b July 24, 1876, d Feb. 21, 1950

Fitzgerald, R. A. (CU & Middx; Sec. MCC 1863–76) b Oct. 1, 1834, d Oct. 28, 1881

Fitzroy-Newdegate, Hon. J. M. (Northants) b March 20, 1897, d May 7, 1976

*Flavell, J. A. (Worcs; *CY 1965*) b May 15, 1929

*Fleetwood-Smith, L. O'B. (Vic.) b March 30, 1908, d March 16, 1971

Fletcher, D. A. G. (Rhod. & Zimb.; Eng. coach) b Sept. 27, 1948

Fletcher, D. G. W. (Surrey) b July 6, 1924

*Fletcher, K. W. R. OBE (Essex; *CY 1974*; Eng. manager) b May 20, 1944

Fletcher, S. D. (Yorks & Lancs) b June 8, 1964

*Floquet, C. E. (Tvl) b Nov. 3, 1884, d Nov. 22, 1963

*Flowers, W. (Notts) b Dec. 7, 1856, d Nov. 1, 1926

*Foley, H. (Wgtn) b Jan. 28, 1906, d Oct. 16, 1948

Folley, I. (Lancs & Derbys) b Jan. 9, 1963, d Aug. 30, 1993

Forbes, C. (Notts) b Aug. 9, 1936

*Ford, F. G. J. (CU & Middx) b Dec. 14, 1866, d Feb. 7, 1940

Ford, G. X. (Natal; SA coach) b Nov. 16, 1960

Fordham, A. (Northants) b Nov. 9, 1964

Foreman, D. J. (W. Prov. & Sussex) b Feb. 1, 1933

*Foster, F. R. (Warwicks; *CY 1912*) b Jan. 31, 1889, d May 3, 1958

Foster, G. N. (OU, Worcs & Kent) b Oct. 16, 1884, d Aug. 11, 1971

Foster, H. K. (OU & Worcs; *CY 1911*) b Oct. 30, 1873, d June 23, 1950

Foster, M. K. (Worcs) b Jan. 1, 1889, d Dec. 3, 1940

*Foster, M. L. C. (Jam.) b May 9, 1943

*Foster, N. A. (Essex & Tvl; *CY 1988*) b May 6, 1962

*Foster, R. E. (OU & Worcs; *CY 1901*) b April 16, 1878, d May 13, 1914

*Fothergill, A. J. (Som) b Aug. 26, 1854, d Aug. 1, 1932

Fowke, G. H. S. (Leics) b Oct. 14, 1880, d June 24, 1946

Fowler, G. (Lancs & Durham) b April 20, 1957

Francis, B. C. (NSW & Essex) b Feb. 18, 1948

Francis, D. A. (Glam) b Nov. 29, 1953

*Francis, G. N. (B'dos) b Dec. 11, 1897, d Jan. 7, 1942

*Francis, H. H. (Glos & W. Prov.) b May 26, 1868, d Jan. 7, 1936

Francis, K. T. (Test umpire) b Oct. 15, 1949

Francke, F. M. (SL & Qld) b March 29, 1941

*Francois, C. M. (Griq. W.) b June 20, 1897, d May 26, 1944

*Frank, C. N. (Tvl) b Jan. 27, 1891, d Dec. 25, 1961

*Frank, W. H. B. (SA) b Nov. 23, 1872, d Feb. 16, 1945

*Franklin, T. J. (Auck.) b March 18, 1962

*Frederick, M. (B'dos, Derbys & Jam.) b May 6, 1927

*Fredericks, R. C. (†Guyana & Glam; *CY 1974*) b Nov. 11, 1942, d Sept. 5, 2000

*Freeman, A. P. (Kent; *CY 1923*) b May 17, 1888, d Jan. 28, 1965

*Freeman, D. L. (Wgtn) b Sept. 8, 1914, d May 31, 1994

*Freeman, E. W. (S. Aust.) b July 13, 1944

Freeman, J. R. (Essex) b Sept. 3, 1883, d Aug. 8, 1958

Freer, F. W. (Vic.) b Dec. 4, 1915, d Nov. 2 1998

French, B. N. (Notts) b Aug. 13, 1959

Frindall, W. H. (statistician) b March 3, 1939

Frith, David E. J. (Writer) b March 16, 1937

Frost, G. (Notts) b Jan. 15, 1947

Fry, C. B. (OU, Sussex & Hants; *CY 1895*) b April 25, 1872, d Sept. 7, 1956

Fuller, E. R. H. (W. Prov.) b Aug. 2, 1931

Fuller, R. L. (Jam.) b Jan. 30, 1913, d May 3, 1987

Fullerton, G. M. (Tvl) b Dec. 8, 1922, d Nov. 19, 2002

Funston, K. J. (NE Tvl, OFS & Tvl) b Dec. 3, 1925

*Furlonge, H. A. (T/T) b June 19, 1934

Gabriel, R. S. (T/T) b June 5, 1952

Gadkari, C. V. (M'tra & Ind. Serv.) b Feb. 3, 1928, d Jan. 11, 1998

Gaekwad, A. D. (Baroda; Ind. coach) b Sept. 23, 1952

Gaekwad, D. K. (Baroda) b Oct. 27, 1928

Gaekwad, H. G. (†M. Pradesh) b Aug. 29, 1923

Gale, R. A. (Middx) b Dec. 10, 1933

Gallichan, N. (Wgtn) b June 3, 1906, d March 25, 1969

Gamage, J. C. (Colts & Galle) b April 17, 1964

Gamsy, D. (Natal) b Feb. 17, 1940

Gandotra, A. (Delhi & Bengal) b Nov. 24, 1948

Gannon, J. B. (W. Aust.) b Feb. 8, 1947

Ganteaume, A. G. (T/T) b Jan. 22, 1921

Gard, T. (Som) b June 2, 1957

Gardiner, Howard (ICC referee) b Jan. 1, 1944

Gardner, F. C. (Warwicks) b June 4, 1922, d Jan. 12, 1979

Gardner, L. R. (Leics) b Feb. 23, 1934

Garland-Wells, H. M. (OU & Surrey) b Nov. 14, 1907, d May 28, 1993

Garlick, R. G. (Lancs & Northants) b April 11, 1917, d May 16, 1988

*Garner, J. MBE (B'dos, Som & S. Aust.; *CY 1980*) b Dec. 16, 1952

Garnham, M. A. (Glos, Leics & Essex) b Aug. 20, 1960

*Garrett, T. W. (NSW) b July 26, 1858, d Aug. 6, 1943

*Gaskin, B. B. M. (BG) b March 21, 1908, d May 1, 1979

*Gatting, M. W. OBE (Middx; *CY 1984*) b June 6, 1957

*Gaunt, R. A. (W. Aust. & Vic.) b Feb. 26, 1934

*Gavaskar, S. M. (Bombay & Som; *CY 1980*) b July 10, 1949

*Gay, L. H. (CU, Hants & Som) b March 24, 1871, d Nov. 1, 1949

*Geary, G. (Leics; *CY 1927*) b July 9, 1893, d March 6, 1981

*Gedye, S. G. (Auck.) b May 2, 1929

*Gehrs, D. R. A. (S. Aust.) b Nov. 29, 1880, d June 25, 1953

*Germon, L. K. (Cant.) b Nov. 4, 1968

Ghai, R. S. (Punjab) b June 12, 1960

*Ghavri, K. D. (S'tra & Bombay) b Feb. 28, 1951

*Ghazali, M. E. Z. (M'tra & Pak. Serv.) b June 15, 1924

*Ghorpade, J. M. (Baroda) b Oct. 2, 1930, d March 29, 1978

*Ghulam Abbas (Kar., NBP & PIA) b May 1, 1947

*Ghulam Ahmed (H'bad) b July 4, 1922, d Oct. 28, 1998

*Gibb, P. A. (CU, Scotland, Yorks & Essex) b July 11, 1913, d Dec. 7, 1977

Gibbons, H. H. (Worcs) b Oct. 10, 1904, d Feb. 16, 1973

*Gibbs, G. L. (BG) b Dec. 27, 1925, d Feb. 21, 1979

*Gibbs, L. R. (†Guyana, S. Aust. & Warwicks; *CY 1972*) b Sept. 29, 1934

Gibbs, P. J. K. (OU & Derbys) b Aug. 17, 1944

*Gibson, C. H. (Eton, CU & Sussex; *CY 1918*) b Aug. 23, 1900, d Dec. 31, 1976

Gibson, D. (Surrey) b May 1, 1936

*Gibson, O. D. (B'dos, Border, Glam, Griq. W. & Gauteng) b March 16, 1969

*Giffen, G. (S. Aust.; *CY 1894*) b March 27, 1859, d Nov. 29, 1927

*Giffen, W. F. (S. Aust.) b Sept. 20, 1861, d June 29, 1949

*Gifford, N. MBE (Worcs & Warwicks; *CY 1975*) b March 30, 1940

*Gilbert, D. R. (NSW, Tas. & Glos) b Dec. 29, 1960

*Gilchrist, R. (Jam. & H'bad) b June 28, 1934, d July 18, 2001

Giles, R. J. (Notts) b Oct. 17, 1919

Gilhouley, K. (Yorks & Notts) b Aug. 8, 1934

*Gillespie, S. R. (Auck.) b March 2, 1957

Gilliat, R. M. C. (OU & Hants) b May 20, 1944

*Gilligan, A. E. R. (CU, Surrey & Sussex; *CY 1924*; Pres. MCC 1967–68) b Dec. 23, 1894, d Sept. 5, 1976

*Gilligan, A. H. H. (Sussex) b June 29, 1896, d May 5, 1978

Gilligan, F. W. (OU & Essex) b Sept. 20, 1893, d May 4, 1960

Gillingham, Canon F. H. (Essex) b Sept. 6, 1875, d April 1, 1953

*Gilmour, G. J. (NSW) b June 26, 1951

*Gimblett, H. (Som; *CY 1953*) b Oct. 19, 1914, d March 30, 1978

Gladstone, G. (*see* Marais, G. G.)

*Gladwin, Cliff (Derbys) b April 3, 1916, d April 10, 1988

*Gleeson, J. W. (NSW & E. Prov.) b March 14, 1938

*Gleeson, R. A. (E. Prov.) b Dec. 6, 1873, d Sept. 27, 1919

Glover, A. C. S. (Warwicks) b April 19, 1872, d May 22, 1949

*Glover, G. K. (Kimberley & Griq. W.) b May 13, 1870, d Nov. 15, 1938

*Goddard, J. D. C. OBE (B'dos) b April 21, 1919, d Aug. 26, 1987

*Goddard, T. L. (Natal & NE Tvl) b Aug. 1, 1931

*Goddard, T. W. (Glos; *CY 1938*) b Oct. 1, 1900, d May 22, 1966

Goel, R. (Patiala & Haryana) b Sept. 29, 1942

*Gomes, H. A. (T/T & Middx; *CY 1985*) b July 13, 1953

*Gomez, G. E. (T/T) b Oct. 10, 1919, d Aug. 6, 1996

*Gooch, G. A. OBE (Essex & W. Prov.; *CY 1980*) b July 23, 1953

Goodwin, H. (Lancs) b June 25, 1938

Goodwin, T. J. (Leics) b Jan. 22, 1929

Goonatillake, F. R. M. de S. (SL) b Aug. 15, 1951

*Goonatillake, H. M. (SL) b Aug. 16, 1952

Goonesena, G. (Ceylon, Notts, CU & NSW) b Feb. 16, 1931

*Gopalan, M. J. (Madras) b June 6, 1909

*Gopinath, C. D. (Madras) b March 1, 1930

*Gordon, N. (Tvl) b Aug. 6, 1911

Gore, A. C. (Eton & Army; *CY 1919*) b May 14, 1900, d June 7, 1990

Gould, I. J. (Middx, Auck. & Sussex) b Aug. 19, 1957

*Gover, A. R. MBE (Surrey; *CY 1937*) b Feb. 29, 1908, d Oct. 7, 2001

*Gower, D. I. OBE (Leics & Hants; *CY 1979*) b April 1, 1957

Grace, C. B. (London County; son of W. G.) b March 1882, d June 6, 1938

*Grace, Dr E. M. (Glos; brother of W. G.) b Nov. 28, 1841, d May 20, 1911

*Grace, G. F. (Glos; brother of W. G.) b Dec. 13, 1850, d Sept. 22, 1880

Grace, Dr Henry (Glos; brother of W. G.) b Jan. 31, 1833, d Nov. 15, 1895

Grace, Dr H. M. (father of W. G.) b Feb. 21, 1808, d Dec. 23, 1871

Grace, Mrs H. M. (mother of W. G.) b July 18, 1812, d July 25, 1884

*Grace, Dr W. G. (Glos; *CY 1896*) b July 18, 1848, d Oct. 23, 1915

Grace, W. G., jun. (CU & Glos; son of W. G.) b July 6, 1874, d March 2, 1905

Graf, S. F. (Vic., W. Aust. & Hants) b May 19, 1957

*Graham, H. (Vic. & Otago) b Nov. 22, 1870, d Feb. 7, 1911

Graham, J. N. (Kent) b May 8, 1943

*Graham, R. W. (Prov.) b Sept. 16, 1877, d April 21, 1946

*Grant, G. C. (CU, T/T & Rhod.) b May 9, 1907, d Oct. 26, 1978

*Grant, R. S. (CU & T/T) b Dec. 15, 1909, d Oct. 18, 1977

Graveney, D. A. (Glos, Som & Durham; Chairman Eng. selectors) b Jan. 2, 1953

Graveney, J. K. (Glos) b Dec. 16, 1924

*Graveney, T. W. OBE (Glos, Worcs & Qld; *CY 1953*) b June 16, 1927

Graves, P. J. (Sussex & OFS) b May 19, 1946

*Gray, A. H. (T/T, Surrey & W. Tvl) b May 23, 1963

*Gray, E. J. (Wgtn) b Nov. 18, 1954

Gray, J. R. (Hants) b May 19, 1926

Gray, L. H. (Middx) b Dec. 15, 1915, d Jan. 3, 1983

Gray, M. A. (Pres. ICC 2000–   ) b May 30, 1940

*Greatbatch, M. J. (C. Dist.) b Dec. 11, 1963

Green, A. M. (Sussex & OFS) b May 28, 1960

Green, D. M. (OU, Lancs & Glos; *CY 1969*) b Nov. 10, 1939

Green, Major L. (Lancs) b Feb. 1, 1890, d March 2, 1963

*Greenhough, T. (Lancs) b Nov. 9, 1931

*Greenidge, A. E. (B'dos) b Aug. 20, 1956

*Greenidge, C. G. MBE (Hants & B'dos; *CY 1977*; Bang. coach) b May 1, 1951

*Greenidge, G. A. (B'dos & Sussex) b May 26, 1948

Greensmith, W. T. (Essex) b Aug. 16, 1930

*Greenwood, A. (Yorks) b Aug. 20, 1847, d Feb. 12, 1889

Greetham, C. (Som) b Aug. 28, 1936

*Gregory, D. W. (NSW; first Australian captain) b April 15, 1845, d Aug. 4, 1919

*Gregory, E. J. (NSW) b May 29, 1839, d April 22, 1899

*Gregory, J. M. (NSW; *CY 1922*) b Aug. 14, 1895, d Aug. 7, 1973

*Gregory, R. G. (Vic.) b Feb. 28, 1916, d June 10, 1942

Gregory, R. J. (Surrey) b Aug. 26, 1902, d Oct. 6, 1973

*Gregory, S. E. (NSW; *CY 1897*) b April 14, 1870, d Aug. 1, 1929

*Greig, A. W. (Border, E. Prov. & Sussex; *CY 1975*) b Oct. 6, 1946

*Greig, I. A. (CU, Border, Sussex & Surrey) b Dec. 8, 1955

*Grell, M. G. (T/T) b Dec. 18, 1899, d Jan. 11, 1976

*Grieve, B. A. F. (Eng.) b May 28, 1864, d Nov. 19, 1917

Grieves, K. J. (NSW & Lancs) b Aug. 27, 1925, d Jan. 3, 1992

*Grieveson, R. E. OBE (Tvl) b Aug. 24, 1909, d July 24, 1998

*Griffin, G. M. (Natal & Rhod.) b June 12, 1939

*Griffith, A. F. G. (B'dos) b Nov. 19, 1971

*Griffith, C. C. (B'dos; *CY 1964*) b Dec. 14, 1938

Griffith, G. ("Ben") (Surrey & Utd England XI) b Dec. 20, 1833, d May 3, 1879

*Griffith, H. C. (B'dos) b Dec. 1, 1893, d March 18, 1980

Griffith, M. G. (CU & Sussex) b Nov. 25, 1943

*Griffith, S. C. CBE (CU, Surrey & Sussex; Sec. MCC 1962–74; Pres. MCC 1979–80) b June 16, 1914, d April 7, 1993

Griffiths, B. J. (Northants) b June 13, 1949

*Grimmett, C. V. (Wgtn, Vic., & S. Aust.; *CY 1931*) b Dec. 25, 1891, d May 2, 1980

*Groube, T. U. (Vic.) b Sept. 2, 1857, d Aug. 5, 1927

*Grout, A. T. W. (Qld) b March 30, 1927, d Nov. 9, 1968

Grove, C. W. (Warwicks & Worcs) b Dec. 16, 1912, d Feb. 15, 1982

Grundy, James (Notts & Utd England XI) b March 5, 1824, d Nov. 24, 1873

*Guard, G. M. (Bombay & Guj.) b Dec. 12, 1925, d March 13, 1978

*Guest, C. E. J. (Vic. & W. Aust.) b Oct. 7, 1937

*Guha, S. (Bengal) b Jan. 31, 1946

**Guillen, S. C. (T/T & Cant.) b Sept. 24, 1924

**Gul Mahomed (N. Ind., Baroda, H'bad, Punjab & Lahore) b Oct. 15, 1921, d May 8, 1992

*Gunasekera, Y. (SL) b Nov. 8, 1957

Gunawardene, A. A. W. (SSC & Moors) b March 31, 1969

*Guneratne, R. P. W. (Nomads) b Jan. 26, 1962

*Gunn, G. (Notts; *CY 1914*) b June 13, 1879, d June 29, 1958

Gunn, G. V. (Notts) b June 21, 1905, d Oct. 14, 1957

*Gunn, J. (Notts; *CY 1904*) b July 19, 1876, d Aug. 21, 1963

*Gunn, W. (Notts; *CY 1890*) b Dec. 4, 1858, d Jan. 29, 1921

*Gupte, B. P. (Bombay, Bengal & Ind. Rlwys) b Aug. 30, 1934

*Gupte, S. P. (Bombay, Bengal, Raja. & T/T) b Dec. 11, 1929, d May 31, 2002

*Gursharan Singh (Punjab) b March 8, 1963

*Gurusinha, A. P. (SSC & NCC) b Sept. 16, 1966

*Guy, J. W. (C. Dist., Wgtn, Northants, Cant., Otago & N. Dist.) b Aug. 29, 1934

Haafiz Shahid (WAPDA) b May 10, 1963

Hadlee, B. G. (Cant.) b Dec. 14, 1941

*Hadlee, D. R. (Cant.) b Jan. 6, 1948

*Hadlee, Sir Richard J. (Cant., Notts & Tas.; *CY 1982*) b July 3, 1951

*Hadlee, W. A. CBE (Cant. & Otago) b June 4, 1915

*Hafeez, A. (*see* Kardar)

*Haig, N. E. (Middx) b Dec. 12, 1887, d Oct. 27, 1966

*Haigh, S. (Yorks; *CY 1901*) b March 19, 1871, d Feb. 27, 1921

Hair, D. B. (Test umpire) b Sept. 30, 1952

Halfyard, D. J. (Kent & Notts) b April 3, 1931, d Aug. 23, 1996

*Hall, A. E. (Tvl & Lancs) b Jan. 23, 1896, d Jan. 1, 1964

*Hall, G. G. (NE Tvl & E. Prov.) b May 24, 1938, d June 26, 1987

Hall, I. W. (Derbys) b Dec. 27, 1939

Hall, L. (Yorks; *CY 1890*) b Nov. 1, 1852, d Nov. 19, 1915

*Hall, W. W. (B'dos, T/T & Qld) b Sept. 12, 1937

Hallam, A. W. (Lancs & Notts; *CY 1908*) b Nov. 12, 1869, d July 24, 1940

Hallam, M. R. (Leics) b Sept. 10, 1931, d Jan. 1, 2000

Halliday, H. (Yorks) b Feb. 9, 1920, d Aug. 27, 1967

*Halliwell, E. A. (Tvl & Middx; *CY 1905*) b Sept. 7, 1864, d Oct. 2, 1919

*Hallows, C. (Lancs; *CY 1928*) b April 4, 1895, d Nov. 10, 1972

Hallows, J. (Lancs; *CY 1905*) b Nov. 14, 1873, d May 20, 1910

*Halse, C. G. (Natal) b Feb. 28, 1935

*Hamence, R. A. (S. Aust.) b Nov. 25, 1915

Hamer, A. (Yorks & Derbys) b Dec. 8, 1916, d Nov. 3, 1993

Hammond, H. E. (Sussex) b Nov. 7, 1907, d June 16, 1985

*Hammond, J. R. (S. Aust.) b April 19, 1950

*Hammond, W. R. (Glos; *CY 1928*) b June 19, 1903, d July 1, 1965

*Hampshire, J. H. (Yorks, Derbys & Tas.; Test umpire; Zimb. coach) b Feb. 10, 1941
*Hands, P. A. M. (W. Prov.) b March 18, 1890, d April 27, 1951
*Hands, R. H. M. (W. Prov.) b July 26, 1888, d April 20, 1918
*Hanif Mohammad (B'pur, Kar. & PIA; *CY 1968*) b Dec. 21, 1934
*Hanley, M. A. (Border & W. Prov.) b Nov. 10, 1918, d June 2, 2000
*Hanumant Singh (M. Pradesh & Raja.; ICC referee) b March 29, 1939
Harden, R. J. (Som, Yorks & C. Dist.) b Aug. 16, 1965
Hardie, B. R. (Scotland & Essex) b Jan. 14, 1950
*Hardikar, M. S. (Bombay) b Feb. 8, 1936, d Feb. 4, 1995
*Hardinge, H. T. W. (Kent; *CY 1915*) b Feb. 25, 1886, d May 8, 1965
*Hardstaff, J. (Notts; Test umpire) b Nov. 9, 1882, d April 2, 1947
*Hardstaff, J., jun. (Notts, Auck.; *CY 1938*) b July 3, 1911, d Jan. 1, 1990
Hardy, J. J. E. (Hants, Som, W. Prov. & Glos) b Oct. 2, 1960
*Harford, N. S. (C. Dist. & Auck.) b Aug. 30, 1930, d March 30, 1981
*Harford, R. I. (Auck.) b May 30, 1936
Hargreave, S. (Warwicks) b Sept. 22, 1875, d Jan. 1, 1929
Harman, R. (Surrey) b Dec. 28, 1941
*Haroon Rashid (Kar., Sind, NBP, PIA & UBL; Pak. coach) b March 25, 1953
*Harper, D. J. (ICC umpire) b Oct. 23, 1951
*Harper, R. A. (Guyana & Northants; WI coach) b March 17, 1963
*Harris, 4th Lord (OU & Kent; Pres. MCC 1895) b Feb. 3, 1851, d March 24, 1932
Harris, C. B. (Notts) b Dec. 6, 1907, d Aug. 8, 1954
Harris, David (Hants & All-England) b 1755, d May 19, 1803
Harris, J. H. (Som; umpire) b Feb. 13, 1936
Harris, M. J. (Middx, Notts, E. Prov. & Wgtn) b May 25, 1944
*Harris, P. G. Z. (Cant.) b July 18, 1927, d Dec. 1, 1991
*Harris, R. M. (Auck.) b July 27, 1933
*Harris, T. A. (Griq. W. & Tvl) b Aug. 27, 1916, d March 7, 1993
Harrison, L. (Hants) b June 8, 1922
*Harry, J. (Vic.) b Aug. 1, 1857, d Oct. 27, 1919
Hart, R. T. (C. Dist. & Wgtn) b Nov. 7, 1961
*Hartigan, G. P. D. (Border) b Dec. 30, 1884, d Jan. 7, 1955
*Hartigan, R. J. (NSW & Qld) b Dec. 12, 1879, d June 7, 1958
*Hartkopf, A. E. V. (Vic.) b Dec. 28, 1889, d May 20, 1968

*Hartland, B. R. (Cant.) b Oct. 22, 1966
Hartley, A. (Lancs; *CY 1911*) b April 11, 1879, d Oct. 9, 1918
*Hartley, J. C. (OU & Sussex) b Nov. 15, 1874, d March 8, 1963
Hartley, P. J. (Warwicks, Yorks & Hants) b April 18, 1960
Hartley, S. N. (Yorks & OFS) b March 18, 1956
Harvey, J. F. (Derbys) b Sept. 27, 1939
*Harvey, M. R. (Vic.) b April 29, 1918, d March 20, 1995
Harvey, P. F. (Notts) b Jan. 15, 1923
*Harvey, R. L. (Natal) b Sept. 14, 1911, d July 20, 2000
*Harvey, R. N. MBE (Vic. & NSW; *CY 1954*) b Oct. 8, 1928
Hasan Jamil (Kalat, Kar., Pak. Us & PIA) b July 25, 1952
*Haseeb Ahsan (Peshawar, Pak. Us, Kar. & PIA) b July 15, 1939
Hassan, B. (Notts) b March 24, 1944
*Hassett, A. L. MBE (Vic.; *CY 1949*) b Aug. 28, 1913, d June 16, 1993
*Hastings, B. F. (Wgtn, C. Dist. & Cant.; ICC referee) b March 23, 1940
*Hathorn, C. M. H. (Tvl) b April 7, 1878, d May 17, 1920
*Hawke, 7th Lord (CU & Yorks; *CY 1909*; Pres. MCC 1914–18) b Aug. 16, 1860, d Oct. 10, 1938
*Hawke, N. J. N. (W. Aust., S. Aust. & Tas.) b June 27, 1939, d Dec. 25, 2000
Hawkins, D. G. (Glos) b May 18, 1935
*Hayes, E. G. (Surrey & Leics; *CY 1907*) b Nov. 6, 1876, d Dec. 2, 1953
*Hayes, F. C. (Lancs) b Dec. 6, 1946
*Hayes, J. A. (Auck. & Cant.) b Jan. 11, 1927
Hayes, R. L. (N. Dist.) b May 9, 1971
Haygarth, A. (Sussex; Historian) b Aug. 4, 1825, d May 1, 1903
Hayhurst, A. N. (Lancs, Som & Derbys) b Nov. 23, 1962
*Haynes, D. L. (B'dos, Middx & W. Prov.; *CY 1991*) b Feb. 15, 1956
Haynes, G. R. (Worcs) b Sept. 29, 1969
Haynes, R. C. (Jam.) b Nov. 2, 1964
Hayward, T. (Cambs. & All-England) b March 21, 1835, d July 21, 1876
*Hayward, T. W. (Surrey; *CY 1895*) b March 29, 1871, d July 19, 1939
*Hazare, V. S. (M'tra, C. Ind. & Baroda) b March 11, 1915
Hazell, H. L. (Som) b Sept. 30, 1909, d March 31, 1990
Hazlerigg, Sir A. G. Bt (later 1st Lord) (Leics) b Nov. 17, 1878, d May 25, 1949
Hazlitt, G. R. (Vic. & NSW) b Sept. 4, 1888, d Oct. 30, 1915
*Headley, D. W. (Middx & Kent) b Jan. 27, 1970

*Headley, G. A. MBE (Jam.; *CY 1934*) b May 30, 1909, d Nov. 30, 1983

*Headley, R. G. A. (Worcs & Jam.) b June 29, 1939

*Healy, I. A. (Qld; *CY 1994*) b April 30, 1964

Heane, G. F. H. (Notts) b Jan. 2, 1904, d Oct. 24, 1969

Heap, J. S. (Lancs) b Aug. 12, 1882, d Jan. 30, 1951

Hearn, P. (Kent) b Nov. 18, 1925

*Hearne, A. (Kent; *CY 1894*) b July 22, 1863, d May 16, 1952

**Hearne, F. (Kent & W. Prov.) b Nov. 23, 1858, d July 14, 1949

*Hearne, G. A. L. (W. Prov.) b March 27, 1888, d Nov. 13, 1978

*Hearne, G. G. (Kent) b July 7, 1856, d Feb. 13, 1932

*Hearne, J. T. (Middx; *CY 1892*) b May 3, 1867, d April 17, 1944

*Hearne, J. W. (Middx; *CY 1912*) b Feb. 11, 1891, d Sept. 14, 1965

Hearne, T. (Middx) b Sept. 4, 1826, d May 13, 1900

Heath, G. E. M. (Hants) b Feb. 20, 1913, d March 6, 1994

Heath, M. (Hants) b March 9, 1934

Hedges, B. (Glam) b Nov. 10, 1927

Hedges, L. P. (Tonbridge, OU, Kent & Glos; *CY 1919*) b July 13, 1900, d Jan. 12, 1933

*Heine, P. S. (NE Tvl, OFS & Tvl) b June 28, 1928

*Hemmings, E. E. (Warwicks, Notts & Sussex) b Feb. 20, 1949

Hemsley, E. J. O. (Worcs) b Sept. 1, 1943

*Henderson, M. (Wgtn) b Aug. 2, 1895, d June 17, 1970

Henderson, R. (Surrey; *CY 1890*) b March 30, 1865, d Jan. 29, 1931

*Hendren, E. H. (Middx; *CY 1920*) b Feb. 5, 1889, d Oct. 4, 1962

*Hendrick, M. (Derbys & Notts; *CY 1978*) b Oct. 22, 1948

*Hendriks, J. L. (Jam.; ICC referee) b Dec. 21, 1933

*Hendry, H. L. (NSW & Vic.) b May 24, 1895, d Dec. 16, 1988

*Henry, O. (W. Prov., Boland, OFS & Scotland) b Jan. 23, 1952

Herman, O. W. (Hants) b Sept. 18, 1907, d June 24, 1987

Herman, R. S. (Middx, Border, Griq. W. & Hants) b Nov. 30, 1946

Heron, J. G. (Zimb.) b Nov. 8, 1948

*Heseltine, C. (Hants) b Nov. 26, 1869, d June 13, 1944

Hever, N. G. (Middx & Glam) b Dec. 17, 1924, d Sept. 11, 1987

Hewett, H. T. (OU & Som; *CY 1893*) b May 25, 1864, d March 4, 1921.

Heyhoe-Flint, Rachael (England Women) b June 11, 1939

Heyn, P. D. (SL) b June 26, 1945

*Hibbert, P. A. (Vic.) b July 23, 1952

Hide, M. E. (Molly) (England Women) b Oct. 24, 1913, d Sept. 10, 1995

*Higgs, J. D. (Vic.) b July 11, 1950

*Higgs, K. (Lancs & Leics; *CY 1968*) b Jan. 14, 1937

Hignell, A. J. (CU & Glos) b Sept. 4, 1955

*Hilditch, A. M. J. (NSW & S. Aust.) b May 20, 1956

Hill, Alan (Derbys & OFS) b June 29, 1950

*Hill, Allen (Yorks) b Nov. 14, 1843, d Aug. 29, 1910

*Hill, A. J. L. (CU & Hants) b July 26, 1871, d Sept. 6, 1950

*Hill, C. (S. Aust.; *CY 1900*) b March 18, 1877, d Sept. 5, 1945

Hill, E. (Som) b July 9, 1923

Hill, G. (Hants) b April 15, 1913

*Hill, J. C. (Vic.) b June 25, 1923, d Aug. 11, 1974

Hill, M. (Notts, Derbys & Som) b Sept. 14, 1935

Hill, N. W. (Notts) b Aug. 22, 1935

Hill, W. A. (Warwicks) b April 27, 1910, d Aug. 11, 1995

Hill-Wood, Sir Samuel H. (Derbys) b March 21, 1872, d Jan. 4, 1949

Hillyer, W. R. (Kent & Surrey) b March 5, 1813, d Jan. 8, 1861

Hilton, C. (Lancs & Essex) b Sept. 26, 1937

*Hilton, M. J. (Lancs; *CY 1957*) b Aug. 2, 1928, d July 8, 1990

*Hime, C. F. W. (Natal) b Oct. 24, 1869, d Dec. 6, 1940

*Hindlekar, D. D. (Bombay) b Jan. 1, 1909, d March 30, 1949

Hinks, S. G. (Kent & Glos) b Oct. 12, 1960

Hipkin, A. B. (Essex) b Aug. 8, 1900, d Feb. 11, 1957

*Hirst, G. H. (Yorks; *CY 1901*) b Sept. 7, 1871, d May 10, 1954

*Hitch, J. W. (Surrey; *CY 1914*) b May 7, 1886, d July 7, 1965

Hitchcock, R. E. (Cant. & Warwicks) b Nov. 28, 1929

*Hoad, E. L. G. (B'dos) b Jan. 29, 1896, d March 5, 1986

*Hoare, D. E. (W. Aust.) b Oct. 19, 1934

*Hobbs, Sir John B. "Jack" (Surrey; *CY 1909, special portrait 1926, Cricketer of the Century 2000*) b Dec. 16, 1882, d Dec. 21, 1963

*Hobbs, R. N. S. (Essex & Glam) b May 8, 1942

*Hodges, J. R. (Vic.) b Aug. 11, 1855, death unknown

Hodgson, A. (Northants) b Oct. 27, 1951

Hodgson, G. D. (Glos) b Oct. 22, 1966

*Hunt, W. A. (NSW) b Aug. 26, 1908, d Dec. 30, 1983

*Hunte, Sir Conrad C. (B'dos; *CY 1964*) b May 9, 1932, d Dec. 3, 1999

*Hunte, E. A. C. (T/T) b Oct. 3, 1905, d June 26, 1967

Hunter, D. (Yorks) b Feb. 23, 1860, d Jan. 11, 1927

Hunter, J. (Yorks) b Aug. 3, 1855, d Jan. 4, 1891

Hurst, A. G. (Vic.) b July 15, 1950

Hurst, R. J. (Middx) b Dec. 29, 1933, d Feb. 10, 1996

Hurwood, A. (Qld) b June 17, 1902, d Sept. 26, 1982

Hutchings, K. L. (Kent; *CY 1907*) b Dec. 7, 1882, d Sept. 3, 1916

Hutchinson, J. M. (Derbys; *believed to be longest-lived first-class cricketer at 103 years 344 days*) b Nov. 29, 1896, d Nov. 7, 2000

Hutchinson, P. (SA) b Jan. 26, 1862, d Sept. 30, 1925

Hutton, Sir Leonard (Yorks; *CY 1938*) b June 23, 1916, d Sept. 6, 1990

Hutton, R. A. (CU, Yorks & Tvl) b Sept. 6, 1942

Hylton, L. G. (Jam.) b March 29, 1905, d May 17, 1955

Ibadulla, K. (Punjab, Warwicks, Tas. & Otago) b Dec. 20, 1935

Ibrahim, K. C. (Bombay) b Jan. 26, 1919

Iddison, R. (Yorks & Lancs) b Sept. 15, 1834, d March 19, 1890

Iddon, J. (Lancs) b Jan. 8, 1902, d April 17, 1946

Igglesden, A. P. (Kent & W. Prov.) b Oct. 8, 1964

Ijaz Ahmed, sen. (Gujranwala, PACO, HBL, I'bad & Lahore) b Sept. 20, 1968

Ijaz Butt (Pak. Us, Punjab, Lahore, R'pindi & Multan) b March 10, 1938

Ijaz Faqih (Kar., Sind, PWD & MCB) b March 24, 1956

Ikin, J. T. (Lancs) b March 7, 1918, d Sept. 15, 1984

Illingworth, R. CBE (Yorks & Leics; *CY 1960*; Chairman Eng. selectors; Eng. manager) b June 8, 1932

Illingworth, R. K. (Worcs, Natal & Derbys) b Aug. 23, 1963

Imran Khan (Lahore, Dawood, Worcs, OU, PIA, Sussex & NSW; *CY 1983*) b Nov. 25, 1952

Imtiaz Ahmed (N. Ind., Comb. Us, NWFP, Pak. Servs, Peshawar & PAF) b Jan. 5, 1928

Imtiaz Ali (T/T) b July 28, 1954

Inchmore, J. D. (Worcs & N. Tvl) b Feb. 22, 1949

Indrajitsinhji, K. S. (S'tra & Delhi) b June 15, 1937

Ingle, R. A. (Som) b Nov. 5, 1903, d Dec. 19, 1992

Ingleby-Mackenzie, A. C. D. (Hants; Pres. MCC 1996–98) b Sept. 15, 1933

Inman, C. C. (Ceylon & Leics) b Jan. 29, 1936

*Inshan Ali (T/T) b Sept. 25, 1949, d June 24, 1995

*Insole, D. J. CBE (CU & Essex; *CY 1956*; Chairman TCCB 1975–78) b April 18, 1926

*Intikhab Alam (Kar., PIA, Surrey, PWD, Sind, Punjab; ICC referee; Pak. manager) b Dec. 28, 1941

*Inverarity, R. J. (W. Aust. & S. Aust.) b Jan. 31, 1944

*Iqbal Qasim (Kar., Sind & NBP) b Aug. 6, 1953

Iqbal Sikandar (PIA, Kar. & H'bad) b Dec. 19, 1958

*Irani, J. K. (Sind) b Aug. 18, 1923, d Feb. 25, 1982

*Iredale, F. A. (NSW) b June 19, 1867, d April 15, 1926

Iremonger, J. (Notts; *CY 1903*) b March 5, 1876, d March 25, 1956

*Ironmonger, H. (Qld & Vic.) b April 7, 1882, d June 1, 1971

*Ironside, D. E. J. (Tvl) b May 2, 1925

*Irvine, B. L. (W. Prov., Natal, Essex & Tvl) b March 9, 1944

Isaacs, E. (ICC referee) b Jan. 26, 1945

*Israr Ali (S. Punjab, B'pur & Multan) b May 1, 1927

*Iverson, J. B. (Vic.) b July 27, 1915, d Oct. 24, 1973

*Jack, S. D. (Tvl) b Aug. 4, 1970

*Jackman, R. D. (Surrey, W. Prov. & Rhod.; *CY 1981*) b Aug. 13, 1945

*Jackson, A. A. (NSW) b Sept. 5, 1909, d Feb. 16, 1933

Jackson, A. B. (Derbys) b Aug. 21, 1933

*Jackson, Rt Hon. Sir F. Stanley (CU & Yorks; *CY 1894*; Pres. MCC 1921) b Nov. 21, 1870, d March 9, 1947

Jackson, G. R. (Derbys) b June 23, 1896, d Feb. 21, 1966

*Jackson, H. L. (Derbys; *CY 1959*) b April 5, 1921

Jackson, J. (Notts & All-England) b May 21, 1833, d Nov. 4, 1901

Jackson, P. F. (Worcs) b May 11, 1911, d April 27, 1999

Jackson, V. E. (NSW & Leics) b Oct. 25, 1916, d Jan. 30, 1965

*Jadeja, A. (Haryana & J/K) b Feb. 1, 1971

Jahangir Alam Talukdar (Biman) b Dec. 4, 1968

*Jahangir Khan (N. Ind. & CU) b Feb. 1, 1910, d July 23, 1988

*Jai, L. P. (Bombay) b April 1, 1902, d Jan. 29, 1968
*Jaisimha, M. L. (H'bad) b March 3, 1939, d July 6, 1999
Jakeman, F. (Yorks & Northants) b Jan. 10, 1920, d May 18, 1986
*Jalal-ud-Din (PWD, Kar., IDBP & Allied Bank) b June 12, 1959
James, A. E. (Sussex) b Aug. 7, 1924
James, C. L. R. (Writer) b Jan. 4, 1901, d May 31, 1989
*James, K. C. (Wgtn & Northants) b March 12, 1904, d Aug. 21, 1976
James, K. D. (Middx, Wgtn & Hants) b March 18, 1961
James, W. R. (Mat.) b Aug. 27, 1965
Jameson, J. A. (Warwicks) b June 30, 1941
*Jamshedji, R. J. (Bombay) b Nov. 18, 1892, d April 5, 1976
*Jardine, D. R. (OU & Surrey; CY 1928) b Oct. 23, 1900, d June 18, 1958
*Jarman, B. N. (S. Aust.; ICC referee) b Feb. 17, 1936
*Jarvis, A. H. (S. Aust.) b Oct. 19, 1860, d Nov. 15, 1933
Jarvis, K. B. S. (Kent & Glos) b April 23, 1953
*Jarvis, M. P. (Mash.) b Dec. 6, 1955
*Jarvis, P. W. (Yorks, Sussex & Som) b June 29, 1965
*Jarvis, T. W. (Auck. & Cant.) b July 29, 1944
*Javed Akhtar (R'pindi & Pak. Serv.; Test umpire) b Nov. 21, 1940
Javed Qadir (PIA & Kar.) b Aug. 25, 1976
*Javed Miandad (Kar., Sind, Sussex, HBL & Glam; CY 1982; Pak. coach) b June 12, 1957
*Jayantilal, K. (H'bad) b Jan. 13, 1948
Jayaprakash, A. V. (Test umpire) b March 14, 1950
*Jayasekera, R. S. A. (SL) b Dec. 7, 1957
Jayasinghe, S. (Ceylon & Leics) b Jan. 19, 1931
Jayasinghe, S. A. (SL) b July 15, 1955, d April 20, 1995
Jeeves, P. (Warwicks) b March 5, 1888, d July 22, 1916
Jefferies, S. T. (W. Prov., Derbys, Lancs, Hants & Boland) b Dec. 8, 1959
*Jeganathan, S. (SL) b July 11, 1951, d May 14, 1996
*Jenkins, R. O. (Worcs; CY 1950) b Nov. 24, 1918, d July 21, 1995
*Jenner, T. J. (W. Aust. & S. Aust.) b Sept. 8, 1944
Jephson, D. L. A. (CU & Surrey) b Feb. 23, 1871, d Jan. 19, 1926

Jepson, A. (Notts; Test umpire) b July 12, 1915, d July 17, 1997
*Jessop, G. L. (CU & Glos; CY 1898) b May 19, 1874, d May 11, 1955
Jesty, T. E. (Hants, Border, Griq. W., Cant., Surrey & Lancs; CY 1983) b June 2, 1948
Jewell, Major M. F. S. (Worcs & Sussex) b Sept. 15, 1885, d May 28, 1978
*John, V. B. (SL) b May 27, 1960
*Johnson, C. L. (Tvl) b 1871, d May 31, 1908
*Johnson, D. J. (Karn.) b Oct. 16, 1971
Johnson, G. W. (Kent & Tvl) b Nov. 8, 1946
*Johnson, H. H. H. (Jam.) b July 13, 1910, d June 24, 1987
Johnson, H. L. (Derbys) b Nov. 8, 1927
*Johnson, I. W. OBE (Vic.) b Dec. 8, 1917, d Oct. 9, 1998
Johnson, L. A. (Northants) b Aug. 12, 1936
*Johnson, L. J. (Qld) b March 18, 1919, d April 20, 1977
Johnson, P. R. (CU & Som) b Aug. 5, 1880, d July 1, 1959
*Johnson, T. F. (T/T) b Jan. 10, 1917, d April 5, 1985
Johnston, Brian A. CBE (Broadcaster) b June 24, 1912, d Jan. 5, 1994
*Johnston, W. A. (Vic.; CY 1949) b Feb. 26, 1922
Jones, A. MBE (Glam, W. Aust., N. Tvl & Natal; CY 1978) b Nov. 4, 1938
Jones, A. A. (Sussex, Som, Middx, Glam, N. Tvl & OFS) b Dec. 9, 1947
*Jones, A. H. (Wgtn & C. Dist.) b May 9, 1959
Jones, A. L. (Glam) b June 1, 1957
Jones, A. N. (Sussex, Border & Som) b July 22, 1961
*Jones, A. O. (Notts & CU; CY 1900) b Aug. 16, 1872, d Dec. 21, 1914
*Jones, C. M. (BG) b Nov. 3, 1902, d Dec. 10, 1959
*Jones, D. M. (Vic., Durham & Derbys; CY 1990) b March 24, 1961
*Jones, Ernest (S. Aust. & W. Aust.) b Sept. 30, 1869, d Nov. 23, 1943
Jones, E. C. (Glam) b Dec. 14, 1911, d April 14, 1989
Jones, E. W. (Glam) b June 25, 1942
*Jones, I. J. (Glam) b Dec. 10, 1941
Jones, K. V. (Middx) b March 28, 1942
*Jones, P. E. (T/T) b June 6, 1917, d Nov. 21, 1991
Jones, P. H. (Kent) b June 19, 1935
*Jones, S. P. (NSW, Qld & Auck.) b Aug. 1, 1861, d July 14, 1951
Jones, W. E. (Glam) b Oct. 31, 1916, d July 25, 1996
Jordon, R. C. (Vic.) b Feb. 17, 1937
*Joseph, D. R. E. (Leewards) b Nov. 15, 1969
*Joshi, P. G. (M'tra) b Oct. 27, 1926, d Jan. 8, 1987

Joshi, U. C. (S'tra, Ind. Rlwys, Guj. & Sussex) b Dec. 23, 1944

*Joslin, L. R. (Vic.) b Dec. 13, 1947

*Julian, B. P. (W. Aust. & Surrey) b Aug. 10, 1970

Julian, R. (Leics) b Aug. 23, 1936

*Julien, B. D. (T/T & Kent) b March 13, 1950

*Jumadeen, R. R. (T/T) b April 12, 1948

*Jupp, H. (Surrey) b Nov. 19, 1841, d April 8, 1889

*Jupp, V. W. C. (Sussex & Northants; *CY 1928*) b March 27, 1891, d July 9, 1960

*Jurangpathy, B. R. (CCC) b June 25, 1967

*Kallicharran, A. I. (Guyana, Warwicks, Qld, Tvl & OFS; *CY 1983*) b March 21, 1949

*Kaluperuma, L. W. (SL) b May 25, 1949

*Kaluperuma, S. M. S. (SL) b Oct. 22, 1961

*Kanhai, R. B. (†Guyana, T/T, W. Aust., Warwicks & Tas.; *CY 1964; WI manager) b Dec. 26, 1935

*Kanitkar, H. S. (M'tra) b Dec. 8, 1942

*Kapil Dev (Haryana, Northants & Worcs; *CY 1983;* Ind. coach) b Jan. 6, 1959

**Kardar, A. H. (formerly Abdul Hafeez) (N. Ind., OU, Warwicks & Pak. Serv.) b Jan. 17, 1925, d April 21, 1996

*Karim, S. S. (Bihar & Bengal) b Nov. 14, 1967

Karnain, S. H. U. (NCC & Moors) b Aug. 11, 1962

*Keeton, W. W. (Notts; *CY 1940*) b April 30, 1905, d Oct. 10, 1980

*Keith, H. J. (Natal) b Oct. 25, 1927, d Nov. 17, 1997

*Kelleway, C. (NSW) b April 25, 1886, d Nov. 16, 1944

*Kelly, J. J. (NSW; *CY 1903*) b May 10, 1867, d Aug. 14, 1938

Kelly, J. M. (Lancs & Derbys) b March 19, 1922, d Nov. 13, 1979

*Kelly, T. J. D. (Vic.) b May 3, 1844, d July 20, 1893

*Kempis, G. A. (Natal) b Aug. 4, 1865, d May 19, 1890

*Kendall, T. (Vic. & Tas.) b Aug. 24, 1851, d Aug. 17, 1924

Kennedy, A. (Lancs) b Nov. 4, 1949

*Kennedy, A. S. (Hants; *CY 1933*) b Jan. 24, 1891, d Nov. 15, 1959

Kennedy, R. J. (Otago & Wgtn) b June 3, 1972

*Kenny, R. B. (Bombay & Bengal) b Sept. 29, 1930, d Nov. 21, 1985

*Kent, M. F. (Qld) b Nov. 23, 1953

*Kentish, E. S. M. (Jam. & OU) b Nov. 21, 1916

*Kenyon, D. (Worcs; *CY 1963*) b May 15, 1924, d Nov. 12, 1996

*Kenyon, M. N. (Lancs) b Dec. 25, 1886, d Nov. 21, 1960

*Kerr, J. L. (Cant.) b Dec. 28, 1910

*Kerr, R. B. (Qld) b June 16, 1961

Key, Sir Kingsmill J. (Surrey & OU) b Oct. 11, 1864, d Aug. 9, 1932

*Khalid Hassan (Punjab & Lahore) b July 14, 1937

*Khalid Wazir (Pak.) b April 27, 1936

*Khan Mohammad (N. Ind., Pak. Us, Som, B'pur, Sind, Kar. & Lahore) b Jan. 1, 1928

Khanna, S. C. (Delhi) b June 3, 1956

Killick, E. H. (Sussex) b Jan. 17, 1875, d Sept. 29, 1948

*Killick, Rev. E. T. (CU & Middx) b May 9, 1907, d May 18, 1953

Kilner, N. (Yorks & Warwicks) b July 21, 1895, d April 28, 1979

*Kilner, R. (Yorks; *CY 1924*) b Oct. 17, 1890, d April 5, 1928

King, B. P. (Worcs & Lancs) b April 22, 1915, d March 31, 1970

*King, C. L. (B'dos, Glam, Worcs & Natal) b June 11, 1951

*King, F. M. (B'dos) b Dec. 8, 1926, d Dec. 23, 1990

King, J. B. (Philadelphia) b Oct. 19, 1873, d Oct. 17, 1965

*King, J. H. (Leics) b April 16, 1871, d Nov. 18, 1946

*King, L. A. (Jam. & Bengal) b Feb. 27, 1939, d July 9, 1998

*Kinneir, S. P. (Warwicks; *CY 1912*) b May 13, 1871, d Oct. 16, 1928

*Kippax, A. F. (NSW) b May 25, 1897, d Sept. 4, 1972

Kirby, D. (CU & Leics) b Jan. 18, 1939

*Kirmani, S. M. H. (†Karn.) b Dec. 29, 1949

*Kirsten, P. N. (W. Prov., Sussex, Derbys & Border) b May 14, 1955

*Kischenchand, G. (W. Ind., Guj. & Baroda) b April 14, 1925, d April 16, 1997

Kitchen, M. J. (Som; Test umpire) b Aug. 1, 1940

*Kline, L. F. (Vic.) b Sept. 29, 1934

*Knight, A. E. (Leics; *CY 1904*) b Oct. 8, 1872, d April 25, 1946

*Knight, B. R. (Essex & Leics) b Feb. 18, 1938

*Knight, D. J. (OU & Surrey; *CY 1915*) b May 12, 1894, d Jan. 5, 1960

Knight, R. D. V. (CU, Surrey, Glos & Sussex; Sec. MCC 1994–) b Sept. 6, 1946

Knight, W. H. (Editor of *Wisden* 1870–79) b Nov. 29, 1812, d Aug. 16, 1879

*Knott, A. P. E. (Kent & Tas.; *CY 1970*) b April 9, 1946

Knott, C. J. (Hants) b Nov. 26, 1914

Knowles, J. (Notts) b March 25, 1910

*Knox, N. A. (Surrey; *CY 1907*) b Oct. 10, 1884, d March 3, 1935

Koertzen, R. E. (ICC umpire) b March 26, 1949

Kortright, C. J. (Essex) b Jan. 9, 1871, d Dec. 12, 1952

*Kotze, J. J. (Tvl & W. Prov.) b Aug. 7, 1879, d July 7, 1931

*Kripal Singh, A. G. (Madras & H'bad) b Aug. 6, 1933, d July 23, 1987

*Krishnamurthy, P. (H'bad) b July 12, 1947, d Jan. 28, 1999

*Kuggeleijn, C. M. (N. Dist.) b May 10, 1956

*Kuiper, A. P. (W. Prov., Derbys & Boland) b Aug. 24, 1959

*Kulkarni, N. M. (†Mumbai) b April 3, 1973

*Kulkarni, R. R. (Bombay) b Sept. 25, 1962

*Kulkarni, U. N. (Bombay) b March 7, 1942

*Kumar, V. V. (†TN) b June 22, 1935

*Kunderan, B. K. (Ind. Rlwys & Mysore) b Oct. 2, 1939

*Kuruppu, D. S. B. P. (BRC) b Jan. 5, 1962

*Kuruppuarachchi, A. K. (NCC) b Nov. 1, 1964

*Kuruvilla, A. (†Mumbai) b Aug. 8, 1968

*Kuys, F. (W. Prov.) b March 21, 1870, d Sept. 12, 1953

Kynaston, R. (Middx; Sec. MCC 1846–58) b Nov. 5, 1805, d June 21, 1874

*Labrooy, G. F. (CCC; ICC referee) b June 7, 1964

Lacey, Sir Francis E. (CU & Hants; Sec. MCC 1898–1926) b Oct. 19, 1859, d May 26, 1946

*Laird, B. M. (W. Aust.) b Nov. 21, 1950

*Laker, J. C. (Surrey, Auck. & Essex; *CY 1952*) b Feb. 9, 1922, d April 23, 1986

*Lall Singh (S. Punjab) b Dec. 16, 1909, d Nov. 19, 1985

*Lamb, A. J. (W. Prov., Northants & OFS; *CY 1981*) b June 20, 1954

Lamb, T. M. (OU, Middx & Northants; Chief Exec. ECB, 1997–) b March 24, 1953

*Lamba, R. (Delhi) b Jan. 2, 1960, d Feb. 23, 1998

*Lambert, C. B. (Guyana & N. Tvl) b Feb. 10, 1962

Lambert, G. E. (Glos & Som) b May 11, 1918, d Oct. 31, 1991

Lambert, R. H. (Ireland) b July 18, 1874, d March 24, 1956

Lambert, Wm (Surrey) b 1779, d April 19, 1851

Lampitt, S. R. (Worcs) b July 29, 1966

*Lance, H. R. (NE Tvl & Tvl) b June 6, 1940

Langdon, T. (Glos) b Jan. 8, 1879, d Nov. 30, 1944

Langford, B. A. (Som) b Dec. 17, 1935

*Langley, G. R. A. (S. Aust.; *CY 1957*) b Sept. 14, 1919, d May 14, 2001

*Langridge, James (Sussex; *CY 1932*) b July 10, 1906, d Sept. 10, 1966

Langridge, John G. MBE (Sussex; Test umpire; *CY 1950*) b Feb. 10, 1910, d June 27, 1999

Langridge, R. J. (Sussex) b April 13, 1939

*Langton, A. B. C. (Tvl) b March 2, 1912, d Nov. 27, 1942

*Larkins, W. (Northants, E. Prov. & Durham) b Nov. 22, 1953

*Larsen, G. R. (Wgtn) b Sept. 27, 1962

*Larter, J. D. F. (Northants) b April 24, 1940

*Larwood, H. MBE (Notts; *CY 1927*) b Nov. 14, 1904, d July 22, 1995

*Lashley, P. D. (B'dos) b Feb. 11, 1937

Latchman, H. C. (Middx & Notts) b July 26, 1943

*Latham, R. T. (Cant.) b June 12, 1961

*Lathwell, M. N. (Som) b Dec. 26, 1971

*Laughlin, T. J. (Vic.) b Jan. 30, 1951

*Laver, F. (Vic.) b Dec. 7, 1869, d Sept. 24, 1919

Lavis, G. (Glam) b Aug. 17, 1908, d July 29, 1956

*Lawrence, D. V. (Glos) b Jan. 28, 1964

*Lawrence, G. B. (Rhod. & Natal) b March 31, 1932

Lawrence, J. (Som) b March 29, 1914, d Dec. 10, 1988

*Lawry, W. M. (Vic.; *CY 1962*) b Feb. 11, 1937

*Lawson, G. F. (NSW & Lancs) b Dec. 7, 1957

Lawton, A. E. (Derbys & Lancs) b March 31, 1879, d Dec. 25, 1955

Leach, G. (Sussex) b July 18, 1881, d Jan. 10, 1945

Leadbeater, B. (Yorks) b Aug. 14, 1943

*Leadbeater, E. (Yorks & Warwicks) b Aug. 15, 1927

Leary, S. E. (Kent) b April 30, 1933, d Aug. 21, 1988

Lee, C. (Yorks & Derbys) b March 17, 1924, d Sept. 3, 1999

Lee, F. S. (Middx & Som; Test umpire) b July 24, 1905, d March 30, 1982

Lee, G. M. (Notts & Derbys) b June 7, 1887, d Feb. 29, 1976

Lee, H. W. (Middx) b Oct. 26, 1890, d April 21, 1981

Lee, J. W. (Middx & Som) b Feb. 1, 1904, d June 20, 1944

Lee, P. G. (Northants & Lancs; *CY 1976*) b Aug. 27, 1945

*Lee, P. K. (S. Aust.) b Sept. 15, 1904, d Aug. 9, 1980

*Lees, W. K. MBE (Otago; NZ coach) b March 19, 1952

*Lees, W. S. (Surrey; *CY 1906*) b Dec. 25, 1875, d Sept. 10, 1924

Lefebvre, R. P. (Holland, Som, Cant. & Glam) b Feb. 7, 1963

*Legall, R. (B'dos & T/T) b Dec. 1, 1925

*Leggat, I. B. (C. Dist.) b June 7, 1930

*Leggat, J. G. (Cant.) b May 27, 1926, d March 9, 1973

*Legge, G. B. (OU & Kent) b Jan. 26, 1903, d Nov. 21, 1940

Lenham, L. J. (Sussex) b May 24, 1936

Lenham, N. J. (Sussex) b Dec. 17, 1965

*le Roux, F. L. (Tvl & E. Prov.) b Feb. 5, 1882, d Sept. 22, 1963

le Roux, G. S. (W. Prov. & Sussex) b Sept. 4, 1955

*Leslie, C. F. H. (OU & Middx) b Dec. 8, 1861, d Feb. 12, 1921

Lester, E. (Yorks) b Feb. 18, 1923

Lester, G. (Leics) b Dec. 27, 1915, d Jan. 26, 1998

Lester, Dr J. A. (Philadelphia) b Aug. 1, 1871, d Sept. 3, 1969

*Lever, J. K. MBE (Essex & Natal; *CY 1979*) b Feb. 24, 1949

*Lever, P. (Lancs & Tas.) b Sept. 17, 1940

*Leveson Gower, Sir H. D. G. (OU & Surrey) b May 8, 1873, d Feb. 1, 1954

*Levett, W. H. V. (Kent) b Jan. 25, 1908, d Nov. 30, 1995

*Lewis, A. R. CBE (Glam & CU; Pres. MCC 1998–2000; writer & broadcaster) b July 6, 1938

Lewis, A. E. (Som) b Jan. 20, 1877, d Feb. 22, 1956

Lewis, C. BEM (Kent) b July 27, 1908, d April 26, 1993

*Lewis, C. C. (Leics, Notts & Surrey) b Feb. 14, 1968

*Lewis, D. M. (Jam.) b Feb. 21, 1946

Lewis, E. J. (Glam & Sussex) b Jan. 31, 1942

*Lewis, P. T. (W. Prov.) b Oct. 2, 1884, d Jan. 30, 1976

*Leyland, M. (Yorks; *CY 1929*) b July 20, 1900, d Jan. 1, 1967

*Liaqat Ali (Kar., Sind, HBL & PIA) b May 21, 1955

Lightfoot, A. (Northants) b Jan. 8, 1936

*Lillee, D. K. MBE (W. Aust., Tas. & Northants; *CY 1973*) b July 18, 1949

Lilley, A. A. (Warwicks; *CY 1897*) b Nov. 28, 1866, d Nov. 17, 1929

Lilley, A. W. (Essex) b May 8, 1959

Lilley, B. (Notts) b Feb. 11, 1895, d Aug. 4, 1950

Lillywhite, Fred (Sussex; Editor of *Lillywhite's Guide to Cricketers*) b July 23, 1829, d Sept. 15, 1866

Lillywhite, F. W. ("William") (Sussex) b June 13, 1792, d Aug. 21, 1854

*Lillywhite, James, jun. (Sussex) b Feb. 23, 1842, d Oct. 25, 1929

*Lindsay, D. T. (NE Tvl, N. Tvl & Tvl; ICC referee) b Sept. 4, 1939

*Lindsay, J. D. (Tvl & NE Tvl) b Sept. 8, 1908, d Aug. 31, 1990

*Lindsay, N. V. (Tvl & OFS) b July 30, 1886, d Feb. 2, 1976

*Lindwall, R. R. MBE (NSW & Qld; *CY 1949*) b Oct. 3, 1921, d June 22, 1996

*Ling, W. V. S. (Griq. W. & E. Prov.) b Oct. 3, 1891, d Sept. 26, 1960

*Lissette, A. F. (Auck. & N. Dist.) b Nov. 6, 1919, d Jan. 24, 1973

Lister, W. H. L. (CU & Lancs) b Oct. 7, 1911, d July 29, 1998

Livingston, L. (NSW & Northants) b May 3, 1920, d Jan. 16, 1998

Livingstone, D. A. (Hants) b Sept. 21, 1933, d Sept. 8, 1988

Livsey, W. H. (Hants) b Sept. 23, 1893, d Sept. 12, 1978

*Llewellyn, C. B. (Natal & Hants; *CY 1911*) b Sept. 26, 1876, d June 7, 1964

Llewellyn, M. J. (Glam) b Nov. 27, 1953

Lloyd, B. J. (Glam) b Sept. 6, 1953

*Lloyd, C. H. OBE (†Guyana & Lancs; *CY 1971*; WI manager; ICC referee) b Aug. 31, 1944

*Lloyd, D. (Lancs; Eng. coach) b March 18, 1947

*Lloyd, T. A. (Warwicks & OFS) b Nov. 5, 1956

Lloyds, J. W. (Som, OFS & Glos) b Nov. 17, 1954

*Loader, P. J. (Surrey & W. Aust.; *CY 1958*) b Oct. 25, 1929

Lobb, B. (Warwicks & Som) b Jan. 11, 1931, d May 3, 2000

*Lock, A. C. I. (Mash.) b Sept. 10, 1962

*Lock, G. A. R. (Surrey, W. Aust. & Leics; *CY 1954*) b July 5, 1929, d March 29, 1995

Lock, H. C. (Surrey; first TCCB pitch inspector) b May 8, 1903, d May 19, 1978

Lockwood, Ephraim (Yorks) b April 4, 1845, d Dec. 19, 1921

*Lockwood, W. H. (Notts & Surrey; *CY 1899*) b March 25, 1868, d April 26, 1932

Lockyer, T. (Surrey & All-England) b Nov. 1, 1826, d Dec. 22, 1869

Logan, J. D., jun. (SA) b June 24, 1880, d Jan. 3, 1960

*Logie, A. L. (T/T) b Sept. 28, 1960

*Lohmann, G. A. (Surrey, W. Prov. & Tvl; *CY 1889*) b June 2, 1865, d Dec. 1, 1901

Lomax, J. G. (Lancs & Som) b May 5, 1925, d May 21, 1992

Long, A. (Surrey & Sussex) b Dec. 18, 1940

Longrigg, E. F. (Som & CU) b April 16, 1906, d July 23, 1974

Lord, Thomas (Middx; founder of Lord's) b Nov. 23, 1755, d Jan. 13, 1832

*Love, H. S. B. (NSW & Vic.) b Aug. 10, 1895, d July 22, 1969

Love, J. D. (Yorks) b April 22, 1955

*Loveridge, G. R. (C. Dist. & CU) b Jan. 15, 1975

*Lowry, T. C. (Wgtn, CU & Som) b Feb. 17, 1898, d July 20, 1976
*Lowson, F. A. (Yorks) b July 1, 1925, d Sept. 8, 1984
*Loxton, S. J. E. (Vic.) b March 29, 1921
*Lucas, A. P. (CU, Surrey, Middx & Essex) b Feb. 20, 1857, d Oct. 12, 1923
Luckes, W. T. (Som) b Jan. 1, 1901, d Oct. 27, 1982
*Luckhurst, B. W. (Kent; *CY 1971*) b Feb. 5, 1939
Lumb, R. G. (Yorks) b Feb. 27, 1950
*Lundie, E. B. (E. Prov., W. Prov. & Tvl) b March 15, 1888, d Sept. 12, 1917
Lupton, A. W. (Yorks) b Feb. 23, 1879, d April 14, 1944
Lynch, M. A. (Surrey, Glos & Guyana) b May 21, 1958
Lyon, B. H. (OU & Glos; *CY 1931*) b Jan. 19, 1902, d June 22, 1970
Lyon, M. D. (CU & Som) b April 22, 1898, d Feb. 17, 1964
*Lyons, J. J. (S. Aust.) b May 21, 1863, d July 21, 1927
*Lyttelton, Hon. Alfred (CU & Middx; Pres. MCC 1898) b Feb. 7, 1857, d July 5, 1913
Lyttelton, Rev. Hon. C. F. (CU & Worcs) b Jan. 26, 1887, d Oct. 3, 1931
Lyttelton, Hon. C. G. (CU) b Oct. 27, 1842, d June 9, 1922
Lyttelton, Hon. C. J. (*see* 10th Visct Cobham)

*McAlister, P. A. (Vic.) b July 11, 1869, d May 10, 1938
*Macartney, C. G. (NSW & Otago; *CY 1922*) b June 27, 1886, d Sept. 9, 1958
*Macaulay, G. G. (Yorks; *CY 1924*) b Dec. 7, 1897, d Dec. 13, 1940
*Macaulay, M. J. (Tvl, W. Prov., OFS, NE Tvl & E. Prov.) b April 1939
*MacBryan, J. C. W. (CU & Som; *CY 1925*) b July 22, 1892, d July 14, 1983
*McCabe, S. J. (NSW; *CY 1935*) b July 16, 1910, d Aug. 25, 1968
*McCague, M. J. (W. Aust. & Kent) b May 24, 1969
*McCarthy, C. N. (Natal & CU) b March 24, 1929, d Aug. 14, 2000
*McConnon, J. E. (Glam) b June 21, 1922, d Jan. 26, 2003
*McCool, C. L. (NSW, Qld & Som) b Dec. 9, 1916, d April 5, 1986
McCorkell, N. (Hants) b March 23, 1912
*McCormick, E. L. (Vic.) b May 16, 1906, d June 28, 1991
*McCosker, R. B. (NSW; *CY 1976*) b Dec. 11, 1946
McCurdy, R. J. (Vic., Derbys, S. Aust., E. Prov. & Natal) b Dec. 30, 1959
*McDermott, C. J. (Qld; *CY 1986*) b April 14, 1965
*McDonald, C. C. (Vic.) b Nov. 17, 1928

*McDonald, E. A. (Tas., Vic. & Lancs; *CY 1922*) b Jan. 6, 1891, d July 22, 1937
*McDonnell, P. S. (Vic., NSW & Qld) b Nov. 13, 1858, d Sept. 24, 1896
McEwan, K. S. (E. Prov., W. Prov., Essex & W. Aust.; *CY 1978*) b July 16, 1952
*McEwan, P. E. (Cant.) b Dec. 19, 1953
*McGahey, C. P. (Essex; *CY 1902*) b Feb. 12, 1871, d Jan. 10, 1935
*MacGibbon, A. R. (Cant.) b Aug. 28, 1924
McGilvray, A. D. (NSW; broadcaster) b Dec. 6, 1909, d July 16, 1996
*McGirr, H. M. (Wgtn) b Nov. 5, 1891, d April 14, 1964
*McGlew, D. J. (Natal; *CY 1956*) b March 11, 1929, d June 9, 1998
*MacGregor, G. (CU & Middx; *CY 1891*) b Aug. 31, 1869, d Aug. 20, 1919
*McGregor, S. N. (Otago) b Dec. 18, 1931
*McIlwraith, J. (Vic.) b Sept. 7, 1857, d July 5, 1938
*McIntyre, A. J. (Surrey; *CY 1958*) b May 14, 1918
*Mackay, K. D. MBE (Qld) b Oct. 24, 1925, d June 13, 1982
McKechnie, B. J. (Otago) b Nov. 6, 1953
*McKenzie, G. D. (W. Aust. & Leics; *CY 1965*) b June 24, 1941
*McKibbin, T. R. (NSW) b Dec. 10, 1870, d Dec. 15, 1939
*McKinnon, A. H. (E. Prov. & Tvl) b Aug. 20, 1932, d Dec. 1, 1983
*MacKinnon, F. A. (CU & Kent; *believed to be longest-lived Test cricketer*) b April 9, 1848, d Feb. 27, 1947
*MacLaren, A. C. (Lancs; *CY 1895*) b Dec. 1, 1871, d Nov. 17, 1944
*McLaren, J. W. (Qld) b Dec. 24, 1886, d Nov. 17, 1921
MacLaurin of Knebworth, Lord (Chairman ECB 1997–2002) b March 30, 1937
*Maclean, J. A. (Qld) b April 27, 1946
*McLean, R. A. (Natal; *CY 1961*) b July 9, 1930
MacLeay, K. H. (W. Aust. & Som) b April 2, 1959
*McLeod, C. E. (Vic.) b Oct. 24, 1869, d Nov. 26, 1918
*McLeod, E. G. (Auck. & Wgtn) b Oct. 14, 1900, d Sept. 14, 1989
*McLeod, R. W. (Vic.) b Jan. 19, 1868, d June 14, 1907
McMahon, J. W. (Surrey & Som) b Dec. 28, 1919, d May 8, 2001
McMahon, T. G. (Wgtn) b Nov. 8, 1929
*McMaster, J. E. P. (Eng.) b March 16, 1861, d June 7, 1929
*McMillan, B. M. (Tvl, W. Prov. & Warwicks) b Dec. 22, 1963
*McMillan, Q. (Tvl) b June 23, 1904, d July 3, 1948

McMorris, E. D. A. (Jam.) b April 4, 1935

McRae, D. A. N. (Cant.) b Dec. 25, 1912, d Aug. 10, 1986

McShane, P. G. (Vic.) b April 18, 1858, d Dec. 11, 1903

McSweeney, E. B. (C. Dist. & Wgtn) b March 8, 1957

McVicker, N. M. (Warwicks & Leics) b Nov. 4, 1940

McWatt, C. A. (BG) b Feb. 1, 1922, d July 12, 1997

Madan Lal (Punjab & Delhi; Ind. coach) b March 20, 1951

Maddocks, L. V. (Vic. & Tas.) b May 24, 1926

Madondo, T. N. (Mash.) b Nov. 22, 1976, d June 11, 2001

Madray, I. S. (BG) b July 2, 1934

Madugalle, R. S. (NCC; ICC referee) b April 22, 1959

Madurasinghe, M. A. W. R. (Kurunegala) b Jan. 30, 1961

Mafizur Rehman (Bangladesh) b Nov. 10, 1978

Maguire, J. N. (Qld, E. Prov. & Leics) b Sept. 15, 1956

Mahanama, R. S. (CCC & Bloom.) b May 31, 1966

Mahbubur Rahman (Dhaka Div.) b Feb. 1, 1969

Maher, B. J. M. (Derbys) b Feb. 11, 1958

Mahmood Hussain (Pak. Us, Punjab, Kar., E. Pak. & NTB) b April 2, 1932, d Dec. 25, 1991

Mailey, A. A. (NSW; writer) b Jan. 3, 1886, d Dec. 31, 1967

*Majid Khan (Lahore, Pak. Us, CU, Glam, PIA, Qld, Punjab; *CY 1970;* Pak. manager) b Sept. 28, 1946

Maka, E. S. (Bombay) b March 5, 1922, dead

Makepeace, H. (Lancs) b Aug. 22, 1881, d Dec. 19, 1952

Malhotra, A. (Haryana, Bengal & Delhi) b Jan. 26, 1957

Mallender, N. A. (Northants, Otago & Som) b Aug. 13, 1961

Mallett, A. A. (S. Aust.) b July 13, 1945

Malone, M. F. (W. Aust. & Lancs) b Oct. 9, 1950

Maninder Singh (Delhi) b June 13, 1965

Manjrekar, V. L. (Bombay, Bengal, Andhra, U. Pradesh, Raja. & M'tra) b Sept. 26, 1931, d Oct. 18, 1983

Manjrekar, S. V. (†Mumbai) b July 12, 1965

Mankad, A. V. (Bombay) b Oct. 12, 1946

Mankad, V. (M. H.) (W. Ind., Naw., M'tra, Guj., Bengal, Bombay & Raja.; *CY 1947*) b April 12, 1917, d Aug. 21, 1978

Mann, A. L. (W. Aust.) b Nov. 8, 1945

Mann, F. G. CBE (CU & Middx; Chairman TCCB 1978–83; Pres. MCC 1984–85) b Sept. 6, 1917, d Aug. 8, 2001

*Mann, F. T. (CU & Middx) b March 3, 1888, d Oct. 6, 1964

*Mann, N. B. F. (Natal & E. Prov.) b Dec. 28, 1920, d July 31, 1952

Manning, J. S. (S. Aust. & Northants) b June 11, 1924, d May 5, 1988

Manning, T. E. (Northants) b Sept. 2, 1884, d Nov. 22, 1975

*Mansell, P. N. F. MBE (Rhod.) b March 16, 1920, d May 9, 1995

*Mansoor Akhtar (Kar., UBL & Sind) b Dec. 25, 1957

Mansur Ali Khan (*see* Pataudi, Mansur Ali, Nawab of)

*Mantri, M. K. (Bombay & M'tra) b Sept. 1, 1921

Manuel, P. (Test umpire) b Nov. 18, 1950

Manzoor Akhtar (Kar., Allied Bank, I'bad & Biman) b April 16, 1968

*Manzoor Elahi (Multan, Pak. Rlwys, Lahore & ADBP) b Sept. 15, 1963

*Maqsood Ahmed (S. Punjab, R'pindi, B'pur & Kar.) b March 26, 1925, d Jan. 4, 1999

Maqsood Rana (Lahore, R'pindi & NBP) b Aug. 1, 1972

*Marais, G. G. ("G. Gladstone") (Jam.) b Jan. 14, 1901, d May 19, 1978

Marchant, F. (Kent & CU) b May 22, 1864, d April 13, 1946

*Markham, L. A. (Natal) b Sept. 12, 1924, d Aug. 5, 2000

Marks, V. J. (OU, Som & W. Aust.; writer & broadcaster) b June 25, 1955

Marlar, R. G. (CU & Sussex; writer) b Jan. 2, 1931

Marlow, F. W. (Sussex) b Oct. 8, 1867, d Aug. 7, 1952

Marner, P. T. (Lancs & Leics) b March 31, 1936

*Marr, A. P. (NSW) b March 28, 1862, d March 15, 1940

*Marriott, C. S. (CU, Lancs & Kent) b Sept. 14, 1895, d Oct. 13, 1966

Marsden, Tom (Eng.) b 1805, d Feb. 27, 1843

*Marsh, G. R. (W. Aust.; Aust. & Zimb. coach) b Dec. 31, 1958

Marsh, R. W. MBE (W. Aust.; *CY 1982*) b Nov. 4, 1947

Marsh, S. A. (Kent) b Jan. 27, 1961

Marshal, Alan (Qld & Surrey; *CY 1909*) b June 12, 1883, d July 23, 1915

*Marshall, M. D. (B'dos, Hants & Natal; *CY 1983;* WI coach) b April 18, 1958, d Nov. 4, 1999

*Marshall, N. E. (B'dos & T/T) b Feb. 27, 1924

*Marshall, R. E. (B'dos & Hants; *CY 1959*) b April 25, 1930, d Oct. 27, 1992

Marsham, C. H. B. (OU & Kent) b Feb. 10, 1879, d July 19, 1928

Martin, E. J. (Notts) b Aug. 17, 1925

*Martin, F. (Kent; *CY 1892*) b Oct. 12, 1861, d Dec. 13, 1921

*Martin, F. R. (Jam.) b Oct. 12, 1893, d Nov. 23, 1967

Martin, G. C. (Mash.) b May 30, 1966

*Martin, J. W. (NSW & S. Aust.) b July 28, 1931, d July 16, 1992

*Martin, J. W. (Kent) b Feb. 16, 1917, d Jan. 4, 1987

Martin, S. H. (Worcs, Natal & Rhod.) b Jan. 11, 1909, d Feb. 17, 1988

*Martindale, E. A. (B'dos) b Nov. 25, 1909, d March 17, 1972

Martin-Jenkins, Christopher (Writer & broadcaster) b Jan. 20, 1945

Maru, R. J. (Middx & Hants) b Oct. 28, 1962

Marx, W. F. E. (Tvl) b July 4, 1895, d June 2, 1974

*Mason, J. R. (Kent; *CY 1898*) b March 26, 1874, d Oct. 15, 1958

*Masood Anwar (UBL, Multan, F'bad & Lahore) b Dec. 12, 1967

Masood Iqbal (Lahore, Punjab U., Pak. Us & HBL) b April 17, 1952

*Massie, H. H. (NSW) b April 11, 1854, d Oct. 12, 1938

*Massie, R. A. L. (W. Aust.; *CY 1973*) b April 14, 1947

*Matambanadzo, E. Z. (Mash.) b April 13, 1976

*Matheson, A. M. (Auck.) b Feb. 27, 1906, d Dec. 31, 1985

Mathias, Wallis (Sind, Kar. & NBP) b Feb. 4, 1935, d Sept. 1, 1994

*Matthews, A. D. G. (Northants & Glam) b May 3, 1904, d July 29, 1977

*Matthews, C. D. (W. Aust. & Lancs) b Sept. 22, 1962

*Matthews, C. R. (W. Prov.) b Feb. 15, 1965

*Matthews, G. R. J. (NSW) b Dec. 15, 1959

*Matthews, T. J. (Vic.) b April 3, 1884, d Oct. 14, 1943

*Mattis, E. H. (Jam.) b April 11, 1957

*May, P. B. H. CBE (CU & Surrey; *CY 1952*; Pres. MCC 1980–81) b Dec. 31, 1929, d Dec. 27, 1994

*May, T. B. A. (S. Aust.) b Jan. 26, 1962

Mayer, J. H. (Warwicks) b March 2, 1902, d Sept. 6, 1981

Maynard, C. (Warwicks & Lancs) b April 8, 1958

*Mayne, E. R. (S. Aust. & Vict.) b July 2, 1882, d Oct. 26, 1961

*Mayne, L. C. (W. Aust.) b Jan. 23, 1942

*Mead, C. P. (Hants; *CY 1912*) b March 9, 1887, d March 26, 1958

*Mead, W. (Essex; *CY 1904*) b April 1, 1868, d March 18, 1954

Meads, E. A. (Notts) b Aug. 17, 1916

*Meale, T. (Wgtn) b Nov. 11, 1928

*Meckiff, I. (Vic.) b Jan. 6, 1935

Medlycott, K. T. (Surrey & N. Tvl) b May 12, 1965

*Meherhomji, K. R. (W. Ind. & Bombay) b Aug. 9, 1911, d Feb. 10, 1982

*Mehra, V. L. (E. Punjab, Ind. Rlwys & Delhi) b March 12, 1938

*Meintjes, D. J. (Tvl) b June 9, 1890, d July 17, 1979

*Melle, M. G. (Tvl & W. Prov.) b June 3, 1930

*Melville, A. (OU, Sussex, Natal & Tvl; *CY 1948*) b May 19, 1910, d April 18, 1983

Meman, M. A. (Zimb.) b June 26, 1952

Mendis, G. D. (Sussex & Lancs) b April 20, 1955

*Mendis, L. R. D. (SSC) b Aug. 25, 1952

*Mendonca, I. L. (BG) b July 13, 1934

Mercer, J. (Sussex, Glam & Northants; *CY 1927*) b April 22, 1895, d Aug. 31, 1987

*Merchant, V. M. (Bombay; *CY 1937*) b Oct. 12, 1911, d Oct. 27, 1987

*Merritt, W. E. (Cant. & Northants) b Aug. 18, 1908, d June 9, 1977

*Merry, C. A. (T/T) b Jan. 20, 1911, d April 19, 1964

Metcalfe, A. A. (Yorks & Notts) b Dec. 25, 1963

Metson, C. P. (Middx & Glam) b July 2, 1963

*Meuleman, K. D. (Vic. & W. Aust.) b Sept. 5, 1923

*Meuli, E. M. (C. Dist.) b Feb. 20, 1926

Meyer, B. J. (Glos; Test umpire) b Aug. 21, 1932

Meyer, R. J. O. OBE (CU, Som & W. Ind.) b March 15, 1905, d March 9, 1991

Mian Mohammad Aslam (Test umpire) b April 1, 1949

Mian Mohammed Saeed (N. India, Patiala & S. Punjab) b Aug. 31, 1910, d Aug. 23, 1979

*Middleton, J. (W. Prov.) b Sept. 30, 1865, d Dec. 23, 1913

Middleton, T. C. (Hants) b Feb. 1, 1964

**Midwinter, W. E. (Vic. & Glos) b June 19, 1851, d Dec. 3, 1890

*Milburn, B. D. (Otago) b Nov. 24, 1943

*Milburn, C. (Northants & W. Aust.; *CY 1967*) b Oct. 23, 1941, d Feb. 28, 1990

*Milkha Singh, A. G. (Madras) b Dec. 31, 1941

*Miller, A. M. (Eng.) b Oct. 19, 1869, d June 26, 1959

Miller, F. P. (Surrey) b July 29, 1828, d Nov. 22, 1875

*Miller, G. (Derbys, Natal & Essex) b Sept. 8, 1952

*Miller, K. R. MBE (Vic., NSW & Notts; *CY 1954*) b Nov. 28, 1919

*Miller, L. S. M. (C. Dist. & Wgtn) b March 31, 1923, d Dec. 17, 1996

Miller, R. (Warwicks) b Jan. 6, 1941, d May 7, 1996

*Miller, R. C. (Jam.) b Dec. 24, 1924

*Milligan, F. W. (Yorks) b March 19, 1870, d March 31, 1900

*Millman, G. (Notts) b Oct. 2, 1934

Millmow, J. P. (Wgtn) b Sept. 22, 1967

Millns, D. J. (Notts, Leics, Tas & Boland) b Feb. 27, 1965

*Mills, C. H. (Surrey, Kimberley & W. Prov.) b Nov. 26, 1867, d July 26, 1948

*Mills, J. E. (Auck.) b Sept. 3, 1905, d Dec. 11, 1972

Mills, P. T. (Glos) b May 7, 1879, d Dec. 8, 1950

*Milton, C. A. (Glos; *CY 1959*) b March 10, 1928

*Milton, Sir William H. (W. Prov.) b Dec. 3, 1854, d March 6, 1930

*Minnett, R. B. (NSW) b June 13, 1888, d Oct. 21, 1955

Minshull, John (scorer of first recorded century) b *circa* 1741, d Oct. 1793

*Miran Bux (Pak. Serv., Punjab & R'pindi) b April 20, 1907, d Feb. 8, 1991

*Misson, H. M. (NSW) b Nov. 19, 1938

*Mitchell, A. (Yorks) b Sept. 13, 1902, d Dec. 25, 1976

*Mitchell, B. (Tvl; *CY 1936*) b Jan. 8, 1909, d July 2, 1995

**Mitchell, F. (CU, Yorks & Tvl; *CY 1902*) b Aug. 13, 1872, d Oct. 11, 1935

*Mitchell, T. B. (Derbys) b Sept. 4, 1902, d Jan. 27, 1996

*Mitchell-Innes, N. S. (OU & Som) b Sept. 7, 1914

Mitchley, C. J. (Tvl; Test umpire & ICC referee) b July 4, 1938

*Modi, R. S. (Bombay) b Nov. 11, 1924, d May 17, 1996

*Mohammad Akram (R'pindi, Allied Bank & Northants) b Sept 10, 1974

*Mohammad Aslam (N. Ind. & Pak. Rlwys) b Jan. 5, 1920

*Mohammad Farooq (Kar.) b April 8, 1938

*Mohammad Ilyas (Lahore & PIA) b March 19, 1946

*Mohammad Munaf (Sind, E. Pak., Kar. & PIA) b Nov. 2, 1935

*Mohammad Nazir (Pak. Rlwys) b March 8, 1946

*Mohammad Zahid (PIA) b Aug. 2, 1976

*Mohsin Kamal (Lahore, Allied Bank & PNSC; Bang. coach) b June 16, 1963

*Mohsin Khan (Pak. Rlwys, Kar., Sind, Pak. Us & HBL) b March 15, 1955

Moin-ul-Atiq (Kar., UBL, HBL & Peshawar) b Aug. 5, 1964

*Moir, A. M. (Otago) b July 17, 1919, d June 17, 2000

*Mold, A. (Lancs; *CY 1892*) b May 27, 1863, d April 29, 1921

Moles, A. J. (Warwicks & Griq. W.) b Feb. 12, 1961

*Moloney, D. A. R. (Wgtn, Otago & Cant.) b Aug. 11, 1910, d July 15, 1942

*Moodie, G. H. (Jam.) b Nov. 25, 1915, d June 8, 2002

*Moody, T. M. (W. Aust., Warwicks & Worcs; *CY 2000*) b Oct. 2, 1965

*Moon, L. J. (CU & Middx) b Feb. 9, 1878, d Nov. 23, 1916

*Mooney, F. L. H. (Wgtn) b May 26, 1921

Moore, H. I. (Notts) b Feb. 28, 1941

Moore, R. H. (Hants) b Nov. 14, 1913, d March 1, 2002

Moores, P. (Worcs & Sussex) b Dec. 18, 1962

Moorhouse, R. (Yorks) b Sept. 7, 1866, d Jan. 7, 1921

*More, K. S. (Baroda) b Sept. 4, 1962

Morgan, D. C. (Derbys) b Feb. 26, 1929

Morgan, F. D. (Chairman ECB 2003–) b Oct. 6, 1937

*Morgan, R. W. (Auck.) b Feb. 12, 1941

*Morkel, D. P. B. (W. Prov.) b Jan. 25, 1906, d Oct. 6, 1980

*Morley, F. (Notts) b Dec. 16, 1850, d Sept. 28, 1884

*Moroney, J. (NSW) b July 24, 1917, d July 1, 1999

*Morris, A. R. MBE (NSW; *CY 1949*) b Jan. 19, 1922

*Morris, H. (Glam) b Oct. 5, 1963

Morris, H. M. (Essex & CU) b April 16, 1898, d Nov. 18, 1984

*Morris, J. E. (Derbys, Griq. W., Durham & Notts) b April 1, 1964

*Morris, S. (Vic.) b June 22, 1855, d Sept. 20, 1931

*Morrison, B. D. (Wgtn) b Dec. 17, 1933

*Morrison, D. K. (Auck. & Lancs) b Feb. 3, 1966

*Morrison, J. F. M. (C. Dist. & Wgtn; ICC referee) b Aug. 27, 1947

Morshed Ali Khan (Dhaka Met.) b May 14, 1972

Mortensen, O. H. (Denmark & Derbys) b Jan. 29, 1958

*Mortimore, J. B. (Glos) b May 14, 1933

Mortlock, W. (Surrey & Utd Eng. XI) b July 18, 1832, d Jan. 23, 1884

Morton, A., jun. (Derbys) b May 7, 1883, d Dec. 19, 1935

*Moseley, E. A. (B'dos, Glam, E. Prov. & N. Tvl) b Jan. 5, 1958

Moseley, H. R. (B'dos & Som) b May 28, 1948

*Moses, H. (NSW) b Feb. 13, 1858, d Dec. 7, 1938

*Moss, A. E. (Middx) b Nov. 14, 1930

*Moss, J. K. (Vic.) b June 29, 1947

*Motz, R. C. (Cant.; *CY 1966*) b Jan. 12, 1940

*Moule, W. H. (Vic.) b Jan. 31, 1858, d Aug. 24, 1939

*Moxon, M. D. (Yorks & Griq. W.; *CY 1993*) b May 4, 1960

*Mudassar Nazar (Lahore, Punjab, Pak. Us, HBL, PIA & UBL; Pak. manager) b April 6, 1956

*Muddiah, V. M. (Mysore & Ind. Servs) b June 8, 1929

*Mufasir-ul-Haq (Kar., Dacca, PWD, E. Pak. & NBP) b Aug. 16, 1944, d July 27, 1983

Mujahid Jamshed (Lahore, HBL, Gujranwala, Sargodha & Sheikhupura) b Dec. 1, 1971

Mukherjee, S. P. (Bengal) b Dec. 5, 1964

*Muller, S. A. (Qld) b July 11, 1971

Munasinghe, A. M. N. (SSC) b Dec. 10, 1971

Muncer, B. L. (Glam & Middx) b Oct. 23, 1913, d Jan. 18, 1982

Munden, V. S. (Leics) b Jan. 2, 1928

*Munir Malik (Punjab, R'pindi, Pak. Serv. & Kar.) b July 10, 1934

*Munton, T. A. (Warwicks & Derbys; *CY 1995*) b July 30, 1965

**Murdoch, W. L. (NSW & Sussex) b Oct. 18, 1854, d Feb. 18, 1911

*Murray, A. R. A. (E. Prov.) b April 30, 1922, d April 17, 1995

*Murray, B. A. G. (Wgtn) b Sept. 18, 1940

*Murray, D. A. (B'dos) b Sept. 29, 1950

*Murray, D. J. (Cant.) b Sept. 4, 1967

*Murray, D. L. (T/T, CU, Notts & Warwicks) b May 20, 1943

*Murray, J. T. MBE (Middx; *CY 1967*) b April 1, 1935

Murray-Wood, W. (OU & Kent) b June 30, 1917, d Dec. 21, 1968

Murrell, H. R. (Kent & Middx) b Nov. 19, 1879, d Aug. 15, 1952

*Musgrove, H. (Vic.) b Nov. 27, 1860, d Nov. 2, 1931

*Mushtaq Ali, S. (C. Ind., Guj., †M. Pradesh & U. Pradesh) b Dec. 17, 1914

*Mushtaq Mohammad (Kar., Northants & PIA; *CY 1963*; Pak. coach) b Nov. 22, 1943

Mynn, Alfred (Kent & All-Eng.) b Jan. 19, 1807, d Nov. 1, 1861

*Nadeem Abbasi (R'pindi & KRL) b April 15, 1964

*Nadeem Ghauri (Lahore, Pak. Rlwys & HBL) b Oct. 12, 1962

*Nadkarni, R. G. (M'tra & Bombay) b April 4, 1932

Naeem Ahmed (Kar., Pak Us, NBP, UBL & PIA) b Sept. 20, 1952

Naeem Ashraf (Lahore & NBP) b Nov. 10, 1972

*Nagel, L. E. (Vic.) b March 6, 1905, d Nov. 23, 1971

*Naik, S. S. (Bombay) b Feb. 21, 1945

*Nanan, R. (T/T) b May 29, 1953

*Naoomal Jeoomal, M. (N. Ind. & Sind) b April 17, 1904, d July 18, 1980

*Narasimha Rao, M. V. (H'bad) b Aug. 11, 1954

Naseer Malik (Khairpair & NBP) b Feb. 1, 1950, d Aug. 1, 1999

*Nash, L. J. (Tas. & Vic.) b May 2, 1910, d July 24, 1986

Nash, M. A. (Glam) b May 9, 1945

*Nasim-ul-Ghani (Kar., Pak. Us, Dacca, E. Pak., PWD & NBP) b May 14, 1941

*Naushad Ali (Kar., E. Pak., R'pindi, Peshawar, NWFP, Punjab & Pak. Serv.; ICC referee) b Oct. 1, 1943

*Naved Anjum (Railways, Lahore, UBL & HBL) b July 27, 1963

*Navle, J. G. (Rajputana, C. Ind., Holkar & Gwalior) b Dec. 7, 1902, d Sept. 7, 1979

*Nayak, S. V. (Bombay) b Oct. 20, 1954

*Nayudu, Col. C. K. (C. Ind., Andhra, U. Pradesh & Holkar; *CY 1933*) b Oct. 31, 1895, d Nov. 14, 1967

*Nayudu, C. S. (C. Ind., Holkar, Baroda, Bengal, Andhra & U. Pradesh) b April 18, 1914, d Nov 22, 2002

*Nazar Mohammad (N. Ind. & Punjab) b March 5, 1921, d July 12, 1996

*Nazir Ali, S. (S. Punjab & Sussex) b Jan. 8, 1906, d Feb 18, 1975

Neale, P. A. (Worcs; *CY 1989*) b June 5, 1954

Neale, W. L. (Glos) b March 3, 1904, d Oct. 26, 1955

*Neblett, J. M. (B'dos & BG) b Nov. 13, 1901, d March 28, 1959

Needham, A. (Surrey & Middx) b March 23, 1957

*Nel, J. D. (W. Prov.) b July 10, 1928

Nelson, R. P. (Middx, CU & Northants) b Aug. 7, 1912, d Oct. 29, 1940

*Newberry, C. (Tvl) b 1889, d Aug. 1, 1916

Newell, M. (Notts) b Feb. 25, 1965

*Newham, W. (Sussex) b Dec. 12, 1860, d June 26, 1944

Newland, Richard (Sussex) b *circa* 1718, d May 29, 1791

*Newman, Sir Jack (Wgtn & Cant.) b July 3, 1902, d Sept. 23, 1996

Newman, J. A. (Hants & Cant.) b Nov. 12, 1884, d Dec. 21, 1973

Newman, P. G. (Derbys) b Jan. 10, 1959

*Newport, P. J. (Worcs. Boland & N. Tvl) b Oct. 11, 1962

*Newson, E. S. OBE (Tvl & Rhod.) b Dec. 2, 1910, d April 24, 1988

Newstead, J. T. (Yorks; *CY 1909*) b Sept. 8, 1877, d March 25, 1952

Newton, A. E. (OU & Som) b Sept. 12, 1862, d Sept. 15, 1952

*Niaz Ahmed (Dacca, E. Pak., PWD & Pak. Rlwys) b Nov. 11, 1945

Nicholas, M. C. J. (Hants; broadcaster) b Sept. 29, 1957

Nicholls, D. (Kent) b Dec. 8, 1943

Nicholls, E. A. (Test umpire) b Dec. 10, 1947
Nicholls, R. B. (Glos) b Dec. 4, 1933, d July 21, 1994
*Nichols, M. S. (Essex; *CY 1934*) b Oct. 6, 1900, d Jan. 26, 1961
Nicholson, A. G. (Yorks) b June 25, 1938, d Nov. 4, 1985
*Nicholson, F. (Griq. W.) b Sept. 17, 1909, d July 30, 1982
*Nicolson, J. F. W. (Natal & OU) b July 19, 1899, d Dec. 13, 1935
*Nissar, Mahomed (Patiala, S. Punjab & U. Pradesh) b Aug. 1, 1910, d March 11, 1963
*Nitschke, H. C. (S. Aust.) b April 14, 1905, d Sept. 29, 1982
*Noble, M. A. (NSW; *CY 1900*) b Jan. 28, 1873, d June 22, 1940
*Noblet, G. (S. Aust.) b Sept. 14, 1916
*Noreiga, J. M. (T/T) b April 15, 1936
Norman, M. E. J. C. (Northants & Leics) b Jan. 19, 1933
*Norton, N. O. (W. Prov. & Border) b May 11, 1881, d June 27, 1968
*Nothling, O. E. (NSW & Qld) b Aug. 1, 1900, d Sept. 26, 1965
*Nourse, A. D. ("Dudley") (Natal; *CY 1948*) b Nov. 12, 1910, d Aug. 14, 1981
*Nourse, A. W. ("Dave") (Natal, Tvl & W. Prov.) b Jan. 26, 1878, d July 8, 1948
*Nunes, R. K. (Jam.) b June 7, 1894, d July 22, 1958
*Nupen, E. P. (Tvl) b Jan. 1, 1902, d Jan. 29, 1977
*Nurse, S. M. (B'dos; *CY 1967*) b Nov. 10, 1933
Nutter, A. E. (Lancs & Northants) b June 28, 1913, d June 3, 1996
*Nyalchand, S. (W. Ind., Kathiawar, Guj., & S'tra) b Sept. 14, 1919, d Jan. 3, 1997
Nyren, John (Hants) b Dec. 15, 1764, d June 28, 1837
Nyren, Richard (Hants & Sussex; Proprietor Bat & Ball Inn, Broadhalfpenny Down) b 1734, d April 25, 1797

Oakes, C. (Sussex) b Aug. 10, 1912
Oakes, J. (Sussex) b March 3, 1916, d July 4, 1997
*Oakman, A. S. M. (Sussex) b April 20, 1930
Oates, T. W. (Notts) b Aug. 9, 1875, d June 18, 1949
Oates, W. F. (Yorks & Derbys) b June 11, 1929, d May 15, 2001
*O'Brien, L. P. J. (Vic.) b July 2, 1907, d March 13, 1997
*O'Brien, Sir Timothy C. (OU & Middx) b Nov. 5, 1861, d Dec. 9, 1948
*Ochse, A. E. (Tvl) b March 11, 1870, d April 11, 1918
*Ochse, A. L. (E. Prov.) b Oct. 11, 1899, d May 5, 1949

*O'Connor, J. (Essex) b Nov. 6, 1897, d Feb. 22, 1977
*O'Connor, J. D. A. (NSW & S. Aust.) b Sept. 9, 1875, d Aug. 23, 1941
*O'Donnell, S. P. (Vic.) b Jan. 26, 1963
*Ogilvie, A. D. (Qld) b June 3, 1951
*Gorman, T. J. G. (Derbys) b May 15, 1967
*O'Keeffe, K. J. (NSW & Som) b Nov. 25, 1949
*Old, C. M. (Yorks, Warwicks & N. Tvl; *CY 1979*) b Dec. 22, 1948
*Oldfield, N. (Lancs & Northants; Test umpire) b May 5, 1911, d April 19, 1996
*Oldfield, W. A. MBE (NSW; *CY 1927*) b Sept. 9, 1894, d Aug. 10, 1976
Oldham, S. (Yorks & Derbys) b July 26, 1948
Oldroyd, E. (Yorks) b Oct. 1, 1888, d Dec. 27, 1964
*O'Linn, S. (Kent, W. Prov. & Tvl) b May 5, 1927
Oliver, L. (Derbys) b Oct. 18, 1886, d Jan. 22, 1944
*O'Neill, N. C. (NSW; *CY 1962*) b Feb. 19, 1937
Ontong, R. C. (Border, Tvl, N. Tvl & Glam) b Sept. 9, 1955
Onyango, L. (Kenya) b Sept. 22, 1973
Opatha, A. R. M. (SL) b Aug. 5, 1947
Orchard, D. L. (Natal; ICC umpire) b June 24, 1948
Ord, J. S. (Warwicks) b July 12, 1912, d Jan. 14, 2001
*O'Reilly, W. J. OBE (NSW; *CY 1935*) b Dec. 20, 1905, d Oct. 6, 1992
Ormrod, J. A. (Worcs & Lancs) b Dec. 22, 1942
Oscroft, W. (Notts) b Dec. 16, 1843, d Oct. 10, 1905
O'Shaughnessy, S. J. (Lancs & Worcs) b Sept. 9, 1961
Oslear, D. O. (Test umpire) b March 3, 1929
*O'Sullivan, D. R. (C. Dist. & Hants) b Nov. 16, 1944
Outschoorn, L. (Worcs) b Sept. 26, 1918, d Jan. 9, 1994
*Overton, G. W. F. (Otago) b June 8, 1919, d Sept. 7, 1993
Owen, H. G. P. (CU & Essex) b May 19, 1859, d Oct. 20, 1912
*Owens, M. B. (Cant.) b Nov. 11, 1969
*Owen-Smith, H. G. (W. Prov., OU & Middx; *CY 1930*) b Feb. 18, 1909, d Feb. 28, 1990
Owen-Thomas, D. R. (CU & Surrey) b Sept. 20, 1948
*Oxenham, R. K. (Qld) b July 28, 1891, d Aug. 16, 1939

*Padgett, D. E. V. (Yorks) b July 20, 1934
*Padmore, A. L. (B'dos) b Dec. 17, 1946
Page, J. C. T. (Kent) b May 20, 1930, d Dec. 14, 1990

Page, M. H. (Derbys) b June 17, 1941

*Page, M. L. (Cant.) b May 8, 1902, d Feb. 13, 1987

*Pai, A. M. (Bombay) b April 28, 1945

*Paine, G. A. E. (Middx & Warwicks; *CY 1935*) b June 11, 1908, d March 30, 1978

*Pairaudeau, B. H. (BG & N. Dist.) b April 14, 1931

*Palairet, L. C. H. (OU & Som; *CY 1893*) b May 27, 1870, d March 27, 1933

Palairet, R. C. N. (OU & Som) b June 25, 1871, d Feb. 11, 1955

*Palia, P. E. (Parsis, Madras, U. Prov., Bombay, Mysore & Bengal) b Sept. 5, 1910, d Sept. 9, 1981

*Palm, A. W. (W. Prov.) b June 8, 1901, d Aug. 17, 1966

*Palmer, C. H. CBE (Worcs & Leics; Pres. MCC 1978–79; Chairman TCCB 1983–85) b May 15, 1919

*Palmer, G. E. (Vic. & Tas.) b Feb. 22, 1859, d Aug. 22, 1910

*Palmer, K. E. MBE (Som; Test umpire) b April 22, 1937

Palmer, R. (Som; Test umpire) b July 12, 1942

*Pandit, C. S. (†Mumbai, Assam & M. Pradesh) b Sept. 30, 1961

Paranjpe, J. V. (†Mumbai) b April 17, 1972

Pardon, Charles F. (Editor of *Wisden* 1887–90) b March 28, 1850, d April 18, 1890

Pardon, Sydney H. (Editor of *Wisden* 1891–1925) b Sept. 23, 1855, d Nov. 20, 1925

*Parfitt, P. H. (Middx; *CY 1963*) b Dec. 8, 1936

Paris, C. G. A. (Hants; Chairman TCCB 1968–75; Pres. MCC 1975–76) b Aug. 20, 1911, d April 4, 1998

Parish, R. J. (Aust. Administrator) b May 7, 1916

*Park, Dr R. L. (Vic.) b July 30, 1892, d Jan. 23, 1947

*Parkar, G. A. (Bombay) b Oct. 24, 1955

*Parkar, R. D. (Bombay) b Oct. 31, 1946, d Aug. 11, 1999

Parkar, Z. (Bombay) b Nov. 22, 1957

*Parker, C. W. L. (Glos; *CY 1923*) b Oct. 14, 1882, d July 11, 1959

*Parker, G. M. (SA) b May 27, 1899, d May 1, 1969

Parker, J. F. (Surrey) b April 23, 1913, d Jan. 27, 1983

*Parker, J. M. (N. Dist. & Worcs) b Feb. 21, 1951

*Parker, N. M. (Otago & Cant.) b Aug. 28, 1948

*Parker, P. W. G. (CU, Sussex, Natal & Durham) b Jan. 15, 1956

*Parkhouse, W. G. A. (Glam) b Oct. 12, 1925, d Aug. 02, 2000

*Parkin, C. H. (Yorks & Lancs; *CY 1924*) b Feb. 18, 1886, d June 15, 1943

*Parkin, D. C. (E. Prov., Tvl & Griq. W.) b Feb. 20, 1873, d March 20, 1936

Parks, H. W. (Sussex) b July 18, 1906, d May 7, 1984

*Parks, J. H. (Sussex & Cant.; *CY 1938*) b May 12, 1903, d Nov. 21, 1980

*Parks, J. M. (Sussex & Som; *CY 1968*) b Oct. 21, 1931

Parks, R. J. (Hants & Kent) b June 15, 1959

Parr, George (Notts & All-England) b May 22, 1826, d June 23, 1891

*Parry, D. R. (Comb. Is. & Leewards) b Dec. 22, 1954

*Parsana, D. D. (S'tra, Ind. Rlwys & Guj.) b Dec. 2, 1947

Parsons, A. B. D. (CU & Surrey) b Sept. 20, 1933, d Feb. 11, 1999

Parsons, G. J. (Leics, Warwicks, Boland, Griq. W. & OFS) b Oct. 17, 1959

Parsons, Canon J. H. (Warwicks) b May 30, 1890, d Feb. 2, 1981

*Partridge, J. T. (Rhod.) b Dec. 9, 1932, d June 7, 1988

Partridge, N. E. (Malvern, CU & Warwicks; *CY 1919*) b Aug. 10, 1900, d March 10, 1982

Partridge, R. J. (Northants) b Feb. 11, 1912, d Feb. 1, 1997

Parvez Mir (R'pindi, Lahore, Punjab, Pak. Us, Derbys, HBL & Glam) b Sept. 24, 1953

*Pascoe, L. S. (NSW) b Feb. 13, 1950

Pasqual, S. P. (SL) b Oct. 15, 1961

*Passailaigue, C. C. (Jam.) b Aug. 1902, d Jan. 7, 1972

*Patankar, C. T. (Bombay) b Nov. 24, 1930

**Pataudi, Iftiqar Ali, Nawab of (OU, Worcs, Patiala, N. Ind. & S. Punjab; *CY 1932*) b March 16, 1910, d Jan. 5, 1952

*Pataudi, Mansur Ali, Nawab of (Sussex, OU, Delhi & H'bad; *CY 1968*) b Jan. 5, 1941

Patel, A. K. (S'tra) b March 6, 1957

*Patel, B. P. (Karn.) b Nov. 24, 1952

*Patel, D. N. (Worcs & Auck.) b Oct. 25, 1958

*Patel, J. M. (Guj.) b Nov. 26, 1924, d Dec. 12, 1992

*Patel, R. G. M. (Baroda) b June 1, 1964

Paterson, G. A. (Zimb.) b June 9, 1960

*Patiala, Maharaja of (N. Ind., Patiala & S. Punjab) b Jan. 17, 1913, d June 17, 1974

*Patil, S. M. (Bombay & M. Pradesh; Ind. coach) b Aug. 18, 1956

*Patil, S. R. (M'tra) b Oct. 10, 1933

*Patterson, B. P. (Jam., Tas. & Lancs) b Sept. 15, 1961

Patterson, W. H. (OU & Kent) b March 11, 1859, d May 3, 1946

*Payne, T. R. O. (B'dos) b Feb. 13, 1957

*Paynter, E. (Lancs; *CY 1938*) b Nov. 5, 1901, d Feb. 5, 1979

Payton, W. R. D. (Notts) b Feb. 13, 1882, d May 2, 1943

Peach, H. A. (Surrey) b Oct. 6, 1890, d Oct. 8, 1961

*Peall, S. G. (MCD) b Sept. 2, 1969

Pearce, T. N. (Essex) b Nov. 3, 1905, d April 10, 1994

*Pearse, O. C. (Natal) b Oct. 10, 1884, d May 7, 1953

Pearson, F. (Worcs & Auck.) b Sept. 23, 1880, d Nov. 10, 1963

*Peate, E. (Yorks) b March 2, 1855, d March 11, 1900

Peckover, G. E. (Zimb.) b June 2, 1955

*Peebles, I. A. R. (OU, Middx & Scotland; writer; CY 1931) b Jan. 20, 1908, d Feb. 28, 1980

*Peel, R. (Yorks; CY 1889) b Feb. 12, 1857, d Aug. 12, 1941

*Pegler, S. J. (Tvl) b July 28, 1888, d Sept. 10, 1972

*Pellew, C. E. (S. Aust.) b Sept. 21, 1893, d May 9, 1981

Penn, C. (Kent) b June 19, 1963

*Penn, F. (Kent) b March 7, 1851, d Dec. 26, 1916

Penney, T. L. (Boland, Warwicks & Mash.) b June 12, 1968

Pepper, C. G. (NSW & Aust. Serv.; umpire) b Sept. 15, 1916, d March 24, 1993

Perkins, H. (CU & Cambs; Sec. MCC 1876–97) b Dec. 10, 1832, d May 6, 1916

*Perks, R. T. D. (Worcs) b Oct. 4, 1911, d Nov. 22, 1977

Perrin, P. A. (Essex; CY 1905) b May 26, 1876, d Nov. 20, 1945

Perry, N. O. (Jam.) b June 16, 1968

Perryman, S. P. (Warwicks & Worcs) b Oct. 22, 1955

*Pervez Sajjad (Lahore, PIA & Kar.) b Aug. 30, 1942

*Petherick, P. J. (Otago & Wgtn) b Sept. 25, 1942

*Petrie, E. C. (Auck. & N. Dist.) b May 22, 1927

Petrie, R. G. (Wgtn) b Aug. 23, 1967

Pettiford, J. (NSW & Kent) b Nov. 29, 1919, d Oct. 11, 1964

*Phadkar, D. G. (M'tra, Bombay, Bengal & Ind. Rlwys) b Dec. 10, 1925, d March 17, 1985

Phebey, A. H. (Kent) b Oct. 1, 1924, d June 28, 1998

Phelan, P. J. (Essex) b Feb. 9, 1938

*Philipson, H. (OU & Middx) b June 8, 1866, d Dec. 4, 1935

*Phillip, N. (Comb. Is., Windwards & Essex) b June 12, 1948

Phillips, H. (Sussex) b Oct. 14, 1844, d July 3, 1919

Phillips, R. B. (NSW & Qld) b May 23, 1954

*Phillips, W. B. (S. Aust.) b March 1, 1958

*Phillips, W. N. (Vic.) b Nov. 7, 1962

Phillipson, C. P. (Sussex) b Feb. 10, 1952

Phillipson, W. E. (Lancs; Test umpire) b Dec. 3, 1910, d Aug. 24, 1991

*Philpott, P. I. (NSW) b Nov. 21, 1934

Pick, R. A. (Notts & Wgtn) b Nov. 19, 1963

Pienaar, R. F. (Tvl, Northerns, W. Prov. & Kent) b July 17, 1961

Pieris, H. S. M. (SL) b Feb. 16, 1946

*Pierre, L. R. (T/T) b June 5, 1921, d April 14, 1989

Pierson, A. R. K. (Warwicks, Leics, Som & Derbys) b July 21, 1963

*Pigott, A. C. S. (Sussex, Wgtn & Surrey) b June 4, 1958

Pilch, Fuller (Norfolk & Kent) b March 17, 1804, d May 1, 1870

Pilling, H. (Lancs) b Feb. 23, 1943

*Pilling, R. (Lancs; CY 1891) b July 5, 1855, d March 28, 1891

*Pithey, A. J. (Rhod. & W. Prov.) b July 17, 1933

*Pithey, D. B. (Rhod., OU, Northants, W. Prov., Natal & Tvl) b Oct. 4, 1936

*Place, W. (Lancs) b Dec. 7, 1914, d Jan. 25, 2002

Platt, R. K. (Yorks & Northants) b Dec. 21, 1932

*Playle, W. R. (Auck. & W. Aust.) b Dec. 1, 1938

Pleass, J. E. (Glam) b May 21, 1923

Plews, N. T. (Test umpire) b Sept. 5, 1934

*Plimsoll, J. B. (W. Prov. & Natal) b Oct. 27, 1917, d Nov. 11, 1999

*Pocock, B. A. (Auck. & N. Dist.) b June 18, 1971

Pocock, N. E. J. (Hants) b Dec. 15, 1951

*Pocock, P. I. (Surrey & N. Tvl) b Sept. 24, 1946

Pollard, P. R. (Notts & Worcs) b Sept. 24, 1968

*Pollard, R. (Lancs) b June 19, 1912, d Dec. 16, 1985

Pollard, V. (C. Dist. & Cant.) b Sept. 7, 1945

*Pollock, P. M. (E. Prov.; CY 1966) b June 30, 1941

*Pollock, R. G. (E. Prov. & Tvl; CY 1966) b Feb. 27, 1944

*Ponsford, W. H. MBE (Vic.; CY 1935) b Oct. 19, 1900, d April 6, 1991

Pont, K. R. (Essex) b Jan. 16, 1953

*Poole, C. J. (Notts) b March 13, 1921, d Feb. 11, 1996

Pooley, E. (Surrey & first England tour) b Feb. 13, 1842, d July 18, 1907

*Poore, M. B. (Cant.) b June 1, 1930

*Poore, Brig.-Gen. R. M. (Hants & SA; CY 1900) b March 20, 1866, d July 14, 1938

Pope, A. V. (Derbys) b Aug. 15, 1909, d May 11, 1996

*Pope, G. H. (Derbys) b Jan. 27, 1911, d Oct. 29, 1993

*Ranatunga, S. (SSC, Colts & NCC) b April 25, 1969

*Ranchod, U. (Mash.) b May 17, 1969

*Randall, D. W. (Notts; *CY 1980*) b Feb. 24, 1951

Randhir Singh (Orissa & Bihar) b Aug. 16, 1957

*Rangachari, C. R. (Madras) b April 14, 1916, d Oct. 9, 1993

*Rangnekar, K. M. (M'tra, Bombay & †M. Pradesh) b June 27, 1917, d Oct. 11, 1984

*Ranjane, V. B. (M'tra & Ind. Rlwys) b July 22, 1937

*Ranjitsinhji, K. S., (later H. H. the Jam Sahib of Nawanagar) (CU & Sussex; *CY 1897*) b Sept. 10, 1872, d April 2, 1933

*Ransford, V. S. (Vic.; *CY 1910*) b March 20, 1885, d March 19, 1958

Raqibul Hassan (Bangladesh; ICC referee) b Jan. 1, 1953

*Rashid Khan (PWD, Kar. & PIA) b Dec. 15, 1959

Ratcliffe, J. D. (Warwicks & Surrey) b June 19, 1969

Ratnayake, N. L. K. (SSC) b Nov. 22, 1968

*Ratnayake, R. J. (NCC) b Jan. 2, 1964

*Ratnayeke, J. R. (NCC) b May 2, 1960

Rawlin, J. T. (Yorks & Middx) b Nov. 10, 1856, d Jan. 19, 1924

Rawson, P. W. E. (Zimb. & Natal) b May 25, 1957

Rayment, A. W. H. (Hants) b May 29, 1928

*Razdan, V. (Delhi) b Aug. 25, 1969

*Read, H. D. (Surrey & Essex) b Jan. 28, 1910, d Jan. 5, 2000

*Read, J. M. (Surrey; *CY 1890*) b Feb. 9, 1859, d Feb. 17, 1929

*Read, W. W. (Surrey; *CY 1893*) b Nov. 23, 1855, d Jan. 6, 1907

*Reddy, B. (TN) b Nov. 12, 1954

*Redmond, R. E. (Wgtn & Auck.) b Dec. 29, 1944

*Redpath, I. R. MBE (Vic.) b May 11, 1941

Reed, B. L. (Hants) b Sept. 17, 1937

*Reedman, J. C. (S. Aust.) b Oct. 9, 1865, d March 25, 1924

Rees, A. (Glam) b Feb. 17, 1938

*Reeve, D. A. OBE (Sussex & Warwicks; *CY 1996*) b April 2, 1963

Reeves, W. (Essex; Test umpire) b Jan. 22, 1875, d March 22, 1944

*Rege, M. R. (M'tra) b March 18, 1924

*Rehman, S. F. (Punjab, Pak. Us & Lahore) b June 11, 1935

*Reid, B. A. (W. Aust.) b March 14, 1963

*Reid, J. F. (Auck.) b March 3, 1956

*Reid, J. R. OBE (Wgtn & Otago; *CY 1959*; ICC referee) b June 3, 1928

*Reid, N. (W. Prov.) b Dec. 26, 1890, d June 6, 1947

Reid, R. B. (Wgtn & Auck.) b Dec. 3, 1958

Reidy, B. W. (Lancs) b Sept. 18, 1953

*Relf, A. E. (Sussex & Auck.; *CY 1914*) b June 26, 1874, d March 26, 1937

Relf, R. R. (Sussex) b Sept. 1, 1883, d April 28, 1965

*Renneberg, D. A. (NSW) b Sept. 23, 1942

*Rennie, J. A. (Mat.) b July 29, 1970

Revill, A. C. (Derbys & Leics) b March 27, 1923, d July 6, 1998

Reynolds, B. L. (Northants) b June 10, 1932

Rhodes, A. E. G. (Derbys; Test umpire) b Oct. 10, 1916, d Oct. 18, 1983

*Rhodes, H. J. (Derbys) b July 22, 1936

*Rhodes, W. (Yorks; *CY 1899*) b Oct. 29, 1877, d July 8, 1973

Riazuddin (Test umpire) b Dec. 15, 1958

Rice, C. E. B. (Tvl & Notts; *CY 1981*) b July 23, 1949

Rice, J. M. (Hants) b Oct. 23, 1949

Rice, Sir Timothy M. B. (Pres. MCC 2002–03) b Nov. 10, 1944

*Richards, A. R. (W. Prov.) b Dec. 14, 1867, d Jan. 9, 1904

*Richards, B. A. (Natal, Glos, Hants & S. Aust.; *CY 1969*) b July 21, 1945

*Richards, C. J. (Surrey & OFS) b Aug. 10, 1958

Richards, D. L. (Chief Exec. ICC 1993–2001) b July 28, 1946

Richards, G. (Glam) b Nov. 29, 1951

*Richards, Sir Vivian (I. V. A.) OBE (Comb. Is., Leewards, Som, Qld & Glam; *CY 1977, Cricketer of the Century 2000*; WI coach) b March 7, 1952

*Richards, W. H. (SA) b March 26, 1862, d Jan. 4, 1903

*Richardson, A. J. (S. Aust.) b July 24, 1888, d Dec. 23, 1973

Richardson, A. W. (Derbys) b March 4, 1907, d July 29, 1983

*Richardson, D. J. (E. Prov & N. Tvl) b Sept. 16, 1959

*Richardson, D. W. (Worcs) b Nov. 3, 1934

*Richardson, P. E. (Worcs & Kent; *CY 1957*) b July 4, 1931

*Richardson, R. B. (Leewards, Yorks, Northerns, Windwards & WI B; *CY 1992*) b Jan. 12, 1962

*Richardson, T. (Surrey & Som; *CY 1897*) b Aug. 11, 1870, d July 2, 1912

*Richardson, V. Y. (S. Aust.) b Sept. 7, 1894, d Oct. 29, 1969

Riches, N. V. H. (Glam) b June 9, 1883, d Nov. 6, 1975

*Richmond, T. L. (Notts) b June 23, 1890, d Dec. 29, 1957

*Rickards, K. R. (Jam. & Essex) b Aug. 23, 1923, d Aug. 21, 1995

Riddington, A. (Leics) b Dec. 22, 1911, d Feb. 25, 1998

*Ridgway, F. (Kent) b Aug. 10, 1923

*Rigg, K. E. (Vic.) b May 21, 1906, d Feb. 28, 1995
*Ring, D. T. (Vic.) b Oct. 14, 1918
Ripley, D. (Northants) b Sept. 13, 1966
*Ritchie, G. M. (Qld) b Jan. 23, 1960
*Rixon, S. J. (NSW; NZ coach) b Feb. 25, 1954
*Rizwan-uz-Zaman (Kar. & PIA) b Sept. 4, 1961
*Roach, C. A. (T/T) b March 13, 1904, d April 16, 1988
*Roberts, A. D. G. (N. Dist.) b May 6, 1947, d Oct. 26, 1989
*Roberts, A. M. E. CBE (Comb. Is., Leewards, Hants, NSW & Leics; CY 1975; WI coach) b Jan. 29, 1951
*Roberts, A. T. (Windwards & T/T) b Sept. 18, 1937, d July 24, 1996
*Roberts, A. W. (Cant. & Otago) b Aug. 20, 1909, d May 13, 1978
Roberts, D. (Tvl & Derbys) b May 30, 1962
Roberts, F. G. (Glos) b April 1, 1862, d April 7, 1936
Roberts, S. J. (Cant.) b March 22, 1965
Roberts, W. B. (Lancs & Victory Tests) b Sept. 27, 1914, d Aug. 24, 1951
*Robertson, G. K. (C. Dist.) b July 15, 1960
*Robertson, G. R. (NSW) b May 28, 1966
*Robertson, J. B. (W. Prov.) b June 5, 1906, d July 5, 1985
*Robertson, J. D. (Middx; CY 1948) b Feb. 22, 1917, d Oct. 12, 1996
*Robertson, W. R. (Vic.) b Oct. 6, 1861, d June 24, 1938
Robertson-Glasgow, R. C. (OU & Som; writer) b July 15, 1901, d March 4, 1965
Robins, D. H. (Warwicks) b June 26, 1914
*Robins, R. W. V. (CU & Middx; CY 1930) b June 3, 1906, d Dec. 12, 1968
Robinson, D. C. (Glos & Essex) b April 20, 1884, d July 29, 1963
Robinson, E. (Yorks) b Nov. 16, 1883, d Nov. 17, 1969
Robinson, E. P. (Yorks & Som) b Aug. 10, 1911, d Nov. 10, 1998
Robinson, Sir Foster G. (Glos) b Sept. 19, 1880, d Oct. 31, 1967
Robinson, I. D. (Test umpire) b March 11, 1947
Robinson, P. E. (Yorks & Leics) b Aug. 3, 1963
Robinson, P. J. (Worcs & Som) b Feb. 9, 1943
*Robinson, R. D. (Vic.) b June 8, 1946
*Robinson, R. H. (NSW, S. Aust. & Otago) b March 26, 1914, d Aug. 10, 1965
*Robinson, R. T. (Notts; CY 1986) b Nov. 21, 1958
Robson, C. (Hants) b June 20, 1859, d Sept. 27, 1943
Robson, E. (Som) b May 1, 1870, d May 23, 1924
*Rodriguez, W. V. (T/T) b June 25, 1934

Roe, B. (Som) b Jan. 27, 1939
Roebuck, P. M. (CU & Som; CY 1988; writer) b March 6, 1956
Rogers, N. H. (Hants) b March 9, 1918
Rogers, S. S. (Eur. & Som) b March 18, 1923, d Nov. 6, 1969
Romaines, P. W. (Northants, Glos & Griq. W.) b Dec. 25, 1955
*Roope, G. R. J. (Surrey & Griq. W.) b July 12, 1946
*Root, C. F. (Derbys & Worcs) b April 16, 1890, d Jan. 20, 1954
*Rorke, G. F. (NSW) b June 27, 1938
*Rose, B. C. (Som; CY 1980) b June 4, 1950
Roseberry, M. A. (Middx & Durham) b Nov. 28, 1966
*Rose-Innes, A. (Kimberley & Tvl) b Feb. 16, 1868, d Nov. 22, 1946
Rotherham, G. A. (Rugby, CU, Warwicks & Wgtn.; CY 1918) b May 28, 1899, d Jan. 31, 1985
Rouse, S. J. (Warwicks) b Jan. 20, 1949
*Routledge, T. W. (W. Prov. & Tvl) b April 18, 1867, d May 9, 1927
*Rowan, A. M. B. (Tvl) b Feb. 7, 1921, d Feb. 21, 1998
*Rowan, E. A. B. (Tvl; CY 1952) b July 20, 1909, d April 30, 1993
Rowbotham, J. (Yorks; Test umpire) b July 8, 1831, d Dec. 22, 1899
*Rowe, C. G. (Wgtn & C. Dist.) b June 30, 1915, d June 9, 1995
Rowe, C. J. C. (Kent & Glam) b Nov. 11, 1951
Rowe, E. J. (Notts) b July 21, 1920, d Dec. 17, 1989
*Rowe, G. A. (W. Prov.) b June 15, 1874, d Jan. 8, 1950
*Rowe, L. G. (Jam. & Derbys) b Jan. 8, 1949
*Roy, A. (Bengal) b June 5, 1945, d Sept. 19, 1997
*Roy, Pankaj (Bengal) b May 31, 1928, d Feb. 4, 2001
*Roy, Pranab (Bengal) b Feb. 10, 1957
*Royle, Rev. V. P. F. A. (OU & Lancs) b Jan. 29, 1854, d May 21, 1929
*Rumsey, F. E. (Worcs, Som & Derbys) b Dec. 4, 1935
Rundle, D. B. (W. Prov.) b Sept. 25, 1965
Rushby, T. (Surrey) b Sept. 6, 1880, d July 13, 1962
*Rushmere, M. W. (E. Prov & Tvl) b Jan. 7, 1965
*Russell, A. C. (Essex; CY 1923) b Oct. 7, 1887, d March 23, 1961
Russell, P. E. (Derbys) b May 9, 1944
Russell, S. E. J. (Middx & Glos) b Oct. 4, 1937, d June 18, 1994
*Russell, W. E. (Middx) b July 3, 1936
*Rutherford, J. W. (W. Aust.) b Sept. 25, 1929

*Rutherford, K. R. (Otago & †Gauteng) b Oct. 26, 1965

Ryan, F. (Hants & Glam) b Nov. 14, 1888, d Jan. 5, 1954

Ryan, M. (Yorks) b June 23, 1933

*Ryder, J. (Vic.) b Aug. 8, 1889, d April 3, 1977

Saadat Ali (Lahore, UBL & HBFC) b Feb. 6, 1955

*Sadiq Mohammad (Kar., PIA, Tas., Essex, Glos & UBL) b May 3, 1945

*Saeed Ahmed (Punjab, Pak. Us, Lahore, PIA, Kar., PWD & Sind) b Oct. 1, 1937

Saeed Azad (Kar. & NBP) b Aug. 14, 1966

*Saggers, R. A. (NSW) b May 15, 1917, d March 17, 1987

Saiful Islam (Bangladesh) b April 14, 1969

Sainsbury, P. J. (Hants; CY 1974) b June 13, 1934

*St Hill, E. L. (T/T) b March 9, 1904, d May 21, 1957

*St Hill, W. H. (T/T) b July 6, 1893, d circa 1957

Sajjad Akbar (Lahore, PNSC & Sargodha) b March 1, 1961

*Salah-ud-Din (Kar., PIA & Pak. Us) b Feb. 14, 1947

*Saleem Altaf (Lahore & PIA) b April 19, 1944

*Saleem Jaffer (Kar. & UBL) b Nov. 19, 1962

Salim Badar (Test umpire) b May 16, 1953

*Salim Malik (Lahore, HBL & Essex; CY 1988) b April 16, 1963

Salim Pervez (NBP) b Sept. 9, 1947

*Salim Yousuf (Sind, Kar., IDBP, Allied Bank & Customs) b Dec. 7, 1959

Samaranayake, A. D. A. (SL) b Feb. 25, 1962

*Samarasekera, M. A. R. (CCC) b Aug. 5, 1961

Sampson, H. (Yorks & All-England) b March 13, 1813, d March 29, 1885

*Samuelson, S. V. (Natal) b Nov. 21, 1883, d Nov. 18, 1958

*Sandham, A. (Surrey; CY 1923) b July 6, 1890, d April 20, 1982

*Sandhu, B. S. (Bombay) b Aug. 3, 1956

Santall, F. R. (Warwicks) b July 12, 1903, d Nov. 3, 1950

Santall, S. (Warwicks) b June 10, 1873, d March 19, 1957

*Sardesai, D. N. (Bombay) b Aug. 8, 1940

*Sarfraz Nawaz (Lahore, Punjab, Northants, Pak. Rlwys & UBL) b Dec. 1, 1948

*Sarwate, C. T. (CP & B, M'tra, Bombay & †M. Pradesh) b June 22, 1920

*Saunders, J. V. (Vic. & Wgtn) b March 21, 1876, d Dec. 21, 1927

Savage, J. S. (Leics & Lancs) b March 3, 1929

Savill, L. A. (Essex) b June 30, 1935

Saville, G. J. (Essex) b Feb. 5, 1944

Saxelby, K. (Notts) b Feb. 23, 1959

*Saxena, R. C. (Delhi & Bihar) b Sept. 20, 1944

Sayer, D. M. (OU & Kent) b Sept. 19, 1936

*Scarlett, R. O. (Jam.) b Aug. 15, 1934

*Schultz, B. N. (E. Prov. & W. Prov) b Aug. 26, 1970

*Schultz, S. S. (CU & Lancs) b Aug. 29, 1857, d Dec. 18, 1937

*Schwarz, R. O. (Middx & Natal; CY 1908) b May 4, 1875, d Nov. 18, 1918

*Scott, A. P. H. (Jam.) b July 29, 1934

Scott, C. J. (Glos) b May 1, 1919, d Nov. 22, 1992

Scott, C. W. (Notts & Durham) b Jan. 23, 1964

*Scott, H. J. H. (Vic.) b Dec. 26, 1858, d Sept. 23, 1910

Scott, M. E. (Northants) b May 8, 1936

*Scott, O. C. (Jam.) b Aug. 14, 1892, d June 15, 1961

*Scott, R. H. (Cant.) b March 6, 1917

Scott, S. W. (Middx; CY 1893) b March 24, 1854, d Dec. 8, 1933

*Scott, V. J. (Auck.) b July 31, 1916, d Aug. 2, 1980

*Scotton, W. H. (Notts) b Jan. 15, 1856, d July 9, 1893

*Sealey, B. J. (T/T) b Aug. 12, 1899, d Sept. 12, 1963

*Sealy, J. E. D. (B'dos & T/T) b Sept. 11, 1912, d Jan. 3, 1982

*Seccull, A. W. (Kimberley, W. Prov. & Tvl) b Sept. 14, 1868, d July 20, 1945

*Sekar, T. A. P. (TN) b March 28, 1955

*Selby, J. (Notts) b July 1, 1849, d March 11, 1894

Sellers, A. B. MBE (Yorks; CY 1940) b March 5, 1907, d Feb. 20, 1981

*Sellers, R. H. D. (S. Aust.) b Aug. 20, 1940

*Selvey, M. W. W. (CU, Surrey, Middx, Glam & OFS; writer) b April 25, 1948

Semple, K. F. (Guyana) b Aug. 21, 1970

*Sen, P. (Bengal) b May 31, 1926, d Jan. 27, 1970

*Sen Gupta, A. K. (Ind. Serv.) b Aug. 3, 1939

*Senanayake, C. P. (CCC) b Dec. 19, 1962

*Serjeant, C. S. (W. Aust.) b Nov. 1, 1951

Seymour, James (Kent) b Oct. 25, 1879, d Sept. 30, 1930

*Seymour, M. A. (W. Prov.) b June 5, 1936

*Shackleton, D. (Hants; CY 1959) b Aug. 12, 1924

*Shafiq Ahmed (Lahore, Punjab, NBP & UBL) b March 28, 1949

*Shafqat Rana (Lahore & PIA) b Aug. 10, 1943

*Shah, A. H. (Mash.) b Aug. 7, 1959

Shahid Anwar (Lahore & NBP) b July 5, 1968

*Shahid Israr (Kar. & Sind) b March 1, 1950

*Shahid Mahboob (Kar., Quetta, R'pindi, I'bad, PACO & Allied Bank) b Aug. 25, 1962

*Shahid Mahmoud (Kar., Pak. Us & PWD) b March 17, 1939

*Shahid Saeed (HBFC, Lahore & PACO) b Jan. 6, 1966

*Shahriar Hossain (Dhaka Div.) b June 1, 1976

*Shakeel Ahmed, jun. (R'pindi, Peshawar, HBL, Gujranwala & Easterns) b Nov. 12, 1971

Shakeel Khan (WAPDA, HBL, R'pindi & I'bad) b May 28, 1968

*Shalders, W. A. (Griq. W. & Tvl) b Feb. 12, 1880, d March 18, 1917

Shariful Haq (Biman) b Jan. 15, 1976

*Sharma, Ajay (Delhi & H. Pradesh) b April 3, 1964

*Sharma, Chetan (Haryana & Bengal) b Jan. 3, 1966

*Sharma, Gopal (U. Pradesh) b Aug. 3, 1960

*Sharma, P. (Raja.) b Jan. 5, 1948

Sharp, G. (Northants; Test umpire) b March 12, 1950

Sharp, H. P. (Middx) b Oct. 6, 1917, d Jan. 15, 1995

*Sharp, J. (Lancs) b Feb. 15, 1878, d Jan. 28, 1938

Sharp, K. (Yorks & Griq. W.) b April 6, 1959

*Sharpe, D. (Punjab, Pak. Rlwys, Lahore & S. Aust.) b Aug. 3, 1937

*Sharpe, J. W. (Surrey & Notts; *CY 1892*) b Dec. 9, 1866, d June 19, 1936

*Sharpe, P. J. (Yorks & Derbys; *CY 1963*) b Dec. 27, 1936

*Shastri, R. J. (Bombay & Glam) b May 27, 1962

*Shaw, Alfred (Notts & Sussex) b Aug. 29, 1842, d Jan. 16, 1907

Shaw, T. G. (E. Prov.) b July 5, 1959

*Sheahan, A. P. (Vic.) b Sept. 30, 1946

Sheffield, J. R. (Essex & Wgtn) b Nov. 19, 1906, d Nov. 16, 1997

Sheikh Salahuddin (Bangladesh) b Feb. 10, 1969

*Shepherd, B. K. (W. Aust.) b April 23, 1937, d Sept. 17, 2001

Shepherd, D. J. (Glam; *CY 1970*) b Aug. 12, 1927

Shepherd, D. R. MBE (Glos; ICC umpire) b Dec. 27, 1940

*Shepherd, J. N. (B'dos, Kent, Rhod. & Glos; *CY 1979*) b Nov. 9, 1943

Shepherd, T. F. (Surrey) b Dec. 5, 1889, d Feb. 13, 1957

*Sheppard, Rt Rev. D. S. (Bishop of Liverpool; later Baron Sheppard) (CU & Sussex; *CY 1953*) b March 6, 1929

*Shepstone, G. H. (Tvl) b April 9, 1876, d July 3, 1940

*Sherwell, P. W. (Tvl) b Aug. 17, 1880, d April 17, 1948

*Sherwin, M. (Notts; *CY 1891*) b Feb. 26, 1851, d July 3, 1910

Shields, J. (Leics) b Feb. 1, 1882, d May 11, 1960

*Shillingford, G. C. (Comb. Is. & Windwards; Chief Exec. WICB) b Sept. 25, 1944

*Shillingford, I. T. (Comb. Is. & Windwards) b April 18, 1944

*Shinde, S. G. (Baroda, M'tra & Bombay) b Aug. 18, 1923, d June 22, 1955

Shine, K. J. (Hants, Middx & Somerset) b Feb. 22, 1969

Shipman, A. W. (Leics) b March 7, 1901, d Dec. 12, 1979

Shipston, F. W. (Notts; *believed to be oldest living first-class cricketer at end of 2002*) b July 29, 1906

Shirreff, A. C. (CU, Hants, Kent & Som) b Feb. 12, 1919

*Shivnarine, S. (Guyana) b May 13, 1952

*Shodhan, R. H. (Guj. & Baroda) b Oct. 18, 1928

*Shrewsbury, A. (Notts; *CY 1890*) b April 11, 1856, d May 19, 1903

*Shrimpton, M. J. F. (C. Dist. & N. Dist.) b June 23, 1940

*Shuja-ud-Din, Col. (N. Ind., Pak. Us, Pak. Serv., B'pur & R'pindi) b April 10, 1930

*Shukla, R. C. (Bihar & Delhi) b Feb. 4, 1948

*Shuter, J. (Kent & Surrey) b Feb. 9, 1855, d July 5, 1920

*Shuttleworth, K. (Lancs & Leics) b Nov. 13, 1944

Sibbles, F. M. (Lancs) b March 15, 1904, d July 20, 1973

Siddons, J. D. (Vic & S. Aust.) b April 25, 1964

*Sidebottom, A. (Yorks & OFS) b April 1, 1954

*Sidhu, N. S. (Punjab) b Oct. 20, 1963

Sidwell, T. E. (Leics) b Jan. 30, 1888, d Dec. 8, 1958

Siedle, I. J. (Natal) b Jan. 11, 1903, d Aug. 24, 1982

*Sievers, M. W. (Vic.) b April 13, 1912, d May 10, 1968

*Sikander Bakht (PWD, PIA, Sind, Kar. & UBL) b Aug. 25, 1957

Silk, D. R. W. CBE (CU & Som; Pres. MCC 1992–94; Chairman TCCB 1994–96) b Oct. 8, 1931

*Silva, K. J. (Bloom. & SSC) b June 2, 1973

*Silva, S. A. R. (NCC) b Dec. 12, 1960

Sime, W. A. MBE (OU & Notts) b Feb. 8, 1909, d May 5, 1983

Simmons, J. MBE (Lancs & Tas.; *CY 1985*) b March 28, 1941

*Simmons, P. V. (T/T, Leics & Easterns; *CY 1997*) b April 18, 1963

Simons, E. O. (W. Prov. & N. Tvl; SA coach) b March 9, 1962

*Simpson, R. B. (NSW & W. Aust.; *CY 1965*; Aust. coach) b Feb. 3, 1936

*Simpson, R. T. (Sind & Notts; *CY 1950*) b Feb. 27, 1920

*Simpson-Hayward, G. H. (Worcs) b June 7, 1875, d Oct. 2, 1936

Sims, Sir Arthur (Cant.) b July 22, 1877, d April 27, 1969

*Sims, J. M. (Middx) b May 13, 1903, d April 27, 1973

*Sinclair, B. W. (Wgtn) b Oct. 23, 1936

*Sinclair, I. M. (Cant.) b June 1, 1933

*Sinclair, J. H. (Tvl) b Oct. 16, 1876, d Feb. 23, 1913

*Sincock, D. J. (S. Aust.) b Feb. 1, 1942

*Sinfield, R. A. (Glos) b Dec. 24, 1900, d March 17, 1988

*Singh, Charan K. (T/T) b Nov. 27, 1935

*Singh, R. (Delhi) b Jan. 1, 1970

Singh, R. P. (U. Pradesh) b Jan. 6, 1963

Singleton, A. P. (OU, Worcs & Rhod.) b Aug. 5, 1914, d March 22, 1999

*Sivaramakrishnan, L. (TN & Baroda) b Dec. 31, 1965

Skelding, A. (Leics; umpire) b Sept. 5, 1886, d April 17, 1960

*Slack, W. N. (Middx & Windwards) b Dec. 12, 1954, d Jan. 15, 1989

Slade, D. N. F. (Worcs) b Aug. 24, 1940

Slater, A. G. (Derbys) b Nov. 22, 1890, d July 22, 1949

*Slater, K. N. (W. Aust.) b March 12, 1935

Sleep, P. R. (S. Aust.) b May 4, 1957

*Slight, J. (Vic.) b Oct. 20, 1855, d Dec. 9, 1930

Slocombe, P. A. (Som) b Sept. 6, 1954

*Smailes, T. F. (Yorks) b March 27, 1910, d Dec. 1, 1970

Smales, K. (Yorks & Notts) b Sept. 15, 1927

*Small, G. C. (Warwicks & S. Aust.) b Oct. 18, 1961

Small, John, sen. (Hants & All-England) b April 19, 1737, d Dec. 31, 1826

*Small, J. A. (T/T) b Nov. 3, 1892, d April 26, 1958

*Small, M. A. (B'dos) b Feb. 12, 1964

Smart, C. C. (Warwicks & Glam) b July 23, 1898, d May 21, 1975

Smart, J. A. (Warwicks) b April 12, 1891, d Oct. 3, 1979

Smedley, M. J. (Notts) b Oct. 28, 1941

*Smith, A. C. CBE (OU & Warwicks; Chief Exec. TCCB 1987–96; ICC referee) b Oct. 25, 1936

*Smith, Sir C. Aubrey (CU, Sussex & Tvl) b July 21, 1863, d Dec. 20, 1948

*Smith, C. I. J. (Middx; *CY 1935*) b Aug. 25, 1906, d Feb. 9, 1979

*Smith, C. J. E. (Tvl) b Dec. 25, 1872, d March 27, 1947

*Smith, C. L. (Natal, Glam & Hants; *CY 1984*) b Oct. 15, 1958

Smith, C. L. A. (Sussex) b Jan. 1, 1879, d Nov. 22, 1949

Smith, C. S. (later Sir Colin Stansfield-) (CU & Lancs) b Jan. 1, 1932

*Smith, C. W. (B'dos; ICC referee) b July 29, 1933

*Smith, Denis (Derbys; *CY 1936*) b Jan. 24, 1907, d Sept. 12, 1979

*Smith, D. B. M. (Vic.) b Sept. 14, 1884, d July 29, 1963

Smith, D. H. K. (Derbys & OFS) b June 29, 1940

*Smith, D. M. (Surrey, Worcs & Sussex) b Jan. 9, 1956

*Smith, D. R. (Glos) b Oct. 5, 1934

*Smith, D. V. (Sussex) b June 14, 1923

Smith, Edwin (Derbys) b Jan. 2, 1934

*Smith, Ernest (OU & Yorks) b Oct. 19, 1869, d April 9, 1945

*Smith, E. J. (Warwicks) b Feb. 6, 1886, d Aug. 31, 1979

*Smith, F. B. (Cant.) b March 13, 1922, d July 6, 1997

*Smith, F. W. (Tvl) b unknown, d April 17, 1914, aged 53

Smith, G. J. (Essex) b April 2, 1935

*Smith, Harry (Glos) b May 21, 1890, d Nov. 12, 1937

Smith, H. A. (Leics) b March 29, 1901, d Aug. 7, 1948

*Smith, H. D. (Otago & Cant.) b Jan. 8, 1913, d Jan. 25, 1986

*Smith, I. D. S. MBE (C. Dist. & Auck.) b Feb. 28, 1957

Smith, K. D. (Warwicks) b July 9, 1956

Smith, M. J. (Middx) b Jan. 4, 1942

*Smith, M. J. K. OBE (Leics, OU & Warwicks; *CY 1960*) b June 30, 1933

Smith, N. (Yorks & Essex) b April 1, 1949

*Smith, O. G. ("Collie") (Jam.; *CY 1958*) b May 5, 1933, d Sept. 9, 1959

Smith, P. A. (Warwicks) b April 5, 1964

Smith, Ray (Essex) b Aug. 10, 1914, d Feb. 21, 1996

Smith, Roy (Som) b April 14, 1930

Smith, R. C. (Leics) b Aug. 3, 1935, d Dec. 12, 2001

*Smith, S. B. (NSW & Tvl) b Oct. 18, 1961

Smith, S. G. (T/T, Northants & Auck.; *CY 1915*) b Jan. 15, 1881, d Oct. 25, 1963

*Smith, T. P. B. (Essex; *CY 1947*) b Oct. 30, 1908, d Aug. 4, 1967

*Smith, V. I. (Natal) b Feb. 23, 1925

Smith, W. A. (Surrey) b Sept. 15, 1937

Smith, W. C. (Surrey; *CY 1911*) b Oct. 4, 1877, d July 16, 1946

*Smithson, G. A. (Yorks & Leics) b Nov. 1, 1926, d Sept. 6, 1970

*Snedden, C. A. (Auck.) b Jan. 7, 1918

*Snedden, M. C. (Auck.) b Nov. 23, 1958

*Snell, R. P. (Natal, Tvl, Somerset & Gauteng) b Sept. 12, 1968

Snellgrove, K. L. (Lancs) b Nov. 12, 1941

*Snooke, S. D. (W. Prov. & Tvl) b Nov. 11, 1878, d April 6, 1959

*Snooke, S. J. (Border, W. Prov. & Tvl) b Feb. 1, 1881, d Aug. 14, 1966

*Snow, J. A. (Sussex; *CY 1973*) b Oct. 13, 1941

*Sobers, Sir Garfield S. (B'dos, S. Aust. & Notts; *CY 1964, Cricketer of the Century 2000*) b July 28, 1936

Sohail Fazal (HBL) b Nov. 11, 1967

*Sohoni, S. W. (M'tra, Baroda & Bombay) b March 5, 1918, d May 19, 1993

*Solkar, E. D. (Bombay & Sussex) b March 18, 1948

*Solomon, J. S. (BG) b Aug. 26, 1930

*Solomon, W. R. (Tvl & E. Prov.) b April 23, 1872, d July 12, 1964

*Sood, M. M. (Delhi) b July 6, 1939

Southern, J. W. (Hants) b Sept. 2, 1952

*Southerton, James (Surrey, Hants & Sussex) b Nov. 16, 1827, d June 16, 1880

Southerton, S. J. (Editor of *Wisden* 1934–35) b July 7, 1874, d March 12, 1935

*Sparling, J. T. (Auck.) b July 24, 1938

Speak, N. J. (Lancs & Durham) b Nov. 21, 1966

Speed, M. W. (Chief Exec. ICC 2001–) b Sept. 14, 1948

Speight, M. P. (Sussex, Wgtn & Durham) b Oct. 24, 1967

Spencer, C. T. (Leics) b Aug. 18, 1931

Spencer, J. (CU & Sussex) b Oct. 6, 1949

Spencer, T. W. OBE (Kent; Test umpire) b March 22, 1914, d Nov. 1, 1995

Sperry, J. (Leics) b March 19, 1910, d April 21, 1997

*Spofforth, F. R. (NSW & Vic.) b Sept. 9, 1853, d June 4, 1926

*Spooner, R. H. (Lancs; *CY 1905*) b Oct. 21, 1880, d Oct. 2, 1961

*Spooner, R. T. (Warwicks) b Dec. 30, 1919, d Dec. 20, 1997

Springall, J. D. (Notts) b Sept. 19, 1932

Sprot, E. M. (Hants) b Feb. 4, 1872, d Oct. 8, 1945

Squires, H. S. (Surrey) b Feb. 22, 1909, d Jan. 24, 1950

*Srikkanth, K. (TN) b Dec. 21, 1959

*Srinivasan, T. E. (TN) b Oct. 26, 1950

*Stackpole, K. R. MBE (Vic.; *CY 1973*) b July 10, 1940

Standen, J. A. (Worcs) b May 30, 1935

Stanyforth, Lt.-Col. R. T. (Yorks) b May 30, 1892, d Feb. 20, 1964

Staples, A. (Notts) b Feb. 4, 1899, d Sept. 9, 1965

*Staples, S. J. (Notts; *CY 1929*) b Sept. 18, 1892, d June 4, 1950

*Statham, J. B. CBE (Lancs; *CY 1955*) b June 17, 1930, d June 10, 2000

*Stayers, S. C. (†Guyana & Bombay) b June 9, 1937

Stead, B. (Yorks, Essex, Notts & N. Tvl) b June 21, 1939, d April 15, 1980

*Steel, A. G. (CU & Lancs; Pres. MCC 1902) b Sept. 24, 1858, d June 15, 1914

*Steele, D. S. OBE (Northants & Derbys; *CY 1976*) b Sept. 29, 1941

Steele, J. F. (Leics, Natal & Glam) b July 23, 1946

Stephens, E. J. (Glos) b March 23, 1909, d April 3, 1983

Stephenson, F. D. (B'dos, Glos, Tas., Notts, Sussex & †FS; *CY 1989*) b April 8, 1959

Stephenson, G. R. (Derbys & Hants) b Nov. 19, 1942

Stephenson, H. H. (Surrey & All-England) b May 3, 1832, d Dec. 17, 1896

Stephenson, H. W. (Som) b July 18, 1920

Stephenson, Lt.-Col. J. R. CBE (Sec. MCC 1987–93) b Feb. 25, 1931

Stephenson, Lt.-Col. J. W. A. (Essex, Worcs, Army, Europeans & Victory Tests) b Aug. 1, 1907, d May 20, 1982

Stevens, Edward ("Lumpy") (Hants) b *circa* 1735, d Sept. 7, 1819

*Stevens, G. B. (S. Aust.) b Feb. 29, 1932

*Stevens, G. T. S. (UCS, OU & Middx; *CY 1918*) b Jan. 7, 1901, d Sept. 19, 1970

*Stevenson, G. B. (Yorks & Northants) b Dec. 16, 1955

Stevenson, K. (Derbys & Hants) b Oct. 6, 1950

*Stewart, M. J. OBE (Surrey; *CY 1958;* Eng. manager) b Sept. 16, 1932

*Stewart, R. B. (SA) b Sept. 3, 1856, d Sept. 12, 1913

Stewart, W. J. (Warwicks & Northants) b Oct. 31, 1934

*Steyn, P. J. R. (Griq. W., OFS, Natal & Northerns) b June 30, 1967

*Stirling, D. A. (C. Dist.) b Oct. 5, 1961

Stocks, F. W. (Notts) b Nov. 6, 1918, d Feb. 23, 1996

*Stoddart, A. E. (Middx; *CY 1893*) b March 11, 1863, d April 3, 1915

*Stollmeyer, J. B. (T/T) b April 11, 1921, d Sept. 10, 1989

*Stollmeyer, V. H. (T/T) b Jan. 24, 1916, d Sept. 21, 1999

Stone, J. (Hants & Glam) b Nov. 29, 1876, d Nov. 15, 1942

Storer, H. jun. (Derbys) b Feb. 2, 1898, d Sept. 1, 1967

*Storer, W. (Derbys; *CY 1899*) b Jan. 25, 1867, d Feb. 28, 1912

Storey, S. J. (Surrey & Sussex) b Jan. 6, 1941

Stott, L. W. (Auck.) b Dec. 8, 1946

Stott, W. B. (Yorks) b July 18, 1934

Stovold, A. W. (Glos & OFS) b March 19, 1953

*Strang, B. C. (MCD & Mash.) b June 9, 1972

*Street, G. B. (Sussex) b Dec. 6, 1889, d April 24, 1924

*Stricker, L. A. (Tvl) b May 26, 1884, d Feb. 5, 1960

*Strudwick, H. (Surrey; *CY 1912*) b Jan. 28, 1880, d Feb. 14, 1970

Stuart, A. M. (NSW) b Jan. 2, 1970

*Studd, C. T. (CU & Middx) b Dec. 2, 1860, d July 16, 1931

*Studd, G. B. (CU & Middx) b Oct. 20, 1859, d Feb. 13, 1945

Studd, Sir J. E. Kynaston (Middx & CU; Pres. MCC 1930) b July 26, 1858, d Jan. 14, 1944

*Su'a, M. L. (N. Dist. & Auck.) b Nov. 7, 1966

*Subba Row, R. CBE (CU, Surrey & Northnts; *CY 1961;* Chairman TCCB 1985–90; ICC referee) b Jan. 29, 1932

*Subramanya, V. (Mysore) b July 16, 1936

*Such, P. M. (Notts, Leics & Essex) b June 12, 1964

Sudhakar Rao, R. (Karn.) b Aug. 8, 1952

Sueter, T. (Hants & Surrey) b *circa* 1749, d Feb. 17, 1827

*Sugg, F. H. (Yorks, Derbys & Lancs; *CY 1890*) b Jan. 11, 1862, d May 29, 1933

Sullivan, J. (Lancs) b Feb. 5, 1945

Sully, H. (Som & Northnts) b Nov. 1, 1939

Sultan Rana (Pak. Us, Lahore, Punjab & HBL; ICC referee) b Nov. 3, 1951

*Sunderram, G. (Bombay & Raja.) b March 29, 1930

*Surendranath, R. (Ind. Serv.) b Jan. 4, 1937

Surridge, W. S. (Surrey; *CY 1953*) b Sept. 3, 1917, d April 13, 1992

*Surti, R. F. (Guj., Raja., & Qld) b May 25, 1936

*Susskind, M. J. (CU, Middx & Tvl) b June 8, 1891, d July 9, 1957

*Sutcliffe, B. MBE (Auck., Otago & N. Dist.; *CY 1950*) b Nov. 17, 1923, d April 20, 2001

*Sutcliffe, H. (Yorks; *CY 1920*) b Nov. 24, 1894, d Jan. 22, 1978

Sutcliffe, W. H. H. (Yorks) b Oct. 10, 1926, d Sept. 16, 1998

Suttle, K. G. (Sussex) b Aug. 25, 1928

Swamy, V. N. (Ind. Serv.) b May 23, 1924, d May 1, 1983

Swanton, E. W. CBE (Middx; writer & broadcaster) b Feb. 11, 1907, d Jan. 22, 2000

Swarbrook, F. W. (Derbys, Griq. W. & OFS) b Dec. 17, 1950

Swart, P. D. (Rhod., W. Prov., Glam & Boland) b April 27, 1946, d March 13, 2000

*Swetman, R. (Surrey, Notts & Glos) b Oct. 25, 1933

Sydenham, D. A. D. (Surrey) b April 6, 1934

*Symcox, P. L. (Griq. W., Natal & N. Tvl) b April 14, 1960

*Taber, H. B. (NSW) b April 29, 1940

*Taberer, H. M. (OU & Natal) b Oct. 7, 1870, d June 5, 1932

*Tahir Naqqash (Servis Ind., MCB, Punjab & Lahore) b July 6, 1959

Tait, A. R. (N. Dist.) b June 13, 1972

*Talat Ali (Lahore, PIA & UBL; ICC referee) b May 29, 1950

*Tallon, D. (Qld; *CY 1949*) b Feb. 17, 1916, d Sept. 7, 1984

*Tamhane, N. S. (Bombay) b Aug. 4, 1931, d March 19, 2002

*Tancred, A. B. (Kimberley, Griq. W. & Tvl) b Aug. 20, 1865, d Nov. 23, 1911

*Tancred, L. J. (Tvl) b Oct. 7, 1876, d July 28, 1934

*Tancred, V. M. (Tvl) b July 7, 1875, d June 3, 1904

Tanvir Mehdi (Lahore & UBL) b Nov. 7, 1972

*Tapscott, G. L. (Griq. W.) b Nov. 7, 1889, d Dec. 13, 1940

*Tapscott, L. E. (Griq. W.) b March 18, 1894, d July 7, 1934

*Tarapore, K. K. (Bombay) b Dec. 17, 1910, d June 15, 1986

Tarbox, C. V. (Worcs) b July 2, 1891, d June 15, 1978

*Tarrant, F. A. (Vic., Middx & Patiala; *CY 1908*) b Dec. 11, 1880, d Jan. 29, 1951

Tarrant, G. F. (Cambs. & All-England) b Dec. 7, 1838, d July 2, 1870

*Taslim Arif (Kar., Sind & NBP) b May 1, 1954

*Tate, F. W. (Sussex) b July 24, 1867, d Feb. 24, 1943

*Tate, M. W. (Sussex; *CY 1924*) b May 30, 1895, d May 18, 1956

*Tattersall, R. (Lancs) b Aug. 17, 1922

*Tauseef Ahmed (PWD, UBL, Kar. & Customs) b May 10, 1958

*Tavaré, C. J. (OU, Kent & Som) b Oct. 27, 1954

*Tayfield, H. J. (Natal, Rhod. & Tvl; *CY 1956*) b Jan. 30, 1929, d Feb. 25, 1994

Taylor, A. I. (Tvl) b July 25, 1925

Taylor, B. (Essex; *CY 1972*) b June 19, 1932

*Taylor, B. R. (Cant. & Wgtn) b July 12, 1943

Taylor, C. G. (CU & Middx) b Nov. 21, 1816, d Sept. 10, 1869

*Taylor, Daniel (Natal) b Jan. 9, 1887, d Jan. 24, 1957

*Taylor, D. D. (Auck. & Warwicks) b March 2, 1923, d Dec. 5, 1980

Taylor, D. J. S. (Surrey, Som & Griq. W.) b Nov. 12, 1942

*Taylor, H. W. (Natal, Tvl & W. Prov.; *CY 1925*) b May 5, 1889, d Feb. 8, 1973

*Tuckett, L. (OFS) b Feb. 6, 1919
*Tuckett, L. R. (Natal & OFS) b April 19, 1885, d April 8, 1963
*Tufnell, N. C. (CU & Surrey) b June 13, 1887, d Aug. 3, 1951
Tunnicliffe, C. J. (Derbys) b Aug. 11, 1951
Tunnicliffe, J. (Yorks; *CY 1901*) b Aug. 26, 1866. d July 11, 1948
*Turnbull, M. J. (CU & Glam; *CY 1931*) b March 16, 1906, d Aug. 5, 1944
*Turner, A. (NSW) b July 23, 1950
Turner, C. (Yorks) b Jan. 11, 1902, d Nov. 19, 1968
*Turner, C. T. B. (NSW; *CY 1889*) b Nov. 16, 1862, d Jan. 1, 1944
Turner, D. R. (Hants & W. Prov.) b Feb. 5, 1949
Turner, F. M. MBE (Leics) b Aug. 8, 1934
*Turner, G. M. (Otago, N. Dist. & Worcs; *CY 1971*; NZ coach) b May 26, 1947
Turner, S. (Essex & Natal) b July 18, 1943
*Twentyman-Jones, Sir Percy S. (W. Prov.) b Sept. 13, 1876, d March 8, 1954
*Twose, R. G. (Warwicks, N. Dist., C. Dist. & Wgtn) b April 17, 1968
*Tyldesley, E. (Lancs; *CY 1920*) b Feb. 5, 1889, d May 5, 1962
*Tyldesley, J. T. (Lancs; *CY 1902*) b Nov. 22, 1873, d Nov. 27, 1930
*Tyldesley, R. K. (Lancs; *CY 1925*) b March 11, 1897, d Sept. 17, 1943
*Tylecote, E. F. S. (OU & Kent) b June 23, 1849, d March 15, 1938
*Tyler, E. J. (Som) b Oct. 13, 1864, d Jan. 25, 1917
*Tyson, F. H. (Northants; *CY 1956*) b June 6, 1930

Ufton, D. G. (Kent) b May 31, 1928
*Ulyett, G. (Yorks) b Oct. 21, 1851, d June 18, 1898
*Umrigar, P. R. (Bombay & Guj.) b March 28, 1926
*Underwood, D. L. MBE (Kent; *CY 1969*) b June 8, 1945

Vaidya, P. S. (Bengal) b Sept. 23, 1967
*Valentine, A. L. (Jam.; *CY 1951*) b April 28, 1930
*Valentine, B. H. (CU & Kent) b Jan. 17, 1908, d Feb. 2, 1983
*Valentine, V. A. (Jam.) b April 4, 1908, d July 6, 1972
*Vance, R. H. (Wgtn) b March 31, 1955
*van der Bijl, P. G. (W. Prov. & OU) b Oct. 21, 1907, d Feb. 16, 1973
van der Bijl, V. A. P. (Natal, Middx & Tvl; *CY 1981*) b March 19, 1948
*Van der Merwe, E. A. (Tvl) b Nov. 9, 1904, d Feb. 26, 1971

*Van der Merwe, P. L. (W. Prov. & E. Prov.; ICC referee) b March 14, 1937
van Geloven, J. (Yorks & Leics) b Jan. 4, 1934
*Van Ryneveld, C. B. (W. Prov. & OU) b March 19, 1928
van Zyl, C. J. P. G. (OFS & Glam) b Oct. 1, 1961
*Varnals, G. D. (E. Prov., Tvl & Natal) b July 24, 1935
*Vaughan, J. T. C. (Auck.) b Aug. 30, 1967
*Veivers, T. R. (Qld) b April 6, 1937
*Veletta, M. R. J. (W. Aust.) b Oct. 30, 1963
*Vengsarkar, D. B. (Bombay; *CY 1987*) b April 6, 1956
*Venkataraghavan, S. (†TN & Derbys; ICC umpire) b April 21, 1946
*Venkataramana, M. (TN) b April 24, 1966
*Verity, H. (Yorks; *CY 1932*) b May 18, 1905, d July 31, 1943
*Vernon, G. F. (Middx) b June 20, 1856, d Aug. 10, 1902
Vials, G. A. T. (Northants) b March 18, 1887, d April 26, 1974
Vigar, F. H. (Essex) b July 7, 1917
*Viljoen, K. G. (Griq. W., OFS & Tvl) b May 14, 1910, d Jan. 21, 1974
*Vincent, C. L. (Tvl) b Feb. 16, 1902, d Aug. 24, 1968
*Vine, J. (Sussex; *CY 1906*) b May 15, 1875, d April 25, 1946
*Vintcent, C. H. (Tvl & Griq. W.) b Sept. 2, 1866, d Sept. 28, 1943
Virgin, R. T. (Som, Northants & W. Prov.; *CY 1971*) b Aug. 26, 1939
*Viswanath, G. R. (†Karn.; ICC referee) b Feb. 12, 1949
*Viswanath, S. (Karn.) b Nov. 29, 1962
*Vivian, G. E. (Auck.) b Feb. 28, 1946
*Vivian, H. G. (Auck.) b Nov. 4, 1912, d Aug. 12, 1983
*Vizianagram, Maharaj Kumar of, Sir Vijay A., (U. Prov.) b Dec. 28, 1905, d Dec. 2, 1965
*Voce, W. (Notts; *CY 1933*) b Aug. 8, 1909, d June 6, 1984
*Vogler, A. E. E. (Middx, Natal, Tvl & E. Prov.; *CY 1908*) b Nov. 28, 1876, d Aug. 9, 1946
Vonhagt, D. M. (Moors) b March 31, 1965

*Waddington, A. (Yorks) b Feb. 4, 1893, d Oct. 28, 1959
*Wade, H. F. (Natal) b Sept. 14, 1905, d Nov. 23, 1980
Wade, T. H. (Essex) b Nov. 24, 1910, d July 25, 1987
*Wade, W. W. (Natal) b June 18, 1914
*Wadekar, A. L. (Bombay; Ind. manager) b April 1, 1941
*Wadsworth, K. J. (C. Dist. & Cant.) b Nov. 30, 1946, d Aug. 19, 1976
*Wainwright, E. (Yorks; *CY 1894*) b April 8, 1865, d Oct. 28, 1919

*Waite, J. H. B. (E. Prov. & Tvl) b Jan. 19, 1930

*Waite, M. G. (S. Aust.) b Jan. 7, 1911, d Dec. 16, 1985

*Walcott, Sir Clyde L. (B'dos & BG; *CY 1958;* Chairman ICC 1993–97) b Jan. 17, 1926

*Walcott, L. A. (B'dos) b Jan. 18, 1894, d Feb. 27, 1984

Walden, F. (Northants; Test umpire) b March 1, 1888, d May 3, 1949

Walker, A. (Northants & Durham) b July 7, 1962

Walker, C. (Yorks & Hants) b June 27, 1919, d Dec. 3, 1992

Walker, I. D. (Middx) b Jan. 8, 1844, d July 6, 1898

*Walker, M. H. N. (Vic.) b Sept. 12, 1948

*Walker, P. M. (Glam, Tvl & W. Prov.) b Feb. 17, 1936

Walker, V. E. (Middx) b April 20, 1837, d Jan. 3, 1906

Walker, W. (Notts) b Nov. 24, 1892, d Dec. 3, 1991

*Wall, T. W. (S. Aust.) b May 13, 1904, d March 25, 1981

*Wallace, W. M. (Auck.) b Dec. 19, 1916

*Waller, A. C. (Mash.) b Sept. 25, 1959

Waller, C. E. (Surrey & Sussex) b Oct. 3, 1948

*Walsh, C. A. (Jam. & Glos; *CY 1987*) b Oct. 30, 1962

Walsh, J. E. (NSW & Leics) b Dec. 4, 1912, d May 20, 1980

*Walter, K. A. (Tvl) b Nov. 5, 1939

*Walters, C. F. (Glam & Worcs; *CY 1934*) b Aug. 28, 1905, d Dec. 23, 1992

*Walters, F. H. (Vic. & NSW) b Feb. 9, 1860, d June 1, 1922

*Walters, K. D. MBE (NSW) b Dec. 21, 1945

*Waqar Hassan (Pak. Us, Punjab, Pak. Serv. & Kar.) b Sept. 12, 1932

*Ward, Alan (Derbys, Leics & Border) b Aug. 10, 1947

*Ward, Albert (Yorks & Lancs; *CY 1890*) b Nov. 21, 1865, d Jan. 6, 1939

Ward, B. (Essex) b Feb. 28, 1944

Ward, D. (Glam) b Aug. 30, 1934

Ward, D. M. (Surrey) b Feb. 10, 1961

*Ward, F. A. (S. Aust.) b Feb. 23, 1906, d March 25, 1974

*Ward, J. T. (Cant.) b March 11, 1937

*Ward, T. A. (Tvl) b Aug. 2, 1887, d Feb. 16, 1936

Ward, William (MCC & Hants) b July 24, 1787, d June 30, 1849

*Wardle, J. H. (Yorks; *CY 1954*) b Jan. 8, 1923, d July 23, 1985

*Warnapura, B. (SL; ICC referee) b March 1, 1953

*Warnaweera, K. P. J. (Galle & Singha) b Nov. 23, 1960

Warner, A. E. (Worcs & Derbys) b May 12, 1959

*Warner, Sir Pelham F. (OU & Middx; *CY 1904, special portrait 1921;* Pres. MCC 1950–51) b Oct. 2, 1873, d Jan. 30, 1963

*Warr, J. J. (CU & Middx; Pres. MCC 1987–88) b July 16, 1927

*Warren, A. R. (Derbys) b April 2, 1875, d Sept. 3, 1951

*Washbrook, C. CBE (Lancs; *CY 1947*) b Dec. 6, 1914, d April 27, 1999

*Wasim Bari (Kar., PIA & Sind) b March 23, 1948

Wasim Haider (F'bad & PIA) b June 6, 1967

*Wasim Raja (Lahore, Sargodha, Pak. Us, PIA, Punjab & NBP; Pak. coach; ICC referee) b July 3, 1952

Wass, T. G. (Notts; *CY 1908*) b Dec. 26, 1873, d Oct. 27, 1953

*Wassan, A. S. (Delhi) b March 23, 1968

Wassell, A. (Hants) b April 15, 1940

*Watkin, S. L. (Glam: *CY 1994*) b Sept. 15, 1964

*Watkins, A. J. (Glam) b April 21, 1922

*Watkins, J. C. (Natal) b April 10, 1923

*Watkins, J. R. (NSW) b April 16, 1943

*Watkinson, M. (Lancs) b Aug. 1, 1961

Watson, A. (Lancs) b Nov. 4, 1844, d Oct. 26, 1920

*Watson, C. (Jam. & Delhi) b July 1, 1938

Watson, F. (Lancs) b Sept. 17, 1898, d Feb. 1, 1976

*Watson, G. D. (Vic., W. Aust. & NSW) b March 8, 1945

Watson, G. S. (Kent & Leics) b April 10, 1907, d April 1, 1974

*Watson, W. (Yorks & Leics; *CY 1954*) b March 7, 1920

*Watson, W. (Auck.) b Aug. 31, 1965

*Watson, W. J. (NSW) b Jan. 31, 1931

Watt, A. E. (Kent) b June 19, 1907, d Feb. 3, 1974

*Watt, L. (Otago) b Sept. 17, 1924, d Nov. 15, 1996

Watts, E. A. (Surrey) b Aug. 1, 1911, d May 2, 1982

Watts, P. D. (Northants & Notts) b March 31, 1938

Watts, P. J. (Northants) b June 16, 1940

*Wazir, Ali, S. (C. Ind., S. Punjab & Patiala) b Sept. 15, 1903, d June 17, 1950

*Wazir Mohammad (B'pur & Kar.) b Dec. 22, 1929

*Webb, M. G. (Otago & Cant.) b June 22, 1947

*Webb, P. N. (Auck.) b July 14, 1957

Webb, R. J. (Otago) b Sept. 15, 1952

Webb, R. T. (Sussex) b July 11, 1922

*Webbe, A. J. (OU & Middx) b Jan. 16, 1855, d Feb. 19, 1941

Webber, Roy (Statistician) b July 23, 1914, d Nov. 14, 1962

*Weekes, Sir Everton D. (B'dos; *CY 1951*) b Feb. 26, 1925

*Weekes, K. H. (Jam.) b Jan. 24, 1912, d Feb. 9, 1998

Weeks, R. T. (Warwicks) b April 30, 1930

Weerakkody, A. P. (NCC) b Oct. 1, 1970

*Weerasinghe, C. D. U. S. (TU & NCC) b March 1, 1968

Weigall, G. J. V. (CU & Kent) b Oct. 19, 1870, d May 17, 1944

*Weir, G. L. (Auck.; *oldest living Test cricketer at end of 2002*) b June 2, 1908

*Wellard, A. W. (Som; *CY 1936*) b April 8, 1902, d Dec. 31, 1980

*Wellham, D. M. (NSW, Tas. & Qld) b March 13, 1959

*Wells, A. P. (Sussex, Border & Kent) b Oct. 2, 1961

Wells, B. D. (Glos & Notts) b July 27, 1930

Wells, C. M. (Sussex, Border, W. Prov. & Derbys) b March 3, 1960

Wells, W. (Northants) b March 14, 1881, d March 18, 1939

Wenman, E. G. (Kent & England) b Aug. 18, 1803, d Dec. 31, 1879

Wensley, A. F. (Sussex, Auck., Naw. & Eur.) b May 23, 1898, d June 17, 1970

*Wesley, C. (Natal) b Sept. 5, 1937

**Wessels, K. C. (OFS, W. Prov., N. Tvl, Sussex, Qld, E. Prov. & Griq. W.; *CY 1995*) b Sept 14, 1957

West, G. H. (Editor of *Wisden* 1880–86) b 1851, d Oct. 6, 1896

*Westcott, R. J. (W. Prov.) b Sept. 19, 1927

Weston, M. J. (Worcs) b April 8, 1959

*Wettimuny, M. D. (SL) b June 11, 1951

*Wettimuny, S. (SL; *CY 1985;* ICC referee) b Aug. 12, 1956

Wettimuny, S. R. de S. (SL) b Feb. 7, 1949

*Wharton, A. (Lancs & Leics) b April 30, 1923, d Aug. 26, 1993

*Whatmore, D. F. (Vic.; SL coach) b March 16, 1954

Wheatley, O. S. CBE (CU, Warwicks & Glam; *CY 1969*) b May 28, 1935

Whitaker, Haddon OBE (Editor of *Wisden* 1940–43) b Aug. 30, 1908, d Jan. 5, 1982

*Whitaker, J. J. (Leics; *CY 1987*) b May 5, 1962

*White, A. F. T. (CU, Warwicks & Worcs) b Sept. 5, 1915, d March 16, 1993

White, Sir Archibald W. 4th Bt (Yorks) b Oct. 14, 1877, d Dec. 16, 1945

*White, D. J. (N. Dist.) b June 26, 1961

*White, D. W. (Hants & Glam) b Dec. 14, 1935

*White, G. C. (Tvl) b Feb. 5, 1882, d Oct. 17, 1918

*White, J. C. (Som; *CY 1929*) b Feb. 19, 1891, d May 2, 1961

White, Hon. L. R. (5th Lord Annaly) (Middx & Victory Test) b March 15, 1927, d Sept. 30, 1990

White, R. A. (Middx & Notts) b Oct. 6, 1936

White, R. C. (CU, Glos & Tvl) b Jan. 29, 1941

*White, W. A. (B'dos) b Nov. 20, 1938

Whitehead, A. G. T. (Som; Test umpire) b Oct. 28, 1940

Whitehead, H. (Leics) b Sept. 19, 1874, d Sept. 14, 1944

Whitehouse, J. (Warwicks) b April 8, 1949

*Whitelaw, P. E. (Auck.) b Feb. 10, 1910, d Aug. 28, 1988

Whiteside, J. P. (Lancs & Leics) b June 11, 1861, d March 8, 1946

Whitfield, E. W. (Surrey & Northants) b May 31, 1911, d Aug. 10, 1996

Whitington, R. S. (S. Aust. & Victory Tests; writer) b June 30, 1912, d March 13, 1984

*Whitney, M. R. (NSW & Glos) b Feb. 24, 1959

Whittaker, G. J. (Surrey) b May 29, 1916, d April 20, 1997

*Whittall, A. R. (CU & Mat.) b March 28, 1973

Whitticase, P. (Leics) b March 15, 1965

Whittingham, N. B. (Notts) b Oct. 22, 1940

*Whitty, W. J. (S. Aust.) b Aug. 15, 1886, d Jan. 30, 1974

*Whysall, W. W. (Notts; *CY 1925*) b Oct. 31, 1887, d Nov. 11, 1930

*Wickremasinghe, A. G. D. (NCC) b Dec. 27, 1965

*Wiener, J. M. (Vic.) b May 1, 1955

*Wight, C. V. (BG) b July 28, 1902, d Oct. 4, 1969

*Wight, G. L. (BG) b May 28, 1929

Wight, P. B. (BG, Som & Cant.) b June 25, 1930

*Wijegunawardene, K. I. W. (CCC) b Nov. 23, 1964

*Wijesuriya, R. G. C. E. (Mor. & Colts) b Feb. 18, 1960

*Wijetunge, P. K. (SSC & Moors) b Aug. 6, 1971

Wilcox, D. R. (Essex & CU) b June 4, 1910, d Feb. 6, 1953

Wild, D. J. (Northants) b Nov. 28, 1962

*Wiles, C. A. (B'dos & T/T) b Aug. 11, 1892, d Nov. 4, 1957

Wilkins, C. P. (Derbys, Border, E. Prov. & Natal) b July 31, 1944

Wilkinson, C. T. A. (Surrey) b Oct. 4, 1884, d Dec. 16, 1970

*Wilkinson, L. L. (Lancs) b Nov. 5, 1916, d Sept. 3, 2002

Willatt, G. L. (CU, Notts & Derbys) b May 7, 1918

*Willett, E. T. (Comb. Is. & Leewards) b May 1, 1953

Yachad, M. (Tvl) b Nov. 17, 1960
*Yadav, N. S. (H'bad) b Jan. 26, 1957
*Yadav, V. S. (Haryana) b March 14, 1967
*Yajurvindra Singh (M'tra & S'tra) b Aug. 1, 1952
*Yallop, G. N. (Vic.) b Oct. 7, 1952
*Yardley, B. (W. Aust.; SL coach) b Sept. 5, 1947
*Yardley, N. W. D. (CU & Yorks; *CY 1948*) b March 19, 1915, d Oct. 4, 1989
Yardley, T. J. (Worcs & Northants) b Oct. 27, 1946
Yarnold, H. (Worcs) b July 6, 1917, d Aug. 13, 1974
*Yashpal Sharma (Punjab) b Aug. 11, 1954
Yawar Saeed (Som & Punjab) b Jan. 22, 1935
*Yograj Singh (Haryana & Punjab) b March 25, 1958
Young, A. (Som) b Nov. 6, 1890, d April 2, 1936
*Young, B. A. (N. Dist. & Auck.) b Nov. 3, 1964
Young, D. M. (Worcs & Glos) b April 15, 1924, d June 18, 1993
Young, H. I. (Essex) b Feb. 5, 1876, d Dec. 12, 1964

*Young, J. A. (Middx) b Oct. 14, 1912, d Feb. 5, 1993
*Young, R. A. (CU & Sussex) b Sept. 16, 1885, d July 1, 1968
*Younis Ahmed (Lahore, Kar., Surrey, PIA, S. Aust., Worcs & Glam) b Oct. 20, 1947
*Yuile, B. W. (C. Dist.) b Oct. 29, 1941

Zafar Iqbal (Kar. & NBP) b March 6, 1969
*Zaheer Abbas (Kar., Glos, PWD, Dawood Ind., Sind & PIA; *CY 1972*) b July 24, 1947
Zahid Ahmed (PIA & H'bad) b Nov. 15, 1961
*Zahid Fazal (PACO, PIA, Lahore & Gujranwala) b Nov. 10, 1973
Zakir Hassan (Dhaka Div.) b Dec. 1, 1972
*Zakir Khan (Sind, Peshawar & ADBP) b April 3, 1963
Zesers, A. K. (S. Aust.) b March 11, 1967
*Zoehrer, T. J. (W. Aust.) b Sept. 25, 1961
*Zulch, J. W. (Tvl) b Jan. 2, 1886, d May 19, 1924
*Zulfiqar Ahmed (B'pur & PIA) b Nov. 22, 1926
*Zulqarnain (Pak. Rlwys, Lahore, HBFC & PACO) b May 25, 1962

PRESIDENTS OF MCC SINCE 1946

1946	General Sir Ronald Adam, Bart	1972-73	A. M. Crawley
1947	Captain Lord Cornwallis	1973-74	Lord Caccia
1948	Brig.-Gen. The Earl of Gowrie	1974-75	HRH The Duke of Edinburgh
1949	HRH The Duke of Edinburgh	1975-76	C. G. A. Paris
1950	Sir Pelham Warner	1976-77	W. H. Webster
1951-52	W. Findlay	1977-78	D. G. Clark
1952-53	The Duke of Beaufort	1978-79	C. H. Palmer
1953-54	The Earl of Rosebery	1979-80	S. C. Griffith
1954-55	Viscount Cobham	1980-81	P. B. H. May
1955-56	Field Marshal Earl Alexander of Tunis	1981-82	G. H. G. Doggart
		1982-83	Sir Anthony Tuke
1956-57	Viscount Monckton of Brenchley	1983-84	A. H. A. Dibbs
1957-58	The Duke of Norfolk	1984-85	F. G. Mann
1958-59	Marshal of the RAF Viscount Portal of Hungerford	1985-86	J. G. W. Davies
		1986-87	M. C. Cowdrey
1959-60	H. S. Altham	1987-88	J. J. Warr
1960-61	Sir Hubert Ashton	1988-89	Field Marshal The Lord Bramall
1961-62	Col. Sir William Worsley, Bart	1989-90	The Hon. Sir Denys Roberts
1962-63	Lt-Col. Lord Nugent	1990-91	The Rt Hon. The Lord Griffiths
1963-64	G. O. B. Allen	1991-92	M. E. L. Melluish
1964-65	R. H. Twining	1992-94	D. R. W. Silk
1965-66	Lt-Gen. Sir Oliver Leese, Bart	1994-96	The Hon. Sir Oliver Popplewell
1966-67	Sir Alec Douglas-Home	1996-98	A. C. D. Ingleby-Mackenzie
1967-68	A. E. R. Gilligan	1998-2000	A. R. Lewis
1968-69	R. Aird	2000-01	Lord Alexander of Weedon
1969-70	M. J. C. Allom	2001-02	E. R. Dexter
1970-71	Sir Cyril Hawker	2002-03	Sir Timothy Rice
1971-72	F. R. Brown		

Since 1951, Presidents of MCC have taken office on October 1. Previously they took office immediately after the annual general meeting at the start of the season. From 1992 to 2000, Presidents were eligible for two consecutive years of office; since then the period has reverted to one year.

REGISTER OF CURRENT PLAYERS

 This list includes all players who appeared during 2001-02 or 2002 in:
- Tests or one-day internationals for a Test-playing country
- County Championship
- Pura Cup, SuperSport Series, Busta Cup and Duleep Trophy
- first-class domestic cricket, who previously played Tests or one-day internationals
- one-day internationals for Kenya and Holland
- first-class cricket for their country's senior touring team or A-team

Underlining indicates that a player is known by that name.

Teams are those played for in 2001-02 and/or 2002, or the last domestic team for which that player appeared.

Countries are those for which players are qualified.

Country of birth is given if it is not the one for which a player is qualified. It is also given to differentiate between nations in the Leeward and Windward Islands, and where it is essential for clarity.

* Test player

	Team	Country	Born	Birthplace
Aamer Hanif	Allied Bank	P	4.10.71	Karachi
* **Aamir Nazir**	Allied Bank	P	2.1.71	Lahore
Ababu Josephat Sorongo	Kenya	K	15.4.80	Kenya
* **Abdul Razzaq**	PIA/Middlesex	P	2.12.79	Lahore
Abrahams Shafiek	Northerns	SA	4.3.68	Port Elizabeth
Abrahams Umar	Eastern Province	SA	7.2.81	Port Elizabeth
Abrahim Zahir Ahmed	Griqualand West	SA	5.6.72	Robertson
* **Ackerman** Hylton Deon	Western Province	SA	14.2.73	Cape Town
* **Adams** Andre Ryan	Auckland	NZ	17.7.75	Auckland
* **Adams** Christopher John	Sussex	E	6.5.70	Whitwell
Adams Fabian <u>Alex</u>	Leeward Islands	WI	7.1.75	The Valley, Anguilla
Adams James Clive	Free State	WI	9.1.68	Port Maria
Adams James Henry Kenneth	Hampshire	E	23.9.80	Winchester
* **Adams** Paul Regan	Western Province	SA	20.1.77	Cape Town
* **Adcock** Nathan Tennyson	South Australia	A	22.4.78	Campbelltown
Adeel Raja	Holland	H	15.8.80	Lahore, Pakistan
* **Afzaal** Usman	Nottinghamshire	E	9.6.77	Rawalpindi, Pakistan
* **Agarkar** Ajit Bhalchandra	Mumbai	I	4.12.77	Bombay
Ahmed Kamal	Khulna	B	28.12.77	Court Para
Ahsanullah Hasan	Chittagong	B	15.10.79	Comilla
Akhtar Sarfraz	Peshawar/National Bank	P	20.2.76	Peshawar
* **Akram** Khan	Chittagong	B	1.11.68	Chittagong
* **Akram Raza**	Habib Bank	P	22.11.64	Lahore
* **Alamgir Kabir**	Rajshahi	B	10.1.81	Nababganj
Albertyn Wallace Andrew	Boland	SA	26.5.81	Alberton
Alexander Camilus Christopher	West Indies B	WI	20.10.81	Grenada
Ali Kabir	Worcestershire	E	24.11.80	Moseley
Ali Zaheer Reaz	Trinidad & Tobago	WI	17.1.81	Bamboo Village, Trinidad
* **Ali Naqvi**	Islamabad/KRL	P	19.3.77	Lahore
Alleyne David	Middlesex	E	17.4.76	York
Alleyne Mark Wayne	Gloucestershire	E	23.5.68	Tottenham
Ally-Haniff Azib	Guyana	WI	8.11.78	Port Mourant
* **Alok Kapali**	Sylhet	B	1.1.84	Sylhet
* **Al Sahariar**	Dhaka	B	23.4.78	Dhaka
Ambrose Timothy Raymond	Sussex	E	1.12.82	Newcastle, Australia

	Team	Country	Born	Birthplace
Amerasinghe Merenna Koralage Don Ishara	Nondescripts	SL	5.3.78	*Colombo*
Aminul Islam, jun.	Rajshahi	B	1.4.75	*Rajshahi*
* **Aminul Islam**, sen.	Dhaka	B	2.2.68	*Dhaka*
Amla Ahmed Mahomed	KwaZulu-Natal	SA	15.9.79	*Durban*
Amla Hashim Mahomed	KwaZulu-Natal	SA	31.3.83	*Durban*
Anderson James Michael	Lancashire	E	30.7.82	*Burnley*
Anderson Ricaldo Sherman Glenroy	Northamptonshire	E	22.9.76	*Hammersmith*
Angara Joseph Oduol	Kenya	K	8.11.71	*Nairobi*
* **Angel** Jo	Western Australia	A	22.4.68	*Mount Lawley*
Anisur Rahman	Barisal	B	1.3.71	*Dhaka*
Anwar Hossain (Monir)	Bangladesh A	B	31.12.81	*Munshiganj*
Anwar Hossain (Piju)	Bangladesh A	B	10.12.83	*Lalbagh*
Aphale Kaushik Dattatray	Maharashtra	I	18.11.78	*Pune*
* **Aqib Javed**	Allied Bank	P	5.8.72	*Sheikhupura*
Arendse Rayno Garth	Free State	SA	8.12.78	*Worcester*
Arjune Krishna	West Indies B	WI	3.9.80	*Unity Village, Guyana*
Arjune Vishal	West Indies B	WI	24.10.81	*Unity Village, Guyana*
Armstrong Sean Hussain	Barbados	WI	11.5.73	*Bayfield*
Arnberger Jason Lee	Victoria	A	18.11.72	*Penrith*
* **Arnold** Russel Premakumaran	Nondescripts	SL	25.10.73	*Colombo*
* **Arshad Khan**	Peshawar/Allied Bank	P	22.3.71	*Peshawar*
* **Asif Mujtaba**	Karachi/PIA	P	4.11.67	*Karachi*
* **Astle** Nathan John	Canterbury	NZ	15.9.71	*Christchurch*
* **Atapattu** Marvan Samson	Sinhalese	SL	22.11.70	*Kalutara*
* **Ata-ur-Rehman**	Allied Bank	P	28.3.75	*Lahore*
* **Atiq-uz-Zaman**	Karachi/Habib Bank	P	20.7.75	*Karachi*
Austin Ryan Anthony	Barbados	WI	15.11.81	*Arima, Trinidad*
Averis James Maxwell Michael	Gloucestershire	E	28.5.74	*Bristol*
Aymes Adrian Nigel	Hampshire	E	4.6.64	*Southampton*
* **Azhar Mahmood**	Islamabad/PIA/Surrey	P	28.2.75	*Rawalpindi*
* **Bacher** Adam Marc	Gauteng	SA	29.10.73	*Johannesburg*
* **Badani** Hemang Kamal	Tamil Nadu	I	14.11.76	*Madras*
Badree Samuel	Trinidad & Tobago	WI	8.3.81	*Barrackpore*
* **Bahutule** Sairaj Vasant	Mumbai	I	6.1.73	*Bombay*
Bailey Mark David	Northern Districts	NZ	26.11.70	*Hamilton*
Bailey Rupert	Easterns	SA	20.2.80	*Paarl*
Bailey Tobin Michael Barnaby	Northamptonshire	E	28.8.76	*Kettering*
Bakkes Herman Charles	Free State	SA	24.12.69	*Port Elizabeth*
Balaji Lakshmipathy	Tamil Nadu	I	27.9.81	*Madras*
Ball Martyn Charles John	Gloucestershire	E	26.4.70	*Bristol*
* **Bandara** Charitha Malinga	Nondescripts	SL	31.12.79	*Kalutara*
* **Bandaratilleke** Mapa Rallage Chandima Niroshan	Tamil Union	SL	16.5.75	*Colombo*
* **Bangar** Sanjay Bapusaheb	Railways	I	11.10.72	*Beed*
Banks Omari Ahmed Clemente	Leeward Islands	WI	17.7.82	*Anguilla*
Barik Ajay	Orissa	I	10.1.76	*Cuttack*
* **Barnett** Kim John	Gloucestershire	E	17.7.60	*Stoke-on-Trent*
Bassano Christopher Warwick Godfrey	Derbyshire	E	11.9.75	*East London, SA*
Bastow Jonathan Edward	KwaZulu-Natal	SA	12.2.74	*Pietermaritzburg*
Batty Gareth Jon	Worcestershire	E	13.10.77	*Bradford*
Batty Jonathan Neil	Surrey	E	18.4.74	*Chesterfield*
Baugh Carlton	West Indies B	WI	26.6.82	*Kingston*
Bedade Atul Chandrakant	Baroda	I	24.9.66	*Bombay*
Bell Ian Ronald	Warwickshire	E	11.4.82	*Walsgrave*
* **Bell** Matthew David	Wellington	NZ	25.2.77	*Dunedin*
Benfield Mark Rowland	Eastern Province	SA	3.12.76	*Potgietersrus*

	Team	Country	Born	Birthplace
Benkenstein Dale Martin	KwaZulu-Natal	SA	9.6.74	*Salisbury, Rhodesia*
Benn Sulieman Jamaal	Barbados	WI	22.7.81	*Haynesville*
Bennett Bevan Leon	Border	SA	9.9.81	*East London*
Bernard David Eddison	Jamaica	WI	19.7.81	*Kingston*
Berry Darren Shane	Victoria	A	10.12.69	*Melbourne*
Best Tino la Bertram	Barbados	WI	26.8.81	*Richmond Gap*
Betts Melvyn Morris	Warwickshire	E	26.3.75	*Sacriston*
Beukes Jonathan Alan	Free State	SA	15.3.79	*Kimberley*
* **Bevan** Michael Gwyl	New South Wales/Leics	A	8.5.70	*Belconnen*
Bhandari Amit	Delhi	I	1.10.78	*Delhi*
* **Bharadwaj** Raghvendrarao Vijay	Karnataka	I	15.8.75	*Bangalore*
Bhatia Vishal	Himachal Pradesh	I	6.12.81	*Hamirpur*
Bhoite Ajit Prataprao	Baroda	I	9.10.76	*Baroda*
* **Bichel** Andrew John	Queensland/Worcestershire	A	27.8.70	*Laidley*
Bicknell Darren John	Nottinghamshire	E	24.6.67	*Guildford*
* **Bicknell** Martin Paul	Surrey	E	14.1.69	*Guildford*
* **Bikash Ranjan Das**	Dhaka	B	14.7.82	*Dhaka*
Bishop Justin Edward	Essex/Durham UCCE	E	4.1.82	*Bury St Edmunds*
* **Black** Marlon Ian	Trinidad & Tobago	WI	7.6.75	*Trinidad*
Blackwell Ian David	Somerset	E	10.6.78	*Chesterfield*
Blain John Angus Rae	Northamptonshire	S	4.1.79	*Edinburgh*
* **Blakey** Richard John	Yorkshire	E	15.1.67	*Huddersfield*
* **Blewett** Gregory Scott	South Australia	A	29.10.71	*Adelaide*
Bloomfield Timothy Francis	Middlesex	E	31.5.73	*Ashford, Middlesex*
Bodi Ghulam Hussain	KwaZulu-Natal	SA	4.1.79	*Hathuran, India*
* **Boje** Nico	Free State/Nottinghamshire	SA	20.3.73	*Bloemfontein*
* **Bond** Shane Edward	Canterbury/Warwickshire	NZ	7.6.75	*Christchurch*
Bopara Ravinder Singh	Essex	E	4.5.85	*Forest Gate*
Bosman Lungile Loots	Griqualand West	SA	14.4.77	*Kimberley*
Bossenger Wendell	Griqualand West	SA	23.10.76	*Cape Town*
Boteju Jayawardene Welathanthrige Hemantha Devapriya	Colombo	SL	3.11.77	*Colombo*
Botha Anthony Greyvensteyn	Easterns	SA	17.11.76	*Pretoria*
Botha Johan	Eastern Province	SA	2.5.82	*Johannesburg*
Botha Peterus Johannes	Border	SA	28.9.66	*Vereeniging*
* **Boucher** Mark Verdon	Border	SA	3.12.76	*East London*
Bowler Peter Duncan	Somerset	E	30.7.63	*Plymouth*
Bracken Nathan Wade	New South Wales	A	12.9.77	*Penrith*
* **Bradburn** Grant Eric	Northern Districts	NZ	26.5.66	*Hamilton*
Bradfield Carl Crispin	Eastern Province	SA	18.1.75	*Grahamstown*
Bradshaw Ian David Russell	Barbados	WI	9.7.74	*Hopewell*
Brand Derek	Easterns	SA	29.5.75	*Bellville*
Brandy Damian Gareth	Leicestershire	E	14.9.81	*Highgate*
Brant Scott Andrew	Queensland	A	26.1.83	*Harare*
Bravo Dwayne James John	Trinidad & Tobago	WI	7.10.83	*Santa Cruz*
Breese Gareth Rohan	Jamaica	WI	9.1.76	*Montego Bay*
* **Brent** Gary Bazil	Manicaland	Z	13.1.76	*Sinoia*
Bridge Graeme David	Durham	E	4.9.80	*Sunderland*
Brooker Jason	Griqualand West	SA	16.1.77	*Kimberley*
Brophy Gerard Louis	Northamptonshire	SA	26.11.75	*Welkom, South Africa*
Brown Alistair Duncan	Surrey	E	11.2.70	*Beckenham*
Brown Darryl	Trinidad & Tobago	WI	18.12.73	*McBean*
Brown Duncan Loudon	KwaZulu-Natal	SA	23.6.79	*Durban*
Brown Douglas Robert	Warwickshire	E	29.10.69	*Stirling, Scotland*
Brown Jason Fred	Northamptonshire	E	10.10.74	*Newcastle-under-Lyme*
* **Brown** Simon John Emmerson	Durham	E	29.6.69	*Cleadon*
* **Browne** Courtney Oswald	Barbados	WI	7.12.70	*Lambeth, England*
Browne Patrick Anderson	West Indies B	WI	26.1.82	*Bayfield, Barbados*
Bruyns Mark Lloyd	Border	SA	8.11.73	*Pietermaritzburg*
Bryant James Douglas Campbell	Eastern Province	SA	4.2.76	*Durban*

	Team	Country	Born	Birthplace
Bryson Rudi Edwin	Easterns	SA	25.7.68	Springs
Buch Valmik Nalinkant	Baroda	I	29.8.75	Rajkot
Bula Thando Andrew	North West	SA	1.1.81	Whittlesea
Bulbeck Matthew Paul Leonard	Somerset	E	8.11.79	Taunton
Bundela Devendra Singh	Madhya Pradesh	I	22.2.77	Indore
Burger Shane	Gauteng	SA	31.8.82	Johannesburg
Burns Michael	Somerset	E	6.2.69	Barrow-in-Furness
Burns Neil David	Leicestershire	E	19.9.65	Chelmsford
* **Butcher** Mark Alan	Surrey	E	23.8.72	Croydon
Butler Deighton Calvin	Windward Islands	WI	14.7.74	South Rivers, St Vincent
* **Butler** Ian Gareth	Northern Districts	NZ	24.11.81	Middlemore
Buxton-Forman Jon	Gauteng	SA	15.11.74	Pietermaritzberg
Byas David	Lancashire	E	26.8.63	Kilham
* **Caddick** Andrew Richard	Somerset	E	21.11.68	Christchurch, NZ
* **Cairns** Christopher Lance	Canterbury	NZ	13.6.70	Picton
Callaghan David John	Eastern Province	SA	1.2.65	Queenstown
* **Campbell** Alistair Douglas Ross	Manicaland	Z	23.9.72	Salisbury
Campbell Ryan John	Western Australia	A	7.2.72	Osborne Park
* **Campbell** Sherwin Legay	Barbados	WI	1.11.70	Bridgetown
Carberry Michael Alexander	Surrey	E	29.9.80	Croydon
* **Carlisle** Stuart Vance	Mashonaland A	Z	10.5.72	Salisbury
Carr William Niall	Victoria	A	1.6.76	Melbourne
Carseldine Lee Andrew	Queensland	A	17.11.75	Nambour
Carter Neil Miller	Warwickshire	E	29.1.75	Cape Town, South Africa
Cary Sean Ross	Western Australia	A	10.3.71	Subiaco
Casimir Kirsten Nicole	Windward Islands	WI	28.5.78	Dominica
Cassar Matthew Edward	Northamptonshire	E	16.10.72	Sydney, Australia
Cassell Jerry Lee	Queensland	A	12.1.75	Mona Vale
* **Chandana** Umagiliya Durage Upul	Tamil Union	SL	7.5.72	Galle
* **Chanderpaul** Shivnarine	Guyana	WI	16.8.74	Unity Village
Chapple Glen	Lancashire	E	23.1.74	Skipton
Chattergoon Sewnarine	Guyana	WI	3.4.81	Fyrish
Chatterjee Utpal	Bengal	I	13.7.64	Calcutta
Cherry Daniel David	Glamorgan	E	7.2.80	Newport
Chilton Mark James	Lancashire	E	2.10.76	Sheffield
Chopra Akash	Delhi	I	19.9.77	Agra
* **Chopra** Nikhil	Uttar Pradesh	I	26.12.73	Allahabad
Christopher Ricky Joseph	Leeward Islands	WI	26.3.75	Antigua
Cilliers Grant	North West	SA	13.12.78	Ermelo
Clapp Dominic Adrian	Sussex	E	25.5.80	Southport
Clark Anthony Michael	New South Wales	A	23.3.77	St Leonards
Clark Michael Wayne	Western Australia	A	31.3.78	Mount Lawley
Clark Stuart Rupert	New South Wales	A	28.9.75	Sutherland
Clarke Andrew John	Essex	E	9.11.75	Brentwood
Clarke Michael John	New South Wales	A	2.4.81	Liverpool
Clarke Rikki	Surrey	E	29.9.81	Orsett
Clarke Shirley MacDonald	Barbados	WI	21.1.77	Baywoods
Clifford Jeffrey Ian	Warwickshire	E	12.10.82	Birmingham
Clingeleffer Sean Geoffrey	Tasmania	A	9.5.80	Hobart
Clinton Richard Selvey	Essex	E	1.9.81	Sidcup
Collingwood Paul David	Durham	E	26.5.76	Shotley Bridge
* **Collins** Pedro Tyrone	Barbados	WI	12.8.76	Boscobelle
* **Collymore** Corey Dalanelo	Barbados	WI	21.12.77	Boscobelle
Conrad Siraaj	Gauteng	SA	25.2.78	Cape Town
Cook Jeffrey William	Northamptonshire	E	2.2.72	Sydney, Australia
Cook Stephen Craig	Gauteng	SA	29.11.82	Johannesburg
Cook Simon James	Middlesex	E	15.1.77	Oxford
* **Cork** Dominic Gerald	Derbyshire	E	7.8.71	Newcastle-under-Lyme
Cornwall Wilden Winston	Leeward Islands	WI	29.4.73	Liberta, Antigua

	Team	Country	Born	Birthplace
Cosker Dean Andrew	Glamorgan	E	7.1.78	Weymouth
Cottey Phillip Anthony	Sussex	E	2.6.66	Swansea
Cousins Darren Mark	Northamptonshire	E	24.9.71	Cambridge
Cowan Ashley Preston	Essex	E	7.5.75	Hitchin
Cox Jamie	Tasmania/Somerset	A	15.10.69	Burnie
Craven Victor John	Yorkshire	E	31.7.80	Harrogate
* **Crawley** John Paul	Hampshire	E	21.9.71	Maldon
* **Croft** Robert Damien Bale	Glamorgan	E	25.5.70	Morriston
Crookes Derek Norman	Easterns	SA	5.3.69	Mariannhill
Crowe Carl Daniel	Leicestershire	E	25.11.75	Leicester
Cuff Wayne Everton	Jamaica	WI	26.12.71	Kingston
* **Cuffy** Cameron Eustace	Windward Islands	WI	8.2.70	South Rivers, St Vincent
* **Cullinan** Daryll John	Gauteng	SA	4.3.67	Kimberley
Cunliffe Robert John	Leicestershire	E	8.11.73	Oxford
Cunningham Ryan Orlando	Jamaica	WI	29.5.78	Kingston
Currency Romel Kwesi	Windward Islands	WI	7.5.82	St Vincent
Cush Lennox Joseph	Guyana	WI	12.12.74	Georgetown
Cyster Andrew William	Boland	SA	31.3.79	Stellenbosch
Dagnall Charles Edward	Leicestershire	E	10.7.76	Bury
* **Dahiya** Vijay	Delhi	I	10.5.73	Delhi
Dakin Jonathan Michael	Essex	E	28.2.73	Hitchin
* **Dale** Adam Craig	Queensland	A	30.12.68	Ivanhoe
Dale Adrian	Glamorgan	E	24.10.68	Germiston, South Africa
Daley James Arthur	Durham	E	24.9.73	Sunderland
Dalrymple James William Murray	Middx/Oxford UCCE	E	21.1.81	Nairobi, Kenya
Daniel Gerald Ian	Bloomfield	SL	17.8.81	Colombo
* **Danish** Kaneria	Karachi/Habib Bank	P	16.12.80	Karachi
Darlington Kevin Godfrey	Guyana	WI	26.4.72	New Amsterdam
Das Parag Kumar	Assam	I	29.10.76	Gauhati
Das Subhomoy Gupinath	Bengal	I	26.12.81	Calcutta
* **Das** Shiv Sunder	Orissa	I	5.11.77	Bhubaneswar
* **Dasgupta** Deep	Bengal	I	7.6.77	Calcutta
Davids Henry	Boland	SA	19.1.80	Stellenbosch
Davies Anthony Mark	Durham	E	4.10.80	Stockton-on-Tees
Davies Andrew Philip	Glamorgan	E	7.11.76	Neath
Davies Christopher James	South Australia	A	15.11.78	Adelaide
Davis Mark Jeffrey Gronow	Sussex	E	10.10.71	Port Elizabeth, SA
Dawes Joseph Henry	Queensland	A	29.8.70	Herston
Dawson Alan Charles	Western Province	SA	27.11.69	Cape Town
* **Dawson** Richard Kevin James	Yorkshire	E	4.8.80	Doncaster
Dean Kevin James	Derbyshire	E	16.10.75	Derby
de Bruyn Pierre	Easterns	SA	31.3.77	Pretoria
* **DeFreitas** Phillip Anthony Jason	Leicestershire	E	18.2.66	Scotts Head, Dominica
Deitz Shane Andrew	South Australia	A	4.5.75	Bankstown
de Lange Con de Wet	Boland	SA	11.2.81	Bellville
De Leede Timotheus Bernardus Maria	Holland	H	25.1.68	Leidschendam
Dempsey Darren Michael	South Australia	A	17.10.75	Mount Gambier
Denton Gerard John	Tasmania	A	7.8.75	Mount Isa
Deonarine Narsingh	Guyana	WI	8.8.83	New Amsterdam
* **de Saram** Samantha Indika	Tamil Union	SL	2.9.73	Matara
* **de Silva** Karunakalage Sajeewa Chanaka	Burgher	SL	11.1.71	Kalutara
* **de Silva** Pinnaduwage Aravinda	Nondescripts	SL	17.10.65	Colombo
* **de Silva** Sanjeewa Kumara Lanka	Burgher	SL	29.7.75	Kurunegala
* **de Silva** Weddikkara Ruwan Sujeewa	Sebastianites	SL	7.10.79	Beruwala
de Vos Dirk Johannes Jacobus	North West	SA	15.6.75	Pretoria
de Wet Friedel	Northerns	SA	26.6.80	Rustenburg
de Wett Burton Christopher	Border	SA	25.12.80	East London
Dharmani Pankaj	Punjab	I	27.9.74	Delhi

	Team	Country	Born	Birthplace
* **Dharmasena** Handunnettige Deepthi Priyantha <u>Kumar</u>	Bloomfield	SL	24.4.71	*Colombo*
Dighe Samir Sudhakar	Mumbai	I	8.10.68	*Bombay*
Dighton Michael Gray	Tasmania	A	24.4.76	*Toowoomba*
Dillon Mervyn	Trinidad & Tobago	WI	5.6.74	*Toco*
* **Dilshan** Tillekeratne Mudiyanselage	Bloomfield	SL	14.10.76	*Kalutara*
Dipha Lazola	Eastern Province	SA	17.10.82	*Port Elizabeth*
* **Dippenaar** Hendrik Human	Free State	SA	14.6.77	*Kimberley*
Di Venuto Michael James	Tasmania/Derbyshire	A	12.12.73	*Hobart*
Dladla Nhlanhla	KwaZulu-Natal	SA	9.8.80	*Pietermaritzberg*
Dobson Derrick Kevin	Griqualand West	SA	23.9.78	*Kimberley*
Doherty Xavier John	Tasmania	A	22.11.82	*Scottsdale*
* **Donald** Allan Anthony	Free State/Worcestershire	SA	20.10.66	*Bloemfontein*
* **Doull** Simon Blair	Northern Districts	NZ	6.8.69	*Pukekohe*
Dowlin Travis Montague	Guyana	WI	24.2.77	*Georgetown*
Dowman Mathew Peter	Derbyshire	E	10.5.74	*Grantham*
Downton Andrew Graham	Tasmania	A	17.7.77	*Auburn*
Drakes Vasbert Conniel	Border	WI	5.8.69	*Springhead, Barbados*
* **Dravid** Rahul	Karnataka	I	11.1.73	*Indore*
Dreyer Jan Nicolaas	North West	SA	9.9.76	*Amanzimtoti*
Driver Ryan Craig	Lancashire	E	30.4.79	*Truro*
Dros Gerald	Northerns	SA	2.4.73	*Pretoria*
* **Drum** Christopher James	Auckland	NZ	10.7.74	*Auckland*
Duckworth Kevin Dion	Eastern Province	SA	27.3.74	*Salisbury, Rhodesia*
Dugmore Warren Alan	Gauteng	SA	27.2.77	*Johannesburg*
Dumelow Nathan Robert Charles	Derbyshire	E	30.4.81	*Derby*
Duminy Jean-Paul	Western Province	SA	14.4.84	*Strandfontein*
Dutch Keith Philip	Somerset	E	21.3.73	*Harrow*
du Toit Willem Johannes	Boland	SA	18.3.81	*Cape Town*
* **Ealham** Mark Alan	Kent	E	27.8.69	*Willesborough*
* **Ebrahim** Dion Digby	Mashonaland	Z	7.8.80	*Bulawayo*
Edwards Fidel Henderson	Barbados	WI	6.2.82	*Gays*
* **Ehsanul Haque**	Chittagong	B	1.12.79	*Chittagong*
* **Eksteen** Clive Edward	Gauteng	SA	2.12.66	*Johannesburg*
Elliott Grant David	Gauteng	SA	21.3.79	*Johannesburg*
* **Elliott** Matthew Thomas Gray	Victoria/Yorkshire	A	28.9.71	*Chelsea*
Elstub Christopher John	Yorkshire	E	3.2.81	*Dewsbury*
* **Elworthy** Steven	Northerns	SA	23.2.65	*Bulawayo, Rhodesia*
* **Enamul Haque**	Chittagong	B	27.2.67	*Comilla*
Enslin Christian Thinus	North West	SA	16.9.75	*Klerksdorp*
Ervine Sean Michael	Midlands	Z	6.12.82	*Harare*
Esmeijer Jacob-Jan	Holland	H	28.5.72	*Rotterdam*
Eugene John	Windward Islands	WI	16.8.70	*St Lucia*
* **Evans** Craig Neil	Mashonaland	Z	29.11.69	*Salisbury*
* **Fahim Muntasir**	Dhaka	B	1.11.80	*Mymensingh*
* **Fairbrother** Neil Harvey	Lancashire	E	9.9.63	*Warrington*
* **Faisal Iqbal**	Karachi/PIA	P	30.12.81	*Karachi*
* **Fazl-e-Akbar**	Peshawar/PIA	P	20.10.80	*Peshawar*
Fellows Gary Matthew	Yorkshire	E	30.7.78	*Halifax*
Feris Christo Edward	Free State	SA	18.1.76	*Upington*
Fernando Conganige Randhi <u>Dilhara</u>	Sinhalese	SL	19.7.79	*Colombo*
Fernando Charith Sylvester	Chilaw Marians	SL	30.12.82	*Badulla*
Fernando Kandage <u>Hasantha</u> Ruwan Kumara	Sebastianites	SL	14.10.79	*Panadura*
* **Fernando** Thudellage <u>Charitha Buddhika</u>	Panadura	SL	22.8.80	*Panadura*
Fernando Upekha Ashantha	Sinhalese	SL	17.12.79	*Colombo*
Ferreira Lloyd Douglas	Western Province	SA	6.5.74	*Johannesburg*
Fisher Ian Douglas	Gloucestershire	E	31.5.76	*Bradford*

	Team	Country	Born	Birthplace
Fitzgerald David Andrew	South Australia	A	30.11.72	Osborne Park
* **Fleming** Damien William	Victoria	A	24.4.70	Bentley
Fleming Matthew Valentine	Kent	E	12.12.64	Macclesfield
Fleming Stephen Paul	Wellington	NZ	1.4.73	Christchurch
* **Flintoff** Andrew	Lancashire	E	6.12.77	Preston
* **Flower** Andrew	Mashonaland/Essex	Z	28.4.68	Cape Town, SA
* **Flower** Grant William	Mashonaland A/Leics	Z	20.12.70	Salisbury
Flusk Gareth Edward	Easterns	SA	8.11.74	Johannesburg
* **Foster** James Savin	Essex	E	15.4.80	Whipps Cross
Francis John Daniel	Hampshire	E	13.11.80	Bromley
Francis Simon Richard George	Somerset	E	15.8.78	Bromley
* **Franklin** James Edward Charles	Wellington	NZ	7.11.80	Wellington
Franks Paul John	Nottinghamshire	E	3.2.79	Mansfield
* **Fraser** Angus Robert Charles	Middlesex	E	8.8.65	Billinge
Friderichs Bruce Ronald	Eastern Province	SA	27.9.79	King William's Town
* **Friend** Travis John	Midlands	Z	7.1.81	Kwekwe
Frost Tony	Warwickshire	E	17.11.75	Stoke-on-Trent
Fulton David Paul	Kent	E	15.11.71	Lewisham
Gait Andrew Ian	Derbyshire	SA	19.12.78	Bulawayo, Rhodesia
* **Gallage** Indika Sanjeewa	Burgher	SL	22.11.75	Panadura
* **Gallian** Jason Edward Riche	Nottinghamshire	E	25.6.71	Sydney, Australia
Gamage Janak Champika	Kurunegala Youth	SL	17.4.64	Matara
Gambhir Gautam	Delhi	I	14.10.81	Delhi
Gamiet Laden Liep	Border	SA	23.1.78	East London
* **Gandhi** Devang Jayant	Bengal	I	6.9.71	Bhavnagar
Ganegama Withanaarchchige Chamara Akalanka	Nondescripts	SL	29.3.81	Colombo
* **Ganesh** Doddanarasiah	Karnataka	I	30.6.73	Bangalore
Ganga Daren	Trinidad & Tobago	WI	14.1.79	Barrackpore
* **Ganguly** Sourav Chandidas	Bengal	I	8.7.72	Calcutta
Gannon Benjamin Ward	Gloucestershire	E	5.9.75	Oxford
* **Garrick** Leon Vivian	Jamaica	WI	11.11.76	St Ann
Gavaskar Rohan Sunil	Bengal	I	20.2.76	Kanpur
* **Gayle** Christopher Henry	Jamaica	WI	21.9.79	Kingston
George Mulligan Frank	Northerns	SA	10.9.76	Cape Town
* **Germon** Lee Kenneth	Otago	NZ	4.11.68	Christchurch
Ghulam Ali	Karachi/PIA	P	8.9.66	Karachi
* **Gibbs** Herschelle Herman	Western Province	SA	23.2.74	Cape Town
* **Giddins** Edward Simon Hunter	Surrey	E	20.7.71	Eastbourne
Gidley Martyn Ian	Griqualand West	SA	30.9.68	Leicester, England
Gidman Alexander Peter Richard	Gloucestershire	E	22.6.81	High Wycombe
* **Gilchrist** Adam Craig	Western Australia	A	14.11.71	Bellingen
Gilder Gary Michael	KwaZulu-Natal	SA	6.7.74	Salisbury, Rhodesia
* **Giles** Ashley Fraser	Warwickshire	E	19.3.73	Chertsey
* **Gillespie** Jason Neil	South Australia	A	19.4.75	Darlinghurst
Gobind Rivash	KwaZulu-Natal	SA	20.4.82	Durban
Godbole Niranjan Ajit	Maharashtra	I	26.11.76	Nagpur
Golding James Mathew	Kent	E	19.7.77	Canterbury
Gonsalves Andrew	Guyana	WI	31.5.78	Suddie
* **Goodwin** Murray William	W. Australia/Sussex	Z	11.12.72	Salisbury, Rhodesia
* **Gough** Darren	Yorkshire	E	18.9.70	Barnsley
Gough Michael Andrew	Durham	E	18.12.79	Hartlepool
Gowda Yere	Railways	I	27.11.71	Raichur
Grace Graham Vernon	North West	SA	16.8.75	Salisbury, Rhodesia
Grandia Victor D.	Holland	H	10.1.79	Amsterdam
Grant Joseph Benjamin	Essex	WI	17.12.68	Montego Bay, Jamaica
Gray Andrew Kenneth Donovan	Yorkshire	E	19.5.74	Armadale
Grayson Adrian Paul	Essex	E	31.3.71	Ripon
Greenidge Carl Gary	Northamptonshire	E	20.4.78	Basingstoke

	Team	Country	Born	Birthplace
Griffith Reon	West Indies B	WI	8.1.79	*Guyana*
* **Gripper** Trevor Raymond	Mashonaland	Z	28.12.75	*Salisbury*
Grove Jamie Oliver	Leicestershire	E	3.7.79	*Bury St Edmunds*
Gunaratne Pulasthi Waruna	Antonians	SL	27.9.73	*Colombo*
* **Gunawardene** Dihan <u>Avishka</u>	Sinhalese	SL	26.5.77	*Colombo*
Gupta Sandeep Kumar	Kenya	K	7.4.67	*Nairobi*
* **Habib** Aftab	Essex	E	7.2.72	*Reading*
* **Habibul Bashar**	Biman	B	17.8.72	*Kushtia*
Haddin Bradley James	New South Wales	A	23.10.77	*Cowra*
Hall Andrew James	Easterns	SA	31.7.75	*Johannesburg*
Hamblin James Rupert Christopher	Hampshire	E	16.8.78	*Pembury*
Hamilton Gavin Mark	Yorkshire	E	16.9.74	*Broxburn*
Hancock Timothy Harold Coulter	Gloucestershire	E	20.4.72	*Reading*
Haniff Azeemul	Guyana	WI	24.10.77	*Hampton Court*
* **Hannan Sarkar**	Barisal	B	1.12.82	*Dhaka*
* **Harbhajan Singh**	Punjab	I	3.7.80	*Jullundur*
* **Harmison** Stephen James	Durham	E	23.10.78	*Ashington*
Harris Andrew James	Nottinghamshire	E	26.6.73	*Ashton-under-Lyne*
* **Harris** Chris Zinzan	Canterbury	NZ	20.11.69	*Christchurch*
Harris Paul Lee	Western Province	SA	2.11.78	*Salisbury, Rhodesia*
Harris Ryan James	South Australia	A	11.10.79	*Nowra*
Harrison David Stuart	Glamorgan	E	30.7.81	*Newport*
Harrity Mark Andrew	South Australia	A	9.3.74	*Semaphore*
* **Hart** Matthew Norman	Northern Districts	NZ	16.5.72	*Hamilton*
* **Hart** Robert Garry	Northern Districts	NZ	2.12.74	*Hamilton*
Harunur Rashid	Barisal	B	30.11.68	*Mymensingh*
Harvey Ian Joseph	Victoria/Gloucestershire	A	10.4.72	*Wonthaggi*
Harvey Kade Murray	Western Australia	A	7.10.75	*Subiaco*
* **Harvinder Singh**	Railways	I	23.12.77	*Amritsar*
* **Hasan Raza**	Karachi/Habib Bank	P	11.3.82	*Karachi*
Hasanuzzaman	Khulna	B	15.1.75	*Jessore*
* **Hasibul Hussain**	Sylhet	B	3.6.77	*Dhaka*
* **Haslam** Mark James	Auckland	NZ	26.9.72	*Bury, England*
Hatch Nicholas Guy	Durham	E	21.4.79	*Darlington*
* **Hathurusinghe** Upul <u>Chandika</u>	Moors	SL	13.9.68	*Colombo*
Hauritz Nathan Michael	Queensland	A	18.10.81	*Wondai*
* **Hayden** Matthew Lawrence	Queensland	A	29.10.71	*Kingaroy*
Haynes Jamie Jonathan	Lancashire	E	5.7.74	*Bristol*
* **Hayward** Mornantau	Eastern Province	SA	6.3.77	*Uitenhage*
Hector Benjamin	Boland	SA	5.8.79	*Durban*
* **Hegg** Warren Kevin	Lancashire	E	23.2.68	*Whitefield*
Hemp David Lloyd	Glamorgan	E	8.11.70	*Hamilton, Bermuda*
* **Henderson** Claude William	Western Province	SA	14.6.72	*Worcester*
Henderson James Michael	Boland	SA	6.8.75	*Worcester*
Henderson Tyron	Border	SA	1.8.74	*Durban*
* **Herath** Herath Mudiyanselage Rangana Keerthi Bandara	Moors	SL	19.3.78	*Kurunegala*
* **Hettiarachchi** Dinuka	Colts	SL	15.7.76	*Colombo*
Hewett Ian Stephen Louis	Victoria	A	24.1.76	*East Melbourne*
Hewitt Glen Michael	North West	SA	16.4.73	*Johannesburg*
Hewitt James Peter	Kent	E	26.2.76	*Southwark*
Hewson Dominic Robert	Derbyshire	E	3.10.74	*Cheltenham*
Hibbert Keith Hugh	Jamaica	WI	14.6.80	*St Catherine*
* **Hick** Graeme Ashley	Worcestershire	E	23.5.66	*Salisbury, Rhodesia*
Higgins Benjamin Hugh	South Australia	A	8.3.72	*Adelaide*
Higgs Mark Anthony	New South Wales	A	30.6.76	*Queanbeyan*
Hills Dene Fleetwood	Tasmania	A	27.8.70	*Wynyard*
* **Hinds** Ryan O'Neal	Barbados	WI	17.2.81	*Holders Hill*
* **Hinds** Wavell Wayne	Jamaica	WI	7.9.76	*Kingston*

	Team	Country	Born	Birthplace
Hinkel Warwick Robert	Border	SA	18.6.81	East London
* **Hirwani** Narendra Deepchand	Madhya Pradesh	I	18.10.68	Gorakhpur
Hitchcock Paul Anthony	Wellington	NZ	23.1.75	Whangarei
Hockley James Bernard	Kent	E	16.4.79	Beckenham
Hodge Bradley John	Victoria/Durham	A	29.12.74	Sandringham
Hodge Chaka Jara Kwahme	West Indies B	WI	20.11.82	The Valley, Anguilla
* **Hogg** George Bradley	Western Australia	A	6.2.71	Narrogin
Hogg Kyle William	Lancashire	E	2.7.83	Birmingham
* **Hoggard** Matthew James	Yorkshire	E	31.12.76	Leeds
* **Holder** Roland Irwin Christopher	West Indies B	WI	22.12.67	Port-of-Spain, Trinidad
* **Hollioake** Adam John	Surrey	E	5.9.71	Melbourne, Australia
* **Hollioake** Benjamin Caine	Surrey	E	11.11.77	Melbourne, Australia
Died March 23, 2002.				
Holloway Piran Charles Laity	Somerset	E	1.10.70	Helston
Holmes Matthew Keith	North West	SA	8.12.73	Cape Town
Homani Zwelibanzi	Eastern Province	SA	12.12.83	Port Elizabeth
* **Hondo** Douglas Tafadzwa	Mashonaland A	Z	7.7.79	Bulawayo
* **Hooper** Carl Llewellyn	Guyana	WI	15.12.66	Georgetown
Hopes James Redfern	Queensland	A	24.10.78	Townsville
Hopkinson Carl Daniel	Sussex	E	14.9.81	Brighton
* **Horne** Matthew Jeffery	Auckland	NZ	5.12.70	Takapuna
Howell Llorne Gregory	Auckland	NZ	8.7.72	Napier
Hughes Jonathan	Glamorgan	E	30.6.81	Pontypridd
* **Humayun Farhat**	Lahore City/Allied Bank	P	24.1.81	Lahore
Hunter Ian David	Durham	E	11.9.79	Durham
* **Hussain** Nasser	Essex	E	28.3.68	Madras, India
Hussey Michael Edward Killeen	W. Australia/Northants	A	27.5.75	Morley
Hutchison Paul Michael	Sussex	E	9.6.77	Leeds
Hutton Benjamin Leonard	Middlesex	E	29.1.77	Johannesburg, S. Africa
* **Ijaz Ahmed**, jun.	Faisalabad/Allied Bank	P	2.2.69	Lyallpur
* **Ilott** Mark Christopher	Essex	E	27.8.70	Watford
Imran Abbas	Gujranwala/ADBP	P	25.3.78	Gujranwala
* **Imran Farhat**	Lahore City/Habib Bank	P	20.5.82	Lahore
* **Imran Nazir**	Sheikhupura/National Bank	P	16.12.81	Gujranwala
Ingty Mark Julien Vernon	Assam	I	16.9.76	Shillong
Innes Kevin John	Sussex	E	24.9.75	Wellingborough
Inness Mathew William Hunter	Victoria/Northamptonshire	A	13.1.78	East Melbourne
* **Inzamam-ul-Haq**	National Bank	P	3.3.70	Multan
* **Irani** Ronald Charles	Essex	E	26.10.71	Leigh, Lancashire
Irfan Bhatti	Islamabad	P	28.9.64	Peshawar
* **Irfan Fazil**	Lahore City/Habib Bank	P	2.11.81	Lahore
Jackson Andy S.	Trinidad & Tobago	WI	4.3.79	Trinidad
Jackson Ivan Orlanzo	Windward Islands	WI	16.6.74	St Vincent
Jackson Kenneth Charles	Boland	SA	16.8.64	Kitwe, Zambia
Jacobs Arno	North West	SA	13.3.77	Potchefstroom
Jacobs David Johan	North West	SA	4.11.82	Potchefstroom
* **Jacobs** Ridley Detamore	Leeward Islands	WI	26.11.67	Swetes Village, Antigua
Jahangir Alam	Dhaka	B	5.3.73	Narayanganj
James Denzil	Trinidad & Tobago	WI	12.12.82	Moruga
* **James** Stephen Peter	Glamorgan	E	7.9.67	Lydney
Jan Asif Iqbal	Trinidad & Tobago	WI	11.2.79	Mafeking Village
Jan Imran Haniff	Trinidad & Tobago	WI	11.2.79	Mafeking Village
Jaques Philip Anthony	New South Wales	A	3.5.79	Wollongong
* **Javed Omar**	Dhaka	B	25.11.76	Dhaka
* **Jayasuriya** Sanath Teran	Bloomfield	SL	30.6.69	Matara
* **Jayawardene** Denagamage Proboth Mahela De Silva	Sinhalese	SL	27.5.77	Colombo

	Team	Country	Born	Birthplace
* **Jayawardene** Hewasandatchige Asiri Prasanna Wishwanath	Colombo	SL	10.9.79	*Colombo*
Jeffers Shane Melvon	West Indies B	WI	12.9.81	*St Kitts*
Jefferson William Ingleby	Essex/Durham UCCE	E	25.10.79	*Derby*
Jennings Dylan	Easterns	SA	14.9.79	*Johannesburg*
Jeremy Kerry Clifford Bryan	Leeward Islands	WI	6.2.80	*Antigua*
Jewell Nicholas	Victoria	A	27.8.77	*Melbourne*
Jhalani Rohit Banwarilal	Rajasthan	I	1.9.78	*Jaipur*
Johnson Benjamin Andrew	South Australia	A	1.8.73	*Naracoorte*
Johnson Mitchell Guy	Queensland	A	2.11.81	*Townsville*
* **Johnson** Neil Clarkson	W. Province/Hants	Z	24.1.70	*Salisbury*
Johnson Paul	Nottinghamshire	E	24.4.65	*Newark*
Johnson Richard Leonard	Somerset	E	29.12.74	*Chertsey*
Jones Geraint Owen	Kent	E	14.7.76	*Kundiawa, Papua N.G.*
Jones Ian	Middlesex	E	11.3.77	*Edmonton*
Jones Philip Steffan	Somerset	E	9.2.74	*Llanelli*
* **Jones** Simon Philip	Glamorgan	E	25.12.78	*Swansea*
Joseph David Rolston Emmanuel	Leeward Islands	WI	15.11.69	*Antigua*
Joseph Sylvester Cleofoster	Leeward Islands	WI	5.9.78	*New Winthorpes, Antigua*
* **Joshi** Sunil Bandacharya	Karnataka	I	6.6.69	*Gadag*
Joubert Pierre	Northerns	SA	2.5.78	*Pretoria*
Joyce Edmund Christopher	Middlesex	E	22.9.78	*Dublin, Ireland*
Jurgensen Shane John	Tasmania	A	28.4.76	*Redcliffe*
* **Kabir Khan**	Peshawar/Habib Bank	P	12.4.74	*Peshawar*
* **Kaif** Mohammad	Uttar Pradesh/Leics	I	1.12.80	*Allahabad*
Kale Abhijit Vasant	Maharashtra	I	3.7.73	*Ahmednagar*
* **Kallis** Jacques Henry	Western Province	SA	16.10.75	*Cape Town*
Kalpage Ruwan Senani	Nondescripts	SL	19.2.70	*Kandy*
* **Kaluwitharana** Romesh Shantha	Colts	SL	24.11.69	*Colombo*
Kamande James Kabatha	Kenya	K	12.12.78	*Muranga*
* **Kambli** Vinod Ganpat	Mumbai	I	18.1.72	*Bombay*
Kanhai Aneil	Trinidad & Tobago	WI	12.4.82	*Diego Martin*
* **Kanitkar** Hrishikesh Hemant	Maharashtra	I	14.11.74	*Poona*
Kanwat Rahul Jagdish	Rajasthan	I	21.10.74	*Jaipur*
* **Kapoor** Aashish Rakesh	Tamil Nadu	I	25.3.71	*Madras*
* **Kartik** Murali	Railways	I	11.9.76	*Madras*
Kashif Raza	Sheikhupura/WAPDA	P	26.12.79	*Sheikhupura*
* **Kasprowicz** Michael Scott	Queensland/Glamorgan	A	10.2.72	*South Brisbane*
* **Katich** Simon Mathew	Western Australia/Yorkshire	A	21.8.75	*Middle Swan*
Kavaljit Singh	Jammu and Kashmir	I	11.11.73	*Jammu*
Keedy Gary	Lancashire	E	27.11.74	*Wakefield*
Keegan Chad Blake	Middlesex	E	30.7.79	*Santon, South Africa*
* **Kemp** Justin Miles	Eastern Province	SA	2.10.77	*Queenstown*
Kendall William Salwey	Hampshire	E	18.12.73	*Wimbledon*
Kent John Carter	KwaZulu-Natal	SA	7.5.79	*Cape Town*
Kenway Derek Anthony	Hampshire	E	12.6.78	*Fareham*
Kerr Jason Ian Douglas	Derbyshire	E	7.4.74	*Bolton*
* **Key** Robert William Trevor	Kent	E	12.5.79	*East Dulwich*
* **Khaled Mahmud**	Dhaka	B	26.7.71	*Dhaka*
* **Khaled Masud**	Rajshahi	B	8.2.76	*Rajshahi*
Khan Amjad	Kent	E	14.10.80	*Copenhagen*
Khoda Gagan Kishanlal	Rajasthan	I	24.10.74	*Barmer*
Khurasiya Amay Ramsevak	Madhya Pradesh	I	18.5.72	*Jabalpur*
Kidwell Errol Wayne	Griqualand West	SA	6.6.75	*Vereeniging*
Killeen Neil	Durham	E	17.10.75	*Shotley Bridge*
* **King** Reon Dane	Guyana	WI	6.10.75	*Georgetown*
Kirby Steven Paul	Yorkshire	E	4.10.77	*Bury*
* **Kirsten** Gary	Western Province	SA	23.11.67	*Cape Town*
Kirtley Robert James	Sussex	E	10.1.75	*Eastbourne*

	Team	Country	Born	Birthplace
Klinger Michael	Victoria	A	4.7.80	Kew
Kloppenburg Jan Feiko	Holland	H	19.6.74	Haarlem
* **Klusener** Lance	KwaZulu-Natal/Notts	SA	4.9.71	Durban
* **Knight** Nicholas Verity	Warwickshire	E	28.11.69	Watford
Koch Donovan Marius	Boland	SA	11.10.76	Somerset West
Koen Louis Johannes	Boland	SA	28.3.67	Paarl
Koenig Sven Gaetan	Middlesex	SA	9.12.73	Durban, South Africa
Koortzen Pieter Petrus Johannes	Griqualand West	SA	24.9.79	Kimberley
Kops Brent Bjorn	Eastern Province	SA	1.11.82	Port Elizabeth
Kotak Shitanshu Hargovindbhai	Saurashtra	I	19.10.72	Rajkot
Kremerskothen Scott Paul	Tasmania	A	5.1.79	Launceston
Kreusch Justin Peter	Border	SA	27.9.79	East London
Krikken Karl Matthew	Derbyshire	E	9.4.69	Bolton
Kruger Alan Kevin	Griqualand West	SA	16.2.81	Kimberley
Kruger Garnett John-Peter	Eastern Province	SA	5.1.77	Port Elizabeth
Kruis Gideon Jacobus	Griqualand West	SA	9.5.74	Pretoria
Kumaran Thirunavukkarasu	Tamil Nadu	I	30.12.75	Madras
* **Kumble** Anil	Karnataka	I	17.10.70	Bangalore
Lahiri Saurasish Sukanta	Bengal	I	9.9.81	Howrah
Lake Anthony Jermaine Alphonso	Leeward Islands	WI	22.3.74	Antigua
* **Lakshitha** Materba Kanatha Gamage Chamila Premanath	Air Force	SL	4.1.79	Unawatuna
Also known as Chamila Gamage.				
Lambert Grant Michael	New South Wales	A	5.8.77	Parramatta
Laney Jason Scott	Hampshire	E	27.4.73	Winchester
* **Langer** Justin Lee	Western Australia	A	21.11.70	Perth
Langeveldt Charl Kenneth	Boland	SA	17.12.74	Stellenbosch
* **Lara** Brian Charles	Trinidad & Tobago	WI	2.5.69	Santa Cruz
Laraman Aaron William	Middlesex	E	10.1.79	Enfield
Law Danny Richard	Durham	E	15.7.75	Lambeth
* **Law** Stuart Grant	Queensland/Lancashire	A	18.10.68	Herston
Lawson Jermaine Jay Charles	Jamaica	WI	13.1.82	Spanish Town
* **Laxman** Vangipurappu Venkata Sai	Hyderabad	I	1.11.74	Hyderabad
Leatherdale David Antony	Worcestershire	E	26.11.67	Bradford
* **Lee** Brett	New South Wales	A	8.11.76	Wollongong
Lee Shane	New South Wales/Worcs	A	8.8.73	Wollongong
Lefebvre Roland Philippe	Holland	H	7.2.63	Rotterdam
* **Lehmann** Darren Scott	South Australia/Yorkshire	A	5.2.70	Gawler
Lewis Jonathan	Gloucestershire	E	26.8.75	Aylesbury
Lewis Jonathan James Benjamin	Durham	E	21.5.70	Isleworth
Lewis Michael Llewellyn	Victoria	A	29.6.74	Greensborough
Lewis Mohammad Rasheed	Free State	SA	24.4.75	Cape Town
* **Lewis** Rawl Nicholas	Windward Islands	WI	5.9.74	Union Village, Grenada
Lewry Jason David	Sussex	E	2.4.71	Worthing
* **Liebenberg** Gerhardus Frederick Johannes	Free State	SA	7.4.72	Upington
Light Craig	North West	SA	23.9.72	Randburg
Liptrot Christopher George	Worcestershire	E	13.2.80	Wigan
* **Liyanage** Dulip Kapila	Colts	SL	6.6.72	Kalutara
Lloyd Graham David	Lancashire	E	1.7.69	Accrington
Logan Richard James	Nottinghamshire	E	28.1.80	Stone
Lokuarachchi Kaushal Samaraweera	Bloomfield	SL	20.5.82	Colombo
Lopez Carlitos Fernando	West Indies B	WI	10.12.80	Johnson Road, Barbados
Louw Johann	Griqualand West	SA	12.4.79	Cape Town
Love Geoff Terry	Border	SA	19.9.76	Port Elizabeth
Love Martin Lloyd	Queensland/Durham	A	30.3.74	Mundubbera
Loye Malachy Bernard	Northamptonshire	E	27.9.72	Northampton
Lumb Michael John	Yorkshire	E	12.2.80	Johannesburg
Lungley Tom	Derbyshire	E	25.7.79	Derby

	Team	Country	Born	Birthplace
Mabuya Anthony Phakamile Tebogo	Griqualand West	SA	15.7.77	*Kimberley*
McCullum Brendon Barrie	Otago	NZ	27.9.81	*Dunedin*
McDonald Andrew Barry	Victoria	A	15.6.81	*Wodonga*
McGain Bryce Edward	Victoria	A	25.3.72	*Mornington*
* **McGarrell** Neil Christopher	Guyana	WI	12.7.72	*Georgetown*
McGarry Andrew Charles	Essex	E	8.11.81	*Basildon*
* **MacGill** Stuart Charles Glyndwr	New South Wales/Notts	A	25.2.71	*Mount Lawley*
McGrath Anthony	Yorkshire	E	6.10.75	*Bradford*
* **McGrath** Glenn Donald	New South Wales	A	9.2.70	*Dubbo*
McIntyre Peter Edward	South Australia	A	27.4.66	*Gisborne*
Mackay Angus James	Mashonaland	Z	13.6.67	*Salisbury*
MacKenzie Damien Robert	Queensland	A	21.7.80	*Brisbane*
* **McKenzie** Neil Douglas	Northerns	SA	24.11.75	*Johannesburg*
McLaren Adrian Peter	Griqualand West	SA	21.4.80	*Kimberley*
McLean Johnathan James	Western Province	SA	11.7.80	*Johannesburg*
* **McLean** Nixon Alexei McNamara	KwaZulu-Natal	WI	20.7.73	*Stubbs, St Vincent*
McMahon Paul Joseph	Nottinghamshire	E	12.3.83	*Wigan*
Macmillan Campbell	Midlands	Z	16.4.82	*Harare*
* **McMillan** Craig Douglas	Canterbury	NZ	13.9.76	*Christchurch*
MacQueen Robert Bruce	KwaZulu-Natal	SA	6.9.77	*Durban*
* **Maddy** Darren Lee	Leicestershire	E	23.5.74	*Leicester*
Madhukar Nekkanti	Andhra	I	18.5.76	*Vijayawada*
Mafa Johnson Tumelo	Gauteng	SA	5.2.78	*Johannesburg*
Magiet Rashaad	Western Province	SA	30.5.79	*Cape Town*
Maher James Patrick	Queensland	A	27.2.74	*Innistail*
Mahmood Hamid	PIA	P	19.1.69	*Karachi*
Mahmood Sajid Iqbal	Lancashire	E	21.12.81	*Bolton*
Mail Gregory John	New South Wales	A	29.4.78	*Penrith*
Mais Dwight Hugh	Jamaica	WI	27.10.77	*St Catherine*
Makalima Dumisa Liko	Border	SA	29.12.80	*King William's Town*
Maketa Malibongwe	Border	SA	6.10.80	*Port Elizabeth*
Malao Jacob Malekane Moses	North West	SA	19.1.72	*Soweto*
Malcolm Devon Eugene	Leicestershire	E	22.2.63	*Kingston, Jamaica*
Malik Muhammad Nadeem	Nottinghamshire	E	6.10.82	*Nottingham*
Mall Ashraf	KwaZulu-Natal	SA	8.10.78	*Durham*
Manack Hussein Ahmed	Gauteng	SA	10.4.68	*Pretoria*
Mane Vinayak Ramesh	Mumbai	I	10.6.82	*Bombay*
Manhas Mithun	Delhi	I	12.9.77	*Jammu*
* **Manjurul Islam**	Khulna	B	7.11.79	*Khulna*
Manou Graham Allan	South Australia	A	23.4.79	*Modbury*
Mansoor Rana	ADBP	P	27.12.62	*Lahore*
Maregwede Alester	Mashonaland A	Z	5.8.81	*Harare*
* **Marillier** Douglas Anthony	Midlands	Z	24.6.78	*Salisbury*
Marsh Daniel James	Tasmania	A	14.6.73	*Subiaco*
Marshall Hamish John Hamilton	Northern Districts	NZ	15.2.79	*Warkworth*
* **Martin** Christopher Stewart	Canterbury	NZ	10.12.74	*Christchurch*
Martin Jacob Joseph	Baroda	I	11.5.72	*Baroda*
Martin Kenroy Denroy	West Indies B	WI	18.1.79	*St Vincent*
* **Martin** Peter James	Lancashire	E	15.11.68	*Accrington*
Martin-Jenkins Robin Simon Christopher	Sussex	E	28.10.75	*Guildford*
* **Martyn** Damien Richard	Western Australia	A	21.10.71	*Darwin*
* **Masakadza** Hamilton	Mashonaland	Z	9.8.83	*Harare*
Mascarenhas Adrian Dimitri	Hampshire	E	30.10.77	*Chiswick*
Masengemi Sandile	Gauteng	SA	30.12.83	*Kagiso*
* **Mashrafe bin Mortaza**	Khulna	B	5.10.83	*Norail*
Masimula Walter Bafana	Gauteng	SA	23.10.75	*Johannesburg*
Died April 19, 2002.				
Mason Keno Anthony	Trinidad & Tobago	WI	13.11.72	*Trinidad*
Mason Matthew Sean	Worcestershire	E	20.3.74	*Claremont*

	Team	Country	Born	Birthplace
Mason Scott Robert	Tasmania	A	27.7.76	Launceston
Masters David Daniel	Kent	E	22.4.78	Chatham
Mataboge Tshepo Khotso	Gauteng	SA	18.11.78	Soweto
Mayers Antonio Nigel	West Indies B	WI	23.10.79	Horse Hill, Barbados
* **Maynard** Matthew Peter	Glamorgan	E	21.3.66	Oldham
Mazharul Haque	Dhaka	B	3.7.80	Narayanganj
* **Mbangwa** Mpumelelo	Matabeleland	Z	26.6.76	Plumtree
* **Mehrab Hossain**	Dhaka Metropolis	B	22.9.78	Dhaka
Mendis Chaminda	Colts	SL	28.12.68	Galle
Merchant Altaf Azizbhai	Saurashtra	I	30.4.78	Maliya
Meuleman Scott William	Western Australia	A	17.7.80	Subiaco
Meyer Esias Engelbertus	Griqualand West	SA	18.4.78	Bethal
Meyer Lyall	Eastern Province	SA	23.3.82	Port Elizabeth
* **Mhambrey** Paras Laxmikant	Mumbai	I	20.6.72	Bombay
Middlebrook James Daniel	Essex	E	13.5.77	Leeds
* **Miller** Colin Reid	Victoria	A	6.2.64	Footscray
Mills Kyle David	Auckland	NZ	15.3.79	Auckland
Minhazul Abedin	Chittagong	B	25.9.65	Chittagong
* **Misbah-ul-Haq**	Sargodha/KRL	P	28.5.74	Mianwali
Mishra Amit	Haryana	I	24.11.82	Delhi
Mitchell Ian	Border	SA	14.12.77	Johannesburg
Mitchum Junie Alexander	Leeward Islands	WI	22.11.73	St Kitts
Modeste Theodore Jay	Trinidad & Tobago	WI	4.7.79	Trinidad
Modi Hitesh Subhash	Kenya	K	13.10.71	Kisumu
Modi Nilesh Dinesh	Gujarat	I	11.7.73	Nadiad
Mohammad Ali	Derbyshire	E	8.11.73	Bahawalpur
* **Mohammad Ashraful**	Dhaka	B	9.9.84	Dhaka
* **Mohammad Hussain**	Lahore City/Sui Gas	P	8.10.76	Lahore
* **Mohammad Rafiq**	Dhaka	B	15.5.70	Dhaka
* **Mohammad Ramzan**	Faisalabad/KRL	P	25.12.70	Lyallpur
* **Mohammad Sami**	National Bank	P	24.2.81	Karachi
* **Mohammad Sharif**	Dhaka	B	12.12.85	Narayanganj
Mohammad Sheikh	Kenya	K	29.8.80	Nairobi
* **Mohammad Wasim**	Rawalpindi/KRL	P	8.8.77	Rawalpindi
Mohammed Azeem Ashraf	Gauteng	SA	13.10.75	Nelspruit
Mohammed Dave	Trinidad & Tobago	WI	8.10.79	Trinidad
* **Mohanty** Debasis Sarbeswar	Orissa	I	20.7.76	Bhubaneshwar
* **Moin Khan**	Karachi/PIA	P	23.9.71	Rawalpindi
Mol Hendrik-Jan C.	Holland	H	29.3.77	The Hague
Moleon Eugene Owen	North West	SA	2.3.77	Cape Town
Mongia Dinesh	Punjab	I	17.4.77	Chandigarh
* **Mongia** Nayan Ramlal	Baroda	I	19.12.69	Baroda
Montgomerie Richard Robert	Sussex	E	3.7.71	Rugby
Moreeng Hylton Kgosimang	Free State	SA	1.2.78	Kimberley
Morgan McNeil Junior	Windward Islands	WI	18.10.70	St Vincent
Morkel Johannes Albertus	Easterns	SA	10.6.81	Vereeniging
Morris Alexander Corfield	Hampshire	E	4.10.76	Barnsley
Morton Runako Shaku	Leeward Islands	WI	22.7.78	Nevis
Mosaddek Hossain	Dhaka	B	25.11.83	Mymensingh
Moss Jonathon	Victoria	A	4.5.75	Manly
Mott Matthew Peter	Victoria	A	3.10.73	Charleville
Mpitsang Phenyo Victor	Free State	SA	28.3.80	Kimberley
* **Mubarak** Jehan	Colombo	SL	10.1.81	Washington
Muchall Gordon James	Durham	E	2.11.82	Newcastle upon Tyne
Mudalige Chamikara Ravinda Bentota	Colombo	SL	5.7.76	Galle
* **Mullally** Alan David	Hampshire	E	12.7.69	Southend-on-Sea
Mullick Pravanjan Madhabnanda	Orissa	I	12.9.76	Bhubaneswar
Munnik Renier	Western Province	SA	7.1.78	Cape Town
* **Muralitharan** Muttiah	Tamil Union	SL	17.4.72	Kandy
* **Murphy** Brian Andrew	Mashonaland A	Z	1.12.76	Salisbury, Rhodesia

	Team	Country	Born	Birthplace
Murphy Brian Samuel	Jamaica	WI	7.4.73	Jamaica
Murray Denys Wayne	Eastern Province	SA	29.7.77	Graaff-Reinet
* **Murray** Junior Randalph	Windward Islands	WI	20.1.68	St Georges, Grenada
Murtagh Timothy James	Surrey	E	2.8.81	Lambeth
* **Mushfiqur Rehman**	Rajshahi	B	1.1.80	Rajshahi
* **Mushtaq Ahmed**	Rest of Punjab/	P	28.6.70	Sahiwal
	National Bank/Surrey			
* **Mutendera** David Travolta	Mashonaland A	Z	25.1.79	Salisbury
* **Muzumdar** Amol Anil	Mumbai	I	11.11.74	Bombay
Myburgh Johannes Gerhardus	Northerns	SA	22.10.80	Pretoria
* **Nadeem Khan**	PIA	P	10.12.69	Rawalpindi
Nafis Iqbal	Chittagong	B	31.1.85	Chittagong
* **Nagamootoo** Mahendra Veeren	Guyana	WI	9.10.75	Whim
Naidoo Satish	West Indies B	WI	14.12.83	Couva, Trinidad
* **Naimur Rahman**	Dhaka	B	19.9.74	Dhaka
Nandakishore Ammanabrole	Hyderabad	I	10.7.70	Warangal
Napier Graham Richard	Essex	E	6.1.80	Colchester
Nash Brendan Paul	Queensland	A	14.12.77	Attadale
Nash Christopher David	Sussex	E	19.5.83	Cuckfield
Nash Donald Anthony	New South Wales	A	29.3.78	Dubbo
Nash David Charles	Middlesex	E	19.1.78	Chertsey
* **Nash** Dion Joseph	Auckland	NZ	20.11.71	Auckland
* **Naved Ashraf**	Rawalpindi	P	4.9.74	Rawalpindi
* **Naved Latif**	Allied Bank	P	21.2.76	Sargodha
* **Nawaz** Mohamed *Naveed*	Nondescripts	SL	20.9.73	Colombo
Neeyamur Rashid	Dhaka	B	1.1.75	Pabna
* **Nehra** Ashish	Delhi	I	29.4.79	Delhi
* **Nel** Andre	Easterns	SA	15.7.77	Germiston
Nelani Siyabulela Michael	Border	SA	12.5.79	East London
Nevin Christopher John	Wellington	NZ	3.8.75	Dunedin
Newman Scott Alexander	Surrey	E	3.11.79	Epsom
* **Ngam** Mfuneko	Eastern Province	SA	29.1.79	Middledrift
* **Nicholson** Matthew James	Western Australia	A	2.10.74	St Leonards
Niewoudt Riaan	North West	SA	8.5.76	Cradock
Nissanka Ratnayake Arachchige				
Prabath	Bloomfield	SL	25.10.80	Ambalantota
Nixon Paul Andrew	Kent	E	21.10.70	Carlisle
* **Nkala** Mluleki Luke	Matabeleland	Z	1.4.81	Bulawayo
Noffke Ashley Allan	Queensland/Middlesex	A	30.4.77	Nambour
North Marcus James	Western Australia	A	28.7.79	Pakenham
* **Ntini** Makhaya	Border	SA	6.7.77	Zwelitsha
Nurse Martin Andre	Barbados	WI	11.6.85	Durants
Nurse Ryan Paul Omar	West Indies B	WI	24.4.83	Mapps College, Barbados
O'Brien Aaron Warren	New South Wales	A	2.10.81	St Leonards
Obuya Collins Omondi	Kenya	K	27.7.81	Nairobi
Also known as C. O. Otieno.				
Obuya David Oluoch	Kenya	K	14.8.79	Nairobi
Also known as D. O. Otieno.				
Obuya Kennedy Otieno (see K. O. Otieno)				
Ochieng Peter	Kenya	K	10.2.77	Nairobi
Also known as P. J. Ongondo.				
* **O'Connor** Shayne Barry	Otago	NZ	15.11.73	Hastings
Odoyo Thomas Migai	Kenya	K	12.5.78	Nairobi
Odumbe Maurice Omondi	Kenya	K	15.6.69	Nairobi
Oldroyd Bradley John	Western Australia	A	5.11.73	Bentley
* **Olonga** Henry Khaaba	Mashonaland A	Z	3.7.76	Lusaka, Zambia
Ondik Otieno Suji (see T. O. Suji)				
Ongondo Peter Jimmy (see P. Ochieng)				

	Team	Country	Born	Birthplace
* **Ontong** Justin Lee	Boland	SA	4.1.80	Paarl
Onyango Lameck Ngoche	Kenya	K	22.9.73	Nairobi
Oram Jacob David Philip	Central Districts	NZ	28.7.78	Palmerston North
* **Ormond** James	Surrey	E	20.8.77	Walsgrave
Ostler Dominic Piers	Warwickshire	E	15.7.70	Solihull
Otieno Collins Omondi (see C. O. Obuya)				
Otieno David Oluoch (see D. O. Obuya)				
Otieno Kennedy Obuya	Kenya	K	11.3.72	Nairobi
Also known as K. O. Obuya.				
Otto Johannes Marthinus	Gauteng	SA	4.9.80	Pretoria
Pagnis Amit Anil	Railways	I	18.9.78	Bombay
Pagon Donovan Jomo	West Indies B	WI	13.9.82	Kingston, Jamaica
Palframan Steven John	Boland	SA	12.5.70	East London
Pandey Gyanendrakumar Kedarnath	Uttar Pradesh	I	12.8.72	Lucknow
Pandey Sanjay	Madhya Pradesh	I	14.12.76	Bhopal
Panesar Mudhsuden Singh	Northamptonshire	E	25.4.82	Luton
Parchment Brenton Anthony	Jamaica	WI	24.6.82	St Elizabeth
Parida Kulamani Shankar	Railways	I	9.3.77	Cuttack
Parida Rashmi Ranjan	Orissa	I	7.9.74	Bhubaneshwar
Parkin Owen Thomas	Glamorgan	E	24.9.72	Coventry
* **Parore** Adam Craig	Auckland	NZ	23.1.71	Auckland
Parsons Keith Alan	Somerset	E	2.5.73	Taunton
Patel Brijal Jagdish	Kenya	K	14.11.77	Nairobi
* **Patel** Minal Mahesh	Kent	E	7.7.70	Bombay, India
* **Patel** Parthiv Ajay	Gujarat	I	9.3.85	Ahmedabad
Patel Rakesh Bhanuprasad	Baroda	I	23.10.78	Ahmedabad
Pathan Irfan Khan	Baroda	I	27.10.84	Baroda
Pattison Ian	Durham	E	5.5.82	Ryhope
Payne Daniel Martin	Queensland	A	27.10.78	Brisbane
Paynter David Edward	Northamptonshire	E	25.1.81	Truro
Pearson James Alexander	Gloucestershire	E	11.9.83	Bristol
Penberthy Anthony Leonard	Northamptonshire	E	1.9.69	Troon, Cornwall
Peng Nicky	Durham	E	18.9.82	Newcastle upon Tyne
Penn Andrew Jonathan	Wellington	NZ	27.7.74	Wanganui
Percival Andre Ricardo	Guyana	WI	5.1.75	New Amsterdam
* **Perera** Anhettige Suresh Asanka	Sinhalese	SL	16.2.78	Colombo
Perera Kahawelage Gamini	Galle	SL	22.5.64	Colombo
* **Perera** Panagodage Don Ruchira Laksiri	Sinhalese	SL	6.4.77	Colombo
Perera Watuthantrige Malintha Sandesh Mihira	Sinhalese	SL	20.10.74	Colombo
Perren Clinton Terrence	Queensland	A	22.2.75	Herston
Persad Mukesh	Trinidad & Tobago	WI	1.5.70	Trinidad
Peters Keon Kenroy	Windward Islands	WI	24.2.82	St Vincent
Peters Stephen David	Worcestershire	E	10.12.78	Harold Wood
Petersen Alviro Nathan	Northerns	SA	25.11.80	Port Elizabeth
Peterson Robin John	Eastern Province	SA	4.8.79	Port Elizabeth
Pettini Mark Lewis	Essex	E	2.8.83	Brighton
Phelps Matthew James	New South Wales	A	1.9.72	Lismore
Phillips Nicholas Charles	Durham	E	10.5.74	Pembury
Phillips Timothy James	Essex/Durham UCCE	E	13.3.81	Cambridge
Pietersen Charl	Griqualand West	SA	6.1.83	Kimberley
Pietersen Kevin Peter	Nottinghamshire	E	27.6.80	Pietermaritzburg, SA
Pilon Nathan Steven	New South Wales	A	27.10.76	Bulli
Pipe David James	Worcestershire	E	16.12.77	Bradford
Piper Keith John	Warwickshire	E	18.12.69	Leicester
* **Pollock** Shaun Maclean	KwaZulu-Natal/Warwicks	SA	16.7.73	Port Elizabeth
* **Ponting** Ricky Thomas	Tasmania	A	19.12.74	Launceston
Pooran Homchand	Guyana	WI	14.2.79	Port Mourant

	Team	Country	Born	Birthplace
Pope Steven Charles	Border	SA	15.11.72	*East London*
Pothas Nic	Hampshire	SA	18.11.73	*Johannesburg, SA*
Powar Kiran Rajaram	Goa	I	6.4.76	*Bombay*
Powar Ramesh Rajaram	Mumbai	I	20.5.78	*Bombay*
Powell Darren Brentlyle	Jamaica	WI	15.4.78	*Jamaica*
Powell Elsroy Junior	West Indies B	WI	9.11.81	*St Kitts*
Powell Mark John	Northamptonshire	E	4.11.80	*Northampton*
Powell Michael James	Warwicks/Griqualand W.	E	5.4.75	*Bolton*
Powell Michael John	Glamorgan	E	3.2.77	*Abergavenny*
Powell Ricardo Lloyd	Jamaica	WI	16.12.78	*St Elizabeth*
Prasad Bapu Krishnarao Venkatesh	Karnataka	I	5.8.69	*Bangalore*
Prasad Mannava Sri Kanth	Andhra	I	24.4.75	*Guntur*
Prasad Raja Vasireddy Chandramouli	Andhra	I	30.5.74	*Madras*
Pratt Andrew	Durham	E	4.3.75	*Helmington Row*
Pratt Gary Joseph	Durham	E	22.12.81	*Bishop Auckland*
Pretorius Dewald	Free State	SA	6.12.77	*Pretoria*
Price Michael Lynn	Eastern Province	SA	6.10.81	*Grahamstown*
Price Raymond William	Midlands	Z	12.6.76	*Salisbury*
Prince Ashwell Gavin	Western Province	SA	28.5.77	*Port Elizabeth*
Prince Goldwyn Terrence	Leeward Islands	WI	18.6.74	*Antigua*
Pringle Andrew Alexander Welsh	Boland	SA	7.2.78	*Bedford*
Prior Matthew James	Sussex	E	26.2.82	*Johannesburg, SA*
Prittipaul Lawrence Roland	Hampshire	E	19.10.79	*Portsmouth*
Pushpakumara Karuppiahage Ravindra	Nondescripts	SL	21.7.75	*Panadura*
Pushpakumara Muthumudalige	Colts	SL	26.9.81	*Colombo*
Puttick Andrew George	Western Province	SA	11.12.80	*Cape Town*
Pyemont James Patrick	Derbyshire	E	10.4.78	*Eastbourne*
Qaiser Abbas	Sheikhupura/N. Bank	P	7.5.82	*Muridke*
Raja Ali	Railways	I	5.7.76	*Bhopal*
Rajiv Kumar	Bihar	I	2.12.76	*Patna*
Raju Sagi Lakshmi Venkatapathy	Hyderabad	I	9.7.69	*Hyderabad*
Ramanayake Champaka Priyadarshana Hewage	Galle	SL	8.1.65	*Colombo*
Ramesh Sadagoppan	Tamil Nadu	I	16.10.75	*Madras*
Ramnarine Dinanath	Trinidad & Tobago	WI	4.6.75	*Chaguanas*
Rampaul Ravindranath	Trinidad & Tobago	WI	15.10.84	*Preysal*
Ramprakash Mark Ravin	Surrey	E	5.9.69	*Bushey*
Randall Stephen John	Nottinghamshire	E	9.6.80	*Nottingham*
Ranjan Das (see *Bikash Ranjan Das*)				
Rashid Latif	Allied Bank	P	14.10.68	*Karachi*
Rashid Umer Bin Abdul *Died April 1, 2002*	Sussex	E	6.2.76	*Southampton*
Rathore Vikram	Punjab	I	26.3.69	*Jullundur*
Ratra Ajay	Haryana	I	13.12.81	*Faridabad*
Raul Sanjay Susanta	Orissa	I	6.10.76	*Cuttack*
Rawnsley Matthew James	Worcestershire	E	8.6.76	*Birmingham*
Read Christopher Mark Wells	Nottinghamshire	E	10.8.78	*Paignton*
Reddy Brendon Leigh	Easterns	SA	6.11.83	*Durban*
Rees Timothy Martyn	Lancashire	E	4.9.84	*Loughborough*
Reifer Floyd Lamonte	Barbados	WI	23.7.72	*Parish Land*
Reiffel Paul Ronald	Victoria	A	19.4.66	*Box Hill*
Rennie Gavin James	Mashonaland A	Z	12.1.76	*Fort Victoria*
Rhodes Jonathan Neil	KwaZulu-Natal	SA	27.7.69	*Pietermaritzburg*
Rhodes Steven John	Worcestershire	E	17.6.64	*Bradford*
Richards Corey John	New South Wales	A	25.8.75	*Camden*
Richardson Alan	Warwickshire	E	6.5.75	*Newcastle-under-Lyme*
Richardson Mark Hunter	Auckland	NZ	11.6.71	*Hastings*

	Team	Country	Born	Birthplace
Richardson Scott Andrew	Yorkshire	E	5.9.77	*Oldham*
Rindel Michael John Raymond	Easterns	SA	9.2.63	*Durban*
* **Roberts** Lincoln Abraham	Trinidad & Tobago	WI	4.9.74	*Accord, Antigua*
Roberts Timothy William	Lancashire	E	4.3.78	*Kettering*
Robinson Darren David John	Essex	E	2.3.73	*Braintree*
Robinson Mark Andrew	Sussex	E	23.11.66	*Hull*
Roe Garth Anthony	North West	SA	9.7.73	*Port Elizabeth*
Rofe Paul Cameron	South Australia	A	16.1.81	*Adelaide*
Rogers Barney Guy	Mashonaland	Z	20.8.82	*Harare*
Rogers Christopher John Llewellyn	Western Australia	A	31.8.77	*St George*
Rollins Adrian Stewart	Northamptonshire	E	8.2.72	*Barking*
* **Rose** Franklyn Albert	Gauteng	WI	1.2.72	*St Ann's Bay, Jamaica*
Rose Graham David	Somerset	E	12.4.64	*Tottenham*
Rowland Barrington Marquis	Karnataka	I	8.1.80	*Bangalore*
Rudolph Jacobus Andries	Northerns	SA	4.5.81	*Springs*
Rummans Graeme Clifford	New South Wales	A	13.12.76	*Camperdown*
* **Russell** Robert Charles (Jack)	Gloucestershire	E	15.8.63	*Stroud*
* **Saeed Anwar**	ADBP	P	6.9.68	*Karachi*
Saggers Martin John	Kent	E	23.5.72	*King's Lynn*
Sahabuddin Khatib Syeb	Andhra	I	1.1.79	*Kadiri*
Saiful Islam	Dhaka	B	14.4.69	*Mymensingh*
Sajid Ali	National Bank	P	1.7.63	*Karachi*
Sajjad Ahmed	Dhaka	B	20.5.74	*Dhaka*
Saker David James	Tasmania	A	29.5.66	*Oakleigh*
Salahuddin Ahmed	Khulna	B	10.2.69	*Khulna*
Sales David John	Northants/Wellington	E	3.12.77	*Carshalton*
* **Salim Elahi**	Lahore City/Habib Bank	P	21.11.76	*Sahiwal*
* **Salisbury** Ian David Kenneth	Surrey	E	21.1.70	*Northampton*
Salvi Aavishkar Madhav	Mumbai	I	20.10.81	*Bombay*
* **Samaraweera** Dulip Prasanna	Colts	SL	12.2.72	*Colombo*
* **Samaraweera** Thilan Thusara	Sinhalese	SL	22.9.76	*Colombo*
Sampson Philip James	Surrey	E	6.9.80	*Manchester*
* **Samuels** Marlon Nathaniel	Jamaica	WI	5.1.81	*Los Angeles, USA*
* **Samuels** Robert George	Jamaica	WI	13.3.71	*Kingston*
* **Sanford** Adam	Leeward Islands	WI	12.7.76	*Dominica*
* **Sangakkara** Kumar Chokshanada	Nondescripts	SL	27.10.77	*Matale*
* **Sanghvi** Rahul Laxman	Delhi	I	3.9.74	*Surat*
Sangram Singh	Himachal Pradesh	I	30.1.78	*Nahan*
Sanson Audley Algan	Jamaica	WI	5.11.74	*Clarendon*
* **Sanuar Hossain**	Barisal	B	5.8.73	*Mymensingh*
* **Saqlain Mushtaq**	PIA/Surrey	P	29.12.76	*Lahore*
* **Sarandeep Singh**	Delhi	I	21.10.79	*Amritsar*
* **Sarwan** Ramnaresh Ronnie	Guyana	WI	23.6.80	*Wakenaam*
Schiferli Edgar	Holland	H	17.5.76	
* **Schofield** Christopher Paul	Lancashire	E	6.10.78	*Rochdale*
Schofield James Edward Knowle	Hampshire	E	1.11.78	*Blackpool*
Scholte Reinout Hans	Holland	H	10.8.67	*The Hague*
Sealy Anderson Wendle Leandro	West Indies B	WI	10.7.82	*Government Hill*
Seccombe Wade Anthony	Queensland	A	30.10.71	*Murgon*
* **Sehwag** Virender	Delhi	I	20.10.78	*Delhi*
Sekhoto Mpho Remofiloe	Easterns	SA	2.3.82	*Johannesburg*
Selwood Steven Andrew	Derbyshire	E	24.11.79	*Barnet*
Senekal Dewald Meyer	Northerns	SA	12.1.81	*Uitenhage*
Sewell David Graham	Otago	NZ	20.10.77	*Christchurch*
Seymore Andre Johan	Easterns	SA	16.2.75	*Rustenburg*
Shabbir Ahmed	Rest of Punjab/National Bank	P	21.4.76	*Khanewal*
* **Shadab Kabir**	Karachi/Customs	P	12.11.77	*Karachi*
Shafayat Bilal Mustafa	Nottinghamshire	E	10.7.84	*Nottingham*
Shafiq Khan	Haryana	I	11.10.79	*Faridabad*

	Team	Country	Born	Birthplace
Shafiuddin Ahmed	Chittagong	B	1.6.73	*Dhaka*
Shah Owais Alam	Middlesex	E	22.10.78	*Karachi, Pakistan*
Shah Ravindu Dhirajlal	Kenya	K	28.8.72	*Nairobi*
Shahid Nadeem	Surrey	E	23.4.69	*Karachi, Pakistan*
* **Shahid Afridi**	Karachi/Habib Bank	P	1.3.80	*Khyber Agency*
* **Shahid Nazir**	Faisalabad/Habib Bank	P	4.12.77	*Faisalabad*
* **Shakeel Ahmed**, sen.	Rawalpindi/KRL	P	12.2.66	*Kuwait City, Kuwait*
Shakti Singh	Himachal Pradesh	I	19.5.68	*Mandi*
Sharath Sridharan	Tamil Nadu	I	31.10.72	*Madras*
Sharif Zoheb Khalid	Essex	E	22.2.83	*Leytonstone*
* **Sharma** Sanjeev	Rajasthan	I	25.8.65	*Delhi*
Sharma Vineet	Punjab	I	8.10.80	*Jullundur*
Sheikh Mohamed Avez	Warwickshire	E	2.7.73	*Birmingham*
Sheriyar Alamgir	Worcestershire	E	15.11.73	*Birmingham*
Shillingford Shane	Windward Islands	WI	23.2.83	*Dominica*
* **Shoaib Akhtar**	KRL	P	13.8.75	*Rawalpindi*
* **Shoaib Malik**	Sialkot/PIA	P	1.2.82	*Sialkot*
* **Shoaib Mohammad**	PIA	P	8.1.61	*Karachi*
Shukla Laxmi Ratan	Bengal	I	6.5.81	*Howrah*
Siddiqui Iqbal	Maharashtra	I	26.12.74	*Aurangabad*
* **Sidebottom** Ryan Jay	Yorkshire	E	15.6.78	*Huddersfield*
Sillence Roger John	Gloucestershire	E	29.6.77	*Salisbury*
Silva Lindamlilage Prageeth Chamara	Panadura	SL	14.12.79	*Panadura*
* **Silverwood** Christopher Eric Wilfred	Yorkshire	E	5.3.75	*Pontefract*
Simmonds Joel McKenzie	Leeward Islands	WI	27.1.76	*Nevis*
Simmons Lendl Mark Platter	Trinidad & Tobago	WI	25.1.85	*Port of Spain*
* **Sinclair** Mathew Stuart	Central Districts	NZ	9.11.75	*Katherine, Australia*
Singh Anurag	Worcestershire	E	9.9.75	*Kanpur, India*
* **Singh** Rabindra Ramanarayan (Robin)	Tamil Nadu	I	14.9.63	*Princes Town, Trinidad*
Singh Tejinder Pal	Railways	I	16.1.78	*Amritsar*
* **Slater** Michael Jonathon	New South Wales	A	21.2.70	*Wagga Wagga*
Smethurst Michael Paul	Lancashire	E	11.10.76	*Oldham*
Smit Willem Johannes	Boland	SA	1.8.74	*Calvinia*
* **Smith** Andrew Michael	Gloucestershire	E	1.10.67	*Dewsbury*
Smith Benjamin Francis	Worcs/Central Districts	E	3.4.72	*Corby*
Smith Dwayne Romel	Barbados	WI	12.1.83	*Storey Gap*
Smith Devon Sheldon	Windward Islands	WI	21.10.81	*Grenada*
Smith Edward Thomas	Kent	E	19.7.77	*Pembury*
* **Smith** Graeme Craig	Western Province	SA	1.2.81	*Johannesburg*
Smith Gregory James	Northerns/Notts	E	30.10.71	*Pretoria, SA*
Smith Michael John	South Australia	A	17.7.73	*Rose Park*
Smith Neil Michael Knight	Warwickshire	E	27.7.67	*Birmingham*
Smith Richard Andrew Mortimer	Trinidad & Tobago	WI	17.7.71	*Trinidad*
* **Smith** Robin Arnold	Hampshire	E	13.9.63	*Durban, South Africa*
Snape Jeremy Nicholas	Gloucestershire	E	27.4.73	*Stoke-on-Trent*
Sodhi Reetinder Singh	Punjab	I	18.10.80	*Patiala*
Solanki Vikram Singh	Worcestershire	E	1.4.76	*Udaipur, India*
Somasunder Sujith	Saurashtra	I	2.12.72	*Bangalore*
* **Spearman** Craig Murray	Gloucestershire	NZ	4.7.72	*Auckland, NZ*
Spires James Ashley	Warwickshire	E	12.11.79	*Solihull*
* **Srinath** Javagal	Leicestershire	I	31.8.69	*Mysore*
Srinivas Mumbai Rangachary	Tamil Nadu	I	24.10.79	*Bombay*
Sriram Sridharan	Tamil Nadu	I	21.2.76	*Madras*
Srivastava Shalabh Jagdishprasad	Uttar Pradesh	I	22.9.81	*Allahabad*
* **Stead** Gary Raymond	Canterbury	NZ	9.1.72	*Christchurch*
Stemp Richard David	Leicestershire	E	11.12.67	*Birmingham*
* **Stephenson** John Patrick	Essex	E	14.3.65	*Stebbing*
Stevens Darren Ian	Leicestershire	E	30.4.76	*Leicester*

	Team	Country	Born	Birthplace
* Stewart Alec James	Surrey	E	8.4.63	Merton
Stewart Errol Leslie Rae	KwaZulu-Natal	SA	30.7.69	Durban
* Strang Paul Andrew	Manicaland	Z	28.7.70	Bulawayo
Strauss Andrew John	Middlesex	E	2.3.77	Johannesburg, SA
* Streak Heath Hilton	Matabeleland	Z	16.3.74	Bulawayo
Street Matthew Russell	Gauteng	SA	17.12.78	Johannesburg
Strydom Johannes Gerhardus	Boland	SA	6.9.79	Cape Town
Strydom Morne	North West	SA	20.2.74	Port Elizabeth
* Strydom Pieter Coenraad	Border	SA	10.6.69	Somerset East
* Stuart Colin Ellsworth Laurie	Guyana	WI	28.9.73	Georgetown
Stubbings Stephen David	Derbyshire	E	31.3.78	Huddersfield
Styris Scott Bernard	Northern Districts	NZ	10.7.75	Brisbane, Australia
Sudarshana Tuduwa Kankanamge Dhammika	Galle	SL	19.6.76	Galle
Sugden Craig Brian	Border	SA	7.3.74	Durban
Suji Martin Armon	Kenya	K	2.6.71	Nairobi
Suji Tony Ondik	Kenya	K	5.2.76	Nairobi
Also known as O. S. Ondik.				
Sulzberger Glen Paul	Central Districts	NZ	14.3.73	Kaponga
Suppiah Arul Vivasvan	Somerset	E	30.8.83	Kuala Lumpur, Malaysia
Suresh Kumar Mani	Kerala	I	19.4.73	Alleppey
Sutane Paresh Hemant	Vidarbha	I	14.4.75	Nagpur
Sutcliffe Iain John	Leicestershire	E	20.12.74	Leeds
Sutton Luke David	Derbyshire	E	4.10.76	Keynsham
Swan Gavin Graham	Western Australia	A	30.10.70	Subiaco
Swanepoel Adriaan Johannes	Griqualand West	SA	19.3.72	Kimberley
Swann Alec James	Lancashire	E	26.10.76	Northampton
Swann Graeme Peter	Northamptonshire	E	24.3.79	Northampton
Sylvester Kester Kenneth	Windward Islands	WI	5.12.73	St David
Symington Marc Joseph	Durham	E	10.1.80	Newcastle upon Tyne
Symonds Andrew	Queensland/Kent	A	9.6.75	Birmingham, England
* Taibu Tatenda	Mashonaland A	Z	14.5.83	Harare
* Talha Jubair	Bangladesh A	B	10.12.85	Faridpur
* Tapash Baisya	Sylhet	B	25.12.82	Sylhet
Tareq Aziz	Chittagong	B	4.9.83	Chittagong
Tatton Craig Ross	Griqualand West	SA	29.1.75	Bulawayo, Rhodesia
* Taufeeq Umar	Habib Bank	P	20.6.81	Lahore
Taylor Billy Victor	Sussex	E	11.1.77	Southampton
Taylor Christopher Glyn	Gloucestershire	E	27.9.76	Bristol
Taylor Christopher Robert	Yorkshire	E	21.2.81	Pudsey
Telemachus Roger	Western Province	SA	27.3.73	Stellenbosch
Telesford Clyde T.	Windward Islands	WI		
* Tendulkar Sachin Ramesh	Mumbai	I	24.4.73	Bombay
* Terbrugge David John	Gauteng	SA	31.1.77	Ladysmith
Thomas Alfonso Clive	North West	SA	9.2.77	Cape Town
Thomas Antonio Omar	Barbados	WI	21.10.82	Sion Hill
Thomas Bradley John	Tasmania	A	18.1.72	Hobart
Thomas Fernix	Windward Islands	WI	26.9.80	Dominica
Thomas Ian James	Glamorgan	E	9.5.79	Newport
Thomas Stuart Darren	Glamorgan	E	25.1.75	Morriston
Thornicroft Nicholas David	Yorkshire	E	23.1.85	York
Thorpe Ashley Michael	Durham	E	2.4.75	Kiama, Australia
* Thorpe Graham Paul	Surrey	E	1.8.69	Farnham
Tikolo Stephen Ogomji	Kenya	K	25.6.71	Nairobi
* Tillekeratne Hashan Prasantha	Nondescripts	SL	14.7.67	Colombo
Tittle Keithroy Ian	Leeward Islands	WI	28.10.73	Antigua
Tomlinson James Andrew	Hampshire	E	12.6.82	Winchester
Townsend David Hume	Northerns	SA	22.12.77	Port Elizabeth
Toyana Geoffrey	Gauteng	SA	27.2.74	Soweto

	Team	Country	Born	Birthplace
Trainor Nicholas James	Gauteng	E	29.6.75	Gateshead
Tredwell James Cullum	Kent	E	27.2.82	Ashford
Trego Peter David	Somerset	E	12.6.81	Weston-super-Mare
Tremlett Christopher Timothy	Hampshire	E	2.9.81	Southampton
* **Trescothick** Marcus Edward	Somerset	E	25.12.75	Keynsham
Trott Benjamin James	Kent	E	14.3.75	Wellington
Trott Ian Jonathan Leonard	Western Province	SA	22.4.81	Cape Town
Troughton Jamie Oliver	Warwickshire	E	2.3.79	Camden
Tsamaisi Elton Selbui	Griqualand West	SA	18.12.80	Kimberley
Tsolekile Thami Lungisa	Western Province	SA	9.10.80	Cape Town
Tubb Shannon Ben	Tasmania	A	11.5.80	Launceston
Tucker Brett Hurst	Griqualand West	SA	4.4.79	Johannesburg
* **Tudor** Alex Jeremy	Surrey	E	23.10.77	Kensington
Tuffey Daryl Raymond	Northern Districts	NZ	11.6.78	Milton
* **Tufnell** Philip Charles Roderick	Middlesex	E	29.4.66	Barnet
Turner Dale Andrew	New South Wales	A	30.1.74	Bankstown
Turner Robert Julian	Somerset	E	25.11.67	Malvern
* **Tushar Imran**	Khulna	B	10.12.83	Kharki
Tweedie Andrew Neil Walter	KwaZulu-Natal	SA	27.11.75	Durban
Udal Shaun David	Hampshire	E	18.3.69	Farnborough, Hants
* **Upashantha** Kalutarage Eric Amila	Colts	SL	10.6.72	Kurunegala
Uys Johannes	Easterns	SA	14.2.78	Benoni
* **Vaas** Warnakulasuriya Patabendige Ushantha Joseph Chaminda	Colts	SL	27.1.74	Mattumagala
van Bunge Daan L. S.	Holland	H	19.10.82	Voorburg
van Deinsen Brett Paul	New South Wales	A	28.12.77	Camperdown
van den Berg Adolf Matthys	Easterns	SA	9.3.78	Randfontein
van der Wath Johannes Jacobus	Free State	SA	10.1.78	Newcastle
* **Vandort** Michael Graydon	Colombo	SL	19.1.80	Colombo
van Jaarsveld Martin	Northerns	SA	18.6.74	Klerksdorp
van Oosterom Robert Frank	Holland	H	16.10.68	The Hague
van Troost Lucas Petrus	Holland	H	28.12.69	Schiedam
van Wyk Cornelius Francois Kruger	Northerns	SA	2.7.80	Wolmaransstad
van Wyk Jacques Merlin	Boland	SA	27.1.78	Stellenbosch
van Wyk Morne Nico	Free State	SA	20.3.79	Bloemfontein
Vaughan Jeffrey Mark	South Australia	A	26.3.74	Blacktown
* **Vaughan** Michael Paul	Yorkshire	E	29.10.74	Manchester
Venter Jacobus Francois	Free State	SA	1.10.69	Bloemfontein
Venter Martin Colin	North West	SA	12.12.68	East London
Ventura Mario Dimitri	Jamaica	WI	21.4.74	Kingston
Venugopala Rao Yalaka	Andhra	I	26.2.82	Vishakhapatnam
Vermeulen Mark Andrew	Mashonaland A	Z	2.3.79	Salisbury
* **Vettori** Daniel Luca	Northern Districts	NZ	27.1.79	Auckland
* **Viljoen** Dirk Peter	Midlands	Z	11.3.77	Salisbury
Vinay Kumar Devishetty	Hyderabad	I	21.4.77	Delhi
* **Vincent** Lou	Auckland	NZ	12.11.78	Auckland
Visagie Wayne Rodger	Free State	SA	12.5.79	Bloemfontein
Wagg Graham Grant	Warwickshire	E	28.4.83	Rugby
Wagh Mark Anant	Warwickshire	E	20.10.76	Birmingham
* **Wajahatullah Wasti**	Peshawar/Allied Bank	P	11.11.74	Peshawar
* **Walker** Brooke Graeme Keith	Auckland	NZ	25.3.77	Auckland
Walker George William	Leicestershire	E	12.5.84	Norwich
Walker Matthew Jonathan	Kent	E	2.1.74	Gravesend
Wallace Mark Alexander	Glamorgan	E	19.11.81	Abergavenny
* **Wallace** Philo Alphonso	Barbados	WI	2.8.70	Haynesville

	Team	Country	Born	Birthplace
* **Walmsley** Kerry Peter	Otago	NZ	23.8.73	*Dunedin*
Wanasinghe Wasala Mudiyanselage Pasan Nirmitha	Galle	SL	30.9.70	*Colombo*
* **Waqar Younis**	National Bank	P	16.11.71	*Vehari*
* **Ward** Ian James	Surrey	E	30.9.72	*Plymouth*
Ward Trevor Robert	Leicestershire	E	18.1.68	*Farningham*
* **Warne** Shane Keith	Victoria	A	13.9.69	*Ferntree Gully*
Warren Russell John	Northamptonshire	E	10.9.71	*Northampton*
* **Wasim Akram**	PIA	P	3.6.66	*Lahore*
* **Wasim Jaffer**	Mumbai	I	16.2.78	*Bombay*
* **Watambwa** Brighton Tonderai	Mashonaland	Z	9.6.77	*Salisbury*
Watekar Hemal Haribhai	Andhra	I	1.12.77	*Vishakhapatnam*
Watson Douglas James	KwaZulu-Natal	SA	15.5.73	*Pietermaritzburg*
Watson Shane Robert	Tasmania	A	17.6.81	*Ipswich*
* **Waugh** Mark Edward	New South Wales/Essex	A	2.6.65	*Sydney*
* **Waugh** Stephen Rodger	Kent	A	2.6.65	*Sydney*
Weekes Paul Nicholas	Middlesex	E	8.7.69	*Hackney*
Weeraratne Kaushalya	Colts	SL	29.1.81	*Gampola*
Welch Graeme	Derbyshire	E	21.3.72	*Durham*
Wells Vincent John	Leicestershire	E	6.8.65	*Dartford*
Welton Guy Edward	Nottinghamshire	E	4.5.78	*Grimsby*
Weston Robin Michael Swann	Middlesex	E	7.6.75	*Durham*
Weston William Philip Christopher	Worcestershire	E	16.6.73	*Durham*
Wharf Alexander George	Glamorgan	E	4.6.75	*Bradford*
Wharton Lian James	Derbyshire	E	21.2.77	*Holbrook*
Whiley Matthew Jeffrey Allen	Leicestershire	E	6.5.80	*Nottingham*
* **White** Craig	Yorkshire	E	16.12.69	*Morley*
White Cameron Leon	Victoria	A	18.8.83	*Bairnsdale*
White Giles William	Hampshire	E	23.3.72	*Barnstaple*
White Robert Allan	Northamptonshire	E	15.10.79	*Chelmsford*
* **Whittall** Guy James	Manicaland	Z	5.9.72	*Chipinga*
Wiblin Wayne	Border	SA	13.2.69	*Grahamstown*
Wickremaratne Ranasinghe Pattikirikoralalage Aruna Hemantha	Sinhalese	SL	21.2.71	*Colombo*
* **Wickremasinghe** Gallage Pramodya	Tamil Union	SL	14.8.71	*Matara*
Wigley David Harry	Yorkshire	E	26.10.81	*Bradford*
Wilkinson Kurt Jason	Barbados	WI	14.8.81	*Applethwaites*
Wilkinson Louis Johannes	Free State	SA	19.11.66	*Vereeniging*
Willett Tonito Akanni	Leeward Islands	WI	6.2.83	*Nevis*
Williams Brad Andrew	Western Australia	A	20.11.74	*Frankston*
Williams Connor Cecil	Baroda	I	7.8.73	*Baroda*
Williams Henry Smith	Boland	SA	11.6.67	*Stellenbosch*
Williams Jason Lester	Leeward Islands	WI	5.9.76	*St Kitts*
Williams Laurie Rohan	Jamaica	WI	12.12.68	*Jamaica*
Died September 8, 2002.				
* **Williams** Stuart Clayton	Leeward Islands	WI	12.8.69	*Government Road, Nevis*
Williams Vaughan Morgan	New South Wales	A	19.12.77	*Blaxland*
Willoughby Charl Myles	Western Province	SA	3.12.74	*Cape Town*
* **Wilson** Paul	South Australia	A	12.1.72	*Newcastle*
Wilson Sheldon Greg	Windward Islands	WI	23.8.72	*St Lucia*
Windows Matthew Guy Norman	Gloucestershire	E	5.4.73	*Bristol*
* **Wiseman** Paul John	Canterbury	NZ	4.5.70	*Auckland*
* **Wishart** Craig Brian	Midlands	Z	9.1.74	*Salisbury*
Wisneski Warren Anthony	Canterbury	NZ	19.2.69	*New Plymouth*
Wolmarans Johannes Georg Botha	North West	SA	30.7.82	*Orkney*
Wood John	Lancashire	E	22.7.70	*Crofton*
Wood Matthew James	Yorkshire	E	6.4.77	*Huddersfield*
Wood Matthew James	Somerset	E	30.9.80	*Exeter*
Wright Ashley Spencer	Leicestershire	E	21.10.80	*Grantham*
Wright Damien Geoffrey	Tasmania	A	25.7.75	*Casino*

	Team	Country	Born	Birthplace
Yadav Arjun Shivlal	Hyderabad	I	23.12.81	*Palghat*
Yadav Jai Prakash	Railways	I	7.8.74	*Bhopal*
Yadav Jyoti Prasad	Uttar Pradesh	I	26.9.77	*Allahabad*
Yardy Michael Howard	Sussex	E	27.11.80	*Pembury*
Yashpal Singh	Services	I	27.11.81	*Delhi*
Yasir Arafat	Rawalpindi/KRL	P	12.3.82	*Rawalpindi*
Yates Gary	Lancashire	E	20.9.67	*Ashton-under-Lyne*
Yohannan Tinu	Kerala	I	18.2.79	*Quilon*
Young Bradley Evan	South Australia	A	23.2.73	*Semaphore*
Young Shaun	Tasmania	A	13.6.70	*Burnie*
Younis Khan	Habib Bank	P	29.11.77	*Mardan*
Yousuf Youhana	PIA	P	27.8.74	*Lahore*
Yuvraj Singh	Punjab	I	12.12.81	*Chandigarh*
Zaheer Khan	Baroda	I	7.10.78	*Shrirampur*
Zahoor Elahi	Faisalabad/ADBP	P	1.3.71	*Sahiwal*
Zondeki Monde	Border	SA	25.7.82	*King William's Town*
Zoysa Demuni Nuwan Tharanga	Sinhalese	SL	13.5.78	*Colombo*
Zuffri Syed Zakaria	Assam	I	12.10.75	*Guwahati*
Zuiderent Bastiaan	Sussex/Holland	E/H	3.3.77	*Utrecht, Holland*

CRICKETERS OF THE YEAR, 1889–2003

1889	*Six Great Bowlers of the Year:* J. Briggs, J. J. Ferris, G. A. Lohmann, R. Peel, C. T. B. Turner, S. M. J. Woods.
1890	*Nine Great Batsmen of the Year:* R. Abel, W. Barnes, W. Gunn, L. Hall, R. Henderson, J. M. Read, A. Shrewsbury, F. H. Sugg, A. Ward.
1891	*Five Great Wicket-Keepers:* J. McC. Blackham, G. MacGregor, R. Pilling, M. Sherwin, H. Wood.
1892	*Five Great Bowlers:* W. Attewell, J. T. Hearne, F. Martin, A. W. Mold, J. W. Sharpe.
1893	*Five Batsmen of the Year:* H. T. Hewett, L. C. H. Palairet, W. W. Read, S. W. Scott, A. E. Stoddart.
1894	*Five All-Round Cricketers:* G. Giffen, A. Hearne, F. S. Jackson, G. H. S. Trott, E. Wainwright.
1895	*Five Young Batsmen of the Season:* W. Brockwell, J. T. Brown, C. B. Fry, T. W. Hayward, A. C. MacLaren.
1896	W. G. Grace.
1897	*Five Cricketers of the Season:* S. E. Gregory, A. A. Lilley, K. S. Ranjitsinhji, T. Richardson, H. Trumble.
1898	*Five Cricketers of the Year:* F. G. Bull, W. R. Cuttell, N. F. Druce, G. L. Jessop, J. R. Mason.
1899	*Five Great Players of the Season:* W. H. Lockwood, W. Rhodes, W. Storer, C. L. Townsend, A. E. Trott.
1900	*Five Cricketers of the Season:* J. Darling, C. Hill, A. O. Jones, M. A. Noble, Major R. M. Poore.
1901	*Mr R. E. Foster and Four Yorkshiremen:* R. E. Foster, S. Haigh, G. H. Hirst, T. L. Taylor, J. Tunnicliffe.
1902	L. C. Braund, C. P. McGahey, F. Mitchell, W. G. Quaife, J. T. Tyldesley.
1903	W. W. Armstrong, C. J. Burnup, J. Iremonger, J. J. Kelly, V. T. Trumper.
1904	C. Blythe, J. Gunn, A. E. Knight, W. Mead, P. F. Warner.
1905	B. J. T. Bosanquet, E. A. Halliwell, J. Hallows, A. Perrin, R. H. Spooner.
1906	D. Denton, W. S. Lees, G. J. Thompson, J Vine, L. G. Wright.
1907	J. N. Crawford, A. Fielder, E. G. Hayes, K. L. Hutchings, N. A. Knox.
1908	A. W. Hallam, R. O. Schwarz, F. A. Tarrant, A. E. E. Vogler, T. G. Wass.
1909	*Lord Hawke and Four Cricketers of the Year:* W. Brearley, Lord Hawke, J. B. Hobbs, A. Marshal, J. T. Newstead.
1910	W. Bardsley, S. F. Barnes, D. W. Carr, A. P. Day, V. S. Ransford.
1911	H. K. Foster, A. Hartley, C. B. Llewellyn, W. C. Smith, F. E. Woolley.
1912	*Five Members of the MCC's Team in Australia:* F. R. Foster, J. W. Hearne, S. P. Kinneir, C. P. Mead, H. Strudwick.
1913	John Wisden: Personal Recollections.
1914	M. W. Booth, G. Gunn, J. W. Hitch, A. E. Relf, Hon. L. H. Tennyson.
1915	J. W. H. T. Douglas, P. G. H. Fender, H. T. W. Hardinge, D. J. Knight, S. G. Smith.
1916–17	No portraits appeared.
1918	*School Bowlers of the Year:* H. L. Calder, J. E. D'E. Firth, C. H. Gibson, G. A. Rotherham, G. T. S. Stevens.
1919	*Five Public School Cricketers of the Year:* P. W. Adams, A. P. F. Chapman, A. C. Gore, L. P. Hedges, N. E. Partridge.
1920	*Five Batsmen of the Year:* A. Ducat, E. H. Hendren, P. Holmes, H. Sutcliffe, E. Tyldesley.
1921	P. F. Warner.
1922	H. Ashton, J. L. Bryan, J. M. Gregory, C. G. Macartney, E. A. McDonald.
1923	A. W. Carr, A. P. Freeman, C. W. L. Parker, A. C. Russell, A. Sandham.
1924	*Five Bowlers of the Year:* A. E. R. Gilligan, R. Kilner, G. G. Macaulay, C. H. Parkin, M. W. Tate.
1925	R. H. Catterall, J. C. W. MacBryan, H. W. Taylor, R. K. Tyldesley, W. W. Whysall.
1926	J. B. Hobbs.

1927   G. Geary, H. Larwood, J. Mercer, W. A. Oldfield, W. M. Woodfull.
1928   R. C. Blunt, C. Hallows, W. R. Hammond, D. R. Jardine, V. W. C. Jupp.
1929   L. E. G. Ames, G. Duckworth, M. Leyland, S. J. Staples, J. C. White.
1930   E. H. Bowley, K. S. Duleepsinhji, H. G. Owen-Smith, R. W. V. Robins, R. E. S. Wyatt.
1931   D. G. Bradman, C. V. Grimmett, B. H. Lyon, I. A. R. Peebles, M. J. Turnbull.
1932   W. E. Bowes, C. S. Dempster, James Langridge, Nawab of Pataudi sen., H. Verity.
1933   W. E. Astill, F. R. Brown, A. S. Kennedy, C. K. Nayudu, W. Voce.
1934   A. H. Bakewell, G. A. Headley, M. S. Nichols, L. F. Townsend, C. F. Walters.
1935   S. J. McCabe, W. J. O'Reilly, G. A. E. Paine, W. H. Ponsford, C. I. J. Smith.
1936   H. B. Cameron, E. R. T. Holmes, B. Mitchell, D. Smith, A. W. Wellard.
1937   C. J. Barnett, W. H. Copson, A. R. Gover, V. M. Merchant, T. S. Worthington.
1938   T. W. J. Goddard, J. Hardstaff jun., L. Hutton, J. H. Parks, E. Paynter.
1939   H. T. Bartlett, M. A. Brown, D. C. S. Compton, K. Farnes, A. Wood.
1940   L. N. Constantine, W. J. Edrich, W. W. Keeton, A. B. Sellers, D. V. P. Wright.
1941–46 No portraits appeared.
1947   A. V. Bedser, L. B. Fishlock, V. (M. H.) Mankad, T. P. B. Smith, C. Washbrook.
1948   M. P. Donnelly, A. Melville, A. D. Nourse, J. D. Robertson, N. W. D. Yardley.
1949   A. L. Hassett, W. A. Johnston, R. R. Lindwall, A. R. Morris, D. Tallon.
1950   T. E. Bailey, R. O. Jenkins, John Langridge, R. T. Simpson, H. Sutcliffe.
1951   T. G. Evans, S. Ramadhin, A. L. Valentine, E. D. Weekes, F. M. M. Worrell.
1952   R. Appleyard, H. E. Dollery, J. C. Laker, P. B. H. May, E. A. B. Rowan.
1953   H. Gimblett, T. W. Graveney, D. S. Sheppard, W. S. Surridge, F. S. Trueman.
1954   R. N. Harvey, G. A. R. Lock, K. R. Miller, J. H. Wardle, W. Watson.
1955   B. Dooland, Fazal Mahmood, W. E. Hollies, J. B. Statham, G. E. Tribe.
1956   M. C. Cowdrey, D. J. Insole, D. J. McGlew, H. J. Tayfield, F. H. Tyson.
1957   D. Brookes, J. W. Burke, M. J. Hilton, G. R. A. Langley, P. E. Richardson.
1958   P. J. Loader, A. J. McIntyre, O. G. Smith, M. J. Stewart, C. L. Walcott.
1959   H. L. Jackson, R. E. Marshall, C. A. Milton, J. R. Reid, D. Shackleton.
1960   K. F. Barrington, D. B. Carr, R. Illingworth, G. Pullar, M. J. K. Smith.
1961   N. A. T. Adcock, E. R. Dexter, R. A. McLean, R. Subba Row, J. V. Wilson.
1962   W. E. Alley, R. Benaud, A. K. Davidson, W. M. Lawry, N. C. O'Neill.
1963   D. Kenyon, Mushtaq Mohammad, P. H. Parfitt, P. J. Sharpe, F. J. Titmus.
1964   D. B. Close, C. C. Griffith, C. C. Hunte, R. B. Kanhai, G. S. Sobers.
1965   G. Boycott, P. J. Burge, J. A. Flavell, G. D. McKenzie, R. B. Simpson.
1966   K. C. Bland, J. H. Edrich, R. C. Motz, P. M. Pollock, R. G. Pollock.
1967   R. W. Barber, B. L. D'Oliveira, C. Milburn, J. T. Murray, S. M. Nurse.
1968   Asif Iqbal, Hanif Mohammad, K. Higgs, J. M. Parks, Nawab of Pataudi jun.
1969   J. G. Binks, D. M. Green, B. A. Richards, D. L. Underwood, O. S. Wheatley.
1970   B. F. Butcher, A. P. E. Knott, Majid Khan, M. J. Procter, D. J. Shepherd.
1971   J. D. Bond, C. H. Lloyd, B. W. Luckhurst, G. M. Turner, R. T. Virgin.
1972   G. G. Arnold, B. S. Chandrasekhar, L. R. Gibbs, B. Taylor, Zaheer Abbas.
1973   G. S. Chappell, D. K. Lillee, R. A. L. Massie, J. A. Snow, K. R. Stackpole.
1974   K. D. Boyce, B. E. Congdon, K. W. R. Fletcher, R. C. Fredericks, P. J. Sainsbury.
1975   D. L. Amiss, M. H. Denness, N. Gifford, A. W. Greig, A. M. E. Roberts.
1976   I. M. Chappell, P. G. Lee, R. B. McCosker, D. S. Steele, R. A. Woolmer.
1977   J. M. Brearley, C. G. Greenidge, M. A. Holding, I. V. A. Richards, R. W. Taylor.
1978   I. T. Botham, M. Hendrick, A. Jones, K. S. McEwan, R. G. D. Willis.
1979   D. I. Gower, J. K. Lever, C. M. Old, C. T. Radley, J. N. Shepherd.
1980   J. Garner, S. M. Gavaskar, G. A. Gooch, D. W. Randall, B. C. Rose.
1981   K. J. Hughes, R. D. Jackman, A. J. Lamb, C. E. B. Rice, V. A. P. van der Bijl.
1982   T. M. Alderman, A. R. Border, R. J. Hadlee, Javed Miandad, R. W. Marsh.
1983   Imran Khan, T. E. Jesty, A. I. Kallicharran, Kapil Dev, M. D. Marshall.
1984   M. Amarnath, J. V. Coney, J. E. Emburey, M. W. Gatting, C. L. Smith.
1985   M. D. Crowe, H. A. Gomes, G. W. Humpage, J. Simmons, S. Wettimuny.
1986   P. Bainbridge, R. M. Ellison, C. J. McDermott, N. V. Radford, R. T. Robinson.
1987   J. H. Childs, G. A. Hick, D. B. Vengsarkar, C. A. Walsh, J. J. Whitaker.
1988   J. P. Agnew, N. A. Foster, D. P. Hughes, P. M. Roebuck, Salim Malik.
1989   K. J. Barnett, P. J. L. Dujon, P. A. Neale, F. D. Stephenson, S. R. Waugh.

1990	S. J. Cook, D. M. Jones, R. C. Russell, R. A. Smith, M. A. Taylor.
1991	M. A. Atherton, M. Azharuddin, A. R. Butcher, D. L. Haynes, M. E. Waugh.
1992	C. E. L. Ambrose, P. A. J. DeFreitas, A. A. Donald, R. B. Richardson, Waqar Younis.
1993	N. E. Briers, M. D. Moxon, I. D. K. Salisbury, A. J. Stewart, Wasim Akram.
1994	D. C. Boon, I. A. Healy, M. G. Hughes, S. K. Warne, S. L. Watkin.
1995	B. C. Lara, D. E. Malcolm, T. A. Munton, S. J. Rhodes, K. C. Wessels.
1996	D. G. Cork, P. A. de Silva, A. R. C. Fraser, A. Kumble, D. A. Reeve.
1997	S. T. Jayasuriya, Mushtaq Ahmed, Saeed Anwar, P. V. Simmons, S. R. Tendulkar.
1998	M. T. G. Elliott, S. G. Law, G. D. McGrath, M. P. Maynard, G. P. Thorpe.
1999	I. D. Austin, D. Gough, M. Muralitharan, A. Ranatunga, J. N. Rhodes.
2000	C. L. Cairns, R. Dravid, L. Klusener, T. M. Moody, Saqlain Mushtaq.
Cricketers of the Century D. G. Bradman, G. S. Sobers, J. B. Hobbs, S. K. Warne, I. V. A. Richards.	
2001	M. W. Alleyne, M. P. Bicknell, A. R. Caddick, J. L. Langer, D. S. Lehmann.
2002	A. Flower, A. C. Gilchrist, J. N. Gillespie, V. V. S. Laxman, D. R. Martyn.
2003	M. L. Hayden, A. J. Hollioake, N. Hussain, S. M. Pollock, M. P. Vaughan.

CRICKETERS OF THE YEAR: AN ANALYSIS

The five players selected to be Cricketers of the Year for 2003 bring the number chosen since selection began in 1889 to 522. They have been chosen from 37 different teams as follows:

Derbyshire	13	Nottinghamshire	25	South Africans	22	Eton College	2
Essex	23	Somerset	17	West Indians	23	Malvern College	1
Glamorgan	10	Surrey	48	New Zealanders	8	Rugby School	1
Gloucestershire	16	Sussex	20	Indians	13	Tonbridge School	1
Hampshire	14	Warwickshire	19	Pakistanis	11	Univ. Coll. School	1
Kent	25	Worcestershire	15	Sri Lankans	4	Uppingham School	1
Lancashire	31	Yorkshire	41	Zimbabweans	1	Winchester College	1
Leicestershire	8	Oxford Univ.	6	Staffordshire	1		
Middlesex	26	Cambridge Univ.	10	Cheltenham College	1		
Northants	13	Australians	25	Cranleigh School	1		

Notes: Schoolboys were chosen in 1918 and 1919 when first-class cricket was suspended due to war. The total of sides comes to 540 because 18 players played regularly for two teams (England excluded) in the year for which they were chosen. John Wisden, listed as a Sussex player, retired 50 years before his posthumous selection.

Types of Players

Of the 522 Cricketers of the Year, 263 are best classified as batsmen, 148 as bowlers, 77 as all-rounders and 34 as wicket-keepers or wicket-keeper/batsmen.

Nationalities

At the time they were chosen, 329 players (63.02 per cent) were qualified to play for England, 78 for Australia, 36 West Indies, 32 South Africa, 14 Pakistan, 14 India, 12 New Zealand, 5 Sri Lanka and 2 Zimbabwe.

Note: Nationalities and teams are not necessarily identical.

Ages

On April 1 in the year of selection

Youngest: 17 years 67 days H. L. Calder, 1918. The youngest first-class cricketer was Mushtaq Mohammad, 19 years 130 days in 1963.

Oldest: 48 years 228 days Lord Hawke, 1909. (This excludes John Wisden, whose portrait appeared 87 years after his birth and 29 years after his death.)

An analysis of post-war Cricketers of the Year may be found in Wisden *1998, page 174.*

Research: Robert Brooke

4

RECORDS

At the double: Nathan Astle on his way to the fastest Test 200 ever, Christchurch, March 2002. England in New Zealand, page 1163. *Picture by Andrew Cornaga, Reuters*.

PART FOUR: RECORDS

First-class and limited-overs records by PHILIP BAILEY
Test match records by PHILIP BAILEY and GORDON VINCE

This section covers
- first-class records to September 21, 2002, the end of the season in England (pages 264–304)
- Test records to September 9, 2002, the end of the England v India series (pages 305–341)
- Test records series by series (pages 342–438)
- limited-overs international records to September 30, 2002, the end of the ICC Champions Trophy (pages 443–456)
- miscellaneous other records to September 21, 2002, the end of the season in England (pages 456–460)

The sequence
- Test series records begin with those involving England, arranged in the order their opponents entered Test cricket (Australia, South Africa, West Indies, New Zealand, India, Pakistan, Sri Lanka, Zimbabwe, Bangladesh). Next come all remaining series involving Australia, then South Africa – and so on until Zimbabwe v Bangladesh records appear on pages 437–438

Notes
- Unless otherwise stated, all records apply only to first-class cricket. This is considered to have started in 1815, after the Napoleonic War
- mid-year seasons taking place outside England are given simply as 2002, 2001, etc.
- (E), (A), (SA), (WI), (NZ), (I), (P), (SL), (Z) or (B) indicates the nationality of a player or the country in which a record was made

See also
- up-to-date Test records on www.wisden.com
- Features of 2002 (pages 462–466)
- Overseas Features of 2001-02 and 2002 (pages 1130–1138)

NOTES ON THE RECORDS

By HUGH CHEVALLIER

Some records are just records, astonishing one-offs. Others tell a story, and a table on page 316 shows clearly how Test cricket is changing. It lists the ten fastest Test double-hundreds ever recorded in terms of balls faced. These innings – doubles at the double, if you like – are innings of power, class, sustained dynamism, even genius. In the last 15 years of the 20th century, the table did not change at all. Yet no fewer than four of the top ten were blasted in the 12 months covered by this book. They encapsulate how Test cricket is evolving, how action-packed entertainment is no longer the preserve of the one-day game. Nathan Astle didn't just break the world record with his tour de force against England, he hammered it all round Christchurch: his 200 came up in 153 balls, beating the previous best, set by Ian Botham in 1982, by 67 balls, and setting new standards for clean hitting and gob-smacking audacity.

Another of those four doubles came from the flailing bat of Aravinda de Silva and formed part of a colossal team feat. Sri Lanka racked up 509 runs against Bangladesh at Colombo (PSS), more than any other team had managed in a day (page 336). The standard of cricket played by an emerging Test nation may cast both achievements in a duller light, but there can be no doubting the general move towards attacking play spearheaded by Steve Waugh's Australians. Adam Gilchrist, the epitome of the new style, smashed the world's second-best team to smithereens with his 212-ball double-century at Cape Town. Next year there will be another new entry: early in 2003, also at Cape Town, South Africa's Herschelle Gibbs reached 200 off 211 balls against Pakistan.

Last year, these records included a new table – Best Career Strike-Rates – listing the 36 bowlers (with at least 75 wickets) who had taken a wicket every 55 balls or quicker. The arrival of Brett Lee makes it 37 this year, but the strike-rates of all bar two of the nine current players in the table have worsened, confirming that most bowlers had a tough time in 2002. The trend-buckers are Waqar Younis, whose rate of one wicket every 43 balls remains truly exceptional, and Chris Cairns.

The bowlers still had their moments. Muttiah Muralitharan bamboozled nine Zimbabwean batsmen at Kandy to pocket the fifth-best figures in international cricket (page 320). His Sri Lankan team-mate, Chaminda Vaas, supplanted him as the bowler with the best return in one-day internationals: eight for 19 against those bamboozled Zimbabweans, at Colombo (SSC). Vaas also plundered 14 wickets in a Test when he scattered West Indies on the same ground. In that match, Brian Lara hit 221 from 354 balls in the first innings (never mind the pace, feel the quality) and amassed 351 runs in the match, the highest by anyone on the losing side in a Test. Meanwhile his captain, Carl Hooper, joined an even more select club of all-rounders – Ian Botham and Garry Sobers are the only other members – to hit 5,000 runs, take 100 wickets and hold 100 catches. At 122, Hooper's strike-rate was the worst by any bowler with 75 wickets to his name, but that was fair enough for a fill-in bowler. And he has a distinction all his own. Unlike Botham and Sobers, he has completed the all-rounders' treble in *both* forms of the game.

For all Hooper's achievements, though, his career has coincided with a long-term decline in West Indian cricket. Now, for the first time, they have slipped to third in the table of all one-day international results (page 444), behind Australia as well as South Africa. When the table was introduced in *Wisden 1991*, West Indies' win rate was almost 73 per cent. Twelve years on, it has sunk to around 59 per cent. As the 2002-03 season began, South Africa's lead remained large, but Australia were making up ground fast.

This year there are three new tables in the limited-overs international records. One gives the fastest scoring-rates for batsmen with 500 runs or more and is home for the world's most explosive batsmen, so tread softly as you wander past the likes of Virender Sehwag, Shahid Afridi, Adam Gilchrist and Lance Klusener. But top of this volatile chart is Lance Cairns, father of Chris, who larruped his 987 runs at a rate of nearly 105 per 100 balls. His son is in the table too, with a strike-rate of 81.

As with all the best statistical tables, there is more to be gleaned than just the headline data. Look carefully and you'll see how the one-day game too has changed in recent years. Of the 22 players who have career strike-rates of 85 or higher, 14 were playing in the past year. And of the eight who did not, all bar one – Sir Viv was always ahead of the game – usually batted at No. 6 or lower. In the days before the 15-over rule, the slog came low down the order. Nowadays attack begins with the new ball: there are six regular openers in today's 14, none in yesterday's eight.

Common sense says it must have become a harder business to contain batsmen – and so it is. Another new table (page 449) lists all one-day international bowlers to have taken 50 wickets and conceded less than four an over. Thirty qualify, but a mere four are current players, the meanest of today's generation: Shaun Pollock, Murali, Wasim Akram and Glenn McGrath. Five of the stingiest seven are West Indians of a past generation.

The last addition (page 448) measures the power of bowlers to take wickets. Here the spread of current and former players is pretty much even, so the expansive strokeplay of the modern batsman has not made his wicket easier to come by. Speed can be crucial here, with arguably the two fastest bowlers the world has produced – Shoaib Akhtar and Brett Lee – topping the list. Pakistan have five current bowlers in this company, Australia four, West Indies none.

Chaminda Vaas traps Abdul Fazil Sattaur lbw as Canada plummet to 36 all out during the 2003 World Cup – the lowest-ever total in a one-day international. The previous low was set in December 2001, when Vaas took a world-record eight for 19, and Sri Lanka skittled Zimbabwe for 38. *Picture by Clive Mason, Getty Images.*

As the amount of international cricket reaches absurd levels, a cricketer can climb up a career-aggregate ladder almost unnoticed. Mark Boucher, for example, who only turned 25 during the 2001-02 season, is sixth in the list of most successful one-day wicket-keepers, eighth equal in Tests. The demand for umpires has shot up commensurately, and Steve Bucknor has quietly replaced Dickie Bird as the most experienced on the Test circuit. Something else you might have missed in 2002 was another world Test record: Mithali Raj hit 214 for India against England at Taunton, the best ever by a woman.

Taunton has long been a batting paradise, and it wasn't just Raj who enjoyed a trip to nirvana by the Quantocks in 2002. Between them, Somerset and Surrey totted up 1,815 runs in their Championship fixture, the most for any first-class match in England. Taunton, too, was where Somerset lost their last wicket at 453, the highest total to tie a match in first-class cricket. West Indies A shared the honours.

Two cricketers hit hundreds on first-class debut during the English season. But while one signed up to stay at The Oval for five more years, the other had apparently played his only first-class innings. Rikki Clarke made his century for Surrey against Cambridge UCCE and went on to join the England squad for the ICC Champions Trophy. Stuart Moffat, after hitting 169 for Cambridge in the Varsity Match, preferred to try his luck in the world of rugby. Both, though, have their place here, in *Wisden's* records.

CONTENTS

FIRST-CLASS RECORDS

BATTING RECORDS

BOWLING RECORDS

ALL-ROUND RECORDS

WICKET-KEEPING RECORDS

FIELDING RECORDS

TEAM RECORDS

TEST RECORDS

BATTING RECORDS

BOWLING RECORDS

ALL-ROUND RECORDS

WICKET-KEEPING RECORDS

FIELDING RECORDS

TEAM RECORDS

PLAYERS

UMPIRES

TEST SERIES

LIMITED-OVERS INTERNATIONAL RECORDS

MISCELLANEOUS

FIRST-CLASS RECORDS

BATTING RECORDS

HIGHEST INDIVIDUAL INNINGS

501*	B. C. Lara	Warwickshire v Durham at Birmingham	1994
499	Hanif Mohammad	Karachi v Bahawalpur at Karachi	1958-59
452*	D. G. Bradman	NSW v Queensland at Sydney	1929-30
443*	B. B. Nimbalkar	Maharashtra v Kathiawar at Poona	1948-49
437	W. H. Ponsford	Victoria v Queensland at Melbourne	1927-28
429	W. H. Ponsford	Victoria v Tasmania at Melbourne	1922-23
428	Aftab Baloch	Sind v Baluchistan at Karachi	1973-74
424	A. C. MacLaren	Lancashire v Somerset at Taunton	1895
405*	G. A. Hick	Worcestershire v Somerset at Taunton	1988
394	Naved Latif	Sargodha v Gujranwala at Gujranwala	2000-01
385	B. Sutcliffe	Otago v Canterbury at Christchurch	1952-53
383	C. W. Gregory	NSW v Queensland at Brisbane	1906-07
377	S. V. Manjrekar	Bombay v Hyderabad at Bombay	1990-91
375	B. C. Lara	West Indies v England at St John's	1993-94
369	D. G. Bradman	South Australia v Tasmania at Adelaide	1935-36
366	N. H. Fairbrother	Lancashire v Surrey at The Oval	1990
366	M. V. Sridhar	Hyderabad v Andhra at Secunderabad	1993-94
365*	C. Hill	South Australia v NSW at Adelaide	1900-01
365*	G. S. Sobers	West Indies v Pakistan at Kingston	1957-58
364	L. Hutton	England v Australia at The Oval	1938
359*	V. M. Merchant	Bombay v Maharashtra at Bombay	1943-44
359	R. B. Simpson	NSW v Queensland at Brisbane	1963-64
357*	R. Abel	Surrey v Somerset at The Oval	1899
357	D. G. Bradman	South Australia v Victoria at Melbourne	1935-36
356	B. A. Richards	South Australia v Western Australia at Perth	1970-71
355*	G. R. Marsh	Western Australia v South Australia at Perth	1989-90
355	B. Sutcliffe	Otago v Auckland at Dunedin	1949-50
353	V. V. S. Laxman	Hyderabad v Karnataka at Bangalore	1999-2000
352	W. H. Ponsford	Victoria v NSW at Melbourne	1926-27
350	Rashid Israr	Habib Bank v National Bank at Lahore	1976-77
345	C. G. Macartney	Australians v Nottinghamshire at Nottingham	1921
344*	G. A. Headley	Jamaica v Lord Tennyson's XI at Kingston	1931-32
344	W. G. Grace	MCC v Kent at Canterbury	1876
343*	P. A. Perrin	Essex v Derbyshire at Chesterfield	1904
341	G. H. Hirst	Yorkshire v Leicestershire at Leicester	1905
340*	D. G. Bradman	NSW v Victoria at Sydney	1928-29
340	S. M. Gavaskar	Bombay v Bengal at Bombay	1981-82
340	S. T. Jayasuriya	Sri Lanka v India at Colombo	1997-98
338*	R. C. Blunt	Otago v Canterbury at Christchurch	1931-32
338	W. W. Read	Surrey v Oxford University at The Oval	1888
337*	Pervez Akhtar	Railways v Dera Ismail Khan at Lahore	1964-65
337*	D. J. Cullinan	Transvaal v Northern Transvaal at Johannesburg	1993-94
337	Hanif Mohammad	Pakistan v West Indies at Bridgetown	1957-58
336*	W. R. Hammond	England v New Zealand at Auckland	1932-33
336	W. H. Ponsford	Victoria v South Australia at Melbourne	1927-28
334*	M. A. Taylor	Australia v Pakistan at Peshawar	1998-99
334	D. G. Bradman	Australia v England at Leeds	1930
333	K. S. Duleepsinhji	Sussex v Northamptonshire at Hove	1930
333	G. A. Gooch	England v India at Lord's	1990
332	W. H. Ashdown	Kent v Essex at Brentwood	1934
331*	J. D. Robertson	Middlesex v Worcestershire at Worcester	1949
329*	M. E. K. Hussey	Northamptonshire v Essex at Northampton	2001
329	Inzamam-ul-Haq	Pakistan v New Zealand at Lahore	2002

325*	H. L. Hendry	Victoria v New Zealanders at Melbourne	1925-26
325	A. Sandham	England v West Indies at Kingston	1929-30
325	C. L. Badcock	South Australia v Victoria at Adelaide	1935-36
324*	D. M. Jones	Victoria v South Australia at Melbourne	1994-95
324	J. B. Stollmeyer	Trinidad v British Guiana at Port-of-Spain	1946-47
324	Waheed Mirza	Karachi Whites v Quetta at Karachi	1976-77
323	A. L. Wadekar	Bombay v Mysore at Bombay	1966-67
323	D. Gandhi	Bengal v Assam at Gauhati	1998-99
322*	M. B. Loye	Northamptonshire v Glamorgan at Northampton	1998
322	E. Paynter	Lancashire v Sussex at Hove	1937
322	I. V. A. Richards	Somerset v Warwickshire at Taunton	1985
321	W. L. Murdoch	NSW v Victoria at Sydney	1881-82
320	R. Lamba	North Zone v West Zone at Bhilai	1987-88
319	Gul Mahomed	Baroda v Holkar at Baroda	1946-47
318*	W. G. Grace	Gloucestershire v Yorkshire at Cheltenham	1876
317	W. R. Hammond	Gloucestershire v Nottinghamshire at Gloucester	1936
317	K. R. Rutherford	New Zealanders v D. B. Close's XI at Scarborough	1986
316*	J. B. Hobbs	Surrey v Middlesex at Lord's	1926
316*	V. S. Hazare	Maharashtra v Baroda at Poona	1939-40
316	R. H. Moore	Hampshire v Warwickshire at Bournemouth	1937
315*	T. W. Hayward	Surrey v Lancashire at The Oval	1898
315*	P. Holmes	Yorkshire v Middlesex at Lord's	1925
315*	A. F. Kippax	NSW v Queensland at Sydney	1927-28
315*	G. A. Hick	Worcestershire v Durham at Worcester	2002
315	M. A. Wagh	Warwickshire v Middlesex at Lord's	2001
314*	C. L. Walcott	Barbados v Trinidad at Port-of-Spain	1945-46
314*	Wasim Jaffer	Mumbai v Saurashtra at Rajkot	1996-97
313*	S. J. Cook	Somerset v Glamorgan at Cardiff	1990
313	H. Sutcliffe	Yorkshire v Essex at Leyton	1932
313	W. V. Raman‡	Tamil Nadu v Goa at Panjim	1988-89
312*	W. W. Keeton	Nottinghamshire v Middlesex at The Oval†	1939
312*	J. M. Brearley	MCC Under-25 v North Zone at Peshawar	1966-67
312	R. Lamba	Delhi v Himachal Pradesh at Delhi	1994-95
312	J. E. R. Gallian	Lancashire v Derbyshire at Manchester	1996
311*	G. M. Turner	Worcestershire v Warwickshire at Worcester	1982
311	J. T. Brown	Yorkshire v Sussex at Sheffield	1897
311	R. B. Simpson	Australia v England at Manchester	1964
311	Javed Miandad	Karachi Whites v National Bank at Karachi	1974-75
310*	J. H. Edrich	England v New Zealand at Leeds	1965
310*	M. E. K. Hussey	Northamptonshire v Gloucestershire at Bristol	2002
310	H. Gimblett	Somerset v Sussex at Eastbourne	1948
309*	S. P. James	Glamorgan v Sussex at Colwyn Bay	2000
309	V. S. Hazare	The Rest v Hindus at Bombay	1943-44
308*	F. M. M. Worrell	Barbados v Trinidad at Bridgetown	1943-44
308	D. Mongia	Punjab v Jammu and Kashmir at Jullundur	2000-01
307*	T. N. Lazard	Boland v W. Province at Worcester, Cape Province	1993-94
307	M. C. Cowdrey	MCC v South Australia at Adelaide	1962-63
307	R. M. Cowper	Australia v England at Melbourne	1965-66
306*	A. Ducat	Surrey v Oxford University at The Oval	1919
306*	E. A. B. Rowan	Transvaal v Natal at Johannesburg	1939-40
306*	D. W. Hookes	South Australia v Tasmania at Adelaide	1986-87
306	M. H. Richardson	New Zealanders v Zimbabwe A at Kwekwe	2000-01
305*	F. E. Woolley	MCC v Tasmania at Hobart	1911-12
305*	F. R. Foster	Warwickshire v Worcestershire at Dudley	1914
305*	W. H. Ashdown	Kent v Derbyshire at Dover	1935
305*	P. Dharmani	Punjab v Jammu and Kashmir at Ludhiana	1999-2000
304*	A. W. Nourse	Natal v Transvaal at Johannesburg	1919-20
304*	P. H. Tarilton	Barbados v Trinidad at Bridgetown	1919-20
304*	E. D. Weekes	West Indians v Cambridge University at Cambridge	1950
304	R. M. Poore	Hampshire v Somerset at Taunton	1899
304	D. G. Bradman	Australia v England at Leeds	1934

303*	W. W. Armstrong	Australians v Somerset at Bath	1905
303*	Mushtaq Mohammad	Karachi Blues v Karachi University at Karachi	1967-68
303*	Abdul Azeem	Hyderabad v Tamil Nadu at Hyderabad	1986-87
303*	S. Chanderpaul	Guyana v Jamaica at Kingston	1995-96
303*	G. A. Hick	Worcestershire v Hampshire at Southampton	1997
303*	D. J. Sales	Northamptonshire v Essex at Northampton	1999
302	P. Holmes	Yorkshire v Hampshire at Portsmouth	1920
302*	W. R. Hammond	Gloucestershire v Glamorgan at Bristol	1934
302*	Arjan Kripal Singh‡	Tamil Nadu v Goa at Panjim	1988-89
302	W. R. Hammond	Gloucestershire v Glamorgan at Newport	1939
302	L. G. Rowe	West Indies v England at Bridgetown	1973-74
301*	E. H. Hendren	Middlesex v Worcestershire at Dudley	1933
301*	V. V. S. Laxman	Hyderabad v Bihar at Jamshedpur	1997-98
301	W. G. Grace	Gloucestershire v Sussex at Bristol	1896
300*	V. T. Trumper	Australians v Sussex at Hove	1899
300*	F. B. Watson	Lancashire v Surrey at Manchester	1928
300*	Imtiaz Ahmed	PM's XI v Commonwealth XI at Bombay	1950-51
300*	G. K. Khoda	Central Zone v South Zone at Panaji	2000-01
300	J. T. Brown	Yorkshire v Derbyshire at Chesterfield	1898
300	D. C. S. Compton	MCC v N. E. Transvaal at Benoni	1948-49
300	R. Subba Row	Northamptonshire v Surrey at The Oval	1958
300	Ramiz Raja	Allied Bank v Habib Bank at Lahore	1994-95

† *Played at The Oval because Lord's was required for Eton v Harrow.*

‡ *W. V. Raman and Arjan Kripal Singh scored triple-hundreds in the same innings, a unique occurrence.*

DOUBLE-HUNDRED ON DEBUT

227	T. Marsden	Sheffield & Leicester v Nottingham at Sheffield	1826
207	N. F. Callaway†	New South Wales v Queensland at Sydney	1914-15
240	W. F. E. Marx	Transvaal v Griqualand West at Johannesburg	1920-21
200*	A. Maynard	Trinidad v MCC at Port-of-Spain	1934-35
232*	S. J. E. Loxton	Victoria v Queensland at Melbourne	1946-47
215*	G. H. G. Doggart	Cambridge University v Lancashire at Cambridge	1948
202	J. Hallebone	Victoria v Tasmania at Melbourne	1951-52
230	G. R. Viswanath	Mysore v Andhra at Vijayawada	1967-68
260	A. A. Muzumdar	Bombay v Haryana at Faridabad	1993-94
209*	A. Pandey	Madhya Pradesh v Uttar Pradesh at Bhilai	1995-96
210*	D. J. Sales	Northants v Worcestershire at Kidderminster	1996
200*	M. J. Powell	Glamorgan v Oxford University at Oxford	1997

† *In his only first-class innings. He was killed in action in France in 1917.*

TWO SEPARATE HUNDREDS ON DEBUT

148 and 111	A. R. Morris	New South Wales v Queensland at Sydney	1940-41
152 and 102*	N. J. Contractor	Gujarat v Baroda at Baroda	1952-53
132* and 110	Aamer Malik	Lahore A v Railways at Lahore	1979-80

HUNDRED ON DEBUT IN ENGLAND

This does not include players who have previously appeared in first-class cricket outside the British Isles. The following have achieved the feat since 1990. For fuller lists please see earlier *Wisdens*.

116*	J. J. B. Lewis	Essex v Surrey at The Oval	1990
117	J. D. Glendenen	Durham v Oxford University at Oxford	1992
109	J. R. Wileman	Nottinghamshire v Cambridge University at Nottingham	1992
123	A. J. Hollioake†	Surrey v Derbyshire at Ilkeston	1993
101	E. T. Smith	Cambridge University v Glamorgan at Cambridge	1996
110	S. D. Peters	Essex v Cambridge University at Cambridge	1996
210*	D. J. Sales†	Northamptonshire v Worcestershire at Kidderminster	1996

200*	M. J. Powell	Glamorgan v Oxford University at Oxford	1997
104	C. G. Taylor	Gloucestershire v Middlesex at Lord's	2000
107*	R. Clarke	Surrey v Cambridge UCCE at Cambridge	2002
169	J. S. D. Moffat	Cambridge University v Oxford University at Oxford	2002

† *In his second innings.*

TWO DOUBLE-HUNDREDS IN A MATCH

A. E. Fagg	244	202*	Kent v Essex at Colchester	1938

TRIPLE-HUNDRED AND HUNDRED IN A MATCH

G. A. Gooch	333	123	England v India at Lord's	1990

DOUBLE-HUNDRED AND HUNDRED IN A MATCH

C. B. Fry	125	229	Sussex v Surrey at Hove	1900
W. W. Armstrong	157*	245	Victoria v South Australia at Melbourne	1920-21
H. T. W. Hardinge	207	102*	Kent v Surrey at Blackheath	1921
C. P. Mead	113	224	Hampshire v Sussex at Horsham	1921
K. S. Duleepsinhji	115	246	Sussex v Kent at Hastings	1929
D. G. Bradman	124	225	Woodfull's XI v Ryder's XI at Sydney	1929-30
B. Sutcliffe	243	100*	New Zealanders v Essex at Southend	1949
M. R. Hallam	210*	157	Leicestershire v Glamorgan at Leicester	1959
M. R. Hallam	203*	143*	Leicestershire v Sussex at Worthing	1961
Hanumant Singh	109	213*	Rajasthan v Bombay at Bombay	1966-67
Salah-ud-Din	256	102*	Karachi v East Pakistan at Karachi	1968-69
K. D. Walters	242	103	Australia v West Indies at Sydney	1968-69
S. M. Gavaskar	124	220	India v West Indies at Port-of-Spain	1970-71
L. G. Rowe	214	100*	West Indies v New Zealand at Kingston	1971-72
G. S. Chappell	247*	133	Australia v New Zealand at Wellington	1973-74
L. Baichan	216*	102	Berbice v Demerara at Georgetown	1973-74
Zaheer Abbas	216*	156*	Gloucestershire v Surrey at The Oval	1976
Zaheer Abbas	230*	104*	Gloucestershire v Kent at Canterbury	1976
Zaheer Abbas	205*	108*	Gloucestershire v Sussex at Cheltenham	1977
Saadat Ali	141	222	Income Tax v Multan at Multan	1977-78
Talat Ali	214*	104	PIA v Punjab at Lahore	1978-79
Shafiq Ahmad	129	217*	National Bank v MCB at Karachi	1978-79
D. W. Randall	209	146	Nottinghamshire v Middlesex at Nottingham	1979
Zaheer Abbas	215*	150*	Gloucestershire v Somerset at Bath	1981
Qasim Omar	210*	110	MCB v Lahore at Lahore	1982-83
A. I. Kallicharran	200*	117*	Warwickshire v Northants at Birmingham	1984
Rizwan-uz-Zaman	139	217*	PIA v PACO at Lahore	1989-90
G. A. Hick	252*	100*	Worcestershire v Glamorgan at Abergavenny	1990
N. R. Taylor	204	142	Kent v Surrey at Canterbury	1990
N. R. Taylor	111	203*	Kent v Sussex at Hove	1991
W. V. Raman	226	120	Tamil Nadu v Haryana at Faridabad	1991-92
A. J. Lamb	209	107	Northants v Warwicks at Northampton	1992
G. A. Gooch	101	205	Essex v Worcestershire at Worcester	1994
P. A. de Silva	255	116	Kent v Derbyshire at Maidstone	1995
M. C. Mendis	111	200*	Colts CC v Singha SC at Colombo	1995-96
A. M. Bacher	210	112*	Transvaal v Griqualand West at Kimberley	1996-97
H. H. Gibbs	200*	171	South Africans v India A at Nagpur	1996-97
M. L. Hayden	235*	119	Hampshire v Warwickshire at Southampton	1997
G. S. Blewett	169*	213*	Australian XI v England XI at Hobart	1998-99
A. Jadeja	136	202*	Haryana v Saurashtra at Rajkot	1998-99
J. Cox	216	129*	Somerset v Hampshire at Southampton	1999
Mohammad Ramzan	205	102*	Faisalabad v Sargodha at Faisalabad	2000-01
M. W. Goodwin	115	203*	Sussex v Nottinghamshire at Nottingham	2001
D. P. Fulton	208*	104*	Kent v Somerset at Canterbury	2001
B. C. Lara	221	130	West Indies v Sri Lanka at Colombo	2001-02
Minhazul Abedin	210	110	Chittagong v Dhaka at Mymensingh	2001-02

TWO SEPARATE HUNDREDS IN A MATCH

Eight times: Zaheer Abbas.
Seven times: W. R. Hammond.
Six times: J. B. Hobbs, G. M. Turner.
Five times: C. B. Fry, G. A. Gooch, R. T. Ponting.
Four times: D. G. Bradman, G. S. Chappell, J. Cox, J. H. Edrich, L. B. Fishlock, T. W. Graveney, C. G. Greenidge, H. T. W. Hardinge, E. H. Hendren, G. A. Hick, Javed Miandad, G. L. Jessop, H. Morris, M. H. Parmar, P. A. Perrin, M. R. Ramprakash, B. Sutcliffe, H. Sutcliffe.
Three times: Agha Zahid, L. E. G. Ames, Basit Ali, G. Boycott, I. M. Chappell, D. C. S. Compton, S. J. Cook, M. C. Cowdrey, D. Denton, P. A. de Silva, K. S. Duleepsinhji, R. E. Foster, R. C. Fredericks, S. M. Gavaskar, W. G. Grace, G. Gunn, M. R. Hallam, Hanif Mohammad, M. J. Harris, M. L. Hayden, T. W. Hayward, V. S. Hazare, D. W. Hookes, L. Hutton, A. Jones, D. M. Jones, P. N. Kirsten, R. B. McCosker, P. B. H. May, M. P. Maynard, C. P. Mead, T. M. Moody, Rizwan-uz-Zaman, R. T. Robinson, A. C. Russell, Sadiq Mohammad, J. T. Tyldesley, K. C. Wessels.

Notes: W. Lambert scored 107 and 157 for Sussex v Epsom at Lord's in 1817, and it was not until W. G. Grace made 130 and 102* for South of the Thames v North of the Thames at Canterbury in 1868 that the feat was repeated.

C. J. B. Wood, 107* and 117* for Leicestershire v Yorkshire at Bradford in 1911, and S. J. Cook, 120* and 131* for Somerset v Nottinghamshire at Nottingham in 1989, are alone in carrying their bats and scoring hundreds in each innings.

FOUR HUNDREDS OR MORE IN SUCCESSION

Six in succession: D. G. Bradman 1938-39; C. B. Fry 1901; M. J. Procter 1970-71.
Five in succession: B. C. Lara 1993-94/1994; E. D. Weekes 1955-56.
Four in succession: C. W. J. Athey 1987; M. Azharuddin 1984-85; M. G. Bevan 1990-91; G. S. Blewett 1998-99; A. R. Border 1985; D. G. Bradman 1931-32, 1948/1948-49; D. C. S. Compton 1946-47; N. J. Contractor 1957-58; S. J. Cook 1989; K. S. Duleepsinhji 1931; C. B. Fry 1911; C. G. Greenidge 1986; W. R. Hammond 1936-37, 1945/1946; H. T. W. Hardinge 1913; T. W. Hayward 1906; G. A. Hick 1998; J. B. Hobbs 1920, 1925; D. W. Hookes 1976-77; Ijaz Ahmed, jun. 1994-95; R. S. Kaluwitharana 1996-97; P. N. Kirsten 1976-77; J. G. Langridge 1949; C. G. Macartney 1921; K. S. McEwan 1977; P. B. H. May 1956-57; V. M. Merchant 1941-42; A. Mitchell 1933; Nawab of Pataudi sen. 1931; Rizwan-uz-Zaman 1989-90; L. G. Rowe 1971-72; Pankaj Roy 1962-63; Sadiq Mohammad 1976; Saeed Ahmed 1961-62; M. V. Sridhar 1990-91/1991-92; H. Sutcliffe 1931, 1939; S. R. Tendulkar 1994-95; E. Tyldesley 1926; I. J. Ward 2002; W. W. Whysall 1930; F. E. Woolley 1929; Younis Khan 1999-2000; Zaheer Abbas 1970-71, 1982-83.

Notes: T. W. Hayward (Surrey v Nottinghamshire and Leicestershire) and D. W. Hookes (South Australia v Queensland and New South Wales) are the only players listed above to score two hundreds in two successive matches. Hayward scored his in six days, June 4-9, 1906.

The most fifties in consecutive innings is ten – by E. Tyldesley in 1926, by D. G. Bradman in the 1947-48 and 1948 seasons and by R. S. Kaluwitharana in 1994-95.

MOST HUNDREDS IN A SEASON

Eighteen: D. C. S. Compton 1947.
Sixteen: J. B. Hobbs 1925.
Fifteen: W. R. Hammond 1938.
Fourteen: H. Sutcliffe 1932.
Thirteen: G. Boycott 1971, D. G. Bradman 1938, C. B. Fry 1901, W. R. Hammond 1933 and 1937, T. W. Hayward 1906, E. H. Hendren 1923, 1927 and 1928, C. P. Mead 1928, H. Sutcliffe 1928 and 1931.

Since 1969 (excluding G. Boycott – above)

Twelve: G. A. Gooch 1990.
Eleven: S. J. Cook 1991, Zaheer Abbas 1976.
Ten: G. A. Hick 1988, H. Morris 1990, M. R. Ramprakash 1995, G. M. Turner 1970, Zaheer Abbas 1981.

Note: The most achieved outside England is eight by D. G. Bradman in Australia (1947-48), D. C. S. Compton (1948-49), R. N. Harvey and A. R. Morris (both 1949-50) in South Africa, M. D. Crowe in New Zealand (1986-87), Asif Mujtaba in Pakistan (1995-96) and V. V. S. Laxman in India (1999-2000).

MOST DOUBLE-HUNDREDS IN A SEASON

Six: D. G. Bradman 1930.
Five: K. S. Ranjitsinhji 1900; E. D. Weekes 1950.
Four: Arun Lal 1986-87; C. B. Fry 1901; W. R. Hammond 1933, 1934; E. H. Hendren 1929-30; V. M. Merchant 1944-45; G. M. Turner 1971-72.
Three: L. E. G. Ames 1933; Arshad Pervez 1977-78; D. G. Bradman 1930-31, 1931-32, 1934, 1935-36, 1936-37, 1938, 1939-40; W. J. Edrich 1947; C. B. Fry 1903, 1904; M. W. Gatting 1994; G. A. Gooch 1994; W. R. Hammond 1928, 1928-29, 1932-33, 1938; J. Hardstaff jun. 1937, 1947; V. S. Hazare 1943-44; E. H. Hendren 1925; J. B. Hobbs 1914, 1926; M. E. K. Hussey 2001; L. Hutton 1949; D. M. Jones 1991-92; A. I. Kallicharran 1982; V. G. Kambli 1992-93; P. N. Kirsten 1980; R. S. Modi 1944-45; D. Mongia 2000-01; Nawab of Pataudi sen. 1933; W. H. Ponsford 1927-28, 1934; W. V. Raman 1988-89; M. R. Ramprakash 1995; K. S. Ranjitsinhji 1901; I. V. A. Richards 1977; R. B. Simpson 1963-64; P. R. Umrigar 1952, 1959; F. B. Watson 1928.

MOST HUNDREDS IN A CAREER

(35 or more)

		Total	Total 100th 100					
		Total	Inns	Season	Inns	400s	300s	200s
1	J. B. Hobbs	197	1,315	1923	821	0	1	15
2	E. H. Hendren	170	1,300	1928-29	740	0	1	21
3	W. R. Hammond	167	1,005	1935	679	0	4	32
4	C. P. Mead	153	1,340	1927	892	0	0	13
5	G. Boycott	151	1,014	1977	645	0	0	10
6	H. Sutcliffe	149	1,088	1932	700	0	1	16
7	F. E. Woolley	145	1,532	1929	1,031	0	1	8
8	L. Hutton	129	814	1951	619	0	1	10
9	G. A. Gooch	128	990	1992-93	820	0	1	12
10	W. G. Grace	126	1,493	1895	1,113	0	3	10
11	D. C. S. Compton . . .	123	839	1952	552	0	1	8
12	T. W. Graveney	122	1,223	1964	940	0	0	7
13	**G. A. Hick**	**121**	**725**	**1998**	**574**	**1**	**2**	**11**
14	D. G. Bradman	117	338	1947-48	295	1	5	31
15	I. V. A. Richards	114	796	1988-89	658	0	1	9
16	Zaheer Abbas	108	768	1982-83	658	0	0	10
17	{ A. Sandham	107	1,000	1935	871	0	1	10
	{ M. C. Cowdrey	107	1,130	1973	1,035	0	1	2
19	T. W. Hayward	104	1,138	1913	1,076	0	1	7
20	{ G. M. Turner	103	792	1982	779	0	1	9
	{ J. H. Edrich	103	979	1977	945	0	1	3
22	{ L. E. G. Ames	102	951	1950	915	0	0	9
	{ E. Tyldesley	102	961	1934	919	0	0	7
	{ D. L. Amiss	102	1,139	1986	1,081	0	0	3

E. H. Hendren, D. G. Bradman and I. V. A. Richards scored their 100th hundreds in Australia; G. A. Gooch scored his in India. His record includes his century in South Africa in 1981-82, which is no longer accepted by ICC. Zaheer Abbas scored his 100th in Pakistan. Zaheer Abbas and G. Boycott did so in Test matches.

Most double-hundreds scored by batsmen not included in the above list:

Sixteen: C. B. Fry. **Fourteen:** C. G. Greenidge, K. S. Ranjitsinhji. **Thirteen:** W. H. Ponsford (including two 400s and two 300s), J. T. Tyldesley. **Twelve:** P. Holmes, Javed Miandad, R. B. Simpson. **Eleven:** J. W. Hearne, V. M. Merchant. **Ten:** S. M. Gavaskar, J. Hardstaff, jun., V. S. Hazare, A. Shrewsbury, R. T. Simpson.

J. W. Hearne	96
C. B. Fry	94
M. W. Gatting	94
C. G. Greenidge	92
A. J. Lamb	89
A. I. Kallicharran	87
W. J. Edrich	86
G. S. Sobers	86
J. T. Tyldesley	86
P. B. H. May	85
R. E. S. Wyatt	85
J. Hardstaff, jun.	83
R. B. Kanhai	83
S. M. Gavaskar	81
M. E. Waugh	**81**
Javed Miandad	80
M. Leyland	80
B. A. Richards	80
C. H. Lloyd	79
K. F. Barrington	76
J. G. Langridge	76
C. Washbrook	76
H. T. W. Hardinge	75
R. Abel	74
G. S. Chappell	74
D. Kenyon	74
K. S. McEwan	74
Majid Khan	73
Mushtaq Mohammad	72
J. O'Connor	72
W. G. Quaife	72
K. S. Ranjitsinhji	72
D. Brookes	71
M. D. Crowe	71
A. C. Russell	71
A. R. Border	70
D. Denton	69
M. J. K. Smith	69
D. C. Boon	68
R. E. Marshall	68
S. R. Waugh	**68**
R. N. Harvey	67
P. Holmes	67
J. D. Robertson	67
P. A. Perrin	66
K. C. Wessels	66
S. J. Cook	64
T. M. Moody	64
R. G. Pollock	64
R. T. Simpson	64
K. W. R. Fletcher	63
R. T. Robinson	63
G. Gunn	62
K. J. Barnett	**61**
D. L. Haynes	61
D. S. Lehmann	**61**
R. A. Smith	**61**
V. S. Hazare	60
G. H. Hirst	60
C. L. Hooper	**60**
M. R. Ramprakash	**60**
R. B. Simpson	60
P. F. Warner	60

I. M. Chappell	59
A. L. Hassett	59
W. Larkins	59
A. Shrewsbury	59
J. G. Wright	59
A. E. Fagg	58
P. H. Parfitt	58
W. Rhodes	58
P. N. Kirsten	57
L. B. Fishlock	56
A. Jones	56
S. G. Law	**56**
C. A. Milton	56
C. W. J. Athey	55
M. G. Bevan	**55**
C. Hallows	55
Hanif Mohammad	55
M. L. Hayden	**55**
D. M. Jones	55
J. L. Langer	**55**
D. B. Vengsarkar	55
W. Watson	55
M. A. Atherton	54
M. Azharuddin	54
D. J. Insole	54
W. W. Keeton	54
S. R. Tendulkar	**54**
W. Bardsley	53
B. F. Davison	53
A. E. Dipper	53
D. I. Gower	53
G. L. Jessop	53
H. Morris	53
James Seymour	53
Shafiq Ahmad	53
E. H. Bowley	52
D. B. Close	52
A. Ducat	52
J. E. Morris	52
D. W. Randall	52
E. R. Dexter	51
M. P. Maynard	**51**
J. M. Parks	51
W. W. Whysall	51
B. C. Broad	50
G. Cox, jun.	50
H. E. Dollery	50
K. S. Duleepsinhji	50
H. Gimblett	50
W. M. Lawry	50
Sadiq Mohammad	50
F. B. Watson	50
C. G. Macartney	49
M. J. Stewart	49
K. G. Suttle	49
P. R. Umrigar	49
W. M. Woodfull	49
C. J. Barnett	48
M. R. Benson	48
W. Gunn	48
E. G. Hayes	48

B. W. Luckhurst	48
M. J. Procter	48
C. E. B. Rice	48
A. J. Stewart	**48**
C. J. Tavaré	48
R. J. Bailey	48
N. H. Fairbrother	**47**
N. Hussain	**47**
S. P. James	**47**
A. C. MacLaren	47
P. W. G. Parker	47
W. H. Ponsford	47
C. L. Smith	47
A. R. Butcher	46
J. Iddon	46
A. R. Morris	46
C. T. Radley	46
A. P. Wells	46
Younis Ahmed	46
W. W. Armstrong	45
Asif Iqbal	45
L. G. Berry	45
J. M. Brearley	45
A. W. Carr	45
C. Hill	45
B. C. Lara	**45**
M. D. Moxon	45
N. C. O'Neill	45
E. Paynter	45
Rev. D. S. Sheppard	45
N. R. Taylor	45
K. D. Walters	45
J. Cox	**44**
H. H. Gibbons	44
V. M. Merchant	44
A. Mitchell	44
P. E. Richardson	44
B. Sutcliffe	44
G. R. Viswanath	44
P. Willey	44
Asif Mujtaba	**43**
E. J. Barlow	43
T. S. Curtis	43
P. A. de Silva	**43**
B. L. D'Oliveira	43
J. H. Hampshire	43
A. F. Kippax	43
J. W. H. Makepeace	43
Rizwan-uz-Zaman	43
Salim Malik	43
G. P. Thorpe	**43**
P. D. Bowler	**42**
J. P. Crawley	**42**
James Langridge	42
Mudassar Nazar	42
H. W. Parks	42
T. F. Shepherd	42
V. T. Trumper	42
M. J. Harris	41
G. D. Mendis	41
K. R. Miller	41
A. D. Nourse	41

J. H. Parks 41	F. L. Bowley. 38	M. A. Noble. 37
R. M. Prideaux 41	P. J. Burge 38	B. P. Patel 37
G. Pullar 41	J. F. Crapp 38	R. B. Richardson 37
W. E. Russell 41	**D. J. Cullinan** **38**	H. S. Squires 37
M. A. Taylor 41	D. Lloyd 38	R. T. Virgin 37
G. S. Blewett **40**	V. L. Manjrekar 38	C. J. B. Wood 37
R. C. Fredericks 40	A. W. Nourse 38	N. F. Armstrong 36
J. Gunn 40	N. Oldfield 38	**M. S. Atapattu** **36**
P. Johnson **40**	Rev. J. H. Parsons 38	G. Fowler. 36
M. J. Smith 40	W. W. Read 38	**Inzamam-ul-Haq** **36**
C. L. Walcott 40	**Sajid Ali** **38**	M. C. J. Nicholas 36
D. M. Young 40	Ajay Sharma 38	E. Oldroyd 36
Arshad Pervez 39	J. Sharp 38	W. Place 36
W. H. Ashdown 39	**Shoaib Mohammad** . . . **38**	A. L. Wadekar 36
D. J. Bicknell **39**	V. P. Terry 38	E. D. Weekes 36
J. B. Bolus 39	L. J. Todd 38	C. S. Dempster 35
W. A. Brown 39	J. J. Whitaker 38	**M. T. G. Elliott** **35**
R. J. Gregory 39	J. Arnold 37	D. R. Jardine 35
M. A. Lynch 39	G. Brown 37	T. E. Jesty 35
W. R. D. Payton 39	G. Cook 37	K. R. Rutherford 35
R. T. Ponting **39**	**R. Dravid** **37**	J. D. Siddons 35
J. R. Reid 39	G. M. Emmett 37	B. H. Valentine 35
F. M. M. Worrell 39	**G. Kirsten** **37**	G. M. Wood 35
I. T. Botham 38	H. W. Lee 37	

Bold type denotes those who played in 2001-02 or 2002 season.

MOST RUNS IN A SEASON

	Season	I	NO	R	HS	100s	Avge
D. C. S. Compton	1947	50	8	3,816	246	18	90.85
W. J. Edrich	1947	52	8	3,539	267*	12	80.43
T. W. Hayward	1906	61	8	3,518	219	13	66.37
L. Hutton	1949	56	6	3,429	269*	12	68.58
F. E. Woolley	1928	59	4	3,352	198	12	60.94
H. Sutcliffe	1932	52	7	3,336	313	14	74.13
W. R. Hammond	1933	54	5	3,323	264	13	67.81
E. H. Hendren	1928	54	7	3,311	209*	13	70.44
R. Abel	1901	68	8	3,309	247	7	55.15

Notes: 3,000 in a season has been surpassed on 19 other occasions (a full list can be found in *Wisden* 1999 and earlier editions). W. R. Hammond, E. H. Hendren and H. Sutcliffe are the only players to achieve the feat three times. M. J. K. Smith (3,245 in 1959) and W. E. Alley (3,019 in 1961) are the only players except those listed above to have reached 3,000 since World War II.

2,000 RUNS IN A SEASON

Since reduction of Championship matches in 1969

Five times: G. A. Gooch 2,746 (1990), 2,559 (1984), 2,324 (1988), 2,208 (1985), 2,023 (1993).
Three times: D. L. Amiss 2,239 (1984), 2,110 (1976), 2,030 (1978); S. J. Cook 2,755† (1991), 2,608 (1990), 2,241 (1989); M. W. Gatting 2,257 (1984), 2,057 (1991), 2,000 (1992); G. A. Hick 2,713 (1988), 2,347 (1990), 2,004 (1986); G. M. Turner 2,416 (1973), 2,379 (1970), 2,101 (1981).
Twice: G. Boycott 2,503 (1971), 2,051 (1970); J. H. Edrich 2,238 (1969), 2,031 (1971); A. I. Kallicharran 2,301 (1984), 2,120 (1982); Zaheer Abbas 2,554 (1976), 2,306 (1981).
Once: M. Azharuddin 2,016 (1991); J. B. Bolus 2,143 (1970); P. D. Bowler 2,044 (1992); B. C. Broad 2,226 (1990); A. R. Butcher 2,116 (1990); C. G. Greenidge 2,035 (1986); M. J. Harris 2,238 (1971); D. L. Haynes 2,346 (1990); M. E. K. Hussey 2,055 (2001); Javed Miandad 2,083 (1981); A. J. Lamb 2,049 (1981); B. C. Lara 2,066 (1994); K. S. McEwan 2,176 (1983); Majid Khan 2,074 (1972); A. A. Metcalfe 2,047 (1990); H. Morris 2,276 (1990); M. R. Ramprakash 2,258 (1995); D. W. Randall 2,151 (1985); I. V. A. Richards 2,161 (1977); R. T. Robinson 2,032 (1984); M. A. Roseberry 2,044 (1992); C. L. Smith 2,000 (1985); R. T. Virgin 2,223 (1970); D. M. Ward 2,072 (1990); M. E. Waugh 2,072 (1990).

Notes: W. G. Grace scored 2,739 runs in 1871 – the first batsman to reach 2,000 runs in a season. He made ten hundreds and twice exceeded 200, with an average of 78.25 in all first-class matches.

† *Highest since the reduction of Championship matches in 1969.*

1,000 RUNS IN A SEASON MOST TIMES

Includes overseas tours and seasons

28 times: W. G. Grace 2,000 (6); F. E. Woolley 3,000 (1), 2,000 (12).

27 times: M. C. Cowdrey 2,000 (2); C. P. Mead 3,000 (2), 2,000 (9).

26 times: G. Boycott 2,000 (3); J. B. Hobbs 3,000 (1), 2,000 (16).

25 times: E. H. Hendren 3,000 (3), 2,000 (12).

24 times: D. L. Amiss 2,000 (3); W. G. Quaife 2,000 (1); H. Sutcliffe 3,000 (3), 2,000 (12).

23 times: A. Jones.

22 times: T. W. Graveney 2,000 (7); W. R. Hammond 3,000 (3), 2,000 (9).

21 times: D. Denton 2,000 (5); J. H. Edrich 2,000 (6); G. A. Gooch 2,000 (5); W. Rhodes 2,000 (2).

20 times: D. B. Close; K. W. R. Fletcher; M. W. Gatting 2,000 (3); G. Gunn; T. W. Hayward 3,000 (2), 2,000 (8); James Langridge 2,000 (1); J. M. Parks 2,000 (3); A. Sandham 2,000 (8); M. J. K. Smith 3,000 (1), 2,000 (5); C. Washbrook 2,000 (2).

19 times: J. W. Hearne 2,000 (4); G. H. Hirst 2,000 (3); D. Kenyon 2,000 (7); E. Tyldesley 3,000 (1), 2,000 (5); J. T. Tyldesley 3,000 (1), 2,000 (4).

18 times: L. G. Berry 2,000 (1); H. T. W. Hardinge 2,000 (5); G. A. Hick 2,000 (3); R. E. Marshall 2,000 (6); P. A. Perrin; G. M. Turner 2,000 (3); R. E. S. Wyatt 2,000 (5).

17 times: L. E. G. Ames 3,000 (1), 2,000 (5); T. E. Bailey 2,000 (1); D. Brookes 2,000 (6); D. C. S. Compton 3,000 (1), 2,000 (5); C. G. Greenidge 2,000 (1); L. Hutton 3,000 (1), 2,000 (8); J. G. Langridge 2,000 (11); M. Leyland 2,000 (5); I. V. A. Richards 2,000 (1); K. G. Suttle 2,000 (1); Zaheer Abbas 2,000 (5).

16 times: K. J. Barnett; D. G. Bradman 2,000 (4); D. E. Davies 2,000 (1); E. G. Hayes 2,000 (2); C. A. Milton 2,000 (1); J. O'Connor 2,000 (4); C. T. Radley; James Seymour 2,000 (1); C. J. Tavaré.

15 times: G. Barker; K. F. Barrington 2,000 (3); E. H. Bowley 2,000 (4); M. H. Denness; A. E. Dipper 2,000 (5); H. E. Dollery 2,000 (2); W. J. Edrich 3,000 (1), 2,000 (8); J. H. Hampshire; P. Holmes 2,000 (7); Mushtaq Mohammad; R. B. Nicholls 2,000 (1); P. H. Parfitt 2,000 (3); W. G. A. Parkhouse 2,000 (1); B. A. Richards 2,000 (1); J. D. Robertson 2,000 (9); G. S. Sobers; M. J. Stewart 2,000 (1).

Notes: F. E. Woolley reached 1,000 runs in 28 consecutive seasons (1907-1938), C. P. Mead in 27 (1906-1936).

Outside England, 1,000 runs in a season has been reached most times by D. G. Bradman (in 12 seasons in Australia).

Three batsmen have scored 1,000 runs in a season in each of four different countries: G. S. Sobers in West Indies, England, India and Australia; M. C. Cowdrey and G. Boycott in England, South Africa, West Indies and Australia.

HIGHEST AGGREGATES OUTSIDE ENGLAND

	Season	I	NO	R	HS	100s	Avge
In Australia D. G. Bradman	1928-29	24	6	1,690	340*	7	93.88
In South Africa J. R. Reid	1961-62	30	2	1,915	203	7	68.39
In West Indies E. H. Hendren	1929-30	18	5	1,765	254*	6	135.76
In New Zealand M. D. Crowe	1986-87	21	3	1,676	175*	8	93.11
In India C. G. Borde	1964-65	28	3	1,604	168	6	64.16
In Pakistan Saadat Ali	1983-84	27	1	1,649	208	4	63.42

	Season	I	NO	R	HS	100s	Avge
In Sri Lanka							
R. P. Arnold	1995-96	24	3	1,475	217*	5	70.23
In Zimbabwe							
G. W. Flower	1994-95	20	3	983	201*	4	57.82
In Bangladesh							
Minhazul Abedin	2001-02	15	1	1,012	210	3	72.28

Note: In more than one country, the following aggregates of over 2,000 runs have been recorded:

M. Amarnath (P/I/WI)	1982-83	34	6	2,234	207	9	79.78
J. R. Reid (SA/A/NZ)	1961-62	40	2	2,188	203	7	57.57
S. M. Gavaskar (I/P)	1978-79	30	6	2,121	205	10	88.37
R. B. Simpson (I/P/A/WI).	1964-65	34	4	2,063	201	8	68.76
M. H. Richardson (Z/SA/NZ) . .	2000-01	34	3	2,030	306	4	65.48

LEADING BATSMEN IN AN ENGLISH SEASON

(Qualification: 8 completed innings)

Season	Leading scorer	Runs	Avge	Top of averages	Runs	Avge
1946	D. C. S. Compton . . .	2,403	61.61	W. R. Hammond	1,783	84.90
1947	D. C. S. Compton . . .	3,816	90.85	D. C. S. Compton . . .	3,816	90.85
1948	L. Hutton	2,654	64.73	D. G. Bradman	2,428	89.92
1949	L. Hutton	3,429	68.58	J. Hardstaff	2,251	72.61
1950	R. T. Simpson	2,576	62.82	E. D. Weekes	2,310	79.65
1951	J. D. Robertson. . . .	2,917	56.09	P. B. H. May	2,339	68.79
1952	L. Hutton	2,567	61.11	D. S. Sheppard	2,262	64.62
1953	W. J. Edrich	2,557	47.35	R. N. Harvey	2,040	65.80
1954	D. Kenyon	2,636	51.68	D. C. S. Compton . . .	1,524	58.61
1955	D. J. Insole	2,427	42.57	D. J. McGlew	1,871	58.46
1956	T. W. Graveney . . .	2,397	49.93	K. Mackay	1,103	52.52
1957	T. W. Graveney . . .	2,361	49.18	P. B. H. May	2,347	61.76
1958	P. B. H. May	2,231	63.74	P. B. H. May	2,231	63.74
1959	M. J. K. Smith	3,245	57.94	V. L. Manjrekar . . .	755	68.63
1960	M. J. K. Smith	2,551	45.55	R. Subba Row	1,503	55.66
1961	W. E. Alley	3,019	56.96	W. M. Lawry	2,019	61.18
1962	J. H. Edrich	2,482	51.70	R. T. Simpson	867	54.18
1963	J. B. Bolus	2,190	41.32	G. S. Sobers	1,333	47.60
1964	T. W. Graveney . . .	2,385	54.20	K. F. Barrington . . .	1,872	62.40
1965	J. H. Edrich	2,319	62.67	M. C. Cowdrey	2,093	63.42
1966	A. R. Lewis	2,198	41.47	G. S. Sobers	1,349	61.31
1967	C. A. Milton	2,089	46.42	K. F. Barrington . . .	2,059	68.63
1968	B. A. Richards	2,395	47.90	G. Boycott	1,487	64.65
1969	J. H. Edrich	2,238	69.93	J. H. Edrich	2,238	69.93
1970	G. M. Turner	2,379	61.00	G. S. Sobers	1,742	75.73
1971	G. Boycott	2,503	100.12	G. Boycott	2,503	100.12
1972	Majid Khan	2,074	61.00	G. Boycott	1,230	72.35
1973	G. M. Turner	2,416	67.11	G. M. Turner	2,416	67.11
1974	R. T. Virgin	1,936	56.94	C. H. Lloyd	1,458	63.39
1975	G. Boycott	1,915	73.65	R. B. Kanhai	1,073	82.53
1976	Zaheer Abbas	2,554	75.11	Zaheer Abbas	2,554	75.11
1977	I. V. A. Richards . . .	2,161	65.48	G. Boycott	1,701	68.04
1978	D. L. Amiss	2,030	53.42	C. E. B. Rice	1,871	66.82
1979	K. C. Wessels.	1,800	52.94	G. Boycott	1,538	102.53
1980	P. N. Kirsten	1,895	63.16	A. J. Lamb	1,797	66.55
1981	Zaheer Abbas	2,306	88.69	Zaheer Abbas	2,306	88.69
1982	A. I. Kallicharran . . .	2,120	66.25	G. M. Turner	1,171	90.07
1983	K. S. McEwan	2,176	64.00	I. V. A. Richards . . .	1,204	75.25
1984	G. A. Gooch	2,559	67.34	C. G. Greenidge	1,069	82.23
1985	G. A. Gooch	2,208	71.22	I. V. A. Richards . . .	1,836	76.50
1986	C. G. Greenidge	2,035	67.83	C. G. Greenidge	2,035	67.83

Season	Leading scorer	Runs	Avge	Top of averages	Runs	Avge
1987	G. A. Hick	1,879	52.19	M. D. Crowe.	1,627	67.79
1988	G. A. Hick	2,713	77.51	R. A. Harper.	622	77.75
1989	S. J. Cook	2,241	60.56	D. M. Jones	1,510	88.82
1990	G. A. Gooch	2,746	101.70	G. A. Gooch	2,746	101.70
1991	S. J. Cook	2,755	81.02	C. L. Hooper	1,501	93.81
1992	{ P. D. Bowler	2,044	65.93	Salim Malik	1,184	78.93
	M. A. Roseberry. . .	2,044	56.77			
1993	G. A. Gooch	2,023	63.21	D. C. Boon	1,437	75.63
1994	B. C. Lara	2,066	89.82	J. D. Carr.	1,543	90.76
1995	M. R. Ramprakash . .	2,258	77.86	M. R. Ramprakash . . .	2,258	77.86
1996	G. A. Gooch	1,944	67.03	S. C. Ganguly	762	95.25
1997	S. P. James	1,775	68.26	G. A. Hick	1,524	69.27
1998	J. P. Crawley	1,851	74.04	J. P. Crawley	1,851	74.04
1999	S. G. Law	1,833	73.32	S. G. Law	1,833	73.32
2000	D. S. Lehmann	1,477	67.13	M. G. Bevan	1,124	74.93
2001	M. E. K. Hussey. . . .	2,055	79.03	D. R. Martyn	942	104.66
2002	I. J. Ward	1,759	62.82	R. Dravid	773	96.62

Notes: The highest average recorded in an English season was 115.66 (2,429 runs, 26 innings) by D. G. Bradman in 1938.

In 1953, W. A. Johnston averaged 102.00 from 17 innings, 16 not out.

25,000 RUNS

Dates in italics denote the first half of an overseas season; i.e. *1945* denotes the 1945-46 season.

		Career	R	I	NO	HS	100s	Avge
1	J. B. Hobbs	1905-34	61,237	1,315	106	316*	197	50.65
2	F. E. Woolley.	1906-38	58,969	1,532	85	305*	145	40.75
3	E. H. Hendren	1907-38	57,611	1,300	166	301*	170	50.80
4	C. P. Mead	1905-36	55,061	1,340	185	280*	153	47.67
5	W. G. Grace	1865-1908	54,896	1,493	105	344	126	39.55
6	W. R. Hammond	1920-51	50,551	1,005	104	336*	167	56.10
7	H. Sutcliffe	1919-45	50,138	1,088	123	313	149	51.95
8	G. Boycott	1962-86	48,426	1,014	162	261*	151	56.83
9	T. W. Graveney	1948-*71*	47,793	1,223	159	258	122	44.91
10	G. A. Gooch	1973-2000	44,846	990	75	333	128	49.01
11	T. W. Hayward	1893-1914	43,551	1,138	96	315*	104	41.79
12	D. L. Amiss	1960-87	43,423	1,139	126	262*	102	42.86
13	M. C. Cowdrey	1950-76	42,719	1,130	134	307	107	42.89
14	A. Sandham	1911-*37*	41,284	1,000	79	325	107	44.82
15	L. Hutton	1934-60	40,140	814	91	364	129	55.51
16	M. J. K. Smith.	1951-75	39,832	1,091	139	204	69	41.84
17	W. Rhodes	1898-1930	39,802	1,528	237	267*	58	30.83
18	J. H. Edrich.	1956-78	39,790	979	104	310*	103	45.47
19	R. E. S. Wyatt	1923-57	39,405	1,141	157	232	85	40.04
20	D. C. S. Compton. . . .	1936-64	38,942	839	88	300	123	51.85
21	E. Tyldesley.	1909-36	38,874	961	106	256*	102	45.46
22	J. T. Tyldesley	1895-1923	37,897	994	62	295*	86	40.66
23	K. W. R. Fletcher . . .	1962-88	37,665	1,167	170	228*	63	37.77
24	C. G. Greenidge.	1970-92	37,354	889	75	273*	92	45.88
25	J. W. Hearne	1909-36	37,252	1,025	116	285*	96	40.98
26	L. E. G. Ames	1926-51	37,248	951	95	295	102	43.51
27	D. Kenyon	1946-67	37,002	1,159	59	259	74	33.63
28	W. J. Edrich	1934-58	36,965	964	92	267*	86	42.39
29	J. M. Parks	1949-76	36,673	1,227	172	205*	51	34.76
30	M. W. Gatting	1975-98	36,549	861	123	258	94	49.52
31	D. Denton	1894-1920	36,479	1,163	70	221	69	33.37
32	G. H. Hirst	1891-1929	36,323	1,215	151	341	60	34.13
33	I. V. A. Richards	*1971*-93	36,212	796	63	322	114	49.40
34	A. Jones	1957-83	36,049	1,168	72	204*	56	32.89
35	W. G. Quaife	1894-1928	36,012	1,203	185	255*	72	35.37

		Career	R	I	NO	HS	100s	Avge
36	R. E. Marshall	1945-72	35,725	1,053	59	228*	68	35.94
37	**G. A. Hick**	*1983-2002*	**35,246**	**725**	**69**	**405***	**121**	**53.72**
38	G. Gunn	1902-32	35,208	1,061	82	220	62	35.96
39	D. B. Close	1949-86	34,994	1,225	173	198	52	33.26
40	Zaheer Abbas.	1965-86	34,843	768	92	274	108	51.54
41	J. G. Langridge	1928-55	34,380	984	66	250*	76	37.45
42	G. M. Turner	1964-82	34,346	792	101	311*	103	49.70
43	C. Washbrook	1933-64	34,101	906	107	251*	76	42.67
44	M. Leyland	1920-48	33,660	932	101	263	80	40.50
45	H. T. W. Hardinge. . .	1902-33	33,519	1,021	103	263*	75	36.51
46	R. Abel.	1881-1904	33,124	1,007	73	357*	74	35.46
47	A. I. Kallicharran . . .	1966-90	32,650	834	86	243*	87	43.64
48	A. J. Lamb	1972-95	32,502	772	108	294	89	48.94
49	C. A. Milton	1948-74	32,150	1,078	125	170	56	33.73
50	J. D. Robertson. . . .	1937-59	31,914	897	46	331*	67	37.50
51	J. Hardstaff, jun. . . .	1930-55	31,847	812	94	266	83	44.35
52	James Langridge . . .	1924-53	31,716	1,058	157	167	42	35.20
53	K. F. Barrington	1953-68	31,714	831	136	256	76	45.63
54	C. H. Lloyd	1963-86	31,232	730	96	242*	79	49.26
55	Mushtaq Mohammad .	1956-85	31,091	843	104	303*	72	42.07
56	C. B. Fry	1892-1921	30,886	658	43	258*	94	50.22
57	D. Brookes	1934-59	30,874	925	70	257	71	36.10
58	P. Holmes	1913-35	30,573	810	84	315*	67	42.11
59	R. T. Simpson	1944-63	30,546	852	55	259	64	38.32
60	{ L. G. Berry	1924-51	30,225	1,056	57	232	45	30.25
	{ K. G. Suttle	1949-71	30,225	1,064	92	204*	49	31.09
62	P. A. Perrin	1896-1928	29,709	918	91	343*	66	35.92
63	P. F. Warner	1894-1929	29,028	875	75	244	60	36.28
64	R. B. Kanhai	1954-81	28,774	669	82	256	83	49.01
65	J. O'Connor	1921-39	28,764	903	79	248	72	34.90
66	Javed Miandad	1973-93	28,647	631	95	311	80	53.44
67	T. E. Bailey	1945-67	28,641	1,072	215	205	28	33.42
68	**K. J. Barnett**	*1979-2002*	**28,593**	**784**	**76**	**239***	**61**	**40.38**
69	D. W. Randall	1972-93	28,456	827	81	237	52	38.14
70	E. H. Bowley.	1912-34	28,378	859	47	283	52	34.94
71	B. A. Richards	1964-82	28,358	576	58	356	80	54.74
72	G. S. Sobers	1952-74	28,315	609	93	365*	86	54.87
73	A. E. Dipper	1908-32	28,075	865	69	252*	53	35.27
74	D. G. Bradman	1927-48	28,067	338	43	452*	117	95.14
75	J. H. Hampshire	1961-84	28,059	924	112	183*	43	34.55
76	P. B. H. May	1948-63	27,592	618	77	285*	85	51.00
77	R. T. Robinson	1978-99	27,571	739	85	220*	63	42.15
78	B. F. Davison	1967-87	27,453	766	79	189	53	39.96
79	Majid Khan	1961-84	27,444	700	62	241	73	43.01
80	A. C. Russell	1908-30	27,358	717	59	273	71	41.57
81	E. G. Hayes	1896-1926	27,318	896	48	276	48	32.21
82	A. E. Fagg	1932-57	27,291	803	46	269*	58	36.05
83	James Seymour	1900-26	27,237	911	62	218*	53	32.08
84	W. Larkins	1972-95	27,142	842	54	252	59	34.44
85	A. R. Border	1976-95	27,131	625	97	205	70	51.38
86	P. H. Parfitt	1956-73	26,924	845	104	200*	58	36.33
87	G. L. Jessop	1894-1914	26,698	855	37	286	53	32.63
88	K. S. McEwan	1972-91	26,628	705	67	218	74	41.73
89	D. E. Davies	1924-54	26,564	1,032	80	287*	32	27.90
90	A. Shrewsbury	1875-1902	26,505	813	90	267	59	36.65
91	M. J. Stewart	1954-72	26,492	898	93	227*	49	32.90
92	C. T. Radley	1964-87	26,441	880	134	200	46	35.44
93	D. I. Gower	1975-93	26,339	727	70	228	53	40.08
94	C. E. B. Rice	1969-93	26,331	766	123	246	48	40.95
95	Younis Ahmed	1961-86	26,073	762	118	221*	46	40.48
96	P. E. Richardson	1949-65	26,055	794	41	185	44	34.60

		Career	R	I	NO	HS	100s	Avge
97	D. L. Haynes	1976-96	26,030	639	72	255*	61	45.90
98	M. H. Denness	1959-80	25,886	838	65	195	33	33.48
99	S. M. Gavaskar	1966-87	25,834	563	61	340	81	51.46
100	J. W. H. Makepeace. .	1906-30	25,799	778	66	203	43	36.23
101	**M. E. Waugh . . . . . .**	**1985-2002**	**25,715**	**553**	**70**	**229***	**81**	**53.24**
102	W. Gunn	1880-1904	25,691	850	72	273	48	33.02
103	W. Watson	1939-64	25,670	753	109	257	55	39.86
104	G. Brown	1908-33	25,649	1,012	52	232*	37	26.71
105	**R. A. Smith . . . .**	**1980-2002**	**25,633**	**702**	**86**	**209***	**61**	**41.61**
106	G. M. Emmett	1936-59	25,602	865	50	188	37	31.41
107	J. B. Bolus	1956-75	25,598	833	81	202*	39	34.03
108	W. E. Russell	1956-72	25,525	796	64	193	41	34.87
109	C. W. J. Athey	1976-97	25,453	784	71	184	55	35.69
110	C. J. Barnett	1927-53	25,389	821	45	259	48	32.71
111	L. B. Fishlock	1931-52	25,376	699	54	253	56	39.34
112	D. J. Insole	1947-63	25,241	743	72	219*	54	37.61
113	J. M. Brearley	1961-83	25,185	768	102	312*	45	37.81
114	J. Vine	1896-1922	25,171	920	79	202	34	29.92
115	R. M. Prideaux	1958-74	25,136	808	75	202*	41	34.29
116	J. H. King	1895-1925	25,122	988	69	227*	34	27.33
117	**A. J. Stewart. . . . . .**	**1981-2002**	**25,085**	**705**	**77**	**271***	**48**	**39.94**
118	J. G. Wright.	1975-92	25,073	636	44	192	59	42.35

Bold type denotes those who played in 2001-02 or 2002 season.

Note: Some works of reference provide career figures which differ from those in this list, owing to the exclusion or inclusion of matches recognised or not recognised as first-class by *Wisden*.

Other Current Players with 20,000 Runs

	Career	R	I	NO	HS	100s	Avge
M. P. Maynard	1985-2002	22,576	589	57	243	51	42.43
M. R. Ramprakash	1987-2002	21,779	537	66	235	60	46.23
S. R. Waugh	1984-2002	21,351	492	81	216*	68	51.94
C. L. Hooper.	1984-2001	20,801	487	46	236*	60	47.16
N. H. Fairbrother	1982-2002	20,612	580	80	366	47	41.22
P. Johnson.	1982-2002	20,534	624	60	187	40	36.40

CAREER AVERAGE OVER 50

(Qualification: 10,000 runs)

Avge		Career	I	NO	R	HS	100s
95.14	D. G. Bradman	1927-48	338	43	28,067	452*	117
71.22	V. M. Merchant	1929-51	229	43	13,248	359*	44
67.46	Ajay Sharma	1984-2000	166	16	10,120	259*	38
65.18	W. H. Ponsford	1920-34	235	23	13,819	437	47
64.99	W. M. Woodfull	1921-34	245	39	13,388	284	49
61.83	**S. R. Tendulkar**	**1988-2002**	**295**	**29**	**16,448**	**233***	**54**
58.24	A. L. Hassett	1932-53	322	32	16,890	232	59
58.19	V. S. Hazare	1934-66	365	45	18,621	316*	60
58.11	**V. V. S. Laxman**	**1992-2002**	**195**	**21**	**10,112**	**353**	**32**
57.22	A. F. Kippax	1918-35	256	33	12,762	315*	43
56.94	**R. Dravid**	**1990-2002**	**277**	**38**	**13,609**	**217**	**37**
56.83	G. Boycott	1962-86	1,014	162	48,426	261*	151
56.78	**D. S. Lehmann**	**1987-2002**	**356**	**23**	**18,909**	**255**	**61**

Avge		Career	I	NO	R	HS	100s
56.55	C. L. Walcott	1941-63	238	29	11,820	314*	40
56.48	**M. G. Bevan**	**1989-2002**	**344**	**61**	**15,985**	**203***	**55**
56.37	K. S. Ranjitsinhji	1893-1920	500	62	24,692	285*	72
56.22	R. B. Simpson	1952-77	436	62	21,029	359	60
56.10	W. R. Hammond	1920-51	1,005	104	50,551	336*	167
56.02	M. D. Crowe	1979-95	412	62	19,608	299	71
55.51	L. Hutton	1934-60	814	91	40,140	364	129
55.34	E. D. Weekes	1944-64	241	24	12,010	304*	36
55.11	S. V. Manjrekar	1984-97	217	31	10,252	377	31
54.87	G. S. Sobers	1952-74	609	93	28,315	365*	86
54.74	B. A. Richards	1964-82	576	58	28,358	356	80
54.72	**R. T. Ponting**	**1992-2001**	**240**	**35**	**11,218**	**233**	**39**
54.67	R. G. Pollock	1960-86	437	54	20,940	274	64
54.37	**A. Flower**	**1986-2002**	**241**	**50**	**10,385**	**232***	**30**
54.24	F. M. M. Worrell	1941-64	326	49	15,025	308*	39
53.78	R. M. Cowper	1959-69	228	31	10,595	307	26
53.72	**G. A. Hick**	**1983-2002**	**725**	**69**	**35,246**	**405***	**121**
53.67	A. R. Morris	1940-63	250	15	12,614	290	46
53.44	Javed Miandad	1973-93	631	95	28,647	311	80
53.25	**M. L. Hayden**	**1991-2001**	**362**	**36**	**17,361**	**235***	**55**
53.24	**M. E. Waugh**	**1985-2002**	**553**	**70**	**25,715**	**229***	**81**
52.86	D. B. Vengsarkar	1975-91	390	52	17,868	284	55
52.32	Hanif Mohammad	1951-75	371	45	17,059	499	55
52.27	P. R. Umrigar	1944-67	350	41	16,154	252*	49
52.20	G. S. Chappell	1966-83	542	72	24,535	247*	74
51.98	M. Azharuddin	1981-99	343	38	15,855	226	54
51.95	H. Sutcliffe	1919-45	1,088	123	50,138	313	149
51.94	**S. R. Waugh**	**1984-2002**	**492**	**81**	**21,351**	**216***	**68**
51.85	D. M. Jones	1981-97	415	45	19,188	324*	55
51.85	D. C. S. Compton	1936-64	839	88	38,942	300	123
51.54	Zaheer Abbas	1965-86	768	92	34,843	274	108
51.53	A. D. Nourse	1931-52	269	27	12,472	260*	41
51.46	S. M. Gavaskar	1966-87	563	61	25,834	340	81
51.44	W. A. Brown	1932-49	284	15	13,838	265*	39
51.38	A. R. Border	1976-95	625	97	27,131	205	70
51.31	**Inzamam-ul-Haq**	**1985-2002**	**308**	**47**	**13,392**	**329**	**36**
51.24	**J. L. Langer**	**1991-2001**	**372**	**40**	**17,012**	**274***	**55**
51.00	P. B. H. May	1948-63	618	77	27,592	285*	85
50.95	N. C. O'Neill	1955-67	306	34	13,859	284	45
50.93	R. N. Harvey	1946-62	461	35	21,699	231*	67
50.90	W. M. Lawry	1955-71	417	49	18,734	266	50
50.90	A. V. Mankad	1963-82	326	71	12,980	265	31
50.80	E. H. Hendren	1907-38	1,300	166	57,611	301*	170
50.65	J. B. Hobbs	1905-34	1,315	106	61,237	316*	197
50.61	**M. S. Atapattu**	**1988-2002**	**265**	**46**	**11,085**	**253***	**36**
50.58	K. C. Wessels	1973-99	539	50	24,738	254	66
50.58	S. J. Cook	1972-94	475	57	21,143	313*	64
50.22	C. B. Fry	1892-1921	658	43	30,886	258*	94
50.13	**H. P. Tillekeratne**	**1984-2002**	**290**	**70**	**11,029**	**204***	**32**

Note: G. A. Headley (*1927-1954*) scored 9,921 runs, average 69.86.

Bold type denotes those who played in 2001-02 or 2002 season.

FASTEST FIFTIES

Minutes			
11	C. I. J. Smith (66)	Middlesex v Gloucestershire at Bristol	1938
13	Khalid Mahmood (56)	Gujranwala v Sargodha at Gujranwala	2000-01
14	S. J. Pegler (50)	South Africans v Tasmania at Launceston	1910-11
14	F. T. Mann (53)	Middlesex v Nottinghamshire at Lord's	1921

Minutes

14	H. B. Cameron (56)	Transvaal v Orange Free State at Johannesburg . . .	1934-35
14	C. I. J. Smith (52)	Middlesex v Kent at Maidstone	1935

Note: The following fast fifties were scored in contrived circumstances when runs were given from full tosses and long hops to expedite a declaration: C. C. Inman (8 minutes), Leicestershire v Nottinghamshire at Nottingham, 1965; G. Chapple (10 minutes), Lancashire v Glamorgan at Manchester, 1993; T. M. Moody (11 minutes), Warwickshire v Glamorgan at Swansea, 1990; A. J. Stewart (14 minutes), Surrey v Kent at Dartford, 1986; M. P. Maynard (14 minutes), Glamorgan v Yorkshire at Cardiff, 1987.

FASTEST HUNDREDS

Minutes

35	P. G. H. Fender (113*)	Surrey v Northamptonshire at Northampton	1920
40	G. L. Jessop (101)	Gloucestershire v Yorkshire at Harrogate.	1897
40	Ahsan-ul-Haq (100*)	Muslims v Sikhs at Lahore	1923-24
42	G. L. Jessop (191)	Gentlemen of South v Players of South at Hastings	1907
43	A. H. Hornby (106)	Lancashire v Somerset at Manchester.	1905
43	D. W. Hookes (107)	South Australia v Victoria at Adelaide	1982-83
44	R. N. S. Hobbs (100)	Essex v Australians at Chelmsford.	1975

Notes: The fastest recorded authentic hundred in terms of balls received was scored off 34 balls by D. W. Hookes (above).

Research of the scorebook has shown that P. G. H. Fender scored his hundred from between 40 and 46 balls. He contributed 113 to an unfinished sixth-wicket partnership of 171 in 42 minutes with H. A. Peach.

E. B. Alletson (Nottinghamshire) scored 189 out of 227 runs in 90 minutes against Sussex at Hove in 1911. It has been estimated that his last 139 runs took 37 minutes.

The following fast hundreds were scored in contrived circumstances when full tosses, long hops etc were bowled deliberately to expedite a declaration: G. Chapple (21 minutes), Lancashire v Glamorgan at Manchester, 1993; T. M. Moody (26 minutes), Warwickshire v Glamorgan at Swansea, 1990; S. J. O'Shaughnessy (35 minutes), Lancashire v Leicestershire at Manchester, 1983; C. M. Old (37 minutes), Yorkshire v Warwickshire at Birmingham, 1977; N. F. M. Popplewell (41 minutes), Somerset v Gloucestershire at Bath, 1983.

FASTEST DOUBLE-HUNDREDS

Minutes

113	R. J. Shastri (200*)	Bombay v Baroda at Bombay	1984-85
120	G. L. Jessop (286)	Gloucestershire v Sussex at Hove	1903
120	C. H. Lloyd (201*)	West Indians v Glamorgan at Swansea	1976
130	G. L. Jessop (234)	Gloucestershire v Somerset at Bristol	1905
131	V. T. Trumper (293)	Australians v Canterbury at Christchurch	1913-14

FASTEST TRIPLE-HUNDREDS

Minutes

181	D. C. S. Compton (300)	MCC v N. E. Transvaal at Benoni	1948-49
205	F. E. Woolley (305*)	MCC v Tasmania at Hobart	1911-12
205	C. G. Macartney (345)	Australians v Nottinghamshire at Nottingham	1921
213	D. G. Bradman (369)	South Australia v Tasmania at Adelaide	1935-36

300 RUNS IN A DAY BY ONE BATSMAN

390*	B. C. Lara	Warwickshire v Durham at Birmingham	1994
345	C. G. Macartney	Australians v Nottinghamshire at Nottingham	1921
334	W. H. Ponsford	Victoria v New South Wales at Melbourne	1926-27
333	K. S. Duleepsinhji	Sussex v Northamptonshire at Hove	1930
331*	J. D. Robertson	Middlesex v Worcestershire at Worcester	1949
325*	B. A. Richards	S. Australia v W. Australia at Perth	1970-71
322†	E. Paynter	Lancashire v Sussex at Hove.	1937

322	I. V. A. Richards	Somerset v Warwickshire at Taunton	1985
318	C. W. Gregory	New South Wales v Queensland at Brisbane	1906-07
317	K. R. Rutherford	New Zealanders v D. B. Close's XI at Scarborough.	1986
316†	R. H. Moore	Hampshire v Warwickshire at Bournemouth	1937
315*	R. C. Blunt	Otago v Canterbury at Christchurch	1931-32
312*	J. M. Brearley	MCC Under-25 v North Zone at Peshawar.	1966-67
311*	G. M. Turner	Worcestershire v Warwickshire at Worcester	1982
311*	N. H. Fairbrother	Lancashire v Surrey at The Oval	1990
309*	D. G. Bradman	Australia v England at Leeds.	1930
307*	W. H. Ashdown	Kent v Essex at Brentwood.	1934
306*	A. Ducat	Surrey v Oxford University at The Oval	1919
305*	F. R. Foster	Warwickshire v Worcestershire at Dudley.	1914

† *E. Paynter's 322 and R. H. Moore's 316 were scored on the same day: July 28, 1937.*

These scores do not necessarily represent the complete innings. See pages 264–266.

LONGEST INNINGS

Mins
1,015	R. Nayyar (271)	Himachal Pradesh v Jammu and Kashmir at Chamba	1999-2000
970	Hanif Mohammad (337)	Pakistan v West Indies at Bridgetown	1957-58
	Hanif believes he batted 999 minutes.		
878	G. Kirsten (275)	South Africa v England at Durban	1999-2000
799	S. T. Jayasuriya (340)	Sri Lanka v India at Colombo	1997-98
797	L. Hutton (364)	England v Australia at The Oval	1938

1,000 RUNS IN MAY

	Runs	*Avge*
W. G. Grace, May 9 to May 30, 1895 (22 days):		
13, 103, 18, 25, 288, 52, 257, 73*, 18, 169	1,016	112.88
Grace was 46 years old.		
W. R. Hammond, May 7 to May 31, 1927 (25 days):		
27, 135, 108, 128, 17, 11, 99, 187, 4, 30, 83, 7, 192, 14	1,042	74.42
Hammond scored his 1,000th run on May 28, thus equalling		
Grace's record of 22 days.		
C. Hallows, May 5 to May 31, 1928 (27 days):		
100, 101, 51*, 123, 101*, 22, 74, 104, 58, 34*, 232	1,000	125.00

1,000 RUNS IN APRIL AND MAY

	Runs	*Avge*
T. W. Hayward, April 16 to May 31, 1900:		
120*, 55, 108, 131*, 55, 193, 120, 5, 6, 3, 40, 146, 92	1,074	97.63
D. G. Bradman, April 30 to May 31, 1930:		
236, 185*, 78, 9, 48*, 66, 4, 44, 252*, 32, 47*	1,001	143.00
On April 30 Bradman was 75 not out.		
D. G. Bradman, April 30 to May 31, 1938:		
258, 58, 137, 278, 2, 143, 145*, 5, 30*	1,056	150.85
Bradman scored 258 on April 30, and his 1,000th run on May 27.		
W. J. Edrich, April 30 to May 31, 1938:		
104, 37, 115, 63, 20*, 182, 71, 31, 53*, 45, 15, 245, 0, 9, 20*	1,010	84.16
Edrich was 21 not out on April 30. All his runs were scored at Lord's.		
G. M. Turner, April 24 to May 31, 1973:		
41, 151*, 143, 85, 7, 8, 17*, 81, 13, 53, 44, 153*, 3, 2, 66*, 30, 10*, 111	1,018	78.30
G. A. Hick, April 17 to May 29, 1988:		
61, 37, 212, 86, 14, 405*, 8, 11, 6, 7, 172	1,019	101.90
Hick scored a record 410 runs in April, and his 1,000th run on May 28.		

1,000 RUNS IN TWO SEPARATE MONTHS

Only four batsmen, C. B. Fry, K. S. Ranjitsinhji, H. Sutcliffe and L. Hutton, have scored over 1,000 runs in each of two months in the same season. L. Hutton, by scoring 1,294 in June 1949, made more runs in a single month than anyone else. He also made 1,050 in August 1949.

MOST RUNS SCORED OFF AN OVER

(All instances refer to six-ball overs)

36	G. S. Sobers	off M. A. Nash, Nottinghamshire v Glamorgan at Swansea (six sixes)	1968
36	R. J. Shastri	off Tilak Raj, Bombay v Baroda at Bombay (six sixes)	1984-85
34	E. B. Alletson	off E. H. Killick, Nottinghamshire v Sussex at Hove (46604446; including two no-balls)	1911
34	F. C. Hayes	off M. A. Nash, Lancashire v Glamorgan at Swansea (646666)	1977
34†	A. Flintoff	off A. J. Tudor, Lancashire v Surrey at Manchester (64444660; including two no-balls)	1998
32	I. T. Botham	off I. R. Snook, England XI v Central Districts at Palmerston North (466466)	1983-84
32	P. W. G. Parker	off A. I. Kallicharran, Sussex v Warwickshire at Birmingham (466664)	1982
32	I. R. Redpath	off N. Rosendorff, Australians v Orange Free State at Bloemfontein (666644)	1969-70
32	C. C. Smart	off G. Hill, Glamorgan v Hampshire at Cardiff (664664)	1935
32	Khalid Mahmood	off Naved Latif, Gujranwala v Sargodha at Gujranwala (666662)	2000-01

† *Altogether 38 runs were scored off this over, the two no-balls counting for two extra runs each under ECB regulations.*

Notes: The following instances have been excluded from the above table because of the bowlers' compliance: 34 – M. P. Maynard off S. A. Marsh, Glamorgan v Kent at Swansea, 1992; 34 – G. Chapple off P. A. Cottey, Lancashire v Glamorgan at Manchester, 1993; 34 – F. B. Touzel off F. J. J. Viljoen, Western Province B v Griqualand West at Kimberley, 1993-94; 32 – C. C. Inman off N. W. Hill, Leicestershire v Nottinghamshire at Nottingham, 1965; 32 – T. E. Jesty off R. J. Boyd-Moss, Hampshire v Northamptonshire at Southampton, 1984; 32 – M. A. Ealham off G. D. Hodgson, Kent v Gloucestershire at Bristol, 1992; 32 – G. Chapple off P. A. Cottey, Lancashire v Glamorgan at Manchester, 1993. Chapple's 34 and 32 came off successive overs from Cottey.

There were 35 runs off an over received by A. T. Reinholds off H. T. Davis, Auckland v Wellington at Auckland 1995-96, but this included six no-balls (counting as two runs each), four byes and only 19 off the bat.

In a Shell Trophy match against Canterbury at Christchurch in 1989-90, R. H. Vance (Wellington), acting on the instructions of his captain, deliberately conceded 77 runs in an over of full tosses which contained 17 no-balls and, owing to the umpire's understandable miscalculation, only five legitimate deliveries.

The greatest number of runs scored off an eight-ball over is 34 (40446664) by R. M. Edwards off M. C. Carew, Governor-General's XI v West Indians at Auckland, 1968-69.

MOST SIXES IN AN INNINGS

16	A. Symonds (254*)	Gloucestershire v Glamorgan at Abergavenny	1995
15	J. R. Reid (296)	Wellington v Northern Districts at Wellington	1962-63
14	Shakti Singh (128)	Himachal Pradesh v Haryana at Dharmsala	1990-91
13	Majid Khan (147*)	Pakistanis v Glamorgan at Swansea	1967
13	C. G. Greenidge (273*)	D. H. Robins' XI v Pakistanis at Eastbourne	1974
13	C. G. Greenidge (259)	Hampshire v Sussex at Southampton	1975
13	G. W. Humpage (254)	Warwickshire v Lancashire at Southport	1982
13	R. J. Shastri (200*)	Bombay v Baroda at Bombay	1984-85
12	Gulfraz Khan (207)	Railways v Universities at Lahore	1976-77
12	I. T. Botham (138*)	Somerset v Warwickshire at Birmingham	1985

12	R. A. Harper (234)	Northamptonshire v Gloucestershire at Northampton .	1986
12	D. M. Jones (248)	Australians v Warwickshire at Birmingham.	1989
12	U. N. K. Fernando (160)	Sinhalese SC v Sebastianites C and AC at Colombo..	1990-91
12	D. N. Patel (204)	Auckland v Northern Districts at Auckland.	1991-92
12	W. V. Raman (206)	Tamil Nadu v Kerala at Madras	1991-92
12	G. D. Lloyd (241)	Lancashire v Essex at Chelmsford	1996
12	Wasim Akram (257*)	Pakistan v Zimbabwe at Sheikhupura.	1996-97
11	C. K. Nayudu (153)	Hindus v MCC at Bombay	1926-27
11	C. J. Barnett (194)	Gloucestershire v Somerset at Bath	1934
11	R. Benaud (135)	Australians v T. N. Pearce's XI at Scarborough	1953
11	R. Bora (126)	Assam v Tripura at Gauhati	1987-88
11	G. A. Hick (405*)	Worcestershire v Somerset at Taunton	1988
11	A. S. Jayasinghe (183)	Tamil Union v Burgher RC at Colombo	1996-97
11	N. J. Astle (222)	New Zealand v England at Christchurch	2001-02

Note: F. B. Touzel (128*) hit 13 sixes for Western Province B v Griqualand West in contrived circumstances at Kimberley in 1993-94.

MOST SIXES IN A MATCH

| 20 | A. Symonds (254*, 76) | Gloucestershire v Glamorgan at Abergavenny . . . . . . | 1995 |
| 17 | W. J. Stewart (155, 125) | Warwickshire v Lancashire at Blackpool . . . . | 1959 |

MOST SIXES IN A SEASON

80	I. T. Botham	1985		49	I. V. A. Richards	1985
66	A. W. Wellard.	1935		48	A. W. Carr.	1925
57	A. W. Wellard.	1936		48	J. H. Edrich	1965
57	A. W. Wellard.	1938		48	A. Symonds.	1995
51	A. W. Wellard.	1933				

MOST BOUNDARIES IN AN INNINGS

	4s/6s			
72	62/10	B. C. Lara (501*)	Warwickshire v Durham at Birmingham.	1994
68	68/–	P. A. Perrin (343*)	Essex v Derbyshire at Chesterfield	1904
65	64/1	A. C. MacLaren (424)	Lancashire v Somerset at Taunton	1895
64	64/–	Hanif Mohammad (499)	Karachi v Bahawalpur at Karachi	1958-59
57	52/5	J. H. Edrich (310*)	England v New Zealand at Leeds	1965
57	52/5	Naved Latif (394)	Sargodha v Gujranwala at Gujranwala . .	2000-01
55	55/–	C. W. Gregory (383)	NSW v Queensland at Brisbane	1906-07
55	51/3†	S. V. Manjrekar (377)	Bombay v Hyderabad at Bombay	1990-91
55	53/2	G. R. Marsh (355*)	W. Australia v S. Australia at Perth	1989-90
54	53/1	G. H. Hirst (341)	Yorkshire v Leicestershire at Leicester . .	1905
53	51/2	V. V. S. Laxman (353)	Hyderabad v Karnataka at Bangalore . . .	1999-2000
53	53/–	A. W. Nourse (304*)	Natal v Transvaal at Johannesburg.	1919-20
53	45/8	K. R. Rutherford (317)	New Zealanders v D. B. Close's XI at Scarborough	1986
52	47/5	N. H. Fairbrother (366)	Lancashire v Surrey at The Oval	1990
51	51/–	W. G. Grace (344)	MCC v Kent at Canterbury	1876
51	47/4	C. G. Macartney (345)	Australians v Notts at Nottingham	1921
51	50/1	B. B. Nimbalkar (443*)	Maharashtra v Kathiawar at Poona	1948-49
51	49/2	G. A. Hick (315*)	Worcestershire v Durham at Worcester. . .	2002
50	46/4	D. G. Bradman (369)	S. Australia v Tasmania at Adelaide. . . .	1935-36
50	47/–‡	A. Ducat (306*)	Surrey v Oxford U. at The Oval	1919
50	35/15	J. R. Reid (296)	Wellington v N. Districts at Wellington .	1962-63
50	42/8	I. V. A. Richards (322)	Somerset v Warwickshire at Taunton . . .	1985

† *Plus one five.*
‡ *Plus three fives.*

PARTNERSHIPS OVER 500

577 for 4th	V. S. Hazare (288) and Gul Mahomed (319), Baroda v Holkar at Baroda..	1946-47
576 for 2nd	S. T. Jayasuriya (340) and R. S. Mahanama (225), Sri Lanka v India at Colombo.......................................	1997-98
574* for 4th	F. M. M. Worrell (255*) and C. L. Walcott (314*), Barbados v Trinidad at Port-of-Spain.............................	1945-46
561 for 1st	Waheed Mirza (324) and Mansoor Akhtar (224*), Karachi Whites v Quetta at Karachi..................................	1976-77
555 for 1st	P. Holmes (224*) and H. Sutcliffe (313), Yorkshire v Essex at Leyton...	1932
554 for 1st	J. T. Brown (300) and J. Tunnicliffe (243), Yorkshire v Derbyshire at Chesterfield..................................	1898
502* for 4th	F. M. M. Worrell (308*) and J. D. C. Goddard (218*), Barbados v Trinidad at Bridgetown............................	1943-44

HIGHEST PARTNERSHIPS FOR EACH WICKET

The following lists include all stands above 400; otherwise the top ten for each wicket.

First Wicket

561	Waheed Mirza and Mansoor Akhtar, Karachi Whites v Quetta at Karachi ...	1976-77
555	P. Holmes and H. Sutcliffe, Yorkshire v Essex at Leyton	1932
554	J. T. Brown and J. Tunnicliffe, Yorkshire v Derbyshire at Chesterfield......	1898
490	E. H. Bowley and J. G. Langridge, Sussex v Middlesex at Hove...........	1933
464	R. Sehgal and R. Lamba, Delhi v Himachal Pradesh at Delhi.............	1994-95
459	Wasim Jaffer and S. K. Kulkarni, Mumbai v Saurashtra at Rajkot	1996-97
456	E. R. Mayne and W. H. Ponsford, Victoria v Queensland at Melbourne ...	1923-24
451*	S. Desai and R. M. H. Binny, Karnataka v Kerala at Chikmagalur........	1977-78
431	M. R. J. Veletta and G. R. Marsh, Western Australia v South Australia at Perth	1989-90
428	J. B. Hobbs and A. Sandham, Surrey v Oxford University at The Oval.....	1926
425*	L. V. Garrick and C. H. Gayle, Jamaica v West Indies B at Montego Bay...	2000-01
424	I. J. Siedle and J. F. W. Nicolson, Natal v Orange Free State at Bloemfontein	1926-27
421	S. M. Gavaskar and G. A. Parkar, Bombay v Bengal at Bombay..........	1981-82
418	Kamal Najamuddin and Khalid Alvi, Karachi v Railways at Karachi	1980-81
413	V. Mankad and Pankaj Roy, India v New Zealand at Madras	1955-56
406*	D. J. Bicknell and G. E. Welton, Notts v Warwickshire at Birmingham....	2000
405	C. P. S. Chauhan and M. S. Gupte, Maharashtra v Vidarbha at Poona	1972-73
403	Rizwan-uz-Zaman and Shoaib Mohammad, PIA v Hyderabad at Hyderabad .	1999-2000

Second Wicket

576	S. T. Jayasuriya and R. S. Mahanama, Sri Lanka v India at Colombo.....	1997-98
475	Zahir Alam and L. S. Rajput, Assam v Tripura at Gauhati...............	1991-92
465*	J. A. Jameson and R. B. Kanhai, Warwicks v Gloucestershire at Birmingham	1974
455	K. V. Bhandarkar and B. B. Nimbalkar, Maharashtra v Kathiawar at Poona ..	1948-49
451	W. H. Ponsford and D. G. Bradman, Australia v England at The Oval.....	1934
446	C. C. Hunte and G. S. Sobers, West Indies v Pakistan at Kingston	1957-58
429*	J. G. Dewes and G. H. G. Doggart, Cambridge U. v Essex at Cambridge ..	1949
426	Arshad Pervez and Mohsin Khan, Habib Bank v Income Tax at Lahore	1977-78
417	K. J. Barnett and T. A. Tweats, Derbyshire v Yorkshire at Derby	1997
415	A. Jadeja and S. V. Manjrekar, Indians v Bowl XI at Springs	1992-93
403	G. A. Gooch and P. J. Prichard, Essex v Leicestershire at Chelmsford	1990

Third Wicket

467	A. H. Jones and M. D. Crowe, New Zealand v Sri Lanka at Wellington	1990-91
456	Khalid Irtiza and Aslam Ali, United Bank v Multan at Karachi	1975-76
451	Mudassar Nazar and Javed Miandad, Pakistan v India at Hyderabad	1982-83
445	P. E. Whitelaw and W. N. Carson, Auckland v Otago at Dunedin	1936-37
438*	G. A. Hick and T. M. Moody, Worcestershire v Hampshire at Southampton .	1997
436	S. S. Das and S. S. Raul, Orissa v Bengal at Baripada	2001-02
434	J. B. Stollmeyer and G. E. Gomez, Trinidad v British Guiana at Port-of-Spain	1946-47
424*	W. J. Edrich and D. C. S. Compton, Middlesex v Somerset at Lord's	1948
413	D. J. Bicknell and D. M. Ward, Surrey v Kent at Canterbury...........	1990
410*	R. S. Modi and L. Amarnath, India in England v The Rest at Calcutta	1946-47
409	V. V. S. Laxman and R. Dravid, South Zone v West Zone at Surat	2000-01
406*	R. S. Gavaskar and S. J. Kalyani, Bengal v Tripura at Agartala	1999-2000
405	A. Jadeja and A. S. Kaypee, Haryana v Services at Faridabad	1991-92

Fourth Wicket

577	V. S. Hazare and Gul Mahomed, Baroda v Holkar at Baroda...........	1946-47
574*	C. L. Walcott and F. M. M. Worrell, Barbados v Trinidad at Port-of-Spain...	1945-46
502*	F. M. M. Worrell and J. D. C. Goddard, Barbados v Trinidad at Bridgetown. .	1943-44
470	A. I. Kallicharran and G. W. Humpage, Warwicks v Lancs at Southport	1982
462*	D. W. Hookes and W. B. Phillips, South Australia v Tasmania at Adelaide ..	1986-87
448	R. Abel and T. W. Hayward, Surrey v Yorkshire at The Oval	1899
436	S. Abbas Ali and P. K. Dwevedi, Madhya Pradesh v Railways at Indore	1997-98
425*	A. Dale and I. V. A. Richards, Glamorgan v Middlesex at Cardiff	1993
424	I. S. Lee and S. O. Quin, Victoria v Tasmania at Melbourne	1933-34
411	P. B. H. May and M. C. Cowdrey, England v West Indies at Birmingham ..	1957
410	G. Abraham and P. Balan Pandit, Kerala v Andhra at Palghat	1959-60
402	W. Watson and T. W. Graveney, MCC v British Guiana at Georgetown	1953-54
402	R. B. Kanhai and K. Ibadulla, Warwicks v Notts at Nottingham.........	1968

Fifth Wicket

464*	M. E. Waugh and S. R. Waugh, New South Wales v Western Australia at Perth	1990-91
405	S. G. Barnes and D. G. Bradman, Australia v England at Sydney.........	1946-47
401	M. B. Loye and D. Ripley, Northamptonshire v Glamorgan at Northampton ..	1998
397	W. Bardsley and C. Kelleway, New South Wales v South Australia at Sydney .	1920-21
393	E. G. Arnold and W. B. Burns, Worcestershire v Warwickshire at Birmingham.	1909
391	A. Malhotra and S. Dogra, Delhi v Services at Delhi...............	1995-96
385	S. R. Waugh and S. S. Blewett, Australia v South Africa at Johannesburg ...	1996-97
381	R. Nayyar and V. Sehwag, North Zone v South Zone at Agartala	1999-2000
377*	G. P. Thorpe and M. R. Ramprakash, England XI v South Australia at Adelaide	1998-99
376	V. V. S. Laxman and R. Dravid, India v Australia at Kolkata	2000-01

Sixth Wicket

487*	G. A. Headley and C. C. Passailaigue, Jamaica v Lord Tennyson's XI at Kingston	1931-32
428	W. W. Armstrong and M. A. Noble, Australians v Sussex at Hove	1902
411	R. M. Poore and E. G. Wynyard, Hampshire v Somerset at Taunton	1899
376	R. Subba Row and A. Lightfoot, Northamptonshire v Surrey at The Oval	1958
372*	K. P. Pietersen and J. E. Morris, Nottinghamshire v Derbyshire at Derby....	2001
371	V. M. Merchant and R. S. Modi, Bombay v Maharashtra at Bombay.......	1943-44
365	B. C. Lara and R. D. Jacobs, West Indians v Australia A at Hobart	2000-01
356	W. V. Raman and A. Kripal Singh, Tamil Nadu v Goa at Panjim	1988-89
353	Salah-ud-Din and Zaheer Abbas, Karachi v East Pakistan at Karachi.......	1968-69
346	J. H. W. Fingleton and D. G. Bradman, Australia v England at Melbourne ...	1936-37

Seventh Wicket

460	Bhupinder Singh, jun. and P. Dharmani, Punjab v Delhi at Delhi	1994-95
347	D. St E. Atkinson and C. C. Depeiza, West Indies v Australia at Bridgetown .	1954-55
344	K. S. Ranjitsinhji and W. Newham, Sussex v Essex at Leyton	1902
340	K. J. Key and H. Philipson, Oxford University v Middlesex at Chiswick Park	1887
336	F. C. W. Newman and C. R. N. Maxwell, Sir J. Cahn's XI v Leicestershire at Nottingham	1935
335	C. W. Andrews and E. C. Bensted, Queensland v New South Wales at Sydney	1934-35
325	G. Brown and C. H. Abercrombie, Hampshire v Essex at Leyton	1913
323	E. H. Hendren and L. F. Townsend, MCC v Barbados at Bridgetown	1929-30
308	Waqar Hassan and Imtiaz Ahmed, Pakistan v New Zealand at Lahore	1955-56
301	C. C. Lewis and B. N. French, Nottinghamshire v Durham at Chester-le-Street	1993

Eighth Wicket

433	V. T. Trumper and A. Sims, A. Sims' Aust. XI v Canterbury at Christchurch	1913-14
313	Wasim Akram and Saqlain Mushtaq, Pakistan v Zimbabwe at Sheikhupura . .	1996-97
292	R. Peel and Lord Hawke, Yorkshire v Warwickshire at Birmingham	1896
291	R. S. C. Martin-Jenkins and M. J. G. Davis, Sussex v Somerset at Taunton . .	2002
270	V. T. Trumper and E. P. Barbour, New South Wales v Victoria at Sydney. . . .	1912-13
263	D. R. Wilcox and R. M. Taylor, Essex v Warwickshire at Southend	1946
255	E. A. V. Williams and E. A. Martindale, Barbados v Trinidad at Bridgetown. .	1935-36
253	N. J. Astle and A. C. Parore, New Zealand v Australia at Perth	2001-02
249*	Shaukat Mirza and Akram Raza, Habib Bank v PNSC at Lahore	1993-94
246	L. E. G. Ames and G. O. B. Allen, England v New Zealand at Lord's	1931

Ninth Wicket

283	J. Chapman and A. Warren, Derbyshire v Warwickshire at Blackwell	1910
268	J. B. Commins and N. Boje, South Africa A v Mashonaland at Harare	1994-95
251	J. W. H. T. Douglas and S. N. Hare, Essex v Derbyshire at Leyton.	1921
249*†	A. S. Srivastava and K. Seth, Madhya Pradesh v Vidarbha at Indore	2000-01
245	V. S. Hazare and N. D. Nagarwalla, Maharashtra v Baroda at Poona	1939-40
244*	Arshad Ayub and M. V. Ramanamurthy, Hyderabad v Bihar at Hyderabad . . .	1986-87
239	H. B. Cave and I. B. Leggat, Central Districts v Otago at Dunedin	1952-53
232	C. Hill and E. Walkley, South Australia v New South Wales at Adelaide	1900-01
231	P. Sen and J. Mitter, Bengal v Bihar at Jamshedpur	1950-51
230	D. A. Livingstone and A. T. Castell, Hampshire v Surrey at Southampton . . .	1962

† 276 unbeaten runs were scored for this wicket in two separate partnerships; after Srivastava retired hurt, Seth and N. D. Hirwani added 27.

Tenth Wicket

307	A. F. Kippax and J. E. H. Hooker, New South Wales v Victoria at Melbourne	1928-29
249	C. T. Sarwate and S. N. Banerjee, Indians v Surrey at The Oval	1946
235	F. E. Woolley and A. Fielder, Kent v Worcestershire at Stourbridge	1909
233	Ajay Sharma and Maninder Singh, Delhi v Bombay at Bombay	1991-92
230	R. W. Nicholls and W. Roche, Middlesex v Kent at Lord's	1899
228	R. Illingworth and K. Higgs, Leicestershire v Northamptonshire at Leicester .	1977
218	F. H. Vigar and T. P. B. Smith, Essex v Derbyshire at Chesterfield	1947
214	N. V. Knight and A. Richardson, Warwickshire v Hampshire at Birmingham . .	2002
211	M. Ellis and T. J. Hastings, Victoria v South Australia at Melbourne.	1902-03
196*	Nadim Yousuf and Maqsood Kundi, MCB v National Bank at Lahore	1981-82

UNUSUAL DISMISSALS

Handled the Ball

J. Grundy	MCC v Kent at Lord's	1857
G. Bennett	Kent v Sussex at Hove	1872
W. H. Scotton	Smokers v Non-Smokers at East Melbourne	1886-87
C. W. Wright	Nottinghamshire v Gloucestershire at Bristol	1893
E. Jones	South Australia v Victoria at Melbourne	1894-95
A. W. Nourse	South Africans v Sussex at Hove	1907
E. T. Benson	MCC v Auckland at Auckland	1929-30
A. W. Gilbertson	Otago v Auckland at Auckland	1952-53
W. R. Endean	South Africa v England at Cape Town	1956-57
P. J. Burge	Queensland v New South Wales at Sydney	1958-59
Dildar Awan	Services v Lahore at Lahore	1959-60
M. Mehra	Railways v Delhi at Delhi	1959-60
Mahmood-ul-Hasan	Karachi University v Railways-Quetta at Karachi	1960-61
Ali Raza	Karachi Greens v Hyderabad at Karachi	1961-62
Mohammad Yusuf	Rawalpindi v Peshawar at Peshawar	1962-63
A. Rees	Glamorgan v Middlesex at Lord's	1965
Pervez Akhtar	Multan v Karachi Greens at Sahiwal	1971-72
Javed Mirza	Railways v Punjab at Lahore	1972-73
R. G. Pollock	Eastern Province v Western Province at Cape Town	1973-74
C. I. Dey	Northern Transvaal v Orange Free State at Bloemfontein	1973-74
Nasir Valika	Karachi Whites v National Bank at Karachi	1974-75
Haji Yousuf	National Bank v Railways at Lahore	1974-75
Masood-ul-Hasan	PIA v National Bank B at Lyallpur	1975-76
Hanif Solangi	Hyderabad v Karachi B at Hyderabad	1977-78
D. K. Pearse	Natal v Western Province at Cape Town	1978-79
A. M. J. Hilditch	Australia v Pakistan at Perth	1978-79
Musleh-ud-Din	Railways v Lahore at Lahore	1979-80
Jalal-ud-Din	IDBP v Habib Bank at Bahawalpur	1981-82
Mohsin Khan	Pakistan v Australia at Karachi	1982-83
D. L. Haynes	West Indies v India at Bombay	1983-84
K. Azad	Delhi v Punjab at Amritsar	1983-84
Athar A. Khan	Allied Bank v HBFC at Sialkot	1983-84
A. N. Pandya	Saurashtra v Baroda at Baroda	1984-85
G. L. Linton	Barbados v Windward Islands at Bridgetown	1985-86
R. B. Gartrell	Tasmania v Victoria at Melbourne	1986-87
R. Nayyar	Himachal Pradesh v Punjab at Una	1988-89
R. Weerawardene	Moratuwa v Nomads SC at Colombo	1988-89
A. M. Kane	Vidarbha v Railways at Nagpur	1989-90
P. Bali	Jammu and Kashmir v Services at Delhi	1991-92
M. J. G. Davis	Northern Transvaal B v OFS B at Bloemfontein	1991-92
J. T. C. Vaughan	Emerging Players v England XI at Hamilton	1991-92
G. A. Gooch	England v Australia at Manchester	1993
A. C. Waller	Mashonaland CD v Mashonaland Under-24 at Harare	1994-95
K. M. Krikken	Derbyshire v Indians at Derby	1996
A. Badenhorst	Eastern Province B v North West at Fochville	1998-99
S. R. Waugh	Australia v India at Chennai	2000-01
M. P. Vaughan	England v India at Bangalore	2001-02
Tushar Imran	Bangladesh A v Jamaica at Spanish Town	2001-02

Obstructing the Field

C. A. Absolom	Cambridge University v Surrey at The Oval	1868
T. Straw	Worcestershire v Warwickshire at Worcester	1899
T. Straw	Worcestershire v Warwickshire at Birmingham	1901
J. P. Whiteside	Leicestershire v Lancashire at Leicester	1901
L. Hutton	England v South Africa at The Oval	1951
J. A. Hayes	Canterbury v Central Districts at Christchurch	1954-55
D. D. Deshpande	Madhya Pradesh v Uttar Pradesh at Benares	1956-57
K. Ibadulla	Warwickshire v Hampshire at Coventry	1963

Qaiser Khan	Dera Ismail Khan v Railways at Lahore	1964-65
Ijaz Ahmed	Lahore Greens v Lahore Blues at Lahore	1973-74
Qasim Feroze	Bahawalpur v Universities at Lahore	1974-75
T. Quirk	Northern Transvaal v Border at East London	1978-79
Mahmood Rashid	United Bank v Muslim Commercial Bank at Bahawalpur	1981-82
Arshad Ali	Sukkur v Quetta at Quetta	1983-84
H. R. Wasu	Vidarbha v Rajasthan at Akola	1984-85
Khalid Javed	Railways v Lahore at Lahore	1985-86
C. Binduhewa	Singha SC v Sinhalese SC at Colombo	1990-91
S. J. Kalyani	Bengal v Orissa at Calcutta	1994-95
R. C. Rupasinghe	Rio v Kurunegala Youth at Colombo	2001-02

Hit the Ball Twice

G. Rawlins	Sheffield v Nottingham at Nottingham	1827
H. E. Bull	MCC v Oxford University at Lord's	1864
H. R. J. Charlwood	Sussex v Surrey at Hove	1872
R. G. Barlow	North v South at Lord's	1878
P. S. Wimble	Transvaal v Griqualand West at Kimberley	1892-93
G. B. Nicholls	Somerset v Gloucestershire at Bristol	1896
A. A. Lilley	Warwickshire v Yorkshire at Birmingham	1897
J. H. King	Leicestershire v Surrey at The Oval	1906
A. P. Binns	Jamaica v British Guiana at Georgetown	1956-57
K. Bhavana	Andhra v Mysore at Guntur	1963-64
Zaheer Abbas	PIA A v Karachi Blues at Karachi	1969-70
Anwar Miandad	IDBP v United Bank at Lahore	1979-80
Anwar Iqbal	Hyderabad v Sukkur at Hyderabad	1983-84
Iqtidar Ali	Allied Bank v Muslim Commercial Bank at Lahore	1983-84
Aziz Malik	Lahore Division v Faisalabad at Sialkot	1984-85
Javed Mohammad	Multan v Karachi Whites at Sahiwal	1986-87
Shahid Pervez	Jammu and Kashmir v Punjab at Srinagar	1986-87
Ali Naqvi	PNSC v National Bank at Faisalabad	1998-99
A. George	Tamil Nadu v Maharashtra at Pune	1998-99
Maqsood Raza	Lahore Division v PNSC at Sheikhupura	1999-2000

Timed Out

| H. Yadav | Tripura v Orissa at Cuttack | 1997-98 |

BOWLING RECORDS

TEN WICKETS IN AN INNINGS

	O	M	R		
E. Hinkly (Kent)				v England at Lord's	1848
*J. Wisden (North)				v South at Lord's	1850
V. E. Walker (England)	43	17	74	v Surrey at The Oval	1859
V. E. Walker (Middlesex)	44.2	5	104	v Lancashire at Manchester	1865
G. Wootton (All England)	31.3	9	54	v Yorkshire at Sheffield	1865
W. Hickton (Lancashire)	36.2	19	46	v Hampshire at Manchester	1870
S. E. Butler (Oxford)	24.1	11	38	v Cambridge at Lord's	1871
James Lillywhite (South)	60.2	22	129	v North at Canterbury	1872
A. Shaw (MCC)	36.2	8	73	v North at Lord's	1874
E. Barratt (Players)	29	11	43	v Australians at The Oval	1878
G. Giffen (Australian XI)	26	10	66	v The Rest at Sydney	1883-84
W. G. Grace (MCC)	36.2	17	49	v Oxford University at Oxford	1886
G. Burton (Middlesex)	52.3	25	59	v Surrey at The Oval	1888
†A. E. Moss (Canterbury)	21.3	10	28	v Wellington at Christchurch	1889-90
S. M. J. Woods (Cambridge U.)	31	6	69	v Thornton's XI at Cambridge	1890
T. Richardson (Surrey)	15.3	3	45	v Essex at The Oval	1894
H. Pickett (Essex)	27	11	32	v Leicestershire at Leyton	1895

	O	M	R		
E. J. Tyler (Somerset)	34.3	15	49	v Surrey at Taunton	1895
W. P. Howell (Australians)	23.2	14	28	v Surrey at The Oval	1899
C. H. G. Bland (Sussex)	25.2	10	48	v Kent at Tonbridge	1899
J. Briggs (Lancashire)	28.5	7	55	v Worcestershire at Manchester	1900
A. E. Trott (Middlesex)	14.2	5	42	v Somerset at Taunton	1900
A. Fielder (Players)	24.5	1	90	v Gentlemen at Lord's	1906
E. G. Dennett (Gloucestershire)	19.4	7	40	v Essex at Bristol	1906
A. E. E. Vogler (E. Province)	12	2	26	v Griqualand W. at Johannesburg	1906-07
C. Blythe (Kent)	16	7	30	v Northants at Northampton	1907
J. B. King (Philadelphia)	18.1	7	53	v Ireland at Haverford‡	1909
A. Drake (Yorkshire)	8.5	0	35	v Somerset at Weston-s-Mare.	1914
W. Bestwick (Derbyshire)	19	2	40	v Glamorgan at Cardiff	1921
A. A. Mailey (Australians)	28.4	5	66	v Gloucestershire at Cheltenham	1921
C. W. L. Parker (Glos.)	40.3	13	79	v Somerset at Bristol	1921
T. Rushby (Surrey)	17.5	4	43	v Somerset at Taunton	1921
J. C. White (Somerset)	42.2	11	76	v Worcestershire at Worcester	1921
G. C. Collins (Kent)	19.3	4	65	v Nottinghamshire at Dover	1922
H. Howell (Warwickshire)	25.1	5	51	v Yorkshire at Birmingham	1923
A. S. Kennedy (Players)	22.4	10	37	v Gentlemen at The Oval	1927
G. O. B. Allen (Middlesex)	25.3	10	40	v Lancashire at Lord's	1929
A. P. Freeman (Kent)	42	9	131	v Lancashire at Maidstone	1929
G. Geary (Leicestershire)	16.2	8	18	v Glamorgan at Pontypridd	1929
C. V. Grimmett (Australians)	22.3	8	37	v Yorkshire at Sheffield	1930
A. P. Freeman (Kent)	30.4	8	53	v Essex at Southend	1930
H. Verity (Yorkshire)	18.4	6	36	v Warwickshire at Leeds	1931
A. P. Freeman (Kent)	36.1	9	79	v Lancashire at Manchester	1931
V. W. C. Jupp (Northants)	39	6	127	v Kent at Tunbridge Wells	1932
H. Verity (Yorkshire)	19.4	16	10	v Nottinghamshire at Leeds	1932
T. W. Wall (South Australia)	12.4	2	36	v New South Wales at Sydney	1932-33
T. B. Mitchell (Derbyshire)	19.1	4	64	v Leicestershire at Leicester	1935
J. Mercer (Glamorgan)	26	10	51	v Worcestershire at Worcester	1936
T. W. J. Goddard (Glos.)	28.4	4	113	v Worcestershire at Cheltenham	1937
T. F. Smailes (Yorkshire)	17.1	5	47	v Derbyshire at Sheffield	1939
A. E. Watts (Surrey)	24.1	8	67	v Warwickshire at Birmingham	1939
*W. E. Hollies (Warwickshire)	20.4	4	49	v Notts at Birmingham	1946
J. M. Sims (East)	18.4	2	90	v West at Kingston	1948
T. E. Bailey (Essex)	39.4	9	90	v Lancashire at Clacton	1949
J. K. Graveney (Glos.)	18.4	2	66	v Derbyshire at Chesterfield	1949
R. Berry (Lancashire)	36.2	9	102	v Worcestershire at Blackpool	1953
S. P. Gupte (President's XI)	24.2	7	78	v Combined XI at Bombay	1954-55
J. C. Laker (Surrey)	46	18	88	v Australians at The Oval	1956
J. C. Laker (England)	51.2	23	53	v Australia at Manchester	1956
G. A. R. Lock (Surrey)	29.1	18	54	v Kent at Blackheath	1956
K. Smales (Nottinghamshire)	41.3	20	66	v Gloucestershire at Stroud	1956
P. M. Chatterjee (Bengal)	19	11	20	v Assam at Jorhat	1956-57
J. D. Bannister (Warwickshire)	23.3	11	41	v Comb. Services at Birmingham§	1959
A. J. G. Pearson (Cambridge U.)	30.3	8	78	v Leics at Loughborough	1961
N. I. Thomson (Sussex)	34.2	19	49	v Warwickshire at Worthing	1964
P. J. Allan (Queensland)	15.6	3	61	v Victoria at Melbourne	1965-66
I. J. Brayshaw (W. Australia)	17.6	4	44	v Victoria at Perth	1967-68
Shahid Mahmood (Karachi Whites)	25	5	58	v Khairpur at Karachi	1969-70
E. E. Hemmings (International XI)	49.3	14	175	v West Indies XI at Kingston	1982-83
P. Sunderam (Rajasthan)	22	5	78	v Vidarbha at Jodhpur	1985-86
S. T. Jefferies (W. Province)	22.5	7	59	v Orange Free State at Cape Town	1987-88
Imran Adil (Bahawalpur)	22.5	3	92	v Faisalabad at Faisalabad	1989-90
G. P. Wickremasinghe (Sinhalese)	19.2	5	41	v Kalutara at Colombo	1991-92
R. L. Johnson (Middlesex)	18.5	6	45	v Derbyshire at Derby	1994
Naeem Akhtar (Rawalpindi B)	21.3	10	28	v Peshawar at Peshawar	1995-96
A. Kumble (India)	26.3	9	74	v Pakistan at Delhi	1998-99
D. S. Mohanty (East Zone)	19	5	46	v South Zone at Agartala	2000-01

Note: The following instances were achieved in 12-a-side matches:

	O	M	R		
E. M. Grace (MCC)	32.2	7	69	v Gents of Kent at Canterbury	1862
W. G. Grace (MCC)	46.1	15	92	v Kent at Canterbury	1873
†D. C. S. Hinds (A. B. St Hill's XII)	19.1	6	36	v Trinidad at Port-of-Spain	1900-01

* *J. Wisden and W. E. Hollies achieved the feat without the direct assistance of a fielder. Wisden's ten were all bowled; Hollies bowled seven and had three lbw.*
† *On debut in first-class cricket.*   ‡ *Pennsylvania.*   § *Mitchells & Butlers Ground.*

OUTSTANDING BOWLING ANALYSES

	O	M	R	W		
H. Verity (Yorkshire)	19.4	16	10	10	v Nottinghamshire at Leeds	1932
G. Elliott (Victoria)	19	17	2	9	v Tasmania at Launceston	1857-58
Ahad Khan (Railways)	6.3	4	7	9	v Dera Ismail Khan at Lahore	1964-65
J. C. Laker (England)	14	12	2	8	v The Rest at Bradford	1950
D. Shackleton (Hampshire)	11.1	7	4	8	v Somerset at Weston-s-Mare	1955
E. Peate (Yorkshire)	16	11	5	8	v Surrey at Holbeck	1883
F. R. Spofforth (Australians)	8.3	6	3	7	v England XI at Birmingham	1884
W. A. Henderson (North-Eastern Transvaal)	9.3	4	4	7	v Orange Free State at Bloemfontein	1937-38
Rajinder Goel (Haryana)	7	4	4	7	v Jammu and Kashmir at Chandigarh	1977-78
V. I. Smith (South Africans)	4.5	3	1	6	v Derbyshire at Derby	1947
S. Costick (Victoria)	21.1	20	1	6	v Tasmania at Melbourne	1868-69
Israr Ali (Bahawalpur)	11	10	1	6	v Dacca U. at Bahawalpur	1957-58
A. D. Pougher (MCC)	3	3	0	5	v Australians at Lord's	1896
G. R. Cox (Sussex)	6	6	0	5	v Somerset at Weston-s-Mare	1921
R. K. Tyldesley (Lancashire)	5	5	0	5	v Leicestershire at Manchester	1924
P. T. Mills (Gloucestershire)	6.4	6	0	5	v Somerset at Bristol	1928

MOST WICKETS IN A MATCH

19-90	J. C. Laker	England v Australia at Manchester	1956
17-48†	C. Blythe	Kent v Northamptonshire at Northampton†	1907
17-50	C. T. B. Turner	Australians v England XI at Hastings	1888
17-54	W. P. Howell	Australians v Western Province at Cape Town	1902-03
17-56	C. W. L. Parker	Gloucestershire v Essex at Gloucester	1925
17-67	A. P. Freeman	Kent v Sussex at Hove	1922
17-89	W. G. Grace	Gloucestershire v Nottinghamshire at Cheltenham	1877
17-89	F. C. L. Matthews	Nottinghamshire v Northants at Nottingham	1923
17-91	H. Dean	Lancashire v Yorkshire at Liverpool	1913
17-91†	H. Verity	Yorkshire v Essex at Leyton	1933
17-92	A. P. Freeman	Kent v Warwickshire at Folkestone	1932
17-103	W. Mycroft	Derbyshire v Hampshire at Southampton	1876
17-106	G. R. Cox	Sussex v Warwickshire at Horsham	1926
17-106†	T. W. J. Goddard	Gloucestershire v Kent at Bristol	1939
17-119	W. Mead	Essex v Hampshire at Southampton	1895
17-137	W. Brearley	Lancashire v Somerset at Manchester	1905
17-159	S. F. Barnes	England v South Africa at Johannesburg	1913-14
17-201	G. Giffen	South Australia v Victoria at Adelaide	1885-86
17-212	J. C. Clay	Glamorgan v Worcestershire at Swansea	1937

† *Achieved in a single day.*

FOUR WICKETS WITH CONSECUTIVE BALLS

J. Wells	Kent v Sussex at Brighton	1862
G. Ulyett	Lord Harris's XI v New South Wales at Sydney	1878-79
G. Nash	Lancashire v Somerset at Manchester	1882
J. B. Hide	Sussex v MCC and Ground at Lord's	1890
F. J. Shacklock	Nottinghamshire v Somerset at Nottingham	1893
A. D. Downes	Otago v Auckland at Dunedin	1893-94
F. Martin	MCC and Ground v Derbyshire at Lord's	1895
A. W. Mold	Lancashire v Nottinghamshire at Nottingham	1895
W. Brearley†	Lancashire v Somerset at Manchester	1905
S. Haigh	MCC v Army XI at Pretoria	1905-06
A. E. Trott‡	Middlesex v Somerset at Lord's	1907
F. A. Tarrant	Middlesex v Gloucestershire at Bristol	1907
A. Drake	Yorkshire v Derbyshire at Chesterfield	1914
S. G. Smith	Northamptonshire v Warwickshire at Birmingham	1914
H. A. Peach	Surrey v Sussex at The Oval	1924
A. F. Borland	Natal v Griqualand West at Kimberley	1926-27
J. E. H. Hooker†	New South Wales v Victoria at Sydney	1928-29
R. K. Tyldesley†	Lancashire v Derbyshire at Derby	1929
R. J. Crisp	Western Province v Griqualand West at Johannesburg	1931-32
R. J. Crisp	Western Province v Natal at Durban	1933-34
A. R. Gover	Surrey v Worcestershire at Worcester	1935
W. H. Copson	Derbyshire v Warwickshire at Derby	1937
W. A. Henderson	N.E. Transvaal v Orange Free State at Bloemfontein	1937-38
F. Ridgway	Kent v Derbyshire at Folkestone	1951
A. K. Walker§	Nottinghamshire v Leicestershire at Leicester	1956
D. Robins†	South Australia v New South Wales at Adelaide	1965-66
S. N. Mohol	President's XI v Combined XI at Poona	1965-66
P. I. Pocock	Surrey v Sussex at Eastbourne	1972
S. S. Saini†	Delhi v Himachal Pradesh at Delhi	1988-89
D. Dias	W. Province (Suburbs) v Central Province at Colombo	1990-91
Ali Gauhar	Karachi Blues v United Bank at Peshawar	1994-95
K. D. James**	Hampshire v Indians at Southampton	1996
G. P. Butcher	Surrey v Derbyshire at The Oval	2000
Fazl-e-Akbar	PIA v Habib Bank at Lahore	2001-02

† *Not all in the same innings.*
‡ *Trott achieved another hat-trick in the same innings of this, his benefit match.*
§ *Having bowled Firth with the last ball of the first innings, Walker achieved a unique feat by dismissing Lester, Tompkin and Smithson with the first three balls of the second.*
** *James also scored a century, a unique double.*

Notes: In their match with England at The Oval in 1863, Surrey lost four wickets in the course of a four-ball over from G. Bennett.

Sussex lost five wickets in the course of the final (six-ball) over of their match with Surrey at Eastbourne in 1972. P. I. Pocock, who had taken three wickets in his previous over, captured four more, taking in all seven wickets with 11 balls, a feat unique in first-class matches. (The eighth wicket fell to a run-out.)

HAT-TRICKS

Double Hat-Trick

Besides Trott's performance, which is given in the preceding section, the following instances are recorded of players having performed the hat-trick twice in the same match, Rao doing so in the same innings.

A. Shaw	Nottinghamshire v Gloucestershire at Nottingham	1884
T. J. Matthews	Australia v South Africa at Manchester	1912
C. W. L. Parker	Gloucestershire v Middlesex at Bristol	1924
R. O. Jenkins	Worcestershire v Surrey at Worcester	1949
J. S. Rao	Services v Northern Punjab at Amritsar	1963-64
Amin Lakhani	Combined XI v Indians at Multan	1978-79

Five Wickets in Six Balls

W. H. Copson	Derbyshire v Warwickshire at Derby	1937
W. A. Henderson	N.E. Transvaal v Orange Free State at Bloemfontein	1937-38
P. I. Pocock	Surrey v Sussex at Eastbourne	1972

Most Hat-Tricks

Seven times: D. V. P. Wright.
Six times: T. W. J. Goddard, C. W. L. Parker.
Five times: S. Haigh, V. W. C. Jupp, A. E. G. Rhodes, F. A. Tarrant.
Four times: R. G. Barlow, A. P. Freeman, J. T. Hearne, J. C. Laker, G. A. R. Lock, G. G. Macaulay, T. J. Matthews, M. J. Procter, T. Richardson, F. R. Spofforth, F. S. Trueman.
Three times: W. M. Bradley, H. J. Butler, S. T. Clarke, W. H. Copson, R. J. Crisp, J. W. H. T. Douglas, J. A. Flavell, G. Giffen, D. W. Headley, K. Higgs, A. Hill, W. A. Humphreys, R. D. Jackman, R. O. Jenkins, A. S. Kennedy, W. H. Lockwood, E. A. McDonald, T. L. Pritchard, J. S. Rao, A. Shaw, J. B. Statham, M. W. Tate, H. Trumble, Wasim Akram, D. Wilson, G. A. Wilson.
Twice (current players only): D. G. Cork, K. J. Dean, Fazl-e-Akbar, D. Gough, A. Kumble, J. D. Lewry, A. Sheriyar, J. Srinath, Waqar Younis.

Hat-Trick on Debut

H. Hay	South Australia v Lord Hawke's XI at Unley, Adelaide	1902-03
H. A. Sedgwick . . .	Yorkshire v Worcestershire at Hull	1906
R. Wooster.	Northamptonshire v Dublin University at Northampton	1925
J. C. Treanor	New South Wales v Queensland at Brisbane	1954-55
V. B. Ranjane	Maharashtra v Saurashtra at Poona	1956-57
Arshad Khan	Dacca University v East Pakistan B at Dacca	1957-58
N. Fredrick	Ceylon v Madras at Colombo	1963-64
J. S. Rao	Services v Jammu and Kashmir at Delhi	1963-64
Mehboodullah	Uttar Pradesh v Madhya Pradesh at Lucknow	1971-72
R. O. Estwick	Barbados v Guyana at Bridgetown	1982-83
S. A. Ankola	Maharashtra v Gujarat at Poona	1988-89
J. Srinath	Karnataka v Hyderabad at Secunderabad	1989-90
S. P. Mukherjee . . .	Bengal v Hyderabad at Secunderabad	1989-90

Notes: R. R. Phillips (Border) took a hat-trick in his first over in first-class cricket (v Eastern Province at Port Elizabeth, 1939-40) having previously played in four matches without bowling.
J. S. Rao took two more hat-tricks in his next match.

250 WICKETS IN A SEASON

	Season	O	M	R	W	Avge
A. P. Freeman	1928	1,976.1	423	5,489	304	18.05
A. P. Freeman	1933	2,039	651	4,549	298	15.26
T. Richardson	1895‡	1,690.1	463	4,170	290	14.37
C. T. B. Turner	1888†	2,427.2	1,127	3,307	283	11.68
A. P. Freeman	1931	1,618	360	4,307	276	15.60
A. P. Freeman	1930	1,914.3	472	4,632	275	16.84
T. Richardson	1897‡	1,603.4	495	3,945	273	14.45
A. P. Freeman	1929	1,670.5	381	4,879	267	18.27
W. Rhodes	1900	1,553	455	3,606	261	13.81
J. T. Hearne	1896‡	2,003.1	818	3,670	257	14.28
A. P. Freeman	1932	1,565.5	404	4,149	253	16.39
W. Rhodes	1901	1,565	505	3,797	251	15.12

† *Indicates 4-ball overs.* ‡ *5-ball overs.*

Notes: In four consecutive seasons (1928-31), A. P. Freeman took 1,122 wickets, and in eight consecutive seasons (1928-35), 2,090 wickets. In each of these eight seasons he took over 200 wickets.
T. Richardson took 1,005 wickets in four consecutive seasons (1894-97).
In 1896, J. T. Hearne took his 100th wicket as early as June 12. In 1931, C. W. L. Parker did the same and A. P. Freeman obtained his 100th wicket a day later.

LEADING BOWLERS IN AN ENGLISH SEASON

(Qualification: 10 wickets in 10 innings)

Season	Leading wicket-taker	Wkts	Avge	Top of averages	Wkts	Avge
1946	W. E. Hollies	184	15.60	A. Booth	111	11.61
1947	T. W. J. Goddard	238	17.30	J. C. Clay	65	16.44
1948	J. E. Walsh	174	19.56	J. C. Clay	41	14.17
1949	R. O. Jenkins	183	21.19	T. W. J. Goddard	160	19.18
1950	R. Tattersall	193	13.59	R. Tattersall	193	13.59
1951	R. Appleyard	200	14.14	R. Appleyard	200	14.14
1952	J. H. Wardle	177	19.54	F. S. Trueman	61	13.78
1953	B. Dooland	172	16.58	C. J. Knott	38	13.71
1954	B. Dooland	196	15.48	J. B. Statham	92	14.13
1955	G. A. R. Lock	216	14.49	R. Appleyard	85	13.01
1956	D. J. Shepherd	177	15.36	G. A. R. Lock	155	12.46
1957	G. A. R. Lock	212	12.02	G. A. R. Lock	212	12.02
1958	G. A. R. Lock	170	12.08	H. L. Jackson	143	10.99
1959	D. Shackleton	148	21.55	J. B. Statham	139	15.01
1960	F. S. Trueman	175	13.98	J. B. Statham	135	12.31
1961	J. A. Flavell	171	17.79	J. A. Flavell	171	17.79
1962	D. Shackleton	172	20.15	C. Cook	58	17.13
1963	D. Shackleton	146	16.75	C. C. Griffith	119	12.83
1964	D. Shackleton	142	20.40	J. A. Standen	64	13.00
1965	D. Shackleton	144	16.08	H. J. Rhodes	119	11.04
1966	D. L. Underwood	157	13.80	D. L. Underwood	157	13.80
1967	T. W. Cartwright	147	15.52	D. L. Underwood	136	12.39
1968	R. Illingworth	131	14.36	O. S. Wheatley	82	12.95
1969	R. M. H. Cottam	109	21.04	A. Ward	69	14.82
1970	D. J. Shepherd	106	19.16	Majid Khan	11	18.81
1971	L. R. Gibbs	131	18.89	G. G. Arnold	83	17.12
1972	T. W. Cartwright	98	18.64	I. M. Chappell	10	10.60
	B. Stead	98	20.38			
1973	B. S. Bedi	105	17.94	T. W. Cartwright	89	15.84
1974	A. M. E. Roberts	119	13.62	A. M. E. Roberts	119	13.62
1975	P. G. Lee	112	18.45	A. M. E. Roberts	57	15.80
1976	G. A. Cope	93	24.13	M. A. Holding	55	14.38
1977	M. J. Procter	109	18.04	R. A. Woolmer	19	15.21
1978	D. L. Underwood	110	14.49	D. L. Underwood	110	14.49
1979	D. L. Underwood	106	14.85	J. Garner	55	13.83
	J. K. Lever	106	17.30			
1980	R. D. Jackman	121	15.40	J. Garner	49	13.93
1981	R. J. Hadlee	105	14.89	R. J. Hadlee	105	14.89
1982	M. D. Marshall	134	15.73	R. J. Hadlee	61	14.57
1983	J. K. Lever	106	16.28	Imran Khan	12	7.16
	D. L. Underwood	106	19.28			
1984	R. J. Hadlee	117	14.05	R. J. Hadlee	117	14.05
1985	N. V. Radford	101	24.68	R. M. Ellison	65	17.20
1986	C. A. Walsh	118	18.17	M. D. Marshall	100	15.08
1987	N. V. Radford	109	20.81	R. J. Hadlee	97	12.64
1988	F. D. Stephenson	125	18.31	M. D. Marshall	42	13.16
1989	D. R. Pringle	94	18.64	T. M. Alderman	70	15.64
	S. L. Watkin	94	25.09			
1990	N. A. Foster	94	26.61	I. R. Bishop	59	19.05
1991	Waqar Younis	113	14.65	Waqar Younis	113	14.65
1992	C. A. Walsh	92	15.96	C. A. Walsh	92	15.96
1993	S. L. Watkin	92	22.80	Wasim Akram	59	19.27
1994	M. M. Patel	90	22.86	C. E. L. Ambrose	77	14.45
1995	A. Kumble	105	20.40	A. A. Donald	89	16.07

Season	Leading wicket-taker	Wkts	Avge	Top of averages	Wkts	Avge
1996	C. A. Walsh	85	16.84	C. E. L. Ambrose	43	16.67
1997	A. M. Smith	83	17.63	A. A. Donald	60	15.63
1998	C. A. Walsh.	106	17.31	V. J. Wells	36	14.27
1999	A. Sheriyar	92	24.70	Saqlain Mushtaq	58	11.37
2000	G. D. McGrath.	80	13.21	C. A. Walsh	40	11.42
2001	R. J. Kirtley.	75	23.32	G. D. McGrath	40	15.60
2002	{ M. J. Saggers.	83	21.51			
	{ K. J. Dean.	83	23.50	C. P. Schofield	18	18.38

100 WICKETS IN A SEASON

(Since reduction of Championship matches in 1969)

Five times: D. L. Underwood 110 (1978), 106 (1979), 106 (1983), 102 (1971), 101 (1969).
Four times: J. K. Lever 116 (1984), 106 (1978), 106 (1979), 106 (1983).
Twice: B. S. Bedi 112 (1974), 105 (1973); T. W. Cartwright 108 (1969), 104 (1971); N. A. Foster 105 (1986), 102 (1991); N. Gifford 105 (1970), 104 (1983); R. J. Hadlee 117 (1984), 105 (1981); P. G. Lee 112 (1975), 101 (1973); M. D. Marshall 134 (1982), 100 (1986); M. J. Procter 109 (1977), 108 (1969); N. V. Radford 109 (1987), 101 (1985); F. J. Titmus 105 (1970), 104 (1971); C. A. Walsh 118 (1986), 106 (1998).
Once: J. P. Agnew 101 (1987); I. T. Botham 100 (1978); A. R. Caddick 105 (1998); K. E. Cooper 101 (1988); R. M. H. Cottam 109 (1969); D. R. Doshi 101 (1980); J. E. Emburey 103 (1983); L. R. Gibbs 131 (1971); R. N. S. Hobbs 102 (1970); Intikhab Alam 104 (1971); R. D. Jackman 121 (1980); A. Kumble 105 (1995); A. M. E. Roberts 119 (1974); P. J. Sainsbury 107 (1971); Sarfraz Nawaz 101 (1975); M. W. W. Selvey 101 (1978); D. J. Shepherd 106 (1970); F. D. Stephenson 125 (1988); Waqar Younis 113 (1991); D. Wilson 102 (1969).

100 WICKETS IN A SEASON MOST TIMES

(Includes overseas tours and seasons)

23 times: W. Rhodes 200 wkts (3).
20 times: D. Shackleton (In successive seasons – 1949 to 1968 inclusive).
17 times: A. P. Freeman 300 wkts (1), 200 wkts (7).
16 times: T. W. J. Goddard 200 wkts (4), C. W. L. Parker 200 wkts (5), R. T. D. Perks, F. J. Titmus.
15 times: J. T. Hearne 200 wkts (3), G. H. Hirst 200 wkts (1), A. S. Kennedy 200 wkts (1).
14 times: C. Blythe 200 wkts (1), W. E. Hollies, G. A. R. Lock 200 wkts (2), M. W. Tate 200 wkts (3), C. W. L. White.
13 times: J. B. Statham.
12 times: J. Briggs, E. G. Dennett 200 wkts (1), C. Gladwin, D. J. Shepherd, N. I. Thomson, F. S. Trueman.
11 times: A. V. Bedser, G. Geary, S. Haigh, J. C. Laker, M. S. Nichols, A. E. Relf.
10 times: W. Attewell, W. G. Grace, R. Illingworth, H. L. Jackson, V. W. C. Jupp, G. G. Macaulay 200 wkts (1), W. Mead, T. B. Mitchell, T. Richardson 200 wkts (3), J. Southerton 200 wkts (1), R. K. Tyldesley, D. L. Underwood, J. H. Wardle, T. G. Wass, D. V. P. Wright.

100 WICKETS IN A SEASON OUTSIDE ENGLAND

W		Season	Country	R	Avge
116	M. W. Tate	1926-27	India/Ceylon	1,599	13.78
113	Kabir Khan	1998-99	Pakistan	1,706	15.09
107	Ijaz Faqih	1985-86	Pakistan	1,719	16.06
106	C. T. B. Turner	1887-88	Australia	1,441	13.59
106	R. Benaud	1957-58	South Africa	2,056	19.39
105	Murtaza Hussain	1995-96	Pakistan	1,882	17.92
104	S. F. Barnes	1913-14	South Africa	1,117	10.74
104	Sajjad Akbar	1989-90	Pakistan	2,328	22.38
103	Abdul Qadir	1982-83	Pakistan	2,367	22.98

1,500 WICKETS

Dates in italics denote the first half of an overseas season; i.e. *1970* denotes the 1970-71 season.

		Career	W	R	Avge
1	W. Rhodes	1898-1930	4,187	69,993	16.71
2	A. P. Freeman	1914-36	3,776	69,577	18.42
3	C. W. L. Parker	1903-35	3,278	63,817	19.46
4	J. T. Hearne	1888-1923	3,061	54,352	17.75
5	T. W. J. Goddard	1922-52	2,979	59,116	19.84
6	W. G. Grace	1865-1908	2,876	51,545	17.92
7	A. S. Kennedy	1907-36	2,874	61,034	21.23
8	D. Shackleton	1948-69	2,857	53,303	18.65
9	G. A. R. Lock	1946-*70*	2,844	54,709	19.23
10	F. J. Titmus	1949-82	2,830	63,313	22.37
11	M. W. Tate	1912-37	2,784	50,571	18.16
12	G. H. Hirst	1891-1929	2,739	51,282	18.72
13	C. Blythe	1899-1914	2,506	42,136	16.81
14	D. L. Underwood	1963-87	2,465	49,993	20.28
15	W. E. Astill	1906-39	2,431	57,783	23.76
16	J. C. White	1909-37	2,356	43,759	18.57
17	W. E. Hollies	1932-57	2,323	48,656	20.94
18	F. S. Trueman	1949-69	2,304	42,154	18.29
19	J. B. Statham	1950-68	2,260	36,999	16.37
20	R. T. D. Perks	1930-55	2,233	53,770	24.07
21	J. Briggs	1879-1900	2,221	35,431	15.95
22	D. J. Shepherd	1950-72	2,218	47,302	21.32
23	E. G. Dennett	1903-26	2,147	42,571	19.82
24	T. Richardson	1892-1905	2,104	38,794	18.43
25	T. E. Bailey	1945-67	2,082	48,170	23.13
26	R. Illingworth	1951-83	2,072	42,023	20.28
27 {	N. Gifford	1960-88	2,068	48,731	23.56
	F. E. Woolley	1906-38	2,068	41,066	19.85
29	G. Geary	1912-38	2,063	41,339	20.03
30	D. V. P. Wright	1932-57	2,056	49,307	23.98
31	J. A. Newman	1906-30	2,032	51,111	25.15
32	†A. Shaw	1864-97	2,027	24,580	12.12
33	S. Haigh	1895-1913	2,012	32,091	15.94
34	H. Verity	1930-39	1,956	29,146	14.90
35	W. Attewell	1881-1900	1,951	29,896	15.32
36	J. C. Laker	1946-*64*	1,944	35,791	18.41
37	A. V. Bedser	1939-60	1,924	39,279	20.41
38	W. Mead	1892-1913	1,916	36,388	18.99
39	A. E. Relf	1900-21	1,897	39,724	20.94
40	P. G. H. Fender	1910-36	1,894	47,458	25.05
41	J. W. H. T. Douglas	1901-30	1,893	44,159	23.32
42	J. H. Wardle	1946-*67*	1,846	35,027	18.97
43	G. R. Cox	1895-1928	1,843	42,136	22.86
44	G. A. Lohmann	1884-*97*	1,841	25,295	13.73
45	J. W. Hearne	1909-36	1,839	44,926	24.42
46	G. G. Macaulay	1920-35	1,837	32,440	17.65
47	M. S. Nichols	1924-39	1,833	39,666	21.63
48 {	J. B. Mortimore	1950-75	1,807	41,904	23.18
	C. A. Walsh	*1981-2000*	1,807	39,233	21.71
50	C. Cook	1946-64	1,782	36,578	20.52
51	R. Peel	1882-99	1,752	28,442	16.23
52	H. L. Jackson	1947-63	1,733	30,101	17.36
53	J. K. Lever	1967-89	1,722	41,772	24.25
54	T. P. B. Smith	1929-52	1,697	45,059	26.55
55	J. Southerton	1854-79	1,681	24,290	14.44
56	A. E. Trott	*1892*-1911	1,674	35,317	21.09

		Career	W	R	Avge
57	A. W. Mold	1889-1901	1,673	26,010	15.54
58	T. G. Wass	1896-1920	1,666	34,092	20.46
59	V. W. C. Jupp	1909-38	1,658	38,166	23.01
60	C. Gladwin	1939-58	1,653	30,265	18.30
61	M. D. Marshall	*1977-95*	1,651	31,548	19.10
62	W. E. Bowes	1928-47	1,639	27,470	16.76
63	A. W. Wellard	1927-50	1,614	39,302	24.35
64	J. E. Emburey	1973-97	1,608	41,958	26.09
65	P. I. Pocock	1964-86	1,607	42,648	26.53
66	N. I. Thomson	1952-72	1,597	32,867	20.58
67	J. Mercer	1919-47	1,591	37,210	23.38
	G. J. Thompson	1897-1922	1,591	30,058	18.89
69	J. M. Sims	1929-53	1,581	39,401	24.92
70	T. Emmett	1866-88	1,571	21,314	13.56
	Intikhab Alam	*1957-82*	1,571	43,474	27.67
72	B. S. Bedi	*1961-81*	1,560	33,843	21.69
73	W. Voce	1927-52	1,558	35,961	23.08
74	A. R. Gover	1928-48	1,555	36,753	23.63
75	T. W. Cartwright	1952-77	1,536	29,357	19.11
	K. Higgs	1958-86	1,536	36,267	23.61
77	James Langridge	1924-53	1,530	34,524	22.56
78	J. A. Flavell	1949-67	1,529	32,847	21.48
79	E. E. Hemmings	1966-95	1,515	44,403	29.30
80	C. F. Root	1910-33	1,512	31,933	21.11
	F. A. Tarrant	*1898-1936*	1,512	26,450	17.49
82	R. K. Tyldesley	1919-35	1,509	25,980	17.21

† *The figures for A. Shaw exclude one wicket for which no analysis is available.*

Note: Some works of reference provide career figures which differ from those in this list, owing to the exclusion or inclusion of matches recognised or not recognised as first-class by *Wisden*.

Current Players with 1,000 Wickets

	Career	W	R	Avge
A. A. Donald	*1985-2002*	1,187	26,937	22.69
P. A. J. DeFreitas	1985-2002	1,145	31,896	27.85
P. C. R. Tufnell	1986-2002	1,057	31,026	29.35
D. E. Malcolm	1984-2002	1,040	31,615	30.39
Wasim Akram	*1984-2001*	1,022	22,046	21.57

ALL-ROUND RECORDS

HUNDRED AND TEN WICKETS IN AN INNINGS

V. E. Walker, England v Surrey at The Oval; 20*, 108, ten for 74, and four for 17 . .   1859
W. G. Grace, MCC v Oxford University at Oxford; 104, two for 60, and ten for 49 . .   1886

Note: E. M. Grace, for MCC v Gentlemen of Kent in a 12-a-side match at Canterbury in 1862, scored 192* and took five for 77 and ten for 69.

DOUBLE-HUNDRED AND 16 WICKETS

G. Giffen, South Australia v Victoria at Adelaide; 271, nine for 96, and seven for 70 . .   1891-92

HUNDRED IN EACH INNINGS AND FIVE WICKETS TWICE

G. H. Hirst, Yorkshire v Somerset at Bath; 111, 117*, six for 70, and five for 45 . . .   1906

HUNDRED IN EACH INNINGS AND TEN WICKETS

B. J. T. Bosanquet, Middlesex v Sussex at Lord's; 103, 100*, three for 75, and eight for 53. 1905

F. D. Stephenson, Nottinghamshire v Yorkshire at Nottingham; 111, 117, four for 105, and seven for 117 1988

HUNDRED AND FOUR WICKETS WITH CONSECUTIVE BALLS

K. D. James, Hampshire v Indians at Southampton; 103 and five for 74 including four wickets with consecutive balls. 1996

HUNDRED AND HAT-TRICK

G. Giffen, Australians v Lancashire at Manchester	1884
W. E. Roller, Surrey v Sussex at The Oval. *Unique instance of 200 and hat-trick*. . .	1885
W. B. Burns, Worcestershire v Gloucestershire at Worcester.	1913
V. W. C. Jupp, Sussex v Essex at Colchester.	1921
R. E. S. Wyatt, MCC v Ceylon at Colombo	1926-27
L. N. Constantine, West Indians v Northamptonshire at Northampton	1928
D. E. Davies, Glamorgan v Leicestershire at Leicester.	1937
V. M. Merchant, Dr C. R. Pereira's XI v Sir Homi Mehta's XI at Bombay	1946-47
M. J. Procter, Gloucestershire v Essex at Westcliff-on-Sea.	1972
M. J. Procter, Gloucestershire v Leicestershire at Bristol.	1979

SEASON DOUBLES

2,000 Runs and 200 Wickets

1906   G. H. Hirst   2,385 runs and 208 wickets

3,000 Runs and 100 Wickets

1937   J. H. Parks   3,003 runs and 101 wickets

2,000 Runs and 100 Wickets

	Season	R	W		Season	R	W
W. G. Grace.	1873	2,139	106	F. E. Woolley.	1914	2,272	125
W. G. Grace.	1876	2,622	130	J. W. Hearne	1920	2,148	142
C. L. Townsend	1899	2,440	101	V. W. C. Jupp	1921	2,169	121
G. L. Jessop	1900	2,210	104	F. E. Woolley.	1921	2,101	167
G. H. Hirst	1904	2,501	132	F. E. Woolley.	1922	2,022	163
G. H. Hirst	1905	2,266	110	F. E. Woolley.	1923	2,091	101
W. Rhodes	1909	2,094	141	L. F. Townsend	1933	2,268	100
W. Rhodes	1911	2,261	117	D. E. Davies	1937	2,012	103
F. A. Tarrant	1911	2,030	111	James Langridge	1937	2,082	101
J. W. Hearne	1913	2,036	124	T. E. Bailey.	1959	2,011	100
J. W. Hearne	1914	2,116	123				

1,000 Runs and 200 Wickets

	Season	R	W		Season	R	W
A. E. Trott	1899	1,175	239	M. W. Tate.	1923	1,168	219
A. E. Trott	1900	1,337	211	M. W. Tate.	1924	1,419	205
A. S. Kennedy	1922	1,129	205	M. W. Tate.	1925	1,290	228

1,000 Runs and 100 Wickets

Sixteen times: W. Rhodes.
Fourteen times: G. H. Hirst.
Ten times: V. W. C. Jupp.
Nine times: W. E. Astill.
Eight times: T. E. Bailey, W. G. Grace, M. S. Nichols, A. E. Relf, F. A. Tarrant, M. W. Tate†, F. J. Titmus, F. E. Woolley.
Seven times: G. E. Tribe.

† M. W. Tate also scored 1,193 runs and took 116 wickets for MCC in first-class matches on the 1926-27 MCC tour of India and Ceylon.

Note: R. J. Hadlee (1984) and F. D. Stephenson (1988) are the only players to perform the feat since the reduction of County Championship matches. A complete list of those performing the feat before then will be found on page 202 of the 1982 *Wisden*.

Wicket-Keeper's Double

	Season	R	D		Season	R	D
L. E. G. Ames. . . .	1928	1,919	122	L. E. G. Ames . .	1932	2,482	104
L. E. G. Ames. . . .	1929	1,795	128	J. T. Murray	1957	1,025	104

20,000 RUNS AND 2,000 WICKETS

	Career	R	Avge	W	Avge	Doubles
W. E. Astill	1906-39	22,731	22.55	2,431	23.76	9
T. E. Bailey	1945-67	28,641	33.42	2,082	23.13	8
W. G. Grace	1865-1908	54,896	39.55	2,876	17.92	8
G. H. Hirst	1891-1929	36,323	34.13	2,739	18.72	14
R. Illingworth	1951-83	24,134	28.06	2,072	20.28	6
W. Rhodes	1898-1930	39,802	30.83	4,187	16.71	16
M. W. Tate	1912-37	21,717	25.01	2,784	18.16	8†
F. J. Titmus	1949-82	21,588	23.11	2,830	22.37	8
F. E. Woolley	1906-38	58,969	40.75	2,068	19.85	8

† Plus one double overseas (see above).

Current Player with 10,000 Runs and 1,000 Wickets

	Career	R	Avge	W	Avge	Doubles
P. A. J. DeFreitas	1985-2002	10,042	23.03	1,145	27.85	–

WICKET-KEEPING RECORDS

MOST DISMISSALS IN AN INNINGS

9 (8ct, 1st)	Tahir Rashid	Habib Bank v PACO at Gujranwala	1992-93
9 (7ct, 2st)	W. R. James*	Matabeleland v Mashonaland CD at Bulawayo. . . .	1995-96
8 (all ct)	A. T. W. Grout	Queensland v Western Australia at Brisbane	1959-60
8 (all ct)†	D. E. East	Essex v Somerset at Taunton	1985
8 (all ct)	S. A. Marsh‡	Kent v Middlesex at Lord's	1991
8 (6ct, 2st)	T. J. Zoehrer	Australians v Surrey at The Oval.	1993
8 (7ct, 1st)	D. S. Berry	Victoria v South Australia at Melbourne	1996-97

8 (7ct, 1st)	Y. S. S. Mendis	Bloomfield v Kurungala Youth at Colombo	2000-01
8 (7ct, 1st)	S. Nath§	Assam v Tripura at Guwahati	2001-02
7 (4ct, 3st)	E. J. Smith	Warwickshire v Derbyshire at Birmingham	1926
7 (6ct, 1st)	W. Farrimond	Lancashire v Kent at Manchester.	1930
7 (all ct)	W. F. F. Price	Middlesex v Yorkshire at Lord's	1937
7 (3ct, 4st)	D. Tallon	Queensland v Victoria at Brisbane	1938-39
7 (all ct)	R. A. Saggers	New South Wales v Combined XI at Brisbane	1940-41
7 (1ct, 6st)	H. Yarnold	Worcestershire v Scotland at Dundee	1951
7 (4ct, 3st)	J. Brown	Scotland v Ireland at Dublin	1957
7 (6ct, 1st)	N. Kirsten	Border v Rhodesia at East London	1959-60
7 (all ct)	M. S. Smith	Natal v Border at East London	1959-60
7 (all ct)	K. V. Andrew	Northamptonshire v Lancashire at Manchester	1962
7 (all ct)	A. Long	Surrey v Sussex at Hove	1964
7 (all ct)	R. M. Schofield	Central Districts v Wellington at Wellington	1964-65
7 (all ct)	R. W. Taylor	Derbyshire v Glamorgan at Derby	1966
7 (6ct, 1st)	H. B. Taber	New South Wales v South Australia at Adelaide. . .	1968-69
7 (6ct, 1st)	E. W. Jones	Glamorgan v Cambridge University at Cambridge. .	1970
7 (6ct, 1st)	S. Benjamin	Central Zone v North Zone at Bombay.	1973-74
7 (all ct)	R. W. Taylor	Derbyshire v Yorkshire at Chesterfield	1975
7 (6ct, 1st)	Shahid Israr	Karachi Whites v Quetta at Karachi.	1976-77
7 (4ct, 3st)	Wasim Bari	PIA v Sind at Lahore	1977-78
7 (all ct)	J. A. Maclean	Queensland v Victoria at Melbourne	1977-78
7 (5ct, 2st)	Taslim Arif	National Bank v Punjab at Lahore	1978-79
7 (all ct)	Wasim Bari	Pakistan v New Zealand at Auckland	1978-79
7 (all ct)	R. W. Taylor	England v India at Bombay	1979-80
7 (all ct)	D. L. Bairstow	Yorkshire v Derbyshire at Scarborough	1982
7 (6ct, 1st)	R. B. Phillips	Queensland v New Zealanders at Bundaberg	1982-83
7 (3ct, 4st)	Masood Iqbal	Habib Bank v Lahore at Lahore	1982-83
7 (3ct, 4st)	Arif-ud-Din	United Bank v PACO at Sahiwal	1983-84
7 (6ct, 1st)	R. J. East	OFS v Western Province B at Cape Town	1984-85
7 (all ct)	B. A. Young	Northern Districts v Canterbury at Christchurch . . .	1986-87
7 (all ct)	D. J. Richardson	Eastern Province v OFS at Bloemfontein	1988-89
7 (6ct, 1st)	Dildar Malik	Multan v Faisalabad at Sahiwal	1988-89
7 (all ct)	W. K. Hegg	Lancashire v Derbyshire at Chesterfield	1989
7 (all ct)	Imran Zia	Bahawalpur v Faisalabad at Faisalabad	1989-90
7 (all ct)	I. D. S. Smith	New Zealand v Sri Lanka at Hamilton	1990-91
7 (all ct)	J. F. Holyman	Tasmania v Western Australia at Hobart	1990-91
7 (all ct)	P. J. L. Radley	OFS v Western Province at Cape Town.	1990-91
7 (all ct)	C. P. Metson	Glamorgan v Derbyshire at Chesterfield	1991
7 (all ct)	H. M. de Vos	W. Transvaal v E. Transvaal at Potchefstroom . . .	1993-94
7 (all ct)	P. Kirsten	Griqualand West v W. Transvaal at Potchefstroom. .	1993-94
7 (6ct, 1st)	S. A. Marsh	Kent v Durham at Canterbury.	1994
7 (all ct)	K. J. Piper	Warwickshire v Essex at Birmingham	1994
7 (6ct, 1st)	K. J. Piper	Warwickshire v Derbyshire at Chesterfield.	1994
7 (all ct)	H. H. Devapriya	Colts v Sinhalese at Colombo.	1995-96
7 (all ct)	D. J. R. Campbell	Mashonaland CD v Matabeleland at Bulawayo	1995-96
7 (all ct)	A. C. Gilchrist	Western Australia v South Australia at Perth	1995-96
7 (all ct)	C. W. Scott	Durham v Yorkshire at Chester-le-Street	1996
7 (all ct)	Zahid Umar	WAPDA v Habib Bank at Sheikhupura	1997-98
7 (all ct)	K. S. M. Iyer	Vidarbha v Uttar Pradesh at Allahabad	1997-98
7 (all ct)	W. M. Noon	Nottinghamshire v Kent at Nottingham	1999
7 (all ct)	Aamer Iqbal	Pakistan Customs v Karachi Whites at Karachi . . .	1999-2000
7 (all ct)	H. A. P. W. Jayawardene	Sebastianites v Sinhalese at Colombo.	1999-2000
7 (all ct)	R. D. Jacobs	West Indies v Australia at Melbourne.	2000-01
7 (all ct)	N. D. Burns	Leicestershire v Somerset at Leicester	2001
7 (all ct)	R. J. Turner	Somerset v Northamptonshire at Taunton	2001
7 (all ct)	W. A. Seccombe	Queensland v New South Wales at Brisbane	2001-02
7 (all ct)	M. G. Croy	Otago v Auckland at Auckland	2001-02

* W. R. James also scored 99 and 99 not out.   *† The first eight wickets to fall.*
‡ S. A. Marsh also scored 108 not out.   *§ On first-class debut.*

WICKET-KEEPERS' HAT-TRICKS

W. H. Brain, Gloucestershire v Somerset at Cheltenham, 1893 – three stumpings off successive balls from C. L. Townsend.

G. O. Dawkes, Derbyshire v Worcestershire at Kidderminster, 1958 – three catches off successive balls from H. L. Jackson.

R. C. Russell, Gloucestershire v Surrey at The Oval, 1986 – three catches off successive balls from C. A. Walsh and D. V. Lawrence (2).

MOST DISMISSALS IN A MATCH

13 (11ct, 2st)	W. R. James*	Matabeleland v Mashonaland CD at Bulawayo ..	1995-96
12 (8ct, 4st)	E. Pooley	Surrey v Sussex at The Oval	1868
12 (9ct, 3st)	D. Tallon	Queensland v New South Wales at Sydney.....	1938-39
12 (9ct, 3st)	H. B. Taber	New South Wales v South Australia at Adelaide .	1968-69
11 (all ct)	A. Long	Surrey v Sussex at Hove..................	1964
11 (all ct)	R. W. Marsh	Western Australia v Victoria at Perth.........	1975-76
11 (all ct)	D. L. Bairstow	Yorkshire v Derbyshire at Scarborough........	1982
11 (all ct)	W. K. Hegg	Lancashire v Derbyshire at Chesterfield	1989
11 (all ct)	A. J. Stewart	Surrey v Leicestershire at Leicester	1989
11 (all ct)	T. J. Nielsen	South Australia v Western Australia at Perth	1990-91
11 (10ct, 1st)	I. A. Healy	Australians v N. Transvaal at Verwoerdburg	1993-94
11 (10ct, 1st)	K. J. Piper	Warwickshire v Derbyshire at Chesterfield	1994
11 (all ct)	D. S. Berry	Victoria v Pakistanis at Melbourne	1995-96
11 (10ct, 1st)	W. A. Seccombe	Queensland v Western Australia at Brisbane	1995-96
11 (all ct)	R. C. Russell	England v South Africa (2nd Test) at Johannesburg	1995-96
11 (10ct, 1st)	D. S. Berry	Victoria v South Australia at Melbourne.......	1996-97
11 (all ct)	Wasim Yousufi	Peshawar v Bahawalpur at Peshawar	1997-98
11 (all ct)	Aamer Iqbal	Pakistan Customs v Karachi Whites at Karachi ...	1999-2000
11 (10ct, 1st)	S. Nath†	Assam v Tripura at Guwahati..............	2001-02

* W. R. James also scored 99 and 99 not out. † On first-class debut.

100 DISMISSALS IN A SEASON

128 (79ct, 49st)	L. E. G. Ames...	1929		104 (82ct, 22st)	J. T. Murray....	1957
122 (70ct, 52st)	L. E. G. Ames...	1928		102 (69ct, 33st)	F. H. Huish	1913
110 (63ct, 47st)	H. Yarnold.....	1949		102 (95ct, 7st)	J. T. Murray....	1960
107 (77ct, 30st)	G. Duckworth ...	1928		101 (62ct, 39st)	F. H. Huish	1911
107 (96ct, 11st)	J. G. Binks	1960		101 (85ct, 16st)	R. Booth......	1960
104 (40ct, 64st)	L. E. G. Ames...	1932		100 (91ct, 9st)	R. Booth	1964

1,000 DISMISSALS

Dates in italics denote the first half of an overseas season; i.e. *1914* denotes the 1914-15 season.

			Career	*M*	*Ct*	*St*
1	1,649	R. W. Taylor	1960-88	639	1,473	176
2	1,527	J. T. Murray	1952-75	635	1,270	257
3	1,497	H. Strudwick........	1902-27	675	1,242	255
4	1,344	A. P. E. Knott......	1964-85	511	1,211	133
5	1,310	F. H. Huish.........	1895-1914	497	933	377
6	1,294	B. Taylor	1949-73	572	1,083	211
7	**1,282**	**R. C. Russell**	**1981-2002**	**452**	**1,158**	**124**
8	1,253	D. Hunter	1889-1909	548	906	347
9	1,228	H. R. Butt	1890-1912	550	953	275
10	1,207	J. H. Board.........	1891-*1914*	525	852	355
11	1,206	H. Elliott	1920-47	532	904	302
12	1,181	J. M. Parks	1949-76	739	1,088	93
13	**1,175**	**S. J. Rhodes**	**1981-2002**	**412**	**1,057**	**118**

			Career	M	Ct	St
14	1,126	R. Booth	1951-70	468	948	178
15	1,121	L. E. G. Ames	1926-51	593	703	418†
16	1,099	D. L. Bairstow.	1970-90	459	961	138
17	1,096	G. Duckworth	1923-47	504	753	343
18	1,082	H. W. Stephenson. . . .	1948-64	462	748	334
19	1,071	J. G. Binks	1955-75	502	895	176
20	1,066	T. G. Evans	1939-69	465	816	250
21	1,046	A. Long.	1960-80	452	922	124
22	1,043	G. O. Dawkes	1937-61	482	895	148
23	1,037	R. W. Tolchard	1965-83	483	912	125
24	1,017	W. L. Cornford	1921-47	496	675	342

Bold type denotes those who played in 2001-02 or 2002 season.

† Record.

Other Current Players with 500 Dismissals

		Career	M	Ct	St
828	W. K. Hegg	1986-2002	305	747	81
802	R. J. Blakey	1985-2002	335	746	56
669	P. A. Nixon.	1989-2002	236	619	50
595	R. J. Turner.	1988-2002	209	555	40
560	A. N. Aymes.	1987-2002	215	516	44
556	K. M. Krikken	*1988-2002*	213	525	31
556	Tahir Rashid	*1979-2001*	178	495	61
545	D. S. Berry.	*1989-2001*	138	500	45
523	K. J. Piper	1989-2002	195	490	33
516	N. D. Burns	1985-2002	205	478	38
502	A. C. Gilchrist	*1992-2001*	118	474	28

Note: A. J. Stewart has had 669 catches and 31 stumpings in 428 matches from 1981 to 2002, but 212 of his catches were taken as a fielder.

FIELDING RECORDS
excluding wicket-keepers

MOST CATCHES IN AN INNINGS

7	M. J. Stewart	Surrey v Northamptonshire at Northampton.	1957
7	A. S. Brown	Gloucestershire v Nottinghamshire at Nottingham. . .	1966

MOST CATCHES IN A MATCH

10	W. R. Hammond†	Gloucestershire v Surrey at Cheltenham	1928
8	W. B. Burns	Worcestershire v Yorkshire at Bradford.	1907
8	F. G. Travers	Europeans v Parsees at Bombay	1923-24
8	A. H. Bakewell	Northamptonshire v Essex at Leyton	1928
8	W. R. Hammond	Gloucestershire v Worcestershire at Cheltenham	1932
8	K. J. Grieves	Lancashire v Sussex at Manchester	1951
8	C. A. Milton	Gloucestershire v Sussex at Hove	1952
8	G. A. R. Lock	Surrey v Warwickshire at The Oval	1957
8	J. M. Prodger	Kent v Gloucestershire at Cheltenham	1961
8	P. M. Walker	Glamorgan v Derbyshire at Swansea	1970
8	Masood Anwar	Rawalpindi v Lahore Division at Rawalpindi	1983-84
8	M. C. J. Ball	Gloucestershire v Yorkshire at Cheltenham	1994
8	J. D. Carr	Middlesex v Warwickshire at Birmingham	1995

† Hammond also scored a hundred in each innings.

MOST CATCHES IN A SEASON

78	W. R. Hammond	1928	69	P. M. Walker	1960
77	M. J. Stewart	1957	66	J. Tunnicliffe	1895
73	P. M. Walker	1961	65	W. R. Hammond	1925
71	P. J. Sharpe	1962	65	P. M. Walker	1959
70	J. Tunnicliffe	1901	65	D. W. Richardson	1961
69	J. G. Langridge	1955			

Note: The most catches by a fielder since the reduction of County Championship matches in 1969 is 49 by C. J. Tavaré in 1978.

750 CATCHES

Dates in italics denote the first half of an overseas season; i.e. *1970* denotes the 1970-71 season.

			M					M
1,018	F. E. Woolley	1906-38	979	784	J. G. Langridge	1928-55	574
887	W. G. Grace	1865-1908	879	764	W. Rhodes	1898-1930	1,107
830	G. A. R. Lock	1946-*70*	654	758	C. A. Milton	1948-74	620
819	W. R. Hammond	1920-51	634	754	E. H. Hendren	1907-38	833
813	D. B. Close	1949-86	786				

Note: The most catches by a current player is 552 by G. A. Hick (*1983*-2002).

TEAM RECORDS

HIGHEST INNINGS TOTALS

1,107	Victoria v New South Wales at Melbourne	1926-27
1,059	Victoria v Tasmania at Melbourne	1922-23
952-6 dec.	Sri Lanka v India at Colombo	1997-98
951-7 dec.	Sind v Baluchistan at Karachi	1973-74
944-6 dec.	Hyderabad v Andhra at Secunderabad	1993-94
918	New South Wales v South Australia at Sydney	1900-01
912-8 dec.	Holkar v Mysore at Indore	1945-46
912-6 dec.†	Tamil Nadu v Goa at Panjim	1988-89
910-6 dec.	Railways v Dera Ismail Khan at Lahore	1964-65
903-7 dec.	England v Australia at The Oval	1938
887	Yorkshire v Warwickshire at Birmingham	1896
868†	North Zone v West Zone at Bhilai	1987-88
863	Lancashire v Surrey at The Oval	1990
855-6 dec.†	Bombay v Hyderabad at Bombay	1990-91
849	England v West Indies at Kingston	1929-30
843	Australians v Oxford & Cambridge U P & P at Portsmouth	1893
839	New South Wales v Tasmania at Sydney	1898-99
826-4	Maharashtra v Kathiawar at Poona	1948-49
824	Lahore Greens v Bahawalpur at Lahore	1965-66
821-7 dec.	South Australia v Queensland at Adelaide	1939-40
815	New South Wales v Victoria at Sydney	1908-09
811	Surrey v Somerset at The Oval	1899
810-4 dec.	Warwickshire v Durham at Birmingham	1994
807	New South Wales v South Australia at Adelaide	1899-1900
805	New South Wales v Victoria at Melbourne	1905-06
803-4 dec.	Kent v Essex at Brentwood	1934

803	Non-Smokers v Smokers at East Melbourne	1886-87
802-8 dec.	Karachi Blues v Lahore City at Peshawar	1994-95
802	New South Wales v South Australia at Sydney.	1920-21
801	Lancashire v Somerset at Taunton	1895
798	Maharashtra v Northern India at Poona.	1940-41
793	Victoria v Queensland at Melbourne	1927-28
791-6 dec.	Karnataka v Bengal at Calcutta.	1990-91
790-3 dec.	West Indies v Pakistan at Kingston	1957-58
786	New South Wales v South Australia at Adelaide.	1922-23
784	Baroda v Holkar at Baroda.	1946-47
783-8 dec.	Hyderabad v Bihar at Secunderabad.	1986-87
781-7 dec.	Northamptonshire v Nottinghamshire at Northampton	1995
780-8	Punjab v Delhi at Delhi.	1994-95
777	Canterbury v Otago at Christchurch.	1996-97
775	New South Wales v Victoria at Sydney.	1881-82

† Tamil Nadu's total of 912-6 dec. included 52 penalty runs from their opponents' failure to meet the required bowling rate. North Zone's total of 868 included 68, and Bombay's total of 855-6 dec. included 48.

HIGHEST FOURTH-INNINGS TOTALS

654-5	England v South Africa at Durban	1938-39
	After being set 696 to win. The match was left drawn on the tenth day.	
604	Maharashtra (*set 959 to win*) v Bombay at Poona	1948-49
576-8	Trinidad (*set 672 to win*) v Barbados at Port-of-Spain	1945-46
572	New South Wales (*set 593 to win*) v South Australia at Sydney	1907-08
529-9	Combined XI (*set 579 to win*) v South Africans at Perth.	1963-64
518	Victoria (*set 753 to win*) v Queensland at Brisbane	1926-27
507-7	Cambridge University v MCC and Ground at Lord's	1896
506-6	South Australia v Queensland at Adelaide	1991-92
502-6	Middlesex v Nottinghamshire at Nottingham.	1925
502-8	Players v Gentlemen at Lord's	1900
500-7	South African Universities v Western Province at Stellenbosch	1978-79

Note: Unless otherwise stated, the side making the runs won the match.

HIGHEST AGGREGATES IN A MATCH

Runs	Wkts		
2,376	37	Maharashtra v Bombay at Poona	1948-49
2,078	40	Bombay v Holkar at Bombay	1944-45
1,981	35	England v South Africa at Durban	1938-39
1,945	18	Canterbury v Wellington at Christchurch.	1994-95
1,929	39	New South Wales v South Australia at Sydney.	1925-26
1,911	34	New South Wales v Victoria at Sydney.	1908-09
1,905	40	Otago v Wellington at Dunedin	1923-24

The entire Sri Lankan team – coach and physio included – began pulling off the covers at the first sight of sun. At least one was removed without the help or consent of the ambling Lahore groundstaff.
Pakistan v Sri Lanka, page 1190

In Britain

Runs	Wkts		
1,815	28	Surrey v Somerset at Taunton	2002
1,808	20	Sussex v Essex at Hove	1993
1,795	34	Somerset v Northamptonshire at Taunton.	2001
1,723	31	England v Australia at Leeds	1948
1,706	23	Hampshire v Warwickshire at Southampton	1997
1,665	33	Warwickshire v Yorkshire at Birmingham	2002
1,655	25	Derbyshire v Nottinghamshire at Derby.	2001
1,650	19	Surrey v Lancashire at The Oval	1990
1,642	29	Nottinghamshire v Kent at Nottingham	1995
1,641	16	Glamorgan v Worcestershire at Abergavenny	1990
1,614	30	England v India at Manchester	1990
1,614	26	Gloucestershire v Northamptonshire at Bristol	2002
1,606	34	Somerset v Derbyshire at Taunton	1996
1,603	28	England v India at Lord's	1990
1,601	29	England v Australia at Lord's	1930
1,601	35	Kent v Surrey at Canterbury.	1995

LOWEST INNINGS TOTALS

12†	Oxford University v MCC and Ground at Oxford.	1877
12	Northamptonshire v Gloucestershire at Gloucester	1907
13	Auckland v Canterbury at Auckland	1877-78
13	Nottinghamshire v Yorkshire at Nottingham	1901
14	Surrey v Essex at Chelmsford.	1983
15	MCC v Surrey at Lord's	1839
15†	Victoria v MCC at Melbourne	1903-04
15†	Northamptonshire v Yorkshire at Northampton	1908
15	Hampshire v Warwickshire at Birmingham	1922
	Following on, Hampshire scored 521 and won by 155 runs.	
16	MCC and Ground v Surrey at Lord's.	1872
16	Derbyshire v Nottinghamshire at Nottingham	1879
16	Surrey v Nottinghamshire at The Oval	1880
16	Warwickshire v Kent at Tonbridge	1913
16	Trinidad v Barbados at Bridgetown	1942-43
16	Border v Natal at East London (first innings)	1959-60
17	Gentlemen of Kent v Gentlemen of England at Lord's	1850
17	Gloucestershire v Australians at Cheltenham	1896
18	The Bs v England at Lord's	1831
18†	Kent v Sussex at Gravesend	1867
18	Tasmania v Victoria at Melbourne	1868-69
18†	Australians v MCC and Ground at Lord's.	1896
18	Border v Natal at East London (second innings)	1959-60
19	Sussex v Surrey at Godalming	1830
19†	Sussex v Nottinghamshire at Hove.	1873
19	MCC and Ground v Australians at Lord's.	1878
19	Wellington v Nelson at Nelson	1885-86
19	Matabeleland v Mashonaland at Harare	2000-01

† *One man absent.*

Note: At Lord's in 1810, The Bs, with one man absent, were dismissed by England for 6.

LOWEST TOTALS IN A MATCH

34	(16 and 18) Border v Natal at East London	1959-60
42	(27 and 15) Northamptonshire v Yorkshire at Northampton	1908

Note: Northamptonshire batted one man short in each innings.

LOWEST AGGREGATE IN A COMPLETED MATCH

Runs	Wkts		
105	31	MCC v Australians at Lord's	1878

Note: The lowest aggregate since 1900 is 157 for 22 wickets, Surrey v Worcestershire at The Oval, 1954.

LARGEST VICTORIES

Largest Innings Victories

Inns and 851 runs:	Railways (910-6 dec.) v Dera Ismail Khan at Lahore	1964-65
Inns and 666 runs:	Victoria (1,059) v Tasmania at Melbourne	1922-23
Inns and 656 runs:	Victoria (1,107) v New South Wales at Melbourne	1926-27
Inns and 605 runs:	New South Wales (918) v South Australia at Sydney	1900-01
Inns and 579 runs:	England (903-7 dec.) v Australia at The Oval	1938
Inns and 575 runs:	Sind (951-7 dec.) v Baluchistan at Karachi	1973-74
Inns and 527 runs:	New South Wales (713) v South Australia at Adelaide	1908-09
Inns and 517 runs:	Australians (675) v Nottinghamshire at Nottingham	1921

Largest Victories by Runs Margin

685 runs:	New South Wales (235 and 761-8 dec.) v Queensland at Sydney	1929-30
675 runs:	England (521 and 342-8 dec.) v Australia at Brisbane	1928-29
638 runs:	New South Wales (304 and 770) v South Australia at Adelaide	1920-21
609 runs:	Muslim Commercial Bank (575 and 282-0 dec.) v WAPDA at Lahore. . .	1977-78
585 runs:	Sargodha (336 and 416) v Lahore Municipal Corporation at Faisalabad . .	1978-79
573 runs:	Sinhalese SC (395-7 dec. and 350-2 dec.) v Sebastianites C and AC	
	at Colombo	1990-91
571 runs:	Victoria (304 and 649) v South Australia at Adelaide	1926-27
562 runs:	Australia (701 and 327) v England at The Oval	1934
556 runs:	Nondescripts (397-8 dec. and 313-6 dec.) v Matara at Colombo	1998-99

Victory Without Losing a Wicket

Lancashire (166-0 dec. and 66-0) beat Leicestershire by ten wickets at Manchester . .   1956
Karachi A (277-0 dec.) beat Sind A by an innings and 77 runs at Karachi   1957-58
Railways (236-0 dec. and 16-0) beat Jammu and Kashmir by ten wickets at Srinagar .   1960-61
Karnataka (451-0 dec.) beat Kerala by an innings and 186 runs at Chikmagalur   1977-78

TIED MATCHES

Since 1948 a tie has been recognised only when the scores are level with all the wickets down in the fourth innings.

The following are the instances since then:

Hampshire v Kent at Southampton	1950
Sussex v Warwickshire at Hove	1952
Essex v Lancashire at Brentwood	1952
Northamptonshire v Middlesex at Peterborough	1953
Yorkshire v Leicestershire at Huddersfield	1954
Sussex v Hampshire at Eastbourne	1955
Victoria v New South Wales at Melbourne	1956-57
T. N. Pearce's XI v New Zealanders at Scarborough	1958
Essex v Gloucestershire at Leyton	1959
Australia v West Indies (First Test) at Brisbane	1960-61
Bahawalpur v Lahore B at Bahawalpur	1961-62
Hampshire v Middlesex at Portsmouth	1967
England XI v England Under-25 XI at Scarborough	1968

Yorkshire v Middlesex at Bradford	1973
Sussex v Essex at Hove	1974
South Australia v Queensland at Adelaide	1976-77
Central Districts v England XI at New Plymouth	1977-78
Victoria v New Zealanders at Melbourne	1982-83
Muslim Commercial Bank v Railways at Sialkot	1983-84
Sussex v Kent at Hastings	1984
Northamptonshire v Kent at Northampton	1984
Eastern Province B v Boland at Albany SC, Grahamstown	1985-86
Natal B v Eastern Province B at Pietermaritzburg	1985-86
India v Australia (First Test) at Madras	1986-87
Gloucestershire v Derbyshire at Bristol	1987
Bahawalpur v Peshawar at Bahawalpur	1988-89
Wellington v Canterbury at Wellington	1988-89
Sussex v Kent at Hove	1991
Nottinghamshire v Worcestershire at Nottingham	1993
Somerset v West Indies A at Taunton	†2002

† *Somerset (453) made the highest total to tie a first-class match.*

MATCHES COMPLETED ON FIRST DAY

(Since 1946)

Derbyshire v Somerset at Chesterfield, June 11	1947
Lancashire v Sussex at Manchester, July 12	1950
Surrey v Warwickshire at The Oval, May 16	1953
Somerset v Lancashire at Bath, June 6 (H. F. T. Buse's benefit)	1953
Kent v Worcestershire at Tunbridge Wells, June 15	1960

THE ASHES

"In affectionate remembrance of English cricket which died at The Oval, 29th August, 1882. Deeply lamented by a large circle of sorrowing friends and acquaintances, R.I.P. N.B. The body will be cremated and the ashes taken to Australia."

Australia's first victory on English soil over the full strength of England, on August 29, 1882, inspired a young London journalist, Reginald Shirley Brooks, to write this mock obituary. It appeared in the *Sporting Times*.

Before England's defeat at The Oval, by seven runs, arrangements had already been made for the Hon. Ivo Bligh, afterwards Lord Darnley, to lead a team to Australia. Three weeks later they set out, now with the popular objective of recovering the Ashes. In the event, Australia won the First Test by nine wickets, but with England winning the next two it became generally accepted that they brought back the Ashes.

It was long believed that the real Ashes – a small urn thought to contain the ashes of a bail used in the third match – were presented to Bligh by a group of Melbourne women. In 1998, Lord Darnley's 82-year-old daughter-in-law said they were the remains of her mother-in-law's veil, not a bail. Other evidence suggests a ball. The certain origin of the Ashes, therefore, is the subject of some dispute.

After Lord Darnley's death in 1927, the urn was given to MCC by his Australian-born widow, Florence. It can be seen in the cricket museum at Lord's, together with a red and gold velvet bag, made specially for it, and the scorecard of the 1882 match.

TEST RECORDS

Note: This section covers all Tests up to September 9, 2002.

BATTING RECORDS

HIGHEST INDIVIDUAL INNINGS

375	B. C. Lara	West Indies v England at St John's	1993-94
365*	G. S. Sobers	West Indies v Pakistan at Kingston	1957-58
364	L. Hutton	England v Australia at The Oval	1938
340	S. T. Jayasuriya	Sri Lanka v India at Colombo (RPS)	1997-98
337	Hanif Mohammad	Pakistan v West Indies at Bridgetown	1957-58
336*	W. R. Hammond	England v New Zealand at Auckland	1932-33
334*	M. A. Taylor	Australia v Pakistan at Peshawar	1998-99
334	D. G. Bradman	Australia v England at Leeds	1930
333	G. A. Gooch	England v India at Lord's	1990
329	Inzamam-ul-Haq	Pakistan v New Zealand at Lahore	2002
325	A. Sandham	England v West Indies at Kingston	1929-30
311	R. B. Simpson	Australia v England at Manchester	1964
310*	J. H. Edrich	England v New Zealand at Leeds	1965
307	R. M. Cowper	Australia v England at Melbourne	1965-66
304	D. G. Bradman	Australia v England at Leeds	1934
302	L. G. Rowe	West Indies v England at Bridgetown	1973-74
299*	D. G. Bradman	Australia v South Africa at Adelaide	1931-32
299	M. D. Crowe	New Zealand v Sri Lanka at Wellington	1990-91
291	I. V. A. Richards	West Indies v England at The Oval	1976
287	R. E. Foster	England v Australia at Sydney	1903-04
285*	P. B. H. May	England v West Indies at Birmingham	1957
281	V. V. S. Laxman	India v Australia at Kolkata	2000-01
280*	Javed Miandad	Pakistan v India at Hyderabad	1982-83
278	D. C. S. Compton	England v Pakistan at Nottingham	1954
277	B. C. Lara	West Indies v Australia at Sydney	1992-93
275*	D. J. Cullinan	South Africa v New Zealand at Auckland	1998-99
275	G. Kirsten	South Africa v England at Durban	1999-2000
274	R. G. Pollock	South Africa v Australia at Durban	1969-70
274	Zaheer Abbas	Pakistan v England at Birmingham	1971
271	Javed Miandad	Pakistan v New Zealand at Auckland	1988-89
270*	G. A. Headley	West Indies v England at Kingston	1934-35
270	D. G. Bradman	Australia v England at Melbourne	1936-37
268	G. N. Yallop	Australia v Pakistan at Melbourne	1983-84
267*	B. A. Young	New Zealand v Sri Lanka at Dunedin	1996-97
267	P. A. de Silva	Sri Lanka v New Zealand at Wellington	1990-91
266	W. H. Ponsford	Australia v England at The Oval	1934
266	D. L. Houghton	Zimbabwe v Sri Lanka at Bulawayo	1994-95
262*	D. L. Amiss	England v West Indies at Kingston	1973-74
261	F. M. M. Worrell	West Indies v England at Nottingham	1950
260	C. C. Hunte	West Indies v Pakistan at Kingston	1957-58
260	Javed Miandad	Pakistan v England at The Oval	1987
259	G. M. Turner	New Zealand v West Indies at Georgetown	1971-72
258	T. W. Graveney	England v West Indies at Nottingham	1957
258	S. M. Nurse	West Indies v New Zealand at Christchurch	1968-69
257*	Wasim Akram	Pakistan v Zimbabwe at Sheikhupura	1996-97
256	R. B. Kanhai	West Indies v India at Calcutta	1958-59
256	K. F. Barrington	England v Australia at Manchester	1964
255*	D. J. McGlew	South Africa v New Zealand at Wellington	1952-53
254	D. G. Bradman	Australia v England at Lord's	1930
251	W. R. Hammond	England v Australia at Sydney	1928-29
250	K. D. Walters	Australia v New Zealand at Christchurch	1976-77
250	S. F. A. F. Bacchus	West Indies v India at Kanpur	1978-79

Note: The highest individual innings for Bangladesh is 145 by Aminul Islam against India at Dhaka in 2000-01.

HUNDRED ON TEST DEBUT

C. Bannerman (165*)	Australia v England at Melbourne	1876-77
W. G. Grace (152)	England v Australia at The Oval	1880
H. Graham (107)	Australia v England at Lord's	1893
†K. S. Ranjitsinhji (154*)	England v Australia at Manchester	1896
†P. F. Warner (132*)	England v South Africa at Johannesburg	1898-99
†R. A. Duff (104)	Australia v England at Melbourne	1901-02
R. E. Foster (287)	England v Australia at Sydney	1903-04
G. Gunn (119)	England v Australia at Sydney	1907-08
†R. J. Hartigan (116)	Australia v England at Adelaide	1907-08
†H. L. Collins (104)	Australia v England at Sydney	1920-21
W. H. Ponsford (110)	Australia v England at Sydney	1924-25
A. A. Jackson (164)	Australia v England at Adelaide	1928-29
†G. A. Headley (176)	West Indies v England at Bridgetown	1929-30
J. E. Mills (117)	New Zealand v England at Wellington	1929-30
Nawab of Pataudi sen. (102)	England v Australia at Sydney	1932-33
B. H. Valentine (136)	England v India at Bombay	1933-34
†L. Amarnath (118)	India v England at Bombay	1933-34
†P. A. Gibb (106)	England v South Africa at Johannesburg	1938-39
S. C. Griffith (140)	England v West Indies at Port-of-Spain	1947-48
A. G. Ganteaume (112)	West Indies v England at Port-of-Spain	1947-48
†J. W. Burke (101*)	Australia v England at Adelaide	1950-51
P. B. H. May (138)	England v South Africa at Leeds	1951
R. H. Shodhan (110)	India v Pakistan at Calcutta	1952-53
B. H. Pairaudeau (115)	West Indies v India at Port-of-Spain	1952-53
†O. G. Smith (104)	West Indies v Australia at Kingston	1954-55
A. G. Kripal Singh (100*)	India v New Zealand at Hyderabad	1955-56
C. C. Hunte (142)	West Indies v Pakistan at Bridgetown	1957-58
C. A. Milton (104*)	England v New Zealand at Leeds	1958
†A. A. Baig (112)	India v England at Manchester	1959
Hanumant Singh (105)	India v England at Delhi	1963-64
Khalid Ibadulla (166)	Pakistan v Australia at Karachi	1964-65
B. R. Taylor (105)	New Zealand v India at Calcutta	1964-65
K. D. Walters (155)	Australia v England at Brisbane	1965-66
J. H. Hampshire (107)	England v West Indies at Lord's	1969
†G. R. Viswanath (137)	India v Australia at Kanpur	1969-70
G. S. Chappell (108)	Australia v England at Perth	1970-71
‡L. G. Rowe (214, 100*)	West Indies v New Zealand at Kingston	1971-72
A. I. Kallicharran (100*)	West Indies v New Zealand at Georgetown	1971-72
R. E. Redmond (107)	New Zealand v Pakistan at Auckland	1972-73
†F. C. Hayes (106*)	England v West Indies at The Oval	1973
†C. G. Greenidge (107)	West Indies v India at Bangalore	1974-75
†L. Baichan (105*)	West Indies v Pakistan at Lahore	1974-75
G. J. Cosier (109)	Australia v West Indies at Melbourne	1975-76
S. Amarnath (124)	India v New Zealand at Auckland	1975-76
Javed Miandad (163)	Pakistan v New Zealand at Lahore	1976-77
†A. B. Williams (100)	West Indies v Australia at Georgetown	1977-78
†D. M. Wellham (103)	Australia v England at The Oval	1981
†Salim Malik (100*)	Pakistan v Sri Lanka at Karachi	1981-82
K. C. Wessels (162)	Australia v England at Brisbane	1982-83
W. B. Phillips (159)	Australia v Pakistan at Perth	1983-84
§M. Azharuddin (110)	India v England at Calcutta	1984-85
D. S. B. P. Kuruppu (201*)	Sri Lanka v New Zealand at Colombo (CCC)	1986-87
†M. J. Greatbatch (107*)	New Zealand v England at Auckland	1987-88
M. E. Waugh (138)	Australia v England at Adelaide	1990-91
A. C. Hudson (163)	South Africa v West Indies at Bridgetown	1991-92
R. S. Kaluwitharana (132*)	Sri Lanka v Australia at Colombo (SSC)	1992-93
D. L. Houghton (121)	Zimbabwe v India at Harare	1992-93
P. K. Amre (103)	India v South Africa at Durban	1992-93

†G. P. Thorpe (114*)	England v Australia at Nottingham	1993
G. S. Blewett (102*).	Australia v England at Adelaide	1994-95
S. C. Ganguly (131)	India v England at Lord's	1996
†Mohammad Wasim (109*). .	Pakistan v New Zealand at Lahore	1996-97
Ali Naqvi (115)	Pakistan v South Africa at Rawalpindi	1997-98
Azhar Mahmood (128*). . . .	Pakistan v South Africa at Rawalpindi	1997-98
M. S. Sinclair (214)	New Zealand v West Indies at Wellington	1999-2000
†Younis Khan (107)	Pakistan v Sri Lanka at Rawalpindi	1999-2000
Aminul Islam (145)	Bangladesh v India at Dhaka	2000-01
†H. Masakadza (119)	Zimbabwe v West Indies at Harare	2001
T. T. Samaraweera (103*). . .	Sri Lanka v India at Colombo (SSC)	2001
Taufeeq Umar (104)	Pakistan v Bangladesh at Multan.	2001-02
†Mohammad Ashraful (114). .	Bangladesh v Sri Lanka at Colombo (SSC)	2001-02
V. Sehwag (105).	India v South Africa at Bloemfontein.	2001-02
L. Vincent (104).	New Zealand v Australia at Perth	2001-02
S. B. Styris (107)	New Zealand v West Indies at St George's	2002

† *In his second innings of the match.*
‡ *L. G. Rowe is the only batsman to score a hundred in each innings on debut.*
§ *M. Azharuddin is the only batsman to score hundreds in each of his first three Tests.*

Notes: L. Amarnath and S. Amarnath were father and son.
  Ali Naqvi and Azhar Mahmood achieved the feat in the same innings.
  Only Bannerman, Houghton and Aminul Islam scored hundreds in their country's first Test.

300 RUNS IN FIRST TEST

314	L. G. Rowe (214, 100*)	West Indies v New Zealand at Kingston	1971-72
306	R. E. Foster (287, 19)	England v Australia at Sydney.	1903-04

TRIPLE-HUNDRED AND HUNDRED IN A TEST

G. A. Gooch (England)   333 and 123 v India at Lord's   1990

The only instance in first-class cricket. M. A. Taylor (Australia) scored 334* and 92 v Pakistan at Peshawar in 1998-99.

DOUBLE-HUNDRED AND HUNDRED IN A TEST

K. D. Walters (Australia)	242 and 103 v West Indies at Sydney	1968-69
S. M. Gavaskar (India)	124 and 220 v West Indies at Port-of-Spain	1970-71
†L. G. Rowe (West Indies)	214 and 100* v New Zealand at Kingston	1971-72
G. S. Chappell (Australia)	247* and 133 v New Zealand at Wellington	1973-74
B. C. Lara (West Indies)	221 and 130 v Sri Lanka at Colombo (SSC)	2001-02

† *On Test debut.*

TWO SEPARATE HUNDREDS IN A TEST

Three times: S. M. Gavaskar.
Twice in one series: C. L. Walcott v Australia (1954-55).
Twice: †A. R. Border; G. S. Chappell; ‡P. A. de Silva; G. A. Headley; H. Sutcliffe.
Once: W. Bardsley; D. G. Bradman; I. M. Chappell; D. C. S. Compton; R. Dravid; A. Flower; G. W. Flower; G. A. Gooch; C. G. Greenidge; A. P. Gurusinha; W. R. Hammond; Hanif Mohammad; V. S. Hazare; G. P. Howarth; Javed Miandad; A. H. Jones; D. M. Jones; R. B. Kanhai; G. Kirsten; B. C. Lara; A. Melville; L. R. D. Mendis; B. Mitchell; J. Moroney; A. R. Morris; E. Paynter; §L. G. Rowe; A. C. Russell; R. B. Simpson; G. S. Sobers; A. J. Stewart; G. M. Turner; Wajahatullah Wasti; K. D. Walters; S. R. Waugh; E. D. Weekes.

† *A. R. Border scored 150* and 153 against Pakistan in 1979-80 to become the first to score 150 in each innings of a Test match.*
‡ *P. A. de Silva scored 138* and 103* against Pakistan in 1996-97 to become the first to score two not out hundreds in a Test match.*
§ *L. G. Rowe's two hundreds were on his Test debut.*

MOST HUNDREDS

	Total	200+	Inns	E	A	SA	WI	NZ	I	P	SL	Z	B
S. M. Gavaskar (I)	34	4	214	4	8	–	13	2	–	5	2	–	–
S. R. Tendulkar (I)	**30**	**2**	**160**	**6**	**6**	**3**	**2**	**3**	**–**	**1**	**6**	**3**	**0**
D. G. Bradman (A)	29	12	80	19	–	4	2	–	–	4	–	–	–
A. R. Border (A)	27	2	265	8	–	0	3	5	4	6	1	–	–
S. R. Waugh (A)	**27**	**1**	**233**	**9**	**–**	**2**	**6**	**2**	**2**	**2**	**3**	**1**	**–**
G. S. Sobers (WI)	26	2	160	10	4	–	–	1	8	3	–	–	–
G. S. Chappell (A)	24	4	151	9	–	–	5	3	1	6	0	–	–
I. V. A. Richards (WI)	24	3	182	8	5	–	–	1	8	2	–	–	–
Javed Miandad (P)	23	6	189	2	6	–	2	7	5	–	1	–	–
M. Azharuddin (I)	22	0	147	6	2	4	0	2	–	3	5	0	–
G. Boycott (E)	22	1	193	–	7	1	5	2	4	3	–	–	–
M. C. Cowdrey (E)	22	0	188	–	5	3	6	2	3	3	–	–	–
W. R. Hammond (E)	22	7	140	–	9	6	1	4	2	–	–	–	–
D. C. Boon (A)	21	1	190	7	–	–	3	3	6	1	1	–	–
R. N. Harvey (A)	21	2	137	6	–	8	3	–	4	0	–	–	–
K. F. Barrington (E)	20	1	131	–	5	2	3	3	3	4	–	–	–
P. A. de Silva (SL)	**20**	**2**	**159**	**2**	**1**	**0**	**0**	**2**	**5**	**8**	**–**	**1**	**1**
G. A. Gooch (E)	20	2	215	–	4	–	5	4	5	1	1	–	–
M. E. Waugh (A)	**20**	**0**	**205**	**6**	**–**	**4**	**4**	**1**	**1**	**3**	**1**	**0**	**–**

Notes: The most hundreds for New Zealand is 17 by M. D. Crowe in 131 innings, for South Africa **14** by D. J. Cullinan in 115 innings and **G. Kirsten** in 148 innings, for Zimbabwe **12** by **A. Flower** in 108 innings, and for Bangladesh **1** by *Aminul Islam* in 24 innings, **Habibul Bashar** in 26 innings and **Mohammad Ashraful** in 14 innings.

The most double-hundreds by a batsman not qualifying for the above list is five by M. S. Atapattu (Sri Lanka).

Bold type denotes those who played Test cricket in 2001-02 or 2002 season. Dashes indicate that a player did not play against the country concerned.

CARRYING BAT THROUGH TEST INNINGS

(Figures in brackets show team's total.)

A. B. Tancred	26*	(47)	South Africa v England at Cape Town	1888-89
J. E. Barrett	67*	(176)†	Australia v England at Lord's	1890
R. Abel	132*	(307)	England v Australia at Sydney	1891-92
P. F. Warner	132*	(237)†	England v South Africa at Johannesburg	1898-99
W. W. Armstrong	159*	(309)	Australia v South Africa at Johannesburg	1902-03
J. W. Zulch	43*	(103)	South Africa v England at Cape Town	1909-10
W. Bardsley	193*	(383)	Australia v England at Lord's	1926
W. M. Woodfull	30*	(66)§	Australia v England at Brisbane	1928-29
W. M. Woodfull	73*	(193)‡	Australia v England at Adelaide	1932-33
W. A. Brown	206*	(422)	Australia v England at Lord's	1938
L. Hutton	202*	(344)	England v West Indies at The Oval	1950
L. Hutton	156*	(272)	England v Australia at Adelaide	1950-51
Nazar Mohammad¶	124*	(331)	Pakistan v India at Lucknow	1952-53
F. M. M. Worrell	191*	(372)	West Indies v England at Nottingham	1957
T. L. Goddard	56*	(99)	South Africa v Australia at Cape Town	1957-58
D. J. McGlew	127*	(292)	South Africa v New Zealand at Durban	1961-62
C. C. Hunte	60*	(131)	West Indies v Australia at Port-of-Spain	1964-65
G. M. Turner	43*	(131)	New Zealand v England at Lord's	1969
W. M. Lawry	49*	(107)	Australia v India at Delhi	1969-70
W. M. Lawry	60*	(116)‡	Australia v England at Sydney	1970-71

G. M. Turner	223* (386)	New Zealand v West Indies at Kingston	1971-72
I. R. Redpath	159* (346)	Australia v New Zealand at Auckland	1973-74
G. Boycott	99* (215)	England v Australia at Perth	1979-80
S. M. Gavaskar . . .	127* (286)	India v Pakistan at Faisalabad	1982-83
Mudassar Nazar¶ . .	152* (323)	Pakistan v India at Lahore	1982-83
S. Wettimuny	63* (144)	Sri Lanka v New Zealand at Christchurch . .	1982-83
D. C. Boon	58* (103)	Australia v New Zealand at Auckland	1985-86
D. L. Haynes	88* (211)	West Indies v Pakistan at Karachi	1986-87
G. A. Gooch	154* (252)	England v West Indies at Leeds	1991
D. L. Haynes	75* (176)	West Indies v England at The Oval	1991
A. J. Stewart	69* (175)	England v Pakistan at Lord's	1992
D. L. Haynes	143* (382)	West Indies v Pakistan at Port-of-Spain . .	1992-93
M. H. Dekker	68* (187)	Zimbabwe v Pakistan at Rawalpindi	1993-94
M. A. Atherton . . .	94* (228)	England v New Zealand at Christchurch . . .	1996-97
G. Kirsten	100* (239)	South Africa v Pakistan at Faisalabad	1997-98
M. A. Taylor	169* (350)	Australia v South Africa at Adelaide	1997-98
G. W. Flower	156* (321)	Zimbabwe v Pakistan at Bulawayo	1997-98
Saeed Anwar	188* (316)	Pakistan v India at Calcutta	1998-99
M. S. Atapattu	216* (428)	Sri Lanka v Zimbabwe at Bulawayo	1999-2000
R. P. Arnold	104* (231)	Sri Lanka v Zimbabwe at Harare	1999-2000
Javed Omar	85* (168)†‡	Bangladesh v Zimbabwe at Bulawayo	2000-01

† *On debut.* ‡ *One man absent.* § *Two men absent.* ¶ *Father and son.*

Notes: G. M. Turner (223*) holds the record for the highest score by a player carrying his bat through a Test innings. He is also the youngest player to do so, being 22 years 63 days old when he first achieved the feat (1969).

  D. L. Haynes, who is alone in achieving this feat on three occasions, also opened the batting and was last man out in each innings for West Indies v New Zealand at Dunedin, 1979-80.

750 RUNS IN A SERIES

	T	I	NO	R	HS	100s	Avge		
D. G. Bradman	5	7	0	974	334	4	139.14	A v E	1930
W. R. Hammond	5	9	1	905	251	4	113.12	E v A	1928-29
M. A. Taylor	6	11	1	839	219	2	83.90	A v E	1989
R. N. Harvey	5	9	0	834	205	4	92.66	A v SA	1952-53
I. V. A. Richards	4	7	0	829	291	3	118.42	WI v E	1976
C. L. Walcott	5	10	0	827	155	5	82.70	WI v A	1954-55
G. S. Sobers	5	8	2	824	365*	3	137.33	WI v P	1957-58
D. G. Bradman	5	9	0	810	270	4	90.00	A v E	1936-37
D. G. Bradman	5	5	1	806	299*	4	201.50	A v SA	1931-32
B. C. Lara	5	8	0	798	375	2	99.75	WI v E	1993-94
E. D. Weekes	5	7	0	779	194	4	111.28	WI v I	1948-49
†S. M. Gavaskar	4	8	3	774	220	4	154.80	I v WI	1970-71
B. C. Lara	6	10	1	765	179	3	85.00	WI v E	1995
Mudassar Nazar	6	8	2	761	231	4	126.83	P v I	1982-83
D. G. Bradman	5	8	0	758	304	2	94.75	A v E	1934
D. C. S. Compton . . .	5	8	0	753	208	4	94.12	E v SA	1947
‡G. A. Gooch	3	6	0	752	333	3	125.33	E v I	1990

† *Gavaskar's aggregate was achieved in his first Test series.*
‡ *G. A. Gooch is alone in scoring 1,000 runs in Test cricket during an English season with 1,058 runs in 11 innings against New Zealand and India in 1990.*

Ryan Hinds ran out the dangerous Abdul Razzaq – a dismissal momentarily in doubt when the TV umpire managed to switch on both lights at once.
Pakistan v West Indies, page 1273

1,200 RUNS IN A CALENDAR YEAR

	T	I	NO	R	HS	100s	Avge	Year
I. V. A. Richards (WI)	11	19	0	1,710	291	7	90.00	1976
S. M. Gavaskar (I)	18	27	1	1,555	221	5	59.80	1979
M. L. Hayden (A)	14	25	3	1,391	203	5	63.22	2001
G. R. Viswanath (I)	17	26	3	1,388	179	5	60.34	1979
R. B. Simpson (A)	14	26	3	1,381	311	3	60.04	1964
D. L. Amiss (E)	13	22	2	1,379	262*	5	68.95	1974
S. M. Gavaskar (I)	18	32	4	1,310	236*	5	46.78	1983
S. T. Jayasuriya (SL)	11	19	0	1,271	340	3	66.89	1997
G. A. Gooch (E)	9	17	1	1,264	333	4	79.00	1990
D. C. Boon (A)	16	25	5	1,241	164*	4	62.05	1993
B. C. Lara (WI)	12	20	2	1,222	179	4	67.88	1995
A. J. Stewart (E)	16	31	4	1,222	164	2	43.64	1998
P. A. de Silva (SL)	11	19	3	1,220	168	7	76.25	1997
M. A. Taylor (A)	11	20	1	1,219	219	4	64.15	1989†

† *The year of his debut.*

Notes: M. Amarnath reached 1,000 runs in 1983 on May 3.

The only batsman to score 1,000 runs in a year before World War II was C. Hill of Australia; 1,061 in 1902.

Gavaskar's 1,555 excludes 141 scored in December 1978 in a Test spanning two calendar years; he scored 148 on January 2.

By the end of 2002, after the deadline for this section, M. P. Vaughan had reached 1,481 runs and S. R. Tendulkar 1,392.

MOST RUNS

		T	I	NO	R	HS	100s	Avge
1	A. R. Border (Australia)	156	265	44	11,174	205	27	50.56
2	S. M. Gavaskar (India)	125	214	16	10,122	236*	34	51.12
3	**S. R. Waugh (Australia)**	148	233	41	9,600	200	27	50.00
4	G. A. Gooch (England)	118	215	6	8,900	333	20	42.58
5	Javed Miandad (Pakistan) . . .	124	189	21	8,832	280*	23	52.57
6	I. V. A. Richards (West Indies)	121	182	12	8,540	291	24	50.23
7	**S. R. Tendulkar (India)**	100	160	15	8,405	217	30	57.96
8	D. I. Gower (England)	117	204	18	8,231	215	18	44.25
9	G. Boycott (England)	108	193	23	8,114	246*	22	47.72
10	G. S. Sobers (West Indies) . .	93	160	21	8,032	365*	26	57.78
11	**M. E. Waugh (Australia)**	125	205	17	7,949	153*	20	42.28
12	**A. J. Stewart (England)**	122	217	19	7,919	190	15	39.99
13	M. A. Atherton (England) . . .	115	212	7	7,728	185*	16	37.69
14	M. C. Cowdrey (England) . . .	114	188	15	7,624	182	22	44.06
15	**B. C. Lara (West Indies)**	90	157	4	7,572	375	18	49.49
16	C. G. Greenidge (West Indies)	108	185	16	7,558	226	19	44.72
17	M. A. Taylor (Australia)	104	186	13	7,525	334*	19	43.49
18	C. H. Lloyd (West Indies) . . .	110	175	14	7,515	242*	19	46.67
19	D. L. Haynes (West Indies) . .	116	202	25	7,487	184	18	42.29
20	D. C. Boon (Australia)	107	190	20	7,422	200	21	43.65
21	W. R. Hammond (England) . .	85	140	16	7,249	336*	22	58.45
22	G. S. Chappell (Australia) . . .	87	151	19	7,110	247*	24	53.86
23	D. G. Bradman (Australia) . . .	52	80	10	6,996	334	29	99.94
24	L. Hutton (England)	79	138	15	6,971	364	19	56.67
25	D. B. Vengsarkar (India)	116	185	22	6,868	166	17	42.13
26	K. F. Barrington (England) . . .	82	131	15	6,806	256	20	58.67
27	**P. A. de Silva (Sri Lanka)** . . .	93	159	11	6,361	267	20	42.97
28	R. B. Kanhai (West Indies) . . .	79	137	6	6,227	256	15	47.53
29	M. Azharuddin (India)	99	147	9	6,215	199	22	45.03
30	R. N. Harvey (Australia)	79	137	10	6,149	205	21	48.41

		T	I	NO	R	HS	100s	Avge
31	G. R. Viswanath (India)	91	155	10	6,080	222	14	41.93
32	R. B. Richardson (West Indies)	86	146	12	5,949	194	16	44.39
33	**Inzamam-ul-Haq (Pakistan)** .	**81**	**133**	**13**	**5,929**	**329**	**16**	**49.40**
34	D. C. S. Compton (England) . .	78	131	15	5,807	278	17	50.06
35	Salim Malik (Pakistan)	103	154	22	5,768	237	15	43.69
36	**G. Kirsten (South Africa)** . . .	**83**	**148**	**12**	**5,671**	**275**	**14**	**41.69**
37	**C. L. Hooper (West Indies)** . .	**99**	**168**	**15**	**5,638**	**233**	**13**	**36.84**
38	M. D. Crowe (New Zealand) . .	77	131	11	5,444	299	17	45.36
39	J. B. Hobbs (England)	61	102	7	5,410	211	15	56.94
40	K. D. Walters (Australia)	74	125	14	5,357	250	15	48.26

Notes: The leading aggregates for other countries are:

A. Flower (Zimbabwe)		**61**	**108**	**19**	**4,655**	**232***	**12**	**52.30**
Habibul Bashar (Bangladesh) . . .		**13**	**26**	**1**	**884**	**108**	**1**	**35.36**

In 2002-03, after the deadline for this section, S. R. Waugh became the third batsman to score 10,000 Test runs.

Bold type denotes those who played Test cricket in 2001-02 or 2002 season.

2,500 RUNS

ENGLAND

		T	I	NO	R	HS	100s	Avge
1	G. A. Gooch	118	215	6	8,900	333	20	42.58
2	D. I. Gower	117	204	18	8,231	215	18	44.25
3	G. Boycott	108	193	23	8,114	246*	22	47.72
4	**A. J. Stewart**	**122**	**217**	**19**	**7,919**	**190**	**15**	**39.99**
5	M. A. Atherton	115	212	7	7,728	185*	16	37.69
6	M. C. Cowdrey	114	188	15	7,624	182	22	44.06
7	W. R. Hammond	85	140	16	7,249	336*	22	58.45
8	L. Hutton	79	138	15	6,971	364	19	56.67
9	K. F. Barrington	82	131	15	6,806	256	20	58.67
10	D. C. S. Compton	78	131	15	5,807	278	17	50.06
11	J. B. Hobbs	61	102	7	5,410	211	15	56.94
12	I. T. Botham	102	161	6	5,200	208	14	33.54
13	J. H. Edrich	77	127	9	5,138	310*	12	43.54
14	**G. P. Thorpe**	**77**	**140**	**18**	**5,109**	**200***	**11**	**41.87**
15	T. W. Graveney	79	123	13	4,882	258	11	44.38
16	A. J. Lamb	79	139	10	4,656	142	14	36.09
17	H. Sutcliffe	54	84	9	4,555	194	16	60.73
18	P. B. H. May	66	106	9	4,537	285*	13	46.77
19	E. R. Dexter	62	102	8	4,502	205	9	47.89
20	**N. Hussain**	**76**	**134**	**13**	**4,484**	**207**	**12**	**37.05**
21	M. W. Gatting	79	138	14	4,409	207	10	35.55
22	A. P. E. Knott	95	149	15	4,389	135	5	32.75
23	R. A. Smith	62	112	15	4,236	175	9	43.67
24	D. L. Amiss	50	88	10	3,612	262*	11	46.30
25	A. W. Greig	58	93	4	3,599	148	8	40.43
26	E. H. Hendren	51	83	9	3,525	205*	7	47.63
27	G. A. Hick	65	114	6	3,383	178	6	31.32
28	F. E. Woolley	64	98	7	3,283	154	5	36.07
29	K. W. R. Fletcher	59	96	14	3,272	216	7	39.90
30	M. Leyland	41	65	5	2,764	187	9	46.06
31	**M. A. Butcher**	**45**	**83**	**3**	**2,651**	**173***	**5**	**33.13**
32	C. Washbrook	37	66	6	2,569	195	6	42.81

AUSTRALIA

		T	I	NO	R	HS	100s	Avge
1	A. R. Border	156	265	44	11,174	205	27	50.56
2	**S. R. Waugh**	**148**	**233**	**41**	**9,600**	**200**	**27**	**50.00**
3	**M. E. Waugh**	**125**	**205**	**17**	**7,949**	**153***	**20**	**42.28**
4	M. A. Taylor	104	186	13	7,525	334*	19	43.49
5	D. C. Boon	107	190	20	7,422	200	21	43.65
6	G. S. Chappell	87	151	19	7,110	247*	24	53.86
7	D. G. Bradman	52	80	10	6,996	334	29	99.94
8	R. N. Harvey	79	137	10	6,149	205	21	48.41
9	K. D. Walters	74	125	14	5,357	250	15	48.26
10	I. M. Chappell	75	136	10	5,345	196	14	42.42
11	M. J. Slater	74	131	7	5,312	219	14	42.83
12	W. M. Lawry	67	123	12	5,234	210	13	47.15
13	R. B. Simpson	62	111	7	4,869	311	10	46.81
14	I. R. Redpath	66	120	11	4,737	171	8	43.45
15	K. J. Hughes	70	124	6	4,415	213	9	37.41
16	I. A. Healy	119	182	23	4,356	161*	4	27.39
17	R. W. Marsh	96	150	13	3,633	132	3	26.51
18	D. M. Jones	52	89	11	3,631	216	11	46.55
19	A. R. Morris	46	79	3	3,533	206	12	46.48
20	**J. L. Langer**	**51**	**85**	**5**	**3,516**	**223**	**12**	**43.95**
21	**R. T. Ponting**	**56**	**89**	**12**	**3,505**	**197**	**10**	**45.51**
22	C. Hill	49	89	2	3,412	191	7	39.21
23	G. M. Wood	59	112	6	3,374	172	9	31.83
24	V. T. Trumper	48	89	8	3,163	214*	8	39.04
25	C. C. McDonald	47	83	4	3,107	170	5	39.32
26	A. L. Hassett	43	69	3	3,073	198*	10	46.56
27	K. R. Miller	55	87	7	2,958	147	7	36.97
28	W. W. Armstrong	50	84	10	2,863	159*	6	38.68
29	G. R. Marsh	50	93	7	2,854	138	4	33.18
30	K. R. Stackpole	43	80	5	2,807	207	7	37.42
31	N. C. O'Neill	42	69	8	2,779	181	6	45.55
32	G. N. Yallop	39	70	3	2,756	268	8	41.13
33	S. J. McCabe	39	62	5	2,748	232	6	48.21
34	G. S. Blewett	46	79	4	2,552	214	4	34.02

SOUTH AFRICA

		T	I	NO	R	HS	100s	Avge
1	**G. Kirsten**	**83**	**148**	**12**	**5,671**	**275**	**14**	**41.69**
2	D. J. Cullinan	70	115	12	4,554	275*	14	44.21
3	**J. H. Kallis**	**60**	**100**	**16**	**3,971**	**189***	**9**	**47.27**
4	W. J. Cronje	68	111	9	3,714	135	6	36.41
5	B. Mitchell	42	80	9	3,471	189*	8	48.88
6	A. D. Nourse	34	62	7	2,960	231	9	53.81
7	H. W. Taylor	42	76	4	2,936	176	7	40.77
8	**H. H. Gibbs**	**38**	**65**	**2**	**2,551**	**211***	**6**	**40.49**
9	J. N. Rhodes	52	80	9	2,532	117	3	35.66
10	E. J. Barlow	30	57	2	2,516	201	6	45.74
	T. L. Goddard	41	78	5	2,516	112	1	34.46

Note: K. C. Wessels scored 2,788 runs in 40 Tests: 1,761 (average 42.95) in 24 Tests for Australia, and 1,027 (average 38.03) in 16 Tests for South Africa.

It was chaos theory without the theory.
Essex v Warwickshire, page 898

WEST INDIES

		T	I	NO	R	HS	100s	Avge
1	I. V. A. Richards	121	182	12	8,540	291	24	50.23
2	G. S. Sobers	93	160	21	8,032	365*	26	57.78
3	**B. C. Lara**	**90**	**157**	**4**	**7,572**	**375**	**18**	**49.49**
4	C. G. Greenidge	108	185	16	7,558	226	19	44.72
5	C. H. Lloyd	110	175	14	7,515	242*	19	46.67
6	D. L. Haynes	116	202	25	7,487	184	18	42.29
7	R. B. Kanhai	79	137	6	6,227	256	15	47.53
8	R. B. Richardson	86	146	12	5,949	194	16	44.39
9	**C. L. Hooper**	**99**	**168**	**15**	**5,638**	**233**	**13**	**36.84**
10	E. D. Weekes	48	81	5	4,455	207	15	58.61
11	A. I. Kallicharran	66	109	10	4,399	187	12	44.43
12	R. C. Fredericks	59	109	7	4,334	169	8	42.49
13	F. M. M. Worrell	51	87	9	3,860	261	9	49.48
14	C. L. Walcott	44	74	7	3,798	220	15	56.68
15	**S. Chanderpaul**	**58**	**95**	**13**	**3,599**	**140**	**5**	**43.89**
16	P. J. L. Dujon	81	115	11	3,322	139	5	31.94
17	C. C. Hunte	44	78	6	3,245	260	8	45.06
18	H. A. Gomes	60	91	11	3,171	143	9	39.63
19	B. F. Butcher	44	78	6	3,104	209*	7	43.11
20	J. C. Adams	54	90	17	3,012	208*	6	41.26
21	**S. L. Campbell**	**52**	**93**	**4**	**2,882**	**208**	**4**	**32.38**
22	S. M. Nurse	29	54	1	2,523	258	6	47.60

NEW ZEALAND

		T	I	NO	R	HS	100s	Avge
1	M. D. Crowe	77	131	11	5,444	299	17	45.36
2	J. G. Wright	82	148	7	5,334	185	12	37.82
3	**S. P. Fleming**	**71**	**123**	**7**	**4,217**	**174***	**4**	**36.35**
4	B. E. Congdon	61	114	7	3,448	176	7	32.22
5	J. R. Reid	58	108	5	3,428	142	6	33.28
6	**N. J. Astle**	**55**	**95**	**8**	**3,365**	**222**	**8**	**38.67**
7	R. J. Hadlee	86	134	19	3,124	151*	2	27.16
8	G. M. Turner	41	73	6	2,991	259	7	44.64
9	A. H. Jones	39	74	8	2,922	186	7	44.27
10	**A. C. Parore**	**78**	**128**	**19**	**2,865**	**110**	**2**	**26.28**
11	**C. L. Cairns**	**55**	**92**	**5**	**2,853**	**126**	**4**	**32.79**
12	B. Sutcliffe	42	76	8	2,727	230*	5	40.10
13	M. G. Burgess	50	92	6	2,684	119*	5	31.20
14	J. V. Coney	52	85	14	2,668	174*	3	37.57
15	**C. D. McMillan**	**42**	**70**	**7**	**2,588**	**142**	**5**	**41.07**
16	G. P. Howarth	47	83	5	2,531	147	6	32.44

INDIA

		T	I	NO	R	HS	100s	Avge
1	S. M. Gavaskar	125	214	16	10,122	236*	34	51.12
2	**S. R. Tendulkar**	**100**	**160**	**15**	**8,405**	**217**	**30**	**57.96**
3	D. B. Vengsarkar	116	185	22	6,868	166	17	42.13
4	M. Azharuddin	99	147	9	6,215	199	22	45.03
5	G. R. Viswanath	91	155	10	6,080	222	14	41.93
6	**R. Dravid**	**64**	**109**	**11**	**5,335**	**217**	**13**	**54.43**
7	Kapil Dev	131	184	15	5,248	163	8	31.05
8	M. Amarnath	69	113	10	4,378	138	11	42.50
9	**S. C. Ganguly**	**62**	**104**	**11**	**4,022**	**173**	**9**	**43.24**

		T	I	NO	R	HS	100s	Avge
10	R. J. Shastri	80	121	14	3,830	206	11	35.79
11	P. R. Umrigar	59	94	8	3,631	223	12	42.22
12	V. L. Manjrekar	55	92	10	3,208	189*	7	39.12
13	N. S. Sidhu	51	78	2	3,202	201	9	42.13
14	C. G. Borde	55	97	11	3,061	177*	5	35.59
15	Nawab of Pataudi jun.	46	83	3	2,793	203*	6	34.91
16	S. M. H. Kirmani	88	124	22	2,759	102	2	27.04
17	F. M. Engineer	46	87	3	2,611	121	2	31.08

PAKISTAN

		T	I	NO	R	HS	100s	Avge
1	Javed Miandad	124	189	21	8,832	280*	23	52.57
2	**Inzamam-ul-Haq**	**81**	**133**	**13**	**5,929**	**329**	**16**	**49.40**
3	Salim Malik	103	154	22	5,768	237	15	43.69
4	Zaheer Abbas	78	124	11	5,062	274	12	44.79
5	Mudassar Nazar	76	116	8	4,114	231	10	38.09
6	Saeed Anwar	55	91	2	4,052	188*	11	45.52
7	Majid Khan	63	106	5	3,931	167	8	38.92
8	Hanif Mohammad	55	97	8	3,915	337	12	43.98
9	Imran Khan	88	126	25	3,807	136	6	37.69
10	Mushtaq Mohammad	57	100	7	3,643	201	10	39.17
11	Asif Iqbal	58	99	7	3,575	175	11	38.85
12	Ijaz Ahmed, sen.	60	92	4	3,315	211	12	37.67
13	Saeed Ahmed	41	78	4	2,991	172	5	40.41
14	**Wasim Akram**	**104**	**147**	**19**	**2,898**	**257***	**3**	**22.64**
15	Ramiz Raja	57	94	5	2,833	122	2	31.83
16 {	**Yousuf Youhana**	**39**	**64**	**5**	**2,823**	**204***	**9**	**47.84**
	Aamir Sohail	47	83	3	2,823	205	5	35.28
18	Wasim Raja	57	92	14	2,821	125	4	36.16
19	Mohsin Khan	48	79	6	2,709	200	7	37.10
20	Shoaib Mohammad	45	68	7	2,705	203*	7	44.34
21	Sadiq Mohammad	41	74	2	2,579	166	5	35.81

SRI LANKA

		T	I	NO	R	HS	100s	Avge
1	**P. A. de Silva**	**93**	**159**	**11**	**6,361**	**267**	**20**	**42.97**
2	A. Ranatunga	93	155	12	5,105	135*	4	35.69
3	**S. T. Jayasuriya**	**75**	**126**	**12**	**4,757**	**340**	**10**	**41.72**
4	**H. P. Tillekeratne**	**71**	**111**	**23**	**3,864**	**204***	**9**	**43.90**
5	**M. S. Atapattu**	**59**	**103**	**12**	**3,495**	**223**	**10**	**38.40**
6	**D. P. M. D. Jayawardene**	**45**	**71**	**5**	**3,227**	**242**	**9**	**48.89**
7	R. S. Mahanama	52	89	1	2,576	225	4	29.27

ZIMBABWE

		T	I	NO	R	HS	100s	Avge
1	**A. Flower**	**61**	**108**	**19**	**4,655**	**232***	**12**	**52.30**
2	**G. W. Flower**	**61**	**112**	**5**	**3,162**	**201***	**6**	**29.55**
3	A. D. R. Campbell	58	105	4	2,718	103	2	26.91

BANGLADESH: The highest aggregate is **884** (average 35.36) by **Habibul Bashar** in 13 Tests.

Bold type denotes those who played Test cricket in 2001-02 or 2002 season.

CAREER AVERAGE OVER 50

(Qualification: 20 innings)

Avge		*T*	*I*	*NO*	*R*	*HS*	*100s*
99.94	D. G. Bradman (A)	52	80	10	6,996	334	29
60.97	R. G. Pollock (SA)	23	41	4	2,256	274	7
60.83	G. A. Headley (WI)	22	40	4	2,190	270*	10
60.73	H. Sutcliffe (E)	54	84	9	4,555	194	16
60.00	**A. C. Gilchrist (A)**	**31**	**44**	**8**	**2,160**	**204***	**6**
59.23	E. Paynter (E)	20	31	5	1,540	243	4
58.67	K. F. Barrington (E)	82	131	15	6,806	256	20
58.61	E. D. Weekes (WI)	48	81	5	4,455	207	15
58.45	W. R. Hammond (E)	85	140	16	7,249	336*	22
57.96	**S. R. Tendulkar (I)**	**100**	**160**	**15**	**8,405**	**217**	**30**
57.78	G. S. Sobers (WI)	93	160	21	8,032	365*	26
56.94	J. B. Hobbs (E)	61	102	7	5,410	211	15
56.68	C. L. Walcott (WI)	44	74	7	3,798	220	15
56.67	L. Hutton (E)	79	138	15	6,971	364	19
55.00	E. Tyldesley (E)	14	20	2	990	122	3
54.43	**R. Dravid (I)**	**64**	**109**	**11**	**5,335**	**217**	**13**
54.20	C. A. Davis (WI)	15	29	5	1,301	183	4
54.20	V. G. Kambli (I).	17	21	1	1,084	227	4
53.86	G. S. Chappell (A)	87	151	19	7,110	247*	24
53.81	A. D. Nourse (SA)	34	62	7	2,960	231	9
52.57	Javed Miandad (P)	124	189	21	8,832	280*	23
52.30	**A. Flower (Z)**	**61**	**108**	**19**	**4,655**	**232***	**12**
51.62	J. Ryder (A)	20	32	5	1,394	201*	3
51.12	S. M. Gavaskar (I)	125	214	16	10,122	236*	34
50.56	A. R. Border (A)	156	265	44	11,174	205	27
50.29	**D. R. Martyn (A)**	**25**	**40**	**9**	**1,559**	**133**	**5**
50.23	I. V. A. Richards (WI)	121	182	12	8,540	291	24
50.06	D. C. S. Compton (E)	78	131	15	5,807	278	17
50.00	**S. R. Waugh (A)**	**148**	**233**	**41**	**9,600**	**200**	**27**

Bold type denotes those who played Test cricket in 2001-02 or 2002 season.

FASTEST FIFTIES

Minutes			
28	J. T. Brown	England v Australia at Melbourne	1894-95
29	S. A. Durani	India v England at Kanpur.	1963-64
30	E. A. V. Williams	West Indies v England at Bridgetown	1947-48
30	B. R. Taylor	New Zealand v West Indies at Auckland.	1968-69
33	C. A. Roach	West Indies v England at The Oval	1933
33	C. R. Browne	West Indies v England at Georgetown	1929-30

The fastest fifties in terms of balls received (where recorded) are:

Balls			
26	I. T. Botham	England v India at Delhi	1981-82
30	Kapil Dev	India v Pakistan at Karachi (2nd Test)	1982-83
31	W. J. Cronje	South Africa v Sri Lanka at Centurion	1997-98
32	I. V. A. Richards	West Indies v India at Kingston	1982-83
32	I. T. Botham	England v New Zealand at The Oval	1986
33	R. C. Fredericks	West Indies v Australia at Perth	1975-76
33	Kapil Dev	India v Pakistan at Karachi	1978-79
33	Kapil Dev	India v England at Manchester	1982
33	A. J. Lamb	England v New Zealand at Auckland	1991-92
33	A. Flintoff	England v New Zealand at Wellington	2001-02

FASTEST HUNDREDS

Minutes

70	J. M. Gregory	Australia v South Africa at Johannesburg	1921-22
75	G. L. Jessop	England v Australia at The Oval	1902
78	R. Benaud	Australia v West Indies at Kingston	1954-55
80	J. H. Sinclair	South Africa v Australia at Cape Town	1902-03
81	I. V. A. Richards	West Indies v England at St John's	1985-86
86	B. R. Taylor	New Zealand v West Indies at Auckland	1968-69

The fastest hundreds in terms of balls received (where recorded) are:

Balls

56	I. V. A. Richards	West Indies v England at St John's	1985-86
67	J. M. Gregory	Australia v South Africa at Johannesburg	1921-22
71	R. C. Fredericks	West Indies v Australia at Perth	1975-76
74	Majid Khan	Pakistan v New Zealand at Karachi	1976-77
74	Kapil Dev	India v Sri Lanka at Kanpur	1986-87
74	M. Azharuddin	India v South Africa at Calcutta	1996-97
76	G. L. Jessop	England v Australia at The Oval	1902

FASTEST DOUBLE-HUNDREDS

Minutes

214	D. G. Bradman	Australia v England at Leeds	1930
217	N. J. Astle	New Zealand v England at Christchurch	2001-02
223	S. J. McCabe	Australia v England at Nottingham	1938
226	V. T. Trumper	Australia v South Africa at Adelaide	1910-11
234	D. G. Bradman	Australia v England at Lord's	1930
240	W. R. Hammond	England v New Zealand at Auckland	1932-33
241	S. E. Gregory	Australia v England at Sydney	1894-95
245	D. C. S. Compton . . .	England v Pakistan at Nottingham	1954

The fastest double-hundreds in terms of balls received (where recorded) are:

Balls

153	N. J. Astle	New Zealand v England at Christchurch	2001-02
212	A. C. Gilchrist	Australia v South Africa at Johannesburg	2001-02
220	I. T. Botham	England v India at The Oval	1982
229	P. A. de Silva	Sri Lanka v Bangladesh at Colombo (PSS)	2002
231	G. P. Thorpe	England v New Zealand at Christchurch	2001-02
232	C. G. Greenidge	West Indies v England at Lord's	1984
240	C. H. Lloyd	West Indies v India at Bombay	1974-75
241	Zaheer Abbas	Pakistan v India at Lahore	1982-83
242	D. G. Bradman	Australia v England at The Oval	1934
242	I. V. A. Richards	West Indies v Australia at Melbourne	1984-85

FASTEST TRIPLE-HUNDREDS

Minutes

288	W. R. Hammond	England v New Zealand at Auckland	1932-33
336	D. G. Bradman	Australia v England at Leeds	1930

MOST RUNS IN A DAY

309	D. G. Bradman	Australia v England at Leeds	1930
295	W. R. Hammond	England v New Zealand at Auckland	1932-33
273	D. C. S. Compton . . .	England v Pakistan at Nottingham	1954
271	D. G. Bradman	Australia v England at Leeds	1934

SLOWEST INDIVIDUAL BATTING

0	in 101 minutes	G. I. Allott, New Zealand v South Africa at Auckland....	1998-99
5	in 102 minutes	Nawab of Pataudi jun., India v England at Bombay	1972-73
6	in 106 minutes	D. R. Martyn, Australia v South Africa at Sydney	1993-94
7	in 123 minutes	G. Miller, England v Australia at Melbourne............	1978-79
9	in 132 minutes	R. K. Chauhan, India v Sri Lanka at Ahmedabad.......	1993-94
10*	in 133 minutes	T. G. Evans, England v Australia at Adelaide	1946-47
14*	in 165 minutes	D. K. Morrison, New Zealand v England at Auckland....	1996-97
18	in 194 minutes	W. R. Playle, New Zealand v England at Leeds.........	1958
19	in 217 minutes	M. D. Crowe, New Zealand v Sri Lanka at Colombo (SSC)	1983-84
25	in 242 minutes	D. K. Morrison, New Zealand v Pakistan at Faisalabad ...	1990-91
29*	in 277 minutes	R. C. Russell, England v South Africa at Johannesburg..	1995-96
35	in 332 minutes	C. J. Tavaré, England v India at Madras	1981-82
60	in 390 minutes	D. N. Sardesai, India v West Indies at Bridgetown	1961-62
62	in 408 minutes	Ramiz Raja, Pakistan v West Indies at Karachi	1986-87
68	in 458 minutes	T. E. Bailey, England v Australia at Brisbane	1958-59
99	in 505 minutes	M. L. Jaisimha, India v Pakistan at Kanpur............	1960-61
105	in 575 minutes	D. J. McGlew, South Africa v Australia at Durban	1957-58
114	in 591 minutes	Mudassar Nazar, Pakistan v England at Lahore	1977-78
146*	in 635 minutes	N. Hussain, England v South Africa at Durban	1999-2000
163	in 720 minutes	Shoaib Mohammad, Pakistan v New Zealand at Wellington	1988-89
201*	in 777 minutes	D. S. B. P. Kuruppu, Sri Lanka v New Zealand at Colombo (CCC)	1986-87
275	in 878 minutes	G. Kirsten, South Africa v England at Durban.........	1999-2000
337	in 970 minutes	Hanif Mohammad, Pakistan v West Indies at Bridgetown..	1957-58

SLOWEST HUNDREDS

557 minutes	Mudassar Nazar, Pakistan v England at Lahore........	1977-78
545 minutes	D. J. McGlew, South Africa v Australia at Durban.....	1957-58
535 minutes	A. P. Gurusinha, Sri Lanka v Zimbabwe at Harare	1994-95
516 minutes	J. J. Crowe, New Zealand v Sri Lanka at Colombo (CCC)	1986-87
500 minutes	S. V. Manjrekar, India v Zimbabwe at Harare	1992-93
488 minutes	P. E. Richardson, England v South Africa at Johannesburg ..	1956-57

Notes: The slowest hundred for any Test in England is 458 minutes (329 balls) by K. W. R. Fletcher, England v Pakistan, The Oval, 1974.

The slowest double-hundred in a Test was scored in 777 minutes (548 balls) by D. S. B. P. Kuruppu for Sri Lanka v New Zealand at Colombo (CCC), 1986-87, on his debut. It is also the slowest-ever first-class double-hundred.

MOST DUCKS

C. A. Walsh (West Indies) 43; C. E. L. Ambrose (West Indies) 26; S. K. Warne (Australia) 25; G. D. McGrath (Australia) and D. K. Morrison (New Zealand) 24; B. S. Chandrasekhar (India) 23; M. Dillon (West Indies) 21; M. A. Atherton (England) and B. S. Bedi (India) 20.

PARTNERSHIPS OVER 400

576	for 2nd	S. T. Jayasuriya (340)/R. S. Mahanama (225).	SL v I	Colombo (RPS)	1997-98
467	for 3rd	A. H. Jones (186)/M. D. Crowe (299).......	NZ v SL	Wellington	1990-91
451	for 2nd	W. H. Ponsford (266)/D. G. Bradman (244)..	A v E	The Oval	1934
451	for 3rd	Mudassar Nazar (231)/Javed Miandad (280*).	P v I	Hyderabad	1982-83
446	for 2nd	C. C. Hunte (260)/G. S. Sobers (365*).....	WI v P	Kingston	1957-58
413	for 1st	V. Mankad (231)/Pankaj Roy (173)........	I v NZ	Madras	1955-56
411	for 4th	P. B. H. May (285*)/M. C. Cowdrey (154)..	E v WI	Birmingham	1957
405	for 5th	S. G. Barnes (234)/D. G. Bradman (234)....	A v E	Sydney	1946-47

Note: 415 runs were added for the third wicket for India v England at Madras in 1981-82 by D. B. Vengsarkar (retired hurt), G. R. Viswanath and Yashpal Sharma.

HIGHEST PARTNERSHIPS FOR EACH WICKET

The following lists include all stands above 300; otherwise the top ten for each wicket.

First Wicket

413	V. Mankad (231)/Pankaj Roy (173)	. . . .	I v NZ	Madras	1955-56
387	G. M. Turner (259)/T. W. Jarvis (182)	. . . .	NZ v WI	Georgetown	1971-72
382	W. M. Lawry (210)/R. B. Simpson (201)	. . . . .	A v WI	Bridgetown	1964-65
359	L. Hutton (158)/C. Washbrook (195)	. . . . . .	E v SA	Johannesburg	1948-49
335	M. S. Atapattu (207*)/S. T. Jayasuriya (188)	. . . . .	SL v P	Kandy	2000
329	G. R. Marsh (138)/M. A. Taylor (219)	. . . . . .	A v E	Nottingham	1989
323	J. B. Hobbs (178)/W. Rhodes (179)	. . . .	E v A	Melbourne	1911-12
298	C. G. Greenidge (149)/D. L. Haynes (167)	. . . .	WI v E	St John's	1989-90
298	Aamir Sohail (160)/Ijaz Ahmed, sen. (151)	. . . . .	P v WI	Karachi	1997-98
296	C. G. Greenidge (154*)/D. L. Haynes (136)	. . . . .	WI v I	St John's	1982-83

Second Wicket

576	S. T. Jayasuriya (340)/R. S. Mahanama (225)	. . . . .	SL v I	Colombo (RPS)	1997-98
451	W. H. Ponsford (266)/D. G. Bradman (244)	. . . . .	A v E	The Oval	1934
446	C. C. Hunte (260)/G. S. Sobers (365*)	. . . .	WI v P	Kingston	1957-58
382	L. Hutton (364)/M. Leyland (187)	. . . .	E v A	The Oval	1938
369	J. H. Edrich (310*)/K. F. Barrington (163)	. . . . .	E v NZ	Leeds	1965
351	G. A. Gooch (196)/D. I. Gower (157)	. . . .	E v A	The Oval	1985
344*	S. M. Gavaskar (182*)/D. B. Vengsarkar (157*)	. . .	I v WI	Calcutta	1978-79
331	R. T. Robinson (148)/D. I. Gower (215)	. . . . . .	E v A	Birmingham	1985
315*	H. H. Gibbs (211*)/J. H. Kallis (148*)	. . . .	SA v NZ	Christchurch	1998-99
301	A. R. Morris (182)/D. G. Bradman (173*)	. . . . . .	A v E	Leeds	1948

Third Wicket

467	A. H. Jones (186)/M. D. Crowe (299)	. . . .	NZ v SL	Wellington	1990-91
451	Mudassar Nazar (231)/Javed Miandad (280*)	. . . .	P v I	Hyderabad	1982-83
397	Qasim Omar (206)/Javed Miandad (203*)	. . . . . .	P v SL	Faisalabad	1985-86
370	W. J. Edrich (189)/D. C. S. Compton (208)	. . . . .	E v SA	Lord's	1947
352*‡	Ijaz Ahmed, sen. (211)/Inzamam-ul-Haq (200*)	. . .	P v SL	Dhaka	1998-99
341	E. J. Barlow (201)/R. G. Pollock (175)	. . . .	SA v A	Adelaide	1963-64
338	E. D. Weekes (206)/F. M. M. Worrell (167)	. . . . .	WI v E	Port-of-Spain	1953-54
323	Aamir Sohail (160)/Inzamam-ul-Haq (177)	. . . . .	P v WI	Rawalpindi	1997-98
319	A. Melville (189)/A. D. Nourse (149)	. . . .	SA v E	Nottingham	1947
316†	G. R. Viswanath (222)/Yashpal Sharma (140)	. . . .	I v E	Madras	1981-82
308	R. B. Richardson (154)/I. V. A. Richards (178)	. . .	WI v A	St John's	1983-84
308	G. A. Gooch (333)/A. J. Lamb (139)	. . . .	E v I	Lord's	1990
303	I. V. A. Richards (232)/A. I. Kallicharran (97)	. . .	WI v E	Nottingham	1976
303	M. A. Atherton (135)/R. A. Smith (175)	. . . . . .	E v WI	St John's	1993-94

† *415 runs were scored for this wicket in two separate partnerships; D. B. Vengsarkar retired hurt when he and Viswanath had added 99 runs.*
‡ *366 runs were scored for this wicket in two separate partnerships; Inzamam retired ill when he and Ijaz had added 352 runs.*

Fourth Wicket

411	P. B. H. May (285*)/M. C. Cowdrey (154)	. . . . . .	E v WI	Birmingham	1957
399	G. S. Sobers (226)/F. M. M. Worrell (197*)	. . . . .	WI v E	Bridgetown	1959-60
388	W. H. Ponsford (181)/D. G. Bradman (304)	. . . . .	A v E	Leeds	1934
350	Mushtaq Mohammad (201)/Asif Iqbal (175)	. . . . .	P v NZ	Dunedin	1972-73

336	W. M. Lawry (151)/K. D. Walters (242)	A v WI	Sydney	1968-69
322	Javed Miandad (153*)/Salim Malik (165)	P v E	Birmingham	1992
288	N. Hussain (207)/G. P. Thorpe (138).	E v A	Birmingham	1997
287	Javed Miandad (126)/Zaheer Abbas (168)	P v I	Faisalabad	1982-83
283	F. M. M. Worrell (261)/E. D. Weekes (129)	WI v E	Nottingham	1950
281	S. R. Tendulkar (217)/S. C. Ganguly (125)	I v NZ	Ahmedabad	1999-2000

288 runs were scored for this wicket in two separate partnerships for Pakistan v Bangladesh at Multan, 2001-02; Inzamam-ul-Haq retired hurt after adding 123 with Yousuf Youhana, who added a further 165* with Abdul Razzaq.

Fifth Wicket

405	S. G. Barnes (234)/D. G. Bradman (234).	A v E	Sydney	1946-47
385	S. R. Waugh (160)/G. S. Blewett (214).	A v SA	Johannesburg	1996-97
376	V. V. S. Laxman (281)/R. Dravid (180)	I v A	Kolkata	2000-01
332*	A. R. Border (200*)/S. R. Waugh (157*).	A v E	Leeds	1993
327	J. L. Langer (144)/R. T. Ponting (197)	A v P	Perth	1999-2000
322†	B. C. Lara (213)/J. C. Adams (94).	WI v A	Kingston	1998-99
293	C. L. Hooper (233)/S. Chanderpaul (140)	WI v I	Georgetown	2001-02
281	Javed Miandad (163)/Asif Iqbal (166)	P v NZ	Lahore	1976-77
281	S. R. Waugh (199)/R. T. Ponting (104)	A v WI	Bridgetown	1998-99
277*	M. W. Goodwin (166*)/A. Flower (100*)	Z v P	Bulawayo	1997-98

† 344 runs were scored for this wicket in two separate partnerships; P. T. Collins retired hurt when he and Lara had added 22 runs.

Sixth Wicket

346	J. H. Fingleton (136)/D. G. Bradman (270)	A v E	Melbourne	1936-37
317	D. R. Martyn (133)/A. C. Gilchrist (204*).	A v SA	Johannesburg	2001-02
298*	D. B. Vengsarkar (164*)/R. J. Shastri (121*)	I v A	Bombay	1986-87
281	G. P. Thorpe (200*)/A. Flintoff (137)	E v NZ	Christchurch	2001-02
274*	G. S. Sobers (163*)/D. A. J. Holford (105*)	WI v E	Lord's	1966
272	M. Azharuddin (199)/Kapil Dev (163)	I v SL	Kanpur	1986-87
260*	D. M. Jones (118*)/S. R. Waugh (134*)	A v SL	Hobart	1989-90
254	C. A. Davis (183)/G. S. Sobers (142)	WI v NZ	Bridgetown	1971-72
250	C. H. Lloyd (242*)/D. L. Murray (91)	WI v I	Bombay	1974-75
246*	J. J. Crowe (120*)/R. J. Hadlee (151*)	NZ v SL	Colombo (CCC)	1986-87

Seventh Wicket

347	D. St E. Atkinson (219)/C. C. Depeiza (122)	WI v A	Bridgetown	1954-55
308	Waqar Hassan (189)/Imtiaz Ahmed (209).	P v NZ	Lahore	1955-56
248	Yousuf Youhana (203)/Saqlain Mushtaq (101*)	P v NZ	Christchurch	2000-01
246	D. J. McGlew (255*)/A. R. A. Murray (109)	SA v NZ	Wellington	1952-53
235	R. J. Shastri (142)/S. M. H. Kirmani (102)	I v E	Bombay	1984-85
221	D. T. Lindsay (182)/P. L. van der Merwe (76)	SA v A	Johannesburg	1966-67
217	K. D. Walters (250)/G. J. Gilmour (101)	A v NZ	Christchurch	1976-77
217	V. V. S. Laxman (130)/A. Ratra (115*)	I v WI	St John's	2001-02
197	M. J. K. Smith (96)/J. M. Parks (101*).	E v WI	Port-of-Spain	1959-60
194*	H. P. Tillekeratne (136*)/T. T. Samaraweera (103*)	SL v I	Colombo (SSC)	2001

Eighth Wicket

313	Wasim Akram (257*)/Saqlain Mushtaq (79)	P v Z	Sheikhupura	1996-97
253	N. J. Astle (156*)/A. C. Parore (110)	NZ v A	Perth	2001-02
246	L. E. G. Ames (137)/G. O. B. Allen (122).	E v NZ	Lord's	1931
243	R. J. Hartigan (116)/C. Hill (160)	A v E	Adelaide	1907-08
217	T. W. Graveney (165)/J. T. Murray (112)	E v WI	The Oval	1966
173	C. E. Pellew (116)/J. M. Gregory (100).	A v E	Melbourne	1920-21

168	R. Illingworth (107)/P. Lever (88*)	E v I	Manchester	1971
161	M. Azharuddin (109)/A. Kumble (88).	I v SA	Calcutta	1996-97
154	G. J. Bonnor (128)/S. P. Jones (40)	A v E	Sydney	1884-85
154	C. W. Wright (71)/H. R. Bromley-Davenport (84). .	E v SA	Johannesburg	1895-96
154	D. Tallon (92)/R. R. Lindwall (100)	A v E	Melbourne	1946-47

Ninth Wicket

195	M. V. Boucher (78)/P. L. Symcox (108)	SA v P	Johannesburg	1997-98
190	Asif Iqbal (146)/Intikhab Alam (51).	P v E	The Oval	1967
163*	M. C. Cowdrey (128*)/A. C. Smith (69*).	E v NZ	Wellington	1962-63
161	C. H. Lloyd (161*)/A. M. E. Roberts (68)	WI v I	Calcutta	1983-84
161	Zaheer Abbas (82*)/Sarfraz Nawaz (90)	P v E	Lahore	1983-84
154	S. E. Gregory (201)/J. McC. Blackham (74)	A v E	Sydney	1894-95
151	W. H. Scotton (90)/W. W. Read (117).	E v A	The Oval	1884
150	E. A. E. Baptiste (87*)/M. A. Holding (69).	WI v E	Birmingham	1984
149	P. G. Joshi (52*)/R. B. Desai (85)	I v P	Bombay	1960-61
147	Mohammad Wasim (192)/Mushtaq Ahmed (57) . . .	P v Z	Harare	1997-98

Tenth Wicket

151	B. F. Hastings (110)/R. O. Collinge (68*)	NZ v P	Auckland	1972-73
151	Azhar Mahmood (128*)/Mushtaq Ahmed (59)	P v SA	Rawalpindi	1997-98
133	Wasim Raja (71)/Wasim Bari (60*)	P v WI	Bridgetown	1976-77
130	R. E. Foster (287)/W. Rhodes (40*)	E v A	Sydney	1903-04
128	K. Higgs (63)/J. A. Snow (59*).	E v WI	The Oval	1966
127	J. M. Taylor (108)/A. A. Mailey (46*)	A v E	Sydney	1924-25
124	J. G. Bracewell (83*)/S. L. Boock (37).	NZ v A	Sydney	1985-86
120	R. A. Duff (104)/W. W. Armstrong (45*)	A v E	Melbourne	1901-02
118	N. J. Astle (222)/C. L. Cairns (23*)	NZ v E	Christchurch	2001-02
117*	P. Willey (100*)/R. G. D. Willis (24*)	E v WI	The Oval	1980

BOWLING RECORDS

MOST WICKETS IN AN INNINGS

10-53	J. C. Laker	England v Australia at Manchester	1956
10-74	A. Kumble	India v Pakistan at Delhi	1998-99
9-28	G. A. Lohmann	England v South Africa at Johannesburg	1895-96
9-37	J. C. Laker	England v Australia at Manchester	1956
9-51	M. Muralitharan . . .	Sri Lanka v Zimbabwe at Kandy	2001-02
9-52	R. J. Hadlee	New Zealand v Australia at Brisbane	1985-86
9-56	Abdul Qadir	Pakistan v England at Lahore	1987-88
9-57	D. E. Malcolm	England v South Africa at The Oval	1994
9-65	M. Muralitharan . . .	Sri Lanka v England at The Oval	1998
9-69	J. M. Patel	India v Australia at Kanpur	1959-60
9-83	Kapil Dev	India v West Indies at Ahmedabad	1983-84
9-86	Sarfraz Nawaz.	Pakistan v Australia at Melbourne	1978-79
9-95	J. M. Noreiga	West Indies v India at Port-of-Spain	1970-71
9-102	S. P. Gupte	India v West Indies at Kanpur	1958-59
9-103	S. F. Barnes	England v South Africa at Johannesburg	1913-14
9-113	H. J. Tayfield	South Africa v England at Johannesburg	1956-57
9-121	A. A. Mailey	Australia v England at Melbourne	1920-21
8-7	G. A. Lohmann	England v South Africa at Port Elizabeth	1895-96
8-11	J. Briggs	England v South Africa at Cape Town	1888-89
8-29	S. F. Barnes	England v South Africa at The Oval	1912
8-29	C. E. H. Croft	West Indies v Pakistan at Port-of-Spain	1976-77
8-31	F. Laver	Australia v England at Manchester	1909

8-31	F. S. Trueman	England v India at Manchester	1952
8-34	I. T. Botham	England v Pakistan at Lord's	1978
8-35	G. A. Lohmann	England v Australia at Sydney	1886-87
8-38	L. R. Gibbs	West Indies v India at Bridgetown	1961-62
8-38	G. D. McGrath	Australia v England at Lord's	1997
8-43†	A. E. Trott	Australia v England at Adelaide	1894-95
8-43	H. Verity	England v Australia at Lord's	1934
8-43	R. G. D. Willis	England v Australia at Leeds	1981
8-45	C. E. L. Ambrose	West Indies v England at Bridgetown	1989-90
8-51	D. L. Underwood	England v Pakistan at Lord's	1974
8-52	V. Mankad	India v Pakistan at Delhi	1952-53
8-53	G. B. Lawrence	South Africa v New Zealand at Johannesburg	1961-62
8-53†	R. A. L. Massie	Australia v England at Lord's	1972
8-53	A. R. C. Fraser	England v West Indies at Port-of-Spain	1997-98
8-55	V. Mankad	India v England at Madras	1951-52
8-56	S. F. Barnes	England v South Africa at Johannesburg	1913-14
8-58	G. A. Lohmann	England v Australia at Sydney	1891-92
8-58	Imran Khan	Pakistan v Sri Lanka at Lahore	1981-82
8-59	C. Blythe	England v South Africa at Leeds	1907
8-59	A. A. Mallett	Australia v Pakistan at Adelaide	1972-73
8-60	Imran Khan	Pakistan v India at Karachi	1982-83
8-61†	N. D. Hirwani	India v West Indies at Madras	1987-88
8-64†	L. Klusener	South Africa v India at Calcutta	1996-97
8-65	H. Trumble	Australia v England at The Oval	1902
8-68	W. Rhodes	England v Australia at Melbourne	1903-04
8-69	H. J. Tayfield	South Africa v England at Durban	1956-57
8-69	Sikander Bakht	Pakistan v India at Delhi	1979-80
8-70	S. J. Snooke	South Africa v England at Johannesburg	1905-06
8-71	G. D. McKenzie	Australia v West Indies at Melbourne	1968-69
8-71	S. K. Warne	Australia v England at Brisbane	1994-95
8-71	A. A. Donald	South Africa v Zimbabwe at Harare	1995-96
8-72	S. Venkataraghavan	India v New Zealand at Delhi	1964-65
8-75†	N. D. Hirwani	India v West Indies at Madras	1987-88
8-75	A. R. C. Fraser	England v West Indies at Bridgetown	1993-94
8-76	E. A. S. Prasanna	India v New Zealand at Auckland	1975-76
8-79	B. S. Chandrasekhar	India v England at Delhi	1972-73
8-81	L. C. Braund	England v Australia at Melbourne	1903-04
8-83	J. R. Ratnayeke	Sri Lanka v Pakistan at Sialkot	1985-86
8-84†	R. A. L. Massie	Australia v England at Lord's	1972
8-84	Harbhajan Singh	India v Australia at Chennai	2000-01
8-85	Kapil Dev	India v Pakistan at Lahore	1982-83
8-86	A. W. Greig	England v West Indies at Port-of-Spain	1973-74
8-86	J. Srinath	India v Pakistan at Calcutta	1998-99
8-87	M. G. Hughes	Australia v West Indies at Perth	1988-89
8-87	M. Muralitharan	Sri Lanka v India at Colombo (SSC)	2001
8-92	M. A. Holding	West Indies v England at The Oval	1976
8-94	T. Richardson	England v Australia at Sydney	1897-98
8-97	C. J. McDermott	Australia v England at Perth	1990-91
8-103	I. T. Botham	England v West Indies at Lord's	1984
8-104†	A. L. Valentine	West Indies v England at Manchester	1950
8-106	Kapil Dev	India v Australia at Adelaide	1985-86
8-107	B. J. T. Bosanquet	England v Australia at Nottingham	1905
8-107	N. A. Foster	England v Pakistan at Leeds	1987
8-109	P. A. Strang	Zimbabwe v New Zealand at Bulawayo	2000-01
8-112	G. F. Lawson	Australia v West Indies at Adelaide	1984-85
8-126	J. C. White	England v Australia at Adelaide	1928-29
8-141	C. J. McDermott	Australia v England at Manchester	1985
8-143	M. H. N. Walker	Australia v England at Melbourne	1974-75
8-164	Saqlain Mushtaq	Pakistan v England at Lahore	2000-01

† *On Test debut.*

Note: The best for Bangladesh is 6-81 by Manjurul Islam against Zimbabwe at Bulawayo in 2000-01.

OUTSTANDING BOWLING ANALYSES

	O	M	R	W		
J. C. Laker (E)	51.2	23	53	10	v Australia at Manchester	1956
A. Kumble (I)	26.3	9	74	10	v Pakistan at Delhi	1998-99
G. A. Lohmann (E)	14.2	6	28	9	v South Africa at Johannesburg	1895-96
J. C. Laker (E)	16.4	4	37	9	v Australia at Manchester	1956
G. A. Lohmann (E)	9.4	5	7	8	v South Africa at Port Elizabeth . . .	1895-96
J. Briggs (E)	14.2	5	11	8	v South Africa at Cape Town	1888-89
J. Briggs (E)	19.1	11	17	7	v South Africa at Cape Town	1888-89
M. A. Noble (A)	7.4	2	17	7	v England at Melbourne	1901-02
W. Rhodes (E)	11	3	17	7	v Australia at Birmingham	1902
A. E. R. Gilligan (E)	6.3	4	7	6	v South Africa at Birmingham	1924
S. Haigh (E)	11.4	6	11	6	v South Africa at Cape Town	1898-99
Shoaib Akhtar (P)	8.2	4	11	6	v New Zealand at Lahore	2002
D. L. Underwood (E)	11.6	7	12	6	v New Zealand at Christchurch	1970-71
S. L. V. Raju (I)	17.5	13	12	6	v Sri Lanka at Chandigarh	1990-91
H. J. Tayfield (SA)	14	7	13	6	v New Zealand at Johannesburg	1953-54
C. T. B. Turner (A)	18	11	15	6	v England at Sydney	1886-87
M. H. N. Walker (A)	16	8	15	6	v Pakistan at Sydney	1972-73
E. R. H. Toshack (A)	2.3	1	2	5	v India at Brisbane	1947-48
H. Ironmonger (A)	7.2	5	6	5	v South Africa at Melbourne	1931-32
T. B. A. May (A)	6.5	3	9	5	v West Indies at Adelaide	1992-93
Pervez Sajjad (P)	12	8	5	4	v New Zealand at Rawalpindi	1964-65
K. Higgs (E)	9	7	5	4	v New Zealand at Christchurch	1965-66
P. H. Edmonds (E)	8	6	6	4	v Pakistan at Lord's	1978
J. C. White (E)	6.3	2	7	4	v Australia at Brisbane	1928-29
J. H. Wardle (E)	5	2	7	4	v Australia at Manchester	1953
R. Appleyard (E)	6	3	7	4	v New Zealand at Auckland	1954-55
R. Benaud (A)	3.4	3	0	3	v India at Delhi	1959-60

WICKET WITH FIRST BALL IN TEST CRICKET

	Batsman dismissed			
A. Coningham	A. C. MacLaren	A v E	Melbourne	1894-95
W. M. Bradley	F. Laver	E v A	Manchester.	1899
E. G. Arnold	V. T. Trumper	E v A	Sydney	1903-04
G. G. Macaulay	G. A. L. Hearne	E v SA	Cape Town	1922-23
M. W. Tate	M. J. Susskind	E v SA	Birmingham	1924
M. Henderson	E. W. Dawson	NZ v E	Christchurch	1929-30
H. D. Smith	E. Paynter	NZ v E	Christchurch	1932-33
T. F. Johnson	W. W. Keeton	WI v E	The Oval	1939
R. Howorth	D. V. Dyer	E v SA	The Oval	1947
Intikhab Alam	C. C. McDonald	P v A	Karachi	1959-60
R. K. Illingworth	P. V. Simmons	E v WI	Nottingham	1991
N. M. Kulkarni	M. S. Atapattu	I v SL	Colombo (RPS) . .	1997-98
M. K. G. C. P. Lakshitha	Mohammad Ashraful	SL v B	Colombo (SSC) . .	2002

HAT-TRICKS

F. R. Spofforth	Australia v England at Melbourne	1878-79
W. Bates.	England v Australia at Melbourne	1882-83
J. Briggs.	England v Australia at Sydney	1891-92
G. A. Lohmann	England v South Africa at Port Elizabeth	1895-96
J. T. Hearne.	England v Australia at Leeds	1899
H. Trumble	Australia v England at Melbourne	1901-02
H. Trumble	Australia v England at Melbourne	1903-04
T. J. Matthews†	} Australia v South Africa at Manchester	1912
T. J. Matthews		
M. J. C. Allom‡	England v New Zealand at Christchurch	1929-30
T. W. J. Goddard	England v South Africa at Johannesburg	1938-39

P. J. Loader	England v West Indies at Leeds	1957
L. F. Kline	Australia v South Africa at Cape Town	1957-58
W. W. Hall	West Indies v Pakistan at Lahore	1958-59
G. M. Griffin	South Africa v England at Lord's	1960
L. R. Gibbs	West Indies v Australia at Adelaide	1960-61
P. J. Petherick‡	New Zealand v Pakistan at Lahore	1976-77
C. A. Walsh§	West Indies v Australia at Brisbane	1988-89
M. G. Hughes§	Australia v West Indies at Perth	1988-89
D. W. Fleming‡	Australia v Pakistan at Rawalpindi	1994-95
S. K. Warne	Australia v England at Melbourne	1994-95
D. G. Cork	England v West Indies at Manchester	1995
D. Gough	England v Australia at Sydney	1998-99
Wasim Akram¶	Pakistan v Sri Lanka at Lahore	1998-99
Wasim Akram¶	Pakistan v Sri Lanka at Dhaka	1998-99
D. N. T. Zoysa	Sri Lanka v Zimbabwe at Harare	1999-2000
Abdul Razzaq	Pakistan v Sri Lanka at Galle	2000
G. D. McGrath	Australia v West Indies at Perth	2000-01
Harbhajan Singh	India v Australia at Kolkata	2000-01
Mohammad Sami	Pakistan v Sri Lanka at Lahore	2001-02

† *T. J. Matthews did the hat-trick in each innings of the same match.*
‡ *On Test debut.*
§ *Not all in the same innings.*
¶ *Wasim Akram did the hat-trick in successive matches.*

FOUR WICKETS IN FIVE BALLS

M. J. C. Allom	England v New Zealand at Christchurch	1929-30
	On debut, in his eighth over: W-WWW	
C. M. Old	England v Pakistan at Birmingham	1978
	Sequence interrupted by a no-ball: WW-WW	
Wasim Akram	Pakistan v West Indies at Lahore (*WW-WW*)	1990-91

MOST WICKETS IN A TEST

19-90	J. C. Laker	England v Australia at Manchester	1956
17-159	S. F. Barnes	England v South Africa at Johannesburg	1913-14
16-136†	N. D. Hirwani	India v West Indies at Madras	1987-88
16-137†	R. A. L. Massie	Australia v England at Lord's	1972
16-220	M. Muralitharan	Sri Lanka v England at The Oval	1998
15-28	J. Briggs	England v South Africa at Cape Town	1888-89
15-45	G. A. Lohmann	England v South Africa at Port Elizabeth	1895-96
15-99	C. Blythe	England v South Africa at Leeds	1907
15-104	H. Verity	England v Australia at Lord's	1934
15-123	R. J. Hadlee	New Zealand v Australia at Brisbane	1985-86
15-124	W. Rhodes	Australia v England at Melbourne	1903-04
15-217	Harbhajan Singh	India v Australia at Chennai	2000-01
14-90	F. R. Spofforth	Australia v England at The Oval	1882
14-99	A. V. Bedser	England v Australia at Nottingham	1953
14-102	W. Bates	England v Australia at Melbourne	1882-83
14-116	Imran Khan	Pakistan v Sri Lanka at Lahore	1981-82
14-124	J. M. Patel	India v Australia at Kanpur	1959-60
14-144	S. F. Barnes	England v South Africa at Durban	1913-14
14-149	M. A. Holding	West Indies v England at The Oval	1976
14-149	A. Kumble	India v Pakistan at Delhi	1998-99
14-191	W. P. U. J. C. Vaas	Sri Lanka v West Indies at Colombo (SSC)	2001-02
14-199	C. V. Grimmett	Australia v South Africa at Adelaide	1931-32

† *On Test debut.*

Note: The best for South Africa is 13-165 by H. J. Tayfield against Australia at Melbourne, 1952-53, for Zimbabwe 11-255 by A. G. Huckle v New Zealand at Bulawayo, 1997-98, and for Bangladesh 6-81 by Manjurul Islam v Zimbabwe at Bulawayo, 2000-01.

MOST BALLS BOWLED IN A TEST

S. Ramadhin (West Indies) sent down 774 balls in 129 overs against England at Birmingham, 1957. It was the most delivered by any bowler in a Test, beating H. Verity's 766 for England against South Africa at Durban, 1938-39. In this match Ramadhin also bowled the most balls (588) in a Test or first-class innings, since equalled by Arshad Ayub, Hyderabad v Madhya Pradesh at Secunderabad, 1991-92.

MOST WICKETS IN A SERIES

	T	R	W	Avge		
S. F. Barnes	4	536	49	10.93	England v South Africa . . .	1913-14
J. C. Laker	5	442	46	9.60	England v Australia	1956
C. V. Grimmett	5	642	44	14.59	Australia v South Africa . . .	1935-36
T. M. Alderman	6	893	42	21.26	Australia v England	1981
R. M. Hogg	6	527	41	12.85	Australia v England	1978-79
T. M. Alderman	6	712	41	17.36	Australia v England	1989
Imran Khan.	6	558	40	13.95	Pakistan v India	1982-83
A. V. Bedser	5	682	39	17.48	England v Australia	1953
D. K. Lillee	6	870	39	22.30	Australia v England	1981
M. W. Tate	5	881	38	23.18	England v Australia	1924-25
W. J. Whitty	5	632	37	17.08	Australia v South Africa . . .	1910-11
H. J. Tayfield	5	636	37	17.18	South Africa v England . . .	1956-57
A. E. E. Vogler	5	783	36	21.75	South Africa v England . . .	1909-10
A. A. Mailey	5	946	36	26.27	Australia v England	1920-21
G. D. McGrath	6	701	36	19.47	Australia v England	1997
G. A. Lohmann	3	203	35	5.80	England v South Africa . . .	1895-96
B. S. Chandrasekhar	5	662	35	18.91	India v England	1972-73
M. D. Marshall	5	443	35	12.65	West Indies v England . . .	1988

Notes: The most for New Zealand is 33 by R. J. Hadlee against Australia in 1985-86, for Sri Lanka 30 by M. Muralitharan against Zimbabwe in 2001-02, for Zimbabwe 22 by H. H. Streak against Pakistan in 1994-95 (all in three Tests), and for Bangladesh 8 by Mashrafe bin Mortaza against Zimbabwe in 2001-02 (two Tests).

70 WICKETS IN A CALENDAR YEAR

	T	R	W	Avge	5W/i	10W/m	Year
D. K. Lillee (A)	13	1,781	85	20.95	5	2	1981
A. A. Donald (SA)	14	1,571	80	19.63	7	–	1998
M. Muralitharan (SL) . . .	12	1,699	80	21.23	7	4	2001
J. Garner (WI)	15	1,604	77	20.83	4	–	1984
Kapil Dev (I)	18	1,739	75	23.18	5	1	1983
M. Muralitharan (SL) . . .	10	1,463	75	19.50	7	3	2000
Kapil Dev (I)	18	1,720	74	23.24	5	–	1979
M. D. Marshall (WI)	13	1,471	73	20.15	9	1	1984
S. K. Warne (A)	16	1,697	72	23.56	2	–	1993
G. D. McKenzie (A)	14	1,737	71	24.46	4	1	1964
S. K. Warne (A)	10	1,274	70	18.20	6	2	1994

MOST WICKETS

		T	Balls	R	W	Avge	5W/i	10W/m
1	C. A. Walsh (West Indies)	132	30,019	12,688	519	24.44	22	3
2	S. K. Warne (Australia)	101	28,346	11,935	450	26.52	21	5
3	Kapil Dev (India)	131	27,740	12,867	434	29.64	23	2
4	R. J. Hadlee (New Zealand) . . .	86	21,918	9,611	431	22.29	36	9
5	M. Muralitharan (Sri Lanka) . . .	76	25,535	10,030	430	23.32	36	11
6	Wasim Akram (Pakistan)	104	22,627	9,779	414	23.62	25	5
7	C. E. L. Ambrose (West Indies)	98	22,103	8,501	405	20.99	22	3

		T	*Balls*	*R*	*W*	*Avge*	*5W/i*	*10W/m*
8	G. D. McGrath (Australia)...	84	20,149	8,524	389	21.91	23	3
9	I. T. Botham (England)......	102	21,815	10,878	383	28.40	27	4
10	M. D. Marshall (West Indies)..	81	17,584	7,876	376	20.94	22	4
11	Imran Khan (Pakistan)......	88	19,458	8,258	362	22.81	23	6
12 {	Waqar Younis (Pakistan)...	80	15,223	8,158	355	22.98	22	5
{	D. K. Lillee (Australia).....	70	18,467	8,493	355	23.92	23	7
14	A. Kumble (India)	73	22,870	9,381	333	28.17	19	4
15	A. A. Donald (South Africa)..	72	15,519	7,344	330	22.25	20	3
16	R. G. D. Willis (England) ...	90	17,357	8,190	325	25.20	16	–
17	L. R. Gibbs (West Indies) ...	79	27,115	8,989	309	29.09	18	2
18	F. S. Trueman (England)....	67	15,178	6,625	307	21.57	17	3
19	D. L. Underwood (England)...	86	21,862	7,674	297	25.83	17	6
20	C. J. McDermott (Australia)..	71	16,586	8,332	291	28.63	14	2
21	B. S. Bedi (India)	67	21,364	7,637	266	28.71	14	1
22	S. M. Pollock (South Africa)..	63	14,145	5,409	261	20.72	14	1
23	J. Garner (West Indies)	58	13,169	5,433	259	20.97	7	–
24	J. B. Statham (England)	70	16,056	6,261	252	24.84	9	1
25	M. A. Holding (West Indies)..	60	12,680	5,898	249	23.68	13	2
26	R. Benaud (Australia)......	63	19,108	6,704	248	27.03	16	1
27	G. D. McKenzie (Australia)...	60	17,681	7,328	246	29.78	16	3
28	B. S. Chandrasekhar (India)..	58	15,963	7,199	242	29.74	16	2
29 {	A. V. Bedser (England).....	51	15,918	5,876	236	24.89	15	5
{	Abdul Qadir (Pakistan)	67	17,126	7,742	236	32.80	15	5
31	G. S. Sobers (West Indies) ...	93	21,599	7,999	235	34.03	6	–
32	J. Srinath (India)	64	14,786	7,069	232	30.46	10	1
33 {	R. R. Lindwall (Australia)...	61	13,650	5,251	228	23.03	12	–
{	D. Gough (England).......	56	11,503	6,288	228	27.57	9	–
35	C. V. Grimmett (Australia)...	37	14,513	5,231	216	24.21	21	7
36	A. R. Caddick (England)....	58	12,532	6,309	214	29.48	12	–
37	M. G. Hughes (Australia)	53	12,285	6,017	212	28.38	7	1
38 {	A. M. E. Roberts (West Indies)	47	11,135	5,174	202	25.61	11	2
{	J. A. Snow (England)......	49	12,021	5,387	202	26.66	8	1
40 {	J. R. Thomson (Australia)...	51	10,535	5,601	200	28.00	8	–
{	W. P. U. J. C. Vaas (Sri Lanka)	62	13,799	6,056	200	30.28	7	2

Notes: The most wickets for other countries are:

H. H. Streak (Zimbabwe) ...	51	11,236	4,858	180	26.98	6	–
Manjurul Islam (Bangladesh)	11	1,878	1,072	22	48.72	1	–

In 2002-03, after the deadline for this section, McGrath became the eighth bowler to take 400 Test wickets.

Bold type denotes those who played Test cricket in 2001-02 or 2002 season.

100 WICKETS

ENGLAND

		T	*Balls*	*R*	*W*	*Avge*	*5W/i*	*10W/m*
1	I. T. Botham.......	102	21,815	10,878	383	28.40	27	4
2	R. G. D. Willis	90	17,357	8,190	325	25.20	16	–
3	F. S. Trueman	67	15,178	6,625	307	21.57	17	3
4	D. L. Underwood ...	86	21,862	7,674	297	25.83	17	6
5	J. B. Statham	70	16,056	6,261	252	24.84	9	1
6	A. V. Bedser	51	15,918	5,876	236	24.89	15	5
7	D. Gough........	56	11,503	6,288	228	27.57	9	–
8	A. R. Caddick	58	12,532	6,309	214	29.48	12	–
9	J. A. Snow	49	12,021	5,387	202	26.66	8	1
10	J. C. Laker	46	12,027	4,101	193	21.24	9	3

		T	Balls	R	W	Avge	5W/i	10W/m
11	S. F. Barnes	27	7,873	3,106	189	16.43	24	7
12	A. R. C. Fraser	46	10,876	4,836	177	27.32	13	2
13	G. A. R. Lock	49	13,147	4,451	174	25.58	9	3
14	M. W. Tate	39	12,523	4,055	155	26.16	7	1
15	F. J. Titmus	53	15,118	4,931	153	32.22	7	–
16	J. E. Emburey	64	15,391	5,646	147	38.40	6	–
17	W. Verity	40	11,173	3,510	144	24.37	5	2
18	C. M. Old	46	8,858	4,020	143	28.11	4	–
19	A. W. Greig	58	9,802	4,541	141	32.20	6	2
20	P. A. J. DeFreitas	44	9,838	4,700	140	33.57	4	–
21	G. R. Dilley	41	8,192	4,107	138	29.76	6	–
22	T. E. Bailey	61	9,712	3,856	132	29.21	5	1
23	**D. G. Cork**	**37**	**7,678**	**3,906**	**131**	**29.81**	**5**	**–**
24	D. E. Malcolm	40	8,480	4,748	128	37.09	5	2
25	W. Rhodes	58	8,231	3,425	127	26.96	6	1
26	P. H. Edmonds	51	12,028	4,273	125	34.18	2	–
27	D. A. Allen	39	11,297	3,779	122	30.97	4	–
	R. Illingworth	61	11,934	3,807	122	31.20	3	–
29	P. C. R. Tufnell	42	11,288	4,560	121	37.68	5	2
30	J. Briggs	33	5,332	2,095	118	17.75	9	4
31	G. G. Arnold	34	7,650	3,254	115	28.29	6	–
32	G. A. Lohmann	18	3,821	1,205	112	10.75	9	5
33	D. V. P. Wright	34	8,135	4,224	108	39.11	6	1
34	J. H. Wardle	28	6,597	2,080	102	20.39	5	1
35	R. Peel	20	5,216	1,715	101	16.98	5	1
36	C. Blythe	19	4,546	1,863	100	18.63	9	4

AUSTRALIA

		T	Balls	R	W	Avge	5W/i	10W/m
1	**S. K. Warne**	**101**	**28,346**	**11,935**	**450**	**26.52**	**21**	**5**
2	**G. D. McGrath**	**84**	**20,149**	**8,524**	**389**	**21.91**	**23**	**3**
3	D. K. Lillee	70	18,467	8,493	355	23.92	23	7
4	C. J. McDermott	71	16,586	8,332	291	28.63	14	2
5	R. Benaud	63	19,108	6,704	248	27.03	16	1
6	G. D. McKenzie	60	17,681	7,328	246	29.78	16	3
7	R. R. Lindwall	61	13,650	5,251	228	23.03	12	–
8	C. V. Grimmett	37	14,513	5,231	216	24.21	21	7
9	M. G. Hughes	53	12,285	6,017	212	28.38	7	1
10	J. R. Thomson	51	10,535	5,601	200	28.00	8	–
11	A. K. Davidson	44	11,587	3,819	186	20.53	14	2
12	G. F. Lawson	46	11,118	5,501	180	30.56	11	2
13	K. R. Miller	55	10,461	3,906	170	22.97	7	1
	T. M. Alderman	41	10,181	4,616	170	27.15	14	1
15	W. A. Johnston	40	11,048	3,826	160	23.91	7	–
16	W. J. O'Reilly	27	10,024	3,254	144	22.59	11	3
17	H. Trumble	32	8,099	3,072	141	21.78	9	3
18	M. H. N. Walker	34	10,094	3,792	138	27.47	6	–
19	A. A. Mallett	38	9,990	3,940	132	29.84	6	1
20	B. Yardley	33	8,909	3,986	126	31.63	6	1
21	**J. N. Gillespie**	**33**	**6,301**	**3,205**	**123**	**26.05**	**6**	**–**
	R. M. Hogg	38	7,633	3,503	123	28.47	6	2
23	M. A. Noble	42	7,159	3,025	121	25.00	9	2
24	B. A. Reid	27	6,244	2,784	113	24.63	5	2
25	I. W. Johnson	45	8,780	3,182	109	29.19	3	–
26	P. R. Reiffel	35	6,403	2,804	104	26.96	5	–
27	G. Giffen	31	6,457	2,791	103	27.09	7	1
28	A. N. Connolly	29	7,818	2,981	102	29.22	4	–
29	C. T. B. Turner	17	5,179	1,670	101	16.53	11	2

SOUTH AFRICA

		T	Balls	R	W	Avge	5W/i	10W/m
1	**A. A. Donald**	72	15,519	7,344	330	22.25	20	3
2	**S. M. Pollock**	63	14,145	5,409	261	20.72	14	1
3	H. J. Tayfield	37	13,568	4,405	170	25.91	14	2
4	T. L. Goddard	41	11,736	3,226	123	26.22	5	–
5	**J. H. Kallis**	60	7,985	3,518	117	30.06	2	–
6	P. M. Pollock	28	6,522	2,806	116	24.18	9	1
7	**P. R. Adams**	36	6,985	3,353	106	31.63	1	–
8	N. A. T. Adcock	26	6,391	2,195	104	21.10	5	–

WEST INDIES

		T	Balls	R	W	Avge	5W/i	10W/m
1	C. A. Walsh	132	30,019	12,688	519	24.44	22	3
2	C. E. L. Ambrose . . .	98	22,103	8,501	405	20.99	22	3
3	M. D. Marshall	81	17,584	7,876	376	20.94	22	4
4	L. R. Gibbs	79	27,115	8,989	309	29.09	18	2
5	J. Garner	58	13,169	5,433	259	20.97	7	–
6	M. A. Holding	60	12,680	5,898	249	23.68	13	2
7	G. S. Sobers	93	21,599	7,999	235	34.03	6	–
8	A. M. E. Roberts . . .	47	11,135	5,174	202	25.61	11	2
9	W. W. Hall	48	10,421	5,066	192	26.38	9	1
10	I. R. Bishop	43	8,407	3,909	161	24.27	6	–
11	S. Ramadhin	43	13,939	4,579	158	28.98	10	1
12	A. L. Valentine	36	12,953	4,215	139	30.32	8	2
13	C. E. H. Croft	27	6,165	2,913	125	23.30	3	–
14	**C. L. Hooper**	99	13,435	5,445	110	49.50	4	–
15	V. A. Holder	40	9,095	3,627	109	33.27	3	–
16	**M. Dillon**	27	6,181	3,128	101	30.97	2	–

NEW ZEALAND

		T	Balls	R	W	Avge	5W/i	10W/m
1	R. J. Hadlee	86	21,918	9,611	431	22.29	36	9
2	**C. L. Cairns**	55	10,445	5,675	197	28.80	12	1
3	D. K. Morrison	48	10,064	5,549	160	34.68	10	–
4	**D. L. Vettori**	42	10,644	4,707	139	33.86	7	1
5	B. L. Cairns	43	10,628	4,280	130	32.92	6	1
6	E. J. Chatfield	43	10,360	3,958	123	32.17	3	1
7	R. O. Collinge	35	7,689	3,393	116	29.25	3	–
8	B. R. Taylor	30	6,334	2,953	111	26.60	4	–
9	J. G. Bracewell	41	8,403	3,653	102	35.81	4	1
10	R. C. Motz	32	7,034	3,148	100	31.48	5	–

INDIA

		T	Balls	R	W	Avge	5W/i	10W/m
1	Kapil Dev	131	27,740	12,867	434	29.64	23	2
2	**A. Kumble**	73	22,870	9,381	333	28.17	19	4
3	B. S. Bedi	67	21,364	7,637	266	28.71	14	1
4	B. S. Chandrasekhar . .	58	15,963	7,199	242	29.74	16	2
5	**J. Srinath**	64	14,786	7,069	232	30.46	10	1
6	E. A. S. Prasanna . . .	49	14,353	5,742	189	30.38	10	2
7	V. Mankad	44	14,686	5,236	162	32.32	8	2
8	S. Venkataraghavan . .	57	14,877	5,634	156	36.11	3	1

		T	Balls	R	W	Avge	5W/i	10W/m
9	R. J. Shastri	80	15,751	6,185	151	40.96	2	–
10	S. P. Gupte	36	11,284	4,403	149	29.55	12	1
11	**Harbhajan Singh**	**28**	**7,493**	**3,401**	**119**	**28.57**	**9**	**2**
12	D. R. Doshi	33	9,322	3,502	114	30.71	6	–
13	K. D. Ghavri	39	7,042	3,656	109	33.54	4	–
14	N. S. Yadav	35	8,349	3,580	102	35.09	3	–

PAKISTAN

		T	Balls	R	W	Avge	5W/i	10W/m
1	**Wasim Akram**	**104**	**22,627**	**9,779**	**414**	**23.62**	**25**	**5**
2	Imran Khan	88	19,458	8,258	362	22.81	23	6
3	**Waqar Younis**	**80**	**15,223**	**8,158**	**355**	**22.98**	**22**	**5**
4	Abdul Qadir	67	17,126	7,742	236	32.80	15	5
5	Mushtaq Ahmed	50	12,226	5,901	183	32.24	10	3
6	Sarfraz Nawaz	55	13,927	5,798	177	32.75	4	1
7	Iqbal Qasim	50	13,019	4,807	171	28.11	8	2
8	**Saqlain Mushtaq**	**40**	**11,604**	**4,821**	**169**	**28.52**	**12**	**2**
9	Fazal Mahmood	34	9,834	3,434	139	24.70	13	4
10	Intikhab Alam	47	10,474	4,494	125	35.95	5	2

SRI LANKA

		T	Balls	R	W	Avge	5W/i	10W/m
1	**M. Muralitharan**	**76**	**25,535**	**10,030**	**430**	**23.32**	**36**	**11**
2	W. P. U. J. C. Vaas	62	13,799	6,056	200	30.28	7	2

ZIMBABWE

		T	Balls	R	W	Avge	5W/i	10W/m
1	**H. H. Streak**	**51**	**11,236**	**4,858**	**180**	**26.98**	**6**	**–**

BANGLADESH: The highest aggregate is **22** wickets, average 48.72, by **Manjurul Islam** in 11 Tests.

Bold type denotes those who played Test cricket in 2001-02 or 2002 season.

BEST CAREER AVERAGES

(Qualification: 75 wickets)

Avge		T	W	BB	5W/i	10W/m	SR
10.75	G. A. Lohmann (E)	18	112	9-28	9	5	34.11
16.43	S. F. Barnes (E)	27	189	9-103	24	7	41.65
16.53	C. T. B. Turner (A)	17	101	7-43	11	2	51.27
16.98	R. Peel (E)	20	101	7-31	5	1	51.64
17.75	J. Briggs (E)	33	118	8-11	9	4	45.18
18.41	F. R. Spofforth (A)	18	94	7-44	7	4	44.52
18.56	F. H. Tyson (E)	17	76	7-27	4	1	45.42
18.63	C. Blythe (E)	19	100	8-59	9	4	45.46
20.39	J. H. Wardle (E)	28	102	7-36	5	1	64.67
20.53	A. K. Davidson (A)	44	186	7-93	14	2	62.29
20.72	**S. M. Pollock (SA)**	**63**	**261**	**7-87**	**14**	**1**	**54.19**
20.94	M. D. Marshall (WI)	81	376	7-22	22	4	46.76
20.97	J. Garner (WI)	58	259	6-56	7	–	50.84
20.99	C. E. L. Ambrose (WI)	98	405	8-45	22	3	54.57

Avge		T	W	BB	5W/i	10W/m	SR
21.10	N. A. T. Adcock (SA)....	26	104	6-43	5	–	61.45
21.24	J. C. Laker (E)........	46	193	10-53	9	3	62.31
21.51	G. E. Palmer (A).......	17	78	7-65	6	3	57.91
21.57	F. S. Trueman (E)......	67	307	8-31	17	3	49.43
21.78	H. Trumble (A)........	32	141	8-65	9	3	57.43
21.91	**G. D. McGrath (A)..**	**84**	**389**	**8-38**	**23**	**3**	**51.79**
22.25	**A. A. Donald (SA)...**	**72**	**330**	**8-71**	**20**	**3**	**47.02**
22.29	R. J. Hadlee (NZ)	86	431	9-52	36	9	50.85
22.59	W. J. O'Reilly (A)....	27	144	7-54	11	3	69.61
22.73	J. V. Saunders (A)....	14	79	7-34	6	–	45.12
22.81	Imran Khan (P)........	88	362	8-58	23	6	53.75
22.97	K. R. Miller (A)......	55	170	7-60	7	1	61.53
22.98	**Waqar Younis (P)...**	**80**	**355**	**7-76**	**22**	**5**	**42.88**

Bold type denotes those who played Test cricket in 2001-02 or 2002 season.

BEST CAREER STRIKE-RATES

(Qualification: 75 wickets)

SR		T	W	Avge	BB	5W/i	10W/m
34.11	G. A. Lohmann (E).....	18	112	10.75	9-28	9	5
41.65	S. F. Barnes (E)......	27	189	16.43	9-103	24	7
42.88	**Waqar Younis (P)...**	**80**	**355**	**22.98**	**7-76**	**22**	**5**
44.52	F. R. Spofforth (A)...	18	94	18.41	7-44	7	4
45.12	J. V. Saunders (A)...	14	79	22.73	7-34	6	–
45.18	J. Briggs (E)........	33	118	17.75	8-11	9	4
45.42	F. H. Tyson (E)......	17	76	18.56	7-27	4	1
45.46	C. Blythe (E)........	19	100	18.63	8-59	9	4
46.48	**B. Lee (A).........**	**21**	**84**	**26.82**	**5-47**	**4**	**–**
46.76	M. D. Marshall (WI)..	81	376	20.94	7-22	22	4
47.02	**A. A. Donald (SA)...**	**72**	**330**	**22.25**	**8-71**	**20**	**3**
49.32	C. E. H. Croft (WI)...	27	125	23.30	8-29	3	–
49.43	F. S. Trueman (E).....	67	307	21.57	8-31	17	3
50.45	D. Gough (E).........	56	228	27.57	6-42	9	–
50.47	**S. C. G. MacGill (A)**	**17**	**82**	**25.01**	**7-50**	**4**	**1**
50.84	J. Garner (WI).......	58	259	20.97	6-56	7	–
50.85	R. J. Hadlee (NZ)....	86	431	22.29	9-52	36	9
50.92	M. A. Holding (WI)...	60	249	23.68	8-92	13	2
51.10	T. Richardson (A)....	14	88	25.22	8-94	11	4
51.22	**J. N. Gillespie (A).**	**33**	**123**	**26.05**	**7-37**	**6**	**–**
51.27	C. T. B. Turner (A)...	17	101	16.53	7-43	11	2
51.54	G. A. Faulkner (SA)..	25	82	26.58	7-84	4	–
51.64	R. Peel (E)..........	20	101	16.98	7-31	5	1
51.79	**G. D. McGrath (A)..**	**84**	**389**	**21.91**	**8-38**	**23**	**3**
51.92	B. P. Patterson (WI)..	28	93	30.90	5-24	5	–
52.01	D. K. Lillee (A)......	70	355	23.92	7-83	23	7
52.05	A. Cotter (A)........	21	89	28.64	7-148	7	–
52.21	I. R. Bishop (WI).....	43	161	24.27	6-40	6	–
52.67	J. R. Thomson (A)....	51	200	28.00	6-46	8	–
53.02	**C. L. Cairns (NZ)..**	**55**	**197**	**28.80**	**7-27**	**12**	**1**
53.40	R. G. D. Willis (E)...	90	325	25.20	8-43	16	–
53.75	Imran Khan (P).......	88	362	22.81	8-58	23	6
54.14	G. O. B. Allen (E)....	25	81	29.37	7-80	5	1
54.19	**S. M. Pollock (SA)..**	**63**	**261**	**20.72**	**7-87**	**14**	**1**
54.27	W. W. Hall (WI)......	48	192	26.38	7-69	9	1
54.57	C. E. L. Ambrose (WI)..	98	405	20.99	8-45	22	3
54.65	**Wasim Akram (P)...**	**104**	**414**	**23.62**	**7-119**	**25**	**5**

Bold type denotes those who played Test cricket in 2001-02 or 2002 season.

ALL-ROUND RECORDS

HUNDRED AND FIVE WICKETS IN AN INNINGS

England

A. W. Greig	148	6-164	v West Indies . .	Bridgetown . . .	1973-74
I. T. Botham	103	5-73	v New Zealand	Christchurch . . .	1977-78
I. T. Botham	108	8-34	v Pakistan . . .	Lord's.	1978
I. T. Botham	114	6-58 ⎫ 7-48 ⎭	v India	Bombay	1979-80
I. T. Botham	149*	6-95	v Australia. . . .	Leeds	1981
I. T. Botham	138	5-59	v New Zealand	Wellington. . . .	1983-84

Australia

C. Kelleway	114	5-33	v South Africa .	Manchester . . .	1912
J. M. Gregory	100	7-69	v England	Melbourne. . . .	1920-21
K. R. Miller	109	6-107	v West Indies . .	Kingston	1954-55
R. Benaud	100	5-84	v South Africa .	Johannesburg . .	1957-58

South Africa

J. H. Sinclair	106	6-26	v England	Cape Town . . .	1898-99
G. A. Faulkner	123	5-120	v England	Johannesburg . .	1909-10
J. H. Kallis	110	5-90	v West Indies . .	Cape Town . . .	1998-99

West Indies

D. St E. Atkinson	219	5-56	v Australia. . . .	Bridgetown . . .	1954-55
O. G. Smith	100	5-90	v India	Delhi	1958-59
G. S. Sobers	104	5-63	v India	Kingston	1961-62
G. S. Sobers	174	5-41	v England	Leeds	1966

New Zealand

B. R. Taylor†	105	5-86	v India	Calcutta	1964-65

India

V. Mankad	184	5-196	v England	Lord's.	1952
P. R. Umrigar	172*	5-107	v West Indies . .	Port-of-Spain . .	1961-62

Pakistan

Mushtaq Mohammad	201	5-49	v New Zealand	Dunedin	1972-73
Mushtaq Mohammad	121	5-28	v West Indies . .	Port-of-Spain . .	1976-77
Imran Khan	117	6-98 ⎫ 5-82 ⎭	v India	Faisalabad	1982-83
Wasim Akram	123	5-100	v Australia. . . .	Adelaide	1989-90

Zimbabwe

P. A. Strang	106*	5-212	v Pakistan	Sheikhupura. . .	1996-97

† *On debut.*

HUNDRED AND FIVE DISMISSALS IN AN INNINGS

D. T. Lindsay	182	6ct	SA v A	Johannesburg	1966-67
I. D. S. Smith	113*	4ct, 1st	NZ v E	Auckland	1983-84
S. A. R. Silva	111	5ct	SL v I	Colombo (PSS)	1985-86

100 RUNS AND TEN WICKETS IN A TEST

A. K. Davidson	44 80	5-135 } 6-87 }	A v WI	Brisbane	1960-61
I. T. Botham	114	6-58 } 7-48 }	E v I	Bombay	1979-80
Imran Khan	117	6-98 } 5-82 }	P v I	Faisalabad	1982-83

1,000 RUNS AND 100 WICKETS

	Tests	Runs	Wkts	Tests for Double
England				
T. E. Bailey	61	2,290	132	47
†I. T. Botham	102	5,200	383	21
J. E. Emburey	64	1,713	147	46
A. W. Greig	58	3,599	141	37
R. Illingworth	61	1,836	122	47
W. Rhodes	58	2,325	127	44
M. W. Tate	39	1,198	155	33
F. J. Titmus	53	1,449	153	40
Australia				
R. Benaud	63	2,201	248	32
A. K. Davidson	44	1,328	186	34
G. Giffen	31	1,238	103	30
M. G. Hughes	53	1,032	212	52
I. W. Johnson	45	1,000	109	45
R. R. Lindwall	61	1,502	228	38
K. R. Miller	55	2,958	170	33
M. A. Noble	42	1,997	121	27
S. K. Warne	**101**	**2,091**	**450**	**58**
South Africa				
T. L. Goddard	41	2,516	123	36
J. H. Kallis	**60**	**3,971**	**117**	**53**
S. M. Pollock	**63**	**2,242**	**261**	**26**
West Indies				
C. E. L. Ambrose	98	1,439	405	69
†**C. L. Hooper**	**99**	**5,638**	**110**	**90**
M. D. Marshall	81	1,810	376	49
†G. S. Sobers	93	8,032	235	48
New Zealand				
J. G. Bracewell	41	1,001	102	41
C. L. Cairns	**55**	**2,853**	**197**	**33**
R. J. Hadlee	86	3,124	431	28
India				
Kapil Dev	131	5,248	434	25
A. Kumble	**73**	**1,364**	**333**	**56**
V. Mankad	44	2,109	162	23
R. J. Shastri	80	3,830	151	44

	Tests	Runs	Wkts	Tests for Double
Pakistan				
Abdul Qadir	67	1,029	236	62
Imran Khan....................	88	3,807	362	30
Intikhab Alam	47	1,493	125	41
Sarfraz Nawaz	55	1,045	177	55
Wasim Akram	**104**	**2,898**	**414**	**45**
Sri Lanka				
W. P. U. J. C. Vaas...........	**62**	**1,403**	**200**	**47**
Zimbabwe				
H. H. Streak..................	**51**	**1,429**	**180**	**40**

Bold type denotes those who played Test cricket in 2001-02 or 2002 season.

† I. T. Botham (120 catches), C. L. Hooper (110) and G. S. Sobers (109) are the only players to have achieved the treble of 1,000 runs, 100 wickets and 100 catches.

WICKET-KEEPING RECORDS

MOST DISMISSALS IN AN INNINGS

7 (all ct)	Wasim Bari	Pakistan v New Zealand at Auckland	1978-79
7 (all ct)	R. W. Taylor	England v India at Bombay	1979-80
7 (all ct)	I. D. S. Smith	New Zealand v Sri Lanka at Hamilton ..	1990-91
7 (all ct)	R. D. Jacobs	West Indies v Australia at Melbourne ...	2000-01
6 (all ct)	A. T. W. Grout	Australia v South Africa at Johannesburg .	1957-58
6 (all ct)	D. T. Lindsay	South Africa v Australia at Johannesburg .	1966-67
6 (all ct)	J. T. Murray.......	England v India at Lord's	1967
6 (5ct, 1st)	S. M. H. Kirmani ..	India v New Zealand at Christchurch....	1975-76
6 (all ct)	R. W. Marsh	Australia v England at Brisbane	1982-83
6 (all ct)	S. A. R. Silva	Sri Lanka v India at Colombo (SSC)	1985-86
6 (all ct)	R. C. Russell......	England v Australia at Melbourne	1990-91
6 (all ct)	R. C. Russell......	England v South Africa at Johannesburg .	1995-96
6 (all ct)	I. A. Healy	Australia v England at Birmingham	1997
6 (all ct)	A. J. Stewart	England v Australia at Manchester......	1997
6 (all ct)	M. V. Boucher	South Africa v Pakistan at Port Elizabeth .	1997-98
6 (all ct)	Rashid Latif	Pakistan v Zimbabwe at Bulawayo.....	1997-98
6 (all ct)	M. V. Boucher	South Africa v Sri Lanka at Cape Town ..	1997-98
6 (5ct, 1st)	†C. M. W. Read....	England v New Zealand at Birmingham ..	1999

† *On debut.*

MOST STUMPINGS IN AN INNINGS

5	K. S. More	India v West Indies at Madras	1987-88

MOST DISMISSALS IN A TEST

11 (all ct)	R. C. Russell......	England v South Africa at Johannesburg..	1995-96
10 (all ct)	R. W. Taylor	England v India at Bombay	1979-80
10 (all ct)	A. C. Gilchrist	Australia v New Zealand at Hamilton....	1999-2000
9 (8ct, 1st)	G. R. A. Langley ..	Australia v England at Lord's	1956
9 (all ct)	D. A. Murray......	West Indies v Australia at Melbourne....	1981-82
9 (all ct)	R. W. Marsh	Australia v England at Brisbane	1982-83
9 (all ct)	S. A. R. Silva	Sri Lanka v India at Colombo (SSC)	1985-86
9 (8ct, 1st)	S. A. R. Silva	Sri Lanka v India at Colombo (PSS)	1985-86
9 (all ct)	D. J. Richardson....	South Africa v India at Port Elizabeth ...	1992-93

9 (all ct)	Rashid Latif	Pakistan v New Zealand at Auckland	1993-94
9 (all ct)	I. A. Healy	Australia v England at Brisbane	1994-95
9 (all ct)	C. O. Browne	West Indies v England at Nottingham	1995
9 (7ct, 2st)	R. C. Russell	England v South Africa at Port Elizabeth .	1995-96
9 (8ct, 1st)	M. V. Boucher	South Africa v England at Port Elizabeth .	1997-98
9 (8ct, 1st)	R. D. Jacobs	West Indies v Australia at Melbourne	2000-01

Notes: S. A. R. Silva made 18 dismissals in two successive Tests.

The most stumpings in a match is 6 by K. S. More for India v West Indies at Madras in 1987-88.

J. J. Kelly (8ct) for Australia v England in 1901-02 and L. E. G. Ames (6ct, 2st) for England v West Indies in 1933 were the only wicket-keepers to make eight dismissals in a Test before World War II.

MOST DISMISSALS IN A SERIES

(Played in 5 Tests unless otherwise stated)

28 (all ct)	R. W. Marsh	Australia v England	1982-83
27 (25ct, 2st)	R. C. Russell	England v South Africa	1995-96
27 (25ct, 2st)	I. A. Healy	Australia v England (6 Tests)	1997
26 (23ct, 3st)	J. H. B. Waite	South Africa v New Zealand	1961-62
26 (all ct)	R. W. Marsh	Australia v West Indies (6 Tests)	1975-76
26 (21ct, 5st)	I. A. Healy	Australia v England (6 Tests)	1993
26 (25ct, 1st)	M. V. Boucher	South Africa v England	1998
26 (24ct, 2st)	A. C. Gilchrist	Australia v England	2001
25 (23ct, 2st)	I. A. Healy	Australia v England	1994-95

Notes: S. A. R. Silva made 22 dismissals (21ct, 1st) in three Tests for Sri Lanka v India in 1985-86.

H. Strudwick, with 21 (15ct, 6st) for England v South Africa in 1913-14, was the only wicket-keeper to make as many as 20 dismissals in a series before World War II.

100 DISMISSALS

			T	Ct	St
1	395	I. A. Healy (Australia)	119	366	29
2	355	R. W. Marsh (Australia)	96	343	12
3	270	P. J. L. Dujon (West Indies)	79	265	5
4	269	A. P. E. Knott (England)	95	250	19
5	228	Wasim Bari (Pakistan)	81	201	27
6	219	T. G. Evans (England)	91	173	46
7	**213**	**A. J. Stewart (England)**	**71**	**200**	**13**
8	**201**	**M. V. Boucher (South Africa)**	**52**	**196**	**5**
	201	**A. C. Parore (New Zealand)**	**67**	**194**	**7**
10	198	S. M. H. Kirmani (India)	88	160	38
11	189	D. L. Murray (West Indies)	62	181	8
12	187	A. T. W. Grout (Australia)	51	163	24
13	176	I. D. S. Smith (New Zealand)	63	168	8
14	174	R. W. Taylor (England)	57	167	7
15	165	R. C. Russell (England)	54	153	12
16	152	D. J. Richardson (South Africa)	42	150	2
17	**151**	**A. Flower (Zimbabwe)**	**55**	**142**	**9**
18	**148**	**R. D. Jacobs (West Indies)**	**42**	**143**	**5**
19	141	J. H. B. Waite (South Africa)	50	124	17
20	133	Moin Khan (Pakistan)	60	113	20
21	**132**	**A. C. Gilchrist (Australia)**	**31**	**122**	**10**
22	130	K. S. More (India)	49	110	20
	130	W. A. Oldfield (Australia)	54	78	52

			T	Ct	St
24	112	J. M. Parks (England)	43	101	11
25	**108**	**Rashid Latif (Pakistan)**	**31**	**98**	**10**
26	107	N. R. Mongia (India)	44	99	8
27	104	Salim Yousuf (Pakistan)	32	91	13
28	**102**	**J. R. Murray (West Indies)**	**33**	**99**	**3**

Notes: The records for P. J. L. Dujon and J. M. Parks each exclude two catches taken when not keeping wicket in two and three Tests respectively. A. J. Stewart's record excludes 36 catches taken in 51 Tests when not keeping wicket; A. C. Parore's excludes three in 11 Tests, A. Flower's seven in six Tests and Moin Khan's one in three Tests when not keeping wicket.

The most wicket-keeping dismissals for Sri Lanka is 94 (R. S. Kaluwitharana 74ct, 20st in 40 Tests) and for Bangladesh is **16 (Khaled Masud** 16ct in 12 Tests). H. P. Tillekeratne (Sri Lanka) has made 111 dismissals (109ct, 2st) in 71 Tests but only 35 (33ct, 2st) in 12 Tests as wicket-keeper (including one in which he took over during the match).

Bold type denotes those who played Test cricket in 2001-02 or 2002 season.

FIELDING RECORDS

(Excluding wicket-keepers)

MOST CATCHES IN AN INNINGS

5	V. Y. Richardson	Australia v South Africa at Durban	1935-36
5	Yajurvindra Singh	India v England at Bangalore	1976-77
5	M. Azharuddin	India v Pakistan at Karachi	1989-90
5	K. Srikkanth	India v Australia at Perth	1991-92
5	S. P. Fleming	New Zealand v Zimbabwe at Harare	1997-98

MOST CATCHES IN A TEST

7	G. S. Chappell	Australia v England at Perth	1974-75
7	Yajurvindra Singh	India v England at Bangalore	1976-77
7	H. P. Tillekeratne	Sri Lanka v New Zealand at Colombo (SSC)	1992-93
7	S. P. Fleming	New Zealand v Zimbabwe at Harare	1997-98
6	A. Shrewsbury	England v Australia at Sydney	1887-88
6	A. E. E. Vogler	South Africa v England at Durban	1909-10
6	F. E. Woolley	England v Australia at Sydney	1911-12
6	J. M. Gregory	Australia v England at Sydney	1920-21
6	B. Mitchell	South Africa v Australia at Melbourne	1931-32
6	V. Y. Richardson	Australia v South Africa at Durban	1935-36
6	R. N. Harvey	Australia v England at Sydney	1962-63
6	M. C. Cowdrey	England v West Indies at Lord's	1963
6	E. D. Solkar	India v West Indies at Port-of-Spain	1970-71
6	G. S. Sobers	West Indies v England at Lord's	1973
6	I. M. Chappell	Australia v New Zealand at Adelaide	1973-74
6	A. W. Greig	England v Pakistan at Leeds	1974
6	D. F. Whatmore	Australia v India at Kanpur	1979-80
6	A. J. Lamb	England v New Zealand at Lord's	1983
6	G. A. Hick	England v Pakistan at Leeds	1992
6	B. A. Young	New Zealand v Pakistan at Auckland	1993-94
6	J. C. Adams	West Indies v England at Kingston	1993-94
6	S. P. Fleming	New Zealand v Australia at Brisbane	1997-98
6	D. P. M. D. Jayawardene	Sri Lanka v Pakistan at Peshawar	1999-2000
6	M. E. Waugh	Australia v India at Chennai	2000-01
6	V. Sehwag	India v England at Leeds	2002

MOST CATCHES IN A SERIES

15	J. M. Gregory	Australia v England	1920-21
14	G. S. Chappell	Australia v England (6 Tests)	1974-75
13	R. B. Simpson	Australia v South Africa	1957-58
13	R. B. Simpson	Australia v West Indies	1960-61
13	B. C. Lara	West Indies v England (6 Tests)	1997-98

100 CATCHES

Ct	T		Ct	T	
173	**125**	**M. E. Waugh (Australia)**	110	85	W. R. Hammond (England)
157	104	M. A. Taylor (Australia)	**110**	**99**	**C. L. Hooper (West Indies)**
156	156	A. R. Border (Australia)	109	93	G. S. Sobers (West Indies)
122	87	G. S. Chappell (Australia)	108	125	S. M. Gavaskar (India)
122	121	I. V. A. Richards (West Indies)	**107**	**71**	**S. P. Fleming (New Zealand)**
120	102	I. T. Botham (England)	105	75	I. M. Chappell (Australia)
120	114	M. C. Cowdrey (England)	105	99	M. Azharuddin (India)
116	**90**	**B. C. Lara (West Indies)**	103	118	G. A. Gooch (England)
110	62	R. B. Simpson (Australia)	**102**	**148**	**S. R. Waugh (Australia)**

Note: The most catches in the field for other countries are South Africa **70** in 83 Tests (**G. Kirsten**); Pakistan **93** in 124 Tests (Javed Miandad); Sri Lanka **76** in 60 Tests (**H. P. Tillekeratne**); Zimbabwe **55** in 58 Tests (**A. D. R. Campbell**); Bangladesh **9** in 11 Tests (**Al Shariar**) and **9** in 13 Tests (**Habibul Bashar**).

Bold type denotes those who played Test cricket in 2001-02 or 2002 season.

TEAM RECORDS

HIGHEST INNINGS TOTALS

952-6 dec.	Sri Lanka v India at Colombo (RPS)	1997-98
903-7 dec.	England v Australia at The Oval	1938
849	England v West Indies at Kingston	1929-30
790-3 dec.	West Indies v Pakistan at Kingston	1957-58
758-8 dec.	Australia v West Indies at Kingston	1954-55
729-6 dec.	Australia v England at Lord's	1930
708	Pakistan v England at The Oval	1987
701	Australia v England at The Oval	1934
699-5	Pakistan v India at Lahore	1989-90
695	Australia v England at The Oval	1930
692-8 dec.	West Indies v England at The Oval	1995
687-8 dec.	West Indies v England at The Oval	1976
681-8 dec.	West Indies v England at Port-of-Spain	1953-54
676-7	India v Sri Lanka at Kanpur	1986-87
674-6	Pakistan v India at Faisalabad	1984-85
674	Australia v India at Adelaide	1947-48
671-4	New Zealand v Sri Lanka at Wellington	1990-91
668	Australia v West Indies at Bridgetown	1954-55
660-5 dec.	West Indies v New Zealand at Wellington	1994-95

The highest innings for the countries not mentioned above are:

622-9 dec.	South Africa v Australia at Durban	1969-70
563-9 dec.	Zimbabwe v West Indies at Harare	2001
400	Bangladesh v India at Dhaka	2000-01

HIGHEST FOURTH-INNINGS TOTALS

To win

406-4	India (needing 403) v West Indies at Port-of-Spain	1975-76
404-3	Australia (needing 404) v England at Leeds	1948
369-6	Australia (needing 369) v Pakistan at Hobart	1999-2000
362-7	Australia (needing 359) v West Indies at Georgetown	1977-78
348-5	West Indies (needing 345) v New Zealand at Auckland	1968-69
344-1	West Indies (needing 342) v England at Lord's	1984

To tie

347	India v Australia at Madras	1986-87

To draw

654-5	England (needing 696 to win) v South Africa at Durban	1938-39
429-8	India (needing 438 to win) v England at The Oval	1979
423-7	South Africa (needing 451 to win) v England at The Oval	1947
408-5	West Indies (needing 836 to win) v England at Kingston	1929-30

To lose

451	New Zealand (lost by 98 runs) v England at Christchurch	2001-02
445	India (lost by 47 runs) v Australia at Adelaide	1977-78
440	New Zealand (lost by 38 runs) v England at Nottingham	1973
417	England (lost by 45 runs) v Australia at Melbourne	1976-77
411	England (lost by 193 runs) v Australia at Sydney	1924-25
402	Australia (lost by 103 runs) v England at Manchester	1981

MOST RUNS IN A DAY (BOTH SIDES)

588	England (398-6), India (190-0) at Manchester (2nd day)	1936
522	England (503-2), South Africa (19-0) at Lord's (2nd day)	1924
509	Sri Lanka (509-9) v Bangladesh at Colombo (PSS) (2nd day)	2002
508	England (221-2), South Africa (287-6) at The Oval (3rd day)	1935

MOST RUNS IN A DAY (ONE SIDE)

509	Sri Lanka (509-9) v Bangladesh at Colombo (PSS) (2nd day)	2002
503	England (503-2) v South Africa at Lord's (2nd day)	1924
494	Australia (494-6) v South Africa at Sydney (1st day)	1910-11
475	Australia (475-2) v England at The Oval (1st day)	1934
471	England (471-8) v India at The Oval (1st day)	1936
458	Australia (458-3) v England at Leeds (1st day)	1930
455	Australia (455-1) v England at Leeds (2nd day)	1934
450	Australia (450) v South Africa at Johannesburg (1st day)	1921-22

MOST WICKETS IN A DAY

27	England (18-3 to 53 all out and 62) v Australia (60) at Lord's (2nd day)	1888
25	Australia (112 and 48-5) v England (61) at Melbourne (1st day)	1901-02

HIGHEST AGGREGATES IN A TEST

Runs	Wkts			*Days played*
1,981	35	South Africa v England at Durban	1938-39	10†
1,815	34	West Indies v England at Kingston	1929-30	9‡
1,764	39	Australia v West Indies at Adelaide	1968-69	5
1,753	40	Australia v England at Adelaide	1920-21	6
1,723	31	England v Australia at Leeds	1948	5
1,661	36	West Indies v Australia at Bridgetown	1954-55	6

† *No play on one day.*   ‡ *No play on two days.*

LOWEST INNINGS TOTALS

26	New Zealand v England at Auckland	1954-55
30	South Africa v England at Port Elizabeth	1895-96
30	South Africa v England at Birmingham	1924
35	South Africa v England at Cape Town	1898-99
36	Australia v England at Birmingham	1902
36	South Africa v Australia at Melbourne	1931-32
42	Australia v England at Sydney	1887-88
42	New Zealand v Australia at Wellington	1945-46
42†	India v England at Lord's	1974
43	South Africa v England at Cape Town	1888-89
44	Australia v England at The Oval	1896
45	England v Australia at Sydney	1886-87
45	South Africa v Australia at Melbourne	1931-32
46	England v West Indies at Port-of-Spain	1993-94
47	South Africa v England at Cape Town	1888-89
47	New Zealand v England at Lord's	1958

The lowest innings for the countries not mentioned above are:

51	West Indies v Australia at Port-of-Spain	1998-99
62	Pakistan v Australia at Perth	1981-82
63	Zimbabwe v West Indies at Port-of-Spain	1999-2000
71	Sri Lanka v Pakistan at Kandy	1994-95
90	Bangladesh v Sri Lanka at Colombo (SSC)	2001-02

† *Batted one man short.*

Note: In 2002-03, after the deadline for this section, Pakistan were dismissed for 59 and 53 by Australia at Sharjah.

FEWEST RUNS IN A FULL DAY'S PLAY

95	Australia (80), Pakistan (15-2) at Karachi (1st day, 5½ hours)	1956-57
104	Pakistan (0-0 to 104-5) v Australia at Karachi (4th day, 5½ hours)	1959-60
106	England (92-2 to 198) v Australia at Brisbane (4th day, 5 hours)	1958-59
	England were dismissed five minutes before the close of play, leaving no time for Australia to start their second innings.	
111	South Africa (48-2 to 130-6 dec.), India (29-1) at Cape Town (5th day, 5½ hours)	1992-93
112	Australia (138-6 to 187), Pakistan (63-1) at Karachi (4th day, 5½ hours)	1956-57
115	Australia (116-7 to 165 and 66-5 after following on) v Pakistan at Karachi (4th day, 5½ hours)	1988-89
117	India (115-7) v Australia at Madras (1st day, 5½ hours)	1956-57
117	New Zealand (6-0 to 123-4) v Sri Lanka at Colombo (SSC) (5th day, 5¾ hours)	1983-84

In England

151	England (175-2 to 289), New Zealand (37-7) at Lord's (3rd day, 6 hours) . . .	1978
158	England (211-2 to 369-9) v South Africa at Manchester (5th day, 6 hours) . .	1998
159	Pakistan (208-4 to 350), England (17-1) at Leeds (3rd day, 6 hours)	1971

LOWEST AGGREGATES IN A COMPLETED TEST

				Days played
Runs	*Wkts*			
234	29	Australia v South Africa at Melbourne	1931-32	3†
291	40	England v Australia at Lord's	1888	2
295	28	New Zealand v Australia at Wellington	1945-46	2
309	29	West Indies v England at Bridgetown	1934-35	3
323	30	England v Australia at Manchester	1888	2

† *No play on one day.*

LARGEST VICTORIES

Largest Innings Victories

Inns & 579 runs	England (903-7 dec.) v Australia (201 & 123‡) at The Oval . .	1938
Inns & 360 runs	Australia (652-7 dec.) v South Africa (159 & 133) at Johannesburg	2001-02
Inns & 336 runs	West Indies (614-5 dec.) v India (124 & 154) at Calcutta . .	1958-59
Inns & 332 runs	Australia (645) v England (141 & 172) at Brisbane	1946-47
Inns & 324 runs	Pakistan (643) v New Zealand (73 & 246) at Lahore	2002
Inns & 322 runs	West Indies (660-5 dec.) v New Zealand (216 & 122) at Wellington	1994-95
Inns & 285 runs	England (629) v India (302 & 42†) at Lord's	1974
Inns & 264 runs	Pakistan (546-3 dec.) v Bangladesh (134 & 148) at Multan . . .	2001-02
Inns & 259 runs	Australia (549-7 dec.) v South Africa (158 & 132) at Port Elizabeth	1949-50

‡ *Two men absent in both Australian innings.*   † *One man absent in India's second innings.*

Largest Victories by Runs Margin

675 runs	England (521 & 342-8 dec.) v Australia (122 & 66†) at Brisbane	1928-29
562 runs	Australia (701 & 327) v England (321 & 145‡) at The Oval	1934
530 runs	Australia (328 & 578) v South Africa (205 & 171§) at Melbourne . .	1910-11
425 runs	West Indies (211 & 411-5 dec.) v England (71 & 126) at Manchester . .	1976
409 runs	Australia (350 & 460-7 dec.) v England (215 & 186) at Lord's	1948
408 runs	West Indies (328 & 448) v Australia (203 & 165) at Adelaide	1979-80
382 runs	Australia (238 & 411) v England (124 & 143) at Adelaide	1894-95
382 runs	Australia (619 & 394-8 dec.) v West Indies (279 & 352) at Sydney	1968-69
377 runs	Australia (267 & 581) v England (190 & 281) at Sydney	1920-21

† *One man absent in Australia's first innings; two men absent in their second.*
‡ *Two men absent in England's first innings; one man absent in their second.*
§ *One man absent in South Africa's second innings.*

TIED TESTS

West Indies (453 & 284) v Australia (505 & 232) at Brisbane	1960-61
Australia (574-7 dec. & 170-5 dec.) v India (397 & 347) at Madras	1986-87

PLAYERS

YOUNGEST TEST PLAYERS

Years	*Days*			
14	227†	Hasan Raza	Pakistan v Zimbabwe at Faisalabad	1996-97
15	124	Mushtaq Mohammad . . .	Pakistan v West Indies at Lahore	1958-59
15	128	Mohammad Sharif	Bangladesh v Zimbabwe at Bulawayo	2000-01
16	189	Aqib Javed	Pakistan v New Zealand at Wellington	1988-89
16	205	S. R. Tendulkar	India v Pakistan at Karachi	1989-90
16	221	Aftab Baloch	Pakistan v New Zealand at Dacca	1969-70

Years	Days			
16	223	Talha Jubair	Bangladesh v Sri Lanka at Colombo (PSS)	2002
16	248	Nasim-ul-Ghani	Pakistan v West Indies at Bridgetown . . .	1957-58
16	352	Khalid Hassan	Pakistan v England at Nottingham	1954
16	362	Mohammad Ashraful . . .	Bangladesh v Sri Lanka at Colombo (SSC)	2001-02
17	5	Zahid Fazal	Pakistan v West Indies at Karachi	1990-91
17	69	Ata-ur-Rehman	Pakistan v England at Birmingham.	1992
17	78	Imran Nazir	Pakistan v Sri Lanka at Lahore	1998-99
17	118	L. Sivaramakrishnan. . . .	India v West Indies at St John's.	1982-83
17	122	J. E. D. Sealy	West Indies v England at Bridgetown . . .	1929-30
17	129	Fazl-e-Akbar	Pakistan v South Africa at Durban	1997-98
17	152	P. A. Patel	India v England at Nottingham	2002
17	189	C. D. U. S. Weerasinghe .	Sri Lanka v India at Colombo (PSS)	1985-86
17	193	Maninder Singh.	India v Pakistan at Karachi.	1982-83
17	239	I. D. Craig	Australia v South Africa at Melbourne . .	1952-53
17	245	G. S. Sobers	West Indies v England at Kingston	1953-54
17	265	V. L. Mehra	India v New Zealand at Bombay	1955-56
17	265	Harbhajan Singh	India v Australia at Bangalore	1997-98
17	300	Hanif Mohammad	Pakistan v India at Delhi	1952-53
17	341	Intikhab Alam	Pakistan v Australia at Karachi	1959-60
17	352	H. Masakadza	Zimbabwe v West Indies at Harare	2001 (Z)
17	364	Waqar Younis	Pakistan v India at Karachi.	1989-90

† *Hasan Raza's age is in dispute and has been rejected by the Pakistan Cricket Board.*

Note: The youngest Test players for countries not mentioned above are: England – D. B. Close, 18 years 149 days, v New Zealand at Manchester, 1949; New Zealand – D. L. Vettori, 18 years 10 days, v England at Wellington, 1996-97; South Africa – P. R. Adams, 18 years 340 days v England at Port Elizabeth, 1995-96.

OLDEST PLAYERS ON TEST DEBUT

Years	Days			
49	119	J. Southerton	England v Australia at Melbourne	1876-77
47	284	Miran Bux	Pakistan v India at Lahore	1954-55
46	253	D. D. Blackie	Australia v England at Sydney	1928-29
46	237	H. Ironmonger	Australia v England at Brisbane	1928-29
42	242	N. Betancourt	West Indies v England at Port-of-Spain . .	1929-30
41	337	E. R. Wilson	England v Australia at Sydney	1920-21
41	27	R. J. D. Jamshedji.	India v England at Bombay	1933-34
40	345	C. A. Wiles	West Indies v England at Manchester. . .	1933
40	295	O. Henry.	South Africa v India at Durban.	1992-93
40	216	S. P. Kinneir	England v Australia at Sydney	1911-12
40	110	H. W. Lee	England v South Africa at Johannesburg .	1930-31
40	56	G. W. A. Chubb	South Africa v England at Nottingham . .	1951
40	37	C. Ramaswami.	India v England at Manchester	1936

Note: The oldest Test player on debut for New Zealand was H. M. McGirr, 38 years 101 days, v England at Auckland, 1929-30; for Sri Lanka, D. S. de Silva, 39 years 251 days, v England at Colombo (PSS), 1981-82; for Zimbabwe, A. C. Waller, 37 years 84 days, v England at Bulawayo, 1996-97; for Bangladesh, Enamul Haque, 35 years 58 days, v Zimbabwe at Harare, 2000-01. A. J. Traicos was 45 years 154 days old when he made his debut for Zimbabwe (v India at Harare, 1992-93) having played three Tests for South Africa in 1969-70.

OLDEST TEST PLAYERS

(Age on final day of their last Test match)

Years	Days			
52	165	W. Rhodes	England v West Indies at Kingston	1929-30
50	327	H. Ironmonger	Australia v England at Sydney	1932-33
50	320	W. G. Grace	England v Australia at Nottingham	1899

Years	Days			
50	303	G. Gunn	England v West Indies at Kingston	1929-30
49	139	J. Southerton	England v Australia at Melbourne	1876-77
47	302	Miran Bux	Pakistan v India at Peshawar	1954-55
47	249	J. B. Hobbs	England v Australia at The Oval	1930
47	87	F. E. Woolley	England v Australia at The Oval	1934
46	309	D. D. Blackie	Australia v England at Adelaide	1928-29
46	206	A. W. Nourse	South Africa v England at The Oval . . .	1924
46	202	H. Strudwick	England v Australia at The Oval	1926
46	41	E. H. Hendren	England v West Indies at Kingston	1934-35
45	304	A. J. Traicos	Zimbabwe v India at Delhi	1992-93
45	245	G. O. B. Allen	England v West Indies at Kingston	1947-48
45	215	P. Holmes	England v India at Lord's	1932
45	140	D. B. Close	England v West Indies at Manchester . . .	1976

100 TEST APPEARANCES

156	A. R. Border (Australia)		116	D. B. Vengsarkar (India)
148	**S. R. Waugh (Australia)**		115	M. A. Atherton (England)
132	C. A. Walsh (West Indies)		114	M. C. Cowdrey (England)
131	Kapil Dev (India)		110	C. H. Lloyd (West Indies)
125	S. M. Gavaskar (India)		108	G. Boycott (England)
125	**M. E. Waugh (Australia)**		108	C. G. Greenidge (West Indies)
124	Javed Miandad (Pakistan)		107	D. C. Boon (Australia)
122	**A. J. Stewart (England)**		104	M. A. Taylor (Australia)
121	I. V. A. Richards (West Indies)		**104**	**Wasim Akram (Pakistan)**
119	I. A. Healy (Australia)		103	Salim Malik (Pakistan)
118	G. A. Gooch (England)		102	I. T. Botham (England)
117	D. I. Gower (England)		**101**	**S. K. Warne (Australia)**
116	D. L. Haynes (West Indies)		**100**	**S. R. Tendulkar (India)**

Note: The most appearances for Sri Lanka is 93 by **P. A. de Silva** and A. Ranatunga, for New Zealand 86 by R. J. Hadlee, for South Africa **83** by **G. Kirsten**, for Zimbabwe **61** by **A. Flower** and **G. W. Flower** and for Bangladesh **13** by **Habibul Bashar**.

Bold type denotes those who played Test cricket in 2001-02 or 2002 season.

MOST CONSECUTIVE TEST APPEARANCES

153	A. R. Border (Australia)	March 1979 to March 1994
106	S. M. Gavaskar (India)	January 1975 to February 1987
104	M. E. Waugh (Australia)	June 1993 to March 2002
87	G. R. Viswanath (India)	March 1971 to February 1983
85	G. S. Sobers (West Indies)	April 1955 to April 1972
84	S. R. Tendulkar (India)	November 1989 to June 2001
72	D. L. Haynes (West Indies)	December 1979 to June 1988
71	I. M. Chappell (Australia)	January 1966 to February 1976
69	M. Azharuddin (India)	April 1989 to February 1999
66	Kapil Dev (India)	October 1978 to December 1984
65	I. T. Botham (England)	February 1978 to March 1984
65	Kapil Dev (India)	January 1985 to March 1994
65	A. P. E. Knott (England)	March 1971 to August 1977

The most consecutive Test appearances for the countries not mentioned above are:

58†	J. R. Reid (New Zealand)	July 1949 to July 1965
56	A. D. R. Campbell (Zimbabwe)	October 1992 to September 2001
54	J. H. Kallis (South Africa)	December 1995 to March 2002
53	M. S. Atapattu (Sri Lanka)	June 1997 to July 2002
53	Javed Miandad (Pakistan)	December 1977 to January 1984

By February 2003, after the deadline for this section, J. H. Kallis had extended his sequence of consecutive Test appearances to 60. M. E. Waugh's sequence ended at 107 in October 2002.

† *Complete Test career.*

MOST TESTS AS CAPTAIN

	P	W	L	D		P	W	L	D
A. R. Border (A)	93	32	22	38*	G. S. Sobers (WI)	39	9	10	20
C. H. Lloyd (WI)	74	36	12	26	**N. Hussain (E)**	**37**	**14**	**11**	**12**
A. Ranatunga (SL)	56	12	19	25	**S. T. Jayasuriya (SL)**	**37**	**18**	**11**	**8**
M. A. Atherton (E)	54	13	21	20	**S. R. Waugh (A)**	**37**	**26**	**6**	**5**
W. J. Cronje (SA)	53	27	11	15	G. A. Gooch (E)	34	10	12	12
I. V. A. Richards (WI)	50	27	8	15	Javed Miandad (P)	34	14	6	14
M. A. Taylor (A)	50	26	13	11	Kapil Dev (I)	34	4	7	22*
G. S. Chappell (A)	48	21	13	14	J. R. Reid (NZ)	34	3	18	13
Imran Khan (P)	48	14	8	26	D. I. Gower (E)	32	5	18	9
M. Azharuddin (I)	47	14	14	19	J. M. Brearley (E)	31	18	4	9
S. P. Fleming (NZ)	**47**	**17**	**15**	**15**	R. Illingworth (E)	31	12	5	14
A. R. Border (A)	47	9	8	30	I. M. Chappell (A)	30	15	5	10
P. B. H. May (E)	41	20	10	11	E. R. Dexter (E)	30	9	7	14
Nawab of Pataudi jun. (I)	40	9	19	12	G. P. Howarth (NZ)	30	11	7	12
R. B. Simpson (A)	39	12	12	15					

* One match tied.

Most Tests as captain of other countries:

	P	W	L	D
A. Flower (Z)	20	1	10	9
Naimur Rahman (B)	**7**	**0**	**6**	**1**

Notes: A. R. Border captained Australia in 93 consecutive Tests.

W. W. Armstrong (Australia) captained his country in the most Tests without being defeated: ten matches with eight wins and two draws.

I. T. Botham (England) captained his country in the most Tests without ever winning: 12 matches with eight draws and four defeats.

Bold type denotes those who were captains in 2001-02 or 2002 season.

UMPIRES

MOST TESTS

		First Test	*Last Test*
69	**S. A. Bucknor (West Indies)**	**1988-89**	**2002**
66	H. D. Bird (England)	1973	1996
64	**D. R. Shepherd (England)**	**1985**	**2002**
57	**S. Venkataraghavan (India)**	**1992-93**	**2002**
48	F. Chester (England)	1924	1955
44	**D. B. Hair (Australia)**	**1991-92**	**2001-02**
42	C. S. Elliott (England)	1957	1974
39	**R. S. Dunne (New Zealand)**	**1988-89**	**2001-02**
36	D. J. Constant (England)	1971	1988
36	S. G. Randell (Australia)	1984-85	1997-98
34	Khizar Hayat (Pakistan)	1979-80	1996-97
34	**R. E. Koertzen (South Africa)**	**1992-93**	**2002**
33	J. S. Buller (England)	1956	1969
33	A. R. Crafter (Australia)	1978-79	1991-92
32	R. W. Crockett (Australia)	1901-02	1924-25
31	D. Sang Hue (West Indies)	1961-62	1980-81
30	**D. L. Orchard (South Africa)**	**1995-96**	**2002**

Bold type indicates umpires who stood in 2001-02 or 2002 season.

SUMMARY OF TESTS

To September 9, 2002

	Opponents	Tests	E	A	SA	WI	NZ	I	P	SL	Z	B	Tied	Drawn
							Won by							
England	Australia	301	94	121	–	–	–	–	–	–	–	–	–	86
	South Africa	120	50	–	23	–	–	–	–	–	–	–	–	47
	West Indies	126	31	–	–	52	–	–	–	–	–	–	–	43
	New Zealand	85	38	–	–	–	7	–	–	–	–	–	–	40
	India	91	33	–	–	–	–	16	–	–	–	–	–	42
	Pakistan	60	16	–	–	–	–	–	10	–	–	–	–	34
	Sri Lanka	12	7	–	–	–	–	–	–	3	–	–	–	2
	Zimbabwe	4	1	–	–	–	–	–	–	–	0	–	–	3
Australia	South Africa	71	–	39	15	–	–	–	–	–	–	–	–	17
	West Indies	95	–	42	–	31	–	–	–	–	–	–	1	21
	New Zealand	41	–	18	–	–	7	–	–	–	–	–	–	16
	India	60	–	29	–	–	–	13	–	–	–	–	1	17
	Pakistan	46	–	18	–	–	–	–	11	–	–	–	–	17
	Sri Lanka	13	–	7	–	–	–	–	–	1	–	–	–	5
	Zimbabwe	1	–	1	–	–	–	–	–	–	0	–	–	0
South Africa	West Indies	11	–	–	7	2	–	–	–	–	–	–	–	2
	New Zealand	27	–	–	15	–	3	–	–	–	–	–	–	9
	India	14	–	–	7	–	–	2	–	–	–	–	–	5
	Pakistan	7	–	–	3	–	–	–	1	–	–	–	–	3
	Sri Lanka	11	–	–	6	–	–	–	–	1	–	–	–	4
	Zimbabwe	5	–	–	4	–	–	–	–	–	0	–	–	1
West Indies	New Zealand	32	–	–	–	10	7	–	–	–	–	–	–	15
	India	75	–	–	–	30	–	8	–	–	–	–	–	37
	Pakistan	39	–	–	–	13	–	–	12	–	–	–	–	14
	Sri Lanka	6	–	–	–	1	–	–	–	3	–	–	–	2
	Zimbabwe	4	–	–	–	3	–	–	–	–	0	–	–	1
New Zealand	India	40	–	–	–	–	7	14	–	–	–	–	–	19
	Pakistan	43	–	–	–	–	6	–	20	–	–	–	–	17
	Sri Lanka	18	–	–	–	–	7	–	–	4	–	–	–	7
	Zimbabwe	11	–	–	–	–	5	–	–	–	0	–	–	6
	Bangladesh	2	–	–	–	–	2	–	–	–	–	0	–	0
India	Pakistan	47	–	–	–	–	–	5	9	–	–	–	–	33
	Sri Lanka	23	–	–	–	–	–	8	–	3	–	–	–	12
	Zimbabwe	9	–	–	–	–	–	5	–	–	2	–	–	2
	Bangladesh	1	–	–	–	–	–	1	–	–	–	0	–	0
Pakistan	Sri Lanka	28	–	–	–	–	–	–	13	6	–	–	–	9
	Zimbabwe	12	–	–	–	–	–	–	6	–	2	–	–	4
	Bangladesh	3	–	–	–	–	–	–	3	–	–	0	–	0
Sri Lanka	Zimbabwe	13	–	–	–	–	–	–	–	8	0	–	–	5
	Bangladesh	3	–	–	–	–	–	–	–	3	–	0	–	0
Zimbabwe	Bangladesh	4	–	–	–	–	–	–	–	–	3	0	–	1
		1,614	270	275	80	142	51	72	85	32	7	0	2	598

	Tests	Won	Lost	Drawn	Tied	% Won	Toss Won
England	799	270	232	297	–	33.79	385
Australia	628	275	172	179	2	43.78	320
South Africa	266	80	98	88	–	30.07	122
West Indies	388	142	110	135	1	36.59	207
New Zealand	299	51	119	129	–	17.05	151
India	360	72	120	167	1	20.00	182
Pakistan	285	85	69	131	–	29.82	136
Sri Lanka	127	32	49	46	–	25.19	69
Zimbabwe	63	7	33	23	–	11.11	36
Bangladesh	13	0	12	1	–	0.00	6

ENGLAND v AUSTRALIA

Captains

Season	England	Australia	T	E	A	D
1876-77	James Lillywhite	D. W. Gregory	2	1	1	0
1878-79	Lord Harris	D. W. Gregory	1	0	1	0
1880	Lord Harris	W. L. Murdoch	1	1	0	0
1881-82	A. Shaw	W. L. Murdoch	4	0	2	2
1882	A. N. Hornby	W. L. Murdoch	1	0	1	0

THE ASHES

Captains

Season	England	Australia	T	E	A	D	Held by
1882-83	Hon. Ivo Bligh	W. L. Murdoch	4*	2	2	0	E
1884	Lord Harris[1]	W. L. Murdoch	3	1	0	2	E
1884-85	A. Shrewsbury	T. P. Horan[2]	5	3	2	0	E
1886	A. G. Steel	H. J. H. Scott	3	3	0	0	E
1886-87	A. Shrewsbury	P. S. McDonnell	2	2	0	0	E
1887-88	W. W. Read	P. S. McDonnell	1	1	0	0	E
1888	W. G. Grace[3]	P. S. McDonnell	3	2	1	0	E
1890†	W. G. Grace	W. L. Murdoch	2	2	0	0	E
1891-92	W. G. Grace	J. McC. Blackham	3	1	2	0	A
1893	W. G. Grace[4]	J. McC. Blackham	3	1	0	2	E
1894-95	A. E. Stoddart	G. Giffen[5]	5	3	2	0	E
1896	W. G. Grace	G. H. S. Trott	3	2	1	0	E
1897-98	A. E. Stoddart[6]	G. H. S. Trott	5	1	4	0	A
1899	A. C. MacLaren[7]	J. Darling	5	0	1	4	A
1901-02	A. C. MacLaren	J. Darling[8]	5	1	4	0	A
1902	A. C. MacLaren	J. Darling	5	1	2	2	A
1903-04	P. F. Warner	M. A. Noble	5	3	2	0	E
1905	Hon. F. S. Jackson	J. Darling	5	2	0	3	E
1907-08	A. O. Jones[9]	M. A. Noble	5	1	4	0	A
1909	A. C. MacLaren	M. A. Noble	5	1	2	2	A
1911-12	J. W. H. T. Douglas	C. Hill	5	4	1	0	E
1912	C. B. Fry	S. E. Gregory	3	1	0	2	E
1920-21	J. W. H. T. Douglas	W. W. Armstrong	5	0	5	0	A
1921	Hon. L. H. Tennyson[10]	W. W. Armstrong	5	0	3	2	A
1924-25	A. E. R. Gilligan	H. L. Collins	5	1	4	0	A
1926	A. W. Carr[11]	H. L. Collins[12]	5	1	0	4	E
1928-29	A. P. F. Chapman[13]	J. Ryder	5	4	1	0	E
1930	A. P. F. Chapman[14]	W. M. Woodfull	5	1	2	2	A
1932-33	D. R. Jardine	W. M. Woodfull	5	4	1	0	E
1934	R. E. S. Wyatt[15]	W. M. Woodfull	5	1	2	2	A
1936-37	G. O. B. Allen	D. G. Bradman	5	2	3	0	A
1938†	W. R. Hammond	D. G. Bradman	4	1	1	2	A
1946-47	W. R. Hammond[16]	D. G. Bradman	5	0	3	2	A
1948	N. W. D. Yardley	D. G. Bradman	5	0	4	1	A
1950-51	F. R. Brown	A. L. Hassett	5	1	4	0	A
1953	L. Hutton	A. L. Hassett	5	1	0	4	E
1954-55	L. Hutton	I. W. Johnson[17]	5	3	1	1	E
1956	P. B. H. May	I. W. Johnson	5	2	1	2	E
1958-59	P. B. H. May	R. Benaud	5	0	4	1	A
1961	P. B. H. May[18]	R. Benaud[19]	5	1	2	2	A
1962-63	E. R. Dexter	R. Benaud	5	1	1	3	A
1964	E. R. Dexter	R. B. Simpson	5	0	1	4	A
1965-66	M. J. K. Smith	R. B. Simpson[20]	5	1	1	3	A
1968	M. C. Cowdrey[21]	W. M. Lawry[22]	5	1	1	3	A
1970-71†	R. Illingworth	W. M. Lawry[23]	6	2	0	4	E
1972	R. Illingworth	I. M. Chappell	5	2	2	1	E
1974-75	M. H. Denness[24]	I. M. Chappell	6	1	4	1	A

Captains

Season	England	Australia	T	E	A	D	Held by
1975	A. W. Greig[22]	I. M. Chappell	4	0	1	3	A
1976-77‡	A. W. Greig	G. S. Chappell	1	0	1	0	—
1977	J. M. Brearley	G. S. Chappell	5	3	0	2	E
1978-79	J. M. Brearley	G. N. Yallop	6	5	1	0	E
1979-80‡	J. M. Brearley	G. S. Chappell	3	0	3	0	—
1980‡	I. T. Botham	G. S. Chappell	1	0	0	1	—
1981	J. M. Brearley[26]	K. J. Hughes	6	3	1	2	E
1982-83	R. G. D. Willis	G. S. Chappell	5	1	2	2	A
1985	D. I. Gower	A. R. Border	6	3	1	2	E
1986-87	M. W. Gatting	A. R. Border	5	2	1	2	E
1987-88‡	M. W. Gatting	A. R. Border	1	0	0	1	—
1989	D. I. Gower	A. R. Border	6	0	4	2	A
1990-91	G. A. Gooch[27]	A. R. Border	5	0	3	2	A
1993	G. A. Gooch[28]	A. R. Border	6	1	4	1	A
1994-95	M. A. Atherton	M. A. Taylor	5	1	3	1	A
1997	M. A. Atherton	M. A. Taylor	6	2	3	1	A
1998-99	A. J. Stewart	M. A. Taylor	5	1	3	1	A
2001	N. Hussain[29]	S. R. Waugh[30]	5	1	4	0	A

			T	E	A	D	
In Australia	. . . .		155	53	76	26	
In England	. . . .		146	41	45	60	
Totals	. . . .		301	94	121	86	

* *The Ashes were awarded in 1882-83 after a series of three matches which England won 2–1. A fourth match was played and this was won by Australia.*

† *The matches at Manchester in 1890 and 1938 and at Melbourne (Third Test) in 1970-71 were abandoned without a ball being bowled and are excluded.*

‡ *The Ashes were not at stake in these series.*

Notes: The following deputised for the official touring captain or were appointed by the home authority for only a minor proportion of the series:

[1]A. N. Hornby (First). [2]W. L. Murdoch (First), H. H. Massie (Third), J. McC. Blackham (Fourth). [3]A. G. Steel (First). [4]A. E. Stoddart (First). [5]J. McC. Blackham (First). [6]A. C. MacLaren (First, Second and Fifth). [7]W. G. Grace (First). [8]H. Trumble (Fourth and Fifth). [9]F. L. Fane (First, Second and Third). [10]J. W. H. T. Douglas (First and Second). [11]A. P. F. Chapman (Fifth). [12]W. Bardsley (Third and Fourth). [13]J. C. White (Fifth). [14]R. E. S. Wyatt (Fifth). [15]C. F. Walters (First). [16]N. W. D. Yardley (Fifth). [17]A. R. Morris (Second). [18]M. C. Cowdrey (First and Second). [19]R. N. Harvey (Second). [20]B. C. Booth (First and Third). [21]T. W. Graveney (Fourth). [22]B. N. Jarman (Fourth). [23]I. M. Chappell (Seventh). [24]J. H. Edrich (Fourth). [25]M. H. Denness (First). [26]I. T. Botham (First and Second). [27]A. J. Lamb (First). [28]M. A. Atherton (Fifth and Sixth). [29]M. A. Atherton (Second and Third). [30]A. C. Gilchrist (Fourth).

HIGHEST INNINGS TOTALS

For England	in England: 903-7 dec. at The Oval	1938
	in Australia: 636 at Sydney	1928-29

For Australia	in England: 729-6 dec. at Lord's	1930
	in Australia: 659-8 dec. at Sydney	1946-47

LOWEST INNINGS TOTALS

For England	in England: 52 at The Oval	1948
	in Australia: 45 at Sydney	1886-87

For Australia	in England: 36 at Birmingham	1902
	in Australia: 42 at Sydney	1887-88

INDIVIDUAL HUNDREDS

For England (208)

R. Abel (1)
132*‡ Sydney 1891-92

L. E. G. Ames (1)
120 Lord's 1934

M. A. Atherton (1)
105 Sydney 1990-91

R. W. Barber (1)
185 Sydney 1965-66

W. Barnes (1)
134 Adelaide . . . 1884-85

C. J. Barnett (2)
129 Adelaide . . . 1936-37
126 Nottingham . . 1938

K. F. Barrington (5)
132* Adelaide . . . 1962-63
101 Sydney 1962-63
256 Manchester. . 1964
102 Adelaide . . . 1965-66
115 Melbourne . . 1965-66

I. T. Botham (4)
119* Melbourne . . 1979-80
149* Leeds 1981
118 Manchester. . 1981
138 Brisbane . . . 1986-87

G. Boycott (7)
113 The Oval . . . 1964
142* Sydney . . . 1970-71
119* Adelaide . . . 1970-71
107 Nottingham . 1977
191 Leeds 1977
128* Lord's 1980
137 The Oval . . . 1981

L. C. Braund (2)
103* Adelaide . . . 1901-02
102 Sydney 1903-04

J. Briggs (1)
121 Melbourne . . 1884-85

B. C. Broad (4)
162 Perth. 1986-87
116 Adelaide . . . 1986-87
112 Melbourne . . 1986-87
139 Sydney 1987-88

J. T. Brown (1)
140 Melbourne . . 1894-95

M. A. Butcher (2)
116 Brisbane . . . 1998-99
173* Leeds 2001

A. P. F. Chapman (1)
121 Lord's 1930

D. C. S. Compton (5)
102† Nottingham . 1938
147 } Adelaide . . . 1946-47
103* }
184 Nottingham . 1948
145* Manchester. . 1948

M. C. Cowdrey (5)
102 Melbourne . . 1954-55
100* Sydney 1958-59

113 Melbourne . . 1962-63
104 Melbourne . . 1965-66
104 Birmingham . 1968

M. H. Denness (1)
188 Melbourne . . 1974-75

E. R. Dexter (2)
180 Birmingham . 1961
174 Manchester. . 1964

B. L. D'Oliveira (2)
158 The Oval . . . 1968
117 Melbourne . . 1970-71

K. S. Duleepsinhji (1)
173† Lord's 1930

J. H. Edrich (7)
120† Lord's 1964
109 Melbourne . . 1965-66
103 Sydney 1965-66
164 The Oval . . . 1968
115* Perth. 1970-71
130 Adelaide . . . 1970-71
175 Lord's 1975

W. J. Edrich (2)
119 Sydney 1946-47
111 Leeds 1948

K. W. R. Fletcher (1)
146 Melbourne . . 1974-75

R. E. Foster (1)
287† Sydney . . . 1903-04

C. B. Fry (1)
144 The Oval . . . 1905

M. W. Gatting (4)
160 Manchester. . 1985
100* Birmingham . 1985
100 Adelaide . . . 1986-87
117 Adelaide . . . 1994-95

G. A. Gooch (4)
196 The Oval . . . 1985
117 Adelaide . . . 1990-91
133 Manchester. . 1993
120 Nottingham . 1993

D. I. Gower (9)
102 Perth. 1978-79
114 Adelaide . . . 1982-83
166 Nottingham . 1985
215 Birmingham . 1985
157 The Oval . . . 1985
136 Perth. 1986-87
106 Lord's 1989
100 Melbourne . . 1990-91
123 Sydney 1990-91

W. G. Grace (2)
152† The Oval . . . 1880
170 The Oval . . . 1886

T. W. Graveney (1)
111 Sydney 1954-55

A. W. Greig (1)
110 Brisbane . . . 1974-75

G. Gunn (2)
119† Sydney 1907-08
122* Sydney 1907-08

W. Gunn (1)
102* Manchester. . 1893

W. R. Hammond (9)
251 Sydney 1928-29
200 Melbourne . . 1928-29
119* } Adelaide . . . 1928-29
177 }
113 Leeds 1930
112 Sydney 1932-33
101 Sydney 1932-33
231* Sydney 1936-37
240 Lord's 1938

J. Hardstaff jun. (1)
169* The Oval . . . 1938

T. W. Hayward (2)
130 Manchester. . 1899
137 The Oval . . . 1899

J. W. Hearne (1)
114 Melbourne . . 1911-12

E. H. Hendren (3)
127* Lord's 1926
169 Brisbane . . . 1928-29
132 Manchester. . 1934

J. B. Hobbs (12)
126* Melbourne . . 1911-12
187 Adelaide . . . 1911-12
178 Melbourne . . 1911-12
107 Lord's 1912
122 Melbourne . . 1920-21
123 Adelaide . . . 1920-21
115 Sydney 1924-25
154 Melbourne . . 1924-25
119 Adelaide . . . 1924-25
119 Lord's 1926
100 The Oval . . . 1926
142 Melbourne . . 1928-29

N. Hussain (2)
207 Birmingham . 1997
105 Leeds 1997

K. L. Hutchings (1)
126 Melbourne . . 1907-08

L. Hutton (5)
100† Nottingham . 1938
364 The Oval . . . 1938
122* Sydney 1946-47
156*‡ Adelaide . . . 1950-51
145 Lord's 1953

Hon. F. S. Jackson (5)
103 The Oval . . . 1893
118 The Oval . . . 1899
128 Manchester. . 1902
144* Leeds 1905
113 Manchester. . 1905

G. L. Jessop (1)
104   The Oval . . .   1902
A. P. E. Knott (2)
106*   Adelaide   1974-75
135   Nottingham . . .   1977
A. J. Lamb (1)
125   Leeds   1989
M. Leyland (7)
137†   Melbourne . .   1928-29
109   Lord's   1934
153   Manchester. . .   1934
110   The Oval   1934
126   Brisbane   1936-37
111*   Melbourne . .   1936-37
187   The Oval   1938
B. W. Luckhurst (2)
131   Perth.   1970-71
109   Melbourne . .   1970-71
A. C. MacLaren (5)
120   Melbourne . .   1894-95
109   Sydney   1897-98
124   Adelaide   1897-98
116   Sydney   1901-02
140   Nottingham . . .   1905
J. W. H. Makepeace (1)
117   Melbourne . .   1920-21
P. B. H. May (3)
104   Sydney   1954-55
101   Leeds   1956
113   Melbourne . .   1958-59
C. P. Mead (1)
182*   The Oval   1921
Nawab of Pataudi sen. (1)
102†   Sydney   1932-33
E. Paynter (1)
216*   Nottingham . . .   1938
M. R. Ramprakash (1)
133   The Oval   2001
D. W. Randall (3)
174†   Melbourne . .   1976-77

150   Sydney   1978-79
115   Perth.   1982-83
K. S. Ranjitsinhji (2)
154*† Manchester. .   1896
175   Sydney   1897-98
W. W. Read (1)
117   The Oval . . .   1884
W. Rhodes (1)
179   Melbourne . .   1911-12
C. J. Richards (1)
133   Perth.   1986-87
P. E. Richardson (1)
104   Manchester. . .   1956
R. T. Robinson (2)
175†   Leeds   1985
148   Birmingham . .   1985
A. C. Russell (3)
135*   Adelaide   1920-21
101   Manchester. . .   1921
102*   The Oval . . .   1921
R. C. Russell (1)
128*   Manchester. . .   1989
J. Sharp (1)
105   The Oval . . .   1909
Rev. D. S. Sheppard (2)
113   Manchester. . .   1956
113   Melbourne . .   1962-63
A. Shrewsbury (3)
105*   Melbourne . .   1884-85
164   Lord's   1886
106   Lord's   1893
R. T. Simpson (1)
156*   Melbourne . .   1950-51
R. A. Smith (2)
143   Manchester. . .   1989
101   Nottingham . . .   1989
A. G. Steel (2)
135*   Sydney   1882-83
148   Lord's   1884

A. J. Stewart (1)
107   Melbourne . .   1998-99
A. E. Stoddart (2)
134   Adelaide   1891-92
173   Melbourne . .   1894-95
R. Subba Row (2)
112†   Birmingham . .   1961
137   The Oval   1961
H. Sutcliffe (8)
115†   Sydney   1924-25
176
127 } Melbourne . .   1924-25
143   Melbourne . .   1924-25
161   The Oval   1926
135   Melbourne . .   1928-29
161   The Oval   1930
194   Sydney   1932-33
G. P. Thorpe (3)
114*† Nottingham . . .   1993
123   Perth.   1994-95
138   Birmingham . .   1997
J. T. Tyldesley (3)
138   Birmingham . .   1902
100   Leeds   1905
112*   The Oval   1905
G. Ulyett (1)
149   Melbourne . .   1881-82
A. Ward (1)
117   Sydney   1894-95
C. Washbrook (2)
112   Melbourne . .   1946-47
143   Leeds   1948
W. Watson (1)
109†   Lord's   1953
F. E. Woolley (2)
133*   Sydney   1911-12
123   Sydney   1924-25
R. A. Woolmer (3)
149   The Oval   1975
120   Lord's   1977
137   Manchester. .   1977

For Australia (256)

W. W. Armstrong (4)
133*   Melbourne . .   1907-08
158   Sydney   1920-21
121   Adelaide   1920-21
123*   Melbourne . .   1920-21
C. L. Badcock (1)
118   Melbourne . .   1936-37
C. Bannerman (1)
165*† Melbourne . .   1876-77
W. Bardsley (3)
136 }
130 } The Oval . . .   1909
193*‡ Lord's   1926
S. G. Barnes (2)
234   Sydney   1946-47
141   Lord's   1948

G. S. Blewett (3)
102*† Adelaide   1994-95
115   Perth.   1994-95
125   Birmingham . .   1997
G. J. Bonnor (1)
128   Sydney   1884-85
D. C. Boon (7)
103   Adelaide   1986-87
184*   Sydney   1987-88
121   Adelaide   1990-91
164*   Lord's   1993
101   Nottingham . . .   1993
107   Leeds   1993
131   Melbourne . .   1994-95

B. C. Booth (2)
112   Brisbane   1962-63
103   Melbourne . .   1962-63
A. R. Border (8)
115   Perth.   1979-80
123*   Manchester. . .   1981
106*   The Oval   1981
196   Lord's   1985
146*   Manchester. . .   1985
125   Perth.   1986-87
100*   Adelaide   1986-87
200*   Leeds   1993
D. G. Bradman (19)
112   Melbourne . .   1928-29
123   Melbourne . .   1928-29

A. R. Morris (8)

155	Melbourne . .	1946-47
122 124* }	Adelaide	1946-47
105	Lord's	1948
182	Leeds	1948
196	The Oval . . .	1948
206	Adelaide . . .	1950-51
153	Brisbane . . .	1954-55

W. L. Murdoch (2)

153*	The Oval . . .	1880
211	The Oval . . .	1884

M. A. Noble (1)

133	Sydney	1903-04

N. C. O'Neill (2)

117	The Oval . . .	1961
100	Adelaide . . .	1962-63

C. E. Pellew (2)

116	Melbourne . .	1920-21
104	Adelaide . . .	1920-21

W. H. Ponsford (5)

110†	Sydney	1924-25
128	Melbourne . .	1924-25
110	The Oval . . .	1930
181	Leeds	1934
266	The Oval . . .	1934

R. T. Ponting (2)

127†	Leeds	1997
144	Leeds	2001

V. S. Ransford (1)

143*	Lord's	1909

I. R. Redpath (2)

171	Perth	1970-71
105	Sydney	1974-75

A. J. Richardson (1)

100	Leeds	1926

V. Y. Richardson (1)

138	Melbourne . .	1924-25

G. M. Ritchie (1)

146	Nottingham .	1985

J. Ryder (2)

201*	Adelaide . . .	1924-25
112	Melbourne . .	1928-29

H. J. H. Scott (1)

102	The Oval . . .	1884

R. B. Simpson (2)

311	Manchester . .	1964
225	Adelaide . . .	1965-66

M. J. Slater (7)

152	Lord's	1993
176	Brisbane . . .	1994-95
103	Sydney	1994-95
124	Perth	1994-95
113	Brisbane . . .	1998-99
103	Adelaide . . .	1998-99
123	Sydney	1998-99

K. R. Stackpole (3)

207	Brisbane . . .	1970-71
136	Adelaide . . .	1970-71
114	Nottingham .	1972

J. M. Taylor (1)

108	Sydney	1924-25

M. A. Taylor (6)

136†	Leeds	1989
219	Nottingham .	1989
124	Manchester . .	1993
111	Lord's	1993
113	Sydney	1994-95
129	Birmingham .	1997

G. H. S. Trott (1)

143	Lord's	1896

V. T. Trumper (6)

135*	Lord's	1899
104	Manchester . .	1902
185*	Sydney	1903-04
113	Adelaide . . .	1903-04
166	Sydney	1907-08
113	Sydney	1911-12

K. D. Walters (4)

155†	Brisbane . . .	1965-66

115	Melbourne . .	1965-66
112	Brisbane . . .	1970-71
103	Perth	1974-75

M. E. Waugh (6)

138†	Adelaide . . .	1990-91
137	Birmingham .	1993
140	Brisbane . . .	1994-95
121	Sydney	1998-99
108	Lord's	2001
120	The Oval . . .	2001

S. R. Waugh (9)

177*	Leeds	1989
152*	Lord's	1989
157*	Leeds	1993
108 116 }	Manchester . .	1997
112	Brisbane . . .	1998-99
122*	Melbourne . .	1998-99
105	Birmingham .	2001
157*	The Oval . . .	2001

D. M. Wellham (1)

103†	The Oval . . .	1981

K. C. Wessels (1)

162†	Brisbane . . .	1982-83

G. M. Wood (3)

100	Melbourne . .	1978-79
112	Lord's	1980
172	Nottingham .	1985

W. M. Woodfull (6)

141	Leeds	1926
117	Manchester . .	1926
111	Sydney	1928-29
107	Melbourne . .	1928-29
102	Melbourne . .	1928-29
155	Lord's	1930

G. N. Yallop (3)

102†	Brisbane . . .	1978-79
121	Sydney	1978-79
114	Manchester . .	1981

† *On first appearance in England–Australia Tests.*
‡ *Carried his bat.*

Note: D. C. S. Compton and A. R. Morris, on opposing sides, each hit two hundreds at Adelaide in 1946-47, the first time this had happened in Tests.

RECORD PARTNERSHIPS FOR EACH WICKET

For England

323 for 1st	J. B. Hobbs and W. Rhodes at Melbourne		1911-12
382 for 2nd†	L. Hutton and M. Leyland at The Oval		1938
262 for 3rd	W. R. Hammond and D. R. Jardine at Adelaide		1928-29
288 for 4th	N. Hussain and G. P. Thorpe at Birmingham		1997
206 for 5th	E. Paynter and D. C. S. Compton at Nottingham		1938
215 for 6th	{ L. Hutton and J. Hardstaff jun. at The Oval		1938
	{ G. Boycott and A. P. E. Knott at Nottingham		1977
143 for 7th	F. E. Woolley and J. Vine at Sydney		1911-12
124 for 8th	E. H. Hendren and H. Larwood at Brisbane		1928-29
151 for 9th	W. H. Scotton and W. W. Read at The Oval		1884
130 for 10th†	R. E. Foster and W. Rhodes at Sydney		1903-04

For Australia

329 for 1st	G. R. Marsh and M. A. Taylor at Nottingham.	1989
451 for 2nd†	W. H. Ponsford and D. G. Bradman at The Oval	1934
276 for 3rd	D. G. Bradman and A. L. Hassett at Brisbane	1946-47
388 for 4th†	W. H. Ponsford and D. G. Bradman at Leeds	1934
405 for 5th†	S. G. Barnes and D. G. Bradman at Sydney	1946-47
346 for 6th†	J. H. Fingleton and D. G. Bradman at Melbourne	1936-37
165 for 7th	C. Hill and H. Trumble at Melbourne	1897-98
243 for 8th†	R. J. Hartigan and C. Hill at Adelaide	1907-08
154 for 9th†	S. E. Gregory and J. McC. Blackham at Sydney	1894-95
127 for 10th†	J. M. Taylor and A. A. Mailey at Sydney.	1924-25

† *Record partnership against all countries.*

MOST RUNS IN A SERIES

England in England	732 (average 81.33)	D. I. Gower	1985
England in Australia	905 (average 113.12)	W. R. Hammond	1928-29
Australia in England	974 (average 139.14)	D. G. Bradman	1930
Australia in Australia	810 (average 90.00)	D. G. Bradman	1936-37

TEN WICKETS OR MORE IN A MATCH

For England (37)

13-163 (6-42, 7-121)	S. F. Barnes, Melbourne	1901-02
14-102 (7-28, 7-74)	W. Bates, Melbourne	1882-83
10-105 (5-46, 5-59)	A. V. Bedser, Melbourne	1950-51
14-99 (7-55, 7-44)	A. V. Bedser, Nottingham	1953
11-102 (6-44, 5-58)	C. Blythe, Birmingham	1909
11-176 (6-78, 5-98)	I. T. Botham, Perth	1979-80
10-253 (6-125, 4-128)	I. T. Botham, The Oval	1981
11-74 (5-29, 6-45)	J. Briggs, Lord's	1886
12-136 (6-49, 6-87)	J. Briggs, Adelaide	1891-92
10-148 (5-34, 5-114)	J. Briggs, The Oval	1893
10-104 (6-77, 4-27)†	R. M. Ellison, Birmingham	1985
10-179 (5-102, 5-77)†	K. Farnes, Nottingham	1934
10-60 (6-41, 4-19)	J. T. Hearne, The Oval	1896
11-113 (5-58, 6-55)	J. C. Laker, Leeds	1956
19-90 (9-37, 10-53)	J. C. Laker, Manchester	1956
10-124 (5-96, 5-28)	H. Larwood, Sydney	1932-33
11-76 (6-48, 5-28)	W. H. Lockwood, Manchester	1902
12-104 (7-36, 5-68)	G. A. Lohmann, The Oval	1886
10-87 (8-35, 2-52)	G. A. Lohmann, Sydney	1886-87
10-142 (8-58, 2-84)	G. A. Lohmann, Sydney	1891-92
12-102 (6-50, 6-52)†	F. Martin, The Oval.	1890
11-68 (7-31, 4-37)	R. Peel, Manchester	1888
15-124 (7-56, 8-68)	W. Rhodes, Melbourne	1903-04
10-156 (5-49, 5-107)†	T. Richardson, Manchester	1893
11-173 (6-39, 5-134)	T. Richardson, Lord's	1896
13-244 (7-168, 6-76)	T. Richardson, Manchester	1896
10-204 (8-94, 2-110)	T. Richardson, Sydney	1897-98

11-228 (6-130, 5-98)†	M. W. Tate, Sydney.	1924-25
11-88 (5-58, 6-30)	F. S. Trueman, Leeds	1961
11-93 (7-66, 4-27)	P. C. R. Tufnell, The Oval	1997
10-130 (4-45, 6-85)	F. H. Tyson, Sydney	1954-55
10-82 (4-37, 6-45)	D. L. Underwood, Leeds	1972
11-215 (7-113, 4-102)	D. L. Underwood, Adelaide.	1974-75
15-104 (7-61, 8-43)	H. Verity, Lord's	1934
10-57 (6-41, 4-16)	W. Voce, Brisbane	1936-37
13-256 (5-130, 8-126)	J. C. White, Adelaide.	1928-29
10-49 (5-29, 5-20)	F. E. Woolley, The Oval	1912

For Australia (41)

10-151 (5-107, 5-44)	T. M. Alderman, Leeds	1989
10-239 (4-129, 6-110)	L. O'B. Fleetwood-Smith, Adelaide	1936-37
10-160 (4-88, 6-72)	G. Giffen, Sydney.	1891-92
11-82 (5-45, 6-37)†	C. V. Grimmett, Sydney	1924-25
10-201 (5-107, 5-94)	C. V. Grimmett, Nottingham	1930
10-122 (5-65, 5-57)	R. M. Hogg, Perth	1978-79
10-66 (5-30, 5-36)	R. M. Hogg, Melbourne	1978-79
12-175 (5-85, 7-90)†	H. V. Hordern, Sydney.	1911-12
10-161 (5-95, 5-66)	H. V. Hordern, Sydney.	1911-12
10-164 (7-88, 3-76)	E. Jones, Lord's	1899
11-134 (6-47, 5-87)	G. F. Lawson, Brisbane	1982-83
10-181 (5-58, 5-123)	D. K. Lillee, The Oval	1972
11-165 (6-26, 5-139)	D. K. Lillee, Melbourne	1976-77
11-138 (6-60, 5-78)	D. K. Lillee, Melbourne	1979-80
11-159 (7-89, 4-70)	D. K. Lillee, The Oval	1981
11-85 (7-58, 4-27)	C. G. Macartney, Leeds	1909
11-157 (8-97, 3-60)	C. J. McDermott, Perth	1990-91
12-107 (5-57, 7-50)	S. C. G. MacGill, Sydney	1998-99
10-302 (5-160, 5-142)	A. A. Mailey, Adelaide	1920-21
13-236 (4-115, 9-121)	A. A. Mailey, Melbourne	1920-21
16-137 (8-84, 8-53)†	R. A. L. Massie, Lord's	1972
10-152 (5-72, 5-80)	K. R. Miller, Lord's	1956
13-77 (7-17, 6-60)	M. A. Noble, Melbourne	1901-02
11-103 (5-51, 6-52)	M. A. Noble, Sheffield.	1902
10-129 (5-63, 5-66)	W. J. O'Reilly, Melbourne	1932-33
11-129 (4-75, 7-54)	W. J. O'Reilly, Nottingham	1934
10-122 (5-66, 5-56)	W. J. O'Reilly, Leeds.	1938
11-165 (7-68, 4-97)	G. E. Palmer, Sydney	1881-82
10-126 (7-65, 3-61)	G. E. Palmer, Melbourne	1882-83
13-148 (6-97, 7-51)	B. A. Reid, Melbourne	1990-91
13-110 (6-48, 7-62)	F. R. Spofforth, Melbourne	1878-79
14-90 (7-46, 7-44)	F. R. Spofforth, The Oval	1882
11-117 (4-73, 7-44)	F. R. Spofforth, Sydney	1882-83
10-144 (4-54, 6-90)	F. R. Spofforth, Sydney	1884-85
12-89 (6-59, 6-30)	H. Trumble, The Oval	1896
10-128 (4-75, 6-53)	H. Trumble, Manchester	1902
12-173 (8-65, 4-108)	H. Trumble, The Oval	1902
12-87 (5-44, 7-43)	C. T. B. Turner, Sydney	1887-88
10-63 (5-27, 5-36)	C. T. B. Turner, Lord's.	1888
11-110 (3-39, 8-71)	S. K. Warne, Brisbane	1994-95
11-229 (7-165, 4-64)	S. K. Warne, The Oval	2001

† *On first appearance in England–Australia Tests.*

Note: J. Briggs, J. C. Laker, T. Richardson in 1896, R. M. Hogg, A. A. Mailey, H. Trumble and
C. T. B. Turner took ten wickets or more in successive Tests. J. Briggs was omitted, however, from
the England team for the first Test match in 1893.

MOST WICKETS IN A SERIES

England in England	46 (average 9.60)	J. C. Laker	1956
England in Australia	38 (average 23.18)	M. W. Tate	1924-25
Australia in England	42 (average 21.26)	T. M. Alderman (6 Tests)	1981
Australia in Australia	41 (average 12.85)	R. M. Hogg (6 Tests)	1978-79

WICKET-KEEPING – MOST DISMISSALS

	M	Ct	St	Total
†R. W. Marsh (Australia)	42	141	7	148
I. A. Healy (Australia)	33	123	12	135
A. P. E. Knott (England)	34	97	8	105
†W. A. Oldfield (Australia)	38	59	31	90
A. A. Lilley (England)	32	65	19	84
A. T. W. Grout (Australia)	22	69	7	76
T. G. Evans (England)	31	64	12	76

† *The number of catches by R. W. Marsh (141) and stumpings by W. A. Oldfield (31) are respective records in England–Australia Tests.*

SCORERS OF OVER 2,000 RUNS

	T		I		NO		R		HS		Avge
D. G. Bradman	37	..	63	..	7	..	5,028	..	334	..	89.78
J. B. Hobbs	41	..	71	..	4	..	3,636	..	187	..	54.26
A. R. Border	47	..	82	..	19	..	3,548	..	200*	..	56.31
D. I. Gower	42	..	77	..	4	..	3,269	..	215	..	44.78
G. Boycott	38	..	71	..	9	..	2,945	..	191	..	47.50
S. R. Waugh	41	..	65	..	18	..	2,895	..	177*	..	61.59
W. R. Hammond	33	..	58	..	3	..	2,852	..	251	..	51.85
H. Sutcliffe	27	..	46	..	5	..	2,741	..	194	..	66.85
C. Hill	41	..	76	..	1	..	2,660	..	188	..	35.46
J. H. Edrich	32	..	57	..	3	..	2,644	..	175	..	48.96
G. A. Gooch	42	..	79	..	0	..	2,632	..	196	..	33.31
G. S. Chappell	35	..	65	..	8	..	2,619	..	144	..	45.94
M. A. Taylor	33	..	61	..	2	..	2,496	..	219	..	42.30
M. C. Cowdrey	43	..	75	..	4	..	2,433	..	113	..	34.26
L. Hutton	27	..	49	..	6	..	2,428	..	364	..	56.46
R. N. Harvey	37	..	68	..	5	..	2,416	..	167	..	38.34
V. T. Trumper	40	..	74	..	5	..	2,263	..	185*	..	32.79
D. C. Boon	31	..	57	..	8	..	2,237	..	184	..	45.65
W. M. Lawry	29	..	51	..	5	..	2,233	..	166	..	48.54
M. E. Waugh	29	..	51	..	7	..	2,204	..	140	..	50.09
S. E. Gregory	52	..	92	..	7	..	2,193	..	201	..	25.80
W. W. Armstrong	42	..	71	..	9	..	2,172	..	158	..	35.03
I. M. Chappell	30	..	56	..	4	..	2,138	..	192	..	41.11
K. F. Barrington	23	..	39	..	6	..	2,111	..	256	..	63.96
A. R. Morris	24	..	43	..	2	..	2,080	..	206	..	50.73

BOWLERS WITH 100 WICKETS

	T		Balls		R		W		5W/i		Avge
D. K. Lillee	29	..	8,516	..	3,507	..	167	..	11	..	21.00
I. T. Botham	36	..	8,479	..	4,093	..	148	..	9	..	27.65
H. Trumble	31	..	7,895	..	2,945	..	141	..	9	..	20.88
R. G. D. Willis	35	..	7,294	..	3,346	..	128	..	7	..	26.14
S. K. Warne	23	..	7,005	..	2,693	..	118	..	7	..	22.82
M. A. Noble	39	..	6,845	..	2,860	..	115	..	9	..	24.86
R. R. Lindwall	29	..	6,728	..	2,559	..	114	..	6	..	22.44
W. Rhodes	41	..	5,791	..	2,616	..	109	..	6	..	24.00
S. F. Barnes	20	..	5,749	..	2,288	..	106	..	12	..	21.58
C. V. Grimmett	22	..	9,224	..	3,439	..	106	..	11	..	32.44
D. L. Underwood	29	..	8,000	..	2,770	..	105	..	4	..	26.38
A. V. Bedser	21	..	7,065	..	2,859	..	104	..	7	..	27.49
G. Giffen	31	..	6,457	..	2,791	..	103	..	7	..	27.09
W. J. O'Reilly	19	..	7,864	..	2,587	..	102	..	8	..	25.36
R. Peel	20	..	5,216	..	1,715	..	101	..	5	..	16.98
C. T. B. Turner	17	..	5,195	..	1,670	..	101	..	11	..	16.53
T. M. Alderman	17	..	4,717	..	2,117	..	100	..	11	..	21.17
J. R. Thomson	21	..	4,951	..	2,418	..	100	..	5	..	24.18

RESULTS ON EACH GROUND

In England

THE OVAL (33)

England (15)	1880, 1886, 1888, 1890, 1893, 1896, 1902, 1912, 1926, 1938, 1953, 1968, 1985, 1993, 1997.
Australia (6)	1882, 1930, 1934, 1948, 1972, 2001.
Drawn (12)	1884, 1899, 1905, 1909, 1921, 1956, 1961, 1964, 1975, 1977, 1981, 1989.

MANCHESTER (27)

England (7)	1886, 1888, 1905, 1956, 1972, 1977, 1981.
Australia (7)	1896, 1902, 1961, 1968, 1989, 1993, 1997.
Drawn (13)	1884, 1893, 1899, 1909, 1912, 1921, 1926, 1930, 1934, 1948, 1953, 1964, 1985.

The scheduled matches in 1890 and 1938 were abandoned without a ball bowled and are excluded.

LORD'S (32)

England (5)	1884, 1886, 1890, 1896, 1934.
Australia (13)	1888, 1899, 1909, 1921, 1930, 1948, 1956, 1961, 1972, 1985, 1989, 1993, 2001.
Drawn (14)	1893, 1902, 1905, 1912, 1926, 1938, 1953, 1964, 1968, 1975, 1977, 1980, 1981, 1997.

NOTTINGHAM (19)

England (3)	1905, 1930, 1977.
Australia (7)	1921, 1934, 1948, 1981, 1989, 1997, 2001.
Drawn (9)	1899, 1926, 1938, 1953, 1956, 1964, 1972, 1985, 1993.

LEEDS (23)

England (7)	1956, 1961, 1972, 1977, 1981, 1985, 2001.
Australia (8)	1909, 1921, 1938, 1948, 1964, 1989, 1993, 1997.
Drawn (8)	1899, 1905, 1926, 1930, 1934, 1953, 1968, 1975.

BIRMINGHAM (11)

England (4)	1909, 1981, 1985, 1997.
Australia (3)	1975, 1993, 2001.
Drawn (4)	1902, 1961, 1968, 1989.

SHEFFIELD (1)

Australia (1)	1902.

In Australia

MELBOURNE (51)

England (19)	*1876, 1882, 1884*(2), *1894*(2), *1903, 1907, 1911*(2), *1924, 1928, 1950, 1954,*
	1962, 1974, 1982, 1986, 1998.
Australia (25)	*1876, 1878, 1882, 1891, 1897*(2), *1901*(2), *1903, 1907, 1920*(2), *1924, 1928,*
	1932, 1936(2), *1950, 1958*(2), *1976, 1978, 1979, 1990, 1994.*
Drawn (7)	*1881*(2), *1946, 1965*(2), *1970, 1974.*

One scheduled match in 1970-71 was abandoned without a ball bowled and is excluded.

SYDNEY (51)

England (20)	*1882, 1886*(2), *1887, 1894, 1897, 1901, 1903*(2), *1911, 1928, 1932*(2), *1936, 1954,*
	1965, 1970(2), *1978*(2).
Australia (24)	*1881*(2), *1882, 1884*(2), *1891, 1894, 1897, 1901, 1907*(2), *1911, 1920*(2), *1924*(2),
	1946(2), *1950, 1962, 1974, 1979, 1986, 1998.*
Drawn (7)	*1954, 1958, 1962, 1982, 1987, 1990, 1994.*

ADELAIDE (27)

England (8)	*1884, 1891, 1911, 1928, 1932, 1954, 1978, 1994.*
Australia (14)	*1894, 1897, 1901, 1903, 1907, 1920, 1924, 1936, 1950, 1958, 1965, 1974, 1982,*
	1998.
Drawn (5)	*1946, 1962, 1970, 1986, 1990.*

BRISBANE Exhibition Ground (1)

England (1)	*1928.*

BRISBANE Woolloongabba (16)

England (4)	*1932, 1936, 1978, 1986.*
Australia (8)	*1946, 1950, 1954, 1958, 1974, 1982, 1990, 1994.*
Drawn (4)	*1962, 1965, 1970, 1998.*

PERTH (9)

England (1)	*1978.*
Australia (5)	*1974, 1979, 1990, 1994, 1998.*
Drawn (3)	*1970, 1982, 1986.*

For Tests in Australia the first year of the season is given in italics; i.e. 1876 denotes the 1876-77 season.

Shane Warne flew 16 friends and relatives to Cape Town for his 100th Test. They saw him bowl 95 overs, take eight wickets, score a half-century, win the match award – and propel his team to yet another series triumph.

South Africa v Australia, page 1290

ENGLAND v SOUTH AFRICA

Season	England	Captains	South Africa	T	E	SA	D
1888-89	C. A. Smith[1]		O. R. Dunell[2]	2	2	0	0
1891-92	W. W. Read		W. H. Milton	1	1	0	0
1895-96	Lord Hawke[3]		E. A. Halliwell[4]	3	3	0	0
1898-99	Lord Hawke		M. Bisset	2	2	0	0
1905-06	P. F. Warner		P. W. Sherwell	5	1	4	0
1907	R. E. Foster		P. W. Sherwell	3	1	0	2
1909-10	H. D. G. Leveson Gower[5]		S. J. Snooke	5	2	3	0
1912	C. B. Fry		F. Mitchell[6]	3	3	0	0
1913-14	J. W. H. T. Douglas		H. W. Taylor	5	4	0	1
1922-23	F. T. Mann		H. W. Taylor	5	2	1	2
1924	A. E. R. Gilligan[7]		H. W. Taylor	5	3	0	2
1927-28	R. T. Stanyforth[8]		H. G. Deane	5	2	2	1
1929	J. C. White[9]		H. G. Deane	5	2	0	3
1930-31	A. P. F. Chapman		H. G. Deane[10]	5	0	1	4
1935	R. E. S. Wyatt		H. F. Wade	5	0	1	4
1938-39	W. R. Hammond		A. Melville	5	1	0	4
1947	N. W. D. Yardley		A. Melville	5	3	0	2
1948-49	F. G. Mann		A. D. Nourse	5	2	0	3
1951	F. R. Brown		A. D. Nourse	5	3	1	1
1955	P. B. H. May		J. E. Cheetham[11]	5	3	2	0
1956-57	P. B. H. May		C. B. van Ryneveld[12]	5	2	2	1
1960	M. C. Cowdrey		D. J. McGlew	5	3	0	2
1964-65	M. J. K. Smith		T. L. Goddard	5	1	0	4
1965	M. J. K. Smith		P. L. van der Merwe	3	0	1	2
1994	M. A. Atherton		K. C. Wessels	3	1	1	1
1995-96	M. A. Atherton		W. J. Cronje	5	0	1	4
1998	A. J. Stewart		W. J. Cronje	5	2	1	2
1999-2000	N. Hussain		W. J. Cronje	5	1	2	2

			T	E	SA	D
In South Africa	. . . .		68	26	16	26
In England	. . . .		52	24	7	21
Totals	. . . .		120	50	23	47

Notes: The following deputised for the official touring captain or were appointed by the home authority for only a minor proportion of the series:

[1]M. P. Bowden (Second). [2]W. H. Milton (Second). [3]Sir T. C. O'Brien (First). [4]A. R. Richards (Third). [5]F. L. Fane (Fourth and Fifth). [6]L. J. Tancred (Second and Third). [7]J. W. H. T. Douglas (Fourth). [8]G. T. S. Stevens (Fifth). [9]A. W. Carr (Fourth and Fifth). [10]E. P. Nupen (First), H. B. Cameron (Fourth and Fifth). [11]D. J. McGlew (Third and Fourth). [12]D. J. McGlew (Second).

HIGHEST INNINGS TOTALS

For England in England: 554-8 dec. at Lord's 1947
         in South Africa: 654-5 at Durban 1938-39

For South Africa in England: 552-5 dec. at Manchester 1998
            in South Africa: 572-7 at Durban 1999-2000

LOWEST INNINGS TOTALS

For England in England: 76 at Leeds 1907
        in South Africa: 92 at Cape Town 1898-99

For South Africa in England: 30 at Birmingham 1924
        in South Africa: 30 at Port Elizabeth 1895-96

INDIVIDUAL HUNDREDS

For England (96)

R. Abel (1)
120   Cape Town . . 1888-89
L. E. G. Ames (2)
148*   The Oval . . .   1935
115   Cape Town . . 1938-39
M. A. Atherton (3)
185* Johannesburg 1995-96
103   Birmingham   1998
108   Port Elizabeth 1999-00
K. F. Barrington (2)
148* Durban 1964-65
121   Johannesburg 1964-65
G. Boycott (1)
117   Port Elizabeth 1964-65
L. C. Braund (1)
104†   Lord's   1907
M. A. Butcher (1)
116   Leeds   1998
D. C. S. Compton (7)
163†   Nottingham . .   1947
208   Lord's   1947
115   Manchester. .   1947
113   The Oval . .   1947
114   Johannesburg 1948-49
112   Nottingham . .   1951
158   Manchester. .   1955
M. C. Cowdrey (3)
101   Cape Town . . 1956-57
155   The Oval . . .   1960
105   Nottingham . .   1965
D. Denton (1)
104   Johannesburg 1909-10
E. R. Dexter (1)
172   Johannesburg 1964-65
J. W. H. T. Douglas (1)
119†   Durban 1913-14
W. J. Edrich (3)
219   Durban 1938-39
189   Lord's   1947
191   Manchester. .   1947
F. L. Fane (1)
143   Johannesburg 1905-06
C. B. Fry (1)
129   The Oval . . .   1907
P. A. Gibb (2)
106†   Johannesburg 1938-39
120   Durban 1938-39
W. R. Hammond (6)
138* Birmingham   1929
101* The Oval . . .   1929

136* Durban 1930-31
181   Cape Town . . 1938-39
120   Durban 1938-39
140   Durban 1938-39
T. W. Hayward (1)
122   Johannesburg 1895-96
E. H. Hendren (2)
132   Leeds   1924
142   The Oval . . .   1924
G. A. Hick (2)
110   Leeds   1994
141   Centurion. . . 1995-96
A. J. L. Hill (1)
124   Cape Town . . 1895-96
J. B. Hobbs (2)
187   Cape Town . . 1909-10
211   Lord's   1924
N. Hussain (2)
105   Lord's   1998
146* Durban 1999-00
L. Hutton (4)
100   Leeds   1947
158   Johannesburg 1948-49
123   Johannesburg 1948-49
100   Leeds   1951
D. J. Insole (1)
110* Durban 1956-57
M. Leyland (2)
102   Lord's   1929
161   The Oval . . .   1935
F. G. Mann (1)
136* Port Elizabeth 1948-49
P. B. H. May (3)
138†   Leeds   1951
112   Lord's   1955
117   Manchester. .   1955
C. P. Mead (3)
102   Johannesburg 1913-14
117   Port Elizabeth 1913-14
181   Durban 1922-23
P. H. Parfitt (1)
122* Johannesburg 1964-65
J. M. Parks (1)
108* Durban 1964-65
E. Paynter (3)
117*⎫
100 ⎬†Johannesburg 1938-39
243   Durban 1938-39
G. Pullar (1)
175   The Oval . . .   1960

W. Rhodes (1)
152   Johannesburg 1913-14
P. E. Richardson (1)
117†   Johannesburg 1956-57
R. W. V. Robins (1)
108   Manchester. .   1935
A. C. Russell (2)
140 ⎫
111 ⎬ Durban 1922-23
R. T. Simpson (1)
137   Nottingham . .   1951
M. J. K. Smith (1)
121   Cape Town . . 1964-65
R. H. Spooner (1)
119†   Lord's   1912
A. J. Stewart (1)
164   Manchester. .   1998
H. Sutcliffe (6)
122   Lord's   1924
102   Johannesburg 1927-28
114   Birmingham   1929
100   Lord's   1929
104 ⎫
109*⎬ The Oval . . .   1929
M. W. Tate (1)
100* Lord's   1929
E. Tyldesley (2)
122   Johannesburg 1927-28
100   Durban 1927-28
J. T. Tyldesley (1)
112   Cape Town . . 1898-99
B. H. Valentine (1)
112   Cape Town . . 1938-39
P. F. Warner (1)
132*†‡Johannesburg 1898-99
C. Washbrook (1)
195   Johannesburg 1948-49
A. J. Watkins (1)
111   Johannesburg 1948-49
H. Wood (1)
134* Cape Town . . 1891-92
F. E. Woolley (3)
115* Johannesburg 1922-23
134* Lord's   1924
154   Manchester. .   1929
R. E. S. Wyatt (2)
113   Manchester. .   1929
149   Nottingham .   1935

For South Africa (72)

E. J. Barlow (1)
138   Cape Town. .   1964-65
K. C. Bland (2)
144*   Johannesburg   1964-65
127   The Oval . . .   1965
M. V. Boucher (1)
108   Durban   1999-00
R. H. Catterall (3)
120   Birmingham .   1924
120   Lord's   1924
119   Durban   1927-28
W. J. Cronje (1)
126   Nottingham .   1998
D. J. Cullinan (2)
108   Johannesburg   1999-00
120   Cape Town. .   1999-00
E. L. Dalton (2)
117   The Oval . . .   1935
102   Johannesburg   1938-39
W. R. Endean (1)
116*   Leeds   1955
G. A. Faulkner (1)
123   Johannesburg   1909-10
T. L. Goddard (1)
112   Johannesburg   1964-65
C. M. H. Hathorn (1)
102   Johannesburg   1905-06
J. H. Kallis (2)
132   Manchester. .   1998
105   Cape Town. .   1999-00
G. Kirsten (3)
110   Johannesburg   1995-96
210   Manchester. .   1998
275   Durban   1999-00
P. N. Kirsten (1)
104   Leeds   1994

L. Klusener (1)
174   Port Elizabeth   1999-00
D. J. McGlew (2)
104*   Manchester. .   1955
133   Leeds   1955
R. A. McLean (3)
142   Lord's   1955
100   Durban   1956-57
109   Manchester. .   1960
B. M. McMillan (1)
100*   Johannesburg   1995-96
A. Melville (4)
103   Durban   1938-39
189 }
104*} Nottingham .   1947
117   Lord's   1947
B. Mitchell (7)
123   Cape Town. .   1930-31
164*   Lord's   1935
128   The Oval . . .   1935
109   Durban   1938-39
120 }
189*} The Oval . . .   1947
120   Cape Town. .   1948-49
A. D. Nourse (7)
120   Cape Town. .   1938-39
103   Durban   1938-39
149   Nottingham .   1947
115   Manchester. .   1947
112   Cape Town. .   1948-49
129*   Johannesburg   1948-49
208   Nottingham .   1951
H. G. Owen-Smith (1)
129   Leeds   1929
A. J. Pithey (1)
154   Cape Town. .   1964-65
R. G. Pollock (2)
137   Port Elizabeth   1964-65

125   Nottingham .   1965
J. N. Rhodes (1)
117   Lord's   1998
E. A. B. Rowan (2)
156*   Johannesburg   1948-49
236   Leeds   1951
P. W. Sherwell (1)
115   Lord's   1907
I. J. Siedle (1)
141   Cape Town. .   1930-31
J. H. Sinclair (1)
106   Cape Town. .   1898-99
H. W. Taylor (7)
109   Durban   1913-14
176   Johannesburg   1922-23
101   Johannesburg   1922-23
102   Durban   1922-23
101   Johannesburg   1927-28
121   The Oval . . .   1929
117   Cape Town. .   1930-31
P. G. V. van der Bijl (1)
125   Durban   1938-39
K. G. Viljoen (1)
124   Manchester. .   1935
W. W. Wade (1)
125   Port Elizabeth   1948-49
J. H. B. Waite (1)
113   Manchester. .   1955
K. C. Wessels (1)
105†   Lord's   1994
G. C. White (2)
147   Johannesburg   1905-06
118   Durban   1909-10
P. L. Winslow (1)
108   Manchester. .   1955

† On first appearance in England–South Africa Tests. K. C. Wessels had earlier scored 162 on his Test debut for Australia against England at Brisbane in 1982-83.

‡ P. F. Warner carried his bat through the second innings.

Notes: A. Melville's four hundreds were made in successive Test innings. H. Wood scored the only hundred of his career in a Test match.

RECORD PARTNERSHIPS FOR EACH WICKET

For England

359	for 1st†	L. Hutton and C. Washbrook at Johannesburg	1948-49
280	for 2nd	P. A. Gibb and W. J. Edrich at Durban	1938-39
370	for 3rd†	W. J. Edrich and D. C. S. Compton at Lord's	1947
197	for 4th	W. R. Hammond and L. E. G. Ames at Cape Town	1938-39
237	for 5th	D. C. S. Compton and N. W. D. Yardley at Nottingham	1947
206*	for 6th	K. F. Barrington and J. M. Parks at Durban	1964-65
115	for 7th	J. W. H. T. Douglas and M. C. Bird at Durban	1913-14
154	for 8th	C. W. Wright and H. R. Bromley-Davenport at Johannesburg	1895-96
71	for 9th	H. Wood and J. T. Hearne at Cape Town	1891-92
92	for 10th	A. C. Russell and A. E. R. Gilligan at Durban	1922-23

For South Africa

260 for 1st†	B. Mitchell and I. J. Siedle at Cape Town	1930-31
238 for 2nd	G. Kirsten and J. H. Kallis at Manchester	1998
319 for 3rd	A. Melville and A. D. Nourse at Nottingham	1947
214 for 4th†	H. W. Taylor and H. G. Deane at The Oval	1929
192 for 5th†	G. Kirsten and M. V. Boucher at Durban	1999-2000
171 for 6th	J. H. B. Waite and P. L. Winslow at Manchester	1955
123 for 7th	H. G. Deane and E. P. Nupen at Durban	1927-28
119 for 8th	L. Klusener and M. V. Boucher at Port Elizabeth	1999-2000
137 for 9th	E. L. Dalton and A. B. C. Langton at The Oval	1935
103 for 10th†	H. G. Owen-Smith and A. J. Bell at Leeds	1929

† *Record partnership against all countries.*

MOST RUNS IN A SERIES

England in England	753 (average 94.12)	D. C. S. Compton .	1947
England in South Africa	653 (average 81.62)	E. Paynter	1938-39
South Africa in England	621 (average 69.00)	A. D. Nourse	1947
South Africa in South Africa . . .	582 (average 64.66)	H. W. Taylor	1922-23

TEN WICKETS OR MORE IN A MATCH

For England (25)

11-110 (5-25, 6-85)†	S. F. Barnes, Lord's	1912
10-115 (6-52, 4-63)	S. F. Barnes, Leeds	1912
13-57 (5-28, 8-29)	S. F. Barnes, The Oval	1912
10-105 (5-57, 5-48)	S. F. Barnes, Durban	1913-14
17-159 (8-56, 9-103)	S. F. Barnes, Johannesburg	1913-14
14-144 (7-56, 7-88)	S. F. Barnes, Durban	1913-14
12-112 (7-58, 5-54)	A. V. Bedser, Manchester	1951
11-118 (6-68, 5-50)	C. Blythe, Cape Town	1905-06
15-99 (8-59, 7-40)	C. Blythe, Leeds	1907
10-104 (7-46, 3-58)	C. Blythe, Cape Town	1909-10
15-28 (7-17, 8-11)	J. Briggs, Cape Town	1888-89
13-91 (6-54, 7-37)†	J. J. Ferris, Cape Town	1891-92
10-122 (5-60, 5-62)	A. R. C. Fraser, Nottingham	1998
10-207 (7-115, 3-92)	A. P. Freeman, Leeds	1929
12-171 (7-71, 5-100)	A. P. Freeman, Manchester	1929
12-130 (7-70, 5-60)	G. Geary, Johannesburg	1927-28
11-90 (6-7, 5-83)	A. E. R. Gilligan, Birmingham	1924
10-119 (4-64, 6-55)	J. C. Laker, The Oval	1951
15-45 (7-38, 8-7)†	G. A. Lohmann, Port Elizabeth	1895-96
12-71 (9-28, 3-43)	G. A. Lohmann, Johannesburg	1895-96
10-138 (1-81, 9-57)	D. E. Malcolm, The Oval	1994
11-97 (6-63, 5-34)	J. B. Statham, Lord's	1960
12-101 (7-52, 5-49)	R. Tattersall, Lord's	1951
12-89 (5-53, 7-36)	J. H. Wardle, Cape Town	1956-57
10-175 (5-95, 5-80)	D. V. P. Wright, Lord's	1947

For South Africa (7)

11-127 (6-53, 5-74)	A. A. Donald, Johannesburg	1999-2000
11-112 (4-49, 7-63)†	A. E. Hall, Cape Town	1922-23
11-150 (5-63, 6-87)	E. P. Nupen, Johannesburg	1930-31
10-87 (5-53, 5-34)	P. M. Pollock, Nottingham	1965
12-127 (4-57, 8-70)	S. J. Snooke, Johannesburg	1905-06

| 13-192 (4-79, 9-113) | H. J. Tayfield, Johannesburg | 1956-57 |
| 12-181 (5-87, 7-94) | A. E. E. Vogler, Johannesburg | 1909-10 |

† *On first appearance in England–South Africa Tests.*

Notes: S. F. Barnes took ten wickets or more in his first five Tests v South Africa and in six of his seven Tests v South Africa. A. P. Freeman and G. A. Lohmann took ten wickets or more in successive matches.

MOST WICKETS IN A SERIES

England in England	34 (average 8.29)	S. F. Barnes	1912
England in South Africa	49 (average 10.93)	S. F. Barnes	1913-14
South Africa in England	33 (average 19.78)	A. A. Donald	1998
South Africa in South Africa	37 (average 17.18)	H. J. Tayfield	1956-57

ENGLAND v WEST INDIES

Captains

Season	England	West Indies	T	E	WI	D
1928	A. P. F. Chapman	R. K. Nunes	3	3	0	0
1929-30	Hon. F. S. G. Calthorpe	E. L. G. Hoad¹	4	1	1	2
1933	D. R. Jardine²	G. C. Grant	3	2	0	1
1934-35	R. E. S. Wyatt	G. C. Grant	4	1	2	1
1939	W. R. Hammond	R. S. Grant	3	1	0	2
1947-48	G. O. B. Allen³	J. D. C. Goddard⁴	4	0	2	2
1950	N. W. D. Yardley⁵	J. D. C. Goddard	4	1	3	0
1953-54	L. Hutton	J. B. Stollmeyer	5	2	2	1
1957	P. B. H. May	J. D. C. Goddard	5	3	0	2
1959-60	P. B. H. May⁶	F. C. M. Alexander	5	1	0	4

THE WISDEN TROPHY

Captains

Season	England	West Indies	T	E	WI	D	Held by
1963	E. R. Dexter	F. M. M. Worrell	5	1	3	1	WI
1966	M. C. Cowdrey⁷	G. S. Sobers	5	1	3	1	WI
1967-68	M. C. Cowdrey	G. S. Sobers	5	1	0	4	E
1969	R. Illingworth	G. S. Sobers	3	2	0	1	E
1973	R. Illingworth	R. B. Kanhai	3	0	2	1	WI
1973-74	M. H. Denness	R. B. Kanhai	5	1	1	3	WI
1976	A. W. Greig	C. H. Lloyd	5	0	3	2	WI
1980	I. T. Botham	C. H. Lloyd⁸	5	0	1	4	WI
1980-81‡	I. T. Botham	C. H. Lloyd	4	0	2	2	WI
1984	D. I. Gower	C. H. Lloyd	5	0	5	0	WI
1985-86	D. I. Gower	I. V. A. Richards	5	0	5	0	WI
1988	J. E. Emburey⁹	I. V. A. Richards	5	0	4	1	WI
1989-90‡	G. A. Gooch¹⁰	I. V. A. Richards¹¹	4	1	2	1	WI
1991	G. A. Gooch	I. V. A. Richards	5	2	2	1	WI
1993-94	M. A. Atherton	R. B. Richardson¹²	5	1	3	1	WI
1995	M. A. Atherton	R. B. Richardson	6	2	2	2	WI
1997-98	M. A. Atherton	B. C. Lara	6	1	3	2	WI
2000	N. Hussain¹³	J. C. Adams	5	3	1	1	E

			T	E	WI	D
	In England		70	21	29	20
	In West Indies		56	10	23	23
	Totals		126	31	52	43

† *The Second Test, at Georgetown, was cancelled owing to political pressure and is excluded.*
‡ *The Second Test, at Georgetown, was abandoned without a ball being bowled and is excluded.*

Notes: The following deputised for the official touring captain or were appointed by the home authority for only a minor proportion of the series:

[1]N. Betancourt (Second), M. P. Fernandes (Third), R. K. Nunes (Fourth). [2]R. E. S. Wyatt (Third). [3]K. Cranston (First). [4]G. A. Headley (First), G. E. Gomez (Second). •[5]F. R. Brown (Fourth). [6]M. C. Cowdrey (Fourth and Fifth). [7]M. J. K. Smith (First), D. B. Close (Fifth). [8]I. V. A. Richards (Fifth). [9]M. W. Gatting (First), C. S. Cowdrey (Fourth), G. A. Gooch (Fifth). [10]A. J. Lamb (Fourth and Fifth). [11]D. L. Haynes (Third). [12]C. A. Walsh (Fifth). [13]A. J. Stewart (Second).

HIGHEST INNINGS TOTALS

For England in England: 619-6 dec. at Nottingham	. . . .	1957
in West Indies: 849 at Kingston	. . . .	1929-30
For West Indies in England: 692-8 dec. at The Oval	. . . .	1995
in West Indies: 681-8 dec. at Port-of-Spain	. . . .	1953-54

LOWEST INNINGS TOTALS

For England in England: 71 at Manchester	. . . .	1976
in West Indies: 46 at Port-of-Spain	. . . .	1993-94
For West Indies in England: 54 at Lord's	. . . .	2000
in West Indies: 102 at Bridgetown	. . . .	1934-35

INDIVIDUAL HUNDREDS

For England (100)

L. E. G. Ames (3)
105 Port-of-Spain 1929-30
149 Kingston . . . 1929-30
126 Kingston . . . 1934-35

D. L. Amiss (4)
174 Port-of-Spain 1973-74
262* Kingston . . . 1973-74
118 Georgetown 1973-74
203 The Oval . . . 1976

M. A. Atherton (4)
144 Georgetown . 1993-94
135 St John's . . . 1993-94
113 Nottingham . 1995
108 The Oval . . . 2000

A. H. Bakewell (1)
107† The Oval . . . 1933

K. F. Barrington (3)
128† Bridgetown . 1959-60
121 Port-of-Spain 1959-60
143 Port-of-Spain 1967-68

G. Boycott (5)
116 Georgetown . 1967-68
128 Manchester . 1969
106 Lord's 1969
112 Port-of-Spain 1973-74
104* St John's . . 1980-81

D. C. S. Compton (2)
120† Lord's 1939
133 Port-of-Spain 1953-54

M. C. Cowdrey (6)
154† Birmingham . 1957
152 Lord's 1957
114 Kingston . . . 1959-60
119 Port-of-Spain 1959-60
101 Kingston . . . 1967-68
148 Port-of-Spain 1967-68

E. R. Dexter (2)
136*† Bridgetown . 1959-60
110 Georgetown . 1959-60

J. H. Edrich (1)
146 Bridgetown . 1967-68

T. G. Evans (1)
104 Manchester . 1950

K. W. R. Fletcher (1)
129* Bridgetown . 1973-74

G. Fowler (1)
106 Lord's 1984

G. A. Gooch (5)
123 Lord's 1980
116 Bridgetown . 1980-81
153 Kingston . . . 1980-81
146 Nottingham . 1988
154*‡ Leeds 1991

D. I. Gower (1)
154* Kingston . . . 1980-81

T. W. Graveney (5)
258 Nottingham . 1957
164 The Oval . . . 1957
109 Nottingham . 1966

165 The Oval . . . 1966
118 Port-of-Spain 1967-68

A. W. Greig (3)
148 Bridgetown . 1973-74
121 Georgetown . 1973-74
116 Leeds 1976

S. C. Griffith (1)
140† Port-of-Spain 1947-48

W. R. Hammond (1)
138 The Oval . . . 1939

J. H. Hampshire (1)
107† Lord's 1969

F. C. Hayes (1)
106*† The Oval . . . 1973

E. H. Hendren (2)
205* Port-of-Spain 1929-30
123 Georgetown . 1929-30

G. A. Hick (1)
118* Nottingham . 1995

J. B. Hobbs (1)
159 The Oval . . . 1928

N. Hussain (1)
106 St John's . . . 1997-98

L. Hutton (5)
196† Lord's 1939
165* The Oval . . . 1939
202*‡ The Oval . . . 1950
169 Georgetown . 1953-54
205 Kingston . . . 1953-54

R. Illingworth (1)
113 Lord's . . 1969
D. R. Jardine (1)
127 Manchester . . 1933
A. P. E. Knott (1)
116 Leeds 1976
A. J. Lamb (6)
110 Lord's 1984
100 Leeds 1984
100* Manchester . . 1984
113 Lord's 1988
132 Kingston . . . 1989-90
119 Bridgetown . . 1989-90
P. B. H. May (3)
135 Port-of-Spain 1953-54
285* Birmingham . 1957
104 Nottingham . . 1957
C. Milburn (1)
126* Lord's 1966
J. T. Murray (1)
112† The Oval . . . 1966

J. M. Parks (1)
101*† Port-of-Spain 1959-60
W. Place (1)
107 Kingston . . . 1947-48
M. R. Ramprakash (1)
154 Bridgetown . . 1997-98
P. E. Richardson (2)
126 Nottingham . . 1957
107 The Oval . . . 1957
J. D. Robertson (1)
133 Port-of-Spain 1947-48
A. Sandham (2)
152† Bridgetown . 1929-30
325 Kingston . . . 1929-30
M. J. K. Smith (1)
108 Port-of-Spain 1959-60
R. A. Smith (3)
148* Lord's 1991
109 The Oval . . . 1991
175 St John's . . . 1993-94

D. S. Steele (1)
106† Nottingham . . 1976
A. J. Stewart (3)
118 ⎱ Bridgetown . 1993-94
143 ⎰
105 Manchester . . 2000
R. Subba Row (1)
100† Georgetown . . 1959-60
G. P. Thorpe (1)
103 Bridgetown . . 1997-98
E. Tyldesley (1)
122† Lord's 1928
C. Washbrook (2)
114† Lord's 1950
102 Nottingham . . 1950
W. Watson (1)
116† Kingston . . . 1953-54
P. Willey (1)
100* The Oval . . . 1980
102* St John's . . . 1980-81

For West Indies (111)

J. C. Adams (1)
137 Georgetown . 1993-94
K. L. T. Arthurton (1)
126 Kingston . . . 1993-94
I. Barrow (1)
105 Manchester . . 1933
C. A. Best (1)
164 Bridgetown . 1989-90
B. F. Butcher (2)
133 Lord's 1963
209* Nottingham . . 1966
G. M. Carew (1)
107 Port-of-Spain 1947-48
S. Chanderpaul (1)
118 Georgetown . 1997-98
C. A. Davis (1)
103 Lord's 1969
P. J. L. Dujon (1)
101 Manchester . . 1984
R. C. Fredericks (3)
150 Birmingham . 1973
138 Lord's 1976
109 Leeds 1976
A. G. Ganteaume (1)
112† Port-of-Spain 1947-48
H. A. Gomes (2)
143 Birmingham . 1984
104* Leeds 1984
C. G. Greenidge (7)
134 ⎱ Manchester . 1976
101 ⎰
115 Leeds 1976
214* Lord's 1984
223 Manchester . . 1984
103 Lord's 1988
149 St John's . . . 1989-90

D. L. Haynes (5)
184 Lord's 1980
125 The Oval . . . 1984
131 St John's . . . 1985-86
109 Bridgetown . . 1989-90
167 St John's . . . 1989-90
G. A. Headley (8)
176† Bridgetown . . 1929-30
114 ⎱ Georgetown . 1929-30
112 ⎰
223 Kingston . . . 1929-30
169* Manchester . . 1933
270* Kingston . . . 1934-35
106 ⎱ Lord's 1939
107 ⎰
D. A. J. Holford (1)
105* Lord's 1966
J. K. Holt (1)
166 Bridgetown . 1953-54
C. L. Hooper (3)
111 Lord's 1991
127 The Oval . . . 1995
108* St John's . . . 1997-98
C. C. Hunte (3)
182 Manchester . . 1963
108* The Oval . . . 1963
135 Manchester . . 1966
B. D. Julien (1)
121 Lord's 1973
A. I. Kallicharran (2)
158 Port-of-Spain 1973-74
119 Bridgetown . 1973-74
R. B. Kanhai (5)
110 Port-of-Spain 1959-60
104 The Oval . . . 1966
153 Port-of-Spain 1967-68

**150 Georgetown . 1967-68
157 Lord's 1973
C. B. Lambert (1)
104 St John's . . . 1997-98
B. C. Lara (6)
167 Georgetown . 1993-94
375 St John's . . . 1993-94
145 Manchester . . 1995
152 Nottingham . . 1995
179 The Oval . . . 1995
112 Manchester . . 2000
C. H. Lloyd (5)
118* Port-of-Spain 1967-68
113* Bridgetown . . 1967-68
132 The Oval . . . 1973
101 Manchester . . 1980
100 Bridgetown . 1980-81
S. M. Nurse (2)
137 Leeds 1966
136 Port-of-Spain 1967-68
A. F. Rae (2)
106 Lord's 1950
109 The Oval . . . 1950
I. V. A. Richards (8)
232† Nottingham . . 1976
135 Manchester . . 1976
291 The Oval . . . 1976
145 Lord's 1980
182* Bridgetown . 1980-81
114 St John's . . . 1980-81
117 Birmingham . . 1984
110* St John's . . . 1985-86
R. B. Richardson (4)
102 Port-of-Spain 1985-86
160 Bridgetown . 1985-86
104 Birmingham . 1991
121 The Oval . . . 1991

C. A. Roach (2)			145	Georgetown	1959-60
122	Bridgetown	1929-30	102	Leeds	1963
209	Georgetown	1929-30	161	Manchester	1966
L. G. Rowe (3)			163*	Lord's	1966
120	Kingston	1973-74	174	Leeds	1966
302	Bridgetown	1973-74	113*	Kingston	1967-68
123	Port-of-Spain	1973-74	152	Georgetown	1967-68
O. G. Smith (2)			150*	Lord's	1973
161†	Birmingham	1957	**C. L. Walcott** (4)		
168	Nottingham	1957	220	Bridgetown	1953-54
G. S. Sobers (10)			124	Port-of-Spain	1953-54
226	Bridgetown	1959-60	116	Kingston	1953-54
147	Kingston	1959-60			

E. D. Weekes (3)			
141	Kingston	1947-48	
129	Nottingham	1950	
206	Port-of-Spain	1953-54	
K. H. Weekes (1)			
137	The Oval	1939	
F. M. M. Worrell (6)			
131*	Georgetown	1947-48	
261	Nottingham	1950	
138	The Oval	1950	
167	Port-of-Spain	1953-54	
191*‡	Nottingham	1957	
197*	Bridgetown	1959-60	

† *On first appearance in England–West Indies Tests. S. C. Griffith is the only England player to hit his maiden century in first-class cricket in his first Test.*

‡ *Carried his bat.*

RECORD PARTNERSHIPS FOR EACH WICKET

For England

212	for 1st	C. Washbrook and R. T. Simpson at Nottingham	1950
266	for 2nd	P. E. Richardson and T. W. Graveney at Nottingham	1957
303	for 3rd	M. A. Atherton and R. A. Smith at St John's	1993-94
411	for 4th†	P. B. H. May and M. C. Cowdrey at Birmingham	1957
150	for 5th	A. J. Stewart and G. P. Thorpe at Bridgetown	1993-94
205	for 6th	M. R. Ramprakash and G. P. Thorpe at Bridgetown	1997-98
197	for 7th†	M. J. K. Smith and J. M. Parks at Port-of-Spain	1959-60
217	for 8th	T. W. Graveney and J. T. Murray at The Oval	1966
109	for 9th	G. A. R. Lock and P. I. Pocock at Georgetown	1967-68
128	for 10th	K. Higgs and J. A. Snow at The Oval	1966

For West Indies

298	for 1st†	C. G. Greenidge and D. L. Haynes at St John's	1989-90
287*	for 2nd	C. G. Greenidge and H. A. Gomes at Lord's	1984
338	for 3rd†	E. D. Weekes and F. M. M. Worrell at Port-of-Spain	1953-54
399	for 4th†	G. S. Sobers and F. M. M. Worrell at Bridgetown	1959-60
265	for 5th	S. M. Nurse and G. S. Sobers at Leeds	1966
274*	for 6th†	G. S. Sobers and D. A. J. Holford at Lord's	1966
155*	for 7th‡	G. S. Sobers and B. D. Julien at Lord's	1973
99	for 8th	C. A. McWatt and J. K. Holt at Georgetown	1953-54
150	for 9th	E. A. E. Baptiste and M. A. Holding at Birmingham	1984
70	for 10th	I. R. Bishop and D. Ramnarine at Georgetown	1997-98

† *Record partnership against all countries.*

‡ *231 runs were added for this wicket in two separate partnerships: G. S. Sobers retired ill and was replaced by K. D. Boyce when 155 had been added.*

TEN WICKETS OR MORE IN A MATCH

For England (12)

11-98 (7-44, 4-54)	T. E. Bailey, Lord's		1957
11-110 (8-53, 3-57)	A. R. C. Fraser, Port-of-Spain		1997-98
10-93 (5-54, 5-39)	A. P. Freeman, Manchester		1928
13-156 (8-86, 5-70)	A. W. Greig, Port-of-Spain		1973-74

11-48 (5-28, 6-20)	G. A. R. Lock, The Oval	1957
10-137 (4-60, 6-77)	D. E. Malcolm, Port-of-Spain	1989-90
11-96 (5-37, 6-59)†	C. S. Marriott, The Oval	1933
10-142 (4-82, 6-60)	J. A. Snow, Georgetown	1967-68
10-195 (5-105, 5-90)†	G. T. S. Stevens, Bridgetown.	1929-30
11-152 (6-100, 5-52)	F. S. Trueman, Lord's	1963
12-119 (5-75, 7-44)	F. S. Trueman, Birmingham	1963
11-149 (4-79, 7-70)	W. Voce, Port-of-Spain	1929-30

For West Indies (15)

10-127 (2-82, 8-45)	C. E. L. Ambrose, Bridgetown	1989-90
11-84 (5-60, 6-24)	C. E. L. Ambrose, Port-of-Spain	1993-94
10-174 (5-105, 5-69)	K. C. G. Benjamin, Nottingham	1995
11-147 (5-70, 6-77)†	K. D. Boyce, The Oval	1973
11-229 (5-137, 6-92)	W. Ferguson, Port-of-Spain	1947-48
11-157 (5-59, 6-98)†	L. R. Gibbs, Manchester	1963
10-106 (5-37, 5-69)	L. R. Gibbs, Manchester	1966
14-149 (8-92, 6-57)	M. A. Holding, The Oval	1976
10-96 (5-41, 5-55)†	H. H. H. Johnson, Kingston	1947-48
10-92 (6-32, 4-60)	M. D. Marshall, Lord's	1988
11-152 (5-66, 6-86)	S. Ramadhin, Lord's	1950
10-123 (5-60, 5-63)	A. M. E. Roberts, Lord's	1976
11-204 (8-104, 3-100)†	A. L. Valentine, Manchester	1950
10-160 (4-121, 6-39)	A. L. Valentine, The Oval.	1950
10-117 (4-43, 6-74)	C. A. Walsh, Lord's.	2000

† *On first appearance in England–West Indies Tests.*

Note: F. S. Trueman took ten wickets or more in successive matches.

ENGLAND v NEW ZEALAND

Captains

Season	England	New Zealand	T	E	NZ	D
1929-30	A. H. H. Gilligan	T. C. Lowry	4	1	0	3
1931	D. R. Jardine	T. C. Lowry	3	1	0	2
1932-33	D. R. Jardine¹	M. L. Page	2	0	0	2
1937	R. W. V. Robins	M. L. Page	3	1	0	2
1946-47	W. R. Hammond	W. A. Hadlee	1	0	0	1
1949	F. G. Mann²	W. A. Hadlee	4	0	0	4
1950-51	F. R. Brown	W. A. Hadlee	2	1	0	1
1954-55	L. Hutton	G. O. Rabone	2	2	0	0
1958	P. B. H. May	J. R. Reid	5	4	0	1
1958-59	P. B. H. May	J. R. Reid	2	1	0	1
1962-63	E. R. Dexter	J. R. Reid	3	3	0	0
1965	M. J. K. Smith	J. R. Reid	3	3	0	0
1965-66	M. J. K. Smith	B. W. Sinclair³	3	0	0	3
1969	R. Illingworth	G. T. Dowling	3	2	0	1
1970-71	R. Illingworth	G. T. Dowling	2	1	0	1
1973	R. Illingworth	B. E. Congdon	3	2	0	1
1974-75	M. H. Denness	B. E. Congdon	2	1	0	1
1977-78	G. Boycott	M. G. Burgess	3	1	1	1
1978	J. M. Brearley	M. G. Burgess	3	3	0	0
1983	R. G. D. Willis	G. P. Howarth	4	3	1	0
1983-84	R. G. D. Willis	G. P. Howarth	3	0	1	2
1986	M. W. Gatting	J. V. Coney	3	0	1	2
1987-88	M. W. Gatting	J. J. Crowe⁴	3	0	0	3
1990	G. A. Gooch	J. G. Wright	3	1	0	2

Season	England	New Zealand	T	E	NZ	D
1991-92	G. A. Gooch	M. D. Crowe	3	2	0	1
1994	M. A. Atherton	K. R. Rutherford	3	1	0	2
1996-97	M. A. Atherton	L. K. Germon[5]	3	2	0	1
1999	N. Hussain[6]	S. P. Fleming	4	1	2	1
2001-02	N. Hussain	S. P. Fleming	3	1	1	1

	T	E	NZ	D
In New Zealand	41	16	3	22
In England	44	22	4	18
Totals	85	38	7	40

Notes: The following deputised for the official touring captain or were appointed by the home authority for only a minor proportion of the series:

[1]R. E. S. Wyatt (Second). [2]F. R. Brown (Third and Fourth). [3]M. E. Chapple (First). [4]J. G. Wright (Third). [5]S. P. Fleming (Third). [6]M. A. Butcher (Third).

HIGHEST INNINGS TOTALS

For England in England: 567-8 dec. at Nottingham 1994
in New Zealand: 593-6 dec. at Auckland 1974-75

For New Zealand in England: 551-9 dec. at Lord's 1973
in New Zealand: 537 at Wellington. 1983-84

LOWEST INNINGS TOTALS

For England in England: 126 at Birmingham 1999
in New Zealand: 64 at Wellington. 1977-78

For New Zealand in England: 47 at Lord's. 1958
in New Zealand: 26 at Auckland 1954-55

INDIVIDUAL HUNDREDS

For England (86)

G. O. B. Allen (1)
122† Lord's 1931
L. E. G. Ames (2)
137† Lord's 1931
103 Christchurch . 1932-33
D. L. Amiss (2)
138*† Nottingham . 1973
164* Christchurch . 1974-75
M. A. Atherton (4)
151† Nottingham . 1990
101 Nottingham . 1994
111 Manchester. . 1994
118 Christchurch . 1996-97

T. E. Bailey (1)
134* Christchurch . 1950-51
K. F. Barrington (3)
126† Auckland. . . 1962-63
137 Birmingham . 1965
163 Leeds 1965
I. T. Botham (3)
103 Christchurch . 1977-78
103 Nottingham . 1983
138 Wellington . . 1983-84
E. H. Bowley (1)
109 Auckland . . . 1929-30

G. Boycott (2)
115 Leeds 1973
131 Nottingham . 1978
B. C. Broad (1)
114† Christchurch . 1987-88
D. C. S. Compton (2)
114 Leeds 1949
116 Lord's 1949
M. C. Cowdrey (2)
128* Wellington . . 1962-63
119 Lord's 1965
M. H. Denness (1)
181 Auckland . . . 1974-75

E. R. Dexter (1)
141 Christchurch. 1958-59

B. L. D'Oliveira (1)
100 Christchurch. 1970-71

K. S. Duleepsinhji (2)
117 Auckland... 1929-30
109 The Oval... 1931

J. H. Edrich (3)
310*† Leeds 1965
115 Lord's..... 1969
155 Nottingham . 1969

W. J. Edrich (1)
100 The Oval... 1949

K. W. R. Fletcher (2)
178 Lord's..... 1973
216 Auckland... 1974-75

A. Flintoff (1)
137† Christchurch. 2001-02

G. Fowler (1)
105† The Oval... 1983

M. W. Gatting (1)
121 The Oval... 1986

G. A. Gooch (4)
183 Lord's..... 1986
154 Birmingham. 1990
114 Auckland... 1991-92
210 Nottingham . 1994

D. I. Gower (4)
111† The Oval... 1978
112* Leeds 1983
108 Lord's..... 1983
131 The Oval... 1986

A. W. Greig (1)
139† Nottingham . 1973

W. R. Hammond (4)
100* The Oval.... 1931
227 Christchurch. 1932-33
336* Auckland.... 1932-33
140 Lord's..... 1937

J. Hardstaff jun. (2)
114† Lord's..... 1937
103 The Oval ... 1937

N. Hussain (1)
106 Christchurch. 2001-02

L. Hutton (3)
100 Manchester... 1937
101 Leeds 1949
206 The Oval.... 1949

B. R. Knight (1)
125† Auckland... 1962-63

A. P. E. Knott (1)
101 Auckland... 1970-71

A. J. Lamb (3)
102*† The Oval... 1983
137* Nottingham . 1983
142 Wellington .. 1991-92

G. B. Legge (1)
196 Auckland... 1929-30

P. B. H. May (3)
113* Leeds 1958
101 Manchester.. 1958
124* Auckland... 1958-59

C. A. Milton (1)
104*† Leeds 1958

P. H. Parfitt (1)
131*† Auckland... 1962-63

C. T. Radley (1)
158 Auckland.... 1977-78

D. W. Randall (2)
164 Wellington .. 1983-84
104 Auckland... 1983-84

P. E. Richardson (1)
100† Birmingham. 1958

J. D. Robertson (1)
121† Lord's..... 1949

P. J. Sharpe (1)
111 Nottingham . 1969

R. T. Simpson (1)
103† Manchester... 1949

A. J. Stewart (4)
148 Christchurch. 1991-92
107 Wellington .. 1991-92
119 Lord's..... 1994
173 Auckland... 1996-97

H. Sutcliffe (2)
117† The Oval... 1931
109* Manchester... 1931

C. J. Tavaré (1)
109† The Oval... 1983

G. P. Thorpe (3)
119† Auckland... 1996-97
108 Wellington .. 1996-97
200* Christchurch. 2001-02

C. Washbrook (1)
103* Leeds 1949

For New Zealand (44)

N. J. Astle (3)
102*† Auckland... 1996-97
101 Manchester.. 1999
222 Christchurch. 2001-02

J. G. Bracewell (1)
110 Nottingham . 1986

M. G. Burgess (2)
104 Auckland... 1970-71
105 Lord's..... 1973

J. V. Coney (1)
174* Wellington .. 1983-84

B. E. Congdon (3)
104 Christchurch. 1965-66
176 Nottingham . 1973
175 Lord's..... 1973

J. J. Crowe (1)
128 Auckland... 1983-84

M. D. Crowe (5)
100 Wellington .. 1983-84
106 Lord's..... 1986
143 Wellington .. 1987-88
142 Lord's..... 1994
115 Manchester.. 1994

C. S. Dempster (2)
136 Wellington .. 1929-30
120 Lord's..... 1931

M. P. Donnelly (1)
206 Lord's..... 1949

S. P. Fleming (1)
129 Auckland... 1996-97

T. J. Franklin (1)
101 Lord's..... 1990

M. J. Greatbatch (1)
107*† Auckland... 1987-88

W. A. Hadlee (1)
116 Christchurch. 1946-47

M. J. Horne (1)
100 Lord's..... 1999

G. P. Howarth (3)
122 } Auckland... 1977-78
102 }
123 Lord's..... 1978

A. H. Jones (1)
143 Wellington .. 1991-92

C. D. McMillan (1)
107* Manchester.. 1999

J. E. Mills (1)
117† Wellington .. 1929-30

M. L. Page (1)
104 Lord's..... 1931

J. M. Parker (1)
121 Auckland... 1974-75

V. Pollard (2)
116 Nottingham . 1973
105* Lord's..... 1973

J. R. Reid (1)
100 Christchurch. 1962-63

K. R. Rutherford (1)
107* Wellington .. 1987-88

B. W. Sinclair (1)
114 Auckland... 1965-66

I. D. S. Smith (1)
113* Auckland... 1983-84

B. Sutcliffe (2)
101 Manchester.. 1949
116 Christchurch. 1950-51

J. G. Wright (4)
130 Auckland.... 1983-84
119 The Oval ... 1986
103 Auckland... 1987-88
116 Wellington .. 1991-92

† *On first appearance in England–New Zealand Tests.*

RECORD PARTNERSHIPS FOR EACH WICKET

For England

223	for 1st	G. Fowler and C. J. Tavaré at The Oval....................	1983
369	for 2nd	J. H. Edrich and K. F. Barrington at Leeds	1965
245	for 3rd	J. Hardstaff jun. and W. R. Hammond at Lord's	1937
266	for 4th	M. H. Denness and K. W. R. Fletcher at Auckland	1974-75
242	for 5th	W. R. Hammond and L. E. G. Ames at Christchurch	1932-33
281	for 6th†	G. P. Thorpe and A. Flintoff at Christchurch...............	2001-02
149	for 7th	A. P. E. Knott and P. Lever at Auckland	1970-71
246	for 8th†	L. E. G. Ames and G. O. B. Allen at Lord's	1931
163*	for 9th†	M. C. Cowdrey and A. C. Smith at Wellington	1962-63
59	for 10th	A. P. E. Knott and N. Gifford at Nottingham	1973

For New Zealand

276	for 1st	C. S. Dempster and J. E. Mills at Wellington	1929-30
241	for 2nd†	J. G. Wright and A. H. Jones at Wellington	1991-92
210	for 3rd	B. A. Edgar and M. D. Crowe at Lord's	1986
155	for 4th	M. D. Crowe and M. J. Greatbatch at Wellington	1987-88
180	for 5th	M. D. Crowe and S. A. Thomson at Lord's	1994
141	for 6th	M. D. Crowe and A. C. Parore at Manchester...............	1994
117	for 7th	D. N. Patel and C. L. Cairns at Christchurch	1991-92
104	for 8th	D. A. R. Moloney and A. W. Roberts at Lord's.............	1937
118	for 9th	J. V. Coney and B. L. Cairns at Wellington	1983-84
118	for 10th	N. J. Astle and C. L. Cairns at Christchurch	2001-02

† *Record partnership against all countries.*

TEN WICKETS OR MORE IN A MATCH

For England (8)

11-140 (6-101, 5-39)	I. T. Botham, Lord's	1978
10-149 (5-98, 5-51)	A. W. Greig, Auckland......................	1974-75
11-65 (4-14, 7-51)	G. A. R. Lock, Leeds	1958
11-84 (5-31, 6-53)	G. A. R. Lock, Christchurch	1958-59
11-147 (4-100, 7-47)†	P. C. R. Tufnell, Christchurch	1991-92
11-70 (4-38, 7-32)†	D. L. Underwood, Lord's	1969
12-101 (6-41, 6-60)	D. L. Underwood, The Oval	1969
12-97 (6-12, 6-85)	D. L. Underwood, Christchurch	1970-71

For New Zealand (5)

10-144 (7-74, 3-70)	B. L. Cairns, Leeds........................	1983
10-140 (4-73, 6-67)	J. Cowie, Manchester.......................	1937
10-100 (4-74, 6-26)	R. J. Hadlee, Wellington....................	1977-78
10-140 (6-80, 4-60)	R. J. Hadlee, Nottingham	1986
11-169 (6-76, 5-93)	D. J. Nash, Lord's	1994

† *On first appearance in England–New Zealand Tests.*

Note: D. L. Underwood took 12 wickets in successive matches against New Zealand in 1969 and 1970-71.

ENGLAND v INDIA

Captains

Season	England	India	T	E	I	D
1932	D. R. Jardine	C. K. Nayudu	1	1	0	0
1933-34	D. R. Jardine	C. K. Nayudu	3	2	0	1
1936	G. O. B. Allen	Maharaj of Vizianagram	3	2	0	1
1946	W. R. Hammond	Nawab of Pataudi sen.	3	1	0	2
1951-52	N. D. Howard[1]	V. S. Hazare	5	1	1	3
1952	L. Hutton	V. S. Hazare	4	3	0	1
1959	P. B. H. May[2]	D. K. Gaekwad[3]	5	5	0	0
1961-62	E. R. Dexter	N. J. Contractor	5	0	2	3
1963-64	M. J. K. Smith	Nawab of Pataudi jun.	5	0	0	5
1967	D. B. Close	Nawab of Pataudi jun.	3	3	0	0
1971	R. Illingworth	A. L. Wadekar	3	0	1	2
1972-73	A. R. Lewis	A. L. Wadekar	5	1	2	2
1974	M. H. Denness	A. L. Wadekar	3	3	0	0
1976-77	A. W. Greig	B. S. Bedi	5	3	1	1
1979	J. M. Brearley	S. Venkataraghavan	4	1	0	3
1979-80	J. M. Brearley	G. R. Viswanath	1	1	0	0
1981-82	K. W. R. Fletcher	S. M. Gavaskar	6	0	1	5
1982	R. G. D. Willis	S. M. Gavaskar	3	1	0	2
1984-85	D. I. Gower	S. M. Gavaskar	5	2	1	2
1986	M. W. Gatting[4]	Kapil Dev	3	0	2	1
1990	G. A. Gooch	M. Azharuddin	3	1	0	2
1992-93	G. A. Gooch[5]	M. Azharuddin	3	0	3	0
1996	M. A. Atherton	M. Azharuddin	3	1	0	2
2001-02	N. Hussain	S. C. Ganguly	3	0	1	2
2002	N. Hussain	S. C. Ganguly	4	1	1	2
	In England		45	23	4	18
	In India		46	10	12	24
	Totals.		91	33	16	42

Notes: The 1932 Indian touring team was captained by the Maharaj of Porbandar but he did not play in the Test match.

The following deputised for the official touring captain or were appointed by the home authority for only a minor proportion of the series:

[1]D. B. Carr (Fifth). [2]M. C. Cowdrey (Fourth and Fifth). [3]Pankaj Roy (Second). [4]D. I. Gower (First). [5]A. J. Stewart (Second).

HIGHEST INNINGS TOTALS

For England in England: 653-4 dec. at Lord's 1990
in India: 652-7 dec. at Madras 1984-85

For India in England: 628-8 dec. at Leeds 2002
in India: 591 at Bombay 1992-93

LOWEST INNINGS TOTALS

For England in England: 101 at The Oval 1971
in India: 102 at Bombay 1981-82

For India in England: 42 at Lord's 1974
in India: 83 at Madras 1976-77

INDIVIDUAL HUNDREDS

For England (83)

D. L. Amiss (2)
188   Lord's   1974
179   Delhi   1976-77
M. A. Atherton (2)
131   Manchester. .   1990
160   Nottingham . .   1996
K. F. Barrington (3)
151* Bombay . . .   1961-62
172   Kanpur   1961-62
113* Delhi   1961-62
I. T. Botham (5)
137   Leeds   1979
114   Bombay . . .   1979-80
142   Kanpur   1981-82
128   Manchester. .   1982
208   The Oval . . .   1982
G. Boycott (4)
246*† Leeds   1967
155   Birmingham .   1979
125   The Oval . . .   1979
105   Delhi   1981-82
M. C. Cowdrey (3)
160   Leeds   1959
107   Calcutta . . .   1963-64
151   Delhi   1963-64
J. P. Crawley (1)
100*† Lord's   2002
M. H. Denness (2)
118   Lord's   1974
100   Birmingham .   1974
E. R. Dexter (1)
126* Kanpur   1961-62
B. L. D'Oliveira (1)
109† Leeds   1967
J. H. Edrich (1)
100* Manchester. .   1974
T. G. Evans (1)
104   Lord's   1952
K. W. R. Fletcher (2)
113   Bombay . . .   1972-73
123* Manchester. .   1974
G. Fowler (1)
201   Madras   1984-85

M. W. Gatting (3)
136   Bombay. . . .   1984-85
207   Madras   1984-85
183* Birmingham .   1986
G. A. Gooch (5)
127   Madras   1981-82
114   Lord's   1986
333 }
123 } Lord's   1990
116   Manchester. .   1990
D. I. Gower (2)
200*† Birmingham .   1979
157* The Oval . . .   1990
T. W. Graveney (2)
175† Bombay . . .   1951-52
151   Lord's   1967
A. W. Greig (3)
148   Bombay . . .   1972-73
106   Lord's   1974
103   Calcutta . . .   1976-77
W. R. Hammond (2)
167   Manchester. .   1936
217   The Oval . . .   1936
J. Hardstaff jun. (1)
205* Lord's   1946
G. A. Hick (1)
178   Bombay . . .   1992-93
N. Hussain (4)
128† Birmingham .   1996
107* Nottingham .   1996
155   Lord's   2002
110   Leeds   2002
L. Hutton (2)
150   Lord's   1952
104   Manchester. .   1952
R. Illingworth (1)
107   Manchester. .   1971
B. R. Knight (1)
127   Kanpur   1963-64
A. J. Lamb (3)
107   The Oval . . .   1982
139   Lord's   1990
109   Manchester. .   1990

A. R. Lewis (1)
125   Kanpur   1972-73
C. C. Lewis (1)
117   Madras   1992-93
D. Lloyd (1)
214* Birmingham .   1974
B. W. Luckhurst (1)
101   Manchester. .   1971
P. B. H. May (1)
106   Nottingham .   1959
P. H. Parfitt (1)
121   Kanpur   1963-64
G. Pullar (2)
131   Manchester. .   1959
119   Kanpur   1961-62
D. W. Randall (1)
126   Lord's   1982
R. T. Robinson (1)
160   Delhi   1984-85
R. C. Russell (1)
124   Lord's   1996
D. S. Sheppard (1)
119   The Oval . . .   1952
M. J. K. Smith (1)
100† Manchester. .   1959
R. A. Smith (2)
100*† Lord's   1990
121* Manchester. .   1990
C. J. Tavaré (1)
149   Delhi   1981-82
B. H. Valentine (1)
136† Bombay . . .   1933-34
M. P. Vaughan (3)
100   Lord's   2002
197   Nottingham .   2002
195   The Oval . . .   2002
C. F. Walters (1)
102   Madras   1933-34
A. J. Watkins (1)
137*† Delhi   1951-52
C. White (1)
121   Ahmedabad .   2001-02
T. S. Worthington (1)
128   The Oval . . .   1936

For India (73)

A. B. Agarkar (1)
109*† Lord's   2002
L. Amarnath (1)
118† Bombay . . .   1933-34
M. Azharuddin (6)
110† Calcutta . . .   1984-85
105   Madras   1984-85
122   Kanpur   1984-85
121   Lord's   1990
179   Manchester. .   1990

182   Calcutta   1992-93
A. A. Baig (1)
112† Manchester. .   1959
D. Dasgupta (1)
100† Mohali   2001-02
R. Dravid (3)
115   Nottingham .   2002
148   Leeds   2002
217   The Oval . . .   2002

F. M. Engineer (1)
121   Bombay. . . .   1972-73
S. C. Ganguly (3)
131† Lord's   1996
136   Nottingham .   1996
128   Leeds   2002
S. M. Gavaskar (4)
101   Manchester. .   1974
108   Bombay. . . .   1976-77

221	The Oval . . .	1979
172	Bangalore . .	1981-82

Hanumant Singh (1)

105†	Delhi	1963-64

V. S. Hazare (2)

164*	Delhi	1951-52
155	Bombay. . . .	1951-52

M. L. Jaisimha (2)

127	Delhi	1961-62
129	Calcutta. . . .	1963-64

V. G. Kambli (1)

224	Bombay. . . .	1992-93

Kapil Dev (2)

116	Kanpur	1981-82
110	The Oval . . .	1990

S. M. H. Kirmani (1)

102	Bombay. . . .	1984-85

B. K. Kunderan (2)

192	Madras	1963-64
100	Delhi	1963-64

V. L. Manjrekar (3)

133	Leeds	1952
189*	Delhi	1961-62
108	Madras	1963-64

V. Mankad (1)

184	Lord's	1952

V. M. Merchant (3)

114	Manchester. .	1936
128	The Oval . . .	1946
154	Delhi	1951-52

Mushtaq Ali (1)

112	Manchester. .	1936

R. G. Nadkarni (1)

122*	Kanpur	1963-64

Nawab of Pataudi jun. (3)

103	Madras	1961-62
203*	Delhi	1963-64
148	Leeds	1967

S. M. Patil (1)

129*	Manchester. .	1982

D. G. Phadkar (1)

115	Calcutta. . . .	1951-52

Pankaj Roy (2)

140	Bombay. . . .	1951-52
111	Madras	1951-52

V. Sehwag (1)

106	Nottingham .	2002

R. J. Shastri (4)

142	Bombay. . . .	1984-85
111	Calcutta. . . .	1984-85
100	Lord's	1990
187	The Oval . . .	1990

N. S. Sidhu (1)

106	Madras	1992-93

S. R. Tendulkar (6)

119*	Manchester. .	1990
165	Madras	1992-93
122	Birmingham .	1996
177	Nottingham .	1996
103	Ahmedabad .	2001-02
193	Leeds	2002

P. R. Umrigar (3)

130*	Madras	1951-52
118	Manchester. .	1959
147*	Kanpur	1961-62

D. B. Vengsarkar (5)

103	Lord's	1979
157	Lord's	1982
137	Kanpur	1984-85
126*	Lord's	1986
102*	Leeds	1986

G. R. Viswanath (4)

113	Bombay. . . .	1972-73
113	Lord's	1979
107	Delhi	1981-82
222	Madras	1981-82

Yashpal Sharma (1)

140	Madras	1981-82

† *On first appearance in England–India Tests.*

Notes: G. A. Gooch's match aggregate of 456 (333 and 123) for England at Lord's in 1990 is the record in Test matches and the only instance of a batsman scoring a triple-hundred and a hundred in the same first-class match. His 333 is the highest innings in any match at Lord's.

    M. Azharuddin scored hundreds in each of his first three Tests.

RECORD PARTNERSHIPS FOR EACH WICKET

For England

225 for 1st	G. A. Gooch and M. A. Atherton at Manchester	1990
241 for 2nd	G. Fowler and M. W. Gatting at Madras	1984-85
308 for 3rd	G. A. Gooch and A. J. Lamb at Lord's	1990
266 for 4th	W. R. Hammond and T. S. Worthington at The Oval	1936
254 for 5th†	K. W. R. Fletcher and A. W. Greig at Bombay	1972-73
171 for 6th	I. T. Botham and R. W. Taylor at Bombay	1979-80
125 for 7th	D. W. Randall and P. H. Edmonds at Lord's	1982
168 for 8th	R. Illingworth and P. Lever at Manchester	1971
103 for 9th	C. White and M. J. Hoggard at Nottingham	2002
70 for 10th	P. J. W. Allott and R. G. D. Willis at Lord's	1982

For India

213 for 1st	S. M. Gavaskar and C. P. S. Chauhan at The Oval	1979
192 for 2nd	F. M. Engineer and A. L. Wadekar at Bombay	1972-73
316 for 3rd†‡	G. R. Viswanath and Yashpal Sharma at Madras	1981-82
249 for 4th	S. R. Tendulkar and S. C. Ganguly at Leeds	2002
214 for 5th	M. Azharuddin and R. J. Shastri at Calcutta	1984-85
130 for 6th	S. M. H. Kirmani and Kapil Dev at The Oval	1982
235 for 7th†	R. J. Shastri and S. M. H. Kirmani at Bombay	1984-85
128 for 8th	R. J. Shastri and S. M. H. Kirmani at Delhi	1981-82

| 104 for 9th | R. J. Shastri and Madan Lal at Delhi . . . . | 1981-82 |
| 63 for 10th | A. B. Agarkar and A. Nehra at Lord's . . . . | 2002 |

† *Record partnership against all countries.*

‡ *415 runs were added between the fall of the 2nd and 3rd wickets: D. B. Vengsarkar retired hurt when he and Viswanath had added 99 runs.*

TEN WICKETS OR MORE IN A MATCH

For England (7)

10-78 (5-35, 5-43)†	G. O. B. Allen, Lord's	1936
11-145 (7-49, 4-96)†	A. V. Bedser, Lord's	1946
11-93 (4-41, 7-52)	A. V. Bedser, Manchester	1946
13-106 (6-58, 7-48)	I. T. Botham, Bombay	1979-80
11-163 (6-104, 5-59)†	N. A. Foster, Madras	1984-85
10-70 (7-46, 3-24)†	J. K. Lever, Delhi	1976-77
11-153 (7-49, 4-104)	H. Verity, Madras	1933-34

For India (5)

10-177 (6-105, 4-72)	S. A. Durani, Madras	1961-62
10-233 (7-115, 3-118)	A. Kumble, Ahmedabad	2001-02
12-108 (8-55, 4-53)	V. Mankad, Madras	1951-52
10-188 (4-130, 6-58)	Chetan Sharma, Birmingham	1986
12-181 (6-64, 6-117)†	L. Sivaramakrishnan, Bombay	1984-85

† *On first appearance in England–India Tests.*

Note: A. V. Bedser took 11 wickets in a match in each of the first two Tests of his career.

ENGLAND v PAKISTAN

Season	England		*Captains* Pakistan	T	E	P	D
1954	L. Hutton[1]		A. H. Kardar	4	1	1	2
1961-62	E. R. Dexter		Imtiaz Ahmed	3	1	0	2
1962	E. R. Dexter[2]		Javed Burki	5	4	0	1
1967	D. B. Close		Hanif Mohammad	3	2	0	1
1968-69	M. C. Cowdrey		Saeed Ahmed	3	0	0	3
1971	R. Illingworth		Intikhab Alam	3	1	0	2
1972-73	A. R. Lewis		Majid Khan	3	0	0	3
1974	M. H. Denness		Intikhab Alam	3	0	0	3
1977-78	J. M. Brearley[3]		Wasim Bari	3	0	0	3
1978	J. M. Brearley		Wasim Bari	3	2	0	1
1982	R. G. D. Willis[4]		Imran Khan	3	2	1	0
1983-84	R. G. D. Willis[5]		Zaheer Abbas	3	0	1	2
1987	M. W. Gatting		Imran Khan	5	0	1	4
1987-88	M. W. Gatting		Javed Miandad	3	0	1	2
1992	G. A. Gooch		Javed Miandad	5	1	2	2
1996	M. A. Atherton		Wasim Akram	3	0	2	1
2000-01	N. Hussain		Moin Khan	3	1	0	2
2001	N. Hussain[6]		Waqar Younis	2	1	1	0
	In England			39	14	8	17
	In Pakistan			21	2	2	17
	Totals			60	16	10	34

Notes: The following deputised for the official touring captain or were appointed by the home authority for only a minor proportion of the series:

[1]D. S. Sheppard (Second and Third). [2]M. C. Cowdrey (Third). [3]G. Boycott (Third). [4]D. I. Gower (Second). [5]D. I. Gower (Second and Third). [6]A. J. Stewart (Second).

HIGHEST INNINGS TOTALS

For England in England: 558-6 dec. at Nottingham 1954
in Pakistan: 546-8 dec. at Faisalabad 1983-84

For Pakistan in England: 708 at The Oval 1987
in Pakistan: 569-9 dec. at Hyderabad 1972-73

LOWEST INNINGS TOTALS

For England in England: 130 at The Oval 1954
in Pakistan: 130 at Lahore 1987-88

For Pakistan in England: 87 at Lord's 1954
in Pakistan: 158 at Karachi 2000-01

INDIVIDUAL HUNDREDS

For England (52)

D. L. Amiss (3)
112 Lahore 1972-73
158 Hyderabad . 1972-73
183 The Oval . . 1974
M. A. Atherton (1)
125 Karachi 2000-01
C. W. J. Athey (1)
123 Lord's 1987
K. F. Barrington (4)
139† Lahore . . . 1961-62
148 Lord's 1967
109* Nottingham . 1967
142 The Oval . . 1967
I. T. Botham (2)
100† Birmingham . 1978
108 Lord's 1978
G. Boycott (3)
121* Lord's 1971
112 Leeds 1971
100* Hyderabad . 1977-78
B. C. Broad (1)
116 Faisalabad . 1987-88
D. C. S. Compton (1)
278 Nottingham . 1954
M. C. Cowdrey (3)
159† Birmingham . 1962
182 The Oval . . 1962
100 Lahore . . . 1968-69
J. P. Crawley (1)
106 The Oval . . 1996

E. R. Dexter (2)
205 Karachi 1961-62
172 The Oval . . 1962
B. L. D'Oliveira (1)
114* Dacca 1968-69
K. W. R. Fletcher (1)
122 The Oval . . 1974
M. W. Gatting (2)
124 Birmingham . 1987
150* The Oval . . 1987
G. A. Gooch (1)
135 Leeds 1992
D. I. Gower (2)
152 Faisalabad . 1983-84
173* Lahore . . . 1983-84
T. W. Graveney (3)
153 Lord's 1962
114 Nottingham . 1962
105 Karachi . . . 1968-69
N. V. Knight (1)
113 Leeds 1996
A. P. E. Knott (1)
116 Birmingham . 1971
B. W. Luckhurst (1)
108*† Birmingham . 1971
C. Milburn (1)
139 Karachi . . . 1968-69
P. H. Parfitt (4)
111 Karachi . . . 1961-62

101* Birmingham . 1962
119 Leeds 1962
101* Nottingham . 1962
G. Pullar (1)
165 Dacca 1961-62
C. T. Radley (1)
106† Birmingham . 1978
D. W. Randall (1)
105 Birmingham . 1982
R. T. Robinson (1)
166† Manchester . 1987
R. T. Simpson (1)
101 Nottingham . 1954
R. A. Smith (1)
127† Birmingham . 1992
A. J. Stewart (2)
190† Birmingham . 1992
170 Leeds 1996
G. P. Thorpe (2)
118 Lahore . . . 2000-01
138 Manchester . 2001
M. E. Trescothick (1)
117 Manchester . 2001
M. P. Vaughan (1)
120 Manchester . 2001

For Pakistan (43)

Aamir Sohail (1)
205 Manchester . 1992
Abdul Razzaq (1)
100* Faisalabad . 2000-01
Alim-ud-Din (1)
109 Karachi . . . 1961-62
Asif Iqbal (3)
146 The Oval . . 1967

104* Birmingham . 1971
102 Lahore . . . 1972-73
Hanif Mohammad (3)
111 } Dacca 1961-62
104 }
187* Lord's 1967
Haroon Rashid (2)
122† Lahore . . . 1977-78
108 Hyderabad . 1977-78

Ijaz Ahmed, sen. (1)
141 Leeds 1996
Imran Khan (1)
118 The Oval . . 1987
Intikhab Alam (1)
138 Hyderabad . 1972-73
Inzamam-ul-Haq (3)
148 Lord's 1996

142	Karachi	2000-01
114	Manchester. .	2001

Javed Burki (3)

138†	Lahore	1961-62
140	Dacca	1961-62
101	Lord's	1962

Javed Miandad (2)

260	The Oval . . .	1987
153*	Birmingham .	1992

Mohsin Khan (2)

200	Lord's	1982
104	Lahore	1983-84

Moin Khan (1)

| 105 | Leeds . . . . . | 1996 |

Mudassar Nazar (3)

114†	Lahore	1977-78
124	Birmingham .	1987
120	Lahore	1987-88

Mushtaq Mohammad (3)

100*	Nottingham .	1962
100	Birmingham .	1971
157	Hyderabad . .	1972-73

Nasim-ul Ghani (1)

| 101 | Lord's . . . . | 1962 |

Sadiq Mohammad (1)

| 119 | Lahore . . . . | 1972-73 |

Saeed Anwar (1)

| 176 | The Oval . . . | 1996 |

Salim Malik (4)

116	Faisalabad . .	1983-84
102	The Oval . . .	1987
165	Birmingham .	1992
100*	The Oval . . .	1996

Wasim Raja (1)

| 112 | Faisalabad . . | 1983-84 |

Yousuf Youhana (2)

124†	Lahore	2000-01
117	Karachi	2000-01

Zaheer Abbas (2)

274†	Birmingham .	1971
240	The Oval . . .	1974

† *On first appearance in England–Pakistan Tests.*

Note: Three batsmen – Majid Khan, Mushtaq Mohammad and D. L. Amiss – were dismissed for 99 at Karachi, 1972-73: the only instance in Test matches.

RECORD PARTNERSHIPS FOR EACH WICKET

For England

198 for 1st	G. Pullar and R. W. Barber at Dacca	1961-62
248 for 2nd	M. C. Cowdrey and E. R. Dexter at The Oval	1962
267 for 3rd	M. P. Vaughan and G. P. Thorpe at Manchester.	2001
188 for 4th	E. R. Dexter and P. H. Parfitt at Karachi	1961-62
192 for 5th	D. C. S. Compton and T. E. Bailey at Nottingham	1954
166 for 6th	G. P. Thorpe and C. White at Lahore	2000-01
167 for 7th	D. I. Gower and V. J. Marks at Faisalabad	1983-84
99 for 8th	P. H. Parfitt and D. A. Allen at Leeds	1962
76 for 9th	T. W. Graveney and F. S. Trueman at Lord's	1962
79 for 10th	R. W. Taylor and R. G. D. Willis at Birmingham.	1982

For Pakistan

173 for 1st	Mohsin Khan and Shoaib Mohammad at Lahore	1983-84
291 for 2nd†	Zaheer Abbas and Mushtaq Mohammad at Birmingham	1971
180 for 3rd	Mudassar Nazar and Haroon Rashid at Lahore	1977-78
322 for 4th	Javed Miandad and Salim Malik at Birmingham	1992
197 for 5th	Javed Burki and Nasim-ul-Ghani at Lord's	1962
145 for 6th	Mushtaq Mohammad and Intikhab Alam at Hyderabad	1972-73
112 for 7th	Asif Mujtaba and Moin Khan at Leeds	1996
130 for 8th	Hanif Mohammad and Asif Iqbal at Lord's	1967
190 for 9th†	Asif Iqbal and Intikhab Alam at The Oval	1967
62 for 10th	Sarfraz Nawaz and Asif Masood at Leeds	1974

† *Record partnership against all countries.*

TEN WICKETS OR MORE IN A MATCH

For England (2)

11-83 (6-65, 5-18)†	N. G. B. Cook, Karachi	1983-84
13-71 (5-20, 8-51)	D. L. Underwood, Lord's	1974

For Pakistan (6)

10-194 (5-84, 5-110)	Abdul Qadir, Lahore	1983-84
10-211 (7-96, 3-115)	Abdul Qadir, The Oval	1987
13-101 (9-56, 4-45)	Abdul Qadir, Lahore	1987-88
10-186 (5-88, 5-98)	Abdul Qadir, Karachi	1987-88
12-99 (6-53, 6-46)	Fazal Mahmood, The Oval	1954
10-77 (3-37, 7-40)	Imran Khan, Leeds	1987

† *On first appearance in England–Pakistan Tests.*

ENGLAND v SRI LANKA

	Captains					
Season	*England*	*Sri Lanka*	*T*	*E*	*SL*	*D*
1981-82	K. W. R. Fletcher	B. Warnapura	1	1	0	0
1984	D. I. Gower	L. R. D. Mendis	1	0	0	1
1988	G. A. Gooch	R. S. Madugalle	1	1	0	0
1991	G. A. Gooch	P. A. de Silva	1	1	0	0
1992-93	A. J. Stewart	A. Ranatunga	1	0	1	0
1998	A. J. Stewart	A. Ranatunga	1	0	1	0
2000-01	N. Hussain	S. T. Jayasuriya	3	2	1	0
2002	N. Hussain	S. T. Jayasuriya	3	2	0	1
	In England		7	4	1	2
	In Sri Lanka		5	3	2	0
	Totals		12	7	3	2

HIGHEST INNINGS TOTALS

For England in England: 545 at Birmingham	2002
in Sri Lanka: 387 at Kandy	2000-01
For Sri Lanka in England: 591 at The Oval	1998
in Sri Lanka: 470-5 dec. at Galle	2000-01

LOWEST INNINGS TOTALS

For England in England: 181 at The Oval	1998
in Sri Lanka: 189 at Galle	2000-01
For Sri Lanka in England: 162 at Birmingham	2002
in Sri Lanka: 81 at Colombo (SSC)	2000-01

INDIVIDUAL HUNDREDS

For England (15)

M. A. Butcher (2)
105   Lord's   2002
123   Manchester . .   2002
J. P. Crawley (1)
156*† The Oval . . .   1998
G. A. Gooch (1)
174   Lord's   1991
G. A. Hick (1)
107   The Oval . . .   1998

N. Hussain (1)
109   Kandy   2000-01
A. J. Lamb (1)
107† Lord's   1984
R. A. Smith (1)
128   Colombo (SSC) 1992-93
A. J. Stewart (2)
113*† Lord's   1991
123   Manchester . .   2002

G. P. Thorpe (2)
113* Colombo (SSC) 2000-01
123   Birmingham .   2002
M. E. Trescothick (2)
122† Galle   2000-01
161   Birmingham .   2002
M. P. Vaughan (1)
115   Lord's   2002

For Sri Lanka (11)

R. P. Arnold (1)
109   Manchester . .   2002
M. S. Atapattu (2)
201* Galle   2000-01
185   Lord's   2002
P. A. de Silva (2)
152   The Oval . . .   1998

106   Galle   2000-01
S. T. Jayasuriya (1)
213   The Oval . . .   1998
D. P. M. D. Jayawardene (2)
101   Kandy   2000-01
107   Lord's   2002

L. R. D. Mendis (1)
111   Lord's   1984
S. A. R. Silva (1)
102*† Lord's   1984
S. Wettimuny (1)
190   Lord's   1984

† *On first appearance in England–Sri Lanka Tests.*

RECORD PARTNERSHIPS FOR EACH WICKET

For England

168 for 1st	M. E. Trescothick and M. P. Vaughan at Lord's	2002
202 for 2nd	M. E. Trescothick and M. A. Butcher at Birmingham.	2002
167 for 3rd	N. Hussain and G. P. Thorpe at Kandy	2000-01
128 for 4th	G. A. Hick and M. R. Ramprakash at The Oval	1998
92 for 5th	M. A. Butcher and A. J. Stewart at Manchester.	2002
87 for 6th	{ A. J. Lamb and R. M. Ellison at Lord's	1984
	{ A. J. Stewart and C. White at Kandy	2000-01
63 for 7th	A. J. Stewart and R. C. Russell at Lord's.	1991
102 for 8th	A. J. Stewart and A. F. Giles at Manchester	2002
53 for 9th	M. R. Ramprakash and D. Gough at The Oval	1998
91 for 10th	G. P. Thorpe and M. J. Hoggard at Birmingham	2002

For Sri Lanka

99 for 1st‡	R. S. Mahanama and U. C. Hathurusinghe at Colombo (SSC)	1992-93
92 for 2nd	M. S. Atapattu and K. C. Sangakkara at Galle	2000-01
243 for 3rd†	S. T. Jayasuriya and P. A. de Silva at The Oval.	1998
148 for 4th	S. Wettimuny and A. Ranatunga at Lord's.	1984
150 for 5th†	S. Wettimuny and L. R. D. Mendis at Lord's	1984
138 for 6th	S. A. R. Silva and L. R. D. Mendis at Lord's	1984
93 for 7th	K. C. Sangakkara and H. D. P. K. Dharmasena at Kandy	2000-01
53 for 8th	H. D. P. K. Dharmasena and W. P. U. J. C. Vaas at Kandy	2000-01
83 for 9th†	H. P. Tillekeratne and M. Muralitharan at Colombo (SSC)	1992-93
64 for 10th	J. R. Ratnayeke and G. F. Labrooy at Lord's	1988

† *Record partnership against all countries.*
‡ *107 runs were scored for Sri Lanka's first wicket at Manchester in 2002, in two partnerships: M. S. Atapattu and R. P. Arnold put on 48 before Atapattu retired hurt, then Arnold and K. C. Sangakkara added a further 59.*

TEN WICKETS OR MORE IN A MATCH

For Sri Lanka (1)

16-220 (7-155, 9-65)	M. Muralitharan at The Oval	1998

Note: The best match figures by an England bowler are 8-95 (5-28, 3-67) by D. L. Underwood at Colombo (PSS), 1981-82.

ENGLAND v ZIMBABWE

		Captains				
Season	*England*	*Zimbabwe*	*T*	*E*	*Z*	*D*
1996-97	M. A. Atherton	A. D. R. Campbell	2	0	0	2
2000	N. Hussain	A. Flower	2	1	0	1
	In England		2	1	0	1
	In Zimbabwe...............		2	0	0	2
	Totals.		4	1	0	3

HIGHEST INNINGS TOTALS

For England in England: 415 at Lord's		2000
in Zimbabwe: 406 at Bulawayo.		1996-97
For Zimbabwe in England: 285-4 dec. at Nottingham		2000
in Zimbabwe: 376 at Bulawayo		1996-97

LOWEST INNINGS TOTALS

For England in England: 147 at Nottingham 2000
             in Zimbabwe: 156 at Harare 1996-97

For Zimbabwe in England: 83 at Lord's 2000
               in Zimbabwe: 215 at Harare 1996-97

INDIVIDUAL HUNDREDS

For England (6)

M. A. Atherton (1)	**G. A. Hick** (1)	**A. J. Stewart** (2)
136 Nottingham . 2000	101† Lord's 2000	101* Harare 1996-97
J. P. Crawley (1)	**N. Hussain** (1)	124* Lord's 2000
112† Bulawayo . . . 1996-97	113† Bulawayo . . . 1996-97	

For Zimbabwe (2)

A. Flower (1)	**M. W. Goodwin** (1)
112† Bulawayo . . . 1996-97	148* Nottingham . 2000

† *On first appearance in England–Zimbabwe Tests.*

HUNDRED PARTNERSHIPS

For England

121	for 1st	M. A. Atherton and M. R. Ramprakash at Nottingham	2000
137	for 2nd	N. V. Knight and A. J. Stewart at Bulawayo.	1996-97
149	for 4th	G. A. Hick and A. J. Stewart at Lord's.	2000
106*	for 4th	A. J. Stewart and G. P. Thorpe at Harare	1996-97
148	for 5th	N. Hussain and J. P. Crawley at Bulawayo.	1996-97
114	for 5th	A. J. Stewart and N. V. Knight at Lord's.	2000

For Zimbabwe

127	for 2nd	G. W. Flower and A. D. R. Campbell at Bulawayo	1996-97
129	for 3rd	M. W. Goodwin and N. C. Johnson at Nottingham	2000
122	for 4th	M. W. Goodwin and A. Flower at Nottingham	2000

BEST MATCH BOWLING ANALYSES

For England

7-42 (5-15, 2-27)†   E. S. H. Giddins, Lord's   2000

For Zimbabwe

7-186 (5-123, 2-63)†   P. A. Strang, Bulawayo 1996-97

† *On first appearance in England–Zimbabwe Tests.*

AUSTRALIA v SOUTH AFRICA

Captains

Season	Australia	South Africa	T	A	SA	D
1902-03S	J. Darling	H. M. Taberer[1]	3	2	0	1
1910-11A	C. Hill	P. W. Sherwell	5	4	1	0
1912E	S. E. Gregory	F. Mitchell[2]	3	2	0	1
1921-22S	H. L. Collins	H. W. Taylor	3	1	0	2
1931-32A	W. M. Woodfull	H. B. Cameron	5	5	0	0
1935-36S	V. Y. Richardson	H. F. Wade	5	4	0	1
1949-50S	A. L. Hassett	A. D. Nourse	5	4	0	1
1952-53A	A. L. Hassett	J. E. Cheetham	5	2	2	1
1957-58S	I. D. Craig	C. B. van Ryneveld[3]	5	3	0	2
1963-64A	R. B. Simpson[4]	T. L. Goddard	5	1	1	3
1966-67S	R. B. Simpson	P. L. van der Merwe	5	1	3	1
1969-70S	W. M. Lawry	A. Bacher	4	0	4	0
1993-94A	A. R. Border	K. C. Wessels[5]	3	1	1	1
1993-94S	A. R. Border	K. C. Wessels	3	1	1	1
1996-97S	M. A. Taylor	W. J. Cronje	3	2	1	0
1997-98A	M. A. Taylor	W. J. Cronje	3	1	0	2
2001-02A	S. R. Waugh	S. M. Pollock	3	3	0	0
2001-02S	S. R. Waugh	M. V. Boucher	3	2	1	0
	In South Africa		39	20	10	9
	In Australia		29	17	5	7
	In England		3	2	0	1
	Totals		71	39	15	17

S Played in South Africa. A Played in Australia. E Played in England.

Notes: The following deputised for the official touring captain or were appointed by the home authority for only a minor proportion of the series:
[1]J. H. Anderson (Second), E. A. Halliwell (Third). [2]L. J. Tancred (Third). [3]D. J. McGlew (First).
[4]R. Benaud (First). [5]W. J. Cronje (Third).

HIGHEST INNINGS TOTALS

For Australia in Australia: 578 at Melbourne		1910-11
in South Africa: 652-7 dec. at Johannesburg		2001-02
For South Africa in Australia: 595 at Adelaide		1963-64
in South Africa: 622-9 dec. at Durban		1969-70

LOWEST INNINGS TOTALS

For Australia in Australia: 111 at Sydney		1993-94
in South Africa: 75 at Durban		1949-50
For South Africa in Australia: 36† at Melbourne		1931-32
in South Africa: 85‡ at Johannesburg		1902-03
85‡ at Cape Town		1902-03

† *Scored 45 in the second innings, giving the smallest aggregate of 81 (12 extras) in Test cricket.*
‡ *In successive innings.*

Warne compared his marathon stint to "a big night out, when you think you've gone several times, but you get a couple of second winds".
South Africa v Australia, page 1290

INDIVIDUAL HUNDREDS

For Australia (77)

W. W. Armstrong (2)
159*‡ Johannesburg 1902-03
132 Melbourne 1910-11
W. Bardsley (3)
132† Sydney 1910-11
121 Manchester. . 1912
164 Lord's 1912
R. Benaud (2)
122 Johannesburg 1957-58
100 Johannesburg 1957-58
G. S. Blewett (1)
214‡ Johannesburg 1996-97
B. C. Booth (2)
169† Brisbane 1963-64
102* Sydney 1963-64
D. G. Bradman (4)
226† Brisbane 1931-32
112 Sydney 1931-32
167 Melbourne 1931-32
299* Adelaide 1931-32
W. A. Brown (1)
121 Cape Town 1935-36
J. W. Burke (1)
189 Cape Town 1957-58
A. G. Chipperfield (1)
109† Durban 1935-36
H. L. Collins (1)
203 Johannesburg 1921-22
J. H. Fingleton (3)
112 Cape Town 1935-36
108 Johannesburg 1935-36
118 Durban 1935-36
A. C. Gilchrist (2)
204* Johannesburg 2001-02
138* Cape Town 2001-02
J. M. Gregory (1)
119 Johannesburg 1921-22
R. N. Harvey (8)
178 Cape Town 1949-50

151* Durban . . . 1949-50
100 Johannesburg 1949-50
116 Port Elizabeth 1949-50
109 Brisbane . . . 1952-53
190 Sydney 1952-53
116 Adelaide . . . 1952-53
205 Melbourne . . 1952-53
A. L. Hassett (3)
112† Johannesburg 1949-50
167 Port Elizabeth 1949-50
163 Adelaide . . . 1952-53
M. L. Hayden (4)
131 Adelaide . . . 2001-02
138 Melbourne . . 2001-02
105 Sydney 2001-02
122 Johannesburg 2001-02
C. Hill (3)
142† Johannesburg 1902-03
191 Sydney 1910-11
100 Melbourne . . 1910-11
C. Kelleway (2)
114 Manchester. . 1912
102 Lord's 1912
J. L. Langer (2)
116† Adelaide . . . 2001-02
126 Sydney 2001-02
W. M. Lawry (1)
157 Melbourne . . 1963-64
S. J. E. Loxton (1)
101* Johannesburg 1949-50
C. G. Macartney (2)
137 Sydney 1910-11
116 Durban 1921-22
S. J. McCabe (2)
149 Durban 1935-36
189* Johannesburg 1935-36
C. C. McDonald (1)
154 Adelaide . . . 1952-53

D. R. Martyn (3)
124* Adelaide . . . 2001-02
117 Sydney 2001-02
133 Johannesburg 2001-02
J. Moroney (2)
118 }
101* } Johannesburg 1949-50
A. R. Morris (2)
111 Johannesburg 1949-50
157 Port Elizabeth 1949-50
R. T. Ponting (2)
105† Melbourne . . 1997-98
100* Cape Town. . 2001-02
K. E. Rigg (1)
127† Sydney 1931-32
J. Ryder (1)
142 Cape Town . . 1921-22
R. B. Simpson (1)
153 Cape Town . . 1966-67
K. R. Stackpole (1)
134 Cape Town . . 1966-67
M. A. Taylor (2)
170† Melbourne . . 1993-94
169*‡ Adelaide . . . 1997-98
V. T. Trumper (2)
159 Melbourne . . 1910-11
214* Sydney 1910-11
M. E. Waugh (4)
113* Durban 1993-94
116 Port Elizabeth 1996-97
100 Sydney 1997-98
115* Adelaide . . . 1997-98
S. R. Waugh (2)
164† Adelaide . . . 1993-94
160 Johannesburg 1996-97
W. M. Woodfull (1)
161 Melbourne . . 1931-32

For South Africa (42)

E. J. Barlow (5)
114† Brisbane . . . 1963-64
109 Melbourne . . 1963-64
201 Adelaide . . . 1963-64
127 Cape Town . . 1969-70
110 Johannesburg 1969-70
K. C. Bland (1)
126 Sydney 1963-64
W. J. Cronje (1)
122 Johannesburg 1993-94
W. R. Endean (1)
162* Melbourne . . 1952-53
G. A. Faulkner (3)
204 Melbourne . . 1910-11
115 Adelaide . . . 1910-11

122* Manchester. . 1912
C. N. Frank (1)
152 Johannesburg 1921-22
H. H. Gibbs (1)
104 Durban 2001-02
A. C. Hudson (1)
102 Cape Town. . 1993-94
B. L. Irvine (1)
102 Port Elizabeth 1969-70
J. H. Kallis (1)
101 Melbourne . . 1997-98
G. Kirsten (2)
108* Adelaide . . . 1997-98
153 Sydney 2001-02

D. T. Lindsay (3)
182 Johannesburg 1966-67
137 Durban 1966-67
131 Johannesburg 1966-67
D. J. McGlew (2)
108 Johannesburg 1957-58
105 Durban 1957-58
A. D. Nourse (2)
231 Johannesburg 1935-36
114 Cape Town . . 1949-50
A. W. Nourse (1)
111 Johannesburg 1921-22
R. G. Pollock (5)
122 Sydney 1963-64

175	Adelaide . . .	1963-64	**E. A. B. Rowan** (1)			**K. G. Viljoen** (1)		
209	Cape Town . .	1966-67	143	Durban	1949-50	111	Melbourne . .	1931-32
105	Port Elizabeth	1966-67	**J. H. Sinclair** (2)			**J. H. B. Waite** (2)		
274	Durban	1969-70	101	Johannesburg	1902-03	115	Johannesburg	1957-58
B. A. Richards (2)			104	Cape Town . .	1902-03	134	Durban	1957-58
140	Durban	1969-70	**S. J. Snooke** (1)			**J. W. Zulch** (2)		
126	Port Elizabeth	1969-70	103	Adelaide . . .	1910-11	105	Adelaide . . .	1910-11
						150	Sydney	1910-11

† *On first appearance in Australia–South Africa Tests.*
‡ *Carried his bat.*

RECORD PARTNERSHIPS FOR EACH WICKET

For Australia

233 for 1st	J. H. Fingleton and W. A. Brown at Cape Town	1935-36
275 for 2nd	C. C. McDonald and A. L. Hassett at Adelaide	1952-53
242 for 3rd	C. Kelleway and W. Bardsley at Lord's	1912
169 for 4th	M. A. Taylor and M. E. Waugh at Melbourne	1993-94
385 for 5th	S. R. Waugh and G. S. Blewett at Johannesburg	1996-97
317 for 6th	D. R. Martyn and A. C. Gilchrist at Johannesburg	2001-02
160 for 7th	R. Benaud and G. D. McKenzie at Sydney	1963-64
83 for 8th	A. G. Chipperfield and C. V. Grimmett at Durban	1935-36
78 for 9th	{ D. G. Bradman and W. J. O'Reilly at Adelaide	1931-32
	{ K. D. Mackay and I. Meckiff at Johannesburg	1957-58
82 for 10th	V. S. Ransford and W. J. Whitty at Melbourne	1910-11

For South Africa

176 for 1st	D. J. McGlew and T. L. Goddard at Johannesburg	1957-58
173 for 2nd	L. J. Tancred and C. B. Llewellyn at Johannesburg	1902-03
341 for 3rd†	E. J. Barlow and R. G. Pollock at Adelaide	1963-64
206 for 4th	C. N. Frank and A. W. Nourse at Johannesburg	1921-22
129 for 5th	J. H. B. Waite and W. R. Endean at Johannesburg	1957-58
200 for 6th†	R. G. Pollock and H. R. Lance at Durban	1969-70
221 for 7th	D. T. Lindsay and P. L. van der Merwe at Johannesburg	1966-67
124 for 8th	A. W. Nourse and E. A. Halliwell at Johannesburg	1902-03
85 for 9th	R. G. Pollock and P. M. Pollock at Cape Town	1966-67
74 for 10th	B. M. McMillan and P. L. Symcox at Adelaide	1997-98

† *Record partnership against all countries.*

TEN WICKETS OR MORE IN A MATCH

For Australia (7)

14-199 (7-116, 7-83)	C. V. Grimmett, Adelaide.	1931-32
10-88 (5-32, 5-56)	C. V. Grimmett, Cape Town	1935-36
10-110 (3-70, 7-40)	C. V. Grimmett, Johannesburg	1935-36
13-173 (7-100, 6-73)	C. V. Grimmett, Durban	1935-36
11-24 (5-6, 6-18)	H. Ironmonger, Melbourne.	1931-32
12-128 (7-56, 5-72)	S. K. Warne, Sydney	1993-94
11-109 (5-75, 6-34)	S. K. Warne, Sydney	1997-98

For South Africa (3)

10-123 (4-80, 6-43)	P. S. de Villiers, Sydney	1993-94
10-116 (5-43, 5-73)	C. B. Llewellyn, Johannesburg	1902-03
13-165 (6-84, 7-81)	H. J. Tayfield, Melbourne	1952-53

Note: C. V. Grimmett took ten wickets or more in three consecutive matches in 1935-36.

AUSTRALIA v WEST INDIES

Captains

Season	Australia	West Indies	T	A	WI	T	D
1930-31*A*	W. M. Woodfull	G. C. Grant	5	4	1	0	0
1951-52*A*	A. L. Hassett[1]	J. D. C. Goddard[2]	5	4	1	0	0
1954-55*W*	I. W. Johnson	D. St E. Atkinson[3]	5	3	0	0	2

THE FRANK WORRELL TROPHY

Captains

Season	Australia	West Indies	T	A	WI	T	D	Held by
1960-61*A*	R. Benaud	F. M. M. Worrell	5	2	1	1	1	A
1964-65*W*	R. B. Simpson	G. S. Sobers	5	1	2	0	2	WI
1968-69*A*	W. M. Lawry	G. S. Sobers	5	3	1	0	1	A
1972-73*W*	I. M. Chappell	R. B. Kanhai	5	2	0	0	3	A
1975-76*A*	G. S. Chappell	C. H. Lloyd	6	5	1	0	0	A
1977-78*W*	R. B. Simpson	A. I. Kallicharran[4]	5	1	3	0	1	WI
1979-80*A*	G. S. Chappell	C. H. Lloyd[5]	3	0	2	0	1	WI
1981-82*A*	G. S. Chappell	C. H. Lloyd	3	1	1	0	1	WI
1983-84*W*	K. J. Hughes	C. H. Lloyd[6]	5	0	3	0	2	WI
1984-85*A*	A. R. Border[7]	C. H. Lloyd	5	1	3	0	1	WI
1988-89*A*	A. R. Border	I. V. A. Richards	5	1	3	0	1	WI
1990-91*W*	A. R. Border	I. V. A. Richards	5	1	2	0	2	WI
1992-93*A*	A. R. Border	R. B. Richardson	5	1	2	0	2	WI
1994-95*W*	M. A. Taylor	R. B. Richardson	4	2	1	0	1	A
1996-97*A*	M. A. Taylor	C. A. Walsh	5	3	2	0	0	A
1998-99*W*	S. R. Waugh	B. C. Lara	4	2	2	0	0	A
2000-01*A*	S. R. Waugh[8]	J. C. Adams	5	5	0	0	0	A
In Australia.			57	30	18	1	8	
In West Indies			38	12	13	0	13	
Totals			95	42	31	1	21	

A Played in Australia.   W Played in West Indies.

Notes: The following deputised for the official touring captain or were appointed by the home authority for only a minor proportion of the series:
[1]A. R. Morris (Third). [2]J. B. Stollmeyer (Fifth). [3]J. B. Stollmeyer (Second and Third). [4]C. H. Lloyd (First and Second). [5]D. L. Murray (First). [6]I. V. A. Richards (Second). [7]K. J. Hughes (First and Second). [8]A. C. Gilchrist (Third).

HIGHEST INNINGS TOTALS

For Australia in Australia: 619 at Sydney.	1968-69
in West Indies: 758-8 dec. at Kingston	1954-55
For West Indies in Australia: 616 at Adelaide	1968-69
in West Indies: 573 at Bridgetown	1964-65

LOWEST INNINGS TOTALS

For Australia in Australia: 76 at Perth	1984-85
in West Indies: 90 at Port-of-Spain.	1977-78
For West Indies in Australia: 78 at Sydney.	1951-52
in West Indies: 51 at Port-of-Spain	1998-99

INDIVIDUAL HUNDREDS
For Australia (86)

R. G. Archer (1)
128   Kingston . . .   1954-55
R. Benaud (1)
121   Kingston . . .   1954-55
D. C. Boon (3)
149   Sydney   1988-89
109*   Kingston . . .   1990-91
111   Brisbane . . .   1992-93
B. C. Booth (1)
117   Port-of-Spain   1964-65
A. R. Border (3)
126   Adelaide . . .   1981-82
100*   Port-of-Spain   1983-84
110   Melbourne . .   1992-93
D. G. Bradman (2)
223   Brisbane . . .   1930-31
152   Melbourne . .   1930-31
G. S. Chappell (5)
106   Bridgetown . .   1972-73
123 }
109* } ‡Brisbane . .   1975-76
182*   Sydney   1975-76
124   Brisbane . . .   1979-80
I. M. Chappell (5)
117†   Brisbane . . .   1968-69
165   Melbourne . .   1968-69
106*   Bridgetown . .   1972-73
109   Georgetown . .   1972-73
156   Perth   1975-76
G. J. Cosier (1)
109†   Melbourne . .   1975-76
R. M. Cowper (2)
143   Port-of-Spain   1964-65
102   Bridgetown . .   1964-65
J. Dyson (1)
127*† Sydney   1981-82
R. N. Harvey (3)
133   Kingston . . .   1954-55
133   Port-of-Spain   1954-55
204   Kingston . . .   1954-55
A. L. Hassett (2)
132   Sydney   1951-52
102   Melbourne . .   1951-52

M. L. Hayden (1)
125   Adelaide . . .   1996-97
I. A. Healy (1)
161*   Brisbane . . .   1996-97
A. M. J. Hilditch (1)
113†   Melbourne . .   1984-85
K. J. Hughes (2)
130*† Brisbane . . .   1979-80
100*   Melbourne . .   1981-82
D. M. Jones (1)
216   Adelaide . . .   1988-89
A. F. Kippax (1)
146†   Adelaide . . .   1930-31
J. L. Langer (1)
127   St John's . . .   1998-99
W. M. Lawry (4)
210   Bridgetown . .   1964-65
105   Brisbane . . .   1968-69
205   Melbourne . .   1968-69
151   Sydney   1968-69
R. R. Lindwall (1)
118   Bridgetown . .   1954-55
R. B. McCosker (1)
109*   Melbourne . .   1975-76
C. C. McDonald (2)
110   Port-of-Spain   1954-55
127   Kingston . . .   1954-55
K. R. Miller (4)
129   Sydney   1951-52
147   Kingston . . .   1954-55
137   Bridgetown . .   1954-55
109   Kingston . . .   1954-55
A. R. Morris (1)
111   Port-of-Spain   1954-55
N. C. O'Neill (1)
181†   Brisbane . . .   1960-61
W. B. Phillips (1)
120   Bridgetown . .   1983-84
W. H. Ponsford (2)
183   Sydney   1930-31
109   Brisbane . . .   1930-31
R. T. Ponting (1)
104   Bridgetown . .   1998-99

I. R. Redpath (4)
132   Sydney   1968-69
102   Melbourne . .   1975-76
103   Adelaide . . .   1975-76
101   Melbourne . .   1975-76
C. S. Serjeant (1)
124   Georgetown . .   1977-78
R. B. Simpson (1)
201   Bridgetown . .   1964-65
M. J. Slater (1)
106   Port-of-Spain   1998-99
K. R. Stackpole (1)
142   Kingston . . .   1972-73
M. A. Taylor (1)
144   St John's . . .   1990-91
P. M. Toohey (1)
122   Kingston . . .   1977-78
A. Turner (1)
136   Adelaide . . .   1975-76
K. D. Walters (6)
118   Sydney   1968-69
110   Adelaide . . .   1968-69
242 }
103 } Sydney   1968-69
102*   Bridgetown . .   1972-73
112   Port-of-Spain   1972-73
M. E. Waugh (4)
139*   St John's . . .   1990-91
112   Melbourne . .   1992-93
126   Kingston . . .   1994-95
119   Perth   2000-01
S. R. Waugh (6)
100   Sydney   1992-93
200   Kingston . . .   1994-95
100   Kingston . . .   1998-99
199   Bridgetown . .   1998-99
121*   Melbourne . .   2000-01
103   Sydney   2000-01
K. C. Wessels (1)
173   Sydney   1984-85
G. M. Wood (2)
126   Georgetown . .   1977-78
111   Perth   1988-89

For West Indies (86)

F. C. M. Alexander (1)
108   Sydney   1960-61
K. L. T. Arthurton (1)
157*† Brisbane . . .   1992-93
D. St E. Atkinson (1)
219   Bridgetown . .   1954-55
B. F. Butcher (3)
117   Port-of-Spain   1964-65
101   Sydney   1968-69
118   Adelaide . . .   1968-69

S. L. Campbell (2)
113   Brisbane . . .   1996-97
105   Adelaide . . .   1998-99
C. C. Depeiza (1)
122   Bridgetown . .   1954-55
P. J. L. Dujon (2)
130   Port-of-Spain   1983-84
139   Perth   1984-85
M. L. C. Foster (1)
125†   Kingston . . .   1972-73

R. C. Fredericks (1)
169   Perth   1975-76
H. A. Gomes (6)
101†   Georgetown . .   1977-78
115   Kingston . . .   1977-78
126   Sydney   1981-82
124*   Adelaide . . .   1981-82
127   Perth   1984-85
120*   Adelaide . . .   1984-85

C. G. Greenidge (4)

120*	Georgetown	1983-84
127	Kingston	1983-84
104	Adelaide	1988-89
226	Bridgetown	1990-91

D. L. Haynes (5)

103*	Georgetown	1983-84
145	Bridgetown	1983-84
100	Perth	1988-89
143	Sydney	1988-89
111	Georgetown	1990-91

G. A. Headley (2)

102*	Brisbane	1930-31
105	Sydney	1930-31

C. L. Hooper (1)

102	Brisbane	1996-97

C. C. Hunte (1)

110	Melbourne	1960-61

A. I. Kallicharran (4)

101	Brisbane	1975-76
127	Port-of-Spain	1977-78
126	Kingston	1977-78
106	Adelaide	1979-80

R. B. Kanhai (5)

117 }	Adelaide	1960-61
115 }		
129	Bridgetown	1964-65
121	Port-of-Spain	1964-65
105	Bridgetown	1972-73

B. C. Lara (6)

277	Sydney	1992-93
132	Perth	1996-97
213	Kingston	1998-99
153*	Bridgetown	1998-99
100	St John's	1998-99
182	Adelaide	2000-01

C. H. Lloyd (6)

129†	Brisbane	1968-69
178	Georgetown	1972-73
149	Perth	1975-76
102	Melbourne	1975-76
121	Adelaide	1979-80
114	Brisbane	1984-85

F. R. Martin (1)

123*	Sydney	1930-31

S. M. Nurse (2)

201	Bridgetown	1964-65
137	Sydney	1968-69

I. V. A. Richards (5)

101	Adelaide	1975-76
140	Brisbane	1979-80
178	St John's	1983-84
208	Melbourne	1984-85
146	Perth	1988-89

R. B. Richardson (9)

131*	Bridgetown	1983-84
154	St John's	1983-84
138	Brisbane	1984-85
122	Melbourne	1988-89

106	Adelaide	1988-89
104*	Kingston	1990-91
182	Georgetown	1990-91
109	Sydney	1992-93
100	Kingston	1994-95

L. G. Rowe (1)

107	Brisbane	1975-76

P. V. Simmons (1)

110	Melbourne	1992-93

O. G. Smith (1)

104†	Kingston	1954-55

G. S. Sobers (4)

132	Brisbane	1960-61
168	Sydney	1960-61
110	Adelaide	1968-69
113	Sydney	1968-69

J. B. Stollmeyer (1)

104	Sydney	1951-52

C. L. Walcott (5)

108	Kingston	1954-55
126 }	Port-of-Spain	1954-55
110 }		
155 }	Kingston	1954-55
110 }		

E. D. Weekes (1)

139	Port-of-Spain	1954-55

A. B. Williams (1)

100†	Georgetown	1977-78

F. M. M. Worrell (1)

108	Melbourne	1951-52

† *On first appearance in Australia–West Indies Tests.*

‡ *G. S. Chappell is the only player to score hundreds in both innings of his first Test as captain.*

Note: F. C. M. Alexander and C. C. Depeiza scored the only hundreds of their first-class careers in a Test match.

RECORD PARTNERSHIPS FOR EACH WICKET

For Australia

382 for 1st†	W. M. Lawry and R. B. Simpson at Bridgetown	1964-65
298 for 2nd	W. M. Lawry and I. M. Chappell at Melbourne	1968-69
295 for 3rd†	C. C. McDonald and R. N. Harvey at Kingston	1954-55
336 for 4th	W. M. Lawry and K. D. Walters at Sydney	1968-69
281 for 5th	S. R. Waugh and R. T. Ponting at Bridgetown	1998-99
206 for 6th	K. R. Miller and R. G. Archer at Bridgetown	1954-55
134 for 7th	A. K. Davidson and R. Benaud at Brisbane	1960-61
137 for 8th	R. Benaud and I. W. Johnson at Kingston	1954-55
114 for 9th	D. M. Jones and M. G. Hughes at Adelaide	1988-89
97 for 10th	T. G. Hogan and R. M. Hogg at Georgetown	1983-84

 The approaches to the dressing-rooms were watched by CCTV cameras, though these seemed superfluous, because there were so few spectators that every single one was identifiable.
Pakistan v West Indies at Sharjah, page 1267

For West Indies

250* for 1st	C. G. Greenidge and D. L. Haynes at Georgetown.		1983-84
297 for 2nd	D. L. Haynes and R. B. Richardson at Georgetown.		1990-91
308 for 3rd	R. B. Richardson and I. V. A. Richards at St John's.		1983-84
198 for 4th	L. G. Rowe and A. I. Kallicharran at Brisbane.		1975-76
322 for 5th†‡	B. C. Lara and J. C. Adams at Kingston.		1998-99
165 for 6th	R. B. Kanhai and D. L. Murray at Bridgetown.		1972-73
347 for 7th†	D. St E. Atkinson and C. C. Depeiza at Bridgetown.		1954-55
87 for 8th	P. J. L. Dujon and C. E. L. Ambrose at Port-of-Spain.		1990-91
122 for 9th	D. A. J. Holford and J. L. Hendriks at Adelaide.		1968-69
56 for 10th	J. Garner and C. E. H. Croft at Brisbane.		1979-80

† *Record partnership against all countries.*

‡ *344 runs were added between the fall of the 4th and 5th wickets: P. T. Collins retired hurt when he and Lara had added 22 runs.*

TEN WICKETS OR MORE IN A MATCH

For Australia (15)

10-113 (4-31, 6-82)	M. G. Bevan, Adelaide.		1996-97
11-96 (7-46, 4-50)	A. R. Border, Sydney.		1988-89
11-222 (5-135, 6-87)†	A. K. Davidson, Brisbane.		1960-61
11-183 (7-87, 4-96)†	C. V. Grimmett, Adelaide.		1930-31
10-115 (6-72, 4-43)	N. J. N. Hawke, Georgetown.		1964-65
10-144 (6-54, 4-90)	R. G. Holland, Sydney.		1984-85
13-217 (5-130, 8-87)	M. G. Hughes, Perth.		1988-89
11-79 (7-23, 4-56)	H. Ironmonger, Melbourne.		1930-31
11-181 (8-112, 3-69)	G. F. Lawson, Adelaide.		1984-85
10-127 (7-83, 3-44)	D. K. Lillee, Melbourne.		1981-82
10-78 (5-50, 5-28)	G. D. McGrath, Port-of-Spain.		1998-99
10-27 (6-17, 4-10)	G. D. McGrath, Brisbane.		2000-01
10-159 (8-71, 2-88)	G. D. McKenzie, Melbourne.		1968-69
10-113 (5-81, 5-32)	C. R. Miller, Adelaide.		2000-01
10-185 (3-87, 7-98)	B. Yardley, Sydney.		1981-82

For West Indies (4)

10-120 (6-74, 4-46)	C. E. L. Ambrose, Adelaide.		1992-93
10-113 (7-55, 3-58)	G. E. Gomez, Sydney.		1951-52
11-107 (5-45, 6-62)	M. A. Holding, Melbourne.		1981-82
10-107 (5-69, 5-38)	M. D. Marshall, Adelaide.		1984-85

† *On first appearance in Australia–West Indies Tests.*

AUSTRALIA v NEW ZEALAND

Captains

Season	Australia	New Zealand	T	A	NZ	D
1945-46*A*	W. A. Brown	W. A. Hadlee	1	1	0	0
1973-74*N*	I. M. Chappell	B. E. Congdon	3	2	0	1
1973-74*N*	I. M. Chappell	B. E. Congdon	3	1	1	1
1976-77*N*	G. S. Chappell	G. M. Turner	2	1	0	1
1980-81*A*	G. S. Chappell	G. P. Howarth[1]	3	2	0	1
1981-82*N*	G. S. Chappell	G. P. Howarth	3	1	1	1

TRANS-TASMAN TROPHY

Season	Australia	Captains New Zealand	T	A	NZ	D	Held by
1985-86*A*	A. R. Border	J. V. Coney	3	1	2	0	NZ
1985-86*N*	A. R. Border	J. V. Coney	3	0	1	2	NZ
1987-88*A*	A. R. Border	J. J. Crowe	3	1	0	2	A
1989-90*A*	A. R. Border	J. G. Wright	1	0	0	1	A
1989-90*N*	A. R. Border	J. G. Wright	1	0	1	0	NZ
1992-93*N*	A. R. Border	M. D. Crowe	3	1	1	1	NZ
1993-94*A*	A. R. Border	M. D. Crowe[2]	3	2	0	1	A
1997-98*A*	M. A. Taylor	S. P. Fleming	3	2	0	1	A
1999-2000*N*	S. R. Waugh	S. P. Fleming	3	3	0	0	A
2001-02*A*	S. R. Waugh	S. P. Fleming	3	0	0	3	A
In Australia			22	10	2	10	
In New Zealand			19	8	5	6	
Totals			41	18	7	16	

A Played in Australia. N Played in New Zealand.

Notes: The following deputised for the official touring captain: [1]M. G. Burgess (Second). [2]K. R. Rutherford (Second and Third).

HIGHEST INNINGS TOTALS

For Australia in Australia: 607-6 dec. at Brisbane	1993-94
in New Zealand: 552 at Christchurch	1976-77
For New Zealand in Australia: 553-7 dec. at Brisbane	1985-86
in New Zealand: 484 at Wellington	1973-74

LOWEST INNINGS TOTALS

For Australia in Australia: 162 at Sydney	1973-74
in New Zealand: 103 at Auckland	1985-86
For New Zealand in Australia: 121 at Perth	1980-81
in New Zealand: 42 at Wellington	1945-46

INDIVIDUAL HUNDREDS

For Australia (40)

D. C. Boon (3)
143 Brisbane ... 1987-88
200 Perth...... 1989-90
106 Hobart..... 1993-94
A. R. Border (5)
152* Brisbane ... 1985-86
140 ⎫
114*⎭ Christchurch. 1985-86
205 Adelaide ... 1987-88
105 Brisbane ... 1993-94
G. S. Chappell (3)
247*⎫
133 ⎭ Wellington .. 1973-74
176 Christchurch. 1981-82
I. M. Chappell (2)
145 ⎫
121 ⎭ Wellington .. 1973-74

M. T. G. Elliott (1)
114 Hobart 1997-98
A. C. Gilchrist (1)
118 Brisbane ... 2001-02
G. J. Gilmour (1)
101 Christchurch. 1976-77
M. L. Hayden (1)
136 Brisbane ... 2001-02
I. A. Healy (1)
113* Perth...... 1993-94
J. L. Langer (3)
122* Hamilton ... 1999-00
104 Brisbane ... 2001-02
123 Hobart 2001-02
G. R. Marsh (1)
118 Auckland ... 1985-86

R. W. Marsh (1)
132 Adelaide ... 1973-74
G. R. J. Matthews (2)
115† Brisbane ... 1985-86
130 Wellington .. 1985-86
R. T. Ponting (1)
157* Hobart 2001-02
I. R. Redpath (1)
159*‡ Auckland ... 1973-74
M. J. Slater (2)
168 Hobart 1993-94
143 Wellington .. 1999-00
K. R. Stackpole (1)
122† Melbourne .. 1973-74
M. A. Taylor (2)
142* Perth...... 1993-94
112 Brisbane ... 1997-98

K. D. Walters (3)
104* Auckland . . . 1973-74
250 Christchurch . 1976-77
107 Melbourne . . 1980-81

M. E. Waugh (1)
111 Hobart 1993-94
S. R. Waugh (2)
147* Brisbane . . . 1993-94

151* Wellington . . 1999-00
G. M. Wood (2)
111† Brisbane . . . 1980-81
100 Auckland . . . 1981-82

For New Zealand (25)

N. J. Astle (1)
156* Perth 2001-02
C. L. Cairns (1)
109 Wellington . . 1999-00
J. V. Coney (1)
101* Wellington . . 1985-86
B. E. Congdon (2)
132 Wellington . . 1973-74
107* Christchurch . 1976-77
M. D. Crowe (3)
188 Brisbane . . . 1985-86
137 Christchurch . 1985-86
137 Adelaide . . . 1987-88
B. A. Edgar (1)
161 Auckland . . . 1981-82

S. P. Fleming (1)
105 Perth 2001-02
M. J. Greatbatch (1)
146*† Perth 1989-90
B. F. Hastings (1)
101 Wellington . . 1973-74
M. J. Horne (1)
133† Hobart 1997-98
A. H. Jones (2)
150 Adelaide . . . 1987-88
143 Perth 1993-94
J. F. M. Morrison (1)
117 Sydney 1973-74
J. M. Parker (1)
108 Sydney 1973-74

A. C. Parore (1)
110 Perth 2001-02
J. F. Reid (1)
108† Brisbane . . . 1985-86
K. R. Rutherford (1)
102 Christchurch . 1992-93
G. M. Turner (2)
101 }
110*} Christchurch . 1973-74
L. Vincent (1)
104† Perth 2001-02
J. G. Wright (2)
141 Christchurch . 1981-82
117* Wellington . . 1989-90

† *On first appearance in Australia–New Zealand Tests.*
‡ *Carried his bat.*

Note: G. S. and I. M. Chappell each hit two hundreds at Wellington in 1973-74, the only instance of two batsmen on the same side scoring twin hundreds in the same Test.

RECORD PARTNERSHIPS FOR EACH WICKET

For Australia

224 for 1st	J. L. Langer and M. L. Hayden at Brisbane	2001-02
235 for 2nd	M. J. Slater and D. C. Boon at Hobart.	1993-94
264 for 3rd	I. M. Chappell and G. S. Chappell at Wellington	1973-74
153 for 4th	M. E. Waugh and S. R. Waugh at Perth.	1997-98
213 for 5th	G. M. Ritchie and G. R. J. Matthews at Wellington	1985-86
197 for 6th	A. R. Border and G. R. J. Matthews at Brisbane	1985-86
217 for 7th†	K. D. Walters and G. J. Gilmour at Christchurch	1976-77
135 for 8th	A. C. Gilchrist and B. Lee at Brisbane	2001-02
69 for 9th	I. A. Healy and C. J. McDermott at Perth.	1993-94
60 for 10th	K. D. Walters and J. D. Higgs at Melbourne	1980-81

For New Zealand

111 for 1st	M. J. Greatbatch and J. G. Wright at Wellington	1992-93
132 for 2nd	M. J. Horne and A. C. Parore at Hobart.	1997-98
224 for 3rd	J. F. Reid and M. D. Crowe at Brisbane	1985-86
229 for 4th	B. E. Congdon and B. F. Hastings at Wellington	1973-74
97 for 5th	S. P. Fleming and C. D. McMillan at Hobart	2001-02
110 for 6th	S. P. Fleming and C. L. Cairns at Wellington	1999-2000
132* for 7th	J. V. Coney and R. J. Hadlee at Wellington	1985-86
253 for 8th†	N. J. Astle and A. C. Parore at Perth	2001-02
73 for 9th	H. J. Howarth and D. R. Hadlee at Christchurch	1976-77
124 for 10th	J. G. Bracewell and S. L. Boock at Sydney	1985-86

† *Record partnership against all countries.*

TEN WICKETS OR MORE IN A MATCH

For Australia (2)

10-174 (6-106, 4-68)	R. G. Holland, Sydney	1985-86
11-123 (5-51, 6-72)	D. K. Lillee, Auckland	1976-77

For New Zealand (5)

10-106 (4-74, 6-32)	J. G. Bracewell, Auckland	1985-86
15-123 (9-52, 6-71)	R. J. Hadlee, Brisbane	1985-86
11-155 (5-65, 6-90)	R. J. Hadlee, Perth	1985-86
10-176 (5-109, 5-67)	R. J. Hadlee, Melbourne	1987-88
12-149 (5-62, 7-87)	D. L. Vettori, Auckland	1999-2000

AUSTRALIA v INDIA

		Captains						
Season	*Australia*		*India*	*T*	*A*	*I*	*T*	*D*
1947-48*A*	D. G. Bradman		L. Amarnath	5	4	0	0	1
1956-57*I*	I. W. Johnson[1]		P. R. Umrigar	3	2	0	0	1
1959-60*I*	R. Benaud		G. S. Ramchand	5	2	1	0	2
1964-65*I*	R. B. Simpson		Nawab of Pataudi jun.	3	1	1	0	1
1967-68*A*	R. B. Simpson[2]		Nawab of Pataudi jun.[3]	4	4	0	0	0
1969-70*I*	W. M. Lawry		Nawab of Pataudi jun.	5	3	1	0	1
1977-78*A*	R. B. Simpson		B. S. Bedi	5	3	2	0	0
1979-80*I*	K. J. Hughes		S. M. Gavaskar	6	0	2	0	4
1980-81*A*	G. S. Chappell		S. M. Gavaskar	3	1	1	0	1
1985-86*A*	A. R. Border		Kapil Dev	3	0	0	0	3
1986-87*I*	A. R. Border		Kapil Dev	3	0	0	1	2
1991-92*A*	A. R. Border		M. Azharuddin	5	4	0	0	1

THE BORDER–GAVASKAR TROPHY

		Captains							
Season	*Australia*		*India*	*T*	*A*	*I*	*T*	*D*	*Held by*
1996-97*I*	M. A. Taylor		S. R. Tendulkar	1	0	1	0	0	I
1997-98*I*	M. A. Taylor		M. Azharuddin	3	1	2	0	0	I
1999-2000*A*	S. R. Waugh		S. R. Tendulkar	3	3	0	0	0	A
2000-01*I*	S. R. Waugh		S. C. Ganguly	3	1	2	0	0	I
	In Australia			28	19	3	0	6	
	In India			32	10	10	1	11	
	Totals			60	29	13	1	17	

A Played in Australia.   I Played in India.

Notes: The following deputised for the official touring captain or were appointed by the home authority for only a minor proportion of the series:
[1]R. R. Lindwall (Second). [2]W. M. Lawry (Third and Fourth). [3]C. G. Borde (First).

HIGHEST INNINGS TOTALS

For Australia in Australia: 674 at Adelaide		1947-48
in India: 574-7 dec. at Madras		1986-87
For India in Australia: 600-4 dec. at Sydney		1985-86
in India: 657-7 dec. at Kolkata		2000-01

LOWEST INNINGS TOTALS

For Australia in Australia: 83 at Melbourne		1980-81
in India: 105 at Kanpur		1959-60
For India in Australia: 58 at Brisbane		1947-48
in India: 135 at Delhi		1959-60

INDIVIDUAL HUNDREDS

For Australia (61)

S. G. Barnes (1)
112   Adelaide   1947-48
D. C. Boon (6)
123†   Adelaide   1985-86
131   Sydney   1985-86
122   Madras   1986-87
129*   Sydney   1991-92
135   Adelaide   1991-92
107   Perth.   1991-92
A. R. Border (4)
162†   Madras   1979-80
124   Melbourne . . .   1980-81
163   Melbourne . . .   1985-86
106   Madras   1986-87
D. G. Bradman (4)
185†   Brisbane   1947-48
132 ⎱
127* ⎰   Melbourne . .   1947-48
201   Adelaide   1947-48
J. W. Burke (1)
161   Bombay.   1956-57
G. S. Chappell (1)
204†   Sydney   1980-81
I. M. Chappell (2)
151   Melbourne . . .   1967-68
138   Delhi   1969-70
R. M. Cowper (2)
108   Adelaide   1967-68
165   Sydney   1967-68
L. E. Favell (1)
101   Madras   1959-60
A. C. Gilchrist (1)
122   Mumbai.   2000-01

R. N. Harvey (4)
153   Melbourne . .   1947-48
140   Bombay. . . .   1956-57
114   Delhi   1959-60
102   Bombay. . . .   1959-60
A. L. Hassett (1)
198*   Adelaide   1947-48
M. L. Hayden (2)
119†   Mumbai. . . .   2000-01
203   Chennai. . . .   2000-01
K. J. Hughes (2)
100   Madras   1979-80
213   Adelaide   1980-81
D. M. Jones (2)
210†   Madras   1986-87
150*   Perth.   1991-92
J. L. Langer (1)
223   Sydney   1999-00
W. M. Lawry (1)
100   Melbourne . . .   1967-68
A. L. Mann (1)
105   Perth.   1977-78
G. R. Marsh (1)
101   Bombay. . . .   1986-87
G. R. J. Matthews (1)
100*   Melbourne . . .   1985-86
T. M. Moody (1)
101†   Perth.   1991-92
A. R. Morris (1)
100*   Melbourne . . .   1947-48

N. C. O'Neill (2)
163   Bombay. . . .   1959-60
113   Calcutta. . . .   1959-60
R. T. Ponting (2)
125   Adelaide   1999-00
141*   Sydney   1999-00
G. M. Ritchie (1)
128†   Adelaide   1985-86
A. P. Sheahan (1)
114   Kanpur   1969-70
R. B. Simpson (4)
103   Adelaide   1967-68
109   Melbourne . . .   1967-68
176   Perth.   1977-78
100   Adelaide   1977-78
K. R. Stackpole (1)
103†   Bombay. . . .   1969-70
M. A. Taylor (2)
100   Adelaide   1991-92
102*   Bangalore . . .   1997-98
K. D. Walters (1)
102   Madras   1969-70
M. E. Waugh (1)
153*   Bangalore . . .   1997-98
S. R. Waugh (2)
150   Adelaide   1999-00
110   Kolkata   2000-01
G. M. Wood (1)
125   Adelaide   1980-81
G. N. Yallop (2)
121†   Adelaide   1977-78
167   Calcutta. . . .   1979-80

For India (44)

M. Amarnath (2)
100   Perth.   1977-78
138   Sydney   1985-86
M. Azharuddin (2)
106   Adelaide   1991-92
163*   Calcutta. . . .   1997-98
N. J. Contractor (1)
108   Bombay. . . .   1959-60
R. Dravid (1)
180   Kolkata   2000-01
S. M. Gavaskar (8)
113†   Brisbane   1977-78
127   Perth.   1977-78
118   Melbourne . . .   1977-78
115   Delhi   1979-80
123   Bombay. . . .   1979-80
166*   Adelaide   1985-86
172   Sydney   1985-86

103   Bombay. . . .   1986-87
V. S. Hazare (2)
116 ⎱
145 ⎰   Adelaide   1947-48
M. L. Jaisimha (1)
101   Brisbane   1967-68
Kapil Dev (1)
119   Madras   1986-87
S. M. H. Kirmani (1)
101*   Bombay. . . .   1979-80
V. V. S. Laxman (2)
167   Sydney   1999-00
281   Kolkata   2000-01
V. Mankad (2)
116   Melbourne . . .   1947-48
111   Melbourne . . .   1947-48
N. R. Mongia (1)
152†   Delhi   1996-97

Nawab of Pataudi jun. (1)
128*†   Madras   1964-65
S. M. Patil (1)
174   Adelaide   1980-81
D. G. Phadkar (1)
123   Adelaide   1947-48
G. S. Ramchand (1)
109   Bombay. . . .   1956-57
R. J. Shastri (2)
121*   Bombay. . . .   1986-87
206   Sydney   1991-92
K. Srikkanth (1)
116   Sydney   1985-86
S. R. Tendulkar (6)
148*   Sydney   1991-92
114   Perth.   1991-92
155*   Chennai. . . .   1997-98
177   Bangalore . . .   1997-98

116	Melbourne . .	1999-00	164*	Bombay	1986-87
126	Chennai	2000-01	**G. R. Viswanath (4)**		
D. B. Vengsarkar (2)			137†	Kanpur	1969-70
112	Bangalore . .	1979-80	161*	Bangalore . .	1979-80

131	Delhi	1979-80
114	Melbourne . .	1980-81
Yashpal Sharma (1)		
100*	Delhi	1979-80

† *On first appearance in Australia–India Tests.*

RECORD PARTNERSHIPS FOR EACH WICKET

For Australia

217	for 1st	D. C. Boon and G. R. Marsh at Sydney	1985-86
236	for 2nd	S. G. Barnes and D. G. Bradman at Adelaide	1947-48
222	for 3rd	A. R. Border and K. J. Hughes at Madras	1979-80
178	for 4th	D. M. Jones and A. R. Border at Madras	1986-87
239	for 5th	S. R. Waugh and R. T. Ponting at Adelaide	1999-2000
197	for 6th	M. L. Hayden and A. C. Gilchrist at Mumbai	2000-01
108	for 7th	S. R. Waugh and S. K. Warne at Adelaide	1999-2000
73	for 8th	T. R. Veivers and G. D. McKenzie at Madras	1964-65
133	for 9th	S. R. Waugh and J. N. Gillespie at Kolkata	2000-01
77	for 10th	A. R. Border and D. R. Gilbert at Melbourne	1985-86

For India

192	for 1st	S. M. Gavaskar and C. P. S. Chauhan at Bombay	1979-80
224	for 2nd	S. M. Gavaskar and M. Amarnath at Sydney	1985-86
159	for 3rd	S. M. Gavaskar and G. R. Viswanath at Delhi	1979-80
159	for 4th	D. B. Vengsarkar and G. R. Viswanath at Bangalore	1979-80
376	for 5th†	V. V. S. Laxman and R. Dravid at Kolkata	2000-01
298*	for 6th†	D. B. Vengsarkar and R. J. Shastri at Bombay	1986-87
132	for 7th	V. S. Hazare and H. R. Adhikari at Adelaide	1947-48
127	for 8th	S. M. H. Kirmani and K. D. Ghavri at Bombay	1979-80
81	for 9th	S. R. Tendulkar and K. S. More at Perth	1991-92
94	for 10th	S. M. Gavaskar and N. S. Yadav at Adelaide	1985-86

† *Record partnership against all countries.*

TEN WICKETS OR MORE IN A MATCH

For Australia (12)

11-105 (6-52, 5-53)	R. Benaud, Calcutta	1956-57
12-124 (5-31, 7-93)	A. K. Davidson, Kanpur	1959-60
12-166 (5-99, 7-67)	G. Dymock, Kanpur	1979-80
10-168 (5-76, 5-92)	C. J. McDermott, Adelaide	1991-92
10-103 (5-48, 5-55)	G. D. McGrath, Sydney	1999-2000
10-91 (6-58, 4-33)†	G. D. McKenzie, Madras	1964-65
10-151 (7-66, 3-85)	G. D. McKenzie, Melbourne	1967-68
10-144 (5-91, 5-53)	A. A. Mallett, Madras	1969-70
10-249 (5-103, 5-146)	G. R. J. Matthews, Madras	1986-87
12-126 (6-66, 6-60)	B. A. Reid, Melbourne	1991-92
11-31 (5-2, 6-29)†	E. R. H. Toshack, Brisbane	1947-48
11-95 (4-68, 7-27)	M. R. Whitney, Perth	1991-92

For India (8)

10-194 (5-89, 5-105)	B. S. Bedi, Perth	1977-78
12-104 (6-52, 6-52)	B. S. Chandrasekhar, Melbourne	1977-78
10-130 (7-49, 3-81)	Ghulam Ahmed, Calcutta	1956-57
13-196 (7-123, 6-73)	Harbhajan Singh, Kolkata.	2000-01
15-217 (7-133, 8-84)	Harbhajan Singh, Chennai	2000-01
11-122 (5-31, 6-91)	R. G. Nadkarni, Madras.	1964-65
14-124 (9-69, 5-55)	J. M. Patel, Kanpur	1959-60
10-174 (4-100, 6-74)	E. A. S. Prasanna, Madras	1969-70

† *On first appearance in Australia–India Tests.*

AUSTRALIA v PAKISTAN

		Captains				
Season	*Australia*	*Pakistan*	*T*	*A*	*P*	*D*
1956-57*P*	I. W. Johnson	A. H. Kardar	1	0	1	0
1959-60*P*	R. Benaud	Fazal Mahmood[1]	3	2	0	1
1964-65*P*	R. B. Simpson	Hanif Mohammad	1	0	0	1
1964-65*A*	R. B. Simpson	Hanif Mohammad	1	0	0	1
1972-73*A*	I. M. Chappell	Intikhab Alam	3	3	0	0
1976-77*A*	G. S. Chappell	Mushtaq Mohammad	3	1	1	1
1978-79*A*	G. N. Yallop[2]	Mushtaq Mohammad	2	1	1	0
1979-80*P*	G. S. Chappell	Javed Miandad	3	0	1	2
1981-82*A*	G. S. Chappell	Javed Miandad	3	2	1	0
1982-83*P*	K. J. Hughes	Imran Khan	3	0	3	0
1983-84*A*	K. J. Hughes	Imran Khan[3]	5	2	0	3
1988-89*P*	A. R. Border	Javed Miandad	3	0	1	2
1989-90*A*	A. R. Border	Imran Khan	3	1	0	2
1994-95*P*	M. A. Taylor	Salim Malik	3	0	1	2
1995-96*A*	M. A. Taylor	Wasim Akram	3	2	1	0
1998-99*P*	M. A. Taylor	Aamir Sohail	3	1	0	2
1999-2000*A*	S. R. Waugh	Wasim Akram	3	3	0	0
	In Pakistan		20	3	7	10
	In Australia		26	15	4	7
	Totals		46	18	11	17

A Played in Australia. P Played in Pakistan.

Notes: The following deputised for the official touring captain or were appointed by the home authority for only a minor proportion of the series:
[1]Imtiaz Ahmed (Second). [2]K. J. Hughes (Second). [3]Zaheer Abbas (First, Second and Third).

HIGHEST INNINGS TOTALS

For Australia in Australia: 585 at Adelaide	1972-73
in Pakistan: 617 at Faisalabad	1979-80
For Pakistan in Australia: 624 at Adelaide	1983-84
in Pakistan: 580-9 dec. at Peshawar	1998-99

LOWEST INNINGS TOTALS

For Australia in Australia: 125 at Melbourne	1981-82
in Pakistan: 80 at Karachi.	1956-57
For Pakistan in Australia: 62 at Perth	1981-82
in Pakistan: 134 at Dacca	1959-60

INDIVIDUAL HUNDREDS

For Australia (53)

J. Benaud (1)
142 Melbourne . . 1972-73

D. C. Boon (1)
114* Karachi 1994-95

A. R. Border (6)
105† Melbourne . . 1978-79
150*⎫
153 ⎭ Lahore 1979-80
118 Brisbane 1983-84
117* Adelaide 1983-84
113* Faisalabad . . 1988-89

G. S. Chappell (6)
116* Melbourne . . 1972-73
121 Melbourne . . 1976-77
235 Faisalabad . . 1979-80
201 Brisbane 1981-82
150* Brisbane 1983-84
182 Sydney 1983-84

I. M. Chappell (1)
196 Adelaide 1972-73

G. J. Cosier (1)
168 Melbourne . . 1976-77

I. C. Davis (1)
105† Adelaide 1976-77

A. C. Gilchrist (1)
149* Hobart 1999-00

K. J. Hughes (2)
106 Perth. 1981-82

J. Benaud column continues right:

106 Adelaide . . . 1983-84

D. M. Jones (2)
116 ⎫
121*⎭ Adelaide . . . 1989-90

J. L. Langer (3)
116 Peshawar . . . 1998-99
127 Hobart 1999-00
144 Perth. 1999-00

R. B. McCosker (1)
105 Melbourne . . 1976-77

R. W. Marsh (1)
118† Adelaide 1972-73

N. C. O'Neill (1)
134 Lahore 1959-60

W. B. Phillips (1)
159† Perth. 1983-84

R. T. Ponting (1)
197 Perth. 1999-00

I. R. Redpath (1)
135 Melbourne . . 1972-73

G. M. Ritchie (1)
106* Faisalabad . . 1982-83

A. P. Sheahan (1)
127 Melbourne . . 1972-73

R. B. Simpson (2)
153 ⎫
115 ⎭ †Karachi 1964-65

M. J. Slater (3)
110 Rawalpindi. . 1994-95
108 Rawalpindi. . 1998-99
169 Brisbane 1999-00

M. A. Taylor (4)
101† Melbourne . . 1989-90
101* Sydney 1989-90
123 Hobart 1995-96
334* Peshawar . . . 1998-99

K. D. Walters (1)
107 Adelaide 1976-77

M. E. Waugh (3)
116 Sydney 1995-96
117 Karachi 1998-99
100 Brisbane 1999-00

S. R. Waugh (2)
112* Brisbane 1995-96
157 Rawalpindi. . 1998-99

K. C. Wessels (1)
179 Adelaide 1983-84

G. M. Wood (1)
100 Melbourne . . 1981-82

G. N. Yallop (3)
172 Faisalabad . . 1979-80
141 Perth. 1983-84
268 Melbourne . . 1983-84

For Pakistan (44)

Aamir Sohail (2)
105 Lahore 1994-95
133 Karachi 1998-99

Asif Iqbal (3)
152* Adelaide . . . 1976-77
120 Sydney 1976-77
134* Perth. 1978-79

Hanif Mohammad (2)
101* Karachi 1959-60
104 Melbourne . . 1964-65

Ijaz Ahmed, sen. (6)
122 Faisalabad . . 1988-89
121 Melbourne . . 1989-90
137 Sydney 1995-96
155 Peshawar . . . 1998-99
120* Karachi 1998-99
115 Perth. 1999-00

Imran Khan (1)
136 Adelaide . . . 1989-90

Inzamam-ul-Haq (1)
118 Hobart 1999-00

Javed Miandad (6)
129* Perth. 1978-79

106* Faisalabad . . 1979-80
138 Lahore 1982-83
131 Adelaide . . . 1983-84
211 Karachi 1988-89
107 Faisalabad . . 1988-89

Khalid Ibadulla (1)
166† Karachi 1964-65

Majid Khan (3)
158 Melbourne . . 1972-73
108 Melbourne . . 1978-79
110* Lahore 1979-80

Mansoor Akhtar (1)
111 Faisalabad . . 1982-83

Mohsin Khan (3)
135 Lahore 1982-83
149 Adelaide . . . 1983-84
152 Melbourne . . 1983-84

Moin Khan (1)
115*† Lahore 1994-95

Mushtaq Mohammad (1)
121 Sydney 1972-73

Qasim Omar (1)
113 Adelaide . . . 1983-84

Sadiq Mohammad (2)
137 Melbourne . . 1972-73
105 Melbourne . . 1976-77

Saeed Ahmed (1)
166 Lahore 1959-60

Saeed Anwar (3)
145 Rawalpindi. . 1998-99
126 Peshawar . . . 1998-99
119 Brisbane 1999-00

Salim Malik (2)
237 Rawalpindi. . 1994-95
143 Lahore 1994-95

Taslim Arif (1)
210* Faisalabad . . 1979-80

Wasim Akram (1)
123 Adelaide . . . 1989-90

Zaheer Abbas (2)
101 Adelaide . . . 1976-77
126 Faisalabad . . 1982-83

† *On first appearance in Australia–Pakistan Tests.*

RECORD PARTNERSHIPS FOR EACH WICKET

For Australia

269 for 1st	M. J. Slater and G. S. Blewett at Brisbane		1999-2000
279 for 2nd	M. A. Taylor and J. L. Langer at Peshawar		1998-99
203 for 3rd	G. N. Yallop and K. J. Hughes at Melbourne		1983-84
217 for 4th	G. S. Chappell and G. N. Yallop at Faisalabad		1979-80
327 for 5th	J. L. Langer and R. T. Ponting at Perth		1999-2000
238 for 6th	J. L. Langer and A. C. Gilchrist at Hobart		1999-2000
185 for 7th	G. N. Yallop and G. R. J. Matthews at Melbourne		1983-84
117 for 8th	G. J. Cosier and L. J. O'Keeffe at Melbourne		1976-77
83 for 9th	J. R. Watkins and R. A. L. Massie at Sydney		1972-73
86 for 10th	S. K. Warne and S. A. Muller at Brisbane		1999-2000

For Pakistan

249 for 1st	Khalid Ibadulla and Abdul Kadir at Karachi		1964-65
233 for 2nd	Mohsin Khan and Qasim Omar at Adelaide		1983-84
223* for 3rd	Taslim Arif and Javed Miandad at Faisalabad		1979-80
177 for 4th	Saeed Anwar and Yousuf Youhana at Brisbane		1999-2000
186 for 5th	Javed Miandad and Salim Malik at Adelaide		1983-84
196 for 6th	Salim Malik and Aamir Sohail at Lahore		1994-95
104 for 7th	Intikhab Alam and Wasim Bari at Adelaide		1972-73
111 for 8th	Majid Khan and Imran Khan at Lahore		1979-80
120 for 9th	Saeed Anwar and Mushtaq Ahmed at Rawalpindi		1998-99
87 for 10th	Asif Iqbal and Iqbal Qasim at Adelaide		1976-77

TEN WICKETS OR MORE IN A MATCH

For Australia (4)

10-111 (7-87, 3-24)†	R. J. Bright, Karachi	1979-80
10-135 (6-82, 4-53)	D. K. Lillee, Melbourne	1976-77
11-118 (5-32, 6-86)†	C. G. Rackemann, Perth	1983-84
11-77 (7-23, 4-54)	S. K. Warne, Brisbane	1995-96

For Pakistan (6)

11-218 (4-76, 7-142)	Abdul Qadir, Faisalabad	1982-83
13-114 (6-34, 7-80)†	Fazal Mahmood, Karachi	1956-57
12-165 (6-102, 6-63)	Imran Khan, Sydney	1976-77
11-118 (4-69, 7-49)	Iqbal Qasim, Karachi	1979-80
11-125 (2-39, 9-86)	Sarfraz Nawaz, Melbourne	1978-79
11-160 (6-62, 5-98)†	Wasim Akram, Melbourne	1989-90

† *On first appearance in Australia–Pakistan Tests.*

AUSTRALIA v SRI LANKA

		Captains				
Season	*Australia*	*Sri Lanka*	*T*	*A*	*SL*	*D*
1982-83*S*	G. S. Chappell	L. R. D. Mendis	1	1	0	0
1987-88*A*	A. R. Border	R. S. Madugalle	1	1	0	0
1989-90*A*	A. R. Border	A. Ranatunga	2	1	0	1
1992-93*S*	A. R. Border	A. Ranatunga	3	1	0	2
1995-96*A*	M. A. Taylor	A. Ranatunga[1]	3	3	0	0
1999-2000*S*	S. R. Waugh	S. T. Jayasuriya	3	0	1	2
	In Australia		6	5	0	1
	In Sri Lanka		7	2	1	4
	Totals.		13	7	1	5

A Played in Australia.   S Played in Sri Lanka.

Note: The following deputised for the official touring captain:
[1]P. A. de Silva (Third).

HIGHEST INNINGS TOTALS

For Australia in Australia: 617-5 dec. at Perth	1995-96
in Sri Lanka: 514-4 dec. at Kandy	1982-83
For Sri Lanka in Australia: 418 at Brisbane.	1989-90
in Sri Lanka: 547-8 dec. at Colombo (SSC).	1992-93

LOWEST INNINGS TOTALS

For Australia in Australia: 224 at Hobart	1989-90
in Sri Lanka: 140 at Kandy	1999-2000
For Sri Lanka in Australia: 153 at Perth	1987-88
in Sri Lanka: 164 at Colombo (SSC)	1992-93

INDIVIDUAL HUNDREDS

For Australia (16)

D. C. Boon (1)	100* Colombo (KS) 1992-93	108 Hobart 1989-90
110 Melbourne . . 1995-96	**T. M. Moody** (1)	**M. E. Waugh** (1)
A. R. Border (1)	106† Brisbane . . . 1989-90	111 Perth. 1995-96
106 Moratuwa . . 1992-93	**R. T. Ponting** (1)	**S. R. Waugh** (3)
D. W. Hookes (1)	105* Colombo (SSC) 1999-00	134* Hobart 1989-90
143*† Kandy. 1982-83	**M. J. Slater** (1)	131* Melbourne . . 1995-96
D. M. Jones (3)	219† Perth. 1995-96	170 Adelaide . . . 1995-96
102† Perth. 1987-88	**M. A. Taylor** (2)	**K. C. Wessels** (1)
118* Hobart 1989-90	164† Brisbane . . . 1989-90	141† Kandy. 1982-83

For Sri Lanka (7)

P. A. de Silva (1)
167   Brisbane . . .   1989-90
A. P. Gurusinha (2)
137   Colombo (SSC)   1992-93
143   Melbourne . .   1995-96

S. T. Jayasuriya (1)
112   Adelaide . . .   1995-96
R. S. Kaluwitharana (1)
132*† Colombo (SSC)   1992-93

A. Ranatunga (1)
127   Colombo (SSC)   1992-93
H. P. Tillekeratne (1)
119   Perth.   1995-96

† *On first appearance in Australia–Sri Lanka Tests.*

RECORD PARTNERSHIPS FOR EACH WICKET

For Australia

228	for 1st	M. J. Slater and M. A. Taylor at Perth	1995-96
170	for 2nd	K. C. Wessels and G. N. Yallop at Kandy	1982-83
158	for 3rd	T. M. Moody and A. R. Border at Brisbane	1989-90
163	for 4th	M. A. Taylor and A. R. Border at Hobart	1989-90
155*	for 5th	D. W. Hookes and A. R. Border at Kandy	1982-83
260*	for 6th	D. M. Jones and S. R. Waugh at Hobart.	1989-90
129	for 7th	G. R. J. Matthews and I. A. Healy at Moratuwa.	1992-93
107	for 8th	R. T. Ponting and J. N. Gillespie at Kandy	1999-2000
45	for 9th	I. A. Healy and S. K. Warne at Colombo (SSC)	1992-93
49	for 10th	I. A. Healy and M. R. Whitney at Colombo (SSC).	1992-93

For Sri Lanka

110	for 1st	R. S. Mahanama and U. C. Hathurusinghe at Colombo (KS)	1992-93
92	for 2nd	R. S. Mahanama and A. P. Gurusinha at Colombo (SSC).	1992-93
125	for 3rd	S. T. Jayasuriya and S. Ranatunga at Adelaide.	1995-96
230	for 4th	A. P. Gurusinha and A. Ranatunga at Colombo (SSC).	1992-93
116	for 5th	H. P. Tillekeratne and A. Ranatunga at Moratuwa.	1992-93
96	for 6th	A. P. Gurusinha and R. S. Kaluwitharana at Colombo (SSC) . . .	1992-93
144	for 7th	P. A. de Silva and J. R. Ratnayeke at Brisbane	1989-90
33	for 8th	A. Ranatunga and C. P. H. Ramanayake at Perth	1987-88
46	for 9th	H. D. P. K. Dharmasena and G. P. Wickremasinghe at Perth. . . .	1995-96
27	for 10th	P. A. de Silva and C. P. H. Ramanayake at Brisbane	1989-90

BEST MATCH BOWLING ANALYSES

For Australia

8-156 (3-68, 5-88)	M. G. Hughes, Hobart	1989-90

For Sri Lanka

8-157 (5-82, 3-75)	C. P. H. Ramanayake, Moratuwa.	1992-93

AUSTRALIA v ZIMBABWE

		Captains				
Season	Australia	Zimbabwe	T	A	Z	D
1999-2000Z	S. R. Waugh	A. D. R. Campbell	1	1	0	0

Z Played in Zimbabwe.

HIGHEST INNINGS TOTALS

For Australia: 422 at Harare 1999-2000

For Zimbabwe: 232 at Harare 1999-2000

INDIVIDUAL HUNDRED

For Australia (1)

S. R. Waugh (1)
151*† Harare 1999-00

Highest score for Zimbabwe: 91 by M. W. Goodwin at Harare, 1999-2000.

† *On first appearance in Australia–Zimbabwe Tests.*

HIGHEST PARTNERSHIPS

For Australia

114 for 8th   S. R. Waugh and D. W. Fleming at Harare 1999-2000

For Zimbabwe

98 for 2nd   T. R. Gripper and M. W. Goodwin at Harare 1999-2000

BEST MATCH BOWLING ANALYSES

For Australia

6-90 (3-44, 3-46)   G. D. McGrath, Harare 1999-2000

For Zimbabwe

5-93 (5-93)   H. H. Streak, Harare 1999-2000

SOUTH AFRICA v WEST INDIES

Season	South Africa	Captains					
		West Indies	T	SA	WI	D	
1991-92*W*	K. C. Wessels	R. B. Richardson	1	0	1	0	
1998-99*S*	W. J. Cronje	B. C. Lara	5	5	0	0	

SIR VIVIAN RICHARDS TROPHY

Season	South Africa	Captains					
		West Indies	T	SA	WI	D	Held by
2000-01*W*	S. M. Pollock	C. L. Hooper	5	2	1	2	SA
	In South Africa		5	5	0	0	
	In West Indies		6	2	2	2	
	Totals		11	7	2	2	

S Played in South Africa. W Played in West Indies.

HIGHEST INNINGS TOTALS

For South Africa in South Africa: 406-8 dec. at Cape Town 1998-99
in West Indies: 454 at Bridgetown. 2000-01

For West Indies in South Africa: 271 at Cape Town. 1998-99
in West Indies: 387 at Bridgetown 2000-01

LOWEST INNINGS TOTALS

For South Africa in South Africa: 195 at Port Elizabeth 1998-99
in West Indies: 141 at Kingston 2000-01

For West Indies in South Africa: 121 at Port Elizabeth 1998-99
in West Indies: 140 at St John's 2000-01

INDIVIDUAL HUNDREDS

For South Africa (10)

M. V. Boucher (1)
100   Centurion. . . 1998-99
D. J. Cullinan (3)
168   Cape Town. . 1998-99
103   Port-of-Spain 2000-01
134   Bridgetown . 2000-01

A. C. Hudson (1)
163† Bridgetown . 1991-92
J. H. Kallis (1)
110   Cape Town. . 1998-99
G. Kirsten (2)
134   Centurion .. 1998-99

150   Georgetown . 2000-01
S. M. Pollock (1)
106* Bridgetown . 2000-01
J. N. Rhodes (1)
103* Centurion . . 1998-99

For West Indies (1)

R. D. Jacobs (1)
113* Bridgetown . 2000-01

† *On first appearance in South Africa–West Indies Tests.*

RECORD PARTNERSHIPS FOR EACH WICKET

For South Africa

97 for 1st	G. Kirsten and H. H. Gibbs at Durban 1998-99
146 for 2nd	G. Kirsten and J. H. Kallis at Georgetown 2000-01
235 for 3rd	J. H. Kallis and D. J. Cullinan at Cape Town 1998-99
149 for 4th	D. J. Cullinan and N. D. McKenzie at Bridgetown. 2000-01
115 for 5th	G. Kirsten and J. N. Rhodes at Centurion 1998-99
92 for 6th	J. N. Rhodes and S. M. Pollock at Port Elizabeth 1998-99
92 for 7th	J. H. Kallis and M. V. Boucher at Centurion. 1998-99
75 for 8th	S. M. Pollock and N. Boje at St John's 2000-01
132 for 9th	S. M. Pollock and A. A. Donald at Bridgetown. 2000-01
25 for 10th	P. L. Symcox and D. J. Terbrugge at Johannesburg 1998-99

For West Indies

99 for 1st	D. L. Haynes and P. V. Simmons at Bridgetown 1991-92
88 for 2nd	C. H. Gayle and M. N. Samuels at Georgetown 2000-01
160 for 3rd	S. Chanderpaul and B. C. Lara at Durban 1998-99
91 for 4th	S. Chanderpaul and C. L. Hooper at Johannesburg 1998-99
116 for 5th	B. C. Lara and C. L. Hooper at Bridgetown. 2000-01
92 for 6th	R. R. Sarwan and C. L. Hooper at Port-of-Spain. 2000-01
81 for 7th	R. D. Jacobs and N. A. M. McLean at Centurion 1998-99
65 for 8th	R. D. Jacobs and N. A. M. McLean at Cape Town 1998-99
71 for 9th	R. D. Jacobs and M. Dillon at Port-of-Spain 2000-01
64 for 10th	R. D. Jacobs and M. Dillon at Cape Town 1998-99

BEST MATCH BOWLING ANALYSES

For South Africa

9-94 (5-28, 4-66)   S. M. Pollock, Kingston.......................... 2000-01

For West Indies

8-79 (2-28, 6-51)   C. E. L. Ambrose, Port Elizabeth.................. 1998-99

SOUTH AFRICA v NEW ZEALAND

		Captains					
Season	South Africa	New Zealand	T	SA	NZ	D
1931-32*N*	H. B. Cameron	M. L. Page	2	2	0	0
1952-53*N*	J. E. Cheetham	W. M. Wallace	2	1	0	1
1953-54*S*	J. E. Cheetham	G. O. Rabone[1]	5	4	0	1
1961-62*S*	D. J. McGlew	J. R. Reid	5	2	2	1
1963-64*N*	T. L. Goddard	J. R. Reid	3	0	0	3
1994-95*S*	W. J. Cronje	K. R. Rutherford	3	2	1	0
1994-95*N*	W. J. Cronje	K. R. Rutherford	1	1	0	0
1998-99*N*	W. J. Cronje	D. J. Nash	3	1	0	2
2000-01*S*	S. M. Pollock	S. P. Fleming	3	2	0	1
	In New Zealand		11	5	0	6
	In South Africa		16	10	3	3
	Totals		27	15	3	9

N Played in New Zealand.   S Played in South Africa.

Note: The following deputised for the official touring captain:
[1]B. Sutcliffe (Fourth and Fifth).

HIGHEST INNINGS TOTALS

For South Africa in South Africa: 471-9 dec. at Bloemfontein 2000-01
in New Zealand: 621-5 dec. at Auckland 1998-99

For New Zealand in South Africa: 505 at Cape Town...................... 1953-54
in New Zealand: 364 at Wellington.................... 1931-32

LOWEST INNINGS TOTALS

For South Africa in South Africa: 148 at Johannesburg 1953-54
in New Zealand: 223 at Dunedin..................... 1963-64

For New Zealand in South Africa: 79 at Johannesburg.................... 1953-54
in New Zealand: 138 at Dunedin 1963-64

INDIVIDUAL HUNDREDS

For South Africa (23)

X. C. Balaskas (1)			**H. H. Gibbs** (2)			**R. A. McLean** (2)	
122*	Wellington . .	1931-32	211*	Christchurch.	1998-99	101	Durban	1953-54
J. A. J. Christy (1)			120	Wellington . .	1998-99	113	Cape Town. .	1961-62
103†	Christchurch.	1931-32	**J. H. Kallis** (2)			**B. Mitchell** (1)	
W. J. Cronje (2)			148*	Christchurch.	1998-99	113†	Christchurch.	1931-32
112	Cape Town. .	1994-95	160	Bloemfontein	2000-01	**A. R. A. Murray** (1)	
101	Auckland. . .	1994-95	**G. Kirsten** (1)			109†	Wellington . .	1952-53
D. J. Cullinan (2)			128	Auckland. . .	1998-99	**D. J. Richardson** (1)	
275*	Auckland. . .	1998-99	**D. J. McGlew** (3)			109	Cape Town. .	1994-95
152	Wellington . .	1998-99	255*†	Wellington . .	1952-53	**J. H. B. Waite** (1)	
H. H. Dippenaar (1)			127*‡	Durban	1961-62	101	Johannesburg	1961-62
100	Johannesburg	2000-01	120	Johannesburg	1961-62		
W. R. Endean (1)			**N. D. McKenzie** (1)				
116	Auckland. . .	1952-53	120	Port Elizabeth	2000-01		

For New Zealand (8)

P. T. Barton (1)			**J. R. Reid** (2)			**M. S. Sinclair** (1)	
109	Port Elizabeth	1961-62	135	Cape Town. .	1953-54	150	Port Elizabeth	2000-01
P. G. Z. Harris (1)			142	Johannesburg	1961-62	**H. G. Vivian** (1)	
101	Cape Town. .	1961-62	**B. W. Sinclair** (1)			100†	Wellington . .	1931-32
G. O. Rabone (1)			138	Auckland. . .	1963-64		
107	Durban	1953-54					

† *On first appearance in South Africa–New Zealand Tests.*
‡ *Carried his bat.*

RECORD PARTNERSHIPS FOR EACH WICKET

For South Africa

196	for 1st	J. A. J. Christy and B. Mitchell at Christchurch.	1931-32
315*	for 2nd†	H. H. Gibbs and J. H. Kallis at Christchurch	1998-99
183	for 3rd	G. Kirsten and D. J. Cullinan at Auckland	1998-99
145	for 4th	D. J. Cullinan and W. J. Cronje at Wellington	1998-99
141	for 5th	D. J. Cullinan and J. N. Rhodes at Auckland	1998-99
126*	for 6th	D. J. Cullinan and S. M. Pollock at Auckland	1998-99
246	for 7th†	D. J. McGlew and A. R. A. Murray at Wellington	1952-53
136	for 8th	N. D. McKenzie and N. Boje at Port Elizabeth	2000-01
60	for 9th	P. M. Pollock and N. A. T. Adcock at Port Elizabeth	1961-62
47	for 10th	D. J. McGlew and H. D. Bromfield at Port Elizabeth	1961-62

For New Zealand

126	for 1st	G. O. Rabone and M. E. Chapple at Cape Town	1953-54
90	for 2nd	M. J. Horne and J. Astle at Auckland	1998-99
94	for 3rd	M. B. Poore and B. Sutcliffe at Cape Town	1953-54
171	for 4th	B. W. Sinclair and S. N. McGregor at Auckland	1963-64
176	for 5th	J. R. Reid and J. E. F. Beck at Cape Town	1953-54
100	for 6th	H. G. Vivian and F. T. Badcock at Wellington	1931-32
84	for 7th	J. R. Reid and G. A. Bartlett at Johannesburg	1961-62
74	for 8th	S. A. Thomson and D. J. Nash at Johannesburg	1994-95
69	for 9th	C. F. W. Allcott and I. B. Cromb at Wellington	1931-32
57	for 10th	S. B. Doull and R. P. de Groen at Johannesburg	1994-95

† *Record partnership against all countries.*

TEN WICKETS OR MORE IN A MATCH

For South Africa (1)

11-196 (6-128, 5-68)†   S. F. Burke, Cape Town   1961-62

† *On first appearance in South Africa–New Zealand Tests.*

Note: The best match figures for New Zealand are 8-134 (3-57, 5-77) by M. N. Hart at Johannesburg, 1994-95.

SOUTH AFRICA v INDIA

	Captains					
Season	*South Africa*	*India*	*T*	*SA*	*I*	*D*
1992-93*S*	K. C. Wessels	M. Azharuddin	4	1	0	3
1996-97*I*	W. J. Cronje	S. R. Tendulkar	3	1	2	0
1996-97*S*	W. J. Cronje	S. R. Tendulkar	3	2	0	1
1999-2000*I*	W. J. Cronje	S. R. Tendulkar	2	2	0	0
2001-02*S*†	S. M. Pollock	S. C. Ganguly	2	1	0	1
	In South Africa		9	4	0	5
	In India		5	3	2	0
	Totals		14	7	2	5

S Played in South Africa. I Played in India.

† *The Third Test at Centurion was stripped of its official status by the ICC after a disciplinary dispute and is excluded.*

HIGHEST INNINGS TOTALS

For South Africa in South Africa: 563 at Bloemfontein   2001-02
          in India: 479 at Bangalore   1999-2000

For India in South Africa: 410 at Johannesburg   1996-97
       in India: 400-7 dec. at Kanpur.   1996-97

LOWEST INNINGS TOTALS

For South Africa in South Africa: 235 at Durban   1996-97
          in India: 105 at Ahmedabad   1996-97

For India in South Africa: 66 at Durban   1996-97
       in India: 113 at Mumbai   1999-2000

INDIVIDUAL HUNDREDS

For South Africa (13)

W. J. Cronje (1)	196 Port Elizabeth 2001-02	**L. Klusener** (2)
135 Port Elizabeth 1992-93	**A. C. Hudson** (1)	102* Cape Town. . 1996-97
D. J. Cullinan (2)	146 Calcutta. . . . 1996-97	108 Bloemfontein 2001-02
153* Calcutta. . . . 1996-97	**G. Kirsten** (3)	**B. M. McMillan** (1)
122* Johannesburg 1996-97	102 ⎫ Calcutta. . . . 1996-97	103* Cape Town. . 1996-97
H. H. Gibbs (2)	133 ⎭	**K. C. Wessels** (1)
107 Bloemfontein 2001-02	103 Cape Town. . 1996-97	118† Durban 1992-93

For India (11)

P. K. Amre (1)			102	Bangalore . .	1999-00	**V. Sehwag** (1)
103†	Durban	1992-93	**R. Dravid** (1)			105† Bloemfontein 2001-02
M. Azharuddin (4)			148	Johannesburg	1996-97	**S. R. Tendulkar** (3)
109	Calcutta. . . .	1996-97	**Kapil Dev** (1)			111 Johannesburg 1992-93
163*	Kanpur	1996-97	129	Port Elizabeth	1992-93	169 Cape Town. . 1996-97
115	Cape Town. .	1996-97				155 Bloemfontein 2001-02

† *On first appearance in South Africa–India Tests.*

RECORD PARTNERSHIPS FOR EACH WICKET

For South Africa

236	for 1st	A. C. Hudson and G. Kirsten at Calcutta	. . . .	1996-97
212	for 2nd	G. Kirsten and D. J. Cullinan at Calcutta	. . . .	1996-97
130	for 3rd	J. H. Kallis and N. D. McKenzie at Bloemfontein	. . . .	2001-02
105	for 4th	H. H. Gibbs and H. H. Dippenaar at Port Elizabeth	. . . . . .	2001-02
164	for 5th	J. H. Kallis and L. Klusener at Bangalore	. . . .	1999-2000
112	for 6th	B. M. McMillan and S. M. Pollock at Johannesburg	. . . . . .	1996-97
121	for 7th	L. Klusener and M. V. Boucher at Bloemfontein	. . . .	2001-02
147*	for 8th	B. M. McMillan and L. Klusener at Cape Town	. . . .	1996-97
60	for 9th	P. S. de Villiers and A. A. Donald at Ahmedabad	. . . .	1996-97
74	for 10th	B. M. McMillan and A. A. Donald at Durban	. . . .	1996-97

For India

90	for 1st	V. Rathore and N. R. Mongia at Johannesburg.	. . . .	1996-97
171	for 2nd	D. Dasgupta and R. Dravid at Port Elizabeth.	. . . .	2001-02
54	for 3rd	R. Dravid and S. R. Tendulkar at Johannesburg	. . . .	1996-97
145	for 4th	R. Dravid and S. C. Ganguly at Bloemfontein.	. . . .	2001-02
220	for 5th	S. R. Tendulkar and V. Sehwag at Bloemfontein	. . . .	2001-02
222	for 6th	S. R. Tendulkar and M. Azharuddin at Cape Town	. . . .	1996-97
76	for 7th	R. Dravid and J. Srinath at Johannesburg	. . . .	1996-97
161	for 8th†	M. Azharuddin and A. Kumble at Calcutta	. . . .	1996-97
80	for 9th	V. V. S. Laxman and A. Kumble at Port Elizabeth	. . . .	2001-02
52	for 10th	A. B. Agarkar and M. Kartik at Mumbai	. . . .	1999-2000

† *Record partnership against all countries.*

TEN WICKETS OR MORE IN A MATCH

For South Africa (2)

12-139 (5-55, 7-84)	A. A. Donald, Port Elizabeth	1992-93
10-147 (4-91, 6-56)	S. M. Pollock, Bloemfontein	2001-02

For India (1)

10-153 (5-60, 5-93)	B. K. V. Prasad, Durban	1996-97

SOUTH AFRICA v PAKISTAN

		Captains				
Season	South Africa	Pakistan	T	SA	P	D
1994-95S	W. J. Cronje	Salim Malik	1	1	0	0
1997-98P	W. J. Cronje	Saeed Anwar	3	1	0	2
1997-98S	W. J. Cronje[1]	Rashid Latif[2]	3	1	1	1
	In South Africa		4	2	1	1
	In Pakistan		3	1	0	2
	Totals...................		7	3	1	3

S Played in South Africa.   P Played in Pakistan.

Notes: The following deputised for the official touring captain or were appointed by the home authority for only a minor proportion of the series:
[1]G. Kirsten (First). [2]Aamir Sohail (First and Second).

HIGHEST INNINGS TOTALS

For South Africa: 460 at Johannesburg   1994-95

For Pakistan: 456 at Rawalpindi   1997-98

LOWEST INNINGS TOTALS

For South Africa: 214 at Faisalabad   1997-98

For Pakistan: 92 at Faisalabad   1997-98

INDIVIDUAL HUNDREDS

For South Africa (3)

G. Kirsten (1)	**B. M. McMillan** (1)	**P. L. Symcox** (1)
100*‡ Faisalabad . . 1997-98	113† Johannesburg 1994-95	108 Johannesburg 1997-98

For Pakistan (5)

Ali Naqvi (1)	**Azhar Mahmood** (3)	**Saeed Anwar** (1)
115† Rawalpindi. . 1997-98	128*† Rawalpindi. . 1997-98	118 Durban 1997-98
	136 Johannesburg 1997-98	
	132 Durban 1997-98	

† *On first appearance in South Africa–Pakistan Tests.*
‡ *Carried his bat.*

RECORD PARTNERSHIPS FOR EACH WICKET

For South Africa

135 for 1st	G. Kirsten and A. M. Bacher at Sheikhupura	1997-98
114 for 2nd	G. Kirsten and J. H. Kallis at Rawalpindi	1997-98
83 for 3rd	J. H. Kallis and H. D. Ackerman at Durban	1997-98
79 for 4th	G. Kirsten and W. J. Cronje at Johannesburg	1994-95
43 for 5th	P. L. Symcox and W. J. Cronje at Faisalabad	1997-98

57 for 6th	J. N. Rhodes and B. M. McMillan at Johannesburg	1994-95
06 for 7th	S. M. Pollock and D. J. Richardson at Rawalpindi.	1997-98
24 for 8th	G. Kirsten and P. L. Symcox at Faisalabad	1997-98
95 for 9th†	M. V. Boucher and P. L. Symcox at Johannesburg	1997-98
71 for 10th	P. S. de Villiers and A. A. Donald at Johannesburg	1994-95

For Pakistan

01 for 1st	Saeed Anwar and Aamir Sohail at Durban	1997-98
69 for 2nd	Ali Naqvi and Mohammad Ramzan at Rawalpindi	1997-98
72 for 3rd	Ijaz Ahmed, sen. and Mohammad Wasim at Johannesburg	1997-98
93 for 4th	Asif Mujtaba and Inzamam-ul-Haq at Johannesburg.	1994-95
44 for 5th	Ali Naqvi and Mohammad Wasim at Rawalpindi	1997-98
44 for 6th	Inzamam-ul-Haq and Moin Khan at Faisalabad	1997-98
35 for 7th	Salim Malik and Wasim Akram at Johannesburg	1994-95
40 for 8th	Inzamam-ul-Haq and Kabir Khan at Johannesburg	1994-95
80 for 9th	Azhar Mahmood and Shoaib Akhtar at Durban	1997-98
51 for 10th†	Azhar Mahmood and Mushtaq Ahmed at Rawalpindi	1997-98

Record partnership against all countries.

TEN WICKETS OR MORE IN A MATCH

For South Africa (1)

0-108 (6-81, 4-27)†	P. S. de Villiers, Johannesburg.	1994-95

For Pakistan (1)

0-133 (6-78, 4-55)	Waqar Younis, Port Elizabeth	1997-98

On first appearance in South Africa–Pakistan Tests.

SOUTH AFRICA v SRI LANKA

	Captains					
Season	*South Africa*	*Sri Lanka*	*T*	*SA*	*SL*	*D*
993-94*SL*	K. C. Wessels	A. Ranatunga	3	1	0	2
997-98*SA*	W. J. Cronje	A. Ranatunga	2	2	0	0
000*SL*	S. M. Pollock	S. T. Jayasuriya	3	1	1	1
000-01*SA*	S. M. Pollock	S. T. Jayasuriya	3	2	0	1
	In South Africa		5	4	0	1
	In Sri Lanka		6	2	1	3
	Totals		11	6	1	4

A Played in South Africa. SL Played in Sri Lanka.

HIGHEST INNINGS TOTALS

or South Africa in South Africa: 504-7 dec. at Cape Town		2000-01
in Sri Lanka: 495 at Colombo (SSC)		1993-94
or Sri Lanka in South Africa: 306 at Cape Town (in each innings)		1997-98
in Sri Lanka: 522 at Galle		2000

LOWEST INNINGS TOTALS

For South Africa in South Africa: 200 at Centurion 1997-98
in Sri Lanka: 231 at Kandy 2000

For Sri Lanka in South Africa: 95 at Cape Town 2000-01
in Sri Lanka: 119 at Colombo (SSC) 1993-94

INDIVIDUAL HUNDREDS

For South Africa (11)

W. J. Cronje (1)			114*	Galle	2000	**N. D. McKenzie** (1)		
122	Colombo (SSC)	1993-94	112	Cape Town . .	2000-01	103	Centurion . .	2000-01
D. J. Cullinan (5)			**G. Kirsten** (1)			**S. M. Pollock** (1)		
102	Colombo (PSS)	1993-94	180	Durban	2000-01	111	Centurion . .	2000-01
113	Cape Town . .	1997-98	**L. Klusener** (1)			**J. N. Rhodes** (1)		
103	Centurion . . .	1997-98	118*	Kandy	2000	101*†	Moratuwa . .	1993-94

For Sri Lanka (5)

M. S. Atapattu (1)			**D. P. M. D. Jayawardene** (2)			**A. Ranatunga** (1)		
120	Kandy	2000	167†	Galle	2000	131†	Moratuwa . .	1993-94
S. T. Jayasuriya (1)			101*	Colombo (SSC)	2000			
148	Galle	2000						

† *On first appearance in South Africa–Sri Lanka Tests.*

RECORD PARTNERSHIPS FOR EACH WICKET

For South Africa

137 for 1st	K. C. Wessels and A. C. Hudson at Colombo (SSC)	1993-94
96 for 2nd	G. Kirsten and J. H. Kallis at Cape Town	2000-01
116 for 3rd	J. H. Kallis and D. J. Cullinan at Cape Town	1997-98
116 for 4th	G. Kirsten and W. J. Cronje at Centurion	1997-98
86 for 5th	D. J. Cullinan and M. V. Boucher at Cape Town	2000-01
124 for 6th	L. Klusener and M. V. Boucher at Kandy	2000
95 for 7th	S. M. Pollock and M. V. Boucher at Cape Town	1997-98
150 for 8th†	N. D. McKenzie and S. M. Pollock at Centurion	2000-01
45 for 9th	N. Boje and P. R. Adams at Kandy	2000
43 for 10th	L. Klusener and M. Hayward at Kandy	2000

For Sri Lanka

193 for 1st	M. S. Atapattu and S. T. Jayasuriya at Galle	2000
103 for 2nd	S. T. Jayasuriya and R. P. Arnold at Colombo (SSC)	2000
168 for 3rd	K. C. Sangakkara and D. P. M. D. Jayawardene at Durban	2000-01
118 for 4th	R. S. Mahanama and A. Ranatunga at Centurion	1997-98
121 for 5th	P. A. de Silva and A. Ranatunga at Moratuwa	1993-94
103 for 6th	A. Ranatunga and H. P. Tillekeratne at Moratuwa	1993-94
43 for 7th	P. A. de Silva and G. P. Wickremasinghe at Centurion	1997-98
117 for 8th	D. P. M. D. Jayawardene and W. P. U. J. C. Vaas at Galle	2000
48 for 9th	G. P. Wickremasinghe and M. Muralitharan at Cape Town	1997-98
22 for 10th	W. P. U. J. C. Vaas and M. Muralitharan at Galle	2000

† *Record partnership against all countries.*

TEN WICKETS OR MORE IN A MATCH

For Sri Lanka (2)

-171 (6-87, 7-84)	M. Muralitharan at Galle	2000
-161 (5-122, 6-39)	M. Muralitharan at Durban.	2000-01

te: The best match figures for South Africa are 9-106 (5-48, 4-58) by B. N. Schultz at Colombo
SC), 1993-94.

SOUTH AFRICA v ZIMBABWE

	Captains					
ason	South Africa	Zimbabwe	T	SA	Z	D
95-96Z	W. J. Cronje	A. Flower	1	1	0	0
99-2000S	W. J. Cronje	A. D. R. Campbell	1	1	0	0
99-2000Z	W. J. Cronje	A. Flower	1	1	0	0
01-02Z	S. M. Pollock	H. H. Streak	2	1	0	1
	In Zimbabwe		4	3	0	1
	In South Africa		1	1	0	0
	Totals		5	4	0	1

Played in South Africa.   Z Played in Zimbabwe.

HIGHEST INNINGS TOTALS

r South Africa in South Africa: 417 at Bloemfontein	1999-2000
in Zimbabwe: 600-3 dec. at Harare	2001-02
r Zimbabwe in South Africa: 212 at Bloemfontein.	1999-2000
in Zimbabwe: 419-9 dec. at Bulawayo	2001-02

LOWEST INNINGS TOTALS

r South Africa in South Africa: 417 at Bloemfontein	1999-2000
in Zimbabwe: 346 at Harare	1995-96
r Zimbabwe in South Africa: 192 at Bloemfontein.	1999-2000
in Zimbabwe: 102 at Harare.	1999-2000

INDIVIDUAL HUNDREDS

For South Africa (7)

, V. Boucher (1)		**A. C. Hudson** (1)		157*	Harare.	2001-02
5	Harare. 1999-00	135†	Harare. 1995-96	189*	Bulawayo. . .	2001-02
H. Gibbs (1)		**J. H. Kallis** (3)		**G. Kirsten** (1)		
7†	Harare. 2001-02	115	Harare. 1999-00	220	Harare.	2001-02

For Zimbabwe (2)

A. Flower (2)

142 }
199*} Harare. 2001-02

On first appearance in South Africa–Zimbabwe Tests.

RECORD PARTNERSHIPS FOR EACH WICKET

For South Africa

256 for 1st	H. H. Gibbs and G. Kirsten at Harare	2001-02
199 for 2nd	G. Kirsten and J. H. Kallis at Harare	2001-02
181 for 3rd	J. H. Kallis and N. D. McKenzie at Bulawayo	2001-02
100 for 4th	J. H. Kallis and W. J. Cronje at Harare	1999-2000
60 for 5th	A. C. Hudson and J. N. Rhodes at Harare	1995-96
101 for 6th	A. C. Hudson and B. M. McMillan at Harare	1995-96
44 for 7th	M. V. Boucher and L. Klusener at Harare	1999-2000
148 for 8th	M. V. Boucher and S. M. Pollock at Harare	1999-2000
79 for 9th	B. M. McMillan and A. A. Donald at Harare	1995-96
54 for 10th	M. V. Boucher and P. R. Adams at Bloemfontein	1999-2000

For Zimbabwe

152 for 1st	A. D. R. Campbell and D. D. Ebrahim at Bulawayo	2001-02
51 for 2nd	M. H. Dekker and A. D. R. Campbell at Harare	1995-96
29 for 3rd	M. W. Goodwin and N. C. Johnson at Harare	1999-2000
186 for 4th	H. Masakadza and A. Flower at Harare	2001-02
97 for 5th	A. Flower and G. J. Whittall at Harare	1995-96
17 for 6th	A. Flower and G. J. Whittall at Harare	2001-02
47 for 7th	G. J. Whittall and H. H. Streak at Bulawayo	2001-02
43 for 8th	C. B. Wishart and H. H. Streak at Harare	1995-96
75 for 9th	A. Flower and T. J. Friend at Harare	2001-02
47 for 10th	A. Flower and D. T. Hondo at Harare	2001-02

TEN WICKETS OR MORE IN A MATCH

For South Africa (1)

11-113 (3-42, 8-71)†   A. A. Donald, Harare 1995-96

Note: The best match figures for Zimbabwe are 5-105 (3-68, 2-37) by A. C. I. Lock at Harare, 1995-96.

† *On first appearance in South Africa–Zimbabwe Tests.*

WEST INDIES v NEW ZEALAND

		Captains				
Season	*West Indies*	*New Zealand*	*T*	*WI*	*NZ*	*D*
1951-52N	J. D. C. Goddard	B. Sutcliffe	2	1	0	1
1955-56N	D. St E. Atkinson	J. R. Reid[1]	4	3	1	0
1968-69N	G. S. Sobers	G. T. Dowling	3	1	1	1
1971-72W	G. S. Sobers	G. T. Dowling[2]	5	0	0	5
1979-80N	C. H. Lloyd	G. P. Howarth	3	0	1	2
1984-85W	I. V. A. Richards	G. P. Howarth	4	2	0	2
1986-87N	I. V. A. Richards	J. V. Coney	3	1	1	1
1994-95N	C. A. Walsh	K. R. Rutherford	2	1	0	1
1995-96W	C. A. Walsh	L. K. Germon	2	1	0	1
1999-2000N	B. C. Lara	S. P. Fleming	2	0	2	0
2002W	C. L. Hooper	S. P. Fleming	2	0	1	1
	In New Zealand		19	7	6	6
	In West Indies		13	3	1	9
	Totals		32	10	7	15

N Played in New Zealand. W Played in West Indies.

Notes: The following deputised for the official touring captain or were appointed by the home authority for only a minor proportion of the series:
[1] H. B. Cave (First). [2] B. E. Congdon (Third, Fourth and Fifth).

HIGHEST INNINGS TOTALS

For West Indies in West Indies: 564-8 at Bridgetown   1971-72
     in New Zealand: 660-5 dec. at Wellington   1994-95

For New Zealand in West Indies: 543-3 dec. at Georgetown   1971-72
      in New Zealand: 518-9 dec. at Wellington   1999-2000

LOWEST INNINGS TOTALS

For West Indies in West Indies: 107 at Bridgetown   2002
     in New Zealand: 77 at Auckland   1955-56

For New Zealand in West Indies: 94 at Bridgetown   1984-85
      in New Zealand: 74 at Dunedin   1955-56

INDIVIDUAL HUNDREDS

By West Indies (34)

J. C. Adams (2)
151 Wellington . . . 1994-95
208* St John's 1995-96
S. L. Campbell (2)
208 Bridgetown . . 1995-96
170 Hamilton . . . 1999-00
M. C. Carew (1)
109† Auckland . . . 1968-69
C. A. Davis (1)
183 Bridgetown . 1971-72
R. C. Fredericks (1)
163 Kingston . . . 1971-72
C. H. Gayle (1)
204 St George's . 2002
C. G. Greenidge (2)
100 Port-of-Spain 1984-85
213 Auckland . . . 1986-87
A. F. G. Griffith (1)
114† Hamilton . . . 1999-00

D. L. Haynes (3)
105† Dunedin . . . 1979-80
122 Christchurch . 1979-80
121 Wellington . . 1986-87
A. I. Kallicharran (2)
100*† Georgetown . 1971-72
101 Port-of-Spain 1971-72
C. L. King (1)
100* Christchurch . 1979-80
B. C. Lara (1)
147 Wellington . . 1994-95
J. R. Murray (1)
101* Wellington . . 1994-95
S. M. Nurse (2)
168† Auckland . . . 1968-69
258 Christchurch . 1968-69
I. V. A. Richards (1)
105 Bridgetown . 1984-85
R. B. Richardson (1)
185 Georgetown . 1984-85

L. G. Rowe (3)
214 }
100* }†Kingston . . 1971-72
100 Christchurch . 1979-80
R. G. Samuels (1)
125 St John's . . . 1995-96
G. S. Sobers (1)
142 Bridgetown . 1971-72
J. B. Stollmeyer (1)
152 Auckland . . . 1951-52
C. L. Walcott (1)
115 Auckland . . . 1951-52
E. D. Weekes (3)
123 Dunedin . . . 1955-56
103 Christchurch . 1955-56
156 Wellington . . 1955-56
F. M. M. Worrell (1)
100 Auckland . . . 1951-52

By New Zealand (23)

N. J. Astle (2)
125† Bridgetown . 1995-96
103 St John's . . . 1995-96
M. G. Burgess (1)
101 Kingston . . . 1971-72
B. E. Congdon (2)
166* Port-of-Spain 1971-72
126 Bridgetown . 1971-72
J. J. Crowe (1)
112 Kingston . . . 1984-85
M. D. Crowe (3)
188 Georgetown . 1984-85
119 Wellington . . 1986-87
104 Auckland . . . 1986-87

B. A. Edgar (1)
127 Auckland . . . 1979-80
S. P. Fleming (1)
130 Bridgetown . 2002
R. J. Hadlee (1)
103 Christchurch . 1979-80
B. F. Hastings (2)
117* Christchurch . 1968-69
105 Bridgetown . 1971-72
G. P. Howarth (1)
147 Christchurch . 1979-80
T. W. Jarvis (1)
182 Georgetown . 1971-72

A. C. Parore (1)
100*† Christchurch . 1994-95
M. S. Sinclair (1)
214† Wellington . . 1999-00
S. B. Styris (1)
107† St George's . 2002
B. R. Taylor (1)
124† Auckland . . . 1968-69
G. M. Turner (2)
223*‡ Kingston . . . 1971-72
259 Georgetown . 1971-72
J. G. Wright (1)
138 Wellington . . 1986-87

† *On first appearance in West Indies–New Zealand Tests.* ‡ *Carried his bat.*

Notes: E. D. Weekes in 1955-56 made three hundreds in consecutive innings.
 L. G. Rowe and A. I. Kallicharran each scored hundreds in their first two innings in Test cricket.
Rowe is the only batsman to do so in his first match.

RECORD PARTNERSHIPS FOR EACH WICKET

For West Indies

276 for 1st	A. F. G. Griffith and S. L. Campbell at Hamilton	1999-2000
269 for 2nd	R. C. Fredericks and L. G. Rowe at Kingston	1971-72
221 for 3rd	B. C. Lara and J. C. Adams at Wellington	1994-95
162 for 4th {	E. D. Weekes and O. G. Smith at Dunedin	1955-56
	C. G. Greenidge and A. I. Kallicharran at Christchurch	1979-80
189 for 5th	F. M. M. Worrell and C. L. Walcott at Auckland	1951-52
254 for 6th	C. A. Davis and G. S. Sobers at Bridgetown	1971-72
143 for 7th	D. St E. Atkinson and J. D. C. Goddard at Christchurch	1955-56
83 for 8th	I. V. A. Richards and M. D. Marshall at Bridgetown	1984-85
70 for 9th	M. D. Marshall and J. Garner at Bridgetown	1984-85
31 for 10th	T. M. Findlay and G. C. Shillingford at Bridgetown	1971-72

For New Zealand

387 for 1st†	G. M. Turner and T. W. Jarvis at Georgetown	1971-72
210 for 2nd	G. P. Howarth and J. J. Crowe at Kingston	1984-85
241 for 3rd	J. G. Wright and M. D. Crowe at Wellington	1986-87
189 for 4th	M. S. Sinclair and N. J. Astle at Wellington	1999-2000
144 for 5th	N. J. Astle and J. T. C. Vaughan at Bridgetown	1995-96
220 for 6th	G. M. Turner and K. J. Wadsworth at Kingston	1971-72
143 for 7th	M. D. Crowe and I. D. S. Smith at Georgetown	1984-85
136 for 8th	B. E. Congdon and R. S. Cunis at Port-of-Spain	1971-72
62* for 9th	V. Pollard and R. S. Cunis at Auckland	1968-69
45 for 10th	D. K. Morrison and R. J. Kennedy at Bridgetown	1995-96

† *Record partnership against all countries.*

TEN WICKETS OR MORE IN A MATCH

For West Indies (2)

11-120 (4-40, 7-80)	M. D. Marshall, Bridgetown	1984-85
13-55 (7-37, 6-18)	C. A. Walsh, Wellington	1994-95

For New Zealand (4)

10-100 (3-73, 7-27)†	C. L. Cairns, Hamilton	1999-2000
10-124 (4-51, 6-73)†	E. J. Chatfield, Port-of-Spain	1984-85
11-102 (5-34, 6-68)†	R. J. Hadlee, Dunedin	1979-80
10-166 (4-71, 6-95)	G. B. Troup, Auckland	1979-80

† *On first appearance in West Indies–New Zealand Tests.*

WEST INDIES v INDIA

Captains

Season	West Indies	India	T	WI	I	D
1948-49*I*	J. D. C. Goddard	L. Amarnath	5	1	0	4
1952-53*W*	J. B. Stollmeyer	V. S. Hazare	5	1	0	4
1958-59*I*	F. C. M. Alexander	Ghulam Ahmed[1]	5	3	0	2
1961-62*W*	F. M. M. Worrell	N. J. Contractor[2]	5	5	0	0
1966-67*I*	G. S. Sobers	Nawab of Pataudi jun.	3	2	0	1
1970-71*I*	G. S. Sobers	A. L. Wadekar	5	0	1	4
1974-75*I*	C. H. Lloyd	Nawab of Pataudi jun.[3]	5	3	2	0

Captains

Season	West Indies	India	T	WI	I	D
1975-76W	C. H. Lloyd	B. S. Bedi	4	2	1	1
1978-79I	A. I. Kallicharran	S. M. Gavaskar	6	0	1	5
1982-83W	C. H. Lloyd	Kapil Dev	5	2	0	3
1983-84I	C. H. Lloyd	Kapil Dev	6	3	0	3
1987-88I	I. V. A. Richards	D. B. Vengsarkar[4]	4	1	1	2
1988-89I	I. V. A. Richards	D. B. Vengsarkar	4	3	0	1
1994-95I	C. A. Walsh	M. Azharuddin	3	1	1	1
1996-97W	C. A. Walsh[5]	S. R. Tendulkar	5	1	0	4
2001-02W	C. L. Hooper	S. C. Ganguly	5	2	1	2
	In India		37	14	5	18
	In West Indies		38	16	3	19
	Totals		75	30	8	37

I Played in India. W Played in West Indies.

Notes: The following deputised for the official touring captain or were appointed by the home authority for only a minor proportion of the series:
[1]P. R. Umrigar (First), V. Mankad (Fourth), H. R. Adhikari (Fifth). [2]Nawab of Pataudi jun. (Third, Fourth and Fifth). [3]S. Venkataraghavan (Second). [4]R. J. Shastri (Fourth). [5]B. C. Lara (Third).

HIGHEST INNINGS TOTALS

For West Indies in West Indies: 631-8 dec. at Kingston 1961-62
    in India: 644-8 dec. at Delhi 1958-59

For India in West Indies: 513-9 dec. at St John's. 2001-02
    in India: 644-7 dec. at Kanpur 1978-79

LOWEST INNINGS TOTALS

For West Indies in West Indies: 140 at Bridgetown 1996-97
    in India: 127 at Delhi 1987-88

For India in West Indies: 81 at Bridgetown. 1996-97
    in India: 75 at Delhi 1987-88

INDIVIDUAL HUNDREDS

For West Indies (90)

J. C. Adams (2)
125* Nagpur 1994-95
174* Mohali 1994-95
S. F. A. F. Bacchus (1)
250 Kanpur 1978-79
B. F. Butcher (2)
103 Calcutta 1958-59
142 Madras 1958-59
S. Chanderpaul (4)
137* Bridgetown . 1996-97
140 Georgetown . 2001-02
101* Bridgetown . 2001-02
136* St John's . . 2001-02
R. J. Christiani (1)
107† Delhi 1948-49

C. A. Davis (2)
125* Georgetown . 1970-71
105 Port-of-Spain 1970-71
P. J. L. Dujon (1)
110 St John's . . . 1982-83
R. C. Fredericks (2)
100 Calcutta . . . 1974-75
104 Bombay. . . . 1974-75
H. A. Gomes (1)
123 Port-of-Spain 1982-83
G. E. Gomez (1)
101† Delhi 1948-49
C. G. Greenidge (5)
107† Bangalore . 1974-75
154* St John's . . 1982-83
194 Kanpur . . . 1983-84

141 Calcutta. . . . 1987-88
117 Bridgetown . 1988-89
D. L. Haynes (2)
136 St John's . . 1982-83
112* Bridgetown . 1988-89
W. W. Hinds (1)
113 Kingston . . . 2001-02
J. K. Holt (1)
123 Delhi 1958-59
C. L. Hooper (5)
100* Calcutta. . . . 1987-88
129 Kingston . . 1996-97
233 Georgetown . 2001-02
115 Bridgetown . 2001-02
136 St John's . . 2001-02

C. C. Hunte (1)
101 Bombay.... 1966-67
R. D. Jacobs (1)
118 St John's.... 2001-02
A. I. Kallicharran (3)
124† Bangalore.. 1974-75
103* Port-of-Spain 1975-76
187 Bombay.... 1978-79
R. B. Kanhai (4)
256 Calcutta.... 1958-59
138 Kingston... 1961-62
139 Port-of-Spain 1961-62
158* Kingston... 1970-71
B. C. Lara (1)
103 St John's... 1996-97
C. H. Lloyd (7)
163 Bangalore.. 1974-75
242* Bombay.... 1974-75
102 Bridgetown. 1975-76
143 Port-of-Spain 1982-83
106 St John's... 1982-83
103 Delhi..... 1983-84
161* Calcutta.... 1983-84
A. L. Logie (2)
130 Bridgetown. 1982-83
101 Calcutta.... 1987-88

E. D. A. McMorris (1)
125† Kingston... 1961-62
B. H. Pairaudeau (1)
115* Port-of-Spain 1952-53
A. F. Rae (2)
104 Bombay.... 1948-49
109 Madras.... 1948-49
I. V. A. Richards (8)
192* Delhi..... 1974-75
142 Bridgetown. 1975-76
130 Port-of-Spain 1975-76
177 Port-of-Spain 1975-76
109 Georgetown. 1982-83
120 Bombay.... 1983-84
109* Delhi..... 1987-88
110 Kingston... 1988-89
R. B. Richardson (2)
194 Georgetown. 1988-89
156 Kingston... 1988-89
O. G. Smith (1)
100 Delhi..... 1958-59
G. S. Sobers (8)
142*† Bombay.... 1958-59
198 Kanpur.... 1958-59
106* Calcutta.... 1958-59
153 Kingston... 1961-62
104 Kingston... 1961-62

108* Georgetown. 1970-71
178* Bridgetown. 1970-71
132 Port-of-Spain 1970-71
J. S. Solomon (1)
100* Delhi..... 1958-59
J. B. Stollmeyer (2)
160 Madras.... 1948-49
104* Port-of-Spain 1952-53
C. L. Walcott (4)
152† Delhi..... 1948-49
108 Calcutta.... 1948-49
125 Georgetown. 1952-53
118 Kingston... 1952-53
E. D. Weekes (7)
128† Delhi..... 1948-49
194 Bombay.... 1948-49
162 } Calcutta.... 1948-49
101 }
207 Port-of-Spain 1952-53
161 Port-of-Spain 1952-53
109 Kingston... 1952-53
A. B. Williams (1)
111 Calcutta.... 1978-79
S. C. Williams (1)
128 Port-of-Spain 1996-97
F. M. M. Worrell (1)
237 Kingston... 1952-53

For India (63)

H. R. Adhikari (1)
114*† Delhi..... 1948-49
M. Amarnath (3)
101* Kanpur.... 1978-79
117 Port-of-Spain 1982-83
116 St John's... 1982-83
M. L. Apte (1)
163* Port-of-Spain 1952-53
C. G. Borde (3)
109 Delhi..... 1958-59
121 Bombay.... 1966-67
125 Madras.... 1966-67
R. Dravid (1)
144* Georgetown. 2001-02
S. A. Durani (1)
104 Port-of-Spain 1961-62
F. M. Engineer (1)
109 Madras.... 1966-67
A. D. Gaekwad (1)
102 Kanpur.... 1978-79
S. M. Gavaskar (13)
116 Georgetown. 1970-71
117* Bridgetown. 1970-71
124 } Port-of-Spain 1970-71
220 }
156 Port-of-Spain 1975-76
102 Port-of-Spain 1975-76
205 Bombay.... 1978-79
107 } Calcutta.... 1978-79
182*}
120 Delhi..... 1978-79

147* Georgetown. 1982-83
121 Delhi..... 1983-84
236* Madras.... 1983-84
V. S. Hazare (2)
134* Bombay.... 1948-49
122 Bombay.... 1948-49
Kapil Dev (3)
126* Delhi..... 1978-79
100* Port-of-Spain 1982-83
109 Madras.... 1987-88
V. V. S. Laxman (1)
130 St John's... 2001-02
S. V. Manjrekar (1)
108 Bridgetown. 1988-89
V. L. Manjrekar (1)
118 Kingston... 1952-53
R. S. Modi (1)
112 Bombay.... 1948-49
Mushtaq Ali (1)
106† Calcutta.... 1948-49
B. P. Patel (1)
115* Port-of-Spain 1975-76
M. Prabhakar (1)
120 Mohali.... 1994-95
A. Ratra (1)
115* St John's... 2001-02
Pankaj Roy (1)
150 Kingston... 1952-53
D. N. Sardesai (3)
212 Kingston... 1970-71

112 Port-of-Spain 1970-71
150 Bridgetown. 1970-71
R. J. Shastri (2)
102 St John's... 1982-83
107 Bridgetown. 1988-89
N. S. Sidhu (3)
116 Kingston... 1988-89
107 Nagpur.... 1994-95
201 Port-of-Spain 1996-97
E. D. Solkar (1)
102 Bombay.... 1974-75
S. R. Tendulkar (2)
179 Nagpur.... 1994-95
117 Port-of-Spain 2001-02
P. R. Umrigar (3)
130 Port-of-Spain 1952-53
117 Kingston... 1952-53
172* Port-of-Spain 1961-62
D. B. Vengsarkar (6)
157* Calcutta.... 1978-79
109 Delhi..... 1978-79
159 Delhi..... 1983-84
100 Bombay.... 1983-84
102 Delhi..... 1987-88
102* Calcutta.... 1987-88
G. R. Viswanath (4)
139 Calcutta.... 1974-75
112 Port-of-Spain 1975-76
124 Madras.... 1978-79
179 Kanpur.... 1978-79

† *On first appearance in West Indies–India Tests.*

RECORD PARTNERSHIPS FOR EACH WICKET

For West Indies

296	for 1st	C. G. Greenidge and D. L. Haynes at St John's	1982-83
55	for 2nd	E. D. A. McMorris and R. B. Kanhai at Kingston	1961-62
20	for 3rd	I. V. A. Richards and A. I. Kallicharran at Bridgetown	1975-76
67	for 4th	C. L. Walcott and G. E. Gomez at Delhi	1948-49
93	for 5th	C. L. Hooper and S. Chanderpaul at Georgetown	2001-02
50	for 6th	C. H. Lloyd and D. L. Murray at Bombay	1974-75
30	for 7th	C. G. Greenidge and M. D. Marshall at Kanpur	1983-84
24	for 8th	I. V. A. Richards and K. D. Boyce at Delhi	1974-75
61	for 9th†	C. H. Lloyd and A. M. E. Roberts at Calcutta	1983-84
98*	for 10th	F. M. M. Worrell and W. W. Hall at Port-of-Spain	1961-62

For India

53	for 1st	S. M. Gavaskar and C. P. S. Chauhan at Bombay	1978-79
44*	for 2nd†	S. M. Gavaskar and D. B. Vengsarkar at Calcutta	1978-79
77	for 3rd	N. S. Sidhu and S. R. Tendulkar at Nagpur	1994-95
72	for 4th	G. R. Viswanath and A. D. Gaekwad at Kanpur	1978-79
204	for 5th	S. M. Gavaskar and B. P. Patel at Port-of-Spain	1975-76
70	for 6th	S. M. Gavaskar and R. J. Shastri at Madras	1983-84
17	for 7th	V. V. S. Laxman and A. Ratra at St John's	2001-02
20*	for 8th	R. Dravid and Sarandeep Singh at Georgetown	2001-02
43*	for 9th	S. M. Gavaskar and S. M. H. Kirmani at Madras	1983-84
64	for 10th	J. Srinath and S. L. V. Raju at Mohali.	1994-95

Record partnership against all countries.

TEN WICKETS OR MORE IN A MATCH

For West Indies (4)

11-126 (6-50, 5-76)	W. W. Hall, Kanpur	1958-59
11-89 (5-34, 6-55)	M. D. Marshall, Port-of-Spain	1988-89
12-121 (7-64, 5-57)	A. M. E. Roberts, Madras	1974-75
10-101 (6-62, 4-39)	C. A. Walsh, Kingston	1988-89

For India (4)

11-235 (7-157, 4-78)†	B. S. Chandrasekhar, Bombay	1966-67
10-223 (9-102, 1-121)	S. P. Gupte, Kanpur	1958-59
16-136 (8-61, 8-75)†	N. D. Hirwani, Madras	1987-88
10-135 (1-52, 9-83)	Kapil Dev, Ahmedabad	1983-84

On first appearance in West Indies–India Tests.

WEST INDIES v PAKISTAN

Captains

Season	West Indies	Pakistan	T	WI	P	D
1957-58W	F. C. M. Alexander	A. H. Kardar	5	3	1	1
1958-59P	F. C. M. Alexander	Fazal Mahmood	3	1	2	0
1974-75P	C. H. Lloyd	Intikhab Alam	2	0	0	2
1976-77W	C. H. Lloyd	Mushtaq Mohammad	5	2	1	2
1980-81P	C. H. Lloyd	Javed Miandad	4	1	0	3
1986-87P	I. V. A. Richards	Imran Khan	3	1	1	1
1987-88W	I. V. A. Richards[1]	Imran Khan	3	1	1	1

	Captains					
Season	*West Indies*	*Pakistan*	*T*	*WI*	*P*	*D*
1990-91*P*	D. L. Haynes	Imran Khan	3	1	1	1
1992-93*W*	R. B. Richardson	Wasim Akram	3	2	0	1
1997-98*P*	C. A. Walsh	Wasim Akram	3	0	3	0
1999-2000*W*	J. C. Adams	Moin Khan	3	1	0	2
2001-02*U*	C. L. Hooper	Waqar Younis	2	0	2	0
	In West Indies		19	9	3	7
	In Pakistan		18	4	7	7
	In United Arab Emirates		2	0	2	0
	Totals		39	13	12	14

P Played in Pakistan. W Played in West Indies. U Played in United Arab Emirates.

Note: The following was appointed by the home authority for only a minor proportion of the series:

¹C. G. Greenidge (First).

HIGHEST INNINGS TOTALS

For West Indies in West Indies: 790-3 dec. at Kingston 1957-58
in Pakistan: 493 at Karachi 1974-75
in United Arab Emirates: 366 at Sharjah 2001-02

For Pakistan in West Indies: 657-8 dec. at Bridgetown 1957-58
in Pakistan: 471 at Rawalpindi 1997-98
in United Arab Emirates: 493 at Sharjah 2001-02

LOWEST INNINGS TOTALS

For West Indies in West Indies: 127 at Port-of-Spain 1992-93
in Pakistan: 53 at Faisalabad 1986-87
in United Arab Emirates: 171 at Sharjah 2001-02

For Pakistan in West Indies: 106 at Bridgetown 1957-58
in Pakistan: 77 at Lahore 1986-87
in United Arab Emirates: 472 at Sharjah 2001-02

INDIVIDUAL HUNDREDS

For West Indies (26)

L. Baichan (1)
105*† Lahore 1974-75
P. J. L. Dujon (1)
106* Port-of-Spain 1987-88
R. C. Fredericks (1)
120 Port-of-Spain 1976-77
C. G. Greenidge (1)
100 Kingston . . . 1976-77
D. L. Haynes (3)
117 Karachi 1990-91
143*‡ Port-of-Spain 1992-93
125 Bridgetown . 1992-93
W. W. Hinds (1)
165 Bridgetown . 1999-00

C. L. Hooper (3)
134 Lahore 1990-91
178* St John's . . . 1992-93
106 Karachi 1997-98
C. C. Hunte (3)
142† Bridgetown . 1957-58
260 Kingston . . . 1957-58
114 Georgetown . 1957-58
B. D. Julien (1)
101 Karachi 1974-75
A. I. Kallicharran (1)
115 Karachi 1974-75
R. B. Kanhai (1)
217 Lahore 1958-59

C. H. Lloyd (1)
157 Bridgetown . 1976-77
I. V. A. Richards (2)
120* Multan 1980-81
123 Port-of-Spain 1987-88
I. T. Shillingford (1)
120 Georgetown . 1976-77
G. S. Sobers (3)
365* Kingston . . . 1957-58
125 }
109*} Georgetown . 1957-58
C. L. Walcott (1)
145 Georgetown . 1957-58
E. D. Weekes (1)
197† Bridgetown . 1957-58

For Pakistan (30)

Aamir Sohail (2)
160 Rawalpindi . . . 1997-98
160 Karachi 1997-98
Asif Iqbal (1)
135 Kingston . . . 1976-77
Hanif Mohammad (2)
337† Bridgetown . 1957-58
103 Karachi 1958-59
Ijaz Ahmed, sen. (1)
151 Karachi 1997-98
Imran Khan (1)
123 Lahore 1980-81
Imran Nazir (1)
131† Bridgetown . 1999-00
Imtiaz Ahmed (1)
122 Kingston . . . 1957-58

Inzamam-ul-Haq (3)
123 St John's . . . 1992-93
177 Rawalpindi . . 1997-98
135 Georgetown . 1999-00
Javed Miandad (2)
114 Georgetown . 1987-88
102 Port-of-Spain 1987-88
Majid Khan (2)
100 Karachi 1974-75
167 Georgetown . 1976-77
Mushtaq Mohammad (2)
123 Lahore 1974-75
121 Port-of-Spain 1976-77
Rashid Latif (1)
150 Sharjah 2001-02
Saeed Ahmed (1)
150 Georgetown . 1957-58

Salim Malik (1)
102 Karachi 1990-91
Shahid Afridi (1)
107† Sharjah 2001-02
Wasim Raja (2)
107* Karachi 1974-75
117* Bridgetown . 1976-77
Wazir Mohammad (2)
106 Kingston . . . 1957-58
189 Port-of-Spain 1957-58
Younis Khan (1)
153 Sharjah 2001-02
Yousuf Youhana (3)
115 Bridgetown . 1999-00
103* St John's . . . 1999-00
146 Sharjah 2001-02

† *On first appearance in West Indies–Pakistan Tests.*
‡ *Carried his bat.*

RECORD PARTNERSHIPS FOR EACH WICKET

For West Indies

182	for 1st	R. C. Fredericks and C. G. Greenidge at Kingston	1976-77
446	for 2nd†	C. C. Hunte and G. S. Sobers at Kingston	1957-58
169	for 3rd	D. L. Haynes and B. C. Lara at Port-of-Spain	1992-93
188*	for 4th	G. S. Sobers and C. L. Walcott at Kingston	1957-58
185	for 5th	E. D. Weekes and O. G. Smith at Bridgetown	1957-58
151	for 6th	C. H. Lloyd and D. L. Murray at Bridgetown	1976-77
74	for 7th	S. Chanderpaul and N. A. M. McLean at Georgetown	1999-2000
60	for 8th	C. L. Hooper and A. C. Cummins at St John's	1992-93
61*	for 9th	P. J. L. Dujon and W. K. M. Benjamin at Bridgetown . . .	1987-88
106	for 10th†	C. L. Hooper and C. A. Walsh at St John's.	1992-93

For Pakistan

298	for 1st†	Aamir Sohail and Ijaz Ahmed, sen. at Karachi	1997-98
190	for 2nd	Shahid Afridi and Younis Khan at Sharjah	2001-02
323	for 3rd	Aamir Sohail and Inzamam-ul-Haq at Rawalpindi	1997-98
174	for 4th	Shoaib Mohammad and Salim Malik at Karachi	1990-91
88	for 5th	Basit Ali and Inzamam-ul-Haq at St John's	1992-93
206	for 6th	Inzamam-ul-Haq and Abdul Razzaq at Georgetown	1999-2000
128	for 7th‡	Wasim Raja and Wasim Bari at Karachi	1974-75
94	for 8th	Salim Malik and Salim Yousuf at Port-of-Spain	1987-88
96	for 9th	Inzamam-ul-Haq and Nadeem Khan at St John's	1992-93
133	for 10th	Wasim Raja and Wasim Bari at Bridgetown	1976-77

† *Record partnership against all countries.*
‡ *Although Pakistan's seventh wicket added 168 runs against West Indies at Lahore in 1980-81, this comprised two partnerships. Imran Khan added 72* with Abdul Qadir (retired hurt) and a further 96 with Sarfraz Nawaz.*

Harbhajan's final spell brought five wickets for six runs, followed by a chaste kiss of the pendant around his neck.
India v England, page 1148

TEN WICKETS OR MORE IN A MATCH

For Pakistan (4)

12-100 (6-34, 6-66)	Fazal Mahmood, Dacca	1958-59
11-121 (7-80, 4-41)	Imran Khan, Georgetown	1987-88
10-106 (5-35, 5-71)	Mushtaq Ahmed, Peshawar	1997-98
11-110 (6-61, 5-49)	Wasim Akram, St John's	1999-2000

Note: The best match figures for West Indies are 9-95 (8-29, 1-66) by C. E. H. Croft at Port-of-Spain, 1976-77.

WEST INDIES v SRI LANKA

Captains

Season	West Indies	Sri Lanka	T	WI	SL	D
1993-94*S*	R. B. Richardson	A. Ranatunga	1	0	0	1
1996-97*W*	C. A. Walsh	A. Ranatunga	2	1	0	1
2001-02*S*	C. L. Hooper	S. T. Jayasuriya	3	0	3	0
	In West Indies		2	1	0	1
	In Sri Lanka		4	0	3	1
	Totals		6	1	3	2

W Played in West Indies.   S Played in Sri Lanka.

HIGHEST INNINGS TOTALS

For West Indies in West Indies: 343 at St Vincent	1996-97
in Sri Lanka: 448 at Galle	2001-02
For Sri Lanka in West Indies: 233-8 at St Vincent	1996-97
in Sri Lanka: 627-9 dec. at Colombo (SSC)	2001-02

LOWEST INNINGS TOTALS

For West Indies in West Indies: 147 at St Vincent	1996-97
in Sri Lanka: 144 at Galle	2001-02
For Sri Lanka in West Indies: 152 at St John's	1996-97
in Sri Lanka: 190 at Moratuwa	1993-94

INDIVIDUAL HUNDREDS

For West Indies (4)

B. C. Lara (4)

115	St Vincent . .	1996-97	221	} Colombo (SSC) 2001-02
178	Galle	2001-02	130	

For Sri Lanka (3)

K. C. Sangakkara (1)   **H. P. Tillekeratne (2)**

140†	Galle	2001-02	105* Galle 2001-02
			204* Colombo (SSC) 2001-02

† On first appearance in West Indies–Sri Lanka Tests.

RECORD PARTNERSHIPS FOR EACH WICKET

For West Indies

160 for 1st	S. L. Campbell and S. C. Williams at St John's		1996-97
80 for 2nd	D. Ganga and R. R. Sarwan at Galle		2001-02
194 for 3rd	R. R. Sarwan and B. C. Lara at Colombo (SSC)		2001-02
153 for 4th	B. C. Lara and C. L. Hooper at Galle		2001-02
84 for 5th	R. B. Richardson and C. L. Hooper at Moratuwa		1993-94
41 for 6th	B. C. Lara and R. D. Jacobs at Kandy		2001-02
59 for 7th	M. N. Samuels and M. Dillon at Kandy		2001-02
53 for 8th	R. I. C. Holder and C. E. L. Ambrose at St Vincent		1996-97
13 for 9th	W. K. M. Benjamin and C. E. L. Ambrose at Moratuwa		1993-94
10 for 10th	B. C. Lara and C. E. L. Stuart at Kandy		2001-02

For Sri Lanka

89 for 1st	M. S. Atapattu and S. T. Jayasuriya at Kandy		2001-02
109 for 2nd	M. S. Atapattu and K. C. Sangakkara at Galle		2001-02
162 for 3rd	K. C. Sangakkara and D. P. M. D. Jayawardene at Galle		2001-02
110 for 4th	S. T. Jayasuriya and A. Ranatunga at St John's		1996-97
141 for 5th	R. P. Arnold and H. P. Tillekeratne at Colombo (SSC)		2001-02
165 for 6th	H. P. Tillekeratne and T. T. Samaraweera at Colombo (SSC)		2001-02
51 for 7th	R. S. Kalpage and P. B. Dassanayake at Moratuwa		1993-94
19 for 8th	H. P. Tillekeratne and D. N. T. Zoysa at Colombo (SSC)		2001-02
42 for 9th	H. P. Tillekeratne and M. R. C. N. Bandaratilleke at Colombo (SSC)		2001-02
16* for 10th	H. P. Tillekeratne and M. Muralitharan at Colombo (SSC)		2001-02

TEN WICKETS OR MORE IN A MATCH

For Sri Lanka (3)

11-170 (6-126, 5-44)	M. Muralitharan, Galle		2001-02
10-135 (4-54, 6-81)	M. Muralitharan, Kandy		2001-02
14-191 (7-120, 7-71)	W. P. U. J. C. Vaas, Colombo (SSC)		2001-02

Note: The best match figures for West Indies are 8-78 (5-37, 3-41) by C. E. L. Ambrose at St John's, 1996-97.

WEST INDIES v ZIMBABWE

		Captains				
Season	*West Indies*	*Zimbabwe*	*T*	*WI*	*Z*	*D*
1999-2000*W*	J. C. Adams	A. Flower	2	2	0	0
2001*Z*	C. L. Hooper	H. H. Streak	2	1	0	1
	In West Indies		2	2	0	0
	In Zimbabwe		2	1	0	1
	Totals		4	3	0	1

W Played in West Indies. Z Played in Zimbabwe.

HIGHEST INNINGS TOTALS

For West Indies in West Indies: 339 at Kingston 1999-2000
in Zimbabwe: 559-6 dec. at Bulawayo 2001

For Zimbabwe in West Indies: 308 at Kingston 1999-2000
in Zimbabwe: 563-9 dec. at Harare 2001

LOWEST INNINGS TOTALS

For West Indies in West Indies: 147 at Port-of-Spain.   1999-2000
　　　　　　　　　 in Zimbabwe: 347 at Harare.   2001

For Zimbabwe in West Indies: 63 at Port-of-Spain   1999-2000
　　　　　　　　 in Zimbabwe: 131 at Harare.   2001

INDIVIDUAL HUNDREDS

For West Indies (3)

J. C. Adams (1)	**C. H. Gayle** (1)	**C. L. Hooper** (1)
101*　Kingston . . .　1999-00	175　Bulawayo. . .　2001	149†　Bulawayo. . .　2001

For Zimbabwe (4)

A. D. R. Campbell (1)	**M. W. Goodwin** (1)
103　Bulawayo. . .　2001	113　Kingston . . .　1999-00
A. Flower (1)	**H. Masakadza** (1)
113*†　Port-of-Spain　1999-00	119†　Harare. . . . .　2001

† *On first appearance in West Indies–Zimbabwe Tests.*

RECORD PARTNERSHIPS FOR EACH WICKET

For West Indies

214 for 1st	D. Ganga and C. H. Gayle at Bulawayo	2001
100 for 2nd	D. Ganga and S. Chanderpaul at Harare	2001
37 for 3rd	S. L. Campbell and S. Chanderpaul at Port-of-Spain.	1999-2000
131 for 4th	R. R. Sarwan and C. L. Hooper at Bulawayo	2001
100 for 5th	C. L. Hooper and M. N. Samuels at Bulawayo	2001
39 for 6th	J. C. Adams and R. D. Jacobs at Kingston	1999-2000
50 for 7th	R. R. Sarwan and N. C. McGarrell at Harare	2001
147 for 8th†	J. C. Adams and F. A. Rose at Kingston.	1999-2000
12 for 9th	W. W. Hinds and R. D. King at Port-of-Spain	1999-2000
26 for 10th	W. W. Hinds and C. A. Walsh at Port-of-Spain	1999-2000

For Zimbabwe

164 for 1st†	D. D. Ebrahim and A. D. R. Campbell at Bulawayo	2001
91 for 2nd	A. D. R. Campbell and H. Masakadza at Harare	2001
169 for 3rd	H. Masakadza and C. B. Wishart at Harare.	2001
176 for 4th	M. W. Goodwin and A. Flower at Kingston.	1999-2000
25 for 5th	G. J. Whittall and G. W. Flower at Bulawayo.	2001
34 for 6th	G. W. Flower and H. H. Streak at Harare	2001
154 for 7th†	H. H. Streak and A. M. Blignaut at Harare	2001
23 for 8th	G. J. Whittall and T. Taibu at Harare	2001
28 for 9th	H. H. Streak and B. C. Strang at Harare	2001
54 for 10th	S. V. Carlisle and H. K. Olonga at Kingston	1999-2000

† *Record partnership against all countries.*

BEST MATCH BOWLING ANALYSES

For West Indies

7-50 (4-42, 3-8)	C. E. L. Ambrose, Port-of-Spain	1999-2000

For Zimbabwe

9-72 (4-45, 5-27)	H. H. Streak, Port-of-Spain	1999-2000

NEW ZEALAND v INDIA

		Captains				
Season	*New Zealand*	*India*	*T*	*NZ*	*I*	*D*
1955-56*I*	H. B. Cave	P. R. Umrigar[1]	5	0	2	3
1964-65*I*	J. R. Reid	Nawab of Pataudi jun.	4	0	1	3
1967-68*N*	G. T. Dowling[2]	Nawab of Pataudi jun.	4	1	3	0
1969-70*I*	G. T. Dowling	Nawab of Pataudi jun.	3	1	1	1
1975-76*N*	G. M. Turner	B. S. Bedi[3]	3	1	1	1
1976-77*I*	G. M. Turner	B. S. Bedi	3	0	2	1
1980-81*N*	G. P. Howarth	S. M. Gavaskar	3	1	0	2
1988-89*I*	J. G. Wright	D. B. Vengsarkar	3	1	2	0
1989-90*N*	J. G. Wright	M. Azharuddin	3	1	0	2
1993-94*N*	K. R. Rutherford	M. Azharuddin	1	0	0	1
1995-96*I*	L. K. Germon	M. Azharuddin	3	0	1	2
1998-99*N*†	S. P. Fleming	M. Azharuddin	2	1	0	1
1999-2000*I*	S. P. Fleming	S. R. Tendulkar	3	0	1	2
	In India		24	2	10	12
	In New Zealand		16	5	4	7
	Totals		40	7	14	19

I Played in India.   N Played in New Zealand.

† *The First Test at Dunedin was abandoned without a ball being bowled and is excluded.*

Notes: The following deputised for the official touring captain or were appointed by the home authority for a minor proportion of the series:
[1]Ghulam Ahmed (First). [2]B. W. Sinclair (First). [3]S. M. Gavaskar (First).

HIGHEST INNINGS TOTALS

For New Zealand in New Zealand: 502 at Christchurch 1967-68
in India: 462-9 dec. at Calcutta 1964-65

For India in New Zealand: 482 at Auckland 1989-90
in India: 583-7 dec. at Ahmedabad 1999-2000

LOWEST INNINGS TOTALS

For New Zealand in New Zealand: 100 at Wellington 1980-81
in India: 124 at Hyderabad 1988-89

For India in New Zealand: 81 at Wellington 1975-76
in India: 83 at Mohali 1999-2000

INDIVIDUAL HUNDREDS

For New Zealand (22)

C. L. Cairns (1)
126　Hamilton . . . 1998-99
M. D. Crowe (1)
113　Auckland . . . 1989-90
G. T. Dowling (3)
129　Bombay 1964-65
143　Dunedin . . . 1967-68

239　Christchurch . 1967-68
J. W. Guy (1)
102†　Hyderabad . . 1955-56
G. P. Howarth (1)
137*　Wellington . . 1980-81
A. H. Jones (1)
170*　Auckland . . . 1989-90

J. M. Parker (1)
104　Bombay 1976-77
J. F. Reid (1)
123*　Christchurch . 1980-81
J. R. Reid (2)
119*　Delhi 1955-56
120　Calcutta 1955-56

I. D. S. Smith (1)
173 Auckland... 1989-90
B. Sutcliffe (3)
137*† Hyderabad .. 1955-56
230* Delhi 1955-56

151* Calcutta.... 1964-65
B. R. Taylor (1)
105† Calcutta.... 1964-65
G. M. Turner (2)
117 Christchurch. 1975-76

113 Kanpur 1976-77
J. G. Wright (3)
110 Auckland... 1980-81
185 Christchurch. 1989-90
113* Napier..... 1989-90

For India (32)

S. Amarnath (1)
124† Auckland... 1975-76
M. Azharuddin (2)
192 Auckland... 1989-90
103* Wellington .. 1998-99
C. G. Borde (1)
109 Bombay.... 1964-65
R. Dravid (3)
190 }
103*} Hamilton ... 1998-99
144 Mohali 1999-00
S. C. Ganguly (2)
101* Hamilton ... 1998-99
125 Ahmedabad . 1999-00
S. M. Gavaskar (2)
116† Auckland... 1975-76
119 Bombay.... 1976-77

A. G. Kripal Singh (1)
100*† Hyderabad .. 1955-56
V. L. Manjrekar (3)
118† Hyderabad .. 1955-56
177 Delhi 1955-56
102* Madras 1964-65
V. Mankad (2)
223 Bombay.... 1955-56
231 Madras 1955-56
Nawab of Pataudi jun. (2)
153 Calcutta.... 1964-65
113 Delhi 1964-65
G. S. Ramchand (1)
106* Calcutta.... 1955-56
S. Ramesh (1)
110 Ahmedabad . 1999-00
Pankaj Roy (2)
100 Calcutta.... 1955-56

173 Madras 1955-56
D. N. Sardesai (2)
200* Bombay.... 1964-65
106 Delhi 1964-65
N. S. Sidhu (1)
116† Bangalore .. 1988-89
S. R. Tendulkar (3)
113 Wellington .. 1998-99
126* Mohali 1999-00
217 Ahmedabad . 1999-00
P. R. Umrigar (1)
223† Hyderabad .. 1955-56
G. R. Viswanath (1)
103* Kanpur 1976-77
A. L. Wadekar (1)
143 Wellington .. 1967-68

† *On first appearance in New Zealand–India Tests. B. R. Taylor is the only New Zealand player to hit his maiden hundred in first-class cricket in his first Test.*

RECORD PARTNERSHIPS FOR EACH WICKET

For New Zealand

149	for 1st	T. J. Franklin and J. G. Wright at Napier	1989-90
155	for 2nd	G. T. Dowling and B. E. Congdon at Dunedin	1967-68
222*	for 3rd	B. Sutcliffe and J. R. Reid at Delhi	1955-56
160	for 4th	R. G. Twose and C. D. McMillan at Hamilton	1998-99
140	for 5th	C. D. McMillan and A. C. Parore at Hamilton	1998-99
137	for 6th	C. D. McMillan and C. L. Cairns at Wellington	1998-99
163	for 7th	B. Sutcliffe and B. R. Taylor at Calcutta.	1964-65
137	for 8th	D. J. Nash and D. L. Vettori at Wellington	1998-99
136	for 9th†	I. D. S. Smith and M. C. Snedden at Auckland	1989-90
61	for 10th	J. T. Ward and R. O. Collinge at Madras	1964-65

For India

413	for 1st†	V. Mankad and Pankaj Roy at Madras	1955-56
204	for 2nd	S. M. Gavaskar and S. Amarnath at Auckland	1975-76
238	for 3rd	P. R. Umrigar and V. L. Manjrekar at Hyderabad	1955-56
281	for 4th†	S. R. Tendulkar and S. C. Ganguly at Ahmedabad	1999-2000
127	for 5th	V. L. Manjrekar and G. S. Ramchand at Delhi.	1955-56
193*	for 6th	D. N. Sardesai and Hanumant Singh at Bombay	1964-65
128	for 7th	S. R. Tendulkar and K. S. More at Napier	1989-90
144	for 8th	R. Dravid and J. Srinath at Hamilton	1998-99
105	for 9th	{ S. M. H. Kirmani and B. S. Bedi at Bombay	1976-77
		{ S. M. H. Kirmani and N. S. Yadav at Auckland	1980-81
57	for 10th	R. B. Desai and B. S. Bedi at Dunedin	1967-68

† *Record partnership against all countries.*

TEN WICKETS OR MORE IN A MATCH

For New Zealand (2)

11-58 (4-35, 7-23)	R. J. Hadlee, Wellington	1975-76
10-88 (6-49, 4-39)	R. J. Hadlee, Bombay	1988-89

For India (3)

10-134 (4-67, 6-67)	A. Kumble, Kanpur	1999-2000
11-140 (3-64, 8-76)	E. A. S. Prasanna, Auckland	1975-76
12-152 (8-72, 4-80)	S. Venkataraghavan, Delhi	1964-65

NEW ZEALAND v PAKISTAN

		Captains				
Season	*New Zealand*	*Pakistan*	*T*	*NZ*	*P*	*D*
1955-56*P*	H. B. Cave	A. H. Kardar	3	0	2	1
1964-65*N*	J. R. Reid	Hanif Mohammad	3	0	0	3
1964-65*P*	J. R. Reid	Hanif Mohammad	3	0	2	1
1969-70*P*	G. T. Dowling	Intikhab Alam	3	1	0	2
1972-73*N*	B. E. Congdon	Intikhab Alam	3	0	1	2
1976-77*P*	G. M. Turner[1]	Mushtaq Mohammad	3	0	2	1
1978-79*N*	M. G. Burgess	Mushtaq Mohammad	3	0	1	2
1984-85*P*	J. V. Coney	Zaheer Abbas	3	0	2	1
1984-85*N*	G. P. Howarth	Javed Miandad	3	2	0	1
1988-89*N*†	J. G. Wright	Imran Khan	2	0	0	2
1990-91*P*	M. D. Crowe	Javed Miandad	3	0	3	0
1992-93*N*	K. R. Rutherford	Javed Miandad	1	0	1	0
1993-94*N*	K. R. Rutherford	Salim Malik	3	1	2	0
1995-96*N*	L. K. Germon	Wasim Akram	1	0	1	0
1996-97*P*	L. K. Germon	Saeed Anwar	2	1	1	0
2000-01*N*	S. P. Fleming	Moin Khan[2]	3	1	1	1
2002*P*‡	S. P. Fleming	Waqar Younis	1	0	1	0
	In Pakistan		21	2	13	6
	In New Zealand		22	4	7	11
	Totals		43	6	20	17

N Played in New Zealand. P Played in Pakistan.

† *The First Test at Dunedin was abandoned without a ball being bowled and is excluded.*
‡ *The Second Test at Karachi was cancelled owing to civil disturbances.*

Note: The following deputised for the official touring captain:
[1]J. M. Parker (Third). [2]Inzamam-ul-Haq (Third).

HIGHEST INNINGS TOTALS

For New Zealand in New Zealand: 492 at Wellington	1984-85
in Pakistan: 482-6 dec. at Lahore	1964-65
For Pakistan in New Zealand: 616-5 dec. at Auckland	1988-89
in Pakistan: 643 at Lahore	2002

LOWEST INNINGS TOTALS

For New Zealand in New Zealand: 93 at Hamilton	1992-93
in Pakistan: 70 at Dacca	1955-56
For Pakistan in New Zealand: 104 at Hamilton	2000-01
in Pakistan: 102 at Faisalabad	1990-91

INDIVIDUAL HUNDREDS

For New Zealand (24)

M. D. Bell (1)
105   Hamilton . . .   2000-01
M. G. Burgess (2)
119*   Dacca   1969-70
111   Lahore   1976-77
J. V. Coney (1)
111*   Dunedin . .   1984-85
M. D. Crowe (2)
174   Wellington . .   1988-89
108*   Lahore . . .   1990-91
B. A. Edgar (1)
129†   Christchurch .   1978-79
M. J. Greatbatch (1)
133   Hamilton . . .   1992-93
B. F. Hastings (1)
110   Auckland . . .   1972-73

G. P. Howarth (1)
114   Napier.   1978-79
W. K. Lees (1)
152   Karachi . . .   1976-77
S. N. McGregor (1)
111   Lahore   1955-56
R. E. Redmond (1)
107†   Auckland . . .   1972-73
J. F. Reid (3)
106   Hyderabad . .   1984-85
148   Wellington . .   1984-85
158*   Auckland . . .   1984-85
J. R. Reid (1)
128   Karachi   1964-65
M. H. Richardson (1)
106   Hamilton . . .   2000-01

B. W. Sinclair (1)
130   Lahore   1964-65
M. S. Sinclair (1)
204*   Christchurch .   2000-01
S. A. Thomson (1)
120*   Christchurch .   1993-94
G. M. Turner (1)
110†   Dacca   1969-70
J. G. Wright (1)
107   Karachi   1984-85
B. A. Young (1)
120   Christchurch .   1993-94

For Pakistan (47)

Asif Iqbal (3)
175   Dunedin . . .   1972-73
166   Lahore   1976-77
104   Napier.   1978-79
Basit Ali (1)
103   Christchurch .   1993-94
Hanif Mohammad (3)
103   Dacca   1955-56
100*   Christchurch .   1964-65
203*   Lahore   1964-65
Ijaz Ahmed, sen. (2)
103   Christchurch .   1995-96
125   Rawalpindi. . .   1996-97
Imran Nazir (1)
127†   Lahore   2002
Imtiaz Ahmed (1)
209   Lahore   1955-56
Inzamam-ul-Haq (3)
135*   Wellington . .   1993-94
130   Christchurch .   2000-01
329   Lahore   2002
Javed Miandad (7)
163†   Lahore   1976-77
206   Karachi   1976-77

160*   Christchurch .   1978-79
104 }
103*} Hyderabad . .   1984-85
118   Wellington . .   1988-89
271   Auckland . . .   1988-89
Majid Khan (3)
110   Auckland . . .   1972-73
112   Karachi   1976-77
119*   Napier.   1978-79
Mohammad Ilyas (1)
126   Karachi   1964-65
Mohammad Wasim (1)
109*†   Lahore   1996-97
Mudassar Nazar (1)
106   Hyderabad . .   1984-85
Mushtaq Mohammad (3)
201   Dunedin . . .   1972-73
101   Hyderabad . .   1976-77
107   Karachi   1976-77
Sadiq Mohammad (2)
166   Wellington . .   1972-73
103*   Hyderabad . .   1976-77
Saeed Ahmed (1)
172   Karachi   1964-65

Saeed Anwar (2)
169   Wellington . .   1993-94
149   Rawalpindi. .   1996-97
Salim Malik (2)
119*   Karachi   1984-85
140   Wellington . .   1993-94
Saqlain Mushtaq (1)
101*   Christchurch .   2000-01
Shoaib Mohammad (5)
163   Wellington . .   1988-89
112   Auckland . . .   1988-89
203*   Karachi   1990-91
105   Lahore   1990-91
142   Faisalabad . .   1990-91
Waqar Hassan (1)
189   Lahore   1955-56
Younis Khan (1)
149*†   Auckland . . .   2000-01
Yousuf Youhana (1)
203   Christchurch .   2000-01
Zaheer Abbas (1)
135   Auckland . . .   1978-79

† *On first appearance in New Zealand–Pakistan Tests.*

Note: Mushtaq and Sadiq Mohammad both hit hundreds at Hyderabad in 1976-77, the fourth time
– after the Chappells (thrice) – that brothers had each scored hundreds in the same Test innings.

RECORD PARTNERSHIPS FOR EACH WICKET

For New Zealand

181 for 1st	M. H. Richardson and M. D. Bell at Hamilton	2000-01
195 for 2nd	J. G. Wright and G. P. Howarth at Napier	1978-79
178 for 3rd	B. W. Sinclair and J. R. Reid at Lahore.	1964-65

147 for 4th	C. D. McMillan and S. P. Fleming at Hamilton.............	2000-01
183 for 5th	M. G. Burgess and R. W. Anderson at Lahore..............	1976-77
145 for 6th	J. F. Reid and R. J. Hadlee at Wellington...............	1984-85
186 for 7th†	W. K. Lees and R. J. Hadlee at Karachi................	1976-77
100 for 8th	B. W. Yuile and D. R. Hadlee at Karachi	1969-70
96 for 9th	M. G. Burgess and R. S. Cunis at Dacca...............	1969-70
151 for 10th†	B. F. Hastings and R. O. Collinge at Auckland............	1972-73

For Pakistan

172 for 1st	Ramiz Raja and Shoaib Mohammad at Karachi	1990-91
262 for 2nd	Saeed Anwar and Ijaz Ahmed, sen. at Rawalpindi.........	1996-97
248 for 3rd	Shoaib Mohammad and Javed Miandad at Auckland	1988-89
350 for 4th†	Mushtaq Mohammad and Asif Iqbal at Dunedin...........	1972-73
281 for 5th†	Javed Miandad and Asif Iqbal at Lahore...............	1976-77
217 for 6th†	Hanif Mohammad and Majid Khan at Lahore.............	1964-65
308 for 7th†	Waqar Hassan and Imtiaz Ahmed at Lahore.............	1955-56
89 for 8th	Anil Dalpat and Iqbal Qasim at Karachi...............	1984-85
78 for 9th	Inzamam-ul-Haq and Shoaib Akhtar at Lahore...........	2002
65 for 10th	Salah-ud-Din and Mohammad Farooq at Rawalpindi	1964-65

† *Record partnership against all countries.*

TEN WICKETS OR MORE IN A MATCH

For New Zealand (1)

11-152 (7-52, 4-100)	C. Pringle, Faisalabad	1990-91

For Pakistan (10)

10-182 (5-91, 5-91)	Intikhab Alam, Dacca	1969-70
11-130 (7-52, 4-78)	Intikhab Alam, Dunedin.	1972-73
11-130 (4-64, 7-66)†	Mohammad Zahid, Rawalpindi	1996-97
10-171 (3-115, 7-56)	Mushtaq Ahmed, Christchurch.	1995-96
10-143 (4-59, 6-84)	Mushtaq Ahmed, Lahore	1996-97
10-106 (3-20, 7-86)	Waqar Younis, Lahore	1990-91
12-130 (7-76, 5-54)	Waqar Younis, Faisalabad	1990-91
10-128 (5-56, 5-72)	Wasim Akram, Dunedin	1984-85
11-179 (4-60, 7-119)	Wasim Akram, Wellington	1993-94
11-79 (5-37, 6-42)†	Zulfiqar Ahmed, Karachi	1955-56

† *On first appearance in New Zealand–Pakistan Tests.*

Note: Waqar Younis's performances were in successive matches.

NEW ZEALAND v SRI LANKA

Season	New Zealand	*Captains* Sri Lanka	T	NZ	SL	D
1982-83N	G. P. Howarth	D. S. de Silva	2	2	0	0
1983-84S	G. P. Howarth	L. R. D. Mendis	3	2	0	1
1986-87S†	J. J. Crowe	L. R. D. Mendis	1	0	0	1
1990-91N	M. D. Crowe¹	A. Ranatunga	3	0	0	3

	Captains					
Season	*New Zealand*	*Sri Lanka*	*T*	*NZ*	*SL.*	*D*
1992-93*S*	M. D. Crowe	A. Ranatunga	2	0	1	1
1994-95*N*	K. R. Rutherford	A. Ranatunga	2	0	1	1
1996-97*N*	S. P. Fleming	A. Ranatunga	2	2	0	0
1997-98*S*	S. P. Fleming	A. Ranatunga	3	1	2	0
	In New Zealand		9	4	1	4
	In Sri Lanka		9	3	3	3
	Totals		18	7	4	7

N Played in New Zealand.   S Played in Sri Lanka.

† *The Second and Third Tests were cancelled owing to civil disturbances.*

Note: The following was appointed by the home authority for only a minor proportion of the series:

¹I. D. S. Smith (Third).

HIGHEST INNINGS TOTALS

For New Zealand in New Zealand: 671-4 at Wellington 1990-91
in Sri Lanka: 459 at Colombo (CCC) 1983-84

For Sri Lanka in New Zealand: 497 at Wellington 1990-91
in Sri Lanka: 397-9 dec. at Colombo (CCC) 1986-87

LOWEST INNINGS TOTALS

For New Zealand in New Zealand: 109 at Napier 1994-95
in Sri Lanka: 102 at Colombo (SSC) 1992-93

For Sri Lanka in New Zealand: 93 at Wellington 1982-83
in Sri Lanka: 97 at Kandy 1986-87

INDIVIDUAL HUNDREDS

For New Zealand (13)

J. J. Crowe (1)
120*   Colombo (CCC) 1986-87
M. D. Crowe (2)
299   Wellington . . 1990-91
107   Colombo (SSC) 1992-93
S. P. Fleming (1)
174*   Colombo (RPS) 1997-98
R. J. Hadlee (1)
151*   Colombo (CCC) 1986-87

A. H. Jones (3)
186   Wellington . . 1990-91
122 }
100* } Hamilton . . . 1990-91
C. D. McMillan (1)
142†   Colombo (RPS) 1997-98
J. F. Reid (1)
180   Colombo (CCC) 1983-84

K. R. Rutherford (1)
105   Moratuwa . . 1992-93
J. G. Wright (1)
101   Hamilton . . . 1990-91
B. A. Young (1)
267*   Dunedin . . . 1996-97

Gilchrist was playing with them like a cat keeping a half-dead mouse alive for entertainment. And it was only the second day of the series.
South Africa v Australia, page 1287

For Sri Lanka (12)

P. A. de Silva (2)
267†   Wellington . .   1990-91
123   Auckland . . .   1990-91
R. L. Dias (1)
108†   Colombo (SSC)   1983-84
A. P. Gurusinha (3)
119 ⎫
102 ⎭   Hamilton . . .   1990-91

127   Dunedin . . .   1994-95
D. P. M. D. Jayawardene (1)
167   Galle.   1997-98
R. S. Kaluwitharana (1)
103†   Dunedin . . .   1996-97
D. S. B. P. Kuruppu (1)
201*†   Colombo (CCC) 1986-87

R. S. Mahanama (2)
153   Moratuwa . .   1992-93
109   Colombo (SSC) 1992-93
H. P. Tillekeratne (1)
108   Dunedin . . .   1994-95

† *On first appearance in New Zealand–Sri Lanka Tests.*

Note: A. H. Jones and A. P. Gurusinha, on opposing sides, each hit two hundreds at Hamilton in 1990-91, the second time this had happened in Tests, after D. C. S. Compton and A. R. Morris, for England and Australia at Adelaide in 1946-47.

RECORD PARTNERSHIPS FOR EACH WICKET

For New Zealand

161	for 1st	T. J. Franklin and J. G. Wright at Hamilton	1990-91
140	for 2nd	B. A. Young and M. J. Horne at Dunedin.	1996-97
467	for 3rd†‡	A. H. Jones and M. D. Crowe at Wellington.	1990-91
240	for 4th	S. P. Fleming and C. D. McMillan at Colombo (RPS)	1997-98
151	for 5th	K. R. Rutherford and C. Z. Harris at Moratuwa	1992-93
246*	for 6th†	J. J. Crowe and R. J. Hadlee at Colombo (CCC)	1986-87
47	for 7th	D. N. Patel and M. L. Su'a at Dunedin	1994-95
79	for 8th	J. V. Coney and W. K. Lees at Christchurch	1982-83
43	for 9th	A. C. Parore and P. J. Wiseman at Galle	1997-98
52	for 10th	W. K. Lees and E. J. Chatfield at Christchurch	1982-83

For Sri Lanka

102	for 1st	R. S. Mahanama and U. C. Hathurusinghe at Colombo (SSC)	1992-93
138	for 2nd	R. S. Mahanama and A. P. Gurusinha at Moratuwa	1992-93
159*	for 3rd§	S. Wettimuny and R. L. Dias at Colombo (SSC).	1983-84
192	for 4th	A. P. Gurusinha and H. P. Tillekeratne at Dunedin.	1994-95
130	for 5th	R. S. Madugalle and D. S. de Silva at Wellington	1982-83
109*	for 6th¶	R. S. Madugalle and A. Ranatunga at Colombo (CCC).	1983-84
137	for 7th	R. S. Kaluwitharana and W. P. U. J. C. Vaas at Dunedin.	1996-97
73	for 8th	H. P. Tillekeratne and G. P. Wickremasinghe at Dunedin	1996-97
31	for 9th	⎧ G. F. Labrooy and R. J. Ratnayake at Auckland	1990-91
		⎩ S. T. Jayasuriya and R. J. Ratnayake at Auckland	1990-91
71	for 10th	R. S. Kaluwitharana and M. Muralitharan at Colombo (SSC)	1997-98

† *Record partnership against all countries.*
‡ *Record third-wicket partnership in first-class cricket.*
§ *163 runs were added for this wicket in two separate partnerships: S. Wettimuny retired hurt and was replaced by J. R. Ratnayeke when 159 had been added.*
¶ *119 runs were added for this wicket in two separate partnerships: R. S. Madugalle retired hurt and was replaced by D. S. de Silva when 109 had been added.*

TEN WICKETS OR MORE IN A MATCH

For New Zealand (1)

10-102 (5-73, 5-29)   R. J. Hadlee, Colombo (CCC)   1983-84

For Sri Lanka (1)

10-90 (5-47, 5-43)†   W. P. U. J. C. Vaas, Napier   1994-95

† *On first appearance in New Zealand–Sri Lanka Tests.*

NEW ZEALAND v ZIMBABWE

		Captains				
Season	*New Zealand*	*Zimbabwe*	*T*	*NZ*	*Z*	*D*
1992-93*Z*	M. D. Crowe	D. L. Houghton	2	1	0	1
1995-96*N*	L. K. Germon	A. Flower	2	0	0	2
1997-98*Z*	S. P. Fleming	A. D. R. Campbell	2	0	0	2
1997-98*N*	S. P. Fleming	A. D. R. Campbell	2	2	0	0
2000-01*Z*	S. P. Fleming	H. H. Streak	2	2	0	0
2000-01*N*	S. P. Fleming	H. H. Streak	1	0	0	1
	In New Zealand		5	2	0	3
	In Zimbabwe		6	3	0	3
	Totals		11	5	0	6

N Played in New Zealand.   Z Played in Zimbabwe.

HIGHEST INNINGS TOTALS

For New Zealand in New Zealand: 487-7 dec. at Wellington   2000-01
in Zimbabwe: 465 at Harare   2000-01

For Zimbabwe in New Zealand: 340-6 dec. at Wellington   2000-01
in Zimbabwe: 461 at Bulawayo   1997-98

LOWEST INNINGS TOTALS

For New Zealand in New Zealand: 251 at Auckland   1995-96
in Zimbabwe: 207 at Harare   1997-98

For Zimbabwe in New Zealand: 170 at Auckland   1997-98
in Zimbabwe: 119 at Bulawayo   2000-01

INDIVIDUAL HUNDREDS

For New Zealand (11)

N. J. Astle (2)
114   Auckland . . .   1997-98
141   Wellington . .   2000-01
C. L. Cairns (2)
120   Auckland . . .   1995-96
124   Harare   2000-01

M. D. Crowe (1)
140   Harare   1992-93
M. J. Horne (2)
157   Auckland . . .   1997-98
110   Bulawayo . . .   2000-01
R. T. Latham (1)
119†   Bulawayo . . .   1992-93

C. D. McMillan (2)
139†   Wellington . .   1997-98
142   Wellington . .   2000-01
C. M. Spearman (1)
112   Auckland . . .   1995-96

For Zimbabwe (6)

K. J. Arnott (1)
101*†   Bulawayo . . .   1992-93
G. W. Flower (2)
104 }
151 }   Harare   1997-98

D. L. Houghton (1)
104*   Auckland . . .   1995-96
G. J. Whittall (2)
203*   Bulawayo . . .   1997-98
188*   Harare   2000-01

† On first appearance in New Zealand–Zimbabwe Tests.

RECORD PARTNERSHIPS FOR EACH WICKET

For New Zealand

214	for 1st	C. M. Spearman and R. G. Twose at Auckland		1995-96
127	for 2nd	R. T. Latham and A. H. Jones at Bulawayo		1992-93
71	for 3rd	A. H. Jones and M. D. Crowe at Bulawayo		1992-93
243	for 4th†	M. J. Horne and N. J. Astle at Auckland		1997-98
222	for 5th†	N. J. Astle and C. D. McMillan at Wellington		2000-01
82*	for 6th	A. C. Parore and L. K. Germon at Hamilton		1995-96
108	for 7th	C. D. McMillan and D. J. Nash at Wellington		1997-98
144	for 8th	C. L. Cairns and D. J. Nash at Harare		2000-01
78	for 9th	A. C. Parore and D. L. Vettori at Bulawayo		2000-01
27	for 10th	C. D. McMillan and S. B. Doull at Auckland		1997-98

For Zimbabwe

156	for 1st	G. J. Rennie and G. W. Flower at Harare		1997-98
107	for 2nd	K. J. Arnott and A. D. R. Campbell at Harare		1992-93
70	for 3rd	A. Flower and G. J. Whittall at Bulawayo		1997-98
130	for 4th	G. J. Rennie and A. Flower at Wellington		2000-01
131	for 5th	A. Flower and G. J. Whittall at Harare		2000-01
151	for 6th	G. J. Whittall and H. H. Streak at Harare		2000-01
91	for 7th	G. J. Whittall and P. A. Strang at Hamilton		1995-96
94	for 8th	A. D. R. Campbell and H. H. Streak at Wellington		1997-98
46	for 9th	G. J. Crocker and M. G. Burmester at Harare		1992-93
40	for 10th	G. J. Whittall and E. Z. Matambanadzo at Bulawayo		1997-98

† *Record partnership against all countries.*

TEN WICKETS OR MORE IN A MATCH

For Zimbabwe (2)

11-255 (6-109, 5-146)	A. G. Huckle, Bulawayo	1997-98
10-158 (8-109, 2-49)	P. A. Strang, Bulawayo	2000-01

Note: The best match figures for New Zealand are 8-85 (4-35, 4-50) by S. B. Doull at Auckland, 1997-98.

NEW ZEALAND v BANGLADESH

		Captains				
Season	*New Zealand*	*Bangladesh*	*T*	*NZ*	*B*	*D*
2001-02N	S. P. Fleming	Khaled Masud	2	2	0	0

N Played in New Zealand.

HIGHEST INNINGS TOTALS

For New Zealand: 365-9 dec. at Hamilton 2001-02

For Bangladesh: 205 at Hamilton 2001-02

LOWEST INNINGS TOTAL

For Bangladesh: 108 at Hamilton 2001-02

INDIVIDUAL HUNDREDS

For New Zealand (2)

C. D. McMillan (1)

106† Hamilton . . . 2001-02

M. H. Richardson (1)

143† Hamilton . . . 2001-02

Highest score for Bangladesh: 61 by Habibul Bashar at Hamilton, 2001-02.

† *On first appearance in New Zealand–Bangladesh Tests.*

HIGHEST PARTNERSHIPS

For New Zealand

190 for 5th	M. H. Richardson and C. D. McMillan at Hamilton.	2001-02
130 for 4th	S. P. Fleming and C. D. McMillan at Wellington.	2001-02
104 for 1st	M. H. Richardson and M. J. Horne at Wellington	2001-02

For Bangladesh

60 for 3rd	Habibul Bashar and Aminul Islam at Hamilton	2001-02

BEST MATCH BOWLING ANALYSES

For New Zealand

8-108 (1-55, 7-53)	C. L. Cairns, Hamilton	2001-02

For Bangladesh

3-99 (3-99)	Manjurul Islam, Wellington.	2001-02

INDIA v PAKISTAN

Season	India	Pakistan	T	I	P	D
		Captains				
1952-53*I*	L. Amarnath	A. H. Kardar	5	2	1	2
1954-55*P*	V. Mankad	A. H. Kardar	5	0	0	5
1960-61*I*	N. J. Contractor	Fazal Mahmood	5	0	0	5
1978-79*P*	B. S. Bedi	Mushtaq Mohammad	3	0	2	1
1979-80*I*	S. M. Gavaskar[1]	Asif Iqbal	6	2	0	4
1982-83*P*	S. M. Gavaskar	Imran Khan	6	0	3	3
1983-84*I*	Kapil Dev	Zaheer Abbas	3	0	0	3
1984-85*P*	S. M. Gavaskar	Zaheer Abbas	2	0	0	2
1986-87*I*	Kapil Dev	Imran Khan	5	0	1	4
1989-90*P*	K. Srikkanth	Imran Khan	4	0	0	4
1998-99*I*	M. Azharuddin	Wasim Akram	2	1	1	0
1998-99*I*†	M. Azharuddin	Wasim Akram	1	0	1	0
	In India		27	5	4	18
	In Pakistan		20	0	5	15
	Totals		47	5	9	33

I Played in India.   P Played in Pakistan.

† *This Test was part of the Asian Test Championship and was not counted as part of the preceding bilateral series.*

Note: The following was appointed by the home authority for only a minor proportion of the series:
  [1]G. R. Viswanath (Sixth).

HIGHEST INNINGS TOTALS

For India in India: 539-9 dec. at Madras 1960-61
    in Pakistan: 509 at Lahore 1989-90

For Pakistan in India: 487-9 dec. at Madras 1986-87
    in Pakistan: 699-5 at Lahore 1989-90

LOWEST INNINGS TOTALS

For India in India: 106 at Lucknow. 1952-53
    in Pakistan: 145 at Karachi 1954-55

For Pakistan in India: 116 at Bangalore 1986-87
    in Pakistan: 158 at Dacca 1954-55

INDIVIDUAL HUNDREDS

For India (32)

M. Amarnath (4)
109* Lahore 1982-83
120 Lahore 1982-83
103* Karachi . . . 1982-83
101* Lahore 1984-85
M. Azharuddin (3)
141 Calcutta. . . 1986-87
110 Jaipur 1986-87
109 Faisalabad . 1989-90
C. G. Borde (1)
177* Madras . . . 1960-61
A. D. Gaekwad (1)
201 Jullundur . . 1983-84
S. M. Gavaskar (5)
111
137 } Karachi 1978-79

166 Madras 1979-80
127*‡ Faisalabad . . 1982-83
103* Bangalore . . 1983-84
V. S. Hazare (1)
146* Bombay. . . . 1952-53
S. V. Manjrekar (2)
113*† Karachi 1989-90
218 Lahore 1989-90
S. M. Patil (1)
127 Faisalabad . 1984-85
R. J. Shastri (3)
128 Karachi 1982-83
139 Faisalabad . 1984-85
125 Jaipur 1986-87
R. H. Shodhan (1)
110† Calcutta. . . . 1952-53

K. Srikkanth (1)
123 Madras 1986-87
S. R. Tendulkar (1)
136 Chennai. . . . 1998-99
P. R. Umrigar (5)
102 Bombay. . . . 1952-53
108 Peshawar . . 1954-55
115 Kanpur 1960-61
117 Madras 1960-61
112 Delhi 1960-61
D. B. Vengsarkar (2)
146* Delhi 1979-80
109 Ahmedabad . 1986-87
G. R. Viswanath (1)
145† Faisalabad . . 1978-79

For Pakistan (43)

Aamer Malik (2)
117 Faisalabad . . 1989-90
113 Lahore 1989-90
Alim-ud-Din (1)
103* Karachi 1954-55
Asif Iqbal (1)
104† Faisalabad . . 1978-79
Hanif Mohammad (2)
142 Bahawalpur . 1954-55
160 Bombay. . . . 1960-61
Ijaz Faqih (1)
105† Ahmedabad . 1986-87
Imran Khan (3)
117 Faisalabad . . 1982-83
135* Madras 1986-87
109* Karachi 1989-90
Imtiaz Ahmed (1)
135 Madras 1960-61
Javed Miandad (5)
154*† Faisalabad . . 1978-79
100 Karachi 1978-79

126 Faisalabad . . 1982-83
280* Hyderabad . . 1982-83
145 Lahore 1989-90
Mohsin Khan (1)
101*† Lahore 1982-83
Mudassar Nazar (6)
126 Bangalore . . 1979-80
119 Karachi 1982-83
231 Hyderabad . . 1982-83
152*‡ Lahore 1982-83
152 Karachi 1982-83
199 Faisalabad . . 1984-85
Mushtaq Mohammad (1)
101 Delhi 1960-61
Nazar Mohammad (1)
124*‡ Lucknow . . . 1952-53
Qasim Omar (1)
210 Faisalabad . . 1984-85
Ramiz Raja (1)
114 Jaipur 1986-87
Saeed Ahmed (2)
121† Bombay. . . . 1960-61

103 Madras 1960-61
Saeed Anwar (1)
188*‡ Calcutta. . . . 1998-99
Salim Malik (3)
107 Faisalabad . . 1982-83
102* Faisalabad . . 1984-85
102* Karachi 1989-90
Shahid Afridi (1)
141† Chennai. . . . 1998-99
Shoaib Mohammad (2)
101 Madras 1986-87
203* Lahore 1989-90
Wasim Raja (1)
125 Jullundur . . . 1983-84
Zaheer Abbas (6)
176† Faisalabad . . 1978-79
235* Lahore 1978-79
215 Lahore 1982-83
186 Karachi 1982-83
168 Faisalabad . . 1982-83
168* Lahore 1984-85

* On first appearance in India–Pakistan Tests.
‡ Carried his bat.

RECORD PARTNERSHIPS FOR EACH WICKET

For India

200 for 1st	S. M. Gavaskar and K. Srikkanth at Madras	. . . .	1986-87
135 for 2nd	N. S. Sidhu and S. V. Manjrekar at Karachi	. . . .	1989-90
190 for 3rd	M. Amarnath and Yashpal Sharma at Lahore	. . . .	1982-83
186 for 4th	S. V. Manjrekar and R. J. Shastri at Lahore	. . . .	1989-90
200 for 5th	S. M. Patil and R. J. Shastri at Faisalabad	. . . .	1984-85
143 for 6th	M. Azharuddin and Kapil Dev at Calcutta	. . . .	1986-87
155 for 7th	R. M. H. Binny and Madan Lal at Bangalore	. . . .	1983-84
122 for 8th	S. M. H. Kirmani and Madan Lal at Faisalabad	. . . .	1982-83
149 for 9th†	P. G. Joshi and R. B. Desai at Bombay	. . . .	1960-61
109 for 10th†	H. R. Adhikari and Ghulam Ahmed at Delhi	. . . .	1952-53

For Pakistan

162 for 1st	Hanif Mohammad and Imtiaz Ahmed at Madras	. . . .	1960-61
250 for 2nd	Mudassar Nazar and Qasim Omar at Faisalabad	. . . .	1984-85
451 for 3rd†	Mudassar Nazar and Javed Miandad at Hyderabad.	. . . . . .	1982-83
287 for 4th	Javed Miandad and Zaheer Abbas at Faisalabad	. . . .	1982-83
213 for 5th	Zaheer Abbas and Mudassar Nazar at Karachi	. . . .	1982-83
207 for 6th	Salim Malik and Imran Khan at Faisalabad	. . . .	1982-83
154 for 7th	Imran Khan and Ijaz Faqih at Ahmedabad	. . . .	1986-87
112 for 8th	Imran Khan and Wasim Akram at Madras	. . . .	1986-87
60 for 9th	Wasim Bari and Iqbal Qasim at Bangalore	. . . .	1979-80
104 for 10th	Zulfiqar Ahmed and Amir Elahi at Madras	. . . .	1952-53

† *Record partnership against all countries.*

TEN WICKETS OR MORE IN A MATCH

For India (5)

11-146 (4-90, 7-56)	Kapil Dev, Madras	. . . .	1979-80
14-149 (4-75, 10-74)	A. Kumble, Delhi	. . . .	1998-99
10-126 (7-27, 3-99)	Maninder Singh, Bangalore	. . . .	1986-87
13-131 (8-52, 5-79)†	V. Mankad, Delhi	. . . .	1952-53
13-132 (5-46, 8-86)	J. Srinath, Calcutta	. . . .	1998-99

For Pakistan (7)

12-94 (5-52, 7-42)	Fazal Mahmood, Lucknow	. . . .	1952-53
11-79 (3-19, 8-60)	Imran Khan, Karachi	. . . .	1982-83
11-180 (6-98, 5-82)	Imran Khan, Faisalabad	. . . .	1982-83
10-175 (4-135, 6-40)	Iqbal Qasim, Bombay	. . . .	1979-80
10-187 (5-94, 5-93)†	Saqlain Mushtaq, Chennai	. . . .	1998-99
10-216 (5-94, 5-122)	Saqlain Mushtaq, Delhi	. . . .	1998-99
11-190 (8-69, 3-121)	Sikander Bakht, Delhi	. . . .	1979-80

† *On first appearance in India–Pakistan Tests.*

INDIA v SRI LANKA

Captains

eason	*India*	*Sri Lanka*	*T*	*I*	*SL*	*D*
982-83I	S. M. Gavaskar	B. Warnapura	1	0	0	1
985-86S	Kapil Dev	L. R. D. Mendis	3	0	1	2
986-87I	Kapil Dev	L. R. D. Mendis	3	2	0	1
990-91I	M. Azharuddin	A. Ranatunga	1	1	0	0
993-94S	M. Azharuddin	A. Ranatunga	3	1	0	2
993-94I	M. Azharuddin	A. Ranatunga	3	3	0	0
997-98S	S. R. Tendulkar	A. Ranatunga	2	0	0	2
997-98I	S. R. Tendulkar	A. Ranatunga	3	0	0	3
998-99S†	M. Azharuddin	A. Ranatunga	1	0	0	1
001S	S. C. Ganguly	S. T. Jayasuriya	3	1	2	0
	In India		11	6	0	5
	In Sri Lanka		12	2	3	7
	Totals		23	8	3	12

Played in India.   S Played in Sri Lanka.

This Test was part of the Asian Test Championship.

HIGHEST INNINGS TOTALS

or India in India: 676-7 at Kanpur	1986-87
in Sri Lanka: 537-8 dec. at Colombo (RPS)	1997-98
or Sri Lanka in India: 420 at Kanpur	1986-87
in Sri Lanka: 952-6 dec. at Colombo (RPS)	1997-98

LOWEST INNINGS TOTALS

or India in India: 288 at Chandigarh	1990-91
in Sri Lanka: 180 at Galle	2001
or Sri Lanka in India: 82 at Chandigarh	1990-91
in Sri Lanka: 198 at Kandy	1985-86

INDIVIDUAL HUNDREDS

For India (30)

¹. Amarnath (2)		**S. M. Gavaskar (2)**		124	Lucknow . . .	1993-94
⁴6*	Kandy 1985-86	155†	Madras 1982-83	111	Colombo (RPS) 1997-98
⁴1	Nagpur . . . 1986-87	176	Kanpur 1986-87	131	Mohali 1997-98
¹. Azharuddin (5)		**V. G. Kambli (2)**		**S. R. Tendulkar (6)**	
⁰9	Kanpur 1986-87	125	Colombo (SSC) 1993-94	104*	Colombo (SSC) 1993-94
⁰8	Bangalore . . 1993-94	120	Colombo (PSS) 1993-94	142	Lucknow . . . 1993-94
⁵2	Ahmedabad . 1993-94	**Kapil Dev (1)**		143	Colombo (RPS) 1997-98
²6	Colombo (RPS) 1997-98	163	Kanpur . . . 1986-87	139	Colombo (SSC) 1997-98
⁰8*	Colombo (SSC) 1997-98	**S. M. Patil (1)**		148	Mumbai 1997-98
. Dravid (1)		114*†	Madras 1982-83	124*	Colombo (SSC) 1998-99
⁰7	Colombo (SSC) 1998-99	**S. Ramesh (1)**		**D. B. Vengsarkar (2)**	
C. Ganguly (3)		143†	Colombo (SSC) 1998-99	153	Nagpur 1986-87
⁴7	Colombo (SSC) 1997-98	**N. S. Sidhu (4)**		166	Cuttack 1986-87
⁴9	Mohali 1997-98	104	Colombo (SSC) 1993-94		
⁷3	Mumbai 1997-98				

For Sri Lanka (25)

M. S. Atapattu (2)			
108	Mohali	1997-98	
108	Colombo (SSC)	2001	
P. A. de Silva (5)			
148	Colombo (PSS)	1993-94	
126	Colombo (RPS)	1997-98	
146 }	Colombo (SSC)	1997-98	
120 }			
110*	Mohali	1997-98	
R. L. Dias (1)			
106	Kandy	1985-86	
S. T. Jayasuriya (3)			
340	Colombo (RPS)	1997-98	
199	Colombo (SSC)	1997-98	

111	Galle.	2001
D. P. M. D. Jayawardene (3)		
242	Colombo (SSC)	1998-99
104	Kandy	2001
139	Colombo (SSC)	2001
R. S. Madugalle (1)		
103	Colombo (SSC)	1985-86
R. S. Mahanama (2)		
151	Colombo (PSS)	1993-94
225	Colombo (RPS)	1997-98
L. R. D. Mendis (3)		
105 }	†Madras	1982-83
105 }		
124	Kandy	1985-86

A. Ranatunga (1)		
111	Colombo (SSC)	1985-86
T. T. Samaraweera (1)		
103*†	Colombo (SSC)	2001
K. C. Sangakkara (1)		
105*†	Galle.	2001
S. A. R. Silva (1)		
111	Colombo (PSS)	1985-86
H. P. Tillekeratne (1)		
136*	Colombo (SSC)	2001

† *On first appearance in India–Sri Lanka Tests.*

RECORD PARTNERSHIPS FOR EACH WICKET

For India

171	for 1st	M. Prabhakar and N. S. Sidhu at Colombo (SSC)		1993-94
232	for 2nd	S. Ramesh and R. Dravid at Colombo (SSC)		1998-99
173	for 3rd	M. Amarnath and D. B. Vengsarkar at Nagpur		1986-87
256	for 4th	S. C. Ganguly and S. R. Tendulkar at Mumbai.		1997-98
150	for 5th	S. R. Tendulkar and S. C. Ganguly at Colombo (SSC).		1997-98
272	for 6th	M. Azharuddin and Kapil Dev at Kanpur.		1986-87
78*	for 7th	S. M. Patil and Madan Lal at Madras.		1982-83
70	for 8th	Kapil Dev and L. Sivaramakrishnan at Colombo (PSS).		1985-86
89	for 9th	S. C. Ganguly and A. Kuruvilla at Mohali.		1997-98
30	for 10th	Zaheer Khan and B. K. V. Prasad at Colombo (SSC)		2001

For Sri Lanka

159	for 1st	S. Wettimuny and J. R. Ratnayeke at Kanpur		1986-87
576	for 2nd†	S. T. Jayasuriya and R. S. Mahanama at Colombo (RPS)		1997-98
218	for 3rd	S. T. Jayasuriya and P. A. de Silva at Colombo (SSC)		1997-98
216	for 4th	R. L. Dias and L. R. D. Mendis at Kandy		1985-86
144	for 5th‡	R. S. Madugalle and A. Ranatunga at Colombo (SSC)		1985-86
103	for 6th	P. A. de Silva and H. D. P. K. Dharmasena at Mohali		1997-98
194*	for 7th†	H. P. Tillekeratne and T. T. Samaraweera at Colombo (SSC) . . .		2001
48	for 8th	P. A. de Silva and M. Muralitharan at Colombo (SSC)		1997-98
60	for 9th	H. P. Tillekeratne and A. W. R. Madurasinghe at Chandigarh . . .		1990-91
64	for 10th	M. Muralitharan and P. D. R. L. Perera at Kandy		2001

† *Record partnership against all countries.*
‡ *Although Sri Lanka's fifth wicket added 176 runs against India at Colombo (SSC) in 1998-99, this comprised two partnerships. D. P. M. D. Jayawardene added 115* with A. Ranatunga (retired hurt) and a further 61 with H. P. Tillekeratne.*

TEN WICKETS OR MORE IN A MATCH

For India (3)

11-128 (4-69, 7-59)	A. Kumble, Lucknow.	1993-94
10-107 (3-56, 7-51)	Maninder Singh, Nagpur	1986-87
11-125 (5-38, 6-87)	S. L. V. Raju, Ahmedabad	1993-94

For Sri Lanka (1)

11-196 (8-87, 3-109)	M. Muralitharan, Colombo (SSC)	2001

INDIA v ZIMBABWE

Captains

Season	India	Zimbabwe	T	I	Z	D
1992-93*Z*	M. Azharuddin	D. L. Houghton	1	0	0	1
1992-93*I*	M. Azharuddin	D. L. Houghton	1	1	0	0
1998-99*Z*	M. Azharuddin	A. D. R. Campbell	1	0	1	0
2000-01*I*	S. C. Ganguly	H. H. Streak	2	1	0	1
2001*Z*	S. C. Ganguly	H. H. Streak	2	1	1	0
2001-02*I*	S. C. Ganguly	S. V. Carlisle	2	2	0	0
	In India		5	4	0	1
	In Zimbabwe		4	1	2	1
	Totals		9	5	2	2

I Played in India.   Z Played in Zimbabwe.

HIGHEST INNINGS TOTALS

For India in India: 609-6 dec. at Nagpur 2000-01
        in Zimbabwe: 318 at Bulawayo 2001

For Zimbabwe in India: 503-6 at Nagpur 2000-01
        in Zimbabwe: 456 at Harare 1992-93

LOWEST INNINGS TOTALS

For India in India: 354 at Delhi 2001-02
        in Zimbabwe: 173 at Harare 1998-99

For Zimbabwe in India: 146 at Delhi 2001-02
        in Zimbabwe: 173 at Bulawayo 2001

INDIVIDUAL HUNDREDS

For India (12)

S. B. Bangar (1)
100*† Nagpur 2001-02
S. S. Das (2)
110 Nagpur 2000-01
105 Nagpur 2001-02
R. Dravid (3)
118† Harare 1998-99
200* Delhi 2000-01
162 Nagpur 2000-01
S. C. Ganguly (1)
136 Delhi 2001-02
V. G. Kambli (1)
227† Delhi 1992-93
S. V. Manjrekar (1)
104† Harare 1992-93
S. R. Tendulkar (3)
122 Delhi 2000-01
201* Nagpur 2000-01
176 Nagpur 2001-02

For Zimbabwe (6)

A. D. R. Campbell (1)
102 Nagpur 2000-01
A. Flower (3)
115 Delhi 1992-93
183* Delhi 2000-01
232* Nagpur 2000-01
G. W. Flower (1)
106* Nagpur 2000-01
D. L. Houghton (1)
121† Harare 1992-93

† *On first appearance in India–Zimbabwe Tests.*

RECORD PARTNERSHIPS FOR EACH WICKET

For India

79	for 1st	S. S. Das and D. Dasgupta at Nagpur........................	2001-02
155	for 2nd	S. S. Das and R. Dravid at Nagpur.........................	2000-01
249	for 3rd	R. Dravid and S. R. Tendulkar at Nagpur	2000-01
110*	for 4th	R. Dravid and S. C. Ganguly at Delhi.....................	2000-01
120	for 5th	S. C. Ganguly and V. Sehwag at Delhi	2001-02
171	for 6th	S. R. Tendulkar and S. B. Bangar at Nagpur	2001-02
44	for 7th	R. Dravid and R. R. Singh at Harare	1998-99
72	for 8th	S. S. Dighe and Harbhajan Singh at Bulawayo	2001
19	for 9th	H. K. Badani and J. Srinath at Harare....................	2001
40	for 10th	J. Srinath and Harbhajan Singh at Harare.................	1998-99

For Zimbabwe

138	for 1st	G. J. Rennie and C. B. Wishart at Harare	1998-99
106	for 2nd	S. V. Carlisle and A. D. R. Campbell at Nagpur	2001-02
119	for 3rd	S. V. Carlisle and A. D. R. Campbell at Delhi	2000-01
209	for 4th	A. D. R. Campbell and A. Flower at Nagpur	2000-01
96	for 5th	A. Flower and G. W. Flower at Nagpur	2000-01
165	for 6th†	D. L. Houghton and A. Flower at Harare	1992-93
98*	for 7th	A. Flower and H. H. Streak at Nagpur	2000-01
46	for 8th	A. Flower and B. A. Murphy at Delhi	2000-01
59	for 9th	T. J. Friend and R. W. Price at Nagpur	2001-02
97*	for 10th†	A. Flower and H. K. Olonga at Delhi	2000-01

† *Record partnership against all countries.*

BEST MATCH BOWLING ANALYSES

For India

9-141 (4-81, 5-60)	J. Srinath, Delhi	2000-01

For Zimbabwe

7-115 (3-69, 4-46)	H. H. Streak, Harare	2001

INDIA v BANGLADESH

Season	India		Bangladesh	*T*	*I*	*B*	*D*
2000-01*B*	S. C. Ganguly		Naimur Rahman	1	1	0	0

B Played in Bangladesh.

HIGHEST INNINGS TOTALS

For India: 429 at Dhaka 2000-01

For Bangladesh: 400 at Dhaka 2000-01

INDIVIDUAL HUNDRED

For Bangladesh (1)

Aminul Islam (1)
145† Dhaka 2000-01

Highest score for India: 92 by S. B. Joshi at Dhaka, 2000-01.

† *On first appearance in India–Bangladesh Tests.*

HIGHEST PARTNERSHIPS

For India

121 for 7th S. C. Ganguly and S. B. Joshi at Dhaka 2000-01

For Bangladesh

93 for 7th Aminul Islam and Khaled Masud at Dhaka 2000-01

BEST MATCH BOWLING ANALYSES

For India

8-169 (5-142, 3-27) S. B. Joshi, Dhaka 2000-01

For Bangladesh

6-154 (6-132, 0-22) Naimur Rahman, Dhaka 2000-01

PAKISTAN v SRI LANKA

Captains

Season	Pakistan	Sri Lanka	T	P	SL	D
1981-82*P*	Javed Miandad	B. Warnapura[1]	3	2	0	1
1985-86*P*	Javed Miandad	L. R. D. Mendis	3	2	0	1
1985-86*S*	Imran Khan	L. R. D. Mendis	3	1	1	1
1991-92*P*	Imran Khan	P. A. de Silva	3	1	0	2
1994-95*S*†	Salim Malik	A. Ranatunga	2	2	0	0
1995-96*P*	Ramiz Raja	A. Ranatunga	3	1	2	0
1996-97*S*	Ramiz Raja	A. Ranatunga	2	0	0	2
1998-99*P*‡	Wasim Akram	H. P. Tillekeratne	1	0	0	1
1998-99*B*‡	Wasim Akram	P. A. de Silva	1	1	0	0
1999-2000*P*	Saeed Anwar[2]	S. T. Jayasuriya	3	1	2	0
2000*S*	Moin Khan	S. T. Jayasuriya	3	2	0	1
2001-02*P*‡	Waqar Younis	S. T. Jayasuriya	1	0	1	0
	In Pakistan		17	7	5	5
	In Sri Lanka		10	5	1	4
	In Bangladesh		1	1	0	0
	Totals.		28	13	6	9

P Played in Pakistan. S Played in Sri Lanka. B Played in Bangladesh.

† *One Test was cancelled owing to the threat of civil disturbances following a general election.*
‡ *These Tests were part of the Asian Test Championship.*

Note: The following deputised for the official touring captain or were appointed by the home authority for only a minor proportion of the series:
[1]L. R. D. Mendis (Second). [2]Moin Khan (Third).

HIGHEST INNINGS TOTALS

For Pakistan in Pakistan: 555-3 at Faisalabad. 1985-86
        in Sri Lanka: 600-8 dec. at Galle. 2000
        in Bangladesh: 594 at Dhaka 1998-99

For Sri Lanka in Pakistan: 528 at Lahore 2001-02
        in Sri Lanka: 467-5 at Kandy 2000

LOWEST INNINGS TOTALS

For Pakistan in Pakistan: 182 at Rawalpindi 1999-2000
        in Sri Lanka: 132 at Colombo (CCC). 1985-86

For Sri Lanka in Pakistan: 149 at Karachi 1981-82
        in Sri Lanka: 71 at Kandy 1994-95

INDIVIDUAL HUNDREDS

For Pakistan (23)

Haroon Rashid (1)
153†   Karachi 1981-82
Ijaz Ahmed, sen. (2)
113†   Colombo (RPS) 1996-97
211   Dhaka 1998-99
Inzamam-ul-Haq (4)
100*   Kandy 1994-95
200*   Dhaka 1998-99
138   Karachi 1999-00
112   Galle. 2000
Javed Miandad (1)
203*   Faisalabad . . 1985-86
Mohsin Khan (1)
129   Lahore 1981-82

Moin Khan (1)
117*   Sialkot 1995-96
Qasim Omar (1)
206†   Faisalabad . . 1985-86
Ramiz Raja (1)
122   Colombo (PSS) 1985-86
Saeed Anwar (2)
136†   Colombo (PSS) 1994-95
123   Galle. 2000
Salim Malik (3)
100*† Karachi 1981-82
101   Sialkot 1991-92
155   Colombo (SSC) 1996-97

Wajahatullah Wasti (2)
133 } †Lahore 1998-99
121*}
Wasim Akram (1)
100   Galle. 2000
Younis Khan (2)
107†   Rawalpindi . . 1999-00
116   Galle. 2000
Zaheer Abbas (1)
134†   Lahore 1981-82

For Sri Lanka (20)

R. P. Arnold (1)
123   Lahore 1998-99
M. S. Atapattu (1)
207*   Kandy 2000
P. A. de Silva (8)
122†   Faisalabad . . 1985-86
105   Karachi 1985-86
127   Colombo (PSS) 1994-95
105   Faisalabad . . 1995-96
168   Colombo (RPS) 1996-97

138*} Colombo (SSC) 1996-97
103*}
112   Rawalpindi . . 1999-00
R. L. Dias (1)
109   Lahore 1981-82
A. P. Gurusinha (1)
116*   Colombo (PSS) 1985-86
S. T. Jayasuriya (2)
113   Colombo (SSC) 1996-97
188   Kandy 2000

R. S. Kaluwitharana (1)
100   Lahore 1998-99
A. Ranatunga (1)
135*   Colombo (PSS) 1985-86
K. C. Sangakkara (1)
230†   Lahore 2001-02
H. P. Tillekeratne (2)
115   Faisalabad . . 1995-96
103   Colombo (PSS) 1996-97
S. Wettimuny (1)
157   Faisalabad . . 1981-82

† *On first appearance in Pakistan–Sri Lanka Tests.*

RECORD PARTNERSHIPS FOR EACH WICKET

For Pakistan

56 for 1st	Wajahatullah Wasti and Shahid Afridi at Lahore	....	1998-99
51 for 2nd	Mohsin Khan and Majid Khan at Lahore	....	1981-82
97 for 3rd	Qasim Omar and Javed Miandad at Faisalabad	....	1985-86
78 for 4th	Wajahatullah Wasti and Yousuf Youhana at Lahore	.....	1998-99
32 for 5th	Salim Malik and Imran Khan at Sialkot	....	1991-92
24 for 6th	Inzamam-ul-Haq and Younis Khan at Karachi	....	1999-2000
20 for 7th	Younis Khan and Wasim Akram at Galle	....	2000
88 for 8th	Moin Khan and Waqar Younis at Karachi	....	1999-2000
45 for 9th	Younis Khan and Wasim Akram at Rawalpindi	....	1999-2000
90 for 10th	Wasim Akram and Arshad Khan at Colombo (SSC)	......	2000

For Sri Lanka

35 for 1st†	M. S. Atapattu and S. T. Jayasuriya at Kandy	....	2000
17 for 2nd	S. Wettimuny and R. L. Dias at Faisalabad	....	1981-82
76 for 3rd	U. C. Hathurusinghe and P. A. de Silva at Faisalabad	...	1995-96
40* for 4th†	A. P. Gurusinha and A. Ranatunga at Colombo (PSS)	...	1985-86
43 for 5th	R. P. Arnold and R. S. Kaluwitharana at Lahore	....	1998-99
21 for 6th	A. Ranatunga and P. A. de Silva at Faisalabad	....	1985-86
31 for 7th	H. P. Tillekeratne and R. S. Kalpage at Kandy	....	1994-95
76 for 8th	P. A. de Silva and W. P. U. J. C. Vaas at Colombo (SSC)	....	1996-97
52 for 9th	P. A. de Silva and R. J. Ratnayake at Faisalabad	......	1985-86
73 for 10th†	H. P. Tillekeratne and K. S. C. de Silva at Dhaka	.....	1998-99

Record partnership against all countries.

TEN WICKETS OR MORE IN A MATCH

For Pakistan (2)

14-116 (8-58, 6-58)	Imran Khan, Lahore	1981-82
11-119 (6-34, 5-85)	Waqar Younis, Kandy	1994-95

For Sri Lanka (1)

10-148 (4-77, 6-71)	M. Muralitharan, Peshawar	1999-2000

PAKISTAN v ZIMBABWE

		Captains				
Season	*Pakistan*		*Zimbabwe*	*T*	*P*	*Z*	*D*
1993-94*P*	Wasim Akram[1]		A. Flower	3	2	0	1
1994-95*Z*	Salim Malik		A. Flower	3	2	1	0
1996-97*P*	Wasim Akram	A. D. R. Campbell	2	1	0	1
1997-98*Z*	Rashid Latif	A. D. R. Campbell	2	1	0	1
1998-99*P*†	Aamir Sohail[2]	A. D. R. Campbell	2	0	1	1
In Pakistan	....			7	3	1	3
In Zimbabwe	....			5	3	1	1
Totals	...			12	6	2	4

P Played in Pakistan.   Z Played in Zimbabwe.

The Third Test at Faisalabad was abandoned without a ball being bowled and is excluded.

Notes: The following were appointed by the home authority for only a minor proportion of the series:

[1]Waqar Younis (First).   [2]Moin Khan (Second).

HIGHEST INNINGS TOTALS

For Pakistan in Pakistan: 553 at Sheikhupura	1996-97
in Zimbabwe: 354 at Harare	1997-98
For Zimbabwe in Pakistan: 375 at Sheikhupura	1996-97
in Zimbabwe: 544-4 dec. at Harare	1994-95

LOWEST INNINGS TOTALS

For Pakistan in Pakistan: 103 at Peshawar	1998-99
in Zimbabwe: 158 at Harare	1994-95
For Zimbabwe in Pakistan: 133 at Faisalabad	1996-97
in Zimbabwe: 139 at Harare	1994-95

INDIVIDUAL HUNDREDS

For Pakistan (4)

Inzamam-ul-Haq (1)
101 Harare 1994-95
Mohammad Wasim (1)
192† Harare 1997-98

Wasim Akram (1)
257* Sheikhupura . 1996-97
Yousuf Youhana (1)
120* Lahore 1998-99

For Zimbabwe (9)

A. Flower (2)
156 Harare 1994-95
100* Bulawayo . . 1997-98
G. W. Flower (3)
201* Harare 1994-95
110 Sheikhupura . 1996-97

156*‡ Bulawayo . . . 1997-98
M. W. Goodwin (1)
166*† Bulawayo . . . 1997-98
N. C. Johnson (1)
107† Peshawar . . . 1998-99

P. A. Strang (1)
106* Sheikhupura . 1996-97
G. J. Whittall (1)
113* Harare 1994-95

† *On first appearance in Pakistan–Zimbabwe Tests.*
‡ *Carried his bat.*

RECORD PARTNERSHIPS FOR EACH WICKET

For Pakistan

95	for 1st	Aamir Sohail and Shoaib Mohammad at Karachi (DS)	1993-94
118*	for 2nd	Shoaib Mohammad and Asif Mujtaba at Lahore	1993-94
83	for 3rd	Shoaib Mohammad and Javed Miandad at Karachi (DS)	1993-94
118	for 4th	Ijaz Ahmed, sen. and Yousuf Youhana at Peshawar	1998-99
110	for 5th	Yousuf Youhana and Moin Khan at Bulawayo	1997-98
96	for 6th	Inzamam-ul-Haq and Rashid Latif at Harare	1994-95
120	for 7th	Ijaz Ahmed, sen. and Inzamam-ul-Haq at Harare	1994-95
313	for 8th†	Wasim Akram and Saqlain Mushtaq at Sheikhupura	1996-97
147	for 9th	Mohammad Wasim and Mushtaq Ahmed at Harare	1997-98
50*	for 10th	Yousuf Youhana and Waqar Younis at Lahore	1998-99

For Zimbabwe

48*	for 1st	G. J. Rennie and G. W. Flower at Lahore	1998-99
135	for 2nd†	M. H. Dekker and A. D. R. Campbell at Rawalpindi	1993-94
84	for 3rd	G. W. Flower and D. L. Houghton at Sheikhupura	1996-97
269	for 4th†	G. W. Flower and A. Flower at Harare	1994-95
277*	for 5th†	M. W. Goodwin and A. Flower at Bulawayo	1997-98

72	for 6th	M. H. Dekker and G. J. Whittall at Rawalpindi.		1993-94
131	for 7th	G. W. Flower and P. A. Strang at Sheikhupura		1996-97
110	for 8th†	G. J. Whittall and B. C. Strang at Harare.		1997-98
87	for 9th†	P. A. Strang and B. C. Strang at Sheikhupura.		1996-97
29	for 10th	E. A. Brandes and S. G. Peall at Rawalpindi		1993-94

† *Record partnership against all countries.*

TEN WICKETS OR MORE IN A MATCH

For Pakistan (2)

13-135 (7-91, 6-44)†	Waqar Younis, Karachi (DS)	1993-94
10-106 (6-48, 4-58)	Wasim Akram, Faisalabad	1996-97

Note: The best match figures for Zimbabwe are 9-105 (6-90, 3-15) by H. H. Streak at Harare, 1994-95.

† *On first appearance in Pakistan–Zimbabwe Tests.*

PAKISTAN v BANGLADESH

		Captains					
Season	*Pakistan*	*Bangladesh*	*T*	*P*	*B*	*D*	
2001-02*P*†	Waqar Younis	Naimur Rahman	1	1	0	0	
2001-02*B*	Waqar Younis	Khaled Masud	2	2	0	0	
	In Pakistan		1	1	0	0	
	In Bangladesh		2	2	0	0	
	Totals.		3	3	0	0	

P Played in Pakistan. B Played in Bangladesh.

† *This Test was part of the Asian Test Championship.*

HIGHEST INNINGS TOTALS

For Pakistan in Pakistan: 546-3 dec. at Multan 2001-02
in Bangladesh: 490-9 dec. at Dhaka. 2001-02

For Bangladesh in Pakistan: 148 at Multan. 2001-02
in Bangladesh: 160 at Dhaka 2001-02

LOWEST INNINGS TOTALS

For Bangladesh in Pakistan: 134 at Multan. 2001-02
in Bangladesh: 148 at Chittagong (in both innings) 2001-02

INDIVIDUAL HUNDREDS

For Pakistan (8)

Abdul Razzaq (2)
110*† Multan 2001-02
134 Dhaka 2001-02
Inzamam-ul-Haq (1)
105*† Multan 2001-02

Saeed Anwar (1)
101† Multan 2001-02
Taufeeq Umar (1)
104† Multan 2001-02

Younis Khan (1)
119 Chittagong . . 2001-02
Yousuf Youhana (2)
102*† Multan 2001-02
204* Chittagong . . 2001-02

Highest score for Bangladesh: 56* by Habibul Bashar at Multan, 2001-02.

† *On first appearance in Pakistan–Bangladesh Tests.*

HIGHEST PARTNERSHIPS

For Pakistan

175	for 6th	Abdul Razzaq and Rashid Latif at Dhaka.	2001-02
168	for 1st	Saeed Anwar and Taufeeq Umar at Multan	2001-02
165*	for 4th‡	Yousuf Youhana and Abdul Razzaq at Multan	2001-02
123*	for 4th‡	Inzamam-ul-Haq and Yousuf Youhana at Multan.	2001-02
100	for 1st	Taufeeq Umar and Shadab Kabir at Dhaka	2001-02

‡ *A total of 288 runs was added between the fall of Pakistan's third wicket and the end of the innings: Inzamam-ul-Haq retired hurt when he and Yousuf Youhana had added 123 runs.*

For Bangladesh

69	for 5th	Habibul Bashar and Sanuar Hossain at Chittagong	2001-02

TEN WICKETS OR MORE IN A MATCH

For Pakistan (1)

12-94 (6-42, 6-52)†	Danish Kaneria, Multan	2001-02

Note: The best match figures for Bangladesh are 4-98 (4-98) by Mohammad Sharif at Chittagong, 2001-02.

† *On first appearance in Pakistan–Bangladesh Tests.*

SRI LANKA v ZIMBABWE

		Captains				
Season	Sri Lanka	Zimbabwe	T	SL	Z	D
1994-95Z	A. Ranatunga	A. Flower	3	0	0	3
1996-97S	A. Ranatunga	A. D. R. Campbell	2	2	0	0
1997-98S	A. Ranatunga	A. D. R. Campbell	2	2	0	0
1999-2000Z	S. T. Jayasuriya	A. Flower	3	1	0	2
2001-02S	S. T. Jayasuriya	S. V. Carlisle	3	3	0	0
	In Sri Lanka		7	7	0	0
	In Zimbabwe		6	1	0	5
	Totals		13	8	0	5

S Played in Sri Lanka. Z Played in Zimbabwe.

HIGHEST INNINGS TOTALS

For Sri Lanka in Sri Lanka: 586-6 dec. at Colombo (SSC)		2001-02
in Zimbabwe: 432 at Harare		1999-2000
For Zimbabwe in Sri Lanka: 338 at Kandy		1997-98
in Zimbabwe: 462-9 dec. at Bulawayo		1994-95

LOWEST INNINGS TOTALS

For Sri Lanka in Sri Lanka: 225 at Colombo (SSC).		1997-98
in Zimbabwe: 218 at Bulawayo		1994-95
For Zimbabwe in Sri Lanka: 79 at Galle.		2001-02
in Zimbabwe: 174 at Harare.		1999-2000

INDIVIDUAL HUNDREDS

For Sri Lanka (14)

R. P. Arnold (1)	**T. M. Dilshan** (1)	100* Bulawayo . . . 1994-95
104*‡ Harare 1999-00	163* Harare 1999-00	**T. T. Samaraweera** (1)
M. S. Atapattu (3)	**A. P. Gurusinha** (1)	123*‡ Colombo (SSC) 2001-02
223† Kandy 1997-98	128† Harare 1994-95	**K. C. Sangakkara** (1)
216*‡ Bulawayo . . . 1999-00	**S. T. Jayasuriya** (1)	128† Colombo (SSC) 2001-02
100* Galle 2001-02	139 Kandy 2001-02	**H. P. Tillekeratne** (2)
P. A. de Silva (1)	**S. Ranatunga** (2)	116 Harare 1994-95
143* Colombo (SSC) 1997-98	118† Harare 1994-95	126* Colombo (SSC) 1996-97

For Zimbabwe (4)

A. Flower (2)	**D. L. Houghton** (2)	
105* Colombo (SSC) 1997-98	266 Bulawayo . . . 1994-95	
129 Harare 1999-00	142 Harare 1994-95	

† *On first appearance in Sri Lanka–Zimbabwe Tests.*
‡ *Carried his bat.*

RECORD PARTNERSHIPS FOR EACH WICKET

For Sri Lanka

85 for 1st	M. S. Atapattu and S. T. Jayasuriya at Bulawayo	1999-2000
217 for 2nd	A. P. Gurusinha and S. Ranatunga at Harare	1994-95
140 for 3rd	M. S. Atapattu and P. A. de Silva at Kandy	1997-98
178 for 4th	D. P. M. D. Jayawardene and T. M. Dilshan at Harare	1999-2000
114 for 5th	A. P. Gurusinha and H. P. Tillekeratne at Colombo (SSC)	1996-97
189* for 6th†	P. A. de Silva and A. Ranatunga at Colombo (SSC)	1997-98
136* for 7th	T. T. Samaraweera and W. P. U. J. C. Vaas at Colombo (SSC) . .	2001-02
146 for 8th	T. T. Samaraweera and U. D. U. Chandana at Galle	2001-02
30 for 9th	R. P. Arnold and G. P. Wickremasinghe at Harare	1999-2000
25 for 10th	H. D. P. K. Dharmasena and M. Muralitharan at Bulawayo	1994-95

For Zimbabwe

153 for 1st	S. V. Carlisle and T. R. Gripper at Galle	2001-02
40 for 2nd	G. J. Rennie and M. W. Goodwin at Colombo (SSC)	1997-98
194 for 3rd†	A. D. R. Campbell and D. L. Houghton at Harare	1994-95
121 for 4th	D. L. Houghton and A. Flower at Bulawayo	1994-95
101 for 5th	M. W. Goodwin and A. Flower at Harare	1999-2000
100 for 6th	D. L. Houghton and W. R. James at Bulawayo	1994-95
125 for 7th	A. Flower and G. J. Whittall at Harare	1999-2000
84 for 8th	D. L. Houghton and J. A. Rennie at Bulawayo	1994-95
43 for 9th	J. A. Rennie and S. G. Peall at Bulawayo	1994-95
35 for 10th	T. J. Friend and H. K. Olonga at Kandy	2001-02

† *Record partnership against all countries.*

TEN WICKETS OR MORE IN A MATCH

For Sri Lanka (2)

12-117 (5-23, 7-94)	M. Muralitharan, Kandy	1997-98
13-115 (9-51, 4-64)	M. Muralitharan, Kandy	2001-02

Note: The best match figures for Zimbabwe are 6-112 (2-28, 4-84) by H. H. Streak at Colombo (SSC), 1997-98.

SRI LANKA v BANGLADESH

Season	*Sri Lanka*	*Bangladesh*	*T*	*SL*	*B*	*D*
2001-02*S*†	S. T. Jayasuriya	Naimur Rahman	1	1	0	0
2002*S*	S. T. Jayasuriya	Khaled Masud	2	2	0	0
	Totals		3	3	0	0

Captains

S Played in Sri Lanka.

† *This Test was part of the Asian Test Championship.*

HIGHEST INNINGS TOTALS

For Sri Lanka: 555-5 dec. at Colombo (SSC)   2001-02

For Bangladesh: 328 at Colombo (SSC).   2001-02

LOWEST INNINGS TOTALS

For Sri Lanka: 373 at Colombo (SSC).   2002

For Bangladesh: 90 at Colombo (SSC)   2001-02

INDIVIDUAL HUNDREDS

For Sri Lanka (5)

M. S. Atapattu (1)	**S. T. Jayasuriya** (1)	**M. G. Vandort** (1)
201† Colombo (SSC) 2001-02	145 Colombo (PSS) 2002	140 Colombo (SSC) 2002
P. A. de Silva (1)	**D. P. M. D. Jayawardene** (1)	
206† Colombo (PSS) 2002	150† Colombo (SSC) 2001-02	

For Bangladesh (1)

Mohammad Ashraful (1)
114†   Colombo (SSC)   2001-02

† *On first appearance in Sri Lanka–Bangladesh Tests.*

HUNDRED PARTNERSHIPS

For Sri Lanka

234 for 5th†	P. A. de Silva and S. T. Jayasuriya at Colombo (PSS)	2002
172 for 2nd	M. G. Vandort and M. N. Nawaz at Colombo (SSC)	2002
171 for 3rd	M. S. Atapattu and D. P. M. D. Jayawardene at Colombo (SSC). . . .	2001-02
150 for 4th	K. C. Sangakkara and P. A. de Silva at Colombo (PSS)	2002
144 for 1st	M. S. Atapattu and S. T. Jayasuriya at Colombo (SSC).	2001-02
127 for 5th	S. T. Jayasuriya and T. T. Samaraweera at Colombo (SSC)	2002
125 for 2nd	M. S. Atapattu and K. C. Sangakkara at Colombo (SSC)	2001-02

For Bangladesh

126 for 5th†	Aminul Islam and Mohammad Ashraful at Colombo (SSC).	2001-02

† *Record partnership against all countries.*

TEN WICKETS OR MORE IN A MATCH

For Sri Lanka (2)

10-111 (5-13, 5-98)	M. Muralitharan, Colombo (SSC)	2001-02
10-98 (5-39, 5-59)	M. Muralitharan, Colombo (PSS).	2002

Note: The best match figures for Bangladesh are 4-144 (4-144) by Enamul Haque at Colombo (PSS), 2002.

ZIMBABWE v BANGLADESH

		Captains				
Season	*Zimbabwe*	*Bangladesh*	*T*	*Z*	*B*	*D*
2000-01*Z*	H. H. Streak	Naimur Rahman	2	2	0	0
2001-02*B*	B. A. Murphy[1]	Naimur Rahman	2	1	0	1
	In Zimbabwe		2	2	0	0
	In Bangladesh		2	1	0	1
	Totals		4	3	0	1

Z Played in Zimbabwe.   B Played in Bangladesh.

Note: The following deputised for the official touring captain:

[1]S. V. Carlisle (Second).

HIGHEST INNINGS TOTALS

For Zimbabwe in Zimbabwe: 457 at Bulawayo	2000-01
in Bangladesh: 542-7 dec. at Chittagong	2001-02
For Bangladesh in Zimbabwe: 266 at Harare.	2000-01
in Bangladesh: 301 at Chittagong	2001-02

LOWEST INNINGS TOTALS

For Zimbabwe in Zimbabwe: 457 at Bulawayo	2000-01
in Bangladesh: 431 at Dhaka.	2001-02
For Bangladesh in Zimbabwe: 168 at Bulawayo.	2000-01
in Bangladesh: 107 at Dhaka	2001-02

INDIVIDUAL HUNDREDS

For Zimbabwe (4)

A. Flower (1)			**G. J. Whittall** (1)		
114*	Chittagong . .	2001-02	119†	Bulawayo. . .	2000-01
T. R. Gripper (1)			**C. B. Wishart** (1)		
112	Chittagong . .	2001-02	114	Chittagong . .	2001-02

For Bangladesh (1)

Habibul Bashar (1)
108   Chittagong . .   2001-02

† *On first appearance in Zimbabwe–Bangladesh Tests.*

HUNDRED PARTNERSHIPS

For Zimbabwe

149 for 4th	G. J. Whittall and A. Flower at Bulawayo	2000-01
137 for 6th	C. B. Wishart and D. A. Marillier at Dhaka	2001-02
133 for 6th	G. W. Flower and H. H. Streak at Harare	2000-01
123 for 6th‡	C. B. Wishart and D. A. Marillier at Chittagong	2001-02
120 for 6th	G. W. Flower and H. H. Streak at Bulawayo	2000-01
108 for 8th	H. H. Streak and T. J. Friend at Dhaka	2001-02
108 for 1st	D. D. Ebrahim and T. R. Gripper at Chittagong	2001-02

For Bangladesh

122 for 2nd†	Javed Omar and Habibul Bashar at Chittagong	2001-02
114 for 4th†	Mehrab Hossain and Habibul Bashar at Harare	2000-01
102 for 2nd	Javed Omar and Habibul Bashar at Dhaka	2001-02

† *Record partnership against all countries.*
‡ *189 runs were added for Zimbabwe's sixth wicket in two separate partnerships. A. Flower retired hurt after adding 66* with Wishart.*

BEST MATCH BOWLING ANALYSES

For Zimbabwe

8-104 (4-41, 4-63)	G. W. Flower, Chittagong	2001-02

For Bangladesh

6-81 (6-81)	Manjurul Islam, Bulawayo	2000-01

TEST GROUNDS

in chronological order

	City and Ground	*First Test Match*		*Tests*
1	Melbourne, Melbourne Cricket Ground	March 15, 1877	A v E	94
2	London, Kennington Oval	September 6, 1880	E v A	85
3	Sydney, Sydney Cricket Ground (No. 1)	February 17, 1882	A v E	88
4	Manchester, Old Trafford	July 11, 1884	E v A	68
5	London, Lord's	July 21, 1884	E v A	104
6	Adelaide, Adelaide Oval	December 12, 1884	A v E	60
7	Port Elizabeth, St George's Park	March 12, 1889	SA v E	20
8	Cape Town, Newlands	March 25, 1889	SA v E	34
9	Johannesburg, Old Wanderers	March 2, 1896	SA v E	22
	Now the site of Johannesburg Railway Station.			
10	Nottingham, Trent Bridge	June 1, 1899	E v A	49
11	Leeds, Headingley	June 29, 1899	E v A	63
12	Birmingham, Edgbaston	May 29, 1902	E v A	38
13	Sheffield, Bramall Lane	July 3, 1902	E v A	1
	Sheffield United Football Club have built a stand over the cricket pitch.			
14	Durban, Lord's	January 21, 1910	SA v E	4
	Ground destroyed and built on.			
15	Durban, Kingsmead	January 18, 1923	SA v E	29
16	Brisbane, Exhibition Ground	November 30, 1928	A v E	2
	No longer used for cricket.			
17	Christchurch, Lancaster Park	January 10, 1930	NZ v E	38
	Ground also known under sponsors' names; currently Jade Stadium.			

	City and Ground	First Test Match		Tests
18	Bridgetown, Kensington Oval	January 11, 1930	WI v E	39
19	Wellington, Basin Reserve	January 24, 1930	NZ v E	39
20	Port-of-Spain, Queen's Park Oval	February 1, 1930	WI v E	51
21	Auckland, Eden Park	February 17, 1930	NZ v E	44
22	Georgetown, Bourda	February 21, 1930	WI v E	28
23	Kingston, Sabina Park	April 3, 1930	WI v E	37
24	Brisbane, Woolloongabba	November 27, 1931	A v SA	44
25	Bombay, Gymkhana Ground	December 15, 1933	I v E	1
	No longer used for first-class cricket.			
26	Calcutta (*now Kolkata*), Eden Gardens	January 5, 1934	I v E	31
27	Madras (*now Chennai*), Chepauk (Chidambaram Stadium)	February 10, 1934	I v E	25
28	Delhi, Feroz Shah Kotla	November 10, 1948	I v WI	27
29	Bombay, Brabourne Stadium	December 9, 1948	I v WI	17
	Rarely used for first-class cricket.			
30	Johannesburg, Ellis Park	December 27, 1948	SA v E	6
	Mainly a rugby stadium, no longer used for cricket.			
31	Kanpur, Green Park (Modi Stadium)	January 12, 1952	I v E	18
32	Lucknow, University Ground	October 25, 1952	I v P	1
	Ground destroyed, now partly under a river bed.			
33	Dacca (*now Dhaka*), Dacca (now Bangabandhu) Stadium	January 1, 1955	P v I	11
	Originally in East Pakistan, now Bangladesh.			
34	Bahawalpur, Dring (now Bahawal) Stadium	January 15, 1955	P v I	1
	Still used for first-class cricket.			
35	Lahore, Lawrence Gardens (Bagh-i-Jinnah)	January 29, 1955	P v I	3
	Still used for club and occasional first-class matches.			
36	Peshawar, Services Ground	February 13, 1955	P v I	1
	Superseded by new stadium.			
37	Karachi, National Stadium	February 26, 1955	P v I	35
38	Dunedin, Carisbrook	March 11, 1955	NZ v E	10
39	Hyderabad, Fateh Maidan (Lal Bahadur Stadium)	November 19, 1955	I v NZ	3
40	Madras, Corporation Stadium	January 6, 1956	I v NZ	9
	Superseded by rebuilt Chepauk Stadium.			
41	Johannesburg, Wanderers	December 24, 1956	SA v E	23
42	Lahore, Gaddafi Stadium	November 21, 1959	P v A	33
43	Rawalpindi, Pindi Club Ground	March 27, 1965	P v NZ	1
	Superseded by new stadium.			
44	Nagpur, Vidarbha C.A. Ground	October 3, 1969	I v NZ	7
45	Perth, Western Australian C.A. Ground	December 11, 1970	A v E	29
46	Hyderabad, Niaz Stadium	March 16, 1973	P v E	5
47	Bangalore, Karnataka State C.A. Ground (Chinnaswamy Stadium)	November 22, 1974	I v WI	14
48	Bombay (*now Mumbai*), Wankhede Stadium	January 23, 1975	I v WI	18
49	Faisalabad, Iqbal Stadium	October 16, 1978	P v I	20
50	Napier, McLean Park	February 16, 1979	NZ v P	3
51	Multan, Ibn-e-Qasim Bagh Stadium	December 30, 1980	P v WI	1
52	St John's (Antigua), Recreation Ground	March 27, 1981	WI v E	17
53	Colombo, P. Saravanamuttu Stadium	February 17, 1982	SL v E	7
54	Kandy, Asgiriya Stadium	April 22, 1983	SL v A	14
55	Jullundur, Burlton Park	September 24, 1983	I v P	1
56	Ahmedabad, Gujarat Stadium	November 12, 1983	I v WI	6
57	Colombo, Sinhalese Sports Club Ground	March 16, 1984	SL v NZ	22
58	Colombo, Colombo Cricket Club Ground	March 24, 1984	SL v NZ	3
59	Sialkot, Jinnah Stadium	October 27, 1985	P v SL	4
60	Cuttack, Barabati Stadium	January 4, 1987	I v SL	2
61	Jaipur, Sawai Mansingh Stadium	February 21, 1987	I v P	1
62	Hobart, Bellerive Oval	December 16, 1989	A v SL	6

	City and Ground	*First Test Match*		*Tests*
63	Chandigarh, Sector 16 Stadium	November 23, 1990	I v SL	1
	Superseded by Mohali ground.			
64	Hamilton, Seddon Park	February 22, 1991	NZ v SL	10
	Ground also known under various sponsors' names, including Trust Bank Park; currently Westpac Trust Park.			
65	Gujranwala, Municipal Stadium	December 20, 1991	P v SL	1
66	Colombo, R. Premadasa (Khettarama) Stadium	August 28, 1992	SL v A	5
67	Moratuwa, Tyronne Fernando Stadium	September 8, 1992	SL v A	4
68	Harare, Harare Sports Club	October 18, 1992	Z v I	20
69	Bulawayo, Bulawayo Athletic Club	November 1, 1992	Z v NZ	1
	Superseded by Queens Sports Club ground.			
70	Karachi, Defence Stadium	December 1, 1993	P v Z	1
71	Rawalpindi, Rawalpindi Cricket Stadium	December 9, 1993	P v Z	7
72	Lucknow, K. D. "Babu" Singh Stadium	January 18, 1994	I v SL	1
73	Bulawayo, Queens Sports Club	October 20, 1994	Z v SL	11
74	Mohali, Punjab Cricket Association Stadium	December 10, 1994	I v WI	4
75	Peshawar, Arbab Niaz Stadium	September 8, 1995	P v SL	5
76	Centurion (*formerly Verwoerdburg*), Centurion Park	November 16, 1995	SA v E	6
77	Sheikhupura, Municipal Stadium	October 17, 1996	P v Z	2
78	St Vincent, Arnos Vale	June 20, 1997	WI v SL	1
79	Galle, International Stadium	June 3, 1998	SL v NZ	8
80	Springbok Park, Bloemfontein	October 29, 1999	SA v Z	3
	Ground also known under sponsor's name; currently Goodyear Park.			
81	Multan, Multan Cricket Stadium	August 29, 2001	P v B	1
82	Chittagong, Chittagong Stadium	November 15, 2001	B v Z	2
83	Sharjah, Sharjah Cricket Association Stadium	January 31, 2002	P v WI	2
84	St George's, Queen's Park New Stadium	June 28, 2002	WI v NZ	1

FAMILIES IN TEST CRICKET

GRANDFATHER, FATHER AND SON

G. A. Headley (West Indies, 22 Tests, 1929-30–1953-54), R. G. A. Headley (West Indies, 2 Tests, 1973) and D. W. Headley (England, 15 Tests, 1997–1999).

FATHERS AND SONS

England
A. R. Butcher (1 Test, 1979) and M. A. Butcher (45 Tests, 1997–2002).
M. C. Cowdrey (114 Tests, 1954-55–1974-75) and C. S. Cowdrey (6 Tests, 1984-85–1988).
J. Hardstaff (5 Tests, 1907-08) and J. Hardstaff jun. (23 Tests, 1935–1948).
L. Hutton (79 Tests, 1937–1954-55) and R. A. Hutton (5 Tests, 1971).
F. T. Mann (5 Tests, 1922-23) and F. G. Mann (7 Tests, 1948-49–1949).
J. H. Parks (1 Test, 1937) and J. M. Parks (46 Tests, 1954–1967-68).
A. Sidebottom (1 Test, 1985) and R. J. Sidebottom (1 Test, 2001).
M. J. Stewart (8 Tests, 1962–1963-64) and A. J. Stewart (122 Tests, 1989-90–2002).
F. W. Tate (1 Test, 1902) and M. W. Tate (39 Tests, 1924–1935).
C. L. Townsend (2 Tests, 1899) and D. C. H. Townsend (3 Tests, 1934-35).
I. J. Jones (15 Tests, 1963-64–1967-68) and S. P. Jones (1 Test, 2002).

Australia
E. J. Gregory (1 Test, 1876-77) and S. E. Gregory (58 Tests, 1890–1912).

South Africa
F. Hearne (4 Tests, 1891-92–1895-96) and G. A. L. Hearne (3 Tests, 1922-23–1924).
 F. Hearne also played 2 Tests for England in 1888-89.
J. D. Lindsay (3 Tests, 1947) and D. T. Lindsay (19 Tests, 1963-64–1969-70).
A. W. Nourse (45 Tests, 1902-03–1924) and A. D. Nourse (34 Tests, 1935–1951).
P. M. Pollock (28 Tests, 1961-62–1969-70) and S. M. Pollock (63 Tests, 1995-96–2001-02).
L. R. Tuckett (1 Test, 1913-14) and L. Tuckett (9 Tests, 1947–1948-49).

West Indies

O. C. Scott (8 Tests, 1928–1930-31) and A. P. H. Scott (1 Test, 1952-53).

New Zealand

W. M. Anderson (1 Test, 1945-46) and R. W. Anderson (9 Tests, 1976-77–1978).

W. P. Bradburn (2 Tests, 1963-64) and G. E. Bradburn (7 Tests, 1990-91–2000-01).

B. L. Cairns (43 Tests, 1973-74–1985-86) and C. L. Cairns (55 Tests, 1989-90–2001-02).

W. A. Hadlee (11 Tests, 1937–1950-51) and D. R. Hadlee (26 Tests, 1969–1977-78); R. J. Hadlee (86 Tests, 1972-73–1990).

P. G. Z. Harris (9 Tests, 1955-56–1964-65) and C. Z. Harris (23 Tests, 1993-94–2001-02).

H. G. Vivian (7 Tests, 1931–1937) and G. E. Vivian (5 Tests, 1964-65–1971-72).

India

L. Amarnath (24 Tests, 1933-34–1952-53) and M. Amarnath (69 Tests, 1969-70–1987-88); S. Amarnath (10 Tests, 1975-76–1978-79).

D. K. Gaekwad (11 Tests, 1952–1960-61) and A. D. Gaekwad (40 Tests, 1974-75–1984-85).

H. S. Kanitkar (2 Tests, 1974-75) and H. H. Kanitkar (2 Tests, 1999-2000).

Nawab of Pataudi (Iftikhar Ali Khan) (3 Tests, 1946) and Nawab of Pataudi (Mansur Ali Khan) (46 Tests, 1961-62–1974-75).
   Nawab of Pataudi sen. also played 3 Tests for England, 1932-33–1934.

V. L. Manjrekar (55 Tests, 1951-52–1964-65) and S. V. Manjrekar (37 Tests, 1987-88–1996-97).

V. Mankad (44 Tests, 1946–1958-59) and A. V. Mankad (22 Tests, 1969-70–1977-78).

Pankaj Roy (43 Tests, 1951-52–1960-61) and Pranab Roy (2 Tests, 1981-82).

India and Pakistan

M. Jahangir Khan (4 Tests, 1932–1936) and Majid Khan (63 Tests, 1964-65–1982-83).

S. Wazir Ali (7 Tests, 1932–1936) and Khalid Wazir (2 Tests, 1954).

Pakistan

Hanif Mohammad (55 Tests, 1952-53–1969-70) and Shoaib Mohammad (45 Tests, 1983-84–1995-96).

Nazar Mohammad (5 Tests, 1952-53) and Mudassar Nazar (76 Tests, 1976-77–1988-89).

GRANDFATHER AND GRANDSONS

Australia

V. Y. Richardson (19 Tests, 1924-25–1935-36) and G. S. Chappell (87 Tests, 1970-71–1983-84); I. M. Chappell (75 Tests, 1964-65–1979-80); T. M. Chappell (3 Tests, 1981).

GREAT-GRANDFATHER AND GREAT-GRANDSON

Australia

W. H. Cooper (2 Tests, 1881-82 and 1884-85) and A. P. Sheahan (31 Tests, 1967-68–1973-74).

BROTHERS IN SAME TEST TEAM

England

E. M., G. F. and W. G. Grace: 1 Test, 1880; C. T. and G. B. Studd: 4 Tests, 1882-83; A. and G. G. Hearne: 1 Test, 1891-92. *F. Hearne, their brother, played in this match for South Africa;* D. W. and P. E. Richardson: 1 Test, 1957; A. J. and B. C. Hollioake: 1 Test, 1997.

Australia

E. J. and D. W. Gregory: 1 Test, 1876-77; C. and A. C. Bannerman: 1 Test, 1878-79; G. and W. F. Giffen: 2 Tests, 1891-92; G. H. S. and A. E. Trott: 3 Tests, 1894-95; I. M. and G. S. Chappell: 43 Tests, 1970-71–1979-80; S. R. and M. E. Waugh: 105 Tests, 1990-91–2001-02 – the only instance of twins appearing together.

South Africa

S. J. and S. D. Snooke: 1 Test, 1907; D. and H. W. Taylor: 2 Tests, 1913-14; R. H. M. and P. A. M. Hands: 1 Test, 1913-14; E. A. B. and A. M. B. Rowan: 9 Tests, 1948-49–1951; P. M. and R. G. Pollock: 23 Tests, 1963-64–1969-70; A. J. and D. B. Pithey: 5 Tests, 1963-64; P. N. and G. Kirsten (half-brothers): 7 Tests, 1993-94–1994.

West Indies

G. C. and R. S. Grant: 4 Tests, 1934-35; J. B. and V. H. Stollmeyer: 1 Test, 1939; D. St E. and E. St E. Atkinson: 1 Test, 1957-58.

New Zealand

D. R. and R. J. Hadlee: 10 Tests, 1973–1977-78; H. J. and G. P. Howarth: 4 Tests, 1974-75–1976-77; J. M. and N. M. Parker: 3 Tests, 1976-77; B. P. and J. G. Bracewell: 1 Test, 1980-81; J. J. and M. D. Crowe: 34 Tests, 1983–1989-90.

India

S. Wazir Ali and S. Nazir Ali: 2 Tests, 1932–1933-34; L. Ramji and Amar Singh: 1 Test, 1933-34; C. K. and C. S. Nayudu: 4 Tests, 1933-34–1936; A. G. Kripal Singh and A. G. Milkha Singh: 1 Test, 1961-62; S. and M. Amarnath: 8 Tests, 1975-76–1978-79.

Pakistan

Wazir and Hanif Mohammad: 18 Tests, 1952-53–1959-60; Wazir and Mushtaq Mohammad: 1 Test, 1958-59; Hanif and Mushtaq Mohammad: 19 Tests, 1960-61–1969-70; Hanif, Mushtaq and Sadiq Mohammad: 1 Test, 1969-70; Mushtaq and Sadiq Mohammad: 26 Tests, 1969-70–1978–79; Wasim and Ramiz Raja: 2 Tests, 1983-84; Moin and Nadeem Khan: 1 Test, 1998-99; Humayun and Imran Farhat: 1 Test, 2000-01.

Sri Lanka

M. D. and S. Wettimuny: 2 Tests, 1982-83; A. and D. Ranatunga: 2 Tests, 1989-90; A. and S. Ranatunga: 8 Tests, 1994-95–1996-97.

Zimbabwe

A. and G. W. Flower: 59 Tests, 1992-93–2001-02; J. A. and G. J. Rennie: 1 Test, 1997-98; P. A. and B. C. Strang: 14 Tests, 1994-95–2000-01.

BROTHERS SCORING HUNDREDS IN THE SAME TEST INNINGS

I. M. Chappell (118) and G. S. Chappell (113)	Australia v England at The Oval	1972
I. M. Chappell (145) and G. S. Chappell (247*)	Australia v New Zealand at Wellington (first innings)	1973-74
I. M. Chappell (121) and G. S. Chappell (133)	Australia v New Zealand at Wellington (second innings)	1973-74
Sadiq Mohammad (103*) and Mushtaq Mohammad (101)	Pakistan v New Zealand at Hyderabad	1976-77
G. W. Flower (201*) and A. Flower (156)	Zimbabwe v Pakistan at Harare	1994-95
M. E. Waugh (126) and S. R. Waugh (200)	Australia v West Indies at Kingston . .	1994-95
M. E. Waugh (120) and S. R. Waugh (157*)	Australia v England at The Oval	2001

Note: The Chappells are the only batsmen to score twin hundreds for the same side in a Test.

BROTHERS SCORING HUNDREDS IN THE SAME TEST MATCH

G. S. Chappell (106) and I. M. Chappell (106*)	Australia v West Indies at Bridgetown	1972-73
G. W. Flower (156*) and A. Flower (100*)	Zimbabwe v Pakistan at Bulawayo . . .	1997-98
G. W. Flower (106*) and A. Flower (232*)	Zimbabwe v India at Nagpur	2000-01

Note: The brother scoring his hundred in the first innings is listed first.

LIMITED-OVERS INTERNATIONAL RECORDS

Matches in this section do not have first-class status.

SUMMARY OF LIMITED-OVERS INTERNATIONALS

1970-71 to September 30, 2002

	Opponents	Matches	E	A	SA	WI	NZ	I	P	SL	Z	B	Ass	Tied	NR
England	Australia	70	31	37	–	–	–	–	–	–	–	–	–	1	1
	South Africa	23	7	–	16	–	–	–	–	–	–	–	–	–	–
	West Indies	61	26	–	–	32	–	–	–	–	–	–	–	–	3
	New Zealand	52	25	–	–	–	23	–	–	–	–	–	–	1	3
	India	47	23	–	–	–	–	22	–	–	–	–	–	–	2
	Pakistan	49	28	–	–	–	–	–	20	–	–	–	–	–	1
	Sri Lanka	26	15	–	–	–	–	–	–	11	–	–	–	–	–
	Zimbabwe	22	15	–	–	–	–	–	–	–	7	–	–	–	–
	Bangladesh	1	1	–	–	–	–	–	–	–	–	0	–	–	–
	Associates	5	5	–	–	–	–	–	–	–	–	–	0	–	–
Australia	South Africa	56	–	29	24	–	–	–	–	–	–	–	–	3	–
	West Indies	98	–	43	–	52	–	–	–	–	–	–	–	2	1
	New Zealand	85	–	57	–	–	25	–	–	–	–	–	–	–	3
	India	67	–	39	–	–	–	25	–	–	–	–	–	–	3
	Pakistan	66	–	36	–	–	–	–	26	–	–	–	–	1	3
	Sri Lanka	44	–	28	–	–	–	–	–	14	–	–	–	–	2
	Zimbabwe	19	–	18	–	–	–	–	–	–	1	–	–	–	–
	Bangladesh	3	–	3	–	–	–	–	–	–	–	0	–	–	–
	Associates	5	–	5	–	–	–	–	–	–	–	–	0	–	–
South Africa	West Indies	26	–	–	18	8	–	–	–	–	–	–	–	–	–
	New Zealand	33	–	–	22	–	8	–	–	–	–	–	–	–	3
	India	43	–	–	27	–	–	15	–	–	–	–	–	–	1
	Pakistan	31	–	–	21	–	–	–	10	–	–	–	–	–	–
	Sri Lanka	28	–	–	14	–	–	–	–	13	–	–	–	–	1
	Zimbabwe	15	–	–	12	–	–	–	–	–	2	–	–	–	1
	Associates	9	–	–	9	–	–	–	–	–	–	–	0	–	–
West Indies	New Zealand	35	–	–	–	22	10	–	–	–	–	–	–	–	3
	India	69	–	–	–	42	–	25	–	–	–	–	–	1	1
	Pakistan	98	–	–	–	60	–	–	36	–	–	–	–	2	–
	Sri Lanka	35	–	–	–	22	–	–	–	12	–	–	–	–	1
	Zimbabwe	19	–	–	–	14	–	–	–	–	5	–	–	–	–
	Bangladesh	3	–	–	–	3	–	–	–	–	–	0	–	–	–
	Associates	6	–	–	–	5	–	–	–	–	–	–	1*	–	–
New Zealand	India	61	–	–	–	–	27	31	–	–	–	–	–	–	3
	Pakistan	64	–	–	–	–	22	–	40	–	–	–	–	1	1
	Sri Lanka	52	–	–	–	–	27	–	–	22	–	–	–	1	2
	Zimbabwe	25	–	–	–	–	16	–	–	–	7	–	–	1	1
	Bangladesh	3	–	–	–	–	3	–	–	–	–	0	–	–	–
	Associates	4	–	–	–	–	4	–	–	–	–	–	0	–	–
India	Pakistan	85	–	–	–	–	–	29	52	–	–	–	–	–	4
	Sri Lanka	75	–	–	–	–	–	39	–	29	–	–	–	–	7
	Zimbabwe	42	–	–	–	–	–	32	–	–	8	–	–	2	–
	Bangladesh	8	–	–	–	–	–	8	–	–	–	0	–	–	–
	Associates	12	–	–	–	–	–	10	–	–	–	–	2†	–	–
Pakistan	Sri Lanka	96	–	–	–	–	–	–	58	35	–	–	–	1	2
	Zimbabwe	24	–	–	–	–	–	–	21	–	2	–	–	1	–
	Bangladesh	11	–	–	–	–	–	–	10	–	–	1	–	–	–
	Associates	9	–	–	–	–	–	–	9	–	–	–	0	–	–
Sri Lanka	Zimbabwe	27	–	–	–	–	–	–	–	21	5	–	–	–	1
	Bangladesh	9	–	–	–	–	–	–	–	9	–	0	–	–	–
	Associates	4	–	–	–	–	–	–	–	4	–	–	0	–	–
Zimbabwe	Bangladesh	10	–	–	–	–	–	–	–	–	10	0	–	–	–
	Associates	11	–	–	–	–	–	–	–	–	10	–	0	–	1
Bangladesh	Associates	7	–	–	–	–	–	–	–	–	–	2	5‡	–	–
Associates	Associates	1	–	–	–	–	–	–	–	–	–	–	1§	–	–
		1,889	176	295	163	260	165	236	282	170	57	3	9	18	55

* *Kenya beat West Indies in the 1996 World Cup.*
† *Kenya beat India at Gwalior, 1997-98 and at Port Elizabeth, 2001-02.*
‡ *Kenya beat Bangladesh five times in 1997-98 and 1998-99.*
§ *United Arab Emirates beat Holland in the 1996 World Cup.*

Note: Current Associate Members of ICC who have played one-day internationals are Canada, East Africa, Holland, Kenya, Scotland and United Arab Emirates. Sri Lanka, Zimbabwe and Bangladesh also played one-day internationals before being given Test status; these are not included among the Associates' results.

RESULTS SUMMARY OF LIMITED-OVERS INTERNATIONALS

1970-71 to 2002 (1,889 matches)

	Matches	Won	Lost	Tied	No Result	% Won (excl. NR)
South Africa	264	163	92	3	6	63.75
Australia	513	295	198	7	13	59.70
West Indies	450	260	176	5	9	59.52
Pakistan	533	282	234	6	11	54.59
England	356	176	168	2	10	51.15
India	509	236	249	3	21	48.66
Sri Lanka	396	170	208	2	16	45.00
New Zealand	414	165	226	4	19	42.27
Zimbabwe	214	57	149	4	4	28.09
Kenya	49	8	40	–	1	16.66
United Arab Emirates . .	7	1	6	–	–	14.28
Bangladesh	55	3	52	–	–	5.45
Canada	3	–	3	–	–	–
East Africa	3	–	3	–	–	–
Holland	7	–	7	–	–	–
Scotland	5	–	5	–	–	–

Note: Matches abandoned without a ball bowled are not included. Those called off after play began are counted as official internationals in their own right, even when replayed, according to the ICC's ruling. In the percentages of matches won, ties are counted as half a win.

BATTING RECORDS

5,000 RUNS

		M	I	NO	R	HS	100s	Avge
1	S. R. Tendulkar (India)	300	291	30	11,544	186*	33	44.22
2	M. Azharuddin (India)	334	308	54	9,378	153*	7	36.92
3	P. A. de Silva (Sri Lanka)	288	278	30	8,803	145	11	35.49
4	Inzamam-ul-Haq (Pakistan) . .	274	259	37	8,712	137*	8	39.24
5	D. L. Haynes (West Indies) . . .	238	237	28	8,648	152*	17	41.37
6	Saeed Anwar (Pakistan)	242	239	18	8,605	194	19	38.93
7	M. E. Waugh (Australia)	244	236	20	8,500	173	18	39.35
8	S. T. Jayasuriya (Sri Lanka) . .	275	267	10	8,182	189	13	31.83
9	S. C. Ganguly (India)	206	198	15	7,950	183	19	43.44
10	S. R. Waugh (Australia)	325	288	58	7,569	120*	3	32.90
11	B. C. Lara (West Indies)	203	198	21	7,549	169	15	42.64
12	A. Ranatunga (Sri Lanka)	269	255	47	7,456	131*	4	35.84
13	Javed Miandad (Pakistan)	233	218	41	7,381	119*	8	41.70
14	Salim Malik (Pakistan)	283	256	38	7,170	102	5	32.88
15	I. V. A. Richards (West Indies) .	187	167	24	6,721	189*	11	47.00
16	Ijaz Ahmed, sen. (Pakistan) . . .	250	232	29	6,564	139*	10	32.33
17	A. R. Border (Australia)	273	252	39	6,524	127*	3	30.62
18	G. Kirsten (South Africa)	177	177	15	6,498	188*	12	40.11
19	R. B. Richardson (West Indies) .	224	217	30	6,249	122	5	33.41

		M	I	NO	R	HS	100s	Avge
20	**A. Flower (Zimbabwe)**	**197**	**194**	**14**	**6,176**	**145**	**4**	**34.31**
21	D. M. Jones (Australia)	164	161	25	6,068	145	7	44.61
22	D. C. Boon (Australia)	181	177	16	5,964	122	5	37.04
23	Ramiz Raja (Pakistan)	198	197	15	5,841	119*	9	32.09
24	**M. G. Bevan (Australia)**	**186**	**161**	**55**	**5,807**	**108***	**6**	**54.78**
25	**R. Dravid (India)**	**182**	**167**	**17**	**5,765**	**153**	**7**	**38.43**
26	J. N. Rhodes (South Africa) . . .	233	211	48	5,692	121	2	34.92
27	**G. W. Flower (Zimbabwe)** . . .	**184**	**182**	**14**	**5,607**	**142***	**5**	**33.37**
28	**J. H. Kallis (South Africa)** . . .	**158**	**153**	**26**	**5,583**	**113***	**8**	**43.96**
29	W. J. Cronje (South Africa) . . .	188	175	31	5,565	112	2	38.64
30	**C. L. Hooper (West Indies)** . . .	**215**	**195**	**40**	**5,551**	**113***	**7**	**35.81**
31	**M. S. Atapattu (Sri Lanka)** . . .	**167**	**165**	**20**	**5,477**	**132***	**6**	**37.77**
32	A. Jadeja (India)	196	179	36	5,359	119	6	37.47
33	**R. T. Ponting (Australia)**	**148**	**147**	**19**	**5,274**	**145**	**9**	**41.20**
34	**N. J. Astle (New Zealand)**	**162**	**159**	**8**	**5,204**	**122***	**12**	**34.46**
35	R. S. Mahanama (Sri Lanka) . . .	213	198	23	5,162	119*	4	29.49
36	C. G. Greenidge (West Indies) . .	128	127	13	5,134	133*	11	45.03
37	**A. D. R. Campbell (Zimbabwe)**	**179**	**175**	**14**	**5,055**	**131***	**7**	**31.39**

Note: The leading aggregates for other Test-playing countries are:

	M	I	NO	R	HS	100s	Avge
A. J. Stewart (England)	**155**	**148**	**14**	**4,315**	**116**	**4**	**32.20**
Akram Khan (Bangladesh)	38	38	2	857	65	0	23.80

Bold type denotes those who played limited-overs international cricket in 2001-02 or 2002 season.

BEST CAREER STRIKE-RATES BY BATSMEN

(Runs per 100 balls. Qualification: 500 runs)

SR		Position	M	I	R	Avge
104.88	B. L. Cairns (NZ)	9/8	78	65	987	16.72
101.95	**V. Sehwag (I)**	**2**	**43**	**41**	**1,252**	**34.77**
101.31	**Shahid Afridi (P)**	**2**	**164**	**160**	**3,783**	**24.72**
99.86	**A. Symonds (A)**	**7**	**49**	**35**	**750**	**25.86**
99.43	I. D. S. Smith (NZ)	8	98	77	1,055	17.29
95.07	Kapil Dev (I)	7/6	225	198	3,783	23.79
92.89	**R. L. Powell (WI)**	**6**	**51**	**47**	**1,006**	**22.86**
90.23	**A. B. Agarkar (I)**	**8**	**102**	**62**	**665**	**16.62**
90.20	I. V. A. Richards (WI)	4	187	167	6,721	47.00
89.93	**Yuvraj Singh (I)**	**6/5**	**45**	**37**	**983**	**30.71**
89.84	**L. Klusener (SA)**	**8/3**	**140**	**116**	**3,184**	**42.45**
89.81	**A. C. Gilchrist (A)**	**2**	**144**	**139**	**4,507**	**33.63**
89.60	Manzoor Elahi (P)	6	54	46	741	22.45
89.56	**S. T. Jayasuriya (SL)**	**1**	**275**	**267**	**8,182**	**31.83**
89.43	S. B. Joshi (I)	8	69	45	584	17.17
88.87	**A. Flintoff (E)**	**6**	**46**	**38**	**847**	**24.20**
88.75	**M. E. Trescothick (E)**	**1**	**46**	**46**	**1,729**	**38.42**
87.95	**Wasim Akram (P)**	**8/7**	**343**	**270**	**3,564**	**16.27**
87.34	**N. Boje (SA)**	**9/3**	**80**	**49**	**1,077**	**27.61**
86.80	R. J. Ratnayake (SL)	9/8	70	55	612	16.54
86.56	**S. R. Tendulkar (I)**	**2**	**300**	**291**	**11,544**	**44.22**
85.71	W. B. Phillips (A)	6	48	41	852	24.34
84.80	Zaheer Abbas (P)	3	62	60	2,572	47.62
83.89	**J. Srinath (I)**	**9/10**	**205**	**107**	**844**	**11.25**
83.84	I. A. Healy (A)	7	168	120	1,764	21.00
83.83	P. A. J. DeFreitas (E)	8/9	103	66	690	16.04
83.61	P. L. Symcox (SA)	8/9	80	54	694	16.92

SR		Position	M	I	R	Avge
83.54	S. M. Patil (I)	5/4	45	42	1,005	24.51
82.67	**M. Kaif (I)**	**7/5**	**23**	**16**	**582**	**52.90**
82.26	R. W. Marsh (A)	7	92	76	1,225	20.08
81.54	**C. L. Cairns (NZ)**	**5**	**151**	**138**	**3,614**	**29.14**
81.41	A. P. Kuiper (SA).	5/4	25	23	539	33.68
81.39	**D. S. Lehmann (A)**	**4**	**81**	**73**	**2,083**	**35.30**
81.29	**S. M. Pollock (SA)**	**7/8**	**167**	**111**	**1,656**	**23.00**
81.22	C. H. Lloyd (WI).	5	87	69	1,977	39.54
81.19	**P. A. de Silva (SL)**.	**4**	**288**	**278**	**8,803**	**35.49**
81.09	Moin Khan (P)	7	190	159	2,853	23.00
81.04	**S. B. Styris (NZ)**.	**9/8**	**47**	**37**	**620**	**19.37**
80.96	S. P. O'Donnell (A)	7	87	64	1,242	25.34
80.91	**Saeed Anwar (P)**.	**1**	**242**	**239**	**8,605**	**38.93**
80.65	**J. N. Rhodes (SA)**	**5**	**233**	**211**	**5,692**	**34.92**
80.30	Ijaz Ahmed, sen. (P).	3	250	232	6,564	32.33

Note: Position means a batsman's most usual position in the batting order.

Bold type denotes those who played limited-overs international cricket in 2001-02 or 2002 season.

HIGHEST INDIVIDUAL INNINGS

194	Saeed Anwar	Pakistan v India at Chennai	1996-97
189*	I. V. A. Richards	West Indies v England at Manchester	1984
189	S. T. Jayasuriya	Sri Lanka v India at Sharjah.	2000-01
188*	G. Kirsten	South Africa v UAE at Rawalpindi.	1995-96
186*	S. R. Tendulkar	India v New Zealand at Hyderabad	1999-2000
183	S. C. Ganguly	India v Sri Lanka at Taunton.	1999
181	I. V. A. Richards	West Indies v Sri Lanka at Karachi	1987-88
175*	Kapil Dev	India v Zimbabwe at Tunbridge Wells.	1983
173	M. E. Waugh	Australia v West Indies at Melbourne	2000-01
171*	G. M. Turner	New Zealand v East Africa at Birmingham	1975
169*	D. J. Callaghan	South Africa v New Zealand at Verwoerdburg	1994-95
169	B. C. Lara	West Indies v Sri Lanka at Sharjah	1995-96
167*	R. A. Smith	England v Australia at Birmingham	1993
161	A. C. Hudson	South Africa v Holland at Rawalpindi.	1995-96
159*	D. Mongia	India v Zimbabwe at Guwahati	2001-02
158	D. I. Gower	England v New Zealand at Brisbane	1982-83
154	A. C. Gilchrist	Australia v Sri Lanka at Melbourne	1998-99
153*	I. V. A. Richards	West Indies v Australia at Melbourne	1979-80
153*	M. Azharuddin	India v Zimbabwe at Cuttack	1997-98
153*	S. C. Ganguly	India v New Zealand at Gwalior	1999-2000
153	B. C. Lara	West Indies v Pakistan at Sharjah	1993-94
153	R. Dravid	India v New Zealand at Hyderabad	1999-2000
152*	D. L. Haynes	West Indies v India at Georgetown.	1988-89
152	C. H. Gayle	West Indies v Kenya at Nairobi.	2001
151*	S. T. Jayasuriya	Sri Lanka v India at Mumbai	1996-97
150	S. Chanderpaul	West Indies v South Africa at East London	1998-99

Note: The highest individual scores for other Test-playing countries are:

145	A. Flower	Zimbabwe v India at Colombo (RPS).	2002
101	Mehrab Hossain	Bangladesh v Zimbabwe at Dhaka	1998-99

TEN HUNDREDS

Total								*Opponents*				
		E	A	SA	WI	NZ	I	P	SL	Z	B	Ass
33	**S. R. Tendulkar (India)**	1	6	3	2	3	–	2	7	5	0	4
19	**S. C. Ganguly (India)**	1	1	3	0	3	–	2	4	3	1	1
19	Saeed Anwar (Pakistan)	0	1	0	2	3	–	2	4	3	1	1
18	**M. E. Waugh (Australia)** . . .	1	–	2	3	3	3	1	1	3	0	1
17	D. L. Haynes (West Indies) . . .	2	6	0	–	2	2	4	1	0	–	
15	**B. C. Lara (West Indies)** . . .	1	3	2	–	2	0	4	1	0	1	1
13	**S. T. Jayasuriya (Sri Lanka)** . .	1	0	0	0	3	4	3	–	1	1	3
12	**N. J. Astle (New Zealand)** . . .	2	1	1	0	–	4	2	0	1	1	0
12	**G. Kirsten (South Africa)** . . .	1	2	–	0	2	4	1	0	0	–	2
11	**P. A. de Silva (Sri Lanka)** . . .	0	2	0	0	3	3	–	2	0	1	
11	C. G. Greenidge (West Indies) . .	0	1	–	–	3	3	2	1	1	–	
11	I. V. A. Richards (West Indies). .	3	3	–	–	1	3	0	1	0	–	
10	Ijaz Ahmed, sen. (Pakistan). . .	1	1	2	0	0	2	–	1	2	1	0

Note: Ass = Associate Members.

Bold type denotes those who played limited-overs international cricket in 2001-02 or 2002 season.
Dashes indicate that a player did not play against the country concerned.

HIGHEST PARTNERSHIP FOR EACH WICKET

258	for 1st	S. C. Ganguly and S. R. Tendulkar	I v K	Paarl	2001-02
331	for 2nd	S. R. Tendulkar and R. Dravid	I v NZ	Hyderabad	1999-2000
237*	for 3rd	R. Dravid and S. R. Tendulkar	I v K	Bristol	1999
275*	for 4th	M. Azharuddin and A. Jadeja	I v Z	Cuttack	1997-98
223	for 5th	M. Azharuddin and A. Jadeja	I v SL	Colombo (RPS)	1997-98
161	for 6th	M. O. Odumbe and A. V. Vadher	K v SL	Southampton	1999
130	for 7th	A. Flower and H. H. Streak	Z v NZ	Harare	2001-02
119	for 8th	P. R. Reiffel and S. K. Warne	A v SA	Port Elizabeth	1993-94
126*	for 9th	Kapil Dev and S. M. H. Kirmani	I v Z	Tunbridge Wells	1983
106*	for 10th	I. V. A. Richards and M. A. Holding	WI v E	Manchester	1984

BOWLING RECORDS

150 WICKETS

		M	Balls	R	W	BB	4W/i	Avge
1	**Wasim Akram (Pakistan)**	343	17,559	11,411	479	5-15	21	23.82
2	**Waqar Younis (Pakistan)** . . .	248	12,128	9,396	395	7-36	26	23.78
3	A. Kumble (India)	233	12,551	8,872	299	6-12	9	29.67
4	**M. Muralitharan (Sri Lanka)** . .	200	10,813	6,916	297	7-30	13	23.28
5	**S. K. Warne (Australia)**	189	10,373	7,347	285	5-33	13	25.77
6	**J. Srinath (India)**	205	10,685	8,000	276	5-23	7	28.98
7	Saqlain Mushtaq (Pakistan). .	156	8,131	5,792	271	5-20	16	21.37
8	**G. D. McGrath (Australia)** . .	163	8,722	5,697	253	5-14	12	22.51
9	Kapil Dev (India)	225	11,202	6,945	253	5-43	4	27.45
10	**A. A. Donald (South Africa)** . .	149	7,824	5,373	252	6-23	13	21.32
11	**W. P. U. J. C. Vaas (Sri Lanka)**	197	9,519	6,672	242	8-19	5	27.57
12	**S. M. Pollock (South Africa)** . .	167	8,778	5,592	235	6-35	11	23.79
13	C. A. Walsh (West Indies)	205	10,822	6,918	227	5-1	7	30.47
14	C. E. L. Ambrose (West Indies) . .	176	9,353	5,429	225	5-17	10	24.12
15	**S. T. Jayasuriya (Sri Lanka)** . .	275	9,953	7,975	225	6-29	8	35.44
16	C. J. McDermott (Australia). . .	138	7,461	5,018	203	5-44	5	24.71
17	**B. K. V. Prasad (India)**	161	8,129	6,332	196	5-27	4	32.30
18	**S. R. Waugh (Australia)**	325	8,883	6,761	195	4-33	3	34.67
19	C. Z. Harris (New Zealand) . . .	216	9,724	6,995	192	5-42	3	36.43
20	C. L. Hooper (West Indies) . .	215	9,093	6,561	188	4-34	3	34.89

		M	Balls	R	W	BB	4W/i	Avge
21	**H. H. Streak (Zimbabwe)** . . .	**149**	**7,491**	**5,698**	**183**	**5-32**	**6**	**31.13**
22	Imran Khan (Pakistan)	175	7,461	4,844	182	6-14	4	26.61
23	Aqib Javed (Pakistan)	163	8,012	5,721	182	7-37	6	31.43
24	**D. Gough (England)**	**111**	**6,091**	**4,380**	**174**	**5-44**	**9**	**25.17**
25	**L. Klusener (South Africa)** . .	**140**	**6,092**	**4,754**	**166**	**6-49**	**6**	**28.63**
26	Mushtaq Ahmed (Pakistan) . . .	143	7,483	5,296	161	5-36	4	32.89
27	R. J. Hadlee (New Zealand) . .	115	6,182	3,407	158	5-25	6	21.56
28	M. Prabhakar (India)	130	6,360	4,535	157	5-33	6	28.88
29	M. D. Marshall (West Indies) . .	136	7,175	4,233	157	4-18	6	26.96
30	**A. B. Agarkar (India)**	**102**	**5,212**	**4,452**	**156**	**4-25**	**7**	**28.53**
31	C. L. Cairns (New Zealand) . .	151	6,278	4,914	154	5-42	3	31.90
32	**Abdul Razzaq (Pakistan)**	**114**	**5,176**	**3,787**	**151**	**6-35**	**7**	**25.07**

Note: The most wickets for Bangladesh is:

	M	Balls	R	W	BB	4W/i	Avge
Khaled Mahmud	31	1,456	1,181	30	3-31	0	39.36

Bold type denotes those who played limited-overs international cricket in 2001-02 or 2002 season.

BEST CAREER STRIKE-RATES BY BOWLERS

(Balls per wicket. Qualification: 1,500 balls)

SR		M	Balls	W	BB	4W/i	Avge
27.38	Shoaib Akhtar (P)	70	3,149	115	6-16	4	20.39
29.03	**B. Lee (A)**	**46**	**2,381**	**82**	**5-27**	**5**	**23.29**
29.38	G. I. Allott (NZ)	31	1,528	52	4-35	4	23.21
29.58	L. S. Pascoe (A)	29	1,568	53	5-30	5	20.11
30.00	**Saqlain Mushtaq (P)** . . .	**156**	**8,131**	**271**	**5-20**	**16**	**21.37**
30.70	**Waqar Younis (P)**	**248**	**12,128**	**395**	**7-36**	**26**	**23.78**
31.04	**A. A. Donald (SA)**	**149**	**7,824**	**252**	**6-23**	**13**	**21.32**
31.13	K. S. C. de Silva (SL) . .	38	1,619	52	3-18	0	25.44
32.17	C. Pringle (NZ)	64	3,314	103	5-45	3	23.87
33.18	Zaheer Khan (I)	49	2,522	76	4-42	4	26.60
33.41	**A. B. Agarkar (I)**	**102**	**5,212**	**156**	**4-25**	**7**	**28.53**
33.88	B. P. Patterson (WI) . . .	59	3,050	90	6-29	2	24.51
34.01	R. D. King (WI)	48	2,483	73	4-25	2	23.23
34.03	C. G. Rackemann (A) . . .	52	2,791	82	5-16	4	22.35
34.27	**Abdul Razzaq (P)**	**114**	**5,176**	**151**	**6-35**	**7**	**25.07**
34.41	**J. N. Gillespie (A)**	**44**	**2,409**	**70**	**5-22**	**4**	**24.80**
34.47	D. W. Fleming (A)	88	4,619	134	5-36	5	25.38
34.47	**G. D. McGrath (A)**	**163**	**8,722**	**253**	**5-14**	**12**	**22.51**
34.73	R. Telemachus (SA)	33	1,702	49	4-43	1	27.59
34.88	D. K. Lillee (A)	63	3,593	103	5-34	6	20.82
35.00	**D. Gough (E)**	**111**	**6,091**	**174**	**5-44**	**9**	**25.17**
35.01	D. S. Mohanty (I)	45	1,996	57	4-56	1	29.15
35.54	S. Lee (A)	45	1,706	48	5-33	2	25.93
35.54	**C. White (E)**	**42**	**1,884**	**53**	**5-21**	**2**	**26.13**
35.89	A. M. E. Roberts (WI) . . .	56	3,123	87	5-22	3	20.35
36.39	**S. K. Warne (A)**	**189**	**10,373**	**285**	**5-33**	**13**	**25.77**
36.39	D. K. Morrison (NZ) . . .	96	4,586	126	5-34	3	27.53
36.40	**M. Muralitharan (SL)** . .	**200**	**10,813**	**297**	**7-30**	**13**	**23.28**
36.45	A. R. Border (A)	273	2,661	73	3-20	0	28.36
36.50	J. Garner (WI)	98	5,330	146	5-31	5	18.84
36.65	**Wasim Akram (P)**	**343**	**17,559**	**479**	**5-15**	**21**	**23.82**
36.69	**L. Klusener (SA)**	**140**	**6,092**	**166**	**6-49**	**6**	**28.63**
36.71	I. R. Bishop (WI)	84	4,332	118	5-25	9	26.50
36.75	C. J. McDermott (A) . . .	138	7,461	203	5-44	5	24.71

Bold type denotes those who played limited-overs international cricket in 2001-02 or 2002 season.

BEST CAREER ECONOMY RATES

(Runs per six balls. Qualification: 50 wickets)

ER		M	Balls	R	W	BB	Avge
.09	J. Garner (WI)	98	5,330	2,752	146	5-31	18.84
.28	R. G. D. Willis (E)	64	3,595	1,968	80	4-11	24.60
.30	R. J. Hadlee (NZ)	115	6,182	3,407	158	5-25	21.56
.32	M. A. Holding (WI)	102	5,473	3,034	142	5-26	21.36
.40	A. M. E. Roberts (WI)	56	3,123	1,771	87	5-22	20.35
.48	C. E. L. Ambrose (WI)	176	9,353	5,429	225	5-17	24.12
.53	M. D. Marshall (WI)	136	7,175	4,233	157	4-18	26.96
.57	P. S. de Villiers (SA)	83	4,422	2,636	95	4-27	27.74
.57	E. J. Chatfield (NZ)	114	6,065	3,618	140	5-34	25.84
.58	D. K. Lillee (A)	63	3,593	2,145	103	5-34	20.82
.63	Sarfraz Nawaz (P)	45	2,412	1,463	63	4-27	23.22
.65	G. F. Lawson (A)	79	4,259	2,592	88	4-26	29.45
.65	T. M. Alderman (A)	65	3,371	2,056	88	5-17	23.36
.71	Kapil Dev (I)	225	11,202	6,945	253	5-43	27.45
.76	G. R. Larsen (NZ)	121	6,368	4,000	113	4-24	35.39
.82	**S. M. Pollock (SA)**	**167**	**8,778**	**5,592**	**235**	**6-35**	**23.79**
.83	C. A. Walsh (WI)	205	10,822	6,918	227	5-1	30.47
.83	**M. Muralitharan (SL)**	**200**	**10,813**	**6,916**	**297**	**7-30**	**23.28**
.84	A. D. Mullally (E)	50	2,699	1,728	63	4-18	27.42
.89	Imran Khan (P)	175	7,461	4,844	182	6-14	26.61
.89	**Wasim Akram (P)**	**343**	**17,559**	**11,411**	**479**	**5-15**	**23.82**
.91	**G. D. McGrath (A)**	**163**	**8,722**	**5,697**	**253**	**5-14**	**22.51**
.92	P. R. Reiffel (A)	92	4,732	3,096	106	4-13	29.20
.94	C. G. Rackemann (A)	52	2,791	1,833	82	5-16	22.35
.94	R. M. Hogg (A)	71	3,677	2,418	85	4-29	28.44
.94	C. R. Matthews (SA)	56	3,003	1,975	79	4-10	25.00
.95	Maninder Singh (I)	59	3,133	2,066	66	4-22	31.30
.96	I. T. Botham (E)	116	6,271	4,139	145	4-31	28.54
.96	P. A. J. DeFreitas (E)	103	5,712	3,775	115	4-35	32.82
.97	R. A. Harper (WI)	105	5,175	3,431	100	4-40	34.31

Bold type denotes those who played limited-overs international cricket in 2001-02 or 2002 season.

BEST BOWLING ANALYSES

-19	W. P. U. J. C. Vaas	Sri Lanka v Zimbabwe at Colombo (SSC)	2001-02
-30	M. Muralitharan	Sri Lanka v India at Sharjah	2000-01
-36	Waqar Younis	Pakistan v England at Leeds	2001
-37	Aqib Javed	Pakistan v India at Sharjah	1991-92
-51	W. W. Davis	West Indies v Australia at Leeds	1983
-12	A. Kumble	India v West Indies at Calcutta	1993-94
-14	G. J. Gilmour	Australia v England at Leeds	1975
-14	Imran Khan	Pakistan v India at Sharjah	1984-85
-15	C. E. H. Croft	West Indies v England at St Vincent	1980-81
-16	Shoaib Akhtar	Pakistan v New Zealand at Karachi	2002
-18	Azhar Mahmood	Pakistan v West Indies at Sharjah	1999-2000
-19	H. K. Olonga	Zimbabwe v England at Cape Town	1999-2000
-20	B. C. Strang	Zimbabwe v Bangladesh at Nairobi (Aga Khan)	1997-98
-23	A. A. Donald	South Africa v Kenya at Nairobi (Gymkhana)	1996-97
-25	S. B. Styris	New Zealand v West Indies at Port-of-Spain	2002
-26	Waqar Younis	Pakistan v Sri Lanka at Sharjah	1989-90
-29	B. P. Patterson	West Indies v India at Nagpur	1987-88
-29	S. T. Jayasuriya	Sri Lanka v England at Moratuwa	1992-93
-30	Waqar Younis	Pakistan v New Zealand at Auckland	1993-94
-35	S. M. Pollock	South Africa v West Indies at East London	1998-99
-35	Abdul Razzaq	Pakistan v Bangladesh at Dhaka	2001-02

6-39	K. H. MacLeay	Australia v India at Nottingham	1983
6-41	I. V. A. Richards	West Indies v India at Delhi	1989-90
6-44	Waqar Younis	Pakistan v New Zealand at Sharjah	1996-97
6-49	L. Klusener	South Africa v Sri Lanka at Lahore	1997-98
6-50	A. H. Gray	West Indies v Australia at Port-of-Spain	1990-91
6-59	Waqar Younis	Pakistan v Australia at Nottingham	2001

Note: The best analyses for other Test-playing countries are:

| 5-15 | M. A. Ealham | England v Zimbabwe at Kimberley . . . . | 1999-2000 |
| 4-36 | Saiful Islam | Bangladesh v Sri Lanka at Sharjah . . . . | 1994-95 |

HAT-TRICKS

Jalal-ud-Din	Pakistan v Australia at Hyderabad	1982-83
B. A. Reid	Australia v New Zealand at Sydney	1985-86
Chetan Sharma	India v New Zealand at Nagpur	1987-88
Wasim Akram	Pakistan v West Indies at Sharjah	1989-90
Wasim Akram	Pakistan v Australia at Sharjah	1989-90
Kapil Dev	India v Sri Lanka at Calcutta	1990-91
Aqib Javed	Pakistan v India at Sharjah	1991-92
D. K. Morrison	New Zealand v India at Napier	1993-94
Waqar Younis	Pakistan v New Zealand at East London	1994-95
Saqlain Mushtaq†	Pakistan v Zimbabwe at Peshawar	1996-97
E. A. Brandes	Zimbabwe v England at Harare	1996-97
A. M. Stuart	Australia v Pakistan at Melbourne	1996-97
Saqlain Mushtaq	Pakistan v Zimbabwe at The Oval	1999
W. P. U. J. C. Vaas	Sri Lanka v Zimbabwe at Colombo (SSC)	2001-02
Mohammad Sami	Pakistan v West Indies at Sharjah	2001-02

† *Four wickets in five balls.*

WICKET-KEEPING AND FIELDING RECORDS

SIX DISMISSALS IN AN INNINGS

6 (all ct)	A. C. Gilchrist	Australia v South Africa at Cape Town	1999-2000
6 (all ct)	A. J. Stewart	England v Zimbabwe at Manchester	2000
6 (5ct, 1st)	R. D. Jacobs	West Indies v Sri Lanka at Colombo (RPS) .	2001-02

100 DISMISSALS

			M	*Ct*	*St*
1	257	Moin Khan (Pakistan).	190	191	66
2	**236**	**A. C. Gilchrist (Australia)**.	144	202	34
3	234	I. A. Healy (Australia).	168	195	39
4	204	P. J. L. Dujon (West Indies).	169	183	21
5	**197**	**R. S. Kaluwitharana (Sri Lanka)**.	174	126	71
6	**179**	**M. V. Boucher (South Africa)**.	125	170	9
7	**176**	**Rashid Latif (Pakistan)**.	140	142	34
8	**166**	**A. Flower (Zimbabwe)**.	190	134	32
9	165	D. J. Richardson (South Africa)	122	148	17
10	154	N. R. Mongia (India).	140	110	44
11	**147**	**R. D. Jacobs (West Indies)**.	102	125	22
12	**144**	**A. J. Stewart (England)**.	123	131	13
13	**136**	**A. C. Parore (New Zealand)**.	150	111	25
14	124	R. W. Marsh (Australia).	92	120	4
15	103	Salim Yousuf (Pakistan).	86	81	22

Notes: The most for Bangladesh is **44** (35 ct, 9 st) in 44 matches by **Khaled Masud.**

A. J. Stewart's record excludes 11 catches taken in 32 limited-overs internationals when not keeping wicket; A. C. Parore's excludes 5 in 29; A. Flower's 4 in 7; and R. S. Kaluwitharana's 1 in 3. R. Dravid (India) has made 104 dismissals (96 ct, 8 st) in 182 limited-overs internationals, but only 29 (21 ct, 8 st) in 23 as wicket-keeper.

Bold type denotes those who played limited-overs international cricket in 2001-02 or 2002 season.

FOUR CATCHES IN AN INNINGS

(Excluding wicket-keepers)

5	J. N. Rhodes	South Africa v West Indies at Bombay		1993-94
4	Salim Malik	Pakistan v New Zealand at Sialkot		1984-85
4	S. M. Gavaskar	India v Pakistan at Sharjah		1984-85
4	R. B. Richardson	West Indies v England at Birmingham		1991
4	K. C. Wessels	South Africa v West Indies at Kingston		1991-92
4	M. A. Taylor	Australia v West Indies at Sydney		1992-93
4	C. L. Hooper	West Indies v Pakistan at Durban		1992-93
4	K. R. Rutherford	New Zealand v India at Napier		1994-95
4	P. V. Simmons	West Indies v Sri Lanka at Sharjah		1995-96
4	M. Azharuddin	India v Pakistan at Toronto		1997-98
4	S. R. Tendulkar	India v Pakistan at Dhaka		1997-98
4	R. Dravid	India v West Indies at Toronto		1999-2000
4	G. J. Whittall	Zimbabwe v England at The Oval		2000
4	C. Z. Harris	New Zealand v India at Colombo (RPS)		2001

Note: While fielding as substitute, J. G. Bracewell held 4 catches for New Zealand v Australia at Adelaide, 1980-81.

100 CATCHES

Ct	M		Ct	M	
156	334	M. Azharuddin (India)	100	187	I. V. A. Richards (West Indies)
127	273	A. R. Border (Australia)			
111	**325**	**S. R. Waugh (Australia)**			*Most catches for other Test-playing countries:*
110	**215**	**C. L. Hooper (West Indies)**	90	250	Ijaz Ahmed, sen. (Pakistan)
109	213	R. S. Mahanama (Sri Lanka)	**87**	**216**	**C. Z. Harris (New Zealand)**
108	**244**	**M. E. Waugh (Australia)**	71	179	A. D. R. Campbell (Zimbabwe)
101	**233**	**J. N. Rhodes (South Africa)**	64	120	G. A. Hick (England)
			13	**39**	**Aminul Islam (Bangladesh)**

Bold type denotes those who played limited-overs international cricket in 2001-02 or 2002 season.

ALL-ROUND RECORDS

2,000 RUNS AND 100 WICKETS

	M	R	W
Abdul Razzaq (Pakistan)	**114**	**2,048**	**151**
I. T. Botham (England)	116	2,113	145
C. L. Cairns (New Zealand)	**151**	**3,614**	**154**
W. J. Cronje (South Africa)	188	5,565	114
C. Z. Harris (New Zealand)	**216**	**3,955**	**192**
C. L. Hooper (West Indies)	**215**	**5,551**	**188**
Imran Khan (Pakistan)	175	3,709	182
S. T. Jayasuriya (Sri Lanka)	**275**	**8,182**	**225**
J. H. Kallis (South Africa)	**158**	**5,583**	**147**
Kapil Dev (India)	225	3,783	253
L. Klusener (South Africa)	**140**	**3,184**	**166**
Mudassar Nazar (Pakistan)	122	2,653	111
I. V. A. Richards (West Indies)	187	6,721	118
Shahid Afridi (Pakistan)	**164**	**3,783**	**118**
R. J. Shastri (India)	150	3,108	129
S. R. Tendulkar (India)	**300**	**11,544**	**110**
Wasim Akram (Pakistan)	**343**	**3,564**	**479**
S. R. Waugh (Australia)	**325**	**7,569**	**195**

Bold type denotes those who played limited-overs international cricket in 2001-02 or 2002 season.

1,000 RUNS AND 100 DISMISSALS

	M	R	W
M. V. Boucher (South Africa)	**125**	**1,578**	**179**
R. Dravid (Pakistan)	**182**	**5,765**	**104**
P. J. L. Dujon (West Indies)	169	1,945	204
A. Flower (Zimbabwe)	**197**	**6,176**	**170**
A. C. Gilchrist (Australia)	**144**	**4,507**	**236**
I. A. Healy (Australia)	168	1,764	234
R. D. Jacobs (West Indies)	**102**	**1,594**	**147**
R. S. Kaluwitharana (Sri Lanka)	**177**	**3,463**	**198**
R. W. Marsh (Australia)	92	1,225	124
Moin Khan (Pakistan)	190	2,853	257
N. R. Mongia (India)	140	1,272	154
A. C. Parore (New Zealand)	**179**	**3,314**	**141**
Rashid Latif (Pakistan)	**140**	**1,332**	**176**
A. J. Stewart (England)	**155**	**4,315**	**155**

Bold type denotes those who played limited-overs international cricket in 2001-02 or 2002 season.

TEAM RECORDS

HIGHEST INNINGS TOTALS

398-5	(50 overs)	Sri Lanka v Kenya at Kandy	1995-96
376-2	(50 overs)	India v New Zealand at Hyderabad	1999-2000
373-6	(50 overs)	India v Sri Lanka at Taunton	1999
371-9	(50 overs)	Pakistan v Sri Lanka at Nairobi (Gymkhana)	1996-97
363-3	(50 overs)	South Africa v Zimbabwe at Bulawayo	2001-02
363-7	(55 overs)	England v Pakistan at Nottingham	1992
360-4	(50 overs)	West Indies v Sri Lanka at Karachi	1987-88
354-3	(50 overs)	South Africa v Kenya at Cape Town	2001-02
351-3	(50 overs)	India v Kenya at Paarl	2001-02
349-6	(50 overs)	Australia v New Zealand at Auckland	1999-2000
349-9	(50 overs)	Sri Lanka v Pakistan at Singapore	1995-96
349-9	(50 overs)	New Zealand v India at Rajkot	1999-2000
348-8	(50 overs)	New Zealand v India at Nagpur	1995-96
347-3	(50 overs)	Kenya v Bangladesh at Nairobi (Gymkhana)	1997-98
339-4	(50 overs)	Sri Lanka v Pakistan at Mohali	1996-97
338-4	(50 overs)	New Zealand v Bangladesh at Sharjah	1989-90
338-4	(50 overs)	Australia v India at Vishakhapatnam	2000-01
338-5	(60 overs)	Pakistan v Sri Lanka at Swansea	1983
337-7	(50 overs)	Australia v Pakistan at Sydney	1999-2000

Note: The highest totals by other Test-playing countries are:

325-6	(50 overs)	Zimbabwe v Kenya at Dhaka	1998-99
272-8	(50 overs)	Bangladesh v Zimbabwe at Bulawayo	2000-01

HIGHEST TOTALS BATTING SECOND

330-7	(49.1 overs)	Australia v South Africa at Port Elizabeth	2001-02
		(*Won by 3 wickets*)	
329	(49.3 overs)	Sri Lanka v West Indies at Sharjah	1995-96
		(*Lost by 4 runs*)	
326-8	(49.3 overs)	India v England at Lord's	2002
		(*Won by 2 wickets*)	
316-7	(47.5 overs)	India v Pakistan at Dhaka	1997-98
		(*Won by 3 wickets*)	

316-4	(48.5 overs)	Australia v Pakistan at Lahore..............	1998-99
		(*Won by 6 wickets*)	
315	(49.4 overs)	Pakistan v Sri Lanka at Singapore	1995-96
		(*Lost by 34 runs*)	
313-7	(49.2 overs)	Sri Lanka v Zimbabwe at New Plymouth............	1991-92
		(*Won by 3 wickets*)	
310	(48.5 overs)	India v South Africa at Nagpur	1999-2000
		(*Lost by 10 runs*)	

HIGHEST MATCH AGGREGATES

664-19	(99.4 overs)	Pakistan v Sri Lanka at Singapore	1995-96
662-17	(99.3 overs)	Sri Lanka v West Indies at Sharjah.............	1995-96
660-19	(99.5 overs)	Pakistan v Sri Lanka at Nairobi (Gymkhana)	1996-97
656-10	(99.1 overs)	South Africa v Australia at Port Elizabeth	2001-02
655-19	(97 overs)	India v New Zealand at Rajkot	1999-2000
652-12	(100 overs)	Sri Lanka v Kenya at Kandy	1995-96
651-13	(99.3 overs)	England v India at Lord's................	2002
650-15	(100 overs)	New Zealand v Australia at Auckland	1999-2000

LOWEST INNINGS TOTALS

38	(15.4 overs)	Zimbabwe v Sri Lanka at Colombo (SSC)	2001-02
43	(19.5 overs)	Pakistan v West Indies at Cape Town	1992-93
45	(40.3 overs)	Canada v England at Manchester	1979
54	(26.3 overs)	India v Sri Lanka at Sharjah	2000-01
55	(28.3 overs)	Sri Lanka v West Indies at Sharjah............	1986-87
63	(25.5 overs)	India v Australia at Sydney	1980-81
64	(35.5 overs)	New Zealand v Pakistan at Sharjah............	1985-86
68	(31.3 overs)	Scotland v West Indies at Leicester	1999
69	(28 overs)	South Africa v Australia at Sydney	1993-94
70	(25.2 overs)	Australia v England at Birmingham	1977
70	(26.3 overs)	Australia v New Zealand at Adelaide	1985-86

Note: This section does not take into account those matches in which the number of overs was reduced.

The lowest totals by other Test-playing countries are:

76	(30.1 overs)	Bangladesh v Sri Lanka at Colombo (SSC)	2002
86	(32.4 overs)	England v Australia at Manchester	2001
87	(29.3 overs)	West Indies v Australia at Sydney	1992-93

LARGEST VICTORIES

245 runs	Sri Lanka (299-5 in 50 overs) v India (54 in 26.3 overs) at Sharjah ...	2000-01
233 runs	Pakistan (320-3 in 50 overs) v Bangladesh (87 in 34.2 overs) at Dhaka .	1999-2000
232 runs	Australia (323-2 in 50 overs) v Sri Lanka (91 in 35.5 overs) at Adelaide	1984-85
224 runs	Australia (332-5 in 50 overs) v Pakistan (108 in 36 overs) at Nairobi ..	2002
217 runs	Pakistan (295-6 in 50 overs) v Sri Lanka (78 in 16.5 overs) at Sharjah .	2001-02
208 runs	South Africa (354-3 in 50 overs) v Kenya (146 in 45.3 overs) at Cape Town	
		2001-02
206 runs	New Zealand (276-7 in 50 overs) v Australia (70 in 26.3 overs) at Adelaide	1985-86
206 runs	Sri Lanka (292-5 in 50 overs) v Holland (86 in 29.3 overs) at Colombo (RPS)....................	
		2002
202 runs	England (334-4 in 60 overs) v India (132-3 in 60 overs) at Lord's	1975
202 runs	South Africa (305-8 in 50 overs) v Kenya (103 in 25.1 overs) at Nairobi	1996-97
202 runs	Zimbabwe (325-6 in 50 overs) v Kenya (123 in 36.5 overs) at Dhaka ..	1998-99

By ten wickets: there have been 15 instances of victory by ten wickets.

TIED MATCHES

West Indies (222-5 in 50 overs) v Australia (222-9 in 50 overs) at Melbourne 1983-84
England (226-5 in 55 overs) v Australia (226-8 in 55 overs) at Nottingham. 1989
West Indies (186-5 in 39 overs) v Pakistan (186-9 in 39 overs) at Lahore 1991-92
India (126 in 47.4 overs) v West Indies (126 in 41 overs) at Perth 1991-92
Australia (228-7 in 50 overs) v Pakistan (228-9 in 50 overs) at Hobart 1992-93
Pakistan (244-6 in 50 overs) v West Indies (244-5 in 50 overs) at Georgetown. . . . 1992-93
India (248-5 in 50 overs) v Zimbabwe (248 in 50 overs) at Indore 1993-94
Pakistan (161-9 in 50 overs) v New Zealand (161 in 49.4 overs) at Auckland 1993-94
Zimbabwe (219-9 in 50 overs) v Pakistan (219 in 49.5 overs) at Harare 1994-95
New Zealand (169-8 in 50 overs) v Sri Lanka (169 in 48 overs) at Sharjah 1996-97
Zimbabwe (236-8 in 50 overs) v India (236 in 49.5 overs) at Paarl 1996-97
New Zealand (237 in 49.4 overs) v England (237-8 in 50 overs) at Napier 1996-97
Zimbabwe (233-8 in 50 overs) v New Zealand (233-9 in 50 overs) at Bulawayo. . . 1997-98
West Indies (173-5 in 30 overs) v Australia (173-7 in 30 overs) at Sydney 1998-99
Australia (213 in 49.2 overs) v South Africa (213 in 49.4 overs) at Birmingham . . . 1999
Pakistan (196 in 49.4 overs) v Sri Lanka (196 in 49.1 overs) at Sharjah 1999-2000
South Africa (226 in 50 overs) v Australia (226-9 in 50 overs) at Melbourne (CS). . 2000
South Africa (259-7 in 50 overs) v Australia (259-9 in 50 overs) at Potchefstroom . 2001-02

OTHER RECORDS

200 APPEARANCES

	Total	E	A	SA	WI	NZ	I	P	SL	Z	B	Ass
Wasim Akram (P) . .	343	31	48	21	64	38	47	–	59	23	6	6
M. Azharuddin (I). . .	334	24	43	33	43	40	–	64	53	22	7	5
S. R. Waugh (A) . . .	325	30	–	47	50	60	53	43	24	14	2	2
S. R. Tendulkar (I). .	300	25	33	41	31	31	–	43	50	31	6	9
P. A. de Silva (SL) . .	288	13	31	21	27	36	57	75	–	15	9	4
Salim Malik (P) . . .	283	26	26	16	46	43	52	–	53	13	3	5
S. T. Jayasuriya (SL) .	275	16	26	27	23	32	51	65	–	25	6	4
Inzamam-ul-Haq (P)	274	18	26	24	38	36	44	–	56	18	9	5
A. R. Border (A) . . .	273	43	–	15	61	52	38	34	23	5	1	1
A. Ranatunga (SL) . .	269	18	33	16	22	35	56	67	–	15	4	3
Ijaz Ahmed, sen. (P) .	250	19	34	20	38	27	53	–	39	13	4	3
Waqar Younis (P). . .	248	13	29	27	43	37	25	–	51	13	4	6
M. E. Waugh (A) . . .	244	21	–	42	47	39	27	29	23	13	1	2
Saeed Anwar (P) . . .	242	10	30	24	17	32	49	–	52	14	6	8
D. L. Haynes (WI) . . .	238	35	64	8	–	13	36	65	14	3	–	–
Javed Miandad (P) . .	233	27	35	3	64	24	35	–	35	6	1	3
A. Kumble (I)	233	26	21	37	21	26	–	30	39	21	4	8
J. N. Rhodes (SA) . .	233	21	55	–	24	29	31	25	27	14	–	7
Kapil Dev (I).	225	23	41	13	42	29	–	32	34	9	2	–
R. B. Richardson (WI)	224	35	51	9	–	11	32	61	21	3	–	1
C. Z. Harris (NZ) . .	216	22	32	30	19	–	27	33	30	19	2	2
C. L. Hooper (WI). .	215	25	40	23	–	11	39	49	19	5	–	4
R. S. Mahanama (SL)	213	11	26	15	22	22	45	52	–	14	4	2
S. C. Ganguly (I). . .	206	15	20	23	18	20	–	35	33	30	4	8
J. Srinath (I).	205	20	27	33	18	22	–	35	27	16	2	5
C. A. Walsh (WI) . . .	205	31	36	5	–	38	16	52	22	2	1	2
B. C. Lara (WI) . . .	203	19	32	23	–	22	31	39	19	12	3	3
M. Muralitharan (SL)	200	11	13	24	17	24	34	48	–	19	6	4

Note: The most appearances for other Test-playing countries are:

A. Flower (Z)	197	22	15	15	15	23	35	24	27	–	10	11
A. J. Stewart (E) . . .	155	–	23	15	25	19	19	21	18	11	1	3
Khaled Masud (B) . .	45	1	2	–	3	2	6	9	6	9	–	7

Bold type denotes those who played limited-overs international cricket in 2001-02 or 2002 season.

CAPTAINS

England (356 matches; 23 captains)

G. A. Gooch 50; M. A. Atherton 43; **N. Hussain 42;** A. J. Stewart 40; M. W. Gatting 37; R. G. D. Willis 29; J. M. Brearley 25; D. I. Gower 24; A. J. Hollioake 14; M. H. Denness 12; I. T. Botham 9; K. W. R. Fletcher 5; J. E. Emburey 4; A. J. Lamb 4; D. B. Close 3; R. Illingworth 3; G. P. Thorpe 3; G. Boycott 2; N. Gifford 2; A. W. Greig 2; J. H. Edrich 1; A. P. E. Knott 1; **M. E. Trescothick 1**.

Australia (513 matches; 16 captains)

A. R. Border 178; **S. R. Waugh 106;** M. A. Taylor 67; G. S. Chappell 49; K. J. Hughes 49; **R. T. Ponting 17;** I. M. Chappell 11; S. K. Warne 11; I. A. Healy 8; **A. C. Gilchrist 4;** G. R. Marsh 4; G. N. Yallop 4; R. B. Simpson 2; R. J. Bright 1; D. W. Hookes 1; W. M. Lawry 1.

South Africa (264 matches; 4 captains)

W. J. Cronje 138; **S. M. Pollock 71;** K. C. Wessels 52; C. E. B. Rice 3.

West Indies (450 matches; 15 captains)

I. V. A. Richards 108; R. B. Richardson 87; C. H. Lloyd 81; B. C. Lara 44; C. A. Walsh 43; **C. L. Hooper 37;** J. C. Adams 26; C. G. Greenidge 8; D. L. Haynes 7; M. A. Holding 2; R. B. Kanhai 2; D. L. Murray 2; S. L. Campbell 1; P. J. L. Dujon 1; A. I. Kallicharran 1.

New Zealand (414 matches; 16 captains)

S. P. Fleming 122; G. P. Howarth 60; M. D. Crowe 44; K. R. Rutherford 37; L. K. Germon 36; J. G. Wright 31; J. V. Coney 25; J. J. Crowe 16; M. G. Burgess 8; **C. D. McMillan 8;** G. M. Turner 8; D. J. Nash 7; B. E. Congdon 6; G. R. Larsen 3; A. H. Jones 2; **C. L. Cairns 1**.

India (509 matches; 17 captains)

M. Azharuddin 174; **S. C. Ganguly 77;** Kapil Dev 74; S. R. Tendulkar 73; S. M. Gavaskar 37; D. B. Vengsarkar 18; A. Jadeja 13; K. Srikkanth 13; R. J. Shastri 11; S. Venkataraghavan 7; B. S. Bedi 4; R. Dravid 2; A. L. Wadekar 2; M. Amarnath 1; S. M. H. Kirmani 1; **A. Kumble 1;** G. R. Viswanath 1.

Pakistan (533 matches; 18 captains)

Imran Khan 139; Wasim Akram 110; Javed Miandad 62; **Waqar Younis 48;** Moin Khan 34; Salim Malik 34; Aamir Sohail 22; Ramiz Raja 22; Rashid Latif 13; Zaheer Abbas 13; Saeed Anwar 10; Asif Iqbal 6; Abdul Qadir 5; Wasim Bari 5; Mushtaq Mohammad 4; Intikhab Alam 3; Majid Khan 2; Sarfraz Nawaz 1.

Sri Lanka (396 matches; 11 captains)

A. Ranatunga 193; **S. T. Jayasuriya 93;** L. R. D. Mendis 61; P. A. de Silva 18; R. S. Madugalle 13; B. Warnapura 8; A. P. B. Tennekoon 4; **M. S. Atapattu 2;** R. S. Mahanama 2; D. S. de Silva 1; J. R. Ratnayeke 1.

Zimbabwe (214 matches; 10 captains)

A. D. R. Campbell 78; A. Flower 52; **H. H. Streak 34;** D. L. Houghton 17; **S. V. Carlisle 12;** D. A. G. Fletcher 6; A. J. Traicos 6; **B. A. Murphy 4;** **G. J. Whittall 4;** G. W. Flower 1.

Bangladesh (55 matches; 6 captains)

Aminul Islam 16; Akram Khan 15; **Khaled Masud 11;** Gazi Ashraf 7; Naimur Rahman 4; Minhazul Abedin 2.

Associate Members (74 matches; 9 captains)

A. Y. Karim (Kenya) 21; **M. O. Odumbe (Kenya) 20; S. O. Tikolo (Kenya) 8;** Sultan M. Zarawani (UAE) 7; G. Salmond (Scotland) 5; S. W. Lubbers (Holland) 4; **R. P. Lefebvre (Holland) 3;** B. M. Mauricette (Canada) 3; Harilal R. Shah (East Africa) 3.

Bold type denotes those who captained in a limited-overs international in 2001-02 or 2002 season.

WORLD CUP FINALS

1975	WEST INDIES (291-8) beat Australia (274) by 17 runs	Lord's
1979	WEST INDIES (286-9) beat England (194) by 92 runs	Lord's
1983	INDIA (183) beat West Indies (140) by 43 runs	Lord's
1987-88	AUSTRALIA (253-5) beat England (246-8) by seven runs	Calcutta
1991-92	PAKISTAN (249-6) beat England (227) by 22 runs.	Melbourne
1995-96	SRI LANKA (245-3) beat Australia (241-7) by seven wickets.	Lahore
1999	AUSTRALIA (133-2) beat Pakistan (132) by eight wickets	Lord's

Note: The 2002-03 World Cup is included in the Stop Press section at the end of this book.

MISCELLANEOUS RECORDS

LARGE ATTENDANCES

Test Series

943,000	Australia v England (5 Tests)	1936-37
In England		
549,650	England v Australia (5 Tests)	1953

Test Matches

†‡465,000	India v Pakistan, Calcutta	1998-99
350,534	Australia v England, Melbourne (Third Test)	1936-37

Note: Attendance at India v England at Calcutta in 1981-82 may have exceeded 350,000.

In England		
158,000+	England v Australia, Leeds	1948
137,915	England v Australia, Lord's	1953

Test Match Day

‡100,000	India v Pakistan, Calcutta (first four days).	1998-99
90,800	Australia v West Indies, Melbourne (Fifth Test, second day). . .	1960-61

Other First-Class Matches in England

93,000	England v Australia, Lord's (Fourth Victory Match, 3 days)	1945
80,000+	Surrey v Yorkshire, The Oval (3 days)	1906
78,792	Yorkshire v Lancashire, Leeds (3 days)	1904
76,617	Lancashire v Yorkshire, Manchester (3 days)	1926

Limited-Overs Internationals

‡100,000	India v South Africa, Calcutta	. . . .	1993-94
‡100,000	India v West Indies, Calcutta	. . . .	1993-94
‡100,000	India v West Indies, Calcutta	. . . .	1994-95
‡100,000	India v Sri Lanka, Calcutta (World Cup semi-final)	. . . .	1995-96
‡90,000	India v Pakistan, Calcutta	. . . .	1986-87
‡90,000	India v South Africa, Calcutta	. . . .	1991-92
87,182	England v Pakistan, Melbourne (World Cup final)	. . . .	1991-92
86,133	Australia v West Indies, Melbourne	. . . .	1983-84

† *Estimated.*

‡ *No official attendance figures were issued for these games, but capacity is believed to have reached 100,000 following rebuilding in 1993.*

LORD'S CRICKET GROUND

Lord's and the Marylebone Cricket Club were founded in London in 1787. The Club has enjoyed an uninterrupted career since that date, but there have been three grounds known as Lord's. The first (1787–1810) was situated where Dorset Square now is; the second (1809–13), at North Bank, had to be abandoned owing to the cutting of the Regent's Canal; and the third, opened in 1814, is the present one at St John's Wood. It was not until 1866 that the freehold of Lord's was secured by MCC. The present pavilion was erected in 1890 at a cost of £21,000.

HIGHEST INDIVIDUAL SCORES MADE AT LORD'S

333	G. A. Gooch	. . . . England v India	. . . .	1990
316*	J. B. Hobbs	. . . . Surrey v Middlesex	. . . .	1926
315*	P. Holmes	. . . . Yorkshire v Middlesex	. . . .	1925
315	M. A. Wagh	. . . . Warwickshire v Middlesex	. . . .	2001

Notes: The longest innings in a first-class match at Lord's was played by S. Wettimuny (636 minutes, 190 runs) for Sri Lanka v England, 1984. Wagh batted for 630 minutes.

HIGHEST TOTALS AT LORD'S

First-Class Matches

729-6 dec.	Australia v England	1930
665	West Indians v Middlesex	1939
653-4 dec.	England v India	1990
652-8 dec.	West Indies v England	1973

Minor Match

735-9 dec.	MCC and Ground v Wiltshire	1888

BIGGEST HIT AT LORD'S

The only known instance of a batsman hitting a ball over the present pavilion at Lord's occurred when A. E. Trott, appearing for MCC against Australians on July 31, August 1, 2, 1899, drove M. A. Noble so far and high that the ball struck a chimney pot and fell behind the building.

MINOR CRICKET

HIGHEST INDIVIDUAL SCORES

628*	A. E. J. Collins, Clark's House v North Town at Clifton College.	
	A junior house match. His innings of 6 hours 50 minutes was spread over	
	four afternoons	1899
566	C. J. Eady, Break-o'-Day v Wellington at Hobart	1901-02
515	D. R. Havewalla, B. B. and C. I. Railways v St Xavier's at Bombay	1933-34
506*	J. C. Sharp, Melbourne GS v Geelong College at Melbourne	1914-15
502*	Chaman Lal, Mehandra Coll., Patiala v Government Coll., Rupar at Patiala	1956-57
485	A. E. Stoddart, Hampstead v Stoics at Hampstead	1886
475*	Mohammad Iqbal, Muslim Model HS v Islamia HS, Sialkot at Lahore	1958-59
466*	G. T. S. Stevens, Beta v Lambda (University College School house match) at	
	Neasden	1919
459	J. A. Prout, Wesley College v Geelong College at Geelong	1908-09

Note: The highest score in a Minor County match is 323* by F. E. Lacey for Hampshire v Norfolk at Southampton in 1887; the highest in the Minor Counties Championship is 282 by E. Garnett for Berkshire v Wiltshire at Reading in 1908.

HIGHEST PARTNERSHIP

664* for 3rd	V. G. Kambli and S. R. Tendulkar, Sharadashram Vidyamandir School	
	v St Xavier's High School at Bombay	1987-88

Note: Kambli was 16 year old, Tendulkar 14. Tendulkar made his Test debut 21 months later.

RECORD HIT

The Rev. W. Fellows, while at practice on the Christ Church ground at Oxford in 1856, drove a ball bowled by Charles Rogers 175 yards from hit to pitch.

THROWING THE CRICKET BALL

140 yards 2 feet, Robert Percival, on the Durham Sands racecourse, Co. Durham	c1882
140 yards 9 inches, Ross Mackenzie, at Toronto	1872
140 yards, "King Billy" the Aborigine, at Clermont, Queensland	1872

Note: Extensive research by David Rayvern Allen has shown that these traditional records are probably authentic, if not necessarily wholly accurate. Modern competitions have failed to produce similar distances although Ian Pont, the Essex all-rounder who also played baseball, was reported to have thrown 138 yards in Cape Town in 1981. There have been speculative reports attributing throws of 150 yards or more to figures as diverse as the South African Test player Colin Bland, the Latvian javelin thrower Janis Lusis, who won a gold medal for the Soviet Union in the 1968 Olympics, and the British sprinter Charley Ransome. The definitive record is still awaited.

COUNTY CHAMPIONSHIP

MOST APPEARANCES

762	W. Rhodes	Yorkshire	1898-1930
707	F. E. Woolley	Kent	1906-38
668	C. P. Mead	Hampshire	1906-36
617	N. Gifford	Worcestershire (484), Warwickshire (133)	1960-88
611	W. G. Quaife	Warwickshire	1895-1928
601	G. H. Hirst	Yorkshire	1891-1921

MOST CONSECUTIVE APPEARANCES

423	K. G. Suttle	Sussex	1954-69
412	J. G. Binks	Yorkshire	1955-69

Notes: J. Vine made 417 consecutive appearances for Sussex in all first-class matches (399 of them in the Championship) between July 1900 and September 1914.

J. G. Binks did not miss a Championship match for Yorkshire between making his debut in June 1955 and retiring at the end of the 1969 season.

UMPIRES

MOST COUNTY CHAMPIONSHIP APPEARANCES

569	T. W. Spencer	1950-1980		481	P. B. Wight	1966-1995
533	F. Chester	1922-1955		462	J. Moss	1899-1929
516	H. G. Baldwin	1932-1962		457	A. Skelding	1931-1958

MOST SEASONS ON FIRST-CLASS LIST

34	**D. J. Constant**	**1969-2002**		28	F. Chester	1922-1955
33	**A. G. T. Whitehead**	**1970-2002**		27	J. Moss	1899-1929
31	**K. E. Palmer**	**1972-2002**		26	W. A. J. West	1896-1925
31	T. W. Spencer	1950-1980		25	H. G. Baldwin	1932-1962
30	R. Julian	1972-2001		25	A. Jepson	1960-1984
30	P. B. Wight	1966-1995		25	J. G. Langridge	1956-1980
29	H. D. Bird	1970-1998		25	B. J. Meyer	1973-1997

Bold type denotes umpires who stood in the 2002 season.

WOMEN'S TEST RECORDS

Amended by MARION COLLIN to the end of the 2002 season in England

HIGHEST INDIVIDUAL SCORES

214	M. Raj	India v England at Taunton	2002
209*	K. L. Rolton	Australia v England at Leeds	2001
204	K. E. Flavell	New Zealand v England at Scarborough	1996
204	M. A. J. Goszko	Australia v England at Shenley Park	2001
200	J. Broadbent	Australia v England at Guildford	1998
193	D. A. Annetts	Australia v England at Collingham	1987
190	S. Agarwal	India v England at Worcester	1986
189	E. A. Snowball	England v New Zealand at Christchurch	1934-35
179	R. Heyhoe-Flint	England v Australia at The Oval	1976
176*	K. L. Rolton	Australia v England at Worcester	1998

1,000 RUNS IN A CAREER

R	T		R	T	
1,935	27	J. A. Brittin (England)	1,110	13	S. Agarwal (India)
1,594	22	R. Heyhoe-Flint (England)	1,078	12	E. Bakewell (England)
1,301	19	D. A. Hockley (New Zealand)	1,007	14	M. E. Maclagan (England)
1,164	18	C. A. Hodges (England)			

BEST BOWLING ANALYSES

8-53	N. David	India v England at Jamshedpur	1995-96
7-6	M. B. Duggan .	England v Australia at Melbourne	1957-58
7-7	E. R. Wilson . .	Australia v England at Melbourne	1957-58
7-10	M. E. Maclagan	England v Australia at Brisbane	1934-35
7-18	A. Palmer	Australia v England at Brisbane	1934-35

11 WICKETS IN A MATCH

11-16	E. R. Wilson	Australia v England at Melbourne	1957-58
11-63	J. Greenwood . . .	England v West Indies at Canterbury	1979

50 WICKETS IN A CAREER

W	T		W	T	
77	17	M. B. Duggan (England)	60	19	S. Kulkarni (India)
68	11	E. R. Wilson (Australia)	57	16	R. H. Thompson (Australia)
63	20	D. F. Edulji (India)	55	15	J. Lord (New Zealand)
60	14	M. E. Maclagan (England)	50	12	E. Bakewell (England)

SIX DISMISSALS IN AN INNINGS

8	(6ct, 2st)	L. Nye	England v New Zealand at New Plymouth	1991-92
6	(2ct, 4st)	B. A. Brentnall .	New Zealand v South Africa at Johannesburg . . .	1971-72

EIGHT DISMISSALS IN A MATCH

9	(8ct, 1st)	C. Matthews . .	Australia v India at Adelaide	1990-91
8	(6ct, 2st)	L. Nye	England v New Zealand at New Plymouth	1991-92

25 DISMISSALS IN A CAREER

		T	Ct	St
58	C. Matthews (Australia)	20	46	12
36	S. A. Hodges (England)	11	19	17
28	B. A. Brentnall (New Zealand)	10	16	12

HIGHEST INNINGS TOTALS

569-6 dec.	Australia v England at Guildford	1998
525	Australia v India at Ahmedabad	1983-84
517-8	New Zealand v England at Scarborough	1996
503-5 dec.	England v New Zealand at Christchurch	1934-35

LOWEST INNINGS TOTALS

35	England v Australia at Melbourne	1957-58
38	Australia v England at Melbourne	1957-58
44	New Zealand v England at Christchurch	1934-35
47	Australia v England at Brisbane	1934-35

5

ENGLISH
CRICKET

Perfect finish: Ian Ward, who won two matches for Surrey with fourth-innings hundreds and did much to help secure the Championship. Surrey, page 751. *Picture by Graham Morris.*

PART FIVE: ENGLISH CRICKET IN 2002

FEATURES OF 2002

Double-Hundreds (22)

315*	G. A. Hick	Worcestershire v Durham at Worcester.
310*	M. E. K. Hussey	Northamptonshire v Gloucestershire at Bristol.
277§	R. A. White	Northamptonshire v Gloucestershire at Northampton.
272	J. P. Crawley	Hampshire v Kent at Canterbury.
255*‡	N. V. Knight	Warwickshire v Hampshire at Birmingham.
254*	K. P. Pietersen	Nottinghamshire v Middlesex at Nottingham.
251†	M. L. Love	Durham v Middlesex at Lord's.
250	S. S. Das	Indians v Essex at Chelmsford.
249	S. P. James	Glamorgan v Essex at Chelmsford.
245*‡	N. V. Knight	Warwickshire v Sussex at Birmingham.
230	M. J. Di Venuto	Derbyshire v Northamptonshire at Derby.
225	D. P. Ostler	Warwickshire v Yorkshire at Birmingham.
218	S. G. Law	Lancashire v Sussex at Manchester.
218‡	M. R. Ramprakash	Surrey v Somerset at Taunton.
217	C. J. Adams	Sussex v Lancashire at Manchester.
217	R. Dravid	India v England (Fourth Test) at The Oval.
216	D. S. Lehmann	Yorkshire v Sussex at Arundel.
210*‡	M. R. Ramprakash	Surrey v Warwickshire at The Oval.
208	A. J. Hollioake	Surrey v Leicestershire at The Oval.
207*	R. C. Irani	Essex v Northamptonshire at Ilford.
205*	R. S. C. Martin-Jenkins	Sussex v Somerset at Taunton.
203*	Abdul Razzaq	Middlesex v Glamorgan at Cardiff.

† County record.
‡ Knight and Ramprakash each scored two double-hundreds.
§ White's 277 was his maiden first-class hundred.

Hundred on First-Class Debut

107*	R. Clarke	Surrey v Cambridge UCCE at Cambridge.
169	J. S. D. Moffat	Cambridge University v Oxford University at Oxford.
	In his only first-class innings.	

Four Hundreds in Successive Innings

I. J. Ward (Surrey)	114 v Warwickshire at Birmingham;
	112 and 156 v Hampshire at Southampton;
	118 v Leicestershire at The Oval.

Hundred in Each Innings of a Match

M. J. Di Venuto	192*	113	Derbyshire v Middlesex at Lord's.
M. B. Loye	105	104*	Northamptonshire v Nottinghamshire at Northampton.
M. P. Maynard	140	118*	Glamorgan v Gloucestershire at Cheltenham.
I. J. Ward	112	156	Surrey v Hampshire at Southampton.
M. J. Wood	106	131	Somerset v Surrey at Taunton.

Carrying Bat through Completed Innings

K. J. Barnett	182*	Gloucestershire (388) v Middlesex at Southgate.
M. J. Di Venuto	192*	Derbyshire (414) v Middlesex at Lord's.
M. A. Gough	75*	Durham (187) v Essex at Chester-le-Street.
W. S. Kendall	53*	Hampshire (146) v Leicestershire at Southampton.
N. V. Knight	255*	Warwickshire (472) v Hampshire at Birmingham.
N. V. Knight	245*	Warwickshire (493) v Sussex at Birmingham.
R. R. Montgomerie	122*	Sussex (247) v Leicestershire at Horsham.
C. M. Spearman	180*	Gloucestershire (293) v Glamorgan at Cheltenham.
I. J. Sutcliffe	125*	Leicestershire (259) v Kent at Canterbury.
A. J. Swann	84*	Lancashire (163) v Hampshire at Manchester.

Hundred with a Runner

133	N. V. Knight	Warwickshire v Surrey at Birmingham.
127*	D. L. Maddy	Leicestershire v Surrey at The Oval.
124	S. J. Rhodes	Worcestershire v Nottinghamshire at Nottingham.
100	D. C. Nash	Middlesex v Worcestershire at Worcester.

Fastest Hundred

M. V. Fleming	66 balls	Kent v Sri Lankans at Canterbury.

Hundred before Lunch

G. P. Swann	(58* to 172*)	Northamptonshire v Gloucestershire at Bristol (3rd day).
R. A. White	(107*)	Northamptonshire v Gloucestershire at Northampton (1st day).

White also scored 97* between lunch and tea.

Most Runs in Boundaries

208 (49×4, 2×6)	G. A. Hick (315*)	Worcestershire v Durham at Worcester.

First to 1,000 Runs

M. E. K. Hussey (Northamptonshire) on July 19.

Long Innings

Mins

653	M. E. K. Hussey (310*)	Northamptonshire v Gloucestershire at Bristol.
629	R. Dravid (217)	India v England (Fourth Test) at The Oval.
616	N. V. Knight (255*)	Warwickshire v Hampshire at Birmingham.

Unusual Dismissals

Stumped by a Substitute

G. W. Flower (7)	Leicestershire v Warwickshire at Birmingham.

Retired Out

R. Dravid (40)	Indians v Derbyshire at Derby.
M. E. K. Hussey (52)	Northamptonshire v Oxford UCCE at Oxford.
B. F. Smith (137)	Worcestershire v Oxford UCCE at Oxford.

Highest Partnerships

First Wicket
375† R. A. White/M. J. Powell, Northamptonshire v Gloucestershire at Northampton.
290   M. E. K. Hussey/M. B. Loye, Northamptonshire v Worcestershire at Northampton.
266   D. P. Fulton/R. W. T. Key, Kent v Hampshire at Canterbury.

Second Wicket
252† M. P. Maynard/D. L. Hemp, Glamorgan v Northamptonshire at Cardiff.
251   M. L. Love/G. J. Muchall, Durham v Middlesex at Lord's.

Third Wicket
317   A. McGrath/D. S. Lehmann, Yorkshire v Lancashire at Leeds.

Fourth Wicket
316   D. J. Bicknell/K. P. Pietersen, Nottinghamshire v Middlesex at Nottingham.

Fifth Wicket
320   E. C. Joyce/Abdul Razzaq, Middlesex v Glamorgan at Cardiff.
282   A. D. Brown/A. J. Hollioake, Surrey v Leicestershire at The Oval.
262   A. D. Brown/N. Shahid, Surrey v Sussex at The Oval.

Sixth Wicket
318   M. E. K. Hussey/G. P. Swann, Northamptonshire v Gloucestershire at Bristol.

Seventh Wicket
256† D. A. Leatherdale/S. J. Rhodes, Worcestershire v Nottinghamshire at Nottingham.
207   R. C. Russell/I. D. Fisher, Gloucestershire v Essex at Gloucester.

Eighth Wicket
291† R. S. C. Martin-Jenkins/M. J. G. Davis, Sussex v Somerset at Taunton.
164   M. W. Alleyne/I. D. Fisher, Gloucestershire v Essex at Chelmsford.
161   R. C. Russell/R. J. Sillence, Gloucestershire v Derbyshire at Bristol.

Tenth Wicket
214† N. V. Knight/A. Richardson, Warwickshire v Hampshire at Birmingham.
145   S. G. Law/G. Keedy, Lancashire v Sussex at Manchester.
119   N. M. Carter/J. A. Spires, Warwickshire v Sussex at Hove.

† *County record.*

Eight Wickets in an Innings (8)

9-93   A. J. Bichel . . . .   Worcestershire v Gloucestershire at Worcester.
8-24   A. A. Noffke . . . .   Middlesex v Derbyshire at Derby.
8-46   A. Richardson . . . .   Warwickshire v Sussex at Birmingham.
8-53   G. J. Smith . . . .   Nottinghamshire v Essex at Nottingham.
8-61   Azhar Mahmood . . . .   Surrey v Lancashire at The Oval.
8-63   S. J. Cook . . . .   Middlesex v Northamptonshire at Northampton.
8-66   P. C. R. Tufnell . . . .   Middlesex v Gloucestershire at Cheltenham.
8-111   S. C. G. MacGill . . . .   Nottinghamshire v Middlesex at Nottingham.

Twelve Wickets in a Match (4)

14-165   S. C. G. MacGill . . . . .   Nottinghamshire v Middlesex at Nottingham.
12-108   A. A. Noffke . . . .   Middlesex v Derbyshire at Derby.
12-131   J. Lewis . . . .   Gloucestershire v Worcestershire at Worcester.
12-216   A. F. Giles . . . .   Warwickshire v Kent at Birmingham.

Hat-Trick (1)

J. Srinath . . . .   Leicestershire v Surrey at The Oval.

100 Wickets

No bowler took 100 wickets. The highest aggregate was 83 by K. J. Dean (Derbyshire) and M. J. Saggers (Kent).

Six Wicket-Keeping Dismissals in an Innings

6 ct. . . . . . . R. C. Russell   Gloucestershire v Durham at Bristol.

Equalling county record.

Nine Wicket-Keeping Dismissals in a Match

9 ct, 1 st . . . A. J. Stewart   Surrey v Lancashire at The Oval.
9 ct. . . . . . . R. C. Russell   Gloucestershire v Durham at Bristol.

Five Catches in an Innings in the Field

M. E. K. Hussey . . . .   Northamptonshire v Oxford UCCE at Oxford.

Equalling county record.

Six Catches in a Match in the Field

7   M. E. K. Hussey . . . .   Northamptonshire v Oxford UCCE at Oxford.
6   D. P. Fulton . . . .   Kent v Somerset at Canterbury.
6   V. Sehwag . . . .   India v England (Third Test) at Leeds.

No Byes Conceded in Total of 500 or More

A. N. Aymes/N. Pothas   Hampshire v Kent (577-7 dec.) at Canterbury.
Pothas took over at 383-4.
A. Flower . . . .   Essex v Northamptonshire (632) at Northampton.
B. J. Hyam . . . .   Essex v Indians (516) at Chelmsford.
D. C. Nash . . . .   Middlesex v Worcestershire (502-4 dec.) at Lord's.
P. A. Nixon . . . . . .   Kent v Leicestershire (530) at Canterbury.
A. Pratt. . . . .   Durham v Worcestershire (643-7 dec.) at Worcester.
R. C. Russell† . . . .   Gloucestershire v Northamptonshire (746-9 dec.) at Bristol.
K. C. Sangakkara . . .   Sri Lanka v England (545) (Second Test) at Birmingham.
R. J. Turner . . . . . .   Somerset v Surrey (608-6 dec.) at Taunton.
R. J. Turner . . . . . .   Somerset v Sussex (644) at Taunton.

† *World record total without byes.*

Highest Innings Totals

746-9 dec. . . . .   Northamptonshire v Gloucestershire at Bristol.
671 . . . .   Hampshire v Kent at Canterbury.
            One batsman retired hurt and one absent hurt.
645-6 dec.† . . . .   Durham v Middlesex at Lord's.
644 . . . .   Sussex v Somerset at Taunton.
643-7 dec. . . . .   Worcestershire v Durham at Worcester.
633-7 dec. . . . .   Middlesex v Glamorgan at Cardiff.
632 . . . .   Northamptonshire v Essex at Northampton.
631-6 dec. . . . .   Sussex v Hampshire at Hove.
628-8 dec. . . . .   India v England (Third Test) at Leeds.
617 . . . .   England v India (Second Test) at Nottingham.
614-5 dec. . . . .   Northamptonshire v Worcestershire at Northampton.
608-6 dec. . . . .   Surrey v Somerset at Taunton.
604 . . . .   Cambridge University v Oxford University at Oxford.
601-9 dec. . . . .   Warwickshire v Yorkshire at Birmingham.

† *County record.*

Lowest Team Total

71 . . . .   Somerset v Lancashire at Blackpool.

Highest Fourth-Innings Totals

453 . . . . Somerset v West Indies A at Taunton (set 454).
410-8 . . . . Surrey v Kent at Canterbury (set 410).
405-7 . . . . Warwickshire v Sussex at Hove (set 401).

Match Aggregate of 1,500 Runs

1,815 for 28† . Surrey (608-6 dec. and 324-5 dec.) v Somerset (554 and 329-7) at Taunton.
1,665 for 33 . . Warwickshire (601-9 dec. and 232-4) v Yorkshire (351 and 481) at Birmingham.
1,614 for 26 . . Gloucestershire (422 and 446-7) v Northamptonshire (746-9 dec.) at Bristol.
1,575 for 33 . . Northamptonshire (632 and 155) v Essex (497-7 dec. and 291-6) at Northampton.
1,557 for 38 . . Surrey (418 and 422-8 dec.) v Hampshire (327 and 390) at Southampton.
1,548 for 33 . . Glamorgan (348 and 528-7 dec.) v Northamptonshire (430 and 242-6) at Cardiff.

† *National record.*

Most Runs Per Wicket in a Match

74.26 (1,411-19)   Kent (577-7 dec. and 163-4 dec.) v Hampshire (671) at Canterbury.
One Hampshire batsman retired hurt and one absent hurt.

Seven Fifties in an Innings

Northamptonshire (632) v Essex at Northampton:
    M. E. K. Hussey (140), A. S. Rollins (89), R. J. Warren (87), J. W. Cook (90), A. L. Penberthy (50), T. M. B. Bailey (64), R. S. G. Anderson (51).

Large Margin of Victory

Surrey (494 and 492-9 dec.) beat Leicestershire (361 and 142) by 483 runs at The Oval.

Victory after Following On

Warwickshire (293 and 350) beat Surrey (475 and 137) by 31 runs at The Oval.

Tied Match

West Indies A (370 and 266-7 dec.) v Somerset (183 and 453) at Taunton.

Most Extras in an Innings

b	l-b	w	n-b		
64	1	15	8	40	Gloucestershire (577-9 dec.) v Derbyshire at Bristol.
64	13	11	16	24	Worcestershire (523-6 dec.) v Oxford UCCE at Oxford.
64	23	24	9	8	Yorkshire (515-5 dec.) v Lancashire at Leeds.
62	17	10	21	14	Lancashire (425) v Sussex at Hove.
60	12	14	0	34	Gloucestershire (438) v Glamorgan at Cheltenham.
60	16	12	2	30	Leicestershire (523) v Warwickshire at Leicester.
60	0	13	12	30	(pen 5) Leicestershire (530) v Kent at Canterbury.

Career Aggregate Milestones

35,000 runs . . . . G. A. Hick.
25,000 runs . . . . R. A. Smith, A. J. Stewart.
20,000 runs . . . . P. Johnson.
15,000 runs . . . . D. Byas, J. Cox, P. A. de Silva, S. P. James.
10,000 runs . . . . A. D. Brown, P. A. J. DeFreitas, M. J. Di Venuto, A. Flower, V. V. S. Laxman, D. P. Ostler, M. P. Vaughan.
1,000 wickets . . . . . . D. E. Malcolm.
500 wickets . . . . J. Srinath.
500 dismissals . . . . . N. D. Burns.

FIRST-CLASS AVERAGES, 2002

BATTING

(Qualification: 8 completed innings)

† *Left-handed batsman.*

		M	I	NO	R	HS	100s	50s	Avge	Ct/St
1	R. Dravid (*Indians*)	7	9	1	773	217	3	3	96.62	14
2	†N. V. Knight (*Warwicks*)	10	19	3	1,520	255*	5	5	95.00	10
3	M. P. Vaughan (*Yorks & England*)	9	15	2	976	197	4	3	75.07	5
4	S. R. Tendulkar (*Indians*)	6	8	0	573	193	2	2	71.62	2
5	†M. E. Trescothick (*Som. & England*)	6	11	2	622	161	2	4	69.11	5
6	†M. E. K. Hussey (*Northants*)	13	23	2	1,442	310*	5	6	68.66	21
7	A. J. Hollioake (*Surrey*)	9	13	2	738	208	2	5	67.09	10
8	†D. S. Lehmann (*Yorks*)	10	18	1	1,136	216	3	7	66.82	5
9	†M. G. Bevan (*Leics*)	9	14	3	697	146	2	4	63.36	4
10	D. P. M. D. Jayawardene (*Sri Lankans*)	6	11	2	567	125*	3	1	63.00	3
11	†I. J. Ward (*Surrey*)	17	31	3	1,759	168*	7	7	62.82	10
12	K. P. Pietersen (*Notts*)	12	17	3	871	254*	4	0	62.21	12
13	†M. J. Di Venuto (*Derbys*)	15	28	3	1,538	230	4	9	61.52	29
14	R. C. Irani (*Essex*)	12	19	3	977	207*	3	3	61.06	0
15	M. R. Ramprakash (*Surrey*)	15	25	4	1,194	218	4	6	56.85	6
16	G. A. Hick (*Worcs*)	18	30	4	1,453	315*	6	5	55.88	30
17	M. P. Maynard (*Glam*)	13	20	1	1,058	151	3	6	55.68	14
18	†M. T. G. Elliott (*Yorks*)	5	10	1	487	127	1	4	54.11	7
19	J. P. Crawley (*Hants & England*)	15	25	4	1,130	272	2	7	53.80	8
20	A. J. Stewart (*Surrey & England*)	11	16	2	751	123	1	5	53.64	34/4
21	K. J. Barnett (*Glos*)	8	15	3	641	182*	1	3	53.41	1
22	P. D. Collingwood (*Durham*)	7	12	0	636	190	1	4	53.00	5
23	S. P. James (*Glam*)	14	22	1	1,111	249	4	3	52.90	7
24	S. G. Law (*Lancs*)	15	26	3	1,216	218	2	6	52.86	21
25	†E. C. Joyce (*Middx*)	18	27	3	1,267	129	4	6	52.79	17
26	†P. N. Weekes (*Middx*)	18	25	6	990	127*	4	5	52.10	23
27	M. A. Gough (*Durham*)	8	14	2	616	103	1	3	51.33	6
28	†J. O. Troughton (*Warwicks*)	14	24	3	1,067	131*	3	5	50.80	8
29	R. Clarke (*Surrey*)	10	16	2	711	153*	2	4	50.78	9
30	A. D. Brown (*Surrey*)	16	26	2	1,211	188	5	3	50.45	18
31	M. J. Powell (*Glam*)	16	26	3	1,152	135	3	7	50.08	7
32	†A. Flower (*Essex*)	16	29	6	1,151	172*	2	6	50.04	35/1
33	P. A. de Silva (*Sri Lankans*)	8	12	2	500	88	0	6	50.00	0
34	V. Sehwag (*Indians*)	8	13	0	640	142	3	1	49.23	13
35	C. M. Spearman (*Glos*)	17	34	4	1,444	180*	5	7	48.13	16
36	†A. J. Strauss (*Middx & MCC*)	17	27	2	1,202	141	3	5	48.08	16
37	†S. C. Ganguly (*Indians*)	7	11	1	477	128	1	4	47.70	3
38	D. L. Maddy (*Leics*)	16	29	4	1,187	156	2	8	47.48	22
39	M. S. Atapattu (*Sri Lankans*)	7	12	1	522	185	2	1	47.45	1
40	R. J. Blakey (*Yorks*)	16	29	7	1,041	103	1	8	47.31	29/1
41	O. A. Shah (*Middx & MCC*)	17	26	3	1,084	172*	3	6	47.13	5
42	†M. A. Butcher (*Surrey & England*)	13	21	1	936	123	3	5	46.80	8
43	†D. S. Smith (*West Indies A*)	6	10	0	465	181	1	2	46.50	4
44	†S. G. Koenig (*Middx*)	18	29	2	1,251	141*	4	7	46.33	6
45	D. C. Nash (*Middx*)	15	19	5	646	100	1	4	46.14	36/1
46	D. D. J. Robinson (*Essex*)	18	34	2	1,474	175	5	6	46.06	17
47	†H. P. Tillekeratne (*Sri Lankans*)	8	13	5	366	81	0	2	45.75	8
48	†U. Afzaal (*Notts & MCC*)	18	32	4	1,275	134	5	6	45.53	12
49	†R. C. Russell (*Glos*)	17	28	6	991	119*	3	5	45.04	39/2
50	C. J. Adams (*Sussex*)	10	19	0	848	217	3	3	44.63	2

		M	I	NO	R	HS	100s	50s	Avge	Ct/St
51	B. F. Smith (*Worcs*)	18	30	3	1,202	137	4	6	44.51	6
52	A. Habib (*Essex*)	15	25	3	964	123	2	8	43.81	12
53	D. P. Fulton (*Kent & MCC*)	17	33	2	1,358	177	4	8	43.80	33
54	D. J. J. Bravo (*West Indies A*)	6	11	3	350	77*	0	3	43.75	4
55	I. J. Harvey (*Glos*)	6	10	1	390	123	1	2	43.33	6
56	D. A. Leatherdale (*Worcs*)	14	23	4	823	154	2	4	43.31	6
57	D. P. Ostler (*Warwicks*)	14	25	1	1,039	225	2	5	43.29	24
58	†R. P. Arnold (*Sri Lankans*)	9	12	0	518	112	2	3	43.16	5
59	C. White (*Yorks & England*)	13	24	2	947	161	2	7	43.04	6
60	V. S. Solanki (*Worcs*)	16	26	4	944	153*	2	5	42.90	18
61	M. E. Cassar (*Northants*)	7	9	1	343	101*	1	2	42.87	4
62	C. W. G. Bassano (*Derbys*)	14	26	1	1,063	152	1	8	42.52	13
63	M. W. Goodwin (*Sussex*)	16	28	0	1,179	162	5	3	42.10	13
64	R. S. C. Martin-Jenkins (*Sussex*)	16	28	4	1,008	205*	1	5	42.00	1
65	†I. J. Sutcliffe (*Leics*)	16	29	3	1,088	125*	2	5	41.84	4
66	R. W. T. Key (*Kent, MCC & England*)	17	31	1	1,255	160	3	6	41.83	12
	V. V. S. Laxman (*Indians*)	8	13	1	502	85	0	3	41.83	5
68	A. S. Rollins (*Northants*)	6	12	1	460	107	1	2	41.81	6
69	J. E. R. Gallian (*Notts*)	16	29	3	1,087	171	4	6	41.80	16
70	S. D. Peters (*Worcs*)	10	16	0	667	146	2	3	41.68	6
71	†A. L. Penberthy (*Northants*)	16	25	3	909	130*	1	4	41.31	9
72	E. T. Smith (*Kent*)	17	32	2	1,239	154	2	8	41.30	4
73	J. W. M. Dalrymple (*Oxford UCCE, British Us & Middx*)	8	14	1	535	148	2	1	41.15	2
74	N. Hussain (*Essex & England*)	8	12	0	483	155	2	2	40.25	8
75	M. M. Patel (*Kent*)	16	20	6	561	82	0	5	40.07	9
76	S. J. Rhodes (*Worcs*)	15	22	6	636	124	1	2	39.75	37/4
77	A. Symonds (*Kent*)	12	24	2	858	118	2	4	39.00	16
78	P. J. Martin (*Lancs*)	14	16	5	422	117*	1	1	38.36	4
79	†I. D. Blackwell (*Somerset*)	14	23	0	879	154	3	3	38.21	4
80	R. R. Montgomerie (*Sussex*)	16	28	1	1,026	196	2	4	38.00	16
	T. R. Ambrose (*Sussex*)	13	22	1	798	149	2	4	38.00	9
82	†P. A. Nixon (*Kent*)	16	30	7	865	103	1	6	37.60	49/4
83	†G. P. Thorpe (*Surrey & England*)	8	14	0	526	143	2	1	37.57	6
84	B. M. Shafayat (*Notts*)	7	13	1	450	104	1	2	37.50	5
85	N. Shahid (*Surrey*)	13	20	1	712	150	2	3	37.47	24
86	G. D. Lloyd (*Lancs*)	7	13	1	449	80	0	5	37.41	4
87	M. Burns (*Somerset*)	16	30	2	1,047	99	0	9	37.39	14
88	A. Dale (*Glam*)	16	24	1	859	127*	1	6	37.34	7
89	V. J. Wells (*Leics*)	11	17	2	558	150	1	3	37.20	9
90	A. J. Swann (*Lancs*)	18	31	2	1,073	128	2	6	37.00	12
91	R. J. Warren (*Northants*)	6	11	1	369	150*	1	1	36.90	16
92	G. E. Welton (*Notts*)	16	28	2	954	115	2	6	36.69	16
93	M. G. N. Windows (*Glos*)	17	31	2	1,062	145	2	7	36.62	6
94	M. B. Loye (*Northants*)	13	22	1	768	139	4	1	36.57	7
95	A. Singh (*Worcs*)	18	32	0	1,167	187	2	6	36.46	11
96	R. D. B. Croft (*Glam*)	17	24	3	747	101*	1	5	35.57	4
97	†J. W. Cook (*Northants*)	15	24	3	746	90	0	4	35.52	4
98	B. J. Hodge (*Durham*)	4	8	0	284	73	0	2	35.50	3
99	J. N. Batty (*Surrey*)	13	23	2	742	151	2	3	35.33	41/5
100	J. P. Stephenson (*Essex*)	13	24	8	562	100*	1	2	35.12	7
101	M. A. Ealham (*Kent*)	14	24	7	594	83*	0	3	34.94	14
102	A. P. R. Gidman (*Glos*)	10	17	1	558	117	1	4	34.87	5
103	M. J. Wood (*Somerset*)	15	28	0	971	196	3	5	34.67	5
104	R. A. Smith (*Hants*)	15	25	1	832	104	2	3	34.66	6
105	C. M. W. Read (*Notts & MCC*)	18	28	5	797	127	1	4	34.65	66/2
106	A. P. Grayson (*Essex*)	7	9	0	309	105	1	1	34.33	7
107	G. P. Swann (*Northants*)	11	16	0	539	183	2	1	33.68	5
108	P. D. Bowler (*Somerset*)	14	25	2	766	94	0	7	33.30	22

		M	I	NO	R	HS	100s	50s	Avge	Ct/St
109	A. W. Laraman (*Middx*)	11	13	3	330	82*	0	1	33.00	3
110	†P. C. L. Holloway (*Somerset*)	7	13	0	428	88	0	3	32.92	4
111	†C. P. Schofield (*Lancs*)	7	9	1	262	91	0	2	32.75	4
112	†N. D. Burns (*Leics*)	16	24	2	720	101	1	5	32.72	61/2
113	D. I. Stevens (*Leics & MCC*)	17	29	3	850	125	1	6	32.69	16
114	W. I. Jefferson (*Durham UCCE, British Us & Essex*)	15	29	4	815	165*	2	3	32.60	17
115	A. McGrath (*Yorks*)	14	26	1	803	165	1	3	32.12	5
116	†D. J. Bicknell (*Notts*)	13	23	0	734	112	2	2	31.91	5
117	K. J. Innes (*Sussex*)	13	22	7	478	60*	0	2	31.86	3
118	P. A. Cottey (*Sussex*)	13	22	0	699	137	3	1	31.77	5
119	†N. C. Johnson (*Hants*)	17	29	2	857	117	1	6	31.74	27
120	J. Cox (*Somerset*)	13	25	2	724	176	1	3	31.47	6
121	M. J. Prior (*Sussex*)	16	27	3	741	102*	1	5	30.87	39/2
122	T. Frost (*Warwicks*)	7	11	1	308	103	1	1	30.80	6/2
123	A. I. Gait (*Derbys*)	17	33	1	983	175	1	8	30.71	14
124	A. B. Agarkar (*Indians*)	7	9	1	244	109*	1	0	30.50	0
125	A. J. Bichel (*Worcs*)	9	11	2	274	78*	0	3	30.44	7
126	D. G. Cork (*Derbys & England*)	11	16	0	487	80	0	5	30.43	12
127	P. Johnson (*Notts*)	14	25	3	662	96	0	5	30.09	7
128	M. J. Powell (*Warwicks*)	17	31	2	872	103	1	6	30.06	13
129	R. J. Turner (*Somerset*)	16	27	4	691	83*	0	4	30.04	50/1
130	J. I. D. Kerr (*Derbys*)	7	12	2	299	68	0	3	29.90	2
131	†D. Byas (*Lancs*)	15	25	2	684	101	1	4	29.73	15
132	M. S. Kasprowicz (*Glam*)	12	19	7	352	72*	0	1	29.33	7
133	†N. Boje (*Notts*)	9	16	2	409	84	0	2	29.21	10
134	S. B. Bangar (*Indians*)	7	11	1	291	74	0	3	29.10	2
135	{ P. A. J. DeFreitas (*Leics*)	16	23	2	609	114	1	3	29.00	10
	T. H. C. Hancock (*Glos*)	9	17	3	406	112	1	2	29.00	1
137	†M. H. Yardy (*Sussex*)	10	17	0	492	93	0	2	28.94	11
138	†B. L. Hutton (*Middx*)	11	19	1	518	116	1	4	28.77	19
139	M. P. Bicknell (*Surrey*)	10	14	5	258	35*	0	0	28.66	6
140	A. Flintoff (*Lancs & England*)	7	10	0	284	137	1	1	28.40	8
141	D. R. Law (*Durham*)	6	10	1	253	72*	0	2	28.11	2
142	†T. J. Phillips (*Durham UCCE & Essex*)	8	13	3	281	75	0	1	28.10	6
143	†D. L. Hemp (*Glam*)	12	20	2	505	108	1	2	28.05	6
144	D. R. Brown (*Warwicks*)	16	28	4	671	79*	0	3	27.95	9
145	M. A. Wagh (*Warwicks*)	10	18	0	503	109	1	2	27.94	3
146	†G. J. Pratt (*Durham*)	16	27	0	746	78	0	4	27.62	12
147	G. M. Fellows (*Yorks*)	10	18	0	493	109	1	1	27.38	9
148	{ R. S. Morton (*West Indies A*)	5	8	0	218	79	0	2	27.25	4
	Harbhajan Singh (*Indians*)	8	10	2	218	54	0	1	27.25	1
150	M. J. Chilton (*Lancs*)	17	29	1	761	107	1	4	27.17	15
151	†S. T. Jayasuriya (*Sri Lankans*)	8	12	0	322	57	0	3	26.83	4
152	†M. J. Lumb (*Yorks*)	16	30	1	777	124	1	4	26.79	8
153	†K. C. Sangakkara (*Sri Lankans*)	9	15	2	345	113	1	1	26.53	12/1
154	{ †M. A. Wallace (*Glam*)	17	25	4	553	106*	1	2	26.33	58/3
	M. J. G. Davis (*Sussex*)	15	22	4	474	111	1	2	26.33	7
	R. M. S. Weston (*Middx*)	9	11	2	237	72	0	2	26.33	4
157	S. D. Udal (*Hants*)	17	26	6	516	88	0	1	25.80	9
158	G. Welch (*Derbys*)	14	23	5	460	64	0	3	25.55	8
159	Saqlain Mushtaq (*Surrey*)	10	13	2	278	60	0	2	25.27	4
160	M. W. Alleyne (*Glos*)	14	25	3	555	142*	1	2	25.22	12
161	†P. J. Franks (*Notts*)	10	14	2	301	67	0	3	25.08	2
162	D. J. Sales (*Northants*)	14	22	0	551	179	1	3	25.04	11
163	{ S. M. Pollock (*Warwicks*)	10	18	1	425	66	0	4	25.00	13
	J. Hughes (*Glam*)	7	10	1	225	74	0	1	25.00	2
165	†I. D. Fisher (*Glos*)	16	26	3	568	103*	1	4	24.69	8
166	C. G. Taylor (*Glos*)	15	29	2	664	126	1	2	24.59	15

	M	I	NO	R	HS	100s	50s	Avge	Ct/St
167 G. J. Muchall (*Durham*)	15	25	0	613	127	1	3	24.52	14
168 †I. R. Bell (*Warwicks*)	16	28	1	658	77	0	3	24.37	6
169 W. S. Kendall (*Hants*)	17	31	0	705	88	0	4	24.31	12
170 †W. P. C. Weston (*Worcs*)	8	15	2	315	82	0	3	24.23	7
171 K. A. Parsons (*Somerset*)	15	26	2	581	68	0	4	24.20	16
172 N. Peng (*Durham*)	12	21	0	508	108	1	2	24.19	4
173 Wasim Jaffer (*Indians*)	7	13	1	290	53	0	2	24.16	9
174 †S. A. Selwood (*Derbys*)	10	19	0	457	99	0	2	24.05	1
175 A. D. Mascarenhas (*Hants*)	16	26	2	574	94	0	4	23.91	8
176 N. Pothas (*Hants*)	16	26	1	597	99	0	5	23.88	30/4
177 J. J. B. Lewis (*Durham*)	11	18	1	402	102	1	2	23.64	2
178 M. M. Betts (*Warwicks*)	9	16	5	259	56	0	1	23.54	2
179 A. P. Cowan (*Essex*)	10	15	2	305	60*	0	2	23.46	6
180 †V. J. Craven (*Yorks*)	11	21	2	439	72	0	3	23.10	8
181 T. R. Ward (*Leics*)	14	24	0	554	89	0	4	23.08	7
182 †J. D. Francis (*Hants & British Univs*)	10	17	0	391	82	0	3	23.00	6
183 N. C. Phillips (*Durham*)	10	16	6	226	58*	0	1	22.60	4
184 †N. H. Fairbrother (*Lancs*)	12	19	1	406	101	1	0	22.55	10
A. A. Noffke (*Middx*)	8	10	1	203	76	0	1	22.55	3
186 †S. D. Stubbings (*Derbys*)	11	20	1	428	128	1	1	22.52	5
187 C. T. Tremlett (*Hants*)	11	14	6	180	40*	0	0	22.50	4
188 N. M. K. Smith (*Warwicks*)	8	15	0	337	96	0	2	22.46	7
189 G. Chapple (*Lancs*)	16	23	1	493	65	0	4	22.40	6
190 R. L. Johnson (*Somerset*)	9	17	4	290	61	0	1	22.30	2
191 J. S. Laney (*Leics*)	7	13	0	289	89	0	1	22.23	7
192 L. D. Sutton (*Derbys*)	10	19	1	400	80	0	3	22.22	30/1
193 R. K. J. Dawson (*Yorks & MCC*)	15	24	1	511	87	0	2	22.21	2
194 A. F. Giles (*Warwicks & England*)	9	12	0	264	68	0	1	22.00	3
195 T. M. B. Bailey (*Northants*)	17	25	4	457	68	0	4	21.76	43/6
196 G. J. Batty (*Worcs*)	18	27	4	491	74	0	3	21.34	9
197 †M. P. Dowman (*Derbys*)	8	14	0	298	71	0	1	21.28	6
198 †J. M. Dakin (*Essex*)	14	20	3	359	57	0	1	21.11	3
199 G. R. Napier (*Essex*)	9	13	2	230	54*	0	1	20.90	6
200 †A. M. Thorpe (*Durham*)	7	13	0	271	95	0	2	20.84	5
201 D. R. Hewson (*Derbys*)	11	20	1	393	102*	1	1	20.68	7
202 †A. Pratt (*Durham*)	17	30	3	556	93	0	3	20.59	42/3
203 †K. J. Dean (*Derbys & MCC*)	17	26	9	347	54*	0	2	20.41	6
204 A. Ratra (*Indians*)	7	11	2	183	101*	1	0	20.33	14/2
205 W. K. Hegg (*Lancs*)	16	23	2	416	62	0	1	19.80	44/2
206 †I. J. Thomas (*Glam*)	9	15	1	273	76	0	2	19.50	2
G. W. White (*Hants*)	8	14	2	234	36	0	0	19.50	6
208 †M. J. Walker (*Kent*)	12	23	3	382	46	0	0	19.10	3
209 †J. J. Sayers (*Oxford UCCE*)	4	8	0	152	55	0	1	19.00	1
210 I. D. K. Salisbury (*Surrey*)	14	20	2	340	59	0	1	18.88	11
211 C. R. Taylor (*Yorks*)	5	9	1	150	52*	0	2	18.75	4
212 G. J. Smith (*Notts*)	15	20	7	243	39*	0	0	18.69	4
213 I. D. Hunter (*Durham*)	8	12	1	204	65	0	1	18.54	2
214 D. A. Kenway (*Hants*)	8	15	2	238	54	0	1	18.30	15
215 †S. P. Jones (*Glam, MCC & England*)	13	18	6	218	44	0	0	18.16	5
216 K. P. Dutch (*Somerset*)	16	27	3	432	74	0	2	18.00	20
J. R. C. Hamblin (*Hants*)	5	9	0	162	50	0	1	18.00	4
218 †M. P. L. Bulbeck (*Somerset*)	16	27	7	359	53*	0	1	17.95	3
219 J. D. Middlebrook (*Essex*)	18	28	4	417	67	0	1	17.37	7
220 J. Wood (*Lancs*)	8	11	0	185	64	0	1	16.81	2
221 S. J. Cook (*Middx*)	15	18	2	267	43*	0	0	16.68	4
222 C. E. W. Silverwood (*Yorks*)	12	19	2	283	44*	0	0	16.64	3
223 R. S. G. Anderson (*Northants*)	5	10	0	166	51	0	1	16.60	0
224 A. Richardson (*Warwicks*)	10	12	4	132	91	0	1	16.50	5
225 K. J. Piper (*Warwicks*)	8	12	2	163	64*	0	1	16.30	14/1
226 †D. D. Cherry (*Glam*)	5	8	0	129	47	0	0	16.12	4

		M	I	NO	R	HS	100s	50s	Avge	Ct/St
227 {	M. J. Symington (*Durham*)	10	16	2	224	42	0	0	16.00	6
	J. Ormond (*Surrey*)	15	17	4	208	43*	0	0	16.00	6
229	Kabir Ali (*Worcs*)	17	21	4	271	51*	0	1	15.94	3
230	A. J. Tudor (*Surrey & England*)	10	14	0	222	61	0	1	15.85	2
231	†G. Keedy (*Lancs*)	16	22	8	219	57	0	1	15.64	6
232	A. Khan (*Kent*)	16	19	5	213	58	0	1	15.21	5
233	Mohammad Ali (*Derbys*)	15	24	2	333	53	0	1	15.13	5
234	J. N. Snape (*Glos*)	5	8	0	117	28	0	0	14.62	2
235	J. Lewis (*Glos*)	16	25	6	273	57	0	1	14.36	6
236	C. D. Crowe (*Leics*)	12	16	4	172	34	0	0	14.33	4
237	G. D. Bridge (*Durham*)	10	15	2	184	49	0	0	14.15	4
238	R. J. Cunliffe (*Leics*)	5	10	1	121	30	0	0	13.44	1
239	†S. D. Thomas (*Glam*)	16	22	1	274	47	0	0	13.04	4
240	†T. Lungley (*Derbys*)	7	13	0	168	44	0	0	12.92	4
241	R. J. Kirtley (*Sussex & MCC*)	11	15	3	146	36*	0	0	12.16	4
242	†K. W. Hogg (*Lancs*)	7	9	0	109	50	0	1	12.11	1
243	M. J. Wood (*Yorks*)	9	17	0	201	43	0	0	11.82	12
244	A. J. Harris (*Notts*)	14	20	7	151	41*	0	0	11.61	6
245	D. M. Cousins (*Northants*)	11	16	7	103	23*	0	0	11.44	4
246	K. M. Krikken (*Derbys*)	9	16	1	169	48	0	0	11.26	26
247	A. M. Davies (*Durham*)	14	24	7	184	33	0	0	10.82	3
248	N. Killeen (*Durham*)	15	22	5	178	27*	0	0	10.47	5
249	D. A. Cosker (*Glam*)	10	13	2	115	37	0	0	10.45	4
250	J. M. M. Averis (*Glos*)	5	8	0	83	43	0	0	10.37	3
251	J. B. Hockley (*Kent*)	5	9	1	82	46	0	0	10.25	1
252	S. P. Kirby (*Yorks*)	10	17	3	141	57	0	1	10.07	0
253	D. E. Malcolm (*Leics*)	16	22	8	138	44	0	0	9.85	4
254	A. Sheriyar (*Worcs*)	18	20	9	107	18	0	0	9.72	1
255	†R. J. Sidebottom (*Yorks*)	13	21	7	135	28	0	0	9.64	4
256	R. J. Logan (*Notts*)	13	19	4	143	32	0	0	9.53	5
257	C. G. Greenidge (*Northants*)	15	19	2	160	46	0	0	9.41	7
258	†J. D. Lewry (*Sussex*)	10	15	5	91	21*	0	0	9.10	5
259	S. R. G. Francis (*Somerset*)	10	16	8	67	17	0	0	8.37	0
260	J. B. Grant (*Essex*)	11	12	4	64	30	0	0	8.00	2
261	†L. J. Wharton (*Derbys*)	14	23	12	83	16	0	0	7.54	7
262	A. R. Caddick (*Somerset & England*)	14	14	2	89	16	0	0	7.41	2
263	†J. M. Anderson (*Lancs*)	13	16	8	58	16	0	0	7.25	2
264	S. J. Harmison (*Durham & England*)	11	18	3	88	19*	0	0	5.86	4
265	†B. V. Taylor (*Sussex*)	10	14	2	70	18*	0	0	5.83	1
	C. B. Keegan (*Middx*)	9	10	0	58	24	0	0	5.80	3
267	M. J. Saggers (*Kent*)	16	19	6	73	16*	0	0	5.61	6
268	A. D. Mullally (*Hants*)	13	16	5	54	23	0	0	4.90	1

BOWLING

(Qualification: 10 wickets)

		Style	O	M	R	W	BB	5W/i	Avge
1	Azhar Mahmood (*Surrey*)	RFM	109.2	27	345	20	8-61	1	17.25
2	C. P. Schofield (*Lancs*)	LBG	122.2	27	331	18	4-35	0	18.38
3	J. Srinath (*Leics*)	RFM	179.2	29	561	30	5-25	2	18.70
4	D. G. Cork (*Derbys & England*)	RFM	403.4	101	1,210	64	6-51	5	18.90
5	I. J. Harvey (*Glos*)	RM	152.2	29	533	28	6-68	3	19.03
6	R. C. Irani (*Essex*)	RM	227.5	72	591	29	6-71	1	20.37
7	P. J. Martin (*Lancs*)	RFM	452	143	1,126	53	5-54	1	21.24
8	R. L. Johnson (*Somerset*)	RFM	307.1	66	914	43	7-43	2	21.25
9	M. J. Saggers (*Kent*)	RFM	571	111	1,786	83	6-39	2	21.51
10	A. J. Harris (*Notts*)	RFM	413.4	93	1,475	67	7-54	3	22.01
11	V. J. Wells (*Leics*)	RM	155	41	421	19	5-39	1	22.15

		Style	O	M	R	W	BB	5W/i	Avge
12	J. M. Anderson (*Lancs*)	RFM	326.4	61	1,114	50	6-23	3	22.28
13	M. P. Dowman (*Derbys*)	RM	72	24	223	10	4-28	0	22.30
14	J. P. Stephenson (*Essex*)	RM	295.4	59	1,082	48	7-44	1	22.54
15	R. J. Kirtley (*Sussex & MCC*)	RFM	379	94	1,199	53	6-107	4	22.62
16	S. C. G. MacGill (*Notts*)	LBG	227.4	37	930	40	8-111	4	23.25
17	K. J. Dean (*Derbys & MCC*)	LFM	590	148	1,951	83	7-42	3	23.50
18	D. L. Maddy (*Leics*)	RM	334.3	78	1,025	43	5-37	2	23.83
19	T. Lungley (*Derbys*)	RM	117.4	32	416	17	3-43	0	24.47
20	M. I. Black (*West Indies A*)	RFM	113.1	32	344	14	4-32	0	24.57
21	N. Boje (*Notts*)	SLA	238	58	671	27	6-128	2	24.85
22	T. J. Murtagh (*British Univs & Surrey*)	RFM	122.1	23	424	17	5-39	1	24.94
23	A. Richardson (*Warwicks*)	RFM	300.2	64	951	38	8-46	2	25.02
24	A. J. Bichel (*Worcs*)	RFM	297	77	902	36	9-93	1	25.05
25	A. A. Noffke (*Middx*)	RFM	305.1	57	1,128	45	8-24	3	25.06
26	Kabir Ali (*Worcs*)	RFM	547.1	129	1,781	71	7-43	5	25.08
27	A. D. Mullally (*Hants*)	LFM	463.2	145	1,156	46	6-56	1	25.13
28	P. J. Franks (*Notts*)	RFM	234.5	53	813	32	5-51	1	25.40
29	P. D. R. L. Perera (*Sri Lankans*)	LFM	115	13	433	17	4-66	0	25.47
30	M. N. Malik (*Notts*)	RFM	146.4	29	562	22	5-67	1	25.54
31	G. Welch (*Derbys*)	RM	486.1	157	1,409	55	6-60	2	25.61
32	Saqlain Mushtaq (*Surrey*)	OB	488.4	112	1,359	53	6-121	3	25.64
33	P. D. Collingwood (*Durham*)	RM	96.4	24	258	10	4-31	0	25.80
34	A. M. Davies (*Durham*)	RM	357.5	106	942	36	5-61	1	26.16
35	S. M. Pollock (*Warwicks*)	RFM	301.3	101	733	28	4-37	0	26.17
36	G. J. Smith (*Notts*)	LFM	400.1	85	1,275	48	8-53	1	26.56
37	M. S. Kasprowicz (*Glam*)	RFM	418.4	78	1,413	53	6-47	4	26.66
38	A. J. Tudor (*Surrey & England*)	RFM	322	74	1,124	42	5-66	1	26.76
39	J. J. C. Lawson (*West Indies A*)	RFM	123.4	19	484	18	6-76	1	26.88
40	S. J. Cook (*Middx*)	RFM	367.2	71	1,305	48	8-63	2	27.18
41	A. P. Cowan (*Essex*)	RFM	276.1	70	843	31	5-68	1	27.19
42	A. R. Caddick (*Somerset & England*)	RFM	423.3	87	1,313	48	6-84	4	27.35
43	S. E. Bond (*Durham*)	RF	95.4	23	330	12	5-64	1	27.50
44	S. P. Jones (*Glam, MCC & England*)	RF	323.5	53	1,101	40	6-45	2	27.52
45	R. C. Driver (*Lancs*)	RM	105	28	331	12	5-70	1	27.58
46	A. Kumble (*Indians*)	LBG	212	51	607	22	4-58	0	27.59
47	Harbhajan Singh (*Indians*)	OB	243.2	43	773	28	7-83	2	27.60
48	A. McGrath (*Yorks*)	OB	174.3	38	498	18	4-49	0	27.66
49	L. J. Wharton (*Derbys*)	SLA	208.5	45	695	25	6-62	2	27.80
50	M. S. Mason (*Worcs*)	RFM	224.4	55	613	22	5-50	1	27.86
51	A. P. Davies (*Glam*)	RM	116.2	14	420	15	5-79	1	28.00
52	R. D. King (*West Indies A*)	RFM	151	31	451	16	4-48	0	28.18
53	S. B. Bangar (*Indians*)	RM	132.5	25	395	14	4-40	0	28.21
54	G. P. Swann (*Northants*)	OB	270.5	60	884	31	6-126	1	28.51
55	G. G. Wagg (*Warwicks*)	LM	82.5	13	343	12	4-43	0	28.58
56	M. W. H. Inness (*Northants*)	LFM	116.4	25	429	15	7-90	1	28.60
57	K. J. Innes (*Sussex*)	RM	268.3	65	834	29	4-41	0	28.75
58	A. Sheriyar (*Worcs*)	RFM	616.2	160	1,905	66	6-71	5	28.86
59	M. E. Cassar (*Northants*)	RFM	113.3	18	464	16	6-34	1	29.00
60	R. J. Sidebottom (*Yorks*)	LFM	380.5	85	1,190	41	5-60	1	29.02
61	Abdul Razzaq (*Middx*)	RFM	206.3	25	757	26	7-133	2	29.11
62	C. T. Tremlett (*Hants*)	RFM	336	83	1,061	36	5-57	2	29.47
63	G. Chapple (*Lancs*)	RFM	539.3	128	1,594	54	6-30	3	29.51
64	A. M. Smith (*Glos*)	LFM	270	55	916	31	5-69	1	29.54
65	D. B. Powell (*West Indies A*)	RFM	81	19	303	10	3-55	0	30.30
66	S. J. Harmison (*Durham & England*)	RF	324.2	75	1,001	33	5-65	1	30.33
67	D. E. Malcolm (*Leics*)	RF	477.5	79	1,826	60	7-76	4	30.43
68	J. M. Dakin (*Leics*)	RM	360.2	77	1,233	40	4-17	0	30.82
69	A. D. Mascarenhas (*Hants*)	RFM	420.5	144	1,141	37	5-87	1	30.83
70	P. C. R. Tufnell (*Middx*)	SLA	514.5	104	1,390	45	8-66	4	30.88
71	G. J. Batty (*Worcs*)	OB	613.1	162	1,733	56	6-71	3	30.94

	Style	O	M	R	W	BB	5W/i	Avge
72 P. A. J. DeFreitas (*Leics*)	RM	566.4	150	1,594	51	6-101	2	31.25
73 M. P. Bicknell (*Surrey*)	RFM	326	78	1,067	34	6-42	2	31.38
74 S. D. Thomas (*Glam.*)	RFM	467.1	66	1,637	52	7-33	3	31.48
75 N. Killeen (*Durham*)	RFM	391.1	108	1,165	37	4-26	0	31.48
76 C. G. Greenidge (*Northants*)	RFM	431	67	1,681	53	6-40	3	31.71
77 A. Khan (*Kent*)	RFM	485	75	2,004	63	6-52	4	31.80
78 G. R. Napier (*Essex*)	RM	172	33	639	20	3-47	0	31.95
79 N. C. Phillips (*Durham*)	OB	210	47	671	21	4-103	0	31.95
80 I. D. K. Salisbury (*Surrey*)	LBG	341.3	50	1,192	37	4-59	0	32.21
81 B. V. Taylor (*Sussex*)	RFM	318.5	73	1,041	32	5-90	1	32.53
82 M. S. Panesar (*British Univs & Northants*)	SLA	190.5	55	554	17	4-42	0	32.58
83 K. W. Hogg (*Lancs*)	RFM	175	41	621	19	5-48	1	32.68
84 C. E. W. Silverwood (*Yorks*)	RF	306.1	68	985	30	4-28	0	32.83
85 J. B. Grant (*Essex*)	RFM	267.5	50	1,086	33	5-38	1	32.90
86 D. R. Brown (*Warwicks.*)	RFM	493.4	75	1,716	52	7-110	2	33.00
87 S. D. Udal (*Hants*)	OB	627.1	146	1,858	56	5-56	4	33.17
88 J. M. M. Averis (*Glos*)	RM	128	33	432	13	5-51	1	33.23
89 D. A. Leatherdale (*Worcs*)	RM	140.3	22	535	16	4-23	0	33.43
90 M. P. L. Bulbeck (*Somerset*)	LFM	534	93	1,940	58	6-93	1	33.44
91 E. S. H. Giddins (*Surrey*)	RFM	232.5	49	736	22	4-113	0	33.45
92 M. M. Patel (*Kent*)	SLA	525.3	152	1,206	36	5-56	1	33.50
93 R. O. Hinds (*West Indies A*)	SLA	105.1	18	338	10	3-54	0	33.80
94 S. R. G. Francis (*Somerset*)	RFM	222.3	26	947	28	5-73	1	33.82
95 A. F. Giles (*Warwicks & England*)	SLA	419.1	67	1,222	36	7-142	3	33.94
96 R. J. Logan (*Notts*)	RFM	319.3	71	1,191	35	4-64	0	34.02
97 J. A. Spires (*Warwicks*)	SLA	171.4	25	613	18	5-165	1	34.05
98 M. A. Ealham (*Kent*)	RM	351	107	954	28	3-22	0	34.07
99 A. W. Laraman (*Middx*)	RFM	262.4	47	920	27	4-55	0	34.07
100 S. P. Kirby (*Yorks*)	RFM	331.1	68	1,262	37	5-129	1	34.10
101 N. M. K. Smith (*Warwicks*)	OB	126	27	411	12	5-42	1	34.25
102 R. J. Sillence (*Glos*)	RFM	100	11	449	13	5-63	1	34.53
103 M. J. Symington (*Durham*)	RM	147	29	590	17	4-27	0	34.70
104 M. J. Hoggard (*Yorks & England*)	RFM	364	71	1,250	36	5-92	1	34.72
105 J. Ormond (*Surrey*)	RFM	485.1	87	1,780	51	5-62	2	34.90
106 J. Wood (*Lancs*)	RFM	180.5	34	631	18	4-17	0	35.05
107 J. C. Tredwell (*Kent*)	OB	124.2	29	358	10	4-103	0	35.80
108 R. S. C. Martin-Jenkins (*Sussex*)	RFM	470.2	100	1,477	41	7-51	2	36.02
109 G. D. Bridge (*Durham*)	SLA	248.5	61	761	21	4-50	0	36.23
110 Mohammad Ali (*Derbys*)	LFM	405	42	1,708	47	3-48	0	36.34
111 N. C. Johnson (*Hants*)	RFM	242.2	52	814	22	3-22	0	37.00
112 C. D. Crowe (*Leics*)	OB	193.2	51	593	16	4-63	0	37.06
113 J. D. Lewry (*Sussex*)	LFM	304.4	45	1,227	33	5-88	1	37.18
114 D. D. Masters (*Kent*)	RFM	243.1	46	864	23	4-36	0	37.56
115 I. D. Blackwell (*Somerset*)	SLA	312.5	83	830	22	5-49	1	37.72
116 J. Lewis (*Glos*)	RFM	536.1	137	1,662	44	6-54	2	37.77
117 M. C. J. Ball (*Glos*)	OB	287	66	876	23	6-54	1	38.08
118 M. J. G. Davis (*Sussex*)	OB	347.2	71	1,081	28	6-97	1	38.60
119 I. D. Hunter (*Durham*)	RFM	206	42	775	20	3-44	0	38.75
120 R. K. J. Dawson (*Yorks & MCC*)	OB	488.5	104	1,551	40	5-42	2	38.77
121 K. A. Parsons (*Somerset*)	RM	216.3	30	830	21	3-44	0	39.52
122 G. Keedy (*Lancs*)	SLA	437.4	102	1,313	33	5-122	1	39.78
123 M. C. Ilott (*Essex*)	LFM	193.5	45	639	16	4-67	0	39.93
124 M. A. Wagh (*Warwicks*)	OB	203	43	604	15	5-137	1	40.26
125 M. Burns (*Somerset*)	RM	101.4	14	444	11	3-54	0	40.36
126 J. F. Brown (*Northants*)	OB	352.5	76	1,138	28	4-88	0	40.64
127 J. I. D. Kerr (*Derbys*)	RFM	147.2	29	652	16	4-32	0	40.75
128 R. Clarke (*Surrey*)	RFM	94.3	15	451	11	3-41	0	41.00
129 B. W. Gannon (*Glos*)	RFM	162	36	626	15	3-41	0	41.73
130 D. N. T. Zoysa (*Sri Lankans*)	LFM	110.2	15	421	10	3-93	0	42.10

		Style	O	M	R	W	BB	5W/i	Avge
131	C. White (*Yorks & England*)	RFM	193.5	33	634	15	4-49	0	42.26
132	R. D. B. Croft (*Glam*)	OB	619	138	1,701	40	5-71	1	42.52
133	J. E. Bishop (*Durham UCCE & Essex*)	LFM	120	17	470	11	3-59	0	42.72
134	A. Nehra (*Indians*)	LFM	114	14	473	11	4-85	0	43.00
135	Zaheer Khan (*Indians*)	LFM	147	32	483	11	3-90	0	43.90
136	A. P. R. Gidman (*Glos*)	RM	99	16	442	10	3-33	0	44.20
137	P. S. Jones (*Somerset*)	RFM	239.2	43	845	19	6-110	1	44.47
138	C. B. Keegan (*Middx*)	RFM	211.5	32	855	19	4-47	0	45.00
139	J. D. Middlebrook (*Essex*)	OB	555.2	121	1,736	38	4-38	0	45.68
140	A. B. Agarkar (*Indians*)	RFM	162.3	32	640	14	4-55	0	45.71
141	A. Symonds (*Kent*)	RM/OB	187.2	34	602	13	6-105	1	46.30
142	D. M. Cousins (*Northants*)	RFM	311.2	67	1,024	22	4-75	0	46.54
143	T. J. Phillips (*Durham UCCE & Essex*)	SLA	209.5	32	844	18	4-102	0	46.88
144	N. M. Carter (*Warwicks*)	LFM	228.1	35	957	20	4-46	0	47.85
145	A. L. Penberthy (*Northants*)	RM	292	76	833	17	3-21	0	49.00
146	M. J. A. Whiley (*Leics*)	LFM	175.4	28	803	16	3-60	0	50.18
147	D. A. Cosker (*Glam*)	SLA	317.5	60	1,012	20	4-135	0	50.60
148	M. M. Betts (*Warwicks*)	RFM	248.4	34	1,023	20	3-75	0	51.15
149	M. W. Alleyne (*Glos*)	RM	266	59	876	17	3-76	0	51.52
150	T. C. B. Fernando (*Sri Lankans*) . . .	RFM	113.5	14	524	10	4-72	0	52.40
151	I. D. Fisher (*Glos*)	SLA	514	103	1,725	32	5-87	1	53.90
152	A. Flintoff (*England & Lancs*)	RFM	251	53	768	14	2-22	0	54.85
153	K. P. Dutch (*Somerset*)	OB	268.3	59	852	15	3-104	0	56.80
154	J. A. R. Blain (*Northants*)	RFM	192.4	21	909	16	4-144	0	56.81
155	P. N. Weekes (*Middx*)	OB	397	61	1,198	21	3-27	0	57.04
156	J. A. Tomlinson (*British Univs & Hants*)	LM	168.3	14	748	12	2-55	0	62.33
157	S. J. Marshall (*Cambridge UCCE*) . .	LB	215.2	42	657	10	6-128	1	65.70

BOWLING STYLES

LB	Leg-breaks (1)	**RF**	Right-arm fast (5)
LBG	Leg-breaks and googlies (4)	**RFM**	Right-arm fast medium (67)
LFM	Left-arm fast medium (18)	**RM**	Right-arm medium (27)
LM	Left-arm medium (2)	**SLA**	Slow left-arm (14)
OB	Off-breaks (20)		

Note: The total comes to 158, because A. Symonds has two styles of bowling.

INDIVIDUAL SCORES OF 100 AND OVER

There were 301 three-figure innings in 177 first-class matches in 2002, 13 fewer than in 2001 when 168 first-class matches were played. Of these, 22 were double-hundreds, compared with 19 in 2001. The list includes 240 hundreds hit in the County Championship, compared with 264 in 2001.

* Signifies not out.

I. J. Ward (7)
106   Surrey v Lancs, Manchester
168* Surrey v Kent, Canterbury
124* Surrey v Yorks, Guildford
114   Surrey v Warwicks, Birmingham
112 }
156 } Surrey v Hants, Southampton
118   Surrey v Leics, The Oval

U. Afzaal (5)
111* MCC v Sri Lankans, Chesterfield
103   Notts v Durham, Chester-le-Street
104* Notts v Glam, Colwyn Bay
103   Notts v Durham, Nottingham
134   Notts v Essex, Chelmsford

A. D. Brown (5)
177   Surrey v Sussex, The Oval
188   Surrey v Kent, The Oval
104   Surrey v Leics, Leicester
135   Surrey v Hants, The Oval
107   Surrey v Leics, The Oval

M. W. Goodwin (5)
162   Sussex v Somerset, Hove
135   Sussex v Kent, Hove
100   Sussex v Surrey, Hove
119   Sussex v Hants, Hove
111   Sussex v Warwicks, Hove

M. E. K. Hussey (5)
170   Northants v Worcs, Northampton
150   Northants v Derbys, Derby
140   Northants v Essex, Northampton
174   Northants v Worcs, Worcester
310* Northants v Glos, Bristol

N. V. Knight (5)
130   Warwicks v Leics, Leicester
255* Warwicks v Hants, Birmingham
245* Warwicks v Sussex, Birmingham
109   Warwicks v Yorks, Leeds
133   Warwicks v Surrey, Birmingham

D. D. J. Robinson (5)
100* Essex v Cambridge UCCE, Cambridge
131   Essex v Glos, Chelmsford
175   Essex v Glos, Gloucester
119   Essex v Glam, Chelmsford
115   Essex v Derbys, Derby

C. M. Spearman (5)
111   Glos v Worcs, Worcester
118   Glos v Notts, Bristol
180* Glos v Glam, Cheltenham
107   Glos v Northants, Northampton
114* Glos v Durham, Bristol

M. J. Di Venuto (4)
230   Derbys v Northants, Derby
192* }
113 } Derbys v Middx, Lord's
175* Derbys v Glos, Bristol

D. P. Fulton (4)
116   Kent v Sri Lankans, Canterbury
116   Kent v Lancs, Liverpool
101   Kent v Warwicks, Maidstone
177   Kent v Lancs, Canterbury

J. E. R. Gallian (4)
111* Notts v Northants, Nottingham
100   Notts v Northants, Northampton
111* Notts v Derbys, Derby
171   Notts v Glam, Colwyn Bay

G. A. Hick (4)
164   Worcs v Oxford UCCE, Oxford
315* Worcs v Durham, Worcester
126   Worcs v Notts, Kidderminster
101   Worcs v Middx, Worcester

S. P. James (4)
121   Glam v Durham, Cardiff
118   Glam v Middx, Cardiff
249   Glam v Essex, Chelmsford
184   Glam v Notts, Colwyn Bay

E. C. Joyce (4)
119   Middx v Notts, Lord's
129   Middx v Glam, Cardiff
129   Middx v Derbys, Lord's
125   Middx v Worcs, Worcester

S. G. Koenig (4)
141* Middx v Cambridge UCCE, Cambridge
100   Middx v Durham, Chester-le-Street
101   Middx v Northants, Northampton
113   Middx v Essex, Southgate

M. B. Loye (4)
139 Northants v Worcs, Northampton
109 Northants v Derbys, Derby
105 }
104* } Northants v Notts, Northampton

K. P. Pietersen (4)
133 Notts v Durham UCCE, Nottingham
103* Notts v Derbys, Derby
254* Notts v Middx, Nottingham
116 Notts v Glos, Nottingham

M. R. Ramprakash (4)
119* Surrey v Lancs, The Oval
121 Surrey v Cambridge UCCE, Cambridge
218 Surrey v Somerset, Taunton
210* Surrey v Warwicks, The Oval

B. F. Smith (4)
137 Worcs v Oxford UCCE, Oxford
129 Worcs v Glos, Worcester
124 Worcs v Middx, Lord's
108 Worcs v Northants, Worcester

M. P. Vaughan (4)
115 England v Sri Lanka, Lord's
100 England v India, Lord's
197 England v India, Nottingham
195 England v India, The Oval

P. N. Weekes (4)
100* Middx v Cambridge UCCE, Cambridge
107 Middx v Northants, Northampton
127* Middx v Worcs, Lord's
102 Middx v Glos, Cheltenham

C. J. Adams (3)
114 Sussex v Surrey, The Oval
101 Sussex v Somerset, Hove
217 Sussex v Lancs, Manchester

K. J. Barnett (3)
100* Glos v Essex, Chelmsford
106 Glos v Essex, Gloucester
182* Glos v Middx, Southgate

I. D. Blackwell (3)
114 Somerset v Yorks, Taunton
114 Somerset v Sussex, Taunton
110 Somerset v Warwicks, Taunton

M. A. Butcher (3)
105 England v Sri Lanka, Lord's
123 England v Sri Lanka, Manchester
116 Surrey v Leics, Leicester

P. A. Cottey (3)
114 Sussex v Surrey, The Oval
120 Sussex v Somerset, Taunton
137 Sussex v Warwicks, Birmingham

R. Dravid (3)
115 India v England, Nottingham
148 India v England, Leeds
217 India v England, The Oval

R. C. Irani (3)
101 Essex v Derbys, Chelmsford
207* Essex v Northants, Ilford
182* Essex v Middx, Southgate

D. P. M. D. Jayawardene (3)
119 Sri Lankans v Kent, Canterbury
125* Sri Lankans v Middx, Shenley Park
107 Sri Lanka v England, Lord's

R. W. T. Key (3)
160 Kent v Hants, Canterbury
114 Kent v Yorks, Canterbury
127 Kent v Leics, Leicester

D. S. Lehmann (3)
119* Yorks v Leics, Leicester
216 Yorks v Sussex, Arundel
187 Yorks v Lancs, Leeds

M. P. Maynard (3)
140 }
118* } Glam v Glos, Cheltenham
151 Glam v Northants, Cardiff

M. J. Powell (3)
122 Glam v Middx, Lord's
135 Glam v Glos, Cardiff
113 Glam v Northants, Cardiff

R. C. Russell (3)
107 Glos v Essex, Gloucester
104* Glos v Northants, Bristol
119* Glos v Derbys, Bristol

V. Sehwag (3)
106 India v England, Nottingham
142 Indians v Essex, Chelmsford
104 Indians v Derbys, Derby

O. A. Shah (3)
112 Middx v Durham, Lord's
148* Middx v Essex, Southgate
172* Middx v Northants, Lord's

A. J. Strauss (3)
121 Middx v Cambridge UCCE, Cambridge
141 Middx v Glam, Cardiff
110 Middx v Notts, Nottingham

J. O. Troughton (3)
131* Warwicks v Hants, Southampton
130 Warwicks v Leics, Birmingham
115 Warwicks v Kent, Birmingham

M. J. Wood (3)
106 ⎫
131 ⎬ Somerset v Surrey, Taunton
196   Somerset v Kent, Taunton

T. R. Ambrose (2)
149 Sussex v Yorks, Leeds
124 Sussex v Kent, Hove

R. P. Arnold (2)
112 Sri Lankans v Durham,
       Chester-le-Street
109 Sri Lanka v England, Manchester

M. S. Atapattu (2)
100 Sri Lankans v British Universities,
       Northampton
185 Sri Lanka v England, Lord's

J. N. Batty (2)
104 Surrey v Lancs, Manchester
151 Surrey v Somerset, Taunton

M. G. Bevan (2)
146 Leics v Warwicks, Leicester
142 Leics v Yorks, Leicester

D. J. Bicknell (2)
108 Notts v Middx, Nottingham
112 Notts v Worcs, Nottingham

R. Clarke (2)
107* Surrey v Cambridge UCCE,
        Cambridge
153* Surrey v Somerset, Taunton

J. P. Crawley (2)
272 Hants v Kent, Canterbury
100* England v India, Lord's

A. Dale (2)
109 Glam v Notts, Colwyn Bay
127* Glam v Worcs, Cardiff

J. W. M. Dalrymple (2)
148 Oxford UCCE v Glos, Oxford
137 Oxford U. v Cambridge U., Oxford

A. Flower (2)
103* Essex v Northants, Northampton
172* Essex v Glam, Chelmsford

D. Ganga (2)
139* West Indies A v Lancs, Liverpool
131* West Indies A v Warwicks,
        Birmingham

A. Habib (2)
117 Essex v Worcs, Worcester
123 Essex v Durham, Chester-le-Street

A. J. Hollioake (2)
122* Surrey v Kent, Canterbury
208 Surrey v Leics, The Oval

N. Hussain (2)
155 England v India, Lord's
110 England v India, Leeds

W. I. Jefferson (2)
109 Essex v Glam, Chelmsford
165* Essex v Notts, Chelmsford

S. G. Law (2)
218 Lancs v Sussex, Manchester
147 Lancs v Sussex, Hove

D. A. Leatherdale (2)
154 Worcs v Northants, Northampton
120 Worcs v Notts, Nottingham

M. L. Love (2)
101* Durham v Middx, Chester-le-Street
251 Durham v Middx, Lord's

D. L. Maddy (2)
156 Leics v Kent, Canterbury
127* Leics v Surrey, The Oval

R. R. Montgomerie (2)
122* Sussex v Leics, Horsham
196 Sussex v Hants, Hove

D. P. Ostler (2)
175 Warwicks v Somerset, Birmingham
225 Warwicks v Yorks, Birmingham

A. L. Penberthy (2)
106* Northants v Notts, Nottingham
130* Northants v Glam, Cardiff

S. D. Peters (2)
146 Worcs v Northants, Northampton
130 Worcs v Glam, Cardiff

M. J. Powell (2)
107 Northants v Glos, Northampton
108* Northants v Glam, Cardiff

N. Shahid (2)
150 Surrey v Sussex, The Oval
116 Surrey v Warwicks, Birmingham

A. Singh (2)
187 Worcs v Glos, Bristol
124 Worcs v Essex, Southend

E. T. Smith (2)
141* Kent v Sussex, Hove
154 Kent v Somerset, Taunton

R. A. Smith (2)
104 Hants v Kent, Southampton
104 Hants v Leics, Leicester

V. S. Solanki (2)
153* Worcs v Middx, Lord's
116 Worcs v Northants, Worcester

I. J. Sutcliffe (2)
103 Leics v Kent, Leicester
125* Leics v Kent, Canterbury

A. J. Swann (2)
128 Lancs v Yorks, Leeds
112 Lancs v Yorks, Manchester

G. P. Swann (2)
109 Northants v Durham, Northampton
183 Northants v Glos, Bristol

A. Symonds (2)
116* Kent v Lancs, Liverpool
118 Kent v Surrey, Canterbury

S. R. Tendulkar (2)
169 Indians v Worcs, Worcester
193 India v England, Leeds

G. P. Thorpe (2)
123 England v Sri Lanka, Birmingham
143 Surrey v Hants, Southampton

M. E. Trescothick (2)
134 Somerset v Yorks, Taunton
161 England v Sri Lanka, Birmingham

C. White (2)
104 Yorks v Kent, Canterbury
161 Yorks v Leics, Scarborough

M. G. N. Windows (2)
145 Glos v Oxford UCCE, Oxford
144 Glos v Derbys, Bristol

The following each played one three-figure innings:

Abdul Razzaq, 203*, Middx v Glam, Cardiff; A. B. Agarkar, 109*, India v England, Lord's; M. W. Alleyne, 142*, Glos v Essex, Chelmsford.

C. W. G. Bassano, 152, Derbys v Essex, Derby; R. J. Blakey, 103, Yorks v Warwicks, Birmingham; G. L. Brophy, 110, Northants v Glam, Cardiff; N. D. Burns, 101, Leics v Hants, Leicester; D. Byas, 101, Lancs v Warwicks, Manchester.

M. A. Carberry, 153*, Surrey v Cambridge UCCE, Cambridge; N. M. Carter, 103, Warwicks v Sussex, Hove; M. E. Cassar, 101*, Northants v Glos, Northampton; M. J. Chilton, 107, Lancs v Durham UCCE, Durham; R. S. Clinton, 107, Essex v Cambridge UCCE, Cambridge; P. D. Collingwood, 190, Durham v Sri Lankans, Chester-le-Street; J. Cox, 176, Somerset v Leics, Taunton; R. D. B. Croft, 101*, Glam v Glos, Cardiff.

S. S. Das, 250, Indians v Essex, Chelmsford; M. J. G. Davis, 111, Sussex v Somerset, Taunton; P. A. J. DeFreitas, 114, Leics v Kent, Leicester.

M. T. G. Elliott, 127, Yorks v Warwicks, Birmingham.

N. H. Fairbrother, 101, Lancs v West Indies A, Liverpool; G. M. Fellows, 109, Yorks v Lancs, Manchester; I. D. Fisher, 103*, Glos v Essex, Gloucester; M. V. Fleming, 102, Kent v Sri Lankans, Canterbury; A. Flintoff, 137, Lancs v Surrey, The Oval; T. Frost, 103, Warwicks v Yorks, Birmingham.

A. I. Gait, 175, Derbys v Northants, Northampton; S. C. Ganguly, 128, India v England, Leeds; A. P. R. Gidman, 117, Glos v Northants, Bristol; M. A. Gough, 103, Durham v Essex, Colchester; A. P. Grayson, 105, Essex v Cambridge UCCE, Cambridge.

T. H. C. Hancock, 112, Glos v Middx, Cheltenham; M. A. Hardinges, 172, Glos v Oxford UCCE, Oxford; I. J. Harvey, 123, Glos v Glam, Cardiff; D. L. Hemp, 108, Glam v Northants, Cardiff; D. R. Hewson, 102*, Derbys v Glam, Cardiff; B. L. Hutton, 116, Middx v Northants, Lord's.

N. C. Johnson, 117, Hants v Kent, Canterbury.

J. J. B. Lewis, 102, Durham v Durham UCCE, Chester-le-Street; M. J. Lumb, 124, Yorks v Surrey, Guildford.

A. McGrath, 165, Yorks v Lancs, Leeds; P. J. Martin, 117*, Lancs v Warwicks, Manchester; R. S. C. Martin-Jenkins, 205*, Sussex v Somerset, Taunton; J. S. D. Moffat, 169, Cambridge U. v Oxford U., Oxford; G. J. Muchall, 127, Durham v Middx, Lord's.

D. C. Nash, 100, Middx v Worcs, Worcester; S. A. Newman, 183, Surrey v Leics, The Oval; P. A. Nixon, 103, Kent v Warwicks, Birmingham.

N. Peng, 108, Durham v Derbys, Derby; M. J. Powell, 103, Warwicks v Sussex, Hove; M. J. Prior, 102*, Sussex v Hants, Hove.

A. Ratra, 101*, Indians v Derbys, Derby; C. M. W. Read, 127, Notts v Northants, Northampton; S. J. Rhodes, 124, Worcs v Notts, Nottingham; A. S. Rollins, 107, Northants v Middx, Northampton.

D. J. Sales, 179, Northants v Notts, Northampton; K. C. Sangakkara, 113, Sri Lankans v Glam, Cardiff; B. M. Shafayat, 104, Notts v Worcs, Nottingham; A. A. Shankar, 143, Cambridge U. v Oxford U., Oxford; R. J. Sillence, 101, Glos v Derbys, Bristol; D. S. Smith, 181, West Indies A v Lancs, Liverpool; J. P. Stephenson, 100*, Essex v Durham, Colchester; D. I. Stevens, 125, Leics v Warwicks, Leicester; A. J. Stewart, 123, England v Sri Lanka, Manchester; S. D. Stubbings, 128, Derbys v Glam, Cardiff.

C. G. Taylor, 126, Glos v Glam, Cheltenham; P. D. Trego, 140, Somerset v West Indies A, Taunton.

M. A. Wagh, 109, Warwicks v Kent, Birmingham; M. A. Wallace, 106*, Glam v Derbys, Cardiff; R. J. Warren, 150*, Northants v Worcs, Northampton; M. E. Waugh, 117, Essex v Durham, Chester-le-Street; S. R. Waugh, 146, Kent v Yorks, Leeds; V. J. Wells, 150, Leics v Hants, Southampton; G. E. Welton, 115, Notts v Glam, Nottingham; R. A. White, 277, Northants v Glos, Northampton.

TEN WICKETS IN A MATCH

There were 26 instances of bowlers taking ten or more wickets in first-class cricket in 2002, eight more than in 2001. The list includes 25 in the County Championship. Twice, two bowlers achieved the feat in the same match, when J. Lewis took 12 wickets for Gloucestershire and A. J. Bichel ten for Worcestershire at Worcester, and when K. J. Dean took ten wickets for Derbyshire and A. A. Noffke 12 for Middlesex at Derby.

Kabir Ali (2)
10-88, Worcs v Oxford UCCE, Oxford; 10-66, Worcs v Glos, Bristol.

K. J. Dean (2)
10-109, Derbys v Glam, Derby; 10-125, Derbys v Middx, Derby.

A. J. Harris (2)
11-122, Notts v Northants, Nottingham; 10-171, Notts v Worcs, Nottingham.

The following each took ten wickets in a match on one occasion:

A. J. Bichel, 10-131, Worcs v Glos, Worcester.
M. E. Cassar, 10-134, Northants v Glos, Bristol; G. Chapple, 10-127, Lancs v Sussex, Hove; D. G. Cork, 10-126, Derbys v Durham, Derby.
A. F. Giles, 12-216, Warwicks v Kent, Birmingham.
I. J. Harvey, 11-154, Glos v Essex, Gloucester.
R. L. Johnson, 10-75, Somerset v Hants, Bath; P. S. Jones, 10-156, Somerset v Warwicks, Birmingham.
M. S. Kasprowicz, 11-105, Glam v Durham, Chester-le-Street; R. J. Kirtley, 10-90, Sussex v Yorks, Leeds.
J. Lewis, 12-131, Glos v Worcs, Worcester.
S. C. G. MacGill, 14-165, Notts v Middx, Nottingham; D. E. Malcolm, 10-148, Leics v Yorks, Leicester.
A. A. Noffke, 12-108, Middx v Derbys, Derby.
J. Ormond, 10-178, Surrey v Warwicks, The Oval.
Saqlain Mushtaq, 11-180, Surrey v Hants, The Oval; G. J. Smith, 11-74, Notts v Essex, Nottingham; J. P. Stephenson, 10-104, Essex v Worcs, Worcester; G. P. Swann, 10-238, Northants v Derbys, Northampton.
S. D. Thomas, 10-83, Glam v Durham, Cardiff.

THE SRI LANKANS IN ENGLAND, 2002

Review by ROB SMYTH

In their 21st year as a Test-playing nation, Sri Lanka's adulthood was finally recognised with the present they most wanted: a first full tour of England. But the party hardly got going at all. They were without Muttiah Muralitharan for the first part of the tour; when he did arrive, they lost the last two Tests comprehensively. England played so well that a 2–0 victory did not flatter them, but Sri Lanka certainly helped gift-wrap it. And the whole thing was conducted in the shadow of a bigger, better jamboree – the football World Cup.

Failure to reach the final of the triangular one-day series compounded an unhappy tour, which was in total contrast to the giddy, all-conquering stopover in 1998. When Sri Lanka's coach, Dav Whatmore, said at the end, "I've seen some positives but we haven't got what it takes to win abroad," only the first bit was debatable.

Sanath Jayasuriya, a lugubrious figure throughout, set the tone, though he wasn't the only one sporting a furrowed brow. Sri Lanka's Australian bowling coach, Daryl Foster, resigned in an argument over travel expenses, Aravinda de Silva was robbed of £3,000 at a Chesterfield hotel, and the tour manager, Chandra Schaffter, found out during the Third Test that his contract would not be renewed.

It was a tour of three distinct parts. Sri Lanka started like a side counting the days until Murali recovered from a dislocated shoulder, rallied briefly to dominate the drawn First Test without him, and then, when he was back in the side, played just as the book says subcontinental sides should in an English May and June. They didn't win a single first-class match, not even against British Universities.

England won their first Test series since going to Sri Lanka 15 months earlier and completed their first double on the ICC Test Championship table. Never had the present generation of England players dominated a rubber quite so extensively: this was England's first 2–0 win in a home series since 1978. From the start of the second innings at Lord's, England averaged 65 per wicket, Sri Lanka just 27.

If England had gone "round the brick wall" in that series in Sri Lanka, as Scyld Berry put it, this time they huffed and puffed until the house fell down. While Ashley Giles, left out at Lord's on the basis of precedent rather than pitch, kept a rein on things, the seamers pounded Sri Lanka's strokemakers into submission with relentless discipline, especially on an Australian-style pitch at Old Trafford.

Enjoying the luxury of not having to penny-pinch to make the best of modest scores, Nasser Hussain's captaincy was at its most sparkling. Not once in the field did he have to defend a total of less than 500, and he allowed himself treats he couldn't usually afford. His declaration gave the First Test a kick when most captains would have happily kept their feet up, and most of his field placings came off too: when Hussain put himself at leg gully for de Silva at Old Trafford, the ball followed him within an over. He even started winning the toss.

Sri Lanka arrived in April on the back of nine consecutive Test wins – a record surpassed only by the two great sides of modern cricket history, the 1980s West Indies and the present-day Australians – yet few people took that statistic seriously. Eight of the wins had been at home, the other in Lahore. It was widely believed that outside the subcontinent, and especially in a dank English spring, the limitations of their angled bats and flashy strokes would be exposed.

Their early form did nothing to confound that opinion. Most of the batsmen could hardly buy a run, and when Kent hammered 419 in only 63.3 overs, the bowlers needed Murali like never before. Sri Lanka were ripe for a hammering, but someone forgot to tell the MCC groundsman – or the elements. The first two days of the series were Lord's in May by name, Colombo in February by nature. A featherbed pitch and sultry heat provided the fuel for Sri Lanka to pass 500 in the first innings for the eighth time in ten Tests. England, by contrast, hadn't managed it even once in five years and 60 Tests – although that wrong would soon be righted.

England responded to the unique challenge of facing three left-arm seamers with some cack-handed batting. Despite having a long, strong line-up with Andrew Flintoff at No. 8, they collapsed and followed on as nature took the course it so often does when a big total is on the board. The man who started the rot, Ruchira Perera, was all over the papers the next morning – but it had nothing to do with the fact that he dismissed Michael Vaughan and Graham Thorpe with successive deliveries. Channel 4 footage cast doubts on his energetic, slingy action, and many viewers agreed that it looked dodgy. Perera was ultimately reported by the umpires after the match for a suspect action and played little further part in the tour, though he did leave Mark Butcher £1,500 out of pocket, after Butcher told his ghost-writer at the *Croydon Advertiser*, "when [Perera] bowls short he just runs up and throws it at you. I can't believe someone gets away with it."

If Butcher was loose with tongue and wealth, he was frugality personified with the bat. His 291-ball century in the second innings at Lord's was the soothing rhetoric that persuaded England that the only demons were in their mind, not the pitch. With the first of five 500-plus totals in the season, England exposed as fanciful the notion of Sri Lanka winning a Test without Murali.

From there the series followed its preordained script. Sri Lanka batted first again at Edgbaston, but this time there were two key differences: Hussain put them in, and Andy Caddick, lethargy incarnate at Lord's, got out of the right side of the bed. Bowled out inside 53 overs, Sri Lanka were never in the game as England built up their biggest first-innings lead since 1967.

It was Marcus Trescothick's turn to help himself this time, with a career-best 161. Even the return of Murali, who toiled through 64 overs for his regulation five-for and denied Butcher a second (and ultimately third) consecutive hundred with a mirror image of Shane Warne's Ball of the Century, couldn't stem the tide. A serene last-wicket partnership of 91 between Graham Thorpe and Matthew Hoggard, in which Hoggard actually took more of the strike, was a microcosm of the morale of both sides throughout the series.

In the swing: **Marcus Trescothick, top-scorer in the Sri Lankan series, hammers Murali past Mahela Jayawardene during the Edgbaston Test.** *Picture by Patrick Eagar.*

The Third Test wasn't far off a carbon-copy. With James Foster ready to return following a broken arm, there were suggestions that Alec Stewart's 118th Test would be his last. Not a bit of it. Sometimes with Stewart you just know a century is in the post: here he was equalling Graham Gooch as England's most-capped player, and England were playing Denmark in the second round of the World Cup when he resumed on 57 on the third day. A patriot and football fan, Stewart waited while most of the crowd watched the Denmark game on the £10,000 big screen that the ECB erected behind the Stretford End – even sneaking the odd glance himself – then, as they funnelled back in, belted four consecutive fours to move from 86 to 102. For a man whose public face can be wooden, Stewart has an acute sense of theatre.

After Giles took the final two wickets at almost the last possible moment that could keep a result alive, England were left chasing 50 off six overs. Yet, for them, this was a penalty shoot-out without the suffocating pressure: the series was already won. Vaughan and Trescothick found top gear straight away and romped to a thrilling victory with an over to spare as Jayasuriya failed to work out that if he spread the field, they could get them in singles. At 7.35, it was one of the latest finishes to a Test in England.

This was a very bad tour for Jayasuriya, whose one-dimensional strategy – bat first, score 500, bowl Murali after about ten overs – suffered in comparison with the invention of Hussain. His batting, lacking any of its usual *joie de vivre*, fell apart to the extent that he dropped down the order for the last Test, and after mopping up 16 English wickets a year earlier, he took none now. His body language was never the same once he dropped Vaughan twice in four overs on the fourth morning at Lord's, and one of the most infectious smiles in world cricket had disappeared long before the end.

Kumar Sangakkara, who arrived with a Test average of 53 and a big reputation as the face of the new, hard-nosed Sri Lanka, wasn't much better. Like Jayasuriya, he failed to make a half-century in the Tests, and with the runs went his angry-young-man routine. Mahela Jayawardene got to grips with the conditions better than anyone, making three first-class centuries including – finally – his first in an overseas Test, while Marvan Atapattu, as in the series between the sides 15 months earlier, put all his eggs in one big, First Test hundred.

If anything, the bowlers were even more disappointing. A lot was expected of Chaminda Vaas, but he struggled to get any reverse swing and the final step from 196 Test wickets to 200 took him a whopping 137 overs. In all, he bowled 35 more overs than he had against England in 2000-01 for a quarter of the wickets: he seemed to miss Mike Atherton. And while England never truly mastered Murali, they certainly muzzled him. Against the left-handers, Trescothick, Butcher and Thorpe, his wickets cost 93 runs and came every 35 overs. Murali's overall strike-rate was a wicket every 95 balls – only the second time in ten series that it had been over 60. The other time had also been against England, testimony to the effectiveness of the forward press that Duncan Fletcher had taught the batsmen to use against spin.

Dilhara Fernando, sidelined until the last Test with a stress fracture, did show raw pace and a confidence trickster of a slower ball that sucked in Vaughan and Hussain, but that was as good as it got. As a consequence, it was a series of plenty for England's batsmen. Vaughan, after a feverish performance in New Zealand, added a drop of discretion to his game and arrived as a Test opener, while Trescothick and Butcher, like left-handed incarnations of Graham Gooch and David Boon minus the bristle, gathered run after run in their contrasting ways.

Only in their selection for Lord's did England take a backward step. The public expected Alex Tudor and Ian Bell… and got Dominic Cork and John Crawley. Both lasted one Test, though they would return later in the summer. England started the series with *Dad's Army* and ended it with *The Young Ones*. When Tudor, Hoggard – who came back well from a butterfly-stomach display at Lord's – and Flintoff won the final Test with an almost Australian relentlessness on a rock-hard Old Trafford pitch, the future looked bright indeed. It was the first time since 1996 that England had won a Test without Caddick, who broke down in his sixth over, or Darren Gough.

Hoggard, Tudor and Flintoff appeared on the cover of *Wisden Cricket Monthly* in August, and a nation dreamed of them sharing the wickets in Australia and bringing home the Ashes. It didn't quite work out like that – they shared nothing more than eight wickets, six stitches and a dodgy hernia. The Sri Lankans weren't alone in realising that the script is one thing, fantasy entirely another.

Rob Smyth covered the series as assistant editor of Wisden Online.

SRI LANKAN TOUR PARTY

S. T. Jayasuriya (Bloomfield) (*captain*), M. S. Atapattu (Sinhalese) (*vice-captain*), M. K. D. I. Amerasinghe (Nondescripts), R. P. Arnold (Nondescripts), U. D. U. Chandana (Tamil Union), P. A. de Silva (Nondescripts), C. R. D. Fernando (Sinhalese), T. C. B. Fernando (Panadura), D. P. M. D. Jayawardene (Sinhalese), H. A. P. W. Jayawardene (Colombo), M. Muralitharan (Tamil Union), P. D. R. L. Perera (Sinhalese), T. T. Samaraweera (Sinhalese), K. C. Sangakkara (Nondescripts), H. P. Tillekeratne (Nondescripts), K. E. A. Upashantha (Colts), W. P. U. J. C. Vaas (Colts), D. N. T. Zoysa (Sinhalese).

Muralitharan and C. R. D. Fernando arrived late because of injuries. K. S. C. de Silva (Burgher) and W. M. P. N. Wanasinghe (Galle) appeared in one match. D. A. Gunawardene (Sinhalese), R. S. Kaluwitharana (Colts), M. N. Nawaz (Nondescripts), L. P. C. Silva (Panadura) and G. P. Wickremasinghe (Tamil Union) replaced Amerasinghe, P. A. de Silva, H. A. P. W. Jayawardene, Perera, Samaraweera, Tillekeratne and Upashantha for the one-day tournament that followed the Tests, but Samaraweera returned when Muralitharan went home with an injured shoulder.

Coach: D. F. Whatmore.   *Manager:* C. T. A. Schaffter.   *Bowling coach:* D. H. Foster.
Batting coach: B. A. Richards.   *Physiotherapist:* A. Kontouri.

SRI LANKAN TOUR RESULTS

Test matches – Played 3: Lost 2, Drawn 1.
First-class matches – Played 9: Lost 2, Drawn 7.
Losses – England (2).
Draws – England, Kent, British Universities, Durham, Middlesex, Glamorgan, MCC.
One-day internationals – Played 6: Won 1, Lost 5. *Win* – England. *Losses* – England (2), India (3).
Other non-first-class matches – Played 4: Won 3, Lost 1. *Wins* – West Indies A, Gloucestershire, Northamptonshire. *Loss* – Somerset.

TEST MATCH AVERAGES

ENGLAND – BATTING

	T	I	NO	R	HS	100s	50s	Avge	Ct/St
M. E. Trescothick	3	5	1	354	161	1	2	88.50	5
M. A. Butcher	3	4	0	339	123	2	1	84.75	1
M. P. Vaughan	3	5	1	285	115	1	1	71.25	2
G. P. Thorpe	3	4	0	247	123	1	1	61.75	3
A. J. Stewart	3	4	1	163	123	1	0	54.33	9/1
N. Hussain	3	4	0	163	68	0	2	40.75	2
M. J. Hoggard	3	3	2	24	17*	0	0	24.00	1
A. Flintoff	3	3	0	42	29	0	0	14.00	4
A. R. Caddick	3	3	1	18	13	0	0	9.00	0

Played in two Tests: A. F. Giles 0, 45 (1 ct); A. J. Tudor 3, 19 (1 ct). Played in one Test: D. G. Cork 0; J. P. Crawley 31, 41*.

BOWLING

	O	M	R	W	BB	5W/i	Avge
A. J. Tudor	64.5	18	159	9	4-65	0	17.66
D. G. Cork	35.3	11	93	3	3-93	0	31.00
A. F. Giles	77.3	11	190	6	4-62	0	31.66
M. J. Hoggard	133	22	449	14	5-92	1	32.07
A. R. Caddick	93	20	276	7	3-47	0	39.42
A. Flintoff	107	20	312	6	2-27	0	52.00

Also bowled: M. A. Butcher 3–0–17–0; M. P. Vaughan 16–2–44–0.

SRI LANKA – BATTING

	T	I	NO	R	HS	100s	50s	Avge	Ct
M. S. Atapattu	3	6	1	277	185	1	1	55.40	0
D. P. M. D. Jayawardene	3	6	1	272	107	1	1	54.40	2
R. P. Arnold	3	5	0	226	109	1	2	45.20	1
H. P. Tillekeratne	3	5	2	128	39	0	0	42.66	5
P. A. de Silva	3	5	0	203	88	0	1	40.60	0
K. C. Sangakkara	3	6	1	105	40	0	0	21.00	10
S. T. Jayasuriya	3	5	0	99	35	0	0	19.80	2
D. N. T. Zoysa	2	3	1	29	28	0	0	14.50	1
W. P. U. J. C. Vaas	3	5	0	72	28	0	0	14.40	2
T. C. B. Fernando	2	3	1	19	13	0	0	9.50	1
M. Muralitharan	2	3	1	6	6	0	0	3.00	1

Played in one Test: C. R. D. Fernando 6*, 4; K. E. A. Upashantha 1, 3. P. D. R. L. Perera did not bat.

BOWLING

	O	M	R	W	BB	5W/i	Avge
P. D. R. L. Perera	41	4	138	5	3-48	0	27.60
M. Muralitharan	126	32	297	8	5-143	1	37.12
D. N. T. Zoysa	77	12	259	6	3-93	0	43.16
C. R. D. Fernando	31.2	2	177	3	3-154	0	59.00
T. C. B. Fernando	69.5	8	271	4	3-83	0	67.75
W. P. U. J. C. Vaas	145.1	23	434	4	2-121	0	108.50

Also bowled: R. P. Arnold 4–1–7–0; P. A. de Silva 36–7–98–1; S. T. Jayasuriya 39–10–108–0; H. P. Tillekeratne 1–1–0–0; K. E. A. Upashantha 8–0–65–1.

SRI LANKAN TOUR AVERAGES – FIRST-CLASS MATCHES

BATTING

	M	I	NO	R	HS	100s	50s	Avge	Ct/St
D. P. M. D. Jayawardene	6	11	2	567	125*	3	1	63.00	3
P. A. de Silva	8	12	2	500	88	0	6	50.00	0
M. S. Atapattu	7	12	1	522	88	0	6	45.75	0
H. P. Tillekeratne	8	13	5	366	185	2	1	47.45	1
R. P. Arnold	9	12	0	518	112	2	3	43.16	5
S. T. Jayasuriya	8	12	0	322	57	0	3	26.83	4
K. C. Sangakkara	9	15	2	345	113	1	1	26.53	12/1
W. P. U. J. C. Vaas	5	7	1	138	50*	0	1	23.00	2
T. T. Samaraweera	5	5	0	101	57	0	1	20.20	3
T. C. B. Fernando	5	6	3	60	20*	0	0	20.00	1
P. D. R. L. Perera	5	4	2	15	5*	0	0	7.50	2
D. N. T. Zoysa	4	5	1	29	28	0	0	7.25	2
K. E. A. Upashantha	5	6	0	43	25	0	0	7.16	1

Played in three matches: M. K. D. I. Amerasinghe 0; U. D. U. Chandana 0, 1, 0 (1 ct); C. R. D. Fernando 3, 6*, 4. Played in two matches: H. A. P. W. Jayawardene 12*, 7 (1 ct); M. Muralitharan)*, 6, 0 (1 ct). Played in one match: W. M. P. N. Wanasinghe 6*. K. S. C. de Silva did not bat.

BOWLING

	O	M	R	W	BB	5W/i	Avge
P. D. R. L. Perera	115	13	433	17	4-66	0	25.47
M. Muralitharan	126	32	297	8	5-143	1	37.12
D. N. T. Zoysa	110.2	15	421	10	3-93	0	42.10
C. R. D. Fernando	49.2	5	230	5	3-154	0	46.00
T. C. B. Fernando	113.5	14	524	10	4-72	0	52.40
K. E. A. Upashantha	57	5	341	6	3-85	0	56.83
W. P. U. J. C. Vaas	186.1	30	543	9	3-79	0	60.33

Also bowled: M. K. D. I. Amerasinghe 26–2–159–3; R. P. Arnold 4–1–7–0; U. D. U. Chandana 35–9–109–2; P. A. de Silva 42–7–142–2; S. T. Jayasuriya 45–10–130–0; D. P. M. D. Jayawardene 13–1–59–1; T. T. Samaraweera 43–5–178–1; H. P. Tillekeratne 5–1–33–0.

Note: Matches in this section which were not first-class are signified by a dagger.

KENT v SRI LANKANS

At Canterbury, April 26, 27, 28. Drawn. Toss: Sri Lankans.

With the first day washed out because of rain, there was never any real possibility of a definite result. On the final afternoon, Fleming entertained the spectators with a typically belligerent innings, putting himself in pole position to win the Walter Lawrence Trophy for the fastest first-class hundred – and he did. He needed only 66 balls, and hit 12 fours and three sixes, as he shared a sixth-wicket stand of 176 in 20 overs with Geraint Jones, the reserve wicket-keeper. Fulton had earlier reached his hundred from 99 balls with 17 fours and a six, as Kent recovered from the early loss of Key and Smith. Jayawardene made the first hundred of a high-scoring contest, off 113 balls, while de Silva, given a warm ovation on his return to the county he served in 1995, responded with an impressive half-century before Golding polished off the tail, following an expensive first spell.

Close of play: First day, No play; Second day, Sri Lankans 375.

Sri Lankans

M. S. Atapattu c Patel b Saggers	20
*S. T. Jayasuriya c Jones b Saggers	0
†K. C. Sangakkara lbw Jones b Trott	19
D. P. M. D. Jayawardene c Saggers b Trott	119
P. A. de Silva c Fulton b Saggers	63
R. P. Arnold c Fulton b Golding	81
T. T. Samaraweera c Fulton b Saggers	57
D. N. T. Zoysa b Golding	0
T. C. B. Fernando c Jones b Golding	2
M. K. D. I. Amerasinghe c Jones b Golding	0
P. D. R. L. Perera not out	5
B 5, l-b 3, w 1	9
1/1 (2) 2/34 (1) 3/54 (3) 4/205 (5)	375
5/245 (4) 6/332 (6) 7/344 (8)	
8/352 (9) 9/354 (10) 10/375 (7)	

Bowling: Saggers 23.3–2–84–4; Trott 18–1–109–2; Fleming 15–1–41–0; Golding 22–4–76–4; Walker 9–0–41–0; Patel 3–0–16–0.

Kent

*D. P. Fulton b Perera	116
R. W. T. Key b Perera	7
E. T. Smith c Jayawardene b Zoysa	6
M. J. Walker lbw b Samaraweera	40
J. B. Hockley c Samaraweera b Perera	2
†G. O. Jones not out	76
M. V. Fleming b de Silva	102
J. M. Golding not out	18
B 1, l-b 10, w 1, n-b 40	52
1/27 (2) 2/34 (3)	(6 wkts dec.) 419
3/198 (1) 4/200 (4)	
5/204 (5) 6/380 (7)	

M. M. Patel, M. J. Saggers and B. J. Trott did not bat.

Bowling: Zoysa 13–2–64–1; Perera 12–1–45–3; Fernando 12.3–1–119–0; Amerasinghe 9–1–83–0; Samaraweera 14–3–63–1; de Silva 3–0–34–1.

Umpires: M. J. Kitchen and P. Willey.

BRITISH UNIVERSITIES v SRI LANKANS

At Northampton, May 2, 3, 4. Drawn. Toss: British Universities. First-class debuts: J. H. K. Adams, J. A. Tomlinson.

This match was an early contender for non-event of the season. The weather was either cold or wet or both, the atmosphere non-existent and a result never likely. Between the showers, five Sri Lankans reached 50 and Atapattu went on to a meticulous hundred, but it was hard to know how much it meant: the pitch was greenish, the bowling greener still. None of the students passed 40, although there were some polished strokes from John Francis and Jamie Dalrymple. Vaas kept beating the outside edge, but the rest of the Sri Lankan attack was almost as modest as the opposition.

Close of play: First day, Sri Lankans 318-7 (Vaas 11, Upashantha 0); Second day, British Universities 37-2 (Francis 10, Dalrymple 0).

Sri Lankans

M. S. Atapattu c Francis b Panesar	100		
*S. T. Jayasuriya c Adams b Tournier	15	– c Porter b Tournier	52
†K. C. Sangakkara c Brown b Tomlinson	15	– (1) not out	51
H. P. Tillekeratne c Brown b Tournier	18	– (3) not out	12
P. A. de Silva b Panesar	57		
R. P. Arnold c Tomlinson b Tournier	43		
T. T. Samaraweera c Jefferson b Tournier	21		
W. P. U. J. C. Vaas not out	50		
K. E. A. Upashantha c Porter b Tournier	0		
T. C. B. Fernando not out	19		
B 10, l-b 9, w 12, n-b 14	45	B 4, l-b 5, w 2, n-b 2	13

1/60 (2) 2/100 (3) 3/127 (4)   (8 wkts dec.) 383   1/89 (2)   (1 wkt dec.) 128
4/238 (5) 5/247 (1) 6/305 (6)
7/309 (7) 8/319 (9)

M. K. D. I. Amerasinghe did not bat.

Bowling: *First Innings*—Tournier 28–4–88–5; Tomlinson 15–0–80–1; Murtagh 20–6–68–0; Ferley 8–1–49–0; Panesar 13–4–43–2; Dalrymple 10–1–36–0. *Second Innings*—Tournier 8–1–37–1; Tomlinson 7–1–31–0; Murtagh 7–1–34–0; Panesar 3–1–9–0; Ferley 1–0–8–0.

British Universities

W. I. Jefferson (*Durham*) c Samaraweera b Vaas	1	
J. H. K. Adams (*Loughborough*) c Arnold b Vaas	12	
J. D. Francis (*Loughborough*) lbw b Amerasinghe	33	
*J. W. M. Dalrymple (*Oxford*) c Sangakkara b Upashantha	40	
J. J. Porter (*Oxford Brookes*) lbw b Upashantha	37	
†M. J. Brown (*Durham*) run out	25	
R. S. Ferley (*Durham*) c Tillekeratne b Fernando	0	
T. J. Murtagh (*St Mary's UC*) c Atapattu b Amerasinghe	3	
J. A. Tomlinson (*Cardiff*) c Samaraweera b Amerasinghe	4	
M. A. Tournier (*Loughborough*) not out	10	
M. S. Panesar (*Loughborough*) b Fernando	0	
B 5, l-b 8, w 7, n-b 34	54	

1/6 (1) 2/25 (2) 3/109 (3) 4/120 (4)   216
5/170 (6) 6/172 (7) 7/189 (8)
8/191 (9) 9/215 (5) 10/216 (11)

Bowling: Vaas 19–5–30–2; Upashantha 14–3–65–2; Fernando 13.3–1–62–2; Amerasinghe 12–1–46–3.

Umpires: T. E. Jesty and R. A. Kettleborough.

DURHAM v SRI LANKANS

At Chester-le-Street, May 7, 8, 9. Drawn. Toss: Durham. First-class debuts: P. Mustard, A. M. Thorpe.

The craftsman upstaged the apprentice as Paul Collingwood amassed a flawless career-best 190 after Gordon Muchall of England Under-19 survived a sketchy start to complete his maiden first-class half-century. Other than the Test left-armers Vaas and Zoysa, the bowling was modest and Durham's third-wicket pair rattled along at six an over. Collingwood's innings was the highest by a Durham batsman on home soil. He faced 212 balls and hit 22 fours and five sixes before miscuing Ruchira Perera to deep square. The reserve wicket-keeper, Phil Mustard, joined in the fun with a run-a-ball 75 on his first-class debut. In cold, windy conditions, 74 overs were lost on the first two days, and the Sri Lankans warmed to their task only after following on, with Russel Arnold making a sparkling 112.

Close of play: First day, Durham 219-4 (Collingwood 103, Thorpe 6); Second day, Sri Lankans 92-3 (Atapattu 40, de Silva 10).

Durham

*J. J. B. Lewis b Vaas	9	†P. Mustard b Vaas	75
G. J. Pratt c Sangakkara b Vaas	4	G. D. Bridge c Perera b Zoysa	21
G. J. Muchall c Arnold b Zoysa	69	N. G. Hatch not out	6
P. D. Collingwood c sub b Perera	190	B 4, l-b 7, n-b 14	25
N. Peng c Arnold b Zoysa	17		
A. M. Thorpe c Zoysa b Perera	29	1/16 (1) 2/17 (2) 3/146 (3) 4/195 (5)	469
M. J. Symington lbw b Perera	8	5/270 (6) 6/279 (7) 7/298 (8)	
I. D. Hunter st Sangakkara b Jayawardene	16	8/428 (4) 9/451 (9) 10/469 (10)	

Bowling: Vaas 22–2–79–3; Zoysa 20.2–1–98–3; Perera 22–2–112–3; Amerasinghe 5–0–30–0; Samaraweera 9–0–54–0; de Silva 3–0–10–0; Jayawardene 9–0–45–1; Tillekeratne 3–0–30–0.

Sri Lankans

*M. S. Atapattu c Thorpe b Hatch	40	– c Thorpe b Bridge	23
R. P. Arnold c Mustard b Hunter	4	– c Pratt b Hatch	112
†K. C. Sangakkara c Muchall b Hunter	5	– b Bridge	17
D. P. M. D. Jayawardene c Hatch b Symington	28	– c Pratt b Muchall	11
P. A. de Silva c Mustard b Symington	53	– not out	63
H. P. Tillekeratne lbw b Hunter	8	– not out	33
T. T. Samaraweera c Muchall b Symington	6		
W. P. U. J. C. Vaas b Pratt b Hatch	16		
D. N. T. Zoysa lbw b Symington	0		
P. D. R. L. Perera not out	0		
M. K. D. I. Amerasinghe absent hurt			
B 1, l-b 6	7	B 16, l-b 3, w 1, n-b 3	23
1/11 (2) 2/19 (3) 3/72 (1) 4/92 (1)	167	1/109 (1) 2/138 (3) (4 wkts)	282
5/119 (6) 6/142 (7) 7/161 (5)		3/157 (4) 4/196 (2)	
8/161 (9) 9/167 (8)			

Bowling: *First Innings*—Hunter 15–3–44–3; Hatch 16.5–4–63–2; Symington 12–5–27–4; Thorpe 2–0–14–0; Bridge 3–0–12–0. *Second Innings*—Hunter 11–2–66–0; Symington 11–3–38–0; Hatch 11–0–63–1; Bridge 12–1–40–2; Muchall 8–0–36–1; Thorpe 6–0–18–0; Peng 1–0–2–0.

Umpires: J. W. Holder and R. T. Robinson.

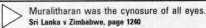

Muralitharan was the cynosure of all eyes.
Sri Lanka v Zimbabwe, page 1240

MIDDLESEX v SRI LANKANS

At Shenley Park, May 11, 12, 13. Drawn. Toss: Sri Lankans.

The weather had the last word, washing out the final day and, with the First Test only three days away, depriving the Sri Lankans of much-needed match practice. On a good pitch, they started as though they were going to score 400 by the close but, as the shine wore off the ball, it started to reverse-swing and Hutton took full advantage to return career-best figures. Jayasuriya and Chandana gave him some help by not offering a stroke. Strauss, in his first match as county captain following the retirement of Angus Fraser, ran out de Silva and Tillekeratne, both with direct hits. When Middlesex batted, Joyce again showed his abundant promise and came close to his second century in two matches. The Sri Lankans, with an 88-run deficit on first innings, once again lost wickets through a cavalier approach, and they were only 14 ahead when the fourth wicket fell. Jayawardene, with his second century of the tour, realised that batting had to be taken more seriously, and they had added an unbroken 179 by the end of the second day.

Close of play: First day, Middlesex 178-6 (Joyce 65, Alleyne 7); Second day, Sri Lankans 281-4 (Jayawardene 125, Tillekeratne 71).

Sri Lankans

M. S. Atapattu c Alleyne b Laraman	46	– c Hutton b Bloomfield	16
*S. T. Jayasuriya b Hutton	52	– b Bloomfield	31
†K. C. Sangakkara c Alleyne b Laraman	1	– lbw b Laraman	13
D. P. M. D. Jayawardene c Alleyne b Laraman	12	– not out	125
P. A. de Silva run out	0	– c Shah b Bloomfield	7
H. P. Tillekeratne run out	15	– not out	71
R. P. Arnold c Alleyne b Hutton	3		
U. D. U. Chandana lbw b Hutton	0		
K. E. A. Upashantha c Joyce b Hutton	25		
T. C. B. Fernando not out	20		
P. D. R. L. Perera lbw b Hunt	5		
L-b 2, w 3, n-b 2	7	B 4, l-b 7, w 4, n-b 3	18
	186	(4 wkts)	**281**

1/81 (1) 2/94 (3) 3/111 (2) 4/113 (4)
5/114 (5) 6/123 (7) 7/123 (6)
8/136 (6) 9/161 (9) 10/186 (11)

1/44 (1) 2/65 (3)   (4 wkts) 281
3/67 (2) 4/102 (5)

Bowling: *First Innings*—Bloomfield 11–0–43–0; Hunt 13.4–1–68–1; Laraman 9–1–32–3; Hutton 16–7–37–4; Weekes 1–0–4–0. *Second Innings*—Bloomfield 17–4–45–3; Hunt 10–1–58–0; Laraman 10–2–55–1; Hutton 16–4–43–0; Weekes 11–1–54–0; Shah 2–0–15–0.

Middlesex

*A. J. Strauss lbw b Fernando	27	A. W. Laraman not out	39
S. G. Koenig lbw b Perera	0	T. A. Hunt c Upashantha b Perera	3
R. M. S. Weston b Fernando	0	T. F. Bloomfield lbw b Chandana	0
O. A. Shah c Jayasuriya b Upashantha	65	L-b 2, n-b 11	13
E. C. Joyce lbw b Fernando	93		
B. L. Hutton lbw b Upashantha	0		**274**
P. N. Weekes lbw b Upashantha	3		
†D. Alleyne b Fernando	31		

1/6 (2) 2/14 (3) 3/45 (1) 4/159 (4)
5/159 (6) 6/164 (7) 7/225 (5)
8/244 (8) 9/272 (10) 10/274 (11)

Bowling: Perera 16–3–39–2; Fernando 18–4–72–4; Upashantha 17–2–85–3; Chandana 18–5–53–1; Jayawardene 4–1–14–0; Jayasuriya 1–0–9–0.

Umpires: G. I. Burgess and P. J. Hartley.

Leicestershire's modest summer on the field was followed by a shambolic winter off it.

Leicestershire, page 681

ENGLAND v SRI LANKA

First npower Test

At Lord's, May 16, 17, 18, 19, 20. Drawn. Toss: Sri Lanka.

Sri Lanka had won nine straight Tests when they took the field at Lord's, but English commentators still felt compelled to patronise them. The assumption was that their victories in Asia would be no guide to their form on damp days and seaming wickets in May. The absence of Muttiah Muralitharan, who was being treated for a dislocated shoulder in Melbourne after a bad fall in the field in an inconsequential one-day game in Sharjah, was commonly expected to be decisive. However, on the first day of the series the buds of May were blossoming and Lord's was like a summer idyll. The sun shone, the less than capacity crowd wore their lightest clothes, and the wicket was as flat as Norfolk. After two days of their first fairly full series in England, the only team with a realistic chance of winning was Sri Lanka, and the pundits had turned their attention to the elegance and fluency of their batsmen.

Hussain, who lost the toss for the 19th time in 22, led a team in which, disappointingly, no room was found for the promising young players who had graduated from the Academy in Adelaide; no Ian Bell or Alex Tudor, who had at least made the squad. The recall of Crawley and Cork brought cries of *Dad's Army*, although neither man had turned 31. Stewart's return at 39 was less controversial only because James Foster, his replacement in India, had broken his arm.

Sri Lanka chose to bat and started as their critics expected them to go on. Sanath Jayasuriya's series began disastrously when he misjudged a third run and was out for 18. Sangakkara edged Hoggard to slip, just as forecast, and Sri Lanka were 55 for two. But they had not studied the script, because nearly four hours later that was 261 for three and England were reeling.

Atapattu and Jayawardene batted sumptuously, displaying style and finesse in a stand of 206. Atapattu had already shown his skills before a Lord's audience, whereas Jayawardene was a revelation. He had eight Test centuries to his name, but this was statistical excellence made flesh. When he was on 47, a ball from Flintoff badly bruised his left hip. A runner was called for, but his power and precision did not desert him. Only the jingoists in the crowd were pleased when he was out for 107, playing Flintoff casually to Trescothick at short mid-wicket. At the close Sri Lanka were 314 for three and Duncan Fletcher had unkind words for all his bowlers bar Flintoff. Caddick, and England, had failed yet again when the tone needed to be set, but some of the responsibility lay with the management, who had taken a policy decision to bowl a full length: between them, Caddick and Hoggard bowled 75 full deliveries on day one, and they went for 103 runs.

The policy did not last into the second day, when the bowling was shorter, Sri Lanka added 241 runs less gloriously and Atapattu failed by only 15 to make his sixth Test double-century. De Silva dug in for 88 in one of his less attractive innings at Lord's. England's bowling figures were grim. Cork improved his with a couple of late wickets, but Caddick remained empty-handed and the most expensive of all was Hoggard, whom Hussain humiliated by taking him off after bowling the first over on day two. England lost Trescothick in the eight remaining overs and 329 runs were still needed just to save the follow-on.

But the openers would be back in again the next evening as England collapsed abysmally and failed by 81 runs to make Sri Lanka bat next. The weather had changed overnight and was sufficiently overcast and damp to delay the third-day start by 20 minutes. Butcher soon fell but Vaughan and Hussain took advantage of the benign wicket. Hussain had 11 boundaries in his 57, and there was no rational explanation for what happened after their stand of 106 was broken. Crawley said later that conditions overhead were difficult, but that did not explain Vaughan's undignified heave to fine leg, or the absence of any contribution from Stewart, Flintoff or Cork in what should have been a long batting order.

Action replay: Marvan Atapattu dominated England's attack on the opening day of the series just as he had at Galle 15 months earlier, but the quality of Sri Lanka's cricket was soon overshadowed by the furore of Ruchira Perera's elbow. *Pictures by Patrick Eagar.*

Sri Lanka's four-man seam attack – with only one right-hander (Buddhika Fernando) among them – had been competent, especially considering that Murali was not there to bowl his usual unfair share. Ruchira Perera was accused of chucking on both radio and TV during the day and at the end of the game his action was referred to the ICC, but his three wickets came from poor shots rather than illegal deliveries.

The result may well have been decided in the first 20 minutes of the bright, fine morning of the fourth day. Jayasuriya, at first slip, dropped Vaughan twice. Both were easy chances. His colleagues consoled their captain after the first, but left him alone after the second, presumably because he was inconsolable. Vaughan, who had apologised to his team-mates for his first-innings indiscretion, added 168 for the first wicket with Trescothick and made a fluent, upright second Test century; theirs were the only wickets to fall that day. England were effectively 41 for two and early wickets on the last morning might have set off a panic, but in the second over Jayasuriya sent four men to the boundary; three more patrolled the covers and there was just one slip. Sri Lanka had accepted the draw.

Butcher knuckled down, suppressing his natural game and taking six and a half hours to score 105. When he was out, the score was 432 and the game had been saved. England batted on to make their first 500 since January 1997 in Auckland (Sri Lanka's 500 had been their eighth in ten Tests), but showed little interest in putting their opponents under pressure. Thirteen overs were left when they finally declared and the only news was that Caddick, typically, bowled better second time around and Hussain declined to open with Hoggard. His confidence was a casualty of the First Test, but the greater casualty was Sri Lanka's ambition and self-belief. **Stephen Fay**

Man of the Match: M. S. Atapattu. *Attendance:* 86,612; *receipts* £1,440,000.

Close of play: First day, Sri Lanka 314-3 (Atapattu 133, de Silva 24); Second day, England 27-1 (Vaughan 4, Butcher 7); Third day, England 53-0 (Trescothick 31, Vaughan 20); Fourth day, England 321-2 (Butcher 55, Hussain 51).

Sri Lanka

M. S. Atapattu c Trescothick b Cork	185	– c Butcher b Caddick	7
*S. T. Jayasuriya run out	18		
†K. C. Sangakkara c Flintoff b Hoggard	10	– (2) not out	6
D. P. M. D. Jayawardene c Trescothick b Flintoff	107	– (3) not out	14
P. A. de Silva c Stewart b Cork	88		
R. P. Arnold c Trescothick b Hoggard	50		
H. P. Tillekeratne not out	17		
W. P. U. J. C. Vaas c Trescothick b Cork	6		
D. N. T. Zoysa c Stewart b Flintoff	28		
T. C. B. Fernando not out	6		
B 1, l-b 13, w 1, n-b 25	40	B 5, l-b 2, n-b 8	15

1/38 (2) 2/55 (3) 3/261 (4)   (8 wkts dec.) 555   1/16 (1)   (1 wkt) 42
4/407 (1) 5/492 (6) 6/492 (5)
7/505 (8) 8/540 (9)

P. D. R. L. Perera did not bat.

Bowling: *First Innings*—Caddick 38.3–8–135–0; Hoggard 39–4–160–2; Cork 35.3–11–93–3; Flintoff 39–8–101–2; Butcher 3–0–17–0; Vaughan 14–2–35–0. *Second Innings*—Caddick 7–2–10–1; Flintoff 5–0–18–0; Hoggard 1–0–7–0.

England

M. E. Trescothick c Jayasuriya b Zoysa	13	– lbw b Zoysa	76
M. P. Vaughan c Zoysa b Perera	64	– c Sangakkara b Perera	115
M. A. Butcher c Jayawardene b Fernando	17	– run out	105
*N. Hussain c Sangakkara b Zoysa	57	– lbw b Perera	68
G. P. Thorpe lbw b Perera	27	– c Fernando b de Silva	65
J. P. Crawley c Sangakkara b Vaas	31	– not out	41
†A. J. Stewart run out	7	– not out	26
A. Flintoff c Sangakkara b Fernando	12		
D. G. Cork c Sangakkara b Fernando	0		
A. R. Caddick c Sangakkara b Perera	13		
M. J. Hoggard not out	0		
B 4, l-b 7, w 9, n-b 14	34	B 1, l-b 9, w 1, n-b 22	33

1/17 (1) 2/43 (3) 3/149 (4) 4/203 (2)   275   1/168 (1) 2/213 (2)   (5 wkts dec.) 529
5/203 (5) 6/214 (7) 7/237 (8)   3/372 (4) 4/432 (3)
8/237 (9) 9/267 (10) 10/275 (6)   5/483 (5)

Bowling: *First Innings*—Vaas 21.1–4–51–1; Zoysa 19–3–82–2; Fernando 22–5–83–3; Perera 11–0–48–3. *Second Innings*—Vaas 44–8–113–0; Zoysa 34–6–84–1; Perera 30–4–90–2; de Silva 27–7–63–1; Fernando 26–1–96–0; Jayasuriya 25–6–66–0; Arnold 4–1–7–0; Tillekeratne 1–1–0–0.

Umpires: D. J. Harper (Australia) and S. Venkataraghavan (India).
Third umpire: J. W. Lloyds. Referee: G. R. Viswanath (India).

GLAMORGAN v SRI LANKANS

At Cardiff, May 23, 24, 25, 26. Drawn. Toss: Glamorgan.

Rain continued to dog the Sri Lankans and play was possible only on the first day. Simon Jones opened the bowling at the request of the England coach, Duncan Fletcher, who was there to watch, but struggled to extract life from a slow pitch. Jayasuriya scythed 48 of his 57 in boundaries, before making it clear he did not like the decision that undid him. Sangakkara – who had been slow to adapt to English conditions – played decisively square of the wicket to reach a chanceless century and add 175 with Tillekeratne. Glamorgan were eventually rewarded for their persistence as five wickets fell for 37. Wharf, returning after two heel operations, showed impressive stamina, as well as resilience after some early hammer. As the rain fell, eyes turned to Muralitharan, who bowled in the indoor nets, prompting speculation that he would play in the Second Test. He did; Jones did not.

Close of play: First day, Sri Lankans 337-7 (Jayawardene 12, Wanasinghe 6); Second day, No play; Third day, No play.

Sri Lankans

*S. T. Jayasuriya c Wallace b Wharf . . . 57	K. E. A. Upashantha c Powell b Jones . . 6
R. P. Arnold lbw b Wharf 46	W. M. P. N. Wanasinghe not out 6
†K. C. Sangakkara c Wallace	
b S. D. Thomas . 113	B 3, l-b 3, w 2 8
H. P. Tillekeratne c Wallace b Wharf . . . 81	
T. T. Samaraweera c Dale b Wharf . . . 7	1/97 (1) 2/108 (2) 3/283 (3) (7 wkts) 337
U. D. U. Chandana c Wallace b Croft. . . 1	4/299 (5) 5/306 (6)
H. A. P. W. Jayawardene not out 12	6/312 (4) 7/320 (8)

C. R. D. Fernando and K. S. C. de Silva did not bat.

Bowling: Jones 20–1–79–1; S. D. Thomas 20–1–102–1; Wharf 25–2–71–4; Croft 27–11–61–1; Dale 7–3–18–0.

Glamorgan

*S. P. James, D. L. Hemp, I. J. Thomas, M. J. Powell, A. Dale, J. Hughes, R. D. B. Croft, S. D. Thomas, †M. A. Wallace, A. G. Wharf and S. P. Jones.

Umpires: M. Dixon and J. W. Lloyds.

ENGLAND v SRI LANKA

Second npower Test

At Birmingham, May 30, 31, June 1, 2. England won by an innings and 111 runs. Toss: England.

The crucial moment came towards the close of the third day. Not the third day here at Edgbaston, but a fortnight earlier at Lord's, when England had at last roused themselves and remembered how to play cricket. They went on to make a stack of runs and, briefly, bowled with fire in their hearts. Whatever Duncan Fletcher and Nasser Hussain had said as they contemplated the follow-on, it was enough for England to retain an Australian intensity for the duration of the Second Test. For the first time in many a moon, England dictated terms throughout, barely suffering so much as a bad session. Their victory was as clinical as it was crushing.

For the tourists, there was just one selection issue: would Muralitharan be fit to play? He wasn't, but he played anyway, increasing the burden on his injured shoulder. Sri Lanka had won none of the 12 Tests he had missed since his 1992-93 debut and ached to have him back. So out went Ruchira Perera, undergoing remedial work on a suspect action, and in came Murali – against his wishes, it was rumoured. England also brought in a spinner, Giles, who replaced Crawley in a more balanced side of five specialist batsmen and four specialist bowlers, with Stewart and Flintoff in between. Hussain and Fletcher stuck by Hoggard, though not before his poor Lord's showing had earned him a public dressing-down, and Tudor replaced Cork.

Rain claimed the morning session but, more unusually, Hussain claimed the toss. Given the chance to exploit a dampish pitch, the England attack did so with consummate skill – or rather Caddick did. Awkward, rearing, seaming deliveries were the rule for him, the exception for his colleagues. His bounce, especially nasty for the left-handers,

Wrong-footed: Sanath Jayasuriya never really found his feet on tour – something Matthew Hoggard was happy to exploit in Sri Lanka's second innings at Edgbaston. *Picture by Patrick Eagar.*

soon had the out-of-sorts Jayasuriya caught behind. Hoggard had already evicted Atapattu in similar fashion, leaving Sri Lanka 23 for two. The third wicket dug in to add 53 before a moment of rank idiocy prompted Sangakkara to chase a delivery from Flintoff so wide it seemed to be hurtling towards gully. Stewart somehow clung on to take his 200th dismissal as a Test wicket-keeper. Jayawardene, class running through his veins, was undone by a Caddick classic: the ball pitched short and around off stump, bucked, seamed, caught the edge and flew to second slip. After that, a farrago of feckless shots, as well as incisive bowling, hustled Sri Lanka out for 162.

The weather stole more play after tea, though there was time enough for England to face seven overs; time enough, too, for Murali to bowl a couple, and for Vaughan to hit his 1,000th Test run. The next day revealed the true value of the toss. Under a warm summer sun and on an impeccable pitch, runs simply flowed as the opening pair sailed merrily along at five an over. Trescothick should have been lbw to Buddhika Fernando when 29, but that went England's way, like everything else, until Vaughan top-edged a sweep. Butcher scratched about before settling, but soon after lunch England eased into the lead with nine wickets in hand. By the time Trescothick slammed Vaas into mid-wicket's hands on the stroke of tea, the score was 294. He and Butcher had added 202, a record for any English wicket against Sri Lanka. Trescothick showed no pity: his highest Test innings contained an array of rasping, forceful shots, including three sixes biffed over the bowler's head and 23 fours, none involving unnecessary risk.

Before the match, Jayasuriya conceded that Murali would need mollycoddling. His injured left shoulder hurt so much that each appeal turned his winsome grin into a wince of pain, yet on the second day, he still totted up 42 overs. Trescothick had kept him at bay with ease, though the ball which removed Butcher for a solid, sometimes elegant 94 was a beauty: one to replay in the mind on long winter evenings. It pitched 18 inches outside leg, spat off the pitch and clipped the off bail. Despite losing Hussain soon afterwards, England were right on top at 341 for four. Not that there was any dominance in the next passage of play. Stewart was as unable to read Murali's variations as escape his clutches, and he writhed and squirmed for an hour. It was a mercy for all when he was put out of his misery.

England began Saturday at 401 for five but, after umpire Harper hallucinated an edge from Flintoff's increasingly confident bat, subsided to 454 for nine, as Zoysa used his height and new-found aggression in a passable impression of a left-arm Caddick. Thorpe, with 5,000 Test runs under his belt, interpreted Hoggard's arrival as a sign of impending doom, and turned down countless singles rather than risk losing strike. Two hours later, it was Hoggard, batting out of his skin, who ran out of partners. On his way to a highest Test score, he helped steer England past 500 for the second consecutive innings and saw Thorpe from 61 to a canny century. Together, they put on 91 (a tenth-wicket record between these sides) and it was Hoggard who faced more balls. Murali, whose mollycoddling restricted him to a mere 64 overs, took five wickets, yet he struggled against England's troika of left-handers; between them, they made three-quarters of the runs from the bat.

When a demoralised Sri Lanka began their second innings, 383 behind, matters took an immediate turn for the worse. Hoggard, straight back in the thick of the action and brimful of confidence, castled Jayasuriya, then despatched Sangakkara, who had kept wicket in exemplary fashion for almost two days. Sri Lanka's centurions from Lord's, Atapattu and Jayawardene, batted through the extended evening session to kindle hopes of a fightback, but next morning, Edgbaston resembled the *Mary Celeste*. The ball everyone was watching was being kicked by David Beckham and co as the England football team began their World Cup campaign. The crucial ball, though, was the one Atapattu dragged on to his stumps. Caddick, hitting a relentlessly menacing length, removed Jayawardene shortly afterwards. Sri Lanka showed more gumption this time, though not once the new ball was taken. Murali, who briefly batted one-handed on the first day, chose to stay in the pavilion, and England were one up in a series they had begun atrociously. **Hugh Chevallier**

Man of the Match: M. J. Hoggard.   *Attendance*: 51,600; *receipts* £770,000.

Close of play: First day, England 24-0 (Trescothick 9, Vaughan 14); Second day, England 401-5 (Thorpe 30, Flintoff 14); Third day, Sri Lanka 132-2 (Atapattu 56, Jayawardene 45).

Sri Lanka

M. S. Atapattu c Stewart b Hoggard	13	– b Hoggard 56
*S. T. Jayasuriya c Stewart b Caddick	8	– b Hoggard 12
†K. C. Sangakkara c Stewart b Flintoff	16	– lbw b Hoggard 1
D. P. M. D. Jayawardene c Flintoff b Caddick .	47	– c Thorpe b Caddick 59
P. A. de Silva c Trescothick b Hoggard	10	– c Thorpe b Caddick 47
H. P. Tillekeratne lbw b Tudor	20	– b Caddick 39
R. P. Arnold c Flintoff b Caddick	1	– c Giles b Hoggard 4
W. P. U. J. C. Vaas b Flintoff	23	– st Stewart b Giles 28
D. N. T. Zoysa c Hoggard b Tudor	0	– (10) not out 1
T. C. B. Fernando run out	13	– (9) b Hoggard 0
M. Muralitharan not out	0	– absent hurt
B 1, n-b 10	11	B 4, l-b 4, n-b 17 25

1/23 (1) 2/23 (2) 3/76 (3) 4/96 (5)   162   1/28 (2) 2/30 (3) 3/135 (1)   272
5/100 (4) 6/108 (7) 7/141 (6)   4/156 (4) 5/233 (6) 6/238 (5)
8/141 (9) 9/159 (8) 10/162 (10)   7/247 (7) 8/247 (9) 9/272 (8)

Bowling: *First Innings*—Caddick 17–4–47–3; Hoggard 17–4–55–2; Giles 4–1–7–0; Tudor 9.5–3–25–2; Flintoff 5–0–27–2. *Second Innings*—Caddick 25–4–67–3; Hoggard 23.2–2–92–5; Flintoff 6–0–23–0; Giles 26.1–3–57–1; Tudor 9–1–25–0.

England

M. E. Trescothick c Tillekeratne b Vaas . 161	A. J. Tudor c Tillekeratne b Zoysa 3
M. P. Vaughan c Jayasuriya	A. F. Giles c Sangakkara b Zoysa 0
b Muralitharan . . 46	A. R. Caddick c Sangakkara b Zoysa . . . 3
M. A. Butcher b Muralitharan. 94	M. J. Hoggard not out. 17
*N. Hussain b Muralitharan. 22	L-b 19, w 6, n-b 15. 40
G. P. Thorpe c Vaas b Fernando 123	
†A. J. Stewart c Tillekeratne	1/92 (2) 2/294 (1) 3/338 (3) 4/341 (4) 545
b Muralitharan . 7	5/368 (6) 6/426 (7) 7/436 (8)
A. Flintoff c Tillekeratne b Muralitharan . 29	8/444 (9) 9/454 (10) 10/545 (5)

Bowling: Vaas 41–3–141–1; Zoysa 24–3–93–3; Muralitharan 64–12–143–5; Fernando 21.5–2–92–1; Jayasuriya 6–2–27–0; de Silva 7–0–30–0.

Umpires: D. J. Harper (Australia) and S. Venkataraghavan (India).
Third umpire: P. Willey.   Referee: G. R. Viswanath (India).

MCC v SRI LANKANS

At Chesterfield, June 6, 7, 8. Drawn. Toss: MCC.

Soggy run-ups and light mist hanging in the encircling trees meant Chesterfield, without first-class cricket for four years, had to wait one more day. When play finally started, as the groundstaff finished trowelling the goose turds from the outfield, Robert Key's bludgeoning back-foot shots into the leg side and crisp drives into the off were punctuated by loud gasps from fans glued to England's famous win over Argentina in the football World Cup. Key hurried MCC to 87 from 12 overs but the tempo fell after his uncharacteristically meek cut to slip. Afzaal's century contained far fewer imperious strokes but only Dilhara Fernando, surprisingly rapid after six months out with a stress fracture of the back, was incisive on a green-tinged pitch. After Fulton declared on the last morning, it would have taken a pair of forfeited innings to breathe life back into the match. They didn't come and, with the draw inevitable, even Sri Lanka's spectacular collapse to 127 all out failed to get pulses racing. Kirtley took two early wickets amid a barrage of big shots and Dean found swing to remove Arnold and Tillekeratne. De Silva, whose unbeaten 54 included five fours, three sixes, and one ball lost in the lake, provided a diversion as the game dribbled away in splendid late-afternoon sunshine.

Close of play: First day, No play; Second day, MCC 270-6 (Afzaal 80, Dawson 10).

MCC

A. J. Strauss c Chandana b Fernando 32	– (2) not out.	37
R. W. T. Key c Tillekeratne b Chandana 77		
*D. P. Fulton c Jayawardene b Perera 29	– (1) not out.	47
O. A. Shah c Perera b Fernando 0		
U. Afzaal not out 111		
D. I. Stevens c Tillekeratne b Perera 3		
†C. M. W. Read c Jayasuriya b Perera 24		
R. K. J. Dawson c Arnold b Perera 15		
K. J. Dean not out 14		
L-b 7, w 1, n-b 13 21	L-b 1, n-b 8.	9

1/95 (1) 2/148 (3) 3/148 (2) (7 wkts dec.) 326 (no wkt dec.) 93
4/148 (4) 5/170 (6)
6/238 (7) 7/287 (8)

S. P. Jones and R. J. Kirtley did not bat.

Bowling: *First Innings*—Perera 20–3–66–4; Upashantha 12–0–96–0; Fernando 18–3–53–2; Samaraweera 16–2–46–0; Chandana 15–4–45–1; Jayasuriya 5–0–13–0. *Second Innings*—Perera 4–0–33–0; Upashantha 6–0–30–0; Samaraweera 4–0–15–0; Chandana 2–0–11–0; Tillekeratne 1–0–3–0.

Sri Lankans

*S. T. Jayasuriya c Read b Kirtley	16	K. E. A. Upashantha c Read b Jones	8
K. C. Sangakkara lbw b Kirtley	6	C. R. D. Fernando c Read b Kirtley	3
R. P. Arnold c Afzaal b Dean	3	P. D. R. L. Perera c Jones b Dawson	5
H. P. Tillekeratne b Dean	0		
T. T. Samaraweera c Dawson b Jones	10	B 5, l-b 8, w 1, n-b 1	15
U. D. U. Chandana run out	0		
†H. A. P. W. Jayawardene c Read b Dean	7	1/22 (1) 2/23 (2) 3/24 (4) 4/25 (3)	127
P. A. de Silva not out	54	5/30 (6) 6/43 (7) 7/45 (5)	
		8/57 (9) 9/116 (10) 10/127 (11)	

Bowling: Kirtley 13–4–47–3; Dean 12–3–29–3; Jones 6–2–23–2; Dawson 4.3–1–15–1.

Umpires: A. Hill and A. G. T. Whitehead.

ENGLAND v SRI LANKA

Third npower Test

At Manchester, June 13, 14, 15, 16, 17. England won by ten wickets. Toss: England.

A Test that had crept along in the shadow of football's World Cup sprang dramatically into life in the equivalent of extra time. As darkness began to fall on the final evening, Giles winkled out Sri Lanka's last two wickets in two balls to leave England a target of 50 in six overs, a penalty shoot-out of a different kind. Vaughan and Trescothick kept their nerve to launch a blistering assault and seal a 2–0 series win with an over to spare. Cricket wasn't quite coming home, but the feeling of optimism that had evaporated the previous summer filled the air once more.

England's victory was a triumph of patience and timing. For an unprecedented third innings in a row they racked up 500. Then, on a pitch that was more pancake than pudding, and without the experience of Caddick, who pulled up in his sixth over, they gritted their teeth, bent their backs, and went for the jugular. Flintoff was the sledgehammer, driving the batsmen on to the back foot; Hoggard the scalpel, swinging the ball both ways with subtlety and incision. But it was Tudor, man of the match for his sustained hostility and seven wickets, who provided the class. And when the quicks slowed, Giles stepped in.

Sri Lanka had been losing momentum ever since the middle of the First Test, and here, with the exception of Arnold and Muralitharan, they were a shambles. Jayasuriya's captaincy was unimaginative, while his failure to stem the singles during England's run-sprint was simply negligent. With the ship rudderless, the crew floundered. Upashantha and Dilhara Fernando, who came in for the injured Zoysa and Buddhika Fernando, had games to forget. Upashantha gifted England's openers a dream start after Hussain had won the toss, then handed Trescothick a life after lunch by dropping a sitter at square leg. Fernando leaked almost a run a ball. Worse, only Arnold, on a batsman's pitch, passed 40.

There was unrest off the field too. The news that Chandra Schaffter, the Sri Lankan manager, would not have his contract renewed at the end of the tour came as no surprise. But the resignation of their Australian bowling coach, Daryl Foster, after an argument with the Sri Lankan board about the plane fare to Perth to visit a sick grandchild, certainly did.

England's confidence after Edgbaston was reflected by an unchanged side and another remorseless display with the bat. The fifty came up in the tenth over and, after Vaughan fell to Fernando's slower ball, Trescothick motored on, crashing ten fours in his half-century. The in-form Butcher helped add 126 for the second wicket before Trescothick edged to slip, the first time he had fallen to Murali in 350 balls in Tests.

Rain lopped 18 overs off the first day and allowed just 28 on the second, but it didn't stop Steve Bucknor leading the players on to the field twice when drizzle was

The feel-good factor: the ecstasy of victory is written on **Michael Vaughan's** face as England complete their dash to glory at Old Trafford. *Picture by Patrick Eagar.*

MOST INTERNATIONAL RUNS AT THE AGE OF 35 OR OLDER

		Avge	*Tests*	*ODIs*
6,245	G. A. Gooch (E)	42.19	4,563 at 48.54	1,682 at 31.14
4,775	**A. J. Stewart (E)**	**34.85**	**3,034 at 38.40**	**1,741 at 30.01**
4,671	C. G. Greenidge (WI)	40.61	2,525 at 38.84	2,146 at 42.92
4,500	G. Boycott (E)	46.39	3,535 at 47.77	965 at 41.95
4,414	C. H. Lloyd (WI)	45.97	2,921 at 52.16	1,493 at 37.32
3,796	S. M. Gavaskar (I)	43.63	1,728 at 45.47	2,068 at 42.20
3,765	I. V. A. Richards (WI)	39.63	2,107 at 43.00	1,658 at 36.04
3,734	A. R. Border (A)	35.56	2,473 at 42.63	1,261 at 26.82
3,605	D. L. Haynes (WI)	39.61	1,578 at 45.08	2,027 at 36.19
3,445	Zaheer Abbas (P)	52.19	2,039 at 52.28	1,406 at 52.07
3,189	E. H. Hendren (E)	53.15	3,189 at 53.15	
2,961	Imran Khan (P)	44.19	1,037 at 61.00	1,924 at 38.48

Up to January 31, 2003.

Alec Stewart is now behind only Graham Gooch, his one-time opening partner and role model, in the list of elderly run-makers. Stewart has the lowest average of those on the list, whether in Tests or all internationals, but the others were not being asked to keep wicket. This is a list not dominated by Australians: longevity belongs largely to Englishmen, West Indians and Pakistanis. The highest average in Tests is by Imran, in one-dayers Zaheer. Patsy Hendren gets in without the benefit of one-day internationals; Jack Hobbs is bubbling under, with 2,945 Test runs at 56.63.

Research: Chris Ryan

---

falling, in his 67th Test – a world record, surpassing Dickie Bird. Nor did it stop Butcher, who timed the ball exquisitely off his pads, moving to his fifth Test century, and his third in five Tests in England. He had barely played a false stroke when Vaas trapped him leg-before. Flintoff was freakishly run out by a deflection on to the stumps at the bowler's end, but now Stewart, dropped in the gully on nought, took over. He was equalling Graham Gooch's England record of 118 Test caps, but had gone into the match with his career in the balance. He came out fighting, which was typical, showed authority against Muralitharan, which was not, and began the third day on 57. Stewart first lost Tudor, who flashed to second slip to give Vaas his 200th Test wicket, and then about 5,000 spectators, who drifted off behind the Stretford End to watch England's footballers take on Denmark on a giant screen provided by the ECB at a cost of £10,000. A keen football fan himself, Stewart celebrated England's first goal with a glorious drive through extra cover off Muralitharan, and brought up his 15th Test century in style with four consecutive fours off Fernando – two pulls, a cover drive and a punch down the ground. It had taken him just 146 balls and soon after he moved past Colin Cowdrey into fifth place on England's list of leading Test run-scorers. He and Giles helped top 500 once more by adding 102 for the eighth wicket.

Sri Lanka's reply got off to a frenetic start: Caddick limped off with a side strain, only for Flintoff to take Atapattu out of the equation too with a stinging blow to his right hand. But Arnold, opening in place of the still out-of-sorts Jayasuriya, counter-attacked skilfully, and Sri Lanka ended the third evening on 130 for one. They reached 219 for four next day, but accurate bowling, clever captaincy, slapdash strokeplay and the second new ball combined to see off the remaining five wickets – Atapattu was absent injured – for just 34.

Sri Lanka followed on for the first time against England, 259 behind, but luck seemed to be going their way on the final day when, two overs before lunch, Jayawardene flicked Flintoff to Hoggard at deep backward square, only for umpire Orchard, who had just moved from square leg to point, to signal no-ball. Orchard had spotted that Hoggard had accidentally become the third fielder behind square on the leg side – along with Vaughan at leg slip and Simon Jones, on as substitute, at fine leg. England

were downcast. Jayawardene added just ten more runs, but with Arnold reaching a
patient five-and-a-half-hour century to take Sri Lanka to 253 for four at tea, the game
was heading for a draw.

Again, the second new ball proved crucial. Arnold drove expansively at Tudor, Vaas
was beaten by Hoggard's nip-backer, and Upashantha heaved at Flintoff. Fernando held
out for 44 minutes; then a heavily bandaged Atapattu emerged to keep Tillekeratne
company until, with time running out, he played back fatally to Giles, who then snaffled
Muralitharan first ball.

The race was on, but Fernando's first over cost 16, and when Trescothick slog-swept
Muralitharan for six, there was only one team in it. England had won only their second
Test at Old Trafford since 1981. For an evening, at least, it was almost possible to
forget about the football. **Lawrence Booth**

Man of the Match: A. J. Tudor.   *Attendance*: 45,089; *receipts* £370,000.

Men of the Series: England – M. A. Butcher; Sri Lanka – D. P. M. D. Jayawardene.

Close of play: First day, England 273-4 (Butcher 85, Stewart 7); Second day, England
377-6 (Stewart 57, Tudor 6); Third day, Sri Lanka 130-1 (Sangakkara 33, Jayawardene 11); Fourth
day, Sri Lanka 63-1 (Arnold 26, Sangakkara 9).

England

M. E. Trescothick c Jayawardene b Muralitharan	81	– not out	23
M. P. Vaughan c Vaas b Fernando	36	– not out	24
M. A. Butcher lbw b Vaas	123		
*N. Hussain c Muralitharan b Fernando	16		
G. P. Thorpe c Sangakkara b Upashantha	32		
†A. J. Stewart c Tillekeratne b Muralitharan	123		
A. Flintoff run out	1		
A. J. Tudor c Arnold b Vaas	19		
A. F. Giles c Sangakkara b Muralitharan	45		
A. R. Caddick not out	2		
M. J. Hoggard lbw b Fernando	7		
B 5, l-b 10, n-b 12	27	L-b 2, n-b 1	3

1/66 (2) 2/192 (1) 3/219 (4) 4/262 (5)   512   (no wkt) 50
5/354 (3) 6/361 (7) 7/400 (8)
8/502 (9) 9/503 (6) 10/512 (11)

Bowling: *First Innings*—Vaas 38–8–121–2; Upashantha 8–0–65–1; Fernando 29.2–2–154–3;
Muralitharan 60–20–137–3; de Silva 2–0–5–0; Jayasuriya 8–2–15–0. *Second Innings*—Vaas
1–0–8–0; Fernando 2–0–23–0; Muralitharan 2–0–17–0.

Sri Lanka

M. S. Atapattu retired hurt	10	– (10) lbw b Giles	6
R. P. Arnold c Vaughan b Tudor	62	– (1) c Stewart b Tudor	109
†K. C. Sangakkara c Thorpe b Hoggard	40	– lbw b Tudor	32
D. P. M. D. Jayawardene c and b Tudor	17	– c Hussain b Giles	28
P. A. de Silva c Hussain b Flintoff	18	– c Vaughan b Tudor	40
*S. T. Jayasuriya lbw b Hoggard	35	– (2) b Hoggard	26
H. P. Tillekeratne c Flintoff b Giles	20	– (6) not out	32
W. P. U. J. C. Vaas lbw b Hoggard	14	– (7) lbw b Hoggard	2
K. E. A. Upashantha c Stewart b Tudor	1	– (8) c Stewart b Flintoff	1
C. R. D. Fernando not out	6	– (9) lbw b Giles	4
M. Muralitharan c Stewart b Tudor	6	– c sub (M. J. Powell) b Giles	0
B 1, l-b 3, n-b 20	24	B 9, l-b 9, w 2, n-b 7	27

1/107 (2) 2/142 (4) 3/149 (3)   253   1/44 (2) 2/110 (3) 3/170 (4)   308
4/171 (5) 5/219 (7) 6/227 (6)   4/233 (5) 5/263 (1) 6/264 (7)
7/228 (9) 8/240 (9) 9/253 (11)   7/270 (8) 8/285 (9)
                                                        9/308 (10) 10/308 (11)

In the first innings, Atapattu retired hurt at 48.

Bowling: *First Innings*—Caddick 5.3–2–17–0; Hoggard 16–4–38–3; Flintoff 23–5–65–1; Tudor 25–8–65–4; Giles 23–3–64–1. *Second Innings*—Hoggard 37–8–97–2; Flintoff 29–7–78–1; Giles 24.2–4–62–4; Tudor 21–6–44–3; Vaughan 2–0–9–0.

Umpires: S. A. Bucknor (West Indies) and D. L. Orchard (South Africa).
Third umpire: N. A. Mallender. Referee: G. R. Viswanath (India).

At Hove, June 19 (day/night). SRI LANKANS beat WEST INDIES A by seven wickets (see West Indies A tour section).

†SOMERSET v SRI LANKANS

At Taunton, June 21. Somerset won by 63 runs. Toss: Somerset.

This was hardly the preparation Sri Lanka needed as the triangular series approached. It did not help their balance or state of mind that Muralitharan had been sent home because of fears of long-term damage to his suspect shoulder. Burns, leading Somerset in the absence of the injured Cox and the vice-captain Trescothick, appropriately provided the backbone of the innings, with good support from Parsons. The target still did not seem an excessive one for the Sri Lankans, though only Nawaz held out any real hopes for them. Their last seven wickets crumbled miserably for 52. Especially reassuring for Somerset was the bowling of Matt Bulbeck, who had been seriously troubled by his back over the past two seasons. He recovered from a shaky start to take four wickets, and Dutch also took four with his off-breaks, but the crowd was thin and the game devoid of atmosphere.

Somerset

P. D. Bowler b Zoysa	18
I. D. Blackwell c Sangakkara b Zoysa	27
M. J. Wood lbw b Vaas	3
†R. J. Turner b Wickremasinghe	6
*M. Burns c Arnold b Wickremasinghe	63
K. A. Parsons c Sangakkara b Zoysa	50
P. C. L. Holloway c Silva b Zoysa	9
K. P. Dutch c Jayawardene b Wickremasinghe	32
M. P. L. Bulbeck lbw b Jayasuriya	12
P. S. Jones run out	8
S. R. G. Francis not out	0
B 2, l-b 4, w 3, n-b 4	13
	241

1/41 (2) 2/48 (1) 3/58 (3)   (48 overs) 241
4/75 (4) 5/159 (5) 6/184 (7)
7/186 (6) 8/214 (9)
9/237 (10) 10/241 (8)

Bowling: Vaas 9–0–48–1; Zoysa 10–1–49–4; Wickremasinghe 9–1–37–3; Chandana 10–0–51–0; Jayasuriya 10–0–50–1.

Sri Lankans

*S. T. Jayasuriya lbw b Bulbeck	0
D. A. Gunawardene lbw b Bulbeck	8
†K. C. Sangakkara c Turner b Jones	33
M. N. Nawaz b Bulbeck	61
L. P. C. Silva c Turner b Dutch	25
D. P. M. D. Jayawardene c Dutch b Bulbeck	12
R. P. Arnold not out	14
U. D. U. Chandana b Dutch	5
W. P. U. J. C. Vaas c Holloway b Dutch	1
D. N. T. Zoysa c and b Dutch	5
G. P. Wickremasinghe run out	3
L-b 3, w 8	11
	178

1/1 (1) 2/16 (2) 3/75 (3)   (42 overs) 178
4/126 (5) 5/145 (6)
6/150 (4) 7/157 (8) 8/161 (9)
9/169 (10) 10/178 (11)

Bowling: Bulbeck 10–0–36–4; Jones 7–0–40–1; Francis 7–0–35–0; Blackwell 8–0–34–0; Dutch 10–1–30–4.

Umpires: R. T. Robinson and D. R. Shepherd.

†GLOUCESTERSHIRE v SRI LANKANS

At Bristol, June 23. Sri Lankans won by 93 runs. Toss: Sri Lankans.

Deciding to bat first on a good-looking wicket brought Jayasuriya the boost he needed as he took a relaxed half-century off 44 balls with two sixes over cover and five fours. Jayawardene stroked 42 off 43 balls and the Sri Lankans were racing away until Alleyne and Harvey pulled them back to 140 for five. Gloucestershire's window of opportunity was slammed shut as Arnold and Nawaz delighted a biggish crowd with a blend of smoothness and power that brought 97 in 15 overs. Arnold had made 80 off 86 balls before underhitting to deep mid-wicket, while Nawaz was on 64 off 64 when he was held at mid-off in the final over. Gloucestershire got the quick start they needed from an enterprising dash by Spearman, dotted with 11 boundaries, but there was little back-up and the final wicket fell at the start of the 37th over.

Sri Lankans

*S. T. Jayasuriya c Russell b Alleyne . . .	53	D. N. T. Zoysa not out 7
†R. S. Kaluwitharana c Ball b Alleyne . .	14	G. P. Wickremasinghe not out 0
M. S. Atapattu run out	6	
D. P. M. D. Jayawardene c Russell b Harvey .	42	B 1, l-b 1, w 2, n-b 2 6
R. P. Arnold c Spearman b Alleyne	80	
L. P. C. Silva c Ball b Harvey	0	1/53 (2) 2/74 (1) (8 wkts, 50 overs) 275
M. N. Nawaz c Ball b Harvey	64	3/81 (3) 4/140 (4)
U. D. U. Chandana c Hardinges b Harvey	3	5/140 (6) 6/237 (5)
		7/253 (8) 8/274 (7)

C. R. D. Fernando did not bat.

Bowling: Lewis 9–1–46–0; Averis 10–0–58–0; Alleyne 8–0–46–3; Hardinges 9–0–48–0; Ball 7–0–40–0; Harvey 7–0–35–4.

Gloucestershire

C. G. Taylor c Kaluwitharana b Fernando	3	†R. C. Russell c Nawaz b Zoysa 10
C. M. Spearman c Chandana b Jayasuriya .	76	J. M. M. Averis b Zoysa 20
I. J. Harvey b Fernando	17	J. Lewis not out 0
M. G. N. Windows b Zoysa	2	L-b 3, w 5, n-b 4 12
A. P. R. Gidman c Nawaz b Fernando . .	10	
M. A. Hardinges run out	16	1/9 (1) 2/35 (3) 3/49 (4) (36.1 overs) 182
M. C. J. Ball c Zoysa b Chandana	4	4/81 (5) 5/118 (6) 6/140 (2)
*M. W. Alleyne c and b Chandana	12	7/142 (7) 8/157 (8)
		9/169 (9) 10/182 (10)

Bowling: Zoysa 7.1–0–43–3; Fernando 8–0–46–3; Wickremasinghe 7–1–33–0; Chandana 10–1–40–2; Jayasuriya 4–0–17–1.

Umpires: J. W. Lloyds and N. A. Mallender.

†NORTHAMPTONSHIRE v SRI LANKANS

At Northampton, June 24 (day/night). Sri Lankans won by eight wickets. Toss: Northamptonshire. County debut: T. M. Baker.

The floodlights had no sooner begun to take effect than the match was over. By 9.15, the Sri Lankans had overwhelmed a half-hearted Northamptonshire attack thanks to a dazzling, stroke-filled innings from Kaluwitharana, which lasted 135 balls and featured two sixes as well as 18 fours. Jayawardene, who played the supporting role to perfection, helped him add 180 in 29 overs, and only Cousins was able to exercise any restraint. Northamptonshire shaped well enough with the bat as Loye hit a six and 13 fours in his 123 from 151 deliveries. Sales joined him in a second-wicket stand of 150, and much of the Sri Lankans' bowling and fielding was appreciably below international standard. When they replied, however, it was a very different story. A local sponsor proclaimed Loye man of the match, but a more objective observer would have found it impossible to resist the claims of Kaluwitharana.

Northamptonshire

*M. E. K. Hussey c Jayawardene b Fernando .	10
M. B. Loye c Kaluwitharana b Vaas . . .	123
D. J. Sales c and b Arnold	65
M. E. Cassar b Fernando	10
J. W. Cook c Jayawardene b Arnold	13
A. L. Penberthy not out	11

G. P. Swann not out	0
L-b 8, w 3, n-b 3	14
1/13 (1) 2/163 (3) (5 wkts, 50 overs) 246	
3/187 (4) 4/208 (5)	
5/239 (2)	

†T. M. B. Bailey, T. M. Baker, D. M. Cousins and J. F. Brown did not bat.

Bowling: Vaas 10–1–49–1; Fernando 10–1–36–2; Wickremasinghe 9–1–46–0; Chandana 8–0–40–0; Jayawardene 3–0–17–0; Arnold 10–0–50–2.

Sri Lankans

D. A. Gunawardene b Cousins	8
†R. S. Kaluwitharana not out	140
*M. S. Atapattu c Swann b Penberthy . .	20
D. P. M. D. Jayawardene not out	67
B 4, l-b 6, w 4	14

1/29 (1) 2/69 (3)   (2 wkts, 43.1 overs) 249

R. P. Arnold, M. N. Nawaz, K. C. Sangakkara, U. D. U. Chandana, W. P. U. J. C. Vaas, T. C. B. Fernando and G. P. Wickremasinghe did not bat.

Bowling: Cousins 8–0–31–1; Baker 10–0–56–0; Penberthy 10–0–57–1; Cassar 2–0–18–0; Brown 7–0–30–0; Swann 5–0–37–0; Cook 1.1–0–10–0.

Umpires: B. Dudleston and K. J. Lyons.

Sri Lanka's matches against England and India in the NatWest Series (June 27–July 11) appear on pages 532–543.

VODAFONE ENGLAND PLAYER OF THE YEAR AWARDS

The Vodafone England Cricketer of the Year Award was won in May 2002 by England captain Nasser Hussain. The women's award went to Clare Connor, the England women's captain. Both received £15,000. Mark Butcher's match-winning 173 not out for England against Australia, at Leeds in August 2001, was named the Outstanding Individual Performance of the Year, and won him £5,000. An equivalent award for the Outstanding Women's Performance was shared by Caroline Atkins and Arran Thompson, for their Test record opening partnership of 200 for England against India at Lucknow in January 2002. An Outstanding Achievement award was made to Mike Atherton, who was presented with a silver bat, engraved with details of his 16 Test centuries.

THE INDIANS IN ENGLAND, 2002

Review by RAHUL BHATTACHARYA

A series of more than three Tests is a rare thing these days. Its shifting dynamics embrace such abstractions as momentum, luck, form, intensity – karma, even – as if it were a universe in itself. India's tour of England in 2002 captured the ebb and flow, the up and down, of this strange and enchanting realm. The series was played out by sides that were evenly matched at the start, became absurdly superior to one another at different points, and ended exactly level as if to reconcile themselves to the truth of the original equation. Life, it appeared, had come a complete circle within the space of four Tests.

The scoreline, 1–1, was frustrating but fair. Michael Vaughan, who came of age with three princely hundreds, did not deserve to be on the losing side; nor did Rahul Dravid, who matched him for excellence if not for excitement. The series was India's first of more than three Tests in England since 1979, and in those 23 years Indian ready-meals had sprung up in Marks & Spencer, chicken tikka masala had overtaken fish and chips as the national dish and Britain had become more multicultural, or more comfortable in its multiculturalism. On hoardings and TV screens, the summer was branded as Indian: there were more Indian movie festivals than anyone could possibly attend, plus the opening season of Andrew Lloyd Webber's musical *Bombay Dreams*. And the lasting flavour of the cricket was Indian.

It was India who made the larger gains, and did so in more valiant fashion. This may seem harsh on England, who at different times were without three, four, even six of their first-choice players. But that must be weighed against India's entire cricket history, which reveals that winning a single Test outside the subcontinent, let alone drawing a series of four matches, is a less frequent occurrence than national elections. India had never drawn a series in England, and although they had won two, in 1971 and 1986, they had lost the other 11 for a combined tally of 41 Tests played, three won and 22 lost.

By the time they finished this, their second long tour in a row following the five-Test series in the Caribbean, India were barking more regularly outside their own border than at any time since 1971. They showed in the one-day triangular series before the Tests, and again in a magnificent fightback from 1–0 down, that they were coming to terms with the mechanisms of digging deep, scrapping and winning against the odds more than ever before. The new, harder India that the captain, Sourav Ganguly, and coach, John Wright, were determined to create was becoming more than just a good idea.

Admittedly, circumstances played their part in making India's effort appear more heroic. Their best efforts came from positions of despair, and from the Second Test onwards, a messy and prolonged row over personal sponsorship twisted and turned till its fortunes were followed back home with as much interest as the cricket. India's cricketers were battling not just against the England cricket team, but the ICC and the Board of Control for Cricket in India as well.

The cricket itself, 19 days of it, could be divided into three sets, each shorter than the one before: a first set of almost nine days, a second of about six and a last of four. In the first, Nasser Hussain and Duncan Fletcher flexed their brains, the England batsmen flexed their muscles and India simply did not know what to do. It began with the First Test at Lord's where, in strangely subcontinental conditions, Hussain employed the grand choke upon the free-scoring Indian middle order, and especially Sachin Tendulkar, to carve out a comprehensive win.

The Indians could not be placated even when Ajit Agarkar, a bowling all-rounder who usually did too little with the bat to justify the title, stroked a frilly second-innings century, bringing a high backlift down in lashing arcs like a lesser Brian Lara. They were still ruing the decision to leave out their greatest perpetrator of batting collapses, Harbhajan Singh, on a pitch that would have encouraged him even though it lacked the bounce that he thrives on. Not even an announcement by Graham Thorpe at the end of the match that he was pulling out of all cricket in an effort to resolve his domestic problems could dampen England's joy at winning three consecutive Tests.

The first set carried over to the first 11 sessions of the next Test, at Trent Bridge, where England batted like Australia to hammer out a 260-run lead. Four Englishmen had scored centuries by this point, and the runs had flowed at four an over. India were not even in the frame.

The second set began in the second over of India's second innings in the Second Test, when they lost their second wicket with the total barely into double figures. India were in danger of losing the match by an innings, putting a series win beyond their reach. Dravid and Tendulkar came together. A spectacular sun came angling out through the clouds late on the fourth evening. Trent Bridge looked beautiful. Now was the time.

By the next evening, the Test had been saved. Tendulkar made 92 runs of bona-fide brilliance, Ganguly scraped an equally crucial 99, and Dravid's 115 occupied almost as many deliveries as both put together, which was a fair indication of its value. Even little Parthiv Patel, the 17-year-old debutant wicket-keeper with bright wide eyes and chubby cheeks, hung around for an hour and a half at the end, a performance stirring enough for the battle-hardened Alec Stewart, 22 years his elder, to put a fatherly arm around him as the players made their way off the pitch. Like an alcoholic who had hit rock bottom, Team India had risen and reformed themselves.

They took this self-belief to Headingley where, given usual conditions, it was all but written in stone that they must lose. Here they made a series of bold decisions. First, they committed themselves to two spinners knowing full well the history of a ground where even Shane Warne had an average of 90-odd. Second, they resisted the urge to recall the opener Shiv Sunder Das, who had just made 250 in a tour game, preferring the utility man Sanjay Bangar, who could offer back-up as third seamer. Third, in order to give the spinners last use of the pitch, they batted first on winning the toss, well aware that the first day would be no tea party.

Every piece fell into place: defensive batting and then attacking batting, seam bowling and then spin bowling, close catching and outfield catching. Dravid and Bangar guarded their wickets on the opening day as if the hopes

Great guns: Michael Vaughan and Rahul Dravid lorded it over the bowlers all summer long. *Pictures by Patrick Eagar.*

of a billion hinged on them, then Tendulkar and Ganguly steamed to a tantalising 249-run partnership at more than four an over. They rattled England, who proceeded to drop four catches in an hour on the third morning. Robert Key, the chunky opener playing his second Test, dropped two more on top of one the previous evening, as his red face kept turning steadily redder.

When it was time to bowl, Anil Kumble produced his greatest performance away from home, and for the first time in a 12-year international career, reaped the rewards. India won by an innings and 46 runs, their largest overseas win. Such was the power of belief. The questions about the mettle of his team that had been asked of Ganguly were now hurled at Hussain. It was one of the great turnarounds.

The third set, which should have been the decider, was the least remarkable. The teams went to The Oval tired and tired, and left tied and tired. On a surface good for little else than batting for long periods, both sides did exactly that. England finished the first day well placed on 336 for two, and Headingley in reverse was a possibility. But they lost the remaining eight wickets for 179 runs, mostly because of the middle order's unwillingness to seize the initiative as the openers had done. When India passed the follow-on mark, the fate of the series was sealed. The game was a washout even before the last day was rained off.

From Vaughan and Dravid, though, who made 195 and 217 respectively, there were batting masterclasses. This series was meant to revolve around Tendulkar. Speculation at every juncture certainly did. After his three failures at Lord's – in the final of the NatWest series and twice in the First Test – all India was beginning to question his big-occasion temperament. Typically, imperturbably, Tendulkarly, he ended the tour with an average of 66.83 and his reputation restored. But it was Dravid who emerged from the shadows to play the central role. He batted for more than 30 hours and compiled 602 studious and utterly critical runs. If Tendulkar remained India's greatest batsman, Dravid was now established as the one you would want to bat for your life – Steve Waugh with more style. When he lifted the helmet off his sweat-drenched face to kiss the Indian crescent upon reaching his third successive century, you could feel the weight of his efforts, the scrupulous diligence behind every run.

Vaughan scored even more than Dravid, more beautifully, and at a much faster rate. If Dravid showed classical mastery of the art of keeping out the seaming ball, Vaughan was the attacking man of the series. He and Trescothick, when fit, gave England flying starts against the slender Indian seamers, and barely slowed down when the spinners came on. The enduring image of Vaughan was of his driving – with the spin of Harbhajan at Trent Bridge, and more deliciously, against the spin of Kumble at The Oval, where he demonstrated just how a line outside the leg stump to a packed leg-side field must be dealt with. He could even produce the odd magic ball, like the one that pitched way outside Tendulkar's off stump at Trent Bridge, drew him forward for the drive, and then squeezed in through the gate to hit the stumps. Vaughan's one weakness was a vulnerability in the nervous 190s. With weaknesses like that, who needed strengths? It was a summer he will never forget, and neither will those who were fortunate enough to watch him.

For the bowlers, it was a poor series. No bowler who played in more than two Tests averaged less than 30, and the highest wicket-takers, Kumble and Matthew Hoggard, managed just 14 each. There was only one five-for: Harbhajan's at The Oval, which contained just two top-order wickets. Against this were the batting statistics, with 13 players averaging in excess of 40. Through the summer, England managed five scores over 500 in seven Tests, and India scored more than 350 every time but the first. The generally flat pitches could take some of the blame, but not all of it. It would be more accurate to conclude that, as suspected all along, both teams had better batsmen than bowlers.

A game of doubles: John Crawley, Nasser Hussain, Sourav Ganguly and Sachin Tendulkar air their views at Lord's. *Picture by Patrick Eagar.*

Bowling cost England more than it did India, because it failed them at the most decisive periods. Not at first: when England wore India down and bowled them out for 221 in the heat, and some dust, of the first innings at Lord's, a semi-makeshift attack carried out Hussain's plan to perfection. Perhaps it was too successful for its own good. The strategy had been to frustrate the batsmen out either by bowling wide of off stump to seven–two or eight–one fields, or by digging in short from round the wicket. Defence, when applied like this, was the best form of attack.

But when the time came to use conventional attacking methods – bowling at the batsmen, making them play as many balls as possible to let movement in the air or off the pitch do the trick – the English bowlers could not do it. They were twice handed a golden opportunity, on the opening day at Trent Bridge and again at Headingley. But they failed to hit the fuller length that greener, more English conditions demanded. It's unclear whether this was part of the strategy; Hussain said during the Headingley Test that "it's not as if there's been any naivety in the dressing-room – we've tried to tell them [the seamers] to pitch it up a bit, but when they have, they've been a bit floaty and hittable". Yet Hussain surely had to take some blame for the line, as he set off-side fields that dissuaded the bowlers from aiming at the stumps for fear of being worked away to leg. And when they did find the correct line, the Indians used judgment. The centuries by Virender Sehwag and Dravid were worth double because they came on the first day, in the most testing conditions of the series.

And so, in his longest summer of captaincy, Hussain was found to be perhaps a little short of ideas, and his stock, feverishly high after the Lord's win, had sunk to normal by the end of the series. There had been a belated recognition of a characteristic found among intense individuals, the benefit of which had hardly ever been granted to Ganguly, least of all by sections of the British press: that their strengths could be, almost in equal measure, their weaknesses. With Ganguly, this meant that the quality which could come across as petulance also provided his team with a rugged, streetfighter edge which they could not previously summon. And so with Hussain, the obsession with attrition as a match-winning tactic, the endless tinkering with fields and continual chat with the bowler could go too far and sometimes be too intellectual and too defensive.

This is not to say that Hussain suddenly ceased to be an excellent captain; just that the warts were now more exposed. Vaughan apart, Hussain had no spark of individual genius to fall back upon, as Ganguly could. This could often manifest itself in little ways. At Headingley, Harbhajan reduced England from 164 for four to 164 for six in two balls to ensure that they could not escape the follow-on. (Hoggard had taken two in two at Lord's, but the second wicket, Ganguly's, had more to do with umpiring.) Then Tendulkar and Ganguly conjured 96 runs in 11 overs amid the gloom on the second evening. An English pair, if they had stayed on the field at all, might have managed around 60.

In the end, Ganguly had hard evidence to throw into Hussain's face. He pointed out that the two teams had squared off on a home-and-away basis within a year and, in the Tests, India had won in India and drawn in England;

in the one-dayers, India had drawn in India and won in England. So in his eyes, there was no disputing the winner.

With the bat, too, Ganguly edged past his counterpart, though both showed the ability to score important runs, and score them in more than one gear. Hussain set the tone with a characteristic, fighting hundred on the opening day at Lord's, and followed it with an even more back-to-the-wall century in the last innings at Headingley. Ganguly, however, had a few more runs, and a decidedly higher average, despite being the victim of two dicey decisions. He could rarely summon the seductive grace of his golden coming in England six summers earlier, but as the captain in him has demonstrated, there is more to cricket than charm.

So how far forward or backward had England gone in the series? The columnist Marcus Berkmann spoke for a puzzled nation when he asked whether England were a good team that sometimes played abjectly, or a useless team that occasionally played above itself. At the end of the summer of 1999, England were in the second category. Hussain and Fletcher lifted them from those depths. Now they belonged to the first category, but were finding that the pressure there was greater. For one, they were required to make things happen, rather than stalling till an opportunity presented itself. They weren't there yet; still, it was a tribute to the team's ascent that the nation expected more.

The last day of each Test had an unmistakable Indian flavour, with the tricolours and drumbeats providing an electric, chaotic sense of occasion. Even the MCC, who did their best to maintain the funereal sobriety they believe must accompany cricket by banning flags and instruments, could not quite repress the spirit. So it was ironic that the most glaring security breach of the summer occurred at Lord's, when a 24-year-old Australian scampered playfully on to the field from the members' area and put a sympathetic arm around Tendulkar as he trudged back after being dismissed in the second innings. Unlike the previous summer, though, pitch invasions were by and large non-existent.

The last-day Indian presence indicated a general preference among Asians for one-day cricket over Tests. They book their one-day games in advance, as they did during the NatWest tri-series, but prefer to wait and watch before buying Test tickets. This means their time comes on Monday, when tickets are reasonably priced – and available at the gate.

On each fifth day, the Indian team responded to their support. At Lord's came a great revival in a losing cause, at Trent Bridge a great escape, at Headingley a great victory. And at The Oval it rained great showers, which coincided almost perfectly with the end of the monsoon season back home. It was like some grand, cosmic levelling – with a whiff of India. It went well with the series.

Rahul Bhattacharya, assistant editor of Wisden Asia Cricket *magazine, reported on the series for* The Guardian.

INDIAN TOURING PARTY

S. C. Ganguly (Bengal) (*captain*), R. Dravid (Karnataka) (*vice-captain*), A. Agarkar (Mumbai), S. B. Bangar (Railways), S. S. Das (Orissa), Harbhajan Singh (Punjab), M. Kaif (Uttar Pradesh), A. Kumble (Karnataka), V. V. S. Laxman (Hyderabad), D. Mongia (Punjab), A. Nehra (Delhi), P. A. Patel (Gujarat), A. Ratra (Haryana), V. Sehwag (Delhi), S. R. Tendulkar (Mumbai), Wasim Jaffer (Mumbai) T. Yohannan (Kerala), Zaheer Khan (Baroda).

Yuvraj Singh (Punjab) left after the one-day tournament, when Bangar, Das, Patel and Wasim Jaffer arrived for the first-class programme. Kaif and Mongia, who were originally to go home after the one-day games, remained as cover for injuries, while Yuvraj departed because he was injured himself.

Coach: J. G. Wright.　　　　*Manager:* M. Ranga Reddy.　　　　*Physiotherapist:* A. Leipus.

INDIAN TOUR RESULTS

Test matches – Played 4: Won 1, Lost 1, Drawn 2.
First-class matches – Played 9: Won 2, Lost 1, Drawn 6.
Wins – England, Hampshire.
Loss – England.
Draws – England (2), West Indies A, Worcestershire, Essex, Derbyshire.
One-day internationals – Played 7: Won 5, Lost 1, No result 1. *Wins* – England (2), Sri Lanka (3).
　　Loss – England. *No result* – England.
Other non-first-class matches – Played 3: Won 2, Lost 1. *Wins* – Sussex, Leicestershire. *Loss* – Kent.

TEST MATCH AVERAGES

ENGLAND – BATTING

	T	I	NO	R	HS	100s	50s	Avge	Ct/St
C. White	2	3	2	153	94*	0	2	153.00	1
M. P. Vaughan	4	7	1	615	197	3	1	102.50	3
A. J. Stewart	4	6	1	287	87	0	2	57.40	7/1
N. Hussain	4	6	0	315	155	2	0	52.50	4
J. P. Crawley	4	6	1	237	100*	1	1	47.40	0
M. A. Butcher	4	6	0	212	54	0	2	35.33	4
R. W. T. Key	2	3	0	81	34	0	0	27.00	2
A. F. Giles	3	4	0	85	31	0	0	21.25	1
A. Flintoff	3	5	0	99	59	0	1	19.80	3
M. J. Hoggard	4	5	2	43	32	0	0	14.33	2
A. R. Caddick	2	3	1	18	14*	0	0	9.00	0
A. J. Tudor	2	3	0	24	21	0	0	8.00	0

Played in two Tests: D. G. Cork 31, 52 (1 ct). Played in one Test: S. J. Harmison 3; S. P. Jones 44; G. P. Thorpe 4, 1 (2 ct); M. E. Trescothick 57, 58*.

BOWLING

	O	M	R	W	BB	5W/i	Avge
S. J. Harmison	49	12	120	5	3-57	0	24.00
M. P. Vaughan	40	8	120	4	2-71	0	30.00
S. P. Jones	38	3	129	4	2-61	0	32.25
C. White	48.4	7	178	5	2-46	0	35.60
A. R. Caddick	83.1	16	264	7	4-114	0	37.71
M. J. Hoggard	160	35	533	14	4-87	0	38.07
D. G. Cork	45	9	166	4	2-54	0	41.50
A. F. Giles	126	23	354	5	2-98	0	70.80
A. Flintoff	112	25	357	5	2-22	0	71.40

Also bowled: M. A. Butcher 1–1–0–0; A. J. Tudor 55–12–226–2.

INDIA – BATTING

	T	I	NO	R	HS	100s	50s	Avge	Ct/St
R. Dravid	4	6	0	602	217	3	1	100.33	10
S. R. Tendulkar	4	6	0	401	193	1	2	66.83	1
S. C. Ganguly	4	6	0	351	128	1	3	58.50	2
A. B. Agarkar	4	6	1	210	109*	1	0	42.00	0
V. V. S. Laxman	4	6	1	199	74	0	1	39.80	3
V. Sehwag	4	6	0	237	106	1	1	39.50	6
P. A. Patel	2	3	2	26	19*	0	0	26.00	2
Harbhajan Singh	3	4	0	90	54	0	1	22.50	0
Zaheer Khan	4	5	3	44	14*	0	0	22.00	0
Wasim Jaffer	2	4	0	59	53	0	1	14.75	5
A. Kumble	3	3	0	22	15	0	0	7.33	0
A. Nehra	2	3	0	19	19	0	0	6.33	0
A. Ratra	2	3	0	10	8	0	0	3.33	5/2

Played in two Tests: S. B. Bangar 68, 21 (1 ct).

BOWLING

	O	M	R	W	BB	5W/i	Avge
S. B. Bangar	43	11	117	4	2-48	0	29.25
Harbhajan Singh	135.4	23	410	12	5-115	1	34.16
A. Kumble	174.1	42	504	14	4-66	0	36.00
Zaheer Khan	147	32	483	11	3-90	0	43.90
A. B. Agarkar	118.3	20	488	8	2-59	0	61.00
A. Nehra	76	8	319	5	2-80	0	63.80

Also bowled: S. C. Ganguly 12–2–64–0; V. Sehwag 19–1–63–1; S. R. Tendulkar 10–0–33–0.

INDIAN TOUR AVERAGES – FIRST-CLASS MATCHES

BATTING

	M	I	NO	R	HS	100s	50s	Avge	Ct/St
R. Dravid	7	9	1	773	217	3	3	96.62	14
S. R. Tendulkar	6	8	0	573	193	2	2	71.62	2
S. S. Das	3	5	0	349	250	1	0	69.80	4
V. Sehwag	8	13	0	640	142	3	3	49.23	13
S. C. Ganguly	7	11	1	477	128	1	4	47.70	3
V. V. S. Laxman	8	13	1	502	85	0	3	41.83	5
A. B. Agarkar	7	9	1	244	109*	1	0	30.50	0
S. B. Bangar	7	11	1	291	74	0	3	29.10	2
Harbhajan Singh	8	10	2	218	54	0	1	27.25	1
Wasim Jaffer	7	13	1	290	53	0	2	24.16	9
Zaheer Khan	4	5	3	44	14*	0	0	22.00	0
A. Ratra	7	11	2	183	101*	1	0	20.33	14/2
P. A. Patel	5	8	2	97	32	0	0	16.16	5
A. Kumble	5	5	0	77	47	0	0	15.40	0

Played in four matches: A. Nehra 0, 19, 0; T. Yohannan 0*, 0*, 4*. Played in one match: M. Kaif 7*, 77; D. Mongia 87, 27.

BOWLING

	O	M	R	W	BB	5W/i	Avge
S. C. Ganguly	21	4	95	5	3-10	0	19.00
A. Kumble	212	51	607	22	4-58	0	27.59
Harbhajan Singh	243.2	43	773	28	7-83	2	27.60
S. B. Bangar	132.5	25	395	14	4-40	0	28.21
A. Nehra	114	14	473	11	4-85	0	43.00
Zaheer Khan	147	32	483	11	3-90	0	43.90
A. B. Agarkar	162.3	32	640	14	4-55	0	45.71
T. Yohannan	73	16	293	5	1-27	0	58.60

Also bowled: S. S. Das 2–0–8–0; D. Mongia 1–0–7–0; P. A. Patel 3–0–9–0; V. Sehwag 65.4–8–232–4; S. R. Tendulkar 10–0–33–0; Wasim Jaffer 4–0–16–0.

Note: Matches in this section which were not first-class are signified by a dagger.

†SUSSEX v INDIANS

At Hove, June 22 (day/night). Indians won by three wickets. Toss: Sussex.

Under lights and serenaded by horns, the Indians began their warm-up for the NatWest Series with a win. However, they were made to work hard by an understrength Sussex attack, and only Tendulkar mastered a slow pitch, eschewing his normal flamboyance to guide his side home with seven balls to spare. Goodwin, Montgomerie and Carpenter – making a rare first-team outing – all got started without producing a telling contribution, and Sussex were left 20 short of a competitive total. Nehra's zippy fast-medium suggested he could be a handful in English conditions.

Sussex

M. H. Yardy b Nehra	5
*R. R. Montgomerie c Laxman b Zaheer Khan .	44
M. W. Goodwin b Sehwag	49
J. R. Carpenter not out	43
B. Zuiderent b Nehra	13
W. J. House c Laxman b Nehra	3
†T. R. Ambrose b Nehra	3
K. J. Innes run out	10
M. J. G. Davis b Agarkar	12
B. V. Taylor not out	3
L-b 11, w 6, n-b 1	18

J. D. Lewry did not bat.

1/24 (1) 2/75 (2) (8 wkts, 50 overs) 203
3/118 (3) 4/141 (5)
5/149 (6) 6/155 (7)
7/174 (8) 8/199 (9)

Bowling: Nehra 10–0–27–4; Zaheer Khan 10–0–45–1; Agarkar 9–1–30–1; Kumble 10–0–43–0; Tendulkar 3–0–15–0; Sehwag 8–0–32–1.

Indians

D. Mongia c Carpenter b House	56
V. Sehwag c and b Innes	26
M. Kaif c Ambrose b Yardy	2
S. R. Tendulkar not out	75
*†R. Dravid b House	6
Yuvraj Singh c and b Davis	4
V. V. S. Laxman b Innes	18
A. B. Agarkar lbw b Innes	5
Zaheer Khan not out	6
L-b 2, w 5	7

A. Kumble and A. Nehra did not bat.

1/60 (2) 2/69 (3) (7 wkts, 48.5 overs) 205
3/126 (1) 4/144 (5)
5/155 (6) 6/185 (7)
7/193 (8)

Bowling: Lewry 4–0–32–0; Taylor 10–2–33–0; Innes 10–2–35–3; Yardy 6–1–30–1; Davis 10–0–33–1; House 8.5–0–40–2.

Umpires: A. Clarkson and R. A. Kettleborough.

†KENT v INDIANS

At Canterbury, June 24. Kent won by 21 runs. Toss: Kent.

Kent's early scoring was electric: Key pounded the ball off the back foot, Symonds pulled with savage power, and at 165 for two in the 27th over they were aiming above 300. Ealham continued the barrage with a rapid 74, hitting five sixes in all, three in Yohannan's last over, which went for 28. One blow even cleared the recently pruned lime tree, and another smashed a windscreen. However, his partners all wilted quickly, leaving India's starry batting line-up to chase 285. Ganguly and Sehwag began disdainfully, putting on 85 in 13 overs, but guts and good fielding paid off for Kent. Golding bowled rifle-barrel straight, frustrating three victims into reckless shots and exposing the tail, before Ealham's dobbers took four wickets at the death to slam the door firmly shut. It meant an unsuccessful return to Canterbury for John Wright, who had been Kent's coach before becoming India's. For Kent, who had just beaten West Indies A, it was a second win over international opposition in two days.

Kent

J. B. Hockley c Dravid b Yohannan	1
R. W. T. Key st Dravid	
b Harbhajan Singh .	76
A. Symonds run out	75
*D. P. Fulton b Kumble	7
M. J. Walker c and b Harbhajan Singh . .	3
M. A. Ealham not out	74
†G. O. Jones lbw b Kumble	20
J. M. Golding c Mongia b Zaheer Khan .	3

J. C. Tredwell lbw b Zaheer Khan	1
A. Khan b Zaheer Khan	7
M. J. Saggers b Zaheer Khan	0
L-b 10, w 4, n-b 3	17

1/10 (1) 2/138 (2)   (50 overs) 284
3/165 (4) 4/167 (3)
5/183 (5) 6/225 (7) 7/234 (8)
8/237 (6) 9/284 (10) 10/284 (11)

Bowling: Yohannan 8–0–73–1; Zaheer Khan 8–0–38–4; Ganguly 4–0–41–0; Kumble 10–0–28–2; Tendulkar 2–0–12–0; Harbhajan Singh 10–0–56–2; Sehwag 4–0–16–0; Yuvraj Singh 4–0–10–0.

Indians

*S. C. Ganguly run out	64
V. Sehwag c Saggers b Golding	45
D. Mongia c Jones b Golding	37
S. R. Tendulkar b Golding	15
†R. Dravid c Khan b Ealham	34
Yuvraj Singh c Fulton b Golding	3
M. Kaif c Ealham b Saggers	19
Harbhajan Singh c Fulton b Ealham . . .	17
Zaheer Khan st Jones b Ealham	5

A. Kumble c Hockley b Ealham	9
T. Yohannan not out	1
L-b 3, w 11	14

1/85 (2) 2/136 (1)   (48.5 overs) 263
3/166 (4) 4/172 (3)
5/179 (6) 6/220 (7) 7/247 (8)
8/249 (6) 9/262 (9) 10/263 (10)

Bowling: Saggers 9–0–58–1; Khan 7–0–40–0; Ealham 9.5–1–45–4; Golding 9–0–42–4; Tredwell 4–0–24–0; Symonds 10–0–51–0.

Umpires: A. Clarkson and A. Hill.

There cannot have been many more assured and enjoyable (unaided) autobiographies by a leading international cricketer written so soon after he had unbuckled his pads for the last time.
Frank Keating on Mike Atherton: Cricket Books, page 1669

†LEICESTERSHIRE v INDIANS

At Leicester, June 26. Indians won by 54 runs. Toss: Indians.

A big crowd, a magnificent atmosphere and a feast of runs turned this into a memorable occasion and a perfect rehearsal for the eventual winners of the triangular one-day series. Ganguly and Sehwag had Leicestershire running for cover with an opening stand of 132 in 13 overs, prompting thoughts of 400. But once the partnership was broken and then Sehwag run out for 98, India had to settle for a mere 315. Leicestershire responded in kind with 95 from Ward in an opening stand of 136, but finished well short as Ganguly used nine bowlers.

Indians

*S. C. Ganguly c Flower b Crowe	68	Harbhajan Singh not out	8
V. Sehwag run out	98		
V. V. S. Laxman c Adshead b Grove	15	B 5, l-b 13, w 17, n-b 1	36
Yuvraj Singh c Ward b Flower	1		
M. Kaif c Maddy b Grove	52	1/132 (1) 2/187 (3) (7 wkts, 50 overs) 315	
D. Mongia c Wright b Stevens	8	3/190 (4) 4/204 (2)	
A. B. Agarkar c Stevens b Whiley	21	5/231 (6) 6/294 (7)	
†A. Ratra not out	8	7/299 (5)	

A. Nehra and T. Yohannan did not bat.

Bowling: Whiley 10–0–57–1; Grove 10–1–58–2; Maddy 4–0–40–0; Crowe 10–1–62–1; Flower 7–0–34–1; Stevens 9–0–46–1.

Leicestershire

T. R. Ward c Ganguly b Yuvraj Singh	95	C. D. Crowe not out	2
*I. J. Sutcliffe run out	50		
D. I. Stevens c Kaif b Yuvraj Singh	3	L-b 3, w 12, n-b 3	18
D. L. Maddy c and b Harbhajan Singh	30		
G. W. Flower c and b Yuvraj Singh	26	1/136 (2) 2/143 (3) (7 wkts, 50 overs) 261	
R. J. Cunliffe not out	28	3/167 (1) 4/210 (5)	
A. S. Wright c Agarkar	9	5/228 (4) 6/246 (7)	
†S. J. Adshead lbw b Mongia	0	7/251 (8)	

J. O. Grove and M. J. A. Whiley did not bat.

Bowling: Nehra 9–0–41–0; Yohannan 4–0–24–0; Agarkar 8–0–39–1; Ganguly 3–0–23–0; Harbhajan Singh 10–0–50–1; Yuvraj Singh 10–0–48–3; Sehwag 4–0–18–0; Mongia 1–0–5–1; Kaif 1–0–10–0.

Umpires: A. Hill and B. Leadbeater.

India's matches against England and Sri Lanka in the NatWest Series (June 29–July 13) appear on pages 532–543.

INDIANS v WEST INDIES A

At Arundel, July 16, 17, 18. Drawn. Toss: Indians.

After the frenetic finale of the NatWest Series, the Indians were looking to switch tempo for the forthcoming Tests. Watchful batting and polite clapping replaced the rasping drives and blaring hooters of Lord's. Laxman, captain while Ganguly and Dravid rested, played with his usual dreamy elegance on a slow pitch, but then presided over a feeble display in the field which led to six missed chances in the first innings. Ryan Hinds and Dwayne Bravo capitalised, butchering Harbhajan's off-spin as West Indies reached 266 in less than 60 overs. Jermaine Lawson then took six wickets with his sharp fast-medium, and for the second time in a week India needed Kaif to dig them out of a hole. He proved the man for the small occasion as well as the big.

Close of play: First day, Indians 253-7 (Kaif 7); Second day, Indians 87-3 (Wasim Jaffer 43, Patel 0).

Indians

S. S. Das lbw b Hinds	29	– c Hibbert b King	0
Wasim Jaffer c Hibbert b Black	5	– c Hinds b Lawson	52
*V. V. S. Laxman c Simmons b Gayle	85	– (6) c Simmons b Black	17
D. Mongia b Hinds	87	– (8) c Black b Lawson	27
S. B. Bangar c Smith b Gayle	0	– (3) lbw b Lawson	27
†A. Ratra lbw b King	15	– (4) c sub b Hinds	8
M. Kaif not out	7	– c Ganga b Lawson	77
P. A. Patel b Black	12	– (5) c Simmons b Lawson	20
A. B. Agarkar (did not bat)		– lbw b Lawson	0
Harbhajan Singh (did not bat)		– c Simmons b King	5
T. Yohannan (did not bat)		– not out	0
B 4, w 2, n-b 7	13	B 8, l-b 5, w 2, n-b 7	22

1/10 (2) 2/69 (1) 3/155 (3)   (7 wkts dec.) 253
4/161 (5) 5/232 (4)
6/235 (6) 7/253 (8)

1/0 (1) 2/63 (3) 3/86 (4)   255
4/115 (5) 5/130 (2) 6/149 (6)
7/234 (8) 8/234 (9)
9/253 (10) 10/255 (7)

Bowling: First Innings—King 23–7–53–1; Black 16.5–7–35–2; Lawson 19–4–67–0; Hinds 17–2–60–2; Bravo 2–0–4–0; Gayle 12–2–30–2. *Second Innings*—King 18–2–62–2; Black 16–3–56–1; Lawson 22.4–4–76–6; Hinds 19–4–42–1; Gayle 2–0–6–0.

West Indies A

*D. Ganga c Ratra b Agarkar	4	– b Agarkar	4
D. S. Smith run out	69	– c Patel b Yohannan	19
D. J. Pagon lbw b Agarkar	4	– lbw b Bangar	18
L. M. P. Simmons c Ratra b Yohannan	4	– c Patel b Harbhajan Singh	4
R. O. Hinds c Ratra b Agarkar	62	– not out	10
D. J. J. Bravo lbw b Harbhajan Singh	55	– not out	15
C. H. Gayle lbw b Agarkar	0		
†K. H. Hibbert b Harbhajan Singh	17		
M. I. Black c Bangar b Harbhajan Singh	9		
J. J. C. Lawson b Harbhajan Singh	14		
R. D. King not out	2		
B 7, l-b 9, w 9, n-b 5	30	B 1, l-b 5, w 2, n-b 3	11

1/8 (1) 2/25 (3) 3/64 (4) 4/109 (2)   266
5/210 (6) 6/211 (7) 7/236 (5)
8/237 (8) 9/257 (10) 10/266 (9)

1/7 (1) 2/49 (2)   (4 wkts) 81
3/55 (3) 4/57 (4)

Bowling: First Innings—Agarkar 16–3–55–4; Yohannan 13–2–63–1; Bangar 16–2–46–0; Harbhajan Singh 13.4–2–79–4; Mongia 1–0–7–0. *Second Innings*—Agarkar 6–3–18–1; Yohannan 8–0–27–1; Bangar 7–3–11–1; Harbhajan Singh 5–0–19–1.

Umpires: N. J. Llong and N. A. Mallender.

HAMPSHIRE v INDIANS

At Southampton, July 20, 21, 22. Indians won by 66 runs. Toss: Indians.

India's last match before the First Test was marred by controversy over the pitch. The Indian tour management even considered calling off the match on the second day when some balls were lifting and others shooting on a drier than normal surface. The ECB sent their pitch consultant, Chris Woods, to look at the strip with the groundsman, Nigel Gray, at the end of the match, 14 balls after lunch on the last day. All the major Indian batsmen except Dravid struggled with the wicket's uncertainties in the first innings even though Hampshire had rested their new-ball bowlers, Mullally and Tremlett. Bangar's medium-pace provided the Indians with a healthy first-innings lead, and when Tendulkar and Dravid decided not to risk batting a second time, the uneasy Ganguly declared after only 41.2 overs. Crawley was absent with food poisoning as Hampshire chased 253, and only some lusty hitting from Udal and the young bowler, James Tomlinson, prevented a quicker demise. Bangar finished with match figures of seven for 67.

Close of play: First day, Hampshire 33-1 (Johnson 30, Crawley 1); Second day, Hampshire 43-2 (Smith 19, Francis 10).

Indians

Wasim Jaffer c Aymes b Tomlinson	13	– c Aymes b Prittipaul	32
V. Sehwag b Udal	41	– c Hamblin b Udal	22
R. Dravid b Mascarenhas	78		
S. R. Tendulkar c Mascarenhas b Udal	3		
*S. C. Ganguly c Aymes b Udal	21	– (6) not out	1
V. V. S. Laxman c Johnson b Udal	38	– (5) c and b Hamblin	0
†A. Ratra lbw b Hamblin	1	– (4) c Johnson b Hamblin	26
S. B. Bangar c Crawley b Udal	4	– (3) not out	52
A. Kumble c Prittipaul b Johnson	8		
Harbhajan Singh c and b Tomlinson	18		
T. Yohannan not out	0		
B 2, l-b 5, n-b 4	11	B 2, l-b 1, w 1, n-b 2	6

1/39 (1) 2/99 (2) 3/103 (4) 4/154 (5)   236   1/29 (2) 2/63 (1)   (4 wkts dec.) 139
5/164 (3) 6/175 (7) 7/184 (8)   3/125 (4) 4/132 (5)
8/216 (9) 9/222 (6) 10/236 (10)

Bowling: *First Innings*—Mascarenhas 11–6–26–1; Tomlinson 15.1–1–55–2; Hamblin 13–3–41–1; Johnson 11–2–45–1; Udal 29–5–59–5; Prittipaul 2–0–3–0. *Second Innings*—Mascarenhas 2–1–5–0; Hamblin 7–0–44–2; Udal 19.5–5–43–1; Kendall 5.2–2–13–0; Prittipaul 8–2–31–1.

Hampshire

N. C. Johnson b Bangar	45	– c Sehwag b Bangar	0
W. S. Kendall c Sehwag b Bangar	0	– c Dravid b Bangar	7
J. P. Crawley b Yohannan	15	– absent ill	
*R. A. Smith c Ratra b Bangar	6	– (3) lbw b Bangar	19
J. D. Francis c Tendulkar b Ganguly	10	– (4) c Ratra b Yohannan	19
L. R. Prittipaul c Dravid b Bangar	0	– (5) b Kumble	32
†A. N. Aymes c Sehwag b Ganguly	2	– (6) b Kumble	18
A. D. Mascarenhas c Ratra b Kumble	18	– (7) c Ratra b Harbhajan Singh	5
S. D. Udal c Dravid b Ganguly	0	– (8) not out	36
J. R. C. Hamblin run out	13	– (9) lbw b Kumble	2
J. A. Tomlinson not out	1	– (10) lbw b Kumble	23
B 8, n-b 5	13	B 14, l-b 4, n-b 7	25

1/3 (2) 2/59 (3) 3/63 (1) 4/80 (4)   123   1/2 (1) 2/18 (2) 3/43 (3)   186
5/80 (6) 6/89 (5) 7/100 (7)   4/80 (4) 5/104 (5) 6/109 (7)
8/101 (9) 9/120 (10) 10/123 (8)   7/127 (6) 8/129 (9) 9/186 (10)

Bowling: *First Innings*—Bangar 10–0–40–4; Yohannan 10–3–30–1; Kumble 8.3–4–20–1; Harbhajan Singh 5–1–15–0; Ganguly 4–1–10–3. *Second Innings*—Bangar 10–1–27–3; Yohannan 7–1–28–1; Harbhajan Singh 12–3–55–1; Kumble 17.2–1–58–4.

Umpires: N. G. Cowley and P. Willey.

Ashley Giles, beset by heel and Achilles problems, trundled up to the crease like an old wheelie-bin.
India v England, page 1151

ENGLAND v INDIA

First npower Test

At Lord's, July 25, 26, 27, 28, 29. England won by 170 runs. Toss: England. Test debut: S. P. Jones.

England went into the four-Test series against India with a depleted team – no Gough, Caddick or Trescothick, and Thorpe visibly distressed by marital problems – and several scores to settle. They had lost the one-day final here two weeks earlier, they had lost the Test series in India in the winter, and they had lost the only game in which the teams met on India's previous visit, for the 1999 World Cup. In the 12 years since Graham Gooch's 333 at Lord's, England had managed to win only one Test against India, home or away. But you would never have known it from this match. On a pitch that could have been cooked up by Sourav Ganguly's personal chef, England weren't merely greater than the sum of their parts: they were greater than the sum of India's.

It was a personal triumph for Nasser Hussain. He won his third Test in succession, made his highest Test score for five years and spiked India's big guns with rigorous game plans. His team showed a spirit that radiated all the way from the middle to the stands, enthusing the crowd, who in turn inspired the players with the will to take 20 wickets on a blandly unresponsive surface. All England's stand-ins stood out – John Crawley with the two biggest partnerships of the match, Craig White with runs and wickets, Simon Jones with pace and a taste for the big occasion. India, by contrast, were tentative and drifty. Ganguly made one crucial error, opting to play a third seamer and leave out Harbhajan Singh, who had won the home series against England on day one. It was a classic case of compromising a strength in a vain attempt to patch up a weakness.

The match wasn't as one-sided as it ended up looking. Zaheer Khan was superb at the start, when England stuttered to 78 for three. Hussain and Crawley, making his second comeback of the summer, were forced to dig in: Hussain's first 60 runs took 50 overs. He might have stayed in second gear had he not been struck by cramp, but its effect was to bring out the strokemaker in him and he raced to 100 in another 12 overs. A wave of the bat is good for most ailments, and Hussain settled again to reach 120 overnight. When Zaheer removed Stewart, his third big wicket, England were 263 for five and could easily have crumpled. It was largely the bowlers who gave themselves something to work with. Flintoff finally showed a home Test crowd the effortless power of his driving in a partnership of 93 with Hussain. When they fell, almost simultaneously, White played the spinners with his usual panache and Jones slogged like the village blacksmith. The tail had wagged and wasted no time: a run-rate of under three on Thursday gave way to nearly four and a half on Friday.

The Indians took the cue, hitting first Hoggard and then Giles out of the attack as Sehwag, opening for the first time in a Test, rattled along to 84 in 96 balls. There was talk of The Oval 1998, when, on a similar pitch, England made 445 batting first and lost to Sri Lanka. But Hussain had not been captain then. He brought back Giles, conscious that "Sehwag treats spinners as if they shouldn't exist"; Sehwag's eyes duly lit up. On Saturday morning, against Dravid and Tendulkar, Hussain nannied his young bowlers into rising to the challenge. Jones flogged bounce out of the pitch without losing control, Flintoff and Hoggard stuck to the game plan (off-theory) in their contrasting styles, the ball reverse-swung from around the 35th over, and the runs dried up. Tendulkar tried to knuckle down, but after Dravid got a lifter, he could resist temptation no longer. Once Ganguly fell to Flintoff, who had taken on Gough's roles of celebrator-in-chief and opening bowler, a hefty lead was assured.

Hussain opted to give the bowlers a rest rather than impose the follow-on, and after a brief wobble, echoing the first day, the third innings was like 1990 all over again, with a hundred there for those who really wanted one. Vaughan got there in

Security breach: Matthew Hoggard found a rare gap in Sachin Tendulkar's defences in the second innings at Lord's; as he walked off, Tendulkar found himself accompanied by an Australian interloper. *Picture by Patrick Eagar.*

140 balls with a crisp composure that still only hinted at the wonders to come. Crawley, all wristy intelligence, needed only 132 balls: in his first Test against India, he lifted his average against subcontinental teams to 97, compared with 25 against the rest.

If Hussain's declaration was cautious, setting India 568 to win, it allowed his field settings not to be. India reached 110 for one but only Dravid threatened to pull off the big salvage act that was needed, and eventually he picked the wrong ball from Giles to cut. Hoggard showed that England could bowl as well as bore Tendulkar out by slipping him three out-swingers, all left alone, followed by the one that came back. On the last day, English supporters lost interest – they weren't used to seeing their team dominate like this – and there was suddenly a different atmosphere, exuberantly Indian, which inspired Agarkar to show off his backlift and become one of history's more improbable centurions. The only cloud for England was that Jones bowled on when clearly struggling with a side strain. It was a minor blemish on an outstanding team performance. **Tim de Lisle**

Man of the Match: N. Hussain.   *Attendance:* 107,390; *receipts* £2,450,000.

Close of play: First day, England 257-4 (Hussain 120, Stewart 19); Second day, India 130-3 (Dravid 33); Third day, England 184-3 (Vaughan 81, Crawley 56); Fourth day, India 232-6 (Laxman 38, Agarkar 28).

England

M. A. Butcher c Wasim Jaffer b Kumble	29	– lbw b Kumble	18
M. P. Vaughan lbw b Zaheer Khan	0	– c Wasim Jaffer b Nehra	100
*N. Hussain c Ratra b Agarkar	155	– c Ratra b Agarkar	12
G. P. Thorpe b Zaheer Khan	4	– c Ganguly b Kumble	1
J. P. Crawley c Dravid b Sehwag	64	– not out	100
†A. J. Stewart lbw b Zaheer Khan	19	– (7) st Ratra b Kumble	33
A. Flintoff c Ratra b Agarkar	59	– (6) c Tendulkar b Nehra	7
C. White st Ratra b Kumble	53	– not out	6
A. F. Giles b Nehra	19		
S. P. Jones c Dravid b Kumble	44		
M. J. Hoggard not out	10		
B 11, l-b 11, w 2, n-b 7	31	B 5, l-b 14, n-b 5	24

1/0 (2) 2/71 (1) 3/78 (4) 4/223 (5)   487   1/32 (1) 2/65 (3)   (6 wkts dec.) 301
5/263 (6) 6/356 (7) 7/357 (3)   3/76 (4) 4/213 (2)
8/390 (9) 9/452 (10) 10/487 (8)   5/228 (6) 6/287 (7)

Bowling: *First Innings*—Nehra 30–4–101–1; Zaheer Khan 36–13–90–3; Agarkar 21–3–98–2; Kumble 42.2–9–128–3; Ganguly 3–1–16–0; Sehwag 10–0–32–1. *Second Innings*—Nehra 14–1–80–2; Zaheer Khan 11–1–41–0; Kumble 24–1–84–3; Agarkar 11.4–1–53–1; Tendulkar 2–0–14–0; Sehwag 2–0–10–0.

India

Wasim Jaffer b Hoggard	1	– c Hussain b Vaughan	53
V. Sehwag b Giles	84	– b Jones	27
R. Dravid c Vaughan b Hoggard	46	– b Giles	63
A. Nehra lbw b Flintoff	0	– (11) c Thorpe b White	19
S. R. Tendulkar c Stewart b White	16	– (4) b Hoggard	12
*S. C. Ganguly c Vaughan b Flintoff	5	– (5) lbw b Hoggard	0
V. V. S. Laxman not out	43	– (6) c Vaughan b Jones	74
†A. Ratra c Stewart b Jones	1	– (7) c Butcher b Hoggard	109
A. B. Agarkar c Flintoff b Jones	2	– (8) not out	15
A. Kumble b White	0	– (9) c and b Hoggard	15
Zaheer Khan c Thorpe b Hoggard	3	– (10) c Stewart b White	7
B 4, l-b 8, n-b 8	20	B 4, l-b 3, w 2, n-b 8	17

1/2 (1) 2/128 (2) 3/130 (4) 4/162 (3)   221   1/61 (2) 2/110 (1) 3/140 (4)   397
5/168 (5) 6/177 (6) 7/191 (8)   4/140 (5) 5/165 (3) 6/170 (7)
8/196 (9) 9/209 (10) 10/221 (11)   7/296 (6) 8/320 (9)
                                       9/334 (10) 10/397 (11)

Bowling: *First Innings*—Hoggard 16.5–4–33–3; Giles 9–1–47–1; Jones 21–2–61–2; White 16–3–46–2. *Second Innings*—Hoggard 24–7–87–4; Flintoff 17–2–87–0; White 16.4–2–61–2; Jones 17–1–68–2; Giles 29–7–75–1; Vaughan 6–2–12–1.

Umpires: R. E. Koertzen (South Africa) and R. B. Tiffin (Zimbabwe).
Third umpire: P. Willey. Referee: M. J. Procter (South Africa).

WORCESTERSHIRE v INDIANS

At Worcester, July 31, August 1, 2, 3. Drawn. Toss: Indians.

The opening two days were washed out, but there was still time for Tendulkar to play himself back into form after his double failure at Lord's. The Indians retained their Test top five, and they were made to work hard as Matt Mason extracted considerable bounce early on. Gareth Batty's two wickets in two balls reduced India to 99 for two; Tendulkar played and missed at the hat-trick ball and exercised exaggerated caution for his first 50, off 118 balls, before accelerating and delighting the crowd with a succession of powerful drives. His second came off 76 balls, the third off just 43, and his 169 off 246 balls contained 30 fours before he became Ben Smith's third first-class victim. Sheriyar claimed four wickets, but Mason deserved better than none for 32 off 20 overs. After India declared overnight, Peters and Anurag Singh figured in a trouble-free opening stand of 84. Wickets then fell at regular intervals before rain returned to force an abandonment at tea.

Close of play: First day, No play; Second day, No play; Third day, Indians 417-8 (Dravid 53, Harbhajan Singh 32).

Indians

Wasim Jaffer c Pipe b Batty	43	A. B. Agarkar c Hick b Ali	14
V. Sehwag c Mason b Batty	42	Harbhajan Singh not out	32
S. B. Bangar c Pipe b Sheriyar	0		
S. R. Tendulkar b Smith	169	B 10, l-b 12, n-b 8	30
*S. C. Ganguly c Pipe b Sheriyar	24		
†P. A. Patel b Sheriyar	6	1/99 (2) 2/99 (1) 3/99 (3) (8 wkts dec.)	417
R. Dravid not out	53	4/160 (5) 5/168 (6)	
A. Ratra lbw b Sheriyar	4	6/292 (8) 7/327 (9) 8/395 (4)	

A. Nehra did not bat.

Dravid, when 41, retired at 246 and resumed at 395.

Bowling: Mason 20–8–32–0; Sheriyar 25–3–109–4; Ali 19–4–99–1; Batty 18–2–68–2; Rawnsley 13–1–42–0; Smith 10–2–45–1.

Worcestershire

S. D. Peters lbw b Nehra	50	†D. J. Pipe c Harbhajan Singh b Ganguly	12
A. Singh c Sehwag b Ganguly	46	Kabir Ali not out	0
*G. A. Hick lbw b Harbhajan Singh	27	B 4, l-b 4, n-b 17	25
B. F. Smith c Sehwag b Nehra	5		
V. S. Solanki c Dravid b Agarkar	5	1/84 (2) 2/126 (1) 3/136 (4) (6 wkts)	200
G. J. Batty not out	30	4/147 (5) 5/163 (3) 6/200 (7)	

M. S. Mason, M. J. Rawnsley and A. Sheriyar did not bat.

Bowling: Nehra 15–2–69–2; Agarkar 13–5–29–1; Bangar 10–1–37–0; Harbhajan Singh 11–2–36–1; Ganguly 5–1–21–2.

Umpires: R. A. Kettleborough and G. Sharp.

ENGLAND v INDIA

Second npower Test

At Nottingham, August 8, 9, 10, 11, 12. Drawn. Toss: India. Test debuts: S. J. Harmison, R. W. T. Key; P. A. Patel.

It is not uncommon on the Monday of a Test match for the stewards to outnumber spectators, but the policy of reducing admission prices, and the prospect of England going 2–0 up, produced a final-day full house to see India bat through for a draw.

England ultimately came to look back with regret at their disappointing opening-day bowling performance, when India, having won the toss, made 210 for four in conditions ideal for seam and, in particular, swing. Hussain went into the game with five quick bowlers, basing his decision partly on the pitch, but also on the ten-green-bottles theory of having at least one of them still able to bowl come the final day.

With the attrition rate in the fast-bowling department beginning to make Hussain feel like Field Marshal Haig, selection was by now revolving around who was fit enough rather than good enough, and Simon Jones of Glamorgan had already proved his England credentials by ending an impressive debut at Lord's with a side strain. Curiously, in what might have been regarded as compassionate leave, England's physiotherapist had gone away on holiday, but his back-up staff were for once relatively underworked, with only Dominic Cork – who sustained minor knee damage attempting a run-out – requiring a visit to the couch. There was, none the less, a mass breakdown in the radar department, with only Matthew Hoggard able to locate the length and line required for the conditions. England opened with two swing bowlers, which doesn't happen very often these days. Ironically, Hoggard swung the ball far too much at times, and Trent Bridge's recent reputation for offering movement in the air – put down by some to altered aerodynamics after the addition of two new stands – did not actually produce many wickets.

Ganguly fought his way back to form and finally came up with something resembling a captain's innings, while first Agarkar and then Harbhajan showed that even tailenders could score at six an over with the ball swinging, as long as England were the opposition. With Steve Harmison producing bounce and hostility on his debut, England might still have won this match had it not been for the loss of a whole day over the first four days, to a combination of rain and bad light. However, this proved controversial in itself, with the umpires constantly peering at their light meters like Indiana Jones trying to negotiate an underground cavern armed with a box of matches, and regarding every passing cotton-wool cloud as a potential eclipse of the sun. For the most part, their myriad offers of the light were hopelessly out of synch with the clause requiring physical danger to be an essential part of the equation, and it reached laughable proportions when England's batsmen left the field on Saturday evening in what most people would have construed as bright sunshine.

By that time England were in a commanding position and seeking to secure four consecutive Test victories for the first time since 1991-92. A handsome and even occasionally restrained second Test century from Virender Sehwag had led to a no more than useful first innings for India, but a majestic 197 from Michael Vaughan had provided England with the launch pad to something colossal. This was Vaughan's third Test century of the summer, and with each one his strokeplay blossomed a little more. Having acquired a mindset of merely protecting his wicket early in his Test career, Vaughan was now unfurling off-side strokes to put Yorkshire's cricketing public in mind of Hutton, although in other areas – a Lancashire birthplace and a preference for a glass of Chardonnay over a pint of Tetley's – he was more a son of the adopted variety. His scoring-rate didn't have Yorkshire written all over it either: one more run would have given him 100 between lunch and tea, and all told his 197, a career-best, came off only 258 balls with 23 fours in 354 minutes.

Alec Stewart's frisky 87 off 92 balls took him past Mike Atherton's total of 7,728 Test runs and to fourth in the all-time England list. And Craig White narrowly missed out on a century as for the second match in a row, England's tail remembered how to wag. When India lost both openers early on in the second innings, they were effectively minus 249 for two and England on course to put the series in their pocket. India needed at least three of their big four to come good, and they did. With the pitch playing progressively easier, Tendulkar, Dravid and Ganguly made the game virtually safe, although it still required an unbeaten 19 in 84 minutes from the 17-year-old wicket-keeper Parthiv Patel to eliminate any chance of England snatching victory via a frantic run-chase. **Martin Johnson**

Man of the Match: M. P. Vaughan.   *Attendance:* 65,569; *receipts* £1,190,000.
Close of play: First day, India 210-4 (Ganguly 29, Laxman 22); Second day, India 302-8 (Harbhajan Singh 13, Zaheer Khan 1); Third day, England 341-5 (Stewart 30, Flintoff 2); Fourth day, India 99-2 (Dravid 34, Tendulkar 56).

India

Wasim Jaffer b Hoggard	0	– (2) lbw b Flintoff	5
V. Sehwag b White	106	– (1) lbw b Hoggard	0
R. Dravid c Key b Hoggard	13	– lbw b Cork	115
S. R. Tendulkar b Cork	34	– b Vaughan	92
*S. C. Ganguly c Stewart b Hoggard	68	– b Harmison	99
V. V. S. Laxman c Key b Flintoff	22	– c White b Cork	14
A. B. Agarkar c Butcher b Harmison	34	– lbw b Vaughan	32
†P. A. Patel c Flintoff b Harmison	0	– not out	19
Harbhajan Singh c Hussain b Harmison	54	– b Harmison	1
Zaheer Khan not out	14	– not out	14
A. Nehra c Stewart b Hoggard	0		
B 1, l-b 8, w 2, n-b 1	12	B 5, l-b 12, w 4, n-b 12	33

1/6 (1) 2/34 (3) 3/108 (4) 4/179 (2)   357   1/0 (1) 2/11 (2)   (8 wkts dec.) 424
5/218 (6) 6/285 (7) 7/287 (8)   3/174 (4) 4/309 (3)
8/295 (5) 9/356 (9) 10/357 (11)   5/339 (6) 6/378 (5)
                                   7/395 (7) 8/396 (9)

Bowling: *First Innings*—Hoggard 35.1–10–105–4; Cork 11–3–45–1; Harmison 20–7–57–3; Flintoff 27–6–85–1; White 8–0–56–1. *Second Innings*—Hoggard 23–0–109–1; Flintoff 22–2–95–1; Harmison 29–5–63–2; Cork 12–1–54–2; Vaughan 21–5–71–2; White 8–2–15–0.

England

R. W. T. Key b Nehra	17	D. G. Cork c Wasim Jaffer	
M. P. Vaughan c Patel b Agarkar	197	b Harbhajan Singh	31
M. A. Butcher c Dravid		M. J. Hoggard b Dravid b Nehra	32
b Harbhajan Singh	53	S. J. Harmison c Wasim Jaffer	
*N. Hussain c Patel b Harbhajan Singh	3	b Agarkar	3
J. P. Crawley c Wasim Jaffer		B 9, l-b 17, w 4, n-b 15	45
b Zaheer Khan	22		
†A. J. Stewart b Zaheer Khan	87	1/56 (1) 2/221 (3) 3/228 (4) 4/272 (5)	617
A. Flintoff b Zaheer Khan	33	5/335 (2) 6/432 (7) 7/433 (6)	
C. White not out	94	8/493 (9) 9/596 (10) 10/617 (11)	

Bowling: Nehra 32–3–138–2; Zaheer Khan 26–4–110–3; Agarkar 24.5–3–93–2; Harbhajan Singh 45–3–175–3; Ganguly 5–0–42–0; Tendulkar 6–0–15–0; Sehwag 6–1–18–0.

Umpires: R. E. Koertzen (South Africa) and R. B. Tiffin (Zimbabwe).
Third umpire: J. W. Lloyds.   Referee: C. H. Lloyd (West Indies).

ESSEX v INDIANS

At Chelmsford, August 14, 15, 16, 17. Drawn. Toss: Indians.

On a benign pitch, the game meandered to a predictable draw as India made it clear they were only interested in batting practice ahead of the Third Test. Their forgotten man, Shiv Sunder Das, made the second highest score by an Indian touring batsman in England, not quite pipping Polly Umrigar's 252 against Cambridge University in 1959. Das struck 32 fours and four sixes during his 380-ball innings, before he was last out. "I have waited a long time for this opportunity," he said; he had also spent a long time making use of it – he had been at the crease for nine hours. Half-centuries from Robinson and Flower gave the Essex reply some respectability before both succumbed to the guile of Harbhajan Singh, who finished with seven wickets. An explosive 142 from Sehwag, off only 156 deliveries, lit up the embers of the match, along with an unbeaten 47 from the 17-year-old Ravinder Bopara.

Close of play: First day, Indians 331-6 (Das 165, Ganguly 3); Second day, Essex 173-3 (Flower 45, Phillips 4); Third day, Indians 231-2 (Bangar 73, Laxman 9).

Indians

S. S. Das c Ilott b Phillips	250		
S. B. Bangar b Middlebrook	21	– (1) lbw b Ilott	74
V. Sehwag lbw b Middlebrook	37	– c and b Bopara	142
V. V. S. Laxman c Robinson b Grant	46	– c and b Phillips	42
Wasim Jaffer c Flower b Middlebrook	19	– lbw b Ilott	4
P. A. Patel c Flower b Grant	32	– (2) c Phillips b Ilott	1
†A. Ratra lbw b Ilott	1	– (6) not out	17
*S. C. Ganguly st Hyam b Middlebrook	74	– (7) c and b Ilott	6
A. B. Agarkar st Hyam b Phillips	20		
Harbhajan Singh c sub b Phillips	0	– (8) not out	29
T. Yohannan not out	4		
B 4, l-b 3, n-b 5	12	L-b 7, w 3, n-b 2	12
	516	(6 wkts dec.)	327

1/60 (2) 2/106 (3) 3/191 (4) 4/234 (5)   516
5/310 (6) 6/326 (7) 7/431 (8)
8/509 (9) 9/509 (10) 10/516 (1)

1/8 (2) 2/217 (3)   (6 wkts dec.) 327
3/237 (1) 4/241 (5)
5/280 (4) 6/296 (7)

Bowling: *First Innings*—Dakin 23–6–85–0; Ilott 26–4–103–1; Grant 23–10–69–2; Middlebrook 36–5–164–4; Phillips 15.4–2–70–3; Bopara 6–1–18–0. *Second Innings*—Grant 20–8–46–0; Ilott 17–3–67–4; Dakin 16–3–54–0; Bopara 8–0–43–1; Phillips 18–3–62–1; Middlebrook 9–1–48–0.

Essex

D. D. J. Robinson c Wasim Jaffer			
b Harbhajan Singh .	59		
R. S. Clinton b Yohannan	23	– (1) c Wasim Jaffer b Sehwag	53
A. Flower c Ganguly b Harbhajan Singh . . .	29	– retired hurt	23
R. S. Bopara c Wasim Jaffer b Harbhajan Singh	29	– not out	47
T. J. Phillips c Laxman b Bangar	8		
*R. C. Irani c Ratra b Harbhajan Singh . . .	20		
J. M. Dakin c Patel b Harbhajan Singh	4	– (5) c Ratra b Sehwag	6
†B. J. Hyam lbw b Harbhajan Singh	12	– (6) not out	16
J. D. Middlebrook lbw b Harbhajan Singh	13	– (2) c Das b Harbhajan Singh	24
M. C. Ilott not out	3		
J. B. Grant b Sehwag	30		
B 5, l-b 5, w 1, n-b 8	19	B 5, l-b 5, w 1, n-b 6	17
	279	(3 wkts)	186

1/55 (2) 2/108 (1) 3/164 (4) 4/187 (5)   279
5/193 (3) 6/209 (7) 7/230 (6)
8/240 (8) 9/247 (9) 10/279 (11)

1/46 (2) 2/97 (1)   (3 wkts) 186
3/137 (5)

In the second innings, Flower retired hurt at 108.

Bowling: *First Innings*—Yohannan 9–2–28–1; Agarkar 9–1–50–0; Bangar 15–2–55–1; Harbhajan Singh 32–5–83–7; Sehwag 10.4–0–53–1. *Second Innings*—Yohannan 12–3–41–0; Bangar 9–3–27–0; Harbhajan Singh 8–2–23–1; Sehwag 18–6–52–2; Wasim Jaffer 4–0–16–0; Das 2–0–8–0; Patel 3–0–9–0.

Umpires: P. Adams and D. J. Constant.

ENGLAND v INDIA

Third npower Test

At Leeds, August 22, 23, 24, 25, 26. India won by an innings and 46 runs. Toss: India.
England can usually rely on Headingley for home comforts. So it was a nasty shock that this year the old girl turned against them, embracing instead India – out-of-form, contract-disputing India. It was they who were invited to Geoffrey Boycott's pre-match curry buffet and it was they who breathed in the dank Leeds air, looked up at the

Finishing the job: Ganguly clings on to an edge from Caddick and rounds off a triumph which began with his brave decision to bat first. *Picture by Patrick Eagar.*

furious age-old leaden skies, mastered the demons in the pitch, and served up a win by an innings – something they hadn't achieved overseas since routing a Packer-scarred Australia at Sydney in 1977-78.

It was a magnificent performance, built on a sublime first-day century by Dravid which Hussain graciously described as one of the finest he had seen. With that in the vaults, Tendulkar and Ganguly had the licence to play, and play they did – Tendulkar smoothing his way to his highest Test score against England, and Ganguly producing a knockabout hundred that would have been at home in a seaside cabaret. It was the first time all three had made a century in the same innings, though they had come close only two weeks earlier at Trent Bridge with two nineties and a hundred; Tendulkar passed David Gower to go seventh on the all-time Test runs list. The really unexpected part of the tale was that this excellent batting was matched by wise, wily bowling from an attack much mocked even at home. Anil Kumble, who famously struggles away from his dust-bowls, merrily spun his buoyant leg-breaks along to seven wickets and thoroughly deserved his first Test victory outside the subcontinent in 12 years. Agarkar, Bangar and Zaheer Khan did much of the rest – out-Englanding the England bowlers in their mastery of line, length, accuracy and patience.

For England it was a big step backwards. Seemingly weary from the start, they were outfoxed on the opening day by the Indians, who Boycottishly refused to play at any balls they did not have to, and then took the opportunity to pile frustration on frustration. There were more runs from Vaughan, though not on the heroic scale that he was increasingly favouring, and that England needed here; there were valiant efforts from Stewart and an innings of angry defiance from Hussain on the final afternoon, but it was not enough after the initiative had been lost so clearly on the first two days. The return of Caddick, which had been sung joyfully from the treetops, made no difference: he was wayward and looked in desperate need of a few rounds on the gallops. It had become rare to see England drop so many catches – four in 35 minutes on a slapdash

Saturday morning, including Parthiv Patel three times in his 11-ball innings. The watching Western Terrace, never ones to suffer in silence, vacillated between disbelief and hysteria, and the laughter that followed each drop, and each of the four consecutive fours Harbhajan Singh heaved off Alex Tudor, cannot have helped the mood when England eventually padded up.

The game had started slowly after Ganguly, fearlessly going against all Headingley precedent by picking two spinners, won the toss and batted. Sehwag gloved a catch in the seventh over; Dravid and Bangar settled back and worked to rule – the first 50 came up ten minutes before lunch, to much foot-shuffling in the crowd. Dravid was immaculate from the start, watching each ball like a seamstress and ignoring the ones which thudded into his shoulder, helmet or chest. Bangar was an admirable sidekick but his demise was greeted with excitement as the crowd prepared for Tendulkar, Yorkshire's prodigal son, who despite his year here as a 19-year-old had never made a first-class century at Headingley. Now, in his 99th Test, as visitors quaffed champagne in the hospitality box Yorkshire had named after him, he did it, overtaking Don Bradman's total of 29 Test hundreds as he stroked the ball round the ground. But the highlight of the match was not the moment of his longed-for century; it was the silly session late on Friday afternoon when, as the skies darkened, he and Ganguly saw four lights on the scoreboard, disdained them, and ran amok, scoring 96 off the first 11 overs of the third new ball. Together they added 249, an Indian fourth-wicket record against England. Ganguly, swinging his bat like Thor, celebrated his hundred by slamming the next two balls for six.

India's total was their highest against England when Ganguly declared. England began brightly, as if not missing Marcus Trescothick at all. Vaughan again dashed on to the attack, but after he drove loosely at the skinny Agarkar, England stalled. All the main batsmen bar Flintoff got a start, but nobody came close to the big hundred the situation demanded. India had batted for two days before losing their fifth wicket; England managed less than four hours. Stewart was admirable in his defence and hit 11 fours with typical flourish, but there is only so much you can do when just one of the last five makes more than a single.

England's follow-on wasn't necessarily doomed, but India were showing intensity in the field and somebody was going to have to produce the big innings that had thwarted Sri Lanka in a similar situation at Lord's in May. Vaughan couldn't help for once, Butcher lost patience after a solid start and Crawley completed a double failure, so it was left to the old sweats, Hussain and Stewart.

They came together in rich late-afternoon sunshine on Sunday and by the close Hussain had 90, Stewart had 40 and England had a chance. Hussain, reckless at times in his willingness to take the aerial route, was outstanding – 66 of those 90 runs had come in boundaries. He went on to his hundred the next morning but fell soon afterwards, and with him went England's hopes of going to The Oval with a lead still in their pockets. Kumble and Harbhajan twirled and fizzed and showed that spin could be a weapon anywhere in the right hands. Stewart struck around without ever finding his fluency and Flintoff, who had bowled 27 overs when clearly unfit, completed a forlorn pair. Hussain admitted afterwards that it had been "almost unprofessional" to pick him.

Before the match Geoffrey Boycott, Fred Trueman, Ray Illingworth and Brian Close gritted their teeth and posed together to open the new East Stand – though such was the financial mess at Yorkshire that no one had much of an idea who was going to pay for it. But the most poignant moment came on Saturday afternoon when the ground stood in complete silence, in memory of Holly Wells and Jessica Chapman, the schoolgirls from Soham whose disappearance had captured the sympathy of the nation. **Tanya Aldred**

Man of the Match: R. Dravid.   *Attendance:* 56,351; *receipts* £840,000.

Close of play: First day, India 236-2 (Dravid 110, Tendulkar 18); Second day, India 584-4 (Tendulkar 185); Third day, England 264-9 (Stewart 71, Hoggard 0); Fourth day, England 239-4 (Hussain 90, Stewart 40).

India

S. B. Bangar c Stewart b Flintoff	68	Harbhajan Singh c Hoggard b Caddick	18	
V. Sehwag c Flintoff b Hoggard	8			
R. Dravid st Stewart b Giles	148	B 14, l-b 13, w 5, n-b 18	50	
S. R. Tendulkar lbw b Caddick	193			
*S. C. Ganguly b Tudor	128	1/15 (2) 2/185 (1)	(8 wkts dec.) 628	
V. V. S. Laxman c Hussain b Tudor	6	3/335 (3) 4/584 (5)		
A. B. Agarkar b Caddick	2	5/596 (4) 6/602 (7)		
†P. A. Patel not out	7	7/604 (6) 8/628 (9)		

Zaheer Khan and A. Kumble did not bat.

Bowling: Hoggard 36–12–102–1; Caddick 40.1–5–150–3; Tudor 36–10–146–2; Flintoff 27–6–68–1; Giles 39–3–134–1; Butcher 1–1–0–0; Vaughan 1–0–1–0.

England

R. W. T. Key c Laxman b Zaheer Khan	30	– lbw b Kumble	34	
M. P. Vaughan c Sehwag b Agarkar	61	– lbw b Agarkar	15	
M. A. Butcher lbw b Kumble	16	– c Dravid b Bangar	42	
*N. Hussain lbw b Zaheer Khan	25	– c Sehwag b Kumble	110	
J. P. Crawley c Laxman b Harbhajan Singh	13	– c Sehwag b Bangar	12	
†A. J. Stewart not out	78	– c Dravid b Kumble	47	
A. Flintoff lbw b Harbhajan Singh	0	– c Dravid b Zaheer Khan	0	
A. J. Tudor c Sehwag b Agarkar	1	– c Sehwag b Harbhajan Singh	21	
A. F. Giles lbw b Kumble	25	– run out	10	
A. R. Caddick b Harbhajan Singh	1	– c Ganguly b Kumble	3	
M. J. Hoggard c Sehwag b Kumble	0	– not out	1	
B 1, l-b 12, n-b 10	23	B 3, l-b 5, n-b 6	14	
	273		**309**	

1/67 (1) 2/109 (3) 3/130 (2) 4/140 (4)   1/28 (2) 2/76 (1) 3/116 (3)
5/164 (5) 6/164 (7) 7/185 (8)   4/148 (5) 5/265 (4) 6/267 (7)
8/255 (9) 9/258 (10) 10/273 (11)   7/267 (6) 8/299 (9)
                                      9/307 (8) 10/309 (10)

Bowling: *First Innings*—Zaheer Khan 19–3–59–2; Agarkar 15–4–59–2; Bangar 4–1–9–0; Kumble 33–7–93–3; Harbhajan Singh 18–6–40–3. *Second Innings*—Zaheer Khan 22–7–63–1; Agarkar 18–5–59–1; Bangar 13–2–54–2; Kumble 29.5–12–66–4; Harbhajan Singh 27–7–56–1; Sehwag 1–0–3–0.

Umpires: E. A. R. de Silva (Sri Lanka) and D. L. Orchard (South Africa).
Third umpire: P. Willey. Referee: C. H. Lloyd (West Indies).

DERBYSHIRE v INDIANS

At Derby, August 28, 29, 30. Drawn. Toss: Indians. First-class debut: C. J. Warn.
After their triumph at Headingley, the Indians were not in search of a taxing match, and Derbyshire obliged by including only two of the team that beat Middlesex the previous week. Cork intended to play but had a cracked finger from practice before the Third Test. Ratra, who would keep wicket at The Oval following an injury to Patel, took the opportunity to score an untroubled century in the Indians' highest total against Derbyshire. Rawait Khan, in his second match for the county, almost emulated him but fell short on the last morning. Sehwag reached his hundred in what was little more than extended practice. During the match, it became clear to Derbyshire supporters that Colin Wells, an absentee at Lord's a week earlier, was no longer acting as cricket manager.
Close of play: First day, Indians 301-5 (Ratra 50, Dravid 40); Second day, Derbyshire 228-3 (Khan 77, Dowman 0).

Indians

S. B. Bangar c Hewson b Kerr	17	– c Warn b Dowman	7
V. Sehwag b Gunter	15	– c Gunter b Selwood	104
S. S. Das b Dowman	18	– c Aldred b Pyemont	52
V. V. S. Laxman c Warn b Kerr	75		
Wasim Jaffer c Warn b Kerr	49	– (4) not out	14
†A. Ratra not out	101		
*R. Dravid retired out	40		
A. Kumble b Aldred	47		
Harbhajan Singh c Dumelow b Gunter	44		
B 15, l-b 6, w 18	39	L-b 2, w 2, n-b 1	5

1/21 (2) 2/58 (1) 3/62 (3)	(8 wkts dec.) 445	1/69 (1) 2/128 (2) (3 wkts dec.) 182
4/164 (5) 5/233 (4) 6/301 (7)		3/182 (3)
7/375 (8) 8/445 (9)		

T. Yohannan and A. Nehra did not bat.

Bowling: *First Innings*—Gunter 23.1–7–76–2; Aldred 35–9–109–1; Kerr 25–9–97–3; Dowman 12–4–28–1; Dumelow 24–5–110–0; Hewson 2–1–4–0. *Second Innings*—Aldred 8–1–35–0; Gunter 7–3–24–0; Dowman 3–0–11–1; Kerr 3–0–10–0; Pyemont 4.3–1–37–1; Hewson 8–3–13–0; Selwood 7–2–35–1; Khan 3–0–15–0.

Derbyshire

S. D. Stubbings b Harbhajan Singh	66	†C. J. Warn run out	1
R. M. Khan c Laxman b Nehra	91	N. E. L. Gunter b Bangar	0
D. R. Hewson c Wasim Jaffer b Kumble	66		
P. Aldred c Das b Kumble	2	B 5, l-b 15, n-b 15	35
*M. P. Dowman lbw b Nehra	16		
J. P. Pyemont c Sehwag b Nehra	43	1/131 (1) 2/225 (3) 3/227 (4)	358
S. A. Selwood c Sehwag b Kumble	9	4/254 (5) 5/273 (2) 6/299 (7)	
N. R. C. Dumelow b Nehra	23	7/345 (8) 8/356 (6)	
J. I. D. Kerr not out	6	9/358 (10) 10/358 (11)	

Bowling: Nehra 23–4–85–4; Yohannan 14–5–76–0; Bangar 12.5–2–35–1; Sehwag 18–1–64–0; Harbhajan Singh 21–5–53–1; Kumble 12–4–25–3.

Umpires: A. A. Jones and K. Shuttleworth.

ENGLAND v INDIA

Fourth npower Test

At The Oval, September 5, 6, 7, 8, 9. Drawn. Toss: England.

This match was the thriller that never was. It was Tendulkar's 100th Test, and an absorbing series was there for the taking. Beforehand few people expected a draw, but a tranquil pitch and two fearful sides ensured there was never much danger of anything but. It was the series in miniature. Vaughan and Dravid played epic innings – sharing almost 19 hours at the crease in a match where nobody else lasted four; both sides passed 500 as bat suffocated ball, and neither was better than the other. The result was dull, but fair.

Weary limbs and faint hearts spoiled what should have been an intoxicating broth. Only 20 wickets fell in 353 overs, before a last-day washout saved everyone from some end-of-term torpor. It was the first Oval draw since 1995, when a series decider against West Indies proved similarly unproductive. At the end there were no recriminations, no tears or jeers: England, savaged by injury, were happy to cut their losses and limp off unbeaten, while India, even though they had again failed to win their first series outside Asia since 1986, would have taken a draw after being well beaten at Lord's.

Back in the groove: Marcus Trescothick hit twin fifties on his return after a broken thumb.
Picture by Patrick Eagar.

England made two changes from the side mangled at Headingley. Trescothick was rushed back in place of Key, despite having played no first-class cricket since breaking his thumb seven weeks earlier, and Flintoff's overdue hernia operation brought another stay of execution for Cork. India recalled Ratra, fresh from a century against Derbyshire, for the injured 17-year-old Patel.

Once Hussain won an apparently critical toss, he and a sell-out crowd were able to put their feet up and savour another Vaughan masterclass as England stormed to 336 for two at the close. Vaughan had made 182 of those, mostly with drives that were both pristine and urgent. His first 100 came off 195 balls, and the last 82 off only 71 as he persecuted Kumble, depositing him time and again through mid-wicket against

ENGLAND'S 175 CLUB

With scores of 197 and 195 against India, Michael Vaughan passed 175 twice in a month. No other England player since Graham Gooch had done it twice in a Test career. Then, in Australia, Vaughan did it twice more. This made it 12 instances of a batsman reaching 175 for England in their 147 Tests since January 1, 1990 – and Vaughan had hit four of them in the space of eight Tests.

333	G. A. Gooch v India at Lord's.	1990
190	A. J. Stewart v Pakistan at Birmingham.	1992
178	G. A. Hick v India at Bombay	1992-93
175	R. A. Smith v West Indies at St John's	1993-94
210	G. A. Gooch v New Zealand at Nottingham	1994
185*	M. A. Atherton v South Africa at Johannesburg	1995-96
207	N. Hussain v Australia at Birmingham	1997
200*	G. P. Thorpe v New Zealand at Christchurch	2001-02
197	M. P. Vaughan v India at Nottingham.	2002
195	M. P. Vaughan v India at The Oval	2002
177	M. P. Vaughan v Australia at Adelaide	2002-03
183	M. P. Vaughan v Australia at Sydney	2002-03

what little spin there was. At least one Indian might have grudgingly approved: Laxman had done just the same to Warne during his classic 281.

Vaughan became the sixth man to make four Test hundreds in an English summer after Herbert Sutcliffe, Don Bradman, Denis Compton, Allan Lamb and Graham Gooch. Not since Gower had an Englishman played with such radiance, but the similarity extended to anticlimactic dismissals when, in the fourth over of the second morning, Vaughan fished at a good one from Zaheer Khan and was caught behind for 195, his second attack of the nervous 190s in three Tests. His dismissal induced England to blunder wretchedly through the second day. Only 179 runs came off 65 overs for the loss of eight wickets, and it was hard to recall such an imposing score – they passed 500 for the fifth time in the summer, having not done so for five years before that – being accompanied by such a fear of failure. Only Cork showed any oomph. Pumped up by suggestions that he was out of his depth at No. 7, he celebrated his third Test fifty with a seven-fingered salute to the press box.

India did bowl well: Bangar's cunning out-swingers gave the middle order just enough rope to hang themselves, and Harbhajan Singh, who took his ninth Test five-for, was far too good for a hard-handed tail. In direct contravention of the laws of spin bowling, all nine of those five-fors had come when India fielded first.

Sehwag went early, again proclaiming his limitations as an opener, but the glimmer of light England saw soon vanished as Dravid unfurled a mercilessly dead bat. They simply never looked like making multiple incisions. The main man should have been Giles, but on a turning pitch he would not take a wicket until his 46th over, another sounding of the death knell for the English finger-spinner. Tudor bowled himself out of the Ashes tour, which Cork, picked to kiss the pitch in Hussain's words, preferred to pummel it.

All the while Dravid ground on and on, false strokes as rare as a steak tartare, to become the first Indian to make centuries in three consecutive Test innings in the same series since Sunil Gavaskar in 1970-71. He also took his crease occupation for the series past 30 hours – an entire Test match, or eight showings of the Oscar-nominated *Lagaan* – and eventually made his highest first-class score, in ten and a half hours.

What he didn't do was dominate, or even accelerate. If Headingley was his arthouse classic – an innings the connoisseur knows will not be bettered – this was Dravid's blockbuster: grander in scale and spectacle, but a colder, more deliberate affair which never set the pulse racing. It was an innings of limited ambition, four hours longer than Vaughan's, and not nearly as good.

The enchantment instead came from Tendulkar, who at 29 became the youngest man to play a century of Tests. He received a standing ovation as he came to the crease, and as he breezed to a boundary-laden 54, nothing looked surer than a second, louder ovation when he reached 100. Then, in the blink of an eye, Caddick – England's best bowler by a long way – trapped Tendulkar lbw on the full, and a disbelieving crowd came to realise the fun was over.

India settled for sedate progress and England for containment, as Hussain's field placings and fed-up body language evoked Atherton more than Brearley. Dravid was finally run out for 217 after a poor call from Ratra – it really was the only way England were going to see him off – and stalemate ensued. Any thoughts of Harbhajan and Kumble making merry as Chandrasekhar had here 31 years earlier were soon dispelled by Trescothick, who made a second beefy fifty, and the inevitable Vaughan. They launched another jet-propelled century partnership, and blew away the last vestige of a positive result.

The last day might have brought Vaughan a record-breaking fifth hundred but nobody was too disappointed. It had been a long, taxing summer; Test cricket had never before been played in England as late as September 9, and still hasn't. Most people were happy to go home and put their feet up. The spectators could, anyway: most of the players were due in Colombo for the Champions Trophy three days later. **Rob Smyth**

Man of the Match: R. Dravid.   *Attendance:* 71,225; *receipts* £1,580,000.
Men of the Series: England – M. P. Vaughan; India – R. Dravid.

Close of play: First day, England 336-2 (Vaughan 182, Crawley 16); Second day, India 66-1 (Bangar 17, Dravid 31); Third day, India 315-4 (Dravid 131, Laxman 14); Fourth day, England 114-0 (Trescothick 58, Vaughan 47).

England

M. E. Trescothick c Bangar b Zaheer Khan....	57	– not out..................	58
M. P. Vaughan c Ratra b Zaheer Khan.......	195	– not out..................	47
M. A. Butcher c Dravid b Harbhajan Singh....	54		
J. P. Crawley lbw b Bangar...............	26		
*N. Hussain c Laxman b Bangar............	10		
†A. J. Stewart c Ratra b Harbhajan Singh.....	23		
D. G. Cork lbw b Harbhajan Singh.........	52		
A. J. Tudor c Dravid b Harbhajan Singh......	2		
A. F. Giles c Dravid b Kumble............	31		
A. R. Caddick not out..................	14		
M. J. Hoggard lbw b Harbhajan Singh.......	0		
B 12, l-b 31, w 1, n-b 7..........	51	B 4, n-b 5............	9
	515	(no wkt)	**114**

1/98 (1) 2/272 (3) 3/349 (2) 4/367 (4)
5/372 (5) 6/434 (6) 7/446 (8)
8/477 (7) 9/514 (9) 10/515 (11)

Bowling: First Innings—Zaheer Khan 28–4–83–2; Agarkar 24–4–111–0; Bangar 24–8–48–2; Harbhajan Singh 38.4–6–115–5; Kumble 35–11–105–1; Ganguly 4–1–6–0; Tendulkar 2–0–4–0.
Second Innings—Zaheer Khan 5–0–37–0; Bangar 2–0–6–0; Kumble 10–2–28–0; Harbhajan Singh 7–1–24–0; Agarkar 4–0–15–0.

India

S. B. Bangar c Butcher b Hoggard....	21	A. Kumble c Hussain b Giles........	7
V. Sehwag c Cork b Caddick........	12	Harbhajan Singh b Giles...........	17
R. Dravid run out..............	217	Zaheer Khan not out............	6
S. R. Tendulkar lbw b Caddick......	54	B 10, l-b 6, n-b 28........	44
*S. C. Ganguly c Stewart b Cork.....	51		
V. V. S. Laxman c Giles b Caddick....	40	1/18 (2) 2/87 (1) 3/178 (4) 4/283 (5)	**508**
A. B. Agarkar b Vaughan..........	31	5/396 (6) 6/465 (7) 7/473 (3)	
†A. Ratra c Butcher b Caddick.......	8	8/477 (8) 9/493 (9) 10/508 (10)	

Bowling: Hoggard 25–2–97–1; Caddick 43–11–114–4; Giles 49–12–98–2; Tudor 19–2–80–0; Cork 22–5–67–1; Vaughan 12–1–36–1.

Umpires: E. A. R. de. Silva (Sri Lanka) and D. L. Orchard (South Africa).
Third umpire: N. A. Mallender. Referee: C. H. Lloyd (West Indies).

THE NATWEST SERIES, 2002

BY LAWRENCE BOOTH

This tournament was defined by one game. Fortunately, that game was the final. Before the third NatWest Series got under way, India's only previous one-day meeting with England at Lord's had been the notorious World Cup game of 1975. On that occasion, Sunil Gavaskar had responded to England's 334 for four by batting out 60 overs for 36 runs as India crawled to 132 for three. This time, England passed 300 once more, only to have the trophy wrenched from their grasp by two innings of audacious brilliance from Yuvraj Singh and Mohammad Kaif, whose combined age of 41 was just two more than the England wicket-keeper, Alec Stewart. Not since November 1998, when they beat Zimbabwe in the Coca-Cola Champions Trophy at Sharjah, had India won a one-day final. It had taken ten bites at the cherry, and – with memories of Andrew Flintoff's bare-chested rampage round Mumbai's Wankhede Stadium in February still fresh in Indian minds – tasted all the sweeter for it.

It was a fairytale finale. A story circulated that back in Allahabad, when India crashed to 146 for five, Mohammad Kaif's parents had given up all hope and disappeared to the cinema, only to discover later that their son was a hero. The 20-year-old Yuvraj Singh, a powerfully built left-hander with the eye of an eagle, proved a big hit too. For the third time in the series, he had averted an Indian crisis, and he ended the third-highest run-scorer, with 254.

For whatever reason, it was quite a series for left-handers. Marcus Trescothick bludgeoned 362 runs at the frightening strike-rate of nearly 108 and played three memorable innings: 86 off 78 balls in the group game against India at Lord's, 82 off 60 to inspire a stunning victory over Sri Lanka at Headingley, and 109 off 100 in the final. The leading wicket-taker was the Indian left-arm seamer, Zaheer Khan, with 14, while Chaminda Vaas, Sri Lanka's left-arm opening bowler, was joint third with nine. Even the most economical front-line bowler was a left-hander: Ashish Nehra of India conceded just 4.16 per over.

But it was the unrivalled flair and depth of the Indian batting – Kaif was a regular at No. 7 – that helped them win five of their six completed matches. They were aided by pitches which, with the exception of Edgbaston, encouraged strokeplay. Familiar concerns about facing the white ball in English conditions failed to materialise, and the average 15-over score was a more-than-healthy 85 for two. Only once, when England were chasing a big Sri Lankan total at Headingley, did a side lose more than three wickets in the first 15 overs.

England's passage to Lord's was built around a nucleus of seven players – Trescothick, Nick Knight, Nasser Hussain, Paul Collingwood, Stewart, Flintoff and Ronnie Irani – who appeared in every game. Flintoff finally lived up to the hype on home soil with 190 runs at a strike-rate of 129 and nine wickets, while Irani made up for his lack of natural flair with sheer guts to turn in the performance of a lifetime at The Oval. But doubts continued to surround the role of Hussain, who managed just 129 runs at less than 26 and a strike-rate of 66 before his cathartic century from the controversial No. 3 position in the final. And with Caddick injured, Gough not fully fit and Hoggard lacking in confidence, England often missed a consistent bowler at the death.

Sri Lanka, demoralised after losing the Tests 2–0, barely showed up. For them, this felt like a series too far, and their chances of reaching Lord's vanished with three group matches still to go. Jayasuriya and, briefly, Sangakkara sparkled with the bat, but the absence of the injured Muttiah Muralitharan cost them dear. The ten-game format would have worked better had Sri Lanka not taken until their fifth match to win, but the jury was still out on the day/night experiment in England, mainly because only three were played under lights, one of which was rained off. In any case, the

The airborne division: Mohammad Kaif celebrates an Indian victory in the final after blitzing England's 325. *Picture by Clive Mason, Getty Images.*

three most gripping games – India's two wins at Lord's and England's enthralling run-chase at Headingley – were played in daylight. In the end, Yuvraj and Kaif dazzled all by themselves.

Note: Matches in this section were not first-class.

ENGLAND v SRI LANKA

At Nottingham, June 27 (day/night). England won by 44 runs. England 4 pts. Toss: England.

Cheeky innovation from Stewart and glorious violence from Flintoff left Sri Lanka with a mini-mountain to climb. But razor-sharp English fielding prevented them from gaining more than a fleeting foothold. Hussain dived breathtakingly to his left at short cover to dismiss a disbelieving Jayasuriya; Irani got rid of the fluent Atapattu with an athletic one-handed effort at mid-off; and Thorpe held on superbly at short mid-wicket to defuse Kaluwitharana's explosiveness. At 214 for four in the 41st over, Sri Lanka still had an outside chance, but Arnold was run out by Hoggard's deflection on to the stumps at the non-striker's end, and Flintoff and Kirtley then did the rest. England's total of 293 was an unexpected bonus after Fernando had removed Hussain and Thorpe in the same over to make it 104 for four. First Stewart showed off his new-found confidence against the spinners with a sequence of searing cuts and delicate dabs. Then, after Irani's patient and crucial 39, Flintoff combined power, timing and placement to belt a brutal half-century in just 28 balls, the quickest by an England player in one-day internationals. It was the sort of innings England fans had been waiting for.

Man of the Match: A. Flintoff.   *Attendance*: 15,149; *receipts* £380,000.

England

M. E. Trescothick c Sangakkara b Vaas	26	P. D. Collingwood not out	10
N. V. Knight lbw b Zoysa	20		
*N. Hussain b Fernando	32	B 4, l-b 4, w 3, n-b 4	15
G. P. Thorpe b Fernando	18		
†A. J. Stewart b Vaas	83	1/39 (2) 2/47 (1) (6 wkts, 50 overs)	293
R. C. Irani c Jayawardene b Arnold	39	3/103 (3) 4/104 (4)	
A. Flintoff not out	50	5/199 (6) 6/283 (5)	
		15 overs: 87-2	

A. F. Giles, R. J. Kirtley and M. J. Hoggard did not bat.

Bowling: Vaas 9–0–58–2; Zoysa 7–0–46–1; Fernando 8–0–46–2; Chandana 10–0–43–0; Jayasuriya 10–0–51–0; Arnold 6–0–41–1.

Sri Lanka

*S. T. Jayasuriya c Hussain b Hoggard	12	D. N. T. Zoysa b Kirtley	0
†R. S. Kaluwitharana c Thorpe		C. R. D. Fernando not out	5
b Collingwood	52		
M. S. Atapattu c Irani b Flintoff	47	B 1, l-b 10, w 10, n-b 6	27
D. P. M. D. Jayawardene b Collingwood	29		
R. P. Arnold run out	29	1/19 (1) 2/91 (3) (9 wkts, 50 overs)	249
K. C. Sangakkara c Kirtley b Flintoff	22	3/149 (2) 4/152 (4)	
U. D. U. Chandana c Thorpe b Flintoff	1	5/214 (5) 6/215 (6)	
M. N. Nawaz not out	15	7/215 (7) 8/238 (9)	
W. P. U. J. C. Vaas b Kirtley	10	9/238 (10)	
		15 overs: 73-1	

Bowling: Hoggard 10–0–49–1; Kirtley 10–0–40–2; Irani 10–0–39–0; Flintoff 10–0–49–3; Giles 5–0–30–0; Collingwood 5–0–31–2.

Umpires: D. L. Orchard (South Africa) and D. R. Shepherd.
Third umpire: N. A. Mallender.   Referee: M. J. Procter (South Africa).

ENGLAND v INDIA

At Lord's, June 29. India won by six wickets. India 4 pts. Toss: England.

A classy, unbroken stand of 131 in 21 overs between Dravid and Yuvraj eased India home with seven balls to spare after a mid-innings collapse almost handed the game to England. Sehwag had hurried India to 109 in the 18th over, but when he picked out Trescothick on the mid-wicket boundary, the innings threatened to unravel. Mongia and Tendulkar followed cheaply, before Ganguly fell victim to one of the greatest catches ever held at Lord's. Launching Giles towards

In-flight entertainment: James Kirtley pulls off one of the greatest catches seen at Lord's. *Picture by Tom Shaw, Getty Images.*

wide long-on, he watched in horror as Kirtley hared round the boundary, dived at full stretch and clung on with his left hand an inch above the turf. England would have been favourites had Stewart not dropped Dravid on 23, and were left to rue the profligacy of their young seamers: Hoggard, Kirtley and Flintoff leaked 175 runs in 26.5 overs; Giles and Irani conceded just 72 in 20. Their batsmen were culpable too, after failing to convert Trescothick's thumping 78-ball 86 into something closer to 300. Yuvraj chiselled away at the middle order with his underrated left-arm spin, before providing a batting masterclass in how to finish a job properly.

Man of the Match: Yuvraj Singh.   *Attendance:* 25,760; *receipts* £740,000.

England

M. E. Trescothick c Dravid b Ganguly	86	A. F. Giles not out		2
N. V. Knight run out	31			
*N. Hussain st Dravid b Yuvraj Singh	54	B 2, l-b 6, w 8, n-b 2		18
A. Flintoff c Mongia b Yuvraj Singh	22			
G. P. Thorpe c Sehwag b Yuvraj Singh	12	1/86 (2) 2/153 (1)	(7 wkts, 50 overs)	271
†A. J. Stewart not out	28	3/201 (4) 4/217 (5)		
R. C. Irani run out	12	5/222 (3) 6/256 (7)		
P. D. Collingwood c Dravid b Zaheer Khan	6	7/267 (8)		15 overs: 90-1

R. J. Kirtley and M. J. Hoggard did not bat.

Bowling: Zaheer Khan 9–0–48–1; Agarkar 8–0–49–0; Harbhajan Singh 10–0–50–0; Kumble 10–0–46–0; Ganguly 6–0–31–1; Yuvraj Singh 7–0–39–3.

India

*S. C. Ganguly c Kirtley b Giles	43	Yuvraj Singh not out		64
V. Sehwag c Trescothick b Giles	71	L-b 12, w 3, n-b 4		19
D. Mongia b Giles	1			
S. R. Tendulkar lbw b Irani	1	1/109 (2) 2/111 (3)	(4 wkts, 48.5 overs)	272
†R. Dravid not out	73	3/118 (4) 4/141 (1)		15 overs: 102-0

M. Kaif, A. B. Agarkar, Harbhajan Singh, A. Kumble and Zaheer Khan did not bat.

Bowling: Hoggard 8.5–0–62–0; Kirtley 10–0–57–0; Flintoff 8–0–56–0; Giles 10–1–39–3; Irani 10–0–33–1; Collingwood 2–0–13–0.

Umpires: S. A. Bucknor (West Indies) and N. A. Mallender.
Third umpire: J. W. Lloyds.   Referee: M. J. Procter (South Africa).

INDIA v SRI LANKA

At The Oval, June 30. India won by four wickets. India 4 pts. Toss: Sri Lanka.

India completed the second win of their London weekend thanks to a mature sixth-wicket partnership between Yuvraj, one of the heroes from the previous day, and Kaif. With India tottering at 135 for five in pursuit of 203, the pair added 60 at almost a run a ball to make the result a formality. Vaas had hinted at a return to form by removing both openers, but Tendulkar responded with typical authority. One square cut hit an unsuspecting pigeon, which was carried off the field by Jayawardene; it later recovered. Sri Lanka had been given a flying start by Jayasuriya, who chose to bat first on his 33rd birthday, and quickly cut Zaheer Khan for six over third man. But Agarkar removed Kaluwitharana with his first ball, added the scalp of Jayasuriya – his 150th wicket in one-day internationals – and then got rid of Arnold. From 97 for five, Sri Lanka relied on Jayawardene's patience to get them to 200. But with Muralitharan still injured, it looked at least 30 below par.

Man of the Match: A. B. Agarkar.   *Attendance:* 18,500; *receipts* £290,000.

Sri Lanka

*S. T. Jayasuriya c Dravid b Agarkar . . .	36	D. N. T. Zoysa c Kaif b Zaheer Khan . .	4
†R. S. Kaluwitharana c Dravid b Agarkar	15	T. C. B. Fernando not out	4
M. S. Atapattu b Zaheer Khan	7		
D. P. M. D. Jayawardene		L-b 8, w 4, n-b 1	13
c and b Zaheer Khan .	62		
R. P. Arnold c Dravid b Agarkar	6	1/42 (2) 2/65 (1) (8 wkts, 50 overs) 202	
M. N. Nawaz c Sehwag b Ganguly	11	3/65 (3) 4/78 (5)	
U. D. U. Chandana c Kaif b Nehra	18	5/97 (6) 6/140 (7)	
W. P. U. J. C. Vaas not out	26	7/182 (4) 8/186 (9) 15 overs: 78-3	

C. R. D. Fernando did not bat.

Bowling: Nehra 10–0–29–1; Zaheer Khan 10–1–48–3; Agarkar 9–2–44–3; Ganguly 10–1–28–1; Kumble 10–0–43–0; Sehwag 1–0–2–0.

India

*S. C. Ganguly lbw b Vaas	7	M. Kaif not out	38
V. Sehwag c Jayasuriya b Vaas	12	A. B. Agarkar not out	7
D. Mongia c Vaas b C. R. D. Fernando .	33	L-b 2, w 9, n-b 7	18
S. R. Tendulkar c Kaluwitharana b Zoysa	49		
†R. Dravid b Chandana	8	1/17 (1) 2/26 (2) (6 wkts, 45.2 overs) 203	
Yuvraj Singh c sub (L. P. C. Silva)		3/97 (3) 4/113 (5)	
b C. R. D. Fernando .	31	5/135 (4) 6/195 (6) 15 overs: 76-2	

A. Kumble, Zaheer Khan and A. Nehra did not bat.

Bowling: Vaas 10–1–38–2; Zoysa 10–0–46–1; C. R. D. Fernando 10–0–53–2; T. C. B. Fernando 3–0–11–0; Chandana 10–1–46–1; Jayasuriya 2–0–5–0; Arnold 0.2–0–2–0.

Umpires: D. L. Orchard (South Africa) and P. Willey.
Third umpire: N. A. Mallender.   Referee: M. J. Procter (South Africa).

ENGLAND v SRI LANKA

At Leeds, July 2. England won by three wickets. England 4 pts. Toss: England.

A match reduced to 32 overs a side by rain was promptly hit by two hurricanes. Jayasuriya smashed five sixes in a murderous 87-ball 112, and Trescothick responded with 82 from 60, before England's batting depth won the day. After putting Sri Lanka in on a grey Yorkshire afternoon, Hussain could only watch as Jayasuriya, merciless off his legs, dismembered his attack en route to a 78-ball hundred, the second-fastest in a one-day international in England and his 12th in all. Hoggard bowled the joint-most expensive four-over spell in history. Needing more than seven and a half an over, England lost Knight to Vaas's fourth ball, stumbled to 126 for five, but were kept in the hunt by Trescothick, who had sped to a half-century in 39 deliveries. When he finally picked out long-on, Collingwood and Stewart added a feisty 66 in less than nine overs. With the light fading and time running out, Gough, back at last after a knee injury, hit the winning runs in front of his home crowd to crown a pulsating afternoon.

Man of the Match: S. T. Jayasuriya.   *Attendance:* 8,793; *receipts* £200,000.

Sri Lanka

*S. T. Jayasuriya c Kirtley b Hoggard	112	K. C. Sangakkara not out	1
†R. S. Kaluwitharana c Hussain b Gough	7		
M. S. Atapattu c Stewart b Flintoff	18	L-b 11, w 13, n-b 3	27
D. P. M. D. Jayawardene b Flintoff	4		
D. A. Gunawardene run out	20	1/26 (2) 2/118 (3) (7 wkts, 32 overs)	240
U. D. U. Chandana lbw b Gough	30	3/132 (4) 4/171 (5)	
R. P. Arnold not out	17	5/201 (1) 6/225 (6)	
W. P. U. J. C. Vaas b Gough	4	7/233 (8)	
		9 overs: 65-1	

D. N. T. Zoysa and C. R. D. Fernando did not bat.

Bowling: Gough 7–0–45–3; Hoggard 4–0–53–1; Kirtley 6–1–37–0; Flintoff 7–0–18–2; Collingwood 5–0–49–0; Irani 3–0–27–0.

England

M. E. Trescothick c Vaas b Jayasuriya	82	D. Gough not out	3
N. V. Knight c and b Vaas	0		
R. C. Irani c Jayawardene b Vaas	27	L-b 3, w 10, n-b 5	18
A. Flintoff c Jayawardene b Arnold	20		
*N. Hussain c Gunawardene b Fernando	0	1/1 (2) 2/69 (3) (7 wkts, 31.2 overs)	241
G. P. Thorpe run out	15	3/97 (4) 4/98 (5)	
P. D. Collingwood b Fernando	38	5/126 (6) 6/171 (1)	
†A. J. Stewart not out	38	7/237 (7)	
		9 overs: 70-2	

R. J. Kirtley and M. J. Hoggard did not bat.

Bowling: Vaas 6–0–39–2; Zoysa 5.2–0–54–0; Arnold 5–0–42–1; Fernando 6–0–38–2; Chandana 5–0–40–0; Jayasuriya 4–0–25–1.

Umpires: S. A. Bucknor (West Indies) and N. A. Mallender.
Third umpire: P. Willey.   Referee: M. J. Procter (South Africa)

ENGLAND v INDIA

At Chester-le-Street, July 4 (day/night). No result. England 2 pts, India 2 pts. Toss: India.

India's 500th one-day international turned into a damp squib after Tendulkar had lit up proceedings with a dazzling century. With India in trouble on a slow pitch at 52 for three, he moved serenely to his first fifty in 72 balls before expanding his repertoire – including a couple of reverse sweeps off Giles – to smash his second in just 34. It was his 32nd one-day international hundred, but his first against England in 22 attempts. Tendulkar added 169 for the fourth wicket with the more cautious Dravid, and a ferocious 64 in 33 balls with Yuvraj. But persistent drizzle meant England were unable to bat for the 25 overs needed for a result. Earlier, Gough had become only the third England bowler – after Ian Botham and Bob Willis – to take 400 wickets in all internationals when he trapped Ganguly with the first ball of the match.

Attendance: 13,500; *receipts* £340,000.

India

*S. C. Ganguly lbw b Gough	0	Yuvraj Singh not out	40
V. Sehwag c Trescothick b Kirtley	16	L-b 8, w 5, n-b 2	15
D. Mongia c Flintoff b Gough	27		
S. R. Tendulkar not out	105	1/0 (1) 2/48 (2) (4 wkts, 50 overs)	285
†R. Dravid c Flintoff b Collingwood	82	3/52 (3) 4/221 (5)	
		15 overs: 68-3	

M. Kaif, A. B. Agarkar, A. Kumble, Zaheer Khan and A. Nehra did not bat.

Bowling: Gough 10–0–52–2; Kirtley 10–0–77–1; Flintoff 10–0–36–0; Irani 10–1–23–0; Collingwood 5–0–48–1; Giles 5–0–41–0.

England

M. E. Trescothick lbw b Zaheer Khan . .   23
N. V. Knight not out   17
*N. Hussain not out   9
         L-b 1, w 3   4

1/30 (1)   (1 wkt, 12.3 overs) 53

M. P. Vaughan, †A. J. Stewart, R. C. Irani, A. Flintoff, P. D. Collingwood, A. F. Giles, R. J. Kirtley and D. Gough did not bat.

Bowling: Nehra 6–0–21–0; Zaheer Khan 6–0–31–1; Agarkar 0.3–0–0–0.

Umpires: D. L. Orchard (South Africa) and D. R. Shepherd.
Third umpire: J. W. Lloyds. Referee: M. J. Procter (South Africa)

INDIA v SRI LANKA

At Birmingham, July 6. India won by four wickets. India 4 pts. Toss: India.

Sri Lanka's slim chances of reaching the final came to an end after a dismal collapse against a disciplined Indian attack on a pitch that helped the seamers. Heavy overnight rain persuaded Ganguly to bowl first, only for Atapattu and Jayawardene to bat Sri Lanka into a position of strength at 125 for two. But Kumble removed both in successive overs, and the last eight wickets fell for just 62. India lost a wicket to the first ball of their innings for the second match in succession, and when Tendulkar was confounded by Fernando's slower ball to make it 59 for four, Sri Lanka had the advantage. If Fernando hadn't ruined things by overstepping moments before Dravid popped a leading edge to cover, they might even have won. Dravid had just nine at the time, but went on to compile another cool match-winning stand, of 91, with Yuvraj. Sri Lanka were left to regret the extravagance of their bowlers, and the winning run came, appropriately enough, courtesy of a wide, the 17th of the innings to go with five no-balls.

Man of the Match: R. Dravid.   *Attendance:* 19,433; *receipts* £370,000.

Sri Lanka

*S. T. Jayasuriya b Nehra 22	W. P. U. J. C. Vaas c Ganguly
†R. S. Kaluwitharana c Dravid b Agarkar 8	b Zaheer Khan . 26
M. S. Atapattu b Kumble 50	G. P. Wickremasinghe run out 2
D. P. M. D. Jayawardene c Nehra	C. R. D. Fernando not out 2
b Kumble . 36	B 4, l-b 4, w 2, n-b 4 14
D. A. Gunawardene c Yuvraj Singh	
b Zaheer Khan . 7	1/33 (1) 2/41 (2) 3/125 (4) (48.2 overs) 187
R. P. Arnold run out 13	4/129 (3) 5/146 (5) 6/150 (7)
T. T. Samaraweera c Sehwag b Nehra . . 3	7/153 (6) 8/182 (9) 9/185 (8)
U. D. U. Chandana c Nehra b Agarkar . . 4	10/187 (10) 15 overs: 55-2

Bowling: Nehra 10–2–28–2; Zaheer Khan 8.2–0–36–2; Agarkar 9–1–31–2; Ganguly 6–0–30–0; Tendulkar 5–0–18–0; Kumble 10–0–36–2.

India

V. Sehwag b Vaas 0	M. Kaif not out 7
*S. C. Ganguly c Kaluwitharana	A. B. Agarkar not out 7
b Wickremasinghe . 24	L-b 3, w 17, n-b 5 25
D. Mongia c Jayasuriya b Vaas 5	
S. R. Tendulkar c Atapattu b Fernando . . 19	1/0 (1) 2/30 (3) (6 wkts, 48.1 overs) 188
†R. Dravid run out 64	3/33 (2) 4/59 (4)
Yuvraj Singh c Chandana b Fernando . . 37	5/150 (6) 6/179 (5) 15 overs: 36-3

Zaheer Khan, A. Kumble and A. Nehra did not bat.

Bowling: Vaas 10–1–26–2; Fernando 10–0–22–2; Wickremasinghe 9–0–47–1; Chandana 6.1–0–32–0; Samaraweera 10–1–35–0; Jayasuriya 3–0–23–0.

Umpires: S. A. Bucknor (West Indies) and N. A. Mallender.
Third umpire: P. Willey. Referee: M. J. Procter (South Africa).

ENGLAND v SRI LANKA

At Manchester, July 7. Sri Lanka won by 23 runs. Sri Lanka 4 pts. Toss: Sri Lanka.

On a slow, dusting pitch, Sri Lanka's spinners exposed old English failings against the turning ball. After racing to 100 for two in the 19th over, England were kept in check by Chandana, Samaraweera and Jayasuriya, who between them bowled nearly 29 overs and took five for 90 as the batsmen failed to adjust to the lack of pace; three were run out in the ensuing panic. Earlier, Sri Lanka had collapsed to spin too after an inventive 70 off 79 deliveries from Sangakkara. Vaughan, with just 130 balls' experience in one-day internationals behind him, picked up four for seven in 15 deliveries with his looping off-breaks to help hurry out the last seven wickets for just 44. The batsmen on both sides weren't the only ones to get in a tangle. Umpire Dave Orchard missed the first four overs of the match after turning up late because he thought it was a day/nighter. The third umpire, Jeremy Lloyds, stepped in. Tudor finally made his one-day debut, almost four years after playing his first Test.

Man of the Match: K. C. Sangakkara.   *Attendance:* 18,414; *receipts* £350,000.

Sri Lanka

M. S. Atapattu run out	34	W. P. U. J. C. Vaas b Vaughan		0
*S. T. Jayasuriya c Hussain b Tudor	23	D. N. T. Zoysa c Knight b Gough		9
†K. C. Sangakkara lbw b Vaughan	70	G. P. Wickremasinghe not out		3
D. P. M. D. Jayawardene run out	42	L-b 9, w 5, n-b 1		15
R. P. Arnold c and b Snape	6			
L. P. C. Silva c Collingwood b Vaughan	9	1/59 (2) 2/73 (1) 3/162 (4) (49.4 overs) 229		
T. T. Samaraweera st Stewart b Vaughan	3	4/185 (5) 5/191 (3) 6/200 (7)		
U. D. U. Chandana c sub	15	7/205 (6) 8/205 (9)		
(A. F. Giles) b Flintoff	8	9/224 (10) 10/229 (8) 15 overs: 79-2		

Bowling: Gough 10–0–51–1; Tudor 8–1–44–1; Flintoff 5.4–0–29–1; Irani 10–0–40–0; Snape 10–2–34–1; Vaughan 6–1–22–4.

England

M. E. Trescothick b Zoysa	27	A. J. Tudor c Atapattu b Jayasuriya		6
N. V. Knight b Zoysa	29	D. Gough run out		0
*N. Hussain run out	28			
M. P. Vaughan c and b Chandana	14	B 1, l-b 10, w 4		15
†A. J. Stewart c Chandana				
b Samaraweera	8	1/37 (1) 2/76 (2) 3/100 (4) (47.4 overs) 206		
R. C. Irani c Zoysa b Jayasuriya	28	4/108 (3) 5/118 (5)		
A. Flintoff b Jayasuriya	7	6/135 (7) 7/160 (6)		
P. D. Collingwood run out	29	8/186 (8) 9/200 (10)		
J. N. Snape not out	11	10/206 (11) 15 overs: 84-2		

Bowling: Vaas 6–0–29–0; Zoysa 7–0–42–2; Wickremasinghe 1–0–10–0; Arnold 5–0–24–0; Chandana 9.4–1–25–1; Samaraweera 10–1–27–1; Jayasuriya 9–0–38–3.

Umpires: D. L. Orchard (South Africa) and P. Willey.
Third umpire: J. W. Lloyds.   Referee: M. J. Procter (South Africa).

ENGLAND v INDIA

At The Oval, July 9. England won by 64 runs. England 5 pts. Toss: India.

A dress rehearsal for the final was settled by a centre-stage performance from Irani. He followed an energetic 53 from 55 balls with a bustling five for 26 – both career-bests – then brought down the curtain by holding the winning catch at long-on. Only Graeme Hick, against Zimbabwe at Harare in February 2000, had scored fifty and taken five wickets in the same one-day international for England before. Until Irani's remarkable spell of four wickets for one in ten balls midway through the Indian innings, the game had been in the balance. But when Hoggard persuaded an in-form Tendulkar to edge a booming drive to the keeper, it was all but over. Not even an entertaining last-wicket flurry could prevent India's only defeat. In another game reduced to 32 overs a side by the weather, England were inserted in damp conditions but still managed to rack up an imposing 229. Irani, dropped by Kaif off Yuvraj on 20, was all industry, Flintoff biffed a half-century from 35 deliveries, and Vaughan added an exquisite 17-ball cameo that included an impudent flick for six over backward square leg off Zaheer. Neither England's late collapse nor Sehwag's early fireworks were enough to save India.

Man of the Match: R. C. Irani.   *Attendance:* 18,500; *receipts* £460,000.

England

M. E. Trescothick b Kumble	9	A. J. Tudor not out			3
N. V. Knight c Kaif b Yuvraj Singh	31	D. Gough not out			7
R. C. Irani b Kumble	53				
A. Flintoff c Nehra b Agarkar	51	L-b 6, w 18, n-b 6			30
M. P. Vaughan c Yuvraj Singh					
b Zaheer Khan	30	1/52 (1) 2/72 (2)	(8 wkts, 32 overs)	229
*N. Hussain c Kaif b Zaheer Khan	6	3/148 (4) 4/196 (5)		
P. D. Collingwood b Nehra	9	5/202 (3) 6/219 (7)		
†A. J. Stewart b Zaheer Khan	0	7/219 (6) 8/219 (8)		9 overs: 54-1

M. J. Hoggard did not bat.

Bowling: Nehra 5–0–28–1; Zaheer Khan 7–0–53–3; Kumble 7–0–39–2; Agarkar 4–0–38–1; Yuvraj Singh 6–0–37–1; Sehwag 1–0–9–0; Ganguly 1–0–10–0; Tendulkar 1–0–9–0.

India

V. Sehwag c Stewart b Irani	46	Zaheer Khan c Gough b Flintoff			2
*S. C. Ganguly c Flintoff b Tudor	6	A. Nehra c Irani b Tudor			24
V. V. S. Laxman c Hoggard					
b Collingwood	14	L-b 1, w 7			8
S. R. Tendulkar c Stewart b Hoggard	36				
Yuvraj Singh st Stewart b Irani	5	1/31 (2) 2/62 (1) 3/78 (3)	(29.1 overs)	165
M. Kaif b Irani	1	4/100 (5) 5/114 (6)		
†A. Ratra c Stewart b Irani	2	6/118 (7) 7/118 (8)		
A. B. Agarkar c Collingwood b Irani	0	8/120 (4) 9/127 (10)		
A. Kumble not out	21	10/165 (11)		9 overs: 60-1

Bowling: Gough 4–0–19–0; Tudor 4.1–0–30–2; Flintoff 4–0–33–1; Irani 7–1–26–5; Collingwood 5–0–31–1; Hoggard 5–0–25–1.

Umpires: S. A. Bucknor (West Indies) and P. Willey.
Third umpire: N. A. Mallender.   Referee: M. J. Procter (South Africa).

INDIA v SRI LANKA

At Bristol, July 11 (day/night). India won by 63 runs. India 5 pts. Toss: India.

The highlight of a meaningless match was a sublime innings from Tendulkar, who resumed his fleeting love affair with Nevil Road to the delight of a flag-waving crowd. On India's only other visit to Bristol, for a World Cup game in 1999 against Kenya, Tendulkar had creamed an unbeaten 140, and this time he drove with elan to make 113 off just 102 balls with 12 fours and a six. It was his 33rd one-day international century and his seventh against Sri Lanka. Tendulkar drove his first and fifth balls to the cover boundary and never looked back, reaching his half-century in 46 deliveries and his hundred in just 93. He shared stands of 99 in 16 overs with Mongia and 74 in 11 with Kaif to help India past 300, as he had done three years earlier. Sri Lanka raced to 50 in the sixth over and were well-placed at 160 for two in the 26th, but Harbhajan came back to snuff out the lower-middle order as the last eight wickets fell for just 81 with almost six overs still to go.

Man of the Match: S. R. Tendulkar.   *Attendance:* 10,000; *receipts* £170,000.

India

*S. C. Ganguly run out	9	A. Nehra b Fernando	3
V. Sehwag run out	39	T. Yohannan not out	5
D. Mongia b Samaraweera	48		
S. R. Tendulkar c Chandana b Vaas	113	L-b 6, w 12, n-b 7	25
†R. Dravid lbw b Chandana	13		
Yuvraj Singh lbw b Samaraweera	8	1/32 (1) 2/73 (2) 3/172 (3) (50 overs) 304
M. Kaif c Silva b Zoysa	41	4/199 (5) 5/210 (6) 6/284 (4)
Harbhajan Singh run out	0	7/286 (8) 8/288 (9)
Zaheer Khan b Fernando	0	9/296 (10) 10/304 (10) 15 overs: 100-2

Bowling: Vaas 10–0–64–1; Zoysa 10–0–66–1; Fernando 10–1–55–2; Chandana 8–0–44–1; Jayasuriya 2–0–14–0; Jayawardene 2–0–16–0; Samaraweera 8–0–39–2.

Sri Lanka

*S. T. Jayasuriya lbw b Zaheer Khan	5	U. D. U. Chandana c Nehra	
M. S. Atapattu run out	53	b Harbhajan Singh	1
†K. C. Sangakkara st Dravid		W. P. U. J. C. Vaas not out	4
b Harbhajan Singh	66	C. R. D. Fernando run out	3
D. P. M. D. Jayawardene c Nehra		B 1, l-b 5, w 5, n-b 6	17
b Yuvraj Singh	31		
D. N. T. Zoysa c Mongia b Ganguly	8	1/11 (1) 2/96 (3) 3/160 (4) (44.1 overs) 241
R. P. Arnold run out	8	4/165 (2) 5/171 (5)
L. P. C. Silva st Dravid		6/188 (6) 7/210 (8)
b Harbhajan Singh	30	8/221 (9) 9/233 (7)
T. T. Samaraweera b Harbhajan Singh	15	10/241 (11) 15 overs: 104-2

Bowling: Nehra 7–0–28–0; Zaheer Khan 8.1–0–52–1; Yohannan 5–0–39–0; Ganguly 10–0–40–1; Harbhajan Singh 10–0–46–4; Yuvraj Singh 2–0–12–1; Mongia 1–0–8–0; Sehwag 1–0–10–0.

Umpires: D. L. Orchard (South Africa) and D. R. Shepherd.
Third umpire: J. W. Lloyds. Referee: M. J. Procter (South Africa).

QUALIFYING TABLE

	Played	Won	Lost	No result	Bonus points	Points	Net run-rate
India	6	4	1	1	1	19	0.18
England	6	3	2	1	1	15	0.39
Sri Lanka	6	1	5	0	0	4	–0.44

Win = 4 pts. One bonus point awarded for achieving victory with a run-rate 1.25 times that of the opposition. When two or more teams finish with an equal number of points, the positions are decided by (a) most wins (b) most wins in head-to-head matches (c) most bonus points (d) highest net run-rate. Net run-rate is calculated by subtracting runs conceded per over from runs scored per over.

FINAL

ENGLAND v INDIA

At Lord's, July 13. India won by two wickets. Toss: England.

This game wasn't merely a case of saving the best until last: it was one of the most thrillingly topsy-turvy limited-overs internationals ever played. At 146 in pursuit of 326 – more than they had ever scored batting second – India were down and out. Their four senior batsmen were all back in the pavilion, and only Yuvraj Singh, aged 20, and Mohammad Kaif, 21, stood between England's bowlers and the tail. But Yuvraj played some punishing strokes off the back foot, Kaif

Three-figure salute: Nasser Hussain, batting at No. 3, gestures pointedly towards the press centre on reaching his first hundred in his 72nd one-day international innings. *Picture by Clive Mason, Getty Images.*

was all wrists through mid-wicket, and the pair added 121 in less than 18 overs. When Yuvraj topedged a sweep to short fine leg, Harbhajan helped add a quick 47 with Kaif to take India to the brink, but Flintoff tilted the balance once more with two wickets in the 48th over. Even so, India needed just 11 runs off 12 balls. Kaif thick-edged Gough to the third-man boundary to reduce the target to two off six, and Zaheer Khan stole the winning runs with three balls remaining courtesy of an overthrow. As England's players wandered off in a daze, the Indians celebrated in style. In an echo of Flintoff's antics at Mumbai five months earlier, Ganguly whipped off his shirt and whirled it round his head on the players' balcony, before running through the Long Room to kiss the Lord's turf and embrace Kaif. The capacity crowd, many of them Indians, stood and cheered. After nine consecutive defeats in one-day finals, India had made it tenth time lucky.

But for most of the match their losing streak had seemed certain to continue. England's innings of 325 for five, their fourth-highest in this form of the game, had inspired drama of its own. In his 72nd innings, Hussain reached his first one-day international century, a dogged but scratchy innings, full of miscues and failed reverse sweeps. When he reached three figures, from 118 balls, he embarked on an impassioned series of gestures to the press box, where several commentators – "ex-players", Hussain later said – had questioned his position in the batting order. Hussain held up three fingers and gesticulated angrily to the No. 3 on the back of his shirt. It was pure theatre, and almost overshadowed an outstanding display from Trescothick, who added a joyous 185 for the second wicket with Hussain in just 177 balls. Trescothick moved to a 40-ball half-century, his most memorable shot a flick for six over mid-wicket off Zaheer, and motored to his third one-day century in 89 balls with some hammer-on-anvil cover-drives. Flintoff bullied 40 off 32, and England had rewarded Hussain's decision to make first use of a belter.

Needing six and a half an over, India came racing out of the blocks too. Ganguly pummelled his way to fifty in just 35 deliveries, and his opening partnership with the dashing Sehwag had reached 106 in the 15th over when Ganguly aimed an ambitious slog at Tudor and was bowled. It was the first of five wickets to fall for 40 runs in less than ten overs – including Tendulkar, bowled as he made room. The game seemed over. But England had reckoned without the youthful daring and verve of Yuvraj and Kaif.

Man of the Match: M. Kaif.
Man of the Series: M. E. Trescothick.   *Attendance:* 25,919; *receipts* £760,000.

England

M. E. Trescothick b Kumble	109	R. C. Irani not out	10
N. V. Knight b Zaheer Khan	14	B 2, l-b 16, w 7, n-b 6	31
*N. Hussain b Nehra	115		
A. Flintoff b Zaheer Khan	40	1/42 (2) 2/227 (1)	(5 wkts, 50 overs) 325
M. P. Vaughan c Mongia b Zaheer Khan	3	3/307 (4) 4/312 (3)	
P. D. Collingwood not out	3	5/312 (5)	15 overs: 90-1

†A. J. Stewart, A. F. Giles, A. J. Tudor and D. Gough did not bat.

Bowling: Nehra 10–0–66–1; Zaheer Khan 10–1–62–3; Kumble 10–0–54–1; Harbhajan Singh 10–0–53–0; Ganguly 3–0–28–0; Sehwag 4–0–26–0; Yuvraj Singh 3–0–18–0.

India

V. Sehwag b Giles	45	A. Kumble c Stewart b Flintoff	0
*S. C. Ganguly b Tudor	60	Zaheer Khan not out	4
D. Mongia c Stewart b Irani	9	B 3, l-b 8, w 6, n-b 1	18
S. R. Tendulkar b Giles	14		
†R. Dravid c Knight b Irani	5	1/106 (2) 2/114 (1)	(8 wkts, 49.3 overs) 326
Yuvraj Singh c Tudor b Collingwood	69	3/126 (3) 4/132 (5)	
M. Kaif not out	87	5/146 (4) 6/267 (6)	
Harbhajan Singh b Flintoff	15	7/314 (8) 8/314 (9)	15 overs: 108-1

A. Nehra did not bat.

Bowling: Gough 10–1–63–0; Tudor 9–0–62–1; Flintoff 7.3–0–55–2; Irani 10–0–64–2; Giles 10–0–47–2; Collingwood 3–0–24–1.

Umpires: S. A. Bucknor (West Indies) and D. R. Shepherd.
Third umpire: P. Willey.   Referee: M. J. Procter (South Africa).

WEST INDIES A IN ENGLAND, 2002

This A tour was a bad-tempered, unproductive meander round the backwaters of English cricket rather than an exhilarating fast stream to the top. The West Indians' learning curve hardly made it above the horizontal and, for some of the younger tourists, it threatened to duck beneath the x-axis as their behaviour made more impact than their cricket. The counties set the tone of ennui by picking sides of fresh-faced teenagers and second-teamers, apathy which was doubly deplorable given the flak the West Indies board had taken when they admitted England A to the 2000-01 Busta Cup. It was ludicrous to claim these fixtures provided a bridge to Test cricket – and no one tried. Nottinghamshire even sent most of their first team on a trip to Guernsey while their second string took the field. Set such an example, too many of the West Indians were happy to follow suit. One win in six first-class matches was far from a glittering achievement, while a 2–1 series defeat by Canada (where they played three limited-overs games on their way home) was a humiliation.

There were few brighter moments. In the only first-class match against quality opposition, West Indies A gave the Indians a scare, and of their six one-day games in England, they won four. But any veneer of success was thin. In their day-nighter against the Sri Lankans, West Indies were routed before the floodlights came on, and the only first-class win followed a generous Warwickshire declaration.

Though the West Indians blamed injuries for their request that games against Nottinghamshire and Somerset be cut from four days to three, it seemed to confirm a lack of appetite for cricket. Their fielding was often lackadaisical, sometimes incompetent, and team spirit got lost in transit. Runako Morton – already the problem child of Caribbean cricket after being expelled from the West Indies Academy – was accused of insubordination, the Barbadians Sulieman Benn and Tino Best feuded openly with their captain, Daren Ganga, and inter-island rivalries resurfaced. Best also became embroiled in a spat with Graham Lloyd of Lancashire, which culminated in him hurling a beamer at Lloyd, who threw his bat down the pitch in anger. In short, the side often looked more like a rag-tag collection of freebooters than a cricket team. The manager, Joel Garner, later admitted the general standard of behaviour was not acceptable; Gus Logie, their coach, went further: "At times there was a breakdown in respect for one another."

Once back in the Caribbean, Benn, Best and Morton reaped the whirlwind. All three were fined ten per cent of their tour fee – the maximum allowable – for a litany of offences. At the same hearing, Morton was banned for a year from all matches organised by the WICB, though this punishment was primarily for later crimes. Called up to the West Indies squad for the Champions Trophy in Sri Lanka, he flew home early after telling officials his grandmother had died. Morton already had a rap sheet as long as Joel Garner's arm, and the management didn't take him at his word: it turned out that one grandmother had been dead for 16 years and the other was alive and well in Antigua. Morton had simply got fed up sitting on the sidelines. As well as the ban, he was sent for a stint on the counsellor's couch – where Benn would soon join him.

All of which helps explain why, though there were some good individual performances, they did not translate into winning team displays. Ganga topped the averages with 325 runs at more than 54 and showed tenacity: his limpet-like powers would earn him a Test recall. Chris Gayle blasted 236 at 47 in contrasting fashion, but he was already a regular Test player and a known quantity. However, the form of 20-year-old Devon Smith, a rumbustious left-hander from the Windward Islands who had destroyed England Under-19 in 2001, showed that the conveyor belt of West Indies talent had not creaked to a total standstill. He crunched 465 in ten innings, including a patient 181 against Lancashire.

In the field, West Indies A conceded more than 287 only once in seven completed innings – the last, when they allowed Somerset to belt 453 in 90 overs and pinch a thrilling tie. And, while not inspiring dread like West Indian quicks of years gone by, Marlon Black, Jermaine Lawson and Reon King all showed they had waspish pace. The 20-year-old Lawson whipped out 18 first-class wickets in four matches, kept it tidy in the one-day games and continued to shine in the Bangladesh Tests.

But it was a gloomy tour, which demonstrated how badly the gleaming pride of past West Indies sides had rusted. Logie, wicket-keeper to the great teams of the 1980s, concluded with a stark warning: "If the players don't buy into the philosophies, we'll have to rethink the selection process." **Paul Coupar**

WEST INDIES A TOURING PARTY

D. Ganga (Trinidad & Tobago) (*captain*), S. J. Benn (Barbados), T. L. Best (Barbados), M. I. Black (Trinidad & Tobago), D. J. J. Bravo (Trinidad & Tobago), G. R. Breese (Guyana), C. H. Gayle (Jamaica), K. H. Hibbert (Jamaica), R. O. Hinds (Barbados), R. D. King (Jamaica), J. J. C. Lawson (Jamaica), R. S. Morton (Leeward Islands), D. J. Pagon (West Indies B), D. B. Powell (Jamaica), L. M. P. Simmons (Trinidad & Tobago), D. S. Smith (Windward Islands).
Coach: A. L. Logie. *Manager:* J. Garner. *Trainer:* D. Cumberbatch.

WEST INDIES A TOUR RESULTS

First-class matches – Played 6: Won 1, Lost 1, Drawn 3, Tied 1.
Win – Warwickshire.
Loss – Derbyshire.
Draws – Nottinghamshire, Lancashire, Indians.
Tie – Somerset.
Non-first-class matches – Played 8: Won 5, Lost 2, No result 1. Abandoned 1. *Wins* – Ireland, British Universities, Sussex, Yorkshire, Gloucestershire. *Losses* – Sri Lankans, Kent. *No result* – Ireland. *Abandoned* – Ireland.

WEST INDIES A TOUR AVERAGES – FIRST-CLASS MATCHES

BATTING

	M	I	NO	R	HS	100s	50s	Avge	Ct/St
D. Ganga	5	8	2	325	139*	2	0	54.16	3
C. H. Gayle	3	5	0	236	94	0	3	47.20	3
D. S. Smith	6	10	0	465	181	1	2	46.50	4
D. J. J. Bravo	6	11	3	350	77*	0	3	43.75	4
R. O. Hinds	5	9	2	289	75	0	3	41.28	2
K. H. Hibbert	4	6	2	140	83*	0	1	35.00	4
R. S. Morton	5	8	0	218	79	0	2	27.25	4
L. M. P. Simmons	5	8	1	176	81	0	1	25.14	7/2
S. J. Benn	3	5	0	75	31	0	0	15.00	4
R. D. King	4	5	4	11	8	0	0	11.00	0
J. J. C. Lawson	4	4	0	37	17	0	0	9.25	0
M. I. Black	4	4	0	33	16	0	0	8.25	2
D. J. Pagon	4	6	0	37	18	0	0	6.16	0

Played in three matches: T. L. Best 8; D. B. Powell 11, 1, 7* (2 ct). Played in two matches: G. R. Breese 54*, 38, 0.

BOWLING

	O	M	R	W	BB	5W/i	Avge
C. H. Gayle	24	2	89	4	2-30	0	22.25
M. I. Black	113.1	32	344	14	4-32	0	24.57
J. J. C. Lawson	123.4	19	484	18	6-76	1	26.88
R. D. King	151	31	451	16	4-48	0	28.18
D. B. Powell	81	19	303	10	3-55	0	30.30
R. O. Hinds	105.1	18	338	10	3-54	0	33.80
T. L. Best	69.4	14	249	6	2-40	0	41.50
S. J. Benn	98	20	322	7	2-52	0	46.00

Also bowled: D. J. J. Bravo 5–0–17–0; G. R. Breese 29.5–2–103–3; D. Ganga 1–0–1–0.

Note: Matches in this section which were not first-class are signified by a dagger.

†At Eglinton, June 12. **Ireland v West Indies A. No result (abandoned).**

†At Malahide, June 13. **No result. West Indies A 220** (46.2 overs) (R. S. Morton 116; A. R. White four for 23) **v Irish President's XI.**

†At Rathmines, June 14. **West Indies A won by 82 runs.** Toss: West Indies A. **West Indies A 268 for six** (50 overs) (D. Ganga 86, D. J. Pagon 62, D. J. J. Bravo 35; A. R. White three for 49); **Ireland 186** (49.1 overs) (P. G. Gillespie 88; M. I. Black three for 23, S. J. Benn three for 24).

†At Oxford, June 17. **West Indies A won by 85 runs.** Toss: British Universities. **West Indies A 225 for six** (50 overs) (D. Ganga 41, D. J. Pagon 46, R. S. Morton 57, K. H. Hibbert 39 not out); **British Universities 140** (44.2 overs) (J. J. C. Lawson three for 13, D. J. J. Bravo three for 28).

†At Hove, June 19 (day/night). **Sri Lankans won by seven wickets.** Toss: West Indies A. **West Indies A 77** (26.1 overs) (T. C. B. Fernando four for 30, U. D. U. Chandana three for seven); **Sri Lankans 82 for three** (13 overs) (K. C. Sangakkara 35).
    A supposedly floodlit match was over by 5.45 p.m., with the sun still shining, after the West Indians collapsed from 21 for one to 27 for five. They scraped only 55 from the bat and the Sri Lankans knocked off the runs with the field restrictions still in place.

†At Hove, June 21. **West Indies A won by three wickets.** Toss: Sussex. **Sussex 124** (35.5 overs) (D. A. Clapp 43; J. J. C. Lawson three for 29, S. J. Benn three for 23); **West Indies A 125 for seven** (46.3 overs).
    First-team debuts: J. A. G. Green, A. J. Hodd.

†At Canterbury, June 23. **Kent won by six wickets.** Toss: West Indies A. **West Indies A 257 for six** (50 overs) (R. S. Morton 126, D. J. J. Bravo 40; J. M. Golding three for 58); **Kent 258 for four** (49.1 overs) (J. C. Tredwell 30, E. T. Smith 87, M. J. Walker 75 not out).

DERBYSHIRE v WEST INDIES A

At Derby, June 26, 27, 28. Derbyshire won by 145 runs. Toss: Derbyshire. First-class debut: N. E. L. Gunter.
    The West Indians' slapdash second-innings batting and sloppy fielding left a poor impression and they were well beaten by a Derbyshire side including only three capped players. The tourists began with a bang, as King and Black bent their backs and troubled batsmen on a slow pitch, but Sutton organised a Derbyshire recovery, helping the last four wickets add 162. In reply, Hibbert reached a fluent 83 and glimpsed a maiden hundred, only to be left stranded when Dowman's

medium-pace flummoxed the lower order. Dowman followed up his career-best four for 28 with a caressed 71 as Derbyshire stretched their lead, before West Indies A threw the match away. Left 252 to win, an embarrassing array of shots cost them six wickets inside 12 overs. All involved the 21-year-old Neil Gunter, who took four himself and held two fine catches at long leg. Bravo hit boldly but never threatened Derbyshire's first win against a West Indian team since 1906.

Close of play: First day, West Indies A 21-1 (Ganga 3, Pagon 8); Second day, Derbyshire 112-4 (Hewson 24, Pyemont 0).

Derbyshire

S. D. Stubbins c Hibbert b Black	25	– lbw b King	0
A. I. Gait c Benn b King	13	– c Simmons b Lawson	9
*M. P. Dowman b Lawson	17	– c Hibbert b Black	71
D. R. Hewson c Smith b Black	0	– b Lawson	47
J. P. Pyemont b King	7	– (6) b Lawson	34
S. A. Selwood c Hibbert b King	0	– (7) c Black b Benn	7
†L. D. Sutton c Hibbert b Black	80	– (8) run out	28
T. Lungley lbw b Black	19	– (9) lbw b Benn	4
P. Aldred c Hibbert b Lawson	29	– (10) not out	9
N. E. L. Gunter b Benn	18	– (11) lbw b Black	0
L. J. Wharton not out	1	– (5) b Black	0
B 8, l-b 5, w 4, n-b 12	29	B 5, l-b 7, n-b 12	24

1/40 (2) 2/50 (1) 3/50 (4) 4/76 (5)   **238**   1/1 (1) 2/57 (2) 3/110 (3)   **233**
5/76 (3) 6/76 (6) 7/138 (8)   4/110 (5) 5/169 (4) 6/184 (7)
8/191 (9) 9/230 (10) 10/238 (7)   7/186 (6) 8/201 (9)
                                                      9/229 (8) 10/233 (11)

Bowling: First Innings—Black 18.2–7–32–4; King 20–4–63–3; Lawson 22–4–84–2; Bravo 1–0–4–0; Benn 20–4–42–1. *Second Innings*—Black 18–7–64–3; King 17–4–41–1; Lawson 15–3–63–3; Benn 23–6–52–2; Ganga 1–0–1–0.

West Indies A

*D. Ganga c Wharton b Dowman	26	– c Gunter b Lungley	0
D. S. Smith lbw b Lungley	0	– (3) lbw b Gunter	0
D. J. Pagon c Sutton b Gunter	12	– (2) lbw b Gunter	6
D. J. J. Bravo lbw b Gunter	0	– (5) lbw b Aldred	48
L. M. P. Simmons b Wharton	42	– (6) c Aldred b Gunter	2
†K. H. Hibbert not out	83	– (7) b Gunter	4
R. S. Morton c Dowman b Aldred	22	– (4) c Gunter b Lungley	0
M. I. Black b Dowman	0	– lbw b Aldred	16
S. J. Benn lbw b Dowman	0	– b Wharton	9
J. J. C. Lawson c Pyemont b Dowman	0	– b Wharton	6
R. D. King lbw b Aldred	8	– not out	1
B 2, l-b 5, w 4, n-b 8	19	B 8, l-b 6	14

1/11 (2) 2/34 (3) 3/48 (4) 4/68 (1)   **220**   1/0 (1) 2/0 (3) 3/11 (2) 4/11 (4)   **106**
5/151 (5) 6/188 (7) 7/203 (8)   5/21 (6) 6/33 (7) 7/82 (8)
8/203 (9) 9/203 (10) 10/220 (11)   8/91 (5) 9/103 (9) 10/106 (10)

Bowling: First Innings—Lungley 18–5–57–1; Aldred 22.2–8–37–2; Gunter 13–4–39–2; Dowman 13–6–28–4; Wharton 13–5–52–1. *Second Innings*—Lungley 8–3–24–2; Gunter 8–4–14–4; Aldred 8–1–30–2; Dowman 4–2–15–0; Wharton 3.2–0–9–2.

Umpires: J. H. Hampshire and R. T. Robinson.

Some press reports claimed the players blamed ill-fitting trousers.
The Khaleej Times Trophy, page 1353

NOTTINGHAMSHIRE v WEST INDIES A

At Nottingham, July 3, 4, 5. Drawn. Toss: Nottinghamshire. First-class debuts: V. Atri, S. R. Patel, W. R. Smith. County debut: T. E. Savill.

At the request of the injury-hit West Indians, a scheduled fourth day was chopped, and any chance of a decent contest disappeared down the Trent Bridge drain when rain lopped off more than half the first day and all of the third. With most of their senior squad in Guernsey on a club trip, Noon was Nottinghamshire's only capped player. Among the debutants, the calm and compact Vikram Atri caught the eye, before he trudged off dejectedly, two shy of a century in his maiden first-class knock. A hugely entertaining, if not always convincing, innings followed from West Indies A as they hurtled towards a declaration at a run a ball. Hinds's half-century was a memorable highlight, and Paul McMahon's off-spin claimed his first first-class victims, albeit at some cost. Then came rain.

Close of play: First day, Nottinghamshire 149-3 (Atri 57, Patel 11); Second day, Nottinghamshire 38-0 (Welton 8, Shafayat 18).

Nottinghamshire

G. E. Welton b Best	43	– not out		8
V. Atri c Morton b Hinds	98			
B. M. Shafayat lbw b Lawson	27	– (2) not out		18
K. P. Pietersen b Lawson	1			
S. R. Patel c Bravo b Best	35			
W. R. Smith not out	38			
G. D. Clough b Hinds	5			
*†W. M. Noon lbw b Lawson	15			
T. E. Savill b Lawson	0			
P. J. McMahon lbw b Hinds	0			
B 6, l-b 5, n-b 14	25	B 1, l-b 7, n-b 4		12

1/55 (1) 2/117 (3) 3/119 (4) (9 wkts. dec.) 287 (no wkt) 38
4/213 (5) 5/229 (2) 6/241 (7)
7/284 (8) 8/284 (9) 9/287 (10)

M. N. Malik did not bat.

Bowling: *First Innings*—Black 17–2–62–0; Best 21–7–69–2; Lawson 20–1–91–4; Hinds 18.3–1–54–3. *Second Innings*—Black 4–0–18–0; Lawson 3–0–12–0; Best 0.4–0–0–0.

West Indies A

*D. Ganga c Noon b Savill	10	†K. H. Hibbert b McMahon	6
D. J. Pagon lbw b Savill	1	M. I. Black lbw b McMahon	8
D. S. Smith c Atri b Malik	31	L-b 2, n-b 18	20
R. S. Morton c Atri b Clough	33		
R. O. Hinds c Shafayat b Clough	73	1/10 (2) 2/53 (3) 3/57 (1) (8 wkts. dec.) 223
D. J. J. Bravo b Malik	21	4/108 (4) 5/157 (6)
L. M. P. Simmons not out	20	6/195 (5) 7/215 (8) 8/223 (9)

T. L. Best and J. J. C. Lawson did not bat.

Bowling: Malik 13–2–84–2; Savill 5–1–42–2; Clough 13–1–61–2; Shafayat 3–0–12–0; McMahon 3.5–0–22–2.

Umpires: M. Dixon and R. Palmer.

†At Leeds, July 7. **West Indies A won by eight wickets.** Toss: Yorkshire. **Yorkshire 139** (39.2 overs) (M. J. Wood 48; J. J. C. Lawson four for 24); **West Indies A 140 for two** (29.5 overs) (D. Ganga 57 not out, C. H. Gayle 49).

First-team debut: J. L. Sadler.

LANCASHIRE v WEST INDIES A

At Liverpool, July 10, 11, 12, 13. Drawn. Toss: West Indies A. First-class debut: M. R. Currie.

Driver, striving for a place in Lancashire's Championship side, swung the ball disconcertingly on the first day, taking five wickets, but batsmen enjoyed themselves thereafter. Devon Smith made a composed 181 in West Indies' first innings, and Gayle thwacked an unbeaten 139 in their second. In between, Fairbrother nurdled his 47th first-class hundred, which would prove to be his last before retiring. It ended uncharacteristically when muddled running cost him his wicket. When Lancashire batted again, needing to hold out for a full day to salvage a draw, they survived comfortably, although Mark Currie suffered a broken finger two runs short of a half-century on debut. Not always the friendliest of friendlies, the match briefly caught alight in Lancashire's first innings, when a flurry of boundaries by Lloyd induced a beamer from Tino Best. Lloyd, incandescent, responded in kind by hurling his bat halfway down the pitch.

Close of play: First day, West Indies A 355-8 (Smith 167, Best 8); Second day, West Indies A 38-0 (Ganga 11, Gayle 23); Third day, West Indies A 361-5 (Ganga 139, Hibbert 15).

West Indies A

*D. Ganga c Haynes b Anderson	11	– not out		139
C. H. Gayle b Driver	50	– c Fairbrother b Anderson		94
D. S. Smith c Driver b Smethurst	181	– (6) c Driver b Smethurst		17
R. S. Morton c Hogg b Driver	14	– (3) c sub b Driver		53
R. O. Hinds lbw b Driver	14	– (4) c Hogg b Driver		5
D. J. J. Bravo lbw b Driver	7	– (5) run out		4
†K. H. Hibbert b Keedy	15	– not out		15
S. J. Benn b Driver	31			
D. B. Powell c Haynes b Anderson	11			
T. L. Best b Anderson	8			
R. D. King not out	5			
B 3, l-b 6, w 2, n-b 26	37	B 13, l-b 1, w 12, n-b 8 . . .		34

1/58 (1) 2/86 (2) 3/90 (4) 4/136 (5)   369   1/149 (2) 2/258 (3)   (5 wkts dec.) 361
5/156 (6) 6/200 (7) 7/302 (8)   3/268 (4) 4/296 (5)
8/337 (9) 9/363 (10) 10/369 (3)   5/326 (6)

Bowling: *First Innings*—Anderson 20–1–83–3; Smethurst 20.4–1–87–1; Hogg 10–1–73–0; Driver 21–3–70–5; Keedy 14–2–47–1. *Second Innings*—Anderson 17–3–49–1; Smethurst 16–4–76–1; Keedy 26–6–77–0; Hogg 17–3–82–0; Driver 19–6–63–2.

Lancashire

M. R. Currie c Benn b Powell	2	– retired hurt		48
A. J. Swann c and b Powell	14	– b Powell		45
D. Byas c Hibbert b Best	11	– b Best		39
N. H. Fairbrother run out	101			
*G. D. Lloyd run out	68	– (4) b Hinds		77
R. C. Driver run out	5	– (5) not out		16
†J. J. Haynes c Morton b King	6	– (6) not out		7
K. W. Hogg b Benn	6			
G. Keedy not out	2			
J. M. Anderson c Smith b King	6			
M. P. Smethurst c Bravo b Benn	13			
B 7, l-b 6, w 6, n-b 28	47	B 12, l-b 9, w 8, n-b 4 . . .		33

1/11 (1) 2/22 (2) 3/74 (3) 4/232 (4)   279   1/115 (2) 2/234 (3)   (3 wkts) 265
5/232 (5) 6/246 (6) 7/251 (7)   3/242 (4)
8/251 (8) 9/266 (10) 10/279 (11)

In the second innings Currie retired hurt at 99.

Bowling: *First Innings*—King 20–4–74–2; Powell 16–5–61–2; Best 10–3–47–1; Benn 12–3–57–2; Hinds 8–3–27–0. *Second Innings*—King 14–5–20–0; Powell 16–5–48–1; Best 19–1–61–1; Benn 14–0–54–0; Bravo 2–0–9–0; Hinds 15–3–51–1; Gayle 1–0–1–0.

Umpires: G. I. Burgess and N. G. Cowley.

Quicksilver: the pace bowling of Jermaine Lawson, who sped his way to 18 wickets, more than any of his West Indies A colleagues, was one of the few sunny moments of a gloomy tour. *Picture by Graham Morris*

At Arundel, July 16, 17, 18. WEST INDIES A drew with INDIANS (See Indian tour section).

WARWICKSHIRE v WEST INDIES A

At Birmingham, July 20, 21, 22. West Indies A won by 119 runs. Toss: West Indies A. First-class debuts: A. P. W. Allen, N. A. Warren.

West Indies A managed the only first-class win of a glum tour – and they had the Warwickshire captain to thank for it. After rain sullied half of the first day, Michael Powell declared on the second, with his weakened Warwickshire side still 235 behind. The declaration breathed life into the match: West Indies bashed quick runs, stretched their lead to 370 and declared on the final morning. Surviving 75 overs for a draw was clearly Warwickshire's priority, and Wagh's spirited 188-ball 86, in his second match back after a serious knee injury, took them within sight. But despite graft by Sandy Allen (called up late to replace Piper as keeper), the West Indians winkled out the last wicket with 14 balls to spare. The win reflected West Indies' early domination. An assured century from Ganga helped them to 358 for three declared in their first innings, before his fellow Test player, Black, destroyed Warwickshire's top order with three wickets in his opening two overs. But without Powell's declaration, there would have been no win.

Close of play: First day, West Indies A 123-1 (Ganga 51, Bravo 14); Second day, West Indies A 72-3 (Breese 28, Bravo 2).

West Indies A

*D. Ganga not out	131		
D. S. Smith lbw b Sheikh	46		
D. J. J. Bravo c Wagh b Spires	51	– (5) not out	37
R. S. Morton c and b Richardson	79		
R. O. Hinds not out	19	– (3) b Spires	31
†L. M. P. Simmons (did not bat)		– (1) c Powell b Warren	7
D. J. Pagon (did not bat)		– (2) b Warren	0
G. R. Breese (did not bat)		– (4) not out	54
B 4, l-b 22, w 2, n-b 4	32	B 1, l-b 3, n-b 2	6
1/83 (2) 2/196 (3) 3/334 (4) (3 wkts dec.)	358	1/0 (2) 2/15 (1) (3 wkts dec.) 3/70 (3)	135

M. I. Black, D. B. Powell and T. L. Best did not bat.

Bowling: *First Innings*—Brown 10–1–61–0; Wagg 13–2–66–0; Warren 9–0–42–0; Richardson 17–7–32–1; Sheikh 8–2–20–1; Spires 9–0–41–1; Wagh 8–1–37–0; Troughton 2–0–21–0; Powell 3–0–12–0. *Second Innings*—Richardson 4–1–14–0; Warren 11–3–48–2; Wagg 3–0–18–0; Spires 2–0–16–1; Wagh 1–0–1–0; Brown 6–0–29–0; Powell 1–0–5–0.

Warwickshire

*M. J. Powell b Black	0	– lbw b Powell	14
M. A. Wagh b Black	0	– lbw b Breese	86
J. O. Troughton b Powell	5	– c Simmons b Powell	10
D. P. Ostler b Black	0	– b Best	31
D. R. Brown b Breese	65	– c Ganga b Hinds	35
M. A. Sheikh c Ganga b Hinds	10	– (7) b Best	16
G. G. Wagg not out	18	– (6) b Powell	0
N. A. Warren not out	2	– run out	11
†A. P. W. Allen (did not bat)		– not out	18
A. Richardson (did not bat)		– b Black	0
J. A. Spires (did not bat)		– lbw b Hinds	10
B 1, l-b 2, w 6, n-b 14	23	B 8, l-b 5, n-b 6	19
1/0 (1) 2/5 (2) 3/11 (4) (6 wkts dec.)	123	1/17 (1) 2/37 (3) 3/74 (4)	251
4/21 (3) 5/74 (6) 6/102 (5)		4/158 (5) 5/163 (6) 6/199 (7)	
		7/218 (2) 8/227 (8)	
		9/231 (10) 10/251 (11)	

Bowling: *First Innings*—Black 9–1–35–3; Powell 7–2–21–1; Best 8–1–32–0; Hinds 6–1–26–1; Breese 3–0–6–1. *Second Innings*—Black 14–5–42–1; Powell 15–1–55–3; Hinds 15.4–4–47–2; Best 11–2–40–2; Breese 17–2–54–1.

Umpires: P. Adams and K. E. Palmer.

SOMERSET v WEST INDIES A

At Taunton, July 24, 25, 26. Tied. Toss: West Indies A. First-class debuts: W. J. Durston, N. J. Edwards, C. M. Gazzard, A. V. Suppiah.

Somerset's remarkable run-chase reached an appropriately remarkable end. They began the nail-biting final over needing eight to win, with nine wickets down; by the final delivery they needed a single. With close fielders swarming, Rose tried a reverse sweep but only chipped a catch to Benn: Somerset's tenth wicket had fallen to the last possible ball of the match and the game was tied. For a young, experimental Somerset side to get so close to chasing down a daunting 454 in 90 overs was most impressive. Their buoyant innings owed much to a maiden century from Trego – often seen as low as No. 9 in the Championship side – and to well-paced innings by Holloway and the debutant Wes Durston, who cracked fifty in 40 balls. But it was the West Indians who had had the better of the first two days. Against some lukewarm bowling and fielding, Gayle smashed 75, including a six that sailed out of the ground off Durston's left-arm spin. Somerset slumped in reply, before rapid West Indies scoring set up a declaration – and a compelling final day.

Close of play: First day, Somerset 60-0 (Wood 28, Edwards 29); Second day, West Indies A 266-7 (Bravo 77, Powell 7).

West Indies A

C. H. Gayle c Gazzard b Bulbeck	75	– b Bulbeck	17
D. S. Smith c Gazzard b Dutch	65	– c Durston b Dutch	29
D. J. J. Bravo c Gazzard b Bulbeck	35	– (5) not out	77
R. S. Morton lbw b Bulbeck	4	– lbw b Parsons	23
*R. O. Hinds c and b Bulbeck	0	– (3) c sub b Durston	75
G. R. Breese c Suppiah b Dutch	38	– c Parsons b Suppiah	0
†L. M. P. Simmons c Edwards b Dutch	81	– b Suppiah	16
S. J. Benn b Parsons	25	– st Gazzard b Suppiah	10
D. B. Powell c Bulbeck b Parsons	1	– not out	7
J. J. C. Lawson c sub b Parsons	17		
R. D. King not out	0		
B 8, l-b 10, w 7, n-b 4	29	B 1, l-b 5, n-b 6	12

1/138 (2) 2/174 (1) 3/180 (4) 4/180 (5)	**370**	1/30 (1) 2/67 (2) (7 wkts dec.) 266
5/217 (3) 6/241 (6) 7/328 (8)		3/118 (4) 4/177 (3)
8/330 (9) 9/370 (10) 10/370 (7)		5/178 (6) 6/243 (7) 7/253 (8)

Bowling: *First Innings*—Bulbeck 18–3–47–4; Rose 6–0–31–0; Trego 9–1–62–0; Parsons 12–0–59–3; Dutch 26.1–5–104–3; Durston 10–0–40–0; Suppiah 5–2–9–0. *Second Innings*—Bulbeck 12.4–4–34–1; Trego 12–2–77–0; Dutch 11–2–54–1; Parsons 7–1–24–1; Suppiah 10–2–46–3; Durston 4–0–25–1.

When the team in control are South Africa, the fat lady thinks twice before opening her mouth.
India v South Africa, page 1418

Somerset

M. J. Wood c Morton b Powell	51	– c Benn b King	12
N. J. Edwards c Gayle b King	31	– c Simmons b Powell	27
P. C. L. Holloway c Bravo b Lawson	4	– b Lawson	88
*K. A. Parsons c Hinds b Lawson	3	– (5) c Gayle b Powell	17
A. V. Suppiah b King	1	– (6) st Simmons b Benn	5
K. P. Dutch c Gayle b King	6	– (7) run out	12
W. J. Durston run out	26	– (8) b King	55
†C. M. Gazzard c Bravo b Benn	24	– (9) c Powell b King	7
P. D. Trego not out	12	– (4) c Morton b Gayle	140
G. D. Rose c Smith b King	8	– c Benn b Gayle	32
M. P. L. Bulbeck st Simmons b Breese	4	– not out	11
B 6, l-b 5, n-b 2	13	B 11, l-b 24, w 8, n-b 4	47

1/63 (2) 2/76 (3) 3/84 (4) 4/91 (5)   **183**   1/16 (1) 2/73 (2) 3/196 (3)   **453**
5/103 (6) 6/116 (1) 7/154 (7)   4/250 (5) 5/275 (6) 6/330 (7)
8/155 (8) 9/178 (10) 10/183 (11)   7/354 (8) 8/364 (9)
                                            9/431 (8) 10/453 (10)

Bowling: First Innings—King 19–3–48–4; Powell 7–0–51–1; Benn 12–4–26–1; Hinds 1–0–1–0; Lawson 9–1–33–2; Breese 3.5–0–13–1. *Second Innings*—King 20–2–90–3; Powell 20–6–67–2; Lawson 13–2–58–1; Benn 17–3–91–1; Breese 6–0–30–0; Hinds 5–0–30–0; Gayle 9–0–52–2.

Umpires: B. Dudleston and J. W. Lloyds.

†At Cheltenham, July 29. **West Indies A won by 44 runs**. Toss: West Indies A. **West Indies A 279** (49.4 overs) (C. H. Gayle 83, R. S. Morton 41, R. O. Hinds 68, D. J. J. Bravo 38; R. J. Sillence four for 35); **Gloucestershire 235** (45 overs) (M. G. N. Windows 41, J. N. Snape 55, A. P. R. Gidman 36, Extras 34; R. O. Hinds six for 46).

First-team debut: J. A. Pearson.

FRIZZELL COUNTY CHAMPIONSHIP, 2002

Review by PAT GIBSON

SURREY
COUNTY CRICKET CLUB

Adam Hollioake

Nick Knight, hopping around the crease like Long John Silver as he used his bat for a crutch because of a groin injury, defied Surrey for nearly six and a half hours at Edgbaston to make them wait another week before they claimed their third Championship in four years. Martin Saggers of Kent took 79 Championship wickets to take his aggregate to 199 in three seasons and was not alone in wondering why consistent form and fitness had not earned him selection for the England tour of Australia ahead of several other fast bowlers who could point to neither. Ian Ward, virtually written off by England a year earlier, became the first Surrey batsman since Jack Hobbs to score four centuries in successive Championship innings, while Jimmy Anderson of Lancashire, Jim Troughton of Warwickshire, Ed Joyce of Middlesex and Rikki Clarke of Surrey all emerged as players of international potential.

And Mike Atherton and Nasser Hussain, England captains past and present, tell us that the very system that gave them their professional opportunities (and lucrative benefits) does not produce players tough enough, ambitious enough or talented enough to play Test cricket. Perhaps they should get out more – and take Duncan Fletcher with them. The England coach does do the rounds of the county circuit but it is more in the guise of a family doctor checking on the progress of his private patients than a dedicated specialist with an overall interest in the health of the domestic game.

If he stayed longer instead of hurrying away to his next appointment with a shin splint or a groin strain, watched more play and spent time with the county captains and coaches, he might come to realise that English cricket is not quite as anaemic as some make it out to be. For a second opinion, he could speak to Steve Waugh, Shane Warne, Glenn McGrath or the other Australians who have been only too happy to play here – and not just for the money. Waugh, who furthered his education with Somerset and took a refresher course with Kent in 2002, thinks the standard is similar to state cricket and that it has helped many of his countrymen expand their games. If they can benefit from county cricket, why can't their English counterparts?

The system has changed in recent times, of course. The introduction of two divisions has deprived half the counties of any chance of winning the title itself while central contracts for England players have turned it into more of a handicap (the Duncan Fletcher Handicap, perhaps) than a classic. Yet it is still the best way, arguably the only way, of developing cricketers to play for England.

At least David Morgan, the new chairman of the England and Wales Cricket Board, appears to have a better grasp of that basic truth than Lord MacLaurin, his predecessor, who pushed through these changes with little appreciation of the damage they might do a cherished institution. One of the first things Morgan did when he took over in 2003 was order a review of the entire structure, which may make the absurdity of a Championship in which Yorkshire do not play Lancashire a short-lived phenomenon.

COUNTY CHAMPIONSHIP TABLE

Division One	Matches	Won	Lost	Drawn	Bonus Points Batting	Bowling	Penalty	Points
1 – Surrey (**4**)	16	10	2	4	59	48	0.25	242.75
2 – Warwickshire (**3**) . . .	16	7	2	7	42	44	0	198
3 – Kent (**3**)	16	7	4	5	48	44	0.50	195.50
4 – Lancashire (**6**)	16	6	4	6	33	43	0	172
5 – Leicestershire (**5**) . . .	16	5	5	6	42	46	1	171
6 – Sussex (*1*)	16	3	6	7	43	47	0	154
7 – Hampshire (*2*)	16	2	5	9	35	44	8*	131
8 – Somerset (**2**)	16	1	7	8	39	44	0.25	126.75
9 – Yorkshire (*1*)	16	2	8	6	35	45	3.25	124.75

Division Two	Matches	Won	Lost	Drawn	Bonus Points Batting	Bowling	Penalty	Points
1 – Essex (*9*).	16	10	3	3	42	46	1	219
2 – Middlesex (*5*).	16	7	3	6	61	43	0.25	211.75
3 – Nottinghamshire (*7*). .	16	8	5	3	47	48	1.25	201.75
4 – Worcestershire (*6*). . .	16	7	4	5	53	43	0	200
5 – Glamorgan (**8**)	16	5	5	6	41	44	0	169
6 – Derbyshire (*9*)	16	7	7	2	37	48	9.25*	167.75
7 – Northamptonshire (*7*).	16	5	7	4	46	41	0.50	162.50
8 – Gloucestershire (*4*) . .	16	2	7	7	42	44	1.50	136.50
9 – Durham (*9*)	16	1	11	4	21	42	0.25	90.75

2001 positions are shown in brackets: Division One in bold, Division Two in italic.

Win = 12 pts; draw = 4 pts.

* *Eight points deducted for a poor pitch.*

It was Yorkshire's downfall in 2002 that most vividly illustrated the inequity of the present format. There was nothing wrong with the fact that a team which had walked away with the Championship the year before could be so abruptly overthrown, because it showed how fierce the competition can be. On the other hand, relegation, with all the financial consequences of second-division status at a time when the club needed every penny it could get, was too high a price to pay for one wretched Championship season in which they were weakened by England calls and injuries. The same thing nearly happened to Surrey the previous season. They had won the title in 1999 and 2000 but almost went down in 2001 before reconfirming that they were the best side in the land in a way that left no room for argument – except from the counties who never had the chance to play against them.

It is probably fair to say that two divisions have created more general interest, particularly towards the end of the season, but the joy of Essex, Middlesex and Nottinghamshire in going up was tempered by the despair of Yorkshire, Somerset and Hampshire in going down.

The Championship does not need such extremes. Fear of failure afflicts too many counties in the first division if not the second. They should all start the season with a theoretical chance of winning the title, with tiered prize money from first to 18th to keep them motivated when all hope has gone. Not that they should need much motivating, anyway. It is still one of the great privileges of living in England that you are never far away from a first-class match in the summer and it would be a sad day if that were to change through negligence or neglect on the part of players and administrators.

Surrey had dedicated their season to Ben Hollioake, the young England all-rounder killed in a car crash in Australia in March, and there was a fervour about their cricket, especially after Adam, Ben's grieving elder brother, returned to lead the side in June, that was quite moving. Adam himself was to score 738 runs in nine matches at almost a run a ball, although by then Surrey had already established their supremacy under the captaincy of Mark Butcher and Ward. They had a lot of England calls, too, but the performances of Nadeem Shahid and Jon Batty emphasised their strength in depth.

Surrey's destiny – and Yorkshire's – was signalled as early as April 26 when the champions were thrashed by an innings and 168 runs inside three days at Headingley, leaving most of the other counties in the first division preoccupied with the other end of the table. Warwickshire made the biggest strides, despite Ian Bell's nasty attack of second-season-itis, which suggested that the fond notion of players going straight from the National Academy into the Test side needs much more thought. So, for that matter, does the premature promotion of gifted young men like James Foster and Richard Dawson.

Kent, Lancashire and, against all expectations, Leicestershire also did well, and with Sussex, another county in mourning following the tragic loss of Umer Rashid, showing great togetherness, it was Hampshire and Somerset who went down with Yorkshire. In Hampshire's case, the soccer-style sacking of Jimmy Cook, the coach, made little difference as relegation loomed, but in the second division similar, albeit swifter, action brought instant success. The demanding Clive Rice was replaced as Nottinghamshire coach by the more sympathetic Mick Newell and the players responded by beating Worcestershire to the third promotion place.

Essex, galvanised by the shrewd guidance of Graham Gooch, the influential leadership of Ronnie Irani and the exemplary influence of Andy Flower, took the title ahead of Middlesex, who secured first-division cricket for Lord's with a rich crop of youngsters under the supervision of John Emburey.

It is the dedication of coaches like Gooch, Emburey and Newell, the achievements of players such as Ward, Knight and Saggers and the emergence of exciting new talent that showed why the Championship deserves more respect than it often gets from people who really ought to know better.

County cricket has its problems and always has done. The finances will always be a worry, the pitches must still be improved, the dearth of spin bowlers has to be addressed and the growing dependence on overseas players carefully monitored. Even in its present state, however, the Championship must still be the bedrock of English cricket. You never know. If it was properly maintained, properly promoted and properly recognised, the England team might become more representative of the English game than it often was in Australia in the winter of 2002-03.

SUMMARY OF RESULTS, 2002

DIVISION ONE

	Hampshire	Kent	Lancashire	Leicestershire	Somerset	Surrey	Sussex	Warwickshire	Yorkshire
Hampshire	–	W	L	L	W	L	D	D	L
Kent	D	–	W	D	W	L	W	D	W
Lancashire	D	L	–	W	W	D	D	D	L
Leicestershire	D	L	D	–	W	L	W	W	W
Somerset	D	D	L	D	–	D	L	D	W
Surrey	W	W	W	W	D	–	W	L	W
Sussex	D	D	L	D	W		–	L	D
Warwickshire	D	W	L	W	W	D	W	–	W
Yorkshire	D	L	D	D	D	L	L	D	–

DIVISION TWO

	Derbyshire	Durham	Essex	Glamorgan	Middlesex	Nottinghamshire	Northamptonshire	Nottinghamshire	Worcestershire
Derbyshire	–	W	L	W	D	L	W	L	L
Durham	W	–	L	L	D	L	L	L	D
Essex	W	W	–	D	D	W	W	W	L
Glamorgan	L	W	W	–	D	L	W	D	L
Gloucestershire	D	W	L	L	–	D	D	W	D
Middlesex	L	D	D	D	W	–	D	W	D
Northamptonshire	L	W	L	W	W	L	–	W	W
Nottinghamshire	L	D	W	W	W	W	W	–	W
Worcestershire	W	W	W	L	W	L	W	D	–

Home teams listed on left, away teams across top; results are for home teams.

Leaders: *Division One* – from April 27 Surrey; June 3 Leicestershire; June 15 Surrey. Surrey became champions on September 7.
Division Two – from April 27 Middlesex; May 11 Derbyshire; May 18 Middlesex; June 3 Derbyshire; June 29 Essex; July 13 Middlesex; September 21 Essex. Essex became champions on September 21.

Bottom place: *Division One* – from April 27 Yorkshire; May 11 Warwickshire; May 18 Yorkshire; May 27 Warwickshire; June 15 Yorkshire.
Division Two – from April 27 Nottinghamshire; May 11 Durham; May 27 Northamptonshire; June 29 Durham.

Prize money

Division One
£105,000 for winners: SURREY.
£50,000 for runners-up: WARWICKSHIRE.

Division Two
£40,000 for winners: ESSEX.
£25,000 for runners-up: MIDDLESEX.

Winners of each match (both divisions): £2,000.

Scoring of Points

(a) For a win, 12 points plus any points scored in the first innings.

(b) In a tie, each side scores six points, plus any points scored in the first innings.

(c) In a drawn match, each side scores four points, plus any points scored in the first innings (see also paragraph (f)).

(d) If the scores are equal in a drawn match, the side batting in the fourth innings scores six points, plus any points scored in the first innings, and the opposing side scores four points plus any points scored in the first innings.

(e) First-innings points (awarded only for performances in the first 130 overs of each first innings and retained whatever the result of the match).

(i) A maximum of five batting points to be available: 200 to 249 runs – 1 point; 250 to 299 runs – 2 points; 300 to 349 runs – 3 points; 350 to 399 runs – 4 points; 400 runs or over – 5 points. Penalty runs awarded within the first 130 overs of each first innings count towards the award of bonus points.

(ii) A maximum of three bowling points to be available: 3 to 5 wickets taken – 1 point; 6 to 8 wickets taken – 2 points; 9 to 10 wickets taken – 3 points.

(*f*) If play starts when less than eight hours' playing time remains and a one-innings match is played, no first-innings points shall be scored. The side winning on the one innings scores 12 points. In a tie, each side scores six points. In a drawn match, each side scores four points. If the scores are equal in a drawn match, the side batting in the second innings scores six points and the opposing side scores four points.

(*g*) If a match is abandoned without a ball being bowled, each side scores four points.

(*h*) The side which has the highest aggregate of points shall be the Champion County of their respective Division. Should any sides in the Championship table be equal on points, the following tie-breakers will be applied in the order stated: most wins, fewest losses, team achieving most points in head-to-head contests between teams level on points, most wickets taken, most runs scored. At the end of the season, the top three teams from the second division will be promoted and the bottom three teams from the first division will be relegated.

(*i*) The minimum over-rate to be achieved by counties will be 16 overs per hour. Overs will be calculated at the end of the match and penalties applied on a match-by-match basis. For each over (ignoring fractions) that a side has bowled short of the target number, 0.25 points will be deducted from their Championship total.

(*j*) A county which is adjudged to have prepared a pitch unfit for four-day first-class cricket will have 20 points deducted. A county adjudged to have prepared a poor pitch will have eight points deducted. This penalty will rise to 12 points if the county has prepared a poor or unfit pitch within the previous 12 months.

Under ECB playing conditions, two extras were scored for every no-ball and wide bowled whether scored off or not. Any runs scored off the bat were credited to the batsman, while byes and leg-byes were counted as no-balls or wides, as appropriate, in accordance with Law 24.13, in addition to the initial penalty

CONSTITUTION OF COUNTY CHAMPIONSHIP

At least four possible dates have been given for the start of county cricket in England. The first, patchy, references began in 1825. The earliest mention in any cricket publication is in 1864 and eight counties have come to be regarded as first-class from that date, including Cambridgeshire, who dropped out after 1871. For many years, the County Championship was considered to have started in 1873, when regulations governing qualification first applied; indeed, a special commemorative stamp was issued by the Post Office in 1973. However, the Championship was not formally organised until 1890 and before then champions were proclaimed by the press; sometimes publications differed in their views and no definitive list of champions can start before that date. Eight teams contested the 1890 competition – Gloucestershire, Kent, Lancashire, Middlesex, Nottinghamshire, Surrey, Sussex and Yorkshire. Somerset joined in the following year, and in 1895 the Championship began to acquire something of its modern shape when Derbyshire, Essex, Hampshire, Leicestershire and Warwickshire were added. At that point MCC officially recognised the competition's existence. Worcestershire, Northamptonshire and Glamorgan were admitted to the Championship in 1899, 1905 and 1921 respectively and are regarded as first-class from these dates. An invitation in 1921 to Buckinghamshire to enter the Championship was declined, owing to the lack of necessary playing facilities, and an application by Devon in 1948 was unsuccessful. Durham were admitted to the Championship in 1992 and were granted first-class status prior to their pre-season tour of Zimbabwe.

In 2000, the Championship was split for the first time into two divisions, on the basis of counties' standings in the 1999 competition. From 2000 onwards, the bottom three teams in Division One were relegated at the end of the season, and the top three teams in Division Two promoted.

COUNTY CHAMPIONS

The title of champion county is unreliable before 1890. In 1963, *Wisden* formally accepted the list of champions "most generally selected" by contemporaries, as researched by the late Rowland Bowen (See *Wisden 1959*, pp 91–98). This appears to be the most accurate available list but has no official status. The county champions from 1864 to 1889 were, according to Bowen:

1864 Surrey; 1865 Nottinghamshire; 1866 Middlesex; 1867 Yorkshire; 1868 Nottinghamshire; 1869 Nottinghamshire and Yorkshire; 1870 Yorkshire; 1871 Nottinghamshire; 1872 Nottinghamshire; 1873 Gloucestershire and Nottinghamshire; 1874 Gloucestershire; 1875 Nottinghamshire; 1876 Gloucestershire; 1877 Gloucestershire; 1878 undecided; 1879 Lancashire and Nottinghamshire; 1880 Nottinghamshire; 1881 Lancashire; 1882 Lancashire and Nottinghamshire; 1883 Nottinghamshire; 1884 Nottinghamshire; 1885 Nottinghamshire; 1886 Nottinghamshire; 1887 Surrey; 1888 Surrey; 1889 Lancashire, Nottinghamshire and Surrey.

Official champions

1890	Surrey	1929	Nottinghamshire	1969	Glamorgan
1891	Surrey	1930	Lancashire	1970	Kent
1892	Surrey	1931	Yorkshire	1971	Surrey
1893	Yorkshire	1932	Yorkshire	1972	Warwickshire
1894	Surrey	1933	Yorkshire	1973	Hampshire
1895	Surrey	1934	Lancashire	1974	Worcestershire
1896	Yorkshire	1935	Yorkshire	1975	Leicestershire
1897	Lancashire	1936	Derbyshire	1976	Middlesex
1898	Yorkshire	1937	Yorkshire	1977	Middlesex / Kent
1899	Surrey	1938	Yorkshire		
1900	Yorkshire	1939	Yorkshire	1978	Kent
1901	Yorkshire	1946	Yorkshire	1979	Essex
1902	Yorkshire	1947	Middlesex	1980	Middlesex
1903	Middlesex	1948	Glamorgan	1981	Nottinghamshire
1904	Lancashire	1949	Middlesex / Yorkshire	1982	Middlesex
1905	Yorkshire			1983	Essex
1906	Kent	1950	Lancashire / Surrey	1984	Essex
1907	Nottinghamshire			1985	Middlesex
1908	Yorkshire	1951	Warwickshire	1986	Essex
1909	Kent	1952	Surrey	1987	Nottinghamshire
1910	Kent	1953	Surrey	1988	Worcestershire
1911	Warwickshire	1954	Surrey	1989	Worcestershire
1912	Yorkshire	1955	Surrey	1990	Middlesex
1913	Kent	1956	Surrey	1991	Essex
1914	Surrey	1957	Surrey	1992	Essex
1919	Yorkshire	1958	Surrey	1993	Middlesex
1920	Middlesex	1959	Yorkshire	1994	Warwickshire
1921	Middlesex	1960	Yorkshire	1995	Warwickshire
1922	Yorkshire	1961	Hampshire	1996	Leicestershire
1923	Yorkshire	1962	Yorkshire	1997	Glamorgan
1924	Yorkshire	1963	Yorkshire	1998	Leicestershire
1925	Yorkshire	1964	Worcestershire	1999	Surrey
1926	Lancashire	1965	Worcestershire	2000	Surrey
1927	Lancashire	1966	Yorkshire	2001	Yorkshire
1928	Lancashire	1967	Yorkshire	2002	Surrey
		1968	Yorkshire		

Notes: Since the Championship was constituted in 1890 it has been won outright as follows: Yorkshire 30 times, Surrey 18, Middlesex 10, Lancashire 7, Essex and Kent 6, Warwickshire and Worcestershire 5, Nottinghamshire 4, Glamorgan and Leicestershire 3, Hampshire 2, Derbyshire 1.
   The title has been shared three times since 1890, involving Middlesex twice, Kent, Lancashire, Surrey and Yorkshire.

Wooden Spoons: since the major expansion of the Championship from nine teams to 14 in 1895, the counties have finished outright bottom as follows: Derbyshire 12; Northamptonshire and Somerset 11; Glamorgan 9; Nottinghamshire and Sussex 8; Gloucestershire and Leicestershire 7; Worcestershire 6; Hampshire 5; Durham 4; Warwickshire 3; Essex and Kent 2; Yorkshire 1. Lancashire, Middlesex and Surrey have never finished bottom. Leicestershire have also shared bottom place twice, once with Hampshire and once with Somerset.

From 1977 to 1983 the Championship was sponsored by Schweppes, from 1984 to 1998 by Britannic Assurance, from 1999 to 2000 by PPP healthcare, in 2001 by CricInfo, and from 2002 by Frizzell.

COUNTY CHAMPIONSHIP – FINAL POSITIONS, 1890–2002

	Derbyshire	Essex	Glamorgan	Gloucestershire	Hampshire	Kent	Lancashire	Leicestershire	Middlesex	Northamptonshire	Nottinghamshire	Somerset	Surrey	Sussex	Warwickshire	Worcestershire	Yorkshire
1890	–	–	–	6	–	3	2	–	7	–	5	–	1	8	–	–	3
1891	–	–	–	9	–	5	2	–	3	–	4	5	1	7	–	–	8
1892	–	–	–	7	–	7	4	–	5	–	2	3	1	9	–	–	6
1893	–	–	–	9	–	4	2	–	3	–	6	8	5	7	–	–	1
1894	–	–	–	9	–	4	4	–	3	–	7	6	1	8	–	–	2
1895	5	9	–	4	10	14	2	12	6	–	12	8	1	11	6	–	3
1896	7	5	–	10	8	9	2	13	3	–	6	11	4	14	12	–	1
1897	14	3	–	5	9	12	1	13	8	–	10	11	2	6	7	–	4
1898	9	5	–	3	12	7	6	13	2	–	8	13	4	9	9	–	1
1899	15	6	–	9	10	8	4	13	2	–	10	13	1	5	7	12	3
1900	13	10	–	7	15	3	2	14	7	–	5	11	7	3	6	12	1
1901	15	10	–	14	7	7	3	12	2	–	9	12	6	4	5	11	1
1902	10	13	–	14	15	7	5	11	12	–	3	7	4	2	6	9	1
1903	12	8	–	13	14	8	4	14	1	–	5	10	11	2	7	6	3
1904	10	14	–	9	15	3	1	7	4	–	5	12	11	6	7	13	2
1905	14	12	–	8	16	6	2	5	11	13	10	15	4	3	7	8	1
1906	16	7	–	9	8	1	4	15	11	11	5	11	3	10	6	14	2
1907	16	7	–	10	12	8	6	11	5	15	1	14	4	13	9	2	2
1908	14	11	–	10	9	2	7	13	4	15	8	16	3	5	12	6	1
1909	15	14	–	16	8	1	2	13	6	7	10	11	5	4	12	8	3
1910	15	11	–	12	6	1	4	10	3	9	5	16	2	7	14	13	8
1911	14	6	–	12	11	2	4	15	3	10	8	16	5	13	1	9	7
1912	12	15	–	11	6	3	4	13	5	2	8	14	7	10	9	16	1
1913	13	15	–	9	10	1	8	14	6	4	5	16	3	7	11	12	2
1914	12	8	–	16	5	3	11	13	2	9	10	15	1	6	7	14	4
1919	9	14	–	8	7	2	5	9	13	12	3	5	4	11	15	–	1
1920	16	9	–	8	11	5	2	13	1	14	7	10	3	6	12	15	4
1921	12	15	17	7	6	4	5	11	1	13	8	10	2	9	16	14	3
1922	11	8	16	13	6	4	5	14	7	15	2	10	3	9	12	17	1
1923	10	13	16	11	7	5	3	14	8	17	2	9	4	6	12	15	1
1924	17	15	13	6	12	5	4	11	2	16	6	8	3	10	9	14	1
1925	14	7	17	10	9	5	3	12	6	11	4	15	2	13	8	16	1
1926	11	9	8	15	7	3	1	13	6	16	4	14	5	10	11	17	2
1927	5	8	15	12	13	4	1	7	9	16	2	14	6	10	11	17	3
1928	10	16	15	5	12	2	1	9	8	13	3	14	6	7	11	17	4
1929	7	12	17	4	11	8	2	9	6	13	1	15	10	4	14	16	2
1930	9	6	11	2	13	5	1	12	16	17	4	13	8	7	15	10	3
1931	7	10	15	12	12	3	6	16	11	17	5	13	8	4	9	14	1
1932	10	14	15	13	8	3	6	12	10	16	4	7	5	2	9	17	1
1933	6	4	16	10	14	3	5	17	12	13	8	11	9	2	7	15	1
1934	3	8	13	7	14	5	1	12	10	17	9	15	11	2	4	16	5
1935	2	9	13	15	16	10	4	6	3	17	5	14	11	7	8	12	1
1936	1	9	16	4	10	8	11	15	2	17	5	7	6	14	13	12	3
1937	3	6	7	4	14	12	9	16	2	17	10	13	8	5	11	15	1
1938	5	6	16	10	14	9	4	15	2	17	12	7	3	8	13	11	1
1939	9	4	13	3	15	5	6	17	2	16	12	14	8	10	11	7	1
1946	15	8	6	5	10	6	3	11	2	16	13	4	11	17	14	8	1
1947	5	11	9	2	16	4	3	14	1	17	11	11	6	9	15	7	7
1948	6	13	1	8	9	15	5	11	3	17	14	12	2	16	7	10	4
1949	15	9	8	7	16	13	11	17	1	6	11	9	5	13	4	3	1
1950	5	17	11	7	12	9	1	16	14	10	15	7	1	13	4	6	3

	Derbyshire	Durham	Essex	Glamorgan	Gloucestershire	Hampshire	Kent	Lancashire	Leicestershire	Middlesex	Northamptonshire	Nottinghamshire	Somerset	Surrey	Sussex	Warwickshire	Worcestershire	Yorkshire
1951	11	–	8	5	12	9	16	3	15	7	13	17	14	6	10	1	4	2
1952	4	–	10	7	9	12	15	3	6	5	8	16	17	1	13	10	14	2
1953	6	–	12	10	6	14	16	3	3	5	11	8	17	1	2	9	15	2
1954	3	–	15	4	13	14	11	10	16	7	7	5	17	1	2	9	15	12
1955	8	–	14	16	12	3	13	9	6	5	7	11	17	1	4	9	15	2
1956	12	–	11	13	3	6	16	2	17	5	4	8	15	1	9	14	9	7
1957	4	–	5	9	12	13	14	6	17	7	2	15	8	1	9	11	16	3
1958	5	–	6	15	14	2	8	7	12	10	4	17	3	1	13	16	9	11
1959	7	–	9	6	2	8	13	5	16	10	11	17	12	3	15	4	14	1
1960	5	–	6	11	8	12	10	2	17	3	9	16	14	7	4	15	13	1
1961	7	–	6	14	5	1	11	16	17	13	3	16	17	10	15	8	12	4
1962	7	–	9	14	4	10	11	16	17	13	8	15	6	5	12	3	2	1
1963	17	–	12	2	8	10	13	15	16	6	7	9	3	11	4	4	14	1
1964	12	–	10	11	17	12	7	14	16	6	3	15	8	4	9	2	1	5
1965	9	–	15	3	10	12	5	13	14	2	5	17	7	8	16	11	1	4
1966	9	–	16	14	15	11	4	6	12	8	12	5	17	3	7	10	2	1
1967	6	–	15	14	17	12	2	11	2	7	9	10	13	4	8	13	5	1
1968	8	–	14	3	16	5	2	6	9	10	13	4	12	15	17	11	7	1
1969	16	–	6	1	2	5	10	15	14	11	9	8	17	3	7	4	12	13
1970	7	–	12	2	17	10	1	3	15	16	14	11	13	5	9	7	6	4
1971	17	–	10	16	8	9	4	3	5	6	14	12	7	1	11	2	15	13
1972	17	–	5	13	3	9	2	15	6	8	4	11	12	16	1	7	10	14
1973	16	–	8	11	5	1	4	2	9	13	3	17	10	2	15	7	6	14
1974	17	–	12	16	14	2	10	8	4	6	3	15	5	7	13	9	1	11
1975	15	–	6	7	9	16	3	5	4	1	8	13	12	6	17	14	10	2
1976	15	–	6	17	3	12	14	16	4	1	2	13	7	9	10	5	11	8
1977	7	–	6	14	3	11	1	16	5	1	9	2	13	7	4	10	5	11
1978	14	–	2	13	10	8	1	12	6	3	17	7	5	16	9	11	15	4
1979	16	–	1	17	10	12	5	13	6	14	11	9	8	3	4	15	2	7
1980	9	–	8	13	7	8	16	15	10	1	12	3	5	2	4	14	11	6
1981	12	–	5	14	13	7	9	6	8	4	15	1	3	6	2	17	11	10
1982	11	–	7	16	15	3	13	12	2	1	9	4	6	5	8	17	14	10
1983	9	–	1	15	12	3	7	12	4	3	11	2	6	5	8	11	14	17
1984	12	–	3	12	13	17	15	5	3	2	6	14	10	8	11	5	16	17
1985	13	–	4	12	3	2	9	14	16	1	10	8	17	6	7	15	5	11
1986	11	–	1	17	2	6	8	15	7	12	9	4	16	3	14	12	5	10
1987	6	–	12	13	10	5	14	2	9	8	16	7	1	11	4	17	15	9
1988	14	–	3	17	10	15	2	9	8	7	1	5	11	4	16	6	1	13
1989	6	–	2	17	9	6	15	4	13	3	5	11	14	12	10	8	1	16
1990	12	–	2	8	13	3	16	6	7	1	5	11	13	15	9	17	5	4
1991	3	–	1	12	13	9	8	16	15	10	4	1	13	5	11	2	6	14
1992	5	18	1	14	10	15	2	12	8	11	3	4	9	13	7	6	17	16
1993	15	18	11	3	17	13	8	13	9	1	7	5	6	10	16	2	12	12
1994	17	16	6	18	12	13	9	10	2	4	5	3	11	7	8	1	15	13
1995	14	17	5	16	6	13	18	4	7	1	9	16	11	3	12	8	7	6
1996	2	18	5	10	13	14	4	15	1	9	16	17	11	12	15	1	8	6
1997	16	17	8	1	7	14	2	11	10	4	15	13	12	8	18	4	3	6
1998	10	14	18	12	4	6	11	2	1	17	15	16	9	5	7	8	13	3
1999	9	8	12	14	18	7	5	2	3	16	13	17	4	1	11	10	15	6
2000	**9**	**8**	*2*	*3*	*4*	**7**	**6**	**2**	**4**	*8*	*1*	*7*	**5**	**1**	*9*	*6*	*5*	**3**
2001	*9*	*8*	**2**	*8*	*4*	**7**	**3**	**4**	**5**	*2*	**7**	*7*	**5**	**1**	*9*	*6*	*1*	**3**
2002	*6*	*9*	*1*	*5*	*8*	*7*	**3**	**4**	**5**	*2*	**7**	*3*	**8**	**1**	**6**	**2**	*4*	**9**

Note: For the 2000–2002 Championships, Division One placings are shown in bold, Division Two in italic.

MATCH RESULTS, 1864–2002

County	Years of Play	Played	Won	Lost	Tied	Drawn
Derbyshire	1871–87; 1895–2002	2,323	579	855	1	888
Durham	1992–2002	188	29	105	0	54
Essex	1895–2002	2,285	663	668	5	949
Glamorgan	1921–2002	1,819	405	617	0	797
Gloucestershire . . .	1870–2002	2,559	758	948	2	851
Hampshire	1864–85; 1895–2002	2,394	623	823	4	944
Kent	1864–2002	2,683	968	804	5	906
Lancashire	1865–2002	2,758	1,026	577	3	1,152
Leicestershire	1895–2002	2,252	516	815	1	920
Middlesex	1864–2002	2,462	913	624	5	920
Northamptonshire .	1905–2002	2,020	498	704	3	815
Nottinghamshire . .	1864–2002	2,592	781	702	1	1,108
Somerset	1882–85; 1891–2002	2,293	543	912	3	835
Surrey	1864–2002	2,839	1,130	625	4	1,080
Sussex	1864–2002	2,732	762	945	6	1,019
Warwickshire	1895–2002	2,265	621	653	1	990
Worcestershire . . .	1899–2002	2,207	557	761	2	887
Yorkshire	1864–2002	2,860	1,267	501	2	1,090
Cambridgeshire . . .	1864–69; 1871	19	8	8	0	3
		20,775	12,647	12,647	24	8,104

Notes: Matches abandoned without a ball bowled are wholly excluded.
Counties participated in the years shown, except that there were no matches in the years 1915–18 and 1940–45; Hampshire did not play inter-county matches in 1868–69, 1871–74 and 1879; Worcestershire did not take part in the Championship in 1919.

COUNTY CHAMPIONSHIP STATISTICS FOR 2002

County	Runs	For Wickets	Avge	Runs	Against Wickets	Avge	RPF
Derbyshire (6)	8,078	277	29.16	8,103	298	27.19	1.07
Durham (9)	6,670	265	25.16	7,030	206	34.12	0.73
Essex (1)	8,527	236	36.13	8,866	271	32.71	1.10
Glamorgan (5)	8,262	244	33.86	8,305	233	35.64	0.94
Gloucestershire (8) . .	8,675	263	32.98	8,731	217	40.23	0.81
Hampshire (7)	7,133	248	28.76	7,692	220	34.96	0.82
Kent (3)	8,524	244	34.93	8,765	268	32.70	1.06
Lancashire (4)	7,131	239	29.83	7,479	262	28.54	1.04
Leicestershire (5) . . .	7,807	242	32.26	8,310	260	31.96	1.00
Middlesex (2)	8,570	212	40.42	8,326	235	35.42	1.14
Northamptonshire (7)	8,560	236	36.27	9,085	224	40.55	0.89
Nottinghamshire (3) .	8,117	243	33.40	7,605	266	28.59	1.16
Somerset (8)	8,079	268	30.14	8,601	245	35.10	0.85
Surrey (1)	10,143	235	43.16	8,907	296	30.09	1.43
Sussex (6)	8,742	259	33.75	8,106	230	35.24	0.95
Warwickshire (2) . . .	9,271	253	36.64	9,137	264	34.60	1.05
Worcestershire (4). . .	8,510	230	37.00	7,918	256	30.92	1.19
Yorkshire (9)	8,539	276	30.93	8,372	219	38.22	0.80
	149,338	4,470	33.40	149,338	4,470	33.40	

*2002 Championship positions are shown in brackets; Division One in bold, Division Two in italic.
Relative performance factor (RPF) is determined by dividing the average runs scored per wicket by the average runs conceded per wicket.*

RUNS SCORED PER 100 BALLS IN THE COUNTY CHAMPIONSHIP, 2002

County	Run-rate/100 balls	County	Run-rate/100 balls
Derbyshire (*6*)	58.72	Middlesex (**2**)	56.20
Durham (*9*)	55.97	Northamptonshire (*7*)	62.83
Essex (*1*)	53.26	Nottinghamshire (*3*)	58.24
Glamorgan (*5*)	61.21	Somerset (**8**)	59.59
Gloucestershire (*8*)	56.88	Surrey (**1**)	65.06
Hampshire (**7**)	51.93	Sussex (*6*)	55.34
Kent (**3**)	57.06	Warwickshire (**2**)	56.79
Lancashire (**4**)	56.45	Worcestershire (*4*)	63.61
Leicestershire (*5*)	55.52	Yorkshire (*9*)	53.11
		2002 average rate	57.58

2002 Championship positions are shown in brackets: Division One in bold, Division Two in italic.

ECB PITCHES TABLE OF MERIT

First-Class Matches, Under-19 Tests and UCCE Matches

		Points	Matches	Average in 2002	Average in 2001
1	Surrey (4)	96	9	5.33	5.15
2	Gloucestershire (9)	83	8	5.19	4.75
3	Middlesex (10=)	113	11	5.14	4.70
4	Kent (5)	102	10	5.10	4.94
5	Somerset (1)	100	10	5.00	5.33
6	Lancashire (2)	99	10	4.95	5.29
7	Nottinghamshire (7=)	104	11	4.73	4.82
8	Glamorgan (12=)	103	11	4.68	4.65
9	Northamptonshire (3)	92	10	4.60	5.17
10	Worcestershire (16)	82	9	4.56	4.30
11	Sussex (10=)	89	10	4.45	4.70
12	Essex (6)	78	9	4.33	4.89
13	Durham (12=)	86	10	4.30	4.65
14	Leicestershire (7=)	77	9	4.28	4.82
15	Warwickshire (14)	94	11	4.27	4.61
16	Yorkshire (17)	85	10	4.25	4.28
17	Derbyshire (15)	89	11	4.05	4.55
18	Hampshire (18)	92	12	3.83	4.22
	Oxford UCCE	74	7	5.29	5.00
	Durham UCCE	40	4	5.00	4.67
	Loughborough UCCE	20	2	5.00	5.00
	Bradford/Leeds UCCE	20	2	5.00	4.75
	Cambridge UCCE	48	5	4.80	5.08

ECB PITCHES TABLE OF MERIT

One-Day Matches

		Points	Matches	Average in 2002	Average in 2001
1	Nottinghamshire (8)	124	12	5.17	4.58
2	Surrey (5)	134	13	5.15	4.77
3	Somerset (1)	161	16	5.03	5.08
4	Gloucestershire (12)	156	16	4.88	4.36
5	Middlesex (10)	153	16	4.78	4.44
6	Lancashire (17)	113	12	4.71	4.15
7	Kent (9)	141	15	4.70	4.45
8 {	Leicestershire (7)	112	12	4.67	4.63
	Northamptonshire (2=)	112	12	4.67	5.00
10	Warwickshire (13)	102	11	4.64	4.29
11	Glamorgan (4)	99	11	4.50	4.85
12	Durham (6)	115	13	4.42	4.64
13	Hampshire (11)	78	9	4.33	4.36
14	Sussex (14)	121	14	4.32	4.25
15	Essex (2=)	135	16	4.22	5.00
16	Worcestershire (18)	81	10	4.05	3.96
17	Derbyshire (16)	77	10	3.85	4.18
18	Yorkshire (15)	96	13	3.69	4.20

In both tables 2001 positions are shown in brackets. Each umpire in a game marks the pitch on the following scale of merit: 6 – very good; 5 – good; 4 – above average; 3 – below average; 2 – poor; 1 – unfit.

The tables, provided by the ECB, cover major matches, including Tests, Under-19 internationals, women's internationals and UCCE games, played on grounds under the county or UCCE's jurisdiction. Middlesex pitches at Lord's are the responsibility of MCC.

The ECB points out that the tables of merit are not a direct assessment of the groundsmen's ability. Marks may be affected by many factors including weather, soil conditions and the resources available.

GROUNDSMEN OF THE YEAR

Paul Brind of Surrey had a double success in the ECB's Groundsmen of the Year awards. For his work at The Oval, he shared the award for four-day pitches with Mike Grantham at St Lawrence Ground, Canterbury, and he won the one-day award outright, with Steve Birks of Trent Bridge coming second. Geoff Swift of Cheltenham won the award for county outgrounds for the second year running with Steve Martin of Southgate named the runner-up. The award for the best UCCE ground was won by Richard Sula of The Parks, Oxford, with Craig Thompson second for the Racecourse Ground, Durham.

DERBYSHIRE
ON THE UP
AT LAST

Ch'ship 6th in Division 2
C&G 3rd round
B&H group stage
NUL 4th in Division 2

Player of the season: Michael Di Venuto

Derbyshire began 2002 with such a bang, winning five of their first six Championship matches, that to miss promotion on two fronts was deeply frustrating. A deduction of eight points for a poor pitch in the final home game, against Middlesex, did nothing to improve the mood, although the decision was accepted as just. Given time to reflect, however, Derbyshire saw past the immediate disappointment and could claim significant progress, even if they failed to win a game in the knockout competitions. The two previous seasons had been so dreadful that members were initially relieved to see the team simply competing. It was strange, if typical of Derbyshire, that the cricket manager, Colin Wells, should survive two years of failure only to be dismissed when there were clear signs of revival.

Wells, it appeared, was no longer in harmony with the captain, Dominic Cork, whose enthusiasm for all things Derbyshire extended to greeting callers to the club over the winter with a switchboard message all his own. He and Wells were offered a further year but, after a series of urgent committee meetings, Wells's offer was withdrawn. By bungling the situation and under-estimating a problem that had been a topic of County Ground gossip for months, Derbyshire landed themselves with a compensation claim.

On the field, the central figures were easy to identify: Cork and Kevin Dean with the ball; Michael Di Venuto, the vice-captain, with the bat. Cork bowled magnificently and batted effectively to earn yet another England recall. In 16 innings for Derbyshire he never failed to take a wicket, but he did not play in the Championship after July. While counties accept the increased programme of domestic internationals, there was general disquiet about the timing of the ICC Champions Trophy in Sri Lanka. Dean, finally free of the back injury that had hampered him for years, enjoyed a tremendous summer and was the Championship's leading wicket-taker with 80, one more than Martin Saggers of Kent.

The peaks for Di Venuto came with an intimidating 230 against Northamptonshire and two centuries at Lord's, where he led Derbyshire to their only victory without Cork. Di Venuto added consistency to his charac-teristic aggression and averaged 61.52, scoring most runs and holding most catches in Division Two. For the first time he was fully on terms with English pitches; at the County Ground they were invariably slow.

The leading players enjoyed more support than recently. Chris Bassano confirmed the promise of his early appearances in 2001 and completed 1,000 runs. He and Luke Sutton were capped after the end of the season. Andrew Gait, engaged from Free State in South Africa, also lent stability to the batting but Dominic Hewson, who hit a century on his Derbyshire debut, was curiously starved of opportunities when he returned from injury. Nor did Sutton add the runs expected when he took over from Karl Krikken as the regular wicket-keeper in the second half of the season. For all the desire to further Sutton's career, it was an odd decision to ignore Krikken's class. Steve Selwood completed his degree at Loughborough University and became increasingly important in the middle order as he adapted to the county game. Jason Kerr, however, found himself in the role of one-day specialist.

Graeme Welch again showed exemplary professionalism with the ball and was so set on promotion that he gave up alcohol in the last two months of the season. From such a sociable player, this was a significant gesture. Mohammad Ali, who already had first-class experience in Pakistan and arrived as a windfall after Glamorgan were unable to offer him a contract, often disconcerted batsmen with his awkward left-arm line and skiddy pace. But he may need more in his repertoire to sustain his impact. The left-arm spinner Lian Wharton produced match-winning performances in away games against Glamorgan and Middlesex, but must be used more intelligently if he is to develop rhythm. When Nottinghamshire were scoring 323 for nine to earn a crucial and dramatic victory at the County Ground, it was absurd that Wharton did not bowl until after lunch on the final day.

Two distinguished players, Rob Bailey and Tim Munton, retired during the season. Their significant careers were elsewhere – Bailey with Northamptonshire, Munton with Warwickshire – but they added mature stability at a time of turmoil. Munton was troubled by a persistent Achilles tendon injury, but Bailey should have been offered the chance to stiffen the batting. The game plan seemed set in stone.

Two more capped players were released. Mathew Dowman was unable to translate fluent strokes into significant innings often enough and Paul Aldred could not regain a place, though his enthusiasm was of great value to the Second Eleven. They finished runners-up in their Championship under the sensible coaching of Adrian Pierson, who was promoted to first-team coach in the close season on a one-year contract. James Pyemont also left the staff, but there were encouraging moments from younger players such as Neil Gunter and Tom Lungley. The quest for a second overseas player hit problems when Nathan Astle, New Zealand's explosive middle-order batsman, announced he would not be able to fulfil his June-to-September contract because of a long-term knee injury. The even more explosive Shahid Afridi was signed up for April to June.

The Grandstand, for so long the dominant feature of the County Ground, was demolished before the start of the season. Concerns that the place would look bare without it proved unfounded. The Grandstand was in its pomp when race meetings were held at Derby before World War II but had become a symbol of decay. Derbyshire are better off without it; their performances gave them a reason to look ahead with optimism. **Gerald Mortimer**

DERBYSHIRE 2002

Back row: A. R. K. Pierson (*assistant coach*), J. M. Brown (*scorer*), N. R. C. Dumelow, S. A. Selwood, N. E. L. Gunter, J. P. Pyemont, A. I. Gait, R. M. Khan, L. J. Wharton. *Middle row:* D. R. Hewson, M. P. Dowman, J. I. D. Kerr, S. D. Stubbings, C. W. G. Bassano, T. Lungley, L. D. Sutton, C. Ranson (*physiotherapist*). *Front row:* C. M. Wells (*cricket manager*), P. Aldred, R. J. Bailey, K. J. Dean, D. G. Cork (*captain*), K. M. Krikken, G. Welch, T. A. Munton, J. T. Smedley (*chief executive*). *Inset:* M. J. Di Venuto. *Main picture by John Grainger.*

DERBYSHIRE RESULTS

All first-class matches – Played 18: Won 8, Lost 7, Drawn 3.
County Championship matches – Played 16: Won 7, Lost 7, Drawn 2.

COUNTY CHAMPIONSHIP AVERAGES: BATTING AND FIELDING

Cap		M	I	NO	R	HS	100s	50s	Avge	Ct/St
2000	M. J. Di Venuto§ . . .	15	28	3	1,538	230	4	7	61.52	29
2002	C. W. G. Bassano . . .	14	26	1	1,063	152	1	8	42.52	13
	A. I. Gait	16	31	1	961	175	1	8	32.03	14
1993	D. G. Cork	8	13	0	404	80	0	4	31.07	11
	J. I. D. Kerr	6	11	1	293	68	0	3	29.30	2
	S. A. Selwood	8	16	0	441	99	0	2	27.56	1
2001	G. Welch	14	23	5	460	64	0	3	25.55	8
2001	S. D. Stubbings	9	17	1	337	128	1	0	21.06	5
1998	K. J. Dean†	16	25	8	333	54*	0	2	19.58	6
2002	L. D. Sutton	9	17	1	292	58	0	2	18.25	29/1
2000	M. P. Dowman	6	11	0	194	41	0	0	17.63	5
	D. R. Hewson	9	17	1	280	102*	1	0	17.50	6
	Mohammad Ali	15	24	2	333	53	0	1	15.13	5
	T. Lungley†	6	11	0	145	44	0	0	13.18	4
1992	K. M. Krikken	9	16	1	169	48	0	0	11.26	26
	J. P. Pyemont	2	4	0	37	33	0	0	9.25	1
	L. J. Wharton†	13	21	11	82	16	0	0	8.20	6

Also batted: N. R. C. Dumelow† (1 match) 1, 56.

† *Born in Derbyshire.*   § *Overseas player.*

BOWLING

	O	M	R	W	BB	5W/i	Avge
D. G. Cork	323.1	81	951	57	6-51	5	16.68
T. Lungley	91.4	24	335	14	3-43	0	23.92
K. J. Dean	578	145	1,922	80	7-42	3	24.02
G. Welch	486.1	157	1,409	55	6-60	2	25.61
L. J. Wharton	192.3	40	634	22	6-62	2	28.81
Mohammad Ali	405	63	1,708	47	3-48	0	36.34
J. I. D. Kerr	119.2	20	545	13	4-32	0	41.92

Also bowled: M. P. Dowman 40–12–141–4; N. R. C. Dumelow 6–0–35–0; D. R. Hewson 3–0–16–0; J. P. Pyemont 11–1–33–0; S. A. Selwood 6–1–32–1.

COUNTY RECORDS

Highest score for:	274	G. Davidson v Lancashire at Manchester	1896
Highest score against:	343*	P. A. Perrin (Essex) at Chesterfield	1904
Best bowling for:	10-40	W. Bestwick v Glamorgan at Cardiff	1921
Best bowling against:	10-45	R. L. Johnson (Middlesex) at Derby	1994
Highest total for:	645	v Hampshire at Derby	1898
Highest total against:	662	by Yorkshire at Chesterfield	1898
Lowest total for:	16	v Nottinghamshire at Nottingham	1879
Lowest total against:	23	by Hampshire at Burton upon Trent	1958

COUNTY OFFICERS

Captain D. G. Cork • **Cricket manager** 2002 – C. M. Wells
First-team coach 2003 – A. R. K. Pierson
President 2002 – Sir Nigel Rudd; 2003 – D. K. Arnott • **Chairman** G. T. Bowring
Chief executive J. T. Smedley • **Chairman, cricket committee** 2002 – L. C. Elliott
Head groundsman N. Godrich • **Scorer** J. M. Brown

At Cardiff, April 19, 20, 21, 22. DERBYSHIRE beat GLAMORGAN by 163 runs.

DERBYSHIRE v DURHAM

At Derby, April 24, 25, 26, 27. Derbyshire won by two runs. Derbyshire 17 pts, Durham 5 pts. Toss: Durham. County debut: Mohammad Ali.

After two mundane days and a washed-out third, the fourth produced a spine-tingling finish. Chasing 235 in 61 overs, Durham were on target until Daley was pinned by the fiery left-armer Mohammad Ali and retired hurt. Cork snatched four for six in 21 balls as six wickets tumbled for 21. Only once – when they beat Gloucestershire by one run in 1939 – had Derbyshire cut it finer. Cork called it "probably the most exciting Championship victory I've played in". Earlier, Ali's rapid 53 helped Cork give Derbyshire's first innings a late boost, and despite an assured century by Peng, Durham ended up five runs behind. They reasserted their grip through steady swing bowling, but the last four wickets pinched a vital 109, including Dean's maiden fifty. It proved just enough.

Close of play: First day, Durham 102-3 (Collingwood 40, Peng 4); Second day, Derbyshire 190-9 (Dean 19, Wharton 1); Third day, No play.

Derbyshire

S. D. Stubbings c Pratt b Davies	19	– c Love b Killeen	4
M. J. Di Venuto c Collingwood b Killeen	56	– c Collingwood b Davies	46
A. I. Gait c Harmison b Bridge	22	– b Killeen	35
D. R. Hewson lbw b Killeen	0	– c Muchall b Collingwood	7
L. D. Sutton c Pratt b Davies	9	– c Pratt b Collingwood	8
*D. G. Cork c and b Killeen	56	– b Collingwood	2
†K. M. Krikken c Pratt b Davies	0	– lbw b Davies	18
J. I. D. Kerr st Pratt b Bridge	28	– b Harmison	18
Mohammad Ali c Bridge b Collingwood	53	– c Collingwood b Harmison	16
K. J. Dean c Collingwood b Killeen	0	– c Peng b Collingwood	50
L. J. Wharton not out	3	– not out	8
B 5, l-b 4, w 8	17	B 8, l-b 7, w 2	17
	263		**229**

1/60 (1) 2/107 (2) 3/107 (3) 4/107 (4)   263
5/144 (5) 6/144 (7) 7/199 (8)
8/213 (6) 9/225 (10) 10/263 (9)

1/9 (1) 2/75 (3) 3/86 (4)   229
4/110 (5) 5/112 (6) 6/120 (3)
7/144 (8) 8/164 (9) 9/168 (7) 10/229 (10)

Bonus points – Derbyshire 2, Durham 3.

Bowling: *First Innings*—Harmison 13–3–50–0; Killeen 19–4–52–4; Collingwood 7.4–1–22–1; Davies 12–3–51–3; Bridge 24–9–79–2. *Second Innings*—Harmison 12–1–71–2; Killeen 18–1–55–2; Davies 20–5–57–2; Collingwood 12–2–31–4.

Durham

*J. J. B. Lewis lbw b Cork	7	– c Gait b Cork	12
J. A. Daley lbw b Cork	5	– not out	59
M. L. Love b Kerr	43	– c Cork b Mohammad Ali	19
P. D. Collingwood lbw b Dean	42	– c Di Venuto b Kerr	76
N. Peng c Gait b Dean	108	– c Hewson b Kerr	9
†A. Pratt b Mohammad Ali	0	– c Krikken b Mohammad Ali	14
G. J. Muchall c Gait b Dean	18	– b Mohammad Ali	12
G. D. Bridge c Sutton b Dean	1	– c Di Venuto b Cork	1
N. Killeen lbw b Mohammad Ali	0	– c Di Venuto b Cork	7
A. M. Davies not out	15	– c Sutton b Cork	0
S. J. Harmison c Krikken b Cork	0	– c Sutton b Cork	0
B 1, l-b 6, w 2, n-b 10	19	L-b 4, n-b 10	14
	258		**232**

1/10 (1) 2/25 (2) 3/95 (3) 4/112 (4)   258
5/136 (6) 6/167 (7) 7/168 (8)
8/181 (9) 9/254 (5) 10/258 (11)

1/30 (1) 2/60 (3) 3/187 (5)   232
4/191 (4) 5/211 (7) 6/216 (6)
7/216 (8) 8/231 (9)
9/232 (10) 10/232 (11)

Bonus points – Durham 2, Derbyshire 3.

In the second innings Daley, when 59, retired hurt at 174 and resumed at 232-9.

Bowling: *First Innings*—Cork 23.1–7–72–5; Dean 26–9–53–2; Mohammad Ali 22–4–81–2; Kerr 8–2–34–1; Wharton 1–0–11–0. *Second Innings*—Cork 14.3–3–54–5; Dean 14–2–62–0; Mohammad Ali 17–1–69–3; Kerr 9–1–34–2; Wharton 1–0–9–0.

Umpires: R. Palmer and A. G. T. Whitehead.

DERBYSHIRE v NORTHAMPTONSHIRE

At Derby, May 8, 9, 10. Derbyshire won by eight wickets. Derbyshire 19.75 pts, Northamptonshire 3 pts. Toss: Northamptonshire.

After Di Venuto and Cork utterly dominated the first two days, Northamptonshire rescued some respect, if not the match. On the first morning Derbyshire were put in on a damp pitch, but by the close they were 487 for seven, a county record for runs in a day. Di Venuto cracked a 254-ball, six-hour 230, his maiden double-century, which contained 32 fours hit to all corners. Northamptonshire's early batting was as threadbare as their attack and Cork's swing nipped out four for one in 21 balls. A humiliating 25 for seven was boosted to an inadequate 131, including seven ducks, and they followed on 407 behind. Hussey and Loye showed application in an opening partnership of 231, but Derbyshire had runs to spare and slowly worked their way to victory in three days. With three consecutive wins, it was their best start to a season since 1954.

Close of play: First day, Derbyshire 487-7 (Sutton 22, Welch 1); Second day, Northamptonshire 100-0 (Hussey 56, Loye 40).

Derbyshire

S. D. Stubbings lbw b Blain	8	– not out	12
M. J. Di Venuto c and b Swann	230		
A. I. Gait c Sales b Cousins	53	– (2) c Hussey b Blain	3
D. R. Hewson c Swann b Anderson	13	– (3) c Bailey b Greenidge	17
C. W. G. Bassano run out	41	– (4) not out	0
*D. G. Cork lbw b Anderson	60		
†L. D. Sutton lbw b Cousins	24		
J. I. D. Kerr b Anderson	8		
G. Welch c Sales b Greenidge	26		
Mohammad Ali b Anderson	11		
K. J. Dean not out	11		
B 2, l-b 9, w 19, n-b 23	53	L-b 1	1

1/12 (1) 2/216 (3) 3/256 (4) 4/381 (5)   538   1/11 (2) 2/32 (3)   (2 wkts) 33
5/415 (2) 6/462 (6) 7/480 (8)
8/503 (7) 9/526 (10) 10/538 (9)

Bonus points – Derbyshire 5, Northamptonshire 3.

Bowling: *First Innings*—Blain 20–1–128–1; Cousins 27–9–64–2; Greenidge 18.2–0–95–1; Anderson 20–6–97–4; Penberthy 18–3–74–0; Swann 16–2–69–1. *Second Innings*—Blain 4.4–1–26–1; Greenidge 4–2–6–1.

As a character in Tom Stoppard's play *Shipwreck* says, "Nature doesn't disdain what lives only for a day. It pours the whole of itself into each moment... Life's bounty is in its flow; later is too late."
Obituary of Ben Hollioake, page 1636

Northamptonshire

*M. E. K. Hussey lbw b Cork	13	– c Di Venuto b Welch	150
M. B. Loye b Cork	0	– c Gait b Dean	109
R. J. Warren c Gait b Cork	0	– lbw b Welch	20
D. J. Sales b Cork	0	– b Cork	16
G. P. Swann c Bassano b Welch	44	– c Di Venuto b Mohammad Ali	62
A. L. Penberthy c Cork b Dean	0	– c Gait b Welch	17
†T. M. B. Bailey lbw b Dean	0	– c Sutton b Mohammad Ali	21
R. S. G. Anderson lbw b Dean	0	– lbw b Welch	4
C. G. Greenidge b Kerr	46	– c Sutton b Dean	1
J. A. R. Blain c Sutton b Welch	0	– lbw b Mohammad Ali	4
D. M. Cousins not out	18	– not out	4
B 4, l-b 4, w 2	10	B 2, l-b 11, w 8, n-b 10	31

1/1 (2) 2/1 (3) 3/3 (4) 4/14 (1)   **131**   1/231 (2) 2/288 (1) 3/295 (3)   **439**
5/15 (6) 6/25 (7) 7/25 (8)   4/327 (4) 5/366 (6) 6/412 (5)
8/87 (5) 9/97 (10) 10/131 (9)   7/424 (7) 8/424 (8)
9/435 (10) 10/439 (9)

Bonus points – Derbyshire 3.

Bowling: *First Innings*—Cork 11–3–29–4; Dean 10–2–28–3; Welch 12–5–29–2; Mohammad Ali 7–4–14–0; Kerr 5.5–0–23–1. *Second Innings*—Cork 25–7–61–1; Dean 27.1–10–57–2; Welch 34–11–107–4; Kerr 15–2–95–0; Mohammad Ali 21–3–106–3.

Umpires: I. J. Gould and G. Sharp.

At Derby, May 15, 16, 17 (not first-class). **Drawn.** Toss: Derbyshire. **Derbyshire 335 for seven dec.** (A. I. Gait 39, M. P. Dowman 101, C. W. G. Bassano 43, L. D. Sutton 40, J. I. D. Kerr 42) **and 413 for seven** (S. D. Stubbings 71, A. I. Gait 77, D. R. Hewson 77, C. W. G. Bassano 86 not out, Extras 31; R. A. White four for 104); **Loughborough UCCE 315 for nine dec.** (J. D. Francis 128, S. A. Selwood 66; P. Aldred three for 55).

At Chelmsford, May 26, 27, 28, 29. DERBYSHIRE lost to ESSEX by six wickets.

DERBYSHIRE v GLAMORGAN

At Derby, May 31, June 1. Derbyshire won by nine wickets. Derbyshire 18.25 pts, Glamorgan 3 pts. Toss: Glamorgan.

A two-day win put Derbyshire back on top of Division Two. On a slow, grassy pitch, Glamorgan did not bowl well enough to justify James's decision to field. Di Venuto again set a brisk tempo, crashing 17 fours in 107 balls with several meaty drives and pulls, and a confident 63 from Welch – plus a generous ration of no-balls – maintained the pace. Cork whipped out James and Ian Thomas on the first evening and, even if the odd ball scuttled through, Glamorgan batted poorly as 19 wickets tumbled the next day. After back trouble in 2001, Dean continued to play a big part in Derbyshire's rousing start, grabbing seven wickets in the first innings on the way to match figures of ten for 109. Cork's swing and Welch's steady medium-pace provided good support, although for the second time in three games Derbyshire were punished for their slow over-rate. Stubbings completed a pair, but they strolled home on the second evening.

Close of play: First day, Glamorgan 22-2 (Hemp 8).

Derbyshire

S. D. Stubbings lbw b Kasprowicz	0	– lbw b Kasprowicz	0
M. J. Di Venuto b S. D. Thomas	98	– not out	1
A. I. Gait lbw b Kasprowicz	37	– not out	4
C. W. G. Bassano c Powell b Kasprowicz	35		
M. P. Dowman lbw b S. D. Thomas	0		
*D. G. Cork c Wallace b Jones	28		
†K. M. Krikken c Wallace b Dale	9		
G. Welch not out	63		
Mohammad Ali c James b Croft	5		
K. J. Dean c Wallace b Jones	21		
L. J. Wharton c Wallace b Jones	5		
B 4, l-b 9, w 8, n-b 32	53		

1/0 (1) 2/158 (3) 3/166 (2) 4/166 (5)   354   1/0 (1)   (1 wkt) 5
5/211 (6) 6/232 (7) 7/282 (4)
8/291 (9) 9/342 (10) 10/354 (11)

Bonus points – Derbyshire 4, Glamorgan 3.

Bowling: *First Innings*—Kasprowicz 22–4–101–3; S. D. Thomas 22–3–81–2; Jones 19.3–1–75–3; Dale 9–0–44–1; Croft 20–10–40–1. *Second Innings*—Kasprowicz 1–1–0–1; S. D. Thomas 0.5–0–5–0.

Glamorgan

*S. P. James lbw b Cork	11	– lbw b Welch	26
D. L. Hemp c Di Venuto b Dean	26	– b Dean	7
I. J. Thomas lbw b Dean	0	– c Gait b Dean	0
M. J. Powell c Welch b Mohammad Ali	17	– c Wharton b Mohammad Ali	33
A. Dale b Dean	0	– c Krikken b Cork	40
J. Hughes lbw b Dean	5	– lbw b Welch	4
†M. A. Wallace c Cork b Dean	21	– c Krikken b Cork	34
R. D. B. Croft c Wharton b Dean	34	– c Di Venuto b Dean	15
S. D. Thomas b Dean	0	– c Welch b Cork	1
M. S. Kasprowicz lbw b Dean	0	– c Stubbings b Cork	11
S. P. Jones not out	2	– not out	2
B 13, l-b 12, w 6, n-b 10	41	B 1, l-b 9, n-b 12, p 5	27

1/18 (1) 2/22 (3) 3/44 (2) 4/44 (5)   157   1/26 (2) 2/26 (3) 3/52 (1)   200
5/60 (6) 6/91 (4) 7/150 (7)   4/74 (4) 5/85 (6) 6/149 (5)
8/150 (9) 9/150 (10) 10/157 (8)   7/176 (7) 8/184 (9)
                                                                        9/194 (8) 10/200 (10)

Bonus points – Derbyshire 3.

Bowling: *First Innings*—Cork 16–3–36–2; Dean 17.4–7–42–7; Welch 12–7–19–0; Mohammad Ali 10–4–35–1. *Second Innings*—Cork 14.5–3–50–4; Dean 14–3–67–3; Welch 12–4–35–2; Mohammad Ali 5.3–1–25–1; Wharton 4.3–2–8–0.

Umpires: M. J. Harris and V. A. Holder.

At Nottingham, June 12, 13, 14, 15. DERBYSHIRE beat NOTTINGHAMSHIRE by four wickets.

At Derby, June 26, 27, 28. DERBYSHIRE beat WEST INDIES A by 145 runs (see West Indies A tour section).

DERBYSHIRE v GLOUCESTERSHIRE

At Derby, July 3, 4, 5, 6. Drawn. Derbyshire 11 pts, Gloucestershire 7 pts. Toss: Derbyshire. First-class debut: A. P. R. Gidman.

Gloucestershire slumped to 39 for five on a rain-blighted first day and owed their partial revival to a typically obstinate Russell and the debutant Alex Gidman, who grew in confidence after an uncertain start. Cork's bustling aggression on a blameless pitch won him a fifth five-for of the season; it included Barnett, whose edge behind led to frenzied celebrations from his former protégé. Gait and Bassano then batted Derbyshire into a strong position, but the game foundered when the third day was washed out. On the fourth morning, Cork chose a push for full batting points rather than a bold declaration but, despite his belligerent 67, Derbyshire fell two runs short. Gloucestershire looked set to save the game comfortably, but when Cork ended Spearman's excellent innings their confidence was rattled. However, Gidman again showed nerve, and Gloucestershire clung on, leaving Derbyshire to wonder about their decision not to declare.

Close of play: First day, Gloucestershire 79-5 (Russell 20, Gidman 15); Second day, Derbyshire 226-4 (Bassano 63, Lungley 9); Third day, No play.

Gloucestershire

K. J. Barnett c Krikken b Cork	9	– (2) b Welch	49
C. M. Spearman c Di Venuto b Dean	12	– (1) lbw b Cork	95
C. G. Taylor b Cork	1	– c Stubbings b Welch	15
M. G. N. Windows c Hewson b Dean	4	– lbw b Cork	10
*M. W. Alleyne c Krikken b Cork	1	– lbw b Welch	0
†R. C. Russell c Welch b Cork	26	– c Krikken b Dean	2
A. P. R. Gidman c Krikken b Welch	67	– not out	5
I. D. Fisher b Cork	5	– b Dean	0
J. Lewis c Dean b Lungley	17	– not out	0
B. W. Gannon c Cork b Lungley	6		
A. M. Smith not out	0		
L-b 7, w 10, n-b 12	29	B 2, l-b 5, w 2, n-b 40	49

1/14 (1) 2/30 (3) 3/30 (2)   **179**
4/35 (5) 5/39 (4) 6/101 (6) 7/123 (8)
8/157 (9) 9/179 (7) 10/179 (10)

1/115 (2) 2/147 (3)   (7 wkts) **225**
3/191 (4) 4/191 (5)
5/196 (6) 6/222 (1) 7/223 (8)

Bonus points – Derbyshire 3.

Bowling: *First Innings*—Cork 25–7–67–5; Dean 19–6–51–2; Welch 10–6–27–1; Mohammad Ali 1–0–7–0; Lungley 3.2–1–20–2. *Second Innings*—Cork 17–7–44–3; Dean 18–4–74–2; Mohammad Ali 9–0–50–0; Welch 10–1–50–2.

Derbyshire

S. D. Stubbings c Russell b Gidman	32	Mohammad Ali c Taylor b Fisher	8
M. J. Di Venuto lbw b Smith	3	G. Welch not out	29
A. I. Gait b Smith	88	K. J. Dean b Smith	0
C. W. G. Bassano lbw b Smith	78	B 10, l-b 14, w 2, n-b 14	40
D. R. Hewson c Taylor b Gannon	7		
T. Lungley lbw b Fisher	38	1/4 (2) 2/78 (1) 3/164 (3) 4/195 (5) **398**
*D. G. Cork c Taylor b Lewis	67	5/269 (4) 6/287 (6) 7/318 (8)
†K. M. Krikken c Gidman b Lewis	8	8/333 (9) 9/396 (7) 10/398 (11)

Bonus points – Derbyshire 4, Gloucestershire 3.

Bowling: Lewis 30–7–94–2; Smith 24.2–4–87–4; Gidman 9–3–24–1; Gannon 17–5–67–1; Alleyne 10–2–33–0; Fisher 14–1–69–2.

Umpires: B. Leadbeater and N. J. Llong.

At Darlington, July 10, 11, 12. DERBYSHIRE lost to DURHAM by 89 runs.

DERBYSHIRE v NOTTINGHAMSHIRE

At Derby, July 19, 20, 21, 22. Nottinghamshire won by one wicket. Nottinghamshire 16 pts, Derbyshire 7 pts. Toss: Nottinghamshire.

Gallian's calm but unyielding concentration ground Nottinghamshire to an astonishing win. As the ball began to shoot through low and his partners fell in worrying bursts, Gallian ploughed relentlessly on, scoring at less than a run an over for much of his unbeaten 111. His efforts nearly went unrewarded when a collapse left Nottinghamshire nine down, 46 short and in trouble, but Smith saw them home. It capped a gritty fightback. Di Venuto's breezy 91 and more cautious fifties from Gait and Bassano helped Derbyshire's first innings reach 353, and only a shaky partnership of 99 between Afzaal and Pietersen – twice dropped in his 103 – plus resistance from Harris saved the follow-on. Boje then found slow turn and preyed on Derbyshire batsmen looking for quick runs, leaving Nottinghamshire a target of 323. Given Boje's success, it was puzzling that Wharton's left-arm spin was not used before 2 p.m. on the last afternoon. The defeat was Derbyshire's second in two games as their early-season momentum faded.

Close of play: First day, Derbyshire 324-7 (Welch 14, Dean 2); Second day, Nottinghamshire 182-8 (Pietersen 72, Smith 1); Third day, Nottinghamshire 39-0 (Gallian 10, Johnson 27).

Derbyshire

A. I. Gait c Read b Logan	76	– c and b Boje	53
M. J. Di Venuto lbw b Boje	91	– b Harris	2
C. W. G. Bassano c Welton b Boje	83	– c Read b Harris	14
M. P. Dowman c Gallian b Boje	9	– b Franks	40
S. A. Selwood b Franks	21	– c Welton b Boje	15
*D. G. Cork c Read b Franks	1	– c Gallian b Franks	19
G. Welch c Read b Harris	16	– b Franks	20
†K. M. Krikken c Welton b Boje	2	– c Welton b Boje	8
K. J. Dean not out	10	– (10) b Boje	4
Mohammad Ali c Read b Harris	11	– (9) c Logan b Boje	4
L. J. Wharton b Smith	6	– not out	6
B 4, l-b 7, w 12, n-b 4	27	L-b 15, w 9	24
	353		**209**

1/147 (2) 2/201 (1) 3/220 (4) 4/299 (3) 5/299 (5) 6/312 (6) 7/315 (8) 8/326 (7) 9/342 (10) 10/353 (11)

1/4 (2) 2/24 (3) 3/101 (1) 4/125 (5) 5/147 (4) 6/166 (6) 7/191 (8) 8/195 (7) 9/201 (9) 10/209 (10)

Bonus points – Derbyshire 4, Nottinghamshire 3.

Bowling: First Innings—Harris 24–2–87–2; Franks 24–9–67–2; Smith 12.3–3–46–1; Logan 17–2–85–1; Boje 25–9–45–4; Pietersen 3–1–12–0. *Second Innings*—Smith 11–3–20–0; Harris 10–2–38–2; Franks 17–4–47–3; Boje 23.2–5–66–5; Logan 6–0–23–0.

Nottinghamshire

*J. E. R. Gallian lbw b Cork	4	– not out	111
G. E. Welton c Krikken b Mohammad Ali	27	– (3) c Krikken b Dean	4
P. Johnson lbw b Dean	6	– (2) lbw b Dean	39
U. Afzaal b Dowman	58	– c Dean b Mohammad Ali	3
K. P. Pietersen not out	103	– c Cork b Welch	30
N. Boje lbw b Cork	0	– c Mohammad Ali b Wharton	22
†C. M. W. Read c Welch b Cork	0	– lbw b Cork	47
P. J. Franks c Di Venuto b Dowman	1	– lbw b Cork	0
R. J. Logan c Mohammad Ali b Dowman	0	– (10) c Wharton b Welch	1
G. J. Smith lbw b Cork	3	– (11) not out	16
A. J. Harris b Mohammad Ali	23	– lbw b Mohammad Ali	0
B 1, l-b 6, n-b 8	15	B 5, l-b 19, w 8, n-b 8	40
	240		(9 wkts) **323**

1/14 (1) 2/25 (3) 3/57 (2) 4/156 (4) 5/157 (6) 6/157 (7) 7/168 (8) 8/170 (9) 9/190 (10) 10/240 (11)

1/58 (2) 2/68 (3) 3/73 (4) 4/124 (5) 5/170 (6) 6/256 (7) 7/256 (9) 8/259 (9) 9/277 (10)

Bonus points – Nottinghamshire 1, Derbyshire 3.

Bowling: *First Innings*—Cork 25–11–55–4; Dean 11–0–60–1; Welch 21–7–53–0; Mohammad Ali 12.1–1–49–2; Dowman 9–5–16–3. *Second Innings*—Cork 31.4–8–68–2; Dean 26–7–81–2; Welch 18–4–57–2; Mohammad Ali 23–4–74–2; Wharton 6–1–19–1.

Umpires: G. I. Burgess and I. J. Gould.

At Northampton, July 25, 26, 27. DERBYSHIRE beat NORTHAMPTONSHIRE by 177 runs.

DERBYSHIRE v ESSEX

At Derby, August 7, 8, 9, 10. Essex won by 140 runs. Essex 17 pts, Derbyshire 6 pts. Toss: Derbyshire.

Essex did not take a firm grip on the match until the last day, when they fired out Derbyshire in 53 overs and shot past them in the race for promotion, returning to second after a winless July. After steaming to 153 for one by lunch on the first day, Essex were restricted to 268 by Welch and Lungley. Derbyshire struggled in reply until Bassano took control with an unflustered century, his first since his two on Championship debut. Sutton – preferred to Krikken as wicket-keeper because of his batting – joined him in a stand of 125, but lethargic bowling allowed Essex to snatch back the initiative. Robinson and Flower took their partnership to 157 on a shortened third day, with Robinson going on to a neat hundred; Welch was again the best bowler. Derbyshire were set 292, but – with Bassano restricted by illness – their innings had neither shape nor substance. They had still to win in the Championship without Cork, who was away with England.

Close of play: First day, Derbyshire 89-3 (Bassano 48, Selwood 12); Second day, Essex 75-2 (Robinson 38, Flower 11); Third day, Essex 227-4 (Robinson 82, Bopara 0).

Essex

D. D. J. Robinson c Sutton b Dowman	69	– c Sutton b Welch		115
W. I. Jefferson b Mohammad Ali	59	– c Di Venuto b Mohammad Ali		12
J. P. Stephenson c Sutton b Lungley	28	– lbw b Dean		8
†A. Flower lbw b Lungley	10	– c Lungley b Welch		75
*R. C. Irani c Dowman b Welch	6	– lbw b Welch		18
R. S. Bopara c Sutton b Welch	11	– c Sutton b Welch		20
J. D. Middlebrook c Bassano b Mohammad Ali	40	– (9) b Lungley		3
A. P. Cowan c Sutton b Welch	12	– c Di Venuto b Lungley		22
G. R. Napier c Dowman b Selwood	11	– (7) c Dowman b Welch		9
J. E. Bishop c Sutton b Mohammad Ali	0	– c Sutton b Mohammad Ali		3
J. B. Grant not out	1	– not out		1
L-b 3, w 8, n-b 10	21	B 4, l-b 8, w 2, n-b 24		38

1/118 (1) 2/162 (3) 3/166 (2) 4/182 (4)   268
5/188 (5) 6/205 (6) 7/219 (8)
8/258 (9) 9/259 (10) 10/268 (7)

1/26 (2) 2/47 (3) 3/204 (4)   324
4/226 (5) 5/275 (1) 6/286 (6)
7/293 (7) 8/303 (9)
9/318 (8) 10/324 (10)

Bonus points – Essex 2, Derbyshire 3.

Bowling: *First Innings*—Dean 15–3–78–0; Mohammad Ali 16.1–1–71–3; Welch 23–10–34–3; Lungley 15–5–46–2; Dowman 4–0–28–1; Selwood 2–1–8–1. *Second Innings*—Dean 16–1–60–1; Mohammad Ali 15.4–2–65–2; Welch 29–11–66–5; Lungley 14–3–59–2; Dowman 16–4–53–0; Selwood 1–0–9–0.

Derbyshire

	First Innings		Second Innings	
A. I. Gait	lbw b Irani	2	c Robinson b Middlebrook	10
*M. J. Di Venuto	c Flower b Cowan	9	lbw b Grant	22
C. W. G. Bassano	c Bopara b Middlebrook	152	(8) b Grant	0
M. P. Dowman	c Middlebrook b Napier	6	lbw b Irani	15
S. A. Selwood	c Flower b Irani	23	lbw b Middlebrook	24
S. D. Stubbings	lbw b Cowan	4	(3) c Flower b Grant	3
†L. D. Sutton	b Grant	58	(6) lbw b Napier	14
T. Lungley	lbw b Middlebrook	6	(9) c Bopara b Irani	7
G. Welch	not out	17	(7) b Grant	7
Mohammad Ali	c Bishop b Middlebrook	2	not out	20
K. J. Dean	c Bopara b Middlebrook	0	b Middlebrook	0
	B 1, l-b 11, w 2, n-b 8	22	B 8, l-b 9, w 4, n-b 8	29
		301		**151**

1/15 (2) 2/17 (1) 3/32 (4) 4/121 (5) 301
5/128 (6) 6/253 (3) 7/273 (8)
8/293 (7) 9/296 (10) 10/301 (11)

1/36 (1) 2/40 (2) 3/43 (3) 151
4/64 (4) 5/92 (6) 6/116 (7)
7/118 (8) 8/118 (5)
9/144 (9) 10/151 (11)

Bonus points – Derbyshire 3, Essex 3.

Bowling: *First Innings*—Cowan 14–4–47–2; Irani 22–6–60–2; Napier 13–5–43–1; Bishop 9–0–38–0; Middlebrook 20.1–1–67–4; Grant 12–3–34–1. *Second Innings*—Cowan 5–1–11–0; Irani 12–5–15–2; Napier 6–0–35–1; Middlebrook 20.1–7–28–3; Grant 9–1–45–4.

Umpires: J. H. Hampshire and J. W. Holder.

DERBYSHIRE v WORCESTERSHIRE

At Derby, August 14, 15, 16. Worcestershire won by nine wickets. Worcestershire 18 pts, Derbyshire 3 pts. Toss: Derbyshire.

A good County Ground pitch persuaded Di Venuto to bat – the first captain to do so here in the 2002 Championship – but Derbyshire's innings lay in ruins by lunch, and they never recovered. Against some less than obdurate batting, Sheriyar hit his rhythm, found some swing and took five for 15 in 30 balls. Bassano and Welch fought back with a stand of 127, before Worcestershire tightened their hold as Rhodes squeezed 104 from the tail to give them a 130-run lead. Derbyshire failed again in their second innings, this time against a spinner, though Batty did not find much turn as he reduced them to 101 for eight. Selwood played outstandingly, falling one short of a deserved first hundred, before Dean and Wharton, both much-improved batsmen, added 50 for the last wicket. They only delayed the inevitable: chasing 114, Solanki wasted no time, hitting 81 in 56 balls, and Worcestershire won before lunch on the third day.

Close of play: First day, Worcestershire 189-5 (Lee 33, Rhodes 12); Second day, Derbyshire 193-8 (Selwood 99, Dean 30).

This was a case not of rain stopped play, but of lack of rain stopped viewing.
The Asian Test Championship, page 1185

Derbyshire

A. I. Gait c Rhodes b Sheriyar	0	– c Singh b Batty	21
*M. J. Di Venuto c Rawnsley b Sheriyar	3	– lbw b Ali	1
C. W. G. Bassano c Solanki b Mason	85	– lbw b Sheriyar	0
J. P. Pyemont lbw b Sheriyar	0	– c Singh b Batty	1
S. A. Selwood c Hick b Sheriyar	1	– c Rhodes b Ali	99
†L. D. Sutton b Sheriyar	1	– c and b Rawnsley	7
G. Welch c Batty b Mason	64	– b Batty	9
T. Lungley c Solanki b Sheriyar	3	– b Batty	0
Mohammad Ali b Ali	20	– b Batty	6
K. J. Dean lbw b Ali	2	– not out	54
L. J. Wharton not out	0	– b Sheriyar	16
B 4, l-b 1, w 2, n-b 4	11	B 9, l-b 8, w 2, n-b 10	29
	190		**243**

1/1 (1) 2/6 (2) 3/6 (4) 4/24 (5)   1/8 (2) 2/9 (3) 3/18 (4) 4/39 (1)
5/36 (6) 6/163 (7) 7/164 (3)   5/50 (6) 6/83 (7) 7/83 (8)
8/182 (8) 9/187 (10) 10/190 (9)   8/101 (9) 9/193 (5) 10/243 (11)

Bonus points – Worcestershire 3.

Bowling: *First Innings*—Mason 12–3–37–2; Sheriyar 15–2–71–6; Ali 9.5–2–20–2; Batty 6–1–30–0; Rawnsley 3–0–22–0; Solanki 1–0–5–0. *Second Innings*—Sheriyar 12.3–4–36–2; Ali 23–6–80–2; Batty 34–14–74–5; Rawnsley 11–4–26–1; Solanki 4–0–10–0.

Worcestershire

V. S. Solanki lbw b Dean	22	– not out	81
A. Singh c Sutton b Mohammad Ali	41	– lbw b Lungley	14
*G. A. Hick c Di Venuto b Dean	0	– not out	4
B. F. Smith c Pyemont b Wharton	49		
S. Lee c Mohammad Ali b Dean	48		
G. J. Batty c Di Venuto b Mohammad Ali	2		
†S. J. Rhodes c Dean b Mohammad Ali	83		
Kabir Ali c Di Venuto b Welch	8		
M. J. Rawnsley c Sutton b Welch	7		
M. S. Mason c Lungley b Wharton	11		
A. Sheriyar not out	5		
B 6, l-b 12, n-b 26	44	B 4, n-b 12	16
	320		**(1 wkt) 115**

1/30 (1) 2/32 (3) 3/124 (4) 4/134 (2)   1/94 (2)
5/146 (6) 6/216 (5) 7/237 (8)
8/261 (9) 9/302 (10) 10/320 (7)

Bonus points – Worcestershire 3, Derbyshire 3.

Bowling: *First Innings*—Dean 25–7–69–3; Mohammad Ali 15.5–1–71–3; Welch 23–6–66–2; Wharton 20–0–69–2; Lungley 3–0–19–0; Pyemont 3–0–8–0. *Second Innings*—Welch 8–2–35–0; Dean 0.2–0–0–0; Mohammad Ali 3.4–0–34–0; Wharton 2–0–29–0; Lungley 1.2–0–13–1.

Umpires: M. R. Benson and N. G. Cowley.

At Lord's, August 21, 22, 23, 24. DERBYSHIRE beat MIDDLESEX by 204 runs.

At Derby, August 28, 29, 30. DERBYSHIRE drew with INDIANS (see Indian tour section).

At Bristol, September 4, 5, 6, 7. DERBYSHIRE drew with GLOUCESTERSHIRE.

DERBYSHIRE v MIDDLESEX

At Derby, September 11, 12, 13. Middlesex won by 73 runs. Middlesex 17 pts, Derbyshire –5 pts. Toss: Middlesex.

While Middlesex celebrated promotion, Derbyshire were left defeated and in disarray. The wicket they chose to play on had been recently relaid and was so green that the ECB pitch liaison officer could not tell which one was actually being used. There were few complaints about the eight-point penalty, though it rubbed salt into their wounds; they had already been dumped out of the promotion race. Derbyshire bowled too short – and fielded too shoddily – to take advantage of unreliable bounce and sharp seam movement on the first day. On the second, Noffke hit the right areas and bowled a startling spell of seven for six in 39 balls. It helped give Middlesex a 155-run lead, which they extended to 305 after Weekes and Alleyne dragged their second innings out of trouble. Di Venuto, who passed 1,500 runs for the season, briefly alarmed Middlesex in pursuit of the highest total of the match but a shrewd spell by Tufnell, backed by excellent catching, settled it. Noffke took 12 for 108 in the match; Dean ten for 125.

Close of play: First day, Middlesex 291-8 (Cook 5, Keegan 6); Second day, Derbyshire 45-1 (Di Venuto 24, Bassano 21).

Middlesex

*S. G. Koenig lbw b Mohammad Ali	72	– c Bassano b Kerr	11
R. M. S. Weston c Sutton b Dean	1	– b Dean	18
B. L. Hutton c Kerr b Mohammad Ali	4	– c Sutton b Kerr	17
E. C. Joyce lbw b Dean	21	– b Dean	0
P. N. Weekes c Gait b Welch	88	– c Di Venuto b Dean	33
J. W. M. Dalrymple c Di Venuto b Welch	33	– lbw b Kerr	0
†D. Alleyne lbw b Dean	13	– not out	49
A. A. Noffke lbw b Dean	13	– b Welch	0
S. J. Cook lbw b Dean	5	– c Di Venuto b Welch	0
C. B. Keegan c Di Venuto b Dean	7	– lbw b Dean	4
P. C. R. Tufnell not out	0	– b Dean	4
B 8, l-b 7, w 2, n-b 18	35	B 1, l-b 5, w 2, n-b 6	14

1/1 (2) 2/10 (3) 3/72 (4) 4/176 (1) 292
5/247 (5) 6/254 (6) 7/273 (8)
8/284 (7) 9/291 (9) 10/292 (10)

1/29 (2) 2/33 (1) 3/33 (4) 150
4/48 (3) 5/54 (6) 6/104 (5)
7/105 (8) 8/105 (9)
9/134 (10) 10/150 (11)

Bonus points – Middlesex 2, Derbyshire 3.

Bowling: First Innings—Dean 25.3–8–59–6; Mohammad Ali 18–3–51–2; Kerr 23–4–84–0; Welch 34–16–52–2; Wharton 7–2–31–0. *Second Innings*—Dean 15.5–3–66–4; Kerr 9–3–32–4; Mohammad Ali 3–0–20–0; Welch 9–3–26–2.

Derbyshire

A. I. Gait c Joyce b Cook	0	– c Tufnell b Cook	0
*M. J. Di Venuto c Hutton b Noffke	4	– b Tufnell	71
C. W. G. Bassano c Weekes b Noffke	49	– c Weston b Tufnell	44
D. R. Hewson c Joyce b Hutton	36	– c Alleyne b Noffke	15
S. A. Selwood c Weekes b Noffke	13	– c Noffke b Tufnell	14
†L. D. Sutton c Alleyne b Noffke	0	– c Hutton b Noffke	1
J. I. D. Kerr b Noffke	0	– b Tufnell	28
G. Welch lbw b Noffke	2	– c Hutton b Noffke	23
Mohammad Ali not out	21	– c Hutton b Noffke	8
K. J. Dean c Cook b Noffke	0	– c Hutton b Tufnell	0
L. J. Wharton b Noffke	0	– not out	0
B 4, l-b 5, w 2	11	B 18, l-b 6, w 2, n-b 2	28

1/0 (1) 2/10 (2) 3/81 (4) 4/113 (3) 137
5/113 (6) 6/113 (5) 7/116 (5)
8/127 (8) 9/137 (10) 10/137 (11)

1/0 (1) 2/124 (3) 3/131 (2) 232
4/157 (4) 5/163 (6) 6/167 (5)
7/220 (8) 8/228 (7)
9/228 (10) 10/232 (9)

Bonus points – Middlesex 3.

Bowling: *First Innings*—Cook 11–1–44–1; Noffke 15–6–24–8; Keegan 7–0–36–0; Hutton 9–4–24–1. *Second Innings*—Cook 21–6–64–1; Noffke 23.3–7–84–4; Hutton 4–2–7–0; Keegan 4–0–18–0; Tufnell 23–10–35–5.

Umpires: D. J. Constant and T. E. Jesty.

At Worcester, September 18, 19, 20, 21. DERBYSHIRE lost to WORCESTERSHIRE by one wicket.

LORDS AND COMMONS RESULTS, 2002

Matches 17: Won 3, Lost 11, Drawn 3.

At St Paul's School, Barnes, April 24. St Paul's won by 112 runs. St Paul's 197 for two dec. (B. Duncan 54, J. Loftdall 53); Lords and Commons 85 (E. Poland four for three).

At Bank of England Ground, Roehampton, May 16. Parliamentary Staff won by eight wickets. Lords and Commons 194 for three (J. Wrathmell 100 not out); Parliamentary Staff 198 for two (A. M. F. Mellows-Facer 120 not out).

At Civil Service Ground, Chiswick, May 21. ACAS won by six wickets. Lords and Commons 157 for eight dec. (A. George 49); ACAS 158 for four (G. Boyce 95).

At Civil Service Ground, Chiswick, June 12. Mandarins won by four wickets. Lords and Commons 147 for five dec. (A. Shantry 85, Lord Naseby 45); Mandarins 148 for six (C. Healy 69).

At Stowell Park, Gloucestershire, June 16. Drawn. Gloucestershire Gypsies 211 for four dec. (C. Hall 46, D. Terrington 43); Lords and Commons 191 for six (H. Bellingham 68, M. Green 60).

At Burton Court, June 19. Drawn. Lords and Commons 256 for six dec. (W. Boone 83, M. Boobbyer 58); Brigade of Guards 184 for nine (M. Boobbyer six for 41).

At Hayfield, Derbyshire, June 23. Derbyshire & Cheshire Cricket League won by 72 runs. Derbyshire & Cheshire Cricket League 184 (A. Burgoyne 50 not out); Lords and Commons 112 (S. Goodwin four for 16).

At Burton Court, June 27. MCC won by 57 runs. MCC 228 for five dec. (J. Brennan 108 not out, S. Henderson 80); Lords and Commons 171 (M. Spelman 45; J. C. Huntingdon four for 35).

At Hurlingham, June 28. Lords and Commons won by seven wickets. Dutch Parliament 245 (Westendorb 41; H. Robertson four for 47); Lords and Commons 246 for three (C. Blunt 106 not out, D. Bingham 51).

At Englefield Park, Reading, June 30. Lords and Commons won by four wickets. Dutch Parliament 209 for three dec. (E. de Moura Correia 80 not out, N. de Lanoy Meijer 51); Lords and Commons 213 for six (H. Bellingham 95).

At Durrant's, Rickmansworth, July 4. Fleet Street won by 33 runs. Fleet Street 238 for two dec. (P. Webster 109, A. Rose 90); Lords and Commons 205 (C. Blunt 121; B. Clark four for 65).

At Highclere, July 14. Lords and Commons won by three wickets. Lord Carnarvon's XI 292 for four dec. (K. Storey 100, R. Bairamain 96 not out); Lords and Commons 293 for seven (P. Oborne 86 not out, Lord Mackintosh 76, J. Wrathmell 62; R. Daniels five for 70).

At Burton Court, July 17. Eton Ramblers won by four wickets. Lords and Commons 253 for seven dec. (H. Scott-Gall 60, A. Rawlinson 59, C. Blunt 50, R. Daniels four for 53); Eton Ramblers 257 for six (E. Inkin 49; H. Scott-Gall five for 89).

At Old Emanuel CC, New Malden, July 23. Law Society won by three wickets. Lords and Commons 164 (R. Evans 76); Law Society 165 for seven (J. Egan 44).

At Bank of England Ground, Roehampton, August 20. Drawn. England Women's XI 288 for five dec. (H. Lloyd 68, C. Taylor 54, C. Connor 50); Lords and Commons 49 for two.

At Harrow School, September 6. Harrow Wanderers won by seven wickets. Lords and Commons 217 for four dec. (M. Neal 85, H. Robertson 54 not out); Harrow Wanderers 221 for three (W. Gillions 110, L. Jones 63 not out).

At Moulton, Lincolnshire, September 15. Moulton Harrox Irregulars won by 93 runs. Moulton Harrox Irregulars 186 for eight; Lords and Commons 93.

DURHAM
BROKEN BONES, INJURED PRIDE

Ch'ship 9th in Division 2
C&G 4th round
B&H group stage
NUL 8th in Division 1 – relegated

Player of the season: Gary Pratt

It was a cruel summer for Durham. From the moment Murphy's Law ruled out Danny Law for the start of the season, they were hit by an injury jinx that developed a momentum of its own. Simon Brown and Nicky Phillips succumbed in the opening Championship match, and in the next game, at Derby, Jimmy Daley suffered the seventh broken finger of his career. Several mishaps later, Durham's walking wounded had finished bottom of Division Two and been relegated from Division One of the Norwich Union League.

Neither Daley nor Brown made another first-team appearance. The release of both players severed the final link with Durham's original first-class squad from 1992 and was tinged with sadness. No one will ever know how good Daley might have been, granted better fortune, while Brown, previously known for staying fit, had always been Durham's spearhead until he began to struggle with injuries in 2001. His 518 first-class wickets for the county were twice as many as his nearest rival, and he topped 50 wickets seven times. This time Neil Killeen led the way with a mere 37.

If the bowling lacked potency, it was the batting that again lay at the root of Durham's troubles. The top run-scorer was Gary Pratt with just 746, and the batsmen mustered a measly 21 bonus points, ten of them in two games in May against Gloucestershire and Middlesex. Durham enforced the follow-on in both matches, and Martin Love scored 78 and 251 – a county record – but he broke a finger trying to take a slip catch in the next game against Worcestershire and didn't bat again in the Championship. His replacement, Brad Hodge from Victoria, duly broke his left thumb in the nets after just one match. The captain, Jon Lewis, then developed a groin injury and missed the last six games, while Graeme Bridge, the left-arm spinner, was out for almost half the season with a broken finger.

Much was expected of Paul Collingwood following his winter of one-day success with England, while Nicky Peng and Stephen Harmison had impressed at the ECB Academy. But Collingwood suffered knee and neck injuries and made only five Championship appearances, Harmison, who had just recovered from a shoulder problem, was out for six weeks with a side strain, and Peng went into steep decline after a tremendous start, prompting the coach, Martyn Moxon, to suggest he was suffering from burn-out.

Harmison's winter at the Academy had clearly helped him off the field, but improvement on it wasn't instantly apparent. When he returned from injury, however, there was a steady improvement in his accuracy, and by the end of the season in which he made his Test debut he was looking more worthy of his Ashes tour place. Collingwood was sadly missed. A career-best 190 against the Sri Lankans and a maiden one-day century against Nottinghamshire showed what he could do, but, with Durham short of all-rounders, it is to be hoped that his neck problem does not threaten his future as a bowler.

The result of this gruesome sick-list was that Durham lost 11 games out of 16 in the Championship, and, after promotion the previous season, won only two out of their first 11 in the Norwich Union League. Three wins in the last five came too late to save them from relegation.

Even so, three bright lights emerged from the gloom, and a fourth was rekindled. The improving batting and brilliant ground fielding of Gary Pratt, still only 20, earned him the members' vote as Player of the Year in succession to his wicket-keeping brother, Andrew, the one ever-present player in the Championship. Gordon Muchall began as though to the manner born, contributing 127 to a stand of 251 with Love at Lord's, and his 254 in an Under-19 Test against India led to a call-up to the ECB Academy. And Mark Davies, a 21-year-old seamer whose 2001 season had been ended by a collapsed lung, often proved Durham's most accurate bowler. After two difficult years, Michael Gough, the former England Under-19 captain, began to look like a master of his craft once more. He played only two Championship games before the start of August, but finished with 616 runs at 51.33 and shared seven half-century opening stands with Gary Pratt in the last six matches.

Law was crucial to the balance of the side, in theory at least. He managed two good innings but bowled poorly, especially in one-day games, and probably has one season left in which to fulfil the potential which neither Sussex nor Essex could harness. Law's malfunctioning gave Marc Symington plenty of opportunities, but wholehearted effort failed to mask modest talent and he was released. The other departure was James Brinkley, who asked to go in late July, shortly before it was announced that the South African paceman Dewald Pretorius would be the second overseas player in 2003, with Love returning for a third season. Durham also signed the 37-year-old Vince Wells from Leicestershire on a two-year contract.

The solitary Championship win came against Derbyshire at Durham's happiest hunting ground, Darlington. After spending 2001 entirely at Riverside, Durham went back to an outground because temporary stands were being dismantled after the one-day international against India. An indoor school was finally built at Riverside during the winter and the amount of permanent seating was increased ahead of the ground's first Test, involving Zimbabwe, scheduled for June 2003 – cricket politics permitting. But the chairman, Bill Midgley, felt compelled to warn that it was no good developing top-class facilities without having a team to match. There were times when Durham fielded nine home-grown players, but the message was clear: improve or you're out. **Tim Wellock**

DURHAM 2002

Standing: B. Hunt *(first-team scorer)*, C. Sanctuary *(sports scientist)*, A. Walker *(second-team coach)*, G. D. Bridge, M. J. Symington, I. Pattison, G. J. Pratt, N. Peng, M. A. Gough, N. G. Hatch, J. E. Brinkley, A. M. Davies, I. D. Hunter, C. Mann, A. M. Thorpe, G. M. Scott, N. A. Kent *(physiotherapist)*, D. W. Graham *(second-team scorer)*. *Seated:* S. J. Harmison, D. R. Law, N. Killeen, P. D. Collingwood, M. L. Love, J. J. B. Lewis *(captain)*, M. D. Moxon *(first-team coach)*, S. J. E. Brown, N. C. Phillips, J. A. Daley, A. Pratt. *Inset:* G. J. Muchall. *Main picture by Ian Dobson Photography.*

DURHAM RESULTS

All first-class matches – Played 18: Won 1, Lost 11, Drawn 6.
County Championship matches – Played 16: Won 1, Lost 11, Drawn 4.

COUNTY CHAMPIONSHIP AVERAGES: BATTING AND FIELDING

Cap		M	I	NO	R	HS	100s	50s	Avge	Ct/St
2001	M. L. Love§	6	8	1	576	251	2	2	82.28	3
	M. A. Gough†	8	14	0	616	103	1	3	51.33	6
1998	P. D. Collingwood† . .	5	9	0	371	99	0	3	41.22	4
	B. J. Hodge§	4	8	0	284	73	0	2	35.50	3
2001	D. R. Law	5	8	1	227	72*	0	2	32.42	1
	G. J. Pratt†	14	24	0	713	78	0	4	29.70	9
1999	J. A. Daley†	2	4	1	85	59*	0	1	28.33	0
	G. J. Muchall	14	24	0	544	127	1	2	22.66	12
2001	N. Peng	10	18	0	384	108	1	1	21.33	8
2001	N. C. Phillips	9	15	5	211	58*	0	1	21.10	4
	A. M. Thorpe	6	12	0	242	95	0	2	20.16	3
2001	A. Pratt†	16	28	2	523	93	0	3	20.11	40/3
1998	J. J. B. Lewis	9	15	0	289	71	0	2	19.26	2
	I. D. Hunter†	7	11	1	188	65	0	1	18.80	2
	M. J. Symington . . .	9	15	2	216	42	0	0	16.61	6
	G. D. Bridge†	9	14	2	163	49	0	0	13.58	4
	A. M. Davies	13	23	7	171	33	0	0	10.68	3
	I. Pattison†	3	6	0	61	27	0	0	10.16	1
1999	N. Killeen†	14	21	4	151	23	0	0	8.88	5
1999	S. J. Harmison	9	17	3	85	19*	0	0	6.07	4

Also batted: N. G. Hatch† (3 matches) 1*, 5, 0 (1 ct). S. J. E. Brown† (cap 1998) (1 match) did not bat.

† *Born in Durham.* § *Overseas player.*

BOWLING

	O	M	R	W	BB	5W/i	Avge
A. M. Davies	336.5	95	910	33	5-61	1	27.57
N. C. Phillips	169	36	581	20	4-103	0	29.05
N. Killeen	366.1	100	1,084	35	4-26	0	30.97
S. J. Harmison	257.4	57	836	26	5-65	1	32.15
G. D. Bridge	233.5	60	709	19	4-50	0	37.31
I. D. Hunter	180	37	665	17	3-62	0	39.11
M. J. Symington	124	21	525	13	3-43	0	40.38

Also bowled: S. J. E. Brown 18.4–3–65–2; P. D. Collingwood 83.4–17–231–8; M. A. Gough 41–9–132–2; N. G. Hatch 96–22–318–6; B. J. Hodge 22.4–4–102–1; D. R. Law 66–13–272–4; G. J. Muchall 35–6–158–3; I. Pattison 35–9–159–4; G. J. Pratt 1.3–0–8–0.

COUNTY RECORDS

Highest score for:	251	M. L. Love v Middlesex at Lord's	2002
Highest score against:	501*	B. C. Lara (Warwickshire) at Birmingham	1994
Best bowling for:	9-64	M. M. Betts v Northamptonshire at Northampton .	1997
Best bowling against:	8-22	D. Follett (Middlesex) at Lord's	1996
Highest total for:	645-6 dec.	v Middlesex at Lord's	2002
Highest total against:	810-4 dec.	by Warwickshire at Birmingham	1994
Lowest total for:	67	v Middlesex at Lord's	1996
Lowest total against:	67	by Durham UCCE at Chester-le-Street	2001

COUNTY OFFICERS

Captain J. J. B. Lewis • **Head coach** M. D. Moxon
President 2002 – J. D. Robson; 2003 – M. Pratt • **Chairman** D. W. Midgley
Chief executive D. Harker • **Chairman, cricket committee** R. Jackson
Director of cricket G. Cook • **Head groundsman** D. Measor • **Scorer** B. Hunt

DURHAM v DURHAM UCCE

At Chester-le-Street, April 13, 14, 15. Drawn. Toss: Durham. First-class debuts: A. M. Davies; A. P. Hollingsworth, W. A. Kirby, M. A. Souter.

A deserved draw meant the university side remained unbeaten in first-class cricket. In the corresponding fixture in 2001 the students had been routed for 67, but this time they provided good opposition: Martyn Moxon, the Durham coach, said the match was "excellent preparation" for the Championship. On a remarkably dry April pitch, Lewis made a century in Durham's first innings, though Peng played more fluently. In reply, Tim Phillips unfurled some assured drives, Michael Brown also impressed and the university avoided the follow-on. Mark Davies, on his first-class debut, was the pick of Durham's bowlers and his bustling medium-pace earned him a long run in the side. After Lewis's last-day declaration, the students easily held out for the draw.

Close of play: First day, Durham 415-8 (Killeen 27, Phillips 15); Second day, Durham UCCE 264-9 (Ferley 13, Bruce 0).

Durham

*J. J. B. Lewis c Thorburn b Loudon	102	– (7) not out		2
G. J. Pratt c Brown b Souter	13	– c Brown b Thorburn		16
J. A. Daley lbw b Ferley	17	– (1) lbw b Bruce		28
P. D. Collingwood c Kirby b Ferley	74	– (6) lbw b Hollingsworth		1
N. Peng c Souter b Hollingsworth	82	– (3) c Loudon b Hollingsworth		25
D. R. Law c Banes b Phillips	11	– (4) b Hollingsworth		15
†A. Pratt c Ferley b Thorburn	15	– (5) not out		18
A. M. Davies b Thorburn	13			
N. Killeen not out	27			
N. C. Phillips not out	15			
B 6, l-b 9, w 9, n-b 22	46	B 7, l-b 4, w 12, n-b 10		33

1/36 (2) 2/57 (3) 3/199 (4) (8 wkts dec.) 415
4/273 (1) 5/314 (6) 6/338 (5)
7/356 (7) 8/384 (8)

1/33 (2) 2/80 (3) (5 wkts dec.) 138
3/106 (1) 4/110 (4)
5/114 (6)

S. J. Harmison did not bat.

Bowling: *First Innings*—Bruce 6–1–17–0; Thorburn 18–4–69–2; Souter 12–3–54–1; Ferley 29–7–94–2; Phillips 27–5–85–1; Banes 3–0–13–0; Loudon 7–2–41–1; Hollingsworth 5–1–27–1. *Second Innings*—Thorburn 6–2–19–1; Souter 8–2–29–0; Bruce 10–1–37–1; Hollingsworth 11–1–35–3; Ferley 3–0–7–0.

Durham UCCE

†M. J. Brown c Collingwood b Harmison	57	– lbw b Killeen		4
W. I. Jefferson lbw b Davies	11	– b Killeen		5
*M. J. Banes lbw b Davies	39	– c A. Pratt b Collingwood		27
A. G. R. Loudon c Daley b Davies	4	– b Collingwood		11
T. J. Phillips c and b Law	75	– not out		19
W. A. Kirby lbw b Phillips	7	– not out		9
A. P. Hollingsworth lbw b Law	24			
R. S. Ferley not out	15			
M. Thorburn b Law	4			
M. A. Souter c A. Pratt b Harmison	1			
J. T. A. Bruce not out	0			
B 5, l-b 6, w 14, n-b 6	31	L-b 3, w 3, n-b 2		8

1/33 (2) 2/115 (1) 3/133 (4) (9 wkts dec.) 268
4/136 (3) 5/183 (6) 6/236 (7)
7/245 (5) 8/255 (9) 9/263 (10)

1/7 (1) 2/12 (2) (4 wkts) 83
3/44 (4) 4/65 (3)

Bowling: *First Innings*—Killeen 14–3–56–0; Harmison 15.4–6–37–2; Davies 16–8–22–3; Phillips 37–10–82–1; Law 12–3–41–3; G. J. Pratt 1–0–4–0; Collingwood 6–3–15–0. *Second Innings*—Harmison 2–0–8–0; Killeen 11–5–25–2; Davies 5–3–10–0; Law 7–1–17–0; Collingwood 7–4–12–2; Phillips 4–1–8–0.

Umpires: B. Dudleston and R. A. Kettleborough.

DURHAM v MIDDLESEX

At Chester-le-Street, April 19, 20, 21. Middlesex won by ten wickets. Middlesex 18 pts, Durham 3 pts. Toss: Middlesex. First-class debut: G. J. Muchall. County debut: A. A. Noffke. Championship debuts: A. M. Davies, S. G. Koenig.

Durham began their county season with a stinging defeat. On his Championship debut Sven Koenig compiled a neat century, putting on 103 with the flashier Strauss. Particularly strong off his legs, Strauss had cracked 12 fours before Koenig – a South African with a Scandinavian name and an Italian passport – drove his second. In reply, Durham fell apart. On a docile pitch, Cook and Ashley Noffke, Middlesex's stand-in overseas player, proved the value of bowling straight and full, though Durham could claim to be unlucky: two wickets fell to run-outs at the bowler's end, and both Brown and Phillips were hindered by injuries picked up in the Middlesex innings. Gordon Muchall made his mark by matching Peng's bold strokeplay in a stand of 88, but there was little other resistance. Durham followed on 187 behind, and although Love, who batted almost throughout, and Pratt avoided a two-day defeat, Middlesex completed a routine win when play resumed on the third afternoon.

Close of play: First day, Middlesex 326-8 (Nash 55, Fraser 14); Second day, Durham 140-5 (Love 57, Pratt 35).

Middlesex

A. J. Strauss c Pratt b Harmison	70	– not out	19
S. G. Koenig lbw b Phillips	100	– not out	3
R. M. S. Weston c Muchall b Brown	8		
O. A. Shah c Pratt b Collingwood	34		
E. C. Joyce c and b Davies	14		
P. N. Weekes c Pratt b Harmison	3		
†D. C. Nash not out	66		
A. A. Noffke c Muchall b Phillips	4		
S. J. Cook lbw b Brown	7		
*A. R. C. Fraser c Peng b Harmison	16		
P. C. R. Tufnell c Lewis b Davies	8		
B 1, l-b 8, w 8	17	B 4, l-b 1	5
	347	(no wkt)	**27**

1/103 (1) 2/122 (3) 3/206 (4) 4/229 (2) 5/232 (6) 6/255 (5) 7/270 (8) 8/289 (9) 9/336 (10) 10/347 (11)

Bonus points – Middlesex 3, Durham 3.

Bowling: *First Innings*—Brown 18.4–3–65–2; Harmison 27–7–72–3; Collingwood 16–2–49–1; Davies 22–4–77–2; Phillips 27–6–75–2. *Second Innings*—Harmison 2–1–9–0; Davies 2–0–13–0.

Durham

*J. J. B. Lewis lbw b Cook	15	– c Koenig b Noffke	11
J. A. Daley c Nash b Noffke	21	– lbw b Fraser	0
M. L. Love c Weekes b Cook	0	– not out	101
P. D. Collingwood b Cook	7	– c Nash b Cook	19
N. Peng c Nash b Noffke	47	– c Strauss b Fraser	6
G. J. Muchall lbw b Tufnell	48	– run out	0
†A. Pratt c Weekes b Noffke	8	– b Noffke	49
A. M. Davies c Joyce b Tufnell	4	– b Noffke	0
S. J. Harmison run out	0	– c Weston b Tufnell	10
N. C. Phillips not out	0	– absent hurt	
S. J. E. Brown absent hurt		– absent hurt	
B 2, l-b 2, n-b 6	10	B 4, l-b 5, n-b 8	17
	160		**213**

1/36 (1) 2/36 (2) 3/36 (3) 4/47 (4) 5/135 (5) 6/147 (7) 7/155 (6) 8/160 (9) 9/160 (8)

1/3 (2) 2/29 (1) 3/64 (4) 4/81 (5) 5/81 (6) 6/168 (7) 7/178 (8) 8/213 (9)

Bonus points – Middlesex 3.

Bowling: *First Innings*—Fraser 14–5–32–0; Noffke 18–5–51–3; Cook 12–3–37–3; Tufnell 10.3–2–36–2. *Second Innings*—Fraser 20–6–65–2; Noffke 15–4–63–3; Cook 10–2–36–1; Tufnell 8.5–2–19–1; Weekes 3–0–21–0.

Umpires: J. F. Steele and P. Willey.

At Derby, April 24, 25, 26, 27. DURHAM lost to DERBYSHIRE by two runs.

At Chester-le-Street, May 7, 8, 9. DURHAM drew with SRI LANKANS (see Sri Lankan tour section).

At Cardiff, May 15, 16, 17, 18. DURHAM lost to GLAMORGAN by five wickets.

DURHAM v GLOUCESTERSHIRE

At Chester-le-Street, May 24, 25, 26, 27. Drawn. Durham 12 pts, Gloucestershire 6 pts. Toss: Durham.

Durham finally managed a draw; it could easily have been a win. Having followed on 338 behind, Gloucestershire were 177 for seven midway through the last afternoon, but Russell made good use of his famous leave shot, held out doggedly for almost four hours, and saved the game. At the other end he was well supported by Averis for 39 overs, and by Lewis for the last ten. Durham lost their most penetrative bowler when Hunter suffered an abdominal injury on the last afternoon shortly after he had Russell dropped by Love at third slip. Earlier, Gary Pratt and his brother Andrew had both made career-best scores, as Durham reached their highest total at Chester-le-Street and achieved maximum batting points for the first time in nearly two years. But Russell, and rain that cost nearly a day's play, stymied them. Lewis, the Durham captain, missed his first Championship game since 1999 with a back injury, and Collingwood led the side for the first time.

Close of play: First day, Durham 238-3 (Collingwood 47, Peng 1); Second day, Gloucestershire 95-6 (Gannon 0, Russell 0); Third day, Gloucestershire 44-2 (Barnett 20, Windows 13).

Durham

M. A. Gough lbw b Alleyne	32	G. D. Bridge not out	12
G. J. Pratt st Russell b Fisher	66	A. M. Davies not out	1
M. L. Love b Alleyne	78	L-b 15, w 2, n-b 2	19
*P. D. Collingwood c Russell b Alleyne	65		
N. Peng lbw b Fisher	19	1/71 (1) 2/152 (2)	(8 wkts dec.) 470
G. J. Muchall lbw b Snape	52	3/235 (3) 4/267 (4)	
†A. Pratt run out	93	5/275 (5) 6/382 (6)	
I. D. Hunter c Averis b Snape	33	7/452 (8) 8/459 (7)	

N. Killeen did not bat.

Bonus points – Durham 5, Gloucestershire 2 (130 overs: 423-6).

Bowling: Lewis 30–10–62–0; Averis 19–3–71–0; Fisher 36–10–118–2; Gannon 17–3–74–0; Alleyne 24–3–76–3; Snape 14–1–54–2.

Gloucestershire

K. J. Barnett b Hunter	2	– (2) lbw b Hunter	31
C. M. Spearman c Muchall b Killeen	4	– (1) b Hunter	4
C. G. Taylor lbw b Davies	37	– lbw b Hunter	2
M. G. N. Windows run out	1	– run out	73
*M. W. Alleyne c Gough b Killeen	18	– lbw b Bridge	19
J. N. Snape c A. Pratt b Hunter	28	– lbw b Bridge	19
B. W. Gannon c Love b Davies	14		
†R. C. Russell b Bridge	15	– (7) not out	78
I. D. Fisher c Bridge b Hunter	6	– (8) c Muchall b Bridge	0
J. M. M. Averis b Bridge	0	– (9) b Bridge	14
J. Lewis not out	0	– (10) not out	6
B 1, l-b 2, n-b 4	7	B 5, l-b 6, n-b 4	15

1/7 (1) 2/9 (2) 3/10 (4) 4/43 (5)   **132**   1/8 (1) 2/18 (3) 3/63 (2) (8 wkts) **261**
5/95 (3) 6/95 (6) 7/111 (7)   4/130 (5) 5/146 (4)
8/128 (8) 9/132 (9) 10/132 (10)   6/177 (6) 7/177 (8) 8/233 (9)

Bonus points – Durham 3.

Bowling: *First Innings*—Killeen 18–7–34–2; Hunter 16–5–62–3; Collingwood 3–2–4–0; Davies 14–6–28–2; Bridge 2.2–1–1–2. *Second Innings*—Hunter 23–5–68–3; Killeen 26–12–31–0; Davies 24–6–49–0; Collingwood 12–2–37–0; Bridge 35–14–50–4; Gough 7–4–15–0.

Umpires: D. J. Constant and B. Leadbeater.

At Lord's, May 31, June 1, 2, 3. DURHAM drew with MIDDLESEX.

DURHAM v WORCESTERSHIRE

At Chester-le-Street, June 12, 13, 14, 15. Drawn. Durham 8 pts, Worcestershire 9 pts. Toss: Worcestershire.

Bad weather cost the game nearly two full days and reduced it to stalemate. Donald relied on skill more than pace to take five for 77 on what would prove to be his only Championship appearance as a stand-in for Bichel. Earlier, Hatch's towering height brought bounce and a career-best four for 61, and Batty hit a maiden fifty. It was brought up with an edge that broke Love's finger at third slip as the ball flew to the boundary. The finger had to be pinned, and Love didn't play again all season.

Close of play: First day, Worcestershire 153-5 (Leatherdale 32, Batty 27); Second day, Durham 195-4 (A. Pratt 63, Law 33); Third day, Durham 206-5 (Law 37, Bridge 0).

Worcestershire

W. P. C. Weston c A. Pratt b Hatch	13	– (6) not out	1
A. Singh lbw b Hatch	29	– b Killeen	16
*G. A. Hick c Killeen b Hatch	6	– c Symington b Killeen	14
B. F. Smith lbw b Davies	22	– c Symington b Killeen	14
V. S. Solanki b Symington	12	– (1) b Killeen	17
D. A. Leatherdale b Symington	63	– (5) lbw b Law	9
G. J. Batty b Hatch	56	– not out	0
†S. J. Rhodes b Davies	10		
Kabir Ali c sub b Symington	0		
A. A. Donald not out	5		
A. Sheriyar c and b Davies	15		
B 1, l-b 6, n-b 12	19	L-b 1, n-b 2	3

1/33 (1) 2/43 (3) 3/50 (2) 4/86 (5)   **250**   1/30 (1) 2/32 (3) 3/35 (2) (5 wkts) **60**
5/90 (4) 6/195 (6) 7/221 (6)   4/52 (4) 5/59 (5)
8/225 (8) 9/225 (10) 10/250 (11)

Bonus points – Worcestershire 2, Durham 3.

Bowling: *First Innings*—Killeen 17–3–69–0; Hatch 22–7–61–4; Davies 17.5–5–39–3; Symington 12–3–43–3; Law 6–1–28–0; Bridge 3–2–3–0. *Second Innings*—Killeen 9–1–26–4; Hatch 5–0–14–0; Law 4–1–17–1; Symington 1.4–0–2–0.

Durham

*J. J. B. Lewis c Rhodes b Donald	0	N. Killeen c Hick b Donald	4
G. J. Pratt c Hick b Sheriyar	20	N. G. Hatch not out	1
G. J. Muchall c Rhodes b Donald	46	M. L. Love absent hurt	
M. J. Symington c Rhodes b Batty	20	B 5, l-b 2, w 2, n-b 8	17
†A. Pratt c Ali b Donald	67		
D. R. Law c Weston b Batty	68		243
G. D. Bridge b Batty	0		
A. M. Davies b Donald	0		

1/0 (1) 2/34 (2) 3/83 (3)
4/91 (4) 5/205 (5) 6/206 (7)
7/217 (8) 8/223 (9) 9/243 (6)

Bonus points – Durham 1, Worcestershire 3.

Bowling: Donald 24–3–77–5; Sheriyar 19–6–46–1; Ali 21–6–55–0; Leatherdale 3–0–16–0; Batty 15.3–4–42–3.

Umpires: I. J. Gould and T. E. Jesty.

At Worcester, June 26, 27, 28. DURHAM lost to WORCESTERSHIRE by an innings and 308 runs.

At Northampton, July 3, 4, 5, 6. DURHAM lost to NORTHAMPTONSHIRE by one wicket.

DURHAM v DERBYSHIRE

At Darlington, July 10, 11, 12. Durham won by 89 runs. Durham 15 pts, Derbyshire 3 pts. Toss: Durham.

With the County Ground being dismantled after an England–India one-day match, Durham decamped to an outground for the first time in two years. The last occasion also brought a three-day win over Derbyshire at Darlington. By the end of the first day 20 wickets had fallen, and a pitch inspector had been called for, but the damage was done by poor technique in swinging conditions, not the Feethams strip. Durham emerged from the opening-day carnage in the stronger position, with a lead of 158 and ten second-innings wickets in hand. A disciplined innings by Peng widened the gap on the second day, before Dean's left-arm swing removed the remaining four batsmen on the third morning. Needing 299 to win, Derbyshire reduced the target to below 100 with four wickets left, after first Di Venuto and Bassano, then Welch played bright, attacking innings. But Phillips, bowling for the first time in the match, found immediate turn with his off-spin and took three wickets in four overs at no cost, all to bat-pad catches. Derbyshire's second defeat of the season again came in a match when Cork was absent on England duty; despite their first win, Durham remained rooted at the foot of the table.

Close of play: First day, Durham 63-0 (Lewis 31, G. J. Pratt 23); Second day, Durham 169-6 (Bridge 6, Phillips 0).

Durham

*J. J. B. Lewis lbw b Dean	6	– lbw b Welch	31
G. J. Pratt c Welch b Dean	1	– lbw b Welch	46
G. J. Muchall b Welch	29	– c Krikken b Welch	0
N. Peng lbw b Lungley	21	– c Hewson b Mohammad Ali	57
M. J. Symington c Di Venuto b Lungley	8	– lbw b Lungley	5
†A. Pratt c Krikken b Welch	1	– lbw b Lungley	2
G. D. Bridge lbw b Dean	49	– lbw b Dean	6
N. C. Phillips run out	22	– not out	18
A. M. Davies c Wharton b Dean	33	– b Dean	4
N. Killeen not out	3	– c Di Venuto b Dean	0
S. J. Harmison c Krikken b Mohammad Ali	0	– c Di Venuto b Dean	7
L-b 6, n-b 12	18	L-b 9, w 4, n-b 14	27
	191		**203**

1/1 (2) 2/8 (1) 3/60 (4) 4/60 (3)
5/72 (5) 6/76 (6) 7/108 (8)
8/177 (9) 9/186 (7) 10/191 (11)

1/63 (1) 2/63 (3) 3/106 (2)
4/129 (5) 5/143 (6) 6/169 (4)
7/169 (7) 8/175 (9)
9/175 (10) 10/203 (11)

Bonus points – Derbyshire 3.

Bowling: *First Innings*—Dean 19–4–65–4; Mohammad Ali 13–1–57–1; Welch 15–4–40–2; Lungley 9–5–23–2. *Second Innings*—Dean 24.2–8–67–4; Mohammad Ali 9–4–25–1; Welch 29–10–71–3; Lungley 11–4–21–2; Wharton 3–1–10–0.

Derbyshire

S. D. Stubbings lbw b Killeen	0	– lbw b Davies	30
*M. J. Di Venuto c Lewis b Symington	57	– c A. Pratt b Harmison	40
A. I. Gait b Killeen	0	– c A. Pratt b Harmison	0
C. W. G. Bassano c A. Pratt b Killeen	1	– lbw b Symington	49
D. R. Hewson run out	4	– lbw b Bridge	18
T. Lungley c A. Pratt b Davies	2	– b Harmison	20
†K. M. Krikken run out	1	– c Peng b Phillips	1
G. Welch b Davies	0	– c A. Pratt b Phillips	44
Mohammad Ali run out	0	– c Peng b Phillips	0
K. J. Dean not out	8	– c and b Bridge	2
L. J. Wharton c G. J. Pratt b Symington	13	– not out	0
L-b 8, n-b 2	10	B 2, l-b 1, w 2	5
	96		**209**

1/2 (1) 2/30 (3) 3/48 (4) 4/56 (5)
5/64 (6) 6/71 (7) 7/71 (8)
8/71 (9) 9/76 (10) 10/96 (11)

1/58 (2) 2/58 (3) 3/111 (1)
4/123 (4) 5/160 (6) 6/162 (5)
7/206 (7) 8/206 (9)
9/207 (8) 10/209 (10)

Bonus points – Durham 3.

Bowling: *First Innings*—Killeen 10–3–27–3; Harmison 6–2–25–0; Bridge 1–0–6–0; Davies 6–2–18–2; Symington 3.5–0–12–2. *Second Innings*—Killeen 6–0–47–0; Harmison 17–6–54–3; Davies 12–4–34–1; Symington 7–1–36–1; Bridge 10.5–1–35–2; Phillips 4–4–0–3.

Umpires: D. J. Constant and K. E. Palmer.

DURHAM v NOTTINGHAMSHIRE

At Chester-le-Street, July 24, 25, 26. Nottinghamshire won by eight wickets. Nottinghamshire 19 pts, Durham 3 pts. Toss: Nottinghamshire. County debut: B. J. Hodge.

Nottinghamshire's revival gathered pace with their third win in succession. Gallian won the toss and made a flawless 75, before Afzaal's flowing century and Franks's clattered 60 took Nottinghamshire to 362. Durham's reply was a calamity. On a blameless pitch they slid from 34 without loss to 116 all out: Logan's three-wicket burst smashed through a fragile middle order and Smith bowled fuller than in his opening spell to fire out the tail. Only Brad Hodge – an Australian drafted in to replace Love, whose badly broken finger had still not healed after six weeks – survived more than 29 balls. Durham followed on 246 behind, and their openers cracked some back-foot boundaries before Law and Davies showed grit. But the task was too big, and Nottinghamshire won before tea on the third day. The day after, Hodge broke his left thumb going for a return catch in the nets, and he didn't return until September.

Close of play: First day, Nottinghamshire 362; Second day, Durham 184-2 (Hodge 42, Collingwood 0).

Nottinghamshire

G. E. Welton c A. Pratt b Davies	27	– (2) not out			42
*J. E. R. Gallian b Phillips	75	– (1) c Symington b Killeen			11
P. Johnson c Hodge b Law	0	– c A. Pratt b Harmison			11
U. Afzaal run out	103	– not out			12
K. P. Pietersen c A. Pratt b Davies	37				
N. Boje lbw b Phillips	2				
†C. M. W. Read c A. Pratt b Harmison	39				
P. J. Franks c Phillips b Harmison	60				
R. J. Logan run out	0				
G. J. Smith lbw b Killeen	10				
A. J. Harris not out	0				
L-b 5, w 2, n-b 2	9	L-b 3, w 2, n-b 2			7

1/70 (1) 2/71 (3) 3/147 (2) 4/214 (5)   362   1/28 (1) 2/43 (3)   (2 wkts) 83
5/223 (6) 6/261 (4) 7/335 (7)
8/345 (9) 9/360 (10) 10/362 (8)

Bonus points – Nottinghamshire 4, Durham 3.

Bowling: *First Innings*—Killeen 17–2–72–1; Harmison 24.1–2–81–2; Davies 19–5–48–2; Law 12–2–45–1; Collingwood 8–2–30–0; Phillips 21–2–81–2. *Second Innings*—Killeen 5–0–28–1; Harmison 7–1–22–1; Davies 4–1–9–0; Law 3–0–13–0; Hodge 1.4–1–8–0.

Durham

*J. J. B. Lewis lbw b Smith	15	– b Harris			70
G. J. Pratt lbw b Harris	17	– b Logan			42
B. J. Hodge c Afzaal b Franks	21	– c Boje b Smith			44
P. D. Collingwood c Read b Logan	14	– c Pietersen b Harris			34
M. J. Symington b Logan	0	– lbw b Harris			7
†A. Pratt c Boje b Logan	5	– c Pietersen b Smith			8
D. R. Law c Franks b Smith	14	– c Gallian b Boje			36
N. C. Phillips c Boje b Smith	5	– b Harris			0
A. M. Davies c Read b Smith	3	– c Johnson b Logan			25
N. Killeen c Pietersen b Harris	4	– c Read b Logan			18
S. J. Harmison not out	6	– not out			3
L-b 2, w 4, n-b 6	12	L-b 25, w 8, n-b 8			41

1/34 (2) 2/38 (1) 3/53 (4) 4/53 (5)   116   1/72 (2) 2/184 (1) 3/201 (3)   328
5/73 (6) 6/83 (3) 7/100 (7)   4/218 (5) 5/237 (6) 6/237 (4)
8/101 (8) 9/108 (10) 10/116 (9)   7/237 (8) 8/290 (7)
                                                9/321 (10) 10/328 (9)

Bonus points – Nottinghamshire 3.

Bowling: *First Innings*—Smith 11.5–4–24–4; Harris 9–1–33–2; Logan 9–3–36–3; Franks 7–0–21–1. *Second Innings*—Smith 20–4–81–2; Harris 18–7–60–4; Franks 9–1–36–0; Logan 20.2–3–73–3; Boje 22–11–40–1; Pietersen 3–1–13–0.

Umpires: M. J. Harris and B. Leadbeater.

DURHAM v GLAMORGAN

At Chester-le-Street, August 16, 17. Glamorgan won by ten wickets. Glamorgan 16 pts, Durham 3 pts. Toss: Durham. First-class debut: I. Pattison. Championship debut: A. M. Thorpe.

Durham's first innings was bad, their second worse, and within five sessions the players were packing to leave. The damage was done by Kasprowicz, who bewildered a green batting line-up with his out-swing and ended the match with 11 for 105. Six came on the opening day, when Durham slumped to 124 all out; Kasprowicz even managed to beat Ian Pattison six times in one over. There was little wrong with the pitch, and though Glamorgan lost eight wickets before the close – to make it 18 for the day – the umpires instructed Lord's not to send an inspector. On the second morning, Gough and Gary Pratt took a bite out of Glamorgan's 109-run lead, before Durham astonishingly lost all ten wickets for 37. Kasprowicz grabbed five, including four in 13 balls, Croft preyed on a clueless lower order, and the last six to fall all made ducks. It was Durham's fastest first-class defeat and Glamorgan's earliest finish in a four-day game.

Close of play: First day, Glamorgan 196-8 (Kasprowicz 7, Davies 0).

Durham

M. A. Gough c I. J. Thomas b Kasprowicz	30	– c Maynard b Kasprowicz	37
G. J. Pratt c and b S. D. Thomas	8	– lbw b S. D. Thomas	35
A. M. Thorpe c Cosker b Kasprowicz	4	– b Kasprowicz	5
N. Peng b Kasprowicz	5	– c Wallace b Kasprowicz	11
D. R. Law c Wallace b Kasprowicz	6	– c Maynard b Kasprowicz	0
I. Pattison c Croft b S. D. Thomas	6	– c Wallace b Kasprowicz	0
†A. Pratt lbw b S. D. Thomas	40	– not out	10
*N. C. Phillips c Cosker b S. D. Thomas	3	– c Powell b Croft	0
A. M. Davies b Kasprowicz	0	– c Wallace b Croft	0
N. Killeen not out	4	– c Maynard b Croft	0
S. J. Harmison c Wallace b Kasprowicz	6	– c Wallace b Croft	0
B 4, l-b 4, w 2, n-b 2	12	L-b 2, n-b 14	16
	124		**114**

1/21 (3) 2/41 (4) 3/44 (1) 4/49 (5) 1/77 (2) 2/82 (1) 3/99 (3)
5/84 (6) 6/88 (2) 7/107 (8) 4/102 (4) 5/102 (6) 6/105 (5)
8/114 (7) 9/114 (9) 10/124 (11) 7/106 (8) 8/110 (9)
 9/114 (10) 10/114 (11)

Bonus points – Glamorgan 3.

In the first innings G. J. Pratt, when 4, retired hurt at 11 and resumed at 84.

Bowling: *First Innings*—Kasprowicz 15.1–3–47–6; Davies 9–1–32–0; S. D. Thomas 13–6–23–4; Dale 4–2–11–0; Croft 1–0–3–0. *Second Innings*—Kasprowicz 13–0–58–5; Davies 4–1–17–0; Croft 15–3–20–4; S. D. Thomas 6–0–17–1.

Glamorgan

*S. P. James b Law b Davies	47	– not out	6
I. J. Thomas c A. Pratt b Davies	15	– not out	3
A. Dale c and b Harmison	35		
M. J. Powell b Gough b Davies	1		
M. P. Maynard run out	15		
†M. A. Wallace c Killeen b Harmison	18		
R. D. B. Croft b Phillips	33		
S. D. Thomas c G. J. Pratt b Davies	11		
M. S. Kasprowicz not out	26		
A. P. Davies lbw b Davies	0		
D. A. Cosker c A. Pratt b Harmison	12		
B 1, l-b 9, w 8, n-b 2	20		
	233		(no wkt) **9**

1/43 (2) 2/100 (1) 3/106 (3) 4/106 (4) **233**
5/127 (5) 6/168 (7) 7/189 (6)
8/191 (8) 9/200 (10) 10/233 (11)

Bonus points – Glamorgan 1, Durham 3.

Bowling: *First Innings*—Harmison 24.5–1–75–3; Killeen 14–2–34–0; Davies 22–7–61–5; Law 3–0–22–0; Pattison 3–1–25–0; Phillips 4–2–6–1. *Second Innings*—Pattison 2–1–1–0; G. J. Pratt 1.3–0–8–0.

Umpires: N. A. Mallender and P. Willey.

At Colchester, August 21, 22, 23, 24. DURHAM lost to ESSEX by four wickets.

DURHAM v NORTHAMPTONSHIRE

At Chester-le-Street, August 27, 28, 29. Northamptonshire won by seven wickets. Northamptonshire 16 pts, Durham 4 pts. Toss: Northamptonshire.

Two injury-hit teams from the lowest reaches of the Championship met on a treacherous pitch and the result was mediocre cricket. Fighting innings down the order for Durham, and Brophy's gritty 61 for Northamptonshire, left the sides nearly level after the first innings, before another abject Durham collapse decided the game. After a switch of ends, Greenidge found rhythm, line and length and whipped out four batsmen in six overs, including Gough for a sturdy 67. He cleaned up quickly on the next morning to improve his career-best figures for the second consecutive game. Northamptonshire were left 141 to chase, and White and Powell blasted 96 of them in less than 13 overs. A duel developed as Harmison tried to lure White into a miscued hook, but the wider contest was over.

Close of play: First day, Northamptonshire 60-1 (Powell 24, Panesar 0); Second day, Durham 129-8 (Davies 5, Killeen 0).

Durham

M. A. Gough c Cook b Cassar	35	– c Bailey b Greenidge	67
G. J. Pratt c Powell b Inness	18	– lbw b Cassar	23
G. J. Muchall c Sales b Penberthy	10	– lbw b Penberthy	0
N. Peng lbw b Inness	22	– b Penberthy	8
A. M. Thorpe c Cassar b Greenidge	2	– c Bailey b Penberthy	0
M. J. Symington lbw b Cassar	25	– lbw b Greenidge	10
†A. Pratt c and b Inness	19	– b Greenidge	6
*N. C. Phillips b Panesar	47	– b Greenidge	0
A. M. Davies not out	14	– not out	6
N. Killeen c and b Inness	11	– c Powell b Greenidge	5
S. J. Harmison c Bailey b Panesar	17	– c Powell b Greenidge	1
L-b 14, w 2, n-b 4	20	B 1, l-b 7, n-b 2	10

1/52 (2) 2/59 (1) 3/77 (3) 4/93 (5)	240	1/62 (2) 2/65 (3) 3/81 (4) 4/87 (5) 136
5/103 (4) 6/133 (7) 7/164 (6)		5/112 (6) 6/121 (1) 7/121 (8)
8/202 (8) 9/219 (10) 10/240 (11)		8/124 (7) 9/134 (10) 10/136 (11)

Bonus points – Durham 1, Northamptonshire 3.

Bowling: *First Innings*—Greenidge 13–0–52–1; Inness 22–4–60–4; Penberthy 14–7–33–1; Cassar 13–4–38–2; Panesar 15.3–7–31–2; Cook 7–2–12–0. *Second Innings*—Greenidge 15.1–4–40–6; Inness 12–3–39–0; Cassar 8–1–28–1; Penberthy 10–3–21–3.

Northamptonshire

R. A. White c Thorpe b Harmison	19	– c A. Pratt b Symington	45
M. J. Powell c G. J. Pratt b Davies	28	– lbw b Muchall	39
M. S. Panesar c Peng b Harmison	0		
D. J. Sales c A. Pratt b Harmison	0	– (3) c Harmison b Muchall	24
J. W. Cook b Killeen	44	– (4) not out	14
G. L. Brophy not out	61	– (5) not out	0
*A. L. Penberthy c Gough b Killeen	3		
M. E. Cassar c A. Pratt b Killeen	0		
†T. M. B. Bailey b Phillips	30		
C. G. Greenidge b Phillips	0		
M. W. H. Inness c Gough b Harmison	21		
B 4, l-b 6, w 4, n-b 16	30	L-b 3, w 6, n-b 10	19
	236	**(3 wkts)**	**141**

1/60 (1) 2/64 (2) 3/64 (3) 4/65 (4)
5/119 (5) 6/149 (7) 7/153 (8)
8/205 (9) 9/205 (10) 10/236 (11)

1/96 (1) 2/96 (2) 3/137 (3)

Bonus points – Northamptonshire 1, Durham 3.

Bowling: *First Innings*—Harmison 22.5–5–83–4; Killeen 12–4–34–3; Davies 16–6–39–1; Symington 3–0–21–0; Muchall 3–0–12–0; Phillips 12–3–37–2. *Second Innings*—Harmison 6–0–45–0; Killeen 4–0–30–0; Muchall 8–2–52–2; Symington 6.3–3–11–1.

Umpires: I. J. Gould and V. A. Holder.

At Nottingham, September 6, 7, 8, 9. DURHAM drew with NOTTINGHAMSHIRE.

DURHAM v ESSEX

At Chester-le-Street, September 11, 12, 13, 14. Essex won by ten wickets. Essex 20 pts, Durham 3 pts. Toss: Essex.

Essex were pushing hard for promotion, while Durham were well adrift at the bottom. The gap showed. With Andy Flower on international duty, Essex welcomed back Mark Waugh after seven years, and he repeatedly found time to step back and stroke Durham's three spinners through the off side on his way to 117. Badly dropped on 25, he and Habib gradually wound up the tempo after Essex had stalled, losing three wickets on 83. Together they added 218 – which turned out to be 31 more than Durham's entire first innings. Gough dropped anchor and became the third Durham batsman (after Wayne Larkins and Jon Lewis) to carry his bat through a first-class innings, but the others again subsided meekly. When Durham followed on 276 behind, Gough played well before Stephenson seized three for none in seven balls. Though Hodge and the chunky left-hander Thorpe put on 136 for the fourth wicket, the damage was done. The win left Essex needing only one point to guarantee an immediate return to the first division.

Close of play: First day, Essex 368-5 (Grayson 21, Foster 5); Second day, Durham 99-4 (Gough 41, Pattison 7); Third day, Durham 264-7 (Killeen 7, Hunter 10).

Essex

D. D. J. Robinson b Pattison		33	– not out	16
W. I. Jefferson b Harmison		46	– not out	22
J. P. Stephenson c A. Pratt b Hunter		0		
M. E. Waugh c Harmison b Phillips		117		
A. Habib c A. Pratt b Killeen		123		
*A. P. Grayson c G. J. Pratt b Hunter		36		
†J. S. Foster c Phillips b Harmison		11		
J. M. Dakin not out		38		
G. R. Napier st A. Pratt b Pattison		21		
J. D. Middlebrook c and b Pattison		12		
J. B. Grant run out		0		
B 3, l-b 23		26	L-b 4	4
		463	(no wkt)	42

1/83 (2) 2/83 (1) 3/83 (3) 4/301 (4)
5/358 (5) 6/390 (6) 7/398 (7)
8/429 (9) 9/455 (10) 10/463 (11)

Bonus points – Essex 5, Durham 3 (130 overs: 460-9).

Bowling: *First Innings*—Harmison 29–10–74–2; Hunter 28–4–107–2; Killeen 20–8–55–1; Pattison 16.3–6–41–3; Phillips 20–4–80–1; Gough 4–0–20–0; Hodge 8–0–41–0; Muchall 5–0–19–0. *Second Innings*—Harmison 4–1–11–0; Hunter 4–0–21–0; Pattison 0.3–0–6–0.

Durham

M. A. Gough not out		75	– c and b Stephenson	46
G. J. Pratt b Napier		20	– c Dakin b Stephenson	28
B. J. Hodge b Napier		2	– c Napier b Grayson	56
G. J. Muchall c Foster b Grant		7	– lbw b Stephenson	0
A. M. Thorpe c Waugh b Grayson		14	– c Waugh b Middlebrook	95
I. Pattison c Foster b Dakin		7	– b Napier	0
†A. Pratt st Foster b Middlebrook		10	– c sub b Grayson	8
I. D. Hunter c Habib b Middlebrook		7	– (9) c Foster b Dakin	12
*N. C. Phillips lbw b Middlebrook		5	– (10) b Middlebrook	5
N. Killeen lbw b Grant		11	– (8) c Waugh b Grayson	23
S. J. Harmison c Waugh b Middlebrook		0	– not out	19
B 6, l-b 8, n-b 8		22	B 15, l-b 5, n-b 2	22
		187		314

1/36 (2) 2/42 (3) 3/58 (4) 4/86 (5)
5/99 (6) 6/129 (7) 7/153 (8)
8/169 (9) 9/186 (10) 10/187 (11)

1/78 (2) 2/81 (1) 3/81 (4)
4/217 (3) 5/222 (6) 6/247 (5)
7/247 (7) 8/279 (9)
9/284 (10) 10/314 (8)

Bonus points – Essex 3.

Bowling: *First Innings*—Dakin 12–3–26–1; Napier 11–2–48–2; Grant 13–2–38–2; Stephenson 3–0–12–0; Grayson 9–5–11–1; Middlebrook 18.4–6–38–4. *Second Innings*—Dakin 15–4–49–1; Napier 9–1–40–1; Grant 3–0–27–0; Middlebrook 27–3–94–2; Stephenson 11–2–31–3; Grayson 15.1–3–39–3; Waugh 4–1–14–0.

Umpires: A. Clarkson and M. J. Harris.

At Bristol, September 18, 19, 20. DURHAM lost to GLOUCESTERSHIRE by ten wickets.

ESSEX
DISCIPLINE + FUN = PROMOTION × 2

Ch'ship	winners of Division 2 – promoted
C&G	quarter-finalists
B&H	finalists
NUL	3rd in Division 2 – promoted

When Graham Gooch was appointed head coach at the end of an acrimonious 2001, he promised to bring back discipline and enjoyment to the Essex dressing-room. Only then, he declared, could they hope to rediscover winning ways. His plan worked a treat. Essex bounced back from a disastrous season to top Division Two of the Championship, win promotion in the Norwich Union League and reach the final of the last Benson and Hedges Cup. Albeit at a lower level, it was the sort of season Gooch had been used to in his playing days.

The decision to sign Andy Flower, Zimbabwe's star player, as successor to Stuart Law proved a master stroke. Flower said he was disappointed not to have scored more than two centuries and 1,151 first-class runs before leaving early for the ICC Champions Trophy in Sri Lanka, but an average of over 50 in both Championship and one-day cricket spoke volumes for his consistency. He was just as impressive as wicket-keeper, a role he filled virtually all season after James Foster broke his arm in May and his left thumb in July. Flower's eagerness to encourage his team-mates made him a popular character in the dressing-room too. "Although you can pin a world-class label on Andy," said Gooch, "you still won't find anyone who works harder at his game." Essex were delighted that Flower agreed to return in 2003.

When it came to self-belief, none could match Ronnie Irani, who led from the front and enjoyed his most successful season yet. His all-round deeds provided the springboard for the B&H Cup run, and in the Championship he followed a career-best 207 not out against Northamptonshire with an unbeaten 182 against Middlesex. His effervescence carried him back into the England one-day team and all the way to the World Cup.

Darren Robinson was another player who benefited from Gooch's influence. He collected 1,000 runs in a season for the first time, and went on to be Essex's leading run-scorer with 1,474, including five centuries. With Paul Grayson missing ten Championship matches after knee surgery, Robinson's journey from promise to fulfilment could not have been better timed. Aftab Habib began his Essex career well, but missed the whole of August with a finger injury before returning to score more than 300 runs in the last three matches; an aggregate of 964 at nearly 44 showed what a fine acquisition he was. Seven years after his last appearance, Mark Waugh, one of Essex's most distinguished players, returned as a two-week stopgap for Flower and responded with 242 in two matches, including a century against Durham and a majestic 76 against Nottinghamshire which helped land the title.

After taking just ten first-class wickets in the first half of the season, the former Yorkshire off-spinner James Middlebrook grew in confidence to claim 28 in the second. Jon Dakin emerged as a valuable all-rounder after he was dropped mid-season when Gooch questioned his fitness and attitude. But the surprise package was John Stephenson who, rejoining Essex after seven years with Hampshire, exceeded all expectations at the age of 37. Brought back to captain the Second Eleven, he was called upon in May for the Championship match at Worcester, took ten for 104, and became a regular member of the first team. He finished as Essex's leading wicket-taker, with 48, and scored nearly 600 runs at 35.12, including a match-winning unbeaten century against Durham.

The victory over Worcestershire began a sequence of five wins, but Essex's challenge hit stormy waters in July when heavy defeats at Swansea and Southend were followed by two draws. Their title aspirations were reignited by a hostile spell from Joe Grant, which set up victory over Derbyshire; Grant's energy and enthusiasm were never in doubt, even if his accuracy was sometimes awry. Wins over Durham, twice, and Middlesex followed to set the scene for a memorable clash against Nottinghamshire at Chelmsford in the last game of the season. Both sides secured the necessary points to clinch promotion during the first two days, but the title remained up for grabs.

When Essex found themselves chasing 340 on a pitch offering encouragement to the bowlers, who included the in-form leg-spinner Stuart MacGill, the odds favoured Nottinghamshire. But Will Jefferson played the innings of his young life: an unbeaten 165 from 214 balls. It won him his county cap, and confirmed the potential he had shown during a match-saving century against Glamorgan in July. The progress of Jefferson, plus encouraging performances from the teenagers Mark Pettini and Ravinder Bopara, helped explain why Richard Clinton's contract was not renewed, even though he started the season with a maiden century against Cambridge UCCE.

Also on his way out was Mark Ilott, whose 14-year career brought him 633 first-class wickets and five Test caps. Unfortunately, a succession of injuries had restricted his appearances over the past few seasons, but a substantial benefit cheque will no doubt make the parting of the ways easier. With Ashley Cowan restricted to a handful of outings in the second half of the season because of a knee problem, Essex bolstered their seam attack by giving one-year contracts to Nick Denning, who had been at Berkshire, and Adrian McCoubrey, a 22-year-old from Normthern Ireland. They sprang a surprise by signing as their second overseas player Scott Brant, a 20-year-old left-arm swing bowler, who had emigrated from Zimbabwe to Australia and played a handful of games for Queensland. **Nigel Fuller**

ESSEX 2002

Standing: J. Davis *(physiotherapist),* G. R. Napier, J. B. Grant, M. L. Pettini, A. C. McGarry, A. J. Clarke, R. S. Clinton, J. D. Middlebrook, Z. K. Sharif, R. S. Bopara. *Seated:* J. M. Dakin, B. J. Hyam, J. P. Stephenson *(second-team coach and captain),* M. C. Ilott, N. Hussain *(club captain),* R. C. Irani *(team captain),* A. P. Grayson, D. D. J. Robinson, A. P. Cowan, J. S. Foster, A. Habib. *Inset:* A. Flower. *Pictures by Bill Smith.*

ESSEX RESULTS

All first-class matches – Played 18: Won 11, Lost 3, Drawn 4.
County Championship matches – Played 16: Won 10, Lost 3, Drawn 3.

COUNTY CHAMPIONSHIP AVERAGES: BATTING AND FIELDING

Cap		M	I	NO	R	HS	100s	50s	Avge	Ct/St
1994	R. C. Irani	10	17	3	920	207*	3	1	65.71	0
2002	A. Flower§	14	25	5	1,048	172*	2	5	52.40	32/1
1997	D. D. J. Robinson†	16	31	1	1,289	175	4	5	42.96	15
2002	A. Habib	14	24	3	900	123	2	7	42.85	9
2002	W. I. Jefferson	12	24	4	783	165*	2	2	39.15	14
1989	J. P. Stephenson†	13	24	8	562	100*	1	2	35.12	7
	M. L. Pettini	3	6	0	157	64	0	1	26.16	2
1996	A. P. Grayson	6	8	0	204	83	0	1	25.50	5
1997	A. P. Cowan	9	13	1	293	60*	0	2	24.41	6
	J. M. Dakin	12	16	2	300	57	0	1	21.42	1
1993	M. C. Ilott	5	4	2	42	28	0	0	21.00	2
	T. J. Phillips	4	7	2	105	42	0	0	21.00	4
	G. R. Napier†	9	13	2	230	54*	0	1	20.90	6
2001	J. S. Foster‡	4	4	0	80	36	0	0	20.00	9/1
	J. D. Middlebrook	16	24	4	378	67	0	1	18.90	7
	R. S. Bopara	3	5	0	89	48	0	0	17.80	5
	A. J. Clarke†	2	4	1	42	31	0	0	14.00	1
	R. S. Clinton	3	4	1	40	24	0	0	13.33	1
	J. E. Bishop	5	8	1	52	23*	0	0	7.42	2
	J. B. Grant	9	11	4	34	15	0	0	4.85	0

Also batted: N. Hussain‡ (cap 1989) (1 match) 1, 4 (2 ct); A. C. McGarry† (2 matches) 5*, 0, 0 (1 ct); Z. K. Sharif (2 matches) 42; M. E. Waugh§ (cap 1989) (2 matches) 117, 49, 76 (4 ct).

† *Born in Essex.*   ‡ *ECB contract.*   § *Overseas player.*

BOWLING

	O	M	R	W	BB	5W/i	Avge
R. C. Irani	220.5	71	570	26	6-71	1	21.92
J. P. Stephenson	295.4	59	1,082	48	7-44	1	22.54
J. M. Dakin	307.2	63	1,048	38	4-17	0	27.57
A. P. Cowan	255.1	60	817	29	5-68	1	28.17
G. R. Napier	172	33	639	20	3-47	0	31.95
J. B. Grant	196.1	26	898	25	4-45	0	35.92
J. E. Bishop	113	16	449	11	3-59	0	40.81
M. C. Ilott	150.5	38	469	11	2-25	0	42.63
T. J. Phillips	113.1	16	472	11	4-102	0	42.90
J. D. Middlebrook	492.2	109	1,463	33	4-38	0	44.33

Also bowled: R. S. Bopara 2–0–13–0; A. J. Clarke 36.3–5–113–7; A. Flower 6–0–19–0; A. P. Grayson 64.1–17–155–5; A. C. McGarry 33.5–7–136–0; D. D. J. Robinson 9–1–54–0; Z. K. Sharif 31–0–164–4; M. E. Waugh 4–1–14–0.

COUNTY RECORDS

Highest score for:	343*	P. A. Perrin v Derbyshire at Chesterfield	1904
Highest score against:	332	W. H. Ashdown (Kent) at Brentwood	1934
Best bowling for:	10-32	H. Pickett v Leicestershire at Leyton	1895
Best bowling against:	10-40	E. G. Dennett (Gloucestershire) at Bristol	1906
Highest total for:	761-6 dec.	v Leicestershire at Chelmsford	1990
Highest total against:	803-4 dec.	by Kent at Brentwood	1934
Lowest total for:	30	v Yorkshire at Leyton	1901
Lowest total against:	14	by Surrey at Chelmsford	1983

COUNTY OFFICERS

Club captain N. Hussain • **Team captain** R. C. Irani • **Head coach** G. A. Gooch
President D. J. Insole • **Chairman** N. R. A. Hilliard • **Chief executive** D. E. East
Chairman, cricket committee G. J. Saville • **Head groundsman** S. Kerrison • **Scorer** D. J. Norris

At Cambridge, April 20, 21, 22. ESSEX beat CAMBRIDGE UCCE by 258 runs.

ESSEX v GLOUCESTERSHIRE

At Chelmsford, April 24, 25, 26, 27. Drawn. Essex 11 pts, Gloucestershire 11 pts. Toss: Gloucestershire. Championship debut: A. Flower.

After the entire third day was lost to rain, the match drifted to a predictable draw. Essex, newly relegated from Division One, and Gloucestershire, who finished fourth in Division Two, had proved well-matched, each reaching 379 in their first innings, though in very different styles. Gloucestershire relied on a late rally: only Spearman held their early innings together and they lost seven wickets in reaching 150. But Alleyne was put down at slip soon afterwards and he went on to a brawny 142, adding 164 with Fisher, who proved a jaunty No. 9. By contrast, Essex began magisterially. On an increasingly benign pitch, Robinson drove with authority on both sides of the wicket and Flower improvised neatly as he swept his way to 91. But Harvey's out-swingers and slower balls bewitched the tail and Essex lost their last seven wickets for 79. Barnett then hit an unbeaten hundred as the game meandered to a close.

Close of play: First day, Gloucestershire 336-9 (Alleyne 125, Lewis 0); Second day, Essex 305-4 (Robinson 127, Middlebrook 0); Third day, No play.

Gloucestershire

K. J. Barnett c Grayson b Irani	3	– (2) not out	100
C. M. Spearman c Flower b Irani	80	– (1) b Grant	0
C. G. Taylor lbw b Cowan	0	– b Dakin	29
M. G. N. Windows c Habib b Grant	13	– lbw b Dakin	5
I. J. Harvey lbw b Dakin	4		
*M. W. Alleyne not out	142	– not out	33
J. N. Snape c Robinson b Cowan	5	– (5) c Clinton b Grant	11
†R. C. Russell b Cowan	6		
I. D. Fisher c Robinson b Dakin	65		
J. M. M. Averis c Flower b Dakin	6		
J. Lewis b Dakin	26		
B 1, l-b 10, w 2, n-b 16	29	B 1, l-b 4, n-b 12	17
	379	(4 wkts dec.)	**195**

1/33 (1) 2/34 (3) 3/80 (4) 4/85 (5)   1/0 (1) 2/49 (3)   (4 wkts dec.)
5/124 (2) 6/129 (7) 7/145 (8)   3/61 (4) 4/94 (5)
8/309 (9) 9/331 (10) 10/379 (11)

Bonus points – Gloucestershire 4, Essex 3.

Bowling: *First Innings*—Cowan 26–6–96–3; Irani 23–8–56–2; Grant 16–3–59–1; McGarry 15–3–62–0; Dakin 23.3–4–62–4; Middlebrook 2–0–21–0; Grayson 5–0–12–0. *Second Innings*—Grant 10–0–68–2; McGarry 4–0–25–0; Dakin 7–3–8–2; Cowan 5–1–23–0; Grayson 9–3–18–0; Middlebrook 13–1–48–0.

Essex

D. D. J. Robinson c Russell b Harvey	131	A. P. Cowan c Taylor b Averis	7
A. P. Grayson lbw b Harvey	18	A. C. McGarry not out	5
R. S. Clinton b Fisher	24	J. B. Grant lbw b Harvey	3
A. Habib c Harvey b Alleyne	18	L-b 17, w 6, n-b 10	33
†A. Flower lbw b Lewis	91		
J. D. Middlebrook lbw b Harvey	0		**379**
*R. C. Irani c Alleyne b Harvey	35		
J. M. Dakin lbw b Harvey	14		

1/29 (2) 2/77 (3) 3/136 (4) 4/300 (5)   379
5/305 (6) 6/328 (1) 7/350 (8)
8/369 (9) 9/371 (7) 10/379 (11)

Bonus points – Essex 4, Gloucestershire 3.

Bowling: Lewis 24–11–41–1; Averis 23–6–60–1; Harvey 25.2–6–68–6; Fisher 27–10–95–1; Alleyne 17–5–51–1; Snape 10–0–47–0.

Umpires: N. J. Llong and K. E. Palmer.

At Nottingham, May 8, 9, 10. ESSEX lost to NOTTINGHAMSHIRE by seven wickets.

At Worcester, May 15, 16, 17, 18. ESSEX beat WORCESTERSHIRE by five wickets.

ESSEX v DERBYSHIRE

At Chelmsford, May 26, 27, 28, 29. Essex won by six wickets. Essex 15 pts, Derbyshire 3 pts. Toss: Essex.

A brilliant, strongarm hundred by Irani transformed a game dominated by seamers. Chasing 190 in 40 overs on a pitch losing its early juice, Essex stumbled to a precarious 26 for three – in effect 26 for four when Clinton injured. However, Irani flayed a nerveless century from only 70 balls, including three sixes in five deliveries – two driven off Dean and one meatily pulled off Mohammad Ali. Flower, who made a relatively understated 55 and added 155 with Irani, watched the carnage from the other end; Essex breezed home with seven overs to spare. Earlier, the seamers had injected life into a match that should have been dead. Rain wiped out nearly two-thirds of the first three days, but the pitch offered zip to the quicker bowlers and no one reached 50 in the first three innings. Stephenson was unlucky to take just two wickets as Derbyshire folded to 158 all out, Essex managed just ten more as Ali's skiddy left-armers ripped out their top order – and broke Clinton's wrist – before Krikken and Dean batted tenaciously to set up the dramatic finish.

Close of play: First day, No play; Second day, Essex 93-3 (Robinson 39); Third day, Derbyshire 73-5 (Kerr 4, Dean 0).

Derbyshire

S. D. Stubbings lbw b Stephenson	41	– lbw b Cowan	0
*M. J. Di Venuto lbw b Irani	25	– c Flower b Irani	41
A. I. Gait lbw b Stephenson	0	– lbw b Cowan	8
D. R. Hewson c Robinson b Cowan	10	– c Middlebrook b Irani	9
C. W. G. Bassano lbw b Irani	0	– lbw b Irani	9
J. I. D. Kerr c Napier b Cowan	23	– b Stephenson	6
†K. M. Krikken lbw b Ilott	0	– (8) lbw b Dakin	48
G. Welch c Flower b Cowan	4	– (9) c Flower b Dakin	9
Mohammad Ali c Robinson b Dakin	38	– (10) c Napier b Dakin	16
K. J. Dean not out	9	– (7) c Napier b Stephenson	48
L. J. Wharton c Flower b Dakin	0	– not out	0
B 2, l-b 2, w 4	8	L-b 5	5
	158		**199**

1/67 (2) 2/68 (3) 3/71 (1) 4/72 (5)   1/0 (1) 2/26 (3) 3/52 (4)
5/91 (4) 6/92 (7) 7/108 (6)   4/62 (5) 5/69 (2) 6/83 (6)
8/108 (8) 9/158 (9) 10/158 (11)   7/150 (7) 8/177 (9)
                                      9/195 (10) 10/199 (8)

Bonus points – Essex 3.

Bowling: *First Innings*—Cowan 12–1–41–3; Ilott 13–3–64–1; Irani 13–6–27–2; Stephenson 8–5–9–2; Dakin 3.4–0–13–2. *Second Innings*—Cowan 5 2–21–2; Ilott 11–3–41–0; Irani 18–5–33–3; Stephenson 18–5–47–2; Dakin 10–2–33–3; Middlebrook 13–5–19–0.

Essex

D. D. J. Robinson c Dean b Mohammad Ali . . .	43	– c Gait b Dean	16
R. S. Clinton retired hurt	10		
A. Habib c Krikken b Mohammad Ali	1	– (6) not out	5
†A. Flower c Krikken b Mohammad Ali	8	– not out	55
*R. C. Irani c Welch b Wharton	28	– c Bassano b Dean	101
J. M. Dakin c Di Venuto b Dean	7		
G. R. Napier b Dean	2	– (3) run out	1
J. P. Stephenson lbw b Dean	0	– (2) c Krikken b Mohammad Ali . .	7
J. D. Middlebrook c Krikken b Welch	15		
A. P. Cowan b Kerr	40		
M. C. Ilott not out	0		
B 4, l-b 2, w 6, n-b 2	14	B 5, l-b 1, w 2	8
	168		193

1/26 (3) 2/40 (4) 3/93 (5) 4/99 (1) 168
5/105 (6) 6/105 (8) 7/112 (7)
8/160 (9) 9/168 (10)

1/16 (1) 2/26 (3) (4 wkts) 193
3/26 (2) 4/181 (5)

Bonus points – Derbyshire 3.

In the first innings, Clinton retired hurt at 24.

Bowling: *First Innings*—Dean 19–9–58–3; Mohammad Ali 18–5–48–3; Kerr 6.3–0–39–1; Welch 8–4–13–1; Wharton 1–0–4–1. *Second Innings*—Dean 10–0–57–2; Mohammad Ali 9–1–56–1; Kerr 5–0–38–0; Welch 9–1–36–0.

Umpires: M. R. Benson and N. A. Mallender.

At Northampton, May 31, June 1, 2, 3. ESSEX beat NORTHAMPTONSHIRE by four wickets.

ESSEX v NORTHAMPTONSHIRE

At Ilford, June 12, 13, 14, 15. Essex won by nine wickets. Essex 20 pts, Northamptonshire 3 pts. Toss: Northamptonshire.

An emphatic Essex victory was built on a magnificent unbeaten 207 from Irani, who calmed his usual effervescence to play a disciplined, confident and chanceless innings. His maiden double-century lasted 407 minutes and 307 balls and included 21 fours and three sixes. On a moist pitch, Essex had subsided to 22 for three as Greenidge found nippy swing and seam, but Jefferson's solid driving and Flower's cheeky reverse-sweeps helped Irani piece the innings back together. When Northamptonshire took their turn, Essex proved too good as the accurate Cowan picked up four wickets. Forced to follow on, Northamptonshire ran into further trouble against Middlebrook, who found slow turn, and Stephenson. Bailey fought hard and Hussey – who hit 140 against Essex a fortnight before – made two half-centuries, but it was not enough. Essex's fourth consecutive win lifted them to second; Northamptonshire, who had now lost five in a row, remained bottom.

Close of play: First day, Essex 322-5 (Irani 121, Napier 27); Second day, Northamptonshire 138-5 (Penberthy 8, Bailey 2); Third day, Northamptonshire 269-6 (Bailey 16, Anderson 8).

There was a rest day, the first in Tests since 1997. The cause was a full moon, observed as a *poya* day by Buddhists.
Sri Lanka v Zimbabwe, page 1237

Essex

D. D. J. Robinson c Cook b Greenidge	3	– b Anderson	16
W. I. Jefferson c Bailey b Penberthy	59	– not out	33
J. D. Middlebrook c Bailey b Greenidge	0	– not out	9
A. Habib c Hussey b Anderson	6		
†A. Flower st Bailey b Brown	85		
*R. C. Irani not out	207		
G. R. Napier c Rollins b Greenidge	43		
J. M. Dakin c Bailey b Penberthy	17		
J. P. Stephenson b Greenidge	22		
A. P. Cowan c Hussey b Cook	22		
M. C. Ilott not out	4		
B 5, l-b 11, w 8, n-b 6	30	B 4, l-b 4, n-b 2	10

1/7 (1) 2/7 (3) 3/22 (4)   (9 wkts dec.) 498   1/35 (1)   (1 wkt) 68
4/118 (2) 5/255 (5) 6/353 (7)
7/383 (8) 8/430 (9) 9/486 (10)

Bonus points – Essex 5, Northamptonshire 2 (130 overs: 401-7).

Bowling: *First Innings*—Cousins 29–8–89–0; Greenidge 34–10–86–4; Anderson 29–5–102–1; Penberthy 33–12–82–2; Brown 27–3–86–1; Cook 10–2–37–1. *Second Innings*—Cousins 2–1–3–0; Greenidge 2–0–13–0; Brown 5–0–14–0; Anderson 4–1–19–1; Cook 1–0–11–0.

Northamptonshire

*M. E. K. Hussey c Middlebrook b Stephenson	67	– (2) c Flower b Middlebrook	71
A. S. Rollins c Middlebrook b Ilott	1	– (1) c Jefferson b Stephenson	34
M. B. Loye lbw b Ilott	0	– c Robinson b Middlebrook	24
R. J. Warren c Napier b Cowan	28	– c Robinson b Cowan	34
J. W. Cook c Robinson b Middlebrook	23	– c Robinson b Cowan	43
A. L. Penberthy c Flower b Stephenson	37	– c Habib b Middlebrook	25
†T. M. B. Bailey c Jefferson b Cowan	16	– b Middlebrook	68
R. S. G. Anderson c Flower b Cowan	1	– b Stephenson	35
C. G. Greenidge c Flower b Cowan	14	– b Stephenson	8
D. M. Cousins not out	6	– c Habib b Stephenson	5
J. F. Brown b Middlebrook	0	– not out	0
B 1, l-b 4, w 2, n-b 4	11	B 3, l-b 1, w 4, n-b 6	14

1/6 (2) 2/6 (3) 3/63 (4) 4/122 (5)   204   1/74 (1) 2/125 (3) 3/158 (2)   361
5/136 (1) 6/177 (6) 7/183 (7)   4/182 (4) 5/245 (5) 6/245 (6)
8/192 (8) 9/203 (9) 10/204 (11)   7/313 (8) 8/327 (9)
                                                    9/355 (10) 10/361 (7)

Bonus points – Northamptonshire 1, Essex 3.

Bowling: *First Innings*—Cowan 18–4–62–4; Ilott 17–5–43–2; Stephenson 19–5–64–2; Napier 2–0–15–0; Middlebrook 9–1–15–2. *Second Innings*—Ilott 13–2–51–0; Stephenson 23–4–87–4; Cowan 20–6–57–2; Middlebrook 42.3–9–122–4; Dakin 5–0–22–0; Napier 5–1–18–0.

Umpires: J. W. Lloyds and P. Willey.

At Gloucester, June 26, 27, 28, 29. ESSEX beat GLOUCESTERSHIRE by three wickets.

At Swansea, July 3, 4, 5, 6. ESSEX lost to GLAMORGAN by eight wickets.

ESSEX v WORCESTERSHIRE

At Southend, July 10, 11, 12, 13. Worcestershire won by eight wickets. Worcestershire 19 pts, Essex 3 pts. Toss: Essex.

On an agonisingly slow pitch, Essex's spinners could not match Batty's control, their batsmen lacked Singh's fluency, and Worcestershire won comfortably. After Essex chose to bat, even Flower became mired, taking 48 overs for his 41. Batty's relentlessly accurate off-spin slowed the scoring to a crawl and he bowled a marathon 34 overs off the reel to claim a career-best six for 71, though it must have been a difficult introduction to cricket for a visiting coachload of French schoolchildren. In reply, Singh found a balance between torpor and recklessness during his 124, unleashing controlled off-side drives and hitting six more fours than Essex managed in total. Solanki played freely too, and Rhodes scored a lively fifty as Middlebrook struggled to direct his off-breaks. Pettini then defied a bevy of close fielders to make 58, and Cowan led some brave lower-order resistance to force Worcestershire to bat again. But with plenty of time left victory was a formality. Worcestershire edged past Essex in the promotion race.

Close of play: First day, Worcestershire 16-0 (Weston 9, Singh 5); Second day, Worcestershire 332-6 (Rhodes 45, Bichel 19); Third day, Essex 115-5 (Flower 14, Cowan 2).

Essex

*D. D. J. Robinson lbw b Bichel	0	– c Hick b Rawnsley	15
W. I. Jefferson b Sheriyar	3	– lbw b Sheriyar	0
M. L. Pettini c Rhodes b Bichel	38	– c Singh b Batty	58
A. Habib st Rhodes b Batty	38	– b Ali	13
†A. Flower lbw b Ali	41	– c Solanki b Batty	17
J. D. Middlebrook b Batty	9	– b Batty	0
A. P. Cowan c Hick b Batty	16	– c Rhodes b Ali	53
J. P. Stephenson c Bichel b Batty	44	– c Rhodes b Sheriyar	1
T. J. Phillips c Rhodes b Batty	3	– lbw b Bichel	24
J. E. Bishop b Batty	0	– not out	23
A. J. Clarke not out	11	– c sub b Ali	31
L-b 7, n-b 5	19	B 3, l-b 9, w 2, n-b 8	22

1/0 (1) 2/10 (2) 3/24 (3) 4/84 (4)   **197**   1/2 (2) 2/55 (1) 3/87 (4)   **257**
5/114 (6) 6/122 (5) 7/140 (7)   4/98 (3) 5/98 (6) 6/121 (5)
8/156 (9) 9/160 (10) 10/197 (8)   7/122 (8) 8/192 (7)
                                      9/204 (9) 10/257 (11)

Bonus points – Worcestershire 3.

Bowling: First Innings—Bichel 18–6–48–2; Sheriyar 14–7–28–1; Ali 15–4–28–1; Batty 34.2–9–71–6; Rawnsley 6–1–15–0. *Second Innings*—Bichel 15–4–46–1; Sheriyar 14–3–30–2; Ali 11.1–2–32–3; Batty 43–12–71–3; Solanki 2–0–5–0; Rawnsley 31–12–61–1.

Worcestershire

W. P. C. Weston lbw b Middlebrook	39	– not out	20
A. Singh c Flower b Bishop	124	– lbw b Bishop	0
*G. A. Hick c Middlebrook b Clarke	9	– c Cowan b Phillips	34
B. F. Smith c Cowan b Stephenson	20	– not out	23
V. S. Solanki c Cowan b Stephenson	56		
G. J. Batty lbw b Cowan	0		
†S. J. Rhodes c Phillips b Bishop	56		
A. J. Bichel c Jefferson b Bishop	30		
Kabir Ali lbw b Cowan	3		
M. J. Rawnsley not out	9		
A. Sheriyar c Phillips b Cowan	2		
B 6, l-b 7, n-b 12	25	L-b 1, w 2, n-b 2	5

1/82 (1) 2/105 (3) 3/150 (4) 4/226 (2)   **373**   1/4 (2) 2/44 (3)   (2 wkts) **82**
5/227 (6) 6/301 (5) 7/347 (8)
8/350 (9) 9/366 (7) 10/373 (11)

Bonus points – Worcestershire 4, Essex 3.

Bowling: *First Innings*—Cowan 30.5–13–51–3; Clarke 13–4–34–1; Middlebrook 28–8–81–1; Phillips 12–0–51–0; Stephenson 15–0–84–2; Bishop 18–3–59–3. *Second Innings*—Cowan 5–2–9–0; Bishop 4–0–27–1; Phillips 7.4–0–26–1; Middlebrook 7–1–19–0.

Umpires: T. E. Jesty and B. Leadbeater.

At Southgate, July 18, 19, 20, 21. ESSEX drew with MIDDLESEX.

ESSEX v GLAMORGAN

At Chelmsford, July 24, 25, 26, 27. Drawn. Essex 8 pts, Glamorgan 12 pts. Toss: Essex.

Essex began their second innings 344 behind and needing to bat for nearly two days to earn a draw; when the captains shook hands at 5.20 on the final evening, they had held out for 171 overs and lost just four wickets. Jefferson kept the fielders busy between mid-on and cover, Robinson became the first Englishman to pass 1,000 runs, and both made fine centuries – in Jefferson's case, his first. Flower then saw out the last day with unwavering concentration, making an unbeaten 172 on a friendly pitch. The stalemate was disappointing for Glamorgan, who had earlier built an impregnable lead. On the first day their seamers took advantage of muggy conditions and undisciplined batting to dismiss Essex for 231. James responded with the innings of the match, a mammoth 249 in 318 balls and nearly seven and a half hours, which was his sixth double-hundred. He hit 32 fours as Maynard and Croft dished out further punishment at the other end. Foster broke his thumb on the second day; his comeback after breaking his arm in May had lasted a week.

Close of play: First day, Glamorgan 6-0 (Cosker 6, James 0); Second day, Glamorgan 505-6 (James 235, Croft 37); Third day, Essex 281-2 (Flower 36).

Essex

D. D. J. Robinson c Wallace b Thomas.	48	– b Thomas	119
W. I. Jefferson c Maynard b Wharf.	6	– c Thomas b Parkin	109
A. Habib c Maynard b Wharf.	0	– (5) c Cherry b Croft	31
A. Flower lbw b Wharf.	5	– (3) not out.	172
*R. C. Irani c Maynard b Dale.	34	– (4) c Cosker b Thomas	18
†J. S. Foster c Cosker b Thomas.	4		
J. D. Middlebrook c Cherry b Croft.	42		
T. J. Phillips c Cosker b Parkin.	14		
J. P. Stephenson not out.	46	– (6) not out.	29
J. E. Bishop c James b Parkin	19		
J. B. Grant c Cherry b Croft	10		
B 2, l-b 1	3	B 12, l-b 14, w 4, n-b 6.	36

1/16 (2) 2/16 (3) 3/38 (4) 4/89 (1)	231	1/185 (2) 2/281 (1) (4 wkts dec.) 514
5/93 (5) 6/97 (6) 7/122 (8)		3/331 (4) 4/410 (5)
8/167 (7) 9/211 (10) 10/231 (11)		

Bonus points – Essex 1, Glamorgan 3.

Bowling: *First Innings*—Parkin 18–5–47–2; Wharf 22–2–54–3; Dale 14–5–39–1; Thomas 16.1–3–46–2; Croft 20–7–23–2; Cosker 12.5–3–19–0. *Second Innings*—Parkin 25–5–58–1; Wharf 21–1–65–0; Croft 54–8–164–1; Cosker 40–7–108–0; Thomas 24–4–72–2; Dale 5–0–13–0; Powell 1–0–8–0; Cherry 1–1–0–0.

Glamorgan

D. A. Cosker c Foster b Bishop	37	S. D. Thomas not out	24

D. A. Cosker c Foster b Bishop 37
*S. P. James lbw b Bishop 249
D. D. Cherry lbw b Bishop 1
A. Dale b Phillips 12
M. J. Powell lbw b Middlebrook 46
M. P. Maynard c and b Stephenson 76
†M. A. Wallace b Irani 34
R. D. B. Croft lbw b Grant 62

S. D. Thomas not out 24
A. G. Wharf b Grant 6
O. T. Parkin b Phillips 0
          B 2, l-b 8, w 2, n-b 16 28
                                                      ───
                                                      575

1/75 (1) 2/89 (3) 3/115 (4) 4/227 (5)
5/383 (6) 6/442 (7) 7/528 (2)
8/552 (8) 9/574 (10) 10/575 (11)

Bonus points – Glamorgan 5, Essex 3.

Bowling: Grant 18–1–108–2; Irani 25–6–67–1; Bishop 25–4–103–3; Stephenson 20–0–99–1; Phillips 18.3–2–98–2; Middlebrook 19–0–90–1.

Umpires: G. I. Burgess and R. Palmer.

At Derby, August 7, 8, 9, 10. ESSEX beat DERBYSHIRE by 140 runs.

At Chelmsford, August 14, 15, 16, 17. ESSEX drew with INDIANS (see Indian tour section).

ESSEX v DURHAM

At Colchester, August 21, 22, 23, 24. Essex won by four wickets. Essex 17 pts, Durham 5 pts. Toss: Durham.

Stephenson, once an England opener, now coach of Essex's Second Eleven, continued his dazzling comeback. With Essex chasing 321 in 91 overs, his cut to the rope in the 87th brought up a hundred and concluded a perfectly judged pursuit. Along the way, Pettini, aged 19, cracked several penetrating drives in his 64, though Phillips's off-breaks should have created more pressure with the pitch helping spin. Stephenson's century took his total since breaking into the Championship team in May to 475 runs at over 43 (along with 40 wickets at under 24). Earlier, Gough had anchored Durham's first innings with a measured maiden Championship hundred. In reply, Hunter and Killeen had Essex on the slide to 96 for six, before Napier's pyrotechnic 54 and Bopara's calm 48 boosted them to a lead of 12. Durham then took advantage of indifferent bowling and sloppy catching to leave a testing target.

Close of play: First day, Essex 25-3 (Stephenson 12, Ilott 5); Second day, Durham 65-1 (G. J. Pratt 26, Muchall 1); Third day, Durham 323-8 (Phillips 50, Davies 4).

Durham

M. A. Gough c Flower b Stephenson 103
G. J. Pratt c Flower b Ilott 0
G. J. Muchall c Robinson b Napier 27
N. Peng c Ilott b Dakin 9
A. M. Thorpe lbw b Stephenson 9
M. J. Symington lbw b Grant 4
†A. Pratt lbw b Ilott 14
I. D. Hunter b Middlebrook 32
*N. C. Phillips run out 0
A. M. Davies not out 17
N. Killeen c Flower b Grant 17
          B 2, l-b 11, w 2, n-b 12 27

– c Robinson b Napier 34
– c Bopara b Napier 65
– c Napier b Stephenson 16
– lbw b Stephenson 0
– c Bopara b Dakin 61
– c Jefferson b Napier 6
– c Jefferson b Dakin 51
– b Grant 10
– not out 58
– c Flower b Dakin 5
– lbw b Ilott 0
          B 3, l-b 9, w 2, n-b 12 26

1/3 (2) 2/79 (3) 3/94 (4) 4/107 (5)   259
5/112 (6) 6/132 (7) 7/191 (8)
8/195 (9) 9/228 (1) 10/259 (11)

1/64 (1) 2/113 (3) 3/117 (4)   332
4/131 (2) 5/143 (6) 6/241 (7)
7/256 (5) 8/280 (8)
9/329 (10) 10/332 (11)

Bonus points – Durham 2, Essex 3.

Bowling: *First Innings*—Ilott 11–3–44–2; Grant 19.1–4–75–2; Dakin 18–4–47–1; Napier 13–3–37–1; Stephenson 14–6–20–2; Middlebrook 11–4–23–1. *Second Innings*—Dakin 15–0–73–3; Ilott 11.5–4–20–1; Middlebrook 23–8–58–0; Napier 16–3–47–3; Grant 13–0–66–1; Stephenson 13–4–43–2; Bopara 2–0–13–0.

Essex

*D. D. J. Robinson c A. Pratt b Hunter	0	– c Symington b Phillips	48
W. I. Jefferson c A. Pratt b Killeen	0	– lbw b Symington	39
J. P. Stephenson c Muchall b Phillips	39	– not out	100
†A. Flower c Gough b Hunter	6	– c Killeen b Davies	27
M. C. Ilott b Muchall b Killeen	28		
M. L. Pettini c Gough b Symington	2	– (5) b Phillips	64
R. S. Bopara c Phillips b Hunter	48	– (6) c A. Pratt b Phillips	8
J. M. Dakin c Thorpe b Phillips	38	– (7) c A. Pratt b Phillips	12
J. D. Middlebrook c Muchall b Killeen	4	– (8) not out	3
G. R. Napier not out	54		
J. B. Grant lbw b Killeen	15		
B 8, l-b 7, w 12, n-b 10	37	B 8, l-b 5, w 6, n-b 2	21

1/2 (2) 2/4 (1) 3/20 (4) 4/62 (5)   271   1/77 (2) 2/134 (1)   (6 wkts) 322
5/69 (6) 6/96 (3) 7/172 (8)   3/186 (4) 4/283 (5)
8/179 (9) 9/218 (7) 10/271 (11)   5/293 (6) 6/309 (7)

Bonus points – Essex 2, Durham 3.

Bowling: *First Innings*—Hunter 21–2–67–3; Killeen 19–7–49–4; Davies 15–3–44–0; Symington 12–3–30–1; Phillips 25–8–66–2. *Second Innings*—Hunter 7–0–40–0; Killeen 14–4–53–0; Symington 18–4–51–1; Davies 15–2–39–1; Phillips 27–3–103–4; Gough 6–0–23–0.

Umpires: J. H. Evans and G. Sharp.

ESSEX v MIDDLESEX

At Chelmsford, September 4, 5, 6. Essex won by six wickets. Essex 17 pts, Middlesex 5 pts. Toss: Essex.

A Middlesex victory would have virtually guaranteed promotion; instead Essex's third successive win dragged the leaders back into a ruckus of five teams scrapping for three spots. After two evenly balanced days, the turning point came on the third, when Essex's seamers demolished Middlesex for 93. Dakin and Irani exploited some bungled batting on a placid pitch, and Grant wrapped things up with three wickets in 13 balls. Set 111, Essex wobbled briefly before Flower finished the job. On the first morning, Irani was released from England's Test squad too late to toss up, and Grayson's decision to bowl looked to have misfired when the openers put on 108. But Middlebrook winkled both out, and Essex made regular inroads. In reply, Cook was lively, the spinners found turn and only Habib's well-constructed 65 prevented Middlesex taking a lead of more than 17. But, as the second day drew to a close, Essex took three quick wickets – and a grip they never relinquished.

Close of play: First day, Middlesex 283-7 (Nash 26, Cook 20); Second day, Middlesex 21-3 (Cook 1, Shah 12).

The approach to the 17th green at Waitikiri Golf Club has been known as the Brittenden bypass ever since he holed it in one.
Obituary of Dick Brittenden, page 1616

Middlesex

B. L. Hutton lbw b Middlebrook	85	– lbw b Irani	0
S. G. Koenig c Flower b Middlebrook	26	– lbw b Dakin	5
J. W. M. Dalrymple c Stephenson b Grant	17	– c Flower b Dakin	25
*O. A. Shah lbw b Irani	47	– (5) lbw b Napier	25
E. C. Joyce c Flower b Dakin	15	– (6) c Flower b Dakin	3
P. N. Weekes c Jefferson b Grant	12	– (7) c Flower b Irani	0
†D. C. Nash b Napier	26	– (8) c Jefferson b Grant	33
A. A. Noffke st Flower b Grayson	19	– (9) b Grant	22
S. J. Cook c Stephenson b Dakin	25	– (4) lbw b Dakin	1
C. B. Keegan c Habib b Napier	5	– lbw b Grant	0
P. C. R. Tufnell not out	2	– not out	0
B 1, l-b 5, w 6, n-b 4	16	L-b 2	2

1/108 (2) 2/133 (3) 3/135 (1) 4/193 (5)   295   1/0 (1) 2/7 (3) 3/8 (2) 4/25 (4)   93
5/203 (4) 6/218 (6) 7/243 (8)   5/29 (6) 6/32 (7) 7/47 (5)
8/283 (7) 9/289 (9) 10/295 (10)   8/90 (8) 9/92 (10) 10/93 (9)

Bonus points – Middlesex 2, Essex 3.

Bowling: *First Innings*—Dakin 23–4–60–2; Grant 21–4–76–2; Napier 17–3–45–2; Middlebrook 27–8–60–2; Irani 11–4–21–1; Grayson 7–3–10–1; Stephenson 3–0–17–0. *Second Innings*—Irani 12–5–22–2; Dakin 9–3–17–4; Napier 4–2–11–1; Grant 6.1–1–19–3; Grayson 7–1–22–0.

Essex

D. D. J. Robinson c Nash b Cook	20	– b Cook	4
W. I. Jefferson b Cook	14	– lbw b Cook	4
J. P. Stephenson lbw b Cook	10	– hit wicket b Cook	8
†A. Flower lbw b Cook	32	– not out	43
*R. C. Irani c Joyce b Weekes	43	– c and b Weekes	42
A. Habib lbw b Tufnell	65	– not out	9
A. P. Grayson c and b Weekes	5		
J. M. Dakin c Keegan b Weekes	6		
J. D. Middlebrook st Nash b Tufnell	33		
G. R. Napier not out	38		
J. B. Grant c Nash b Tufnell	0		
L-b 4, n-b 8	12	L-b 1	1

1/26 (2) 2/39 (1) 3/52 (3) 4/91 (4)   278   1/8 (2) 2/9 (1)   (4 wkts) 111
5/170 (5) 6/180 (7) 7/190 (8)   3/28 (3) 4/95 (5)
8/214 (6) 9/268 (9) 10/278 (11)

Bonus points – Essex 2, Middlesex 3.

Bowling: *First Innings*—Noffke 20–1–88–0; Keegan 10–2–33–0; Cook 12–4–27–4; Tufnell 22–1–58–3; Weekes 21–1–59–3; Hutton 3–0–9–0. *Second Innings*—Noffke 8–2–23–0; Cook 10–3–26–3; Tufnell 8.5–1–25–0; Keegan 4–1–20–0; Weekes 3–0–16–1.

Umpires: J. H. Evans and J. W. Lloyds.

At Chester-le-Street, September 11, 12, 13, 14. ESSEX beat DURHAM by ten wickets.

ESSEX v NOTTINGHAMSHIRE

At Chelmsford, September 18, 19, 20, 21. Essex won by seven wickets. Essex 16.5 pts, Nottinghamshire 6 pts. Toss: Essex.

After weeks of jostling, the race for the title reached a superb finale. A win for either side here would almost certainly make them champions, while for Essex, six bonus points plus a draw would suffice; any other stalemate would leave Middlesex top. On the opening day, Afzaal belted anything wide during an aggressive 134 and Read cut and pulled his way to a dashing 73. Fiery pace from Harris then helped give Nottinghamshire a lead of 59. With both teams now assured of promotion, the fight was for first place – and a £40,000 cheque. Nottinghamshire were favourites after Shafayat stroked an elegant 70 to leave Essex chasing a tricky 340. But, on a last-day pitch offering turn, MacGill dropped too short too often, and Jefferson, Waugh and Habib hit 198 flowing runs in the morning session alone. Jefferson went on to a magnificent, hard-hit 165 and Essex secured their fifth consecutive win with surprising ease. The last ball was a gentle off-spinner from Johnson, who had earlier been given a rousing ovation as he walked to the crease for the last time before retirement.

Close of play: First day, Essex 2-0 (Robinson 0, Jefferson 0); Second day, Nottinghamshire 39-1 (Gallian 8, Harris 1); Third day, Essex 129-2 (Jefferson 71, Waugh 29).

Nottinghamshire

*J. E. R. Gallian lbw b Stephenson	23	– (2) c Jefferson b Dakin	12
G. E. Welton c Jefferson b Dakin	1	– (1) b Middlebrook	23
D. J. Bicknell lbw b Napier	53	– (4) lbw b Stephenson	31
U. Afzaal c Jefferson b Middlebrook	134	– (5) c Foster b Grant	0
B. M. Shafayat lbw b Stephenson	4	– (6) b Dakin	70
P. Johnson c Foster b Dakin	16	– (7) c Foster b Napier	13
†C. M. W. Read c Middlebrook b Dakin	73	– (8) b Dakin	18
P. J. Franks b Habib b Middlebrook	1	– (9) c Grayson b Stephenson	33
S. C. G. MacGill c Grayson b Middlebrook	0	– (11) not out	9
G. J. Smith c Stephenson b Napier	4	– c Habib b Middlebrook	16
A. J. Harris not out	16	– (3) lbw b Stephenson	17
B 8, l-b 1, n-b 8	17	B 5, l-b 9, w 6, n-b 18	38

1/7 (2) 2/50 (1) 3/160 (3) 4/195 (5)   341   1/34 (1) 2/43 (2) 3/90 (3)   280
5/238 (6) 6/250 (4) 7/250 (8)   4/93 (4) 5/99 (5) 6/123 (7)
8/250 (9) 9/265 (10) 10/341 (7)   7/149 (8) 8/236 (9)
                                      9/262 (6) 10/280 (10)

Bonus points – Nottinghamshire 3, Essex 3.

Bowling: *First Innings*—Dakin 18.5–2–87–3; Napier 15–3–65–2; Stephenson 11–2–42–2; Grant 15–2–62–0; Middlebrook 25–8–69–3; Grayson 2–0–7–0. *Second Innings*—Dakin 19–3–49–3; Napier 14–2–50–1; Middlebrook 11.3–3–37–2; Grant 14–0–66–1; Stephenson 13–4–45–3; Grayson 5–1–19–0.

Essex

D. D. J. Robinson c MacGill b Smith	41	– b Franks	22
W. I. Jefferson lbw b Harris	0	– not out	165
J. P. Stephenson c Read b Harris	65	– b MacGill	4
M. E. Waugh b Franks	49	– c Gallian b Franks	76
A. Habib c Harris b MacGill	50	– not out	57
*A. P. Grayson c Read b MacGill	2		
†J. S. Foster c Shafayat b Franks	29		
J. M. Dakin c Read b Harris	1		
J. D. Middlebrook not out	25		
G. R. Napier lbw b Franks	0		
J. B. Grant lbw b MacGill	0		
B 1, l-b 5, n-b 14	20	L-b 9, n-b 10	19

1/2 (2) 2/87 (1) 3/144 (3) 4/213 (4)   282   1/57 (1) 2/70 (3)   (3 wkts) 343
5/222 (6) 6/233 (5) 7/244 (8)   3/205 (4)
8/281 (7) 9/281 (10) 10/282 (11)

Bonus points – Essex 2, Nottinghamshire 3.

Bowling: *First Innings*—Smith 17–3–60–1; Harris 20–10–42–3; Franks 21–7–50–3; MacGill 28.4–4–116–3; Shafayat 2–0–8–0. *Second Innings*—Smith 11–1–63–0; Harris 11–2–65–0; MacGill 25–1–121–1; Franks 14–5–54–2; Shafayat 6–0–19–0; Johnson 1.2–0–12–0.

Umpires: B. Leadbeater and J. F. Steele.

GLAMORGAN
SUNDAY
BEST

Ch'ship 5th in Division 2
C&G 4th round
B&H group stage
NUL winners of Division 1

Player of the season: Robert Croft

Glamorgan's disappointment at failing to gain promotion to Division One of the Championship was tempered by winning the Norwich Union League. As in 1993, when Glamorgan first won the one-day league, the title was sealed at Canterbury and, on the penultimate Sunday of the season, the hordes of travelling support once more gathered under the pavilion at the St Lawrence ground to pay tribute to their team. If the supporters were happy travellers, so were the players: they had won every game away from home.

The trophy confirmed the progress Glamorgan had made in the one-day game in 2001, when they claimed the Division Two title, so it was bizarre that, for the second year in a row, they lost every single game in the Benson and Hedges Cup. They also played their part in one of the most astonishing one-day games ever seen. Set a massive 439 to beat Surrey in the fourth round of the C&G at The Oval, they failed heroically by just ten runs.

Their Championship form was less impressive. Only two sides gained fewer batting points, and too often Glamorgan failed to make a commanding total in the first innings. The decision to sign Mike Kasprowicz as the overseas player instead of Jimmy Maher – the Australian one-day batsman who led the averages in 2001 – paid off on the bowling front but left Steve James without an established opening partner. David Hemp, who returned after five years with Warwickshire, fell a long way short of expectations as an opening bat, while Ian Thomas and Dan Cherry failed to make the most of their chances. However, Thomas did establish himself as a one-day opener, and Glamorgan were sufficiently impressed to offer him and Cherry two-year contracts.

James missed three Championship games through injury but scored over 1,000 runs and averaged 52.90 with four centuries. He struck 249 against Essex at Chelmsford and later made 184 to continue his remarkable record both at Colwyn Bay and against Nottinghamshire. It was his eighth century against them – two were for Cambridge University – and his fifth at Colwyn Bay. Matthew Maynard also missed three games after breaking a bone in his hand early on but bounced back to pass 1,000 runs for the first time since 1997 and play some thrilling innings. The second of his twin hundreds at Cheltenham – a feat he had achieved 11 years earlier – was a superb effort as Glamorgan successfully chased 317 on a turning pitch. Maynard became only the fourth batsman – after Emrys Davies, Gilbert Parkhouse and Alan Jones – to score 20,000 first-class runs for the county, and said at the end of the season that he was "playing as well as I have ever done".

Michael Powell also passed 1,000 runs and averaged 50. After being left out of the game at Colwyn Bay because of a training-ground spat with a team-mate, Powell ended the season with a flourish. He made six successive half-centuries, played some important one-day innings and won the match award for his 74 at Canterbury. He was unlucky to miss out on a place at the England Academy: "I would willingly pay my own way," he said, "to go there and improve my game."

Robert Croft and Mark Wallace, who was picked for the Academy, lent solid support to the front-line batsmen. Croft scored 747 Championship runs, his best yet, and Wallace hit a maiden century, against Derbyshire. Jonathan Hughes, a 21-year-old batsman from Pontypridd, played only six Championship games, but his 74 against Worcestershire transformed Glamorgan's first innings after they had slumped to 106 for six. He has an uninhibited approach and should soon be challenging for a regular place.

Kasprowicz led the attack superbly. He was the leading wicket-taker with 53 at 26.66 and was voted the Clubman of the Year by his team-mates for his enthusiasm and willingness to help the younger bowlers. Despite offers from two other counties, he agreed to stay with Glamorgan for two more years. Simon Jones's rapid pace and improved control were recognised by the England selectors, who picked him for the Lord's Test against India and the Ashes tour. But the agonising cruciate-ligament injury he sustained on the Brisbane outfield on the first day of the series meant he was expected to miss the whole of the 2003 season. Darren Thomas passed 50 first-class wickets, including a Championship-best of seven for 33 against Durham, while David Harrison, a 21-year-old seamer, showed considerable promise at the end of the season and claimed a five-for against Yorkshire in the League. Croft's 39 Championship wickets were expensive, but few pitches across the country assisted finger-spinners. He did, however, play a major part in the Norwich Union triumph, finishing as the competition's third-highest wicket-taker and forming an effective partnership with the left-arm spinner, Dean Cosker.

John Derrick succeeded Jeff Hammond as county coach and was an unqualified success. A former Glamorgan player and someone who commands respect, Derrick is supportive of his team but not blindly so: when they capitulated to 144 on a good Northampton pitch, he quickly told them a few home truths.

Glamorgan have now won three major titles in the past decade and the squad has strength in depth. The Second Eleven, under the guidance of the academy director Steve Watkin and the captain Adrian Shaw, finished fourth as the club carried on their commendable policy of producing home-grown talent instead of signing overseas players with European passports. The future looks bright. **Edward Bevan**

GLAMORGAN 2002

Back row: D. D. Cherry, M. A. Wallace, L. A. Smith, S. P. Jones, D. S. Harrison, I. J. Thomas, J. Hughes, R. E. Watkins, T. D. Evison. *Middle row:* G. N. Lewis *(first-team scorer)*, A. W. Evans, K. Newell, O. T. Parkin, A. G. Wharf, M. J. Powell, D. A. Cosker, A. P. Davies, E. Mustafa *(physiotherapist)*. *Front row:* J. Derrick *(club coach)*, D. L. Hemp, S. D. Thomas, A. Dale, S. P. James *(captain)*, R. D. B. Croft *(vice-captain)*, M. P. Maynard, A. D. Shaw *(second-team captain/coach)*, M. S. Kasprowicz, S. L. Watkin *(academy director)*. *Picture by Huw John.*

GLAMORGAN RESULTS

All first-class matches – Played 17: Won 5, Lost 5, Drawn 7.
County Championship matches – Played 16: Won 5, Lost 5, Drawn 6.

COUNTY CHAMPIONSHIP AVERAGES: BATTING AND FIELDING

Cap		M	I	NO	R	HS	100s	50s	Avge	Ct/St
1987	M. P. Maynard	13	20	1	1,058	151	3	6	55.68	14
1992	S. P. James	13	22	1	1,111	249	4	3	52.90	7
2000	M. J. Powell†	15	26	3	1,152	135	3	7	50.08	6
1992	A. Dale	15	24	1	859	127*	2	3	37.34	6
1992	R. D. B. Croft† . . .	16	24	3	747	101*	1	5	35.57	8
2002	M. S. Kasprowicz§ . .	12	19	7	352	72*	0	1	29.33	7
1994	D. L. Hemp	11	20	2	505	108	1	2	28.05	6
	M. A. Wallace† . . .	16	25	4	553	106*	1	2	26.33	54/3
	J. Hughes†	6	10	1	225	74	0	1	25.00	2
	I. J. Thomas†	8	15	1	273	76	0	2	19.50	2
	D. D. Cherry†	5	8	0	129	47	0	0	16.12	4
2002	S. P. Jones†	10	17	6	174	26	0	0	15.81	4
1997	S. D. Thomas†	15	22	1	274	47	0	0	13.04	4
2000	D. A. Cosker.	10	13	2	115	37	0	0	10.45	8
	A. P. Davies†	5	6	0	58	30	0	0	9.66	0

Also batted: D. S. Harrison† (1 match) 0; O. T. Parkin (3 matches) 0, 7, 16 (1 ct); A. G. Wharf (cap 2000) (2 matches) 0, 6.

† *Born in Wales.*   § *Overseas player.*

BOWLING

	O	M	R	W	BB	5W/i	Avge
S. P. Jones	259.5	47	870	33	6-45	2	26.36
M. S. Kasprowicz	418.4	78	1,413	53	6-47	4	26.66
A. P. Davies	116.2	14	420	15	5-79	1	28.00
S. D. Thomas	447.1	65	1,535	51	7-33	3	30.09
R. D. B. Croft.	592	127	1,640	39	5-71	1	42.05
D. A. Cosker	317.5	60	1,012	20	4-135	0	50.60

Also bowled: D. D. Cherry 3–3–0–0; A. Dale 118–22–441–6; D. S. Harrison 39–6–132–3; M. P. Maynard 1–0–5–0; O. T. Parkin 83.4–19–247–7; M. J. Powell 6–0–21–0; I. J. Thomas 6.1–0–30–1; A. G. Wharf 61–7–195–3.

COUNTY RECORDS

Highest score for:	309*	S. P. James v Sussex at Colwyn Bay	2000
Highest score against:	322*	M. B. Loye (Northamptonshire) at Northampton. .	1998
Best bowling for:	10-51	J. Mercer v Worcestershire at Worcester	1936
Best bowling against:	10-18	G. Geary (Leicestershire) at Pontypridd	1929
Highest total for:	718-3 dec.	v Sussex at Colwyn Bay	2000
Highest total against:	712	by Northamptonshire at Northampton	1998
Lowest total for:	22	v Lancashire at Liverpool	1924
Lowest total against:	33	by Leicestershire at Ebbw Vale	1965

COUNTY OFFICERS

Captain S. P. James • **First-team coach** J. Derrick • **President** A. R. Lewis
Chairman G. Elias • **Chief executive** M. J. Fatkin
Chairman, cricket committee R. Needham • **Cricket secretary** Mrs C. L. Watkins
Head groundsman L. A. Smith • **Scorer** G. N. Lewis

GLAMORGAN v DERBYSHIRE

At Cardiff, April 19, 20, 21, 22. Derbyshire won by 163 runs. Derbyshire 16 pts, Glamorgan 3 pts. Toss: Derbyshire. County debuts: M. S. Kasprowicz; A. I. Gait, D. R. Hewson, J. I. D. Kerr.

A rejuvenated Derbyshire took just one game to match their previous summer's total of Championship wins. Three new recruits – Andrew Gait, an ECB-qualified Zimbabwean with first-class experience for Free State, Hewson from Gloucestershire and Kerr from Somerset – all made contributions to a resounding victory. After choosing to bat, Derbyshire were discomfited by Jones, who was appreciably quicker after a winter with the ECB Academy and claimed a career-best six for 45. But a bravura bowling performance from Cork dragged Derbyshire back into contention; his victims included Hemp, out first ball on his return to Glamorgan after five years with Warwickshire. Derbyshire, 42 ahead, batted much better in their second innings. Stubbings shared a partnership of 192 with Gait, and Hewson made an unbeaten century to help set a nominal target of 505 in five sessions. Wallace, who made the first hundred by a Glamorgan wicket-keeper since Eifion Jones in 1979, and James – whose 78 included a six that sailed into the press box – held things up, but Wharton's career-best six for 103 won the day.

Close of play: First day, Glamorgan 163-8 (Kasprowicz 0, Cosker 1); Second day, Derbyshire 353-4 (Hewson 35, Cork 7); Third day, Glamorgan 281-7 (Wallace 84, Kasprowicz 32).

Derbyshire

S. D. Stubbings lbw b Thomas	4	– c Croft b Thomas	128
M. J. Di Venuto c Wallace b Jones	38	– b Maynard b Cosker	62
A. I. Gait c Croft b Jones	24	– run out	80
D. R. Hewson c Wallace b Jones	0	– not out	102
L. D. Sutton lbw b Jones	7	– c Kasprowicz b Jones	15
*D. G. Cork c Hemp b Dale	33	– b Thomas	22
†K. M. Krikken b Croft	20	– c Hemp b Croft	25
J. I. D. Kerr b Jones	58	– not out	2
G. Welch b Jones	0		
K. J. Dean not out	7		
L. J. Wharton lbw b Croft	1		
B 10, l-b 5, n-b 10	25	B 10, l-b 8, n-b 8	26
	217	(6 wkts dec.)	**462**

1/25 (1) 2/57 (2) 3/57 (4) 4/69 (5)
5/88 (3) 6/120 (6) 7/209 (7)
8/209 (8) 9/214 (9) 10/217 (11)

1/96 (2) 2/288 (3) (6 wkts dec.) 462
3/289 (1) 4/329 (5)
5/375 (6) 6/443 (7)

Bonus points – Derbyshire 1, Glamorgan 3.

Bowling: *First Innings*—Kasprowicz 17–3–67–0; Thomas 13–1–56–1; Croft 6.3–2–17–2; Jones 14–4–45–6; Dale 7–3–17–1. *Second Innings*—Kasprowicz 24–1–104–0; Thomas 21–2–78–2; Jones 23–3–65–1; Cosker 20–4–91–1; Croft 38–11–91–1; Dale 2–0–15–0.

Glamorgan

*S. P. James c Hewson b Dean	15	– lbw b Wharton	78
D. L. Hemp b Cork	0	– c Cork b Dean	8
A. Dale b Kerr	56	– b Cork	6
M. J. Powell c Stubbings b Cork	16	– lbw b Wharton	33
M. P. Maynard b Cork	0	– b Cork	6
R. D. B. Croft b Cork	46	– c Cork b Wharton	0
†M. A. Wallace lbw b Kerr	0	– not out	106
S. D. Thomas c Gait b Dean	12	– c Sutton b Kerr	6
M. S. Kasprowicz lbw b Cork	8	– b Wharton	36
D. A. Cosker not out	4	– c Hewson b Wharton	8
S. P. Jones c Krikken b Cork	0	– c Stubbings b Wharton	18
L-b 2, n-b 16	18	B 13, l-b 5, n-b 18	36
	175		**341**

1/3 (2) 2/25 (1) 3/64 (4) 4/64 (5)
5/136 (3) 6/136 (7) 7/162 (6)
8/162 (8) 9/175 (9) 10/175 (11)

1/18 (2) 2/39 (3) 3/102 (4)
4/113 (5) 5/114 (6) 6/193 (1)
7/206 (8) 8/291 (9)
9/319 (10) 10/341 (11)

Bonus points – Derbyshire 3.

Bowling: *First Innings*—Cork 17.4–3–51–6; Dean 14–4–45–2; Welch 10–2–44–0; Kerr 7–2–33–2. *Second Innings*—Cork 19–3–70–2; Dean 11–2–42–1; Welch 11–3–35–0; Kerr 20–5–73–1; Wharton 29–5–103–6.

Umpires: A. Clarkson and G. Sharp.

At Cardiff, April 24, 25 (not first-class). **Glamorgan won by ten wickets.** Toss: Cardiff UCCE. **Cardiff UCCE 216** (A. N. Bressington 58, T. Sud 31 not out; O. T. Parkin four for 55) **and 145** (A. N. French 45, N. J. K. Creed 30 not out; A. P. Davies three for 32); **Glamorgan 353** (D. L. Hemp 70, I. J. Thomas 31, M. A. Wallace 106, A. P. Davies 47 not out, Extras 31; J. A. Tomlinson three for 45, T. Sud four for 63) **and 12 for no wkt.**

At Worcester, May 8, 9, 10, 11. GLAMORGAN beat WORCESTERSHIRE by 110 runs.

GLAMORGAN v DURHAM

At Cardiff, May 15, 16, 17, 18. Glamorgan won by five wickets. Glamorgan 16 pts, Durham 3 pts. Toss: Glamorgan.

Glamorgan's target of 201 was far from straightforward, as both sets of bowlers found swing throughout the match, but James led the chase confidently, compiling a chanceless century and standing sentinel until only two runs were needed. Glamorgan also had to contend with bad weather, which cost almost all of the third day and an hour of the fourth, but wickets had tumbled so quickly early in the match that they still won with 20 overs to spare. Fifteen batsmen fell on the opening day alone — seven to Darren Thomas, who went on to take ten in a match for the first time. It triggered a visit from A. C. Smith, a pitch liaison officer, but he chose not to criticise a green-tinged and slightly damp wicket. By the second afternoon Durham were in disarray at 41 for four, still two behind, and only Collingwood and Muchall, in his third Championship game, prevented the game being settled straight away. They put on 140 to leave Glamorgan a tricky chase. Unusually, 19 of the 22 players had learned their game in the county they represented.

Close of play: First day, Glamorgan 117-5 (Powell 30, Hughes 0); Second day, Durham 239-9 (Davies 12, Killeen 5); Third day, Durham 243.

Durham

*J. J. B. Lewis c and b Kasprowicz	9	– lbw b Kasprowicz	0
G. J. Pratt c James b Jones	16	– lbw b S. D. Thomas	0
M. L. Love c Wallace b S. D. Thomas	71	– c Hughes b Kasprowicz	13
P. D. Collingwood c Powell b S. D. Thomas	15	– c Wallace b Kasprowicz	99
N. Peng c Hemp b S. D. Thomas	8	– lbw b S. D. Thomas	4
G. J. Muchall c Wallace b S. D. Thomas	6	– c Croft b Jones	77
†A. Pratt lbw b Kasprowicz	7	– b Jones	8
I. D. Hunter c James b S. D. Thomas	0	– c Kasprowicz b Croft	0
G. D. Bridge not out	5	– b Jones	2
A. M. Davies c Wallace b S. D. Thomas	4	– lbw b S. D. Thomas	15
N. Killeen b S. D. Thomas	0	– not out	5
L-b 9, w 4, n-b 8	21	B 12, l-b 4, n-b 4	20
	162		**243**

1/12 (1) 2/73 (2) 3/120 (4) 4/131 (3)
5/138 (5) 6/153 (6) 7/153 (8)
8/153 (7) 9/160 (10) 10/162 (11)

1/0 (1) 2/2 (2) 3/30 (3)
4/41 (5) 5/181 (4) 6/217 (7)
7/218 (8) 8/220 (6)
9/221 (9) 10/243 (10)

Bonus points – Glamorgan 3.

Bowling: *First Innings*—Kasprowicz 18–4–55–2; S. D. Thomas 15.2–6–33–7; Dale 3–0–15–0; Jones 8–0–37–1; Croft 7–4–13–0. *Second Innings*—Kasprowicz 19–3–61–3; S. D. Thomas 14.1–4–50–3; Croft 14–1–33–1; Jones 13–1–42–3; Dale 7–2–41–0.

Glamorgan

*S. P. James lbw b Hunter	2	– st A. Pratt b Bridge	121
D. L. Hemp lbw b Killeen	31	– c Peng b Hunter	16
I. J. Thomas lbw b Davies	39	– c G. J. Pratt b Davies	18
M. J. Powell not out	62	– lbw b Davies	1
A. Dale b Hunter	5	– c Love b Bridge	16
M. S. Kasprowicz c A. Pratt b Davies	0		
J. Hughes b Collingwood	30	– (6) not out	26
†M. A. Wallace c Muchall b Bridge	0	– (7) not out	4
R. D. B. Croft c Muchall b Collingwood	3		
S. D. Thomas run out	0		
S. P. Jones c Davies b Bridge	12		
B 2, l-b 11, w 8	21	B 1, l-b 1	2

1/9 (1) 2/72 (2) 3/93 (3) 4/114 (5)	**205**	1/57 (2) 2/103 (3) （5 wkts) **204**
5/115 (6) 6/181 (7) 7/186 (8)		3/109 (4) 4/152 (5)
8/193 (9) 9/193 (10) 10/205 (11)		5/199 (1)

Bonus points – Glamorgan 1, Durham 3.

Bowling: *First Innings*—Killeen 20–6–37–1; Hunter 24–8–67–2; Collingwood 17–5–36–2; Davies 15–6–20–2; Bridge 13–5–32–2. *Second Innings*—Killeen 11–2–44–0; Hunter 10–0–62–1; Collingwood 8–1–22–0; Davies 11–3–29–2; Bridge 11–1–45–2.

Umpires: G. I. Burgess and M. J. Harris.

At Cardiff, May 23, 24, 25, 26. GLAMORGAN drew with SRI LANKANS (see Sri Lankan tour section).

At Derby, May 31, June 1. GLAMORGAN lost to DERBYSHIRE by nine wickets.

At Lord's, June 12, 13, 14, 15. GLAMORGAN drew with MIDDLESEX.

GLAMORGAN v MIDDLESEX

At Cardiff, June 26, 27, 28, 29. Middlesex won by eight wickets. Middlesex 20 pts, Glamorgan 2 pts. Toss: Middlesex.

While Middlesex took full advantage of a placid pitch, Glamorgan's batting flopped, and the 398-run lead proved too big to close. After choosing to bat, Middlesex stacked up 633, their best in this fixture: Strauss set a rapid tempo, cracking the ball square of the wicket, before Abdul Razzaq and Joyce put on a gargantuan 320 – Middlesex's highest partnership against Glamorgan. Both innings were career-bests: Razzaq drove aggressively in his unbeaten 203, lasting 296 balls and 345 minutes, and hit 19 fours and two sixes; Joyce's 129 was more restrained. After Strauss declared early on the second afternoon, only James and Maynard played Middlesex's spinners with any ease and Tufnell took five wickets for the 50th time. On such a good pitch a total of 235 was a poor effort. Glamorgan fought harder after following on, as James showed concentration and the middle order batted resolutely on the final morning. But, with only 84 to chase, Middlesex completed their win comfortably. Maximum points took them second in Division Two.

Close of play: First day, Middlesex 408-4 (Joyce 50, Abdul Razzaq 88); Second day, Glamorgan 173-7 (Maynard 57); Third day, Glamorgan 301-5 (Wallace 37, Croft 9).

Middlesex

*A. J. Strauss lbw b Croft	141	– c Croft b Cosker	48
S. G. Koenig lbw b Croft	30	– b Cosker	27
R. M. S. Weston lbw b Cosker	17	– not out	0
O. A. Shah lbw b Jones	62	– not out	4
E. C. Joyce c Maynard b Croft	129		
Abdul Razzaq not out	203		
S. J. Cook c Wallace b Croft	5		
P. N. Weekes c Kasprowicz b Cosker	17		
†D. C. Nash not out	1		
B 6, l-b 10, n-b 12	28	W 2, n-b 4	6

1/54 (2) 2/104 (3) 3/253 (4) (7 wkts dec.) 633 1/81 (1) 2/81 (2) (2 wkts) 85
4/261 (1) 5/581 (5)
6/600 (7) 7/623 (8)

P. C. R. Tufnell and C. B. Keegan did not bat.

Bonus points – Middlesex 5, Glamorgan 1 (130 overs: 500-4).

Bowling: *First Innings*—Kasprowicz 28–4–109–0; Thomas 27–1–108–0; Croft 43–5–151–4; Jones 26–5–90–1; Cosker 39.1–2–159–2. *Second Innings*—Kasprowicz 3–0–33–0; Croft 8–1–26–0; Jones 3–1–10–0; Cosker 3.2–1–16–2.

Glamorgan

*S. P. James c Nash b Keegan	40	– b Abdul Razzaq	118
D. L. Hemp lbw b Tufnell	19	– c sub b Keegan	8
A. Dale b Tufnell	8	– b Weekes	46
M. J. Powell lbw b Tufnell	9	– b Cook	18
M. P. Maynard c sub b Tufnell	66	– c sub b Tufnell	41
†M. A. Wallace lbw b Weekes	16	– c Weekes b Tufnell	59
R. D. B. Croft c Joyce b Weekes	6	– c Nash b Abdul Razzaq	75
S. D. Thomas c Strauss b Weekes	6	– b Weekes	47
M. S. Kasprowicz not out	17	– b Abdul Razzaq	9
D. A. Cosker b Tufnell	0	– not out	10
S. P. Jones c Cook b Tufnell	26	– b Keegan	9
B 4, l-b 4, n-b 14	22	B 8, l-b 3, w 8, n-b 19	38

1/52 (2) 2/76 (3) 3/80 (1) 4/94 (4) 235 1/21 (2) 2/107 (3) 3/148 (4) 481
5/135 (6) 6/147 (7) 7/173 (8) 4/232 (5) 5/274 (1) 6/340 (6)
8/201 (5) 9/201 (10) 10/235 (11) 7/420 (8) 8/451 (9)
9/472 (7) 10/481 (11)

Bonus points – Glamorgan 1, Middlesex 3.

Bowling: *First Innings*—Abdul Razzaq 9–0–42–0; Cook 3–0–23–0; Tufnell 25–5–96–6; Keegan 12–4–39–1; Weekes 7–1–27–3. *Second Innings*—Keegan 17–2–70–2; Cook 20–4–57–1; Tufnell 45–7–133–2; Weekes 34–6–106–2; Abdul Razzaq 24–3–104–3.

Umpires: M. J. Harris and N. J. Llong.

GLAMORGAN v ESSEX

At Swansea, July 3, 4, 5, 6. Glamorgan won by eight wickets. Glamorgan 18 pts, Essex 5 pts. Toss: Essex. First-class debut: A. J. Clarke.

Essex came into the match on a run of five straight wins, two the result of rousing second-innings rallies. Now, however, a second-innings failure cost them dear. They began 28 behind, but Kasprowicz, playing against his old county, took two wickets with the first two balls, both perfect out-swingers, and Essex ended the third day in effect 32 for five. Flower and Napier denied Glamorgan for most of the next morning, eking out 56 in 34 overs, but Jones finished things quickly after lunch. In a venomous 16-ball burst he took the last four wickets for just eight runs, leaving Glamorgan to chase 112, which they reached just after tea. On the first day, a wet outfield had made quick scoring difficult, though Essex finished on a healthy 208 for three. However, a hostile spell by Thomas on the second morning and deceptive flight from Croft reduced them to 283 all out. When Glamorgan replied against a depleted attack, Andrew Clarke took five for 54 on debut with his medium-fast but Powell survived a rocky start to help his team to a small lead.

Close of play: First day, Essex 208-3 (Habib 27, Flower 13); Second day, Glamorgan 197-5 (Powell 57, Croft 20); Third day, Essex 60-5 (Flower 2, Bishop 0).

Essex

*D. D. J. Robinson lbw b Croft	72	– lbw b Kasprowicz		0
W. I. Jefferson lbw b Croft	43	– b Kasprowicz		26
J. D. Middlebrook c Jones b Cosker	32	– c Wallace b Kasprowicz		0
A. Habib c Wallace b Thomas	61	– b Croft		20
†A. Flower lbw b Croft	16	– c Wallace b Jones		33
M. L. Pettini c Wallace b Thomas	19	– c Wallace b Jones		1
G. R. Napier b Thomas	1	– (8) c Kasprowicz b Jones		26
J. P. Stephenson not out	10	– (9) c Wallace b Jones		5
T. J. Phillips c Kasprowicz b Jones	2	– (10) not out		0
J. E. Bishop c Wallace b Croft	0	– (7) c Maynard b Croft		7
A. J. Clarke b Croft	0	– c Wallace b Jones		0
B 4, l-b 5, n-b 18	27	B 8, l-b 3, n-b 10		21

1/95 (2) 2/161 (1) 3/180 (3) 4/211 (5)   **283**
5/262 (4) 6/264 (7) 7/271 (6)
8/282 (9) 9/283 (10) 10/283 (11)

1/0 (1) 2/0 (3) 3/43 (4)   **139**
4/51 (2) 5/59 (6) 6/72 (7)
7/128 (8) 8/138 (9)
9/139 (5) 10/139 (11)

Bonus points – Essex 2, Glamorgan 3.

Bowling: *First Innings*—Kasprowicz 19–7–43–0; Thomas 21–3–43–3; Cosker 35–9–75–1; Jones 15–3–42–1; Croft 33–11–71–5. *Second Innings*—Kasprowicz 13–4–27–3; Thomas 12–2–39–0; Croft 26–14–28–2; Jones 14.4–4–28–5; Cosker 4–1–6–0.

Glamorgan

*S. P. James b Napier	1	– c Bishop b Phillips		56
D. D. Cherry c Pettini b Clarke	26	– c Flower b Clarke		11
D. L. Hemp c Robinson b Clarke	25	– not out		23
M. J. Powell c Jefferson b Stephenson	90	– not out		13
M. P. Maynard c Pettini b Clarke	16			
†M. A. Wallace lbw b Stephenson	37			
R. D. B. Croft c Phillips b Bishop	35			
S. D. Thomas c and b Clarke	11			
M. S. Kasprowicz not out	19			
D. A. Cosker b Phillips	3			
S. P. Jones b Clarke	24			
B 4, l-b 4, w 2, n-b 14	24	L-b 1, n-b 8		9

1/3 (1) 2/53 (2) 3/57 (3) 4/89 (5)   **311**
5/172 (6) 6/233 (7) 7/261 (4)
8/263 (9) 9/273 (10) 10/311 (11)

1/35 (2) 2/90 (1)   (2 wkts) **112**

Bonus points – Glamorgan 3, Essex 3.

Bowling: *First Innings*—Bishop 11–0–55–1; Napier 20–3–69–1; Clarke 17.3–1–54–5; Stephenson 18–0–74–2; Middlebrook 9–4–21–0; Phillips 9–3–30–1. *Second Innings*—Bishop 3–0–20–0; Clarke 6–0–25–1; Middlebrook 13.2–3–28–0; Phillips 9–0–38–1.

Umpires: V. A. Holder and M. J. Kitchen.

At Nottingham, July 10, 11, 12. GLAMORGAN lost to NOTTINGHAMSHIRE by seven wickets.

At Cheltenham, July 19, 20, 21, 22. GLAMORGAN beat GLOUCESTERSHIRE by two wickets.

At Chelmsford, July 24, 25, 26, 27. GLAMORGAN drew with ESSEX.

GLAMORGAN v GLOUCESTERSHIRE

At Cardiff, August 7, 8, 9, 10. Drawn. Glamorgan 12 pts, Gloucestershire 11 pts. Toss: Glamorgan.
There was little prospect of a positive result after rain cost nearly two days' play. However, Glamorgan did manage maximum bonus points, which kept them in touch with the teams chasing promotion; Gloucestershire took 11 but their hopes of going up had already faded. James chose to bowl first but, despite a mid-innings stutter, there was little to vindicate his decision. Harvey launched a violent assault on the Glamorgan attack to score a century off only 72 balls, and Russell coaxed 73 from the last three wickets before Glamorgan quickly lost both openers to Smith's out-swing. Powell and Maynard were charging when rain cut short the second day, but when play finally resumed on the final afternoon the contest was already dead. Powell went on to a punishing century, while Croft reached 101 – his second Championship hundred – to guide Glamorgan to their final batting point.
Close of play: First day, Glamorgan 6-1 (Cherry 3); Second day, Glamorgan 189-3 (Powell 94, Maynard 33); Third day, No play.

Gloucestershire

T. H. C. Hancock c Wallace b Thomas	40	– (2) not out	0
C. M. Spearman c Dale b Thomas	32	– (1) not out	7
C. G. Taylor retired hurt	74		
M. G. N. Windows c Maynard b Davies	20		
*M. W. Alleyne b Davies	4		
A. P. R. Gidman b Davies	6		
I. J. Harvey lbw b Cosker	123		
†R. C. Russell lbw b Parkin	52		
I. D. Fisher c Powell b Cosker	0		
J. Lewis b Parkin	11		
A. M. Smith not out	9		
B 8, l-b 9, w 2, n-b 6	25		

1/67 (1) 2/80 (2) 3/118 (4)   396   (no wkt)   7
4/130 (5) 5/146 (6) 6/323 (7)
7/323 (9) 8/361 (10) 9/396 (8)

Bonus points – Gloucestershire 4, Glamorgan 3.

In the first innings, Taylor retired hurt at 317.

Bowling: *First Innings*—Parkin 17.4–3–66–2; Davies 25–5–90–3; Thomas 21–3–98–2; Dale 3–0–20–0; Croft 11–1–57–0; Cosker 21–9–48–2. *Second Innings*—Powell 3–0–7–0; Cherry 2–2–0–0.

Glamorgan

*S. P. James c Lewis b Smith	3	A. P. Davies b Smith	30
D. D. Cherry c sub b Smith	3	D. A. Cosker c Fisher b Harvey	3
A. Dale c and b Alleyne	36	O. T. Parkin b Harvey	1
M. J. Powell b Harvey	135	B 16, l-b 15, n-b 16	47
M. P. Maynard lbw b Lewis	33		
†M. A. Wallace c Taylor b Smith	0	1/6 (1) 2/8 (2) 3/118 (3) 4/190 (5)	407
R. D. B. Croft not out	101	5/191 (6) 6/257 (4) 7/283 (8)	
S. D. Thomas c Fisher b Harvey	9	8/376 (9) 9/391 (10) 10/407 (11)	

Bonus points – Glamorgan 5, Gloucestershire 2.

Bowling: Smith 27–5–83–4; Lewis 21–3–94–1; Harvey 20–5–71–4; Gidman 3–1–10–0; Alleyne 11–0–61–1; Fisher 18–2–57–0.

Umpires: T. E. Jesty and M. J. Kitchen.

At Chester-le-Street, August 16, 17. GLAMORGAN beat DURHAM by ten wickets.

At Northampton, August 21, 22, 23. GLAMORGAN lost to NORTHAMPTONSHIRE by eight wickets.

GLAMORGAN v NOTTINGHAMSHIRE

At Colwyn Bay, August 27, 28, 29, 30. Drawn. Glamorgan 10 pts, Nottinghamshire 12 pts. Toss: Nottinghamshire.

A slow pitch, described as "a turgid strip of rolled mud" by one Nottinghamshire source, conspired with rain to produce stalemate. The match began badly for Glamorgan: Jones, whose pace might have squeezed some life from the wicket, managed just one over before straining his ribs. Nottinghamshire's openers duly put on 172 and Gallian reached an impeccable 162 by the close. But the perseverance of the spinners Cosker and Croft was rewarded on the second morning as seven wickets fell for 136. Glamorgan then lost two early wickets themselves, but this proved

---

STEVE JAMES AT COLWYN BAY

8 and 152*	v Lancashire (drawn)	1992
10 and 32	v Durham (won by 113 runs)	1993
12 and 3	v Lancashire (lost by 220 runs).	1994
6 and 84	v Middlesex (lost by eight wickets)	1995
162	v Nottinghamshire (drawn)	1997
259*	v Nottinghamshire (won by an innings and 118 runs)	1999
309*	v Sussex (won by an innings and 60 runs)	2000
184	v Nottinghamshire (drawn).	**2002**

Total: 1,221 runs at an average of 135.66.

Research: Andrew Hignell

---

deceptive, and Nottinghamshire found the going just as hard. James drove sweetly through the off side, punched to leg and maintained his astonishing record at Colwyn Bay, while Dale ended a wait of over a year – since his last visit here – for a hundred. Boje took six well-earned wickets, but Glamorgan still made 495 – a lead of 31. Rain lopped more than 60 overs from the last two days and, in a dull conclusion, Afzaal and Boje improved their batting averages against an attack missing Kasprowicz, who had sore shins.

Close of play: First day, Nottinghamshire 325-3 (Gallian 162, Randall 2); Second day, Glamorgan 248-3 (James 143, Dale 27); Third day, Glamorgan 495.

Nottinghamshire

G. E. Welton c Wallace b Kasprowicz	92	– (2) lbw b Cosker		33
*J. E. R. Gallian c James b S. D. Thomas	171	– (1) c Hemp b Dale		1
D. J. Bicknell c James b Cosker	20	– c Hemp b Cosker		16
U. Afzaal c Wallace b Kasprowicz.	40	– not out		104
S. J. Randall c Wallace b S. D. Thomas	5			
B. M. Shafayat c I. J. Thomas b Cosker	44	– (5) b Cosker		31
N. Boje b Croft	31	– (6) c James b I. J. Thomas		70
†C. M. W. Read not out	31	– (7) not out		0
P. J. Franks b Cosker	5			
R. J. Logan lbw b Cosker	0			
G. J. Smith c Dale b Croft.	5			
B 5, l-b 9, w 4, n-b 2	20	B 7, l-b 8, w 4		19

1/172 (1) 2/225 (3) 3/317 (4) 4/328 (5)   **464**   1/1 (1) 2/54 (3) 3/71 (2)   (5 wkts) **274**
5/341 (2) 6/419 (7) 7/419 (6)   4/131 (5) 5/274 (6)
8/443 (9) 9/457 (10) 10/464 (11)

Bonus points – Nottinghamshire 5, Glamorgan 1 (130 overs: 414-5).

Bowling: *First Innings*—Kasprowicz 32–10–69–2; Jones 1–0–4–0; S. D. Thomas 23–3–83–2; Croft 39.4–1–136–2; Dale 4–0–23–0; Cosker 43–4–135–4. *Second Innings*—S. D. Thomas 5–0–11–0; Dale 5–2–15–1; Cosker 29–6–101–3; Croft 33–3–106–0; I. J. Thomas 6–0–26–1.

Glamorgan

*S. P. James st Read b Boje	184	M. S. Kasprowicz not out		35
I. J. Thomas b Smith	4	D. A. Cosker c Welton b Logan		1
D. L. Hemp b Smith	4	S. P. Jones b Boje		12
M. P. Maynard c Bicknell b Boje	56	B 5, l-b 16, w 2, n-b 4		27
A. Dale b Boje	109			
†M. A. Wallace lbw b Boje	21	1/13 (2) 2/21 (3) 3/154 (4) 4/371 (5)		495
R. D. B. Croft c Read b Boje	9	5/380 (1) 6/404 (7) 7/421 (6)		
S. D. Thomas c Randall b Logan	33	8/461 (8) 9/474 (10) 10/495 (11)		

Bonus points – Glamorgan 5, Nottinghamshire 3 (130 overs: 483-9).

Bowling: Smith 22–5–73–2; Logan 24–6–99–2; Franks 16–1–62–0; Boje 42–6–128–6; Randall 22–5–89–0; Afzaal 2–0–10–0; Shafayat 3–0–13–0.

Umpires: N. G. Cowley and J. F. Steele.

GLAMORGAN v WORCESTERSHIRE

At Cardiff, September 5, 6, 7, 8. Drawn. Glamorgan 12 pts, Worcestershire 11 pts. Toss: Glamorgan.

With every point crucial to Worcestershire's promotion push, and the first three days blighted by rain, Hick faced a dilemma on the third evening: gamble on victory by declaring behind to set up a run-chase, or play safe by pushing on for three more bonus points? He played safe, a decision he may have regretted two games later when Worcestershire narrowly missed promotion. As it turned out, they didn't take full bonus points either: Peters, with his second Championship century of the season, and Solanki put on 167 for the fourth wicket, but there was little resistance from the others and Worcestershire were all out for 381. Davies, who opened the bowling in Kasprowicz's absence, took a career-best five for 79. Earlier, Glamorgan had racked up 447 as Dale scored a second successive century and Powell, reinstated after an argument with a team-mate had cost him his place, hit a stylish 84.

Close of play: First day, Glamorgan 290-4 (Dale 50, Hughes 12); Second day, Worcestershire 99-1 (Peters 39, Hick 38); Third day, Worcestershire 288-3 (Peters 108, Solanki 83).

Glamorgan

I. J. Thomas c Solanki b Ali	56	– (2) c Pipe b Sheriyar		2
M. P. Maynard c Leatherdale b Sheriyar	37	– (1) c Peters b Ali		31
D. L. Hemp run out	33	– not out		69
M. J. Powell c Pipe b Sheriyar	84	– not out		60
A. Dale not out	127			
J. Hughes c Smith b Sheriyar	31			
†M. A. Wallace c Pipe b Ali	9			
*R. D. B. Croft b Ali	17			
S. D. Thomas b Batty	2			
A. P. Davies lbw b Batty	0			
O. T. Parkin c Solanki b Sheriyar	16			
B 9, l-b 12, w 4, n-b 10	35	B 5, l-b 2, w 6, n-b 6		19

1/77 (2) 2/112 (1) 3/175 (3) 4/267 (4)   447   1/6 (2) 2/60 (1)   (2 wkts) 181
5/335 (6) 6/369 (7) 7/391 (8)
8/408 (9) 9/408 (10) 10/447 (11)

Bonus points – Glamorgan 5, Worcestershire 3 (130 overs: 446-9).

Bowling: *First Innings*—Mason 28–6–119–0; Sheriyar 30.5–9–81–4; Ali 24–6–70–3; Batty 32–7–104–2; Hick 5–0–19–0; Leatherdale 11–2–33–0. *Second Innings*—Mason 8–0–17–0; Sheriyar 8–0–34–1; Batty 17–3–39–0; Ali 5–0–15–1; Solanki 10–2–43–0; Hick 7–3–21–0; Leatherdale 1–0–5–0.

Worcestershire

S. D. Peters st Wallace b Dale	130	
A. Singh lbw b Parkin	20	
*G. A. Hick c Wallace b Davies	58	
B. F. Smith b Davies	10	
V. S. Solanki st Wallace b Croft	94	
D. A. Leatherdale c Maynard b Croft	8	
G. J. Batty b Davies	4	
†D. J. Pipe b Davies	26	

Kabir Ali c and b Parkin 3
M. S. Mason c S. D. Thomas b Davies . . 12
A. Sheriyar not out 6
    B 2, l-b 4, w 2, n-b 2 10

1/37 (2) 2/132 (3) 3/146 (4)   381
4/313 (5) 5/329 (6) 6/329 (1) 7/344 (7)
8/351 (9) 9/374 (10) 10/381 (8)

Bonus points – Worcestershire 4, Glamorgan 3.

Bowling: Parkin 23–6–76–2; Davies 23.4–3–79–5; Dale 11–1–47–1; S. D. Thomas 16–0–91–0; Croft 32–10–82–2.

Umpires: D. J. Constant and I. J. Gould.

GLAMORGAN v NORTHAMPTONSHIRE

At Cardiff, September 18, 19, 20, 21. Drawn. Glamorgan 10 pts, Northamptonshire 12 pts. Toss: Northamptonshire.

Neither side was challenging for promotion and the season's last match brought free-wheeling batting and 1,548 runs – the highest first-class aggregate at Sophia Gardens. On a true pitch, Michael Powell set the tone with a vigorous 113, ended by a rearing ball from Northamptonshire's replacement overseas player, Inness, who finished with a hard-earned seven for 90. When Northamptonshire replied, White, fresh from scoring 277 against Gloucestershire, hit a half-century which brimmed with aggression, before Penberthy's watchful 130 and Brophy's punchier 110 rebuilt a sagging innings. Northamptonshire led by 82, but they were soon back in the red. Maynard was unstoppable as he crashed a 95-ball hundred and Hemp was not much slower: in 43 overs together they hit 252 – a county record for the second wicket. Croft's declaration on 528 left a stiff target of 447 in 87 overs. After losing early wickets Northamptonshire concentrated on survival; Mark Powell's second hundred, in only his fourth Championship match, ensured they made it.

Close of play: First day, Northamptonshire 3-0 (White 3, Powell 0); Second day, Northamptonshire 409-8 (Penberthy 120, Inness 25); Third day, Glamorgan 470-5 (Powell 82, Croft 43).

Glamorgan

M. P. Maynard lbw b Penberthy	50	– st Bailey b White	151
†M. A. Wallace b Inness	12	– c Bailey b Greenidge	1
D. L. Hemp c Bailey b Inness	12	– b White	108
M. J. Powell c Bailey b Inness	113	– b Greenidge	92
A. Dale c Greenidge b Cook	29	– c Powell b Brown	50
J. Hughes lbw b White	26	– c Sales b Brown	3
*R. D. B. Croft not out	59	– not out	71
S. D. Thomas c Brown b Inness	22	– c Powell b Greenidge	17
D. S. Harrison b Inness	0		
A. P. Davies b Inness	18		
D. A. Cosker c and b Inness	0		
B 1, l-b 2, w 4	7	B 8, l-b 5, w 12, n-b 10	35

1/26 (2) 2/46 (3) 3/87 (1) 4/149 (5)   348
5/226 (6) 6/254 (4) 7/304 (8)
8/312 (9) 9/348 (10) 10/348 (11)

1/23 (2) 2/275 (3)   (7 wkts dec.) 528
3/286 (1) 4/375 (5)
5/385 (6) 6/482 (4) 7/528 (8)

Bonus points – Glamorgan 3, Northamptonshire 3.

Bowling: *First Innings*—Greenidge 18–3–73–0; Inness 26–5–90–7; Cassar 12–0–50–0; Penberthy 14–5–30–1; Brown 16–5–45–0; Cook 10.2–2–38–1; White 4–0–19–1. *Second Innings*—Greenidge 15–0–108–3; Inness 14–1–63–0; Cassar 16–1–85–0; Penberthy 5–0–22–0; Brown 32–2–124–2; Cook 12–0–71–0; White 10–0–42–2.

Northamptonshire

R. A. White c Dale b Thomas	69	– c Wallace b Davies	6
M. J. Powell c Wallace b Thomas	7	– not out	108
D. J. Sales b Davies	14	– b Harrison	5
J. W. Cook c Wallace b Harrison	23	– c Cosker b Croft	30
*A. L. Penberthy not out	130	– c Wallace b Thomas	5
M. E. Cassar c Hughes b Thomas	8	– c Cosker b Croft	41
G. L. Brophy c Croft b Harrison	110	– lbw b Cosker	5
†T. M. B. Bailey lbw b Cosker	4	– not out	24
C. G. Greenidge c Maynard b Davies	4		
M. W. H. Inness c Powell b Thomas	25		
J. F. Brown c Maynard b Thomas	11		
B 3, l-b 10, w 6, n-b 6	25	B 5, l-b 5, w 8	18

1/34 (2) 2/61 (3) 3/96 (4) 4/125 (1)   430   1/20 (1) 2/31 (3)   (6 wkts) 242
5/145 (6) 6/319 (7) 7/329 (8)   3/69 (4) 4/74 (5)
8/355 (9) 9/410 (10) 10/430 (11)   5/147 (6) 6/152 (7)

Bonus points – Northamptonshire 5, Glamorgan 3.

Bowling: *First Innings*—Harrison 23–0–79–2; Thomas 23.3–3–104–5; Davies 21–0–95–2; Cosker 18–5–61–1; Dale 3–0–9–0; Croft 19–5–63–0; Powell 2–0–6–0. *Second Innings*—Davies 20–3–54–1; Harrison 16–6–53–1; Thomas 13–2–39–1; Croft 19–4–59–2; Cosker 12–3–22–1; Dale 2–2–0–0; Maynard 1–0–5–0.

Umpires: J. W. Holder and A. A. Jones.

COUNTY MEMBERSHIP

	1992	2001	2002	Variation
Derbyshire	1,976	1,877	2,019	+142
Durham	6,566	5,678	6,161	+483
Essex	8,642	6,181	7,827	+1,646
Glamorgan	3,680	7,680	7,119	−561
Gloucestershire	4,699	5,800	6,134	+334
Hampshire	5,494	4,839	5,233	+394
Kent	4,986	7,259	7,390	+131
Lancashire	13,644	11,674	10,431	−1,243
Leicestershire	2,564	4,619	4,411	−208
Middlesex	8,597	8,533	8,290	−243
Northamptonshire	2,223	3,822	3,441	−381
Nottinghamshire	4,574	6,759	6,272	−487
Somerset	4,973	6,605	6,901	+296
Surrey	5,247	8,777	8,875	+98
Sussex	4,305	5,409	5,129	−280
Warwickshire	11,170	12,106	11,535	−571
Worcestershire	5,225	5,285	6,325	+1,040
Yorkshire	7,920	15,331	15,056	−275
MCC	19,277	20,187	22,102	+1,915
	125,762	148,421	150,651	+2,230

Note: All the first-class counties now quote their membership in terms of the total number of individuals affiliated to their clubs. Until 1999, Derbyshire, Kent and Yorkshire registered corporate or joint membership as representing one person.

GLOUCESTERSHIRE
NEAR-MUTINY, SOME BOUNTY

Ch'ship 8th in Division 2
C&G quarter-finalists
B&H quarter-finalists
NUL winners of Division 2 – promoted

Player of the season: Jack Russell

Every ten years or so, a seismic shock rocks Gloucestershire's foundations, only for things to return gradually to normal. So it was in 2002. John Bracewell, the director of cricket, had built a highly successful one-day side based on a strong team ethic, but found himself at odds with a few senior players, and came close to being overwhelmed by their personal ambitions.

It was a problem Bracewell had seen coming, and it was partly the result of his belief that players could be selected or dropped according to circumstance: the type of competition, the strengths of the opposition and the need to develop young players all influenced selection at various stages of the season. Jeremy Snape and Martyn Ball, the two off-spinning all-rounders who had earned England recognition, did not take well to the suggestion that they were not automatic choices; the old head of Kim Barnett shook in disbelief; and the overseas player, Ian Harvey, appeared to agree with him. The battle of cricket ideologies quickly burst from the confines of the dressing-room and soon Mark Alleyne was saying publicly that he would give up the captaincy unless he had the full backing of his team.

For Alan Haines, the new chairman, and Tony Brown, the cricket chairman, it was a testing time. They refused to air their views in public, but at a Cheltenham Festival riddled with rumour, the county acted decisively by extending the contracts of both Bracewell and Alleyne. The rebellion was over. Barnett, top of the batting averages at the time, didn't play again and left the club during the winter with a year left on his contract. Snape, who spun just 50 first-class overs all summer, had already been banished to the sidelines; he managed to keep his place in the England one-day squad, but in November he opted to join Leicestershire. Ball, in his benefit year, got his head down, battled for his spot with Ian Fisher, the left-arm spinner who had been signed from Yorkshire, and agreed a new contract. But whispers continued to circulate about the future of Harvey. Some inside the club felt that after four years they had seen the best of him, but the crowd were on his side and remained captivated by his barnstorming approach. Finally, a deal was drawn up and accepted: Gloucestershire retained an established match-winner to go with their enterprising signing for 2003, Jonty Rhodes.

So much for the turmoil. On the field, the stated ambition was to win a one-day trophy and gain promotion in the Championship. For once the knockouts passed Gloucestershire by, though they won Division Two of the Norwich Union League with style and purpose. But the Championship was a shambles. Gloucestershire won just two matches all season as a promising start evaporated amid the internecine strife. This led to accusations that some of the players were not trying, albeit wrapped in euphemisms such as "we just didn't compete" and "we failed to build partnerships".

It was ironic, then, that the first-class season ended with a record 12 players making a hundred and seven taking five or more wickets in an innings. Three of the centuries came from newcomers: Alex Gidman and Roger Sillence – who were brought into the side under Bracewell's development strategy – and Fisher. All three were selected principally as bowlers but Gidman averaged 34.87 with the bat from ten matches, Fisher 24.69 from 16, and Sillence's hundred came in only his third game. Five centuries flowed from the bat of Craig Spearman, the former New Zealand Test opener who qualified to play in England through his Welsh mother. Although he was often vulnerable early in an innings, he was a spectator's delight, and his fresh, uncompromising approach and wide range of shots made him lethal once he had played himself in. Despite having to adjust to half a dozen different opening partners, Spearman finished with 1,444 runs.

The sadness was that Barnett, who notched up his 61st hundred in a career that began with Derbyshire in 1979, failed to stay as his regular partner. On the eve of his 42nd birthday, he was still adjusting his technique, holding the bat higher up the handle to give greater leverage to the clean shots which are his hallmark. Before his season ended so abruptly at Cheltenham he was averaging 53.41 and was well on course to pass 1,000 runs in a season for the 17th time. Matt Windows, though, did reach 1,000, for a third time. Runs were not a problem, but wickets were: just three counties were bowled out twice, and only Jon Lewis, with 44, claimed more than 31 victims in the Championship.

Amid the turmoil stood Jack Russell, the wicket-keeper with the crumpled sunhat and irrepressible enthusiasm, who responded to adversity with three centuries. He missed 1,000 runs by a whisker; his 1,016th dismissal for Gloucestershire, in the last game, left him needing just one more to beat the county record. The guard of honour he received from the players at the final match was well earned.

Success in the Norwich Union League could not disguise the fact it was a year of underachievement. But at least there was a promising glimpse of the future in November, when Gloucestershire officially opened their new academy, under the directorship of their former captain, Tony Wright.

Graham Russell

GLOUCESTERSHIRE 2002

Back row: D. Harris (*physiotherapist*), I. D. Fisher, M. A. Hardinges, R. J. Sillence, B. W. Gannon, A. P. R. Gidman, S. P. Pope. *Middle row:* J. G. Bracewell (*first-team coach*), A. J. Wright (*second-team coach*), C. M. Spearman, K. J. Barnett, J. M. M. Averis, J. N. Snape, C. G. Taylor, A. W. Stovold (*director of development*), K. T. Gerrish (*scorer*). *Front row:* J. Lewis, M. G. N. Windows, T. H. C. Hancock, M. W. Alleyne (*captain*), A. H. Haines (*chairman*), R. C. Russell, A. M. Smith, M. C. J. Ball, I. J. Harvey. *Picture by Martin Bennet.*

GLOUCESTERSHIRE RESULTS

All first-class matches – Played 17: Won 3, Lost 7, Drawn 7.
County Championship matches – Played 16: Won 2, Lost 7, Drawn 7.

COUNTY CHAMPIONSHIP AVERAGES: BATTING AND FIELDING

Cap		M	I	NO	R	HS	100s	50s	Avge	Ct/St
2002	C. M. Spearman . . .	16	32	4	1,388	180*	5	6	49.57	15
1999	K. J. Barnett	7	14	2	586	182*	3	0	48.83	1
1999	I. J. Harvey§	6	10	1	390	123	1	2	43.33	6
1985	R. C. Russell†	16	27	5	928	119*	3	4	42.18	36/2
	A. P. R. Gidman . . .	10	17	1	558	117	1	4	34.87	5
1998	M. G. N. Windows† . .	16	30	2	917	144	1	7	32.75	6
1998	T. H. C. Hancock . . .	9	17	3	406	112	1	2	29.00	1
	I. D. Fisher	15	25	3	560	103*	1	4	25.45	2
1990	M. W. Alleyne	14	25	3	555	142*	1	2	25.22	12
	R. J. Sillence	4	7	0	167	101	1	0	23.85	2
2001	C. G. Taylor†	14	27	1	616	126	1	2	23.69	14
	J. A. Pearson†	3	6	1	114	51	0	1	22.80	2
1996	M. C. J. Ball†	6	9	2	117	63	0	0	16.71	3
1999	J. N. Snape	4	7	0	101	28	0	0	14.42	1
1998	J. Lewis	16	25	6	273	57	0	1	14.36	6
1995	A. M. Smith	9	13	6	92	21	0	0	13.14	3
2001	J. M. M. Averis† . . .	5	8	0	83	43	0	0	10.37	3
	B. W. Gannon	6	8	4	31	14	0	0	7.75	1

† *Born in Gloucestershire.*   § *Overseas player.*

BOWLING

	O	M	R	W	BB	5W/i	Avge
I. J. Harvey	152.2	29	533	28	6-68	3	19.03
A. M. Smith	270	55	916	31	5-69	1	29.54
J. M. M. Averis	128	33	432	13	5-51	1	33.23
R. J. Sillence	85	8	397	11	5-63	1	36.09
J. Lewis	536.1	137	1,662	44	6-54	2	37.77
A. P. R. Gidman	99	16	442	10	3-33	0	44.20
B. W. Gannon	137	30	521	11	3-41	0	47.36
M. W. Alleyne	266	59	876	17	3-76	0	51.52
I. D. Fisher	478.1	93	1,643	30	5-87	1	54.76
M. C. J. Ball	233	45	784	14	3-74	0	56.00

Also bowled: K. J. Barnett 12.4–1–67–1; J. N. Snape 26–1–111–2; C. G. Taylor 10–1–36–0;
M. G. N. Windows 3.2–0–20–0.

COUNTY RECORDS

Highest score for:	318*	W. G. Grace v Yorkshire at Cheltenham	1876
Highest score against:	310*	M. E. K. Hussey (Northamptonshire) at Bristol . .	2002
Best bowling for:	10-40	E. G. Dennett v Essex at Bristol	1906
Best bowling against:	{10-66	A. A. Mailey (Australians) at Cheltenham	1921
	10-66	K. Smales (Nottinghamshire) at Stroud	1956
Highest total for:	653-6 dec.	v Glamorgan at Bristol	1928
Highest total against:	774-7 dec.	by Australians at Bristol	1948
Lowest total for:	17	v Australians at Cheltenham	1896
Lowest total against:	12	by Northamptonshire at Gloucester	1907

COUNTY OFFICERS

Captain M. W. Alleyne • **Director of cricket** J. G. Bracewell
Director of development A. W. Stovold • **President** G. F. Collis • **Chairman** A. H. Haines
Chief executive T. E. M. Richardson • **Chairman, cricket committee** A. S. Brown
Head groundsman S. Williams • **Scorer** K. T. Gerrish

At Worcester, April 19, 20, 21. 22. GLOUCESTERSHIRE lost to WORCESTERSHIRE by 206 runs.

At Chelmsford, April 24, 25, 26, 27. GLOUCESTERSHIRE drew with ESSEX.

At Oxford, May 8, 9, 10. GLOUCESTERSHIRE beat OXFORD UCCE by 159 runs.

GLOUCESTERSHIRE v NOTTINGHAMSHIRE

At Bristol, May 15, 16, 17. Gloucestershire won by seven wickets. Gloucestershire 18 pts, Nottinghamshire 3 pts. Toss: Nottinghamshire.

Gloucestershire's first win was threatened more by rain on the third day than by their opponents. They dominated from the start, as Averis took five wickets and Gannon flummoxed the Nottinghamshire batsmen with a slower ball that they seemed to lose above the sightscreen. Around 50 spectators were moved as a result, but it had little effect and Nottinghamshire crashed to 197. They then failed to run out Spearman on nought, and were given plenty of time to ponder the miss while he cut and drove a meaty 118. Windows was more attritional, but his 53 on the second morning was equally important and held Gloucestershire together against an ageing ball that was beginning to swing. A lively partnership between Fisher and Averis boosted the lead to 150. Hopes of a Nottinghamshire revival grew as Welton made an unflustered 68 in their second innings – and faded when he hooked to square leg. Pietersen and a 90-minute break for rain dragged things out, but his five partners scraped only 20, and Gloucestershire were left a trifling target.

Close of play: First day, Gloucestershire 165-2 (Spearman 99, Windows 25); Second day, Nottinghamshire 108-5 (Harris 0).

Nottinghamshire

*D. J. Bicknell b Alleyne	38	– c Spearman b Lewis	0
G. E. Welton lbw b Averis	0	– c Lewis b Alleyne	68
U. Afzaal c Taylor b Gannon	34	– lbw b Lewis	4
P. Johnson b Gannon	0	– b Gannon	18
N. Boje c Alleyne b Averis	36	– c Russell b Alleyne	15
K. P. Pietersen c Russell b Lewis	29	– (7) not out	46
†C. M. W. Read c Windows b Averis	16	– (8) c Alleyne b Averis	9
R. J. Logan c Taylor b Averis	3	– (9) c Taylor b Gannon	0
A. J. Harris lbw b Averis	9	– (6) c Russell b Lewis	5
G. J. Smith not out	9	– b Averis	6
M. N. Malik lbw b Gannon	0	– c Taylor b Averis	0
B 1, l-b 6, w 10, n-b 6	23	B 4, l-b 3, w 4	11

1/4 (2) 2/75 (3) 3/81 (4) 4/85 (1)   197   1/0 (1) 2/4 (3) 3/50 (4)   182
5/134 (6) 6/163 (7) 7/172 (5)   4/99 (5) 5/108 (2) 6/124 (6)
8/183 (8) 9/192 (9) 10/197 (11)   7/140 (8) 8/157 (9)
     9/178 (10) 10/182 (11)

Bonus points – Gloucestershire 3.

Bowling: *First Innings*—Lewis 17–0–61–1; Averis 16–4–51–5; Gannon 12–2–41–3; Alleyne 12–4–37–1. *Second Innings*—Lewis 21–8–59–3; Averis 15.5–8–34–3; Gannon 11–2–33–2; Fisher 9–1–34–0; Alleyne 12–6–15–2.

Gloucestershire

C. M. Spearman lbw b Boje	118	– (2) c Harris b Boje	0
K. J. Barnett c Logan b Malik	4	– (1) c Read b Malik	23
C. G. Taylor lbw b Smith	20	– lbw b Malik	0
M. G. N. Windows b Logan	53	– not out	4
*M. W. Alleyne c Boje b Harris	13	– not out	6
J. N. Snape c Read b Harris	3		
†R. C. Russell c Read b Logan	16		
I. D. Fisher c Read b Malik	41		
J. M. M. Averis c Welton b Malik	43		
J. Lewis c Logan b Malik	1		
B. W. Gannon not out	2		
B 4, l-b 12, w 4, n-b 13	33		
	347	**(3 wkts)**	**33**

1/20 (2) 2/104 (3) 3/185 (1) 4/214 (5)   347   1/23 (1) 2/23 (2) 3/23 (3)   (3 wkts) 33
5/218 (6) 6/243 (4) 7/268 (7)
8/339 (8) 9/343 (10) 10/347 (9)

Bonus points – Gloucestershire 3, Nottinghamshire 3.

Bowling: *First Innings*—Smith 23–4–69–1; Malik 18–4–55–4; Harris 20–5–69–2; Logan 25–6–81–2; Boje 21–4–48–1; Pietersen 2–0–9–0. *Second Innings*—Logan 2–0–14–0; Malik 3.4–1–14–2; Boje 2–1–5–1.

Umpires: A. A. Jones and N. A. Mallender.

At Chester-le-Street, May 24, 25, 26, 27. GLOUCESTERSHIRE drew with DURHAM.

GLOUCESTERSHIRE v WORCESTERSHIRE

At Bristol, May 31, June 1, 2. Worcestershire won by 304 runs. Worcestershire 17 pts, Gloucestershire 3 pts. Toss: Worcestershire.

John Bracewell, Gloucestershire's director of cricket, criticised a "two-paced" wicket though in truth his side were embarrassingly off the boil. After choosing to bat, Hick put Worcestershire in control with a typically authoritative 79 but when he and Weston fell the innings spluttered to a halt. It didn't matter: Gloucestershire were soon shot out for 130 in 56 overs, and, after Hick chose not to impose the follow-on, Worcestershire cruised to 324 for three in just 62. Singh's flowing 187, off 190 balls, was a career-best and his brisk tempo allowed a declaration with nearly two days left. Gloucestershire needed 482, but their confidence had gone and it was all over in less than 57 overs, as Ali again ripped through their line-up. The sides swapped places in the table, with Gloucestershire slipping to fifth from fourth, but there was one ray of hope: after a year wrecked by a groin injury, Mike Smith, the left-arm seamer, took four for 61 in Worcestershire's first innings.

Close of play: First day, Worcestershire 287; Second day, Worcestershire 243-1 (Singh 139, Hick 44).

Worcestershire

W. P. C. Weston lbw b Gannon	82	– b Smith	54
A. Singh b Smith	16	– c Lewis b Barnett	187
*G. A. Hick b Gannon	79	– b Alleyne	72
B. F. Smith lbw b Smith	25	– not out	4
V. S. Solanki b Alleyne	41		
D. A. Leatherdale c Russell b Gannon	2		
G. J. Batty c Russell b Smith	16		
†S. J. Rhodes lbw b Lewis	7		
A. J. Bichel c Russell b Smith	0		
Kabir Ali not out	9		
A. Sheriyar lbw b Lewis	2		
B 4, l-b 2, n-b 2	8	B 2, l-b 5	7

1/20 (2) 2/142 (3) 3/194 (4) 4/219 (1)   287   1/148 (1) 2/313 (3)   (3 wkts dec.) 324
5/225 (6) 6/260 (5) 7/275 (7)   3/324 (2)
8/275 (9) 9/281 (8) 10/287 (11)

Bonus points – Worcestershire 2, Gloucestershire 3.

Bowling: *First Innings*—Lewis 23.2–9–65–2; Smith 23–8–61–4; Alleyne 19–5–48–1; Gannon 17–4–50–3; Ball 20–7–57–0. *Second Innings*—Lewis 12–1–63–0; Smith 11–2–51–1; Gannon 11–0–83–0; Alleyne 16–1–59–1; Barnett 11.4–1–61–1.

Gloucestershire

C. M. Spearman c Batty b Ali	18	– (2) c sub b Ali	55
T. H. C. Hancock c Rhodes b Ali	12	– (1) c Weston b Ali	6
K. J. Barnett lbw b Ali	0	– c Batty b Sheriyar	25
M. G. N. Windows c Rhodes b Ali	15	– lbw b Ali	5
C. G. Taylor c and b Bichel	25	– run out	0
*M. W. Alleyne lbw b Sheriyar	1	– c Smith b Leatherdale	29
†R. C. Russell not out	32	– c sub b Leatherdale	20
M. C. J. Ball c Solanki b Bichel	2	– absent hurt	
J. Lewis c Solanki b Ali	5	– (8) b Ali	17
A. M. Smith c Hick b Bichel	7	– (9) b Ali	4
B. W. Gannon b Sheriyar	4	– (10) not out	0
L-b 3, w 2, n-b 4	9	B 1, l-b 3, w 6, n-b 6	16

1/34 (1) 2/34 (3) 3/45 (2) 4/60 (4)   130   1/28 (1) 2/79 (3)   177
5/70 (6) 6/78 (5) 7/84 (8)   3/98 (4) 4/101 (2)
8/89 (9) 9/108 (10) 10/130 (11)   5/104 (5) 6/146 (6)
                                       7/171 (8) 8/171 (7) 9/177 (9)

Bonus points – Worcestershire 3.

Bowling: *First Innings*—Bichel 20–4–50–3; Sheriyar 18.5–7–44–2; Ali 16–6–32–5; Leatherdale 1–0–1–0. *Second Innings*—Bichel 4–0–13–0; Sheriyar 18–4–65–1; Ali 13.5–4–34–5; Leatherdale 8–2–40–2; Batty 13–4–21–0.

Umpires: G. I. Burgess and R. Palmer.

At Bristol, June 23. GLOUCESTERSHIRE lost to SRI LANKANS by 93 runs (see Sri Lankan tour section).

GLOUCESTERSHIRE v ESSEX

At Gloucester, June 26, 27, 28, 29. Essex won by three wickets. Essex 18 pts, Gloucestershire 7 pts. Toss: Gloucestershire.

Gloucestershire claimed the first three days only to be pickpocketed on the last, as Essex once again chased down an improbable target. The pitch offered Cowan seam movement on the first day, but Barnett's century – his 60th, dotted with perfectly struck cover-drives – and a rally from Alleyne and Ball gave Gloucestershire control. They tightened their grip on the second day as shirt sleeves gave way to extra sweaters and Harvey caused trouble with his bustling fast-medium, although a neat 66 by Habib and irksome lower-order resistance kept Essex in the game. The tide turned again as Russell and Fisher, with his first hundred, obdurately boosted Gloucestershire's lead, but, set 381 in a minimum of 80 overs, Essex attacked with gusto. Robinson drove powerfully to all corners, added 111 with Jefferson and 180 with Habib, and charged to a high-quality 175. By the time a reinvigorated Harvey was recalled, it was too late. Alleyne, the despondent home captain, admitted that defeat ended his promotion hopes. After the King's School groundsman had been taken ill a month earlier, the pitch – which easily lasted four days – was prepared by his 18-year-old apprentice, Richard Bowman.

Close of play: First day, Essex 11-0 (Robinson 9, Jefferson 2); Second day, Essex 283-9 (Cowan 30, Ilott 0); Third day, Gloucestershire 245-6 (Russell 74, Fisher 74).

Gloucestershire

C. M. Spearman c Robinson b Cowan	0	– (2) c Jefferson b Stephenson 15
K. J. Barnett b Cowan	106	– (1) b Ilott 5
C. G. Taylor c Jefferson b Cowan	5	– c and b Stephenson 36
M. G. N. Windows c Middlebrook b Napier	21	– lbw b Ilott 12
I. J. Harvey c sub b Napier	56	– lbw b Stephenson 0
*M. W. Alleyne lbw b Ilott	87	– lbw b Napier 11
†R. C. Russell b Napier	0	– c Flower b Middlebrook 107
I. D. Fisher lbw b Stephenson	1	– not out 103
M. C. J. Ball lbw b Cowan	63	– not out 5
J. Lewis b Cowan	11	
B. W. Gannon not out	0	
B 6, l-b 7, w 4, n-b 16	33	B 4, l-b 12, w 4, n-b 8 28

1/0 (1) 2/16 (3) 3/117 (4) 4/171 (2)   **383**   1/5 (1) 2/41 (2)   (7 wkts dec.) **322**
5/207 (5) 6/211 (7) 7/214 (8)   3/70 (4) 4/71 (5)
8/372 (6) 9/374 (9) 10/383 (10)   5/84 (3) 6/90 (6) 7/297 (7)

Bonus points – Gloucestershire 4, Essex 3.

Bowling: *First Innings*—Cowan 20.2–6–68–5; Ilott 22–6–53–1; Stephenson 12–1–58–1; Dakin 5–0–30–0; Middlebrook 20–2–58–0; Napier 11–1–70–3; Sharif 6–0–33–0. *Second Innings*—Cowan 11–0–40–0; Ilott 12–5–25–2; Stephenson 29–5–105–3; Napier 16–4–46–1; Middlebrook 25–9–57–1; Sharif 5–0–33–0.

Essex

*D. D. J. Robinson c Russell b Gannon	33	– b Harvey 175
W. I. Jefferson lbw b Lewis	2	– b Ball 47
J. D. Middlebrook c Barnett b Lewis	4	– (5) lbw b Harvey 9
A. Habib run out	66	– (3) b Harvey 82
†A. Flower c Russell b Harvey	7	– (4) c Windows b Harvey 13
G. R. Napier c Fisher b Harvey	3	– b Harvey 20
J. M. Dakin c Gannon b Harvey	29	– (8) not out 6
J. P. Stephenson c Lewis b Harvey	57	– (9) not out 4
Z. K. Sharif b Lewis	42	
A. P. Cowan not out	60	– (7) b Harvey 3
M. C. Ilott lbw b Harvey	10	
L-b 9, w 4, n-b 2	15	B 1, l-b 19, n-b 2 22

1/11 (2) 2/23 (3) 3/47 (1) 4/56 (5)   **325**   1/111 (2) 2/291 (3)   (7 wkts) **381**
5/60 (6) 6/100 (7) 7/172 (4)   3/315 (4) 4/327 (5)
8/232 (8) 9/271 (9) 10/325 (11)   5/365 (6) 6/371 (7) 7/376 (1)

Bonus points — Essex 3, Gloucestershire 3.

Bowling: *First Innings*—Lewis 34–11–79–3; Gannon 23–7–56–1; Harvey 22.1–5–64–5; Ball 23–6–57–0; Fisher 18–6–45–0; Alleyne 7–3–15–0. *Second Innings*—Lewis 16–1–63–0; Harvey 17.5–1–90–6; Ball 12–3–62–1; Gannon 5–1–28–0; Alleyne 15–2–54–0; Fisher 12–0–58–0; Barnett 1–0–6–0.

Umpires: A. Clarkson and I. J. Gould.

At Derby, July 3, 4, 5, 6. GLOUCESTERSHIRE drew with DERBYSHIRE.

At Southgate, July 10, 11, 12, 13. GLOUCESTERSHIRE lost to **MIDDLESEX** by five wickets.

GLOUCESTERSHIRE v GLAMORGAN

At Cheltenham, July 19, 20, 21, 22. Glamorgan won by two wickets. Glamorgan 20 pts, Gloucestershire 8 pts. Toss: Gloucestershire.

This match belonged to Maynard. His first lustrous century kept Glamorgan in the contest, and his second clinched it. Upright, and ruthless on anything wide or over-pitched, he guided Glamorgan past the 317 they needed with two overs to spare. On a very quick pitch he batted mostly in a cap for an unbeaten 104-ball 118, and the big crowd – divided in loyalty but united in delight at his skill and sense of adventure – responded with a standing ovation. The match had got off to a fiery start when Hancock and Harvey were poleaxed by Kasprowicz and taken to hospital for head scans; Hancock, bowled off his helmet, was doubly unfortunate. Taylor, Russell and Fisher showed guts and skill thereafter, but were overshadowed by Maynard. His 140 came off 166 balls and kept Gloucestershire's first-innings lead down to 23. The gap should have been stretched beyond Glamorgan's reach as Spearman carried his bat for a thrilling career-best 180, but his team-mates managed just 82 between them. Then came Maynard.

Close of play: First day, Gloucestershire 363-5 (Russell 75, Fisher 38); Second day, Glamorgan 204-4 (Maynard 48, Wallace 30); Third day, Gloucestershire 184-5 (Spearman 125, Fisher 19).

Gloucestershire

T. H. C. Hancock b Kasprowicz	14	– (2) c Wallace b Jones	6
C. M. Spearman c Wallace b Kasprowicz	13	– (1) not out	180
C. G. Taylor lbw b Croft	126	– c Wallace b Kasprowicz	12
M. G. N. Windows c Maynard b Kasprowicz	10	– lbw b Kasprowicz	0
I. J. Harvey retired hurt	19	– (11) c and b Cosker	18
A. P. R. Gidman b Jones	14	– (5) b Thomas	9
*†R. C. Russell c Jones b Thomas	84	– (6) lbw b Croft	0
I. D. Fisher not out	79	– (7) c Wallace b Thomas	27
M. C. J. Ball b Thomas	0	– (8) c Croft b Jones	2
J. Lewis c Jones b Croft	19	– (9) b Jones	0
A. M. Smith lbw b Croft	0	– (10) b Jones	8
B 12, l-b 14, n-b 34	60	B 18, l-b 1, w 8, n-b 4	31
	438		**293**

1/27 (2) 2/28 (1) 3/44 (4) 4/120 (6) 5/299 (3) 6/393 (7) 7/393 (9) 8/438 (10) 9/438 (11)

1/7 (2) 2/61 (3) 3/61 (4) 4/109 (5) 5/114 (6) 6/201 (7) 7/210 (8) 8/210 (9) 9/258 (10) 10/293 (11)

Bonus points – Gloucestershire 5, Glamorgan 3.

In the first innings, Harvey retired hurt at 71.

Bowling: *First Innings*—Jones 31–9–93–1; Kasprowicz 30–6–120–3; Thomas 29–3–66–2; Dale 4–0–15–0; Croft 26.5–8–73–3; Cosker 8–1–45–0. *Second Innings*—Jones 14–3–67–4; Kasprowicz 15.4–3–40–2; Thomas 17.2–1–66–2; Croft 25–2–84–1; Cosker 6.3–2–17–1.

Glamorgan

*S. P. James c Smith b Gidman	16	– c Spearman b Fisher	74
D. D. Cherry c Spearman b Ball	47	– c Ball b Smith	10
A. Dale lbw b Smith	25	– b Ball	49
M. J. Powell st Russell b Ball	20	– c Russell b Ball	3
M. P. Maynard c and b Smith	140	– not out	118
†M. A. Wallace c and b Fisher	69	– c Spearman b Fisher	11
R. D. B. Croft b Lewis	21	– c Harvey b Fisher	6
S. D. Thomas c Russell b Lewis	11	– run out	11
M. S. Kasprowicz c Ball b Lewis	25	– c Spearman b Ball	1
D. A. Cosker b Smith	1		
S. P. Jones not out	8	– (10) not out	11
B 3, l-b 11, n-b 18	32	B 6, l-b 12, w 2, n-b 6	26

1/34 (1) 2/83 (3) 3/111 (2) 4/154 (4)	**415**	1/24 (2) 2/146 (3) (8 wkts) **320**
5/317 (6) 6/356 (5) 7/377 (8)		3/156 (1) 4/172 (4)
8/378 (7) 9/387 (10) 10/415 (9)		5/203 (6) 6/245 (7)
		7/292 (8) 8/309 (9)

Bonus points – Glamorgan 5, Gloucestershire 3.

Bowling: *First Innings*—Smith 29–7–122–3; Lewis 24.4–8–94–3; Gidman 13–2–48–1; Ball 27–2–102–2; Fisher 11–1–35–1. *Second Innings*—Lewis 10–3–36–0; Smith 9–0–39–1; Gidman 4–0–23–0; Fisher 26.2–3–111–3; Ball 23–1–93–3.

Umpires: B. Dudleston and A. G. T. Whitehead.

GLOUCESTERSHIRE v MIDDLESEX

At Cheltenham, July 24, 25, 26, 27. Drawn. Gloucestershire 12 pts, Middlesex 10 pts. Toss: Gloucestershire.

Before the match Gloucestershire sent a clear message to those players involved in ructions with John Bracewell by extending his contract. Neither Kim Barnett, reported to have a sore calf, nor Jeremy Snape (finger injury) played, and Barnett would not be selected again in 2002. On the field, Gloucestershire's early hold was loosened in the second innings by the magnificent Tufnell, who lured eight batsmen to their downfall. Left to chase 362, Middlesex soon contented themselves with the draw, which left them 15 points clear at the top of the table. There was a special moment for Russell when he caught Strauss and completed his 1,000th first-class dismissal for Gloucestershire – 900 catches and 100 stumpings. Earlier, Hancock's first hundred since 1998 carried them to 196 for one and, although Abdul Razzaq induced a mid-innings stutter, they still ended up with 494. In reply, Middlesex contrived to lose six wickets for 191 on a true pitch and it took a powerful 102 by Weekes to keep Gloucestershire's lead to 131.

Close of play: First day, Gloucestershire 367-6 (Gidman 18, Fisher 18); Second day, Middlesex 218-6 (Weekes 22, Nash 10); Third day, Gloucestershire 175-8 (Lewis 5, Spearman 8).

Out fishing before dawn with Andrew Symonds, Hayden's boat hit a sandbar and sank. They had to swim for an hour to safety through waters they knew to be infested by sharks. "It was a good life lesson," Hayden said.
Greg Baum on Matthew Hayden, page 71

Gloucestershire

T. H. C. Hancock c Nash b Laraman	112	– c Weekes b Tufnell	28
C. M. Spearman c Nash b Laraman	12	– (10) not out	35
C. G. Taylor lbw b Abdul Razzaq	67	– c Hutton b Tufnell	32
M. G. N. Windows c Strauss b Abdul Razzaq	55	– c Strauss b Tufnell	21
*M. W. Alleyne b Abdul Razzaq	62	– c Weekes b Tufnell	23
A. P. R. Gidman b Abdul Razzaq	94	– c Hutton b Tufnell	6
†R. C. Russell c Weekes b Abdul Razzaq	4	– (2) b Tufnell	34
I. D. Fisher c Weekes b Tufnell	18	– (7) c Strauss b Weekes	5
M. C. J. Ball b Cook	33	– (8) c Strauss b Tufnell	3
J. Lewis c Hutton b Cook	8	– (9) c Cook b Tufnell	30
B. W. Gannon not out	5	– lbw b Abdul Razzaq	0
L-b 2, n-b 22	24	– L-b 4, n-b 9	13
	494		**230**

1/43 (2) 2/196 (1) 3/216 (3) 4/323 (5)
5/330 (4) 6/334 (7) 7/367 (8)
8/444 (9) 9/474 (10) 10/494 (6)

1/64 (2) 2/71 (1) 3/115 (4)
4/128 (3) 5/140 (5) 6/153 (7)
7/155 (5) 8/158 (8)
9/229 (9) 10/230 (11)

Bonus points – Gloucestershire 5, Middlesex 2 (130 overs: 447-8).

Bowling: *First Innings*—Abdul Razzaq 34.2–3–125–5; Laraman 33–5–99–2; Cook 17–3–103–2; Tufnell 28–8–64–1; Hutton 3–0–16–0; Weekes 23–3–74–0; Joyce 1–0–11–0. *Second Innings*—Abdul Razzaq 10.3–0–55–1; Laraman 2–0–10–0; Tufnell 39–12–66–8; Weekes 31–4–95–1.

Middlesex

*A. J. Strauss c Windows b Gidman	49	– c Russell b Fisher	26
S. G. Koenig c Russell b Alleyne	33	– lbw b Ball	53
B. L. Hutton run out	22	– c Alleyne b Gannon	88
O. A. Shah run out	65	– (5) c Lewis b Gidman	5
E. C. Joyce c Gidman b Fisher	5	– (6) not out	32
Abdul Razzaq c Spearman b Fisher	0	– (4) c Russell b Gidman	14
P. N. Weekes b Gidman	102	– not out	37
†D. C. Nash lbw b Lewis	43		
S. J. Cook c Taylor b Gidman	13		
A. W. Laraman c Russell b Lewis	2		
P. C. R. Tufnell not out	0		
B 2, l-b 3, w 6, n-b 18	29	B 5, l-b 5	10
	363		**265**

1/76 (1) 2/98 (2) 3/125 (3) 4/146 (5)
5/146 (6) 6/191 (4) 7/305 (8)
8/350 (9) 9/359 (10) 10/363 (7)

1/37 (1) 2/126 (2)   (5 wkts) 265
3/146 (4) 4/158 (5)
5/214 (3)

Bonus points – Middlesex 4, Gloucestershire 3.

Bowling: *First Innings*—Lewis 24–8–87–2; Gannon 16–4–66–0; Alleyne 17–3–58–1; Gidman 13–3–33–3; Ball 17–4–60–0; Fisher 21–6–54–2. *Second Innings*—Lewis 7–1–23–0; Gidman 10–2–18–2; Ball 30–7–68–1; Fisher 25–2–123–1; Gannon 8–2–23–1.

Umpires: J. H. Hampshire and G. Sharp.

At Cheltenham, July 29. GLOUCESTERSHIRE lost to WEST INDIES A by 44 runs (see West Indies A tour section).

At Cardiff, August 7, 8, 9, 10. GLOUCESTERSHIRE drew with GLAMORGAN.

GLOUCESTERSHIRE v NORTHAMPTONSHIRE

At Bristol, August 15, 16, 17, 18. Drawn. Gloucestershire 10 pts, Northamptonshire 12 pts. Toss: Gloucestershire. First-class debut: J. A. Pearson.

A year after his 329 against Essex, Hussey produced another magisterial triple-century, the first against Gloucestershire. He took 13 overs to reach double figures while he sized up an impeccable wicket and a short boundary, and went on to bat for 653 minutes, hitting two sixes and 38 fours in an unbeaten 433-ball 310. Swann made an impressive 183, adding 318 with his captain and belting 114 on the third morning, but the innings will be remembered for the sheer authority of Hussey's cuts and drives. When he finally called a halt, at 746 for nine, Russell hadn't conceded a single bye, a world record. At 99 for four in their second innings, Gloucestershire were still 225 behind, but managed to claw their way back. Gidman hit an orthodox first century, Russell compiled one that was anything but, and they salvaged a draw. On the first day, Harvey's 57-ball 79 had given an early idea of the nature of the pitch. Three other half-centuries included a dogged 51 by James Pearson on debut, while Cassar took six for 34, the first part of a maiden ten-wicket haul. But both achievements were soon dwarfed by Hussey.

Close of play: First day, Northamptonshire 15-0 (Hussey 4, Loye 10); Second day, Northamptonshire 471-5 (Hussey 203, Swann 58); Third day, Gloucestershire 172-4 (Gidman 42, Harvey 33).

Gloucestershire

*C. M. Spearman c Panesar b Cassar	71	– (2) b Cassar	15
J. A. Pearson lbw b Cassar	51	– (1) lbw b Blain	0
C. G. Taylor b Cassar	9	– c Bailey b Cassar	42
M. G. N. Windows c Loye b Cassar	83	– lbw b Blain	21
A. P. R. Gidman lbw b Blain	28	– c Bailey b Swann	117
I. J. Harvey st Bailey b Panesar	79	– c Hussey b Cassar	41
†R. C. Russell c Bailey b Panesar	16	– not out	104
I. D. Fisher lbw b Swann	22	– c Bailey b Cassar	69
M. C. J. Ball not out	6		
J. Lewis c Loye b Cassar	0		
A. M. Smith b Cassar	0		
B 5, l-b 8, w 10, n-b 34	57	B 7, l-b 10, w 2, n-b 18	37

1/137 (1) 2/146 (2) 3/173 (3) 4/218 (5)   **422**
5/329 (6) 6/371 (7) 7/416 (8)
8/416 (4) 9/416 (10) 10/422 (11)

1/17 (1) 2/42 (2) 3/93 (3)   **(7 wkts) 446**
4/99 (4) 5/184 (6)
6/309 (5) 7/446 (8)

Bonus points – Gloucestershire 5, Northamptonshire 3.

Bowling: *First Innings*—Greenidge 18–2–63–0; Blain 13–0–117–1; Cook 12–3–53–0; Penberthy 12–0–47–0; Cassar 10.3–4–34–6; Swann 14–3–39–1; Panesar 18–5–56–2. *Second Innings*—Greenidge 18–2–78–0; Blain 19–2–82–2; Panesar 40–13–80–0; Cassar 21.5–1–100–4; Cook 6–1–33–0; Swann 26–5–50–1; Penberthy 4–1–5–0; Loye 2–1–1–0.

Northamptonshire

*M. E. K. Hussey not out	310	J. A. R. Blain c Smith b Ball	8
M. B. Loye c Pearson b Lewis	16	M. S. Panesar not out	2
D. J. Sales lbw b Ball	70		
J. W. Cook c Harvey b Fisher	32	L-b 9, w 2, n-b 14	25
A. L. Penberthy b Harvey	61		
M. E. Cassar lbw b Harvey	11	1/21 (2) 2/140 (3) (9 wkts dec.) 746	
G. P. Swann c Gidman b Smith	183	3/210 (4) 4/337 (5)	
†T. M. B. Bailey c Taylor b Gidman	26	5/353 (6) 6/671 (7)	
C. G. Greenidge lbw b Fisher	2	7/713 (8) 8/721 (9) 9/736 (10)	

Bonus points – Northamptonshire 5, Gloucestershire 1 (130 overs: 582-5).

Bowling: Lewis 29–7–95–1; Smith 31–3–113–1; Harvey 25–4–106–2; Gidman 20–2–121–1; Ball 32–2–157–2; Fisher 27–2–129–2; Windows 3–0–16–0.

Umpires: N. J. Llong and R. Palmer.

At Nottingham, August 21, 22, 23. GLOUCESTERSHIRE lost to NOTTINGHAMSHIRE by an innings and 84 runs.

GLOUCESTERSHIRE v DERBYSHIRE

At Bristol, September 4, 5, 6, 7. Drawn. Gloucestershire 7 pts, Derbyshire 7 pts. Toss: Gloucestershire.

The match had a peculiar, back-to-front feel, with wickets falling like ninepins in the first innings and batsmen cavorting in the second. On the first morning, Gloucestershire's openers put on an untroubled 93, before Welch induced mayhem by grabbing six for 60 with late swing, and all ten wickets crashed for 99. On a friendly pitch, Derbyshire floundered too, as Smith took five wickets for the first time since 2000. Then, with a three-day finish looming, the game exploded into runs. Windows pulled and cut his way to a sparkling 126-ball century, and Roger Sillence, playing as a pace bowler in his third Championship match, crashed a full-blooded 101 off 113 balls. Russell jabbed his way to a contrasting hundred – his third of the season – to give Gloucestershire their highest second-innings total and leave Derbyshire staring at a mammoth 583 to win. Amid last-day showers, a handsome 175 by Di Venuto made sure of a draw that was crucial to maintaining their push for promotion.

Close of play: First day, Derbyshire 153-6 (Sutton 24, Welch 10); Second day, Gloucestershire 290-5 (Windows 143, Russell 37); Third day, Derbyshire 155-1 (Di Venuto 92, Bassano 17).

Gloucestershire

T. H. C. Hancock c Di Venuto b Welch	54	– (2) c Bassano b Mohammad Ali	15
C. M. Spearman c Sutton b Welch	30	– (1) b Dean	26
C. G. Taylor c Sutton b Welch	22	– b Welch	12
M. G. N. Windows c Bassano b Welch	8	– c Bassano b Mohammad Ali	144
*M. W. Alleyne lbw b Dean	13	– c Gait b Welch	12
A. P. R. Gidman c Di Venuto b Dean	2	– b Wharton	9
†R. C. Russell b Dowman b Mohammad Ali	26	– not out	119
I. D. Fisher c Mohammad Ali b Welch	0	– c Sutton b Welch	0
R. J. Sillence c Sutton b Welch	0	– c Bassano b Mohammad Ali	101
J. Lewis c Welch b Dean	1	– c Dean b Wharton	57
A. M. Smith not out	2	– not out	18
L-b 9, w 9, n-b 16	34	B 1, l-b 15, w 8, n-b 40	64

1/93 (1) 2/106 (2) 3/128 (4) 4/151 (5)   **192**   1/43 (1) 2/43 (2)   (9 wkts dec.) **577**
5/155 (6) 6/155 (3) 7/161 (8)   3/84 (3) 4/110 (5)
8/161 (9) 9/162 (10) 10/192 (7)   5/178 (6) 6/292 (4)
                                    7/292 (8) 8/453 (9) 9/543 (10)

Bonus points – Derbyshire 3.

Bowling: *First Innings*—Dean 24–9–63–3; Mohammad Ali 12.2–3–60–1; Welch 20–7–60–6; Dowman 1–1–0–0. *Second Innings*—Welch 33–8–147–3; Dean 21–3–105–1; Mohammad Ali 35–4–170–3; Dowman 8–2–36–0; Wharton 29–9–87–2; Hewson 3–0–16–0.

Having dismissed Cork for a golden duck on the first day, Swann admitted he was especially pleased, describing him as "not the most popular guy on the circuit". Cork's response was both dramatic and predictable.
Northamptonshire v Derbyshire, page 718

Derbyshire

A. I. Gait c Spearman b Lewis	24	– c Russell b Lewis	33
*M. J. Di Venuto c Hancock b Smith	8	– not out	175
C. W. G. Bassano lbw b Smith	4	– lbw b Fisher	51
M. P. Dowman c Gidman b Silence	16	– (6) b Silence	3
S. A. Selwood lbw b Smith	37	– c Alleyne b Silence	10
D. R. Hewson b Lewis	12	– (4) c Russell b Silence	7
†L. D. Sutton b Smith	46	– not out	6
G. Welch c and b Lewis	11		
Mohammad Ali c Russell b Lewis	0		
K. J. Dean c Spearman b Smith	9		
L. J. Wharton not out	0		
W 2, n-b 18	20	B 2, l-b 8, w 2, n-b 22	34

1/36 (2) 2/40 (1) 3/40 (3) 4/68 (4)   187   1/95 (1) 2/224 (3)   (5 wkts) 319
5/92 (6) 6/136 (5) 7/157 (8)   3/265 (4) 4/283 (5)
8/157 (9) 9/180 (10) 10/187 (7)   5/295 (6)

Bonus points – Gloucestershire 3.

Bowling: *First Innings*—Lewis 20–5–63–4; Smith 20.4–6–69–5; Silence 6–0–36–1; Alleyne 7–2–19–0. *Second Innings*—Lewis 24–5–78–1; Smith 13–2–44–0; Gidman 6–1–50–0; Alleyne 5–2–33–0; Fisher 25.2–7–54–1; Silence 13–4–50–3.

Umpires: M. J. Harris and P. Willey.

At Northampton, September 11, 12, 13. GLOUCESTERSHIRE lost to NORTHAMPTONSHIRE by an innings and 59 runs.

GLOUCESTERSHIRE v DURHAM

At Bristol, September 18, 19, 20. Gloucestershire won by ten wickets. Gloucestershire 19 pts, Durham 4 pts. Toss: Durham.

Losing the contest between the Championship's two weakest sides summed up Durham's season. They began the match with three batting points from their last seven games, and it showed, as Silence bowled fast and straight to take five for 63. In reply, Harmison also took five wickets, but the pitch was benign and Spearman's aggressive 89 and Gidman's elegant 96 built a lead of 143. Durham's first century opening stand of 2002 eroded the deficit, and at lunch on the third day they were well placed, with a lead of 107 and only four wickets down. But brilliant catches by Alleyne and Fisher accelerated yet another collapse. The final wicket was Russell's 1,016th first-class dismissal for Gloucestershire, drawing him level with Jack Board's county record (set between 1891 and 1914). In the first innings, he had also equalled the county record of six in an innings, and he finished with nine in the match. He left the field with a guard of honour and a tip of his famous sunhat. Chasing 170, Spearman destroyed the Durham attack and secured victory with an unbeaten century – his fifth of the season.

Close of play: First day, Gloucestershire 144-4 (Spearman 80); Second day, Durham 120-1 (Gough 70, Hodge 2).

Durham

M. A. Gough b Sillence	. . . .	33	– c Russell b Lewis	. . . .	78
G. J. Pratt c Russell b Smith	. . . .	6	– c Alleyne b Fisher	. . . .	41
*B. J. Hodge c Russell b Sillence	. . . . .	73	– c Russell b Alleyne	. . . .	39
G. J. Muchall c Russell b Fisher	. . . . . .	6	– c Spearman b Alleyne	. . . .	29
A. M. Thorpe c Spearman b Lewis	. . . .	1	– c Alleyne b Fisher	. . . .	31
I. Pattison c Spearman b Sillence	. . . .	27	– c Windows b Fisher	. . . .	21
†A. Pratt c Russell b Sillence	. . . .	25	– b Smith	. . . .	1
I. D. Hunter c Russell b Sillence	. . . . .	2	– (10) not out	. . . .	20
G. D. Bridge c Russell b Smith	. . . . . .	17	– (8) c Fisher b Smith	. . . .	4
A. M. Davies not out	. . . .	4	– (9) lbw b Sillence	. . . .	5
S. J. Harmison c Windows b Lewis	. . . .	1	– c Russell b Fisher	. . . .	15
B 3, l-b 2, w 4, n-b 12	. . . . . .	21	B 5, l-b 3, w 2, n-b 18	. . . .	28

1/10 (2) 2/68 (1) 3/93 (4) 4/94 (5)   216   1/112 (2) 2/147 (1) 3/198 (3)   312
5/163 (3) 6/178 (6) 7/190 (8)   4/205 (4) 5/258 (5) 6/259 (7)
8/195 (7) 9/211 (9) 10/216 (11)   7/263 (8) 8/271 (6)
                                                               9/279 (9) 10/312 (11)

Bonus points – Durham 1, Gloucestershire 3.

Bowling: *First Innings*—Lewis 15.3–2–59–2; Smith 12–2–29–2; Sillence 15–1–63–5; Fisher 23–7–58–1; Alleyne 3–1–2–0. *Second Innings*—Lewis 14–3–42–1; Smith 18–3–44–2; Alleyne 17–4–64–2; Sillence 16–1–79–1; Fisher 21.4–5–67–4; Gidman 1–0–8–0.

Gloucestershire

C. M. Spearman c A. Pratt b Harmison	. . . . .	89	– not out	. . . .	114
J. A. Pearson c Hodge b Davies	. . . .	19	– retired hurt	. . . .	18
T. H. C. Hancock c A. Pratt b Harmison	. . . .	3	– not out	. . . .	23
M. G. N. Windows c Pattison b Hodge	. . . .	38		
*M. W. Alleyne c Hodge b Harmison	. . . .	0		
A. P. R. Gidman c Muchall b Gough	. . . . .	96		
†R. C. Russell c A. Pratt b Pattison	. . . . .	35		
I. D. Fisher c A. Pratt b Harmison	. . . . . .	37		
R. J. Sillence c Thorpe b Gough	. . . .	9		
J. Lewis c A. Pratt b Harmison	. . . .	13		
A. M. Smith not out	. . . .	7		
B 4, l-b 5, w 2, n-b 2	. . . .	13	B 8, l-b 2, n-b 6	. . . .	16

1/38 (2) 2/41 (3) 3/144 (4) 4/144 (5)   359   (no wkt) 171
5/159 (1) 6/279 (7) 7/304 (6)
8/314 (9) 9/344 (10) 10/359 (8)

Bonus points – Gloucestershire 4, Durham 3.

In the second innings Pearson retired hurt at 95.

Bowling: *First Innings*—Harmison 22.5–5–65–5; Hunter 7–0–35–0; Davies 17–3–63–1; Bridge 21–5–68–0; Pattison 10–1–69–1; Hodge 10–3–28–1; Gough 11–4–22–2. *Second Innings*—Harmison 11–3–20–0; Davies 5–2–18–0; Pattison 3–0–17–0; Hunter 3–1–17–0; Bridge 5.2–0–38–0; Hodge 3–0–25–0; Muchall 3–0–26–0.

Umpires: N. G. Cowley and G. Sharp.

HAMPSHIRE
NO BED
OF ROSES

Ch'ship 7th in Division 1 – relegated
C&G 4th round
B&H group stage
NUL 7th in Division 2

Player of the season: Shaun Udal

Hampshire began the season with high expectations. John Crawley had been lured south on the back of promotion in the Championship; the development of the Rose Bowl continued with the opening of a £7m pavilion; and news that the ground would be granted international status for 2003 led to a share issue designed to raise a further £4m.

Those expectations were never fulfilled. Hampshire won only 12 games out of 40 in all cricket, were promptly relegated in the Championship, and made very little impact in any one-day competition. The chairman of the newly created Hampshire Cricket, Rod Bransgrove, who carries much of the county's financial burden, expressed his discontent by sacking Jimmy Cook as coach with a third of the season remaining. Cook, who shouldered the blame for a team that rarely functioned as a unit or even as individuals, was a convenient scapegoat, and results did not improve after his undignified departure.

He had not been helped by the fact that Alex Morris played in only two first-class matches, and that injuries to the durable Adrian Aymes and, later, Chris Tremlett reduced his options. However, there was one other excuse for a season of solid underachievement, and that was the pitch. Only the three most experienced hands, the captain Robin Smith, the overseas player Neil Johnson and Crawley, made first-class centuries. Three of the four they made came away from home. And only the off-spinner Shaun Udal, again overlooked by England, passed the modest target for a front-line bowler of 50 wickets.

With 500 runs as well, Udal was one of the few players who could look back on 2002 with satisfaction. Others, not least Derek Kenway, who like Tremlett spent the winter at the ECB Academy in Adelaide, failed to live up to their promise and master the combination of Division One attacks and the demons in the Rose Bowl wicket. The batting was stiffened by the return in mid-season from Loughborough University of John Francis, who hinted at what might lie ahead by twice improving his best score in the Norwich Union League. But more seasoned batsmen did not take their opportunities, and it was no surprise when Jason Laney and Giles White were allowed to leave; neither had realised his undoubted potential.

With Aymes injured, Hampshire turned to Nic Pothas, possibly the only person in the world with a Greek passport and three one-day caps for South Africa, as his long-term replacement. Pothas, aged 28 and with a first-class batting average of 36, responded with some reliable performances behind the stumps, but it was not until the final Championship innings that he revealed the full extent of his batting ability, scoring 99 against Surrey. Aymes later announced that he would be retiring a year early to become joint-manager of Fleet Town, a local football team in the Dr Martens League.

Alan Mullally was often troubled by a side strain but, when fit, was Hampshire's most dangerous bowler, while Tremlett was on course for another winter at the Academy until he broke a bone in his foot. Johnson, was a big disappointment. Exceptional at slip, he flourished only spasmodically with bat and ball and was never a match-winner. Smith hit centuries against Kent and Leicestershire, and unleashed a few brutal cameos elsewhere, but at 39 he was clearly no longer the batsman of his magnificent prime, and it was in belated acknowledgement of his fading powers that he stepped down from the captaincy after five years in charge. At least the signing of Crawley from Lancashire was a significant plus. He began with 272 at Canterbury and gathered enough runs in the early stages of the season to spend much of the rest of it away with England. Only ten of his 15 first-class matches were for Hampshire and his absence was keenly felt: no one managed 1,000 runs.

After Hampshire were eliminated in the early stages of both the C&G and B&H, the overriding issue of the summer was the unpredictable state of the Rose Bowl surface in its second full season. At best it was low and slow; at worst, close to unplayable. The Indian tourists considered abandoning their game on the second day because they felt it was too dangerous, and eight precious points were docked by the ECB inspectors after all 40 wickets in the Lancashire match tumbled in seven sessions for just 629 runs. The groundsman, Nigel Gray, had been an award-winner in the run-filled days at the old County Ground, but a dry middle-and-late summer did not help his preparations, and the frail confidence of the home batsmen was plainly undermined by the pitch's vagaries.

Once relegation had been confirmed, Bransgrove, an omnipotent figure at the Hampshire helm, wasted no time in reorganising the club. He appointed Paul Terry, who had spent 20 years opening the batting for Hampshire but now lived in Australia, as Cook's successor, and rehired Shane Warne, this time as captain. But when in early 2003, Warne was banned from cricket for using restricted drugs, Bransgrove was forced to rethink. While holding out the possibility of Warne leading Hampshire in 2004, he turned to another high-profile bowler, Pakistan's Shoaib Akhtar, subject to a stringent medical. There had been talk of bringing in Mark Waugh as the county's second overseas player, but Terry wanted a younger name and ended up signing the new vice-captain of New South Wales, Simon Katich, to bolster the batting. The bowling will be strengthened by the arrival of Ed Giddins from Surrey, joining his fourth county on a two-year contract. Even so, Terry faces a daunting task. Hampshire may be an ambitious club with a wealthy chairman and a superb new stadium, but in 2002, they had neither the team nor the pitch to match. **Pat Symes**

HAMPSHIRE 2002

Back row: C. G. van der Gucht, J. E. K. Schofield, J. R. C. Hamblin, I. Brunnschweiler, L. R. Prittipaul, D. A. Kenway Middle row: T. M. Tremlett (director of cricket), P. Farhart (physiotherapist/fitness coach), D. Newman (physiotherapist), P. J. Hartley, I. H. Shah, N. Pothas, C. T. Tremlett, A. D. Mascarenhas, S. J. Cook (county coach), T. C. Middleton (second-team coach). Front row: J. P. Crawley, A. N. Aymes, W. S. Kendall (vice-captain), R. A. Smith (captain), S. D. Udal, G. W. White, J. S. Laney. A. C. Morris. Insets: N. C. Johnson, A. D. Mullally.

HAMPSHIRE RESULTS

All first-class matches – Played 17: Won 2, Lost 6, Drawn 9.
County Championship matches – Played 16: Won 2, Lost 5, Drawn 9.

COUNTY CHAMPIONSHIP AVERAGES: BATTING AND FIELDING

Cap		M	I	NO	R	HS	100s	50s	Avge	Ct/St
2002	J. P. Crawley	9	16	2	806	272	1	6	57.57	7
1985	R. A. Smith	14	23	1	807	104	2	3	36.68	6
2001	N. C. Johnson§	16	27	2	812	117	1	6	32.48	25
1999	W. S. Kendall	16	29	2	698	88	0	4	25.85	12
	J. H. K. Adams†	2	4	1	76	48	0	0	25.33	2
1992	S. D. Udal†	16	24	5	480	88	0	1	25.26	9
1998	A. D. Mascarenhas . .	15	24	2	551	94	0	2	25.04	7
	N. Pothas	16	26	1	597	99	0	5	23.88	30/4
	J. D. Francis	8	14	0	329	82	0	5	23.50	5
	C. T. Tremlett†	11	14	6	180	40*	0	0	22.50	4
1996	J. S. Laney†	7	13	0	289	89	0	1	22.23	7
	J. R. C. Hamblin . . .	4	7	0	147	50	0	1	21.00	2
	G. W. White	8	14	2	234	36	0	0	19.50	6
2001	D. A. Kenway†	8	15	2	238	54	0	1	18.30	15
1991	A. N. Aymes†	4	5	2	32	22*	0	0	10.66	13/1
2000	A. D. Mullally	13	16	5	54	23	0	0	4.90	1
	L. R. Prittipaul†	2	4	0	13	7	0	0	3.25	0
	J. A. Tomlinson†	4	7	4	9	5	0	0	3.00	0

Also batted: A. C. Morris (cap 2001) (2 matches) 12, 24; J. E. K. Schofield (1 match) 0, 18*.

† *Born in Hampshire.*   § *Overseas player.*

BOWLING

	O	M	R	W	BB	5W/i	Avge
A. D. Mullally	463.2	145	1,156	46	6-56	1	25.13
C. T. Tremlett	336	83	1,061	36	5-57	2	29.47
A. D. Mascarenhas	407.5	137	1,110	36	5-87	1	30.83
S. D. Udal	579.1	136	1,756	50	5-56	3	35.12
N. C. Johnson	231.2	50	769	21	3-22	0	36.61

Also bowled: J. H. K. Adams 21–4–102–2; J. D. Francis 2–1–1–1; J. R. C. Hamblin 61–6–288–3;
W. S. Kendall 58.2–12–173–3; D. A. Kenway 1–0–8–0; A. C. Morris 29–5–112–0; L. R. Prittipaul
28.3–8–74–2; J. E. K. Schofield 53–14–192–6; J. A. Tomlinson 131.2–12–582–9; G. W. White
12.1–1–64–1.

COUNTY RECORDS

Highest score for:	316	R. H. Moore v Warwickshire at Bournemouth . . .	1937
Highest score against:	303*	G. A. Hick (Worcestershire) at Southampton	1997
Best bowling for:	9-25	R. M. H. Cottam v Lancashire at Manchester	1965
Best bowling against:	10-46	W. Hickton (Lancashire) at Manchester	1870
Highest total for:	672-7 dec.	v Somerset at Taunton	1899
Highest total against:	742	by Surrey at The Oval	1909
Lowest total for:	15	v Warwickshire at Birmingham	1922
Lowest total against:	23	by Yorkshire at Middlesbrough	1965

COUNTY OFFICERS

Captain 2002 – R. A. Smith • **First-team manager** 2002 – S. J. Cook; 2003 – V. P. Terry
President A. C. D. Ingleby-Mackenzie • **Chairman** R. G. Bransgrove
Chief executive G. M. Walker • **Managing director** N. S. Pike
Chairman, Members Committee R. J. Treherne • **Head groundsman** N. Gray
Scorer V. H Isaacs

At Canterbury, April 19, 20, 21, 22. HAMPSHIRE drew with KENT.

HAMPSHIRE v LEICESTERSHIRE

At Southampton, April 24, 25, 26, 27. Leicestershire won by an innings and nine runs. Leicestershire 20 pts, Hampshire 5 pts. Toss: Leicestershire.

Leicestershire were superior with both bat and ball. On a sunny first day, Wells cut and drove his way to an unbeaten 149 against an underpowered home attack. Though Leicestershire added only 39 the next morning, Hampshire's reply was soon in trouble; amid sporadic resistance, Crawley, on his home debut, showed much more patience than most. Play was briefly halted in mid-afternoon when a swarm of bees invaded the Rose Bowl: as players dived for cover and seats were evacuated, a Hampshire member, known as "the Honeyman", was called from the stands and, with the help of council workers, he removed the culprits. On the third morning, Hampshire crept agonisingly towards the follow-on target, only for Mullally to run himself out six short. In their second innings, Malcolm found bounce where others had failed, and Maddy continued to get movement off the seam. He ended with match figures of nine for 74 and, while Kendall carried his bat, Hampshire quickly subsided to their first first-class defeat at the Rose Bowl.

Close of play: First day, Leicestershire 389-6 (Wells 149, DeFreitas 24); Second day, Hampshire 245-8 (Hamblin 33, Tremlett 13); Third day, Hampshire 81-2 (Kendall 24, Hamblin 1).

Leicestershire

T. R. Ward c Mascarenhas b Mullally	10	C. D. Crowe c Johnson b Tremlett		3
I. J. Sutcliffe c Kenway b Johnson	35	C. E. Dagnall not out		4
D. L. Maddy c Kenway b Hamblin	0	D. E. Malcolm c Udal b Tremlett		0
M. G. Bevan c Kenway b Udal	34	B 1, l-b 14, w 6, n-b 12		33
*V. J. Wells c Kenway b Mullally	150			
D. I. Stevens c sub b Mullally	82	1/16 (1) 2/33 (3) 3/72 (2) 4/145 (4)		428
†N. D. Burns lbw b Tremlett	26	5/294 (6) 6/352 (7) 7/391 (5)		
P. A. J. DeFreitas c Pothas b Mullally	51	8/424 (8) 9/426 (9) 10/428 (11)		

Bonus points – Leicestershire 5, Hampshire 3.

Bowling: Mullally 34–12–88–3; Hamblin 21–2–104–1; Tremlett 25–7–87–3; Mascarenhas 0.4–0–4–0; Kendall 4.2–1–8–1; Johnson 11–3–41–1; Udal 24–5–81–1.

Hampshire

D. A. Kenway lbw b DeFreitas	9	– c Burns b Dagnall		10
W. S. Kendall c Stevens b Dagnall	18	– not out		53
J. P. Crawley c Sutcliffe b Dagnall	80	– c Burns b Crowe		35
*R. A. Smith c Crowe b Maddy	44	– (5) b Maddy		1
N. C. Johnson lbw b Maddy	0	– (6) c Wells b Maddy		0
†N. Pothas lbw b Maddy	6	– (7) c and b Malcolm		3
S. D. Udal c Maddy b Dagnall	19	– (8) c Wells b Maddy		8
J. R. C. Hamblin lbw b DeFreitas	46	– (4) c Burns b Malcolm		2
A. D. Mascarenhas lbw b Maddy	11	– b Malcolm.		16
C. T. Tremlett not out	28	– b Maddy		2
A. D. Mullally run out	0	– b Maddy		0
B 5, l-b 5, w 2	12	B 4, l-b 8, w 2, n-b 2		16
1/25 (1) 2/37 (2) 3/107 (4) 4/123 (5)	273	1/13 (1) 2/73 (3) 3/83 (4)		146
5/131 (6) 6/179 (7) 7/190 (3)		4/96 (5) 5/96 (6) 6/99 (7)		
8/216 (9) 9/268 (8) 10/273 (11)		7/108 (8) 8/131 (9)		
		9/140 (10) 10/146 (11)		

Bonus points – Hampshire 2, Leicestershire 3.

Bowling: *First Innings*—Malcolm 21–1–77–0; DeFreitas 22.4–8–46–2; Wells 8–0–27–0; Dagnall 18–3–55–3; Maddy 17–4–37–4; Crowe 10–3–20–0; Stevens 1–0–1–0. *Second Innings*—DeFreitas 10.4–4–18–0; Dagnall 11–4–29–1; Maddy 17–7–37–5; Wells 5–3–9–0; Crowe 4–2–2–1; Malcolm 13–4–39–3.

Umpires: J. W. Holder and N. A. Mallender.

HAMPSHIRE v KENT

At Southampton, May 8, 9, 10. Hampshire won by eight wickets. Hampshire 18 pts, Kent 3 pts. Toss: Hampshire.

After the feast of runs at Canterbury in April, the return match lasted less than three days. Although the wicket became progressively less difficult, Kent's attack, and Saggers in particular, found darting movement on the first morning. Hampshire were reduced to 160 for seven, only to be rescued by Robin Smith, who repeatedly – and bravely – lunged on to the front foot. The recovery continued thanks to Udal's composure and Hamblin's hard hitting. Kent responded meekly to seam movement from Mascarenhas and swing from Mullally. However, after following on 227 behind, they batted with more assurance, as solid innings by Ed Smith and Nixon contrasted with a dashing knock from Patel. But it was not enough. Hampshire needed just 111, and Crawley reasserted his recent dominance over Kent with an 83-ball half-century. It took Hampshire to a first win against Kent since 1994 and helped earn Crawley a recall to the England squad announced the next day.

Close of play: First day, Hampshire 303-9 (Hamblin 12, Mullally 0); Second day, Kent 148-4 (Smith 61, Nixon 8).

Hampshire

D. A. Kenway b Fleming	18	– lbw b Saggers		11
W. S. Kendall c Fulton b Saggers	10	– c Khan b Saggers		6
J. P. Crawley lbw b Saggers	2	– not out		50
*R. A. Smith c Symonds b Saggers	104			
N. C. Johnson c Fulton b Saggers	0			
G. W. White c Nixon b Khan	17	– (4) not out		27
†N. Pothas c Nixon b Trott	24			
A. D. Mascarenhas c Fulton b Trott	0			
S. D. Udal lbw b Trott	88			
J. R. C. Hamblin b Saggers	50			
A. D. Mullally not out	4			
B 8, l-b 11, w 9	28	B 2, l-b 5, w 10		17

1/21 (2) 2/29 (3) 3/33 (1) 4/34 (5)　　　　　345　　1/17 (2) 2/56 (1)　　　(2 wkts) 111
5/86 (6) 6/160 (7) 7/160 (8)
8/269 (4) 9/302 (10) 10/345 (10)

Bonus points – Hampshire 3, Kent 3.

Bowling: *First Innings*—Saggers 30.1–5–74–5; Trott 22–6–83–3; Fleming 14–6–25–1; Khan 18–2–80–1; Patel 21–3–45–0; Symonds 7–3–19–0. *Second Innings*—Saggers 9–0–35–2; Trott 4–0–13–0; Khan 5–0–27–0; Fleming 1–0–11–0; Patel 4–1–10–0; Symonds 3.2–1–8–0.

Kent

*D. P. Fulton c Crawley b Mascarenhas	6	– c Johnson b Mullally		11
R. W. T. Key c Pothas b Mullally	3	– c Smith b Mascarenhas		29
E. T. Smith b Mascarenhas	20	– c Johnson b Mascarenhas		77
A. Symonds c Crawley b Mascarenhas	39	– b Johnson		21
M. J. Walker c Smith b Udal	2	– c Johnson b Udal		2
†P. A. Nixon c White b Mascarenhas	4	– not out		77
M. V. Fleming c Hamblin b Johnson	25	– c Kenway b Mascarenhas		12
M. M. Patel c Kenway b Mullally	4	– b Mullally		58
M. J. Saggers c Johnson b Udal	4	– (11) lbw b Mascarenhas		1
A. Khan not out	5	– (9) lbw b Johnson		1
B. J. Trott c Pothas b Johnson	0	– (10) run out		1
L-b 4, w 2, n-b 4	10	B 1, l-b 7, w 6, n-b 8		22

1/7 (1) 2/11 (2) 3/39 (3) 4/47 (5)　　　　　118　　1/20 (1) 2/68 (2) 3/109 (4)　　　　337
5/65 (6) 6/86 (4) 7/105 (8)　　　　　　　　　　　　4/126 (5) 5/190 (3) 6/206 (7)
8/109 (7) 9/113 (9) 10/118 (11)　　　　　　　　　　7/295 (8) 8/333 (9)
　　　　　　　　　　　　　　　　　　　　　　　　　9/335 (10) 10/337 (11)

Bonus points – Hampshire 3.

Bowling: *First Innings*—Mullally 17–5–49–2; Mascarenhas 14–4–49–4; Udal 3–2–2–2; Hamblin 2–0–11–0; Johnson 3–1–3–2. *Second Innings*—Mullally 24–6–62–2; Mascarenhas 25.4–5–73–4; Johnson 16–5–54–2; Udal 31–6–100–1; Kendall 3–0–14–0; Hamblin 7–1–26–0.

Umpires: A. Clarkson and K. E. Palmer.

At Birmingham, May 15, 16, 17, 18. HAMPSHIRE drew with WARWICKSHIRE.

At Leeds, May 24, 25, 26, 27. HAMPSHIRE drew with YORKSHIRE.

HAMPSHIRE v WARWICKSHIRE

At Southampton, May 31, June 1, 2, 3. Drawn. Hampshire 9 pts, Warwickshire 9 pts. Toss: Warwickshire.

Bad weather, shoddy catching and resolute batting from Hampshire's lower order denied Warwickshire a first Championship win. A slow pitch of uneven bounce made for little entertainment over the first three days and the match only spluttered into life on the last morning. Powell's declaration left Hampshire needing an improbable 303 in 83 overs, but stoppages meant only 50 were bowled, and, after Hampshire were reduced to 129 for seven, White and Udal managed to hold out. Warwickshire dropped three important catches, including Smith on one. On the first three days, some torpid cricket was relieved by flashes of menace from Mullally and two innings of great elan by Troughton. He was the only batsman to master an untrustworthy pitch, and he played with freedom and maturity to score a maiden first-class century. On the second day, Warwickshire's coach, Bob Woolmer, and overseas player, Pollock, learned of the death of their friend, the former South African captain, Hansie Cronje. Both teams wore black armbands in his memory.

Close of play: First day, Warwickshire 241–7 (Frost 28); Second day, Hampshire 245–7 (Mascarenhas 18, Udal 13); Third day, Warwickshire 267–5 (Troughton 107, Brown 5).

Warwickshire

*M. J. Powell c Crawley b Udal	92	– lbw b Mascarenhas	24
N. V. Knight c Johnson b Tremlett	14	– lbw b Mascarenhas	31
I. R. Bell c Pothas b Mullally	2	– st Pothas b Udal	37
D. P. Ostler c Crawley b Mascarenhas	1	– c Kendall b Tremlett	9
J. O. Troughton c Pothas b Mullally	63	– not out	131
†T. Frost c Kendall b Tremlett	28	– (9) c Pothas b Johnson	0
S. M. Pollock c Udal b Mullally	16	– (6) c Pothas b Mullally	37
D. R. Brown c White b Mullally	5	– (7) b Mullally	23
N. M. K. Smith c Pothas b Mullally	0	– (8) b Mullally	18
M. M. Betts not out	7	– not out	2
A. Richardson c Kenway b Mullally	0		
B 3, l-b 1, w 12, n-b 6	22	B 6, l-b 5, w 6	17

1/35 (2) 2/47 (3) 3/50 (4) 4/168 (5)	250	1/56 (2) 2/59 (1) (8 wkts dec.)	329
5/196 (1) 6/225 (7) 7/241 (8)		3/81 (4) 4/171 (3)	
8/241 (9) 9/241 (6) 10/250 (11)		5/259 (6) 6/285 (7)	
		7/325 (8) 8/326 (9)	

Bonus points – Warwickshire 2, Hampshire 3.

Bowling: *First Innings*—Mullally 27.2–7–56–6; Mascarenhas 17–2–54–1; Tremlett 23–10–38–2; Udal 24–9–62–1; Johnson 12–2–34–0; Kendall 8–6–2–0. *Second Innings*—Mullally 34–15–87–3; Tremlett 21–5–56–1; Mascarenhas 21–10–60–2; Johnson 4–0–17–1; Kendall 7–1–20–0; Udal 13–0–63–1; White 3–0–15–0.

Hampshire

D. A. Kenway c Bell b Pollock	14	– b Richardson	16
W. S. Kendall lbw b Brown	27	– c Frost b Betts	14
J. P. Crawley c Knight b Brown	60	– lbw b Richardson	16
*R. A. Smith lbw b Brown	5	– c Powell b Betts	41
N. C. Johnson c Smith b Bell	33	– c Troughton b Brown	3
G. W. White b Pollock	21	– not out	10
†N. Pothas c Powell b Betts	1	– b Brown	6
A. D. Mascarenhas c Frost b Pollock	27	– c Bell b Brown	11
S. D. Udal b Betts	23	– not out	5
C. T. Tremlett b Pollock	4		
A. D. Mullally not out	5		
B 6, l-b 9, w 6, n-b 36	57	N-b 20	20
	277	(7 wkts)	**142**

1/40 (1) 2/81 (2) 3/93 (4) 4/170 (5)   1/33 (1) 2/37 (2)   (7 wkts) 142
5/196 (3) 6/203 (7) 7/217 (6)   3/85 (3) 4/100 (5)
8/259 (8) 9/269 (9) 10/277 (10)   5/102 (4) 6/115 (7) 7/129 (8)

Bonus points – Hampshire 2, Warwickshire 3.

Bowling: *First Innings*—Pollock 17–3–37–4; Betts 24–3–84–2; Richardson 16–2–63–0; Brown 23–7–44–3; Smith 5–0–12–0; Bell 19–6–22–1. *Second Innings*—Pollock 11–5–25–0; Betts 13.4–3–48–2; Richardson 13–2–36–2; Brown 12–2–33–3.

Umpires: I. J. Gould and J. F. Steele.

At Bath, June 12, 13, 14, 15. HAMPSHIRE drew with SOMERSET.

At Southampton, June 25, 26, 27 (not first-class). **Hampshire won by three wickets.** Toss: Loughborough UCCE. **Loughborough UCCE 371 for five dec.** (J. H. K. Adams 53, V. Atri 35, M. J. Powell 124 not out, R. A. White 44, C. C. Benham 54 not out, Extras 47) **and 220 for eight dec.** (C. D. Nash 70, R. Wilkinson 36; J. A. Tomlinson four for 66); **Hampshire 283 for seven dec.** (D. A. Kenway 57, J. S. Laney 35, W. S. Kendall 100 not out) **and 309 for seven** (J. S. Laney 98, G. W. White 40, W. S. Kendall 62, J. R. C. Hamblin 49; D. H. Wigley five for 71).

County debuts: I. J. Hilsum, J. A. Tomlinson.

HAMPSHIRE v SUSSEX

At Southampton, July 3, 4, 5, 6. Drawn. Hampshire 7 pts, Sussex 8 pts. Toss: Sussex.
Adams was left fuming after a wet outfield prevented any play on the third day and killed hopes of a Sussex win. Rain meant only ten and a half overs were possible on the first day, but by the end of the second, Martin-Jenkins had swung the match Sussex's way. On another pitch showing uneven bounce, he batted watchfully for three hours and anchored their first innings, then gave a superb display of seam bowling when Hampshire's batsmen took their turn. They were 88 for six – and in deep trouble – at the close of the second day, before the conditions halted Sussex's charge. Adams clearly thought the lengthy stoppage was unnecessary: "When the groundstaff finally started work on the field after lunch it dried up considerably." On the last morning a forthright 49 from Mascarenhas left Hampshire 83 behind, and, although Sussex declared, Hampshire made no effort to indulge in a chase. The match was called off with a possible 11 overs remaining.
Close of play: First day, Sussex 30-2 (Adams 10, Yardy 6); Second day, Hampshire 88-6 (White 17, Mascarenhas 19); Third day, No play.

Sussex

R. R. Montgomerie run out	10	– (2) c Johnson b Mullally	20
M. W. Goodwin c Kenway b Mullally	3	– (1) c Pothas b Mullally	5
*C. J. Adams b Mullally	27	– c Johnson b Udal	20
M. H. Yardy st Pothas b Udal	34	– c White b Udal	39
T. R. Ambrose c Pothas b Mullally	49	– not out	17
R. S. C. Martin-Jenkins not out	80	– not out	1
†M. J. Prior c Mascarenhas b Udal	10		
K. J. Innes c Kendall b Udal	1		
M. J. G. Davis lbw b Johnson	8		
J. D. Lewry c Kendall b Udal	4		
B. V. Taylor c Smith b Udal	7		
B 1, l-b 6, w 2, n-b 4	13	B 4, l-b 1, w 2, n-b 2	9

1/9 (2) 2/13 (1) 3/50 (3) 4/108 (4)   246   1/16 (1) 2/39 (2)   (4 wkts dec.) 111
5/158 (5) 6/179 (7) 7/198 (8)   3/61 (3) 4/110 (4)
8/215 (9) 9/226 (10) 10/246 (11)

Bonus points – Sussex 1, Hampshire 3.

Bowling: *First Innings*—Mullally 19–5–44–3; Tremlett 14–2–60–0; Mascarenhas 15–3–41–0; Johnson 13–1–38–1; Udal 24.4–7–56–5. *Second Innings*—Mullally 14–4–28–2; Tremlett 10–2–27–0; Mascarenhas 6–3–11–0; Udal 9–3–19–2; White 2–0–18–0; Johnson 1.3–0–3–0.

Hampshire

D. A. Kenway lbw b Martin-Jenkins	4	– not out	29
W. S. Kendall lbw b Lewry	4	– not out	17
J. P. Crawley b Martin-Jenkins	4		
*R. A. Smith b Taylor	9		
N. C. Johnson c Innes b Martin-Jenkins	3		
G. W. White lbw b Martin-Jenkins	17		
†N. Pothas c Prior b Taylor	10		
A. D. Mascarenhas c Prior b Innes	49		
S. D. Udal lbw b Martin-Jenkins	16		
C. T. Tremlett not out	18		
A. D. Mullally c and b Davis	1		
B 6, l-b 2, w 2, n-b 18	28	L-b 2, n-b 8	10

1/15 (2) 2/19 (1) 3/32 (3) 4/36 (5)   163   (no wkt) 56
5/46 (4) 6/60 (7) 7/88 (6)
8/118 (9) 9/162 (8) 10/163 (11)

Bonus points – Sussex 3.

Bowling: *First Innings*—Lewry 16–3–56–1; Martin-Jenkins 15–7–37–5; Taylor 16–6–46–2; Innes 5–1–13–1; Davis 1.3–0–3–1. *Second Innings*—Lewry 6–2–26–0; Martin-Jenkins 3–1–9–0; Davis 3–0–14–0; Taylor 1–0–5–0.

Umpires: K. E. Palmer and G. Sharp.

At Leicester, July 10, 11, 12, 13. HAMPSHIRE drew with LEICESTERSHIRE.

At Southampton, July 20, 21, 22. HAMPSHIRE lost to INDIANS by 66 runs (see Indian tour section).

HAMPSHIRE v LANCASHIRE

At Southampton, July 25, 26, 27. Lancashire won by 111 runs. Lancashire 15 pts, Hampshire
−5 pts. Toss: Lancashire.

With good-length balls thudding into batsmen's pads at ankle height one moment and rapping
fingers the next, Hampshire's eight-point penalty for a "poor" pitch was no surprise. Twelve wickets
tumbled on the first day, 22 on the second, and the match was over before lunch on the third.
After Lancashire chose to bat, Tremlett took advantage of a dry, heavily cracked surface, grabbing
four wickets with lifters and one with a shooter. Without Swann's diligence they would have
struggled to reach even 183. In reply, Anderson caused real uncertainty with his accuracy and
sharp pace to help Lancashire to a crucial 51-run lead. Udal took five wickets in Lancashire's
second innings, and nine all told, with some skilful off-spin, but Law and Fairbrother grafted
sensibly to leave Hampshire chasing 239. Given the conditions, it always looked beyond them,
and they were duly skittled in under 34 overs. Anderson ended the match with nine for 50.

Close of play: First day, Hampshire 45-2 (Kendall 18, Udal 0); Second day, Hampshire
54-4 (Francis 20).

Lancashire

M. J. Chilton	b Tremlett	8	– c Aymes b Udal		22
A. J. Swann	c Pothas b Udal	66	– c Pothas b Mullally		0
D. Byas	c Johnson b Mullally	29	– c Johnson b Tremlett		0
S. G. Law	b Tremlett	22	– st Aymes b Udal		38
N. H. Fairbrother	c Mascarenhas b Udal	0	– c Kendall b Udal		39
G. Chapple	c Aymes b Tremlett	0	– c Kendall b Udal		31
R. C. Driver	c Pothas b Udal	0	– c Aymes b Mullally		5
*†W. K. Hegg	c Aymes b Tremlett	5	– c Kendall b Udal		23
J. Wood	c Aymes b Udal	26	– c Aymes b Mullally		3
G. Keedy	b Tremlett	5	– not out		16
J. M. Anderson	not out	1	– c Johnson b Udal		1
	B 3, l-b 10, w 2, n-b 6	21	B 2, l-b 3, w 4		9
		183			187

1/21 (1) 2/99 (3) 3/128 (2) 4/128 (5)
5/139 (6) 6/142 (7) 7/142 (4)
8/159 (8) 9/181 (9) 10/183 (10)

1/1 (2) 2/2 (3) 3/58 (1) 4/61 (4)
5/131 (6) 6/141 (5) 7/143 (7)
8/147 (9) 9/179 (8) 10/187 (11)

Bonus points – Hampshire 3.

Bowling: *First Innings*—Mullally 16–6–28–1; Tremlett 22.2–4–68–5; Mascarenhas
14–3–38–0; Johnson 5–2–11–0; Udal 19–5–25–4. *Second Innings*—Mullally 13–3–36–3;
Tremlett 11–1–36–2; Mascarenhas 7–1–22–0; Udal 23–3–59–5; Johnson 6–0–29–0.

Hampshire

G. W. White	b Wood	1	– c Fairbrother b Wood		1
W. S. Kendall	b Anderson	54	– lbw b Wood		3
J. D. Francis	c Hegg b Anderson	10	– b Keedy		27
S. D. Udal	lbw b Wood	2	– (5) b Anderson		7
*R. A. Smith	c Hegg b Chapple	4	– (4) c Fairbrother b Anderson		12
N. C. Johnson	c Hegg b Anderson	14	– st Hegg b Keedy		28
N. Pothas	b Wood	18	– c and b Chapple		9
†A. N. Aymes	c Hegg b Anderson	0	– lbw b Anderson		1
A. D. Mascarenhas	c Hegg b Anderson	1	– b Wood		13
C. T. Tremlett	c Swann b Anderson	3	– not out		2
A. D. Mullally	not out	1	– b Wood		0
	B 9, l-b 1, n-b 6	16	B 14, l-b 8, w 2		24
		132			127

1/7 (1) 2/40 (3) 3/47 (4) 4/66 (5)
5/94 (6) 6/117 (2) 7/123 (8)
8/127 (7) 9/129 (9) 10/132 (10)

1/5 (1) 2/22 (2) 3/46 (4)
4/54 (5) 5/81 (3) 6/92 (7)
7/108 (8) 8/108 (6)
9/127 (9) 10/127 (11)

Bonus points – Lancashire 3.

Bowling: *First Innings*—Chapple 13–6–21–1; Wood 17–3–53–3; Anderson 14–6–23–6; Driver 7–3–18–0; Keedy 2–0–7–0. *Second Innings*—Chapple 13–2–39–1; Wood 4.5–0–17–4; Anderson 9–2–27–3; Keedy 7–1–22–2.

Umpires: A. A. Jones and A. G. T. Whitehead.

At Manchester, August 8, 9, 10, 11. HAMPSHIRE drew with LANCASHIRE.

HAMPSHIRE v SOMERSET

At Southampton, August 14, 15, 16, 17. Hampshire won by four wickets. Hampshire 16 pts, Somerset 5 pts. Toss: Somerset.

After losing eight of their previous nine matches in all cricket, Hampshire sacked their South African coach, Jimmy Cook, immediately before the game. He turned up to watch anyway as Somerset, his old county, took a 42-run first-innings lead thanks to Richard Johnson and Blackwell, whose slow left-arm won him a career-best five for 49 on a sluggish surface that offered turn from the first day. But they frittered the advantage with some weak batting second time round, when only Holloway and Turner showed enough fight, and Hampshire were handed a huge 134 overs to score a gettable 233. Neil Johnson and Laney made a flying start, only for Hampshire to falter during a fiery 13-over spell from Caddick on the final morning and find themselves six wickets down, 20 runs short and facing a nervous lunch. But after the break Mascarenhas made sure with some bold hitting. The victory was Hampshire's first in the Championship since May 10.

Close of play: First day, Hampshire 15-0 (Johnson 5, Laney 10); Second day, Somerset 14-2 (Burns 3, Bulbeck 2); Third day, Hampshire 136-2 (Kendall 18, Smith 8).

Somerset

*J. Cox lbw b Mullally	31	– (2) c Laney b Udal	5
M. J. Wood c Tremlett b Mascarenhas	9	– (1) c Aymes b Mullally	3
M. Burns c Aymes b Udal	31	– c Francis b Mascarenhas	11
P. C. L. Holloway lbw b Mullally	17	– (5) c Johnson b Tremlett	48
K. A. Parsons c Aymes b Udal	51	– (6) c Udal b Tremlett	6
I. D. Blackwell c and b Udal	0	– (7) b Tremlett	6
†R. J. Turner c Aymes b Mullally	57	– (8) lbw b Udal	34
M. P. L. Bulbeck c Aymes b Johnson	4	– (4) c Kendall b Mascarenhas	26
R. L. Johnson c Udal b Mullally	61	– b Johnson	6
A. R. Caddick b Mascarenhas	1	– b Udal	16
S. R. G. Francis not out	0	– not out	2
L-b 14, w 2	16	B 7, l-b 14, w 2, n-b 6	29
	278		**190**

1/21 (2) 2/66 (3) 3/90 (1) 4/101 (4)   278   1/8 (1) 2/8 (2) 3/44 (3) 4/57 (4)   190
5/102 (6) 6/201 (5) 7/206 (8)   5/69 (6) 6/79 (7) 7/148 (8)
8/265 (7) 9/278 (9) 10/278 (10)   8/163 (9) 9/184 (10) 10/190 (5)

Bonus points – Somerset 2, Hampshire 3.

Bowling: *First Innings*—Mullally 25–8–58–4; Tremlett 14–5–30–0; Mascarenhas 17.5–7–48–2; Johnson 12–3–39–1; Udal 28–6–89–3. *Second Innings*—Mullally 3–1–6–1; Tremlett 16.4–3–42–3; Udal 35–9–74–3; Mascarenhas 13–7–23–2; Johnson 7–1–24–1.

Hampshire

N. C. Johnson lbw b Johnson	10	– c Turner b Parsons	57
J. S. Laney c Turner b Caddick	15	– c Johnson b Francis	46
W. S. Kendall c Turner b Blackwell	46	– c Turner b Caddick	25
*R. A. Smith b Blackwell	52	– lbw b Caddick	34
J. D. Francis c Caddick b Blackwell	53	– c Turner b Francis	10
N. Pothas c Turner b Caddick	5	– lbw b Johnson	17
†A. N. Aymes c Turner b Blackwell	8	– (8) not out	1
A. D. Mascarenhas b Bulbeck	3	– (7) not out	27
S. D. Udal lbw b Johnson	10		
C. T. Tremlett not out	16		
A. D. Mullally c Wood b Blackwell	3		
B 1, l-b 4, w 2, n-b 8	15	L-b 8, w 2, n-b 6	16

1/25 (1) 2/25 (2) 3/108 (4) 4/149 (3)   236   1/97 (2) 2/119 (1)   (6 wkts) 233
5/154 (6) 6/171 (7) 7/182 (8)   3/169 (3) 4/176 (4)
8/206 (9) 9/224 (5) 10/236 (11)   5/199 (6) 6/213 (5)

Bonus points – Hampshire 1, Somerset 3.

Bowling: *First Innings*—Caddick 22–5–61–2; Johnson 22–6–53–2; Francis 8–2–32–0; Bulbeck 10–1–22–1; Blackwell 31–12–49–5; Parsons 3–0–14–0. *Second Innings*—Caddick 23–4–69–2; Johnson 15.1–3–50–1; Bulbeck 9–1–40–0; Blackwell 10–1–28–0; Francis 9–0–20–2; Parsons 7–2–18–1.

Umpires: G. I. Burgess and M. J. Kitchen.

At The Oval, August 22, 23, 24, 25. HAMPSHIRE lost to SURREY by an innings and 60 runs.

HAMPSHIRE v YORKSHIRE

At Southampton, August 27, 28, 29. Yorkshire won by seven wickets. Yorkshire 17 pts, Hampshire 5 pts. Toss: Hampshire.

A second successive win provided a lifeline for Yorkshire, while for Hampshire, also fighting relegation, defeat was a hammer blow. The sides were evenly matched over the first two innings: McGrath's part-time swing knocked out Hampshire's middle order but, when Yorkshire responded, the tenacious Udal troubled everyone except Elliott. The key to the game was the second evening, when limp batting by Hampshire cost them four wickets for four runs. From 91 for six overnight there was no way back, despite resistance from Mascarenhas and Udal. On a pitch that offered gentle turn and ever-lower bounce, Dawson finished with five for 49. Needing 151, Yorkshire made no mistake, with Craven smashing sixes off Johnson and Udal, and the reliable Elliott continuing his first-innings dominance. With Aymes already injured, Pothas started as keeper; when he twisted his knee, Laney took over; when he in turn bruised his finger, the 17-year-old Tom Burrows kept wicket in Yorkshire's second innings. He held a catch, did not concede a bye and even signed autographs.

Close of play: First day, Yorkshire 53-2 (Elliott 30, Kirby 0); Second day, Hampshire 91-6 (Kendall 1, Mascarenhas 0).

Hampshire

N. C. Johnson c Blakey b Sidebottom	37	– c Elliott b McGrath	18
J. S. Laney c Taylor b Sidebottom	10	– lbw b Sidebottom	10
J. P. Crawley b McGrath	21	– c Sidebottom b Dawson	26
*R. A. Smith lbw b Kirby	58	– lbw b Kirby	18
J. D. Francis c sub b McGrath	0	– (6) lbw b Dawson	0
W. S. Kendall c Elliott b McGrath	36	– (7) c Taylor b Dawson	1
†N. Pothas b McGrath	6	– (9) c Taylor b Dawson	2
A. D. Mascarenhas c Blakey b Sidebottom	15	– not out	32
S. D. Udal b Kirby	40	– (10) lbw b Dawson	24
J. R. C. Hamblin c Elliott b Dawson	23	– (5) c Blakey b Kirby	0
J. A. Tomlinson not out	0	– c Elliott b McGrath	5
B 2, l-b 11, n-b 10	23	B 9, l-b 12, w 4	25

1/59 (1) 2/68 (2) 3/90 (3) 4/92 (5)	**269**	1/26 (2) 2/53 (1) 3/83 (4)	**161**
5/168 (6) 6/174 (7) 7/197 (8)		4/83 (5) 5/84 (6) 6/87 (3) 7/92 (7)	
8/209 (4) 9/269 (10) 10/269 (9)		8/102 (9) 9/140 (10) 10/161 (11)	

Bonus points – Hampshire 2, Yorkshire 3.

Bowling: *First Innings*—Silverwood 5–2–14–0; Kirby 19.2–3–80–2; Sidebottom 20–4–48–3; Dawson 22–6–52–1; McGrath 16–3–49–4; Fellows 1–0–13–0. *Second Innings*—Kirby 18–6–45–2; Sidebottom 10–2–39–1; McGrath 5.4–1–7–2; Dawson 22–4–49–5.

Yorkshire

V. J. Craven c Crawley b Mascarenhas	6	– c Hamblin b Udal	72
C. R. Taylor c Kendall b Udal	16	– lbw b Mascarenhas	7
M. T. G. Elliott lbw b Mascarenhas	92	– not out	52
S. P. Kirby c sub b Udal	2		
A. McGrath b Udal	31	– (4) c sub b Tomlinson	4
M. J. Lumb b Tomlinson	18	– (5) not out	13
G. M. Fellows c Mascarenhas b Johnson	35		
*†R. J. Blakey not out	34		
R. K. J. Dawson b Johnson b Udal	19		
C. E. W. Silverwood c Smith b Hamblin	3		
R. J. Sidebottom lbw b Udal	5		
B 5, l-b 7, w 3, n-b 4	19	L-b 4	4

1/7 (1) 2/52 (2) 3/64 (4)	**280**	1/10 (2) 2/120 (1)	(3 wkts)	**152**
4/120 (5) 5/147 (6) 6/212 (3) 7/214 (7)		3/128 (4)		
8/242 (9) 9/251 (10) 10/280 (11)				

Bonus points – Yorkshire 2, Hampshire 3.

Bowling: *First Innings*—Tomlinson 17–1–73–1; Mascarenhas 23–7–56–2; Udal 29–6–69–5; Hamblin 10–1–44–1; Johnson 9–1–26–1. *Second Innings*—Udal 16–3–53–1; Mascarenhas 9–2–18–1; Johnson 5–1–21–0; Hamblin 5–0–22–0; Tomlinson 6.4–0–34–1.

Umpires: J. H. Evans and J. W. Lloyds.

At Hove, September 5, 6, 7, 8. HAMPSHIRE drew with SUSSEX.

HAMPSHIRE v SURREY

At Southampton, September 11, 12, 13, 14. Surrey won by 123 runs. Surrey 20 pts, Hampshire 6 pts. Toss: Surrey.

With Surrey confirmed as champions, and Hampshire already relegated, media attention focused on Graham Thorpe. He had just been named in the Ashes squad but after a summer of personal problems and self-imposed exile he was playing his first match for more than seven weeks. After a rusty 19 in the first innings, he hit crisply to all corners in the second, going on to an authoritative

143. Ward was no less imposing. On an uncharacteristically benign Rose Bowl pitch which yielded 1,557 runs, he cut and drove his way to centuries in each innings, as Surrey ruthlessly exposed an inexperienced attack. Hampshire's task was to score an unlikely 514 in a day, and Bicknell snuffed out any hope with four early wickets. But Johnson, Mascarenhas and Pothas, with his best score of the season, cracked plenty of boundaries, and ensured some dignity in defeat. It was their eighth in succession against Surrey.

Close of play: First day, Surrey 348-7 (Brown 59, Saqlain Mushtaq 11); Second day, Hampshire 327; Third day, Surrey 422-8 (Saqlain Mushtaq 15).

Surrey

*I. J. Ward run out	112	– st Pothas b Adams	156
S. A. Newman c Adams b Schofield	4	– lbw b Schofield	15
N. Shahid c Udal b Schofield	82	– c Pothas b Mascarenhas	20
G. P. Thorpe b Udal	19	– c Adams b Tomlinson	143
A. D. Brown lbw b Mascarenhas	60	– lbw b Adams	0
†J. N. Batty c Johnson b Udal	0	– c Johnson b Schofield	13
M. P. Bicknell c Crawley b Udal	25	– c Pothas b Tomlinson	28
I. D. K. Salisbury c Pothas b Tomlinson	7	– b Schofield	16
Saqlain Mushtaq b Tomlinson	55	– not out	15
J. Ormond c Johnson b Schofield	4		
T. J. Murtagh not out	15		
B 12, l-b 13, w 8, n-b 2	35	B 8, l-b 4, w 2, n-b 2	16

1/8 (2) 2/205 (3) 3/225 (1) 4/239 (4)   **418**   1/27 (2) 2/93 (3)   (8 wkts dec.) **422**
5/239 (6) 6/305 (7) 7/312 (8)   3/332 (1) 4/332 (5)
8/350 (5) 9/361 (10) 10/418 (9)   5/360 (6) 6/360 (6)
                                         7/396 (8) 8/422 (7)

Bonus points – Surrey 5, Hampshire 3.

Bowling: *First Innings*—Tomlinson 26.2–3–118–2; Schofield 30–7–98–3; Johnson 8–2–16–0; Mascarenhas 29–9–79–1; Udal 34–6–82–3. *Second Innings*—Schofield 23–7–94–3; Tomlinson 23.2–3–112–2; Mascarenhas 12–5–39–1; Udal 25–6–69–0; Adams 18–3–81–2; Kendall 2–0–15–0.

Hampshire

N. C. Johnson c Murtagh b Saqlain Mushtaq	32	– b Salisbury	86
J. S. Laney b Ormond	48	– c Batty b Bicknell	8
J. H. K. Adams c Newman b Ormond	17	– lbw b Bicknell	8
J. P. Crawley c Newman b Saqlain Mushtaq	82	– c and b Bicknell	0
*W. S. Kendall c Ward b Bicknell	38	– b Bicknell	23
J. D. Francis c Batty b Ormond	59	– lbw b Bicknell	28
†N. Pothas c Murtagh b Saqlain Mushtaq	4	– c Brown b Salisbury	99
A. D. Mascarenhas c sub b Salisbury	30	– lbw b Ward	67
S. D. Udal not out	8	– b Salisbury	28
J. E. K. Schofield b Ormond	0	– not out	18
J. A. Tomlinson lbw b Salisbury	1	– c Newman b Salisbury	2
L-b 4, n-b 4	8	B 4, l-b 7, w 4, n-b 4	23

1/79 (1) 2/80 (2) 3/109 (3) 4/209 (4)   **327**   1/13 (2) 2/27 (3) 3/27 (4)   **390**
5/231 (5) 6/246 (7) 7/314 (6)   4/65 (5) 5/141 (6) 6/189 (1)
8/316 (8) 9/318 (10) 10/327 (11)   7/287 (8) 8/335 (9)
                                          9/384 (7) 10/390 (11)

Bonus points – Hampshire 3, Surrey 3.

Bowling: *First Innings*—Bicknell 17–2–92–1; Ormond 20–1–87–4; Murtagh 9–1–52–0; Saqlain Mushtaq 20–1–68–3; Salisbury 10–2–24–2. *Second Innings*—Bicknell 14–3–56–5; Ormond 14–2–52–0; Murtagh 11–1–54–0; Saqlain Mushtaq 16–0–100–0; Salisbury 25.2–1–116–4; Ward 1–0–1–1.

Umpires: J. W. Holder and J. F. Steele.

KENT
THE NEARLY MEN

Ch'ship 3rd in Division 1
C&G semi-finalists
B&H group stage
NUL 5th in Division 1

Player of the season: Martin Saggers

In sport, the line between success and failure is always thin, and for Kent it has a habit of being thinner still. They finished third in the Championship for the second season in a row, fifth in the Norwich Union League, and were beaten semi-finalists in the C&G. The verdict was familiar: good, but could do better.

Being in contention in three of the four competitions meant it was never a dull summer, but at the end everyone involved with the club was left with mixed emotions. In the Championship, Kent turned potential victories against Sussex, Leicestershire and Surrey into two draws and a defeat. Losing to Surrey was hardest to take: set a massive 410 to win, Surrey, who led the table, reached their seemingly unassailable target shortly after lunch on the final day. Despite that setback, Kent entered the final week with a chance of claiming the £50,000 prize for second place. They pulled off a three-day win over Yorkshire, who had already been relegated, but were powerless to prevent Warwickshire chasing more than 400 to beat Sussex on the final day at Hove and nab the cheque. Kent were left to reflect on crucial batting points they missed against Somerset and Lancashire.

Their inconsistency extended to the Norwich Union League, which they had won the year before. They were forced to play catch-up from the start after losing to Yorkshire in the opening fixture and managing only a tie at Cardiff in a game they should have won. Kent stayed in touch with the leaders, but defeat by Worcestershire at New Road put a second successive title beyond them and they drifted to fifth. The most disappointing defeat of the one-day season came in the semi-final of the C&G at Taunton. An undistinguished display by the bowlers had allowed Somerset to amass 344, but at 336 for six Kent had done all the hard work and a place in the final seemed a formality. Astonishingly, they lost four wickets for three runs to snatch defeat from the jaws of victory.

After the narrow failure to reach the knockout stages of the B&H earlier in the season, Matthew Fleming, the retiring one-day captain, was unable to celebrate his last season with a trophy. Fleming's walk back to the pavilion in the final home game of the season was a tearful affair. He would dearly have loved to swap places with the Glamorgan captain, Robert Croft, who was soon celebrating winning the title. After 14 seasons with Kent, Fleming was honoured with a lifetime achievement award and also won the Walter Lawrence Trophy for the fastest first-class century of the season – 66 balls against the Sri Lankans at Canterbury in April. The unprecedented decision to appoint two captains had worked well, although David Fulton has assumed both roles for 2003.

Fulton and Robert Key again formed an effective opening partnership with six century stands in the Championship and 1,000 runs each. Key's forthright strokeplay earned him two home Tests and a late call-up to the Ashes squad in place of Graham Thorpe. Ed Smith made 1,000 too, and Andrew Symonds might have done if Australia had not summoned him to the ICC Champions Trophy in Sri Lanka. He returns in 2003, but was replaced for the final five weeks of 2002 by Steve Waugh, who struggled at first but set up victory over Yorkshire in the final Championship game of the season with 146. Waugh averaged nearly 40 in one-day cricket. Paul Nixon produced some important scores, and news of his release came as a shock. Kent decided not to renew his contract because they wanted to bring on the highly promising but inexperienced Geraint Jones, so Nixon, in his prime at 32, signed for his old club Leicestershire on a three-year contract.

Matthew Walker saved his best innings for one-day cricket, while Min Patel batted impressively in the Championship but lost his role as preferred one-day slow bowler to the 20-year-old off-spinner, James Tredwell. The seamer James Hewitt, a fresh arrival from Middlesex, never established himself in the pecking order and made just one Championship appearance.

The real success story, though, was the performance of Martin Saggers and Amjad Khan. Between them, they took 146 first-class wickets, with ten individual five-wicket hauls. Saggers racked up 83 wickets in first-class cricket – equal highest for the season with Kevin Dean – 111 in all first-team cricket and thoroughly deserved his four Player of the Year awards. The coach, Ian Brayshaw, confirmed he had put Saggers's name forward to the national selectors, but he had to make do with representing England in the Hong Kong Sixes in November. Khan, born in Copenhagen of Pakistani extraction, enjoyed a great season. He worked hard on eradicating his overstepping problem, and his 63 wickets won him an award as Kent's most improved player.

Even so, Kent decided to bolster their seam attack with the close-season signing of Alamgir Sheriyar, the Worcestershire and England A left-armer, on a two-year contract. They also recruited two recent England Under-19 stars, Peter Trego, the Somerset all-rounder, and the Surrey opener Michael Carberry. Martin McCague was released after 12 years and many fiery spells with the new ball, and James Hockley and James Golding did not have their contracts renewed. Matthew Banes escaped the axe after a productive winter playing grade cricket in Australia. **Andrew Gidley**

654

KENT 2002

Back row: J. C. Tredwell, J. B. Hockley, G. O. Jones, M. J. Walker. *Middle row:* M. J. Saggers, J. P. Hewitt, J. M. Golding, B. J. Trott, D. D. Masters, E. T. Smith, R. W. T. Key, A. Khan. *Front row:* M. M. Patel, M. A. Ealham, M. V. Fleming *(limited-overs captain),* D. P. Fulton *(Championship captain),* M. J. McCague, P. A. Nixon. *Inset:* A. Symonds. Main picture by Terry Mahoney.

KENT RESULTS

All first-class matches – Played 17: Won 7, Lost 4, Drawn 6.
County Championship matches – Played 16: Won 7, Lost 4, Drawn 5.

COUNTY CHAMPIONSHIP AVERAGES: BATTING AND FIELDING

Cap		M	I	NO	R	HS	100s	50s	Avge	Ct/St
	J. M. Golding†	3	4	2	95	32	0	0	47.50	0
2002	S. R. Waugh§	4	6	1	224	146	1	0	44.80	3
2001	R. W. T. Key	13	26	1	1,090	160	3	5	43.60	10
2001	E. T. Smith†	16	31	2	1,233	154	3	5	42.51	4
1998	D. P. Fulton	15	30	1	1,166	177	3	4	40.20	30
1994	M. M. Patel	15	20	6	561	82	0	5	40.07	8
1999	A. Symonds§	12	24	2	858	118	2	4	39.00	16
2000	P. A. Nixon	16	30	7	865	103	1	6	37.60	49/4
1992	M. A. Ealham†	14	24	7	594	83*	0	3	34.94	14
	J. C. Tredwell†	4	6	0	161	61	0	2	26.83	8
1990	M. V. Fleming	4	7	1	109	42*	0	0	18.16	0
2000	M. J. Walker	11	22	3	342	46	0	0	18.00	3
	D. D. Masters†	8	7	0	117	68	0	1	16.71	3
	A. Khan	16	19	5	213	58	0	1	15.21	5
	J. B. Hockley†	4	8	1	80	46	0	0	11.42	1
2001	M. J. Saggers	15	19	6	73	16*	0	0	5.61	5

Also batted: J. P. Hewitt (1 match) 48*; G. O. Jones (3 matches) 40, 28, 19 (2 ct); B. J. Trott (2 matches) 0, 1, 26.

† *Born in Kent.* § *Overseas player.*

BOWLING

	O	M	R	W	BB	5W/i	Avge
M. J. Saggers	547.3	109	1,702	79	6-39	6	21.54
A. Khan	485	75	2,004	63	6-52	4	31.80
M. M. Patel	522.3	152	1,190	36	5-56	1	33.05
M. A. Ealham	351	107	954	28	3-22	0	34.07
J. C. Tredwell	124.2	29	358	10	4-103	0	35.80
D. D. Masters	243.1	46	864	23	4-36	0	37.56
A. Symonds	187.2	34	602	13	6-105	1	46.30

Also bowled: M. V. Fleming 87–18–251–6; J. M. Golding 38.1–6–119–2; J. P. Hewitt 26–5–92–0; P. A. Nixon 0.3–0–8–0; B. J. Trott 40–7–151–5; M. J. Walker 15.3–4–57–0; S. R. Waugh 3–0–15–0.

COUNTY RECORDS

Highest score for:	332	W. H. Ashdown v Essex at Brentwood	1934
Highest score against:	344	W. G. Grace (MCC) at Canterbury	1876
Best bowling for:	10-30	C. Blythe v Northamptonshire at Northampton. . . .	1907
Best bowling against:	10-48	C. H. G. Bland (Sussex) at Tonbridge	1899
Highest total for:	803-4 dec.	v Essex at Brentwood	1934
Highest total against:	676	by Australians at Canterbury.	1921
Lowest total for:	18	v Sussex at Gravesend	1867
Lowest total against:	16	by Warwickshire at Tonbridge.	1913

COUNTY OFFICERS

Captain 2002 – D. P. Fulton/M. V. Fleming; 2003 – D. P. Fulton
Director of cricket I. J. Brayshaw
President 2002 – The Rt Hon. Lord Kingsdown; 2003 – R. H. B. Neame
Chairman C. F. Openshaw • **Chief executive** P. E. Millman
Chairman, cricket committee M. H. Denness • **Head groundsman** M. Grantham
Scorer J. C. Foley

At Canterbury, April 13, 14, 15 (not first-class). **Drawn.** Toss: Kent. **Kent 443 for six dec.** (R. W. T. Key 141, E. T. Smith 56, M. J. Walker 117 not out, J. B. Hockley 77, Extras 39; M. S. Panesar four for 138); **Loughborough UCCE 213** (J. H. K. Adams 103, V. Atri 33; M. V. Fleming four for 18) **and 331 for eight** (J. H. K. Adams 113, J. D. Francis 48, D. F. Watts 59 not out, Extras 36; A. Khan three for 63).

County debut: J. P. Hewitt. Jimmy Adams, who had yet to make his first-class debut, scored a hundred in each innings. From 2003, Loughborough's matches against the counties will be first-class.

KENT v HAMPSHIRE

At Canterbury, April 19, 20, 21, 22. Drawn. Kent 10 pts, Hampshire 11 pts. Toss: Kent. County debuts: J. P. Crawley, N. Pothas. Championship debut: A. Khan.

Neither attack had the subtlety to succeed on a hard, even pitch, and the match produced 1,411 runs and a glut of batting records. In his first innings for Hampshire after an acrimonious departure from Lancashire, Crawley hit 272 – his sixth double-hundred and the highest score for the county since the war. He batted for nine and a half hours, faced 451 balls and hit 36 fours. His masterpiece

MOST SCORES OF 250 OR ABOVE

		Career
16	D. G. Bradman (4 for NSW, 3 for Australians, 5 for Australia, 4 for South Australia)	*1927–48*
13	W. R. Hammond (10 for Gloucestershire, 2 for England, 1 for MCC)	1920–51
7	W. G. Grace (4 for Gloucestershire, 2 for South, 1 for MCC)	1865–1908
7	W. H. Ponsford (5 for Victoria, 1 for Australians, 1 for Australia)	*1920–34*
6	P. Holmes (all for Yorkshire)	1913–35
5	**J. P. Crawley (1 for England A, 3 for Lancashire, 1 for Hampshire)**	1990–
5	L. Hutton (4 for Yorkshire, 1 for England)	1934–60

of determined accumulation was finally, and freakishly, ended when Patel deflected a drive on to the non-striker's stumps. Hampshire, though, went on to a gargantuan 671, one short of their best first-class total but the highest by any county against Kent. This followed Kent's own 577 for seven declared, after Key scythed and pulled his way to a career-best 160, and Symonds blasted anything within reach. With three Hampshire players absent injured on the last afternoon, their coach Jimmy Cook and his son Stephen were both used as substitute fielders.

Close of play: First day, Kent 340-2 (Smith 41, Symonds 21); Second day, Hampshire 136-2 (Crawley 56, Smith 17); Third day, Hampshire 490-4 (Crawley 223, Pothas 32).

Kent

*D. P. Fulton c Tremlett b Johnson	98	– c sub b Tremlett	24
R. W. T. Key run out	160	– c Kenway b Mullally	33
E. T. Smith b Tremlett	52	– c sub b Tremlett	44
A. Symonds c Smith b Tremlett	89	– not out	25
M. J. Walker c Aymes b Tremlett	0	– c Pothas b Johnson	11
†P. A. Nixon c sub b Udal	52	– not out	11
M. V. Fleming c Kenway b Tremlett	1		
M. M. Patel not out	50		
J. P. Hewitt not out	48		
L-b 5, w 22	27	L-b 1, w 4, n-b 10	15

1/266 (2) 2/294 (1) 3/368 (3) (7 wkts dec.) 577   1/39 (2) 2/96 (1) (4 wkts dec.) 163
4/368 (5) 5/451 (4) 3/107 (3) 4/135 (5)
6/455 (7) 7/501 (6)

D. D. Masters and A. Khan did not bat.

Bonus points – Kent 5, Hampshire 2 (130 overs: 496-6).

Bowling: *First Innings*—Mullally 37–9–120–0; Morris 29–5–112–0; Johnson 10–2–33–1; Tremlett 31–5–129–4; Udal 37–6–178–1. *Second Innings*—Mullally 7–1–27–1; Tremlett 10–2–63–2; Kendall 14–2–45–0; Johnson 5–0–19–1; Kenway 1–0–8–0.

Hampshire

D. A. Kenway c Symonds b Khan	18	C. T. Tremlett not out 40
W. S. Kendall c Fulton b Patel	21	A. D. Mullally c Walker b Masters 23
J. P. Crawley run out	272	†A. N. Aymes absent hurt
*R. A. Smith lbw b Khan	31	B 1, l-b 11, n-b 41 53
N. C. Johnson c Fulton b Fleming	117	
N. Pothas st Nixon b Patel	48	671
S. D. Udal retired hurt	36	
A. C. Morris c Masters b Khan	12	

1/35 (1) 2/81 (2) 3/178 (4)
4/410 (5) 5/551 (6) 6/559 (3)
7/585 (8) 8/671 (10)

Bonus points – Hampshire 5, Kent 1 (130 overs: 434-4).

Udal retired hurt at 609.

Bowling: Masters 28–6–92–1; Khan 37–2–165–3; Patel 48–13–130–2; Hewitt 26–5–92–0; Fleming 27–3–81–1; Symonds 26–5–93–0; Walker 3–2–6–0.

Umpires: J. H. Evans and I. J. Gould.

At Canterbury, April 26, 27, 28. KENT drew with SRI LANKANS (see Sri Lankan tour section).

At Southampton, May 8, 9, 10. KENT lost to HAMPSHIRE by eight wickets.

KENT v YORKSHIRE

At Canterbury, May 15, 16, 17, 18. Kent won by four wickets. Kent 20 pts, Yorkshire 4 pts. Toss: Yorkshire.

On the final afternoon Kent came close to losing a match they should have strolled. Key and Smith were cruising towards a target of 168 when five wickets fell for 11 runs. Kent still needed 73 and, with nerves jittery and just four wickets left, Yorkshire were suddenly marginal favourites. However, Fleming restored confidence to the chase, helped settle Walker and made a match-winning 42. Earlier, Khan had taken important wickets at important times, and Key had scored a second domineering hundred of the season; together they inspired Kent to a 179-run first-innings lead. A three-day thrashing looked likely when Yorkshire's second innings collapsed to 151 for six, but Blakey and Dawson made a nuisance of themselves by grinding out 162 in 66 overs and seeing off the second new ball. After starting the season poorly, Yorkshire and Kent had been left at the bottom of the first division; now they parted company decisively.

Close of play: First day, Kent 61-0 (Fulton 25, Key 19); Second day, Yorkshire 22-2 (White 9, Lehmann 6); Third day, Yorkshire 323-7 (Blakey 88, Silverwood 6).

Somerset retrieved the initiative in the dying overs with an ebullience and opportunistic style that will live with the timeless thrills and optical illusions in the history of West Country cricket.
Somerset, page 738

Yorkshire

M. J. Wood c Fulton b Khan	12	– (2) c Nixon b Saggers	7
C. White c Ealham b Patel	104	– (1) c Nixon b Saggers	9
M. J. Lumb b Ealham	17	– c Key b Saggers	0
*D. S. Lehmann lbw b Khan	31	– c Fulton b Patel	72
A. McGrath c Nixon b Khan	0	– lbw b Patel	24
G. M. Fellows b Patel	42	– b Patel	0
†R. J. Blakey c Key b Khan	13	– b Khan	90
R. K. J. Dawson lbw b Patel	4	– c Symonds b Patel	87
C. E. W. Silverwood c Nixon b Khan	0	– b Saggers	10
R. J. Sidebottom not out	1	– not out	6
S. P. Kirby b Khan	1	– c Nixon b Saggers	1
B 5, l-b 7, n-b 2	14	B 4, l-b 22, w 10, n-b 4	40

1/25 (1) 2/66 (3) 3/145 (4) 4/147 (5)   239
5/195 (2) 6/232 (6) 7/234 (7)
8/234 (9) 9/238 (8) 10/239 (11)

1/11 (2) 2/11 (3) 3/22 (1)   346
4/104 (5) 5/104 (6) 6/151 (4)
7/313 (8) 8/327 (9)
9/341 (7) 10/346 (11)

Bonus points – Yorkshire 1, Kent 3.

Bowling: *First Innings*—Saggers 19–2–68–0; Khan 21.2–7–52–6; Ealham 14–5–36–1; Fleming 14–2–45–0; Symonds 5–1–15–0; Patel 14–7–11–3. *Second Innings*—Saggers 30.1–8–82–5; Khan 32–13–63–1; Ealham 14–4–36–0; Patel 35–11–82–4; Symonds 9–0–36–0; Fleming 8–2–21–0.

Kent

*D. P. Fulton c Wood b Silverwood	71	– c White b Kirby	13
R. W. T. Key c Wood b Sidebottom	114	– b Silverwood	37
E. T. Smith lbw b Silverwood	22	– b Lehmann	26
A. Symonds c Fellows b Kirby	48	– lbw b Lehmann	0
M. J. Walker b Sidebottom	0	– not out	31
†P. A. Nixon c Wood b Dawson	28	– lbw b Lehmann	10
M. A. Ealham c Sidebottom b Dawson	34	– lbw b Silverwood	0
M. V. Fleming lbw b Silverwood	15	– not out	42
M. M. Patel not out	29		
A. Khan lbw b Silverwood	0		
M. J. Saggers c Fellows b Sidebottom	9		
B 6, l-b 10, w 2, n-b 30	48	B 4, l-b 2, n-b 4	10

1/198 (1) 2/238 (3) 3/238 (2) 4/238 (5)   418
5/318 (4) 6/347 (6) 7/370 (7)
8/389 (8) 9/389 (10) 10/418 (11)

1/31 (1) 2/84 (3)   (6 wkts) 169
3/84 (2) 4/84 (4)
5/94 (6) 6/95 (7)

Bonus points – Kent 5, Yorkshire 3.

Bowling: *First Innings*—Silverwood 21–4–82–4; Kirby 17–3–87–1; Dawson 12–0–53–2; Sidebottom 20.3–2–82–3; White 14–1–39–0; Lehmann 14–3–35–0; Fellows 7–1–24–0. *Second Innings*—Silverwood 16–4–38–2; Fellows 3–0–13–0; Kirby 8–2–28–1; Dawson 10–1–27–0; Lehmann 18–5–40–3; White 3–0–9–0; McGrath 0.2–0–8–0.

Umpires: J. H. Evans and V. A. Holder.

KENT v SUSSEX

At Tunbridge Wells, May 31, June 1, 2, 3. Kent won by four wickets. Kent 18 pts, Sussex 3 pts. Toss: Kent.

The Nevill Ground was still drying after a recent flood, but it was swing rather than a capricious pitch that scuppered Sussex's first innings. Saggers bowled superbly to reduce a promising 89 for one to a poor 180 all out; a second turning point came when Ealham and Trott redeemed Kent's reply by cracking a demoralising 77 for the last wicket. It gave them a first-innings lead of 163, but Sussex's openers wiped out 146 before Symonds's off-breaks snared Montgomerie. On a pitch taking spin, only Prior played consistently against Symonds, who went on to a career-best six for 105 as Sussex slowly subsided. Kent needed 192, and Smith took them most of the way with a selection of classical drives before he became the first of three wickets in the space of seven overs. But they were already close enough. Walker – using a runner after spraining his ankle – and Patel swatted Davis's ineffective off-spin to complete a win that lifted Kent out of the bottom three.

Close of play: First day, Kent 156-3 (Symonds 53, Saggers 0); Second day, Sussex 117-0 (Montgomerie 68, Goodwin 41); Third day, Kent 134-3 (Smith 74, Nixon 23).

Sussex

M. W. Goodwin lbw b Saggers	18	– (2) c Fulton b Symonds	76
R. R. Montgomerie c Fulton b Ealham	35	– (1) c Fulton b Symonds	79
M. H. Yardy b Saggers	28	– c Key b Patel	10
P. A. Cottey c Symonds b Saggers	17	– c Fulton b Symonds	2
T. R. Ambrose b Saggers	0	– lbw b Symonds	9
R. S. C. Martin-Jenkins c Ealham b Saggers	7	– c Key b Symonds	19
†M. J. Prior lbw b Saggers	10	– c Saggers b Khan	67
K. J. Innes lbw b Ealham	13	– c Key b Symonds	28
M. J. G. Davis not out	24	– lbw b Patel	18
*R. J. Kirtley c Ealham b Trott	1	– c Fulton b Trott	14
J. D. Lewry c and b Patel	0	– not out	7
B 8, l-b 11, w 6, n-b 2	27	B 17, l-b 6, w 2	25
	180		**354**

1/24 (1) 2/89 (2) 3/96 (3) 4/100 (5)
5/124 (6) 6/133 (7) 7/140 (7)
8/173 (8) 9/175 (10) 10/180 (11)

1/146 (1) 2/169 (2) 3/179 (3)
4/179 (4) 5/194 (5) 6/219 (6)
7/275 (8) 8/314 (9)
9/346 (10) 10/354 (7)

Bonus points – Kent 3.

Bowling: *First Innings*—Saggers 18–6–39–6; Khan 12–3–34–0; Trott 8–1–22–1; Symonds 9–3–20–0; Ealham 11–2–30–2; Patel 10–5–16–1. *Second Innings*—Saggers 10–2–38–0; Trott 6–0–33–1; Patel 33–4–99–2; Khan 8.4–0–47–1; Symonds 31–3–105–6; Walker 4–1–9–0.

Kent

*D. P. Fulton lbw b Innes	20	– c Goodwin b Lewry	20
R. W. T. Key c Yardy b Martin-Jenkins	39	– c Goodwin b Kirtley	13
E. T. Smith c Montgomerie b Kirtley	89	– c and b Kirtley	82
A. Symonds c Lewry b Martin-Jenkins	89	– c Kirtley b Lewry	0
M. J. Saggers lbw b Kirtley	2		
M. J. Walker lbw b Lewry	14	– (7) not out	13
†P. A. Nixon b Kirtley	6	– (5) c Prior b Davis	32
M. A. Ealham not out	83	– (6) c Prior b Kirtley	17
M. M. Patel b Lewry	7	– (8) not out	13
A. Khan lbw b Lewry	8		
B. J. Trott c Yardy b Kirtley	26		
B 7, l-b 8, w 4, n-b 8	27	L-b 3, w 2	5
	343	(6 wkts)	**195**

1/69 (2) 2/75 (1) 3/152 (3) 4/158 (5)
5/209 (4) 6/209 (6) 7/233 (7)
8/238 (9) 9/266 (10) 10/343 (11)

1/26 (2) 2/59 (1)
3/59 (4) 4/143 (3)
5/161 (5) 6/173 (6)

Bonus points – Kent 3, Sussex 3.

Bowling: *First Innings*—Lewry 27–5–90–3; Kirtley 30.4–8–88–4; Martin-Jenkins 26–5–84–2; Innes 15–7–31–1; Yardy 4–1–24–0; Davis 4–1–11–0. *Second Innings*—Lewry 6–0–36–2; Kirtley 16–5–39–3; Martin-Jenkins 13–4–35–0; Davis 17.5–4–66–1; Innes 3–0–16–0.

Umpires: A. A. Jones and B. Leadbeater.

At The Oval, June 12, 13, 14. KENT lost to SURREY by nine wickets.

At Canterbury, June 23. KENT beat WEST INDIES A by six wickets (see West Indies A tour section).

At Canterbury, June 24. KENT beat INDIANS by 21 runs (see Indian tour section).

At Liverpool, June 26, 27, 28, 29. KENT beat LANCASHIRE by six wickets.

KENT v WARWICKSHIRE

At Maidstone, July 3, 4, 5, 6. Drawn. Kent 10 pts, Warwickshire 7 pts. Toss: Kent.
Both teams were left chasing bonus points after the first and third days were completely washed out. Fulton made his 12th first-class hundred since the beginning of the 2001 season, and Kent, 179 for one on the second afternoon, were on course for an intimidating total before they collapsed to 229 for six. Patel and Golding edged them past 300 to earn a third batting point, but the momentum was lost. On the last day, Warwickshire struggled against Patel, who got significant turn and took a season's-best five for 56, but a draw was the only conceivable result. Brown missed the game after bruising his foot during a kickabout on the outfield. It was Warwickshire's second football-related injury, after Wagh injured his knee in pre-season training.

Close of play: First day, No play; Second day, Warwickshire 29-2 (Bell 3, Betts 6); Third day, No play.

Kent

*D. P. Fulton lbw b Wagg	101	– c Smith b Pollock	7
R. W. T. Key c Clifford b Spires	62	– lbw b Carter	8
E. T. Smith lbw b Wagg	7	– b Carter	0
A. Symonds st Clifford b Spires	9	– c Clifford b Carter	16
M. J. Walker c Powell b Smith	43	– c Troughton b Spires	20
†P. A. Nixon lbw b Smith	7	– not out	34
M. A. Ealham lbw b Betts	7	– not out	24
J. M. Golding c Bell b Pollock	32		
M. M. Patel c Wagg b Spires	17		
A. Khan b Wagg	2		
M. J. Saggers not out	1		
B 1, l-b 3, n-b 14	18	B 6, l-b 1, n-b 2	9

1/140 (2) 2/179 (3) 3/180 (1)   **306**   1/14 (2) 2/14 (3)   (5 wkts dec.) **118**
4/194 (4) 5/208 (6) 6/229 (7) 7/266 (5)   3/32 (1) 4/32 (4)
8/301 (9) 9/304 (10) 10/306 (8)   5/83 (5)

Bonus points – Kent 3, Warwickshire 3.

Bowling: *First Innings*—Pollock 16.4–7–18–1; Betts 13–0–54–1; Wagg 14–2–38–3; Carter 8–0–47–0; Smith 13–2–62–2; Powell 2–0–15–0; Spires 28–8–68–3. *Second Innings*—Pollock 8–1–23–1; Carter 10–3–24–3; Spires 9–2–32–1; Smith 4–0–10–0; Troughton 4–0–9–0; Ostler 1–0–13–0; Powell 1–1–0–0.

Warwickshire

*M. J. Powell lbw b Patel	. . . .	6
†I. J. Clifford lbw b Saggers	. . . . . .	4
I. R. Bell c Fulton b Patel	. . . .	31
M. M. Betts b Patel	. . . .	22
D. P. Ostler c Nixon b Ealham	. . . . . .	21
J. O. Troughton not out	. . . .	30
S. M. Pollock c Symonds b Khan	. . . . .	5
G. G. Wagg b Patel	. . . .	18
N. M. K. Smith b Ealham	. . . .	8
N. M. Carter b Patel	. . . .	1
J. A. Spires b Ealham	. . . .	2
B 5, l-b 3, n-b 16		24
		172

1/11 (2) 2/21 (1) 3/69 (4)
4/84 (3) 5/102 (5) 6/118 (7) 7/151 (8)
8/164 (9) 9/165 (10) 10/172 (11)

Bonus points – Kent 3.

Bowling: Saggers 13–2–36–1; Khan 16–3–50–1; Patel 20–6–56–5; Ealham 11.3–2–22–3.

Umpires: M. J. Harris and J. W. Holder.

At Hove, July 10, 11, 12, 13. KENT drew with SUSSEX.

KENT v SURREY

At Canterbury, July 19, 20, 21, 22. Surrey won by two wickets. Surrey 16 pts, Kent 7 pts. Toss: Kent.

A remarkable game ended in an astonishing win for Surrey, and proved to be a turning point in the struggle for the Championship. Kent dominated the first three days, only to be mugged on the last, when Ward and two tailenders cobbled together the highest successful run-chase in Surrey's history. With 410 needed, defeat looked a formality at 208 for seven, but what began as futile but entertaining hitting from Saqlain Mushtaq grew into a real worry for Kent as he and Ward put on 105. Nervous bowlers lost control of their line, allowing Ormond to make 43 at No. 10, without which Ward's immaculately judged, chanceless career-best 168 would have been in vain. Kent, though, should have been out of sight long before the final day. Their first innings had begun in style, as Fulton and Key built their fifth century opening stand of the season and Symonds walloped a hundred of fearsome power. Surrey's spinners then took control and 285 for three became 374 all out. Kent's second innings also stalled – four middle-order wickets fell for 15 – but after a miserable first attempt from Surrey, it didn't seem to matter. With Saggers and Khan finding swing, only Hollioake resisted, crashing an unbeaten 122 despite a chipped bone in his finger and an injured knee. Kent would have gone second, eight points behind Surrey, if they had won; instead, they remained fourth, and Surrey moved 24 points clear.

Close of play: First day, Surrey 20-1 (Butcher 5, Salisbury 2); Second day, Kent 174-6 (Key 63, Golding 12); Third day, Surrey 264-7 (Ward 115, Saqlain Mushtaq 31).

Kent

*D. P. Fulton c Clarke b Saqlain Mushtaq	. . . .	62
R. W. T. Key lbw b Saqlain Mushtaq	. . . .	57
E. T. Smith run out	. . . .	19
A. Symonds b Saqlain Mushtaq	. . . .	118
J. B. Hockley st Batty b Salisbury	. . . .	46
†P. A. Nixon c Giddins b Salisbury	. . . .	8
M. A. Ealham c Batty b Salisbury	. . . .	18
J. M. Golding not out	. . . .	24
M. M. Patel b Salisbury	. . . .	1
A. Khan lbw b Saqlain Mushtaq	. . . .	1
M. J. Saggers b Saqlain Mushtaq	. . . .	0
B 6, l-b 4, w 6, n-b 4		20
		374

– c Batty b Giddins 11
– c Batty b Ormond 68
– c Ramprakash b Ormond 6
– c Ward b Saqlain Mushtaq 51
– c Ward b Saqlain Mushtaq 8
– c Batty b Saqlain Mushtaq 1
– b Salisbury 0
– lbw b Giddins 26
– not out 43
– lbw b Salisbury 11
– lbw b Saqlain Mushtaq 2
B 5, l-b 16, w 2, n-b 10 . . 33
260

1/121 (1) 2/122 (2) 3/155 (3) 4/285 (5)
5/321 (6) 6/329 (4) 7/371 (7)
8/373 (9) 9/374 (10) 10/374 (11)

1/18 (1) 2/33 (3) 3/130 (4)
4/142 (5) 5/144 (6) 6/145 (7)
7/189 (2) 8/203 (8)
9/255 (10) 10/260 (11)

Bonus points – Kent 4, Surrey 3.

Bowling: *First Innings*—Giddins 17–5–39–0; Ormond 14–2–80–0; Clarke 8–0–56–0; Saqlain Mushtaq 33.5–8–122–5; Hollioake 2–0–8–0; Salisbury 17–3–59–4. *Second Innings*—Giddins 15–3–40–2; Ormond 17–3–61–2; Clarke 4–0–23–0; Saqlain Mushtaq 19.5–3–60–4; Salisbury 18–1–55–2.

Surrey

M. A. Butcher c Fulton b Khan	34	– c Symonds b Saggers	20
I. J. Ward c Nixon b Khan.	7	– not out	168
I. D. K. Salisbury b Saggers	2	– (8) b Ealham	5
M. R. Ramprakash c Nixon b Saggers	0	– (3) c Nixon b Saggers	2
R. Clarke c Nixon b Khan	5	– (4) c Hockley b Symonds.	66
A. D. Brown b Saggers	9	– (5) c Ealham b Symonds	0
*A. J. Hollioake not out	122	– (6) c Nixon b Saggers	8
†J. N. Batty c Symonds b Golding	8	– (7) c Key b Symonds	0
Saqlain Mushtaq b Saggers	4	– c Patel b Khan	60
J. Ormond b Khan	4	– not out	43
E. S. H. Giddins c Symonds b Saggers	1		
L-b 13, w 2, n-b 14.	29	B 17, l-b 13, w 2, n-b 6 . .	38
	225	(8 wkts)	**410**

1/16 (2) 2/29 (3) 3/29 (4) 4/34 (5)
5/59 (1) 6/77 (6) 7/126 (8)
8/169 (9) 9/184 (10) 10/225 (11)

1/52 (1) 2/54 (3)
3/177 (4) 4/181 (5)
5/190 (6) 6/191 (7)
7/208 (8) 8/313 (9)

Bonus points – Surrey 1, Kent 3.

Bowling: *First Innings*—Saggers 13.5–3–66–5; Khan 16–2–91–4; Patel 6–3–21–0; Golding 8–2–13–1; Ealham 6–2–21–0; Symonds 1–1–0–0. *Second Innings*—Saggers 31–6–85–3; Khan 20–3–91–1; Symonds 28–5–85–3; Ealham 19.3–7–42–1; Golding 8–1–27–0; Patel 20–6–50–0.

Umpires: D. J. Constant and T. E. Jesty.

At Leicester, July 24, 25, 26, 27. KENT beat LEICESTERSHIRE by six wickets.

KENT v SOMERSET

At Canterbury, August 7, 8, 9, 10. Kent won by 153 runs. Kent 17 pts, Somerset 4 pts. Toss: Kent.

Kent left themselves 86 overs to bowl out Somerset, but required only 49 after Saggers burst through the top order. From 67 for five, only Parsons and Turner delayed the defeat – which came with Fulton's sixth catch of the match. Earlier, Fulton's controlled 89 and a brutal 69 from Symonds had given Kent's first innings solid foundations, but Caddick, returning after seven weeks out with a side strain, found steep bounce, took wickets in each of his three spells and kept Kent in check. In reply, Khan's raw pace quickly picked off Cox and Burns, and he later returned to accelerate a helter-skelter collapse of six for 32. However, Johnson dragged Somerset within 44 of Kent's total by hammering 49 off just 29 balls before rain lopped 82 overs off the third day. But the match slipped away from Somerset as Patel quickly boosted Kent's lead on the final morning to set up an early declaration.

Close of play: First day, Somerset 64-2 (Wood 26, Bowler 17); Second day, Kent 176-5 (Smith 54, Ealham 35); Third day, Kent 221-6 (Ealham 53, Patel 25).

Kent

*D. P. Fulton c Turner b Caddick	89	– c Turner b Caddick	35
M. J. Walker lbw b Johnson	13	– c Turner b Bulbeck	24
E. T. Smith c Parsons b Caddick	14	– c Bowler b Bulbeck	55
A. Symonds c Caddick b Johnson	69	– lbw b Johnson	19
J. B. Hockley c Bowler b Caddick	1	– c Parsons b Caddick	4
†P. A. Nixon c Parsons b Bulbeck	9	– c Bowler b Caddick	1
M. A. Ealham not out	36	– c Turner b Johnson	60
M. M. Patel c Dutch b Burns	15	– not out	71
A. Khan c Turner b Bulbeck	6	– not out	7
D. D. Masters c Bowler b Caddick	3		
M. J. Saggers lbw b Caddick	0		
L-b 4, w 6, n-b 6	16	L-b 4, n-b 6	10
	271	(7 wkts dec.)	286

1/28 (2) 2/49 (3) 3/166 (4) 4/175 (5)
5/202 (1) 6/212 (6) 7/253 (8)
8/266 (9) 9/271 (10) 10/271 (11)

1/49 (2) 2/79 (1)   (7 wkts dec.) 286
3/108 (4) 4/113 (5)
5/115 (6) 6/182 (3) 7/252 (7)

Bonus points – Kent 2, Somerset 3.

Bowling: *First Innings*—Caddick 22–5–65–5; Johnson 18–2–62–2; Bulbeck 16–3–68–2; Burns 6–1–21–1; Parsons 12–3–30–0; Blackwell 4–0–21–0. *Second Innings*—Caddick 29–4–108–3; Johnson 24–4–79–2; Bulbeck 17–2–50–2; Parsons 7–2–29–0; Dutch 3–1–7–0; Blackwell 3–0–7–0; Burns 2–1–2–0.

Somerset

*J. Cox lbw b Khan	1	– lbw b Saggers	3
M. J. Wood b Khan	55	– c Fulton b Khan	5
M. Burns c Fulton b Khan	4	– c Symonds b Saggers	10
P. D. Bowler c Fulton b Ealham	50	– c and b Saggers	6
K. A. Parsons lbw b Khan	11	– c Walker b Ealham	52
I. D. Blackwell c Ealham b Patel	0	– c Nixon b Masters	12
†R. J. Turner c Smith b Symonds	19	– lbw b Saggers	35
K. P. Dutch c Fulton b Khan	0	– c Symonds b Ealham	0
M. P. L. Bulbeck c Fulton b Saggers	2	– c Nixon b Khan	16
R. L. Johnson not out	49	– not out	18
A. R. Caddick c Saggers b Masters	7	– c Fulton b Saggers	7
L-b 11, n-b 18	29	L-b 5, n-b 8	13
	227		177

1/1 (1) 2/7 (3) 3/124 (4) 4/143 (5)
5/146 (2) 6/146 (6) 7/147 (8)
8/156 (9) 9/198 (7) 10/227 (11)

1/4 (1) 2/18 (3) 3/26 (2) 4/38 (4)   177
5/67 (6) 6/123 (5) 7/123 (8)
8/148 (7) 9/156 (9) 10/177 (11)

Bonus points – Somerset 1, Kent 3.

Bowling: *First Innings*—Saggers 19–4–48–1; Khan 18–3–76–5; Masters 12.5–3–35–1; Ealham 12–5–29–1; Symonds 5–1–25–1; Patel 4–2–3–1. *Second Innings*—Saggers 10.3–2–42–5; Khan 14–1–54–2; Patel 8–1–22–0; Symonds 5–1–10–0; Masters 5–1–23–1; Ealham 6–2–21–2.

Umpires: K. E. Palmer and D. R. Shepherd.

At Birmingham, August 14, 15, 16, 17. KENT lost to WARWICKSHIRE by ten wickets.

KENT v LEICESTERSHIRE

At Canterbury, August 22, 23, 24, 25. Drawn. Kent 11 pts, Leicestershire 9 pts. Toss: Leicestershire. First-class debut: G. W. Walker. Championship debut: A. S. Wright.

Determined resistance, centred on a gritty hundred from Maddy, frustrated Kent. With 66 overs to go, Leicestershire led by 164 with only four wickets left, but Maddy shrugged off two wince-inducing blows and hung on, and DeFreitas made the game safe with an incendiary 94. The draw left Kent a purely mathematical chance of winning the title. After Leicestershire chose to bat, only Sutcliffe denied Saggers and the sparky Ealham for long, and he carried his bat for a stubborn century. In reply, Waugh's much-heralded return to Championship cricket was an anticlimax: he retired hurt for six hours after his finger was split open by Malcolm and scored just 16. However, Smith, mixing the streaky and the sumptuous, Nixon and Patel all made eighties, which set Kent on course for a win. They might have got one, had Saggers not dropped a simple chance when Maddy had 87. Leicestershire's 18-year-old left-arm spinner, George Walker, hit an unbeaten 37.

Close of play: First day, Leicestershire 240-9 (Sutcliffe 119); Second day, Kent 217-4 (Nixon 74, Ealham 0); Third day, Leicestershire 169-3 (Maddy 41, Wright 16).

Leicestershire

T. R. Ward c Walker b Saggers	3	– c Ealham b Saggers	66
*I. J. Sutcliffe not out	125	– c Nixon b Patel	21
D. L. Maddy lbw b Saggers	9	– c Patel b Masters	156
D. I. Stevens b Ealham	8	– c Patel b Saggers	0
A. S. Wright c Waugh b Patel	1	– b Ealham	28
†N. D. Burns c Fulton b Saggers	23	– c Ealham b Patel	24
R. J. Cunliffe b Ealham	23	– lbw b Khan	0
P. A. J. DeFreitas c Smith b Ealham	18	– c Waugh b Khan	94
J. Srinath b Patel	15	– st Nixon b Patel	90
G. W. Walker c Fulton b Masters	7	– not out	37
D. E. Malcolm b Saggers	9	– b Patel	44
B 6, l-b 3, w 2, n-b 7	18	L-b 13, w 12, n-b 30, p 5	60

1/6 (1) 2/16 (3) 3/48 (4) 4/55 (5)   259
5/89 (6) 6/153 (7) 7/173 (8)
8/217 (9) 9/240 (10) 10/259 (11)

1/69 (2) 2/132 (1) 3/132 (4)   530
4/222 (5) 5/268 (6) 6/271 (7)
7/410 (3) 8/441 (8)
9/441 (9) 10/530 (11)

Bonus points – Leicestershire 2, Kent 3.

Bowling: *First Innings*—Saggers 19–4–68–4; Khan 16–5–50–0; Patel 23–13–30–2; Ealham 18–8–37–3; Masters 15–2–65–1. *Second Innings*—Saggers 23–5–66–2; Khan 24–0–170–2; Masters 21–2–116–1; Patel 52.5–18–99–4; Walker 3–0–17–0; Ealham 15–7–44–1.

Kent

*D. P. Fulton c Burns b Srinath	13	– not out	41
M. J. Walker c Walker b Malcolm	1	– not out	11
E. T. Smith lbw b Srinath	87		
S. R. Waugh c Maddy b Srinath	16		
†P. A. Nixon b DeFreitas	86		
M. A. Ealham c Burns b Srinath	0		
G. O. Jones c Burns b Maddy	40		
M. M. Patel c and b DeFreitas	82		
D. D. Masters c Cunliffe b DeFreitas	7		
A. Khan c Wright b Malcolm	3		
M. J. Saggers not out	0		
B 1, l-b 16, w 12, n-b 15	44	W 6	6

1/14 (1) 2/14 (2) 3/197 (3) 4/211 (4)   379
5/217 (6) 6/251 (5) 7/344 (7)
8/372 (9) 9/377 (8) 10/379 (10)

(no wkt) 58

Bonus points – Kent 4, Leicestershire 3.

In the first innings Waugh, when 12, retired hurt at 26 and resumed at 197.

Bowling: *First Innings*—Srinath 26–8–70–4; Malcolm 20.2–0–98–2; DeFreitas 32–8–71–3; Maddy 20–3–83–1; Walker 5–0–26–0; Stevens 6–1–14–0. *Second Innings*—Stevens 4–1–16–0; Walker 8–2–24–0; Ward 3–0–15–0; Sutcliffe 1–0–3–0.

Umpires: J. W. Holder and T. E. Jesty.

At Taunton, September 4, 5, 6, 7. KENT drew with SOMERSET.

KENT v LANCASHIRE

At Canterbury, September 11, 12, 13, 14. Kent won by six wickets. Kent 19 pts, Lancashire 2 pts. Toss: Kent.

With the title already decided, Kent were scrapping for second place – and a £50,000 cheque. On a flat pitch Fulton and Key completed their sixth century partnership of the summer, and Fulton went on to a careful 177, Kent's best score in 2002. They lost their way on the second morning as eight wickets tumbled for 119, but below-par batting by Lancashire handed back control. Byas perished after changing his mind about a third run; Saggers found dangerous away swing to take three for four in 18 balls; and Lancashire were forced to follow on 208 behind. Chilton and Law gave them hope with a diligent century stand, and Hegg and Schofield added 75, but Kent were left to chase only 144. They won with more than seven overs to spare, completing a double against Lancashire. Fairbrother was greeted warmly on his last appearance at Canterbury.

Close of play: First day, Kent 286-2 (Fulton 137, Waugh 0); Second day, Lancashire 164-8 (Martin 19, Keedy 0); Third day, Lancashire 224-3 (Chilton 89, Keedy 2).

Kent

*D. P. Fulton c and b Keedy	177	– c Chilton b Chapple	6
R. W. T. Key b Chapple	75	– b Martin	37
E. T. Smith st Hegg b Keedy	68	– lbw b Schofield	68
S. R. Waugh lbw b Chapple	5	– not out	20
†P. A. Nixon c Hegg b Martin	1	– c Law b Schofield	6
M. A. Ealham b Anderson	33	– not out	3
G. O. Jones c Hegg b Anderson	18		
M. M. Patel run out	15		
J. C. Tredwell lbw b Anderson	2		
A. Khan not out	0		
M. J. Saggers c Swann b Martin	1		
L-b 10	10	L-b 2, n-b 2	4
	405	**(4 wkts)**	**144**

1/148 (2) 2/286 (3) 3/295 (4) 4/302 (5)   1/8 (1) 2/67 (2)
5/361 (1) 6/371 (6) 7/394 (7)   3/135 (3) 4/141 (5)
8/398 (9) 9/403 (8) 10/405 (11)

Bonus points – Kent 4, Lancashire 2 (130 overs: 398-7).

Bowling: *First Innings*—Martin 25.4–4–69–2; Chapple 22–5–48–2; Chilton 12–2–26–0; Anderson 22–3–88–3; Keedy 28–5–93–2; Schofield 18–2–59–0; Law 3–1–2–0; Fairbrother 3–0–10–0. *Second Innings*—Chapple 9–0–27–1; Anderson 9.2–0–42–0; Martin 7–0–34–1; Keedy 8–3–23–0; Schofield 5–0–16–2.

Lancashire

M. J. Chilton c Nixon b Ealham	23	– b Saggers	90
A. J. Swann c Nixon b Saggers	38	– b Khan	8
D. Byas run out	6	– b Khan	2
S. G. Law c Nixon b Ealham	13	– c Smith b Tredwell	90
N. H. Fairbrother c Nixon b Saggers	10	– (6) b Tredwell	13
G. Chapple c Tredwell b Khan	14	– (7) lbw b Saggers	17
C. P. Schofield c Jones b Saggers	14	– (8) c Key b Patel	33
*†W. K. Hegg c Nixon b Khan	13	– (9) c Khan b Saggers	43
P. J. Martin lbw b Saggers	25	– (10) lbw b Saggers	0
G. Keedy not out	16	– (5) c Nixon b Khan	3
J. M. Anderson c Waugh b Tredwell	5	– not out	2
B 12, l-b 8, n-b 14	34	B 17, l-b 11, w 6, n-b 16	50
	197		**351**

1/57 (1) 2/65 (3) 3/94 (4) 4/102 (2)   1/29 (2) 2/55 (3) 3/219 (4)
5/111 (5) 6/111 (7) 7/139 (8)   4/225 (1) 5/229 (5) 6/258 (7)
8/158 (6) 9/177 (9) 10/197 (11)   7/272 (6) 8/347 (9)
    9/347 (8) 10/351 (10)

Bonus points – Kent 3.

Bowling: *First Innings*—Saggers 21–5–34–4; Khan 14–0–67–2; Ealham 20–7–47–2; Patel 14–7–20–0; Tredwell 2.2–0–9–1. *Second Innings*—Saggers 20.4–3–64–4; Ealham 17–3–57–0; Khan 17–3–63–3; Patel 49–16–73–1; Tredwell 40–15–66–2.

Umpires: R. Palmer and A. G. T. Whitehead.

At Leeds, September 18, 19, 20. KENT beat YORKSHIRE by eight wickets.

WALTER LAWRENCE TROPHY

The Walter Lawrence Trophy for the fastest first-class century in 2002 was won by Matthew Fleming of Kent, who reached 100 in 66 balls against the Sri Lankans at Canterbury in April. His nearest rival was Neil Carter of Warwickshire, who reached his maiden hundred in 67 balls against Sussex at Hove in September. Fleming, who retired from first-class cricket at the end of the season, received £5,000 from the trophy's sponsors, Aon.

ERRATA

WISDEN, 1987
Page 394   S. J. Base's highest innings in the Championship season was 15*, not 13*.

WISDEN, 2001
Page 56   Darren Lehmann married Craig White's sister Andrea in 1999.
Pages 1396-7   In the Ranji final, Mumbai's seventh wicket fell at 377 in their second innings, and Hyderabad's seventh wicket fell at 186 in their first. Hyderabad's second-innings Extras consisted of five byes, three leg-byes and six no-balls.

WISDEN, 2002
Page 28   The picture of the Bradman Museum in Bowral was supplied back to front.
Page 709   In Yorkshire's Championship averages, J. D. Middlebrook made two catches and S. P. Kirby four.
Page 714   R. K. J. Dawson made his Championship debut against Leicestershire; he had made his first-class debut for British Universities v Zimbabweans in June 2000.
Page 745   In Yorkshire's C&G quarter-final against Warwickshire on July 25, S. P. Kirby was bowled by Drakes, not caught behind.
Page 1575   We believe that Alf Gover was the first Surrey fast bowler to take 200 wickets in a season since Tom Richardson in 1897.

LANCASHIRE
ACCENTUATE THE POSITIVE

Ch'ship 4th in Division 1
C&G 4th round
B&H semi-finalists
NUL 5th in Division 2

Player of the season: Glen Chapple

They battled to avoid relegation in the Championship and failed to climb out of Division Two of the League. They suffered an embarrassing defeat in the C&G and a nerve-shredding one in the B&H. But what a good season Lancashire had.

Three new signings made their mark, and five young players broke into the side. Mike Watkinson, the manager, and Warren Hegg, the captain, improved organisation and team spirit in their first year in charge, and the players stuck to a charter encouraging positive thought and action. A lengthy dispute with John Crawley, the previous captain, ended with him buying out the last three years of his contract for a five-figure sum. But after a troubled winter the new regime created a happy dressing-room. Watkinson impressed the players with his communication skills and business-like approach and, with Hegg, underlined the importance of having fun. "The dressing-room *craic* hasn't been as good as this for years," said Peter Martin.

There were lows, however, none worse than the last-ball defeat in the B&H semi-final when the Warwickshire No. 11, Neil Carter, audaciously grabbed the winning runs to stun the Old Trafford crowd and players. Hegg, who called it the worst moment of his career, threw himself to the ground and pummelled the grass in anguish. The knock-on effect was huge: just 12 days later, Lancashire were humiliated in the C&G at Chelmsford, prompting a group of angry fans to stomp out of the ground shouting "rubbish". Essex had just beaten them in the Norwich Union League too, and it would be another month before Lancashire won again.

Those two cup defeats were part of a dismal run of 12 winless games which brought a slump into the bottom four in both leagues. David Byas, who missed the bulk of that period with a broken knuckle, returned to score a painstaking 78 and help beat Derbyshire in the Norwich Union League. It proved a turning point: Lancashire lost only four more matches all season. Byas, Yorkshire captain only a year earlier, scored fewer runs than expected but made an invaluable contribution to a team in transition. Watkinson had sparked off controversy on both sides of the Pennines by luring him out of retirement, but it proved a sound move. In December, though, Byas announced he had turned down Lancashire's offer of another season to devote himself to his farming business.

Two other signings, Stuart Law and Alec Swann, were successes. Both passed 1,000 runs – no surprise in the case of Law, but a real achievement from Swann after six modest seasons at Northamptonshire. He formed a reliable opening partnership with Mark Chilton, hit a century in each of his first two Roses matches, and carried his bat against Hampshire. But the Player of the Year was Glen Chapple, who missed only one game in the four competitions. Never the luckiest of bowlers, he sent down 100 first-class overs at one stage without a wicket, but finished with 54 in the Championship, as well as 493 runs after being promoted to No. 6. Martin's testimonial year was a productive one with 53 wickets, while his 117 against Warwickshire was the highest score ever made by a Lancashire No. 10. Chris Schofield regained his confidence in the Second Eleven before bouncing back with some sparkling batting to win his county cap, while Andrew Flintoff was limited by England call-ups and injury to a single Championship appearance, when he hit 137 against Surrey. Harbhajan Singh, India's exceptional young off-spinner, was signed as the second overseas player for 2003.

The 2002 season will be best remembered for the exciting emergence of Lancashire's young brigade, led by the teenagers Kyle Hogg and Jimmy Anderson. Hogg, a third-generation Lancashire player as the son of the fast bowler Willie Hogg and grandson of the great West Indian spinner Sonny Ramadhin, took five for 48 in the opening game and hit a half-century in the last. A promising left-handed bat and a seamer with a smooth bowling action, he had risen through England's junior ranks. The progress of Anderson was more of a surprise. Nicknamed the Burnley Express, he had been struggling in the Second Eleven in 2001, but quickly had the critics drooling over his pace and accuracy and claimed 24 wickets in five mid-season Championship matches. Both were chosen for the England Academy, and as England's injuries multiplied, Anderson was rushed into the one-day squad. He took the new ball in the VB Series, was England's joint leading wicket-taker with 13, broke the record for the most economical figures against Australia in a one-day international with 10–6–12–1 at Adelaide, and went off to the World Cup with more one-day games for England under his belt (nine) than for Lancashire (three).

Lancashire also gave first-class debuts to Mark Currie, an opener, Tim Rees, a middle-order batsman, and Sajid Mahmood, an all-rounder, but released Tim Roberts and Ryan Driver. With an eye on the future, they opened their academy, with John Stanworth as director.

The retirement of Neil Fairbrother and Graham Lloyd confirmed the end of an era: only Hegg, Martin, Chapple and Gary Yates (now Second Eleven coach) remain from the glittering 1990s. The holes in the batting were filled by signing Mal Loye from Northamptonshire and Iain Sutcliffe from Leicestershire. With 36 seasons' service between them, Fairbrother and Lloyd received a warm send-off at Old Trafford in the Norwich Union League game against Northamptonshire. It had perhaps been a season too many for Fairbrother, and he was never fully fit after a knee operation caused him to miss the first four Championship games. Among the many peaks of a career stretching back 21 seasons were seven triumphant cup finals at Lord's and some of England's canniest one-day innings. **Colin Evans**

LANCASHIRE 2002

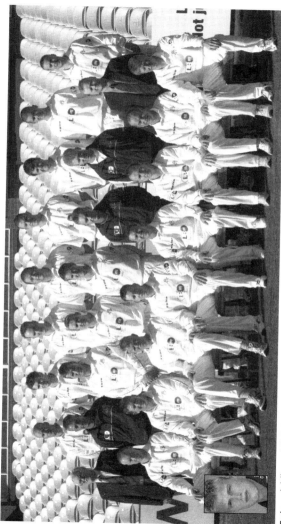

Back row: J. J. Haynes, J. M. Anderson, R. C. Driver, J. Wood, M. P. Smethurst, A. J. Swann, K. W. Hogg, T. W. Roberts. *Middle row:* A. West (*first-team scorer*), M. Watkinson (*cricket manager*), D. Byas, C. P. Schofield, M. J. Chilton, B. Robinson (*physiotherapist*), G. Rodgers (*fitness coach*), D. White (*second-team scorer*). *Front row:* G. Keedy, G. Yates, P. J. Martin, S. G. Law, W. K. Hegg (*captain*), N. H. Fairbrother, G. D. Lloyd, G. Chapple. *Inset:* A. Flintoff. *Main picture by John Dawson Cricket Images.*

LANCASHIRE RESULTS

All first-class matches – Played 18: Won 6, Lost 4, Drawn 8.
County Championship matches – Played 16: Won 6, Lost 4, Drawn 6.

COUNTY CHAMPIONSHIP AVERAGES: BATTING AND FIELDING

Cap		M	I	NO	R	HS	100s	50s	Avge	Ct/St
2002	S. G. Law§	15	26	3	1,216	218	2	6	52.86	21
2002	A. J. Swann	16	28	2	1,006	128	2	3	38.69	12
1994	P. J. Martin†	12	16	5	422	117*	1	1	38.36	4
2002	C. P. Schofield†	6	8	0	262	91	0	1	32.75	3
1992	G. D. Lloyd†	6	11	1	304	80	0	3	30.40	4
2002	D. Byas	14	23	2	634	101	1	4	30.19	15
2002	M. J. Chilton	16	28	1	654	90	0	4	24.22	15
1994	G. Chapple	16	23	6	493	65	0	4	22.40	6
1985	N. H. Fairbrother†	11	18	1	305	39	0	0	17.94	9
1989	W. K. Hegg†	15	22	2	354	43	0	0	17.70	43/2
	J. Wood	7	11	0	185	64	0	1	16.81	2
2000	G. Keedy	14	21	7	217	57	0	0	15.50	4
	R. C. Driver	3	5	0	67	56	0	1	13.40	3
	K. W. Hogg	6	8	0	105	50	0	1	13.12	1
	J. M. Anderson†	11	15	8	52	16	0	0	7.42	2

Also batted: A. Flintoff†‡ (cap 1998) (1 match) 137, 6 (1 ct); J. J. Haynes (1 match) 4 (1 ct);
S. I. Mahmood† (1 match) 18; T. M. Rees (1 match) 3; T. W. Roberts (1 match) 2 (1 ct);
M. P. Smethurst† (2 matches) 13, 0*, 6* (1 ct); G. Yates† (cap 1994) (1 match) 3, 14.

† *Born in Lancashire.*   ‡ *ECB contract.*   § *Overseas player.*

BOWLING

	O	M	R	W	BB	5W/i	Avge
C. P. Schofield	99.2	18	298	16	4-35	0	18.62
J. M. Anderson	275.4	53	934	46	6-23	3	20.30
P. J. Martin	452	143	1,126	53	5-54	1	21.24
K. W. Hogg	148	37	466	19	5-48	1	24.52
G. Chapple	539.3	128	1,594	54	6-30	3	29.51
J. Wood	168.5	27	618	17	4-17	0	36.35
G. Keedy	382.4	87	1,161	31	5-122	1	37.45

Also bowled: M. J. Chilton 70–17–224–3; R. C. Driver 51–16–157–4; N. H. Fairbrother
6–0–27–0; A. Flintoff 32–8–99–3; S. G. Law 24.4–5–72–1; S. I. Mahmood 2–1–6–0; T. W.
Roberts 2–0–6–0; M. P. Smethurst 53.2–8–248–6; A. J. Swann 8–1–40–0; G. Yates 29–7–76–0.

COUNTY RECORDS

Highest score for:	424	A. C. MacLaren v Somerset at Taunton	1895
Highest score against:	315*	T. W. Hayward (Surrey) at The Oval	1898
Best bowling for:	10-46	W. Hickton v Hampshire at Manchester	1870
Best bowling against:	10-40	G. O. B. Allen (Middlesex) at Lord's	1929
Highest total for:	863	v Surrey at The Oval	1990
Highest total against:	707-9 dec.	by Surrey at The Oval	1990
Lowest total for:	25	v Derbyshire at Manchester	1871
Lowest total against:	22	by Glamorgan at Liverpool	1924

COUNTY OFFICERS

Captain W. K. Hegg • **Cricket manager** M. Watkinson • **President** J. F. Blackledge
Chairman J. Simmons • **Chief executive** J. Cumbes
Chairman, cricket committee G. Ogden • **Head groundsman** P. Marron • **Scorer** A. West

LANCASHIRE v LEICESTERSHIRE

At Manchester, April 19, 20, 21, 22. Lancashire won by one wicket. Lancashire 17 pts, Leicestershire 6 pts. Toss: Leicestershire. Championship debut: K. W. Hogg. County debuts: D. Byas, S. G. Law, A. J. Swann; M. G. Bevan.

Lancashire scrabbled to 388 for nine to complete their highest run-chase since the Second World War. In the nerve-jangling final stages, three wickets tumbled for six, leaving the last pair to make six more. Smethurst, a true No. 11, somehow held out, before Keedy drove a Malcolm full toss down the ground for four, then grabbed the two needed to complete a memorable win. A shattered Leicestershire also lost a point for their slow over-rate. Earlier, they had bossed the match. DeFreitas led a middle-order blitz with a brutal 22-ball fifty, before finding sufficient swing to seize six wickets and become only the second current player (after Allan Donald) to take 1,100 in first-class cricket. Leicestershire's first-innings lead was stretched from 110 to 387 by a controlled innings from Maddy and another late rally by Burns and DeFreitas. But the good work was undone by loose bowling on the last day, which let Law and Lloyd piece together a telling 137. David Byas began his Lancashire career with a dropped catch and a golden duck; Kyle Hogg and Alec Swann were more successful: Hogg bowled with a high, efficient action to take a five-for on Championship debut and Swann played two key innings.

Close of play: First day, Lancashire 9-0 (Chilton 0, Swann 5); Second day, Leicestershire 94-3 (Maddy 37, Crowe 1); Third day, Lancashire 132-1 (Chilton 51, Byas 23).

Leicestershire

R. J. Cunliffe b Martin	9	– lbw b Chapple		19
I. J. Sutcliffe c Law b Chapple	27	– b Martin		8
D. L. Maddy c Law b Smethurst	6	– lbw b Martin		66
M. G. Bevan c Hegg b Martin	66	– b Hogg		27
*V. J. Wells c Byas b Keedy	74	– (6) b Hogg		0
D. I. Stevens c Hegg b Smethurst	74	– (7) lbw b Martin		28
†N. D. Burns c Hegg b Hogg	51	– (8) c Martin b Hogg		62
P. A. J. DeFreitas c Hegg b Chilton	51	– (9) c Swann b Hogg		41
C. D. Crowe c Hegg b Chapple	7	– (5) c Smethurst b Hogg		6
C. E. Dagnall lbw b Chapple	2	– c Byas b Keedy		8
D. E. Malcolm not out	2	– not out		0
L-b 6, n-b 10	16	B 4, l-b 6, n-b 2		12

1/14 (1) 2/27 (3) 3/65 (2) 4/184 (5)   **385**
5/285 (7) 6/354 (8) 7/366 (6)
8/381 (9) 9/383 (4) 10/385 (10)

1/19 (2) 2/40 (1) 3/85 (4)   **277**
4/115 (5) 5/115 (6) 6/150 (7)
7/161 (3) 8/260 (8)
9/270 (9) 10/277 (10)

Bonus points – Leicestershire 4, Lancashire 3.

In the first innings Bevan, when 53, retired hurt at 179 and resumed at 354.

Bowling: *First Innings*—Martin 24–8–52–2; Chapple 23.5–7–61–3; Smethurst 14–2–74–2; Hogg 16–3–67–1; Keedy 16–1–79–1; Chilton 6–1–46–1. *Second Innings*—Martin 22–8–69–3; Chapple 19–5–64–1; Smethurst 18–2–73–0; Hogg 16–3–48–5; Keedy 6.5–3–13–1.

On a very quick pitch, Maynard batted mostly in a cap for an unbeaten 118, and the big crowd – divided in loyalty but united in delight at his skill and sense of adventure – responded with a standing ovation.
Gloucestershire v Glamorgan, page 631

Lancashire

M. J. Chilton c Burns b DeFreitas	13	lbw b DeFreitas	53
A. J. Swann c Burns b Wells	80	c Dagnall b Crowe	49
D. Byas lbw b DeFreitas	0	lbw b DeFreitas	24
S. G. Law c Burns b Maddy	22	c Maddy b Wells	69
G. D. Lloyd c Burns b DeFreitas	51	b Wells	73
*†W. K. Hegg c Crowe b DeFreitas	8	c Wells b Malcolm	34
G. Chapple b DeFreitas	15	c Burns b Malcolm	38
K. W. Hogg c Stevens b DeFreitas	6	c Stevens b Dagnall	11
P. J. Martin not out	21	lbw b Dagnall	1
G. Keedy c and b Maddy	3	not out	7
M. P. Smethurst b Malcolm	13	not out	0
B 5, l-b 6, n-b 32	43	B 16, l-b 11, n-b 2	29

1/52 (1) 2/52 (3) 3/107 (4) 4/192 (5)   275   1/104 (2) 2/135 (1)   (9 wkts) 388
5/204 (6) 6/204 (2) 7/226 (7)   3/150 (3) 4/287 (5)
8/243 (8) 9/248 (10) 10/275 (11)   5/288 (4) 6/351 (7)
    7/376 (6) 8/377 (9) 9/382 (8)

Bonus points – Lancashire 2, Leicestershire 3.

Bowling: *First Innings*—Malcolm 14.3–4–64–1; DeFreitas 23–4–101–6; Dagnall 10–3–26–0; Maddy 13–4–52–2; Wells 6–3–21–1. *Second Innings*—Malcolm 24.3–3–100–2; Dagnall 27–10–66–2; Wells 8–3–30–2; Maddy 8–0–35–0; DeFreitas 24–4–67–2; Crowe 13–2–52–1; Bevan 2–0–11–0.

Umpires: V. A. Holder and B. Leadbeater.

At Birmingham, April 24, 25, 26. LANCASHIRE beat WARWICKSHIRE by six wickets.

At The Oval, May 8, 9, 10, 11. LANCASHIRE lost to SURREY by three wickets.

LANCASHIRE v SUSSEX

At Manchester, May 15, 16, 17, 18. Drawn. Lancashire 11 pts, Sussex 12 pts. Toss: Sussex.

An exciting match was lit up by double-centuries from Adams and Law that will linger long in the memory. Adams made a typically dashing start and, though hampered by a calf injury, battered 26 fours, together with three sixes off Keedy's left-arm spin. His 217 came from 369 balls and had lasted seven and a half hours when he perished driving hard to mid-off. In reply, Lancashire looked certain to follow on after Lewry's late swing reduced them to 221 for nine. But Keedy, with a reputation as a stubborn tailender, stuck to his task grimly, allowing Law to stroke his way effortlessly from 116 to 218. Law's innings lasted 473 minutes and 346 balls and included 29 fours. Their partnership of 145, one run short of the record tenth-wicket stand at Old Trafford, dragged Lancashire back into contention. And if Chilton had not dropped Montgomerie on 18, they could have been pushing for a win when rain ended the last day after only 11 overs.

Close of play: First day, Sussex 345-7 (Adams 159, Davis 4); Second day, Lancashire 279-9 (Law 149, Keedy 15); Third day, Sussex 186-6 (Prior 10, Kirtley 0).

Sussex

R. R. Montgomerie c Hegg b Martin	14	– (2) c Hegg b Martin	80
M. W. Goodwin lbw b Hogg	5	– (1) lbw b Martin	14
*C. J. Adams c Law b Keedy	217	– c Hegg b Keedy	15
P. A. Cottey b Hogg	17	– c Byas b Schofield	29
M. H. Yardy b Keedy	41	– lbw b Keedy	19
R. S. C. Martin-Jenkins b Keedy	44	– lbw b Martin	8
†M. J. Prior c Keedy b Hogg	24	– b Martin	14
K. J. Innes lbw b Chilton	11	– (9) not out	24
M. J. G. Davis c Hegg b Martin	8		
R. J. Kirtley c Chilton b Martin	5	– (8) not out	7
J. D. Lewry not out	9		
B 13, l-b 7, w 2, n-b 6	28	B 1, l-b 4, w 2, n-b 4	11

1/16 (1) 2/40 (2) 3/101 (4) 4/168 (5) 423 1/36 (1) 2/61 (3) (7 wkts) 221
5/247 (6) 6/298 (7) 7/335 (8) 3/110 (4) 4/145 (5)
8/365 (9) 9/381 (10) 10/423 (3) 5/172 (6) 6/185 (2) 7/190 (7)

Bonus points – Sussex 5, Lancashire 3 (130 overs: 402-9).

Bowling: *First Innings*—Martin 33–6–97–3; Chapple 28–3–94–0; Hogg 19–5–39–3; Chilton 6–3–12–1; Keedy 39.3–8–121–3; Schofield 10–1–40–0. *Second Innings*—Martin 21–6–53–4; Chapple 18–5–55–0; Hogg 8–2–27–0; Keedy 30–8–54–2; Schofield 8–1–27–1.

Lancashire

M. J. Chilton lbw b Lewry	0	K. W. Hogg c Montgomerie b Lewry	8
A. J. Swann c Montgomerie b Davis	51	P. J. Martin lbw b Lewry	4
D. Byas c Goodwin b Lewry	0	G. Keedy not out	25
S. G. Law c Lewry b Davis	218	B 7, l-b 10, n-b 8	25
G. D. Lloyd c Prior b Kirtley	15		
C. P. Schofield b Kirtley	4	1/0 (1) 2/0 (3) 3/132 (2) 4/161 (5) 366
*†W. K. Hegg c Yardy b Davis	5	5/169 (6) 6/178 (7) 7/199 (8)
G. Chapple b Lewry	11	8/213 (9) 9/221 (10) 10/366 (4)

Bonus points – Lancashire 4, Sussex 3.

Bowling: Lewry 27–5–88–5; Kirtley 27–3–117–2; Davis 30.5–7–71–3; Innes 5–0–15–0; Martin-Jenkins 21–0–58–0.

Umpires: N. J. Llong and P. Willey.

LANCASHIRE v SURREY

At Manchester, May 31, June 1, 2, 3. Drawn. Lancashire 6 pts, Surrey 10 pts. Toss: Surrey. First-class debut: J. M. Anderson. Championship debut: R. Clarke.

Ward's decision not to impose the follow-on let Lancashire out of jail. Despite a first-innings lead of 188 and the prospect of rain, Surrey chose to bat again, hoping Lancashire would succumb to the spin of Saqlain Mushtaq and Salisbury on the final day. Ward hit a considered hundred, then set Lancashire 116 overs to chase 435 – too cautious given the poor weather forecast and the fact that no county had made more than 416 in the fourth innings against Surrey. Rain duly had the last laugh, lopping 20 overs off the third day and allowing only two hours' play on the last. Two new faces added zest to a hard-fought game. The lively Jimmy Anderson, 19, fired out Carberry and Ramprakash in successive balls, while Rikki Clarke, fresh from a stylish century on first-class debut at Fenner's, struck the ball straight and hard. On the first day, Martin bowled magnificently, conceding 28 from 22 overs, yet somehow failed to take a wicket; on the second, Batty built Surrey's strong position with a determined hundred. This draw, and a win for Leicestershire, knocked Surrey off the top – the only week all season they didn't lead the table.

Close of play: First day, Surrey 292-7 (Batty 55); Second day, Lancashire 163-7 (Chapple 35, Martin 0); Third day, Surrey 246-6 dec.

Surrey

*I. J. Ward c Hegg b Anderson	61	– c Chilton b Hogg	106
M. A. Carberry c Law b Hogg	10	– c Hegg b Anderson	24
M. R. Ramprakash run out	71	– lbw b Anderson	0
N. Shahid lbw b Keedy	0	– c Hegg b Chapple	1
A. D. Brown b Keedy	28	– c Chapple b Keedy	30
R. Clarke c Law b Anderson	41	– c Swann b Hogg	24
†J. N. Batty b Keedy	104	– not out	12
M. P. Bicknell b Keedy	5	– not out	29
I. D. K. Salisbury c Law b Keedy	19		
Saqlain Mushtaq not out	19		
J. Ormond c Fairbrother b Martin	2		
B 4, l-b 16, n-b 2	22	B 10, l-b 6, w 4	20

1/18 (2) 2/143 (3) 3/143 (4) 4/167 (1)   **382**   1/98 (2) 2/98 (3)   (6 wkts dec.) **246**
5/177 (5) 6/279 (6) 7/292 (8)   3/101 (4) 4/155 (5)
8/332 (9) 9/377 (7) 10/382 (11)   5/193 (1) 6/205 (6)

Bonus points – Surrey 3, Lancashire 2 (130 overs: 340-8).

Bowling: *First Innings*—Martin 30–17–36–1; Chapple 28–6–72–0; Hogg 20–4–54–1; Anderson 19–4–65–2; Keedy 45–13–122–5; Chilton 3–0–10–0; Swann 2–1–3–0. *Second Innings*—Martin 11–4–17–0; Chapple 15–5–36–1; Hogg 9–0–46–2; Anderson 9–1–22–2; Keedy 17–0–84–1; Chilton 5–0–14–0; Law 1–0–11–0.

Lancashire

M. J. Chilton c Batty b Ormond	13	– lbw b Ormond	23
A. J. Swann run out	18	– lbw b Bicknell	3
N. H. Fairbrother b Saqlain Mushtaq	35	– lbw b Bicknell	38
S. G. Law c Batty b Bicknell	18	– not out	33
G. D. Lloyd c Batty b Ormond	9	– not out	6
*†W. K. Hegg c Shahid b Saqlain Mushtaq	1		
G. Chapple c Brown b Salisbury	51		
K. W. Hogg c Ward b Saqlain Mushtaq	16		
P. J. Martin c Batty b Salisbury	7		
G. Keedy b Saqlain Mushtaq	3		
J. M. Anderson not out	0		
L-b 11, w 2, n-b 10	23	L-b 1, w 2, n-b 6	9

1/33 (2) 2/36 (1) 3/87 (4) 4/103 (3)   **194**   1/9 (2) 2/49 (1) 3/85 (3)   (3 wkts) **112**
5/107 (5) 6/109 (6) 7/161 (8)
8/189 (7) 9/194 (10) 10/194 (9)

Bonus points – Surrey 3.

Bowling: *First Innings*—Bicknell 17–6–43–1; Ormond 15–3–47–2; Saqlain Mushtaq 29–10–43–4; Clarke 5–0–34–0; Salisbury 10.1–2–16–2. *Second Innings*—Bicknell 11–2–52–2; Ormond 12–2–58–1; Saqlain Mushtaq 3–2–1–0.

Umpires: D. J. Constant and N. G. Cowley.

At Durham, June 12, 13, 14. LANCASHIRE drew with DURHAM UCCE.

The match had a bizarre start, when its fifth over was completed by three bowlers.
Sri Lanka v West Indies, page 1224

LANCASHIRE v KENT

At Liverpool, June 26, 27, 28, 29. Kent won by six wickets. Kent 15.5 pts, Lancashire 4 pts. Toss: Lancashire.

Lancashire were left kicking themselves after a spate of dropped chances allowed Kent to overhaul a tough target of 360 with six wickets to spare, thanks to chalk-and-cheese centuries from Fulton and Symonds. Before Kent took over on the final day, this had been a ding-dong struggle. Khan, born in Copenhagen of Pakistani parents, carved through Lancashire's top order in the opening session with a series of sharply lifting deliveries. But Martin turned the tables with five for 54, and then made an unbeaten 80 in the second innings. Batting at No. 10, he put on 109 with Chapple as Fulton's bowlers lost control in blustery conditions. Key, watched by the England selector, Geoff Miller, stroked the ball confidently to kickstart Kent's victory bid before holing out to mid-on. But Fulton, his opening partner, was dropped three times by Lloyd as he ground his way to 116. By contrast, Symonds – almost timed out before reaching the crease – was far more fluent. His unbeaten hundred included a six that cannoned off the pavilion with such force that it scattered spectators.

Close of play: First day, Kent 102-4 (Walker 23, Nixon 20); Second day, Lancashire 197-7 (Chapple 7, Wood 10); Third day, Kent 174-2 (Fulton 82, Symonds 1).

Lancashire

M. J. Chilton c Nixon b Khan	4	– c Nixon b Saggers 60
A. J. Swann c Fulton b Khan	7	– lbw b Khan 85
N. H. Fairbrother c Ealham b Khan	12	– c Nixon b Ealham 9
S. G. Law c and b Patel	75	– (6) lbw b Ealham 4
G. D. Lloyd c Symonds b Ealham	8	– (4) b Ealham 0
R. C. Driver b Khan	56	– (5) lbw b Khan 1
*†W. K. Hegg c Nixon b Khan	10	– c and b Khan 11
G. Chapple c Key b Ealham	4	– c Ealham b Saggers 55
J. Wood b Khan b Saggers	24	– b Saggers 14
P. J. Martin not out	11	– not out 80
G. Keedy c Nixon b Golding	7	– c Fulton b Patel 10
B 5, l-b 3	8	B 7, l-b 4, w 6, n-b 2 . . . 18

1/7 (1) 2/22 (2) 3/29 (3) 4/40 (5) 226
5/139 (6) 6/155 (7) 7/164 (8)
8/203 (4) 9/209 (9) 10/226 (11)

1/118 (1) 2/156 (3) 3/156 (4) 347
4/157 (5) 5/166 (6) 6/170 (2)
7/179 (7) 8/204 (9)
9/313 (8) 10/347 (11)

Bonus points – Lancashire 1, Kent 3.

Bowling: *First Innings*—Saggers 19–5–49–1; Khan 18–0–74–5; Ealham 11–2–54–2; Golding 6.1–1–27–1; Patel 7–2–14–1. *Second Innings*—Saggers 25–2–86–3; Khan 22–3–92–3; Ealham 25–7–53–3; Symonds 5–1–27–0; Patel 8.2–0–22–1; Golding 16–2–52–0; Walker 1–0–5–0.

Kent

*D. P. Fulton c Hegg b Chapple	27	– c Swann b Keedy 116
R. W. T. Key c Lloyd b Chapple	0	– c Driver b Keedy 78
E. T. Smith c Driver b Martin	14	– c Lloyd b Chapple 6
A. Symonds c Law b Driver	12	– not out 116
M. J. Walker c Hegg b Martin	42	– lbw b Martin 10
†P. A. Nixon run out	49	– not out 19
M. A. Ealham c Keedy b Chapple	24	
J. M. Golding not out	13	
M. M. Patel c Lloyd b Martin	20	
A. Khan c Hegg b Martin	0	
M. J. Saggers c Chilton b Martin	0	
B 1, l-b 4, w 4, n-b 4	13	B 6, l-b 2, w 7 15

1/8 (2) 2/37 (1) 3/41 (3) 4/66 (4) 214
5/144 (5) 6/178 (7) 7/178 (6)
8/214 (9) 9/214 (10) 10/214 (11)

1/140 (2) 2/159 (3) (4 wkts) 360
3/270 (1) 4/315 (5)

Bonus points – Kent 1, Lancashire 3.

Bowling: *First Innings*—Martin 22–7–54–5; Chapple 23–6–58–3; Wood 17–3–68–0; Driver 9–4–29–1. *Second Innings*—Martin 30–4–96–1; Chapple 25–4–81–1; Wood 12–3–55–0; Driver 11–1–56–0; Keedy 24–9–58–2; Chilton 3–1–6–0.

Umpires: D. J. Constant and J. H. Evans.

At Leicester, July 3, 4, 5, 6. LANCASHIRE drew with LEICESTERSHIRE.

At Liverpool, July 10, 11, 12, 13. LANCASHIRE drew with WEST INDIES A (see West Indies A tour section).

At Leeds, July 19, 20, 21, 22. LANCASHIRE drew with YORKSHIRE.

At Southampton, July 25, 26, 27. LANCASHIRE beat HAMPSHIRE by 111 runs.

LANCASHIRE v HAMPSHIRE

At Manchester, August 8, 9, 10, 11. Drawn. Lancashire 6 pts, Hampshire 7 pts. Toss: Lancashire. First-class debut: S. I. Mahmood.

On a turbulent first day, Swann's patience helped him become the first Lancashire player to carry his bat since Gehan Mendis in 1988, and the first at Old Trafford since John Ikin in 1949. Seventeen wickets fell in the day, and though the ball moved in the air and off the pitch, many batsmen played rash shots. Not so Swann, who batted four times longer than anyone else. He and the debutant Sajid Mahmood, a 20-year-old from Bolton, played sensibly, adding 54 before Mahmood was knocked over by Tremlett, who grabbed a career-best five for 57 with his awkward seamers. Hampshire were in a similar plight by the close but rain wrecked the rest of the game and, when play finally resumed on the final afternoon, the sides were left to scrap for bonus points. By declaring the moment the eighth wicket fell, Kendall denied Lancashire a third bowling point.

Close of play: First day, Hampshire 84-7 (Aymes 9, Udal 0); Second day, No play; Third day, No play.

Lancashire

M. J. Chilton c Mullally b Tremlett	2	– not out	18
A. J. Swann not out	84	– not out	29
D. Byas c Johnson b Tremlett	1		
S. G. Law lbw b Johnson	9		
N. H. Fairbrother c Pothas b Mascarenhas	5		
G. Chapple c Johnson b Tremlett	3		
*†W. K. Hegg c Kendall b Mullally	7		
J. Wood c Aymes b Udal	14		
S. I. Mahmood c Laney b Tremlett	18		
G. Keedy c Laney b Tremlett	1		
J. M. Anderson c Mascarenhas b Udal	0		
B 4, l-b 7, w 2, n-b 6	19	B 1, n-b 4	5
	163	(no wkt)	**52**

1/13 (1) 2/18 (3) 3/29 (4) 4/38 (5)
5/56 (6) 6/65 (7) 7/84 (8)
8/138 (9) 9/140 (10) 10/163 (11)

Bonus points – Hampshire 3.

Bowling: *First Innings*—Mullally 17–9–32–1; Tremlett 17–2–57–5; Johnson 5–3–14–1; Mascarenhas 11–5–25–1; Udal 13–5–24–2. *Second Innings*—Mullally 4–2–11–0; Tremlett 5–2–4–0; Johnson 6–1–20–0; Mascarenhas 5–2–16–0.

Hampshire

J. S. Laney c Law b Chapple	9	A. D. Mascarenhas c and b Wood	7
*W. S. Kendall c Chilton b Chapple	1	S. D. Udal c Chapple b Keedy	24
J. D. Francis c Fairbrother b Anderson	4	L-b 2, n-b 2	4
N. C. Johnson b Chapple	1		
N. Pothas c Chilton b Anderson	26	1/3 (2) 2/10 (3) 3/14 (1) (8 wkts dec.) 122	
A. C. Morris c Fairbrother b Anderson	24	4/15 (4) 5/58 (5) 6/67 (6)	
†A. N. Aymes not out	22	7/78 (8) 8/122 (9)	

C. T. Tremlett and A. D. Mullally did not bat.

Bonus points – Lancashire 2.

Bowling: Chapple 10–2–33–3; Anderson 14–3–59–3; Wood 10–5–16–1; Mahmood 2–1–6–0; Keedy 5.1–1–6–1.

Umpires: B. Dudleston and N. J. Llong.

LANCASHIRE v YORKSHIRE

At Manchester, August 14, 15, 16, 17. Yorkshire won by 150 runs. Yorkshire 17 pts, Lancashire 6 pts. Toss: Yorkshire. First-class debut: N. D. Thornicroft. County debut: M. T. G. Elliott.

With both teams battling for their first-division lives, this was a Roses battle to savour. It ended with Dawson clinching Yorkshire's first win of the season, and reminding England of his potential, with five for 42. It had begun with a sterling individual performance from a Yorkshire player too, as one Australian left-hander seamlessly replaced another. Matthew Elliott took over from Lehmann and produced a debut innings of great authority. His 83, plus a gritty 77 from Blakey, shored up an innings in danger of being undermined by Anderson's pace and accuracy. In reply, Swann drove fluently in his 112, and became the first Lancashire batsman to hit hundreds in each of his first two Roses matches, but the support was poor. Nick Thornicroft made a nervous start to his first-class career, but recovered to take two wickets. Lancashire could manage a lead of only seven – thanks to Hegg, who came in at No. 11 despite a dislocated finger to ensure a third batting point. It looked more than enough when Yorkshire slumped to 85 for five, but McGrath fought back aggressively. He was helped by Fellows, who made a crucial first hundred, felling Chilton at short leg with a sweep into his ribs along the way. Facing a difficult target, Lancashire went down tamely with two sessions to spare as Dawson rediscovered his bite.

Close of play: First day, Yorkshire 272-8 (Blakey 68, Kirby 7); Second day, Yorkshire 3-1 (Craven 1, Kirby 1); Third day, Lancashire 36-2 (Chilton 16).

Yorkshire

V. J. Craven c Byas b Chapple	36	– (2) c Byas b Anderson	6
C. R. Taylor c Law b Anderson	0	– (1) c Chilton b Chapple	0
M. T. G. Elliott lbw b Anderson	83	– (4) run out	8
A. McGrath c Keedy b Chapple	17	– (5) run out	86
M. J. Lumb c Law b Wood	15	– (6) c Chilton b Keedy	14
G. M. Fellows c Chilton b Keedy	0	– (7) c sub b Keedy	109
*†R. J. Blakey c sub b Anderson	77	– (8) b Wood	13
R. K. J. Dawson c Fairbrother b Anderson	14	– (9) not out	27
C. E. W. Silverwood c Anderson b Chapple	14	– (10) c Chapple b Keedy	9
S. P. Kirby lbw b Anderson	16	– (3) c sub b Anderson	10
N. D. Thornicroft not out	4	– b Law	0
B 3, l-b 15	18	L-b 9, w 8, n-b 6	23

1/4 (2) 2/68 (1) 3/131 (3) 4/146 (4)	294
5/149 (6) 6/173 (5) 7/207 (8)	
8/243 (9) 9/289 (7) 10/294 (10)	

1/0 (1) 2/21 (3) 3/24 (2) 4/39 (4)	305
5/85 (6) 6/180 (5) 7/211 (8)	
8/291 (7) 9/305 (10) 10/305 (11)	

Bonus points – Yorkshire 2, Lancashire 3.

Bowling: *First Innings*—Chapple 21–6–63–3; Anderson 28–8–61–5; Wood 19–1–56–1; Keedy 31–11–54–1; Yates 16–5–42–0. *Second Innings*—Chapple 15–3–41–1; Anderson 15–1–70–2; Wood 15–3–64–1; Keedy 24–3–63–3; Yates 13–2–34–0; Law 9.4–1–24–1.

Lancashire

M. J. Chilton b Kirby	45	– b Kirby	16
A. J. Swann c Blakey b McGrath	112	– b Silverwood	12
D. Byas c Lumb b Dawson	4	– (4) b McGrath	14
S. G. Law c McGrath b Kirby	47	– (5) b Dawson	13
N. H. Fairbrother c Fellows b Thornicroft	27	– (6) c Fellows b Kirby	38
G. Chapple c Fellows b Thornicroft	9	– (7) c McGrath b Dawson	11
G. Yates lbw b Dawson	3	– (8) c Taylor b Dawson	14
J. Wood b Silverwood	22	– (9) c Elliott b Dawson	11
G. Keedy c Elliott b Silverwood	4	– (3) c Lumb b Dawson	6
J. M. Anderson not out	5	– not out	4
*†W. K. Hegg not out	6	– absent hurt	
B 5, l-b 10, n-b 2	17	L-b 3, w 2, n-b 4	9

1/140 (1) 2/161 (3) 3/193 (2)   (9 wkts dec.) 301
4/244 (4) 5/253 (5) 6/256 (7)
7/260 (6) 8/290 (9) 9/291 (8)

1/29 (2) 2/36 (3) 3/36 (1)   148
4/59 (5) 5/92 (4) 6/116 (6)
7/120 (7) 8/139 (8) 9/148 (9)

Bonus points – Lancashire 3, Yorkshire 3.

Bowling: *First Innings*—Silverwood 19–2–66–2; Kirby 15–2–52–2; Thornicroft 14–4–51–2; Dawson 32.4–9–97–2; Elliott 1–0–7–0; McGrath 6–1–13–1. *Second Innings*—Silverwood 13–5–44–1; Kirby 12–4–27–2; Dawson 14.3–5–42–5; McGrath 6–1–18–1; Thornicroft 4–0–14–0.

Umpires: J. W. Holder and J. F. Steele.

At Hove, August 22, 23, 24, 25. LANCASHIRE beat SUSSEX by seven wickets.

LANCASHIRE v SOMERSET

At Blackpool, August 27, 28, 29. Lancashire won by 336 runs. Lancashire 17 pts, Somerset 3 pts. Toss: Lancashire.

The match was dominated by incisive quick bowling but lost by feeble Somerset batting. On a sluggish pitch, Somerset's last eight wickets crashed in nine overs as they plummeted to 71 all out, the lowest of the season, and a crushing defeat. "This was one of the poorest performances I've seen from us," said their coach, Kevin Shine. "We just rolled over." Somerset's problems began in Lancashire's first innings when Johnson, who swung and seamed his way to six for 47, had Law dropped in the slips on nought. Law went on to 77, an innings studded with cover-drives, before Anderson blew Somerset away to give Lancashire a lead of 111. Caddick bowled long and hard in the second innings, found his rhythm and earned six for 84, but could not get the better of Byas, who hit a dogged 81, or Schofield, who fidgeted to 77. Somerset were left to chase a daunting 408 – and surrendered abjectly. Chapple bowled beautifully on the third day and became the fourth seamer to take six wickets in an innings; he found movement from a full length to finish with a career-best six for 30. The collapse gave Somerset an extra day and a half to prepare for the C&G final.

Close of play: First day, Somerset 91-5 (Turner 8, Dutch 10); Second day, Somerset 21-1 (Wood 16, Francis 0).

There were times when Durham fielded nine home-grown players, but the chairman's message was clear: improve or you're out.
Durham, page 581

Lancashire

M. J. Chilton b Johnson	1	– b Caddick	3
A. J. Swann c Burns b Caddick	36	– lbw b Johnson	1
D. Byas c Turner b Johnson	6	– c Turner b Caddick	81
S. G. Law b Francis	77	– b Francis	24
N. H. Fairbrother c Parsons b Johnson	23	– c Parsons b Francis	17
G. Chapple c Turner b Johnson	1	– c Parsons b Francis	10
C. P. Schofield b Parsons	40	– c Turner b Johnson	77
*†W. K. Hegg c Johnson b Caddick	22	– lbw b Caddick	9
P. J. Martin c Parsons b Johnson	12	– c Turner b Caddick	39
G. Keedy c Dutch b Johnson	10	– not out	18
J. M. Anderson not out	8	– b Caddick	2
L-b 3, n-b 12	15	B 2, l-b 5, n-b 8	15
	251		**296**

1/5 (1) 2/25 (3) 3/69 (2) 4/146 (5)
5/152 (4) 6/176 (6) 7/209 (7)
8/221 (8) 9/232 (9) 10/251 (10)

1/6 (1) 2/6 (2) 3/41 (4) 4/67 (5)
5/83 (6) 6/205 (3) 7/219 (8)
8/234 (7) 9/294 (9) 10/296 (11)

Bonus points – Lancashire 2, Somerset 3.

Bowling: *First Innings*—Caddick 23–5–81–2; Johnson 18.1–5–47–6; Francis 9–1–50–1; Parsons 12–1–51–1; Burns 4–0–18–0; Dutch 1–0–1–0. *Second Innings*—Caddick 23.1–3–84–6; Johnson 19–2–73–2; Francis 14–0–51–2; Parsons 4–0–23–0; Blackwell 16–4–40–0; Dutch 6–2–18–0.

Somerset

*J. Cox c Chilton b Anderson	20	– (2) lbw b Martin	1
M. J. Wood b Martin	10	– (1) lbw b Chapple	16
P. D. Bowler lbw b Chapple	7	– (4) b Anderson	18
K. A. Parsons b Anderson	27	– (5) c Law b Chapple	0
I. D. Blackwell c and b Schofield	4	– (6) lbw b Chapple	0
†R. J. Turner lbw b Martin	8	– (8) lbw b Chapple	5
K. P. Dutch lbw b Anderson	35	– (9) c Law b Anderson	0
M. Burns lbw b Anderson	18	– (7) c Schofield b Chapple	3
R. L. Johnson c Chapple b Anderson	3	– (10) not out	7
A. R. Caddick c Hegg b Anderson	2	– (11) c Hegg b Chapple	0
S. R. G. Francis not out	0	– (3) c Law b Anderson	7
B 2	2	B 8, l-b 2, n-b 4	14
	140		**71**

1/23 (2) 2/32 (3) 3/57 (1) 4/72 (5)
5/76 (4) 6/96 (6) 7/134 (7)
8/135 (8) 9/140 (9) 10/140 (10)

1/17 (2) 2/21 (1) 3/44 (3) 4/49 (5)
5/49 (6) 6/55 (7) 7/55 (4)
8/55 (9) 9/71 (8) 10/71 (11)

Bonus points – Lancashire 3.

Bowling: *First Innings*—Martin 16–5–43–2; Chapple 14–9–28–1; Chilton 6–2–18–0; Anderson 11.5–2–41–6; Schofield 4–2–8–1. *Second Innings*—Martin 11–7–15–1; Chapple 12.3–1–30–6; Anderson 7–1–16–3.

Umpires: M. R. Benson and M. J. Harris.

LANCASHIRE v WARWICKSHIRE

At Manchester, September 4, 5, 6, 7. Drawn. Lancashire 12 pts, Warwickshire 9 pts. Toss: Lancashire.

A rain-ruined draw was memorable only for some sparkling Lancashire batting. Byas hit a composed hundred and became the second player to score centuries for each of the Roses counties after Roger Iddison, another Yorkshire captain, who played in the 1860s. Martin smashed an unbeaten 117, the highest by a Lancashire No. 10, off just 121 balls with six sixes, and Schofield manoeuvred the ball into some strange places and made a career-best 91. Lancashire's 598 was their highest against Warwickshire. However, the second afternoon was cut short, and more bad weather on the last two days ruined any chance of a result. This was Neil Fairbrother's last Championship match at Old Trafford. He and Graham Lloyd, who had already lost his place, announced they would retire at the end of the season.

Close of play: First day, Lancashire 352-6 (Schofield 4, Keedy 4); Second day, Warwickshire 38-1 (Powell 15, Bell 7); Third day, Warwickshire 126-4 (Ostler 31).

Lancashire

M. J. Chilton c Frost b Richardson	38	*†W. K. Hegg c Troughton b Richardson	12
A. J. Swann c Bell b Brown	62	P. J. Martin not out	117
D. Byas c Ostler b Carter	101	J. M. Anderson b Spires	16
S. G. Law c Frost b Brown	28	B 5, l-b 27, w 4, n-b 20	56
N. H. Fairbrother c Ostler b Powell	7		
G. Chapple c Spires b Carter	65	1/79 (1) 2/126 (2) 3/158 (4) 4/198 (5)	598
C. P. Schofield lbw b Wagh	91	5/343 (6) 6/347 (3) 7/362 (8)	
G. Keedy c Frost b Richardson	5	8/402 (9) 9/511 (7) 10/598 (11)	

Bonus points – Lancashire 5, Warwickshire 2 (130 overs: 492-8).

Bowling: Carter 34–6–165–2; Wagg 5–1–16–0; Richardson 28–4–102–3; Brown 35–6–117–2; Spires 20.5–2–91–1; Powell 15–3–48–1; Wagh 15–5–27–1.

Warwickshire

*M. J. Powell c Hegg b Martin	21	N. M. Carter c Chapple b Schofield	70
M. A. Wagh b Chapple	10	A. Richardson c Fairbrother b Schofield	0
I. R. Bell b Anderson	10	J. A. Spires c Byas b Schofield	4
D. P. Ostler lbw b Martin	63	L-b 15, w 2, n-b 2	19
J. O. Troughton c Hegg b Chapple	43		
D. R. Brown not out	68	1/16 (2) 2/47 (3) 3/57 (1) 4/126 (5)	328
†T. Frost run out	2	5/187 (4) 6/189 (7) 7/218 (8)	
G. G. Wagg b Anderson	18	8/323 (9) 9/323 (10) 10/328 (11)	

Bonus points – Warwickshire 3, Lancashire 3.

Bowling: Martin 24–8–67–2; Chapple 17–1–80–2; Anderson 20–3–70–2; Keedy 16–6–50–0; Schofield 8.2–2–25–3; Law 4–2–21–0.

Umpires: G. I. Burgess and T. E. Jesty.

At Canterbury, September 11, 12, 13, 14. LANCASHIRE lost to KENT by six wickets.

At Taunton, September 18, 19. LANCASHIRE beat SOMERSET by eight wickets.

CRICKET SOCIETY AWARDS, 2002

Gordon Muchall won the Cricket Society's Most Promising Young Cricketer Award. The A. A. Thomson Fielding Prize, for the best schoolboy fielder, went to Robert Woodman, of Castle School, Taunton. The Sir John Hobbs Jubilee Memorial Prize, for the outstanding Under-16 schoolboy, was won by Phillip Holdsworth of Northallerton College. The Don Rowan Memorial Trophy, for primary schools promoting cricket, was given to Henry Fawcett Junior School, in south-east London, and the Christopher Box-Grainger Memorial Trophy for schools promoting cricket to underprivileged children to the Phoenix School, Box. Darren Maddy of Leicestershire won the Wetherell award for the outstanding all-rounder in the first-class game. A new award for the Most Promising Young Woman Cricketer of the Year was given to Jenny Gunn of Nottinghamshire.

LEICESTERSHIRE
A MESSY DIVORCE

Ch'ship	5th in Division 1
C&G	4th round
B&H	quarter-final
NUL	6th in Division 1

Player of the season: Darren Maddy

Leicestershire's modest summer on the field was followed by a shambolic winter off it. Though the trophy cabinet remained bare, they could be forgiven for feeling satisfied at staying up in both leagues after starting the season as undisputed favourites to go down. They and Kent are now alone in having avoided relegation in either form of the game. But their performances veered between the admirable and the abject, and not everyone agreed that congratulations were in order. A letter in the local paper summed up the feelings of a section of the membership. "There are celebrations at Grace Road at retaining Division One status," it said, "but it is a celebration of mediocrity. Leicestershire looked what they were, an ageing team. What is needed is a shake-up." By January, there had been one. Having already lost four key players – James Ormond, Ben Smith, Aftab Habib and Jon Dakin – at the end of the 2001 season, they now lost more, in ugly circumstances.

Perhaps the most contentious departure was that of the wicket-keeper Neil Burns. Though approaching 37, he had enjoyed another excellent season: his 63 dismissals were the most in Division One, and he scored 720 runs at nearly 33. Even so, he was not offered a new contract. He found the explanation given by the club unsatisfactory and resolved to take his case to an industrial tribunal.

Controversy surrounded the captaincy too. Vince Wells, who had led the side for three years, was dogged by niggling injuries and endured a difficult summer. He occasionally recaptured the form of the Championship-winning days of the late 1990s – he hit a magnificent 150 against Hampshire and took eight wickets against Yorkshire – but was no longer the same all-round force. At the end of the summer, the club sacked him as captain; Wells said he had been given an oral offer of the job, and he turned down a one-year playing contract in disgust, preferring to move to Durham. The captaincy was duly offered to Iain Sutcliffe, who was expected to be a vital part of Leicestershire's future. But Sutcliffe was so disillusioned by the treatment of Wells that he abandoned the county that had groomed him for eight years and joined Lancashire. Phillip DeFreitas, the senior pro, was asked to plug the gap in 2003.

The role of James Whitaker, formerly one of the county's most successful captains, sowed confusion. He was negotiating contracts and helping decide on the retained list despite having announced his resignation as secretary/ general manager well before the end of the season. The Professional Cricketers' Association were not happy at this, and called a meeting with Kevin Hill, the new general manager, to discuss how the players' contracts had been handled. Shortly afterwards, the club took the unusual step of issuing a statement to explain their side of the story. But many members remained unhappy, and in January 2003 a public gathering of dissatisfied voices ran to about 300 – bigger than some attendances at Grace Road.

All the while, the dressing-room door was revolving. Out went the batsman Ashley Wright, the off-spinner Carl Crowe, and the wicket-keeper Stephen Adshead. In came the recent England tourist Paul Nixon, for his second spell at the county, and the seamer David Masters (both from Kent), and Jeremy Snape, Gloucestershire and England's off-spinning all-rounder. The slow left-armer Rupesh Amin joined from Surrey, and one-year contracts were given to two 21-year-old left-handed batsmen: John Maunders, who had been at Middlesex, and Yorkshire's John Sadler.

On the field, it was a big year for Darren Maddy. Once regarded as a future England opener, Maddy reinvented himself as a genuine all-rounder, passing 1,000 runs from the middle order and taking 43 Championship wickets with his medium-pace swingers. Only the two evergreens, Devon Malcolm and DeFreitas, took more. At the age of 39, Malcolm claimed 60 wickets for the second successive season, while DeFreitas, a relative youngster at 36, deserved more than 51. When Javagal Srinath (aged 33 by August) became the club's fourth overseas player for the season, Leicestershire boasted not only the oldest attack on the circuit but one of the best. Srinath was a joy to watch and bowled beautifully to claim 30 wickets at under 19 in just five Championship matches. Srinath's compatriot, the explosive Virender Sehwag, looks an astute overseas signing for 2003; Brad Hodge, the all-rounder from Victoria, may be too.

The original 2002 import, Michael Bevan, averaged over 60 in the Championship (from just nine games), and in both the Norwich Union League and the B&H. His seven-hour 146 against Warwickshire in the opening home four-day fixture was a batting masterclass. But he was also an integral part of Australia's one-day squad and his stay in England was cut short. A full season from him or Srinath would have improved Leicestershire's chances in all competitions.

Sutcliffe benefited from Bevan's tutelage, completing 1,000 first-class runs for a second consecutive summer, but it was a benchmark that only he and Maddy reached. Darren Stevens came close with 847 and sparkled in the Norwich Union, where he was top-scorer with 651 at 43. He fully deserved his place in the England Academy during the winter. But Leicestershire's newcomers made little impact. Charlie Dagnall's season was wrecked by a hip injury which limited him to just four Championship games, and there were few opportunities for Rob Cunliffe or Jamie Grove.

After the winter ructions, supporters were left wondering what would happen next. It was hard to fathom whether Leicestershire were in a state of turmoil and decline or rehabilitation and development. **Neville Foulger**

683

LEICESTERSHIRE 2002

Back row: H. Eaton (*physiotherapist*), T. J. New, L. J. Wright, D. S. Brignull, D. G. Brandy, R. J. Cunliffe, D. Ayriss (*second-team scorer*), G. A. York (*first-team scorer*), D. I. Stevens, S. J. Adshead, C. E. Dagnall, J. O. Grove, M. J. A. Whiley, C. D. Crowe, A. S. S. Wright. *Middle row*: N. D. Burns, D. E. Malcolm, I. J. Sutcliffe, B. G. Groves (*chairman*), P. Whitticase (*head coach*), B. A. F. Smith (*president*), V. J. Wells (*captain*), J. J. Whitaker (*secretary/general manager*), D. L. Maddy, P. A. J. DeFreitas, T. R. Ward. *Front row*:

LEICESTERSHIRE RESULTS

All first-class matches – Played 16: Won 5, Lost 5, Drawn 6.
County Championship matches – Played 16: Won 5, Lost 5, Drawn 6.

COUNTY CHAMPIONSHIP AVERAGES: BATTING AND FIELDING

Cap		M	I	NO	R	HS	100s	50s	Avge	Ct/St
2002	M. G. Bevan§	9	14	3	697	146	2	4	63.36	4
1996	D. L. Maddy†	16	29	4	1,187	156	2	8	47.48	22
1997	I. J. Sutcliffe	16	29	3	1,088	125*	2	5	41.84	4
1994	V. J. Wells	11	17	2	558	150	1	3	37.20	9
2002	D. I. Stevens†	16	28	3	847	125	1	6	33.88	16
2001	N. D. Burns	16	24	2	720	101	1	5	32.72	61/2
1986	P. A. J. DeFreitas . . .	16	23	2	609	114	1	3	29.00	10
2001	T. R. Ward	14	24	0	554	89	0	4	23.08	7
	C. D. Crowe†	12	16	4	172	34	0	0	14.33	4
2002	J. Srinath§	5	7	0	98	52	0	1	14.00	2
	R. J. Cunliffe	5	10	1	121	30	0	0	13.44	1
	A. S. Wright	5	8	1	94	28	0	0	13.42	1
2001	D. E. Malcolm	16	22	8	138	44	0	0	9.85	4
	C. E. Dagnall	4	5	1	33	16	0	0	8.25	1
	M. J. A. Whiley. . . .	7	9	2	41	13*	0	0	5.85	1
	J. O. Grove.	2	4	0	13	6	0	0	3.25	0

Also batted: D. G. Brandy (2 matches) 5, 23, 0 (1 ct); G. W. Flower§ (1 match) (cap 2002) 75, 7 (1 ct); M. Kaif (cap 2002) (1 match) 13, 43; R. D. Stemp (1 match) 8*, 0; G. W. Walker (1 match) 7, 37* (1 ct).

† *Born in Leicestershire.*   § *Overseas player.*

BOWLING

	O	M	R	W	BB	5W/i	Avge
J. Srinath	179.2	29	561	30	5-25	2	18.70
V. J. Wells	155	41	421	19	5-39	1	22.15
D. L. Maddy.	334.3	78	1,025	43	5-37	2	23.83
D. E. Malcolm	477.5	79	1,826	60	7-76	4	30.43
P. A. J. DeFreitas	566.4	150	1,594	51	6-101	2	31.25
C. D. Crowe	193.2	51	593	16	4-63	0	37.06
M. J. A. Whiley	175.4	28	803	16	3-60	0	50.18

Also bowled: M. G. Bevan 33–1–118–3; D. G. Brandy 17–0–114–2; R. J. Cunliffe 1.1–0–3–0; C. E. Dagnall 91–24–270–7; G. W. Flower 35–12–98–6; J. O. Grove 35–6–152–1; M. Kaif 7–0–43–0; R. D. Stemp 17–2–59–1; D. I. Stevens 49–3–201–1; I. J. Sutcliffe 7–0–39–0; G. W. Walker 13–2–50–0; T. R. Ward 11–0–47–1.

COUNTY RECORDS

Highest score for:	261	P. V. Simmons v Northamptonshire at Leicester . .	1994
Highest score against:	341	G. H. Hirst (Yorkshire) at Leicester	1905
Best bowling for:	10-18	G. Geary v Glamorgan at Pontypridd	1929
Best bowling against:	10-32	H. Pickett (Essex) at Leyton	1895
Highest total for:	701-4 dec.	v Worcestershire at Worcester	1906
Highest total against:	761-6 dec.	by Essex at Chelmsford	1990
Lowest total for:	25	v Kent at Leicester	1912
Lowest total against:	{ 24	by Glamorgan at Leicester	1971
	24	by Oxford University at Oxford.	1985

COUNTY OFFICERS

Captain 2002 – V. J. Wells; 2003 – P. A. J. DeFreitas • **Head coach** P. Whitticase
President B. A. F. Smith • **Chairman** B. G. Groves
General Mgr. 2002 – J. J. Whitaker; 2003 – K. P. Hill • **Chm., cricket c'tee** P. R. Haywood
Head groundsmen A. Ward and A. Whiteman • **Scorer** G. A. York

At Leicester, April 13, 14 (not first-class). **Leicestershire won by an innings and 316 runs.** Toss: Bradford/Leeds UCCE. **Bradford/Leeds UCCE 93** (C. E. Dagnall three for 29) **and 158** (J. W. N. Lucas 37, C. J. Elstub 58 not out; C. D. Crowe seven for 52); **Leicestershire 567 for seven dec.** (I. J. Sutcliffe 160, D. L. Maddy 112, D. I. Stevens 46, V. J. Wells 48, N. D. Burns 76, P. A. J. DeFreitas 63, Extras 31; R. G. R. Barlow three for 108).

County debuts: R. J. Cunliffe, C. E. Dagnall.

At Manchester, April 19, 20, 21, 22. LEICESTERSHIRE lost to LANCASHIRE by one wicket.

At Southampton, April 24, 25, 26, 27. LEICESTERSHIRE beat HAMPSHIRE by an innings and nine runs.

LEICESTERSHIRE v WARWICKSHIRE

At Leicester, May 8, 9, 10, 11. Leicestershire won by seven wickets. Leicestershire 19 pts, Warwickshire 1 pt. Toss: Warwickshire.

In a dramatic conclusion, Leicestershire were left to scurry 94 off only 16 overs; guided by Bevan, cricket's most lethal nurdler, they eased home with nine balls to spare. Earlier, Bevan had also paved the way for victory with a superb 146, which delighted James Whitaker, the club's general manager, who had bet on him reaching three figures. After Leicestershire had been inserted on a grudging pitch and tumbled to 45 for two, Bevan's innings was a masterpiece of forbearance: his first fifty included 11 fours but came from 134 balls, which meant that only six runs came from the other 123. Stevens, with an equally impressive 125, kept Warwickshire in the field until the middle of the second afternoon, and when the visitors responded to 523 they slumped to 177. But they gathered themselves and produced a much better effort in the second innings: a determined century from Knight, a well-measured fifty from Troughton and clean hitting by Pollock set up the tense finale.

Close of play: First day, Leicestershire 292-4 (Bevan 99, Stevens 26); Second day, Warwickshire 36-3 (Knight 11); Third day, Warwickshire 197-2 (Knight 75, Troughton 17).

Leicestershire

T. R. Ward c Knight b Pollock	7	
I. J. Sutcliffe lbw b Bell	71	– run out 15
D. L. Maddy lbw b Brown	12	– (5) not out ... 1
M. G. Bevan st Piper b Giles	146	– (1) not out ... 38
*V. J. Wells c Pollock b Giles	33	
D. I. Stevens b Giles	125	– (3) run out ... 15
†N. D. Burns b Betts	16	– (4) b Richardson ... 15
P. A. J. DeFreitas not out	39	
C. D. Crowe c Piper b Richardson	0	
D. E. Malcolm b Giles	14	
M. J. A. Whiley lbw b Giles	0	
B 16, l-b 12, w 2, n-b 30	60	B 2, n-b 10 ... 12

1/14 (1) 2/45 (3) 3/172 (2)   **523**   1/47 (2) 2/68 (3) 3/92 (4)   (3 wkts) 94
4/241 (5) 5/404 (4) 6/431 (7) 7/493 (6)
8/500 (9) 9/523 (10) 10/523 (11)

Bonus points – Leicestershire 4, Warwickshire 1 (130 overs: 382-4).

Bowling: *First Innings*—Pollock 24–8–37–1; Betts 28–6–87–1; Richardson 31–9–84–1; Brown 28–6–101–1; Giles 38.5–7–126–5; Smith 2–0–16–0; Bell 11–2–44–1. *Second Innings*—Pollock 4–0–27–0; Betts 3–0–20–0; Richardson 4–0–29–1; Giles 3.3–0–16–0.

Warwickshire

*M. J. Powell lbw b DeFreitas	0	– c Burns b DeFreitas	67
N. V. Knight b Bevan	11	– lbw b Whiley	130
I. R. Bell c DeFreitas b Malcolm	5	– c Stevens b Maddy	13
J. O. Troughton lbw b Bevan	12	– lbw b DeFreitas	66
M. M. Betts c Ward b Bevan	7	– (10) b Malcolm	1
D. R. Brown c Wells b Whiley	33	– (5) c DeFreitas b Malcolm	14
S. M. Pollock lbw b DeFreitas	59	– (6) c Burns b Maddy	66
N. M. K. Smith c Burns b Whiley	24	– (7) b Whiley	21
†K. J. Piper c Burns b Whiley	1	– (8) c Maddy b Whiley	0
A. F. Giles c Ward b Crowe	1	– (9) b Maddy	17
A. Richardson not out	5	– not out	0
L-b 1, w 14, n-b 4	19	B 13, l-b 9, w 10, n-b 12	44

1/0 (1) 2/11 (3) 3/36 (4) 4/39 (2)   177   1/113 (1) 2/150 (3) 3/289 (4)   439
5/60 (5) 6/89 (6) 7/129 (8)   4/306 (5) 5/344 (2) 6/395 (7)
8/147 (9) 9/148 (10) 10/177 (7)   7/395 (8) 8/436 (9)
                                    9/439 (6) 10/439 (10)

Bonus points – Leicestershire 3.

Bowling: *First Innings*—DeFreitas 14–4–43–2; Malcolm 15–5–30–1; Whiley 17–2–64–3; Crowe 3–1–14–1; Bevan 7–1–25–3. *Second Innings*—DeFreitas 26–6–83–2; Malcolm 27.1–7–91–2; Maddy 26–6–59–3; Wells 3–0–12–0; Whiley 22–3–108–3; Crowe 25–11–26–0; Bevan 8–0–37–0; Sutcliffe 1–0–1–0.

Umpires: B. Leadbeater and P. Willey.

At Taunton, May 15, 16, 17, 18. LEICESTERSHIRE drew with SOMERSET.

At Horsham, May 24, 25, 26, 27. LEICESTERSHIRE drew with SUSSEX.

LEICESTERSHIRE v YORKSHIRE

At Leicester, May 31, June 1, 2, 3. Leicestershire won by five wickets. Leicestershire 18 pts, Yorkshire 5.5 pts. Toss: Yorkshire.

Outstanding fast bowling from Malcolm and another sublime century by Bevan took Leicestershire top of the Championship for a week. As Malcolm thundered in, arced the ball toward the slips and wrapped up Yorkshire's first innings for 310, he passed a milestone that few bowlers ever glimpse: 1,000 first-class wickets. Only four current players had done it before him. Among them was Malcolm's opening partner, DeFreitas, who was one of the first to offer smiling congratulations when Craven was castled. In reply, Bevan pulled and cut his way to a high-quality 142 to give Leicestershire a lead of 36. When Yorkshire batted again Malcolm blasted out four more batsmen, making it ten in the match, while DeFreitas found late swing and snatched five for 38. Only Lehmann kept them at bay, hitting a precise 119. Thanks once more to Bevan, who stroked an unbeaten 76, Leicestershire made light work of chasing 204. After a game in which his temper often got the better of him, Kirby became the first player to collect three points under the new disciplinary code.

Close of play: First day, Yorkshire 296-8 (Blakey 34, Sidebottom 0); Second day, Yorkshire 1-0 (White 1, Wood 0); Third day, Leicestershire 33-1 (Sutcliffe 17, Crowe 1).

Yorkshire

M. J. Wood c Burns b Maddy	23	– (2) c Burns b Malcolm	1
C. White c Wells b Malcolm	62	– (1) c Sutcliffe b Malcolm	8
M. J. Lumb c Burns b Malcolm	21	– c and b Malcolm	46
*D. S. Lehmann c Stevens b Wells	51	– not out	119
A. McGrath lbw b Wells	25	– lbw b DeFreitas	18
V. J. Craven b Malcolm	13	– c Burns b DeFreitas	0
†R. J. Blakey not out	48	– c Burns b DeFreitas	10
R. K. J. Dawson c Maddy b Malcolm	8	– c Bevan b DeFreitas	0
C. E. W. Silverwood c DeFreitas b Maddy	33	– c sub b Maddy	6
R. J. Sidebottom lbw b Malcolm	0	– c sub b Malcolm	12
S. P. Kirby c and b Malcolm	0	– lbw b DeFreitas	0
B 2, l-b 14, w 4, n-b 6	26	B 1, l-b 10, w 4, n-b 4	19
	310		**239**

1/62 (1) 2/112 (2) 3/123 (3) 4/194 (5) 310
5/203 (4) 6/227 (6) 7/241 (8)
8/292 (9) 9/310 (10) 10/310 (11)

1/3 (2) 2/14 (1) 3/105 (3) 239
4/153 (5) 5/153 (6) 6/167 (7)
7/167 (8) 8/174 (9)
9/204 (10) 10/239 (11)

Bonus points – Yorkshire 3, Leicestershire 3.

Bowling: *First Innings*—Malcolm 26.4–5–72–6; DeFreitas 19–7–53–0; Maddy 20–5–49–2; Dagnall 20–3–70–0; Crowe 13–4–43–0; Wells 7–3–7–2. *Second Innings*—Malcolm 23–3–76–4; DeFreitas 22.4–10–38–5; Maddy 14–1–50–1; Wells 12–0–42–0; Crowe 12–4–22–0.

Leicestershire

T. R. Ward b Kirby	4	– lbw b Silverwood	8
I. J. Sutcliffe lbw b Kirby	14	– c Blakey b Kirby	36
D. L. Maddy c White b Sidebottom	61	– (4) c White b Dawson	58
M. G. Bevan b White	142	– (5) not out.	76
*V. J. Wells b Sidebottom	0	– (6) c White b Kirby	0
D. I. Stevens c Dawson b McGrath	31	– (7) not out.	0
†N. D. Burns c Wood b McGrath	5		
P. A. J. DeFreitas c Blakey b McGrath	0		
C. D. Crowe lbw b Kirby	29	– (3) c Blakey b Silverwood	6
C. E. Dagnall c Craven b White	16		
D. E. Malcolm not out	6		
B 5, l-b 4, w 7, n-b 22	38	B 2, l-b 9, w 6, n-b 6	23
	346		**207**

1/7 (1) 2/55 (2) 3/131 (3) 4/135 (5) 346
5/194 (6) 6/212 (7) 7/218 (8)
8/282 (9) 9/327 (10) 10/346 (4)

1/26 (1) 2/42 (3) (5 wkts) 207
3/63 (2) 4/198 (4)
5/202 (6)

Bonus points – Leicestershire 3, Yorkshire 3.

Bowling: *First Innings*—Silverwood 18–3–52–0; Kirby 21–3–86–3; Sidebottom 19–5–60–2; Dawson 14–3–37–0; White 9.4–0–53–2; McGrath 12–1–33–3; Lehmann 2–0–16–0. *Second Innings*—Silverwood 14–4–30–2; Kirby 11–3–35–2; Sidebottom 10–3–47–0; Dawson 7–1–19–1; Lehmann 4–3–16–0; White 8–2–26–0; McGrath 4–1–23–0.

Umpires: J. W. Lloyds and A. G. T. Whitehead.

At Birmingham, June 12, 13, 14, 15. LEICESTERSHIRE lost to WARWICKSHIRE by 144 runs.

At Leicester, June 26. LEICESTERSHIRE lost to INDIANS by 54 runs (see Indian tour section).

LEICESTERSHIRE v LANCASHIRE

At Leicester, July 3, 4, 5, 6. Drawn. Leicestershire 8 pts, Lancashire 7 pts. Toss: Lancashire.

Bad weather wiped out both the first day and the third, so contrived declarations provided the only hope of a positive result. But neither side wanted to risk defeat, and they settled for a draw. On a green pitch the ball darted off the seam, and Leicestershire struggled against an accurate attack. Martin's control and Anderson's pace forced Maddy to battle for his half-century. Lancashire's batsmen fared no better: only their top three reached double figures as Malcolm again found swing and picked up another five wickets – giving him 100 for Leicestershire in only 24 games. The final day was little more than batting practice, as every Lancashire player bar Byas and Hegg turned their arm over. Maddy and Wells made the most of it.

Close of play: First day, No play; Second day, Lancashire 126-3 (Byas 15); Third day, No play.

Leicestershire

T. R. Ward c Driver b Martin	0	– c Chilton b Martin	4
I. J. Sutcliffe b Driver	36	– c Martin b Wood	38
D. L. Maddy c Fairbrother b Martin	59	– not out	79
M. G. Bevan lbw b Anderson	4		
*V. J. Wells lbw b Anderson	18	– c Hegg b Driver	50
D. I. Stevens c Hegg b Chapple	21	– not out	15
†N. D. Burns c Hegg b Driver	2	– (4) c Roberts b Wood	0
P. A. J. DeFreitas b Anderson	25		
C. D. Crowe not out	20		
M. J. A. Whiley c Fairbrother b Wood	5		
D. E. Malcolm b Anderson	0		
B 4, l-b 13, w 2, n-b 10	29	B 4, l-b 4, w 2, n-b 10	20
	219	**(4 wkts dec.)**	**206**

1/0 (1) 2/76 (2) 3/81 (4) 4/131 (5)   1/6 (1) 2/75 (2)   (4 wkts dec.) 206
5/140 (3) 6/157 (6) 7/173 (7)   3/81 (4) 4/177 (5)
8/201 (8) 9/212 (10) 10/219 (11)

Bonus points – Leicestershire 1, Lancashire 3.

Bowling: *First Innings*—Martin 16–6–41–3; Chapple 15–5–63–1; Wood 13–2–41–1; Anderson 14–4–33–3; Driver 8–3–22–2; Fairbrother 1–0–2–0. *Second Innings*—Martin 10–4–21–1; Chapple 12–2–34–0; Driver 16–5–32–1; Anderson 5–1–12–0; Wood 5–1–13–2; Chilton 5–0–28–0; Swann 6–0–37–0; Roberts 2–0–6–0; Fairbrother 2–0–15–0.

Lancashire

M. J. Chilton lbw b Maddy	57	P. J. Martin c Burns b Malcolm	8
A. J. Swann lbw b Wells	20	J. M. Anderson not out	1
D. Byas c Burns b DeFreitas	48		
J. Wood b Wells	3	L-b 9, w 8, n-b 16	33
N. H. Fairbrother c DeFreitas b Malcolm	3		
T. W. Roberts c Maddy b Malcolm	2		**180**
R. C. Driver lbw b DeFreitas	5	1/71 (2) 2/113 (1) 3/126 (4)	
*†W. K. Hegg c Maddy b Malcolm	0	4/146 (5) 5/148 (6) 6/153 (7)	
G. Chapple c DeFreitas b Malcolm	0	7/154 (8) 8/160 (9)	
		9/172 (10) 10/180 (3)	

Bonus points – Leicestershire 3.

Bowling: Malcolm 16–6–52–5; DeFreitas 18.4–9–39–2; Wells 11–7–18–2; Whiley 6–0–53–0; Maddy 4–1–9–1.

Umpires: J. H. Evans and A. A. Jones.

LEICESTERSHIRE v HAMPSHIRE

At Leicester, July 10, 11, 12, 13. Drawn. Leicestershire 10 pts, Hampshire 10 pts. Toss: Hampshire.
Rain on the second day, and Hampshire's lack of adventure on the fourth, condemned the match to stalemate. On a demanding pitch both teams needed vital contributions from the lower order as their first innings crumbled. Hampshire were in disarray at 113 for five, then lost Crawley, bowled for 60 with bat held high, and it took a defiant 63 from Pothas – helped by 17 no-balls from Whiley – to steady the ship. Replying to 311, Leicestershire were in a worse mess at 81 for five – and in serious danger of being made to follow on. But Bevan crawled to a 204-ball fifty, Burns eked out a four-hour century and DeFreitas cracked a valuable 44. In the end, Sutcliffe could even afford to declare. However, there would be no declaration from Smith, and he and Francis plodded into the last afternoon. When Maddy finally cleaned up the tail, Leicestershire had just 36 overs to score an unrealistic 295. The predictable draw meant Leicestershire stayed second in the table, Hampshire third.

Close of play: First day, Hampshire 311; Second day, Leicestershire 98-5 (Bevan 29, Burns 7); Third day, Hampshire 102-4 (Smith 40, Francis 9).

Hampshire

G. W. White lbw b Maddy	28	– lbw b DeFreitas	19
W. S. Kendall c Sutcliffe b Whiley	19	– c Stevens b DeFreitas	0
J. P. Crawley b Whiley	60	– c Burns b DeFreitas	0
*R. A. Smith c DeFreitas b Crowe	12	– lbw b Maddy	104
N. C. Johnson st Burns b Crowe	4	– c Burns b Crowe	25
J. D. Francis c Bevan b Crowe	2	– c Maddy b Malcolm	82
†N. Pothas c Burns b Malcolm	63	– b Maddy	0
A. D. Mascarenhas lbw b DeFreitas	22	– c Burns b Maddy	9
S. D. Udal c Bevan b Malcolm	23	– b Maddy	1
C. T. Tremlett b Maddy	28	– c Burns b Whiley	13
A. D. Mullally not out	1	– not out	3
B 4, l-b 5, w 4, n-b 36	49	B 6, l-b 5, w 10, n-b 6	27

1/52 (1) 2/58 (2) 3/81 (4) 4/93 (5)   311   1/17 (2) 2/17 (3) 3/28 (1)   283
5/113 (6) 6/185 (3) 7/235 (8)   4/83 (5) 5/207 (4) 6/207 (7)
8/247 (7) 9/305 (9) 10/311 (10)   7/241 (8) 8/247 (9)
9/273 (6) 10/283 (10)

Bonus points – Hampshire 3, Leicestershire 3.

Bowling: *First Innings*—DeFreitas 20–8–33–1; Malcolm 22–2–72–2; Maddy 17.3–7–45–2; Whiley 18–4–89–2; Crowe 19–6–63–3. *Second Innings*—DeFreitas 32–11–79–3; Malcolm 17–3–59–1; Crowe 17–6–56–1; Maddy 17–4–37–4; Whiley 8.4–2–22–1; Bevan 7–0–19–0.

Leicestershire

T. R. Ward c Pothas b Mullally	0	– b Udal	18
*I. J. Sutcliffe c Johnson b Mascarenhas	18	– (4) not out	11
D. L. Maddy c Pothas b Tremlett	12	– (5) c White b Francis	9
M. G. Bevan b Tremlett	62		
D. I. Stevens c Pothas b Udal	1	– (3) c Francis b Kendall	11
R. J. Cunliffe b Mascarenhas	23	– not out	5
†N. D. Burns c Johnson b Mullally	101		
P. A. J. DeFreitas c Tremlett b Udal	44	– (2) b Mullally	15
C. D. Crowe not out	18		
D. E. Malcolm c Francis b Mullally	1		
M. J. A. Whiley not out	4		
L-b 10, w 6	16	L-b 3	3

1/0 (1) 2/26 (3) 3/35 (2)   (9 wkts. dec.) 300   1/19 (2) 2/45 (1)   (4 wkts) 72
4/36 (5) 5/81 (6) 6/188 (4)   3/51 (3) 4/64 (5)
7/271 (7) 8/283 (8) 9/284 (10)

Bonus points – Leicestershire 3, Hampshire 3.

Bowling: *First Innings*—Mullally 27–7–54–3; Mascarenhas 29–17–39–2; Tremlett 26–4–80–2; Udal 29.2–11–78–2; Johnson 10–1–39–0. *Second Innings*—Mullally 4–1–7–1; Tremlett 5–0–24–0; Mascarenhas 4–1–7–0; Johnson 3–1–6–0; Udal 5–4–4–1; Kendall 5–1–12–1; Francis 2–1–1–1; White 1–0–8–0.

Umpires: B. Dudleston and M. J. Harris.

LEICESTERSHIRE v KENT

At Leicester, July 24, 25, 26, 27. Kent won by six wickets. Kent 18 pts, Leicestershire 3 pts. Toss: Kent.

Hugely disappointing batting on the opening day lay at the heart of Leicestershire's first home defeat. After being put in, they were flummoxed by Saggers's swing and Masters's sharp seam movement and tumbled to 131 all out an hour after lunch. The wicket was sometimes uneven, but Kent soon put Leicestershire's traumas in perspective: the ECB's pitch inspector arrived in time to watch Key and Symonds crash 99 in just 16 overs. Key drove sumptuously to reach an excellent century and contributions throughout the order gave Kent a 208-run lead. In reply, Sutcliffe and Ward began with a blaze of shots, before settling down to put on 161. Saggers and Masters shot through the middle order but Kent were stopped in their tracks by DeFreitas's clean-hit 114, which gave Leicestershire an outside chance of victory. But time was never an issue, and Kent eased home.

Close of play: First day, Kent 183-4 (Key 103, Nixon 6); Second day, Leicestershire 151-0 (Ward 66, Sutcliffe 74); Third day, Kent 66-1 (Walker 27, Saggers 10).

Leicestershire

T. R. Ward lbw b Saggers	1	– c Ealham b Saggers	70
I. J. Sutcliffe c Patel b Masters	17	– c Symonds b Masters	103
D. L. Maddy lbw b Ealham	15	– c Nixon b Saggers	0
M. G. Bevan c Nixon b Masters	0	– lbw b Khan	61
*V. J. Wells c Nixon b Masters	0	– lbw b Masters	8
D. I. Stevens b Saggers	23	– c Symonds b Masters	4
†N. D. Burns not out	40	– lbw b Patel	4
P. A. J. DeFreitas c Nixon b Saggers	2	– c Ealham b Saggers	114
C. D. Crowe lbw b Saggers	0	– not out	16
M. J. A. Whiley c Nixon b Masters	6	– b Symonds	0
D. E. Malcolm b Saggers	12	– b Saggers	0
B 4, l-b 5, n-b 6	15	B 6, l-b 4, n-b 10	20
	131		**400**

1/12 (1) 2/38 (2) 3/42 (4) 4/46 (5) 5/56 (3) 6/89 (6) 7/97 (8) 8/103 (9) 9/110 (10) 10/131 (11)

1/161 (1) 2/165 (3) 3/200 (2) 4/216 (5) 5/220 (6) 6/225 (7) 7/353 (4) 8/398 (8) 9/399 (10) 10/400 (11)

Bonus points – Kent 3.

Bowling: *First Innings*—Saggers 17.2–6–44–5; Khan 6–1–20–0; Masters 16–6–36–4; Ealham 9–7–5–1; Symonds 4–0–17–0. *Second Innings*—Saggers 21.4–7–68–4; Khan 12–4–48–1; Masters 29–8–86–3; Ealham 26–9–62–0; Patel 44–16–95–1; Symonds 11–3–31–1.

Kent

M. J. Walker lbw b DeFreitas	4	– c Wells b Malcolm	46
R. W. T. Key c Ward b Wells	127	– lbw b Maddy	18
E. T. Smith c Maddy b Whiley	10	– (4) not out	48
A. Symonds b Maddy	45	– (5) b Maddy	25
J. B. Hockley c Wells b Maddy	0	– (6) not out	15
†P. A. Nixon lbw b Whiley	41		
M. A. Ealham c Ward b Malcolm	22		
*M. M. Patel lbw b Crowe	20		
A. Khan not out	18		
D. D. Masters c Bevan b Crowe	4		
M. J. Saggers lbw b Whiley	6	– (3) lbw b Wells	16
B 14, l-b 10, n-b 18	42	B 2, l-b 7, n-b 16	25

1/10 (1) 2/52 (3) 3/151 (4) 4/155 (5)   **339**   1/45 (2) 2/81 (3)   **(4 wkts) 193**
5/244 (6) 6/252 (2) 7/303 (8)   3/109 (4) 4/158 (5)
8/323 (7) 9/328 (10) 10/339 (11)

Bonus points – Kent 3, Leicestershire 3.

Bowling: *First Innings*—DeFreitas 21–7–46–1; Malcolm 21–2–100–1; Wells 15–3–38–1; Maddy 16–4–52–2; Whiley 17–3–60–3; Crowe 5–1–19–2. *Second Innings*—Malcolm 9–1–43–1; DeFreitas 11–1–49–0; Maddy 13–4–38–2; Whiley 7.5–2–33–0; Wells 8–2–16–1; Stevens 1–0–5–0.

Umpires: N. G. Cowley and V. A. Holder.

LEICESTERSHIRE v SURREY

At Leicester, August 14, 15, 16. Surrey won by seven wickets. Surrey 20 pts, Leicestershire 5 pts. Toss: Surrey. County debut: M. Kaif.

Surrey, looking like certain champions, totally dominated and won with a day to spare. In truth, Leicestershire were only in the match for the first morning, when Whiley's left-arm seam reduced Surrey to 74 for three. Their hopes were quickly dashed as Butcher and Brown laid into the bowling and piled on 211 in 37 madcap overs; Brown smashed 104 off 97 balls, while Butcher's 116 included 84 in boundaries. Leicestershire's misery continued as Hollioake blazed 80 off 74 balls and Clarke eased 95. Maddy's improving medium-pace brought him a second five-for of the season, but it was small consolation. In reply to a huge 540, Leicestershire were forced to follow on, foxed by Mushtaq Ahmed's leg-spin. His victims included Mohammad Kaif, like him a locum overseas player. Though Maddy and Sutcliffe twice scrapped hard on a flat pitch, their team-mates let them down, and Surrey were left a paltry 40 to win. John Major, the ex-Prime Minister, enjoyed his visit to Grace Road so much that he wrote out a cheque for Leicestershire membership before he left.

Close of play: First day, Surrey 454-6 (Clarke 52, Tudor 8); Second day, Leicestershire 265-6 (Burns 16, DeFreitas 8).

Atherton in the end became resigned to his bowlers' and fielders' fallibility; Hussain has barked at every foible and thought up new ways to dismiss batsmen.
Scyld Berry on Nasser Hussain, page 75

Surrey

I. J. Ward lbw b Whiley	28	– c Maddy b Whiley	6
†J. N. Batty lbw b Maddy	28	– c Maddy b Malcolm	4
M. A. Butcher c Burns b Maddy	116	– c Burns b Malcolm	8
M. R. Ramprakash c Maddy b Whiley	0	– not out	5
A. D. Brown c Ward b Maddy	104	– not out	14
*A. J. Hollioake c Burns b Ward	80		
R. Clarke c Burns b Maddy	95		
A. J. Tudor lbw b DeFreitas	8		
Mushtaq Ahmed c Burns b DeFreitas	12		
M. P. Bicknell not out	23		
J. Ormond b Maddy	6		
B 2, l-b 6, w 16, n-b 16	40	L-b 1, w 2, n-b 2	5

1/61 (1) 2/63 (2) 3/74 (4) 4/285 (5)   540   1/8 (1) 2/12 (2) 3/21 (3)   (3 wkts) 42
5/342 (3) 6/419 (6) 7/458 (8)
8/474 (9) 9/526 (7) 10/540 (11)

Bonus points – Surrey 5, Leicestershire 3.

Bowling: *First Innings*—DeFreitas 34–6–91–2; Malcolm 22–3–114–0; Grove 10–0–63–0; Maddy 25.4–4–104–5; Whiley 22–4–85–2; Kaif 7–0–43–0; Ward 8–0–32–1. *Second Innings*—Whiley 3.1–0–34–1; Malcolm 3–0–7–2.

Leicestershire

T. R. Ward c Brown b Tudor	39	– lbw b Bicknell	16
*I. J. Sutcliffe c Batty b Mushtaq Ahmed	48	– c Brown b Bicknell	64
D. L. Maddy lbw b Mushtaq Ahmed	81	– lbw b Ormond	94
D. I. Stevens b Bicknell	15	– c Ward b Mushtaq Ahmed	14
M. Kaif lbw b Mushtaq Ahmed	13	– lbw b Tudor	43
R. J. Cunliffe b Ormond	8	– (7) c Brown b Tudor	4
†N. D. Burns not out	29	– (6) c sub b Mushtaq Ahmed	11
P. A. J. DeFreitas b Mushtaq Ahmed	8	– c Butcher b Tudor	0
J. O. Grove b Mushtaq Ahmed	4	– b Tudor	3
M. J. A. Whiley run out	0	– st Batty b Mushtaq Ahmed	13
D. E. Malcolm c Batty b Ormond	4	– not out	4
B 10, l-b 11, w 6, n-b 14	41	B 8, l-b 5, n-b 10	23

1/65 (1) 2/167 (2) 3/196 (4) 4/225 (5)   290   1/26 (1) 2/182 (2) 3/203 (4)   289
5/234 (3) 6/240 (6) 7/271 (8)   4/219 (3) 5/250 (6) 6/267 (7)
8/283 (9) 9/285 (10) 10/290 (11)   7/269 (8) 8/270 (5)
                                         9/285 (10) 10/289 (9)

Bonus points – Leicestershire 2, Surrey 3.

Bowling: *First Innings*—Bicknell 15–1–76–1; Tudor 18–6–58–1; Ormond 21.3–9–46–2; Hollioake 2–0–18–0; Mushtaq Ahmed 30–7–71–5; Butcher 1–1–0–0. *Second Innings*—Bicknell 16–2–41–2; Tudor 17.1–2–54–4; Butcher 3–1–22–0; Mushtaq Ahmed 33–7–115–3; Ormond 14–2–44–1.

Umpires: M. J. Harris and A. A. Jones.

At Canterbury, August 22, 23, 24, 25. LEICESTERSHIRE drew with KENT.

LEICESTERSHIRE v SUSSEX

At Leicester, August 27, 28, 29. Leicestershire won by eight wickets. Leicestershire 16 pts, Sussex 4 pts. Toss: Sussex.

Leicestershire finally rediscovered the art of winning and pulled clear of the relegation dogfight. Without a win since June 3, they were bowled to a comfortable victory by their thirty-something attack of Malcolm, DeFreitas and Srinath – their fourth overseas player of the summer. Sussex had chosen to bat but were dismissed cheaply as Malcolm took five for 38 with booming out-swingers and Srinath made incisions with his surprise in-ducker. Only Martin-Jenkins played confidently but – with the exception of Sutcliffe's grinding and invaluable 75 – Leicestershire's batsmen struggled too, and it took heavy hitting by Malcolm at No. 11 to muster a slim but helpful lead of 32. Leicestershire's trio of golden oldies then had Sussex in disarray once more, and they were left only 111 to chase. Sutcliffe again dropped anchor, and they made it with four sessions to spare.

Close of play: First day, Leicestershire 50-2 (Sutcliffe 21); Second day, Sussex 58-5 (Ambrose 24, Kirtley 1).

Sussex

M. W. Goodwin lbw b Srinath	5	– (2) lbw b Srinath	14
R. R. Montgomerie lbw b Malcolm	10	– (1) lbw b Srinath	2
P. A. Cottey b Srinath	21	– lbw b DeFreitas	3
*C. J. Adams c and b DeFreitas	60	– c Burns b DeFreitas	0
T. R. Ambrose c Burns b Malcolm	34	– c Burns b DeFreitas	30
R. S. C. Martin-Jenkins b Maddy	62	– c Burns b Maddy	8
†M. J. Prior b Malcolm	0	– (8) b Srinath	4
K. J. Innes lbw b Malcolm	0	– (9) not out	49
M. J. G. Davis not out	6	– (6) b DeFreitas	7
R. J. Kirtley c Ward b Maddy	0	– (7) c Maddy b Malcolm	12
B. V. Taylor c Burns b Malcolm	2	– c Burns b Malcolm	3
B 4, l-b 1, n-b 10	15	L-b 6, n-b 4	10

1/9 (1) 2/21 (2) 3/103 (3) 4/125 (4)   **215**   1/2 (1) 2/21 (3) 3/21 (4) 4/23 (2)   **142**
5/172 (5) 6/176 (7) 7/178 (8)   5/41 (6) 6/69 (5) 7/76 (8)
8/209 (6) 9/213 (10) 10/215 (11)   8/92 (7) 9/115 (10) 10/142 (11)

Bonus points – Sussex 1, Leicestershire 3.

Bowling: *First Innings*—Malcolm 16.2–6–38–5; Srinath 19–5–47–2; Maddy 15–2–50–2; Wells 11–2–32–0; DeFreitas 16–6–25–1; Crowe 3–0–18–0. *Second Innings*—Srinath 17–1–48–3; DeFreitas 19–7–42–4; Maddy 6–3–17–1; Malcolm 13.5–5–29–2.

Leicestershire

T. R. Ward c Cottey b Kirtley	0	– b Innes	26
I. J. Sutcliffe c and b Davis	75	– not out	30
D. L. Maddy lbw b Innes	29	– lbw b Kirtley	23
D. I. Stevens lbw b Kirtley	7	– not out	31
*V. J. Wells c Montgomerie b Davis	36		
A. S. Wright c Montgomerie b Taylor	0		
†N. D. Burns lbw b Taylor	4		
P. A. J. DeFreitas c Kirtley b Innes	16		
J. Srinath c Montgomerie b Kirtley	18		
C. D. Crowe b Kirtley	34		
D. E. Malcolm not out	24		
B 4, n-b 4	8	B 1	1

1/0 (1) 2/50 (3) 3/63 (4) 4/131 (5)   **247**   1/37 (1) 2/71 (3)   **(2 wkts) 111**
5/132 (6) 6/132 (7) 7/168 (8)
8/170 (2) 9/202 (9) 10/247 (10)

Bonus points – Leicestershire 1, Sussex 3.

Bowling: *First Innings*—Kirtley 26–6–89–4; Martin-Jenkins 15–4–60–0; Taylor 15–4–31–2; Innes 20–8–36–2; Davis 25–15–27–2. *Second Innings*—Kirtley 13.4–3–47–1; Martin-Jenkins 4–0–19–0; Innes 4–2–15–1; Taylor 4–1–5–0; Davis 6–1–24–0.

Umpires: A. Clarkson and N. A. Mallender.

At Scarborough, September 4, 5, 6, 7. LEICESTERSHIRE drew with YORKSHIRE.

LEICESTERSHIRE v SOMERSET

At Leicester, September 12, 13. Leicestershire won by an innings and 18 runs. Leicestershire 18 pts, Somerset 2.75 pts. Toss: Leicestershire. First-class debut: D. G. Brandy.

Leicestershire started their penultimate match embroiled in the mid-table mêlée, with both second spot and relegation still possible. Somerset needed a convincing win to stand a chance of avoiding the drop, but instead capitulated in sorry style, going down in under five sessions. The rout began as Srinath and DeFreitas bowled beautifully in Somerset's first innings, exploiting early moisture to find seam movement and swing. Michael Burns, who had already made 99, 98 and 95 in 2002, was left stranded on 97 not out, having scored more than half of Somerset's total. In reply, Ward's excellent 84 gave Leicestershire a 119-run lead. It hardly looked enough for an innings victory but none of Somerset's top seven reached double figures and they were skittled in less than 30 overs, as Srinath gave another exhibition of high-quality bowling. Helped by brilliant catching – including Damian Brandy's wonderful effort at long leg to dismiss Holloway – he claimed five for 25.

Close of play: First day, Leicestershire 207-5 (Burns 8, Crowe 5).

Somerset

*J. Cox lbw b Srinath	4	– (2) c Burns b Srinath	4
M. J. Wood lbw b Srinath	1	– (1) run out	2
M. Burns not out	97	– lbw b Srinath	4
P. D. Bowler c Burns b Srinath	8	– c Maddy b DeFreitas	6
P. C. L. Holloway c Sutcliffe b DeFreitas	15	– c Brandy b Srinath	8
P. D. Trego c Burns b DeFreitas	15	– c Crowe b Srinath	9
†R. J. Turner c Stevens b DeFreitas	0	– c Crowe b Srinath	0
K. P. Dutch c Burns b Crowe	4	– not out	14
M. P. L. Bulbeck c Burns b Srinath	22	– b Maddy	18
R. L. Johnson lbw b Maddy	18	– c Maddy b Malcolm	18
S. R. G. Francis b Maddy	0	– lbw b Maddy	17
L-b 1, n-b 6	7	B 1, l-b 1, w 2, n-b 4	8

1/4 (1) 2/17 (2) 3/37 (4) 4/72 (5)　　　191　　1/7 (2) 2/10 (1) 3/20 (4) 4/30 (3)　　101
5/98 (6) 6/106 (7) 7/114 (8)　　　　　　　5/41 (5) 6/41 (6) 7/42 (7)
8/160 (9) 9/191 (10) 10/191 (11)　　　　　8/67 (9) 9/82 (10) 10/101 (11)

Bonus points – Leicestershire 3.

Bowling: *First Innings*—Srinath 14–1–60–4; Malcolm 10–1–51–0; DeFreitas 10–3–35–3; Maddy 5.3–0–29–2; Crowe 3–0–15–1. *Second Innings*—Srinath 11–4–25–5; DeFreitas 10–3–28–1; Maddy 4.5–1–20–2; Malcolm 4–0–26–1.

Leicestershire

T. R. Ward c Turner b Trego	84	P. A. J. DeFreitas not out	38
*I. J. Sutcliffe lbw b Bulbeck	17	J. Srinath c Dutch b Johnson	3
D. L. Maddy c Bowler b Trego	36	D. E. Malcolm c Turner b Johnson	0
D. I. Stevens c Turner b Johnson	8	B 4, l-b 19, w 8, n-b 8	39
A. S. Wright b Bulbeck	25		
†N. D. Burns lbw b Trego	46	1/42 (2) 2/130 (3) 3/147 (4) 4/190 (5)	310
C. D. Crowe c Dutch b Bulbeck	9	5/200 (1) 6/215 (7) 7/222 (8)	
D. G. Brandy c Turner b Francis	5	8/303 (6) 9/310 (10) 10/310 (11)	

Bonus points – Leicestershire 3, Somerset 3.

Bowling: Johnson 23.4–3–71–3; Bulbeck 21–4–69–3; Dutch 9–2–17–0; Francis 11–1–65–1; Trego 17–2–65–3.

Umpires: J. H. Hampshire and N. J. Llong.

At The Oval, September 18, 19, 20, 21. LEICESTERSHIRE lost to SURREY by 483 runs.

MIDDLESEX
BEATING THE BLIP

Ch'ship 2nd in Division 2 – promoted
C&G 3rd round
B&H 5th in South Group
NUL 9th in Division 2

Player of the season: Ed Joyce

There was a period last season when Middlesex must have suffered an uncomfortable feeling of *déjà vu*. Back in August 2001, a loss of form had cost them a place in the promotion race, and they eventually finished fifth in Division Two of the Championship. At the time, most observers agreed that Middlesex had probably overachieved for much of the season and were not yet ready to go up anyway. When a similar blip a year later looked as if it would cost them promotion once more, the same observers were not quite so philosophical, and there was concern that a wonderful opportunity was about to be missed. In the event, vital wins at Worcester and Derby ensured a happy ending: they made it to Division One after all.

The early portents were not good. Angus Fraser decided that the laptop was mightier than the ball, and played just six matches before accepting an offer to become the cricket correspondent of *The Independent*. His retirement meant the captaincy passed abruptly to the inexperienced Andrew Strauss. The success of Sven Koenig, a South African left-hander with an Italian passport, helped Strauss retain his batting form (he made 985 Championship runs at 44) and gave consistency to the opening partnership. But batting wasn't the problem: a lack of penetration made it a difficult attack to manage and there were too many occasions when Strauss showed an excessively defensive mindset. With experience, presumably, will come adventure.

Victory in the first three matches represented Middlesex's best start to a Championship season since 1988. Ashley Noffke, the Queensland fast bowler who was filling in until the arrival of the Pakistan all-rounder Abdul Razzaq, played an important part in these early wins, taking 19 wickets at 23. But his departure exposed the shortcomings of the other bowlers, and Razzaq, whose signing had seemed inspired at the time, was something of a disappointment. He did manage 26 wickets in only six appearances, but he always seemed to be bowling well within himself and neither of his best returns (seven for 133 against Essex and five for 125 against Gloucestershire) led to victory. He showed his ability with the bat in a spectacular, hard-hit 203 not out at Cardiff, but that was his only score above 38. Better things are hoped for in 2003, when Razzaq will be available from the start of the season. On his return, Noffke took a couple of weeks to regain his fitness and rhythm before picking up 20 wickets in the wins at Worcester, where he also scored a career-best 76, and Derby. His presence for the whole of 2003 should ensure that the Middlesex attack commands a little more respect from the opposition.

There was little wrong with the batting, and Middlesex earned 61 bonus points from a possible 80 – more than any other side in the country. They reached 400 ten times, and eight batsmen averaged over 40. Ed Joyce, a Dubliner in his first full season, scored 1,166 Championship runs at 53, and Koenig and Owais Shah also topped 1,000. Paul Weekes did not allow his benefit to distract him and had his best season for some years, hitting 887 at nearly 50. David Nash continued to keep wicket well and also made runs at important times, particularly with his hundred at Worcester. Ben Hutton made five ducks in seven innings at one stage but also scored a century and four fifties, hit the ball hard and registered the most sixes in Division Two. Without Noffke, the seam bowling lacked a cutting edge, and the spinners fared little better: Weekes was too expensive and Phil Tufnell too often ineffective, although he played an important part in the crucial win at Derby with five for 35.

Yet again, it is best to draw a veil over Middlesex's one-day form. They failed to qualify for the knockout stage of the B&H, winning only one of their five group matches, and lost interest in the C&G at the first hurdle after being unable to defend 291 at Chelmsford. The Norwich Union produced just four wins and some embarrassing performances, notably the game against Northamptonshire at Lord's, when they were dismissed for 72. But there was some consolation in the last home League match of the season when Nick Compton scored a stylish and entertaining 86 not out against Lancashire at the Denis Compton Oval, Shenley – the ground named after his illustrious grandfather. With Hutton – the grandson of Len – already on the staff, Middlesex added another big name when they signed Mali Richards, son of Sir Viv, on a part-time contract. The 19-year-old Richards, a left-handed batsman, was born in England and had attracted offers from other counties, but will be available for Middlesex for certain games in 2003 while continuing his education.

Many will say that reaching Division One was the easy part and staying there will not be so straightforward. But Strauss has almost a year's captaincy experience behind him, the depth of the batting remains strong, and Noffke and Razzaq are expected to be available for the whole season. It won't be straightforward, but it is certainly possible. **Norman de Mesquita**

MIDDLESEX 2002

Back row: S. G. Koenig, C. B. Keegan, S. Nikitaras, E. C. Joyce, J. K. Maunders, M. J. Brown. *Middle row:* J. C. Pooley *(assistant coach),* J. E. Emburey *(head coach),* M. J. Smith *(first-team scorer),* B. L. Hutton, S. J. Cook, D. Alleyne, A. W. Laraman, N. R. D. Compton, A. J. Coleman, T. A. Hunt, A. Jones *(second-team scorer),* A. Herd *(fitness adviser),* A. Scott *(physiotherapist).* *Front row:* T. F. Bloomfield, O. A. Shah *(vice-captain),* P. C. R. Tufnell, A. J. Strauss, A. R. C. Fraser *(captain),* P. N. Weekes, D. C. Nash, R. M. S. Weston. *Insets:* Abdul Razzaq, A. A. Noffke. *Pictures by Bill Smith.*

MIDDLESEX RESULTS

All first-class matches – Played 18: Won 8, Lost 3, Drawn 7.
County Championship matches – Played 16: Won 7, Lost 3, Drawn 6.

COUNTY CHAMPIONSHIP AVERAGES: BATTING AND FIELDING

Cap		M	I	NO	R	HS	100s	50s	Avge	Ct/St
	Abdul Razzaq§	6	9	3	364	203*	1	0	60.66	1
2002	E. C. Joyce	16	25	3	1,166	129	4	5	53.00	13
2000	D. C. Nash	14	18	5	642	100	1	4	49.38	34/1
1993	P. N. Weekes	16	23	5	887	127*	3	3	49.27	22
2000	O. A. Shah	15	24	3	1,019	172*	3	5	48.52	4
2001	A. J. Strauss	14	23	1	985	141	2	5	44.77	12
2002	S. G. Koenig	16	27	1	1,110	113	3	7	42.69	6
	B. L. Hutton	9	17	1	512	116	1	4	32.00	19
	A. W. Laraman	9	11	2	249	82*	0	1	27.66	3
	A. A. Noffke§	8	10	1	203	76	0	1	22.55	3
2001	R. M. S. Weston . . .	7	9	1	170	72	0	1	21.25	4
	S. J. Cook	14	17	1	224	38*	0	0	14.00	4
	J. W. M. Dalrymple . .	3	5	0	66	33	0	0	13.20	1
1990	P. C. R. Tufnell	14	15	8	89	45	0	0	12.71	3
	C. B. Keegan	8	10	0	58	24	0	0	5.80	1

Also batted: D. Alleyne (2 matches) 13, 49* (4 ct); T. F. Bloomfield (cap 2001) (2 matches) 31*, 26*; A. R. C. Fraser (cap 1988) (2 matches) 16, 20; I. Jones (1 match) 29.

§ *Overseas player.*

BOWLING

	O	M	R	W	BB	5W/i	Avge
A. A. Noffke	305.1	57	1,128	45	8-24	3	25.06
Abdul Razzaq	206.3	25	757	26	7-133	2	29.11
P. C. R. Tufnell	514.5	104	1,390	45	8-66	4	30.88
S. J. Cook	344.2	65	1,243	39	8-63	1	31.87
A. W. Laraman	226.4	41	775	20	4-55	0	38.75
C. B. Keegan	193.5	31	806	18	4-47	0	44.77
P. N. Weekes	367.3	52	1,100	18	3-27	0	61.11

Also bowled: T. F. Bloomfield 65.1–15–252–4; J. W. M. Dalrymple 12–4–33–0; A. R. C. Fraser 72–26–190–7; B. L. Hutton 51–9–182–5; I. Jones 22.3–3–100–4; E. C. Joyce 14–2–54–0.

COUNTY RECORDS

Highest score for:	331*	J. D. Robertson v Worcestershire at Worcester . . .	1949
Highest score against:	316*	J. B. Hobbs (Surrey) at Lord's	1926
Best bowling for:	10-40	G. O. B. Allen v Lancashire at Lord's	1929
Best bowling against:	9-38	R. C. Robertson-Glasgow (Somerset) at Lord's . .	1924
Highest total for:	642-3 dec.	v Hampshire at Southampton	1923
Highest total against:	665	by West Indians at Lord's	1939
Lowest total for:	20	v MCC at Lord's	1864
Lowest total against:	{ 31	by Gloucestershire at Bristol	1924
	{ 31	by Glamorgan at Cardiff	1997

COUNTY OFFICERS

Captain A. J. Strauss • **Head coach** J. E. Emburey • **President** R. A. Gale
Chairman P. H. Edmonds • **Secretary/chief executive** V. J. Codrington
Chairman, cricket committee D. Bennet
Head groundsmen M. Hunt (Lord's); S. Martin (Southgate) • **Scorer** M. J. Smith

At Cambridge, April 13, 14, 15. MIDDLESEX beat CAMBRIDGE UCCE by 282 runs.

At Chester-le-Street, April 19, 20, 21. MIDDLESEX beat DURHAM by ten wickets.

MIDDLESEX v NOTTINGHAMSHIRE

At Lord's, April 24, 25, 26, 27. Middlesex won by an innings and 31 runs. Middlesex 20 pts, Nottinghamshire 2.5 pts. Toss: Middlesex. County debut: L. Klusener.

Shortly after lunch on the final day, Noffke completed Middlesex's second resounding win in succession. Filling in as overseas player until the arrival of Abdul Razzaq, he bowled with unfriendly pace and unerring control, and took a career-best seven for 100 as Nottinghamshire collapsed for the second time. Fraser, in his last Championship appearance before retiring, had done the damage in their first innings with his first five-wicket return since 2000, though Middlesex were helped by three visiting batsmen who fell leg-before without offering a shot. Apart from graft by Bicknell, and some late aggression from Klusener and Smith, there was a strange lack of resolve in both Nottinghamshire innings. The win was set up by glorious Middlesex batting in first-day sunshine: Koenig and Strauss put together another century opening partnership, and Joyce scored a superb hundred, brought up with two audacious sixes. Nottinghamshire became the first team to play at Lord's with numbers on their white shirts, but since these did not correspond to the scorecard they simply caused confusion.

Close of play: First day, Middlesex 433-6 (Weekes 50); Second day, Nottinghamshire 90-1 (Bicknell 37, Welton 41); Third day, Nottinghamshire 156-4 (Randall 8, Klusener 24).

Middlesex

A. J. Strauss c Gallian b Smith	62		S. J. Cook b Logan		4
S. G. Koenig c Gallian b Malik	47		*A. R. C. Fraser c Klusener b Smith		20
R. M. S. Weston b Klusener	24		P. C. R. Tufnell not out		0
O. A. Shah b Logan	63		B 6, l-b 11, w 8, n-b 26		51
E. C. Joyce c Afzaal b Smith	119				
P. N. Weekes lbw b Logan	50		1/103 (1) 2/138 (2) 3/162 (3) 4/316 (4)		462
†D. C. Nash c Read b Logan	21		5/376 (5) 6/433 (7) 7/438 (6)		
A. A. Noffke c Pietersen b Smith	1		8/438 (8) 9/454 (9) 10/462 (10)		

Bonus points – Middlesex 5, Nottinghamshire 3.

Bowling: Smith 23.2–6–70–4; Malik 24–4–79–1; Logan 28–7–105–4; Klusener 20–4–88–1; Randall 11–1–51–0; Afzaal 4–0–23–0; Pietersen 4–0–29–0.

Nottinghamshire

D. J. Bicknell lbw b Fraser	48	– c Strauss b Noffke		46
*J. E. R. Gallian c Shah b Fraser	16	– c Koenig b Noffke		0
G. E. Welton c Cook b Noffke	13	– lbw b Noffke		51
U. Afzaal lbw b Cook	4	– c Nash b Noffke		11
L. Klusener b Cook	0	– (6) c Shah b Cook		42
K. P. Pietersen lbw b Fraser	1	– (7) lbw b Noffke		10
†C. M. W. Read not out	26	– (8) c Weekes b Tufnell		20
R. J. Logan c Nash b Fraser	18	– (9) retired hurt		2
S. J. Randall c Weekes b Fraser	0	– (5) b Noffke		8
G. J. Smith lbw b Tufnell	0	– not out		39
M. N. Malik c Nash b Noffke	9	– c Nash b Noffke		18
L-b 8, n-b 16	24	B 4, l-b 7, n-b 14		25
1/53 (2) 2/77 (3) 3/88 (4) 4/96 (5)	159	1/9 (2) 2/107 (1) 3/118 (3)		272
5/96 (1) 6/97 (6) 7/127 (8)		4/125 (4) 5/165 (5) 6/183 (6)		
8/135 (9) 9/136 (10) 10/159 (11)		7/187 (7) 8/237 (8) 9/272 (11)		

Bonus points – Middlesex 3.

In the second innings, Logan retired hurt at 190.

Bowling: *First Innings*—Fraser 22–9–61–5; Noffke 16.4–2–57–2; Cook 10–5–10–2; Tufnell 12–5–23–1. *Second Innings*—Noffke 23.2–3–100–7; Cook 14–1–53–1; Fraser 16–6–32–0; Tufnell 19–4–40–1; Weekes 12–2–36–0.

Umpires: M. R. Benson and A. A. Jones.

At Shenley Park, May 11, 12, 13. MIDDLESEX drew with SRI LANKANS (see Sri Lankan tour section).

At Northampton, May 15, 16, 17. MIDDLESEX beat NORTHAMPTONSHIRE by an innings and two runs.

MIDDLESEX v DURHAM

At Lord's, May 31, June 1, 2, 3. Drawn. Middlesex 9 pts, Durham 11 pts. Toss: Durham. Championship debut: Abdul Razzaq.

Durham took full advantage of first use of an easy-paced pitch to make their highest-ever total, and the best in a Championship match at Lord's. In the fifth over, Gough ducked into a lifter from Abdul Razzaq and was knocked out, but after that neither the pitch nor the Middlesex attack showed much menace. Love led the way with a career-best 251 – Durham's highest individual score – which came from 335 balls, lasted nearly seven hours and included 39 fours. Muchall kept pace to hit a maiden first-class hundred, and together they added 251. Strauss and Koenig replied with their fourth century partnership of the season before Shah showed a determination so often lacking, batting six hours for his 112. Even so, Middlesex could not avert the follow-on and were soon in trouble at 29 for three. But Shah and Joyce stayed together for 32 overs and Durham had to settle for a draw. In a busy match for Tufnell, he was officially reprimanded for swearing at umpire Kitchen on the first day, and later bombarded by Symington – who was warned for intimidation.

Close of play: First day, Durham 456-2 (Love 221, Lewis 34); Second day, Middlesex 167-2 (Nash 18, Shah 12); Third day, Middlesex 443-9 (Laraman 35, Tufnell 3).

Durham

M. A. Gough retired hurt	6	G. D. Bridge c Abdul Razzaq b Cook	22
G. J. Pratt b Laraman	42	A. M. Davies not out	4
M. L. Love c Nash b Laraman	251	B 3, l-b 21, w 4, n-b 10	38
G. J. Muchall c Weekes b Tufnell	127		
*J. J. B. Lewis lbw b Abdul Razzaq	71	1/97 (2) 2/348 (4)	(6 wkts dec.) 645
†A. Pratt b Weekes	43	3/498 (3) 4/554 (5)	
M. J. Symington not out	41	5/592 (6) 6/635 (8)	

N. Killeen and N. G. Hatch did not bat.

Bonus points – Durham 5, Middlesex 1 (130 overs: 555-4).

Gough retired hurt at 14.

Bowling: Abdul Razzaq 26–4–91–1; Keegan 15–1–87–0; Cook 26–1–108–1; Laraman 23–5–89–2; Tufnell 35–1–137–1; Weekes 28–3–109–1.

Middlesex

*A. J. Strauss c Davies	96	– lbw b Killeen	18
S. G. Koenig b Killeen	29	– run out	4
†D. C. Nash run out	44	– c A. Pratt b Killeen	0
O. A. Shah c A. Pratt b Davies	112	– lbw b Symington	37
E. C. Joyce c A. Pratt b Hatch	44	– c Bridge b Muchall	71
Abdul Razzaq lbw b Symington	15	– not out	20
P. N. Weekes c G. J. Pratt b Bridge	22	– not out	29
S. J. Cook c Symington b Killeen	1		
A. W. Laraman not out	45		
C. B. Keegan c Hatch b Davies	4		
P. C. R. Tufnell c A. Pratt b Hatch	15		
B 1, l-b 9, w 8, n-b 20	38	B 3, l-b 2, w 6, n-b 4	15

1/118 (2) 2/147 (1) 3/212 (3) 4/303 (5)   465
5/332 (6) 6/364 (7) 7/369 (8)
8/407 (4) 9/423 (10) 10/465 (11)

1/13 (2) 2/14 (3)   (5 wkts) 194
3/29 (1) 4/130 (4)
5/145 (5)

Bonus points – Middlesex 4, Durham 2 (130 overs: 385-7).

Bowling: *First Innings*—Killeen 33–10–69–2; Hatch 38–9–121–2; Davies 33–15–69–3; Symington 21–3–100–1; Bridge 36–14–66–1; Gough 3–0–17–0; Muchall 3–0–13–0. *Second Innings*—Killeen 12–5–23–2; Hatch 8–4–12–0; Symington 12–2–44–1; Davies 7–2–28–0; Bridge 15–2–41–0; Muchall 11–3–28–1; Gough 5–1–13–0.

Umpires: J. W. Holder and M. J. Kitchen.

MIDDLESEX v GLAMORGAN

At Lord's, June 12, 13, 14, 15. Drawn. Middlesex 12 pts, Glamorgan 11 pts. Toss: Middlesex.
The chances of a positive result were slim after water leaked under the covers, delaying the start until 2.30 on the second day. Despite the moisture, a slow pitch offered less assistance than Strauss hoped when he put Glamorgan in. Powell hit hard and straight to score a century, and Maynard was within ten of achieving a full set of hundreds against all 17 English counties. With Glamorgan batting on the third afternoon, Middlesex were left with one objective: to reach 400 and gain maximum bonus points. For much of the time it looked straightforward, but indiscretions meant that 64 were still needed when the eighth wicket fell. Cook and Nash took Middlesex to 399, when a run-out put the pressure on Tufnell. He responded by stroking a drive to the cover boundary.

Close of play: First day, No play; Second day, Glamorgan 228-3 (Powell 89, Maynard 86); Third day, Middlesex 131-1 (Koenig 65, Weston 20).

Glamorgan

*S. P. James b Abdul Razzaq	6	S. D. Thomas c Weston b Cook	32
D. L. Hemp b Laraman	18	A. G. Wharf b Abdul Razzaq	0
A. Dale b Cook	19	M. S. Kasprowicz not out	10
M. J. Powell c Weston b Tufnell	122	L-b 5, w 2, n-b 10	17
M. P. Maynard c Nash b Laraman	90		
J. Hughes lbw b Laraman	0		
*M. A. Wallace c Nash b Cook	37	1/8 (1) 2/43 (3) 3/61 (2) 4/249 (5) 369
R. D. B. Croft b Abdul Razzaq	18	5/257 (6) 6/275 (4) 7/320 (8)
		8/358 (7) 9/359 (10) 10/369 (9)

Bonus points – Glamorgan 4, Middlesex 3.

Bowling: Abdul Razzaq 28–4–91–3; Cook 24.2–5–116–3; Laraman 19–5–55–3; Tufnell 9–4–70–1; Weekes 11–1–32–0.

Middlesex

*A. J. Strauss c Wallace b Kasprowicz	. .	38
S. G. Koenig c Dale b Thomas	. . . . .	86
R. M. S. Weston c Wallace b Croft	. . . .	25
O. A. Shah lbw b Kasprowicz	. . . .	23
E. C. Joyce c Maynard b Dale	. . . . . .	73
Abdul Razzaq c Kasprowicz b Croft	. . .	38
P. N. Weekes c Wallace b Kasprowicz	. .	17
†D. C. Nash not out	. . . .	44
A. W. Laraman lbw b Kasprowicz	. . . . .	5

S. J. Cook run out 34
P. C. R. Tufnell not out 4

B 1, l-b 5, n-b 10 16

(9 wkts. dec.) 403

1/60 (1) 2/147 (3)
3/171 (2) 4/198 (4)
5/289 (5) 6/302 (6)
7/328 (7) 8/336 (9) 9/399 (10)

Bonus points – Middlesex 5, Glamorgan 3.

Bowling: Kasprowicz 32–6–108–4; Thomas 27.5–5–97–1; Dale 8–0–29–1; Wharf 18–4–76–0; Croft 31–6–87–2.

Umpires: B. Leadbeater and R. Palmer.

At Cardiff, June 26, 27, 28, 29. MIDDLESEX beat GLAMORGAN by eight wickets.

MIDDLESEX v WORCESTERSHIRE

At Lord's, July 3, 4, 5, 6. Drawn. Middlesex 10 pts, Worcestershire 11 pts. Toss: Worcestershire. With Middlesex second in the table and Worcestershire fourth, this was always likely to be a hard-fought match. Rain delayed the start until 3.30 on the first day, but batting conditions were near perfect as Smith hit a forceful century and Solanki – out of form till now – a graceful one. Worcestershire's declaration was cautious, and they seemed more concerned with batting Middlesex out of the game than victory. Still, a win remained possible when Bichel found some zest in the pitch to help reduce Middlesex to 158 for five. But Weekes played superbly under pressure, and received crucial support from Joyce and the lower order. Cook confirmed his improvement as a batsman with a rapid 33, allowing Strauss to declare at the fall of the eighth wicket and deny his opponents the chance of maximum bowling points. Despite signs of spin and a flurry of Worcestershire wickets, there was never a prospect of a positive result.

Close of play: First day, Worcestershire 95-1 (Weston 48, Hick 37); Second day, Middlesex 15-0 (Strauss 6, Koenig 1); Third day, Middlesex 229-5 (Joyce 43, Weekes 39).

Worcestershire

W. P. C. Weston c sub b Abdul Razzaq	. . . . .	52	– c Strauss b Abdul Razzaq	. . . . . .	0
A. Singh c Nash b Abdul Razzaq	. . . .	7	– b Abdul Razzaq		12
*G. A. Hick c sub b Keegan	. . . .	88			
B. F. Smith c Joyce b Cook	. . . .	124	– (3) b Abdul Razzaq	. . . .	0
V. S. Solanki not out	. . . .	153	– (4) not out.	. . . .	42
D. A. Leatherdale not out	. . . .	59	– (5) b Tufnell		16
G. J. Batty (did not bat)	. . . .		– (6) c Joyce b Tufnell		5
†S. J. Rhodes (did not bat)	. . . .		– (7) not out.	. . . .	10
L-b 9, w 2, n-b 8	. . . .	19	B 4, l-b 2, n-b 2	. . . . . .	8

1/15 (2) 2/112 (1)   (4 wkts. dec.) 502   1/0 (1) 2/13 (2) 3/20 (3)   (5 wkts) 99
3/178 (3) 4/379 (4)   4/59 (5) 5/69 (6)

A. J. Bichel, Kabir Ali and A. Sheriyar did not bat.

Bonus points – Worcestershire 5, Middlesex 1.

Bowling: *First Innings*—Abdul Razzaq 33–5–86–2; Keegan 29–3–139–1; Cook 26–2–126–1; Weekes 14–2–57–0; Tufnell 18–2–71–0; Joyce 3–0–14–0. *Second Innings*—Abdul Razzaq 7–2–28–3; Cook 7–1–24–0; Joyce 4–0–12–0; Tufnell 7–1–15–2; Weekes 3–0–14–0.

Middlesex

*A. J. Strauss lbw b Bichel	19	S. J. Cook b Batty 33
S. G. Koenig c Rhodes b Ali	63	
R. M. S. Weston b Bichel	5	B 1, l-b 13, w 4, n-b 24 42
O. A. Shah lbw b Ali	4	
E. C. Joyce b Batty	70	(8 wkts dec.) 417
Abdul Razzaq b Batty	28	
P. N. Weekes not out	127	
†D. C. Nash c Sheriyar b Bichel	26	

1/42 (1) 2/78 (3)
3/91 (4) 4/118 (2)
5/158 (6) 6/281 (5)
7/368 (8) 8/417 (9)

C. B. Keegan and P. C. R. Tufnell did not bat.

Bonus points – Middlesex 5, Worcestershire 2.

Bowling: Bichel 32–11–102–3; Ali 29–10–82–2; Sheriyar 24–1–127–0; Batty 30.2–11–84–3; Solanki 2–0–8–0.

Umpires: A. Clarkson and B. Dudleston.

MIDDLESEX v GLOUCESTERSHIRE

At Southgate, July 10, 11, 12, 13. Middlesex won by five wickets. Middlesex 18 pts, Gloucestershire 7 pts. Toss: Gloucestershire.

A generous declaration by Alleyne and a maiden half-century by Laraman transformed the game. Needing a win to revive their season, Gloucestershire set Middlesex a gettable target of 240 from a minimum of 55 overs. Having seen their left-handers struggle against the spinners Ball and Fisher in the first innings, Strauss shuffled the batting order, and his faith was repaid by Laraman, whose powerful drives included three sixes. On a turning pitch, he and Shah added 149 for the fourth wicket at nearly a run a ball. They took Middlesex to within seven runs of victory, which duly came with three overs to spare. Gloucestershire, though, had the best of the first three days. Barnett scored a chanceless hundred, carrying his bat for the fourth time in his career, and Gloucestershire's spinners initially had the edge on Tufnell – who briefly refused to bowl when the umpires decided not to replace the ball on the first day – and Weekes. But on the final day they could not recapture their rhythm and effectiveness. Middlesex's fifth win of the season took them top of the second division.

Close of play: First day, Gloucestershire 270-4 (Barnett 119, Russell 9); Second day, Middlesex 98-0 (Strauss 56, Koenig 32); Third day, Middlesex 297-9 (Cook 38, Tufnell 0).

Gloucestershire

C. M. Spearman c Nash b Cook	46	– (2) b Cook	1
K. J. Barnett not out	182	– (1) c Weekes b Jones	47
T. H. C. Hancock c Nash b Laraman	16	– not out	63
M. G. N. Windows c Hutton b Weekes	11	– not out	30
*M. W. Alleyne lbw b Hutton	45		
†R. C. Russell c Hutton b Jones	22		
A. P. R. Gidman c Joyce b Jones	7		
I. D. Fisher c sub b Cook	7		
M. C. J. Ball c Laraman b Weekes	3		
J. Lewis c Strauss b Weekes	0		
A. M. Smith c Tufnell b Jones	16		
B 2, l-b 17, n-b 14	33	B 1, l-b 2, n-b 8	11

1/76 (1) 2/106 (3) 3/144 (4) 4/244 (5)   388   1/6 (2) 2/66 (1)   (2 wkts dec.) 152
5/306 (6) 6/316 (7) 7/344 (8)
8/353 (9) 9/353 (10) 10/388 (11)

Bonus points – Gloucestershire 4, Middlesex 3 (130 overs: 356-9).

Bowling: *First Innings*—Jones 16.3–2–72–3; Laraman 27–5–62–1; Cook 24–2–88–2; Tufnell 41–9–83–0; Weekes 26–5–50–3; Hutton 7–0–14–1. *Second Innings*—Laraman 5–0–25–0; Cook 11–1–42–1; Jones 6–1–28–1; Tufnell 7–1–30–0; Weekes 6–0–16–0; Hutton 1–0–8–0.

Middlesex

*A. J. Strauss b Fisher	82	– c Spearman b Ball		30
S. G. Koenig lbw b Ball	59	– c Spearman b Alleyne		38
B. L. Hutton c and b Ball	29	– (7) not out		0
O. A. Shah c Alleyne b Ball	13	– (5) lbw b Lewis		63
E. C. Joyce lbw b Fisher	21	– (6) c Russell b Lewis		0
P. N. Weekes b Fisher	10			
†D. C. Nash lbw b Fisher	2			
S. J. Cook not out	38	– (3) c Alleyne b Ball		10
A. W. Laraman lbw b Fisher	0	– (4) not out		82
I. Jones c Russell b Smith	29			
P. C. R. Tufnell not out	4			
B 4, l-b 2, w 4, n-b 4	14	B 4, l-b 5, w 5, n-b 4		18

1/142 (1) 2/158 (2) 3/178 (4)   (9 wkts dec.) 301   1/66 (2) 2/81 (1) 3/84 (3)   (5 wkts) 241
4/197 (3) 5/220 (6) 6/225 (5)   4/233 (5) 5/233 (6)
7/232 (7) 8/232 (9) 9/297 (10)

Bonus points – Middlesex 3, Gloucestershire 3.

Bowling: *First Innings*—Lewis 22–6–62–0; Smith 20–8–48–1; Gidman 4–1–20–0; Ball 39–12–74–3; Fisher 38–12–87–5; Windows 0.2–0–4–0. *Second Innings*—Lewis 10–2–36–2; Smith 5–0–30–0; Alleyne 13–2–39–1; Fisher 14–0–73–0; Ball 10–1–54–2.

Umpires: V. A. Holder and J. F. Steele.

MIDDLESEX v ESSEX

At Southgate, July 18, 19, 20, 21. Drawn. Middlesex 12 pts, Essex 11 pts. Toss: Middlesex.

A bad-tempered game finally petered out into one of the most boring draws imaginable. The second-division leaders, Middlesex, were so determined not to let third-placed Essex gain any ground that they batted until tea on the final day, setting a meaningless target of 524. Essex had already registered disgust by sitting down in the outfield to eat ice creams during a pointedly unhurried afternoon drinks break. Before the tedium had come rancour. On the first day, Cowan was warned for intimidatory bowling, and on the second both teams became embroiled as Tufnell and Irani traded abuse. The umpires had to intervene, and the sides were reported for bad behaviour. Before the cricket lost all meaning, Koenig's undemonstrative hundred and some fierce driving and pulling by Hutton – who hit four sixes in his 65 – proved the friendliness of another good Southgate pitch. Even Tufnell joined in with two sixes and four fours. Essex's reply was anchored by Irani, who came in at seven for three and stuck around until the end.

Close of play: First day, Middlesex 376-6 (Weekes 67, Nash 22); Second day, Essex 239-4 (Irani 109, Foster 33); Third day, Middlesex 116-1 (Strauss 55, Hutton 44).

Middlesex

*A. J. Strauss lbw b Dakin	1	– b Phillips		59
S. G. Koenig c Cowan b Phillips	113	– c Phillips b Bishop		5
B. L. Hutton c Foster b Bishop	65	– run out		57
O. A. Shah lbw b Bishop	60	– not out		148
E. C. Joyce b Phillips	1	– b Phillips		81
Abdul Razzaq lbw b Phillips	11	– not out		35
P. N. Weekes c Foster b Dakin	71			
†D. C. Nash not out	81			
S. J. Cook b Middlebrook	19			
A. W. Laraman lbw b Phillips	21			
P. C. R. Tufnell c Flower b Dakin	45			
B 12, l-b 8, w 2, n-b 28	50	B 11, l-b 4, w 10, n-b 16		41

1/7 (1) 2/168 (3) 3/234 (2) 4/246 (5)   538   1/18 (2) 2/122 (1)   (4 wkts dec.) 426
5/272 (6) 6/310 (4) 7/388 (7)   3/148 (3) 4/349 (5)
8/438 (9) 9/467 (10) 10/538 (11)

Bonus points – Middlesex 5, Essex 2 (130 overs: 462-8).

Bowling: *First Innings*—Cowan 21–5–77–0; Dakin 31.2–7–103–3; Bishop 29–4–110–2; Middlebrook 35–7–126–1; Phillips 25–6–102–4. *Second Innings*—Dakin 18–4–72–0; Bishop 14–5–37–1; Middlebrook 29–5–102–0; Phillips 32–5–127–2; Flower 6–0–19–0; Robinson 9–1–54–0.

Essex

D. D. J. Robinson lbw b Abdul Razzaq	73	– b Abdul Razzaq	0
W. I. Jefferson lbw b Laraman	0	– not out	31
A. Habib b Abdul Razzaq	0		
A. Flower b Abdul Razzaq	1		
*R. C. Irani not out	182		
†J. S. Foster c Nash b Abdul Razzaq	36		
J. M. Dakin c Nash b Abdul Razzaq	27		
J. D. Middlebrook b Abdul Razzaq	21		
A. P. Cowan lbw b Tufnell	6		
T. J. Phillips c Hutton b Weekes	42	– (3) not out	20
J. E. Bishop b Abdul Razzaq	0		
B 5, l-b 2, w 2, n-b 44	53	L-b 2	2

1/4 (2) 2/7 (3) 3/7 (4) 4/174 (1)   **441**   1/0 (1)   **(1 wkt) 53**
5/246 (6) 6/290 (7) 7/352 (8)
8/370 (9) 9/440 (10) 10/441 (11)

Bonus points – Essex 5, Middlesex 3.

Bowling: *First Innings*—Abdul Razzaq 33.4–4–133–7; Laraman 25–5–88–1; Tufnell 27–3–96–1; Cook 17–5–39–0; Weekes 27–2–78–1. *Second Innings*—Abdul Razzaq 1–0–2–1; Laraman 5–2–11–0; Cook 4–1–7–0; Weekes 7–2–14–0; Joyce 6–2–17–0.

Umpires: M. R. Benson and J. W. Holder.

At Cheltenham, July 24, 25, 26, 27. MIDDLESEX drew with GLOUCESTERSHIRE.

MIDDLESEX v NORTHAMPTONSHIRE

At Lord's, August 7, 8, 9, 10. Drawn. Middlesex 12 pts, Northamptonshire 6 pts. Toss: Northamptonshire.

Yet again, rain was the deciding factor. Only 103 overs were bowled on the first three days and, with no chance of a positive result, the match became a battle for bonus points. Between the downpours, Middlesex had dominated. For the third time in 2002, Hussey watched his opponents score heavily after putting them in: Derbyshire had made 538, Essex 498 and now Middlesex racked up 400. Shah continued his run of form as he cut and drove his way to 172; Hutton was less aggressive, though he did crack a remarkable cut for six to reach his first century of the summer. After Middlesex took their fifth batting point and promptly declared on the last morning, Northamptonshire's reply was undistinguished. Strauss seemed reluctant to attack, but they were still bowled out for 231. Noffke was unlucky on his return as Middlesex's overseas player but Hutton grabbed two wickets in an over, Tufnell found turn and Northamptonshire subsided inside 77 overs.

Close of play: First day, Middlesex 206-2 (Hutton 69, Shah 78); Second day, Middlesex 360-3 (Shah 148, Joyce 30); Third day, No play.

Middlesex

*A. J. Strauss c Loye b Panesar	43	P. N. Weekes not out		2
S. G. Koenig lbw b Blain	8	L-b 4, w 6, n-b 6		16
B. L. Hutton c Blain b Penberthy	116			
O. A. Shah not out	172	1/26 (2) 2/91 (1)	(4 wkts dec.)	400
E. C. Joyce c Bailey b Cook	43	3/289 (3) 4/393 (5)		

†D. Alleyne, A. W. Laraman, S. J. Cook, A. A. Noffke and P. C. R. Tufnell did not bat.

Bonus points – Middlesex 5, Northamptonshire 1.

Bowling: Greenidge 24–3–101–0; Blain 26–1–88–1; Penberthy 22–12–29–1; Cassar 3–0–19–0; Panesar 20.5–2–99–1; Cook 10–1–38–1; Swann 6–3–22–0.

Northamptonshire

*M. E. K. Hussey c Alleyne b Laraman	9	C. G. Greenidge c Koenig b Laraman		15
M. B. Loye c Weekes b Hutton	30	J. A. R. Blain c sub b Tufnell		7
D. J. Sales lbw b Cook	7	M. S. Panesar not out		2
J. W. Cook c Laraman b Tufnell	46	B 3, l-b 7, w 4, n-b 18		32
A. L. Penberthy lbw b Hutton	2			
M. E. Cassar c Hutton b Laraman	58	1/33 (1) 2/52 (3) 3/54 (2) 4/58 (5)		231
G. P. Swann c Laraman b Tufnell	23	5/124 (4) 6/172 (7) 7/172 (8)		
†T. M. B. Bailey c Alleyne b Cook	0	8/202 (9) 9/223 (6) 10/231 (10)		

Bonus points – Northamptonshire 1, Middlesex 3.

Bowling: Noffke 16–5–71–0; Laraman 18–4–48–3; Cook 18–8–32–2; Hutton 4–0–17–2; Tufnell 20.2–6–53–3.

Umpires: G. I. Burgess and B. Leadbeater.

At Nottingham, August 14, 15, 16. MIDDLESEX lost to NOTTINGHAMSHIRE by an innings and 73 runs.

MIDDLESEX v DERBYSHIRE

At Lord's, August 21, 22, 23, 24. Derbyshire won by 204 runs. Derbyshire 20 pts, Middlesex 6 pts. Toss: Derbyshire.

Derbyshire owed much to Di Venuto, who hit two polished centuries, but also to a Middlesex display so lacking in confidence that it raised fears of a repeat of 2001, when a late-season slump cost them promotion. After winning the toss, Di Venuto was light on his feet and chose his gaps against a wayward attack, eventually carrying his bat for 192. In reply to 414, a superb spell of left-arm swing from Dean reduced Middlesex to five for three, before Joyce's third century of the season kept the deficit to 110. As Derbyshire stretched their lead on the third day, Di Venuto made another silky hundred, though Tufnell's turn and bounce slowed scoring and delayed the declaration until the last morning. A draw looked likely. Instead, injudicious shots from Middlesex's middle order helped Wharton to a career-best six for 62 and brought Derbyshire to the brink of victory. But the last pair, Tufnell and Noffke, resisted stubbornly for nearly an hour and a half until, with 11 balls to go, Welch trapped Tufnell, who slunk off in disappointment. Derbyshire climbed to third, while despite two hefty losses Middlesex clung on to first place.

Close of play: First day, Derbyshire 375-8 (Di Venuto 173, Dean 5); Second day, Middlesex 275-6 (Joyce 126, Laraman 32); Third day, Derbyshire 259-6 (Welch 25, Lungley 15).

Derbyshire

A. I. Gait lbw b Noffke	3	– lbw b Tufnell	8
*M. J. Di Venuto not out	192	– c Hutton b Tufnell	113
C. W. G. Bassano c Joyce b Keegan	26	– c Hutton b Weekes	34
J. P. Pyemont c Hutton b Noffke	3	– lbw b Tufnell	33
S. A. Selwood b Nash b Tufnell	21	– c Hutton b Tufnell	0
†L. D. Sutton c Nash b Noffke	32	– b Tufnell	11
G. Welch c Tufnell b Noffke	50	– not out	36
T. Lungley c Nash b Laraman	14	– c Shah b Keegan	44
Mohammad Ali c Weekes b Noffke	13		
K. J. Dean c Nash b Noffke	23		
L. J. Wharton c Hutton b Tufnell	1		
B 2, l-b 12, n-b 22	36	L-b 20, n-b 2	22

1/10 (1) 2/53 (3) 3/62 (4) 4/108 (5) 414   1/39 (1) 2/118 (3) (7 wkts dec.) 301
5/177 (6) 6/307 (7) 7/348 (8)   3/184 (2) 4/184 (5)
8/367 (9) 9/409 (10) 10/414 (11)   5/210 (6) 6/221 (4) 7/301 (8)

Bonus points – Derbyshire 5, Middlesex 3.

Bowling: *First Innings*—Noffke 33–0–138–6; Laraman 20–4–67–1; Keegan 16–3–84–1; Tufnell 36.5–7–91–2; Weekes 11–4–20–0. *Second Innings*—Noffke 18–2–69–0; Keegan 6–0–28–1; Tufnell 38.3–11–80–5; Weekes 33.3–5–104–1.

Middlesex

*A. J. Strauss c Sutton b Dean	1	– st Sutton b Wharton	21
S. G. Koenig lbw b Dean	1	– b Mohammad Ali	0
B. L. Hutton lbw b Dean	0	– c Bassano b Welch	27
O. A. Shah c Gait b Welch	9	– b Wharton	20
E. C. Joyce lbw b Welch	129	– c Sutton b Mohammad Ali	51
P. N. Weekes c Di Venuto b Wharton	28	– c Sutton b Wharton	17
†D. C. Nash b Wharton	55	– b Wharton	0
A. W. Laraman b Welch	36	– c Welch b Wharton	6
A. A. Noffke lbw b Dean	6	– not out	31
C. B. Keegan c Di Venuto b Welch	11	– lbw b Wharton	3
P. C. R. Tufnell not out	0	– lbw b Welch	7
B 4, l-b 4, w 2, n-b 18	28	B 2, l-b 2, n-b 20	24

1/4 (1) 2/4 (3) 3/5 (2) 4/37 (4) 304   1/0 (2) 2/45 (1) 3/61 (3) 4/97 (4) 207
5/91 (6) 6/211 (7) 7/279 (8)   5/133 (6) 6/133 (7) 7/153 (8)
8/284 (5) 9/302 (10) 10/304 (9)   8/153 (5) 9/156 (10) 10/207 (11)

Bonus points – Middlesex 3, Derbyshire 3.

Bowling: *First Innings*—Dean 26.4–6–73–4; Mohammad Ali 14–3–64–0; Lungley 10–1–42–0; Welch 25–8–61–4; Wharton 24–5–44–2; Pyemont 5–0–12–0. *Second Innings*—Dean 13–7–18–0; Mohammad Ali 21–4–73–2; Wharton 31–11–62–6; Welch 10.1–2–21–2; Lungley 6–1–16–0; Pyemont 3–1–13–0.

Umpires: K. E. Palmer and R. Palmer.

At Worcester, August 27, 28, 29, 30. MIDDLESEX beat WORCESTERSHIRE by six wickets.

At Chelmsford, September 4, 5, 6. MIDDLESEX lost to ESSEX by six wickets.

At Derby, September 11, 12, 13. MIDDLESEX beat DERBYSHIRE by 73 runs.

NORTHAMPTONSHIRE
BAD TO WORSE

Ch'ship 7th in Division 2
C&G 4th round
B&H group stage
NUL 6th in Division 2

Player of the season:
Carl Greenidge

If double relegation in 2001 indicated that Northamptonshire did not possess the strength in depth to compete with the best counties, their results in 2002 hinted at even starker shortcomings. A return to both top divisions had naturally been the target, but promotion in the Championship was ruled out as a serious possibility in July, while the chances of a top-three finish in the Norwich Union League evaporated with the loss of the last six matches.

It was depressing enough to finish seventh in Division Two of the Championship, three off the bottom of the one-day league, and suffer early exits from both the B&H and C&G. But other issues gave substance to the perception that Northamptonshire were an increasingly accident-prone club. One of their longest-serving players, Russell Warren, was dropped in June following a domestic imbroglio, apparently involving a team-mate's fiancée, of which the management had been aware for some months. Then, a fortnight before the end of the season, Mal Loye, Warren's near-contemporary, announced his intention to leave after 13 years on the staff. The breakdown in his working relationship with the director of cricket, Bob Carter, was at the heart of Loye's decision. He later agreed a four-year deal with Lancashire; Warren left for Nottinghamshire.

Of Carter's six close-season signings, only one – the fast bowler Carl Greenidge, from Surrey – made much of an impact in the first team. He missed just two matches and captured 49 Championship wickets; no one else managed 30. Gerry Brophy scored a century in the final game of the season, against Glamorgan, but Ricky Anderson, Michael Cawdron and Tom Baker played the bulk of their cricket in the second team, while the luckless Ben Phillips spent most of the summer recovering from a shoulder injury.

These factors combined to convince the committee that a change of direction was required, and Carter was sacked in September with a year of his contract remaining. An official statement said that performances and results "had not justified [the committee's] support and the significant financial investment made". A thorough review of the coaching and cricket management set-up was promised, and in December the former Australian batsman and South African captain Kepler Wessels was hired as Carter's replacement on a two-year contract.

Carter could claim, with some justification, that he had not been helped by the absence of the new captain, Mike Hussey, called away by Australia A for the last five weeks of the season. Hussey followed his 2,055 first-class runs in 2001 with 1,442 in 13 matches, including an unbeaten 310 at Bristol, and once again set a magnificent example in the field. His departure coincided with the team's loss of one-day form, although the players he left behind then won three successive Championship matches, even if the surge came too late to reignite their chances of promotion. Hussey's vice-captain, Tony Penberthy, scored runs consistently in his benefit year, but of the other batsmen only Loye and Jeff Cook exceeded 600 in four-day cricket, while David Sales found form elusive in his first full season since a serious knee injury threatened his career.

The limitations of the attack were readily apparent. Darren Cousins, as wholehearted as ever but never fully fit, missed the closing weeks, and although Mathew Inness – the Victorian left-arm pace bowler signed as Hussey's replacement – shone with a seven-wicket haul at Cardiff, the admirable Greenidge lacked incisive support. Matthew Cassar, rarely seen in the first team since Carter signed him ahead of the 2001 season, demonstrated his all-round ability by returning match figures of ten for 134 and then hitting 101 not out in the two matches against Gloucestershire. But it was not enough to earn him another contract. The three front-line spinners – Jason Brown, Graeme Swann and Monty Panesar – all had their moments, and Panesar earned a place at the National Academy in 2002-03. But on pitches that didn't help the slow men, especially in the early part of the summer, Northamptonshire were toothless. The decision to sign the South African fast bowler Andre Nel for 2003 was a step in the right direction.

Without doubt, though, the most positive aspect of 2002 was the emergence of Rob White and Mark Powell, two young products of the county's development structure. White, named the club's most promising player in 2001, and Powell, a successful captain of the Loughborough UCCE team, injected much-needed optimism as they compiled a record opening partnership of 375 against Gloucestershire in the final home game. White's exhilarating strokeplay, redolent of a less careworn era, was a revelation to supporters unfamiliar with his methods, while Powell's more measured approach brought him centuries in consecutive matches, the second of which, against Glamorgan, saved Northamptonshire from likely defeat. The fact that neither had previously made more than a solitary Championship appearance provided, in the eyes of some, further evidence of flawed selection.

Both were rewarded in September with new, long-term contracts. White and Powell had given the faithful some reason to believe in the future. The rest of the season offered precious little cause for celebration aside from a memorable dinner to mark the 70-year association of Dennis Brookes – still Northamptonshire's leading run-scorer – with the club. **Andrew Radd**

NORTHAMPTONSHIRE 2002

Back row: G. L. Brophy, C. G. Greenidge, T. M. B. Bailey, J. A. R. Blain, R. S. G. Anderson, M. E. Cassar. *Middle row:* N. G. B. Cook (*second-team coach*), D. M. Cousins, A. S. Rollins, J. W. Cook, B. J. Phillips, M. J. Cawdron, T. M. Baker, R. M. Carter (*director of cricket*). *Front row:* G. P. Swann, D. J. Sales, A. L. Penberthy (*vice-captain*), M. E. K. Hussey (*captain*), M. B. Loye, R. J. Warren, J. F. Brown. *Picture by Bill Smith.*

NORTHAMPTONSHIRE RESULTS

All first-class matches – Played 17: Won 6, Lost 7, Drawn 4.
County Championship matches – Played 16: Won 5, Lost 7, Drawn 4.

COUNTY CHAMPIONSHIP AVERAGES: BATTING AND FIELDING

Cap		M	I	NO	R	HS	100s	50s	Avge	Ct/St
2001	R. A. White	4	7	1	556	277	1	3	92.66	1
	M. E. K. Hussey§ . .	12	21	2	1,379	310*	5	3	72.57	14
	M. J. Powell†	3	5	1	289	108*	2	0	72.25	4
	G. L. Brophy	4	8	3	246	110	1	1	49.20	5
	M. E. Cassar.	7	9	1	343	101*	1	3	42.87	4
1994	A. L. Penberthy . . .	16	25	3	909	130*	1	3	41.31	9
	A. S. Rollins	5	10	0	389	107	1	2	38.90	5
1995	R. J. Warren†	6	11	1	369	150*	1	1	36.90	1
1994	M. B. Loye†	12	20	1	700	139	4	0	36.84	6
	J. W. Cook	14	23	3	717	90	0	4	35.85	3
1999	G. P. Swann†	10	14	0	487	183	2	1	34.78	5
	D. J. Sales	13	21	0	500	179	1	2	23.80	9
	M. W. H. Inness§ . .	4	4	1	66	25	0	0	22.00	5
	T. M. B. Bailey† . .	16	23	2	389	68	0	3	18.52	41/6
	R. S. G. Anderson . .	5	10	0	166	51	0	1	16.60	0
2000	D. M. Cousins	10	16	7	103	23*	0	0	11.44	4
2000	J. F. Brown	8	11	5	64	19	0	0	10.66	2
	D. E. Paynter	2	4	1	32	20	0	0	10.66	2
	C. G. Greenidge . . .	14	18	1	147	46	0	0	8.64	7
	J. A. R. Blain	6	8	2	47	17*	0	0	7.83	2
	M. S. Panesar	5	5	2	4	2*	0	0	1.33	3

† *Born in Northamptonshire.* § *Overseas player.*

BOWLING

	O	M	R	W	BB	5W/i	Avge
M. W. H. Inness	116.4	25	429	15	7-90	1	28.60
M. E. Cassar	113.3	18	464	16	6-34	1	29.00
G. P. Swann	252.1	52	854	26	6-126	1	32.84
C. G. Greenidge	404.1	62	1,613	49	6-40	3	32.91
M. S. Panesar	174.5	50	502	15	4-42	0	33.46
J. F. Brown	352.5	76	1,138	28	4-88	0	40.64
A. L. Penberthy	292	76	833	17	3-21	0	49.00
D. M. Cousins	290.2	58	988	20	4-75	0	49.40
J. A. R. Blain	173.4	17	861	14	4-144	0	61.50

Also bowled: R. S. G. Anderson 143–29–550–9; J. W. Cook 119–24–447–6; M. B. Loye 2–1–1–0; R. A. White 26.4–3–91–5.

COUNTY RECORDS

Highest score for:	329*	M. E. K. Hussey v Essex at Northampton	2001
Highest score against:	333	K. S. Duleepsinhji (Sussex) at Hove	1930
Best bowling for:	10-127	V. W. C. Jupp v Kent at Tunbridge Wells	1932
Best bowling against:	10-30	C. Blythe (Kent) at Northampton	1907
Highest total for:	781-7 dec.	v Nottinghamshire at Northampton	1995
Highest total against:	670-9 dec.	by Sussex at Hove	1921
Lowest total for:	12	v Gloucestershire at Gloucester	1907
Lowest total against:	33	by Lancashire at Northampton	1977

COUNTY OFFICERS

Captain M. E. K. Hussey • **Director of cricket** 2002 – R. M. Carter
First-team coach 2003 – K. C. Wessels • **President** L. A. Wilson
Chairman S. G. Schanschieff • **Chief executive** S. P. Coverdale
Chairman, cricket c'ttee J. A. Scopes • **Head groundsman** D. Bates • **Scorer** A. C. Kingston

At Oxford, April 18, 19, 20. NORTHAMPTONSHIRE beat OXFORD UCCE by 207 runs.

NORTHAMPTONSHIRE v WORCESTERSHIRE

At Northampton, April 24, 25, 26, 27. Drawn. Northamptonshire 11 pts, Worcestershire 10 pts. Toss: Worcestershire.

For the second year running, the opening match at Northampton was a high-scoring, rain-affected draw which delighted record-keepers considerably more than bowlers. Even on a pitch more liberally grassed than usual, Worcestershire's decision to bat first was straightforward. Peters, who hit a maiden Championship century, and the punchy Leatherdale pierced the field regularly while adding 239 for the fourth wicket. The innings ended fittingly when Kabir Ali pulled Penberthy out of the ground to reach fifty and prompt the declaration. Northamptonshire's reply was just as strong. Hussey was immovable during his 170, while Loye hit a remarkable 114 of his 139 in boundaries, and the score had reached a demoralising 290 before they were parted – Northamptonshire's third-best opening partnership in the Championship. The last two days were interrupted by the weather, but Warren's well-crafted 150 meant that, for the first time, Northamptonshire's top three had all scored centuries.

Close of play: First day, Worcestershire 398-5 (Leatherdale 147, Rawnsley 4); Second day, Northamptonshire 254-0 (Hussey 120, Loye 120); Third day, Northamptonshire 380-2 (Warren 49, Sales 0).

Worcestershire

S. D. Peters c and b Penberthy	146	†S. J. Rhodes not out			34
A. Singh c Bailey b Greenidge	8	Kabir Ali not out			51
*G. A. Hick c Penberthy b Blain	8	B 4, l-b 15, w 6, n-b 12			37
B. F. Smith lbw b Blain	24				
D. A. Leatherdale b Blain	154	1/16 (2) 2/43 (3)		(8 wkts dec.)	524
G. J. Batty c Bailey b Blain	33	3/77 (4) 4/316 (1)			
M. J. Rawnsley c and b Greenidge	4	5/389 (6) 6/398 (7)			
A. J. Bichel c Bailey b Greenidge	25	7/430 (5) 8/432 (8)			

A. Sheriyar did not bat.

Bonus points – Worcestershire 5, Northamptonshire 2.

Bowling: Cousins 17–4–46–0; Greenidge 33–7–124–3; Blain 29–5–144–4; Cook 15–6–48–0; Penberthy 21.1–3–71–1; Swann 13–2–72–0.

Northamptonshire

*M. E. K. Hussey c Batty b Ali	170	J. W. Cook not out			12
M. B. Loye c Hick b Batty	139	B 9, l-b 16, w 6, n-b 21			52
R. J. Warren not out	150				
D. J. Sales b Ali	16	1/290 (2) 2/374 (1)		(5 wkts dec.)	614
G. P. Swann c Rhodes b Batty	12	3/426 (4) 4/458 (5)			
A. L. Penberthy b Leatherdale	63	5/573 (6)			

†T. M. B. Bailey, C. G. Greenidge, J. A. R. Blain and D. M. Cousins did not bat.

Bonus points – Northamptonshire 5, Worcestershire 1 (130 overs: 457-3).

Bowling: Bichel 29–8–81–0; Sheriyar 29–8–84–0; Ali 23–2–102–2; Batty 38–7–131–2; Rawnsley 29–10–108–0; Hick 7–2–16–0; Leatherdale 16–2–53–1; Smith 3–0–14–0.

Umpires: J. H. Evans and B. Leadbeater.

At Derby, May 8, 9, 10. NORTHAMPTONSHIRE lost to DERBYSHIRE by eight wickets.

NORTHAMPTONSHIRE v MIDDLESEX

At Northampton, May 15, 16, 17. Middlesex won by an innings and two runs. Middlesex 20 pts, Northamptonshire 4 pts. Toss: Middlesex.

Northamptonshire lost 16 wickets on the third day to hand Middlesex a conclusive win. On another grassy pitch, Middlesex were indebted to Simon Cook, who bowled with lively pace and intelligence to take a career-best eight for 63 in the first innings. But conditions were far from unplayable, and for the third game in a row Northamptonshire conceded over 500. Strauss departed early, but Koenig put on 157 with Weston and went on to a compact 101, before Weekes and Nash preyed on a wayward attack and added 133. Northamptonshire's openers launched the reply positively by stroking 167 in 32 overs, but the remaining batsmen succumbed meekly as Simon Cook made regular incisions. The last six wickets tumbled for 34 in nine overs and Northamptonshire followed on 255 adrift. Resolution was in even shorter supply second time around and, after Hussey fell, only Jeff Cook and Bailey showed much spirit. Their efforts were not enough to avoid an innings defeat inside three days.

Close of play: First day, Middlesex 367-5 (Weekes 92, Nash 38); Second day, Northamptonshire 202-4 (Rollins 69, Penberthy 8).

Middlesex

*A. J. Strauss lbw b Cousins	2	A. A. Noffke b Cousins	31
S. G. Koenig c Bailey b Cook	101	T. F. Bloomfield not out	31
R. M. S. Weston b Penberthy	72		
O. A. Shah c Bailey b Blain	2	B 7, l-b 8, w 8, n-b 16	39
E. C. Joyce b Swann	29		
P. N. Weekes c and b Blain	107		541
†D. C. Nash lbw b Anderson	55		
S. J. Cook c Sales b Cook	29		
A. W. Laraman lbw b Anderson	43		

1/2 (1) 2/159 (3) 3/170 (4)
4/198 (2) 5/259 (5) 6/392 (6)
7/404 (7) 8/469 (8)
9/488 (9) 10/541 (10)

Bonus points – Middlesex 5, Northamptonshire 2 (130 overs: 438-7).

Bowling: Cousins 32.3–7–90–2; Blain 31–2–129–2; Penberthy 27–6–67–1; Anderson 33–4–129–2; Cook 15–3–47–2; Swann 20–3–64–1.

Northamptonshire

*M. E. K. Hussey c Nash b Cook	84	– (2) lbw b Laraman		27
A. S. Rollins lbw b Cook	107	– (1) lbw b Cook		28
R. J. Warren c Weekes b Cook	0	– c Joyce b Noffke		2
D. J. Sales c Weekes b Cook	0	– c Nash b Laraman		0
G. P. Swann b Noffke	10	– c Shah b Laraman		0
A. L. Penberthy c Koenig b Cook	18	– b Bloomfield		19
J. W. Cook lbw b Cook	4	– b Noffke		84
†T. M. B. Bailey c Nash b Bloomfield	11	– lbw b Bloomfield		34
R. S. G. Anderson c Noffke b Cook	8	– lbw b Laraman		10
J. A. R. Blain c Weekes b Cook	1	– not out		8
D. M. Cousins not out	0	– c Koenig b Noffke		5
		B 10, l-b 12, w 6, n-b 8		36
B 9, l-b 6, w 6, n-b 22	43			

1/167 (1) 2/167 (3) 3/169 (4) 4/186 (5)   286
5/252 (2) 6/256 (7) 7/273 (6)
8/283 (9) 9/286 (10) 10/286 (8)

1/39 (2) 2/48 (3) 3/57 (4)   253
4/57 (5) 5/69 (1) 6/103 (6)
7/189 (8) 8/223 (9)
9/247 (7) 10/253 (11)

Bonus points – Northamptonshire 2, Middlesex 3.

Bowling: *First Innings*—Noffke 22–5–89–1; Bloomfield 15.1–5–57–1; Laraman 8–1–43–0; Weekes 7–1–19–0; Cook 18–3–63–8. *Second Innings*—Bloomfield 16–5–39–2; Cook 13–2–42–1; Noffke 20.4–4–77–3; Laraman 19–5–55–4; Weekes 7–1–18–0.

Umpires: A. Clarkson and A. G. T. Whitehead.

At Nottingham, May 24, 25, 26, 27. NORTHAMPTONSHIRE lost to NOTTINGHAMSHIRE by seven wickets.

NORTHAMPTONSHIRE v ESSEX

At Northampton, May 31, June 1, 2, 3. Essex won by four wickets. Essex 19 pts, Northamptonshire 7 pts. Toss: Northamptonshire. First-class debut: R. S. Bopara.

When Stephenson cut the winning runs on the last afternoon, he created an extraordinary piece of cricketing history: no side had scored more than Northamptonshire's 632 in an innings and gone on to lose. Left 291 to chase in 52 overs, Essex's openers provided a purposeful start but the dramatic final day belonged to Flower. With clouds gathering, the pitch wearing and wickets falling he did the leg-work with a run-a-ball, unbeaten 92. His reverse-sweeping against Brown's off-spin was so devastating that the bowler was at a loss to know what to try next. Flower and

HIGHEST INNINGS TOTALS BY LOSING TEAMS

632	**Northamptonshire (632 and 155) v Essex (497-7 dec. and 291-6) at**	
	Northampton	**2002**
614	New South Wales (614 and 152) v Victoria (502 and 265-3) at Sydney	1924-25
608	Wellington (608-9 dec. and 35-1 dec.) v Northern Districts (323-5 dec. and	
	322-7) at Hamilton	1998-99
604†	Maharashtra (407 and 604) v Bombay (651 and 714-8 dec.) at Poona	1948-49
597	Essex (597 and 97) v Derbyshire (548 and 149-1) at Chesterfield.	1904
591	Sussex (591 and 312-3 dec.) v Essex (493-4 dec. and 412-3) at Hove.	1993
589	Otago (161 and 589) v Canterbury (472 and 279-7) at Christchurch	1931-32
589†	Lancashire (83 and 589) v Derbyshire (490-8 dec. and 186-7) at Blackpool	1994
588	New South Wales (287 and 588) v Queensland (577 and 300-5) at Sydney	1926-27
587	Lancashire (587-9 dec. and 174-3 dec.) v Derbyshire (473-8 dec. and 289-8) at	
	Manchester	1996
586	Australia (586 and 166) v England (325 and 437) at Sydney	1894-95

† *Losing team batted second.*

Research: Robert Brooke.

Dakin added 111 in only 18 overs, Stephenson rounded off his excellent all-round contribution with 25 from 22 balls and Essex secured an outstanding win with 13 balls to spare. It was an emphatic reversal of the opening day, when Northamptonshire took control on a perfect batting pitch. Hussey drove crisply and put on 185 with Rollins, before Warren and Cook meted out more punishment in the afternoon. In all, seven batsmen passed fifty, a county record. Flower starred as Essex responded with similar authority, and Irani kept the match alive by declaring 135 behind. His enterprise paid off handsomely: Northamptonshire collapsed to Dakin and Stephenson and, despite the loss of 44 minutes of the last day to rain, Essex took up the chase with relish.

Close of play: First day, Northamptonshire 451-5 (Penberthy 16, Bailey 5); Second day, Essex 186-2 (Middlebrook 55, Habib 25); Third day, Northamptonshire 58-2 (Hussey 32, Warren 6).

In 2001, he conducted a club inquiry into the conspicuous good fortune enjoyed by senior Lancashire officials' wives in winning players' benefit raffles four years on the trot.
Obituary of Sir Patrick Russell, page 1653

Northamptonshire

*M. E. K. Hussey b Sharif	140	– (2) c Stephenson b Ilott	41
A. S. Rollins lbw b Irani	89	– (1) c Jefferson b Dakin	1
M. B. Loye b Irani	0	– c Habib b Middlebrook	17
R. J. Warren lbw b Stephenson	87	– c Robinson b Dakin	6
J. W. Cook lbw b Ilott	90	– c Flower b Dakin	9
A. L. Penberthy c Flower b Stephenson	50	– b Stephenson	23
†T. M. B. Bailey b Sharif	64	– lbw b Stephenson	15
R. S. G. Anderson b Sharif	51	– b Stephenson	31
J. A. R. Blain not out	17	– lbw b Middlebrook	2
D. M. Cousins lbw b Sharif	4	– c Ilott b Stephenson	1
J. F. Brown lbw b Stephenson	12	– not out	2
L-b 6, w 6, n-b 16	28	L-b 1, w 2, n-b 4	7

1/185 (2) 2/191 (3) 3/275 (1) 4/417 (5)   **632**   1/5 (1) 2/43 (3) 3/62 (4) 4/76 (5)   **155**
5/436 (4) 6/507 (6) 7/596 (7)   5/76 (2) 6/93 (7) 7/140 (6)
8/601 (8) 9/607 (10) 10/632 (11)   8/145 (9) 9/150 (10) 10/155 (8)

Bonus points – Northamptonshire 5, Essex 2 (130 overs: 575-6).

Bowling: *First Innings*—Irani 19–6–61–2; Ilott 27–3–100–1; Dakin 23–4–108–0; Stephenson 25.2–4–116–3; Middlebrook 32–4–143–0; Sharif 20–0–98–4. *Second Innings*—Ilott 13–4–28–1; Dakin 18–6–75–3; Middlebrook 6–1–26–2; Stephenson 7.2–2–25–4.

Essex

D. D. J. Robinson c Warren b Anderson	68	– st Bailey b Brown	31
W. I. Jefferson c sub b Penberthy	22	– run out	41
J. D. Middlebrook b Brown	67	– (7) c Hussey b Cousins	8
A. Habib lbw b Blain	93	– (5) lbw b Brown	5
†A. Flower not out	103	– (3) not out	92
*R. C. Irani st Bailey b Brown	54	– (4) c Loye b Penberthy	7
R. S. Bopara c Rollins b Brown	1		
J. M. Dakin c Hussey b Blain	0	– (6) run out	57
J. P. Stephenson not out	37	– (8) not out	25
B 9, l-b 7, w 4, n-b 30	50	B 4, l-b 3, w 14, n-b 4	25

1/68 (2) 2/138 (1) 3/206 (3)   (7 wkts dec.) **497**   1/85 (1) 2/89 (2)   (6 wkts) **291**
4/303 (4) 5/401 (6)   3/104 (4) 4/114 (5)
6/413 (7) 7/414 (8)   5/225 (6) 6/245 (7)

Z. K. Sharif and M. C. Ilott did not bat.

Bonus points – Essex 5, Northamptonshire 2 (130 overs: 422-7).

Bowling: *First Innings*—Cousins 30–6–100–0; Blain 28–4–127–2; Anderson 29–8–82–1; Penberthy 10.5–5–31–1; Brown 51–11–130–3; Cook 2–0–11–0. *Second Innings*—Cousins 11–0–67–1; Blain 3–1–20–0; Anderson 7–0–46–0; Penberthy 12–0–49–1; Brown 16.5–2–102–2.

Umpires: N. J. Llong and G. Sharp.

At Ilford, June 12, 13, 14, 15. NORTHAMPTONSHIRE lost to ESSEX by nine wickets.

At Northampton, June 24 (day/night). NORTHAMPTONSHIRE lost to SRI LANKANS by eight wickets (see Sri Lankan tour section).

NORTHAMPTONSHIRE v NOTTINGHAMSHIRE

At Northampton, June 26, 27, 28, 29. Northamptonshire won by six wickets. Northamptonshire 20 pts, Nottinghamshire 8 pts. Toss: Nottinghamshire. First-class debut: P. J. McMahon.

Nottinghamshire batted themselves into a seemingly unassailable position in their first innings, then spent the second half of the match watching it crumble. Their 489 was a topsy-turvy affair: the first six batsmen contributed 165 – including an unruffled hundred from Gallian – while their last five totalled 282, centred on Read's 127. But Loye and Sales, who unleashed his full range of shots and cracked 179 after a month out of the Championship side, restricted their lead to 69. By the third day, the recently used strip was dusting and offering turn and bounce to the slow bowlers, and Nottinghamshire's hold slipped as Brown and Swann snared six batsmen. They were bundled out for 172 early on the fourth day. Northamptonshire stuttered to 79 for three, but the spinners McMahon and Boje didn't show much menace, and Loye, with a second stylish century, and Cook ensured Northamptonshire's first win of the season. It ended a run of five successive defeats – their worst losing streak since 1961.

Close of play: First day, Nottinghamshire 339-6 (Read 106, Franks 40); Second day, Northamptonshire 248-2 (Loye 105, Sales 61); Third day, Nottinghamshire 169-8 (Logan 12, Harris 4).

Nottinghamshire

G. E. Welton b Greenidge	3	– b Cousins		0
*J. E. R. Gallian c Bailey b Cousins	100	– c Hussey b Greenidge		2
P. Johnson run out	12	– c Greenidge b Swann		70
U. Afzaal st Bailey b Brown	13	– c Bailey b Brown		34
N. Boje lbw b Cousins	37	– b Swann		18
B. M. Shafayat b Swann	0	– c Penberthy b Brown		0
†C. M. W. Read lbw b Swann	127	– c Rollins b Brown		6
P. J. Franks c Penberthy b Greenidge	67	– c Rollins b Swann		15
R. J. Logan c Rollins b Brown	32	– c Loye b Greenidge		13
A. J. Harris not out	41	– not out		4
P. J. McMahon c Bailey b Brown	15	– lbw b Greenidge		0
B 17, l-b 16, w 5, n-b 4	42	B 7, l-b 3		10
	489			**172**

1/7 (1) 2/33 (3) 3/57 (4) 4/122 (5)
5/125 (6) 6/231 (2) 7/365 (7)
8/419 (9) 9/421 (8) 10/489 (11)

1/0 (1) 2/10 (2) 3/97 (4)
4/121 (3) 5/121 (6) 6/131 (5)
7/133 (8) 8/159 (8)
9/172 (9) 10/172 (11)

Bonus points – Nottinghamshire 5, Northamptonshire 3 (130 overs: 429-9).

Bowling: *First Innings*—Cousins 29–3–103–2; Greenidge 24–4–95–2; Brown 40.1–16–105–3; Penberthy 20–5–56–0; Swann 31–5–94–2; Cook 3–2–3–0. *Second Innings*—Cousins 8–4–21–1; Greenidge 9.4–0–27–3; Brown 22–6–59–3; Swann 20–5–55–3.

Northamptonshire

*M. E. K. Hussey c Johnson b Logan	39	– (2) lbw b Harris		4
A. S. Rollins lbw b Boje	23	– (1) c Welton b Logan		39
M. B. Loye run out	105	– not out		104
D. J. Sales c Johnson b Logan	179	– run out		1
J. W. Cook lbw b Boje	0	– c Gallian b Harris		68
A. L. Penberthy c Boje b Logan	2	– not out		5
G. P. Swann c Shafayat b Logan	12			
†T. M. B. Bailey c Read b Harris	8			
C. G. Greenidge lbw b Boje	7			
D. M. Cousins c Boje b Harris	13			
J. F. Brown not out	3			
B 9, l-b 4, w 4, n-b 8	29	B 4, l-b 8, n-b 9		21
	420		(4 wkts)	**242**

1/61 (1) 2/62 (2) 3/256 (3) 4/256 (5)
5/265 (6) 6/277 (7) 7/303 (8)
8/330 (9) 9/373 (10) 10/420 (4)

1/15 (2) 2/78 (1)
3/79 (4) 4/214 (5)

Bonus points – Northamptonshire 5, Nottinghamshire 3.

Bowling: *First Innings*—Harris 29–4–107–2; Franks 16–3–77–0; Boje 31–7–115–3; Logan 16.1–2–64–4; McMahon 8–1–29–0; Afzaal 4–0–11–0. *Second Innings*—Harris 11.3–3–36–2; Franks 4–1–32–0; Boje 18–2–51–0; Logan 10–1–45–1; McMahon 11–1–52–0; Afzaal 4.3–1–14–0.

Umpires: N. G. Cowley and J. W. Holder.

NORTHAMPTONSHIRE v DURHAM

At Northampton, July 3, 4, 5, 6. Northamptonshire won by one wicket. Northamptonshire 15 pts, Durham 4 pts. Toss: Durham. First-class debut: D. E. Paynter.

Both sides were desperate to resurrect a dire season, and their willingness to flirt with defeat in pursuit of victory produced a tense finish. Only 12 overs were possible on the first day, but some unusually solid batting by Durham took them to 352 on the second, though they still relied on powerful drives and pulls from Hunter at No. 8. More rain washed out the third, and a run-chase was contrived, leaving Northamptonshire a target of 353 in 96 overs. On another pitch clearly prepared to help the home spinners (rough patches on a length were evident before the start), the match was edging Durham's way at 181 for five. But Penberthy and Swann added 110, and Swann powered on to his first Championship century since 1998, smashing six sixes and ten fours off only 82 balls. He perished trying to finish the match in emphatic style against the persevering Bridge, but Northamptonshire's final pair scraped the last four runs.

Close of play: First day, Durham 35-0 (Lewis 6, G. J. Pratt 23); Second day, Northamptonshire 0-0 (Hussey 0, Paynter 0); Third day, No play.

Durham

*J. J. B. Lewis c Bailey b Cousins	7	
G. J. Pratt b Swann	78	
G. J. Muchall c Paynter b Brown	33	
N. Peng c Hussey b Swann	29	
M. J. Symington c Hussey b Swann	42	
†A. Pratt c Cousins b Swann	0	
D. R. Law c Sales b Cousins	31	
I. D. Hunter c Greenidge b Cousins	65	

G. D. Bridge c Bailey b Cousins	5
N. C. Phillips not out	21
N. Killeen lbw b Brown	13
B 4, l-b 18, w 2, n-b 4	28
	352

1/46 (1) 2/133 (3) 3/133 (2) 4/200 (4)
5/200 (6) 6/217 (5) 7/298 (7)
8/313 (8) 9/321 (9) 10/352 (11)

Bonus points – Durham 4, Northamptonshire 3.

Bowling: Cousins 22–7–75–4; Greenidge 20–2–95–0; Penberthy 9–2–20–0; Brown 29.4–10–59–2; Swann 29–9–81–4.

Durham forfeited their second innings.

Northamptonshire

*M. E. K. Hussey not out	0	– b Hunter	15
D. E. Paynter not out	0	– c G. J. Pratt b Killeen	20
M. B. Loye (did not bat)		– c Phillips b Bridge	19
D. J. Sales (did not bat)		– b Bridge	74
J. W. Cook (did not bat)		– c Peng b Bridge	29
A. L. Penberthy (did not bat)		– lbw b Phillips	47
G. P. Swann (did not bat)		– c Hunter b Bridge	109
†T. M. B. Bailey (did not bat)		– c Killeen b Phillips	12
C. G. Greenidge (did not bat)		– lbw b Phillips	2
D. M. Cousins (did not bat)		– not out	2
J. F. Brown (did not bat)		– not out	2
		B 3, l-b 19	22

(no wkt dec.)	0	(9 wkts) 353

1/39 (1) 2/43 (2)
3/111 (3) 4/156 (4)
5/181 (5) 6/291 (6)
7/340 (8) 8/343 (9) 9/349 (7)

Bowling: *First Innings*—Killeen 1–1–0–0. *Second Innings*—Killeen 13–3–41–1; Hunter 13–5–36–1; Law 11–2–43–0; Bridge 26.2–3–102–4; Phillips 17–1–94–3; Symington 2–0–15–0.

Umpires: J. H. Hampshire and T. E. Jesty.

At Worcester, July 19, 20, 21. NORTHAMPTONSHIRE lost to WORCESTERSHIRE by eight wickets.

NORTHAMPTONSHIRE v DERBYSHIRE

At Northampton, July 25, 26, 27. Derbyshire won by 177 runs. Derbyshire 19 pts, Northamptonshire 4 pts. Toss: Derbyshire.

Spurred on by ill-advised comments in the local press from Graeme Swann, Derbyshire completed a double over Northamptonshire. Having dismissed Cork for a golden duck on the first day, Swann admitted he was especially pleased, describing him as "not the most popular guy on the circuit". Cork's response was both dramatic and predictable. He launched a ferocious second-innings assault on Swann's off-spin, hitting four sixes on the way to 80 from 81 balls, and then killed off Northamptonshire's faint hopes of scoring 461 for victory by dismissing Hussey first ball. After that – and the embarrassing run-out of the chastened Swann – only Penberthy and Bailey prevented humiliation. Even by his standards, it had been a humdinging three days for Cork. On the first evening he was on the phone to the ECB about a pitch that had been shaved at both ends to help spinners, only to be told that the practice was legal, if not encouraged. But the strip didn't harm Derbyshire's progress, as Gait's careful career-best hundred helped them to a healthy 388. Northamptonshire's reply was, with the exception of Cook, an irresolute affair and, after Cork chose not to impose the follow-on, his second-innings fireworks set up the win.

Close of play: First day, Derbyshire 388; Second day, Derbyshire 188-6 (Selwood 24, Cork 20).

Derbyshire

A. I. Gait c Brophy b Swann	175	– b Greenidge	5
M. J. Di Venuto c Brophy b Cousins	30	– c Greenidge b Swann	24
C. W. G. Bassano c Cousins b Greenidge	57	– c Brophy b Brown	69
M. P. Dowman c Brophy b Cook	28	– lbw b Brown	41
S. A. Selwood c Brophy b Brown	32	– lbw b Swann	32
T. Lungley lbw b Swann	8	– c Loye b Swann	3
*D. G. Cork c Hussey b Swann	0	– (8) c Cousins b Brown	80
†K. M. Krikken c Sales b Swann	0	– (9) c Swann b Greenidge	3
Mohammad Ali c Greenidge b Swann	26	– (10) c Cousins b Brown	12
K. J. Dean c Hussey b Swann	6	– (11) not out	2
L. J. Wharton not out	4	– (7) lbw b Swann	0
B 8, l-b 8, n-b 6	22	B 1, l-b 4, w 2, n-b 4	11

1/47 (2) 2/203 (3) 3/294 (4) 4/330 (1)   388   1/7 (1) 2/51 (2) 3/140 (4)   282
5/346 (6) 6/346 (7) 7/348 (8)   4/141 (3) 5/158 (6) 6/158 (7)
8/364 (5) 9/378 (9) 10/388 (10)   7/206 (5) 8/211 (9)
                                     9/276 (8) 10/282 (10)

Bonus points – Derbyshire 4, Northamptonshire 3.

Bowling: *First Innings*—Cousins 12–5–31–1; Greenidge 15–2–69–1; Penberthy 12–3–44–0; Brown 26–6–88–1; Swann 27.1–3–126–6; Cook 10–2–14–1. *Second Innings*—Cousins 5–0–26–0; Greenidge 10–2–37–2; Brown 25.1–5–88–4; Swann 26–6–112–4; Cook 4–0–14–0.

Northamptonshire

	First innings		Second innings	
*M. E. K. Hussey lbw b Cork	13	– c Lungley b Cork	0
M. B. Loye c Krikken b Dean	1	– lbw b Dean	34
D. J. Sales c Krikken b Cork	8	– c Di Venuto b Dean	29
G. L. Brophy c Gait b Mohammad Ali	18	– lbw b Cork	8
J. W. Cook c Krikken b Mohammad Ali	88	– c Lungley b Dean	21
A. L. Penberthy lbw b Cork	29	– b Wharton	62
G. P. Swann c Gait b Lungley	15	– run out	12
†T. M. B. Bailey c Krikken b Lungley	0	– not out	50
C. G. Greenidge c Di Venuto b Lungley	0	– lbw b Wharton	0
D. M. Cousins run out	2	– c Di Venuto b Mohammad Ali	1
J. F. Brown not out	0	– b Mohammad Ali	15
B 4, l-b 7, w 2, n-b 23	36	B 8, l-b 8, n-b 35	51
	210		**283**

1/8 (2) 2/18 (1) 3/31 (3) 4/69 (4)
5/154 (6) 6/202 (5) 7/208 (7)
8/208 (9) 9/210 (10) 10/210 (8)

1/0 (1) 2/47 (3) 3/78 (7)
4/102 (2) 5/113 (5) 6/143 (7)
7/218 (6) 8/230 (9)
9/241 (10) 10/283 (11)

Bonus points – Northamptonshire 1, Derbyshire 3.

Bowling: *First Innings*—Cork 15–2–56–3; Dean 15–6–33–1; Mohammad Ali 8–0–37–2; Lungley 8–1–43–3; Wharton 4–0–15–0; Selwood 3–0–15–0. *Second Innings*—Cork 13–1–71–2; Dean 15–4–48–3; Lungley 11–3–33–0; Mohammad Ali 14–2–72–2; Wharton 11–2–43–2.

Umpires: M. J. Kitchen and J. F. Steele.

At Lord's, August 7, 8, 9, 10. NORTHAMPTONSHIRE drew with MIDDLESEX.

At Bristol, August 15, 16, 17, 18. NORTHAMPTONSHIRE drew with GLOUCESTERSHIRE.

NORTHAMPTONSHIRE v GLAMORGAN

At Northampton, August 21, 22, 23. Northamptonshire won by eight wickets. Northamptonshire 19 pts, Glamorgan 3 pts. Toss: Glamorgan. County debut: M. W. H. Inness.

Northamptonshire took control on the first day by dismissing Glamorgan cheaply on a blameless pitch. Greenidge swung the new ball impressively and Mathew Inness, a left-arm seamer from Victoria signed to replace Hussey, soon found his range, but their task was made easier by Glamorgan's lack of application. In reply, Northamptonshire moved rapidly into the lead as Rob White dominated a century opening partnership. In only his second Championship appearance, he hooked Jones for two sixes during an aggressive 66-ball fifty, before Penberthy's authoritative 99 pressed home the advantage. Kasprowicz and Davies mopped up the last six wickets in 46 balls, but Northamptonshire took a lead of 231, and Glamorgan lost eight men in clearing the arrears. A bold counter-attack from Kasprowicz helped add 110 for the last two wickets and avert an innings defeat, but this was only mildly irritating for Northamptonshire, who won with five sessions to spare.

Close of play: First day, Northamptonshire 205-3 (Cook 21, Penberthy 17); Second day, Glamorgan 164-6 (Croft 0, Kasprowicz 1).

Glamorgan

*S. P. James c Bailey b Greenidge	20	– c Bailey b Greenidge	12
I. J. Thomas b Greenidge	0	– c Bailey b Inness	10
A. Dale c Swann b Penberthy	37	– c White b Swann	52
M. J. Powell c Bailey b Greenidge	12	– c Inness b Panesar	33
M. P. Maynard c Swann b Cassar	43	– c Inness b Panesar	19
†M. A. Wallace c and b Penberthy	4	– c Panesar b Swann	25
R. D. B. Croft c Cook b Greenidge	7	– lbw b Panesar	14
M. S. Kasprowicz not out	8	– not out	72
A. P. Davies lbw b Greenidge	4	– b Swann	6
D. A. Cosker lbw b Inness	0	– b Greenidge	36
S. P. Jones c Panesar b Inness	2	– c Bailey b Greenidge	17
B 1, l-b 4, n-b 2	7	B 4, l-b 2, w 2, n-b 8	16

1/6 (2) 2/23 (1) 3/45 (4) 4/103 (3)   144   1/26 (1) 2/26 (2) 3/80 (4)   312
5/121 (5) 6/121 (6) 7/133 (7)   4/122 (5) 5/162 (6) 6/163 (3)
8/141 (9) 9/142 (10) 10/144 (11)   7/183 (7) 8/202 (9)
                                        9/260 (10) 10/312 (11)

Bonus points – Northamptonshire 3.

Bowling: *First Innings*—Inness 11.4–3–33–2; Greenidge 12–3–44–5; Penberthy 9–2–31–2; Cassar 8–2–31–1. *Second Innings*—Greenidge 14–3–68–3; Inness 7–2–32–1; Penberthy 4–1–9–0; Cassar 4–2–7–0; Panesar 30–3–120–3; Swann 24–6–70–3.

Northamptonshire

M. B. Loye c Wallace b Kasprowicz	41	– b Kasprowicz	3
R. A. White b Davies	80	– not out	60
D. J. Sales c Powell b Cosker	37	– st Wallace b Cosker	8
J. W. Cook lbw b Croft	21	– not out	13
*A. L. Penberthy lbw b Kasprowicz	99		
M. E. Cassar c Wallace b Kasprowicz	68		
G. P. Swann c Wallace b Davies	5		
†T. M. B. Bailey c Wallace b Davies	0		
C. G. Greenidge not out	4		
M. S. Panesar lbw b Kasprowicz	0		
M. W. H. Inness b Davies	0		
B 3, l-b 13, w 2, n-b 2	20		

1/104 (1) 2/165 (3) 3/167 (2) 4/205 (4)   375   1/38 (1) 2/61 (3)   (2 wkts) 84
5/355 (5) 6/362 (7) 7/362 (8)
8/374 (6) 9/374 (10) 10/375 (11)

Bonus points – Northamptonshire 4, Glamorgan 3.

Bowling: *First Innings*—Kasprowicz 23–2–63–4; Davies 13.4–1–53–4; Croft 19–2–68–1; Jones 16–4–58–0; Cosker 22–3–88–1; Dale 4–0–29–0. *Second Innings*—Kasprowicz 5–2–16–1; Jones 4–0–26–0; Cosker 4–0–21–1; Croft 4–1–17–0; Thomas 0.1–0–4–0.

Umpires: M. R. Benson and A. Clarkson.

At Chester-le-Street, August 27, 28, 29. NORTHAMPTONSHIRE beat DURHAM by seven wickets.

NORTHAMPTONSHIRE v GLOUCESTERSHIRE

At Northampton, September 11, 12, 13. Northamptonshire won by an innings and 59 runs. Northamptonshire 20 pts, Gloucestershire 4 pts. Toss: Northamptonshire.

Northamptonshire's Loughborough student openers, Rob White, 22, and Mark Powell, 21, grabbed the headlines by putting on a county-record 375 for the first wicket. With just seven Championship appearances between them, they passed the 372 set by Mal Loye and Richard

Montgomerie against Yorkshire in 1996 with a flurry of powerful shots. Both made maiden centuries. White faced 325 balls in 379 minutes for his superb, nimble-footed 277, and hit two sixes and 41 fours. White made a dashing hundred before lunch, 204 by tea, and seemed surprised at the attention this brought. Meanwhile, Powell played the supporting role to perfection, facing 241 balls for 107. The contrast in styles prompted comparisons with Wayne Larkins and Geoff Cook, Northamptonshire's openers during the 1980s. Cassar's first century for the county piled on more misery and, in reply Gloucestershire had little stomach for the fight once Spearman and Windows were parted after adding 185. The last eight wickets fell for 68 to the spin of Brown and Panesar, and they did the damage again during the follow-on. White, bowling leg-breaks, rounded off a remarkable performance with his first two first-class wickets. Despite three wins on the trot, Northamptonshire remained seventh in Division Two.

Close of play: First day, Northamptonshire 417-4 (Cook 5, Penberthy 6); Second day, Gloucestershire 149-2 (Spearman 64, Windows 53).

Northamptonshire

R. A. White lbw b Smith	277	C. G. Greenidge c Sillence b Fisher	16	
M. J. Powell b Fisher	107	M. W. H. Inness not out	20	
D. J. Sales c Russell b Gidman	0	B 3, l-b 9, n-b 16	28	
J. W. Cook b Smith	8			
M. S. Panesar b Smith	0	1/375 (2) 2/390 (3)	(8 wkts dec.)	592
*A. L. Penberthy c Gidman b Sillence	33	3/411 (1) 4/411 (5)		
M. E. Cassar not out	101	5/426 (4) 6/467 (6)		
†T. M. B. Bailey c and b Fisher	2	7/472 (8) 8/530 (9)		

J. F. Brown did not bat.

Bonus points – Northamptonshire 5, Gloucestershire 2 (130 overs: 481-7).

Bowling: Lewis 29–9–75–0; Smith 27–5–96–3; Sillence 18–2–84–1; Fisher 58.1–9–172–3; Alleyne 12–1–72–0; Taylor 10–1–36–0; Gidman 11–0–45–1.

Gloucestershire

T. H. C. Hancock b Greenidge	10	– (2) lbw b Inness		1
C. M. Spearman b Brown	107	– (1) c Bailey b Brown		64
C. G. Taylor c Bailey b Greenidge	16	– b Greenidge		3
M. G. N. Windows c Penberthy b Panesar	89	– c Sales b Panesar		52
*M. W. Alleyne c Powell b Brown	1	– b Brown		0
A. P. R. Gidman c Penberthy b Brown	0	– b Panesar		66
†R. C. Russell c Brown b Panesar	5	– b Brown		14
I. D. Fisher c sub b Brown	3	– c Penberthy b White		8
R. J. Sillence c Cassar b Panesar	21	– c Bailey b Panesar		3
J. Lewis not out	13	– c Greenidge b White		13
A. M. Smith lbw b Panesar	21	– not out		0
L-b 7, n-b 6	13	B 6, w 2, n-b 2		10

1/24 (1) 2/46 (3) 3/231 (2) 4/235 (5)	299	1/18 (2) 2/51 (3) 3/76 (1)	234
5/235 (6) 6/235 (4) 7/242 (8)		4/84 (5) 5/155 (4) 6/179 (7)
8/252 (7) 9/265 (9) 10/299 (11)		7/217 (8) 8/217 (6)
		9/228 (9) 10/234 (10)

Bonus points – Gloucestershire 2, Northamptonshire 3.

Bowling: *First Innings*—Greenidge 16–2–67–2; Inness 16–5–64–0; Cassar 3–0–13–0; Panesar 28.3–14–42–4; Brown 26–4–106–4. *Second Innings*—Greenidge 7–0–29–1; Inness 8–2–48–1; Brown 15–3–47–3; Panesar 22–6–74–3; White 12.4–3–30–2.

Umpires: J. H. Evans and K. E. Palmer.

At Cardiff, September 18, 19, 20, 21. NORTHAMPTONSHIRE drew with GLAMORGAN.

NOTTINGHAMSHIRE
A VICTORY FOR DEMOCRACY

Ch'ship 3rd in Division 2 – promoted
C&G 4th round
B&H group stage
NUL 9th in Division 1 – relegated

Player of the season: Andrew Harris

Two managers, three overseas players, promotion in the Championship and relegation in the Norwich Union League: Nottinghamshire's season was certainly eventful. On top of that, the club opened its impressive new Fox Road Stand and, mainly because of the increase in capacity, signed a staging agreement to secure international cricket at Trent Bridge until 2011.

Members paid tribute to the much-admired and popular Paul Johnson who joined the coaching staff after 22 years' sterling service and dashing strokeplay. He was a natural entertainer, whose arrival at the crease generated an air of expectancy; his diminutive figure will be sadly missed on the circuit. By his exceptional standards, Johnson went out with a whimper, but he did reach the rare double of 20,000 first-class and 10,000 one-day runs.

It was a fitting farewell for him that Nottinghamshire won promotion in the Championship on the strength of an unstinting run of high-class cricket in the second half of the season. The late surge was prompted by the departure of Clive Rice, a Trent Bridge legend, from the manager's post in June. The committee took this toughest of decisions after ignominious exits from both knockout competitions and a miserable run in the Norwich Union. On the field, Rice was the club's most successful captain and arguably its greatest leader-by-example, but he could not exert the same influence from the pavilion. His straight talking and single-minded approach ruffled feathers, and his all-too-frequent practice sessions seemed to lack a clear objective. Few connected with Nottinghamshire cricket dared believe that Rice was the reason for consistent underperformance, but results did point that way.

He was replaced by Mick Newell, who had been in charge of all cricket outside the first team. Where Rice had been autocratic, Newell, a vastly different character, chose group discussion and democracy. His impact was almost immediate: after defeat in the Championship at Northampton, Notts reeled off an unbeaten run of nine games, including six victories. It lifted them from eighth to the brink of the Division Two title, which they would have won had they beaten Essex at Chelmsford on the final day.

Aside from a brief hiccough against Derbyshire, Trent Bridge was a fortress: there were six home wins and only the weather prevented a seventh against Durham. But Newell's magic did not extend to the one-day game.

The South African all-rounder Lance Klusener had an early spell as the overseas player but was not at his best, and this set the tone for a dismal Norwich Union League season, which culminated in relegation. The silver lining was that it presented an ideal opportunity to blood a number of teenagers in senior cricket.

After the injury crisis of 2001, the key players stayed fit and performed to their potential. Andrew Harris profited from an unbroken run in the team to bank 67 first-class wickets. He was accurate, consistent and supported by an ever-reliable foil, the giant left-armer Greg Smith, who followed up 50 wickets in his debut season in England with 48 more; with better luck, he might easily have matched Harris's total. The return to fitness of Paul Franks in mid-July after a year's lay-off was a timely boost. He took nine wickets against Glamorgan in his second game back and was promptly named in the provisional list for the England Academy. He was later excluded, inexplicably because few young players have more talent or would have benefited more from the Academy's fitness schedule than Franks. A place in Adelaide did go to Chris Read, who topped the list of first-class dismissals, made nearly 800 runs and spent some time with the senior one-day squad as Alec Stewart's understudy. The stylish Usman Afzaal shrugged off the disappointment of being ditched by England to pass 1,000 runs for the third season in a row.

The captain, Jason Gallian, earned immense credit for managing to steer the ship through turbulent waters after missing nearly all of 2001 with knee problems. He enjoyed a renaissance with the bat, passing 1,000 runs in his most productive season for Nottinghamshire, and won the games at home to Northamptonshire and at Derby with disciplined centuries of the highest class under intense pressure. After a lean spell early in the season, the precocious Kevin Pietersen stormed back to form. He hit three career-best scores during a run of four hundreds in all cricket in ten memorable days, before his season was cut short by a fractured shin. In December, Nottinghamshire announced they had signed the middle-order batsman Russell Warren from Northamptonshire.

The other pivotal point came in early August when the steady but unspectacular slow left-armer Nicky Boje was succeeded as overseas player by Stuart MacGill, the Australian leg-spinner. Barely over his jetlag, he exploded on to the scene with five wickets at Kidderminster to bolster the promotion push, then seized 14 in the crushing home win over Middlesex, who had been unbeaten. MacGill added eight more in the next game, against Gloucestershire, and by the end of the season had taken 40 wickets in six matches. He was promptly offered a contract for 2003 and 2004 though his availability may be limited by increased international commitments after Shane Warne's one-year ban. Fitness permitting, Chris Cairns will join MacGill as the second overseas player. If both make it on to the field, it is a combination with Rice-and-Hadlee potential which could confirm Nottinghamshire as a major force. **Paul Fearn**

NOTTINGHAMSHIRE 2002

Back row: S. J. Randall, G. D. Clough, M. N. Malik, R. J. Logan, P. J. McMahon, B. M. Shafayat. *Middle row:* W. M. Noon, D. S. Lucas, A. J. Harris, K. P. Pietersen, G. J. Smith, U. Afzaal, G. E. Welton. *Front row:* L. Klusener, P. J. Franks, D. J. Bicknell, C. E. B. Rice *(director of cricket),* J. E. R. Gallian *(captain),* P. Johnson, C. M. W. Read, M. Newell *(second-team coach). Picture by Sam Bowles, Bowles Associates.*

NOTTINGHAMSHIRE RESULTS

All first-class matches – Played 18: Won 9, Lost 5, Drawn 4.
County Championship matches – Played 16: Won 8, Lost 5, Drawn 3.

COUNTY CHAMPIONSHIP AVERAGES: BATTING AND FIELDING

Cap		M	I	NO	R	HS	100s	50s	Avge	Ct/St
2002	K. P. Pietersen	10	15	3	737	254*	3	0	61.41	9
2000	U. Afzaal	16	29	3	1,155	134	4	6	44.42	10
1998	J. E. R. Gallian . . .	15	27	3	1,006	171	4	5	41.91	15
	B. M. Shafayat† . . .	5	9	0	332	104	1	1	36.88	4
1999	C. M. W. Read	16	25	5	694	127	1	3	34.70	60/2
2000	D. J. Bicknell	12	21	0	711	112	2	2	33.85	5
	G. E. Welton	14	25	1	806	115	1	5	33.58	16
1986	P. Johnson†	14	25	3	662	96	0	5	30.09	7
	N. Boje§	9	16	2	409	84	0	2	29.21	10
1999	P. J. Franks†	10	14	2	301	67	0	3	25.08	2
2001	G. J. Smith	15	20	7	243	39*	0	0	18.69	4
2000	A. J. Harris	13	18	6	149	41*	0	0	12.41	5
	R. J. Logan	12	17	2	139	32	0	0	9.26	4
2002	S. C. G. MacGill§ . .	6	7	1	48	22	0	0	8.00	5
	M. N. Malik†	5	7	1	32	18	0	0	5.33	—

Also batted: L. Klusener§ (1 match) 0, 42 (1 ct); P. J. McMahon (1 match) 15, 0; S. J. Randall†
2 matches) 0, 8, 5 (1 ct).

Born in Nottinghamshire.   § *Overseas player.*

BOWLING

	O	M	R	W	BB	5W/i	Avge
A. J. Harris	392.4	84	1,411	63	7-54	3	22.39
S. C. G. MacGill	227.4	37	930	40	8-111	4	23.25
N. Boje	238	58	671	27	6-128	2	24.85
P. J. Franks	234.5	53	813	32	5-51	1	25.40
G. J. Smith	400.1	85	1,275	48	8-53	1	26.56
M. N. Malik	112.4	25	389	14	4-55	0	27.78
R. J. Logan	302.3	64	1,142	35	4-64	0	32.62

Also bowled: U. Afzaal 30.3–2–122–0; P. Johnson 1.2–0–12–0; L. Klusener 20–4–88–1; P. J.
McMahon 19–2–81–0; K. P. Pietersen 30–3–152–2; S. J. Randall 33–6–140–0; B. M. Shafayat
1–0–40–0.

COUNTY RECORDS

Highest score for:	312*	W. W. Keeton v Middlesex at The Oval	1939
Highest score against:	345	C. G. Macartney (Australians) at Nottingham . . .	1921
Best bowling for:	10-66	K. Smales v Gloucestershire at Stroud	1956
Best bowling against:	10-10	H. Verity (Yorkshire) at Leeds	1932
Highest total for:	739-7 dec.	v Leicestershire at Nottingham	1903
Highest total against:	781-7 dec.	by Northamptonshire at Northampton	1995
Lowest total for:	13	v Yorkshire at Nottingham	1901
Lowest total against: {	16	by Derbyshire at Nottingham	1879
	16	by Surrey at The Oval	1880

COUNTY OFFICERS

Captain J. E. R. Gallian • **Director of cricket** 2002 – C. E. B. Rice; 2003 – M. Newell
President The Rt Hon. K. Clarke • **Chairman** A. Bocking
Chief executive D. G. Collier • **Chairman, cricket committee** S. E. Foster
Head groundsman S. Birks • **Scorer** G. Stringfellow

NOTTINGHAMSHIRE v DURHAM UCCE

At Nottingham, April 20, 21, 22. Nottinghamshire won by 191 runs. Toss: Nottinghamshire. First-class debut: M. A. Hazelton.

Nottinghamshire completed their early-season preparations with a comfortable win. Their first innings was dominated by a stand of 205 between Pietersen and Welton, with Pietersen hammering 133 off only 148 balls. Lucas then played an enjoyable cameo, swatting 49 in 47 deliveries. Nadeem Malik, Nottinghamshire's 19-year-old seamer, promptly rattled through Durham's top order until Andrew Hollingsworth provided some stout resistance. He coaxed 89 from the tail before running out of partners. Gallian enjoyed his return to action after a knee problem and a broken knuckle had restricted him to just two matches in 2001, and hit 13 fours in his 68 before declaring and leaving Durham an unlikely 407 to win. Once again their batting folded, plunging them to their first first-class defeat. The part-time spinners Afzaal and Pietersen shouldered the bulk of the work and Harris returned to clean up the tail.

Close of play: First day, Durham UCCE 56-1 (Kirby 33, Ferley 7); Second day, Nottinghamshire 221-5 (Logan 4, Harris 1).

Nottinghamshire

D. J. Bicknell c Loudon b Thorburn	23	– c Loudon b Thorburn	0
*J. E. R. Gallian c Jefferson b Bruce	13	– c Hollingsworth b Loudon	68
U. Afzaal c Brown b Bruce	5	– c Brown b Bruce	4
K. P. Pietersen c Hazelton b Ferley	133		
G. E. Welton c Jefferson b Ferley	97		
B. M. Shafayat b Ferley	2	– (4) c Bruce b Ferley	71
†C. M. W. Read c Hazelton b Ferley	25	– (5) c Kirby b Ferley	54
D. S. Lucas c and b Loudon	49		
R. J. Logan not out	0	– (6) not out	4
A. J. Harris b Loudon	1	– (7) not out	1
B 11, l-b 16, w 4, n-b 16	47	B 7, l-b 3, w 2, n-b 6	19

1/50 (2) 2/54 (1) 3/70 (3) (9 wkts dec.) 395
4/275 (4) 5/278 (6) 6/321 (5)
7/394 (8) 8/394 (9) 9/395 (10)

1/9 (1) 2/24 (3) (5 wkts dec.) 221
3/119 (2) 4/178 (4)
5/219 (5)

M. N. Malik did not bat.

Bowling: *First Innings*—Thorburn 9–1–62–1; Bruce 16–2–76–2; Hazelton 5–1–32–0; Hollingsworth 7–2–24–0; Ferley 21–3–83–4; Phillips 7–0–31–0; Loudon 17.1–3–60–2. *Second Innings*—Bruce 6–1–20–1; Thorburn 9–3–34–1; Hazelton 5–1–26–0; Phillips 13–3–64–0; Loudon 12–0–42–1; Ferley 10–4–24–2.

Durham UCCE

W. I. Jefferson c Read b Malik	9	– (2) b Malik	6
W. A. Kirby c Afzaal b Malik	37	– (6) b Harris	25
R. S. Ferley run out	22	– (8) c Read b Lucas	22
*M. J. Banes c Pietersen b Malik	4	– (3) c Logan b Pietersen	39
A. G. R. Loudon b Malik	2	– (4) c Pietersen b Afzaal	2
T. J. Phillips c Malik b Pietersen	31	– b Afzaal	5
†M. J. Brown lbw b Lucas	1	– (1) b Pietersen	43
A. P. Hollingsworth not out	42	– (7) c Gallian b Afzaal	5
M. A. Hazelton b Malik	11	– lbw b Harris	5
M. Thorburn c Harris b Afzaal	12	– b Harris	0
J. T. A. Bruce c Pietersen b Harris	0	– not out	8
B 8, l-b 3, n-b 28	39	B 12, l-b 12, w 6, n-b 12	42

1/36 (1) 2/67 (2) 3/75 (4) 4/85 (5) 210
5/102 (3) 6/121 (7) 7/142 (6)
8/173 (9) 9/206 (10) 10/210 (11)

1/26 (2) 2/88 (1) 3/103 (4) 215
4/129 (3) 5/145 (5) 6/157 (7)
7/191 (8) 8/200 (6)
9/200 (10) 10/215 (9)

Bowling: *First Innings*—Lucas 13–5–21–1; Logan 12–5–36–0; Malik 16–2–67–5; Harris 9–4–29–1; Afzaal 8–3–26–1; Pietersen 5–1–20–1. *Second Innings*—Logan 5–2–13–0; Malik 5–0–22–1; Harris 12–5–35–3; Lucas 16–6–35–1; Pietersen 27–9–54–2; Afzaal 25–15–32–3.

Umpires: N. J. Llong and J. W. Lloyds.

At Lord's, April 24, 25, 26, 27. NOTTINGHAMSHIRE lost to MIDDLESEX by an innings and 31 runs.

NOTTINGHAMSHIRE v ESSEX

At Nottingham, May 8, 9, 10. Nottinghamshire won by seven wickets. Nottinghamshire 16 pts, Essex 2.5 pts. Toss: Nottinghamshire. County debut: N. Boje.

The toss was vital on a damp, green-tinged wicket, described by an ECB pitch panel as "below average" and by Irani as "downright dangerous". Nottinghamshire were relieved to be able to insert Essex, who were skittled for 130 as swing compounded unpredictable bounce. In reply, Gallian dug in for a gritty half-century before Smith bludgeoned 35 from 31 balls and put together a valuable final-wicket stand that gave Nottinghamshire a useful lead. Irani revelled in the conditions to produce career-best figures of six for 71, but even his outstanding performance was eclipsed by Smith's eight for 53 as Essex struggled again in their second innings. His best bowling figures were reward for unerring accuracy, and only Grayson found the necessary mixture of resolve and luck. Nottinghamshire were left a tricky 188 to win, but Afzaal stroked 17 fours and played magnificently on the drying wicket to secure victory before tea on the third day. Without interruptions for bad light, the match would have been over in two days and 90 minutes.

Close of play: First day, Nottinghamshire 152-5 (Pietersen 14, Read 4); Second day, Essex 215-7 (Middlebrook 16, Cowan 4).

Essex

D. J. Robinson c Afzaal b Harris	7	– c Read b Smith	0
A. P. Grayson lbw b Smith	19	– c Read b Smith	83
N. Hussain c Read b Smith	1	– lbw b Smith	4
A. Habib c Gallian b Harris	20	– c Read b Smith	15
†A. Flower lbw b Smith	4	– c Read b Smith	25
*R. C. Irani lbw b Malik	37	– c Smith b Harris	28
J. M. Dakin c Read b Malik	6	– c Bicknell b Logan	17
J. D. Middlebrook c Gallian b Harris	6	– c Read b Smith	27
A. P. Cowan c Read b Malik	9	– c Afzaal b Smith	42
A. C. McGarry b Harris	0	– (11) b Smith	0
J. B. Grant not out	1	– (10) not out	3
B 5, w 2, n-b 8	15	B 4, l-b 7, w 8, n-b 7	26
	130		**270**

1/19 (1) 2/26 (3) 3/31 (2) 4/35 (5) 5/95 (6) 6/99 (4) 7/115 (7) 8/125 (9) 9/129 (8) 10/130 (10)

1/0 (1) 2/16 (3) 3/80 (4) 4/137 (2) 5/146 (5) 6/189 (6) 7/199 (7) 8/253 (8) 9/270 (9) 10/270 (11)

Bonus points – Nottinghamshire 3.

Bowling: *First Innings*—Smith 10–3–21–3; Malik 17–5–45–3; Harris 14.4–4–41–4; Logan 4–0–15–0; Boje 2–0–3–0. *Second Innings*—Smith 23–6–53–8; Malik 12–0–57–0; Harris 18–2–72–1; Logan 10–1–51–1; Boje 6–1–26–0.

Nottinghamshire

D. J. Bicknell c Cowan b Irani	32	– b Dakin	39
*J. E. R. Gallian c Flower b Cowan	52	– c Flower b Cowan	9
U. Afzaal lbw b Cowan	4	– not out	85
P. Johnson lbw b Grant	16	– c Hussain b Grant	9
N. Boje lbw b Irani	25	– not out	21
K. P. Pietersen c McGarry b Irani	19		
†C. M. W. Read c Hussain b Irani	18		
R. J. Logan lbw b Irani	1		
A. J. Harris c Flower b Cowan	4		
G. J. Smith not out	35		
M. N. Malik c Grayson b Irani	2		
B 2, l-b 1, w 2	5	B 9, l-b 2, n-b 14	25

1/52 (1) 2/56 (3) 3/95 (4) 4/131 (2)   213   1/21 (2) 2/122 (1)   (3 wkts) 188
5/141 (5) 6/168 (6) 7/171 (7)   3/133 (4)
8/174 (8) 9/176 (9) 10/213 (11)

Bonus points – Nottinghamshire 1, Essex 3.

Bowling: *First Innings*—Cowan 24–5–70–3; Irani 23.5–10–71–6; McGarry 8–2–29–0; Dakin 9–2–22–0; Grant 3–1–18–1. *Second Innings*—Cowan 10–0–41–1; Irani 8–1–29–0; Dakin 8–3–16–1; Grant 9–0–71–1; McGarry 6.5–2–20–0.

Umpires: B. Dudleston and M. J. Kitchen.

At Bristol, May 15, 16, 17. NOTTINGHAMSHIRE lost to GLOUCESTERSHIRE by seven wickets.

NOTTINGHAMSHIRE v NORTHAMPTONSHIRE

At Nottingham, May 24, 25, 26, 27. Nottinghamshire won by seven wickets. Nottinghamshire 16 pts, Northamptonshire 3.5 pts. Toss: Northamptonshire.

Undaunted by dressing-room rumblings about Clive Rice's methods and record as coach, Nottinghamshire sneaked a welcome win – despite 15 stoppages over the first three days. Northamptonshire chose to bat but rain freshened the pitch and they were soon deep in trouble at 127 for seven. However, Penberthy feasted on some dire bowling and the last three helped him add 150. Nottinghamshire collapsed too, before persistent rain on day three prevented Northamptonshire pressing home their advantage. With both captains intent on forcing a result, Gallian declared behind on the last morning, and Northamptonshire went for quick runs. They were undone by Harris, who ripped through the middle order with seven wickets in a five-over burst either side of lunch. His seven for 54 was a career-best. Chasing 230 in 63 overs, Nottinghamshire lost two quick wickets, but Gallian played with immense determination to reach his first hundred in 20 months and guide his team home. Minutes later, the rain returned.

Close of play: First day, Northamptonshire 249-9 (Penberthy 83, Cousins 11); Second day, Nottinghamshire 184-7 (Boje 16, Harris 4); Third day, Nottinghamshire 207-8 (Harris 7, Smith 0).

Northamptonshire

*M. E. K. Hussey c Read b Logan	10	– (2) c Read b Smith	36
A. S. Rollins lbw b Smith	7	– (1) c Harris b Malik	60
M. B. Loye lbw b Harris	37	– c Read b Harris	1
R. J. Warren c Read b Smith	42	– lbw b Harris	0
G. P. Swann c Welton b Harris	0	– b Harris	0
A. L. Penberthy not out	106	– c Boje b Harris	31
J. W. Cook b Harris	4	– c Welton b Smith	11
†T. M. B. Bailey run out	4	– c Boje b Harris	0
R. S. G. Anderson c Logan b Boje	26	– c Read b Harris	0
C. G. Greenidge run out	1	– c Afzaal b Harris	9
D. M. Cousins b Harris	16	– not out	2
L-b 14, w 10	24	B 1, l-b 6, n-b 2	9

1/15 (2) 2/23 (1) 3/98 (3) 4/98 (5)   277   1/57 (2) 2/58 (3) 3/62 (4)   159
5/104 (4) 6/121 (7) 7/127 (8)   4/62 (5) 5/118 (1) 6/131 (6)
8/186 (9) 9/196 (10) 10/277 (11)   7/131 (8) 8/141 (9)
                                        9/151 (10) 10/159 (11)

Bonus points – Northamptonshire 2, Nottinghamshire 3.

Bowling: *First Innings*—Smith 23–5–56–2; Malik 10–2–44–0; Logan 14–2–66–1; Harris 20.4–3–68–4; Boje 4–0–29–1. *Second Innings*—Smith 10.3–1–48–2; Harris 11–2–54–7; Malik 5–1–26–1; Logan 4–0–24–0.

Nottinghamshire

D. J. Bicknell lbw b Greenidge	34	– lbw b Cousins	0
*J. E. R. Gallian c Bailey b Cousins	12	– not out	111
G. E. Welton c Hussey b Greenidge	35	– c Bailey b Greenidge	0
U. Afzaal c Bailey b Cousins	21	– c Bailey b Cousins	88
P. Johnson lbw b Greenidge	16	– not out	25
N. Boje lbw b Greenidge	36		
†C. M. W. Read c Hussey b Greenidge	8		
R. J. Logan c Bailey b Penberthy	20		
A. J. Harris not out	7		
G. J. Smith not out	0		
L-b 8, w 10	18	L-b 3, n-b 4	7

1/21 (2) 2/91 (1) 3/96 (3)   (8 wkts dec.) 207   1/0 (1) 2/5 (3) 3/188 (4)   (3 wkts) 231
4/132 (4) 5/132 (5) 6/144 (7)
7/171 (8) 8/207 (6)

M. N. Malik did not bat.

Bonus points – Nottinghamshire 1, Northamptonshire 2.

Bowling: *First Innings*—Cousins 23–2–70–2; Greenidge 20–3–66–5; Anderson 11–2–38–0; Penberthy 8–2–25–1. *Second Innings*—Cousins 18.5–1–88–2; Greenidge 13–1–59–1; Penberthy 9–1–27–0; Anderson 10–3–37–0; Cook 2–0–17–0.

Umpires: K. E. Palmer and J. F. Steele.

NOTTINGHAMSHIRE v DERBYSHIRE

At Nottingham, June 12, 13, 14, 15. Derbyshire won by four wickets. Derbyshire 19 pts, Nottinghamshire 7 pts. Toss: Nottinghamshire.

Faced with an unresponsive pitch and almost certain stalemate, Cork bent his back, ripped through Nottinghamshire and conjured a remarkable win. A draw was odds-on as Nottinghamshire began their second innings at 5.20 on the third evening with a lead of one, but just eight balls after lunch on the last day they were all out – and on their way to defeat. Never one to concede without a scrap, Cork bowled unchanged for nearly 28 overs and grabbed six for 78. His heroics left Derbyshire 65 overs to score 177; thanks to Bassano's solid 79 they needed only 37. But Nottinghamshire should have made the match safe much earlier. A typically dismissive 96 from Johnson and a dashing 84 by Boje gave their first innings solid foundations, but they were rapidly undermined as 374 for five became 393 all out. A commanding 79 from Di Venuto and graft from Stubbings and Bassano took Derbyshire to virtual parity, before a 46-over rain break delayed the start of Nottinghamshire's reply – and appeared to condemn the game to a draw.

Close of play: First day, Derbyshire 18-0 (Stubbings 10, Di Venuto 8); Second day, Derbyshire 298-5 (Bassano 45, Krikken 11); Third day, Nottinghamshire 75-3 (Johnson 11, Pietersen 14).

Nottinghamshire

D. J. Bicknell lbw b Dean	24	– c Krikken b Cork	24
*J. E. R. Gallian c Krikken b Dean	69	– c Stubbings b Cork	20
P. Johnson c Wharton b Mohammad Ali	96	– lbw b Cork	34
U. Afzaal c Wharton b Mohammad Ali	35	– c Cork b Mohammad Ali	2
K. P. Pietersen c Dowman b Welch	34	– lbw b Cork	14
N. Boje lbw b Cork	84	– run out	10
†C. M. W. Read b Cork	6	– lbw b Cork	13
R. J. Logan c Mohammad Ali b Dean	9	– c Krikken b Dean	0
G. J. Smith not out	3	– b Cork	27
A. J. Harris c Cork b Dean	1	– c Cork b Mohammad Ali	11
M. N. Malik c Krikken b Cork	3	– not out	0
L-b 4, w 15, n-b 10	29	B 7, l-b 3, n-b	20

1/55 (1) 2/134 (2) 3/210 (4) 4/251 (3)   **393**   1/44 (1) 2/47 (2) 3/50 (4)   **175**
5/307 (5) 6/374 (6) 7/383 (8)   4/75 (5) 5/102 (6) 6/125 (3)
8/387 (9) 9/390 (10) 10/393 (11)   7/126 (8) 8/128 (7)
                             9/175 (10) 10/175 (9)

Bonus points – Nottinghamshire 4, Derbyshire 3.

Bowling: *First Innings*—Cork 28–9–89–3; Dean 22–3–73–4; Welch 21–4–83–1; Mohammad Ali 15–3–76–2; Wharton 11–2–60–0; Dowman 2–0–8–0. *Second Innings*—Cork 27.2–4–78–6; Dean 16–1–50–1; Mohammad Ali 11–2–37–2.

Derbyshire

S. D. Stubbings c Read b Harris	45	– c Read b Smith	7
M. J. Di Venuto c Read b Malik	79	– c Johnson b Smith	17
A. I. Gait b Logan	52	– b Pietersen	20
C. W. G. Bassano b Harris	64	– b Boje	79
M. P. Dowman c Afzaal b Logan	9	– c Harris b Boje	27
*D. G. Cork b Boje	31	– c Smith b Boje	5
†K. M. Krikken c Read b Malik	14	– not out	12
G. Welch c Read b Malik	0	– not out	0
Mohammad Ali c Read b Logan	43		
K. J. Dean b Boje	16		
L. J. Wharton not out	8		
B 1, l-b 14, w 8, n-b 8	31	B 2, l-b 4, w 2, n-b 6	14

1/125 (2) 2/174 (1) 3/202 (3) 4/222 (5)   **392**   1/18 (2) 2/24 (1)   (6 wkts) **181**
5/276 (4) 6/301 (6) 7/301 (8)   3/106 (3) 4/163 (5)
8/364 (9) 9/366 (10) 10/392 (10)   5/163 (4) 6/174 (6)

Bonus points – Derbyshire 4, Nottinghamshire 3.

Bowling: *First Innings*—Harris 23–7–94–2; Boje 31.4–11–83–2; Smith 16–4–59–0; Logan 18–4–66–3; Malik 18–7–50–3; Pietersen 6–0–25–0. *Second Innings*—Harris 6–1–19–0; Smith 6–0–24–2; Malik 5–1–19–0; Logan 3–0–29–0; Boje 9–1–28–3; Pietersen 4–0–32–1; Afzaal 4–0–24–0.

Umpires: J. H. Evans and A. G. T. Whitehead.

At Northampton, June 26, 27, 28, 29. NOTTINGHAMSHIRE lost to NORTHAMPTONSHIRE by six wickets.

At Nottingham, July 3, 4, 5. NOTTINGHAMSHIRE drew with WEST INDIES A (see West Indies A tour section).

NOTTINGHAMSHIRE v GLAMORGAN

At Nottingham, July 10, 11, 12. Nottinghamshire won by seven wickets. Nottinghamshire 18 pts, Glamorgan 4 pts. Toss: Glamorgan.

After a year out with a knee injury and with only a rusty return against Northamptonshire behind him, Franks hit top gear. His accuracy proved lethal on an uneven pitch and his nine wickets were vital to Nottinghamshire's third win of the summer. After electing to bat, Glamorgan made a flying start but were pegged back by the swing of Harris and the consistency of Franks: a prosperous 114 for one suddenly became a precarious 149 for six. Welton then showed concentration and grit to reach a long-overdue second hundred, putting on 201 with the diligent Afzaal and batting Nottinghamshire into a comfortable lead. In reply, Maynard and Dale were on course to set a testing target before another feeble Glamorgan collapse, this time from 196 for five to 211 all out. Franks showed aggression on the fast-wearing pitch, Logan bowled some unplayable balls, and their work left Nottinghamshire's batsmen with a simple chase. Victory was sealed by a punchy half-century from Gallian.

Close of play: First day, Nottinghamshire 133-2 (Welton 55, Afzaal 53); Second day, Glamorgan 69-3 (Powell 18, Kasprowicz 4).

Glamorgan

I. J. Thomas b Harris	76	– c Read b Franks			13
D. D. Cherry b Logan	26	– c Read b Franks			5
D. L. Hemp lbw b Harris	9	– c Read b Smith			25
M. J. Powell b Harris	7	– lbw b Franks			20
M. P. Maynard c Read b Franks	15	– (6) b Franks			55
A. Dale c Read b Harris	3	– (7) b Logan			36
†M. A. Wallace not out	20	– (8) not out			6
*R. D. B. Croft b Logan	15	– (9) lbw b Franks			2
S. D. Thomas c Gallian b Franks	0	– (10) b Logan			6
M. S. Kasprowicz c Boje b Franks	4	– (5) c Read b Harris			27
S. P. Jones b Franks	2	– c Read b Logan			0
L-b 14, w 8, n-b 14	36	B 1, l-b 11, w 2, n-b 2			16

1/91 (2) 2/114 (3) 3/124 (4) 4/131 (1)   213   1/19 (1) 2/22 (2) 3/63 (3)   211
5/149 (6) 6/149 (5) 7/190 (8)   4/76 (4) 5/100 (5) 6/196 (7)
8/191 (9) 9/205 (10) 10/213 (11)   7/196 (6) 8/198 (9)
                                   9/205 (10) 10/211 (11)

Bonus points – Glamorgan 1, Nottinghamshire 3.

Bowling: *First Innings*—Smith 9–2–28–0; Harris 20.4–4–70–4; Franks 15.5–3–46–4; Logan 12–1–55–2. *Second Innings*—Harris 22–3–65–1; Franks 19–3–51–5; Smith 14–3–50–1; Logan 16.1–6–29–3; Boje 1–0–4–0.

Nottinghamshire

G. E. Welton c Wallace b Jones	115	– (2) c Wallace b Kasprowicz	28
*J. E. R. Gallian lbw b Kasprowicz	5	– (1) not out	55
P. Johnson c Dale b Jones	9	– c Hemp b Kasprowicz	0
U. Afzaal b Kasprowicz	88	– c Dale b Jones	11
N. Boje b Kasprowicz	0	– not out	2
K. P. Pietersen b Kasprowicz	31		
†C. M. W. Read c Cherry b Jones	24		
P. J. Franks b Kasprowicz	1		
R. J. Logan c Wallace b S. D. Thomas	7		
G. J. Smith not out	14		
A. J. Harris lbw b Jones	0		
B 10, l-b 10, n-b 14	34	L-b 2, w 2	4
	328	**(3 wkts)**	**100**

1/7 (2) 2/34 (3) 3/235 (4) 4/235 (5)   328   1/73 (2) 2/79 (3)   (3 wkts) 100
5/255 (1) 6/285 (6) 7/289 (8)   3/94 (4)
8/302 (9) 9/328 (7) 10/328 (11)

Bonus points – Nottinghamshire 3, Glamorgan 3.

Bowling: *First Innings*—Kasprowicz 33–5–104–5; S. D. Thomas 20–2–67–1; Jones 25.4–5–72–4; Croft 8–1–27–0; Dale 14–3–38–0. *Second Innings*—Kasprowicz 8.4–0–34–2; Jones 8–1–27–1; S. D. Thomas 6–0–31–0; Croft 2–0–6–0.

Umpires: N. L. Bainton and G. Sharp.

At Derby, July 19, 20, 21, 22. NOTTINGHAMSHIRE beat DERBYSHIRE by one wicket.

At Chester-le-Street, July 24, 25, 26. NOTTINGHAMSHIRE beat DURHAM by eight wickets.

At Kidderminster, August 8, 9, 10, 11. NOTTINGHAMSHIRE drew with WORCESTERSHIRE.

NOTTINGHAMSHIRE v MIDDLESEX

At Nottingham, August 14, 15, 16. Nottinghamshire won by an innings and 73 runs. Nottinghamshire 20 pts, Middlesex 3 pts. Toss: Nottinghamshire.

Middlesex arrived unbeaten but went home humbled. The match ended 20 overs into the third day after outstanding performances from Pietersen and MacGill ensured a comprehensive thrashing. On a tricky wicket, Pietersen seemed to be playing a different game from the others as he thumped towards a chanceless, career-best 254 at a run a ball. Striking with awesome power, he batted for 405 minutes, faced 252 balls, and hit most of his 31 fours and three sixes while several fielders fruitlessly guarded the rope. Bicknell was less fluent, but dug in for a gutsy 108 from 309 balls and helped Pietersen add 316 for the fourth wicket. From then on the story was of Middlesex's utter bamboozlement against MacGill's attacking leg-spin. He ripped out six wickets in their first innings and, despite another century opening stand between Strauss and Koenig, Middlesex proved nearly as clueless after following on, a massive 332 behind. MacGill found sharp turn, showed off his variations and earned match figures of 14 for 165, a career high and the best of the English season. The win was Nottinghamshire's fourth in six Championship games since Mick Newell replaced Clive Rice as coach.

Close of play: First day, Nottinghamshire 416-6 (Pietersen 232, Logan 6); Second day, Middlesex 180-3 (Strauss 101, Shah 18).

Nottinghamshire

G. E. Welton lbw b Keegan	24	S. C. G. MacGill run out	1
*J. E. R. Gallian b Laraman	5	G. J. Smith b Keegan	18
D. J. Bicknell b Weekes	108	A. J. Harris c Strauss b Laraman	3
U. Afzaal c Nash b Laraman	4	B 1, l-b 12, n-b 4	17
K. P. Pietersen not out	254		
†C. M. W. Read b Cook	12	1/31 (2) 2/35 (1) 3/40 (4) 4/356 (3)	470
P. Johnson b Keegan	9	5/382 (6) 6/395 (7) 7/430 (8)	
R. J. Logan c Koenig b Keegan	15	8/431 (9) 9/459 (10) 10/470 (11)	

Bonus points – Nottinghamshire 5, Middlesex 3.

Bowling: Laraman 22.4–0–123–3; Keegan 29–4–113–4; Cook 16–2–76–1; Tufnell 24–2–69–0; Weekes 23–5–49–1; Hutton 4–0–27–0.

Middlesex

*A. J. Strauss c Read b Harris	15	– b MacGill	110
S. G. Koenig b MacGill	30	– c Smith b Logan	52
B. L. Hutton c MacGill b Smith	2	– lbw b MacGill	0
O. A. Shah lbw b Harris	7	– (5) c Read b MacGill	25
E. C. Joyce c Read b MacGill	3	– (7) not out	41
P. N. Weekes b MacGill	21	– (8) b Welton b MacGill	8
†D. C. Nash not out	40	– (6) c Welton b Harris	5
A. W. Laraman lbw b MacGill	4	– (9) b MacGill	5
S. J. Cook c Welton b Smith	0	– (10) lbw b MacGill	0
C. B. Keegan c Read b Smith	0	– (4) c Gallian b MacGill	0
P. C. R. Tufnell lbw b MacGill	0	– c Bicknell b MacGill	0
B 6, l-b 4, w 4, n-b 2	16	B 3, l-b 6, w 2, n-b 2	13

1/17 (1) 2/32 (3) 3/41 (4) 4/56 (5)	138	1/127 (2) 2/136 (3) 3/136 (4)	259
5/69 (2) 6/130 (6) 7/136 (8)		4/192 (5) 5/197 (6) 6/203 (1)	
8/137 (9) 9/138 (10) 10/138 (11)		7/235 (8) 8/249 (9)	
		9/249 (10) 10/259 (11)	

Bonus points – Nottinghamshire 3.

Bowling: *First Innings*—Smith 12–1–30–2; Harris 6–0–30–2; Logan 8–3–14–0; MacGill 12.4–0–54–6. *Second Innings*—Harris 13–4–42–1; Logan 13–3–47–1; MacGill 24.4–2–111–8; Smith 5–2–20–0; Afzaal 7–1–25–0; Pietersen 5–1–5–0.

Umpires: J. H. Evans and T. E. Jesty.

NOTTINGHAMSHIRE v GLOUCESTERSHIRE

At Nottingham, August 21, 22, 23. Nottinghamshire won by an innings and 84 runs. Nottinghamshire 20 pts, Gloucestershire 2.25 pts. Toss: Gloucestershire.

Nottinghamshire grabbed another win, their fifth in six starts, with four sessions to spare and continued their surge for promotion. Alleyne chose to bat on a fast, even pitch but his batsmen played some reckless shots, and Gloucestershire tumbled to 51 for six. Franks was the main destroyer, with an exemplary, accurate spell of seam bowling, and only half-centuries from Russell and Fisher averted complete embarrassment. By contrast, Nottinghamshire cruised to maximum batting points. Afzaal, Johnson and Read made jaunty fifties, but Pietersen was unstoppable. His muscular, straight-batted century was his fourth in succession in all cricket and lifted his run-tally to a stratospheric 639 in ten days. Nottinghamshire's 303-run first-innings lead proved more than enough. MacGill was the star as Gloucestershire failed once more: his leg-spin foxed five batsmen as he became the first Nottinghamshire player to begin his career with five-wicket hauls in each of his first three Championship games.

Close of play: First day, Nottinghamshire 165-3 (Afzaal 38, Pietersen 60); Second day, Gloucestershire 91-5 (Windows 18, Russell 3).

Gloucestershire

C. M. Spearman c Welton b Smith	0	– c Pietersen b Logan	20
J. A. Pearson c Pietersen b Franks	17	– c Pietersen b MacGill	9
C. G. Taylor lbw b Franks	7	– c Read b Logan	15
M. G. N. Windows c Read b Franks	5	– lbw b Smith	40
*M. W. Alleyne c Welton b Logan	0	– lbw b Smith	15
A. P. R. Gidman c Read b Franks	10	– (8) b MacGill	22
†R. C. Russell c Afzaal b Logan	54	– not out	45
I. D. Fisher c Johnson b MacGill	57	– (9) b MacGill	1
R. J. Sillence b MacGill	0	– (10) st Read b MacGill	33
J. M. M. Averis lbw b MacGill	3	– (6) c Read b Smith	0
J. Lewis not out	5	– lbw b MacGill	0
L-b 7, w 6, n-b 2	15	B 7, l-b 12	19

1/0 (1) 2/26 (3) 3/28 (5) 4/38 (4)   173   1/25 (1) 2/55 (2) 3/55 (3)   219
5/51 (6) 6/51 (2) 7/139 (8)   4/81 (5) 5/81 (6) 6/120 (4)
8/151 (9) 9/163 (10) 10/173 (7)   7/155 (8) 8/167 (9)
    9/219 (10) 10/219 (11)

Bonus points – Nottinghamshire 3.

In the first innings Pearson, when 17, retired hurt at 28-2 and resumed at 51-5.

Bowling: *First Innings*—Smith 18–8–31–1; Logan 20.5–3–58–2; Franks 14–4–33–4; MacGill 11–2–44–3. *Second Innings*—Smith 16–4–45–3; Logan 22–11–63–2; MacGill 29–9–92–5.

Nottinghamshire

*J. E. R. Gallian c Fisher b Gidman	34	S. C. G. MacGill c Sillence b Lewis	5
G. E. Welton c Taylor b Lewis	9	R. J. Logan not out	8
D. J. Bicknell c Pearson b Averis	9	G. J. Smith b Fisher	1
U. Afzaal c Taylor b Alleyne	61	B 5, l-b 16, w 13, n-b 10	44
K. P. Pietersen lbw b Alleyne	116		
P. Johnson c Russell b Averis	83	1/17 (2) 2/32 (3) 3/76 (1) 4/230 (4)	476
†C. M. W. Read lbw b Lewis	80	5/271 (5) 6/412 (6) 7/460 (7)	
P. J. Franks c Russell b Fisher	26	8/462 (8) 9/474 (9) 10/476 (11)	

Bonus points – Nottinghamshire 5, Gloucestershire 3.

Bowling: Lewis 32–4–100–3; Averis 20–3–102–2; Sillence 17–0–85–0; Gidman 5–1–42–1; Alleyne 16–2–60–2; Fisher 15.4–2–66–2.

Umpires: I. J. Gould and V. A. Holder.

At Colwyn Bay, August 27, 28, 29, 30. NOTTINGHAMSHIRE drew with GLAMORGAN.

NOTTINGHAMSHIRE v DURHAM

At Nottingham, September 6, 7, 8, 9. Drawn. Nottinghamshire 12 pts, Durham 5.75 pts. Toss: Nottinghamshire.

Nottinghamshire's charge for promotion was stalled as bad weather denied them near-certain victory over Durham. After Gallian chose to bat, Harmison and Hunter wasted helpful conditions by bowling too short during the 20 overs possible on the first day. Nottinghamshire put their foot on the gas on the second in a bid to force a win, and Welton played superbly until he was run out after a bad call by Afzaal – who made amends by completing a century. Gallian declared as soon as Nottinghamshire had banked maximum batting points, leaving five sessions to dismiss Durham twice. But for the weather it would have been ample. Gough perished first ball, and Harris and Franks found bounce and swing to rip through flimsy batting. After following on 268 behind, Durham lost five more wickets only for bad light to curtail the third day, and rain to wash out the last. A win would have taken Nottinghamshire second; instead, they remained fourth.

Close of play: First day, Nottinghamshire 56-1 (Welton 18, Bicknell 26); Second day, Nottinghamshire 306-3 (Afzaal 91, Shafayat 46); Third day, Durham 153-5 (Symington 12, A. Pratt 0).

Nottinghamshire

G. E. Welton run out	77		P. J. Franks not out	15
*J. E. R. Gallian lbw b Hunter	7			
D. J. Bicknell lbw b Symington	54		B 9, l-b 21, w 8, n-b 8	46
U. Afzaal c Hunter b Harmison	103			
B. M. Shafayat lbw b Hunter	48		1/12 (2) 2/121 (3)	(6 wkts dec.) 400
P. Johnson c Symington b Killeen	23		3/193 (1) 4/318 (5)	
†C. M. W. Read not out	27		5/324 (4) 6/369 (6)	

S. C. G. MacGill, G. J. Smith and A. J. Harris did not bat.

Bonus points – Nottinghamshire 5, Durham 2.

Bowling: Harmison 29–9–79–1; Hunter 24–7–83–2; Killeen 18.1–5–67–1; Symington 15–2–72–1; Phillips 12–3–39–0; Muchall 2–1–8–0; Gough 5–0–22–0.

Durham

M. A. Gough lbw b Smith	0	– c and b MacGill	40
G. J. Pratt lbw b Harris	9	– b MacGill	65
B. J. Hodge c Shafayat b Franks	48	– c MacGill b Franks	1
G. J. Muchall c Read b Harris	0	– b Franks	12
A. M. Thorpe c Gallian b Harris	8	– lbw b MacGill	12
M. J. Symington lbw b MacGill	16	– not out	12
†A. Pratt b Franks	5	– not out	0
I. D. Hunter c Bicknell b Franks	7		
*N. C. Phillips not out	20		
N. Killeen b MacGill	5		
S. J. Harmison b Harris	0		
B 4, l-b 4, w 6	14	B 1, l-b 6, w 2, n-b 2	11

1/0 (1) 2/34 (2) 3/34 (4) 4/54 (5)		132
5/81 (3) 6/95 (7) 7/95 (6)		
8/105 (9) 9/131 (10) 10/132 (11)		

1/79 (1) 2/80 (3)		(5 wkts) 153
3/110 (4) 4/134 (2)		
5/153 (5)		

Bonus points – Nottinghamshire 3.

Bowling: *First Innings*—Smith 12–3–40–1; Harris 13.3–5–40–4; Franks 10–3–30–3; MacGill 11–6–14–2. *Second Innings*—Smith 6–0–39–0; Harris 4–1–25–0; MacGill 10–2–52–3; Franks 3–1–15–2; Afzaal 5–0–15–0.

Umpires: B. Dudleston and K. E. Palmer.

NOTTINGHAMSHIRE v WORCESTERSHIRE

At Nottingham, September 11, 12, 13, 14. Nottinghamshire won by 114 runs. Nottinghamshire 20 pts, Worcestershire 7 pts. Toss: Nottinghamshire.

This was a crunch match in the fight for promotion, as Worcestershire began in third place with a paper-thin advantage over Nottinghamshire. After choosing to bat, Nottinghamshire achieved their first target – full batting points – thanks to a precise hundred from Bicknell and some expert farming of the strike by Franks. Worcestershire soon slumped to 120 for six, before a heroic stand between Leatherdale and Rhodes dragged them back into contention. Feasting on some erratic bowling by MacGill, both scored hundreds in a partnership of 256, a county seventh-wicket record. Rhodes made a career-best 124 despite a thigh strain which forced him to use a runner. But Harris quickly shot out the tail, and the 18-year-old Shafayat then shored up a rickety Nottinghamshire reply. Knowing his team's season could hang on his efforts, he drove and whipped his way to a maiden first-class hundred and played with immense maturity. Worcestershire were left to chase a tricky 249 but managed only 134, as Hick and Solanki fell early on the final morning and the tail capitulated. Harris ended the match with ten wickets. Worcestershire would come to rue seven vital runs that got away here: Nottinghamshire's first innings scraped past 400 to earn an extra bonus point, while Worcestershire, all out for 397, just failed. In the final table, Worcestershire were 1.75 points behind Nottinghamshire – and missed promotion because of it.

Close of play: First day, Nottinghamshire 344-7 (Franks 15, MacGill 0); Second day, Worcestershire 362-6 (Leatherdale 110, Rhodes 122); Third day, Worcestershire 40-4 (Hick 24, Solanki 0).

Nottinghamshire

*J. E. R. Gallian lbw b Batty	62	– (2) c sub b Sheriyar	4
G. E. Welton c Rhodes b Mason	16	– (1) c sub b Mason	38
D. J. Bicknell lbw b Sheriyar	112	– c sub b Sheriyar	2
U. Afzaal c Rhodes b Mason	4	– c sub b Mason	2
B. M. Shafayat c Singh b Ali	31	– c Batty b Mason	104
P. Johnson c Leatherdale b Batty	36	– c Smith b Batty	13
†C. M. W. Read lbw b Batty	50	– c Singh b Sheriyar	4
P. J. Franks not out	57	– c and b Batty	21
S. C. G. MacGill c Hick b Ali	9	– run out	2
G. J. Smith c Rhodes b Ali	0	– c Singh b Mason	35
A. J. Harris c and b Ali	8	– not out	2
B 2, l-b 11, n-b 6	19	B 5, l-b 3, w 2, n-b 4	14
	404		**241**

1/42 (2) 2/144 (1) 3/151 (4) 4/205 (5)
5/256 (6) 6/309 (3) 7/340 (7)
8/388 (9) 9/390 (10) 10/404 (11)

1/6 (2) 2/10 (3) 3/15 (4)
4/100 (1) 5/131 (6) 6/140 (7)
7/179 (8) 8/185 (9)
9/233 (5) 10/241 (10)

Bonus points – Nottinghamshire 5, Worcestershire 3.

Bowling: *First Innings*—Mason 32–6–94–2; Sheriyar 28–7–79–1; Ali 28.4–7–117–4; Batty 28–8–94–3; Solanki 2–0–7–0. *Second Innings*—Mason 17.3–5–37–4; Sheriyar 20–4–70–3; Ali 15–1–65–0; Batty 22–6–53–2; Leatherdale 2–1–8–0.

Worcestershire

S. D. Peters c and b Harris	8	– c Gallian b Harris	1
A. Singh c Read b Franks	44	– b Smith	4
*G. A. Hick c Welton b Harris	25	– c Read b Harris	39
B. F. Smith c Afzaal b Franks	14	– c Welton b MacGill	8
V. S. Solanki c Read b MacGill	9	– (6) c Gallian b Smith	8
D. A. Leatherdale b Smith	120	– (7) not out	30
G. J. Batty b Franks	3	– (5) lbw b MacGill	0
†S. J. Rhodes b Harris	124	– c Bicknell b Harris	15
Kabir Ali c Read b Harris	9	– c Smith b Harris	4
M. S. Mason not out	8	– b Harris	0
A. Sheriyar c Shafayat b Harris	4	– c Afzaal b MacGill	16
L-b 15, w 6, n-b 8	29	L-b 7, w 2	9
	397		**134**

1/15 (1) 2/62 (3) 3/90 (4) 4/109 (2)
5/113 (5) 6/120 (7) 7/376 (6)
8/376 (8) 9/393 (9) 10/397 (11)

1/3 (1) 2/7 (2) 3/35 (4) 4/35 (5)
5/59 (6) 6/63 (3) 7/83 (8)
8/91 (9) 9/91 (10) 10/134 (11)

Bonus points – Worcestershire 4, Nottinghamshire 3.

Bowling: *First Innings*—Smith 23–4–65–1; Harris 26.5–4–115–5; Franks 19–3–76–3; MacGill 30–2–126–1. *Second Innings*—Smith 9–1–21–2; Harris 15–2–56–5; MacGill 6–2–29–3; Franks 7–1–21–0.

Umpires: I. J. Gould and J. W. Lloyds.

At Chelmsford, September 18, 19, 20, 21. NOTTINGHAMSHIRE lost to ESSEX by seven wickets

SOMERSET
A SORRY STORY

Ch'ship 8th in Division 1 – relegated
C&G finalists
B&H group stage
NUL 7th in Division 1 – relegated

Player of the season: Ian Blackwell

Explanations do not come easily for Somerset's embarrassing decline. By the end of the season they had been relegated in both the Championship and the Norwich Union League. Their chief executive, Peter Anderson, was sufficiently mystified by the team's miserable form to send a letter of apology to each member. "Too many of our performances," he wrote, "seemed to lack enthusiasm, urgency, and the requisite application expected of professional players." He said some members might feel puzzled or even resentful that such a successful team in 2001 should underperform so badly. In uncompromising tones, he added that every coach and player within the club was being interviewed. The message was simple: "You got us down, now you get us up." The players were left smarting by this very public rebuke.

The previous season had been the best in Somerset's history. They finished second in the Championship, higher than ever before. But for a reason that was never quite discernible they completely lost backbone and fibre during 2002. Some of the batting was inept and devoid of technical efficiency; the last two Championship matches were lost in two days. In Victorian and Edwardian days, Somerset were hardly renowned for their fielding, and far too many catches were put down again this undulating season. What had happened, the fans wondered, to the collective verve that had characterised their approach 12 months earlier? It is true that they missed Marcus Trescothick and Andy Caddick, but so they had the year before. Certainly injuries among the seamers seriously stretched their resources. The Taunton pitch, as lovingly and expertly tended as ever, led to one prevalent theory that the batsmen, spoilt by the luxuries of this amiable track, were lost when confronted with less friendly squares elsewhere.

The supporters, among the most loyal in the country, were beginning to get restive long before autumn. Richard Parsons, the county's long-standing chairman, retired, while Jamie Cox stipulated that when he returned from Tasmania for another season, it would not be as captain. In that role he had been conscientious and accessible, rejecting excuses for his team's short-comings – and indeed at times his own. He scored a single hundred in 2002, a fine one against Leicestershire in May, but was a shadow of the attractive batsman who first arrived at Taunton. Like a disproportionate number of his players, he was affected by injury – a broken thumb in his case – and he struggled for consistency and the kind of buoyant leadership that was needed. The new captain will be Michael Burns, again no extrovert, but a dedicated, down-to-earth cricketer who hopes to lead by example from high in the order. Somerset confirmed the signing of the West Indian fast bowler Nixon McLean, as well as the seamer Aaron Laraman from Middlesex. James Bryant, an ECB-qualified South African from Eastern Province, arrives to strengthen the top-order batting.

Burns alone passed 1,000 runs, and only just. Matthew Wood was a mere 29 short and his sustained promise was one of the few highlights. Another was Matthew Bulbeck, the gifted left-arm swing bowler who narrowly missed out on an Academy place. His control was apt to vary but at his best he was well worth his 58 wickets. Ian Blackwell's sturdy forearms remained very much to the liking of the home fans. Here, by some distance, was Somerset's most exciting player: Taunton's short boundaries seemed even more inviting whenever he was at the crease. England noticed him and he battered 82 off 68 balls in his second one-day international, against India in Sri Lanka. This left members holding their breath and fearing that he too might be lost to the lure of central contracts. Rob Turner continued to keep well, though Keith Parsons, with a modest record, lost his place at one stage. His strength, however, was in the one-day matches; his Championship form still needs more refining, but he is essentially an orthodox batsman. The most correct and experienced remains Bowler, even if his aggregate was disappointing at under 800. Peter Trego had a forgettable season apart from hitting 140 in a memorable run-chase against West Indies A when Somerset scored 453, the highest to tie a first-class match. Trego later moved to Kent.

Too frequently, the limited-overs game appeared an alien one for Somerset, and it took them until August to discover how to start winning again. There was, of course, their progress in the C&G. That they reached the Lord's final was directly attributable to Kent's aberration in the semi-final, a wondrous match at Taunton, full of handsome cricket. Somerset retrieved the initiative in the dying overs with an ebullience and opportunistic style that will live with the timeless thrills and optical illusions in the history of West Country cricket.

On they went to Lord's, to be beaten by Yorkshire, and especially by Matthew Elliott who was standing in for Darren Lehmann. It was a fine match, watched by virtually a full house. Somerset never had quite enough runs, but there wasn't so much between them, and success would have done much to obscure so many of the other overall failings. The turning point was the wonderful one-handed catch by Michael Vaughan that accounted for Trescothick, who had taken on Matthew Hoggard. He was bravely belting the ball in all directions with great aplomb, unmindful of his bandaged left thumb and intent on making up for lost time after his Somerset absences. He looked as though he was going to win the trophy on his own. Alas, there were too few such images of grandeur to savour. **David Foot**

SOMERSET 2002

Back row: A. V. Suppiah, P. D. Trego, S. R. G. Francis, M. P. L. Bulbeck, I. D. Blackwell, C. M. Gazzard. *Middle row:* K. P. Dutch, P. C. L. Holloway, J. P. Tucker, M. J. Wood, T. Webley, K. A. Parsons. *Front row:* R. J. Turner, G. D. Rose, P. S. Jones, M. Burns, M. E. Trescothick, R. L. Johnson. *Insets:* J. Cox (*captain*), A. R. Caddick, P. D. Bowler.

SOMERSET RESULTS

All first-class matches – Played 17: Won 1, Lost 7, Drawn 8, Tied 1.
County Championship matches – Played 16: Won 1, Lost 7, Drawn 8.

COUNTY CHAMPIONSHIP AVERAGES: BATTING AND FIELDING

Cap		M	I	NO	R	HS	100s	50s	Avge	Ct/St
1999	M. E. Trescothick†‡	2	4	0	153	134	1	0	38.25	0
2001	I. D. Blackwell	14	23	0	879	114	3	3	38.21	4
1999	M. Burns	16	30	2	1,047	99	0	9	37.39	14
	M. J. Wood	14	26	0	908	196	3	4	34.92	5
1995	P. D. Bowler	14	25	2	766	94	0	7	33.30	22
1999	J. Cox§	13	25	2	724	176	1	3	31.47	6
1997	P. C. L. Holloway	6	11	0	336	77	0	2	30.54	4
1994	R. J. Turner	16	27	4	691	83*	0	4	30.04	50/1
1999	K. A. Parsons†	14	24	2	561	68	0	4	25.50	15
2001	R. L. Johnson	9	17	4	290	61	0	1	22.30	2
	P. D. Trego†	3	6	0	118	47	0	0	19.66	2
2001	K. P. Dutch	15	25	3	414	74	0	2	18.81	20
2002	M. P. L. Bulbeck†	15	25	6	344	53*	0	1	18.10	1
2001	P. S. Jones	7	8	3	76	37*	0	0	15.20	0
	S. R. G. Francis	10	16	8	67	17	0	0	8.37	0
1992	A. R. Caddick‡	5	8	0	53	16	0	0	6.62	2

Also batted: G. D. Rose (cap 1988) (2 matches) 20, 24 (1 ct); A. V. Suppiah (1 match) 0, 21.

† *Born in Somerset.*   ‡ *ECB contract.*   § *Overseas player.*

BOWLING

	O	M	R	W	BB	5W/i	Avge
R. L. Johnson	307.1	66	914	43	7-43	2	21.25
A. R. Caddick	247.2	53	773	34	6-84	4	22.73
S. R. G. Francis	222.3	26	947	28	5-73	1	33.82
M. P. L. Bulbeck	504	86	1,859	53	6-93	1	35.07
I. D. Blackwell	312.5	83	830	22	5-49	1	37.72
M. Burns	101.4	14	444	11	3-54	0	40.36
K. A. Parsons	197.3	29	747	17	3-44	0	43.94
P. S. Jones	239.2	43	845	19	6-110	1	44.47
K. P. Dutch	231.2	52	694	11	2-42	0	63.09

Also bowled: P. D. Bowler 7–1–23–1; G. D. Rose 24–10–64–0; P. D. Trego 42–3–218–5.

COUNTY RECORDS

Highest score for:	322	I. V. A. Richards v Warwickshire at Taunton	1985
Highest score against:	424	A. C. MacLaren (Lancashire) at Taunton	1895
Best bowling for:	10-49	E. J. Tyler v Surrey at Taunton	1895
Best bowling against:	10-35	A. Drake (Yorkshire) at Weston-super-Mare	1914
Highest total for:	675-9 dec.	v Hampshire at Bath	1924
Highest total against:	811	by Surrey at The Oval	1899
Lowest total for:	25	v Gloucestershire at Bristol	1947
Lowest total against:	22	by Gloucestershire at Bristol	1920

COUNTY OFFICERS

Captain 2002 – J. Cox; 2003 – M. Burns • **First-team coach** K. J. Shine
President M. F. Hill • **Chairman** 2002 – M. F. Hill; 2003 – C. G. Clarke
Chief executive P. W. Anderson • **Chairman, cricket committee** V. J. Marks
Head groundsman P. Frost • **Scorer** G. A. Stickley

At Millfield School, April 13, 14, 15 (not first-class). **Somerset won by 221 runs.** Toss: Cardiff UCCE. **Somerset 389 for nine dec.** (M. J. Wood 98, K. A. Parsons 81, K. P. Dutch 97; J. A. Tomlinson five for 104) **and 129 for eight dec.** (M. P. L. Bulbeck 60; N. J. K. Creed four for 61); **Cardiff UCCE 189** (E. Brown 62, J. A. Tomlinson 30 not out; M. P. L. Bulbeck three for 64, P. S. Jones three for 18, S. R. G. Francis three for 56) **and 108** (A. N. French 30; K. P. Dutch four for eight).

First-team debut: C. M. Gazzard (Somerset). County debut: S. R. G. Francis. Cardiff reduced Somerset to 47 for six in their second innings.

At Hove, April 24, 25, 26, 27. SOMERSET drew with SUSSEX.

SOMERSET v YORKSHIRE

At Taunton, May 8, 9, 10. Somerset won by seven wickets. Somerset 16 pts, Yorkshire 4 pts. Toss: Somerset.

Last season's runners-up beat the champions in a fascinating match. On a true wicket tinged with green, Trescothick chose to bowl first, Caddick showed his stamina and seaming skills, and Yorkshire were all out by mid-afternoon. Only Lumb played fluently, driving hard through the off side. In reply, Silverwood gave Yorkshire the best of starts by taking the first three wickets for one run, but Blackwell's boisterous blows brought a recovery. His 114 included four hooked fours and three sixes off two Hoggard overs. When they batted again, Yorkshire failed miserably to build on the work of Lumb and White, losing their last eight wickets for 94 in a collapse that ultimately cost them the match. A stylish and aggressive century from Trescothick made a potentially tricky chase look simple, and he and Bowler put on 167 to shut out Yorkshire. In one of his rare Somerset appearances, Caddick became the first player to be reprimanded under the ECB's new code of conduct after his fuming reaction to an unsuccessful lbw appeal against White.

Close of play: First day, Somerset 186-6 (Blackwell 104, Dutch 30); Second day, Yorkshire 280-9 (McGrath 48, Hoggard 2).

Yorkshire

C. White b Bulbeck	16	– c Turner b Francis	69
M. P. Vaughan c Dutch b Caddick	3	– c Bowler b Bulbeck	19
M. J. Lumb c Parsons b Caddick	66	– b Parsons	62
*D. S. Lehmann lbw b Caddick	12	– lbw b Blackwell	43
A. McGrath lbw b Francis	13	– not out	48
G. M. Fellows lbw b Bulbeck	13	– lbw b Caddick	9
†R. J. Blakey c Turner b Caddick	7	– c Cox b Parsons	4
R. K. J. Dawson c Burns b Parsons	23	– c Dutch b Caddick	3
C. E. W. Silverwood not out	44	– c Turner b Parsons	4
R. J. Sidebottom c Parsons b Francis	3	– c Turner b Francis	6
M. J. Hoggard c Bowler b Caddick	5	– c Parsons b Caddick	2
L-b 6, n-b 2	8	B 1, l-b 10	11

1/19 (2) 2/25 (1) 3/48 (4) 4/100 (5)   213   1/48 (2) 2/106 (1) 3/186 (4)   280
5/123 (6) 6/127 (3) 7/146 (7)   4/208 (3) 5/230 (6) 6/239 (7)
8/179 (8) 9/204 (10) 10/213 (11)   7/248 (8) 8/253 (9)
                                  9/275 (10) 10/280 (11)

Bonus points – Yorkshire 1, Somerset 3.

Bowling: *First Innings*—Caddick 23.3–5–72–5; Bulbeck 18–2–90–2; Francis 12–1–37–2; Parsons 3–0–8–1. *Second Innings*—Caddick 26.4–6–73–3; Bulbeck 18–1–71–1; Francis 10–2–44–2; Parsons 16–2–44–3; Dutch 9–1–27–0; Blackwell 6–2–10–1.

Somerset

J. Cox b Silverwood	4	– b Silverwood	17
*M. E. Trescothick c Lehmann b Silverwood	. . .	– c Silverwood b Dawson	134
M. Burns b Hoggard	32	– c Blakey b Hoggard	6
P. D. Bowler lbw b Silverwood	0	– not out	79
K. A. Parsons lbw b Fellows	6	– not out	13
I. D. Blackwell c Lehmann b Sidebottom	114		
†R. J. Turner c McGrath b Hoggard	0		
K. P. Dutch c and b Sidebottom	46		
M. P. L. Bulbeck lbw b Hoggard	1		
A. R. Caddick b Fellows b Silverwood	5		
S. R. G. Francis not out	13		
L-b 3, n-b 8	11	B 4, l-b 10	14

1/4 (2) 2/13 (1) 3/19 (4) 4/26 (5) 232 1/32 (1) 2/66 (3) (3 wkts) 263
5/75 (3) 6/75 (7) 7/206 (8) 3/233 (2)
8/207 (9) 9/217 (6) 10/232 (10)

Bonus points – Somerset 1, Yorkshire 3.

Bowling: *First Innings*—Hoggard 24–5–104–3; Silverwood 10.1–4–28–4; Fellows 5–0–25–1; Sidebottom 14–4–37–2; White 6–2–25–0; Dawson 2–1–10–0. *Second Innings*—Silverwood 12–0–42–1; Hoggard 14–3–51–1; Sidebottom 7–1–17–0; Dawson 16–4–64–1; Lehmann 2–0–6–0; White 4–1–25–0; Fellows 6–2–23–0; Vaughan 3.2–0–21–0.

Umpires: D. J. Constant and R. Palmer.

SOMERSET v LEICESTERSHIRE

At Taunton, May 15, 16, 17, 18. Drawn. Somerset 11 pts, Leicestershire 8 pts. Toss: Somerset.

On a baking first day, Somerset breezed away, grateful for first use of an amiable track. Cox's hundred was full of confident attacking strokes: he batted for most of the day, surviving one chance in the seventies, and shared an assertive partnership with the promising Wood. They helped Somerset reach a formidable total, but their efforts with the bat counted for little: fewer than ten overs were possible on the third day, and none on the fourth. For Leicestershire, Sutcliffe hit a dozen crisp boundaries, but most of the batting that followed was too casual and too adventurous. Even against a Somerset attack weakened by the absence of Johnson, Jones and Caddick, Leicestershire's chances of avoiding the follow-on were not good when play was abandoned.

Close of play: First day, Somerset 390-3 (Bowler 45, Parsons 7); Second day, Leicestershire 241-7 (Stevens 40, Crowe 4); Third day, Leicestershire 288-8 (Crowe 8, Malcolm 4).

Somerset

*J. Cox b Maddy	176	M. P. L. Bulbeck st Burns b Crowe	8
M. J. Wood c Maddy b Crowe	79	S. R. G. Francis not out	0
M. Burns c Stevens b DeFreitas	52		
P. D. Bowler c Stevens b Malcolm	60	B 4, l-b 10, w 8, n-b 21	43
K. A. Parsons b Wells	7		
I. D. Blackwell c Burns b DeFreitas	6	1/184 (2) 2/298 (3) 3/376 (1)	565
†R. J. Turner c Wells b Whiley	44	4/390 (5) 5/401 (6) 6/427 (4)	
K. P. Dutch b Crowe	70	7/475 (7) 8/549 (8)	
G. D. Rose c Burns b Crowe	20	9/560 (9) 10/565 (10)	

Bonus points – Somerset 5, Leicestershire 2 (130 overs: 487-7).

Bowling: DeFreitas 30–4–101–2; Malcolm 26–3–101–1; Whiley 23–3–123–1; Wells 20–5–52–1; Maddy 22–4–88–1; Bevan 8–0–23–0; Crowe 17.2–3–63–4.

Leicestershire

T. R. Ward c Dutch b Bulbeck	7	C. D. Crowe not out	8
I. J. Sutcliffe lbw b Bulbeck	73	D. E. Malcolm not out	4
D. L. Maddy c Bowler b Dutch	22		
M. G. Bevan lbw b Bulbeck	9		
*V. J. Wells c Bowler b Francis	35	L-b 10, w 2, n-b 6	18
D. I. Stevens lbw b Burns	73		
†N. D. Burns b Francis	33	1/14 (1) 2/79 (3) 3/96 (4) (8 wkts) 288	
P. A. J. DeFreitas c Cox b Burns	6	4/137 (2) 5/168 (5)	
		6/222 (7) 7/229 (8) 8/284 (6)	

Bonus points – Leicestershire 2, Somerset 2.

M. J. A. Whiley did not bat.

Bowling: Bulbeck 22–4–69–3; Francis 13–0–102–2; Rose 13–5–42–0; Dutch 3–3–0–1; Blackwell 1–1–0–0; Burns 11–1–53–2; Parsons 2.2–0–12–0.

Umpires: N. G. Cowley and I. J. Gould.

At The Oval, May 24, 25, 26, 27. SOMERSET drew with SURREY.

SOMERSET v HAMPSHIRE

At Bath, June 12, 13, 14, 15. Drawn. Somerset 7 pts, Hampshire 9 pts. Toss: Somerset.

Miserable weather and negative publicity sank the annual Bath Festival in an aura of gloom. Shortly before the match, Cox said that playing at Bath was like an extra away game, and that it worked against the county. Yet, amid the rain and recurring bad light, Somerset came close to sneaking an unlikely win. In a bold move late on the third day, Cox declared 91 behind, a step which led to the umpires being loudly abused by the crowd, who mistakenly believed Somerset had come off for bad light. Cox's gamble very nearly paid off: helped by a variable pitch, Richard Johnson persuaded Kenway to mishook his first ball to fine leg, then had White caught behind. After ending the third day on three for four, which became 16 for six next morning, Hampshire progressed uneasily to 98. Johnson's seven for 43 was his best for the county. Somerset needed 190 at a little more than three an over, but in dodgy batting conditions, it proved too much.

Close of play: First day, Hampshire 149-3 (Kendall 70, Johnson 31); Second day, Somerset 79-5 (Blackwell 24, Turner 2); Third day, Hampshire 3-4 (Johnson 0, Pothas 0).

Hampshire

D. A. Kenway c Bowler b Johnson	4	– c Bulbeck b Johnson	0
W. S. Kendall c Burns b Bulbeck	88	– c Bowler b Bulbeck	1
G. W. White c Dutch b Francis	33	– c Turner b Johnson	2
*R. A. Smith b Francis	6	– (8) not out	41
N. C. Johnson c Bowler b Bulbeck	35	– (4) b Bulbeck	2
J. S. Laney c Turner b Bulbeck	0	– (5) lbw b Bulbeck	0
†N. Pothas c Turner b Burns	22	– (6) b Johnson	0
A. D. Mascarenhas c Burns b Johnson	28	– (7) c Cox b Johnson	31
S. D. Udal b Burns	12	– lbw b Johnson	3
C. T. Tremlett not out	9	– b Johnson	9
A. D. Mullally c Blackwell b Johnson	2	– lbw b Johnson	2
L-b 7, n-b 8	15	L-b 1, w 2, n-b 4	7
1/6 (1) 2/88 (3) 3/98 (4) 4/153 (5) 252		1/0 (1) 2/3 (3) 3/3 (2) 4/3 (5) 98	
5/163 (6) 6/178 (2) 7/213 (7)		5/4 (6) 6/16 (4) 7/44 (7)	
8/229 (9) 9/247 (8) 10/252 (11)		8/56 (9) 9/92 (10) 10/98 (11)	

Bonus points – Hampshire 3, Somerset 3.

Bowling: *First Innings*—Johnson 19.3–6–32–3; Bulbeck 19–2–68–3; Francis 16–2–69–2; Parsons 9–2–31–0; Dutch 4–1–16–0; Burns 9–2–29–2. *Second Innings*—Johnson 14.2–5–43–7; Bulbeck 11–2–31–3; Burns 3–1–6–0; Francis 4–0–12–0; Dutch 4–2–5–0.

Somerset

*J. Cox lbw b Mullally	8	– lbw b Mullally	27
M. J. Wood c Kenway b Mascarenhas	25	– c Kenway b Tremlett	0
M. Burns c White b Johnson	9	– c Pothas b Tremlett	3
P. D. Bowler lbw b Mullally	4	– b Johnson	48
K. A. Parsons c Pothas b Mullally	0	– (6) c Kenway b Tremlett	22
I. D. Blackwell c Udal b Mascarenhas	42	– (5) c Udal b Mullally	15
†R. J. Turner c Kenway b Mullally	33	– c Laney b Johnson	0
K. P. Dutch lbw b Johnson	24	– not out	15
R. L. Johnson b Johnson	9	– c Pothas b Johnson	20
M. P. L. Bulbeck not out	0	– not out	13
S. R. G. Francis not out	0		
L-b 3, n-b 4	7	B 3, l-b 7	10

1/14 (1) 2/38 (3) 3/43 (4)   (9 wkts dec.) 161   1/4 (2) 2/14 (3) 3/48 (1)   (8 wkts) 173
4/47 (5) 5/51 (6) 6/100 (6)   4/82 (5) 5/118 (6)
7/141 (8) 8/157 (9) 9/161 (7)   6/118 (4) 7/119 (7) 8/141 (9)

Bonus points – Hampshire 3.

Bowling: *First Innings*—Mullally 27–10–64–4; Tremlett 17–7–41–0; Mascarenhas 16–10–23–2; Johnson 11–5–22–3. *Second Innings*—Mullally 19–4–51–2; Tremlett 16–8–45–3; Mascarenhas 12–6–31–0; Johnson 11.5–5–36–3; Udal 2–2–0–0.

Umpires: D. J. Constant and G. Sharp.

At Taunton, June 21. SOMERSET beat SRI LANKANS by 63 runs (see Sri Lankan tour section).

At Birmingham, June 26, 27, 28, 29. SOMERSET lost to WARWICKSHIRE by 88 runs.

SOMERSET v SURREY

At Taunton, July 3, 4, 5, 6. Drawn. Somerset 11 pts, Surrey 12 pts. Toss: Somerset.

An astounding aggregate of 1,815 runs was the highest ever for a first-class match in England. Though the ball swung occasionally, the pitch was a traditional Taunton belter and the bat utterly dominated. After Surrey were put in, Ramprakash scored a typically neat and well-measured double-hundred, striking 28 fours in seven and a half hours from 339 balls, and Clarke impressed the watching chairman of selectors, David Graveney, with a maiden Championship century that glistened with promise. Replying to a mammoth 608 for six, Somerset fought back bravely. Led by Wood and Holloway, who shared an opening stand of 202, and bolstered by Burns, their stand-in captain, they cut the lead to 54. Runs continued to pour in Surrey's second innings, with a century from the wicket-keeper, Batty. Things were made even easier for them when Francis broke his finger in the field and Bulbeck limped off. Hollioake, in his first Championship game of the season, asked Somerset to score an unlikely 379 from 57 overs and, with the pitch still true, the match meandered to a draw. There was still time for Wood to give more evidence of his burgeoning talent as he hit his second hundred of the month and the fifth in all.

Close of play: First day, Surrey 448-5 (Ramprakash 199, Clarke 60); Second day, Somerset 304-3 (Burns 51, Parsons 13); Third day, Surrey 96-0 (Ward 31, Batty 63).

Surrey

I. J. Ward c Bowler b Francis	13	– c Turner b Bulbeck	75
†J. N. Batty lbw b Jones	0	– c Wood b Parsons	151
M. R. Ramprakash b Jones	218	– b Blackwell	53
N. Shahid lbw b Blackwell	51	– (6) not out	8
A. D. Brown c Turner b Francis	10		
*A. J. Hollioake c Parsons b Francis	87		
R. Clarke not out	153	– (5) c Burns b Parsons	22
I. D. K. Salisbury not out	46	– (4) c Turner b Parsons	2
L-b 10, w 12, n-b 8	30	B 1, l-b 6, w 2, n-b 4	13

1/0 (2) 2/32 (1) 3/162 (4) (6 wkts dec.) 608
4/179 (5) 5/317 (6) 6/527 (3)

1/153 (1) 2/258 (3) (5 wkts dec.) 324
3/261 (4) 4/309 (5)
5/324 (2)

Saqlain Mushtaq, J. Ormond and E. S. H. Giddins did not bat.

Bonus points – Surrey 5, Somerset 2 (130 overs: 596-6).

Bowling: *First Innings*—Bulbeck 28–4–141–0; Jones 33.1–6–157–2; Francis 25.5–2–104–3; Parsons 7–0–37–0; Blackwell 24.5–3–89–1; Dutch 12–1–70–0. *Second Innings*—Jones 17–4–59–0; Bulbeck 17.4–3–63–1; Dutch 9–3–35–0; Parsons 17.1–4–91–3; Blackwell 9–0–69–1.

Somerset

P. C. L. Holloway c Hollioake b Ormond	77	– c Shahid b Salisbury	33
M. J. Wood b Ormond	106	– st Batty b Saqlain Mushtaq	131
*M. Burns lbw b Clarke	99	– c Clarke b Saqlain Mushtaq	68
P. D. Bowler lbw b Giddins	19	– (8) run out	6
K. A. Parsons lbw b Clarke	47	– not out	33
I. D. Blackwell c sub b Clarke	34	– (4) st Batty b Saqlain Mushtaq	22
†R. J. Turner not out	56	– b Hollioake	5
K. P. Dutch c Salisbury b Ormond	2	– (6) c Clarke b Saqlain Mushtaq	6
M. P. L. Bulbeck c Batty b Saqlain Mushtaq	27	– not out	1
P. S. Jones c Batty b Salisbury	23		
S. R. G. Francis c sub b Saqlain Mushtaq	8		
B 11, l-b 8, w 9, n-b 28	56	B 4, l-b 8, w 6, n-b 6	24

1/202 (2) 2/217 (1) 3/261 (4) 4/378 (5) 554
5/401 (3) 6/440 (6) 7/443 (8)
8/506 (9) 9/537 (10) 10/554 (11)

1/75 (1) 2/216 (3) (7 wkts) 329
3/247 (4) 4/286 (2)
5/300 (6) 6/316 (7) 7/324 (8)

Bonus points – Somerset 5, Surrey 3 (130 overs: 537-9).

Bowling: *First Innings*—Giddins 21–5–83–1; Ormond 33–3–137–3; Clarke 20–2–104–3; Salisbury 22–4–85–1; Saqlain Mushtaq 35.2–8–110–2; Hollioake 3–0–16–0. *Second Innings*—Giddins 5–0–29–0; Ormond 13–1–65–0; Saqlain Mushtaq 23.4–3–111–4; Salisbury 11–0–79–1; Hollioake 4–0–33–1.

Umpires: I. J. Gould and A. G. T. Whitehead.

At Scarborough, July 10, 11, 12, 13. SOMERSET drew with YORKSHIRE.

SOMERSET v SUSSEX

At Taunton, July 19, 20, 21. Sussex won by an innings and one run. Sussex 20 pts, Somerset 4 pts. Toss: Somerset.

With some style and few false strokes, Martin-Jenkins paraded his merits as an all-rounder, and hit a first double-hundred. His crucial stand with Davis, whose century was also a first, produced 291 runs – an eighth-wicket record for Sussex. Together they saved their team from repeating the blunder Somerset had already made, when they recklessly failed to take advantage of a friendly strip. Although Bulbeck mocked his lowly status in the order with two straight sixes in an entertaining half-century, there were plenty of daft shots from his team-mates. They showed slightly more application second time round: Burns was out two short of a fighting hundred, and Blackwell muscled his way to three figures after surviving two chances. Again Bulbeck, this time with the last man, Jones, offered a beefy finale but it was not enough to make Sussex bat again. Lewry and the vivacious Taylor both took four wickets.

Close of play: First day, Sussex 164-2 (Cottey 52); Second day, Sussex 589-7 (Martin-Jenkins 171, Davis 91).

Somerset

*J. Cox c Prior b Taylor	27	– b Lewry	0
M. J. Wood c Ambrose b Taylor	31	– c sub b Lewry	13
M. Burns c Taylor b Innes	26	– c sub b Davis	98
P. D. Bowler c Yardy b Innes	0	– lbw b Lewry	20
K. A. Parsons b Lewry	17	– b Lewry	0
I. D. Blackwell b Innes	18	– c Ambrose b Taylor	114
†R. J. Turner lbw b Lewry	9	– lbw b Taylor	31
K. P. Dutch b Goodwin b Davis	30	– c and b Davis	2
P. D. Trego b Davis	26	– b Taylor	4
M. P. L. Bulbeck not out	53	– c Ambrose b Taylor	22
P. S. Jones c Ambrose b Lewry	6	– not out	37
L-b 5, w 8, n-b 14	27	B 5, l-b 13, w 6, n-b 8	32

1/51 (1) 2/82 (2) 3/94 (3) 4/94 (4)   270   1/0 (1) 2/23 (2) 3/63 (4)   373
5/116 (6) 6/138 (7) 7/153 (5)   4/63 (5) 5/191 (3) 6/276 (7)
8/206 (9) 9/207 (8) 10/270 (11)   7/299 (8) 8/305 (6)
                                    9/306 (9) 10/373 (10)

Bonus points – Somerset 2, Sussex 3.

Bowling: *First Innings*—Lewry 16.2–3–84–3; Martin-Jenkins 20–2–67–0; Taylor 20–8–56–2; Innes 4–0–28–3; Yardy 4–0–10–0; Davis 4–1–20–2. *Second Innings*—Lewry 22–1–112–4; Martin-Jenkins 14–3–43–0; Innes 13–4–44–0; Taylor 20.2–3–68–4; Davis 19–0–88–2.

Sussex

*R. R. Montgomerie c Bowler b Trego	25	B. V. Taylor c Turner b Jones	1
M. W. Goodwin c Turner b Burns	42	J. D. Lewry c Wood b Jones	0
P. A. Cottey c Trego b Parsons	120		
M. H. Yardy c Bowler b Blackwell	36	L-b 11, w 2, n-b 12	25
T. R. Ambrose c Bowler b Parsons	68		
R. S. C. Martin-Jenkins not out	205	1/60 (2) 2/94 (1) 3/287 (5)	644
†M. J. Prior st Turner b Parsons	8	4/288 (4) 5/308 (3) 6/330 (7)	
K. J. Innes c Turner b Trego	3	7/351 (8) 8/642 (9) 9/644 (10)	
M. J. G. Davis c Bowler b Jones	111	10/644 (11)	

Bonus points – Sussex 5, Somerset 2 (130 overs: 555-7).

Yardy, when 35, retired hurt at 164 and resumed at 287.

Bowling: Bulbeck 13–1–66–0; Jones 37.3–6–147–3; Burns 17–3–77–1; Parsons 19–2–67–3; Trego 17–1–110–2; Blackwell 33–9–124–1; Dutch 15–1–42–0.

Umpires: J. H. Evans and M. J. Kitchen.

At Taunton, July 24, 25, 26. SOMERSET tied with WEST INDIES A (see West Indies A tour section).

At Canterbury, August 7, 8, 9, 10. SOMERSET lost to KENT by 153 runs.

At Southampton, August 14, 15, 16, 17. SOMERSET lost to HAMPSHIRE by four wickets.

SOMERSET v WARWICKSHIRE

At Taunton, August 21, 22, 23, 24. Drawn. Somerset 12 pts, Warwickshire 10 pts. Toss: Somerset.

Somerset stepped up their game, showed greater resolve, and came agonisingly close to victory. In the end they were frustrated by Warwickshire's last pair, Bond and Carter, who remained doggedly at the crease for the final 12 overs, though both were dropped during the tense conclusion to go with two other missed chances. Earlier, the match appeared to be swinging Somerset's way. Blackwell bludgeoned his third Championship hundred of the season and Burns made 95 before falling to a fine catch – by Knight, who would also just miss a century on the most benign of pitches. Warwickshire's reply came up 104 short as Francis bowled a good length to return five wickets for the first time. Bond's pace bowling was equally impressive when Somerset resumed, particularly a rapid 11-over spell of four for 29. But in the end, his batting proved just as vital, as Warwickshire crumbled chasing a mighty 499. The draw loosened Somerset's weak hold on the first division.

Close of play: First day, Somerset 403-9 (Bulbeck 26, Francis 8); Second day, Somerset 35-0 (Wood 7, Cox 22); Third day, Warwickshire 42-1 (Knight 24, Wagh 9).

Somerset

*J. Cox lbw b Brown	29	– (2) c Clifford b Carter	44
M. J. Wood lbw b Bond	0	– (1) b Bond	68
M. Burns c Knight b Wagg	95	– lbw b Bond	80
P. D. Bowler lbw b Brown	31	– lbw b Bond	12
K. A. Parsons c Clifford b Smith	25	– b Bond	0
I. D. Blackwell c Smith b Powell	110	– c Carter	81
†R. J. Turner c Knight b Powell	35	– lbw b Carter	37
K. P. Dutch b Wagg	0	– (9) c Clifford b Bond	1
M. P. L. Bulbeck c Clifford b Wagg	31	– (11) c Clifford b Wagg	9
R. L. Johnson b Wagg	2	– (8) c Smith b Carter	10
S. R. G. Francis not out	8	– (10) not out	4
B 4, l-b 1, w 2, n-b 17	24	B 22, l-b 20, w 2, n-b 4	48
	408		**394**

1/3 (2) 2/79 (1) 3/167 (4) 4/169 (3)   **408**   1/96 (2) 2/194 (1) 3/227 (3)   **394**
5/227 (5) 6/342 (6) 7/361 (7)   4/233 (5) 5/238 (4) 6/357 (7)
8/365 (8) 9/369 (10) 10/408 (9)   7/375 (8) 8/379 (9)
                                       9/385 (6) 10/394 (11)

Bonus points – Somerset 5, Warwickshire 3.

Bowling: *First Innings*—Bond 13–3–77–1; Carter 14–2–65–0; Brown 29–5–84–2; Wagg 17.2–5–62–4; Smith 20–5–73–1; Wagh 5–3–13–0; Powell 8–1–29–2. *Second Innings*—Bond 26–7–64–5; Wagg 16.3–1–72–1; Brown 20–1–84–0; Carter 11–0–46–4; Powell 23–1–86–0.

When Sri Lanka's coach, Dav Whatmore, said, "I've seen some positives but we haven't got what it takes to win abroad," only the first bit was debatable.
The Sri Lankans in England, page 480

Warwickshire

*M. J. Powell c Turner b Francis	26	– c Blackwell b Bulbeck	7
N. V. Knight lbw b Francis	98	– c Burns b Bulbeck	28
M. A. Wagh c Parsons b Francis	4	– c Burns b Johnson	11
I. R. Bell c Blackwell b Johnson	31	– c Dutch b Francis	77
D. P. Ostler lbw b Burns	23	– b Francis	55
D. R. Brown lbw b Bulbeck	24	– c Turner b Dutch	30
G. G. Wagg c Dutch b Francis	4	– c Parsons b Johnson	9
N. M. K. Smith c Dutch b Bulbeck	39	– lbw b Johnson	17
†J. I. Clifford b Bulbeck	4	– lbw b Johnson	4
S. E. Bond c Dutch b Francis	20	– not out	29
N. M. Carter not out	17	– not out	27
L-b 4, w 6, n-b 4	14	B 1, l-b 7, w 2, n-b 6	16

1/50 (1) 2/54 (3) 3/132 (4) 4/173 (5)   304   1/17 (1) 2/46 (2) 3/50 (3)   (9 wkts) 310
5/197 (2) 6/207 (7) 7/241 (6)   4/147 (5) 5/212 (6)
8/267 (9) 9/270 (8) 10/304 (10)   6/228 (4) 7/232 (7)
                                                                          8/247 (8) 9/268 (9)

Bonus points – Warwickshire 3, Somerset 3.

Bowling: *First Innings*—Johnson 20–3–61–1; Bulbeck 19.4–4–75–3; Francis 18.1–0–73–5; Burns 17.2–3–62–1; Parsons 7–0–29–0. *Second Innings*—Johnson 33–11–60–4; Bulbeck 23–7–60–2; Blackwell 9–5–14–0; Francis 25–7–87–2; Burns 7–0–24–0; Dutch 20–7–57–1.

Umpires: B. Dudleston and A. A. Jones.

At Blackpool, August 27, 28, 29. SOMERSET lost to LANCASHIRE by 336 runs.

SOMERSET v KENT

At Taunton, September 4, 5, 6, 7. Drawn. Somerset 11 pts, Kent 12 pts. Toss: Kent.

In a high-scoring match, the timing of Somerset's declaration was tricky: they eventually set Kent 377 in what would have been a minimum of 80 overs but for two rain interruptions. Francis took three wickets in an over to offer fleeting hope but it all ended in a predictable draw. After being put in, Somerset's early batsmen had set off in sturdy style. Wood, the 21-year-old Devonian, showed off a repertoire of fine shots to reach a career-best 196, before Masters undid him with an excellent one-handed catch at mid-wicket. But Khan's pace blasted Kent back into the match on the second morning and, in reply, Smith's capable century and contrasting innings by Nixon and Tredwell took them to 400. Fulton declared behind to try and inject some life into the match, but the pitch stayed good, and Cox and Bowler accumulated steadily. After the second declaration, Nixon and Ealham were content to drop anchor as the game – and Somerset's hopes of avoiding relegation – petered out.

Close of play: First day, Somerset 433-5 (Blackwell 30, Bulbeck 5); Second day, Kent 300-3 (Smith 115, Nixon 79); Third day, Somerset 265-4 (Bowler 77, Blackwell 13).

Somerset

*J. Cox lbw b Ealham	62	– (2) lbw b Patel 79
M. J. Wood c Masters b Khan	196	– (1) c Fulton b Tredwell 25
M. Burns c Tredwell b Saggers	6	– c and b Tredwell 21
P. D. Bowler c Jones b Masters	31	– c Ealham b Saggers 81
K. A. Parsons b Saggers	68	– c Nixon b Tredwell 36
I. D. Blackwell c Nixon b Khan	39	– lbw b Saggers 13
M. P. L. Bulbeck c Tredwell b Khan	5	– (7) c Fulton b Masters 10
†R. J. Turner not out	9	– (7) c Ealham b Masters 11
K. P. Dutch lbw b Saggers	1	– (8) not out 19
S. R. G. Francis b Khan	4	– c Fulton b Masters 6
P. S. Jones c Fulton b Saggers	4	
B 9, l-b 5, w 7, n-b 14	35	B 5, l-b 4, w 4, n-b 2 . . . 15

1/150 (1) 2/177 (3) 3/275 (4) 4/396 (2)	**460**	1/64 (1) 2/98 (3) (9 wkts dec.) 316
5/398 (5) 6/434 (7) 7/447 (6)		3/186 (2) 4/241 (5)
8/450 (9) 9/455 (10) 10/460 (11)		5/265 (6) 6/270 (4)
		7/282 (7) 8/300 (9) 9/316 (10)

Bonus points – Somerset 5, Kent 3.

Bowling: *First Innings*—Saggers 22.5–6–87–4; Khan 21–2–88–4; Masters 18–1–68–1; Ealham 20–4–62–1; Patel 16–0–84–0; Tredwell 11–1–42–0; Waugh 3–0–15–0. *Second Innings*—Saggers 16–3–64–2; Khan 7–2–17–0; Ealham 5–3–13–0; Tredwell 29–4–112–3; Patel 19–1–52–1; Masters 15.4–2–49–3.

Kent

*D. P. Fulton b Francis	35	– c Parsons b Francis 26
J. C. Tredwell c Turner b Blackwell	58	– b Francis 22
E. T. Smith c Turner b Bulbeck	154	– c Parsons b Francis 0
S. R. Waugh c Bowler b Jones	0	– c Turner b Jones 37
†P. A. Nixon c Burns b Bulbeck	88	– not out 51
M. A. Ealham not out	15	– not out 26
G. O. Jones lbw b Blackwell	28	
M. M. Patel not out	6	
L-b 3, w 3, n-b 10	16	B 4, l-b 5 9

1/52 (1) 2/135 (2) 3/138 (4)	(6 wkts dec.) 400	1/49 (1) 2/49 (3) (4 wkts) 171
4/334 (5) 5/355 (3) 6/393 (7)		3/50 (1) 4/116 (4)

A. Khan, D. D. Masters and M. J. Saggers did not bat.

Bonus points – Kent 5, Somerset 2.

Bowling: *First Innings*—Bulbeck 24–7–89–2; Francis 25–4–93–1; Jones 24–5–73–1; Parsons 8–2–24–0; Blackwell 19–1–70–2; Dutch 20–3–48–0. *Second Innings*—Francis 16–3–44–3; Bulbeck 15–5–40–0; Jones 10–1–37–1; Dutch 11–1–27–0; Blackwell 8–5–11–0; Bowler 1–0–3–0.

Umpires: G. Sharp and J. F. Steele.

At Leicester, September 12, 13. SOMERSET lost to LEICESTERSHIRE by an innings and 18 runs.

SOMERSET v LANCASHIRE

At Taunton, September 18, 19. Lancashire won by eight wickets. Lancashire 16 pts, Somerset pts. Toss: Lancashire. First-class debut: T. M. Rees. Championship debut: A. V. Suppiah.

Somerset lost in two days, just as they had in their previous fixture. It was a miserable conclusion o a season bereft of success or much sign of team buoyancy; not for the first time, the batting aved in and catches were dropped. Trego and Turner held their first innings together, but only

Holloway resisted in the second, as Martin and Schofield – with his best return for two years – each grabbed four wickets. Somerset's last five batsmen tumbled in 17 balls and, left to chase 123, Byas and Law belted the runs in only 17 overs. Lancashire were hardly favourites at the end of the first day, when they were tottering at 88 for six. But they were allowed to recover through a determined stand of 82 between Hogg and Martin. Like the perplexed home supporters, they must have been surprised at how easily they won. There were few consolations for Somerset, though Bulbeck turned in an impressive career-best six for 93, and Johnson produced his most challenging fast bowling of the summer. After 31 seasons as a Championship umpire, Ken Palmer stood in his last match, on his old home ground.

Close of play: First day, Lancashire 88-6 (Chapple 17, Hegg 0).

Somerset

*J. Cox b Martin	24	– (2) b Martin	5
M. J. Wood b Hogg	22	– (1) lbw b Chapple	12
M. Burns c Hegg b Martin	32	– c Rees b Schofield	19
P. C. L. Holloway c Swann b Hogg	0	– (5) c Hegg b Martin	45
A. V. Suppiah c Hegg b Martin	0	– (4) c Hegg b Schofield	25
P. D. Trego c Swann b Martin	47	– b Schofield	17
†R. J. Turner lbw b Schofield	45	– (8) not out	7
K. P. Dutch c Schofield b Anderson	23	– (7) lbw b Schofield	1
M. P. L. Bulbeck not out	18	– c Swann b Martin	0
R. L. Johnson c Swann b Anderson	2	– c Hegg b Martin	0
S. R. G. Francis run out	0	– c Hogg b Anderson	0
N-b 8	8	N-b 2	2

1/46 (1) 2/46 (2) 3/46 (4) 4/47 (5)   **221**   1/17 (2) 2/17 (1) 3/49 (4)   **129**
5/122 (3) 6/137 (6) 7/197 (8)   4/68 (3) 5/116 (6) 6/122 (5)
8/213 (7) 9/216 (10) 10/221 (11)   7/126 (10) 8/127 (9)
                                    9/127 (10) 10/129 (11)

Bonus points – Somerset 1, Lancashire 3.

Bowling: *First Innings*—Martin 19-3-52-4; Chapple 10-2-44-0; Hogg 13-4-52-2; Anderson 10-2-37-2; Schofield 9.4-1-36-1. *Second Innings*—Martin 14-7-29-4; Chapple 10-3-37-1; Hogg 5-1-14-0; Anderson 6.3-2-14-1; Schofield 11-3-35-4.

Lancashire

M. J. Chilton b Johnson	0	– b Johnson	0
A. J. Swann lbw b Bulbeck	4	– c Dutch b Bulbeck	1
D. Byas b Johnson	15	– not out	63
S. G. Law c Holloway b Bulbeck	18	– not out	57
T. M. Rees lbw b Bulbeck	16		
G. Chapple b Johnson	36		
C. P. Schofield c Trego b Bulbeck	16		
*†W. K. Hegg c Holloway b Johnson	24		
K. W. Hogg c Turner b Bulbeck	50		
P. J. Martin not out	34		
J. M. Anderson c Dutch b Bulbeck	3		
L-b 12	12	L-b 1, n-b 2	3

1/4 (2) 2/6 (1) 3/21 (3) 4/47 (4)   **228**   1/0 (1) 2/8 (2)   (2 wkts) **124**
5/54 (5) 6/84 (7) 7/125 (8)
8/138 (6) 9/220 (9) 10/228 (11)

Bonus points – Lancashire 1, Somerset 3.

Bowling: *First Innings*—Johnson 22-4-68-4; Bulbeck 24.3-3-93-6; Francis 3-0-32-0; Trego 6-0-23-0. *Second Innings*—Johnson 5-1-23-1; Bulbeck 6-0-48-1; Francis 3.3-1-32-0; Trego 2-0-20-0.

Umpires: J. W. Lloyds and K. E. Palmer.

SURREY
OUT OF GRIEF, TRIUMPH

Ch'ship	winners
C&G	semi-finalists
B&H	group stage
NUL	2nd in Division 2 – promoted

Player of the season: Ian Ward

The death of Ben Hollioake cast a dark cloud over the start of the season, yet the tragedy had a silver lining. The whole club was drawn closer together, and the collective sense of purpose and spirit played a big hand in Surrey's success – a third Championship title in four years, and promotion in the Norwich Union League. Almost as exciting was the rapid rise of two stars of the future: Rikki Clarke and Scott Newman both scored maiden hundreds, and Clarke looked useful with the ball too.

The early part of the season took place without the captain, Adam Hollioake, who remained with his family in Australia until June, by which time his wife Sherryn had given birth to their daughter, Bennaya. When he did return, he played with unfettered ease and confirmed his reputation as one of the most astute, innovative and flexible captains in the modern game. His philosophy was to entertain, and several sensational innings rekindled memories of the way he had burst on the scene in the early 1990s. His unbeaten 117 in the C&G at Hove was not unlike his brother Ben at his best: brutal but beautiful. "Adam played," wrote one observer, "like a man possessed." Nor were his fireworks confined to the short game. He thrashed 738 Championship runs off just 812 balls, scoring 66 per cent of his runs – 86 fours and 24 sixes – in boundaries. He crowned his season with a magnificent maiden double-hundred against Leicestershire in the final Championship innings, and his deceptive, varied medium-pacers were back to their best with two one-day five-fors. Throughout one of the most traumatic periods of his life, Hollioake displayed dignity, composure and professionalism, and these qualities filtered through to the whole squad.

The frequent absences of Saqlain Mushtaq on international duty were a blessing in disguise because his replacements, both fellow Pakistanis, proved astute signings. Azhar Mahmood claimed 20 wickets in three Championship matches, including a stunning eight-wicket haul to beat Lancashire. And near the end of the season, Mushtaq Ahmed's leg-spin was crucial in the victory at Leicester. Not even a cruel injury to Martin Bicknell – out for eight weeks from late June after stumbling in his delivery stride against Sussex and breaking his right wrist – could stop an exhilarating team from lifting the title. They headed the table after every round save one.

The C&G campaign was crammed with excitement, records and entertainment. It ended in the semi-final at Headingley, but only after an unprecedented decision to designate a fourth day for the tie. For reasons best known to themselves, Yorkshire switched pitches from the original choice, and cantered to victory. Before that, Surrey had produced some scintillating cricket, particularly against Glamorgan at The Oval, where both sides topped 400 – a world record – and Alistair Brown yet again blazed his way into the history books with a phenomenal 268 from just 160 balls. The performance in the B&H Cup was understandably muted, coming so soon after the loss of Ben Hollioake, who more than anyone had won it for Surrey in 1997 and 2001.

In the Championship, Newman's five innings revealed a powerful strokemaker of the highest calibre. He became only the third Surrey player to hit 99 in his first Championship innings, but needed just three more attempts to score a century, and a big one at that: 183 against Leicestershire at The Oval. Clarke followed a maiden first-class hundred on debut, against Cambridge, with a fine unbeaten 153 at Taunton, produced some promising spells of fast-medium bowling, and was rewarded with a winter at the ECB Academy. He was named Young Cricketer of the Year by the Cricket Writers' Club, and Surrey were delighted when he signed a new, five-year contract. The emergence of Tim Murtagh and Philip Sampson as promising seamers means that, when Bicknell eventually retires, there are others capable of assuming his onerous mantle.

Once again, Surrey's success could not be laid at the door of any one individual. This was a team effort, beginning with the stand-in captain, Mark Butcher, who enjoyed an unbeaten run of four Championship matches before handing over to Ian Ward. In the win at Canterbury, when Surrey successfully chased over 400, Ward hit a vital hundred. He made six others in the Championship – including four in as many innings at the end of the season – and was the country's highest first-class run-scorer with 1,759. Brown was often in explosive form, hammering five Championship centuries to go with his world-record 268, and passing 1,000 runs for the sixth time. Jonathan Batty, for so long an unsung hero, caught the eye with two thoroughly good centuries, the second coming when he was not just standing in for Alec Stewart but also deputising as opener for Butcher. Behind the stumps he was as tidy as his team-mates could have wished. Mark Ramprakash also passed 1,000 runs, with double-hundreds in successive matches, and Nadeem Shahid was a stand-in who would have been a linchpin at many counties.

Surrey picked up maximum bowling points in every Championship match. Generally, the wickets were shared around, although Saqlain and Ian Salisbury took 90 between them. In his first season with Surrey, Jimmy Ormond passed 50 wickets, and against Warwickshire took ten in a match for the first time. Bicknell and a resurgent Alex Tudor picked up more than 30 each, but Ed Giddins disappointed in the final year of his contract and left in November to join Hampshire. The slow left-armer Rupesh Amin, released in 2001, was re-signed, only to be re-released at the end of the season; he joined Leicestershire. **David Llewellyn**

SURREY 2002

Back row: T. J. Murtagh, S. A. Newman, R. Clarke, P. J. Sampson, B. J. M. Scott. *Middle row:* K. R. Booth (*scorer*), N. Walker (*physiotherapist*), D. Naylor (*physiotherapist*), R. M. Amin, J. Ormond, E. S. H. Giddins, M. A. Carberry, K. T. Medlycott (*cricket manager*), A. R. Butcher (*coach*). *Front row:* I. J. Ward, A. J. Tudor, J. D. Ratcliffe, A. D. Brown, M. P. Bicknell, A. J. Stewart, M. A. Butcher, G. P. Thorpe, I. D. K. Salisbury, N. Shahid, M. R. Ramprakash, J. N. Batty. *Insets:* A. J. Hollioake (*captain*), Saqlain Mushtaq, Azhar Mahmood. *Main picture by EMPICS.*

SURREY RESULTS

All first-class matches – Played 17: Won 10, Lost 2, Drawn 5.
County Championship matches – Played 16: Won 10, Lost 2, Drawn 4.

COUNTY CHAMPIONSHIP AVERAGES: BATTING AND FIELDING

Cap		M	I	NO	R	HS	100s	50s	Avge	Ct/St
1995	A. J. Hollioake	9	13	2	738	208	2	5	67.09	10
2000	I. J. Ward	16	29	3	1,708	168*	7	7	65.69	9
	S. A. Newman†. . . .	3	5	0	322	183	1	1	64.40	3
2002	M. R. Ramprakash. .	14	24	4	1,073	218	3	6	53.65	6
1994	A. D. Brown	16	26	2	1,211	188	5	3	50.45	18
1985	A. J. Stewart†.	4	6	0	301	99	0	3	50.16	18/2
	R. Clarke	9	14	1	580	153*	1	4	44.61	7
1996	M. A. Butcher†‡ . . .	6	11	1	385	116	1	2	38.50	3
2001	J. N. Batty	12	22	2	740	151	2	3	37.00	41/5
1998	N. Shahid.	12	19	1	647	150	2	2	35.94	23
1991	G. P. Thorpe†‡	4	8	0	274	143	1	0	34.25	1
	Azhar Mahmood§ . .	3	4	1	96	64*	0	1	32.00	3
1989	M. P. Bicknell†	10	14	5	258	35*	0	0	28.66	6
1998	Saqlain Mushtaq§ . .	10	13	2	278	60	0	2	25.27	4
	T. J. Murtagh	3	5	3	41	22	0	0	20.50	2
1999	A. J. Tudor	6	9	0	176	61	0	1	19.55	1
1998	I. D. K. Salisbury . .	14	20	2	340	59	0	1	18.88	11
	J. Ormond	15	17	4	208	43*	0	0	16.00	6
	E. S. H. Giddins . . .	6	7	4	23	9	0	0	7.66	1

Also batted: M. A. Carberry† (1 match) 10, 24; Mushtaq Ahmed§ (2 matches) 7, 47, 12 (1 ct);
P. J. Sampson (1 match) 0, 1*.

† *Born in Surrey.*   ‡ *ECB contract.*   § *Overseas player.*

BOWLING

	O	M	R	W	BB	5W/i	Avge
Azhar Mahmood	109.2	27	345	20	8-61	1	17.25
T. J. Murtagh	74.1	11	276	13	5-39	1	21.23
A. J. Tudor	202.1	44	739	31	5-66	1	23.83
Saqlain Mushtaq	488.4	112	1,359	53	6-121	3	25.64
M. P. Bicknell.	326	78	1,067	34	6-42	2	31.38
I. D. K. Salisbury	341.3	50	1,192	37	4-59	0	32.21
J. Ormond	485.1	87	1,780	51	5-62	2	34.90
E. S. H. Giddins	208.5	41	696	19	4-113	0	36.63
R. Clarke	76.3	7	398	10	3-41	0	39.80

Also bowled: A. D. Brown 3–0–7–0; M. A. Butcher 8–2–43–0; A. J. Hollioake 37–1–178–5;
Mushtaq Ahmed 105–23–305–8; M. R. Ramprakash 2–0–2–0; P. J. Sampson 21–4–101–5;
N. Shahid 22–1–72–1; I. J. Ward 3–1–5–2.

COUNTY RECORDS

Highest score for:	357*	R. Abel v Somerset at The Oval	1899
Highest score against:	366	N. H. Fairbrother (Lancashire) at The Oval	1990
Best bowling for:	10-43	T. Rushby v Somerset at Taunton	1921
Best bowling against:	10-28	W. P. Howell (Australians) at The Oval.	1899
Highest total for:	811	v Somerset at The Oval.	1899
Highest total against:	863	by Lancashire at The Oval	1990
Lowest total for:	14	v Essex at Chelmsford.	1983
Lowest total against:	16	by MCC at Lord's	1872

COUNTY OFFICERS

Captain A. J. Hollioake • **Cricket manager** K. T. Medlycott
President 2002 – The Rt Hon. J. Major; 2003 – B. G. K. Downing
Chairman 2002 – M. J. Soper; 2003 – D. Stewart • **Chief executive** P. C. J. Sheldon
Cricket secretary A. Gibson • **Head groundsman** P. D. Brind • **Scorer** K. R. Booth

SURREY v SUSSEX

At The Oval, April 19, 20, 21, 22. Surrey won by ten wickets. Surrey 19.75 pts, Sussex 5 pts.
Toss: Surrey. County debuts: Azhar Mahmood; P. M. Hutchison.

The match began with a two-minute silence to remember Surrey's Ben Hollioake and Sussex's Umer Rashid, who died in separate accidents before the season started. Once play was under way, the Surrey batsmen demonstrated why they were favourites for the Championship and hit 384 in boundaries alone. Brown brought up both his fifty and his century with straight sixes, Shahid made an equally brutal career-best 150 and Stewart – looking to regain his England place – scored 99. Kirtley, after remodelling his action in the close season, was the only Sussex bowler who was better than innocuous. When Sussex replied, Tudor, much-improved after a winter at the Academy, made batting tricky, and there was a promising start from Surrey's stand-in overseas player Azhar Mahmood; together they ensured Sussex followed on. Adams made a strongarm century, full of crushing drives through the covers, and Cottey a grafting one, but it was not enough.

Close of play: First day, Surrey 461-4 (Brown 132, Shahid 132); Second day, Sussex 308-9 (Kirtley 10, Hutchison 1); Third day, Surrey 23-0 (Butcher 14, Ward 9).

Surrey

*M. A. Butcher b Kirtley	15	– not out		68
I. J. Ward lbw b Kirtley	12	– not out		43
M. R. Ramprakash c Prior b Hutchison	56			
†A. J. Stewart c Prior b Hutchison	99			
A. D. Brown b Lewry	177			
N. Shahid c Prior b Kirtley	150			
Azhar Mahmood lbw b Lewry	16			
A. J. Tudor c Martin-Jenkins b Hutchison	1			
M. P. Bicknell not out	28			
B 1, l-b 14, w 4, n-b 2	21	B 1, w 2, n-b 2		5

1/26 (2) 2/33 (1) 3/176 (3)   (8 wkts dec.) 575   (no wkt) 116
4/229 (4) 5/491 (6) 6/533 (7)
7/538 (8) 8/575 (5)

I. D. K. Salisbury and J. Ormond did not bat.

Bonus points – Surrey 5, Sussex 2.

Bowling: *First Innings*—Lewry 19–4–89–2; Kirtley 32–8–122–3; Hutchison 28–0–146–3; Martin-Jenkins 24–4–112–0; Davis 12–2–44–0; Adams 4–0–19–0; Yardy 7–0–28–0. *Second Innings*—Lewry 4.2–1–20–0; Kirtley 8–0–43–0; Hutchison 7–0–43–0; Davis 2–0–9–0.

Sussex

R. R. Montgomerie c Azhar Mahmood b Tudor	27	– (2) lbw b Tudor		0
M. W. Goodwin c Shahid b Ormond	36	– (1) c Shahid b Salisbury		34
*C. J. Adams c Stewart b Tudor	11	– b Tudor		114
P. A. Cottey c Azhar Mahmood b Tudor	2	– c Stewart b Salisbury		114
M. H. Yardy c Salisbury b Azhar Mahmood	93	– lbw b Ormond		10
R. S. C. Martin-Jenkins b Tudor	24	– c Ramprakash b Azhar Mahmood		8
†M. J. Prior c Brown b Ormond	35	– c Ramprakash b Azhar Mahmood		2
M. J. G. Davis c Ormond b Azhar Mahmood	28	– c Shahid b Salisbury		14
R. J. Kirtley lbw b Salisbury	10	– b Tudor		34
J. D. Lewry c Stewart b Azhar Mahmood	0	– not out		21
P. M. Hutchison not out	1	– c Salisbury b Bicknell		0
B 1, l-b 4, w 8, n-b 28	41	B 4, l-b 13, n-b 10		27

1/33 (1) 2/61 (3) 3/67 (4) 4/111 (2)   308   1/0 (2) 2/110 (1) 3/198 (3)   379
5/170 (6) 6/217 (7) 7/293 (5)   4/214 (5) 5/231 (6) 6/237 (7)
8/296 (8) 9/298 (10) 10/308 (9)   7/262 (8) 8/317 (9)
                                                          9/372 (4) 10/379 (11)

Bonus points – Sussex 3, Surrey 3.

Bowling: *First Innings*—Bicknell 17–3–48–0; Tudor 16–1–84–4; Ormond 16–4–52–2; Azhar Mahmood 16–5–59–3; Salisbury 15.2–2–60–1. *Second Innings*—Bicknell 19–8–60–1; Tudor 21–2–81–3; Azhar Mahmood 23–3–95–2; Ormond 13–6–33–1; Salisbury 19–0–93–3.

Umpires: N. G. Cowley and B. Dudleston.

At Leeds, April 24, 25, 26. SURREY beat YORKSHIRE by an innings and 168 runs.

SURREY v LANCASHIRE

At The Oval, May 8, 9, 10, 11. Surrey won by three wickets. Surrey 16 pts, Lancashire 6 pts. Toss: Lancashire.

Surrey gave Lancashire a big head start, but two performances of genuine class from Azhar Mahmood and Ramprakash secured a remarkable home win. Lancashire had gained a first-innings lead of 104 thanks to a ferocious 75-ball century by Flintoff and waspish seam bowling by Chapple. In the second half of the match, however, they were totally outplayed. Azhar, with a masterful display of whippy, swing bowling, was set to take all ten wickets in Lancashire's second innings until Ormond trapped Wood lbw, prompting sheepish apologies. Even so, Azhar grabbed eight for 61 to take his total as stopgap overseas player to 20 wickets at just over 17. Needing 305, Surrey were never in trouble, as Ramprakash produced a lordly selection of drives, cuts and glances. Victory had barely seemed possible after first-innings misadventures left Tudor having to bat heroically simply to save the follow-on. Stewart claimed five victims in each innings.

Close of play: First day, Surrey 106-7 (Salisbury 1, Tudor 14); Second day, Lancashire 124-5 (Law 21, Hegg 7); Third day, Surrey 200-4 (Ramprakash 71, Stewart 25).

Lancashire

M. J. Chilton c and b Salisbury	26	– lbw b Azhar Mahmood	35
A. J. Swann run out	18	– c Stewart b Azhar Mahmood	11
D. Byas b Tudor	31	– c Stewart b Azhar Mahmood	12
S. G. Law c Salisbury b Tudor	137	– lbw b Azhar Mahmood	39
A. Flintoff st Stewart b Salisbury	137	– b Azhar Mahmood	6
G. D. Lloyd c Stewart b Ormond	29	– c Stewart b Azhar Mahmood	15
*†W. K. Hegg c Stewart b Azhar Mahmood	9	– b Ormond	43
G. Chapple c Stewart b Salisbury	16	– c Stewart b Azhar Mahmood	1
K. W. Hogg c Azhar Mahmood b Bicknell	1	– c Stewart b Azhar Mahmood	4
J. Wood c Stewart b Bicknell	4	– lbw b Ormond	10
G. Keedy not out	0	– not out	0
B 4, l-b 4, w 6, n-b 8	22	B 2, l-b 6, w 2, n-b 14	24
	320		**200**

1/31 (2) 2/79 (1) 3/99 (3) 4/134 (4) 5/197 (6) 6/220 (7) 7/283 (8) 8/296 (9) 9/320 (10) 10/320 (5) — **320**

1/41 (2) 2/60 (1) 3/65 (3) 4/75 (5) 5/109 (6) 6/154 (4) 7/166 (8) 8/180 (9) 9/181 (10) 10/200 (7) — **200**

Bonus points – Lancashire 3, Surrey 3.

Bowling: *First Innings*—Bicknell 20–4–68–2; Tudor 14–3–79–2; Azhar Mahmood 14–2–79–1; Ormond 12–0–56–1; Salisbury 10.1–3–30–3. *Second Innings*—Bicknell 19–4–41–0; Tudor 14–2–48–0; Ormond 13.4–1–42–2; Azhar Mahmood 25–5–61–8.

Surrey

*M. A. Butcher c Flintoff b Chapple	12	– lbw b Hogg	16
I. J. Ward run out	48	– c Swann b Wood	37
M. R. Ramprakash c Hegg b Chapple	5	– not out	119
G. P. Thorpe lbw b Chapple	0	– c Hogg b Wood	20
A. D. Brown c Chilton b Flintoff	16	– c Byas b Flintoff	10
†A. J. Stewart c Hegg b Flintoff	0	– c Byas b Chilton	46
I. D. K. Salisbury b Chapple	7		
Azhar Mahmood c Byas b Hogg	1	– (7) c Hegg b Wood	15
A. J. Tudor lbw b Chapple	61	– (8) lbw b Keedy	8
M. P. Bicknell c Byas b Keedy	18	– (9) not out	7
J. Ormond not out	35		
L-b 4, w 6, n-b 6	13	B 10, l-b 5, w 2, n-b 14	31
	216	(7 wkts)	309

1/24 (1) 2/40 (3) 3/40 (4) 4/88 (2)
5/88 (6) 6/89 (5) 7/92 (8)
8/129 (7) 9/164 (10) 10/216 (9)

1/42 (1) 2/78 (2) (7 wkts) 309
3/104 (4) 4/139 (5)
5/248 (6) 6/281 (7) 7/290 (8)

Bonus points – Surrey 1, Lancashire 3.

Bowling: *First Innings*—Chapple 18.3–1–65–5; Flintoff 13–4–32–2; Wood 11–2–41–0; Hogg 14–7–26–1; Keedy 8–0–51–1. *Second Innings*—Chapple 26–4–91–0; Flintoff 19–4–67–1; Hogg 10–2–32–1; Wood 14–0–52–3; Keedy 9.4–0–42–1; Chilton 7–3–10–1.

Umpires: V. A. Holder and J. W. Lloyds.

At Cambridge, May 15, 16, 17. SURREY drew with CAMBRIDGE UCCE.

SURREY v SOMERSET

At The Oval, May 24, 25, 26, 27. Drawn. Surrey 8 pts, Somerset 9 pts. Toss: Surrey.

The loss of the third day to rain, and Butcher's unwillingness to set Somerset a realistic target, reduced the match to stalemate. His decision to bat on brought slow hand-clapping from a few disgruntled home supporters, but it ensured that Somerset gained no ground on Surrey, who were top of the table. On a pitch that had sweated under covers, Caddick, playing his seventh Championship match in three seasons, found rhythm and seam movement, while Bulbeck swung the ball dangerously. Together they took nine wickets to put Somerset in a strong position on the first evening, only for their batsmen to squander it. Tudor caused most problems, removing the top three, and only Blackwell showed much fight, thumping Somerset into a modest lead. But rain intervened, leaving a dogged half-century from Stewart and a second sixty from Ward to pad out a meaningless final day.

Close of play: First day, Somerset 10-0 (Cox 8, Trescothick 1); Second day, Surrey 87-3 (Ward 34, Salisbury 0); Third day, No play.

A miserable week for Yorkshire began with the news that the fraud squad were investigating the disappearance of up to £100,000 from the club shop, and ended with a thrashing.
Yorkshire v Surrey, page 814

Surrey

*M. A. Butcher b Caddick	4	– lbw b Caddick	9
I. J. Ward b Dutch c Bulbeck	62	– c Bowler b Dutch	67
M. R. Ramprakash c Burns b Bulbeck	1	– run out	7
G. P. Thorpe c Burns b Caddick	19	– c Burns b Blackwell	29
A. D. Brown c Turner b Caddick	30	– (6) lbw b Dutch	48
†A. J. Stewart c Bowler b Caddick	7	– (7) lbw b Bulbeck	53
A. J. Tudor b Jones	24	– (8) b Blackwell	44
M. P. Bicknell b Caddick	9	– (9) not out	35
I. D. K. Salisbury c Turner b Bulbeck	26	– (5) c Burns b Bulbeck	4
Saqlain Mushtaq lbw b Bulbeck	21	– c Bowler b Blackwell	10
J. Ormond not out	7	– c Dutch b Parsons	0
L-b 6, w 4	10	L-b 10, n-b 16	26
	220		**332**

1/4 (1) 2/7 (3) 3/56 (4) 4/106 (5)   220
5/120 (6) 6/128 (2) 7/153 (8)
8/169 (7) 9/209 (10) 10/220 (9)

1/26 (1) 2/34 (3) 3/84 (4)   332
4/91 (5) 5/174 (2) 6/191 (6)
7/278 (7) 8/307 (8)
9/331 (10) 10/332 (11)

Bonus points – Surrey 1, Somerset 3.

Bowling: *First Innings*—Caddick 28–10–66–5; Bulbeck 20.1–2–60–4; Jones 17–3–69–1; Parsons 4–0–19–0. *Second Innings*—Caddick 27–6–94–1; Bulbeck 20–3–80–2; Jones 15–2–40–0; Blackwell 15–8–19–3; Dutch 13–1–52–2; Parsons 11–1–37–1.

Somerset

J. Cox b Tudor	34	– not out	14
*M. E. Trescothick c Stewart b Tudor	7	– c Stewart b Tudor	12
M. Burns c Brown b Tudor	13	– not out	10
P. D. Bowler c Thorpe b Saqlain Mushtaq	21		
K. A. Parsons lbw b Bicknell	5		
I. D. Blackwell lbw b Salisbury	98		
†R. J. Turner c Tudor b Bicknell	34		
K. P. Dutch c Ramprakash b Bicknell	3		
M. P. L. Bulbeck b Bicknell	4		
A. R. Caddick st Stewart b Saqlain Mushtaq	15		
P. S. Jones not out	4		
B 1, l-b 10, w 2, n-b 2	15	L-b 5, n-b 4	9
	253	(1 wkt)	**45**

1/28 (2) 2/52 (3) 3/61 (1) 4/69 (5)   253
5/111 (4) 6/217 (7) 7/221 (8)
8/225 (9) 9/237 (6) 10/253 (10)

1/28 (2)   (1 wkt) 45

Bonus points – Somerset 2, Surrey 3.

Bowling: *First Innings*—Bicknell 22–4–72–4; Tudor 19–7–64–3; Ormond 13–2–53–0; Saqlain Mushtaq 13.2–3–31–2; Salisbury 13–3–22–1. *Second Innings*—Ormond 5–1–17–0; Tudor 4–1–22–1; Ramprakash 1–0–1–0.

Umpires: G. I. Burgess and J. W. Holder.

At Manchester, May 31, June 1, 2, 3. SURREY drew with LANCASHIRE.

SURREY v KENT

At The Oval, June 12, 13, 14. Surrey won by nine wickets. Surrey 19 pts, Kent 3 pts. Toss: Surrey.
   As play should have been resuming on the second day, Kent had two players at The Oval and ten stuck in traffic: a burst water main in Buckingham Palace Road, roadworks and an accident had conspired to cause gridlock. The umpires spoke to Alan Fordham, the ECB cricket operations manager, and decided to delay the start and make up lost time later. Play began 90 minutes late, with Kent forced to field a 12th man until 1.30, when Patel, whose BMW had overheated, finally arrived. Kent's day did not improve on the field. Brown, who had come in the previous evening at 39 for three, made a savage 188, with 29 fours and a six, before he was last man out. He consolidated a strong position: on the opening day Bicknell had hit a nagging length and darted the ball off the seam to undermine Kent. His six for 42 meant he had taken five or more in an innings against the other 17 counties. Kent fared little better second time round. Fulton fell to an astonishing catch in the gully, but many of the middle order made bad errors of judgment. Khan's resistance was entertaining, but futile.
   Close of play: First day, Surrey 111-5 (Brown 49, Bicknell 8); Second day, Kent 79-1 (Fulton 41, Smith 32).

Kent

*D. P. Fulton lbw b Bicknell	2	– c Salisbury b Giddins	48
R. W. T. Key c Batty b Bicknell	15	– b Ormond	4
E. T. Smith c Ward b Bicknell	20	– lbw b Giddins	44
A. Symonds c Salisbury b Ormond	1	– run out	14
M. J. Walker c Clarke b Ormond	6	– c Ormond b Bicknell	18
†P. A. Nixon c Saqlain Mushtaq b Bicknell	54	– c and b Bicknell	23
M. A. Ealham lbw b Giddins	25	– c Ormond b Saqlain Mushtaq	21
M. V. Fleming c Batty b Ormond	12	– c Ward b Saqlain Mushtaq	2
M. M. Patel c Shahid b Bicknell	0	– c Batty b Giddins	37
A. Khan c Salisbury b Bicknell	0	– not out	42
M. J. Saggers not out	5	– c Shahid b Ormond	7
B 4, l-b 1, w 6, n-b 2	13	B 2, l-b 2, n-b 4	8

1/4 (1) 2/27 (2) 3/32 (4) 4/38 (5)   153   1/6 (2) 2/94 (1) 3/99 (3)   268
5/48 (3) 6/100 (7) 7/129 (8)   4/130 (5) 5/133 (4) 6/159 (7)
8/138 (9) 9/140 (10) 10/153 (6)   7/162 (8) 8/202 (9)
                                         9/234 (6) 10/268 (11)

Bonus points – Surrey 3.

   Bowling: *First Innings*—Bicknell 13–5–42–6; Ormond 14–2–56–3; Giddins 9–2–37–1; Clarke 4–2–6–0; Saqlain Mushtaq 3–0–7–0. *Second Innings*—Bicknell 23–7–78–2; Ormond 14.4–4–44–2; Saqlain Mushtaq 15–0–62–2; Giddins 18–3–80–3.

Surrey

*I. J. Ward c Nixon b Khan	0	– b Patel	15
†J. N. Batty c Symonds b Fleming	24	– not out	32
M. R. Ramprakash lbw b Khan	1	– not out	11
N. Shahid c Nixon b Fleming	20		
A. D. Brown c Key b Patel	188		
R. Clarke c Khan b Fleming	5		
M. P. Bicknell c Nixon b Fleming	27		
I. D. K. Salisbury c Symonds b Khan	13		
Saqlain Mushtaq c Nixon b Saggers	25		
J. Ormond b Ealham	33		
E. S. H. Giddins not out	4		
B 4, l-b 13, w 2, n-b 2	21	L-b 1, w 2	3

1/3 (1) 2/5 (3) 3/39 (4) 4/58 (2)   361   1/35 (1)   3
5/80 (6) 6/166 (7) 7/231 (8)   (1 wkt) 61
8/287 (9) 9/333 (10) 10/361 (5)

Bonus points – Surrey 4, Kent 3.

Bowling: *First Innings*—Saggers 22–2–96–1; Khan 16–2–81–3; Fleming 23–5–68–4; Ealham 15–4–68–1; Patel 11.1–3–31–1. *Second Innings*—Saggers 4–0–15–0; Khan 6–2–15–0; Patel 5–2–8–1; Ealham 4–1–7–0; Walker 3.3–1–15–0.

Umpires: B. Dudleston and J. F. Steele.

At Taunton, July 3, 4, 5, 6. SURREY drew with SOMERSET.

SURREY v WARWICKSHIRE

At The Oval, July 10, 11, 12, 13. Warwickshire won by 31 runs. Warwickshire 17 pts, Surrey 8 pts. Toss: Surrey.

For the first time, Warwickshire won after following on. A remarkable rescue effort began in their second innings, when Powell, with a grinding 95, and Troughton, who made a jauntier 94, cancelled out Surrey's 182-run lead. Their fourth-wicket stand of 113 was not well supported, but it was enough to leave Surrey an awkward target of 169 in 34 overs. Thanks to immaculate bowling by Pollock, and canny field placings which built up stifling pressure, they were fired out 11 balls short of safety. Pollock dismissed Batty and Ramprakash in his first over, before the needless loss of Ally Brown, run out when called for a quick single by Hollioake, sparked a dramatic collapse. The last six wickets fell in 71 balls. The astonishing result eclipsed three days of Surrey dominance, and overshadowed Ramprakash's double-hundred – the seventh of his career and his second in consecutive matches, lasting eight and three-quarter hours and 308 balls, with 32 fours and a six – as well as Ormond's first ten-wicket haul.

Close of play: First day, Surrey 191-5 (Ramprakash 57, Clarke 9); Second day, Warwickshire 120-5 (Pollock 13, Brown 0); Third day, Warwickshire 165-3 (Powell 66, Troughton 15).

Surrey

I. J. Ward c Ostler b Brown	34	– c Piper b Carter			7
†J. N. Batty lbw b Pollock	16	– lbw b Pollock			0
M. R. Ramprakash not out	210	– c Piper b Pollock			0
N. Shahid c Ostler b Brown	2	– c Pollock b Carter			15
A. D. Brown lbw b Brown	0	– run out			33
*A. J. Hollioake b Betts	56	– c Carter b Brown			52
R. Clarke lbw b Brown	79	– lbw b Brown			5
I. D. K. Salisbury c Smith b Carter	30	– c Piper b Pollock			1
Saqlain Mushtaq c and b Brown	0	– lbw b Pollock			9
J. Ormond c Powell b Brown	13	– lbw b Smith			0
E. S. H. Giddins c and b Brown	9	– not out			9
B 3, l-b 17, w 2, n-b 4	26	B 1, l-b 4, n-b 4			9

1/57 (2) 2/57 (1) 3/59 (4) 4/59 (5)   475   1/5 (2) 2/5 (3) 3/21 (1) 4/32 (4)   137
5/147 (6) 6/322 (7) 7/404 (8)   5/103 (5) 6/111 (7) 7/126 (8)
8/405 (9) 9/435 (10) 10/475 (11)   8/126 (6) 9/129 (9) 10/137 (10)

Bonus points – Surrey 5, Warwickshire 3.

Bowling: *First Innings*—Pollock 22–11–37–1; Carter 21–1–114–1; Brown 33.5–7–110–7; Betts 17–0–106–1; Smith 12–1–49–0; Wagh 4–1–9–0; Bell 4–0–23–0; Troughton 2–0–7–0. *Second Innings*—Pollock 12–2–44–4; Carter 9–1–37–2; Brown 8–1–26–2; Troughton 3–0–25–0; Smith 0.1–0–0–1.

Warwickshire

*M. J. Powell b Ormond	2	– lbw b Giddins	95
M. A. Wagh c Batty b Ormond	17	– lbw b Salisbury	43
I. R. Bell c Shahid b Saqlain Mushtaq	39	– lbw b Salisbury	8
D. P. Ostler b Saqlain Mushtaq	22	– c Shahid b Saqlain Mushtaq	13
J. O. Troughton lbw b Saqlain Mushtaq	12	– c Saqlain Mushtaq b Ormond	94
S. M. Pollock lbw b Ormond	50	– c Brown b Ormond	24
D. R. Brown b Ormond	16	– c Hollioake b Ormond	5
N. M. K. Smith c Shahid b Saqlain Mushtaq	74	– b Ormond	6
†K. J. Piper c Brown b Ormond	3	– not out	25
M. M. Betts c Batty b Giddins	18	– b Ormond	4
N. M. Carter not out	7	– c Shahid b Saqlain Mushtaq	2
B 4, l-b 11, n-b 18	33	B 2, l-b 8, w 10, n-b 6, p 5	31

1/17 (1) 2/26 (2) 3/79 (4) 4/98 (3)   **293**
5/119 (5) 6/162 (7) 7/237 (6)
8/261 (9) 9/281 (8) 10/293 (10)

1/85 (2) 2/113 (3) 3/132 (4)   **350**
4/245 (1) 5/284 (6) 6/293 (7)
7/309 (8) 8/327 (5)
9/337 (10) 10/350 (11)

Bonus points – Warwickshire 2, Surrey 3.

Bowling: *First Innings*—Giddins 8.5–2–32–1; Ormond 23–5–116–5; Saqlain Mushtaq 29–3–97–4; Clarke 3–0–8–0; Salisbury 8–0–25–0. *Second Innings*—Ormond 18–2–62–5; Giddins 19–1–63–1; Clarke 4–0–24–0; Saqlain Mushtaq 43.2–14–90–2; Salisbury 26–4–95–2; Hollioake 1–0–1–0.

Umpires: A. Clarkson and J. H. Hampshire.

At Canterbury, July 19, 20, 21, 22. SURREY beat KENT by two wickets.

SURREY v YORKSHIRE

At Guildford, July 24, 25, 26, 27. Surrey won by six wickets. Surrey 19 pts, Yorkshire 3 pts. Toss: Yorkshire. First-class debut: D. H. Wigley.

Surrey's performance was as tight as Yorkshire's was wayward and, for the second match in a row, an unbeaten hundred by Ward clinched victory. The second ball of the game reared freakishly, caught the shoulder of Wood's bat and looped to gully, but this was not a spiteful pitch. Clarke then underlined his talent with a polished fifty as Surrey sailed to a 210-run lead and, despite a quality century from Lumb, Yorkshire were unable to muster enough second-innings runs to set a challenging target. They might have put more pressure on Surrey had it not been for a bizarre interlude when Blakey swept a four into the press tent. After the ball was fetched, Hollioake noticed some tooth marks; the culprit, it transpired, was Bumper, a labrador who belonged to Geoffrey Dean from *The Times*. The damage prompted Hollioake to take the new ball – 21 overs after it had become available – and Surrey's seamers quickly despatched the Yorkshire tail. Ward calmly picked off the 237 needed, while Salisbury gave superb support.

Close of play: First day, Surrey 207-5 (Batty 78, Hollioake 1); Second day, Yorkshire 254-3 (Lehmann 55, Lumb 68); Third day, Surrey 110-3 (Ward 67, Salisbury 0).

Yorkshire

M. J. Wood c Salisbury b Giddins	0	– c Batty b Giddins	43
V. J. Craven c Batty b Giddins	21	– c Batty b Ormond	56
A. McGrath lbw b Giddins	26	– c Batty b Giddins	13
*D. S. Lehmann c Clarke b Ormond	7	– lbw b Giddins	61
M. J. Lumb c Saqlain Mushtaq b Ormond	16	– c Shahid b Salisbury	124
G. M. Fellows c Shahid b Clarke	16	– c Batty b Hollioake	33
†R. J. Blakey c Shahid b Saqlain Mushtaq	23	– c Brown b Clarke	50
R. K. J. Dawson c Brown b Clarke	15	– c Brown b Ormond	20
C. E. W. Silverwood c Hollioake b Clarke	2	– c Brown b Giddins	6
R. J. Sidebottom not out	6	– b Clarke	1
D. H. Wigley c Clarke b Saqlain Mushtaq	15	– not out	4
B 4, l-b 7, w 2, n-b 12	25	L-b 17, w 4, n-b 14	35
	172		**446**

1/0 (1) 2/53 (2) 3/64 (3) 4/74 (4)   1/83 (1) 2/117 (3) 3/117 (2)
5/85 (5) 6/125 (6) 7/141 (7)   4/269 (4) 5/337 (6) 6/366 (5)
8/150 (9) 9/151 (8) 10/172 (11)   7/413 (8) 8/422 (9)
     9/433 (10) 10/446 (7)

Bonus points – Surrey 3.

Bowling: *First Innings*—Giddins 15–3–48–3; Ormond 13–3–51–2; Saqlain Mushtaq 10–1–21–2; Clarke 8–0–41–3. *Second Innings*—Giddins 35–6–113–4; Ormond 29–4–106–2; Clarke 9.3–2–39–2; Saqlain Mushtaq 29–4–82–0; Hollioake 7–1–27–1; Salisbury 13–2–62–1.

Surrey

I. J. Ward c Blakey b Silverwood	12	– not out	124
†J. N. Batty b Sidebottom	99	– b Sidebottom	16
M. R. Ramprakash b Silverwood	8	– lbw b Silverwood	16
N. Shahid c Fellows b Sidebottom	45	– c Lumb b Dawson	7
A. D. Brown c Craven b Fellows	50	– (6) not out	5
I. D. K. Salisbury b Fellows	0	– (5) c Blakey b Lehmann	59
*A. J. Hollioake c Blakey b Sidebottom	5		
R. Clarke b McGrath	56		
Saqlain Mushtaq c Craven b Wigley	44		
J. Ormond c Wood b Silverwood	39		
E. S. H. Giddins not out	8		
B 5, l-b 7, n-b 12	24	L-b 6, n-b 4	10
	382	(4 wkts)	**237**

1/24 (1) 2/24 (3) 3/101 (4) 4/193 (5)   1/52 (2) 2/98 (3)
5/195 (6) 6/215 (7) 7/250 (2)   3/109 (4) 4/209 (5)
8/297 (8) 9/351 (10) 10/382 (9)

Bonus points – Surrey 4, Yorkshire 3.

Bowling: *First Innings*—Silverwood 21–5–71–3; Sidebottom 22–7–57–3; Wigley 10.4–0–71–1; McGrath 15–3–55–1; Dawson 12–0–68–0; Fellows 5–1–21–2; Lehmann 9–3–27–0. *Second Innings*—Silverwood 17–7–45–1; Sidebottom 13–2–39–1; Dawson 16–3–57–1; Wigley 10–2–45–0; Lehmann 9.3–1–43–1; McGrath 3–1–2–0.

Umpires: N. J. Llong and K. E. Palmer.

At Hove, August 8, 9, 10, 11. SURREY lost to SUSSEX by four wickets.

At Leicester, August 14, 15, 16. SURREY beat LEICESTERSHIRE by seven wickets.

SURREY v HAMPSHIRE

At The Oval, August 22, 23, 24, 25. Surrey won by an innings and 60 runs. Surrey 20 pts, Hampshire 2 pts. Toss: Hampshire. First-class debut: S. A. Newman. Championship debut: J. A. Tomlinson.

On a bone-dry pitch, eight Hampshire wickets fell to spin on the first day, which led to a visit from an ECB pitch liaison officer. But his trip was rendered superfluous by the Surrey reply. A belligerent hundred from Brown, and 99 on first-class debut by Scott Newman – an innings littered with bold strokeplay before a fatal decision not to offer a shot – made a mockery of Hampshire's earlier caution and the umpires' fears about the pitch. When Hampshire tried again, Saqlain Mushtaq's subtleties and variations were backed up by off-spin from Ormond, who switched from his usual fast-medium and succeeded in bowling Laney. The defeat was Hampshire's seventh in a row against Surrey. Saqlain marked his return from international duty with a tenth ten-wicket haul for Surrey; by contrast, Hampshire's off-spinner, Udal, conceded 213 – the most expensive analysis for the county in a Championship innings.

Close of play: First day, Hampshire 190; Second day, Surrey 410-5 (Brown 103, Batty 36); Third day, Hampshire 303-8 (Mascarenhas 75, Hamblin 13).

Hampshire

N. C. Johnson c Batty b Ormond	15	– lbw b Saqlain Mushtaq	32
J. S. Laney c Shahid b Saqlain Mushtaq	5	– b Ormond	39
W. S. Kendall c Hollioake b Saqlain Mushtaq	36	– c Shahid b Saqlain Mushtaq	36
*R. A. Smith c Hollioake b Saqlain Mushtaq	7	– c Shahid b Saqlain Mushtaq	28
J. D. Francis c Batty b Ormond	6	– c Shahid b Saqlain Mushtaq	0
†N. Pothas c Shahid b Saqlain Mushtaq	58	– lbw b Saqlain Mushtaq	24
L. R. Prittipaul lbw b Salisbury	0	– lbw b Saqlain Mushtaq	5
A. D. Mascarenhas c Batty b Salisbury	20	– c Ormond b Salisbury	94
S. D. Udal lbw b Salisbury	4	– st Batty b Salisbury	18
J. R. C. Hamblin c Hollioake b Saqlain Mushtaq	10	– c and b Salisbury	16
J. A. Tomlinson not out	1	– not out	0
B 6, l-b 10, w 4, n-b 8	28	B 6, l-b 14, w 2, n-b 12	34
	190		**326**

1/16 (2) 2/36 (1) 3/55 (4) 4/72 (5)   1/51 (1) 2/87 (6) 3/142 (4)
5/88 (3) 6/93 (7) 7/161 (8)   4/142 (5) 5/157 (3) 6/167 (7)
8/177 (9) 9/177 (6) 10/190 (10)   7/208 (6) 8/247 (9)
                              9/317 (10) 10/326 (8)

Bonus points – Surrey 3.

Bowling: *First Innings*—Bicknell 13–2–28–0; Ormond 18–7–41–2; Saqlain Mushtaq 34.2–12–59–5; Salisbury 18–4–44–3; Hollioake 1–0–1–0; Ramprakash 1–0–1–0. *Second Innings*—Bicknell 10–3–30–0; Ormond 14–1–51–1; Saqlain Mushtaq 39–9–121–6; Salisbury 27.4–5–104–3.

Surrey

I. J. Ward c Johnson b Udal	87	Saqlain Mushtaq c Francis b Prittipaul	18
S. A. Newman lbw b Tomlinson	99	J. Ormond not out	1
M. R. Ramprakash c Francis b Udal	38		
N. Shahid c Mascarenhas b Hamblin	22	B 8, l-b 1, w 10, n-b 8	27
A. D. Brown c Laney b Udal	135		
*A. J. Hollioake c Johnson b Tomlinson	9	1/198 (2) 2/202 (1) 3/249 (4)	**576**
†J. N. Batty lbw b Prittipaul	89	4/295 (3) 5/316 (6)	
M. P. Bicknell c Laney b Udal	24	6/470 (5) 7/495 (8)	
I. D. K. Salisbury c Laney		8/542 (9) 9/575 (10)	
b Mascarenhas	27	10/576 (7)	

Bonus points – Surrey 5, Hampshire 2 (130 overs: 542-8).

Bowling: Tomlinson 28–0–91–2; Mascarenhas 21–3–94–1; Udal 47–7–213–4; Prittipaul 13.3–4–43–2; Hamblin 16–2–81–1; Johnson 10–0–45–0.

Umpires: N. A. Mallender and A. G. T. Whitehead.

At Birmingham, August 27, 28, 29, 30. SURREY drew with WARWICKSHIRE.

At Southampton, September 11, 12, 13, 14. SURREY beat HAMPSHIRE by 123 runs.

SURREY v LEICESTERSHIRE

At The Oval, September 18, 19, 20, 21. Surrey won by 483 runs. Surrey 20 pts, Leicestershire 7 pts. Toss: Surrey. Championship debut: P. J. Sampson.

It was fitting that Surrey should wind up a stunning season with a huge victory. Hollioake's apparently strange decision to bat well into the last day left Leicestershire needing to survive less than two sessions, but Murtagh skittled them within 39 overs. It had been a landmark-strewn match. As Surrey roared to 494 in their first innings, Ward became the third batsman, after Jack Hobbs (twice) and Tom Hayward, to hit four consecutive Championship hundreds for the county,

LARGEST CHAMPIONSHIP WINS BY RUNS

483	**Surrey (494 and 492-9 dec.) beat Leicestershire (361 and 142) at The Oval** . .	**2002**
470	Sussex (309 and 307-5 dec.) beat Gloucestershire (66 and 80) at Hove	1913
429	Kent (224 and 343-4 dec.) beat Northamptonshire (92 and 46) at Dover.	1933
423	Lancashire (277 and 405) beat Somerset (193 and 66) at Liverpool	1911
419	Somerset (344 and 264-6 dec.) beat Kent (116 and 73) at Bath	1937

All except Surrey v Leicestershire were three-day matches.

Research: Philip Bailey

but was upstaged by Newman's muscular maiden century. Srinath then removed Hollioake and Philip Sampson in consecutive balls to grab an unwitting hat-trick: he had forgotten that Ormond had fallen to the final ball of his previous over. And, after Maddy, batting with a runner, and Sutcliffe had provided the backbone of Leicestershire's 361, Hollioake crowned his remarkable season with an incendiary maiden double-century, his first hundred coming between lunch and tea. In all, he batted five hours, struck 21 fours and three sixes in 252 balls and shared a 282-run stand with Brown. At the close of the first day, Hollioake was presented with the Championship trophy, in front of 2,000 fans.

Close of play: First day, Surrey 397-3 (Thorpe 9, Shahid 0); Second day, Leicestershire 303-5 (Maddy 109, Cunliffe 0); Third day, Surrey 335-4 (Brown 89, Hollioake 146).

Surrey

I. J. Ward c Maddy b DeFreitas	118	– c Stevens b Srinath	22
S. A. Newman c Burns b Srinath	183	– c Maddy b Crowe	21
†J. N. Batty c Srinath b Malcolm	74	– (7) lbw b Srinath	0
G. P. Thorpe c Srinath b DeFreitas	44	– b Malcolm.	0
N. Shahid lbw b DeFreitas.	2	– (3) c Burns b Malcolm	28
A. D. Brown c Malcolm b Crowe	34	– (5) c Burns b Stevens	107
*A. J. Hollioake b Srinath	20	– (6) c DeFreitas b Brandy	208
I. D. K. Salisbury b Srinath	0	– not out	36
J. Ormond c Stevens b Srinath	0	– b Brandy	9
T. J. Murtagh not out	0	– c Stevens b Srinath	22
P. J. Sampson b Srinath.	0	– not out	1
L-b 5, n-b 14	19	L-b 6, w 20, n-b 12	38

1/227 (1) 2/352 (2) 3/397 (3) 4/419 (5)   **494**   1/35 (1) 2/89 (3)   (9 wkts dec.) **492**
5/456 (4) 6/490 (6) 7/493 (8)   3/89 (4) 4/89 (2)
8/493 (9) 9/494 (7) 10/494 (11)   5/371 (5) 6/374 (7)
                                            7/445 (6) 8/455 (9) 9/491 (10)

Bonus points – Surrey 5, Leicestershire 3.

Bowling: *First Innings*—Srinath 26.2–1–114–5; Malcolm 13–0–70–1; Crowe 28–4–100–1; DeFreitas 28–3–121–3; Maddy 5–0–16–0; Brandy 4–0–28–0; Stevens 7–0–40–0. *Second Innings*—DeFreitas 17–1–74–0; Srinath 26–1–89–3; Malcolm 6–1–41–2; Crowe 7–2–33–1; Stevens 30–1–125–1; Sutcliffe 5–0–35–0; Brandy 13–0–86–2; Cunliffe 1.1–0–3–0.

Leicestershire

A. S. Wright c Batty b Sampson	22	– c sub b Sampson 7
*I. J. Sutcliffe c Ward b Salisbury	72	– (6) lbw b Salisbury 24
D. L. Maddy not out.	127	– (7) lbw b Murtagh 12
D. I. Stevens c Ward b Shahid	53	– lbw b Murtagh 0
D. G. Brandy c Ormond b Hollioake	23	– (3) b Murtagh 0
†N. D. Burns b Hollioake	7	– (5) c and b Hollioake 68
R. J. Cunliffe c Batty b Sampson	30	– (2) c Hollioake b Sampson 0
P. A. J. DeFreitas c Salisbury b Sampson	4	– b Murtagh 9
J. Srinath c Batty b Murtagh	1	– c Shahid b Salisbury 9
C. D. Crowe c Batty b Murtagh	4	– lbw b Murtagh 8
D. E. Malcolm c Batty b Murtagh.	0	– not out 0
B 6, l-b 4, w 4, n-b 4	18	L-b 3, n-b 2. 5
	361	**142**

1/60 (1) 2/140 (2) 3/217 (4) 4/277 (5)   1/4 (2) 2/5 (3) 3/7 (1) 4/11 (4)
5/300 (6) 6/348 (7) 7/352 (8)   5/99 (5) 6/105 (6) 7/123 (7)
8/353 (9) 9/361 (10) 10/361 (11)   8/124 (8) 9/142 (10) 10/142 (9)

Bonus points – Leicestershire 4, Surrey 3.

Bowling: *First Innings*—Ormond 13–2–49–0; Murtagh 18.5–2–62–3; Sampson 11–1–52–3; Salisbury 26–4–94–1; Shahid 16–1–55–1; Hollioake 9–0–39–2. *Second Innings*—Murtagh 12–2–39–5; Sampson 10–3–49–2; Salisbury 12.5–4–28–2; Hollioake 4–0–23–1.

Umpires: M. R. Benson and N. J. Llong.

DATES OF WINNING COUNTY CHAMPIONSHIP

The dates on which the County Championship has been settled since 1979 are as follows:

			Final margin
1979	Essex	August 21	77 pts
1980	Middlesex	September 2	13 pts
1981	Nottinghamshire	September 14	2 pts
1982	Middlesex	September 11	39 pts
1983	Essex	September 13	16 pts
1984	Essex	September 11	14 pts
1985	Middlesex	September 17	18 pts
1986	Essex	September 10	28 pts
1987	Nottinghamshire	September 14	4 pts
1988	Worcestershire	September 16	1 pt
1989	Worcestershire	August 31	6 pts
1990	Middlesex	September 20	31 pts
1991	Essex	September 19	13 pts
1992	Essex	September 3	41 pts
1993	Middlesex	August 30	36 pts
1994	Warwickshire	September 2	42 pts
1995	Warwickshire	September 16	32 pts
1996	Leicestershire	September 21	27 pts
1997	Glamorgan	September 20	4 pts
1998	Leicestershire	September 19	15 pts
1999	Surrey	September 2	56 pts
2000	Surrey	September 13	20 pts
2001	Yorkshire	August 24	16 pts
2002	Surrey	September 7	44.75 pts

Note: The earliest date on which the Championship has been won since it was expanded in 1895 was August 12, 1910, by Kent.

SUSSEX
STAYING POWER

Ch'ship	6th in Division 1
C&G	quarter-finalists
B&H	quarter-finalists
NUL	8th in Division 2

Player of the season: Robin Martin-Jenkins

The feat of staying in Division One of the Championship may have lacked the euphoria that marked promotion in 2001, but the captain, Chris Adams, stressed how much bigger an accomplishment he felt it was. Sixth place was Sussex's best for 18 years and, at the end of a traumatic season, Adams was more than happy. "It's always nice to lift trophies," he said, "but we've become one of the top six clubs in the country. That is a magnificent achievement."

The season began in tragedy. Within ten days of the death of Surrey's Ben Hollioake, Sussex lost their gifted all-rounder Umer Rashid, who drowned trying to save his younger brother, Burhan, during the club's pre-season tour to Grenada. The county cap that would have been given to Rashid was presented to his father, Mirza, in a moving ceremony when Sussex played Angus Fraser's XI in a memorial match for the brothers. Adams called Rashid "probably the most naturally gifted player on the staff", and his memory will live on at Hove in the form of a new spin clinic and the refurbished main scoreboard, which has been named after him.

Sussex were without three key players for a third of the season and won only three Championship games, but it was a tribute to the team spirit Rashid helped engender that they pulled through. Adams, James Kirtley and Jason Lewry were all hit by injury. Adams suffered a calf strain as a reaction to knee surgery, and missed most of June after scoring a double-hundred against Lancashire, while Kirtley, his deputy, missed six games. He broke his hand halfway through the NatWest Series but he was delighted just to be back in the England side. During their trip to Zimbabwe in October 2001 his action had been queried by the referee and he spent three months in the new year remodelling his delivery with the help of the Sussex coach, Peter Moores, and the ECB's bowling advisor, Bob Cottam, before being cleared by an ECB panel. His England recall came after he had rushed to 29 wickets in his first six games; despite his hand injury, he took 50 wickets for the fourth successive summer.

Lewry was troubled by a knee problem early on and restricted to just ten games in his benefit season, while shin splints limited his fellow left-armer Paul Hutchison, who had joined from Yorkshire, to three Championship matches. The uncapped Billy Taylor stepped up to underline his promise and finished as Sussex's leading one-day wicket-taker with 42.

Murray Goodwin and Richard Montgomerie, such an effective opening pair in 2001, quickly discovered the greater potency of Division One attacks but both still reached 1,000 runs. All five of Goodwin's hundreds came at Hove, while Montgomerie scored 792 one-day runs and helped send Hampshire down with a career-best 196 in the Championship. Robin Martin-Jenkins, who played in every Championship game, joined them on 1,000 runs and almost took 50 wickets after a winter of diligence in the gym. Tim Ambrose, Australian-born but ECB-qualified, made notable progress, hit a maiden hundred against Yorkshire and added another, against Kent. And when Matthew Prior made his first century, against Hampshire, it was the first by a Sussex wicket-keeper for five years. Prior was the eighth Sussex player to score a first-class hundred in 2002, and their survival was due in no small part to lower-order grit.

The acquisition of Kevin Innes was a vital boost. After just 21 first-class appearances in eight seasons with Northamptonshire, he revelled in the new challenge, filling Rashid's all-rounder's slot and adding half a yard of pace. Mark Davis shouldered the slow-bowling duties and once again proved his value down the order with his maiden first-class century. Tony Cottey showed glimpses of his best form with successive hundreds after winning back his place in mid-July.

After a strong start in the B&H, with Montgomerie, Adams and Taylor starring, Sussex lost to the eventual winners, Warwickshire, in the quarter-finals. They went out at the same stage of the C&G and had another bleak year in the Norwich Union League. They trimmed their staff by releasing Jamie Carpenter, Dominic Clapp and Paul Havell, while Will House decided to retire and take up a job in the City. After failing to lure Harbhajan Singh, Sussex signed the experienced Pakistani leg-spinner Mushtaq Ahmed as their second overseas player, in addition to Goodwin.

Off the field, the chairman, Don Trangmar, resigned three years ahead of schedule, severed all links and was replaced by the semi-retired businessman David Green. Trangmar had been chairman for four years and in his work for the ECB had played a key role in the introduction of central contracts. Green insisted there were "no warring factions" when he took over and later appointed Hugh Griffiths, who had been operations manager, as acting chief executive. He replaced Nigel Russell, who left by mutual consent just three months into the job.

Sussex have completed the first stage of redeveloping Hove with a new five-lane indoor school, and were major beneficiaries of the will of the former president Spen Cama, who left £7m (£4.3m after deductions) of his £23m estate to the club. Green says most will be spent on ground improvements, although a sum will be ring-fenced to ensure the club's long-term financial security. **Andy Arlidge and Bruce Talbot**

SUSSEX 2002

Back row: S. Osborne (*physiotherapist*), J. Carmichael (*physiotherapist*), P. M. R. Havell, J. R. Carpenter, B. V. Taylor, B. Zuiderent, P. M. Hutchison, R. Harley (*fitness consultant*). *Middle row*: C. D. Hopkinson, M. J. G. Davis, M. J. Prior, T. R. Ambrose, W. J. House, D. A. Clapp, M. H. Yardy. *Front row*: J. D. Lewry, R. S. C. Martin-Jenkins, M. A. Robinson, R. J. Kirtley, C. J. Adams (*captain*), P. Moores (*first-team coach*), P. A. Cottey, R. R. Montgomerie. *Picture by Roger Ockenden.*

SUSSEX RESULTS

All first-class matches – Played 16: Won 3, Lost 6, Drawn 7.
County Championship matches – Played 16: Won 3, Lost 6, Drawn 7.

COUNTY CHAMPIONSHIP AVERAGES: BATTING AND FIELDING

Cap		M	I	NO	R	HS	100s	50s	Avge	Ct/St
1998	C. J. Adams	10	19	0	848	217	3	3	44.63	2
2001	M. W. Goodwin§	16	28	0	1,179	162	5	3	42.10	13
2000	R. S. C. Martin-Jenkins	16	28	4	1,008	205*	1	5	42.00	1
1999	R. R. Montgomerie . . .	16	28	1	1,026	196	2	4	38.00	16
	T. R. Ambrose	13	22	1	798	149	2	2	38.00	9
	K. J. Innes	13	22	7	478	60*	0	1	31.86	3
1999	P. A. Cottey	13	22	0	699	137	3	1	31.77	5
	M. J. Prior	16	27	3	741	102*	1	5	30.87	39/2
	M. H. Yardy	10	17	0	492	93	0	2	28.94	11
2002	M. J. G. Davis	15	22	4	474	111	1	2	26.33	8
1998	R. J. Kirtley†	10	15	3	146	36*	0	0	12.16	4
	P. M. Hutchison	3	5	2	29	20*	0	0	9.66	0
1996	J. D. Lewry†	10	15	5	91	21*	0	0	9.10	5
	B. V. Taylor	10	14	2	70	18*	0	0	5.83	4

Also batted: D. A. Clapp (1 match) 6; C. D. Hopkinson† (1 match) 33, 9 (2 ct); C. D. Nash†
(1 match) 0, 0* (1 ct); M. A. Robinson (cap 1997) (1 match) 6, 4*; B. Zuiderent (1 match) 0, 10.

† *Born in Sussex.* § *Overseas player.*

BOWLING

	O	M	R	W	BB	5W/i	Avge
R. J. Kirtley	366	90	1,152	50	6-107	4	23.04
K. J. Innes	268.3	65	834	29	4-41	0	28.75
B. V. Taylor	318.5	73	1,041	32	5-90	1	32.53
R. S. C. Martin-Jenkins	470.2	100	1,477	41	7-51	2	36.02
J. D. Lewry	304.4	45	1,227	33	5-88	1	37.18
M. J. G. Davis	347.2	71	1,081	28	6-97	1	38.60

Also bowled: C. J. Adams 7–1–24–0; T. R. Ambrose 1–0–1–0; P. A. Cottey 16.2–5–33–0;
M. W. Goodwin 2–1–1–0; C. D. Hopkinson 7–0–35–1; P. M. Hutchison 79–6–389–6; R. R.
Montgomerie 6–2–10–0; C. D. Nash 35–1–171–2; M. A. Robinson 40–8–138–5; M. H. Yardy
58–9–231–2.

COUNTY RECORDS

Highest score for:	333	K. S. Duleepsinhji v Northamptonshire at Hove . .	1930
Highest score against:	322	E. Paynter (Lancashire) at Hove	1937
Best bowling for:	10-48	C. H. G. Bland v Kent at Tonbridge	1899
Best bowling against:	9-11	A. P. Freeman (Kent) at Hove	1922
Highest total for:	705-8 dec.	v Surrey at Hastings	1902
Highest total against:	726	by Nottinghamshire at Nottingham	1895
Lowest total for:	{ 19	v Surrey at Godalming	1830
	{ 19	v Nottinghamshire at Hove	1873
Lowest total against:	18	by Kent at Gravesend	1867

COUNTY OFFICERS

Captain C. J. Adams • **Director of cricket** P. Moores
President 2002 – The Rt Rev. Lord Sheppard; 2003 – J. M. Parks
Chairman D. E. Green • **Chief executive** H. H. Griffiths
Chairman, cricket committee J. R. T. Barclay • **Head groundsman** D. J. Traill
Scorer J. Hartridge

At The Oval, April 19, 20, 21, 22. SUSSEX lost to SURREY by ten wickets.

SUSSEX v SOMERSET

At Hove, April 24, 25, 26, 27. Drawn. Sussex 10 pts, Somerset 12 pts. Toss: Sussex.

Hove was sunk in sea fret as play began, but a wayward Somerset attack squandered the best bowling conditions of the match. Goodwin was scintillating: cutting and pulling balls of good length, he drove crisply as soon as the bowlers overcompensated. His hundred came ten minutes after lunch, and he went on to hit 26 fours and two sixes in 168 balls while the rest of the batsmen came and went in a procession. In reply, Cox and Wood built a stylish century stand, before Bowler – once much desired by Sussex – dropped anchor. Kirtley's five wickets were reward for perseverance in superb batting conditions. With the pitch still flat, the loss of 57 overs to rain on the third day ended any chance of a positive result. Sussex began the last day in effect 114 for three, but Adams insured his team against defeat, Martin-Jenkins played a series of handsome leg-side shots and, in the end, they could afford the luxury of a declaration.

Close of play: First day, Somerset 4-0 (Cox 1, Wood 1); Second day, Somerset 380-8 (Johnson 13, Bulbeck 0); Third day, Sussex 178-3 (Adams 68, Yardy 29).

Sussex

R. R. Montgomerie c Dutch b Jones	37	– (2) c Turner b Johnson	27
M. W. Goodwin lbw b Bulbeck	162	– (1) b Parsons	29
*C. J. Adams b Bulbeck	8	– c Blackwell b Bulbeck	101
P. A. Cottey c Turner b Johnson	19	– c Cox b Parsons	6
M. H. Yardy lbw b Bulbeck	5	– c Turner b Burns	73
R. S. C. Martin-Jenkins c Cox b Burns	25	– c Cox b Johnson	86
†M. J. Prior b Burns	5	– not out	37
M. J. G. Davis lbw b Johnson	3	– lbw b Bulbeck	1
R. J. Kirtley not out	36	– not out	5
J. D. Lewry b Bulbeck	1		
P. M. Hutchison b Burns	7		
L-b 9, w 4, n-b 16	29	B 3, l-b 8, w 4, n-b 16	31

1/102 (1) 2/126 (3) 3/217 (4)   337   1/47 (2) 2/90 (1)   (7 wkts dec.) 396
4/242 (5) 5/259 (2) 6/286 (6) 7/286 (7)   3/130 (4) 4/225 (3)
8/308 (8) 9/309 (10) 10/337 (11)   5/287 (5) 6/380 (6) 7/389 (8)

Bonus points – Sussex 3, Somerset 3.

Bowling: *First Innings*—Johnson 23–3–92–2; Bulbeck 28–3–104–4; Jones 14–3–58–1; Dutch 12–4–20–0; Burns 13.2–2–54–3. *Second Innings*—Johnson 26–8–87–2; Bulbeck 25–5–75–2; Parsons 18–3–74–2; Burns 10–0–85–1; Blackwell 14–1–38–0; Dutch 5–1–26–0.

Somerset

*J. Cox c and b Davis	65	– not out	40
M. J. Wood c Prior b Martin-Jenkins	54	– b Martin-Jenkins	4
M. Burns b Davis	33	– c Goodwin b Kirtley	38
P. D. Bowler c Montgomerie b Kirtley	94	– not out	8
K. A. Parsons lbw b Lewry	29		
I. D. Blackwell c Cottey b Kirtley	24		
†R. J. Turner c Adams b Yardy	20		
K. P. Dutch lbw b Kirtley	23		
R. L. Johnson c Davis b Kirtley	24		
M. P. L. Bulbeck lbw b Kirtley	9		
P. S. Jones not out	1		
B 4, l-b 11, w 4, n-b 6	25	N-b 4	4

1/102 (2) 2/153 (3) 3/174 (1) 4/220 (5)   401   1/8 (2) 2/76 (3)   (2 wkts) 94
5/253 (6) 6/301 (7) 7/365 (8)
8/378 (4) 9/392 (10) 10/401 (9)

Bonus points – Somerset 5, Sussex 3.

Bowling: *First Innings*—Lewry 26–3–89–1; Kirtley 27.5–4–90–5; Hutchison 13–2–56–0; Martin-Jenkins 19–2–74–1; Davis 20–4–60–2; Yardy 6–2–17–1. *Second Innings*—Lewry 8–2–27–0; Martin-Jenkins 7–0–19–1; Kirtley 4–1–10–1; Yardy 8–2–33–0; Adams 3–1–5–0; Montgomerie 2–2–0–0.

Umpires: M. J. Harris and T. E. Jesty.

At Hastings, May 8, 9, 10 (not first-class). **Sussex won by 200 runs.** Toss: Sussex. **Sussex 400 for nine dec.** (B. Zuiderent 41, M. J. Prior 151, K. J. Innes 53, J. D. Lewry 42 not out, Extras 41; S. Noach five for 85) **and 163 for five dec.** (B. Zuiderent 84, C. D. Hopkinson 36 not out); **Bradford/Leeds UCCE 164** (J. W. Payn 42, J. W. N. Lucas 49; J. D. Lewry four for 28, W. J. House four for ten) **and 199** (J. W. N. Lucas 35, S. Noach 52, Extras 31; J. D. Lewry five for 35).
First-team debuts: D. A. Clapp, C. F. Mumby, K. R. Singh. County debut: K. J. Innes.

At Manchester, May 15, 16, 17, 18. SUSSEX drew with LANCASHIRE.

SUSSEX v LEICESTERSHIRE

At Horsham, May 24, 25, 26, 27. Drawn. Sussex 8 pts, Leicestershire 9 pts. Toss: Leicestershire. First-class debut: D. A. Clapp.

The Horsham festival was battered by high winds and blighted by rain, and no play was possible on the last two days. By then, Leicestershire had built a useful lead in seamer-friendly conditions. But it was a Sussex bowler, the tall Robin Martin-Jenkins, who was first to profit, bowling accurately and with a zip boosted by the strong tail wind: seven for 51 was a career-best, on his club ground. Only Wells and Stevens batted with authority. In reply, Malcolm pounded in like a charging bull to claim seven wickets and take his first-class total to 997. Sussex had been struggling at 57 for five but Montgomerie was limpet-like, becoming the first Sussex batsman in eight years to carry his bat. Simple but effective, with lots of tucks through square leg, it was one of his best innings for the county. The deficit was kept down to 17, but Leicestershire were slowly stretching the gap again when the rain returned. The Horsham club – who had paid £10,000 to stage the game – were left facing a loss.

Close of play: First day, Leicestershire 257-7 (Wells 85, Crowe 4); Second day, Leicestershire 94-2 (Maddy 31, Bevan 28); Third day, No play.

Leicestershire

T. R. Ward c Yardy b Martin-Jenkins	48	– c Prior b Martin-Jenkins	24
I. J. Sutcliffe c Lewry b Martin-Jenkins	12	– lbw b Kirtley	8
D. L. Maddy st Prior b Davis	21	– not out	31
M. G. Bevan c Yardy b Martin-Jenkins	4	– not out	28
*V. J. Wells not out	86		
D. I. Stevens c Lewry b Yardy	50		
†N. D. Burns b Davis	0		
P. A. J. DeFreitas c Prior b Martin-Jenkins	26		
C. D. Crowe lbw b Martin-Jenkins	4		
C. E. Dagnall c Prior b Martin-Jenkins	3		
D. E. Malcolm b Martin-Jenkins	0		
L-b 8, w 2	10	L-b 3	3

1/46 (2) 2/82 (1) 3/84 (3) 4/96 (4)   **264**   1/20 (2) 2/34 (1)   (2 wkts) **94**
5/199 (6) 6/207 (7) 7/250 (8)
8/258 (9) 9/264 (10) 10/264 (11)

Bonus points – Leicestershire 2, Sussex 3.

Bowling: *First Innings*—Lewry 10–0–51–0; Kirtley 19–4–62–0; Martin-Jenkins 16.4–4–51–7; Yardy 7–1–36–1; Davis 18–2–56–2. *Second Innings*—Lewry 4–0–9–0; Kirtley 11–5–26–1; Martin-Jenkins 8–3–32–1; Davis 6–1–24–0.

Sussex

R. R. Montgomerie not out	122	M. J. G. Davis c Burns b Malcolm	34
M. W. Goodwin lbw b Malcolm	4	*R. J. Kirtley b Malcolm	3
D. A. Clapp c Ward b Malcolm	6	J. D. Lewry b Malcolm	5
P. A. Cottey c Burns b Malcolm	6	B 5, l-b 3	8
M. H. Yardy c Burns b Wells	8		
T. R. Ambrose lbw b Dagnall	0	1/12 (2) 2/30 (3) 3/45 (4) 4/54 (5)	247
R. S. C. Martin-Jenkins b Malcolm	22	5/57 (6) 6/109 (7) 7/165 (8)	
†M. J. Prior b DeFreitas	29	8/217 (9) 9/233 (10) 10/247 (11)	

Bonus points – Sussex 1, Leicestershire 3.

Bowling: DeFreitas 13–2–43–1; Malcolm 19.5–4–76–7; Wells 12–3–31–1; Dagnall 5–1–24–1; Crowe 14–2–47–0; Bevan 1–0–3–0; Maddy 5–0–15–0.

Umpires: V. A. Holder and G. Sharp.

At Tunbridge Wells, May 31, June 1, 2, 3. SUSSEX lost to KENT by four wickets.

At Leeds, June 12, 13, 14, 15. SUSSEX beat YORKSHIRE by an innings and 94 runs.

At Hove, June 21. SUSSEX lost to WEST INDIES A by three wickets (see West Indies A tour section).

At Hove, June 22. SUSSEX lost to INDIANS by three wickets (see Indian tour section).

SUSSEX v YORKSHIRE

At Arundel, June 26, 27, 28, 29. Drawn. Sussex 11 pts, Yorkshire 9 pts. Toss: Yorkshire.

Yorkshire failed to finish the job after Lehmann transformed the match with a gutsy double-century in their second innings. When he arrived Yorkshire were still 123 behind, and two wickets down; when he left, they were 213 ahead and pushing for victory. After being bowled by a Robinson no-ball on 17, Lehmann scored efficiently with cuts and leg-side clips. He batted six hours and hit 25 fours and a six off 302 balls, and put on 238 with Lumb; the Sussex attack, missing both Kirtley and Lewry for the first time in a Championship match since 1997, was toothless. Set a target of 322 on a turning pitch, Sussex could only scrap for survival. In a thrilling finish, Prior and Innes defied Yorkshire's slow-bowling triumvirate, before Robinson – a renowned rabbit – blocked 11 balls to scrape a deserved draw. Sussex had expected more after forging a first-innings lead of 137, thanks in part to Prior's best first-class score. Fears that an escapee from the nearby Ford prison had melted into the crowd led to a strong police presence on the second day.

Close of play: First day, Sussex 23-0 (Montgomerie 14, Goodwin 8); Second day, Sussex 392; Third day, Yorkshire 357-4 (Lumb 89, Gray 0).

Yorkshire

C. White c Goodwin b Taylor	7	– lbw b Taylor	0
M. J. Wood c Yardy b Martin-Jenkins	15	– c Prior b Martin-Jenkins	9
A. McGrath c Yardy b Robinson	7	– c Montgomerie b Davis	33
*D. S. Lehmann c Prior b Innes	71	– lbw b Taylor	216
M. J. Lumb lbw b Robinson	0	– c Prior b Taylor	92
V. J. Craven b Robinson	37	– (9) c Montgomerie b Davis	1
†R. J. Blakey b Innes	14	– not out	28
R. K. J. Dawson lbw b Taylor	33	– c Adams b Robinson	7
A. K. D. Gray c Prior b Martin-Jenkins	40	– (6) c Davis b Robinson	40
C. J. Elstub not out	0	– not out	18
R. J. Sidebottom lbw b Martin-Jenkins	0		
B 1, l-b 11, n-b 19	31	B 4, l-b 4, n-b 6	14

1/12 (1) 2/33 (2) 3/41 (3) 4/41 (5)   255
5/137 (6) 6/162 (4) 7/183 (7)
8/255 (8) 9/255 (9) 10/255 (11)

1/0 (1) 2/14 (2)   (8 wkts dec.) 458
3/112 (3) 4/350 (4)
5/371 (5) 6/414 (6)
7/427 (8) 8/429 (9)

Bonus points – Yorkshire 2, Sussex 3.

Bowling: *First Innings*—Taylor 20–6–51–2; Martin-Jenkins 15.5–3–46–3; Robinson 20–6–57–3; Innes 17–4–45–2; Davis 17–5–35–0; Yardy 4–1–9–0. *Second Innings*—Taylor 28–8–82–3; Martin-Jenkins 25–4–77–1; Robinson 20–2–81–2; Innes 12–0–57–0; Davis 31.1–4–111–2; Yardy 8–0–34–0; Montgomerie 2–0–8–0.

Sussex

R. R. Montgomerie b White	78	– (2) run out	10
M. W. Goodwin lbw b White	35	– (1) c White b Elstub	2
*C. J. Adams lbw b White	10	– b Sidebottom	23
M. H. Yardy c Lumb b Lehmann	38	– c Blakey b Dawson	8
T. R. Ambrose c Lumb b Gray	19	– c McGrath b Gray	18
R. S. C. Martin-Jenkins lbw b Dawson	35	– c Wood b Dawson	32
†M. J. Prior c Blakey b Sidebottom	85	– not out	70
K. J. Innes b Dawson	0	– c McGrath b Lehmann	28
M. J. G. Davis not out	70	– b Gray	1
B. V. Taylor lbw b Sidebottom	1	– c White b Gray	5
M. A. Robinson lbw b White	6	– not out	2
B 6, l-b 7, n-b 2	15	B 5, l-b 5, w 4	14

1/85 (2) 2/109 (3) 3/142 (1) 4/173 (5)   392
5/196 (4) 6/269 (6) 7/269 (8)
8/357 (7) 9/363 (10) 10/392 (11)

1/2 (1) 2/36 (3) 3/36 (2)   (9 wkts) 216
4/53 (4) 5/96 (5) 6/102 (6)
7/159 (8) 8/170 (9) 9/206 (10)

Bonus points – Sussex 4, Yorkshire 3.

Bowling: *First Innings*—Sidebottom 19–2–87–2; Elstub 16–3–66–0; Dawson 24–3–86–2; Gray 25–5–65–1; White 17.2–5–49–4; Lehmann 10–1–26–1. *Second Innings*—Elstub 8–3–16–1; Sidebottom 11–1–33–1; Dawson 24–7–55–2; Lehmann 11–3–24–1; Gray 20–2–62–3; White 5–0–16–0.

Umpires: N. L. Bainton and G. I. Burgess.

At Southampton, July 3, 4, 5, 6. SUSSEX drew with HAMPSHIRE.

SUSSEX v KENT

At Hove, July 10, 11, 12, 13. Drawn. Sussex 7 pts, Kent 10 pts. Toss: Kent.

After dominating the first two days, Kent ended up grateful for a draw. Sussex began their second innings 204 behind, but Goodwin and Ambrose both scored centuries to lead a dogged fightback. They took advantage of a pitch that had become less tricky after starting damp, and added 236, though Goodwin was dropped on 29 by the substitute Martyn Sigley – Kent's physio and a first-class cricketer in his native New Zealand – and Ambrose survived a big appeal for a catch off bat and pad when on 92. Pointedly, the Kent players did not applaud his century. Entertaining cameos from Prior and Innes made the match safe for Sussex before Kent lost five wickets in the last session in pursuit of a notional target. Earlier, Fulton's decision to bowl first was vindicated when Khan settled into a probing off-stump line, found darting seam movement and seized six wickets. In reply, Smith's careful, seven-hour vigil left Kent with a big lead. It wasn't a stylish innings, but it should have been a match-winning one.

Close of play: First day, Kent 152-5 (Smith 63, Ealham 12); Second day, Sussex 114-3 (Goodwin 47, Ambrose 26); Third day, Sussex 256-3 (Goodwin 108, Ambrose 101).

Sussex

R. R. Montgomerie lbw b Masters	14	– (2) lbw b Khan	2
M. W. Goodwin lbw b Masters	12	– (1) c Ealham b Patel	135
*C. J. Adams lbw b Khan	18	– (4) lbw b Masters	10
M. H. Yardy c Nixon b Khan	33	– (3) lbw b Khan	14
T. R. Ambrose c Fulton b Khan	4	– c Symonds b Saggers	124
R. S. C. Martin-Jenkins c Nixon b Khan	1	– c Nixon b Patel	8
†M. J. Prior b Khan	0	– c Saggers b Masters	53
K. J. Innes lbw b Saggers	17	– c Key b Saggers	56
M. J. G. Davis b Saggers	1	– lbw b Patel	1
B. V. Taylor not out	11	– c Nixon b Saggers	0
J. D. Lewry b Khan	20	– not out	15
L-b 6, n-b 8	14	B 5, l-b 9, w 8, n-b 10	32

1/32 (2) 2/33 (1) 3/72 (3) 4/76 (5)   145   1/8 (2) 2/30 (3) 3/54 (4)   450
5/78 (6) 6/78 (7) 7/109 (4)   4/290 (5) 5/313 (6) 6/336 (1)
8/113 (8) 9/114 (9) 10/145 (11)   7/400 (7) 8/412 (9)
                                                             9/413 (10) 10/450 (8)

Bonus points – Kent 3.

Bowling: *First Innings*—Saggers 17–4–44–2; Khan 15–4–56–6; Masters 7–0–19–2; Ealham 8–3–10–0; Patel 3–0–10–0. *Second Innings*—Saggers 32.2–6–93–3; Khan 23–2–111–2; Masters 29–7–86–2; Symonds 31–6–82–0; Patel 31–8–51–3; Walker 1–0–5–0; Ealham 4–1–8–0.

Kent

*D. P. Fulton c Prior b Lewry	14	– c Montgomerie b Martin-Jenkins	1
R. W. T. Key b Taylor	6	– lbw b Lewry	25
E. T. Smith not out	141	– c Prior b Martin-Jenkins	0
A. Symonds c Martin-Jenkins	32	– c sub b Taylor	6
M. J. Walker lbw b Innes	11	– c Prior b Lewry	20
†P. A. Nixon b Lewry	0	– not out	19
M. A. Ealham lbw b Lewry	27	– not out	5
M. M. Patel c Yardy b Davis	28		
A. Khan c Prior b Davis	58		
M. J. Saggers lbw b Martin-Jenkins	0		
D. D. Masters b Taylor	5		
B 4, l-b 9, w 6, n-b 8	27	B 4, l-b 1, n-b 4	9

1/24 (2) 2/30 (1) 3/72 (4) 4/95 (5)   349   1/2 (1) 2/2 (3) 3/17 (4)   (5 wkts) 85
5/100 (6) 6/186 (7) 7/237 (8)   4/53 (2) 5/58 (5)
8/327 (9) 9/334 (10) 10/349 (11)

Bonus points – Kent 3, Sussex 3.

Bowling: *First Innings*—Lewry 25–4–82–3; Martin-Jenkins 31–10–81–2; Taylor 27.4–7–86–2; Innes 16–4–36–1; Yardy 3–1–11–0; Davis 17–3–40–2. *Second Innings*—Martin-Jenkins 5–1–12–2; Lewry 11–2–44–2; Taylor 6–1–20–1; Goodwin 2–1–1–0; Davis 5–2–3–0.

Umpires: A. A. Jones and K. J. Lyons.

At Taunton, July 19, 20, 21. SUSSEX beat SOMERSET by an innings and one run.

At Birmingham, July 24, 25, 26, 27. SUSSEX lost to WARWICKSHIRE by 208 runs.

SUSSEX v SURREY

At Hove, August 8, 9, 10, 11. Sussex won by four wickets. Sussex 16 pts, Surrey 3 pts. Toss: Sussex. County debut: Mushtaq Ahmed.

Goodwin's tenth century for Sussex – and arguably his most important – decided a compelling contest. Chasing 287, Sussex crawled from 85 for two to 145 for three on a tense final morning, as Tudor and Mushtaq Ahmed, standing in for fellow-Pakistan spinner Saqlain, produced spells of Test quality. Crucially, however, Sussex lost only one wicket, which allowed Goodwin and the belligerent Adams to launch a thrilling counter-attack in the afternoon. Both departed in quick succession, but they had brought the target within reach, and the middle order finished the job. Although 17 wickets crashed on the first day, when Innes's medium-pace won him career-best figures and Surrey tumbled to their lowest first-innings total of the season, the umpires blamed flimsy batting rather than a slow, seaming pitch. In reply, Sussex were revived by their tailenders, and the match seesawed as Ward and Ramprakash batted sublimely to put Surrey back in control. But Davis, using crafty variation in flight, took six wickets, the last four bowled, to leave Sussex a gettable target.

Close of play: First day, Sussex 139-7 (Innes 6, Davis 18); Second day, Surrey 261-8 (Mushtaq Ahmed 17, Murtagh 4); Third day, Sussex 85-2 (Goodwin 42, Prior 0).

Surrey

I. J. Ward lbw b Taylor	28	– c Prior b Davis	76
†J. N. Batty run out	16	– c sub b Davis	46
M. R. Ramprakash lbw b Kirtley	32	– st Prior b Innes	64
N. Shahid c Prior b Kirtley	28	– b Kirtley	5
A. D. Brown c Davis b Kirtley	49	– b Davis	7
*A. J. Hollioake lbw b Martin-Jenkins	9	– b Davis	0
R. Clarke lbw b Innes	17	– b Davis	2
A. J. Tudor c Goodwin b Innes	0	– b Davis	28
Mushtaq Ahmed lbw b Innes	7	– c Goodwin b Kirtley	47
T. J. Murtagh not out	0	– b Kirtley	4
E. S. H. Giddins c Prior b Innes	0	– not out	1
L-b 7	7	B 6, l-b 4, n-b 6	16
	193		**296**

1/29 (2) 2/60 (1) 3/94 (3) 4/111 (4)   193   1/121 (2) 2/142 (1) 3/147 (4)   296
5/136 (6) 6/157 (7) 7/165 (8)   4/176 (5) 5/176 (6) 6/190 (7)
8/189 (5) 9/193 (9) 10/193 (11)   7/240 (3) 8/242 (8)
                     9/267 (10) 10/296 (9)

Bonus points – Sussex 3.

Bowling: *First Innings*—Kirtley 15–7–49–3; Martin-Jenkins 16–6–34–1; Innes 14.4–5–41–4; Taylor 11–1–44–1; Davis 2–0–18–0. *Second Innings*—Kirtley 17.2–4–59–3; Martin-Jenkins 15–2–53–0; Taylor 6–0–29–0; Innes 13–3–48–1; Davis 26–2–97–6.

Sussex

M. W. Goodwin b Tudor	3	– (2) lbw b Murtagh	100
R. R. Montgomerie c Shahid b Giddins	1	– (1) c Batty b Giddins	10
P. A. Cottey run out	35	– lbw b Murtagh	22
*C. J. Adams c Mushtaq Ahmed b Giddins	21	– (5) c sub b Tudor	62
T. R. Ambrose c Ramprakash b Tudor	25	– (6) lbw b Murtagh	16
R. S. C. Martin-Jenkins c Batty b Murtagh	23	– (7) not out	23
†M. J. Prior c Brown b Tudor	0	– (4) b Tudor	20
K. J. Innes not out	41	– not out	12
M. J. G. Davis c Brown b Tudor	30		
R. J. Kirtley c Hollioake b Tudor	8		
B. V. Taylor c Batty b Murtagh	5		
B 3, l-b 4, n-b 4	11	L-b 9, n-b 14	23
	203	(6 wkts)	**288**

1/4 (2) 2/4 (1) 3/58 (3) 4/70 (4) 203 1/15 (1) 2/77 (3) (6 wkts) 288
5/112 (5) 6/112 (6) 7/112 (7) 3/128 (4) 4/234 (5)
8/158 (9) 9/172 (10) 10/203 (11) 5/238 (2) 6/265 (6)

Bonus points – Sussex 1, Surrey 3.

Bowling: *First Innings*—Tudor 22–4–66–5; Giddins 21–4–68–2; Mushtaq Ahmed 13–3–40–0; Murtagh 10.1–2–22–2. *Second Innings*—Tudor 23–5–80–2; Giddins 25–7–64–1; Clarke 3–0–9–0; Murtagh 13.1–3–47–3; Mushtaq Ahmed 29–6–79–0.

Umpires: R. Palmer and P. Willey.

SUSSEX v LANCASHIRE

At Hove, August 22, 23, 24, 25. Lancashire won by seven wickets. Lancashire 20 pts, Sussex 4 pts. Toss: Lancashire.

Lancashire's victory was thoroughly deserved. For a while it looked as if Law's decision to bowl first might backfire as Goodwin and Ambrose took Sussex to 190 for three. But Chapple's pace broke the stand, Schofield's leg-spin bewildered the tail and Sussex lost seven for 50. The malaise spread to their bowling. Lewry had a torrid time, and Law, aided by Byas, put Lancashire in a commanding position. Initially even Law struggled to time the ball on a two-paced pitch, but he went on to crack his first hundred since May. Sussex, trailing by 185, needed at least one batsman to stick around; none did. Chapple's control earned him a match haul of ten wickets, before Law guided Lancashire past a small target. On the third morning, the Sussex coach, Peter Moores, briefly stood at square leg when umpire John Hampshire, recently bereaved, had to leave the field after the minute's silence for the murdered schoolgirls, Holly Wells and Jessica Chapman.

Close of play: First day, Lancashire 116-1 (Chilton 39, Byas 20); Second day, Sussex 12-1 (Montgomerie 5, Kirtley 4); Third day, Sussex 276-9 (Davis 5).

Sussex

M. W. Goodwin c Haynes b Chapple	87	– (2) lbw b Chapple	1
R. R. Montgomerie lbw b Chapple	0	– (1) run out	43
P. A. Cottey c Law b Chapple	6	– (4) lbw b Schofield	41
*C. J. Adams lbw b Martin	36	– (5) c Swann b Chapple	61
T. R. Ambrose c Byas b Chapple	60	– (6) c Martin b Anderson	39
R. S. C. Martin-Jenkins b Martin	22	– (7) b Chapple	55
†M. J. Prior c and b Martin	7	– (8) lbw b Chapple	0
K. J. Innes lbw b Schofield	0	– (9) c Law b Chapple	7
M. J. G. Davis b Schofield	8	– (10) not out	5
R. J. Kirtley c Law b Schofield	1	– (3) c Swann b Chapple	4
J. D. Lewry not out	1	– b Martin	0
B 3, l-b 7, w 2	12	B 2, l-b 9, w 8	19
	240		**277**

1/2 (2) 2/8 (3) 3/92 (4) 4/190 (5) 240 1/4 (2) 2/20 (3) 3/98 (1) 4/101 (4) 277
5/207 (1) 6/229 (7) 7/230 (8) 5/172 (6) 6/242 (5) 7/242 (8)
8/230 (6) 9/235 (10) 10/240 (9) 8/261 (7) 9/276 (9) 10/277 (11)

Bonus points – Sussex 1, Lancashire 3.

Bowling: *First Innings*—Martin 22–10–45–3; Chapple 15–1–61–4; Anderson 10–2–54–0; Chilton 7–4–11–0; Keedy 7–0–38–0; Schofield 13.2–6–21–3. *Second Innings*—Martin 26.2–12–45–1; Chapple 31–14–66–6; Anderson 17–1–58–1; Keedy 20–5–38–0; Schofield 12–0–31–1; Chilton 3–1–14–0; Law 7–1–14–0.

Lancashire

M. J. Chilton c Ambrose b Innes	44	– c Prior b Kirtley	0
A. J. Swann lbw b Martin-Jenkins	23	– lbw b Kirtley	4
D. Byas c Prior b Davis	71	– c Kirtley b Martin-Jenkins	24
*S. G. Law lbw b Innes	147	– not out	45
N. H. Fairbrother lbw b Kirtley	16	– not out	13
G. Chapple not out	36		
C. P. Schofield c Prior b Lewry	1		
†J. J. Haynes lbw b Lewry	4		
P. J. Martin c Goodwin b Martin-Jenkins	14		
G. Keedy c Goodwin b Martin-Jenkins	7		
J. M. Anderson lbw b Kirtley	0		
B 17, l-b 10, w 21, n-b 14	62	L-b 3, w 4.	7
	425	(3 wkts)	**93**

1/69 (2) 2/130 (1) 3/260 (3) 4/326 (5) 5/366 (4) 6/373 (7) 7/379 (8) 8/400 (9) 9/420 (10) 10/425 (11)

1/5 (2) 2/6 (1) 3/60 (3)

Bonus points – Lancashire 5, Sussex 3.

Bowling: *First Innings*—Lewry 25–4–118–2; Kirtley 34–6–94–2; Martin-Jenkins 26–2–67–3; Innes 20–6–53–2; Davis 19–1–66–1. *Second Innings*—Kirtley 5–3–10–2; Lewry 6–1–23–0; Martin-Jenkins 8–0–25–1; Innes 4–1–10–0; Davis 2–0–17–0; Cottey 0.2–0–5–0.

Umpires: J. H. Hampshire and M. J. Kitchen.

At Leicester, August 27, 28, 29. SUSSEX lost to LEICESTERSHIRE by eight wickets.

SUSSEX v HAMPSHIRE

At Hove, September 5, 6, 7, 8. Drawn. Sussex 12 pts, Hampshire 10 pts. Toss: Hampshire. County debut: J. H. K. Adams.

Sussex condemned Hampshire to the second division after burying them under a mountain of runs. The two teams began the match either side of the relegation cut-off: Sussex, 20 points ahead, took no risks and produced the flattest Hove pitch of the summer. They couldn't have imagined they would get first use of it after losing the toss, but Smith was seduced by green tinges and low sea mist. He could only watch helplessly as Montgomerie rediscovered his nimble footwork and sureness of touch in a career-best 196, Goodwin crashed through the off side, and Prior brought up the quickest hundred of the three, his first, in only 105 balls. Sussex finally declared on the second afternoon with a mammoth 631 for six, but their bowlers found it hard work. Rain frustrated them, Laney organised spirited resistance and Hampshire had only 43 overs to survive in their second innings. They succeeded, but it was not enough to save them from the drop.

Close of play: First day, Sussex 399-3 (Montgomerie 168, Ambrose 21); Second day, Hampshire 69-1 (Laney 14); Third day, Hampshire 276-4 (Smith 19, Francis 31).

Sussex

M. W. Goodwin lbw b Mascarenhas	119	†M. J. Prior not out	102
R. R. Montgomerie c Pothas b Tomlinson	196	K. J. Innes not out	17
P. A. Cottey c Pothas b Johnson	28	B 7, l-b 8, w 10, n-b 14	39
*C. J. Adams c and b Udal	34		
T. R. Ambrose c Kendall b Mascarenhas	32	1/193 (1) 2/264 (3)	(6 wkts dec.) 631
R. S. C. Martin-Jenkins c Johnson		3/349 (4) 4/425 (5)	
b Kendall	64	5/460 (2) 6/580 (6)	

M. J. G. Davis, R. J. Kirtley and B. V. Taylor did not bat.

Bonus points – Sussex 5, Hampshire 1 (130 overs: 485-5).

Bowling: Mullally 28–6–82–0; Tomlinson 30–5–154–1; Mascarenhas 31–8–114–2; Johnson 19–3–78–1; Udal 34–7–121–1; Adams 3–1–21–0; Kendall 11–1–46–1.

Hampshire

N. C. Johnson c Prior b Martin-Jenkins	51	– not out	51
J. S. Laney lbw b Kirtley	89	– c Montgomerie b Davis	10
J. H. K. Adams c Ambrose b Kirtley	48	– not out	3
W. S. Kendall b Kirtley	4		
*R. A. Smith b Kirtley	60		
J. D. Francis c Montgomerie b Innes	48		
†N. Pothas c Montgomerie b Innes	8		
A. D. Mascarenhas c Goodwin b Martin-Jenkins	36		
S. D. Udal lbw b Kirtley	11		
A. D. Mullally c Goodwin b Kirtley	0		
J. A. Tomlinson not out	0		
L-b 16, w 4, n-b 26	46	L-b 3	3

1/69 (1) 2/208 (2) 3/212 (4) 4/213 (3)	401	1/47 (2)	(1 wkt) 67
5/317 (6) 6/335 (7) 7/363 (5)			
8/393 (9) 9/401 (8) 10/401 (10)			

Bonus points – Hampshire 5, Sussex 3.

Bowling: *First Innings*—Kirtley 29.2–7–107–6; Martin-Jenkins 27–3–111–2; Taylor 22–6–74–0; Davis 25–11–45–0; Innes 18–5–48–2. *Second Innings*—Kirtley 6–2–10–0; Martin-Jenkins 6–2–14–0; Davis 11–2–26–1; Innes 2–0–7–0; Cottey 9–5–4–0; Montgomerie 2–0–2–0; Ambrose 1–0–1–0.

Umpires: V. A. Holder and B. Leadbeater.

SUSSEX v WARWICKSHIRE

At Hove, September 18, 19, 20, 21. Warwickshire won by three wickets. Warwickshire 17 pts, Sussex 7 pts. Toss: Sussex. First-class debut: C. D. Hopkinson.

As the last day began, Sussex looked clear favourites: only once had Warwickshire, who resumed on 103 for three, scored a fourth-innings total of more than the 401 they needed. But Powell hit his first hundred in 59 first-class innings, Ostler crunched 90 and Brown's six-strewn firework display ensured victory just after tea. It was a thrilling end to a match of punch and counter-punch. Sussex had chosen to bat on a slow, seaming pitch, and Goodwin's watchful 93, together with a late rally, took them to 352. In reply, Carter reached a maiden hundred in 67 balls – the quickest of the 2002 Championship, with six sixes and a riot of savage pulls and blistering drives. He and Spires, the No. 11, joined forces 29 short of the follow-on. They managed 119. Goodwin's more studious century in Sussex's second innings boosted their lead and, after Carl Hopkinson snared Bell with his brisk medium-pace, Bob Woolmer, Warwickshire's departing coach, admitted his team would have to "bat out of their skins" to win. Aided by some very ordinary bowling and a ridiculous 51-yard boundary, they did just that, pipping Kent to second place in the Championship and the £50,000 prize money.

Close of play: First day, Warwickshire 20-0 (Powell 6, Wagh 7); Second day, Sussex 166-4 (Ambrose 8); Third day, Warwickshire 103-3 (Powell 39, Ostler 5).

Sussex

*R. R. Montgomerie c Piper b Brown	34	– (2) c Piper b Sheikh	43
M. W. Goodwin c Wagh b Brown	93	– (1) c Ostler b Wagh	111
P. A. Cottey c Richardson b Brown	5	– run out	0
M. J. Prior c Piper b Richardson	10	– c Richardson b Sheikh	3
†T. R. Ambrose c Piper b Brown	26	– lbw b Sheikh	30
R. S. C. Martin-Jenkins c Spires b Richardson	33	– c Ostler b Wagh	9
C. D. Hopkinson lbw b Richardson	33	– c Ostler b Sheikh	9
K. J. Innes not out	60	– c Piper b Brown	40
M. J. G. Davis c Ostler b Richardson	4	– c Carter b Brown	66
P. M. Hutchison c Ostler b Brown	0	– not out	20
B. V. Taylor c Piper b Carter	10	– b Brown	0
B 13, l-b 7, w 4, n-b 20	44	L-b 6, n-b 4	10

1/45 (1) 2/53 (3) 3/94 (4) 4/177 (5)   352
5/222 (2) 6/228 (6) 7/305 (7)
8/323 (9) 9/326 (10) 10/352 (11)

1/128 (2) 2/130 (3) 3/146 (4)   341
4/166 (1) 5/176 (6) 6/203 (7)
7/212 (5) 8/264 (8)
9/341 (9) 10/341 (11)

Bonus points – Sussex 4, Warwickshire 3.

Bowling: *First Innings*—Sheikh 27–5–82–0; Carter 13.1–1–59–1; Brown 29–4–103–5; Richardson 23–4–76–4; Spires 3–1–12–0. *Second Innings*—Carter 8–0–46–0; Richardson 16–2–61–0; Sheikh 31–8–78–4; Brown 15–3–55–3; Spires 7–0–39–0; Wagh 26–6–56–2.

Warwickshire

*M. J. Powell c Hopkinson b Martin-Jenkins	15	– c Cottey b Hutchison	103
M. A. Wagh b Martin-Jenkins	8	– b Martin-Jenkins	6
T. Frost b Taylor	73	– c Goodwin b Taylor	28
I. R. Bell c Cottey b Taylor	5	– b Hopkinson	18
D. P. Ostler c Hopkinson b Hutchison	0	– c Montgomerie b Innes	90
D. R. Brown c Ambrose b Hutchison	0	– not out	79
M. A. Sheikh b Taylor	34	– b Davis	43
†K. J. Piper b Taylor	0	– c Ambrose b Martin-Jenkins	15
N. M. Carter b Martin-Jenkins	103	– not out	0
A. Richardson lbw b Taylor	0		
J. A. Spires not out	37		
L-b 2, w 6, n-b 12	20	B 10, l-b 3, w 4, n-b 6	23

1/29 (2) 2/38 (1) 3/48 (4) 4/59 (5)   293
5/61 (6) 6/143 (3) 7/143 (8)
8/174 (7) 9/174 (10) 10/293 (9)

1/10 (2) 2/56 (3)   (7 wkts) 405
3/97 (4) 4/249 (5)
5/288 (1) 6/363 (7) 7/399 (8)

Bonus points – Warwickshire 2, Sussex 3.

Bowling: *First Innings*—Hutchison 12–1–52–2; Martin-Jenkins 15.4–3–56–3; Davis 13–1–66–0; Innes 9–3–27–0; Taylor 17–2–90–5. *Second Innings*—Hutchison 19–3–92–1; Martin-Jenkins 23–7–68–2; Innes 17–3–69–1; Taylor 22.2–5–96–1; Hopkinson 7–0–35–1; Davis 8–2–32–1.

Umpires: J. H. Evans and I. J. Gould.

THE CRICKET SOCIETY LITERARY AWARD

The Cricket Society Literary Award has been presented since 1970 to the author of the cricket book judged as best of the year. The 2002 award, sponsored by the *Daily Telegraph*, was won by Stephen Chalke for *At The Heart of English Cricket: The life and memories of Geoffrey Howard*. The shortlist for the 2003 award was: *Opening up: My Autobiography* by Mike Atherton; *The Father of Modern Sport: The Life and Times of Charles W. Alcock* by Keith Booth; *A Corner of a Foreign Field: The Indian History of a British Sport* by Ramachandra Guha; and *Rain Stops Play: Cricketing Climates* by Andrew Hignell.

WARWICKSHIRE
GOOD RESULTS, BAD BLOOD

Ch'ship 2nd in Division 1
C&G 4th round
B&H winners
NUL 3rd in Division 1

Player of the season: Nick Knight

Warwickshire enjoyed their best summer since 1995, winning the last Benson and Hedges Cup and finishing as runners-up in their first season in Division One of the Championship – all of it against a background of unsettling political intrigue. Victory over Essex at Lord's allowed Bob Woolmer to end his second spell as director of coaching as he had his first – with a trophy, the county's first in five years – and to leave with some dignity. But there was nothing dignified about the machinations that led to his departure. Within two weeks of the B&H triumph, Woolmer announced that he would not be seeking a renewal of his contract. This was ostensibly because he wanted to spend more time at home in Cape Town, but it soon became apparent that he had jumped before he was pushed. Warwickshire had repeatedly stalled Woolmer's requests to discuss his future and when no extension to his initial three-year contract was forthcoming, it was obvious that they were already casting around for his successor. John Inverarity, the former Australian all-rounder, was appointed as his replacement before the end of the season.

The captain, Michael Powell, and the vice-captain, Dougie Brown, both owed their appointments to Woolmer, and tried to persuade the cricket committee to reconsider. Woolmer's parting shot told a tale. "I have found the last three years very educational," he said, "but I can't pretend that they have been the most enjoyable three years of my career." His supporters in the dressing-room were in a clear minority, but it was the strained relationship between him and M. J. K. Smith, who announced his retirement after 12 years as chairman, that proved most damaging. Woolmer's tenure had come to a messy end, but his reputation as Warwickshire's most successful coach remained intact.

Warwickshire did not always produce the consistent cricket that Woolmer aspired to, particularly in the one-day game. A mid-season slump triggered an early exit from the C&G and prevented a sustained challenge in the Norwich Union. Qualification for the knockout stages of the B&H came through the back door as they finished third in their group, but they then played purposeful and resilient cricket to dispose of Sussex, Lancashire and Essex. The competition brought the best out of Ian Bell, who won Gold Awards for his composed half-centuries in both the quarter-final and final.

But his Championship form was wretched: he failed to justify the early-season rave reviews, scraping 658 runs, and looked jaded after four years of non-stop cricket. Bell was also handicapped by a stress fracture of the back; the end of the season could not come quickly enough.

Mark Wagh also struggled to build on his 2001 form, mainly because he damaged knee ligaments playing football in pre-season training and missed three months of the summer. But his absence created an opening for Jim Troughton, a positive, swashbuckling left-hander from a well-known theatrical family. He leapt at the opportunity, hit 1,000 Championship runs in his first full season and won a place at the England Academy. Dominic Ostler topped 1,000 runs despite missing three matches with a broken finger. But Nick Knight towered above everyone and needed only ten matches to compile 1,520 runs. So often branded a one-day specialist, Knight enjoyed far more success in the Championship, where he set out his stall to bat for at least a day. His five centuries included two marathons: an unbeaten 245 against Sussex and a career-best 255 against Hampshire.

In the Hampshire game, Knight shared a county-record last-wicket stand of 214 with Alan Richardson, who had begun the season hoping to beat his career-best 17 not out; he ended up with 91, more than his career aggregate. Richardson later took eight for 46 against Sussex, Warwickshire's best return in 25 years. The irrepressible Brown completed the modern double of 500 runs and 50 wickets, and there was enough promise from Graham Wagg, a spiky all-rounder from Rugby, to secure a place in both the England Under-19 side and the Academy. But Melvyn Betts lost form, confidence and his bowling action, and was banished to the Second Eleven for most of the latter half of the season.

England duty allowed Ashley Giles only four Championship matches, although he was still Warwickshire's leading spinner. Neil Smith claimed his best return for seven years, against Leicestershire in June, but was given surprisingly little first-class cricket after that. Even so, he was offered a new one-year contract. Shaun Pollock produced a moderate 28 wickets and 425 runs, but contributed to the wins over Leicestershire and Surrey – Warwickshire's first ever after following on – with withering opening spells and "took wickets at the other end" in Woolmer's view. Shane Bond, the New Zealand strike bowler, did enough in his three games as a locum to be offered a contract for 2003, but Damien Fleming enjoyed one of history's briefest spells as a county overseas player: he bowled just four one-day overs before returning to Australia with a damaged shoulder.

Pollock's major contribution was in the dressing-room where his experience proved invaluable to Powell, who again struggled with the twin demands of captaincy and opening the batting. At one stage, Powell dropped himself from the National League side, but eventually he came good in the Championship with match-winning innings under pressure against Yorkshire and Sussex to help secure the £50,000 runners-up cheque. His tactics veered between the inspired and the inexplicable, but he always led from the front and usually managed to pull things together when it mattered. In a season full of off-field distractions, he kept the players focused throughout. **Paul Bolton**

WARWICKSHIRE 2002

Back row: N. Tahir, J. O. Troughton, J. A. Spires, N. A. Warren, E. J. Wilson. *Middle row*: D. L. Amiss (*chief executive*), R. N. Abberley (*head coach, indoor cricket centre*), M. A. Sheikh, M. A. Wagh, A. Richardson, N. M. Carter, M. M. Betts, T. Frost, G. Mostert (*physiotherapist*), S. J. Hollyhead (*fitness and conditioning coach*), M. J. K. Smith (*chairman*). *Front row*: S. P. Perryman (*second-team coach*), I. R. Bell, T. L. Penney, N. M. K. Smith, D. R. Brown (*vice-captain*), M. J. Powell (*captain*), R. A. Woolmer (*director of coaching*), N. V. Knight, A. F Giles, D. P. Ostler, K. J. Piper. *Insets*: S. M. Pollock, G. G. Wagg. *Pictures by Roger Wootton.*

WARWICKSHIRE RESULTS

All first-class matches – Played 17: Won 7, Lost 3, Drawn 7.
County Championship matches – Played 16: Won 7, Lost 2, Drawn 7.

COUNTY CHAMPIONSHIP AVERAGES: BATTING AND FIELDING

Cap		M	I	NO	R	HS	100s	50s	Avge	Ct/St
1995	N. V. Knight	10	19	3	1,520	255*	5	10	95.00	10
2002	J. O. Troughton	13	22	3	1,052	131*	3	6	55.36	8
1991	D. P. Ostler†	13	23	1	1,008	225	2	5	45.81	24
	N. M. Carter	9	12	5	305	103	1	1	43.57	4
	M. A. Sheikh†	4	6	2	152	43	0	0	38.00	1
1999	M. J. Powell	16	29	2	858	103	1	6	31.77	12
	T. Frost	7	11	1	308	103	1	1	30.80	6/2
	G. G. Wagg†	4	6	1	142	51	0	1	28.40	1
2000	M. A. Wagh†	9	16	0	417	109	1	1	26.06	2
1995	D. R. Brown	15	26	4	571	79*	0	2	25.95	9
	S. M. Pollock§	10	18	1	425	66	0	4	25.00	13
2001	I. R. Bell†	16	28	1	658	77	0	3	24.37	6
2001	M. M. Betts	9	16	5	259	56	0	1	23.54	2
1993	N. M. K. Smith†	8	15	0	337	96	0	2	22.46	7
1996	A. F. Giles‡	4	6	0	134	68	0	1	22.33	1
	S. E. Bond§	3	4	1	64	29*	0	0	21.33	1
	J. A. Spires†	5	6	3	60	37*	0	0	20.00	3
2002	A. Richardson	9	11	4	132	91	0	1	18.85	4
1992	K. J. Piper	8	12	2	163	64*	0	1	16.30	14/1
	J. I. Clifford†	4	6	0	20	7	0	0	3.33	15/1

† *Born in Warwickshire.*   ‡ *ECB contract.*   § *Overseas player.*

BOWLING

	O	M	R	W	BB	5W/i	Avge
G. G. Wagg	66.5	11	259	12	4-43	0	21.58
A. Richardson	279.2	56	905	37	8-46	2	24.45
S. M. Pollock	301.3	101	733	28	4-37	0	26.17
A. F. Giles	215.4	33	678	25	7-142	3	27.12
S. E. Bond	95.4	23	330	12	5-64	1	27.50
D. R. Brown	477.4	74	1,626	52	7-110	2	31.26
N. M. K. Smith	126	27	411	12	5-42	1	34.25
J. A. Spires	160.4	25	556	16	5-165	1	34.75
M. A. Wagh	194	42	566	15	5-137	1	37.73
N. M. Carter	228.1	35	957	20	4-46	0	47.85
M. M. Betts	248.4	34	1,023	20	3-75	0	51.15

Also bowled: I. R. Bell 34–8–89–2; T. Frost 1–0–9–0; D. P. Ostler 1–0–13–0; M. J. Powell 53–7–193–3; M. A. Sheikh 122.3–23–376–5; J. O. Troughton 16–0–68–0.

COUNTY RECORDS

Highest score for:	501*	B. C. Lara v Durham at Birmingham	1994
Highest score against:	322	I. V. A. Richards (Somerset) at Taunton	1985
Best bowling for:	10-41	J. D. Bannister v Combined Services at Birmingham	1959
Best bowling against:	10-36	H. Verity (Yorkshire) at Leeds	1931
Highest total for:	810-4 dec.	v Durham at Birmingham	1994
Highest total against:	887	by Yorkshire at Birmingham	1896
Lowest total for:	16	v Kent at Tonbridge	1913
Lowest total against:	15	by Hampshire at Birmingham	1922

COUNTY OFFICERS

Captain M. J. Powell • **Director of coaching** 2002 – R. A. Woolmer; 2003 – J. Inverarity
President The Rt Hon. Lord Guernsey
Chairman 2002 – M. J. K. Smith; 2003 – W. N. Houghton • **Chief executive** D. L. Amiss
Chairman, cricket c'ttee T. A. Lloyds • **Head groundsman** S. J. Rouse • **Scorer** D. Wainright

At Birmingham, April 20, 21, 22 (not first-class). **Warwickshire won by 580 runs.** Toss: Warwickshire. **Warwickshire 477 for six dec.** (T. Frost 90, I. R. Bell 107, D. P. Ostler 94, D. R. Brown 93 not out, N. M. K. Smith 41) **and 411 for eight dec.** (N. V. Knight 117, M. A. Sheikh 67, J. O. Troughton 44, N. M. K. Smith 62, I. R. Bell 54, Extras 37; A. N. French four for 116), **Cardiff UCCE 144** (A. N. Bressington 40; N. A. Warren five for 39) **and 164** (P. J. Evans 38 J. A. Tomlinson 36 not out; J. A. Spires five for 55).

First-team debut: N. A. Warren.

WARWICKSHIRE v LANCASHIRE

At Birmingham, April 24, 25, 26. Lancashire won by six wickets. Lancashire 17 pts, Warwickshire 5 pts. Toss: Warwickshire.

Warwickshire were lucky not to end their first match with negative points after 17 wickets fell on the second day. An inspection panel spent five hours deliberating whether a grassy pitch warranted an eight-point penalty. They decided not, but the bounce was unpredictable and only Byas played with confidence. His unbeaten 83 in Lancashire's second innings, from just 92 balls, made a tricky chase look straightforward. Earlier, Warwickshire had clawed their way from 136 for seven to 297 thanks to a belligerent 96 from Smith and Betts's first fifty since leaving Durham. Lloyd, given two lives, then held Lancashire together with his third consecutive half-century. Pollock – who flew in from South Africa on the morning of the match – bowled well for little reward, but it was Richardson who caused most damage. His five for 59 brought his county cap. Lancashire's seamers then made light work of Warwickshire's second innings despite Knight's defiance. Ostler suffered a broken finger in his first game back after missing the end of the previous season with an elbow injury.

Close of play: First day, Lancashire 48-0 (Chilton 14, Swann 28); Second day, Warwickshire 124-7 (Piper 7, Betts 10).

Warwickshire

*M. J. Powell c Hogg b Smethurst	14	– c Hegg b Martin	6
N. V. Knight c Hegg b Martin	38	– c Law b Martin	49
I. R. Bell c Hegg b Martin	11	– c Byas b Smethurst	22
D. P. Ostler c Byas b Martin	15	– (10) not out	2
D. R. Brown c Chilton b Martin	4	– c Law b Hogg	0
J. O. Troughton lbw b Chapple	2	– (4) c Hegg b Hogg	19
S. M. Pollock lbw b Chapple	16	– (6) lbw b Hogg	0
N. M. K. Smith c Law b Smethurst	96	– (7) c Lloyd b Martin	5
†K. J. Piper b Keedy	13	– (8) b Martin	13
M. M. Betts c Chilton b Smethurst	56	– (9) c Byas b Chapple	22
A. Richardson not out	0	– c Hegg b Chapple	0
B 4, l-b 4, w 12, n-b 12.	32	B 6, l-b 3, n-b 2.	11

1/43 (1) 2/80 (2) 3/89 (3) 4/93 (5)   **297**   1/10 (1) 2/51 (3) 3/93 (4)   **150**
5/119 (6) 6/120 (7) 7/136 (4)   4/93 (5) 5/97 (6) 6/103 (2)
8/188 (9) 9/289 (10) 10/297 (8)   7/112 (7) 8/142 (8)
                                                9/146 (10) 10/150 (11)

Bonus points – Warwickshire 2, Lancashire 3.

In the first innings Ostler, when 1, retired hurt at 93-4 and resumed at 120.

Bowling: *First Innings*—Martin 21–7–77–4; Chapple 20–7–58–2; Smethurst 13.2–2–68–3; Hogg 10–1–45–0; Keedy 12–4–35–1; Chilton 2–0–6–0. *Second Innings*—Martin 20–5–41–4; Chapple 17.4–4–51–2; Smethurst 8–2–33–1; Hogg 8–5–16–3.

Lancashire

M. J. Chilton b Richardson	45	– c Knight b Pollock	12
A. J. Swann c Pollock b Brown	29	– lbw b Richardson	27
D. Byas c Piper b Betts	4	– not out	83
S. G. Law b Richardson	30	– c Pollock b Richardson	2
G. D. Lloyd b Richardson	80	– c sub b Richardson	18
*†W. K. Hegg lbw b Richardson	10	– not out	34
G. Chapple b Richardson	9		
K. W. Hogg c Smith b Brown	9		
P. J. Martin lbw b Brown	2		
G. Keedy c Knight b Brown	4		
M. P. Smethurst not out	6		
B 4, l-b 5, n-b 14	23	B 9, n-b 12	21

1/50 (2) 2/83 (3) 3/99 (1) 4/192 (4) 251   1/38 (1) 2/71 (2) (4 wkts) 197
5/218 (6) 6/228 (7) 7/229 (5) 3/103 (4) 4/127 (5)
8/236 (9) 9/240 (10) 10/251 (8)

Bonus points – Lancashire 2, Warwickshire 3.

Bowling: *First Innings*—Pollock 16–6–38–0; Betts 17–4–67–1; Brown 24.2–4–78–4; Richardson 21–4–59–5. *Second Innings*—Pollock 13.4–3–56–1; Betts 7–1–28–0; Richardson 11–1–62–3; Brown 8–1–42–0.

Umpires: N. G. Cowley and B. Dudleston.

At Leicester, May 8, 9, 10, 11. WARWICKSHIRE lost to LEICESTERSHIRE by seven wickets.

WARWICKSHIRE v HAMPSHIRE

At Birmingham, May 15, 16, 17, 18. Drawn. Warwickshire 10 pts, Hampshire 10 pts. Toss: Warwickshire.

This match will be remembered for an astonishing last-wicket stand between Knight and Richardson worth 214. Richardson, a true No. 11 with a previous career-best of 17, reached double figures for only the third time and went on to 91; Knight carried his bat and finished unbeaten on 255. He batted ten hours 16 minutes, faced 493 balls and hit 31 fours and three sixes. The prodigious partnership was a county record, the fifth-highest in Championship history and the eighth-best ever. It was also thoroughly demoralising for Hampshire. Despite solid batting here and there, they fell 21 short of the follow-on target, and were 50 behind and three down at the end of the third day. But the pitch flattened out, rain snatched an hour, Warwickshire drifted in the field, taking just two wickets on the final day, and Johnson and Pothas saved the game. During the match, Robin Smith became the fourth current player to pass 25,000 first-class runs.

Close of play: First day, Warwickshire 274-9 (Knight 151, Richardson 1); Second day, Hampshire 89-3 (Smith 10, Johnson 8); Third day, Hampshire 120-3 (Smith 33, Johnson 3).

Warwickshire

*M. J. Powell c Kenway b Mullally	19	M. M. Betts c Pothas b Mascarenhas	4
N. V. Knight not out	255	A. Richardson st Pothas b White	91
. R. Bell c Tremlett b Mullally	22		
. O. Troughton b Tremlett	0	B 2, l-b 4, w 4, n-b 8	18
*T. Frost lbw b Tremlett	5		
D. R. Brown c Johnson b Mascarenhas	15	1/55 (1) 2/107 (3) 3/108 (4)	472
S. M. Pollock lbw b Mascarenhas	4	4/118 (5) 5/154 (6) 6/170 (7)	
A. F. Giles c Smith b Johnson	20	7/214 (8) 8/253 (9)	
K. J. Piper c Pothas b Mullally	19	9/258 (10) 10/472 (11)	

Bonus points – Warwickshire 3, Hampshire 3 (130 overs: 347-9).

Bowling: Mullally 38–14–92–3; Mascarenhas 24.5–11–59–3; Tremlett 23–8–69–2; Udal 44.1–7–140–0; Johnson 12–3–47–1; Prittipaul 15–4–31–0; Kendall 4–0–11–0; White 2.1–0–17–1.

Hampshire

D. A. Kenway lbw b Betts	1	– lbw b Brown	54
W. S. Kendall c Brown b Giles	25	– c Frost b Richardson	21
G. W. White c Bell b Giles	36	– lbw b Richardson	0
*R. A. Smith c Pollock b Giles	44	– c Bell b Giles	43
N. C. Johnson lbw b Betts	79	– not out	74
L. R. Prittipaul b Brown	1	– lbw b Betts	7
†N. Pothas b Richardson	59	– not out	71
A. D. Mascarenhas c Brown b Betts	0		
S. D. Udal not out	27		
C. T. Tremlett c Pollock b Richardson	1		
A. D. Mullally c Richardson b Pollock	5		
L-b 8, n-b 16	24	B 9, l-b 7, n-b 20	36

1/1 (1) 2/48 (2) 3/81 (3) 4/162 (4)   302   1/43 (2) 2/45 (3)   (5 wkts dec.) 306
5/163 (6) 6/250 (5) 7/250 (8)   3/110 (1) 4/152 (4)
8/277 (7) 9/279 (10) 10/302 (11)   5/169 (6)

Bonus points – Hampshire 3, Warwickshire 3.

Bowling: *First Innings*—Pollock 18.5–7–31–1; Betts 22–5–75–3; Giles 35–9–96–3; Richardson 18–3–61–2; Brown 12–2–31–1. *Second Innings*—Pollock 20–6–47–0; Betts 15–2–59–1; Giles 33–4–90–1; Richardson 21–6–41–2; Brown 15–3–38–1; Powell 4–1–15–0.

Umpires: M. R. Benson and R. Palmer.

At Southampton, May 31, June 1, 2, 3. WARWICKSHIRE drew with HAMPSHIRE.

WARWICKSHIRE v LEICESTERSHIRE

At Birmingham, June 12, 13, 14, 15. Warwickshire won by 144 runs. Warwickshire 20 pts, Leicestershire 6 pts. Toss: Warwickshire. Championship debut: G. W. Flower.

Warwickshire's bowlers slowly strangled Leicestershire: Smith flighted his off-spin cleverly, Pollock was precision-perfect and Leicestershire fell 145 short of their target. Incredibly, Pollock bowled ten consecutive maidens, while Smith's five for 42 was his best in seven years. Warwickshire had grafted to 462 after batting first. Bell's gritty 72 was followed by more fluent innings from Ostler and Troughton, who won his cap with a second consecutive century full of languid offside drives. Leicestershire avoided the follow-on but Pollock's belligerent 65 allowed Powell to make a challenging declaration; Smith's guile and Pollock's control finished the job. Warwickshire used four wicket-keepers in one innings: Frost broke a finger and was replaced first by Powell, then by Keith Piper – called up from the Second XI – and finally by Ian Clifford, a 19-year-old, who impressed with five catches and a stumping in all. Warwickshire's first win, in their fifth match, and a victory for Surrey, knocked Leicestershire from the top of the Championship.

Close of play: First day, Warwickshire 295-4 (Troughton 65, Frost 7); Second day, Leicestershire 205-4 (Flower 37, Stevens 21); Third day, Warwickshire 118-4 (Troughton 18, Pollock 39).

Warwickshire

*M. J. Powell c Stevens b DeFreitas	0	– b Malcolm	2
N. V. Knight c Stevens b Flower	47	– b Malcolm	13
I. R. Bell c Burns b Grove	72	– c Maddy b DeFreitas	11
D. P. Ostler c Burns b Flower	81	– c Burns b DeFreitas	25
J. O. Troughton b Flower	130	– c Burns b DeFreitas	37
†T. Frost run out	18		
S. M. Pollock b Malcolm	11	– (6) c Whiley b Flower	65
D. R. Brown c and b Flower	35	– (7) not out	26
N. M. K. Smith c Stevens b Maddy	0	– (8) c Maddy b Flower	7
M. M. Betts not out	21	– (9) not out	10
N. M. Carter c Stevens b Malcolm	12		
L-b 15, w 4, n-b 16	35	L-b 6, w 2, n-b 2	10

1/1 (1) 2/91 (2) 3/187 (3) 4/261 (4)　　　462　　　1/14 (2) 2/15 (1) 3/41 (3) 4/60 (4)　(7 wkts dec.) 206
5/312 (6) 6/325 (7) 7/410 (8)　　　　　　　　　　 5/149 (5) 6/164 (6) 7/176 (8)
8/411 (9) 9/433 (10) 5/10/462 (11)

Bonus points – Warwickshire 5, Leicestershire 2 (130 overs: 400-6).

Bowling: *First Innings*—Malcolm 12.4–2–55–2; DeFreitas 32–8–100–1; Whiley 23–3–94–0; Maddy 23–6–57–1; Grove 22–6–75–1; Flower 30–11–66–4. *Second Innings*—DeFreitas 22–7–53–3; Malcolm 21–4–63–2; Whiley 8–2–38–0; Grove 3–0–14–0; Flower 5–1–32–2.

Leicestershire

T. R. Ward c Pollock b Smith	89	– b Pollock	18
I. J. Sutcliffe b Betts	31	– c sub b Pollock	6
D. L. Maddy c sub b Carter	16	– c sub b Carter	22
G. W. Flower b Pollock	75	– st sub b Smith	7
*V. J. Wells c Carter b Betts	5	– c sub b Pollock	43
D. I. Stevens c Troughton b Brown	38	– c sub b Smith	20
†N. D. Burns c sub b Carter	64	– b Smith	34
P. A. J. DeFreitas b Pollock	5	– c Pollock b Smith	1
J. O. Grove b Betts	6	– lbw b Smith	0
D. E. Malcolm c sub b Pollock	0	– (11) not out	2
M. J. A. Whiley not out	13	– (10) b Betts	0
L-b 5, n-b 10	15	L-b 1	1

1/108 (2) 2/128 (1) 3/148 (3) 4/164 (5)　　370　　1/23 (2) 2/24 (1) 3/53 (3)　　　　154
5/227 (6) 6/321 (4) 7/331 (8)　　　　　　　　 4/53 (4) 5/89 (6) 6/121 (5)
8/346 (7) 9/346 (9) 10/370 (10)　　　　　　　 7/122 (8) 8/124 (9)
　　　　　　　　　　　　　　　　　　　　　 9/142 (10) 10/154 (7)

Bonus points – Leicestershire 4, Warwickshire 3.

Bowling: *First Innings*—Betts 25–3–115–3; Carter 17–3–60–2; Pollock 22.2–7–36–3; Brown 19–2–78–1; Smith 27–7–56–1; Troughton 5–0–20–0. *Second Innings*—Pollock 16–10–23–3; Betts 14–2–58–1; Smith 23.1–11–42–5; Carter 7–2–30–1.

Umpires: G. I. Burgess and N. J. Llong.

WARWICKSHIRE v SOMERSET

At Birmingham, June 26, 27, 28, 29. Warwickshire won by 88 runs. Warwickshire 16 pts, Somerset 4 pts. Toss: Warwickshire. First-class debuts: J. I. Clifford, G. G. Wagg.

After 23 wickets had fallen in just over four sessions, Ostler bucked the trend with a brutal 175, Graham Wagg weighed in with an aggressive 51 on debut, and together they put the match beyond Somerset. Although brisk half-centuries by Blackwell and Burns injected some momentum and Turner hung in for an unbeaten 83, a target of 446 proved too big. Earlier, Wagg had cracked

42 and hustled out the Somerset tail to help Warwickshire to a 22-run first-innings lead; Ostler, venting his frustration after being omitted from the Benson and Hedges Cup final four days earlier, did the rest. A depleted Warwickshire side included three players – Wagg, Jamie Spires and Ian Clifford – with just one Championship appearance between them. Clifford kept tidily but struggled as a makeshift opener, while Spires took two important wickets in the second innings. For Somerset, Jones shouldered an extra burden after Johnson pulled a hamstring, and he bowled heroically to take ten wickets for the first time.

Close of play: First day, Somerset 121-3 (Bowler 54, Jones 0); Second day, Warwickshire 236-5 (Ostler 110, Brown 5); Third day, Somerset 248-6 (Turner 26, Dutch 3).

Warwickshire

*M. J. Powell lbw b Parsons	28	– b Jones	3
†J. I. Clifford lbw b Johnson	1	– b Bulbeck	0
I. R. Bell c Wood b Jones	46	– c Holloway b Jones	42
D. P. Ostler lbw b Parsons	11	– c Burns b Jones	175
J. O. Troughton b Blackwell	42	– b Blackwell	52
S. M. Pollock lbw b Bulbeck	9	– c Bowler b Jones	10
D. R. Brown c Turner b Jones	10	– b Jones	38
N. M. K. Smith c Turner b Dutch	13	– lbw b Dutch	9
G. G. Wagg not out	42	– c Wood b Dutch	51
M. M. Betts c Holloway b Jones	23	– b Jones	15
J. A. Spires c Turner b Jones	0	– not out	9
B 4, l-b 1	5	B 8, l-b 11	19
	230		**423**

1/9 (2) 2/70 (1) 3/78 (4) 4/95 (4)   230
5/122 (6) 6/140 (7) 7/165 (8)
8/165 (5) 9/230 (10) 10/230 (11)

1/1 (2) 2/19 (1) 3/60 (3)   423
4/183 (5) 5/210 (6) 6/334 (7)
7/337 (4) 8/396 (8)
9/401 (9) 10/423 (10)

Bonus points – Warwickshire 1, Somerset 3.

Bowling: *First Innings*—Johnson 4.2–0–13–1; Bulbeck 17–4–62–1; Jones 16.1–2–46–4; Parsons 15–3–38–2; Burns 2–0–13–0; Dutch 8–2–34–1; Blackwell 6–2–19–1. *Second Innings*—Bulbeck 19–2–106–1; Jones 33.3–5–110–6; Parsons 12–2–51–0; Blackwell 42–12–95–1; Dutch 14–4–42–2.

Somerset

P. C. L. Holloway c Powell b Pollock	0	– lbw b Betts	28
M. J. Wood c Clifford b Betts	4	– c Ostler b Smith	32
*M. Burns b Brown	54	– c Ostler b Spires	54
P. D. Bowler lbw b Brown	57	– c Ostler b Spires	16
P. S. Jones c Clifford b Pollock	0	– (10) b Pollock	1
K. A. Parsons c Ostler b Betts	31	– (5) c Smith b Pollock	16
I. D. Blackwell c Ostler b Wagg	15	– (6) c Betts b Brown	64
†R. J. Turner lbw b Wagg	11	– (7) not out	83
K. P. Dutch c Clifford b Wagg	0	– (8) lbw b Pollock	3
M. P. L. Bulbeck c Powell b Wagg	12	– (9) c Clifford b Brown	4
R. L. Johnson not out	12	– c Spires b Smith	38
B 1, l-b 1, n-b 10	12	B 1, l-b 5, w 2, n-b 10	18
	208		**357**

1/0 (1) 2/6 (2) 3/110 (4) 4/121 (5)   208
5/125 (4) 6/173 (7) 7/173 (6)
8/178 (9) 9/191 (8) 10/208 (10)

1/48 (1) 2/85 (2) 3/123 (3)   357
4/142 (4) 5/162 (5) 6/239 (6)
7/264 (8) 8/297 (9)
9/302 (10) 10/357 (11)

Bonus points – Somerset 1, Warwickshire 3.

Bowling: *First Innings*—Pollock 15–7–33–2; Betts 13–3–46–2; Wagg 10–2–43–4; Brown 13–3–57–2; Smith 5–0–27–0; Spires 1–1–0–0. *Second Innings*—Pollock 25–5–97–3; Betts 13–0–54–1; Wagg 4–0–28–0; Brown 20–1–58–2; Smith 14.4–1–64–2; Spires 12–2–50–2.

Umpires: T. E. Jesty and J. F. Steele.

At Maidstone, July 3, 4, 5, 6. WARWICKSHIRE drew with KENT.

At The Oval, July 10, 11, 12, 13. WARWICKSHIRE beat SURREY by 31 runs.

At Birmingham, July 20, 21, 22. WARWICKSHIRE lost to WEST INDIES A by 119 runs (see West Indies A tour section).

WARWICKSHIRE v SUSSEX

At Birmingham, July 24, 25, 26, 27. Warwickshire won by 208 runs. Warwickshire 20 pts, Sussex 7 pts. Toss: Sussex. First-class debut: C. D. Nash.

Warwickshire completed their fourth win in five matches thanks to two outstanding individual performances. Knight became the first Warwickshire batsman since Alvin Kallicharran in 1983 to score two double-centuries in a season – for good measure he carried his bat both times – and Richardson earned their best figures in 25 years as he made short work of Sussex on the final day. After choosing to bowl on a damp, slow pitch, Sussex paid heavily for Prior's fumbled catch off Innes when Knight had 37. He went on to an unbeaten 245 in eight and a half hours of expert judgment, hitting a six and 30 fours from 390 balls. Sussex struggled in reply, but Cottey unleashed some authoritative drives to establish a measure of control. His 137 helped avoid the follow-on, before Knight guided Warwickshire to a lead of 400. Sussex made no attempt to push for a win as Richardson exploited some increasingly variable bounce. He took eight for 46 as Sussex subsided; only Cottey and Martin-Jenkins offered resistance. Sussex's 19-year-old off-spinner, Chris Nash, took two wickets on a difficult debut.

Close of play: First day, Warwickshire 368-7 (Knight 198, Piper 4); Second day, Sussex 237-4 (Cottey 105, Martin-Jenkins 20); Third day, Sussex 5-1 (Montgomerie 5, Taylor 0).

Warwickshire

*M. J. Powell c Prior b Innes	57	– b Taylor	5
N. V. Knight not out	245	– lbw b Innes	97
M. A. Wagh c Innes b Lewry	4	– c Ambrose b Lewry	39
I. R. Bell c Prior b Innes	12	– c Prior b Nash	30
D. P. Ostler c Prior b Nash	6	– c Lewry b Taylor	45
J. O. Troughton c Cottey b Lewry	45	– c Prior b Taylor	16
S. M. Pollock b Taylor	29	– not out	19
D. R. Brown c Montgomerie b Lewry	2	– not out	14
†K. J. Piper c Prior b Lewry	4		
N. M. Carter c Nash b Innes	38		
A. Richardson b Taylor	28		
L-b 4, w 6, n-b 13	23	L-b 6, w 13	19
	493	(6 wkts dec.)	**284**

1/95 (1) 2/113 (3) 3/146 (4) 4/186 (5)   1/11 (1) 2/60 (3)
5/290 (6) 6/343 (7) 7/362 (8)   3/109 (4) 4/194 (5)
8/368 (9) 9/425 (10) 10/493 (11)   5/233 (6) 6/263 (2)

Bonus points – Warwickshire 5, Sussex 3.

Bowling: *First Innings*—Lewry 38–4–151–4; Martin-Jenkins 5.1–0–32–0; Innes 28.5–2–106–3; Taylor 35.3–4–110–2; Nash 20–0–90–1. *Second Innings*—Lewry 8–1–32–1; Taylor 21–3–83–3; Innes 10–1–34–1; Martin-Jenkins 6–2–24–0; Nash 15–1–81–1; Cottey 7–0–24–0.

Sussex

M. W. Goodwin b Brown	16	– (2) lbw b Richardson	0
*R. R. Montgomerie c Ostler b Pollock	51	– (1) lbw b Richardson	45
P. A. Cottey c Ostler b Carter	137	– (4) lbw b Richardson	64
B. Zuiderent lbw b Pollock	0	– (5) c Powell b Wagh	10
T. R. Ambrose lbw b Wagh	42	– (6) c Pollock b Richardson	7
R. S. C. Martin-Jenkins b Wagh	34	– (7) b Richardson	40
†M. J. Prior c Powell b Carter	47	– (8) c Ostler b Richardson	16
K. J. Innes not out	30	– (9) c Ostler b Wagh	7
C. D. Nash lbw b Carter	0	– (10) not out	0
B. V. Taylor c Pollock b Brown	9	– (3) c Pollock b Richardson	1
J. D. Lewry b Brown	8	– c Piper b Richardson	0
B 1, l-b 2	3	L-b 2	2

1/40 (1) 2/90 (2) 3/90 (3) 4/181 (5)   377   1/0 (2) 2/6 (3) 3/111 (4)   192
5/257 (6) 6/325 (3) 7/330 (7)   4/114 (1) 5/126 (6) 6/150 (5)
8/330 (9) 9/357 (10) 10/377 (11)   7/183 (8) 8/192 (9)
                                      9/192 (7) 10/192 (11)

Bonus points – Sussex 4, Warwickshire 3.

Bowling: *First Innings*—Pollock 19–6–60–2; Carter 20–3–77–3; Brown 20.2–3–72–3; Richardson 21–6–72–0; Wagh 28–4–86–2; Troughton 2–0–7–0. *Second Innings*—Carter 9–5–14–0; Richardson 23.5–10–46–8; Brown 10–0–45–0; Wagh 24–3–85–2.

Umpires: D. J. Constant and J. W. Holder.

At Leeds, August 7, 8, 9, 10. WARWICKSHIRE drew with YORKSHIRE.

WARWICKSHIRE v KENT

At Birmingham, August 14, 15, 16, 17. Warwickshire won by ten wickets. Warwickshire 20 pts, Kent 3 pts. Toss: Warwickshire.

After Powell chose to bat, the cracked pitch showed some variable bounce and the ball swung in the air, but the Kent bowlers pitched wastefully short. Their inaccuracy allowed Wagh to flay an aggressive – if slightly streaky – hundred, Troughton to score his third century of the summer and Warwickshire to reach 565. Shane Bond, the New Zealand fast bowler and Warwickshire's stand-in overseas player, then ripped open Kent's top order with a fiery opening spell. Despite a battling century by Nixon, some subtle left-arm spin from Giles made sure Warwickshire enforced the follow-on. In Kent's second innings Giles was supported by electric close catching and, on a pitch offering increasing turn, he grabbed seven for 142, his best for two years. Ealham's boisterous 83 and a maiden fifty from Masters avoided a three-day defeat with a ninth-wicket stand of 108, but Warwickshire needed just 30 balls on the fourth morning to complete the rout. Their fifth win in seven games left them 37 points behind Surrey with a game in hand.

Close of play: First day, Warwickshire 387-5 (Troughton 64, Giles 2); Second day, Kent 191-8 (Nixon 70, Masters 1); Third day, Kent 304-9 (Masters 60, Saggers 0).

Warwickshire

*M. J. Powell c Nixon b Khan	1	– not out	8
N. V. Knight b Masters	69	– not out	0
M. A. Wagh c Nixon b Symonds	109		
I. R. Bell c Tredwell b Khan	0		
D. P. Ostler st Nixon b Tredwell	80		
J. O. Troughton c and b Saggers	115		
D. R. Brown c Nixon b Tredwell	44		
A. F. Giles b Symonds	68		
S. E. Bond st Nixon b Tredwell	8		
N. M. Carter not out	13		
†J. I. Clifford c and b Tredwell	7		
B 11, l-b 12, n-b 28	51		

1/3 (1) 2/147 (2) 3/158 (4) 4/233 (3) 　　**565**　　(no wkt) **8**
5/297 (5) 6/508 (8) 7/533 (7)
8/541 (6) 9/547 (9) 10/565 (11)

Bonus points – Warwickshire 5, Kent 1 (130 overs: 499-5).

In the first innings Brown, when 31, retired hurt at 384 and resumed at 508.

Bowling: *First Innings*—Saggers 33–6–95–1; Khan 24–1–129–2; Masters 25–6–110–1; Tredwell 34–8–103–4; Ealham 22–3–76–0; Symonds 7–0–29–2. *Second Innings*—Nixon 0.3–0–8–0.

Kent

*D. P. Fulton c Clifford b Bond	20	– (3) c Ostler b Brown	44
R. W. T. Key c Carter b Bond	22	– lbw b Giles	26
E. T. Smith c and b Bond	0	– (4) c Clifford b Brown	23
A. Symonds c Brown b Giles	14	– (5) lbw b Giles	0
J. B. Hockley c Clifford b Brown	0	– (6) c Brown b Giles	6
†P. A. Nixon c and b Giles	103	– (1) c Brown b Giles	26
M. A. Ealham c Powell b Giles	25	– c Troughton b Wagh	83
J. C. Tredwell c Clifford b Giles	1	– c Ostler b Giles	17
A. Khan b Bond	15	– c Troughton b Giles	7
D. D. Masters c Ostler b Giles	13	– c Knight b Giles	68
M. J. Saggers not out	16	– not out	5
B 1, l-b 10, n-b 12	23	B 4, l-b 4, w 2, n-b 2	12

1/32 (1) 2/32 (3) 3/47 (2) 4/57 (5) 　　**252**　　1/50 (1) 2/61 (2) 3/102 (4)　　**317**
5/85 (4) 6/141 (7) 7/147 (8) 　　　　　　4/105 (5) 5/121 (6) 6/143 (3)
8/186 (9) 9/225 (10) 10/252 (6) 　　　　7/178 (8) 8/196 (9)
　　　　　　　　　　　　　　　　　　　9/304 (7) 10/317 (10)

Bonus points – Kent 2, Warwickshire 3.

Bowling: *First Innings*—Bond 19–4–70–4; Carter 9–1–26–0; Giles 30.5–6–74–5; Brown 22–2–60–1; Wagh 5–1–11–0. *Second Innings*—Bond 14–1–59–0; Carter 19–7–51–0; Giles 40.3–3–142–7; Brown 12–2–54–2; Wagh 6–4–3–1.

Umpires: A. Clarkson and J. W. Lloyds.

At Taunton, August 21, 22, 23, 24. WARWICKSHIRE drew with SOMERSET.

WARWICKSHIRE v SURREY

At Birmingham, August 27, 28, 29, 30. Drawn. Warwickshire 9 pts, Surrey 12 pts. Toss: Warwickshire.

Knight overcame a groin injury to hobble to his fifth first-class century of the season and salvage an unlikely draw, which kept Surrey waiting for the Championship. But his stoical innings of nearly six and a half hours was not enough for Warwickshire, who badly needed a win to maintain their title challenge. Their first-innings 345, built round a defiant fifty from Knight and a dashing one from Troughton, was too small on a benign pitch, and Surrey rushed past with just three down. Ward scored a gritty hundred, Ramprakash became Surrey's fourth player of the summer to fall on 99, and Surrey plundered 183 before lunch on the third morning as Shahid ended a long lean spell with a splendid century. But the cricket became more attritional as Warwickshire struggled to avoid defeat. Thanks to Knight's vigilance – and determined innings by Frost, who took 53 balls to score, and Troughton – they made it. Using his bat as a crutch between deliveries, Knight had a runner throughout, and gave only one chance, when he was dropped at leg slip on 83.

Close of play: First day, Warwickshire 300-9 (Sheikh 9, Betts 14); Second day, Surrey 319-3 (Shahid 43, Brown 25); Third day, Warwickshire 154-3 (Troughton 30, Knight 14).

Warwickshire

*M. J. Powell lbw b Saqlain Mushtaq	36	– c Shahid b Saqlain Mushtaq	48
N. V. Knight c Batty b Ormond	74	– (5) b Ward	133
M. A. Wagh c Hollioake b Saqlain Mushtaq	3	– (2) lbw b Saqlain Mushtaq	39
I. R. Bell c Batty b Bicknell	34	– c Batty b Ormond	4
J. O. Troughton lbw b Bicknell	61	– (4) lbw b Salisbury	63
S. M. Pollock c Brown b Ormond	2	– c Shahid b Saqlain Mushtaq	3
D. R. Brown c Clarke b Saqlain Mushtaq	6	– c Batty b Saqlain Mushtaq	20
†T. Frost b Saqlain Mushtaq	35	– c Batty b Clarke	13
A. F. Giles b Ormond	3	– c Ormond b Clarke	25
M. A. Sheikh not out	19	– not out	7
M. M. Betts c Saqlain Mushtaq b Ormond	47	– not out	0
L-b 3, w 4, n-b 18	25	B 2, l-b 14, w 8, n-b 25	49
	345	(9 wkts dec.)	404

1/79 (2) 2/87 (3) 3/146 (4) 4/179 (2)   1/86 (2) 2/105 (3)   (9 wkts dec.) 404
5/185 (6) 6/196 (7) 7/251 (5)   3/105 (1) 4/214 (4)
8/271 (8) 9/279 (9) 10/345 (11)   5/225 (6) 6/257 (7)
  7/330 (8) 8/376 (9) 9/403 (5)

Bonus points – Warwickshire 3, Surrey 3.

Bowling: *First Innings*—Bicknell 24–6–87–2; Ormond 30.2–5–108–4; Saqlain Mushtaq 49–16–94–4; Clarke 1–0–5–0; Salisbury 14–2–48–0. *Second Innings*—Bicknell 20–5–71–0; Ormond 24–2–95–1; Saqlain Mushtaq 43–15–80–4; Salisbury 25–4–53–1; Shahid 6–0–17–0; Hollioake 4–0–12–0; Clarke 7–1–49–2; Brown 3–0–7–0; Ward 2–1–4–1.

Surrey

I. J. Ward c Knight b Pollock	114	Saqlain Mushtaq c Betts b Brown	6
†J. N. Batty c Pollock b Betts	8	J. Ormond c and b Brown	0
M. R. Ramprakash lbw b Brown	99		
N. Shahid c Pollock b Giles	114	B 1, l-b 4, w 7, n-b 32	44
A. D. Brown st Frost b Giles	57		
*A. J. Hollioake not out	82		544
R. Clarke st Frost b Giles	10	1/32 (2) 2/236 (3) 3/251 (1)	
M. P. Bicknell c Brown b Giles	0	4/397 (5) 5/474 (4) 6/502 (7)	
I. D. K. Salisbury lbw b Brown	44	7/502 (8) 8/525 (9)	
		9/543 (10) 10/544 (11)	

Bonus points – Surrey 5, Warwickshire 2 (130 overs: 524-7).

Bowling: Pollock 21–7–64–1; Betts 24–2–122–1; Sheikh 26–7–79–0; Giles 34–4–134–4; Brown 28.1–1–124–4; Wagh 3–1–16–0.

Umpires: M. J. Kitchen and B. Leadbeater.

At Manchester, September 4, 5, 6, 7. WARWICKSHIRE drew with LANCASHIRE.

WARWICKSHIRE v YORKSHIRE

At Birmingham, September 12, 13, 14, 15. Warwickshire won by six wickets. Warwickshire 20 pts, Yorkshire 6 pts. Toss: Warwickshire.

Warwickshire's win confirmed Yorkshire's relegation, 12 months after they were crowned champions. Yorkshire badly needed a win to keep their hopes alive, but they didn't get a sniff. Powell and Wagh put on 175 against a dispirited attack, as Warwickshire cruised to victory with three overs of a possible 51 unused. Earlier, Warwickshire had made a mammoth 601: Frost, a keeper filling in as a specialist batsman, hit a composed maiden Championship hundred, but it was soon eclipsed by Ostler's career-best 225. Disdainful at times, he faced just 240 balls in 321 minutes, and hit 40 fours and a six. When Yorkshire replied, Warwickshire's spinners, Spires and Wagh, could afford to attack, and both recorded career-best figures. After Powell imposed the follow-on, Elliott and McGrath added an untroubled 172 for the second wicket, Blakey cut his way to a first hundred in three years, and Fellows resisted for three hours. But by then it was too late.

Close of play: First day, Warwickshire 374-5 (Ostler 126, Sheikh 8); Second day, Yorkshire 261-6 (Blakey 36, Dawson 14); Third day, Yorkshire 304-5 (Fellows 22, Blakey 19).

Warwickshire

*M. J. Powell lbw b Sidebottom	58	– not out	92
M. A. Wagh b Kirby	2	– c Lumb b Elliott	90
T. Frost lbw b McGrath	103	– (6) not out	3
I. R. Bell c Fellows b Thornicroft	15	– c Fellows b Dawson	6
D. P. Ostler c Blakey b Dawson	225	– c Craven b Dawson	9
D. R. Brown c Lumb b Sidebottom	28	– (3) lbw b Dawson	17
M. A. Sheikh c Lumb b Thornicroft	33		
†K. J. Piper not out	64		
N. M. Carter run out	15		
A. Richardson b Dawson	0		
J. A. Spires not out	8		
B 5, l-b 7, w 2, n-b 36	50	B 1, l-b 10, w 2, n-b 2	15

1/17 (2) 2/157 (1) 3/193 (4)   (9 wkts dec.) 601   1/175 (2) 2/206 (3)   (4 wkts) 232
4/226 (3) 5/338 (6) 6/446 (7)   3/212 (4) 4/228 (5)
7/550 (5) 8/583 (9) 9/585 (10)

Bonus points – Warwickshire 5, Yorkshire 2 (130 overs: 532-6).

Bowling: *First Innings*—Kirby 30–2–161–1; Sidebottom 26–3–129–2; Thornicroft 21–5–104–2; McGrath 17–6–33–1; Dawson 42–10–121–2; Craven 2–0–7–0; Fellows 6–0–28–0; Elliott 1–0–6–0. *Second Innings*—Kirby 9–4–35–0; Sidebottom 4–0–23–0; Dawson 17–0–85–3; Elliott 14–1–64–1; McGrath 4–0–14–0.

Yorkshire

M. T. G. Elliott b Spires	74	– b Wagh	127
V. J. Craven c Ostler b Carter	5	– c Piper b Spires	19
A. McGrath lbw b Wagh	46	– c Powell b Spires	66
C. White c Ostler b Spires	53	– lbw b Spires	2
M. J. Lumb c Powell b Wagh	1	– b Wagh	11
G. M. Fellows c Powell b Spires	11	– b Richardson	88
*†R. J. Blakey c Ostler b Wagh	70	– c Sheikh b Richardson	103
R. K. J. Dawson lbw b Spires	50	– lbw b Richardson	9
R. J. Sidebottom c Richardson b Wagh	12	– b Spires	2
S. P. Kirby b Wagh	0	– not out	3
N. D. Thornicroft not out	0	– c Wagh b Spires	1
B 6, l-b 17, w 2, n-b 4	29	B 25, l-b 13, n-b 12	50

1/23 (2) 2/120 (3) 3/140 (1) 4/143 (5)   351   1/39 (2) 2/211 (3) 3/213 (4)   481
5/180 (6) 6/227 (4) 7/320 (7)   4/246 (5) 5/261 (1) 6/436 (6)
8/345 (9) 9/351 (10) 10/351 (8)   7/460 (8) 8/467 (9)
    9/475 (7) 10/481 (11)

Bonus points – Yorkshire 4, Warwickshire 3.

Bowling: *First Innings*—Carter 7–0–41–1; Brown 3–1–18–0; Sheikh 3–0–13–0; Wagh 36–7–137–5; Spires 35.1–5–99–4; Richardson 1–0–11–0; Frost 1–0–9–0. *Second Innings*—Carter 12–0–55–0; Richardson 8–1–29–3; Wagh 28–1–97–2; Spires 44.4–4–165–5; Sheikh 17–3–44–0; Brown 19–3–53–0.

Umpires: V. A. Holder and P. Willey.

At Hove, September 18, 19, 20, 21. WARWICKSHIRE beat SUSSEX by three wickets.

THE DUCKWORTH/LEWIS METHOD

In 1997, the ECB's one-day competitions adopted a new method to revise targets in interrupted games, devised by Frank Duckworth of the Royal Statistical Society and Tony Lewis of the University of the West of England. The method was gradually taken up by other countries and in 1999 the ICC decided to incorporate it into the standard playing conditions for one-day internationals.

The system aims to preserve any advantage that one team has established before the interruption. It uses the idea that teams have two resources from which they make runs – an allocated number of overs, and ten wickets. It also takes into account when the interruption occurs, because of the different scoring-rates typical of different stages of an innings. Traditional run-rate calculations relied only on the overs available, and ignored wickets lost.

After modifications, the system now uses one table with 50 rows, covering matches of any length up to 50 overs, and ten columns, from nought to nine wickets down. Each figure in the table gives the percentage of the total runs in an innings that would, on average, be scored with a certain number of overs left and wickets lost.

If overs are lost, the table is used to calculate the percentage of runs the team would be expected to score in those missing overs. This is obtained by reading off the figure for the number of overs left and wickets down when play stops and subtracting from it the corresponding figure for the number of overs remaining when it resumes.

If the suspension of play occurs between innings, and the second team's allocation of overs is reduced, then their target is obtained by calculating the appropriate percentage for the reduced number of overs with all ten wickets standing. For instance, if the second team's innings halves from 50 overs to 25, the table shows that they still have 66.5 per cent of their resources left, so have to beat two-thirds of the first team's total, rather than half.

If the first innings is complete and the second innings is interrupted or prematurely terminated, the target to be beaten is reduced by the percentage of the innings lost. In the World Cup match between South Africa and Sri Lanka at Durban on March 3, 2003, South Africa's run-chase was ended by rain after 45 overs, when they were 229 for six. The Duckworth/Lewis tables showed that, with five overs left and four wickets standing, South Africa had used 85.7 per cent of their run-scoring resources, and 14.3 per cent remained unused. Multiplying Sri Lanka's 50-over total, 268, by 85.7 per cent produced a figure of 229.67. This was rounded down to 229 to give the par score (the target to tie), and the target to win became par plus one – 230 in 45 overs. Under old-fashioned average run-rate per over, the target would have been 242; South Africa benefited because they had preserved wickets into the final stages. (If they had lost one more wicket, par would have been 233; one fewer, 226.) As South Africa had equalled par exactly, the match was tied, the points were split, and they failed to qualify for the Super Six stage of the tournament.

The system also covers interruptions to the first innings, multiple interruptions and innings terminated by rain. The tables were revised slightly in September 2002, taking account of rising scoring-rates; the average 50-over total in a one-day international is now taken to be 235, rather than 225.

WORCESTERSHIRE
WITHIN A
WHISKER

Ch'ship	4th in Division 2
C&G	quarter-finalists
B&H	semi-finalists
NUL	2nd in Division 1

Player of the season: Ben Smith

Two near misses by the narrowest of margins left Worcestershire to reflect on an ultimately disappointing season. The biggest setback came when a late surge from Nottinghamshire edged them out of the third promotion spot in the Championship by one and three-quarter points. And it was the same in Division One of the National League: Worcestershire, fresh from promotion, at one stage led the table by eight points, only for Glamorgan to beat them twice and pip them to the honours. A thumping defeat at Chelmsford in the semi-final of the B&H and a quarter-final loss at Taunton in the C&G added to the feeling of what might have been.

The departure of Andy Bichel in July to join Australia, and the arrival of Stuart MacGill at Trent Bridge, proved crucial. Worcestershire won only two more Championship matches – both against Derbyshire – and although Kabir Ali, Alamgir Sheriyar and Matt Mason strove to fill the breach, the lack of a cutting edge in the final third of the season counted against them. Bichel was replaced by another Australian, the all-rounder Shane Lee but the move backfired: rusty after knee surgery and a long lay-off, Lee broke down in his third match; all told, his 3.2 overs cost 47 runs and he left after just three weeks. Meanwhile, MacGill was starting to fizz: he collected 40 wickets in six games to spearhead Nottinghamshire's charge. Worcestershire were left as the only county apart from Gloucestershire who had still to reach Division One of the Championship.

There was a further and unexpected blow in October when Sheriyar, who shone once more with 66 first-class wickets, was granted a request to be released from the final year of his contract. He had made the same move two years earlier after a fall-out with Bill Athey, coach at the time, only to return after Athey's resignation. This time, Sheriyar felt that his efforts were not receiving the recognition they deserved from the club's hierarchy. With Bichel likely to be kept away by international commitments, Worcestershire filled the holes in their new-ball attack by signing the fiery fast bowler Nantie Hayward, who was sufficiently disenchanted with South Africa's Test selectors to forgo the chance of a tour of England, and Mark Harrity, a South Australian left-arm seamer with a British passport. The other overseas signing is the South African Test all-rounder Andrew Hall.

The director of cricket, Tom Moody, went into 2003 believing the county's fortunes were on the up after several seasons of stagnation following the break-up of the successful side of the 1980s and 1990s. Moody brought in four new faces for 2002 and all succeeded to varying degrees. Ben Smith ended more than a decade's service with Leicestershire and provided extra quality – and competition for places – in the middle order. He scored more than 1,200 first-class runs, proved an expert at masterminding one-day chases – no one in the country managed more than his 654 runs at 65.40 in the National League – and richly deserved Worcestershire's Player of the Year award. In November, Smith was appointed captain in place of Graeme Hick, who was asked to step down after three years in charge.

Gareth Batty arrived hungry to make his mark in the first-class game after being used primarily as a one-day player at Surrey. He became the first Worcestershire spinner to take more than 50 Championship wickets in a season since Richard Illingworth in 1990, and made some telling contributions with the bat. A place at the ECB Academy was followed by a surprise call-up to the injury-hit England squad, and Batty soon found himself thrown in at the deep end against Australia at Sydney and Melbourne. Stephen Peters quickly replaced Phil Weston as opener after arriving from Essex and averaged 41 either side of a hand injury which sidelined him for six weeks. The fourth newcomer was the Western Australian paceman Matt Mason, who qualified as a non-overseas player via an EU passport, and turned in some promising performances in the final third of the season.

The other player to make big strides was the former England Under-19 seamer Kabir Ali. In his first full season of county cricket he gained 71 first-class wickets and a place in the Academy squad. The efforts of Kabir, Batty and Sheriyar meant that, for the first time since Illingworth, Stuart Lampitt and Phil Newport in 1990, three Worcestershire players took 50 Championship wickets in the same season.

Hick was not as consistent as he had often been, but an unbeaten 315 against a second-string Durham attack – the highest score by a Worcestershire batsman at New Road – and a big century against Oxford University helped him to a healthy 1,453 runs. The opener Anurag Singh passed 1,000 for the second season in a row following his switch from Warwickshire, although he tailed off dramatically. David Leatherdale began and ended the season with a flourish, and made some useful contributions with the ball in one-day cricket; he deserves his benefit in 2003. But it was disappointing that the classy Vikram Solanki failed to reach four figures again, particularly given the improved nature of the New Road pitch under the new head groundsman, Tim Packwood.

One loyal servant who finally said farewell after 17 years' sterling service was the unsung all-rounder Lampitt. He has taken up a full-time appointment as the Worcestershire Cricket Board's development officer. **John Curtis**

WORCESTERSHIRE 2002

Back row: D. J. Pipe, N. W. Round, P. R. Pollard, D. N. Catterall, D. B. Patel, G. S. Kandola, Kadeer Ali. *Middle row:* M. S. Mason, M. J. Rawnsley, C. G. Liptrot, Kabir Ali, S. D. Peters, A. Singh, G. J. Batty, B. F. Smith, L. Stephenson (*physiotherapist*). *Front row:* D. B. D'Oliveira (*assistant coach*). V. S. Solanki, D. A. Leatherdale, S. J. Rhodes, G. A. Hick (*captain*), T. M. Moody (*director of cricket*), S. R. Lampitt, W. P. C. Weston, A. Sheriyar. *Inset:* A. J. Bichel. *Main picture by Mike Pollard.*

WORCESTERSHIRE RESULTS

All first-class matches – Played 18: Won 8, Lost 4, Drawn 6.
County Championship matches – Played 16: Won 7, Lost 4, Drawn 5.

COUNTY CHAMPIONSHIP AVERAGES: BATTING AND FIELDING

Cap		M	I	NO	R	HS	100s	50s	Avge	Ct/St
1986	G. A. Hick	16	28	4	1,262	315*	3	6	52.58	28
1994	D. A. Leatherdale . .	13	21	4	812	154	2	4	47.76	4
2002	B. F. Smith.	16	28	3	1,060	129	3	6	42.40	5
1986	S. J. Rhodes	14	20	5	627	124	1	2	41.80	36/3
1998	V. S. Solanki.	14	23	3	832	153*	2	4	41.60	18
2002	S. D. Peters	9	15	0	617	146	2	2	41.13	6
	A. Singh	16	29	0	1,074	187	2	6	37.03	11
2001	A. J. Bichel§.	9	11	2	274	78*	0	2	30.44	7
1995	W. P. C. Weston . . .	7	13	2	311	82	0	3	28.27	6
2002	G. J. Batty	16	24	2	395	74	0	3	17.95	9
2002	M. S. Mason.	6	8	2	107	50	0	1	17.83	0
	Kabir Ali	15	19	2	246	51*	0	1	14.47	3
1997	A. Sheriyar.	16	19	8	90	18	0	0	8.18	1

Also batted: A. A. Donald§ (1 match) 5*; S. Lee§ (2 matches) 32, 48; C. G. Liptrot (1 match) 6, 16; D. J. Pipe (2 matches) 26, 14, 12 (9 ct, 1 st); M. J. Rawnsley (3 matches) 4, 9*, 7 (2 ct).

§ *Overseas player.*

BOWLING

	O	M	R	W	BB	5W/i	Avge
A. J. Bichel	297	77	902	36	9-93	1	25.05
M. S. Mason	204.4	47	581	22	5-50	1	26.40
Kabir Ali	497.5	116	1,594	60	5-32	4	26.56
A. Sheriyar.	555.2	144	1,715	57	6-71	4	30.08
D. A. Leatherdale	129.3	18	502	16	4-23	0	31.37
G. J. Batty	571.5	152	1,614	51	6-71	3	31.64

Also bowled: A. A. Donald 24–3–77–5; G. A. Hick 21–5–71–0; S. Lee 0.2–0–8–0; C. G. Liptrot 27–0–141–2; M. J. Rawnsley 80–27–232–2; B. F. Smith 7–0–32–0; V. S. Solanki 39–6–128–0.

COUNTY RECORDS

Highest score for:	405*	G. A. Hick v Somerset at Taunton	1988
Highest score against:	331*	J. D. Robertson (Middlesex) at Worcester	1949
Best bowling for:	9-23	C. F. Root v Lancashire at Worcester	1931
Best bowling against:	10-51	J. Mercer (Glamorgan) at Worcester	1936
Highest total for:	670-7 dec.	v Somerset at Worcester	1995
Highest total against:	701-4 dec.	by Leicestershire at Worcester.	1906
Lowest total for:	24	v Yorkshire at Huddersfield.	1903
Lowest total against:	30	by Hampshire at Worcester	1903

COUNTY OFFICERS

Captain 2002 – G. A. Hick; 2003 – B. F. Smith • **Director of cricket** T. M. Moody
President M. G. Jones • **Chairman** J. W. Elliott
Chief executive M. Newton • **Head groundsman** T. R. Packwood • **Scorer** W. Clarke

At Oxford, April 13, 14, 15. WORCESTERSHIRE beat OXFORD UCCE by 332 runs.

WORCESTERSHIRE v GLOUCESTERSHIRE

At Worcester, April 19, 20, 21, 22. Worcestershire won by 206 runs. Worcestershire 18 pts, Gloucestershire 5 pts. Toss: Worcestershire. County debuts: S. D. Peters; I. D. Fisher, C. M. Spearman.

Remarkable bowling from Bichel, who collected Worcestershire's first nine-wicket haul since Neal Radford in 1986, helped settle a match between the bookmakers' favourites for promotion. However, the platform for victory had been laid by Ben Smith who, on a wicket of surprising pace and bounce after winter floods, became the first player to score centuries in his opening two first-class games for Worcestershire. Driving with authority, he added 142 for the fifth wicket with Leatherdale, before the first of two excellent, accurate performances from Lewis, returning from a stress fracture of the back, restricted them to 333. At 177 for two, with Craig Spearman – a New Zealand international with a Welsh mother – unbeaten on 111, Gloucestershire were strongly placed, but Bichel's hostile fast-medium triggered a collapse to 268. Hick's commanding 92 stretched Worcestershire's lead to 360, which Gloucestershire gave up chasing once Sheriyar and Kabir Ali made early incisions. Without Hancock, who had a broken finger, they tumbled to defeat shortly after lunch on the last day.

Close of play: First day, Worcestershire 302-7 (Batty 11, Rhodes 12); Second day, Gloucestershire 233-6 (Snape 19, Russell 1); Third day, Gloucestershire 15-1 (Spearman 8, Fisher 1).

Worcestershire

W. P. C. Weston c Russell b Lewis	6	– c Taylor b Lewis	15
A. Singh c Spearman b Harvey	35	– lbw b Lewis	13
*G. A. Hick c Snape b Harvey	2	– lbw b Lewis	92
B. F. Smith c Russell b Harvey	129	– c Harvey b Lewis	4
S. D. Peters c Harvey b Lewis	34	– c Averis b Harvey	26
D. A. Leatherdale c Spearman b Lewis	55	– not out	49
G. J. Batty c Alleyne b Lewis	11	– lbw b Lewis	0
A. J. Bichel lbw b Harvey	0	– c Windows b Lewis	27
†S. J. Rhodes not out	38	– lbw b Averis	31
Kabir Ali c Alleyne b Lewis	5	– c Averis b Alleyne	13
A. Sheriyar c Harvey b Lewis	0	– c sub b Averis	2
B 3, l-b 5, w 4, n-b 6	18	B 6, l-b 7, w 2, n-b 8	23
	333		**295**

1/16 (1) 2/33 (3) 3/48 (2) 4/133 (5) 5/275 (6) 6/287 (4) 7/287 (8) 8/319 (7) 9/325 (10) 10/333 (11)

1/25 (2) 2/71 (1) 3/79 (4) 4/121 (5) 5/174 (3) 6/174 (7) 7/202 (8) 8/277 (9) 9/292 (10) 10/295 (11)

Bonus points – Worcestershire 3, Gloucestershire 3.

The infamous ball which Mike Atherton allegedly rubbed in soil from his trouser pocket, and which later became the property of the ICC referee Peter Burge, sold for £1,600.
Cricketana, page 1701

Bowling: *First Innings*—Lewis 29.4–9–77–6; Averis 18–4–56–0; Harvey 29–8–85–4; Alleyne 19–5–44–0; Fisher 21–5–53–0; Snape 2–0–10–0. *Second Innings*—Lewis 17–4–54–6; Averis 16.1–5–58–2; Fisher 17–2–85–0; Harvey 13–0–49–1; Alleyne 14–6–36–1.

Gloucestershire

C. M. Spearman c Hick b Bichel	111	– (2) lbw b Ali	14
T. H. C. Hancock lbw b Bichel	3	– absent hurt	
C. G. Taylor lbw b Bichel	1	– (4) b Sheriyar	8
M. G. N. Windows c Hick b Bichel	60	– (5) lbw b Ali	12
I. J. Harvey st Rhodes b Batty	9	– (6) b Batty	41
*M. W. Alleyne c Hick b Bichel	7	– (7) b Batty	13
J. N. Snape c Singh b Bichel	24	– (8) run out	11
†R. C. Russell c Weston b Bichel	12	– (1) c Peters b Bichel	0
I. D. Fisher not out	1	– (3) lbw b Sheriyar	5
J. M. M. Averis c Weston b Bichel	0	– (9) c Hick b Batty	17
J. Lewis c Weston b Bichel	4	– (10) not out	16
B 3, l-b 11, w 6, n-b 16	36	L-b 9, w 4, n-b 4	17

1/9 (2) 2/17 (3) 3/177 (1) 4/198 (4)   268   1/10 (1) 2/25 (3) 3/30 (2)   154
5/204 (5) 6/214 (6) 7/257 (7)   4/46 (5) 5/58 (4) 6/102 (6)
8/258 (8) 9/260 (10) 10/268 (11)   7/114 (8) 8/117 (7) 9/154 (9)

Bonus points – Gloucestershire 2, Worcestershire 3.

Bowling: *First Innings*—Bichel 23.1–4–93–9; Sheriyar 15–2–56–0; Ali 21–6–60–0; Leatherdale 3–0–18–0; Batty 11–3–27–1. *Second Innings*—Bichel 16–4–38–1; Ali 11–2–32–2; Sheriyar 11–3–42–2; Batty 7.4–1–33–3.

Umpires: M. R. Benson and M. J. Kitchen.

At Northampton, April 24, 25, 26, 27. WORCESTERSHIRE drew with NORTHAMPTONSHIRE.

WORCESTERSHIRE v GLAMORGAN

At Worcester, May 8, 9, 10, 11. Glamorgan won by 110 runs. Glamorgan 17 pts, Worcestershire 5 pts. Toss: Worcestershire.

Glamorgan won their first competitive game of the season after twice clawing back a match that was slipping away. They lost two wickets in Bichel's opening over and were listing badly at 106 for six before Jonathan Hughes, in only his second Championship match, turned things round. Scoreless for 35 balls, he needed only 76 more to hammer 74 as he and Croft doubled the total. Glamorgan lurched into trouble again when Worcestershire's openers rode their luck on a sluggish, seaming pitch to put on 156, but again they came back fighting. Darren Thomas found swing and took five wickets to keep the lead down to 12, before consistent batting, including Powell's second fifty, left Worcestershire facing a testing target of 337. Once Peters and Solanki fell to Croft in successive overs, they never looked likely to make it. Kasprowicz had failed to take a wicket in his first match, but ended with seven here.

Close of play: First day, Worcestershire 29-0 (Peters 9, Singh 18); Second day, Glamorgan 38-0 (James 15, Hemp 16); Third day, Worcestershire 25-0 (Peters 8, Singh 17).

Glamorgan

*S. P. James c Rhodes b Bichel	1	– lbw b Sheriyar	25
D. L. Hemp c Peters b Bichel	0	– lbw b Batty	64
I. J. Thomas lbw b Ali	18	– c Hick b Sheriyar	8
M. J. Powell c Rhodes b Ali	53	– c Bichel b Batty	59
A. Dale c Rhodes b Bichel	24	– c Hick b Sheriyar	39
J. Hughes c Batty b Ali	74	– b Sheriyar	26
†M. A. Wallace lbw b Ali	0	– c Singh b Bichel	9
R. D. B. Croft c and b Bichel	59	– c Leatherdale b Ali	39
S. D. Thomas lbw b Batty	0	– c Bichel b Sheriyar	13
M. S. Kasprowicz b Ali	33	– b Ali	8
S. P. Jones not out	7	– not out	22
B 7, l-b 6, w 2, n-b 2	17	B 4, l-b 9, w 8, n-b 4	25

1/1 (2) 2/2 (1) 3/36 (3) 4/102 (5)   286
5/106 (4) 6/106 (7) 7/212 (6)
8/213 (9) 9/278 (8) 10/286 (10)

1/67 (1) 2/87 (3) 3/136 (2)   348
4/220 (5) 5/224 (4) 6/262 (7)
7/262 (6) 8/284 (9)
9/301 (10) 10/348 (8)

Bonus points – Glamorgan 2, Worcestershire 3.

Bowling: *First Innings*—Bichel 24–10–39–4; Sheriyar 19–3–66–0; Ali 23.4–5–80–5; Leatherdale 6–0–33–0; Batty 19–3–55–1. *Second Innings*—Bichel 32–9–93–1; Sheriyar 30–6–86–5; Ali 23–6–67–2; Batty 21–5–74–2; Hick 2–0–15–0.

Worcestershire

S. D. Peters c Wallace b S. D. Thomas	71	– b Croft	40
A. Singh c Wallace b S. D. Thomas	81	– b Kasprowicz	26
*G. A. Hick c Wallace b S. D. Thomas	8	– b S. D. Thomas	4
B. F. Smith b Croft	3	– lbw b Kasprowicz	61
V. S. Solanki lbw b Jones	25	– b Croft	4
D. A. Leatherdale b Jones	29	– c Wallace b S. D. Thomas	24
G. J. Batty b S. D. Thomas	17	– c S. D. Thomas b Kasprowicz	10
A. J. Bichel c Croft b Kasprowicz	8	– c Wallace b S. D. Thomas	8
†S. J. Rhodes not out	20	– b Kasprowicz	7
Kabir Ali b S. D. Thomas	10	– c Jones b Kasprowicz	19
A. Sheriyar b Kasprowicz	1	– not out	4
B 3, l-b 14, w 2, n-b 6	25	B 5, l-b 12, w 2	19

1/156 (2) 2/164 (3) 3/175 (4) 4/177 (1) 298
5/228 (6) 6/243 (5) 7/258 (8)
8/279 (7) 9/289 (10) 10/298 (11)

1/47 (2) 2/62 (3) 3/95 (1)   226
4/99 (5) 5/161 (4) 6/183 (7)
7/192 (8) 8/193 (6)
9/222 (10) 10/226 (9)

Bonus points – Worcestershire 2, Glamorgan 3.

Bowling: *First Innings*—Kasprowicz 24.1–7–77–2; S. D. Thomas 25–5–77–5; Jones 18–3–59–2; Dale 6–2–14–0; Croft 23–6–54–1. *Second Innings*—Kasprowicz 23–3–77–5; S. D. Thomas 15–3–54–3; Croft 14–0–41–2; Jones 6–0–30–0; Dale 3–0–7–0.

Umpires: N. G. Cowley and N. A. Mallender.

WORCESTERSHIRE v ESSEX

At Worcester, May 15, 16, 17, 18. Essex won by five wickets. Essex 19 pts, Worcestershire 6 pts. Toss: Worcestershire.

An evenly poised game was tilted Essex's way by John Stephenson, who had been brought back to his first county primarily as Second Eleven coach, but picked up seven wickets in the second innings and ten in all. Worcestershire slumped to 130 for five after choosing to bat on an uneven pitch, but were revived by Smith's resolute 61 and lively lower-order resistance, centred on Bichel's clean-hit 65. By contrast, Essex reached 321 for four on the back of a grinding hundred by Habib – his first since leaving Leicestershire – only to falter badly to 373. Stephenson then changed the game in the blink of an eye. Called up only because of a long injury list, he cut the ball in sharply to the right-handers and took four wickets in four overs as Worcestershire nose-dived to 63 for five. He finished with a career-best seven for 44. Needing just 135, Essex wobbled badly, but Flower's experience brought calm. Fittingly, it was Stephenson who hit the runs to complete their first Championship win. During the match, Allan Donald, the South African fast bowler, who had played for Warwickshire for 11 seasons, was unveiled as Worcestershire's locum overseas player. "I'd rather be a pear than a bear," he told the crowd.

Close of play: First day, Essex 9-0 (Robinson 6, Grayson 3); Second day, Essex 316-4 (Habib 96, Irani 46); Third day, Worcestershire 98-6 (Rhodes 14).

Worcestershire

S. D. Peters lbw b Dakin	24	– absent hurt	
A. Singh b Stephenson	60	– lbw b Stephenson	23
*G. A. Hick lbw b Irani	30	– lbw b Irani	10
B. F. Smith lbw b Stephenson	61	– b Stephenson	14
V. S. Solanki b Irani	0	– (1) c Flower b Stephenson	15
D. A. Leatherdale lbw b Stephenson	0	– (5) lbw b Stephenson	1
G. J. Batty c Grayson b Grant	32	– (6) b Stephenson	4
†S. J. Rhodes lbw b Dakin	30	– (7) c Robinson b Stephenson	22
A. J. Bichel c Cowan b Grant	65	– not out	2
Kabir Ali c Habib b Cowan	40	– (8) lbw b Stephenson	24
A. Sheriyar not out	0	– (10) run out	4
B 1, l-b 6, w 4, n-b 14	25	B 8, l-b 5, w 2, n-b 6	21

1/50 (1) 2/111 (2) 3/125 (3) 4/125 (5)	367	1/43 (1) 2/54 (2) 3/58 (3)	140
5/130 (6) 6/215 (7) 7/229 (4)		4/59 (5) 5/63 (6) 6/98 (4)	
8/300 (8) 9/364 (10) 10/367 (9)		7/129 (7) 8/134 (8) 9/140 (10)	

Bonus points – Worcestershire 4, Essex 3.

Bowling: *First Innings*—Cowan 21–4–72–1; Grant 14.5–4–66–2; Irani 19–4–60–2; Dakin 16–5–76–2; Stephenson 19–5–60–3; Middlebrook 5–2–9–0; Grayson 5–1–17–0. *Second Innings*—Cowan 7–0–31–0; Middlebrook 1–0–4–0; Irani 15–5–48–1; Stephenson 14–5–44–7.

Essex

D. D. J. Robinson c Peters b Leatherdale	71	– b Ali	0
A. P. Grayson c Rhodes b Sheriyar	15	– c Rhodes b Sheriyar	26
R. S. Clinton c Bichel b Batty	4	– lbw b Sheriyar	2
A. Habib run out	117	– c Leatherdale b Sheriyar	4
†A. Flower c Peters b Sheriyar	45	– lbw b Ali	47
*R. C. Irani lbw b Sheriyar	48	– not out	32
J. P. Stephenson c Hick b Sheriyar	0	– not out	13
J. M. Dakin b Batty	24		
J. D. Middlebrook not out	1		
A. P. Cowan c Hick b Sheriyar	1		
J. B. Grant b Batty	0		
B 1, l-b 18, w 4, n-b 21	44	B 4, l-b 5, n-b 2	11

1/50 (2) 2/80 (3) 3/139 (1) 4/218 (5)	373	1/0 (1) 2/9 (3) 3/13 (4) (5 wkts) 135	
5/321 (6) 6/321 (7) 7/367 (8)		4/66 (2) 5/117 (5)	
8/368 (4) 9/372 (10) 10/373 (11)			

Bonus points – Essex 4, Worcestershire 2 (130 overs: 368-8).

Bowling: *First Innings*—Bichel 12–6–22–0; Sheriyar 42–15–111–5; Ali 32–9–75–0; Batty 41.5–13–109–3; Leatherdale 8–1–37–1. *Second Innings*—Ali 16–5–52–2; Sheriyar 11.4–3–46–3; Batty 4–0–18–0; Leatherdale 3–0–10–0.

Umpires: K. E. Palmer and J. F. Steele.

At Bristol, May 31, June 1, 2. WORCESTERSHIRE beat GLOUCESTERSHIRE by 304 runs.

Frizzell County Championship Division 2 – Worcestershire

803

At Chester-le-Street, June 12, 13, 14, 15. WORCESTERSHIRE drew with DURHAM.

WORCESTERSHIRE v DURHAM

At Worcester, June 26, 27, 28. Worcestershire won by an innings and 308 runs. Worcestershire 20 pts, Durham 2 pts. Toss: Durham.

Two weeks after holding their own against the same opponents, a drastically depleted Durham side suffered the biggest thrashing in their first-class history. After winning the toss, they reached 49 without loss on the first morning; it proved to be their high point. On a true pitch, Bichel and Kabir Ali took advantage of nervy batting to demolish the innings inside 40 overs and, when Hick took his turn against an attack missing several first-choice bowlers, the contest had the inevitability of a man batting against boys. In more than nine hours at the crease he played and missed once, on 213, and shared hundred partnerships with Singh, Smith and Batty. When he finally declared, Hick was unbeaten on a majestic 315, his third triple-century, which lasted nine hours 10 minutes and 386 balls, with two sixes and 49 fours, the majority creamed through the covers. Worcestershire's total of 643 was the second-highest in their history. Resuming a massive 523 behind, Durham were again undone by Bichel and Ali, and only Law put up prolonged resistance. It was Worcestershire's biggest win.

Close of play: First day, Worcestershire 264-2 (Hick 119, Smith 31); Second day, Durham 50-0 (Lewis 15, G. J. Pratt 23).

Durham

*J. J. B. Lewis c Rhodes b Bichel	13	– c Solanki b Ali	22
G. J. Pratt c and b Bichel	34	– lbw b Ali	33
G. J. Muchall b Ali	1	– b Rhodes b Bichel	4
N. Peng c Hick b Ali	21	– c Solanki b Ali	0
M. J. Symington lbw b Ali	16	– c Rhodes b Bichel	4
†A. Pratt c Singh b Batty	12	– c Solanki b Ali	1
D. R. Law c Rhodes b Sheriyar	0	– not out	72
G. D. Bridge c Batty b Bichel	6	– c Rhodes b Sheriyar	33
A. M. Davies c Hick b Ali	0	– c Solanki b Bichel	3
N. Killeen not out	5	– c Rhodes b Sheriyar	16
N. G. Hatch c Singh b Bichel	5	– b Batty	0
L-b 1, n-b 6	7	L-b 1, w 4, n-b 22	27
	120		**215**

1/49 (2) 2/50 (3) 3/62 (1) 4/74 (4)
5/94 (6) 6/95 (7) 7/108 (8)
8/108 (5) 9/113 (9) 10/120 (11)

1/57 (1) 2/74 (2) 3/74 (4)
4/78 (3) 5/81 (6) 6/83 (5)
7/152 (8) 8/169 (9)
9/214 (10) 10/215 (11)

Bonus points – Worcestershire 3.

Bowling: *First Innings*—Bichel 12.5–2–58–4; Sheriyar 12–6–23–1; Ali 10–2–31–4; Batty 5–3–7–1. *Second Innings*—Bichel 21–4–84–3; Sheriyar 14–6–26–2; Ali 18–2–77–4; Batty 5.3–2–11–1; Solanki 1–1–0–0; Leatherdale 3–1–16–0.

Worcestershire

W. P. C. Weston lbw b Killeen	4	†S. J. Rhodes c G. J. Pratt b Symington	27
A. Singh c Peng b Law	88	A. J. Bichel not out	78
*G. A. Hick not out	315	L-b 14, w 2, n-b 16	32
B. F. Smith c A. Pratt b Law	83		
V. S. Solanki c Muchall b Killeen	11	1/10 (1) 2/200 (2) (7 wkts dec.) **643**
D. A. Leatherdale b Davies	5	3/371 (4) 4/404 (5)
G. J. Batty c b G. J. Pratt b Killeen	0	5/415 (6) 6/420 (7) 7/505 (8)

Kabir Ali and A. Sheriyar did not bat.

Bonus points – Worcestershire 5, Durham 2 (130 overs: 505-6).

Bowling: Killeen 30–10–107–3; Hatch 23–2–110–0; Davies 28–5–77–1; Law 27–7–104–2; Bridge 30–3–143–0; Symington 10–0–88–1.

Umpires: V. A. Holder and A. A. Jones.

At Lord's, July 3, 4, 5, 6. WORCESTERSHIRE drew with MIDDLESEX.

At Southend, July 10, 11, 12, 13. WORCESTERSHIRE beat ESSEX by eight wickets.

WORCESTERSHIRE v NORTHAMPTONSHIRE

At Worcester, July 19, 20, 21. Worcestershire won by eight wickets. Worcestershire 19 pts, Northamptonshire 7 pts. Toss: Northamptonshire. County debut: G. L. Brophy. Championship debut: M. S. Mason.

After two hard-fought days, Northamptonshire collapsed dramatically on the third to hand Worcestershire a comfortable win. Once again, Hussey underpinned Northamptonshire's first innings, batting more than seven hours for 174, his ninth hundred in only 25 Championship matches. It made him the first batsman to pass 1,000 first-class runs in the season. Easing drives and cracking cuts and pulls, he was supported staunchly by the middle order – including Gerard Brophy, a South African with a British passport – as Northamptonshire recovered from 49 for three to 387. Worcestershire replied positively: Singh reached 50 in 46 balls, and Smith and Solanki added 195 for the fourth wicket. But the match changed tack on the third morning. Cloud cover helped swing, the bounce became more inconsistent and Worcestershire lost seven for 103 in search of quick runs. Even so, few would have envisaged Northamptonshire being bowled out for 77. Bichel's pace and the extra bounce of Matt Mason, an Australian with a British passport, inflicted the early damage before Leatherdale mopped up the tail. Worcestershire needed only 82, and Hick steered them home in rapid time.

Close of play: First day, Northamptonshire 339-7 (Hussey 163, Greenidge 5); Second day, Worcestershire 273-3 (Smith 104, Solanki 91).

Northamptonshire

*M. E. K. Hussey c Rhodes b Bichel	174	– c Rhodes b Sheriyar	6
D. E. Paynter lbw b Sheriyar	2	– b Bichel	10
M. B. Loye c Rhodes b Sheriyar	16	– lbw b Bichel	4
D. J. Sales b Mason	0	– c Rhodes b Mason	12
A. L. Penberthy c Solanki b Mason	41	– c Hick b Mason	1
G. L. Brophy b Leatherdale	30	– not out	14
M. E. Cassar lbw b Bichel	55	– lbw b Leatherdale	1
†T. M. B. Bailey lbw b Sheriyar	0	– c Hick b Leatherdale	0
C. G. Greenidge c Smith b Bichel	17	– lbw b Mason	1
D. M. Cousins not out	23	– b Leatherdale	1
J. F. Brown c Solanki b Mason	0	– c Weston b Leatherdale	19
B 4, l-b 9, w 12, n-b 4	29	L-b 8	8

1/6 (2) 2/40 (3) 3/49 (4) 4/127 (5)   387   1/13 (1) 2/20 (3) 3/21 (2) 4/23 (5)   77
5/193 (6) 6/321 (7) 7/328 (8)   5/40 (4) 6/41 (7) 7/41 (8)
8/356 (9) 9/364 (1) 10/387 (11)   8/50 (9) 9/51 (10) 10/77 (11)

Bonus points – Northamptonshire 4, Worcestershire 3.

Bowling: *First Innings*—Bichel 29–3–119–3; Sheriyar 28–9–69–3; Mason 21–4–59–3; Leatherdale 9–1–48–1; Batty 18–3–61–0; Smith 4–0–18–0. *Second Innings*—Bichel 9–2–16–2; Sheriyar 10–4–15–1; Mason 9–4–15–3; Leatherdale 7.3–2–23–4.

Worcestershire

W. P. C. Weston c Cassar b Greenidge	7	– c Penberthy b Greenidge	18
A. Singh c and b Cassar	51	– c Bailey b Greenidge	5
*G. A. Hick lbw b Greenidge	8	– not out	36
B. F. Smith c Bailey b Cousins	108	– not out	18
V. S. Solanki b Cassar	116		
D. A. Leatherdale lbw b Greenidge	5		
G. J. Batty c Sales b Penberthy	3		
†S. J. Rhodes c Hussey b Penberthy	6		
A. J. Bichel c Paynter b Cousins	31		
M. S. Mason c Bailey b Cousins	18		
A. Sheriyar not out	5		
B 12, l-b 11, n-b 2	25	B 1, l-b 4	5

1/43 (1) 2/59 (3) 3/85 (2) 4/280 (4)   **383**   1/10 (2) 2/39 (1)   **(2 wkts) 82**
5/291 (6) 6/304 (7) 7/320 (5)
8/332 (8) 9/374 (10) 10/383 (9)

Bonus points – Worcestershire 4, Northamptonshire 3.

Bowling: *First Innings*—Cousins 20–1–91–3; Greenidge 25–6–90–3; Cassar 14–3–59–2; Penberthy 18–3–60–2; Brown 18–3–60–0. *Second Innings*—Cousins 4–0–24–0; Greenidge 6–1–28–2; Brown 3–0–25–0; Cassar 0.1–0–0–0.

Umpires: M. J. Harris and R. Palmer.

At Worcester, July 31, August 1, 2, 3. WORCESTERSHIRE drew with INDIANS (see Indian tour section).

WORCESTERSHIRE v NOTTINGHAMSHIRE

At Kidderminster, August 8, 9, 10, 11. Drawn. Worcestershire 8 pts, Nottinghamshire 7 pts. Toss: Worcestershire. County debut: S. C. G. MacGill.

Worcestershire lacked the cutting edge to force victory, a failure that would prove crucial when Nottinghamshire eventually pipped them to the last promotion spot. Even so, the bowlers had bossed both first innings. MacGill spun his leg-breaks hard on a slow, grudging pitch, and became only the third Nottinghamshire bowler in 75 years – after Bill Voce and Garry Sobers – to take five wickets on his Championship debut. But Nottinghamshire also found batting tricky. In an inspired spell, Sheriyar nipped the ball both ways to seize the top five wickets. From 42 for five, Johnson's defiant and unbeaten 52 boosted the total to 161, but he ran out of partners as the tall Mason polished off the last five. On the third day the sun shone, and Hick and Smith cashed in; on the fourth, Batty's explosive 66 boosted Worcestershire's lead to 376 and set up a declaration. Victory for either side seemed unlikely given the nature of the pitch, and Johnson's second fifty of the game and Afzaal's 91 helped Nottinghamshire bat out 86 overs in relative comfort.

Close of play: First day, Nottinghamshire 5-1 (Gallian 0); Second day, Nottinghamshire 112-7 (Johnson 31, Smith 2); Third day, Worcestershire 253-4 (Hick 126, Batty 11).

Worcestershire

S. D. Peters c MacGill b Harris	5	– c Read b Smith	10
A. Singh b Harris	57	– c Afzaal b Smith	13
*G. A. Hick c Read b Harris	13	– c and b Pietersen	126
B. F. Smith c Johnson b MacGill	32	– c Johnson b Smith	65
V. S. Solanki c Read b MacGill	0	– lbw b Harris	5
S. Lee c Pietersen b Smith	32		
G. J. Batty c Gallian b MacGill	2	– (6) not out	66
†S. J. Rhodes lbw b MacGill	34	– (7) not out	24
Kabir Ali b Smith	0		
M. S. Mason not out	1		
A. Sheriyar c Franks b MacGill	4		
L-b 6, w 10, p 5	21	B 5, l-b 6, w 10, n-b 6	27
	201	(5 wkts dec.)	**336**

1/13 (1) 2/47 (3) 3/121 (4) 4/121 (5)
5/121 (2) 6/124 (7) 7/185 (6)
8/193 (9) 9/195 (8) 10/201 (11)

1/14 (1) 2/38 (2)
3/198 (4) 4/216 (5)
5/253 (3)

Bonus points – Worcestershire 1, Nottinghamshire 3.

Bowling: *First Innings*—Smith 15–3–45–2; Harris 14–4–43–3; Franks 6–0–39–0; MacGill 18.4–5–63–5. *Second Innings*—Smith 21–2–94–3; Franks 13–4–56–0; MacGill 21–2–108–0; Harris 13–2–40–1; Pietersen 3–0–27–1.

Nottinghamshire

G. E. Welton c Rhodes b Sheriyar	4	– (2) c Peters b Sheriyar	76
*J. E. R. Gallian lbw b Sheriyar	8	– (1) b Batty	27
D. J. Bicknell lbw b Sheriyar	13	– c Rhodes b Batty	8
U. Afzaal c Solanki b Sheriyar	0	– c Hick b Batty	91
K. P. Pietersen lbw b Sheriyar	13	– lbw b Sheriyar	0
P. Johnson not out	52	– not out	56
†C. M. W. Read c Solanki b Mason	26	– not out	14
P. J. Franks c Hick b Mason	0		
G. J. Smith b Mason	2		
S. C. G. MacGill b Mason	22		
A. J. Harris b Mason	0		
B 2, l-b 9, w 4, n-b 6	21	B 14, l-b 4, w 2	20
	161	(5 wkts)	**292**

1/5 (1) 2/26 (2) 3/26 (4) 4/33 (3)
5/42 (5) 6/103 (7) 7/103 (8)
8/137 (9) 9/161 (10) 10/161 (11)

1/69 (1) 2/87 (3)
3/139 (2) 4/139 (5)
5/256 (4)

Bonus points – Worcestershire 3.

Bowling: *First Innings*—Mason 16.4–3–50–5; Sheriyar 17–6–59–5; Ali 7–1–29–0; Lee 0.2–0–8–0; Batty 1.4–0–4–0. *Second Innings*—Mason 16–1–42–0; Sheriyar 11–3–42–2; Ali 16–4–64–0; Batty 32–9–97–3; Solanki 11–1–29–0.

Umpires: D. J. Constant and A. G. T. Whitehead.

At Derby, August 14, 15, 16. WORCESTERSHIRE beat DERBYSHIRE by nine wickets.

WORCESTERSHIRE v MIDDLESEX

At Worcester, August 27, 28, 29, 30. Middlesex won by six wickets. Middlesex 19.75 pts, Worcestershire 5 pts. Toss: Middlesex.

Worcestershire fought back in the second innings but ultimately paid the penalty for ragged bowling in the first. Kabir Ali took three early wickets in four balls, but Joyce – who caressed a hundred and passed 1,000 Championship runs for the season – plundered the bowling along with Nash, who needed a runner, and Noffke as the attack toiled in the sweltering heat. Replying to an intimidating 531 on an inconsistent wicket, Worcestershire began confidently, but it was a different story on the third morning. As the sun disappeared, Noffke and Keegan found swing, Hick failed to add to a crisp 101 (his 121st first-class century), which took him past 35,000 runs, and eight wickets tumbled for 81. Worcestershire followed on 212 behind and defeat looked imminent when they began the final day in effect 39 for five. However, the lower order battled hard to leave Middlesex a target of 190 in 56 overs. They hiccoughed their way to 70 for three, but Joyce and Weekes held their nerve. The win pulled Middlesex 24 points clear at the top of the table; Worcestershire were precariously perched at third.

Close of play: First day, Middlesex 374-7 (Nash 67, Noffke 9); Second day, Worcestershire 231-2 (Hick 101, Smith 38); Third day, Worcestershire 251-5 (Leatherdale 30, Batty 11).

Middlesex

*A. J. Strauss c Hick b Ali	8	– c Smith b Leatherdale	27
S. G. Koenig c Rhodes b Ali	81	– c Hick b Ali	33
B. L. Hutton lbw b Ali	0	– c Rhodes b Sheriyar	0
O. A. Shah b Ali	0	– c Ali b Liptrot	19
E. C. Joyce st Rhodes b Leatherdale	125	– not out	46
P. N. Weekes lbw b Liptrot	46	– not out	40
†D. C. Nash c Hick b Batty	100		
J. W. M. Dalrymple c Hick b Ali	14		
A. A. Noffke c Hick b Leatherdale	76		
C. B. Keegan c Rhodes b Sheriyar	24		
T. F. Bloomfield not out	26		
B 3, l-b 12, w 10, n-b 6	31	B 5, l-b 13, w 4, n-b 6	28

1/25 (1) 2/25 (3) 3/25 (4) 4/167 (2)   **531**
5/264 (5) 6/305 (6) 7/338 (8)
8/477 (7) 9/485 (9) 10/531 (10)

1/56 (1) 2/68 (2)   (4 wkts) **193**
3/70 (3) 4/114 (4)

Bonus points – Middlesex 5, Worcestershire 2 (130 overs: 470-7).

Bowling: *First Innings*—Sheriyar 31.3–8–119–1; Ali 33.9–9–100–5; Liptrot 21.0–105–1; Batty 34–10–126–1; Leatherdale 24–4–61–2; Solanki 2–1–5–0. *Second Innings*—Ali 17.4–2–54–1; Sheriyar 13–0–54–1; Leatherdale 9–1–31–1; Liptrot 6–0–36–1.

Worcestershire

S. D. Peters c Joyce b Bloomfield	13	– c Nash b Noffke	14
A. Singh c Weekes b Noffke	50	– c Nash b Noffke	40
*G. A. Hick c Weekes b Noffke	101	– b Keegan	69
B. F. Smith c Nash b Noffke	50	– c and b Noffke	60
V. S. Solanki c Joyce b Noffke	24	– lbw b Keegan	4
D. A. Leatherdale c Hutton b Keegan	39	– c Strauss b Weekes	42
G. J. Batty c Joyce b Keegan	3	– c Strauss b Keegan	33
†S. J. Rhodes c Joyce b Keegan	2	– run out	47
Kabir Ali c Nash b Keegan	0	– c Hutton b Keegan	35
C. G. Liptrot b Hutton	6	– c Dalrymple b Noffke	16
A. Sheriyar not out	0	– not out	2
B 4, l-b 13, w 2, n-b 12	31	B 13, l-b 22, w 2, n-b 2	39

1/35 (1) 2/103 (2) 3/238 (3) 4/265 (4)   **319**
5/268 (5) 6/296 (7) 7/302 (8)
8/302 (9) 9/319 (10) 10/319 (6)

1/30 (1) 2/69 (2) 3/186 (3)   **401**
4/194 (5) 5/217 (4) 6/291 (6)
7/293 (7) 8/355 (9)
9/395 (10) 10/401 (8)

Bonus points – Worcestershire 3, Middlesex 3.

Bowling: *First Innings*—Noffke 26–5–84–4; Bloomfield 20–4–100–1; Keegan 20.1–8–47–4; Hutton 12–2–42–1; Weekes 9–2–21–0; Dalrymple 3–1–8–0. *Second Innings*—Noffke 30–6–110–4; Bloomfield 14–1–56–0; Hutton 4–1–18–0; Keegan 24.4–3–92–4; Weekes 21–2–65–1; Dalrymple 9–3–25–0.

Umpires: J. H. Hampshire and A. G. T. Whitehead.

At Cardiff, September 5, 6, 7, 8. WORCESTERSHIRE drew with GLAMORGAN.

At Nottingham, September 11, 12, 13, 14. WORCESTERSHIRE lost to NOTTINGHAMSHIRE by 114 runs.

WORCESTERSHIRE v DERBYSHIRE

At Worcester, September 18, 19, 20, 21. Worcestershire won by one wicket. Worcestershire 17 pts, Derbyshire 3.75 pts. Toss: Derbyshire.

The match reached a dramatic climax when Hick defied a broken thumb and came to the crease at No. 11 to help Leatherdale squeeze a narrow victory. But it was a hollow triumph. Needing at least four batting points (350 runs) to maintain a chance of beating Nottinghamshire to the third promotion place, Worcestershire stumbled to 75 for three against Dean. After Solanki's aggressive innings came to an end they never threatened to make it. Derbyshire batted with vigour in their second innings to open up a lead of 372, and it looked like Worcestershire's season would end with a whimper as they slumped to 97 for four. But Leatherdale, with a perfectly paced 89, engineered an unexpected triumph. Batty cracked 74, Mason bludgeoned 50 off 27 balls, and Hick, after breaking his thumb in the field, made a brave ten to secure victory. Batty's five for 60 in Derbyshire's first innings made him the first Worcestershire spinner since Richard Illingworth in 1990 to take 50 Championship wickets.

Close of play: First day, Worcestershire 52-1 (Peters 32, Hick 9); Second day, Derbyshire 98-2 (Gait 46); Third day, Worcestershire 36-1 (Peters 23, Smith 2).

Derbyshire

A. I. Gait b Batty	58	– lbw b Leatherdale	67
*†L. D. Sutton c Pipe b Ali	51	– lbw b Mason	2
C. W. G. Bassano c Pipe b Ali	0	– b Leatherdale	39
D. R. Hewson c Pipe b Mason	9	– c Solanki b Batty	14
S. A. Selwood lbw b Batty	22	– b Leatherdale	77
G. Welch c Hick b Batty	2	– (7) lbw b Sheriyar	27
J. I. D. Kerr c Pipe b Ali	54	– (6) c Solanki b Leatherdale	68
N. R. C. Dumelow c Solanki b Ali	1	– c Batty b Mason	56
Mohammad Ali st Pipe b Batty	0	– c Pipe b Ali	0
K. J. Dean not out	40	– c Pipe b Sheriyar	11
L. J. Wharton c Singh b Batty	0	– not out	11
B 1, l-b 2, w 4, n-b 2	9	B 9, l-b 4, w 2, n-b 4	19
	246		391

1/103 (2) 2/107 (3) 3/125 (1) 4/137 (4)   246
5/140 (6) 6/159 (5) 7/160 (8)
8/165 (9) 9/227 (7) 10/246 (11)

1/15 (2) 2/98 (1) 3/118 (4)   391
4/151 (1) 5/282 (5) 6/291 (6)
7/328 (7) 8/329 (9)
9/344 (10) 10/391 (8)

Bonus points – Derbyshire 1, Worcestershire 3.

Bowling: *First Innings*—Mason 21–7–49–1; Sheriyar 14–3–43–0; Ali 19–3–72–4; Leatherdale 4–0–19–0; Batty 30–10–60–5. *Second Innings*—Mason 23.3–8–62–2; Sheriyar 25–5–63–2; Ali 16–4–69–1; Batty 28–4–118–1; Leatherdale 11–1–50–4; Solanki 4–1–16–0.

Worcestershire

S. D. Peters c Selwood b Mohammad Ali	72	– b Dean	23
A. Singh c Kerr b Dean	5	– b Dean	5
*G. A. Hick b Dean	16	– (11) not out	10
B. F. Smith c Bassano b Dean	2	– (3) c Bassano b Dean	27
V. S. Solanki c Hewson b Welch	81	– (4) c Sutton b Welch	12
D. A. Leatherdale b Kerr	13	– (5) not out	89
G. J. Batty c Sutton b Welch	21	– (6) lbw b Welch	74
†D. J. Pipe b sub b Mohammad Ali	14	– (7) b Welch	12
Kabir Ali c Bassano b Mohammad Ali	4	– (8) c Bassano b Welch	9
M. S. Mason c Sutton b Dean	7	– (9) b Dean	50
A. Sheriyar not out	0	– (10) c Gait b Dean	18
L-b 16, w 2, n-b 12	30	B 8, l-b 18, w 6, n-b 12	44

1/21 (2) 2/67 (3) 3/75 (4) 4/143 (1)   265
5/174 (6) 6/226 (5) 7/253 (7)
8/258 (8) 9/259 (9) 10/265 (10)

1/33 (2) 2/36 (1) 3/77 (3) (9 wkts) 373
4/97 (4) 5/219 (6)
6/231 (7) 7/265 (8)
8/328 (9) 9/360 (10)

Bonus points – Worcestershire 2, Derbyshire 3.

Bowling: *First Innings*—Dean 19.3–4–75–4; Mohammad Ali 14–2–48–3; Welch 23–7–57–2; Wharton 7–0–26–0; Kerr 5–0–43–1. *Second Innings*—Dean 28–3–143–5; Mohammad Ali 11.4–0–63–0; Welch 17–4–85–4; Kerr 6–1–17–0; Dumelow 6–0–35–0; Wharton 1–0–4–0.

Umpires: G. I. Burgess and A. Clarkson.

PROFESSIONAL CRICKETERS' ASSOCIATION AWARDS

At the Professional Cricketers' Association annual dinner in September 2002, Michael Vaughan of Yorkshire was named Cater Allen Private Bank Player of the Year for 2002. Kabir Ali of Worcestershire was the Costcutter PCA Young Player of the Year. Alistair Brown of Surrey, whose 268 against Glamorgan in the C&G Trophy was the highest one-day score ever, won the Slazenger Sheer Instinct Award. For the second year running, Neil Mallender received the Accenture PCA Umpire of the Year award and Glamorgan won the MCC Spirit of Cricket Award. Phil Frost of Somerset was the Mitsubishi Motors PCA Groundsman of the Year. The Jardine Lloyd Thompson PCA in the Community Award went to Wasim Khan. Benson and Hedges, whose three decades of sponsoring one-day cricket had just ended, received a special ECB award.

YORKSHIRE
TOP TO
BOTTOM

Ch'ship 9th in Division 1 – relegated
C&G winners
B&H quarter-finalists
NUL 4th in Division 1

Player of the season: Richard Blakey

In sharp contrast with normal practice, Yorkshire's latest revolution broke out during the season rather than waiting for the winter months. Their fortunes fluctuated wildly both on and off the field. After the long-awaited Championship triumph in 2001 came humble pie: anchored to the bottom of the table from early June, Yorkshire raised their game a little but could not avoid relegation. Some compensation came in the form of a Lord's cup win in the C&G – just like the 2001 Championship, it came after a 33-year gap – but it was the spectacular failure to defend their Championship crown that lingered in the memory. The coach, Wayne Clark from Western Australia, refused to offer excuses and acknowledged that dreadful form early on had left them with too much to do. He did, however, concede that the players had not been able to concentrate 100 per cent on their game because of problems elsewhere. It was a valid point. But in January 2003, it was announced that Clark, who had turned down the position of bowling coach after failing to agree a revised contract, was leaving the club by mutual consent a year early. His replacements were expected to be Kevin Sharp, as batting coach, and Arnie Sidebottom for the bowling, as Yorkshire turned back to their own.

Dark clouds had gathered over Headingley at the annual meeting the previous March when the treasurer, Peter Townend, apologised to members for "our abysmal failure to conduct business successfully last year". He also admitted that the wiping out of profits in the marketing department had highlighted several serious deficiencies in the way the club shop was run. Soon afterwards, the fraud squad were called in to investigate a black hole of up to £100,000. No evidence was found of criminal wrongdoing, but there were mounting fears that Yorkshire were heading for bankruptcy. On August 12, it was announced that the chairman, Keith Moss, had agreed to stand down and that a new, four-strong management team had, at the bank's insistence and with the committee's approval, taken over the running of the club's affairs (the management team was confirmed at a meeting in December). Later in August, an extraordinary general meeting voted in a rule change which allowed the club's borrowing ceiling to rise to £10m in order to meet the spiralling costs of Headingley's redevelopment.

It was against this backcloth that Yorkshire lost five of their first six Championship matches. They were surprised how much they missed the discipline and runs of David Byas, who had retired after being told he would no longer be captain, only to resurface with arch-rivals Lancashire. Yorkshire toughened up in the second half of the season, but they knew they were going down long before survival became impossible with defeat in their penultimate game at Edgbaston. The weaknesses were plain to see. The almost permanent absence of Michael Vaughan and Matthew Hoggard on England duty – not to mention the injured Darren Gough – was keenly felt, and when Craig White was not involved in the Tests he was often unable to bowl because of a side strain. Gavin Hamilton developed psychological problems which prevented him from bowling more than a dozen overs. Matthew Wood, who had completed 1,000 Championship runs the previous season, managed only 201 in 17 innings before being discarded; there was no ideal replacement. Ryan Sidebottom was the top wicket-taker with 41, but he was steady rather than spectacular, as were Steven Kirby, who failed to match the exploits of his debut season in 2001, and Richard Dawson. Chris Silverwood was distinctly quick but seldom fully fit.

On the credit side, Darren Lehmann was as consistent as ever – at one stage he made consecutive scores of 51, 119 not out, 71, 216, 64, 75 and 187 – and when his compatriot Matthew Elliott replaced him later in the season, he was just as enthusiastic and reliable. But it was typical of Yorkshire's *annus horribilis* that Lehmann was to find himself in hot water after a racist outburst during a one-day international against Sri Lanka in January 2003. The ICC banned him for five matches, and Yorkshire, after initially appearing to excuse his behaviour, eventually issued a statement that condemned it but announced his position at the club was unaffected. The choice of Anthony McGrath as captain for 2003 apparently had more to do with Lehmann's international commitments than his much-publicised misdemeanour. In March, it was agreed Lehmann would not return in 2003. Elliott was again signed to replace him. No second overseas player was hired; given that the club had just reported spectacular losses of £1.3m, this was understandable.

Richard Blakey deserved real admiration for the way he shouldered the burden of captaincy after Lehmann's departure without losing the new-found batting form that brought him 1,041 runs going in almost exclusively at No. 7. It was under Blakey's command that Yorkshire pulled off their two wins but they still went through the summer without a home victory for the first time since 1983, when they also ended up bottom (of 17 counties, not nine). Blakey was also in charge for the hard-fought C&G final against Somerset, when Elliott was the conquering hero with a peerless unbeaten 128. Victory was the culmination of a journey full of twists and turns. Yorkshire squeezed past Essex in the quarter-finals after a middle-order rally, and then thrashed Surrey at Headingley after rain had prevented play on any of the three scheduled days. The ECB turned a blind eye to the regulations by allowing the game to be played the following Sunday rather than go to a bowl-out in the indoor school. The decision enabled White to hit a sumptuous century, but Surrey later complained that a damp pitch had been used and not the one originally prepared. After the season they'd had, Yorkshire were in no mood to sympathise. **David Warner**

YORKSHIRE 2002

Back row: T. T. Bresnan, S. M. Guy, C. J. Elstub, D. H. Wigley, G. M. Fellows, J. L. Sadler, R. A. Stead. *Middle row:* M. Carrico (*first-team physiotherapist*), S. Oldham (*cricket development manager*), S. P. Kirby, V. J. Craven, M. J. Lumb, W. M. Clark (*first-team coach*), C. R. Taylor, R. K. J. Dawson, S. A. Richardson, A. K. D. Gray, A. Sidebottom (*second-team coach*). *Front row:* M. J. Wood, M. J. Hoggard, A. McGrath, C. E. W. Silverwood, C. White, D. S. Lehmann (*captain*), M. P. Vaughan, D. Gough, R. J. Blakey, G. M. Hamilton, R. J. Sidebottom.

YORKSHIRE RESULTS

All first-class matches – Played 16: Won 2, Lost 8, Drawn 6.
County Championship matches – Played 16: Won 2, Lost 8, Drawn 6.

COUNTY CHAMPIONSHIP AVERAGES: BATTING AND FIELDING

Cap		M	I	NO	R	HS	100s	50s	Avge	Ct/St
1997	D. S. Lehmann§	10	18	1	1,136	216	3	7	66.82	5
	M. T. G. Elliott§	5	10	1	487	127	1	3	54.11	7
1987	R. J. Blakey†	16	29	7	1,041	103	1	8	47.31	29/1
	A. K. D. Gray.	4	6	1	193	74*	0	1	38.60	0
1993	C. White†	11	21	0	794	161	2	5	37.80	5
1999	A. McGrath†	14	26	1	803	165	1	3	32.12	7
	G. M. Fellows†	10	18	0	493	109	1	1	27.38	9
	M. J. Lumb	16	30	1	777	124	1	4	26.79	8
	V. J. Craven†	11	21	2	439	72	0	3	23.10	8
	R. K. J. Dawson† . . .	14	23	1	496	87	0	2	22.54	1
	C. R. Taylor†	5	9	1	150	52*	0	2	18.75	4
1996	C. E. W. Silverwood†	12	19	2	283	44*	0	0	16.64	3
2001	M. J. Wood†	9	17	0	201	43	0	0	11.82	12
	S. A. Richardson . . .	2	4	0	45	29	0	0	11.25	2
	S. P. Kirby	10	17	3	141	57	0	1	10.07	0
2000	R. J. Sidebottom† . . .	13	21	7	135	28	0	0	9.64	4
1998	G. M. Hamilton. . . .	2	4	0	23	11	0	0	5.75	0
	N. D. Thornicroft† . .	3	6	3	9	4*	0	0	3.00	0

Also batted: C. J. Elstub† (2 matches) 0*, 18*, 4* (1 ct); M. J. Hoggard†‡ (cap 2000) (2 matches) 5, 2, 21*; S. M. Katich§ (1 match) 21, 16 (1 ct); M. P. Vaughan‡ (cap 1995) (2 matches) 3, 19, 54; D. H. Wigley† (1 match) 15, 4*. D Gough†‡ (cap 1993) (1 match) did not bat.

† *Born in Yorkshire.* ‡ *ECB contract.* § *Overseas player.*

BOWLING

	O	M	R	W	BB	5W/i	Avge
A. McGrath	174.3	38	498	18	4-49	0	27.66
R. J. Sidebottom	380.5	85	1,190	41	5-60	1	29.02
C. E. W. Silverwood. . . .	306.1	68	985	30	4-28	0	32.83
S. P. Kirby	331.1	68	1,262	37	5-129	1	34.10
R. K. J. Dawson	484.2	103	1,536	39	5-42	2	39.38
C. White	145.1	26	456	10	4-49	0	45.60

Also bowled: V. J. Craven 15–3–56–1; M. T. G. Elliott 16–1–77–1; C. J. Elstub 41–7–181–1; G. M. Fellows 73.5–9–315–8; D. Gough 19.3–3–85–2; A. K. D. Gray 97–17–297–5; G. M. Hamilton 12–2–65–1; M. J. Hoggard 71–14–268–8; S. M. Katich 2–0–25–0; D. S. Lehmann 133.2–32–346–9; M. J. Lumb 3–0–16–0; N. D. Thornicroft 61.1–14–248–4; M. P. Vaughan 3.2–0–21–0; D. H. Wigley 20.4–2–116–1.

COUNTY RECORDS

Highest score for:	341	G. H. Hirst v Leicestershire at Leicester 1905
Highest score against:	318*	W. G. Grace (Gloucestershire) at Cheltenham. 1876
Best bowling for:	10-10	H. Verity v Nottinghamshire at Leeds 1932
Best bowling against:	10-37	C. V. Grimmett (Australians) at Sheffield 1930
Highest total for:	887	v Warwickshire at Birmingham. 1896
Highest total against:	681-7 dec.	by Leicestershire at Bradford 1996
Lowest total for:	23	v Hampshire at Middlesbrough 1965
Lowest total against:	13	by Nottinghamshire at Nottingham 1901

COUNTY OFFICERS

Captain 2002 – D. S. Lehmann; 2003 – A. McGrath
First-team coach 2002 – W. M. Clark; 2003 – K. Sharp (batting) • **President** R. A. Smith
Chairman 2002 – K. H. Moss • **Chief executive** 2002 – C. D. Hassell; 2003 – C. J. Graves
Chairman, cricket c'ttee 2002 – R. K. Platt • **Director of cricket** 2003 – G. A. Copes
Head groundsman A. W. Fogarty • **Scorer** J. T. Potter

At Leeds, April 20, 21, 22 (not first-class). **Yorkshire won by an innings and 61 runs.** Toss: Yorkshire. **Bradford/Leeds UCCE 165** (J. W. Payn 31, H. Marambe 35, Extras 43; C. E. W. Silverwood four for 21, R. K. J. Dawson three for 21) **and 158** (H. Marambe 33, Extras 49; R. J. Sidebottom three for 22, G. M. Fellows four for 12); **Yorkshire 384 for four dec.** (M. J. Wood 31, S. A. Richardson 121, M. J. Lumb 121, C. R. Taylor 44 not out, G. M. Fellows 40).

YORKSHIRE v SURREY

At Leeds, April 24, 25, 26. Surrey won by an innings and 168 runs. Surrey 20 pts, Yorkshire 3 pts. Toss: Surrey.

A miserable week for Yorkshire began with news that the fraud squad were investigating the disappearance of up to £100,000 from the club shop, and ended with a thrashing. Surrey's pace attack were faultless on the first day as they reduced the champions to tentative, ineffective prodding. Stewart was far more fluent when Surrey replied, showing impeccable timing and coming within a whisker of a century for the second innings in a row. Brown was the only top-order batsman not to contribute and, though Kirby was rewarded for his big heart with five wickets, Yorkshire badly missed the five capped players either injured or withheld by England. Surrey attacked hard after taking a lead of 370, and a clutch of slips lurked from first ball to last. Chris Taylor hit a maiden fifty, but the game was already lost.

Close of play: First day, Surrey 115-0 (Butcher 53, Ward 51); Second day, Yorkshire 0-2 (Sidebottom 0).

Yorkshire

M. J. Wood c Bicknell b Tudor	0	– c Stewart b Bicknell	0
S. A. Richardson c Butcher b Azhar Mahmood	16	– b Tudor	0
M. J. Lumb c Stewart b Tudor	30	– (4) c Bicknell b Tudor	15
*D. S. Lehmann c Ramprakash b Bicknell	16	– (5) c and b Bicknell	1
C. R. Taylor c Bicknell b Tudor	8	– (6) not out	52
G. M. Fellows c Stewart b Bicknell	15	– (7) lbw b Ormond	24
G. M. Hamilton lbw b Tudor	0	– (8) lbw b Azhar Mahmood	7
†R. J. Blakey c Brown b Ormond	16	– (9) c Brown b Ormond	31
C. E. W. Silverwood c Butcher b Azhar Mahmood	3	– (10) b Azhar Mahmood	38
R. J. Sidebottom not out	15	– (3) b Bicknell	14
S. P. Kirby c Stewart b Azhar Mahmood	7	– lbw b Azhar Mahmood	2
B 1, l-b 5, w 2, n-b 6	14	B 1, l-b 7, w 2, n-b 8	18
	140		**202**

1/5 (1) 2/41 (2) 3/57 (3)   1/0 (1) 2/0 (2) 3/20 (3)
4/74 (4) 5/80 (5) 6/80 (7) 7/102 (6)   4/28 (5) 5/32 (4) 6/67 (7) 7/80 (8)
8/109 (9) 9/119 (8) 10/140 (11)   8/129 (9) 9/188 (10) 10/202 (11)

Bonus points – Surrey 3.

Bowling: *First Innings*—Bicknell 22–7–39–2; Tudor 19–8–31–4; Ormond 17–6–31–1; Azhar Mahmood 17.5–7–33–3. *Second Innings*—Bicknell 14–4–43–3; Tudor 15–3–72–2; Ormond 11–2–40–2; Azhar Mahmood 13.3–5–18–3; Butcher 4–0–21–0.

Surrey

*M. A. Butcher c Wood b Kirby	83	I. D. K. Salisbury c Sidebottom b Fellows	27
I. J. Ward b Silverwood	70	J. Ormond b Fellows	3
M. R. Ramprakash c Blakey b Kirby	65	B 8, l-b 5, w 10, n-b 22	45
†A. J. Stewart c Wood b Fellows	96		
A. D. Brown c Silverwood b Hamilton	10		**510**
N. Shahid c Richardson b Kirby	45		
J. Ormond not out	64		
A. J. Tudor lbw b Kirby	2		
M. P. Bicknell lbw b Kirby	0		

1/161 (2) 2/172 (1) 3/309 (3)
4/335 (5) 5/381 (4) 6/431 (6)
7/443 (8) 8/443 (9)
9/496 (10) 10/510 (11)

Bonus points – Surrey 5, Yorkshire 3.

Bowling: Silverwood 23–2–124–1; Kirby 27–2–129–5; Sidebottom 28–6–71–0; 11–2–48–1; Fellows 27.5–5–90–3; Lehmann 11–1–35–0.

Umpires: G. I. Burgess and I. J. Gould.

At Taunton, May 8, 9, 10. YORKSHIRE lost to SOMERSET by seven wickets.

At Canterbury, May 15, 16, 17, 18. YORKSHIRE lost to KENT by four wickets.

YORKSHIRE v HAMPSHIRE

At Leeds, May 24, 25, 26, 27. Drawn. Yorkshire 12 pts, Hampshire 11 pts. Toss: Hampshire.
   Yorkshire gained some comfort from this rain-ruined game: a draw ended a run of three defeats, and determined tail-end batting won maximum bonus points. On the first day, gale-force winds meant even umpire Kitchen's heavy set of lignum vitae bails wouldn't stay put, so none were used after 2.15. This possibly led to a reprieve for Kendall when Blakey was convinced a ball from Silverwood clipped the off stump. However, the weather, which cost 199 overs on the middle two days, killed off the match. Between the showers, there were signs that Hoggard was regaining form and confidence; in reply, Wood collected his fourth Headingley duck in a row and White showed how well he had adapted to opening. He and three other top-order batsmen fell to Mascarenhas as Yorkshire slipped to 275 for eight. A polished 83 by Blakey and some meaty hitting in Kirby's maiden fifty then dragged them to 400 – and full batting points.
   Close of play: First day, Hampshire 273-7 (Pothas 8, Udal 0); Second day, Yorkshire 174-4 (White 49, Lumb 14); Third day, Yorkshire 207-5 (Lumb 21, Blakey 0).

Hampshire

D. A. Kenway c Blakey b Hoggard	20	– not out	30
W. S. Kendall b Hoggard	67	– lbw b Kirby	4
J. P. Crawley b Dawson	79	– not out	19
*R. A. Smith c Blakey b Silverwood	41		
N. C. Johnson c Blakey b Hoggard	5		
G. W. White b Silverwood	22		
†N. Pothas b Kirby	8		
A. D. Mascarenhas b Kirby	2		
S. D. Udal not out	43		
C. T. Tremlett b Hoggard	7		
A. D. Mullally c Lehmann b Kirby	6		
B 8, l-b 8, w 2, n-b 36	54	B 4, l-b 1, n-b 4	9

1/36 (1) 2/181 (3) 3/185 (2) 4/201 (5) 354 1/16 (2) (1 wkt) 62
5/251 (6) 6/260 (4) 7/269 (8)
8/276 (7) 9/321 (10) 10/354 (11)

Bonus points – Hampshire 4, Yorkshire 3.

Bowling: *First Innings*—Hoggard 27–5–93–4; Silverwood 20–9–50–2; Kirby 23.3–4–93–3; McGrath 9–3–20–0; Dawson 17–3–52–1; White 11–2–30–0; Lehmann 2–2–0–0. *Second Innings*—Hoggard 6–1–20–0; Kirby 4–2–18–1; Dawson 5–3–3–0; Lumb 3–0–16–0.

Yorkshire

A. J. Wood c Crawley b Mullally	0
C. White b Mascarenhas	67
M. P. Vaughan lbw b Tremlett	54
*D. S. Lehmann lbw b Mascarenhas	21
A. McGrath c White b Mascarenhas	10
M. J. Lumb c and b Mascarenhas	25
†R. J. Blakey c Johnson b Tremlett	83
R. K. J. Dawson c Pothas b Udal	15

C. E. W. Silverwood c Kendall b Udal . .	18
S. P. Kirby c Pothas b Mascarenhas	57
M. J. Hoggard not out	21
B 3, l-b 7, w 16, n-b 26	52
	423

1/0 (1) 2/76 (3) 3/118 (4) 4/136 (5)
5/207 (2) 6/218 (6) 7/247 (8)
8/275 (9) 9/366 (7) 10/423 (10)

Bonus points – Yorkshire 5, Hampshire 3 (130 overs: 406-9).

Bowling: Mullally 29–10–74–1; Tremlett 29–6–105–2; Mascarenhas 29.5–6–87–5; Johnson 16–4–54–0; Udal 27–6–87–2; White 4–1–6–0.

Umpires: A. A. Jones and M. J. Kitchen.

At Leicester, May 31, June 1, 2, 3. YORKSHIRE lost to LEICESTERSHIRE by five wickets.

YORKSHIRE v SUSSEX

At Leeds, June 12, 13, 14, 15. Sussex won by an innings and 94 runs. Sussex 20 pts, Yorkshire 4 pts. Toss: Yorkshire.

Neither team had yet won a Championship match, but Sussex were vastly superior. They never looked back after the 19-year-old Tim Ambrose and Matt Prior, 20, put on 191 to ensure a hefty first-innings total. Ambrose cut and drove delightfully on his way to his first century, while Prior, Ambrose's rival for the wicket-keeping gloves, was equally convincing. Yorkshire's bowling was ragged and Hamilton, back after a severe breakdown in confidence, gained widespread sympathy when his first over contained five wides and a no-ball. He couldn't bring himself to bowl again – and it proved to be his last over of the season. On a pitch that offered seam movement, Kirtley then gave a lesson in accuracy as Sussex enforced the follow-on. Menacing in both innings, he grabbed match figures of ten for 90. Rain lopped 78 overs off the third day, but Yorkshire never looked remotely like saving the game, and defeat sent them to the bottom of the table.

Close of play: First day, Sussex 375-6 (Ambrose 146, Innes 26); Second day, Yorkshire 195-6 (Blakey 41, Hamilton 9); Third day, Yorkshire 8-0 (Wood 5, White 2).

Sussex

M. W. Goodwin lbw b Silverwood	18
R. R. Montgomerie lbw b Kirby	11
M. H. Yardy b Silverwood	3
P. A. Cottey c Katich b Sidebottom	5
T. R. Ambrose c Wood b Kirby	149
R. S. C. Martin-Jenkins c Wood b Kirby	30
†M. J. Prior c Blakey b White	83
K. J. Innes lbw b Sidebottom	34

M. J. G. Davis c Blakey b White	22
*R. J. Kirtley b Sidebottom	4
B. V. Taylor not out	18
B 7, l-b 9, w 26, n-b 16	58
	435

1/16 (2) 2/39 (3) 3/40 (1) 4/70 (4)
5/121 (6) 6/312 (7) 7/388 (5)
8/390 (8) 9/398 (10) 10/435 (9)

Bonus points – Sussex 5, Yorkshire 3.

Bowling: Silverwood 26–2–87–2; Kirby 35–9–113–3; Sidebottom 29–8–78–3; Hamilton 1–0–17–0; McGrath 16–2–55–0; White 20.1–4–44–2; Katich 2–0–25–0.

Yorkshire

C. White b Kirtley	12	– (2) c Prior b Kirtley	7
M. J. Wood b Martin-Jenkins	20	– (1) lbw b Kirtley	18
M. J. Lumb lbw b Kirtley	0	– c Prior b Kirtley	1
S. M. Katich lbw b Innes	21	– lbw b Kirtley	16
A. McGrath lbw b Taylor	71	– b Innes	18
V. J. Craven c Prior b Innes	6	– b Innes	2
*†R. J. Blakey lbw b Martin-Jenkins	52	– b Prior	28
G. M. Hamilton c Prior b Kirtley	11	– c Yardy b Taylor	5
C. E. W. Silverwood c Montgomerie b Kirtley	6	– b Martin-Jenkins	11
S. P. Kirby not out	2	– c Innes b Martin-Jenkins	9
R. J. Sidebottom c Yardy b Kirtley	0	– not out	0
B 4, l-b 7, w 2, n-b 2	15	L-b 6, n-b 4	10
	216		**125**

1/32 (1) 2/32 (3) 3/36 (2) 4/98 (4)   1/13 (2) 2/19 (3) 3/34 (1)
5/104 (6) 6/176 (5) 7/201 (8)   4/47 (4) 5/57 (6) 6/70 (5) 7/85 (8)
8/213 (9) 9/215 (7) 10/216 (11)   8/101 (9) 9/125 (10) 10/125 (7)

Bonus points – Yorkshire 1, Sussex 3.

Bowling: *First Innings*—Kirtley 27.5–9–49–5; Martin-Jenkins 25–13–47–2; Taylor 19–8–37–1; Yardy 7–1–29–0; Innes 12–4–35–2; Davis 2–0–8–0. *Second Innings*—Kirtley 16.2–5–41–5; Martin-Jenkins 15–3–30–2; Taylor 7–0–28–1; Innes 6–2–20–2.

Umpires: M. J. Harris and D. R. Shepherd.

At Arundel, June 26, 27, 28, 29. YORKSHIRE drew with SUSSEX.

At Leeds, July 7. YORKSHIRE lost to WEST INDIES A by eight wickets (see West Indies A tour section).

YORKSHIRE v SOMERSET

At Scarborough, July 10, 11, 12, 13. Drawn. Yorkshire 9 pts, Somerset 11 pts. Toss: Somerset.

Somerset's aim was to grind out a score big enough to prevent defeat, the Yorkshire attack was enthusiastic but blunt – and the result was utter tedium. On a slow pitch that offered gentle turn, the spin of Dawson and Andy Gray proved ineffective, allowing Somerset's innings to sprawl into the 166th over, the longest against Yorkshire since 1998. In reply, Bulbeck, the game's outstanding pace bowler, found swing, and Yorkshire were forced to follow on, despite good work from the left-handers in their middle order. Second time round, White and Wood put on 77 for the first wicket, before both fell to Dutch's off-spin. A second fifty from Lehmann put Yorkshire in the lead, and by the time he was snared by Blackwell, the game was dead. Somerset didn't bother to claim the extra half-hour.

Close of play: First day, Somerset 299-5 (Blackwell 34, Turner 8); Second day, Yorkshire 46-1 (White 15, McGrath 2); Third day, Yorkshire 258-6 (Blakey 12, Dawson 4).

Somerset

P. C. L. Holloway c Wood b Dawson	65	G. D. Rose st Blakey b Dawson	24
M. J. Wood c McGrath b Silverwood	5	M. P. L. Bulbeck not out	29
*M. Burns c Wood b Sidebottom	21	B 6, l-b 12, w 2, n-b 10	30
P. D. Bowler b Dawson	84		
K. A. Parsons b Lehmann	59	1/17 (2) 2/49 (3)	(9 wkts dec.) 498
I. D. Blackwell c Blakey b Sidebottom	44	3/161 (1) 4/246 (4)	
†R. J. Turner b Sidebottom	63	5/278 (5) 6/310 (6)	
K. P. Dutch lbw b Dawson	74	7/440 (8) 8/453 (7) 9/498 (9)	

P. S. Jones did not bat.

Bonus points – Somerset 4, Yorkshire 2 (130 overs: 369-6).

Bowling: Silverwood 26–5–75–1; Sidebottom 30–8–59–3; White 23–6–55–0; McGrath 7–0–14–0; Dawson 40.1–7–154–4; Gray 18–3–70–0; Lehmann 21–4–53–1.

Yorkshire

C. White b Bulbeck	19	– c and b Dutch	40
M. J. Wood lbw b Bulbeck	18	– b Dutch	30
A. McGrath b Bulbeck	16	– lbw b Blackwell	5
*D. S. Lehmann c and b Dutch	64	– c Burns b Blackwell	75
M. J. Lumb lbw b Blackwell	57	– lbw b Bowler	15
V. J. Craven c Dutch b Bulbeck	51	– not out	12
†R. J. Blakey c Turner b Blackwell	26	– not out	20
R. K. J. Dawson c Turner b Dutch	42		
C. E. W. Silverwood c Rose b Blackwell	8		
A. K. D. Gray lbw b Blackwell	1		
R. J. Sidebottom not out	0		
B 2, l-b 13, w 4, n-b 2	21	B 3, l-b 11, n-b 2	16

1/39 (2) 2/50 (1) 3/89 (3) 4/159 (4)　　　　323　　1/77 (2) 2/82 (1) 3/92 (3)　(5 wkts) 213
5/239 (5) 6/252 (6) 7/285 (7)　　　　　　　　　　　　4/155 (5) 5/184 (4)
8/315 (9) 9/321 (10) 10/323 (8)

Bonus points – Yorkshire 3, Somerset 3 (130 overs: 322-9).

Bowling: *First Innings*—Bulbeck 34–7–94–4; Jones 17–4–46–0; Blackwell 37–13–49–4; Dutch 28.2–6–77–2; Rose 11–5–22–0; Parsons 4–0–20–0. *Second Innings*—Bulbeck 9–4–25–0; Jones 5–2–3–0; Blackwell 25–4–78–2; Dutch 25–6–73–2; Bowler 6–1–20–1.

Umpires: I. J. Gould and J. W. Holder.

YORKSHIRE v LANCASHIRE

At Leeds, July 19, 20, 21, 22. Drawn. Yorkshire 11 pts, Lancashire 10 pts. Toss: Yorkshire.

After a fine rally had saved Lancashire from the follow-on, the game was almost turned on its head during the final afternoon when Yorkshire slumped to 73 for seven, just 110 ahead. But Blakey and Silverwood calmed nerves and ensured a draw. Earlier, Lehmann had built Yorkshire's strong position. Dropped on 22, he went on to cruise past 50 for the seventh Championship innings in a row and ended with 187. Driving fluently despite a lively pitch, Lehmann and the more cautious McGrath put on a colossal 317, Yorkshire's best for any wicket at Headingley. When Lancashire batted, Gough fired out Chilton and Byas, but Swann, given lives on four and 67, glued the innings together with a meticulous century. Resistance by Chapple, Wood and Keedy – all Yorkshire-born – further frustrated their native county, before Chapple raced in to take quick wickets. Gough, in his only Championship match of the season, had aimed to prove his fitness before the Test series against India. He limped off on the third evening, not to reappear.

Close of play: First day, Yorkshire 163-2 (McGrath 55, Lehmann 68); Second day, Lancashire 89-2 (Swann 31, Law 32); Third day, Lancashire 330-6 (Swann 121, Martin 39).

Yorkshire

C. White lbw b Martin	11	– c Byas b Chapple	1
M. J. Wood b Martin	5	– c Anderson b Chapple	0
A. McGrath b Keedy	165	– (5) b Wood	1
*D. S. Lehmann c Wood b Anderson	187	– (7) c Byas b Keedy	14
M. J. Lumb c Chilton b Keedy	43	– (3) c Law b Keedy	24
V. J. Craven not out	36	– (4) b Chapple	14
†R. J. Blakey not out	4	– (8) not out	18
R. K. J. Dawson (did not bat)		– (6) lbw b Anderson	7
C. E. W. Silverwood (did not bat)		– not out	30
B 23, l-b 24, w 9, n-b 8	64	B 8, l-b 3, n-b 4	15

1/19 (2) 2/24 (1) 3/341 (4)　　　(5 wkts dec.) 515　　1/1 (2) 2/1 (1) 3/25 (4)　　(7 wkts) 124
4/426 (5) 5/497 (3)　　　　　　　　　　　　　　　　4/28 (5) 5/39 (6)
　　　　　　　　　　　　　　　　　　　　　　　　　　6/68 (7) 7/73 (3)

D. Gough and R. J. Sidebottom did not bat.

Bonus points – Yorkshire 5, Lancashire 1.

Bowling: *First Innings*—Martin 27–5–73–2; Chapple 26–6–73–0; Anderson 24–4–109–1; Wood 25–3–113–0; Keedy 16.3–3–77–2; Chilton 5–0–23–0. *Second Innings*—Chapple 12–3–20–3; Anderson 11–3–33–1; Wood 6–1–29–1; Keedy 10–3–31–2.

Lancashire

M. J. Chilton b Gough	3	J. Wood c Lehmann b McGrath	64
A. J. Swann c and b Silverwood	128	G. Keedy c Blakey b McGrath	57
D. Byas b Gough	15	J. M. Anderson not out	4
S. G. Law b Sidebottom	51	B 6, l-b 10, w 2, n-b 6	24
N. H. Fairbrother c Blakey b Sidebottom	0		
G. Chapple c Blakey b White	60	1/4 (1) 2/28 (3) 3/113 (4) 4/113 (5)	478
*†W. K. Hegg b White	25	5/206 (6) 6/271 (7) 7/347 (2)	
P. J. Martin lbw b Sidebottom	47	8/347 (8) 9/467 (10) 10/478 (9)	

Bonus points – Lancashire 5, Yorkshire 2 (130 overs: 418-8).

Bowling: Gough 19–3–85–2; Sidebottom 27–6–81–3; Silverwood 20–5–67–1; White 24–3–85–2; Dawson 39–10–118–0; Lehmann 12–6–18–0; McGrath 4.3–1–8–2.

Umpires: A. Clarkson and J. F. Steele.

At Guildford, July 24, 25, 26, 27. YORKSHIRE lost to SURREY by six wickets.

YORKSHIRE v WARWICKSHIRE

At Leeds, August 7, 8, 9, 10. Drawn. Yorkshire 10 pts, Warwickshire 8 pts. Toss: Warwickshire. County debut: S. E. Bond.

A draw was inevitable after large chunks of the game, including the whole of the third day, were lost to the weather. Warwickshire chose to bat and struggled against Silverwood, hurtling in after another England snub. He removed Powell second ball, but it was McGrath who would have picked up a hat-trick had Ostler not survived a big lbw shout. Knight, though, hit a slick 79, taking him past 1,000 runs in only 12 innings. Lehmann and Taylor then defied some fierce bowling from the New Zealander, Shane Bond, and helped give Yorkshire a lead of 80. Rain had killed the game by the time Warwickshire started their second innings, and Knight and Bell cashed in. Lehmann, playing his last match before joining the Australian one-day squad for Kenya, broke his finger in the field.

Close of play: First day, Yorkshire 29-1 (Taylor 11, McGrath 10); Second day, Yorkshire 304-9 (Gray 6, Elstub 2); Third day, No play.

Warwickshire

*M. J. Powell c Blakey b Silverwood	0	– b Dawson	23
N. V. Knight c Lehmann b Dawson	79	– c Craven b Fellows	109
M. A. Wagh c Craven b McGrath	23	– b Dawson	9
I. R. Bell lbw b McGrath	0	– not out	55
D. P. Ostler b Silverwood	35	– b Fellows	2
J. O. Troughton c Elstub b Gray	19	– not out	0
D. R. Brown lbw b Dawson	15		
M. A. Sheikh c Craven b Lehmann	18		
†K. J. Piper lbw b Silverwood	6		
S. E. Bond c McGrath b Lehmann	7		
A. Richardson not out	7		
B 1, l-b 7, n-b 16	24	B 3, l-b 5, w 2, n-b 8	18

1/0 (1) 2/96 (3) 3/100 (4) 4/140 (2)   233   1/47 (1) 2/79 (3)   (4 wkts) 216
5/154 (5) 6/189 (7) 7/193 (6)   3/213 (2) 4/215 (5)
8/219 (9) 9/219 (8) 10/233 (10)

Bonus points – Warwickshire 1, Yorkshire 3.

Bowling: *First Innings*—Silverwood 17–3–49–3; Elstub 7–0–47–0; McGrath 9–3–24–2; Fellows 4–0–17–0; Dawson 22–5–65–2; Gray 11–3–16–1; Lehmann 3.5–0–7–2. *Second Innings*—Silverwood 8–2–21–0; Elstub 10–1–52–0; McGrath 13–4–28–0; Dawson 23–6–50–2; Gray 11–3–27–0; Craven 2–0–7–0; Fellows 5–0–23–2.

Yorkshire

V. J. Craven lbw b Sheikh	4	A. K. D. Gray c sub b Bond	13
C. R. Taylor c Knight b Richardson	50	C. J. Elstub not out	4
A. McGrath b Brown	34		
*D. S. Lehmann c Piper b Brown	75	B 8, l-b 5, w 6, n-b 16	35
M. J. Lumb c Knight b Richardson	2		
G. M. Fellows lbw b Brown	24	1/5 (1) 2/88 (3) 3/129 (2)	313
†R. J. Blakey c Troughton b Bond	20	4/145 (5) 5/207 (6)	
R. K. J. Dawson run out	14	6/212 (4) 7/231 (8)	
C. E. W. Silverwood c Troughton		8/294 (7) 9/298 (9)	
b Richardson	38	10/313 (10)	

Bonus points – Yorkshire 3, Warwickshire 3.

Bowling: Bond 23.4–8–60–2; Sheikh 18.3–0–80–1; Richardson 23.3–2–73–3; Brown 19–4–61–3; Wagh 14–6–26–0.

Umpires: N. A. Mallender and G. Sharp.

At Manchester, August 14, 15, 16, 17. YORKSHIRE beat LANCASHIRE by 150 runs.

At Southampton, August 27, 28, 29. YORKSHIRE beat HAMPSHIRE by seven wickets.

YORKSHIRE v LEICESTERSHIRE

At Scarborough, September 4, 5, 6, 7. Drawn. Yorkshire 8 pts, Leicestershire 9 pts. Toss: Yorkshire. County debut: R. D. Stemp.

Yorkshire, at the foot of the table, desperately needed a win, but had to be content with another home draw. White's sumptuous 161 was cancelled out by muscular hitting from the Leicestershire lower order, and Yorkshire began their second innings three behind. Fine swing bowling by Wells zipped out the top order and had them deep in trouble at 198 for eight, before Blakey and Gray dragged them out. Together they scrabbled 149, Yorkshire's best ninth-wicket stand for 31 years. During the stand, Blakey was warned for deliberately scuffing the pitch, with an eye to helping his spinners in the fourth innings. The ploy didn't work, and while Maddy and Stevens were cracking 128 in 26 overs off some listless bowling, a surprise Leicestershire win looked possible. Rain then left the match to fizzle out. Leicestershire had hurriedly registered Stemp before the game, but his left-arm spin made little impact. Despite two spinners of their own, Yorkshire were docked a point for a slow over-rate.

Close of play: First day, Leicestershire 32-1 (Sutcliffe 12, Maddy 9); Second day, Yorkshire 137-3 (White 34, Sidebottom 1); Third day, Leicestershire 6-1 (Sutcliffe 1, Stemp 0).

Yorkshire

V. J. Craven c DeFreitas b Malcolm	2	– lbw b Wells	40
C. R. Taylor c Burns b Srinath	6	– c and b Wells	11
M. T. G. Elliott b Srinath	2	– b Stemp	31
C. White b Malcolm	161	– c Burns b Srinath	36
M. J. Lumb c Burns b Wells	17	– (6) c Maddy b Wells	24
G. M. Fellows c Burns b Malcolm	9	– (7) b Wells	17
G. *†R. J. Blakey lbw b Malcolm	0	– (8) not out	63
R. K. J. Dawson lbw b Srinath	3	– (9) c Burns b Wells	2
A. K. D. Gray lbw b Wells	25	– (10) not out	74
S. P. Kirby c Burns b Wells	22		
R. J. Sidebottom not out	4	– (5) c Maddy b DeFreitas	10
B 4, l-b 4, w 7, n-b 10	25	B 5, l-b 14, w 4, n-b 16	39

1/2 (1) 2/5 (3) 3/22 (2) 4/66 (5)	276	1/54 (1) 2/63 (2)	(8 wkts dec.) 347
5/99 (6) 6/99 (7) 7/118 (8)		3/124 (3) 4/139 (4)	
8/225 (9) 9/254 (4) 10/276 (10)		5/171 (5) 6/183 (6)	
		7/194 (7) 8/198 (9)	

Bonus points – Yorkshire 2, Leicestershire 3.

Bowling: *First Innings*—Malcolm 21–2–95–4; Srinath 18–7–38–3; DeFreitas 15–6–31–0; Wells 12–1–47–3; Maddy 6–2–16–0; Stemp 10–1–41–0. *Second Innings*—Srinath 22–1–70–1; DeFreitas 24–3–84–1; Wells 17–6–39–5; Malcolm 19–2–87–0; Stemp 7–1–18–1; Maddy 14–6–30–0.

Leicestershire

T. R. Ward lbw b Sidebottom	11	– lbw b Kirby	1
I. J. Sutcliffe c Elliott b Dawson	27	– lbw b Dawson	26
D. L. Maddy lbw b Craven	44	– (4) b Kirby	86
*V. J. Wells lbw b Kirby	13	– (6) not out	7
A. S. Wright c Craven b Sidebottom	11	– (7) not out	0
D. I. Stevens b Sidebottom	22	– (5) c Blakey b Kirby	80
†N. D. Burns lbw b Sidebottom	59		
P. A. J. DeFreitas b Sidebottom	0		
J. Srinath c Blakey b Kirby	52		
R. D. Stemp not out	8	– (3) b Sidebottom	0
D. E. Malcolm b Kirby	1		
B 1, l-b 12, w 4, n-b 14	31	B 10, l-b 5, w 10, n-b 6	31

1/17 (1) 2/93 (2) 3/93 (3) 4/116 (4)   279   1/4 (1) 2/6 (3) 3/54 (2)   (5 wkts) 231
5/143 (6) 6/150 (5) 7/150 (8)   4/182 (5) 5/231 (4)
8/243 (7) 9/271 (9) 10/279 (11)

Bonus points – Leicestershire 2, Yorkshire 3.

Bowling: *First Innings*—Kirby 23.2–4–71–3; Sidebottom 21–8–60–5; Dawson 20–3–67–1; Craven 8–3–25–1; Fellows 1–0–9–0; Gray 6–0–34–0. *Second Innings*—Kirby 21–6–56–3; Sidebottom 17–6–48–1; Dawson 13–4–43–1; Craven 3–0–17–0; Gray 6–1–23–0; Fellows 3–0–29–0.

Umpires: M. J. Kitchen and R. Palmer.

At Birmingham, September 12, 13, 14, 15. YORKSHIRE lost to WARWICKSHIRE by six wickets.

YORKSHIRE v KENT

At Leeds, September 18, 19, 20. Kent won by eight wickets. Kent 19 pts, Yorkshire 2.25 pts. Toss: Yorkshire.

Steve Waugh's cussedness was the difference between the sides. On a pitch that favoured bowlers, he battled through an unconvincing start and punched his way to a thoroughly professional 146. It ended a long lean streak: five innings for Kent had brought just 78, and it was only his second century since the memorable one-legged 157 against England in August 2001. Saggers rammed home the advantage, finding bounce and jagging away movement, and Yorkshire, already relegated, followed on 181 behind. At 74 for five, an innings defeat loomed, but Blakey hit back with a defiant 94, taking him past 1,000 runs for the sixth time. Chasing 103, Kent galloped home enthusiastically in 22 overs. The three-day defeat meant Yorkshire, who again had points docked for a slow over-rate, ended the season without a home win for the first time since 1983. Kent's win kept them on course for the £50,000 runners-up cheque, but they were pipped next day by Warwickshire.

Close of play: First day, Kent 332-6 (Waugh 136, Tredwell 37); Second day, Yorkshire 13-1 (Richardson 3, Elliott 10).

Kent

*D. P. Fulton c Blakey b McGrath	16	– lbw b Sidebottom	12
R. W. T. Key lbw b Kirby	1	– not out	33
E. T. Smith lbw b Sidebottom	67	– lbw b Sidebottom	30
S. R. Waugh c Blakey b Kirby	146		
†P. A. Nixon run out	5	– (4) not out	14
M. A. Ealham c Richardson b Sidebottom	6		
M. M. Patel lbw b Dawson	52		
J. C. Tredwell lbw b Kirby	61		
D. D. Masters lbw b Sidebottom	17		
A. Khan b Sidebottom	4		
M. J. Saggers not out	2		
B 5, l-b 11, w 4, n-b 2	22	L-b 10, n-b 4	14

1/5 (2) 2/49 (1) 3/105 (3) 4/114 (5)   399   1/25 (1) 2/67 (3)   (2 wkts) 103
5/132 (6) 6/233 (7) 7/353 (4)
8/376 (8) 9/388 (10) 10/399 (9)

Bonus points – Kent 4, Yorkshire 3.

Bowling: *First Innings*—Kirby 29–9–109–3; Sidebottom 25.2–7–61–4; Thornicroft 20–4–66–0; McGrath 24–6–85–1; Dawson 18–5–62–1. *Second Innings*—Kirby 8–0–37–0; Sidebottom 8–0–34–2; McGrath 3–1–9–0; Thornicroft 2.1–1–13–0.

Yorkshire

S. A. Richardson lbw b Saggers	0	– c Fulton b Khan	29
M. J. Lumb c Patel b Khan	8	– lbw b Khan	0
M. T. G. Elliott c Nixon b Saggers	8	– c Patel b Saggers	10
A. McGrath c Nixon b Saggers	17	– lbw b Khan	9
C. White b Saggers	62	– b Patel	48
*†R. J. Blakey lbw b Ealham	2	– (7) c Nixon b Masters	94
G. M. Fellows c Masters b Khan	34	– (6) c Nixon b Saggers	14
R. K. J. Dawson b Patel	47	– b Ealham	47
R. J. Sidebottom c Tredwell b Ealham	28	– run out	10
S. P. Kirby c Tredwell b Ealham	4	– not out	5
N. D. Thornicroft not out	0	– c Smith b Masters	4
L-b 4, n-b 4	8	B 6, l-b 7	13

1/0 (1) 2/16 (3) 3/20 (2) 4/54 (4)   218   1/0 (2) 2/13 (3) 3/38 (4) 4/53 (1)   283
5/69 (6) 6/121 (5) 7/150 (7)   5/74 (6) 6/147 (5) 7/245 (8)
8/196 (9) 9/208 (10) 10/218 (8)   8/271 (7) 9/279 (9) 10/283 (11)

Bonus points – Yorkshire 1, Kent 3.

Bowling: *First Innings*—Saggers 13–2–44–4; Khan 11–1–52–2; Ealham 16–3–55–3; Masters 9–1–23–0; Patel 9.1–2–32–1; Tredwell 2–1–8–0. *Second Innings*—Saggers 17–3–72–2; Khan 15–4–41–3; Tredwell 6–0–18–0; Patel 7–2–24–1; Ealham 22–6–59–1; Masters 12.4–1–56–2.

Umpires: B. Dudleston and N. A. Mallender.

WOMBWELL CRICKET LOVERS' SOCIETY AWARDS, 2002

Michael Vaughan, the Yorkshire batsman who scored four centuries for England during the summer of 2002, was voted George Spofforth Cricketer of the Year by members of the Wombwell Cricket Lovers' Society. Vaughan also won the Learie Constantine Award for Best Fielder in the C&G Final. Other award-winners were: C. B. Fry Young Cricketer of the Year – Jimmy Anderson; Brian Sellers County Captain of the Year – Adam Hollioake of Surrey; Arthur Wood Wicket-keeper of the Year – Chris Read of Nottinghamshire; Les Bailey Best Yorkshire Newcomer – Tim Bresnan; Dr Leslie Taylor Award for Best Performance in the Roses Matches – Anthony McGrath; J. M. Kilburn Cricket Writer of the Year – Robert Mills of the *Yorkshire Post*; Ted Umbers Services to Yorkshire Cricket – Alan Shaw.

CHELTENHAM & GLOUCESTER TROPHY, 2002

Ally Brown

The second Cheltenham & Gloucester Trophy was a vintage year. Not because Yorkshire defeated Somerset in a classic final – it wasn't – but because in the fourth round Surrey and Glamorgan fought out one of the most staggering battles in one-day cricket. Years hence, people who weren't within 100 miles of The Oval will brag about a match they never actually saw, and pub-quiz aficionados will recall the deeds that sent statisticians into transports of delight. Quite simply, the game made cricket history.

Ally Brown, the only person to have hit a double-hundred in the Sunday League – he did it when it was a 40-over competition – went ballistic, smashing the bowlers and the record books to all corners. He scored an outrageous 268 as Surrey racked up an astounding 438. But the passion and audacity with which Robert Croft and his Glamorgan team came within two shots of victory took this game beyond mere figures and into the realms of greatness. Even allowing for a flat pitch and a short boundary, this was limited-overs cricket at its absolute best.

Beside this, the rest of the C&G was something of a comedown, though it had its moments. Those moments, however, were rather spread out, since the 2002 competition had begun three days before Somerset got their hands on the 2001 Trophy. The aim was to ease early-season fixture congestion by moving the two preliminary rounds to the tail-end of the previous summer. The performances of this proto-competition came from Bedfordshire's David Clarke, who hit 176, and Ryan Minter, a seamer playing for the Kent Board XI, who scythed through Leicestershire's recreational cricketers to take six for eight.

The tightest finish was at Horsford, where Holland lost to Norfolk off the last ball: a single would have reversed the result. Norfolk were leading a charmed life, and in the next round they won on a technicality, or rather a simplification. The ECB had adopted the Duckworth/Lewis method for all disrupted games involving first-class sides, but they dared not let scorers further down the ladder wrestle with its complexities. So when rain cut short the Somerset Board XI's innings, the nice-and-simple scoring-rate method pronounced Norfolk the winners. Had it been a third-round game, Somerset would have won, courtesy of those tricky Duckworth/Lewis tables.

When the competition resumed, eight months on, none of the minor sides could quite capture a major scalp, though Suffolk came tantalisingly close to ousting Northamptonshire. That astonishing encounter at The Oval aside, the fourth round produced little to write home about. Leicestershire were going great guns against Sussex until they turned them on themselves and plummeted from 204 for one to 233 all out: the last four Leicestershire lemmings added a single. At Trent Bridge, Nottinghamshire's mauling by Worcestershire spelled the end of Clive Rice's unhappy reign as coach.

In the quarter-finals, Yorkshire belied their wretched Championship form and ended a roller-coaster tussle with Essex, a team in prime one-day touch, with the scores level.

Yorkshire won through on the wickets-lost rule to set up an appetising tie against Surrey, who had just overcome Sussex. Adam Hollioake had played the Ally Brown role to perfection, walloping a glorious 52-ball hundred. Inviting though the Yorkshire–Surrey semi-final was, it almost didn't happen. Only the persistence of the umpires rescued it from a watery grave and the ignominy of a bowl-out. The ignominy was left for Surrey, who were knocked senseless by a phenomenal all-round performance from Craig White.

Somerset, the trophy-holders, strode past Hampshire and Worcestershire into the semis, where they faced Kent, led by Matthew Fleming. He had dreamed of contesting a one-day final in his last season and surely thought he had achieved it when Kent, apparently undaunted by a target of 345, needed nine to win with two and a half overs and four wickets in hand. But dream became nightmare when the bowlers kept their cool – and the batsmen lost theirs. It set up a final between Yorkshire and Somerset, 2001's county champions against 2001's C&G winners. But both were ending dire seasons, their confidence sagging, and it was a perfectly paced hundred from Matthew Elliott, newly arrived from Australia, that won the day. Yorkshire had some consolation for a miserable summer. Somerset had none. **Hugh Chevallier**

Prize money

£53,000 for winners: YORKSHIRE.
£27,000 for runners-up: SOMERSET.
£16,500 for each losing semi-finalist: KENT, SURREY.
£11,500 for each losing quarter-finalist: ESSEX, GLOUCESTERSHIRE, SUSSEX, WORCESTERSHIRE.

Man of the match award winners received £1,750 in the final, £550 in the semi-finals, £500 in the quarter-finals, £450 in the fourth round, £350 in the third round, £325 in the second round and £300 in the first round. The prize money was unchanged from the 2001 competition.

*In the following scores, * by the name of a team indicates that they won the toss.*

FIRST ROUND

At Dunstable, August 29, 2001. **Bedfordshire won by 185 runs. Bedfordshire* 367 for three** (50 overs) (A. R. Roberts 113, D. R. Clarke 176 not out, Extras 35); **Derbyshire Board XI 182** (36.3 overs) (J. R. Benstead 65, W. J. L. Bagshawe 44; N. A. Stanley three for 48, A. R. Roberts five for 40).
　Man of the Match: A. R. Roberts.
　Andy Roberts, the former Northamptonshire leg-spinner, and David Clarke put on 193 for the second wicket. Clarke's undefeated 176 was the best for a Minor County and, at the time, the seventh-highest score in the competition. He faced 131 balls, hit 20 fours and four sixes.

At Dinton, August 29, 2001. **Buckinghamshire won by 39 runs. Buckinghamshire 224 for seven** (50 overs) (M. Bowyer 35, P. R. Sawyer 43, Z. A. Sher 40 not out); **Worcestershire Board XI* 185** (47 overs) (D. Manning 48; J. D. Batty three for 51).
　Man of the Match: Z. A. Sher.

At Chester Boughton Hall, August 29, 2001. **Cheshire won by eight wickets. Lancashire Board XI* 128** (46.2 overs) (J. P. Whittaker three for 18); **Cheshire 131 for two** (19.4 overs) (P. R. J. Bryson 31 not out, P. C. McKeown 30, R. G. Hignett 54 not out).
　Man of the Match: C. S. Lamb.
　For Cheshire, Lamb's figures were 10–3–16–2.

At Millom, August 29, 2001. **Warwickshire Board XI won by 17 runs. Warwickshire Board XI 212 for seven** (50 overs) (J. O. Troughton 115 not out; D. B. Pennett three for 35); **Cumberland* 195** (48.4 overs) (A. A. Metcalfe 50, S. J. O'Shaughnessy 50; J. O. Troughton four for 23).
　Man of the Match: J. O. Troughton.

At Chelmsford, August 29, 2001. **Sussex Board XI won by six wickets. Essex Board XI* 237 for nine** (50 overs) (G. W. Ecclestone 66, A. C. Richards 64; A. R. Cornford three for 38, R. G. Halsall four for 34); **Sussex Board XI 243 for four** (44 overs) (G. R. A. Campbell 65, D. J. Hussey 118 not out).

Man of the Match: D. J. Hussey.

Dave Hussey, from Western Australia, is the younger brother of Mike, a Western Australia regular and captain of Northamptonshire.

At Welwyn Garden City, August 29, 2001. **Staffordshire won by 161 runs. Staffordshire 268** (49.2 overs) (M. C. Longmore 40, G. F. Archer 53, P. F. Shaw 62, O. D. Gibson 41; B. J. Frazer three for 56); **Hertfordshire* 107** (34.4 overs) (D. Follett four for 17, R. A. Cooper five for 42).

Man of the Match: D. Follett.

At Godmanchester, August 29, 2001. **Gloucestershire Board XI won by five wickets. Huntingdonshire Board XI* 180 for eight** (50 overs) (W. Larkins 50; J. P. Rendell three for 36); **Gloucestershire Board XI 183 for five** (42.1 overs) (N. C. Stovold 33, N. A. Stovold 75).

Man of the Match: N. A. Stovold.

Nick (N. C.) and Neil (N. A.), both sons of Andy Stovold, Gloucestershire's director of development, shared a fourth-wicket partnership of 112.

At Barwell, August 29, 2001. **Leicestershire Board XI won by seven wickets. Northamptonshire Board XI* 212** (49 overs) (R. E. Falkner 37, Extras 54; N. J. Pullen three for 25); **Leicestershire Board XI 213 for three** (33.3 overs) (N. J. Pullen 88, N. G. Patel 62, Extras 38).

Man of the Match: N. J. Pullen.

At Lincoln Lindum, August 29, 2001. **Lincolnshire won by 86 runs. Lincolnshire* 243 for eight** (50 overs) (J. Trower 76, M. A. Fell 75 not out; J. K. Barrow four for 31); **Berkshire 157** (41.5 overs) (R. P. Davis 56; R. J. Chapman four for 18).

Man of the Match: M. A. Fell.

At Southgate, August 29, 2001. **Scotland won by 24 runs. Scotland* 245 for eight** (50 overs) (N. J. MacRae 83, D. G. Wright 55; K. H. A. Powell three for 49); **Middlesex Board XI 221** (50 overs) (S. J. Price 85, I. J. Boyton 31, P. E. Wellings 32, M. L. Creese 34; S. J. Davidson four for 43).

Man of the Match: D. G. Wright.

Damien Wright, from Tasmania, also dismissed both Middlesex Board XI openers to take two for 37.

At Horsford, August 29, 2001. **Norfolk won by virtue of losing fewer wickets. Norfolk* 245 for three** (50 overs) (C. J. Rogers 139 not out, J. R. Walker 76); **Holland 245** (50 overs) (H. J. C. Mol 56, D. J. Reekers 53, L. P. van Troost 35; P. J. Bradshaw four for 30).

Man of the Match: C. J. Rogers.

Carl Rogers hit 15 fours and two sixes, and faced 173 balls for his unbeaten 139. He and James Walker put on 180 for the second wicket. Holland's No. 11, Nadeem Abbas, was run out off the last ball attempting the single that would have won the match.

At Christ Church, Oxford, August 29, 2001. **Oxfordshire won by five wickets. Nottinghamshire Board XI 248 for five** (50 overs) (C. M. Tolley 78, M. W. Creed 77, T. E. Savill 35 not out); **Oxfordshire* 249 for five** (47.3 overs) (C. A. Haupt 126 not out, G. P. Savin 31 not out, Extras 37).

Man of the Match: C. A. Haupt.

Chris Tolley and Murray Creed, a South African from Eastern Province, shared a third-wicket stand of 132. Craig Haupt faced 150 balls for his unbeaten 126, and hit one six and 18 fours. Aged 15 years 277 days, Mark Footit was believed to have been the tournament's youngest player – beating his team-mate in the Board XI, Aaron Thomas, who was 83 days older when he first appeared in May 2001.

At Copdock, August 29, 2001. **Suffolk won by seven wickets. Denmark* 112** (28.4 overs) (I. D. Graham four for 17); **Suffolk 114 for three** (33.4 overs) (A. M. Brown 44 not out, D. J. Callaghan 49).

Man of the Match: D. J. Callaghan.

Dave Callaghan, who played 29 one-day internationals for South Africa, also took two for 26.

At South Wilts CC, August 29, 2001. **Ireland won by 85 runs. Ireland* 247** (50 overs) (D. Joyce 67, P. G. Gillespie 66, Extras 35; R. J. Bates three for 58); **Wiltshire 162** (40.2 overs) (S. M. Perrin 34; P. J. K. Mooney four for 34).

Man of the Match: P. G. Gillespie.

Ireland recovered from 25 for three, then 78 for five, before Dominick Joyce and Peter Gillespie added 125 for the sixth wicket.

SECOND ROUND

At Beaconsfield, September 13, 14, 2001. **Buckinghamshire won by 21 runs. Buckinghamshire 187** (47.3 overs) (P. D. Atkins 50; M. J. North four for 26); **Durham Board XI* 166** (46.1 overs) (G. J. Pratt 32, Q. J. Hughes 31, Extras 35; A. W. Thomas three for 47, Z. A. Sher three for 23). *Close of play:* Durham Board XI 11-0 (2.4 overs).

Man of the Match: P. D. Atkins.

At March, September 13, 14, 2001. **Warwickshire Board XI won by 75 runs. Warwickshire Board XI 232** (49.1 overs) (I. J. Westwood 55, J. O. Troughton 51, N. V. Humphrey 32, Extras 40; A. Akhtar four for 29); **Cambridgeshire* 157** (40 overs) (R. J. Rollins 50, Extras 30; T. Mees three for 19, B. Joshi three for nine). *Close of play:* Cambridgeshire 44-2 (10 overs).

Man of the Match: T. Mees.

At Toft, September 13, 14, 2001. **Cornwall won by 65 runs. Cornwall 216 for eight** (45 overs) (J. M. Hands 30, S. C. Pope 59, B. P. Price 74; A. Kuruvilla four for 21); **Cheshire* 151** (43.3 overs) (N. T. Wood 50; J. M. Hands three for 25).

Man of the Match: S. C. Pope.

There was no play on the first day; on the reserve day, the game was reduced to 45 overs a side. Steven Pope, a South African from Border, also had figures of 9–2–16–2.

At Exmouth, September 13, 2001. **Devon won by three wickets. Bedfordshire* 266 for eight** (50 overs) (A. R. Roberts 50, N. A. Stanley 69, A. J. Trott 41 not out, Extras 35); **Devon 268 for seven** (46.2 overs) (G. T. J. Townsend 36, R. I. Dawson 88, J. J. Williams 40, P. M. Roebuck 30 not out, Extras 40; A. R. Roberts four for 26).

Man of the Match: R. I. Dawson.

For Bedfordshire, Andy Roberts and Neil Stanley put on 129 for the first wicket. Robert Dawson and Jeremy Williams added 100 for Devon's fifth.

At Bristol, September 13, 2001. **Yorkshire Board XI won by four wickets. Gloucestershire Board XI 185 for nine** (50 overs) (C. R. J. Budd 65; S. J. Foster five for 33); **Yorkshire Board XI* 186 for six** (49.1 overs) (R. Wilkinson 36).

Man of the Match: S. J. Foster.

At Southampton, September 13, 2001. **Ireland won by 32 runs. Ireland* 241 for seven** (50 overs) (P. J. Davy 30, A. C. Botha 75, D. Heasley 66 not out); **Hampshire Board XI 209** (50 overs) (R. K. Kenway 47, R. J. E. Hindley 38, P. N. Gover 34; A. C. Botha three for 30, W. K. McCallan three for 42).

Man of the Match: A. C. Botha.

At Hinckley, September 13, 2001. **Kent Board XI won by 189 runs. Kent Board XI* 280 for nine** (50 overs) (M. J. Banes 82, A. G. R. Loudon 53, L. J. P. Jenkins 50 not out, Extras 46; N. J. Pullen four for 61); **Leicestershire Board XI 91** (26.5 overs) (R. J. Minter six for eight).

Man of the Match: R. J. Minter.

Matthew Banes and Alex Loudon put on 132 for Kent Board XI's third wicket. Ryan Minter, right-arm fast-medium, had figures of 7–2–8–6.

At Bourne, September 13, 14, 2001. **Lincolnshire won by 94 runs. Lincolnshire 244 for nine** (50 overs) (J. Clarke 47, O. E. Burford 55, M. A. Fell 39, Extras 34; A. P. Hollingsworth three for 36); **Surrey Board XI* 150** (31 overs) (S. A. Newman 49, Extras 47; D. J. Pipes three for 24, S. Trower three for six). *Close of play:* Surrey Board XI 108-4 (17.3 overs).

Man of the Match: O. E. Burford.

At Horsford, September 13, 14, 2001. **Norfolk won on scoring-rate. Norfolk 173** (48.1 overs) (C. Amos 42; M. P. L. Bulbeck five for 18); **Somerset Board XI* 61 for two** (22 overs) (K. G. Sedgbeer 30 not out).

Man of the Match: M. P. L. Bulbeck.

Play was not possible on the reserve day. Under C&G playing conditions, the Duckworth/Lewis method is not used to determine results of interrupted matches in rounds one and two. Had it been, Somerset Board XI would have won by two runs.

At Jesmond, September 13, 14, 2001. **Staffordshire won by seven wickets. Northumberland 233 for nine** (50 overs) (S. Chapman 40, J. A. Graham 55, J. B. Windows 52 not out; R. A. Cooper three for 46); **Staffordshire* 234 for three** (45.1 overs) (G. F. Archer 89 not out, O. D. Gibson 102 not out). *Close of play:* Staffordshire 21-0 (6 overs).

Man of the Match: G. F. Archer.

All three Staffordshire wickets fell at 36. Graeme Archer, once of Nottinghamshire, and Ottis Gibson, the former West Indian Test all-rounder, then added an unbroken 198. Gibson had earlier taken two for 49.

At Linlithgow, September 13, 14, 2001. **Scotland won by ten wickets. Dorset 101** (43 overs) (C. L. Park 35; D. J. Cox three for 28, S. J. Davidson three for 15); **Scotland* 103 for no wkt** (15.5 overs) (B. M. W. Patterson 40 not out, D. G. Wright 53 not out). *Close of play:* Dorset 91-8 (39.1 overs).

Man of the Match: D. G. Wright.

Dorset collapsed from 88 for four. Damien Wright also had figures of 7–2–14–1.

At Shifnal, September 13, 14, 2001. **Shropshire won by eight runs. Shropshire 200 for eight** (50 overs) (D. Williamson 49, A. B. Byram 32 not out); **Oxfordshire* 192 for nine** (50 overs) (B. J. Thompson 42, G. P. Savin 37, Extras 30; G. J. Byram three for 33). *Close of play:* Shropshire 79-3 (24.5 overs).

Man of the Match: A. B. Byram.

At Bury St Edmunds, September 13, 14, 2001. **Suffolk won by 103 runs. Suffolk 254 for seven** (50 overs) (C. P. Seal 41, C. J. Warn 52 not out, Extras 48); **Herefordshire* 151** (41.4 overs) (C. W. Boroughs 59 not out; D. J. Callaghan three for 28). *Close of play:* Herefordshire 83-5 (25.2 overs).

Man of the Match: C. J. Warn.

Christopher Warn, who hit 52 from 40 balls, also held three catches and made a stumping.

At Hastings, September 13, 2001. **Wales won by three runs. Wales 238** (50 overs) (A. J. Jones 50, P. V. Simmons 51, R. W. Sylvester 51; J. R. Morgan four for 55); **Sussex Board XI* 235** (49.3 overs) (G. R. A. Campbell 57, J. Snashall 56; A. D. Towse three for 24, P. V. Simmons three for 34, A. N. French three for 35).

Man of the Match: P. V. Simmons.

Sussex Board XI lost their last five wickets for 13 runs. Phil Simmons, the former West Indian all-rounder, took the last three.

THIRD ROUND

ESSEX v MIDDLESEX

At Chelmsford, May 24. Essex won by five wickets. Toss: Essex.

A true pitch brought a run-glut, and the main reason Essex won with 11 balls unused was Middlesex's dawdling start. They should have had more than 24 after ten overs, and it wasn't until the halfway stage that their innings took off. Koenig, dropped three times, strode to his century by striking his 102nd ball for six, but he was pedestrian beside Cook's rip-roaring 39 off 15. The last four overs yielded 57. Essex gambled by batting Dakin and Cowan at Nos 3 and 4. They failed, but others didn't. Hussain, who was in consummate touch, hit an effortless 96, while Irani had crashed five sixes (and no fours) by the time he zoomed past 50. Essex's invincible start to the one-day season continued: this made it seven wins out of seven.

Man of the Match: R. C. Irani.

Middlesex

*A. J. Strauss c Flower b Irani	10	S. J. Cook not out	39
S. G. Koenig c Clarke b Irani	116	L-b 1, w 9, n-b 2	12
Abdul Razzaq lbw b Dakin	8		
O. A. Shah c Grayson b Dakin	20	1/11 (1) 2/38 (3) (5 wkts, 50 overs) 291	
E. C. Joyce run out	10	3/78 (4) 4/99 (5)	
P. N. Weekes not out	76	5/234 (2)	

B. L. Hutton, †D. C. Nash, A. W. Laraman and T. F. Bloomfield did not bat.

Bowling: Irani 10–1–47–2; Cowan 10–3–39–0; Dakin 10–1–51–2; Stephenson 5–0–45–0; Grayson 6–1–44–0; Middlebrook 4–0–27–0; Clarke 5–0–37–0.

Essex

N. Hussain b Abdul Razzaq	96	A. Habib not out	29
D. D. J. Robinson b Cook	17	L-b 13, w 2, n-b 2	17
J. M. Dakin lbw b Laraman	4		
A. P. Cowan c Nash b Cook	1	1/42 (2) 2/51 (3) (5 wkts, 48.1 overs) 295	
†A. Flower lbw b Weekes	45	3/68 (4) 4/142 (5)	
*R. C. Irani not out	86	5/228 (1)	

J. P. Stephenson, A. P. Grayson, J. D. Middlebrook and A. J. Clarke did not bat.

Bowling: Abdul Razzaq 10–0–58–1; Cook 10–0–48–2; Laraman 10–2–59–1; Hutton 2–0–16–0; Bloomfield 7.1–1–51–0; Weekes 9–0–50–1.

Umpires: M. R. Benson and P. Willey.

LANCASHIRE v DERBYSHIRE

At Manchester, May 24. Lancashire won by ten wickets. Toss: Lancashire.

Lancashire's second ten-wicket win in the competition was not as painless as it sounded. On a fast, bouncy pitch, three players injured their hands, and all were out of action for around a month. Hewson, the only Derbyshire batsman to come to terms with the testing, blustery conditions, soldiered on and oversaw a spirited recovery from a woeful 39 for six. Selwood, who was sitting his finals at Loughborough University, was struck on his writing hand. Both were hit by the fiery Flintoff. The third patient for the orthopaedic department and the only one to retire hurt, was Byas. But Lancashire barely noticed his departure as Chilton, batting beautifully, and Chapple waltzed home.

Man of the Match: M. J. Chilton.

Derbyshire

A. I. Gait lbw b Martin	0	G. Welch not out	31
M. J. Di Venuto c Law b Martin	10	Mohammad Ali run out	19
M. P. Dowman c Lloyd b Flintoff	10		
D. R. Hewson c Law b Flintoff	63	L-b 6, w 2, n-b 8	16
S. A. Selwood c Law b Hogg	1		
*D. G. Cork c Flintoff b Hogg	0	1/0 (1) 2/21 (2) 3/36 (3) (46.2 overs) 167	
J. I. D. Kerr run out	0	4/37 (5) 5/37 (6) 6/39 (7)	
†L. D. Sutton st Hegg b Schofield	14	7/103 (8) 8/107 (4)	
T. Lungley lbw b Schofield	3	9/136 (9) 10/167 (11)	

Bowling: Martin 9–0–21–2; Chapple 9.2–1–29–0; Flintoff 10–2–46–2; Hogg 6–2–27–2; Wood 5–1–10–0; Schofield 7–0–28–2.

Lancashire

D. Byas retired hurt	. . . .	5
M. J. Chilton not out	. . . .	76
G. Chapple not out	. . . .	81
W 3, n-b 4	. . . .	7

(no wkt, 28.1 overs) 169

S. G. Law, A. Flintoff, G. D. Lloyd, *†W. K. Hegg, C. P. Schofield, K. W. Hogg, P. J. Martin and J. Wood did not bat.

Byas retired hurt at 28.

Bowling: Cork 10–3–36–0; Lungley 3.1–0–28–0; Welch 5.5–0–37–0; Kerr 6.1–0–46–0; Mohammad Ali 3–0–22–0.

Umpires: J. H. Evans and N. A. Mallender.

BUCKINGHAMSHIRE v SUSSEX

At Beaconsfield, May 29. Sussex won by 125 runs. Toss: Buckinghamshire.

Once Buckinghamshire had plummeted to 48 for five in the 17th over, there was little life left in the game. On a grudging pitch that stifled strokeplay from the word go, Sussex had managed to set a stiff target thanks to a responsible 139-ball 95 from Ambrose and a similarly paced fifty from Zuiderent, the Dutchman erroneously introduced on the Tannoy as Sussex's Zimbabwean overseas player. Sher – whose full name is Zaheer Abbas Sher, though he answers to Bobby – took three wickets and later hit a steady half-century, but never threatened to change the outcome.

Man of the Match: T. R. Ambrose.

Sussex

R. R. Montgomerie c Clarke b Saleem . .	27		R. S. C. Martin-Jenkins not out	. . . . . .	1
†T. R. Ambrose c Batty b Saleem	. . . . .	95		B 1, l-b 3, w 5, n-b 6	. . . . . .	15
B. Zuiderent c Bowyer b Sher	. . . . .	50				
M. W. Goodwin c Paskins b Clarke	. . . .	37		1/42 (1) 2/154 (3)	(6 wkts, 50 overs)	268
P. A. Cottey lbw b Sher	. . . .	42		3/217 (4) 4/263 (2)		
W. J. House st Drepaul b Sher	. . . . .	1		5/267 (6) 6/268 (5)		

M. H. Yardy, M. J. G. Davis, *R. J. Kirtley and B. V. Taylor did not bat.

Bowling: Stanway 8–1–44–0; Saleem 8–1–25–2; Batty 10–0–44–0; Clarke 10–1–53–1; Sher 9–0–56–3; Lane 5–0–42–0.

Buckinghamshire

M. Bowyer lbw b Kirtley	. . . .	2		†D. R. Drepaul c Ambrose b Taylor	. . . .	35
R. P. Lane b Kirtley	. . . .	4		A. Saleem not out	. . . .	0
G. D. T. Paskins c Montgomerie b Martin-Jenkins		2		L-b 6, w 11	. . . .	17
R. A. Jones lbw b Taylor	. . . . . .	11				
*P. D. Atkins lbw b Taylor	. . . .	12		1/7 (1) 2/16 (2)	(7 wkts, 50 overs)	143
Z. A. Sher not out	. . . .	55		3/19 (3) 4/42 (4)		
J. D. Batty c Martin-Jenkins b Davis	. .	5		5/48 (5) 6/69 (7) 7/137 (8)		

A. R. Clarke and S. F. Stanway did not bat.

Bowling: Martin-Jenkins 8–0–18–1; Kirtley 8–2–12–2; House 7–0–28–0; Taylor 9–4–23–3; Davis 10–1–28–1; Yardy 5–0–12–0; Cottey 3–0–16–0.

Umpires: V. A. Holder and B. Leadbeater.

CORNWALL v WORCESTERSHIRE

At Truro, May 29, 30. Worcestershire won by 49 runs. Toss: Worcestershire.

Charlie Shreck gave Cornwall a real chance of a first-class scalp when his five for 19 helped restrict Worcestershire to a modest 125 in a 30-overs contest. However, the professional bowlers proved just as adept at exploiting favourable conditions, and the four seamers had combined figures of seven for 21 from 18 overs. Only three Cornish batsmen made it to double figures (as only three Worcestershire batsmen had earlier). Ultimately, it was the 61 added by Hick and Leatherdale that was the difference. The match was switched from St Austell because of a waterlogged pitch, which prevented play on the first day.

Man of the Match: C. E. Shreck.

Worcestershire

V. S. Solanki c Hands b Shreck	4	†S. J. Rhodes not out	4
A. Singh c Price b Shreck	4	Kabir Ali not out	9
*G. A. Hick c Shreck b Hands	36	B 1, l-b 4, w 7	12
B. F. Smith c Edwards b Pope	14		
D. A. Leatherdale c Hands b Shreck	40	1/8 (1) 2/16 (2) (7 wkts, 30 overs) 125	
A. J. Bichel lbw b Shreck	1	3/44 (4) 4/105 (3)	
G. J. Batty b Shreck	1	5/107 (6) 6/110 (5) 7/111 (7)	

S. R. Lampitt and A. Sheriyar did not bat.

Bowling: Shreck 6–2–19–5; Stephens 6–0–19–0; Pope 6–0–30–1; Berryman 6–0–21–0; Hands 6–0–31–1.

Cornwall

J. M. Hands run out	2	C. E. Shreck c Singh b Ali	0
G. M. Thomas lbw b Sheriyar	0	K. P. Berryman lbw b Ali	0
S. C. Pope c Rhodes b Solanki	19		
N. S. Curnow c Leatherdale b Bichel	0	L-b 11	11
B. P. Price b Ali	3		
*T. G. Sharp b Lampitt	0	1/2 (1) 2/2 (2) 3/5 (4) (29.2 overs) 76	
J. P. Kent not out	13	4/19 (5) 5/22 (6) 6/39 (3)	
†G. D. Edwards c and b Batty	27	7/72 (8) 8/76 (9)	
J. C. J. Stephens b Ali	1	9/76 (10) 10/76 (11)	

Bowling: Sheriyar 6–3–8–1; Bichel 4–3–1–1; Lampitt 4–0–10–1; Ali 4.2–2–2–4; Batty 6–2–19–1; Solanki 5–0–25–1.

Umpires: T. E. Jesty and R. Palmer.

DEVON v YORKSHIRE

At Exmouth, May 29. Yorkshire won by 143 runs. Toss: Devon.

White overcame the trials of a sluggish strip to make an attractive 87 from just 73 balls. His top-order colleagues never quite matched his fluency, but his departure barely stemmed the flow of Yorkshire runs. Lehmann, picking up where White left off, ensured a healthy total with a near-run-a-ball fifty. The Devon batsmen had a much harder time: the entire innings contained just 22 in boundaries, compared to 48 from White alone. Robert Dawson, who hit three first-class hundreds for Gloucestershire, hung around, but his namesake, Richard, and Lehmann spun their way through the Devon innings.

Man of the Match: C. White.

Yorkshire

C. White c Williams b Hancock	87	G. M. Fellows not out			18
M. J. Wood c Priscott b Richards	19				
C. E. W. Silverwood c Dawson b Hancock	19	B 2, l-b 2, w 11			15
M. J. Lumb st Williams b Procter	23	1/63 (2) 2/111 (3) (5 wkts, 50 overs)			259
*D. S. Lehmann not out	54	3/148 (1) 4/161 (4)			
A. McGrath c Stoneman b Bishop	24	5/224 (6)			

†R. J. Blakey, R. K. J. Dawson, R. J. Sidebottom and T. T. Bresnan did not bat.

Bowling: Bishop 10–0–60–1; Richards 10–3–35–1; Stoneman 7–0–47–0; Theedom 2–0–20–0; Procter 10–1–43–1; Hancock 10–0–44–2; Dawson 1–0–6–0.

Devon

S. M. Priscott c Blakey b Bresnan	7	I. E. Bishop b Dawson			1
D. F. Lye c Blakey b Lehmann	22	M. C. Theedom b Dawson			0
K. A. O. Barrett c Blakey b Sidebottom	6				
*R. I. Dawson c Wood b Lehmann	31	B 2, l-b 5, w 2			9
†J. J. Williams b Dawson	5				
N. D. Hancock c Sidebottom b Lehmann	20	1/20 (1) 2/33 (3) 3/55 (2) (39.4 overs)			116
S. A. Stoneman b Dawson	2	4/74 (5) 5/92 (4) 6/101 (6)			
M. A. E. Richards not out	11	7/108 (7) 8/113 (9)			
A. J. Procter c Blakey b Lehmann	2	9/116 (10) 10/116 (11)			

Bowling: Silverwood 6–0–15–0; Bresnan 7–1–18–1; Sidebottom 5–1–6–1; White 4–1–10–0; Lehmann 9–0–26–4; Dawson 8.4–0–34–4.

Umpires: K. J. Lyons and J. F. Steele.

IRELAND v NOTTINGHAMSHIRE

At Clontarf, May 29. Nottinghamshire won by eight wickets. Toss: Nottinghamshire.

Without either of the Joyce brothers or an overseas professional, a weakened Ireland never troubled Nottinghamshire. Put in, Ireland had slipped to a shaky 48 for five before Kyle McCallan and Derek Heasley added a painstaking 64. Afzaal eventually removed McCallan for a 90-ball 30 and then finished off the Irish tailenders to snatch a one-day best three for eight. He capped it with a stylish fifty as Nottinghamshire ran out winners with oceans of time to spare.

Man of the Match: U. Afzaal.

Ireland

*J. A. M. Molins lbw b Harris	19	W. J. McGonigle run out			2
†A. D. Patterson c Afzaal b Smith	4	A. G. A. M. McCoubrey st Read b Afzaal			2
A. R. White lbw b Smith	3	B 1, l-b 19, w 10, n-b 6			36
P. J. Davy lbw b Franks	9				
P. G. Gillespie c Gallian b Harris	1	1/31 (2) 2/35 (1) 3/43 (3) (50 overs)			164
W. K. McCallan c Read b Afzaal	30	4/44 (5) 5/48 (4) 6/112 (7)			
D. Heasley c Gallian b Boje	24	7/144 (6) 8/158 (8)			
P. J. K. Mooney st Read b Afzaal	24	9/162 (10) 10/164 (11)			
G. J. Neely not out	8				

Bowling: Smith 10–2–25–2; Malik 2–0–12–0; Harris 8–3–17–2; Franks 6–0–39–1; Boje 10–2–17–1; Pietersen 10–1–26–0; Afzaal 4–0–8–3.

Nottinghamshire

D. J. Bicknell b Heasley 46
*J. E. R. Gallian lbw b Mooney 5
U. Afzaal not out 64
P. Johnson not out 25
        B 1, l-b 4, w 17, n-b 4 26

1/31 (2) 2/108 (1)   (2 wkts, 37.2 overs) 166

K. P. Pietersen, N. Boje, †C. M. W. Read, P. J. Franks, G. J. Smith, A. J. Harris and M. N. Malik did not bat.

Bowling: Mooney 7.2–0–28–1; McCoubrey 3–1–18–0; Neely 8–0–34–0; McCallan 7–1–40–0; McGonigle 4–0–8–0; Heasley 4–0–20–1; White 4–0–13–0.

Umpires: B. Dudleston and N. J. Llong.

KENT BOARD XI v HAMPSHIRE

At Folkestone, May 29, 30. Hampshire won by eight wickets. Toss: Hampshire.

Rain prevented play before 4 p.m. on the first day, but by the close, four hours later, Hampshire were in the box seat. Several of the Kent amateurs made starts only to get themselves out; Hugo Loudon, who played for Hampshire Seconds in 1998 and 1999, survived longest. Pick of the Hampshire attack was Tremlett. The Board XI had an ideal start when Kevin Masters removed Laney with the third ball of the innings. (Masters had turned out for the senior Kent side in the early 1980s, when he gained his singular first-class batting average of 0.16). But with Kenway driving beautifully, Hampshire raced to 46 without further loss before fading light forced them from the field. Next morning, they needed only an hour to wrap things up.

Man of the Match: D. A. Kenway.

Close of play: Hampshire 46-1 (8 overs) (Johnson 18, Kenway 24).

Kent Board XI

J. D. P. Bowden run out 14
J. E. G. Lincoln lbw b Tremlett 10
J. G. C. Rowe lbw b Tremlett 30
J. Hodgson b Kendall 22
*H. Iqbal b Udal 0
H. J. H. Loudon c Pothas b Tremlett . . 38
†K. R. J. Bingham c Kendall b Johnson . 0
D. J. Trigger c Kendall b Udal 3
D. A. Scott c Johnson b Mascarenhas . . . 7
A. Tutt c Johnson b Mullally 0
K. D. Masters not out 2
        L-b 7, w 8, n-b 4 19

1/22 (1) 2/37 (2) 3/69 (3)   (47.5 overs) 145
4/74 (5) 5/109 (4)
6/114 (7) 7/121 (8)
8/135 (9) 9/143 (10) 10/145 (6)

Bowling: Mullally 9–1–16–1; Mascarenhas 10–0–34–1; Tremlett 9.5–3–20–3; Johnson 6–0–27–1; Udal 10–1–33–2; Kendall 3–0–8–1.

Hampshire

J. S. Laney lbw b Masters 0
N. C. Johnson not out 66
D. A. Kenway c Trigger b Scott 76
*R. A. Smith not out 2
        L-b 2, w 4 6

1/0 (1) 2/138 (3)   (2 wkts, 26.3 overs) 150

G. W. White, W. S. Kendall, †N. Pothas, A. D. Mascarenhas, S. D. Udal, C. T. Tremlett and A. D. Mullally did not bat.

Bowling: Masters 9–0–44–1; Tutt 4–0–20–0; Trigger 4–0–34–0; Scott 5.3–0–40–1; Lincoln 4–0–10–0.

Umpires: N. L. Bainton and J. W. Holder.

LINCOLNSHIRE v GLAMORGAN

At Sleaford, May 29. Glamorgan won by six wickets. Toss: Glamorgan.

With Glamorgan homing in on victory, Simon Oakes, one of the quickest on the Minor Counties circuit, bowled what looked like a deliberate beamer at Steve James. Oakes did not apologise, though the umpires had enough doubt about his intent that they made no mention of the incident in their report. However, Lincolnshire were unhappy at the lack of remorse and found Oakes guilty of a level two breach of the code of conduct: an intentional beamer constitutes a level-three offence. It was an ugly end to a game otherwise contested in a good spirit. Earlier, Lincolnshire, lifted from a precarious 21 for four by Simon Webb's patient fifty, managed just 154. Yet when Glamorgan lost their third wicket at 55, there was a chance it could be enough. James and Dale then knuckled down until Oakes – incensed at James surviving an appeal for caught behind – unleashed his beamer. Perhaps it worked: James fell later in the over, but by then Glamorgan were almost there.

Man of the Match: S. Webb.

Lincolnshire

*J. C. Harrison c Wallace b Kasprowicz .	4	K. Adams not out	1
M. A. Fell b Davies	0	S. Oakes b Kasprowicz	2
R. W. J. Howitt b Kasprowicz	8		
J. Trower run out	26	L-b 8, w 3, n-b 6	17
J. Clarke b Davies	1		
S. Webb b Davies	55	1/6 (1) 2/6 (2) 3/20 (3) (46.5 overs) 154
†O. E. Burford b Davies	28	4/21 (5) 5/78 (4) 6/134 (7)
D. A. Christmas c Powell b Thomas	12	7/147 (6) 8/149 (8)
D. J. Pipes lbw b Davies	0	9/151 (9) 10/154 (11)

Bowling: Kasprowicz 8.5–2–28–3; Davies 9–3–19–5; Wharf 10–0–27–0; Thomas 7–0–24–1; Croft 10–0–40–0; Dale 2–0–8–0.

Glamorgan

K. Newell c Burford b Oakes	12	M. J. Powell not out	5
D. L. Hemp b Christmas	9	L-b 3, w 9, n-b 6	18
R. D. B. Croft b Adams	23		
*S. P. James lbw b Oakes	47	1/23 (1) 2/41 (2) (4 wkts, 37.4 overs) 157
A. Dale not out	43	3/55 (3) 4/140 (4)

†M. A. Wallace, S. D. Thomas, M. S. Kasprowicz, A. P. Davies and A. G. Wharf did not bat.

Bowling: Oakes 10–1–37–2; Christmas 10–1–39–1; Pipes 8.4–1–29–0; Adams 6–1–25–1; Howitt 3–0–24–0.

Umpires: K. E. Palmer and K. Shuttleworth.

NORFOLK v KENT

At Horsford, May 29. Kent won by 191 runs. Toss: Norfolk.

Norfolk had won their first-round match on the fewer-wickets-lost rule and their second on the don't-trust-Minor-County-scorers-with-Duckworth/Lewis rule. But their luck ran out against a strong Kent side in which Fleming shone brightest. All the professional batsmen made runs – Fleming's 56 was scorched from 38 balls – as ten sixes whistled over the ropes. Norfolk began their reply at a sedate pace, but preserved their wickets until Carl Rogers's departure proved the catalyst for a catastrophic collapse: seven fell for 15 in a torrent of reckless strokes. Fleming's share of the spoils was three for four.

Man of the Match: M. V. Fleming.

Kent

*M. V. Fleming b Taylor	56	M. J. Walker not out	0
R. W. T. Key c Parlane b Newman	77		
J. B. Hockley c Bradshaw b Brown	39	L-b 2, w 11, n-b 4	17
A. Symonds c Amos b Brown	17		
D. P. Fulton c Parlane b Goldsmith	62	1/79 (1) 2/144 (3) (6 wkts, 50 overs) 341	
M. A. Ealham c Goldsmith b Taylor	47	3/170 (4) 4/228 (2)	
†P. A. Nixon not out	26	5/296 (6) 6/339 (5)	

J. C. Tredwell, A. Khan and M. J. Saggers did not bat.

Bowling: Bradshaw 10–0–78–0; Taylor 10–2–59–2; Goldsmith 10–0–84–1; Brown 10–0–70–2; Newman 10–0–48–1.

Norfolk

C. Amos st Nixon b Tredwell	39	P. J. Bradshaw not out	20
C. J. Rogers c Tredwell b Fleming	17	J. P. Taylor not out	10
M. E. Parlane c and b Fleming	1	B 1, l-b 9, w 13	23
S. C. Goldsmith c Saggers b Fleming	1		
J. R. Walker c Khan b Symonds	4	1/64 (2) 2/66 (1) (8 wkts, 50 overs) 150	
†J. P. Garner st Nixon b Tredwell	1	3/68 (3) 4/69 (4)	
C. R. Borrett b Tredwell	1	5/73 (6) 6/76 (5)	
C. Brown c Khan b Hockley	33	7/79 (7) 8/131 (8)	

*P. G. Newman did not bat.

Bowling: Saggers 8–1–30–0; Khan 6–0–22–0; Ealham 6–1–12–0; Fleming 4–1–4–3; Tredwell 10–5–7–3; Symonds 10–2–24–1; Hockley 4–0–35–1; Walker 2–0–6–0.

Umpires: P. Adams and G. Sharp.

SCOTLAND v SURREY

At Raeburn Place, May 29, 30. Surrey won by 55 runs (D/L method). Toss: Scotland.

Surrey quickly imposed control after a first-day washout. True, they lost Brown before the scoreboard had moved, but Ward and Ramprakash took advantage of any lapse in line or length, sharing an assured century partnership. Shahid provided impetus towards the end of the innings with a brisk sixty, while Ramprakash was solid from start to finish. On a slow, damp pitch, a target of five an over was steeper than it seemed. Halfway through the Scots' stalling reply, with Giddins the wrecker-in-chief, the weather worsened, leaving Duckworth/Lewis to put a figure on the inevitable result.

Man of the Match: M. R. Ramprakash.

Surrey

*I. J. Ward run out	58	
A. D. Brown c Williamson b Thomson	0	
M. R. Ramprakash not out	101	
N. Shahid not out	65	
L-b 5, w 17	22	

1/0 (2) 2/111 (1) (2 wkts, 50 overs) 246

M. A. Carberry, R. Clarke, †J. N. Batty, M. P. Bicknell, E. S. H. Giddins, Saqlain Mushtaq and J. Ormond did not bat.

Bowling: Kent 10–1–42–0; Thomson 10–2–41–1; Davidson 7–0–27–0; Hoffmann 10–0–49–0; Wright 6–0–29–0; Iqbal 3–0–24–0; Stanger 4–0–29–0.

Scotland

J. G. Williamson c Bicknell
               b Saqlain Mushtaq .   22
N. J. MacRae lbw b Bicknell   4
J. C. Kent b Giddins   2
†C. J. O. Smith c Batty b Giddins   1
R. R. Watson not out   14

M. M. Iqbal, I. M. Stanger, K. Thompson, P. J. C. Hoffmann and S. J. Davidson did not bat.

*C. M. Wright not out   9

     L-b 3, w 4, n-b 4   11

1/15 (2) 2/24 (3)   (4 wkts, 24.1 overs) 63
3/26 (4) 4/51 (1)

Bowling: Bicknell 8–1–26–1; Giddins 7–2–9–2; Saqlain Mushtaq 5–0–14–1; Ormond 4.1–0–11–0.

Umpires: A. Clarkson and M. Dixon.

SHROPSHIRE v GLOUCESTERSHIRE

At Shrewsbury School, May 29, 30. Gloucestershire won by seven wickets (D/L method). Toss: Gloucestershire.

The soggy state of the St George's ground at Telford meant this game, reduced to a 32-overs affair, was switched on the reserve day to Shrewsbury School. The sorry state of the Shropshire batting meant it was hardly worth the effort. Hardinges sabotaged their innings by seaming the ball away from the right-handers and sent Shropshire spiralling to 55 for seven. They limped to 98 all out, and Hardinges ended on a one-day best four for 19. The Gloucestershire reply started with a wobble before Barnett, a cool head on experienced shoulders, saw them home.

Man of the Match: M. A. Hardinges.

Shropshire

M. J. Marvell c Smith b Hardinges   26
*J. B. R. Jones c Ball b Averis   5
J. V. Anders b Hardinges   0
D. Williamson c Russell b Smith   2
T. J. Mason b Hardinges   5
J. T. Ralph lbw b Alleyne   0
G. L. Home c Windows b Ball   15
A. B. Byram c Russell b Hardinges   1
†G. J. Mumford b Averis   12

A. M. Shimmons st Russell b Ball   9
A. P. O'Connor not out   0

     B 7, l-b 2, w 14   23

1/19 (2) 2/29 (3) 3/40 (4)   (30.2 overs) 98
4/48 (1) 5/52 (6) 6/53 (5)
7/55 (8) 8/80 (9)
9/97 (7) 10/98 (10)

Bowling: Averis 5–0–29–2; Smith 7–2–9–1; Hardinges 7–2–19–4; Alleyne 6–2–16–1; Ball 5.2–0–16–2.

Gloucestershire

K. J. Barnett not out   54
C. M. Spearman c Ralph b Shimmons . .   4
M. A. Hardinges b Williamson   12
C. G. Taylor st Mumford b Mason   11
M. G. N. Windows not out   13
     L-b 2, w 3   5

1/16 (2) 2/47 (3)   (3 wkts, 27.2 overs) 99
3/66 (4)

*M. W. Alleyne, J. N. Snape, †R. C. Russell, J. M. M. Averis, M. C. J. Ball and A. M. Smith did not bat.

Bowling: O'Connor 6–1–17–0; Shimmons 6–2–20–1; Williamson 5–0–18–1; Mason 7–1–28–1; Byram 3–0–9–0; Anders 0.2–0–5–0.

Umpires: G. I. Burgess and D. J. Constant.

STAFFORDSHIRE v WARWICKSHIRE

At Stone, May 29. Warwickshire won by 50 runs. Toss: Staffordshire.

Damp run-ups delayed the start, while a damp pitch made for slow scoring. Well though the Staffordshire attack performed, class shone through. Knight and later Pollock made sure they collected runs, and were wise enough not to fret at the paltry pace. Pollock followed his dogged innings with a masterclass in containing bowling: his eight overs yielded nine runs, if no wickets. Richardson, a former Staffordshire player, profited most from the pressure, taking a one-day best five for 35 with his medium-pace. Graeme Archer and Paul Shaw put on 55 for the fourth wicket, but there was little resistance once they were parted.

Man of the Match: S. M. Pollock.

Warwickshire

*M. J. Powell c Humphries b Crook	16	†T. Frost c Archer b Womble	9
N. V. Knight b Bulpitt	54	A. Richardson not out	1
I. R. Bell c Humphries b Womble	25		
D. P. Ostler lbw b Cooper	0	B 1, l-b 6, w 5	12
T. L. Penney c Humphries b Cooper	2		
S. M. Pollock b Cooper	47	1/32 (1) 2/70 (3) 3/71 (4) (50 overs) 192
D. R. Brown b Edwards	4	4/89 (5) 5/128 (2) 6/135 (7)	
N. M. K. Smith b Crook	9	7/154 (8) 8/177 (6)	
M. A. Sheikh c Harvey b Womble	13	9/190 (10) 10/192 (9)	

Bowling: Crook 10–0–43–2; Edwards 10–1–28–1; Cooper 10–0–39–3; Womble 10–0–42–3; Bulpitt 10–0–33–1.

Staffordshire

*S. J. Dean c Penney b Brown	13	G. D. Crook b Richardson	0
M. C. Longmore c Brown b Richardson	11	G. Bulpitt b Brown	2
D. R. Womble lbw b Richardson	8		
G. F. Archer c Knight b Smith	34	L-b 10, w 21	31
P. F. Shaw c Richardson b Smith	26		
R. P. Harvey c Frost b Sheikh	2	1/15 (1) 2/34 (3) 3/46 (2) (45.4 overs) 142
†M. I. Humphries not out	10	4/101 (4) 5/118 (6)	
D. J. Edwards b Richardson	5	6/126 (5) 7/134 (8)	
R. A. Cooper b Richardson	0	8/136 (9) 9/136 (10) 10/142 (11)	

Bowling: Pollock 8–4–9–0; Brown 7.4–1–31–2; Sheikh 10–1–32–1; Richardson 10–1–35–5; Smith 10–3–25–2.

Umpires: K. Cobain and I. J. Gould.

SUFFOLK v NORTHAMPTONSHIRE

At Bury St Edmunds, May 29. Northamptonshire won by one wicket. Toss: Northamptonshire.

One wicket separated Suffolk from the upset of the round. When Northamptonshire were eight down 25 short of their target, David looked set to slay Goliath. But Warren and Cousins whittled the deficit down to a single before Warren fell to an excellent catch at mid-wicket by Phil Caley off Kevin Shaw's medium-pace. Next ball – a leg-side wide – evened the scores, but offered a fiendishly difficult stumping chance; Suffolk would have won if Christopher Warn had somehow managed it. Cousins then shattered Suffolk dreams by striking Richard Pineo for four. Earlier, Caley and Shaw had batted resolutely in trying conditions. While Loye was scoring freely, Northamptonshire were heading for a straightforward win, but Gary Kirk and Andrew Hall, the South African Test all-rounder making his Suffolk debut, set up the breathless finish.

Man of the Match: K. G. Shaw.

Suffolk

R. J. Catley b Blain	1	R. W. Pineo c Penberthy b Blain		7
A. J. Hall c Bailey b Cook	16	G. M. Kirk not out		0
A. M. Brown c Loye b Cousins	1			
C. W. J. Athey run out	6	B 1, l-b 2, w 4		7
*P. J. Caley b Brown	35			
†C. J. Warn c sub b Penberthy	7	1/3 (1) 2/14 (3)	(9 wkts, 50 overs)	128
T. M. Smith st Bailey b Brown	6	3/22 (2) 4/28 (4)		
C. A. Swallow st Bailey b Cousins	8	5/43 (6) 6/76 (7)		
K. G. Shaw not out	34	7/77 (5) 8/117 (8) 9/124 (10)		

Bowling: Cousins 8–5–12–2; Blain 10–1–47–2; Cook 5–2–5–1; Penberthy 8–1–17–1; Brown 10–4–20–2; Swann 9–1–24–0.

Northamptonshire

M. B. Loye b Hall	34	D. M. Cousins not out		17
*M. E. K. Hussey c Hall b Kirk	12	J. F. Brown not out		0
D. J. Sales c Shaw b Kirk	9			
R. J. Warren c Caley b Shaw	21	B 1, l-b 1, w 16, n-b 2		20
G. P. Swann c Brown b Kirk	13			
A. L. Penberthy c Warn b Hall	0	1/48 (2) 2/60 (1)	(9 wkts, 39.2 overs)	132
J. W. Cook lbw b Hall	0	3/74 (3) 4/91 (5)		
†T. M. B. Bailey c Warn b Hall	0	5/91 (6) 6/93 (7)		
J. A. R. Blain c Caley b Smith	6	7/97 (8) 8/104 (9) 9/127 (4)		

Bowling: Pineo 9.2–1–34–0; Smith 9–1–44–1; Kirk 10–4–16–3; Hall 10–4–33–4; Shaw 1–0–3–1.

Umpires: M. J. Harris and J. W. Lloyds.

WALES v DURHAM

At Cardiff, May 29. Durham won by 49 runs (D/L method). Toss: Wales.

An opening stand of 159 between Gough and Gary Pratt set the tone for this one-sided match. Despite gales, which prevented cricket before 3.10 p.m. and forced the umpires to dispense with bails, these two played with mounting confidence until Pratt was eventually caught behind. Runs continued to flow for Durham as Gough eased to his first one-day hundred, with his driving through the covers especially strong. The Wales reply stuttered before Jamie Sylvester and Phil Simmons, the former West Indian Test all-rounder, steadied the ship. At the close, halfway through their overs, they had a mammoth task ahead. Rain washed out the reserve day, and Duckworth/Lewis was unambiguous.

Man of the Match: M. A. Gough.

Close of play: First day, Wales 65-2 (25 overs) (J. P. J. Sylvester 18, Simmons 32).

Durham

M. A. Gough c Metson b Simmons	132	M. J. Symington not out		0
G. J. Pratt c Metson b J. P. J. Sylvester	89	L-b 7, w 11, n-b 2		20
M. L. Love c Jones b J. P. J. Sylvester	23			
N. Peng run out	1	1/159 (2) 2/208 (3)	(5 wkts, 50 overs)	301
*J. J. B. Lewis not out	30	3/210 (4) 4/290 (1)		
†A. Pratt st Metson b Davies	6	5/301 (6)		

G. D. Bridge, A. M. Davies, N. Killeen and N. G. Hatch did not bat.

Bowling: Gage 9–1–59–0; Davies 6–0–34–1; Barnsley 3–0–34–0; Simmons 9–0–47–1; R. W. Sylvester 5–0–22–0; Skone 10–0–54–0; J. P. J. Sylvester 8–0–44–2.

Wales

A. J. Jones lbw b Killeen	0
J. P. J. Sylvester not out	18
S. Morris c A. Pratt b Hatch	2
P. V. Simmons not out	32
L-b 5, w 8	13

1/6 (1) 2/13 (3)   (2 wkts, 25 overs) 65

R. W. Sylvester, R. J. Skone, O. A. Dawkins, C. J. Barnsley, N. A. Gage, *†C. P. Metson and J. Davies did not bat.

Bowling: Killeen 4–1–12–1; Hatch 7–3–14–1; Davies 6–1–12–0; Bridge 5–0–15–0; Gough 3–0–7–0.

Umpires: M. J. Kitchen and A. G. T. Whitehead.

WARWICKSHIRE BOARD XI v LEICESTERSHIRE

At Coventry, May 29. Leicestershire won by 26 runs. Toss: Leicestershire.

When the Warwickshire Board XI were qualifying for this tie, late in 2001, they relied on the emerging talent of Jim Troughton. In the interim, though, he had established himself in the senior side. Someone of his calibre might perhaps have tipped the scales in the Board XI's favour, given how well his former colleagues did. The left-armers Graham Wagg and Naheem Sajjad discomfited Leicestershire, and had Westwood not conceded 23 off the 48th over, the Board XI might have been chasing under 200. Huw Jones, an Oxford student, led the fight with the only fifty, a sensible 99-ball innings, but his side were never quite up with the rate.

Man of the Match: H. R. Jones.

Leicestershire

T. R. Ward c Sajjad b Khan	29	P. A. J. DeFreitas c Howell b Wagg	30
I. J. Sutcliffe b Wagg	11	C. D. Crowe not out	0
D. I. Stevens st Clifford b Sajjad	36	B 1, l-b 1, w 11, n-b 6	19
†N. D. Burns c Parker b Sajjad	18		
D. L. Maddy b Sajjad	6	1/25 (2) 2/68 (1) (7 wkts, 50 overs) 208	
*V. J. Wells not out	49	3/104 (4) 4/112 (5)	
A. S. Wright c Khan b Wagg	10	5/119 (3) 6/134 (7) 7/205 (8)	

J. O. Grove and D. E. Malcolm did not bat.

Bowling: Wilson 9–1–25–0; Sajjad 10–3–21–3; Wagg 10–3–35–3; Dalton 5–0–34–0; Khan 10–0–47–1; Westwood 4–0–33–0; Parker 2–0–11–0.

Warwickshire Board XI

W. G. Khan c Wells b Malcolm	27	L. C. Parker not out	6
I. J. Westwood c DeFreitas b Malcolm . .	2	†J. I. Clifford not out	5
*C. R. Howell c Wells b Malcolm	5	L-b 7, w 3	10
H. R. Jones st Burns b Wells	72		
N. V. Humphrey c Malcolm b Wells	30	1/10 (2) 2/36 (1) (8 wkts, 50 overs) 182	
G. G. Wagg c Malcolm b Wells	21	3/39 (3) 4/121 (5)	
N. Sajjad st Burns b Maddy	2	5/163 (6) 6/167 (7)	
D. A. T. Dalton b Maddy	2	7/171 (4) 8/171 (8)	

E. J. Wilson did not bat.

Bowling: Malcolm 10–3–24–3; Grove 4–0–14–0; DeFreitas 7–1–19–0; Maddy 10–0–46–2; Crowe 9–0–40–0; Wells 10–1–32–3.

Umpires: P. J. Hartley and T. E. Jesty.

YORKSHIRE BOARD XI v SOMERSET

At Scarborough, May 29. Somerset won by 87 runs. Toss: Yorkshire Board XI.

The trophy-holders had few problems in breezing past the Yorkshire Board XI. Their substantial total was based on a second-wicket partnership, worth 148, between the experienced pair of Bowler and Cox. Both were dismissed by the 19-year-old Richard Pyrah, who pocketed five for 50 with his medium-pace, though it was another teenage medium-pacer, the 18-year-old South African, Pieter Swanepoel, who finished the innings in emphatic style. His hat-trick, the first in the competition for five years, came off Somerset's last three balls, and dramatically improved his figures. Once three wickets had fallen with the Board XI stalled on nine, the game was effectively over.

Man of the Match: R. M. Pyrah.

Somerset

P. D. Bowler c Harland b Pyrah	104	G. D. Rose b Swanepoel	0
M. J. Wood c Kellaway b Ramsden	6	M. P. L. Bulbeck not out	0
*J. Cox c Ramsden b Pyrah	64	B 1, l-b 2, w 9	12
I. D. Blackwell c Brice b Pyrah	6		
M. Burns c Foster b Pyrah	32	1/11 (2) 2/159 (3) (9 wkts, 50 overs) 255	
K. A. Parsons c Widdup b Swanepoel	27	3/170 (4) 4/203 (1)	
†R. J. Turner c Foster b Pyrah	2	5/234 (5) 6/249 (7)	
K. P. Dutch c and b Swanepoel	2	7/255 (8) 8/255 (6) 9/255 (9)	

P. S. Jones did not bat.

Bowling: Ramsden 6–0–25–1; Gill 7–0–19–0; Foster 10–0–49–0; Swanepoel 8–0–47–3; Brice 10–0–62–0; Pyrah 9–0–50–5.

Yorkshire Board XI

*A. J. Bethel c Turner b Rose	4	C. T. Brice c and b Cox	10
S. Widdup c Cox b Bulbeck	4	N. S. Gill not out	37
S. J. Foster c Burns b Bulbeck	0	L-b 9, w 7, n-b 2	18
D. S. Harland c Turner b Dutch	16		
A. W. Gale c Dutch b Jones	13	1/9 (2) 2/9 (1) (8 wkts, 50 overs) 168	
R. M. Pyrah c and b Dutch	26	3/9 (3) 4/34 (5)	
P. J. Swanepoel st Turner b Dutch	16	5/59 (4) 6/91 (6)	
†M. J. Kellaway not out	24	7/94 (7) 8/111 (9)	

G. Ramsden did not bat.

Bowling: Bulbeck 8–1–16–2; Rose 7–1–13–1; Jones 7–1–26–1; Dutch 10–1–26–3; Blackwell 10–0–25–0; Cox 7–0–33–1; Burns 1–0–20–0.

Umpires: N. G. Cowley and R. A. Kettleborough.

FOURTH ROUND

ESSEX v LANCASHIRE

At Chelmsford, June 19. Essex won by nine wickets. Toss: Essex.

A majestic unbeaten 83 from Hussain – including a gargantuan six walloped over mid-wicket off Flintoff – guided Essex to a thumping win. Lancashire had lost heavily at Ilford in the National League three days earlier, but thoughts of revenge receded as three wickets tumbled in a dozen overs. Chilton and Flintoff, who had little of his usual fluency, briefly arrested the slide until Flintoff, captain instead of the injured Hegg, fell to a magnificent diving catch by Hussain at backward point. Cowan consistently troubled the batsmen with his bounce and gained strong support from a seam attack seldom veering from line and length. Restricting Lancashire to just 166 meant the rest was plain sailing for Hussain and Robinson. By his standards, Irani had a quiet game, though he did shin up a tree to fetch a ball Flintoff had smashed for six.

Man of the Match: N. Hussain.

Lancashire

M. J. Chilton c Hussain b Clarke	42	
†A. J. Swann run out	4	
G. Chapple c Robinson b Cowan	1	
S. G. Law c Flower b Cowan	4	
*A. Flintoff c Hussain b Napier	45	
N. H. Fairbrother lbw b Napier	15	
G. D. Lloyd c Hussain b Dakin	27	
C. P. Schofield run out	13	
K. W. Hogg c Clarke b Cowan	0	

J. Wood c Flower b Cowan 1
P. J. Martin not out 1

L-b 3, w 10 13

1/16 (2) 2/22 (3) 3/38 (4)   (46.5 overs) 166
4/86 (1) 5/117 (5) 6/125 (6)
7/154 (8) 8/154 (9)
9/162 (10) 10/166 (7)

Bowling: Irani 8–0–29–0; Cowan 10–1–27–4; Dakin 8.5–1–22–1; Clarke 8–0–42–1; Grayson 2–0–9–0; Napier 10–0–34–2.

Essex

N. Hussain not out 83
D. D. J. Robinson c Fairbrother
               b Schofield . 59
G. R. Napier not out 12
         B 4, l-b 4, w 3, n-b 2 13

1/142 (2)   (1 wkt, 28.3 overs) 167

†A. Flower, *R. C. Irani, A. Habib, A. P. Grayson, J. M. Dakin, J. P. Stephenson, A. P. Cowan and A. J. Clarke did not bat.

Bowling: Martin 6–1–18–0; Chapple 5–0–32–0; Flintoff 4–0–24–0; Wood 5.3–0–36–0; Hogg 3–0–17–0; Schofield 5–0–32–1.

Umpires: G. I. Burgess and A. G. T. Whitehead.

GLOUCESTERSHIRE v DURHAM

At Bristol, June 19. Gloucestershire won by eight wickets. Toss: Durham.
A year earlier, in this precise fixture, Durham had knocked out a complacent Gloucestershire. Now, without the injured batsmen Love and Collingwood, normal service was resumed. Durham's best moments came when Lewis and Symington shared a fourth-wicket partnership of 59, but both fell in the thirties to Alleyne. On a beautiful wicket, a target of 180 was never likely to tax Gloucestershire, and the Antipodean pair of Harvey and Spearman tore into an attack missing Harmison's pace. Harvey followed his three wickets with a demoralising 27 off 18 balls, while Spearman, driving beautifully, rocketed to his first limited-overs century for Gloucestershire. He reached his fifty from 52 deliveries and his hundred from another 23. No one could rein in the scoring, and Gloucestershire won with 24 overs unused.
Man of the Match: C. M. Spearman.

Durham

N. Peng lbw b Hardinges	23	
G. J. Pratt c Ball b Smith	14	
G. J. Muchall c Taylor b Harvey	3	
M. J. Symington c Smith b Alleyne	34	
*J. J. B. Lewis b Alleyne	31	
†A. Pratt st Russell b Alleyne	13	
D. R. Law c Hardinges b Alleyne	24	
N. C. Phillips b Harvey	10	
G. D. Bridge not out	14	

A. M. Davies c Ball b Averis 2
N. Killeen lbw b Harvey 1

L-b 6, w 4 10

1/27 (2) 2/30 (3) 3/47 (1)   (47.3 overs) 179
4/106 (5) 5/111 (4)
6/146 (7) 7/152 (6)
8/170 (8) 9/173 (10) 10/179 (11)

Bowling: Smith 10–2–40–1; Harvey 8.3–0–25–3; Hardinges 5–1–19–1; Averis 10–2–29–1; Ball 7–0–33–0; Alleyne 7–1–27–4.

Gloucestershire

C. M. Spearman not out	104
K. J. Barnett b Killeen	9
I. J. Harvey c A. Pratt b Law	27
C. G. Taylor not out	29
L-b 2, w 7, n-b 2	11

1/22 (2) 2/63 (3)　　(2 wkts, 26 overs) 180

M. G. N. Windows, *M. W. Alleyne, †R. C. Russell, M. A. Hardinges, M. C. J. Ball, J. M. M. Averis and A. M. Smith did not bat.

Bowling: Killeen 8–1–39–1; Davies 5–1–43–0; Law 4–0–14–1; Phillips 3–0–32–0; Symington 4–0–37–0; Bridge 2–0–13–0.

Umpires: N. J. Llong and D. R. Shepherd.

KENT v WARWICKSHIRE

At Canterbury, June 19. Kent won by 128 runs. Toss: Kent.

This was hardly ideal preparation for the B&H final Warwickshire would contest three days later. First their bowlers failed to contain some effervescent Kent strokeplay, then their batsmen foundered on a strip their opponents had relished. Kent's total was built around a magnificent maiden hundred from James Hockley, who pulled and drove gloriously in his 107-ball innings. He and Key added 157 for the second wicket in 25 overs as Kent – until Powell's career-best five for 40 blew them off course – were headed for a mammoth score. In need of a bright start, Warwickshire sank to 44 for three before their young stars, Bell and Troughton, briefly lit up the reply; gloom returned once they were separated.

Man of the Match: J. B. Hockley.

Kent

A. Khan c Knight b Pollock	13	J. C. Tredwell not out	15
R. W. T. Key c Bell b Carter	64	M. J. Saggers not out	0
J. B. Hockley b Smith	121		
A. Symonds c Carter b Powell	41	L-b 10, w 6	16
*D. P. Fulton c Brown b Powell	6		
†P. A. Nixon c Knight b Powell	21	1/21 (1) 2/178 (2)　(9 wkts, 50 overs) 328	
M. A. Ealham c Powell b Brown	12	3/241 (3) 4/251 (5)	
M. J. Walker c Ostler b Powell	6	5/276 (4) 6/278 (6)	
J. M. Golding c Troughton b Powell	13	7/294 (7) 8/300 (8) 9/318 (9)	

Bowling: Pollock 8–0–40–1; Carter 7–0–45–1; Sheikh 10–0–62–0; Brown 10–0–76–1; Smith 8–0–55–1; Powell 7–0–40–5.

Warwickshire

N. M. Carter c Walker b Khan	6	†K. J. Piper c Nixon b Tredwell	3
N. V. Knight b Saggers	25	M. A. Sheikh run out	14
S. M. Pollock b Khan	9		
I. R. Bell b Symonds	50	B 2, l-b 8, w 5	15
J. O. Troughton c Nixon b Ealham	32		
D. P. Ostler st Nixon b Tredwell	8	1/26 (1) 2/44 (2) 3/44 (3)　(37.1 overs) 200	
*M. J. Powell c and b Symonds	6	4/119 (4) 5/137 (4)	
D. R. Brown lbw b Symonds	4	6/145 (7) 7/149 (8)	
N. M. K. Smith not out	28	8/151 (6) 9/157 (10) 10/200 (11)	

Bowling: Saggers 6–1–16–1; Khan 8–0–50–2; Golding 5.1–0–30–0; Ealham 7–0–33–1; Walker 3–0–16–0; Symonds 4–0–21–3; Tredwell 4–0–24–2.

Umpires: B. Dudleston and J. H. Evans.

LEICESTERSHIRE v SUSSEX

At Leicester, June 19. Sussex won by six wickets. Toss: Leicestershire.

Leicestershire squandered a commanding position with such an inept display of self-destructive strokeplay that it strained belief. Ward and Stevens had put on 171 – a county record for the second wicket in this competition – when Ward holed out to long-on. But instead of building on an ideal platform, the Leicestershire batsmen preferred hara-kiri. In no time, 204 for one in the 43rd over had become 233 all out. Nine wickets fell for 29 in 38 balls, the last five for one in nine, Taylor helping himself to his second one-day hat-trick of the season. Sussex gratefully accepted such profligacy. A beautifully constructed unbeaten 126 from Montgomerie, backed up by Yardy, steered them home with plenty in the tank. Ward's hundred deserved better.

Man of the Match: R. R. Montgomerie.

Leicestershire

T. R. Ward c House b Yardy	112	
I. J. Sutcliffe c Prior b Kirtley	13	
D. I. Stevens b Kirtley	83	
*V. J. Wells c Innes b Yardy	4	
†N. D. Burns b Yardy	6	
P. A. J. DeFreitas b Taylor	5	
G. W. Flower c House b Taylor	3	
D. L. Maddy b Taylor	0	
C. D. Crowe b Kirtley	1	

D. E. Malcolm c House b Taylor	0
M. J. A. Whiley not out	0
L-b 2, w 4	6

1/33 (2) 2/204 (1)   (49.1 overs) 233
3/209 (4) 4/215 (5)
5/225 (6) 6/232 (3) 7/232 (7)
8/232 (8) 9/232 (10) 10/233 (9)

Bowling: Martin-Jenkins 10–3–28–0; Kirtley 9.1–1–46–3; Taylor 9–1–37–4; Innes 6–0–38–0; Davis 10–0–43–0; Yardy 5–0–39–3.

Sussex

R. R. Montgomerie not out	126	
T. R. Ambrose c Maddy b Malcolm	4	
M. H. Yardy st Burns b Flower	52	
M. W. Goodwin c and b Flower	11	
W. J. House b Maddy	18	

R. S. C. Martin-Jenkins not out	13
L-b 4, w 6	10

1/19 (2) 2/147 (3)   (4 wkts, 47.3 overs) 234
3/165 (4) 4/198 (5)

†M. J. Prior, K. J. Innes, M. J. G. Davis, *R. J. Kirtley and B. V. Taylor did not bat.

Bowling: DeFreitas 7–2–30–0; Malcolm 9–0–41–1; Whiley 4–0–27–0; Maddy 8.3–1–51–1; Wells 4–0–32–0; Flower 10–0–33–2; Crowe 2–0–16–0.

Umpires: A. Clarkson and J. W. Lloyds.

NORTHAMPTONSHIRE v YORKSHIRE

At Northampton, June 19. Yorkshire won by 49 runs. Toss: Northamptonshire.

Two teams in dire Championship form – each propped up their division – met in perfect conditions. The game went Yorkshire's way thanks to a powerful batting display which cast doubts on the wisdom of Hussey's surprise decision to bowl. Wood and the pinch-hitter, Silverwood, put on 125 in 20 overs for the second wicket, before Vaughan, who faced only 50 balls, and Katich plundered 86 from the last ten overs as Yorkshire reached a daunting 303. Northamptonshire's chances of mounting a serious challenge evaporated when Loye, Hussey and Warren went for 53, two to Silverwood, who maintained a back-of-a-length off-stump line. Cook hit four huge sixes in a robust 59-ball innings ended by Vaughan's brilliant fielding at cover point. The remaining batsmen contributed little.

Man of the Match: C. E. W. Silverwood.

Yorkshire

M. J. Wood c Cousins b Greenidge	. . . .	91
C. White c Greenidge b Anderson	. . . .	30
C. E. W. Silverwood c Cousins	. . . . . .	61
M. P. Vaughan not out	. . . .	63
S. M. Katich not out	. . . .	40
B 1, l-b 4, w 11, n-b 2	. . . . .	18

1/69 (2) 2/194 (1)   (3 wkts, 50 overs) 303
3/199 (3)

A. McGrath, G. M. Fellows, *†R. J. Blakey, R. K. J. Dawson, M. J. Hoggard and R. J. Sidebottom
  did not bat.

Bowling: Cousins 10–0–52–1; Greenidge 10–0–73–1; Anderson 7–0–53–1; Penberthy
10–0–43–0; Brown 10–1–57–0; Cook 3–0–20–0.

Northamptonshire

*M. E. K. Hussey c Wood b Silverwood	15	D. M. Cousins not out	. . . .	8
M. B. Loye c Vaughan b Hoggard	11	J. F. Brown b Hoggard	. . . .	3
D. J. Sales c Fellows b McGrath	44			
R. J. Warren lbw b Silverwood	6	L-b 9, w 11, n-b 8	. . . .	28
J. W. Cook run out	70			
A. L. Penberthy c Hoggard b Sidebottom	39	1/20 (2) 2/41 (1) 3/53 (4) (48.2 overs) 254		
†T. M. B. Bailey b White	14	4/145 (3) 5/172 (5)		
R. S. G. Anderson run out	4	6/219 (7) 7/225 (6)		
C. G. Greenidge b Sidebottom	12	8/233 (8) 9/249 (9) 10/254 (11)		

Bowling: Hoggard 9.2–0–37–2; Silverwood 10–3–35–2; White 9–0–34–1; Sidebottom
10–0–59–2; Dawson 6–0–47–0; McGrath 4–0–33–1.

Umpires: N. G. Cowley and K. E. Palmer.

NOTTINGHAMSHIRE v WORCESTERSHIRE

At Nottingham, June 19. Worcestershire won by eight wickets. Toss: Nottinghamshire.
  Nottinghamshire's meek submission against a Worcestershire side who had beaten just one first-
class team in this competition since 1994 sealed the fate of Clive Rice, their director of cricket.
Within 48 hours he had left the club. Nottinghamshire's total, including a fine half-century from
Gallian and an even better one, off 46 balls, from Read, appeared respectable enough. It would
have been more still had Donald not been the epitome of consistency on a Trent Bridge beauty,
but it was made to look wholly inadequate as Solanki and Hick tucked in to some inviting bowling.
Both made centuries, Hick's arguably the better. His unbeaten 117 was rattled up off 104 balls
with 15 fours and two sixes, with Solanki's a shade slower. But victory came with six overs to
spare.
  Man of the Match: V. S. Solanki.

Nottinghamshire

G. E. Welton c Batty b Lampitt	. . . .	26	B. M. Shafayat not out	. . . .	28
*J. E. R. Gallian c Hick b Mason	. . . .	69	B 1, l-b 5, w 6, n-b 2	. . . . .	14
U. Afzaal st Rhodes b Leatherdale	. . . . .	42			
K. P. Pietersen lbw b Leatherdale	. . . .	24	1/51 (1) 2/134 (3) (5 wkts, 50 overs) 262		
N. Boje c Leatherdale b Donald	. . . .	8	3/163 (2) 4/175 (5)		
†C. M. W. Read not out	. . . .	51	5/195 (4)		

P. J. Franks, G. J. Smith, A. J. Harris and G. D. Clough did not bat.

Bowling: Mason 10–0–61–1; Ali 10–0–59–0; Lampitt 9–0–57–1; Donald 10–3–24–1; Batty
3–0–20–0; Leatherdale 8–0–35–2.

Worcestershire

V. S. Solanki c Welton b Boje	. . . . . .	108
A. Singh run out	. . . .	9
*G. A. Hick not out	. . . .	117
B. F. Smith not out	. . . .	16
B 1, l-b 5, w 7, n-b 2	. . . . . .	15

1/18 (2) 2/213 (1) (2 wkts, 44 overs) 265

D. A. Leatherdale, G. J. Batty, †S. J. Rhodes, Kabir Ali, S. R. Lampitt, M. S. Mason and A. A. Donald did not bat.

Bowling: Smith 8–0–40–0; Harris 10–0–42–0; Franks 8–0–68–0; Clough 6–0–38–0; Boje 9–0–48–1; Pietersen 3–0–23–0.

Umpires: M. J. Harris and N. A. Mallender.

SOMERSET v HAMPSHIRE

At Taunton, June 19. Somerset won by six wickets. Toss: Hampshire.

This was another attacking, supremely confident one-day batting triumph by Trescothick. Leading by example, he ensured Somerset were never inhibited by Hampshire's challenging target. His 133 came off 115 balls, and most of his 18 boundaries were clean, jaunty strokes – to the delight of the Taunton faithful. Hampshire had themselves been ominously full of runs. Neil Johnson's canny half-century had laid the foundations; then Crawley dominated, handsomely compiling a wristy unbeaten hundred. Somerset's riposte carried the poise of trophy-holders. Bowler was a polished foil to Trescothick, and the innings was paced perfectly. Blackwell carted late sixes to make doubly sure. It proved an uphill day for the 14 bowlers who were tried.

Man of the Match: M. E. Trescothick.

Hampshire

N. C. Johnson c Johnson b Burns	. . . . .	52	†N. Pothas not out	10
D. A. Kenway c Dutch b Johnson	. . . .	30	L-b 1, w 6	7
J. P. Crawley not out	. . . .	113		
*R. A. Smith run out	. . . .	28	1/54 (2) 2/122 (1) (5 wkts, 50 overs) 262
G. W. White c Bowler b Jones	. . . . .	2	3/193 (4) 4/204 (5)
A. D. Mascarenhas b Johnson	. . . .	20	5/238 (6)

W. S. Kendall, S. D. Udal, C. T. Tremlett and A. D. Mullally did not bat.

Bowling: Johnson 10–2–42–2; Bulbeck 3–0–29–0; Jones 10–0–50–1; Parsons 8–0–43–0; Burns 6–0–31–1; Dutch 6–0–26–0; Blackwell 7–0–40–0.

Somerset

P. D. Bowler c Johnson b Mascarenhas	. .	41	K. A. Parsons not out	21
*M. E. Trescothick c Pothas b Mullally	.	133	L-b 5, w 7, n-b 2	14
M. J. Wood c Johnson b Tremlett	. . . . .	19		
M. Burns run out	. . . .	3	1/130 (1) 2/176 (3) (4 wkts, 45.1 overs) 265
I. D. Blackwell not out	. . . .	34	3/202 (4) 4/211 (2)

†R. J. Turner, K. P. Dutch, R. L. Johnson, M. P. L. Bulbeck and P. S. Jones did not bat.

Bowling: Mullally 10–1–53–1; Mascarenhas 8–1–48–1; Tremlett 9–0–52–1; Johnson 4–0–28–0; Udal 10–0–57–0; Kendall 4–0–18–0; White 0.1–0–4–0.

Umpires: T. E. Jesty and A. A. Jones.

SURREY v GLAMORGAN

At The Oval, June 19. Surrey won by nine runs. Toss: Surrey.

This sensational match left a trail of broken records in its wake. Thanks to a belter of a pitch and a 60-yard boundary under the gasometers, it was a batsman's – and statistician's – delight. At its heart was Ally Brown's brilliant, scarcely credible world-record 268, yet this was no one-man show. Perhaps most astonishing was that Glamorgan, not given a prayer by anyone after conceding 438, so nearly won. Robert Croft, acting-captain while Steve James tended his sick daughter, led a never-say-die fightback with a captain's innings that was also a phenomenal feat of pinch-hitting. He smacked Bicknell's first ball for four as he sprinted to 50 in 22 balls. His hundred came up in 59 minutes off 56 balls, whereas Brown's first hundred had taken 98 minutes and 80 balls. Hemp, the game's third centurion, got there in 85 balls and kept the run-rate near the required 8.78; off the last ten overs, Glamorgan needed a just-about-feasible 103.

WORLD LIMITED-OVERS RECORDS SET DURING SURREY v GLAMORGAN

Individual score	**268** by A. D. Brown, beating 222 not out by R. G. Pollock for Eastern Province v Border at East London in 1974-75.
Total	**438-5** by Surrey, beating 413-4* (60 overs) by Somerset v Devon at Torquay in 1990.
Match aggregate	**867** by Surrey (438-5) and Glamorgan (429), beating 754 scored by India Seniors (392-6) and India B (362) at Chennai in 2000-01.
Runs conceded	**108** by S. D. Thomas (9–0–108–3), beating 107 by C. C. Lovell (12–0–107–2) for Cornwall v Warwickshire at St Austell in 1996.

* Superseded as second-highest limited-overs score, first by Glamorgan in this match, then by Buckinghamshire (424-5) v Suffolk at Dinton in the first round of the 2003 C&G Trophy.

Thomas made amends for haemorrhaging 12 runs an over by cracking an unbeaten 71 off only 41 balls. But wickets were falling at the other end, mainly to Hollioake who, with ten runs needed off two balls, bowled Cosker to complete a wonderful contest. The honours, though, went to Brown for his second – and only the sixth ever – one-day double-hundred, following his 203 in a Sunday League game against Hampshire in 1997 (*Wisden 1998*, page 827). His brutal innings contained 192 in boundaries, including 12 sixes, one short of Ian Botham's world record, and his 268 came off only 160 balls, at a strike-rate of 167. His pulling, especially, was perfection, but he also hit 22 fours and two sixes through or over the covers, driving off the back foot as well as the front. "I'm in the best form of my life," he said later. Asked to name his best shots, he chose "the sixes I hit when Darren Thomas pitched it short". Ward made an admirable 97 off 95 balls with four sixes and helped add 286 for the first wicket but he, like everyone else, was eclipsed by Brown.

Man of the Match: A. D. Brown.

Surrey

I. J. Ward b Croft	97	A. J. Stewart not out	2
A. D. Brown b Kasprowicz	268	†J. N. Batty not out	6
M. R. Ramprakash		L-b 8, w 20, n-b 2	30
c and b S. D. Thomas	26		
R. Clarke c Wallace b S. D. Thomas	5	1/286 (1) 2/354 (3) (5 wkts, 50 overs) 438	
*A. J. Hollioake c I. J. Thomas		3/376 (4) 4/424 (5)	
b S. D. Thomas	4	5/431 (2)	

M. P. Bicknell, Saqlain Mushtaq, J. Ormond and E. S. H. Giddins did not bat.

Bowling: Kasprowicz 10–0–53–1; Davies 8–0–88–0; S. D. Thomas 9–0–108–3; Croft 8–0–62–1; Dale 8–0–68–0; Cosker 7–0–51–0.

Glamorgan

*R. D. B. Croft c Ward b Hollioake....	119		A. P. Davies c Ormond b Hollioake....	1
I. J. Thomas run out	23		D. A. Cosker b Hollioake...........	0
D. L. Hemp c Ormond b Bicknell.....	102			
M. P. Maynard c Ramprakash b Giddins.	21		L-b 7, w 6..............	13
A. Dale c Clarke b Hollioake........	49			
M. J. Powell c Giddins b Hollioake....	0		1/113 (2) 2/162 (1) (49.5 overs)	429
S. D. Thomas not out	71		3/197 (4) 4/295 (5)	
†M. A. Wallace c Ramprakash b Bicknell	5		5/295 (6) 6/336 (3) 7/352 (8)	
M. S. Kasprowicz run out	25		8/417 (9) 9/421 (10) 10/429 (11)	

Bowling: Bicknell 10–0–84–2; Giddins 8–0–77–1; Ormond 9–0–72–0; Saqlain Mushtaq 10–0–82–0; Hollioake 8.5–0–77–5; Clarke 4–0–30–0.

Umpires: I. J. Gould and P. Willey.

QUARTER-FINALS

ESSEX v YORKSHIRE

At Chelmsford, July 16. Yorkshire won by virtue of losing fewer wickets. Toss: Essex.

Yorkshire crowned a magnificent recovery by winning more comfortably than the scores suggest. They began the final over knowing three runs would carry them to the semis. McGrath turned Dakin's first ball for two, and a quick single from the fifth let Fellows block the last. Victory looked unlikely when the pair came together at 155 for five in the 32nd over. But they batted with supreme confidence and control, McGrath's polished 72 coming off 70 balls, while the more aggressive Fellows hit eight fours and a six off 59. Earlier, brisk innings from Robinson and Flower had steered Essex to a position of strength only for them to lose their way: their last ten overs brought just 53. Gough, playing his first county match of the summer, came through unscathed despite colliding with Dawson, who in the ensuing mêlée somehow clung on to the ball to dismiss Hussain.

Man of the Match: A. McGrath.

Essex

N. Hussain c Dawson b Hoggard......	7		J. D. Middlebrook not out	6
D. D. J. Robinson c and b Silverwood .	52		T. J. Phillips not out	4
J. M. Dakin run out	17			
†A. Flower c Blakey b White	75		B 9, l-b 11, w 14, n-b 2	36
*R. C. Irani b Gough	32			
A. Habib c White b Lehmann........	40		1/10 (1) 2/82 (3) (9 wkts, 50 overs)	283
G. R. Napier c Fellows b Lehmann	4		3/113 (2) 4/169 (5)	
A. P. Cowan b Gough	7		5/246 (4) 6/258 (6)	
M. L. Pettini c Wood b White.......	3		7/258 (7) 8/268 (8) 9/270 (9)	

Bowling: Gough 10–0–52–2; Hoggard 8–1–45–1; White 10–0–47–2; Silverwood 7–0–40–1; Dawson 9–0–51–0; Lehmann 6–0–28–2.

Yorkshire

C. White c Habib b Irani.........	8		G. M. Fellows not out.............	68
M. J. Wood b Irani.............	22		B 4, l-b 7, w 3, n-b 2	16
C. E. W. Silverwood c Pettini b Napier..	37			
M. P. Vaughan c Flower b Napier....	42		1/12 (1) 2/52 (2) (5 wkts, 50 overs)	283
*D. S. Lehmann b Middlebrook	18		3/82 (3) 4/120 (5)	
A. McGrath not out	72		5/155 (4)	

R. K. J. Dawson, †R. J. Blakey, M. J. Hoggard and D. Gough did not bat.

Bowling: Irani 10–1–53–2; Cowan 10–1–49–0; Dakin 9–1–50–0; Napier 7–0–47–2; Middlebrook 9–0–46–1; Phillips 5–0–27–0.

Umpires: A. A. Jones and R. Palmer.

KENT v GLOUCESTERSHIRE

At Canterbury, July 16. Kent won by five wickets. Toss: Gloucestershire.

Fleming, aged 37 and in his last season before retiring, piloted Kent to just their second C&G semi-final since 1984. Victory arrived by a comfortable margin, though the most eye-catching play came from Barnett and Russell, with a combined age of over 80, and tough and cussed as a pair of Gloucester Old Spots. Once Saggers's third over – a triple-wicket-maiden – had reduced Gloucestershire to 17 for three, they were forced to rely on Barnett's wiles and Russell's improvisation to set a target. Together they put on 100, Russell giving the innings a rousing finale as he hit 66 from 49 balls. The pace barely slackened as Fleming launched Kent's reply: his 53 needed just 42 balls. With such a platform, they barely looked back.

Man of the Match: K. J. Barnett.

Gloucestershire

K. J. Barnett b Fleming	108	M. C. J. Ball not out	1
C. M. Spearman c Ealham b Saggers . . .	6	J. M. M. Averis not out	3
I. J. Harvey c Tredwell b Saggers	0	B 1, l-b 3, w 4	8
T. H. C. Hancock b Saggers	0		
*M. W. Alleyne c Key b Ealham	28	1/17 (2) 2/17 (3) (8 wkts, 50 overs) 232
A. P. R. Gidman c Fleming b Symonds .	11	3/17 (4) 4/82 (5)
†R. C. Russell lbw b Fleming	66	5/120 (6) 6/220 (1)
M. A. Hardinges c Fulton b Fleming . . .	1	7/228 (8) 8/229 (7)

J. Lewis did not bat.

Bowling: Saggers 9–1–41–3; Khan 6–0–33–0; Fleming 10–1–45–3; Ealham 10–0–47–1; Tredwell 9–0–37–0; Symonds 6–0–25–1.

Kent

*M. V. Fleming c Lewis b Alleyne	53	†P. A. Nixon not out	39
R. W. T. Key c Russell b Alleyne	18	L-b 5, w 6	11
J. B. Hockley b Ball	9		
A. Symonds run out	47	1/72 (1) 2/79 (2) (5 wkts, 44.2 overs) 238
D. P. Fulton not out	43	3/106 (3) 4/155 (4)
M. J. Walker c Russell b Barnett	18	5/178 (6)

M. A. Ealham, M. J. Saggers, J. C. Tredwell and A. Khan did not bat.

Bowling: Lewis 8.2–1–39–0; Harvey 8–0–62–0; Averis 3–0–27–0; Alleyne 10–0–46–2; Ball 10–0–36–1; Barnett 5–0–23–1.

Umpires: D. J. Constant and V. A. Holder.

SOMERSET v WORCESTERSHIRE

At Taunton, July 17. Somerset won by four wickets. Toss: Somerset.

Parsons's good-looking 121, his first one-day century, was a composed innings despite coming from just 100 balls. It earned him a standing ovation from a Taunton crowd whose optimism must have been tested by the absence of six seamers, all injured. Paul Jarvis was brought out of retirement, which was not a success, and he was withdrawn from the attack after two costly overs. With Hick scoring ominously quickly – including a fierce cover-drive that broke Trescothick's thumb and put him out for six weeks – Worcestershire had looked set for a huge score; thanks to tight bowling from Jones and Parsons they managed only a good one. Smith played neatly, but they lacked acceleration, and only 113 came in the second half. Somerset's reply began unimpressively before Parsons, with Turner in support, steered them towards a handsome win.

Man of the Match: K. A. Parsons.

Worcestershire

S. D. Peters lbw b Jones	18	S. R. Lampitt c Bulbeck b Blackwell	5
V. S. Solanki c Blackwell b Burns	53	M. S. Mason run out	1
*G. A. Hick b Parsons	39		
B. F. Smith not out	85	B 4, l-b 7, w 18	29
D. A. Leatherdale c Parsons b Burns	5		
G. J. Batty c Cox b Parsons	2	1/37 (1) 2/118 (3) 3/153 (2) (49 overs) 271
A. J. Bichel run out	11	4/163 (5) 5/179 (6)
†S. J. Rhodes c Parsons b Jones	15	6/201 (7) 7/234 (8)
Kabir Ali c Bulbeck b Jones	8	8/252 (9) 9/268 (10) 10/271 (11)

Bowling: Jones 8–0–47–3; Bulbeck 10–0–61–0; Jarvis 2–0–25–0; Parsons 10–0–37–2; Burns 10–0–52–3; Blackwell 9–0–37–1.

Somerset

J. Cox c Hick b Bichel	15	M. P. L. Bulbeck not out	4
P. D. Bowler c Rhodes b Mason	5		
M. Burns b Lampitt	24	L-b 1, w 13	14
K. A. Parsons c Rhodes b Mason	121		
I. D. Blackwell c Rhodes b Leatherdale	30	1/29 (1) 2/36 (2) (6 wkts, 47.3 overs) 273
†R. J. Turner c Rhodes b Ali	47	3/87 (3) 4/145 (5)
K. P. Dutch not out	13	5/251 (4) 6/261 (6)

*M. E. Trescothick, P. W. Jarvis and P. S. Jones did not bat.

Bowling: Bichel 10–1–42–1; Mason 8.3–1–58–2; Ali 7–0–51–1; Lampitt 8–0–45–1; Batty 6–0–30–0; Leatherdale 8–0–46–1.

Umpires: J. H. Evans and I. J. Gould.

SUSSEX v SURREY

At Hove, July 17. Surrey won by 14 runs. Toss: Surrey.

Just 48 hours after the service of thanksgiving for the life of his brother Ben at Southwark Cathedral, Adam Hollioake reminded the world of his own talents. Coming in at 189 for three in the 36th over, he and his largely passive partner, Ramprakash, added 148, all bar 31 to Hollioake. He reached his hundred from his 52nd delivery, and in all faced 59, 11 of which shot for four, five for six. He was especially strong on the leg, his bottom hand regularly powering pull-drives to the rope. Ramprakash's run-a-ball century barely registered. On such a friendly pitch, Sussex's batsmen had a chance and, with classy innings from Montgomerie and Goodwin – the day's third hundred to be scored at better than even time – they came close. Crucially, though, they could not match Hollioake's coruscating strokeplay at the end: 117 came from Surrey's last ten overs, 79 from Sussex's.

Man of the Match: A. J. Hollioake.

Surrey

I. J. Ward c Prior b Martin-Jenkins	12
A. D. Brown c Adams b Martin-Jenkins	36
M. R. Ramprakash not out	107
R. Clarke c Montgomerie b Yardy	55
*A. J. Hollioake not out	117
L-b 5, w 5	10

1/39 (1) 2/48 (2) (3 wkts, 50 overs) 337
3/189 (4)

I. D. K. Salisbury, †A. J. Stewart, J. D. Ratcliffe, Saqlain Mushtaq, J. Ormond and E. S. H. Giddins did not bat.

Bowling: Taylor 10–1–59–0; Martin-Jenkins 10–1–65–2; Yardy 8–0–56–1; Innes 7–0–45–0; Davis 10–0–56–0; Cottey 3–0–23–0; Goodwin 2–0–28–0.

Sussex

R. R. Montgomerie c Stewart b Ratcliffe	88		K. J. Innes c Stewart b Saqlain Mushtaq	1
T. R. Ambrose c Brown b Clarke	12		M. J. G. Davis not out	1
*C. J. Adams c Stewart b Clarke	33		B 1, l-b 1, w 10, n-b 6	18
M. W. Goodwin not out	110			
†M. J. Prior run out	34		1/55 (2) 2/127 (3)	(8 wkts, 50 overs) 323
P. A. Cottey b Holioake	1		3/174 (1) 4/238 (5)	
R. S. C. Martin-Jenkins b Giddins	15		5/240 (6) 6/275 (7)	
M. H. Yardy b Holioake	10		7/311 (8) 8/316 (9)	

B. V. Taylor did not bat.

Bowling: Giddins 10–0–58–1; Ormond 7–0–61–0; Clarke 10–0–56–2; Saqlain Mushtaq 10–0–49–1; Ratcliffe 4–0–33–1; Salisbury 2–0–14–0; Holioake 7–0–50–2.

Umpires: B. Leadbeater and J. F. Steele.

SEMI-FINALS

SOMERSET v KENT

At Taunton, August 1. Somerset won by five runs. Toss: Kent.

Kent must have wondered quite how they lost this enthralling semi-final. Unfazed by Somerset's prodigious total, they batted with brilliant freedom and needed just nine off 15 balls with four wickets in hand. Amid nervous batting, superb fielding and feverish excitement for the 7,000 crowd, Kent lost those wickets in ten balls. In all, this Taunton classic had produced 683 runs. Earlier, Fleming had inserted Somerset, something of a surprise on one of Phil Frost's marvellous run-friendly pitches. Bowler and Burns admirably laid the foundations, while Blackwell, in front of Rod Marsh, the Academy director, gave a rousing display of uninhibited batting, 86 coming from 53 balls. But Kent's reply betrayed no fear. Fleming and Key raised 100 in the 14th over, Symonds faced 41 balls for his 55, and the middle order sustained the tempo. A Kent win was looking routine – until the calamitous collapse. Nixon was run out by a deflection as he backed up, then Francis, fielding in place of Johnson, who had cramp, spectacularly removed Golding. Bulbeck bowled Masters, leaving Ealham to score six from the last over. But he was well caught at mid-wicket off the first ball, and Somerset were back at Lord's.

Man of the Match: I. D. Blackwell.

Somerset

*J. Cox c Nixon b Ealham	31		K. P. Dutch not out	12
P. D. Bowler b Symonds	70		L-b 7, w 13, n-b 2	22
M. Burns c Fleming b Golding	72			
I. D. Blackwell c Symonds b Fleming	86		1/59 (1) 2/150 (2)	(5 wkts, 50 overs) 344
K. A. Parsons run out	32		3/240 (3) 4/294 (4)	
†R. J. Turner not out	19		5/332 (5)	

M. J. Wood, R. L. Johnson, M. P. L. Bulbeck and P. S. Jones did not bat.

Bowling: Saggers 10–0–66–0; Masters 7–0–58–0; Golding 7–1–38–1; Ealham 10–0–40–1; Fleming 10–0–76–1; Symonds 6–0–59–1.

Kent

*M. V. Fleming c Turner b Jones	63		D. D. Masters b Bulbeck	0
R. W. T. Key b Parsons	42		M. J. Saggers not out	0
J. B. Hockley lbw b Parsons	7			
A. Symonds c Cox b Blackwell	55		L-b 14, w 6	20
D. P. Fulton c Wood b Parsons	48			
M. J. Walker c Blackwell b Parsons	35		1/100 (2) 2/112 (1)	(49.1 overs) 339
†P. A. Nixon run out	33		3/122 (3) 4/190 (4)	
M. A. Ealham c Dutch b Jones	36		5/260 (5) 6/262 (6) 7/336 (7)	
J. M. Golding run out	0		8/338 (9) 9/339 (10) 10/339 (8)	

Bowling: Johnson 8–0–47–0; Bulbeck 8–0–54–1; Jones 9.1–0–51–2; Parsons 8–0–55–4; Burns 2–0–19–0; Blackwell 10–0–69–1; Dutch 4–0–30–0.

Umpires: B. Leadbeater and A. G. T. Whitehead.

YORKSHIRE v SURREY

At Leeds, August 4. Yorkshire won by ten wickets (D/L method). Toss: Yorkshire.

In the end, after three postponements, Yorkshire galloped into the final. Torrential rain prevented play on Wednesday, Thursday or Friday, prompting umpires Hampshire and Dudleston to ignore ECB regulations and ask whether the game could be saved from a bowl-out and played on the Sunday. After some hesitation, and once Duncan Fletcher had sanctioned the participation of England's centrally contracted players, Lord's agreed. Hampshire then left to stand in another match. Both teams had League games on the Saturday – Surrey's in Croydon – and Yorkshire controversially prepared a new pitch, believing the original would take too much spin. Surrey felt the replacement was damp, and their batting betrayed their anxieties, though they were not helped by four interruptions. Only Ramprakash, patiently accumulating 63 from 114 balls, hung around for long. Hoggard dismissed both openers, but White wreaked most damage with four for 35. Duckworth/Lewis revised Yorkshire's target to 167 from 42 overs, but it might as well have been twice that. White played a majestic innings, winning the match with a boundary that dashed him to a century off 78 balls, with 16 fours and a six – an exhilarating display containing barely a false stroke. Wood thrashed 18 from Clarke's first four balls, but otherwise he was pedestrian beside his partner.

Man of the Match: C. White.

Surrey

I. J. Ward lbw b Hoggard	2	Saqlain Mushtaq c McGrath b White	5
A. D. Brown c Lumb b Hoggard	9	J. Ormond not out	5
M. R. Ramprakash run out	63	L-b 15, w 12, n-b 2	29
†A. J. Stewart c Blakey b White	3		
N. Shahid c McGrath b Lehmann	21	1/6 (1) 2/25 (2) (8 wkts, 48 overs) 173	
*A. J. Hollioake lbw b White	16	3/50 (4) 4/91 (5)	
R. Clarke c Blakey b White	3	5/124 (6) 6/130 (7)	
A. J. Tudor not out	17	7/152 (3) 8/158 (9)	

E. S. H. Giddins did not bat.

Bowling: Hoggard 10–1–21–2; Silverwood 8–2–23–0; Sidebottom 10–0–35–0; White 10–0–35–4; McGrath 5–0–26–0; Lehmann 5–0–18–1.

Yorkshire

C. White not out	100
M. J. Wood not out	57
L-b 1, w 5, n-b 4	10

(no wkt, 24.1 overs) 167

M. P. Vaughan, *D. S. Lehmann, A. McGrath, G. M. Fellows, M. J. Lumb, †R. J. Blakey, C. E. W. Silverwood, R. J. Sidebottom and M. J. Hoggard did not bat.

Bowling: Tudor 9–0–40–0; Giddins 4–0–42–0; Ormond 4–0–20–0; Clarke 2.1–0–29–0; Saqlain Mushtaq 5–0–35–0.

Umpires: B. Dudleston and J. W. Holder.

There is too much cricket. There has been too much cricket for far too long and if we do not act now to stop the rot, we will all be driven to distraction.
Christopher Martin-Jenkins, page 34

Jaw-dropping: Matthew Elliott sweeps Yorkshire to victory in the C&G final. *Picture by Craig Prentis, Getty Images.*

FINAL

SOMERSET v YORKSHIRE

At Lord's, August 31. Yorkshire won by six wickets. Toss: Somerset.

A close encounter between two teams having a nightmare in the Championship was decided by the one man on the field who had not spent months worrying about relegation. When he strode out to bat in a mini-crisis, Matthew Elliott had been a Yorkshire player for two and a half weeks and had not even followed this year's C&G, let alone played in it. After a watchful start, he rediscovered the booming strokeplay that had rung out in the Lord's Test of 1997. He reminded a capacity crowd why the Australian selectors had once preferred him to Matthew Hayden, and played out a trailer for the Ashes by singling out Caddick for rough treatment. Caddick went wicketless for the third time in four Lord's finals, and the only sign of a cutting edge came in a spell of big-hearted swing from his new-ball partner, Johnson. Somerset, fielding the eleven that had won the cup the year before, were comfortably beaten, and Yorkshire lifted their first Lord's trophy in 15 years.

Spectators had an interesting day rather than a gripping one. On a low, slow, dusty pitch, runs had to be chiselled out, and most of the bowlers tried cutters and slower balls. The match featured nine men who had played for England in the past two years and it began as a duel between two of them – Trescothick, returning hastily after a broken thumb, and Hoggard. When a Hoggard over went for 20, including four off a free-hit, Trescothick was well on top, even though the big shots left him wincing with pain. But he was lured into a loose drive and his England opening partner, Vaughan, hurled himself to his right at short extra to hold on to a scintillating catch.

Bowler and Cox made sure the momentum wasn't lost, and Somerset chugged along at a curiously steady five an over for the rest of the innings. Although England's new one-day biffer, Blackwell, flopped, Parsons and Dutch hustled them to a total that was maybe 20 above par. Blakey, standing in for the absent Lehmann, had shuffled his bowlers shrewdly: Silverwood hit the bat hard, McGrath was frugal and Hoggard, characteristically, was both the most expensive bowler on either side and the most incisive.

Johnson steamed in from the Pavilion End and removed the dangerous White, playing as a batsman, as well as Wood and the pinch-hitter (or not, in this case) Silverwood. Johnson took his sweater with superb figures of three for 20 from seven overs, but then came Elliott. The difference between him and everybody else was simple: he had the power and precision to beat the deep fielders – 16 times, ten more than the next man (Bowler) on a day of twos and threes. The other batsmen had only to keep him company and look for singles. Vaughan saw this and reverted to his sober mode (56 balls, no fours) before the more combative McGrath completed a fine all-round performance. Elliott's hundred was the first by an overseas player in the final of this competition since Viv Richards in 1979, and he finished with 128 off 125 balls, while his English colleagues managed 108 off 164 between them. In Australia, Elliott had acquired a reputation as an awkward character; at Yorkshire, this meant he fitted in perfectly. **Tim de Lisle**

Man of the Match: M. T. G. Elliott.   *Attendance:* 26,231; *receipts* £660,000.

Somerset

P. D. Bowler c Blakey b Hoggard	67	K. P. Dutch not out		13
M. E. Trescothick c Vaughan b Hoggard	27	A. R. Caddick not out		0
*J. Cox lbw b McGrath	34	B 1, l-b 6, w 6, n-b 6		19
M. Burns lbw b Hoggard	21			
I. D. Blackwell b Sidebottom	12	1/41 (2) 2/122 (3)	(8 wkts, 50 overs)	256
K. A. Parsons c Sidebottom b Hoggard	41	3/159 (1) 4/171 (4)		
†R. J. Turner c White b Sidebottom	20	5/191 (6) 6/230 (7)		
R. L. Johnson b Hoggard	2	7/233 (8) 8/250 (6)	15 overs: 82-1	

P. S. Jones did not bat.

Bowling: Silverwood 8–1–30–0; Hoggard 10–0–65–5; Sidebottom 9–0–49–2; McGrath 9–0–37–1; Dawson 10–0–48–0; Vaughan 4–0–20–0.

Yorkshire

C. White c Turner b Johnson	12	A. McGrath not out		46
M. J. Wood b Johnson	19	L-b 7, w 15, n-b 2		24
C. E. W. Silverwood b Johnson	0			
M. T. G. Elliott not out	128	1/19 (1) 2/19 (3)	(4 wkts, 48 overs)	260
M. P. Vaughan lbw b Jones	31	3/64 (2) 4/157 (5)	15 overs: 67-3	

G. M. Fellows, *†R. J. Blakey, R. K. J. Dawson, R. J. Sidebottom and M. J. Hoggard did not bat.

Bowling: Caddick 9–0–53–0; Johnson 10–2–51–3; Parsons 6–0–31–0; Jones 9–0–45–1; Dutch 8–0–43–0; Blackwell 6–0–30–0.

Umpires: J. W. Holder and G. Sharp.

CHELTENHAM & GLOUCESTER TROPHY RECORDS

(Including Gillette Cup, 1963–80, and NatWest Trophy, 1981–2000)

65-over games in 1963; 60-over games 1964–98; 50-over games 1999–2002.
The first two rounds of the 2002 competition, played in 2001, are designated as 2001-02.

Batting

Highest individual scores: 268, A. D. Brown, Surrey v Glamorgan, The Oval, 2002; 206, A. I. Kallicharran, Warwickshire v Oxfordshire, Birmingham, 1984; 201, V. J. Wells, Leicestershire v Berkshire, Leicester, 1996; 180*, T. M. Moody, Worcestershire v Surrey, The Oval, 1994; 179, J. M. Dakin, Leicestershire v Wales, Swansea, 2001; 177, C. G Greenidge, Hampshire v Glamorgan, Southampton, 1975; 177, A. J. Wright, Gloucestershire v Scotland, Bristol, 1997; 176*, D. R. Clarke, Bedfordshire v Derbyshire Board XI, Dunstable, 2001-02; 173*, M. J. Di Venuto, Derbyshire v Derbyshire Board XI, Derby, 2000; 172*, G. A. Hick, Worcestershire v Devon, Worcester, 1987; 165*, V. P. Terry, Hampshire v Berkshire, Southampton, 1985; 162*,

C. J. Tavaré, Somerset v Devon, Torquay, 1990; 162*, I. V. A. Richards, Glamorgan v Oxfordshire, Swansea, 1993. *In the final:* 146, G. Boycott, Yorkshire v Surrey, 1965. (384 hundreds have been scored in the competition. The most hundreds in one tournament was 29 in 2002.)

Most runs: 2,547, G. A. Gooch; 2,364, R. A. Smith; 2,203, K. J. Barnett; 2,148, M. W. Gatting; 2,142, G. A. Hick; 1,998, A. J. Lamb; 1,950, D. L. Amiss.

Fastest hundred: G. D. Rose off 36 balls, Somerset v Devon, Torquay, 1990.

Most hundreds: 8, R. A. Smith; 7, G. A. Hick and C. L. Smith; 6, G. A. Gooch; 5, D. I. Gower, I. V. A. Richards and G. M. Turner.

Highest totals: 438 for five, Surrey v Glamorgan, The Oval, 2002; 429, Glamorgan v Surrey, The Oval, 2002; 413 for four, Somerset v Devon, Torquay, 1990; 406 for five, Leicestershire v Berkshire, Leicester, 1996; 404 for three, Worcestershire v Devon, Worcester, 1987; 392 for five, Warwickshire v Oxfordshire, Birmingham, 1984; 386 for five, Essex v Wiltshire, Chelmsford, 1988; 384 for six, Kent v Berkshire, Finchampstead, 1994; 384 for nine, Sussex v Ireland, Belfast, 1996; 381 for three, Lancashire v Hertfordshire, Radlett, 1999; 373 for seven, Glamorgan v Bedfordshire, Cardiff, 1998; 372 for five, Lancashire v Gloucestershire, Manchester, 1990; 371 for four, Hampshire v Glamorgan, Southampton, 1975. *In the final:* 322 for five, Warwickshire v Sussex, Lord's, 1993.

Highest total by a minor county: 367 for three, Bedfordshire v Derbyshire Board XI, Dunstable, 2001-02.

Highest total by a side batting first and losing: 327 for eight (60 overs), Derbyshire v Sussex, Derby, 1997. *In the final:* 321 for six (60 overs), Sussex v Warwickshire, 1993.

Highest totals by a side batting second: 429 (49.5 overs), Glamorgan lost to Surrey, The Oval, 2002; 350 (59.5 overs), Surrey lost to Worcestershire, The Oval, 1994; 339 for nine (60 overs), Somerset lost to Warwickshire, Birmingham, 1995; 339 (49.1 overs), Kent lost to Somerset, Taunton, 2002; 329 for five (59.2 overs), Sussex beat Derbyshire, Derby, 1997; 326 for nine (60 overs), Hampshire lost to Leicestershire, Leicester, 1987; 323 for eight (50 overs), Sussex lost to Surrey, Hove, 2002; 322 for five (60 overs), Warwickshire beat Sussex, Lord's, 1993 (*in the final*); 319 for nine (59.5 overs), Essex beat Lancashire, Chelmsford, 1992.

Lowest completed totals: 39 (26.4 overs), Ireland v Sussex, Hove, 1985; 41 (20 overs), Cambridgeshire v Buckinghamshire, Cambridge, 1972; 41 (19.4 overs), Middlesex v Essex, Westcliff, 1972; 41 (36.1 overs), Shropshire v Essex, Wellington, 1974. *In the final:* 57 (27.2 overs), Essex v Lancashire, 1996.

Lowest total by a side batting first and winning: 98 (56.2 overs), Worcestershire v Durham, Chester-le-Street, 1968.

Shortest innings: 10.1 overs (60 for one), Worcestershire v Lancashire, Worcester, 1963.

Matches rearranged on a reduced number of overs are excluded from the above.

Record partnerships for each wicket

311	for 1st	A. J. Wright and N. J. Trainor, Gloucestershire v Scotland at Bristol ..	1997
286	for 2nd	I. S. Anderson and A. Hill, Derbyshire v Cornwall at Derby	1986
309*	for 3rd	T. S. Curtis and T. M. Moody, Worcestershire v Surrey at The Oval ...	1994
234*	for 4th	D. Lloyd and C. H. Lloyd, Lancashire v Gloucestershire at Manchester	1978
166	for 5th	M. A. Lynch and G. R. J. Roope, Surrey v Durham at The Oval	1982
226	for 6th	N. J. Llong and M. V. Fleming, Kent v Cheshire at Bowdon	1999
160*	for 7th	C. J. Richards and I. R. Payne, Surrey v Lincolnshire at Sleaford	1983
112	for 8th	A. L. Penberthy and J. E. Emburey, Northamptonshire v Lancashire at Manchester	1996
87	for 9th	M. A. Nash and A. E. Cordle, Glamorgan v Lincolnshire at Swansea ..	1974
81	for 10th	S. Turner and R. E. East, Essex v Yorkshire at Leeds	1982

Bowling

Most wickets: 88, A. A. Donald; 81, G. G. Arnold; 80, C. A. Connor; 79, J. Simmons.

Best bowling (12 overs unless stated): eight for 21 (10.1 overs), M. A. Holding, Derbyshire v Sussex, Hove, 1988; eight for 31 (11.1 overs), D. L. Underwood, Kent v Scotland, Edinburgh, 1987; seven for 15, A. L. Dixon, Kent v Surrey, The Oval, 1967; seven for 15 (9.3 overs), R. P. Lefebvre, Somerset v Devon, Torquay, 1990; seven for 19, N. V. Radford, Worcestershire v Bedfordshire, Bedford, 1991; seven for 27 (9.5 overs), D. Gough, Yorkshire v Ireland, Leeds, 1997; seven for 30, P. J. Sainsbury, Hampshire v Norfolk, Southampton, 1965; seven for 32, S. P. Davis, Durham v Lancashire, Chester-le-Street, 1983; seven for 33, R. D. Jackman, Surrey v Yorkshire, Harrogate, 1970; seven for 35 (10.1 overs), D. E. Malcolm, Derbyshire v Northamptonshire, Derby, 1997; seven for 37, N. A. Mallender, Northamptonshire v Worcestershire, Northampton, 1984. *In the final:* six for 18 (6.2 overs), G. Chapple, Lancashire v Essex, 1996.

Most economical analysis: 12–9–3–1, J. Simmons, Lancashire v Suffolk, Bury St Edmunds, 1985.

Most expensive analysis: 9–0–108–3, S. D. Thomas, Glamorgan v Surrey, The Oval, 2002.

Hat-tricks (13): J. D. F. Larter, Northamptonshire v Sussex, Northampton, 1963; D. A. D. Sydenham, Surrey v Cheshire, Hoylake, 1964; R. N. S. Hobbs, Essex v Middlesex, Lord's, 1968; N. M. McVicker, Warwickshire v Lincolnshire, Birmingham, 1971; G. S. le Roux, Sussex v Ireland, Hove, 1985; M. Jean-Jacques, Derbyshire v Nottinghamshire, Derby, 1987; J. F. M. O'Brien, Cheshire v Derbyshire, Chester, 1988; R. A. Pick, Nottinghamshire v Scotland, Nottingham, 1995; J. E. Emburey, Northamptonshire v Cheshire, Northampton, 1996; A. R. Caddick, Somerset v Gloucestershire, Taunton, 1996; D. Gough, Yorkshire v Ireland, Leeds, 1997; P. J. Swanepoel, Yorkshire Board XI v Somerset, Scarborough, 2002; B. V. Taylor, Sussex v Leicestershire, Leicester, 2002.

Four wickets in five balls: D. A. D. Sydenham, Surrey v Cheshire, Hoylake, 1964.

Wicket-keeping and Fielding

Most dismissals: 93 (78 ct, 15 st), R. C. Russell; 72 (62 ct, 10 st), S. J. Rhodes; 66 (58 ct, 8 st), R. W. Taylor; 65 (59 ct, 6 st), A. P. E. Knott.

Most dismissals in an innings: 8 (all ct), D. J. Pipe, Worcestershire v Hertfordshire, Hertford, 2001; 7 (all ct), A. J. Stewart, Surrey v Glamorgan, Swansea, 1994.

Most catches by a fielder: 27, W. Larkins and J. Simmons; 26, M. W. Gatting and G. A. Gooch; 25, G. Cook and G. A. Hick; 24, N. H. Fairbrother and P. J. Sharpe.

Most catches by a fielder in an innings: 4 – A. S. Brown, Gloucestershire v Middlesex, Bristol, 1963; G. Cook, Northamptonshire v Glamorgan, Northampton, 1972; C. G. Greenidge, Hampshire v Cheshire, Southampton, 1981; D. C. Jackson, Durham v Northamptonshire, Darlington, 1984; T. S. Smith, Hertfordshire v Somerset, St Albans, 1984; H. Morris, Glamorgan v Scotland, Edinburgh, 1988; C. C. Lewis, Nottinghamshire v Worcestershire, Nottingham, 1992; G. Yates, Lancashire v Essex, Manchester, 2000; D. P. Fulton, Kent v Northamptonshire, Canterbury, 2001.

Results

Largest victories in runs: Somerset by 346 runs v Devon, Torquay, 1990; Sussex by 304 runs v Ireland, Belfast, 1996; Worcestershire by 299 runs v Devon, Worcester, 1987; Essex by 291 runs v Wiltshire, Chelmsford, 1988; Worcestershire by 267 runs v Hertfordshire, Hertford, 2001; Sussex by 244 runs v Ireland, Hove, 1985; Lancashire by 241 runs v Gloucestershire, Manchester, 1990.

Victories by ten wickets (23): By Essex, Glamorgan, Hampshire (twice), Holland, Lancashire (twice), Middlesex, Northamptonshire, Nottinghamshire, Scotland, Somerset, Surrey (twice), Sussex (twice), Warwickshire (twice), Yorkshire (five times).

Earliest finishes: both at 2.20 p.m. Worcestershire beat Lancashire by nine wickets at Worcester, 1963; Essex beat Middlesex by eight wickets at Westcliff, 1972.

Scores level (13): Nottinghamshire 215, Somerset 215 for nine at Taunton, 1964; Surrey 196, Sussex 196 for eight at The Oval, 1970; Somerset 287 for six, Essex 287 at Taunton, 1978; Surrey 195 for seven, Essex 195 at Chelmsford, 1980; Essex 149, Derbyshire 149 for eight at Derby, 1981; Northamptonshire 235 for nine, Derbyshire 235 for six at Lord's, 1981 (*in the final*); Middlesex 222 for nine, Somerset 222 for eight at Lord's, 1983; Hampshire 224 for eight, Essex 224 for seven at Southampton, 1985; Essex 307 for six, Hampshire 307 for five at Chelmsford, 1990; Hampshire 204 for nine, Leicestershire 204 for nine at Leicester, 1995; Cheshire 204, Lincolnshire 204 for nine at Chester, 2000; Norfolk 245 for three, Holland 245 at Horsford, 2001-02; Essex 283 for nine, Yorkshire 283 for five at Chelmsford, 2002.

Under competition rules the side which lost fewer wickets won; at Leicester in 1995, Leicester-shire won by virtue of their higher total after 30 overs.

Match Awards

Most awards: 9, G. A. Gooch and R. A. Smith; 8, C. H. Lloyd and C. L. Smith.

WINNERS 1963–2002
Gillette Cup

		Man of the Match
1963	SUSSEX* beat Worcestershire by 14 runs.	N. Gifford†
1964	SUSSEX beat Warwickshire* by eight wickets.	N. I. Thomson
1965	YORKSHIRE beat Surrey* by 175 runs.	G. Boycott
1966	WARWICKSHIRE* beat Worcestershire by five wickets.	R. W. Barber
1967	KENT* beat Somerset by 32 runs.	M. H. Denness
1968	WARWICKSHIRE beat Sussex* by four wickets.	A. C. Smith
1969	YORKSHIRE beat Derbyshire* by 69 runs.	B. Leadbeater
1970	LANCASHIRE* beat Sussex by six wickets.	H. Pilling
1971	LANCASHIRE* beat Kent by 24 runs.	Asif Iqbal†
1972	LANCASHIRE* beat Warwickshire by four wickets.	C. H. Lloyd
1973	GLOUCESTERSHIRE* beat Sussex by 40 runs.	A. S. Brown
1974	KENT* beat Lancashire by four wickets.	A. P. E. Knott
1975	LANCASHIRE* beat Middlesex by seven wickets.	C. H. Lloyd
1976	NORTHAMPTONSHIRE* beat Lancashire by four wickets.	P. Willey
1977	MIDDLESEX* beat Glamorgan by five wickets.	C. T. Radley
1978	SUSSEX* beat Somerset by five wickets.	P. W. G. Parker
1979	SOMERSET beat Northamptonshire* by 45 runs.	I. V. A. Richards
1980	MIDDLESEX* beat Surrey by seven wickets.	J. M. Brearley

NatWest Trophy

1981	DERBYSHIRE* beat Northamptonshire by losing fewer wickets with the scores level.	G. Cook†
1982	SURREY* beat Warwickshire by nine wickets.	D. J. Thomas
1983	SOMERSET beat Kent* by 24 runs.	V. J. Marks
1984	MIDDLESEX beat Kent* by four wickets.	C. T. Radley
1985	ESSEX beat Nottinghamshire* by one run.	B. R. Hardie
1986	SUSSEX* beat Lancashire by seven wickets.	D. A. Reeve
1987	NOTTINGHAMSHIRE* beat Northamptonshire by three wickets.	R. J. Hadlee
1988	MIDDLESEX* beat Worcestershire by three wickets.	M. R. Ramprakash
1989	WARWICKSHIRE beat Middlesex* by four wickets.	D. A. Reeve
1990	LANCASHIRE* beat Northamptonshire by seven wickets.	P. A. J. DeFreitas
1991	HAMPSHIRE* beat Surrey by four wickets.	R. A. Smith

		Man of the Match
1992	NORTHAMPTONSHIRE* beat Leicestershire by eight wickets.	A. Fordham
1993	WARWICKSHIRE* beat Sussex by five wickets.	Asif Din
1994	WORCESTERSHIRE* beat Warwickshire by eight wickets.	T. M. Moody
1995	WARWICKSHIRE beat Northamptonshire* by four wickets.	D. A. Reeve
1996	LANCASHIRE beat Essex* by 129 runs.	G. Chapple
1997	ESSEX* beat Warwickshire by nine wickets.	S. G. Law
1998	LANCASHIRE* beat Derbyshire by nine wickets.	I. D. Austin
1999	GLOUCESTERSHIRE beat Somerset* by 50 runs.	R. C. Russell
2000	GLOUCESTERSHIRE* beat Warwickshire by 22 runs (D/L method).	A. A. Donald†

Cheltenham & Gloucester Trophy

2001	SOMERSET* beat Leicestershire by 41 runs.	K. A. Parsons
2002	YORKSHIRE beat Somerset* by six wickets.	M. T. G. Elliott

* Won toss.   † On losing side.

TEAM RECORDS 1963–2002

	Rounds reached				*Matches*		
	W	F	SF	QF	P	W	L
Derbyshire	1	3	4	13	81*	42	39
Durham	0	0	0	2	49	17	32
Essex	2	3	6	16	89	51	38
Glamorgan	0	1	4	16	86	46	40
Gloucestershire	3	3	7	17	90	52	38
Hampshire	1	1	10	22	101	62	39
Kent	2	5	8	17	94	56	38
Lancashire	7	10	17	23	116	83	33
Leicestershire	0	2	5	16	86	46	40
Middlesex	4	6	13	21	104	68	36
Northamptonshire	2	7	10	21	101	63	38
Nottinghamshire	1	2	3	13	83	44	39
Somerset	3	7	12	20	103	66	37
Surrey	1	4	12	24	104*	65	39
Sussex	4	8	13	20	102	66	36
Warwickshire	5	11	18	23	117	82	35
Worcestershire	1	4	10	16	91	52	39
Yorkshire	3	3	8	19	91	54	37

* Derbyshire and Surrey totals each include a bowling contest after their first-round matches were abandoned in 1991; Derbyshire lost to Hertfordshire and Surrey beat Oxfordshire.

MINOR COUNTY RECORDS

From 1964 to 1979 the previous season's top five Minor Counties were invited to take part in the competition. In 1980 these were joined by Ireland, and in 1983 the competition was expanded to embrace 13 Minor Counties, Ireland and Scotland. The number of Minor Counties dropped to 12 in 1992 when Durham attained first-class status, and 11 in 1995 when Holland were admitted to the competition.

Between 1964 and 1991 Durham qualified 21 times, including 15 years in succession from 1977–91. They reached the second round a record six times.

Up to the 1998 tournament, Staffordshire qualified most among the remaining Minor Counties, 20 times, followed by Devon, 19. Only Hertfordshire have ever reached the quarter-finals, in 1976.

From 1999, the competition was reformed and two preliminary rounds introduced, in which 42 teams compete for the right to join the first-class counties in the third round. They are all 20 Minor Counties (including Wales), plus Huntingdonshire Board XI, the first-class county Board XIs (excluding Glamorgan, who are covered by Wales) and the national teams of Denmark, Holland, Ireland and Scotland. These four national teams did not take part in the 2001 Trophy because of the forthcoming ICC Trophy.

Wins by a minor team over a first-class county (11): Durham v Yorkshire (by five wickets), Harrogate, 1973; Lincolnshire v Glamorgan (by six wickets), Swansea, 1974; Hertfordshire v Essex (by 33 runs), 2nd round, Hitchin, 1976; Shropshire v Yorkshire (by 37 runs), Telford, 1984; Durham v Derbyshire (by seven wickets), Derby, 1985; Buckinghamshire v Somerset (by seven runs), High Wycombe, 1987; Cheshire v Northamptonshire (by one wicket), Chester, 1988; Hertfordshire v Derbyshire (2–1 in a bowling contest after the match was abandoned), Bishop's Stortford, 1991; Scotland v Worcestershire (by four runs), Edinburgh, 1998; Holland v Durham (by five wickets), Amstelveen, 1999; Herefordshire v Middlesex (by three wickets), Kingsland, 2001.

YOUNG CRICKETER OF THE YEAR, 2002
RIKKI CLARKE

Rikki Clarke of Surrey, who had never played a first-class match before 2002, did enough in his first season to be voted Young Cricketer of the Year by members of the Cricket Writers' Club. In September, just before turning 21, he joined the England one-day squad in Sri Lanka, although he didn't get a game. A hard-hitting No.7, Clarke filled the gap left at Surrey by the death of Ben Hollioake and averaged 50 with the bat, as well as taking 11 wickets with his lively medium-pace. He pipped Robert Key of Kent by a single vote; the shortlist also included Ian Bell and Graham Wagg (Warwickshire), Kabir Ali (Worcestershire), Tim Ambrose and Matt Prior (Sussex), Richard Dawson (Yorkshire) and Kyle Hogg (Lancashire). Surrey players have now won the award eight times, Middlesex seven, Lancashire and Yorkshire six apiece. Worcestershire and Durham are the only first-class counties that have not had a winner.

Year	Winner (team) Test, ODI caps
1950	R. Tattersall (Lancs) 16, –
1951	P. B. H. May (Surrey) 66, –
1952	F. S. Trueman (Yorks) 67, –
1953	M. C. Cowdrey (OU & Kent) 114, 1
1954	P. J. Loader (Surrey) 13, –
1955	K. F. Barrington (Surrey) 82, –
1956	B. Taylor (Essex) –, –
1957	M. J. Stewart (Surrey) 8, –
1958	A. C. D. Ingleby-Mackenzie (Hants) –, –
1959	G. Pullar (Lancs) 28, –
1960	D. A. Allen (Glos) 39, –
1961	P. H. Parfitt (Middx) 37, –
1962	P. J. Sharpe (Yorks) 12, –
1963	G. Boycott (Yorks) 108, 36
1964	J. M. Brearley (CU & Middx) 39, 25
1965	A. P. E. Knott (Kent) 95, 20
1966	D. L. Underwood (Kent) 86, 26
1967	A. W. Greig (Sussex) 58, 22
1968	R. M. H. Cottam (Kent) 4, –
1969	A. Ward (Derbys) 5, –
1970	C. M. Old (Yorks) 46, 32
1971	J. Whitehouse (Warwicks) –, –
1972	D. R. Owen-Thomas (CU & Surrey) –, –
1973	M. Hendrick (Derbys) 30, 22
1974	P. H. Edmonds (CU & Middx) 51, 29
1975	A. Kennedy (Lancs) –, –
1976	G. Miller (Derbys) 34, 25

Year	Winner (team) Test, ODI caps
1977	I. T. Botham (Somerset) 102, 116
1978	D. I. Gower (Leics) 117, 114
1979	P. W. G. Parker (Sussex) 1, –
1980†	G. R. Dilley (Kent) 41, 36
1981	M. W. Gatting (Middx) 79, 92
1982	N. G. Cowans (Middx) 19, 23
1983	N. A. Foster (Essex) 29, 48
1984	R. J. Bailey (Northants) 4, 4
1985	D. V. Lawrence (Glos) 5, 1
1986	A. A. Metcalfe (Yorks) –, –
	J. J. Whitaker (Leics) 1, 2
1987	R. J. Blakey (Yorks) 2, 3
1988	M. P. Maynard (Glam) 4, 14
1989	N. Hussain (Essex) 81, 80
1990	M. A. Atherton (Lancs) 115, 54
1991	M. R. Ramprakash (Middx) 52, 18
1992	I. D. K. Salisbury (Sussex) 15, 4
1993	M. N. Lathwell (Somerset) 2, –
1994	J. P. Crawley (Lancs) 37, 13
1995	A. Symonds (Glos) –, 50 for Aus
1996	C. E. W. Silverwood (Yorks) 6, 7
1997	B. C. Hollioake (Surrey) 2, 20
1998	A. Flintoff (Lancs) 21, 46
1999	A. J. Tudor (Surrey) 10, 3
2000	P. J. Franks (Notts) –, 1
2001	O. A. Shah (Middx) –, 15
2002	R. Clarke (Surrey) –, –

Teams are those played for at the time. Caps are up to Jan 14, 2003, and for England unless stated. †An extra award, in memory of Norman Preston, Editor of Wisden 1951–1980, was made to C. W. J. Athey (Yorks, 23, 31).

BENSON AND HEDGES CUP, 2002

Michael Powell

English cricket gave up its long dependence on tobacco in June 2002 when Benson and Hedges, the most faithful sponsors in the game, backed their last match. Warwickshire won, Michael Powell held the cup aloft, and the competition drifted gently into oblivion.

The end had been signalled in 1997 when the new Labour government, more worried about Britain's coughers than sport's coffers, announced a clampdown on tobacco sponsorship. But the competition was not dead yet, and it briefly metamorphosed into the superfluous Benson and Hedges Super Cup, whittled down to just seven games. This proved popular with no one, least of all the 18 first-class counties who had come to rely on their early-season fix of one-day cricket, and so life was breathed back into the corpse for three more years. The group stages were revived, but without any of the minor sides. No slain giants meant no romance, and any magic the B&H once possessed seeped away. In fact, crowds for the final had been dwindling for some years, and few shed a tear at its loss.

The B&H, though always playing second fiddle to its older, posher cousin, the Gillette-cum-NatWest-cum-C&G, still had its moments. Things started with a bang in 1972, when Mike Procter gave the most astounding display of all-round excellence seen in the English one-day game. He followed a take-no-prisoners 154 not out with an irrepressible five for 26 as Gloucestershire thumped Somerset. Four seasons later, in a gesture that hinted at how the game would change in the coming decades, Nottinghamshire's Derek Randall was imaginatively given the Gold Award purely for his fielding, when he had neither held a catch nor run anyone out. And in 1989, Combined Universities came four agonising runs short of gate-crashing the semis after a brilliant hundred from Nasser Hussain and a more surprising four for 42 from his captain, Mike Atherton. The B&H proved a test-bed for innovation too, and in 1993 Surrey's game against Lancashire at The Oval was the first in England to use a third umpire. Capping it all was the closest one-day final yet – the 1987 classic when Yorkshire broke Northamptonshire hearts and won by dint of taking more wickets with the scores level.

There were dark days too, none darker than Brian Rose's calculating declaration at one for no wicket in 1979. It left Worcestershire to refund spectators, cricket badly tarnished, and Somerset in the quarter-finals on a technicality – until they were disqualified for bringing the game into disrepute. Four years later, the weather and a lack of planning conspired to let Middlesex through to the semi-final on the toss of a coin. They went on to win the cup.

The most successful teams over the 31 years were Kent and Lancashire, who finished with identical match records, winning 98 and losing 54 out of 152 completed games. Lancashire, with four victories in the final to Kent's three, won the tie-breaker. Gloucestershire, Leicestershire and Surrey also lifted the cup three times, but it was Essex, with 92 wins and 53 losses, who came third in terms of overall results (full table at end of this section). One player stands head and shoulders above all others, though he was on the Cup-winning side just once, in 1979. Essex's Graham Gooch hit the highest individual innings, scored more runs, made more hundreds, held more catches as a fielder and won more Gold Awards than anyone else. No other player comes close, and it would have felt right if Gooch, now county coach, had steered Essex to success in the 1,424th and last match of a competition he made his own. Essex were facing Warwickshire, also coached by a towering figure in the B&H. Bob Woolmer had been a key member of the Kent side that strutted so confidently through the late 1970s. He had tasted victory during his previous stint at Edgbaston in 1994 and after a less than thrilling finale he tasted it again.

Warwickshire flirted with failure in the league stage. They inched past Northamptonshire into third place in the Midlands group simply because head-to-head results were given more weight than net run-rate. And they had a hair-raising ride in a roller-coaster semi-final when they beat Lancashire by one wicket off the last ball. Ian Bell was their mainstay: in an otherwise thin season, he hit 326 vibrant runs, just three fewer than the leading scorer, Sussex's Richard Montgomerie. It was Essex, though, who had the player of the tournament. Before the final, Ronnie Irani could do no wrong. All told, he filched 20 wickets with his seam bowling and crashed 214 runs, often when his side were up against it. As captain, he always had an answer and – while the ball was in his hand or singing sweetly from his bat – Essex could never be written off.

Without Adam Hollioake, still in Australia after the death of his brother, the cup-holders, Surrey, fell at the first hurdle. Twice the B&H had got the best from Ben when it really mattered – nobody else had two Gold Awards from the final – and the Hollioakes were sorely missed. Gloucestershire, who had reached Lord's for the previous three years, foundered at home to Worcestershire, their first defeat at Bristol in 13 B&H games. Leicestershire, winners of the first cup in 1972, began in awesome form, and looked as if they could give the competition a pleasing symmetry by winning again. They were undefeated in their group matches – and in all limited-overs games – until Lancashire beat them in the quarter-finals. David Byas, batting on a fiendish wicket, was the difference. He had enjoyed his first return to Headingley since leaving at the end of 2001; Yorkshire, who were rolled over for 81, had not.

In that match, Yorkshire lasted just 27.2 overs, 44 balls more than they will be allowed in the B&H's replacement. Called Twenty20, it is aimed at luring younger spectators to all-action battles shoehorned into midsummer-evening slots of under three hours. Either inspired thinking or the worst example of crash–bang–wallop cricket yet dreamt up, the new tournament faces one clear danger. With 45 games scheduled for 12 hectic days, keep your fingers crossed for the weather. **Hugh Chevallier**

Prize money

£52,000 for winners: WARWICKSHIRE.

£26,000 for runners-up: ESSEX.

£15,500 for losing semi-finalists: LANCASHIRE, WORCESTERSHIRE.

£10,500 for losing quarter-finalists: GLOUCESTERSHIRE, LEICESTERSHIRE, SUSSEX, YORKSHIRE.

Gold Award winners received £1,750 in the final, £550 in the semi-finals, £500 in the quarter-finals and £300 in the group matches; these figures were unchanged from the 2001 competition, and the total sponsorship also remained at £850,000.

FINAL GROUP TABLES

	Played	Won	Lost	No result	Points	Net run-rate
Midlands/Wales/West Group						
GLOUCESTERSHIRE	5	4	1	0	8	1.33
WORCESTERSHIRE	5	4	1	0	8	−0.06
WARWICKSHIRE*	5	3	2	0	6	0.01
Northamptonshire	5	3	2	0	6	1.51
Glamorgan	5	0	4	1	1	−1.74
Somerset	5	0	4	1	1	−2.39
North Group						
LEICESTERSHIRE	5	4	0	1	9	0.46
YORKSHIRE	5	3	2	0	6	0.45
LANCASHIRE*	5	2	2	1	5	1.35
Nottinghamshire	5	2	3	0	4	−0.71
Durham	5	2	3	0	4	−0.54
Derbyshire	5	0	3	2	2	−1.46
South Group						
ESSEX	5	4	0	1	9	0.48
SUSSEX	5	4	1	0	8	0.61
Kent	5	2	3	0	4	−0.48
Hampshire	5	2	3	0	4	−0.42
Middlesex	5	1	3	1	3	0.37
Surrey	5	1	4	0	2	−0.29

* Lancashire and Warwickshire qualified as the most successful third-placed teams.

Where two or more counties finished with an equal number of points, the positions were decided by (a) most wins (b) most points in head-to-head matches (c) net run-rate (runs scored per over minus runs conceded per over, revising figures in matches where the Duckworth/Lewis method was used and discounting those not achieving a result) (d) most wickets taken per balls bowled in matches achieving a result.

MIDLANDS/WALES/WEST GROUP

NORTHAMPTONSHIRE v GLAMORGAN

At Northampton, April 28. Northamptonshire won by eight wickets. Toss: Northamptonshire. County debut: M. J. Cawdron.

Glamorgan had not won in the B&H since their 2000 semi-final against Surrey, and reckless batting condemned them to a seventh successive defeat. The pitch offered pace, bounce and some sideways movement, but nothing could justify the strokes – ranging from the ill-advised to the suicidal – that threw away Glamorgan's last six wickets for only 17. Cook cashed in, doubling his previous total of three one-day victims with his occasional medium-pace. Northamptonshire, who scored more than half their runs in boundaries, eased home with nearly 24 overs unused.

Gold Award: J. W. Cook.

Glamorgan

K. Newell c Cawdron b Phillips	12	S. P. Jones c Loye b Cook	4
D. L. Hemp c Bailey b Phillips	13	O. T. Parkin b Penberthy	0
R. D. B. Croft c Swann b Cawdron	33		
*S. P. James c Sales b Cawdron	2	L-b 4, w 5	9
†M. P. Maynard b Cook	32		
M. J. Powell c Bailey b Cook	6	1/20 (2) 2/49 (1) (30.5 overs) 122
A. Dale c Sales b Penberthy	3	3/62 (3) 4/84 (4) 5/105 (5)
S. D. Thomas not out	8	6/106 (6) 7/110 (7) 8/115 (9)
M. S. Kasprowicz lbw b Penberthy	0	9/120 (10) 10/122 (11)

Bowling: Greenidge 8–0–41–0; Phillips 7–1–28–2; Cawdron 5–0–24–2; Penberthy 5.5–3–6–3; Cook 5–0–19–3.

Northamptonshire

*M. E. K. Hussey c Maynard b Newell .	28	
G. P. Swann lbw b Kasprowicz	7	
M. B. Loye not out	53	
D. J. Sales not out	23	
B 1, l-b 6, w 4, n-b 2	13	

1/7 (2) 2/70 (1)   (2 wkts, 26.1 overs) 124

R. J. Warren, A. L. Penberthy, J. W. Cook, †T. M. B. Bailey, B. J. Phillips, M. J. Cawdron and C. G. Greenidge did not bat.

Bowling: Kasprowicz 6–2–16–1; Parkin 5–0–14–0; Thomas 3–0–22–0; Jones 6–0–31–0; Newell 2–0–16–1; Croft 3–0–13–0; Dale 1.1–0–5–0.

Umpires: M. R. Benson and N. G. Cowley.

WARWICKSHIRE v SOMERSET

At Birmingham, April 28. Warwickshire won by 94 runs (D/L method). Toss: Somerset.

Rain breaks and revised targets lent this game an odd pattern. Warwickshire's innings was punctuated by several stoppages before it was finally cut short at 41 overs, yet Knight managed to remain fluent, scoring at more than a run a ball against Somerset bowling that was often pitched too short. Helped by brisk contributions from Smith, Bell and Penney, he guided Warwickshire to an imposing 263, and reached a county-record 13th one-day century. Initially Somerset needed 6.4 an over. After the fifth interruption it was more than eight; after the sixth, nearly 24. Already five wickets down, they chose batting practice, sedately playing out the final five overs in watery sunshine.

Gold Award: N. V. Knight.

Warwickshire

N. V. Knight not out	126	†K. J. Piper not out	11	
N. M. K. Smith b Johnson	28			
D. R. Brown b Trego	13	L-b 4, w 8, n-b 6	18	
I. R. Bell c Turner b Burns	31			
*M. J. Powell c Cox b Burns	7	1/61 (2) 2/92 (3) (6 wkts, 41 overs) 263		
T. L. Penney c Blackwell b Dutch	23	3/156 (4) 4/171 (5)		
S. M. Pollock c Burns b Francis	6	5/217 (6) 6/224 (7)		

M. A. Sheikh, N. M. Carter and A. Richardson did not bat.

Bowling: Johnson 8–1–43–1; Bulbeck 7–0–51–0; Francis 9–0–61–1; Trego 5–0–32–1; Parsons 1–0–5–0; Burns 4–0–27–2; Dutch 7–0–40–1.

Somerset

*J. Cox c Knight b Sheikh	25	†R. J. Turner not out	11	
P. D. Bowler c Penney b Brown	0	L-b 3, w 4, n-b 2	9	
M. Burns c Richardson b Pollock	1			
I. D. Blackwell c Piper b Brown	2	1/5 (2) 2/8 (3) (5 wkts, 19 overs) 78		
P. D. Trego b Brown	5	3/12 (4) 4/28 (5)		
K. A. Parsons not out	25	5/47 (1)		

K. P. Dutch, R. L. Johnson, M. P. L. Bulbeck and S. R. G. Francis did not bat.

Bowling: Pollock 4–0–18–1; Brown 6–0–15–3; Sheikh 3–0–14–1; Richardson 3–0–13–0; Carter 3–0–15–0.

Umpires: A. Clarkson and B. Leadbeater.

WORCESTERSHIRE v GLOUCESTERSHIRE

At Worcester, April 29. Gloucestershire won by six wickets. Toss: Gloucestershire.

Disciplined Gloucestershire bowling on a pitch offering extravagant seam movement produced the B&H's earliest finish: 1.50 p.m. after just 40 overs and two balls. It could have been briefer still: after 15 minutes Worcestershire had slumped to 14 for six, with the tournament's lowest score – 50 by Hampshire at Headingley in 1991 – a distant prospect. The pitch had sweated under covers for 48 hours before the game, and Harvey and Lewis exploited conditions perfectly by keeping the ball up to the bat. Lusty hitting from Kabir Ali lifted Worcestershire to 70 in 22 overs, two balls more than the tournament's shortest completed innings. Batting remained difficult, but Gloucestershire were never in serious danger.

Gold Award: I. J. Harvey.

Worcestershire

S. D. Peters c Spearman b Harvey	0	Kabir Ali lbw b Alleyne		27
V. S. Solanki b Lewis	4	A. Sheriyar not out		2
*G. A. Hick c Russell b Harvey	2			
B. F. Smith b Lewis	0	W 1		1
D. A. Leatherdale b Harvey	1			
G. J. Batty b Lewis	12	1/0 (1) 2/6 (3) 3/6 (2)	(22 overs)	70
A. J. Bichel c Russell b Harvey	3	4/7 (5) 5/9 (4) 6/14 (7)		
†S. J. Rhodes b Lewis	15	7/28 (6) 8/40 (8)		
S. R. Lampitt c Alleyne b Averis	3	9/62 (9) 10/70 (10)		

Bowling: Harvey 10–2–21–4; Lewis 10–0–41–4; Averis 1–0–2–1; Alleyne 1–0–6–1.

Gloucestershire

K. J. Barnett c Hick b Ali	33	*M. W. Alleyne not out		3
C. M. Spearman b Bichel	8	L-b 3, w 1, n-b 2		6
I. J. Harvey c Rhodes b Ali	15			
C. G. Taylor c Batty b Ali	6	1/17 (2) 2/42 (3)	(4 wkts, 18.2 overs)	71
M. G. N. Windows not out	0	3/64 (1) 4/67 (4)		

A. P. R. Gidman, †R. C. Russell, J. N. Snape, J. M. M. Averis and J. Lewis did not bat.

Bowling: Bichel 9.2–1–35–1; Sheriyar 4–2–12–0; Ali 5–0–21–3.

Umpires: J. W. Holder and R. Palmer.

SOMERSET v GLAMORGAN

At Taunton, April 30. No result (abandoned).

GLOUCESTERSHIRE v WARWICKSHIRE

At Bristol, May 1. Gloucestershire won by 149 runs. Toss: Warwickshire.

Well-honed craftsmanship in all departments gave Gloucestershire a second crushing win in three days. Taylor and Windows showed nous and skill against the seaming ball, minimising risk but never getting bogged down, and they put on 144 in almost even time. Looking for nearly six an over on a slow outfield, Warwickshire needed a sprightly start, but were kept on the leash by tight bowling from the Gloucestershire openers. Russell, standing up to the brisk Harvey, gave a masterful wicket-keeping display, catching Knight and, two balls later, Bell to complete Harvey's hat-trick. Warwickshire looked unlikely to recover from 13 for four; Snape and Averis made sure they didn't.

Gold Award: C. G. Taylor.

Gloucestershire

C. M. Spearman lbw b Brown	4	J. N. Snape not out		5
K. J. Barnett c Knight b Pollock	2	L-b 2, w 2		4
I. J. Harvey c Piper b Sheikh	34			
C. G. Taylor lbw b Pollock	93	1/4 (1) 2/18 (2)	(6 wkts, 43 overs)	240
M. G. N. Windows c Penney b Brown	86	3/44 (3) 4/188 (4)		
*M. W. Alleyne b Pollock	12	5/219 (6) 6/240 (5)		

†R. C. Russell, A. P. R. Gidman, J. M. M. Averis and J. Lewis did not bat.

Bowling: Brown 9–0–42–2; Pollock 9–0–44–3; Sheikh 9–1–44–1; Carter 3–0–21–0; Richardson 5–0–43–0; Smith 6–0–26–0; Bell 2–0–18–0.

Warwickshire

N. V. Knight c Russell b Harvey	6	N. M. Carter b Averis		0
N. M. K. Smith c Spearman b Harvey	2	A. Richardson c Alleyne b Snape		5
D. R. Brown c Windows b Harvey	2			
I. R. Bell c Russell b Harvey	0	L-b 6, w 3		9
*M. J. Powell not out	28			
T. L. Penney c Russell b Averis	24	1/7 (1) 2/10 (2) 3/10 (4)	(28.4 overs)	91
S. M. Pollock b Averis	13	4/13 (3) 5/57 (6) 6/71 (7)		
†K. J. Piper lbw b Snape	2	7/78 (8) 8/82 (9)		
M. A. Sheikh lbw b Snape	0	9/86 (10) 10/91 (11)		

Bowling: Lewis 7–1–14–0; Harvey 6–1–12–4; Gidman 4–0–26–0; Averis 6–3–13–3; Alleyne 3–0–13–0; Snape 2.4–1–7–3.

Umpires: I. J. Gould and P. Willey.

NORTHAMPTONSHIRE v WORCESTERSHIRE

At Northampton, May 1. Worcestershire won by five wickets. Toss: Worcestershire.

On a nearby strip, these sides had shared 1,138 runs for 13 wickets in the preceding Championship game. This one was more like the New Road wicket where Worcestershire were routed for 70 two days earlier, though the scores were very different. Worcestershire won the toss and, in a closely fought match, gained an important advantage, allowing Bichel to find swing and seam in the early moisture. Hussey was circumspect, before Penberthy, scoring at nearly a run a ball, and Cook, quicker still, hit out. Penberthy also excelled with the ball – his ten overs cost 18 – and Worcestershire took quick wickets each time Worcestershire looked on course. But the loss of Phillips with a shoulder injury asked too much of the wayward Cawdron.

Gold Award: A. L. Penberthy.

Northamptonshire

*M. E. K. Hussey b Batty	58	†T. M. B. Bailey not out		12
G. P. Swann c Lampitt b Bichel	11	B. J. Phillips not out		3
M. B. Loye b Bichel	2	L-b 3, w 8		11
D. J. Sales c Rhodes b Ali	9			
R. J. Warren c Rhodes b Bichel	23	1/20 (2) 2/27 (3)	(7 wkts, 50 overs)	232
A. L. Penberthy b Sheriyar	53	3/50 (4) 4/88 (5)		
J. W. Cook c Leatherdale b Bichel	50	5/127 (1) 6/195 (7) 7/222 (6)		

M. J. Cawdron and C. G. Greenidge did not bat.

Bowling: Bichel 10–1–38–4; Sheriyar 10–0–68–1; Ali 10–0–49–1; Lampitt 10–2–25–0; Leatherdale 5–0–20–0; Batty 5–0–29–1.

Worcestershire

S. D. Peters lbw b Swann	52	A. J. Bichel not out		27
V. S. Solanki st Bailey b Penberthy	50	B 8, l-b 2, w 10, n-b 2		22
*G. A. Hick lbw b Penberthy	17			
B. F. Smith c Hussey b Cook	19	1/95 (2) 2/129 (3) (5 wkts, 47.3 overs)		233
D. A. Leatherdale c Bailey b Cawdron	33	3/133 (1) 4/183 (4)		
G. J. Batty not out	13	5/183 (5)		

†S. J. Rhodes, S. R. Lampitt, Kabir Ali and A. Sheriyar did not bat.

Bowling: Greenidge 8.3–3–28–0; Phillips 2–1–4–0; Cawdron 8–0–67–1; Cook 10–0–57–1; Penberthy 10–2–18–2; Swann 9–0–49–1.

Umpires: J. W. Holder and V. A. Holder.

GLAMORGAN v GLOUCESTERSHIRE

At Cardiff, May 3. Gloucestershire won by eight wickets. Toss: Glamorgan.

Defeat spelled almost certain elimination for Glamorgan, whose solitary point in three games had come courtesy of the weather. Gloucestershire, meanwhile, enjoyed a third straight victory, thanks in large part to the former New Zealand Test batsman Craig Spearman – ECB-qualified because of his Welsh mother – who hit a confident 73 from 60 balls. On a slow pitch of variable bounce, Glamorgan never got going against an all-seam attack bowling full and straight. Wickets fell regularly, and only Hemp and Dale reached 20. Gloucestershire's ground fielding was outstanding, as was Harvey and Lewis's bowling. Alleyne, who broke Maynard's hand with a ball that spat from a length, later gave permission for Wallace (not in the original 12) to keep wicket.

Gold Award: C. M. Spearman.

Glamorgan

K. Newell c Harvey b Lewis	9	D. A. Cosker b Harvey		6
D. L. Hemp c Lewis b Alleyne	62	S. P. Jones not out		1
R. D. B. Croft b Russell b Averis	4			
*S. P. James b Alleyne	14	L-b 4, w 3		7
†M. P. Maynard retired hurt	1			
M. J. Powell c Hardinges b Lewis	11	1/14 (1) 2/37 (3) (8 wkts, 50 overs)		171
A. Dale c and b Harvey	27	3/72 (4) 4/90 (6)		
S. D. Thomas b Windows b Harvey	10	5/124 (2) 6/138 (7)		
M. S. Kasprowicz not out	19	7/147 (8) 8/170 (10)		

Maynard retired hurt at 74.

Bowling: Lewis 10–1–25–2; Harvey 10–1–32–3; Averis 10–4–41–1; Hardinges 10–0–37–0; Alleyne 10–1–32–2.

Gloucestershire

K. J. Barnett c Hemp b Cosker	29
C. M. Spearman b Croft	73
I. J. Harvey not out	29
C. G. Taylor not out	29
L-b 5, w 8	13

1/109 (1) 2/117 (2) (2 wkts, 29.1 overs) 173

M. G. N. Windows, *M. W. Alleyne, †R. C. Russell, J. N. Snape, M. A. Hardinges, J. M. M. Averis and J. Lewis did not bat.

Bowling: Kasprowicz 7–2–29–0; Thomas 4–0–32–0; Jones 3–0–28–0; Croft 8–0–38–1; Cosker 7.1–0–41–1.

Umpires: V. A. Holder and N. A. Mallender.

SOMERSET v NORTHAMPTONSHIRE

At Taunton, May 3. Northamptonshire won by 145 runs. Toss: Northamptonshire. County debut: R. S. G. Anderson.

For the second time in a row Somerset's batting withered and died in the face of a challenging total. Although embellished by three memorable sixes – Hussey launched two into St James's churchyard and Sales one through the window of the pavilion bar – Northamptonshire's 299 was only slightly above par given a true pitch and lightning outfield. They were kept under 300 largely by the sixth bowler, Blackwell, who teased out Hussey and Loye and reimposed control after his colleagues proved expensive. Needing exactly a run a ball, Somerset lost Cox to the third of the innings and subsided to their heaviest B&H defeat, against a competent but unspectacular Northamptonshire attack.

Gold Award: M. E. K. Hussey.

Northamptonshire

*M. E. K. Hussey c Johnson b Blackwell	87		†T. M. B. Bailey not out	0
G. P. Swann c Trego b Bulbeck	24			
M. B. Loye st Turner b Blackwell	56		L-b 6, w 3	9
D. J. Sales c Francis b Dutch	76			
R. J. Warren b Blackwell	19		1/55 (2) 2/160 (1) (6 wkts, 50 overs) 299	
A. L. Penberthy st Turner b Dutch	20		3/196 (3) 4/242 (5)	
J. W. Cook not out	8		5/272 (6) 6/297 (4)	

R. S. G. Anderson, D. M. Cousins and C. G. Greenidge did not bat.

Bowling: Johnson 6–0–37–0; Bulbeck 10–0–38–1; Trego 6–0–39–0; Dutch 10–0–64–2; Francis 8–0–69–0; Blackwell 10–0–46–3.

Somerset

*J. Cox c Bailey b Greenidge	0		S. R. G. Francis run out	21
P. D. Bowler lbw b Anderson	21		R. L. Johnson not out	1
M. Burns c Bailey b Greenidge	23			
I. D. Blackwell c Cousins b Anderson . .	8		L-b 4, w 9	13
K. A. Parsons b Penberthy	1			
†R. J. Turner c Sales b Swann	33		1/0 (1) 2/33 (3) 3/54 (4) (34.1 overs) 154	
K. P. Dutch lbw b Swann	16		4/56 (2) 5/58 (5) 6/91 (7)	
P. D. Trego b Swann	3		7/105 (8) 8/131 (9)	
M. P. L. Bulbeck st Bailey b Swann . . .	14		9/146 (6) 10/154 (10)	

Bowling: Greenidge 7.1–1–29–2; Cousins 8–1–25–0; Anderson 5–0–21–2; Penberthy 7–1–46–1; Swann 7–2–29–4.

Umpires: J. W. Holder and P. Willey.

WARWICKSHIRE v WORCESTERSHIRE

At Birmingham, May 3. Worcestershire won by three wickets. Toss: Warwickshire. County debut: M. S. Mason.

A pitch of variable bounce made for treacherous batting but fascinating cricket. The wicket used against Somerset five days earlier was revived after water ran on to the intended pitch, with the result that good-length balls jumped alarmingly and short ones scudded through. Bell was the only batsman who played with confidence, while Bichel in Warwickshire's innings and Richardson in Worcestershire's amply demonstrated that full, straight bowling could gain reward. In such circumstances, chasing 130 was never straightforward and, with Worcestershire 73 for seven, Warwickshire were clear favourites. But Leatherdale and Lampitt sensibly looked to score from the occasional medium-pace of Powell, and Worcestershire crawled over the line with nine balls to spare.

Gold Award: D. A. Leatherdale.

Warwickshire

N. V. Knight b Bichel	2
N. M. K. Smith c Ali b Mason	15
D. R. Brown b Ali	13
I. R. Bell c Lampitt b Leatherdale	40
*M. J. Powell c Batty b Bichel	30
T. L. Penney c Lampitt b Bichel	1
J. O. Troughton b Leatherdale	14
S. M. Pollock run out	2
†K. J. Piper run out	7

M. A. Sheikh c Smith b Bichel	3
A. Richardson not out	1
B 1, w 1	2

1/10 (1) 2/20 (2) 3/37 (3)   (44.4 overs) 130
4/99 (5) 5/101 (6) 6/114 (4)
7/119 (7) 8/119 (8)
9/129 (9) 10/130 (10)

Bowling: Bichel 9.4–2–24–4; Mason 8–1–27–1; Ali 7–2–14–1; Lampitt 10–1–27–0; Batty 3–0–19–0; Leatherdale 7–1–18–2.

Worcestershire

V. S. Solanki b Brown	3
G. J. Batty lbw b Richardson	22
S. D. Peters b Sheikh	5
*G. A. Hick b Sheikh	0
B. F. Smith lbw b Richardson	9
D. A. Leatherdale not out	43
A. J. Bichel lbw b Richardson	9

†S. J. Rhodes b Richardson	0
S. R. Lampitt not out	20
L-b 12, w 8	20

1/22 (1) 2/29 (3)   (7 wkts, 48.3 overs) 131
3/29 (4) 4/47 (5)
5/51 (2) 6/73 (7) 7/73 (8)

Kabir Ali and M. S. Mason did not bat.

Bowling: Pollock 10–3–18–0; Brown 10–1–19–1; Sheikh 10–1–28–2; Richardson 10–2–21–4; Powell 6.3–0–27–0; Bell 2–0–6–0.

Umpires: G. I. Burgess and J. W. Lloyds.

GLOUCESTERSHIRE v SOMERSET

At Bristol, May 5. Gloucestershire won by 39 runs. Toss: Gloucestershire.

A match which ebbed and flowed was decided by the nerveless Harvey just when the tide was turning Somerset's way. Alleyne brought him back with Turner and Dutch going well and requiring 48 from 42 balls. Under pressure, Harvey produced his full repertoire of variations, and made clean hitting difficult. He bamboozled Dutch with a very slow delivery to end a partnership of 86 off 54 balls and then guaranteed Gloucestershire a quarter-final place by winning two more lbw decisions, taking his total in the game to five. Earlier, Gloucestershire's battery of all-rounders had resuscitated their innings after a brief wobble at 117 for four. Between them, Alleyne, Snape and Ball hit 119 from 116 balls.

Gold Award: I. J. Harvey.

Gloucestershire

C. M. Spearman c Trescothick b Bulbeck	20
K. J. Barnett b Blackwell	67
I. J. Harvey c Turner b Francis	24
C. G. Taylor c Cox b Dutch	22
M. G. N. Windows c Cox b Parsons . . .	2
*M. W. Alleyne c Wood b Dutch	47
J. N. Snape c Burns b Caddick	35

M. C. J. Ball not out	37
†R. C. Russell not out	1
L-b 8, w 5, n-b 2	15

1/26 (1) 2/67 (3)   (7 wkts, 50 overs) 270
3/111 (4) 4/117 (5)
5/176 (2) 6/221 (6) 7/266 (7)

J. M. M. Averis and J. Lewis did not bat.

Bowling: Bulbeck 10–0–52–1; Caddick 10–2–39–1; Francis 6–0–49–1; Parsons 8–0–39–1; Dutch 9–0–43–2; Blackwell 7–0–40–1.

Somerset

*M. E. Trescothick c Snape b Alleyne	47	
M. J. Wood lbw b Harvey	2	
J. Cox lbw b Harvey	0	
M. Burns c and b Snape	61	
K. A. Parsons b Snape	14	
I. D. Blackwell c Russell b Lewis	8	
†R. J. Turner c and b Ball	36	
K. P. Dutch lbw b Harvey	45	
M. P. L. Bulbeck lbw b Harvey	1	

A. R. Caddick lbw b Harvey	1	
S. R. G. Francis not out	1	
L-b 12, w 1, n-b 2	15	

1/7 (2) 2/9 (3) 3/92 (1)   (45.5 overs) 231
4/117 (5) 5/138 (6)
6/142 (4) 7/228 (8)
8/228 (7) 9/230 (9) 10/231 (10)

Bowling: Harvey 7.5–1–20–5; Lewis 8–1–40–1; Averis 6–0–46–0; Alleyne 9–0–43–1; Ball 9–0–32–1; Snape 6–0–38–2.

Umpires: A. Clarkson and M. J. Kitchen.

WARWICKSHIRE v NORTHAMPTONSHIRE

At Birmingham, May 5. Warwickshire won by six wickets. Toss: Warwickshire.

Powell's first one-day hundred and an accomplished fifty from Bell won the day for Warwickshire, but their task should have been tougher: Northamptonshire were 136 for one, then 179 for three, before their last seven wickets fell for 47. Hussey's misguided attempt to savage Brown after an innings of masterful cuts and pulls was a key moment; a farcical collision between Anderson and Bailey, which ended a promising partnership, was another. Powell promoted himself to open the Warwickshire reply and saw the job through to the end. A Northamptonshire win would have taken them through to the quarter-finals; Warwickshire's victory, though they didn't know it, was just enough to put them third in the group – and on the path to Lord's.

Gold Award: M. J. Powell.

Northamptonshire

*M. E. K. Hussey b Brown	84	
G. P. Swann b Pollock	4	
M. B. Loye lbw b Richardson	57	
D. J. Sales lbw b Giles	13	
J. W. Cook c Knight b Powell	12	
R. J. Warren c Bell b Giles	3	
A. L. Penberthy c and b Powell	9	
†T. M. B. Bailey run out	6	
R. S. G. Anderson b Brown	19	

C. G. Greenidge b Pollock	3	
D. M. Cousins not out	1	
L-b 4, w 11	15	

1/13 (2) 2/136 (3)   (48.5 overs) 226
3/157 (1) 4/179 (4)
5/179 (5) 6/182 (6) 7/197 (7)
8/221 (8) 9/222 (9) 10/226 (10)

Bowling: Pollock 9.5–3–18–2; Brown 9–0–53–2; Richardson 10–0–32–1; Warren 6–0–45–0; Giles 10–0–52–2; Powell 4–0–22–2.

Warwickshire

*M. J. Powell not out	101	
N. V. Knight lbw b Greenidge	8	
S. M. Pollock run out	21	
I. R. Bell b Swann	56	
J. O. Troughton c Sales b Greenidge	14	

T. L. Penney not out	16	
L-b 5, w 3, n-b 4	12	

1/24 (2) 2/82 (3)   (4 wkts, 49.1 overs) 228
3/171 (4) 4/204 (5)

D. R. Brown, A. F. Giles, †K. J. Piper, N. A. Warren and A. Richardson did not bat.

Bowling: Greenidge 10–1–54–2; Cousins 8.1–1–27–0; Anderson 10–0–36–0; Cook 4–0–27–0; Penberthy 10–0–42–0; Swann 7–0–37–1.

Umpires: R. Palmer and J. F. Steele.

This tour made history of a thoroughly undesirable sort.
The Indians in South Africa, page 1200

WORCESTERSHIRE v GLAMORGAN

At Worcester, May 5. Worcestershire won by five wickets. Toss: Worcestershire.

Solanki, often accused of putting style before substance, married the two expertly in a match-winning innings. He cantered to fifty in 41 balls, hit 15 fours – largely with elegant drives through the off side – and steered Worcestershire to the cusp of victory. When he was third out at 151, Worcestershire were 41 short of their target, after Glamorgan failed to pass 200 for the third time in three completed games. Even so, it was a bigger total than might have been expected when Bichel and Mason reduced them to 108 for six.

Gold Award: V. S. Solanki.

Glamorgan

K. Newell lbw b Bichel	13	M. S. Kasprowicz not out	33
D. L. Hemp b Mason	6	A. P. Davies not out	7
R. D. B. Croft b Ali	20	L-b 5, w 3, n-b 2	10
*S. P. James b Bichel	0		
A. Dale c Smith b Mason	42	1/18 (2) 2/35 (1) (8 wkts, 50 overs) 191
M. J. Powell c Batty b Mason	18	3/35 (4) 4/49 (3)
†M. A. Wallace c Hick b Bichel	31	5/107 (5) 6/108 (6)
S. D. Thomas c Smith b Leatherdale	11	7/130 (8) 8/164 (7)
O. T. Parkin did not bat.			

Bowling: Bichel 10–2–24–3; Mason 10–0–49–3; Ali 10–3–28–1; Lampitt 9–0–33–0; Batty 4–0–17–0; Leatherdale 7–0–35–1.

Worcestershire

S. D. Peters c Parkin b Croft	36	A. J. Bichel not out	4
V. S. Solanki c Wallace b Thomas	90	B 1, l-b 6, w 2	9
*G. A. Hick b Thomas	16		
B. F. Smith not out	23	1/112 (1) 2/142 (3) (5 wkts, 39.4 overs) 192
D. A. Leatherdale b Dale	14	3/151 (2) 4/187 (5)
G. J. Batty b Parkin	0	5/188 (6)

†S. J. Rhodes, Kabir Ali, S. R. Lampitt and M. S. Mason did not bat.

Bowling: Kasprowicz 8–2–30–0; Parkin 5.4–0–31–1; Davies 10–0–53–0; Thomas 8–0–34–2; Dale 4–2–15–1; Croft 4–0–22–1.

Umpires: D. J. Constant and B. Dudleston.

GLAMORGAN v WARWICKSHIRE

At Cardiff, May 6. Warwickshire won by 58 runs. Toss: Glamorgan.

Pollock's earlier performances in the group games were merely tidy; this was world-class. Sent in at No. 3 on a wicket that encouraged the bowlers throughout, he drove straight and hard, putting on 109 with his captain, Powell. Glamorgan again started badly, with the top four contributing just 49 runs. Wallace and the other Powell – Michael John of Glamorgan – rallied, but Pollock, now excelling with the ball, suffocated the innings and finished with four for 12. Glamorgan, one of three counties never to win the B&H Cup, suffered a record 70th competition defeat, their tenth in succession.

Gold Award: S. M. Pollock.

Warwickshire

*M. J. Powell c Wallace b Croft	74	A. F. Giles not out 21
N. V. Knight c Dale b Kasprowicz	2	†K. J. Piper not out 13
S. M. Pollock c Hemp b Dale	64	L-b 5, w 7 12
I. R. Bell lbw b Croft	3	
J. O. Troughton c and b Thomas	42	1/20 (2) 2/129 (3) (8 wkts, 50 overs) 261
T. L. Penney run out	1	3/137 (4) 4/191 (1)
D. R. Brown c Powell b Parkin	19	5/193 (6) 6/203 (5)
N. M. K. Smith b Davies	10	7/218 (8) 8/237 (7)

A. Richardson did not bat.

Bowling: Kasprowicz 10–1–49–1; Parkin 9–1–49–1; Davies 8–0–44–1; Thomas 8–2–40–1; Croft 10–0–51–2; Dale 5–0–23–1.

Glamorgan

K. Newell c Piper b Pollock	0	A. P. Davies not out 8
D. L. Hemp c Bell b Giles	36	O. T. Parkin b Pollock 1
R. D. B. Croft c Bell b Brown	13	
*S. P. James b Pollock	0	B 1, l-b 7, w 7 15
A. Dale c Brown b Giles	12	
M. J. Powell run out	51	1/0 (1) 2/21 (3) 3/22 (4) (47 overs) 203
†M. A. Wallace c Bell b Brown	39	4/54 (5) 5/90 (2) 6/154 (7)
S. D. Thomas c Troughton b Pollock	19	7/175 (6) 8/192 (8)
M. S. Kasprowicz c Bell b Brown	9	9/197 (9) 10/203 (11)

Bowling: Pollock 9–3–12–4; Brown 10–1–52–3; Richardson 8–1–31–0; Giles 10–0–46–2; Smith 10–0–54–0.

Umpires: A. Clarkson and N. J. Llong.

NORTHAMPTONSHIRE v GLOUCESTERSHIRE

At Northampton, May 6. Northamptonshire won by 118 runs. Toss: Gloucestershire.

Northamptonshire won a surprising victory over their in-form opponents, but results elsewhere denied them a quarter-final place. Gloucestershire, already assured of theirs, were set for another routine victory when Harvey took advantage of helpful conditions to put Northamptonshire on the slide. Warren and Cook added 116 as batting became easier, but a total of 212 from 44 overs looked vulnerable against an experienced batting line-up on a quick outfield. Blain bowled with pace and accuracy, but Gloucestershire's response was uncharacteristically supine. Russell and Averis resisted doggedly, though there was no recovery from 48 for eight.

Gold Award: J. A. R. Blain.

Northamptonshire

*M. E. K. Hussey lbw b Harvey	9	J. W. Cook not out 45
G. P. Swann c Barnett b Averis	19	B 4, l-b 4, w 4, n-b 2 14
M. B. Loye c Russell b Harvey	1	
D. J. Sales c Ball b Alleyne	17	1/15 (1) 2/23 (3) (5 wkts, 44 overs) 212
R. J. Warren not out	78	3/50 (4) 4/52 (2)
A. L. Penberthy lbw b Averis	29	5/96 (6)

†T. M. B. Bailey, R. S. G. Anderson, D. M. Cousins and J. A. R. Blain did not bat.

Bowling: Lewis 9–1–38–0; Harvey 9–1–33–2; Alleyne 6–0–23–1; Averis 9–1–61–2; Ball 7–0–29–0; Snape 4–0–20–0.

Gloucestershire

K. J. Barnett c Swann b Blain	....	0
C. M. Spearman b Blain	....	17
I. J. Harvey c Bailey b Blain	.....	5
C. G. Taylor lbw b Blain	....	2
M. G. N. Windows c Cook b Penberthy	.	10
*M. W. Alleyne lbw b Penberthy	.....	5
J. N. Snape c Bailey b Anderson	.....	1
†R. C. Russell not out	....	25

M. C. J. Ball b Anderson	....	0
J. M. M. Averis b Blain	....	20
J. Lewis c Cousins b Anderson	......	0
L-b 2, w 3, n-b 4	....	9

1/0 (1) 2/6 (3) 3/8 (4) (24 overs) 94
4/33 (2) 5/46 (6) 6/47 (7)
7/47 (5) 8/48 (9) 9/82 (10) 10/94 (11)

Bowling: Blain 8–1–30–5; Cousins 5–1–18–0; Anderson 7–2–28–3; Penberthy 4–1–16–2.

Umpires: D. J. Constant and J. F. Steele.

SOMERSET v WORCESTERSHIRE

At Taunton, May 6. Worcestershire won by seven wickets (D/L method). Toss: Somerset.

The wisdom of Trescothick's decision to bat on a fresh pitch was debatable, though it was a series of rash shots that reduced Somerset to 60 for six. They eventually hobbled to 126 for nine from 32 overs. Duckworth/Lewis calculations revised Worcestershire's target to 121 from 32, though they required just 19 to complete a comfortable win and take them to the knockout stage for the first time since 1995. Hick, who had managed 85 in his previous nine B&H innings, smashed 39 in 22 balls, while Solanki, with his third significant score of the group matches, eased his way to an unbeaten 48.

Gold Award: A. J. Bichel.

Somerset

*M. E. Trescothick c Ali b Bichel	.....	20
M. J. Wood c Rhodes b Mason	....	4
J. Cox c Rhodes b Mason	......	6
M. Burns c Hick b Mason	....	6
K. A. Parsons c Smith b Bichel	.....	5
I. D. Blackwell b Lampitt	....	2
†R. J. Turner b Lampitt	....	30
K. P. Dutch b Lampitt	....	16
P. D. Trego not out	....	15

M. P. L. Bulbeck c Solanki b Ali	.....	7
A. R. Caddick not out	....	4
L-b 2, w 3, n-b 6	....	11

1/8 (2) 2/26 (1) (9 wkts, 32 overs) 126
3/31 (3) 4/36 (5)
5/51 (4) 6/60 (6)
7/87 (7) 8/98 (8) 9/121 (10)

Bowling: Bichel 7–1–19–2; Mason 6–1–33–3; Ali 7–1–16–1; Lampitt 6–0–28–3; Leatherdale 6–0–28–0.

Worcestershire

S. D. Peters c Bulbeck b Caddick	.....	8
V. S. Solanki not out	....	48
*G. A. Hick c and b Parsons	....	39
B. F. Smith lbw b Trego	....	1
D. A. Leatherdale not out	....	17
W 9	....	9

1/18 (1) 2/77 (3) (3 wkts, 19 overs) 122
3/78 (4)

G. J. Batty, A. J. Bichel, †S. J. Rhodes, Kabir Ali, S. R. Lampitt and M. S. Mason did not bat.

Bowling: Caddick 5–1–39–1; Bulbeck 5–0–27–0; Trego 5–1–39–1; Parsons 4–1–17–1.

Umpires: N. G. Cowley and J. H. Evans.

NORTH GROUP

DERBYSHIRE v LANCASHIRE

At Derby, April 28. No result. Toss: Derbyshire.

The two teams who had propped up the North Group in 2001 had little chance to show they could do better this time. Play was possible only in the early afternoon, and Lancashire had just lost their second wicket when the rain returned. After several more inspections, the game was abandoned.

Lancashire

M. J. Chilton not out	. . . .	3
G. Chapple lbw b Dean	. . . .	4
D. Byas b Cork	. . . .	3
	L-b 1, n-b 6	7

1/8 (2) 2/17 (3)   (2 wkts, 4.3 overs) 17

S. G. Law, G. D. Lloyd, T. W. Roberts, *†W. K. Hegg, C. P. Schofield, K. W. Hogg, J. Wood and M. P. Smethurst did not bat.

Bowling: Cork 2.3–0–10–1; Dean 2–0–6–1.

Derbyshire

S. D. Stubbings, M. J. Di Venuto, *D. G. Cork, S. A. Selwood, C. W. G. Bassano, D. R. Hewson, Mohammad Ali, †K. M. Krikken, T. Lungley, G. Welch and K. J. Dean.

Umpires: B. Dudleston and J. F. Steele.

NOTTINGHAMSHIRE v YORKSHIRE

At Nottingham, April 28. Yorkshire won by two runs (D/L method). Toss: Nottinghamshire.

Klusener, who had already pulled White for six, needed four from his final ball but, to Yorkshire's great relief, managed only a single to third man. As a blustery day had deteriorated, Nottinghamshire's target was revised three times, eventually settling on 71 from 13 overs. In the morning, Smith had reduced Yorkshire to 46 for four in a fiery 15-ball spell, before Lehmann fought back, sharing a 109-run stand with McGrath. The lower order fell away, however, and Nottinghamshire were still favourites at 35 for one after eight overs.

Gold Award: G. J. Smith.

Yorkshire

M. J. Wood b Smith	. . . .	14	T. T. Bresnan not out	. . . .	1
C. White c Read b Smith	. . . .	9	R. J. Sidebottom c Read b Harris	. . . .	1
C. E. W. Silverwood b Smith	. . . .	9			
M. J. Lumb c Afzaal b Smith	. . . .	6		L-b 3, w 9, n-b 6	18
*D. S. Lehmann c Shafayat b Harris	. . .	89			
A. McGrath b Malik	. . . .	48	1/25 (2) 2/34 (1) (47.4 overs) 225		
G. M. Fellows lbw b Clough	. . . .	13	3/37 (3) 4/46 (4) 5/155 (6)		
†R. J. Blakey c Read b Smith	. . . .	9	6/191 (7) 7/215 (5) 8/215 (8)		
R. K. J. Dawson b Harris	. . . .	8	9/223 (9) 10/225 (11)		

Bowling: Smith 10–2–39–5; Malik 8–0–36–1; Harris 9.4–0–52–3; Klusener 8–0–38–0; Clough 5–0–21–1; Pietersen 7–0–36–0.

Nottinghamshire

D. J. Bicknell c and b Sidebottom	. . . . .	10
*J. E. R. Gallian st Blakey b Dawson	. .	22
L. Klusener not out	. . . .	29
K. P. Pietersen c Blakey b White	. . . . . .	2
U. Afzaal not out	. . . .	1
L-b 3, w 1	. . . .	4

1/28 (1) 2/55 (2)   (3 wkts, 13 overs) 68
3/66 (4)

B. M. Shafayat, †C. M. W. Read, A. J. Harris, G. D. Clough, G. J. Smith and M. N. Malik did not bat.

Bowling: Silverwood 4–1–17–0; Bresnan 3–0–8–0; Sidebottom 1–0–7–1; White 2–0–19–1; Dawson 2–0–7–1; Lehmann 1–0–7–0.

Umpires: V. A. Holder and J. W. Lloyds.

LEICESTERSHIRE v DURHAM

At Leicester, April 29. Leicestershire won by 32 runs. Toss: Leicestershire. County debut: J. O. Grove.

A double-century stand between Ward and Bevan propelled Leicestershire to 316 for six, the most conceded by Durham in the competition, beating Leicestershire's own 289 for six in 1996. Bevan, emerging for his home debut after Harmison struck Wells's forearm and forced him off, added 202 in 33 overs with Ward, who hit two sixes and 17 fours in 143 balls and knocked Peng over the rope after striking him in the chest. Bevan swept on to 113 from 102 deliveries. Peng led Durham's reply, but was bowled by Wells, back after a precautionary X-ray. Despite strong support down the order, Leicestershire's attack, without Malcolm and DeFreitas, maintained the advantage.

Gold Award: T. R. Ward.

Leicestershire

T. R. Ward b Collingwood	. . . .	127	R. J. Cunliffe not out	9
I. J. Sutcliffe c A. Pratt b Harmison	. . . .	10	C. D. Crowe not out	7
*V. J. Wells retired hurt	. . . .	0	B 6, l-b 12, w 11	29
M. G. Bevan b Killeen	. . . .	113		
D. L. Maddy c G. J. Pratt b Hunter	. . . .	19	1/34 (2) 2/240 (1) (6 wkts, 50 overs) 316
D. I. Stevens c Peng b Killeen	. . . .	1	3/279 (4) 4/295 (6)
†N. D. Burns c Harmison b Hunter	. . . .	1	5/298 (5) 6/298 (7)

J. O. Grove and M. J. A. Whiley did not bat.

Wells retired hurt at 38.

Bowling: Killeen 10–4–28–2; Harmison 10–1–63–1; Hunter 10–0–68–2; Davies 7–0–52–0; Collingwood 8–1–54–1; Bridge 5–0–33–0.

Durham

N. Peng b Wells	. . . .	67	N. Killeen lbw b Maddy	0
†A. Pratt b Whiley	. . . .	4	A. M. Davies not out	18
M. L. Love c Bevan b Maddy	. . . . . .	25	B 7, l-b 10, w 2, n-b 8	27
P. D. Collingwood c and b Maddy	. . . . .	8		
*J. J. B. Lewis c Crowe	. . . .	31	1/33 (2) 2/80 (3) (8 wkts, 50 overs) 284
G. J. Pratt c Ward b Crowe	. . . .	15	3/96 (4) 4/127 (1)
I. D. Hunter c Maddy b Grove	. . . . . .	39	5/150 (6) 6/162 (5)
G. D. Bridge not out	. . . .	50	7/222 (7) 8/222 (9)

S. J. Harmison did not bat.

Bowling: Grove 9–0–53–1; Whiley 10–1–48–1; Wells 7–0–42–1; Maddy 10–1–53–3; Crowe 10–0–42–2; Bevan 4–0–29–0.

Umpires: N. J. Llong and J. F. Steele.

NOTTINGHAMSHIRE v DERBYSHIRE

At Nottingham, April 30. Nottinghamshire won by ten wickets. Toss: Nottinghamshire.

Rain finally allowed a start at 4.55, with the teams limited to ten overs a side. By the seventh, Derbyshire's openers had raised 52. But once they were parted, Smith yorked three men in five balls, and Nottinghamshire's eventual target was 73. A rush of runs from Read and Klusener secured the points with ten balls to spare.

Gold Award: G. J. Smith.

Derbyshire

S. D. Stubbings c Clough b Klusener	26		C. W. G. Bassano not out		3
M. J. Di Venuto c Pietersen b Clough	30				
*D. G. Cork b Smith	8		B 1, l-b 1, w 1		3
S. A. Selwood c Clough b Harris	2				
D. R. Hewson b Smith	0		1/52 (2) 2/65 (1)	(7 wkts, 10 overs)	72
Mohammad Ali b Smith	0		3/68 (3) 4/68 (5)		
J. I. D. Kerr c Read b Harris	0		5/68 (6) 6/69 (7) 7/72 (4)		

†K. M. Krikken, G. Welch and T. Lungley did not bat.

Bowling: Smith 2–0–8–3; Malik 2–0–10–0; Klusener 2–0–18–1; Pietersen 1–0–11–0; Harris 2–0–17–2; Clough 1–0–6–1.

Nottinghamshire

†C. M. W. Read not out	35
L. Klusener not out	39
L-b 1	1
(no wkt, 8.2 overs)	75

*J. E. R. Gallian, G. E. Welton, U. Afzaal, K. P. Pietersen, B. M. Shafayat, G. D. Clough, A. J. Harris, G. J. Smith and M. N. Malik did not bat.

Bowling: Cork 2–0–18–0; Lungley 2–0–15–0; Ali 2–0–17–0; Welch 1.2–0–20–0; Kerr 1–0–4–0.

Umpires: T. E. Jesty and A. G. T. Whitehead.

DURHAM v LANCASHIRE

At Chester-le-Street, May 1. Durham won by 16 runs (D/L method). Toss: Durham.

Durham claimed their first victory of the summer despite slumping to 67 for six. The later order rallied to 166 before their seamers successfully stifled the Lancashire batsmen. Durham's recovery had been started by Gough, who put on 41 with Hunter. He shared the highest stand of the match – 58 in nine overs – with Bridge, who top-scored with a 33-ball 37 from No. 9. Frequent showers had shortened Durham's innings, and further rain revised Lancashire's target to 171 from 42 overs. Bridge added two wickets with his left-arm spin, while Killeen and Davies matched Hogg's economy earlier in the day; only three Lancastrians reached double figures.

Gold Award: G. D. Bridge.

Durham

N. Peng c Hegg b Chapple	1	I. D. Hunter c Martin b Wood	24
†A. Pratt lbw b Martin	1	G. D. Bridge not out	37
M. L. Love b Wood	34	L-b 8, w 8	16
P. D. Collingwood lbw b Chapple	6		
*J. J. B. Lewis b Hogg	13	1/2 (1) 2/5 (2) (7 wkts, 44 overs) 166
G. J. Pratt c Roberts b Wood	2	3/20 (4) 4/57 (3)
M. A. Gough not out	32	5/65 (6) 6/67 (5) 7/108 (8)

A. M. Davies and N. Killeen did not bat.

Bowling: Martin 9–0–42–1; Chapple 8–1–26–2; Hogg 9–2–13–1; Wood 9–0–33–3; Schofield 8–0–41–0; Chilton 1–0–3–0.

Lancashire

M. J. Chilton c Love b Hunter	9	J. Wood c A. Pratt b Killeen	6
G. Chapple b Killeen	0	P. J. Martin b Collingwood	5
D. Byas c Love b Davies	29		
S. G. Law lbw b Killeen	4	L-b 12, w 9	21
G. D. Lloyd b Collingwood	9		
T. W. Roberts c Lewis b Bridge	33	1/13 (2) 2/36 (1) 3/41 (4) (41 overs) 154
C. P. Schofield b Bridge	6	4/57 (5) 5/85 (3) 6/101 (7)
*†W. K. Hegg c Hunter	26	7/124 (6) 8/138 (8)
K. W. Hogg not out	6	9/147 (10) 10/154 (11)

Bowling: Killeen 8–1–12–3; Hunter 8–0–38–2; Davies 9–2–12–1; Collingwood 8–0–37–2; Bridge 8–0–43–2.

Umpires: A. Clarkson and G. Sharp.

YORKSHIRE v LEICESTERSHIRE

At Leeds, May 1. Leicestershire won by six runs (D/L method). Toss: Leicestershire.

With 36 required from six overs, seven wickets in hand and White closing in on a century, Yorkshire were firm favourites to overhaul a revised target of 221 in 45 overs. But rash strokeplay cost them five wickets and left them needing 14 off the last over. Bevan bowled White for 93 and kept them down to seven. Earlier, Bevan scored 48 and shared a 97-run stand with Sutcliffe, before risky shots sent Leicestershire sliding to 184 for seven. Burns ensured a competitive total by cracking 44 from 29 balls.

Gold Award: M. G. Bevan.

Leicestershire

T. R. Ward run out	15	R. J. Cunliffe c White b Fellows	2
I. J. Sutcliffe c Fellows b White	65	C. D. Crowe not out	2
*V. J. Wells c Blakey b Silverwood	2	L-b 3, w 8	11
M. G. Bevan lbw b Lehmann	48		
D. L. Maddy c Sidebottom b Fellows	19	1/17 (1) 2/25 (3) (7 wkts, 46 overs) 221
D. I. Stevens c Sidebottom b Fellows	6	3/122 (4) 4/157 (2)
†N. D. Burns not out	44	5/166 (5) 6/179 (6) 7/184 (8)

J. O. Grove and M. J. A. Whiley did not bat.

Bowling: Silverwood 8–0–41–1; Bresnan 9–0–29–0; White 9–1–44–1; Lehmann 7–0–26–1; Dawson 2–0–15–0; Sidebottom 6–0–32–0; Fellows 5–0–31–3.

Yorkshire

M. J. Wood c Whiley b Grove	2	R. K. J. Dawson not out	5
C. White b Bevan	93	T. T. Bresnan not out	1
C. E. W. Silverwood c Stevens b Whiley	11	B 2, l-b 12, w 10, n-b 2	26
M. J. Lumb c Bevan b Crowe	43		
*D. S. Lehmann c Maddy b Whiley	25	1/9 (1) 2/24 (3) (8 wkts, 45 overs) 214	
A. McGrath c Grove b Maddy	4	3/134 (4) 4/185 (5)	
G. M. Fellows c Bevan b Crowe	2	5/196 (6) 6/198 (7)	
†R. J. Blakey c Cunliffe b Crowe	2	7/203 (8) 8/210 (2)	

R. J. Sidebottom did not bat.

Bowling: Grove 9–1–33–1; Whiley 9–0–40–2; Maddy 9–0–44–1; Wells 9–0–44–0; Crowe 8–0–35–3; Bevan 1–0–4–1.

Umpires: M. R. Benson and N. A. Mallender.

DURHAM v YORKSHIRE

At Chester-le-Street, May 2. Yorkshire won by 124 runs. Toss: Yorkshire.

White, carrying on where he had left off the previous day, was this time rewarded with victory. His 71, at almost a run a ball, set Yorkshire on the road to a confident 271, bolstered by Lehmann's 72 from 87. Lehmann's left-arm spin later claimed three key wickets as Durham slumped to 147 all out, with Davies absent, after feeling breathless and dizzy during his morning spell. When he trapped Wood lbw, he could not muster the voice to join the fielders' appeal. Davies had suffered a collapsed lung the previous year, but hospital tests suggested a virus was to blame this time.

Gold Award: C. White.

Yorkshire

C. White lbw b Bridge	71	†R. J. Blakey not out	7
M. J. Wood lbw b Davies	8	A. K. D. Gray not out	10
C. E. W. Silverwood b Killeen	16	B 1, l-b 8, w 12	21
*M. J. Lumb run out	25		
*D. S. Lehmann c sub b Killeen	72	1/19 (2) 2/64 (3) (7 wkts, 50 overs) 271	
A. McGrath c sub b Collingwood	37	3/117 (4) 4/143 (1)	
G. M. Fellows run out	4	5/246 (5) 6/252 (6) 7/256 (7)	

T. T. Bresnan and R. J. Sidebottom did not bat.

Bowling: Killeen 10–0–43–2; Davies 3–0–19–1; Hunter 10–0–59–0; Symington 7–0–53–0; Collingwood 10–0–42–1; Bridge 10–0–46–1.

Durham

N. Peng lbw b Silverwood	4	N. Killeen not out	7
†A. Pratt c Silverwood b White	16	A. M. Davies absent ill	
M. L. Love c and b Bresnan	0		
P. D. Collingwood c Wood b Lehmann	33	W 3	3
*J. J. B. Lewis c and b Lehmann	27		
G. J. Pratt b Lehmann	23	1/9 (1) 2/10 (3) (44.4 overs) 147	
M. J. Symington lbw b Fellows	32	3/38 (2) 4/81 (5)	
I. D. Hunter c White b Gray	5	5/88 (4) 6/118 (6)	
G. D. Bridge b Fellows	2	7/119 (8) 8/126 (9) 9/147 (7)	

Bowling: Silverwood 6–1–15–1; Bresnan 7–1–13–1; White 5–0–31–1; Sidebottom 5–2–13–0; Lehmann 8–0–29–3; Gray 10–0–33–1; Fellows 3.4–0–13–2.

Umpires: M. J. Harris and G. Sharp.

DERBYSHIRE v LEICESTERSHIRE

At Derby, May 3. No result (D/L method). Toss: Derbyshire.

Rain halted Leicestershire's innings and then washed out Derbyshire's promising assault on a revised target of 82 from ten overs. They were ahead of the required rate, with Hewson unbeaten on 26 from 14 balls, when they were forced to stop. A share of the points kept Leicestershire top of the North Group – while Derbyshire remained bottom.

Leicestershire

T. R. Ward b Lungley	. . . .	36
I. J. Sutcliffe not out	. . . .	52
*V. J. Wells c Krikken b Lungley	. . .	7
M. G. Bevan not out	. . . .	6
B 5, l-b 11, w 2	. . . .	18

1/73 (1) 2/102 (3)   (2 wkts, 32 overs) 119

D. L. Maddy, D. I. Stevens, M. J. A. Whiley, †N. D. Burns, P. A. J. DeFreitas, C. D. Crowe and J. O. Grove did not bat.

Bowling: Cork 6–2–15–0; Dean 7–1–22–0; Welch 6–1–20–0; Lungley 9–0–31–2; Ali 4–0–15–0.

Derbyshire

*D. G. Cork b Wells	. . . .	12
M. J. Di Venuto c Maddy b Whiley	. . . .	5
D. R. Hewson not out	. . . .	26
C. W. G. Bassano not out	. . . .	3
L-b 2, w 1, n-b 2	. . . .	5

1/8 (2) 2/45 (1)   (2 wkts, 5.1 overs) 51

S. D. Stubbings, S. A. Selwood, †K. M. Krikken, T. Lungley, G. Welch, K. J. Dean and Mohammad Ali did not bat.

Bowling: Grove 2–0–21–0; Whiley 1–0–10–1; Maddy 1–0–14–0; Wells 1–0–3–1; DeFreitas 0.1–0–1–0.

Umpires: D. J. Constant and J. H. Evans.

LANCASHIRE v NOTTINGHAMSHIRE

At Manchester, May 3. Lancashire won by 76 runs (D/L method). Toss: Nottinghamshire.

Chilton's maiden one-day century brought Lancashire their first win of the tournament. He struck nine fours in 120 balls, and enjoyed plenty of help from his colleagues – as well as from Nottinghamshire, who bowled poorly and fielded sloppily. Rain left them to chase 215 in 27 overs, but they were bowled out for 138 as their middle order was wrecked by Wood, who claimed four wickets. Four runs and ten costly overs completed a bad day for Klusener, Nottinghamshire's stopgap overseas player.

Gold Award: M. J. Chilton.

Lancashire

M. J. Chilton c Clough b Klusener	102	*†W. K. Hegg not out	5
G. Chapple c Read b Harris	50	B 2, l-b 16, w 13	31
D. Byas c Clough b Harris	0		
S. G. Law st Read b Afzaal	47	(5 wkts, 50 overs) 297
G. D. Lloyd not out	49	1/89 (2) 2/93 (3)
T. W. Roberts c Pietersen b Smith	13	3/207 (4) 4/237 (1)
		5/281 (6)

C. P. Schofield, K. W. Hogg, P. J. Martin and J. Wood did not bat.

Bowling: Smith 10–0–52–1; Malik 6–0–31–0; Harris 10–0–56–2; Klusener 10–0–65–1; Pietersen 8–0–33–0; Clough 2–0–15–0; Afzaal 4–0–27–1.

Nottinghamshire

D. J. Bicknell c Chilton b Martin	12	A. J. Harris lbw b Hogg	3
†C. M. W. Read c Hegg b Martin	1	M. N. Malik not out	8
U. Afzaal c Chapple b Wood	23		
K. P. Pietersen c Law b Wood	29	L-b 5, w 2	7
L. Klusener b Hogg	4		
*J. E. R. Gallian c Schofield b Wood	25	1/12 (1) 2/23 (2) 3/42 (3)	(26 overs) 138
B. M. Shafayat c Chapple b Schofield	13	4/57 (5) 5/83 (4) 6/103 (6)
G. D. Clough lbw b Wood	2	7/106 (8) 8/126 (7)
G. J. Smith b Schofield	11	9/126 (9) 10/138 (10)

Bowling: Martin 5–1–23–2; Chapple 4–0–24–0; Hogg 5–0–28–2; Wood 6–0–31–4; Schofield 6–0–27–2.

Umpires: A. Clarkson and A. A. Jones.

DERBYSHIRE v YORKSHIRE

At Derby, May 4. Yorkshire won by 131 runs. Toss: Derbyshire.

Wood was stretchered off and needed nine stitches in his forehead after ducking into a delivery from the pacy Mohammad Ali. But he had already completed his first one-day hundred, which proved more than enough to ensure another convincing victory for Yorkshire. Derbyshire subsided for 157, just beating the opening stand of 146 between Wood, with 11 fours in 136 balls, and White, who passed 70 for the third match running. After Silverwood reduced Derbyshire to 35 for three, only Selwood resisted, until he became the first of Dawson's four victims, a one-day best.

Gold Award: M. J. Wood.

Yorkshire

M. J. Wood retired hurt	115	C. E. W. Silverwood c Selwood b Lungley	1
C. White b Selwood	77	R. K. J. Dawson not out	3
M. P. Vaughan c Hewson b Welch	27	L-b 15, w 10, n-b 4	29
*D. S. Lehmann b Ali	18		
A. McGrath lbw b Lungley	1	1/146 (2) 2/192 (3)	(6 wkts, 50 overs) 288
G. M. Fellows not out	13	3/244 (4) 4/253 (5)
†R. J. Blakey run out	4	5/272 (7) 6/274 (8)

T. T. Bresnan and M. J. Hoggard did not bat.

Wood retired hurt at 261.

Bowling: Cork 8–2–23–0; Dean 8–0–43–0; Lungley 9–0–54–2; Welch 8–0–51–1; Ali 7–0–54–1; Selwood 10–1–48–1.

Derbyshire

S. D. Stubbings c White b Silverwood	0	Mohammad Ali st Blakey b Dawson	0
M. J. Di Venuto c Blakey b Hoggard	16	K. J. Dean lbw b Dawson	1
C. W. G. Bassano b Silverwood	8		
D. R. Hewson b Silverwood	9	L-b 7, w 2	9
S. A. Selwood c Fellows b Dawson	62		
*D. G. Cork b Bresnan	19	1/0 (1) 2/13 (3) 3/35 (4) (37.3 overs) 157	
T. Lungley run out	17	4/49 (2) 5/95 (6)	
†K. M. Krikken not out	15	6/134 (7) 7/142 (5)	
G. Welch c and b Dawson	1	8/153 (9) 9/153 (10) 10/157 (11)	

Bowling: Silverwood 8–2–23–3; Hoggard 8–2–22–1; Bresnan 7–1–30–1; White 3–0–20–0; Lehmann 5–0–17–0; Fellows 3–0–25–0; Dawson 3.3–0–13–4.

Umpires: A. A. Jones and J. W. Lloyds.

NOTTINGHAMSHIRE v DURHAM

At Nottingham, May 4. Nottinghamshire won by five runs. Toss: Nottinghamshire.

Klusener redeemed himself in his final home game. First he made 68 in 89 balls, sedate by his standards despite a pulled six off Harmison. Then he claimed two vital wickets, including Peng, who top-scored in the match with 72 before falling to a one-handed catch by Read. Harris dismissed Durham's last two batsmen in the final over to scrape a tight win that kept Nottinghamshire in contention for the knockouts. Their captain, Gallian, had put them on course with a fifty, before Klusener and Read accelerated in a sixth-wicket stand of 68.

Gold Award: L. Klusener.

Nottinghamshire

D. J. Bicknell c Hunter b Killeen	9	†C. M. W. Read not out	36
*J. E. R. Gallian b Bridge	56	L-b 9, w 11, n-b 2	22
U. Afzaal run out	6		
K. P. Pietersen lbw b Killeen	6	1/9 (1) 2/29 (3) (6 wkts, 50 overs) 224	
P. Johnson c A. Pratt b Hunter	21	3/38 (4) 4/90 (5)	
L. Klusener run out	68	5/156 (2) 6/224 (6)	

G. D. Clough, G. J. Smith, A. J. Harris and M. N. Malik did not bat.

Bowling: Harmison 10–0–49–0; Killeen 10–1–30–2; Symington 6–1–29–0; Hunter 7–0–33–1; Bridge 10–0–30–1; Collingwood 7–0–44–0.

Durham

G. J. Pratt c Gallian b Harris	18	N. Killeen lbw b Harris	15
N. Peng c Read b Klusener	72	S. J. Harmison b Harris	0
M. L. Love c Read b Klusener	4		
P. D. Collingwood c Malik b Harris	8	L-b 8, w 6	14
*J. J. B. Lewis c Johnson b Pietersen	27		
†A. Pratt run out	38	1/37 (1) 2/75 (3) 3/88 (4) (49.4 overs) 219	
M. J. Symington c Klusener b Malik	13	4/122 (2) 5/152 (5) 6/193 (7)	
I. D. Hunter lbw b Pietersen	1	7/194 (8) 8/195 (6)	
G. D. Bridge not out	9	9/219 (10) 10/219 (11)	

Bowling: Smith 9–0–43–0; Malik 10–1–47–1; Harris 9.4–1–42–4; Klusener 10–0–31–2; Clough 2–0–12–0; Pietersen 9–0–36–2.

Umpires: B. Dudleston and R. Palmer.

LANCASHIRE v LEICESTERSHIRE

At Manchester, May 5. Leicestershire won by 17 runs. Toss: Leicestershire.

On a pitch bereft of pace but with occasional erratic bounce, Lancashire's unlikely destroyers were the medium-pace pair of Maddy and his captain, Wells, who picked up four wickets each. Flintoff, in his first county game of the year, was the only significant contributor with a steady 47. Leicestershire had been similarly reliant on a third successive fifty from Sutcliffe, the only man to pass 25 after Wells elected to bat. Leicestershire, winners of the first Benson and Hedges Cup, in 1972, were through to the knockout stage; Lancashire's progress was uncertain.

Gold Award: D. L. Maddy.

Leicestershire

T. R. Ward c Law b Martin	6	J. O. Grove not out 9
I. J. Sutcliffe run out	58	M. J. A. Whiley not out 3
*V. J. Wells lbw b Wood	13	
M. G. Bevan b Wood	12	B 1, l-b 2, w 8, n-b 2 13
D. L. Maddy c Law b Schofield	0	
D. I. Stevens c and b Schofield	5	1/23 (1) 2/47 (3) (9 wkts, 50 overs) 175
†N. D. Burns c Law b Martin	25	3/81 (4) 4/82 (5)
P. A. J. DeFreitas c Hegg b Chapple . . .	12	5/99 (2) 6/99 (6) 7/126 (8)
C. D. Crowe b Chapple	19	8/147 (7) 9/169 (9)

Bowling: Martin 8–3–24–2; Chapple 10–1–34–2; Flintoff 10–1–31–0; Wood 10–1–41–2; Schofield 10–0–35–2; Chilton 2–0–7–0.

Lancashire

M. J. Chilton lbw b Maddy	23	J. Wood lbw b Wells 3
G. Chapple b Grove	2	P. J. Martin not out 5
D. Byas b Whiley	10	
S. G. Law c Burns b Maddy	9	B 6, l-b 9, w 11, n-b 2 28
A. Flintoff b Wells	47	
G. D. Lloyd lbw b Maddy	0	1/3 (2) 2/37 (3) 3/49 (4) (47.2 overs) 158
T. W. Roberts lbw b Wells	2	4/58 (1) 5/66 (6) 6/77 (7)
*†W. K. Hegg b Maddy	8	7/89 (8) 8/136 (5)
C. P. Schofield c Burns b Wells	21	9/140 (10) 10/158 (9)

Bowling: Grove 8–1–21–1; Whiley 8–1–20–1; DeFreitas 6–0–19–0; Maddy 10–1–34–4; Wells 9.2–1–32–4; Crowe 6–0–17–0.

Umpires: J. W. Holder and B. Leadbeater.

DURHAM v DERBYSHIRE

At Chester-le-Street, May 6. Durham won by four wickets. Toss: Derbyshire.

Durham's second win in eight matches in 2002 ensured only that it was Derbyshire who were pushed into bottom place in their group. Derbyshire had rested three players, but lost two more when the acting-captain, Di Venuto, and the wicket-keeper, Krikken, were injured. Welch assumed the captaincy, Stubbings the gloves – catching Collingwood, who made the only fifty of the game – while the physio, Craig Ranson, took the field as substitute. Durham's attack was also weakened by injury, but they dismissed Derbyshire for 172 on a chilly day.

Gold Award: P. D. Collingwood.

Derbyshire

S. D. Stubbings c and b Hatch	1
*M. J. Di Venuto c Lewis b Killeen	9
C. W. G. Bassano c Love b Hunter	22
D. R. Hewson run out	46
S. A. Selwood c and b Hatch	33
N. R. C. Dumelow b Bridge	11
†K. M. Krikken b Hunter	4
T. Lungley c and b Bridge	12
P. Aldred b Killeen	7

G. Welch b Collingwood	11
L. J. Wharton not out	2
L-b 9, w 5	14

1/3 (1) 2/27 (2) 3/47 (3)　　(48.2 overs) 172
4/113 (4) 5/132 (5)
6/133 (6) 7/150 (8)
8/152 (7) 9/170 (10) 10/172 (9)

Bowling: Killeen 9.2–2–18–2; Hatch 10–2–37–2; Hunter 10–3–22–2; Symington 5–0–29–0; Collingwood 5–0–22–1; Bridge 9–1–35–2.

Durham

G. J. Pratt c Wharton b Lungley	2
N. Peng c Lungley b Wharton	35
M. L. Love c Krikken b Lungley	14
P. D. Collingwood c Stubbings b Aldred .	51
*J. J. B. Lewis b Lungley	22
†A. Pratt not out	22
M. J. Symington run out	10

I. D. Hunter not out	6
L-b 5, w 3, n-b 4	12

1/9 (1) 2/30 (3)　　(6 wkts, 46.5 overs) 174
3/85 (2) 4/124 (5)
5/142 (4) 6/156 (7)

G. D. Bridge, N. Killeen and N. G. Hatch did not bat.

Bowling: Welch 10–2–27–0; Lungley 10–2–29–3; Aldred 9.5–1–52–1; Hewson 3–0–9–0; Wharton 5–0–24–1; Dumelow 9–1–28–0.

Umpires: A. A. Jones and P. Willey.

LEICESTERSHIRE v NOTTINGHAMSHIRE

At Leicester, May 6. Leicestershire won by eight wickets. Toss: Leicestershire.

Leicestershire secured an easy win in a match reduced to 22 overs a side by the weather. Unbeaten in the qualifying stages, they headed the North Group, but Nottinghamshire's faint hopes of reaching the last eight vanished when they collapsed abjectly for 95. Crowe earned the match award for four overs of intelligent off-spin that cost just seven runs and had Pietersen, the only Nottinghamshire player to reach 20, stumped. Stevens ensured victory with nearly four overs left.

Gold Award: C. D. Crowe.

Nottinghamshire

†C. M. W. Read c Burns b Whiley	10
*J. E. R. Gallian lbw b Grove	0
P. Johnson c Stevens b Grove	13
U. Afzaal run out	14
L. Klusener b Whiley	4
K. P. Pietersen st Burns b Crowe	20
B. M. Shafayat c DeFreitas b Maddy . . .	14
G. D. Clough lbw b DeFreitas	1

A. J. Harris b DeFreitas.	0
G. J. Smith not out	7
M. N. Malik lbw b Maddy.	0
B 1, l-b 8, w 3	12

1/2 (2) 2/24 (1) 3/25 (3)　　(21.4 overs) 95
4/31 (5) 5/62 (4) 6/70 (6)
7/73 (8) 8/73 (9) 9/94 (7) 10/95 (11)

Bowling: Whiley 5–0–20–2; Grove 4–0–22–2; DeFreitas 5–0–25–2; Crowe 4–0–7–1; Maddy 2.4–0–9–2; Wells 1–0–3–0.

Leicestershire

T. R. Ward b Malik	. . . .	9
I. J. Sutcliffe b Afzaal	. . . .	32
D. I. Stevens not out	. . . .	44
†N. D. Burns not out	. . . .	4
L-b 4, w 5	. . . .	9

1/15 (1) 2/90 (2)   (2 wkts, 18.1 overs) 98

*V. J. Wells, A. S. Wright, D. L. Maddy, P. A. J. DeFreitas, C. D. Crowe, J. O. Grove and M. J. A. Whiley did not bat.

Bowling: Smith 3–0–13–0; Malik 3–0–8–1; Klusener 3–0–10–0; Harris 2–0–23–0; Pietersen 3–0–22–0; Afzaal 3.1–1–14–1; Shafayat 1–0–4–0.

Umpires: R. Palmer and A. G. T. Whitehead.

YORKSHIRE v LANCASHIRE

At Leeds, May 6. Lancashire won by eight wickets. Toss: Lancashire.

David Byas's return to Headingley after his controversial departure was keenly awaited, but no one had predicted such a one-sided outcome. Yorkshire were annihilated for 81, their lowest total in the competition's history, on an uneven pitch, and Byas was at the crease when Lancashire, benefiting from four dropped catches, sealed victory. Chapple, another Yorkshire-born Lancastrian, did most of the work with the bat, racing to 42 in 26 balls. Flintoff had dominated earlier, collecting a one-day best four for 11. The entire game lasted only 38.1 overs, and was completed by 2.15. The result enabled Lancashire, as one of the two most successful third-placed teams, to join Yorkshire in the quarter-finals.

Gold Award: G. Chapple.

Yorkshire

C. White b Wood	. . . .	10	S. P. Kirby c Hegg b Hogg	0
M. P. Vaughan c Hegg b Wood	. . . . .	18	M. J. Hoggard not out	7
T. T. Bresnan c Swann b Wood	. . . . .	16		
M. J. Lumb lbw b Chapple	. . . .	0	L-b 6, w 1	7
A. McGrath c Flintoff b Hogg	. . . . . .	2		
G. M. Fellows c Byas b Flintoff	. . . . .	2	1/28 (1) 2/31 (2) 3/32 (4) (27.2 overs) 81	
*D. S. Lehmann b Flintoff	. . . .	4	4/48 (3) 5/50 (5) 6/51 (6)	
†R. J. Blakey c Hogg b Flintoff	. . . . .	14	7/62 (7) 8/64 (9)	
A. K. D. Gray c and b Flintoff	. . . . . .	1	9/65 (10) 10/81 (8)	

Bowling: Chapple 6–2–14–1; Wood 6–0–33–3; Hogg 8–2–17–2; Flintoff 7.2–4–11–4.

Lancashire

M. J. Chilton not out	. . . .	27
G. Chapple c Hoggard b Bresnan	. . . .	42
A. J. Swann c Lehmann b Hoggard	. . . .	1
D. Byas not out	. . . .	3
W 1, n-b 8	. . . .	9

1/67 (2) 2/73 (3)   (2 wkts, 10.5 overs) 82

S. G. Law, G. D. Lloyd, A. Flintoff, C. P. Schofield, *†W. K. Hegg, K. W. Hogg and J. Wood did not bat.

Bowling: Kirby 5–1–43–0; Hoggard 4.5–0–33–1; Bresnan 1–0–6–1.

Umpires: B. Leadbeater and N. A. Mallender.

SOUTH GROUP

ESSEX v SUSSEX

At Chelmsford, April 28. Essex won by 20 runs (D/L method). Toss: Sussex.

An inspired spell of swing bowling from Irani wrested this game from Sussex, who were sitting pretty at 103 for one in search of 207. But when Irani removed Adams, for a bold fifty, and Goodwin in successive balls, the breach was made. The middle order was unable to patch things up, and in no time Sussex were 114 for six; Stephenson, back at Chelmsford after seven summers at Hampshire, chipped in with the wicket of Martin-Jenkins. Minutes later, rain ended play, and Irani had done enough to swing Duckworth/Lewis Essex's way. He had earlier hit a responsible 47 after Kirtley wrecked the top of the Essex innings.

Gold Award: R. C. Irani.

Essex

J. P. Stephenson b Kirtley	0	J. D. Middlebrook c Cottey b Kirtley	9
J. M. Dakin c Ambrose b Kirtley	5	A. J. Clarke not out	2
G. R. Napier lbw b Martin-Jenkins	1		
†A. Flower lbw b Kirtley	2	L-b 10, w 10, n-b 2	22
*R. C. Irani c Ambrose b Yardy	47		
A. Habib c Adams b Taylor	46	1/0 (1) 2/1 (3)	(9 wkts, 50 overs) 206
A. P. Grayson not out	49	3/8 (4) 4/18 (2)	
D. D. J. Robinson c Kirtley b Yardy	8	5/95 (5) 6/154 (6)	
A. P. Cowan b Kirtley	15	7/167 (8) 8/183 (9) 9/199 (10)	

Bowling: Kirtley 10–0–33–5; Martin-Jenkins 10–2–33–1; Taylor 10–0–40–1; Yardy 10–0–44–2; Davis 7–0–28–0; House 3–0–18–0.

Sussex

R. R. Montgomerie not out	44	W. J. House c Napier b Irani	4
†T. R. Ambrose b Irani	5	M. H. Yardy not out	2
*C. J. Adams c Napier b Irani	54	L-b 2, w 7	9
M. W. Goodwin c Flower b Irani	0		
P. A. Cottey c Cowan b Irani	0	1/15 (2) 2/103 (3)	(6 wkts, 31 overs) 120
R. S. C. Martin-Jenkins c Flower		3/103 (4) 4/105 (5)	
b Stephenson	2	5/109 (6) 6/114 (7)	

M. J. G. Davis, R. J. Kirtley and B. V. Taylor did not bat.

Bowling: Cowan 6–0–37–0; Irani 10–2–36–5; Dakin 6–1–12–0; Clarke 3–0–16–0; Stephenson 6–0–17–1.

Umpires: A. A. Jones and N. J. Llong.

MIDDLESEX v SURREY

At Lord's, April 28. Middlesex won by eight wickets. Toss: Middlesex.

Although both sides had enjoyed encouraging starts to the season – each cantering to victory in their two Championship games – Surrey's reckless strokeplay made life easy for Middlesex. Keegan benefited when first Stewart and then Ramprakash fell to attempted drives. Their team-mates shared their impatience, and only Butcher showed conviction in a resolute 81-ball fifty. He was one of four victims for Noffke, whose sharp pace brought him four for 34. Despite three rain stoppages, Hutton and Shah, who breezed to an unbeaten 50 from 46 balls, kept their concentration to ensure defeat for the cup-holders.

Gold Award: M. A. Butcher.

Surrey

*M. A. Butcher b Noffke	51	J. Ormond c Nash b Noffke	3
†A. J. Stewart c Nash b Keegan	6	E. S. H. Giddins not out	5
M. R. Ramprakash c Weekes b Keegan	4		
N. Shahid c Nash b Fraser	5	L-b 9, w 4	13
A. D. Brown c Weekes b Keegan	2		
I. J. Ward run out	3	1/17 (2) 2/37 (3)	(38 overs) 123
Azhar Mahmood lbw b Noffke	10	3/42 (4) 4/45 (5) 5/51 (6)	
A. J. Tudor run out	13	6/79 (7) 7/106 (8) 8/106 (1)	
M. P. Bicknell c Nash b Noffke	8	9/118 (10) 10/123 (9)	

Bowling: Fraser 10–2–22–1; Keegan 8–2–24–3; Noffke 10–3–34–4; Cook 6–0–26–0; Weekes 4–0–8–0.

Middlesex

A. J. Strauss c Azhar Mahmood		O. A. Shah not out	50
b Ormond	24	L-b 1, w 5, n-b 4	10
S. G. Koenig run out	13		
B. L. Hutton not out	27	1/37 (1) 2/42 (3)	(2 wkts, 30.2 overs) 124

E. C. Joyce, P. N. Weekes, †D. C. Nash, A. A. Noffke, S. J. Cook, *A. R. C. Fraser and C. B. Keegan did not bat.

Bowling: Bicknell 5–2–15–0; Tudor 8–0–50–0; Giddins 7–2–12–0; Ormond 6.2–1–17–1; Azhar Mahmood 4–0–29–0.

Umpires: T. E. Jesty and N. A. Mallender.

HAMPSHIRE v KENT

At Southampton, April 29. Kent won by 68 runs. Toss: Hampshire.

Deft exploitation of conditions favouring swing eventually brought Kent a comfortable win that had seemed implausible when Hampshire reduced them to 25 for four, then 64 for five. However, Walker and Nixon, sharing the game's only fifty partnership, watchfully set the recovery in train before Golding gave the innings late impetus with a brisk 34. Even so, Kent's 183 looked inadequate, especially while the pinch-hitter, Hamblin, was walloping the ball to all corners in his 24-ball cameo. Yet it proved more than enough: from 49 for nought, the game became a non-stop clatter of Hampshire wickets as one batsman after another was deceived by the moving ball. All ten departed for 66 as the procession gained embarrassing speed.

Gold Award: P. A. Nixon.

Kent

D. P. Fulton b Johnson	6	J. M. Golding not out	34
R. W. T. Key run out	1	M. J. Saggers not out	10
J. B. Hockley c Kendall b Mullally	3	B 1, l-b 4, w 12, n-b 2	19
E. T. Smith c Pothas b Mullally	10		
A. Symonds b Hamblin	21	1/2 (2) 2/7 (3)	(8 wkts, 50 overs) 183
M. J. Walker b Udal	35	3/25 (1) 4/25 (4)	
†P. A. Nixon c Kenway b Tremlett	42	5/64 (5) 6/118 (6)	
*M. V. Fleming lbw b Tremlett	2	7/121 (8) 8/159 (7)	

D. D. Masters did not bat.

Bowling: Hamblin 10–0–38–1; Mullally 10–3–29–2; Johnson 10–0–46–1; Tremlett 10–0–42–2; Udal 10–2–23–1.

Hampshire

J. R. C. Hamblin lbw b Saggers	39	C. T. Tremlett run out		0
N. C. Johnson c Saggers b Fleming	10	A. D. Mullally not out		2
D. A. Kenway lbw b Masters	25			
J. P. Crawley c Nixon b Fleming	2	B 1, l-b 1, w 7		9
*R. A. Smith b Fleming	4			
W. S. Kendall c Nixon b Symonds	2	1/49 (1) 2/66 (2) 3/75 (4)	(37.2 overs)	115
†N. Pothas lbw b Symonds	2	4/81 (5) 5/89 (6) 6/93 (3)		
G. W. White c Nixon b Masters	8	7/93 (7) 8/109 (8)		
S. D. Udal b Saggers	12	9/110 (10) 10/115 (9)		

Bowling: Saggers 7.2–2–19–2; Masters 10–1–44–2; Golding 8–1–24–0; Fleming 6–2–12–3; Symonds 6–0–14–2.

Umpires: G. I. Burgess and N. A. Mallender.

MIDDLESEX v ESSEX

At Lord's, April 30. No result (abandoned).

KENT v SUSSEX

At Canterbury, May 1. Sussex won by 126 runs. Toss: Sussex.

Sussex had this game in their pocket before the Kent batsmen had reached the crease. The openers, Montgomerie and Ambrose, laid the foundations with a stand of 137, before Goodwin weighed in with a devastating innings. From just 62 balls – four of which disappeared for six – he thumped the demoralised Kent bowlers for an undefeated 85. Goodwin and Adams helped themselves to 128 in 18 overs. Martin-Jenkins, on his way to his best return in limited-overs cricket, then reduced Kent to 65 for five. They had won from there in their last match, but this time they were up against a formidable 282. Kirtley lopped off the tail to give Sussex their biggest victory over Kent in 31 seasons of B&H cricket.

Gold Award: M. W. Goodwin.

Sussex

R. R. Montgomerie st Nixon b Symonds	71
†T. R. Ambrose b Masters	64
*C. J. Adams b Fleming	41
M. W. Goodwin not out	85
W. J. House not out	7
B 4, l-b 7, w 3	14

1/137 (1) 2/141 (2) (3 wkts, 50 overs) 282
3/269 (3)

P. A. Cottey, M. H. Yardy, R. S. C. Martin-Jenkins, M. J. G. Davis, R. J. Kirtley and B. V. Taylor did not bat.

Bowling: Saggers 10–0–46–0; Masters 10–0–61–1; Fleming 10–0–50–1; Golding 9–1–53–0; Symonds 8–0–39–1; Walker 3–0–22–0.

Kent

†P. A. Nixon c Adams b Martin-Jenkins	.	2
R. W. T. Key b Kirtley	.	0
J. B. Hockley c Yardy b Martin-Jenkins	.	16
E. T. Smith b Martin-Jenkins	.	22
A. Symonds lbw b Martin-Jenkins	.	7
M. J. Walker c Adams b Kirtley	.	27
D. P. Fulton run out	.	37
*M. V. Fleming not out	.	20
J. M. Golding lbw b Kirtley	.	0

M. J. Saggers b Kirtley	.	2
D. D. Masters c Kirtley b Yardy	.	0
L-b 17, w 4, n-b 2	.	23

1/2 (2) 2/2 (1) 3/30 (3)   (41 overs) 156
4/42 (5) 5/65 (4) 6/120 (6)
7/138 (7) 8/139 (9)
9/147 (10) 10/156 (11)

Bowling: Martin-Jenkins 10–2–22–4; Kirtley 10–0–34–4; Taylor 7–0–38–0; Yardy 5–0–24–1; Davis 9–1–21–0.

Umpires: J. W. Lloyds and R. Palmer.

SURREY v HAMPSHIRE

At The Oval, May 1. Hampshire won by one run. Toss: Surrey.

Needing two from the final ball – Surrey would have won by dint of losing fewer wickets had the scores finished level – Tudor picked out mid-wicket and snatched just a single. Thanks to wayward bowling from a Surrey attack without Bicknell, resting a sore back, Hampshire passed 100 in the 14th over, and they were reined in only by Azhar Mahmood's steady medium-pace. Smith held the innings together as it threatened to crumple, and helped ensure a decent target. In reply, Stewart and Ramprakash added 70 for the second wicket to build a promising base, before Udal plucked out both on his way to a competition-best four for 36. Azhar did his utmost to rescue Surrey with a 40-ball fifty, but 17 off two overs – 16 if they preserved their wickets – just eluded them.

Gold Award: S. D. Udal.

Hampshire

J. R. C. Hamblin c Butcher b Ormond	.	21
N. C. Johnson c Ward b Tudor	.	46
D. A. Kenway c Salisbury b Azhar Mahmood	.	40
J. P. Crawley c Stewart b Azhar Mahmood	.	0
*R. A. Smith c Tudor b Ormond	.	64
W. S. Kendall lbw b Salisbury	.	0
†N. Pothas lbw b Salisbury	.	0
G. W. White lbw b Ormond	.	24

S. D. Udal not out	.	17
C. T. Tremlett c Stewart b Tudor	.	0
A. D. Mullally run out	.	3
B 1, l-b 18, w 9	.	28

1/53 (1) 2/100 (2) 3/107 (4)   (50 overs) 243
4/138 (5) 5/139 (6)
6/140 (7) 7/207 (8)
8/226 (5) 9/231 (10) 10/243 (11)

Bowling: Ormond 10–0–52–3; Tudor 10–1–44–2; Giddins 10–1–51–0; Azhar Mahmood 10–0–29–2; Salisbury 10–1–48–2.

Surrey

*M. A. Butcher c Pothas b Mullally	.	1
†A. J. Stewart lbw b Udal	.	52
M. R. Ramprakash c Pothas b Udal	.	39
N. Shahid c Kendall b Udal	.	22
A. D. Brown c Smith b Udal	.	15
I. J. Ward c Pothas b Tremlett	.	14
Azhar Mahmood run out	.	50

A. J. Tudor not out	.	28
I. D. K. Salisbury not out	.	4
L-b 10, w 7	.	17

J. Ormond and E. S. H. Giddins did not bat.

1/6 (1) 2/76 (3)   (7 wkts, 50 overs) 242
3/106 (2) 4/127 (5)
5/152 (4) 6/157 (6) 7/226 (7)

Bowling: Mullally 10–2–39–1; Hamblin 8–0–50–0; Tremlett 8–0–47–1; Johnson 4–0–18–0; Udal 10–1–36–4; Kendall 10–1–42–0.

Umpires: B. Dudleston and J. F. Steele.

ESSEX v SURREY

At Chelmsford, May 2. Essex won by four wickets. Toss: Essex.

A third defeat in three games meant that Surrey, winners in 2001, were all but out of the competition. A solid start from their top three – they were 107 for one before Butcher fell for a sharp 62 – should have brought confident strokeplay rather than a timid meander to 223 all out, with Ramprakash unable to wrest the strike from the tail. Irani maintained his irrepressible form with four for 38. Surrey might have been heartened by Bicknell's two early strikes, but they simply hastened the arrival of Flower. When he departed, 212 runs later, aiming to loft Tudor over square leg, he had made a glorious 98, and the game was as good as over.

Gold Award: A. Flower.

Surrey

*M. A. Butcher c and b Grayson	62	I. D. K. Salisbury c Flower b Irani	16
†A. J. Stewart c Irani b Dakin	20	E. S. H. Giddins lbw b Irani	0
M. R. Ramprakash not out	70	
A. D. Brown c Habib b Irani	7	L-b 6, w 8, n-b 4	18
N. Shahid b Irani	0	
I. J. Ward c Flower b Clarke	8	1/61 (2) 2/107 (1) (49.2 overs) 223
Azhar Mahmood c Flower b Cowan	19	3/120 (4) 4/120 (5)
A. J. Tudor b Cowan	3	5/146 (6) 6/181 (7) 7/191 (8)
M. P. Bicknell b Stephenson	0	8/195 (4) 9/221 (10) 10/223 (11)

Bowling: Irani 9.2–2–38–4; Cowan 10–0–50–2; Dakin 5–0–36–1; Stephenson 10–0–36–1; Grayson 10–0–30–1; Clarke 5–0–27–1.

Essex

J. P. Stephenson c Shahid b Bicknell	0	J. M. Dakin not out	0
D. D. J. Robinson c Stewart b Bicknell	4	
G. R. Napier c Shahid b Azhar Mahmood	41	L-b 6, w 11	17
†A. Flower c sub b Tudor	98	
*R. C. Irani c Stewart b Bicknell	30	1/0 (1) 2/8 (2) (6 wkts, 45.2 overs) 224
A. Habib c Brown b Tudor	27	3/77 (3) 4/123 (5)
A. P. Grayson not out	7	5/185 (6) 6/220 (4)

J. D. Middlebrook, A. P. Cowan and A. J. Clarke did not bat.

Bowling: Bicknell 10–3–24–3; Tudor 9.2–2–0–57–2; Giddins 8–0–45–0; Azhar Mahmood 10–0–49–1; Salisbury 6–0–31–0; Butcher 2–0–12–0.

Umpires: N. G. Cowley and A. G. T. Whitehead.

KENT v MIDDLESEX

At Canterbury, May 2. Kent won by seven wickets (D/L method). Toss: Kent.

Rain, which had already reduced the match to a 31-over affair, returned to lop another 12 from the Middlesex innings. Duckworth/Lewis increased Kent's task to 139 from 19, but Fleming, promoting himself to open, and Key made life easy for the middle order by putting on 84 in 11 overs. Hockley, with a calm 33 not out from 32 balls, masterminded the endgame. The Middlesex innings had contained swashbuckling contributions from Cook, who faced 28 balls, and Joyce, just 14, but lost its way once they were separated.

Gold Award: J. B. Hockley.

Middlesex

A. J. Strauss b Golding	16	C. B. Keegan not out	9
S. G. Koenig c Key b Symonds	26		
O. A. Shah b Tredwell	3	L-b 1, w 3	4
S. J. Cook c and b Golding	39		
E. C. Joyce c Hockley b Symonds	27	1/24 (1) 2/45 (3) (6 wkts, 19 overs) 133	
B. L. Hutton c and b Symonds	0	3/53 (2) 4/104 (5)	
P. N. Weekes not out	9	5/105 (6) 6/117 (4)	

†D. C. Nash, A. A. Noffke and *A. R. C. Fraser did not bat.

Bowling: Saggers 4–0–21–0; Golding 4–0–24–2; Tredwell 3–0–26–1; Symonds 4–0–28–3; Fleming 4–0–33–0.

Kent

*M. V. Fleming c and b Noffke	50
R. W. T. Key c Koenig b Weekes	26
J. B. Hockley not out	33
A. Symonds lbw b Weekes	0
E. T. Smith not out	13
B 2, l-b 10, w 3, n-b 2	17

1/84 (2) 2/90 (1) (3 wkts, 18.4 overs) 139
3/91 (4)

D. P. Fulton, M. J. Walker, †P. A. Nixon, J. M. Golding, M. J. Saggers and J. C. Tredwell did not bat.

Bowling: Keegan 3–0–23–0; Fraser 4–0–19–0; Noffke 4–0–34–1; Cook 3.4–0–29–0; Weekes 4–0–22–2.

Umpires: B. Leadbeater and R. Palmer.

SUSSEX v HAMPSHIRE

At Hove, May 3. Sussex won by six wickets. Toss: Hampshire.

With a patient, unbeaten 80, Adams overcame tricky conditions and steered Sussex to a tense win. Chasing an ostensibly modest 204, they had veered off course at 51 for three, all victims for Mascarenhas, the pick of the Hampshire bowlers. As the ball jagged about, Adams and Cottey consolidated at first and when Cottey went, 58 short of victory, Martin-Jenkins atoned for his wayward opening spell – his first two overs cost 31 – to lend vital support to Adams. After its explosive beginning, Hampshire's innings had also lost direction, with the fast-improving Taylor causing most of the problems.

Gold Award: C. J. Adams.

Hampshire

J. R. C. Hamblin c Ambrose b Taylor	33	C. T. Tremlett not out	7
N. C. Johnson c Ambrose b Kirtley	18	A. D. Mullally not out	0
D. A. Kenway c Kirtley b Taylor	20		
J. P. Crawley c Kirtley b Yardy	23	L-b 15, w 8, n-b 2	25
*R. A. Smith c Yardy b Davis	33		
G. W. White c Goodwin b Kirtley	12	1/63 (2) 2/63 (1) (9 wkts, 50 overs) 203	
†N. Pothas run out	8	3/103 (4) 4/130 (4)	
A. D. Mascarenhas lbw b Kirtley	0	5/156 (5) 6/159 (6)	
S. D. Udal b Taylor	24	7/159 (8) 8/180 (7) 9/202 (9)	

Bowling: Martin-Jenkins 10–1–60–0; Kirtley 10–0–41–3; Taylor 10–3–26–3; Yardy 10–0–34–1; Davis 10–1–27–1.

Sussex

R. R. Montgomerie b Mascarenhas	6	R. S. C. Martin-Jenkins not out	26
†T. R. Ambrose c Johnson b Mascarenhas	10	L-b 2, w 3, n-b 2	7
*C. J. Adams not out	80		
M. W. Goodwin c Pothas b Mascarenhas	14	1/12 (1) 2/25 (2) (4 wkts, 49 overs) 204	
P. A. Cottey c White b Mullally	61	3/51 (4) 4/146 (5)	

W. J. House, M. H. Yardy, M. J. G. Davis, R. J. Kirtley and B. V. Taylor did not bat.

Bowling: Mullally 10–2–31–1; Mascarenhas 10–3–19–3; Tremlett 8–0–47–0; Udal 10–1–27–0; Hamblin 6–0–43–0; Johnson 5–0–35–0.

Umpires: M. J. Kitchen and N. J. Llong.

SURREY v KENT

At The Oval, May 4. Surrey won by 44 runs. Toss: Surrey.

Buoyed by the inclusion of Thorpe after five weeks' enforced rest, Surrey at last remembered how to win a limited-overs match. The break seemed to have done Thorpe good: he made a confident 61, sharing a stand of 93 with Brown, whose typically pugnacious 73 came from 58 balls. Crucially, both batsmen were dropped, enabling Surrey to reach a testing total. Kent began badly after Fleming skied the first ball, and only while Key was compiling a well-crafted fifty did they make a fight of it. Tudor's tidy spell kindled speculation of an England recall, and various injuries and mishaps meant the Surrey coach, Keith Medlycott, fielded briefly.

Gold Award: A. D. Brown.

Surrey

A. D. Brown c Nixon b Symonds	73	J. Ormond not out	14
†A. J. Stewart c Hockley b Saggers	5	P. J. Sampson not out	3
M. R. Ramprakash c Nixon b Fleming	5		
G. P. Thorpe c Nixon b Khan	61	B 4, l-b 5, w 4	13
N. Shahid c Saggers b Symonds	12		
*I. J. Ward run out	21	1/12 (2) 2/35 (3) (9 wkts, 50 overs) 257	
Azhar Mahmood c Smith b Tredwell	25	3/128 (1) 4/157 (5)	
A. J. Tudor c and b Tredwell	7	5/161 (4) 6/206 (7)	
I. D. K. Salisbury c Fulton b Symonds	18	7/212 (6) 8/229 (8) 9/251 (9)	

Bowling: Khan 10–0–62–1; Saggers 10–0–52–1; Fleming 10–0–43–1; Tredwell 10–0–44–2; Symonds 10–0–47–3.

Kent

*M. V. Fleming c Tudor b Ormond	0	A. Khan b Tudor	0
R. W. T. Key b Ramprakash	59	M. J. Saggers b Tudor	0
J. B. Hockley b Tudor	7		
E. T. Smith c Ward b Sampson	27	L-b 4, w 11	15
A. Symonds b Sampson	3		
D. P. Fulton b Sampson	42	1/0 (1) 2/23 (3) 3/79 (4) (45.3 overs) 213	
M. J. Walker not out	41	4/85 (5) 5/113 (2) 6/172 (6)	
†P. A. Nixon c sub b Ormond	15	7/189 (8) 8/207 (9)	
J. C. Tredwell c sub b Ormond	4	9/213 (10) 10/213 (11)	

Bowling: Ormond 10–1–65–3; Tudor 8.3–1–28–3; Sampson 10–0–42–3; Azhar Mahmood 9–0–30–0; Ramprakash 6–0–31–1; Ward 2–0–13–0.

Umpires: I. J. Gould and M. J. Harris.

ESSEX v HAMPSHIRE

At Chelmsford, May 5. Essex won by six wickets (D/L method). Toss: Hampshire.

Essex sailed into the quarter-finals for the first time since 1998, the year they trounced Leicestershire in the final. Success now came thanks to a one-day best of five for 28 from Irani and another classy innings from Flower. Duckworth/Lewis ruled that Essex needed 174 after two brief interruptions to the Hampshire innings, but their early assault on an undemanding total lacked conviction, and they lost Stephenson for a third successive duck. Hussain, in his first outing of the summer, looked more at home as he struck both Mascarenhas and Mullally for sixes. Earlier, Stephenson had enjoyed a happier time with the ball against his former team-mates, seizing three valuable wickets at little cost.

Gold Award: A. Flower.

Hampshire

J. R. C. Hamblin c Stephenson b Irani	1	C. T. Tremlett b Irani	3
N. C. Johnson lbw b Stephenson	24	A. D. Mullally c Flower b Irani	7
D. A. Kenway c Flower b Irani	4		
J. P. Crawley c Napier b Stephenson	27	L-b 11, w 7	18
*R. A. Smith c Napier b Irani	15		
†N. Pothas b Clarke	12	1/2 (1) 2/15 (3) 3/57 (2) (46 overs) 174	
W. S. Kendall not out	34	4/78 (5) 5/78 (4) 6/106 (6)	
A. D. Mascarenhas b Clarke	5	7/118 (8) 8/155 (9)	
S. D. Udal c Middlebrook b Stephenson	24	9/164 (10) 10/174 (11)	

Bowling: Irani 9–0–28–5; Cowan 10–0–41–0; Dakin 5–1–15–0; Stephenson 8–1–22–3; Grayson 6–0–25–0; Clarke 8–2–32–2.

Essex

N. Hussain lbw b Udal	47	A. Habib not out	20
J. P. Stephenson b Mascarenhas	0	L-b 2, w 4, n-b 6	12
G. R. Napier lbw b Mascarenhas	15		
†A. Flower not out	79	1/6 (2) 2/29 (3) (4 wkts, 39.4 overs) 176	
*R. C. Irani b Udal	3	3/107 (1) 4/114 (5)	

A. P. Grayson, J. M. Dakin, A. P. Cowan, J. D. Middlebrook and A. J. Clarke did not bat.

Bowling: Mullally 10–3–42–0; Mascarenhas 10–1–32–2; Tremlett 3–0–15–0; Udal 9–0–40–2; Hamblin 4.4–0–31–0; Johnson 2–0–14–0; Kendall 1–1–0–0.

Umpires: M. R. Benson and V. A. Holder.

MIDDLESEX v SUSSEX

At Lord's, May 5. Sussex won by 28 runs. Toss: Sussex.

This was Angus Fraser's farewell appearance at Lord's before becoming cricket correspondent of *The Independent* newspaper. Though repeatedly cheered as he trundled in, he could offer no more than his customary economy as his Middlesex team went down to a decisive defeat. Sussex began assuredly, as their openers racked up 139 in 31 overs – much as they had against Kent – though from such a commanding position Adams would have expected more than 252. Middlesex then reached 39 for one before lurching to 62 for seven with a display of anaemic batting. Nash and Noffke repaired much of the damage with a competition-record eighth-wicket partnership of 112, but never put Middlesex noses in front. Taylor's five for 28 was a career-best.

Gold Award: B. V. Taylor.

Sussex

R. R. Montgomerie run out	85	M. H. Yardy not out		0
†T. R. Ambrose c Shah b Cook	56			
M. W. Goodwin b Cook	29	L-b 9, w 3		12
*C. J. Adams not out	40			
W. J. House c Hutton b Noffke	9	1/139 (2) 2/160 (1)	(6 wkts, 50 overs)	252
P. A. Cottey c Shah b Noffke	8	3/196 (3) 4/216 (5)		
R. S. C. Martin-Jenkins c Nash b Keegan	13	5/237 (6) 6/252 (7)		

M. J. G. Davis, R. J. Kirtley and B. V. Taylor did not bat.

Bowling: Fraser 10–1–40–0; Keegan 10–0–61–1; Noffke 10–1–50–2; Weekes 10–0–46–0; Cook 10–0–46–2.

Middlesex

A. J. Strauss c Yardy b Martin-Jenkins	13	C. B. Keegan b Taylor		24
S. G. Koenig c Montgomerie b Davis	30	*A. R. C. Fraser not out		1
B. L. Hutton c Ambrose b Taylor	3			
O. A. Shah lbw b Taylor	0	L-b 12, w 12		24
E. C. Joyce c Ambrose b Martin-Jenkins	1			
P. N. Weekes b Martin-Jenkins	1	1/16 (1) 2/39 (3) 3/39 (4)	(48.3 overs)	224
†D. C. Nash b Taylor	67	4/42 (5) 5/46 (6) 6/55 (2)		
S. J. Cook c Adams b Taylor	2	7/62 (8) 8/174 (9)		
A. A. Noffke c Kirtley b House	58	9/223 (10) 10/224 (7)		

Bowling: Kirtley 9–2–33–0; Martin-Jenkins 10–2–27–3; Taylor 9.3–1–28–5; Davis 5–0–30–1; Yardy 10–0–52–0; House 5–0–42–1.

Umpires: M. J. Harris and K. E. Palmer.

HAMPSHIRE v MIDDLESEX

At Southampton, May 6. Hampshire won by three runs. Toss: Middlesex.

An improbably huge Middlesex win could theoretically have taken them to the quarter-finals, though with Hampshire unable to progress, this was in reality a dead game. It did at least contain a classy unbeaten hundred from Crawley. He did not score until his 15th delivery, but once he got going, he kept going, and put on 127 with White. In reply, the Middlesex middle order fired sporadically and, by the time Fraser – who in his final game before full-time journalism had earlier taken a useful two for 34 – arrived to face the penultimate ball, six were needed. He signed off with a valedictory bye.

Gold Award: J. P. Crawley.

Hampshire

J. R. C. Hamblin c Weekes b Fraser	4	A. D. Mascarenhas not out		2
N. C. Johnson b Keegan	0	L-b 6, w 8		14
D. A. Kenway c Nash b Noffke	28			
J. P. Crawley not out	103	1/4 (1) 2/4 (2)	(5 wkts, 50 overs)	237
G. W. White c Strauss b Fraser	60	3/41 (3) 4/168 (5)		
†N. Pothas c Joyce b Keegan	26	5/230 (6)		

*W. S. Kendall, S. D. Udal, L. R. Prittipaul and A. D. Mullally did not bat.

Bowling: Fraser 10–1–34–2; Keegan 10–1–47–2; Noffke 10–0–48–1; Cook 10–0–42–0; Hutton 6–0–36–0; Weekes 4–0–24–0.

Middlesex

A. J. Strauss c Pothas b Mullally	3	
S. G. Koenig b Mascarenhas	2	
B. L. Hutton c Kendall b Prittipaul	27	
O. A. Shah c Kenway b Kendall	47	
E. C. Joyce c Mascarenhas b Hamblin	53	
†D. C. Nash c Pothas b Mascarenhas	15	
S. J. Cook c Mascarenhas b Kendall	48	
A. A. Noffke c and b Mascarenhas	0	
P. N. Weekes run out	24	

C. B. Keegan not out	1
*A. R. C. Fraser not out	0

B 1, l-b 7, w 6 14

1/6 (2) 2/6 (1)   (9 wkts, 50 overs) 234
3/63 (3) 4/113 (4)
5/149 (6) 6/165 (5)
7/166 (8) 8/227 (7) 9/232 (9)

Bowling: Mullally 10–1–32–1; Mascarenhas 10–1–33–3; Hamblin 7–0–41–1; Prittipaul 5–0–21–1; Udal 10–0–51–0; Kendall 8–0–48–2.

Umpires: J. W. Lloyds and G. Sharp.

KENT v ESSEX

At Canterbury, May 6. Essex won by two wickets. Toss: Essex.

Irani continued his exquisite B&H touch, this time with the bat, as he rescued Essex's flagging reply with a 34-ball undefeated fifty. Victory, which came with four balls to spare, earned Essex a home tie in the quarter-finals and confirmed Kent's elimination. Fortunes ebbed and flowed after a fine new-ball spell from Cowan helped reduce Kent to 43 for four and give Essex an early advantage. Walker and Fulton fought back only for Clarke to remove them both. Hussain and then Flower threatened to put Kent out of the game, but the pendulum swung back as both fell to straight balls. Had Hockley not dropped Irani in the closing stages, the denouement might have been different.

Gold Award: R. C. Irani.

Kent

*M. V. Fleming lbw b Cowan	13	
R. W. T. Key lbw b Irani	0	
J. B. Hockley lbw b Cowan	12	
A. Symonds lbw b Cowan	0	
M. J. Walker c Habib b Clarke	64	
D. P. Fulton b Clarke	80	
†P. A. Nixon c Irani b Clarke	12	
J. M. Golding run out	18	
J. C. Tredwell c Irani b Clarke	5	

M. J. Saggers not out	4
B. J. Trott not out	0

B 10, l-b 7, w 6 23

1/9 (2) 2/23 (1)   (9 wkts, 50 overs) 231
3/23 (4) 4/43 (3)
5/163 (6) 6/186 (7)
7/202 (6) 8/210 (9) 9/229 (8)

Bowling: Irani 10–0–58–1; Cowan 8–1–19–3; Stephenson 10–0–39–0; Dakin 5–0–21–0; Grayson 7–0–33–0; Clarke 10–0–44–4.

Essex

N. Hussain lbw b Fleming	42	
J. P. Stephenson lbw b Trott	5	
J. M. Dakin c Tredwell b Golding	18	
†A. Flower b Golding	32	
A. Habib lbw b Symonds	22	
A. P. Cowan b Trott	15	
*R. C. Irani not out	50	
A. P. Grayson c Nixon b Trott	9	

D. D. J. Robinson c Saggers b Tredwell	11
J. D. Middlebrook not out	15

L-b 5, w 10 15

1/16 (2) 2/52 (3)   (8 wkts, 49.2 overs) 234
3/76 (1) 4/115 (5)
5/129 (4) 6/162 (6)
7/174 (8) 8/211 (9)

A. J. Clarke did not bat.

Bowling: Saggers 8–0–32–0; Trott 10–0–43–3; Golding 9–1–37–2; Fleming 9.2–1–33–1; Symonds 8–0–44–1; Tredwell 5–0–40–1.

Umpires: G. I. Burgess and K. E. Palmer.

SUSSEX v SURREY

At Hove, May 6. Sussex won by virtue of losing fewer wickets. Toss: Surrey.

A large crowd, enticed more by free admission for children and a £1 charge for adults than by the weather, which reduced the game to a 46-over contest, watched a thriller. Although Sussex were already guaranteed qualification and Surrey denied it, there was some excellent cricket. Brown hit with his customary vim to make 97 from 89 balls and, with Ward – captain in the absence of Butcher and Holloake – gave Surrey a positive start. But they lost their way, and Taylor's hat-trick wrapped up the innings eight balls early. In reply, Montgomerie maintained his majestic form with 66, taking his aggregate in the group stage to 272. Ormond pulled out of the attack with a sore back, leaving Ward to fill in: he grabbed two quick wickets, but his third over cost 15. Sussex's task boiled down to 18 needed off two, then four off the last after Sampson conceded 14. Azhar Mahmood did his best, removing the inventive Davis for a brisk 15, but once the scores were levelled off the penultimate ball, it didn't matter that Kirtley fell to the last.

Gold Award: M. J. G. Davis.

Surrey

M. A. Carberry c Montgomerie b Taylor.	7	P. J. Sampson lbw b Taylor	0
A. D. Brown c and b Davis	97	E. S. H. Giddins c Ambrose b Taylor...	0
†A. J. Stewart c Cottey b Martin-Jenkins.	11		
*I. J. Ward b House	46	L-b 3, w 11	14
N. Shahid c Yardy b Kirtley	14		
Azhar Mahmood c Goodwin b Davis	7	1/29 (1) 2/54 (3) 3/145 (4) (44.4 overs) 220	
S. A. Newman c Ambrose b Kirtley.	14	4/173 (5) 5/185 (6)	
M. P. Bicknell not out	8	6/197 (2) 7/218 (7)	
J. Ormond c Cottey b Taylor	2	8/220 (9) 9/220 (10) 10/220 (11)	

Bowling: Martin-Jenkins 9–0–49–1; Kirtley 9–1–36–2; Taylor 8.4–0–23–4; Davis 9–0–47–2; Yardy 3–0–20–0; House 4–0–30–1; Adams 2–0–12–0.

Sussex

R. R. Montgomerie c Carberry		M. H. Yardy not out	19
b Azhar Mahmood.	66	M. J. G. Davis b Azhar Mahmood	15
†T. R. Ambrose c Sampson b Ormond.	8	R. J. Kirtley c Stewart b Azhar Mahmood	1
*C. J. Adams c Stewart b Bicknell	6		
M. W. Goodwin c Stewart		B 1, l-b 12, w 11, n-b 2	26
b Azhar Mahmood	18		
P. A. Cottey c Carberry b Ward	37	1/16 (2) 2/31 (3) (9 wkts, 46 overs) 220	
R. S. C. Martin-Jenkins b Ward	4	3/68 (4) 4/133 (1)	
W. J. House c Azhar Mahmood		5/163 (5) 6/163 (6)	
b Sampson	20	7/197 (7) 8/218 (9) 9/220 (10)	

B. V. Taylor did not bat.

Bowling: Bicknell 9–2–28–1; Ormond 6–0–26–1; Giddins 9–0–42–0; Azhar Mahmood 10–1–34–4; Sampson 9–0–50–1; Ward 3–0–27–2.

Umpires: M. R. Benson and I. J. Gould.

QUARTER-FINALS

GLOUCESTERSHIRE v WORCESTERSHIRE

At Bristol, May 21, 22. Worcestershire won by eight wickets. Toss: Worcestershire.

Worcestershire, humbled in the group stage three weeks earlier, did something no visiting team had done in the B&H since British Universities in 1998, and brought Gloucestershire's run of 12 home wins in the tournament to an emphatic end. Two sharp gully catches from Hick helped reduce Gloucestershire to 49 for three, before the experienced pair of Barnett and Alleyne overcame a sluggish pitch to add 90 in 23 overs. Although both fell shortly after reaching 50 – Barnett's canny half-century was his 90th in limited-overs cricket – Gloucestershire were in sight of a decent total when rain halted play. Next day, in winds so strong the umpires dispensed with the bails, Bichel, promoted to open and instructed to unsettle the bowlers, did just that, before easing to a measured unbeaten 94. Only Mike Smith showed control as Worcestershire, playing their first B&H quarter-final since 1995, dumped Gloucestershire, finalists for the past three seasons, out of the competition.

Gold Award: A. J. Bichel.

Close of play: Gloucestershire 193-7 (48.4 overs) (Hardinges 29, Averis 0).

Gloucestershire

K. J. Barnett c Singh b Ali	51	J. M. M. Averis not out	7
C. M. Spearman lbw b Bichel	16	J. Lewis not out	1
M. G. N. Windows c Hick b Sheriyar	11	L-b 3, w 7, n-b 2	12
J. N. Snape c Hick b Lampitt	1		
*M. W. Alleyne run out	52	1/26 (2) 2/47 (3) (8 wkts, 50 overs) 203	
M. A. Hardinges b Ali	31	3/49 (4) 4/139 (1)	
†R. C. Russell c Bichel b Leatherdale	13	5/140 (5) 6/169 (7)	
M. C. J. Ball c Leatherdale b Ali	8	7/183 (8) 8/197 (6)	
A. M. Smith did not bat.			

Bowling: Bichel 10–1–41–1; Sheriyar 9–1–39–1; Ali 10–1–39–3; Lampitt 10–2–21–1; Batty 6–0–29–0; Leatherdale 5–0–31–1.

Worcestershire

A. Singh b Smith	30
A. J. Bichel not out	94
*G. A. Hick c Smith b Lewis	66
V. S. Solanki not out	0
L-b 8, w 6	14
1/74 (1) 2/201 (3) (2 wkts, 41.4 overs) 204	

D. A. Leatherdale, B. F. Smith, G. J. Batty, †S. J. Rhodes, Kabir Ali, S. R. Lampitt and A. Sheriyar did not bat.

Bowling: Smith 10–2–29–1; Lewis 7.4–0–36–1; Alleyne 5–0–37–0; Ball 8–0–34–0; Averis 6–0–24–0; Snape 2–0–12–0; Barnett 3–0–24–0.

Umpires: N. G. Cowley and J. H. Evans.

ESSEX v YORKSHIRE

At Chelmsford, May 22. Essex won by seven wickets. Toss: Essex.

Hussain was in such consummate touch that Essex overhauled a stiffish target with five overs to spare. He reserved his most dismissive batting for his England colleague, Hoggard, whose confidence – already rickety after a poor showing in the Lord's Test against Sri Lanka – took another buffeting as his last three overs went for 29. Hussain's magnificent unbeaten 136, off 144 balls and with 18 fours and a six, was a limited-overs best, beating the 118 he made for Combined Universities against Somerset in 1989. Yorkshire had relied on an explosive innings from Silverwood, who hit 40 in boundaries, and Lehmann, whose half-century was more circumspect.

Gold Award: N. Hussain.

Yorkshire

M. J. Wood c Middlebrook b Stephenson	20
C. White c Flower b Cowan	5
C. E. W. Silverwood b Dakin	56
M. P. Vaughan c Flower b Grayson	32
*D. S. Lehmann c Habib b Clarke	59
A. McGrath b Dakin	9
G. M. Fellows lbw b Dakin	0
†R. J. Blakey c Cowan b Clarke	34
A. K. D. Gray c Grayson b Cowan	6

T. T. Bresnan not out	5
M. J. Hoggard not out	1
L-b 6, w 4	10

1/7 (2) 2/84 (3) (9 wkts, 50 overs) 237
3/107 (1) 4/131 (4)
5/149 (6) 6/149 (7)
7/224 (5) 8/226 (8) 9/234 (9)

Bowling: Irani 8–2–32–0; Cowan 10–1–48–2; Dakin 10–0–47–3; Clarke 7–0–39–2; Stephenson 5–0–30–1; Grayson 10–0–35–1.

Essex

N. Hussain not out	136
D. D. J. Robinson c Lehmann b Hoggard	26
J. P. Stephenson b Fellows	27
†A. Flower c Wood b White	22
*R. C. Irani not out	19
L-b 2, w 3, n-b 4	9

1/51 (2) 2/145 (3) (3 wkts, 45 overs) 239
3/200 (4)

J. M. Dakin, A. Habib, A. P. Grayson, J. D. Middlebrook, A. P. Cowan and A. J. Clarke did not bat.

Bowling: Silverwood 6–0–27–0; Hoggard 10–1–65–1; Bresnan 6–0–33–0; White 10–0–51–1; Lehmann 8–0–30–0; Fellows 3–0–14–1; Gray 2–0–17–0.

Umpires: A. Clarkson and T. E. Jesty.

LEICESTERSHIRE v LANCASHIRE

At Leicester, May 22. Lancashire won by four wickets. Toss: Leicestershire.

Leicestershire suffered their first one-day defeat of the season thanks to an innings of great application from Byas and disciplined, naggingly accurate bowling from Lancashire's battery of seamers. Kyle Hogg, a lithe 18-year-old, led the way with an exemplary return of two for 27 from ten overs. On a slow pitch, even the usually fluent Bevan laboured 126 balls over his 67, the major contribution to Leicestershire's disappointing 163. But it proved more of a challenge than Lancashire expected. They too struggled to get the ball away – except for Byas, who almost single-handedly steered them to victory with 91 off 148 balls. None of his colleagues could manage 20.

Gold Award: D. Byas.

Leicestershire

T. R. Ward c Hegg b Martin	7
I. J. Sutcliffe c Hegg b Martin	5
D. I. Stevens c Flintoff b Wood	27
M. G. Bevan c Hegg b Wood	67
*V. J. Wells b Wood	1
D. L. Maddy b Hogg	4
†N. D. Burns b Hogg	5
P. A. J. DeFreitas b Flintoff	15

C. D. Crowe not out	23
J. O. Grove not out	2
L-b 1, w 2, n-b 4	7

1/10 (1) 2/21 (2) (8 wkts, 50 overs) 163
3/50 (3) 4/52 (5)
5/73 (6) 6/91 (7)
7/123 (8) 8/157 (4)

M. J. A. Whiley did not bat.

Bowling: Martin 10–1–40–2; Chapple 10–2–28–0; Flintoff 10–1–34–1; Hogg 10–2–27–2; Wood 10–1–33–3.

Lancashire

D. Byas b Whiley	91		C. P. Schofield not out	15
M. J. Chilton c Burns b Whiley	5			
G. Chapple lbw b Grove	8		L-b 3, w 1	4
S. G. Law c Wells b Maddy	19			
A. Flintoff lbw b Maddy	0		1/9 (2) 2/34 (3)	(6 wkts, 47.4 overs) 164
G. D. Lloyd lbw b DeFreitas	4		3/78 (4) 4/78 (5)	
*†W. K. Hegg not out	18		5/99 (6) 6/147 (1)	

K. W. Hogg, J. Wood and P. J. Martin did not bat.

Bowling: Whiley 10–1–44–2; Grove 10–4–26–1; DeFreitas 10–1–38–1; Maddy 10–1–25–2; Wells 5.4–0–22–0; Crowe 2–0–6–0.

Umpires: M. J. Harris and N. A. Mallender.

SUSSEX v WARWICKSHIRE

At Hove, May 22. Warwickshire won by four wickets. Toss: Sussex.

The decisive moment of a low-scoring match came when Bell, then on 47, should have been stumped by Ambrose. On a desperately slow pitch, Bell had started streakily, though he hung on tenaciously to guide Warwickshire home. Sussex could only reflect on squandered opportunities: Ambrose and Montgomerie had given their innings a solid start, but the middle order lacked the firepower to push on after Montgomerie was bowled by the impressive Giles. It looked as if it would not matter when Martin-Jenkins reduced Warwickshire to eight for three but, despite two rain breaks, Bell maintained his nerve and his concentration. Brown and Smith played cameos around him, and Warwickshire made it with eight balls to spare.

Gold Award: I. R. Bell.

Sussex

R. R. Montgomerie b Giles	57		M. H. Yardy not out	22
†T. R. Ambrose c and b Richardson	87		M. J. G. Davis not out	3
M. W. Goodwin c Frost b Giles	0		L-b 2, w 2	4
B. Zuiderent lbw b Smith	15			
P. A. Cottey run out	5		1/99 (1) 2/99 (3)	(7 wkts, 50 overs) 196
R. S. C. Martin-Jenkins c Ostler b Brown	1		3/123 (4) 4/143 (5)	
W. J. House b Brown	2		5/145 (6) 6/159 (7) 7/185 (2)	

*R. J. Kirtley and B. V. Taylor did not bat.

Bowling: Brown 10–2–27–2; Pollock 10–1–38–0; Richardson 10–0–48–1; Giles 10–0–29–2; Smith 9–0–41–1; Powell 1–0–11–0.

Warwickshire

*M. J. Powell c Goodwin b Martin-Jenkins	0		D. R. Brown b Yardy	26
N. V. Knight c Yardy b Martin-Jenkins	4		N. M. K. Smith not out	28
S. M. Pollock c Goodwin b Martin-Jenkins	0		B 5, l-b 10, n-b 4	19
I. R. Bell not out	85		1/2 (1) 2/6 (3)	(6 wkts, 48.4 overs) 197
D. P. Ostler c Kirtley b Yardy	17		3/8 (2) 4/54 (5)	
T. L. Penney c Ambrose b Yardy	18		5/96 (6) 6/149 (7)	

A. F. Giles, †T. Frost and A. Richardson did not bat.

Bowling: Martin-Jenkins 10–1–29–3; Kirtley 9–2–29–0; Taylor 9.4–0–37–0; Davis 8–0–37–0; Yardy 8–0–30–3; House 4–0–20–0.

Umpires: G. I. Burgess and N. J. Llong.

SEMI-FINALS

ESSEX v WORCESTERSHIRE

At Chelmsford, June 6, 7. Essex won by 138 runs. Toss: Worcestershire.

Irani, whose form in the Benson and Hedges had been little short of miraculous, led Essex to a crushing win. For Hick, the opposing captain, things could barely have gone worse. First he saw the Essex batsmen mock his optimism on winning an ostensibly important toss, then he fell first ball to the ubiquitous Irani as Worcestershire finished a truncated day out for the count at 26 for four. Hussain had given the Essex innings oomph with a rapid 35 – including 18 larruped from an especially wayward Sheriyar over. Flower provided a flowing 45 and Robinson an 87-ball graft, but the batsman to shine in the gloom was Irani, whose half-century came in better than even time. And before bad light ended play, he had shown the Worcestershire seamers just what accuracy could achieve on a helpful pitch. Rhodes hung on doggedly next day, before Clarke mopped up.

Gold Award: R. C. Irani.

Close of play: Worcestershire 26-4 (Leatherdale 5, Batty 6).

Essex

N. Hussain c Singh b Ali	35	J. P. Stephenson c Hick b Ali	6
D. D. J. Robinson run out	46	A. J. Clarke not out	1
G. R. Napier c Lampitt b Sheriyar	18		
†A. Flower run out	45	L-b 13, w 15	28
*R. C. Irani st Rhodes b Sheriyar	57		
A. Habib run out	5	1/55 (1) 2/92 (3) (9 wkts, 50 overs) 262
A. P. Grayson c Rhodes b Ali	0	3/134 (2) 4/198 (4)
J. M. Dakin b Ali	7	5/231 (5) 6/231 (6)
A. P. Cowan not out	14	7/233 (7) 8/248 (8) 9/260 (10)

Bowling: Donald 10–1–54–0; Sheriyar 9–0–70–2; Ali 10–0–34–4; Lampitt 10–1–44–0; Batty 4–0–25–0; Leatherdale 7–0–22–0.

Worcestershire

V. S. Solanki lbw b Cowan	14	A. A. Donald c Napier b Clarke	10
A. Singh lbw b Irani	0	A. Sheriyar not out	3
*G. A. Hick c Napier b Irani	0		
B. F. Smith lbw b Irani	1	L-b 3, w 5	8
D. A. Leatherdale b Dakin	10		
G. J. Batty c Cowan b Stephenson	20	1/7 (2) 2/7 (3) 3/15 (1) (33.4 overs) 124
†S. J. Rhodes c and b Clarke	41	4/15 (4) 5/31 (5) 6/81 (6)
Kabir Ali run out	9	7/94 (8) 8/107 (7)
S. R. Lampitt c Irani b Clarke	8	9/112 (9) 10/124 (10)

Bowling: Irani 8–1–30–3; Cowan 8–4–15–1; Dakin 5–1–12–1; Stephenson 5–0–27–1; Grayson 4–0–24–0; Clarke 3.4–0–13–3.

Umpires: D. J. Constant and J. W. Holder.

LANCASHIRE v WARWICKSHIRE

At Manchester, June 7. Warwickshire won by one wicket. Toss: Lancashire.

Needing two off the last ball to tie the game at 211 for nine – and reach Lord's by dint of a better 15-over score – Warwickshire found a level-headed hero in Neil Carter, their No. 11, who calmly chipped his only ball, from Chapple, for four with a premeditated scoop. Hegg promptly threw himself to the ground, pounding the turf in frustration. The ball before, Flintoff's cannon-like throw from mid-wicket had run out Brown to leave a pulsating game on a knife-edge. Earlier, Chilton had become the only man to score two B&H hundreds in the season, despite managing just four boundaries. Flintoff, with an unusually restrained 40, helped give Lancashire a workable total, despite magnificent bowling from Pollock, who seized four for 27 having just returned from Hansie Cronje's funeral in South Africa. At 131 for six, with 15 overs left and neither batsman off the mark, Warwickshire looked beaten, but Smith and Brown stunned Lancashire with a freewheeling partnership of 60 that set up the classic finale. It was Lancashire's fourth semi-final defeat in three years.

Gold Award: M. J. Chilton.

Lancashire

N. H. Fairbrother c Bell b Carter	1
M. J. Chilton b Pollock	101
G. Chapple c Frost b Carter	0
S. G. Law c Powell b Pollock	11
A. Flintoff c Knight b Brown	40
G. D. Lloyd b Carter	18
*†W. K. Hegg c and b Pollock	11
C. P. Schofield run out	10

J. Wood not out 4
K. W. Hogg b Pollock 0
B 4, l-b 6, w 5 15

1/11 (1) 2/18 (3)   (9 wkts, 50 overs) 211
3/36 (4) 4/122 (5)
5/172 (6) 6/185 (7)
7/200 (8) 8/211 (2) 9/211 (10)

P. J. Martin did not bat.

Bowling: Pollock 10–2–27–4; Carter 10–1–43–3; Brown 10–0–55–1; Giles 10–1–38–0; Smith 10–0–38–0.

Warwickshire

*M. J. Powell c Chilton b Martin	12
N. V. Knight c Hegg b Chapple	0
S. M. Pollock st Hegg b Hogg	22
I. R. Bell c Hogg b Wood	46
J. O. Troughton lbw b Schofield	38
T. L. Penney c Chapple b Flintoff	3
D. R. Brown run out	42
N. M. K. Smith c Chapple b Hogg	29
A. F. Giles c Chilton b Chapple	3

†T. Frost not out 4
N. M. Carter not out 4

L-b 2, w 8 10

1/3 (2) 2/25 (1)   (9 wkts, 50 overs) 213
3/54 (3) 4/114 (5)
5/130 (4) 6/131 (6)
7/191 (8) 8/199 (9) 9/209 (7)

Bowling: Martin 10–1–37–1; Chapple 10–0–39–2; Flintoff 10–2–35–1; Hogg 6–1–27–2; Wood 10–2–40–1; Chilton 1–0–10–0; Schofield 3–0–23–1.

Umpires: K. E. Palmer and G. Sharp.

FINAL

ESSEX v WARWICKSHIRE

At Lord's, June 22. Warwickshire won by five wickets. Toss: Warwickshire.

Under a June sky mottled with blue, white and inky grey, the Benson and Hedges Cup was laid to rest. Only once had the final been played so early in the summer and, when Pollock's second ball kicked off the seam, bruised the shoulder of Hussain's bat and zipped through to Piper, it looked as though a morning of fencing, prodding and jabbing would bring complaints that the toss had decided the match. But the early signs were misleading: the ball that got Hussain was a brilliant freak, the jute-brown pitch proved benign enough, and it was harum-scarum batting from Essex that left the match lop-sided. Later, a composed innings from the 20-year-old Ian Bell made sure they were never back on terms.

Put in, Essex were 86 for six – and in effect out of the match – within 25 overs. The loss of Hussain, who was averaging almost 87 in this year's tournament, brought in Napier, averaging under 19, but apparently intent on overtaking him in one innings. His excitability infected Robinson and, six overs into the game, a below-capacity crowd had already seen a huge six into the Grandstand, a handful of misses – one attempted pull by Napier, aimed towards Father Time, might easily have dislocated his shoulder – four caressed fours and a referral to the third umpire after a direct hit from Penney. Essex played as if 20-over cricket had already arrived, but the excitement quickly blew itself out as shocking shot selection undid their top order.

Napier's dismissal was unforgivable: Troughton at deep mid-wicket lost a mistimed pull, ran away from the ball, recovered, threw and hit the stumps. Although the eye followed the ricochet into the off, it turned out that a dawdling Napier was short of his ground. With pressure building, Warwickshire were relentless. While the styles contrasted – Pollock metronomic, Giles firing in flat deliveries from over the wicket, Smith looping and dipping his off-spinners like a kingfisher swooping to the water – the control of line and length was constant, and Essex panicked. Stephenson faced one ball, which brought a half-hearted prod, an inside edge and his fourth B&H duck in seven innings; Robinson mowed wildly; and Irani, unable to push the ball around, was frustrated into a heave, and caught at mid-off. It was chaos theory without the theory. No one but Flower could impose the necessary calm and, after he leg-glanced too fine, the tail was left to play out time.

Only Surrey, in 1974, had defended a total of 181 or less in a B&H final, and Essex could not upset history. That a routine chase still felt routine after Knight and Powell went within seven overs owed everything to Bell. More Atherton-like than ever – sheepish grin, upturned collar, phlegmatic bearing – he accumulated quietly through nudges and uncomplicated punches into the off. His lack of flourish contrasted with Troughton, who found his timing instantly, hit eight fours from 33 balls and played with a carefree joy that changed the tone of the match. Though Irani huffed and puffed, hair and shirt-tails flapping, his team-mates – Dakin and Clarke in particular – bowled too wide. But the match will be remembered as the grandest showcase yet for the talents of Bell. **Paul Coupar**

Gold Award: I. R. Bell.   *Attendance:* 22,286;   *receipts:* £530,000.

Essex

N. Hussain c Piper b Pollock	0	J. M. Dakin c Powell b Brown 12
D. D. J. Robinson c Brown b Carter	18	A. P. Cowan not out 27
G. R. Napier run out	17	L-b 4, w 4, n-b 4 12
J. P. Stephenson b Carter	0	
†A. Flower c Piper b Smith	30	1/0 (1) 2/33 (3) (8 wkts, 50 overs) 181
*R. C. Irani c Smith b Brown	8	3/33 (4) 4/40 (2)
A. Habib c Knight b Giles	19	5/61 (6) 6/86 (5)
A. P. Grayson not out	38	7/109 (8) 8/134 (9)
		15 overs: 53-4

A. J. Clarke did not bat.

Bowling: Pollock 10–1–32–1; Carter 10–1–45–2; Brown 10–0–32–2; Giles 10–1–28–1; Smith 10–0–40–1.

Warwickshire

*M. J. Powell c Flower b Cowan	11	D. R. Brown not out 12
N. V. Knight c Flower b Irani	9	L-b 6, w 8 14
I. R. Bell not out	65	
J. O. Troughton c Flower b Napier	37	1/19 (1) 2/21 (2) (5 wkts, 36.2 overs) 182
S. M. Pollock c Dakin b Irani	34	3/105 (4) 4/158 (5)
T. L. Penney lbw b Stephenson	0	5/159 (6)
		15 overs: 83-2

N. M. K. Smith, A. F. Giles, †K. J. Piper and N. M. Carter did not bat.

Bowling: Irani 10–2–40–2; Cowan 8–0–37–1; Clarke 2–0–20–0; Dakin 2–0–22–0; Grayson 4–0–11–0; Napier 5.2–0–31–1; Stephenson 5–0–15–1.

Umpires: B. Dudleston and J. H. Hampshire.
Third umpire: B. Leadbeater.

BENSON AND HEDGES CUP RECORDS

55 overs available in all games 1972–95. 50 overs in 1996–2002.
Only eight teams took part in 1999.

Batting

Highest individual scores: 198*, G. A. Gooch, Essex v Sussex, Hove, 1982; 177, S. J. Cook, Somerset v Sussex, Hove, 1990; 173*, C. G. Greenidge, Hampshire v Minor Counties (South), Amersham, 1973; 167*, A. J. Stewart, Surrey v Somerset, The Oval, 1994; 160, A. J. Stewart, Surrey v Hampshire, The Oval, 1996; 158*, B. F. Davison, Leicestershire v Warwickshire, Coventry, 1972; 158, W. J. Cronje, Leicestershire v Lancashire, Manchester, 1995; 157*, M. G. Bevan, Sussex v Essex, Chelmsford, 2000; 155*, M. D. Crowe, Somerset v Hampshire, Southampton, 1987; 155*, R. A. Smith, Hampshire v Glamorgan, Southampton, 1989; 154*, M. J. Procter, Gloucestershire v Somerset, Taunton, 1972; 154*, C. L. Smith, Hampshire v Combined Universities, Southampton, 1990; 151*, M. P. Maynard, Glamorgan v Middlesex, Lord's, 1996; 151, D. L. Maddy, Leicestershire v Minor Counties, Leicester, 1998. *In the final:* 132*, I. V. A. Richards, Somerset v Surrey, 1981. (348 hundreds were scored in the competition. The most in one season was 26 in 1996.)

Most runs: 5,176, G. A. Gooch; 3,347, K. J. Barnett; 3,134, A. J. Stewart; 2,962, G. A. Hick; 2,921, M. W. Gatting; 2,850, N. H. Fairbrother; 2,837, R. J. Bailey; 2,761, C. J. Tavaré; 2,718, W. Larkins; 2,663, D. W. Randall; 2,636, A. J. Lamb; 2,567, R. T. Robinson; 2,551, C. W. J. Athey.

Fastest hundred: M. A. Nash in 62 minutes, Glamorgan v Hampshire at Swansea, 1976.

Most hundreds: 15, G. A. Gooch; 7, G. A. Hick and W. Larkins; 6, M. P. Maynard and N. R. Taylor; 5, C. G. Greenidge, N. V. Knight, A. J. Lamb and R. A. Smith.

Highest totals: 388 for seven, Essex v Scotland, Chelmsford, 1992; 382 for six, Leicestershire v Minor Counties, Leicester, 1998; 371 for six, Leicestershire v Scotland, Leicester, 1997; 369 for eight, Warwickshire v Minor Counties, Jesmond, 1996; 366 for four, Derbyshire v Combined Universities, Oxford, 1991; 361 for eight, Surrey v Nottinghamshire, The Oval, 2001; 359 for seven, Essex v Ireland, Chelmsford, 1998; 353 for seven, Lancashire v Nottinghamshire, Manchester, 1995; 350 for three, Essex v Oxford & Cambridge Univs, Chelmsford, 1979; 349 for seven, Somerset v Ireland, Taunton, 1997; 338 for six, Kent v Somerset, Maidstone, 1996; 333 for four, Essex v Oxford & Cambridge Univs, Chelmsford, 1985; 333 for six, Surrey v Hampshire, The Oval, 1996; 331 for five, Surrey v Hampshire, The Oval, 1990; 331 for five, Essex v British Univs, Chelmsford, 1996; 330 for four, Lancashire v Sussex, Manchester, 1991. *In the final:* 291 for nine, Gloucestershire v Yorkshire, 1999.

Highest total by a side batting second and winning: 318 for five (54.3 overs), Lancashire v Leicestershire (312 for five), Manchester, 1995. *In the final:* 244 for six (55 overs), Yorkshire v Northamptonshire (244 for seven), 1987; 244 for seven (55 overs), Nottinghamshire v Essex (243 for seven), 1989.

Highest total by a side batting second and losing: 303 for seven (55 overs), Derbyshire v Somerset (310 for three), Taunton, 1990. *In the final:* 255 (51.4 overs), Surrey v Essex (290 for six), 1979.

Highest match aggregates: 631 for 15 wickets, Kent (338 for six) v Somerset (293 for nine), Maidstone, 1996; 630 for ten wickets, Leicestershire (312 for five) v Lancashire (318 for five), Manchester, 1995; 629 for 14 wickets, Lancashire (353 for seven) v Nottinghamshire (276 for seven), Manchester, 1995; 628 for 15 wickets, Warwickshire (312 for six) v Lancashire (316 for nine), Manchester, 1996; 626 for ten wickets, British Univs (312 for eight) v Glamorgan (314 for two), Cambridge, 1996; 615 for 11 wickets, Gloucestershire (307 for four) v Surrey (308 for seven), The Oval, 1996; 613 for ten wickets, Somerset (310 for three) v Derbyshire (303 for seven), Taunton, 1990; 610 for eight wickets, Sussex (303 for six) v Kent (307 for two), Hove, 1995; 610 for 14 wickets, Warwickshire (304 for eight) v Kent (306 for six), Canterbury, 1997.

Lowest totals: 50 in 27.2 overs, Hampshire v Yorkshire, Leeds, 1991; 52 in 26.5 overs, Minor Counties v Lancashire, Lakenham, 1998; 56 in 26.2 overs, Leicestershire v Minor Counties, Wellington, 1982; 59 in 34 overs, Oxford & Cambridge Univs v Glamorgan, Cambridge, 1983; 60 in 26 overs, Sussex v Middlesex, Hove, 1978; 61 in 25.3 overs, Essex v Lancashire, Chelmsford, 1992; 62 in 26.5 overs, Gloucestershire v Hampshire, Bristol, 1975. *In the final:* 76 in 27.4 overs, Leicestershire v Essex, 1998.

Shortest completed innings: 21.4 overs (156), Surrey v Sussex, Hove, 1988.

Record partnership for each wicket

252	for 1st	V. P. Terry and C. L. Smith, Hampshire v Combined Universities at Southampton	1990
285*	for 2nd	C. G. Greenidge and D. R. Turner, Hampshire v Minor Counties (South) at Amersham	1973
271	for 3rd	C. J. Adams and M. G. Bevan, Sussex v Essex at Chelmsford	2000
207	for 4th	R. C. Russell and A. J. Wright, Gloucestershire v British Universities at Bristol	1998
160	for 5th	A. J. Lamb and D. J. Capel, Northamptonshire v Leicestershire at Northampton	1986
167*	for 6th	M. G. Bevan and R. J. Blakey, Yorkshire v Lancashire at Manchester. . .	1996
149*	for 7th	J. D. Love and C. M. Old, Yorkshire v Scotland at Bradford.	1981
112	for 8th	D. C. Nash and A. A. Noffke, Middlesex v Sussex at Lord's	2002
83	for 9th	P. G. Newman and M. A. Holding, Derbyshire v Nottinghamshire at Nottingham	1985
80*	for 10th	D. L. Bairstow and M. Johnson, Yorkshire v Derbyshire at Derby	1981

Bowling

Most wickets: 149, J. K. Lever; 132, I. T. Botham.

Best bowling: seven for 12, W. W. Daniel, Middlesex v Minor Counties (East), Ipswich, 1978; seven for 22, J. R. Thomson, Middlesex v Hampshire, Lord's, 1981; seven for 24, Mushtaq Ahmed, Somerset v Ireland, Taunton, 1997; seven for 32, R. G. D. Willis, Warwickshire v Yorkshire, Birmingham, 1981. *In the final:* five for 13, S. T. Jefferies, Hampshire v Derbyshire, 1988.

Hat-tricks (15): G. D. McKenzie, Leicestershire v Worcestershire, Worcester, 1972; K. Higgs, Leicestershire v Surrey in the final, Lord's, 1974; A. A. Jones, Middlesex v Essex, Lord's, 1977; M. J. Procter, Gloucestershire v Hampshire, Southampton, 1977; W. Larkins, Northamptonshire v Oxford & Cambridge Univs, Northampton, 1980; E. A. Moseley, Glamorgan v Kent, Cardiff, 1981; G. C. Small, Warwickshire v Leicestershire, Leicester, 1984; N. A. Mallender, Somerset v Combined Universities, Taunton, 1987; W. K. M. Benjamin, Leicestershire v Nottinghamshire, Leicester, 1987; A. R. C. Fraser, Middlesex v Sussex, Lord's, 1988; S. M. Pollock (four in four balls), Warwickshire v Leicestershire, Birmingham, 1996; Saqlain Mushtaq, Surrey v Lancashire, The Oval, 1998; R. J. Kirtley, Sussex v Hampshire, Southampton, 2001; I. J. Harvey, Gloucestershire v Warwickshire, Bristol, 2002; B. V. Taylor, Sussex v Surrey, Hove, 2002.

Wicket-keeping and Fielding

Most dismissals: 122 (117 ct, 5 st), D. L. Bairstow; 113 (102 ct, 11 st), S. J. Rhodes; 112 (105 ct, 7 st), W. K. Hegg; 101 (86 ct, 15 st), R. C. Russell.

Most dismissals in an innings: 8 (all ct), D. J. S. Taylor, Somerset v Oxford & Cambridge Univs, Taunton, 1982.

Most catches by a fielder: 68, G. A. Gooch; 55, C. J. Tavaré; 53, I. T. Botham; 51, G. A. Hick.

Most catches by a fielder in an innings: 5, V. J. Marks, Oxford & Cambridge Univs v Kent, Oxford, 1976.

Results

Largest victories in runs: Essex by 272 runs v Scotland, Chelmsford, 1992; Leicestershire by 256 runs v Minor Counties, Leicester, 1998; Somerset by 233 runs v Ireland, Eglinton, 1995; Somerset by 221 runs v Ireland, Taunton, 1997; Glamorgan by 217 runs v Combined Universities, Cardiff, 1995; Essex by 214 runs v Oxford & Cambridge Univs, Chelmsford, 1979; Derbyshire by 206 runs v Combined Universities, Oxford, 1991; Warwickshire by 195 runs v Minor Counties, Jesmond, 1996.

Victories by ten wickets (21): By Derbyshire, Essex (twice), Glamorgan, Hampshire, Kent (twice), Lancashire (twice), Leicestershire (twice), Middlesex, Northamptonshire, Nottinghamshire, Somerset, Warwickshire, Worcestershire (twice), Yorkshire (three times).

Gold Awards

Most awards: 22, G. A. Gooch; 11, K. J. Barnett, M. W. Gatting, G. A. Hick, T. E. Jesty and B. Wood.

WINNERS 1972–2002

Gold Award

1972	LEICESTERSHIRE* beat Yorkshire by five wickets.	J. C. Balderstone
1973	KENT* beat Worcestershire by 39 runs.	Asif Iqbal
1974	SURREY* beat Leicestershire by 27 runs.	J. H. Edrich
1975	LEICESTERSHIRE beat Middlesex* by five wickets.	N. M. McVicker
1976	KENT* beat Worcestershire by 43 runs.	G. W. Johnson
1977	GLOUCESTERSHIRE* beat Kent by 64 runs.	A. W. Stovold
1978	KENT beat Derbyshire by six wickets.	R. A. Woolmer
1979	ESSEX beat Surrey* by 35 runs.	G. A. Gooch
1980	NORTHAMPTONSHIRE* beat Essex by six runs.	A. J. Lamb
1981	SOMERSET* beat Surrey by seven wickets.	I. V. A. Richards
1982	SOMERSET* beat Nottinghamshire by nine wickets.	V. J. Marks
1983	MIDDLESEX beat Essex* by four runs.	C. T. Radley
1984	LANCASHIRE* beat Warwickshire by six wickets.	J. Abrahams
1985	LEICESTERSHIRE* beat Essex by five wickets.	P. Willey
1986	MIDDLESEX beat Kent* by two runs.	J. E. Emburey
1987	YORKSHIRE* beat Northamptonshire, having taken more wickets with the scores tied.	J. D. Love
1988	HAMPSHIRE* beat Derbyshire by seven wickets.	S. T. Jefferies
1989	NOTTINGHAMSHIRE beat Essex* by three wickets.	R. T. Robinson
1990	LANCASHIRE beat Worcestershire* by 69 runs.	M. Watkinson
1991	WORCESTERSHIRE beat Lancashire* by 65 runs.	G. A. Hick
1992	HAMPSHIRE beat Kent* by 41 runs.	R. A. Smith
1993	DERBYSHIRE beat Lancashire* by six runs.	D. G. Cork
1994	WARWICKSHIRE* beat Worcestershire by six wickets.	P. A. Smith
1995	LANCASHIRE beat Kent* by 35 runs.	P. A. de Silva†
1996	LANCASHIRE* beat Northamptonshire by 31 runs.	I. D. Austin
1997	SURREY beat Kent* by eight wickets.	B. C. Hollioake
1998	ESSEX beat Leicestershire* by 192 runs.	P. J. Prichard
1999‡	GLOUCESTERSHIRE* beat Yorkshire by 124 runs.	M. W. Alleyne
2000	GLOUCESTERSHIRE beat Glamorgan* by seven wickets.	M. P. Maynard†
2001	SURREY* beat Gloucestershire by 47 runs.	B. C. Hollioake
2002	WARWICKSHIRE* beat Essex by five wickets.	I. R. Bell

* *Won toss.*   † *On losing side.*   ‡ *Super Cup.*

The second Asian Test Championship was a hopeless affair.
The Asian Test Championship, page 1185

WINS BY NON-CHAMPIONSHIP TEAMS

1973	OXFORD beat Northamptonshire at Northampton by two wickets.
1975	{ OXFORD & CAMBRIDGE beat Worcestershire at Cambridge by 66 runs.
	{ OXFORD & CAMBRIDGE beat Northamptonshire at Oxford by three wickets.
1976	OXFORD & CAMBRIDGE beat Yorkshire at Barnsley by seven wickets.
1980	MINOR COUNTIES beat Gloucestershire at Chippenham by three runs.
1981	MINOR COUNTIES beat Hampshire at Southampton by three runs.
1982	MINOR COUNTIES beat Leicestershire at Wellington by 131 runs.
1984	OXFORD & CAMBRIDGE beat Gloucestershire at Bristol by 27 runs.
1986	SCOTLAND beat Lancashire at Perth by three runs.
1987	MINOR COUNTIES beat Glamorgan at Oxford (Christ Church) by seven wickets.
1989	{ COMBINED UNIVERSITIES beat Surrey at Cambridge by nine runs.
	{ COMBINED UNIVERSITIES beat Worcestershire at Worcester by five wickets.
1990	{ COMBINED UNIVERSITIES beat Yorkshire at Leeds by two wickets.
	{ SCOTLAND beat Northamptonshire at Northampton by two wickets.
1992	MINOR COUNTIES beat Sussex at Marlow by 19 runs.
1995	MINOR COUNTIES beat Leicestershire at Leicester by 26 runs.
1997	{ IRELAND beat Middlesex at Dublin (Castle Avenue) by 46 runs.
	{ BRITISH UNIVERSITIES beat Sussex at Cambridge by 19 runs.
1998	BRITISH UNIVERSITIES beat Gloucestershire at Bristol by seven runs.

TEAM RECORDS 1972–2002

	Rounds reached				Matches			
	W	F	SF	QF	P	W	L	NR
Derbyshire	1	3	4	9	136	66	58	12
Durham	0	0	0	3	43	19	22	2
Essex	2	7	10	17	154	92	53	9
Glamorgan	0	1	2	9	132	54	70	8
Gloucestershire	3	4	5	11	141	74	61	6
Hampshire	2	2	5	14	142	66	67	9
Kent	3	8	13	19	160	98	54	8
Lancashire	4	6	12	20	160	98	54	8
Leicestershire	3	5	8	13	148	81	57	10
Middlesex	2	3	5	15	144	70	60	14
Northamptonshire	1	3	6	11	138	64	63	11
Nottinghamshire	1	2	6	14	142	78	56	8
Somerset	2	2	8	14	143	73	63	7
Surrey	3	5	11	16	153	85	59	9
Sussex	0	0	2	13	135	65	64	6
Warwickshire	2	3	9	17	150	83	57	10
Worcestershire	1	5	9	16	148	76	65	7
Yorkshire	1	3	9	16	146	80	58	8
Cambridge University	0	0	0	0	8	0	8	0
Oxford University	0	0	0	0	4	1	3	0
Oxford & Cambridge Universities	0	0	0	0	48	4	42	2
Combined/British Universities	0	0	0	1	47	5	41	1
Minor Counties	0	0	0	0	75	6	65	4
Minor Counties (North)	0	0	0	0	20	0	20	0
Minor Counties (South)	0	0	0	0	20	0	19	1
Minor Counties (East)	0	0	0	0	12	0	12	0
Minor Counties (West)	0	0	0	0	12	0	12	0
Scotland	0	0	0	0	70	2	64	4
Ireland	0	0	0	0	17	1	14	2

Middlesex beat Gloucestershire on the toss of a coin in their quarter-final in 1983. Derbyshire, Kent, Somerset and Warwickshire totals each include a bowling contest; Derbyshire beat Somerset and Warwickshire beat Kent when their quarter-finals, in 1993 and 1994 respectively, were abandoned. In 1999, only eight counties took part; from 2000, the competition was restricted to the 18 first-class counties.

NORWICH UNION LEAGUE, 2002

Robert Croft

As the September sun set over Canterbury, the equation for Glamorgan was simple: avoid leaking ten runs in the last over and win the League. Paul Nixon's desperate dive couldn't prevent him being run out, Kent's tailenders couldn't muster the runs, and Glamorgan began their celebrations. Robert Croft was their *primus inter pares*: 28 wickets, pinch-hitting opener and stand-in captain. The victory over last year's winners, Kent, in the penultimate match of the season, was not just clinching but symbolic: a year before, Glamorgan had been playing in the second division, as had the eventual runners-up, Worcestershire. What's more, the three sides who had never plunged down a division – Kent, Leicestershire and Yorkshire – ended the summer off the pace. In football, the gap between the top league and the next is a chasm; in one-day cricket it looked paper-thin.

The race for the title was less a question of neck-and-neck jostling than of Glamorgan quietly stalking Warwickshire and Worcestershire from third or fourth place, knowing they had enough games in hand to surge past them in the second half of the season. During the first, so many teams had played different numbers of games that a crystal ball and a calculator were needed to find out who was genuinely in contention. Warwickshire, inspired by laser-guided bowling and beefy hitting from Shaun Pollock, began with a bang, before losing four matches from five in late June and July. By September, Glamorgan had sneaked past Worcestershire to head the table, and they extended that lead by beating them, for the second time, on September 3. It gave them a six-point cushion, with two games left. In a sign of the League's place in the pecking order, finishing as runners-up was not enough for Graeme Hick to save his captaincy.

In Division Two the story was very different – Gloucestershire opened up an early lead and never looked back. Their success suggested that the sharp decline in their one-day form after the trophies of 1999 and 2000 had perhaps bottomed out. They finished two points ahead of Surrey, who continued to yo-yo between the divisions after promotion in 2000 and relegation in 2001. The third promotion place was won by a resurgent Essex – with a lot of help from Northamptonshire, who threw away a strong position by failing to win any of their last six games.

In 2003, the climb out of the bottom division will be even steeper, as Scotland join in for the first time. The impact they make may largely depend on money: the Scottish Cricket Union hope to offer up to eight semi-professional contracts to amateur players, and are also planning to land two big names from overseas. But both projects depend on support from sponsors. Scotland are not the only ones in need of commercial support – the League itself needs a new sponsor. Having already gone through more incarnations than a Buddhist lama, the competition will have a new name in 2003, its 12th in 35 years.

NORWICH UNION LEAGUE

Division One

	M	W	L	T	NR	Pts	Net run-rate
1 – Glamorgan Dragons (*1*)	16	12	3	1	0	50	8.35
2 – Worcestershire Royals (*3*)	16	11	3	0	2	48	10.68
3 – Warwickshire Bears (*3*)	16	9	6	0	1	38	8.41
4 – Yorkshire Phoenix (**6**)	16	8	7	0	1	34	1.43
5 – Kent Spitfires (**1**)	16	7	8	1	0	30	5.84
6 – Leicestershire Foxes (**2**)	16	7	8	0	1	30	3.52
7 – Somerset Sabres (**4**)	16	5	10	0	1	22	–3.52
8 – Durham Dynamos (*2*)	16	5	11	0	0	20	–21.17
9 – Nottinghamshire Outlaws (**5**)	16	3	11	0	2	16	–11.28

Division Two

	M	W	L	T	NR	Pts	Net run-rate
1 – Gloucestershire Gladiators (**7**) . . .	16	10	4	0	2	44	12.74
2 – Surrey Lions (**8**)	16	10	5	0	1	42	6.52
3 – Essex Eagles (*7*)	16	10	6	0	0	40	3.93
4 – Derbyshire Scorpions (*9*)	16	8	7	0	1	34	–0.98
5 – Lancashire Lightning (*6*)	16	7	7	0	2	32	–6.96
6 – Northamptonshire Steelbacks (**9**) .	16	7	8	0	1	30	7.60
7 – Hampshire Hawks (*4*)	16	6	9	0	1	26	–2.80
8 – Sussex Sharks (*5*)	16	4	10	0	2	20	–7.42
9 – Middlesex Crusaders (*8*)	16	4	10	0	2	20	–12.51

2001 positions are shown in brackets: Division One in bold, Division Two in italic.

The bottom three teams in Division One are relegated for 2003, the top three teams in Division Two are promoted for 2003. The bottom four teams in Division Two play each other in the third round of the 2003 Cheltenham & Gloucester Trophy.

When two or more counties finished with an equal number of points, the positions were decided by a) most wins, b) higher net run-rate (runs scored per 100 balls minus runs conceded per 100 balls).

Prize money

Division One
£54,000 for winners: GLAMORGAN.
£27,000 for runners-up: WORCESTERSHIRE.

Division Two
£20,000 for winners: GLOUCESTERSHIRE.
£11,000 for runners-up: SURREY.

Winners of each match (both divisions): £600.

Leading run-scorers: B. F. Smith 654, D. I. Stevens 651, *S. G. Law* 561, V. S. Solanki 555, *C. M. Spearman* 542, *M. R. Ramprakash* 537, K. P. Pietersen 515, I. J. Sutcliffe 512, *A. Flower* 506.

Leading wicket-takers: *E. S. H. Giddins* and N. Killeen 30, R. B. D. Croft 28, *A. D. Mascarenhas* and *A. M. Smith* 24, *A. J. Hollioake* and *G. Welch* 23, *J. W. Cook*, P. S. Jones, *B. V. Taylor* and *J. Wood* 22.

Most economical bowlers (runs per over, minimum 100 overs): *A. M. Smith* 3.52, *R. S. C. Martin-Jenkins* 3.56, *A. L. Penberthy* 3.84, *B. V. Taylor* 3.87, *A. D. Mascarenhas* 4.00, *M. J. G. Davis* 4.01, *J. Wood* 4.05, *E. S. H. Giddins* 4.06, *J. I. D. Kerr* 4.13.

Leading wicket-keepers: P. A. Nixon 26 (20 ct, 6 st) and *R. C. Russell* 26 (21 ct, 5 st), *T. M. B. Bailey* 25 (19 ct, 6 st) and A. Pratt 25 (19 ct, 6 st), R. J. Turner 23 (17 ct, 6 st) and M. A. Wallace 23 (17 ct, 6 st).

Leading fielders: *N. C. Johnson* and M. P. Maynard 13, M. J. Powell (Warwickshire) 11, K. P. Dutch and T. R. Ward 10, *A. J. Hollioake* 9.
M. P. Maynard also took one catch as a wicket-keeper.

Players who appeared in Division Two are shown in italics.

DIVISION ONE

DURHAM

DURHAM v WARWICKSHIRE

At Chester-le-Street, May 12. Warwickshire won by 44 runs. Toss: Warwickshire.

On a slow pitch, Knight soon opted for steady accumulation, and Bell followed suit, hitting only two fours in an 85-ball half-century. With Durham chasing 208, Pollock took three quick wickets, before Love and Lewis rallied with a stand of 58. But four wickets fell for eight runs, including three stumpings by Piper, and Durham finished well short.

Warwickshire

*M. J. Powell lbw b Hunter	1	N. M. K. Smith not out	9
N. V. Knight c Lewis b Davies	40	A. F. Giles not out	1
S. M. Pollock c Davies b Hunter	25	L-b 8, w 5	13
I. R. Bell c Hunter b Collingwood	72		
J. O. Troughton c Peng b Bridge	14	1/4 (1) 2/40 (3) (7 wkts, 45 overs) 207
T. L. Penney b Collingwood	29	3/91 (2) 4/120 (5)
D. R. Brown lbw b Killeen	3	5/189 (4) 6/193 (7) 7/205 (6)

†K. J. Piper and M. A. Sheikh did not bat.

Bowling: Killeen 9–1–31–1; Hunter 9–2–42–2; Davies 9–1–38–1; Collingwood 5–0–31–2; Bridge 9–0–35–1; Gough 4–0–22–0.

Durham

G. J. Pratt c Piper b Pollock	1	A. M. Davies not out	31
N. Peng lbw b Pollock	3	N. Killeen not out	9
M. L. Love lbw b Smith	36		
P. D. Collingwood c Piper b Pollock	11	L-b 5, w 3	8
*J. J. B. Lewis st Piper b Smith	26		
†A. Pratt st Piper b Smith	6	1/5 (1) 2/8 (2) (9 wkts, 45 overs) 163
M. A. Gough st Piper b Giles	7	3/22 (4) 4/80 (3)
I. D. Hunter c Powell b Sheikh	7	5/87 (5) 6/88 (6) 7/88 (7)
G. D. Bridge b Brown	24	8/109 (8) 9/138 (9)

Bowling: Pollock 9–1–29–3; Brown 9–0–23–1; Sheikh 9–0–47–1; Giles 9–0–34–1; Smith 9–0–25–3.

Umpires: J. H. Evans and J. W. Holder.

At Cardiff, May 19. DURHAM lost to GLAMORGAN by 20 runs.

At Birmingham, June 4. DURHAM lost to WARWICKSHIRE by seven wickets.

DURHAM v WORCESTERSHIRE

At Chester-le-Street, June 16. Worcestershire won by 121 runs (D/L method). Toss: Worcestershire. Torrential rain seeped under the covers and the match was played on a used practice pitch. It proved treacherous, and Worcestershire's 265 – built round a well-judged 83 from Smith – was daunting. Durham started scratchily and were routed by Leatherdale: after bowling Peng with a shooter, he enticed four more to their downfall, finishing with a career-best five for nine in just three and a half overs. Rain ended play in the 30th over, with Durham hopelessly behind the required rate.

Worcestershire

V. S. Solanki c Peng b Killeen	12	M. J. Rawnsley not out	1
A. Singh c Gough b Hatch	37	A. A. Donald c Davies b Killeen	0
*G. A. Hick b Davies	41		
B. F. Smith b Law	83	B 4, l-b 7, w 8, n-b 2	21
D. A. Leatherdale c A. Pratt b Davies	4		
G. J. Batty b Davies	36	1/25 (1) 2/91 (2) 3/124 (3) (44.4 overs) 265
†S. J. Rhodes c A. Pratt b Killeen	2	4/132 (5) 5/212 (6)
Kabir Ali c Muchall b Law	24	6/215 (7) 7/259 (8)
M. S. Mason c Lewis b Killeen	4	8/262 (4) 9/264 (9) 10/265 (11)

Bowling: Hatch 7–0–40–1; Killeen 8.4–0–48–4; Law 8–0–67–2; Bridge 9–1–33–0; Davies 9–0–41–3; Gough 3–0–25–0.

Durham

M. A. Gough c Solanki b Ali	0	A. M. Davies c Rhodes b Leatherdale	0
G. J. Pratt b Mason	16	N. Killeen not out	0
G. J. Muchall st Rhodes b Rawnsley	28	L-b 2, w 9	11
N. Peng b Leatherdale	29		
*J. J. B. Lewis not out	5	1/1 (1) 2/28 (2) (8 wkts, 29.3 overs) 99
†A. Pratt b Leatherdale	0	3/81 (3) 4/85 (4)
D. R. Law lbw b Leatherdale	10	5/85 (6) 6/97 (7)
G. D. Bridge b Leatherdale	0	7/97 (8) 8/99 (9)

N. G. Hatch did not bat.

Bowling: Ali 6–1–23–1; Mason 7–1–27–1; Donald 6–1–18–0; Rawnsley 7–0–20–1; Leatherdale 3.3–1–9–5.

Umpires: I. J. Gould and T. E. Jesty.

DURHAM v YORKSHIRE

At Chester-le-Street, June 23. Yorkshire won by 30 runs. Toss: Yorkshire. A breathtaking catch by Lehmann stalled Durham just when their chase seemed to be back on track. Lewis and Gary Pratt had added 83 in 14 overs when Lewis blasted Dawson to short extra cover: Lehmann jumped, knocked the ball upwards and grabbed the rebound. Pratt skied a catch in Dawson's next over, and two more quickly followed. Earlier, Lehmann had hit a controlled 70 on his return from international one-day duty. Silverwood crashed 58 off only 32 balls as a pinch-hitter.

Yorkshire

C. White c A. Pratt b Bridge	32	G. M. Fellows not out		9
M. J. Wood c A. Pratt b Killeen	11	L-b 2, w 3, n-b 2		7
C. E. W. Silverwood b Davies	58			
A. McGrath run out	40	1/32 (2) 2/103 (3)	(5 wkts, 45 overs)	269
*D. S. Lehmann c Muchall b Killeen	70	3/109 (4) 4/184 (4)		
M. J. Lumb not out	42	5/234 (5)		

†R. J. Blakey, R. K. J. Dawson, T. T. Bresnan and R. J. Sidebottom did not bat.

Bowling: Killeen 9–2–41–2; Hatch 9–0–60–0; Law 8–0–57–0; Davies 9–0–40–1; Bridge 8–0–57–1; Symington 2–0–12–0.

Durham

N. Peng c Blakey b Bresnan	7	N. Killeen not out		22
G. J. Pratt c Lehmann b Dawson	61	N. G. Hatch not out		20
G. J. Muchall b Bresnan	20			
M. J. Symington c Blakey b White	13	B 5, l-b 6, w 7, n-b 3		21
*J. J. B. Lewis c Lehmann b Dawson	37			
†A. Pratt c Wood b Lehmann	32	1/10 (1) 2/49 (3)	(9 wkts, 45 overs)	239
D. R. Law st Blakey b Lehmann	0	3/64 (4) 4/147 (5)		
G. D. Bridge c Blakey b Dawson	1	5/158 (2) 6/158 (7)		
A. M. Davies st Blakey b Dawson	5	7/161 (8) 8/185 (9) 9/194 (6)		

Bowling: Silverwood 7–1–28–0; Bresnan 7–0–27–2; White 4–0–30–1; Sidebottom 6–0–27–0; Lehmann 8–0–35–2; McGrath 2–0–22–0; Dawson 9–0–37–4; Fellows 2–0–22–0.

Umpires: D. J. Constant and N. G. Cowley.

At Worcester, June 30. DURHAM beat WORCESTERSHIRE by nine wickets (D/L method).

At Maidstone, July 7. DURHAM lost to KENT by 165 runs.

DURHAM v LEICESTERSHIRE

At Chester-le-Street, July 21. Leicestershire won by 85 runs. Toss: Leicestershire.

Two dropped catches at second slip in the fifth and sixth overs by Phillips proved crucial. The reprieved men, Stevens and Ward, smashed a string of boundaries, and Stevens went on to rub more salt into Durham's wounds with a blazing 114-ball 125. In reply, Collingwood, making his first appearance in eight weeks, walloped 44 and built a threatening stand with Muchall. But both fell to leg-side catches in the deep, and Durham's challenge faded.

Leicestershire

T. R. Ward b Davies	33	P. A. J. DeFreitas run out		0
I. J. Sutcliffe c Collingwood b Hunter	6	C. D. Crowe not out		1
D. I. Stevens st A. Pratt b Phillips	125	L-b 6, w 15		21
M. G. Bevan lbw b Collingwood	20			
*V. J. Wells c G. J. Pratt b Phillips	12	1/12 (2) 2/75 (1)	(7 wkts, 45 overs)	266
†N. D. Burns c Lewis b Collingwood	18	3/129 (4) 4/164 (5)		
D. L. Maddy not out	30	5/210 (6) 6/256 (3) 7/259 (8)		

J. O. Grove and M. J. A. Whiley did not bat.

Bowling: Hunter 8–0–46–1; Killeen 9–1–51–0; Davies 9–1–40–1; Law 3–0–24–0; Collingwood 7–0–45–2; Phillips 9–0–54–2.

Durham

N. Peng c Stevens b DeFreitas	10	
†A. Pratt b DeFreitas	2	
D. R. Law c Ward b DeFreitas	9	
P. D. Collingwood c Ward b Whiley	44	
G. J. Muchall c Ward b Crowe	48	
*J. J. B. Lewis c Maddy b Crowe	31	
G. J. Pratt run out	3	
I. D. Hunter st Burns b Crowe	16	
N. C. Phillips b Wells	0	

A. M. Davies lbw b Wells	0
N. Killeen not out	0
L-b 8, w 8, n-b 2	18
	—
	181

1/8 (2) 2/17 (1) 3/26 (3)   (40.2 overs) 181
4/91 (4) 5/139 (5) 6/145 (7)
7/174 (6) 8/175 (9)
9/175 (10) 10/181 (8)

Bowling: DeFreitas 7–0–25–3; Grove 7–1–23–0; Whiley 5–0–31–1; Maddy 5–0–26–0; Crowe 8.2–0–42–3; Wells 8–0–26–2.

Umpires: J. H. Hampshire and N. A. Mallender.

DURHAM v NOTTINGHAMSHIRE

At Chester-le-Street, July 28. Durham won by 44 runs. Toss: Durham.

Collingwood's masterly maiden one-day century propelled Durham to 275, their highest in the League at the Riverside. Gough provided solidity on his recall, putting on 63 with Peng and 104 with Collingwood. Nottinghamshire stumbled to 53 for four before Pietersen and Boje smashed 136 in 20 overs. But the fightback ended when Pietersen fell, and his team-mates went tamely.

Durham

N. Peng b Logan	38
M. A. Gough c Pietersen b Boje	57
P. D. Collingwood not out	118
G. J. Pratt run out	20
*J. J. B. Lewis not out	29
L-b 8, w 5	13

1/63 (1) 2/167 (2)   (3 wkts, 45 overs) 275
3/192 (4)

†A. Pratt, D. R. Law, N. C. Phillips, A. M. Davies, N. Killeen and S. J. Harmison did not bat.

Bowling: Smith 9–2–50–0; Harris 9–0–50–0; Logan 9–0–73–1; Randall 9–0–49–0; Boje 9–0–45–1.

Nottinghamshire

P. Johnson b Killeen	13	
G. E. Welton c Peng b Killeen	7	
U. Afzaal c A. Pratt b Harmison	10	
*J. E. R. Gallian c Collingwood b Davies	10	
N. Boje b Phillips	60	
K. P. Pietersen c A. Pratt b Collingwood	85	
†C. M. W. Read b Killeen	17	
S. J. Randall c Collingwood b Phillips	3	
G. J. Smith lbw b Phillips	3	

R. J. Logan not out	7
A. J. Harris c A. Pratt b Collingwood	3
L-b 3, w 10	13

1/13 (1) 2/33 (2) 3/44 (3)   (44.4 overs) 231
4/53 (4) 5/189 (6) 6/199 (5)
7/205 (8) 8/213 (9)
9/224 (7) 10/231 (11)

Bowling: Harmison 9–0–33–1; Killeen 8–0–31–3; Davies 5–0–25–1; Law 5–0–34–0; Phillips 9–0–52–3; Gough 3–0–23–0; Collingwood 5.4–0–30–2.

Umpires: M. J. Harris and B. Leadbeater.

DURHAM v KENT

At Chester-le-Street, August 3. Kent won by five wickets. Toss: Durham.

A delayed start reduced the game to 37 overs a side. The damp pitch was a medium-pacer's dream, and Golding and the trundling but miserly Ealham reduced Durham from 41 without loss to 95 for six. The result was never in doubt once Fleming had kickstarted Kent's reply with 37 off 22 balls.

Durham

N. Peng c Fleming b Golding	32	A. M. Davies c Ealham b Fleming		3
M. A. Gough c and b Golding	12			
D. R. Law c Fleming b Golding	12	B 1, l-b 9, w 7		17
P. D. Collingwood c Nixon b Ealham	10			
G. J. Pratt b Ealham	6	1/41 (2) 2/55 (1)	(8 wkts, 37 overs)	153
*J. B. Lewis not out	37	3/65 (3) 4/74 (4)		
†A. Pratt c Key b Ealham	7	5/84 (5) 6/95 (7)		
N. C. Phillips run out	17	7/139 (8) 8/153 (9)		

N. Killeen and S. J. Harmison did not bat.

Bowling: Saggers 8–0–28–0; Masters 7–1–42–0; Golding 7–0–23–3; Ealham 8–1–18–3; Fleming 7–0–32–1.

Kent

*M. V. Fleming c Davies b Harmison	37	†P. A. Nixon not out		13
R. W. T. Key b Phillips	20	B 4, l-b 3, w 9		16
J. B. Hockley c Davies b Harmison	29			
A. Symonds c and b Phillips	29	1/51 (1) 2/80 (2)	(5 wkts, 31.3 overs)	154
E. T. Smith c and b Phillips	0	3/122 (3) 4/123 (5)		
M. J. Walker not out	10	5/124 (4)		

M. A. Ealham, J. M. Golding, M. J. Saggers and D. D. Masters did not bat.

Bowling: Killeen 6–0–28–0; Harmison 8–0–45–2; Davies 4–0–20–0; Phillips 8–0–38–3; Gough 3.3–0–9–0; Law 2–0–7–0.

Umpires: A. Clarkson and D. J. Constant.

At Leeds, August 5 (day/night). DURHAM lost to YORKSHIRE by 28 runs.

At Leicester, August 11. DURHAM beat LEICESTERSHIRE by five wickets.

DURHAM v GLAMORGAN

At Chester-le-Street, August 14 (day/night). Glamorgan won by three wickets. Toss: Durham.

Thomas's 14-ball spell of three for five was the shove that began Durham's slide to defeat. On an unthreatening pitch, a healthy 77 for one became a perilous 121 for eight, as successive batsmen gifted their wickets, including two laughable run-outs. Needing 162 to win (and top the table), Glamorgan had one eye on improving their run-rate and lost wickets as a result. But James showed a cool head and skill against the turning ball. His unbeaten 55 saw them home comfortably.

Durham

N. Peng c Wallace b Davies	14	A. M. Davies not out		14
M. A. Gough c Wallace b S. D. Thomas	42	N. Killeen lbw b Croft		11
D. R. Law c Wallace b S. D. Thomas	15			
A. M. Thorpe c Maynard b Cosker	9	L-b 11, w 7, n-b 2		20
G. J. Pratt c Maynard b S. D. Thomas	0			
*J. J. B. Lewis run out	20	1/39 (1) 2/77 (2) 3/85 (3)	(42.5 overs)	161
†A. Pratt run out	0	4/86 (5) 5/109 (4) 6/109 (7)		
I. D. Hunter c Maynard b Croft	3	7/120 (8) 8/121 (6)		
N. C. Phillips b Kasprowicz	13	9/143 (9) 10/161 (11)		

Bowling: Kasprowicz 9–0–20–1; Davies 7–0–33–1; S. D. Thomas 6–0–31–3; Dale 5–1–15–0; Croft 6.5–0–31–2; Cosker 9–2–20–1.

Glamorgan

R. D. B. Croft c G. J. Pratt b Killeen	7	S. D. Thomas c and b Killeen		7
I. J. Thomas c Peng b Davies	8	M. S. Kasprowicz not out		5
M. J. Powell run out	39	L-b 6, w 4		10
M. P. Maynard c Hunter b Phillips	24			
*S. P. James not out	55	1/11 (2) 2/20 (1)	(7 wkts, 34.5 overs)	163
A. Dale b Phillips	0	3/74 (4) 4/114 (3)		
†M. A. Wallace c A. Pratt b Hunter	8	5/116 (6) 6/133 (7) 7/152 (8)		

A. P. Davies and D. A. Cosker did not bat.

Bowling: Killeen 8.5–1–46–2; Davies 7–1–30–1; Hunter 9–2–40–1; Phillips 9–0–38–2; Gough 1–0–3–0.

Umpires: N. A. Mallender and P. Willey.

DURHAM v SOMERSET

At Chester-le-Street, September 2. Durham won by six wickets. Toss: Somerset.

Hodge, Durham's replacement overseas player, returned after a broken left thumb and immediately stiffened their batting. Cutting vigorously, he made an assured 77 and put on 128 with Muchall, who reached his highest one-day score. Trescothick, released by England to prove his fitness ahead of the Fourth Test against India, had earlier cruised to 41 before driving to mid-off. Apart from him, only Dutch showed much gumption in Somerset's innings.

Somerset

*M. E. Trescothick c Gough		M. P. L. Bulbeck lbw b Phillips		8
b Symington	41	S. R. G. Francis not out		10
M. J. Wood c Symington b Killeen	7	P. S. Jones not out		5
K. P. Dutch c Peng b Gough	64	L-b 5, w 6, n-b 2		13
A. V. Suppiah st A. Pratt b Gough	22			
†R. J. Turner run out	24	1/15 (2) 2/85 (1)	(9 wkts, 45 overs)	204
I. D. Blackwell run out	3	3/135 (4) 4/145 (3)		
W. J. Durston run out	0	5/156 (6) 6/157 (7)		
P. D. Trego b Gough	7	7/174 (8) 8/183 (5) 9/196 (9)		

Bowling: Killeen 9–1–31–1; Davies 5–0–30–0; Symington 4–0–31–1; Hunter 5–0–27–0; Phillips 9–0–41–1; Gough 9–1–26–3; Hodge 4–0–14–0.

Durham

N. Peng c Trescothick b Francis	. . . . .	0
M. A. Gough lbw b Bulbeck	. . . .	7
B. J. Hodge st Turner b Blackwell	. . . .	77
G. J. Muchall b Blackwell	. . . .	81
G. J. Pratt not out	. . . .	12

†A. Pratt not out	15
L-b 7, w 9	16

1/4 (1) 2/31 (2)   (4 wkts, 44 overs) 208
3/159 (3) 4/190 (4)

M. J. Symington, I. D. Hunter, *N. C. Phillips, A. M. Davies and N. Killeen did not bat.

Bowling: Bulbeck 9–2–19–1; Francis 7–0–30–1; Dutch 9–0–33–0; Blackwell 7–0–47–2; Suppiah 5–0–26–0; Durston 2–0–19–0; Jones 5–0–27–0.

Umpires: M. R. Benson and M. J. Kitchen.

At Nottingham, September 4 (day/night). DURHAM beat NOTTINGHAMSHIRE by seven wickets.

At Taunton, September 22. DURHAM lost to SOMERSET by 175 runs.

GLAMORGAN

GLAMORGAN v DURHAM

At Cardiff, May 19. Glamorgan won by 20 runs. Toss: Glamorgan.

On a slow pitch, disciplined Glamorgan bowling strangled Durham. First Kasprowicz zipped the ball off the seam to take three for 18 in a seven-over spell; then Croft and Cosker kept the brakes on, conceding just three boundaries from their 18 overs. Glamorgan had also faltered against the new ball, slipping to 49 for five, but Powell and Wallace came to the rescue. Lewis dropped Wallace when he had only ten, a costly miss in a low-scoring game.

Glamorgan

K. Newell c Gough b Killeen	. . . .	4
D. L. Hemp lbw b Hunter	. . . .	5
R. D. B. Croft c Love b Killeen	. . . . . .	16
*S. P. James c Collingwood b Davies	. . .	15
A. Dale lbw b Davies	. . . .	4
M. J. Powell not out	. . . .	47
†M. A. Wallace c Peng b Bridge	. . . . . .	34
S. D. Thomas st A Pratt b Gough	. . . . .	14

M. S. Kasprowicz b Killeen	5
A. P. Davies not out	11
L-b 3, w 3	6

1/11 (1) 2/11 (2)   (8 wkts, 45 overs) 161
3/30 (3) 4/48 (5)
5/49 (4) 6/107 (7)
7/131 (8) 8/139 (9)

D. A. Cosker did not bat.

Bowling: Killeen 9–2–29–3; Hunter 6–0–35–1; Davies 9–2–24–2; Collingwood 7–2–17–0; Bridge 9–0–25–1; Gough 5–0–28–1.

Durham

G. J. Pratt lbw b Kasprowicz	. . . .	11
N. Peng b Kasprowicz	. . . .	0
M. L. Love b Kasprowicz	. . . .	12
P. D. Collingwood c Cosker b Croft	. . . .	9
*J. J. B. Lewis c Cosker b Croft	. . . . . .	13
†A. Pratt c Hemp b Davies	. . . .	42
M. A. Gough c Kasprowicz b Cosker	. . .	21
I. D. Hunter b Davies	. . . .	2
G. D. Bridge not out	. . . .	8

A. M. Davies b Kasprowicz	4
N. Killeen not out	7
L-b 5, w 7	12

1/4 (2) 2/26 (3)   (9 wkts, 45 overs) 141
3/27 (1) 4/41 (4)
5/65 (5) 6/111 (6)
7/118 (8) 8/120 (7) 9/130 (10)

Bowling: Kasprowicz 9–1–28–4; Davies 9–2–17–2; Thomas 9–1–37–0; Croft 9–0–26–2; Cosker 9–0–28–1.

Umpires: G. I. Burgess and M. J. Harris.

At Leicester, June 4. GLAMORGAN beat LEICESTERSHIRE by 45 runs.

GLAMORGAN v KENT

At Cardiff, June 9. Tied. Toss: Kent.

Rain prevented play before 4 p.m. and reduced the match to 23 overs a side. But after the soggy start came a thrilling finish. Kent were favourites at the beginning of the final over, needing six to win with four wickets in hand. But, after failing to score from Dale's first ball, Jones was caught off the next, and when Ealham fell to the fourth, six runs were still required. Golding drove the penultimate ball for four, but managed only a single from the last. Glamorgan had been given a turbo start by Hemp and Croft, and Kent needed to score at almost seven an over. They began well, but failed to capitalise on Key's fluent fifty and a 21-ball 32 from Symonds.

Glamorgan

R. D. B. Croft b Hewitt	23	†M. A. Wallace b Fleming	17
D. L. Hemp c Hockley b Symonds	39	A. G. Wharf not out	5
*S. P. James c Tredwell b Fleming	3	B 4, l-b 4, w 5, n-b 2	15
M. P. Maynard c Nixon b Ealham	6		
A. Dale b Tredwell	17	1/33 (1) 2/48 (3) (7 wkts, 23 overs) 155	
M. J. Powell c Fleming b Tredwell	2	3/55 (4) 4/83 (5)	
S. D. Thomas not out	28	5/91 (6) 6/105 (2) 7/146 (8)	

M. S. Kasprowicz and A. P. Davies did not bat.

Bowling: Golding 2–0–22–0; Hewitt 2–0–20–1; Ealham 5–0–33–1; Fleming 5–0–24–2; Tredwell 5–0–23–2; Symonds 4–0–25–1.

Kent

*M. V. Fleming c and b Davies	15	J. M. Golding not out	5
R. W. T. Key lbw b Croft	51	J. C. Tredwell run out	0
J. B. Hockley b Wharf	6	B 4, l-b 2, w 4	10
A. Symonds c Maynard b Davies	32		
D. P. Fulton run out	2	1/32 (1) 2/38 (3) (9 wkts, 23 overs) 155	
M. A. Ealham c Kasprowicz b Dale	24	3/88 (4) 4/95 (5)	
†P. A. Nixon lbw b Thomas	9	5/121 (2) 6/143 (7)	
G. O. Jones c Maynard b Dale	1	7/150 (8) 8/150 (6) 9/155 (10)	

J. P. Hewitt did not bat.

Bowling: Kasprowicz 4–0–27–0; Davies 5–0–25–2; Wharf 5–0–34–1; Thomas 3–0–24–1; Croft 5–0–34–1; Dale 1–0–5–2.

Umpires: J. H. Hampshire and M. J. Harris.

At Taunton, June 30. GLAMORGAN beat SOMERSET by one wicket (D/L method).

GLAMORGAN v LEICESTERSHIRE

At Swansea, July 7. Leicestershire won by five wickets. Toss: Glamorgan.

Glamorgan suffered their first defeat of the season, ending an unbeaten home run dating from August 2000. Miserly spells from the spinners Croft and Cosker restricted Leicestershire after DeFreitas's 16-ball 25 gave them a whirlwind start. At the death, 12 were needed from eight balls – Burns walloped ten from Thomas's last two deliveries and Leicestershire got home with four balls to spare. DeFreitas had earlier reduced Glamorgan to 28 for three before Dale's well-crafted half-century helped set a challenging total on a turning pitch.

Glamorgan

R. D. B. Croft c Wells b DeFreitas	11	M. S. Kasprowicz c Crowe b DeFreitas	13
*S. P. James b DeFreitas	6	A. P. Davies not out	2
D. L. Hemp lbw b DeFreitas	0	L-b 9, w 6	15
M. P. Maynard c Burns b Wells	38		
A. Dale not out	78	1/9 (2) 2/9 (3) (8 wkts, 45 overs) 220	
M. J. Powell c Whiley b Crowe	18	3/28 (1) 4/72 (4)	
†M. A. Wallace c Whiley b Crowe	15	5/112 (6) 6/147 (7)	
S. D. Thomas c Wells b Malcolm	24	7/193 (8) 8/216 (9)	

D. A. Cosker did not bat.

Bowling: DeFreitas 9–2–24–4; Malcolm 9–1–60–1; Wells 9–1–46–1; Whiley 3–0–18–0; Crowe 9–0–38–2; Maddy 6–0–25–0.

Leicestershire

T. R. Ward c Wallace b Kasprowicz	1	D. L. Maddy not out	17
P. A. J. DeFreitas c Wallace b Kasprowicz	25	B 1, l-b 4, w 7, n-b 2	14
I. J. Sutcliffe c Cosker b Croft	67		
D. I. Stevens c Wallace b Croft	28	1/3 (1) 2/33 (2) (5 wkts, 44.2 overs) 221	
*V. J. Wells b Davies	31	3/84 (4) 4/151 (3)	
†N. D. Burns not out	38	5/171 (5)	

R. J. Cunliffe, C. D. Crowe, D. E. Malcolm and M. J. A. Whiley did not bat.

Bowling: Kasprowicz 8.2–0–47–2; Davies 6–1–39–1; Thomas 6–0–55–0; Croft 9–1–19–2; Cosker 9–0–29–0; Dale 6–0–27–0.

Umpires: V. A. Holder and M. J. Kitchen.

At Nottingham, July 14. GLAMORGAN beat NOTTINGHAMSHIRE by eight wickets.

At Birmingham, July 28. GLAMORGAN beat WARWICKSHIRE by 62 runs.

GLAMORGAN v SOMERSET

At Cardiff, August 3. Somerset won by 107 runs (D/L method). Toss: Glamorgan.

Somerset owed their comprehensive victory to a muscular counter-attack marshalled by Parsons. Their last six and a half overs produced 63 runs, after Glamorgan had reduced them to 101 for five. Parsons and Turner began the revival, before Bulbeck and Dutch iced Somerset's cake by smashing 16 off Dale's final over. Despite an early flurry of boundaries from Croft, Glamorgan wickets were soon tumbling. Bulbeck ripped through the top order and only Powell and Parkin resisted, adding 45 for the tenth wicket – a Glamorgan record in limited-overs matches. But the contest was already over.

Somerset

P. D. Bowler b S. D. Thomas	18	K. P. Dutch not out	26
M. J. Wood c Maynard b Parkin	0	M. P. L. Bulbeck not out	24
*J. Cox c Cosker b Davies	12	B 6, l-b 9, w 14	29
M. Burns c James b S. D. Thomas	25		
K. A. Parsons c Hemp b Croft	70	1/4 (2) 2/34 (3) (7 wkts, 43.3 overs) 245	
D. Blackwell b Dale	10	3/58 (1) 4/78 (4)	
†R. J. Turner c Cosker b Croft	31	5/101 (6) 6/186 (5) 7/192 (7)	

S. R. G. Francis and P. S. Jones did not bat.

Bowling: Davies 8–0–37–1; Parkin 5.3–1–35–1; S. D. Thomas 4–0–22–2; Dale 8–0–48–1; Cosker 9–0–41–0; Croft 9–0–47–2.

Glamorgan

R. D. B. Croft c Dutch b Francis	16	D. A. Cosker b Burns		5
I. J. Thomas c Turner b Bulbeck	6	O. T. Parkin not out		14
D. L. Hemp c Dutch b Bulbeck	0			
†M. P. Maynard c Turner b Bulbeck	11	L-b 3, w 11		14
*S. P. James lbw b Bulbeck	2			
A. Dale c Turner b Francis	4	1/18 (2) 2/28 (1) 3/29 (3)	(22.1 overs)	118
M. J. Powell b Blackwell	46	4/32 (5) 5/41 (6) 6/58 (4)		
S. D. Thomas b Burns	0	7/65 (8) 8/65 (9)		
A. P. Davies lbw b Burns	0	9/73 (10) 10/118 (7)		

Bowling: Francis 6–0–30–2; Bulbeck 7–0–39–4; Burns 4–0–22–3; Jones 4–0–21–0; Blackwell 1.1–0–3–1.

Umpires: R. Palmer and J. F. Steele.

At Worcester, August 4. GLAMORGAN beat WORCESTERSHIRE by 22 runs (D/L method).

GLAMORGAN v YORKSHIRE

At Cardiff, August 11. Glamorgan won by 21 runs (D/L method). Toss: Glamorgan.

Glamorgan kept up their impressive one-day form, with their seventh win in ten league matches. Croft and Thomas gave Glamorgan a rapid start, before rain butted in. After the resumption, lusty lower-order hitting kept the runs flowing. Yorkshire's revised target of 175 off 22 overs, at a run-rate of almost eight, looked reachable as Silverwood slammed 55 from 39 balls. But Croft soon made inroads, taking three wickets in his first two overs, while Cosker grabbed four for 17, his League-best.

Glamorgan

R. D. B. Croft c McGrath b Sidebottom	37	†M. A. Wallace not out		10
I. J. Thomas b Blakey b Gray	40			
M. J. Powell b Dawson	12	L-b 2, w 6, n-b 2		10
M. P. Maynard c Lumb b Gray	3			
*S. P. James lbw b Dawson	0	1/84 (1) 2/91 (2)	(6 wkts, 22 overs)	149
A. Dale not out	18	3/99 (3) 4/99 (5)		
S. D. Thomas c Lumb b Gray	19	5/103 (4) 6/131 (7)		

A. P. Davies, D. A. Cosker and O. T. Parkin did not bat.

Bowling: Silverwood 6–0–34–0; Bresnan 3–0–18–0; Sidebottom 5–0–31–1; Dawson 4–0–31–2; Gray 3–0–23–3; McGrath 1–0–10–0.

Yorkshire

C. E. W. Silverwood c Maynard b Croft	55	T. T. Bresnan b Cosker		4
V. J. Craven c Cosker b Parkin	14	R. J. Sidebottom not out		4
M. J. Wood b Croft	9			
R. K. J. Dawson b Croft	8	L-b 6, w 4, n-b 4		14
A. McGrath c Wallace b Dale	1			
M. J. Lumb lbw b Cosker	14	1/42 (2) 2/86 (3) 3/94 (1)	(21.2 overs)	153
G. M. Fellows st Wallace b Cosker	27	4/98 (4) 5/100 (5)		
*†R. J. Blakey b Cosker	2	6/118 (6) 7/126 (8)		
A. K. D. Gray run out	1	8/135 (9) 9/148 (7) 10/153 (10)		

Bowling: Parkin 5–0–38–1; Davies 3–0–28–0; S. D. Thomas 2–0–18–0; Croft 5–0–27–3; Dale 3–0–19–1; Cosker 3.2–0–17–4.

Umpires: T. E. Jesty and M. J. Kitchen.

At Chester-le-Street, August 14 (day/night). GLAMORGAN beat DURHAM by three wickets.

GLAMORGAN v NOTTINGHAMSHIRE

At Colwyn Bay, August 26. Glamorgan won by five wickets. Toss: Nottinghamshire.

Glamorgan shot back to the top of the first division by chasing down a tricky target. Needing 227 on a slow, low pitch, they set off at a canter, with Ian Thomas blasting 64 from only 56 balls. James then saw them home with a controlled half-century. He shared fifty partnerships with Dale and Wallace, who improvised his way to his best League score. Earlier, Nottinghamshire had stuttered after Bicknell's dismissal, then rallied, hitting 39 runs from the final five overs. But it wasn't enough.

Nottinghamshire

D. J. Bicknell b Dale	51	P. J. Franks not out		15
G. E. Welton b Davies	18	S. J. Randall not out		17
N. Boje st Wallace b Dale	14	B 6, l-b 8, w 3		17
K. P. Pietersen c Croft b Dale	7			
B. M. Shafayat run out	48	1/37 (2) 2/75 (3)	(7 wkts, 45 overs)	226
*J. E. R. Gallian b Cosker	12	3/99 (1) 4/102 (4)		
†C. M. W. Read b Kasprowicz	27	5/124 (6) 6/186 (5) 7/190 (7)		

D. S. Lucas and R. J. Logan did not bat.

Bowling: Kasprowicz 9–0–48–1; Davies 9–1–37–1; S. D. Thomas 3–0–20–0; Dale 9–0–29–3; Croft 9–0–51–0; Cosker 6–0–27–1.

Glamorgan

R. D. B. Croft c Boje b Lucas	14	†M. A. Wallace not out		37
I. J. Thomas st Read b Boje	64	L-b 8, w 7		15
D. L. Hemp c Read b Franks	14			
M. P. Maynard c Pietersen b Boje	15	1/41 (1) 2/92 (3)	(5 wkts, 43 overs)	227
*S. P. James not out	54	3/111 (2) 4/122 (4)		
A. Dale c Randall b Shafayat	14	5/173 (6)		

S. D. Thomas, M. S. Kasprowicz, A. P. Davies and D. A. Cosker did not bat.

Bowling: Logan 8–0–39–0; Lucas 6–0–42–1; Franks 7–0–35–1; Shafayat 5–0–23–1; Boje 9–1–31–2; Randall 8–0–49–0.

Umpires: N. G. Cowley and J. F. Steele.

At Leeds, September 2. GLAMORGAN beat YORKSHIRE by nine wickets.

GLAMORGAN v WORCESTERSHIRE

At Cardiff, September 3 (day/night). Glamorgan won by 103 runs. Toss: Glamorgan.

Glamorgan's win over second-placed Worcestershire stretched their lead to six points with two games to go. They recovered from a poor start to reach an imposing total, built on an imperious 133-run partnership between Powell and Maynard. Worcestershire never looked on track in the face of an accurate attack and outstanding fielding. When Hick and Smith were dismissed in the space of four runs, Worcestershire had slumped to 91 for five. Despite Leatherdale's half-century their innings quickly folded, and the last three wickets fell in three balls.

Glamorgan

R. D. B. Croft lbw b Sheriyar	0
I. J. Thomas c Batty b Sheriyar	12
M. J. Powell run out	71
M. P. Maynard c and b Batty	87
*S. P. James run out	43
A. Dale c Singh b Leatherdale	3
†M. A. Wallace c Lampitt b Leatherdale	21
M. S. Kasprowicz run out	13

D. S. Harrison not out 10

B 2, l-b 4, w 14 20

1/1 (1) 2/24 (2)   (8 wkts, 45 overs) 280
3/157 (3) 4/198 (4)
5/207 (6) 6/249 (7)
7/261 (5) 8/280 (8)

A. P. Davies and D. A. Cosker did not bat.

Bowling: Sheriyar 9–0–55–2; Ali 9–0–61–0; Lampitt 7–0–52–0; Leatherdale 9–0–52–2; Batty 9–0–41–1; Hick 2–0–13–0.

Worcestershire

V. S. Solanki b Dale	27
A. Singh c Maynard b Davies	8
†D. J. Pipe b Kasprowicz	13
*G. A. Hick c Croft b Harrison	26
B. F. Smith run out	10
S. D. Peters c Wallace b Croft	11
D. A. Leatherdale b Croft	53
G. J. Batty st Wallace b Cosker	16
Kabir Ali c Croft b Cosker	1

S. R. Lampitt run out 0
A. Sheriyar not out 0

L-b 7, w 5 12

1/11 (2) 2/31 (3) 3/75 (1)   (36.3 overs) 177
4/87 (4) 5/91 (5) 6/131 (6)
7/175 (7) 8/177 (8)
9/177 (10) 10/177 (9)

Bowling: Kasprowicz 7–1–20–1; Davies 6–1–24–1; Harrison 7–1–35–1; Dale 7–0–31–1; Croft 5–0–32–2; Cosker 4.3–0–28–2.

Umpires: A. Clarkson and B. Leadbeater.

At Canterbury, September 15. GLAMORGAN beat KENT by four runs.

GLAMORGAN v WARWICKSHIRE

At Cardiff, September 22. Warwickshire won by 74 runs. Toss: Warwickshire.

A big crowd celebrated Glamorgan's title win, secured at Canterbury the previous week, despite witnessing their third loss of the season. Warwickshire set a challenging target as Brown and Ostler added 114 in only 13 overs. Glamorgan soon lost their openers, before Maynard and Dale gave them hope. But both were dismissed within three balls and their team-mates subsided with barely a whimper.

Warwickshire

M. A. Wagh c and b Kasprowicz	12
N. M. Carter c Thomas b Kasprowicz	4
D. R. Brown c Thomas b Croft	73
D. P. Ostler c Croft b Dale	97
M. A. Sheikh c Dale b Croft	2
H. R. Jones c Powell b Cosker	6
I. R. Bell c Harrison b Dale	31
*M. J. Powell not out	21
N. M. K. Smith c Maynard b Harrison	7

†K. J. Piper run out 0
T. Frost not out 12

L-b 3, w 1, n-b 6 10

1/11 (2) 2/23 (1)   (9 wkts, 45 overs) 275
3/137 (3) 4/148 (5)
5/174 (6) 6/224 (4)
7/247 (7) 8/259 (9) 9/259 (10)

Bowling: Kasprowicz 9–0–49–2; Davies 7–0–47–0; Harrison 6–0–51–1; Dale 5–0–37–2; Croft 9–0–45–2; Cosker 9–0–43–1.

Glamorgan

*R. D. B. Croft c Powell b Brown	20	A. P. Davies run out	0
I. J. Thomas c Piper b Carter	1	D. A. Cosker not out	1
M. J. Powell c Ostler b Smith	27		
M. P. Maynard lbw b Powell	54	B 8, l-b 1, w 8, n-b 8	25
A. Dale c and b Powell	31		
D. L. Hemp b Smith	24	1/26 (2) 2/30 (1) 3/84 (3) (35.3 overs) 201
†M. A. Wallace b Sheikh	0	4/157 (4) 5/158 (5)
M. S. Kasprowicz c Piper b Powell	10	6/165 (7) 7/184 (8)
D. S. Harrison run out	8	8/197 (9) 9/198 (10) 10/201 (6)

Bowling: Carter 7–0–42–1; Brown 6–0–36–1; Sheikh 9–0–40–1; Smith 6.3–0–30–2; Powell 7–0–44–3.

Umpires: J. W. Holder and A. A. Jones.

KENT

KENT v YORKSHIRE

At Canterbury, May 19. Yorkshire won by five wickets. Toss: Kent.

Kent's title defence began badly. On a slow pitch, only Symonds ever dominated the bowling, smashing five fours in his 18 balls, but he didn't last long enough to make much difference. Despite resistance from Walker and Fulton, Kent's total was barely adequate. Yorkshire's reply was delayed by a Gurkha pipe band, who disregarded the end of the interval and continued marching at long-on, oblivious to the bewildered players and umpires. White, having waited to take strike, was bowled first ball, but a shrewd partnership between Lehmann and Fellows guided Yorkshire home.

Kent

*M. V. Fleming c Wood b Kirby	0	M. J. Saggers lbw b White	1
R. W. T. Key b Bresnan	2	B. J. Trott c Blakey b White	0
J. B. Hockley lbw b Bresnan	20		
A. Symonds b Kirby	22	L-b 5, w 8	13
D. P. Fulton c White b Dawson	30		
M. J. Walker c Lumb b White	54	1/0 (1) 2/12 (2) 3/45 (4) (44.2 overs) 180
M. A. Ealham c McGrath b Lehmann . . .	10	4/51 (3) 5/108 (5)
†P. A. Nixon not out	26	6/127 (7) 7/166 (6)
C. Tredwell run out	2	8/178 (9) 9/180 (10) 10/180 (11)

Bowling: Kirby 9–0–40–2; Bresnan 9–1–27–2; Gray 6–0–28–0; Lehmann 6–0–22–1; White 8.2–0–23–3; Dawson 8–0–30–1; Fellows 1–0–5–0.

Yorkshire

C. White b Saggers	0	G. M. Fellows not out	35
M. J. Wood b Ealham	27	L-b 1, w 10	11
K. J. Dawson b Trott	12		
J. L. Lumb c Tredwell b Trott	6	1/0 (1) 2/23 (3) (5 wkts, 41.2 overs) 181
D. S. Lehmann not out	69	3/36 (4) 4/64 (2)
A. McGrath c Nixon b Saggers	21	5/121 (6)

†R. J. Blakey, A. K. D. Gray, T. T. Bresnan and S. P. Kirby did not bat.

Bowling: Saggers 8–0–37–2; Trott 9–0–39–2; Ealham 9–1–27–1; Tredwell 7–0–30–0; Fleming 5.2–0–28–0; Symonds 3–0–19–0.

Umpires: J. H. Evans and V. A. Holder.

KENT v NOTTINGHAMSHIRE

At Tunbridge Wells, June 4. Kent won by five wickets (D/L method). Toss: Nottinghamshire.
Nottinghamshire lost wickets too regularly to set a challenging target: although several batsmen got a start, none made a telling contribution. Rain during the interval meant Kent faced a revised target of 179 from 39 overs, and a typically belligerent innings from Fleming gave them the perfect beginning. A mini-collapse called for a recovery from Key and Nixon, and their responsible partnership ensured a comfortable win.

Nottinghamshire

D. J. Bicknell c Nixon b Khan	11	A. J. Harris not out	16
*J. E. R. Gallian lbw b Khan	12	M. N. Malik not out	0
U. Afzaal lbw b Fleming	33		
P. Johnson c Hockley b Golding	19	B 1, l-b 10, w 6	17
N. Boje b Symonds	25		
K. P. Pietersen run out	24	1/21 (2) 2/31 (1) (9 wkts, 45 overs) 191	
†C. M. W. Read lbw b Golding	12	3/78 (4) 4/81 (3)	
G. D. Clough c Symonds b Saggers	22	5/119 (6) 6/146 (5)	
G. J. Smith lbw b Golding	0	7/146 (7) 8/146 (9) 9/190 (8)	

Bowling: Saggers 9–0–40–1; Khan 8–0–47–2; Golding 9–1–25–3; Fleming 7–0–27–1; Tredwell 3–0–14–0; Symonds 9–0–27–1.

Kent

*M. V. Fleming b Boje	64	†P. A. Nixon not out	21
R. W. T. Key not out	68	L-b 4, w 3	7
J. B. Hockley b Boje	6		
A. Symonds b Smith	7	1/82 (1) 2/103 (3) (5 wkts, 34.1 overs) 181	
D. P. Fulton st Read b Pietersen	7	3/112 (4) 4/127 (5)	
E. T. Smith c Read b Pietersen	1	5/129 (6)	

J. M. Golding, J. C. Tredwell, A. Khan and M. J. Saggers did not bat.

Bowling: Smith 8–1–26–1; Harris 8–1–41–0; Malik 3–0–19–0; Boje 7–0–34–2; Clough 3–0–28–0; Pietersen 5.1–0–29–2.

Umpires: A. A. Jones and B. Leadbeater.

At Cardiff, June 9. KENT tied with GLAMORGAN.

At Nottingham, June 16. KENT beat NOTTINGHAMSHIRE by 132 runs.

At Birmingham, June 30. KENT lost to WARWICKSHIRE by 19 runs (D/L method).

KENT v DURHAM

At Maidstone, July 7. Kent won by 165 runs. Toss: Kent.
Masters ripped the heart out of Durham's innings with a wicket in his first over and three in four balls in his fourth, finishing with a one-day best of five for 20. The dank, murky conditions brought him disconcerting seam movement, while his pace had Nixon taking the ball above his head. From 19 for five, recovery was impossible. Earlier, Kent's impressive total was founded on half-centuries from Key and Hockley, then boosted by bold hitting from the lower order.

Kent

A. Khan lbw b Killeen	. . . .	6
R. W. T. Key st A. Pratt b Bridge	. . . . .	58
J. B. Hockley c G. J. Pratt b Davies	. . .	58
A. Symonds b Symington	. . . .	31
*D. P. Fulton lbw b Bridge	. . . .	10
M. A. Ealham c A. Pratt b Symington	. .	0
†P. A. Nixon c Muchall b Bridge	. . . . .	7
M. J. Walker b Hunter b Killeen	. . . . .	16
J. M. Golding c Symington b Law	. . . . .	21

M. M. Patel not out	. . . .	12
D. D. Masters not out	. . . .	6
	L-b 11, w 8	19

1/16 (1) 2/118 (2)   (9 wkts, 44 overs) 244
3/134 (3) 4/165 (5)
5/169 (6) 6/178 (4)
7/195 (7) 8/222 (9) 9/237 (8)

Bowling: Killeen 9–0–56–2; Hunter 6–0–51–0; Davies 9–0–33–1; Law 7–0–43–1; Bridge 9–0–33–3; Symington 4–0–17–2.

Durham

N. Peng c Nixon b Masters	. . . .	11
G. J. Pratt c Fulton b Masters	. . . . . .	0
G. J. Muchall b Khan	. . . .	1
M. J. Symington c Nixon b Golding	. . .	22
*J. J. B. Lewis lbw b Masters	. . . .	0
†A. Pratt b Masters	. . . .	0
D. R. Law c Golding b Masters	. . . . . .	10
I. D. Hunter lbw b Ealham	. . . .	2
G. D. Bridge c Ealham b Patel	. . . . . .	24

A. M. Davies st Nixon b Patel	. . . . . .	6
N. Killeen not out	. . . .	0
	W 1, n-b 2	3

1/3 (2) 2/4 (3) 3/19 (1)   (28.2 overs) 79
4/19 (5) 5/19 (6) 6/35 (7)
7/48 (8) 8/54 (4)
9/74 (10) 10/79 (9)

Bowling: Masters 7–0–20–5; Khan 5–1–14–1; Ealham 5–0–15–1; Golding 7–0–24–1; Patel 4.2–3–6–2.

Umpires: M. J. Harris and J. W. Holder.

KENT v WORCESTERSHIRE

At Canterbury, July 14. Worcestershire won by five wickets. Toss: Kent.

An awkward opening spell from Mason condemned Kent to a third defeat in seven games and dented their hopes of retaining the title. After bowling Fleming via his elbow, Mason took three more wickets in 24 balls. Walker hit a crisp 94 from just 77 deliveries, and Nixon compiled a slower 60 to restore some respectability. Worcestershire began scratchily, but Solanki found his fluency, Smith batted doggedly, and Leatherdale reduced the pressure with a jaunty 25.

Kent

*M. V. Fleming b Mason	. . . .	2
R. W. T. Key c Rhodes b Mason	. . . . .	9
J. B. Hockley c Smith b Mason	. . . . .	4
A. Symonds lbw b Bichel	. . . .	1
D. P. Fulton st Rhodes b Lampitt	. . . . .	14
M. J. Walker lbw b Batty	. . . .	94
†P. A. Nixon run out	. . . .	60

J. M. Golding not out	. . . .	28
J. C. Tredwell not out	. . . .	2
	B 1, l-b 4, w 3, n-b 2	10

1/2 (1) 2/10 (3)   (7 wkts, 45 overs) 224
3/11 (4) 4/21 (2)
5/52 (5) 6/168 (6) 7/212 (7)

M. J. Saggers and D. D. Masters did not bat.

Bowling: Mason 9–1–37–3; Bichel 8–1–31–1; Ali 9–0–54–0; Lampitt 9–2–37–1; Batty 5–0–35–1; Leatherdale 5–0–25–0.

Worcestershire

S. D. Peters c Hockley b Golding	19	†S. J. Rhodes not out	4
V. S. Solanki st Nixon b Golding	57	L-b 7, w 4	11
*G. A. Hick c Nixon b Tredwell	44		
B. F. Smith not out	54	1/63 (1) 2/101 (2) (5 wkts, 43 overs) 226	
D. A. Leatherdale c Hockley b Symonds	25	3/155 (3) 4/199 (5)	
G. J. Batty lbw b Saggers	12	5/222 (6)	

A. J. Bichel, Kabir Ali, S. R. Lampitt and M. S. Mason did not bat.

Bowling: Saggers 9–2–53–1; Masters 6–0–36–0; Golding 8–0–36–2; Fleming 8–1–28–0; Symonds 7–0–40–1; Tredwell 5–0–26–1.

Umpires: J. H. Hampshire and M. J. Kitchen.

At Leicester, July 28. KENT lost to LEICESTERSHIRE by 17 runs.

KENT v WARWICKSHIRE

At Canterbury, July 30 (day/night). Kent won by 13 runs (D/L method). Toss: Kent.

In a thrilling contest, Fleming's medium-pace and Nixon's impressive glovework demolished Warwickshire's innings. A mid-innings thunderstorm had heightened the drama, leaving Warwickshire a revised target of 144 from 22 overs, but wickets fell too regularly for them. Earlier, a solid partnership between Walker and Symonds had laid the foundation for Kent's total.

Kent

*M. V. Fleming c Carter b Warren	0	J. C. Tredwell not out	0
R. W. T. Key lbw b Warren	10	M. J. Saggers not out	4
J. B. Hockley c Piper b Warren	21		
A. Symonds b Richardson	46	B 1, l-b 3, w 5, n-b 2	11
M. J. Walker lbw b Brown	75		
†P. A. Nixon c Carter b Brown	34	1/0 (1) 2/26 (2) (9 wkts, 45 overs) 217	
G. O. Jones c Piper b Carter	6	3/35 (3) 4/113 (4)	
J. M. Golding st Piper b Brown	3	5/193 (5) 6/200 (7)	
D. D. Masters c Carter b Brown	7	7/205 (6) 8/213 (9) 9/213 (8)	

Bowling: Warren 5–0–34–3; Carter 9–0–41–2; Richardson 9–1–30–1; Brown 9–0–43–3; Smith 9–0–36–0; Powell 4–0–29–0.

Warwickshire

N. M. Carter b Saggers	18	N. A. Warren c Saggers b Golding	2
N. V. Knight st Nixon b Fleming	21	A. Richardson not out	1
D. R. Brown run out	4		
I. R. Bell st Nixon b Fleming	2	B 4, l-b 9, w 7	20
J. O. Troughton c Nixon b Symonds	24		
*M. J. Powell lbw b Fleming	7	1/36 (1) 2/47 (3) 3/51 (4) (21.2 overs) 130	
T. L. Penney c Nixon b Fleming	0	4/60 (2) 5/83 (6) 6/89 (5)	
N. M. K. Smith b Golding	14	7/89 (7) 8/121 (8)	
†K. J. Piper lbw b Symonds	17	9/123 (10) 10/130 (9)	

Bowling: Masters 4–0–27–0; Saggers 4–1–15–1; Fleming 5–0–22–4; Golding 4–0–30–2; Symonds 4.2–0–23–2.

Umpires: M. J. Kitchen and J. W. Lloyds.

At Chester-le-Street, August 3. KENT beat DURHAM by five wickets.

KENT v SOMERSET

At Canterbury, August 11. Kent won by 126 runs. Toss: Somerset.

An early three-wicket burst by Saggers sparked Somerset's rapid decline, and they were shot out with more than twelve overs remaining. Two run-outs didn't help, and only four players reached double figures in a disappointing performance. Kent gave Smith a rare one-day outing and he responded with a determined 83, while Walker and Ealham upped the momentum. A demoralised Somerset never got within a sniff of the 239 needed, and moved a step closer to relegation.

Kent

*M. V. Fleming c Turner b Bulbeck	31	G. O. Jones not out	12
E. T. Smith c Cox b Jones	83		
J. B. Hockley c Turner b Bulbeck	7	B 1, l-b 2, w 3	6
A. Symonds lbw b Jones	2		
M. J. Walker c Wood b Dutch	45	1/38 (1) 2/53 (3) (6 wkts, 45 overs) 238	
†P. A. Nixon c and b Dutch	8	3/58 (4) 4/153 (5)	
M. A. Ealham not out	44	5/168 (6) 6/191 (2)	

J. M. Golding, J. C. Tredwell and M. J. Saggers did not bat.

Bowling: Francis 5–0–29–0; Bulbeck 7–0–38–2; Jones 9–0–59–2; Parsons 7–0–33–0; Dutch 9–0–34–2; Blackwell 8–0–42–0.

Somerset

P. D. Bowler b Saggers	2	S. R. G. Francis c Saggers b Tredwell	27
M. J. Wood run out	14	P. S. Jones not out	5
*J. Cox run out	14		
M. Burns c Nixon b Saggers	0	B 1, l-b 4, w 6	11
K. A. Parsons c Nixon b Saggers	2		
I. D. Blackwell c Jones b Tredwell	23	1/6 (1) 2/23 (2) 3/25 (4) (32.5 overs) 112	
†R. J. Turner b Ealham	2	4/33 (5) 5/41 (3) 6/50 (7)	
K. P. Dutch c Symonds b Golding	7	7/60 (8) 8/71 (9)	
M. P. L. Bulbeck b Golding	5	9/88 (6) 10/112 (10)	

Bowling: Saggers 7–0–21–3; Fleming 6–1–17–0; Golding 9–1–20–2; Ealham 5–1–15–1; Tredwell 4.5–0–21–2; Symonds 1–0–13–0.

Umpires: K. E. Palmer and D. R. Shepherd.

KENT v LEICESTERSHIRE

At Canterbury, August 21 (day/night). Kent won by five wickets. Toss: Leicestershire. County debuts: S. R. Waugh; J. Srinath.

The stage was set for Steve Waugh and he did not disappoint the 7,000-strong crowd, guiding Kent to victory with a characteristically cool fifty. Fittingly, he even struck the winning runs, with just two balls to spare. Leicestershire had struggled to score, especially against the accurate bowling of Saggers, with Burns and DeFreitas forming the only decent partnership. Kent wobbled in reply, but the nerveless new boy saw them home.

Leicestershire

T. R. Ward b Ealham	24	A. S. Wright not out	18
*I. J. Sutcliffe c Nixon b Saggers	11	J. Srinath not out	2
D. I. Stevens c and b Patel	22	B 1, l-b 6, w 7	14
D. L. Maddy lbw b Fleming	22		
†N. D. Burns b Saggers	35	1/34 (2) 2/47 (1) (7 wkts, 45 overs) 168
R. J. Cunliffe st Nixon b Patel	2	3/78 (3) 4/90 (4)
P. A. J. DeFreitas c Waugh b Saggers	18	5/98 (6) 6/141 (7) 7/161 (5)

C. D. Crowe and J. O. Grove did not bat.

Bowling: Saggers 9–1–22–3; Masters 5–0–21–0; Golding 6–0–30–0; Ealham 8–1–28–1; Fleming 8–2–26–1; Patel 9–1–34–2.

Kent

*M. V. Fleming b Grove	27	†P. A. Nixon not out	33
E. T. Smith c Ward b Grove	6	B 1, l-b 3, w 2, n-b 4	10
D. P. Fulton not out	7		
S. R. Waugh not out	59	1/29 (2) 2/40 (1) (5 wkts, 44.4 overs) 172
M. J. Walker c Maddy b DeFreitas	5	3/46 (3) 4/52 (5)
M. A. Ealham c Srinath b Crowe	25	5/100 (6)

J. M. Golding, M. M. Patel, D. D. Masters and M. J. Saggers did not bat.

Bowling: Srinath 9–0–30–0; Grove 9–1–33–2; DeFreitas 7.4–1–29–1; Maddy 7–0–27–0; Crowe 8–0–30–1; Stevens 4–1–19–0.

Umpires: J. W. Holder and T. E. Jesty.

At Worcester, September 1. KENT lost to WORCESTERSHIRE by three wickets.

At Taunton, September 8. KENT lost to SOMERSET by 118 runs.

KENT v GLAMORGAN

At Canterbury, September 15. Glamorgan won by four runs. Toss: Glamorgan.

Glamorgan squeezed the narrow victory which confirmed them as champions. A jubilant Croft led the celebrations after Kent fell agonisingly short of the ten they needed off the last over. Nixon, playing his final home game before returing to Leicestershire, was run out off the first ball, and the last pair could not pinch a win. Fleming had also said his farewells during an emotional final walk back to the Canterbury pavilion. With the ball, his bits-and-pieces medium-pace had earlier snared a 250th League victim.

Glamorgan

*R. D. B. Croft b Trott	14	M. S. Kasprowicz not out	4
I. J. Thomas c Waugh b Saggers	12	D. S. Harrison not out	0
M. J. Powell c and b Tredwell	74	L-b 5, w 3	8
M. P. Maynard b Ealham	33		
A. Dale b Tredwell	43	1/17 (1) 2/38 (2) (7 wkts, 45 overs) 226
D. L. Hemp b Fleming	37	3/94 (4) 4/157 (3)
†M. A. Wallace st Nixon b Tredwell	1	5/218 (6) 6/221 (7) 7/222 (5)

A. P. Davies and D. A. Cosker did not bat.

Bowling: Saggers 9–1–27–1; Trott 9–0–55–1; Ealham 9–0–42–1; Fleming 8–0–44–1; Waugh 3–0–25–0; Tredwell 7–1–28–3.

Kent

*M. V. Fleming c Hemp b Kasprowicz	2	J. C. Tredwell not out	3
R. W. T. Key c Thomas b Harrison	19	B. J. Trott not out	1
M. A. Ealham c Maynard b Croft	75		
S. R. Waugh b Davies	7	B 1, l-b 8, w 1, n-b 2	12
M. J. Walker st Wallace b Croft	26		
†P. A. Nixon run out	49	1/4 (1) 2/42 (2) (9 wkts, 45 overs) 222	
G. O. Jones c Powell b Harrison	17	3/62 (4) 4/136 (5)	
A. G. R. Loudon c Thomas b Davies	11	5/149 (3) 6/186 (7)	
M. J. Saggers c Croft b Davies	0	7/212 (8) 8/212 (9) 9/218 (6)	

Bowling: Kasprowicz 9–0–42–1; Davies 9–2–37–3; Harrison 9–1–46–2; Croft 9–0–46–2; Dale 5–0–25–0; Cosker 4–0–17–0.

Umpires: R. Palmer and A. G. T. Whitehead.

At Leeds, September 22. KENT lost to YORKSHIRE by 79 runs.

LEICESTERSHIRE

LEICESTERSHIRE v NOTTINGHAMSHIRE

At Leicester, May 12. Leicestershire won by 32 runs. Toss: Leicestershire.

In a thoroughly entertaining match, an exhilarating partnership of 185 in 24 overs between Ward and Stevens set up an emphatic Leicestershire victory. Stevens's 74-ball 91 contained ten fours and a six, and after taking 23 balls to get off the mark, Ward matched him shot-for-shot, rattling the boundary boards 13 times and clearing them once. Bevan then scurried 42 off 41 balls, despite not finding the rope. Nottinghamshire were never quite up with the rate, and only Afzaal's thumping innings provided hope. He hit three sixes – and survived three drops – but his swashbuckling display was not enough.

Leicestershire

T. R. Ward c Harris b Boje	91	P. A. J. DeFreitas not out	31
*I. J. Sutcliffe c Boje b Smith	4	L-b 5, w 4, n-b 2	11
D. I. Stevens c Pietersen b Afzaal	91		
M. G. Bevan not out	42	1/5 (2) 2/190 (3) (5 wkts, 45 overs) 283	
◻. L. Maddy c Malik b Afzaal	9	3/194 (1) 4/219 (5)	
†N. D. Burns run out	4	5/226 (6)	

A. S. Wright, C. D. Crowe, J. O. Grove and M. J. A. Whiley did not bat.

Bowling: Smith 9–1–36–1; Malik 7–1–25–0; Harris 6–0–63–0; Logan 2–0–25–0; Boje 9–1–44–1; Pietersen 7–0–52–0; Afzaal 5–0–33–2.

Nottinghamshire

*D. J. Bicknell b Grove	40	R. J. Logan st Burns b Bevan	2
◻. E. Welton c Bevan b Grove	17	A. J. Harris not out	1
N. Boje lbw b DeFreitas	22	B 1, l-b 4, w 10, n-b 2	17
◻. Afzaal c Grove b Grove	63		
◻. Johnson c Ward b Crowe	13	1/35 (2) 2/68 (1) (8 wkts, 45 overs) 251	
◻. P. Pietersen c Stevens b Maddy	26	3/122 (3) 4/147 (5)	
C. M. W. Read c Grove b Bevan	34	5/188 (4) 6/214 (6)	
◻. J. Smith not out	16	7/238 (7) 8/244 (9)	

◻. N. Malik did not bat.

Bowling: Grove 7–0–32–2; Whiley 7–0–41–0; DeFreitas 7–0–26–1; Maddy 9–0–54–1; Crowe 9–0–55–2; Bevan 6–0–38–2.

Umpires: B. Leadbeater and P. Willey.

LEICESTERSHIRE v GLAMORGAN

At Leicester, June 4. Glamorgan won by 45 runs. Toss: Glamorgan. County debut: G. W. Flower.

Leicestershire needed 68 off the last ten overs, with five wickets standing, but they handed Glamorgan victory with an astonishing collapse. Their remaining wickets fell for 21 runs in slightly more than three overs, with two run-outs adding to the mayhem. Bevan, away on international duty, was sorely missed. A patient innings from James was the cornerstone of Glamorgan's batting. Dale and Croft then bowled tidily enough, but Leicestershire looked in control until they pressed the self-destruct button.

Glamorgan

R. D. B. Croft c Maddy b Whiley	24	†M. A. Wallace not out		1
D. L. Hemp c Burns b Whiley	4			
*S. P. James c Ward b Crowe	86	L-b 3, w 9		12
J. Hughes c Stevens b DeFreitas	9			
A. Dale b Crowe	16	1/21 (2) 2/40 (1)	(6 wkts, 45 overs)	194
M. J. Powell c Sutcliffe b Flower	14	3/64 (4) 4/117 (5)		
S. D. Thomas not out	28	5/150 (6) 6/176 (3)		

M. S. Kasprowicz, A. P. Davies and D. A. Cosker did not bat.

Bowling: Whiley 9–0–37–2; Grove 6–1–26–0; DeFreitas 7–0–23–1; Wells 6–0–28–0; Flower 9–0–43–1; Crowe 8–0–34–2.

Leicestershire

T. R. Ward run out	5	J. O. Grove b Croft		0
I. J. Sutcliffe st Wallace b Cosker	57	M. J. A. Whiley run out		5
D. I. Stevens c Croft b Dale	21			
G. W. Flower lbw b Dale	3	L-b 11, w 5		16
D. L. Maddy lbw b Dale	3			
*V. J. Wells b Croft	19	1/6 (1) 2/68 (3) 3/72 (4)	(39.2 overs)	149
†N. D. Burns run out	7	4/80 (5) 5/118 (6) 6/128 (2)		
P. A. J. DeFreitas b Davies	6	7/136 (8) 8/142 (8)		
C. D. Crowe not out	7	9/143 (10) 10/149 (11)		

Bowling: Kasprowicz 7–2–15–0; Davies 6.2–0–27–1; Thomas 4–0–15–0; Dale 9–1–28–3; Cosker 9–0–36–1; Croft 4–0–17–2.

Umpires: J. W. Lloyds and A. G. T. Whitehead.

LEICESTERSHIRE v WORCESTERSHIRE

At Oakham School, June 9. No result. Toss: Leicestershire.

Only three overs were possible before rain swept in and the game was washed out.

Leicestershire

T. R. Ward not out	9
*I. J. Sutcliffe not out	0
B 1, l-b 1	2

(no wkt, 3 overs) 11

D. I. Stevens, G. W. Flower, D. L. Maddy, A. S. Wright, †N. D. Burns, P. A. J. DeFreitas, C. D. Crowe, J. O. Grove and M. J. A. Whiley did not bat.

Bowling: Donald 2–1–9–0; Sheriyar 1–1–0–0.

Worcestershire

V. S. Solanki, A. Singh, *G. A. Hick, B. F. Smith, D. A. Leatherdale, G. J. Batty, †S. J. Rhodes, Kabir Ali, D. N. Catterall, A. A. Donald and A. Sheriyar.

Umpires: G. I. Burgess and G. Sharp.

At Bath, June 16. LEICESTERSHIRE lost to SOMERSET by seven wickets.

At Nottingham, June 30. LEICESTERSHIRE lost to NOTTINGHAMSHIRE by five wickets.

At Swansea, July 7. LEICESTERSHIRE beat GLAMORGAN by five wickets.

LEICESTERSHIRE v WARWICKSHIRE

At Leicester, July 14. Leicestershire won by four wickets. Toss: Warwickshire.

A decisive 66 by Bevan underlined his status as the master of the chase: he steered Leicestershire home after defeat was staring them in the face. Despite a rollicking start by DeFreitas, they struggled on a sluggish pitch until Bevan brought experience and calm, and they strolled to victory with more than nine overs left. Knight, shaking off his disappointment at England's defeat by India at Lord's the previous day, played Warwickshire's only innings of note.

Warwickshire

*M. J. Powell c Burns b DeFreitas	17	M. A. Sheikh not out		4
N. V. Knight c Ward b Crowe	86	N. M. Carter b Grove		2
S. M. Pollock c Stevens b Maddy	0			
I. R. Bell run out	12	L-b 1, w 11, n-b 2		14
D. P. Ostler c Sutcliffe b Wells	34			
J. O. Troughton b Wells	0	1/41 (1) 2/44 (3) 3/72 (4)	(45 overs)	189
D. R. Brown lbw b Crowe	17	4/136 (5) 5/136 (6) 6/176 (7)		
†N. M. K. Smith b Maddy	2	7/179 (8) 8/181 (2)		
†K. J. Piper b Crowe	1	9/181 (9) 10/189 (11)		

Bowling: DeFreitas 9–0–24–1; Grove 8–0–39–1; Maddy 9–1–34–2; Wells 8–0–37–2; Crowe 9–0–40–3; Stevens 2–0–14–0.

Leicestershire

T. R. Ward c Piper b Carter	2	D. L. Maddy not out		0
P. A. J. DeFreitas b Sheikh	49			
I. J. Sutcliffe c Piper b Pollock	13	L-b 1, w 3		4
D. I. Stevens c Pollock b Sheikh	19			
M. G. Bevan not out	66	1/3 (1) 2/47 (3)	(6 wkts, 35.5 overs)	193
*V. J. Wells lbw b Brown	0	3/86 (4) 4/86 (2)		
†N. D. Burns lbw b Powell	40	5/87 (6) 6/189 (7)		

C. D. Crowe, J. O. Grove and M. J. A. Whiley did not bat.

Bowling: Pollock 7–0–34–1; Carter 5.5–0–35–1; Brown 7–1–33–1; Sheikh 9–3–47–2; Smith 4–0–27–0; Powell 3–1–16–1.

Umpires: B. Dudleston and M. J. Harris.

At Chester-le-Street, July 21. LEICESTERSHIRE beat DURHAM by 85 runs.

LEICESTERSHIRE v KENT

At Leicester, July 28. Leicestershire won by 17 runs. Toss: Leicestershire.

On a slow, low pitch Maddy's unbeaten 50 proved crucial as Leicestershire lost their way after a spectacular start. DeFreitas, relishing his pinch-hitting role, smacked 24 from 18 balls, and he and Ward took 25 runs off the first two overs. Leicestershire slowed as wickets fell, but Stevens and Maddy steadied the ship. In reply, Kent looked beaten at 110 for seven, until Jones and Golding blazed away, crashing the game's only fifty partnership. An upset briefly threatened, but Leicestershire held their nerve.

Leicestershire

T. R. Ward c Golding b Masters	19	J. O. Grove b Fleming 13
P. A. J. DeFreitas c Symonds b Golding	24	M. J. A. Whiley not out 1
I. J. Sutcliffe c Hockley b Golding	2	
D. I. Stevens c and b Symonds	48	L-b 1, w 3 4
M. G. Bevan c and b Ealham	22	
*V. J. Wells b Fleming	2	1/35 (2) 2/46 (3) (9 wkts, 45 overs) 206
†N. D. Burns c Walker b Symonds	13	3/47 (1) 4/89 (5)
D. L. Maddy not out	50	5/92 (6) 6/115 (7)
C. D. Crowe c Nixon b Ealham	8	7/148 (4) 8/168 (9) 9/205 (10)

Bowling: Trott 5–0–37–0; Masters 9–1–44–1; Golding 9–2–33–2; Ealham 9–0–31–2; Fleming 9–0–34–2; Symonds 4–0–26–2.

Kent

*M. V. Fleming lbw b Grove	20	J. M. Golding not out 47
R. W. T. Key lbw b Grove	8	D. D. Masters not out 8
J. B. Hockley run out	4	B 1, l-b 3 4
A. Symonds lbw b DeFreitas	21	
M. J. Walker c and b Crowe	40	1/27 (1) 2/28 (2) (8 wkts, 45 overs) 189
†P. A. Nixon lbw b Maddy	4	3/42 (3) 4/62 (4)
M. A. Ealham run out	6	5/69 (6) 6/86 (7)
G. O. Jones st Burns b Grove	27	7/110 (5) 8/172 (8)

B. J. Trott did not bat.

Bowling: DeFreitas 9–1–30–1; Grove 9–1–29–3; Maddy 9–1–40–1; Wells 9–1–29–0; Crowe 8–0–52–1; Whiley 1–0–5–0.

Umpires: V. A. Holder and R. T. Robinson.

At Birmingham, August 4. LEICESTERSHIRE lost to WARWICKSHIRE by seven wickets (D/L method).

The England coach does do the rounds of the county circuit but it is more in the guise of a family doctor checking on the progress of his private patients than a dedicated specialist with an overall interest in the health of the domestic game.
Pat Gibson on the County Championship, page 554

LEICESTERSHIRE v DURHAM

At Leicester, August 11. Durham won by five wickets. Toss: Leicestershire.

Durham, already on the road to relegation, belied their lowly position to earn a rare but well-deserved victory. It was a subdued and uninspired performance from Leicestershire. Despite half-centuries from Stevens and Wells, they were bowled out inside their 45 overs, largely because of Killeen's splendid four for 12. Peng was bowled offering no shot to the second ball of the innings, but fifties from Gough, Pratt and Lewis sealed the win.

Leicestershire

T. R. Ward c A. Pratt b Davies	23	J. O. Grove not out	4
I. J. Sutcliffe c A. Pratt b Killeen	10	C. E. Dagnall st A. Pratt b Gough	3
P. A. J. DeFreitas b Davies	6		
D. I. Stevens c A. Pratt b Phillips	54	B 4, l-b 2, w 7	13
*V. J. Wells b Thorpe	56		
†N. D. Burns c Davies b Thorpe	29	1/37 (1) 2/39 (2) 3/53 (3) (44.4 overs) 230
D. L. Maddy c Hunter b Killeen	21	4/148 (5) 5/162 (4)
R. J. Cunliffe c and b Killeen	11	6/209 (6) 7/219 (7)
C. D. Crowe lbw b Killeen	0	8/220 (9) 9/225 (8) 10/230 (11)

Bowling: Hunter 5–0–42–0; Killeen 9.2–2–12–4; Davies 7–1–23–2; Law 3–0–29–0; Phillips 9–0–49–1; Thorpe 8–0–49–2; Gough 3.4–0–20–1.

Durham

N. Peng b DeFreitas	0	†A. Pratt not out	2
M. A. Gough c Cunliffe b Crowe	54	B 2, l-b 8, w 8	18
D. R. Law st Burns b Grove	28		
A. M. Thorpe c Burns b Wells	17	1/0 (1) 2/46 (3) (5 wkts, 43.5 overs) 231
G. J. Pratt not out	60	3/78 (4) 4/144 (2)
*J. J. B. Lewis b Maddy	52	5/229 (6)

I. D. Hunter, N. C. Phillips, A. M. Davies and N. Killeen did not bat.

Bowling: DeFreitas 9–2–40–1; Grove 9–0–49–1; Wells 8–1–35–1; Dagnall 5–0–19–0; Maddy 7.5–0–47–1; Crowe 5–0–31–1.

Umpires: J. H. Evans and J. F. Steele.

LEICESTERSHIRE v YORKSHIRE

At Leicester, August 18. Leicestershire won by five wickets. Toss: Yorkshire.

There was drama at the beginning and end of a remarkable match. First, Grove and DeFreitas reduced Yorkshire to one for four in the fifth over, but a magnificent 181-run partnership between Elliott – with 109 from 114 balls – and McGrath stopped the slide. Stevens and the impressive Kaif then took Leicestershire within sight of victory. They needed eight off the last over and DeFreitas settled it with a six.

Yorkshire

V. J. Craven c Burns b Grove	1	*†R. J. Blakey not out	11
M. J. Wood c Kaif b Grove	0		
R. K. J. Dawson lbw b DeFreitas	0	L-b 1, w 5	6
M. T. G. Elliott c Cunliffe b Grove	109		
M. P. Vaughan b DeFreitas	0	1/1 (1) 2/1 (2) (6 wkts, 45 overs) 229
A. McGrath c Maddy b Dagnall	78	3/1 (3) 4/1 (5)
G. M. Fellows not out	24	5/182 (6) 6/204 (4)

T. T. Bresnan, S. P. Kirby and M. J. Hoggard did not bat.

Bowling: DeFreitas 9–2–32–2; Grove 9–2–32–3; Maddy 9–0–57–0; Dagnall 9–0–46–1; Crowe 5–0–37–0; Stevens 4–0–24–0.

Leicestershire

T. R. Ward c Blakey b Hoggard	5	P. A. J. DeFreitas not out		8
*I. J. Sutcliffe lbw b McGrath	36	L-b 2, w 9		11
D. I. Stevens c Craven b Dawson	85			
M. Kaif not out	60	1/8 (1) 2/100 (2)	(5 wkts, 44.4 overs)	231
D. L. Maddy run out	0	3/162 (3) 4/163 (5)		
†N. D. Burns c Blakey b Hoggard	26	5/217 (6)		

R. J. Cunliffe, C. D. Crowe, J. O. Grove and C. E. Dagnall did not bat.

Bowling: Hoggard 9–1–28–2; Bresnan 6.4–0–39–0; Kirby 9–1–50–0; McGrath 9–0–42–1; Dawson 9–0–58–1; Fellows 2–0–12–0.

Umpires: M. J. Harris and A. A. Jones.

At Canterbury, August 21 (day/night). LEICESTERSHIRE lost to KENT by five wickets.

At Scarborough, September 8. LEICESTERSHIRE beat YORKSHIRE by six wickets.

LEICESTERSHIRE v SOMERSET

At Leicester, September 11 (day/night). Somerset won by three wickets. Toss: Leicestershire. First-team debuts: D. G. Brandy; M. Parsons.

With little at stake – Leicestershire were safe and Somerset already relegated – both sides fielded experimental line-ups, and Somerset emerged with credit. They bowled excellently, and Leicestershire's innings was virtually a one-man show by Sutcliffe, who hit 11 fours and three sixes in his first League century. Thanks to a quick-fire start from Cox, Somerset were always ahead of the rate. They won with four balls to spare, despite Maddy's valiant four for 36.

Leicestershire

T. R. Ward c Turner b Bulbeck	0	C. E. Dagnall b Bulbeck	27
*I. J. Sutcliffe not out	104	M. J. A. Whiley not out	1
D. I. Stevens c K. A. Parsons b Bulbeck	0		
D. L. Maddy lbw b K. A. Parsons	20	L-b 1, w 5, n-b 2	8
†N. D. Burns c Cox b Trego	15		
D. G. Brandy st Turner b Dutch	35	1/0 (1) 2/0 (3)	(9 wkts, 45 overs) 215
R. J. Cunliffe c Turner b Suppiah	4	3/54 (4) 4/82 (5)	
C. D. Crowe c Turner b Suppiah	0	5/148 (6) 6/155 (7)	
J. O. Grove c K. A. Parsons b Dutch	1	7/155 (8) 8/156 (9) 9/207 (10)	

Bowling: Bulbeck 9–0–39–3; M. Parsons 5–1–26–0; K. A. Parsons 9–1–30–1; Trego 7–1–38–1; Dutch 9–0–45–2; Suppiah 6–0–36–2.

Somerset

*J. Cox c Ward b Maddy	52	P. D. Trego not out	1
P. C. L. Holloway c Burns b Grove	8	†R. J. Turner not out	8
K. P. Dutch c Grove b Maddy	22	B 2, l-b 4, w 23, n-b 4	33
M. J. Wood b Maddy	10		
K. A. Parsons c Crowe b Dagnall	45	1/60 (2) 2/91 (1)	(7 wkts, 44.2 overs) 216
P. D. Bowler c Maddy b Whiley	35	3/108 (4) 4/109 (3)	
A. V. Suppiah b Maddy	2	5/201 (5) 6/207 (6) 7/207 (7)	

M. P. L. Bulbeck and M. Parsons did not bat.

Bowling: Whiley 8.2–0–48–1; Grove 9–1–43–1; Dagnall 9–0–31–1; Maddy 9–1–36–4; Crowe 6–0–38–0; Stevens 3–0–14–0.

Umpires: J. H. Hampshire and N. J. Llong.

At Worcester, September 22. LEICESTERSHIRE lost to WORCESTERSHIRE by 28 runs.

NOTTINGHAMSHIRE

At Leicester, May 12. NOTTINGHAMSHIRE lost to LEICESTERSHIRE by 32 runs.

NOTTINGHAMSHIRE v WARWICKSHIRE

At Nottingham, May 19. Warwickshire won by 85 runs. Toss: Nottinghamshire.

A high-class all-round display from Pollock helped Warwickshire to a convincing win. First, he took charge with the bat, creaming a stylish 70 from 76 balls, including two towering sixes, after Warwickshire's openers had made a painfully slow start. Then he bowled with accuracy and penetration to ensure Nottinghamshire fell well short. Afzaal managed a determined fifty, but the home side never recovered from their disastrous start.

Warwickshire

*M. J. Powell run out	39	A. F. Giles c Boje b Smith	2
N. V. Knight c Logan b Smith	13	N. M. Carter not out	4
S. M. Pollock c Welton b Boje	70	L-b 4, w 6, n-b 4	14
I. R. Bell c Welton b Boje	14		
D. P. Ostler lbw b Smith	41	1/30 (2) 2/98 (1) (8 wkts, 45 overs) 236	
T. L. Penney not out	34	3/125 (4) 4/156 (3)	
D. R. Brown c Bicknell b Harris	0	5/205 (5) 6/206 (7)	
N. M. K. Smith c Logan b Harris	5	7/223 (8) 8/231 (9)	

†T. Frost did not bat.

Bowling: Smith 9–2–41–3; Malik 9–0–45–0; Harris 8–0–47–2; Logan 6–0–34–0; Boje 9–1–26–2; Afzaal 4–0–39–0.

Nottinghamshire

*D. J. Bicknell c Frost b Pollock	11	A. J. Harris c Pollock b Giles	7
G. E. Welton lbw b Pollock	0	M. N. Malik not out	0
N. Boje c Frost b Carter	0	L-b 2, w 7, n-b 2	11
U. Afzaal b Smith	51		
P. Johnson lbw b Giles	11	1/1 (2) 2/3 (3) 3/13 (1) (41.1 overs) 151	
†C. M. W. Read c and b Pollock	20	4/30 (5) 5/89 (6) 6/107 (4)	
B. M. Shafayat c Powell b Brown	15	7/127 (7) 8/133 (8)	
R. J. Logan c Powell b Carter	15	9/146 (9) 10/151 (10)	
G. J. Smith b Giles	10		

Bowling: Carter 9–1–34–2; Pollock 7–1–12–3; Brown 8–1–31–1; Giles 8.1–1–27–3; Smith 9–1–45–1.

Umpires: M. J. Kitchen and G. Sharp.

At Tunbridge Wells, June 4. NOTTINGHAMSHIRE lost to KENT by five wickets (D/L method).

NOTTINGHAMSHIRE v YORKSHIRE

At Nottingham, June 9. No result (abandoned).

NOTTINGHAMSHIRE v KENT

At Nottingham, June 16. Kent won by 132 runs. Toss: Kent.

Nottinghamshire, still without a win in the League, gave no sign of turning the corner during a massive defeat. Kent rattled along at seven an over, with Fleming, Hockley and Fulton all scoring at more than a run a ball. But even they were outshone by Key's 98-ball 114, including seven fours and four sixes. In contrast, Nottinghamshire wickets fell regularly, and only Franks, playing his first game after more than a year out with injury, pushed their score to something approaching respectability.

Kent

*M. V. Fleming c Shafayat b Malik	49	M. J. Walker not out		4
R. W. T. Key b Franks	114	J. C. Tredwell not out		1
J. B. Hockley c Read b Franks	38	L-b 7, w 14, n-b 2		23
†P. A. Nixon c Malik b Afzaal	34			
A. Symonds st Read b Afzaal	2	1/68 (1) 2/119 (3)	(8 wkts, 45 overs)	317
M. A. Ealham st Read b Afzaal	12	3/210 (4) 4/212 (5)		
D. P. Fulton c Read b Smith	37	5/251 (6) 6/294 (2)		
J. M. Golding b Smith	3	7/301 (8) 8/315 (7)		

M. J. Saggers did not bat.

Bowling: Smith 7–1–53–2; Harris 7–1–39–0; Franks 9–0–52–2; Malik 5–0–48–1; Boje 8–0–45–0; Pietersen 2–0–25–0; Afzaal 7–0–48–3.

Nottinghamshire

P. Johnson c Saggers b Ealham	36	A. J. Harris c Symonds b Tredwell		6
*J. E. R. Gallian c Nixon b Golding	6	M. N. Malik not out		6
U. Afzaal c Hockley b Ealham	30			
K. P. Pietersen b Fleming	19	L-b 3, w 2		5
N. Boje c Walker b Golding	5			
†C. M. W. Read c Nixon b Golding	5	1/19 (2) 2/68 (1) 3/84 (3)	(37 overs)	185
B. M. Shafayat run out	7	4/95 (4) 5/103 (5) 6/103 (6)		
P. J. Franks b Saggers	60	7/131 (7) 8/131 (9)		
G. J. Smith b Symonds	0	9/150 (10) 10/185 (8)		

Bowling: Saggers 9–0–47–1; Golding 5–0–38–3; Ealham 6–0–31–2; Fleming 2–0–6–1; Tredwell 8–0–41–1; Symonds 7–1–19–1.

Umpires: J. H. Evans and A. G. T. Whitehead.

NOTTINGHAMSHIRE v LEICESTERSHIRE

At Nottingham, June 30. Nottinghamshire won by five wickets. Toss: Leicestershire.

This was Mick Newell's first home game as team manager and his troops responded with a thrilling win. After starting an hour late to avoid clashing with the final of the football World Cup, Leicestershire soon got going, thanks to Stevens and Wells. Boje stemmed the flow of runs with an excellent spell of left-arm spin, before DeFreitas smashed 26 from ten balls at the death. At 11 for three, Nottinghamshire were in desperate trouble but Boje and Gallian put on 190 – the county's best League stand for the fourth wicket – before Pietersen and Read finished the job with some lusty blows.

Leicestershire

T. R. Ward c Gallian b Harris	2
I. J. Sutcliffe b Randall	25
D. I. Stevens c Randall b Boje	54
*V. J. Wells b Franks	68
†N. D. Burns lbw b Randall	3
D. L. Maddy c Welton b Afzaal	27
R. J. Cunliffe run out	25

P. A. J. DeFreitas not out	26
L-b 12, w 13, n-b 4	29
1/8 (1) 2/86 (2) (7 wkts, 45 overs) 259	
3/108 (3) 4/118 (5)	
5/173 (6) 6/224 (4) 7/259 (7)	

C. D. Crowe, D. E. Malcolm and M. J. A. Whiley did not bat.

Bowling: Harris 7–0–43–1; Franks 9–0–58–1; Logan 8–0–61–0; Boje 9–1–25–1; Randall 9–0–44–2; Afzaal 3–0–16–1.

Nottinghamshire

P. Johnson c Whiley b Malcolm	7
G. E. Welton c Whiley b DeFreitas	0
U. Afzaal c Burns b Malcolm	0
*J. E. R. Gallian st Burns b Crowe . . .	91
N. Boje c and b Wells	86
K. P. Pietersen not out	30

†C. M. W. Read not out	20
L-b 17, w 10, n-b 2	29
1/6 (2) 2/6 (3) (5 wkts, 44.3 overs) 263	
3/11 (1) 4/201 (4)	
5/220 (5)	

P. J. Franks, S. J. Randall, R. J. Logan and A. J. Harris did not bat.

Bowling: DeFreitas 9–1–32–1; Malcolm 9–1–36–2; Wells 8–0–47–1; Whiley 4–0–29–0; Maddy 7.3–0–59–0; Crowe 7–0–43–1.

Umpires: N. G. Cowley and K. E. Palmer.

NOTTINGHAMSHIRE v GLAMORGAN

At Nottingham, July 14. Glamorgan won by eight wickets. Toss: Glamorgan.

Fragile batting on a perfect pitch plunged Nottinghamshire deeper into relegation trouble and handed Glamorgan a comfortable win. Nottinghamshire belted along but, with wickets tumbling throughout, only Boje and Pietersen managed a half-century stand. Their below-par total proved inadequate. Croft and Thomas stroked a breezy 52 for the first wicket and Maynard thumped 80 from 69 balls to win the game with 49 balls to spare.

Nottinghamshire

P. Johnson run out	26
G. E. Welton b Powell b Kasprowicz . . .	13
U. Afzaal c Wallace b Wharf	31
*J. E. R. Gallian c Hemp b Davies	4
N. Boje b Croft	39
K. P. Pietersen b Cosker	36
†C. M. W. Read b Cosker	6
P. J. Franks b Kasprowicz	23
S. J. Randall b Kasprowicz	19

G. J. Smith run out	4
A. J. Harris not out	1
B 1, l-b 9, w 8	18
1/26 (2) 2/72 (1) 3/76 (4) (45 overs) 220	
4/92 (3) 5/156 (6)	
6/164 (7) 7/170 (5)	
8/202 (8) 9/218 (10) 10/220 (9)	

Bowling: Kasprowicz 9–0–39–3; Davies 9–0–54–1; Wharf 9–0–42–1; Cosker 9–1–33–2; Croft 9–0–42–1.

Glamorgan

*R. D. B. Croft c Read b Harris	36
I. J. Thomas b Boje	34
D. L. Hemp not out	55
M. P. Maynard not out	80
L-b 10, w 9	19

1/52 (1) 2/107 (2)   (2 wkts, 36.5 overs) 224

A. Dale, M. J. Powell, †M. A. Wallace, A. G. Wharf, M. S. Kasprowicz, A. P. Davies and D. A. Cosker did not bat.

Bowling: Smith 7–0–44–0; Harris 7–0–43–1; Franks 6.5–0–50–0; Randall 9–0–31–0; Boje 5–0–31–1; Afzaal 2–0–15–0.

Umpires: M. R. Benson and G. Sharp.

At Chester-le-Street, July 28. NOTTINGHAMSHIRE lost to DURHAM by 44 runs.

At Leeds, August 3. NOTTINGHAMSHIRE lost to YORKSHIRE by four wickets (D/L method).

At Worcester, August 7 (day/night). NOTTINGHAMSHIRE v WORCESTERSHIRE. No result.

NOTTINGHAMSHIRE v SOMERSET

At Nottingham, August 18. Nottinghamshire won by 69 runs. Toss: Nottinghamshire.
Nottinghamshire won this battle of the basement comfortably, thanks largely to the resurgent Pietersen. Having hit a career-best unbeaten 254 in the Championship three days earlier, he crashed his maiden one-day century, which included nine fours and five sixes. Somerset were all but beaten in their opening four overs, when Lucas filched three wickets without conceding a run. Shafayat showed he has rich promise with ball as well as bat, and grabbed four for 35 – his best first-team figures.

Nottinghamshire

*J. E. R. Gallian c Parsons b Dutch	39	S. C. G. MacGill b Jones		4
B. M. Shafayat c Bowler b Caddick	10	S. J. Randall not out		1
U. Afzaal c Cox b Caddick	12	L-b 7, w 2		9
K. P. Pietersen b Jones	122			
P. Johnson run out	1	1/16 (2) 2/43 (3) (9 wkts, 45 overs) 239		
†C. M. W. Read run out	38	3/105 (1) 4/106 (5)		
P. J. Franks c Wood b Francis	3	5/204 (6) 6/213 (7)		
D. S. Lucas b Jones	0	7/215 (8) 8/236 (4) 9/239 (9)		

R. J. Logan did not bat.

Bowling: Caddick 9–1–34–2; Francis 8–2–43–1; Jones 8–1–46–3; Parsons 9–0–38–0; Dutch 9–0–39–1; Blackwell 2–0–32–0.

Somerset

M. Burns c Read b Logan	. . . .	4
P. D. Bowler st Read b Randall	. . . . .	44
*J. Cox c MacGill b Lucas	. . . .	0
I. D. Blackwell b Lucas	. . . .	0
K. A. Parsons lbw b Lucas	. . . .	0
M. J. Wood c Gallian b Shafayat	. . . .	37
†R. J. Turner not out	. . . .	39
K. P. Dutch b Randall	. . . .	2
S. R. G. Francis b Shafayat	. . . . . .	8

P. S. Jones c MacGill b Shafayat	. . . . .	10
A. R. Caddick b Shafayat	. . . .	4
L-b 11, w 11	. . . .	22

1/4 (1) 2/6 (3) 3/11 (4)   (38.4 overs) 170
4/11 (5) 5/91 (2)
6/109 (6) 7/124 (8)
8/133 (9) 9/149 (10) 10/170 (11)

Bowling: Logan 7–1–34–1; Lucas 5–2–13–3; Franks 5–1–20–0; MacGill 4–1–12–0; Randall 9–0–45–2; Shafayat 8.4–0–35–4.

Umpires: J. H. Evans and T. E. Jesty.

At Taunton, August 19 (day/night). NOTTINGHAMSHIRE beat SOMERSET by 59 runs.

At Colwyn Bay, August 26. NOTTINGHAMSHIRE lost to GLAMORGAN by five wickets.

At Birmingham, September 1. NOTTINGHAMSHIRE lost to WARWICKSHIRE by 51 runs.

NOTTINGHAMSHIRE v DURHAM

At Nottingham, September 4 (day/night). Durham won by seven wickets. Toss: Nottinghamshire. Nottinghamshire gave a poor display against a poor side, and stumbled to their fifth straight defeat under the Trent Bridge lights. Bicknell and Afzaal constructed an opening stand of 145, but the middle order failed to push on. In response, Thorpe provided early momentum with a 57-ball 53, and Hodge's punchy 91 saw Durham over the line.

Nottinghamshire

D. J. Bicknell c G. J. Pratt b Phillips	. . .	64
U. Afzaal run out	. . . .	75
†C. M. W. Read c and b Hodge	. . . . .	23
B. M. Shafayat c Hodge b Phillips	. . . .	11
W. R. Smith st A. Pratt b Phillips	. . . .	16
*J. E. R. Gallian run out	. . . .	19

P. J. Franks not out	. . . .	5
L-b 9, w 7	. . . .	16

1/145 (2) 2/155 (1)   (6 wkts, 45 overs) 229
3/179 (4) 4/187 (3)
5/221 (5) 6/229 (6)

S. J. Randall, S. C. G. MacGill, D. S. Lucas and A. J. Harris did not bat.

Bowling: Killeen 6–1–27–0; Hunter 6–0–24–0; Davies 8–0–36–0; Symington 5–0–27–0; Phillips 8–0–39–3; Gough 9–0–52–0; Hodge 3–0–15–1.

Durham

M. A. Gough b Read b Franks	. . . . . .	16
A. M. Thorpe run out	. . . .	53
B. J. Hodge not out	. . . .	91
G. J. Muchall c Smith b MacGill	. . . .	22
G. J. Pratt not out	. . . .	25
L-b 9, w 12, n-b 4	. . . .	25

1/35 (1) 2/122 (2)   (3 wkts, 41.5 overs) 232
3/179 (4)

†A. Pratt, M. J. Symington, *N. C. Phillips, I. D. Hunter, A. M. Davies and N. Killeen did not bat.

Bowling: Lucas 7–0–43–0; Harris 7.5–0–42–0; Franks 7–0–45–1; MacGill 9–0–41–1; Shafayat 2–0–17–0; Randall 9–2–35–0.

Umpires: J. W. Holder and K. E. Palmer.

NOTTINGHAMSHIRE v WORCESTERSHIRE

At Nottingham, September 15. Worcestershire won by 81 runs. Toss: Worcestershire. First-team debut: C. E. Shreck.

Nottinghamshire's Cornish trialist Charlie Shreck made a massive impression with some pumped-up pace bowling, but was let down by his more experienced team-mates. He checked Worcestershire's early progress, but Smith and Leatherdale broke free and hit fine half-centuries. Nottinghamshire made a disastrous start with the bat. Afzaal, Read, Bicknell and Johnson (in his final game at Trent Bridge) fell quickly and already-relegated Nottinghamshire slumped to another dismal defeat. They finished bottom of Division One.

Worcestershire

V. S. Solanki b Shreck	27		†D. J. Pipe not out		3
A. Singh c and b Shreck	21				
*G. A. Hick c Malik b Shreck	23		L-b 6, w 14, n-b 6.		26
B. F. Smith c Shafayat b Shreck	61				
S. D. Peters c Read b Shreck	3		1/48 (1) 2/62 (2)	(6 wkts, 45 overs)	251
D. A. Leatherdale c Randall b Shafayat	66		3/102 (3) 4/106 (5)		
G. J. Batty not out	21		5/192 (4) 6/246 (6)		

Kabir Ali, S. R. Lampitt and M. S. Mason did not bat.

Bowling: Lucas 7–0–62–0; Malik 9–0–62–0; Shreck 9–1–35–5; Randall 9–0–32–0; Shafayat 8–1–36–1; Afzaal 3–0–18–0.

Nottinghamshire

D. J. Bicknell c Smith b Lampitt	22		M. N. Malik b Mason		11
U. Afzaal run out	6		C. E. Shreck not out		1
†C. M. W. Read c Hick b Ali	5				
P. Johnson c and b Ali	4		L-b 1, w 5, n-b 2		8
B. M. Shafayat st Pipe b Batty	24				
*J. E. R. Gallian c Mason b Hick	47		1/20 (2) 2/27 (3) 3/37 (4)	(40.5 overs)	170
W. R. Smith st Pipe b Batty	9		4/45 (1) 5/101 (5) 6/123 (7)		
S. J. Randall c and b Batty	25		7/125 (6) 8/140 (9)		
D. S. Lucas c Pipe b Batty	8		9/163 (8) 10/170 (10)		

Bowling: Mason 6.5–1–22–1; Ali 8–0–40–2; Lampitt 7–0–20–1; Leatherdale 6–2–27–0; Batty 9–0–36–4; Hick 4–0–24–1.

Umpires: I. J. Gould and J. W. Lloyds.

SOMERSET

SOMERSET v YORKSHIRE

At Taunton, May 12. Yorkshire won by one run. Toss: Yorkshire.

It would be hard to conjure up a more exciting match than this – 613 runs and a result resting on the final ball. Lehmann seemed to have put Yorkshire beyond reach with a century that began with scrambled singles and ended with booming blows. Ragged Somerset fielding helped him add 170 with the quieter Wood. Overcoming Trescothick's early dismissal, Cox, Bowler and Blackwell attacked the Yorkshire bowling with thrilling vigour. Dutch needed four off the last ball, but managed only two.

Yorkshire

C. White c Bowler b Jones	25	A. McGrath not out	20
M. J. Wood not out	105	B 2, l-b 11, w 15, n-b 2	30
C. E. W. Silverwood c and b Jones	3		
M. P. Vaughan lbw b Bulbeck	20	1/52 (1) 2/62 (3)	(4 wkts, 45 overs) 307
*D. S. Lehmann b Dutch	104	3/100 (4) 4/270 (5)	

G. M. Fellows, †R. J. Blakey, A. K. D. Gray, R. J. Sidebottom and M. J. Hoggard did not bat.

Bowling: Caddick 9–0–52–0; Bulbeck 6–0–49–1; Jones 9–0–40–2; Parsons 5–0–24–0; Dutch 8–0–54–1; Blackwell 4–0–38–0; Trego 4–0–37–0.

Somerset

*M. E. Trescothick lbw b Hoggard	0	A. R. Caddick b Sidebottom	11
P. D. Bowler c Hoggard b White	53	P. S. Jones not out	3
J. Cox c Lehmann b White	99	L-b 7, w 5	12
I. D. Blackwell b Silverwood	79		
†M. Burns b Hoggard	24	1/0 (1) 2/112 (2)	(8 wkts, 45 overs) 306
K. A. Parsons c Sidebottom b Silverwood	3	3/215 (3) 4/247 (4)	
K. P. Dutch not out	22	5/255 (6) 6/279 (5)	
P. D. Trego b Hoggard	0	7/280 (8) 8/302 (9)	

M. P. L. Bulbeck did not bat.

Bowling: Hoggard 9–1–44–3; Silverwood 9–0–62–2; White 9–0–59–2; Sidebottom 6–0–38–1; Lehmann 6–0–40–0; Gray 4–0–34–0; Fellows 2–0–22–0.

Umpires: D. J. Constant and R. Palmer.

At Worcester, May 19. SOMERSET lost to WORCESTERSHIRE by 127 runs.

At Birmingham, June 9. SOMERSET v WARWICKSHIRE. No result (abandoned).

SOMERSET v LEICESTERSHIRE

At Bath, June 16. Somerset won by seven wickets. Toss: Leicestershire.

A big win cheered up home supporters worried about the future of Bath's festival. Ward gave Leicestershire a brisk start but nothing substantial followed, as Somerset's bowlers settled after a spray-gun first few overs. They were helped by two memorable catches, one by Blackwell at full stretch on the boundary and one by Dutch in his follow-through. In reply, Somerset cruised home with nearly 13 overs to spare, but only after an early stutter. Michael Burns, standing in as captain, and Parsons shared an unbroken stand of 115.

Leicestershire

T. R. Ward c Turner b Jones	62	J. O. Grove b Jones	0
I. J. Sutcliffe lbw b Johnson	2	M. J. A. Whiley not out	14
D. I. Stevens lbw b Johnson	3		
G. W. Flower c Burns b Parsons	19	B 4, l-b 1, w 5	10
*V. J. Wells b Parsons	16		
D. L. Maddy c Turner b Parsons	4	1/14 (2) 2/38 (3) 3/83 (4)	(37.5 overs) 147
†N. D. Burns c Blackwell b Dutch	11	4/90 (1) 5/109 (6) 6/112 (5)	
P. A. J. DeFreitas c and b Dutch	0	7/113 (8) 8/130 (7)	
C. D. Crowe lbw b Jones	6	9/130 (10) 10/147 (9)	

Bowling: Johnson 7–1–19–2; Francis 7–0–46–0; Jones 7.5–1–27–3; Parsons 9–1–29–3; Dutch 7–1–21–2.

Somerset

P. D. Bowler c and b Grove		17
I. D. Blackwell c Burns b Whiley		1
P. C. L. Holloway b Whiley		4
*M. Burns not out		54
K. A. Parsons not out		59
B 1, l-b 1, w 11		13

1/20 (2) 2/20 (1)　　(3 wkts, 32.2 overs) 148
3/33 (3)

M. J. Wood, †R. J. Turner, K. P. Dutch, R. L. Johnson, S. R. G. Francis and P. S. Jones did not bat.

Bowling: Whiley 9–1–39–2; Grove 6–0–31–1; Maddy 2–0–13–0; DeFreitas 5–0–21–0; Flower 5.2–0–19–0; Crowe 5–0–23–0.

Umpires: D. J. Constant and G. Sharp.

SOMERSET v GLAMORGAN

At Taunton, June 30. Glamorgan won by one wicket (D/L method). Toss: Glamorgan.
A fluctuating game ended in controversy. After Glamorgan's innings was twice interrupted by rain they were set a revised target of 209 off 39 overs. But, with one over remaining, the umpires indicated that Somerset would be penalised for a slow over-rate, leaving Glamorgan to score six instead of 12. They scraped home with one ball left, leaving Somerset's coach, Kevin Shine, to claim that miscalculations had cost his side. Earlier, Davies had quickly removed Somerset's top three before the middle order staged a recovery. Glamorgan's innings followed the same pattern, with Dale leading the rescue mission.

Somerset

P. D. Bowler c Hemp b Davies		2
I. D. Blackwell b Davies		9
K. P. Dutch c Wallace b Davies		0
*M. Burns st Wallace b Dale		51
K. A. Parsons c Thomas b Kasprowicz		6
M. J. Wood c Powell b Croft		58
†R. J. Turner run out		33
P. C. L. Holloway c Kasprowicz b Croft		16
G. D. Rose not out		20

S. R. G. Francis b Davies … 11
P. S. Jones not out … 4

L-b 1, w 7, n-b 2 … 10

1/10 (1) 2/13 (2)　　(9 wkts, 45 overs) 220
3/16 (3) 4/40 (5)
5/118 (4) 6/146 (6)
7/183 (7) 8/185 (8) 9/202 (10)

Bowling: Kasprowicz 9–2–24–1; Davies 8–0–33–4; Wharf 7–0–49–0; Thomas 7–0–42–0; Dale 5–0–34–1; Croft 9–0–37–2.

Glamorgan

R. D. B. Croft c Burns b Jones		1
*S. P. James c Turner b Rose		0
D. L. Hemp c Bowler b Jones		3
M. P. Maynard b Jones		36
A. Dale run out		63
M. J. Powell b Francis		32
S. D. Thomas c Rose b Francis		5
†M. A. Wallace c Dutch b Blackwell		13
A. G. Wharf run out		18

M. S. Kasprowicz not out … 8
A. P. Davies not out … 2

B 2, l-b 10, w 8, n-b 2, p 6 … 28

1/1 (2) 2/1 (1)　　(9 wkts, 38.5 overs) 209
3/20 (3) 4/47 (4)
5/122 (6) 6/140 (7)
7/166 (8) 8/192 (5) 9/195 (9)

Bowling: Rose 8–1–29–1; Jones 7.5–0–36–3; Francis 8–0–54–2; Dutch 4–0–21–0; Parsons 3–0–21–0; Blackwell 8–0–30–1.

Umpires: B. Dudleston and B. Leadbeater.

SOMERSET v WORCESTERSHIRE

At Taunton, July 7. Worcestershire won by eight wickets. Toss: Somerset.

Not for the first time, Hick batted with muscular majesty to tear apart the Somerset bowling. At the ground where he blasted 405 in 1988, his first fifty came off 34 balls – and he marched on effortlessly. Solanki and Smith also batted confidently, and Worcestershire hurried home to claim top spot in the table. Blackwell and Turner had both made fifties at better than a run a ball in Somerset's own substantial total, but their bowlers proved far less effective.

Somerset

P. D. Bowler lbw b Bichel	16	G. D. Rose c Smith b Bichel		10
M. J. Wood b Batty	37	P. S. Jones not out		5
I. D. Blackwell b Batty	55	L-b 6, w 9		15
*M. Burns c Batty b Ali	54			
K. A. Parsons b Batty	11	1/45 (1) 2/99 (2)	(8 wkts, 45 overs)	269
P. C. L. Holloway lbw b Lampitt	12	3/131 (3) 4/150 (5)		
†R. J. Turner not out	53	5/182 (6) 6/226 (4)		
K. P. Dutch c Bichel b Mason	1	7/230 (8) 8/253 (9)		

M. P. L. Bulbeck did not bat.

Bowling: Bichel 9–1–34–2; Mason 9–0–60–1; Ali 9–0–63–1; Lampitt 9–0–40–1; Batty 9–0–66–3.

Worcestershire

V. S. Solanki c Burns b Jones	58
A. J. Bichel c Dutch b Bulbeck	0
*G. A. Hick not out	141
B. F. Smith not out	64
L-b 6, w 1	7

1/4 (2) 2/131 (1)   (2 wkts, 40.2 overs) 270

S. D. Peters, D. A. Leatherdale, G. J. Batty, †S. J. Rhodes, Kabir Ali, S. R. Lampitt and M. S. Mason did not bat.

Bowling: Rose 6–0–48–0; Bulbeck 4–0–38–1; Jones 9–0–80–1; Blackwell 9–0–42–0; Dutch 7.2–0–27–0; Parsons 5–0–29–0.

Umpires: I. J. Gould and K. J. Lyons.

At Scarborough, July 14. SOMERSET lost to YORKSHIRE by 135 runs.

At Cardiff, August 3. SOMERSET beat GLAMORGAN by 107 runs (D/L method).

At Canterbury, August 11. SOMERSET lost to KENT by 126 runs.

At Nottingham, August 18. SOMERSET lost to NOTTINGHAMSHIRE by 69 runs.

SOMERSET v NOTTINGHAMSHIRE

At Taunton, August 19 (day/night). Nottinghamshire won by 59 runs. Toss: Nottinghamshire.

Pietersen was dominant, even disdainful as he made Somerset pay for dropping him in the slips by tearing apart their attack and hustling a hundred from 78 balls – his second in two days, both career-bests. Shafayat played confidently in support and Nottinghamshire reached a huge 296. In reply, Somerset again revealed their patchy one-day technique with an early collapse. Johnson's thunderous eight-ball 25, with three fours and two sixes, provided fireworks, but the only resilience came from Parsons and Wood.

Nottinghamshire

P. Johnson c Wood b Francis	21	S. C. G. MacGill not out		2
*J. E. R. Gallian c Dutch b Johnson	3	S. J. Randall not out		1
U. Afzaal c Bowler b Johnson	14	L-b 4, w 7		11
K. P. Pietersen c Francis b Burns	147			
B. M. Shafayat c Jones b Johnson	66	1/17 (2) 2/37 (1)	(7 wkts, 45 overs)	296
†C. M. W. Read b Jones	21	3/49 (3) 4/207 (5)		
P. J. Franks c Dutch b Burns	10	5/267 (6) 6/291 (4) 7/292 (7)		

D. S. Lucas and R. J. Logan did not bat.

Bowling: Johnson 9–0–41–3; Francis 7–1–48–1; Jones 9–0–60–1; Dutch 8–0–56–0; Parsons 6–0–39–0; Burns 6–0–48–2.

Somerset

P. D. Bowler b Logan	0	S. R. G. Francis not out		2
R. L. Johnson b Logan	25	P. S. Jones b Franks		0
*J. Cox lbw b Lucas	2			
M. Burns lbw b Lucas	0	L-b 5, w 10, n-b 8		23
I. D. Blackwell b Lucas	31			
K. A. Parsons lbw b Randall	73	1/0 (1) 2/34 (3) 3/34 (4)	(38.3 overs)	237
M. J. Wood b Franks	61	4/35 (2) 5/80 (5) 6/171 (6)		
†R. J. Turner b Randall	2	7/180 (8) 8/225 (9)		
K. P. Dutch c Logan b Franks	18	9/237 (7) 10/237 (11)		

Bowling: Logan 8–1–62–2; Lucas 6–0–37–3; Franks 5.3–0–31–3; MacGill 7–0–34–0; Randall 9–0–37–2; Shafayat 3–0–31–0.

Umpires: A. Clarkson and V. A. Holder.

SOMERSET v WARWICKSHIRE

At Taunton, August 25. Warwickshire won by eight wickets. Toss: Somerset.

As if already resigned to relegation, Somerset batted badly, bowled without much menace, and dropped their catches. Apart from Cox and Blackwell, less aggressive than usual, their batting was ragged and weary. It was all too easy for Warwickshire – and especially for Pollock on his return. He followed up his penetrative bowling with a well-paced 43. Knight played adventurously, then Ostler saw Warwickshire home on a day that left the Taunton supporters shaking their heads.

Somerset

*J. Cox lbw b Sheikh	64	M. P. L. Bulbeck not out		4
P. D. Trego c Ostler b Pollock	4	P. S. Jones c Ostler b Brown		3
P. C. L. Holloway c Ostler b Pollock	5			
M. Burns c Frost b Brown	4	B 8, l-b 9, w 10		27
K. A. Parsons c Wagg b Sheikh	7			
I. D. Blackwell b Pollock	51	1/19 (2) 2/27 (3) 3/48 (4)	(43.4 overs)	188
K. P. Dutch b Smith	5	4/65 (5) 5/109 (1) 6/129 (7)		
M. J. Wood run out	8	7/151 (8) 8/181 (6)		
†R. J. Turner c Powell b Pollock	6	9/182 (9) 10/188 (11)		

Bowling: Pollock 9–0–36–4; Brown 6.4–0–26–2; Wagg 8–0–34–0; Sheikh 8–1–19–2; Smith 9–0–37–1; Wagh 3–0–19–0.

Warwickshire

M. A. Wagh c Parsons b Dutch	18
N. V. Knight b Jones	45
S. M. Pollock not out	43
D. P. Ostler not out.	77
L-b 1, w 7	8

1/64 (2) 2/75 (1)   (2 wkts, 35 overs) 191

I. R. Bell, *M. J. Powell, D. R. Brown, N. M. K. Smith, G. G. Wagg, †T. Frost and M. A. Sheikh did not bat.

Bowling: Bulbeck 3–0–22–0; Burns 9–0–41–0; Jones 8–0–59–1; Dutch 7–0–31–1; Blackwell 6–0–33–0; Trego 2–0–4–0.

Umpires: B. Dudleston and A. A. Jones.

At Chester-le-Street, September 2. SOMERSET lost to DURHAM by six wickets.

SOMERSET v KENT

At Taunton, September 8. Somerset won by 118 runs. Toss: Kent.

Somerset's innings belonged to Holloway, who batted as though he had a point to prove, which given his limited opportunities in 2002 he probably did. His unbeaten hundred, including four sixes, was followed by news that he was considering his future due to uncertainty over his first-team place. Kent batted carelessly, losing four wickets to stumpings off Blackwell's spin. Waugh crafted a measured half-century, but received scant support. Fleming managed just 16 – but passed 4,000 League runs in the process.

Somerset

*J. Cox c Saggers b Ealham	41	†R. J. Turner not out.	16
P. C. L. Holloway not out	112		
K. P. Dutch c Fulton b Tredwell	34	L-b 2, w 4	6
I. D. Blackwell c Nixon b Tredwell . . .	8		
A. V. Suppiah b Saggers	3	1/72 (1) 2/130 (3) (6 wkts, 45 overs) 244
P. D. Trego b Ealham	24	3/142 (4) 4/157 (5)
W. J. Durston lbw b Saggers	0	5/214 (6) 6/215 (7)

M. P. L. Bulbeck, S. R. G. Francis and P. S. Jones did not bat.

Bowling: Saggers 9–0–48–2; Trott 9–1–52–0; Ealham 9–1–47–2; Fleming 9–1–34–0; Tredwell 6–0–36–2; Waugh 3–0–25–0.

Kent

*M. V. Fleming c Turner b Bulbeck	16	M. J. Saggers st Turner b Blackwell . . .	1
R. W. T. Key st Turner b Blackwell	32	B. J. Trott st Turner b Blackwell	0
S. R. Waugh b Trego	53		
†P. A. Nixon c Francis b Jones	3	L-b 1, w 4	5
M. J. Walker c Suppiah b Jones	0		
D. P. Fulton lbw b Trego	8	1/21 (1) 2/79 (2) 3/86 (4) (34 overs) 126
M. A. Ealham st Turner b Blackwell . . .	1	4/91 (5) 5/101 (6) 6/116 (7)
G. O. Jones not out	5	7/120 (3) 8/124 (9)
J. C. Tredwell c Trego b Dutch	2	9/126 (10) 10/126 (11)

Bowling: Francis 7–2–10–0; Bulbeck 9–0–36–1; Trego 9–0–47–2; Blackwell 6–1–24–4; Jones 2–1–5–2; Dutch 1–0–3–1.

Umpires: G. Sharp and J. F. Steele.

At Leicester, September 11 (day/night). SOMERSET beat LEICESTERSHIRE by three wickets.

SOMERSET v DURHAM

At Taunton, September 22. Somerset won by 175 runs. Toss: Somerset.

With public criticism from the chief executive over their poor performances ringing in their ears, Somerset ended the season with a leisurely triumph against an anaemic-looking Durham. After Wood, Burns, and Parsons steered Somerset to 254, Durham's reply was embarrassingly limp. Trego took three for 14 in four overs, and Dutch didn't concede a run in his 3.2. But an efficient Somerset win couldn't take the sting out of a thoroughly uninspiring season.

Somerset

*J. Cox c A. Pratt b Harmison	7	K. P. Dutch not out	1
P. C. L. Holloway c A. Pratt b Harmison	6		
M. Burns c Phillips b Davies	54	L-b 9, w 10	19
M. J. Wood not out	88		
K. A. Parsons run out	40	1/8 (2) 2/27 (1) (6 wkts, 45 overs) 254
A. V. Suppiah c G. J. Pratt b Gough	18	3/80 (3) 4/164 (5)
†R. J. Turner c Hodge b Killeen	21	5/201 (6) 6/251 (7)

P. D. Trego, M. P. L. Bulbeck and S. R. G. Francis did not bat.

Bowling: Harmison 9–0–39–2; Killeen 8–0–47–1; Davies 6–0–34–1; Pattison 4–1–29–0; Phillips 7–0–35–0; Thorpe 3–0–18–0; Gough 8–0–43–1.

Durham

M. A. Gough lbw b Bulbeck	12	A. M. Davies not out	9
A. M. Thorpe c Parsons b Francis	4	N. Killeen c Burns b Trego	0
*B. J. Hodge c Parsons b Bulbeck	27	S. J. Harmison c and b Dutch	3
G. J. Muchall c Turner b Francis	4	L-b 6, w 7, n-b 2	15
G. J. Pratt b Trego	0		
†A. Pratt c Francis b Dutch	5	1/7 (2) 2/40 (1) 3/54 (3) (21.2 overs) 79
I. Pattison c Burns b Trego	0	4/58 (4) 5/64 (5) 6/64 (7)
N. C. Phillips run out	0	7/64 (8) 8/65 (6) 9/66 (10) 10/79 (11)

Bowling: Francis 7–0–34–2; Bulbeck 7–2–25–2; Trego 4–2–14–3; Dutch 3.2–3–0–2.

Umpires: J. W. Lloyds and K. E. Palmer.

WARWICKSHIRE

At Chester-le-Street, May 12. WARWICKSHIRE beat DURHAM by 44 runs.

At Nottingham, May 19. WARWICKSHIRE beat NOTTINGHAMSHIRE by 85 runs.

WARWICKSHIRE v DURHAM

At Birmingham, June 4. Warwickshire won by seven wickets. Toss: Durham.

Neil Carter was the undoubted star. He swung his way to career-best one-day figures, and later clubbed three sixes in a nine-ball 24 as Warwickshire sped to victory in 67 balls. Another abject batting display by Durham was summed up when Law was run out without facing a ball, in his first competitive innings of the season. A measly 72 was their lowest League score. Despite three early wickets, Pollock made light work of the chase and Warwickshire won before tea. As part of the Jubilee Day celebrations, spectators had only been charged 50p admission, so they could hardly complain about being short-changed.

Durham

N. Peng lbw b Pollock	1
G. J. Pratt c Frost b Carter	1
M. L. Love c Frost b Carter	2
G. J. Muchall b Carter	0
*J. B. Lewis c Pollock b Carter	21
†A. Pratt not out	22
D. R. Law run out	0
G. D. Bridge lbw b Brown	2
A. M. Davies c Frost b Carter	1

N. Killeen b Pollock	6
N. G. Hatch b Pollock	5
L-b 5, w 4, n-b 2	11

1/2 (1) 2/2 (2) 3/3 (4)   (21.2 overs) 72
4/18 (3) 5/40 (5) 6/44 (7)
7/49 (8) 8/50 (9)
9/66 (10) 10/72 (11)

Bowling: Pollock 5.2–2–10–3; Carter 9–0–31–5; Brown 4–1–16–1; Giles 3–0–10–0.

Warwickshire

N. M. Carter c Davies b Killeen	24
N. V. Knight c Love b Killeen	1
D. P. Ostler c A. Pratt b Hatch	0
S. M. Pollock not out	29
J. O. Troughton not out	14
L-b 3, w 2	5

1/28 (1) 2/28 (2)   (3 wkts, 11.1 overs) 73
3/28 (3)

*M. J. Powell, T. L. Penney, D. R. Brown, N. M. K. Smith, †T. Frost and A. F. Giles did not bat.

Bowling: Killeen 6–1–19–2; Hatch 3–1–34–1; Law 2.1–0–17–0.

Umpires: V. A. Holder and K. E. Palmer.

WARWICKSHIRE v SOMERSET

At Birmingham, June 9. No result (abandoned).

At Leeds, June 16. WARWICKSHIRE beat YORKSHIRE by 14 runs (D/L method).

At Worcester, June 24. WARWICKSHIRE lost to WORCESTERSHIRE by four runs.

WARWICKSHIRE v KENT

At Birmingham, June 30. Warwickshire won by 19 runs (D/L method). Toss: Kent.

An intriguing contest was spoiled by the weather, as Warwickshire purposefully pursued a challenging total. Steady drizzle fell throughout their innings but the batsmen's aggression ensured they were well ahead of the rate when play was called off. It redeemed Warwickshire's shabby performance in the field, where they conceded 150 runs in boundaries. Ealham exploited the gaffes expertly, punching a sprightly fifty.

Kent

A. Khan lbw b Brown	21	J. M. Golding not out	8
R. W. T. Key lbw b Sheikh	46	J. C. Tredwell b Wagg	0
J. B. Hockley c Ostler b Sheikh	20	B 1, l-b 10, w 11, n-b 4	26
A. Symonds c Troughton b Wagg	2		
*D. P. Fulton c Clifford b Carter	36	1/56 (1) 2/95 (3) (9 wkts, 45 overs) 266	
M. J. Walker lbw b Wagg	48	3/97 (4) 4/97 (2)	
M. A. Ealham c Clifford b Wagg	53	5/157 (5) 6/243 (6)	
†P. A. Nixon lbw b Pollock	6	7/254 (8) 8/260 (7) 9/266 (10)	

M. J. Saggers did not bat.

Bowling: Pollock 9–1–44–1; Carter 5–0–39–1; Brown 8–0–45–1; Sheikh 9–0–40–2; Wagg 7–1–50–4; Powell 7–0–37–0.

Warwickshire

*M. J. Powell c Nixon b Ealham	34		
N. M. Carter c Symonds b Saggers	10		
D. P. Ostler b Ealham	43		
I. R. Bell not out	29		
J. O. Troughton not out	8		
W 2	2		

1/11 (2) 2/68 (1)   (3 wkts, 20.1 overs) 126
3/109 (3)

S. M. Pollock, D. R. Brown, N. M. K. Smith, G. G. Wagg, M. A. Sheikh and †J. I. Clifford did not bat.

Bowling: Saggers 5.1–0–46–1; Khan 7–0–39–0; Ealham 5–0–22–2; Golding 3–0–19–0.

Umpires: T. E. Jesty and J. F. Steele.

At Leicester, July 14. WARWICKSHIRE lost to LEICESTERSHIRE by four wickets.

WARWICKSHIRE v GLAMORGAN

At Birmingham, July 28. Glamorgan won by 62 runs. Toss: Warwickshire.

Warwickshire's title challenge stalled with a third defeat in four matches. Their attack suffered heavy punishment, as Glamorgan amassed their second-highest total in the competition. There were meaty contributions from Maynard, Dale and especially Ian Thomas, who sped to his best one-day score. Croft's enigmatic variations of pace and flight then kept Warwickshire in check. Only a fightback by young guns Bell and Troughton saved them from a heavier defeat.

Glamorgan

*R. D. B. Croft b Carter	34	A. G. Wharf not out	11
I. J. Thomas c Richardson b Powell	72	D. A. Cosker not out	2
D. L. Hemp c Smith b Brown	14	B 2, l-b 5, w 13, n-b 2	22
M. P. Maynard c Knight b Powell	63		
A. Dale c Knight b Carter	63	1/63 (1) 2/103 (3) (8 wkts, 45 overs) 300	
S. D. Thomas b Powell	12	3/153 (2) 4/220 (4)	
M. J. Powell c Powell b Brown	7	5/277 (6) 6/280 (5)	
†M. A. Wallace run out	0	7/281 (8) 8/296 (7)	

O. T. Parkin did not bat.

Bowling: Brown 9–0–44–2; Carter 9–0–67–2; Richardson 8–0–62–0; Smith 9–0–57–0; Powell 9–0–46–3; Wagh 1–0–17–0.

Warwickshire

N. M. Carter c S. D. Thomas b Wharf . .	1
N. V. Knight c Powell b Wharf	6
M. A. Wagh c Hemp b Wharf	17
D. P. Ostler c Wallace b Parkin	17
I. R. Bell lbw b S. D. Thomas	86
J. O. Troughton c Maynard b Croft	48
*M. J. Powell c Wallace b Croft	9
D. R. Brown c Wharf b Croft	16
N. M. K. Smith c Parkin b Croft	2

†K. J. Piper not out	13
A. Richardson b S. D. Thomas	8
L-b 8, w 7	15

1/5 (1) 2/13 (2) 3/41 (3)   (39.4 overs) 238
4/45 (4) 5/149 (6) 6/175 (7)
7/208 (5) 8/215 (9)
9/220 (8) 10/238 (11)

Bowling: Parkin 7–0–39–1; Wharf 6–0–39–3; S. D. Thomas 7.4–0–42–2; Dale 3–0–23–0; Croft 9–0–40–4; Cosker 7–0–47–0.

Umpires: D. J. Constant and J. W. Holder.

At Canterbury, July 30 (day/night). WARWICKSHIRE lost to KENT by 13 runs (D/L method).

WARWICKSHIRE v LEICESTERSHIRE

At Birmingham, August 4. Warwickshire won by seven wickets (D/L method). Toss: Leicestershire.
 Ostler, dropped for Warwickshire's previous game in the competition, made a spectacular return after the captain Powell boldly decided to omit himself. In true *Boys' Own* fashion, Ostler struck the winning runs to bring up his century. Troughton was a dashing companion, hitting a cavalier 66, and with lightning flashing around the ground, they romped to their revised target of 203. Sutcliffe's measured contribution was the only highlight of a dispirited Leicestershire performance, and after his dismissal they lost all momentum.

Leicestershire

T. R. Ward lbw b Pollock	2
I. J. Sutcliffe run out	98
D. I. Stevens lbw b Sheikh	17
M. G. Bevan c Giles b Brown	32
P. A. J. DeFreitas not out	44
*V. J. Wells b Sheikh	4
†N. D. Burns c Bell b Richardson	29

D. L. Maddy not out	16
L-b 4, w 2, n-b 2	8

1/11 (1) 2/45 (3)   (6 wkts, 45 overs) 250
3/152 (2) 4/152 (4)
5/168 (6) 6/216 (7)

C. D. Crowe, J. O. Grove and M. J. A. Whiley did not bat.

Bowling: Pollock 9–1–40–1; Brown 9–0–60–1; Sheikh 9–0–45–2; Richardson 9–0–45–1; Giles 9–0–56–0.

Warwickshire

N. V. Knight b DeFreitas	0
N. M. K. Smith b Grove	14
D. P. Ostler not out	103
I. R. Bell c Burns b DeFreitas	7
J. O. Troughton not out	66
L-b 6, w 6, n-b 4	16

1/1 (1) 2/43 (2)   (3 wkts, 30.4 overs) 206
3/67 (4)

S. M. Pollock, *D. R. Brown, †K. J. Piper, A. F. Giles, M. A. Sheikh and A. Richardson did not bat.

Bowling: DeFreitas 7.4–0–36–2; Grove 7–0–62–1; Whiley 5–0–31–0; Maddy 4–0–24–0; Crowe 3–0–21–0; Wells 4–0–26–0.

Umpires: M. R. Benson and N. A. Mallender.

WARWICKSHIRE v WORCESTERSHIRE

At Birmingham, August 19 (day/night). Worcestershire won by eight wickets. Toss: Warwickshire.

A vibrant innings from Solanki and a sedate one from Singh helped Worcestershire saunter past a potentially tricky target under lights. Their partnership of 183 – Worcestershire's highest for any wicket in the competition – flourished courtesy of some woeful bowling. Earlier Wagh's stylish 84, his highest one-day score, had given Warwickshire a good foundation, but Leatherdale and Lampitt undermined it. Warwickshire were handicapped by having to bat in twilight for ten overs, before the floodlights were belatedly switched on.

Warwickshire

M. A. Wagh b Leatherdale	84	N. M. Carter not out	1
*N. V. Knight c Rhodes b Lampitt	31	M. A. Sheikh not out	0
D. P. Ostler c Rhodes b Leatherdale	14	B 4, l-b 7, w 9	20
I. R. Bell c Solanki b Lampitt	27		
J. O. Troughton st Rhodes b Leatherdale	7	1/62 (2) 2/96 (3)	(8 wkts, 45 overs) 216
D. R. Brown run out	17	3/151 (4) 4/172 (5)	
N. M. K. Smith lbw b Leatherdale	0	5/185 (1) 6/185 (7)	
†K. J. Piper b Ali	15	7/211 (8) 8/215 (6)	

S. E. Bond did not bat.

Bowling: Sheriyar 9–1–43–0; Ali 9–0–43–1; Lampitt 9–0–40–2; Leatherdale 9–0–37–4; Batty 9–0–42–0.

Worcestershire

V. S. Solanki c Knight b Brown	91
A. Singh not out	75
*G. A. Hick run out	3
B. F. Smith not out	21
B 6, l-b 9, w 12, n-b 2	29

1/183 (1) 2/188 (3)   (2 wkts, 39.2 overs) 219

S. Lee, D. A. Leatherdale, G. J. Batty, †S. J. Rhodes, Kabir Ali, S. R. Lampitt and A. Sheriyar did not bat.

Bowling: Bond 9–2–32–0; Carter 5.2–1–42–0; Sheikh 5–1–26–0; Brown 5–0–32–1; Wagh 9–0–28–0; Smith 6–0–44–0.

Umpires: I. J. Gould and J. H. Hampshire.

At Taunton, August 25. WARWICKSHIRE beat SOMERSET by eight wickets.

WARWICKSHIRE v NOTTINGHAMSHIRE

At Birmingham, September 1. Warwickshire won by 51 runs. Toss: Warwickshire.

Nottinghamshire were relegated after an abject collapse in which they surrendered their last eight wickets for just 43 runs. Read coasted to his one-day best, but panic set in after he pulled to deep mid-wicket. Suicidal running, plus accurate bowling and sharp fielding, contributed to their demise. Warwickshire also found scoring difficult on a slow pitch but Wagh gave them early impetus, and Bell played sensibly, allowing free rein to his more aggressive partners.

Warwickshire

M. A. Wagh c MacGill b Franks	49	M. A. Sheikh st Read b MacGill	0
D. P. Ostler c Shafayat b Logan	2	†T. Frost not out	0
S. M. Pollock c Read b MacGill	39		
I. R. Bell c Randall b Lucas	54	B 6, w 4, n-b 2	12
J. O. Troughton c Welton b Patel	34		
*M. J. Powell c Shafayat b Lucas	22	1/3 (2) 2/79 (1) (9 wkts, 45 overs) 238
D. R. Brown c Franks b Lucas	13	3/95 (3) 4/166 (5)
N. M. K. Smith not out	11	5/205 (6) 6/219 (7)
G. G. Wagg b Logan	2	7/228 (4) 8/231 (9) 9/238 (10)

Bowling: Logan 6–1–31–2; Lucas 9–0–48–3; Franks 7–0–26–1; Shafayat 5–0–31–0; MacGill 9–0–38–2; Randall 5–0–28–0; Patel 4–0–30–1.

Nottinghamshire

G. E. Welton b Brown	13	D. S. Lucas not out	0
U. Afzaal run out	45	R. J. Logan c Smith b Brown	0
†C. M. W. Read c Wagg b Smith	69	B 1, l-b 1, w 7	9
B. M. Shafayat c Frost b Smith	10		
*J. E. R. Gallian c and b Powell	1	1/42 (1) 2/116 (2) (41.4 overs) 187
S. R. Patel run out	18	3/144 (3) 4/146 (5)
P. J. Franks run out	15	5/152 (4) 6/178 (6)
S. C. G. MacGill c Brown b Wagg	6	7/181 (7) 8/187 (8)
S. J. Randall c Powell b Wagg	1	9/187 (9) 10/187 (11)

Bowling: Pollock 7–1–21–0; Wagg 7–1–22–2; Sheikh 6–0–40–0; Brown 7.4–1–33–2; Smith 9–0–38–2; Powell 5–0–31–1.

Umpires: D. J. Constant and N. A. Mallender.

WARWICKSHIRE v YORKSHIRE

At Birmingham, September 10 (day/night). Yorkshire won by eight wickets. Toss: Warwickshire. County debut: D. W. Fleming.

This was another miserable trouncing for Warwickshire under Edgbaston's floodlights. They failed to post a competitive total, and without Brown's defiant career-best would have been in a far sorrier state. Their attack was then hindered by heavy dew, and a shoulder injury to their replacement overseas player, Fleming. He bowled only four expensive overs and flew home two days later. However, with Yorkshire's batsmen in outstanding form, even a fully-fit Fleming would have struggled to alter the result.

Warwickshire

N. M. Carter b Bresnan	0	N. M. K. Smith not out	23
M. A. Wagh c Blakey b Thornicroft	1		
D. P. Ostler c White b Thornicroft	19	L-b 4, w 9, n-b 4	17
I. R. Bell c Fellows b Sidebottom	17		
*M. J. Powell c Blakey b McGrath	15	1/3 (1) 2/7 (2) (6 wkts, 45 overs) 191
D. R. Brown not out	82	3/36 (3) 4/66 (4)
†T. Frost st Blakey b Dawson	17	5/67 (5) 6/104 (7)

D. W. Fleming, M. A. Sheikh and A. Richardson did not bat.

Bowling: Thornicroft 7–2–35–2; Bresnan 9–0–58–1; Sidebottom 9–3–20–1; McGrath 9–3–23–1; Dawson 7–0–28–1; Fellows 4–0–23–0.

Yorkshire

C. White b Richardson	. . . .	36
M. J. Lumb b Carter	. . . .	73
*†R. J. Blakey not out	. . . .	48
M. T. G. Elliott not out	. . . .	25
L-b 4, w 4, n-b 4		12

1/73 (1) 2/153 (2)   (2 wkts, 27.3 overs) 194

M. J. Wood, A. McGrath, G. M. Fellows, T. T. Bresnan, R. K. J. Dawson, N. D. Thornicroft and R. J. Sidebottom did not bat.

Bowling: Fleming 4–0–25–0; Carter 7.3–0–38–1; Richardson 3–0–41–0; Brown 6–1–44–0; Sheikh 2–0–22–0; Smith 3–1–13–0; Wagh 2–0–7–0.

Umpires: G. I. Burgess and V. A. Holder.

At Cardiff, September 22. WARWICKSHIRE beat GLAMORGAN by 74 runs.

WORCESTERSHIRE

WORCESTERSHIRE v SOMERSET

At Worcester, May 19. Worcestershire won by 127 runs. Toss: Worcestershire.

On a sound pitch, Kabir Ali did an impressive demolition job, storming through Somerset's flimsy batting. He removed Bowler and Cox in successive overs, and then took two wickets in two balls to dismiss Burns and Turner. Earlier, Worcestershire had eagerly taken full advantage of Somerset's ineptitude in the field, despite losing Solanki to the very first ball. Singh underpinned the innings with a silky fifty, which allowed Smith and Rhodes to plunder quick runs later on.

Worcestershire

V. S. Solanki c Turner b Bulbeck	. . . . .	0	Kabir Ali not out		4
A. Singh c Dutch b Blackwell	. . . .	65	S. R. Lampitt not out		5
*G. A. Hick c sub b Rose	. . . .	18	L-b 6, w 7		13
B. F. Smith c Burns b Francis	. . . .	66			
D. A. Leatherdale b Francis	. . . .	39	1/0 (1) 2/70 (3) (7 wkts, 45 overs)		254
G. J. Batty c Turner b Francis	. . . .	2	3/101 (2) 4/165 (5)		
†S. J. Rhodes c Turner b Francis	. . . .	42	5/167 (6) 6/245 (4) 7/245 (7)		

M. J. Rawnsley and A. Sheriyar did not bat.

Bowling: Bulbeck 8–1–40–1; Rose 9–0–33–1; Dutch 9–0–54–0; Parsons 1–0–10–0; Blackwell 9–2–41–1; Francis 8–0–60–4; Burns 1–0–10–0.

Somerset

P. D. Bowler b Ali	. . . .	1	M. P. L. Bulbeck b Rawnsley	. . . .	21
M. J. Wood lbw b Sheriyar	. . . .	4	S. R. G. Francis not out	. . . .	6
*J. Cox lbw b Ali	. . . .	7			
M. Burns b Ali	. . . .	11	L-b 1, w 8		9
I. D. Blackwell c Smith b Sheriyar	. . . .	12			
K. A. Parsons c Smith b Rawnsley	. . . .	37	1/1 (1) 2/11 (2) (32.4 overs)		127
†R. J. Turner c Hick b Ali	. . . .	0	3/15 (3) 4/30 (5) 5/40 (4)		
K. P. Dutch c Rhodes b Lampitt	. . . . .	6	6/40 (7) 7/61 (8) 8/88 (9)		
G. D. Rose b Batty	. . . .	13	9/106 (6) 10/127 (10)		

Bowling: Sheriyar 7–0–36–2; Ali 7–2–15–4; Lampitt 5–1–21–1; Batty 9–0–35–1; Rawnsley 4.4–0–19–2.

Umpires: K. E. Palmer and J. F. Steele.

At Leeds, June 4. WORCESTERSHIRE beat YORKSHIRE by six wickets.

At Oakham School, June 9. WORCESTERSHIRE v LEICESTERSHIRE. No result.

At Chester-le-Street, June 16. WORCESTERSHIRE beat DURHAM by 121 runs (D/L method).

WORCESTERSHIRE v WARWICKSHIRE

At Worcester, June 24. Worcestershire won by four runs. Toss: Worcestershire.

An explosive century from Pollock just failed to rescue Warwickshire in a real nail-biter. He needed six off the final ball, but Bichel held his nerve. At 75 for six, Warwickshire had looked gone and forgotten, but Pollock plundered Worcestershire's attack, smacking eight fours and six sixes. He got limping support from Penney, who had to bat with a runner after injuring his hamstring. Earlier, Worcestershire were indebted to a superbly paced century from Solanki, full of deft placement and elegance.

Worcestershire

V. S. Solanki not out 119	Kabir Ali c Powell b Carter	8
A. Singh b Pollock 4	†S. J. Rhodes not out	4
*G. A. Hick c Clifford b Smith 50	L-b 5, w 2	7
A. J. Bichel c Clifford b Brown 1		
B. F. Smith c Powell b Carter 12	1/8 (2) 2/94 (3) (7 wkts, 45 overs) 232
D. A. Leatherdale b Smith 20	3/96 (4) 4/128 (5)
G. J. Batty b Pollock 7	5/169 (6) 6/196 (7) 7/218 (8)

S. R. Lampitt and M. S. Mason did not bat.

Bowling: Pollock 9–1–27–2; Carter 9–0–50–2; Sheikh 9–0–44–0; Brown 9–1–49–1; Smith 9–0–57–2.

Warwickshire

*M. J. Powell b Bichel 39	T. L. Penney b Ali	50
D. P. Ostler b Mason 4	N. M. Carter not out	5
I. R. Bell c Solanki b Ali 5	L-b 3, w 9	12
J. O. Troughton c Hick b Lampitt 0		
S. M. Pollock not out 111	1/6 (2) 2/35 (3) (7 wkts, 45 overs) 228
D. R. Brown st Rhodes b Lampitt 1	3/42 (4) 4/64 (1)
N. M. K. Smith b Lampitt 1	5/71 (6) 6/75 (7) 7/209 (8)

M. A. Sheikh and †J. I. Clifford did not bat.

Bowling: Bichel 9–0–41–1; Mason 8–1–35–1; Ali 9–0–59–2; Lampitt 9–3–35–3; Batty 8–0–43–0; Leatherdale 2–0–12–0.

Umpires: N. J. Llong and R. Palmer.

WORCESTERSHIRE v DURHAM

At Worcester, June 30. Durham won by nine wickets (D/L method). Toss: Worcestershire.

Worcestershire suffered their season's first defeat in the competition. A stoic stand from Smith and Leatherdale was sandwiched between two damaging collapses, and their total always looked paltry. Rain left Durham a revised target of 62 in 13 overs, and their youngsters hurried them home with little trouble.

Worcestershire

V. S. Solanki c Symington b Hunter. . . .	0	S. R. Lampitt not out	3
A. Singh run out	13	M. S. Mason b Killeen	6
*G. A. Hick c A. Pratt b Killeen.	0		
B. F. Smith lbw b Bridge.	54	L-b 8, w 5, n-b 3	16
D. A. Leatherdale c Killeen b Bridge . . .	30		
G. J. Batty lbw b Davies	2	1/13 (2) 2/15 (1) 3/15 (3) (43.1 overs) 144
A. J. Bichel b Symington.	12	4/99 (5) 5/102 (6) 6/106 (4)
†S. J. Rhodes c A. Pratt b Bridge	2	7/111 (8) 8/127 (7)
Kabir Ali b Symington	6	9/128 (9) 10/144 (11)

Bowling: Killeen 8.1–2–23–2; Hunter 8–1–31–1; Davies 9–1–32–1; Law 3–0–17–0; Bridge 9–1–22–3; Symington 6–1–11–2.

Durham

N. Peng not out	32
G. J. Pratt c Bichel b Mason	6
G. J. Muchall not out	24
B 1, l-b 1, w 1	3

1/12 (2)   (1 wkt, 10.4 overs) 65

M. J. Symington, *J. J. B. Lewis, †A. Pratt, D. R. Law, I. D. Hunter, G. D. Bridge, A. M. Davies and N. Killeen did not bat.

Bowling: Bichel 2.4–0–16–0; Mason 3–0–14–1; Lampitt 2–0–14–0; Ali 2–0–13–0; Leatherdale 1–0–6–0.

Umpires: V. A. Holder and A. A. Jones.

At Taunton, July 7. WORCESTERSHIRE beat SOMERSET by eight wickets.

At Canterbury, July 14. WORCESTERSHIRE beat KENT by five wickets.

WORCESTERSHIRE v YORKSHIRE

At Worcester, July 28. Worcestershire won by six wickets. Toss: Yorkshire.

Worcestershire moved eight points clear at the top of the table, thanks to a trademark display by the ever-impressive Bichel. His fiery new-ball spell left Yorkshire reeling; Lehmann restored some calm but they were never on top. In reply, the openers fell cheaply and the game was evenly poised at 99 for four. However, Smith and Batty wore down Yorkshire's depleted attack and carried Worcestershire home.

Yorkshire

V. J. Craven c Hick b Mason	25	A. K. D. Gray b Ali	6
M. J. Wood b Bichel	16	C. J. Elstub not out.	4
R. K. J. Dawson c Rhodes b Bichel . . .	0	B 2, l-b 13, w 3, n-b 2	20
A. McGrath c Rhodes b Bichel.	6		
*D. S. Lehmann c Ali b Leatherdale . . .	56	1/29 (2) 2/29 (3) (8 wkts, 45 overs) 207
G. M. Fellows c Rhodes b Lampitt	28	3/35 (4) 4/65 (1)
M. J. Lumb c Solanki b Leatherdale . . .	32	5/111 (6) 6/169 (5)
†R. J. Blakey not out	14	7/184 (7) 8/200 (9)

R. J. Sidebottom did not bat.

Bowling: Bichel 9–0–30–3; Ali 9–0–47–1; Lampitt 9–2–49–1; Mason 9–1–28–1; Leatherdale 7–1–21–2; Batty 2–0–17–0.

Worcestershire

S. D. Peters c Lehmann b Elstub	2	G. J. Batty not out	54
V. S. Solanki c Blakey b Sidebottom	9	L-b 2, w 13	15
*G. A. Hick lbw b McGrath	29		
B. F. Smith not out	92	1/13 (1) 2/17 (2)	(4 wkts, 42 overs) 208
D. A. Leatherdale st Blakey b Lehmann	7	3/85 (3) 4/99 (5)	

A. J. Bichel, †S. J. Rhodes, Kabir Ali, S. R. Lampitt and M. S. Mason did not bat.

Bowling: Sidebottom 9–2–35–1; Elstub 7–2–31–1; Fellows 8–1–47–0; McGrath 9–0–55–1; Gray 4–0–12–0; Lehmann 5–0–26–1.

Umpires: M. R. Benson and A. Clarkson.

WORCESTERSHIRE v GLAMORGAN

At Worcester, August 4. Glamorgan won by 22 runs (D/L method). Toss: Glamorgan. County debut: S. Lee.

Glamorgan took advantage of some rusty bowling by the Australian all-rounder Shane Lee and overcame their main title rivals. Lee's introduction, with Glamorgan at a precarious 28 for three, turned the game: his hugely expensive spell handed the initiative back, allowing Maynard and James to swing away merrily, and when the clouds burst open, they were well ahead of the required rate. Earlier, Lee had acquitted himself better with the bat, but it was a lone effort as Worcestershire were strangled by some excellent Glamorgan fielding.

Worcestershire

S. D. Peters c Wallace b S. D. Thomas	29	S. R. Lampitt not out	10
V. S. Solanki c James b Davies	13	M. S. Mason not out	1
*G. A. Hick c Maynard b Parkin	10		
B. F. Smith b Davies	25	B 5, l-b 9, w 8, n-b 2	24
S. Lee lbw b Dale	41		
D. A. Leatherdale c Powell b Dale	15	1/20 (2) 2/50 (3)	(9 wkts, 45 overs) 202
G. J. Batty c Wallace b S. D. Thomas	3	3/66 (1) 4/129 (4)	
†S. J. Rhodes c Davies b Dale	14	5/137 (5) 6/147 (7)	
Kabir Ali run out	17	7/155 (6) 8/182 (8) 9/194 (9)	

Bowling: Davies 9–0–44–2; Parkin 8–1–23–1; S. D. Thomas 9–1–33–2; Harrison 6–0–27–0; Croft 4–0–29–0; Dale 9–0–32–3.

Glamorgan

R. D. B. Croft b Mason	15	
I. J. Thomas c Solanki b Ali	6	
M. J. Powell c Lee b Mason	4	
M. P. Maynard not out	32	
*S. P. James not out	41	
B 1, l-b 4, w 5	10	

1/17 (2) 2/26 (1) (3 wkts, 22.1 overs) 108
3/28 (3)

A. Dale, D. S. Harrison, †M. A. Wallace, S. D. Thomas, A. P. Davies and O. T. Parkin did not bat.

Bowling: Mason 7–0–27–2; Ali 5–1–10–1; Lee 3–0–39–0; Lampitt 4.1–0–13–0; Leatherdale 3–0–14–0.

Umpires: A. A. Jones and K. E. Palmer.

WORCESTERSHIRE v NOTTINGHAMSHIRE

At Worcester, August 7 (day/night). No result. Toss: Worcestershire.

Worcestershire posted a challenging total on a pitch of variable bounce, but the rain came before Nottinghamshire could reply. Solanki crafted another finely-judged innings, sharing a steady stand with Hick, and a pacier one with the ultra-aggressive Lee, who thumped three sixes. But the storm had the last word.

Worcestershire

S. D. Peters c Afzaal b Smith	9	Kabir Ali b Smith	16
V. S. Solanki c Lucas b Randall	81	S. R. Lampitt not out	2
*G. A. Hick c Pietersen b Lucas	19	L-b 11, w 4, n-b 2	17
B. F. Smith c Boje b Lucas	1		
S. Lee c Boje b Randall	36	1/13 (1) 2/69 (3)	(8 wkts, 45 overs) 230
D. A. Leatherdale c Pietersen b Boje	10	3/71 (4) 4/141 (5)	
G. J. Batty c Pietersen b Harris	13	5/166 (6) 6/172 (2)	
†S. J. Rhodes not out	26	7/202 (7) 8/226 (9)	

M. S. Mason did not bat.

Bowling: Smith 9–1–33–2; Harris 9–1–56–1; Lucas 9–1–44–2; Randall 9–0–39–2; Boje 9–0–47–1.

Nottinghamshire

D. J. Bicknell, U. Afzaal, N. Boje, K. P. Pietersen, *P. Johnson, †C. M. W. Read, S. R. Patel, D. S. Lucas, S. J. Randall, A. J. Harris and G. J. Smith.

Umpires: D. J. Constant and A. G. T. Whitehead.

At Birmingham, August 19 (day/night). WORCESTERSHIRE beat WARWICKSHIRE by eight wickets.

WORCESTERSHIRE v KENT

At Worcester, September 1. Worcestershire won by three wickets. Toss: Kent.

Graeme Hick passed a milestone only Kim Barnett and Graham Gooch had reached before him – 8,000 League runs – as he guided Worcestershire to a tense last-over victory. Kent had looked set for a big total as Fleming and Key flayed 101 off the first 18 overs. But Batty and Leatherdale pegged them back, and superb Worcestershire fielding contributed to four run-outs. Worcestershire were given a flying start by Solanki, and Hick's stand with Smith seemed to have settled the issue. A late stumble kept things interesting, but Hick had seen it all before.

Kent

*M. V. Fleming c Solanki b Batty	68	M. M. Patel run out	1
R. W. T. Key run out	46	D. D. Masters not out	2
J. M. Golding c Singh b Batty	13	L-b 3, w 5	8
E. T. Smith run out	1		
S. R. Waugh b Leatherdale	3	1/101 (1) 2/131 (3)	(8 wkts, 45 overs) 213
D. P. Fulton not out	41	3/134 (4) 4/137 (2)	
†P. A. Nixon run out	24	5/142 (5) 6/191 (7)	
M. A. Ealham b Ali	6	7/205 (8) 8/208 (9)	

M. J. Saggers did not bat.

Bowling: Ali 9–2–51–1; Sheriyar 7–0–41–0; Lampitt 9–0–35–0; Batty 9–0–39–2; Leatherdale 9–0–29–1; Smith 2–0–15–0.

Worcestershire

V. S. Solanki b Saggers	46		G. J. Batty b Fleming		6
A. Singh b Saggers	6		Kabir Ali not out		8
†D. J. Pipe c Key b Saggers	0		L-b 9, w 7		16
*G. A. Hick not out	77				
B. F. Smith c Nixon b Saggers	46		1/36 (2) 2/40 (3)	(7 wkts, 44.1 overs)	217
S. D. Peters c Nixon b Waugh	12		3/61 (1) 4/155 (5)		
D. A. Leatherdale c Saggers b Waugh	0		5/177 (6) 6/177 (7) 7/193 (8)		

S. R. Lampitt and A. Sheriyar did not bat.

Bowling: Saggers 9–2–37–4; Masters 5–0–33–0; Fleming 9–1–39–1; Ealham 8.1–0–29–0; Patel 8–0–40–0; Golding 3–0–24–0; Waugh 2–0–6–2.

Umpires: B. Leadbeater and P. Willey.

At Cardiff, September 3 (day/night). WORCESTERSHIRE lost to GLAMORGAN by 103 runs.

At Nottingham, September 15. WORCESTERSHIRE beat NOTTINGHAMSHIRE by 81 runs.

WORCESTERSHIRE v LEICESTERSHIRE

At Worcester, September 22. Worcestershire won by 28 runs. Toss: Worcestershire. First-team debut: D. S. Brignull.

The last game of the season was memorable for Stuart Lampitt's farewell to Worcestershire after 18 seasons. Fittingly, he took a wicket in his final over, before leaving the field to a standing ovation. One eye-catching performance came from Kadeer Ali, who gave a hint of his rich promise; the other came from Sheriyar, playing what would prove to be his last match before moving to Kent. Leicestershire found life hard, especially after Ward's first-ball dismissal, and only Stevens batted with real freedom. Sheriyar and the reliable Lampitt kept a tight grip to secure the win.

Worcestershire

V. S. Solanki b Dagnall	15		Kabir Ali c Ward b Dagnall		2
A. Singh c Burns b Dagnall	20		S. R. Lampitt not out		0
*B. F. Smith c Burns b Brignull	27		L-b 2, w 11, n-b 5		18
Kadeer Ali c Burns b Stevens	57				
S. D. Peters c Cunliffe b Brignull	22		1/24 (1) 2/45 (2)	(8 wkts, 45 overs)	255
D. A. Leatherdale not out	60		3/124 (4) 4/135 (3)		
G. J. Batty b Stevens	14		5/156 (5) 6/201 (7)		
†D. J. Pipe run out	20		7/248 (8) 8/251 (9)		

A. Sheriyar did not bat.

Bowling: Dagnall 9–0–56–3; Grove 9–0–60–0; Whiley 9–2–42–0; Brignull 9–0–52–2; Stevens 9–0–43–2.

Leicestershire

T. R. Ward c Pipe b Kabir Ali	0		D. S. Brignull st Pipe b Sheriyar		1
*I. J. Sutcliffe c Solanki b Lampitt	23		M. J. A. Whiley not out		4
R. J. Cunliffe b Lampitt	28				
D. I. Stevens st Pipe b Batty	54		L-b 2, w 9		11
†N. D. Burns c Pipe b Kabir Ali	39				
D. G. Brandy lbw b Lampitt	15		1/0 (1) 2/54 (3) 3/56 (2)	(44.2 overs)	227
A. S. Wright c Leatherdale b Sheriyar	20		4/136 (5) 5/159 (4)		
J. O. Grove b Leatherdale	4		6/174 (6) 7/183 (8)		
C. E. Dagnall c Batty b Sheriyar	28		8/217 (7) 9/223 (9) 10/227 (10)		

Bowling: Kabir Ali 9–1–42–2; Sheriyar 7.2–1–30–3; Lampitt 9–1–33–3; Leatherdale 8–0–43–1; Batty 9–0–60–1; Solanki 2–0–17–0.

Umpires: G. I. Burgess and A. Clarkson.

YORKSHIRE

At Taunton, May 12. YORKSHIRE beat SOMERSET by one run.

At Canterbury, May 19. YORKSHIRE beat KENT by five wickets.

YORKSHIRE v WORCESTERSHIRE

At Leeds, June 4. Worcestershire won by six wickets. Toss: Yorkshire. County debuts: S. M. Katich; A. A. Donald.

Donald's first outing sharpened an already strong Worcestershire attack but it was Kabir Ali who wreaked havoc, ripping through Yorkshire's batting with a one-day best of five for 36. Despite a sprightly start from White, Yorkshire imploded as five wickets tumbled in 16 balls – including that of Katich, who was brilliantly run out first-ball by the Yorkshire reject Batty. Two early wickets from Hoggard were not enough, and Worcestershire cantered home.

Yorkshire

C. White c Rhodes b Ali	45
M. J. Wood c Hick b Ali	8
R. K. J. Dawson c Rhodes b Ali	36
M. P. Vaughan lbw b Lampitt	0
S. M. Katich run out	0
A. McGrath lbw b Ali	0
G. M. Fellows b Lampitt	1
*†R. J. Blakey c Hick b Ali	10
T. T. Bresnan not out	12

R. J. Sidebottom c Solanki b Donald	0
M. J. Hoggard b Donald	0
L-b 3, w 13	16

1/59 (1) 2/70 (2) 3/74 (4)   (33.4 overs) 128
4/74 (5) 5/74 (6) 6/75 (7)
7/109 (3) 8/114 (8)
9/128 (10) 10/128 (11)

Bowling: Sheriyar 7–0–24–0; Donald 7.4–1–27–2; Ali 9–2–36–5; Lampitt 9–0–30–2; Leatherdale 1–0–8–0.

Worcestershire

V. S. Solanki c Wood b Hoggard	0
A. Singh c Fellows b White	33
*G. A. Hick c Blakey b Hoggard	1
B. F. Smith not out	38
D. A. Leatherdale c Katich b Fellows	18

G. J. Batty not out	20
B 1, l-b 5, w 7, n-b 6	19

1/0 (1) 2/4 (3)   (4 wkts, 37.1 overs) 129
3/63 (2) 4/103 (5)

†S. J. Rhodes, Kabir Ali, S. R. Lampitt, A. A. Donald and A. Sheriyar did not bat.

Bowling: Hoggard 9–3–28–2; Bresnan 6–1–11–0; Sidebottom 8–0–19–0; White 7.1–0–36–1; McGrath 4–0–15–0; Fellows 3–1–14–1.

Umpires: J. H. Evans and P. Willey.

At Nottingham, June 9. YORKSHIRE v NOTTINGHAMSHIRE. No result (abandoned).

YORKSHIRE v WARWICKSHIRE

At Leeds, June 16. Warwickshire won by 14 runs (D/L method). Toss: Warwickshire. First-team debut: J. I. Clifford.

Excellent bowling by Pollock helped Warwickshire defend a slim total and preserve their unbeaten record. Chasing 188, Yorkshire looked in control at 85 for two, but suddenly they faltered. First McGrath pushed Pollock to cover for a non-existent single and was undone by Penney's direct hit, then Wood played all around the next delivery. A five-over rain break reduced the target to 177, but Yorkshire fell just short. Earlier, Warwickshire had struggled against tight bowling on a poor one-day pitch, but Brown's perseverance spared their blushes.

Warwickshire

*M. J. Powell c Lumb b Silverwood	15	M. A. Sheikh lbw b Sidebottom	9
N. V. Knight c Fellows b Silverwood	12	N. M. Carter not out	17
S. M. Pollock c Blakey b Bresnan	15	†J. I. Clifford run out	1
I. R. Bell c Blakey b White	13	L-b 8, w 9, n-b 2	19
D. P. Ostler b Dawson	14		
T. L. Penney c Blakey b White	19	1/34 (1) 2/34 (2) 3/51 (3) (44.5 overs) 187	
D. R. Brown c Katich b Sidebottom	37	4/79 (5) 5/89 (4) 6/112 (6)	
N. M. K. Smith c Fellows b Dawson	16	7/137 (8) 8/164 (9) 9/175 (7) 10/187 (11)	

Bowling: Silverwood 9–0–29–2; Bresnan 7–0–41–1; Sidebottom 9–1–32–2; Dawson 9–0–33–2; White 6.5–0–24–2; McGrath 4–0–20–0.

Yorkshire

C. White c Clifford b Pollock	0	T. T. Bresnan lbw b Smith	22
M. J. Wood lbw b Pollock	42	R. J. Sidebottom not out	0
C. E. W. Silverwood b Pollock	12		
A. McGrath run out	25	L-b 2, w 4	6
S. M. Katich not out	39		
M. J. Lumb c Carter b Brown	1	1/0 (1) 2/15 (3) (9 wkts, 40 overs) 162	
G. M. Fellows lbw b Smith	13	3/85 (4) 4/85 (2)	
*†R. J. Blakey b Sheikh	0	5/88 (6) 6/108 (7)	
R. K. J. Dawson b Sheikh	2	7/109 (8) 8/111 (9) 9/161 (10)	

Bowling: Pollock 8–2–20–3; Carter 8–2–21–0; Sheikh 8–0–41–2; Brown 8–1–36–1; Smith 8–0–42–2.

Umpires: M. J. Harris and D. R. Shepherd.

At Chester-le-Street, June 23. YORKSHIRE beat DURHAM by 30 runs.

YORKSHIRE v SOMERSET

At Scarborough, July 14. Yorkshire won by 135 runs. Toss: Yorkshire.

A superb all-round performance from White gave Yorkshire their first win in ten home matches in all cricket. He began with a crisply-struck 64, then crushed Somerset with a series of fast off-breaks to put the result beyond doubt. Somerset's bowling injury list was so long that Paul Jarvis was sent an SOS call. Against his former team he claimed two late wickets, but could make no impact as a pinch-hitter, and Somerset's batsmen subsided quietly.

Yorkshire

C. White c sub b Blackwell	64	R. K. J. Dawson lbw b Jarvis	0
M. J. Wood c Burns b Jones	21	T. T. Bresnan not out	2
C. E. W. Silverwood c Bowler b Blackwell	24	R. J. Sidebottom not out	1
A. McGrath c Burns b Jones	59	L-b 4, w 9, n-b 2	15
*D. S. Lehmann c Turner b Burns	32	1/66 (2) 2/98 (3) (9 wkts, 45 overs) 283	
M. J. Lumb c Parsons b Jones	35	3/146 (1) 4/201 (5)	
G. M. Fellows b Jarvis	25	5/228 (4) 6/258 (6)	
†R. J. Blakey b Jones	5	7/279 (8) 8/280 (9) 9/281 (7)	

Bowling: Bulbeck 5–0–33–0; Jones 9–0–72–4; Jarvis 8–0–54–2; Blackwell 9–1–52–2; Dutch 9–0–39–0; Burns 5–0–29–1.

Somerset

P. D. Bowler c Blakey b Bresnan	10	P. S. Jones b White	1
I. D. Blackwell c Fellows b Bresnan	30	M. P. L. Bulbeck c Silverwood	
P. W. Jarvis c Wood b Silverwood	0	b Lehmann	9
*M. Burns b White	49	B 4, l-b 1, w 1	6
K. A. Parsons b White	30		
M. J. Wood lbw b White	0	1/32 (1) 2/41 (2) 3/41 (3) (27 overs) 148	
P. C. L. Holloway c Blakey b White	0	4/112 (4) 5/112 (6) 6/112 (7)	
†R. J. Turner not out	11	7/125 (5) 8/132 (9)	
K. P. Dutch c Wood b Lehmann	2	9/139 (10) 10/148 (11)	

Bowling: Silverwood 6–1–45–1; Bresnan 7–1–32–2; Sidebottom 3–0–24–0; White 6–0–19–5; Lehmann 5–0–23–2.

Umpires: I. J. Gould and J. W. Holder.

At Worcester, July 28. YORKSHIRE lost to WORCESTERSHIRE by six wickets.

YORKSHIRE v NOTTINGHAMSHIRE

At Leeds, August 3. Yorkshire won by four wickets (D/L method). Toss: Nottinghamshire.

Another batting blitz by White gave Yorkshire a much-needed victory. The Duckworth/Lewis system decreed that Yorkshire should chase 19 more runs than Nottinghamshire managed – off nine fewer overs – but White set about the task with gusto, racing to a 30-ball 48. Earlier, disciplined bowling restricted Nottinghamshire's scoring, and even Gallian's 63 was a stodgy effort. Pietersen provided acceleration before rain abruptly ended the innings.

Nottinghamshire

*J. E. R. Gallian not out	63
B. M. Shafayat c and b Dawson	28
K. P. Pietersen not out	19
L-b 2, w 10, n-b 2	14
1/81 (2) (1 wkt, 35 overs) 124	

W. R. Smith, S. R. Patel, P. Johnson, †C. M. W. Read, P. J. Franks, S. J. Randall, M. N. Malik and A. J. Harris did not bat.

Bowling: Silverwood 6–1–14–0; Bresnan 5–0–23–0; Sidebottom 6–0–25–0; White 5–1–13–0; Dawson 6–0–25–1; Lehmann 7–0–22–0.

Yorkshire

C. White c Read b Shafayat	48	†R. J. Blakey not out	7
M. J. Wood lbw b Harris	0	L-b 2, w 7	9
C. E. W. Silverwood c Read b Shafayat	29		
A. McGrath b Franks	4	1/1 (2) 2/76 (1) (6 wkts, 25 overs) 143	
*D. S. Lehmann c Read b Patel	20	3/87 (4) 4/87 (3)	
G. M. Fellows not out	26	5/126 (5) 6/126 (7)	
M. J. Lumb st Read b Patel	0		

R. K. J. Dawson, R. J. Sidebottom and T. T. Bresnan did not bat.

Bowling: Harris 5–0–33–1; Malik 4–0–30–0; Franks 4–0–33–1; Shafayat 5–0–21–2; Randall 3–0–10–0; Patel 4–1–14–2.

Umpires: G. I. Burgess and J. W. Holder.

YORKSHIRE v DURHAM

At Leeds, August 5 (day/night). Yorkshire won by 28 runs. Toss: Yorkshire.

Silverwood's hostile spell shattered Durham's early batting, Fellows rapidly mopped up the lower order and Yorkshire grabbed a deserved victory. Only staunch batting from the Pratt brothers meant the floodlights were needed at all: Andrew slammed four fours and a six in his half-century, and Gary crafted a more sedate 84. In Yorkshire's innings, Craven had got off to a rattling start, despatching Law's first three balls for 16 runs, and went on to 59, his best one-day innings.

Yorkshire

V. J. Craven c Gough b Killeen	59	R. K. J. Dawson lbw b Killeen		1
M. J. Wood c A. Pratt b Hunter	5	T. T. Bresnan not out		3
C. E. W. Silverwood lbw b Davies	1	R. J. Sidebottom run out		1
A. McGrath c A. Pratt b Law	23	L-b 7, w 19		26
*D. S. Lehmann run out	3			
G. M. Fellows c G. J. Pratt		1/25 (2) 2/30 (3) 3/77 (4)	(45 overs)	222
b Collingwood	50	4/92 (5) 5/125 (1) 6/186 (6)		
M. J. Lumb c Law b Collingwood	32	7/214 (7) 8/217 (8)		
†R. J. Blakey c Collingwood b Killeen	18	9/219 (9) 10/222 (11)		

Bowling: Killeen 9–1–42–3; Hunter 9–0–49–1; Davies 7–1–18–1; Law 3–0–26–1; Phillips 9–0–39–0; Gough 2–0–12–0; Collingwood 6–0–29–2.

Durham

N. Peng b Bresnan	1	A. M. Davies b Fellows		4
M. A. Gough lbw b Silverwood	4	N. Killeen lbw b Fellows		1
D. R. Law c Wood b Silverwood	0	L-b 7, w 5		12
P. D. Collingwood b Silverwood	3			
G. J. Pratt not out	84	1/9 (2) 2/9 (1) 3/11 (3)	(43.5 overs)	194
*J. J. B. Lewis c Wood b McGrath	11	4/17 (4) 5/53 (6) 6/141 (7)		
†A. Pratt c Silverwood b Lehmann	59	7/176 (8) 8/183 (9)		
I. D. Hunter c Bresnan b Fellows	13	9/192 (10) 10/194 (11)		
N. C. Phillips c McGrath b Fellows	2			

Bowling: Silverwood 8–3–15–3; Bresnan 9–1–30–1; McGrath 9–0–33–1; Sidebottom 2–0–6–0; Dawson 7–0–46–0; Lehmann 5–0–38–1; Fellows 3.5–0–19–4.

Umpires: J. W. Lloyds and J. F. Steele.

At Cardiff, August 11. YORKSHIRE lost to GLAMORGAN by 21 runs (D/L method).

At Leicester, August 18. YORKSHIRE lost to LEICESTERSHIRE by five wickets.

YORKSHIRE v GLAMORGAN

At Leeds, September 2. Glamorgan won by nine wickets. Toss: Yorkshire.

A sparkling display by David Harrison won him career-best figures with both bat and ball, and lifted Glamorgan to the top of the table. He ripped the heart out of Yorkshire's batting with a hugely impressive five for 26, before inflicting further pain with a no-nonsense 37. Yorkshire's only high point was a county-record last-wicket stand between Blakey and Sidebottom. Their bowlers then struggled to contain Glamorgan, and Croft and Thomas thrashed away before Harrison put Yorkshire out of their misery.

Yorkshire

C. White c Maynard b Parkin	32	S. P. Kirby lbw b Davies	1
M. J. Wood c Wallace b Parkin	13	R. J. Sidebottom not out	30
T. T. Bresnan c Wallace b Harrison	6		
M. T. G. Elliott c Wallace b Harrison	16	L-b 3, w 6, n-b 2	11
V. J. Craven b Harrison	6		
G. M. Fellows c Cosker b Harrison	0	1/35 (2) 2/48 (1) 3/68 (3)	(44.3 overs) 167
M. J. Lumb c Powell b Harrison	5	4/78 (5) 5/78 (6) 6/83 (4)	
*†R. J. Blakey c Maynard b Croft	47	7/88 (7) 8/92 (9)	
R. K. J. Dawson run out	0	9/103 (10) 10/167 (8)	

Bowling: Parkin 9–1–44–2; Davies 9–0–36–1; Harrison 9–0–26–5; Dale 9–0–24–0; Croft 6.3–1–27–1; Cosker 2–0–7–0.

Glamorgan

R. D. B. Croft b Sidebottom	59
I. J. Thomas not out	55
D. S. Harrison not out	37
B 1, l-b 5, w 5, n-b 6	17
1/102 (1)	(1 wkt, 24.1 overs) 168

M. J. Powell, M. P. Maynard, *S. P. James, A. Dale, †M. A. Wallace, O. T. Parkin, A. P. Davies and D. A. Cosker did not bat.

Bowling: Kirby 8–0–48–0; Bresnan 4.1–0–25–0; Sidebottom 6–1–41–1; Fellows 2–0–21–0; Dawson 4–0–27–0.

Umpires: I. J. Gould and A. G. T. Whitehead.

YORKSHIRE v LEICESTERSHIRE

At Scarborough, September 8. Leicestershire won by six wickets. Toss: Yorkshire.
For the second time in a week, Blakey was involved in a county-record stand (this time for the eighth wicket with Dawson) but still saw his team trounced. Leicestershire won without breaking sweat, as their batsmen stroked the ball around with ease. Yorkshire had found it tougher, after an opening assault from Srinath and Grove left them staggering. Blakey and Dawson rescued them from the depths of 45 for seven, but only delayed the inevitable.

Yorkshire

C. White b Grove	8	S. P. Kirby c Stevens b Wells	1
M. J. Wood c and b Srinath	1	N. D. Thornicroft not out	0
T. T. Bresnan c Sutcliffe b Grove	4		
M. T. G. Elliott c Burns b Srinath	1	L-b 11, w 7	18
A. McGrath c Burns b Wells	14		
V. J. Craven c Burns b Srinath	0	1/9 (2) 2/16 (1) 3/19 (4)	(44.2 overs) 153
G. M. Fellows c Srinath b Dagnall	5	4/21 (3) 5/30 (6) 6/37 (5)	
*†R. J. Blakey run out	60	7/45 (7) 8/134 (9)	
R. K. J. Dawson c Ward b Stemp	41	9/153 (8) 10/153 (10)	

Bowling: Srinath 9–2–18–3; Grove 9–1–22–2; Dagnall 9–2–27–1; Wells 6.2–1–17–2; Maddy 4–0–19–0; Stemp 7–1–39–1.

Leicestershire

T. R. Ward lbw b Thornicroft	7	†N. D. Burns not out 1
I. J. Sutcliffe not out	54	B 4, l-b 1, w 6 11
D. I. Stevens c Fellows b Kirby	30	
*V. J. Wells b Craven	48	1/10 (1) 2/44 (3) (4 wkts, 18.4 overs) 157
D. L. Maddy c Wood b Dawson	6	3/132 (4) 4/147 (5)

R. J. Cunliffe, R. D. Stemp, J. Srinath, J. O. Grove and C. E. Dagnall did not bat.

Bowling: Kirby 7.4–0–59–1; Thornicroft 4–0–23–1; Bresnan 2–0–31–0; Dawson 3–0–18–1; Craven 2–0–21–1.

Umpires: M. J. Kitchen and R. Palmer.

At Birmingham, September 10 (day/night). YORKSHIRE beat WARWICKSHIRE by eight wickets.

YORKSHIRE v KENT

At Leeds, September 22. Yorkshire won by 79 runs. Toss: Kent.

Yorkshire gave their demoralised supporters something to remember over the long winter months with a feast of batting. Elliott and McGrath piled on a rousing 198, with 105 coming off the last ten overs. Elliott's fabulous century was his third in six one-day innings for Yorkshire, and McGrath struck a powerful 85, including three sixes off one over of dobbers from Ealham. Nor were the pair barged out of the limelight when Yorkshire took the field: Elliott removed Waugh with a direct hit from the square-leg boundary, and McGrath's swingers and Gray's spinners fired out a tired-looking Kent.

Yorkshire

C. White c Tredwell b Ealham	19	
M. J. Lumb c and b Ealham	35	
**†R. J. Blakey c Nixon b Ealham	24	
M. T. G. Elliott not out	115	
A. McGrath not out	85	
B 8, l-b 5, w 6, n-b 2	21	

1/58 (2) 2/69 (1)   (3 wkts, 45 overs) 299
3/101 (3)

M. J. Wood, G. M. Fellows, A. K. D. Gray, R. J. Sidebottom, T. T. Bresnan and N. D. Thornicroft did not bat.

Bowling: Saggers 9–1–46–0; Masters 8–0–59–0; Ealham 9–0–59–3; Fleming 9–0–58–0; Tredwell 8–0–46–0; Waugh 2–0–18–0.

Kent

*M. V. Fleming c Sidebottom b Bresnan .	1	D. D. Masters c Lumb b Gray 7
E. T. Smith c McGrath b Gray	43	M. J. Saggers not out 0
M. A. Ealham b Sidebottom	35	
G. O. Jones c Blakey b Gray	28	B 2, l-b 6, w 3 11
S. R. Waugh run out	37	
M. J. Walker c Blakey b McGrath	27	1/7 (1) 2/67 (3) 3/111 (2) (37 overs) 220
†P. A. Nixon lbw b McGrath	10	4/112 (5) 5/171 (5) 6/187 (6)
A. G. R. Loudon c Thornicroft b Gray . .	21	7/204 (7) 8/204 (9)
J. C. Tredwell lbw b McGrath	0	9/220 (10) 10/220 (8)

Bowling: Thornicroft 4–0–31–0; Bresnan 4–0–27–1; McGrath 9–0–39–3; Sidebottom 6–0–46–1; Gray 8–1–34–4; Fellows 6–0–35–0.

Umpires: B. Dudleston and N. A. Mallender.

DIVISION TWO

DERBYSHIRE

DERBYSHIRE v SUSSEX

At Derby, May 12. Derbyshire won by six wickets. Toss: Derbyshire.

Nagging bowling from Derbyshire restricted Sussex to a modest total on a slow pitch, before their top order turned the pursuit into a formality. Di Venuto, fresh from a Championship double-hundred, dominated proceedings. Despite a tight spell by Martin-Jenkins, who went for only one single and one lucky four in his first seven overs, Derbyshire cantered home with three overs to spare.

Sussex

R. R. Montgomerie c Bassano b Kerr	. .	27
†T. R. Ambrose c Cork b Welch	. . . . .	0
*C. J. Adams c Bassano b Cork	. . . . .	26
M. W. Goodwin b Lungley	. . . .	12
P. A. Cottey c Cork b Welch	. . . . . .	26
R. S. C. Martin-Jenkins run out	. . . . .	9
W. J. House c Sutton b Welch	. . . . . .	27
K. J. Innes b Wharton	. . . .	9

B. V. Taylor did not bat.

M. J. G. Davis not out 11
R. J. Kirtley not out 3
L-b 2, w 12, n-b 2 16

1/1 (2) 2/47 (3)   (8 wkts, 45 overs) 166
3/75 (1) 4/75 (4)
5/108 (5) 6/113 (6)
7/139 (8) 8/154 (7)

Bowling: Cork 9–1–20–1; Welch 9–2–45–3; Lungley 9–1–31–1; Kerr 9–1–34–1; Wharton 9–0–34–1.

Derbyshire

A. I. Gait b Innes	. . . .	21
M. J. Di Venuto c House b Kirtley	. . . .	84
C. W. G. Bassano c Goodwin b Kirtley	. .	38
D. R. Hewson lbw b Kirtley	. . . .	5
S. A. Selwood not out	. . . .	3

*D. G. Cork not out 8
L-b 4, w 3, n-b 2 9

1/50 (1) 2/141 (3)   (4 wkts, 42 overs) 168
3/152 (4) 4/157 (2)

†L. D. Sutton, G. Welch, J. I. D. Kerr, T. Lungley and L. J. Wharton did not bat.

Bowling: Kirtley 9–0–49–3; Martin-Jenkins 9–5–12–0; Taylor 3–0–26–0; Innes 5–1–15–1; Davis 7–0–22–0; Cottey 7–0–25–0; Adams 2–0–15–0.

Umpires: I. J. Gould and G. Sharp.

At Chelmsford, May 19. DERBYSHIRE lost to ESSEX by seven wickets.

At Southampton, June 9. DERBYSHIRE v HAMPSHIRE. No result (abandoned).

DERBYSHIRE v NORTHAMPTONSHIRE

At Derby, June 16. Derbyshire won by three wickets. Toss: Derbyshire.

This was a fluctuating game, with thrust followed by counter-thrust. The ball swung from the start, often too far: batting was treacherous, but Derbyshire also conceded 24 wides. Penberthy, Bailey and Anderson hauled Northamptonshire back after a dire start, but Derbyshire's batting was equally uncertain and at 88 for seven they were heading for defeat. But Sutton's watchfulness and Kerr's aggression turned the tables. In 22 overs they compiled a match-winning 94, Derbyshire's League-best for the eighth wicket.

Northamptonshire

*M. E. K. Hussey lbw b Dean	2	C. G. Greenidge b Welch	6
M. B. Loye b Cork	15	D. M. Cousins not out	9
D. J. Sales lbw b Dean	1	L-b 16, w 24, n-b 2	42
R. J. Warren lbw b Cork	1		
J. W. Cook lbw b Dean	6	1/15 (1) 2/26 (2) (8 wkts, 45 overs) 180		
A. L. Penberthy not out	55	3/26 (3) 4/28 (4)		
†T. M. B. Bailey c Sutton b Kerr	21	5/44 (5) 6/98 (7)		
R. S. G. Anderson c Dean b Dowman	22	7/148 (8) 8/157 (9)		

J. F. Brown did not bat.

Bowling: Cork 9–1–20–2; Dean 9–1–29–3; Welch 9–0–37–1; Kerr 9–0–44–1; Dowman 7–1–23–1; Wharton 2–0–11–0.

Derbyshire

S. D. Stubbings c Bailey b Greenidge	11	†L. D. Sutton not out	27
A. I. Gait c Bailey b Cousins	0	J. I. D. Kerr not out	65
G. Welch c Warren b Anderson	23	L-b 7, w 9	16
M. J. Di Venuto c Bailey b Penberthy	22		
*D. G. Cork c Sales b Greenidge	12	1/1 (2) 2/34 (1) (7 wkts, 43.4 overs) 182		
C. W. G. Bassano lbw b Penberthy	5	3/35 (3) 4/63 (4)		
M. P. Dowman lbw b Greenidge	1	5/86 (6) 6/86 (5) 7/88 (7)		

K. J. Dean and L. J. Wharton did not bat.

Bowling: Cousins 9–0–26–1; Greenidge 9–4–25–3; Anderson 4–0–41–1; Penberthy 9–0–25–2; Cook 7–0–32–0; Brown 5.4–0–26–0.

Umpires: M. R. Benson and V. A. Holder.

DERBYSHIRE v LANCASHIRE

At Derby, June 23. Derbyshire won by seven wickets. Toss: Derbyshire.

An unimpressive Lancashire performance was in keeping with their recent poor one-day form. None of the batsmen could manage a meaningful score on a sluggish Derby pitch, and their total was never a challenge to Derbyshire. Stubbings was badly dropped by Fairbrother in the covers on 18, before going on to amass his biggest one-day score, with Cork lending typically boisterous support.

Lancashire

N. H. Fairbrother c Cork b Dean	1	C. P. Schofield not out	18
M. J. Chilton lbw b Cork	13	K. W. Hogg not out	14
G. Chapple b Dean	10	B 1, l-b 8, w 10	19
S. G. Law c and b Kerr	25		
G. D. Lloyd c Sutton b Kerr	20	1/6 (1) 2/22 (2) (7 wkts, 45 overs) 174		
R. C. Driver c Di Venuto b Cork	25	3/48 (3) 4/73 (4)		
*†W. K. Hegg c Cork b Dowman	29	5/90 (5) 6/140 (7) 7/140 (6)		

J. Wood and P. J. Martin did not bat.

Bowling: Cork 9–1–28–2; Dean 9–2–29–2; Welch 9–0–47–0; Kerr 9–1–37–2; Dowman 9–0–24–1.

Derbyshire

S. D. Stubbings not out		98
A. I. Gait b Wood		16
G. Welch lbw b Wood		2
M. J. Di Venuto c Hegg b Martin		11
*D. G. Cork not out		28
B 5, l-b 11, w 8		24

1/52 (2) 2/66 (3)   (3 wkts, 41.1 overs) 179
3/96 (4)

S. A. Selwood, M. P. Dowman, †L. D. Sutton, J. I. D. Kerr, K. J. Dean and L. J. Wharton did not bat.

Bowling: Martin 7.1–1–21–1; Chapple 7–1–27–0; Hogg 6–1–29–0; Wood 9–0–25–2; Driver 8–1–34–0; Chilton 2–0–14–0; Schofield 2–0–13–0.

Umpires: J. W. Holder and G. Sharp.

DERBYSHIRE v GLOUCESTERSHIRE

At Derby, July 7. Derbyshire won by seven runs. Toss: Gloucestershire.

Derbyshire somehow contrived to lose a match they should have strolled. On yet another slow, untrustworthy pitch, Welch bowled outstandingly and, though Harvey injected some dash, Gloucestershire's total was well within sight. Cork's energetic innings should have sealed the win: Derbyshire needed 16 from three overs with five wickets intact. But Alleyne and Harvey bowled with bamboozling variation, Averis kept his head in the final over, and Gloucestershire grabbed victory. Barnett's solitary run during Gloucestershire's innings made him the first batsman to reach 9,000 League runs.

Gloucestershire

K. J. Barnett lbw b Dean	1		J. M. M. Averis not out		20
C. M. Spearman c Lungley b Welch	29		A. M. Smith c Sutton b Cork		1
I. J. Harvey c Sutton b Lungley	43				
†R. C. Russell lbw b Lungley	1		B 2, l-b 7, w 17		26
*M. W. Alleyne c Sutton b Welch	1				
C. G. Taylor c Gait b Welch	0		1/17 (1) 2/74 (2) 3/80 (4)	(40.3 overs)	161
A. P. R. Gidman lbw b Welch	23		4/81 (5) 5/90 (3) 6/96 (6)		
M. A. Hardinges c Sutton b Welch	6		7/120 (7) 8/125 (8)		
M. C. J. Ball b Dowman	10		9/160 (9) 10/161 (11)		

Bowling: Cork 8.3–1–36–1; Dean 9–2–36–1; Lungley 9–0–42–2; Welch 9–3–18–5; Kerr 3–0–16–0; Dowman 2–0–4–1.

Derbyshire

S. D. Stubbings c Hardinges b Smith	16		†L. D. Sutton b Averis		0
A. I. Gait lbw b Hardinges	30		K. J. Dean not out		1
G. Welch c Ball b Hardinges	0				
M. J. Di Venuto c Russell b Alleyne	22		L-b 5, w 6		11
*D. G. Cork b Alleyne	43				
S. A. Selwood c and b Averis	12		1/36 (1) 2/44 (3)	(9 wkts, 45 overs)	154
M. P. Dowman c Harvey b Averis	15		3/74 (2) 4/92 (4)		
J. I. D. Kerr c and b Harvey	1		5/121 (6) 6/147 (5)		
T. Lungley not out	3		7/148 (8) 8/152 (7) 9/152 (10)		

Bowling: Smith 9–2–20–1; Harvey 9–2–27–1; Averis 9–0–44–3; Hardinges 9–1–37–2; Alleyne 9–1–21–2.

Umpires: B. Leadbeater and N. J. Llong.

At Blackpool, July 14. DERBYSHIRE lost to LANCASHIRE by one wicket.

At Northampton, July 24 (day/night). DERBYSHIRE lost to NORTHAMPTONSHIRE by seven wickets.

DERBYSHIRE v HAMPSHIRE

At Derby, August 3. Derbyshire won by two wickets (D/L method). Toss: Hampshire.

Frantic scampering from Derbyshire's tail – and a little help from Duckworth/Lewis – took them home. Rain had reduced Hampshire's innings to 40 overs, in which they managed 143. But the timing of the stoppages meant the calculations left Derbyshire a target six runs smaller – a decision that sent the Hampshire coach Jimmy Cook in grim-faced search of the match manager. The vagaries of the system looked academic when Derbyshire slid to 100 for seven, with only Di Venuto showing conviction on a vividly green pitch, but the lower order scrambled home with an over to spare.

Hampshire

N. C. Johnson c Gait b Dean	14	C. T. Tremlett b Dowman 0
D. A. Kenway lbw b Cork	1	A. D. Mullally not out 9
J. P. Crawley run out	0	
J. D. Francis c Sutton b Welch	8	B 2, l-b 21, w 19, n-b 2 44
*W. S. Kendall lbw b Lungley	1	
L. R. Prittipaul b Welch	4	1/9 (2) 2/13 (3) (9 wkts, 40 overs) 143
†N. Pothas not out	50	3/29 (1) 4/42 (5)
A. D. Mascarenhas b Lungley	0	5/48 (6) 6/49 (4)
S. D. Udal c Cork b Dowman	12	7/50 (8) 8/101 (9) 9/101 (10)

Bowling: Cork 8–4–9–1; Dean 8–1–34–1; Lungley 6–0–30–2; Welch 8–2–20–2; Kerr 3–0–15–0; Dowman 7–2–12–2.

Derbyshire

A. I. Gait c Pothas b Mullally	0	J. I. D. Kerr b Tremlett 14
M. J. Di Venuto c Pothas b Prittipaul . .	37	T. Lungley not out 7
G. Welch c Johnson b Mullally	0	L-b 12, w 23 35
S. D. Stubbings c Johnson b Tremlett . .	10	
*D. G. Cork c Pothas b Johnson	11	1/1 (1) 2/13 (3) (8 wkts, 39 overs) 137
S. A. Selwood run out	5	3/48 (4) 4/71 (5)
†M. P. Dowman b Johnson	6	5/82 (6) 6/98 (7)
†L. D. Sutton not out	12	7/100 (2) 8/126 (9)

K. J. Dean did not bat.

Bowling: Mullally 8–2–17–2; Mascarenhas 8–1–35–0; Tremlett 7.5–1–23–2; Johnson 8–1–29–2; Prittipaul 7.1–1–21–1.

Umpires: M. R. Benson and N. J. Llong.

DERBYSHIRE v ESSEX

At Derby, August 11. Essex won by 49 runs. Toss: Derbyshire.

Essex became the first team to pass 200 at the County Ground in 2002 and it was enough to take them another step towards promotion. Flower's steady half-century provided the backbone, and there was stout support from Stephenson and Dakin, against tight bowling by Welch and Dean. Derbyshire could find nobody to anchor their reply, and the constant fall of wickets scuppered them.

Essex

D. D. J. Robinson lbw b Dean	13	G. R. Napier c Selwood b Dowman	2	
W. I. Jefferson c Sutton b Dean	13	J. D. Middlebrook not out	13	
*R. C. Irani lbw b Dean	0	B 7, l-b 13, w 19	39	
†A. Flower c Sutton b Wharton	52			
M. L. Pettini b Dean	2	1/22 (2) 2/36 (3)	(7 wkts, 45 overs) 209	
J. P. Stephenson lbw b Dowman	30	3/39 (1) 4/61 (5)		
J. M. Dakin not out	45	5/129 (6) 6/160 (4) 7/163 (8)		

J. E. Bishop and A. C. McGarry did not bat.

Bowling: Welch 9–3–19–0; Dean 9–2–33–4; Lungley 7–0–36–0; Kerr 7–0–32–0; Dowman 8–0–43–2; Wharton 5–0–26–1.

Derbyshire

*M. J. Di Venuto lbw b Irani	3	K. J. Dean c Middlebrook b McGarry	2	
C. W. G. Bassano c Pettini b Irani	23	L. J. Wharton run out	1	
S. D. Stubbings lbw b Napier	12	L-b 10, w 13	23	
S. A. Selwood b Bishop	18			
M. P. Dowman b Napier	22	1/13 (1) 2/30 (2) 3/57 (3)	(37.3 overs) 160	
J. I. D. Kerr lbw b Bishop	0	4/77 (4) 5/77 (6) 6/107 (5)		
†L. D. Sutton lbw b McGarry	29	7/122 (7) 8/141 (9)		
G. Welch not out	17	9/151 (10) 10/160 (11)		
T. Lungley b Bishop	10			

Bowling: Irani 7–0–26–2; Dakin 7–0–22–0; Napier 7–0–28–2; McGarry 7.3–1–35–2; Bishop 9–0–39–3.

Umpires: J. H. Hampshire and J. W. Holder.

At The Oval, August 18. DERBYSHIRE beat SURREY by four wickets.

At Lord's, August 25. DERBYSHIRE beat MIDDLESEX by 32 runs.

DERBYSHIRE v SURREY

At Derby, September 2 (day/night). Surrey won by one wicket. Toss: Derbyshire.

A courageous innings from Clarke pushed Surrey nearer to promotion – and dented Derbyshire's hopes. A blow on the thigh from Welch left him limping but, in an exciting floodlit finish, Clarke held on and cut the winning run with two balls to spare. Earlier, Cork and Dumelow, with his first one-day fifty, had combined effectively, until Holliokae engineered a collapse. Derbyshire's bowlers kept them in the hunt, but Clarke's composure made the difference.

Derbyshire

M. J. Di Venuto c Batty b Giddins	1	Mohammad Ali not out	10	
C. W. G. Bassano b Giddins	3	K. J. Dean run out	12	
N. R. C. Dumelow c Bicknell b Salisbury	52	L-b 17, w 14, n-b 4	35	
*D. G. Cork c Batty b Holliokae	51			
S. A. Selwood c Batty b Holliokae	38	1/3 (1) 2/6 (2) 3/117 (3)	(45 overs) 213	
M. P. Dowman c Batty b Holliokae	7	4/162 (4) 5/173 (6) 6/187 (7)		
J. I. D. Kerr b Holliokae	3	7/188 (5) 8/188 (8)		
G. Welch b Murtagh	1	9/190 (9) 10/213 (11)		
†L. D. Sutton run out	0			

Bowling: Bicknell 5–1–29–0; Giddins 7–0–37–2; Murtagh 9–0–46–1; Clarke 9–0–36–0; Salisbury 9–0–25–1; Holliokae 6–0–23–4.

Surrey

I. J. Ward lbw b Cork 2
A. D. Brown b Dean 9
M. R. Ramprakash c Sutton
                 b Mohammad Ali . 28
R. Clarke not out 98
N. Shahid c Kerr b Dowman 20
*A. J. Hollioake b Welch 6
†J. N. Batty lbw b Welch 0
M. P. Bicknell b Dowman 2
I. D. K. Salisbury c Dean
                 b Mohammad Ali . 21

T. J. Murtagh c Kerr
                 b Mohammad Ali . 0
E. S. H. Giddins not out 1

        L-b 8, w 15, n-b 4 27

1/17 (2) 2/17 (1)   (9 wkts, 44.4 overs) 214
3/65 (3) 4/123 (5)
5/151 (6) 6/153 (7)
7/170 (8) 8/210 (9)
9/210 (10)

Bowling: Cork 8.4–3–30–1; Dean 7–0–39–1; Welch 7–0–42–2; Mohammad Ali 9–0–42–3; Kerr 4–0–17–0; Dowman 9–0–36–2.

Umpires: G. I. Burgess and G. Sharp.

At Bristol, September 8. DERBYSHIRE lost to GLOUCESTERSHIRE by 52 runs.

At Hove, September 15. DERBYSHIRE beat SUSSEX by 74 runs.

DERBYSHIRE v MIDDLESEX

At Derby, September 22. Derbyshire won by 22 runs. Toss: Middlesex.
    Victory on the final day raised Derbyshire into fourth place and left Middlesex languishing at the bottom. Selwood confirmed his promise with a mature innings, but the day belonged to Welch. His six for 31 was not only his best one-day return, but also the best by anyone in the League in 2002. Though Joyce and Dalrymple briefly threatened, Middlesex always lagged behind the rate.

Derbyshire

S. D. Stubbings b Bloomfield 18
C. W. G. Bassano b Bloomfield 7
N. R. C. Dumelow b Keegan 0
S. A. Selwood not out 81
D. R. Hewson b Keegan 9
M. P. Dowman c Koenig b Bloomfield . . 33
J. I. D. Kerr lbw b Dalrymple 9
G. Welch c Koenig b Hutton 6

N. E. L. Gunter did not bat.

*†L. D. Sutton c and b Dalrymple 15
K. J. Dean not out 16
      B 2, l-b 7, w 5, n-b 2 16

1/22 (2) 2/29 (3)   (8 wkts, 45 overs) 210
3/29 (1) 4/42 (5)
5/106 (6) 6/138 (7)
7/155 (8) 8/188 (9)

Bowling: Bloomfield 9–2–28–3; Keegan 9–0–49–2; Hunt 5–0–29–0; Hutton 9–0–49–1; Weekes 6–0–21–0; Dalrymple 7–0–25–2.

Middlesex

*S. G. Koenig c Sutton b Welch 0
R. M. S. Weston b Dean 0
P. N. Weekes b Welch 16
N. R. D. Compton c Sutton b Welch . . 12
E. C. Joyce c Dean b Dumelow 58
J. W. M. Dalrymple b Welch 52
B. L. Hutton lbw b Dowman 12
†D. Alleyne lbw b Kerr 12
C. B. Keegan not out 12

T. A. Hunt b Welch 0
T. F. Bloomfield b Welch 10

      L-b 6, w 4 10

1/0 (1) 2/0 (2) 3/33 (4)   (43.3 overs) 188
4/34 (3) 5/132 (5) 6/154 (7)
7/162 (6) 8/170 (6)
9/170 (10) 10/188 (11)

Bowling: Welch 8.3–2–31–6; Dean 9–3–26–1; Kerr 8–0–35–1; Gunter 3–0–11–0; Dumelow 8–0–46–1; Dowman 7–1–33–1.

Umpires: V. A. Holder and T. E. Jesty.

ESSEX

ESSEX v DERBYSHIRE

At Chelmsford, May 19. Essex won by seven wickets. Toss: Derbyshire.

Flower followed up his five victims behind the stumps with a highly entertaining 43 from 37 balls, taking Essex to an effortless victory with eight overs to spare. Derbyshire's batsmen struggled against Essex's accuracy, with Bassano's tortuous 26-ball duck perfectly illustrating their laboriousness. Essex knocked off the runs with little problem.

Derbyshire

A. I. Gait b Irani	12		G. Welch c Habib b Clarke		22
*M. J. Di Venuto lbw b Stephenson	23		L. J. Wharton not out		11
M. P. Dowman c Flower b Cowan	1				
D. R. Hewson c Robinson b Irani	4		B 2, l-b 5, w 9		16
C. W. G. Bassano c Grayson b Dakin	0				
S. A. Selwood c Flower b Clarke	30		1/12 (1) 2/23 (3) 3/28 (4) (44.3 overs) 155		
†L. D. Sutton c Flower b Cowan	10		4/45 (5) 5/46 (2) 6/72 (7)		
J. I. D. Kerr c Flower b Clarke	16		7/102 (8) 8/115 (6)		
T. Lungley c Flower b Cowan	10		9/133 (9) 10/155 (10)		

Bowling: Irani 9–0–54–2; Cowan 9–0–21–3; Stephenson 5–1–17–1; Dakin 5–2–5–1; Clarke 7.3–0–29–3; Grayson 9–0–22–0.

Essex

D. D. J. Robinson c Kerr b Wharton	36
J. P. Stephenson c Gait b Kerr	22
G. R. Napier b Lungley	19
†A. Flower not out	43
*R. C. Irani not out	29
B 2, l-b 3, w 5	10

1/54 (2) 2/78 (1) (3 wkts, 37 overs) 159
3/88 (3)

A. Habib, A. P. Grayson, J. M. Dakin, J. D. Middlebrook, A. P. Cowan and A. J. Clarke did not bat.

Bowling: Welch 9–1–31–0; Lungley 6–0–29–1; Kerr 9–1–37–1; Wharton 9–0–41–1; Dowman 4–0–16–0.

Umpires: M. R. Benson and D. J. Constant.

At Horsham, June 4. ESSEX lost to SUSSEX by 32 runs.

ESSEX v LANCASHIRE

At Ilford, June 16. Essex won by seven wickets. Toss: Lancashire.

Another comprehensive Essex win was secured by Robinson's well-judged 76 and a partnership of contrasts between Flower and Irani. Flower was characteristically neat, while Irani preferred the bludgeon to the scalpel, smashing a 43-ball 51. Earlier, Lancashire were on course to set a more testing target, thanks to Chilton's fluency. But precise Essex bowling undermined his efforts.

Lancashire

M. J. Chilton c Flower b Clarke	84	K. W. Hogg c Cowan b Irani	0
A. J. Swann c Robinson b Irani	13	P. J. Martin b Irani	0
G. Chapple c Dakin b Grayson	33		
S. G. Law c Irani b Napier	28	B 2, l-b 2, w 4	8
N. H. Fairbrother c Irani b Napier	6		
G. D. Lloyd not out	19	1/33 (2) 2/88 (3) 3/144 (4) (44.2 overs) 203
*†W. K. Hegg st Flower b Grayson	7	4/166 (5) 5/178 (1) 6/191 (7)
G. Yates c Flower b Grayson	2	7/197 (8) 8/203 (9)
J. Wood c Grayson b Cowan	3	9/203 (10) 10/203 (11)

Bowling: Irani 7.2–0–29–3; Cowan 9–2–21–1; Stephenson 2–0–26–0; Dakin 1–0–16–0; Clarke 9–1–29–1; Grayson 9–0–45–3; Napier 7–0–33–2.

Essex

D. D. J. Robinson c Hegg b Wood	76
G. R. Napier c Hegg b Martin	1
W. I. Jefferson c Hegg b Martin	0
†A. Flower not out	56
*R. C. Irani not out	51
L-b 5, w 11, n-b 4	20

1/4 (2) 2/4 (3)   (3 wkts, 39 overs) 204
3/133 (1)

A. Habib, A. P. Grayson, J. P. Stephenson, J. M. Dakin, A. P. Cowan and A. J. Clarke did not bat.

Bowling: Martin 9–2–26–2; Chapple 7–0–28–0; Wood 9–0–41–1; Hogg 7–0–51–0; Yates 7–0–53–0.

Umpires: J. W. Lloyds and P. Willey.

At Gloucester, June 30. ESSEX beat GLOUCESTERSHIRE by 12 runs (D/L method).

ESSEX v HAMPSHIRE

At Southend, July 14. Essex won by five runs. Toss: Essex.

Essex pulled off a remarkable victory after looking doomed. Hampshire needed 24 from the last six overs with eight wickets standing, but crumbled in the face of a stunning Essex resurgence. Cowan, who removed the dangerous Johnson, and Middlebrook were the heroes, keeping their nerve right down to the wire. Earlier, only Habib and Robinson had made any impact on a slow pitch, as Tremlett's nagging line and length kept Essex to a mediocre total.

Essex

D. D. J. Robinson run out	44	J. P. Stephenson not out	2
J. M. Dakin b Tremlett	27	T. J. Phillips not out	2
G. R. Napier c Johnson b Tremlett	11		
†A. Flower run out	3	B 3, l-b 5, w 8	16
*R. C. Irani c Johnson b Mascarenhas	0		
A. Habib c Tremlett b Kendall	50	1/48 (2) 2/68 (3) (9 wkts, 45 overs) 200
M. L. Pettini b Tremlett	22	3/82 (4) 4/83 (5)
A. P. Cowan c Tremlett b Udal	4	5/98 (1) 6/151 (7)
J. D. Middlebrook b Tremlett	19	7/156 (8) 8/195 (6) 9/195 (9)

Bowling: Tomlinson 7–0–38–0; Mascarenhas 9–1–37–1; Tremlett 9–1–25–4; Johnson 1–0–10–0; Udal 9–0–32–1; Prittipaul 3–0–18–0; Kendall 7–0–32–1.

Hampshire

N. C. Johnson c Flower b Cowan	83	S. D. Udal st Flower b Middlebrook	2
D. A. Kenway lbw b Napier	38	C. T. Tremlett not out	0
A. D. Mascarenhas st Flower b Phillips	23	B 1, l-b 6, w 1	8
J. P. Crawley c Flower b Napier	30		
L. R. Prittipaul b Middlebrook	0	1/62 (2) 2/120 (3) (8 wkts, 45 overs) 195	
G. W. White lbw b Middlebrook	10	3/177 (4) 4/180 (5)	
†N. Pothas not out	1	5/192 (6) 6/192 (1)	
*W. S. Kendall b Middlebrook	0	7/193 (8) 8/195 (9)	

J. A. Tomlinson did not bat.

Bowling: Irani 7–1–24–0; Cowan 8–1–38–1; Napier 7–1–38–2; Dakin 4–1–8–0; Middlebrook 8–0–33–4; Phillips 9–0–39–1; Stephenson 2–0–8–0.

Umpires: T. E. Jesty and B. Leadbeater.

ESSEX v MIDDLESEX

At Chelmsford, July 22 (day/night). Middlesex won by 41 runs. Toss: Middlesex.

The regular clatter of falling wickets meant Essex never mounted a serious challenge in Chelmsford's first day/night duel. A sedate half-century from Strauss, and a breezy one from Shah, gave Middlesex a good start, which they promptly chucked away by losing four wickets on 150. However, the lower order recovered impressively. None of the Essex batsmen could find similar steel, and their innings gradually faded away.

Middlesex

*A. J. Strauss c Flower b Middlebrook	58	J. W. M. Dalrymple not out	35
A. W. Laraman c Foster b Irani	19	S. J. Cook not out	1
S. G. Koenig run out	0	L-b 1, w 9	10
O. A. Shah c Robinson b Middlebrook	54		
E. C. Joyce b Phillips	9	1/28 (2) 2/32 (3) (8 wkts, 45 overs) 209	
Abdul Razzaq c Foster b Phillips	0	3/122 (4) 4/150 (5)	
P. N. Weekes b Dakin b Middlebrook	0	5/150 (6) 6/150 (1)	
†D. C. Nash c Stephenson b Cowan	23	7/150 (7) 8/207 (8)	

I. Jones did not bat.

Bowling: Irani 9–4–34–1; Cowan 8–1–41–1; Dakin 2–0–15–0; Stephenson 5–0–18–0; Phillips 7–0–36–2; Napier 6–0–24–0; Middlebrook 8–0–40–3.

Essex

D. D. J. Robinson b Laraman	7	J. D. Middlebrook b Dalrymple	2
J. M. Dakin c Nash b Cook	22	T. J. Phillips c Nash b Laraman	5
G. R. Napier c Jones b Cook	14		
A. Flower c Dalrymple b Cook	8	B 4, l-b 12, w 15, n-b 4	35
*R. C. Irani c Weekes b Dalrymple	22		
A. Habib lbw b Abdul Razzaq	5	1/28 (1) 2/38 (2) 3/48 (4) (37.4 overs) 168	
†J. S. Foster c Dalrymple b Weekes	14	4/61 (3) 5/80 (6) 6/88 (5)	
A. P. Cowan c Jones b Weekes	18	7/111 (7) 8/142 (8)	
J. P. Stephenson not out	16	9/156 (10) 10/168 (11)	

Bowling: Jones 3–0–18–0; Laraman 7.4–0–25–2; Cook 5–0–28–3; Abdul Razzaq 7–1–19–1; Dalrymple 9–0–39–2; Weekes 6–1–23–2.

Umpires: A. A. Jones and N. J. Llong.

In the last 100 years there were only 17 worse summers.
Philip Eden on Cricket and the Weather, page 1698

At Guildford, July 28. ESSEX lost to SURREY by 73 runs.

At Lord's, August 4. ESSEX lost to MIDDLESEX by two wickets (D/L method).

At Derby, August 11. ESSEX beat DERBYSHIRE by 49 runs.

At Southampton, August 18. ESSEX lost to HAMPSHIRE by five wickets.

ESSEX v NORTHAMPTONSHIRE

At Colchester, August 25. Essex won by four wickets. Toss: Northamptonshire.

A masterly fifty by Flower, on a pitch that posed problems throughout the game, sealed victory with 19 balls to spare. He steered the ball expertly into the gaps, striking only two fours in his innings. In a low-scoring battle, it was a more impressive performance than the scorebook suggested.

Northamptonshire

M. B. Loye c and b Stephenson	33	C. G. Greenidge run out		1
R. A. White lbw b Dakin	16	M. S. Panesar not out		16
D. J. Sales b Napier	12	L-b 5, w 3, n-b 2		10
M. E. Cassar b Stephenson	13			
J. W. Cook c Dakin b Middlebrook	31	1/18 (2) 2/49 (3)	(8 wkts, 45 overs)	167
*A. L. Penberthy c Napier b Grant	1	3/78 (1) 4/81 (4)		
G. P. Swann b Stephenson	6	5/82 (6) 6/94 (7)		
†T. M. B. Bailey not out	28	7/134 (5) 8/137 (9)		

M. W. H. Inness did not bat.

Bowling: Cowan 9–0–36–0; Dakin 7–1–26–1; Napier 8–2–27–1; Grant 7–0–22–1; Stephenson 6–0–21–3; Middlebrook 8–0–30–1.

Essex

R. S. Clinton c Sales b Inness	11	G. R. Napier not out		16
W. I. Jefferson c sub b Inness	37			
J. P. Stephenson c Bailey b Penberthy	8	B 3, l-b 3, w 3		9
†A. Flower not out	57			
M. L. Pettini c Sales b Penberthy	6	1/44 (2) 2/51 (1)	(6 wkts, 41.5 overs)	168
*A. P. Grayson c Cassar b Penberthy	18	3/71 (3) 4/85 (5)		
J. M. Dakin c and b Cook	6	5/119 (6) 6/135 (7)		

J. D. Middlebrook, A. P. Cowan and J. B. Grant did not bat.

Bowling: Greenidge 8–1–38–0; Inness 7–1–28–2; Penberthy 9–1–31–3; Panesar 9–0–26–0; Cook 4–0–16–1; Swann 1–0–6–0; Cassar 3.5–0–17–0.

Umpires: J. H. Evans and G. Sharp.

ESSEX v GLOUCESTERSHIRE

At Colchester, August 27 (day/night). Essex won by five wickets. Toss: Gloucestershire. County debut: J. Angel.

This match was played on a particularly poor pitch, the ball turning and seaming alarmingly throughout. Gloucestershire arrived as runaway leaders and predictably elected to bat first, but their innings was one of rapid decline. Jo Angel, the one-time Australian Test bowler, made an early strike. But Stephenson, having already taken three wickets, dug in resolutely to anchor Essex's reply, and Grayson's resolve to treat every ball on merit proved a winning formula.

Gloucestershire

I. D. Fisher c Stephenson b Cowan	6
C. M. Spearman c Grant b Cowan	1
J. N. Snape c Jefferson b Grant	30
M. G. N. Windows c Flower b Dakin	1
*M. W. Alleyne c Jefferson b Stephenson	22
C. G. Taylor c Grayson b Grant	0
A. P. R. Gidman lbw b Grant	1
†R. C. Russell b Stephenson	10
J. Angel not out	10

J. M. M. Averis c Clinton b Middlebrook	1
A. M. Smith c Napier b Stephenson	3
L-b 4, w 8	12

1/11 (2) 2/17 (1) 3/22 (4) (33.4 overs) 97
4/50 (3) 5/50 (6)
6/53 (7) 7/78 (8)
8/79 (5) 9/80 (10) 10/97 (11)

Bowling: Cowan 7–1–16–2; Dakin 5–0–20–1; Grant 7–1–13–3; Napier 5–1–23–0; Middlebrook 5–2–7–1; Stephenson 4.4–0–14–3.

Essex

R. S. Clinton c Spearman b Smith	3
W. I. Jefferson c Russell b Angel	2
J. P. Stephenson c Windows b Fisher	44
†A. Flower c Gidman b Averis	3
*A. P. Grayson not out	26
R. S. Bopara run out	0

J. M. Dakin not out	8
L-b 5, w 7	12

1/2 (2) 2/28 (1) (5 wkts, 36.1 overs) 98
3/44 (4) 4/76 (3)
5/83 (6)

G. R. Napier, J. D. Middlebrook, A. P. Cowan and J. B. Grant did not bat.

Bowling: Smith 9–2–17–1; Angel 9–1–31–1; Averis 6–0–14–1; Snape 7–2–12–0; Alleyne 2–0–8–0; Fisher 3.1–0–11–1.

Umpires: B. Dudleston and T. E. Jesty.

At Manchester, September 1. ESSEX beat LANCASHIRE by seven wickets.

ESSEX v SURREY

At Chelmsford, September 8. Surrey won by two runs. Toss: Essex.

If Essex had survived the 39th over they would have won: Surrey's allotted time in which to bowl their overs was about to run out, and Essex would have been credited six runs for each of the six overs not yet bowled, which would have taken them way past their target. But they seemed unaware of this and were bowled out midway through the 38th over. On a Chelmsford minefield, Cowan and Grant had kept Surrey in check. Irani marshalled the chase well, before the lower order lost the plot and guaranteed Surrey's promotion.

Surrey

I. J. Ward b Cowan	5
A. D. Brown c Napier b Irani	2
M. R. Ramprakash b Napier	13
R. Clarke c Grant b Irani	17
N. Shahid c Flower b Grant	18
*A. J. Hollioake c Grant b Cowan	27
†J. N. Batty c Jefferson b Grant	19
M. P. Bicknell b Grant	9
Saqlain Mushtaq b Cowan	28

T. J. Murtagh not out	14
E. S. H. Giddins c Flower b Cowan	2
L-b 2, w 6	8

1/7 (2) 2/7 (1) 3/30 (4) (43.3 overs) 162
4/42 (3) 5/82 (6) 6/92 (5)
7/111 (8) 8/124 (7)
9/156 (9) 10/162 (11)

Bowling: Irani 7–2–19–2; Cowan 8.3–1–16–4; Napier 6–1–32–1; Dakin 5–0–27–0; Stephenson 2–0–11–0; Grant 7–0–28–3; Grayson 8–1–27–0.

Essex

D. D. J. Robinson b Bicknell	2	A. P. Cowan b Giddins	0
W. I. Jefferson c Batty b Murtagh	29	J. B. Grant lbw b Hollioake	0
J. P. Stephenson c Hollioake b Giddins	5		
†A. Flower c Brown b Saqlain Mushtaq	13	L-b 6, w 12, n-b 4	22
*R. C. Irani b Bicknell	41		
A. P. Grayson c Batty b Hollioake	29	1/3 (1) 2/27 (3) 3/61 (4) (38.2 overs) 160
M. L. Pettini b Giddins	6	4/63 (2) 5/137 (5) 6/145 (6)
J. M. Dakin c Batty b Hollioake	8	7/155 (8) 8/159 (7)
G. R. Napier not out	5	9/159 (10) 10/160 (11)

Bowling: Bicknell 9–3–28–2; Giddins 9–2–43–3; Murtagh 6–0–28–1; Saqlain Mushtaq 9–0–35–1; Clarke 2–0–9–0; Hollioake 3.2–1–11–3.

Umpires: J. H. Evans and J. W. Lloyds.

At Northampton, September 15. ESSEX beat NORTHAMPTONSHIRE by 42 runs.

ESSEX v SUSSEX

At Chelmsford, September 22. Essex won by 29 runs (D/L method). Toss: Sussex. First-team debut: N. R. K. Turk.

Habib, Robinson and Dakin were the chief batting contributors for Essex in a 42-over match. Their total looked insufficient as Goodwin and the debutant Neil Turk combined to put Sussex in pole position. But Sussex then faltered through a succession of rash strokes against the spinners to hand victory back to Essex.

Essex

D. D. J. Robinson c Ambrose b Taylor	42	J. D. Middlebrook run out	2
W. I. Jefferson b Hutchison	22	J. B. Grant c Ambrose b Hutchison	2
J. P. Stephenson lbw b Martin-Jenkins	1		
M. E. Waugh lbw b Hutchison	2	L-b 7, w 2	9
A. Habib c Hutchison b Hopkinson	53		
*A. P. Grayson lbw b Taylor	14	1/40 (2) 2/41 (3) 3/44 (4) (38 overs) 189
J. M. Dakin not out	40	4/89 (1) 5/109 (6) 6/172 (5)
†J. S. Foster b Davis	1	7/175 (8) 8/181 (9)
G. R. Napier c Goodwin b Davis	1	9/187 (10) 10/189 (11)

Bowling: Martin-Jenkins 7–2–28–1; Hutchison 8–1–38–3; Taylor 7–1–25–2; Yardy 5–0–28–0; Davis 9–0–47–2; Hopkinson 2–0–16–1.

Sussex

*R. R. Montgomerie lbw b Napier	10	M. J. G. Davis c Napier b Waugh	8
P. A. Cottey c Foster b Napier	3	P. M. Hutchison c Dakin b Waugh	12
M. W. Goodwin c Stephenson b Middlebrook	55	B. V. Taylor not out	2
N. R. K. Turk c Stephenson b Grayson	36	B 1, l-b 5, w 3	9
†T. R. Ambrose run out	3		
R. S. C. Martin-Jenkins c Middlebrook b Grayson	0	1/11 (2) 2/16 (1) 3/99 (3) (38.3 overs) 158
C. D. Hopkinson c Foster b Grayson	12	4/108 (5) 5/109 (6)
M. H. Yardy b Waugh	8	6/122 (4) 7/126 (7)
		8/135 (9) 9/144 (8) 10/158 (10)

Bowling: Dakin 6–0–26–0; Napier 8–0–23–2; Stephenson 1–0–16–0; Grant 2–0–21–0; Middlebrook 9–2–25–1; Grayson 9–1–27–3; Waugh 3.3–0–14–3.

Umpires: B. Leadbeater and J. F. Steele.

GLOUCESTERSHIRE

At Southampton, May 12. GLOUCESTERSHIRE lost to HAMPSHIRE by 46 runs.

GLOUCESTERSHIRE v SURREY

At Bristol, May 19. Gloucestershire won by one wicket. Toss: Gloucestershire.
This was a low-scoring thriller that Gloucestershire's bowlers won with the bat. Barnett, captaining in Alleyne's absence, saw his pleasure at restricting Surrey's batsmen all but vanish as Gloucestershire's own innings fell away. Ball, with his highest League score, led the recovery, but fell with 18 still needed. Lewis was dropped by Ward at slip, and then Smith, who had already survived a close run-out call, scampered the winning single off a misfield. Earlier, Surrey's openers had given them a promising start, but the middle order collapsed spectacularly, thanks to Lewis's best one-day return.

Surrey

*I. J. Ward b Hardinges	27
A. D. Brown b Lewis	54
M. R. Ramprakash c Russell b Lewis . .	3
N. Shahid c Ball b Lewis	0
M. A. Carberry run out	5
A. J. Tudor c Russell b Lewis	6
R. Clarke c Russell b Hardinges	0
M. P. Bicknell b Smith	15
†J. N. Batty not out	28

Saqlain Mushtaq c Smith b Ball	3
E. S. H. Giddins not out	13
L-b 3, w 6	9

1/86 (1) 2/86 (2)   (9 wkts, 45 overs) 163
3/86 (4) 4/97 (3)
5/103 (5) 6/103 (7)
7/103 (6) 8/122 (8) 9/131 (10)

Bowling: Smith 9–0–35–1; Averis 9–1–32–0; Lewis 9–3–22–4; Hardinges 9–1–46–2; Ball 9–0–25–1.

Gloucestershire

C. M. Spearman c Ramprakash b Bicknell	2
*K. J. Barnett lbw b Giddins	3
M. G. N. Windows c Batty b Bicknell . .	9
J. N. Snape c Batty b Giddins	36
M. A. Hardinges c Batty b Giddins	2
†R. C. Russell c Batty b Clarke	2
M. C. J. Ball c Clarke	45
C. G. Taylor lbw b Bicknell	6
J. M. M. Averis c Giddins b Saqlain Mushtaq .	7

J. Lewis not out	27
A. M. Smith not out	4
L-b 9, w 12	21

1/2 (1) 2/7 (2)   (9 wkts, 43.3 overs) 164
3/32 (3) 4/63 (4)
5/64 (5) 6/77 (6)
7/98 (8) 8/115 (9)
9/146 (7)

Bowling: Bicknell 9–2–24–3; Giddins 9–0–31–3; Tudor 8–0–48–0; Clarke 8.3–1–32–2; Saqlain Mushtaq 9–2–20–1.

Umpires: A. A. Jones and N. A. Mallender.

At Manchester, June 4 (day/night). GLOUCESTERSHIRE beat LANCASHIRE by 79 runs.

At Northampton, June 9. GLOUCESTERSHIRE v NORTHAMPTONSHIRE. No result (abandoned).

He could yet be even more successful and flamboyant as a writer than as a cricketer.
Frank Keating on E. T. Smith's literary debut: Cricket Books, page 1676

GLOUCESTERSHIRE v MIDDLESEX

At Bristol, June 16. Gloucestershire won by five wickets. Toss: Middlesex.

On a seaming wicket, Harvey, passed over for Australia's one-day squad, took out his frustration on Middlesex. His 41-ball 60 swept Gloucestershire to victory with more than 20 overs to spare. Middlesex had been in control thanks to a brisk partnership between Strauss and Razzaq, until both fell in the same over. This sparked an astonishing collapse: seven wickets fell in eight overs for 25 runs. Weekes was reported for dissent following his dismissal to cap a miserable match for Middlesex.

Middlesex

*A. J. Strauss c Hardinges b Alleyne	65	B. L. Hutton c and b Ball	1
S. G. Koenig lbw b Smith	1	C. B. Keegan not out	0
E. C. Joyce b Harvey	10		
O. A. Shah c Barnett b Lewis	7	B 4, l-b 3, w 3, n-b 2	12
Abdul Razzaq lbw b Alleyne	24		
S. J. Cook st Russell b Ball	8	1/15 (2) 2/30 (3) 3/56 (4) (37.3 overs) 142	
†D. C. Nash lbw b Alleyne	0	4/117 (1) 5/122 (5)	
P. N. Weekes c Russell b Ball	8	6/124 (7) 7/135 (8)	
A. W. Laraman run out	6	8/136 (6) 9/142 (9) 10/142 (10)	

Bowling: Smith 6–1–22–1; Harvey 6–2–16–1; Hardinges 5–0–19–0; Lewis 7–0–35–1; Alleyne 8–1–30–3; Ball 5.3–0–13–3.

Gloucestershire

K. J. Barnett c Nash b Keegan	0	M. A. Hardinges not out	2
C. M. Spearman b Laraman	8	L-b 6, n-b 6	12
I. J. Harvey c Nash b Laraman	60		
C. G. Taylor c Nash b Abdul Razzaq	9	1/0 (1) 2/22 (2) (5 wkts, 24.2 overs) 144	
M. G. N. Windows c Nash b Keegan	21	3/75 (3) 4/78 (4)	
*M. W. Alleyne not out	32	5/122 (5)	

†R. C. Russell, M. C. J. Ball, A. M. Smith and J. Lewis did not bat.

Bowling: Keegan 7.2–0–44–2; Laraman 5–0–44–2; Cook 5–0–20–0; Abdul Razzaq 7–0–30–1.

Umpires: J. H. Hampshire and A. A. Jones.

GLOUCESTERSHIRE v ESSEX

At Gloucester, June 30. Essex won by 12 runs (D/L method). Toss: Gloucestershire.

Essex stuttered at the start but then 18-year-old Pettini smashed his maiden one-day fifty, as he and the imperious Flower salvaged a decent total on a grey afternoon. Gloucestershire's target was adjusted to 200 from 35 after several showers, and Clarke seemed to have denied them with three wickets in five overs. But a bludgeoning knock from Alleyne reignited the match. He thumped two sixes and six fours before finally miscuing Clarke to long-off.

Essex

*D. J. Robinson b Smith	9	J. E. Bishop not out	2
W. I. Jefferson c Russell b Averis	1	A. J. Clarke not out	0
G. R. Napier run out	9		
†A. Flower lbw b Gidman	80	L-b 2, w 6	8
A. Habib lbw b Alleyne	7		
M. L. Pettini c Smith b Gidman	75	1/12 (2) 2/16 (1) (9 wkts, 42.3 overs) 215	
J. D. Middlebrook b Gidman	11	3/27 (3) 4/48 (5)	
J. P. Stephenson c Hardinges b Smith	7	5/164 (4) 6/194 (7)	
T. J. Phillips c Alleyne b Averis	6	7/205 (6) 8/213 (9) 9/215 (8)	

Bowling: Smith 7.3–1–32–2; Averis 8–0–34–2; Alleyne 9–0–41–1; Hardinges 7–0–30–0; Gidman 7–0–46–3; Ball 4–0–30–0.

Gloucestershire

C. M. Spearman c Clarke b Bishop	0	J. M. M. Averis not out		0
K. J. Barnett c Robinson b Clarke	10	A. M. Smith not out		1
C. G. Taylor b Clarke	23			
†R. C. Russell c Habib b Stephenson	21	L-b 3, w 4		7
M. G. N. Windows c Flower b Clarke	0			
*M. W. Alleyne c Middlebrook b Clarke	76	1/0 (1) 2/32 (2)	(9 wkts, 35 overs)	187
A. P. R. Gidman b Middlebrook	14	3/35 (3) 4/42 (5)		
M. A. Hardinges c Stephenson b Bishop	29	5/74 (4) 6/113 (7)		
M. C. J. Ball run out	6	7/167 (6) 8/183 (8) 9/186 (9)		

Bowling: Bishop 7–0–47–2; Napier 7–0–37–0; Clarke 7–0–30–4; Stephenson 7–0–31–1; Middlebrook 6–0–27–1; Phillips 1–0–12–0.

Umpires: A. Clarkson and I. J. Gould.

At Derby, July 7. GLOUCESTERSHIRE beat DERBYSHIRE by seven runs.

At Southgate, July 14. GLOUCESTERSHIRE beat MIDDLESEX by 78 runs.

GLOUCESTERSHIRE v HAMPSHIRE

At Cheltenham, July 18. Gloucestershire won by 71 runs. Toss: Gloucestershire.

Spearman and Windows unleashed a scoring spree of 171 in 27 overs, punishing anything remotely wayward on a shirt-front of a pitch. Hampshire were put under further pressure as Smith claimed three early wickets, but Francis drove fiercely for a defiant fifty. Udal and Kendall provided great entertainment with a big-hitting partnership, but Gloucestershire were always sure of the win.

Gloucestershire

C. M. Spearman c White b Udal	107	J. M. M. Averis run out		4
T. H. C. Hancock lbw b Mascarenhas	0	A. M. Smith not out		12
I. J. Harvey c Crawley b Mascarenhas	4			
M. G. N. Windows c Pothas b Udal	76	L-b 13, w 11, n-b 6		30
*M. W. Alleyne b Mascarenhas	21			
J. N. Snape not out	38	1/9 (2) 2/17 (3)	(9 wkts, 45 overs)	296
A. P. R. Gidman run out	4	3/188 (1) 4/228 (4)		
†R. C. Russell c Pothas b Mascarenhas	0	5/233 (5) 6/245 (7)		
M. C. J. Ball c Pothas b Johnson	0	7/245 (8) 8/246 (9) 9/259 (10)		

Bowling: Mullally 9–0–45–0; Mascarenhas 9–0–67–4; Tremlett 7–0–65–0; Johnson 9–0–42–1; Udal 9–0–39–2; Kendall 2–0–25–0.

Hampshire

N. C. Johnson b Smith	1	C. T. Tremlett c Gidman b Harvey	6
D. A. Kenway b Harvey	4	A. D. Mullally not out	1
J. P. Crawley c Russell b Smith	13		
G. W. White b Smith	30	L-b 6, w 1, n-b 4	11
J. D. Francis c Hancock b Snape	51		
†N. Pothas c Harvey b Ball	6	1/5 (1) 2/7 (2) (9 wkts, 45 overs) 225	
A. D. Mascarenhas c Harvey b Snape	12	3/33 (3) 4/83 (4)	
*W. S. Kendall not out	32	5/94 (6) 6/123 (7)	
S. D. Udal lbw b Harvey	58	7/126 (5) 8/215 (9) 9/223 (10)	

Bowling: Harvey 9–0–40–3; Smith 9-2–25–3; Alleyne 3–0–23–0; Ball 9–0–43–1; Averis 9–0–52–0; Snape 6–0–36–2.

Umpires: B. Dudleston and A. G. T. Whitehead.

GLOUCESTERSHIRE v SUSSEX

At Cheltenham, July 28. Gloucestershire won by six wickets. Toss: Sussex.

This was all over inside four hours, but a full house had their money's worth as Gloucestershire rushed to victory. Harvey and Smith ripped through Sussex's top order, Ball expertly cleaned up the tail, and there were five catches for Russell, equalling a 31-year-old Gloucestershire record. Spearman and Harvey then blasted 81 in eight scintillating overs. Harvey lashed 13 fours in his 63, and later announced he would like to stay with Gloucestershire. It must have been music to their ears.

Sussex

W. J. House c Russell b Harvey	12	B. V. Taylor c and b Ball	0
*R. R. Montgomerie lbw b Smith	23	M. A. Robinson c Russell b Ball	0
T. R. Ambrose c Alleyne b Harvey	4		
M. W. Goodwin c Russell b Smith	5	W 3, n-b 4	7
†M. J. Prior c Gidman b Averis	18		
P. A. Cottey c Russell b Averis	5	1/16 (1) 2/30 (3) 3/42 (4) (30.5 overs) 116	
R. S. C. Martin-Jenkins lbw b Ball	25	4/50 (2) 5/55 (6) 6/86 (5)	
K. J. Innes not out	16	7/107 (7) 8/110 (9)	
J. D. Lewry c Russell b Ball	1	9/116 (10) 10/116 (11)	

Bowling: Harvey 5–0–25–2; Smith 9–1–33–2; Averis 7–0–26–2; Alleyne 5–0–16–0; Ball 3.5–0–15–4; Snape 1–0–1–0.

Gloucestershire

T. H. C. Hancock c Prior b Robinson	12	J. N. Snape not out	4
C. M. Spearman c Lewry b Taylor	24	L-b 1, w 1, n-b 6	8
I. J. Harvey not out	68		
M. G. N. Windows c House b Lewry	2	1/13 (1) 2/94 (2) (4 wkts, 17.2 overs) 118	
*M. W. Alleyne run out	0	3/107 (4) 4/109 (5)	

A. P. R. Gidman, †R. C. Russell, M. C. J. Ball, J. M. M. Averis and A. M. Smith did not bat.

Bowling: Lewry 6.2–1–29–1; Taylor 8–1–45–1; Robinson 3–0–43–1.

Umpires: J. H. Hampshire and G. Sharp.

 Howard was a natural diplomat: tactful, courteous and – an attribute by no means commonplace in the English cricket establishment of the time – sympathetic to his fellow-man regardless of creed, colour or class.

Obituary of Geoffrey Howard, page 1637

GLOUCESTERSHIRE v LANCASHIRE

At Bristol, August 3. Gloucestershire won by five wickets. Toss: Lancashire.

Smith and Harvey were the early destroyers as Lancashire slumped to 49 for six in the 12th over. Law and Hegg repaired some of the damage with a stoic 85, but it was always a simple target. Lancashire were under immediate pressure as Harvey and Spearman pushed on vigorously. Alleyne played the anchor role, and some sparkling shots from Gidman cemented a convincing win.

Lancashire

G. Chapple lbw b Smith	0	K. W. Hogg not out	23
M. J. Chilton lbw b Harvey	21	M. P. Smethurst not out	1
D. Byas b Smith	11		
S. G. Law c Gidman b Ball	55	B 1, l-b 2, w 4, n-b 2	9
N. H. Fairbrother c Russell b Harvey	0		
G. D. Lloyd b Smith	6	1/0 (1) 2/33 (3) (9 wkts, 45 overs) 183	
R. C. Driver c Russell b Harvey	0	3/34 (2) 4/34 (5)	
*†W. K. Hegg c Snape b Harvey	54	5/47 (6) 6/49 (7)	
G. Yates c Russell b Snape	3	7/134 (4) 8/140 (9) 9/172 (8)	

Bowling: Smith 9–2–36–3; Harvey 9–0–41–4; Averis 8–1–36–0; Alleyne 6–0–21–0; Ball 8–0–30–1; Snape 5–1–16–1.

Gloucestershire

C. M. Spearman run out	54	A. P. R. Gidman not out	20
T. H. C. Hancock c Hogg b Chapple	2	L-b 3, w 5	8
I. J. Harvey c Hegg b Hogg	56		
M. G. N. Windows b Chapple	16	1/25 (2) 2/110 (3) (5 wkts, 35 overs) 185	
*M. W. Alleyne not out	25	3/129 (1) 4/137 (4)	
J. N. Snape lbw b Yates	4	5/148 (6)	

†R. C. Russell, M. C. J. Ball, J. M. M. Averis and A. M. Smith did not bat.

Bowling: Chapple 9–1–36–2; Smethurst 6–0–45–0; Hogg 7–1–35–1; Driver 3–0–17–0; Yates 9–1–37–1; Chilton 1–0–12–0.

Umpires: N. G. Cowley and T. E. Jesty.

At Hove, August 5 (day/night). GLOUCESTERSHIRE v SUSSEX. No result.

GLOUCESTERSHIRE v NORTHAMPTONSHIRE

At Bristol, August 13 (day/night). Gloucestershire won by 55 runs. Toss: Gloucestershire.

A hard-hit hundred from Windows propelled Gloucestershire to a massive total, with typically rumbustious contributions by Harvey and Alleyne. They were particularly severe on the Gloucestershire old boy, Cawdron: his nine overs were savaged for 91, with Windows smacking 24 from the final one. Northamptonshire struggled under the lights, and determined batting from Penberthy and Sales could not save them.

Gloucestershire

C. G. Taylor c Bailey b Cook	. . . .	18
C. M. Spearman c Cassar b Cawdron	. . .	14
I. J. Harvey c Swann b Brown	. . . . . .	52
M. G. N. Windows not out	. . . .	112
*M. W. Alleyne b Cook	. . . .	43
J. N. Snape b Cook	. . . .	13
A. P. R. Gidman lbw b Cook	. . . .	9

M. C. J. Ball not out 0

L-b 5, w 6, n-b 2 13

1/18 (2) 2/79 (1)   (6 wkts, 45 overs) 274
3/96 (3) 4/175 (5)
5/227 (6) 6/250 (7)

†R. C. Russell, J. M. M. Averis and A. M. Smith did not bat.

Bowling: Cousins 2–0–4–0; Cawdron 9–0–91–1; Penberthy 9–0–62–0; Cook 9–0–35–4; Brown 9–1–42–1; Swann 7–0–35–0.

Northamptonshire

*M. E. K. Hussey b Smith	. . . .	10
M. B. Loye b Harvey	. . . .	17
D. J. Sales lbw b Ball	. . . .	51
M. E. Cassar b Alleyne	. . . .	19
J. W. Cook c Averis b Ball	. . . .	13
A. L. Penberthy st Russell b Averis	. . .	64
G. P. Swann run out	. . . .	1
†T. M. B. Bailey c Russell b Averis	. . .	37
M. J. Cawdron c Alleyne b Harvey	. . .	0

J. F. Brown not out 1
D. M. Cousins absent hurt

L-b 2, w 4 6

1/23 (1) 2/28 (2)   (9 wkts, 42 overs) 219
3/87 (4) 4/106 (3)
5/123 (5) 6/127 (7)
7/210 (6) 8/211 (9) 9/219 (8)

Bowling: Harvey 8–0–44–2; Smith 9–1–39–1; Averis 6–0–40–2; Alleyne 5–0–17–1; Ball 9–0–57–2; Snape 5–0–20–0.

Umpires: R. Palmer and G. Sharp.

At Colchester, August 27 (day/night). GLOUCESTERSHIRE lost to ESSEX by five wickets.

GLOUCESTERSHIRE v DERBYSHIRE

At Bristol, September 8. Gloucestershire won by 52 runs. Toss: Derbyshire.

On a day everything else fell into place, Gloucestershire had to wait for a late result from Chelmsford to confirm they were going up as champions. They had been given a flying start when Spearman and Russell streaked away to 100 inside the first 12 overs. Hancock and Alleyne then joined the fun, spurring Gloucestershire to their second-best League score. Derbyshire mounted a strong chase, with Selwood especially threatening, but they suddenly disintegrated as the last four wickets went down in ten balls.

Gloucestershire

†R. C. Russell lbw b Kerr	. . . .	42
C. M. Spearman b Dumelow	. . . .	81
T. H. C. Hancock b Dowman	. . . . . .	45
M. G. N. Windows c Selwood b Dowman		13
*M. W. Alleyne b Kerr	. . . .	54
C. G. Taylor lbw b Dowman	. . . . . .	15
A. P. R. Gidman st Sutton b Welch	. . .	18
J. Lewis b Kerr	. . . .	0

I. D. Fisher not out 3

L-b 6, w 13, n-b 2 21

1/111 (1) 2/173 (2)   (8 wkts, 45 overs) 292
3/185 (3) 4/216 (4)
5/248 (6) 6/276 (5)
7/276 (8) 8/292 (7)

J. Angel and A. M. Smith did not bat.

Bowling: Welch 9–0–80–1; Dean 2–0–22–0; Kerr 9–1–34–3; Gunter 9–0–80–0; Dumelow 9–0–32–1; Dowman 7–0–38–3.

Derbyshire

*M. J. Di Venuto c Russell b Lewis	0	N. E. L. Gunter b Smith	0
C. W. G. Bassano c Taylor b Fisher	61	K. J. Dean b Smith	0
N. R. C. Dumelow run out	13		
S. A. Selwood c Alleyne b Angel	93	B 4, l-b 8, w 6	18
D. R. Hewson b Alleyne	6		
J. I. D. Kerr b Alleyne	3	1/0 (1) 2/54 (3) 3/102 (2) (41.4 overs) 240	
M. P. Dowman b Angel	45	4/112 (5) 5/116 (6)	
G. Welch b Smith	1	6/239 (4) 7/240 (7)	
†L. D. Sutton not out	0	8/240 (8) 9/240 (10) 10/240 (11)	

Bowling: Lewis 9–1–55–1; Smith 7.4–0–33–3; Angel 7–0–40–2; Alleyne 9–0–50–2; Fisher 9–0–50–1.

Umpires: M. J. Harris and P. Willey.

At The Oval, September 22. GLOUCESTERSHIRE lost to SURREY by 79 runs.

HAMPSHIRE

HAMPSHIRE v GLOUCESTERSHIRE

At Southampton, May 12. Hampshire won by 46 runs. Toss: Gloucestershire.

Mascarenhas grabbed hold of this match with a raucous 39 and an accurate spell of seam, which brought him his best one-day return. After Hampshire had started tentatively, he blasted them to a defendable total, adding 62 in the last six overs with Pothas. In Gloucestershire's reply, Mascarenhas deceived Barnett with his first ball and removed Taylor in the same over. Spearman responded fluently but the innings dwindled after his dismissal.

Hampshire

J. R. C. Hamblin c Barnett b Lewis	7	A. D. Mascarenhas not out	39
N. C. Johnson c Russell b Harvey	1	L-b 8, w 12	20
D. A. Kenway lbw b Alleyne	50		
G. W. White c Harvey b Averis	11	1/8 (2) 2/8 (1) (5 wkts, 45 overs) 219	
J. S. Laney c Snape b Ball	38	3/46 (4) 4/101 (3)	
†N. Pothas not out	53	5/157 (5)	

*W. S. Kendall, L. R. Prittipaul, S. D. Udal and A. D. Mullally did not bat.

Bowling: Lewis 6–2–21–1; Harvey 9–0–36–1; Averis 9–0–74–1; Alleyne 9–0–28–1; Ball 9–0–36–1; Snape 3–0–16–0.

Gloucestershire

K. J. Barnett c Johnson b Mascarenhas	0	J. M. M. Averis c Pothas b Mascarenhas	1
C. M. Spearman c Kendall b Prittipaul	82	J. Lewis not out	0
C. G. Taylor c White b Mascarenhas	4		
M. G. N. Windows b Mascarenhas	12	L-b 1, w 6, n-b 2	9
*M. W. Alleyne c and b Udal	22		
J. N. Snape b Prittipaul	6	1/0 (1) 2/5 (3) 3/38 (4) (38.3 overs) 173	
I. J. Harvey c Johnson b Mullally	17	4/115 (5) 5/131 (5)	
†R. C. Russell c Kenway b Prittipaul	17	6/135 (6) 7/158 (7)	
M. C. J. Ball c Hamblin b Mascarenhas	3	8/172 (8) 9/173 (9) 10/173 (10)	

Bowling: Mascarenhas 7.3–1–27–5; Mullally 7–2–23–1; Johnson 5–0–25–0; Hamblin 3–0–23–0; Udal 9–0–41–1; Prittipaul 7–1–33–3.

Umpires: A. Clarkson and K. E. Palmer.

At Lord's, June 4. HAMPSHIRE beat MIDDLESEX by two runs.

HAMPSHIRE v DERBYSHIRE

At Southampton, June 9. No result (abandoned).

HAMPSHIRE v SURREY

At Southampton, June 16. Surrey won by three wickets. Toss: Surrey.

Adam Hollioake returned to the Surrey side three months after the death of his brother Ben. On a damp pitch, Bicknell and Giddins jagged the ball off the seam, and Hollioake found some gentle swing. Only powerful late hitting by Mascarenhas gave Hampshire a competitive score. In reply, Surrey toiled despite the absence of the injured Mullally from Hampshire's attack. But Salisbury finally relieved the pressure, lifting the first ball of the last over from Prittipaul over mid-wicket for six.

Hampshire

J. R. C. Hamblin c Ormond b Giddins . .	5	A. D. Mascarenhas not out	25
N. C. Johnson c Clarke b Bicknell	0	S. D. Udal not out	4
D. A. Kenway b Clarke	9	L-b 7, w 12	19
J. P. Crawley c Batty b Hollioake	34		
L. R. Prittipaul c Batty b Hollioake	20	1/5 (1) 2/7 (2) (8 wkts, 45 overs) 178
G. W. White c Ward b Bicknell.	14	3/39 (3) 4/75 (4)
†N. Pothas c and b Hollioake	27	5/90 (5) 6/102 (6)
*W. S. Kendall c Shahid b Giddins . . .	21	7/146 (8) 8/153 (7)

C. T. Tremlett did not bat.

Bowling: Bicknell 9–1–15–2; Giddins 9–1–34–2; Ormond 9–0–25–0; Clarke 8–1–44–1; Hollioake 9–0–45–3; Ward 1–0–8–0.

Surrey

I. J. Ward b Tremlett.	51	M. P. Bicknell not out.	19
A. D. Brown c and b Tremlett	14	I. D. K. Salisbury not out	15
M. R. Ramprakash run out.	12	B 2, l-b 3, w 12, n-b 2	19
R. Clarke c Johnson b Hamblin	1		
N. Shahid c Pothas b Prittipaul	19	1/27 (2) 2/57 (3) (7 wkts, 44.1 overs) 180
*A. J. Hollioake c Pothas b Mascarenhas	15	3/62 (4) 4/99 (5)
†J. N. Batty lbw b Tremlett	15	5/121 (1) 6/128 (6) 7/155 (7)

J. Ormond and E. S. H. Giddins did not bat.

Bowling: Mascarenhas 9–1–36–1; Tremlett 9–0–25–3; Johnson 9–0–41–0; Hamblin 3–0–13–1; Udal 9–1–27–0; Prittipaul 5.1–0–33–1.

Umpires: B. Leadbeater and R. Palmer.

HAMPSHIRE v SUSSEX

At Southampton, July 7. Hampshire won by 93 runs. Toss: Hampshire. County debut: J. A. Tomlinson.

Sussex's chase never got going. A memorable opening spell by left-arm seamer James Tomlinson removed both openers, then a superb catch by Johnson halted a middle-order fightback, and three more wickets for Udal sealed Hampshire's win. Earlier, Hampshire had ended with a fairly modest total, considering the early impetus provided by Johnson. Taylor's four for 22 kept them on the leash.

Hampshire

N. C. Johnson c Montgomerie b House	92	C. T. Tremlett c Prior b Taylor	10
D. A. Kenway c Goodwin b Taylor	29	J. A. Tomlinson not out	0
J. P. Crawley c Prior b Innes	1		
L. R. Prittipaul c Ambrose b Taylor	4	B 7, l-b 6, w 4	17
G. W. White c Goodwin b Innes	3		
†N. Pothas run out	26	1/78 (2) 2/87 (3) 3/92 (4) (45 overs) 203
A. D. Mascarenhas lbw b Davis	10	4/104 (5) 5/156 (1) 6/172 (7)
*W. S. Kendall c Lewry b Davis	7	7/182 (8) 8/189 (6)
S. D. Udal c Adams b Taylor	4	9/201 (9) 10/203 (10)

Bowling: Martin-Jenkins 9–1–38–0; Lewry 7–0–37–0; Taylor 9–1–22–4; Innes 9–1–30–2; Davis 8–0–45–2; House 3–0–18–1.

Sussex

R. R. Montgomerie c Pothas b Tomlinson	7	B. V. Taylor c Pothas b Udal	1
W. J. House c Pothas b Tomlinson	0	J. D. Lewry not out	0
T. R. Ambrose c Pothas b Mascarenhas	3		
*C. J. Adams c and b Udal	34	L-b 2, w 5	7
M. W. Goodwin Johnson b Udal	32		
R. S. C. Martin-Jenkins b Prittipaul	1	1/2 (2) 2/4 (3) 3/15 (1) (34.2 overs) 110
†M. J. Prior c Pothas b Udal	5	4/66 (5) 5/79 (4) 6/79 (6)
K. J. Innes b Prittipaul	16	7/85 (7) 8/109 (8)
M. J. G. Davis run out	7	9/110 (10) 10/110 (9)

Bowling: Mascarenhas 9–1–19–1; Tomlinson 7–1–15–2; Tremlett 5–1–14–0; Johnson 2–0–12–0; Udal 6.2–0–31–4; Prittipaul 5–1–17–2.

Umpires: K. E. Palmer and G. Sharp.

At Southend, July 14. HAMPSHIRE lost to ESSEX by five runs.

At Cheltenham, July 18. HAMPSHIRE lost to GLOUCESTERSHIRE by 71 runs.

HAMPSHIRE v LANCASHIRE

At Southampton, July 23 (day/night). Lancashire won by 16 runs. Toss: Lancashire.

The ball dominated the bat in a low-scoring game, with only Law coming to terms with the juicy pitch. His quality innings boosted Lancashire's scanty total. Hampshire's aggressive reply faltered when Johnson was caught at third man. The delivery that got him was above head height, but wasn't called a no-ball. It proved a turning point, as Hogg then ran through Hampshire with a one-day best of four for 20.

Lancashire

G. Chapple c Smith b Mascarenhas	10	K. W. Hogg c White b Mullally	4
M. J. Chilton c Pothas b Mascarenhas	10	J. Wood not out	2
D. Byas b Mullally	2		
S. G. Law c Smith b Johnson	66	L-b 12, w 5	17
N. H. Fairbrother c Johnson b Tremlett	0		
G. D. Lloyd c Kendall b Udal	25	1/15 (1) 2/20 (3) 3/50 (2) (39.1 overs) 163
*†W. K. Hegg c Pothas b Johnson	0	4/55 (5) 5/102 (6) 6/103 (7)
G. Yates c Kenway b Johnson	17	7/143 (8) 8/147 (4)
P. J. Martin c Pothas b Tremlett	10	9/161 (10) 10/163 (9)

Bowling: Mullally 8–1–25–2; Mascarenhas 8–0–19–2; Tremlett 7.1–1–23–2; Udal 8–0–39–1; Johnson 8–0–45–3.

Hampshire

N. C. Johnson c Wood b Martin	27	C. T. Tremlett b Hogg	5
D. A. Kenway c Chilton b Hogg	20	A. D. Mullally run out	8
*R. A. Smith c Chilton b Wood	3		
G. W. White c Law b Hogg	6	B 1, l-b 5, w 7	13
J. D. Francis c Hegg b Chapple	25		
†N. Pothas c Wood b Chilton	4	1/37 (1) 2/53 (2) 3/59 (3) (37.4 overs) 147
W. S. Kendall c Byas b Wood	5	4/69 (4) 5/95 (6) 6/95 (5)
A. D. Mascarenhas c Yates b Hogg	7	7/107 (7) 8/112 (8)
S. D. Udal not out	24	9/121 (10) 10/147 (11)

Bowling: Martin 7–1–32–1; Chapple 6.4–0–34–1; Wood 8–0–37–2; Hogg 8–1–20–4; Chilton 8–0–18–1.

Umpires: J. H. Evans and T. E. Jesty.

At Derby, August 3. HAMPSHIRE lost to DERBYSHIRE by two wickets (D/L method).

At Northampton, August 4. HAMPSHIRE lost to NORTHAMPTONSHIRE by 16 runs (D/L method).

At Manchester, August 6 (day/night). HAMPSHIRE lost to LANCASHIRE by four wickets.

HAMPSHIRE v ESSEX

At Southampton, August 18. Hampshire won by five wickets. Toss: Essex.

Francis ended Hampshire's run of six League defeats with a powerful innings – one huge six clearing the 6ft 10in figure of Jefferson at long-on. Francis and Kendall added a composed 132 in 24 overs after a shaky start by the top order. Essex had batted soundly but slowly, and never truly upped the tempo, losing wickets at crucial times.

Essex

*D. D. J. Robinson c Francis b Tomlinson	51	R. S. Clinton not out	1
W. I. Jefferson st Pothas b Udal	48	B 4, l-b 4, w 7	15
†A. Flower b Udal	54		
J. M. Dakin not out	41	1/85 (2) 2/160 (1) (4 wkts, 45 overs) 227
M. L. Pettini c Johnson b Mascarenhas	17	3/176 (3) 4/220 (5)

J. P. Stephenson, G. R. Napier, J. D. Middlebrook, J. E. Bishop and J. B. Grant did not bat.

Bowling: Mascarenhas 9–1–38–1; Tomlinson 9–1–49–1; Tremlett 1.1–0–6–0; Johnson 8–1–46–0; Prittipaul 8.5–0–49–0; Udal 9–0–31–2.

Hampshire

N. C. Johnson c Clinton b Dakin   0
J. S. Laney c Napier b Stephenson 34
J. P. Crawley c Robinson b Dakin 17
J. D. Francis not out 84
*W. S. Kendall lbw b Middlebrook 51
A. D. Mascarenhas b Grant   0

†N. Pothas not out 14
B 3, l-b 5, w 18, n-b 2 28

1/0 (1) 2/39 (3)   (5 wkts, 44 overs) 228
3/65 (2) 4/197 (5)
5/198 (6)

L. R. Prittipaul, S. D. Udal, C. T. Tremlett and J. A. Tomlinson did not bat.

Bowling: Dakin 8–0–37–2; Grant 9–2–27–1; Napier 9–0–64–0; Stephenson 5–0–28–1; Middlebrook 9–0–42–1; Bishop 4–0–22–0.

Umpires: G. I. Burgess and M. J. Kitchen.

At The Oval, August 21 (day/night). HAMPSHIRE lost to SURREY by 70 runs.

HAMPSHIRE v MIDDLESEX

At Southampton, September 1. Hampshire won by 24 runs. Toss: Hampshire.
   Kendall's first century in 110 limited-overs games rescued Hampshire from a disastrous start. Francis and Udal provided valuable support, and Mascarenhas's breezy 24 helped set Middlesex an awkward target. In reply, Middlesex were a threat as Hutton anchored one end and Shah, Joyce and Dalrymple blazed away at the other. But they failed to master the bowling when it mattered, and the task of getting 90 from the last ten overs proved beyond them.

Hampshire

N. C. Johnson run out   0
J. S. Laney c Alleyne b Cook   0
J. H. K. Adams b Cook   3
J. D. Francis c and b Hunt 33
*W. S. Kendall not out 110
S. D. Udal c Keegan b Hutton 58
A. D. Mascarenhas c Joyce b Keegan . . . 24

J. R. C. Hamblin c and b Keegan   0
L. R. Prittipaul not out   2
L-b 7, w 4 11

1/2 (2) 2/5 (1)   (7 wkts, 45 overs) 241
3/6 (3) 4/76 (4)
5/179 (6) 6/234 (7) 7/235 (8)

†I. Brunnschweiler and J. A. Tomlinson did not bat.

Bowling: Keegan 9–4–22–2; Cook 9–0–29–2; Hunt 6–0–24–1; Weekes 8–0–66–0; Hutton 8–0–62–1; Dalrymple 5–0–31–0.

Middlesex

B. L. Hutton lbw b Johnson 63
S. J. Cook lbw b Mascarenhas   0
R. M. S. Weston c Udal b Tomlinson . . .   1
*O. A. Shah c Tomlinson b Udal 30
E. C. Joyce run out 43
J. W. M. Dalrymple b Udal 42
P. N. Weekes not out 12

†D. Alleyne c Brunnschweiler b Tomlinson   2
N. R. D. Compton not out   3
B 1, l-b 10, w 10 21

1/5 (2) 2/12 (3)   (7 wkts, 45 overs) 217
3/104 (4) 4/105 (1)
5/194 (6) 6/203 (5) 7/212 (8)

C. B. Keegan and T. A. Hunt did not bat.

Bowling: Tomlinson 9–0–23–2; Mascarenhas 9–1–35–1; Hamblin 4–0–19–0; Prittipaul 8–0–50–0; Udal 9–0–47–2; Johnson 6–1–32–1.

Umpires: A. Clarkson and N. J. Llong.

At Hove, September 3 (day/night). HAMPSHIRE lost to SUSSEX by seven wickets.

HAMPSHIRE v NORTHAMPTONSHIRE

At Southampton, September 22. Hampshire won by six wickets. Toss: Northamptonshire.

Francis scored his maiden century for Hampshire to give Robin Smith victory in his final match as captain. An easy-paced Rose Bowl wicket provided a feast for run-starved spectators. Sales's aggressive 93 had dominated Northamptonshire's innings, and Crawley and Johnson added worthy contributions for Hampshire. But they were all overshadowed by Francis's style and power, as he guided Hampshire home with just three balls left.

Northamptonshire

R. A. White c Mullally b Tomlinson . . .	14	†T. M. B. Bailey not out	0
M. J. Powell lbw b Prittipaul	64		
D. J. Sales c Kendall b Tomlinson	93	L-b 8, w 10	18
J. W. Cook run out	29		
*A. L. Penberthy c Pothas b Mullally . .	44	1/29 (1) 2/156 (2) (6 wkts, 45 overs) 285
M. E. Cassar not out	22	3/194 (3) 4/233 (4)
G. L. Brophy run out	1	5/275 (5) 6/281 (7)

C. G. Greenidge, M. W. H. Inness and J. F. Brown did not bat.

Bowling: Mascarenhas 7–0–33–0; Tomlinson 7–0–45–2; Mullally 9–0–54–1; Prittipaul 9–0–62–1; Udal 9–0–58–0; Johnson 4–0–25–0.

Hampshire

N. C. Johnson c Cassar b Penberthy . . .	73	S. D. Udal not out	4
*R. A. Smith c Bailey b Greenidge	8	L-b 7, w 9, n-b 2	18
J. P. Crawley lbw b Brown	52		
J. D. Francis not out	103	1/11 (2) 2/109 (3) (4 wkts, 44.3 overs) 289
W. S. Kendall b Cook	31	3/185 (1) 4/284 (5)

A. D. Mascarenhas, L. R. Prittipaul, †N. Pothas, A. D. Mullally and J. A. Tomlinson did not bat.

Bowling: Greenidge 8.3–2–55–1; Inness 9–1–50–0; Cassar 2–0–18–0; Penberthy 7–0–53–1; Brown 9–0–57–1; Cook 9–0–49–1.

Umpires: A. G. T. Whitehead and P. Willey.

LANCASHIRE

At The Oval, May 12. LANCASHIRE lost to SURREY by six wickets.

LANCASHIRE v SUSSEX

At Manchester, May 19. Lancashire won by four wickets. Toss: Lancashire.

Law's well-paced 71 carried Lancashire to victory under leaden skies, but credit was also due to dynamic bowling from Wood and Martin and to sporadically alert fielding. Two run-outs stymied Sussex – Lloyd and Schofield accounting for Cottey and Adams – although Lancashire blotted their copybook by dropping five catches. Batting was never easy but Law's class shone through to brighten the afternoon.

Sussex

R. R. Montgomerie lbw b Martin	3	
M. H. Yardy b Wood	31	
†T. R. Ambrose c Lloyd b Wood	3	
*C. J. Adams run out	21	
M. W. Goodwin c Lloyd b Wood	6	
P. A. Cottey run out	10	
R. S. C. Martin-Jenkins c Hogg b Chilton	13	
W. J. House c Roberts b Martin	31	
M. J. G. Davis c Byas b Hogg	28	

R. J. Kirtley b Chapple	1	
B. V. Taylor not out	0	
L-b 3, w 8, n-b 2	13	

1/4 (1) 2/37 (3) 3/56 (2)   (41.4 overs) 160
4/64 (5) 5/81 (6) 6/89 (4)
7/102 (8) 8/159 (9)
9/159 (8) 10/160 (10)

Bowling: Martin 7–0–22–2; Chapple 4.4–0–12–1; Hogg 8–0–42–1; Wood 9–1–21–3; Chilton 8–0–32–1; Schofield 5–0–28–0.

Lancashire

D. Byas c Adams b Martin-Jenkins	12	
M. J. Chilton c Ambrose b Taylor	16	
G. Chapple c Adams b Yardy	8	
S. G. Law not out	71	
G. D. Lloyd c Martin-Jenkins b Yardy	3	
T. W. Roberts lbw b Yardy	14	
*†W. K. Hegg b Kirtley	11	

C. P. Schofield not out	8	
L-b 11, w 7	18	

1/36 (1) 2/38 (2)   (6 wkts, 40.5 overs) 161
3/60 (3) 4/78 (5)
5/105 (6) 6/141 (7)

K. W. Hogg, P. J. Martin and J. Wood did not bat.

Bowling: Kirtley 9–0–36–1; Martin-Jenkins 9–2–19–1; Taylor 9–1–25–1; Yardy 7–1–36–3; Davis 6.5–0–34–0.

Umpires: N. J. Llong and P. Willey.

LANCASHIRE v MIDDLESEX

At Manchester, May 26. No result (abandoned).

LANCASHIRE v GLOUCESTERSHIRE

At Manchester, June 4 (day/night). Gloucestershire won by 79 runs. Toss: Gloucestershire.

Gloucestershire amassed their biggest League total against Lancashire with solid contributions all down the order. Barnett led the way and Harvey provided acceleration, but Martin bowled with admirable economy and Wood continued his purple patch with a one-day best of five for 49. Gloucestershire's bowlers all exerted pressure and Lancashire were soon floundering on 45 for four. Law and Lloyd restored some respectability before the end, but Gloucestershire were too strong.

Gloucestershire

C. M. Spearman c Martin b Wood	25	
K. J. Barnett c Hegg b Martin	66	
C. G. Taylor lbw b Wood	22	
I. J. Harvey c Hegg b Martin	47	
†R. C. Russell c Lloyd b Flintoff	14	
M. G. N. Windows b Wood	34	
*M. W. Alleyne c Lloyd b Wood	33	
J. N. Snape c Hegg b Wood	6	

M. A. Hardinges not out	10	
J. M. M. Averis not out	1	
L-b 4, w 5, n-b 2	11	

1/60 (1) 2/93 (3)   (8 wkts, 45 overs) 269
3/165 (4) 4/166 (2)
5/180 (5) 6/230 (6)
7/246 (8) 8/261 (7)

J. Lewis did not bat.

Bowling: Martin 9–1–28–2; Chapple 7–0–65–0; Flintoff 9–0–56–1; Wood 9–0–49–5; Hogg 8–0–40–0; Schofield 3–0–27–0.

Lancashire

N. H. Fairbrother lbw b Harvey	14
M. J. Chilton lbw b Harvey	10
G. Chapple b Lewis	10
S. G. Law b Alleyne	39
A. Flintoff c Barnett b Hardinges	1
G. D. Lloyd c Alleyne b Averis	41
*†W. K. Hegg c Taylor b Alleyne	8
C. P. Schofield c Harvey b Averis	20
K. W. Hogg st Russell b Snape	24

J. Wood lbw b Snape	13
P. J. Martin not out	2
L-b 2, w 2, n-b 4	8

1/18 (1) 2/35 (3) 3/43 (2)   (41 overs) 190
4/45 (5) 5/102 (4)
6/114 (7) 7/142 (8)
8/149 (6) 9/181 (9) 10/190 (10)

Bowling: Lewis 9–0–33–1; Harvey 5–1–24–2; Hardinges 7–0–34–1; Averis 7–0–41–2; Alleyne 5–0–17–2; Snape 8–0–39–2.

Umpires: M. R. Benson and M. J. Harris.

At Ilford, June 16. LANCASHIRE lost to ESSEX by seven wickets.

At Derby, June 23. LANCASHIRE lost to DERBYSHIRE by seven wickets.

LANCASHIRE v SURREY

At Manchester, June 30. No result. Toss: Surrey.
    There was time for a typically thumping innings from Brown, who hit seven fours and a six in his half-century, before the rain came.

Surrey

I. J. Ward c Lloyd b Martin	5
A. D. Brown b Chapple	56
M. R. Ramprakash not out	39
R. Clarke st Hegg b Chilton	28
N. Shahid not out	11
L-b 7, w 4, n-b 2	13

1/36 (1) 2/79 (2)   (3 wkts, 31 overs) 152
3/131 (4)

*A. J. Hollioake, †J. N. Batty, I. D. K. Salisbury, Saqlain Mushtaq, J. Ormond and E. S. H. Giddins did not bat.

Bowling: Martin 6–0–26–1; Chapple 6–0–43–1; Wood 4–0–16–0; Driver 8–0–21–0; Schofield 5–0–26–0; Chilton 2–0–13–1.

Lancashire

M. J. Chilton, A. J. Swann, D. Byas, N. H. Fairbrother, G. D. Lloyd, *†W. K. Hegg, R. C. Driver, C. P. Schofield, G. Chapple, J. Wood and P. J. Martin.

Umpires: D. J. Constant and M. Dixon.

At Northampton, July 7. LANCASHIRE lost to NORTHAMPTONSHIRE by 62 runs.

Ponting alarmed drinkers in the Gabba bar by launching a six on to its glass roof.
Australia v South Africa, page 1373

LANCASHIRE v DERBYSHIRE

At Blackpool, July 14. Lancashire won by one wicket. Toss: Derbyshire.

Lancashire began this game on the back of a dismal run of 12 matches without a win in all cricket, yet squeaked home by the narrowest of margins. They had slumped to 82 for six, with Fairbrother run out after a misunderstanding with Byas. However, Byas made amends during his crucial stand with Yates. At the fall of the eighth wicket Lancashire were still 27 short, and there were nervous moments before Martin edged the winning runs.

Derbyshire

S. D. Stubbings c Byas b Hogg	39	K. J. Dean b Wood		9
A. I. Gait c Byas b Martin	0	L. J. Wharton not out		3
G. Welch lbw b Wood	4			
M. J. Di Venuto lbw b Martin	1	B 8, l-b 11, w 12		31
*D. G. Cork b Hogg	11			
S. A. Selwood run out	52	1/1 (2) 2/17 (3) 3/22 (4)	(44.5 overs)	169
M. P. Dowman c Byas b Yates	1	4/62 (5) 5/89 (1) 6/95 (7)		
†L. D. Sutton c Hegg b Hogg	5	7/102 (8) 8/136 (9)		
J. I. D. Kerr c Fairbrother b Wood	13	9/154 (10) 10/169 (6)		

Bowling: Martin 8.5–2–27–2; Wood 9–0–36–3; Hogg 9–0–20–3; Driver 9–1–40–0; Yates 9–1–27–1.

Lancashire

M. J. Chilton b Cork	0	J. Wood not out		12
A. J. Swann lbw b Dean	2	P. J. Martin not out		4
D. Byas lbw b Cork	78			
N. H. Fairbrother run out	0	L-b 3, w 11, n-b 4		18
G. D. Lloyd c Sutton b Dean	11			
R. C. Driver c Di Venuto b Welch	0	1/1 (1) 2/13 (2)	(9 wkts, 40.4 overs)	170
*†W. K. Hegg lbw b Welch	1	3/14 (4) 4/37 (5)		
G. Yates lbw b Wharton	32	5/80 (6) 6/82 (7)		
K. W. Hogg b Kerr	12	7/137 (3) 8/143 (8) 9/166 (9)		

Bowling: Cork 9–0–30–2; Dean 8–1–31–2; Welch 9–1–44–2; Kerr 6.4–0–30–1; Dowman 2–0–14–0; Wharton 6–1–18–1.

Umpires: G. I. Burgess and K. E. Palmer.

At Southampton, July 23 (day/night). LANCASHIRE beat HAMPSHIRE by 16 runs.

At Bristol, August 3. LANCASHIRE lost to GLOUCESTERSHIRE by five wickets.

LANCASHIRE v HAMPSHIRE

At Manchester, August 6 (day/night). Lancashire won by four wickets. Toss: Hampshire. First-team debut: S. I. Mahmood.

Law made his third successive League fifty – with a little help from television. On 23, he edged Tremlett to first slip where Johnson, eyes shut, snapped up what appeared to be a catch and instinctively threw the ball into the air. Law walked but, halfway to the pavilion, the slow-motion replay revealed the ball had bounced and Hampshire called him back. Law and Chilton then knocked off the bulk of the target, and Hegg hammered the winning boundary with two balls to go.

Hampshire

N. C. Johnson c Hegg b Wood	7	C. T. Tremlett run out	18
J. S. Laney lbw b Anderson	71	A. D. Mullally not out	0
J. D. Francis c Hegg b Chapple	3	B 2, l-b 7, w 6	15
S. D. Udal run out	8		
L. R. Prittipaul b Anderson	0	1/22 (1) 2/25 (3)	(8 wkts, 45 overs) 188
†N. Pothas c Hegg b Anderson	6	3/34 (4) 4/34 (5)	
*W. S. Kendall run out	33	5/60 (6) 6/118 (7)	
A. D. Mascarenhas not out	27	7/146 (2) 8/187 (9)	

J. A. Tomlinson did not bat.

Bowling: Chapple 9–1–27–1; Wood 9–0–42–1; Anderson 9–2–42–3; Mahmood 8–0–31–0; Yates 9–0–32–0; Chilton 1–0–5–0.

Lancashire

D. Byas c Kendall b Mascarenhas	1	G. Yates not out	7
M. J. Chilton c Johnson b Tomlinson	66		
S. G. Law run out	64	L-b 3, w 6	9
N. H. Fairbrother c Kendall b Udal	0		
G. D. Lloyd lbw b Tremlett	10	1/4 (1) 2/120 (3)	(6 wkts, 44.4 overs) 189
G. Chapple b Tomlinson	20	3/125 (4) 4/142 (5)	
*†W. K. Hegg not out	12	5/153 (2) 6/171 (6)	

J. Wood, J. M. Anderson and S. I. Mahmood did not bat.

Bowling: Mullally 8–0–29–0; Mascarenhas 9–0–38–1; Tremlett 7–2–21–1; Tomlinson 8.4–1–37–2; Udal 9–0–46–1; Prittipaul 3–0–15–0.

Umpires: I. J. Gould and A. A. Jones.

At Hove, August 20 (day/night). LANCASHIRE beat SUSSEX by four wickets.

LANCASHIRE v ESSEX

At Manchester, September 1. Essex won by seven wickets. Toss: Essex.

Irani returned to his former stamping ground, and celebrated his call-up for the Oval Test squad with two early wickets. It put Lancashire in an early stranglehold and Essex never relinquished their grip. Only Law, awarded his first-team cap earlier, and some late-order defiance gave Lancashire's total a gloss of respectability. Essex marched home with nearly 11 overs to spare, stomping on any Lancashire promotion hopes.

Lancashire

M. J. Chilton c Jefferson b Irani	16	P. J. Martin not out	23
A. J. Swann c Jefferson b Irani	8	G. Keedy not out	10
D. Byas lbw b Dakin	7		
*S. G. Law c Jefferson b Middlebrook	36	B 4, l-b 4, w 6	14
C. P. Schofield lbw b Dakin	7		
G. Chapple b Napier	5	1/13 (2) 2/26 (3)	(9 wkts, 45 overs) 153
†J. J. Haynes c Flower b Napier	2	3/32 (1) 4/43 (5)	
K. W. Hogg c Stephenson b Middlebrook	23	5/49 (6) 6/55 (7)	
J. Wood b Middlebrook	2	7/105 (4) 8/113 (9) 9/116 (8)	

Bowling: Irani 9–1–35–2; Dakin 7–0–32–2; Napier 5–1–14–2; Grant 5–1–16–0; Stephenson 4–0–22–0; Middlebrook 9–2–14–3; Grayson 6–0–12–0.

Essex

D. D. J. Robinson c Byas b Keedy	54
W. I. Jefferson lbw b Chapple	10
J. P. Stephenson run out	35
†A. Flower not out	37
*R. C. Irani not out	12
L-b 3, w 1, n-b 2	6

1/16 (2) 2/98 (1)   (3 wkts, 34.1 overs) 154
3/116 (3)

M. L. Pettini, A. P. Grayson, J. M. Dakin, G. R. Napier, J. D. Middlebrook and J. B. Grant did not bat.

Bowling: Martin 7–0–27–0; Chapple 5–0–15–1; Hogg 5–0–17–0; Schofield 7.1–1–28–0; Keedy 7–0–50–1; Wood 3–0–14–0.

Umpires: V. A. Holder and R. Palmer.

LANCASHIRE v NORTHAMPTONSHIRE

At Manchester, September 8. Lancashire won by 97 runs. Toss: Northamptonshire.
Lancashire's last home match ended on a high note. There were emotional farewells for Fairbrother and Lloyd, who were both retiring, plus a storming innings from Law, the captain for the day. He and Chilton added a marvellous 185 – Lancashire's League-best for the second wicket. Brilliant catching from Lloyd and Haynes, deputising for Hegg, kept Northamptonshire on the rack. Martin again bowled with pace and bounce in an incisive spell to cap a memorable day for Lancashire.

Lancashire

D. Byas c Brown b Greenidge	7	G. Chapple not out	10
M. J. Chilton c Sales b Brown	61	L-b 3, w 1	4
*S. G. Law c Brophy b Penberthy	133		
C. P. Schofield b Cook	33	1/10 (1) 2/195 (2) (5 wkts, 45 overs) 270	
N. H. Fairbrother c Sales b Inness	10	3/213 (3) 4/230 (5)	
G. D. Lloyd not out	12	5/253 (4)	

†J. J. Haynes, K. W. Hogg, J. Wood and P. J. Martin did not bat.

Bowling: Greenidge 8–0–55–1; Inness 9–0–46–1; Penberthy 6–0–36–1; Cassar 4–0–19–0; Cook 8–0–47–1; Brown 9–0–45–1; White 1–0–19–0.

Northamptonshire

G. P. Swann c Haynes b Martin	19	M. W. H. Inness c Law b Schofield	1
R. A. White c Lloyd b Martin	18	J. F. Brown st Haynes b Law	16
D. J. Sales c Martin b Law	41		
M. E. Cassar c Haynes b Martin	3	L-b 1, w 6, n-b 2	9
J. W. Cook b Hogg	16		
*A. L. Penberthy lbw b Hogg	0	1/32 (2) 2/42 (1) 3/47 (4) (41.2 overs) 173	
G. L. Brophy c Haynes b Schofield	6	4/74 (5) 5/74 (6) 6/84 (7)	
†T. M. B. Bailey not out	44	7/122 (3) 8/125 (9)	
C. G. Greenidge c Haynes b Law	0	9/140 (10) 10/173 (11)	

Bowling: Chapple 5–0–33–0; Martin 7–1–18–3; Wood 7–0–26–0; Hogg 5–0–16–2; Schofield 9–0–38–2; Law 8.2–0–41–3.

Umpires: G. I. Burgess and T. E. Jesty.

At Shenley Park, September 15. LANCASHIRE beat MIDDLESEX by six wickets.

MIDDLESEX

At Northampton, May 19. MIDDLESEX lost to NORTHAMPTONSHIRE by six wickets.

At Manchester, May 26. MIDDLESEX v LANCASHIRE. No result (abandoned).

MIDDLESEX v HAMPSHIRE

At Lord's, June 4. Hampshire won by two runs. Toss: Middlesex.

Middlesex's middle order let a winning position slip away. Disciplined bowling supported by keen, aggressive fielding had restricted Hampshire to a modest total and, after Strauss and Koenig struck 69 off 18 overs, it should have been straightforward. But Hutton, Shah and Weekes were all guilty of playing poor strokes, and 14 off the last over proved just beyond Nash.

Hampshire

J. R. C. Hamblin c Nash b Bloomfield	8	S. D. Udal c Bloomfield b Weekes		9
N. C. Johnson lbw b Abdul Razzaq	26	C. T. Tremlett not out		5
D. A. Kenway lbw b Bloomfield	13	L-b 9, w 3		12
J. P. Crawley c Hutton b Abdul Razzaq	31			
G. W. White lbw b Keegan	25	1/8 (1) 2/34 (3)	(8 wkts, 45 overs)	183
†N. Pothas not out	39	3/72 (2) 4/94 (4)		
*W. S. Kendall lbw b Abdul Razzaq	13	5/130 (5) 6/154 (7)		
A. D. Mascarenhas b Weekes	2	7/163 (8) 8/173 (9)		

A. D. Mullally did not bat.

Bowling: Bloomfield 9–0–36–2; Keegan 9–0–30–1; Cook 9–1–41–0; Abdul Razzaq 9–1–25–3; Weekes 9–0–42–2.

Middlesex

*A. J. Strauss c Pothas b Tremlett	35	C. B. Keegan run out		1
S. G. Koenig lbw b Udal	24	T. F. Bloomfield not out		0
B. L. Hutton c Mascarenhas b Johnson	9			
O. A. Shah c Hamblin b Udal	26	B 7, l-b 4, w 7		18
Abdul Razzaq b Johnson	14			
E. C. Joyce lbw b Udal	3	1/69 (2) 2/69 (1)	(9 wkts, 45 overs)	181
P. N. Weekes c Udal b Mullally	4	3/91 (3) 4/120 (5)		
S. J. Cook run out	17	5/123 (6) 6/130 (4)		
†D. C. Nash not out	30	7/131 (7) 8/168 (8) 9/173 (10)		

Bowling: Mascarenhas 9–2–32–0; Mullally 9–0–30–1; Tremlett 9–0–38–1; Udal 9–1–35–3; Johnson 9–0–35–2.

Umpires: J. W. Holder and M. J. Kitchen.

MIDDLESEX v SUSSEX

At Lord's, June 9. No result. Toss: Middlesex.

A grey morning and a poor forecast brought what was believed to be the smallest attendance ever seen for a Sunday League match at Lord's. Play started on time but, 20 minutes and 32 balls later, rain sent the players to the pavilion. Unfortunately, Weekes had chosen this as his benefit game.

Sussex

R. R. Montgomerie not out 12
M. H. Yardy lbw b Keegan 0
M. W. Goodwin not out. 13

1/3 (2)   (1 wkt, 5.2 overs) 25

W. J. House, R. S. C. Martin-Jenkins, B. Zuiderent, K. J. Innes, †M. J. Prior, M. J. G. Davis, *R. J. Kirtley and B. V. Taylor did not bat.

Bowling: Keegan 3–0–11–1; Laraman 2.2–0–14–0.

Middlesex

*A. J. Strauss, S. G. Koenig, O. A. Shah, Abdul Razzaq, E. C. Joyce, B. L. Hutton, P. N. Weekes, S. J. Cook, †D. C. Nash, A. W. Laraman and C. B. Keegan.

Umpires: N. A. Mallender and J. F. Steele.

At Bristol, June 16. MIDDLESEX lost to GLOUCESTERSHIRE by five wickets.

At Arundel, June 30. MIDDLESEX beat SUSSEX by eight wickets.

MIDDLESEX v SURREY

At Southgate, July 7. Surrey won by eight wickets (D/L method). Toss: Surrey.

A brief rain break early in Middlesex's innings reduced the match to 42 overs. Middlesex began badly, limping to 130 for six, and only some late aggression from Shah boosted them to a defendable 194. But Surrey's reply was never in trouble. Ramprakash was unruffled by boos and shouts of "Judas" from the Middlesex crowd, and he and Clarke put on a jaunty 121 to guide Surrey home with ten balls to spare.

Middlesex

*A. J. Strauss c Batty b Murtagh	9	A. W. Laraman not out 8
†D. Alleyne lbw b Murtagh	0	P. N. Weekes not out. 4
S. G. Koenig c Hollioake b Murtagh . . .	16	
E. C. Joyce c Clarke b Ratcliffe	31	L-b 5, w 7 12
O. A. Shah b Clarke	74	
Abdul Razzaq c Batty b Saqlain Mushtaq	3	1/6 (2) 2/22 (1) (8 wkts, 42 overs) 194
J. W. M. Dalrymple c Murtagh		3/34 (3) 4/89 (4)
b Ratcliffe .	16	5/95 (6) 6/130 (7)
S. J. Cook b Giddins	21	7/178 (5) 8/190 (8)

I. Jones did not bat.

Bowling: Giddins 8–1–22–1; Murtagh 9–0–38–3; Clarke 5–0–30–1; Saqlain Mushtaq 8–0–33–1; Ratcliffe 9–0–41–2; Hollioake 3–0–25–0.

Surrey

I. J. Ward c Abdul Razzaq b Cook	....	30
A. D. Brown c Strauss b Jones	....	6
M. R. Ramprakash not out	....	87
R. Clarke not out	....	62
L-b 6, w 2, n-b 4	....	12

1/21 (2) 2/76 (1)   (2 wkts, 40.2 overs) 197

N. Shahid, *A. J. Hollioake, J. D. Ratcliffe, †J. N. Batty, Saqlain Mushtaq, T. J. Murtagh and E. S. H. Giddins did not bat.

Bowling: Jones 8–0–37–1; Laraman 8–0–30–0; Cook 9–0–48–1; Abdul Razzaq 8.2–1–47–0; Weekes 7–0–29–0.

Umpires: A. Clarkson and B. Dudleston.

MIDDLESEX v GLOUCESTERSHIRE

At Southgate, July 14. Gloucestershire won by 78 runs. Toss: Middlesex.

Spearman and Alleyne blasted Gloucestershire to a daunting total that proved well beyond Middlesex's grasping hands. Crucially, Joyce spilled a straightforward chance at square leg when Spearman was on 17. Strauss started Middlesex's reply briskly with 15 off eight balls, but they were undone by outstanding catching – most memorably a brilliantly judged one-handed effort at long leg by Harvey. There was no coming back, as Middlesex were again unable to translate their Championship form to one-day cricket.

Gloucestershire

C. M. Spearman c Shah b Dalrymple	..	78	M. C. J. Ball not out	....	17
K. J. Barnett c Nash b Jones	....	2	†R. C. Russell not out	....	0
I. J. Harvey c Coleman b Laraman	....	1	L-b 2, w 5, n-b 2	....	9
T. H. C. Hancock c Dalrymple b Weekes		22			
*M. W. Alleyne c Joyce b Weekes	....	93	1/3 (2) 2/9 (3) (7 wkts, 45 overs) 272		
A. P. R. Gidman b Cook	....	48	3/103 (4) 4/115 (1)		
M. A. Hardinges c Shah b Cook	....	2	5/229 (6) 6/245 (7) 7/270 (5)		

J. M. M. Averis and A. M. Smith did not bat.

Bowling: Laraman 9–2–48–1; Jones 9–1–47–1; Weekes 9–0–48–2; Cook 9–0–63–2; Dalrymple 6–0–33–1; Coleman 3–0–31–0.

Middlesex

*A. J. Strauss c Russell b Averis	......	15	S. J. Cook c Spearman b Ball	....	2
A. W. Laraman c Hancock b Averis	....	28	A. J. Coleman not out	....	14
S. G. Koenig c Russell b Averis	....	4	L-b 1, w 12, n-b 2	....	15
O. A. Shah c Harvey b Smith	....	2			
E. C. Joyce c Averis b Alleyne	....	19	1/26 (1) 2/32 (3) (8 wkts, 45 overs) 194		
J. W. M. Dalrymple c Barnett b Harvey	.	19	3/49 (4) 4/56 (2)		
P. N. Weekes not out	....	53	5/95 (6) 6/106 (5)		
†D. C. Nash st Russell b Ball	....	16	7/137 (8) 8/144 (9)		

I. Jones did not bat.

Bowling: Smith 6–1–31–1; Averis 9–1–44–3; Hardinges 8–0–36–0; Harvey 8–0–34–1; Ball 9–1–24–2; Alleyne 5–0–24–1.

Umpires: V. A. Holder and J. F. Steele.

At Chelmsford, July 22 (day/night). MIDDLESEX beat ESSEX by 41 runs.

MIDDLESEX v ESSEX

At Lord's, August 4. Middlesex won by two wickets (D/L method). Toss: Middlesex.

Torrential rain at the end of Essex's innings meant Middlesex were set 77 off 10 overs. Shah rose to the challenge with a brief but blazing 25 off 16 balls, and was aided by the scampering Laraman and Dalrymple. Three runs were still needed off the last two deliveries, and Weekes kept his head to smash the winning four off the penultimate ball. The thrilling finish rather overshadowed Jefferson's mature century – the sole highlight of the Essex batting.

Essex

D. D. J. Robinson c Dalrymple b Keegan	8
W. I. Jefferson not out	111
†A. Flower c Weekes b Keegan	1
*R. C. Irani c Joyce b Abdul Razzaq	28
M. L. Pettini c Nash b Abdul Razzaq	0
G. R. Napier c and b Weekes	12
R. S. Bopara run out	0
A. P. Cowan b Dalrymple	2
J. D. Middlebrook run out	10
J. E. Bishop not out	6
L-b 5, w 11	16

A. C. McGarry did not bat.

1/10 (1) 2/12 (3) (8 wkts, 41.5 overs) 194
3/79 (4) 4/79 (5)
5/122 (6) 6/122 (7)
7/131 (8) 8/167 (9)

Bowling: Keegan 9–0–42–2; Laraman 9–2–34–0; Abdul Razzaq 7.5–0–51–2; Cook 5–0–25–0; Weekes 7–0–25–1; Dalrymple 4–0–12–1.

Middlesex

Abdul Razzaq b Cowan	4
A. W. Laraman b Napier	11
O. A. Shah c and b Napier	25
J. W. M. Dalrymple b Middlebrook	16
S. J. Cook c Flower b Napier	0
E. C. Joyce b Middlebrook	8
*A. J. Strauss b Cowan	5
P. N. Weekes not out	5
S. G. Koenig run out	0
C. B. Keegan not out	0
L-b 3	3

†D. C. Nash did not bat.

1/5 (1) 2/39 (2) (8 wkts, 9.5 overs) 77
3/41 (2) 4/41 (5)
5/66 (6) 6/69 (4)
7/73 (7) 8/73 (9)

Bowling: Irani 2–0–9–0; Cowan 1.5–0–8–2; Bishop 2–0–26–0; McGarry 1–0–16–0; Napier 2–0–10–3; Middlebrook 1–0–5–2.

Umpires: J. H. Evans and M. J. Kitchen.

At Whitgift School, August 6. MIDDLESEX beat SURREY by 65 runs.

MIDDLESEX v NORTHAMPTONSHIRE

At Lord's, August 11. Northamptonshire won by 214 runs. Toss: Middlesex.

A rock-solid century from Hussey formed the backbone of Northamptonshire's imposing total, and Cook added some fireworks with his 37-ball 61. Any hopes of a successful Middlesex chase were dashed when the openers fell without a run on the board. Thereafter it was a lemming-like procession as Middlesex completely disintegrated. Cousins, grabbing his one-day best of five for 22, was their main tormentor as Northamptonshire completed a crushing win.

Northamptonshire

*M. E. K. Hussey b Keegan	. . . .	110	
M. B. Loye c and b Weekes	. . . .	56	
D. J. Sales c Alleyne b Hutton	. . . . . .	7	
M. E. Cassar c Bloomfield b Hutton	. .	38	
J. W. Cook c Bloomfield b Keegan	. . .	61	
A. L. Penberthy b Weekes	. . . .	2	
G. P. Swann c Shah b Weekes	. . . . . .	0	

†T. M. B. Bailey not out	 6
M. J. Cawdron not out	 0
L-b 4, n-b 2	 6

1/125 (2) 2/134 (3) (7 wkts, 45 overs) 286
3/194 (4) 4/274 (1)
5/277 (6) 6/277 (7) 7/280 (5)

D. M. Cousins and J. F. Brown did not bat.

Bowling: Bloomfield 6–0–43–0; Keegan 9–1–51–2; Jones 6–0–37–0; Weekes 8–0–44–3; Hutton 9–0–48–2; Dalrymple 7–0–59–0.

Middlesex

*A. J. Strauss b Cousins	. . . .	0
B. L. Hutton c Sales b Cawdron	. . . .	0
M. J. Brown c Hussey b Brown	. . . .	18
O. A. Shah c Swann b Cousins	. . . . . .	5
E. C. Joyce c and b Cousins	. . . .	5
P. N. Weekes b Cousins	. . . .	9
J. W. M. Dalrymple c Bailey b Cousins	.	2
†D. Alleyne lbw b Penberthy	. . . .	12

C. B. Keegan not out	 7
I. Jones run out	 6
T. F. Bloomfield lbw b Penberthy	. . . 5
W 3	3

1/0 (1) 2/0 (2) 3/6 (4) (24 overs) 72
4/17 (5) 5/36 (6) 6/38 (7)
7/50 (3) 8/54 (8) 9/60 (10) 10/72 (11)

Bowling: Cousins 7–2–22–5; Cawdron 7–0–18–1; Brown 5–1–15–1; Penberthy 5–0–17–2.

Umpires: G. I. Burgess and B. Leadbeater.

MIDDLESEX v DERBYSHIRE

At Lord's, August 25. Derbyshire won by 32 runs. Toss: Derbyshire.

Di Venuto won more booty during the last part of a smash-and-grab visit to Lord's, following up his two centuries in the Championship match with a destructive 94. Strong support from Dumelow helped add 98 for the second wicket. Cork bowled superbly, conceding only eight runs in his first seven overs, and despite an impressive 70 by Strauss, Middlesex never looked like achieving their target. This was umpire Ken Palmer's last day at Lord's, and the players formed a guard of honour as he left the field.

Derbyshire

M. J. Di Venuto c and b Dalrymple	. . . .	94	
C. W. G. Bassano c Hutton b Jones	. . . .	11	
N. R. C. Dumelow c Dalrymple			
		b Weekes	. 47
S. D. Stubbings b Dalrymple	. . . .	13	
*D. G. Cork c and b Hutton	. . . .	19	
S. A. Selwood c and b Weekes	. . . . . .	17	
M. P. Dowman not out	. . . .	20	
J. I. D. Kerr b Hutton	. . . .	8	

†L. D. Sutton c Jones b Keegan	 8
G. Welch not out	 6
B 1, l-b 4, w 3	 8

1/32 (2) 2/130 (3) (8 wkts, 45 overs) 243
3/163 (4) 4/172 (1)
5/205 (6) 6/205 (5)
7/205 (8) 8/226 (9)

L. J. Wharton did not bat.

Bowling: Keegan 7–0–49–1; Jones 4–0–29–1; Hunt 4–0–27–0; Hutton 7–0–34–2; Weekes 9–1–37–2; Dalrymple 9–0–42–2; Compton 5–0–20–0.

Middlesex

*A. J. Strauss b Wharton	70	N. R. D. Compton not out	22
B. L. Hutton c Sutton b Cork	11		
O. A. Shah st Sutton b Wharton	17	L-b 6, w 5, n-b 2	13
E. C. Joyce run out	1		
J. W. M. Dalrymple b Welch	39	1/51 (2) 2/100 (3) (6 wkts, 45 overs) 211	
P. N. Weekes run out	6	3/106 (4) 4/109 (1)	
†D. C. Nash not out	32	5/121 (6) 6/173 (5)	

C. B. Keegan, I. Jones and T. A. Hunt did not bat.

Bowling: Cork 9–2–16–1; Welch 9–0–67–1; Kerr 9–0–38–0; Wharton 9–0–38–2; Dumelow 4–0–27–0; Dowman 5–0–19–0.

Umpires: K. E. Palmer and R. Palmer.

At Southampton, September 1. MIDDLESEX lost to HAMPSHIRE by 24 runs.

MIDDLESEX v LANCASHIRE

At Shenley Park, September 15. Lancashire won by six wickets. Toss: Lancashire. First-team debut: T. M. Rees.

This was a day for nostalgia buffs, with three descendants of famous players taking part – Nick Compton and Ben Hutton (grandsons of Denis and Len) for Middlesex, and Kyle Hogg (grandson of Sonny Ramadhin) for Lancashire. In fact, it was Compton, with his highest county score, and Hutton who rescued Middlesex from a perilous position, both exhibiting a pleasing range of classical shots as they added 142, a League record for the sixth wicket. But Chilton's determination and an enterprising fifty by Schofield meant Lancashire reached their target with ease.

Middlesex

R. M. S. Weston c Rees b Anderson	21	B. L. Hutton not out	71
*S. G. Koenig c Schofield b Wood	2	L-b 4, w 3, n-b 2	9
P. N. Weekes c Hegg b Hogg	1		
N. R. D. Compton not out	86	1/12 (2) 2/24 (3) (5 wkts, 45 overs) 198	
E. C. Joyce c Anderson b Schofield	3	3/28 (1) 4/41 (5)	
J. W. M. Dalrymple lbw b Anderson	5	5/56 (6)	

†D. Alleyne, S. J. Cook, T. F. Bloomfield and C. B. Keegan did not bat.

Bowling: Chapple 9–1–31–0; Wood 9–1–41–1; Hogg 9–2–37–1; Anderson 9–1–41–2; Schofield 9–0–44–1.

Lancashire

D. Byas b Bloomfield	11	T. M. Rees not out	7
M. J. Chilton not out	84	L-b 5, w 3	8
S. G. Law c Joyce b Bloomfield	12		
C. P. Schofield c Alleyne b Cook	52	1/18 (1) 2/32 (3) (4 wkts, 40.4 overs) 199	
A. J. Swann lbw b Cook	25	3/131 (4) 4/179 (5)	

*†W. K. Hegg, G. Chapple, K. W. Hogg, J. Wood and J. M. Anderson did not bat.

Bowling: Bloomfield 9–0–27–2; Keegan 9–1–37–0; Hutton 4–0–23–0; Dalrymple 4–0–36–0; Cook 9–0–32–2; Weekes 5.4–0–39–0.

Umpires: B. Dudleston and G. Sharp.

At Derby, September 22. MIDDLESEX lost to DERBYSHIRE by 22 runs.

NORTHAMPTONSHIRE

NORTHAMPTONSHIRE v MIDDLESEX

At Northampton, May 19. Northamptonshire won by six wickets. Toss: Northamptonshire. County debut: Abdul Razzaq.

Middlesex never fully recovered from losing Strauss to the first ball of the match, and only Shah made headway against a disciplined Northamptonshire attack. Cousins was outstanding, claiming a wicket in each of his first three overs, while Bailey kept impressively. Abdul Razzaq, making his first appearance for Middlesex, beat Loye for pace, but Hussey and Sales repaired the damage with a century stand, and Northamptonshire breezed home.

Middlesex

*A. J. Strauss c Bailey b Cousins	0		†D. Alleyne not out		1
S. G. Koenig c Bailey b Cousins	5		T. F. Bloomfield b Cousins		1
Abdul Razzaq lbw b Cousins	4				
O. A. Shah c Bailey b Penberthy	48		L-b 15, w 8, n-b 2		25
E. C. Joyce c Greenidge b Penberthy	12				
B. L. Hutton c Bailey b Swann	10		1/0 (1) 2/4 (3) 3/10 (2)	(40.2 overs)	146
P. N. Weekes c Penberthy b Greenidge	21		4/73 (5) 5/94 (4) 6/96 (6)		
S. J. Cook b Greenidge	16		7/136 (7) 8/143 (8)		
A. W. Laraman c Bailey b Blain	3		9/145 (9) 10/146 (11)		

Bowling: Cousins 6.2–2–13–4; Blain 9–0–42–1; Greenidge 7–0–26–2; Penberthy 9–1–17–2; Swann 9–0–33–1.

Northamptonshire

*M. E. K. Hussey c Joyce b Weekes	56		A. L. Penberthy not out		6
G. P. Swann c Cook b Bloomfield	9		L-b 1, w 3		4
M. B. Loye b Abdul Razzaq	0				
D. J. Sales c Weekes b Cook	66		1/18 (2) 2/22 (3)	(4 wkts, 31.3 overs)	149
R. J. Warren not out	8		3/131 (1) 4/135 (4)		

J. W. Cook, †T. M. B. Bailey, C. G. Greenidge, D. M. Cousins and J. A. R. Blain did not bat.

Bowling: Abdul Razzaq 9–0–45–1; Bloomfield 6–0–36–1; Cook 9–2–34–1; Laraman 2–0–5–0; Hutton 1–0–10–0; Weekes 4.3–1–18–1.

Umpires: A. Clarkson and A. G. T. Whitehead.

NORTHAMPTONSHIRE v SURREY

At Northampton, June 4. Northamptonshire won by five runs. Toss: Northamptonshire.

After a remarkable fightback, Northamptonshire snatched back a match they looked doomed to lose. Surrey, chasing 230, smashed 68 off the first eight overs, courtesy of Ward and Brown. During his 55, Brown passed 5,000 League runs. The Northamptonshire bowlers then recovered from their collective bout of shell shock and picked up regular wickets, despite strong resistance from the highly promising Clarke. Surrey needed six off the final over, but Greenidge trapped Saqlain with the second ball. Northamptonshire were indebted to a sturdy hundred stand by their openers.

Northamptonshire

*M. E. K. Hussey b Giddins	69	R. S. G. Anderson not out	1
M. B. Loye b Bicknell	86		
D. J. Sales lbw b Giddins	0	L-b 4, w 3, n-b 2	9
R. J. Warren c and b Salisbury	17		
J. W. Cook b Salisbury	1	1/127 (1) 2/127 (3) (6 wkts, 45 overs) 229	
A. L. Penberthy run out	38	3/158 (4) 4/160 (5)	
†T. M. B. Bailey not out	8	5/208 (2) 6/224 (6)	

C. G. Greenidge, D. M. Cousins and J. F. Brown did not bat.

Bowling: Bicknell 9–0–47–1; Giddins 9–1–35–2; Clarke 3–0–29–0; Tudor 9–0–46–0; Saqlain Mushtaq 8–0–33–0; Salisbury 7–0–35–2.

Surrey

*I. J. Ward c Hussey b Penberthy	25	Saqlain Mushtaq lbw b Greenidge	0
A. D. Brown c Hussey b Anderson	55	E. S. H. Giddins not out	5
M. R. Ramprakash c Cousins b Anderson	44		
†A. J. Stewart c Penberthy b Anderson	5	L-b 4, w 14	18
N. Shahid st Bailey b Brown	2		
R. Clarke c Cook b Greenidge	52	1/68 (1) 2/84 (2) 3/112 (4) (44.2 overs) 224	
A. J. Tudor c Bailey b Cook	4	4/117 (5) 5/180 (3)	
M. P. Bicknell c Hussey b Cousins	8	6/188 (7) 7/203 (8)	
I. D. K. Salisbury b Greenidge	6	8/215 (6) 9/215 (10) 10/224 (9)	

Bowling: Cousins 9–0–54–1; Greenidge 5.2–0–49–3; Penberthy 9–0–27–1; Anderson 7–0–30–3; Brown 9–0–35–1; Cook 5–0–25–1.

Umpires: N. J. Llong and G. Sharp.

NORTHAMPTONSHIRE v GLOUCESTERSHIRE

At Northampton, June 9. No result (abandoned).

At Derby, June 16. NORTHAMPTONSHIRE lost to DERBYSHIRE by three wickets.

NORTHAMPTONSHIRE v LANCASHIRE

At Northampton, July 7. Northamptonshire won by 62 runs. Toss: Lancashire.

Much interest centred on the personal contest between the Swann brothers – Alec, released by Northamptonshire at the end of the previous season, and Graeme. The former battled to hold Lancashire together with a patient innings, but they fell well short of their target. Northamptonshire had accelerated to perfection, piling on 228 in their last 30 overs. Cook struck four sixes and nine fours in his spectacular century – the first for Northamptonshire in the League since 1998 – before rounding off a good day at the office with three wickets.

Northamptonshire

*M. E. K. Hussey c Schofield b Chapple	12	C. G. Greenidge run out	0
M. B. Loye c Hegg b Wood	11		
D. J. Sales lbw b Schofield	64	L-b 7, w 12	19
D. E. Paynter c Wood b Schofield	11		
J. W. Cook b Wood	102	1/24 (1) 2/24 (2) (8 wkts, 45 overs) 261	
A. L. Penberthy not out	38	3/48 (4) 4/157 (3)	
G. P. Swann b Wood	3	5/252 (5) 6/256 (7)	
†T. M. B. Bailey c Chilton b Martin	1	7/259 (8) 8/261 (9)	

D. M. Cousins and J. F. Brown did not bat.

Bowling: Martin 9–2–27–1; Chapple 5.2–2–17–1; Wood 9–2–40–3; Chilton 3.4–0–27–0; Driver 7–0–50–0; Schofield 8–0–60–2; Fairbrother 2–0–17–0; Swann 1–0–16–0.

Lancashire

M. J. Chilton st Bailey b Brown	34	G. Chapple not out	11
A. J. Swann run out	61	P. J. Martin b Cook	8
D. Byas run out	16		
G. D. Lloyd lbw b Swann	12	L-b 4, w 4, n-b 2	10
N. H. Fairbrother c Greenidge b Paynter	3		
*†W. K. Hegg b Swann	28	1/68 (1) 2/101 (3) (41.2 overs) 199	
C. P. Schofield c Penberthy b Cook	9	3/116 (4) 4/131 (5)	
R. C. Driver st Bailey b Swann	5	5/161 (6) 6/166 (2) 7/170 (7)	
J. Wood st Bailey b Cook	2	8/175 (9) 9/181 (8) 10/199 (11)	

Bowling: Cousins 5–0–9–0; Greenidge 7–0–43–0; Penberthy 9–1–27–0; Brown 9–1–30–1; Swann 7–0–43–3; Paynter 2–0–27–1; Cook 2.2–0–16–3.

Umpires: J. H. Hampshire and T. E. Jesty.

At Hove, July 14. NORTHAMPTONSHIRE lost to SUSSEX by 38 runs.

NORTHAMPTONSHIRE v DERBYSHIRE

At Northampton, July 24 (day/night). Northamptonshire won by seven wickets. Toss: Derbyshire. Northamptonshire climbed to second place in Division Two after an undramatic victory. Derbyshire, without Cork, Di Venuto and Welch, failed to muster a competitive total against some pinpoint bowling. Slapdash running didn't help, and only Kerr showed much flair. Loye and Hussey launched the reply by hammering 20 off the first two overs, and Northamptonshire wrapped up their win in quick time.

Derbyshire

S. D. Stubbings c Sales b Greenidge	2	K. J. Dean c Swann b Greenidge	2
A. I. Gait c Bailey b Greenidge	23	L. J. Wharton run out	0
C. W. G. Bassano lbw b Penberthy	11		
S. A. Selwood c Hussey b Penberthy	11	B 1, l-b 8, w 9	18
*M. P. Dowman c Bailey b Cook	16		
†L. D. Sutton run out	1	1/19 (1) 2/35 (2) 3/52 (4) (43.5 overs) 143	
J. I. D. Kerr run out	45	4/57 (3) 5/63 (6) 6/102 (5)	
T. Lungley not out	12	7/135 (7) 8/140 (9)	
Mohammad Ali run out	2	9/143 (10) 10/143 (11)	

Bowling: Cousins 7–1–23–0; Greenidge 8–2–22–3; Penberthy 9–3–16–2; Brown 9–2–29–0; Cook 5–0–26–1; Swann 5.5–0–18–0.

Northamptonshire

*M. E. K. Hussey not out	72
M. B. Loye c Stubbings b Dean	31
D. J. Sales c Selwood b Kerr	4
G. L. Brophy c Sutton b Mohammad Ali	0
J. W. Cook not out	37
W 4	4

1/53 (2) 2/86 (3) (3 wkts, 27.5 overs) 146
3/88 (4)

A. L. Penberthy, G. P. Swann, †T. M. B. Bailey, C. G. Greenidge, D. M. Cousins and J. F. Brown did not bat.

Bowling: Dean 6–0–39–1; Lungley 5–0–28–0; Mohammad Ali 5–0–24–1; Kerr 5–0–25–1; Wharton 3.5–0–21–0; Dowman 3–1–9–0.

Umpires: M. J. Kitchen and J. F. Steele.

At Whitgift School, August 3. NORTHAMPTONSHIRE beat SURREY by 102 runs (D/L method).

NORTHAMPTONSHIRE v HAMPSHIRE

At Northampton, August 4. Northamptonshire won by 16 runs (D/L method). Toss: Northamptonshire.

Hampshire crashed 19 runs off the first two overs, but that was as good as things got for them. Already without Smith, through chicken-pox, the batting struggled with only Crawley and Pothas offering resistance. Cousins made the early incisions, backed by the impressively economical Brown. The match had originally been reduced to 42 overs and Northamptonshire were well ahead on the Duckworth/Lewis calculation when another downpour prevented any further play.

Hampshire

N. C. Johnson c Bailey b Cousins	14	A. D. Mullally b Swann ... 1
J. S. Laney lbw b Cousins	6	J. A. Tomlinson b Cook ... 1
A. D. Mascarenhas lbw b Cousins	0	
J. P. Crawley st Bailey b Brown	33	L-b 4, w 6, n-b 2 ... 12
J. D. Francis run out	11	
†N. Pothas not out	34	(41.3 overs) 133
L. R. Prittipaul c Hussey b Penberthy	5	1/19 (2) 2/19 (4) 3/32 (1)
*W. S. Kendall b Swann	14	4/72 (5) 5/74 (4) 6/90 (7)
S. D. Udal c Loye b Cook	2	7/115 (8) 8/118 (9)
		9/128 (10) 10/133 (11)

Bowling: Cousins 9–1–36–3; Cawdron 6–1–28–0; Penberthy 9–3–17–1; Brown 8–1–16–1; Cook 5.3–0–17–2; Swann 4–0–15–2.

Northamptonshire

*M. E. K. Hussey not out	18
M. B. Loye not out	31
W 1, n-b 2	3
(no wkt, 14.4 overs)	52

D. J. Sales, M. E. Cassar, J. W. Cook, A. L. Penberthy, G. P. Swann, †T. M. B. Bailey, M. J. Cawdron, D. M. Cousins and J. F. Brown did not bat.

Bowling: Mullally 7–2–21–0; Mascarenhas 6–1–21–0; Tomlinson 1.4–0–10–0.

Umpires: J. H. Hampshire and M. J. Harris.

At Lord's, August 11. NORTHAMPTONSHIRE beat MIDDLESEX by 214 runs.

At Bristol, August 13 (day/night). NORTHAMPTONSHIRE lost to GLOUCESTERSHIRE by 55 runs.

At Colchester, August 25. NORTHAMPTONSHIRE lost to ESSEX by four wickets.

NORTHAMPTONSHIRE v SUSSEX

At Northampton, September 1. Sussex won by six wickets. Toss: Sussex.

Northamptonshire's promotion hopes suffered a heavy blow as bottom-placed Sussex triumphed with some ease. The main talking point in the stands was Loye's bizarrely turgid innings: he managed only six runs in 50 balls. He later announced his intention to leave Northamptonshire at the end of the season, but strenuously denied that this had been a protest against the club. Sales and Cook failed to convert promising starts into substantial scores, and Sussex were driven home by Adams and Ambrose, who cracked 63 in just eight overs. Although named in the home side, Brown took no part in the match after his wife was taken ill.

Northamptonshire

M. B. Loye run out	6	C. G. Greenidge c Davis b Taylor	20
R. A. White c Davis b Kirtley	17	M. W. H. Inness not out	2
D. J. Sales c Goodwin b Innes	36	L-b 3, w 7, n-b 4	14
M. E. Cassar c Carpenter b Taylor.	18		
J. W. Cook c Ambrose b Kirtley	32	1/18 (2) 2/58 (3) (8 wkts, 45 overs) 195
*A. L. Penberthy c Goodwin b Davis. . .	15	3/67 (1) 4/108 (5)	
G. P. Swann c House b Martin-Jenkins. .	1	5/128 (6) 6/129 (7)	
†T. M. B. Bailey not out	34	7/143 (4) 8/190 (9)	
J. F. Brown did not bat.			

Bowling: Kirtley 9–3–32–2; Martin-Jenkins 9–2–29–1; Taylor 9–1–49–2; Innes 9–0–44–1; Davis 9–0–38–1.

Sussex

B. Zuiderent lbw b Cook	39	†T. R. Ambrose not out	33
J. R. Carpenter b Greenidge	8	L-b 3, w 9, n-b 2	14
M. W. Goodwin b White	38		
*C. J. Adams not out	64	1/16 (2) 2/73 (1) (4 wkts, 43.4 overs) 197
W. J. House lbw b White	1	3/128 (3) 4/134 (5)	

R. S. C. Martin-Jenkins, K. J. Innes, M. J. G. Davis, R. J. Kirtley and B. V. Taylor did not bat.

Bowling: Inness 9–1–25–0; Greenidge 8.4–0–34–1; Cassar 5–0–30–0; Penberthy 9–0–42–0; Cook 7–0–45–1; White 5–0–18–2.

Umpires: B. Dudleston and T. E. Jesty.

At Manchester, September 8. NORTHAMPTONSHIRE lost to LANCASHIRE by 97 runs.

NORTHAMPTONSHIRE v ESSEX

At Northampton, September 15. Essex won by 42 runs. Toss: Essex.

This was a vital match for both sides – victory for Essex would secure promotion, while Northamptonshire needed to win to keep alive their own dreams of Division One. Essex's hulking opener, Jefferson, played the decisive innings, hitting 13 fours in a flowing 102, though he was well supported by the purposeful Habib. Northamptonshire's early batting fell apart, leaving Penberthy and Brophy to try and repair the damage. They didn't manage it. This was Northamptonshire's fifth successive defeat and it ensured another season in Division Two.

Essex

D. D. J. Robinson b Greenidge	1	A. P. Cowan not out	9
W. I. Jefferson c Brophy b Inness . . . 102		J. D. Middlebrook not out	0
J. P. Stephenson lbw b Cassar.	24		
M. E. Waugh b Brown	26	L-b 7, w 4	11
A. Habib b Inness	46		
J. M. Dakin run out	14	1/20 (1) 2/87 (3) (9 wkts, 45 overs) 258
*A. P. Grayson b Cook	10	3/117 (4) 4/199 (2)	
G. R. Napier b Cook	10	5/211 (5) 6/226 (6)	
†J. S. Foster b Greenidge	5	7/240 (8) 8/245 (9) 9/258 (7)	

Bowling: Greenidge 9–1–39–2; Inness 9–0–48–2; Cassar 5–0–32–1; Penberthy 9–0–43–0; Brown 8–0–50–1; Cook 5–0–39–2.

Northamptonshire

R. A. White c and b Cowan	5	
M. J. Powell c Cowan b Dakin	2	
D. J. Sales c Foster b Napier	19	
J. W. Cook lbw b Middlebrook	22	
*A. L. Penberthy c Habib b Napier	54	
M. E. Cassar c Cowan b Middlebrook	10	
G. L. Brophy st Foster b Grayson	54	
†T. M. B. Bailey b Stephenson	27	
C. G. Greenidge c Foster b Stephenson	10	

M. W. H. Inness b Grayson 1
J. F. Brown not out 0

L-b 6, w 4, n-b 2 12

1/4 (2) 2/13 (1) 3/46 (3)   (43.1 overs) 216
4/62 (4) 5/80 (6) 6/151 (5)
7/188 (7) 8/215 (9)
9/216 (8) 10/216 (10)

Bowling: Cowan 5.4–1–15–1; Dakin 7–1–27–1; Napier 8–0–50–2; Middlebrook 9–0–35–2; Stephenson 9–0–49–2; Grayson 4.3–0–34–2.

Umpires: J. H. Evans and K. E. Palmer.

At Southampton, September 22. NORTHAMPTONSHIRE lost to HAMPSHIRE by six wickets.

SURREY

SURREY v LANCASHIRE

At The Oval, May 12. Surrey won by six wickets. Toss: Lancashire.

The only thing lightning-like about Lancashire was the speed of their collapse. Under heavy clouds, Bicknell and Giddins swung the ball both ways, their team-mates caught everything going, and Lancashire equalled their lowest total in League cricket. Surrey knocked off the runs in fewer than 12 overs, and it was all over by 4.18.

Lancashire

M. J. Chilton lbw b Bicknell	10	
G. Chapple c Stewart b Giddins	0	
D. Byas c Stewart b Giddins	13	
S. G. Law c Carberry b Bicknell	3	
A. Flintoff c Stewart b Bicknell	3	
G. D. Lloyd c Stewart b Bicknell	1	
T. W. Roberts c Carberry b Bicknell	0	
*†W. K. Hegg c and b Sampson	17	

C. P. Schofield c Shahid b Sampson.... 5
K. W. Hogg not out 3
P. J. Martin c Stewart b Azhar Mahmood 0
L-b 6, w 5, n-b 2 13

1/4 (2) 2/31 (1) 3/33 (3)   (20.4 overs) 68
4/36 (5) 5/39 (4) 6/40 (7)
7/41 (6) 8/49 (9) 9/65 (8) 10/68 (11)

Bowling: Bicknell 9–2–26–5; Giddins 6–2–8–2; Sampson 4–0–18–2; Azhar Mahmood 1.4–0–10–1.

Surrey

*I. J. Ward lbw b Martin	6	
A. D. Brown c Chilton b Martin	8	
M. R. Ramprakash not out	18	
†A. J. Stewart run out	11	
N. Shahid c Byas b Hogg	9	

M. A. Carberry not out 4
L-b 4, w 7, n-b 2 13

1/11 (2) 2/19 (1)   (4 wkts, 11.5 overs) 69
3/50 (4) 4/61 (5)

Azhar Mahmood, M. P. Bicknell, P. J. Sampson, A. J. Tudor and E. S. H. Giddins did not bat.

Bowling: Chapple 5–0–23–0; Martin 4–0–24–2; Hogg 1.5–0–14–1; Flintoff 1–0–4–0.

Umpires: V. A. Holder and T. E. Jesty.

At Bristol, May 19. SURREY lost to GLOUCESTERSHIRE by one wicket.

At Northampton, June 4. SURREY lost to NORTHAMPTONSHIRE by five runs.

At Southampton, June 16. SURREY beat HAMPSHIRE by three wickets.

SURREY v SUSSEX

At The Oval, June 23. Surrey won by six wickets. Toss: Sussex.

Surrey's win came at a cost: Bicknell, starting his sixth over, stumbled in his follow-through and fell heavily. X-rays later revealed a severe wrist fracture, which would keep him out for nearly eight weeks. Giddins found late swing to take a one-day best of five for 20, and though Martin-Jenkins reached a plucky half-century – full of upright straight drives – Sussex's total was below par. After a sticky start Surrey needed 74 from 17 overs, but Hollioake and Shahid had dug them out of worse holes before, and they managed it again.

Sussex

M. H. Yardy c Batty b Giddins	21	
*R. R. Montgomerie c Batty b Giddins .	2	
M. W. Goodwin lbw b Giddins	0	
W. J. House c Salisbury b Giddins	7	
R. S. C. Martin-Jenkins c Clarke		
b Hollioake	50	
B. Zuiderent b Giddins	0	
†M. J. Prior c and b Clarke	10	
K. J. Innes lbw b Hollioake	22	

M. J. G. Davis b Saqlain Mushtaq	6
B. V. Taylor c sub b Clarke	16
M. A. Robinson not out	7
L-b 5, w 2, n-b 2	9
	150

1/12 (2) 2/12 (3)   (43.1 overs) 150
3/27 (4) 4/40 (1)
5/40 (6) 6/53 (7) 7/106 (8)
8/115 (9) 9/137 (10) 10/150 (5)

Bowling: Bicknell 5.1–1–16–0; Giddins 9–1–20–5; Clarke 8.5–0–38–2; Salisbury 5–0–24–0; Saqlain Mushtaq 9–1–32–1; Hollioake 6.1–0–15–2.

Surrey

I. J. Ward b Davis	23	
A. D. Brown c and b Taylor	11	
M. R. Ramprakash c Montgomerie		
b Robinson .	10	
R. Clarke st Prior b Innes	13	
N. Shahid not out.	50	

*A. J. Hollioake not out	42
B 1, l-b 1, w 1	3
	152

1/19 (2) 2/45 (1)   (4 wkts, 38.5 overs) 152
3/45 (3) 4/77 (4)

†J. N. Batty, I. D. K. Salisbury, Saqlain Mushtaq, M. P. Bicknell and E. S. H. Giddins did not bat.

Bowling: Martin-Jenkins 8.5–0–25–0; Taylor 7–0–23–1; Robinson 8–2–55–1; Davis 9–1–19–1; Innes 6–1–28–1.

Umpires: V. A. Holder and A. G. T. Whitehead.

At Manchester, June 30. SURREY v LANCASHIRE. No result.

At Southgate, July 7. SURREY beat MIDDLESEX by eight wickets (D/L method).

Her attacking leg-spin bowling, with its tantalising flight and variations of off-breaks, top-spin and an occasional googly, brought selection for Victoria at 15 and soon led her to be dubbed "the girl Grimmett".
Obituary of Peggy Antonio, page 1613

SURREY v ESSEX

At Guildford, July 28. Surrey won by 73 runs. Toss: Essex.

Free-flowing batting from Ward and Ramprakash helped Surrey amass the highest League total of the season in Division Two. Ratcliffe also waded in, smashing 53 off 31 balls, before taking four vital wickets in Essex's reply. Flower and the promising Pettini played with aggressive intent, until both fell to Ratcliffe. The Essex innings was interrupted when the Surrey coach Keith Medlycott came on to the field to inform Clarke that his father had been taken to hospital with a heart problem. Happily, all proved well, and Clarke returned later to see Surrey complete their win.

Surrey

I. J. Ward c Pettini b Phillips	62	I. D. K. Salisbury not out		19
A. D. Brown b Irani	15	A. J. Tudor not out		1
M. R. Ramprakash c Jefferson b Cowan	74			
R. Clarke c Phillips b Cowan	23	L-b 7, w 12, n-b 4		23
N. Shahid c Flower b Dakin	34			
*A. J. Hollioake c Middlebrook		1/43 (2) 2/120 (1)	(7 wkts, 45 overs)	310
b Stephenson	6	3/178 (4) 4/195 (3)		
J. D. Ratcliffe c Robinson b Cowan	53	5/214 (6) 6/278 (5) 7/302 (7)		

†J. N. Batty and T. J. Murtagh did not bat.

Bowling: Irani 9–0–49–1; Cowan 9–0–57–3; Dakin 3–0–32–1; McGarry 9–0–74–0; Stephenson 5–0–34–1; Phillips 5–0–27–1; Middlebrook 5–0–30–0.

Essex

D. D. J. Robinson b Murtagh	26	T. J. Phillips not out		1
J. M. Dakin c and b Clarke	38	A. C. McGarry st Batty b Salisbury		1
W. I. Jefferson b Murtagh	23			
†A. Flower c Murtagh b Ratcliffe	50	B 6, l-b 6, w 3		15
*R. C. Irani c Ward b Salisbury	1			
M. L. Pettini b Ratcliffe	51	1/42 (1) 2/86 (3) 3/90 (2)	(40.1 overs)	237
A. P. Cowan c Hollioake b Ratcliffe	21	4/95 (5) 5/194 (6) 6/224 (7)		
J. D. Middlebrook st Batty b Salisbury	5	7/224 (4) 8/235 (8)		
J. P. Stephenson c Ramprakash b Ratcliffe	5	9/235 (9) 10/237 (11)		

Bowling: Tudor 7–1–43–0; Murtagh 9–0–41–2; Clarke 5–1–26–1; Salisbury 7.1–0–44–3; Ratcliffe 8–0–44–4; Hollioake 4–0–27–0.

Umpires: J. W. Lloyds and K. E. Palmer.

SURREY v NORTHAMPTONSHIRE

At Whitgift School, August 3. Northamptonshire won by 102 runs (D/L method). Toss: Northamptonshire. First-team debuts: J. G. E. Benning, D. J. Miller, S. A. Newman, B. J. M. Scott.

Surrey's first team were stranded in Yorkshire, waiting to play their ill-fated C&G semi-final, so Salisbury took charge of a motley crew. As well as four debutants, there were recalls for two golden oldies, David Ward and Gary Butcher, plus a rare appearance for Rupesh Amin. Unsurprisingly they lost, but there was glory for Ward in front of the Whitgift schoolboys he now teaches. Six years and six days after his last League appearance – and brandishing a bat he had christened "The Blade of Thrappington" – he thumped a belligerent 78 off 52 balls and reminded an enthusiastic crowd what an entertainer he still is. Earlier, Loye's marvellous hundred and quickfire fifties from Cassar and Sales had ensured a huge Northamptonshire total.

Northamptonshire

*M. E. K. Hussey b Butcher	18	G. P. Swann not out	9
M. B. Loye not out.	101	L-b 7, w 9	16
D. J. Sales c Ward b Benning	67		
M. E. Cassar c Salisbury b Sampson . .	54	1/55 (1) 2/179 (3) (5 wkts, 40 overs) 277
J. W. Cook b Butcher	0	3/249 (4) 4/249 (5)
A. L. Penberthy b Benning.	12	5/267 (6)

†T. M. B. Bailey, C. G. Greenidge, D. M. Cousins and J. F. Brown did not bat.

Bowling: Sampson 9–0–45–1; Miller 7–0–32–0; Butcher 7–0–49–2; Benning 7–0–58–2; Amin 3–0–33–0; Salisbury 7–0–53–0.

Surrey

D. M. Ward c Cousins b Brown	78	D. J. Miller b Swann.	1
S. A. Newman c Bailey b Penberthy . . .	30	R. M. Amin not out	0
M. A. Carberry c Bailey b Brown	19		
†J. N. Batty c Penberthy b Brown	3	L-b 4, w 3	7
J. G. E. Benning b Cook	10		
*I. D. K. Salisbury b Cook	0	1/89 (2) 2/125 (1) 3/135 (4) (27 overs) 162
G. P. Butcher c Cousins b Swann	9	4/136 (3) 5/137 (6) 6/152 (5)
B. J. M. Scott c Loye b Swann	4	7/158 (7) 8/160 (9)
P. J. Sampson b Cook	1	9/162 (8) 10/162 (10)

Bowling: Cousins 4–0–33–0; Greenidge 5–0–40–0; Penberthy 6–0–31–1; Brown 6–1–30–3; Cook 3–0–8–3; Swann 3–0–16–3.

Umpires: I. J. Gould and J. W. Lloyds.

SURREY v MIDDLESEX

At Whitgift School, August 6. Middlesex won by 65 runs. Toss: Surrey.

Surrey's established stars returned but fared little better than their stand-ins in the previous match. Shah was imperious with a sparkling hundred, including four towering sixes and eight fours. Strauss gave him fine support as Middlesex piled on a substantial total. Surrey only came close thanks to a thunderous onslaught from Brown. He hammered 94 off 63 balls, with one of his sixes crashing onto a marquee table, smashing glasses and scattering guests. However, Brown's electrifying effort wasn't enough, and after his dismissal Surrey soon folded.

Middlesex

*A. J. Strauss run out	74	S. J. Cook c Murtagh b Hollioake	11
A. W. Laraman lbw b Giddins	7	†D. C. Nash not out	10
S. G. Koenig c Saqlain Mushtaq			
b Murtagh .	9	B 4, l-b 3, w 6, n-b 4	17
O. A. Shah c Brown b Giddins	110		
E. C. Joyce c Hollioake		1/35 (2) 2/60 (3) (8 wkts, 45 overs) 274
b Saqlain Mushtaq .	15	3/150 (1) 4/194 (5)
P. N. Weekes c Brown b Hollioake . . .	20	5/248 (4) 6/251 (7)
J. W. M. Dalrymple c Brown b Giddins .	1	7/252 (6) 8/274 (8)

I. Jones and C. B. Keegan did not bat.

Bowling: Giddins 9–0–56–3; Murtagh 9–2–26–1; Sampson 4–0–37–0; Clarke 6–0–48–0; Saqlain Mushtaq 9–0–44–1; Hollioake 8–0–56–2.

Surrey

I. J. Ward lbw b Laraman	4	P. J. Sampson b Jones	16
A. D. Brown c Koenig b Weekes	94	E. S. H. Giddins not out	4
M. R. Ramprakash run out	10		
R. Clarke c Keegan b Laraman	10	B 2, l-b 3, w 5, n-b 2	12
N. Shahid run out	6		
*A. J. Hollioake b Dalrymple	15	1/4 (1) 2/27 (3) 3/64 (4) (38.1 overs) 209
†J. N. Batty c and b Weekes	19	4/130 (5) 5/135 (2)
Saqlain Mushtaq c Shah b Weekes	16	6/152 (6) 7/176 (7)
T. J. Murtagh b Dalrymple	3	8/183 (9) 9/187 (8) 10/209 (10)

Bowling: Laraman 7–0–51–2; Keegan 7–0–55–0; Cook 5–0–26–0; Jones 2.1–0–11–1; Weekes 9–1–32–3; Dalrymple 8–1–29–2.

Umpires: D. J. Constant and M. J. Harris.

At Hove, August 7 (day/night). SURREY beat SUSSEX by six wickets.

SURREY v DERBYSHIRE

At The Oval, August 18. Derbyshire won by four wickets. Toss: Surrey.

Surrey's third League defeat in four matches put them under pressure as the promotion race intensified. They had set off at a gallop, with Dean's opening two overs disappearing for 34 and Brown and Ward racing along at nine an over. But, once again, Surrey's impetus faded when Brown departed. With the honourable exception of Ramprakash, who compiled 78, Surrey played as if determined to embrace defeat. In the field they spurned four catches and a run-out chance, and another mature innings by Selwood took Derbyshire to the cusp of victory.

Surrey

I. J. Ward c Krikken b Cork	31	M. P. Bicknell b Kerr	2
A. D. Brown lbw b Cork	19	T. J. Murtagh b Kerr	8
M. R. Ramprakash c Stubbings		E. S. H. Giddins not out	0
b Lungley	78	L-b 4, w 9	13
S. A. Newman c Krikken b Lungley	4		
†A. J. Stewart st Krikken b Dean	11	1/45 (2) 2/65 (1) 3/78 (4) (44.4 overs) 190
N. Shahid b Kerr	1	4/104 (5) 5/107 (6)
*A. J. Hollioake b Dowman	21	6/148 (7) 7/154 (8)
I. D. K. Salisbury b Dowman	2	8/167 (9) 9/181 (10) 10/190 (3)

Bowling: Cork 9–1–33–2; Dean 9–0–62–1; Welch 7–0–16–0; Lungley 6.4–0–29–2; Kerr 9–0–27–3; Dowman 4–0–19–2.

Derbyshire

M. J. Di Venuto c Ramprakash b Bicknell	5	G. Welch not out	0
C. W. G. Bassano b Giddins	19		
S. D. Stubbings c Stewart b Murtagh	26	L-b 11, w 12, n-b 2	25
*D. G. Cork b Brown b Murtagh	32		
S. A. Selwood c Salisbury b Bicknell	50	1/17 (1) 2/38 (2) (6 wkts, 38.5 overs) 193
M. P. Dowman st Stewart b Salisbury	2	3/79 (3) 4/120 (4)
J. I. D. Kerr not out	34	5/128 (6) 6/189 (5)

†K. M. Krikken, T. Lungley and K. J. Dean did not bat.

Bowling: Bicknell 9–0–57–2; Giddins 7–0–34–1; Murtagh 9–1–38–2; Salisbury 9–0–36–1; Hollioake 4.5–0–17–0.

Umpires: B. Dudleston and I. J. Gould.

SURREY v HAMPSHIRE

At The Oval, August 21 (day/night). Surrey won by 70 runs. Toss: Surrey.

Surrey finally rediscovered winning ways, as Hollioake's five-wicket haul ensured an early night. All their batsmen played a part, with Brown's attractive 40-ball cameo catching the eye. Hampshire glided along in reply, but ran out of steam once Hollioake got his hands on the ball. The match was more day/dusk than day/night, after Lambeth Council asked Surrey to begin the game an hour earlier so as to minimise any nuisance the floodlights might cause residents.

Surrey

I. J. Ward c Johnson b Mascarenhas	38	M. P. Bicknell b Mascarenhas		3
A. D. Brown c Adams b Hamblin	49	T. J. Murtagh c Johnson b Mascarenhas		6
M. R. Ramprakash c Mascarenhas		E. S. H. Giddins not out		1
b Johnson	50			
S. A. Newman c Laney b Johnson	37	L-b 3, w 7		10
Mushtaq Ahmed c Mascarenhas				
b Johnson	16	1/76 (1) 2/98 (2) 3/180 (4) (44.5 overs)		262
*A. J. Hollioake c Adams b Prittipaul	18	4/187 (3) 5/200 (5)		
N. Shahid c Francis b Mascarenhas	32	6/248 (6) 7/250 (7)		
†J. N. Batty b Tomlinson	2	8/254 (8) 9/261 (9) 10/262 (10)		

Bowling: Mascarenhas 8.5–0–45–4; Tomlinson 8–0–53–1; Hamblin 5–0–34–1; Prittipaul 8–0–44–1; Udal 9–0–41–0; Johnson 6–0–42–3.

Hampshire

N. C. Johnson b Murtagh	44	†N. Pothas not out		20
J. S. Laney run out	25	L. R. Prittipaul b Hollioake		7
J. R. C. Hamblin run out	13	J. A. Tomlinson b Murtagh		6
J. D. Francis c and b Hollioake	10	B 6, l-b 14, w 6		26
*W. S. Kendall c Brown				
b Mushtaq Ahmed	25	1/64 (2) 2/89 (1) 3/92 (3) (41.3 overs)		192
J. H. K. Adams c and b Hollioake	8	4/109 (4) 5/142 (5)		
S. D. Udal b Hollioake	6	6/152 (6) 7/156 (8)		
A. D. Mascarenhas b Hollioake	2	8/157 (7) 9/175 (10) 10/192 (11)		

Bowling: Bicknell 6–0–25–0; Giddins 7–0–32–0; Murtagh 8.3–0–40–2; Mushtaq Ahmed 9–2–19–1; Hollioake 9–0–43–5; Ramprakash 2–0–13–0.

Umpires: N. A. Mallender and A. G. T. Whitehead.

At Derby, September 2 (day/night). SURREY beat DERBYSHIRE by one wicket.

At Chelmsford, September 8. SURREY beat ESSEX by two runs.

SURREY v GLOUCESTERSHIRE

At The Oval, September 22. Surrey won by 79 runs. Toss: Surrey.

Thorpe hit his sixth League hundred, leaving England supporters confident he was in good form to tackle Australia. But within 24 hours he had executed a U-turn, and announced that he would not tour. Thorpe's stylish knock was the cornerstone of Surrey's innings, as Smith's left-arm swing posed plenty of problems. Their total proved well beyond Gloucestershire's reach. Hollioake's four wickets helped secure the runners-up spot for Surrey, who were already assured of promotion.

Surrey

I. J. Ward b Smith	17
A. D. Brown lbw b Smith	0
M. R. Ramprakash c Spearman b Smith	11
G. P. Thorpe c and b Smith	114
N. Shahid lbw b Lewis	17
*A. J. Hollioake c Windows b Angel	38
†J. N. Batty st Russell b Fisher	30
I. D. K. Salisbury c Hancock b Smith	17

Saqlain Mushtaq not out	4
T. J. Murtagh not out	1
L-b 8, w 4, n-b 2	14

1/5 (2) 2/28 (3) (8 wkts, 45 overs) 263
3/31 (1) 4/58 (5)
5/140 (6) 6/221 (7)
7/252 (8) 8/262 (4)

E. S. H. Giddins did not bat.

Bowling: Smith 9–0–30–5; Angel 9–0–47–1; Lewis 9–0–65–1; Alleyne 7–0–41–0; Fisher 9–0–50–1; Bressington 2–0–22–0.

Gloucestershire

C. M. Spearman c Shahid b Giddins	37
†R. C. Russell c Shahid b Hollioake	31
T. H. C. Hancock c Batty b Hollioake	5
M. G. N. Windows c Giddins b Saqlain Mushtaq	37
R. J. Sillence run out	11
*M. W. Alleyne c Salisbury b Hollioake	1
A. N. Bressington c Giddins b Ramprakash	22
I. D. Fisher c Giddins b Ramprakash	1

J. Angel b Giddins	2
J. Lewis c and b Hollioake	24
A. M. Smith not out	1
B 2, l-b 2, w 6, n-b 2	12

1/68 (1) 2/78 (2) 3/78 (3) (39.2 overs) 184
4/105 (5) 5/108 (6)
6/145 (4) 7/146 (8)
8/151 (9) 9/182 (10) 10/184 (7)

Bowling: Giddins 9–0–44–2; Murtagh 9–0–57–0; Hollioake 6–1–24–4; Saqlain Mushtaq 7–1–17–1; Salisbury 5–0–19–0; Ramprakash 3.2–0–19–2.

Umpires: M. R. Benson and N. J. Llong.

SUSSEX

At Derby, May 12. SUSSEX lost to DERBYSHIRE by six wickets.

At Manchester, May 19. SUSSEX lost to LANCASHIRE by four wickets.

SUSSEX v ESSEX

At Horsham, June 4. Sussex won by 32 runs. Toss: Sussex.

On a difficult batting surface, Essex were bowling Sussex out of the game before Prior punched back with a blistering 73. In reply, Davis took wickets at crucial moments to check Essex's progress. Irani and Jefferson blazed away, trying to drag Essex above the rate needed for a win under Duckworth/Lewis, although the feared abandonment never came. Creditably, the captains and umpires kept the match going through heavy rain in the last hour, as Sussex slipped and slithered to victory.

Sussex

M. H. Yardy b Irani	. . . .	18
R. R. Montgomerie c Jefferson b Clarke	. .	28
M. W. Goodwin c Robinson b Dakin	. . .	19
W. J. House lbw b Dakin	. . . .	21
R. S. C. Martin-Jenkins b Clarke	. . . . .	1
B. Zuiderent run out	. . . .	14
†M. J. Prior c Stephenson b Napier	. . . .	73
K. J. Innes not out	. . . .	41
M. J. G. Davis c Habib b Cowan	. . . . .	3

*R. J. Kirtley c Clarke b Irani	. . . .	3
B. V. Taylor c Napier b Irani	. . . .	0
B 1, l-b 9, w 9	. . . .	19

1/40 (1) 2/56 (2) 3/84 (3) (45 overs) 240
4/92 (5) 5/95 (4) 6/165 (6)
7/214 (7) 8/235 (9)
9/239 (10) 10/240 (11)

Bowling: Irani 9–1–45–3; Cowan 9–0–33–1; Dakin 9–0–41–2; Clarke 9–0–36–2; Napier 5–0–43–1; Middlebrook 4–0–32–0.

Essex

D. D. J. Robinson c Yardy b Kirtley	. . . .	0
J. M. Dakin b Kirtley	. . . .	1
G. R. Napier c Prior b Martin-Jenkins	. .	50
†A. Flower run out	. . . .	49
*R. C. Irani b Yardy	. . . .	51
A. Habib c and b Davis	. . . .	1
W. I. Jefferson c Yardy b Davis	. . . . . .	23
J. P. Stephenson b Davis	. . . .	5
A. P. Cowan not out	. . . .	9

J. D. Middlebrook run out	. . . .	3
A. J. Clarke c Innes b Taylor	. . . .	0
B 1, l-b 6, w 7, n-b 2	. . . . . .	16

1/0 (1) 2/4 (2) 3/105 (4) (40.2 overs) 208
4/119 (3) 5/120 (6)
6/176 (7) 7/191 (8)
8/193 (5) 9/206 (10) 10/208 (11)

Bowling: Kirtley 7–2–37–2; Martin-Jenkins 9–2–47–1; Taylor 7.2–2–22–1; Innes 4–0–39–0; Davis 9–1–40–3; Yardy 4–0–16–1.

Umpires: I. J. Gould and N. A. Mallender.

At Lord's, June 9. SUSSEX v MIDDLESEX. No result.

At The Oval, June 23. SUSSEX lost to SURREY by six wickets.

SUSSEX v MIDDLESEX

At Arundel, June 30. Middlesex won by eight wickets. Toss: Sussex. County debut: I. Jones. Accurate Middlesex bowling on a helpful pitch reduced Sussex's middle order to tatters. Abdul Razzaq and Weekes were the main beneficiaries as Sussex stumbled towards a paltry total. Strauss put the bowling to the sword in a short but entertaining innings, and Koenig and Shah had little trouble polishing off the runs as Sussex's attack struggled.

Sussex

R. R. Montgomerie c Shah b Jones	. . . .	1
T. R. Ambrose run out	. . . .	30
*C. J. Adams c Weekes b Jones	. . . . . .	17
M. W. Goodwin lbw b Abdul Razzaq	. .	3
W. J. House c Cook b Abdul Razzaq	. .	0
R. S. C. Martin-Jenkins c Dalrymple b Weekes	.	19
†M. J. Prior b Abdul Razzaq	. . . .	0
K. J. Innes lbw b Cook	. . . .	24

M. J. G. Davis not out	. . . .	8
B. V. Taylor c Nash b Weekes	. . . . .	1
M. A. Robinson b Weekes	. . . .	6
B 2, l-b 8, w 6	. . . .	16

1/3 (1) 2/31 (3) 3/60 (2) (41.4 overs) 125
4/60 (5) 5/61 (4)
6/63 (7) 7/87 (6)
8/112 (8) 9/115 (10) 10/125 (11)

Bowling: Keegan 9–1–26–0; Jones 9–0–32–2; Abdul Razzaq 7–2–19–3; Cook 9–2–21–1; Weekes 7.4–3–17–3.

Middlesex

*A. J. Strauss c Innes b Martin-Jenkins .	25		
D. Alleyne c Ambrose b Innes	5		
S. G. Koenig not out.	43		
O. A. Shah not out	41		
B 1, l-b 3, w 8	12		

1/34 (1) 2/42 (2)   (2 wkts, 38.5 overs) 126

Abdul Razzaq, †D. C. Nash, S. J. Cook, C. B. Keegan, P. N. Weekes, J. W. M. Dalrymple and
  I. Jones did not bat.

  Bowling: Taylor 7–1–16–0; Martin-Jenkins 9–1–22–1; Innes 7–1–27–1; Robinson 2–0–14–0;
Davis 8–2–29–0; House 5.5–0–14–0.

Umpires: N. L. Bainton and G. I. Burgess.

At Southampton, July 7. SUSSEX lost to HAMPSHIRE by 93 runs.

SUSSEX v NORTHAMPTONSHIRE

At Hove, July 14. Sussex won by 38 runs. Toss: Northamptonshire.
  This was a welcome second win for Sussex. On a bouncy pitch, Adams led the way with a
conservative 41. After Hussey and Loye made a rapid start, 186 was firmly in Northamptonshire's
cross-hairs, but Robinson and Martin-Jenkins each took two wickets in an over to peg them back.
Thereafter the run-chase faltered and Sussex never lost their grip on the game.

Sussex

W. J. House c Cook b Greenidge	26	M. H. Yardy not out	4
R. R. Montgomerie st Bailey b Brown . .	31		
T. R. Ambrose c Bailey b Cook	22	B 1, l-b 7, w 12	20
*C. J. Adams c Penberthy b Cook	41		
M. W. Goodwin c Greenidge b Brown . .	3	1/49 (1) 2/86 (2) (6 wkts, 45 overs) 185	
R. S. C. Martin-Jenkins not out	33	3/96 (3) 4/107 (5)	
†M. J. Prior run out	5	5/165 (4) 6/175 (7)	

M. J. G. Davis, B. V. Taylor and M. A. Robinson did not bat.

  Bowling: Cousins 5–0–37–0; Greenidge 7–0–22–1; Penberthy 9–0–29–0; Cook 9–0–30–2;
Brown 9–0–31–2; Swann 6–0–28–0.

Northamptonshire

*M. E. K. Hussey c Montgomerie		C. G. Greenidge lbw b House	8
b Martin-Jenkins .	27	D. M. Cousins run out	21
M. B. Loye b Robinson	23	J. F. Brown not out.	0
D. J. Sales b Martin-Jenkins	0		
D. E. Paynter c House b Taylor	18	L-b 5, w 10	15
A. L. Penberthy c Montgomerie			
b Robinson .	0	1/54 (1) 2/54 (3) 3/54 (2) (38.3 overs) 147	
G. P. Swann b Davis	18	4/54 (5) 5/91 (6) 6/102 (7)	
J. W. Cook b Adams b Taylor	6	7/106 (4) 8/117 (9)	
†T. M. B. Bailey b Davis	11	9/138 (8) 10/147 (10)	

  Bowling: Martin-Jenkins 7–2–21–2; Taylor 7–2–24–2; Robinson 8–1–38–2; Davis
7.3–0–24–2; Yardy 7–0–27–0; House 2–0–8–1.

Umpires: A. A. Jones and K. J. Lyons.

At Cheltenham, July 28. SUSSEX lost to GLOUCESTERSHIRE by six wickets.

SUSSEX v GLOUCESTERSHIRE

At Hove, August 5 (day/night). No result. Toss: Sussex.

Only ten balls of the first floodlit game of the season at Hove were possible before a torrential storm left the ground flooded.

Sussex

W. J. House not out	. . . .	0
R. R. Montgomerie not out	. . . .	2
L-b 6		6

(no wkt, 1.4 overs) 8

T. R. Ambrose, M. W. Goodwin, P. A. Cottey, †M. J. Prior, R. S. C. Martin-Jenkins, K. J. Innes, M. J. G. Davis, B. V. Taylor and *R. J. Kirtley did not bat.

Bowling: Smith 1–1–0–0; Harvey 0.4–0–2–0.

Gloucestershire

C. M. Spearman, T. H. C. Hancock, I. J. Harvey, C. G. Taylor, *M. W. Alleyne, J. N. Snape, A. P. R. Gidman, †R. C. Russell, M. C. J. Ball, J. M. M. Averis and A. M. Smith.

Umpires: N. G. Cowley and B. Leadbeater.

SUSSEX v SURREY

At Hove, August 7 (day/night). Surrey won by six wickets. Toss: Sussex.

A composed 60 by Adams, on his return from injury, and a doughty half-century from Innes revived Sussex, after Giddins had rattled his former colleagues with a new-ball burst of four for 21. Kirtley, returning to action after a broken hand, took two wickets in ten balls as Surrey's top order slumped to 25 for three. But Ramprakash and Shahid calmed nerves with a sensible fourth-wicket stand, and a fiery cameo from Holliaoke brought victory with 34 balls left.

Sussex

R. R. Montgomerie c Ward b Giddins	. .	1	K. J. Innes not out	50
*C. J. Adams c Holliaoke b Tudor	. .	60	M. J. G. Davis not out	27
M. W. Goodwin c Batty b Giddins	. . . .	3		
P. A. Cottey b Giddins	. . . .	14	L-b 9, w 8	17
†M. J. Prior b Giddins	. . . .	0		
R. S. C. Martin-Jenkins			1/3 (1) 2/13 (3) (7 wkts, 45 overs) 194	
c Saqlain Mushtaq b Murtagh	.	13	3/49 (4) 4/49 (5)	
T. R. Ambrose c Brown b Tudor	. . . . .	9	5/71 (6) 6/101 (7) 7/110 (2)	

R. J. Kirtley and B. V. Taylor did not bat.

Bowling: Tudor 9–0–32–2; Giddins 9–2–39–4; Murtagh 9–0–39–1; Saqlain Mushtaq 9–0–28–0; Clarke 4–0–14–0; Holliaoke 5–0–33–0.

Surrey

I. J. Ward lbw b Kirtley	. . . .	9	*A. J. Holliaoke not out	26
A. D. Brown c Adams b Kirtley	. . . . .	0	B 6, l-b 6, w 2	14
M. R. Ramprakash c Kirtley b Taylor	. .	60		
R. Clarke lbw b Martin-Jenkins	. . . . .	12	1/4 (2) 2/9 (1) (4 wkts, 39.2 overs) 195	
N. Shahid not out	. . . .	74	3/25 (4) 4/156 (3)	

†J. N. Batty, Saqlain Mushtaq, A. J. Tudor, T. J. Murtagh and E. S. H. Giddins did not bat.

Bowling: Martin-Jenkins 9–2–31–1; Kirtley 8.2–2–25–2; Taylor 9–0–47–1; Innes 6–0–41–0; Davis 7–0–39–0.

Umpires: R. Palmer and P. Willey.

SUSSEX v LANCASHIRE

At Hove, August 20 (day/night). Lancashire won by four wickets. Toss: Sussex.

On a slow pitch that inhibited strokeplayers on either side, Lancashire laboured their way to victory. Law and Byas put together what proved to be a match-winning stand, although it needed Schofield's unorthodox hitting at the end to see Lancashire home. Goodwin's 40, plus useful runs from the wagging tail, had given Sussex something to defend. A big crowd of around 3,500 was some consolation.

Sussex

R. R. Montgomerie c Haynes b Chapple .	11
*C. J. Adams lbw b Chapple	10
M. W. Goodwin c Haynes b Hogg	40
P. A. Cottey c Haynes b Chapple	0
W. J. House c Hogg b Wood	2
R. S. C. Martin-Jenkins c Haynes	
b Hogg	10
†M. J. Prior b Schofield	30
K. J. Innes b Martin	15

M. J. G. Davis c Martin b Keedy	18
R. J. Kirtley not out	19
B. V. Taylor b Keedy	0
L-b 9, w 5	14

1/15 (1) 2/22 (2) 3/27 (4)   (45 overs) 169
4/41 (5) 5/77 (6)
6/80 (3) 7/124 (8)
8/126 (7) 9/168 (9) 10/169 (11)

Bowling: Martin 9–1–32–1; Chapple 9–2–26–3; Wood 9–1–30–1; Hogg 6–1–22–2; Keedy 7–0–28–2; Schofield 5–0–22–1.

Lancashire

M. J. Chilton lbw b Martin-Jenkins	28
A. J. Swann lbw b Martin-Jenkins	0
D. Byas b Kirtley	35
*S. G. Law b Davis	29
C. P. Schofield b Taylor	36
G. Chapple c and b Davis	8
†J. J. Haynes not out	7

J. Wood not out	12
L-b 6, w 8, n-b 2	16

1/3 (2) 2/46 (1)   (6 wkts, 44.1 overs) 171
3/102 (4) 4/105 (3)
5/134 (6) 6/156 (5)

K. W. Hogg, G. Keedy and P. J. Martin did not bat.

Bowling: Kirtley 9–0–23–1; Martin-Jenkins 9–0–39–2; Taylor 9–0–35–1; Innes 8.1–0–34–0; Davis 9–0–34–2.

Umpires: N. G. Cowley and M. J. Harris.

At Northampton, September 1. SUSSEX beat NORTHAMPTONSHIRE by six wickets.

SUSSEX v HAMPSHIRE

At Hove, September 3 (day/night). Sussex won by seven wickets. Toss: Sussex.

Sussex won their final floodlit game comfortably. House, who had earlier announced his retirement to take up a job in the City, signed off in style with a huge six on to the pavilion roof to win the match. Innes had taken his best League return, as Hampshire's last six wickets tumbled for 15. Goodwin's classy 76 was Sussex's highest League score of the summer.

Hampshire

J. R. C. Hamblin c Innes		
b Martin-Jenkins	1	
N. C. Johnson c sub b Taylor	26	
J. S. Laney c Carpenter b Taylor	23	
J. H. K. Adams b Davis	17	
J. D. Francis b Davis	11	
*W. S. Kendall b Innes	24	
S. D. Udal c Ambrose b Innes	6	
A. D. Mascarenhas c Ambrose b Innes	0	

L. R. Prittipaul b Kirtley   1
†I. Brunnschweiler c Ambrose b Innes . .   0
J. A. Tomlinson not out   0
    B 3, l-b 4, w 6, n-b 4 17

1/2 (1) 2/56 (2) 3/58 (3)   (33 overs) 126
4/74 (5) 5/111 (4) 6/121 (6)
7/121 (8) 8/126 (7)
9/126 (10) 10/126 (9)

Bowling: Martin-Jenkins 5–0–29–1; Kirtley 6–1–27–1; Taylor 7–2–18–2; Innes 8–1–26–4; Davis 7–0–19–2.

Sussex

B. Zuiderent c Brunnschweiler
    b Mascarenhas .   0
J. R. Carpenter c Brunnschweiler
    b Mascarenhas .   3
M. W. Goodwin not out 76
*C. J. Adams lbw b Mascarenhas . 30

W. J. House not out 11

    L-b 4, w 3   7

1/0 (1) 2/5 (2)   (3 wkts, 25.1 overs) 127
3/100 (4)

†T. R. Ambrose, R. S. C. Martin-Jenkins, K. J. Innes, M. J. G. Davis, R. J. Kirtley and B. V. Taylor did not bat.

Bowling: Mascarenhas 9–3–24–3; Tomlinson 8–0–49–0; Prittipaul 4–0–14–0; Johnson 2–0–12–0; Hamblin 2–0–18–0; Adams 0.1–0–6–0.

Umpires: D. J. Constant and B. Dudleston.

SUSSEX v DERBYSHIRE

At Hove, September 15. Derbyshire won by 74 runs. Toss: Sussex.

Sussex's last home game reached a thoroughly dismal conclusion. The biggest cheer was totally unrelated to League events at Hove, coming when it was announced that results elsewhere had secured the county's place in the first division of the Championship. There certainly wasn't much to applaud on the pitch, with only Taylor exploiting helpful conditions. A target of 241 always looked beyond Sussex, who produced another inglorious batting collapse, losing their last six wickets for 11 runs in only slightly more than two overs.

Derbyshire

*M. J. Di Venuto c Martin-Jenkins
    b Taylor . 22
C. W. G. Bassano c Davis b Taylor 55
N. R. C. Dumelow b Hopkinson b Davis 13
S. A. Selwood c Adams b Robinson. . . . 16
D. R. Hewson c Cottey b Davis 32
M. P. Dowman c Taylor b Robinson . . . 26
J. I. D. Kerr b Taylor 24
G. Welch not out 13

†L. D. Sutton c Hutchison b Taylor   2
K. J. Dean not out   4

    B 4, l-b 6, w 19, n-b 4 33

1/50 (1) 2/101 (2)   (8 wkts, 45 overs) 240
3/101 (3) 4/146 (4)
5/160 (5) 6/210 (6)
7/233 (7) 8/235 (9)

L. J. Wharton did not bat.

Bowling: Hutchison 7–0–38–0; Martin-Jenkins 8–0–44–0; Taylor 9–0–39–4; Robinson 9–0–51–2; Davis 9–0–33–2; Cottey 5–0–25–0.

Sussex

R. R. Montgomerie c Kerr b Dean	. . . .	20
P. A. Cottey c Sutton b Dowman	. . . . . .	43
M. W. Goodwin b Wharton	. . . . . .	45
*C. J. Adams lbw b Dowman	. . . .	0
†T. R. Ambrose b Kerr	. . . .	9
R. S. C. Martin-Jenkins c Selwood		
b Dumelow	. . . .	32
C. D. Hopkinson c Selwood b Dumelow	.	2
M. J. G. Davis c Dowman b Wharton	. .	0

P. M. Hutchison run out	. . . .	1
B. V. Taylor c Dean b Dumelow	. . . . .	2
M. A. Robinson not out	. . . . .	2
B 3, l-b 5, n-b 2	. . . .	10

1/41 (1) 2/78 (2)   (41.4 overs) 166
3/78 (4) 4/93 (5) 5/155 (6)
6/158 (3) 7/158 (8) 8/161 (7)
9/161 (9) 10/166 (10)

Bowling: Welch 6–0–20–0; Dean 7–0–42–1; Dowman 5–0–22–2; Kerr 7–0–20–1; Wharton 9–1–30–2; Dumelow 7.4–0–24–3.

Umpires: N. G. Cowley and M. J. Kitchen.

At Chelmsford, September 22. SUSSEX lost to ESSEX by 29 runs (D/L method).

NORWICH UNION LEAGUE RECORDS

*40 overs available in all games up to 1998, except for 1993, when teams played 50 overs;
45 overs 1999–2002.*

Batting

Highest individual scores: 203, A. D. Brown, Surrey v Hampshire, Guildford, 1997; 191, D. S. Lehmann, Yorkshire v Nottinghamshire, Scarborough, 2001; 176, G. A. Gooch, Essex v Glamorgan, Southend, 1983; 175*, I. T. Botham, Somerset v Northamptonshire, Wellingborough School, 1986.

Most runs: 9,002, K. J. Barnett; 8,573, G. A. Gooch; 8,071, G. A. Hick; 7,526, C. W. J. Athey; 7,499, W. Larkins; 7,225, P. Johnson; 7,062, D. W. Randall; 7,040, D. L. Amiss; 7,031, R. J. Bailey; 6,995, N. H. Fairbrother; 6,950, M. P. Maynard; 6,793, R. A. Smith; 6,695, R. T. Robinson; 6,673, M. W. Gatting. **In a season:** 917, T. M. Moody, Worcestershire, 1991.

Most hundreds: 14, W. Larkins; 12, A. D. Brown, G. A. Gooch and G. A. Hick; 11, C. G. Greenidge; 10, T. M. Moody and R. A. Smith; 9, C. J. Adams, K. S. McEwan and B. A. Richards. 684 hundreds have been scored in the League. The most in one season is 40 in 1990.

Most sixes in an innings: 13, I. T. Botham, Somerset v Northamptonshire, Wellingborough School, 1986. **By a team in an innings:** 18, Derbyshire v Worcestershire, Knypersley, 1985, and Surrey v Yorkshire, Scarborough, 1994. **In a season:** 26, I. V. A. Richards, Somerset, 1977.

Highest total: 375 for four, Surrey v Yorkshire, Scarborough, 1994. **By a side batting second:** 317 for six, Surrey v Nottinghamshire, The Oval, 1993 (50-overs match).

Highest match aggregate: 631 for 13 wickets, Nottinghamshire (314 for seven) v Surrey (317 for six), The Oval, 1993 (50-overs match).

Lowest total: 23 (19.4 overs), Middlesex v Yorkshire, Leeds, 1974.

Shortest completed innings: 16 overs (59), Northamptonshire v Middlesex, Tring, 1974.

Record partnerships for each wicket

239	for 1st	G. A. Gooch and B. R. Hardie, Essex v Nottinghamshire at Nottingham .	1985
273	for 2nd	G. A. Gooch and K. S. McEwan, Essex v Nottinghamshire at Nottingham	1983
223	for 3rd	S. J. Cook and G. D. Rose, Somerset v Glamorgan at Neath	1990
219	for 4th	C. G. Greenidge and C. L. Smith, Hampshire v Surrey at Southampton .	1987
220*	for 5th	C. C. Lewis and P. A. Nixon, Leicestershire v Kent at Canterbury	1999
142*	for 6th	N. R. D. Compton and B. L. Hutton, Middlesex v Lancashire at Shenley	2002
164	for 7th	J. N. Snape and M. A. Hardinges, Gloucestershire v Notts at Nottingham	2001
116*	for 8th	N. D. Burns and P. A. J. DeFreitas, Leicestershire v Northants at Leicester .	2001
105	for 9th	D. G. Moir and R. W. Taylor, Derbyshire v Kent at Derby	1984
82	for 10th	G. Chapple and P. J. Martin, Lancashire v Worcestershire at Manchester .	1996

Bowling

Most wickets: 386, J. K. Lever; 368, J. E. Emburey; 346, D. L. Underwood; 307, J. Simmons; 303, S. Turner; 284, N. Gifford; 281, E. E. Hemmings; 273, R. K. Illingworth; 267, J. N. Shepherd; 261, G. C. Small; 260, A. C. S. Pigott; 256, I. T. Botham; 250, M. V. Fleming. **In a season:** 39, A. J. Hollioake, Surrey, 1996.

Best bowling: eight for 26, K. D. Boyce, Essex v Lancashire, Manchester, 1971; seven for 15, R. A. Hutton, Yorkshire v Worcestershire, Leeds, 1969; seven for 16, S. D. Thomas, Glamorgan v Surrey, Swansea, 1998; seven for 30, M. P. Bicknell, Surrey v Glamorgan, The Oval, 1999; seven for 39, A. Hodgson, Northamptonshire v Somerset, Northampton, 1976; seven for 41, A. N. Jones, Sussex v Nottinghamshire, Nottingham, 1986; six for six, R. W. Hooker, Middlesex v Surrey, Lord's, 1969; six for seven, M. Hendrick, Derbyshire v Nottinghamshire, Nottingham, 1972; six for nine, N. G. Cowans, Middlesex v Lancashire, Lord's, 1991.

Most economical analysis: 8–8–0–0, B. A. Langford, Somerset v Essex, Yeovil, 1969.

Most expensive analyses: 9–0–99–1, M. R. Strong, Northamptonshire v Gloucestershire, Cheltenham, 2001; 8–0–96–1, D. G. Cork, Derbyshire v Nottinghamshire, Nottingham, 2001; 8–0–94–2, P. N. Weekes, Middlesex v Leicestershire, Leicester, 1994; 7.5–0–89–3, G. Miller, Derbyshire v Gloucestershire, Gloucester, 1984; 8–0–88–1, E. E. Hemmings, Nottinghamshire v Somerset, Nottingham, 1983.

Hat-tricks: There have been 32 hat-tricks, four of them for Glamorgan.

Four wickets in four balls: A. Ward, Derbyshire v Sussex, Derby, 1970; V. C. Drakes, Nottinghamshire v Derbyshire, Nottingham, 1999.

Wicket-keeping and Fielding

Most dismissals: 374 (287 ct, 87 st), S. J. Rhodes; 280 (226 ct, 54 st), R. C. Russell; 268 (229 ct, 39 st), W. K. Hegg; 262 (218 ct, 44 st), R. J. Blakey; 257 (234 ct, 23 st), D. L. Bairstow; 236 (187 ct, 49 st), R. W. Taylor; 223 (184 ct, 39 st), E. W. Jones; 220 (197 ct, 23 st), S. A. Marsh. **In a season:** 32 (26 ct, 6 st), R. J. Blakey, Yorkshire, 1999. **In an innings:** 7 (6 ct, 1 st), R. W. Taylor, Derbyshire v Lancashire, Manchester, 1975.

Most catches in an innings: 6, K. Goodwin, Lancashire v Worcestershire, Worcester, 1969; R. W. Taylor, Derbyshire v Lancashire, Manchester, 1975; K. M. Krikken, Derbyshire v Hampshire, Southampton, 1994; and P. A. Nixon, Leicestershire v Essex, Leicester, 1994.

Most stumpings in an innings: 4, S. J. Rhodes, Worcestershire v Warwickshire, Birmingham, 1986, N. D. Burns, Somerset v Kent, Taunton, 1991 and R. J. Turner, Somerset v Kent, Taunton, 2002.

Most catches by a fielder: 107, K. J. Barnett; 103, V. P. Terry; 101, J. F. Steele; 100, G. A. Gooch; 98, C. J. Adams and M. P. Maynard†; 97, M. W. Alleyne† and D. P. Hughes; 95, C. W. J. Athey† and D. Byas. **In a season:** 16, J. M. Rice, Hampshire, 1978. **In an innings:** 5, J. M. Rice, Hampshire v Warwickshire, Southampton, 1978.

† C. W. J. Athey also took two catches as a wicket-keeper, M. W. Alleyne four and M. P. Maynard 11.

Results

Largest victory in runs: Somerset by 220 runs v Glamorgan, Neath, 1990.

Victories by ten wickets (34): By Derbyshire, Durham, Essex (four times), Glamorgan (twice), Hampshire (twice), Kent, Lancashire, Leicestershire (twice), Middlesex (twice), Northamptonshire, Nottinghamshire, Somerset (twice), Surrey (three times), Warwickshire (twice), Worcestershire (six times) and Yorkshire (three times).

This does not include those matches in which the side batting second was set a reduced target but does include matches where both sides faced a reduced number of overs.

Ties: There have been 58 tied matches. Worcestershire have tied 11 times.

Shortest match: 1 hr 53 min (26.3 overs), Surrey v Leicestershire, The Oval, 1996.

WINNERS 1969–2002

John Player's County League

1969	Lancashire

John Player League

1970	Lancashire
1971	Worcestershire
1972	Kent
1973	Kent
1974	Leicestershire
1975	Hampshire
1976	Kent
1977	Leicestershire
1978	Hampshire
1979	Somerset
1980	Warwickshire
1981	Essex
1982	Sussex
1983	Yorkshire

John Player Special League

1984	Essex
1985	Essex
1986	Hampshire

Refuge Assurance League

1987	Worcestershire
1988	Worcestershire
1989	Lancashire
1990	Derbyshire
1991	Nottinghamshire

Sunday League

1992	Middlesex

AXA Equity & Law League

1993	Glamorgan
1994	Warwickshire
1995	Kent
1996	Surrey

AXA Life League

1997	Warwickshire

AXA League

1998	Lancashire

CGU National League

1999	Lancashire

Norwich Union National League

2000	Gloucestershire

Norwich Union League

2001	Kent
2002	Glamorgan

There was something pre-Christian in his explanation, an echo of Greek heroes blaming the gods rather than themselves for their misfortunes.
Obituary of Hansie Cronje, page 1625

MATCH RESULTS 1969–2002

	P	W	L	T	NR	1st	2nd	3rd
			Matches				*League positions*	
Derbyshire	551	222	269	5	55	1	0	1
Durham	183	55	105	3	20	0	0	0
Essex	551	277	219	10	45	3	5*	4
Glamorgan	551	211	276	8	56	2	0	0
Gloucestershire	551	201	281	4	65	1	1	1
Hampshire	551	256	243	7	45	3	1	3
Kent	551	297	194	8	52	5	4	5
Lancashire	551	280	198	10	63	5	2	3
Leicestershire	551	242	238	5	66	2	3*	2
Middlesex	551	237	245	10	59	1	1	3
Northamptonshire	551	218	271	6	56	0	0	2
Nottinghamshire	551	233	264	4	50	1	3	1
Somerset	551	260	235	4	52	1	6*	0
Surrey	551	247	242	5	57	1	0	1
Sussex	551	234	253	6	58	1	2*	1
Warwickshire	551	244	242	7	58	3	2	3
Worcestershire	551	273	214	11	53	3	5	2
Yorkshire	551	250	248	3	50	1	2	1

* *Includes one shared 2nd place in 1976.*

COUNTY CAPS AWARDED IN 2002

Derbyshire	C. W. G. Bassano, L. D. Sutton.
Essex	A. Flower, A. Habib, W. I. Jefferson.
Glamorgan	M. S. Kasprowicz, S. P. Jones.
Gloucestershire	C. M. Spearman.
Hampshire	J. P. Crawley.
Kent	S. R. Waugh.
Lancashire	D. Byas, M. J. Chilton, S. G. Law, C. P. Schofield, A. J. Swann.
Leicestershire	M. G. Bevan, G. W. Flower, M. Kaif, J. Srinath, D. I. Stevens.
Middlesex	E. C. Joyce, S. G. Koenig.
Nottinghamshire	K. P. Pietersen, S. C. G. MacGill.
Somerset	M. P. L. Bulbeck.
Surrey	M. R. Ramprakash.
Sussex	M. J. G. Davis.
Warwickshire	A. Richardson, J. O. Troughton.
Worcestershire	G. J. Batty, M. S. Mason, S. D. Peters, B. F. Smith.

No caps were awarded by Durham, Northamptonshire or Yorkshire.

CAREER FIGURES

Players not expected to appear in county cricket in 2003.

BATTING

	M	I	NO	R	HS	100s	Avge	1,000r/ season
P. Aldred	60	81	12	806	83	0	11.68	0
A. N. Aymes	215	314	79	7,338	133	8	31.22	0
R. J. Bailey	374	628	89	21,844	224*	47	40.52	13
K. J. Barnett	479	784	76	28,593	239*	61	40.38	16
J. E. Brinkley	29	35	7	300	65	0	10.71	0
S. J. E. Brown	159	221	72	1,796	69	0	12.05	0
N. D. Burns	205	307	65	7,376	166	7	30.47	0
D. Byas	283	474	44	15,082	213	29	35.07	5
J. R. Carpenter	13	24	0	383	65	0	15.95	0
M. E. Cassar	63	98	12	2,155	121	2	25.05	0
D. N. Catterall	4	5	0	157	60	0	31.40	0
R. S. Clinton	13	23	2	525	107	1	25.00	0
C. D. Crowe	38	49	10	581	44*	0	14.89	0
J. A. Daley	94	164	13	4,272	159*	4	28.29	0
M. P. Dowman	101	178	11	4,648	149	9	27.83	1
R. C. Driver	25	43	6	686	64	0	18.54	0
C. J. Elstub.	7	9	7	34	18*	0	17.00	0
A. W. Evans	38	63	7	1,503	125	1	26.83	0
N. H. Fairbrother	366	580	80	20,612	366	47	41.22	10
M. V. Fleming	219	348	43	9,206	138	11	30.18	0
D. Follett	18	22	8	87	19	0	6.21	0
A. R. C. Fraser	290	344	82	2,934	92	0	11.19	0
B. W. Gannon	31	36	16	187	28	0	9.35	0
J. M. Golding	11	16	7	224	32	0	24.88	0
J. B. Hockley	19	30	2	423	74	0	15.10	0
B. C. Hollioake†	75	114	6	2,794	163	3	25.87	0
W. J. House	37	57	8	1,443	136	2	29.44	0
M. C. Ilott	192	245	52	2,830	60	0	14.66	0
P. Johnson	371	624	60	20,534	187	40	36.40	9
I. Jones	4	5	1	107	35	0	26.75	0
S. R. Lampitt	236	311	74	5,649	122	1	23.83	0
J. S. Laney	87	153	5	4,414	112	5	29.82	1
M. N. Lathwell	156	272	11	8,727	206	12	33.43	1
G. D. Lloyd	203	323	28	11,279	241	24	38.23	5
M. J. McCague	135	186	45	2,324	72	0	16.48	0
T. A. Munton	252	272	98	1,827	54*	0	10.50	0
K. Newell	72	123	14	2,930	135	5	26.88	0
P. R. Pollard	192	332	24	9,685	180	15	31.44	3
J. P. Pyemont	38	58	4	1,126	124	1	20.85	0
U. B. A. Rashid†	41	63	7	1,421	110	2	25.37	0
J. D. Ratcliffe	136	244	14	6,561	135	5	28.52	0
M. J. Rawnsley	46	56	9	522	39	0	11.10	0
T. W. Roberts	5	7	0	110	49	0	15.71	0
M. A. Robinson	229	259	112	590	27	0	4.01	0
A. S. Rollins	129	233	20	7,331	210	13	34.41	3
G. D. Rose	251	347	63	8,737	191	11	30.76	1
J. E. K. Schofield	4	7	3	43	21*	0	10.75	0
M. P. Smethurst	30	35	13	227	66	0	10.31	0
M. J. Symington	13	19	4	276	42	0	18.40	0
G. W. White	128	223	21	6,195	156	9	30.66	1
A. S. Wright	6	10	1	124	30	0	13.77	0

† *Hollioake died March 23, 2002; Rashid died April 1, 2002.*

BOWLING AND FIELDING

	R	W	BB	Avge	5W/i	10W/m	Ct/St
P. Aldred	4,562	132	7-101	34.56	5	1	34
A. N. Aymes	438	6	2-101	73.00	–	–	516/44
R. J. Bailey	5,144	121	5-54	42.51	2	0	272
K. J. Barnett	7,108	188	6-28	37.80	3	0	284
J. E. Brinkley	2,116	82	6-14	25.80	4	0	12
S. J. E. Brown	15,800	550	7-51	28.72	36	2	42
N. D. Burns	8	0	–	–	–	–	478/38
D. Byas	727	12	3-55	60.58	–	–	366
J. R. Carpenter	81	1	1-50	81.00	–	–	5
M. E. Cassar	2,751	91	6-34	30.23	3	1	20
D. N. Catterall	308	11	4-50	28.00	–	–	1
R. S. Clinton	30	2	2-30	15.00	–	–	4
C. D. Crowe	1,925	57	4-47	33.77	–	–	18
J. A. Daley	81	1	1-12	81.00	–	–	44
M. P. Dowman	1,394	35	4-28	39.82	–	–	56
R. C. Driver	408	14	5-70	29.14	1	–	13
C. J. Elstub	421	11	3-37	38.27	–	–	2
A. W. Evans	5	0	–	–	–	–	24
N. H. Fairbrother	500	7	2-91	71.42	–	–	290
M. V. Fleming	10,415	290	5-51	35.91	2	0	83
D. Follett	1,509	44	8-22	34.29	3	1	5
A. R. C. Fraser	24,277	886	8-53	27.40	36	5	54
B. W. Gannon	2,730	85	6-80	32.11	3	0	8
J. M. Golding	637	14	4-76	45.50	–	–	2
J. B. Hockley	233	3	1-21	77.66	–	–	9
B. C. Hollioake	4,215	126	5-51	33.45	1	0	68
W. J. House	964	4	1-34	241.00	–	–	21
M. C. Ilott	17,537	633	9-19	27.70	27	3	54
P. Johnson	617	6	1-9	102.83	–	–	236/1
I. Jones	441	10	3-72	44.10	–	–	0
S. R. Lampitt	17,224	601	7-45	28.65	20	3	148
J. S. Laney	224	2	1-24	112.00	–	–	72
M. N. Lathwell	721	13	2-21	55.46	–	–	105
G. D. Lloyd	440	2	1-4	220.00	–	–	140
M. J. McCague	12,392	456	9-86	27.17	25	2	75
T. A. Munton	19,065	737	8-89	25.86	35	6	82
K. Newell	1,023	24	4-61	42.62	–	–	25
P. R. Pollard	272	4	2-79	68.00	–	–	158
J. P. Pyemont	743	12	4-101	61.91	–	–	22
U. B. A. Rashid	2,073	49	5-103	42.30	1	0	12
J. D. Ratcliffe	911	27	6-48	33.74	1	0	68
M. J. Rawnsley	3,283	74	6-44	44.36	3	1	23
T. W. Roberts	6	0	–	–	–	–	2
M. A. Robinson	17,807	584	9-37	30.49	13	2	41
A. S. Rollins	122	1	1-19	122.00	–	–	109/1
G. D. Rose	17,963	604	7-47	29.74	15	1	117
J. E. K. Schofield	477	19	4-51	25.10	–	–	1
M. P. Smethurst	2,380	85	7-37	28.00	3	0	5
M. J. Symington	805	24	4-27	33.54	–	–	7
G. W. White	629	12	3-23	52.41	–	–	107/2

Note: A. S. Wright did not bowl and took one catch.

THE UNIVERSITIES, 2002

Loughborough remained the undisputed champions of university cricket in 2002. Fielding a side composed almost exclusively of players on the books of first-class counties, they won the traditional British Universities Championship for the third successive season, and retained their title in the second Inter-UCCE competition, part of the ECB's programme for the six University Centres of Cricketing Excellence. Moreover, their form against the first-class counties had improved enormously since the previous season, when they lost all three of their county fixtures. This time, they lost only one, after declaring to set a target, and put up a fight in all the games. In November, the ECB, whose National Academy was being built at Loughborough, awarded them first-class status, thus putting right the injustice that they had not been elevated in 2001 alongside Durham University. From 2003, in recognition of their "outstanding progress", Loughborough would play on the same footing as their old rivals, Durham, and the original first-class university teams, Oxford and Cambridge.

Durham found fewer rewards for their efforts in 2002. They suffered their first first-class defeat, at Nottingham. Though they reached their sixth successive British Universities final, they lost for the third time running to Loughborough, and unexpectedly finished fourth in the Inter-UCCE table. Instead, it was Oxford who were UCCE runners-up and met Loughborough in the one-day challenge match at Lord's. But Oxford had few other successes, and lost all their county games. Cambridge found it even more difficult to hold their own at first-class level, or even against the other university sides. Their best game was at Oxford, where they scored easily the highest total in the history of the Varsity Match.

Of the non-first-class UCCEs, Cardiff were placed third, behind Oxford, in both the British Universities Southern League and the Inter-UCCE, but Bradford/Leeds finished well behind everyone except Cambridge.

OXFORD

President: A. C. Smith (Brasenose)
Chairman: Dr S. R. Porter (St Cross College)

Captain: J. W. M. Dalrymple (Radley and St Peter's)
Oxford UCCE Captain for 2003: J. J. Sayers (St Mary's RC Menston and Worcester)
Oxford University Captain for 2003: J. W. M. Dalrymple (Radley and St Peter's)

The University Centres of Cricket Excellence were designed to close the gap between students and county cricketers, but a look at Oxford's results in 2002 suggested how far they had to go. Indeed, comparing results from the days when Oxford University played some ten first-class matches to the last couple of years, when the combined forces of Oxford and Oxford Brookes Universities played only three county games, student cricket looked weaker. There were extenuating circumstances, however, for the three heavy defeats.

The matches were all scheduled in the first four weeks of the season, when the counties were keen to put out near full-strength sides to take advantage of The Parks' excellent pitches. In former years, they had often fielded what were virtually second elevens. Even the weather offered Oxford no help: play was possible on all nine scheduled days. Oxford had a single one-day game against Essex Seconds before meeting Worcestershire, and a mere three first-class matches hardly gave the students time to progress before the programme ended in early May.

It has to be asked whether this new format justified first-class status any more than the old system, often ridiculed but probably a better grounding for future county cricketers to learn about the game. There will still be players from universities who go on to county and even international level. Whether they can be described as products of university cricket, or merely cricketers who went to university, is debatable.

Even during this brief season, the captain, Jamie Dalrymple, who was already on Middlesex's staff, demonstrated enormous potential. He averaged 48 against the counties, scoring Oxford's first century against county opposition for four years; he added another against Cambridge, to complete 429 runs at 61 in all first-class matches. Though Dalrymple's off-breaks produced only six wickets in 100 overs, he was bowling on unresponsive pitches against batsmen in full flow, and still kept his economy rate below four an over. Stephen Hawinkels also lifted his batting average to 41, while James Redmayne and Neil Millar were in the thirties.

The leading wicket-takers were Tom Mees and Toby Sharpe, who strove hard to give Oxford's attack respectability and claimed eight victims each. Mees, who played only two games to Sharpe's three, had the best average, and that was 33.75. This lack of penetration and, indeed, lack of economy illustrated the gap between the students and their professional opponents.

Outside the first-class matches, Oxford did well enough in the Inter-UCCE championship to secure the runners-up spot behind Loughborough, after squeezing ahead of Cardiff on a tie-breaker. They were easily beaten by Loughborough in the one-day challenge match at Lord's, despite a century from Huw Jones, of Oxford Brookes, who had scored 97 against Worcestershire.

The high point of the season was also at Lord's, a week earlier, in the one-day Varsity Match. A hundred from Hawinkels helped to ensure an imposing 322, but the Cambridge openers looked like overhauling that until Dalrymple and Hawinkels truncated the chase. Mees and Sharpe, and the other five Brookes players who appeared against the counties, were ineligible, because the Varsity games remained the preserve of the traditional universities. The weakness of Oxford's attack in their absence was further highlighted the next day, when the first-class Varsity match was staged at The Parks. Cambridge ran up the first 600-run total in the fixture's history, and made Oxford follow on. It took Dalrymple's century to ensure the draw against what had appeared the weaker side. **Ralph Dellor**

OXFORD UCCE/UNIVERSITY RESULTS

First-class matches – Played 4: Lost 3, Drawn 1.

FIRST-CLASS AVERAGES

BATTING AND FIELDING

	M	I	NO	R	HS	100s	50s	Avge	Ct/St
J. W. M. Dalrymple	4	8	1	429	148	2	1	61.28	1
S. J. Hawinkels	2	4	0	166	78	0	1	41.50	1
J. R. S. Redmayne	2	4	1	106	75*	0	1	35.33	0
N. Millar	3	6	0	203	67	0	2	33.83	2
H. R. Jones	3	6	0	130	97	0	1	21.66	3
J. J. Porter	2	4	0	86	33	0	0	21.50	2
J. J. Sayers	4	8	0	152	55	0	1	19.00	1
I. J. Hilsum	2	4	0	56	23	0	0	14.00	1
T. C. Hicks	3	6	1	58	38	0	0	11.60	2
A. A. Wyatt	2	3	1	18	10*	0	0	9.00	0
T. Mees	2	4	0	20	13	0	0	5.00	0
T. J. Daniels	2	4	0	18	16	0	0	4.50	4/1
C. C. M. Warren	2	3	0	12	8	0	0	4.00	1
T. J. Sharpe	3	6	2	12	7*	0	0	3.00	4
M. K. Floyd	2	4	0	9	7	0	0	2.25	1

Also batted: P. J. Clark (1 match) 0, 2*; S. H. Dalrymple (1 match) 12, 15* (2 ct); P. P. Evans (1 match) 16 (2 ct); A. F. Gofton (1 match) 25, 16; W. O. F. Howard (1 match) 1, 0 (1 ct); B. M. Vonwiller (1 match) 4* (1 ct).

BOWLING

	O	M	R	W	BB	5W/i	Avge
T. Mees	64	10	270	8	4-55	0	33.75
T. J. Sharpe	95	18	400	8	3-70	0	50.00
J. W. M. Dalrymple	100.4	15	398	6	4-152	0	66.33
T. C. Hicks	84.5	12	324	4	1-56	0	81.00

Also bowled: P. J. Clark 17–1–92–1; A. F. Gofton 18–1–83–1; S. J. Hawinkels 23–1–130–2; I. J. Hilsum 5–1–20–0; N. Millar 48–2–226–2; J. J. Porter 13–0–72–2; J. J. Sayers 3–1–12–0; B. M. Vonwiller 15–2–80–2; A. A. Wyatt 49–7–181–2.

Note: Matches in this section which were not first-class are signified by a dagger.

†At Oxford, April 10. **Essex Second Eleven won by 79 runs.** Toss: Oxford UCCE. **Essex Second Eleven 226 for four** (45 overs) (J. D. Middlebrook 71, J. P. Stephenson 46, M. L. Pettini 43); **Oxford UCCE 147** (36 overs) (J. J. Porter 61; A. C. McGarry six for 24).

OXFORD UCCE v WORCESTERSHIRE

At Oxford, April 13, 14, 15. Worcestershire won by 332 runs. Toss: Oxford UCCE. First-class debuts: P. J. Clark, J. J. Sayers. County debuts: G. J. Batty, B. F. Smith.

The students' season had the most depressing start imaginable. The tone was set when Worcestershire rattled up 523 at six an over – boosted by 64 extras – and still had time to take two wickets that evening. Hick and Smith, in his first match since leaving Leicestershire, fully exploited a good pitch and friendly bowling to add 248. Next day, the first Sunday ever to feature first-class cricket in The Parks, only Millar resisted the county's pace attack. Worcestershire waived the follow-on in favour of more batting practice, though Mees held up their advance with three wickets in nine balls. After Hick declared overnight, 537 ahead, Ali was simply too much of a handful for Oxford. Once he had begun a century stand between Millar and Jones – Ali fell in an agonising three short of a maiden hundred – Ali seized six wickets in 21 balls, to finish with a career-best seven, five bowled and two lbw.

Close of play: First day, Oxford UCCE 10-2 (Sayers 1, Porter 4); Second day, Worcestershire 159-6 (Ali 25, Sheriyar 17).

Worcestershire

W. P. C. Weston c Daniels b Sharpe	0	– c Dalrymple b Mees 4
A. Singh c Porter b Clark	40	– b Mees 7
*G. A. Hick st Daniels b Porter	164	
B. F. Smith retired out	137	
V. S. Solanki c Porter b Sharpe	85	– (4) retired hurt 22
D. A. Leatherdale c Daniels b Mees	11	– (3) b Mees 0
G. J. Batty not out	18	– (5) lbw b Dalrymple 48
†S. J. Rhodes not out	4	– (6) c Daniels b Mees 5
Kabir Ali (did not bat)		– (7) not out 20
C. G. Liptrot (did not bat)		– (8) b Dalrymple 5
A. Sheriyar (did not bat)		– (9) not out 17
B 13, l-b 11, w 16, n-b 24	64	B 7, w 4, n-b 10 21

1/17 (1) 2/95 (2) 3/343 (3)   (6 wkts dec.) 523
4/439 (4) 5/481 (6) 6/508 (5)

1/10 (1) 2/10 (3)   (6 wkts dec.) 159
3/13 (2) 4/64 (6)
5/102 (5) 6/132 (8)

In the second innings Solanki retired hurt at 54.

Bowling: *First Innings*—Mees 19–3–111–1; Sharpe 24–1–138–2; Clark 13–1–72–1; Millar 11–0–54–0; Dalrymple 11–0–90–0; Porter 6–0–34–1. *Second Innings*—Mees 13–0–55–4; Sharpe 7–1–25–0; Dalrymple 13–3–36–2; Clark 4–0–20–0; Millar 4–0–16–0.

Oxford UCCE

M. K. Floyd lbw b Sheriyar	0	– (2) c sub b Liptrot	2
J. J. Sayers lbw b Ali	5	– (1) b Ali	30
*J. W. M. Dalrymple lbw b Sheriyar	4	– c sub b Liptrot	4
J. J. Porter b Sheriyar	9	– c Rhodes b Batty	21
H. R. Jones c Hick b Ali	1	– lbw b Ali	97
N. Millar st Rhodes b Batty	67	– lbw b Ali	34
C. C. M. Warren c Hick b Ali	0	– b Ali	4
†T. J. Daniels b Batty	16	– b Ali	0
T. Mees lbw b Sheriyar	13	– b Ali	0
P. J. Clark c Weston b Sheriyar	0	– not out	2
T. J. Sharpe not out	7	– b Ali	0
B 4, l-b 9, w 8, n-b 2	23	B 4, l-b 3, w 4	11

1/0 (1) 2/4 (3) 3/14 (2) 4/26 (4)   145
5/26 (5) 6/32 (7) 7/82 (8)
8/115 (9) 9/123 (10) 10/145 (6)

1/4 (2) 2/14 (3) 3/51 (1) 4/67 (4)   205
5/195 (6) 6/200 (5) 7/200 (8)
8/200 (9) 9/205 (7) 10/205 (11)

Bowling: *First Innings*—Sheriyar 21–8–46–5; Ali 17–5–45–3; Leatherdale 6–2–16–0; Liptrot 8–4–18–0; Batty 5.2–1–7–2. *Second Innings*—Sheriyar 15–5–35–0; Liptrot 14–1–51–2; Ali 13.2–4–43–7; Batty 18–7–44–1; Leatherdale 5–2–17–0; Hick 3–2–8–0.

Umpires: P. J. Hartley and K. E. Palmer.

OXFORD UCCE v NORTHAMPTONSHIRE

At Oxford, April 18, 19, 20. Northamptonshire won by 207 runs. Toss: Northamptonshire. First-class debuts: I. J. Hilsum, W. O. F. Howard, A. A. Wyatt. County debuts: C. G. Greenidge, B. J. Phillips.

Though Oxford suffered another heavy defeat, there was some comfort from the improving performance of their bowlers. The home attack was led by Mees and Sharpe – two of six Brookes players in the side. By adhering to basic principles, they reduced a strong county line-up to 243 for eight on the opening day. But the attack had lost its discipline by the time Northamptonshire batted again, and the batting showed all-too-familiar failings in both Oxford innings; only Porter reached 30 in either attempt, as Northamptonshire swept to a win that could have been far more difficult. Hussey, their Australian captain, held five catches in the second innings, a county record, and seven in the match.

Close of play: First day, Northamptonshire 243-8 (Bailey 50, Greenidge 13); Second day, Northamptonshire 139-1 (Hussey 52, Rollins 8).

Northamptonshire

*M. E. K. Hussey c Jones b Sharpe	11	– retired out	52
M. B. Loye c Sayers b Mees	4	– b Porter	64
A. S. Rollins c Howard b Sharpe	36	– not out	35
D. J. Sales lbw b Mees	51		
G. P. Swann b Mees	14	– (4) c Sharpe b Hicks	38
J. W. Cook c Jones b Sharpe	29		
†T. M. B. Bailey not out	50	– (5) not out	18
B. J. Phillips c Sharpe b Wyatt	17		
J. A. R. Blain c and b Hicks	0		
C. G. Greenidge not out	13		
L-b 6, w 2, n-b 10	18	B 12, l-b 5, w 2	19

1/21 (1) 2/25 (2) 3/101 (3)   (8 wkts dec.) 243
4/124 (5) 5/131 (4) 6/167 (6)
7/194 (8) 8/201 (9)

1/107 (2) 2/139 (1)   (3 wkts dec.) 226
3/195 (4)

D. M. Cousins did not bat.

Bowling: *First Innings*—Mees 18–5–55–3; Sharpe 24–5–70–3; Wyatt 11–2–33–1; Hicks 20–3–64–1; Dalrymple 2–0–15–0. *Second Innings*—Mees 14–2–49–0; Sharpe 14–8–37–0; Hicks 9–0–58–1; Wyatt 8–1–27–0; Porter 7–0–38–1.

Oxford UCCE

J. J. Sayers c Sales b Blain	17	– c Bailey b Phillips	14
*J. W. M. Dalrymple c Loye b Phillips	29	– c Hussey b Cousins	5
J. R. S. Redmayne b Cook	8	– b Phillips	14
J. J. Porter b Cousins	23	– c Hussey b Swann	33
H. R. Jones c sub b Greenidge	20	– c Hussey b Phillips	8
I. J. Hilsum c Hussey b Swann	23	– c Hussey b Cook	18
T. C. Hicks c Hussey b Greenidge	4	– c Cook b Swann	1
†W. O. F. Howard lbw b Blain	1	– c Bailey b Cook	0
A. A. Wyatt not out	10	– lbw b Greenidge	8
T. Mees c Sales b Swann	0	– c Hussey b Greenidge	7
T. J. Sharpe c Rollins b Swann	0	– not out	3
L-b 12, n-b 2	14	N-b 2	2

1/43 (2) 2/57 (1) 3/60 (3) 4/98 (4)   149   1/7 (2) 2/30 (1) 3/43 (3)   113
5/112 (5) 6/116 (7) 7/117 (8)   4/61 (5) 5/94 (6) 6/94 (4) 7/95 (7)
8/149 (6) 9/149 (10) 10/149 (11)   8/95 (8) 9/110 (9) 10/113 (10)

Bowling: *First Innings*—Cousins 14–8–25–1; Greenidge 15–2–44–2; Phillips 10–3–13–1; Blain 11–4–22–2; Cook 5–2–20–1; Swann 6.4–2–13–3. *Second Innings*—Cousins 7–1–11–1; Greenidge 11.5–3–24–2; Phillips 7–2–28–3; Blain 8–0–26–0; Swann 12–6–17–2; Cook 8–5–7–2.

Umpires: A. Hill and N. A. Mallender.

†At Oxford, April 22, 23. **Oxford UCCE won by 63 runs.** Toss: Northamptonshire Second Eleven. **Oxford UCCE 328 for nine** (J. R. S. Redmayne 72, W. O. F. Howard 71, I. J. Hilsum 51; M. E. Cassar three for 60); **Northamptonshire Second Eleven 265** (G. L. Brophy 100, T. B. Huggins 55, A. J. Shantry 45; J. J. Sayers four for 19, G. N. Bowers three for 59).

†At Oxford, April 26. **Oxford University won by six wickets.** Toss: Oxford University. **Oxfordshire 120 for eight** (35 overs) (C. S. Knightley 37; A. A. Wyatt three for 17); **Oxford University 121 for four** (32.1 overs) (M. K. Floyd 38; A. P. Cook three for 25).

†At Oxford, May 1, 2, 3. **Drawn.** Toss: MCC Young Cricketers. **MCC Young Cricketers 207** (J. E. P. Walford 65; G. N. Bowers five for 53) **and 268 for seven dec.** (P. R. Sawyer 66, M. W. A. van Nierop 57 not out, M. Wilkie 49, F. A. Klokker 39; G. N. Bowers five for 90); **Oxford UCCE 202** (G. Adams 39, M. K. Floyd 34, S. Rana 32; Z. Taylor three for 22, P. R. Sawyer three for 32) **and 161 for eight** (S. Rana 36; B. S. Hooper three for 17, P. R. Sawyer three for 39).

OXFORD UCCE v GLOUCESTERSHIRE

At Oxford, May 8, 9, 10. Gloucestershire won by 159 runs. Toss: Gloucestershire.

Gofton gave Oxford an encouraging start when he dismissed Spearman, the New Zealand Test batsman, in the second over. But the game soon reverted to the usual pattern, with big hundreds from Windows and Hardinges, who hit three sixes each and shared a fourth-wicket stand of 180. Russell pushed the total on to 483 before declaring overnight. Next day, it was Dalrymple's turn. He showed his potential in a formidable maiden century, and added 105 with Sayers, whose valuable fifty carried Oxford past 300 – something they had not achieved against a first-class county for nearly six years. Gloucestershire went for quick runs on the final morning, and set a target of 310. Dalrymple scored another half-century, though he had to drop down the order because of a damaged elbow. But Ball wrecked the middle order and Oxford slid to a 3–0 whitewash by the counties with 13 balls to go.

Close of play: First day, Gloucestershire 483-6 (Russell 63, Ball 0); Second day, Oxford UCCE 306.

Gloucestershire

C. G. Taylor c Daniels b Sharpe	30	– (3) not out	18
C. M. Spearman c Hilsum b Gofton	2	– (1) c Millar b Hawkinels	54
M. G. N. Windows c Floyd b Sharpe	145		
J. N. Snape c and b Millar	16		
M. A. Hardinges c Jones b Hicks	172		
*R. C. Russell not out	63		
I. D. Fisher lbw b Sharpe	8		
M. C. J. Ball not out	0		
K. J. Barnett (did not bat)		– (2) not out	55
B 7, l-b 5, w 19, n-b 16	47	W 3, n-b 2	5

1/4 (2) 2/77 (1) 3/132 (4)   (6 wkts dec.) 483   1/100 (1)   (1 wkt dec.) 132
4/312 (3) 5/443 (5) 6/466 (7)

R. J. Silence and B. W. Gannon did not bat.

Bowling: *First Innings*—Sharpe 22–2–107–3; Gofton 14–1–59–1; Millar 19–0–87–1; Dalrymple 22–1–105–0; Hicks 16–2–56–1; Hawkinels 6–0–37–0; Hilsum 5–1–20–0. *Second Innings*—Sharpe 4–1–23–0; Gofton 4–0–24–0; Hawkinels 7–0–44–1; Millar 2–0–21–0; Hicks 4.5–1–20–0.

Oxford UCCE

M. K. Floyd b Gannon	0	– b Gannon	7
*J. W. M. Dalrymple c Snape b Barnett	148	– (6) not out	54
S. J. Hawkinels c Russell b Silence	36	– c and b Fisher	25
H. R. Jones c Ball b Silence	3	– b Ball	1
N. Millar c Ball b Gannon	17	– b Ball	1
I. J. Hilsum c Russell b Gannon	9	– (7) c Taylor b Ball	6
J. J. Sayers run out	55	– (2) lbw b Ball	23
A. F. Gofton lbw b Ball	25	– lbw b Ball	16
†T. J. Daniels c Russell b Ball	0	– b Ball	2
T. C. Hicks not out	3	– c Spearman b Fisher	2
T. J. Sharpe lbw b Ball	0	– run out	2
B 1, l-b 3, w 2, n-b 4	10	L-b 1, w 8, n-b 2	11

1/4 (1) 2/66 (3) 3/72 (4) 4/114 (5)   306   1/20 (1) 2/58 (2) 3/60 (4)   150
5/148 (6) 6/253 (2) 7/302 (8)   4/64 (3) 5/70 (5) 6/90 (7) 7/118 (6)
8/302 (7) 9/306 (9) 10/306 (11)   8/124 (9) 9/137 (10) 10/150 (11)

Bowling: *First Innings*—Gannon 15–4–66–3; Silence 10–2–41–2; Hardinges 10–1–43–0; Fisher 16–3–48–0; Snape 17–1–59–0; Ball 21–9–38–3; Barnett 10–5–7–1. *Second Innings*—Gannon 10–2–39–1; Silence 5–1–11–0; Ball 33–12–54–6; Hardinges 2–1–2–0; Fisher 19.5–7–34–2; Snape 7–4–9–0.

Umpires: M. Dixon and M. J. Harris.

†At Arundel, May 23. **Oxford University won by one wicket.** Toss: Oxford University. **Earl of Arundel's XI 205 for nine dec.** (A. R. Whittall 58, A. I. C. Dodemaide 51); **Oxford University 207 for nine** (M. K. Floyd 37, J. W. M. Dalrymple 124 not out).

†At Wormsley, May 29. **Drawn.** Toss: Oxford University. **Sir Paul Getty's XI 231 for five dec.** (L. A. Carseldine 91 not out, D. P. Waugh 43, M. Morrison 42; S. J. Hawkinels four for 63); **Oxford University 164 for seven** (M. K. Floyd 38, J. W. M. Dalrymple 53, P. P. Evans 33 not out; D. Slade three for 30).

†At Oxford, May 30. **Hertfordshire won by 80 runs.** Toss: Hertfordshire. **Hertfordshire 283 for five** (50 overs) (F. Moss 137 not out, N. Walker 45); **Oxford University 203** (48.5 overs) (S. J. Hawkinels 63, S. H. Dalrymple 42).

†At Oxford, June 7. **No result.** Toss: Harlequins. **Oxford University 66 for one** (22.1 overs) (C. C. M. Warren 38 not out) **v Harlequins**.

†At Oxford, June 12, 13, 14. **Drawn.** Toss: Combined Services. **Oxford University 305 for two dec.** (M. K. Floyd 117, J. J. Sayers 151) **and 276 for seven dec.** (J. W. M. Dalrymple 61, T. C. Hicks 61 not out; Sgt D. Woodhouse three for 43); **Combined Services 337** (LPT M. Toogood 38, FS G. N. Lumb 142, LCpl K. Ford 37, SSgt N. Palmer 59; T. C. Hicks four for 80).

†At Oxford, June 19, 20, 21. **Oxford University won by three wickets.** Toss: MCC. **MCC 280 for seven dec.** (J. B. R. Jones 89 not out, K. G. Sedgbeer 83 not out; J. W. M. Dalrymple five for 78) **and 308** (J. B. R. Jones 31, K. G. Sedgbeer 57 not out, E. L. Home 50, R. Brewster 53, S. M. Brogan 37; A. A. Wyatt four for 61, T. C. Hicks three for 76); **Oxford University 382 for five dec.** (J. J. Sayers 78, S. J. Hawinkels 137, J. W. M. Dalrymple 46 not out, N. Millar 40) **and 208 for seven** (J. J. Sayers 31, J. W. M. Dalrymple 57 not out, C. C. M. Warren 34; K. G. Sedgbeer three for 51).

Dalrymple started the match with a spell of 9–6–6–5 and ended it by striking the winning six off the penultimate ball.

At Lord's, June 25. OXFORD UNIVERSITY beat CAMBRIDGE UNIVERSITY by 37 runs (See One-Day University Match, 2002).

At Oxford, June 26, 27, 28, 29. OXFORD UNIVERSITY drew with CAMBRIDGE UNIVERSITY (See The University Match, 2002).

CAMBRIDGE

President: Professor A. D. Buckingham (Pembroke)

Captain: J. W. R. Parker (Tonbridge and St Catharine's)
Cambridge UCCE Captain for 2003: S. J. Marshall (Birkenhead and Pembroke)
Cambridge University Captain for 2003: A. Shankar (Bedford and Queens')

Cambridge have been slow in getting to grips with the ECB's grand design for the University Centres of Cricketing Excellence. With Anglia Polytechnic University, the other half of the partnership, only beginning to get their recruitment programme up and running, the 2002 UCCE side continued to rely almost exclusively on players from Cambridge University – which continued to enforce an unyieldingly academic admissions policy.

But though a team with no county-contracted players struggled to match their rivals on the field, off it the signs became more encouraging. Chris Scott, Cambridge's energetic coach, identified several areas for recruitment and, by the end of the summer, there were signs of young cricketers, particularly from London's Asian community, being offered and accepting places at APU. Up to six players from the academies of first-class counties were awarded places for 2002-03, which suggested that, in future, APU would provide the majority of the squad, and Cambridge UCCE should be able to field a team consisting almost entirely of players keen to make a career in first-class cricket.

In the meantime, Cambridge's three matches against first-class counties proved to be uphill battles. The students went down to resounding defeats against Middlesex and Essex before they salvaged some pride by batting out a draw against Surrey, who would be county champions. Bowling was a problem: the leg-spinner Simon Marshall was the only player to claim five wickets in an innings. His performance against Essex was far and away the best of the season in the county games: six for 128 in Essex's first innings, followed by 99 in Cambridge's second. That was the highest individual score, until the Varsity Match, and Cambridge's highest total against the counties was 218. The captain, Jamie Parker, son of Paul Parker of Sussex, was easily the leading scorer, with 284 at 40 in all first-class matches, and only Marshall reached ten wickets.

Cambridge also struggled in the inter-university competitions. But they saved their two best performances for the Varsity matches against Oxford in June. Although they lost the one-day game at Lord's, where their bowling again proved inadequate, it was not without a fight. Oxford set them 323 to win, but Alex Simcox and Duncan Heath opened with 185, and Cambridge began to believe they could overhaul the target. In the end, the pressure of scoring more than six an over proved too much for an inexperienced side. At Oxford next day, however, they scored at will, eventually amassing 604 at nearly four an over, a record total for the Varsity Match. Adrian Shankar scored 143 but the game really belonged to Stuart Moffat, a rugby Blue, who made a dazzling 169 in his first, and what seemed likely to remain his only, first-class innings. He was to take up a professional rugby career with Glasgow Caledonians a fortnight later, and his form won him an international cap for Scotland. Cambridge's joy knew no bounds when they forced Oxford to follow on, 380 runs adrift, but from then on it was hard toil on a flat pitch as the home side fought their way to a draw. **David Hallett**

CAMBRIDGE UCCE/UNIVERSITY RESULTS

First-class matches – Played 4: Lost 2, Drawn 2.

FIRST-CLASS AVERAGES

BATTING AND FIELDING

	M	I	NO	R	HS	100s	50s	Avge	Ct/St
J. W. R. Parker	4	7	0	284	86	0	2	40.57	1
S. J. Marshall	4	7	0	182	99	0	1	26.00	1
A. Shankar	4	7	0	167	143	1	0	23.85	2
T. E. Savill	3	5	2	58	18*	0	0	19.33	2
V. H. Kumar	4	7	0	114	64	0	1	16.28	3/1
F. I. Sharif	2	3	0	46	36	0	0	15.33	2
D. J. Noble	4	6	2	61	21	0	0	15.25	0
D. R. Heath	4	7	1	88	75	0	1	14.66	0
A. D. Simcox	4	7	1	72	30	0	0	12.00	2
J. R. Moyes	3	5	0	51	35	0	0	10.20	6
T. R. Hughes	2	4	2	12	10	0	0	6.00	0

Also batted: M. S. Chapman-Smith (1 match) 7, 3; J. A. Heath (2 matches) 1, 35; J. R. Jordison (1 match) 11, 17; D. E. T. McGrath (1 match) 0; J. S. D. Moffat (1 match) 169.

BOWLING

	O	M	R	W	BB	5W/i	Avge
D. E. T. McGrath	46	9	148	6	3-49	0	24.66
D. R. Heath	72.3	20	230	6	3-28	0	38.33
D. J. Noble	133	24	480	9	3-66	0	53.33
T. E. Savill	81	9	380	6	2-62	0	63.33
S. J. Marshall	215.2	42	657	10	6-128	1	65.70

Also bowled: J. A. Heath 16–7–31–0; T. R. Hughes 45–7–178–1; J. R. Jordison 29–6–96–1; J. W. R. Parker 8–0–39–0; F. I. Sharif 42.3–2–180–1.

Note: Matches in this section which were not first-class are signified by a dagger.

CAMBRIDGE UCCE v MIDDLESEX

At Cambridge, April 13, 14, 15. Middlesex won by 282 runs. Toss: Middlesex. First-class debuts: D. R. Heath, J. R. Jordison, S. J. Marshall, J. R. Moyes, D. J. Noble, T. E. Savill, A. Shankar; T. A. Hunt. County debut: S. G. Koenig.

Cambridge managed a single wicket on a damp first day. By the afternoon, Strauss, assuming the Middlesex captaincy in anticipation of Angus Fraser's retirement, and Sven Koenig, their latest import from South Africa, had put on 200. Strauss finally went for 121, and Koenig completed his own century, batting more than five hours, as he added another 158 with Weston before the declaration. Cook extracted both openers by the close; next day, he returned a career-best five for 11 while Thomas Hunt claimed three wickets on debut and Cambridge were swept away for 111. Middlesex sought more batting practice, though they lost three cheap wickets before Weekes reached an unbeaten century. Strauss promptly declared again, 487 ahead, and took the keeper's gloves because Nash had dislocated a finger. It was his bowlers, however, who were to blame for the bulk of 57 extras, the biggest contribution to Cambridge's total. The students showed more resolution, but subsided for 205.

Close of play: First day, Cambridge UCCE 22-2 (Kumar 3, Parker 9); Second day, Cambridge UCCE 6-0 (Noble 0, Simcox 0).

Middlesex

*A. J. Strauss c Parker b Jordison	121			
S. G. Koenig not out	141			
R. M. S. Weston not out	67	– (1) lbw b Hughes	8
E. C. Joyce (did not bat)		– (2) lbw b Savill	6
B. L. Hutton (did not bat)		– (3) not out	100
P. N. Weekes (did not bat)		– (4) b Savill	4
†D. C. Nash (did not bat)		– (5) c Savill b Noble	42
A. W. Laraman (did not bat)		– (6) not out	43
S. J. Cook (did not bat)			
B 6, l-b 4, w 4, n-b 11	29	B 10, l-b 9, w 18	37

1/200 (1) (1 wkt dec.) 358 1/19 (2) 2/45 (1) (4 wkts dec.) 240
3/58 (4) 4/136 (5)

C. B. Keegan and T. A. Hunt did not bat.

Bowling: *First Innings*—Savill 13–0–74–0; Jordison 18–2–61–1; Noble 11–1–51–0; Hughes 16–1–78–0; Marshall 24–3–80–0. *Second Innings*—Savill 12–0–62–2; Hughes 14–2–49–1; Jordison 11–4–35–0; Marshall 21.5–5–68–0; Noble 3–0–7–1.

Cambridge UCCE

A. D. Simcox c Nash b Cook	4	– (2) c Strauss b Laraman	1
D. R. Heath c Weekes b Cook	0	– (3) c Strauss b Laraman	2
†V. H. Kumar c Nash b Keegan	7	– (4) lbw b Cook	28
*J. W. R. Parker b Cook	10	– (5) b Cook	34
A. Shankar lbw b Cook	6	– (6) c Joyce b Cook	2
S. J. Marshall c Keegan b Hunt	20	– (7) b Joyce	29
J. R. Moyes c Nash b Hunt	4	– (8) c Keegan b Cook	0
J. R. Jordison c Strauss b Hunt	11	– (9) c Strauss b Weekes	17
D. J. Noble c Joyce b Weekes	21	– (1) b Laraman	8
T. E. Savill lbw b Weekes	5	– not out	17
T. R. Hughes not out	0	– b Weekes	10
B 5, l-b 4, n-b 14	23	B 6, l-b 9, w 16, n-b 26	57

1/2 (2) 2/5 (1) 3/31 (3) 4/31 (4) 111 1/20 (2) 2/34 (3) 3/51 (1) 205
5/44 (5) 6/64 (7) 7/73 (6) 4/94 (4) 5/116 (6) 6/125 (5)
8/104 (8) 9/111 (9) 10/111 (10) 7/125 (8) 8/170 (9)
9/180 (7) 10/205 (11)

Bowling: *First Innings*—Keegan 11–1–29–1; Cook 11.5–5–11–5; Hunt 9–0–43–3; Laraman 6–0–18–0; Weekes 3.4–2–1–1. *Second Innings*—Keegan 7–0–20–0; Laraman 11–3–40–3; Hunt 5–1–20–0; Cook 12–1–51–4; Weekes 13.5–6–39–2; Joyce 4–0–20–1.

Umpires: N. L. Bainton and N. G. Cowley.

CAMBRIDGE UCCE v ESSEX

At Cambridge, April 20, 21, 22. Essex won by 258 runs. Toss: Cambridge UCCE. First-class debut: F. I. Sharif. County debuts: J. M. Dakin, A. Flower, A. Habib, J. D. Middlebrook.

Two Cambridge leg-spinners shared the ball on the first afternoon. Faisal Sharif, on first-class debut, found more turn, but could not match the accuracy of Simon Marshall, who claimed six victims. The prize wicket, however, fell to Savill, who yorked Andy Flower, Zimbabwe's greatest batsman, and dismissed him again next day. In between, Irani helped to reduce Cambridge to 37 for five, though Parker salvaged something with a fifty. When Essex batted again, Clinton scored a maiden first-class century, and Robinson was given time to complete one in the morning, before Irani declared. Grant's opening spell took four for 24: Cambridge were 60 for six before lunch. But Marshall and Sharif joined forces once more to add 128. Marshall just missed his hundred, trying to turn Grayson to leg, while Grant took five in an innings for the first time.

Close of play: First day, Cambridge UCCE 17-1 (Shankar 9, Noble 4); Second day, Essex 222-3 (Robinson 97, Dakin 1).

Essex

D. D. J. Robinson c Heath b Marshall	26	– not out	100	
A. P. Grayson st Kumar b Marshall	105			
†A. Flower b Savill	20	– (2) c Shankar b Savill	1	
A. Habib c Moyes b Marshall	64			
*R. C. Irani run out	37			
R. S. Clinton c Savill b Marshall	19	– (3) run out	107	
J. M. Dakin not out	34	– (5) b Noble	15	
J. D. Middlebrook c Kumar b Marshall	2	– (4) b Noble	0	
A. P. Cowan b Marshall	10	– (6) not out	2	
A. C. McGarry not out	11			
B 19, l-b 13, w 2, n-b 8	42	B 14, l-b 4, w 2	20	

1/81 (1) 2/130 (3) 3/207 (2) (8 wkts dec.) 370
4/272 (4) 5/296 (5) 6/307 (6)
7/317 (8) 8/339 (9)

1/7 (2) 2/220 (3) (4 wkts dec.) 245
3/221 (4) 4/237 (5)

J. B. Grant did not bat.

Bowling: First Innings—Savill 21–7–57–1; Hughes 12–3–31–0; Noble 12–0–52–0; Marshall 33–2–128–6; Sharif 13–0–70–0. *Second Innings*—Savill 12–2–27–1; Hughes 3–1–20–0; Marshall 10–0–78–0; Noble 17–1–66–2; Heath 7–0–29–0; Sharif 2.3–0–7–0.

Cambridge UCCE

A. D. Simcox b McGarry	2	– b Grant	4	
A. Shankar b Irani	15	– lbw b Grant	0	
D. J. Noble c Robinson b Irani	4	– (10) b Grayson	12	
†V. H. Kumar c Grayson b Irani	0	– (3) b Grant	15	
*J. W. R. Parker c Dakin b Middlebrook	55	– (4) c Dakin b Grant	0	
D. R. Heath c Clinton b Cowan	1	– (5) c Flower b Dakin	0	
S. J. Marshall c Habib b Dakin	15	– (6) lbw b Grayson	99	
J. R. Moyes lbw b McGarry	2	– (7) c Grayson b Cowan	10	
F. I. Sharif run out	0	– (8) c Habib b Grant	36	
T. E. Savill c Habib b Grant	9	– (9) not out	18	
T. R. Hughes not out	2	– b Grayson	0	
B 4, l-b 7, w 4, n-b 8	23	B 2, l-b 4, w 16, n-b 2	24	

1/9 (1) 2/17 (3) 3/25 (4) 4/34 (2) 139
5/37 (6) 6/68 (7) 7/88 (8)
8/122 (9) 9/126 (5) 10/139 (10)

1/6 (1) 2/6 (3) 3/11 (2) 4/14 (5) 218
5/38 (4) 6/60 (7) 7/188 (8)
8/188 (6) 9/218 (10) 10/218 (11)

Bowling: First Innings—Cowan 11–6–11–1; McGarry 11–1–23–2; Grant 16.4–5–35–1; Irani 7–1–21–3; Dakin 5–3–5–1; Middlebrook 11–5–33–1. *Second Innings*—Grant 12–1–38–5; Dakin 9–2–41–1; McGarry 12–1–69–0; Cowan 10–4–15–1; Middlebrook 7–1–28–0; Grayson 5.5–1–21–3.

Umpires: R. T. Robinson and A. G. T. Whitehead.

†At Cambridge, April 25. **Cambridgeshire won by 26 runs.** Toss: Cambridgeshire. **Cambridgeshire 196 for eight** (50 overs) (N. T. Gadsby 36, S. A. Kellett 45; J. A. Cliffe four for 38); **Cambridge UCCE 170** (47.3 overs) (A. Shankar 37, J. A. Heath 35 not out; P. M. Such three for 24, R. Pryor three for 29).

†At Bishop's Stortford, May 2. **Cambridge UCCE won by 66 runs.** Toss: Hertfordshire. **Cambridge UCCE 259 for two** (50 overs) (A. D. Simcox 34, A. Shankar 80 not out, S. J. Marshall 104 not out); **Hertfordshire 193** (48.3 overs) (N. Gladwin 43, M. A. Everett 49; S. J. Marshall six for 38).

†At Wormsley, May 12. **Sir Paul Getty's XI won by seven wickets.** Toss: Sir Paul Getty's XI. **Cambridge University 187 for seven dec.** (A. D. Simcox 52, M. S. Chapman-Smith 41; W. Morrick three for 26, G. D. Rose three for eight); **Sir Paul Getty's XI 190 for three** (D. M. Ward 80, R. J. Greatorex 38, P. W. G. Parker 31 not out, G. D. Rose 30 not out; S. J. Marshall three for 69).

CAMBRIDGE UCCE v SURREY

At Cambridge, May 15, 16, 17. Drawn. Toss: Surrey. First-class debuts: M. S. Chapman-Smith, J. A. Heath; R. Clarke, P. J. Sampson.

Cambridge managed to hang on for the draw, despite Giddins grabbing three wickets in six overs. The opener, Simcox, batted nearly two and a half hours for 23, supported at the last by Duncan Heath, who came in at No. 7 after leaving the ground for a Russian oral exam. On the first morning, Heath had dismissed both Surrey openers before Ramprakash batted four hours for his century. But the headlines were stolen by 20-year-old Rikki Clarke, who marked his first-class debut with 107 from 160 balls, striking a six and eight fours. The determined Heath steered Cambridge to 146 for two, but the innings fell away: the last eight went for 72 runs. Resuming, Carberry reached his maiden first-class century after 30 balls in the nervous nineties, and was 153 when Ward set a nominal target of 507. Survival was the students' only object, and they achieved it.

Close of play: First day, Cambridge UCCE 25-0 (Simcox 13, D. R. Heath 12); Second day, Surrey 129-3 (Carberry 67, Clarke 5).

Surrey

*I. J. Ward c Sharif b D. R. Heath	27	– (4) b D. R. Heath	24		
M. A. Carberry c Marshall b D. R. Heath	36	– not out	153		
M. R. Ramprakash c Kumar b Marshall	121				
N. Shahid c Shankar b Sharif	65	– b Savill	24		
R. Clarke not out	107	– (1) lbw b Noble	13		
J. D. Ratcliffe not out	3	– (3) lbw b Savill	6		
†J. N. Batty (did not bat)		– (6) c Sharif b Marshall	42		
P. J. Sampson (did not bat)		– (7) c Shankar b Marshall	6		
T. J. Murtagh (did not bat)					
B 4, l-b 3, w 4, n-b 32	43	B 11, l-b 4, w 13, n-b 30	58		

1/81 (2) 2/84 (1)   (4 wkts dec.) 402   1/31 (1) 2/34 (3)   (6 wkts dec.) 322
3/194 (4) 4/386 (3)   3/108 (4) 4/194 (5)
                                          5/300 (6) 6/322 (7)

R. M. Amin and E. S. H. Giddins did not bat.

Bowling: *First Innings*—Savill 9–0–77–0; Noble 13–2–67–0; D. R. Heath 19–4–68–2; Marshall 31–3–102–1; Sharif 20–2–81–1. *Second Innings*—Savill 14–0–83–2; Noble 20–3–90–1; D. R. Heath 6–1–27–1; Marshall 20.3–1–71–2; Parker 3–0–14–0; Sharif 7–0–22–0.

Cambridge UCCE

A. D. Simcox lbw b Ratcliffe	30	— (2) not out	23
D. R. Heath b Clarke	75	— (7) not out	3
A. Shankar b Murtagh	0	— (1) c Carberry b Murtagh	1
*J. W. R. Parker c Murtagh b Sampson	44	— (3) run out	40
†V. H. Kumar c Clarke b Sampson	4	— (4) c Shahid b Giddins	5
S. J. Marshall c Ward b Amin	9	— b Giddins	0
M. S. Chapman-Smith c Carberry b Murtagh	7	— (5) b Giddins	3
J. A. Heath b Murtagh	1		
F. I. Sharif lbw b Ward	5		
T. E. Savill c Clarke b Amin	9		
D. J. Noble not out	15		
B 1, l-b 6, w 8, n-b 4	19	B 5, w 16	21
	218	(5 wkts)	**96**

1/62 (1) 2/74 (3) 3/146 (4) 4/152 (5)
5/170 (2) 6/183 (7) 7/186 (8)
8/191 (6) 9/200 (10) 10/218 (9)

1/21 (1) 2/84 (3) 3/89 (4)
4/93 (5) 5/93 (6)

Bowling: *First Innings*—Giddins 18–5–33–0; Sampson 19–5–54–2; Murtagh 15–2–37–3; Amin 15–4–40–2; Clarke 12–5–25–1; Ratcliffe 3–3–0–1; Ramprakash 6–1–21–0; Ward 1.4–0–1–1. *Second Innings*—Clarke 6–3–28–0; Murtagh 6–3–9–1; Ratcliffe 3–1–14–0; Amin 9–4–15–0; Ward 5–2–13–0; Giddins 6–3–7–3; Sampson 4–2–5–0.

Umpires: R. A. Kettleborough and B. Leadbeater.

---

†At Arundel, May 29. **Cambridge UCCE won by two runs.** Toss: Cambridge UCCE. **Cambridge UCCE 230 for three** (40 overs) (A. D. Akram 82, A. B. Reddy 65, M. S. Chapman-Smith 56); **Earl of Arundel's XI 228 for eight** (40 overs) (R. T. Ragnauth 65, R. Jones 56; J. A. Heath four for 27).

†At Cambridge, June 3. **Cambridge UCCE won by 12 runs.** Toss: Cambridge UCCE. **Cambridge UCCE 249 for five** (50 overs) (A. D. Simcox 70, J. S. D. Moffat 89); **Quidnuncs 237 for nine** (50 overs) (G. J. Dill 100, B. J. Collins 48 not out; D. E. T. McGrath three for 21).

†At Cambridge, June 9. **Drawn.** Toss: Free Foresters. **Free Foresters 117 for four** (C. R. Pimlott 44) v **Cambridge University**.

†At Cambridge, June 11, 12, 13. **MCC won by 95 runs.** Toss: MCC. **MCC 306 for seven dec.** (S. A. A. Block 77, S. G. Hinks 46, D. P. Waugh 76) **and 230 for four dec.** (P. McGlashan 43, M. J. Semmence 86 not out, S. G. Hinks 43); **Cambridge UCCE 257 for dec.** (A. Shankar 95, D. R. Heath 66, M. S. Chapman-Smith 50 not out; M. J. Semmence three for 27) **and 184** (S. J. Marshall 36, M. S. Chapman-Smith 47 not out, A. B. Reddy 46; K. Powell five for 42, D. A. Lees three for 61).

†At Cambridge, June 14. **No result.** Toss: Lashings. **Lashings 109 for one** (17.1 overs) (S. C. Williams 40 not out, M. J. Church 38 not out) v **Cambridge UCCE**.

†At High Wycombe, June 17. **MCC Young Cricketers won by 182 runs.** Toss: Cambridge UCCE. **MCC Young Cricketers 294 for six** (50 overs) (J. M. Hudson 68, P. R. Sawyer 51, A. C. Parker 31 not out; S. J. Marshall three for 42); **Cambridge UCCE 112** (38 overs) (C. T. Peploe three for 24, J. M. Hudson three for 26).

†At Aldershot, June 19, 20, 21. **Combined Services won by five wickets.** Toss: Cambridge UCCE. **Cambridge UCCE 160** (J. S. D. Moffat 60, D. J. Noble 33 not out; Pte T. F. Fabien three for 26, JT M. Bray three for 45) **and 335** (J. S. D. Moffat 47, D. J. Noble 30, D. E. T. McGrath 31, F. I. Sharif 70 not out, A. P. Palladino 57, Extras 42; Pte T. F. Fabien five for 62); **Combined Services 282** (Gnr P. Carlin 61, SSgt N. Palmer 45, Extras 46; D. J. Noble three for 49, S. J. Marshall four for 62) **and 217 for five** (JT M. Bray 38, FS G. N. Lumb 83 not out, SSgt N. Palmer 38 not out; S. J. Marshall three for 103).

In the second innings, Cambridge were 156 for seven; the last three wickets added 179, including 104 for the tenth from Sharif and Palladino.

At Lord's, June 25. CAMBRIDGE UNIVERSITY lost to OXFORD UNIVERSITY by 37 runs (See One-day University Match, 2002).

At Oxford, June 26, 27, 28, 29. CAMBRIDGE UNIVERSITY drew with OXFORD UNIVERSITY (See The University Match, 2002).

ONE-DAY UNIVERSITY MATCH, 2002

†OXFORD UNIVERSITY v CAMBRIDGE UNIVERSITY

At Lord's, June 25. Oxford University won by 37 runs. Toss: Cambridge University.

Oxford's victory in a high-scoring match levelled the one-day Varsity series at 4–4. But Cambridge looked likely to pull further ahead when their openers, Alex Simcox and Duncan Heath, stormed to 185 in 27 overs. They seemed to be cruising towards their target of 323 when the South African seamer, Stephen Hawinkels, broke the partnership. Only one more batsman passed 12 as he and Dalrymple ran through the line-up; Simcox was ninth out, and Cambridge lost with more than four overs to spare. Hawinkels and Dalrymple had also dominated Oxford's batting, adding 158 after Joe Sayers fell in the first over. Neil Millar contributed 70, and the 30 wides donated by Cambridge pushed the total past 300. Next door on the Nursery Ground, Cambridge's women beat Oxford by a single wicket, thanks to 86 from Alys Langdale.

Oxford University

J. J. Sayers (*St Mary's RC Menston and Worcester*) c Moyes b McGrath		0
S. J. Hawinkels (*St Stithians, Island School Hong Kong and University*) b J. A. Heath		103
*J. W. M. Dalrymple (*Radley and St Peter's*) c Moyes b D. R. Heath		78
N. Millar (*Fettes and Christ Church*) st Moyes b Noble		70
J. R. S. Redmayne (*Eton and Trinity*) c McGrath b Noble		16
S. H. Dalrymple (*Radley and Christ Church*) lbw b McGrath		2
C. C. M. Warren (*Sherborne and Worcester*) not out		1
T. C. Hicks (*Lord Wandsworth and St Catherine's*) c Shankar b McGrath		14
L-b 6, w 30, n-b 2		38

1/0 2/158 3/249 4/285 5/304 6/308 7/322   (7 wkts, 50 overs) 322

†P. P. Evans (*Eton and Keble*), C. P. Stearn (*Bedford and Worcester*) and P. J. Clark (*Glenunga IHS, Flinders U. and Balliol*) did not bat.

Bowling: McGrath 10–0–75–3; Hughes 7–1–47–0; Noble 10–0–73–2; Marshall 10–0–42–0; D. R. Heath 10–1–55–1; J. A. Heath 3–0–24–1.

Cambridge University

A. D. Simcox (*Eastbourne C and Robinson*) b J. W. M. Dalrymple		104
D. R. Heath (*Sir John Nelthorpe S, Brigg SFC and Pembroke*) c S. H. Dalrymple		
	b Hawinkels	103
*J. W. R. Parker (*Tonbridge and St Catharine's*) c Millar b Hawinkels		3
S. J. Marshall (*Birkenhead and Pembroke*) b Hawinkels		0
M. S. Chapman-Smith (*King's C. Auckland, Otago U. and Hughes Hall*) c Clark		
	b J. W. M. Dalrymple	32
A. Shankar (*Bedford and Queens'*) run out		2
†J. R. Moyes (*Cockermouth, Durham U. and Hughes Hall*) c Evans b J. W. M. Dalrymple		11
J. A. Heath (*Sir John Nelthorpe S, Brigg SFC and Pembroke*) lbw b J. W. M. Dalrymple		4
D. J. Noble (*Rugby and Emmanuel*) c Sayers b Hawinkels		0
D. E. T. McGrath (*St Joseph's, Queensland U. of Tech. and St Edmund's*) run out		12
T. R. Hughes (*Oldbury Wells and Homerton*) not out		0
L-b 4, w 8, n-b 6		18

1/185 2/189 3/189 4/236 5/243 6/264 7/264 8/265 9/285   (45.4 overs) 285

Bowling: Millar 8–0–56–0; Clark 5–0–26–0; Hawinkels 9–0–55–4; Stearn 5–0–50–0; Hicks 10–0–52–0; J. W. M. Dalrymple 8.4–2–42–4.

Umpires: G. I. Burgess and A. Clarkson.

THE UNIVERSITY MATCH, 2002

OXFORD UNIVERSITY v CAMBRIDGE UNIVERSITY

At Oxford, June 26, 27, 28, 29. Drawn. Toss: Cambridge University. First-class debuts: S. H. Dalrymple, P. P. Evans; D. E. T. McGrath, J. S. D. Moffat.

The first first-class Varsity Match at Oxford since 1850 belonged to a Cambridge debutant, Stuart Moffat. In what promised to be his only first-class innings – he was about to become a rugby professional – he scored 169 in 193 balls, with 17 fours and five sixes. The openers failed after their heroics at Lord's, but Moffat added 159 in 30 overs with Adrian Shankar, who made a more sedate 143, and 130 with Vikram Kumar. His *tour de force* carried Cambridge past the fixture's record total, 513 for six by Oxford in 1996; Cambridge's own best had been a mere 432 for nine in 1936. Oxford badly missed their Brookes-based bowlers, ineligible for Varsity games. Their captain, the off-spinner Jamie Dalrymple, shared the new ball and bowled 52 overs before ending the run-fest at 604. Dropping down the order, he returned to the field with Oxford 65 for four. Cambridge enforced the follow-on in the absence of their captain, Jamie Parker, who was collecting his degree. But Parker was back for the final day, when his attack sweated for just four wickets, while Dalrymple took his stand with Stephen Hawinkels to 166 and completed a century.

Close of play: First day, Cambridge University 389-5 (Moffat 96, Kumar 8); Second day, Oxford University 99-4 (Millar 32, J. W. M. Dalrymple 17); Third day, Oxford University 140-1 (Hawinkels 51, J. W. M. Dalrymple 73).

Cambridge University

A. D. Simcox (*Eastbourne C and Robinson*) c Hawinkels b J. W. M. Dalrymple		8
D. R. Heath (*Sir John Nelthorpe S, Brigg SFC and Pembroke*) c Evans b Vonwiller		7
A. Shankar (*Bedford and Queens'*) b Hawinkels		143
*J. W. R. Parker (*Tonbridge and St Catharine's*) c S. H. Dalrymple b J. W. M. Dalrymple		86
S. J. Marshall (*Birkenhead and Pembroke*) c Evans b Wyatt		10
J. S. D. Moffat (*Edinburgh Academy and St Edmund's*) lbw b Vonwiller		169
V. H. Kumar (*Dulwich and St John's*) c S. H. Dalrymple b Millar		64
†J. R. Moyes (*Cockermouth, Durham U. and Hughes Hall*) c Hicks b J. W. M. Dalrymple		35
J. A. Heath (*Sir John Nelthorpe S, Brigg SFC and Pembroke*) c Vonwiller b Hicks		35
D. J. Noble (*Rugby and Emmanuel*) not out		1
D. E. T. McGrath (*St Joseph's, Queensland U. of Tech. and St Edmund's*)		
	lbw b J. W. M. Dalrymple	0
B 10, l-b 1, n-b 30, p 5		46

1/17 (1) 2/23 (2) 3/203 (4) 4/220 (5) 5/379 (3)   604
6/509 (7) 7/537 (6) 8/603 (9) 9/604 (8) 10/604 (11)

Bowling: Vonwiller 15–2–80–2; J. W. M. Dalrymple 52.4–11–152–4; Millar 12–2–48–1; Hicks 35–6–126–1; Wyatt 30–4–121–1; Hawinkels 10–1–49–1; Sayers 3–1–12–0.

Oxford University

J. J. Sayers (*St Mary's RC Menston and Worcester*) lbw b McGrath .	0	– c D. R. Heath b Noble 8
S. J. Hawinkels (*St Stithians, Island School Hong Kong and University*) c Moyes b Noble .	27	– b Noble 78
J. R. S. Redmayne (*Eton and Trinity*) c Moyes b Noble .	9	– (5) not out 75
N. Millar (*Fettes and Christ Church*) c sub b D. R. Heath .	51	– c Simcox b McGrath 33
C. C. M. Warren (*Sherborne and Worcester*) c Shankar b Marshall .	8	
*J. W. M. Dalrymple (*Radley and St Peter's*) c Moyes b D. R. Heath .	48	– (3) c Moyes b McGrath 137
S. H. Dalrymple (*Radley and Christ Church*) lbw b Noble .	12	– not out 15
T. C. Hicks (*Lord Wandsworth and St Catherine's*) c Moyes b McGrath .	38	– (6) b McGrath 10
†P. P. Evans (*Eton and Keble*) c Kumar b D. R. Heath .	16	
A. A. Wyatt (*Melbourne GS, Melbourne U. and New*) c Simcox b McGrath .	0	
B. M. Vonwiller (*Sydney Shore S, Sydney U. and Trinity*) not out .	4	
B 5, l-b 4, w 2	11	B 14, l-b 2, w 10, n-b 6 . . 32
	224	**(5 wkts) 388**

1/0 (1) 2/11 (3) 3/46 (2) 4/65 (5)
5/139 (4) 6/152 (6) 7/188 (7)
8/206 (8) 9/212 (10) 10/224 (9)

1/15 (1) 2/181 (2)   (5 wkts) 388
3/270 (3) 4/275 (4)
5/305 (6)

Bowling: *First Innings*—McGrath 22–6–49–3; Noble 30–11–66–3; Marshall 35–14–61–1; D. R. Heath 16.3–9–28–3; J. A. Heath 6–1–11–0. *Second Innings*—McGrath 24–3–99–3; D. R. Heath 24–6–78–0; Noble 27–6–81–2; Marshall 40–14–69–0; J. A. Heath 10–6–20–0; Parker 5–0–25–0.

Umpires: K. J. Lyons and R. Palmer.

OXFORD v CAMBRIDGE, NOTES

The University Match dates back to 1827. Altogether there have been 157 official matches, Cambridge winning 56 and Oxford 49, with 52 drawn. Since the war Cambridge have won ten times (1949, 1953, 1957, 1958, 1972, 1979, 1982, 1986, 1992 and 1998) and Oxford ten (1946, 1948, 1951, 1959, 1966, 1976, 1984, 1993, 1995 and 2001). All other matches have been drawn; the 1988 fixture was abandoned without a ball being bowled. The first-class fixture was moved from its traditional venue at Lord's in 2001, to be staged alternately at Cambridge and Oxford, and a one-day game was played instead at Lord's.

One hundred and eleven three-figure innings have been played in the University matches, 52 for Oxford and 59 for Cambridge. For the fullest lists see the 1940 and 1993 *Wisdens*. There have been three double-centuries for Cambridge (211 by G. Goonesena in 1957, 201 by A. Ratcliffe in 1931 and 200 by Majid Khan in 1970) and two for Oxford (238* by Nawab of Pataudi, sen. in 1931 and 201* by M. J. K. Smith in 1954). Ratcliffe's score was a record for the match for only one day, before being beaten by Pataudi's. M. J. K. Smith and R. J. Boyd-Moss (Cambridge) are the only players to score three hundreds.

The highest totals in the fixture are 604 in 2002 by Cambridge, and 513 for six in 1996, 503 in 1900, 457 in 1947, 453 for eight in 1931 and 453 for nine in 1994, all by Oxford. The lowest totals are 32 by Oxford in 1878 and 39 by Cambridge in 1858.

F. C. Cobden, in the Oxford v Cambridge match in 1870, performed the hat-trick by taking the last three wickets and won an extraordinary game for Cambridge by two runs. Other hat-tricks, all for Cambridge, have been achieved by A. G. Steel (1879), P. H. Morton (1880), J. F. Ireland (1911) and R. G. H. Lowe (1926). S. E. Butler, in the 1871 match, took all ten wickets in the Cambridge first innings.

D. W. Jarrett (Oxford 1975, Cambridge 1976), S. M. Wookey (Cambridge 1975-76, Oxford 1978) and G. Pathmanathan (Oxford 1975-78, Cambridge 1983) gained Blues for both Universities.

A full list of Blues from 1837 may be found in Wisdens *published between 1923 and 1939. The lists thereafter were curtailed, covering more recent years only, and dropped after 1992.*

DURHAM

President: Dr J. G. Holland (St Hild and St Bede)
Hon. Treasurer: B. R. Lander (Hatfield)

Captain: M. J. Banes (Tonbridge and Collingwood)
Senior Captain of College Cricket: R. A. Johnson (Hallcross and Stephenson)

Durham University entered their second year of first-class cricket with a strong UCCE side, which retained many players from the previous season. Matt Banes remained captain, providing steady leadership and several key performances with the bat. Will Jefferson, when available, again looked an outstanding prospect; he scored an impressive 154 not out against Cambridge in the Inter-UCCE competition, and went on to make two first-class centuries for Essex later in the summer. Michael Brown was another significant contributor. In addition to opening the batting, he doubled up as wicket-keeper, in the absence of James Foster, who had made his Test debut over the winter but missed most of the 2002 season through injury.

Justin Bishop, the England Under-19 strike bowler, also had a nagging injury, which meant he contributed only 17 overs during the academic season – though he played a remarkable innings in the BUSA final. Most of the bowling duties therefore fell to the indomitable and persistent James Bruce, his fellow-seamer Mark Thorburn and the left-arm spinners Matt Creese and Rob Ferley. Andy Hollingsworth and the former England Under-19 captain, Alex Loudon, made some useful all-round contributions.

Durham drew two of their county matches and lost one – their maiden first-class defeat. In Durham, snow can fall at any time up to the beginning of May but, in 2002, April proved one of the driest and sunniest months of the year, and permitted the students to earn an honourable draw against their neighbours, Durham County, up the road at Chester-le-Street. A few days later, at Trent Bridge, they succumbed by 191 runs to Nottinghamshire, though they managed to pass 200 in both innings. In June, the weather was less pleasant, and Durham shared a damp, single-innings draw with Lancashire.

Away from the county circuit, Durham dropped to fourth in the Inter-UCCE competition, but only because they failed to break a tenth-wicket stand by Cambridge in their opening game. That last wicket would have given them an extra seven first-innings points, which would have put them on top of the tables, with the reward of another Lord's challenge game against Loughborough. Durham did meet Loughborough in the British Universities championship final, but lost to them for the third year running – by two runs, in a game which went to the last ball. The result reversed Durham's six-wicket victory over Loughborough in the competition's league stage.

In the junior British Universities championships, Durham were represented by their Combined Colleges squad (effectively the third and fourth teams), led by the charismatic Rob Johnson, and won both the Trophy Championship and Trophy Shield, as well as the women's title. Johnson left the university with a remarkable record: the Combined Colleges registered 37 victories and no defeats in his two years as senior captain of college cricket.

Many of Durham's most influential players from the UCCE team also graduated at the end of the season. It seems certain that 2003 will be a particularly demanding year, as a fresh group of players face the challenge of first-class opposition and defending Durham's position as one of university cricket's two strongest sides.

DURHAM UCCE RESULTS

First-class matches – Played 3: Lost 1, Drawn 2.

FIRST-CLASS AVERAGES
BATTING AND FIELDING

	M	I	NO	R	HS	100s	50s	Avge	Ct
R. S. Ferley	3	4	2	96	37*	0	0	48.00	1
T. J. Phillips	3	5	1	168	75	0	1	42.00	1
M. J. Banes	3	5	0	178	69	0	1	35.60	1
W. A. Kirby	2	4	1	78	37	0	0	26.00	2
M. J. Brown	3	5	0	120	57	0	1	24.00	4
A. P. Hollingsworth	3	4	1	72	42*	0	0	24.00	1
A. G. R. Loudon	3	5	0	54	35	0	0	10.80	5
J. T. A. Bruce	3	3	2	8	8*	0	0	8.00	2
W. I. Jefferson	2	4	0	31	11	0	0	7.75	2
M. Thorburn	3	3	0	16	12	0	0	5.33	1

Also batted: J. E. Bishop (1 match) 17*; M. L. Creese (1 match) 8; M. A. Hazelton (1 match) 5, 11 (2 ct); A. J. Maiden (1 match) 0; M. A. Souter (1 match) 1 (1 ct).

BOWLING

	O	M	R	W	BB	5W/i	Avge
A. P. Hollingsworth	23	4	86	4	3-35	0	21.50
R. S. Ferley	78	19	246	8	4-83	0	30.75
M. Thorburn	53	12	244	7	2-60	0	34.85
J. T. A. Bruce	48	6	178	5	2-76	0	35.60
A. G. R. Loudon	52.1	10	190	4	2-60	0	47.50
T. J. Phillips	63	11	240	3	2-60	0	80.00

Also bowled: M. J. Banes 3–0–13–0; J. E. Bishop 7–1–21–0; M. L. Creese 3–0–9–0; M. A. Hazelton 10–2–58–0; M. A. Souter 20–5–83–1.

At Chester-le-Street, April 13, 14, 15. DURHAM UCCE drew with DURHAM.

At Nottingham, April 20, 21, 22. DURHAM UCCE lost to NOTTINGHAMSHIRE by 191 runs.

DURHAM UCCE v LANCASHIRE

At Durham, June 12, 13, 14. Drawn. Toss: Durham UCCE. First-class debut: A. J. Maiden. University debuts: J. E. Bishop, M. L. Creese.

The bad weather that bedevilled the previous season's encounter between these teams revisited the Racecourse in 2002. Rain threatened from the outset and caused several interruptions on the first day. Banes claimed first use of an excellent pitch and took advantage with an invaluable half-century, but Durham never found much momentum as they proceeded to 198 in 89 overs. After seeing the poor forecast next morning, the students batted on for just ten overs, adding some quick runs, then declared to give the game a semblance of a chance. Thorburn swiftly removed Swann, but Chilton, one of three Durham alumni appearing for Lancashire, made a three-hour century, ably supported by Haynes and Hegg, whose fifties carried their side into the lead. But the following morning, a pall of grey cloud hung over the ground, and a veil of rain killed off the prospect of further play.

Close of play: First day, Durham UCCE 198-6 (Ferley 19, Creese 8); Second day, Lancashire 279-5 (Driver 25, Schofield 0).

Durham UCCE

†M. J. Brown c Hegg b Schofield	15		M. L. Creese c Haynes b Schofield	8	
A. J. Maiden lbw b Smethurst	0		J. E. Bishop not out	17	
*M. J. Banes lbw b Wood	69		B 8, l-b 9, w 18	35	
T. J. Phillips run out	25				
A. G. R. Loudon b Driver	35			(7 wkts dec.) 242	
A. P. Hollingsworth c Schofield b Keedy	1		1/4 (2) 2/51 (1)		
R. S. Ferley not out	37		3/124 (4) 4/141 (3)		
			5/150 (6) 6/166 (5) 7/199 (8)		

M. Thorburn and J. T. A. Bruce did not bat.

Bowling: Wood 12–7–13–1; Smethurst 20–7–60–1; Anderson 14–4–48–0; Driver 14–3–41–1; Schofield 23–9–33–2; Keedy 15–7–28–1; Chilton 1–0–2–0.

Lancashire

M. J. Chilton b Thorburn	107		C. P. Schofield not out	0	
A. J. Swann lbw b Thorburn	8				
†J. J. Haynes b Phillips	53		B 8, l-b 8, n-b 8	24	
*W. K. Hegg c Loudon b Bruce	62				
T. W. Roberts lbw b Phillips	0		1/14 (2) 2/180 (3) 3/192 (1)	(5 wkts) 279	
R. C. Driver not out	25		4/199 (5) 5/273 (4)		

J. Wood, G. Keedy, M. P. Smethurst and J. M. Anderson did not bat.

Bowling: Bruce 10–1–28–1; Thorburn 11–2–60–2; Bishop 7–1–21–0; Loudon 16–5–47–0; Ferley 15–5–38–0; Phillips 16–3–60–2; Creese 3–0–9–0.

Umpires: M. R. Benson and R. T. Robinson.

OTHER UCCES, 2002

By GRENVILLE HOLLAND

The gulf between the six University Centres of Cricketing Excellence and the first-class counties was even clearer in 2002 than the previous year, if only because better weather allowed more evidence for comparison. Of the 18 three-day games between the counties and the UCCEs, first-class and non-first-class, the counties won 13 and drew five, compared to seven wins, eight draws and three abandoned in 2001.

Loughborough, however, bucked the trend: they were the only UCCE to improve their county record. They were made to follow on by Kent in their first match of the season, but were never bowled out again. The opening batsman, Jimmy Adams, scored twin hundreds to secure the draw against Kent. In the next game, they declared 15 runs behind Derbyshire, in an attempt to create a result. It was another declaration – the third of the match – which led to their defeat by Hampshire in the final county game in June, but the county had seven wickets down when they won, five of them to the Yorkshire seamer, David Wigley. They passed 300 in at least one innings against each of the three counties, and, in addition to Adams, Jon Francis and Mark Powell scored centuries. Loughborough's relative performance factor (average runs scored per wicket divided by average runs conceded per wicket) against the counties was 0.69, some way short of equality (1.00) but well ahead of the first-class universities of

Durham (0.56), Oxford (0.30) and Cambridge (0.25). For comparison, a strong Cambridge team fifty years earlier outperformed their county opponents over 11 first-class games, with an RPF of 1.05.

Cardiff's 2001 county programme was almost drowned out of existence; in 2002, the weather relented, but the counties didn't. All three games, played in April when the professionals were seeking batting practice, ended in crushing defeats. The first two matches were prolonged when Somerset and Warwickshire both waived the follow-on – at Millfield, this enabled Cardiff to enjoy a brief moment of glory, reducing Somerset's second innings to 47 for six – but they went down by ten wickets in two days to their neighbours Glamorgan.

Like Cardiff, Bradford/Leeds lost all three county games, and were clearly out of their depth, with an RPF of 0.26 to Cardiff's 0.37. In successive weeks in April, they suffered innings defeats at the hands of Leicestershire and Yorkshire; in May, against Sussex, the margin was a mere 200 runs. They never reached 200 in any innings, and in the match against Yorkshire, 92 of their combined total of 323 were donated in extras.

Notes: Matches in this section were not first-class. UCCE away games appear in the county sections.

At Canterbury, April 13, 14, 15. LOUGHBOROUGH UCCE drew with KENT.

At Leicester, April 13, 14. BRADFORD/LEEDS UCCE lost to LEICESTERSHIRE by an innings and 316 runs.

At Millfield School, April 13, 14, 15. CARDIFF UCCE lost to SOMERSET by 221 runs.

At Birmingham, April 20, 21, 22. CARDIFF UCCE lost to WARWICKSHIRE by 580 runs.

At Leeds, April 20, 21, 22. BRADFORD/LEEDS UCCE lost to YORKSHIRE by an innings and 61 runs.

At Cardiff, April 24, 25. CARDIFF UCCE lost to GLAMORGAN by ten wickets.

At Hastings, May 8, 9, 10. BRADFORD/LEEDS UCCE lost to SUSSEX by 200 runs.

At Derby, May 15, 16, 17. LOUGHBOROUGH UCCE drew with DERBYSHIRE.

At Southampton, June 25, 26, 27. LOUGHBOROUGH UCCE lost to HAMPSHIRE by three wickets.

INTER-UCCE CRICKET, 2002

By GRENVILLE HOLLAND

This was the second year of the Inter-UCCE competition, in which the six University Centres of Cricketing Excellence played a round robin of two-day games. The points system placed a heavy emphasis on first innings, which often lasted more than 100 overs each, with the same number of points awarded for a first-innings win as an outright win. Tactics inevitably adapted to this structure. In 2001, in 15 games, there were two outright wins, both for Durham, but this time there were none: in fact, only six games managed a first-innings result.

Loughborough headed the table with two of those first-innings wins, over Cambridge and Oxford, thanks to a powerful batting line-up. They passed 300 in every match except for the fixture against Cardiff, which was washed out without a ball being bowled, and another rain-ruined game with Durham, which was called off when they were 72 for three.

Cardiff also completed two first-innings wins, notably against Durham, whom they led by six runs, and later against Cambridge, whom they led by 91 runs, thanks to an outstanding all-round performance by Alex French, who followed six wickets with a century. They tied on points with Oxford, who managed only one first-innings win, over Bradford/Leeds, powered by hundreds from Huw Jones and Joe Porter. But Oxford claimed the runners-up position, because they had taken seven points to Cardiff's five in a rain-affected draw. In fact, Oxford could have headed the table had they scored two more runs against Cambridge in May; they finished one short of Cambridge's first-innings total, which cost them seven points. They had done enough, however, to reach the one-day final at Lord's, where Loughborough once more demonstrated their superiority.

One of the key fixtures turned out to have been the opening game between Durham and Cambridge in April. The home openers, Will Jefferson and Michael Brown, were in commanding form. Both scored centuries and Durham declared at 363 for one. But had they been less intent on butchering some inept bowling and declared earlier, they would almost certainly have claimed a full ten first-innings points against Cambridge – whose team contained players who were not in residence at either the University or at Anglia, but merely intending students on a gap year. In fact, Cambridge hung on desperately, thanks to an undefeated 67 from John Heath, and finished on 173 for nine. That restricted Durham to three first-innings points. At the end of the season, they were six points behind Loughborough – and three behind Oxford and Cardiff. Durham slipped up again in May when they were bowled out six runs short of Cardiff's first-innings 257. Their only first-innings win came against Bradford/Leeds, thanks to a century from Matt Banes and seven wickets from the left-arm spinner Rob Ferley; another four wickets would have converted it into an outright innings win, which would have lifted them to second in the table.

INTER-UCCE CHAMPIONSHIP, 2002

	Played	Won	Lost	Drawn	1st-inns points	Bonus points Batting	Bowling	Points
Loughborough	5	0	0	5*	26	12	11	54
Oxford	5	0	0	5	19	10	22	51
Cardiff	5	0	0	5*	26	10	10	51
Durham	5	0	0	5	19	12	10	48†
Bradford/Leeds	5	0	0	5	19	7	18	30
Cambridge	5	0	0	5	9	10	14	29

Oxford were placed ahead of Cardiff by virtue of gaining more points in their head-to-head match.

* *Includes one match abandoned without a ball bowled.*   † *1 pt deducted for slow over-rate.*

Outright win = 10 pts; 1st-innings lead in a match reaching an outright result = 5 pts; 1st-innings win in a drawn match = 10 pts; no result on 1st innings = 3 pts; abandoned = 5 pts.
Up to four bonus points for batting and bowling were available in each innings, though in the first innings batting points were available only for the first 102 overs (or 50 per cent of the total overs in a shortened match). The first innings of the side batting first could not use more than 60 per cent of the total overs available in the match.

Note: Matches in this section were not first-class.

At Durham, April 29, 30. **Drawn** (no result). **Durham 363 for one** (M. J. Brown 109, W. I. Jefferson 154 not out, M. J. Banes 67 not out); **Cambridge 173 for nine** (J. R. Moyes 41, J. A. Heath 67 not out; J. T. A. Bruce six for 21). *Durham 11 pts, Cambridge 4 pts.*

At Loughborough, April 29, 30. **Drawn** (no result). **Loughborough 303 for six** (J. D. Francis 61, C. D. Nash 61, R. A. White 46, M. C. Rosenberg 69 not out; R. McLean three for 46); **Bradford/Leeds 20 for two.** *Loughborough 7 pts, Bradford/Leeds 5 pts.*

At Oxford, April 29, 30. **Drawn** (no result). **Cardiff 220** (J. Cook 33, A. N. French 36, A. N. Bressington 46, C. J. Yates 39; T. J. Sharpe four for 78, J. W. M. Dalrymple three for 50); **Oxford 39 for no wkt.** *Oxford 7 pts, Cardiff 5 pts.*

At Cambridge, May 8, 9. **Drawn.** Loughborough won by 89 runs on first innings. **Cambridge 219** (D. R. Heath 38, A. Shankar 54, S. J. Marshall 62 not out; M. A. Tournier four for 48, M. S. Panesar five for 62) **and 155 for eight** (J. R. Moyes 47 not out; M. A. Tournier three for 28, M. S. Panesar three for 69); **Loughborough 308 for five** (J. H. K. Adams 79, J. D. Francis 52, M. J. Powell 43, S. A. Selwood 57 not out). *Loughborough 21 pts, Cambridge 6 pts.*

At Cardiff, May 8, 9. **Drawn.** Cardiff won by six runs on first innings. **Cardiff 257** (J. Cook 85; M. Thorburn five for 68) **and 116 for four; Durham 251.** *Cardiff 18 pts, Durham 7 pts.*
    England Women's Caroline Atkins appeared for Durham.

At Oxford, May 15, 16. **Drawn.** Oxford won by 187 runs on first innings. **Oxford 348 for nine dec.** (J. J. Porter 130, H. R. Jones 129; C. J. Elstub six for 57); **Bradford/Leeds 161** (J. O. Siddall 62 not out; G. N. Bowers four for 40, J. W. M. Dalrymple three for 39) **and 175 for seven** (S. Webb 45, J. O. Siddall 41; H. R. Jones three for 27, G. N. Bowers three for 92). *Oxford 21 pts, Bradford/Leeds 7 pts.*

At Oxford, May 21, 22. **Drawn** (no result). **Cambridge 257** (P. Riley 33, S. J. Marshall 102, D. Williams 35; J. W. M. Dalrymple seven for 100); **Oxford 256 for seven** (J. J. Porter 44, P. P. Evans 41, S. H. Dalrymple 79; S. J. Marshall three for 93). *Oxford 10 pts, Cambridge 9 pts.*

At Cambridge, May 25, 26. **Drawn** (no result). **Bradford/Leeds 231** (L. Gordon 69, C. J. Elstub 50; D. J. Noble three for 92, F. I. Sharif seven for 74); **Cambridge 58 for three.** *Cambridge 7 pts, Bradford/Leeds 6 pts.*

At Abergavenny, May 25, 26. **Cardiff v Loughborough. Abandoned** (no result). *Cardiff 5 pts, Loughborough 5 pts.*

At Durham, May 25, 26. **Drawn** (no result). **Durham 170** (M. J. Brown 37, R. S. Ferley 52, J. E. Bishop 45; T. J. Sharpe four for 23, T. C. Hicks four for 60); **Oxford 131 for five** (J. J. Porter 47, H. R. Jones 51). *Durham 6 pts, Oxford 7 pts.*

At Loughborough, June 5, 6. **Drawn** (no result). **Loughborough 72 for three v Durham.** *Loughborough 3 pts, Durham 4 pts.*

At Bradford, June 8, 9. **Drawn** (no result). **Cardiff 206** (J. Cook 84); **Bradford/Leeds 58 for one.** *Bradford/Leeds 7 pts, Cardiff 5 pts.*

At Bradford, June 22, 23. **Drawn.** Durham won by 218 runs on first innings. **Durham 366 for seven dec.** (M. J. Banes 119, W. I. Jefferson 78, T. J. Phillips 63, A. P. Hollingsworth 50); **Bradford/Leeds 148** (R. S. Ferley seven for 38) **and 181 for six.** *Durham 20 pts, Bradford/Leeds 5 pts.*

At Pontypridd, June 22, 23. **Drawn.** Cardiff won by 91 runs on first innings. **Cambridge 209** (A. D. Simcox 56, D. R. Heath 51; A. N. French six for 51) **and 73 for no wkt** (A. D. Simcox 31 not out, D. R. Heath 40 not out); **Cardiff 300 for four dec.** (J. Cook 41, A. N. French 108, C. J. Yates 101 not out). *Cardiff 18 pts, Cambridge 3 pts.*

At Loughborough, June 22, 23. **Drawn.** Loughborough won by 23 runs on first innings. **Loughborough 319 for eight dec.** (C. D. Nash 93, R. A. White 65, D. F. Watts 32; T. Mees four for 54) **and ten for no wkt**; **Oxford 296** (J. W. M. Dalrymple 104, J. R. S. Redmayne 60, T. Mees 31 not out; D. H. Wigley three for 90). *Loughborough 18 pts, Oxford 6 pts.*

ONE-DAY UCCE CHALLENGE

LOUGHBOROUGH v OXFORD

At Lord's, July 2. Loughborough won by 69 runs. Toss: Oxford.

Mark Powell led Loughborough to their second university title in a fortnight when they bowled out Oxford with more than three overs to spare. Their only hiccough came at the start of the match when, asked to bat, their openers were bowled by successive deliveries with the score on ten. After that, Powell made full use of an easy-paced pitch and an undemanding attack, adding 91 with Steve Selwood and 154 with Chris Nash, who hit his last ten balls for 35. A target of nearly six an over was well beyond Oxford when David Wigley reduced them to 30 for four in eight overs. Huw Jones battled to 114 in 110 balls, and struck two sixes before he was eighth out, caught at deep square leg off Monty Panesar's left-arm spin. But it was Powell's match-winning 96 that claimed the prizes.

Man of the Match: M. J. Powell.

Loughborough

J. H. K. Adams b Sharpe	4	C. D. Nash c Hilsum b Mees	85
V. Atri b Mees	5	D. F. Watts not out	3
S. A. Selwood c Howard b J. W. M. Dalrymple	56	B 4, l-b 10, w 13, n-b 8	35
*M. J. Powell not out	96		
R. A. White c Mees b J. W. M. Dalrymple	12	1/10 2/10 3/101 (5 wkts, 50 overs)	296
		4/126 5/280	

D. H. Wigley, †C. P. Coleman, M. A. Tournier and M. S. Panesar did not bat.

Bowling: Mees 10–0–73–2; Sharpe 10–3–26–1; Millar 8–0–66–0; Hicks 10–0–44–0; J. W. M. Dalrymple 10–0–64–2; Sayers 2–0–9–0.

Oxford

J. J. Sayers lbw b Wigley	7	†W. O. F. Howard c Adams b Wigley	23
H. R. Jones c Selwood b Panesar	114	S. H. Dalrymple b Tournier	12
*J. W. M. Dalrymple c Coleman b Wigley	2	T. J. Sharpe not out	1
N. Millar lbw b Wigley	0	L-b 3, w 12, n-b 2	17
J. R. S. Redmayne b Wigley	0		
T. C. Hicks lbw b Watts	14	1/17 2/28 3/28 (46.4 overs)	227
I. J. Hilsum c Coleman b Panesar	28	4/30 5/78 6/156	
T. Mees c White b Panesar	9	7/173 8/200 9/221	

Bowling: Tournier 8–0–43–1; Wigley 8.4–1–52–5; Powell 10–0–46–0; Watts 10–0–45–1; Panesar 10–0–38–3.

Umpires: T. E. Jesty and G. Sharp.

WINNERS

2001	Loughborough	2002	Loughborough

THE HALIFAX BRITISH UNIVERSITIES CHAMPIONSHIP, 2002

By GRENVILLE HOLLAND

Over recent years, the British Universities Sports Association has broadened its base to embrace nearly 100 university cricket clubs, some of whom, like Loughborough and Durham, enter up to four teams in its various competitions. The university season is always a busy one, compressed into less than three months and usually clashing with examinations. It places a heavy administrative burden on the small and dedicated BUSA staff. But it was disappointing to see several university teams scratch at the last moment, even those at the highest level of competition.

In the Southern Premier League, Brunel West London, who were promoted only a year earlier, conceded their last two games, against Bristol and Exeter. Their punishment was to be relegated without the usual play-off against the bottom-placed team from the Northern Premier League. But they were not alone in their transgressions. In the Midlands division of the First Team Shield, Cambridge's eleven, having already profited from Derby's concession in an earlier round, granted Oxford Brookes a walkover. In the Women's Northern Premier League, Bradford/Leeds UCCE "failed to get a team together" against Durham UCCE.

Overall, standards continued to improve, but the gap between the top teams and the rest seemed, if anything, to be widening. The same four contested the semi-finals of the men's premiership as in the previous season – the UCCE teams of Durham, Loughborough and Oxford, and one from outside the UCCE circle, Exeter. Durham reached the final for the sixth year running, Loughborough for the sixth year in seven, and their junior teams won four other titles between them. In the premiership, the spoils went to Loughborough, by the narrowest of margins. A month earlier, Durham had won their league game by six wickets, which enabled them to head the Northern Premier League, with four victories excluding one abandoned match. Nottingham had an impressive season, with away wins over Bradford/Leeds UCCE and Cambridge, thanks to centuries from Robert Mutucumarana and Stephen Cordingley respectively. They finished level on points with Loughborough, but were placed third because they had lost their head-to-head match.

In the Southern Premier League, Exeter carried all before them, winning the three matches they actually played, thanks to the all-round efforts of Steve Moore; one fixture was abandoned in addition to the Brunel walkover. Oxford lost only to Exeter, but the unluckiest team was Cardiff UCCE, who had four games washed out; they won the single fixture which survived the weather, against Bristol.

In the final of the First Team Shield, Loughborough's First Eleven eased past Reading with the minimum of exertion – but since the rules prevented them from joining Loughborough UCCE in the Premier League, Reading returned to the top level after one year. Loughborough's luck ran out in the Trophy Championship, where their Second Eleven lost a fiercely contested final to Durham's Combined Colleges A team. The Combined Colleges B side won the Trophy Shield final against Southampton Second Eleven. The women's team won Durham's third title, in an outstanding campaign which saw them demolish Manchester for just seven runs, Southampton for 30 and, in the semi-final, St Mary's for 65, which England player Caroline Atkins had outscored off her own bat, with an unbeaten 85 in Durham's innings. They met Loughborough, who had just squashed Oxford by ten wickets, in the women's final, two days after their male counterparts had played at Cambridge, and the all-round performance of Ruth Barron brought them a 27-run victory.

BRITISH UNIVERSITIES PREMIER LEAGUES

Northern

	Played	Won	Lost	No result	Points
DURHAM UCCE	5	4	0	1	13
LOUGHBOROUGH UCCE . .	5	3	1	1	10
Nottingham	5	3	1	1	10
Cambridge UCCE	5	1	3	1	4
Bradford/Leeds UCCE	5	1	3	1	4
Liverpool	5	0	4	1	1

Loughborough qualified for the semi-finals by virtue of winning their head-to-head match with Nottingham.

Southern

	Played	Won	Lost	No result	Points
EXETER	5	4*	0	1	13
OXFORD UCCE	5	3	1	1	10
Cardiff UCCE	5	1	0	4	7
St Mary's	5	1	2	2	5
Bristol	5	1*	3	1	4
Brunel West London	5	0	4*	1	-5

* Brunel West London conceded their matches with Exeter and Bristol. They were automatically relegated, and replaced by Reading, the runners-up in the First Team Shield, because Shield winners Loughborough already had a team in the Premier Leagues.

SEMI-FINALS

At Bournemouth, June 10. **Loughborough UCCE won by seven wickets.** Toss: Loughborough UCCE. **Exeter 153** (48.1 overs) (N. Turk 32, R. Marshall 47); **Loughborough UCCE 154 for three** (39.1 overs) (M. J. Powell 45 not out, R. A. White 36 not out).

At Liverpool, June 11. **Durham UCCE won by ten wickets.** Toss: Durham UCCE. **Oxford UCCE 175 for nine** (50 overs) (J. J. Porter 34; R. S. Ferley three for 17); **Durham UCCE 176 for no wkt** (30.4 overs) (W. I. Jefferson 96 not out, M. J. Brown 72 not out).

FINAL

DURHAM UCCE v LOUGHBOROUGH UCCE

At Cambridge, June 18. Loughborough UCCE won by two runs. Toss: Durham UCCE.

Loughborough completed a hat-trick of victories over Durham, but it went to the wire. Justin Bishop needed six to tie off the last ball, and hit four. A close finish seemed unlikely when Monty Panesar claimed Durham's ninth wicket: they were still 56 behind, with eight overs left. But Bishop and James Bruce unfurled the best batting of the day, whittling the target down to 12 by the final over, from David Wigley. They could have won but for Durham's earlier profligacy – 28 extras, 17 in wides and no-balls. Rain had washed out the morning and reduced each innings to 44 overs. The pitch was far from friendly, but Jimmy Adams and his captain, Mark Powell, accumulated patiently, scoring only four boundaries between them. Before Durham's reply reached double figures, Mark Tournier and Wigley had grabbed three wickets. Matt Banes fought back, with a delightful 26-ball 22, and Alex Loudon made a determined 41, but it took the last-wicket pair to give Durham hope of a sensational victory.

Player of the Final: M. J. Powell.

Loughborough UCCE

J. H. K. Adams c and b Loudon	42	†C. P. Coleman not out	8
V. Atri c Banes b Bishop	14	D. H. Wigley not out	6
J. D. Francis c Maiden b Loudon	19	B 2, l-b 9, w 9, n-b 8	28
*M. J. Powell c Banes b Bruce	44		
R. A. White lbw b Ferley	11	1/41 2/90 3/94 (7 wkts, 44 overs) 190	
C. D. Nash lbw b Ferley	10	4/123 5/149	
D. F. Watts c Banes b Ferley	8	6/164 7/179	

M. A. Tournier and M. S. Panesar did not bat.

Bowling: Bruce 7–0–27–1; Thorburn 9–1–27–0; Bishop 7–1–23–1; Loudon 4–0–23–2; Ferley 9–0–40–3; Phillips 8–0–39–0.

Durham UCCE

†M. J. Brown c Francis b Wigley	1	J. E. Bishop not out	42
T. J. Phillips b Tournier	0	M. Thorburn b Panesar	3
A. J. Maiden c Coleman b Wigley	3	J. T. A. Bruce not out	22
*M. J. Banes c White b Watts	22	B 1, l-b 4, w 6, n-b 4	15
A. G. R. Loudon c Tournier b Panesar	41		
A. P. Hollingsworth c Coleman b Watts	1	1/1 2/1 3/8 (9 wkts, 44 overs) 188	
R. S. Ferley c Atri b Panesar	15	4/39 5/41 6/81	
M. L. Creese run out	23	7/104 8/117 9/134	

Bowling: Tournier 9–2–30–1; Wigley 9–1–47–2; Watts 8–1–40–2; Powell 9–2–22–0; Panesar 9–0–44–3.

Umpires: A. Flook and K. Hopley.

WINNERS 1927–2002

The UAU Championship was replaced by the British Universities Championship from 1995.

1927 Manchester	1958 Null and void	1981 Durham
1928 Manchester	1959 Liverpool	1982 Exeter
1929 Nottingham	1960 Loughborough Colls.	1983 Exeter
1930 Sheffield	1961 Loughborough Colls.	1984 Bristol
1931 Liverpool	1962 Manchester	1985 Birmingham
1932 Manchester	1963 Loughborough Colls.	1986 Durham
1933 Manchester	1964 Loughborough Colls.	1987 Durham
1934 Leeds	1965 Hull	1988 Swansea
1935 Sheffield	1966 { Newcastle / Southampton }	1989 Loughborough
1936 Sheffield		1990 Durham
1937 Nottingham	1967 Manchester	1991 Durham
1938 Durham	1968 Southampton	1992 Durham
1939 Durham	1969 Southampton	1993 Durham
1946 Not completed	1970 Southampton	1994 Swansea
1947 Sheffield	1971 Loughborough Colls.	1995 Durham
1948 Leeds	1972 Durham	1996 Loughborough
1949 Leeds	1973 { Leicester / Loughborough Colls. }	1997 Loughborough
1950 Manchester		1998 { Durham / Loughborough }
1951 Manchester	1974 Durham	
1952 Loughborough Colls.	1975 Loughborough Colls.	1999 Durham
1953 Durham	1976 Loughborough	2000 Loughborough
1954 Manchester	1977 Durham	2001 Loughborough
1955 Birmingham	1978 Manchester	2002 Loughborough
1956 Null and void	1979 Manchester	
1957 Loughborough Colls.	1980 Exeter	

MCC MATCHES, 2002

After trips in recent years to Shenley, The Parks and Arundel, the bacon-and-egg ties travelled north for the showcase first-class fixture, where MCC met Sri Lanka at Chesterfield's leafy Queen's Park. An MCC side crammed with young English players who were going places dominated the match and earned full marks from the England management for giving no quarter to the Sri Lankans before the decisive final Test. With the ground a blaze of sunhats, MCC skittled the tourists for 127 on the third day, but soggy run-ups had prevented any play on the first, and there was no chance of a win.

It was not the last time that bad weather would barge in uninvited. Of the 408 matches arranged against clubs and schools, 66 were abandoned without a ball bowled, 17 more than the year before, and seven cancelled. On April 30, rain washed out all seven scheduled matches, and even as late as July 3 just one match of 11 survived. Among 100 draws, 21 were sullied by the weather.

But the dark clouds could not dim some sparkling performances. The MCC won more than twice as many games as they lost – 158 to 74 – and there were plenty of individual heroics. In total, 62 hundreds were scored, including three by Iain Collins and two (on successive days) by Paul Berry, whose 140 against King Edward VII & Queen Mary School, Lytham was MCC's highest score of the summer. The bowling honours went to Paul O'Reilly, once of Hertfordshire, who grabbed eight for 27 against Bishop's Stortford College with his fast-medium.

The year started with three winter tours, which produced the usual mixture of exciting finishes, impressive performances and daft moments. Highlights included two magnificent innings by Steve Tikolo, who helped bat a strong MCC side into submission in Kenya. Four more tours took place later in the year.

Back on home soil, match managers prepared for the new season by dusting off their speech-making skills as well as their pads and whites. The 2002 season marked the beginning of a campaign to spread the gospel of the "Spirit of Cricket" among schoolchildren, and managers gave a talk on the subject at many games. On the field, three thrilling ties set pulses racing, including one against King's School, Macclesfield. The crucial moment came when Bob Cooke's tempting "orbit ball" dismissed Macclesfield's Alan Day for 152. There was more innovation in the match against Magdalen College School, when MCC sent out Neil Hunt as a lunch-watchman. Against St Lawrence College, Simon Willis whipped off his wicket-keeping pads and then nipped out six batsmen as an emergency spinner, while Simon Hughes, Channel 4's The Analyst, showed he had learned a bit about batting and was warmly praised by his captain for showing the boys of his old school, Latymer, a textbook forward defence.

The MCC women's side had their most successful season yet, winning five of their 12 matches, drawing four and losing three. The strides made since their first season in 1999 were clear when they hosted a fixture against the full Indian women's side. A narrow defeat was an impressive effort against a team that had thrashed England in a one-day series over the winter of 2001-02. More new ground was broken when Claire Taylor trotted out alongside Mike Gatting, Mark Nicholas and eight other men to represent MCC against the Duke of Richmond's XI during the Goodwood Club's 300th anniversary.

MCC Young Cricketers won 16 of their 45 games, with six draws, 11 defeats and 12 matches abandoned. Rikki Clarke became the latest in a long line of former Young Cricketers to be called up by England, when he was added to the squad for the Champions Trophy in Sri Lanka.

Note: Matches in this section were not first-class except for the game against the Sri Lankans.

At Exmouth, April 28. **Devon won on scoring-rate.** Toss: Devon. **Devon 226** (50 overs) (K. A. D. Barrett 62, S. A. Stoneman 61); **MCC 121** (35 overs) (N. Hancock five for 16, T. Anning three for 23).

MCC's target had been revised to 182 in 40 overs.

At Bournemouth, May 1. **Dorset won by three wickets.** Toss: MCC. **MCC 202 for five dec.** (J. B. R. Jones 88); **Dorset 204 for seven** (M. G. Miller 55, T. C. Z. Lamb 51; P. N. Unsworth three for 47).

At Lord's, May 2. **No result.** Toss: MCC. **Minor Counties 67 for two** (20 overs) v MCC.

At Lord's, May 8. **MCC won by 72 runs.** Toss: MCC Young Cricketers. **MCC 250 for four dec.** (S. H. Wootton 43, T. W. Harrison 71, J. E. Morris 32, Extras 31); **MCC Young Cricketers 178** (D. M. Rushbrook 44, J. E. P. Walford 32; A. R. Roberts four for 59, T. S. Smith three for 39).

At Ealing, May 29. **Club Cricket Conference won by four wickets.** Toss: MCC. **MCC 147** (42 overs) (J. P. Arscott 35; D. Prasad four for 33, D. Carter three for 14); **Club Cricket Conference 148 for six** (37.2 overs) (B. Hooper four for 45).

At Chesterfield, June 6, 7, 8. MCC drew with SRI LANKANS (see Sri Lankan tour section).

At Cambridge, June 11, 12, 13. MCC beat CAMBRIDGE UNIVERSITY by 95 runs (see The Universities section).

At Durham, June 17, 18, 19. **Drawn.** Toss: MCC. **MCC 405 for five dec.** (G. D. Hodgson 50, G. J. Lord 101, G. Katz 54, M. W. Gatting 114 not out) **and 146 for four dec.; Durham University 294 for six dec.** (B. Kirby 76, J. Howes 60, C. Hey 49; H. Pedrola three for 74) **and 232 for nine** (C. Hey 68, T. Allen 65, S. Polley 47; G. L. Molins four for 87).

At Oxford, June 19, 20, 21. MCC lost to OXFORD UNIVERSITY by three wickets (see The Universities section).

At Shenley Park, June 24. **MCC won by 49 runs.** Toss: MCC. **MCC 279 for four** (45 overs) (B. J. Debenham 70, M. W. Cowell 82, M. Parmar 76 not out); **Cricket Club of India 230 for seven** (45 overs) (K. S. More 55, M. Rajawat 82; S. Burger three for 54).

At Shenley Park, June 26. **England Board XI won by nine wickets.** Toss: England Board XI. **MCC 191 for eight** (50 overs) (S. V. Carlisle 74, J. R. Wileman 40; A. J. Pugh three for 15); **England Board XI 194 for one** (46 overs) (C. M. Mole 78, Q. J. Hughes 54 not out).

At Swansea, July 8, 9, 10. **Wales won by two wickets.** Toss: MCC. **MCC 314 for nine dec.** (S. J. Dean 87, B. J. Debenham 54, A. G. W. Lewin 108; M. Wilkshire four for 75) **and 153 for eight dec.** (P. E. Wellings 60 not out; I. Capon three for 45); **Wales 205** (O. A. Dawkins 57; A. Robinson four for 63, J. D. Batty four for 47) **and 264 for eight** (A. Beasley 64, M. Wilkshire 65; J. D. Batty six for 108).
J. D. Batty took ten for 155 in the match.

At Castleford, July 12. **Sydney University won by 53 runs.** Toss: Sydney University. **Sydney University 231 for seven** (50 overs) (E. Quoyle 66, E. Cowan 55); **MCC 178** (43.2 overs) (P. Murphy four for 47).

At Wormsley, July 21. **Sir Paul Getty's XI won by six wickets.** Toss: Sir Paul Getty's XI. **MCC 160** (W. Morrick six for 51); **Sir Paul Getty's XI 162 for four** (G. Morgan 67; D. J. Terbrugge three for 28).

At Lord's, August 12. **MCC won by six wickets.** Toss: MCC. **Scotland 240** (49.4 overs) (R. E. More 81, C. J. O. Smith 39, D. A. J. Rigby 66, Extras 37; R. Kotkamp four for 31, D. R. Brown three for 36); **MCC 241 for four** (46 overs) (J. E. R. Gallian 36, M. P. Maynard 117 not out, Asif Mujtaba 65).

At Cork, August 13, 14, 15. **Ireland won by five wickets.** Toss: MCC. **MCC 294 for seven dec.** (D. M. Ward 97, T. W. Harrison 46, M. W. Cowell 55) **and forfeited second innings; Ireland forfeited first innings and 297 for five** (N. J. O'Brien 111, A. R. White 76).

At Goodwood, September 1. **MCC won by six wickets.** Toss: Duke of Richmond's XI. **Duke of Richmond's XI 203** (C. S. Cowdrey 68; A. J. R. Bird six for 109); **MCC 204 for four** (M. C. J. Nicholas 47, B. J. Debenham 69, M. W. Gatting 54).

At Scarborough, September 2. **MCC won by six wickets.** Toss: MCC. **Combined Services 102** (45.2 overs) (F/Off T. Adcock 30; B. T. P. Donelan four for 11); **MCC 104 for four** (25.3 overs) (R. K. Lynch 42, N. S. Hartley 31; Cpl S. Cooper three for 18).

OTHER MATCHES, 2002

Note: Matches in this section were not first-class.

At Southampton, April 17, 18, 19, 20. **England Under-19 won by three wickets.** Toss: England Under-19. **Hampshire Second Eleven 376** (G. W. White 118, L. R. Prittipaul 67, Extras 72; G. G. Wagg four for 89) **and 214 for three dec.** (G. W. White 102 not out, J. S. Laney 53); **England Under-19 290** (A. W. Gale 79, S. R. Patel 51; I. H. Shah three for 40) **and 305 for seven** (A. W. Gale 32, Kadeer Ali 96, M. L. Pettini 46, S. R. Patel 38, G. G. Wagg 46 not out; J. R. C. Hamblin three for 58).

This match was the annual fixture between the previous year's Second Eleven Champions and England Under-19.

At Cardiff, June 24. **Wales won by eight wickets.** Toss: Wales. **England XI 189 for nine** (50 overs) (M. E. Trescothick 38, A. J. Stewart 39); **Wales 191 for two** (40.3 overs) (R. D. B. Croft 30, S. P. James 83 not out, D. L. Hemp 57).

Billed as the NatWest Challenge, this was a warm-up match for England's one-day squad before the NatWest Series. Tickets were £25 and the ground was about half full. Wales fielded nine Glamorgan players, South Africa's all-rounder Jacques Kallis (Glamorgan 1999) and Steffan Jones of Somerset, born in Llanelli. Trescothick captained England for the first time in the UK. Croft, who also took two for 36, was Man of the Match.

EUROPEAN CHAMPIONSHIP

At Larne, July 20. **England Board XI won by two runs.** Toss: Scotland. **England Board XI 173 for seven** (50 overs) (Q. J. Hughes 56, I. Dawood 40); **Scotland 171** (49.5 overs) (D. A. J. Rigby 44, R. R. Watson 40; S. J. Foster three for 22, S. Chapman three for 32).

Chasing 174, Scotland were 170 for four with two overs to go, but lost their last six for one run in 11 balls.

At Comber, July 20. **Italy won by one run.** Toss: Holland. **Italy 144** (45.5 overs) (J. C. Scuderi 64; R. P. Lefebvre three for 12, Adeel Raja three for 26); **Holland 143 for nine** (50 overs) (L. P. van Troost 41, N. A. Statham 50; A. G. Corbellari four for 33).

At Stormont, July 20. **Ireland won by 98 runs.** Toss: Denmark. **Ireland 281 for nine** (50 overs) (J. A. M. Molins 57, A. R. White 70, D. Joyce 31, P. G. Gillespie 40; H. Hansen three for 50, L. Hedegaard three for 50); **Denmark 183 for seven** (50 overs) (Aftab Ahmed 36, T. M. Hansen 44 not out; G. J. Neely three for 38, A. R. White three for 35).

At Downpatrick, July 21. **Holland won by 73 runs.** Toss: Holland. **Holland 247** (50 overs) (K. J. J. van Noortwijk 64, L. P. van Troost 96; H. Hansen four for 63); **Denmark 174** (49.4 overs) (L. Hedegaard 52, M. Hedegaard 55 not out; E. Schiferli three for 36, Adeel Raja three for 23).

At Bangor, July 21. **England Board XI won by 62 runs.** Toss: England Board XI. **England Board XI 245 for eight** (50 overs) (S. J. Foster 36, P. S. Lazenbury 46, S. Chapman 57, Extras 39); **Italy 183 for eight** (50 overs) (J. C. Scuderi 32, S. Ketipe 71 not out).

At Lisburn, July 21. **Scotland won by eight wickets.** Toss: Ireland. **Ireland 103** (46.5 overs) (P. J. C. Hoffmann three for 20); **Scotland 104 for two** (26.3 overs) (J. G. Williamson 54).

At Waringstown, July 22. **Scotland won by four wickets.** Toss: Denmark. **Denmark 198 for eight** (50 overs) (L. Hedegaard 48, Extras 31); **Scotland 202 for six** (44.3 overs) (D. R. Lockhart 37, C. J. O. Smith 87).

At Lurgan, July 22. **England Board XI won by five wickets.** Toss: Holland. **Holland 160** (49.1 overs) (T. B. M. de Leede 53; M. A. Sharp three for 11, A. Akhtar three for 34); **England Board XI 161 for five** (48 overs) (S. J. Foster 54, S. Chapman 35 not out, A. J. Pugh 30).

At Comber, July 22. **Ireland won by 28 runs.** Toss: Ireland. **Ireland 231 for eight** (50 overs) (W. K. McCallan 75, D. Heasley 38, Extras 34; H. Jayasena three for 22); **Italy 203** (48.2 overs) (A. Bonora 69, S. Ketipe 51; G. J. Neely five for 30).

At Eglinton, July 23. **Ireland won by 11 runs.** Toss: Holland. **Ireland 193 for eight** (37 overs) (A. R. White 35, W. K. McCallan 34; L. P. van Troost three for 30); **Holland 182 for nine** (37 overs) (T. B. M. de Leede 51, J-J. Esmeijer 31).

At Limavady, July 23. **Scotland won by 137 runs.** Toss: Scotland. **Scotland 247 for seven** (46 overs) (D. R. Lockhart 36, J. G. Williamson 99, C. J. O. Smith 57; H. Jayasena four for 59); **Italy 110 for nine** (46 overs) (Majid Haq three for 33).

At Limavady, July 24. **England Board XI won by ten wickets.** Toss: Denmark. **Denmark 115 for eight** (50 overs) (M. Lund 42 not out; A. Akhtar three for 26, S. Chapman three for 20); **England Board XI 117 for no wkt** (38 overs) (S. J. Foster 56 not out, Q. J. Hughes 51 not out).

At Lurgan, July 25. **Denmark won by nine wickets.** Toss: Italy. **Italy 131 for eight** (46 overs) (J. C. Scuderi 54); **Denmark 132 for one** (23.3 overs) (F. A. Klokker 53 not out, C. R. Pedersen 41).

At Stormont, July 25. **Holland won by three runs.** Toss: Holland. **Holland 183 for seven** (50 overs) (H-J. Mol 35, T. B. M. de Leede 52); **Scotland 180 for eight** (50 overs) (D. R. Lockhart 54, D. A. J. Rigby 56; E. Schiferli three for 34, J-J. Esmeijer three for 21).

At Waringstown, July 25. **England Board XI won by one run.** Toss: Ireland. **England Board XI 226 for eight** (50 overs) (R. W. J. Howitt 83, S. Chapman 44; A. R. White three for 32); **Ireland 225 for nine** (50 overs) (J. A. M. Molins 106, W. K. McCallan 42, N. J. O'Brien 33).

The England Board XI became European champions, with five straight wins. Ireland needed seven runs from the last over, with three wickets left; had they won, they would have tied on eight points with England and been declared champions by virtue of a head-to-head victory. Instead, they were placed third, because Scotland, with whom they tied on six points, had won their head-to-head game.

Division One

	Played	Won	Lost	Points
England	5	5	0	10
Scotland	5	3	2	6
Ireland	5	3	2	6
Holland	5	2	3	4
Denmark	5	1	4	2
Italy	5	1	4	2

Division Two

	Played	Won	Lost	Points
Gibraltar	5	4	1	8
Germany	5	4	1	8
Portugal	5	3	2	6
Israel	5	2	3	4
France	5	2	3	4
Austria	5	0	5	0

When two teams finished with an equal number of points, the positions were decided by the result of their head-to-head match.

Previous European champions were Ireland (1996) and Holland (1998 and 2000).

At Hove, September 13 (day/night). **Angus Fraser's XI won by seven wickets.** Toss: Sussex XI. **Sussex XI 199 for seven** (20 overs) (R. R. Montgomerie 36, W. J. House 76); **Angus Fraser's XI 204 for three** (18.3 overs) (M. A. Roseberry 34, M. W. Gatting 90 not out).

This was a memorial match for Sussex's Umer Rashid and his brother Burhan, who drowned in Grenada in April. Their brother Sultan played for Sussex. Fraser's team included Dr Keith Mitchell, the prime minister of Grenada, who bowled the opening over, and the Surrey captain Adam Hollioake, who missed the penultimate Championship match to play.

POWER CRICKET

At Millennium Stadium, Cardiff, October 4. **Rest of the World won by seven wickets.** Toss: Rest of the World XI. **The Brits 133 for eight** (15 overs) (M. Muralitharan three for 29) **and 155** (15 overs) (A. D. Brown 30, J. P. Crawley 36, M. A. Ealham 31; C. A. Walsh five for 50); **Rest of the World 179 for six** (15 overs) (A. Flower 45) **and 112 for three** (12.4 overs) (N. J. Astle 76 not out).

At Millennium Stadium, Cardiff, October 5. **Rest of the World won by two runs.** Toss: The Brits. **Rest of the World 142 for seven** (15 overs) (P. A. de Silva 61) **and 141** (14.3 overs) (S. P. Fleming 43, Shahid Afridi 35; M. J. Saggers five for 18, M. A. Ealham three for 19); **The Brits 143 for nine** (15 overs) (A. D. Brown 54; C. A. Walsh three for 17) **and 138 for eight** (15 overs) (M. P. Maynard 44; M. Muralitharan three for 32, Wasim Akram three for 30).

These two matches, billed as Power Cricket, were played indoors at Cardiff's Millennium Stadium, which has a capacity of 73,000 – and short side boundaries. The first game attracted 4,000 and the second 7,500. Nasser Hussain captained the Brits and Stephen Fleming the Rest of the World. Each side fielded 16 players, of whom 11 could bat and 11 field. Eight runs were awarded for hitting the ball into the middle tier of the seating and ten for the top tier; Shahid Afridi achieved the maximum 12 for hitting the roof.

SIR PAUL GETTY'S XI RESULTS, 2002

Played 9: Won 4, Lost 2, Drawn 3. Abandoned 2.

April 30	Sri Lankans	Abandoned
May 5	Eton Ramblers	Drawn
May 12	Cambridge University	Won by seven wickets
May 26	I Zingari	Abandoned
May 29	Oxford University	Drawn
June 9	Arabs	Drawn
June 19	Pilgrims	Won by 68 runs
July 21	MCC	Won by six wickets
August 4	Combined Services	Lost by 93 runs
August 28	Minor Counties	Lost by two wickets
September 15	Heartaches	Won by 71 runs

In the match against Minor Counties on August 28, David Ward scored an unbeaten 211 out of 282 for no wicket declared – and still finished on the losing side.

THE MINOR COUNTIES, 2002

A combination of a slow over-rate, rain and a cautious declaration meant Herefordshire could not quite ram home their advantage against Norfolk and, as in 2001, the Minor Counties Championship was shared. It was hard on Kevin Cooper, who gave everything and turned in another magnificent display of fast-medium seam bowling. He was as accurate and penetrating as ever, belying his 44 years, and he seized nine wickets in the final. His glorious season brought 52 at under ten apiece.

The Western Division was a two-horse race: as the last round began Devon, thanks to five straight victories, were top. But while Herefordshire were winning in Cornwall, Devon fell just short in a nerve-shredding run-chase against Berkshire at Torquay. It meant the two leaders had identical records – played six, won five, drawn one – but Herefordshire had one more bonus point. The pity was that they hadn't played each other during the summer. The current Championship system of six three-day games pits each side against the others in their group once home and once away in a three-year cycle, and chance kept Herefordshire and Devon apart in 2002. Devon's failure to reach the final denied their captain, Peter Roebuck, the chance of a fifth Championship in his last season. At the other end of the table, the bottom three teams could not eke out a win between them.

It was very much an East Anglian affair in the Eastern Division, with Norfolk finishing second, Suffolk second and Cambridgeshire third. Norfolk relied on a powerful batting line-up, though they were lucky with the weather. As the last fixtures were about to start, five counties could in theory have won the division. Norfolk, who enjoyed an 11-point cushion, gained another ten from a draw with Northumberland, but could still have been overtaken if Suffolk had won convincingly. They never had the chance: a Mildenhall monsoon washed out all three days of their clash with Buckinghamshire and gave them just six points. Cambridgeshire had a quieter season than in 2001, when they were docked 53 points for fielding an ineligible player and plummeted from first to seventh. The year also marked the nadir in Cumberland's fortunes: they finished last, and were the only county in the division without a victory.

Although the continuation of the experiment with three-day cricket did mean fewer matches were left unfinished – results outnumbered draws in both divisions – there were familiar complaints from counties that it was impossible to play a settled team. As many as 28 different players turned out for Wales, 27 for Cheshire, as cricketers tried to juggle work, family and sport commitments. It was no surprise that neither of those sides could look back on 2002 with much satisfaction. Two that could were the Warwickshire Board XI and Buckinghamshire. The Board XI became the first non-Minor County to win the ECB 38-County Cup, when they squeezed past Devon in the last over of the final, condemning Roebuck to two near misses in his farewell summer. Buckinghamshire's season had been no great shakes until the first round of the 2003 C&G. Then came the great shakes, as David Taylor and Paul Atkins propelled Buckinghamshire to a meteoric 424, the third-highest total in the competition. Unlucky Suffolk were the ones to suffer.

▷ "Come on guys," exhorted McKenzie, as Tweedie took KwaZulu-Natal past 700, "a wicket always falls on 702." But it didn't.
KwaZulu-Natal v Northerns, page 1462

MINOR COUNTIES CHAMPIONSHIP, 2002

Eastern Division

	P	W	L	D	Bonus Points Batting	Bowling	Total Points
Norfolk	6	3	0	3	11	22	93
Suffolk	5	2	1	2	15	17	78*
Cambridgeshire	6	2	0	4	10	19	77
Bedfordshire	6	2	1	3	10	19	77
Staffordshire	6	2	1	3	11	20	75
Lincolnshire	6	1	1	4	20	16	72
Northumberland	6	1	2	3	10	20	68
Hertfordshire	6	1	4	1	16	18	58
Buckinghamshire	5	1	2	2	4	18	54
Cumberland	6	0	3	3	6	21	52*
							39

* Suffolk and Buckinghamshire took six points each from an abandoned match.

Western Division

	P	W	L	D	Bonus Points Batting	Bowling	Total Points
Herefordshire	6	5	0	1	14	22	120
Devon	6	5	0	1	16	19	119
Oxfordshire	6	3	1	2	8	24	88
Cornwall	6	3	2	1	8	23	83
Berkshire	6	2	2	2	12	23	75
Cheshire	6	1	2	3	17	17	62
Shropshire	6	1	3	2	11	22	57
Dorset	6	0	4	2	12	24	44
Wiltshire	6	0	3	3	8	21	41
Wales	6	0	3	3	8	12	32

Final: Herefordshire drew with Norfolk.

Win = 16 points; draw = 4 points.

BEDFORDSHIRE

If rain had not disrupted three of Bedfordshire's last four games, they might have been pressing for top spot. They had Norfolk, who did finish first, a tantalising eight down with 91 still needed – despite losing more than 40 overs on the last day. Andy Roberts was an innovative captain and usually preferred the risk of a run-chase to a drab draw. His hand was strengthened by the arrival of two new players: Dave Roberts (ex-Northamptonshire), who made a pair on debut but went on to average almost 50; and Mark Patterson (of Ireland and Surrey), who tore in at a terrifying pace, spurred Shaun Rashid on to do the same and ended with 20 wickets. James Knott headed the batting averages for the second year running.

Batting

	M	I	NO	R	HS	100s	50s	Avge
J. A. Knott	6	11	3	460	69	0	6	57.50
D. J. Roberts	5	10	2	394	126*	1	3	49.25
A. Shankar	5	9	0	356	104	1	0	39.55
A. R. Roberts	6	11	3	255	79	0	1	31.87
T. R. Bristow	4	7	2	150	60	0	1	30.00
N. A. Stanley	4	7	0	166	67	0	1	23.71
D. J. M. Mercer	4	7	0	119	75	0	1	17.00
A. D. Patterson	5	10	1	148	46	0	0	16.44

Six matches: M. W. Patterson 43 runs, S. Rashid 29, J. A. Green 7. *Five matches:* R. J. Pack 11. *One match:* A. N. Cook 67, J. M. Steadman 64, C. P. Stearn 15, S. J. Watts 0.

Bowling

	O	M	R	W	BB	5W/i	Avge
A. R. Roberts	181.4	66	343	20	7-85	1	17.15
M. W. Patterson	173.1	43	539	20	5-57	1	26.95
S. Rashid	174.4	34	665	23	4-94	0	28.91

Other wicket-takers: R. J. Pack 9, J. A. Green 8.

BERKSHIRE

Inconsistent performances led to mixed results – two wins, two losses, two draws – and a mid-table finish, though there were several individual success stories. Essex were sufficiently impressed by Nick Denning to offer him a year's contract for 2003, while his fellow-seamer, James Theunissen, also looked a good prospect. The batting was led by Jon Perkins, who hit 344 runs in just three games, including 138 not out in the innings defeat by Herefordshire. The former Sussex keeper, Nick Wilton, kept neatly and batted well, and James Morris, a Bradfield College student, shone in his debut season. Berkshire went through the group stages of the 38-County Cup unbeaten, but an inferior net run-rate prevented them from reaching the knockout rounds. Travelling the opposite way from Denning was the ex-Essex batsman, Paul Prichard, who made up for indifferent Championship form with two important innings in the preliminary rounds of the C&G to set up a tie against Durham in May.

Batting

	M	I	NO	R	HS	100s	50s	Avge
J. R. Perkins	3	6	1	344	138*	1	2	68.80
J. C. Morris	4	7	1	251	80	0	3	41.83
N. J. Wilton	5	8	1	278	79	0	2	39.71
J. R. Wood	6	11	2	259	129	1	0	28.77
L. H. Nurse	4	8	0	183	68	0	2	22.87
S. J. Wyatt	6	9	1	167	84*	0	1	20.87
S. M. Brogan	3	5	0	104	61	0	1	20.80
P. J. Prichard	5	7	0	119	80	0	1	17.00

Six matches: J. E. Theunissen 48 runs. *Five matches:* S. P. Naylor 59, N. A. Denning 43. *Three matches:* M. A. Smith 47, L. D. Atkinson 36. *Two matches:* T. D. Fray 86, T. L. Hall 73. *One match:* S. S. Patel 92, T. L. Lambert 43, T. G. Burrows 39, P. R. Carter 22.

Bowling

	O	M	R	W	BB	5W/i	Avge
N. A. Denning	165	49	457	33	8-66	3	13.84
J. R. Wood	83	22	223	13	4-49	0	17.15
J. C. Morris	76.3	11	333	10	2-16	0	33.30
J. E. Theunissen	146	26	606	17	4-42	0	35.64

Other wicket-takers: S. P. Naylor 9, L. D. Atkinson 4, T. L. Lambert 3, M. A. Smith 2, P. R. Carter and S. S. Patel 1.

BUCKINGHAMSHIRE

The most dazzling day of a drear summer came near the end, when in the first round of the 2003 C&G Buckinghamshire blew the Suffolk attack to smithereens. David Taylor, a hard-hitting left-hander, pummelled his way to 147 off 77 balls as Buckinghamshire totalled 424 for five, which would have been the highest score in the competition had Surrey and Glamorgan not gone berserk at The Oval a few weeks earlier. Taylor, who was making a debut to remember, screamed to 100 from 47 balls, believed to be the county's fastest. Paul Atkins, the captain, also made hay with a century, but the day was not typical of Buckinghamshire's season: in the Championship, they managed a measly four batting points, less than anyone else. Atkins was the pick of the batsmen, hitting a hundred in the only win, against Cumberland, and carrying his bat (for the second time) in the defeat by Staffordshire. The leg-spinner Andy Clarke sustained the bowling, and passed 250 Championship wickets during the summer.

Batting

	M	I	NO	R	HS	100s	50s	Avge
P. D. Atkins	5	9	4	351	113*	1	3	70.20
J. D. Batty	3	4	0	117	43	0	0	29.25
G. D. T. Paskins	3	6	0	147	64	0	1	24.50
K. J. Locke	4	8	0	195	52	0	1	24.37
A. J. Ward	4	8	1	163	63*	0	1	23.28
R. P. Lane	3	6	0	131	51	0	1	21.83
D. R. Drepaul	5	10	1	129	65	0	1	14.33

Five matches: A. R. Clarke 45 runs, S. F. Stanway 35. *Three matches:* A. Saleem 81, S. J. Brandon 73, R. A. Jones 54. *Two matches:* A. S. Umpleby 71, M. J. O'Reilly 36, P. S. Lynch 27. *One match:* G. R. Steptoe 46, Z. A. Sher 13, N. Amin 1.

Bowling

	O	M	R	W	BB	5W/i	Avge
R. P. Lane	48	10	110	10	4-31	0	11.00
A. R. Clarke	237.3	58	650	29	5-50	2	22.41
S. F. Stanway	134.5	46	345	10	3-36	0	34.50

Other wicket-takers: A. Saleem and A. S. Umpleby 7, J. D. Batty 6, S. J. Brandon 4, Z. A. Sher 1.

CAMBRIDGESHIRE

The arrival of Peter Such, the former Essex and England off-spinner, helped compensate for the loss of several senior players. His 34 wickets – beaten only by Kevin Cooper of Herefordshire and Cornwall's Charles Shreck – proved crucial in guiding Cambridgeshire to third place in the Eastern Division. Two games were won and none lost. The captain, Ajaz Akhtar, weighed in with 22 wickets and also hit 219 useful runs. The leading batsman was Simon Kellett, who made Cambridgeshire's only two hundreds and totalled over 500. But there were worryingly few signs of talented young players coming through the extensive local coaching system.

Batting

	M	I	NO	R	HS	100s	50s	Avge
S. A. Kellett	6	11	3	516	150*	2	1	64.50
A. Akhtar	6	9	2	219	63	0	2	31.28
C. Jones	6	10	1	271	73*	0	2	30.11
G. D. Freear	6	10	0	284	62	0	3	28.40
I. N. Flanagan	2	4	0	104	92	0	1	26.00
A. J. C. Mutucumarana	6	10	0	116	50	0	1	11.60

Six matches: P. M. Such 38 runs. *Four matches:* I. N. Blanchett 91, E. C. Rodgers 81, G. J. Thatcher 44, M. J. G. Mason 15. *Two matches:* G. J. McDougall 27, S. Shipp 13, M. E. Roberts 9. *One match:* N. T. Gadsby 55, G. W. Ecclestone 29, T. S. Smith 16, M. Peacock 10, J. Outar 5, M. A. Kay 2.

Bowling

	O	M	R	W	BB	5W/i	Avge
P. M. Such	291.3	85	684	34	6-75	4	20.11
A. Akhtar	219.2	72	542	22	6-61	1	24.63
M. J. G. Mason	94	24	308	12	3-45	0	25.66

Other wicket-takers: T. S. Smith 6, I. N. Blanchett 4, I. N. Flanagan 3, M. E. Roberts 2, M. Peacock 1.

Fraser, in his final game before full-time journalism... signed off with a valedictory bye.
Hampshire v Middlesex, page 890

CHESHIRE

The summer of 2002 was a let-down for Cheshire after they had shared the Championship the year before. Cheshire won only once, against Wales, perhaps the weakest team in the division, though there were encouraging performances in the rain-ruined draw with Cornwall. Richard Hignett hit 183 and Danny Leech an unbeaten 152 (both career-bests) as they put on 248, a county fourth-wicket record. Hignett led Cheshire in that match because Andrew Hall – who had himself taken over from his long-term predecessor, Ian Cockbain – had broken a finger. It proved impossible to field a settled side and 27 different players turned out in the Championship. Cheshire had no more success in one-day games, and failed to reach either the third round of the 2003 C&G or the knockout stages of the 38-County Cup.

Batting	M	I	NO	R	HS	100s	50s	Avge
R. G. Hignett	4	5	0	367	183	1	2	73.40
S. Ogilvy	3	4	1	175	82	0	1	58.33
S. J. Renshaw	5	7	1	340	106	1	2	56.66
N. D. Cross.	4	5	2	132	79*	0	1	44.00
D. N. Leech	6	9	2	279	152*	1	1	39.85
N. A. Din	2	3	0	112	96	0	1	37.33
A. J. Hall	4	6	0	147	43	0	0	24.50

Four matches: B. J. Cutbill 62 runs, J. P. Whittaker 40. *Three matches:* M. Makin 70, C. S. Lamb 52, J. A. Daniels 4. *Two matches:* S. J. Marshall 31, A. J. Batterley 17, J. C. A. Powell 9, R. W. Fisher 14, I. S. Spencer 5, C. C. Finegan 0. *One match:* P. J. Berry 26, S. M. Eaton 13, J. K. Knibbs 13, M. J. Knight 12, A. J. W. Carolan 5, E. McCray 4, A. S. Bones 3, P. West 2, D. R. Leech 0.

Bowling	O	M	R	W	BB	5W/i	Avge
C. S. Lamb.	97.1	29	285	16	5-65	2	17.81
S. J. Renshaw	138.1	37	355	17	4-33	0	20.88
J. P. Whittaker	89.2	20	230	11	4-17	0	20.90

Other wicket-takers: B. J. Cutbill 8, R. W. Fisher 5, N. D. Cross and J. C. A. Powell 4, C. C. Finegan, R. G. Hignett, M. Makin and S. J. Marshall 2, J. A. Daniels, N. A. Din, A. J. Hall and D. N. Leech 1.

CORNWALL

The star of the Cornish summer was Charlie Shreck. He took 41 wickets in the Championship, second only to Kevin Cooper of Herefordshire, and was drafted into the Nottinghamshire side for an end of season League game, when he plucked out Worcestershire's top five. Shreck had already taken five for 19 against Worcestershire, in a losing cause, in the C&G third round. He was instrumental in Cornwall winning half their fixtures, something they hadn't done for 25 years, and they finished fourth in the Western Division. The victories came against Dorset, Wales and Shropshire, while the last game ended in defeat by Herefordshire, who won the division. The leading run-scorer was the new captain, Tom Sharp, closely followed by Ben Price, but batting was hardly Cornwall's strength, as eight bonus points showed. No one could quite manage a hundred. Even so, they hit 382 against Shropshire, their highest total since 1955. Cornwall had no success in the 38-County Cup, but did set up a third-round tie with Kent in the 2003 C&G.

Batting	M	I	NO	R	HS	100s	50s	Avge
P. C. L. Holloway	1	2	0	125	84*	0	1	62.50
B. P. Price.	5	8	2	311	74*	0	4	51.83
T. G. Sharp	6	8	0	314	99	0	2	39.25
J. C. J. Stephens	5	7	1	171	70	0	1	28.50

	M	I	NO	R	HS	100s	50s	Avge
J. P. Kent	4	5	0	125	97	0	1	25.00
N. A. Stoddard	6	11	2	201	61	0	1	22.33
A. M. Pearce	6	11	0	242	67	0	1	22.00
G. D. Edwards	4	6	0	130	63	0	1	21.66

Six matches: C. A. Hunkin 60 runs, C. E. Shreck 39. *Four matches:* W. Vincent 54. *Three matches:* N. A. Carter 30. *Two matches:* J. M. Hands 90, B. A. Smeeth 18, M. K. Munday 2. *One match:* C. M. Gazzard 72, T. Edwards 35, N. S. Curnow 6, R. M. Burley 0.

Bowling

	O	M	R	W	BB	5W/i	Avge
C. E. Shreck	232	48	875	41	7-100	5	21.34
C. A. Hunkin	113	29	361	15	4-56	0	24.06
J. C. J. Stephens	161	50	431	17	6-44	1	25.35

Other wicket-takers: B. A. Smeeth 6, J. M. Hands and M. K. Munday 3, N. A. Carter and A. M. Pearce 2.

CUMBERLAND

Cumberland's slump – they were Minor County Champions in 1999, runners-up in 2000 and fifth in their division in 2001 – hit rock bottom when they ended a gloomy season winless and bottom of the eastern table. Prospects had seemed good with the arrival of the former England and Lancashire all-rounder, Ian Austin, but he managed just one fifty and a disappointing, if economical, ten wickets. He and David Pennett were released. In for 2003 comes another ex-Lancashire player, Graham Lloyd, who should add stability to the upper order; only Buckinghamshire managed fewer batting points in either division. One batsman, however, had something to shout about as summer turned to autumn. Steven Knox hit twin unbeaten hundreds in the final game, against Bedfordshire.

Batting

	M	I	NO	R	HS	100s	50s	Avge
S. T. Knox	5	8	2	436	125*	2	3	72.66
O. J. Clayson	5	7	2	200	107	1	0	40.00
G. A. White	5	9	1	297	138	1	0	37.12
A. A. Metcalfe	5	8	1	206	112*	1	0	29.42
J. M. Lewis	6	8	1	195	77	0	2	27.85
I. D. Austin	3	5	0	121	52	0	1	24.20

Five matches: D. B. Pennett 54 runs, P. J. Lawson 31. *Four matches:* M. A. Sharp 19. *Three matches:* R. W. Mason 97, J. Mason 48, G. Mawdsley 20. *Two matches:* S. A. Twigg 84, J. M. Fielding 72, A. S. Williams 54, C. P. Pink 13, D. R. Williams 9, M. Burns 0. *One match:* J. R. Moyes 33, D. Connor 25.

Bowling

	O	M	R	W	BB	5W/i	Avge
I. D. Austin	72.1	30	159	10	5-16	1	15.90
G. Mawdsley	82.2	15	256	14	5-62	1	18.28
J. M. Fielding	116.1	51	225	12	6-57	1	18.75
P. J. Lawson	141.2	20	545	20	5-85	1	27.25

Other wicket-takers: J. M. Lewis, D. B. Pennett and M. A. Sharp 9, G. A. White 5, D. Connor, J. Mason and R. W. Mason 2, A. A. Metcalfe 1.

It was New Zealand's heaviest Test defeat. Fleming called it "a tough day at the office".
Pakistan v New Zealand, page 1319

DEVON

After 11 highly successful seasons, ten as captain, Peter Roebuck announced his retirement from Minor County cricket at the end of 2002. He led Devon to four consecutive Championships, from 1994 to 1997, and four knockout finals, winning two. In the Championship, he totalled 2,939 runs and 297 wickets – and he very nearly went out on a high. Devon had won their first five games of the season and in the last, against Berkshire, came tantalisingly close to a sixth that would have made them winners of the Western Division. Set 202 from 21 overs, they ended on 195 for six, and a single point behind Herefordshire. In that game, Andy Pugh (158) and David Court (58) put on a county-record 172 for the eighth wicket. The batting had strength in depth, and the attack was incisive: three bowlers took more than 20 wickets at under 20 each. One of them, Mark Richards, had a debut to remember when he had match figures of ten for 105 against Wiltshire. Devon also made it to the final of the 38-County Knockout, but lost to Warwickshire Board XI. Their only other defeat all summer came at the hands of Yorkshire in the C&G Trophy.

Batting

	M	I	NO	R	HS	100s	50s	Avge
P. M. Roebuck	6	9	6	237	93*	0	1	79.00
G. T. J. Townsend	1	2	0	131	131	1	0	65.50
A. J. Pugh	2	4	0	257	158	1	0	64.25
J. J. Williams	3	5	2	155	62	0	2	51.66
T. S. Anning	2	3	1	103	75	0	1	51.50
D. E. J. Townsend	4	7	1	268	97	0	3	44.66
M. P. Hunt	4	7	0	289	63	0	3	41.28
R. I. Dawson	6	12	2	381	76*	0	4	38.10
T. A. Wright	3	5	1	108	44*	0	0	27.00
A. J. Procter	6	9	2	137	52	0	1	19.57
D. G. Court	5	8	1	130	58	0	1	18.57

Six matches: I. E. Bishop 10 runs. *Four matches:* R. S. Marshall 84, M. A. E. Richards 53. *Three matches:* D. F. Lye 69. *Two matches:* S. J. Edwards 42, J. G. Willow 32. *One match:* K. A. O. Barrett 90, R. J. Foan 61, M. C. Theedom 0.

Bowling

	O	M	R	W	BB	5W/i	Avge
I. E. Bishop	220.2	69	524	34	5-55	2	15.41
M. A. E. Richards	170.3	67	334	21	6-46	1	15.90
A. J. Procter	207.2	74	421	22	4-35	0	19.13
D. G. Court	125	24	382	14	3-32	0	27.28

Other wicket-takers: P. M. Roebuck 7, A. J. Pugh 3, R. J. Foan 2, D. F. Lye, R. I. Dawson and T. A. Wright 1.

DORSET

Dorset, champions in 2000, ended the season in eighth place and without a win, but things weren't as bad as they seemed. Several times they had the upper hand, though were unable to make it count. Sean Walbridge, a left-arm spinner, grabbed his 200th Championship wicket and was the mainstay of an effective attack: Dorset were one of only two counties to claim maximum bowling points. The batting was less reliable, though Darren Cowley, Peter Deakin and Glyn Treagus (who otherwise had a thin season) all passed 1,000 Championship runs. In the match against Wales at Abergavenny, Dorset made 493 for six, breaking the record set in 1902. In the same game, Darren Cowley and Ben Lawes put on 220, a county-best for the fifth wicket.

Batting

	M	I	NO	R	HS	100s	50s	Avge
D. J. Cowley	4	8	0	311	151	1	1	38.87
S. W. D. Rintoul	6	12	1	411	139	1	3	37.36
B. J. Lawes	2	3	0	107	83	0	1	35.66
P. J. Deakin	5	10	1	297	92*	0	3	33.00
M. G. Miller	4	8	2	186	79	0	2	31.00
T. C. Z. Lamb	6	11	1	307	103	1	2	30.70
M. Swarbrick	6	12	1	235	103	1	0	21.36
G. R. Treagus	6	12	0	135	38	0	0	11.25

Six matches: S. R. Walbridge 77 runs. *Five matches:* M. R. Mixer 14, J. R. Wilson 14. *Two matches:* T. C. Hicks 33, N. J. Thurgood 30. *One match:* D. H. Kerry 23, J. A. Elliot-Square 16, R. L. Keates 15, D. Worrad 14, D. J. Trotter 11, K. J. Wilson 6, J. G. Tizzard 0.

Bowling

	O	M	R	W	BB	5W/i	Avge
J. R. Wilson	178	73	401	22	4-16		18.22
S. R. Walbridge	229	59	594	27	6-38	2	22.00
M. R. Mixer	151	31	474	15	6-49	1	31.60

Other wicket-takers: P. J. Deakin 6, J. A. Elliot-Square and D. Worrad 4, D. J. Trotter 3, D. J. Cowley and G. R. Treagus 2, R. L. Keates and B. J. Lawes 1.

HEREFORDSHIRE

This was the most successful of Herefordshire's 11 seasons as a Minor County. They inched out Devon by a point to win the Western Division for the first time, were within sight of victory over Norfolk in the rain-curtailed Championship final, and had the leading wicket-taker, leading wicket-keeper and second-highest run-scorer in the competition. They won five games and drew the sixth. Kevin Cooper broke his own club record by taking 52 wickets in a season, including 13 for 81 against Dorset. For the second summer running, his was the only single-figure average by a Minor Counties bowler taking ten wickets and, as in 2001, he won the Frank Edwards bowling award. He received whole-hearted support from the former Kent and England seamer, Martin McCague. Ismail Dawood made 26 dismissals and added an unbeaten 148 for good measure, while Paul Lazenbury hit two hundreds as he totalled 585 runs. The captain, Chris Boroughs, picked up the Wilfred Rhodes Trophy for his consistent batting.

Batting

	M	I	NO	R	HS	100s	50s	Avge
C. W. Boroughs	7	10	4	446	96*	0	5	74.33
I. Dawood	7	11	3	438	148*	1	2	54.75
P. S. Lazenbury	7	12	1	585	143	2	2	53.18
A. Farooque	5	8	3	212	85	0	2	42.40
H. V. Patel	6	11	0	352	93	0	2	32.00
M. J. McCague	4	4	0	124	67	0	2	31.00
R. D. Hughes	5	9	1	145	41	0	0	18.12

Six matches: N. M. Davies 61 runs, K. E. Cooper 16. *Five matches:* K. Pearson 52. *Four matches:* P. A. Thomas 28. *Three matches:* D. R. Willetts 82, R. S. Nagra 48, S. A. Roberts 7. *Two matches:* A. N. C. Owen 7. *One match:* S. Pathan 22, A. M. Mason 13, G. M. Roberts 11, M. Horrocks 0.

Bowling

	O	M	R	W	BB	5W/i	Avge
K. E. Cooper	220.2	75	482	52	7-49	5	9.26
M. J. McCague	131.1	46	290	18	4-42	0	16.11
A. Farooque	99.5	25	302	13	4-36	0	23.23
N. M. Davies	102	19	342	14	4-61	0	24.42

Other wicket-takers: P. A. Thomas 9, S. A. Roberts 7, P. S. Lazenbury 5, C. W. Boroughs 2, K. Pearson 1.

HERTFORDSHIRE

Hertfordshire could not build on a promising 2001 season and dropped from fourth to eighth. One problem was the greater commitment required for three-day cricket, and not once were they able to field a first-choice side. The innings defeat by Suffolk was a low point, though Hertfordshire came back strongly in the convincing win over Cumberland. They also smelt the whiff of victory against Lincolnshire and Staffordshire but let their chances slip – perhaps a result of the policy of picking younger players. The other side of the coin was that several less experienced cricketers came good. Stephen Cordingley, Tony Pickett and Simon White all hit maiden Championship hundreds, and in the Cumberland match there were a number of encouraging performances: Ben Frazer yanked out seven batsmen for 36 in the first innings and Matt Smith six for 102 in the second. Smith enjoyed himself with the bat, too, as he and White added 210, more than doubling the old county seventh-wicket record of 104. For 2003, David Ward replaces Martin James as captain.

Batting	M	I	NO	R	HS	100s	50s	Avge
S. P. White	4	7	6	244	110*	1	0	244.00
A. Pickett	3	6	1	256	122	1	1	51.20
S. G. Cordingley	5	10	1	434	133*	1	3	48.22
D. M. Ward	4	8	0	317	92	0	4	39.62
M. E. Smith	2	4	0	127	86	0	1	31.75
M. H. James	6	12	1	333	115	1	1	30.27
S. J. Lowe	5	9	0	267	105	1	1	29.66
B. J. Frazer	5	9	0	265	101	1	1	29.44
M. A. Everett	4	8	2	165	38*	0	0	27.50
T. J. Pearman	6	9	4	121	31	0	0	24.20
T. P. Cranston	3	5	0	110	59	0	1	22.00

Five matches: L. M. Cooper 46 runs. *Four matches:* P. J. O'Reilly 31. *Two matches:* K. Marc 44. *One match:* C. G. Bailey 29, N. G. E. Walker 26, J. E. Fitt 10, K. J. Walls 10, N. Gladwin 9, R. J. Cordingley 7, R. L. Channer 5, J. W. Shaw 0.

Bowling	O	M	R	W	BB	5W/i	Avge
M. E. Smith	73.2	12	214	11	6-102	1	19.45
B. J. Frazer	207.5	30	768	26	7-36	2	29.53
P. J. O'Reilly	120	26	410	13	5-34	0	31.53

Other wicket-takers: L. M. Cooper 8, K. Marc 7, A. Pickett, N. G. E. Walker and S. P. White 4, R. L. Channer 3, J. W. Shaw 2, R. J. Cordingley and T. P. Cranston 1.

LINCOLNSHIRE

Injuries affecting the entire seam attack meant the 2002 season was a difficult one for Lincolnshire. And the absence during the early-season one-day games of the former captain and key batsman, Mark Fell, didn't help. He returned to the side for the three-day matches and was quickly back in the groove, although the most successful batsman – and the only player in the Minor Counties Championship to reach 600 runs – was Richard Howitt, who hit two centuries, including a magnificent unbeaten 153 against Buckinghamshire. But Lincolnshire, though they totted up more batting points than any other county, could win only once, against Hertfordshire. They did beat Cheshire, however, in the preliminary stage of the C&G to set up a third-round tie against Nottinghamshire in 2003.

Batting

	M	I	NO	R	HS	100s	50s	Avge
M. A. Fell.	5	8	3	394	92	0	4	78.80
R. W. J. Howitt	6	10	1	624	153*	2	3	69.33
J. Trower	6	10	0	478	86	0	7	47.80
O. E. Burford	6	9	3	203	91*	0	2	33.83
R. J. Chapman	4	5	1	122	40*	0	0	30.50
M. C. Dobson	6	10	0	284	87	0	3	28.40
J. Clarke	6	10	2	204	84*	0	1	25.50
D. R. Heath	4	7	0	142	68	0	1	20.28

Six matches: D. J. Pipes 31 runs. *Three matches:* J. C. Harrison 66, J. R. Davies 38, S. J. Airey 14. *Two matches:* D. A. Christmas 7, S. Oakes 0. *One match:* S. Webb 32, J. A. Heath 29, S. G. Plumb 12, K. Adams 0.

Bowling

	O	M	R	W	BB	5W/i	Avge
M. C. Dobson	203	49	625	16	4-89	0	39.06
D. J. Pipes	153.5	31	559	11	3-73	0	50.81

Other wicket-takers: R. J. Chapman 7, R. W. J. Howitt 6, J. R. Davies, S. Oakes and J. Trower 5, D. A. Christmas 4, S. J. Airey 1.

NORFOLK

Norfolk won (or in this case, shared) their fifth Minor Counties Championship, 89 years after their fourth. They had their good fortune – in the final Herefordshire ended in much the stronger position– but they headed the Eastern Division thanks to three wins. The most exciting game came against Cumberland, when they sneaked home by three runs, the most emphatic against Buckinghamshire and the most pleasing against Hertfordshire, when the Norfolk openers, Carl Amos and Carl Rogers, put on 335, a Minor Counties first-wicket record. Hertfordshire's nemesis in that game was Chris Brown, whose off-breaks claimed 30 wickets over the summer. Steve Goldsmith, once of Kent and Derbyshire, had a magnificent all-round season, but Paul Taylor, once of England, had a less happy time, and his contract was not renewed.

Batting

	M	I	NO	R	HS	100s	50s	Avge
S. C. Goldsmith	7	14	1	559	167	1	2	43.00
C. J. Rogers	7	14	0	561	153	2	3	40.07
C. R. Borrett	6	12	2	366	77*	0	4	36.60
C. Amos.	7	14	0	467	180	1	1	33.35
L. T. S. Newton	5	9	2	198	39*	0	0	28.28
C. Brown	6	8	0	164	41	0	0	20.50
J. R. Walker	7	14	0	252	67	0	1	18.00
J. M. Spelman	5	10	3	113	41*	0	0	16.14

Seven matches: P. J. Bradshaw 69 runs, P. G. Newman 61. *Five matches:* J. P. Taylor 44. *Three matches:* M. O. Wilkinson 80. *Two matches:* J. P. Garner 49. *One match:* A. M. Watson 7, P. J. Free 6, I. R. Slegg 1.

Bowling

	O	M	R	W	BB	5W/i	Avge
C. Brown	216	58	627	30	5-49	1	20.90
C. J. Rogers	100.1	38	220	10	4-64	0	22.00
P. J. Bradshaw	146	36	380	17	4-36	0	22.35
S. C. Goldsmith.	165	34	526	22	4-13	0	23.90
J. P. Taylor	131.3	24	438	14	3-31	0	31.28

Other wicket-takers: I. R. Slegg 5, P. G. Newman and J. M. Spelman 3, C. R. Borrett 2.

NORTHUMBERLAND

Falling to seventh, four places lower than in 2001, was an unsatisfactory end to a season that began full of optimism. The first game brought a good win over Suffolk, but Northumberland's shallow resources were exposed by the unavailability of senior players, and there were no more victories in the Championship. Batting highlight of the summer was John Windows's magnificent unbeaten 188 against Lincolnshire, the sixth-best score for Northumberland. The off-break bowler, Lee Crozier, did best with the ball, and his 19 wickets were especially gratifying given his absence for most of 2001 through injury. Meanwhile, Iain Purdy, a 16-year-old left-arm spinner, bowled 28 overs off the reel in the last game of the season, and removed five Norfolk batsmen for his pains.

Batting	M	I	NO	R	HS	100s	50s	Avge
J. B. Windows	3	5	2	278	188*	1	0	92.66
B. Parker	4	8	2	326	120*	1	1	54.33
S. Chapman	4	8	1	280	103	1	1	40.00
L. J. Crozier	5	6	2	111	71	0	1	27.75
D. J. Rutherford	4	6	1	121	43	0	0	24.20
J. A. Graham	5	9	1	153	64	0	2	19.12
J. N. Miller	3	6	0	102	47	0	0	17.00
A. T. Heather	6	12	1	175	62*	0	1	15.90

Six matches: P. J. Nicholson 92 runs. *Five matches*: G. Angus 96. *Four matches*: M. J. Turner 89, M. L. Pollard 26. *Two matches*: N. Wood 69, G. Hallam 46, B. Stewart 34, J. M. Callaghan 11, M. A. F. Hynd 9. *One match*: J. A. Benn 35, N. J. Tomlinson 12, I. C. Purdy 4.

Bowling	O	M	R	W	BB	5W/i	Avge
G. Angus	111	29	302	11	4-57	0	27.45
L. J. Crozier	177.5	45	525	19	5-93	1	27.63
D. J. Rutherford	121	30	406	13	5-89	1	31.23

Other wicket-takers: S. Chapman 8, M. L. Pollard and I. C. Purdy 7, J. A. Graham 6, B. Stewart 2, J. M. Callaghan 1.

OXFORDSHIRE

Keith Arnold, as enthusiastic and committed at the age of 42 as ever, led Oxfordshire to a moderately successful season: three wins put them third behind the runaway leaders of the Western Division, Herefordshire and Devon. Charlie Knightley and Ben Thompson were the most successful batsmen, though it was in the bowling that Oxfordshire were strongest. Arnold's fast-medium picked up 32 wickets, though against Dorset he was eclipsed by a newcomer, Simon Launder, who grabbed Oxfordshire's first hat-trick since 1964.

Batting	M	I	NO	R	HS	100s	50s	Avge
C. S. Knightley	5	9	3	393	91	0	4	65.50
B. J. Thompson	4	8	3	262	125	1	1	52.40
I. M. Tew	3	5	1	135	66	0	1	33.75
I. A. Hawtin	6	12	0	333	82	0	2	27.75
A. P. Cook	6	8	1	190	47	0	0	27.14
G. S. Peddy	5	6	0	155	67	0	1	25.83
I. J. Evans	3	6	1	124	50	0	1	24.80
R. W. Hawkins	6	12	0	177	45	0	0	14.75

Six matches: K. A. Arnold 31 runs, S. A. Launder 21. *Five matches*: I. M. Crosby 72. *Four matches*: R. Lynch 73. *Two matches*: R. J. Williams 92, R. D. Brooks 41. *One match*: J. M. Cook 25, M. Rowell 13, S. J. Ali 0.

Bowling

	O	M	R	W	BB	5W/i	Avge
K. A. Arnold	197	55	474	32	6-75	1	14.81
G. S. Peddy	145.5	35	396	19	6-85	1	20.84
S. A. Launder	107.4	16	336	13	4-23	0	25.84
A. P. Cook	180.4	49	564	18	5-106	1	31.33

Other wicket-takers: B. J. Thompson 9, R. Lynch 7, I. J. Evans 2, I. M. Crosby 1.

SHROPSHIRE

There was little to savour in Shropshire's season: a solitary win, against Wiltshire, was outweighed by three defeats, and eighth place was a grave disappointment. Injuries and unavailability caused major headaches for a team coming to terms with the retirement of two experienced hands, Asif Din and Kevin Evans. A major plus, though, was the performance of Anthony O'Connor, a left-arm medium-pacer who topped the bowling in his debut summer. The other success story was Tim Mason, Shropshire's professional. He hit 574 runs and picked up 17 wickets with his off-breaks. In the Wiltshire match he spun Shropshire to victory by scooping seven for 68 – after hitting an unbeaten 146. He put on 144, a county record for the seventh wicket, with Guy Home, who becomes captain in 2003 in place of Bryan Jones.

Batting

	M	I	NO	R	HS	100s	50s	Avge
D. J. Bowett	1	2	1	101	80	0	1	101.00
T. J. Mason	6	12	2	574	146*	2	3	57.40
J. B. R. Jones	6	11	3	311	64*	0	5	38.87
M. J. Marvell	5	10	1	329	103*	1	2	36.55
M. A. Tilt	5	10	1	265	67	0	1	29.44
D. Williamson	3	6	1	138	54*	0	1	27.60
G. L. Home	6	11	1	196	37	0	0	19.60
J. T. Ralph	5	9	1	117	50*	0	1	14.62

Four matches: A. P. O'Connor 21 runs, A. T. O. Dunkerley 10. *Three matches*: A. B. Byram 91. *Two matches*: G. J. Byram 77, I. Gillespie 62, B. W. W. Platt 43, A. M. Shimmons 26, R. P. L. Burton 25, C. J. Lewis 25. *One match*: J. V. Anders 24, G. J. Mumford 21, M. Bamford 19, N. B. Archibald 17, M. A. Downes 10, N. C. Stovold 5.

Bowling

	O	M	R	W	BB	5W/i	Avge
A. P. O'Connor	130	32	419	23	6-66	3	18.21
A. M. Shimmons	108.1	25	353	15	7-81	1	23.53
T. J. Mason	174.3	50	420	17	7-68	2	24.70

Other wicket-takers: D. Williamson 9, A. T. O. Dunkerley 7, A. B. Byram 6, I. Gillespie 5, G. L. Home and B. W. W. Platt 3, M. A. Downes and J. T. Ralph 2, D. J. Bowett and C. J. Lewis 1.

STAFFORDSHIRE

Staffordshire badly missed their experienced opening bowler, David Follett. He missed the first three games with a rib injury, but once he was back he transformed their season, taking ten wickets in the demolition of Northumberland, seven in the win over Buckinghamshire and eight in the draw against Hertfordshire. On average, he picked up a wicket every 26 balls. Steve Dean, who stood down as captain at the end of the summer, had another good season, totting up almost 500 runs to take him within one big innings of 10,000 in the Championship. The batting star, however, was Graeme Archer, formerly of Nottinghamshire, who hit two hundreds. Staffordshire reached the semi-final of the 38-County Cup, where they lost to Warwickshire Board XI, the eventual winners. Dean's successor as captain is Richard Harvey.

Batting

	M	I	NO	R	HS	100s	50s	Avge
G. F. Archer	5	10	2	452	111	2	1	56.50
M. I. Humphries	6	10	5	211	59*	0	1	42.20
R. P. Harvey	3	6	1	207	103*	1	2	41.40
S. J. Dean	6	12	0	492	133	1	1	41.00
G. D. Franklin	4	8	0	306	151	1	1	38.25
P. S. J. Goodwin	4	8	2	171	49	0	0	28.50
R. A. Cooper	6	8	1	146	52	0	1	20.85
D. R. Womble	6	12	1	142	33	0	0	12.90

Six matches: G. Bulpitt 72 runs. *Four matches:* G. D. Crook 38. *Three matches:* G. R. Willott 60, D. Follett 6. *Two matches:* M. C. Longmore 36, P. M. Cheadle 21. *One match:* C. Tranter 33, G. D. Wright 26, P. F. Shaw 22, M. R. Dawson 18, A. J. Jones 15, D. J. Edwards 0.

Bowling

	O	M	R	W	BB	5W/i	Avge
D. Follett	109.4	18	404	25	7-67	3	16.16
G. Bulpitt	190.2	58	384	19	5-42	1	20.21

Other wicket-takers: G. D. Crook 9, R. A. Cooper 8, G. R. Willott and D. R. Womble 7, D. J. Edwards 5, A. J. Jones 2, R. P. Harvey 1.

SUFFOLK

After a scratchy season in 2001, Suffolk got the hang of three-day Championship cricket – and could have won the Eastern Division had a downpour at Mildenhall not washed out the final fixture, against Buckinghamshire. As it was, Suffolk had to settle for second behind arch-rivals, Norfolk. The improvement owed much to three experienced cricketers: the former Derbyshire seamer, Trevor Smith; Andrew Mawson, once of Cumberland, who hit two hundreds from his four Suffolk innings; and the captain, Phil Caley. A fourth, the current South African Test player, Andrew Hall, was recruited for the C&G match against Northamptonshire, who narrowly averted an embarrassing defeat. Paul King, a product of the Suffolk development structure, was player of the season for his steady seam bowling and all-round contribution. The season's one blemish was the crushing defeat in the first round of the 2003 C&G by Buckinghamshire, who rattled up 424.

Batting

	M	I	NO	R	HS	100s	50s	Avge
A. D. Mawson	3	4	0	351	162	2	0	87.75
P. J. Caley	5	6	3	212	87*	0	2	70.66
A. M. Brown	2	3	1	105	59*	0	1	52.50
M. D. Catley	1	2	0	103	54	0	1	51.50
I. S. Morton	3	5	1	178	73	0	2	44.50
R. J. Catley	5	8	1	264	96	0	2	37.71
T. M. Catley	5	7	1	193	88	0	2	32.16
C. J. Warn	5	7	0	220	58	0	2	31.42
T. M. Smith	5	7	1	113	49	0	0	22.60

Five matches: P. D. King 85 runs. *Four matches:* C. A. Swallow 56, K. G. Shaw 51, J. P. East 18. *Two matches:* G. M. Kirk 0. *One match:* M. P. Jones 15, M. R. Geeves 12.

Bowling

	O	M	R	W	BB	5W/i	Avge
P. D. King	109.4	24	364	17	3-23	0	21.41
T. M. Smith	171	42	559	24	6-86	1	23.29

Other wicket-takers: J. P. East and G. M. Kirk 7, C. A. Swallow 6, K. G. Shaw 5, I. S. Morton 4, M. R. Geeves 1.

WALES

Wales had a lousy season. They finished last in their division, losing three and drawing three. The bowling was especially weak, and their total of just 12 bowling points was four fewer than any other team. Unlike the other 19 sides, they had no bowler who reached ten wickets. The batsmen made a better fist of things: Owen Dawkins and Kanal Khanna set a fifth-wicket record when they put on 165 against Oxfordshire at Swansea. Dawkins, who led the side when Colin Metson was absent, went on to 164, his first Championship hundred and the highest individual score for Wales. He also ended the season in some style by hitting twin centuries, against Dorset, only the second time a Wales player had done so, after Jamie Sylvester (also against Dorset, in 1995).

Batting

	M	I	NO	R	HS	100s	50s	Avge
O. A. Dawkins	6	12	2	501	164	3	0	50.10
D. J. Lovell	4	8	0	238	89	0	2	29.75
K. Khanna	5	10	0	235	70	0	1	23.50
O. C. Hopkins	5	10	0	224	70	0	2	22.40
D. M. Lloyd	5	9	1	114	35*	0	0	14.25
C. J. Barnsley	6	11	0	133	30	0	0	12.09

Five matches: J. L. Davies 90 runs. *Three matches:* R. I. Clitheroe 51, R. P. Willey 14. *Two matches:* C. P. Metson 44, R. J. G. Coles 39, S. Morris 34, N. D. Buttigieg 28, A. C. Smith 4. *One match:* I. A. Clayton 80, N. A. Gage 57, J. P. J. Sylvester 38, D. Kreischer 19, G. Rees 19, D. A. Fury 16, M. Evans 14, L. Fury 6, A. J. Jones 6, R. W. Sylvester 5, R. J. Williams 5, T. J. L. Hagger 4, A. H. Thomas 4, J. Richards 0.

No bowler took ten wickets. The wicket-takers were: C. J. Barnsley 9, O. C. Hopkins 6, J. P. J. Sylvester and R. P. Willey 5, A. C. Smith 4, O. A. Dawkins, D. Kreischer, D. J. Lovell and S. Morris 2, N. A. Gage, T. J. L. Hagger and K. Khanna 1.

WILTSHIRE

Three draws and three defeats in the Championship left Wiltshire bottom but one in the Western Division. If the bowlers had managed to finish off wounded opponents things could have been much better: twice, against Oxfordshire and against Cheshire, they were stranded two wickets from victory. The batting was often far stronger in the second innings – when they were usually playing catch-up – so their tally of bonus points was a feeble eight. The opener, Russell Rowe, who replaces Steve Perrin as captain in 2003, hit most runs, despite starting the Championship season with a pair at home to Dorset. Chris Budd and Baqar Rizvi, who also took handy wickets with his fast-medium, both managed 300. Kevin Nash weighed in productively at No. 9 or 10, and topped the bowling with his right-arm seam. Wiltshire began well in the 38-County Competition, only to be routed by Devon.

Batting

	M	I	NO	R	HS	100s	50s	Avge
K. J. Nash	3	6	3	122	40*	0	0	40.66
Baqar Rizvi	4	8	0	300	59	0	2	37.50
K. R. Blackburn	3	6	0	218	59	0	2	36.33
C. R. J. Budd	5	10	0	348	112	1	3	34.80
R. J. Rowe	6	12	0	399	96	0	3	33.25
R. J. Bates	6	12	0	287	60	0	1	23.91
T. N. Shardlow	6	12	1	177	40	0	0	16.09
J. Hibberd	6	12	0	164	35	0	0	13.66

Four matches: J. P. Searle 67 runs, P. R. Bates 38, C. R. Gibbens 38. *Three matches:* J. A. H. Chandler 77. *Two matches:* M. D. Coxon 45, D. M. Chard 14. *One match:* M. J. Glasson 88, S. M. Perrin 31, W. J. Nichols 29, D. J. Goodway 23, C. D. Chaplin 2, M. E. Scully 1, I. R. Richardson 8, D. P. Moore 0.

Bowling

	O	*M*	*R*	*W*	*BB*	*5W/i*	*Avge*
K. J. Nash	102.1	22	351	20	5-33	2	17.55
J. P. Searle	183.5	51	448	18	6-43	1	24.88
R. J. Bates	198.5	51	615	19	7-112	1	32.36
J. Hibberd	107	25	398	11	3-87	0	36.18

Other wicket-takers: C. R. Gibbens 8, Baqar Rizvi 6, D. P. Moore 5, W. J. Nichols 3, I. R. Richardson and P. R. Bates 2, D. M. Chard and C. D. Chaplin 1.

CHAMPIONSHIP FINAL

HEREFORDSHIRE v NORFOLK

At Luctonians, Kingsland, September 8, 9, 10. Drawn. Toss: Herefordshire.

For the second year running – though for only the third time in over a century – the Championship was shared. In 2001, a flat pitch was to blame; this time it was a combination of rain, which nabbed three hours from the second day, and caution from the Herefordshire captain, Chris Boroughs, who did not declare until well into the final afternoon. Norfolk made no attempt on the 331 they were set, and Herefordshire, with a few more than the 45 overs they allowed themselves, would surely have grabbed the last two wickets. On the opening day, Harshad Patel and Boroughs had seen Herefordshire to a healthy total from their 70 overs before the Norfolk Carls, Amos and Rogers, fought back. Next morning, Kevin Cooper's exemplary line and length on a pitch offering swing and uncertain bounce wrought havoc. The top four sank in the space of three runs. Norfolk limped to 217 before Paul Lazenbury and Ismail Dawood extended the lead. Then came the declaration and more Norfolk floundering – they were going under for the second time at 11 for four – before the ninth-wicket pair, Paul Bradshaw and Paul Taylor, played out 23 balls.

Man of the Match: K. E. Cooper.

Close of play: First day, Norfolk 47-0 (Amos 25, Rogers 22); Second day, Herefordshire 13-0 (Patel 4, Lazenbury 7).

Herefordshire

H. V. Patel b Brown	84	– lbw b Goldsmith	26
P. S. Lazenbury lbw b Taylor	6	– c Borrett b Brown	77
R. D. Hughes c Newton b Goldsmith	41	– b Brown	10
†I. Dawood c Walker b Bradshaw	14	– not out	70
*C. W. Boroughs c Newton b Brown	90	– not out	26
M. J. McCague st Newton b Brown	3		
N. M. Davies c Amos b Taylor	26		
A. Farooque b Brown	4		
K. Pearson lbw b Taylor	5		
K. E. Cooper run out	0		
S. A. Roberts not out	1		
L-b 18, w 4, n-b 6	28	B 15, l-b 7, w 8, n-b 6	36

1/8 2/86 3/111 4/256 5/264 (70 overs) 302   1/84 2/111 3/174 (3 wkts dec.) 245
6/265 7/279 8/301 9/301

Bowling: *First Innings*—Bradshaw 13–2–31–1; Taylor 14–2–57–3; Newman 5–1–22–0; Brown 22–1–98–4; Goldsmith 12–2–48–1; Rogers 4–0–28–0. *Second Innings*—Bradshaw 8–1–16–0; Taylor 16.3–1–100–0; Goldsmith 12–3–33–1; Brown 20–2–74–2.

Norfolk

C. Amos c Dawood b Cooper	32	– c Dawood b Cooper	2
C. J. Rogers c Dawood b Cooper	31	– c Dawood b McCague	0
S. C. Goldsmith lbw b McCague	0	– c Boroughs b Cooper	8
C. R. Borrett c Dawood b Cooper	0	– c Davies b McCague	51
J. R. Walker c Cooper b Davies	36	– lbw b Cooper	0
J. M. Spelman c Dawood b Davies	13	– c Dawood b Farooqe	2
†L. T. S. Newton not out	39	– c Boroughs b Roberts	3
C. Brown c Boroughs b Cooper	30	– lbw b Cooper	7
*P. G. Newman c Dawood b Cooper	4		
P. J. Bradshaw not out	12	– (9) not out	18
J. P. Taylor (did not bat)		– (10) not out	0
B 7, l-b 3, w 8, n-b 2	20	L-b 6	6

1/63 2/66 3/66 4/66 5/107   (8 wkts, 70 overs) 217   1/0 2/10 3/11 4/11 5/37   (8 wkts) 97
6/136 7/195 8/200   6/50 7/65 8/95

Bowling: *First Innings*—McCague 15–6–35–1; Cooper 27–9–64–5; Roberts 11–4–29–0; Farooqe 4–0–17–0; Davies 13–1–62–2. *Second Innings*—Cooper 13–4–26–4; McCague 18–11–22–2; Davies 2–0–12–0; Farooqe 8–2–26–1; Roberts 4–1–5–1.

Umpires: K. Coburn and M. P. Moran.

THE MINOR COUNTIES CHAMPIONS

1895 {	Norfolk Durham Worcestershire	1930	Durham	1971	Yorkshire II
		1931	Leicestershire II	1972	Bedfordshire
		1932	Buckinghamshire	1973	Shropshire
1896	Worcestershire	1933	Undecided	1974	Oxfordshire
1897	Worcestershire	1934	Lancashire II	1975	Hertfordshire
1898	Worcestershire	1935	Middlesex II	1976	Durham
1899 {	Northamptonshire Buckinghamshire	1936	Hertfordshire	1977	Suffolk
		1937	Lancashire II	1978	Devon
1900 {	Glamorgan Durham Northamptonshire	1938	Buckinghamshire	1979	Suffolk
		1939	Surrey II	1980	Durham
		1946	Suffolk	1981	Durham
1901	Durham	1947	Yorkshire II	1982	Oxfordshire
1902	Wiltshire	1948	Lancashire II	1983	Hertfordshire
1903	Northamptonshire	1949	Lancashire II	1984	Durham
1904	Northamptonshire	1950	Surrey II	1985	Cheshire
1905	Norfolk	1951	Kent II	1986	Cumberland
1906	Staffordshire	1952	Buckinghamshire	1987	Buckinghamshire
1907	Lancashire II	1953	Berkshire	1988	Cheshire
1908	Staffordshire	1954	Surrey II	1989	Oxfordshire
1909	Wiltshire	1955	Surrey II	1990	Hertfordshire
1910	Norfolk	1956	Kent II	1991	Staffordshire
1911	Staffordshire	1957	Yorkshire II	1992	Staffordshire
1912	In abeyance	1958	Yorkshire II	1993	Staffordshire
1913	Norfolk	1959	Warwickshire II	1994	Devon
1914	Staffordshire†	1960	Lancashire II	1995	Devon
1920	Staffordshire	1961	Somerset II	1996	Devon
1921	Staffordshire	1962	Warwickshire II	1997	Devon
1922	Buckinghamshire	1963	Cambridgeshire	1998	Staffordshire
1923	Buckinghamshire	1964	Lancashire II	1999	Cumberland
1924	Berkshire	1965	Somerset II	2000	Dorset
1925	Buckinghamshire	1966	Lincolnshire	2001 {	Cheshire Lincolnshire
1926	Durham	1967	Cheshire		
1927	Staffordshire	1968	Yorkshire II	2002 {	Herefordshire Norfolk
1928	Berkshire	1969	Buckinghamshire		
1929	Oxfordshire	1970	Bedfordshire		

† Disputed. Most sources claim the Championship was never decided.

THE ECB 38-COUNTY CUP FINAL

DEVON v WARWICKSHIRE BOARD XI

At Worcester, September 3. Warwickshire Board XI won by two wickets. Toss: Devon.

Warwickshire became the first Board XI to win the 38-County Cup since its beginnings in 1983 when they beat Devon in a tight finish. The two innings took a similar course – a substantial opening partnership followed by a middle-order wobble – but the Board XI's Gavin Shephard kept a cool head at the death and, with Nadeem Sajjad, added 44 for the ninth wicket to steer his side home. Devon had looked set for a big total while Gareth Townsend and Mark Hunt were sharing 160, but in no time Mohamed Sheikh's medium-pace had knocked them back to 190 for four. Nick Warren then hit the stumps three times to maintain Warwickshire's momentum, though giving away 70 extras – the highest score on the Devon card – wouldn't have pleased their batsmen. Neil Humphrey and Ian Westwood responded positively with an opening stand of 142, before Andy Procter, seizing four for 35 with his off-breaks, put the game in the melting-pot.

Devon

M. P. Hunt c Westwood b Sheikh	65	S. A. Stoneman not out		14
G. T. J. Townsend c Howell b Sheikh	51	D. G. Court not out		17
A. J. Procter c Howell b Sheikh	12			
†R. I. Dawson c Allen b Sheikh	7	B 4, l-b 21, w 31, n-b 14		70
A. J. Pugh b Warren	6			
D. F. Lye c Humphrey b Khan	2	1/160 2/174 3/188	(8 wkts, 50 overs)	261
*P. M. Roebuck b Warren	5	4/190 5/202 6/207		
M. R. Gribble b Warren	12	7/225 8/232		

I. E. Bishop did not bat.

Bowling: Warren 10–1–42–3; Shephard 1–0–17–0; Dalton 6–0–19–0; Sajjad 10–1–45–0; Sheikh 10–0–37–4; Westwood 4–0–30–0; Khan 9–1–46–1.

Warwickshire Board XI

N. V. Humphrey c and b Bishop	57	N. A. Warren b Procter		4
I. J. Westwood c and b Pugh	67	N. Sajjad not out		19
*C. R. Howell st Dawson b Procter	20			
W. G. Khan lbw b Bishop	0	B 5, l-b 12, w 19		36
H. R. Jones c Dawson b Procter	20			
M. A. Sheikh lbw b Court	9	1/142 2/148 3/148	(8 wkts, 49.1 overs)	266
G. F. Shephard not out	33	4/186 5/196 6/202		
D. A. T. Dalton b Procter	1	7/210 8/222		

†A. P. W. Allen did not bat.

Bowling: Stoneman 10–0–53–0; Court 6–0–36–1; Bishop 9.1–1–39–2; Roebuck 7–0–37–0; Procter 7–0–35–4; Pugh 9–0–40–1; Gribble 1–0–9–0.

Umpires: K. Coburn and M. P. Moran.

WINNERS 1983–2002

1983	Cheshire	1990	Buckinghamshire	1997	Norfolk
1984	Hertfordshire	1991	Staffordshire	1998	Devon
1985	Durham	1992	Devon	1999	Bedfordshire
1986	Norfolk	1993	Staffordshire	2000	Herefordshire
1987	Cheshire	1994	Devon	2001	Norfolk
1988	Dorset	1995	Cambridgeshire	2002	Warwickshire Board XI
1989	Cumberland	1996	Cheshire		

SECOND ELEVEN CHAMPIONSHIP, 2002

Forever bridesmaids in the senior competitions, Kent tripped merrily down the aisle an eyebrow-raising twice in September, albeit in the humbler world of Second Eleven cricket. They played just ten games in the Championship – a couple of counties played half as many again – but won a healthy six and ended with a points average comfortably ahead of their nearest rivals. And in the final of the one-day Trophy, they squeezed past Hampshire, champions of 2001, in the last over, thanks in the main to a responsible hundred from James Tredwell.

The 2002 season was one for batsmen to savour, and three counties made their best totals in the Championship. Worcestershire powered their way to 589 for seven declared against Warwickshire, Sussex scattered the Hampshire bowlers to the winds before calling a halt at 600 for eight, and Warwickshire, in their home fixture with Somerset, piled up 680, a competition record. In that game, at Knowle and Dorridge CC, Trevor Penney finished unbeaten on 255, a county-best and the highest of the season. He and Ian Trott, who was making his debut, shared a mammoth 397 for the fourth wicket, another record. Trott eventually fell for 245 and Warwickshire ran out winners by an innings and 71. There was another batsman's match at Horntye Park, Hastings, when two Sussex players – Carl Hopkinson and Will House – both hit twin hundreds against Northamptonshire, who were beaten by six wickets.

Some of the drawn games included plenty of excitement, too. Gloucestershire, set 353 by Leicestershire, agonisingly ran out of time at 352 for nine, while some last-ditch heroics from Richard Hodgkinson and Paul McMahon guided Nottinghamshire to safety after Derbyshire had asked them to make 560. Coming together at 318 for nine, their stand had reached 125 when stumps were drawn.

The best bowling figures of the season came as Lancashire took on Northamptonshire at Nelson CC in May. The eight for 54 didn't bring Lancashire victory, but they did set Jimmy Anderson on course for a dizzying rise to England selection come the end of the year. Other bowlers with something to shout about were Matt Mason of

SECOND ELEVEN CHAMPIONSHIP, 2002

	P	W	L	D	Bonus points Batting	Bowling	Points	Avge
1 – Kent (6)	10	6	2	2	22	35	137	13.70
2 – Derbyshire (18).	12	5	1	6	38	37	159	13.25
3 – Yorkshire (2)	12	5	1	6	34	39	157	13.08
4 – Glamorgan (16)	11	4	1	6	32	34	138	12.55
5 – Warwickshire (8). . . .	12	5	1	6	26	36	146	12.16
6 – Northamptonshire (5).	15	6	3	6	34	47	177	11.80
7 – Lancashire (9)	13	4	2	7	29	37	142	10.92
8 – Hampshire (1)	11	3	4	4	32	28	112	10.18
9 – Durham (10)	11	3	3	5	21	29	106	9.63
10 – Middlesex (11).	11	2	3	6	28	29	105	9.54
11 – Surrey (7)	13	1	3	9	32	41	121	9.30
12 – Worcestershire (13) . .	11	2	6	3	29	35	100	9.09
13 – Nottinghamshire (3). .	15	3	4	8	23	45	136	9.06
14 – Sussex (17)	12	3	6	3	27	31	106	8.83
15 – Somerset (15).	10	2	3	5	15	25	84	8.40
16 – Gloucestershire (4) . .	11	1	4	6	12	29	79*	7.18
17 – Leicestershire (12). . .	12	1	6	5	17	36	85	7.08
18 – Essex (14)	10	1	4	5	10	21	63	6.30

2001 positions are shown in brackets.

Win = 12 pts; draw = 4 pts.

* Includes 2 pts for a draw in which scores ended level and Gloucestershire were batting last.

Worcestershire and Durham's Ian Pattison, who celebrated the summer's two hat-tricks. Neil Gunter of Derbyshire was the leading wicket-taker with 48. He helped Derbyshire leap 16 places up the table from 18th in 2001 to second in 2002; their points average more than doubled.

Two players passed 1,000 runs for the season, though their careers seemed to be heading in different directions. Scott Newman, after accruing 1,209 for the seconds, looked every inch the part when he stepped up to the Surrey first team and made 322 in just three matches. Wayne Noon, however, is unlikely to do the same for Nottinghamshire unless Chris Read – his rival for the gloves – becomes Alec Stewart's England successor. Another Nottinghamshire player tipped to catch the eye of the England selectors before long was Bilal Shafayat. Starting the season aged just 17, he cracked four hundreds and totted up 638 runs in six games. He was named Second Eleven Player of the Year by the Association of Cricket Statisticians and Historians.

LEADING AVERAGES, 2002

BATTING

(Qualification: 300 runs, average 30.00)

	M	I	NO	R	HS	100s	50s	Avge	Ct/St
T. L. Penney (*Warwicks*)	8	10	3	733	255*	3	2	104.71	2
J. S. Laney (*Hants*)	5	8	2	608	205*	3	1	101.33	12
G. O. Jones (*Kent*)	8	14	5	747	211*	2	3	83.00	28/2
J. H. K. Adams (*Hants*)	6	9	1	615	200*	3	2	76.87	3
Hassan Adnan (*Derbys*)	8	16	4	882	128*	5	2	73.50	8
S. D. Stubbings (*Derbys*)	5	8	1	500	203*	2	1	71.42	2
K. Newell (*Glam*)	5	7	1	420	93	0	5	70.00	1
P. C. L. Holloway (*Somerset*) . .	6	8	2	398	95	0	4	66.33	4
J. R. C. Hamblin (*Hants*)	7	9	2	458	109*	1	4	65.42	1
B. M. Shafayat (*Notts*)	6	11	1	638	194*	1	4	63.80	6/4
B. L. Hutton (*Middx*)	4	6	0	371	143	2	1	61.83	2
M. L. Pettini (*Essex*)	7	12	3	552	123	2	3	61.33	5
S. A. Newman (*Surrey*)	11	20	0	1,209	164	4	5	60.45	13
R. J. Cunliffe (*Leics*)	4	6	0	353	116	1	2	58.83	2
T. Frost (*Warwicks*)	5	6	0	340	144	1	2	56.66	16
R. S. Bopara (*Essex*)	6	11	1	558	164	2	3	55.80	4
G. Yates (*Lancs*)	12	16	4	664	106	1	5	55.33	9
D. Alleyne (*Middx*)	11	19	6	699	200*	3	2	53.76	26/1
R. A. White (*Northants*)	4	8	1	371	151	2	0	53.00	1
V. J. Craven (*Yorks*)	6	10	0	528	138	2	1	52.80	5
A. C. Morris (*Hants*)	10	16	1	784	173*	1	6	52.26	5
J. W. Wade (*Northants*)	6	11	2	460	73	0	5	51.11	2
W. M. Noon (*Notts*)	14	25	4	1,033	166*	2	7	49.19	18/1
D. J. Pipe (*Worcs*)	10	18	4	675	101*	1	5	48.21	24/3
A. D. Shaw (*Glam*)	11	16	3	626	127	1	3	48.15	19/3
P. R. Pollard (*Worcs*)	5	10	2	384	186	1	1	48.00	8
J. G. E. Benning (*Surrey*)	10	18	2	759	105	1	5	47.43	5
J. B. Hockley (*Kent*)	5	9	1	378	103	2	1	47.25	1
W. J. House (*Sussex*)	8	12	1	512	201*	2	0	46.54	3
J. Hughes (*Glam*)	5	7	0	324	140	1	1	46.28	3
B. J. Hyam (*Essex*)	9	13	2	493	94	0	4	44.81	13
C. D. Hopkinson (*Sussex*)	10	17	2	658	215	3	1	43.86	4
T. W. Roberts (*Lancs*)	10	16	3	570	106*	1	4	43.84	10
A. W. Evans (*Glam*)	6	8	0	345	86	0	4	43.12	2
M. E. Cassar (*Northants*)	7	10	2	343	118	1	1	42.87	3
S. A. Cunningham (*Hants, Kent & Somerset*)	8	13	2	469	125*	2	2	42.63	3

	M	I	NO	R	HS	100s	50s	Avge	Ct/St
M. A. Carberry (*Surrey*)	9	17	0	703	169	1	5	41.35	6
J. L. Sadler (*Yorks*)	12	18	3	612	109	3	2	40.80	5
G. G. Wagg (*Warwicks*)	6	10	1	365	103	1	2	40.55	3
P. D. Trego (*Somerset*)	8	11	0	441	188	1	1	40.09	3
G. L. Brophy (*Northants*)	11	17	0	673	166	3	1	39.58	26/3
P. Aldred (*Derbys*)	10	15	5	392	67*	0	3	39.20	9
S. A. Richardson (*Yorks*)	11	19	4	587	125	2	2	39.13	12
J. R. Carpenter (*Sussex*)	11	20	3	664	113*	2	2	39.05	5
M. P. Dowman (*Derbys*)	6	11	0	423	111	1	3	38.45	5
H. R. Jones (*Warwicks*)	8	13	3	379	79*	0	4	37.90	1
K. K. Beazleigh (*Essex*)	7	11	2	337	78	0	3	37.44	1
D. R. Holt (*Middx*)	8	13	3	374	111	1	1	37.40	1
C. C. Benham (*Hants*)	7	12	1	410	88	0	2	37.27	7
J. K. Maunders (*Leics & Middx*)	10	17	1	587	100	1	4	36.68	13
D. A. Clapp (*Sussex*)	11	22	3	697	90*	0	6	36.68	3
G. S. Kandola (*Worcs*)	10	19	3	572	116	1	3	35.75	7
J. P. Pyemont (*Derbys*)	9	15	1	497	104	1	3	35.50	2
M. J. Powell (*Northants*)	6	12	1	390	79	0	2	35.45	2
R. C. Driver (*Lancs*)	10	15	2	446	90	0	4	34.30	5
W. P. C. Weston (*Worcs*)	8	16	1	511	113*	1	3	34.06	6
N. R. C. Dumelow (*Derbys*)	11	17	1	541	112	1	2	33.81	4
N. R. D. Compton (*Middx*)	10	17	1	541	96	0	6	33.81	0
D. G. Brandy (*Leics*)	10	18	2	532	149	1	2	33.25	5
D. D. Cherry (*Glam*)	9	13	1	398	91	0	4	33.16	8
C. R. Taylor (*Yorks*)	7	10	0	330	117	1	1	33.00	6
R. E. Watkins (*Glam*)	9	12	2	330	84	0	3	33.00	8
S. C. Moore (*Surrey, Sussex, & Worcs*)	8	15	0	482	109	1	3	32.13	4
D. E. Paynter (*Northants*)	14	25	3	701	125	1	4	31.86	7
P. Mustard (*Durham*)	9	14	1	410	80	0	3	31.53	17
R. A. Stead (*Yorks*)	11	16	2	438	153	1	1	31.28	3
R. S. G. Anderson (*Northants*)	9	14	3	341	68*	0	3	31.00	1
J. J. Haynes (*Lancs*)	10	15	0	456	106	1	2	30.40	29/1

BOWLING

(Qualification: 10 wickets, average 25.00)

	O	M	R	W	BB	5W/i	Avge
D. A. Cosker (*Glam*)	41.1	14	89	11	4-44	0	8.09
M. C. Ilott (*Essex*)	40	10	99	11	4-39	0	9.00
G. D. Rose (*Somerset*)	82	35	147	13	4-12	0	11.30
J. A. Tomlinson (*Hants*)	92.5	27	234	20	6-47	2	11.70
C. P. Schofield (*Lancs*)	98.5	32	223	16	5-68	1	13.93
J. E. Brinkley (*Durham*)	108	37	289	20	5-61	1	14.45
M. A. Sheikh (*Warwicks*)	153.1	53	327	22	7-42	2	14.86
D. J. Forder (*Glam*)	126.2	25	373	23	5-30	1	16.21
S. R. Lampitt (*Worcs*)	106.3	25	327	20	4-31	0	16.35
I. Pattison (*Durham*)	91.4	25	268	16	6-39	1	16.75
B. J. Trott (*Kent*)	176.4	41	572	33	7-47	3	17.33
T. F. Bloomfield (*Middx*)	89	22	278	16	6-34	1	17.37
C. M. Goode (*Northants*)	60.3	17	174	10	4-21	0	17.40
G. G. Wagg (*Warwicks*)	121.5	31	342	19	5-14	1	18.00
G. Keedy (*Lancs*)	106	36	271	15	5-68	2	18.06
D. S. Harrison (*Glam*)	217	40	622	34	6-49	3	18.29
J. M. Golding (*Kent*)	125.3	38	335	18	4-49	0	18.61
P. J. McMahon (*Notts*)	330.2	105	847	45	5-27	3	18.82

	O	M	R	W	BB	5W/i	Avge
M. S. Mason (*Worcs*)	57.4	12	190	10	6-73	1	19.00
G. M. Hamilton (*Yorks*)	73	15	232	12	5-38	1	19.33
J. M. Anderson (*Lancs*)	145.2	35	414	21	8-54	1	19.71
N. E. L. Gunter (*Derbys*)	277	67	950	48	5-28	2	19.79
P. D. Trego (*Somerset*)	193	43	645	32	7-42	3	20.15
J. P. Pyemont (*Derbys*)	79	17	248	12	5-101	1	20.66
M. J. Cawdron (*Northants*)	256.1	48	869	42	6-21	2	20.69
J. P. Hewitt (*Kent*)	275.5	74	726	35	4-60	0	20.74
P. J. Swanepoel (*Yorks*)	328	88	905	43	6-50	1	21.04
J. M. M. Averis (*Glos*)	78	13	280	13	4-32	0	21.53
B. W. O'Connell (*Derbys, Leics & Sussex*)	236.5	78	562	26	6-16	2	21.61
G. Yates (*Lancs*)	300.4	100	689	31	6-38	2	22.22
O. T. Parkin (*Glam*)	185	42	492	22	5-23	1	22.36
C. D. Hopkinson (*Sussex*)	88.5	20	272	12	3-19	0	22.66
J. A. R. Blain (*Northants*)	130	19	464	20	5-42	1	23.20
P. Aldred (*Derbys*)	339	106	886	38	5-81	1	23.31
M. P. Smethurst (*Essex & Lancs*)	278.5	63	897	37	5-39	2	24.24
J. C. Tredwell (*Kent*)	143	39	391	16	4-43	0	24.43
M. J. Symington (*Durham*)	115.1	30	368	15	4-20	0	24.53
T. A. Hunt (*Middx*)	232.4	46	863	35	6-48	3	24.65
C. E. Dagnall (*Leics*)	92.2	24	273	11	4-49	0	24.81
S. W. T. Jacques (*Somerset*)	81	20	249	10	3-11	0	24.90
C. T. Brice (*Yorkshire*)	223.1	61	673	27	4-18	0	24.92

SECOND ELEVEN CHAMPIONS 1959–2002

1959	Gloucestershire	1974	Middlesex	1988	Surrey
1960	Northamptonshire	1975	Surrey	1989	Middlesex
1961	Kent	1976	Kent	1990	Sussex
1962	Worcestershire	1977	Yorkshire	1991	Yorkshire
1963	Worcestershire	1978	Sussex	1992	Surrey
1964	Lancashire	1979	Warwickshire	1993	Middlesex
1965	Glamorgan	1980	Glamorgan	1994	Somerset
1966	Surrey	1981	Hampshire	1995	Hampshire
1967	Hampshire	1982	Worcestershire	1996	Warwickshire
1968	Surrey	1983	Leicestershire	1997	Lancashire
1969	Kent	1984	Yorkshire	1998	Northamptonshire
1970	Kent	1985	Nottinghamshire	1999	Middlesex
1971	Hampshire	1986	Lancashire	2000	Middlesex
1972	Nottinghamshire	1987	{ Kent / Yorkshire	2001	Hampshire
1973	Essex			2002	Kent

SECOND ELEVEN TROPHY, 2002

A Zone

	Played	Won	Lost	No result	Points	Net run-rate
YORKSHIRE	8	4	1	3	11	13.05
Lancashire	8	3	2	3	9	7.90
Nottinghamshire	8	3	4	1	7	−1.15
Derbyshire	8	2	3	3	7	−7.66
Durham	8	2	4	2	6	−9.09

B Zone

	Played	Won	Lost	No result	Points	Net run-rate
MIDDLESEX	8	7	1	0	14	6.89
Northamptonshire	8	6	1	1	13	15.31
Leicestershire	8	3	4	1	7	−5.75
Minor Counties	8	1	6	1	3	−5.57
Warwickshire	8	1	6	1	3	−9.07

C Zone

	Played	Won	Lost	No result	Points	Net run-rate
HAMPSHIRE..............	8	4	2	2	10	9.89
Glamorgan................	8	5	3	0	10	0.19
Gloucestershire	8	4	3	1	9	−1.28
Worcestershire	8	2	3	3	7	0.79
Somerset	8	1	5	2	4	−10.50

D Zone

	Played	Won	Lost	No result	Points	Net run-rate
KENT..................	8	4	1	3	11	20.46
Surrey..................	8	5	2	1	11	16.03
Sussex	8	3	4	1	7	−12.24
Essex	8	3	3	2	6*	−3.01
MCC Young Cricketers.	8	0	5	3	3	−24.01

* Two points deducted for fielding an unqualified player.

Semi-finals

At Uxbridge, August 12. **Kent won by four wickets.** Toss: Kent. **Middlesex 137** (49.1 overs) (M. J. Brown 44, J. W. M. Dalrymple 54; H. J. H. Loudon three for ten); **Kent 138 for six** (49.1 overs) (J. P. Hewitt 44; A. J. Coleman three for 36).

At Stamford Bridge, August 12. **Hampshire won by 60 runs.** Toss: Hampshire. **Hampshire 278 for five** (50 overs) (J. H. K. Adams 53, A. C. Morris 37, L. R. Prittipaul 61 not out, J. D. Francis 36, J. R. C. Hamblin 38, Extras 40); **Yorkshire 218** (45.5 overs) (S. A. Richardson 40, G. M. Hamilton 76; J. A. Tomlinson three for 35).

Final

At Southampton, September 9, 10. **Kent won by five wickets.** Toss: Kent. **Hampshire 238** (49.1 overs) (J. H. K. Adams 58, A. C. Morris 38, J. D. Francis 49, J. R. C. Hamblin 40); **Kent 241 for five** (49.4 overs) (J. C. Tredwell 111; I. H. Shah three for 45).

LEAGUE CRICKET IN ENGLAND AND WALES IN 2002

By GEOFFREY DEAN

Three years after the introduction of premier league cricket, 25 leagues were accredited by the ECB in 2002. With only one more league, Leicestershire, welcomed into the fold, and no new entrants expected for 2003, it appeared that the steady rise from a starting base of ten in 1999 had reached a plateau. The board was satisfied, however, that it had put in place a national network covering most of the country, with scope for more leagues to join in.

There was one regret. After four years of playing two-day matches over separate weekends, the Kent League, English pioneers of the revered Australian-style grade cricket, decided to revert to one-day games in 2003. No other league had suggested any interest in the longer duration. "We're sorry to see Kent's change, as they'd shown that the two-day format was workable in this country," said Frank Kemp, the ECB's operations manager for recreational cricket. "While the incorporation of Kent professionals had gone smoothly, the consistent problem of pitches of the requisite quality had become an issue, not helped by bad weather. A lot of committees and spectators were also anti the longer duration, as were some older players."

In fact, the change meant that, in 2003, Kent matches would last 110 overs per day rather than 102. Meanwhile, their grant from the ECB would be cut from £2,500 per club to £750. Leagues playing the board's preferred quota of 120 overs per match would continue to receive £1,250 per club, with regional league clubs getting £2,000 each to cover higher travel costs.

The Essex League expressed doubts about 120 overs per day, but elected to carry on with it for another season. There were other problems around the country. The Derbyshire League was to be reduced from 12 clubs to 11 in 2003 because Langley Mill could not raise enough players. The Northern League was still having difficulty in satisfying key ECB criterion for premiership status – a pyramid structure – though the Liverpool Competition was making progress on this front. But their neighbours, the Lancashire and Central Lancashire Leagues, continued to reject any overtures to join the premiership family.

One of the strongest premier leagues, the Birmingham & District, witnessed a remarkable change of fortune. After Dave Manning, captain of Halesowen, had lost the first 13 tosses of the season, he handed over calling duties to Richard Cox, who won the last seven. Halesowen climbed from a mid-table position in late July – 52 points behind the leaders, Himley – to clinch their first title. The reigning champions, Stratford, struggled so badly that they were relegated. The same fate befell Finchampstead, winners of the 2001 Home Counties League; the High Wycombe all-rounder, David Taylor, helped his side to the championship with 550 runs and 42 wickets.

In London, two clubs made flying starts and were never caught. Teddington won their first nine games, a Middlesex League record, and were proclaimed champions with five weeks to go – their first title in six years. Danny Waugh, brother of Australia's Test twins, contributed 40 wickets at 13 each with his left-arm spin, and more than 300 runs. South of the Thames, Wimbledon gained victories in eight of their first nine Surrey Championship matches. Although they stumbled in July, losing four times, they were crowned on August 17. Ronnie Kotkamp, their New Zealand-born swing bowler, enjoyed a change from Reader to Duke's balls so much that he claimed 71 victims, a Surrey premier division record. Other emphatic champions included West Indian Cavaliers, who won the Nottinghamshire League by 92 points.

Gidea Park & Romford won their first Essex League title for 19 years; their only defeat was in their opening match, against newly promoted Orsett. Andy Churchill scored 737 runs for Gidea Park, and Mel Hussain, brother of Nasser, proved a vital signing, with 31 wickets and more than 400 runs. But Orsett lost form, were bowled out for 32 inside 14 overs by Wanstead, and went straight down again. Across the Thames Estuary, Bromley, the Kent League runners-up four times in eight years, finally won the top prize. It was third time lucky for Hastings & St Leonard's, who secured the Sussex League title after two seasons in second place.

The closest finish came in the Liverpool Competition, where Wallasey and Leigh finished with the same number of points and victories: Wallasey became champions as they had gained 28 points to 26 in their two meetings with Leigh. While Darwen went through the season unbeaten to dominate the Northern League, Harrogate relied on a strong finish to stop Sheffield Collegiate retaining their Yorkshire League title, which they themselves last won in 1990. For the second year running, David Byas's 18-year-old Yorkshire League record of 1,394 runs was under threat, this time from Cleethorpes' Australian batsman, Shane Deitz: he needed another 60 in the final game against Scarborough – but made a rare duck.

The Devon League title race went down to the final hour of the season. The leaders, Bovey Tracey, needed 191 to beat second-placed Sidmouth, and appeared to be throwing it away at a parlous 116 for seven, until an unbeaten 40 from Danny Full helped them to victory. Further west, in Cornwall, Charlie Shreck took 84 wickets, and made Truro's title look inevitable.

Outside the premier leagues, in the South Wales Association, Swansea became the first club to do the league and cup double, and Alun Evans of Ammanford the first Welshman in that league to score 1,000 in a season. But one of the most remarkable all-round performances occurred further north, in the Saddleworth League, where Heyside's professional, Melbourne Austin, fell just short of a personal double, combining 1,310 runs with 91 wickets.

ECB PREMIER LEAGUE TABLES, 2002

Birmingham and District Premier Cricket League

	P	W	L	T	Pts
Halesowen	22	9	4	1	269
Himley	22	7	3	0	263
Moseley	22	7	3	1	245
Cannock	22	7	5	0	225
Barnt Green	22	6	6	0	220
Old Hill	22	6	6	0	219
Knowle & Dorridge	22	5	6	0	219
Walsall	22	6	6	0	212
Wolverhampton	22	5	8	0	207
Coventry & N. Warwicks	22	5	7	0	191
Stratford-upon-Avon	22	3	7	0	175
Aston Unity	22	3	10	0	162

Cheshire County Cricket League

	P	W	L	Pts
Bowdon	22	12	4	365
Macclesfield	22	11	3	363
Hyde	22	13	2	353
Oulton Park	22	8	7	330
Bramhall	22	10	5	323
Didsbury	22	10	6	307
Alderley Edge	22	7	10	271
Chester Boughton Hall	22	7	7	251
Nantwich	22	6	10	250
Neston	22	6	10	249
Grappenhall	22	2	14	147
Cheadle Hulme	22	0	14	131

Cornwall Premier League

	P	W	L	T	Pts
Truro	27	17	0	0	433
St Buryan	27	16	2	0	388
Grampound Road	27	9	7	1	323
St Just	27	10	7	0	310
Falmouth	27	9	8	2	305
Callington	27	7	8	2	287
Menheniot	27	6	13	0	250
Mullion	27	4	11	1	232
Troon	27	5	12	0	224
Camborne	27	1	16	0	192

Derbyshire Premier League

	P	W	L	T	Pts
Sandiacre Town	22	15	1	0	427
Ockbrook & Borrowash	22	14	3	0	422
Dunstall	22	11	5	0	388
Ilkeston Rutland	22	9	8	0	296
Langley Mill United	22	8	9	1	296
Denby	22	7	6	0	284
Chesterfield	22	5	10	0	265
Clifton	22	7	6	0	263
Quarndon	22	6	10	1	262
Sawley & Long Eaton Park	22	4	11	0	217
Alvaston & Boulton	22	4	11	0	196
Wirksworth	22	4	14	0	172

Please see note on page 1072.

Devon Cricket League

	P	W	L	T	Pts
Bovey Tracey	18	8	3	1	249
Exeter	18	9	4	1	247
Sidmouth	18	8	5	0	234
Plympton	18	7	5	0	214
Barton	18	9	5	0	212
Paignton	18	8	7	1	193
Sandford	18	6	4	0	186
Torquay	18	3	7	1	174
Exmouth	18	5	8	0	161
Cornwood	18	0	15	0	94

East Anglian Premier Cricket League

	P	W	L	Pts
Vauxhall Mallards	17	7	2	229
Clacton	17	6	1	213
Cambridge Granta	17	4	4	201
Swardeston	17	4	3	180
Cambridge & Godmanchester	17	3	4	171
Bury St Edmunds	17	4	5	160
Norwich	17	3	3	160
Maldon	17	3	6	144
Mildenhall	17	2	5	134
Ramsey	17	2	5	128

Essex Premier League

	P	W	L	Pts
Gidea Park & Romford	18	9	1	254
Wanstead	18	10	3	249
Saffron Walden	18	7	4	214
Loughton	18	6	6	196
Colchester & East Essex	18	5	5	175
Hainault & Clayhall	18	5	7	175
South Woodford	18	6	8	172
Fives & Heronians	18	4	6	165
Orsett	18	4	10	149
Shenfield	18	4	10	138

Home Counties Premier Cricket League

	P	W	L	Pts
High Wycombe	9	6	0	187
Reading	9	4	0	148
Henley	9	4	3	143
Slough	9	4	2	134
Basingstoke & N. Hants	9	4	5	127
Banbury	9	3	2	121
Radlett	9	2	2	116
Beaconsfield	9	3	4	111
Bicester & N. Oxford	9	1	6	62
Finchampstead	9	0	7	58

Kent Cricket League

	P	W	L	Pts
Bromley	9	3	0	298
St Lawrence	9	3	1	277
Sevenoaks Vine	9	4	0	268
The Mote	9	2	0	242
Bexley	9	1	1	211
Lordswood	9	1	2	197
Folkestone	9	2	1	178
Tunbridge Wells	9	1	1	146
Dartford Halls	9	0	3	89
Orpington	9	0	8	70

Leicestershire County Cricket League

	P	W	L	Pts
Loughborough Town	22	17	0	436
Kibworth	22	14	2	423
Market Harborough	22	11	3	376
Lutterworth	22	10	7	320
Leicester Ivanhoe	22	7	7	296
Leicester Banks	22	7	10	264
Illston Abbey	22	6	9	250
Syston Town	22	5	9	241
Stoughton	22	5	11	221
Billesdon	22	3	13	221
Barwell	22	2	11	201
Hinckley Town	22	5	10	134

Lincolnshire Cricket Board Premier League

	P	W	L	Pts	%
Grantham	14	10	1	228	16.29
Bourne	16	10	2	246	15.38
Market Rasen	16	8	2	225	14.06
Sleaford	14	4	3	181	12.93
Market Deeping	15	7	5	175	11.67
Lindum	16	3	8	139	8.69
Messingham	15	3	8	128	8.53
Boston	16	3	7	127	7.94
Grimsby Town	15	3	8	112	7.47
Caistor	15	2	9	107	7.13

Liverpool and District Cricket Competition

	P	W	L	Pts
Wallasey	22	13	5	335
Leigh	22	13	4	335
Bootle	22	12	5	316
Northern	22	10	4	270
Northop Hall	22	10	7	268
Ormskirk	22	8	6	215
Maghull	22	8	10	214
New Brighton	22	7	10	196
Lytham	22	6	11	184
Wigan	22	6	10	183
Sefton Park	22	6	12	180
Worsley	22	1	16	82

Wallasey were champions because they scored 28 points to Leigh's 26 in head-to-head matches.

Middlesex County Cricket League

	P	W	L	Pts
Teddington	18	13	2	142
Richmond	18	6	3	84
Brondesbury	18	5	3	75
Ealing	18	5	6	66
Wembley	18	5	5	64
Finchley	18	5	7	62
Eastcote	18	5	7	59
Stanmore	18	5	7	52
Hampstead	18	3	7	50
Winchmore Hill	18	2	7	44

Northamptonshire Cricket Championship

	P	W	L	Pts
Finedon Dolben	22	13	1	190
Old Northamptonians	22	11	5	159
Bedford Town	22	12	5	152
Peterborough Town	22	10	5	152
Stony Stratford	22	11	7	149
County Colts	22	9	6	135
Brixworth	22	7	11	105
Horton House	22	5	6	99
Wellingborough Town	22	4	10	83
Rothwell Town	22	3	10	75
Northampton Saints	22	2	10	73
Old Wellingburians	22	1	12	52

North East Premier Cricket League

	P	W	L	Pts
Benwell Hill	22	14	1	409
South Northumberland	22	11	4	378
Sunderland	22	9	5	324
Philadelphia	22	7	5	293
Chester-le-Street	22	8	7	288
Gateshead Fell	22	7	5	268
Blaydon	22	5	5	263
Durham Cricket Academy	22	4	6	242
Norton	22	5	10	204
Newcastle	22	3	8	204
Stockton	22	1	8	190
Tynemouth	22	2	12	174

Northern Cricket League

	P	W	L	Pts
Darwen	22	14	0	231
Morecambe	22	15	3	215
Netherfield	22	9	5	171
Kendal	22	7	4	165
Blackpool	22	8	7	145
Chorley	22	8	6	132
St Annes	22	5	6	123
Preston	22	6	11	122
Fleetwood	22	5	9	122
Leyland & Farington	22	4	12	96
Lancaster	22	1	8	89
Leyland Motors	22	2	13	87

North Staffs & South Cheshire League

	P	W	L	Pts
Norton-in-Hales	22	13	5	352
Longton	22	11	4	321
Betley	22	11	6	313
Leek	22	9	5	265
Porthill Park	22	9	7	257
Caverswall	22	8	4	256
Moddershall	22	8	4	256
Barlaston	22	5	9	215
Checkley	22	5	6	213
Audley	22	5	10	208
Knypersley	22	5	10	198
Crewe	22	0	19	94

North Wales Premier League

	P	W	L	Pts
Bangor	22	13	5	332
Brymbo	22	11	3	316
Llandudno	22	11	3	311
Hawarden Park	22	12	5	306
Mold	22	9	6	268
Northop	22	9	7	256
Pontblyddin	22	6	7	210
St Asaph	22	6	12	186
Halkyn	22	5	8	178
Mochdre	22	5	11	175
Marchwiel & Wrexham	22	4	9	170
Connah's Quay	22	1	16	92

Nottinghamshire Cricket Board Premier League

	P	W	L	Pts
West Indian Cavaliers	22	16	2	361
Welbeck Colliery	22	9	5	269
Clifton Village	22	7	4	260
Kimberley Institute	22	11	8	256
Blidworth	22	8	8	249
Bracebridge Heath	22	8	4	241
Wollaton	22	8	8	226
Caythorpe	22	5	10	214
Notts Unity Casuals	22	2	8	193
Southwell	22	4	9	186
Bridon	22	3	9	180
Retford	22	3	9	152

Southern Premier Cricket League

	P	W	L	Pts	Avge
Havant	15	12	2	265	17.67
BAT Sports	16	12	3	279	17.44
Bashley Rydal	15	8	5	220	14.67
South Wiltshire	17	7	8	210	12.35
Bournemouth	13	4	5	155	11.92
Portsmouth	13	4	6	144	11.08
Liphook & Ripsley	16	4	6	170	10.63
Andover	15	6	8	159	10.60
Calmore Sports	16	4	9	137	8.56
Burridge	14	2	11	90	6.43

South Wales Cricket League

	P	W	L	Pts	Avge
Sudbrook	12	8	0	209	17.42
Cardiff Athletic	12	6	4	181	15.08
Pentyrch	15	6	4	226	15.07
St Fagans	14	8	4	206	14.71
Pontypridd	13	6	5	155	11.92
Newport	12	3	2	140	11.67
Usk	14	5	7	154	11.00
Penarth	14	3	7	128	9.14
Abergavenny	14	3	7	125	8.93
Miskin Manor	14	1	9	99	7.07

Surrey Championship

	P	W	L	Pts
Wimbledon	18	13	4	170
Guildford	18	10	2	142
Weybridge	18	8	4	119
Reigate Priory	18	8	9	105
Banstead	18	7	7	102
Cheam	18	7	7	98
Sutton	18	7	9	96
Esher	18	6	7	90
Sunbury	18	4	11	55
Bank of England	18	1	11	22

Sussex Cricket League

	P	W	L	Pts
Hastings & St Leonard's	18	11	2	393
Horsham	18	11	3	386
Three Bridges	18	9	6	342
Brighton & Hove	18	6	5	292
Eastbourne	18	7	7	284
Worthing	18	5	6	240
Chichester Priory Park	18	5	7	221
Steyning	18	4	5	188
St James's Montefiore	18	3	9	182
Haywards Heath	18	1	12	143

Wisden 2002 was inadvertently supplied with the 2000 table for the Derbyshire Premier League. The correct table (*right*) for the 2001 season was:

West of England Premier League

	P	W	L	Pts	Avge
Keynsham	15	10	4	206	13.73
Bath	16	8	3	200	12.50
Corsham	14	8	3	175	12.50
Thornbury	14	7	3	160	11.43
Cheltenham	14	7	3	147	10.50
Optimists & Clifton	14	6	4	144	10.29
Taunton St Andrews	16	6	6	142	8.88
Bristol West Indians	14	5	7	114	8.14
Knowle	16	2	11	62	3.88
Lansdown	17	1	16	20	1.18

Yorkshire ECB County Premier League

	P	W	L	T	Pts
Harrogate	26	18	4	0	155
Sheffield Collegiate	26	20	4	0	152
Doncaster Town	26	15	7	0	128
Sheffield United	26	14	7	0	120
Yorkshire Academy	26	13	8	0	109
Castleford	26	11	12	0	98
Barnsley	26	10	12	0	96
Cleethorpes	26	10	9	1	95
York	26	10	13	0	90
Scarborough	26	11	11	0	89
Hull	26	6	16	1	58
Rotherham Town	26	6	16	0	54
Driffield	26	6	17	0	52
Appleby Frodingham	26	4	18	0	42

Derbyshire Premier League 2001

	P	W	L	Pts
Denby	22	9	2	385
Dunstall	22	10	3	382
Ockbrook & Borrowash	22	13	2	370
Quarndon	22	7	4	336
Sandiacre Town	22	7	6	275
Alvaston & Boulton	22	5	5	265
Ilkeston Rutland	22	5	5	235
Wirksworth	22	5	8	235
Chesterfield	22	4	7	219
Heanor Town	22	3	9	217
Langley Mill United	22	3	11	206
Stainsby Hall	22	2	11	192

OTHER LEAGUE WINNERS, 2002

Airedale & Wharfedale	Adel
Bassetlaw	Cutthorpe
Bolton Association	Spring View
Bolton League	Tonge
Bradford	Pudsey Congs
Central Yorkshire	Birstall
Durham County	Evenwood
Durham Senior	Burnmoor
Hertfordshire	Hemel Hempstead
Huddersfield	Kirkburton
Lancashire County	Denton West
Merseyside Competition	Ainsdale
North Lancs & Cumbria League	Barrow
Norfolk Alliance	Fakenham
Northumberland & Tyneside Senior	Shotley Bridge
North Yorks & South Durham	Guisborough
Pembrokeshire	Haverfordwest
Ribblesdale	Read
Saddleworth	Saddleworth
Shropshire	Bridgnorth
South Wales Association	Swansea
Two Counties	Copdock & Old Ipswichians
West Wales Association	Maesteg
York Senior	Dunnington

THE LANCASHIRE LEAGUES IN 2002

By CHRIS ASPIN

Despite another wet summer, which prevented almost a quarter of the games in the Lancashire leagues from reaching a result, several important records tumbled. Most were for batting, though David Ormerod of Bacup became the first amateur since the war to be the leading wicket-taker in the Lancashire League season. Ormerod claimed 82 at 13.20, in partnership with the Tasmanian professional Shaun Young, who took 64 at 12.09. Bowling unchanged in most games, the pair accounted for 86 per cent of Bacup's wickets. They helped Bacup to their third successive championship, by a margin of 40 points from runners-up Enfield.

In three weeks of July, the South African Jacques Rudolph hit five successive centuries for Lowerhouse: 149 not out against Accrington, 116 against Todmorden, 154 not out and 126 not out against Rishton and 105 not out against Haslingden, an aggregate of 650 runs for once out. Not since Everton Weekes scored three successive centuries for Bacup in 1951 has the league seen such consistency. Rudolph, one of four professionals to pass 1,000 runs, aggregated 1,121 at 86.23, eight behind the Nelson pro, Joe Scuderi, who headed the list with an average of 94.08.

Michael Clarke, a 21-year-old Australian, became the first player to score a double-century in a Lancashire League game. In an unbeaten onslaught, he faced 164 balls and hit 24 fours and seven sixes, reaching 200 out of a Ramsbottom total of 294 for three at Enfield. Clarke shone again in the Worsley Cup semi-finals, scoring 178, in 148 balls, out of 307 for four against Todmorden. In the other semi, his New South Wales team-mate Mark Higgs hammered 168 for Church, who ran up a club record of 328 against Lowerhouse. The final proved much tamer: Ramsbottom dismissed Church for 114, chasing 178, in a rain-affected game which dragged into a third day. Clarke and Higgs both left for home before it finally ended. The recall of overseas professionals meant that the season ended with 11 of the 14 clubs using substitutes. Tushar Arothe, who stood in at Todmorden for several games, set a club record with an unbeaten 189 against Accrington. Peter Sleep, the former Australian Test player, was the leading amateur, with 931 runs and 57 wickets for Rishton. Graham Knowles made 828 runs for Haslingden and Andrew Payne 703 for Rawtenstall. Keith Roscoe, the Rawtenstall left-arm spinner, took 58 wickets at 15.74.

In the Central Lancashire League, Littleborough had to wait until the last over of the season to be sure they had clinched their 18th title. League officials, who had carried the cup to Stand, expecting to make the presentation to their rivals, Radcliffe, had to dash back to Ashton, where Littleborough were playing their final match. They started level on points with Radcliffe, and won their game by seven wickets, but Ashton had denied them the bonus point awarded for bowling the opposition out. Meanwhile, Radcliffe seemed certain to get the bonus point they needed to pull ahead when they ran up a commanding 260 for five and had Stand seven down for 64, with 18 overs to play. The Stand tail wagged, however, reaching 130 for seven before the overs ran out. Radcliffe remained tied on points with Littleborough and had to cede the title as they had fewer wins. Norden beat Rochdale to take the Wood Cup, but Rochdale clinched a keenly contested inter-league competition, dismissing East Lancs for 123 in the final and winning by four wickets. The former Pakistan Test player, Asif Mujtaba, scored 1,588 runs and took 108 wickets for Norden, joining a select group who have achieved the double; five other pros topped a thousand.

Len Wolstenholme, the Middleton spinner, was again the most successful amateur wicket-taker with 80 at 13.35, ahead of Sardar Shah at Radcliffe, who claimed 64 at 3.56. Bobby Cross was the leading amateur run-scorer, with 949 for Heywood at 55.82, and Travis Birt of Radcliffe and David Blake of Walsden also passed 700.

Jim Bradbury and Arnold Pope, who have been umpires since the 1960s, stood in their 1,000th games during 2002. They declared they had no intention of retiring.

TRANSCO LANCASHIRE LEAGUE

	P	W	L	*Bonus* NR Pts	Pts	Professional	Runs	Avge	Wkts	Avge
Bacup	26	19	2	5	31	236	S. Young	637	39.81	64	12.09
Enfield	26	14	5	7	35	196	M. van Jaarsveld . . .	1,068	71.20	49	17.93
Haslingden . . .	26	13	7	6	21	169	I. D. Austin	878	73.16	51	19.07
Rishton	26	11	9	5	18	150*	‡P. R. Adams	93	7.75	37	20.54
Nelson	26	9	12	5	45	150	J. C. Scuderi	1,129	94.08	35	21.68
Rawtenstall . . .	26	11	9	6	18	146	A. J. Hall	723	60.25	33	23.39
Todmorden . . .	26	10	9	7	25	146	*Several professionals appeared for Todmorden.*				
Colne	26	10	12	4	29	141	‡C. K. Langeveldt . .	105	17.50	27	11.92
Burnley	26	9	10	7	30	141	P. Joubert	841	76.45	18	30.50
Ramsbottom . .	26	9	11	6	27	135	M. J. Clarke	883	58.86	18	23.50
East Lancs . . .	26	8	13	5	37	132	‡C. D. de Lange . . .	432	27.00	39	16.97
Church	26	8	12	6	24	122	M. A. Higgs	658	54.83	30	23.60
Lowerhouse . .	26	7	13	5	21	112*†	J. A. Rudolph	1,121	86.23	7	42.14
Accrington . . .	26	4	18	4	23	74†	A. J. Seymore	1,115	61.94	13	30.92

Notes: Ten points awarded for a win; seven for a tie; two points for dismissing the opposition and three for an uncompleted game. A maximum of five bonus points to losing sides for batting and bowling.

* *Includes seven points for a tie.*
† *One point deducted for slow over rate.*
‡ *Did not play the whole season.*

CENTRAL LANCASHIRE LEAGUE

	P	OW	LW	*Losing* L D Pts	Pts	Professional	Runs	Avge	Wkts	Avge
Littleborough	28	11	7	6 4 2	93	L. A. Carseldine	1,319	73.27	44	19.77
Radcliffe . . .	28	12	5	7 4 5	93	S. E. Dearden	462	21.00	59	14.59
Norden	28	12	3	6 6 3	90*	Asif Mujtaba	1,588	79.40	108	13.42
Werneth	28	12	4	7 5 2	88	S. Fernando	1,489	67.68	93	13.91
Rochdale . . .	28	9	7	6 6 3	88	D. J. L. de Vos	926	66.14	40	14.00
Middleton . . .	28	8	7	8 5 4	82	G. R. P. Peiris	1,146	54.57	19	14.89
Oldham	28	8	4	8 8 2	74	G. F. J. Liebenberg . .	899	52.88	34	16.79
Walsden	28	8	3	14 3 9	67	M. R. C. N. Bandaratilleke	312	14.18	97	12.22
Royton	28	6	3	14 5 6	58	‡Iqbal Siddiqui	493	44.81	22	27.90
Milnrow	28	5	4	12 7 3	58	C. T. Perren	1,069	50.90	40	19.85
Crompton . . .	28	6	3	15 3 2	53*	Saeed Anwar, jun. . .	931	40.47	70	19.00
Heywood . . .	28	3	4	14 6 5	51*	C. B. Sugden	1,183	59.15	5	44.40
Ashton	28	4	3	16 5 6	48	A. Rideegammanagedera	811	36.86	60	21.36
Unsworth . . .	28	2	1	16 8 4	37*	W. M. P. N. Wanasinghe	805	40.25	46	25.34
Stand	28	3	0	18 7 3	32	M. Hegg	260	13.68	56	15.96

Notes: Five points awarded for outright win; four points for a limited win; two points for a draw. A team achieves an outright win by bowling out the opposition. One losing point is awarded if a team batting second and losing achieves at least 75 per cent of the first team's total or if the team bowling second and losing takes seven or more wickets. CLL averages include cup games.

* *Includes three points for a tie.*
‡ *Did not play the whole season.*

NATIONAL CLUB CHAMPIONSHIP, 2002

Two first-timers contested the National Club final, and the venue was another change: with the Lord's outfield dug up, and being sold off to the public on the very day of the match, the teams adjourned to Edgbaston. It was a six-mile drive for Barnt Green, winners of their Midlands group. But Saffron Walden – quarter-finalists the previous season, when they won the Essex Premier League – made the long journey home triumphant, thanks to 99 not out from the Cambridgeshire batsman Giles Ecclestone.

Both teams won their semi-finals with a single ball to spare. Saffron Walden had visited Stanmore, who ran up 173 for seven, thanks to an unbeaten fifty from Alastair Fraser, brother of the Test bowler, Angus. Saffron Walden's reply fell away, but the wicket-keeper Neil Gladwin, scored 17 at No. 10, and the last man, Tim Smith, helped him scrape through. On the same day, Barnt Green had a nail-biting trip to Guisborough. Asked to bat, they totalled 169 for five, and Guisborough, the North Yorks & South Durham champions, reached the final over needing seven, with three wickets standing. But Richard Illingworth, the former Test spinner, kept them to four, while two men were run out, and then bowled David Towse for 47 with the fifth ball.

Barnt Green won more comfortably in the first of the national rounds, for the competition's last 16, against Cheshire club Bowdon, but cut it fine in their quarter-final against Bootle, whose captain, Ian Cockbain, steered them to 245 with an unbeaten 94. Illingworth and his old Worcestershire team-mate, Gavin Haynes, helped Barnt Green win with three balls remaining. Saffron Walden cruised to the semis by beating West Indian Cavaliers, the Nottinghamshire champions, and Ealing, with Ecclestone playing a key role.

Neither of the 2001 finalists reached the national knockouts. Bath lost the West and Wales final to Optimists & Clifton, and the title-holders, Bramhall, lost the first match they played, to Ormskirk by a single wicket.

FINAL

BARNT GREEN v SAFFRON WALDEN

At Birmingham, September 5. Saffron Walden won by seven wickets. Toss: Saffron Walden.

Despite Barnt Green's near-home advantage, Saffron Walden become the club knockout's newest champions. They seized the initiative from the start, putting Barnt Green in and running out Richard Hall before he faced a ball. But his team-mates, led by the former Worcestershire all-rounder Gavin Haynes, reached a fluent 192 for three before losing four for 19. Chasing 235, Saffron Walden also lost an opener for nought: their captain, Steve Plumb, trapped second ball. But Ryan Sparrow and Giles Ecclestone played with complete confidence, showing no respect for the ex-England spinner Richard Illingworth as they raised 181 at nearly six an over. Ecclestone was only one short of his hundred, with six runs required for victory, when Simon Williams deprived him of the landmark, hitting Mark Bagley over the square-leg rope to bring up victory with three overs to spare.

Man of the Match: G. W. Ecclestone.

Barnt Green

M. Dallaway c Williams b S. C. Ecclestone .	30	
R. Hall run out	0	
S. Froggatt c G. W. Ecclestone b Smith .	48	
G. R. Haynes c and b Smith	67	
*L. Jones b Mackinlay	41	
R. K. Illingworth lbw b Mackinlay . .	6	

†A. Smith lbw b G. W. Ecclestone 0
C. Bagley not out 16
L. Moncrieffe not out 3
B 1, l-b 12, w 7, n-b 3 23

1/1 2/64 3/107 4/192 (7 wkts, 45 overs) 234
5/207 6/208 7/211

M. Bagley and M. Hind did not bat.

Bowling: Mackinlay 9–1–41–2; R. Sparrow 6–0–26–0; S. C. Ecclestone 9–0–28–1; G. W. Ecclestone 6–0–36–1; Smith 9–1–48–2; Plumb 6–0–42–0.

Saffron Walden

R. Sparrow b Haynes	90	S. Williams not out	6
*S. G. Plumb lbw b Hind	0	L-b 7, w 18, n-b 1	26
G. W. Ecclestone not out	99		
S. C. Ecclestone b M. Bagley	14	1/0 2/181 3/221 (3 wkts, 41.5 overs) 235	

A. Mackinlay, W. Earl, J. Holland, †N. Gladwin, T. Smith and J. Sparrow did not bat.

Bowling: Haynes 9–3–35–1; Hind 7–0–35–1; Moncrieffe 8–0–45–0; Illingworth 6–0–44–0; Jones 3–1–21–0; M. Bagley 8.5–1–48–1.

Umpires: K. Coburn and J. Salisbury.

WINNERS 1969–2002

1969	Hampstead	1981	Scarborough	1993	Old Hill
1970	Cheltenham	1982	Scarborough	1994	Chorley
1971	Blackheath	1983	Shrewsbury	1995	Chorley
1972	Scarborough	1984	Old Hill	1996	Walsall
1973	Wolverhampton	1985	Old Hill	1997	Eastbourne
1974	Sunbury	1986	Stourbridge	1998	Doncaster Town
1975	York	1987	Old Hill	1999	Wolverhampton
1976	Scarborough	1988	Enfield	2000	Sheffield Collegiate
1977	Southgate	1989	Teddington	2001	Bramhall
1978	Cheltenham	1990	Blackpool	2002	Saffron Walden
1979	Scarborough	1991	Teddington		
1980	Moseley	1992	Optimists		

NATIONAL VILLAGE CHAMPIONSHIP, 2002

The National Village final was the last match played on the 188-year-old turf of Lord's before the outfield was dug up before relaying. The game was scheduled a day after the C&G final, with another historic venue, Hambledon, booked in case it needed a reserve day. But fine weather meant Elvaston returned to Lord's for the third year running, to meet Shipton-under-Wychwood, who had fielded Sam Mendes, the future Oscar-winning director, in the 1997 final. Mendes was absent, but his team-mates became the first champions from Oxfordshire.

Shipton had knocked out the title-holders, Ynystawe, but in the quarter-finals they slid to ten for three against Werrington. Two former Oxfordshire players, Phil Garner and Paul Hemming, added 101 before Hemming ensured victory with four wickets. In the semi-final, against Rowledge, Jason Constable pummelled 65 – out of 87 – in seven overs, despite which they scraped through by just two runs. Meanwhile, Elvaston romped through the Derbyshire group, beating Tideswell by 315 runs when their 15-year-old off-spinner, Gareth Charlesworth, claimed four for nine. At Great Eccleston, Paul Birch scored 70, then took seven for 27, with a hat-trick. Elvaston recovered from two for three to beat Colwall, in a repeat of the 2001 quarter-final, to earn another repeat in the semis, against Wolviston; Lee Archer saw them through with 94 not out.

Elsewhere, Iain MacPherson of Halsall in Lancashire followed up 103 against Dalton with seven for 45, including a hat-trick, and 16-year-old Matthew Asbrey, in a Loddington team of nine players, seized six for 23 to rout Great Houghton. A Somerset Under-15 player, James Palmer, plundered an unbeaten 75, with eight sixes, in only 34 balls for Hinton Charterhouse against Failand & Portbury.

The North Yorkshire South final between neighbours Folkton & Flixton and Staxton had a strange conclusion. Staxton's tenth-wicket pair needed three from the last ball; the keeper appealed unsuccessfully for a stumping, then started to celebrate, assuming the ball was dead. The batsmen ran three byes, and the umpires, agreeing play was still in progress, awarded them the match.

FINAL

ELVASTON v SHIPTON-UNDER-WYCHWOOD

At Lord's, September 1. Shipton-under-Wychwood won by five wickets. Toss: Elvaston.

This was Elvaston's third successive final, but they could not regain their title of 2000. Opting to bat, they started badly when 16-year-old Charles Ault was bowled in the first over. Lee Archer and Paul Birch began to rebuild, but Phil Garner, the 56-year-old off-spinner and retired Oxfordshire captain, tightened the screw, and Paul Hemming broke the stand with his fourth ball. Chris Panter went one better, striking with each of his first two deliveries, and an astonishing catch by Steve Bates, stretching out one hand on the long-off boundary, reduced Elvaston to 89 for seven. Only James Bodill's efforts saw them into three figures. After two early wickets for Ian Hall, Bates and Hemming rallied with 60 for Shipton's third wicket, and Shane Duff, a professional footballer with Cheltenham Town, steered them to victory with 16 balls to spare.

Elvaston

C. Ault b Snell	2		A. R. Barrett b Constable		2
†L. D. Archer b Garner	15		I. Hall not out		7
P. E. Birch c Bates b Hemming	22		G. Charlesworth b Panter		2
A. Brear b Panter	16				
*R. D. Johnson st Duff b Hemming	1		B 1, l-b 3, w 10, n-b 1		15
R. Kettlewell c Bates b Hemming	15				
R. A. Torry lbw b Panter	0		1/4 2/47 3/48 4/54 5/77	(40 overs)	121
J. R. Bodill b Constable	24		6/77 7/89 8/98 9/113		

Bowling: Snell 9–1–24–1; Constable 7–1–21–2; Garner 9–0–20–1; Hemming 9–0–26–3; Panter 6–0–26–3.

Shipton-under-Wychwood

J. M. Constable c Kettlewell b Hall	5		C. P. Panter not out		0
S. Bates st Archer b Birch	40				
S. P. Gillett b Hall	1		L-b 4, w 9		13
*P. Hemming c Archer b Barrett	33				
P. J. Garner run out	16		1/11 2/17 3/77	(5 wkts, 37.2 overs)	122
†S. Duff not out	14		4/100 5/112		

I. Lewis, P. Snell, C. Lambert and A. Prior-Wandesforde did not bat.

Bowling: Hall 9–0–34–2; Barrett 9–3–16–1; Charlesworth 4–0–22–0; Bodill 5.2–1–17–0; Birch 9–3–23–1; Kettlewell 1–0–6–0.

Umpires: W. Smith and R. Wylie.

WINNERS 1972–2002

1972	Troon (Cornwall)		1988	Goatacre (Wiltshire)
1973	Troon (Cornwall)		1989	Toft (Cheshire)
1974	Bomarsund (Northumberland)		1990	Goatacre (Wiltshire)
1975	Gowerton (Glamorgan)		1991	St Fagans (Glamorgan)
1976	Troon (Cornwall)		1992	Hursley Park (Hampshire)
1977	Cookley (Worcestershire)		1993	Kington (Herefordshire)
1978	Linton Park (Kent)		1994	Elvaston (Derbyshire)
1979	East Bierley (Yorkshire)		1995	Woodhouse Grange (Yorkshire)
1980	Marchwiel (Clwyd)		1996	Caldy (Cheshire)
1981	St Fagans (Glamorgan)		1997	Caldy (Cheshire)
1982	St Fagans (Glamorgan)		1998	Methley (Yorkshire)
1983	Quarndon (Derbyshire)		1999	Linton Park (Kent)
1984	Marchwiel (Clwyd)		2000	Elvaston (Derbyshire)
1985	Freuchie (Fife)		2001	Ynystawe (Glamorgan)
1986	Forge Valley (Yorkshire)		2002	Shipton-under-Wychwood
1987	Longparish (Hampshire)			(Oxfordshire)

IRISH CRICKET, 2002

By DEREK SCOTT

Ireland came within two runs of winning the European Championship in July 2002. Though inaugural champions in 1996, they had disappointed in the next two tournaments. But with Northern Ireland hosting the biennial competition, the Irish reached the last round knowing that a win against the England Board XI would make them champions – level on points, with the head-to-head result the tie-breaker. Their spinners restricted England to 226 for eight, and they reached 149 with only three men out. But despite a century from Jason Molins, the required rate crept up; Ireland lost by a single run.

The Triple Crown tournament was cancelled in 2002, and the traditional first-class fixture against Scotland did not return. Ireland's season began and ended with the Cheltenham & Gloucester Trophy. They had won two preliminaries in late 2001, so went straight into the third round, in May – and straight out, when Nottinghamshire won easily at Clontarf. West Indies A visited during a wet June, completing only one of three games: a splendid 88 by Peter Gillespie could not save Ireland. In August, MCC came to Cork. After a second-day washout, a last-morning declaration and two innings forfeits set Ireland a target of 295 in 74 overs. They completed their best-ever run-chase thanks to an opening stand of 182 between Andy White and Niall O'Brien, a 20-year-old left-hander, whose 111 was one of the season's highlights. But Ireland finished on a losing note, in the C&G first round, when a fifty from Paul Prichard rescued Berkshire from 57 for six.

Though O'Brien averaged 47.25 from 189 runs in his seven matches, Ireland's leading run-scorer was Kyle McCallan, with 249. Ed Joyce was absent as his career with Middlesex blossomed. Gary Neely spearheaded the attack with 17 wickets at 20.41.

The South team (Leinster and Munster) beat North and North-West to the Senior Interprovincial Championship. For the first time, two Dublin clubs contested the final of the Royal Liver Irish Senior Cup, in its 21st year: Malahide beat their neighbours, Rush. The Dublin Senior League was won by newly promoted Pembroke, who lost the 50-over final to Railway Union. Clontarf's yoyo form led to their second relegation in a seven-year period which had also brought them three Senior League titles; YMCA retained the knockout cup.

For the second season running, Brigade and Donemana tied on points at the head of the North-West League and, again, Brigade won the play-off. Limavady claimed the North-West Cup for the third time in four years – they were beaten finalists in 2001 – when Declan Curry scored twin centuries in the final against Bready. In the Northern Union, North Down claimed their third league title in four seasons, and almost added their third knockout cup in that time, losing the final to Lurgan. They did win the Ulster Cup final, against Downpatrick. In Munster, Cork County retained the cup, but their seven-year reign in the league was ended by Cork Harlequins.

Ireland won the European Cups at Under-17, Under-15 and Under-13 levels, with Eoin Morgan, a left-hander from Malahide, scoring centuries in the Under-17 and Under-15 tournaments. Malahide's women won three titles in Dublin; the national women's team lost one-day series against New Zealand and India.

Ireland's mission in 2003 was to regain their place among the elite of the ICC's Associate Members, after a poor showing in the 2001 ICC Trophy. They were to play in the second division of the Associates' World League at Los Angeles in September; an extra incentive was the prospect of the next ICC Trophy, in 2005, being staged in Ireland.

Winners of Irish Leagues and Cups
Royal Liver Irish Senior Cup: Malahide; **Ulster Cup:** North Down; **Dublin Senior League:** Pembroke; **Dublin Senior Cup:** YMCA; **Munster League:** Cork Harlequins; **Munster Cup:** Cork County; **Northern Union:** North Down; **Northern Union Cup:** Lurgan; **North-West League:** Brigade; **North-West Cup:** Limavady.

SCOTTISH CRICKET, 2002

By NEIL LEITCH

This was a year of transition, as Scotland prepared for their inaugural appearance – under the name of the Scottish Saltires – in the 2003 National Cricket League. The season's centrepiece was the European Championship in Northern Ireland. Scotland finished second, behind an England Board XI, though they could count themselves lucky to come so close after throwing two games away. In their opening match, against England, Scotland required four runs from the last two overs, with six wickets in hand; they contrived to lose all six for a single run, an even more dramatic catastrophe than losing six for 22 to Namibia in the 2001 ICC Trophy, which cost them a World Cup place. Scotland still had a chance of the European title if they won their last match, against Holland: chasing 184, they reached 171 for six before two late wickets halted them. In between, they won three games, but there was more frustration for the opener Greig Williamson, who had over 100 Scotland caps. He was closing in on a maiden international century – 99 against Italy, with eight overs left – when he holed out to long-on.

Scotland's two Cheltenham & Gloucester matches, at opposite ends of the season, were disrupted by rain. In May, Surrey swept through on Duckworth/Lewis calculations, while Scotland eventually got home against the Lancashire Board after a slightly nervy performance in the 2003 preliminaries, staged in September. On a sunnier day at Lord's, where they played a one-day fixture rather than the traditional two days, they lost to a strong MCC side led by their former team-mate, Dougie Brown. Further practice for the National League came in five friendlies against first-class counties, including a deserved win over Nottinghamshire.

Cedric English made a dazzling start: a century against Glamorgan on debut, and a hat-trick against Durham three days later. Another newcomer, Robert More, scored 81 against MCC. The pick of the bowlers was the seamer Paul Hoffmann, with 16 wickets in seven games. He had to retire out after opening the batting against the Lancashire Board, returning to his normal job when play spilled into a second day. Scottish Cricket Limited, which has taken over most of the duties of the Scottish Cricket Union, hoped to sign some international stars for the National League games but had problems securing funding, either for them or for a permanent national coach to replace Jim Love, who resigned the previous year. Greenock's coach, Tony Judd, continued to stand in.

Rain and Greenock dominated the club season. Despite a rule change eliminating the draw from league cricket, atrocious weather meant many matches never reached a result, and the West League Cup's final stages were postponed to 2003. But Greenock managed enough cricket to complete the double of the Scottish National League's premier division and the Scottish Cup. It followed their first-division/Scottish Cup double the previous year, after a controversial 75-point penalty and relegation in 2000. Grange, champions for the last two seasons, were runners-up. Greenock's second team, Glenpark, won the Western Union feeder league – but were ineligible for promotion to the Scottish National League, which eventually went to the East of Scotland champions, Corstorphine, and Dundee HSFP. They replaced Perthshire and Strathmore, two famous clubs with international grounds, sadly out of form. They could only hope to emulate Dundee, who bounced straight back after a year in the Strathmore Union, qualifying for the play-offs when Huntly chose not to seek promotion.

Winners of Scottish Leagues and Cups
Scottish National Cricket League: *Premier Division* – Greenock; *First Division* – Prestwick; *Second Division* – Arbroath United. **Scottish Cup:** Greenock. **SCU Trophy:** Falkland. **Small Clubs' Cup:** Largo. **Border League:** Kelso. **East of Scotland League:** Corstorphine. **Strathmore Union:** Huntly. **Western Union:** Glenpark (Greenock Second XI). **North of Scotland League:** Highland. **Perthshire League:** North Inch (Perthshire Second XI). **West League Cup:** Unfinished. **Rowan Cup:** Uddingston. **Masterton Trophy:** Grange.

INDIA UNDER-19 IN ENGLAND, 2002

By GARETH A. DAVIES

India's third Under-19 tour of England proved a tough assignment. They had won the only one of their previous six Tests in England to reach a conclusion – at Taunton in 1994, a match featuring hundreds from V. V. S. Laxman and Michael Vaughan. But on this trip, with their batsmen taking time to adjust to conditions, they never hit top gear in the Test series, which was won by rampant England batting. They finished on a high note, however, claiming all three one-day internationals.

The sides had last met only 18 months earlier, when India won the Test series – England's first loss overseas since the West Indies in 1994-95 – and the one-day series, which had to be moved after an earthquake in Gujarat. Three members of their victorious team survived in a squad brimming with talent: the captain, Yaleeka Gnaneswara Rao, Alind Naidu, an all-rounder, and the seam bowler Nitin Aggarwal. England fielded four of the 2000-01 tourists: Kadeer Ali, Kyle Hogg, Gordon Muchall and Nadeem Malik.

India's class of 2002 had the usual suspects: eminently talented batsmen, assured on both sides of the wicket, with good footwork, generally favouring the front foot. In attack, they were devastating, but solid starts often petered out. The rough diamond was the diminutive Deepak Chougule, already whispered of as a potential new Gavaskar. He had a junior world record to his name: an unbeaten 400 in a day for Karnataka Under-13 against Goa in 1996-97. There were flashes of Chougule's brilliance on this tour – a beautiful array of shots and a near-perfect technique, which brought him a fine century against ECB Schools and several cameos in the internationals – and he was India's highest run-scorer in the Tests, with 181 at 45.25. But the Indian batsmen disappointed overall, and their inability to build partnerships ultimately cost them the Test series. The left-handed Suresh Raina's aggregate was two short of Chougule's, and the openers, Manvinder Bisla and Paul Valthaty, scored 133 apiece, but only the wicket-keeper, Subhojit Paul, scored a Test century, to go with his 15 dismissals. The bowlers fared little better, excepting Irfan Pathan, whose left-arm pace claimed 15 wickets. The next best on either side was ten, from the England captain and off-spinner, Paul McMahon. Pathan was accurate, hostile, had the ability to move the ball both ways, and also scored useful runs down the order.

It was England's superior batting which won the Test series. In the First Test at Cardiff, Gordon Muchall of Durham scored 254, the third-highest innings for England Under-19, after Mathew Dowman's 267 in 1993 and Kevin Sharp's unbeaten 260 in 1978, both against West Indies. It was the first double-hundred by an England right-hander, though there was another, three weeks later, when Nottinghamshire's Bilal Shafayat made 201 not out in the Third Test at Northampton to set up the series' only win. Remarkably, Shafayat and Kadeer Ali of Worcestershire shared two double-century stands in the match. Shafayat was easily the heaviest scorer of the series, with an outstanding 449 runs at 112.25; Muchall and Ali both passed 360 and averaged over 70.

India found their stride in time for the one-day games, which ended in a whitewash, though all of them went to the wire. Their opener, Ambati Rayudu, played an innings of pure brilliance on the final day of the tour, at Taunton. Chasing a target of 304, India had been reduced to 137 for six in the 22nd over. Then Rayudu, who had scored only 37 in three innings in the Tests, set about the attack. His unbeaten 177 from 137 balls included 22 fours and two sixes, and took India to an improbable victory. It was an indication of what might have been in the Test series, had the tourists acclimatised more quickly.

INDIA UNDER-19 TOURING PARTY

Y. Gnaneswara Rao (Andhra Pradesh) (*captain*), M. S. Bisla (Haryana) (*vice-captain*), N. Aggarwal (Haryana), C. E. Atram (Vidarbha), D. A. Chougule (Karnataka), A. S. Naidu (Vidarbha), T. K. Patel (Gujarat), U. B. Patel (Karnataka), I. K. Pathan (Baroda), Subhojit Paul (Vidarbha), S. Raina (Utter Pradesh), K. Rawat (Delhi), A. T. Rayudu (Hyderabad), A. Sharma (Delhi), P. C. Valthaty (Mumbai), Vivek Yadav (Rajasthan).

Coach: R. R. Singh.   *Manager:* A. Ohri.   *Physiotherapist:* Dr A. S. Rana.

INDIA UNDER-19 TOUR RESULTS

Played 14: Won 9, Lost 1, Drawn 4.

At Wellington College, July 19, 20, 21. **India Under-19 won by an innings and 41 runs.** Toss: ECB Schools XI. **ECB Schools XI 195** (S. C. Hollingsworth 40, C. Salmons 41, S. M. J. Cusden 59 not out; S. Raina three for 13) **and 131** (R. E. King 31 not out; A. Sharma four for 29); **India Under-19 367** (P. C. Valthaty 74, D. A. Chougule 33, S. Raina 44, Subhojit Paul 48, I. K. Pathan 59, C. E. Atram 31 not out; R. E. King three for 46).

At Abergavenny, July 23, 24, 25. **Drawn.** Toss: Development of Excellence XI. **Development of Excellence XI 383 for nine dec.** (A. W. Gale 45, J. A. Pearson 100, J. G. E. Benning 31, P. Mustard 94, L. E. Plunkett 40) **and 221 for seven dec.** (J. A. Pearson 81, J. G. E. Benning 54; N. Aggarwal three for 41, U. B. Patel four for 59); **India Under-19 157** (S. Raina 45, Subhojit Paul 62; L. E. Plunkett four for 24, G. Onions three for 55) **and 285 for three** (M. S. Bisla 123, D. A. Chougule 114).

ENGLAND v INDIA

First Under-19 Test

At Cardiff, July 27, 28, 29, 30. Drawn. Toss: England Under-19.

A double-hundred from Gordon Muchall set the tone for the series. He was the fourth England player to reach 200 at this level, and the first right-hander. Arriving in the 19th over, he survived a couple of early scares, with Pathan bowling fast and moving the ball both ways. By the close, Muchall was 170, and next day he advanced to 254, striking 37 fours and three sixes from 377 balls before he was ninth out, after seven and a half hours. England promptly declared, at 511, and despite a century from Subhojit Paul proceeded to bowl out India 186 behind. But humid weather and regulations limiting the number of overs Under-19 cricketers could bowl in a day persuaded them against enforcing the follow-on. Their second innings was far more laboured. McMahon declared again when rain stopped play on the final morning, leaving India a target of 334. But further rain meant that they faced only 25 overs.

Close of play: First day, England Under-19 351-5 (Muchall 170, Hogg 11); Second day, India Under-19 213-5 (Raina 64, Subhojit Paul 61); Third day, England Under-19 145-7 (Hogg 37, Bresnan 0).

In the hall-of-mirrors world of the bonus point, fewer runs meant a greater chance of reaching the final.
VB Series, page 1368

England Under-19

N. R. D. Compton lbw b Pathan	11	– c Subhojit Paul b Pathan	5
J. J. Sayers c Subhojit Paul b Atram	16	– c Subhojit Paul b Pathan	1
Kadeer Ali c Rayudu b Patel	67	– c Subhojit Paul b Atram	49
G. J. Muchall st Subhojit Paul b Sharma	254	– run out	8
B. M. Shafayat b Pathan	57	– lbw b Bisla	22
G. G. Wagg c Valthaty b Atram	0	– c Valthaty b Bisla	2
K. W. Hogg c Subhojit Paul b Pathan	25	– c Rayudu b Atram	37
†S. P. Pope lbw b Raina	51	– c Subhojit Paul b Atram	5
T. T. Bresnan c Bisla b Sharma	3	– not out	1
*P. J. McMahon not out	1	– not out	1
B 5, l-b 6, w 7, n-b 8	26	B 8, l-b 4, w 4	16

1/22 2/39 3/191 4/329 5/332   (9 wkts dec.) 511
6/367 7/472 8/499 9/511

1/5 2/8 3/25 4/63   (8 wkts dec.) 147
5/69 6/116 7/142 8/145

M. N. Malik did not bat.

Bowling: *First Innings*—Pathan 33–6–122–3; Atram 31–8–83–2; Bisla 23–7–72–0; Valthaty 11–1–30–0; Sharma 22.4–2–96–2; Patel 16–2–66–1; Raina 6–2–31–1. *Second Innings*—Pathan 17–7–24–2; Atram 18–6–28–3; Bisla 13–2–29–2; Sharma 20–7–36–0; Patel 6–0–18–0.

India Under-19

*M. S. Bisla b Hogg	2	– c Compton b Malik	9
P. C. Valthaty lbw b McMahon	52	– lbw b Muchall	43
D. A. Chougule b Malik	9	– not out	19
A. T. Rayudu c Pope b Wagg	15	– not out	9
S. Raina c Ali b Hogg	72		
A. S. Naidu lbw b McMahon	0		
†Subhojit Paul c Compton b Hogg	115		
I. K. Pathan b Bresnan	13		
A. Sharma not out	26		
U. B. Patel c McMahon b Malik	2		
C. E. Atram c Bresnan b Hogg	0		
B 4, l-b 7, w 2, n-b 6	19	B 1, n-b 6	7

1/2 2/27 3/60 4/101 5/101   325
6/232 7/261 8/313 9/317

1/21 2/77   (2 wkts) 87

Bowling: *First Innings*—Hogg 21.3–4–68–4; Malik 21–2–60–2; Wagg 15–0–71–1; Bresnan 16–6–54–1; McMahon 16–3–49–2; Shafayat 3–0–12–0. *Second Innings*—Hogg 5–1–7–0; Malik 5–0–14–1; Wagg 4–0–31–0; Bresnan 4–0–11–0; Muchall 3–0–19–1; McMahon 3–1–3–0; Ali 1–0–1–0.

Umpires: J. H. Evans and N. A. Mallender.

At Arundel, August 1, 2, 3. **Drawn.** Toss: India Under-19. **India Under-19 168** (T. K. Patel 56; S. M. J. Cusden three for 32) **and 188 for five** (P. C. Valthaty 63, D. A. Chougule 58; S. M. J. Cusden three for 37); **Development of Excellence (South) XI 137** (R. S. Bopara 49; T. K. Patel five for 32).

ENGLAND v INDIA

Second Under-19 Test

At Southampton, August 7, 8, 9, 10. Drawn. Toss: England Under-19.

Rain wiped out all play after 5.45 on the second evening, when India trailed by 86 with four first-innings wickets left. Bisla and Chougule had guided them to a confident 169 for one before England, who bowled only one spinner, rifled through the middle order. Seam had also dominated the Indian attack, with Pathan picking up four wickets, while his fellow left-armer Atram and

Aggarwal collected two apiece. Shafayat, who had been promoted to open after Compton and Sayers, the openers in the previous Test, were dropped, gave England a bright start – 90 in their first 25 overs – before steering a short ball from Bisla to second slip. Fifty from Hogg put them back on course after a mini-collapse, but it was an aggressive 60 from Graham Wagg, at No. 9, which lifted England above 300.

Close of play: First day, England Under-19 309-9 (Wagg 48, Malik 10); Second day, India Under-19 237-6 (Subhojit Paul 0, Patel 0); Third day, No play.

England Under-19

B. M. Shafayat c Valthaty b Bisla	51	G. G. Wagg b Pathan		60
M. L. Pettini lbw b Pathan	2	*P. J. McMahon c Subhojit Paul		
Kadeer Ali c Rayudu b Aggarwal	38		b Aggarwal	4
G. J. Muchall c Bisla b Atram	21	M. N. Malik not out		12
J. G. E. Benning b Pathan	16	B-l 11, w 9, n-b 8, p 5		33
K. W. Hogg b Atram	50			
L. E. Plunkett c Subhojit Paul b Pathan	35	1/19 2/90 3/130 4/138 5/156		323
†S. P. Pope c Valthaty b Patel	1	6/221 7/225 8/257 9/275		

Bowling: Pathan 26.4–3–83–4; Atram 22–2–68–2; Aggarwal 20–4–60–2; Bisla 19–3–43–1; Patel 14–3–48–1; Raina 1–0–5–0.

India Under-19

M. S. Bisla c Pettini b Plunkett	78	†Subhojit Paul not out		0
P. C. Valthaty c Hogg b Wagg	10	T. K. Patel not out		0
D. A. Chougule c Pettini b Malik	89	B 4, l-b 5, w 6, n-b 9		24
*Y. Gnaneswara Rao c Pettini b Wagg	1			
S. Raina b Plunkett	22	1/39 2/169 3/177	(6 wkts)	237
A. T. Rayudu b Pope b Muchall	13	4/218 5/233 6/237		

I. K. Pathan, C. E. Atram and N. Aggarwal did not bat.

Bowling: Hogg 10–1–26–0; Malik 16–3–45–1; Wagg 10–3–38–2; Plunkett 12–3–32–2; McMahon 18–4–65–0; Muchall 7.2–1–22–1.

Umpires: A. Clarkson and N. G. Cowley.

ENGLAND v INDIA

Third Under-19 Test

At Northampton, August 13, 14, 15, 16. England Under-19 won by 185 runs. Toss: India Under-19.

Bilal Shafayat and Kadeer Ali set up a crushing victory to win the series. They raised England Under-19's second-wicket record twice in three days; Shafayat became the second Englishman, after Mark Ramprakash, to score two hundreds at this level, and went on to England's fifth double-century. Put in, Pettini was caught behind in the fourth over. But it was four hours before the next breakthrough, when Ali was caught at long-on trying to reach his hundred after adding 212 with Shafayat. Only Muchall backed them up, however, and Chougule and Raina helped reduce India's deficit to 31. Pettini completed a pair, but this time Shafayat and Ali shared a five-hour stand of 256, with Ali reaching his century. Shafayat steamed on to an unbeaten 201, lasting seven and a half hours, and hit 23 fours in 347 balls. India needed an unlikely 434 in 91 overs, and were 145 for eight shortly after tea. Yadav and Udit Patel resisted, adding 84, but McMahon broke their stand with his eighth wicket of the match, and the end came with 12 overs to spare.

Close of play: First day, England Under-19 331-7 (Wagg 7, Bresnan 0); Second day, England Under-19 13-0 (Shafayat 12, Pettini 0); Third day, England Under-19 389-5 (Shafayat 193, Bresnan 11).

England Under-19

B. M. Shafayat c Valthaty b Pathan	118	– not out	201
M. L. Pettini c Subhojit Paul b Aggarwal	0	– c Subhojit Paul b Pathan	0
Kadeer Ali c T. K. Patel b U. B. Patel	97	– c Bisla b Pathan	111
G. J. Muchall c Valthaty b T. K. Patel	67	– run out	19
S. R. Patel c Valthaty b Pathan	8	– run out	2
†S. P. Pope c Subhojit Paul b U. B. Patel	3		
L. E. Plunkett st Subhojit Paul b Pathan	11		
G. G. Wagg st Subhojit Paul b T. K. Patel	13	– (6) c Subhojit Paul b Pathan	18
T. T. Bresnan c Valthaty b Pathan	0	– (7) not out	16
*P. J. McMahon c Raina b T. K. Patel	0		
M. N. Malik not out	4		
B 4, l-b 5, w 10, n-b 1	20	B 10, l-b 10, w 10, n-b 5	35

1/8 2/220 3/236 4/254 5/284   341   1/17 2/273 3/321   (5 wkts dec.) 402
6/321 7/324 8/337 9/337   4/333 5/365

Bowling: *First Innings*—Pathan 25.3–4–83–3; Aggarwal 15–6–49–1; Vivek Yadav 5–1–20–0; U. B. Patel 34–3–98–2; Bisla 14–3–35–0; T. K. Patel 10–1–40–4; Raina 4–2–7–0. *Second Innings*—Pathan 22–4–77–3; Aggarwal 11–3–47–0; T. K. Patel 28–2–89–0; Vivek Yadav 11–1–34–0; U. B. Patel 19–3–46–0; Raina 11–2–44–0; Bisla 11–0–45–0.

India Under-19

M. S. Bisla b Malik	17	– lbw b Wagg	27
P. C. Valthaty b Malik	11	– b Wagg	17
D. A. Chougule c sub b McMahon	62	– c Muchall b Plunkett	2
*Y. Gnaneswara Rao c McMahon b Plunkett	16	– c Pettini b McMahon	27
S. Raina c and b Malik	63	– c Muchall b McMahon	22
†Subhojit Paul c Pope b Plunkett	4	– b McMahon	8
T. K. Patel not out	44	– c Pope b Bresnan	15
I. K. Pathan c Malik b McMahon	0	– c Pope b Bresnan	0
Vivek Yadav c Bresnan b McMahon	1	– not out	49
U. B. Patel lbw b McMahon	23	– c Wagg b McMahon	46
N. Aggarwal b Muchall	17	– c Plunkett b Wagg	5
B 11, l-b 29, n-b 8	53	B 6, l-b 8, w 4, n-b 12	30

1/26 2/32 3/65 4/180 5/205   310   1/51 2/60 3/60 4/101 5/128   248
6/205 7/229 8/229 9/253   6/129 7/142 8/145 9/229

Bowling: *First Innings*—Malik 18–3–75–3; Wagg 15–2–46–0; Bresnan 18–4–56–0; Plunkett 13–3–51–2; Muchall 2.4–0–10–1; McMahon 21–8–47–4; Patel 2–0–9–0. *Second Innings*—Malik 17–1–83–0; Bresnan 14.2–6–40–3; Plunkett 15–2–37–1; Wagg 10–5–14–2; McMahon 21–8–58–4; Muchall 1–0–2–0.

Umpires: B. Leadbeater and A. G. T. Whitehead.

At Sleaford, August 19. **India Under-19 won by 145 runs.** Toss: ECB North Under-19 XI. **India Under-19 321 for six** (50 overs) (P. C. Valthaty 40, M. S. Bisla 145, Subhojit Paul 35, A. T. Rayudu 45; R. E. King three for 51); **ECB North Under-19 176** (43.3 overs) (M. A. K. Lawson 39; Y. Gnaneswara Rao three for 15).

At Sleaford, August 20. **India Under-19 won by seven wickets.** Toss: ECB North Under-19 XI. **ECB North Under-19 212 for five** (50 overs) (T. J. New 70, H. Rashid 41 not out, R. E. King 30); **India Under-19 216 for three** (35.1 overs) (A. T. Rayudu 91, Y. Gnaneswara Rao 59 not out).

At Sleaford, August 21. **India Under-19 won by 65 runs.** Toss: India Under-19. **India Under-19 291 for nine** (45 overs) (Subhojit Paul 115, K. Rawat 33, T. K. Patel 36 not out, U. B. Patel 33; M. A. K. Lawson three for 33); **ECB North Under-19 226** (39.3 overs) (T. J. New 40, N. J. Edwards 39, C. R. Gilbert 30, R. E. King 39; A. Sharma three for 31).

At Bristol, August 23. **India Under-19 won by six wickets.** Toss: Gloucestershire Second Eleven. **Gloucestershire Second Eleven 224 for nine** (50 overs) (J. N. Snape 45, S. Bhatt 63, T. Sharpe 36; I. K. Pathan three for 25, M. S. Bisla four for 40); **India Under-19 225 for four** (37.2 overs) (Y. Gnaneswara Rao 68, D. A. Chougule 37, S. Raina 60 not out).

At King's College, Taunton, August 25. **India Under-19 won by 111 runs.** Toss: India Under-19. **India Under-19 227 for eight** (50 overs) (M. S. Bisla 41, K. Rawat 53, S. Raina 33; N. A. Denning four for 50); **ECB XI 116** (37.5 overs) (T. K. Patel three for 19).

At Bristol, August 27. **First one-day international: India Under-19 won by three wickets.** Toss: England Under-19. **England Under-19 265 for eight** (50 overs) (P. Mustard 45, Kadeer Ali 62, J. G. E. Benning 60); **India Under-19 268 for seven** (49.1 overs) (M. S. Bisla 35, A. T. Rayudu 34, K. Rawat 53 not out, I. K. Pathan 42 not out, Extras 41; L. E. Plunkett three for 46).

At Taunton, August 29. **Second one-day international: India Under-19 won by one wicket (D/L method).** Toss: England Under-19. **England Under-19 269** (50 overs) (J. G. E. Benning 47, K. W. Hogg 103, M. L. Pettini 31); **India Under-19 262 for nine** (47 overs) (M. S. Bisla 59, A. T. Rayudu 80, Extras 30; K. W. Hogg three for 51).

Five England batsmen were run out. India's target was revised to 259 from 47 overs; No. 11 Chandrasekhar Atram hit the last two balls of the match, from Graham Wagg, for four and six.

At Taunton, August 30. **Third one-day international: India Under-19 won by one wicket.** Toss: India Under-19. **England Under-19 303 for seven** (50 overs) (A. W. Gale 77, Kadeer Ali 125, K. W. Hogg 35 not out; P. Mustard 34; T. K. Patel four for 36); **India Under-19 306 for nine** (48.1 overs) (A. T. Rayudu 177 not out, K. Rawat 37; S. R. Patel three for 45).

Kadeer Ali reached his 100 in 85 balls; in all, he hit 15 fours and three sixes in 122 balls. Rayudu reached his in 91, and in all faced 137 balls and hit 22 fours and two sixes. His second six won the match, to give India the series 3–0.

ZONE6 CITY CRICKET

All matches in the Zone6 City Cricket tournament were played at Edgbaston on June 21.

Birmingham won by 33 runs. Bristol 176 (M. P. Maynard 49); **Birmingham 209** (G. A. Hick 64, V. S. Solanki 49).

London won by 42 runs. London 192 (Abdul Razzaq 68; M. J. Saggers three for 40); **Southampton 150** (M. B. Loye 49; Saqlain Mushtaq three for 39).

Manchester won by 91 runs. Manchester 225 (U. Afzaal 54, S. G. Law 45, K. P. Pietersen 20); **Bristol 134 for six.**

Leeds won by ten runs. London 194; Leeds 204 (P. A. de Silva 53).

Birmingham won by nine runs. Manchester 144 (U. Afzaal 33; D. A. Leatherdale three for 15); **Birmingham 153** (G. A. Hick 55).

Leeds won by 25 runs. Southampton 191 (N. C. Johnson 43, R. S. C. Martin-Jenkins 40); **Leeds 216** (P. A. de Silva 75).

Final: Leeds won by three runs. Birmingham 199 (G. A. Hick 68, V. S. Solanki 33); **Leeds 202** (P. A. de Silva 57, D. I. Stevens 33).

The city teams fielded eight players, who could bat or bowl but not both. Matches were eight overs a side, with bowlers limited to three overs each. Teams started with a total of 100 runs, and lost six for every wicket; batsmen were replaced on the captain's decision, rather than dismissed. Extra runs were awarded for hitting runs through one of six "scoring zones". Results were calculated on runs, with no allowance for wickets. Zone6 was organised by the PCA to raise money for the PCA Benevolent Fund.

SCHOOLS CRICKET, 2002

This section covers
- an introduction to the issues and outstanding performances in schools cricket in 2002
- the ECB's East v West Schools match
- Eton v Harrow
- top batting and bowling averages for schools listed in *Wisden*
- schools with notable playing records
- results for the 2002 season from 186 schools – and a report (when provided)
- averages for batsmen with 150 runs and bowlers with ten wickets
- averages for a school's leading run-scorer and wicket-taker if no batsman or bowler qualified

Abbreviations and symbols
- In the result line, A = abandoned without a ball being bowled
- An asterisk next to a name indicates captain

Notes
- Schools provide their own comments
- For your school to be considered for inclusion, please contact Paul Coupar at 13 Old Aylesfield, Froyle Road, Golden Pot, Alton, Hampshire GU34 4BY, or on 01420 83415

See also
- Youth Cricket (pages 1120–1121) for county age-group cricket in 2002

Review by GARETH A. DAVIES

Last year's schools section reported the stresses brought by the new AS-level exams for lower-sixth formers. Already 16 and 18-year-olds faced a summer with plenty of exams and little cricket: now 17-year-olds did too. With pupils reluctant to commit to the team, many masters had found they were forced to cancel games, especially those in midweek. The summer of 2002 brought a shade more optimism. The Department for Education and Skills had scaled down AS-levels, which eased the pressure a little, but many fixture lists remained pruned.

All work and no play?

A few, however, decided enough was enough and took a tough stand against books and study swallowing more and more time. Nick Gandon, a cricket coach at Haileybury, was one. "We will not let exam boards set the agenda. Haileybury expects pupils to manage their academic commitments, but also to immerse themselves in the broader curriculum. We are not prepared to compromise that."

Others believed that if cricket had become incompatible with the current school year, then it was time for the school year to change. Several masters-in-charge wanted public exams moved; Bedford Modern were more radical still, suggesting a year of four terms, with cricket in May, a break for exams in June, a shorter summer holiday and a new school year beginning in early August. Most cricket would be played in August and September, under clearer skies and on harder pitches.

Charterhouse have gone beyond musings and put their ideas, albeit less radical, on paper. The proposal, which they will present to the Headmasters' Conference, is to extend the idea of the Cowdrey Cup – a mini-league set up in 2001 involving Charterhouse, Eton, Harrow, Tonbridge and Wellington – into a national competition for first elevens. Regional leagues would be played before exams, semi-finals and final immediately afterwards.

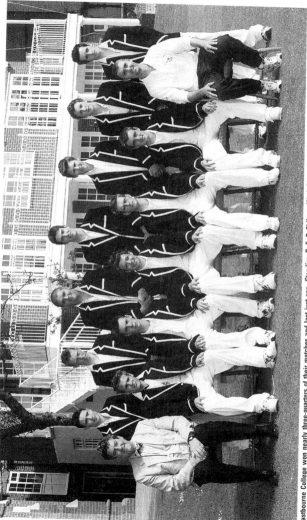

Eastbourne College won nearly three-quarters of their matches and lost just one. *Standing*: R. E. P. Chilcott, W. J. Ripley, H. C. Hassen, J. G. Langridge, J. A. M. Toy, P. J. Morgan, J. P. Reid. *Seated*: N. L. Wheeler (*master-in-charge*), J. C. Farley, S. T. Cooke (*vice-captain*), S. D. Cane Hardy (*captain*), N. J. Reid, O. L. Gale, D. B. Kotze (*coach*).

Simon Crampton (*left*) of Tiffin took 49 wickets – joint second-best in the country – and cracked 514 runs at 57. Bedford's Alastair Cook was the only batsman to pass 1,000 runs, with 1,126 at 93.

To declare or not to declare

But while the vexed debate about scheduling rumbled on, another important break with tradition had already been made. The summer of 2002 saw Oundle became the first English school to adopt National League rules – including coloured kit, white ball and black sightscreens – in midweek matches. The white ball proved a major plus when the light was fading, and the experiment was well received by pupils, who had apparently been put off by the number of draws.

But not everyone was happy. "There is great pressure to play the limited-overs format in afternoon games," complained Mike Askham of Wellingborough. "Oundle rang out of the blue to suggest a National-League style match with coloured clothing. We were disturbed by this development and disappointed to be placed under such pressures."

A *Daily Telegraph* poll of cricket masters showed that this declaration–limited-overs divide ran throughout the country, with equal support for each form of the game. The poll also revealed that masters considered boys and girls just as enthusiastic about cricket as ten years ago, and spotlighted perennial concerns about inadequate equipment, particularly covers, which masters felt would lead to faster, bouncier wickets.

Cricket... but not as we know it

Ultimately, though, the greatest worries must be about the state sector, where cricket has slowly declined. During the summer of 2002, Ian Botham, among others, attacked the lack of cricket in state schools. This brought a strong response from the England and Wales Cricket Board, who denounced the supposed death of cricket in state schools as a myth, citing their own recent survey which concluded that 85 per cent of the 4,000 state secondary schools in England and Wales provide cricket either during or after school. However, their picture of what constitutes "cricket" has been painted with a very broad brush: the 85 per cent includes schools where cricket amounts to just a few PE lessons a year, and schools who play inter-cricket – a new indoor game introduced in 2001. It's cricket, but not as we know it. Perhaps 1,500 – the number of schools who entered the England Schools Cricket Association's Under-15 tournament – is a better estimate of how many play organised, competitive, outdoor cricket.

The ECB seem to have recognised that, with playing fields sold off and teachers over-stretched, long 11-a-side games are often not possible. However, Pete Ackerley, their development officer for secondary schools, insists that, "While school cricket was not in a great position three years ago, there have been significant improvements. We concede that there are areas in the country where schools don't play cricket, and we accept that schools are not playing for six hours on a

Wednesday. But given the constraints on teaching time, we have produced the best set of free educational resources for teachers in the country.

Ackerley is referring to *Howzat!*, a CD-ROM containing 130 video clips and animated drills, delivered to 2,000 state secondary schools. The hope is that, while there might not be time for a game, cricket can still be introduced to schoolchildren. And, with curriculum inspectors now demanding that secondary school students show "striking and fielding" skills, the ECB have made sure that learning the skills from the CD-ROM is one way of getting ticks in the right boxes. But the crucial question remains: will watching Shane's leg-spin, Darren's out-swinger and Alec's off-drive produce new Warnes, Goughs and Stewarts? The package has been well received, but it is no substitute for real coaches and real matches.

Aware of this, the ECB is concentrating on linking schools with clubs, and those without a suitable playing field will be helped to find a club ground. But the problem of busy teachers remains. Meanwhile, promising students will be encouraged to play for local club sides.

Supply and demand

So it seems that the heart of the game rests with a few schools, and the amateur clubs, rather than the mainstream education system. What a pity. While England were losing the 2002-03 Ashes, research conducted by Sports Marketing Surveys at a cross-section of state and independent schools found that plenty of children wanted to play cricket. Of boys and girls who were members of a school sports team, 23 per cent chose to play cricket at school outside the time allocated for PE, 13 per cent had coaching outside school, and 12 per cent were members of amateur clubs. But asked which sport they played most in lesson time, only three per cent said cricket. Even basketball and volleyball came higher, with six per cent. The survey concluded that children wanted to play cricket at school but were not being given the chance. The responsibility for that lies not simply within the corridors of power at the ECB, but also within the corridors of power in Westminster. Governments must recognise the value of supporting our summer game.

The story of 2002

At King Edward's, Birmingham, a Christmas tour of Australia brought significant benefits: 14 wins beat the old school record, set in 1891 and equalled in 1994. Anurag Singh, now at Worcestershire, captained the 1994 side, and his brother, Anirudh, was captain in 2002. He scored 799 runs at 66, principally supported by Daniel Shilvock, who scored 675 at 45.

Tiffin also had a brilliant season, their only defeat coming in the closing stages of a long term. The strength of the side lay in the variety and accuracy of their bowling, and they had a special all-round talent in Arun Harinath. An England Under-15 player, he has already played for Surrey Under-19s. Simon Crampton, the captain, was one of the country's leading all-rounders, finishing with 49 wickets at under nine, and 514 runs at 57.

Eastbourne won 11 of their 15 matches, the third-highest percentage among schools who played more than 12 games. The two who achieved higher ratios (Eton and King Edward's, Birmingham) both lost more matches than Eastbourne, who were beaten only once. A young team fielded brilliantly, inspired by their coach, the Namibian captain Deon Kotze, and were astutely led by Simon Cane Hardy.

Hampton and Leeds GS each had suffered just one defeat in the course of a long season. Tight bowling and tigerish fielding brought Hampton's success, while Alex Blakeborough's 641 at 80 formed the heart of Leeds' batting.

Outstanding all-round performances from opening batsmen Phil Burdon (946 runs and 30 wickets) and Joe Robinson (862 and 39) helped King's, Worcester power to a record 16 wins from their 22 matches. Burdon and Robinson put on eight century partnerships, and King's suffered only one defeat against schools. Wyggeston and Queen Elizabeth I College went one better, going undefeated against schools, colleges and university teams.

RGS Guildford, Christ's Hospital, Eton and Kimbolton also set new school records for wins during impressive seasons. Guildford managed 13 and won all their matches at the RGS Festival at Worcester; Christ's won ten, with a visiting South African student, Andries Kruger, hitting a school-record 835 runs; Eton triumphed in the Cowdrey Cup, though according to their cricket master the results "slightly flattered the real quality of the team". Meanwhile, Kimbolton won 12 matches from 19. Luke Bailey hit 154 against Felsted, the highest by a Kimbolton batsman, while Alex Lacey, the captain and a Northamptonshire Under-19 player, turned in many impressive all-round performances. In his school career he took just under 100 wickets and scored close to 1,500 runs.

Ones to watch

The 2002 season also threw up plenty of names to watch out for in future. Dominic Chambers was the linchpin at St Edmund's, Canterbury, scoring 846 runs (four hundreds, three fifties) at an average of 70, and bringing his total in four full seasons in the first eleven to a staggering 2,701 at 67. He hopes to make a career in cricket with Kent.

Just as impressive was James Toms of Plymouth College, who hit four centuries in 11 innings, including a magnificent unbeaten 201 against an OPM XI. His average of 125 was bettered only by Mark Paine of Simon Langton GS. Tim Stonock of Durham hit the only other double-century, an unbeaten 200 in the game with King's, Tynemouth.

Alastair Cook's feat of scoring five hundreds in consecutive innings for Bedford School (and seven in the season) hinted at impressive powers of concentration. He was the leading run-scorer in the country with 1,126 at almost 94, though he just failed to beat the school record of 1,181 (from several more innings), set by Ian Peck, who went on to play for Cambridge University and – briefly – Northamptonshire in the late 1970s and early 1980s.

Alan Day of King's, Macclesfield, was next with 987, and Phil Burdon of King's, Worcester, third. Meanwhile, Oliver Allen, son of Clive Allen the ex-England footballer, averaged 90 at Brentwood School. Impressive for any schoolboy, it was remarkable for an Under-15.

In fact it was a good season for younger players. Tom Woolsey (St Peter's, York), also an Under-15, was the leading wicket-taker, collecting 51 at 13 with his left-arm spin. Simon Crampton of Tiffin was next with 49 at just under nine, and Nick Lockwood of Bedford Modern third with 49 at just under 12 and a half.

Another left-arm spinner claimed the prize for the country's best bowling average. George Walker of Norwich ended the season with 15 wickets at an astonishing 2.33. After bamboozling schoolboy batsmen – grabbing five for one against Gresham's – he faced a sterner test on his first-class debut for Leicestershire against Kent. Second-best came from Gautham Hariharan (Glasgow Academy) whose pace caused havoc against George Heriot's when he seized five for six. Best average among those to take 20 wickets or more came from Shivan Dave of Merchant Taylors', Northwood, with 41 at 7.51.

Darshan Depala (Christ's College, Finchley) and Mark Willoughby (Chislehurst and Sidcup GS) produced a pair of *Boys' Own* performances. Depala fired out four batsmen from St Ignatius College in four balls, but, perhaps fittingly in a bumper year for spinners, Willoughby went one better, taking five in five across two matches with his leg-breaks. English spin may live again.

Festival finds

There was more good news from Paul Farbrace, the coach of the ECB Under-15 squad. During the 15th Bunbury England Schools Cricket Association festival he spotted a crop of four burgeoning seam bowlers – Mark Footit (West Notts College), Stuart Wedge (Codsall HS, Wolverhampton), David Harrison (West Monmouth Comprehensive School) and David Griffiths (Sandown HS, Isle of Wight). They will be monitored closely and could be fast-tracked into the ECB Cricket Academy inside two seasons. Footit is one of the quickest bowlers seen in this age group, while Harrison, physically strong and also a quality batsman, looks the pick of the bunch at this stage.

Farbrace also selected a highly rated wicket-keeper/batsman in Steve Davis, who has been working with Steve Rhodes at Worcestershire, and, remarkably, two boys not only from the Isle of Wight, but also from the same street – Griffiths and Mark Mitchell, another left-arm spinner. But the player of the tournament was Mark Cummins, an obdurate opener from Wickersley, Rotherham. He scored two hundreds and a 70 in his three innings, to add to two centuries for Yorkshire Under-15s early in July, and was rewarded with a two-week stay at the Adelaide Cricket Academy under Rod Marsh. Cummins is one of three outstanding talents monitored by the ECB since the age of 12. The other two are Arun Harinath (of Tiffin) and wicket-keeper Travis Binnion, from Heritage School in Clowne, Nottinghamshire.

ECB SCHOOLS EAST v ECB SCHOOLS WEST

At Slough, July 9, 10. Drawn. Toss: ECB Schools West.

Rain, and its effect on the pitch, meant the ECB's annual schools try-out was a trial in more ways than one. The first day was washed out, but hard work by the groundstaff allowed a 10 a.m. start on the second. Batting was awkward on a damp track, and the West lost two quick wickets before Ravinder Bopara showed why Essex had offered him a contract. He and Luke Stokes helped rescue their side, but progress was slow: the declaration at 174 for six came after 67 overs. In reply, the East were soon in trouble against the new ball, Thomas Andrews taking three for five from eight overs. But when time was called, Richard King had at least got them to 88 for six in 37 overs. Andrew Parkin-Coates batted for both sides after being run out without facing in his first innings.

ECB Schools West

R. S. Bopara (Barking Abbey S)		
retired out	.	51
R. T. Timms (Millfield) c Fateh b Newby		3
J. L. Denly (Chaucer Technology S,		
Canterbury) c Phythian b King	.	5
R. L. S. Stokes (Millfield) c Newby		
b Wake	.	41
S. G. James (Merchant Taylors',		
Northwood) not out	.	27

C. J. Salmons (Archbishop Tenison's,		
Croydon) retired out	.	33
A. W. Parker-Coates (Worksop C) run out		0
J. C. Hildreth (Millfield) not out	. . . . . .	10
B 2, l-b 1, n-b 1	. . . .	4
1/5 2/30 3/96	(6 wkts dec.)	174
4/105 5/153 6/155		

†J. P. T. Knappett (*East Barnet S*), M. Bagley (*King Charles 1 S, Kidderminster*), T. J. Andrews (*Walton Community S, Peterborough*) and S. M. J. Cusden (*Simon Langton GS*) did not bat.

Bowling: Newby 13–4–30–1; Ede 12–1–35–0; King 8–4–13–1; Edes 7–2–24–0; Mason 0–17–0; Wake 13–4–30–1; Newton 4–0–13–0; Everett 3–0–9–0.

ECB Schools East

A. J. Hewlett (Hereford Cathedral)		
b Andrews	.	13
C. J. Wake (Oundle) c Hildreth		
b Andrews	.	0
A. C. Fateh (Dean Close) c Stokes		
b Bagley	.	15
J. B. Mason (Sedbergh) b Andrews	. . . .	2
A. W. Parkin-Coates (Worksop C)		
c Denly b Salmons	.	16

D. J. Chambers (St Edmund's, Canterbury)		
lbw b James	.	7
R. E. King (Bedford Modern) not out	. . .	22
*W. M. H. Edes (Bradfield) not out	. . . .	2
B 2, l-b 2, w 2, n-b 5	. . . . . .	11
1/7 2/26 3/30	(6 wkts)	88
4/55 5/64 6/65		

†M. J. Phythian (*Oundle*), O. J. Newby (*Myerscough C, Preston*), J. L. Ede (*John Taylor HS, Burton upon Trent*), C. Everett, (*Droitwich Spa HS*) and J. B. Newton (*Campion S, Bugbrooke*) did not bat.

Bowling: Cusden 6–0–16–0; Andrews 8–4–10–3; Hildreth 6–2–16–0; Bagley 6–2–16–1; Salmons 4–3–2–1; James 4–1–17–1; Bopara 3–0–7–0.

Umpires: C. Coburn and A. Price.

ETON v HARROW

At Lord's, May 25. Eton won by 66 runs. Toss: Eton.

Eton's handsome victory was their first at Lord's since 1991, when this fixture was a declaration game rather than limited-overs. Their match-winner was Ben Thompson, who well deserved a century but fell just short in the closing stages. He had hit 12 fours and a six to score 98 out of 149 while he was at the crease. James Mathias grabbed 16 runs off the final over, from Rupert Harmsworth, and Nicholas Defty started Harrow's reply in similar style, smashing Alex de Lisle's first three balls for ten. But when he was lbw and de Lisle struck twice in two balls, Harrow were three down in the third over. They never regained the initiative against some keen fielding. Harmsworth held the innings together, but took 95 balls over 48 (barely half Thompson's scoring-rate). He was last out, seeking a second run to retain the strike, with more than six overs to go.

Eton

A. M. Goldberg c Dunbar b Harmsworth	14	†J. H. Mathias not out	36
A. W. A. Barker c Mahon b Kostoris	22	A. E. M. P. de Lisle not out	3
*T. P. McCall run out	20	L-b 7, w 3, n-b 2	12
B. R. Thompson c Maydon b Harmsworth	98		
E. F. J. Nissen b Moseley	8	1/34 2/49 3/97 (7 wkts, 55 overs) 221
H. W. A. Clarke run out	7	4/115 5/132
C. P. A. Nissen b Roditi	1	6/142 7/198

W. T. Dobson and N. C. R. Westoll did not bat.

Bowling: Moseley 11–3–26–1; Roditi 11–1–52–1; Harmsworth 11–0–53–2; Kostoris 11–0–35–1; Morrison 7–1–32–0; Defty 4–0–16–0.

Harrow

N. E. Defty lbw b Barker	10	A. W. Stileman b Westoll	9
M. B. Mahon c sub (Wallace) b Dobson	31	H. M. Morrison lbw b Westoll	2
*S. R. L. Maydon b de Lisle	0	J. B. K. Roditi lbw b Dobson	3
†P. R. Dunbar c C. P. A. Nissen b de Lisle	0	P. D. Moseley not out	0
J. M. Kostoris c C. P. A. Nissen b Thompson	16	L-b 4, w 6	10
R. V. G. Harmsworth run out	48	1/11 2/12 3/12 (48.3 overs) 155
C. R. Reid run out	26	4/59 5/66 6/122
		7/135 8/139 9/150

Bowling: de Lisle 5–0–37–2; Barker 4–1–14–1; Thompson 6.3–2–16–1; Dobson 11–6–17–2; Goldberg 2–0–4–0; McCall 9–1–20–0; Westoll 11–1–43–2.

Umpires: A. Patel and J. H. Mills.

Of the 164 matches played between the two schools since 1805, Eton have won 53, Harrow 45 and 66 have been drawn. Matches during the two world wars are excluded from the reckoning. The fixture was reduced from a two-day, two-innings-a-side match to one day in 1982, and became a limited-overs fixture from 1999. Forty-nine centuries have been scored, the highest being 183 by D. C. Boles of Eton in 1904; M. C. Bird of Harrow is the only batsman to have made two hundreds in a match, in 1907. The highest score since the First World War is 161 not out by M. K. Fosh of Harrow in 1975. Harrow's last victory before 2000. Since then Eton have won in 1977, 1985, 1990, 1991 and 2002, Harrow in 2000. The 1997, 1999 and 2001 matches were abandoned and all others have been drawn. A full list of centuries since 1918 and results from 1950 can be found in Wisdens prior to 1994.

Note: The following five tables cover those schools listed in the Schools A–Z section.

BATTING

HIGHEST AVERAGE IN SCHOOLS CRICKET

(Qualification: 150 runs, 3 completed innings, average 65.00)

	I	NO	Runs	HS	100s	Avge
M. Paine (*Simon Langton GS*)	5	2	382	103*	1	127.33
J. Toms (*Plymouth College*)	11	5	751	201*	4	125.16
A. N. Cook (*Bedford School*)	15	3	1,126	173*	7	93.83
O. T. Allen (*Brentwood School*)	13	6	635	102	1	90.71
A. N. Russell (*Gordonstoun School*)	14	4	878	159	4	87.80
C. M. G. Harding (*Bethany School*)	9	3	502	121*	2	83.66
Z. Hussain (*Watford GS*)	9	4	403	80*	0	80.60
J. J. R. Bedford (*Woodhouse Grove School*)	13	5	642	109*	2	80.25
A. J. Blakeborough (*Leeds GS*)	12	4	641	133*	2	80.12
P. Buszard (*Gordonstoun School*)	8	5	234	82*	0	78.00
J. J. Ablett (*Lord Wandsworth College*)	14	5	695	138	2	77.22

	I	NO	Runs	HS	100s	Avge
M. J. Stacpoole (*Framlingham College*)	5	2	215	96*	0	71.66
A. W. Parkin-Coates (*Worksop College*)	14	4	715	110	1	71.50
D. Chambers (*St Edmund's School, Canterbury*)	12	0	846	151	4	70.50
R. A. J. Lintott (*Gresham's School*)	16	5	767	115*	1	69.72
J. F. Wildman (*Merchant Taylors' School, Crosby*)	8	2	411	109*	1	68.50
A. Singh (*King Edward's School, Birmingham*)	17	5	799	118*	1	66.58
J. I. Morrison (*Reed's School*)	12	2	655	173	2	65.50

MOST RUNS IN SCHOOLS CRICKET

(Qualification: 750 runs)

	I	NO	HS	100s	Avge	Runs
A. N. Cook (*Bedford School*)	15	3	173*	7	93.83	1,126
A. Day (*King's School, Macclesfield*)	21	3	152	1	54.83	987
P. A. Burdon (*King's School, Worcester*)	22	3	95	0	49.78	946
A. N. Russell (*Gordonstoun School*)	14	4	159	4	87.80	878
J. W. Robinson (*King's School, Worcester*)	22	3	110	1	45.36	862
B. R. Thompson (*Eton College*)	18	3	118	1	56.46	847
I. R. Massey (*Shrewsbury School*)	21	3	92*	0	47.05	847
J. C. F. F. Johnson (*Bancroft's School*)	26	2	112	1	35.29	847
D. Chambers (*St Edmund's School, Canterbury*)	12	0	151	4	70.50	846
C. J. Wake (*Oundle School*)	20	3	105*	2	49.58	843
A. M. Kruger (*Christ's Hospital*)	17	3	122	2	59.64	835
A. C. Fateh (*Dean Close School*)	17	1	152	4	51.18	819
A. Singh (*King Edward's School, Birmingham*)	17	5	118*	1	66.58	799
R. J. Malcolm (*Eltham College*)	18	3	140*	1	51.86	778
A. Dewhurst (*Victoria College, Jersey*)	19	3	151	3	48.50	776
R. A. J. Lintott (*Gresham's School*)	16	5	115*	1	69.72	767
J. Toms (*Plymouth College*)	11	5	201*	4	125.16	751

BOWLING

BEST AVERAGE IN SCHOOLS CRICKET

(Qualification: 10 wickets, average 9.00)

	O	M	R	W	BB	Avge
G. W. Walker (*Norwich School*)	41	26	35	15	5-1	2.33
G. Hariharan (*Glasgow Academy*)	33.2	7	58	12	5-6	4.83
S. Baxter (*Kingston GS*)	27	4	73	12	4-5	6.08
T. M. Hine (*Strathallan School*)	30	7	67	11	5-21	6.09
M. C. Woda (*Chigwell School*)	27	7	71	10	6-32	7.10
B. Coupar (*Strathallan School*)	66.3	26	119	16	3-13	7.43
S. N. Dave (*Merchant Taylors', Northwood*)	154	43	308	41	4-15	7.51
M. J. Bean (*Queen Elizabeth's Hospital*)	29	7	87	11	3-18	7.90
M. A. Bateson (*RGS, Lancaster*)	28.5	5	112	14	7-38	8.00
C. Thompson (*King Edward VII & QM School*)	30.4	7	112	14	4-8	8.00
T. Hamid (*Queen Elizabeth's Hospital*)	69	10	189	23	5-19	8.21
A. Shahzad (*Bradford GS*)	54	15	132	16	3-27	8.25
S. K. Haider (*Merchant Taylors', Northwood*)	41.4	11	84	10	3-10	8.40
M. Van de Ven (*Downside School*)	56	10	196	23	3-22	8.52
W. Stafford (*King's College, Taunton*)	92	12	256	29	5-12	8.82
P. Stephen (*Wellington School*)	89	25	221	25	4-20	8.84
S. G. D. Crampton (*Tiffin School*)	204.4	65	435	49	6-29	8.87
N. Canning (*Bryanston School*)	54.5	12	152	17	3-5	8.94
C. C. Depala (*Christ's College, Finchley*)	71.1	8	243	27	5-18	9.00

MOST WICKETS IN SCHOOLS CRICKET

(Qualification: 40 wickets)

	O	M	R	BB	Avge	W
T. J. Woolsey (*St Peter's School, York*)	222.3	67	677	7-33	13.27	51
S. G. D. Crampton (*Tiffin School*)	204.4	65	435	6-29	8.87	49
N. Lockwood (*Bedford Modern School*)	222.4	51	611	5-17	12.46	49
N. C. R. Westolt (*Eton College*)	188.1	20	707	7-56	14.72	48
E. Buxton (*Forest School*)	170	52	456	5-17	10.36	44
J. R. Bayly (*Hurstpierpoint College*)	196.2	48	491	6-41	11.15	44
T. H. Martin (*Lord Wandsworth College*)	176.1	49	528	6-5	12.00	44
M. E. Westwood (*Brentwood School*)	179.3	23	726	5-42	16.88	43
A. Dewhurst (*Victoria College, Jersey*)	177	32	569	5-30	13.54	42
S. N. Dave (*Merchant Taylors', Northwood*)	154	43	308	4-15	7.51	41
P. R. J. Hazell (*Dulwich College*)	176.2	32	559	7-64	13.63	41
R. J. Malcolm (*Eltham College*)	189.2	45	568	4-36	13.85	41
A. M. McKeever (*Shrewsbury School*)	243.1	67	630	7-23	15.36	41
A. Murphy (*Gordonstoun School*)	131	23	410	6-31	10.25	40
T. J. Jacklin (*Leeds GS*)	143	34	426	6-64	10.65	40

OUTSTANDING SEASONS, 2002

(Qualification: played eight matches)

	P	W	L	D	A	%W
Bristol Grammar School	11	8	3	0	4	72.7
Eastbourne College	15	11	1	3	0	73.3
Eton College	19	14	2	3	0	73.7
Hampton School	14	9	1	4	2	64.3
King Edward's School, Birmingham	19	14	2	3	4	73.7
King's College, Taunton	12	9	3	0	2	75.0
King's School, Macclesfield	20	14	3	3	2	70.0
King's School, Worcester	22	16	4	2	0	72.7
Kingswood School	10	8	2	0	4	80.0
Leeds Grammar School	13	8	1	4	4	61.5
Norwich School	17	12	4	1	2	70.6
St Albans School	11	8	1	2	3	72.7
Sherborne School	15	11	4	0	2	73.3
Tiffin School	18	11	1	6	2	61.1
Wyggeston and Queen Elizabeth I College	11	9	1	1	0	81.8

SCHOOLS A–Z

Abingdon School
P12 W2 L5 D5 A3

Batting J. A. D. Watkins 266 at 33.25; R. W. Balch 187 at 23.37; D. Desai 176 at 22.00; M. T. Armitage* 168 at 16.80.
Bowling D. Desai 22 at 17.13; G. W. A. Stern 11 at 18.45; B. J. L. Garner 10 at 26.20.

Aldenham School
P13 W2 L9 D2 A1

With runs always difficult to come by, an inexperienced team struggled for positive results.
Batting A. Mohindra 252 at 31.50; S. Gray 191 at 21.22; C. Chittleborough 189 at 21.00.
Bowling R. Brant 19 at 16.94; S. Gray 12 at 21.00.

Alleyn's School
P9 W3 L3 D3 A4

Weather and the pressure of exams hindered the progress of a determined young team. None of the players came from the upper sixth, and the leading batsman and bowler were both from the fifth year.

Batting C. Morris 222 at 44.40; F. Baird 158 at 31.60.
Bowling C. McGill 14 at 12.21.

Ampleforth College
P14 W6 L3 D5

In a very pleasing summer, Ben Fitzherbert led by example to score more than 600 runs for the second year running. Archie Woodhead, Toby Fitzherbert and off-spinner Joseph Brennan all bowled extremely well, though the team's major strength was its spirit and character.

Batting B. J. B. Fitzherbert* 636 at 57.81; J. R. W. Pawle 294 at 32.66; J. R. M. Smith 335 at 27.91; C. A. ff. Woodhead 190 at 17.27.
Bowling T. F. J. Fitzherbert 21 at 19.23; C. A. ff. Woodhead 17 at 20.94; W. E. Moore 14 at 22.28; J. E. N. Brennan 22 at 24.27; A. H. J. Kisielewski 10 at 25.10.

Arnold School
P9 W2 L7 D0 A2

Batting B. J. G. Taylor 217 at 27.12; J. Patel 150 at 18.75.
Bowling No one took ten wickets.

Ashville College
P12 W4 L4 D4 A2

The First XI toured Barbados and Antigua in July.
Batting J. A. Chervak 418 at 59.71; J. I. Townsend 319 at 35.44.
Bowling G. N. Randle 17 at 17.52; B. C. Woolman 21 at 21.09; N. R. Gupta 12 at 23.08.

Bancroft's School
P27 W7 L15 D5 A1

Despite disappointing results against strong opposition, a young party learned plenty from a winter tour to South Africa. At home, inexperience meant some games were lost that should have been won. The batting relied heavily on captain Joe Johnson. Matthew Rowland took the school's first hat-trick in 22 years.

Batting J. C. F. F. Johnson* 847 at 35.29; S. C. Miller 320 at 20.00; C. P. Smith 203 at 18.45; P. D. Macleod 220 at 16.92; S. Ganandran 331 at 15.76; J. H. T. Curran 291 at 14.55; M. Rowland 175 at 12.50; R. J. Harrison 219 at 12.16.
Bowling M. Rowland 16 at 18.68; D. Samuel 27 at 22.70; S. Ganandran 28 at 23.46; D. Ossack 31 at 25.12; D. Patel 20 at 26.00; S. C. Miller 11 at 30.54.

Bangor Grammar School
P13 W4 L7 D2 A7

The number of matches lost either to dreadful weather or to opponents through inept play, meant this was an unsatisfactory season.
Batting C. S. Cook 244 at 30.50; S. Cooper 249 at 24.90; P. D. McKenzie* 213 at 21.30.
Bowling P. D. McKenzie 26 at 9.96; G. S. J. Watterson 18 at 15.77; P. J. S. Speers 15 at 16.53; A. C. Mercer 14 at 16.78; C. S. Scott 10 at 18.30.

Barnard Castle School
P10 W1 L3 D6 A1

Despite a poor record, the team played positive cricket and lost several games that might easily have been drawn. Winning, though, was made far less likely by poor catching. Rory Wood led the side admirably for the second year.
Batting M. Brown 358 at 51.14; R. Wood* 226 at 28.25; R. Batty 175 at 21.88.
Bowling R. Batty 13 at 18.00; C. Dawson 10 at 27.00.

Bedford Modern School
P18 W5 L3 D10 A1

Richard King, an upper-sixth student, played for England Schools Under-18.
Batting N. K. P. Choudhury 593 at 45.61; B. N. Campbell 485 at 40.41; L. J. L. Steeden 177 at 35.40; D. N. G. Myers 535 at 33.43; R. W. Cruickshank 160 at 22.85; J. M. Fallows 165 at 12.69; A. L. Chinneck 167 at 10.43; N. Lockwood* 166 at 9.76.
Bowling N. Lockwood 49 at 12.46; A. M. Walker 23 at 14.95; R. A. Kemp 27 at 16.74.

Bedford School

Alastair Cook came within 55 of the school record for runs scored in a season, despite playing seven innings fewer than the current holder. He hit seven centuries, including a run of five in consecutive innings. Nine of the side were due to return for 2003.

Batting A. N. Cook 1,126 at 93.83; C. Soul 318 at 31.80; W. Notley 435 at 31.07; A. Turner 176 at 22.00; C. Fitzpatrick 160 at 12.30.

Bowling A. N. Cook 22 at 16.27; T. Coleman 20 at 23.20; S. Edmunds 15 at 28.26; W. Notley 11 at 30.90; E. Bray 12 at 41.66.

Berkhamsted Collegiate School

Berkhamsted won their last five matches and retained the Castle Bowl. Mark Herring, the captain, batted with flair, if not always care, and his unbeaten 117 against Kimbolton was the best individual performance.

Batting M. Herring* 485 at 40.41; R. Bartholomew 163 at 27.16; B. Ramsden 311 at 25.91; J. Rodwell 235 at 23.50; R. Gaymer 250 at 20.83; T. Chesters 183 at 15.25.

Bowling T. Chesters 21 at 17.19; M. Herring 19 at 27.00.

Bethany School

The team played with commitment and showed great spirit under pressure. They were ably led by Charlie Harding, who scored two hundreds. Tom Reynolds's determined occupation of the crease and marvellous sense of humour will be missed.

Batting C. M. G. Harding* 502 at 83.66; N. M. Khalid 187 at 31.16; G. W. Bright 160 at 20.00.

Bowling N. M. Khalid 10 at 20.10; M. I. Booth 13 at 26.00; A. J. H. Clarke 10 at 27.80.

Bloxham School

Batting J. C. Parker 265 at 37.85; R. F. J. Crofts 252 at 25.20; I. E. Baig 232 at 23.20; A. Baig 208 at 18.90; S. P. B. Whatman 152 at 16.88.

Bowling I. E. Baig 14 at 12.28; R. J. Foxon 19 at 14.63; R. F. J. Crofts 10 at 15.20; T. J. Hill 11 at 15.81; K. A. Rahman 18 at 21.44.

Bradfield College

A young team produced some impressive results, including wins against Harrow, Radley, Marlborough and MCC. James Morris was outstanding, turning in impressive performances with his batting and his leg-spin, while William Edes captained the side admirably. His reliable batting and accurate seam bowling will be sorely missed.

Batting J. C. Morris 687 at 62.45; S. P. J. Brain 426 at 38.72; W. M. H. Edes* 406 at 31.23; W. H. Chaloner 161 at 26.83; N. S. Woodroffe 232 at 25.77.

Bowling M. D. Sydenham 18 at 21.27; J. C. Morris 15 at 24.60; W. M. H. Edes 16 at 27.81.

Bradford Grammar School

In a promising season for a young side, two of the four defeats came when a weakened team toured Holland. The batting was strong, but the bowling sometimes lacked real bite: four games were drawn with the opposition nine down. At 14 years and nine months, Uzair Mahomed scored an unbeaten 110 at St Peter's, York to become the school's youngest century-maker.

Batting U. Mahomed 631 at 48.53; A. Shahzad 474 at 47.40; J. A. S. Benzafar* 433 at 43.30; S. Mahomed 521 at 40.07; T. D. Ambepitiya 246 at 22.36.

Bowling A. Shahzad 16 at 8.25; U. Mahomed 18 at 14.00; S. P. D. Slater 11 at 15.27; A. Aziz 26 at 17.65; S. Mahomed 23 at 17.86; J. N. MacDougall 14 at 23.14; S. J. Beck 10 at 27.20.

Brentwood School

Oliver Allen, who also played at Under-15 level, is the son of the former England footballer, Clive Allen.

Batting O. T. Allen 635 at 90.71; J. G. Redwood* 638 at 42.53; J. Harrison 178 at 35.60; J. C. Turnbull 332 at 27.66; M. E. Westwood 370 at 23.12; C. J. Westwood 242 at 20.16.

Bowling M. E. Westwood 43 at 16.88; J. G. Redwood 33 at 19.75; F. N. Crosby 22 at 23.72; N. J. P. Mead 16 at 26.00.

Brighton College
P16 W10 L2 D4 A3

Rain and the increased pressure of exams meant fewer matches than usual. A youthful side started slowly, but their last ten games brought nine wins and a draw. The batting was especially strong, with four players notching centuries. Brighton played more limited-overs matches this year.
Batting C. M. Grammer 660 at 50.76; M. N. Waller 641 at 45.78; M. Gardner 420 at 38.18; R. L. Young 301 at 37.62; J. S. Gatting 239 at 34.14; T. R. Burton* 345 at 31.36; R. Sekri 183 at 16.63.
Bowling T. R. Burton 25 at 14.52; R. Sekri 14 at 16.00; C. M. Grammer 23 at 17.91; M. T. Sleep 19 at 22.52; M. J. Wood 17 at 23.94; S. Murphy 11 at 30.45; M. N. Waller 13 at 32.76.

Bristol Grammar School
P11 W8 L3 D0 A4

This proved to be a very successful season. Jamie Butt was the linchpin of the side, but both batting and bowling had strength in depth: almost everyone played an important innings at some stage, and a sextet of seamers frequently kept the opposition under 100. James Smith proved an intelligent captain.
Batting J. D. Butt 329 at 36.55; J. R. A. Smith* 165 at 27.50; D. S. Knox 159 at 17.66.
Bowling S. J. Nandha 13 at 10.61; J. D. Butt 19 at 13.47; M. W. Leonard 16 at 13.93; T. D. Westray 11 at 17.36.

Bromsgrove School
P14 W6 L4 D4 A1

There were three Under-15s and four Under-16s in the regular First XI: Sam Robinson and Matthew Mullan were the leading batsmen, while Maneesh Gahir and Jonathan Jones bowled incisively. Ben Dudley provided vital support behind the stumps.
Batting S. Robinson 570 at 51.81; M. J. Mullan 470 at 36.15; O. Woodyatt 183 at 20.33.
Bowling M. Gahir 27 at 12.59; J. Jones 19 at 15.78; S. Robinson 10 at 35.50.

Bryanston School
P13 W6 L5 D2 A1

The summer began brightly with four wins, a draw and two hundreds for Jim Denning. But as the matches got tougher, the loss of wicket-keeper/batsman Mark Pritchard, captain of Wiltshire Under-17, with a knee injury, proved crucial.
Batting J. R. Denning 397 at 39.70; L. C. Bettesworth 221 at 36.83; B. C. Edgell 252 at 31.50; S. R. Martin 175 at 15.90.
Bowling N. Canning 17 at 8.94; S. R. Martin 26 at 13.42; G. M. Evans 13 at 25.38.

Campbell College
P11 W5 L4 D2

Batting A. Nixon 168 at 16.80.
Bowling N. Black 13 at 11.07; A. Coulter 12 at 17.25.

Canford School
P11 W10 L1 D0 A2

Batting T. Cledwyn 395 at 43.88; A. Harms 330 at 36.66; T. Norris 383 at 34.81; C. Martin 317 at 31.70; J. Holt 187 at 26.71.
Bowling K. Rathbone 21 at 15.42; T. Norris 16 at 18.06; R. Tolley 20 at 22.35; R. Scaife 14 at 24.35; J. Pople 11 at 25.36.

Charterhouse
P18 W12 L4 D2

The First XI equalled the school record for wins in a season. In ten of the 12 victories the opposition were bowled out. All-rounder and captain Simon Hollingsworth went on to represent ECB Schools and captain Surrey Under-19s. Tonbridge was beaten for the first time in 19 years.
Batting J. H. P. Hooper 305 at 43.57; S. C. Hollingsworth* 352 at 32.00; L. P. Bernhard 306 at 30.60; J. R. Wood 333 at 30.27; W. H. Young 379 at 23.68; J. A. D. Lumsden 322 at 23.00; M. A. A. Cook 200 at 20.00.
Bowling L. E. Carpenter 23 at 11.95; F. D. Palley 23 at 15.78; S. C. Hollingsworth 22 at 17.36; M. R. Grindy 18 at 18.83; W. H. Young 24 at 21.75; J. A. D. Lumsden 16 at 22.31.

Cheltenham College
P17 W9 L6 D2 A3

Batting M. A. Richards* 694 at 46.26; W. H. Marshall 430 at 33.07; S. D. Davy 249 at 24.90; D. C. Hall 265 at 22.08; B. E. L. Snell 254 at 21.16; C. J. L. Sandbach 291 at 18.18; E. J. L. Richardson 266 at 16.62; T. M. B. Brierley 155 at 15.50.
Bowling M. A. Richards 29 at 16.13; N. J. Abendanon 17 at 20.00; T. M. B. Brierley 33 at 22.21; C. J. L. Sandbach 15 at 22.33; C. S. Luckock 12 at 29.83.

Darshan Depala (*left*) of Christ's College, Finchley took four wickets in four balls; Mark Willoughby of Chislehurst and Sidcup GS went one better, with five in five.

Chigwell School
P14 W9 L3 D2 A2

Batting S. Ditta 331 at 55.16; H. Ditta 336 at 42.00; R. Bhome 488 at 40.66; C. S. Benn 348 at 34.80; R. Gull* 386 at 27.57; M. C. Woda 151 at 25.16.
Bowling M. C. Woda 10 at 7.10; R. Bhome 35 at 14.14; J. Chandrakumar 13 at 19.69; R. Gull 18 at 21.05.

Chislehurst and Sidcup Grammar School
P10 W3 L4 D3 A4

For the first time, the side entered the Kent Schools Under-19 League and under the excellent captaincy of Ben Wiles they finished third in their group. The highlight of the summer was Mark Willoughby taking six wickets in eight balls with his leg-spin.
Batting No batsman scored 150 runs. The leading batsman was P. Grayson, who scored 142 at 20.28.
Bowling M. J. Willoughby 18 at 11.55; L. E. Rogers 10 at 11.80; D. G. Meeking 12 at 12.25.

Christ College, Brecon
P10 W3 L6 D1 A3

A very young side learnt much from a tough season. All but three of the squad should return next year.
Batting C. S. D. James 174 at 17.40.
Bowling D. Wolfe 11 at 15.72; D. J. K. Rees 11 at 15.81.

Christ's College, Finchley
P16 W10 L3 D3 A2

An inexperienced side with a positive attitude improved rapidly. The bowling was of a high standard, while fielding and batting proved better than expected. Darshan Depala, his brother Chetan and his cousin Mayur were effective all-rounders. Darshan took four wickets in four balls against St Ignatius College.
Batting D. C. Depala 423 at 30.21; C. C. Depala 258 at 21.50; M. Depala 150 at 21.42; A. Afzal 261 at 18.64.
Bowling C. C. Depala 27 at 9.00; D. C. Depala 28 at 9.82; R. A. Barney 13 at 11.84; M. Depala 16 at 12.25.

Christ's Hospital
P17 W10 L2 D5 A1

Christ's had an outstanding season and won a school-record ten games. The team was admirably led by Neil Green in his fifth year in the squad. Andries Kruger set a new mark for runs in a season, fielded exceptionally and took 19 wickets before a side strain prevented him bowling. He fully deserved his All-Rounder of the Year award from *Wisden's* schools website.
Batting A. M. Kruger 835 at 59.64; S. Curtin 425 at 38.63; N. J. Green* 430 at 35.83; A. E. J. Woodbridge 183 at 14.07.

Cla{}esmore School

P14 W6 L6 D2 A2

Batting E. J. Calver 267 at 19.07; A. E. Cook 152 at 16.88; E. J. B. Lack 225 at 16.07; W. J. Harding 189 at 14.53; C. A. Haniff* 199 at 14.21; S. J. L. Peters 156 at 13.00.
Bowling C. A. Haniff 22 at 13.22; A. E. Cook 14 at 20.00; S. J. Hughes 11 at 21.72; E. J. Calver 10 at 24.10; T. J. Robertshaw 10 at 24.80; A. G. Merson 10 at 36.30.

Clifton College

P11 W4 L4 D3 A5

Five weeks of near-incessant rain ripped the heart out of the term. Highlights were a nail-biting win against Cheltenham College, and a crushing one against King's, Taunton.
Batting M. Houcke 319 at 35.44; R. Yates 257 at 28.55.
Bowling G. Robinson 12 at 11.33; F. Musa 18 at 12.22; R. Yates 15 at 17.13; C. Lincoln 11 at 21.27.

Colfe's School

P12 W8 L2 D2

Colfe's visit to Cape Town at Easter was the school's largest tour.
Batting S. Cullum 342 at 57.00; T. Holmes 203 at 22.55; J. Davies 153 at 21.85.
Bowling S. Cullum 26 at 10.42; P. Harman 17 at 18.88; G. Houghton 17 at 19.05.

Cranbrook School

P21 W11 L6 D4

A pre-season tour to Barbados was a great success, with both first and second teams playing six matches against stiff opposition.
Batting C. Marriott 444 at 31.71; J. Burgess 329 at 29.90; C. Page 436 at 29.06; C. Sorensen* 355 at 16.90; P. Towner 191 at 13.64.
Bowling P. Towner 32 at 11.21; O. Reynolds 29 at 11.41; T. Cullen 17 at 15.64; D. Allen 13 at 17.07; C. Marriott 28 at 18.82; C. Sorensen 24 at 19.07.

Cranleigh School

P20 W8 L6 D6

An inexperienced attack could not exert pressure on helpful early-season wickets, though this changed as bowlers adjusted to first-team cricket. Edward McGregor was a consistent run-scorer; Sam Worthy, the captain, fought hard with bat and ball and engendered a high standard of fielding.
Batting S. R. Langmead 459 at 35.30; E. G. McGregor 691 at 34.55; D. Hill 402 at 28.71; S. C. Worthy* 261 at 15.35; R. H. Jones 311 at 17.27; J. R. Gates 261 at 13.73.
Bowling S. J. Wicks 10 at 10.90; E. P. C. Prince 14 at 17.14; A. E. Kendrick 13 at 17.23; D. A. C. Lewis 23 at 18.82; D. Hill 18 at 21.83; S. C. Worthy 20 at 27.65.

Culford School

P12 W3 L7 D2 A3

Batting T. E. B. Beaney* 294 at 32.66; R. J. Hobley 204 at 25.50; M. T. Fronicke 175 at 17.50; L. E. J. Cousins 154 at 17.11; N. K. Khagram 151 at 15.10.
Bowling M. T. Fronicke 14 at 22.35; T. E. B. Beaney 10 at 31.00; S. J. G. Perren 10 at 42.40.

Dauntsey's School

P13 W1 L10 D2 A1

Batting E. Poulding 151 at 25.16; E. K. Curtis 188 at 20.88; S. E. Blackford 228 at 19.00.
Bowling S. S. Chaudhry 14 at 18.21; C. T. J. Jones 11 at 22.18; J. E. M. Bayliss 18 at 22.50.

Dean Close School

P17 W8 L6 D3

Batting A. C. Fateh 819 at 51.18; A. Hume 397 at 30.53; J. Jenkins 354 at 27.23; T. A. Judge* 291 at 22.38; A. Carlisle 169 at 18.77.
Bowling A. Carlisle 20 at 14.20; J. Jenkins 34 at 14.67; N. Ball 14 at 19.85; T. A. Judge 20 at 31.10.

Denstone College

P13 W2 L5 D6 A2

Adam Johnson and Matthew Gouldstone recorded maiden centuries. Johnson was largely responsible for Denstone's best victory, against Wickersley, scoring 45 and then taking five for 23 with accurate off-spin. David Soar was the best bowler.
Batting M. A. Gouldstone 389 at 38.90; A. Johnson* 337 at 28.08; S. J. F. Grosvenor 231 at 23.10; A. J. Whiston 201 at 22.33; P. W. Carr 152 at 13.81.
Bowling A. Johnson 10 at 14.10; J. R. Millar-Beards 15 at 17.66; D. G. G. Soar 22 at 24.13; W. B. I. Felton 11 at 31.90.

Dollar Academy

P9 W4 L5 D0 A5

The season started with three consecutive defeats, but hard work in training saw the team to victories over Loretto, Fettes and the XL Club.
Batting J. Barber-Fleming 154 at 25.66; R. Chalmers 171 at 19.00.
Bowling G. Wilson 19 at 12.84; J. Barber-Fleming 14 at 13.42.

Dover College

P11 W0 L7 D4

Captain John Brasier's fine all-round performance helped sustain a young side.
Batting J. Brasier* 281 at 40.14; L. D. Disbury 160 at 17.77.
Bowling J. Brasier 22 at 19.04.

Downside School

P7 W4 L3 D0 A1

Batting B. Parker 202 at 25.25.
Bowling M. Van de Ven 23 at 8.52.

Duke of York's Royal Military School

P8 W5 L1 D2 A6

The side remained unbeaten until the last game of a highly satisfactory season. Tight bowling and fielding made the difference in a number of close games. Owen Donovan's batting was mature and Tom Gilbert and Sebastian Cripps were positive and, at times, inspired. Edward Whiteley bowled probing leg-spin.
Batting O. T. Donovan* 235 at 39.16; T. Gilbert 177 at 35.40; S. Cripps 255 at 31.87.
Bowling E. Whiteley 20 at 14.45.

Dulwich College

P15 W3 L2 D10 A3

New first-team coach Bill Athey instilled a professional attitude and a love of the game perhaps absent in recent years. Though there have been more talented Dulwich sides, they made themselves very hard to beat. Rupert Hazell was the best player, while Tommy Roy's unbeaten 101 against Brighton College was a wonderful innings.
Batting T. T. Askew 572 at 44.00; T. D. Roy 410 at 34.16; P. R. J. Hazell* 385 at 32.08; C. J. Owen 201 at 25.12; T. J. Bevan 181 at 15.08.
Bowling P. R. J. Hazell 41 at 13.63; T. T. Askew 13 at 22.07; T. J. Bevan 31 at 23.16; G. P. Porter 11 at 35.18.

Durham School

P15 W7 L1 D7 A4

The school was well led by Phillip Carleton. The development of the younger players was especially pleasing: Tim Stonock and Jonathan McRedie topped the averages and return next year, while Patrick Dias and Paul Muchall have three years left.
Batting T. Stonock 704 at 58.66; P. Muchall 503 at 38.69; P. Dias 281 at 31.22; N. Duffitt 304 at 21.71; P. Carleton 262 at 20.15; J. McRedie 184 at 15.33; S. Ali 197 at 15.15.
Bowling J. McRedie 34 at 16.20; T. Stonock 19 at 20.00; P. Dias 18 at 21.33; P. Muchall 19 at 23.63; S. Ali 11 at 32.63.

Eastbourne College

P15 W11 L1 D3

A successful team included seven – sometimes eight – Under-16s. Much depended on the astute captaincy and prolific run-scoring of Simon Cane Hardy, and he helped the side retain the Langdale Cup. The fielding was magnificent, thanks to coach Deon Kotze, Namibia's captain for the 2003 World Cup.
Batting S. D. Cane Hardy* 691 at 62.81; O. L. Gale 350 at 35.00; H. C. Hassen 373 at 33.90; J. A. M. Toy 243 at 24.30; J. P. Reid 168 at 24.00.
Bowling W. J. Ripley 21 at 14.23; P. J. Morgan 13 at 15.23; N. J. Reid 10 at 19.40; J. C. Farley 19 at 20.89; S. D. Cane Hardy 18 at 24.83.

Edinburgh Academy

P16 W6 L10 D0 A5

An inexperienced team who gelled well and established an excellent team spirit ensured a good season. The highlight was winning the inaugural Ryden Lothian Schools Cup.
Batting D. W. Blair 392 at 30.15; N. A. Sellar* 313 at 22.35; A. J. Cosh 264 at 17.60; S. G. Cosh 221 at 17.00; F. H. K. Allison 183 at 13.07.
Bowling S. G. Cosh 25 at 13.08; N. A. Sellar 20 at 16.60; F. H. K. Allison 21 at 22.04; M. G. Allison 13 at 30.84.

Elizabeth College, Guernsey
P15 W7 L6 D2

Batting M. J. Watson 402 at 30.92; A. S. Harbour 321 at 26.75; L. J. Gallienne 172 at 21.50; J. D. Warr 191 at 15.91; C. A. Van Vliet 173 at 15.72.
Bowling C. A. Van Vliet 34 at 10.58; J. G. Orme 15 at 16.26; L. J. Gallienne 18 at 20.61; M. J. Watson 15 at 26.26.

Ellesmere College
P11 W4 L4 D3 A3

Nick Watson-Jones's seven for 18 in the win against Liverpool College was the performance of the summer. For two matches, the side contained three pairs of brothers – Sam and Nick Watson-Jones, Max and Guy Stringer and Richard and David Baxter.
Batting R. A. M. Baxter 170 at 42.50.
Bowling N. D. Watson-Jones 25 at 11.08; M. Singh 16 at 20.50.

Eltham College
P19 W13 L4 D2 A1

The College won the Lemon (Kent) Cup.
Batting R. J. Malcolm 778 at 51.86; P. J. Selvey-Clinton* 706 at 47.06; O. J. Willis 265 at 20.38; R. P. Unwin 242 at 18.61; T. J. Goodyear 249 at 17.78.
Bowling R. J. Malcolm 41 at 13.85; P. J. Selvey-Clinton 29 at 15.03; T. J. Goodyear 19 at 25.26; M. L. Dransfield 15 at 27.40; J. P. Campion 10 at 31.50.

Enfield Grammar School
P15 W5 L5 D5 A3

Batting S. Levy 175 at 43.75; E. Barber 348 at 34.80; S. Nabi 262 at 32.75; M. Holly 285 at 23.75.
Bowling E. Barber 16 at 13.68; D. Fuller 14 at 16.57; T. Miller* 14 at 22.85.

Epsom College
P17 W9 L6 D2

Form improved after a poor start. Adam Howard anchored the batting, while Nikin Tanna ended three years in the XI with a total of almost 90 wickets. Re-laying of the square meant all matches in the first half of term were played away.
Batting A. Howard 450 at 32.14; A. Vernon 409 at 25.56; J. Laidler 377 at 25.13; R. Lammiman 303 at 23.30; A. Cama 225 at 17.30; A. Robinson 167 at 10.43.
Bowling N. Tanna 38 at 11.23; D. Hastings 18 at 14.88; R. Pooley 19 at 17.42; A. Cama 20 at 20.90; B. Sears 10 at 35.40.

Eton College
P19 W14 L2 D3

A record number of wins slightly flattered the real quality of the team. Eton won both the Cowdrey Cup (a round-robin involving Tonbridge, Harrow, Charterhouse and Wellington) and the Silk Trophy. The side included only one seamer of note (Benjamin Thompson) but four talented spinners (two leg-break, two off-break). Thompson's batting was highly consistent, and he reached 50 ten times. James Mathias's unbeaten 106 against Carey Grammar School, Melbourne came from 37 balls.
Batting B. R. Thompson 847 at 56.46; E. F. J. Nissen 350 at 43.75; A. W. A. Barker 31 at 29.61; J. H. Mathias 301 at 27.36; T. P. McCall* 442 at 26.00; H. W. A. Clarke 271 at 22.58; A. M. Goldberg 383 at 22.52; C. P. A. Nissen 181 at 16.45.
Bowling N. C. R. Westoll 48 at 14.72; A. W. A. Barker 10 at 17.10; T. P. McCall 25 at 20.96; B. R. Thompson 23 at 22.00; W. T. Dobson 14 at 27.42; A. E. M. P. de Lisle 10 at 37.20.

Exeter School
P13 W7 L5 D1 A5

Rain made this a frustrating season. The side underperformed at times and seven wins from 13 was perhaps disappointing. Captain Dan Saunders scored 405 at a healthy average, and Toby Giles was the pick of the bowlers with 19 wickets at 17.52. Harry Trick kept superbly.
Batting D. Saunders* 405 at 45.00; C. Hampshire 249 at 27.66; J. Lamb 313 at 26.08; A. Milton 263 at 21.91; R. Hooper 162 at 20.25.
Bowling T. Giles 19 at 17.52; J. Fisher 12 at 17.58; B. Cadoux-Hudson 14 at 19.35; R. Berryman 12 at 24.08.

Felsted School
P15 W6 L5 D4 A2

A talented team never realised its potential during the season, despite some impressive individual performances. William Edwards hit a fine hundred but, disappointingly, it was the only one of the summer. Youngsters Joseph Buttleman and Christopher Huntington slotted easily into the side, while Andrew Stothard was a commendable captain.

All-round skills: Christ's Hospital's Andries Kruger (*left*) was among the country's leading run-scorers, took 19 wickets at nearly 13 and proved a talented wicket-keeper, while Edward Buxton grabbed 44 wickets for Forest, and hit 569 runs at nearly 44.

Batting J. E. L. Buttleman 286 at 47.66; W. Edwards 412 at 31.69; C. J. Huntington 376 at 31.33; G. Ladipo 441 at 29.40; A. Stothard* 355 at 25.35; J. Leeder 263 at 23.90; N. Porter 257 at 21.41.
Bowling J. E. L. Buttleman 16 at 22.43; N. Porter 23 at 23.73; A. Stothard 20 at 34.95.

Fettes College   P16 W6 L8 D2

Batting J. F. Jackson 476 at 34.00; C. B. Samuel 194 at 13.85.
Bowling L. G. M. Vieilledent 17 at 13.05; C. B. Samuel 10 at 15.40; A. P. Cadzow 24 at 16.50; J. F. Jackson 23 at 18.60.

Forest School   P15 W7 L3 D5 A1

Edward Buxton opened the batting and bowling and topped both averages; taking 44 wickets at 10.36 is quite an achievement. He also played all of Essex's Under-17 games, along with Nick Rotsey.
Batting E. Buxton 569 at 43.76; N. Rotsey 383 at 27.35; K. Paul* 308 at 25.66; M. Declaiterosse 268 at 22.33; J. Palmer 208 at 18.90.
Bowling E. Buxton 44 at 10.36; F. Gay 12 at 18.83; A. Williams 13 at 24.84; M. Declaiterosse 10 at 27.40.

Framlingham College   P10 W1 L7 D2 A1

The team lacked genuine class, with one or two players having to carry the side. Spencer Veevers-Chorlton achieved fame late in the season when he hit 42 in an over (seven sixes, including one from a no-ball) in a local league fixture. It merited a brief mention in *The Times*.
Batting M. J. Stacpoole 215 at 71.66; S. Veevers-Chorlton 479 at 53.22.
Bowling No one took ten wickets.

Giggleswick School   P13 W7 L6 D0 A2

After a disappointing start to the season, the side benefited from a tour to Barbados, where they won four games from six – and learnt a great deal. In his second year as captain, Jack Hird showed great maturity and organisation. There were pleasing performances from Sam Christian and Nick Hird.
Batting J. W. Hird* 471 at 39.25; S. D. Christian 198 at 19.80; I. T. Bartlett 193 at 16.08.
Bowling B. Topham 18 at 15.16; N. Hird 22 at 16.90; S. D. Christian 20 at 19.25; S. Horsfall 12 at 31.41.

Glasgow Academy
P4 W3 L0 D1

A fixture list savaged by the weather meant that perhaps the strongest side in ten years played only four matches. Among the three wins was a rout of George Heriot's, who were bowled out for 12. Gareth Williams proved an excellent captain, Stuart Ker batted with maturity and the seamer Gautham Hariharan earned impressive figures.

Batting No batsman scored 150 runs. The leading batsman was S. D. Ker, who scored 133 at 44.33.
Bowling G. Hariharan 12 at 4.83.

Glenalmond College
P11 W3 L2 D6 A4

The strength of the side lay in its bowling, which often had to make up for inadequate batting. The team was undefeated by Scottish schools, and Loretto and Fettes were dismissed for 48 and 35 respectively. Paul Stoll, a fifth former, was the find of the season, while James Bruton's seven for 35 against KEQM, Lytham was a tremendous performance. Five of this year's attack should return in 2003.

Batting No batsman scored 150 runs. The leading batsman was R. J. Monro, who scored 111 at 22.20.
Bowling P. A. D. Stoll 19 at 11.47; J. D. Brunton 23 at 12.00; R. S. Stevenson 13 at 12.00.

Gordonstoun School
P17 W11 L2 D4 A2

Gordonstoun, unbeaten by other schools, defeated MCC for the first time in a decade. Robin Pyper, the captain, bowled accurately and economically and Adam Murphy was a consistent wicket-taker. The player of the season was Andrew Russell from Johannesburg, who combined fine keeping skills with a prolific bat.

Batting A. N. Russell 878 at 87.80; P. Buszard 234 at 78.00; M. H. Faizan 156 at 52.00; A. Murphy 239 at 34.14; E. W. F. Paterson 188 at 20.88; G. Crow 165 at 16.50.
Bowling A. Murphy 40 at 10.25; R. S-R. Pyper* 17 at 15.00; P. Buszard 17 at 15.11; D. J. Nisbet 13 at 17.46.

Gresham's School
P16 W7 L3 D6 A2

Rory Lintott hit 767 runs, the school's second-highest aggregate for a season, while Michael Pickett took his total of First XI wickets to 1,509, also second in the school records.

Batting R. A. J. Lintott 767 at 69.72; M. J. Pickett 568 at 37.86; T. B. Farrow 379 at 31.58; A. C. J. Broom 150 at 25.00; O. F. Dudman 168 at 24.00; J. O. Elliott 170 at 21.25; R. M. K. Steward 290 at 19.33.
Bowling J. O. Elliott 15 at 17.73; R. M. K. Steward 24 at 17.83; R. A. J. Lintott 17 at 19.58; S. J. Matthews 18 at 21.33; J. R. A. Pearse 17 at 21.64; H. J. Flower 11 at 29.54.

Haberdashers' Aske's School
P18 W9 L4 D5 A4

Despite bad weather marring the end-of-term tour to Devon, this was a successful season. Nine wins included one-wicket triumphs against local rivals Merchant Taylors', Northwood and Bedford Modern. The captain, Philip Duffy, led by example and gained good support from Alex Theivendra, who hit six fifties. Off-spinner Prabhu Arumugam, who turned out for Hertfordshire Under-19, performed consistently well.

Batting A. M. Theivendra 575 at 44.23; P. B. Duffy* 292 at 41.71; J. S. T. Williams 429 at 30.64; R. Suva-Kumar 408 at 25.50; K. Sethi 199 at 15.30.
Bowling P. B. Duffy 26 at 15.42; G. E. B. FitzGerald 31 at 17.53; A. M. Patel 21 at 18.76; P. Arumugam 24 at 22.62; A. M. Theivendra 10 at 22.70; V. Vaithianathan 13 at 25.92.

Haileybury College
P15 W6 L6 D3

Batting N. Walker 294 at 58.80; C. Scott 259 at 25.90; F. Qureshi 227 at 22.70; D. Stewart* 211 at 19.18.
Bowling D. Gerrard 13 at 12.92; J. Melvill 27 at 15.85; N. Walker 18 at 17.72; F. Qureshi 20 at 18.10; C. Wyles 18 at 28.38.

Hampton School
P14 W9 L1 D4 A2

A strong team relied on a tight and varied bowling attack and excellent fielding. They benefited from a tour to Sri Lanka over New Year 2002, where they learnt to defend modest totals. The side was ably led by Jonny Irons. The core of the team should return next summer.

Batting O. G. K. Roland-Jones 481 at 32.33; S. Patel 216 at 27.00; S. P. G. Morris 321 at 26.75; N. E. Baker 290 at 26.36; J. D. Irons* 252 at 21.00.
Bowling J. D. Irons 34 at 10.52; S. Patel 23 at 11.21; P. J. Sellick 18 at 12.50; W. M. Gaines 16 at 22.43.

Harrow School
P17 W9 L3 D5

Harrow enjoyed an excellent season, though Eton won the annual Lord's match by 66 runs. The strength of the side lay in its accurate bowling, especially the off-spin of James Kostoris and Hamish Morrison. The batsmen underperformed, though Kostoris was consistent. Nicholas Defty's 116 to beat Tonbridge was the best innings.

Batting J. M. Kostoris 438 at 43.80; S. R. L. Maydon* 370 at 28.46; N. E. Defty 408 at 25.50; P. R. Dunbar 327 at 25.15; M. B. Mahon 152 at 16.88.
Bowling J. M. Kostoris 24 at 16.66; H. M. Morrison 21 at 17.61; R. V. G. Harmsworth 25 at 18.40; N. E. Defty 15 at 19.60; J. B. K. Roditi 14 at 24.78; P. D. Moseley 13 at 26.69.

Harvey Grammar School
P12 W3 L2 D7 A7

Batting P. J. Goddard* 280 at 31.11; S. Ireland 307 at 30.70; S. Bentley 160 at 17.77.
Bowling S. Ireland 24 at 9.45; P. Osborne 10 at 15.60; S. Bentley 10 at 16.40.

Hereford Cathedral School
P15 W5 L9 D1 A1

Batting A. M. Nahorniak 509 at 46.27; A. J. Hewlett* 429 at 30.64; M. A. Lowden 305 at 21.78; O. R. Vaughan 180 at 16.36.
Bowling N. A. Townson 24 at 18.66; T. A. Harper 20 at 20.35; C. J. Ball 17 at 20.58.

Highgate School
P12 W4 L8 D0

Batting J. D. M. Atchinson 238 at 34.00; J. A. Whybrow 165 at 15.00.
Bowling J. A. Whybrow 24 at 15.29; A. L. Schlagman 22 at 21.09.

Hurstpierpoint College
P18 W10 L4 D4

The outstanding contributions of a successful summer came from James Bayly, the captain, who took 44 wickets, and from wicket-keeper Lakshyaraj Mewar, who claimed 41 victims.

Batting T. M. Price 244 at 40.66; T. J. Jarvis 423 at 38.45; J. R. Bayly* 213 at 26.62; T. P. Harrison 357 at 25.50; J. C. Andrews 283 at 23.58; A. S. Godhania 340 at 22.66.
Bowling J. R. Bayly 44 at 11.15; D. K. Harris 14 at 13.35; A. S. Godhania 29 at 18.55; A. J. A. Sinclair 20 at 24.40; N. A. Viggor 13 at 26.92; L. B. Tarr 14 at 28.71.

Ipswich School
P16 W5 L4 D7 A3

Batting R. Crowe 343 at 57.16; T. Hembry 385 at 55.00; H. Knights 363 at 33.00; C. Flather 161 at 32.20; I. Swallow* 254 at 18.14.
Bowling T. Caston 33 at 15.48; I. Swallow 31 at 17.93.

John Lyon School
P17 W3 L7 D7

A pleasing start to the season was not maintained. During cricket week, when a clash with exams meant a number of players were unavailable, the team slumped to several defeats. Rhodri James was consistent, passing 50 four times, while Sam Singh took 28 wickets, the best return for 20 years.

Batting R. T. James 445 at 49.44; J. M. H. Silvester 293 at 20.92; S. Singh* 152 at 16.88; N. Panchal 232 at 14.50.
Bowling S. Singh 28 at 14.35; E. Swain 15 at 18.13; N. Rughani 11 at 18.72; A. R. Pankhania 15 at 21.06; R. T. James 10 at 28.70; T. Cook 10 at 30.20.

Kimbolton School
P19 W12 L2 D5 A2

Twelve victories meant this was Kimbolton's best season. Luke Bailey scored 154 against Felsted, the highest score on record. Meanwhile, the captain, Alex Lacey, ended his school career just short of 100 wickets and with almost 1,500 runs to his name; Oliver Huggins, a fourth-former, scored four fifties. Despite exams, nine upper-sixth players played in every game, creating a superb team spirit.

Batting A. Lacey* 743 at 57.15; E. Longmate 618 at 44.14; M. Ralph 354 at 27.23; O. Huggins 412 at 25.75; A. McCarthy 237 at 23.70.
Bowling M. Ellerbeck 36 at 15.19; A. Lacey 29 at 19.68; J. Cooper 21 at 20.33; L. Bailey 16 at 32.87.

King Edward VI College, Stourbridge
P11 W3 L8 D0 A2

A team largely comprising lower-sixth students had a disappointing season. The best performance was Ben Tipping's unbeaten 62 off 32 balls at Bishop Vesey's GS.

Batting W. A. Kazi 176 at 22.00; R. S. Musk 164 at 16.40.
Bowling T. M. Cunningham 11 at 16.18; R. S. Musk 12 at 18.66; A. Dawes 13 at 19.07.

King Edward VI School, Southampton   P14 W8 L5 D1 A3

A strong batting line-up meant that run-scoring was never a problem. Alexander Richardson and
Graham Noble led the assault, but they were let down by some erratic bowling.
Batting J. P. Richardson 291 at 41.57; A. P. Richardson 407 at 40.70; G. H. Noble 394 at 32.83; E. M. Brogan*
257 at 32.12.
Bowling A. R. Brown 11 at 14.63; M. J. Gurd 11 at 16.09; A. R. N. Warrick 17 at 16.23; T. W. Carter 16 at
17.87; M. D. Boyd 13 at 19.15.

King Edward VII & Queen Mary School, Lytham   P19 W8 L9 D2 A1

Highlights included Chris Thompson's four for eight against Glenalmond and Jack Kelliher's
unbeaten 140 on a rain-affected pitch at King's, Macclesfield. The team was excellently led by
Tom Eastham.
Batting J. Kelliher 714 at 54.92; C. Roberts 275 at 39.28; T. Eastham* 682 at 35.89; B. Hall 269 at 29.88;
S. Holliday 282 at 17.62; R. Openshaw 221 at 15.78.
Bowling C. Thompson 14 at 8.00; S. Holliday 37 at 11.83; L. Smith 22 at 19.77; C. Pickles 18 at 20.22; R. Taylor
12 at 21.41; R. Openshaw 12 at 24.16; J. Kelliher 12 at 36.75.

King Edward's School, Birmingham   P19 W14 L2 D3 A4

An Australian tour over Christmas produced clear benefits. Fourteen wins was a school record,
and 11 teams were bowled out. Anirudh Singh, brother of Worcestershire's Anurag, led by example
and scored 799 runs. He was well supported by Daniel Shilvock and Ravi Tiwari. The spin attack
had strength in depth, with two leg-spinners – Shilvock and Andrew Holmes – and a left-arm
spinner, Vikram Banerjee, all taking 20 wickets or more at under 18.
Batting A. Singh* 799 at 66.58; D. J. F. Shilvock 675 at 45.00; S. P. G. Chase 281 at 35.12; R. D. Tiwari 513 at
30.17; N. C. Brandrick 278 at 23.16; B. N. Patel 237 at 19.75.
Bowling A. P. S. Holmes 20 at 11.45; D. J. F. Shilvock 29 at 16.62; R. D. Tiwari 11 at 17.90; V. Banerjee 25 at
17.92; R. Chopra 21 at 19.14; N. C. Brandrick 21 at 19.66; A. P. S. Thind 15 at 29.26.

King Edward's School, Witley   P13 W2 L5 D6 A5

The tragic death of Walter Masimula, King Edward's South African professional, cast a long
shadow over the summer. Once the career period was over, a youthful side that had begun the
season with four defeats and three draws, blossomed. Alex Fitzgerald and Jack Wooldridge
spearheaded the seam attack, though the batsmen never really hit their stride.
Batting R. C. Ledger* 346 at 26.61; B. Bogi 299 at 24.91.
Bowling J. J. Wooldridge 15 at 17.60; A. B. Fitzgerald 16 at 22.87; A. M. W. Manley 12 at 29.83.

King's College, Taunton   P12 W9 L3 D0 A2

A young side that adjusted quickly to First XI cricket enjoyed a successful season. The captain,
Warren Stafford, was outstanding with both bat and ball, while the batting of Chas Sheppard and
the flight and guile of James Excell provided good support.
Batting W. Stafford* 426 at 47.33; C. Sheppard 344 at 43.00; S. Whittaker 211 at 35.16; O. Lewis 180 at 30.00.
Bowling W. Stafford 29 at 8.82; J. Excell 24 at 12.58.

King's College School, Wimbledon   P16 W8 L4 D4 A1

Despite not having played cricket for four years, Blake Hutchins was the leading wicket-taker.
Batting T. W. Eaves 589 at 39.26; G. E. Peck 227 at 28.37; H. F. Jones* 321 at 22.92; O. Fernie 331 at 22.06;
J. J. Corbett 187 at 20.77; O. H. Bretton 169 at 16.90; J. J. Bensohn 186 at 15.50.
Bowling J. C. C. Walton 12 at 10.66; B. Hutchins 26 at 12.88; A. H. Shandro 24 at 13.66; C. T. Foster 24 at
15.87; J. J. Bensohn 23 at 21.04; H. F. Jones 12 at 24.16.

King's School, Bruton   P15 W2 L13 D0 A3

Too many dropped catches meant this was a frustrating season of near misses. Only Andrew
Grazette, the captain, could be relied on for runs. The bowling, however, was strong: Marcus
Savage, Archie Bush, David Ball and Matthew Masters all took at least 20 wickets.
Batting A. J. Grazette 411 at 37.36; T. L. Martin 211 at 15.07; S. J. U. Todd 154 at 12.83; D. Ball 159 at 12.23.
Bowling A. J. Grazette 13 at 13.86; M. Masters 20 at 17.40; D. Ball 20 at 19.10; M. F. Savage 20 at 19.90;
A. J. Bush 21 at 20.71.

King's School, Canterbury
P17 W4 L6 D7 A3

The pace bowling was spearheaded by Toby Humphrey and George Brooke, who between them seized 57 wickets. William Bruce's potent leg-spin added variety.

Batting P. G. Dixey 316 at 22.57; J. D. E. Stubbs 292 at 20.85; P. R. Archer 205 at 20.50; M. E. B. Humphrey 288 at 19.20; G. H. B. Brooke 181 at 18.10; J. A. Ellis* 248 at 16.53; H. L. Doulton 181 at 15.08.

Bowling G. H. B. Brooke 29 at 14.75; T. J. L. Humphrey 28 at 19.25; A. L. Thorne 24 at 21.58; H. L. Doulton 13 at 22.15.

King's School, Chester
P14 W7 L3 D4

Although the bowling lacked penetration, the side enjoyed much success with the bat, including a school-record 267 for seven in 40 overs against King William's College, Isle of Man. Brothers Freddie and Edward Owen topped batting and bowling averages respectively.

Batting F. G. Owen 247 at 61.75; B. R. Jordan 209 at 41.80; G. N. Hughes 308 at 30.80; C. B. Sanderson 206 at 25.75; D. J. Newham 245 at 24.50; E. A. N. Whittaker 248 at 20.66.

Bowling E. L. Owen* 20 at 15.25.

King's School, Ely
P13 W3 L7 D3 A3

A young side, sometimes fielding five Under-15s, made encouraging progress, though the bowling had few teeth. Only once was 14-year-old Ben Howgego dismissed for under 40, and he went on to play for South of England Under-14.

Batting B. H. N. Howgego 345 at 49.28; D. R. F. Cannie* 423 at 38.45; J. W. Payne 178 at 25.42; H. C. Sperling 168 at 24.00.

Bowling L. P. Hayden 16 at 28.18; H. C. Sperling 10 at 30.00.

King's School, Macclesfield
P20 W14 L3 D3 A2

In an excellent season that brought a record number of victories, Tom Isherwood topped both averages. The player of the year, though, was Alan Day, who fell 13 short of 1,000 runs. John Arnfield proved a hostile opening bowler and James Barratt, who also played at Under-14 level, took wickets consistently with his left-arm spin. Stephen Allday scored runs quickly and was an outstanding fielder.

Batting T. Isherwood* 567 at 56.70; A. Day 987 at 54.83; O. Kenyon 555 at 32.64; S. Allday 346 at 28.83; J. Perring 212 at 15.14.

Bowling T. Isherwood 30 at 16.03; T. Davenport 19 at 16.89; J. Arnfield 28 at 17.03; O. Kenyon 16 at 19.75; J. Barratt 26 at 19.88; A. Day 16 at 27.31.

King's School, Rochester
P13 W5 L4 D4 A4

The school had a talented young side, very strong in batting but lacking either a strike bowler or an accurate spinner. Apart from a poor game against MCC, the team remained competitive, and were close to victory in all their drawn games.

Batting J. N. Butler 440 at 55.00; C. A. Maurice 493 at 44.81; M. J. Melford 171 at 42.75; B. D. Phillips 364 at 40.44; S. G. Wakeman 320 at 26.66; R. D. Barrett 168 at 21.00.

Bowling R. Lakhera 14 at 15.00; J. A. W. Warner 14 at 17.85; J. M. Shakespeare 28 at 19.35; C. A. Maurice 18 at 23.72.

King's School, Tynemouth
P11 W1 L8 D2

Although the team endured a tough season, there was great hope for the future. All who appeared in the final three fixtures should return in 2003, and only one player from the upper sixth appeared regularly. Toby Flood led the side with increasing confidence, and Tom Pollock showed he could occupy the crease.

Batting T. J. Pollock 259 at 25.90; T. G. A. Flood* 246 at 24.60; L. R. N. Dobbin 150 at 21.42.

Bowling No one took ten wickets. The leading bowler was T. J. Pollock, who took nine at 16.33.

King's School, Worcester
P22 W16 L4 D2

Outstanding all-round performances from opening batsmen Phil Burdon and Joe Robinson helped King's to a record 16 wins, with only one defeat against other schools. The openers put on eight century partnerships, thrice passing 150. Nicholas Major, the captain, completed a formidable top three.

Batting P. A. Burdon 946 at 49.78; J. W. Robinson 862 at 45.36; N. O. S. Major* 592 at 42.28; H. Dimond 292 at 20.85; O. Fiaz 155 at 19.37; J. R. Gwynne 285 at 17.81.

Alex Lacey (*left*) of Kimbolton averaged 20 with the ball and 57 with the bat. Shivan Dave took 41 wickets at less than eight for Merchant Taylors', Northwood.

Bowling O. Fiaz 30 at 17.56; J. W. Robinson 39 at 17.61; W. B. C. Hardy 10 at 20.90; P. A. Burdon 30 at 26.06; T. P. Cullen 17 at 28.52; W. M. Smith 12 at 32.08.

Kingston Grammar School
P10 W1 L8 D1

The side was capable of good cricket but managed to sustain it only during the win against Sutton. Ben Collier was the only batsman to reach 50 all season. Hanzaq Mir's opening spells had pace and venom, while Sebastian Baxter's medium pace was effective. Against KES, Witley, Ben Collier took six for 20.
Batting B. Collier 179 at 19.88.
Bowling S. Baxter 12 at 6.08; B. Collier 11 at 14.00.

Kingswood School
P10 W8 L2 D0

Another successful season saw Jack Seddon, in his fifth year in the side, hit two hundreds and became Kingswood's leading aggregate run-scorer. He also played for Somerset Under-19s. Daniel Gerrish's wickets came at a miserly cost. Kingswood retained the Bath and Districts League title.
Batting J. Seddon* 628 at 62.80; G. Cooper 222 at 22.20; A. Hola-Peryer 159 at 17.66.
Bowling D. Gerrish 23 at 9.86; G. Cooper 23 at 11.17; C. Magniac 12 at 19.08; J. West 13 at 19.92; B. Booth 14 at 20.78.

Lancing College
P13 W6 L5 D2 A4

Robert Wakeford scored heavily and attractively; he received solid support from Alexander Dodsworth and Jeremy Green. Angus Williams's seam bowling improved significantly.
Batting R. H. Wakeford* 484 at 53.77; J. A. G. Green 309 at 44.14; A. G. Dodsworth 210 at 35.00; J. F. Taylor 158 at 26.33.
Bowling A. D. Williams 14 at 12.28; B. J. M. Hanley 14 at 16.07; R. H. Wakeford 16 at 16.87; J. A. G. Green 13 at 19.53; J. D. Worcester 10 at 21.00.

Leeds Grammar School
P13 W8 L1 D4 A4

Alex Blakeborough, the outstanding batsman of a very good team, was ably supported by younger colleagues. Off-spinner Toby Jacklin had a spectacular first year in the XI and his brother Ben was a superb captain.
Batting A. J. Blakeborough 641 at 80.12; A. M. Guest 192 at 38.40; B. D. Jacklin* 172 at 28.66; D. J. Stokoe 229 at 19.08.
Bowling T. J. Jacklin 40 at 10.65; B. D. Jacklin 23 at 15.56; B. R. Maude 11 at 22.63.

Liverpool College
P11 W1 L8 D2 A2

Though results were poor, this was still an excellent season. The side enjoyed good team spirit, and the problems that theoretically came with the exam period never materialised.
Batting J. Howarth 527 at 52.70.
Bowling M. Melia 20 at 23.70.

Llandovery College
P10 W3 L6 D1

Batting B. Esterhuizen 183 at 18.30.
Bowling B. Esterhuizen 15 at 18.93; O. R. Davies* 14 at 20.28.

Lord Wandsworth College
P14 W8 L1 D5 A2

Ten of the side had played the previous summer and, taken together, these were the two most successful years in the school's history – 20 wins in 37 games. Toby Martin was one of the country's best schoolboy bowlers, taking 127 wickets in his career to break the school record, while Jon Ablett was a capable captain. However, success ultimately derived from teamwork.
Batting J. J. Ablett* 695 at 77.22; M. J. Horn 303 at 37.87; J. D. Irving 306 at 21.85; J. A. D. Colvin 250 at 20.83; L. A. Houghton 183 at 13.07.
Bowling T. H. Martin 44 at 12.00; C. W. Pidgeon 26 at 20.57; J. C. McCardle 13 at 25.76.

Lord Williams's School
P13 W8 L2 D3 A1

First XI opener James Cook scored 203 not out for Oxfordshire Under-17s, a county youth record, and made his Minor County debut.
Batting A. Wynd 353 at 44.12; C. Wynd 327 at 40.87; J. Hewitt 280 at 35.00; J. Cook 229 at 28.62.
Bowling J. Hewitt 15 at 10.40; W. Eason 14 at 12.07; J. Shirley 15 at 12.20.

Loughborough Grammar School
P15 W6 L6 D3 A1

A very young side, consisting of seven fifth years and four fourth-formers, improved dramatically as the season progressed. Sam Underwood bowled with real pace, and the bowling and fielding was generally good. Under-15 Charlie Krarup took his chance and finished top of the batting averages; otherwise, the batting was disappointing.
Batting C. M. Krarup 223 at 55.75; S. J. Bird 298 at 29.80; D. J. Howgate 314 at 24.15; P. S. Broster 215 at 19.54; R. M. Worrall 220 at 16.92.
Bowling S. J. Underwood 16 at 15.31; H. F. Gurney 12 at 25.41; M. Ashcroft 16 at 27.62; F. B. Baker 13 at 28.15.

Malvern College
P19 W12 L4 D3 A1

Malvern stuck to traditional declaration games, played positive cricket and were not afraid to lose: just three of 19 matches were drawn. Charles Tolchard is the son of Roger (Leicestershire and England), Will Murtagh the son of Andy (Hampshire).
Batting W. M. Gifford 738 at 61.50; C. Wood 725 at 48.33; W. A. Murtagh 240 at 34.28; B. W. Edkins 459 at 30.60; H. D. Bailey* 156 at 17.33; C. W. Tolchard 208 at 13.00.
Bowling E. C. Latter 24 at 13.08; M. J. G. King 14 at 14.14; G. P. Vaughan 39 at 15.07; C. W. Tolchard 22 at 15.77; W. M. Gifford 10 at 18.80; H. D. Bailey 16 at 19.25; B. W. Edkins 20 at 22.35.

Manchester Grammar School
P15 W5 L4 D6 A3

Batting D. C. Madden 458 at 41.63; P. C. Martin 277 at 27.70; D. R. Leech 235 at 21.36; R. J. Hodges 157 at 19.62; M. R. A. Tufft* 200 at 16.66.
Bowling R. A. Partington 24 at 19.90; P. C. Martin 28 at 20.89; D. A. Woods 20 at 27.35.

Marlborough College
P14 W7 L4 D3 A1

Marlborough won the Cheltenham Schools Festival and recorded more wins than for several seasons. These were fine achievements for a young team that played naïve cricket early in the season. Later success was based on astute captaincy from Ed Nicholson, tight bowling, excellent fielding and some good run-chases. Robbie Williams, an England Under-15 player, topped both averages.
Batting R. Williams 178 at 29.66; G. Hawley 295 at 26.81; J. Bill 365 at 26.07; E. Nicholson* 306 at 25.50; H. Harvey 256 at 21.33; J. Sinclair 221 at 20.09.
Bowling R. Williams 17 at 12.29; T. Forsythe 19 at 15.73; O. Hextall 30 at 18.16; W. Davies 21 at 19.52.

Merchant Taylors' School, Crosby P12 W5 L2 D5 A2

Batting J. F. Wildman 411 at 68.50; J. Cole 172 at 28.66; G. A. Barry 191 at 27.28.
Bowling G. W. Davies 10 at 9.50; D. M. Trapp 17 at 10.23; J. F. Wildman 18 at 12.33; G. A. Barry 17 at 12.94.

Merchant Taylors' School, Northwood P17 W9 L3 D5

The side was well captained by Steffan James, in his fifth season in the side. Shivan Dave was a capable opening bowler, and Karan Chopra again proved a reliable wicket-keeper/batsman.
Batting R. J. M. Booth 393 at 26.20; S. G. James* 211 at 21.10; V. V. Le Vesconte 165 at 18.33; A. P. Farfan 203 at 16.91; A. Kaul 180 at 12.85.
Bowling S. N. Dave 41 at 7.51; S. K. Haider 10 at 8.40; A. Kaul 13 at 11.61; S. G. James 25 at 13.32; V. Paul 10 at 20.30; R. J. M. Booth 17 at 23.05.

Merchiston Castle School P12 W5 L6 D1 A4

Despite the wettest season in living memory, a young side developed well, with James Welch and Michael Beaumont the cornerstones. Both averaged around 50 – some achievement on damp wickets. Beaumont's seven for 20 against Fettes included a hat-trick; he also took five for 19 in the second innings and scored an unbeaten century.
Batting J. W. Welch 365 at 52.14; M. E. Beaumont 483 at 48.30.
Bowling M. E. Beaumont 33 at 9.81; J. W. Welch 21 at 13.19; R. J. C. Windle 11 at 23.54.

Mill Hill School P13 W8 L4 D1 A1

Batting M. Hirsch* 447 at 40.63; M. Halstead 205 at 22.77; A. Martins-Craig 195 at 21.66; P. Mason 180 at 20.00; M. Stein 216 at 18.00; J. Hutcheson 150 at 13.63.
Bowling A. Martins-Craig 29 at 12.37; J. Hutcheson 19 at 16.15; I. Raja 10 at 20.20; M. Khan 10 at 23.00.

Millfield School P13 W9 L2 D2 A2

A successful season included wins against Exeter University First XI, Somerset Academy, Eton and Tonbridge. Success was based on all-round contributions by all the players. The fielding was outstanding.
Batting I. R. Haley* 320 at 64.00; R. T. Timms 439 at 48.77; L. A. Smith 370 at 46.25; R. L. S. Stokes 353 at 35.30; K. J. Latouf 176 at 29.33.
Bowling J. M-F. Rawson 14 at 12.14; L. A. Smith 15 at 12.60; J. C. Hildreth 17 at 13.05; C. W. N. Taylor 17 at 14.11; J. J. Becher 11 at 17.54.

Monkton Combe P15 W4 L10 D1 A2

An inability to make defendable totals meant this was a disappointing season. However, the side bowled and fielded tidily.
Batting J. Auld 358 at 27.53; P. Auld 170 at 18.88; H. J. H. Williams 201 at 15.46; J. A. Lowde 182 at 15.16.
Bowling T. A. H. Quayle* 19 at 17.31; R. N. B. Baddeley 16 at 22.43.

Monmouth School P14 W5 L5 D4

An excellent victory against MCC was the highlight of an otherwise disappointing season. The opening attack of Ben Pike and Tom Robinson caused trouble all season, and the batting and keeping of Ian Clayton was excellent.
Batting I. A. Clayton 499 at 38.38; M. Robinson 257 at 25.70; J. Richards 284 at 21.84; W. Jacks 186 at 20.66; L. Cronk 159 at 14.45.
Bowling B. R. Pike* 22 at 12.18; T. Robinson 28 at 13.60; L. Cronk 16 at 28.06.

Newcastle-under-Lyme School P14 W6 L4 D4 A1

The school won six matches in convincing style, and two of the four defeats came against exceptionally strong adult sides. Christopher Whalley, an Under-16, took six for 18 against Stockport Grammar School and seven for 22 against Rydal Penrhos. Simon Howland scored an unbeaten 114 against King's, Tynemouth.
Batting A. Merali 168 at 56.00; D. J. Moss* 292 at 29.20; V. Kumar 220 at 27.50; J. D. Wright 308 at 23.69; S. J. P. Howland 278 at 21.38.
Bowling C. D. Whalley 27 at 13.40; B. W. R. Furnival 13 at 15.53; D. J. Moss 17 at 23.52.

Norwich School
P17 W12 L4 D1 A2

Left-arm spinner George Walker played frequently for Leicestershire Second XI and also made his first-class debut against Kent. His absence meant greater responsibilities for the rest of the team, who rose to the challenge and won more games than for many years. The batting was dependent on the prolific Edward Foster and Charles Webster; Mark Proctor took most wickets. The season finished with a testing but successful tour of Antigua.

Batting E. J. Foster 727 at 55.92; C. J. M. Webster 405 at 40.50; P. W. Robinson 235 at 21.36; E. D. Hopkins* 274 at 21.07; A. J. Kelly 195 at 16.25.
Bowling G. W. Walker 15 at 2.33; M. A. M. Riches 13 at 12.69; E. J. Foster 19 at 14.94; C. J. M. Webster 18 at 17.22; M. H. Proctor 25 at 17.28; J. Walton 15 at 23.66; J. O. Atkinson 11 at 30.09.

Nottingham High School
P14 W4 L8 D2 A1

The school fielded a young side, but most should be back next season, under the same captain.
Batting T. R. Chalkley* 439 at 36.58; C. C. J. Nembhard 209 at 29.85; M. Seaton 206 at 20.60; C. P. Saxton 169 at 18.77; J. A. Coupland 193 at 16.08; R. A. Sargent 185 at 14.23.
Bowling C. J. Harrison 23 at 13.08; D. J. Howell 15 at 25.86; T. R. Chalkley 11 at 27.63; J. C. Sharpe 10 at 31.30.

Oakham School
P18 W9 L3 D6

A very strong batting side had a successful season. Against the MCC, the school successfully chased a mammoth 284. Colt Brian Makwana headed the batting averages and two other colts, Paul Cook and Stuart Broad, were the leading wicket-takers. Broad is the son of the England cricketer, Chris.
Batting B. Makwana 493 at 54.77; M. Matthews 294 at 49.00; G. Firmin 556 at 46.33; W. Wright 678 at 42.37; M. Boyce 362 at 36.20; R. Cook 401 at 28.64; S. Taylor 153 at 25.50; P. Cook 164 at 18.22.
Bowling W. Wright 12 at 14.16; P. Cook 27 at 16.37; S. Broad 29 at 16.68; M. Matthews 12 at 27.75; R. Cook 14 at 33.00.

The Oratory School
P16 W9 L6 D1

Batting L. W. Roycroft 422 at 60.28; G. A. Napier 365 at 33.18; R. E. Greenland 211 at 30.14; T. T. Bailey 356 at 25.42.
Bowling L. W. Roycroft 27 at 14.25; R. E. Greenland 18 at 22.50.

Oswestry School
P7 W1 L6 D0

Batting M. S. Leonard 152 at 38.00.
Bowling C. Sproulle* 11 at 19.63.

Oundle School
P24 W11 L4 D9 A3

A young team playing attacking cricket had an outstanding season. Cameron Wake hit most runs and grabbed most wickets, bowling a mixture of leg-spin and seam. Together with wicket-keeper/batsman Mark Phythian, he was selected for the ECB Schools East v West game; Wake also played for ECB Schools Under-18s. Oundle became the first HMC school to play limited-overs games under National League rules, including coloured clothing, a white ball and black sightscreens.
Batting C. J. Wake 843 at 49.58; R. M. Fahrenheim 690 at 38.33; M. J. Phythian* 539 at 31.70; M. L. Austin 368 at 26.28; J. I. Hay 230 at 23.00; T. Newton 248 at 20.66; E. J. Clough 329 at 20.56; C. M. Morris 213 at 15.21.
Bowling P. J. Foster 34 at 16.20; C. M. Morris 29 at 20.13; C. J. Wake 38 at 21.92; R. S. Legget 10 at 23.10; J. I. Hay 22 at 25.50.

The Perse School, Cambridge
P16 W5 L5 D6

The side won the County Cup. Captain Duncan Simmonds's all-round abilities earned him the cricketer of the season trophy.
Batting O. R. Gregory 458 at 32.71; T. Wilkins 367 at 30.58; J. E. Hayden-Smith 367 at 24.46; D. G. M. Simmonds* 262 at 23.81; J. A. M. Crawford 234 at 21.27; B. A. J. Apperly 211 at 17.58.
Bowling D. G. M. Simmonds 18 at 19.38; T. A. Tippen 11 at 20.36; D. E. Howells 14 at 21.35; T. Wilkins 14 at 25.42; J. A. M. Crawford 18 at 26.72; J. E. Hayden-Smith 15 at 27.86.

Plymouth College

P11 W2 L2 D7 A7

Despite severe disruption by the weather, 2002 was a successful season. Captain James Toms hit a magnificent unbeaten 201 – the highest score on the school wicket – and he led the college to victory in the four-counties cricket festival held at Abbotsholme School, Derbyshire.
Batting J. Toms* 751 at 125.16; P. Wass 159 at 19.87.
Bowling J. Toms 24 at 12.25; P. Thorpe 11 at 13.81.

Pocklington School

P15 W7 L3 D5 A2

Richard Owen's three for 53 included a hat-trick.
Batting H. J. Mitchell 698 at 53.69; J. L. T. Bolam 471 at 52.33; R. G. Booth 377 at 41.88; R. J. G. Owen* 190 at 31.66; T. P. Nettleton 348 at 26.76; P. Van Dijk 236 at 26.22.
Bowling R. G. Booth 26 at 14.88; D. J. Mays 16 at 22.56; R. J. G. Owen 16 at 22.62; I. R. L. Gladstone 14 at 27.35; S. A. Boyes 16 at 34.18.

Portsmouth Grammar School

P14 W6 L7 D1 A2

A young side relied heavily on captain Benjamin Morgan for runs and wickets. Useful support came from Edward Dixon-Lowe, who took 20 wickets in his first season.
Batting B. Morgan* 450 at 50.00; D. Neville 173 at 24.71; M. Saunders 224 at 18.66; S. Khoyratty 204 at 17.00.
Bowling E. Dixon-Lowe 20 at 17.65; A. Jessop 14 at 21.64; B. Morgan 11 at 24.45; M. Saunders 10 at 44.80.

Prior Park College

P13 W0 L11 D2 A1

Too much limited-overs cricket left a spirited and committed, though inexperienced, team with an undeserved record.
Batting T. W. Grimshaw 279 at 23.25; A. Creed 210 at 21.00; J. L. Wheeler 180 at 16.36.
Bowling J. L. Wheeler 21 at 17.80; B. J. Todd 10 at 19.80; S. L. Williams 18 at 20.61.

Queen Elizabeth Grammar School, Wakefield

P12 W5 L6 D1 A1

All the defeats came in close contests. This was a young side, with only captain David Sugden in the upper sixth. Daniel Wood and Andrew Rennison played for county Under-15 sides.
Batting D. Wood 389 at 43.22; A. Rennison 306 at 34.00; T. Harrison 182 at 22.75; J. Barkley 163 at 20.37; R. Greatrick 205 at 18.63.
Bowling J. Barkley 11 at 15.18; D. Sugden* 15 at 17.26; J. Bluemink 10 at 18.40; D. Wood 10 at 28.00.

Queen Elizabeth's Hospital

P10 W7 L2 D1 A2

Batting H. J. Hanchet* 404 at 40.40; A. J. Bamber 211 at 21.10; G. T. Humphreys 155 at 14.09.
Bowling M. J. Bean 11 at 7.90; T. Hamid 23 at 8.21; J. R. Burberry 15 at 10.00.

Queen's College, Taunton

P13 W1 L8 D4 A4

A young side struggled through a rain-affected season. Oliver Stewart showed promise as an all-rounder and Lawrence Evans led the batting.
Batting L. M. Evans 292 at 24.33; J. W. M. Butler 220 at 18.33; R. A. Stanley 202 at 16.83; O. J. Stewart 180 at 15.00.
Bowling O. J. Stewart 18 at 13.00; J. A. Kelly 14 at 20.71; A. G. Needs* 10 at 40.30.

Radley College

P14 W4 L4 D6

A very young side – there were three Under-15s and two Under-16s – and a lack of penetration in the bowling made this a tough season. Simon Butler was the leading run-scorer, and he shouldered much of the bowling too, along with Inderneel Singh and George Foxall. Charles Duffell was an outstanding wicket-keeper.
Batting S. M. Butler* 569 at 43.76; D. P. R. Clements 176 at 35.20; J. D. J. Corry 351 at 25.07; M. J. A. Yorke-Long 305 at 21.78; B. S. Dancy 200 at 20.00; T. A. B. Everitt 196 at 19.60.
Bowling G. J. Foxall 14 at 22.50; I. Singh 19 at 28.78; S. M. Butler 13 at 30.69.

Ratcliffe College

P12 W1 L6 D5 A1

This was a very disappointing season, made the more difficult by the premature departure of three Leicestershire Under-16 players and the ever-increasing pressure of exams.
Batting A. J. Smith 188 at 26.85; T. Cabrelli* 260 at 26.00; J. A. Taylor 159 at 17.66.
Bowling A. J. Smith 16 at 21.68; A. Frith 14 at 26.00.

Reading School
P12 W5 L3 D4 A2

Despite the loss of Martin Bushell and Tom Burrows to the Hampshire Academy for several matches, the side enjoyed a reasonably successful season.
Batting J. E. Lloyd 163 at 81.50; M. Bushell 208 at 52.00; T. G. Burrows 182 at 45.50; G. J. Duncan 230 at 25.55.
Bowling M. Ahmed 21 at 11.09; M. R. Jubb* 18 at 11.11; T. J. H. Jacob 12 at 17.41.

Reed's School
P13 W5 L2 D6 A4

An inexperienced attack did surprisingly well and helped give Reed's a pleasing season. James Morrison led by example, topping both averages. His 173 against Lord Wandsworth College was a school record. Reed's beat the MCC for the first time in many years.
Batting J. I. Morrison* 655 at 65.50; J. D. Worrall 257 at 32.12; S. C. Waller 265 at 24.09; S. J. Day 256 at 21.33.
Bowling J. I. Morrison 21 at 16.80; N. J. Davies 19 at 21.05; E. J. Hoadley 16 at 21.12; D. W. Owen 12 at 24.83; J. Dodd 15 at 27.93.

Rendcomb College
P12 W5 L1 D6

A hugely successful season was rounded off with an enjoyable tour to Malta.
Batting S. Hicks 309 at 38.62; L. Baghdadi 227 at 32.42; S. Ward 216 at 30.85.
Bowling S. Hicks 21 at 12.09; R. Burden 10 at 14.40; M. Hutchins 18 at 19.72; J. Raby* 11 at 20.63; C. Jeffreys 12 at 27.50.

Repton School
P15 W4 L7 D4 A1

Batting E. Crowther* 574 at 57.40; M. Pointer 304 at 38.00; E. Corbett 170 at 21.25; M. Pearson 151 at 18.87; O. Dacey 224 at 18.66; M. Edgerton 170 at 14.16.
Bowling S. Chilman 33 at 17.30; E. Corbett 22 at 25.59; T. Henry 19 at 27.57.

Rossall School
P13 W3 L8 D2 A1

Batting I. A. Swaine 163 at 18.11; R. V. Dingle* 197 at 17.90; J. B. Preston 184 at 16.72; P. F. Heald 188 at 14.46; J. A. Heald 173 at 14.41; F. Hameed 166 at 12.76.
Bowling R. V. Dingle 32 at 14.50; J. A. Heald 15 at 20.33; J. B. Preston 24 at 20.75; P. F. Heald 13 at 30.07.

Royal Grammar School, Colchester
P20 W3 L11 D6 A2

In a bowler-friendly season, the team was seriously short of runs, with several senior batsmen producing fewer than expected. The consistent excellence of Peter Smith often salvaged self-respect in defence of low totals, and his season's best of six for 17 secured a rare victory.
Batting J. Warner 507 at 25.35; S. Hummerstone 527 at 25.09; T. W. R. George 464 at 22.09; M. Tyler* 160 at 14.54; N. S. Coles 161 at 13.41.
Bowling P. C. Smith 39 at 17.79; R. A. Lomer 26 at 28.34; T. W. R. George 17 at 29.00; N. S. Coles 16 at 31.50; M. Tyler 17 at 37.47.

Royal Grammar School, Guildford
P19 W13 L2 D4 A1

The side won 13 games, including all their matches at the RGS Festival. The batting was strong and runs were scored consistently by many players. William Sabey spearheaded the bowling, and captain Peter Hosier's leadership was invaluable. The season ended with a successful tour to Barbados and Antigua.
Batting P. Hosier* 344 at 38.22; S. Coomer 388 at 35.27; C. Nelson 204 at 34.00; T. Barford 529 at 33.06; W. Sabey 317 at 31.41; T. Markham 470 at 26.11; S. Barnsley 291 at 20.78.
Bowling M. Ackroyd 26 at 16.30; S. MacLean 11 at 18.09; W. Sabey 32 at 18.96; D. Nelson 27 at 20.03; A. Wilson 20 at 23.25.

Royal Grammar School, Lancaster
P19 W10 L4 D5 A2

Lancaster were undefeated in their home season and held the upper hand in every game. Unusually, weather forced the abandonment of just two matches. All four defeats came at the 16th Sir Garfield Sobers International Schools Tournament in Barbados, where Lancaster won six games to finish the highest-placed English team.
Batting D. J. Hagen 707 at 37.21; T. D. Battarbee 536 at 33.50; G. J. Hiron 317 at 26.41; B. P. Hughes* 356 at 22.25; C. R. Glover 195 at 21.66; D. M. Kidd 232 at 17.84; B. Akrigg 175 at 15.90.
Bowling M. A. Bateson 14 at 8.00; C. R. Glover 37 at 11.24; J. P. Toulmin 29 at 12.75; B. P. Hughes 10 at 12.90; D. Roberts 10 at 15.10; D. M. Kidd 25 at 18.64; W. Quinn 17 at 27.23.

Top of the averages: Mark Paine (*left*) averaged 127 for Simon Langton GS, while James Toms finished second with 125. One of the country's top all-rounders, he also took 24 wickets at 12 for Plymouth College.

Royal Grammar School, Newcastle   P15 W7 L5 D3 A5

Batting M. M. Gray* 427 at 53.37; M. C. Phillips 399 at 33.25; P. T. Burton 380 at 31.66; Z. U. D. Khan 164 at 20.50.
Bowling Z. U. D. Khan 15 at 14.00; I. Maini 16 at 15.56; M. C. Phillips 14 at 15.92; C. J. J. Wilson 18 at 19.05; R. P. Malcolm 11 at 28.00; B. M. Ahmad 11 at 30.81.

Royal Grammar School, Worcester   P20 W7 L12 D1 A2

A young side with a young captain learned plenty during the summer. James Watkins scored the bulk of the runs and displayed sound temperament and technique. The bowling relied on the persistence and accuracy of Miles Illingworth, Oliver Butterworth and Dominic Harris. Illingworth, son of Richard (Worcestershire, Derbyshire and England), maintained a family tradition by bowling accurate left-arm spin.
Batting J. R. Watkins* 671 at 39.47; G. W. Gough 366 at 26.14; M. J. R. Illingworth 231 at 19.25; A. S. Wilkinson 255 at 18.21; D. P. Harris 221 at 17.00; T. G. Payton 269 at 14.94; O. R. C. Butterworth 170 at 13.07.
Bowling O. J. Haines 11 at 12.18; T. J. R. Ohlson 17 at 19.64; G. W. Gough 11 at 21.81; M. J. R. Illingworth 19 at 23.57; O. R. C. Butterworth 18 at 28.00; D. P. Harris 15 at 30.86.

Rugby School   P15 W1 L8 D6 A2

Batting J. F. Noble* 397 at 30.53; R. L. H. Crawford 383 at 29.46; H. Connell 228 at 28.50; S. C. V. Greaves 218 at 19.81.
Bowling O. Benzie 13 at 21.38; S. C. V. Greaves 15 at 31.60; J. F. Nob 18 at 36.27.

Rydal Penrhos, Colwyn Bay   P8 W4 L2 D2 A1

David Watkins captained an experienced team with only one addition from 2001. Against Liverpool College, Watkins and Craig Stock put on an unbeaten 241 for the fourth wicket, a school record. Stock was player of the tournament at Rydal's end-of-season festival. Josh Leach played for Wales Under-14s.
Batting D. M. Watkins* 344 at 57.33; C. D. R. Stock 326 at 46.57; P. J. H. Leach 230 at 46.00.
Bowling P. J. H. Leach 14 at 15.42; S. J. Wilson 11 at 20.90; C. D. R. Stock 12 at 23.83.

St Albans School
P11 W8 L1 D2 A3

A side with an inexperienced bowling attack was well led by Nick Lamb, the youngest captain in 100 years. Lamb, the son of ECB chief executive, Tim, extracted wins in some unlikely circumstances and finished with an excellent record. Next summer the school is due to play on a new 70-acre ground.

Batting N. Lamb* 387 at 35.18; E. Charlesworth 274 at 27.40; M. Searle 265 at 24.09.
Bowling A. Skovberg-Hansen 10 at 26.40.

St Dunstan's College
P11 W1 L7 D3

Batting S. Giddins* 307 at 27.90; A. Darroch 266 at 24.18; W. Taylor 200 at 22.22; A. Mahey 188 at 18.80.
Bowling No one took ten wickets.

St Edmund's College, Ware
P4 W0 L3 D1 A3

The most rain-affected season since 1994.
Batting No one scored 150 runs. The leading batsman was P. Loughrey, who scored 148 at 37.00.
Bowling No one took ten wickets. The leading bowler was T. Gribbin, who took seven at 20.71.

St Edmund's School, Canterbury
P12 W6 L5 D1 A4

Dominic Chambers was once again the linchpin, scoring 864 runs, including four hundreds and three fifties. In four seasons in the First XI, he made a remarkable 2,701 runs at an average of 67, smashing the school record. Kevin Surujlal bowled with pace and aggression, and took six for six against Dover College. He was also an exciting middle-order batsman.

Batting D. Chambers* 846 at 70.50; K. Surujlal 165 at 33.00; A. Cork 288 at 28.80; S. Barda 276 at 25.09; R. Waitt 281 at 23.41.
Bowling K. Surujlal 23 at 18.21; P. Masayavanij 14 at 18.78; A. Cork 16 at 25.25; W. Hilary 10 at 35.30.

St Edward's School, Oxford
P13 W3 L4 D6

Batting M. C. Sutton 450 at 50.00; T. H. Newell* 352 at 35.20; R. W. Abraham 154 at 30.80; J. B. Barrett 391 at 30.07; J. W. H. Gabriel 180 at 18.00.m
Bowling M. C. Sutton 28 at 19.21; J. W. H. Gabriel 21 at 19.52; W. G. F. Myers 12 at 23.83.

St George's College, Weybridge
P18 W6 L7 D5 A2

Batting M. J. Arnot* 558 at 34.87; T. N. J. Doran 411 at 29.35; J. D. Hardman 273 at 17.06; T. M. Grant 223 at 15.92; S. P. Twist 173 at 12.35.
Bowling D. Meers 21 at 14.42; P. L. Haydon 15 at 18.00; B. T. Williams 15 at 27.86; A. J. Wood 10 at 27.90; S. K. Henry 16 at 32.87.

St John's School, Leatherhead
P18 W11 L3 D4

The team won a record number of matches. All the side were in the lower sixth.
Batting P. C. F. Scott 347 at 43.37; T. G. A. Close 221 at 27.62; D. J. Balcombe 357 at 23.80; P. D. Anderson 188 at 23.50; G. D. Littlejohns 206 at 20.60.
Bowling J. R. Amos 22 at 19.50; P. D. Anderson 27 at 21.22; P. M. Cohen 24 at 22.29.

St Lawrence College
P11 W2 L6 D3 A1

Despite several very close matches and two good wins, the team struggled. The batting relied upon the captain and the two Rices, Mark (son of former Nottinghamshire all-rounder, Clive Rice), and his cousin Michael.
Batting M. C. D. Rice 391 at 35.54; M. R. Rice 318 at 28.90; C. P. Baker* 174 at 15.81.
Bowling N. Wake 14 at 16.21; C. P. Baker 13 at 18.69; M. R. Rice 20 at 19.05; M. C. D. Rice 20 at 20.55.

St Paul's School
P15 W6 L7 D2

Ben Duncan played for an ECB Schools XI against India Under-19 and was the dominant performer for St Paul's. Fifteen-year-old Jake Lofdahl had an impressive first season, keeping wicket well and scoring over 400 runs.
Batting B. J. Duncan* 644 at 53.66; J. J. Lofdahl 441 at 31.50; F. W. H. Abrahams 320 at 21.33; A. T. L. Lee 161 at 20.12; P. B. Desai 168 at 15.00.
Bowling E. R. H. Poland 22 at 14.95; B. J. Duncan 20 at 18.10; P. B. Desai 14 at 20.57; I. M. R. Ladak 18 at 21.61; A. T. L. Lee 15 at 25.20; A. S. Charkham 11 at 31.63.

St Peter's School, York
P17 W10 L2 D5 A3

St Peter's had a successful season, winning ten out of 15 completed matches. The team played good, positive cricket and was well captained by James Taylor, the leading batsman. He was supported by all-rounders Tom Main and Tom Bartram and by left-arm spinner Tom Woolsey, an Under-15 who took 51 wickets at 13.27.

Batting J. E. Taylor* 534 at 41.07; T. Main 295 at 32.77; T. S. Bartram 350 at 26.92; A. J. Chalmers 246 at 24.60; M. S. Hodsdon 229 at 17.61.
Bowling T. J. Woolsey 51 at 13.27; T. S. Bartram 28 at 21.28; T. Main 20 at 28.55; J. P. Sweeting 10 at 32.60.

Sedbergh School
P14 W4 L8 D2

This was a better season than the results might suggest. John Mason was the outstanding batsman, while Andrew Robertson, the only centurion, showed promise. Craig Barrington was by far Sedbergh's best bowler, taking 35 wickets at under ten. Christian Howard was also effective. The school defeated the MCC for the second year running.

Batting J. Mason 541 at 49.18; A. Robertson 505 at 38.84; E. Parker 263 at 32.87; T. Laidler 178 at 14.83.
Bowling C. Barrington 35 at 9.77; C. Howard 25 at 17.44.

Sevenoaks School
P12 W1 L10 D1 A3

Batting S. Sharma* 412 at 37.45; K. Shah 276 at 25.09; D. Burden 183 at 15.25.
Bowling G. Alexander 21 at 17.28; S. Sharma 10 at 29.10; E. Davies 11 at 32.00.

Shebbear College
P6 W2 L3 D1 A2

Batting O. Wickett* 214 at 42.80; E. Jones 220 at 36.66.
Bowling J. Corry 11 at 12.27.

Sherborne School
P15 W11 L4 D0 A2

Sherborne bowled better than they batted. All school matches were limited-overs games, so draws were a thing of the past.

Batting W. Russell 441 at 33.92; J. Britten 209 at 26.12; W. Fegen* 299 at 24.91; R. Jordan 252 at 16.80; J. Harding 181 at 16.45.
Bowling W. Fegen 23 at 15.43; C. Dupont 17 at 16.88; W. Dawson 25 at 17.92; H. Lamb 15 at 21.66; A. Budge 10 at 22.30; F. Mead 10 at 25.10.

Shrewsbury School
P22 W11 L5 D6 A1

Shrewsbury enjoyed an excellent season despite the inexperience of the side: 12 of this year's squad should play next summer. Alastair McKeever's return of 41 wickets was pleasing, and included seven for 23 against Manchester Grammar School. Sixteen-year-old Ian Massey scored 847 runs.

Batting I. R. Massey 847 at 47.05; F. C. Argyle 502 at 29.52; A. M. McKeever* 375 at 25.00; M. J. Dwyer 197 at 24.62; T. W. P. Cox 386 at 22.70.
Bowling A. M. McKeever 41 at 15.36; T. J. Owen 20 at 17.50; N. J. Bevan 35 at 18.97; B. M. Pridgeon 15 at 25.86; R. D. T. Nichols 14 at 31.00; M. J. Dwyer 11 at 32.63.

Simon Langton Grammar School
P5 W2 L3 D0 A5

Weather chopped the fixture list in half, allowing only five games to be played. Simon Cusden, who in schools matches hit 205 at 102.50, played for an ECB Schools XI against India and was later selected to tour Australia with England Under-19.

Batting M. Paine* 382 at 127.33.
Bowling No one took ten wickets. The leading bowler was S. M. J. Cusden, who took seven at 13.28.

Solihull School
P17 W7 L6 D4 A1

Solihull's young side had an encouraging campaign, and all bar three should return next year.
Batting C. Bartley 403 at 33.58; J. Hemming 334 at 30.36; J. Pooley* 263 at 26.30; B. Pugh 289 at 24.08; J. Coutts 222 at 22.20; J. Sammons 225 at 20.45; A. Blasdale 284 at 20.28; S. Reddish 232 at 16.57.
Bowling C. Bartley 27 at 10.18; J. Pooley 31 at 19.93; T. Kirtland 21 at 22.14; B. Watson 17 at 23.41; Q. Tchakhotine 12 at 26.83; B. Pugh 13 at 38.38.

South Craven School P7 W3 L3 D1 A3
South Craven had mixed fortunes, but a number of school records were broken: 306 for five declared against Grange Technology College, Bradford was their highest total; 152 by Andrew Sewell the highest individual score; 172 between Sewell and Simon Doane the highest stand for any wicket; and 246 the biggest margin of victory. The wicket-keeper was Anna Spragg of Yorkshire Women, sister of Laura Spragg (England Women).
Batting A. M. Sewell 273 at 45.50.
Bowling C. P. Walker* 13 at 13.46; M. Shuttleworth 10 at 19.30.

Stamford School P17 W3 L14 D0 A1
Batting R. Sabin 327 at 32.70; S. Albinson 163 at 32.60; W. Clough 301 at 21.50; J. Lawrence 206 at 12.87; P. Matthew 166 at 9.76.
Bowling N. Wells 30 at 15.86; C. Talbot 22 at 19.86; T. Goodman 11 at 34.27.

Stockport Grammar School P14 W6 L6 D2
A summer of close finishes brought much entertainment. An end-of-season tour to Malta was an excellent experience, and playing on hard, fast wickets brought confidence to a rather weak batting line-up. Simon Elliott and James Davenport showed star quality.
Batting J. Davenport 226 at 45.20; S. Elliott* 336 at 42.00; L. Bottomley 190 at 17.27.
Bowling J. Woodsmith 12 at 11.66; R. Barrow 12 at 16.16; J. Davenport 16 at 18.87; A. Jennings 12 at 21.33; C. Mercer 11 at 26.72.

Stowe School P12 W1 L7 D4
Fragile batting meant a depressing number of losses. However, Stowe proved they were a competitive side with the ball and in the field and, in Graeme White, had a left-arm spinner of great promise. White went on to play for England Under-15s. Harold Rhodes (Derbyshire and England) retired after six years as professional.
Batting O. Cullingworth 303 at 25.25; G. Sharp* 258 at 23.45; W. Gallimore 241 at 21.90; A. Leon 200 at 20.00; J. Leggett 154 at 12.83.
Bowling G. White 22 at 24.31; H. Sheppard 18 at 28.83; G. Sharp 11 at 31.90.

Strathallan School P6 W3 L1 D2 A9
The worst summer in over a decade saw more than half the scheduled matches lost to the weather, including every game after June 5. Six batsmen scored at least one fifty, while the bowling was dominated by Brad Coupar, a left-arm quick bowler on exchange from Brisbane Boys College. His 16 wickets did not accurately reflect his quality.
Batting B. Coupar 160 at 32.00.
Bowling T. M. Hine 11 at 6.09; B. Coupar 16 at 7.43.

Sutton Valence School P10 W4 L3 D3 A4
Batting N. Chapman 334 at 33.40; J. Varnals 195 at 27.85; P. Stileman* 277 at 27.70; T. Brandreth 169 at 18.77.
Bowling N. Chapman 12 at 13.41; O. Clarkson 18 at 16.16; P. Stileman 18 at 20.72.

Taunton School P9 W3 L6 D0 A3
Batting M. Collins* 390 at 48.75; J. Hayward 208 at 41.60.
Bowling H. Carpenter 11 at 14.72; L. Vassay 10 at 19.40.

Tiffin School P18 W11 L1 D6 A2
This was a spectacular season for Tiffin. Simon Crampton had a marvellous summer, finishing with 49 wickets and 514 runs. His ability to read batsmen allied with an astute cricketing sense won him respect as a captain. The major strength of the side undoubtedly lay in the variety and accuracy of its bowling, and in the all-round skills of Arun Harinath.
Batting S. G. D. Crampton* 514 at 57.11; A. Harinath 621 at 56.45; R. Uthayashanker 376 at 25.06; D. Sellayah 339 at 22.60; H. M. Vanderman 235 at 21.36; B. C. Gibbs 175 at 19.44; K. Balasubramaniam 164 at 13.66.
Bowling S. G. D. Crampton 49 at 8.87; A. Harinath 19 at 16.15; R. Gnanendran 31 at 18.87; R. Kumarasuriyar 10 at 21.30; C. R. Secker 10 at 22.00; J. R. Anderson 11 at 23.72.

Tonbridge School
P15 W3 L8 D4 A2

Batting C. G. Atkinson 627 at 41.80; F. R. Chillcott* 501 at 35.78; D. J. Norman 414 at 25.87; S. Kapila 333 at 25.61; D. H. Odds 168 at 15.27; J. E. G. Burman 167 at 13.91; J. W. K. Beeny 200 at 13.33.
Bowling C. Douglas-Hughes 18 at 17.11; C. G. R. Haire 18 at 22.00; C. G. Atkinson 19 at 26.94; A. J. R. Collier 19 at 28.15; J. E. G. Burman 13 at 37.69.

Trent College
P15 W6 L6 D3

Batting D. Mathias* 324 at 23.14; J. Shelton 227 at 22.70; S. Kelly 226 at 22.60; D. Jones 252 at 19.38; J. Tunnicliffe 251 at 19.30; A. Marshall 205 at 18.63.
Bowling D. Jones 20 at 15.75; D. Wall 13 at 19.38; S. Roberts 15 at 39.80.

Trinity School, Croydon
P16 W2 L8 D6

A very young side contained only two players from 2001. Opponents were often bowled out for under 200, but an inexperienced batting line-up generally fell short of the target. The team relied too much on a couple of strong all-rounders.
Batting A. Savage 341 at 22.73; B. Shorten 271 at 16.93; J. May 186 at 14.30.
Bowling B. Shorten 10 at 15.00; D. Whitehair 16 at 22.62; J. May 12 at 28.16.

Truro School
P10 W3 L4 D3 A2

Batting T. F. Glover 341 at 48.71; D. J. Pollard* 239 at 29.87.
Bowling D. J. Pollard 17 at 11.64; B. T. Pollard 14 at 12.78; M. K. Munday 12 at 21.25; T. F. Glover 10 at 31.10.

University College School
P11 W4 L5 D2 A1

Some excellent victories helped offset disappointing defeats. The highlight was a victory over Berkhamsted, when James Floyd and Nick Jones both scored hundreds. If anything, the side was too dependent on this pair for runs. All the team bar one should return next year.
Batting J. Floyd* 478 at 47.80; N. Jones 370 at 41.11.
Bowling A. Cohen 13 at 14.38; D. Patel 17 at 16.88; B. Kirmani 14 at 19.21.

Uppingham School
P16 W9 L3 D4 A1

The side had its most successful campaign for many years. Duncan Wood was the leading all-rounder, and bowled outstandingly to take ten for 47 in the annual two-day game against Shrewsbury. Will Crowder fell just short of 100 wickets for the First XI, ending with 96 in three fine seasons. All three defeats came in limited-overs matches.
Batting J. T. Branson 348 at 34.80; D. C. Wood 338 at 30.72; H. J. L. Swayne* 259 at 23.54; J. C. J. Sharrock 192 at 17.45; S. Dean 223 at 17.15; H. M. C. Judd 150 at 15.00.
Bowling D. C. Wood 39 at 13.94; D. N. Feit 13 at 14.30; W. E. Crowder 23 at 18.52; T. J. Burwell 14 at 22.28; T. H. Higgs 11 at 24.63.

Victoria College, Jersey
P20 W7 L7 D6

Andrew Dewhurst, the captain, was in scintillating form. In the 44-run win over Elizabeth College, Guernsey he hit 122 and took four for 43; he also scored 151 against Bryanston.
Batting A. Dewhurst* 776 at 48.50; P. Gough 611 at 33.94; P. Gales 285 at 31.66; J. Gough 630 at 31.50; S. Dewhurst 245 at 22.27; O. Hughes 345 at 18.15; T. Minty 203 at 13.53.
Bowling A. Dewhurst 42 at 13.54; H. MacLachlan 21 at 18.33; J. Gough 23 at 20.78; P. Gough 16 at 23.18; T. Minty 21 at 27.52.

Warwick School
P15 W8 L3 D4 A2

Batting D. G. Roots 515 at 64.37; W. R. Warwick 154 at 51.33; O. C. Higgens* 463 at 46.30; T. F. Rigby 225 at 37.50; J. D. Tickle 225 at 37.50; A. R. Wilkinson 405 at 36.81; C. M. Wilson 325 at 27.08.
Bowling O. C. Higgens 15 at 15.33; A. R. Wilkinson 12 at 19.16; C. J. Todd 11 at 25.45; B. E. A. Carr 10 at 26.30.

Watford Grammar School
P9 W2 L2 D5 A1

A young team, well marshalled by Edward Welch, continued to improve. The batting of Zawar Hussain was supported by excellent swing bowling from Matthew Corbridge.
Batting Z. Hussain 403 at 80.60.
Bowling M. Corbridge 19 at 13.26; R. Mukherjee 15 at 19.26.

Wellington College
P16 W8 L4 D4

A good all-round team, well led by Adrian Jarvis, enjoyed a successful term.
Batting A. T. Jarvis* 699 at 63.54; H. T. Y. Shephard 477 at 39.75; P. J. W. Young 399 at 36.27; A. A. Shelley 231 at 28.87; H. R. Streatfield 459 at 28.68; A. W. J. Mills 184 at 23.00; G. R. Tysoe 167 at 16.70.
Bowling C. J. Rylatt 23 at 15.39; A. A. Shelley 34 at 16.50; H. T. Y. Shephard 20 at 17.20; G. R. Tysoe 21 at 22.47; J. R. Coyne 12 at 34.91.

Wellington School
P11 W4 L3 D4 A5

A season that promised much was blighted by poor weather and an inability to wheedle out late-order batsmen.
Batting C. Nicholls 205 at 41.00; J. T. House* 341 at 37.88; G. Sheppard 318 at 35.33.
Bowling P. Short 25 at 8.84; J. T. House 13 at 13.69; R. Rexworthy 13 at 16.38; P. Nicholls 15 at 20.80.

Wells Cathedral School
P13 W2 L6 D5 A2

After last year's undefeated campaign, this was a far tougher season.
Batting G. Oram 350 at 43.75.
Bowling E. Harper 21 at 17.28; G. Oram 18 at 20.50; A. Taylor-Maughan 11 at 31.72; M. Brandon 12 at 34.41.

West Buckland School
P13 W4 L7 D2 A1

The bowling and fielding of a very young side – it contained only one upper-sixth player – was of a very high standard; the batting was not.
Batting J. C. Hickman 272 at 27.20; J. D. Wallace* 188 at 17.09; M. A. Stevens 158 at 15.80; A. M. Laughrane 174 at 13.38.
Bowling C. A. Boulden 20 at 15.80; J. C. Hickman 16 at 18.00; D. J. Higgs 14 at 20.28; J. D. Wallace 14 at 21.85; A. D. Hobbs 13 at 22.15.

Westminster School
P13 W5 L6 D2 A3

Westminster enjoyed a fine season. The bowling was strong, with the off-spin of James Japhet ably supported by Charles Cooke, William Yell and Nick Manners. The batting lacked consistency but Richard Clark showed great potential.
Batting R. L. Pike 205 at 29.28; R. K. Clark 271 at 27.10; J. N. Japhet* 264 at 22.00; W. B. J. Stevenson 210 at 19.09.
Bowling J. N. Japhet 18 at 27.27; C. A. Cooke 10 at 27.30.

Whitgift School
P14 W6 L5 D3

This was a successful season – the more so since it was largely devoted to developing junior players. Four Under-15s and an Under-16 performed admirably. Sam Woodward was included in the Surrey Academy and was named Surrey Under-17 player of the year. David Ward, the joint master in charge, was recalled to play for Surrey in a National League game played on the school ground.
Batting S. Woodward 636 at 63.60; M. Spiegal 365 at 36.50; N. Grant 190 at 27.14; J. Pearce* 349 at 26.84; J. Wright 226 at 20.54.
Bowling J. Pearce 22 at 11.36; A. Bailey 19 at 15.78; N. Grant 18 at 20.44; A. Clarke 15 at 22.00.

Wickersley School and Sports College
P9 W2 L4 D3 A1

Wickersley found the going difficult, and were over-reliant on a small number of players. The early batting performed well but the bowlers struggled to dismiss sides. Elizabeth Lazenby became the first girl to play First XI cricket, while Mark Cummins played for England Under-15s and won the Bunbury Scholarship award, awarded by ECB coaches to a player showing great promise.
Batting M. Cummins 277 at 55.40; L. Heathcote 188 at 26.85.
Bowling M. Cummins 13 at 16.23; L. Heathcote 10 at 31.80.

Winchester College
P15 W3 L4 D8 A1

This was an average season for Winchester. Tom White had a good year with bat and ball, and beat Radley and Wellington almost single-handed with fine bowling displays. However, a lack of runs meant the side struggled to chase targets, and games that should have been won were drawn.
Batting J. Merriot 330 at 30.00; J. Walters 346 at 26.61; J. Mortimer 236 at 21.45; T. White* 234 at 21.27; C. Walters 247 at 20.58; J. Brierly 204 at 17.00.
Bowling T. White 18 at 22.00; J. Pringle 12 at 23.50; E. Foster 13 at 24.38; J. Walters 13 at 27.30.

Wolverhampton Grammar School
P11 W3 L5 D3 A6

A season constantly interrupted by bad weather saw an inexperienced side perform well on occasions. For the second year running, Michael Young was leading wicket-taker; Daniel Bowyer, the captain, took 13 and scored over 350 runs.

Batting C. Mulvihill 286 at 40.85; D. Bowyer* 367 at 36.70; J. Acaster 156 at 17.33.
Bowling D. Bowyer 13 at 15.46; M. Young 16 at 16.81.

Woodbridge School
P12 W3 L5 D4 A2

Batting M. Fernley 388 at 38.80; P. Nicholls 311 at 31.10; J. McNally 212 at 19.27.
Bowling W. Nicholls 16 at 20.62; C. Tunstall 11 at 23.18.

Woodhouse Grove School
P17 W7 L5 D5 A1

Joe Bedford scored 642 runs at 80.25; he also played rugby for England Schools in the spring term. Wicket-keeper Sam Anderson scored 558 runs and captained Yorkshire Schools in their festival at St Peter's, York.

Batting J. R. Bedford 642 at 80.25; M. S. Bottomley* 602 at 35.41; S. R. Anderson 558 at 34.87; R. H. Haslam 225 at 17.30.
Bowling M. S. Druce 16 at 12.75; O. D. Wolfenden 12 at 19.83; H. J. Driver 15 at 22.86; E. C. Haslam 16 at 23.25; A. M. Pearce 14 at 27.57; M. S. Bottomley 10 at 34.40.

Worksop College
P18 W10 L3 D5 A1

Samit Patel played for Nottinghamshire against West Indies A, Andrew Parkin-Coates played for Nottinghamshire Seconds, and Bhavesh Patel represented England Under-17.

Batting A. W. Parkin-Coates 715 at 71.50; L. J. Ambrose 196 at 32.66; S. R. Patel 385 at 32.08; M. T. Palmer 315 at 31.50; T. Corbyn 295 at 22.69; B. Patel 336 at 22.40; J. R. Gray 333 at 19.58.
Bowling S. R. Patel 32 at 10.43; L. J. Ambrose 10 at 11.30; J. R. Gray 26 at 11.57; B. Patel 24 at 15.83; R. M. Davies 16 at 20.06.

Wrekin College
P14 W3 L5 D6 A1

Some good all-round performances gave lustre to an average season. Most matches were declaration games, which Wrekin played as positively as possible. The team included three fourth formers.

Batting A. Rylance* 342 at 28.50; J. Pee 242 at 24.20; R. O'Brien 287 at 23.91; T. Fisher 198 at 18.00; A. Sultan 170 at 17.00; N. Berry 158 at 12.15.
Bowling R. O'Brien 17 at 17.29; J. Pee 21 at 18.90; M. Rhodes 21 at 20.14; A. Sultan 10 at 22.70.

Wycliffe College
P10 W2 L6 D2 A1

Four 15-year-olds made their first-team debuts in a season of mixed fortunes: the pick was Tom Williams, who was the leading wicket-taker. The side was expertly captained by Stuart Gilchriest, who comfortably topped the batting.

Batting S. Gilchriest* 275 at 45.83.
Bowling T. Williams 12 at 18.66.

Wyggeston and Queen Elizabeth I College
P11 W9 L1 D1

The team had its best summer for several years: unbeaten against schools, colleges and university teams, they lost only to an Old Wyggestonians XI. Mohsin Contractor's unbeaten 119 at Rugby was the most stylish innings, while Andrew Fletcher's 114 and Luke Berriman's hat-trick helped win the Leicestershire Under-19 final. Kunal Jogia played for Leicestershire Seconds.

Batting A. H. Fletcher 261 at 43.50; M. Contractor 332 at 41.50; K. Jogia 279 at 39.85; J. Anderson 244 at 34.85.
Bowling A. H. Fletcher 19 at 10.05; I. K. Lodhi 16 at 13.43; M. Khan* 17 at 14.29; L. Berriman 16 at 15.56.

YOUTH CRICKET, 2002

In December 2000, the ECB announced an ambitious goal: to produce by 2007 an England side that was the best in the world. At least part of this world-beating team will be made up of today's 16–19-year-olds, so youth cricket has been targeted as a crucial part of the ECB's drive. Consequently, it has changed more in the past two years than in the preceding 20. Though the National Academy and its director, Rodney Marsh, have grabbed the headlines, a quieter revolution has taken place in the counties. Fifteen ECB-licensed feeder academies have been set up (and three more planned), each carefully monitored by the board. The ECB establishes the programme, trains the full-time director, provides a standard training template and monitors results. It also pays many of the bills. Each academy receives £50,000 a year to fund up to 12 boys aged 13–18, who come in several times a week in the off-season, slightly less in the summer. Every player spends around half his time on technical training (including regular one-to-one sessions with senior county pros), 25 per cent or so on mental development, ten on tactical learning, ten on fitness and five on lifestyle management. The aim is to provide a carefully burnished set of bright young players, ready to slip in quick succession from county cap – via National Academy tracksuit – to England sweater. By 2007, the ECB hope that half the England team will be graduates of the county academies.

UNDER-19 CRICKET

The summer of 2002 was the last for the Under-19 County Championship. Many of the arguments deployed against its senior cousin were also levelled at this competition: too many of the best players were missing, in this case with county Second Elevens, leaving too many who lacked the ability to take the next step up the ladder. No direct replacement for the cash-hungry two-day competition is planned. However, from 2003, the ECB's one-day 38-County tournament will be for under-21s, with just two over-age players allowed.

The final was won by the 1999 champions, Somerset, who beat the 1998 winners, Hampshire, by eight wickets at Nevil Road, Bristol. Hampshire could only limp to 125, with Adam Kelly taking three for 34 and Gareth Andrew two for 17. In response, Somerset, fielding several players off the prolific Millfield production-line, reduced the chase to a 26-over cruise. Tom Webley ended unbeaten on 70.

UNDER-17 CRICKET

Promotion and relegation between two divisions was the ECB's prescription for the senior County Championship, and the recipe has been adapted for the Under-17 competition. From 2003, the country will be split north–south, with three divisions in each area; all will have promotion and/or relegation, and the season will end with a clash between the winners of the two first divisions. The aim is to produce fewer dead matches, and increase the number of closely fought games.

Nottinghamshire were the last champions under the old format, squeezing to an 11-run win against Surrey in a two-day match at Headingley. Their total of 300 was built round fifties by Aquib Afzaal and Tom Chalkley; David Balcombe grabbed four for 39 in 18 overs. On the second day, Bharesh Patel's spin (two for 35 in 25 overs) mired Surrey, before a late spurt gave them a sniff of victory. Their last pair needed 32 but they couldn't quite make it. Staffordshire and Middlesex were the two beaten semi-finalists.

UNDER-15 CRICKET

The 16th annual ESCA/Bunbury Festival was held in July at Billericay CC, and was dominated by the North, who won two group matches and drew one, and by the bat of Yorkshire's Mark Cummins. In three innings, he hit 108, 103 and 71, and he also took four for 36 against the West. But, with Cummins rested, the North were defeated by the Midlands in a nail-biting final. After Chris Brook's 44 helped the Midlands to 212 for six in their 50 overs, Phillip Holdsworth hit 52 and carried the North within sight. But, in the end, they fell an agonising two short. More dramatic still, the South and the West tied in the match for the Chairman's plate, with the South awarded the game on wickets lost. The North's Paul Muchall (brother of Durham's Gordon) hit the only other century of the competition, while the Midlands' Graeme White took four for 37 against the South. But neither could match Cummins, a gritty opening batsman, and he was awarded the Bunbury scholarship, which included three weeks' coaching in Australia.

Yorkshire won the Under-15 County Championship finals at Oundle School, beating Surrey by 26 runs. This time it was Cummins's Yorkshire opening partner, Andrew Rennison, who made the runs, hitting 73 of his side's 209 in 50 overs. Although Surrey's Rory Hamilton-Brown followed up his three for 32 with a sparkling 78, Yorkshire's tight bowling and fielding applied the tourniquet, and Surrey were all out for 183. In a good competition for all-rounders, Hamilton-Brown also shone in the semi-final against Staffordshire, though he was eclipsed by his team-mate, Arun Harinath. Harinath seized two for 40, before cantering to an unbeaten hundred at close to a run a ball. An outstanding talent, his progress has been watched by the ECB since the age of 12. He remains well ahead of most of his peers, having also played for Surrey in the Under-17 final. In the other semi, Wales came within a whisker of upsetting Yorkshire, falling four short of 199.

The Lord's Taverners/*Cricketer* Colts final had a familiar outcome when a Millfield captain claimed the Trophy. Their 89-run win against Driffield from East Yorkshire, the second comprehensive in two seasons to reach the final, was their seventh outright victory in 31 years (they have also shared the trophy twice). Millfield rocketed to 226 for seven in their 40 overs, as Robin Lett made a Trent Bridge final look like a schoolfield knockabout, easing to his third century in successive rounds. Though the hulking, 6ft 3in Andrew Chapman hit some booming extra-cover drives and Russell Robinson made an energetic and unbeaten fifty, Driffield fell short. Sean Parry wheedled out three for 22 with his medium-pace.

UNDER-14 CRICKET

The 2002 Lord's Taverner's Under-14 Festival at Oundle was a rain-blighted affair. Only two of the six scheduled matches escaped the deluge unscathed: Sunil Tailor took four for 25 from 16 overs for the South to help them dismiss the West for 78 and set up a comfortable win, while James Ord hit 99 for the Midlands in their draw with the North. The four top players, each winning two-year Gray-Nicolls kit sponsorships were James Ord (Midlands), Karl Brown (North), Rory Hamilton-Brown (South) and Michael O'Shea (West).

UNDER-13 CRICKET

Yorkshire Under-13s bossed the County Championship finals, played alongside the Under-15 finals at Oundle. In their semi-final they buried Somerset under a pile of runs: the openers Greg Wood and James Clarkson put on 112, and Yorkshire reached an intimidating 241 from 40 overs. It proved enough for an 81-run win. After Essex beat Warwickshire in the corresponding match, Yorkshire dished out more of the same in the final. Their total of 235, with Wood cracking 92, was far beyond the reach of Essex, who managed just 142 in reply. Somerset won the third-place play-off.

After 38 county winners had been sifted down to just two teams, Whitgift won the Under-13 Calypso Cup at a typically rainy Headingley, beating Hymers College after a sensible batting performance.

TEST MATCH SPECIAL UNDER-15 YOUNG CRICKETER OF THE YEAR

Phillip Holdsworth, from Northallerton in Yorkshire, won the third BBC *Test Match Special* Under-15 Young Cricketer of the Year Award. The award was given to him by a panel of ECB national judges after he captained England Under-15, scoring 255 runs at 42.50 and taking 17 wickets at 12.82. The previous winners were Samit Patel of Nottinghamshire and Adam Harrison of Glamorgan.

WOMEN'S CRICKET, 2002

By CAROL SALMON

NEW ZEALAND WOMEN AND INDIAN WOMEN IN ENGLAND, 2002

England welcomed two women's touring teams in the summer of 2002 – New Zealand, the World Cup holders, and India, who had hosted an England tour in January. The three sides contested a triangular one-day tournament, the first of its kind in England, and New Zealand emerged comprehensive winners when the home nation meekly succumbed in the final at Chester-le-Street. In a rain-affected series, with two games washed out completely, only three players passed 50 runs, all New Zealanders, headed by their captain, Emily Drumm, with 134 at 44.66. Rachel Pullar, a tall, accurate, seam bowler, was the fulcrum of their attack, taking 12 wickets for 60 in four games.

Like England, New Zealand were rebuilding – only five of their squad had played in the World Cup final in December 2000 – but their mental strength and organisation remained streets ahead. England's coach, John Harmer, was flabbergasted to find two of his selections, Sarah Collyer and Kathryn Leng, had opted for a sand-and-sunshine holiday in the Canary Islands instead of the intensive pre-series training he had prescribed. Commitment was never in question when Harmer was in charge of the Australian women's squads. Leng and Collyer were swiftly discarded, and Isa Guha and Hannah Lloyd called up to replace them.

The 17-year-old Guha, the first Asian to play for England's women, was an immediate success with her right-arm seamers. She finished the summer as the side's top wicket-taker and was later named BBC Asian Sports Personality of the Year. It was a timely arrival, as England's left-arm seam bowler, Lucy Pearson, suffered a stress fracture during the opening match of the series, which put her out for the rest of the season. The triangular series also spelled the end of the road, at least in the short term, for England's wicket-keeper, Jane Cassar, who had underperformed in India. A virtual ever-present since England won the 1993 World Cup, Cassar had played 70 one-day internationals and claimed a record 80 dismissals.

An out-of-sorts India had a tournament to forget. They had beaten England 5–0 in the recent one-day series on home soil, and had just lost 2–1 in South Africa (though they won the single Test there by ten wickets). But in this series, they never managed to reach 100, and were dismissed for their lowest-ever total, 26 in 19.1 overs, by New Zealand, who had last met them in a World Cup semi-final. Clearly, India did not appreciate the cold and damp conditions, or an itinerary that offered them just one practice match, on the Isle of Wight, which was abandoned. New Zealand had warmed up by touring the Netherlands and Ireland, where only rain denied them a 100 per cent record.

The dreadful summer weather continued after New Zealand departed, as India stayed on to play two Tests following their own Irish trip. When the First Test, at Shenley, was abandoned without a ball bowled, the teams agreed to an extra one-day international, to get some cricket in ahead of the Second Test. By now, only the captain, Clare Connor, her deputy, Clare Taylor, the new wicket-keeper, Mandi Godliman, and Dawn Holden survived from the winter tour party. But Leng was recalled, and enjoyed a 92-run opening stand with Charlotte Edwards to set up victory. England could not maintain their advantage in the Test at Taunton, however, when their slow but solid first-innings effort was eclipsed by the record-breaking feats of India's Mithali Raj. She batted nearly ten hours for 214, the fifth and highest double-century in women's Test cricket. Neetu David, the classy left-arm spinner, took six wickets in the match, and was the pick of the Indian bowlers throughout the tour. But with the run-rate at Taunton rarely rising above two and a half an over, there was plenty of ammunition for those who believe there is no appeal in women's Test cricket.

INDIAN TOURING PARTY

A. Chopra (Air India) (*captain*), M. Raj (Air India) (*vice-captain*), N. Al-Khadeer (Karnataka),
N. David (Railways), J. Goswami (Bengal), B. Goyal (Madhya Pradesh), H. Kala (Railways),
A. Kirkire (Madhya Pradesh), A. M. Corbin (Wellington), D. M. Kulkarni (Railways), M. Maben (Bangalore), S. Naik
(Mumbai), S. A. Paranjpe (Mumbai), A. Sharma (Delhi), J. Sharma (Railways), S. Singh (Railways).
  Coach: Tarak Sinha.   *Manager:* F. Fernandes.   *Administrative Manager:* J. Joshi.

NEW ZEALAND TOURING PARTY

E. C. Drumm (Auckland) (*captain*), K. A. Ramel (Auckland) (*vice-captain*), N. J. Browne (Northern
Districts), A. M. Corbin (Wellington), F. E. Fraser (Canterbury), F. S. King (Wellington), S. J.
McGlashan (Central Districts), A. L. Mason (Central Districts), L. E. Milliken (Northern Districts),
N. Payne (Canterbury), K. L. Pulford (Central Districts), R. J. Pullar (Otago), R. J. Rolls (Auckland),
H. M. Tiffen (Canterbury).
  Coach: M. J. F. Shrimpton.   *Manager:* J. Reynolds.

Note: Matches in this section were not first-class.

Triangular Series

At St Saviour, Jersey, July 10. **England won by six wickets.** Toss: England. **India 59** (35.2 overs)
(L. J. Harper four for 11); **England 60 for four** (30.2 overs) (C. M. Edwards 31 not out).
  *The Grainville Ground hosted the Channel Islands' first cricket international. India scored their
lowest one-day total against England (previously 61 in 1981-82). Clare Taylor became the fourth
bowler – and the first English player – to take 100 international wickets.*

At St Saviour, Jersey, July 11. **New Zealand won by 142 runs.** Toss: India. **New Zealand 168
for nine** (50 overs) (E. C. Drumm 56, H. M. Tiffen 37; J. Goswami three for 45, D. M. Kulkarni
four for 37); **India 26** (19.1 overs) (R. J. Pullar five for ten).
  *This was India's lowest one-day total, beating 37 in 35 overs, also against New Zealand, in
1981-82, and only three above Pakistan's world record low of 23 against Australia in 1996-97.
Their first seven wickets fell for six runs in 35 balls. Jhulan Goswami, at No. 9, and Extras top-
scored with six runs each.*

At St Saviour, Jersey, July 12. **England v New Zealand. No result (abandoned).**

At Durham, July 16. **New Zealand won by seven wickets.** Toss: England. **England 111** (38
overs); **New Zealand 113 for three** (31 overs) (E. C. Drumm 63 not out).
  *England recovered from 66 for eight. Only Isa Guha, at No. 9, and Laura Spragg, at No. 10,
reached double figures.*

At Durham, July 17. **New Zealand won by five wickets.** Toss: India. **India 95** (41.1 overs)
(R. J. Pullar three for ten); **New Zealand 96 for five** (28.4 overs) (H. M. Tiffen 30 not out;
N. David three for 17).

At Chester-le-Street, July 19. **England v India. No result (abandoned).**

New Zealand 14 pts, England 8 pts, India 2 pts.

FINAL

ENGLAND v NEW ZEALAND

At Chester-le-Street, July 20. New Zealand won by 63 runs. Toss: England.

England had good reason to hope that their dreadful run against New Zealand – 14 one-day defeats since the 1993 World Cup final – was coming to an end when they grabbed two wickets in the first two overs. Isa Guha quickly added the series' leading scorer, Emily Drumm, to make it 21 for three. But England's failings in the field soon surfaced, and a determined fifty from Kate Pulford launched New Zealand's recovery before Guha returned to end the innings. It became a thoroughly dispiriting day for home supporters when England began their reply. In 44 tortuous overs, they slid to 98 all out and a 15th defeat. Shot selection and running between the wickets were as bad as they ever had been, prompting questions about the players' cricketing nous, as well as the effectiveness of an extensive programme of coaching.

Player of the Match: K. L. Pulford.

New Zealand

N. Payne c Harper b Guha	0	R. J. Pullar st Godliman b C. E. Taylor . 0
†R. J. Rolls c Godliman b Spragg	0	F. S. King not out	3
*E. C. Drumm c S. C. Taylor b Guha	15	N. J. Browne run out	1
K. L. Pulford c and b Connor	55	L-b 1, w 14, n-b 2	17
H. M. Tiffen c Thompson b Harper	17		
F. E. Fraser lbw b Spragg	14	1/0 (1) 2/0 (2) 3/21 (3) (48.5 overs) 161
S. J. McGlashan c Godliman b C. E. Taylor	19	4/66 (5) 5/109 (6) 6/117 (4)
A. L. Mason c Edwards b Guha	20	7/154 (8) 8/155 (9)
		9/159 (7) 10/161 (11)

Bowling: Guha 7.5–1–28–3; Spragg 10–1–31–2; C. E. Taylor 9–3–26–2; Newton 2–0–18–0; Harper 10–0–25–1; Reynard 5–0–18–0; Connor 5–2–14–1.

England

*C. J. Connor b Pullar	10	†M. C. Godliman lbw b Tiffen	10
S. C. Taylor run out	32	C. E. Taylor not out	7
C. M. Edwards lbw b Tiffen	0		
A. Thompson lbw b King	3	L-b 2, w 11	13
M. A. Reynard st Rolls b Mason	9		
L. K. Newton lbw b Pulford	0	1/19 (1) 2/27 (3) 3/39 (4) (43.4 overs) 98
L. Spragg c Drumm b Pullar	8	4/54 (2) 5/57 (6) 6/75 (7)
L. J. Harper lbw b Mason	4	7/77 (5) 8/80 (8)
I. T. Guha c Browne b Mason	2	9/81 (9) 10/98 (10)

Bowling: Pullar 9–1–19–2; Browne 4–2–6–0; Tiffen 7.4–1–20–2; King 10–3–20–1; Mason 10–3–20–3; Pulford 3–0–11–1.

Umpires: L. E. Elgar and R. A. Kettleborough.
Third umpire: V. Gibbens.

New Zealand in Holland and Ireland

At Utrecht, June 25. **First one-day international: New Zealand won by 169 runs.** Toss: Holland. **New Zealand 245 for seven** (50 overs) (N. Payne 37, R. J. Rolls 33, E. C. Drumm 36, K. L. Pulford 36, Extras 39); **Holland 76** (41 overs) (R. J. Pullar three for ten).

At Amstelveen, June 26. **Second one-day international: New Zealand won by 248 runs.** Toss: Holland. **New Zealand 335 for four** (50 overs) (R. J. Rolls 54, K. L. Pulford 95, K. A. Ramel 37, F. E. Fraser 54 not out, E. C. Drumm 48 not out, Extras 36); **Holland 87** (35 overs) (A. L. Mason four for 26, A. M. Corbin three for 13).

At Utrecht, June 28. **Third one-day international: New Zealand won by 210 runs.** Toss: Holland. **New Zealand 263 for five** (45 overs) (N. Payne 45, H. M. Tiffen 87, S. J. McGlashan 41 not out, F. S. King 31, Extras 31); **Holland 53** (27.1 overs) (F. S. King three for nine, K. L. Pulford four for five).

New Zealand took the series 3–0.

At Clontarf, Dublin, July 1. **First one-day international: No result.** Toss: New Zealand. **New Zealand 249 for six** (42 overs) (N. Payne 60, R. J. Rolls 88); **Ireland 18 for one** (6.1 overs).

At Malahide, Dublin, July 3. **Second one-day international: New Zealand won by eight wickets.** Toss: Ireland. **Ireland 176** (47 overs) (C. M. Beggs 56, Extras 31; F. S. King four for 27, H. M. Tiffen three for 22); **New Zealand 179 for two** (30.3 overs) (R. J. Rolls 86, K. L. Pulford 40, E. C. Drumm not out).

At Trinity College, Dublin, July 6. **Third one-day international: New Zealand won by nine wickets.** Toss: Ireland. **Ireland 90** (38.1 overs) (C. O'Neill 39 not out; N. J. Browne four for 20); **New Zealand 91 for one** (20.4 overs) (N. Payne 32 not out, H. M. Tiffen 33).

New Zealand took the series 2–0.

India in England and Ireland

At Durham, July 15. **India won by 49 runs. India 201 for four** (50 overs) (S. Singh 90 not out, M. Maben 34); **ECB Development XI 152** (49.2 overs) (N. Al-Khadeer three for 38, S. Singh three for 29).

At Rush CC, Dublin, July 24. **First one-day international: India won by eight wickets.** Toss: Ireland. **Ireland 101 for nine** (50 overs) (M. E. Grealey 32; S. A. Paranjpe four for eight); **India 104 for two** (24 overs) (J. Sharma 52).

At Merrion CC, Dublin, July 26. **Second one-day international: India won by 144 runs.** Toss: Ireland. **India 206 for seven** (50 overs) (M. Raj 41, A. Kirkire 58, S. Naik 50); **Ireland 62** (34 overs) (B. Goyal three for three).

At Fox Lodge CC, Strabane, July 28. **Third one-day international: Ireland v India. No result (abandoned).**

India took the series 2–0.

At Reading CC, August 2. **India won by 53 runs.** Toss: ECB Development XI. **India 128 for nine** (50 overs) (S. A. Paranjpe 37; S. J. Collyer three for 31, S. L. Clarke three for 24); **ECB Development XI 75** (40.1 overs) (S. A. Paranjpe four for 17).

At Bradfield College, Reading, August 3. **India won by 32 runs.** Toss: MCC. **India 221 for four** (50 overs) (S. A. Paranjpe 51, J. Sharma 68, M. Raj 59); **MCC 189** (47.3 overs) (S. C. Taylor 35, H. M. Tiffen 49; N. David four for 26).

At Reading CC, August 4. **India won by three runs.** Toss: England Under-21. **India 167 for six** (50 overs) (J. Sharma 33, M. Maben 37 not out, H. Kala 33); **England Under-21 164** (49.1 overs) (S. V. Collyer 47, S. A. Briggs 31; S. Singh three for 24).

ENGLAND v INDIA

First Test Match

At Shenley Park, August 8, 9, 10, 11. **Abandoned.**

At Beaconsfield, August 11. **One-day international: England won by six wickets.** Toss: India. **India 118** (49.5 overs) (H. Kala 38; I. T. Guha three for 28, C. J. Connor three for 25); **England 119 for four** (38.2 overs) (C. M. Edwards 54, K. M. Leng 46).

This match was arranged after the First Test was abandoned to provide the players with practice before the Second Test.

ENGLAND v INDIA

Second Test Match

At Taunton, August 14, 15, 16, 17. Drawn. Toss: India. Test debuts: M. C. Godliman, I. T. Guha; S. Naik, S. A. Paranjpe.

Mithali Raj made the highest score in women's Test cricket to give India a chance of only their second victory at this level. The 19-year-old Raj displayed an excellent technique and a full repertoire of strokes, which brought her 19 fours; she faced 407 balls in nine hours 41 minutes. It was the fifth double-century in a women's Test, all of them scored against England in the last seven seasons: the previous high was Karen Rolton's 209 not out for Australia at Headingley in 2001. Raj added 144 with Hemlata Kala, an Indian fourth-wicket record, and 157 with Jhulan Goswami, a seventh-wicket record for any country. Their efforts helped India to 467, their highest Test total, and a first-innings lead of 138. England had recovered from 27 for three on the first morning, thanks to Laura Newton, who fell just short of a four-hour hundred, with support from Clare Connor and Mandi Godliman, before Neetu David spun out the tail. A second-innings fifty from Charlotte Edwards and another solid contribution from Connor, who had led England with determination and dignity through a difficult summer, ensured the draw. But it was a slow-scoring match throughout.

Players of the Match: L. K. Newton and M. Raj.

Close of play: First day, England 280-7 (Godliman 51, Shaw 10); Second day, India 156-3 (Raj 43, Kala 31); Third day, India 445-6 (Raj 210, Goswami 54).

England

C. M. Edwards c Paranjpe b Singh	1	– st Naik b Goyal	56
K. M. Leng c Chopra b Goswami	10	– c Goswami b Singh	7
C. M. G. Atkins lbw b Goswami	12	– c Raj b Kulkarni	15
S. C. Taylor c Naik b Chopra	27	– b David	16
*C. J. Connor st Naik b David	48	– c Goswami b David	46
L. K. Newton c Raj b Goswami	98	– run out	33
L. J. Harper run out	11	– not out	20
†M. C. Godliman c Singh b David	65	– not out	1
N. J. Shaw b David	27		
I. T. Guha not out	13		
C. E. Taylor c Paranjpe b David	0		
B 10, l-b 6, w 1	17	L-b 3, n-b 1	4

1/1 (1) 2/18 (3) 3/27 (2)   329   1/16 (2) 2/79 (1)   (6 wkts dec.) 198
4/70 (4) 5/126 (5) 6/147 (7) 7/253 (6)   3/100 (4) 4/113 (4)
8/313 (9) 9/328 (8) 10/329 (11)   5/170 (5) 6/184 (6)

Bowling: *First Innings*—Goswami 25–10–51–3; Singh 21–6–58–1; Chopra 4–1–13–1; David 38–15–71–4; Goyal 16–1–62–0; Kulkarni 23–5–58–0; Kala 1–1–0–0. *Second Innings*—Goswami 12–3–31–0; Singh 10–4–13–1; Kala 1–0–10–0; David 27–6–70–2; Goyal 21–8–36–1; Kulkarni 10–1–35–1.

India

S. A. Paranjpe lbw b Shaw	2	B. Goyal not out	1
M. Maben c Godliman b Connor	20	S. Singh b Shaw	0
*A. Chopra c Newton b Leng	52	N. David c Godliman b Guha	7
M. Raj lbw b Guha	214	B 18, l-b 1, w 3, n-b 1	23
H. Kala run out	62		
D. M. Kulkarni c S. C. Taylor b Connor	8	1/2 (1) 2/45 (2) 3/100 (3) 4/244 (5)	467
†S. Naik c Newton b Harper	16	5/275 (6) 6/297 (7) 7/454 (4)	
J. Goswami c and b Shaw	62	8/458 (9) 9/458 (10) 10/467 (11)	

Bowling: Shaw 27–4–74–3; Guha 29.1–6–68–2; Newton 14–3–37–0; Connor 25–9–64–2; C. E. Taylor 18–9–25–0; Harper 34–10–80–1; Leng 14.1–1–44–1; Atkins 3–0–13–0; Edwards 13–1–43–0.

Umpires: V. Gibbens and V. A. Holder.

ENGLISH WOMEN'S CRICKET, 2002

The 2002 domestic season introduced a new competition, intended to provide a much-needed stepping stone from the County Championship to the international stage. The "Super Fours" was the brainchild of England's new coach, the Australian, John Harmer, and Gill McConway, the ECB's executive director of women's cricket, and was the most conspicuous move in a range of ECB initiatives to raise standards. In April, the best 48 players in the country were invited to Trent Bridge for a team-building session; in May and June, the four sides thus created (nicknamed the Braves, the Knight Riders, the Super Strikers and the V Team) met in a mini-league, with six one-day games apiece spread over five weekends. The England captain, Clare Connor, led the Braves to an inaugural win. The matches served as trials for the international programme which began in July. The Super Fours was judged a success, with the players showing excellent spirit and application, and was set to become a regular fixture.

The County Championship was sponsored for the first time, as part of the ECB's four-year agreement with Liverpool Victoria, a friendly society, to sponsor the men's Championship. That meant a new name, the Frizzell County Championship, but it was business as usual on the Cambridge pitches. Unlike their male counterparts, Yorkshire retained the title, winning all the three matches they played – the weather was so bad that, for the first time since the Championship was established in 1980, two entire days and thus two rounds of matches were lost. Kent, boosted by Charlotte Edwards's return from injury and the help of New Zealand international Paula Flannery, scored heavily to bounce straight back from Division Two after the previous season's relegation. Hampshire moved up from Division Three, where Northamptonshire, who won the Emerging Counties competition, replaced Wiltshire.

Yorkshire also dominated the age-group finals, where their Under-19s defeated Sussex by 42 runs and the Under-17s beat Kent by eight wickets. The Under-15 final was contested by two of the newer counties, with Worcestershire beating Essex by 55 runs.

In the Premier League final, Wolverhampton upset Kent Invicta, the favourites and Southern Area champions. Kelly Evenson ran through Invicta's strong batting line-up with five for 22. Clare Connor was in top form as Brighton and Hove won the Knockout Cup final against Wakefield: she took five wickets and followed up with a fifty as Brighton passed their target inside 23 overs.

England won the first Under-21 European Cup, held in Dublin, thanks to an impressive seven-wicket win over Ireland in the decisive game. Holland and Scotland also took part in a tournament badly hit by rain. The ECB planned to send an England side to play in the Australian Under-19 State Championship early in 2003, followed by two age-group internationals. It was only the second time an England age-group side had toured outside Europe; an Under-21 team went to South Africa for the provincial championships and age-group internationals in 1991.

England's senior team had another winter on the road lined up, with a one-day quadrangular series in New Zealand followed by two Tests in Australia, before South Africa arrived to tour England in the summer of 2003. But some England players would be in Australia and New Zealand already. The number of overseas cricketers appearing in English club and county sides has been rising steadily, and many English players have made the reverse journey. At least four of the senior squad were due to spend part of the English winter with New Zealand sides.

Note: Matches in this section were not first-class.

SUPER FOURS, 2002

	Played	Won	Lost	Bonus points Batting	Bonus points Bowling	Points
Braves	6	4	2	2	2	52
Knight Riders	6	3	3	3	1	40
V Team	6	3	3	2	2	40
Super Strikers	6	2	4	5	2	31

FRIZZELL COUNTY CHAMPIONSHIP, 2002

Division One
	Played	Won	Lost	Points
Yorkshire	3	3	0	81.5
Berkshire	3	2	1	70.5
Sussex	3	2	1	66
Nottinghamshire	3	1	2	54
Surrey	3	1	2	49
Staffordshire	3	0	3	40

Division Two
	Played	Won	Lost	Points
Kent	3	3	0	84.5
Lancashire	3	3	0	80.5
Hertfordshire	3	2	1	68
Somerset	3	1	2	52
Middlesex	3	0	3	42.5
Derbyshire	3	0	3	41

Division Three
	Played	Won	Lost	Points
Hampshire	3	3	0	82.5
Warwickshire	3	2	1	68.5
Cheshire	3	2	1	68
Essex	3	1	2	55.5
Durham	3	1	2	54
Wiltshire	3	0	3	36

Staffordshire, Derbyshire and Wiltshire were relegated from their respective divisions; Kent and Hampshire were promoted, with Northamptonshire entering Division Three.

ECB NATIONAL KNOCKOUT FINAL, 2002

At King's College, Taunton, September 7. **Brighton and Hove won by eight wickets.** Toss: Brighton and Hove. **Wakefield 106 for nine** (37 overs) (C. J. Connor five for 28); **Brighton and Hove 108 for two** (22.3 overs) (C. J. Connor 54, H. M. Tiffen 39 not out).
Rain reduced the match to 37 overs a side.

ECB NATIONAL LEAGUE FINAL, 2002

At Derby, September 8. **Wolverhampton won by five wickets.** Toss: Wolverhampton. **Kent Invicta 152** (49 overs) (O. J. Magno 77 not out; K. Evenson five for 22); **Wolverhampton 153 for five** (45 overs) (T. Crump 43 not out).

6
OVERSEAS CRICKET

Helping himself: Inzamam-ul-Haq made 329 at Lahore. New Zealanders in Pakistan, page 1315.
Picture by Mohsin Raza, Reuters.

PART SIX: OVERSEAS CRICKET IN 2001-02 AND 2002

FEATURES OF 2001-02 AND 2002

This section covers
- all international tours outside England in 2001-02 and 2002, i.e. starting between August 29, 2001 and Sept 12, 2002 (pages 1139–1440)
- all first-class overseas domestic competitions (pages 1441–1556)

The sequence
- Features of the overseas year
- Test tours (pages 1139–1336), beginning with England in India and in New Zealand, followed by other tours in order of start date. Where the Test series was accompanied by a one-day series between the same two teams, the one-day series goes with it
- one-day tours and tournaments (pages 1337–1422), beginning with England in Zimbabwe and followed by other one-day series in order of start date
- the England Academy in Australia (pages 1423–1425)
- A-team tours outside England (pages 1426–1428)
- the Under-19 World Cup (pages 1430–1437)
- England Women's tour of India (pages 1438–1440)
- domestic competitions, from Australia, the oldest Test nation, to Bangladesh, the youngest (pages 1441–1556), followed by Kenya, the Netherlands and other non-Test nations (pages 1557–1574)

Notes
- England's tour of India (pages 1139–1162), which took place in two parts – a Test leg before Christmas 2001 and a one-day leg early in the New Year – is treated as a single tour
- series taking place outside England in the middle of the year, which were dated 2001 (SL) or (P) or (Z) in last year's Almanack, are now given as 2001, for simplicity's sake

See also
- World View (pages 86–104) for each country's form and results over the year from September to September, as well as the ICC Test and One-Day Championship tables
- Test Matches, 2002-03 (pages 1712–1723), for brief coverage of all Test series between September 2002 and February 2003, plus the 2003 World Cup

Double-Hundreds (58)

329	Inzamam-ul-Haq	Pakistan v New Zealand (First Test) at Lahore.
274	D. P. M. D. Jayawardene. .	Sinhalese v Tamil Union at Colombo (NCC).
271	J. J. Martin	Baroda v Hyderabad at Baroda.
259	D. M. Benkenstein.	KwaZulu-Natal v Northerns at Durban.
256‡	Hasan Raza	Karachi Whites v Rest of Baluchistan at Karachi.
253†	S. S. Das.	Orissa v Bengal at Baripada.
252*	S. C. Williams	Leeward Islands v Guyana at Albion.
249	V. Rathore	North Zone v East Zone at Delhi.
247	G. J. Whittall	Manicaland v Mashonaland at Mutare.
246	D. S. Lehmann	South Australia v Tasmania at Hobart.
244‡	G. Kirsten	Western Province v Eastern Province at Cape Town.
235*	G. W. Flower	Mashonaland A v Mashonaland at Harare.

235	A. Haniff	Guyana v Bangladesh A at Georgetown.
235	J. A. H. Marshall	Northern Districts v Canterbury at Christchurch.
233‡	C. L. Hooper	West Indies v India (First Test) at Georgetown.
230	K. C. Sangakkara	Sri Lanka v Pakistan (Asia Test Final) at Lahore.
229*	A. G. Puttick	Western Province v Boland at Paarl.
227	Babar Naeem	Rawalpindi v Lahore Blues at Lahore.
223‡	N. J. Astle	New Zealanders v Queensland at Brisbane.
222‡	N. J. Astle	New Zealand v England (First Test) at Christchurch.
222‡	C. L. Hooper	Guyana v Leeward Islands at Albion.
221	B. C. Lara	West Indies v Sri Lanka (Third Test) at Colombo (SSC).
220‡	G. Kirsten	South Africa v Zimbabwe (First Test) at Harare.
218‡	G. Gambhir	Indian Board President's XI v Zimbabweans at Vijayawada.
215*	M. I. Gidley	Griqualand West v Northerns at Centurion.
215*	Sangram Singh	Himachal Pradesh v Services at Una.
214‡	G. Gambhir	Delhi v Railways at Delhi.
214	A. Nandakishore	Hyderabad v Karnataka at Secunderabad.
212*	S. B. Styris	Northern Districts v Otago at Hamilton.
212	S. B. Bangar	Railways v Tamil Nadu at Delhi.
211*	S. C. Joseph	Leeward Islands v West Indies B at Charlestown.
210	C. N. Evans	Mashonaland v Manicaland at Mutare.
210	N. R. Ferreira	Manicaland v Matabeleland at Mutare.
210	Minhazul Abedin	Chittagong v Dhaka at Mymensingh.
210†	S. S. Raul	Orissa v Bengal at Baripada.
210	Usman Tariq	Bahawalpur v Sargodha at Sargodha.
209	J. P. Maher	Queensland v South Australia at Brisbane.
209	Yuvraj Singh	North Zone v South Zone at Faridabad.
207*	R. V. Bharadwaj	Karnataka v Tamil Nadu at Bangalore.
207*	P. M. Mullick	Orissa v Bihar at Baripada.
206	P. A. de Silva	Sri Lanka v Bangladesh (First Test) at Colombo (PSS).
206	Kavaljit Singh	Jammu and Kashmir v Services at Delhi.
204*	A. C. Gilchrist	Australia v South Africa (First Test) at Johannesburg.
204*‡	Misbah-ul-Haq	Sargodha v Bahawalpur at Sargodha.
204*	H. P. Tillekeratne	Sri Lanka v West Indies (Third Test) at Colombo (SSC).
204*	Yousuf Youhana	Pakistan v Bangladesh (Second Test) at Chittagong.
204	C. H. Gayle	West Indies v New Zealand (Second Test) at St George's.
204†	Imran Farhat	Habib Bank v ADBP at Sheikhupura.
203*	M. G. Bevan	New South Wales v Western Australia at Sydney.
202*	M. L. Love	Queensland v South Australia at Adelaide.
202‡	Misbah-ul-Haq	Sargodha v Hyderabad at Sargodha.
202	Yashpal Singh	Services v Punjab at Amritsar.
201*	Khaled Masud	Rajshahi v Khulna at Dhaka.
201*	B. F. Smith	Central Districts v Canterbury at New Plymouth.
201	M. S. Atapattu	Sri Lanka v Bangladesh (Asia Test) at Colombo (SSC).
200*†‡	Hasan Raza	Habib Bank v ADBP at Sheikhupura.
200*	M. J. North	Western Australia v Victoria at Melbourne.
200*	G. P. Thorpe	England v New Zealand (First Test) at Christchurch.

† *Imran Farhat and Hasan Raza scored their double-hundreds in one innings, as did Das and Raul.*
‡ *Astle, Gambhir, Hasan Raza, Hooper, Kirsten, and Misbah-ul-Haq each scored two double-hundreds, Gambhir in successive innings.*

Hundred on First-Class Debut

119	Aariz Kamal	Karachi Whites v Rest of Baluchistan at Karachi.
106	G. F. Barrett	CFX Academy v Manicaland at Mutare.
137	K. D. Duckworth	Eastern Province v Free State at Port Elizabeth.
106*	G. M. Ewing	Matabeleland v Mashonaland at Bulawayo.
113	Faisal Khan	Sialkot v Lahore Whites at Sialkot.
110	D. J. Pagon	West Indies B v Guyana at Albion.
101*	K. I. Tittle	Leeward Islands v West Indies B at Charlestown.

Three Hundreds in Successive Innings

P. Dharmani (Punjab) . . . .
119* v Himachal Pradesh at Mohali;
106 and 127* v Services at Amritsar.

C. L. Hooper (Guyana) . . . .
222 v Leeward Islands at Albion;
149* v Jamaica at Kingston;
233 West Indies v India (First Test) at Georgetown.

Hundred in Each Innings of a Match

J. A. Beukes	105	101*	Free State v Border at East London.
P. Dharmani	106	127*	Punjab v Services at Amritsar.
A. Flower	142	199*	Zimbabwe v South Africa (First Test) at Harare.
A. Flower	114	156*	Mashonaland v Mashonaland A at Harare.
B. J. Hodge	140	110*	Victoria v South Australia at Adelaide.
B. C. Lara	221	130	West Indies v Sri Lanka (Third Test) at Colombo (SSC).
Minhazul Abedin	210	110	Chittagong v Dhaka at Mymensingh.
A. A. Pagnis	126	133*	Railways v Rajasthan at Delhi.
R. T. Ponting	126	154	Tasmania v New South Wales at Sydney.
C. J. L. Rogers	101*	102*	Western Australia v South Australia at Perth.
M. van Jaarsveld	182*	158*	Northerns v Griqualand West at Centurion.
Wasim Jaffer	122	103*	West Zone v Central Zone at Rajkot.

Carrying Bat through Completed Innings

K. Arjune	109*	West Indies B (264) v Trinidad & Tobago at Pointe-à-Pierre.
		One batsman retired hurt.
M. L. Bruyns	102*	Border (170) v Northerns at Centurion.
D. S. Bundela	111*	Madhya Pradesh (274) v Railways at Indore.
A. Chopra	119*	North Zone (253) v West Zone at Pune.
M. U. Dissanayake	98*	Sinhalese (234) v Moors at Colombo (CCC).
B. A. Johnson	121*	South Australia (206) v Western Australia at Adelaide.
B. A. Johnson	138*	South Australia (229) v Victoria at Melbourne.
In consecutive matches.		
G. J. Mail	150*	New South Wales (436) v South Australia at Sydney.
Mohammad Azam	73*	Sheikhupura (247) v Islamabad at Sheikhupura.
S. B. Saikia	29*	Assam (92) v Orissa at Balasore.
C. M. Withanage	54*	Galle (140) v Tamil Union at Colombo (CCC).

High Percentage of Runs in a Completed Innings

69.93%   Rizwan Malik (100*)   Gujranwala (143) v Bahawalpur at Bahawalpur.
Equal lowest completed innings total to include 100.

Hundred before Lunch

D. S. Lehmann . .   31* to 131*   South Australia v Tasmania at Hobart (3rd day).
A. J. Mackay . . .   108   Mashonaland v Matabeleland at Bulawayo (2nd day).

Most Sixes in an Innings

11	N. J. Astle (222)	New Zealand v England (First Test) at Christchurch.
10	A. J. Mackay (108)	Mashonaland v Matabeleland at Bulawayo.
10	S. B. Styris (212*)	Northern Districts v Otago at Hamilton.
10	Yashpal Singh (202)	Services v Punjab at Amritsar.

Most Runs in Boundaries

206 (38×4, 9×6)   Inzamam-ul-Haq (329)   Pakistan v New Zealand (First Test) at Lahore.

Long Innings

Mins
692   G. Gambhir (214) . . . .   Delhi v Railways at Delhi.
680   A. G. Puttick (229*) . . . .   Western Province v Boland at Paarl.
675   S. Chanderpaul (136*) . . . .   West Indies v India (Fourth Test) at St John's.
660   S. S. Das (253) . . . .   Orissa v Bengal at Baripada.
631   S. B. Bangar (212) . . . .   Railways v Tamil Nadu at Delhi.
630   C. L. Hooper (233) . . . .   West Indies v India (First Test) at Georgetown.
629   J. J. Martin (271) . . . .   Baroda v Hyderabad at Baroda.
626   S. Ramesh (126*) . . . .   Tamil Nadu v Kerala at Chennai.

Slow Fifty

Mins
383   S. Ramesh (126*) . . . .   Tamil Nadu v Kerala at Chennai.
     World record.

Slow Hundred

Mins
556   S. Ramesh (126*) . . . .   Tamil Nadu v Kerala at Chennai.
     One minute short of world record.

Unusual Dismissals

Retired Out
M. S. Atapattu (201) . . . .   Sri Lanka v Bangladesh (Asia Test) at Colombo (SSC).
Faisal Hossain (105). . . . .   Chittagong v Dhaka at Mymensingh.
C. H. Gayle (120) . . . .   West Indians v Sri Lanka A at Matara.
D. P. M. D. Jayawardene (150). . . . .   Sri Lanka v Bangladesh (Asia Test) at Colombo (SSC).
Minhazul Abedin (110). . . . . .   Chittagong v Dhaka at Mymensingh.

Obstructing the Field
R. C. Rupasinghe (5) . . . .   Rio v Kurungala Youth at Colombo (Reid Avenue).

Handled the Ball
Tushar Imran (0) . . . .   Bangladesh A v Jamaica at Spanish Town.
M. P. Vaughan (64) . . . .   England v India (Third Test) at Bangalore.

Run Out by the Bowler for Backing Up
R. J. Kanwat (1) . . . .   Rajasthan v Railways at Delhi.

First-Wicket Partnership of 100 in Each Innings

185   125 . . . . .   C. C. Williams/S. S. Parab, Baroda v Maharashtra at Pune.
124   124 . . . . .   S. B. Bangar/A. A. Pagnis, Railways v Bengal at Delhi.
121   101 . . . . .   A. Chopra/G. Gambhir, Delhi v Haryana at Delhi.

Highest Partnerships

First Wicket
340   A. Haniff/S. Chattergoon, Guyana v Bangladesh A at Georgetown.
299   M. D. Bell/R. A. Jones, Wellington v Otago at Dunedin.
283   D. S. Manohar/A. Nandakishore, Hyderabad v Karnataka at Secunderabad.
256   H. H. Gibbs/G. Kirsten, South Africa v Zimbabwe (First Test) at Harare.
252   A. Chopra/G. Gambhir, India A v BCCSL Academy XI at Colombo (RPS).

Second Wicket
386   G. S. Blewett/D. S. Lehmann, South Australia v Tasmania at Hobart.
320   N. D. Modi/H. H. Kanitkar, West Zone v East Zone at Kolkata.
316   N. A. Godbole/H. H. Kanitkar, Maharashtra v Saurashtra at Pune.
294   J. P. Maher/M. L. Love, Queensland v New South Wales at Sydney.

Third Wicket
436† S. S. Das/S. S. Raul, Orissa v Bengal at Baripada.
308   S. N. Wijesinghe/R. H. S. Silva, Sebastianites v Galle at Moratuwa.
296* M. L. Love/B. P. Nash, Queensland v South Australia at Adelaide.
        312 were added in all for this wicket, A. Symonds replacing Love (retired hurt).
282   Aariz Kamal/Hasan Raza, Karachi Whites v Rest of Baluchistan at Karachi.
265   M. J. Horne/A. C. Barnes, Auckland v Bangladeshis at Auckland.
259   Wasim Jaffer/A. A. Muzumdar, Mumbai v Baroda at Baroda.
253   L. J. Cush/S. Chanderpaul, Guyana v Leeward Islands at Albion.

Fourth Wicket
326   T. P. Singh/Raja Ali, Railways v Madhya Pradesh at Indore.
321   D. R. Martyn/M. W. Goodwin, Western Australia v Tasmania at Perth.
306   Asif Mujtaba/Faisal Iqbal, PIA v Pakistan Customs at Karachi.
269   V. Rathore/D. Mongia, Punjab v Himachal Pradesh at Mohali.
255   E. F. M. U. Fernando/K. A. S. Jayasinghe, Ragama v Chilaw Marians at Colombo (Colts).
        288* were added by Inzamam-ul-Haq, Yousuf Youhana and Abdul Razzaq, Pakistan v Bangladesh at Multan; Inzamam-ul-Haq retired hurt after 123 runs were added.

Fifth Wicket
293   C. L. Hooper/S. Chanderpaul, West Indies v India (First Test) at Georgetown.
290   D. Vinay Kumar/A. S. Yadav, Hyderabad v Goa at Panaji.
271   Imran Abbas/Asim Munir, Gujranwala v Faisalabad at Gujranwala.
258   Halim Shah/Mazharul Haque, Dhaka v Barisal at Barisal.

Sixth Wicket
317   D. R. Martyn/A. C. Gilchrist, Australia v South Africa (First Test) at Johannesburg.
302   T. M. Dilshan/U. D. U. Chandana, Sri Lanka A v Kenya at Matara.
281   G. P. Thorpe/A. Flintoff, England v New Zealand (First Test) at Christchurch.

Seventh Wicket
217   V. V. S. Laxman/A. Ratra, India v West Indies (Fourth Test) at St John's.
191   Misbah-ul-Haq/Atiq Ahmed, Sargodha v Bahawalpur at Sargodha.
189   C. N. Evans/D. J. R. Campbell, Mashonaland v Manicaland at Mutare.
179   B. B. J. Griggs/C. J. M. Furlong, Central Districts v Northern Districts at Hamilton.
175   G. B. Hogg/M. J. Nicholson, Western Australia v South Africans at Perth.

Eighth Wicket
253   N. J. Astle/A. C. Parore, New Zealand v Australia (Third Test) at Perth.
184   C. O. Browne/S. J. Benn, Barbados v Windward Islands at Bridgetown.
171   D. M. Benkenstein/G. H. Bodi, KwaZulu-Natal v Northerns at Durban.
167   S. B. Bangar/M. Kartik, Railways v Tamil Nadu at Delhi.
154   D. D. Wickremasinghe/L. D. I. Dilhara, Galle v Ragama at Katunayake.
153   R. J. Nicol/R. A. Young, Auckland v Canterbury at Auckland.

Ninth Wicket
180   D. Jennings/B. L. Reddy, Easterns v Griqualand West at Benoni.
180   R. V. C. Prasad/H. H. Watekar, Andhra v Gujarat at Ahmedabad.
179   Rehan Rafiq/Faisal Elahi, Bahawalpur v Karachi Whites at Bahawalpur.
152   Zulfiqar Jan/Jaffer Nazir, KRL v PWD at Sialkot.

Tenth Wicket
118   N. J. Astle/C. L. Cairns, New Zealand v England (First Test) at Christchurch.
114   D. J. Saker/S. J. Jurgensen, Tasmania v Queensland at Hobart.

† *National record.*

Eight Wickets in an Innings (15)

9-51	M. Muralitharan	Sri Lanka v Zimbabwe (Second Test) at Kandy.
8-21	A. J. Penn	Wellington v Canterbury at Wellington.
8-32	T. P. Gamage	Ragama v Rio at Moratuwa.
8-34	K. A. D. M. Fernando	Sebastianites v Galle at Moratuwa.
8-35	R. W. Price	Midlands v CFX Academy at Kwekwe.
8-40	Abdur Rauf	Sui Gas v ADBP at Faisalabad.
8-47	H. M. R. K. B. Herath	Moors v Galle at Colombo (Reid Avenue).
8-50	J. N. Gillespie	South Australia v New South Wales at Sydney.
8-65	K. S. Parida	Railways v Madhya Pradesh at Indore.
8-68	Fazl-e-Akbar	Peshawar v Islamabad at Peshawar.
8-73	A. G. R. M. S. Ranaweera	Rio v Kandy at Katunayake.
8-80	Arshad Khan	Allied Bank v PWD at Karachi.
8-86	Shafiuddin Ahmed	Chittagong v Rajshahi at Rajshahi.
8-132	S. Pandey	Madhya Pradesh v Railways at Indore.
8-133	L. J. P. Gunaratne	Chilaw Marians v Sebastianites at Colombo (NCC).

Twelve Wickets in a Match (17)

14-98	Abdur Rauf	Sui Gas v ADBP at Faisalabad.
14-116	K. A. D. M. Fernando	Sebastianites v Galle at Moratuwa.
14-191	W. P. U. J. C. Vaas	Sri Lanka v West Indies (Third Test) at Colombo (SSC).
13-55	U. Chatterjee	Bengal v Tripura at Agartala.
13-95	M. Muralitharan	Tamil Union v Burgher at Colombo (RPS).
13-106	Waqas Ahmed	WAPDA v Habib Bank at Lahore.
13-112	P. C. Rofe	South Australia v New South Wales at Adelaide.
13-115	M. Muralitharan	Sri Lanka v Zimbabwe (Second Test) at Kandy.
12-55	A. J. Penn	Wellington v Canterbury at Wellington.
12-73	M. K. G. C. P. Lakshitha	Air Force v Rio at Colombo (BRC).
12-79	R. W. Price	Midlands v CFX Academy at Kwekwe.
12-94	Danish Kaneria	Pakistan v Bangladesh (Asia Test) at Multan.
12-127	Yasir Arafat	KRL v Pakistan Customs at Hyderabad.
12-133	Mohammad Hussain	Lahore Blues v Rest of NWFP at Lahore.
12-134	Fazl-e-Akbar	PIA v Habib Bank at Lahore.
12-134	Fazl-e-Akbar	Peshawar v Islamabad at Peshawar.
12-185	Arshad Khan	Allied Bank v PWD at Karachi.

Hat-Tricks (11)

Asif Mujtaba	PIA v PWD at Karachi.
A. Barik	Orissa v Assam at Balasore.
Faisal Irfan	WAPDA v Habib Bank at Lahore.
Fazl-e-Akbar	PIA v Habib Bank at Lahore.
I. J. Harvey	Victoria v South Australia at Adelaide.
Jaffer Nazir	Sheikhupura v Rest of Punjab at Lahore.
S. J. Jurgensen	Tasmania v New South Wales at Hobart.
A. Mishra	Haryana v Himachal Pradesh at Rohtak.
Mohammad Sami	Pakistan v Sri Lanka (Asia Test Final) at Lahore.
M. Ntini	Border v Free State at Bloemfontein.
C. M. Willoughby	Western Province v Eastern Province at Cape Town.

Four Wickets in Four Balls

Fazl-e-Akbar	PIA v Habib Bank at Lahore.

Four Wickets in Five Balls

D. S. Mohanty	Orissa v Tripura at Kalahandi (*all lbw*).

Wicket with First Ball in First-Class Cricket

B. Ranaweera . . . .   Bloomfield v Galle at Colombo (CCC)
L. J. Woodcock . . . .   Wellington v Otago at Wellington.

Most Overs Bowled in an Innings

79–19–181–5   R. W. Price . . . . . .   Zimbabwe v South Africa (Second Test) at Bulawayo.

Match Double (100 runs and 10 wickets)

Mohammad Hussain   0, 126; 6-60, 6-73   Lahore Blues v Rest of NWFP at Lahore.

Six Wicket-Keeping Dismissals in an Innings

7 ct, 1 st† . .	S. Nath	Assam v Tripura at Guwahati.
7 ct‡	M. G. Croy	Otago v Auckland at Auckland.
7 ct	W. A. Seccombe	Queensland v New South Wales at Brisbane.
6 ct	Aamer Iqbal	Pakistan Customs v Sui Gas at Lahore.
5 ct, 1 st . .	M. V. Boucher	Border v Boland at East London.
6 ct	T. A. Bula	North West v Gauteng at Johannesburg.
5 ct, 1 st . .	T. M. Dilshan	Bloomfield v Chilaw Marians at Colombo (RA).
6 ct	D. J. Jacobs	North West v Easterns at Benoni.
5 ct, 1 st . .	J. R. Murray	Windward Islands v Jamaica at St George's.
5 ct, 1 st . .	S. Ohlan	Haryana v Punjab at Gurgaon.
6 ct	Ravikant Sharma	Himachal Pradesh v Delhi at Bilaspur.
6 ct	M. R. Street	Gauteng v Boland at Paarl.
6 ct	A. A. Velaskar	Goa v Karnataka at Bangalore.

† *National record. It was Nath's first-class debut.*   ‡ *Equalling national record.*

Nine Wicket-Keeping Dismissals in a Match

10 ct, 1 st† . .	S. Nath	Assam v Tripura at Guwahati.
9 ct, 1 st . .	D. Jennings	Easterns v Griqualand West at Benoni.
9 ct	Aamer Iqbal	Pakistan Customs v Sui Gas at Lahore.
9 ct	S. G. Clingeleffer	Tasmania v Queensland at Hobart.
3 ct, 6 st . .	Humayun Farhat	Lahore Blues v Lahore Whites at Lahore.
8 ct, 1 st . .	M. K. P. B. Kularatne	Galle v Colombo at Colombo (CCC).
9 ct	Moin Khan	PIA v WAPDA at Faisalabad.
9 ct	N. S. Pilon	New South Wales v South Australia at Sydney.
9 ct	W. A. Seccombe	Queensland v Tasmania at Brisbane.

† *National record, it was Nath's first-class debut.*

Five Catches in an Innings in the Field

D. N. Crookes . . . .   Easterns v Griqualand West at Benoni.
                        Wicket-keeper D. Jennings caught the other five.
Ehsanul Haque . . .   Bangladesh A v Leeward Islands at St John's.

Six Catches in a Match in the Field

6 J. P. Maher . . .   Queensland v Western Australia at Perth.
6 D. J. Marsh . . .   Tasmania v New South Wales at Hobart.
6 D. R. Martyn . .   Western Australia v Tasmania at Perth.
6 J. Mubarak . . .   Colombo v Air Force at Katunayake.
6 V. C. Naidu . . .   Vidarbha v Madhya Pradesh at Nagpur.

No Byes Conceded in Total of 500 or More

M. S. Dhoni . . . . . . Bihar v Orissa (625-8 dec.) at Baripada.
A. Flower . . . . Zimbabwe v South Africa (600-3 dec.) (First Test) at Harare.
R. D. Jacobs . . . . . West Indies v India (513-9 dec.) (Fourth Test) at St John's.
Khaled Masud . . . . . Bangladesh v Sri Lanka (555-5 dec.) (Asia Test) at Colombo (SSC).
Khaled Masud . . . . . Bangladesh v Sri Lanka (541-9 dec.) (First Test) at Colombo (PSS).
S. Reuben Paul. . . . . Saurashtra v Baroda (509) at Rajkot.
C. F. K. van Wyk . . . Northerns v Griqualand West (529-6 dec.) at Centurion.

Highest Innings Totals

754† . . . . KwaZulu-Natal v Northerns at Durban.
673 . . . . Baroda v Hyderabad at Baroda.
671-6 dec. . . . . Orissa v Bengal at Baripada.
652-7 dec. . . . . Australia v South Africa (First Test) at Johannesburg.
644-9 dec. . . . . Mashonaland v Matabeleland at Bulawayo.
643 . . . . Pakistan v New Zealand (First Test) at Lahore.
629-9 dec. . . . . West Indies v India (Fourth Test) at St John's.
627-9 dec. . . . . Sri Lanka v West Indies (Third Test) at Colombo (SSC).
625-8 dec. . . . . Orissa v Bihar at Baripada.
604-7 dec. . . . . Pakistan Customs v PWD at Karachi.
600-3 dec. . . . . South Africa v Zimbabwe (First Test) at Harare.
600-8 dec. . . . . Western Australia v South Africans at Perth.

† *National record.*

Lowest Innings Totals

27 . . . . Habib Bank v PIA at Lahore.
46 . . . . Pakistan Customs v KRL at Hyderabad.
49 . . . . Rio v Sebastianites at Colombo (Reid Avenue).
56 . . . . Rest of Sindh v Gujranwala at Muridke.
58 . . . . Colombo v Colts at Colombo (PSS).
61 . . . . Habib Bank v WAPDA at Lahore (*One batsman absent*).
62 . . . . Khulna v Sylhet at Jessore.
65 . . . . Sheikhupura v Peshawar at Peshawar *(One batsman absent)*.
65 . . . . Burgher v Nondescripts at Colombo (NCC).
65 . . . . Kandy v Antonians at Katunayake.
71 . . . . Auckland v Central Districts at Palmerston North.
71 . . . . Rio v Chilaw Marians at Colombo (Moors) (1st innings).
72 . . . . Central Districts v Auckland at Palmerston North.
72 . . . . Rio v Chilaw Marians at Colombo (Moors) (2nd innings).
72 . . . . Eastern Province v Easterns at Benoni.
73 . . . . New Zealand v Pakistan (First Test) at Lahore.

Highest Fourth-Innings Total

451 . . . . New Zealand v England (First Test) at Christchurch (set 550).

Match Aggregate of 1,500 Runs

1,529 for 18 . . . . Griqualand West (529-6 dec. and 235-4 dec.) v Northerns
(423-5 dec. and 342-3) at Centurion.
1,522 for 35 . . . . New Zealand (534-9 dec. and 256-9 dec.) v Australia (351 and 381-7)
(Third Test) at Perth.

Four or More Hundreds in an Innings

Pakistan (546-3 dec.) v Bangladesh (Asia Test) at Multan:
  Saeed Anwar 101, Taufeeq Umar 104, Inzamam-ul-Haq 105 retired hurt, Yousuf Youhana 102*,
    Abdul Razzaq 110*.
New Zealand (534-9 dec.) v Australia (Third Test) at Perth:
  L. Vincent (104), S. P. Fleming (105), N. J. Astle (156*), A. C. Parore (110).

Large Margin of Victory

Chilaw Marians (267 and 409-8 dec.) beat Rio (71 and 72) at Colombo (Moors) by 533 runs.

Victory after Following On

Mashonaland (226 and 506) beat Manicaland (513-9 dec. and 146) by 73 runs at Mutare.
Western Australia (175 and 410) beat Victoria (450-6 dec. and 98) by 37 runs at Melbourne.

11 Bowlers in an Innings

Pakistan Customs v PIA (520-4 dec.) at Karachi.
Dhaka v Chittagong (286-5) at Mymensingh.
India v West Indies (629-9 dec.) (Fourth Test) at St John's.

Most Extras in an Innings

b	*l-b*	*w*	*n-b*	
69	29	17	1	22	Bahawalpur (526-8 dec.) v Sargodha at Sargodha.
67	30	8	26	3	Rajshahi (304) v Sylhet at Rajshahi.
63	18	6	11	28	Sialkot (388-9 dec.) v Rest of Punjab at Okara.
63	12	21	7	23	Sheikhupura (429) v Rawalpindi at Sheikhupura.
62	13	13	10	26	Peshawar (335) v Rest of Punjab at Lahore.
60	32	5	4	19	KRL (487) v PIA at Lahore.
60	29	7	12	12	Chittagong (345) v Sylhet at Sylhet.
60	25	6	7	22	Mashonaland (644-9 dec.) v Matabeleland at Bulawayo.
60	11	12	3	34	KRL (410) v Sui Gas at Rawalpindi.

Career Aggregate Milestones

25,000 runs	M. E. Waugh.
20,000 runs	C. L. Hooper.
15,000 runs	M. G. Bevan, S. R. Tendulkar.
10,000 runs	M. S Atapattu, S. T. Jayasuriya, Saeed Anwar, B. F. Smith, H. P. Tillekeratne.
500 wickets	C. L. Hooper, Mohammad Zahid, sen., Murtaza Hussain.
500 dismissals. . . .	A. C. Gilchrist.

ENGLAND IN INDIA, 2001-02

BY DAVID HOPPS

England's first Test tour of India for nine years should have been a delight, an overdue opportunity to sample the cricketing and cultural pleasures of a land seething with life and unpredictability. Instead, it came close to being blighted before a ball was bowled – first by no-shows from three regular players, then by the prickly politics of two countries still carrying plenty of colonial baggage. The cricket might have been incidental, but turned out to be much more interesting than that. Nasser Hussain rose to the challenge of returning to the land of his birth with an inexperienced team and made sure that the Test series, although lost, was close and competitive. The one-day series was even closer, culminating in a dramatic denouement at Mumbai: the abiding image of the tour was of Andrew Flintoff, transformed from a Test reject to a fast-bowling all-rounder, careering round the Wankhede Stadium with his shirt off after clinching a hard-earned 3–3 draw.

Given the overcrowded international programme, it is too easy to carp whenever a player, especially one with children, asks for a break. But it was with sadly predictable timing that the request came from two England players with little inclination to immerse themselves in Indian ways or endure dead Indian pitches. The withdrawal of Alec Stewart and (from the Tests only) Darren Gough left a bitter taste in the mouth which was not assuaged by the fact that both would have returned for the Tests in New Zealand if the management had let them. If Stewart's decision had something to do with needing operations on both elbows, he was also swayed by the allegations – consistently denied – that he had had dealings with illegal Indian book-makers in 1993.

No sooner had the team been picked than September 11 changed the world. For a while it looked as if India's neighbours might be drawn into war and the tour called off altogether; then the ECB announced that it would be left to the individual to decide. Eleven players confirmed that they would go, subject to a (rather token) check on security arrangements by Tim O'Gorman of the Professional Cricketers' Association and John Carr of the ECB. Five expressed doubts – Marcus Trescothick, Andy Caddick, Ashley Giles, Craig White and Robert Croft. On October 30, after the five had been given more time, Caddick and Croft pulled out. Caddick, a father of two, said he had only to cradle his baby (Fraser, born on October 12) in his arms to know he had made the right decision.

The doubters were far from alone – the airline industry worldwide suffered a drastic loss of business, and those who ridiculed the players' jitters often did so as they headed down to the travel agent's to cancel their own holiday. The Foreign Office was advising Europeans in India "to keep a low profile", a phrase that met with disbelief from the players. The ECB was giving out conflicting signals: the chief executive, Tim Lamb, was far more adamant that the tour would proceed than the chairman, Lord MacLaurin. The players were entitled to exercise their freedom of choice, but the wavering seemed to be based less on a realistic assessment of the risks than a vague fear of

Brothers in arms? Sourav Ganguly and Nasser Hussain, the only current Test captains born in the same country, meet at Mohali. *Picture by Graham Morris.*

the unknown. There was a mostly vacuous debate about the dangers of India, where it was imagined that England cricketers might be a target of extremists among the large Muslim minority; and there was some haziness about the proximity of Afghanistan. It was pointed out that the first two Tests were to take place close to the border with Pakistan; it was also pointed out that they could easily be switched, and most Indian cities were further from Kabul than London was from Sarajevo.

When the plane finally landed, matters should have improved. But preparations for the First Test at Mohali were overshadowed by a stand-off between cricket's two most powerful figures: the ICC's Australian chief executive, Malcolm Speed, and the autocratic Indian board president, Jagmohan Dalmiya, whose position was underpinned by Indian TV money. The source of the dispute was India's disgust with the decisions of the ICC referee (and former England captain) Mike Denness in their Test series in South Africa. India had cause to be aggrieved, but to resort to open rebellion against ICC authority, rather than go through the proper channels, was close to anarchy. Speed, determined to present the ICC as a well-run and modern sporting body, had no choice but to assert his authority. When India protested at the one-Test suspension of Virender Sehwag by refusing to accept Denness as referee for the final Test, the ICC had to declare the match unofficial.

Dalmiya embarked, not for the first time, on a display of brinkmanship. It might have played well to India's sense of nationalism and stirred lingering grievances over colonial racism, but it ill served the sport he was supposed to represent. Sehwag had sat out the Centurion match; India insisted that this meant he had served his time, and included him in the squad for the

First Test against England. The ICC said that, if he played, they would rule this Test unofficial too; England should – and, all the indications were, would – go home. A compromise was reached with only three days to go: Sehwag was omitted in exchange for a "referees commission", whose constitution, in due course, Dalmiya successfully challenged.

All this took months. The Test series was only three weeks from start to finish, but was absorbing enough to catch the imagination. England were heavily beaten at Mohali, but fought back to have the better of a draw at Ahmedabad, and were well on top when rain ruined the finale at Bangalore. Hussain proved a shrewd and diplomatic leader, tactically astute, imaginative, yet realistic about his team's limitations. He was a polite, intelligent spin doctor with the media, and immensely loyal to what he never tired of reminding everybody was a young side, largely untutored in Asian conditions.

However, Hussain went too far in his attempts to smother India's star batsman, Sachin Tendulkar. First, he instructed his bowlers to aim wide of off stump, to a seven–two or even eight–one field; then, when Tendulkar still made runs, Hussain told Giles (left-arm over) and Andrew Flintoff (right-arm round) to aim outside leg. The tactics had a touch of Douglas Jardine about them, as another England captain, Mike Brearley, remarked – saying that he felt "a deep uneasiness". To oppose these ploys was to goad Hussain into employing them all the more. To question the ability of the 21-year-old wicket-keeper, James Foster, who for all his sparkiness was prone to error, was to draw from Hussain even louder protestations of loyalty. The debate about the handling of Tendulkar was valid: although his scoring-rate slowed to 49 per 100 balls, he still made more runs at a far higher average than anyone else on either side. The concern about Foster's credentials was equally reasonable. Like Mike Atherton before him, Hussain did not lack a stubborn streak.

Inexperience was particularly acute among the bowlers. Matthew Hoggard, after a couple of Tests, suddenly found himself leading the attack. Early in the tour, White admitted publicly that his pace had been slowed by injury; at the same time, Duncan Fletcher had a hunch that England needed the bang-it-in style of Flintoff, who was summoned from the National Academy in Adelaide. Sharing the new ball in the Second and Third Tests, Hoggard and Flintoff showed great discipline and stamina as India's starry batting line-up twice failed to reach 300. The uncapped off-spinner, Richard Dawson, fresh out of Exeter University, recovered well from a couple of early maulings, and Giles shrugged off a long-term Achilles injury to play his part in Hussain's plan. India's scoring-rate over the series, 2.49 runs per over, was markedly slower than England's 2.93.

England's batsmen were caught cold by India's spinners, Harbhajan Singh and Anil Kumble, at Mohali, where the seamers had been expected to dominate. England played the turning ball with increasing confidence thereafter, pushing Harbhajan and Kumble's joint strike-rate from 36 in the First Test to 58 in the Second and 340 in the Third. Graham Thorpe put up most of the resistance in the closing stages of the First Test, but made an unexpected departure on the eve of the Second. Rarely a contented tourist in recent years, he flew home in a doomed attempt to save his marriage.

The people's game: scooters at Ahmedabad for the Second Test. *Picture by Graham Morris.*

Hussain batted manfully throughout; Mark Butcher, although still prone to unforced errors, conquered his weakness against spin; Marcus Trescothick was his usual no-nonsense self, scoring at 57 runs per 100 balls, faster than anyone in the series bar Sehwag (70). Michael Vaughan's bad luck with injury continued, although he didn't help himself by handling the ball when well set at Bangalore. Mark Ramprakash, although contentedly exploring his Indian ancestry, and looking as relaxed as he ever had in an England shirt, could not translate his good form into more than one significant score. Flintoff flopped horribly with the bat, but White resumed his love affair with the subcontinent, playing the spinners as well as any of the top order and reaching his first Test century.

Winning the series gained a little respite for India's captain Sourav Ganguly and coach John Wright after their troubles in South Africa. The selectors dealt them a curious hand for the First Test, supplying a seam attack that was even greener than England's. If Ganguly lost most of the tactical battles, he won the war. He himself was a weak link in the batting, which leant heavily on Tendulkar, but there were runs at different times from all the other big guns plus Deep Dasgupta, the wicket-keeper and makeshift opener, who batted a great deal better than he kept. Sehwag joined Adam Gilchrist as a Test No. 7 with the ability to take the breath away. Even when the seasoned Javagal Srinath returned, England coped comfortably with the quicker bowlers, whose 12 wickets in the series came at a cost of 50 apiece. After starting the series by fielding three seamers on a turning pitch, India ended up playing three spinners on a surface that seamed. Ganguly took the new ball himself with his little dobbers, awakening memories of Eknath Solkar.

To Ganguly's annoyance, it was England who gained more of the acclaim. When Thorpe departed, Hussain and Fletcher were missing five core members of the team that had won in Pakistan and Sri Lanka a year earlier – Atherton, Thorpe, Stewart, Caddick and Gough – but they showed just how much could be done with a cast of understudies. After two bad sessions in the First Test, they were never embarrassed, and with the tail wagging and the bowlers sticking to the plan, they even achieved two hefty first-innings leads. If victory was beyond them, respectability was not.

Lawrence Booth writes: England carried on the good work in January, when they returned to India – reinforced by Thorpe, the refuseniks Gough and Caddick, and a handful of limited-overs specialists – for a six-match one-day series. Few gave them much hope, and when India's openers ran riot at Kanpur to go into a 3–1 lead, a thrashing was on the cards. But England held their nerve, won the last two games by a whisker and nearly reduced Ganguly to tears as he faced the wrath of the Mumbai crowd at the presentation ceremony. For India, a drawn series felt more like a defeat.

Typically, the cricket had been preceded by politicking behind the scenes. Dalmiya's predecessors had agreed to a five-match series, but he demanded six and also wanted to expand England's next tour, in 2005-06, from three Tests to five. If his demands were denied, he threatened that India would play three Tests, not four, in England later in the year. Negotiations carried on until the end of December, when it was agreed that England would play a sixth international, at Cuttack, in a reshuffled schedule, but they offered no concession on the future tour.

The cricket, played in six different cities and in front of packed houses, was vibrant and enthralling. Trescothick captured the mood by blasting over 300 runs at more than a run a ball, and Sehwag matched him for explosiveness. But the final word went to Flintoff, who had been England's thriftiest bowler throughout. With the crowd bubbling in the Wankhede pressure-cooker, he first gave England a total to defend, then steamed in with the ball to precipitate a fatal Indian collapse. His shirt-off shenanigans may not have pleased everyone, but it was a spontaneous response to a seminal moment. England were no longer one-day pushovers.

ENGLAND TOURING PARTY

N. Hussain (Essex) (*captain*), U. Afzaal (Nottinghamshire), M. C. J. Ball (Gloucestershire), M. A. Butcher (Surrey), R. K. J. Dawson (Yorkshire), A. Flintoff (Lancashire), J. S. Foster (Essex), A. F. Giles (Warwickshire), W. K. Hegg (Lancashire), M. J. Hoggard (Yorkshire), R. L. Johnson (Somerset), J. Ormond (Leicestershire), M. R. Ramprakash (Surrey), G. P. Thorpe (Surrey), M. E. Trescothick (Somerset), M. P. Vaughan (Yorkshire), C. White (Yorkshire).

A. R. Caddick (Somerset) and R. D. B. Croft (Glamorgan) were originally selected for the Test leg of the tour, but withdrew because of security fears and were replaced by Ball and Johnson. Flintoff was called up from the National Academy after the start of the tour. Thorpe flew home for personal reasons before the Second Test, but returned for the limited-overs series. The one-day squad was further reinforced by Caddick, P. D. Collingwood (Durham), D. Gough (Yorkshire),

B. C. Hollioake (Surrey), N. V. Knight (Warwickshire), O. A. Shah (Middlesex) and J. N. Snape (Gloucestershire), replacing Afzaal, Ball, Butcher, Dawson, Hegg, Johnson, Ormond and Ramprakash.

Coach: D. A. G. Fletcher. *Operations manager:* P. A. Neale. *Assistant coaches:* G. R. Dilley and T. J. Boon. *Scorer/video analyst:* M. N. Ashton. *Physiotherapist:* D. O. Conway. *Physiologist:* N. P. Stockill. *Media relations managers:* D. A. Clarke and A. J. Walpole.

ENGLAND TOUR RESULTS

Test matches – Played 3: Lost 1, Drawn 2.
First-class matches – Played 5: Won 1, Lost 1, Drawn 3.
Win – India A.
Loss – India.
Draws – India (2), Indian Board President's XI.
One-day internationals – Played 6: Won 3, Lost 3.
Other non-first-class match – Drawn v Mumbai CA President's XI.

TEST MATCH AVERAGES

INDIA – BATTING

	T	I	NO	R	HS	100s	50s	Avge	Ct
S. R. Tendulkar	3	4	0	307	103	1	2	76.75	4
D. Dasgupta.	3	5	1	177	100	1	1	44.25	6
R. Dravid	3	4	1	122	86	0	1	40.66	3
V. V. S. Laxman	3	3	0	115	75	0	1	38.33	6
S. S. Das	3	4	0	129	58	0	1	32.25	5
S. C. Ganguly	3	4	1	68	47	0	0	22.66	1
A. Kumble	3	3	0	56	37	0	0	18.66	2
Harbhajan Singh.	3	3	0	9	8	0	0	3.00	0

Played in two Tests: V. Sehwag 20, 66 (2 ct); J. Srinath 0, 2*; T. Yohannan 2*, 3* (1 ct). Played in one Test: S. B. Bangar 36; Iqbal Siddiqui 24, 5* (1 ct); Sarandeep Singh 4.

BOWLING

	O	M	R	W	BB	5W/i	Avge
Sarandeep Singh.	21	5	54	3	3-54	0	18.00
A. Kumble	166.1	36	440	19	7-115	2	23.15
Harbhajan Singh.	136.3	35	319	13	5-51	2	24.53
J. Srinath.	71	18	221	6	4-73	0	36.83
T. Yohannan.	56	8	213	4	2-56	0	53.25

Also bowled: S. B. Bangar 5–2–17–0; S. C. Ganguly 16–3–51–0; Iqbal Siddiqui 19–5–48–1; V. Sehwag 5–1–10–0; S. R. Tendulkar 17–3–50–1.

ENGLAND – BATTING

	T	I	NO	R	HS	100s	50s	Avge	Ct/St
M. P. Vaughan	2	3	1	106	64	0	1	53.00	1
M. E. Trescothick	3	6	1	240	99	0	2	48.00	2
M. A. Butcher	3	6	1	215	92	0	2	43.00	5
C. White	3	5	0	205	121	1	0	41.00	0
N. Hussain.	3	5	0	191	85	0	2	38.20	4
M. R. Ramprakash	3	5	0	159	58	0	1	31.80	0
J. S. Foster.	3	5	0	96	48	0	0	19.20	5/1
A. F. Giles	2	3	0	43	28	0	0	14.33	0
R. K. J. Dawson	3	5	1	27	11	0	0	6.75	1
A. Flintoff.	3	5	0	26	18	0	0	5.20	1
M. J. Hoggard	3	5	2	6	4*	0	0	2.00	0

Played in one Test: J. Ormond 3*, 0; G. P. Thorpe 23, 62 (1 ct).

BOWLING

	O	M	R	W	BB	5W/i	Avge
M. J. Hoggard	101.5	29	281	9	4-80	0	31.22
A. Flintoff.	92	31	189	6	4-50	0	31.50
A. F. Giles	108.3	46	198	6	5-67	1	33.00
R. K. J. Dawson	90	15	279	6	4-134	0	46.50

Also bowled: M. A. Butcher 7–1–19–1; J. Ormond 28–8–70–1; C. White 54–17–122–2.

ENGLAND TOUR AVERAGES – FIRST-CLASS MATCHES

BATTING

	M	I	NO	R	HS	100s	50s	Avge	Ct/St
N. Hussain.	5	9	0	374	85	0	3	41.55	5
M. E. Trescothick	4	8	1	277	99	0	2	39.57	3
M. R. Ramprakash	5	9	0	318	105	1	1	35.33	1
M. A. Butcher	5	10	1	309	92	0	2	34.33	6
M. P. Vaughan	4	6	1	168	64	0	1	33.60	1
G. P. Thorpe.	2	4	0	111	62	0	1	27.75	2
C. White	5	9	0	214	121	1	0	23.77	0
J. S. Foster.	5	9	1	137	48	0	0	17.12	13/1
A. F. Giles	3	5	1	55	28	0	0	13.75	1
R. K. J. Dawson	5	8	1	71	24	0	0	10.14	1
A. Flintoff.	4	7	0	66	40	0	0	9.42	1
J. Ormond	2	4	1	14	6	0	0	4.66	0
M. J. Hoggard	4	7	4	11	5*	0	0	3.66	0

Played in one match: M. C. J. Ball 28, 25* (1 ct); R. L. Johnson 5, 0*.

BOWLING

	O	M	R	W	BB	5W/i	Avge
A. Flintoff	126	43	263	12	4-50	0	21.91
C. White	101	28	229	9	5-31	1	25.44
M. J. Hoggard	124.5	33	332	11	4-80	0	30.18
A. F. Giles	125.3	49	246	7	5-67	1	35.14
R. K. J. Dawson	125.5	17	414	8	4-134	0	51.75

Also bowled: M. C. J. Ball 27–4–89–3; M. A. Butcher 19–8–34–1; R. L. Johnson 24.1–5–81–4; J. Ormond 43–10–116–1; M. E. Trescothick 2–1–4–0; M. P. Vaughan 2–0–7–0.

Note: Matches in this section which were not first-class are signified by a dagger.

†At Wankhede Stadium, Mumbai, November 18, 19. **Drawn**. Toss: England XI. **Mumbai CA President's XI 373 for five dec.** (V. R. Mane 33, Wasim Jaffer 99, V. G. Kambli 109, B. J. Thakkar 46, S. V. Bahutule 52 not out); **England XI 370 for five** (M. A. Butcher 33, M. E. Trescothick 60, N. Hussain 70 retired out, G. P. Thorpe 45 retired out, M. R. Ramprakash 58 not out, C. White 79 not out).
Kambli scored 109 in 109 balls, with 19 fours.

INDIAN BOARD PRESIDENT'S XI v ENGLAND XI

At Hyderabad, November 22, 23, 24. Drawn. Toss: England XI.

Elsewhere in India, effigies of Mike Denness, the former England captain, now an ICC referee, were being burned in the street. He had become known as Denness the Menace, but his latest successor, Hussain, had a better day, winning the toss and scoring 46. It was Ramprakash, however, who went on to a century. He batted for three and three-quarter hours, and rescued England from 149 for five. The spinners, Saradeep Singh and Kartik, prospered on a slow pitch, but their English counterparts, Richard Dawson and Martyn Ball, found it heavy going. After Hoggard removed Wasim Jaffer in his first over, Sriram added 202 with Martin and batted most of the second day. Ball's off-spin eventually earned three victims, and the President's XI declared, 19 ahead, with two sessions remaining. England had a scare when Bangar swung his way into the Test team with two wickets in eight balls, and at 122 for six, they led by only 103, with 26 overs to go. But Ball steered them to the draw with an unbeaten 25. It was his first, and possibly last, match for England.

Close of play: First day, England XI 297-9 (Dawson 9, Hoggard 0); Second day, Indian Board President's XI 256-2 (Sriram 120, Martin 83).

England XI

M. A. Butcher c Surendra Singh b Saradeep Singh	41	– c Dharmani b Surendra Singh	12
M. P. Vaughan c Mongia b Bangar	22	– b Yohannan	18
*N. Hussain c Gavaskar b Kartik	46	– c Kartik b Bangar	38
G. P. Thorpe lbw b Kartik	13	– b Bangar	13
M. R. Ramprakash b Kartik	105	– c Dharmani b Kartik	32
C. White b Saradeep Singh	0	– c Dharmani b Bangar	4
†J. S. Foster c Martin b Saradeep Singh	9	– b Bangar	0
M. C. J. Ball c Gavaskar b Saradeep Singh	28	– not out	25
J. Ormond lbw b Saradeep Singh	5	– run out	6
R. K. J. Dawson c Mongia b Bangar	24	– lbw b Bangar	1
M. J. Hoggard not out	5	– not out	0
B 4, l-b 1, w 1, n-b 16	22	B 3, l-b 6, n-b 5	14
	320		**(9 wkts) 163**

1/51 2/104 3/122 4/139 5/149 6/187 7/239 8/265 9/292

1/29 2/48 3/80 4/116 5/120 6/122 7/144 8/157 9/162

Bowling: *First Innings*—Surendra Singh 13–4–37–0; Yohannan 11–1–57–0; Bangar 16.4–3–34–2; Sarandeep Singh 24–0–98–5; Kartik 31–7–84–3; Gavaskar 1–0–5–0. *Second Innings*—Surendra Singh 10–4–22–1; Yohannan 7–1–38–1; Kartik 15–5–29–1; Bangar 14–6–32–5; Sarandeep Singh 6–0–33–0.

Indian Board President's XI

S. Sriram c Foster b White	149	M. Kartik not out	7
Wasim Jaffer c Foster b Hoggard	0	Sarandeep Singh not out	10
D. Mongia c Thorpe b Ball	44		
*J. J. Martin b Hoggard	89	B 2, l-b 3, w 1, n-b 3	9
R. S. Gavaskar c and b Ball	24		
†P. Dharmani lbw b White	5	1/3 2/66 3/268 4/315 (7 wkts dec.) 339	
S. B. Bangar lbw b Ball	2	5/315 6/318 7/322	

T. Yohannan and Surendra Singh did not bat.

Bowling: Hoggard 23–4–51–2; Ormond 15–2–46–0; Ball 27–4–89–3; White 20–5–44–2; Dawson 25–2–97–0; Vaughan 2–0–7–0.

Umpires: K. Parthasarathy and G. A. Pratap Kumar.

INDIA A v ENGLAND XI

At Jaipur, November 27, 28, 29. England XI won by three wickets. Toss: England XI.

The fate of the Test series remained uncertain when the Indian squad, announced during this match, included Virender Sehwag, in defiance of the ICC's edict. But England completed their preparations by winning a seesawing game. It began with a bang – three wickets in Johnson's first eight balls, and a fourth in Flintoff's second over. Then Kale batted for four and a half hours, until his dismissal triggered another collapse: three wickets in 13 balls, including one for Giles, in his first first-class match since July. Next morning, England lost seven men – Iqbal Siddiqui won a Test debut with three for nought in 13 balls – and with nine down after lunch they still trailed by 105. The last pair, Foster and Dawson, reduced that to 63, and White claimed three wickets by the close. On the final day, he and Flintoff, newly arrived from the Academy in Adelaide, needed an hour to demolish the rest. A solid fifty from Hussain and Flintoff's rapid 40 eased England home with 20 overs to spare.

Close of play: First day, England XI 37-0 (Butcher 32, Trescothick 5); Second day, India A 75-3 (Gowda 13, Parida 4).

India A

V. R. Mane c Foster b Johnson	0	– lbw b White	15
G. Gambhir lbw b Johnson	5	– b White	30
Y. Gowda b Johnson	0	– c Foster b Flintoff	13
G. K. Khoda b Flintoff	64	– lbw b White	0
R. R. Parida c Foster b Flintoff	0	– c Hussain b White	13
A. V. Kale c Ramprakash b Dawson	122	– c Butcher b Flintoff	3
R. S. Sodhi c Foster b Flintoff	2	– (8) retired hurt	0
†A. Ratra c Foster b Giles	26	– (7) b White	0
*S. B. Joshi lbw b Dawson	0	– c Trescothick b Flintoff	13
D. Ganesh not out	0	– (11) not out	0
Iqbal Siddiqui (did not bat)		– (10) c Foster b Johnson	1
B 3, l-b 2, n-b 9	14	B 5, l-b 9, w 1, n-b 6	21

1/0 2/0 3/7 4/8 5/122 (9 wkts dec.) 233   1/39 2/64 3/64 4/77 5/86   109
6/134 7/233 8/233 9/233   6/86 7/102 8/105 9/109

In the second innings Sodhi retired hurt at 87.

Bowling: *First Innings*—Johnson 15–3–56–3; Flintoff 17–4–47–3; White 14–3–32–0; Butcher 1–0–3–0; Giles 17–3–48–1; Dawson 10.5–0–38–2; Trescothick 2–1–4–0. *Second Innings*—Johnson 9.1–2–25–1; Flintoff 17–8–27–3; White 13–3–31–5; Butcher 11–7–12–0.

England XI

M. A. Butcher c Kale b Iqbal Siddiqui	37	– c Gambhir b Ganesh	4
M. E. Trescothick c Ratra b Ganesh	7	– c Ratra b Iqbal Siddiqui	30
M. P. Vaughan c Mane b Iqbal Siddiqui	22		
*N. Hussain b Joshi	40	– (3) st Ratra b Gambhir	59
M. R. Ramprakash lbw b Iqbal Siddiqui	0	– (4) b Joshi	22
A. Flintoff c Ratra b Iqbal Siddiqui	0	– (5) c Khoda b Joshi	40
C. White b Sodhi	2	– (6) c and b Gambhir	3
A. F. Giles c Khoda b Joshi	2	– (7) not out	10
†J. S. Foster not out	32	– (8) c Joshi b Gambhir	0
R. L. Johnson b Joshi	5	– (9) not out	0
R. K. J. Dawson lbw b Sodhi	19		
L-b 1, n-b 3	4	L-b 2, w 1, n-b 2	5

1/46 2/46 3/82 4/86 5/90   170   1/5 2/51 3/109 4/151   (7 wkts) 173
6/97 7/100 8/122 9/128   5/157 6/165 7/172

Bowling: First Innings—Ganesh 20–5–65–1; Iqbal Siddiqui 21–5–53–4; Joshi 16–5–39–3; Sodhi 5.3–2–12–2. *Second Innings*—Ganesh 11–3–37–1; Iqbal Siddiqui 15–3–48–1; Joshi 13.1–5–30–2; Khoda 5–0–28–0; Gowda 5–0–16–0; Gambhir 6–1–12–3.

Umpires: V. K. Ramaswamy and A. M. Saheba.

INDIA v ENGLAND

First Test Match

At Mohali, December 3, 4, 5, 6. India won by ten wickets. Toss: India. Test debuts: S. B. Bangar, Iqbal Siddiqui, T. Yohannan; R. K. J. Dawson, J. S. Foster.

The ICC and the Indian board settled their differences just in time for the Test series to get under way, but some things stayed the same, as Hussain lost his 14th successive toss in international cricket. It looked like a vital toss, too: the prospect of early-morning dew and cloud cover at one of India's most northerly grounds had been an enticing one for England's seam bowlers. But India's pace attack, which consisted of three debutants, was found wanting, and in the end they were rescued by their spinners: Harbhajan Singh and Kumble, with 15 wickets between them, set up a ten-wicket defeat shortly after tea on the fourth day. Hussain described them as the best pair of their kind in the world.

When England raced to 200 for three inside two sessions, with Hussain eyeing up a century in his first Test innings in the land of his birth, the spin of a coin hardly seemed to matter. Butcher had been dismissed by the fourth ball of the series, but then India's three newcomers, Sanjay Bangar, Tinu Yohannan and Iqbal Siddiqui – none of whom had been on the recent tour to South Africa – let the excitement get to them, and Hussain batted as slickly as he had for some time. But when he was caught at silly point off Kumble, shortly after being dropped behind the wicket off Harbhajan, England's well-being departed and Harbhajan took control. In 25 overs, they surrendered their last seven wickets for 38. Harbhajan's final spell of 7.3 overs brought five wickets for six runs, followed by a chaste kiss of the pendant around his neck.

England had successfully countered two other world-class off-spinners, Saqlain Mushtaq and Muttiah Muralitharan, on Asian pitches the previous year, but they had drawn on knowledge gleaned in county cricket. Harbhajan, bearing a slightly sad, gnomish expression underneath his patka, was known by reputation alone. He found little turn, but the threat of the ball that fades away from the right-hander spread uncertainty. England's middle and lower order played him with a mixture of misplaced aggression and sheer bewilderment. An hour after tea, they were all out for 238.

Their bowlers responded manfully on the second day, but for scant reward. Their only victims were the night-watchman, Kumble – a first Test wicket with his 12th ball

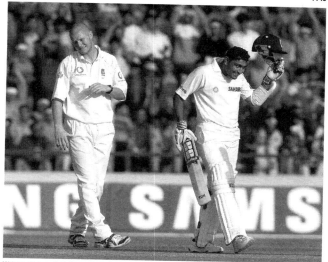

Written all over their faces: Deep Dasgupta, acknowledging his first Test century, with Matthew Hoggard. *Picture by Graham Morris.*

for Richard Dawson, the rookie Yorkshire off-spinner – and Dasgupta, India's sixth wicket-keeper in a year, whose maiden Test hundred in his third match was a masterpiece of self-denial. As in his last Test, in South Africa, Dasgupta went in first, this time because Bangar, the specialist opener, had pulled a muscle. He scored 15 in the morning session, spent more than an hour on 21, and needed nearly three and a half to complete a fifty heavily reliant on deflections behind square. After speeding up slightly to reach a hundred in five and a half hours, he was bowled through the gate by White.

India, 24 ahead at the close of the day, didn't waste their advantage. England's experience of Tendulkar had been limited and, although he had played many bigger Test innings, his unflustered 88 brought gasps of admiration from the bowlers, as well as the usual idolatry from the stands. His on-driving, in particular, was exquisite. His dismissal – a thin edge to a good-length ball from the tidy Hoggard – came as a complete surprise. England stemmed the flow by bowling wide of off stump to packed off-side fields. Hussain was bent upon survival training for a novice attack, and India's 469 took the best part of two days, although it should never have lasted as long as that: England missed four good chances in the field, including two to Foster, who had a debut to forget. Dawson was controlled and self-possessed as he collected four wickets, while an engrossing 18-certificate spat between Flintoff and his former colleague at Lancashire, Ganguly, was passed off as "chirp" by the referee.

On the third evening, England survived their first taste of batting in Test cricket under floodlights, even if it was only for seven overs. Next day they were dazzled by Kumble, whose six wickets removed fears that his shoulder operation nearly a year earlier had reduced his powers for good. Once Ganguly belatedly bowled him and Harbhajan in tandem, after lunch on the fourth day, they tore England apart: the last seven wickets tumbled in 22 overs. Only Thorpe suggested permanence – his 62 in three hours was his first first-class fifty in six injury-hit months – until he chipped Kumble a return catch to be ninth out. India needed only two balls after tea to finish the job.

Kumble had altered little since destroying England in India nine years earlier, and the outcome was disturbingly similar. He rarely beat the outside edge, but whiplashed the pads with the top-spinner that hacked straight on and an even better googly. With Harbhajan, he reigned supreme to give India what proved a winning lead.

Man of the Match: A. Kumble.

Close of play: First day, India 24-1 (Dasgupta 19, Kumble 1); Second day, India 262-3 (Dravid 78, Tendulkar 31); Third day, England 34-0 (Butcher 11, Trescothick 16).

England

M. A. Butcher c Laxman b Yohannan	4	– c sub (J. J. Martin) b Yohannan	18
M. E. Trescothick b Yohannan	66	– c Iqbal Siddiqui b Yohannan	46
*N. Hussain c Laxman b Kumble	85	– b Kumble	12
G. P. Thorpe c Laxman b Iqbal Siddiqui	23	– c and b Kumble	62
M. R. Ramprakash c Das b Harbhajan Singh	17	– lbw b Kumble	28
A. Flintoff c Kumble b Harbhajan Singh	18	– c Ganguly b Kumble	4
C. White c Dravid b Kumble	5	– c Dasgupta b Harbhajan Singh	22
†J. S. Foster lbw b Harbhajan Singh	0	– lbw b Harbhajan Singh	5
J. Ormond not out	3	– b Kumble	0
R. K. J. Dawson c Laxman b Harbhajan Singh	5	– b Kumble	11
M. J. Hoggard c sub (C. C. Williams) b Harbhajan Singh	0	– not out	0
L-b 7, n-b 5	12	B 10, l-b 13, w 1, n-b 3	27
	238		**235**

1/4 (1) 2/129 (2) 3/172 (4) 4/200 (3)   238
5/224 (5) 6/227 (6) 7/229 (8)
8/229 (7) 9/238 (10) 10/238 (11)

1/68 (1) 2/82 (2) 3/87 (3)   235
4/159 (5) 5/163 (6) 6/196 (7)
7/206 (8) 8/207 (9)
9/224 (4) 10/235 (10)

Bowling: First Innings—Yohannan 18–3–75–2; Iqbal Siddiqui 11–2–32–1; Bangar 5–2–17–0; Kumble 19–6–52–2; Tendulkar 4–3–4–0; Harbhajan Singh 19.3–4–51–5. *Second Innings*—Yohannan 17–3–56–2; Iqbal Siddiqui 8–3–16–0; Kumble 28.4–6–81–6; Harbhajan Singh 24–9–59–2.

India

S. S. Das b Butcher	2		
†D. Dasgupta b White	100	– not out	0
A. Kumble c Foster b Dawson	37		
R. Dravid lbw b Ormond	86		
S. R. Tendulkar c Foster b Hoggard	88		
*S. C. Ganguly c Thorpe b Hoggard	47		
V. V. S. Laxman c Hussain b Dawson	28		
S. B. Bangar c and b Dawson	36		
Harbhajan Singh lbw b Dawson	1		
Iqbal Siddiqui b Hoggard	24	– (1) not out	5
T. Yohannan not out	2		
L-b 12, w 2, n-b 4	18		
	469	(no wkt)	**5**

1/23 (1) 2/76 (3) 3/212 (2) 4/290 (4)   469
5/370 (5) 6/378 (6) 7/430 (7)
8/436 (9) 9/449 (8) 10/469 (10)

(no wkt) 5

Bowling: First Innings—Hoggard 32–9–98–3; Ormond 28–8–70–1; Butcher 7–1–19–1; Flintoff 34–11–80–0; White 25–8–56–1; Dawson 43–6–134–4. *Second Innings*—Hoggard 0.2–0–5–0.

Umpires: S. A. Bucknor (West Indies) and S. Venkataraghavan.
Third umpire: K. Murali. Referee: D. T. Lindsay (South Africa).

INDIA v ENGLAND

Second Test Match

At Ahmedabad, December 11, 12, 13, 14, 15. Drawn. Toss: England.

After England's defeat in the opening Test at Mohali, predictions of another Indian whitewash filled the air, but at Ahmedabad Hussain's team proved more resilient than Graham Gooch's nine years earlier. Even without Thorpe, who decided only hours before the start to fly home at once for family reasons, England dominated large tracts of the match, but ultimately lacked the firepower to force the victory that would have levelled the series.

Waiting to be bowled out, 373 ahead, was overly cautious for a side 1–0 down in a three-Test rubber. Hussain was wary of the damage that Tendulkar, in particular, could inflict on his inexperienced attack. He left India's batsmen just over a day to negotiate and, on a comatose pitch that had failed to offer the expected sharp turn, they did this with ease. A ponderous century opening stand between Das and Dasgupta – at barely two an over – directed them to safety at 198 for three. With both captains apparently more interested in avoiding defeat than chasing victory, the final day was virtually unwatchable.

Both sides made two changes from Mohali. Vaughan stepped in for Thorpe, and Giles was welcomed back in place of Ormond. For India, Sehwag returned after his suspension and Srinath after injury, while Iqbal Siddiqui and Bangar dropped out. Hussain won the toss for the first time since the Lahore Test, 13 months before, and Trescothick and Butcher celebrated with a positive century stand for the first wicket. Butcher's eventual dismissal was the first of ten in the match for Kumble, which took him to 299 Test wickets. England repeatedly fell prey to his googly which, allied to the ever-present top-spinner, made playing back to him a dangerous occupation. Four batsmen succumbed to the googly on the first day, including Trescothick, who drove and slog-swept the spinners stoutly, but dabbed to the wicket-keeper on 99.

Hussain, leg-before to a ball snaking down the leg side, and Vaughan, given out caught off bat and pad, were both left cursing umpire Robinson. With Flintoff's technique against spin proving hopelessly unsubtle, England needed a maiden Test century from Craig White to pass 400. Seven and a half years and 23 Tests after his international debut, White's vulnerable yet unquestioned talent finally held sway in an innings that, suitably, was stylish one minute, fretful the next. It had its good fortune – during a 105-run partnership with Foster, Dasgupta failed to stump him, on 44, off Harbhajan, and dropped a simple chance off Srinath when he was 63; in the same over, Kumble dropped a difficult one when White hooked to long leg. For all his wonders with the ball, Kumble was harshly jeered by the crowd as he left for treatment on a damaged hand.

England's first-innings lead of 116 was largely thanks to an indefatigable display by Giles who, beset by heel and Achilles problems, trundled up to the crease like an old wheelie bin, but claimed a Test-best five for 67 from 43.3 overs in sapping heat. Giles had bowled only 17 overs since July, and met each congratulatory huddle as if he feared he might topple over. He judged it the achievement of his career.

Giles made short work of India's last four wickets, the final indignity for a partisan crowd. Earlier, they had hero-worshipped Tendulkar towards his 27th Test hundred – level with Allan Border and Steve Waugh, behind only Bradman and Gavaskar – and then abruptly lost interest from the moment that he drove Hoggard to the juggling Hussain at mid-on shortly before tea. Tendulkar was supreme in the afternoon, ridiculing England's packed off-side fields by whipping balls from outside off through the leg side at will; three such strokes, in one memorable over from Hoggard, brought him 11 runs. Hussain's captaincy was enthusiastic, clear-sighted and, at times, uncompromisingly negative: he never allowed the game to drift, marshalled his limited resources intelligently and posed Tendulkar question upon question, most of which were answered perfectly. It was as compelling as the final hours were dull.

A taste for the subcontinent: after successful tours of Pakistan and Sri Lanka, Craig White moves towards his first Test hundred by lofting Harbhajan Singh for six at Ahmedabad. *Picture by Graham Morris.*

On the fourth day, Butcher defied a stomach bug that had afflicted much of the squad to keep England's victory ambitions alive. Dropped on 59 by the fallible Dasgupta, he gutsed it out for four and a quarter hours until he cut to slip, eight short of a century. But he had done enough to suggest that his demons against spin were becoming a thing of the past. India's fielding was woeful, but England, with Vaughan also unwell, were in no mood to be hurried into a declaration, and the draw grew ever more likely.

Man of the Match: C. White.

Close of play: First day, England 277-6 (White 42, Foster 15); Second day, India 71-2 (Dravid 5, Tendulkar 2); Third day, England 15-0 (Butcher 5, Trescothick 10); Fourth day, India 17-0 (Das 11, Dasgupta 6).

England

M. A. Butcher c Dasgupta b Kumble	51	– c Dravid b Harbhajan Singh	92
M. E. Trescothick c Dasgupta b Kumble	99	– c Das b Srinath	12
*N. Hussain lbw b Kumble	1	– c Sehwag b Harbhajan Singh	50
M. P. Vaughan c Sehwag b Kumble	11	– (7) not out	31
M. R. Ramprakash b Tendulkar	37	– (4) c Tendulkar b Harbhajan Singh .	19
A. Flintoff c Laxman b Kumble	0	– (5) b Kumble	4
C. White b Harbhajan Singh	121	– (6) run out	18
†J. S. Foster c Tendulkar b Kumble	40	– c Yohannan b Kumble	3
A. F. Giles b Kumble	7	– c Das b Harbhajan Singh	8
R. K. J. Dawson c Dasgupta b Srinath	9	– c Tendulkar b Kumble	2
M. J. Hoggard not out	4	– c Das b Harbhajan Singh	1
B 6, l-b 15, w 1, n-b 5	27	B 6, l-b 8, n-b 3	17

1/124 (1) 2/144 (3) 3/172 (4) 4/176 (2)   407   1/21 (2) 2/133 (3) 3/178 (4)   257
5/180 (6) 6/239 (5) 7/344 (8)   4/183 (5) 5/183 (1) 6/225 (6)
8/360 (9) 9/391 (10) 10/407 (7)   7/231 (8) 8/247 (9)
                                         9/253 (10) 10/257 (11)

Bowling: First Innings—Srinath 29-7-105-1; Yohannan 17-2-57-0; Harbhajan Singh 35.3-9-78-1; Kumble 51-13-115-7; Tendulkar 10-0-27-1; Sehwag 2-1-4-0. *Second Innings*—Srinath 9-2-24-1; Yohannan 4-0-25-0; Kumble 38-5-118-3; Harbhajan Singh 30.2-6-71-5; Sehwag 2-0-5-0.

India

S. S. Das c Butcher b Flintoff	41	– run out	58
†D. Dasgupta c Hussain b Giles	17	– c Butcher b Dawson	60
R. Dravid c Foster b Hoggard	7	– not out	26
S. R. Tendulkar c Hussain b Hoggard	103	– c Vaughan b Dawson	26
*S. C. Ganguly c sub (M. C. J. Ball) b Flintoff .	5	– not out	16
V. V. S. Laxman c Butcher b Giles	75		
V. Sehwag lbw b White	20		
A. Kumble b Giles	5		
Harbhajan Singh c Flintoff b Giles	0		
J. Srinath c Butcher b Giles	0		
T. Yohannan not out	3		
B 6, l-b 5, w 1, n-b 3	15	B 12	12

1/54 (2) 2/64 (1) 3/86 (3) 4/93 (5)   291   1/119 (1) 2/124 (2)   (3 wkts) 198
5/211 (4) 6/248 (7) 7/268 (8)   3/168 (4)
8/272 (9) 9/274 (10) 10/291 (6)

Bowling: First Innings—Hoggard 28-7-65-2; Flintoff 22-7-42-2; Giles 43.3-16-67-5; Dawson 15-0-73-0; White 12-2-33-1. *Second Innings*—Hoggard 17-6-33-0; Giles 31-12-57-0; Dawson 32-9-72-2; Flintoff 8-4-17-0; White 9-5-7-0.

Umpires: I. D. Robinson (Zimbabwe) and A. V. Jayaprakash.
Third umpire: Jasbir Singh. Referee: D. T. Lindsay (South Africa).

INDIA v ENGLAND

Third Test Match

At Bangalore, December 19, 20, 21, 22, 23. Drawn. Toss: England.

Dank weather which had more in common with Manchester than Bangalore initially encouraged England to think that they could still pull off a victory to tie the series. But the overcast skies – floodlights were in use throughout – increasingly bore unseasonal rain. As a hard-fought series petered out, the depression clung not just over the Bay of Bengal but also over the England dressing-room.

A chief source of that depression was the criticism of their negative bowling tactics against Tendulkar, apparent throughout the series, but here employed more bloody-mindedly than ever. The unedifying spectacle of Flintoff and, in particular, Giles aiming outside Tendulkar's leg stump left both Hussain and Duncan Fletcher unrepentant and, in Hussain's case, resentful that an inexperienced team's attempts to compete in alien conditions had not been given unreserved support. Denis Lindsay, the ICC referee, needed all his man-management skills to prevent a reasonably well-behaved series spinning out of control at the last.

Tendulkar is a special talent, and the need to curb him encouraged extreme tactics. First Flintoff conjured up memories of Bodyline by banging the ball in short from round the wicket. Then Giles deliberately landed his slow left-armers a foot outside leg stump, where the wicket-keeper, Foster, stood in readiness. On the third morning, 90 per cent of Giles's balls pitched outside leg, and Tendulkar padded away more than half. But even if Hussain felt he could justify his methods, the umpires had the power to rule these persistent negative deliveries as wides; in the broader interests of the game, they should have done. An ICC cricket committee meeting in March agreed that steps should be taken to ensure as much.

It was the buccaneering leg-side blows of his partner and acolyte, Sehwag, that finally tempted Tendulkar into indiscretion, shortly after he passed 1,000 Test runs in the calendar year. When he charged at Giles to be stumped for the first time in his 89-Test career, England were convinced that their suffocating tactics had been successful. But Tendulkar had made 90, and, if he required four and a half hours, then the lost time was to England's disadvantage. They, after all, were chasing the game.

The crowd, for once, were not exclusively obsessed with Tendulkar – they had their own local hero to cheer. By dismissing Hoggard on the second afternoon, lbw as he tried to sweep, Kumble became the second Indian (after Kapil Dev) and fourth spinner (after Shane Warne, Muttiah Muralitharan and Lance Gibbs) to reach 300 Test wickets, achieving the landmark in his 66th game.

Hussain had won the toss again, but the chief talking point on the first day was the controversy when Vaughan became the seventh batsman in Test cricket to be dismissed for handling the ball. His reputation as a perpetually blighted Test batsman – one he would do well to ignore – had arisen largely because of some freakish injuries, but here a mental aberration undid him. Vaughan was batting with more authority than at any time in his Test career when, on 64, he missed a sweep at the off-spinner Sarandeep Singh. As the ball became tangled beneath him, he first smothered it, then brushed it away from his crease, a lapse that would be condemned in a club match. The ball was not heading for the stumps, but that was irrelevant under Law 33. India were entitled to appeal, although Vaughan complained, unwisely, that it was "against the spirit of the game". Hussain's admission that he would have appealed himself "nine times out of ten" put this gripe into perspective. Had Vaughan simply tossed the ball to a fielder, an appeal would have been unlikely.

His dismissal, at 206 for four, demanded retrenchment. Instead, Flintoff naively belted his fourth ball to mid-wicket to extend his miserable sequence to 26 runs in five innings. Ramprakash completed an impressive fifty before he was adjudged caught

The trap is sprung: an exultant **Ashley Giles** celebrates the dismissal of **Sachin Tendulkar**, stumped for the first time in 89 Tests. Many observers found England's leg-side tactics less appealing. *Picture by Graham Morris.*

at slip off Sarandeep. It took another plucky innings by the improving Foster on the second morning to lift England to 336.

A relaid pitch had made selection difficult. India chose three spinners, replacing the last of Mohali's debutants with Sarandeep, and employed Ganguly as a token new-ball bowler, but this was a mistake: it was the swing of Srinath that bore most threat, and England's seamers who forced a 98-run first-innings lead. Flintoff's new-ball bowling, full of heart and skill, was in stark contrast to his leaden batting; Hoggard rediscovered his out-swinger, compared Bangalore to Headingley and stomped happily back to his mark, singing and pulling the strange faces that persuaded his team-mates to nickname him Shrek after the animated green ogre in the children's film. These two each collected four wickets for the first time in a Test innings. But rain, which allowed less than 16 overs during the last two days, ruined everything.

Man of the Match: A. Flintoff.   *Man of the Series:* S. R. Tendulkar.

Close of play: First day, England 255-6 (White 30, Foster 14); Second day, India 99-3 (Tendulkar 50, Dravid 1); Third day, India 218-7 (Kumble 10, Harbhajan Singh 0); Fourth day, England 33-0 (Butcher 23, Trescothick 9).

England

M. A. Butcher run out	27	– not out	23
M. E. Trescothick c Laxman b Srinath	8	– not out	9
*N. Hussain c Dasgupta b Srinath	43		
M. P. Vaughan handled the ball	64		
M. R. Ramprakash c Dravid b Sarandeep Singh	58		
A. Flintoff c Tendulkar b Sarandeep Singh	0		
C. White c Das b Srinath	39		
†J. S. Foster c Dasgupta b Srinath	48		
A. F. Giles lbw b Sarandeep Singh	28		
R. K. J. Dawson not out	0		
M. J. Hoggard lbw b Kumble	1		
B 8, l-b 9, n-b 3	20	B 1	1
	336	(no wkt)	**33**

1/21 (2) 2/68 (1) 3/93 (3) 4/206 (4)
5/206 (6) 6/219 (5) 7/271 (7)
8/334 (8) 9/334 (9) 10/336 (11)

Bowling: *First Innings*—Srinath 29–9–73–4; Ganguly 13–3–39–0; Kumble 29.3–6–74–1; Harbhajan Singh 27–7–59–0; Sarandeep Singh 21–5–54–3; Tendulkar 3–0–19–0; Sehwag 1–0–1–0. *Second Innings*—Srinath 4–0–19–0; Ganguly 3–0–12–0; Harbhajan Singh 0.1–0–1–0.

India

S. S. Das b Flintoff	28	Harbhajan Singh c Hussain b Hoggard	8
†D. Dasgupta c Trescothick b Flintoff	0	Sarandeep Singh run out	4
V. V. S. Laxman b Flintoff	12	J. Srinath not out	2
S. R. Tendulkar st Foster b Giles	90	B 4, l-b 4, n-b 3	11
R. Dravid c Foster b Hoggard	3		
*S. C. Ganguly c Butcher b Hoggard	0	1/8 (2) 2/22 (3) 3/88 (1) 4/121 (5)	**238**
V. Sehwag c Foster b Hoggard	66	5/121 (6) 6/173 (4) 7/218 (7)	
A. Kumble c Trescothick b Flintoff	14	8/228 (8) 9/235 (9) 10/238 (10)	

Bowling: Hoggard 24.3–7–80–4; Flintoff 28–9–50–4; Giles 34–18–74–1; White 8–2–26–0.

Umpires: E. A. R. de Silva (Sri Lanka) and A. V. Jayaprakash.
Third umpire: F. Gomes. Referee: D. T. Lindsay (South Africa).

ONE-DAY SERIES by SIMON BRIGGS

†INDIA v ENGLAND

First One-Day International

At Kolkata, January 19 (day/night). India won by 22 runs. Toss: India. International debut: A. Ratra.
In front of a full house of 92,000, Trescothick scored England's fastest one-day century before his shocking lbw turned the match. Chasing a stiff 282 from 49 overs (one was deducted for a slow over-rate), he kept England well on course with a violent assault on the spinners – even though he was recovering from a gastric virus. He reached 100 in 80 balls (two better than David Gower against New Zealand in 1982-83) and was 121 from 109 when umpire Sharma triggered him out, to a ball pitching perhaps six inches outside leg stump. Though Knight and Hussain could also quibble with their lbws, England were complicit in their downfall, and no one else passed 25. Panic set in when Trescothick fell at 224, but the run-out of Flintoff was almost as critical in a slide of six for 35. Earlier, Flintoff had dismissed Tendulkar and Ganguly just when their opening stand was becoming threatening. In his fifth international, Mongia accumulated a deft 71, but some superb ground fielding headed off a 300-run total. Afterwards, England presented the referee, Denis Lindsay, with a letter about the standard of umpiring.

Man of the Match: M. E. Trescothick.

India

*S. C. Ganguly c Hussain b Flintoff	42	Harbhajan Singh not out	18
S. R. Tendulkar b Flintoff	36	A. Kumble not out	0
D. Mongia b Snape	71	B 1, l-b 9, w 9, n-b 2	21
V. V. S. Laxman c Collingwood b Gough	25		
V. Sehwag b Hoggard	29	1/78 (2) 2/95 (1) (8 wkts, 50 overs) 281	
H. K. Badani run out	35	3/150 (4) 4/193 (5)	
A. B. Agarkar st Foster b Giles	2	5/232 (3) 6/236 (7)	
†A. Ratra not out	2	7/242 (8) 8/280 (6)	
J. Srinath did not bat.		15 overs: 78-1	

Bowling: Gough 10–1–48–1; Hoggard 10–2–48–1; Flintoff 10–0–51–2; Collingwood 3–0–22–0; Snape 10–0–53–1; Giles 6–0–41–1; Vaughan 1–0–8–0.

England

M. E. Trescothick lbw b Srinath	121	D. Gough c and b Agarkar	0
N. V. Knight lbw b Srinath	0	M. J. Hoggard not out	4
*N. Hussain lbw b Kumble	25	B 4, l-b 10, w 11, n-b 2	27
M. P. Vaughan c Agarkar b Kumble	14		
P. D. Collingwood c Tendulkar b Ganguly	21	1/1 (2) 2/64 (3) 3/123 (4) (44 overs) 259	
A. Flintoff run out	24	4/184 (5) 5/224 (1)	
J. N. Snape lbw b Harbhajan Singh	3	6/231 (6) 7/233 (7)	
A. F. Giles c Ganguly b Agarkar	18	8/244 (9) 9/246 (10)	
†J. S. Foster c Ratra b Agarkar	2	10/259 (8) 14 overs: 82-2	

Bowling: Srinath 8–0–42–2; Agarkar 9–0–50–3; Kumble 9–1–54–2; Harbhajan Singh 9–0–49–1; Tendulkar 4–0–23–0; Ganguly 5–0–27–1.

Umpires: K. Hariharan and S. K. Sharma.
Third umpire: S. N. Bandekar. Referee: D. T. Lindsay (South Africa).

Perhaps an Oxford side flush with former servicemen was circumspect about the accuracy of a fast bowler whose tank had reputedly taken out a French cow and run over a wounded British soldier.
Obituary of Lawrence Toynbee, page 1657

†INDIA v ENGLAND

Second One-Day International

At Cuttack, January 22. England won by 16 runs. Toss: India.

England struck lucky with the freak dismissal of Tendulkar, run out backing up by a deflection from the bowler, Hollioake, just when he seemed to be taking control. The ensuing confusion left India reeling at 186 for eight and, despite a late rally by Agarkar and Kumble, they fell 16 short. England had picked Vaughan again ahead of Thorpe, now recovered from a stomach bug, and their faith was rewarded when he scored his first fifty in eight one-day internationals, manoeuvring the ball skilfully into gaps. After one sharp single too many, Vaughan perished, the first of five run-outs in the match; a noisy crowd made calling hazardous. But Collingwood set himself to bat out the overs, and finished with a resourceful 71 from 78 balls. England's task would have been easier had Trescothick not dropped both Tendulkar and Mongia in the slips. Three more chances went down, but the ground fielding was exemplary and, once Tendulkar fell, the Indians struggled to hit boundaries on a slowing pitch. When Gough dismissed Kumble, he became the first England bowler, and the 29th worldwide, to take 150 one-day international wickets.

Man of the Match: P. D. Collingwood.

England

M. E. Trescothick c Mongia b Agarkar..	13	†J. S. Foster not out 3
N. V. Knight c Harbhajan Singh b Srinath	14	
*N. Hussain c Agarkar b Ganguly	46	L-b 6, w 1, n-b 6 13
M. P. Vaughan run out	63	
P. D. Collingwood not out	71	1/24 (1) 2/45 (2) (7 wkts, 50 overs) 250
A. Flintoff b Harbhajan Singh.	5	3/114 (3) 4/176 (4)
B. C. Hollioake b Kumble	0	5/190 (6) 6/193 (7)
J. N. Snape run out	22	7/244 (8) 15 overs: 75-2

D. Gough and M. J. Hoggard did not bat.

Bowling: Srinath 9–0–41–1; Agarkar 8–1–46–1; Kumble 10–0–47–1; Harbhajan Singh 10–1–35–1; Ganguly 5–0–29–1; Tendulkar 6–0–35–0; Sehwag 2–0–11–0.

India

*S. C. Ganguly c Knight b Hoggard . . .	14	A. Kumble c Collingwood b Gough. . . . 20
S. R. Tendulkar run out	45	J. Srinath not out 7
D. Mongia run out	49	L-b 3, w 7, n-b 3 13
V. V. S. Laxman run out	3	
V. Sehwag c Knight b Gough	5	1/20 (1) 2/99 (2) 3/110 (4) (48.4 overs) 234
H. K. Badani c Flintoff b Hollioake. . . .	13	4/121 (5) 5/130 (3)
†A. Ratra lbw b Flintoff	30	6/147 (6) 7/179 (7)
A. B. Agarkar c Foster b Gough	29	8/186 (9) 9/224 (10)
Harbhajan Singh lbw b Snape.	6	10/234 (8) 15 overs: 68-1

Bowling: Gough 9.4–0–46–3; Hoggard 9–0–53–1; Flintoff 10–0–35–1; Hollioake 7–0–34–1; Snape 8–0–39–1; Collingwood 5–0–24–0.

Umpires: K. Parthasarathy and V. K. Ramaswamy.
Third umpire: M. R. Singh. Referee: D. T. Lindsay (South Africa).

†INDIA v ENGLAND

Third One-Day International

At Chennai, January 25 (day/night). India won by four wickets. Toss: England.

On a rare visit to his native city, Hussain won his first toss in ten one-day internationals, but had his homecoming spoiled by an attack of the clones. Ganguly's hamstring trouble prompted the launch of a daring new double act – Tendulkar and the 23-year-old Sehwag, whose every shot seemed modelled on his partner. Chasing a below-par target of 218, the little masters raised 107, virtually settling the match. Hoggard did engineer a middle-order collapse – three wickets in six balls – but the momentum reversed again when Foster dropped Badani in the next over. Ratra's unbeaten 29 finished the job. Earlier, Holliaoke had defied stomach trouble to revive a faltering innings, adding 70 with the versatile Snape. Hussain fell anticlimactically, caught at mid-on for one off Bangar's second delivery in one-day internationals, but the most frustrating dismissal was that of Hoggard, the last man, run out off the seventh ball of the 48th over. The match was tarnished by England's mean-spirited mood: Snape shoved Badani in the back, Hoggard gestured two batsmen back to the pavilion, and Flintoff sledged relentlessly.

Man of the Match: S. R. Tendulkar.

England

M. E. Trescothick c Ratra b Agarkar	. . .	36	D. Gough b Agarkar	7
N. V. Knight c Mongia b Srinath	. . . . .	10	M. J. Hoggard run out	1
*N. Hussain c Harbhajan Singh b Bangar		1		
M. P. Vaughan c Tendulkar b Kumble	. . .	43	L-b 3, w 7, n-b 4	14
P. D. Collingwood c Laxman				
b Harbhajan Singh		13	1/42 (2) 2/53 (1) 3/61 (3) (48 overs) 217	
A. Flintoff c and b Kumble	. . . . . .	8	4/90 (5) 5/104 (6)	
B. C. Holliaoke c Kumble b Agarkar	. . .	37	6/125 (4) 7/195 (8)	
J. N. Snape b Agarkar	. . . .	38	8/202 (7) 9/216 (10)	
†J. S. Foster not out	. . . .	9	10/217 (11) 15 overs: 73-3	

Bowling: Srinath 8–0–50–1; Agarkar 9–0–34–4; Bangar 7–0–40–1; Harbhajan Singh 10–1–34–1; Kumble 10–1–37–2; Tendulkar 1–0–8–0; Badani 3–0–11–0.

India

S. R. Tendulkar lbw b Snape	. . . .	68	A. B. Agarkar not out	6
V. Sehwag c Trescothick b Snape	. . . . .	51		
V. V. S. Laxman b Hoggard	. . . .	26	L-b 4, w 2, n-b 2	7
D. Mongia c Foster b Hoggard	. . . .	21		
H. K. Badani c Foster b Gough	. . . . .	12	1/107 (2) 2/130 (1) (6 wkts, 46.4 overs) 221	
S. B. Bangar c Trescothick b Hoggard	. .	1	3/165 (3) 4/172 (4)	
†A. Ratra not out	. . . .	29	5/174 (6) 6/201 (5) 15 overs: 83-0	

Harbhajan Singh, *A. Kumble and J. Srinath did not bat.

Bowling: Gough 10–0–55–1; Hoggard 10–1–52–3; Flintoff 10–0–27–0; Holliaoke 4–0–17–0; Snape 10–0–47–2; Collingwood 2–0–12–0; Vaughan 0.4–0–7–0.

Umpires: V. Chopra and D. D. Sharma.
Third umpire: B. A. Jamula. Referee: D. T. Lindsay (South Africa).

†INDIA v ENGLAND

Fourth One-Day International

At Kanpur, January 28. India won by eight wickets. Toss: England.

India's new opening pair exploded again, this time with 134 runs at almost eight an over. Though Ganguly returned, he dropped down to No. 3 after another hamstring twinge, leaving Sehwag and Tendulkar to compare strokes. At first, Sehwag farmed the strike audaciously, outscoring his idol by 82 to 47 before scooping a catch to mid-on. But Tendulkar, who became the first player to score 11,000 one-day international runs, stepped up a gear and sealed India's win with a straight six off Snape. Afterwards, Hussain admitted England had "taken a battering, basically". But he also maintained, with some justification, that the umpires had reprieved both openers on nought, Tendulkar after a leg-side nibble at the first ball (signalled wide). England wasted a vibrant start again. Knight reverse-swept niftily in his 74, ending a patch of indifferent form, but his demise, held at point off another backhanded swipe, sparked a collapse of four for 22. Thorpe was forced into damage-limitation mode. Fog and overnight rain reduced the game to 39 overs a side, and Foster's sickness compelled Trescothick to keep wicket.

Man of the Match: V. Sehwag.

England

†M. E. Trescothick c Mongia b Kumble .	18
N. V. Knight c Kumble	
b Harbhajan Singh .	74
A. Flintoff c Tendulkar b Kumble	18
*N. Hussain c and b Harbhajan Singh . .	15
G. P. Thorpe not out	36
M. P. Vaughan b Ganguly	4
P. D. Collingwood b Ganguly	6

B. C. Hollioake c Sehwag b Srinath	13
J. N. Snape not out	9
B 1, l-b 19, w 4, n-b 1	25

1/71 (1) 2/111 (3)   (7 wkts, 39 overs) 218
3/144 (2) 4/151 (4)
5/156 (6) 6/166 (7)
7/197 (8)   11 overs: 72-1

D. Gough and M. J. Hoggard did not bat.

Bowling: Srinath 8–0–31–1; Agarkar 5–0–40–0; Harbhajan Singh 8–0–40–2; Kumble 8–0–44–2; Ganguly 5.1–0–17–2; Sehwag 1–0–9–0; Tendulkar 3.5–0–17–0.

India

S. R. Tendulkar not out	87
V. Sehwag c Hoggard b Collingwood . . .	82
*S. C. Ganguly b Gough	26
D. Mongia not out	17
B 1, l-b 2, w 4	7

1/134 (2) 2/179 (3)   (2 wkts, 29.4 overs) 219

11 overs: 98-0

H. K. Badani, M. Kaif, †A. Ratra, A. B. Agarkar, Harbhajan Singh, A. Kumble and J. Srinath did not bat.

Bowling: Gough 6–0–44–1; Hoggard 5–0–38–0; Flintoff 3–0–25–0; Hollioake 4–0–33–0; Snape 5.4–0–45–0; Collingwood 6–0–31–1.

Umpires: C. R. Mohite and I. Sivaram.
Third umpire: S. V. Ramani.   Referee: D. T. Lindsay (South Africa).

†INDIA v ENGLAND

Fifth One-Day International

At Delhi, January 31. England won by two runs. Toss: India.

Injuries continued to reshape the series, as Snape's damaged hand led to a match-winning return by Giles. He began unpromisingly: 32 runs from his first four overs. When he reappeared, India were nearing victory at 204 for three, but Ganguly charged at his seventh ball, and dragged an attempted six into the hands of long-on. It began a spell of five for nine in 20 deliveries from Giles, whose ten previous internationals had yielded only nine wickets. India were suddenly on the canvas. But Agarkar nearly revived them, carving 36 from 24 balls. They went into Gough's final over needing eight for a series-clinching tie, which became four off the last ball; Giles pulled off a diving boundary save to thwart them. Earlier, Knight had neutralised India's spinners with trusty sweep shots, both conventional and reverse. He scored his fourth one-day hundred, and added 117, England's only century stand of the series, with Hussain. The final flurry brought 107 in 15 overs as Flintoff belted a thrilling 52 in 39 balls. The match was halted briefly when England fielders were struck by pellets thrown from the crowd.

Man of the Match: A. F. Giles.

England

M. E. Trescothick c Sarandeep Singh	M. P. Vaughan not out 7
b Agarkar . 35	
N. V. Knight run out 105	L-b 11, n-b 2 13
*N. Hussain c Ratra b Tendulkar 49	
A. Flintoff c Kaif b Srinath 52	1/51 (1) 2/168 (3) (5 wkts, 50 overs) 271
P. D. Collingwood not out 8	3/248 (2) 4/254 (4)
G. P. Thorpe b Agarkar 2	5/260 (6) 15 overs: 70-1

A. F. Giles, †J. S. Foster, A. R. Caddick and D. Gough did not bat.

Bowling: Srinath 10–0–47–1; Agarkar 10–0–61–2; Kumble 10–0–37–0; Sarandeep Singh 5–0–34–0; Ganguly 3–0–19–0; Tendulkar 9–0–45–1; Sehwag 3–0–17–0.

India

V. Sehwag c Knight b Gough 42	A. Kumble b Giles 2
S. R. Tendulkar c Foster b Caddick 18	Sarandeep Singh not out 6
*S. C. Ganguly c sub (O. A. Shah)	
b Giles . 74	L-b 3, w 9, n-b 1 13
D. Mongia c Foster b Flintoff 20	
M. Kaif c Thorpe b Giles 46	1/39 (2) 2/68 (1) (8 wkts, 50 overs) 269
H. K. Badani c and b Giles 2	3/100 (4) 4/211 (3)
†A. Ratra st Foster b Giles 10	5/212 (5) 6/219 (6)
A. B. Agarkar not out 36	7/227 (7) 8/239 (9)
	15 overs: 76-2

J. Srinath did not bat.

Bowling: Caddick 10–1–39–1; Flintoff 7–1–41–1; Gough 10–0–53–1; Vaughan 7–0–40–0; Giles 10–0–57–5; Collingwood 6–0–36–0.

Umpires: A. Bhattacharjee and S. K. Porel.
Third umpire: B. K. Sadashiva. Referee: D. T. Lindsay (South Africa).

†INDIA v ENGLAND

Sixth One-Day International

At Mumbai, February 3 (day/night). England won by five runs. Toss: England.

Flintoff delighted his team-mates, and the photographers, by ripping off his shirt in celebration after he bowled Srinath to tie the series. It was his third wicket, and he more than earned the match award after nursing England's faltering innings through its last 20 overs. Yet ICC referee Denis Lindsay chose Trescothick instead. Capitalising on a useful toss, Trescothick finished the series as he began it, mangling the seamers' figures in a majestic 95 from 80 balls. But after England collapsed against Harbhajan to a quixotic 174 for seven from 30 overs, it was Flintoff who helped to retrieve the situation, adding 37 with last man Gough. A target of 256 appeared all too attainable as Ganguly creamed four sixes in his 80. Then Giles enjoyed a brief flashback to the previous match, bowling Ganguly to prompt a slide of seven for 59. Fighting for his place, Badani held one end up, but India needed six from two balls when Srinath swished and missed. Against all the odds, England had claimed a share of the spoils.

Man of the Match: M. E. Trescothick.   *Man of the Series:* S. R. Tendulkar.

England

M. E. Trescothick	A. F. Giles c Sehwag b Harbhajan Singh . 0
c and b Harbhajan Singh . 95	†J. S. Foster c and b Harbhajan Singh . . 13
N. V. Knight c Ratra b Srinath 0	A. R. Caddick c Kumble b Tendulkar . . . 7
*N. Hussain c Harbhajan Singh	D. Gough not out 16
b Ganguly . 41	B 2, l-b 3, w 14 19
M. P. Vaughan st Ratra b Ganguly 16	
G. P. Thorpe st Ratra b Harbhajan Singh . 6	1/1 (2) 2/88 (3) 3/153 (4) (49.1 overs) 255
P. D. Collingwood c Sehwag	4/172 (5) 5/173 (1)
b Harbhajan Singh . 2	6/174 (6) 7/174 (8) 8/205 (9)
A. Flintoff c Agarkar b Srinath 40	9/218 (10) 10/255 (7) 15 overs: 107-2

A tie and no shirt: Andrew Flintoff is mobbed by team-mates. *Picture by Rebecca Naden, PA Photos.*

Bowling: Srinath 7.1–0–37–2; Agarkar 5–0–47–0; Kumble 10–0–43–0; Ganguly 8–0–40–2; Harbhajan Singh 10–1–43–5; Tendulkar 7–0–30–1; Badani 2–0–10–0.

India

V. Sehwag c Thorpe b Caddick	31	A. Kumble run out 5
S. R. Tendulkar c Foster b Gough	12	J. Srinath b Flintoff 0
*S. C. Ganguly b Giles	80	
D. Mongia st Foster b Vaughan	35	B 1, l-b 10, w 11, n-b 5 27
M. Kaif c Hussain b Flintoff	20	
H. K. Badani not out	27	1/36 (2) 2/88 (1) 3/155 (4) (49.5 overs) 250
†A. Ratra c Giles b Vaughan	8	4/191 (3) 5/206 (5)
A. B. Agarkar c Foster b Caddick	0	6/224 (7) 7/224 (8)
Harbhajan Singh c Collingwood b Flintoff	5	8/238 (9) 9/250 (10)
		10/250 (11) 15 overs: 102-2

Bowling: Caddick 10–1–61–2; Gough 10–0–56–1; Flintoff 9.5–1–38–3; Giles 10–0–47–1; Vaughan 10–1–37–2.

Umpires: S. C. Gupta and M. S. Mahal.
Third umpire: N. N. Menon. Referee: D. T. Lindsay (South Africa).

ENGLAND IN NEW ZEALAND, 2001-02

By Lawrence Booth

England's increasingly polished performances over the winter lost a coat of varnish on the final afternoon of their travels, when they went down to their first Test defeat in New Zealand for 18 years. The result left the series tied at 1–1: not bad against a side that had given Australia a run for their dollars a few months earlier, but an anticlimax after England had bossed the show until the third evening of the Third Test. They had missed a gilt-edged chance to exact revenge – for their defeat at home to New Zealand in 1999 and for the nail-biting 3–2 loss in the one-day series that preceded the Tests. The lack of ruthlessness that cost England a series win over Pakistan in 2001 again proved fatal.

If the players were physically exhausted after six months' jetting between England, Zimbabwe, India and New Zealand, they flew home with their emotions in tatters too. News arrived during the Second Test that Ben Hollioake, a popular team-mate throughout the winter programme of 16 one-day internationals, had been killed in a car crash in Perth, after an evening out with his family. It would be wrong to speculate on just how much this tragedy affected England's cricket, but their step lost the spring that helped them bounce back from bad defeats in the first two one-dayers and then win the First Test. The tour ended in disappointment and in grief.

The two-month trip was split into two parts. An entertaining one-day series, which boiled down to a winner-takes-all clash at Dunedin, whetted the appetite, but it was the Tests which really got the juices flowing. The psychological sparring in the build-up provided a taste of things to come. Nasser Hussain declared that the 1999 series had been England's for the taking, only for Stephen Fleming to accuse England of not giving New Zealand credit for that victory. And when Chris Cairns joined in by declaring that England's Class of '99 had "disrespected" New Zealand, it was clear the days of Kiwi deference to the mother country were long gone.

England, too, were unwilling to kowtow. They grabbed the First Test by the scruff before Nathan Astle's unforgettable double-century nearly wrenched it from their grasp. Then New Zealand were forced to bat out most of the final day to save the Second Test, and when they were 19 for four in the opening session of the last, England were on course for a third successive 2–0 win here. Fleming's mantra, though, was that his side were at their best when desperate. His point, borne out by their dashing victory in the decisive one-day international, was reinforced in the Third Test, where Chris Harris, Daryl Tuffey and the Eden Park floodlights conspired to deny England their first Test series win since Sri Lanka 12 months earlier.

The use of lights to extend play into the evening and make up for lost time – now obligatory if the lights are there – was not the only innovation to make an impact on the series. The national obsession with rugby union meant that several stadiums hosted both sports, so New Zealand Cricket decided to solve the problem of stud marks on a length by installing drop-in pitches for the Tests at Christchurch and Auckland. They behaved unpredictably. Christchurch

Point made: Andy Caddick removes Craig McMillan at Auckland and takes his 200th Test wicket in the country that he felt overlooked his talents. *Picture by Graham Morris.*

was like a normal wicket in reverse, flattening out as the game wore on, while Auckland turned into something of a lottery: early dampness meant that the ball left pronounced pitch-marks, which hardened up as the sun came out. Hussain likened the effect to corrugated iron. But, as long as rugby paid the bills, cricket had little choice.

The two sides were not just evenly matched, but also had a similar feel. Each had a thoughtful, energetic and well-respected captain, and each was missing a strike bowler (Darren Gough aggravated a knee injury towards the end of a typically effervescent performance in the one-day series but would not have been considered anyway after opting out of the Tests in India, while Shane Bond picked up a stress fracture of the foot on the eve of the one-dayers). Each side also had a tendency to collapse when the pressure was on. And each placed the team ethic ahead of individual glory. If the cricket was not always top-class, it was never third-rate.

New Zealand's injury worries ran deeper than England's, and it was their seam attack that suffered most. Dion Nash, a star on their 1999 tour to England, had not recovered after picking up an injury in Australia, while Cairns tore a muscle in his right knee during the Christchurch Test and missed the chance to add to his three wickets in the first hour of the series. And while New Zealand did not unearth a consistently dangerous new-ball replacement until Tuffey took nine wickets at Auckland, England had a locally born star of their own. After a slow start to the tour – he was savaged in a warm-up game by the pinch-hitter Simon Doull and left out of the last four one-day internationals – Andy Caddick was comfortably the most incisive bowler on either side. An irresistible burst on the first morning at Auckland made him the ninth England bowler to reach 200 Test wickets, and his series haul of 19 at less than 20 should have been the difference between the sides.

While Caddick and the bustling Matthew Hoggard (17 wickets at 23) enjoyed the uneven bounce and lavish early movement, the top-order batsmen did not. None of the first three on either side averaged 30, and it was left to the middle order to provide the memorable batting. At Christchurch, Hussain gave a masterclass in bad-wicket grafting, Graham Thorpe and Andrew Flintoff brought New Zealand's bowlers to their knees, and Astle brought the crowd to their feet. At Wellington, Flintoff flexed his muscles to terrifying effect. At Auckland, Chris Harris quietly and quirkily drove England mad, before Astle and Craig McMillan shone under the lights, to say nothing of the moon.

But in a country where mountains and lakes, ravines and fjords lurk round every corner, not everyone was in the mood to appreciate the scenery. Mark Ramprakash and Michael Vaughan paid the price for over-attacking, and Marcus Trescothick, who complained about burn-out during the match against Otago, endured the first extended slump of his England career, making four ducks in 11 international innings. Trescothick was given the additional burden of replacing James Foster behind the stumps for the last four one-dayers – a move designed to eliminate a weakness, which ended up compromising a strength.

It was a bad time to be a wicket-keeper. When Foster returned for the Test series, he seemed to have a blind spot to his left. Chris Nevin had a shaky one-day series for New Zealand, while Adam Parore was below his best in the Tests and retired from the game after the win at Auckland. So it was ironic that the only keeper to enhance his reputation didn't even play an international match: Warren Hegg returned home with a full set of brownie points after spending much of his time working with Foster in the nets.

There were full marks too – from the locals at least – for the Barmy Army, the eclectic English band of seasoned travelling fans, back-packers

Let there be cricket: the use of floodlights on the fourth evening of the Auckland Test helped guide New Zealand to victory after rain disrupted the first three days. *Picture by Graham Morris.*

and opportunistic hangers-on. Their football-style chants provided virtually all the atmosphere at the half-empty Test grounds, and wound Fleming up to the extent that he was unable to resist a friendly-but-prickly dig at them in his end-of-series speech. The New Zealand board attempted to stage-manage a home-grown response, although the Mad Caps were neither loud nor numerous enough to compete. But the biggest – and most unearthly – sound of the tour came during the one-day international at Wellington, where Peter Jackson, the New Zealand-born director of *The Lord of the Rings*, supervised the crowd in creating battle-scene noises for the second of the trilogy, *The Two Towers*.

The never-say-die attitude instilled by Hussain and Duncan Fletcher was most in evidence during the one-day series. When England were dismissed for 89 to go 2–0 down at Wellington, one local newspaper columnist described them as "a sad joke", but in the next game at Napier, Hussain gave the same eleven the chance to provide their own punchline. They issued the perfect riposte, then squared the series at Auckland to threaten an instant replay of their one-day fightback in India, until a blistering hundred from Astle settled matters.

One question that remained unanswered was whether Hussain should be batting at No. 3 in the one-day side. In the Tests he had continued the renaissance that had begun when he returned from his umpteenth broken finger in August 2001, resolving to attack more. But a one-day series of 129 runs at a strike-rate of only 60.56 was not enough to silence the media mutterings.

It was not the only festering sore in the England camp. Following the draw against Otago, Fletcher admitted he was not happy with the fitness of some of the players who had arrived after the one-day series. No names were mentioned, but the finger of suspicion was pointed immediately at Jimmy Ormond and Usman Afzaal. The British tabloids went to town, and Ormond cut a forlorn – if not very svelte – figure for the rest of the tour.

The cricket, though, will be remembered for one innings. Astle's 222 off 168 balls at the end of the First Test was a once-in-a-lifetime cocktail of daring, power, wit and wonder. It combined the violence of Botham, the swagger of Viv and the precision of Tendulkar. Seven days later came the news of Ben Hollioake, and adrenalin turned to tears. It was a tour where the cricket briefly touched Olympian heights, but where, ultimately, the cricket didn't matter.

ENGLAND TOURING PARTY

N. Hussain (Essex) (*captain*), U. Afzaal (Nottinghamshire), M. A. Butcher (Surrey), A. R. Caddick (Somerset), R. K. J. Dawson (Yorkshire), A. Flintoff (Lancashire), J. S. Foster (Essex), A. F. Giles (Warwickshire), W. K. Hegg (Lancashire), M. J. Hoggard (Yorkshire), J. Ormond (Leicestershire), M. R. Ramprakash (Surrey), G. P. Thorpe (Surrey), M. E. Trescothick (Somerset), M. P. Vaughan (Yorkshire), C. White (Yorkshire).

P. D. Collingwood (Durham), D. Gough (Yorkshire), B. C. Hollioake (Surrey), N. V. Knight (Warwickshire), O. A. Shah (Middlesex) and J. N. Snape (Gloucestershire) were with the party for the one-day series and were replaced by Afzaal, Butcher, Dawson, Hegg, Ormond and Ramprakash for the first-class programme. I. R. Bell (Warwickshire) joined the party as cover for the injured Butcher.

Coach: D. A. G. Fletcher. *Operations manager:* P. A. Neale. *Assistant coaches:* G. R. Dilley and T. J. Boon. *Video analyst:* M. N. Ashton. *Physiotherapist:* D. O. Conway. *Physiologist:* N. P. Stockill. *Media relations manager:* A. J. Walpole.

ENGLAND TOUR RESULTS

Test matches – Played 3: Won 1, Lost 1, Drawn 1.
First-class matches – Played 5: Won 1, Lost 1, Drawn 3.
Win – New Zealand.
Loss – New Zealand.
Draws – New Zealand, Otago, Canterbury.
One-day internationals – Played 5: Won 2, Lost 3.
Other non-first-class matches – Played 2: Won 1, Lost 1. *Win* – Northern Districts. *Loss* – Northern Districts.

TEST MATCH AVERAGES

NEW ZEALAND – BATTING

	T	I	NO	R	HS	100s	50s	Avge	Ct
N. J. Astle	3	6	1	314	222	1	1	62.80	3
C. D. McMillan	3	6	2	213	50*	0	1	53.25	1
M. H. Richardson	3	6	0	172	76	0	2	28.66	3
L. Vincent	3	6	0	160	71	0	2	26.66	1
A. C. Parore	3	5	0	82	45	0	0	16.40	10
M. J. Horne	2	4	0	64	38	0	0	16.00	0
D. L. Vettori	3	5	0	68	42	0	0	13.60	3
S. P. Fleming	3	6	0	76	48	0	0	12.66	6
I. G. Butler	2	3	0	16	12	0	0	5.33	1
C. J. Drum	3	4	2	6	2*	0	0	3.00	3

Played in one Test: A. R. Adams 7, 11 (1 ct); C. L. Cairns 0, 23*; C. Z. Harris 71, 43; C. S. Martin 0* (1 ct); D. R. Tuffey 0, 5.

BOWLING

	O	M	R	W	BB	5W/i	Avge
D. R. Tuffey	35	9	116	9	6-54	1	12.88
A. R. Adams	31.4	5	105	6	3-44	0	17.50
C. L. Cairns	19	4	66	3	3-58	0	22.00
N. J. Astle	52.4	20	115	4	2-32	0	28.75
I. G. Butler	63.3	6	288	9	4-60	0	32.00
C. J. Drum	112.2	25	426	12	3-36	0	35.50
D. L. Vettori	82	8	280	5	3-90	0	56.00

Also bowled: C. D. McMillan 20–1–102–0; C. S. Martin 24–4–98–2.

ENGLAND – BATTING

	T	I	NO	R	HS	100s	50s	Avge	Ct
G. P. Thorpe	3	6	2	274	200*	1	0	68.50	7
N. Hussain	3	6	1	280	106	1	2	56.00	2
J. S. Foster	3	5	3	105	25*	0	0	52.50	9
A. Flintoff	3	6	0	243	137	1	1	40.50	2
M. A. Butcher	3	6	0	176	60	0	1	29.33	3
M. E. Trescothick	3	6	0	172	88	0	1	28.66	1
M. P. Vaughan	3	6	0	131	36	0	0	21.83	1
M. R. Ramprakash	3	5	0	77	31	0	0	15.40	2
A. F. Giles	3	4	1	39	21*	0	0	13.00	4
A. R. Caddick	3	4	0	34	20	0	0	8.50	1
M. J. Hoggard	3	4	1	9	7	0	0	3.00	0

BOWLING

	O	M	R	W	BB	5W/i	Avge
A. R. Caddick	124.3	38	377	19	6-63	2	19.84
M. J. Hoggard	119.2	34	402	17	7-63	1	23.64
A. Flintoff	93	20	313	9	3-49	0	34.77
A. F. Giles	100	20	236	6	4-103	0	39.33

Also bowled: M. A. Butcher 14–5–40–2; M. P. Vaughan 5–1–15–0.

ENGLAND TOUR AVERAGES – FIRST-CLASS MATCHES

BATTING

	M	I	NO	R	HS	100s	50s	Avge	Ct
N. Hussain	4	7	1	349	106	1	3	58.16	4
G. P. Thorpe	4	8	2	285	200*	1	0	47.50	8
M. P. Vaughan	4	7	0	287	156	1	0	41.00	1
J. S. Foster	4	6	3	108	25*	0	0	36.00	10
M. E. Trescothick	4	8	0	246	88	0	2	30.75	1
A. Flintoff	5	9	0	260	137	1	1	28.88	4
M. A. Butcher	5	9	0	235	60	0	1	26.11	4
A. F. Giles	4	5	1	65	26	0	0	16.25	6
M. R. Ramprakash	5	8	0	125	42	0	0	15.62	3
A. R. Caddick	5	7	1	71	20	0	0	11.83	1
M. J. Hoggard	4	4	1	9	7	0	0	3.00	0

Played in two matches: U. Afzaal 0, 30, 19 (1 ct); C. White 9, 0, 73 (1 ct). Played in one match: R. K. J. Dawson 24*, 35*; W. K. Hegg 32, 12 (5 ct); J. Ormond 0, 38.

BOWLING

	O	M	R	W	BB	5W/i	Avge
A. R. Caddick	192.3	60	546	31	6-63	3	17.61
M. J. Hoggard	152.2	42	498	18	7-63	1	27.66
A. Flintoff.	119	27	381	10	3-49	0	38.10
A. F. Giles	135.1	32	304	7	4-103	0	43.42

Also bowled: M. A. Butcher 24–8–75–3; R. K. J. Dawson 7–1–14–0; J. Ormond 27–7–84–1; M. P. Vaughan 5–1–15–0; C. White 39–13–75–4.

Note: Matches in this section which were not first-class are signified by a dagger.

†At Hamilton, February 8 (day/night). **Northern Districts won by three wickets.** Toss: England XI. **England XI 288 for six** (50 overs) (M. E. Trescothick 38, N. V. Knight 126, G. P. Thorpe 40, O. A. Shah 31); **Northern Districts 293 for seven** (49.1 overs) (S. B. Doull 80, M. E. Parlane 79, H. J. H. Marshall 38, G. E. Bradburn 43 not out).
   Knight scored his 126 from 125 balls, with ten fours and four sixes. In reply, Doull opened with 80 in 47 balls, including 11 fours and two sixes.

†At Hamilton, February 10. **England XI won by five wickets.** Toss: Northern Districts. **Northern Districts 160** (49.2 overs) (G. E. Bradburn 46 not out; A. Flintoff three for 20); **England XI 163 for five** (33.4 overs) (A. Flintoff 45 not out; J. A. F. Yovich three for 33).
   Flintoff hit his 45 off 25 balls, with nine fours and a six.

†NEW ZEALAND v ENGLAND

First One-Day International

At Christchurch, February 13 (day/night). New Zealand won by four wickets. Toss: England. International debut: I. G. Butler.
   A match of two collapses eventually went the way of New Zealand, who weathered a stormy spell from Gough to halt a run of five one-day defeats. In a game reduced to 42 overs a side by heavy overnight rain, New Zealand, needing 197, were cruising at 136 for two from 28 overs. But Gough seized four wickets for eight in 11 balls, three of them on 144, and New Zealand were indebted to a fearless unbroken fifty partnership between Astle, badly dropped by Foster on 11, and the explosive Adams. England's collapse had been even more abrupt. At 156 for two in the 27th over, they were heading for 250, but when Tuffey removed Knight for a 70-ball 73, it was the first of eight wickets to fall for 40 in less than 14 overs. England hit the ball in the air too often, and New Zealand's catching was razor-sharp, epitomised by Vincent's diving one-handed swoop at cover to dismiss Flintoff.
   Man of the Match: N. J. Astle.   *Attendance:* 13,683.

In and out: James Foster drops Nathan Astle on his way to a crucial fifty in the first one-day international. Foster himself was dropped for the rest of the series. *Picture by Andrew Cornaga.*

England

M. E. Trescothick lbw b Butler	1	A. R. Caddick c Harris b Adams	2
N. V. Knight c Adams b Tuffey	73	D. Gough not out	5
*N. Hussain c Nevin b Adams	35	L-b 6, w 6, n-b 1	13
G. P. Thorpe run out	41		
A. Flintoff c Vincent b Cairns	12	1/2 (1) 2/84 (3) 3/156 (2) (40.2 overs) 196	
P. D. Collingwood c Tuffey b Vettori	9	4/170 (4) 5/181 (6)	
C. White c Cairns b Vettori	0	6/181 (5) 7/183 (7)	
†J. S. Foster c Vincent b Vettori	3	8/189 (8) 9/189 (9)	
A. F. Giles c Harris b Cairns	2	10/196 (10) 12 overs: 84-2	

Bowling: Butler 5–0–37–1; Tuffey 8–0–48–1; Cairns 9–1–43–2; Adams 6.2–1–25–2; Astle 1–0–9–0; Harris 3–0–11–0; Vettori 8–1–17–3.

New Zealand

†C. J. Nevin c Collingwood b Flintoff	55	A. R. Adams not out	28
N. J. Astle not out	67		
*S. P. Fleming c and b White	10	L-b 9, w 6	15
C. D. McMillan c Foster b Gough	15		
C. L. Cairns b Gough	8	1/99 (1) 2/111 (3) (6 wkts, 38.3 overs) 198	
L. Vincent c Flintoff b Gough	0	3/136 (4) 4/144 (5)	
C. Z. Harris c Foster b Gough	0	5/144 (6) 6/144 (7) 12 overs: 57-0	

D. L. Vettori, D. R. Tuffey and I. G. Butler did not bat.

Bowling: Gough 9–1–44–4; Caddick 7.3–0–51–0; Flintoff 8–0–30–1; White 5–0–36–1; Giles 9–1–28–0.

Umpires: A. L. Hill and E. A. Watkin.
Third umpire: D. M. Quested. Referee: D. T. Lindsay (South Africa).

†NEW ZEALAND v ENGLAND

Second One-Day International

At WestpacTrust Stadium, Wellington, February 16 (day/night). New Zealand won by 155 runs. Toss: England.

England recorded their second-lowest total in 344 one-day internationals, stumbling to 40 for six and only narrowly surpassing their 86 against Australia at Old Trafford eight months earlier. On a sluggish wicket, the damage was done by New Zealand's batting stars from the previous game. Adams wobbled it around to take three for 13, while Astle, whose three wickets cost just four runs, was left on a hat-trick. Only Flintoff passed 12 as Fleming's clever field placings exerted a stranglehold. New Zealand's 244 was held together by McMillan, who swept cheekily for his 69. England experimented by handing the gloves to Trescothick, who occasionally looked out of his depth but would be preferred to Foster for the rest of the series. England's fielding was shoddy and three catches were dropped; Hussain later pointed to a lack of intensity. The crowd had no such problems, particularly during the interval, when Peter Jackson, the director of *The Lord of the Rings*, stood on the pitch with a microphone and persuaded them to make howling, growling, grunting noises for use in battle scenes in *The Two Towers*.

Man of the Match: A. R. Adams.   *Attendance:* 25,390.

New Zealand

†C. J. Nevin c and b Gough	21	A. R. Adams not out		25
N. J. Astle lbw b Gough	7	D. L. Vettori not out		0
B. B. McCullum c Trescothick b Flintoff	9	L-b 5, w 3, n-b 4		12
*S. P. Fleming c Shah b Hoggard	40			
C. D. McMillan c Flintoff b White	69	1/25 (2) 2/34 (1)	(8 wkts, 50 overs)	244
L. Vincent b Hoggard	36	3/52 (3) 4/110 (4)		
C. L. Cairns c Flintoff b White	11	5/194 (5) 6/198 (6)		
C. Z. Harris c Knight b Gough	14	7/206 (7) 8/243 (8)	15 overs: 62-3	
D. R. Tuffey did not bat.				

Bowling: Gough 10–0–47–3; Hoggard 8–1–36–2; Flintoff 10–0–46–1; White 10–1–53–2; Giles 8–0–40–0; Collingwood 4–0–17–0.

England

†M. E. Trescothick c Nevin b Adams	0	D. Gough b Astle		0
N. V. Knight b Adams	9	M. J. Hoggard not out		0
*N. Hussain c Fleming b Tuffey	3			
G. P. Thorpe lbw b Adams	10	L-b 2, w 2, n-b 7		11
O. A. Shah c Fleming b Cairns	7			
P. D. Collingwood c Vettori b Astle	0	1/1 (1) 2/13 (3) 3/18 (2)	(37.2 overs)	89
A. Flintoff c McCullum b Astle	26	4/28 (4) 5/35 (6) 6/40 (5)		
C. White lbw b Harris	11	7/65 (8) 8/89 (9)		
A. F. Giles c Vettori b Harris	12	9/89 (7) 10/89 (10)	15 overs: 34-4	

Bowling: Tuffey 8–3–23–1; Adams 7–0–13–3; Cairns 4–1–11–1; Astle 2.2–0–4–3; Vettori 7–0–18–0; Harris 9–2–18–2.

Umpires: R. S. Dunne and D. M. Quested.
Third umpire: A. L. Hill.   Referee: D. T. Lindsay (South Africa).

†NEW ZEALAND v ENGLAND

Third One-Day International

At Napier, February 20 (day/night). England won by 43 runs. Toss: New Zealand.

Collingwood, whose three one-day international wickets had cost 101 each, surprised even himself by finding prodigious swing under the McLean Park lights. He took four for 38 and ran through New Zealand's middle order with little apparent effort. While Fleming was in quiet control,

New Zealand were on course to seal a series win but, at 128 for three in the 30th over, Vincent cut Collingwood to gully. Soon after, Cairns chipped to deep mid-wicket, and only Fleming held his nerve in the ensuing panic. England started convincingly, with three half-century partnerships: Trescothick finally took the attack to New Zealand with a flashy 41, Knight played the anchor role and Thorpe added an imaginative run-a-ball fifty. Even so, on a ground with enticingly short square boundaries, 244 felt 20 below par. But Astle was given out caught behind despite failing to make contact, and Hoggard completed a searching ten-over spell in the blink of an eye. Then Collingwood swung the game England's way to keep the series alive.

Man of the Match: P. D. Collingwood.   *Attendance:* 12,392.

England

†M. E. Trescothick c Harris b Cairns	41	O. A. Shah not out		0
N. V. Knight c Nevin b Cairns	80	B 1, l-b 5, w 5, n-b 8		19
*N. Hussain b Harris	24			
G. P. Thorpe c Astle b Cairns	52	1/71 (1) 2/127 (3)	(5 wkts, 50 overs)	244
A. Flintoff c Vincent b Adams	19	3/192 (2) 4/231 (4)		
P. D. Collingwood not out	9	5/240 (5)	15 overs: 71-1	

C. White, A. F. Giles, D. Gough and M. J. Hoggard did not bat.

Bowling: Butler 4–0–21–0; Tuffey 10–0–39–0; Cairns 10–1–51–3; Adams 9–1–49–1; Vettori 10–0–49–0; Harris 7–0–29–1.

New Zealand

†C. J. Nevin c sub (B. C. Hollioake) b Hoggard	21	D. L. Vettori lbw b Giles		9
N. J. Astle c Trescothick b Gough	2	D. R. Tuffey b Giles		1
*S. P. Fleming not out	76	I. G. Butler b Gough		3
C. D. McMillan c Collingwood b Hoggard	14	B 2, l-b 15, w 15, n-b 2		34
L. Vincent c White b Collingwood	29	1/10 (2) 2/31 (1) 3/70 (4)	(46.3 overs)	201
C. L. Cairns c Flintoff b Collingwood	7	4/128 (5) 5/140 (6)		
C. Z. Harris lbw b Collingwood	3	6/152 (7) 7/168 (8)		
A. R. Adams c Shah b Collingwood	2	8/180 (9) 9/186 (10)		
		10/201 (11)	15 overs: 67-2	

Bowling: Gough 8.3–0–21–2; Hoggard 10–0–44–2; Flintoff 7–0–34–0; White 3–0–15–0; Giles 10–1–32–2; Collingwood 8–0–38–4.

Umpires: B. F. Bowden and D. B. Cowie.
Third umpire: A. L. Hill.   Referee: D. T. Lindsay (South Africa).

†NEW ZEALAND v ENGLAND

Fourth One-Day International

At Auckland, February 23 (day/night). England won by 33 runs (D/L method). Toss: England. Although Duckworth/Lewis may have given England's series-levelling victory a flattering sheen, there was no doubt the better side won. Set 223 in 40 overs after rain had interrupted England's innings, New Zealand slumped to 86 for six, a sequence including an astonishing catch at third man by Gough, who leapt back at full stretch to dismiss Astle. The combative lower middle order gave England a fright, but, when Collingwood bowled Cairns for a 56-ball 58, they breathed again. Flintoff wrapped things up with miserly career-best figures of four for 17. Earlier, England had lost a wicket third ball when Trescothick lifted Tuffey straight to mid-on, while Hussain was ruled lbw to a delivery comfortably passing over off stump, giving Cairns his 150th wicket in his 150th game. Vaughan, in company with Thorpe, put England back on track with an exquisite 59 from 53 deliveries, only to chuck it away in bizarre fashion: struggling to regain his ground, he dropped his bat, and the bowler, Vettori, threw down the stumps. In the end, though, it didn't matter.

Man of the Match: A. Flintoff.   *Attendance:* 32,307.

England

†M. E. Trescothick c Cairns b Tuffey	0	C. White not out		3
N. V. Knight run out	38			
*N. Hussain lbw b Cairns	17	B 4, l-b 6, w 1		11
G. P. Thorpe not out	59			
M. P. Vaughan run out	59	1/0 (1) 2/40 (3)	(6 wkts, 40 overs)	193
A. Flintoff c Astle b Cairns	2	3/78 (2) 4/167 (5)		
P. D. Collingwood st Nevin b Harris	4	5/170 (6) 6/185 (7)	15 overs: 55-2	

A. F. Giles, D. Gough and M. J. Hoggard did not bat.

Bowling: Tuffey 8–1–32–1; Adams 8–1–36–0; Cairns 8–0–39–2; Vettori 8–0–31–0; Harris 4–0–23–1; Astle 4–0–22–0.

New Zealand

†C. J. Nevin c Trescothick b Hoggard	8	D. L. Vettori c Hoggard b Gough		4
N. J. Astle c Gough b Flintoff	23	D. R. Tuffey b Flintoff		5
B. B. McCullum c Vaughan b Hoggard	5	L-b 7, w 5		12
*S. P. Fleming c Vaughan b Gough	8			
C. D. McMillan c Knight b Flintoff	10	1/9 (1) 2/16 (3) 3/42 (4)	(38 overs)	189
L. Vincent c Giles b Flintoff	7	4/58 (5) 5/60 (2)		
C. L. Cairns b Collingwood	58	6/86 (6) 7/153 (8)		
C. Z. Harris c Flintoff b White	23	8/167 (7) 9/181 (10)		
A. R. Adams not out	26	10/189 (11)	12 overs: 55-3	

Bowling: Gough 7–1–33–2; Hoggard 8–1–27–2; Flintoff 7–1–17–4; Collingwood 6–0–43–1; White 8–0–44–1; Giles 2–0–18–0.

Umpires: D. B. Cowie and A. L. Hill.
Third umpire: B. F. Bowden. Referee: D. T. Lindsay (South Africa).

†NEW ZEALAND v ENGLAND

Fifth One-Day International

At Dunedin, February 26 (day/night). New Zealand won by five wickets. Toss: England.

An expertly paced century from Astle, his 12th in one-day internationals, clinched a 3–2 series win for New Zealand and prevented England from pulling off a second Lazarus-like comeback of the winter. Astle flew out of the blocks, smashing 46 in boundaries to reach his first fifty from 42 balls. But Fleming edged to second slip two balls later to make it 80 for three, forcing Astle to adapt: his second fifty came from 85 deliveries, with his 12th four bringing up both his hundred and a century stand with McMillan. Gough gave England hope by dismissing McMillan and Cairns in the next over with 39 needed. Vincent stayed calm, though, and Astle finished things off with seven balls to spare when he swung Flintoff into the stands – the sixth six in a 150-ball innings. It also took him past 5,000 runs in his 150th limited-overs international. England's 218 for eight was at least 25 below expectations, despite a gutsy fourth-wicket stand of 71 between Hussain, hitting his first one-day international fifty in 13 innings, and Shah, who showed touches of real class. Ben Holligan made his final appearance here, as a substitute, and fielded with his usual athleticism at backward point and fine leg.

Man of the Match: N. J. Astle.   *Attendance*: 13,909.

England

†M. E. Trescothick c Harris b Tuffey	5	A. F. Giles not out	21
N. V. Knight c Harris b Tuffey	24	D. Gough not out	2
*N. Hussain c Cairns b Tuffey	50	L-b 4, w 3, n-b 4	11
G. P. Thorpe b Adams	9		
O. A. Shah lbw b Cairns	57	1/8 (1) 2/43 (2)	(8 wkts, 50 overs) 218
P. D. Collingwood c Fleming b Cairns	21	3/62 (4) 4/133 (3)	
A. Flintoff b Cairns	1	5/170 (5) 6/172 (7)	
C. White c Astle b Adams	17	7/183 (6) 8/214 (8)	15 overs: 65-3

M. J. Hoggard did not bat.

Bowling: Tuffey 9–1–42–3; Adams 10–0–50–2; Cairns 10–0–32–3; Vettori 9–0–48–0; Harris 10–0–35–0; Astle 2–0–7–0.

New Zealand

†C. J. Nevin c Trescothick b Flintoff	15	L. Vincent not out	20
N. J. Astle not out	122	L-b 4, w 5, n-b 5	14
B. B. McCullum b White	7		
*S. P. Fleming c Knight b White	1	1/55 (1) 2/77 (3)	(5 wkts, 48.5 overs) 223
C. D. McMillan lbw b Gough	44	3/80 (4) 4/180 (5)	
C. L. Cairns c Hussain b Gough	0	5/180 (6)	15 overs: 80-3

C. Z. Harris, A. R. Adams, D. L. Vettori and D. R. Tuffey did not bat.

Bowling: Gough 10–0–42–2; Hoggard 6–0–41–0; Flintoff 9.5–0–56–1; White 10–0–30–2; Giles 8–0–37–0; Collingwood 5–0–13–0.

Umpires: R. S. Dunne and D. M. Quested.
Third umpire: E. A. Watkin.   Referee: D. T. Lindsay (South Africa).

OTAGO v ENGLAND XI

At Queenstown, March 2, 3, 4. Drawn. Toss: Otago.
The maiden first-class game at Queenstown's Events Centre, a stunningly picturesque ground nestled between the Remarkables mountain range and Coronet Peak, was blighted by the weather, which limited the first two days' play to 106 overs, but the sides came close to forcing a result. Set 261 on the final afternoon, Otago, who had lost seven consecutive first-class games, were reduced to 61 for six by Caddick and White, and needed a tenacious unbroken stand of 63 between Cumming and Morland to salvage a draw. Earlier, Pryor had taken five wickets with his swinging medium-pace as England, giving Hussain a week off with his family and fielding all six players who had arrived for the Test leg of the tour, tumbled to 153 all out. Hostile bowling from Caddick kept Otago in check before Cumming declared, three behind, on the final morning. Trescothick, England's stand-in captain, slammed his first half-century of the tour, but an embarrassing defeat loomed when they collapsed to 162 for eight against Walmsley's nippy seamers. However, Dawson helped add 95 for the last two wickets, and in the end it was Otago who were hanging on.
Close of play: First day, England XI 82-6 (White 6, Hegg 8); Second day, Otago 150-6 (Pryor 6, Morland 2).

 The toss was vital on a damp, green-tinged wicket, described by an ECB pitch panel as "below average" and by Irani as "downright dangerous".
Nottinghamshire v Essex, page 727

England XI

M. A. Butcher lbw b Pryor	20	– c Pryor b Walmsley	0
*M. E. Trescothick c Pryor b Sewell	6	– c Beare b Sewell	68
G. P. Thorpe c McCullum b Sewell	11	– b Walmsley	0
M. R. Ramprakash b Pryor	1	– c Beare b Walmsley	42
U. Afzaal c Drew b Pryor	0	– c Cumming b Sewell	30
A. Flintoff c Drew b McMillan	16	– lbw b Sewell	0
C. White c Morland b Walmsley	9	– c Lawson b Walmsley	0
†W. K. Hegg c Beare b Pryor	32	– c Drew b Walmsley	12
R. K. J. Dawson not out	24	– not out	35
J. Ormond c Beare b Pryor	0	– c Cumming b Morland	38
A. R. Caddick c Morland b Walmsley	6	– c Gaffaney b Beare	16
L-b 11, w 5, n-b 12	28	B 10, l-b 4, w 1, n-b 1	16
	153		**257**

1/32 2/39 3/50 4/50 5/55
6/69 7/88 8/131 9/131

1/0 2/7 3/106 4/139 5/139
6/148 7/155 8/162 9/224

Bowling: *First Innings*—Walmsley 14.4–3–41–2; McMillan 11–3–25–1; Sewell 12–5–31–2; Pryor 12–1–45–5. *Second Innings*—Walmsley 15–4–51–5; McMillan 7–3–6–0; Sewell 13–2–78–3; Pryor 10–0–58–0; Beare 4.1–0–11–1; Morland 8–1–39–1.

Otago

R. A. Lawson c Butcher b Caddick	18	– c Hegg b Caddick	11
B. B. McCullum c Hegg b Caddick	34	– c Hegg b Ormond	19
*C. D. Cumming c Hegg b White	31	– not out	57
C. B. Gaffaney c Thorpe b Butcher	31	– lbw b Caddick	0
S. P. Beare c Flintoff b Butcher	2	– b Caddick	0
C. R. Pryor not out	6	– c and b White	10
†D. J. Drew b Caddick	2	– c Hegg b White	0
N. D. Morland not out	2	– not out	19
B 1, l-b 19, w 2, n-b 2	24	L-b 6, n-b 2	8
	150		**124**

1/35 2/69 3/119
4/136 5/136 6/143

(6 wkts dec.)

1/30 2/34 3/34
4/34 5/57 6/61

(6 wkts)

K. P. Walmsley, J. M. McMillan and D. G. Sewell did not bat.

Bowling: *First Innings*—Caddick 18–6–42–4; Ormond 15–4–47–0; Flintoff 7–3–12–0; White 8–4–11–1; Butcher 8–3–18–1. *Second Innings*—Caddick 14–3–43–3; Ormond 12–3–37–1; White 7–3–7–2; Butcher 2–0–17–0; Dawson 7–1–14–0.

Umpires: R. S. Dunne and E. A. Watkin.

CANTERBURY v ENGLAND XI

At Hagley Oval, Christchurch, March 7, 8, 9. Drawn. Toss: England XI.

An innings of silky elegance from Vaughan lingered in the memory long after Canterbury's top order had doggedly denied England a confidence-boosting win. In his first outing since injuring his shoulder at Auckland, Vaughan lit up the match with a dazzling 156 and shared a second-wicket stand of 207 with the more sedate Hussain. Vaughan's cover-driving was classically simple, his pulling effortlessly violent, and one square-drive even brought applause from his captain. In four hours, he faced 198 balls and hit 23 fours. His dismissal at 278, to the second of Harris's five catches, triggered a collapse of four for eight, before White made an unsuccessful case to stay in the Test team with a patient 73. On the first day, Caddick, returning to the ground where he played club cricket as a teenager, had threatened to skittle Canterbury by himself, but was thwarted by Robert Frew, whose 44 occupied four and a quarter hours, and by Harris. Frew batted even longer to frustrate England on the final day, when Caddick opened with six maidens but claimed no more wickets on a pitch now devoid of its early life.

Close of play: First day, England XI 28-0 (Butcher 14, Vaughan 13); Second day, England XI 400-8 (White 53, Caddick 4).

Canterbury

R. M. Frew c Flintoff b Caddick	44	– (2) b Giles	72
S. L. Stewart c Hussain b Caddick	0	– (1) c Giles b White	58
M. H. W. Papps c Hussain b Hoggard	7	– not out	30
*G. R. Stead c Foster b Caddick	12		
N. J. Astle c Afzaal b Caddick	6		
C. Z. Harris c Giles b Flintoff	82		
†G. J. Hopkins c Ramprakash b Caddick	3	– (4) not out	2
P. J. Wiseman not out	26		
W. A. Wisneski run out	8		
B 6, l-b 10, n-b 8	24	L-b 10, n-b 3	13

1/5 2/18 3/33 4/39 5/145   (8 wkts dec.) 212   1/112 2/172   (2 wkts) 175
6/149 7/186 8/212

W. A. Cornelius and C. S. Martin did not bat.

Bowling: *First Innings*—Caddick 24–5–69–5; Hoggard 13–5–25–1; Flintoff 13–2–45–1; White 12–3–29–0; Giles 12.1–1–28–0. *Second Innings*—Caddick 12–8–15–0; Hoggard 20–3–71–0; Giles 23–11–40–1; White 12–3–28–1; Flintoff 6–2–11–0.

England XI

M. A. Butcher c Harris b Cornelius	39	A. F. Giles c Harris b Wisneski	26
M. P. Vaughan c Harris b Wiseman	156	A. R. Caddick not out	15
*N. Hussain run out	69		
M. R. Ramprakash c Frew b Wiseman	5	L-b 8, n-b 18	26
U. Afzaal c Cornelius b Wisneski	19		
A. Flintoff c and b Harris	1	1/71 2/278 3/279 (9 wkts dec.) 432	
C. White c Harris b Wiseman	73	4/284 5/286 6/329	
†J. S. Foster b Wisneski	3	7/333 8/383 9/432	

M. J. Hoggard did not bat.

Bowling: Wisneski 20–3–88–3; Martin 23–3–92–0; Cornelius 15–2–85–1; Harris 18–4–45–1; Wiseman 21–2–90–3; Astle 9–2–24–0.

Umpires: R. D. Anderson and D. M. Quested.

NEW ZEALAND v ENGLAND

First Test Match

At Christchurch, March 13, 14, 15, 16. England won by 98 runs. Toss: New Zealand. Test debut: I. G. Butler.

This game will be remembered for perhaps the most glorious failure in the history of Test cricket. When an injured Cairns walked out to join Astle late on the fourth afternoon, New Zealand were 333 for nine, still 217 short of a wildly improbable victory. What happened next had to be seen to be believed. Astle, 134 at the fall of the ninth wicket, proceeded to treat England's attack as if they had been drafted in from the local kindergarten. He smashed his way to by far the fastest double-century in Tests and briefly raised hopes of a jaw-dropping, eye-popping win. In the end, England, thanks to their earlier all-round efforts, prevailed. But this was, and will always be, Astle's match.

A cricket ball had perhaps never been hit so cleanly, so often. Astle's first hundred had come from a brisk 114 deliveries, but he was merely playing himself in. The carnage began in earnest when Hussain took the second new ball: the next four overs,

Follow that: Matthew Hoggard watches forlornly as Nathan Astle heads for Test cricket's fastest double-hundred. Hoggard had the last laugh, when he dismissed Astle to win the match. *Picture by Graham Morris.*

even though they included a wicket maiden from Caddick, yielded 61 runs. Hoggard, unplayable on the second day, was smashed for 41 in two overs – and out of the attack. So Astle turned his attention to Caddick, steaming in with the confidence of a man who had already grabbed six wickets in the innings. But in seven balls spread across two overs, Astle sprayed graffiti all over Caddick's figures by smacking him for 38. One six flew over third man, another landed on the roof of the stand at extra cover, and three more – over cover, mid-wicket, and straight down the ground – came in successive deliveries as the home supporters of the crowd began to sing and dance in disbelief. England's supporters, so raucous moments before, were stunned into silence.

Another six off Flintoff, a gentle sweep for a single off Giles, and Astle had raced from 101 to 200 in a scarcely believable 39 balls. He reached his maiden Test double-century in 153, smashing the record – set by Adam Gilchrist at Johannesburg just three weeks earlier – by 59 deliveries. He had taken 217 minutes, three more than Bradman

MOST SIXES IN A TEST INNINGS

12	Wasim Akram (257*), Pakistan v Zimbabwe at Sheikhupura............	1996-97
11	**N. J. Astle (222), England v New Zealand at Christchurch**............	**2001-02**
10	W. R. Hammond (336*), England v New Zealand at Auckland	1932-33
9	C. L. Cairns (120), New Zealand v Zimbabwe at Auckland	1995-96
9	**Inzamam-ul-Haq (329), Pakistan v New Zealand at Lahore**..........	**2002**
8	N. S. Sidhu (124), India v Sri Lanka at Lucknow...................	1993-94
8	**A. C. Gilchrist (204*), Australia v South Africa at Johannesburg**	**2001-02**
7	B. Sutcliffe (80*), New Zealand v South Africa at Johannesburg	1953-54
7	I. V. A. Richards (110*), West Indies v England at St John's	1985-86
7	C. G. Greenidge (213), West Indies v New Zealand at Auckland	1986-87

FASTEST DOUBLE-HUNDREDS IN TESTS (BALLS RECEIVED)

Balls		
153	**N. J. Astle, New Zealand v England at Christchurch**............	**2001-02**
212	**A. C. Gilchrist, Australia v South Africa at Johannesburg**	**2001-02**
220	I. T. Botham, England v India at The Oval	1982
229	**P. A. de Silva, Sri Lanka v Bangladesh at Colombo (PSS)**	**2002**
231	**G. P. Thorpe, England v New Zealand at Christchurch**	**2001-02**
232	C. G. Greenidge, West Indies v England at Lord's	1984
240	C. H. Lloyd, West Indies v India at Bombay......................	1974-75
241	Zaheer Abbas, Pakistan v India at Lahore	1982-83
242	D. G. Bradman, Australia v England at The Oval	1934
242	I. V. A. Richards, West Indies v Australia at Melbourne............	1984-85

Full statistics are not available for many earlier innings, which were recorded only in terms of minutes batted.

at Leeds in 1930, when the balls were not totted up (but over-rates were generally higher). It was as though Astle had taken two seconds off the 100 metres record.

Two more sixes off Hoggard followed, bringing the deficit down to double figures. England were seriously worried, and Astle later admitted he would have started to look for ones and twos had New Zealand come within 70 runs of victory. So the relief England felt when Astle drove at Hoggard and was caught behind for 222 was palpable. In all, he faced 168 balls in 231 minutes, hitting 28 fours and 11 sixes. He put on 118 with Cairns (in 69 balls), beating his own last-wicket record against England, an unbroken 106 with Danny Morrison at Auckland in 1996-97, and helped New Zealand to the second-highest total in the fourth innings of a Test, bettered only by England's 654 for five against South Africa at Durban in 1938-39. And he had done it all in the twinkling of an eye.

Amid the fireworks, it was easy to forget the mistake Astle made at a critical moment in England's second innings. With wickets falling regularly, Thorpe, on four, edged Drum to second slip, but Astle was unable to cling on. Soon after, England had lurched to 106 for five, leading by a precarious 187. But Thorpe survived, and he and Flintoff embarked on a stand that changed the course of the match.

Flintoff had managed just eight runs in his previous five Test innings, but within 13 deliveries a burst of searing cuts and drives had taken him to 26. The fifty partnership came in 39 balls, and New Zealand, deprived of Cairns, who had injured his right knee while bowling on the first day, began to wilt. England's lead was a seemingly impregnable 370 by the time Thorpe reached his third century in four Tests in New Zealand, from 121 balls. Flintoff, whose previous Test-best was 42, was even quicker, moving to his hundred from 114 balls with a top-edged hook over the keeper's head. The stand had reached 281, a sixth-wicket record for England, overtaking Peter Parfitt and Barry Knight's 240, also against New Zealand, at Auckland in 1962-63, when Flintoff picked out deep mid-wicket and departed for 137. Thorpe rattled on to a 231-ball double-hundred, his first in Tests and briefly the third-fastest in Test history, and finished with 28 fours and four sixes in five and a half hours. The ink had barely dried when Astle forced a rewrite.

The final two days, in which 856 runs were scored at almost five an over, provided a violent counterpoint to the first two, when 438 came at under three. On Lancaster Park's drop-in pitch, England lost two wickets in Cairns's first over. They were rescued by an innings of technical brilliance and masterful driving from Hussain, whose maiden Test hundred was flawed only by a straightforward chance to Fleming at first slip on 52.

Hussain's batting was matched by Hoggard's bowling. Swinging the ball as though playing on the green, green grass of Headingley, Hoggard bewitched New Zealand to claim a career-best seven for 63. Any chance of taking all ten was denied him by a characteristically late flash of inspiration by Caddick, who snapped up three wickets in one rampant over. When England lost five cheap wickets in their second innings, a close finish seemed inevitable – but the game was only just warming up.

Man of the Match: G. P. Thorpe.   *Attendance:* 15,864.

Close of play: First day, New Zealand 9-1 (Horne 0, Vettori 4); Second day, England 63-2 (Butcher 22, Hussain 6); Third day, New Zealand 28-0 (Richardson 20, Horne 3).

England

M. E. Trescothick c Parore b Cairns	0	– c Vettori b Butler	33
M. P. Vaughan c Parore b Cairns	27	– b Butler	0
M. A. Butcher c Butler b Cairns	0	– hit wkt b Butler	34
*N. Hussain lbw b Drum	106	– c Parore b Drum	11
G. P. Thorpe c Fleming b Drum	17	– not out	200
M. R. Ramprakash c Parore b Astle	31	– b Drum	11
A. Flintoff lbw b Astle	0	– c sub (M. N. McKenzie) b Astle	137
†J. S. Foster lbw b Drum	19	– not out	22
A. F. Giles c Drum b Butler	8		
A. R. Caddick lbw b Butler	0		
M. J. Hoggard not out	0		
B 1, l-b 10, n-b 9	20	B 6, l-b 4, n-b 10	20
	228	(6 wkts dec.)	**468**

1/0 (1) 2/0 (3) 3/46 (2) 4/83 (5)   228
5/139 (6) 6/151 (7) 7/196 (8)
8/214 (9) 9/226 (10) 10/228 (4)

1/11 (2) 2/50 (1)   (6 wkts dec.) 468
3/81 (4) 4/85 (3)
5/106 (6) 6/387 (7)

Bowling: *First Innings*—Cairns 15–4–58–3; Drum 20.2–8–36–3; Butler 16–2–59–2; Astle 18–10–32–2; Vettori 9–1–26–0; McMillan 3–1–6–0. *Second Innings*—Drum 32–6–130–2; Butler 23–2–137–3; Cairns 4–0–8–0; McMillan 10–0–66–0; Astle 5.4–0–20–1; Vettori 22–3–97–0.

New Zealand

M. H. Richardson lbw b Hoggard	2	– c Foster b Caddick	76
M. J. Horne c Thorpe b Hoggard	14	– c Foster b Caddick	4
D. L. Vettori c Foster b Hoggard	42	– (8) c Flintoff b Giles	12
L. Vincent b Hoggard	12	– (3) c Butcher b Caddick	0
*S. P. Fleming c Giles b Caddick	12	– (4) c Foster b Flintoff	48
N. J. Astle lbw b Hoggard	10	– (5) c Foster b Hoggard	222
C. D. McMillan c and b Vaughan b Hoggard	40	– (6) c and b Caddick	24
C. L. Cairns c Flintoff b Caddick	0	– (11) not out	23
†A. C. Parore lbw b Caddick	0	– (7) b Caddick	1
C. J. Drum not out	2	– (9) lbw b Flintoff	4
I. G. Butler c Hussain b Hoggard	0	– (10) c Foster b Caddick	4
L-b 5, n-b 8	13	B 9, l-b 11, w 1, n-b 16	37
	147		**451**

1/4 (1) 2/50 (2) 3/65 (3) 4/79 (4)   147
5/93 (6) 6/117 (5) 7/117 (8)
8/117 (9) 9/146 (7) 10/147 (11)

1/42 (2) 2/53 (3) 3/119 (1)   451
4/189 (4) 5/242 (6) 6/252 (7)
7/300 (8) 8/301 (9)
9/333 (10) 10/451 (5)

Bowling: *First Innings*—Caddick 18–8–50–3; Hoggard 21.2–7–63–7; Flintoff 12–2–29–0. *Second Innings*—Caddick 25–8–122–6; Hoggard 24.3–5–142–1; Giles 28–6–73–1; Flintoff 16–1–94–2.

Umpires: E. A. R. de Silva (Sri Lanka) and B. F. Bowden.
Third umpire: D. M. Quested.   Referee: J. L. Hendriks (West Indies).

NEW ZEALAND v ENGLAND

Second Test Match

At Basin Reserve, Wellington, March 21, 22, 23, 24, 25. Drawn. Toss: New Zealand.

Cricket shrivelled into insignificance at half past ten on the third morning, when news filtered through that Ben Hollioake, England's 24-year-old all-rounder, had been killed in a car crash in Western Australia. As the cricket community began to mourn the loss of one of its most gifted players, those on the field – as yet unaware of the tragedy – went about their business as normal. It was only at lunch, with England 199 for four in their first innings, that they heard the news. The New Zealand team and England's batsmen, Hussain and Ramprakash, emerged after the interval with black armbands. Flags were lowered to half-mast, and a reverent hush descended.

It would have taken a heart of steel to condemn England for slumping to 280. That evening, Hussain spoke with dignity and feeling about a friend who had been an integral part of the England dressing-room less than a month earlier, on this same tour. The Test, already blighted by a first-day washout, a curtailed second day and poor pitch covering, felt like an irrelevant sideshow.

But the sideshow had to go on and, after a minute's silence on the fourth morning, it did. England were understandably subdued, and New Zealand – just as understandably – took advantage. After 57 careful overs, Richardson and Vincent had taken them to 135 for one, a position from which they should have dictated terms.

Instead, it was England who took charge. On a pitch with little to offer the seamers, Caddick summoned up real fire, while Giles, aiming into the rough outside the right-hander's leg stump, found turn and bounce. Between them, they grabbed five wickets for 14 in nine overs as the shell-shocked New Zealanders careered to 149 for six. McMillan, left with the tail as he had been in the first innings at Christchurch, unleashed some feisty counter-blows, but the eventual collapse of nine for 83 in the equivalent of a session spoke volumes for England's spirit. Caddick, comfortably the best of the seamers, finished with six for 63, to go with his six for 122 in the previous innings. It was the first time an England bowler had taken consecutive six-fors since Ian Botham's six for 58 and seven for 48 at Bombay in 1979-80.

Before play on the fourth morning of the Wellington Test, both teams observed a minute's silence in memory of Ben Hollioake, whose death was announced the previous day. *Picture by Graham Morris.*

New Zealand's bowling attack had muddled through the first innings without the injured Cairns, but the cracks began to appear on the fourth evening as England went for quick runs. The three main seamers – Butler, Drum and Martin, Cairns's replacement – had just 13 previous Tests between them, while the spinner, Vettori, was troubled by a sore back. England showed no mercy. Vaughan and Trescothick opened with a chancy 79 before Vaughan top-edged a sweep to deep square leg. Then Trescothick at last demonstrated to the New Zealand crowd the havoc he could wreak, and Butcher joined in the fun with some spanking drives and cuts. By the close, England led by 246.

The final morning dawned slate-grey, but was lit up by some pyrotechnics from Flintoff. He came to the crease in the third over of the day after Butcher had picked up mid-off, and launched into a display of violence that scattered players and spectators alike. After Trescothick had swept high to short fine leg, Hussain happily played second fiddle as Flintoff powered his way to a 33-ball half-century. Only Botham (twice) had hit a Test fifty for England in fewer balls, though Allan Lamb had equalled it. A furious innings came to a tame end when Flintoff offered a simple return catch to Vettori, but his 75 off 44 balls, with nine fours and two sixes, enabled Hussain to hasten the declaration.

It left New Zealand needing 356 in 88 overs, but neither side came close to victory. Things might have been different if two key moments had gone England's way. Vincent, who had been reprieved by umpire Dunne on three in the first innings after edging Caddick to short leg via his pad, was given another early life by Dunne when he squeezed Giles, again off bat and pad, to silly point. Vincent had four at the time and went on to a match-saving 71. The decision was typical of a game in which the umpires frequently resembled waxwork dummies.

England could have no complaints about what followed, however. Fleming, on one, nicked Flintoff to Foster who – for the third time in the match – put down a chance diving to his left. Fleming proceeded to grind out an utterly tedious 11 in 142 minutes, one of the slowest Test innings of all time. Vincent and Fleming eventually fell within four overs of one another as Hoggard began to find reverse swing, but Astle and McMillan played out the final hour with ease. It was an anticlimactic end to a Test that never quite emerged from beneath the clouds.

Man of the Match: A. R. Caddick. *Attendance:* 21,582.

Close of play: First day, No play; Second day, England 92-2 (Butcher 24, Hussain 16); Third day, New Zealand 70-1 (Richardson 29, Vincent 30); Fourth day, England 184-1 (Trescothick 77, Butcher 57).

England

M. E. Trescothick c Vincent b Vettori	37	– c Richardson b Vettori	88
M. P. Vaughan c Fleming b Drum	7	– c Drum b Vettori	34
M. A. Butcher c Astle b Drum	47	– c Martin b Drum	60
*N. Hussain c Astle b Vettori	66	– (5) not out	13
G. P. Thorpe c Fleming b Martin	11	– (6) not out	1
M. R. Ramprakash b Butler	24		
A. Flintoff c Drum b Butler	2	– (4) c and b Vettori	75
†J. S. Foster not out	25		
A. F. Giles c McMillan b Butler	10		
A. R. Caddick c Richardson b Martin	10		
M. J. Hoggard c Parore b Butler	7		
B 4, l-b 2, w 6, n-b 22	34	B 5, l-b 13, n-b 4	22
	280	(4 wkts dec.)	**293**

1/26 (2) 2/63 (1) 3/133 (3) 4/163 (5)   1/79 (2) 2/194 (3)   (4 wkts dec.)
5/221 (6) 6/221 (4) 7/223 (7)   3/209 (1) 4/291 (4)
8/238 (9) 9/250 (10) 10/280 (11)

Bowling: First Innings—Butler 18.3–2–60–4; Drum 24–6–85–2; Martin 17–3–58–2; Vettori 25–3–62–2; Astle 1–0–1–0; McMillan 3–0–8–0. *Second Innings*—Butler 6–0–32–0; Drum 16–2–78–1; Vettori 24–1–90–3; Astle 9–4–18–0; Martin 7–1–40–0; McMillan 3–0–17–0.

New Zealand

M. H. Richardson c Giles b Caddick	60	– c Thorpe b Giles	4
M. J. Horne b Caddick	8	– c Foster b Flintoff	38
L. Vincent c Thorpe b Giles	57	– lbw b Hoggard	71
*S. P. Fleming c Thorpe b Caddick	3	– b Hoggard	11
N. J. Astle c Hussain b Giles	4	– not out	11
C. D. McMillan lbw b Caddick	41	– not out	17
†A. C. Parore c Ramprakash b Giles	0		
D. L. Vettori c Thorpe b Caddick	11		
C. J. Drum c Trescothick b Giles	2		
I. G. Butler c Foster b Caddick	12		
C. S. Martin not out	0		
B 2, l-b 9, n-b 9	20	B 3, l-b 1, n-b 2	6
	218	(4 wkts)	**158**

1/16 (2) 2/135 (3) 3/138 (4) 4/143 (1)   1/28 (1) 2/65 (2)   (4 wkts)
5/147 (5) 6/149 (7) 7/178 (8)   3/128 (3) 4/131 (4)
8/201 (6) 9/207 (9) 10/218 (10)

Bowling: First Innings—Caddick 28.3–8–63–6; Hoggard 13–5–32–0; Giles 37–3–103–4; Flintoff 10–4–9–0. *Second Innings*—Caddick 17–6–31–0; Hoggard 13–4–31–2; Giles 33–11–53–1; Flintoff 16–6–24–1; Vaughan 5–1–15–0.

Umpires: D. B. Hair (Australia) and R. S. Dunne.
Third umpire: E. A. Watkin. Referee: J. L. Hendriks (West Indies).

NEW ZEALAND v ENGLAND

Third Test Match

At Auckland, March 30, 31, April 1, 2, 3. New Zealand won by 78 runs. Toss: New Zealand. Test debut: A. R. Adams.

New Zealand dramatically squared the series with their first home Test win over England for 18 years. Time was running out on the fourth afternoon when they were given room to manoeuvre by the Eden Park floodlights, switched on at 5.50 p.m. Play continued until shortly before eight o'clock, by which time the moon was shining and New Zealand were beaming, having extended their lead to a decisive 311. It had been a crucial two hours.

Hussain complained that his players were unable to see the ball clearly against the night sky, and the sight of Afzaal fielding as substitute, curled up like an armadillo to protect himself at deep square leg, lent weight to his argument. But the umpires were prepared to offer the light only to the batsmen: England, who nearly 16 months earlier had been more than happy to pursue victory in the gloom at Karachi, had to get on with it. A series that had been theirs for the taking when rain limited play to 54 overs on the first two days was being snatched from under their noses by opponents who had shown more daring – and, ultimately, more desperation.

New Zealand took calculated risks throughout, starting with three changes to the side that had saved the Second Test (England were again unchanged). Out went Horne, Butler and Martin; in came Daryl Tuffey, to take the new ball, Andre Adams for his Test debut as the all-rounder, and Harris, a one-day regular playing his first Test since November 1999. The gamble paid off handsomely.

Yet a New Zealand victory had looked a distant prospect on the first morning. After winning his third toss of the series, Fleming chose to bat on a damp pitch, then watched in horror as the irresistible Caddick and Hoggard reduced his side to 19 for four. England's faultless performance was epitomised by Thorpe's stunning one-handed catch, low to his left at second slip, to dismiss Astle.

The force was with England, but Harris, batting as a Test No. 4 for the first time, had a plan. With the ball darting all over the place, he lessened the risk of being lbw – and eliminated the possibility of being caught behind – by lunging forward, bat raised like a periscope. England, unamused, began to lose their discipline. When Caddick took his 200th Test wicket, removing McMillan on the stroke of lunch to reduce New Zealand to 86 for five, they had regained the initiative, but they lost it again when Harris, on 28, gloved Hoggard to short leg via his thigh, only for umpire Cowie to turn down the appeal. As England cursed, Harris and Parore took advantage. At close of play, 151 for five represented a real fightback.

Cricket eventually resumed after lunch on the third day, but not before a minute's silence for the Queen Mother, who had died aged 101. Amid the showers, New Zealand extended their total to a respectable 202, and then tore into England with the new ball as the sun began to set. Tuffey removed Trescothick and Butcher in his first five deliveries – to recreate England's scoreline of none for two from the first innings at Christchurch – and Hussain edged Drum to slip, the eighth wicket of a fast-forward day spanning just 28 overs. The game had risen from its watery grave.

The following morning, after a brief flurry from Vaughan and Thorpe, England were picked to pieces by the giant Tuffey, who made the ball misbehave off an unreliable surface to claim a Test-best six wickets, and by the energetic Adams. His 14th ball in Test cricket had Vaughan caught at the wicket, and then Ramprakash produced an aberrant smear against Tuffey. Flintoff began with some booming drives, and was just hitting his stride when umpire Cowie gave him out caught behind – off a ball he missed by six inches; even the bowler, Adams, looked embarrassed. Resistance was gossamer-thin after that and, when Fleming held his 100th Test catch to dismiss Hoggard, England's total of 160 was their lowest for 22 Tests.

Parore, in his 78th and avowedly final Test, opened in place of Vincent, who had pulled a groin muscle, and helped extend New Zealand's lead to 95 before slashing Hoggard to slip immediately before tea on the fourth afternoon. That evening, the lights came on and the floodgates opened. Harris made another valuable contribution, Astle evoked memories of Christchurch by hammering 65 in 51 balls, and McMillan chipped in with a run-a-ball fifty which included three sixes. In all, New Zealand flayed 216 runs in a session of 41.2 manic overs.

Fleming declared overnight to set England 312 in 105 overs, and when Butcher and Hussain advanced to 122 for two in the 28th, anything was possible. But the pitch, another drop-in, was becoming a minefield: indentations left by the ball during the damp first three days had hardened, and the occasional delivery exploded disconcertingly from a length. New Zealand had no complaints, and England feared the worst when Astle got one to pop at Butcher, catch the splice and fly to gully.

Thorpe followed next over, caught behind off Tuffey to make Parore only the eighth wicket-keeper to complete 200 Test dismissals (he had also taken three catches as a fielder), and Flintoff was bowled two balls later. Hussain, who passed 4,000 Test runs with some pristine straight drives, and Foster prolonged the inevitable but, at 2.53 p.m. on the final afternoon, Hoggard flashed Adams to slip and New Zealand had levelled the series. It was no less than they deserved.

Man of the Match: D. R. Tuffey.　　　　　　　　*Attendance:* 24,648.

Close of play: First day, New Zealand 151-5 (Harris 55, Parore 24); Second day, No play; Third day, England 12-3 (Vaughan 8, Thorpe 0); Fourth day, New Zealand 269-9 (McMillan 50).

New Zealand

M. H. Richardson b Caddick	5	– c sub (U. Afzaal) b Butcher	25
L. Vincent b Caddick	10	– (9) c Giles b Hoggard	10
*S. P. Fleming c Ramprakash b Hoggard	1	– b Hoggard	1
C. Z. Harris lbw b Flintoff	71	– lbw b Butcher	43
N. J. Astle c Thorpe b Caddick	2	– c Butcher b Flintoff	65
C. D. McMillan lbw b Caddick	41	– not out	50
†A. C. Parore c sub (U. Afzaal) b Flintoff	45	– (2) c Thorpe b Hoggard	36
D. L. Vettori lbw b Hoggard	3	– c Foster b Flintoff	0
A. R. Adams c Giles b Flintoff	7	– (7) b Flintoff	11
D. R. Tuffey c Butcher b Hoggard	0	– b Hoggard	5
C. J. Drum not out	2		
L-b 10, n-b 5	15	B 3, l-b 9, w 1, n-b 10	23

1/12 (1) 2/17 (3) 3/17 (2) 4/19 (5)　　202　　1/53 (2) 2/55 (3)　　(9 wkts dec.) 269
5/86 (6) 6/172 (4) 7/191 (8)　　　　　　　　　3/91 (1) 4/166 (4)
8/198 (7) 9/200 (9) 10/202 (10)　　　　　　　5/217 (5) 6/232 (7)
　　　　　　　　　　　　　　　　　　　　　　7/235 (8) 8/262 (9) 9/269 (10)

Bowling: *First Innings*—Caddick 25–5–70–4; Hoggard 28.2–10–66–3; Flintoff 16–6–49–3; Butcher 5–3–6–0; Giles 1–0–1–0. *Second Innings*—Caddick 11–3–41–0; Hoggard 19.1–3–68–4; Flintoff 23–1–108–3; Butcher 9–2–34–2; Giles 1–0–6–0.

England

M. E. Trescothick lbw b Tuffey	0	– b Drum	14
M. P. Vaughan c Parore b Adams	27	– c Fleming b Drum	36
M. A. Butcher c Richardson b Tuffey	0	– c sub (B. G. K. Walker) b Astle	35
*N. Hussain c Fleming b Drum	2	– c and b Adams	82
G. P. Thorpe b Tuffey	42	– c Parore b Tuffey	3
M. R. Ramprakash c Parore b Tuffey	9	– (7) b Tuffey	2
A. Flintoff c Parore b Adams	29	– (6) b Tuffey	0
†J. S. Foster not out	16	– c Parore b Adams	23
A. F. Giles lbw b Tuffey	0	– not out	21
A. R. Caddick b Tuffey	20	– c Vettori b Drum	4
M. J. Hoggard c Fleming b Adams	0	– c Astle b Adams	2
B 1, l-b 11, n-b 3	15	B 1, l-b 8, n-b 2	11

1/0 (1) 2/0 (3) 3/11 (4) 4/60 (2)　　160　　1/23 (1) 2/73 (2) 3/122 (3)　　233
5/75 (6) 6/118 (7) 7/122 (5)　　　　　　　　4/125 (5) 5/125 (6) 6/155 (7)
8/124 (9) 9/159 (10) 10/160 (11)　　　　　　7/204 (8) 8/207 (4)
　　　　　　　　　　　　　　　　　　　　　　9/230 (10) 10/233 (11)

Bowling: *First Innings*—Tuffey 19–6–54–6; Drum 10–3–45–1; Adams 15.4–2–44–3; McMillan 1–0–5–0. *Second Innings*—Tuffey 16–3–62–3; Drum 10–0–52–3; Adams 16–3–61–3; Astle 19–6–44–1; Vettori 2–0–5–0.

Umpires: S. Venkataraghavan (India) and D. B. Cowie.
Third umpire: A. L. Hill. Referee: J. L. Hendriks (West Indies).

THE ASIAN TEST CHAMPIONSHIP, 2001-02

The second Asian Test Championship was a hopeless affair. It involved only two decent teams and a total of three matches, spread over seven months. Poor organisation and one-sided cricket did not help, but the killer blow was the withdrawal of India, which undermined the whole point of the exercise, leaving Sri Lanka champions in name only. Rather than rekindle Asian interest in Test cricket, the tournament arguably set it back.

Only a week before the first match, the Delhi government confirmed that no Indian team would play Pakistan until political relations were "normalised". The Championship was effectively dead in the water. With Bangladesh as one of only three participants, a repeat of the 1999 Sri Lanka–Pakistan final was assured, and the group phase was virtually pointless. Deprived of an India–Pakistan showdown, the event lost its commercial lifeblood and its cricketing soul.

The Asian Cricket Council did themselves no favours, however. Even if all four nations had joined in, they might have struggled to sustain interest from August to March. As it was, many of the talking points thrown up had gone stale by the time of the final. In a sign, perhaps, that even the organisers had lost faith, the Pakistan–Sri Lanka group match was summarily scrapped after Bangladesh's two defeats rendered it academic.

So it was no surprise when spectators, sponsors and broadcasters responded with a shrug. Attendances were mostly poor, a main sponsor never materialised, while a shortage of advertising meant the final was one of only a handful of Tests involving the national team not televised in Sri Lanka. The broadcasters blamed the weather – following a dry spell, the island's dependence on hydroelectric power led to the suspension of the electricity supply for five hours a day, which made sponsorship and advertising less effective. This was a case not of rain stopped play, but lack of rain stopped viewing.

Nor could the cricket redeem matters. Bangladesh were nowhere near good enough to compete: two matches, two innings defeats. They took only six wickets by their own efforts, and just one bowler (Naimur Rahman) conceded less than four an over. Seven of their opponents scored centuries, and just two were dismissed for less than fifty. Only Mohammad Ashraful totalled over 100 runs for Bangladesh; his glorious, audacious – and ultimately futile – hundred against Sri Lanka made him Test cricket's youngest centurion, and provided the only glimmer of hope for his team.

The eye-catching performances of the Pakistanis and Sri Lankans held more questionable significance. Impetuous batting certainly helped Danish Kaneria (only the second Hindu to represent Pakistan, after his cousin, Anil Dalpat) take 12 wickets at Multan; his whirling action recalled Abdul Qadir's, without yet affording the same control. In the same match, five Pakistan batsmen reached hundreds, to equal the record for centuries in an innings. In Colombo a week later, Sanath Jayasuriya was confident enough to retire two batsmen out, a move unprecedented at this level, which some felt reduced Test cricket to a practice knockaround.

The final was the first Test in Pakistan since the Bangladesh match more than six months earlier because of the war in Afghanistan. It proved to be another anticlimax. Amid squabbles over the omission of two match-winning bowlers, Wasim Akram and Saqlain Mushtaq, the Pakistanis reverted to the shambles they had often been before Waqar Younis took over. Muttiah Muralitharan claimed eight wickets, to go with ten against Bangladesh, and bowled more than a third of Sri Lanka's overs. But it was the patience and determination of Kumar Sangakkara that made the difference; he batted for longer than either of Pakistan's complete innings. Sri Lanka's total in the final was their seventh above 500 in nine Tests, all of them won by large margins. Jayasuriya said victory would boost morale ahead of the tour of England; the Asian Test Championship as an end in itself seemed less important.

PAKISTAN v BANGLADESH

At Multan Cricket Stadium, Multan, August 29, 30, 31. Pakistan won by an innings and 264 runs. Pakistan 24 pts. Toss: Bangladesh. Test debuts: Shoaib Malik, Taufeeq Umar.

Bangladesh came to the Multan Cricket Stadium, Test cricket's 81st venue, hoping to avoid defeat for the first time in their fourth Test. But before lunch on the third day, they were reflecting on what was then the sixth-biggest thrashing in Test history. The scale of the defeat – they were skittled out twice in the equivalent of a day's play, while five of the six Pakistanis to bat hit hundreds – raised serious questions about the ICC's decision to grant them Test status.

A first-day crowd of around 10,000 gathered in hot sunshine to watch the return of Test cricket to Multan – which staged one Test against West Indies, at the Ibn-e-Qasim Bagh Stadium, in 1980-81 – and to cheer the local hero, Inzamam-ul-Haq. They had to wait for him when Naimur Rahman chose to bat on a wicket which started firm and was expected to turn. Bangladesh soon confirmed that they lacked the technique and patience to counter quality bowling of any variety: 40 minutes before tea, they were dismissed for 134, in just 41.1 overs. Coincidentally, their second innings also lasted 41.1 overs, although it produced 14 more runs. The visitors' batting was cavalier throughout, with the one notable exception of Habibul Bashar's disciplined 56 not out on the third morning.

MOST HUNDREDS IN A TEST INNINGS

5	Australia (758-8 dec.) v West Indies at Kingston.	1954-55
5	**Pakistan (546-3 dec.) v Bangladesh at Multan**.	**2001-02**
4	England (658-8 dec.) v Australia at Nottingham	1938
4	West Indies (631) v India at Delhi	1948-49
4	Pakistan (652) v India at Faisalabad	1982-83
4	West Indies (550) v India at St John's.	1982-83
4	Pakistan (600-8 dec.) v Sri Lanka at Galle.	2000
4	Sri Lanka (610-6 dec.) v India at Colombo (SSC).	2001
4	**New Zealand (534-9 dec.) v Australia at Perth**.	**2001-02**

Pakistan, by contrast, clobbered 82 boundaries and amassed 546 for three at an exhilarating 4.75 runs an over before the inevitable declaration. The bowlers were clueless as Saeed Anwar belted 101 from 104 balls, passing 4,000 Test runs on the way. Taufeeq Umar helped him rattle up an opening stand of 168 in 33 overs, then became the eighth Pakistani to score a century on debut, and the fifth since 1996. Inzamam realised a childhood dream by hitting a hundred on his home ground and celebrated with a four next ball, before promptly tucking his bat under his arm and retiring hurt. Apparently dehydrated, he took no further part in the match. Yousuf Youhana and Abdul Razzaq continued the fusillade with unbeaten centuries, adding 165 in two hours as Razzaq hammered 110 in 100 balls.

Pakistan's bowlers enjoyed themselves too: Danish Kaneria, the wrist-spinner whose two previous Tests, against England in 2000-01, had fetched four wickets at 54 apiece, scooped six in each innings at a total cost of just 94 runs. Tall enough to extract bounce as well as turn, he mesmerised the batsmen. Ten were caught close to the bat, four of them by Younis Khan, who set an innings record for a substitute. Waqar Younis claimed six wickets, though Wasim Akram, who had taken only seven in his previous four Tests, could add no more. Even Shoaib Malik, given just six overs on his debut, found time to remove two Bangladeshis with his off-breaks. The victory margin was then Pakistan's biggest in Tests, but the celebrations were overshadowed when a tearful Saeed Anwar announced that his three-year-old daughter, Bismah, who had been seriously ill, had died that afternoon. – **Samiul Hasan**

Man of the Match: Danish Kaneria.

Close of play: First day, Pakistan 219-2 (Taufeeq Umar 77, Inzamam-ul-Haq 25); Second day, Bangladesh 55-3 (Habibul Bashar 19, Akram Khan 1).

Bangladesh

Javed Omar c Shoaib Malik b Waqar Younis . . .	12	– c Abdul Razzaq b Waqar Younis . .	4
Mehrab Hossain c Faisal Iqbal b Danish Kaneria	19	– c Rashid Latif b Waqar Younis . . .	9
Habibul Bashar c Rashid Latif b Waqar Younis .	13	– not out	56
Aminul Islam b Shoaib Malik	10	– c sub (Younis Khan)	
		b Danish Kaneria .	18
Akram Khan c Yousuf Youhana b Danish Kaneria	12	– c sub (Younis Khan)	
		b Danish Kaneria .	8
*Naimur Rahman c Faisal Iqbal b Danish Kaneria	8	– c sub (Younis Khan)	
		b Danish Kaneria .	4
†Khaled Masud lbw b Danish Kaneria	4	– c and b Danish Kaneria	0
Enamul Haque c Waqar Younis b Danish Kaneria	14	– c Yousuf Youhana b Danish Kaneria	7
Hasibul Hussain c Taufeeq Umar		– c sub (Younis Khan)	
b Danish Kaneria .	18	b Danish Kaneria .	31
Mohammad Sharif b Shoaib Malik	13	– c Rashid Latif b Waqar Younis . . .	3
Manjurul Islam not out	0	– b Waqar Younis	2
L-b 5, w 1, n-b 5	11	L-b 3, n-b 3	6

1/20 (1) 2/50 (3) 3/55 (2) 4/67 (4)   134   1/5 (1) 2/22 (2) 3/52 (4)   148
5/76 (6) 6/83 (5) 7/101 (8)   4/72 (5) 5/84 (6) 6/84 (7) 7/96 (8)
8/107 (7) 9/134 (9) 10/134 (10)   8/141 (9) 9/144 (10) 10/148 (11)

Bonus points – Pakistan 4.

Bowling: *First Innings*—Wasim Akram 10–2–17–0; Waqar Younis 6–0–25–2; Abdul Razzaq 8–1–27–0; Danish Kaneria 13–3–42–6; Shoaib Malik 4.1–0–18–2. *Second Innings*—Wasim Akram 9–1–32–0; Waqar Younis 7.1–1–19–4; Abdul Razzaq 8–0–34–0; Danish Kaneria 15–3–52–6; Shoaib Malik 2–0–8–0.

Pakistan

Saeed Anwar c Hasibul Hussain		Yousuf Youhana not out	102
b Mohammad Sharif .	101	Abdul Razzaq not out	110
Taufeeq Umar c Khaled Masud		B 1, l-b 3, w 3, n-b 8	15
b Hasibul Hussain .	104		
Faisal Iqbal b Mohammad Sharif	9	1/168 (1) 2/178 (3) (3 wkts dec.) 546
Inzamam-ul-Haq retired hurt	105	3/258 (2)

†Rashid Latif, Wasim Akram, *Waqar Younis, Shoaib Malik and Danish Kaneria did not bat.

Bonus points – Pakistan 4 (100 overs: 443-3).

Inzamam-ul-Haq retired hurt at 381.

Bowling: Manjurul Islam 19–2–103–0; Mohammad Sharif 24.5–4–110–2; Hasibul Hussain 31–5–145–1; Naimur Rahman 19–1–77–0; Enamul Haque 16–1–78–0; Aminul Islam 4–0–17–0; Javed Omar 1–0–12–0.

Umpires: D. B. Hair (Australia) and P. T. Manuel (Sri Lanka).
Third umpire: Riazuddin. Referee: J. R. Reid (New Zealand).

Donald conceded 72 in 15.2 overs before his body announced it would no longer play the game for more than a day at a time.
South Africa v Australia, page 1288

SRI LANKA v BANGLADESH

At Sinhalese Sports Club, Colombo, September 6, 7, 8. Sri Lanka won by an innings and 137 runs. Sri Lanka 24 pts. Toss: Sri Lanka. Test debuts: M. G. Vandort; Mohammad Ashraful.

A week after their demolition by Pakistan, Bangladesh took on Sri Lanka, who had just beaten India by an innings. Another hopeless mismatch was widely predicted – and resulted, though not before some Bangladeshi pride was restored. Even before a ball was bowled, the visitors were left in little doubt about their standing in Sri Lankan eyes: attendance was derisory, despite free entry, while Jayasuriya was sure enough of a quick kill to bowl first on a near-perfect batting pitch. And, by the time Muralitharan took the final wicket, before tea on the third afternoon, their assessment had been vindicated: Sri Lanka won by an innings and 137 runs, then their biggest victory in Tests. One Bangladesh player, however, saved the game from complete farce, and his team from total humiliation. Mohammad Ashraful, on debut, became the youngest player to hit a century in Test history.

Jayasuriya's decision to bowl first, variously interpreted as confident or condescending, was unquestionably successful. Bangladesh's batting crumpled inside 37 overs for a paltry 90 – their lowest total, and the lowest by any Test side against Sri Lanka. Ashraful top-scored with a defiant 26, and Muralitharan took five wickets for 13.

YOUNGEST PLAYERS TO SCORE A TEST HUNDRED

Years	Days				
16	364†	**Mohammad Ashraful† . 114**	**Bangladesh v Sri Lanka at Colombo (SSC)**	**2001-02**
17	82	Mushtaq Mohammad. . . 101	Pakistan v India at Delhi	1960-61
17	112	S. R. Tendulkar 119*	India v England at Manchester	1990
17	354	H. Masakadza‡ 119	Zimbabwe v West Indies at Harare . .	2001
18	157	Imran Nazir. 131	Pakistan v West Indies at Bridgetown .	1999-2000
18	328	Salim Malik‡. 100*	Pakistan v Sri Lanka at Karachi	1981-82
18	335	Shahid Afridi 141	Pakistan v India at Chennai	1998-99

† *Mohammad Ashraful's age is in dispute; some sources say he was 17 years 63 days.*

‡ *On Test debut.*

Sri Lanka's innings instantly put even Muralitharan in the shade. In a withering assault on Bangladesh's innocuous medium-pacers, Jayasuriya looked set for the fastest Test century of all, before losing first momentum, then his wicket. Even so, his 89 came from 56 balls and included 68 in boundaries. Atapattu cruised to a double-century, his fifth in 48 Tests, from only eight hundreds. He reached it, with his 27th four, in 256 balls and 320 minutes; three balls later, his captain called him in and, for the first time in 1,561 Tests, the words "retired out" appeared on a scorecard. The same fate met Jayawardene after he had smashed 150 off 115 balls. Reaction was strong: some in the Sri Lankan press claimed Test cricket had been demeaned. On the field, it made little difference, as Sri Lanka sailed on to 555 at an overall rate of 5.36 an over.

With a bone-dry pitch offering Muralitharan increasing turn, the 466 Bangladesh needed to make Sri Lanka bat again was always fanciful, but Ashraful provided a memorable distraction. Strong-wristed, quick-footed and breathtakingly audacious, he crashed a series of bouncers from Vaas through mid-wicket and danced down the track to loft Muralitharan handsomely over the top.

Whatever his exact age – some claimed he would turn 17 the next day, others that he had done so 63 days earlier – his place as Test cricket's youngest centurion, breaking Mushtaq Mohammad's record, was beyond dispute. It was a special performance, even if there was little at stake. Despite the unexpected resistance, Sri Lanka retained control; eventually, they took the last five wickets for 25, including Ashraful for a four-hour 114. For the second time in the game, Murali claimed five wickets, extending his career total to 350 from 66 Tests. No other bowler had reached the landmark so quickly. He generously donated his share of the cheque for the match award to Ashraful. – **Charlie Austin**

Men of the Match: Mohammad Ashraful and M. Muralitharan.

Close of play: First day, Sri Lanka 246-1 (Atapattu 99, Sangakkara 49); Second day, Bangladesh 100-4 (Aminul Islam 19, Mohammad Ashraful 4).

Bangladesh

Javed Omar c Jayasuriya b Vaas	7	– lbw b Muralitharan	40
Mehrab Hossain run out	23	– lbw b Muralitharan	4
Habibul Bashar b Vaas	4	– (5) c Jayawardene b Muralitharan	19
Aminul Islam c Sangakkara b Perera	6	– b Jayasuriya	56
Al Sahariar c Sangakkara b Muralitharan	16	– (3) lbw b Samaraweera	7
*Naimur Rahman b Muralitharan	0	– (7) c Atapattu b Perera	48
Mohammad Ashraful c Jayasuriya b Muralitharan	26	– (6) c and b Perera	114
†Khaled Masud b Muralitharan	0	– lbw b Muralitharan	3
Hasibul Hussain b Muralitharan	2	– c Sangakkara b Perera	0
Mohammad Sharif c Vandort b Vaas	1	– c and b Muralitharan	19
Manjurul Islam not out	3	– not out	1
L-b 1, n-b 1	2	B 5, l-b 5, n-b 7	17

1/10 (1) 2/16 (3) 3/29 (4) 4/57 (5)   **90**
5/58 (2) 6/61 (6) 7/61 (8)
8/67 (9) 9/72 (10) 10/90 (7)

1/31 (2) 2/54 (1) 3/54 (3)   **328**
4/81 (5) 5/207 (4) 6/303 (7)
7/308 (6) 8/308 (8)
9/314 (9) 10/328 (10)

Bonus points – Sri Lanka 4.

Bowling: *First Innings*—Vaas 14–2–47–3; Pushpakumara 7–4–9–0; Perera 5–1–17–1; Muralitharan 9.4–4–13–5; Samaraweera 1–0–3–0. *Second Innings*—Vaas 16–2–71–0; Pushpakumara 8–5–15–0; Muralitharan 35.3–6–98–5; Perera 13–3–40–3; Samaraweera 13–2–42–1; Jayasuriya 16–2–52–1.

Sri Lanka

M. S. Atapattu retired out	201	H. P. Tillekeratne not out	10
*S. T. Jayasuriya lbw b Naimur Rahman	89		
†K. C. Sangakkara c Aminul Islam b Hasibul Hussain	54	L-b 5, w 2, n-b 8	15
D. P. M. D. Jayawardene retired out	150	1/144 (2) 2/269 (3) (5 wkts dec.) 555	
M. G. Vandort c Manjurul Islam b Naimur Rahman	36	3/440 (1) 4/530 (4) 5/555 (5)	

T. T. Samaraweera, W. P. U. J. C. Vaas, K. R. Pushpakumara, P. D. R. L. Perera and M. Muralitharan did not bat.

Bonus points – Sri Lanka 4 (100 overs: 539-4).

Bowling: Manjurul Islam 18–1–94–0; Mohammad Sharif 17–0–120–0; Hasibul Hussain 23–6–122–1; Naimur Rahman 30.3–8–117–2; Mohammad Ashraful 10–0–63–0; Habibul Bashar 5–0–34–0.

Umpires: R. E. Koertzen (South Africa) and Mian Aslam (Pakistan).
Third umpire: Riazuddin (Pakistan).   Referee: J. R. Reid (New Zealand).

QUALIFYING TABLE

	Played	Won	Lost	Drawn	Bonus Points Batting	Bonus Points Bowling	Points
Pakistan	1	1	0	0	4	4	24
Sri Lanka	1	1	0	0	4	4	24
Bangladesh	2	0	2	0	0	0	0

Win = 12 pts; innings win = 16 pts. Bonus points were awarded for the first 100 overs of each first innings as follows: 250–299 runs – 1 pt; 300–349 runs – 2 pts; 350–399 runs – 3 pts; 400 runs and over – 4 pts. 4–5 wickets – 1 pt; 6–7 wickets – 2 pts; 8–9 wickets – 3 pts; 10 wickets – 4 pts.

Bangladesh did not qualify for a bowling point when Sri Lanka were four down in 100 overs, because two of those wickets were retired out.

FINAL

PAKISTAN v SRI LANKA

At Lahore, March 6, 7, 8, 9, 10. Sri Lanka won by eight wickets. Toss: Sri Lanka.

After Sri Lanka and Pakistan had swatted Bangladesh aside, this match at last promised a contest. But it proved just as one-sided as when the same teams met in the first Asian Test Championship final in March 1999. Then, Pakistan won by an innings and 175 runs; this time, it was Sri Lanka's party. The fact that the home side started the last day with hopes of a draw owed more to rain than to their own efforts.

Pakistan's problems were familiar: a fragile batting line-up (they badly missed Saeed Anwar, nursing a hand injury) and reports of a fractious dressing-room. Reckless shots undermined both their innings, whereas Sri Lanka were unified and resolute, as they showed on the fourth afternoon, when the entire team – coach and physio included – began pulling off the covers at the first sign of the sun. At least one was removed without the help or consent of the ambling Lahore groundstaff.

Put in on a hard and even pitch, the Pakistan batsmen required resolve; they offered little. Both openers perished within six overs, before Younis Khan and Inzamam-ul-Haq gained control, adding 86 in as many minutes. Younis trod the thin line between courage and rashness, reeling off a cover drive for four, a six high over mid-wicket and a deft late cut to the rope from consecutive deliveries from Muralitharan, only to paddle the next ball so fine that he played on. Flashes outside the off stump from Inzamam and Yousuf Youhana left Pakistan 127 for five and, despite a few lusty blows from Rashid Latif and Waqar Younis, they were all out an hour after tea.

In reply, Sri Lanka were as steadfast as Pakistan had been shaky. Sangakkara batted for three hours longer than his opponents' entire innings, and all but matched their total. After Atapattu's golden duck, Sangakkara's eight-hour 230, occupying only 327 balls and including 33 fours and three sixes, featured partnerships of 203 with Jayasuriya and 173 with Jayawardene. In the first 123 years of Test cricket, there had been only three double-centuries by wicket-keepers; Sangakkara's innings – full of scything shots off the back foot – was the third in just 16 months.

DOUBLE-HUNDREDS BY WICKET-KEEPERS IN TESTS

232*	A. Flower, Zimbabwe v India at Nagpur..........................	2000-01
230	**K. C. Sangakkara, Sri Lanka v Pakistan at Lahore**	**2001-02**
210*	Taslim Arif, Pakistan v Australia at Faisalabad	1979-80
209	Imtiaz Ahmed, Pakistan v New Zealand at Lahore	1955-56
204*	**A. C. Gilchrist, Australia v South Africa at Johannesburg**	**2001-02**
201*	D. S. B. P. Kuruppu, Sri Lanka v New Zealand at Colombo (CCC)	1986-87

Mohammad Sami finally ended the Sri Lankan reply with a hat-trick – the third in three Asian Championship fixtures between these sides – that straddled lunch on the third day. But the fireworks came too late; the earlier bowling was not incisive, reigniting the debate over why Wasim Akram (taker of the two previous hat-tricks) and Saqlain Mushtaq had been excluded. Captain and selectors were rumoured to have clashed over Wasim's omission, ostensibly on fitness grounds.

Resuming 294 behind, and with nearly eight sessions remaining, Pakistan had to bat well into the fifth day to stand a chance of salvaging a draw, but by the third evening, they were already five down. Again, several batsmen were culpable: Shahid Afridi's charge down the wicket was a familiar conclusion to an unusually guarded innings, while Younis and Youhana fell to impetuous swishes to leg. Pakistani hopes brightened as bruised skies over Lahore brought persistent rain on the fourth day. Only 32 overs were bowled, and Inzamam and Shoaib Malik were still together at the close. Blue skies next morning dashed their first hope, and the dismissal of Inzamam (off what looked like a no-ball) extinguished their last. With their sentinel gone after a watchful, five-hour 99, Pakistan collapsed within 12 overs. Muralitharan finished with eight wickets, lifting his total from seven Tests in Pakistan to 49. Sri Lanka lost both openers, but their ninth consecutive Test victory was never in doubt. – **Samiul Hasan**

Man of the Match: K. C. Sangakkara.

Close of play: First day, Sri Lanka 94-1 (Jayasuriya 47, Sangakkara 39); Second day, Sri Lanka 447-5 (Vaas 0, Tillekeratne 0); Third day, Pakistan 193-5 (Inzamam-ul-Haq 38, Shoaib Malik 6); Fourth day, Pakistan 248-5 (Inzamam-ul-Haq 72, Shoaib Malik 19).

Pakistan

Shahid Afridi run out	9	– st Sangakkara b Muralitharan	70
Taufeeq Umar c Samaraweera b Vaas	6	– b Vaas	19
Younis Khan b Muralitharan	46	– c Samaraweera b Zoysa	19
Inzamam-ul-Haq c Jayasuriya b Fernando	29	– lbw b Vaas	99
Yousuf Youhana c Sangakkara b Fernando	6	– c Atapattu b Muralitharan	7
Abdul Razzaq lbw b Vaas	24	– lbw b Muralitharan	5
Shoaib Malik c Sangakkara b Fernando	13	– c Samaraweera b Zoysa	21
†Rashid Latif c Sangakkara b Muralitharan	36	– c Muralitharan b Vaas	2
*Waqar Younis b Muralitharan	19	– c Tillekeratne b Muralitharan	25
Shoaib Akhtar lbw b Muralitharan	15	– not out	4
Mohammad Sami not out	0	– c Sangakkara b Vaas	0
L-b 4, w 1, n-b 26	31	B 12, l-b 2, w 1, n-b 39	54

1/18 (2) 2/18 (1) 3/104 (3) 4/108 (4) 234
5/127 (5) 6/147 (6) 7/176 (7)
8/216 (9) 9/219 (8) 10/234 (10)

1/31 (2) 2/66 (3) 3/150 (1) 325
4/166 (5) 5/181 (6) 6/281 (4)
7/285 (8) 8/291 (5)
9/321 (9) 10/325 (11)

Bowling: *First Innings*—Vaas 17–2–62–2; Zoysa 9–2–29–0; Fernando 16–1–84–3; Muralitharan 25–9–55–4. *Second Innings*—Vaas 22.5–3–85–4; Zoysa 21–3–54–2; Fernando 14–2–68–0; Muralitharan 34–8–72–4; Jayasuriya 1–0–7–0; Samaraweera 9–1–25–0.

Sri Lanka

M. S. Atapattu c Shoaib Akhtar b Waqar Younis	0	– c Rashid Latif b Mohammad Sami	1
*S. T. Jayasuriya c Rashid Latif b Abdul Razzaq	88	– c Yousuf Youhana b Shoaib Akhtar	1
†K. C. Sangakkara c Younis Khan b Abdul Razzaq	230	– not out	14
D. P. M. D. Jayawardene c Inzamam-ul-Haq b Mohammad Sami	68	– not out	12
R. P. Arnold b Shoaib Akhtar	44		
W. P. U. J. C. Vaas c Taufeeq Umar b Abdul Razzaq	43		
H. P. Tillekeratne not out	19		
T. T. Samaraweera c Rashid Latif b Shoaib Akhtar	8		
T. C. B. Fernando lbw b Mohammad Sami	7		
D. N. T. Zoysa lbw b Mohammad Sami	0		
M. Muralitharan b Mohammad Sami	0		
B 1, l-b 7, w 5, n-b 8	21	L-b 1, w 2, n-b 2	5

1/0 (1) 2/203 (2) 3/376 (4) 4/447 (3) 528
5/447 (5) 6/501 (6) 7/519 (8)
8/528 (9) 9/528 (10) 10/528 (11)

1/1 (1) 2/14 (2) (2 wkts) 33

Bowling: *First Innings*—Waqar Younis 30–4–123–1; Shoaib Akhtar 27–4–114–2; Mohammad Sami 36.5–4–120–4; Abdul Razzaq 29–5–82–3; Shoaib Malik 14–3–55–0; Shahid Afridi 3–0–26–0. *Second Innings*—Shoaib Akhtar 3.2–0–17–1; Mohammad Sami 3–0–15–1.

Umpires: D. J. Harper (Australia) and Athar Zaidi.
Third umpire: Salim Badar. Referee: A. M. Ebrahim (Zimbabwe).

THE BANGLADESHIS IN PAKISTAN, 2001-02

Bangladesh's first Test tour of Pakistan was for the opening match in the Asian Test Championship, which they lost by an innings and 264 runs, their heaviest defeat yet, at Multan. They played one other first-class match.

BANGLADESHI TOURING PARTY

Naimur Rahman (Dhaka) (*captain*), Khaled Masud (Rajshahi) (*vice-captain*), Akram Khan (Chittagong), Al Sahariar (Dhaka), Aminul Islam (Dhaka), Bikash Ranjan Das (Dhaka), Enamul Haque (Chittagong), Habibul Bashar (Khulna), Hasibul Hussain (Sylhet), Javed Omar (Dhaka), Manjurul Islam (Khulna), Mehrab Hossain (Dhaka), Mohammad Ashraful (Dhaka), Mohammad Sharif (Dhaka).

    Coach: T. M. Chappell.   *Manager:* S. A. Chowdhury.

BANGLADESHI TOUR RESULTS

Test match – Played 1: Lost 1.
First-class matches – Played 2: Lost 1, Drawn 1.
Loss – Pakistan.
Draw – Pakistan Cricket Board XI.

At UBL Sports Complex, Karachi, August 24, 25, 26. **Drawn.** Toss: Bangladeshis. **Bangladeshis 161** (Aminul Islam 36; Shabbir Ahmed three for 30, Yasir Arafat three for 17) **and 239 for nine** (Mehrab Hossain 72, Habibul Bashar 33, Akram Khan 53; Shoaib Malik three for 77); **Pakistan Cricket Board XI 268 for seven dec.** (Taufeeq Umar 113, Naved Latif 30, Misbah-ul-Haq 50 not out; Enamul Haque four for 44).

Bangladesh's Test match against Pakistan (August 29–31) appears in the Asian Test Championship section on pages 1185-1191.

THE SOUTH AFRICANS IN ZIMBABWE, 2001-02

By JOHN WARD

South Africa kicked off what should have been a momentous season with their third Test tour to their neighbours. Unlike in 1995-96 and 1999-2000, they played two Test matches, to constitute a series that would count towards the ICC Test Championship. The South Africans' bid to displace Australia at the top made a good start when they overwhelmed Zimbabwe, who did not do themselves justice – with one outstanding exception.

For them, the stupendous batting feats of Andy Flower overshadowed all else. He alone seemed able to shut out his country's political problems and their ongoing disputes with the Zimbabwe Cricket Union. Against stronger bowling and for a much weaker team, he outscored South Africa's Jacques Kallis by 422 to 388. Hamilton Masakadza confirmed the promise of his debut century against West Indies, and opener Dion Ebrahim twice reached 71. But few of the others demonstrated the fighting spirit that an even greener Zimbabwean team had shown during their early years of Test cricket.

South Africa's batting was far too powerful for a lightweight attack. In the First Test, Zimbabwe's specialist bowlers comprised Heath Streak, a shadow of the player he had been, and three youngsters who had taken 14 Test wickets between them. Gary Kirsten helped himself to his third Test double-century; Herschelle Gibbs showed consistency as well as flamboyance, with scores of 147, 74, 125, 69 and 39 in the two series, while Kallis proved immovable in the Tests. He batted for 1,028 minutes in all without being dismissed, breaking Nasser Hussain's record of 1,021. The only criticism was that he failed to accelerate at Bulawayo to press for victory, but that appeared to be team policy. Neil McKenzie played some good innings at No. 4 and Jonty Rhodes scored a brace of fifties when he arrived for the one-day series.

It was in bowling and strategy that the South Africans hinted they might fail to measure up to the Australians. Allan Donald was selected, but it was announced that he would miss the First Test because of flu; in the event, he never came at all, which was not satisfactorily explained. With Mfuneko Ngam and Nantie Hayward injured, the captain Shaun Pollock shared the new ball with the promising but raw Andre Nel. Makhaya Ntini did not find his best form but Claude Henderson successfully filled in for the injured Nicky Boje with his left-arm spin. Pollock himself lacked his usual accuracy, but so handsomely did his batsmen feast that the attack was rarely under pressure.

South Africa won the First Test easily, despite twin hundreds from Flower, but failed to press home their advantage in the Second, after a day was lost to rain. It was the first time Zimbabwe had avoided defeat in a Test against South Africa; Steve Waugh's Australians would surely not have missed that trick.

SOUTH AFRICAN TOURING PARTY

S. M. Pollock (KwaZulu-Natal) (*captain*), M. V. Boucher (Border) (*vice-captain*), H. H. Dippenaar (Free State), H. H. Gibbs (Western Province), C. W. Henderson (Western Province), J. H. Kallis (Western Province), J. M. Kemp (Eastern Province), G. Kirsten (Western Province), L. Klusener (KwaZulu-Natal), C. K. Langeveldt (Boland), N. D. McKenzie (Northerns), A. Nel (Easterns), M. Ntini (Border).

A. A. Donald (Free State), who was originally selected, withdrew through illness and was replaced by Langeveldt. H. D. Ackerman (Western Province) joined the party as cover for Kirsten. J. L. Ontong (Boland) and J. N. Rhodes (KwaZulu-Natal) replaced Ackerman and Langeveldt for the one-day series.

Coach: G. X. Ford.
Assistant coach: C. J. P. G. van Zyl.
Manager: Goolam Rajah.
Physiotherapist: C. Smith.

SOUTH AFRICAN TOUR RESULTS

Test matches – Played 2: Won 1, Drawn 1.
One-day internationals – Played 3: Won 3.
Other non-first-class match – Won v Zimbabwe A.

Note: Matches in this section which were not first-class are signified by a dagger.

ZIMBABWE v SOUTH AFRICA

First Test Match

At Harare, September 7, 8, 9, 10, 11. South Africa won by nine wickets. Toss: South Africa. Test debuts: D. T. Hondo; C. W. Henderson, A. Nel.

Given first use of a beautiful pitch against a weak attack, South Africa's batsmen gorged themselves, with the top three all completing big hundreds. They virtually ensured victory, but the match will be remembered for the exploits of Andy Flower, who batted for 879 minutes in all and scored 341 runs, which was the record for a player on a losing side in a Test until it was surpassed by Brian Lara (see pages 1225–1227).

Kirsten and Gibbs got South Africa off to a flier, scoring 142 by lunch. Gibbs was the main aggressor, reaching a slightly chancy century in 118 balls with 86 runs in boundaries. The bowlers helped by straying frequently in line and length, and the fielding was well below standard. South Africa's opening partnership was just short of their all-time record, 260 by Bruce Mitchell and Jack Siedle against England in 1930-31, when Gibbs, uncharacteristically trying to nudge a ball to third man in preference to one of his flashing pulls or cover drives, edged it on to his stumps.

Kirsten, less spectacular, completed his set of hundreds against each of the eight Test countries he had faced. He survived two hard chances, while one that was taken, when Kallis edged to the keeper, was rejected by umpire Tiffin. The day ended with the visitors on 414. By then, Kirsten had become the first batsman to score 5,000 Test runs for South Africa, just before reaching his third Test double-century.

Zimbabwe's bowling and fielding improved next day; their luck did not. After seven hours and 22 minutes, 286 balls, 33 fours and a six, Kirsten edged the erratic debutant Doug Hondo to the keeper. But Kallis accumulated runs like an automaton and McKenzie had an intriguing battle with Price, who found some spin. Pollock surprisingly declared at 600 for three – in sight of South Africa's record of 622 for nine, against Australia in 1969-70 – and no doubt expected to win by an innings. He would have done but for Andy Flower.

Campbell senselessly hooked at Nel's fourth ball in Test cricket, but Ebrahim showed no fear of Pollock and scored a fine 71 before making a gift of his wicket. After that, it was Flower all the way, a giant among pygmies. His tenth Test century came, as so often, with all about him falling. On the way, he passed 4,000 Test runs; no one else had yet reached 3,000 for Zimbabwe. Apart from Ebrahim, only Friend supported him, in a valuable ninth-wicket stand of 75, before Flower was last out, adjudged lbw despite being hit outside off while playing a stroke.

Three quick wickets in the follow-on meant he was soon in again. This time, Flower found the 18-year-old Masakadza able and willing to put his head down. They added 186, and Masakadza failed by only 15 runs to join the elite few with centuries in both their first two Tests. Shortly afterwards, Flower became the first wicket-keeper to make two hundreds in the same match, and he would surely have turned this one into a double had he not run out of partners. His haste, with last man Hondo in, might have seen him given out lbw on 198, but Hondo himself departed to a less convincing appeal, leaving Flower stranded on 199 after batting ten minutes short of ten hours. He was only the second player, after South Africa's Jimmy Sinclair against England in 1898-99, to score more than half his team's aggregate over two innings in a Test.

After that effort, which took him to the top of the PwC ratings, Flower passed the keeper's gloves to Campbell for South Africa's second innings. Friend trapped Dippenaar lbw first ball before Kirsten and Kallis romped home.

Man of the Match: A. Flower.

Close of play: First day, South Africa 414-1 (Kirsten 202, Kallis 56); Second day, Zimbabwe 143-4 (A. Flower 54, Price 0); Third day, Zimbabwe 97-3 (Masakadza 37, A. Flower 43); Fourth day, Zimbabwe 304-7 (A. Flower 138, Friend 10).

South Africa

H. H. Gibbs b Friend	147				
G. Kirsten c A. Flower b Hondo	220	– not out	31		
J. H. Kallis not out	157	– not out	42		
N. D. McKenzie c Hondo b Friend	52				
L. Klusener not out	8				
H. H. Dippenaar (did not bat)		(1) lbw b Friend	0		
L-b 2, w 6, n-b 8	16	B 5, l-b 1	6		

1/256 (1) 2/455 (2) 3/582 (4)   (3 wkts dec.) 600   1/0 (1)   (1 wkt) 79

†M. V. Boucher, *S. M. Pollock, C. W. Henderson, M. Ntini and A. Nel did not bat.

Bowling: *First Innings*—Streak 34–4–120–0; Friend 27–2–147–2; Hondo 18–0–87–1; Price 42–2–192–0; Whittall 12–2–34–0; G. W. Flower 6–0–18–0. *Second Innings*—Friend 7–0–44–1; Streak 4–2–10–0; Price 3.2–0–19–0; Hondo 1–1–0–0.

Zimbabwe

D. D. Ebrahim st Boucher b Henderson	71	– lbw b Pollock	0		
A. D. R. Campbell c Boucher b Nel	0	– b Kallis	7		
H. Masakadza run out	13	– c Dippenaar b Henderson	85		
C. B. Wishart c Klusener b Kallis	0	– c Klusener b Pollock	6		
†A. Flower lbw b Pollock	142	– not out	199		
R. W. Price c Kirsten b Nel	0	– (10) c McKenzie b Klusener	4		
G. W. Flower c Dippenaar b Nel	0	– (6) c Dippenaar b Ntini	16		
G. J. Whittall b Kallis	16	– (7) lbw b Henderson	3		
*H. H. Streak lbw b Henderson	7	– (8) c Kallis b Pollock	19		
T. J. Friend c Pollock b Nel	30	– (9) b Klusener	17		
D. T. Hondo not out	1	– lbw b Nel	6		
B 4, n-b 2	6	B 10, l-b 9, n-b 10	29		

1/2 (2) 2/43 (3) 3/51 (4) 4/133 (1)   286   1/0 (1) 2/18 (2) 3/25 (4)   391
5/143 (6) 6/143 (7) 7/188 (8)   4/211 (3) 5/243 (6) 6/260 (7)
8/207 (9) 9/282 (10) 10/286 (5)   7/287 (8) 8/326 (9)
    9/344 (10) 10/391 (11)

Bowling: *First Innings*—Pollock 22.3–5–62–1; Nel 16–6–53–4; Ntini 13–2–60–0; Kallis 12–1–39–2; Henderson 24–5–55–2; Klusener 3–0–13–0. *Second Innings*—Pollock 29–5–67–3; Nel 14.5–5–33–1; Kallis 21–5–52–1; Henderson 55–16–122–2; Ntini 23–10–48–1; Klusener 29–9–50–2.

Umpires: D. B. Hair (Australia) and R. B. Tiffin.
Third umpire: Q. J. Goosen.   Referee: Naushad Ali (Pakistan).

ZIMBABWE v SOUTH AFRICA

Second Test Match

At Bulawayo, September 14, 15, 16, 17, 18. Drawn. Toss: Zimbabwe.
    Zimbabwe avoided defeat for the first time in their five Tests against South Africa, thanks partly to the loss of the second day's play, but also to the visitors' reluctance to take risks and a much-improved showing from Andy Flower's team-mates. Streak was able to claim first use of another superb pitch, and the openers Campbell and Ebrahim put on 152 in almost five hours, only to fall in quick succession just before the close. The weather was cold and blustery, very rare for Bulawayo in September, and on the second day, even more surprisingly, it gave way to rain. With Zimbabwe's middle order scoring consistently, if not heavily, it was not until late on the third day that South Africa began their innings.
    The fourth day brought ponderous batting on a placid pitch against a toothless attack, handicapped by an injury to Paul Strang, playing his first Test for ten months. In his first over, he damaged his right hand in a valiant attempt to catch a fierce drive from Gibbs, the only batsman who really tried to force the pace. Although Strang returned later, he could bowl only with great discomfort.

Gibbs earned praise for walking when he edged Price to the keeper; Kallis earned brickbats for his laboriousness. He did briefly show more intent on the final morning, around the time he reached his century (in five and a half hours off 280 balls). It seemed that South Africa might be aiming to declare at lunch on roughly equal terms, and then mount an assault on the fragile Zimbabwean batting; defeat was already impossible. In fact, they continued past the interval, when they were 29 behind, and into the last afternoon, when Pollock and Boucher finally showed some initiative. They hit while Kallis lumbered towards the double-century he never reached, despite batting for 580 minutes in the cushiest conditions he could have wished for. His total for the series was a record 1,028 minutes without dismissal, and his Test average rose from 41.00 to 46.38. The awards he won might have gone to Andy Flower or to Ray Price, who took five good wickets and bowled 79 overs of left-arm spin, beating by ten the Zimbabwean record of his ailing partner, Strang, at Sheikhupura in 1996-97.

Pollock's tardy declaration, 100 to the good, brought about an early tea, and the South Africans, too late, began to apply pressure. Henderson obtained considerable turn, but the tourists missed an effective second spinner. Even so, the batsmen had a difficult time before Masakadza overcame a nervy start and settled in, assisted by the calm presence of Flower, to secure the draw. Had Zimbabwe been required to bat for a full day on the wearing pitch, they would have struggled to survive. South Africa's willingness to sit on a 1–0 lead had let them off lightly.

Man of the Match: J. H. Kallis. *Man of the Series:* J. H. Kallis.

Close of play: First day, Zimbabwe 154-2 (Masakadza 2, Carlisle 0); Second day, No play; Third day, South Africa 26-0 (Gibbs 15, Kirsten 11); Fourth day, South Africa 300-2 (Kallis 81, McKenzie 74).

Zimbabwe

A. D. R. Campbell c Gibbs b Klusener	77	– c Dippenaar b Henderson	20
D. D. Ebrahim c Pollock b Henderson	71	– b Henderson	4
H. Masakadza c Boucher b Nel	13	– not out	42
S. V. Carlisle lbw b Pollock	49	– c Ntini b Henderson	4
†A. Flower c McKenzie b Henderson	67	– not out	14
G. W. Flower run out	44		
G. J. Whittall c Pollock b Henderson	16		
*H. H. Streak c Klusener b Henderson	31		
P. A. Strang not out	38		
T. J. Friend b Pollock	4		
R. W. Price not out	0		
L-b 8, n-b 1	9	B 4, l-b 4, n-b 4	12

1/152 (1) 2/154 (2) 3/175 (3) (9 wkts dec.) 419
4/261 (5) 5/327 (6) 6/330 (4)
7/377 (8) 8/377 (7) 9/406 (10)

1/21 (2) 2/38 (1) (3 wkts) 96
3/58 (4)

Bowling: *First Innings*—Pollock 28–14–40–2; Nel 21–3–73–1; Ntini 25–9–68–0; Klusener 37–10–87–1; Henderson 67–24–143–4. *Second Innings*—Pollock 4–1–8–0; Nel 3–0–9–0; Henderson 18–11–33–3; Ntini 3–0–11–0; Klusener 12–7–21–0; Kirsten 2–1–6–0.

South Africa

H. H. Gibbs c A. Flower b Price	74	C. W. Henderson b Friend	0
G. Kirsten st A. Flower b Price	65		
J. H. Kallis not out	189	B 3, l-b 7	10
N. D. McKenzie lbw b Friend	88		
H. H. Dippenaar c G. W. Flower b Price	11	1/117 (1) 2/162 (2) (8 wkts dec.) 519
L. Klusener c Campbell b Price	27	3/343 (4) 4/368 (5)
*S. M. Pollock c Carlisle b Price	41	5/418 (6) 6/490 (7)
†M. V. Boucher b Friend	14	7/513 (8) 8/519 (9)

M. Ntini and A. Nel did not bat.

Bowling: Streak 25–9–64–0; Friend 30.2–9–87–3; Strang 14.2–2–52–0; Price 79–19–181–5; Whittall 29.4–6–80–0; G. W. Flower 8–0–45–0.

Umpires: J. H. Hampshire (England) and K. C. Barbour.
Third umpire: G. R. Evans. Referee: Naushad Ali (Pakistan).

†At Bulawayo, September 21. **South Africans won by seven wickets.** Toss: South Africans. **Zimbabwe A 128** (42.3 overs) (P. A. Strang 45 not out; A. Nel five for 11); **South Africans 131 for three** (20.1 overs) (H. H. Dippenaar 60).

Of Zimbabwe A's top eight batsmen, only Tatenda Taibu (21) reached double figures; they were 48 for seven when Strang came in.

†ZIMBABWE v SOUTH AFRICA

First One-Day International

At Bulawayo, September 23. South Africa won by 153 runs. Toss: South Africa.

South Africa began here, as in the Tests, with a batting massacre. A total of 363 for three was their best in one-day cricket, beating 328 for three against Holland in the 1996 World Cup. It was also the highest conceded by Zimbabwe, and a half-fit Streak yielded 80 runs, the most by any Zimbabwean bowler. Of his colleagues, only Paul Strang emerged with any credit; seven no-balls and 15 wides indicated their lack of discipline. Kirsten plundered 66 in 59 balls, Gibbs raced on to 125 in 112, with 15 fours and two sixes, and Rhodes was the fastest of all, smashing 54 off 41. After this blitz Zimbabwe could aim only for respectability; Campbell saw to it with 81.

Man of the Match: H. H. Gibbs.

South Africa

G. Kirsten lbw b Strang	66	L. Klusener not out	10
H. H. Gibbs lbw b Streak	125	B 1, l-b 2, w 15, n-b 7	25
J. H. Kallis c A. Flower b Friend	83		
J. N. Rhodes not out	54	1/153 2/244 3/346 (3 wkts, 50 overs) 363

N. D. McKenzie, *S. M. Pollock, †M. V. Boucher, C. W. Henderson, A. Nel and M. Ntini did not bat.

Bowling: Streak 10–0–80–1; Friend 7–0–73–1; Nkala 10–0–72–0; Strang 10–0–56–1; G. W. Flower 6–0–36–0; Whittall 7–0–43–0.

Zimbabwe

A. D. R. Campbell c and b Pollock	81	G. J. Whittall not out	5
D. D. Ebrahim c Klusener b Nel	0		
H. Masakadza run out	11	B 4, w 6, n-b 2	12
†A. Flower run out	34		
C. B. Wishart c Kallis b Henderson	45	1/6 2/43 3/97 (5 wkts, 50 overs) 210
G. W. Flower not out	22	4/157 5/189

*H. H. Streak, P. A. Strang, M. L. Nkala and T. J. Friend did not bat.

Bowling: Pollock 9–0–33–1; Nel 8–1–27–1; Klusener 5–0–22–0; Ntini 10–0–51–0; Henderson 10–0–44–1; Kallis 5–0–22–0; McKenzie 2–0–6–0; Rhodes 1–0–1–0.

Umpires: C. K. Coventry and J. F. Fenwick.
Third umpire: T. J. Tapfumaneyi. Referee: Naushad Ali (Pakistan).

†ZIMBABWE v SOUTH AFRICA

Second One-Day International

At Harare, September 29. South Africa won by 148 runs. Toss: South Africa.

Streak, who was clearly unfit in Bulawayo, dropped out; Whittall assumed the captaincy, while Brent came into the attack and bowled with superb accuracy. Extra bounce in the pitch surprised one or two of the South African batsmen, who could not sustain their dominance. Gibbs still helped them to an ample total with 69 off 77 balls, though the accolades went to Rhodes for his 56 off 45. Promoted to open, Paul Strang gave Zimbabwe a brisk start before four wickets fell in five overs, including Andy Flower's, when Ntini forced him to chop a ball on to his stumps. The dismissal of Carlisle began a terminal slide, with scarcely a shot played in anger thereafter; Henderson was the main beneficiary.

Man of the Match: J. N. Rhodes.

South Africa

G. Kirsten c and b Friend	10	†M. V. Boucher not out	4
H. H. Gibbs c Whittall b Strang	69		
J. H. Kallis b Strang	26	B 1, l-b 7, w 10	18
N. D. McKenzie c Nkala b G. W. Flower	40		
J. N. Rhodes c Strang b G. W. Flower	56	1/24 2/89 3/133	(7 wkts, 50 overs) 272
L. Klusener c Campbell b Whittall	34	4/212 5/225	
*S. M. Pollock c G. W. Flower b Whittall	15	6/253 7/272	

C. W. Henderson, A. Nel and M. Ntini did not bat.

Bowling: Friend 6–0–37–1; Brent 10–0–37–0; Nkala 7–0–48–0; Strang 10–0–56–2; Whittall 10–0–49–2; G. W. Flower 5–0–21–2; Campbell 2–0–16–0.

Zimbabwe

A. D. R. Campbell c Kirsten b Kallis	21	M. L. Nkala b Klusener	5
P. A. Strang c Boucher b Pollock	19	T. J. Friend st Boucher b Henderson	1
H. Masakadza run out	0	G. B. Brent not out	2
†A. Flower b Ntini	2	L-b 7, w 1	8
S. V. Carlisle c Boucher b Henderson	31		
G. W. Flower run out	20	1/38 2/42 3/48	(40.1 overs) 124
D. D. Ebrahim c Pollock b Henderson	15	4/50 5/94 6/101	
*G. J. Whittall c Rhodes b Henderson	0	7/102 8/121 9/121	

Bowling: Pollock 6–1–13–1; Nel 6–0–29–0; Kallis 5–0–24–1; Ntini 6–0–19–1; Henderson 9.1–1–17–4; Klusener 8–3–15–1.

Umpires: Q. J. Goosen and I. D. Robinson.
Third umpire: G. R. Evans.   Referee: Naushad Ali (Pakistan).

†ZIMBABWE v SOUTH AFRICA

Third One-Day International

At Harare, September 30. South Africa won by six wickets. Toss: Zimbabwe.

For the first time in this series, Zimbabwe had the advantage of the toss, but they timidly played for safety rather than launching a daring assault on a somewhat experimental bowling attack. Campbell and Carlisle scored at scarcely three an over in adding 67 for the second wicket, putting intolerable pressure on the later batsmen. Andy Flower sacrificed himself trying to boost the rate, and only his brother, with 28 off 31 balls, rose to the task. A total of 184 never looked defensible, especially against more spray-gun bowling from Zimbabwe (with the honourable exception of Brent). Dubious lbw decisions against Gibbs and Kemp disrupted South Africa's momentum, but McKenzie played with maturity to complete a clean sweep.

Man of the Match: N. D. McKenzie.   *Man of the Series:* H. H. Gibbs.

Zimbabwe

A. D. R. Campbell b Henderson	40	*G. J. Whittall not out	5
H. Masakadza lbw b Kemp	5		
S. V. Carlisle c Klusener b Ontong	51	L-b 5, w 3, n-b 2	10
†A. Flower c Gibbs b Henderson	4		
D. D. Ebrahim run out	41	1/7 2/74 3/92	(6 wkts, 50 overs) 184
G. W. Flower c Dippenaar b Klusener	28	4/119 5/172 6/184	

P. A. Strang, M. L. Nkala, T. J. Friend and G. B. Brent did not bat.

Bowling: Pollock 10–2–29–0; Kemp 9–2–30–1; Kallis 4–0–18–0; Klusener 9–0–35–1; Henderson 10–1–34–2; Ontong 8–1–33–1.

South Africa

H. H. Dippenaar lbw b Brent	22	†M. V. Boucher not out	15
H. H. Gibbs lbw b Nkala	39	L-b 3, w 7	10
J. M. Kemp lbw b Nkala	1		
N. D. McKenzie not out	69	1/64 2/67	
J. L. Ontong c and b G. W. Flower	32	3/67 4/131	(4 wkts, 41 overs) 188

J. H. Kallis, J. N. Rhodes, L. Klusener, *S. M. Pollock and C. W. Henderson did not bat.

Bowling: Friend 6–1–38–0; Brent 10–4–22–1; Nkala 9–1–46–2; Whittall 6–1–27–0; Strang 6–0–35–0; G. W. Flower 4–0–17–1.

Umpires: M. A. Esat and G. R. Evans.
Third umpire: Q. J. Goosen.   Referee: Naushad Ali (Pakistan).

WISDEN, 100 YEARS AGO

Some excerpts from *Wisden* 1903, selected by Christopher Lane. To read the main articles and match reports from the book in full, go to www.wisden.com, click on "Almanack", and put "1903" into the search.

Tests should not be timeless
From Notes by the Editor (Sydney Pardon): "There seems to be a strong feeling in favour of playing Test games in this country out to a finish, irrespective of the time they occupy... I am very doubtful of the wisdom of making cricket altogether independent of a time limit. Desirable as it is to see one side or the other victorious, the result at cricket is not everything... Cricket has already suffered to some extent from the contrast to Association Football, with its hour and a half of concentrated excitement... Time being of no consequence, the game would, I fear, lose its brilliant qualities and become little more than a matter of endurance."

Trumper puts all previous Australians in the shade
From Five Cricketers of the Year: "Victor Trumper, at the present time, by general consent, the best batsman in the world... during the past season... put into the shade everything that had ever before been done in England by Australian batsmen, scoring, despite the bad weather and wet wickets, 2,570 runs... It is safe to say that no one – not even Ranjitsinhji – has been at once so brilliant and so consistent since W. G. Grace was at his best... [Trumper] did everything with such an easy grace of style that his batting was always a delight to the eye."

Successful debut for Edgbaston
From Warwickshire in 1902: "It was peculiarly unfortunate for Warwickshire that the first England and Australia match ever played at Birmingham should, after a successful first day, have been spoilt by rain. The Edgbaston ground proved well fitted for a Test match, and with the assistance, among others, of the Aston Villa Football Club, the committee were able to make excellent arrangements."

A dreary year for Middlesex
From Middlesex in 1902: "Middlesex had a disastrous season in 1902, and dropped from the second to the eleventh place among the counties. Not a single success rewarded their efforts at Lord's... In most respects, indeed, they had a dreary and disheartening season."

England tourists lose 4–1 in Australia – again
From Mr. MacLaren's team in Australia, 1901-02: "In connection with cricket, history has not often repeated itself so curiously as in the experiences of the last two English elevens taken out to the colonies. Mr. Stoddart's second team, which went to Australia in the winter of 1897-8, won the first of their five Test matches and lost the other four, and precisely the same fate befell Mr. MacLaren's eleven in the Australian summer of 1901-2."

For excerpts from Wisden 50 years ago, see page 1208.

THE INDIANS IN SOUTH AFRICA, 2001-02

By DICKY RUTNAGUR

This tour made history of a thoroughly undesirable sort. The final Test, to be played at Centurion from November 23 to 27, was stripped of its official status by the International Cricket Council when India refused to play under the supervision of Mike Denness, the appointed referee. Denness, an England captain of the 1970s, had imposed penalties on six Indian players he had found in breach of the ICC Code of Conduct during the Second Test, which ended in Port Elizabeth on November 20. The list included the captain, Sourav Ganguly, and the people's favourite, Sachin Tendulkar.

When the ICC rejected India's demand for Denness to be replaced, the Indian board threatened to cut short the tour, a drastic action which could have left their South African counterparts facing swingeing financial penalties for not fulfilling commitments to sponsors and broadcasters. This factor, as much as government pressure, persuaded the South African board to agree that the teams should go ahead with an unofficial Test. They also intimated that Denness would not be allowed in the referee's box, whereupon the ICC instructed him to return home, along with the independent umpire from England, George Sharp.

The tourists were mere bystanders while war was waged on their behalf by Jagmohan Dalmiya, newly elected president of the Indian board and also a former president of the ICC. Dalmiya said that, at the ICC executive's next meeting in March, he would press for the Centurion match to be retrospectively recognised as a Test (it was not) and demand a review of the penalties imposed by Denness.

He also ordered the team management to stand down Virender Sehwag, whom Denness had suspended for one Test, from the game at Centurion, stating that he should thus be considered to have served his suspension. The ICC countered that, with the match downgraded, the Test Sehwag was to sit out would be the first between India and England, due to begin on December 3 at Mohali. Clearly, Dalmiya was looking to open another battlefront. Three days before the Mohali Test, he backed down on this issue, but went above the heads of India's selectors by giving Sehwag his personal assurance that he would play the Second Test against England.

Of the six Indians who allegedly breached the Code of Conduct, Sehwag was the most severely penalised, because he was deemed to have committed two offences. In common with Harbhajan Singh, who was bowling, the wicket-keeper Deep Dasgupta and Shiv Sunder Das who, like Sehwag, was fielding close in, he was found guilty of expressing dissent and attempting to intimidate the umpire by charging at him. Sehwag's other transgression was the use of "crude or abusive language". Besides being suspended for one Test – a punishment which had been meted out only once previously, to West Indies' Ridley Jacobs, for an incident in which Sehwag was the victim – he was fined 75 per cent of his match fee. The other three all received the same fine, but their bans, for one Test, were suspended.

Considering that Ganguly had been suspended and/or fined three times in the previous 12 months, he was fortunate to get away with only a suspended ban for not upholding the spirit of the game and failing to control his players' conduct on the field, as required of the captain by the Code, so bringing the game into disrepute.

At the eye of the storm, however, was the allegation against Tendulkar that he too had brought the game into disrepute through "interference with the match ball, thus changing its condition". This statement could only mean that Tendulkar had tampered with the ball and, by implication, he was a cheat. At first, Denness refused to comment on his verdicts or penalties, but he later issued a vague explanation of the Tendulkar case: it suggested he had not tampered with the ball, but had failed to observe the technicality of asking the umpires to supervise removal of mud from the ball. Denness added that there had been no complaint from the umpires; he had acted on his own initiative after scrutiny of video footage. Tendulkar, who hitherto had an unblemished disciplinary record, was fined 75 per cent of his match fee, with a suspended ban for one Test.

The Indian public were outraged at the slight against the character of their idol. There were street protests in towns and cities throughout the country, and scenes of uproar even in parliament. It did not escape notice that Denness had overlooked a highly aggressive appeal by the South African captain, Shaun Pollock; the omission reinforced the general view held in the subcontinent that ICC referees are racially biased. Therefore, Dalmiya had to take a stand – not that he needed much provocation to adopt a bellicose posture. He was presented with an ideal opportunity to settle scores with his old ICC adversaries.

But the new ICC chief executive, Australia's Malcolm Speed, stood his ground against the threat of schism. He offered a "referees commission" which would review Denness's actions and the broader role of referees. That was enough to end the impasse over Sehwag's ban, although, given that the ICC was already planning to reform the referee system, it looked like a face-saver. By March, it had become a "disputes resolution committee", but the Port Elizabeth case was postponed for several more months because Denness was undergoing heart surgery.

Before cricket gave way to controversy, the Test series was predictably one-sided. South Africa won comfortably, thanks to a nine-wicket victory in the First Test at Bloemfontein, even though their pace attack was below full strength and their middle order less sound than when they last met India in March 2000 (the tour which led to Hansie Cronje's downfall). With Allan Donald and the new find, Mfuneko Ngam, ruled out by long-term injuries, Pollock's fast-bowling support came from Nantie Hayward, in his first Test for 15 months, and Makhaya Ntini. Hayward had his moments, but Ntini had an unrewarding series. The extra burden was valiantly borne by Pollock, who scaled the heights with 16 wickets in the two Tests, including ten in the First.

The lack of class in the batting after No. 3 was camouflaged by the dominance of Herschelle Gibbs, voted the Man of the Series for the purpose and flair which brought him a century in each of the two Tests, and the consistency of Jacques Kallis, who collected 202 in four innings, two unbeaten. On the one occasion when South Africa seemed to be losing the initiative, at Bloemfontein, Lance Klusener came up trumps with 108 at No. 6. Pollock reserved his highest score (113 not out) for the unofficial Test, but scored an unbeaten 55 at a crucial stage at Port Elizabeth.

The Indians entered the series in low spirits after their poor performance in the limited-overs triangular that preceded it – hitting rock bottom in a 70-run defeat by Kenya – and some seemed to lack the management's confidence. They were without a second specialist opening batsman; Connor Williams, an uncapped left-hander from Baroda, was called up on the eve of the First Test, but not considered for selection even for the Second, because the intervening first-class game was washed out, leaving him without an innings. His only outing came in the unofficial Test, when Sehwag was omitted and Ganguly was unfit; Williams made the most of it with a gritty 42.

The conundrum of who should go in first with Das severely tested team spirit. Rahul Dravid was persuaded to do so in the First Test, without success. Neither Dravid nor Laxman would accept the role for the Second Test; the night before, Ganguly said he would do it, but this proved no more than a PR exercise. Next day, Deep Dasgupta, who as wicket-keeper was considered the one expendable batsman, was handed the poisoned chalice. He stayed in for 78 minutes in the first innings and, gaining in confidence, scored 63 in the second, batting for 335 minutes to help save the match. Dasgupta was not even supposed to be in the running for a Test place, after keeping indifferently in the one-day games, but his replacement, Samir Dighe, dropped out with a back injury just before the First Test.

There were a couple of glimpses of the Indian batting in all its glory. At Bloemfontein, Tendulkar and Sehwag, making his debut, scored a century apiece and together put on 220 for the fifth wicket in a blazing counter-attack, while V. V. S. Laxman made a dazzling 89 at Port Elizabeth. Ganguly had scored plentifully in the triangular, but found runs hard to come by in the longer game, where his dislike of the short ball outside the off stump was ruthlessly exploited.

Although just back from injury, Javagal Srinath was India's most penetrative bowler, with 13 wickets in two Tests and two five-fors. Despite helpful conditions, the three other pace bowlers – Ashish Nehra, Zaheer Khan and Ajit Agarkar – did not advance their reputations and were dropped for the home series against England. The pitches denied the spinners help, though Harbhajan Singh might have harnessed the bounce available at Bloemfontein, had he not missed the match through illness. Anil Kumble was at least accurate, if not deadly, on his comeback – he had not played a Test since these teams last met, 20 months earlier, following surgery on his shoulder.

If the tourists were due sympathy on any count, it was for being denied a fair opportunity for preparation. Only two first-class matches were scheduled outside the Tests, and both were washed out without a ball bowled.

INDIAN TOURING PARTY

S. C. Ganguly (Bengal) (*captain*), R. Dravid (Karnataka) (*vice-captain*), A. B. Agarkar (Mumbai), S. S. Das (Orissa), D. Dasgupta (Bengal), S. S. Dighe (Mumbai), Harbhajan Singh (Punjab), A. Kumble (Karnataka), V. V. S. Laxman (Hyderabad), A. Nehra (Delhi), B. K. V. Prasad (Karnataka), V. Sehwag (Delhi), J. Srinath (Karnataka), S. R. Tendulkar (Mumbai), C. C. Williams (Baroda), Zaheer Khan (Baroda).

Harvinder Singh (Railways), J. J. Martin (Baroda), R. S. Sodhi (Punjab) and Yuvraj Singh (Punjab) were in the party for the one-day tournament but were replaced for the first-class programme by Dighe, Nehra, Williams and Zaheer Khan. Laxman arrived for the later one-day games; Dighe went home injured without playing.

Coach: J. G. Wright.   *Manager:* Dr M. K. Bhargawa.

INDIAN TOUR RESULTS

Test matches – Played 2: Lost 1, Drawn 1. Cancelled 1.
First-class matches – Played 3: Lost 2, Drawn 1. Abandoned 2, Cancelled 1.
Losses – South Africa (Test), South Africa (unofficial Test).
Draw – South Africa.
Abandoned – UCBSA President's XI, South Africa A.
Cancelled – South Africa.
One-day internationals – Played 7: Won 3, Lost 4. *Wins* – South Africa, Kenya (2). *Losses* – South Africa (3), Kenya.
Other non-first-class matches – Played 2: Won 2. *Wins* – N. F. Oppenheimer's XI, South Africa A.

Note: Matches in this section which were not first-class are signified by a dagger.

†At Randjesfontein, October 1. **Indians won by five wickets.** N. F. Oppenheimer's XI batted first by mutual agreement. **N. F. Oppenheimer's XI 244 for three dec.** (J. A. Rudolph 109, L. L. Bosman 62, G. C. Smith 54); **Indians 245 for five** (S. C. Ganguly 34, S. R. Tendulkar 45, S. S. Das 59 retired out, R. Dravid 48 retired out, V. Sehwag 44).

†At Benoni, October 3 (day/night). **Indians won by three wickets.** Toss: South Africa A. **South Africa A 241 for six** (50 overs) (H. H. Dippenaar 34, M. van Jaarsveld 69, G. Dros 85; A. B. Agarkar three for 46); **Indians 245 for seven** (49.1 overs) (J. J. Martin 54, R. Dravid 35, Yuvraj Singh 46 not out, A. B. Agarkar 49).

India's matches against South Africa and Kenya in the Standard Bank International Series (October 5–26) appear on pages 1344–1352.

At Chatsworth, October 29, 30, 31. **UCBSA President's XI v Indians. Abandoned.**

SOUTH AFRICA v INDIA

First Test Match

At Bloemfontein, November 3, 4, 5, 6. South Africa won by nine wickets. Toss: South Africa. Test debuts: D. Dasgupta, V. Sehwag.

Though the margin of victory did not flatter South Africa, it did understate the strength of India's opposition. For the first three days of this Test, the cricket was combative and, for the most part, spectacular.

The pitch, relaid not many months earlier, was liberally grassed. It was not fast but initially provided bounce and lateral movement. By the fourth day, it became awkward, developing a mosaic of wide cracks at one end. Pollock's decision to bowl earned good returns in the short term – four wickets in 90 minutes – although his own hostility with the new ball brought him less reward than he deserved. However, South Africa's advance was halted by the awesome mastery with which Tendulkar scored his 26th Test hundred, and his partnership of 220 with Virender Sehwag, who made a flawless century in his maiden Test innings. Sehwag might not have played had Harbhajan Singh not been taken ill on the eve of the match.

Tendulkar became comfortably the youngest player to score 7,000 Test runs, at 28 years 193 days in his 85th Test, beating David Gower (who was 31). The range and power of his shots took him to his hundred in only 114 balls; when, to his immense annoyance, he got himself caught off a short delivery, he had hit 23 fours and a six. Watching ball after ball hit the middle of Tendulkar's bat can only have been reassuring for Sehwag, but his composure and the manner in which he shaped his own innings, 105 in 173 balls, including 19 fours, testified to a sound temperament. The adorning feature was his delightful cover driving. He was finally bowled by a true beauty, the first of three victims Pollock claimed with the second new ball.

South Africa's reply began early on the second day and ended six overs after tea on the third. Their eventual 563 beat their previous best against India: 529 for seven at Cape Town in 1996-97. It was founded on a third consecutive century opening stand between Gibbs, who was allowed the freedom to hit 16 fours and two sixes in 107 off 145 balls, and Kirsten. They departed in successive overs but Kallis and McKenzie, both watchful, kept the innings on an even keel.

India fought back and had the better of the third morning: Kumble and Zaheer Khan restrained Kallis and Dippenaar for 50 minutes before three wickets in six overs with the new ball suggested Ganguly should have taken it before the 95th over. When Kallis was caught at second slip, it was his first dismissal in 1,241 minutes of batting (spread over three matches) – then a Test record. Srinath accounted for the next two with consecutive balls to reach 200 wickets in his 54th Test.

With four wickets left, South Africa were still two runs behind. From that point, however, they took decisive control, thanks to Klusener and Boucher, who put on 121. Klusener's bat was more edge than middle to start with but, once his eye was in, it became a lethal bludgeon. He made 108 off 124 balls, with 18 fours and a six, to set up a formidable lead of 184.

India cleared 96 for just one wicket by the end of the third day. But on the fourth there came a sudden and sharp decline, as Pollock's accuracy and incisiveness conspired with the deteriorating pitch and a fair number of batting errors. Nine wickets went down for 129 runs and Pollock earned a Test haul of ten for the first time. Chasing 54, South Africa settled the argument by tea.

Man of the Match: S. M. Pollock.   *Attendance:* 13,896.

Close of play: First day, India 372-7 (Dasgupta 29); Second day, South Africa 327-3 (Kallis 49); Third day, India 96-1 (Das 54, Laxman 25).

India

S. S. Das b Hayward	9	– c Boucher b Hayward	62
R. Dravid c Kallis b Pollock	2	– c Kirsten b Pollock	11
V. V. S. Laxman c Boucher b Hayward	32	– c Kallis b Pollock	29
S. R. Tendulkar c McKenzie b Ntini	155	– c Gibbs b Kallis	15
*S. C. Ganguly c Kirsten b Kallis	14	– c Boucher b Ntini	30
V. Sehwag b Pollock	105	– b Pollock	31
†D. Dasgupta c Boucher b Pollock	34	– c Boucher b Pollock	4
A. Kumble c Boucher b Kallis	6	– lbw b Hayward	4
J. Srinath c Gibbs b Hayward	1	– c McKenzie b Pollock	16
Zaheer Khan c Boucher b Pollock	0	– c Boucher b Pollock	0
A. Nehra not out	0	– not out	17
L-b 7, w 7, n-b 7	21	B 4, l-b 8, n-b 6	18

1/7 (2) 2/43 (1) 3/51 (3) 4/68 (5) 379
5/288 (4) 6/351 (6) 7/372 (8)
8/378 (9) 9/379 (10) 10/379 (9)

1/29 (2) 2/108 (3) 3/108 (1) 237
4/154 (4) 5/188 (5) 6/195 (6)
7/202 (8) 8/206 (7)
9/206 (10) 10/237 (9)

Bowling: *First Innings*—Pollock 27–8–91–4; Hayward 20.3–5–70–3; Kallis 22–6–87–2; Ntini 14.4–2–71–1; Klusener 6–1–32–0; Boje 5–1–21–0. *Second Innings*—Pollock 21.4–10–56–6; Hayward 23–8–74–2; Kallis 15–3–56–1; Ntini 10–3–39–1.

South Africa

H. H. Gibbs c Zaheer Khan b Srinath	107	– lbw b Kumble	1
G. Kirsten b Kumble	73	– not out	30
J. H. Kallis c Laxman b Nehra	68	– not out	21
N. D. McKenzie lbw b Kumble	68		
H. H. Dippenaar b Srinath	20		
L. Klusener c and b Kumble	108		
*S. M. Pollock c Das b Srinath	0		
†M. V. Boucher c Dravid b Srinath	47		
N. Boje c Dasgupta b Nehra	6		
M. Ntini c Dasgupta b Srinath	23		
M. Hayward not out	0		
B 7, l-b 11, w 4, n-b 16, p 5	43	N-b 2	2

1/189 (2) 2/197 (1) 3/327 (4) 4/359 (3) 563
5/377 (5) 6/377 (7) 7/498 (8)
8/517 (9) 9/548 (6) 10/563 (10)

1/6 (1) (1 wkt) 54

Bowling: *First Innings*—Srinath 33–6–140–5; Nehra 22–3–121–2; Zaheer Khan 26–7–98–0; Kumble 50–12–132–3; Tendulkar 7–0–27–0; Sehwag 5–0–22–0. *Second Innings*—Srinath 5–1–13–0; Kumble 4–0–23–1; Nehra 3–0–9–0; Zaheer Khan 2.4–0–9–0.

Umpires: E. A. R. de Silva (Sri Lanka) and D. L. Orchard.
Third umpire: I. L. Howell. Referee: M. H. Denness (England).

At East London, November 10, 11, 12, 13. **South Africa A v Indians. Abandoned.**

SOUTH AFRICA v INDIA

Second Test Match

At Port Elizabeth, November 16, 17, 18, 19, 20. Drawn. Toss: India.

Achievements on the field, even Gibbs's 196, were overshadowed by a furore which snowballed into one of the game's biggest crises. It was triggered by the announcement on the final morning of penalties imposed by the referee, Mike Denness, on six Indian players for alleged breaches of the Code of Conduct. The tourists considered them excessive and, in Tendulkar's case, grossly unfair.

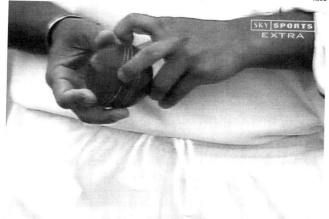

There were so many accusations flying around the Second Test that some mud had to stick. Television found Sachin Tendulkar trying to remove some from the ball without the umpires' approval, an act which earned him a stiff punishment – and threw international cricket into turmoil. *Picture by Sky Sports.*

India started the final day in some peril – 366 behind with one wicket down batting last. But rather than let their emotions over the row undermine them, they resisted gallantly and, with the weather's assistance, secured a comfortable draw.

South Africa were unchanged, while India discarded two seamers, picked another (Agarkar) and welcomed back the off-spinner, Harbhajan Singh. On the first day, they did not gain as much ground as a side opting to bowl would expect. But, by putting South Africa in, India at least avoided a calamitous start themselves. Only Srinath, who took three wickets in the day and six in the innings, exploited a green pitch under a cloudy sky. Without Gibbs, who batted with fluent authority to complete a century off 167 balls, the day would have been desperately tedious. Of the two partners who stayed with him, Kallis took 70 balls over 24 runs and Dippenaar 138 over 29, batting as if he were a relic of the timeless Durban Test of 1938-39.

Warm sunshine on the first afternoon and a strong wind next morning turned the pitch into a batsman's paradise. Gibbs and Boucher revelled in its splendour to add 80 in 17 overs, until Gibbs was caught at gully, cutting loosely in Tendulkar's first over as he tried to reach a double-hundred. India could have ended the stand 39 runs earlier had Dravid held a top-edged steepler that Boucher hoisted off Harbhajan; 31 at the time, Boucher finished unbeaten on 68 off only 70 balls.

Despite the benign pitch, India contrived to lose half their wickets for 69, including a staunch effort as makeshift opener by Dasgupta, digging in for 60 balls, and a rapid, but none too convincing, 42 in 46 balls by Ganguly. Laxman, in at No. 6 and ninth out for 89, was at the heart of a revival. He began by adding 42 with Sehwag and crowned it with a ninth-wicket stand of 80 with Kumble. In three hours of responsible, enterprising batting, Laxman hit 12 fours before he was lbw playing half forward to Pollock.

That was on the third morning, when South Africa swept away India's last two wickets inside half an hour. Nevertheless, the session belonged to the tourists: Srinath, striking twice with the new ball, and Agarkar, producing a deadly breakback to bowl Gibbs, reduced South Africa to 26 for three. India's resurgence lasted until a circumspect Kallis and a belligerent Pollock came together in an unbroken stand of 94 which stretched into the fourth day, when rain permitted only 25 overs in all. It was during the early stages of this partnership, on the third afternoon, when fieldsmen were clustered round the bat, that Harbhajan, Das, Dasgupta and Sehwag allegedly violated the Code of Conduct by charging at the umpire. The third day was also when Tendulkar supposedly "interfered with the match ball", a charge Denness later explained as deriving from a failure to obtain the umpires' permission to clean mud from the seam.

Pollock's cautious declaration set India a target of 395 in a full day plus 41 overs. But only 18 could be bowled before, predictably, bad light ended play again. When Dasgupta and Dravid batted right through an extended first session on the final day, India looked safe. But Hayward dismissed them both with the second new ball, and Pollock bowled a fiery last spell before bad light brought down the curtain on the cricket. The diplomatic drama was only just beginning.

Man of the Match: H. H. Gibbs.
Man of the Series: H. H. Gibbs.
Attendance: 14,722.

Close of play: First day, South Africa 237-5 (Gibbs 155, Pollock 0); Second day, India 182-8 (Laxman 77, Kumble 21); Third day, South Africa 211-5 (Kallis 84, Pollock 38); Fourth day, India 28-1 (Dasgupta 22, Dravid 3).

South Africa

H. H. Gibbs c Sehwag b Tendulkar	196	– b Agarkar			12
G. Kirsten c Laxman b Srinath	4	– c Laxman b Srinath			5
J. H. Kallis b Srinath	24	– not out			89
N. D. McKenzie b Harbhajan Singh	12	– c Dasgupta b Srinath			2
H. H. Dippenaar c Dasgupta b Agarkar	29	– c Sehwag b Harbhajan Singh			28
L. Klusener c Laxman b Srinath	9	– c Sehwag b Harbhajan Singh			29
*S. M. Pollock c Harbhajan Singh b Srinath	3	– not out			55
†M. V. Boucher not out	68				
N. Boje lbw b Kumble	1				
M. Ntini c Das b Srinath	10				
M. Hayward b Srinath	0				
L-b 2, n-b 4	6	B 3, l-b 3, n-b 7			13

1/17 (2) 2/87 (3) 3/116 (4) 4/221 (5)　　362　　1/14 (2) 2/22 (1)　　(5 wkts dec.) 233
5/230 (6) 6/244 (7) 7/324 (1)　　　　　　　　3/26 (4) 4/91 (5)
8/325 (9) 9/353 (10) 10/362 (11)　　　　　　5/139 (6)

Bowling: *First Innings*—Srinath 30–6–76–6; Agarkar 22–2–85–1; Ganguly 2–0–21–0; Kumble 29–10–67–1; Harbhajan Singh 34–6–89–1; Tendulkar 4–0–22–1. *Second Innings*—Srinath 17–9–28–2; Agarkar 23–3–71–1; Ganguly 5–0–17–0; Tendulkar 4–0–10–0; Harbhajan Singh 20–2–79–2; Kumble 9–0–22–0.

India

S. S. Das lbw b Pollock	1	– c Boucher b Pollock			0
†D. Dasgupta b Ntini	13	– c Kallis b Hayward			63
R. Dravid b Pollock	2	– c Boucher b Hayward			87
S. R. Tendulkar c Klusener b Pollock	1	– not out			22
*S. C. Ganguly b Pollock	42	– not out			4
V. V. S. Laxman lbw b Pollock	89				
V. Sehwag c Kirsten b Kallis	13				
A. B. Agarkar c Boucher b Kallis	1				
Harbhajan Singh run out	0				
A. Kumble c Kirsten b Hayward	28				
J. Srinath not out	0				
L-b 3, w 2, n-b 6	11	B 10, l-b 7, w 1, n-b 12			30

1/5 (1) 2/13 (3) 3/15 (4) 4/47 (2)　　201　　1/0 (1) 2/171 (3)　　(3 wkts) 206
5/69 (5) 6/111 (7) 7/119 (8)　　　　　　　　3/184 (2)
8/119 (9) 9/199 (6) 10/201 (10)

Bowling: *First Innings*—Pollock 16–3–40–5; Hayward 17–5–45–1; Ntini 14–3–49–1; Kallis 10–2–50–2; Boje 4–2–8–0; Klusener 1–0–6–0. *Second Innings*—Pollock 26–11–39–1; Hayward 25–6–58–2; Kallis 11.2–5–15–0; Ntini 12–4–25–0; Boje 14–4–33–0; Klusener 7–3–15–0; McKenzie 1–0–4–0.

Umpires: R. B. Tiffin (Zimbabwe) and I. L. Howell.
Third umpire: R. E. Koertzen. Referee: M. H. Denness (England).

SOUTH AFRICA v INDIA

Unofficial Test

At Centurion, November 23, 24, 25, 26, 27. South Africa won by an innings and 73 runs. Toss: South Africa.

This match was neither one thing nor the other. The South African team were told by their board to treat it as unofficial while India were under orders to treat it as a proper Test. Yet it was South Africa who rolled on methodically and relentlessly, and the Indians who were lacklustre and bored and threw the match away with feckless batting and wayward bowling.

With the ICC officials departed, the South African board appointed two home umpires and a home referee, Denis Lindsay, who was to supervise India's series with England in December. Despite withdrawing Test status, the ICC promised no reprisals. They did not, however, accept that Virender Sehwag's omission here fulfilled his one-Test suspension. Ganguly took the opportunity to rest after back spasms; Connor Williams stepped up for his first game of the tour, an international debut of sorts for him and for Jacques Rudolph, both of whom were left, like Alan Jones after the England–Rest of the World series in 1970, in the limbo of the nearly capped.

In the circumstances, it was little surprise that the Indians were overwhelmed by the South African batsmen. Gibbs and Kirsten shared another century opening partnership; Kallis scored 110 in 234 balls, with 18 fours; and finally Pollock moved the game up a couple of gears, dashing to 113 in 109 balls, with nine fours and seven sixes, before declaring 334 ahead on the fourth morning. Williams and Das batted bravely to reach 92 without loss, but both fell before rain brought an early close. The South Africans needed only six more wickets on the final day, as Srinath and Prasad were both injured. Srinath had managed to bowl 27 overs with a broken finger on his left hand (struck by Hayward on the first evening), while Prasad had hurt his neck. Their colleagues – including Tendulkar, who played ludicrously, as though imitating the wild abandon of Harbhajan's batting in the nets – were bowled out with most of two sessions remaining. *Additional reporting by Amit Varma.*

Man of the Match: S. M. Pollock.   Attendance: 34,671.

Close of play: First day, India 221-8 (Prasad 6); Second day, South Africa 261-4 (Kallis 41); Third day, South Africa 566-8 (Pollock 113, Ntini 34); Fourth day, India 118-2 (Dravid 11, Tendulkar 2).

India

S. S. Das c Gibbs b Hayward	46	– b Pollock	48
C. C. Williams lbw b Klusener	5	– c Kallis b Klusener	42
*R. Dravid lbw b Ntini	5	– b Ntini	23
S. R. Tendulkar c Boucher b Kallis	27	– b Hayward	40
V. V. S. Laxman c Kirsten b Kallis	14	– c Gibbs b Ntini	23
†D. Dasgupta c Rudolph b Hayward	36	– lbw b Kallis	27
A. Kumble b Hayward	27	– c Boje b Pollock	8
Harbhajan Singh run out	29	– c Boucher b Hayward	30
J. Srinath retired hurt	8	– absent hurt	
B. K. V. Prasad not out	11	– absent hurt	
A. Nehra c Boje b Hayward	4	– (9) not out	0
B 1, l-b 12, n-b 7	20	B 2, l-b 11, n-b 7	20

1/16 (2) 2/49 (3) 3/90 (4) 4/100 (4)   **232**   1/92 (2) 2/116 (1) 3/130 (3)   **261**
5/107 (5) 6/158 (6) 7/197 (8)   4/188 (4) 5/197 (5) 6/212 (7)
8/221 (7) 9/232 (11)   7/259 (8) 8/261 (6)

In the first innings, Srinath retired hurt at 210.

Bowling: First Innings—Pollock 20–11–21–0; Hayward 28.4–8–74–4; Ntini 17–3–78–1; Klusener 12–6–11–1; Kallis 13–7–15–2; Boje 7–2–20–0. Second Innings—Pollock 14–2–40–2; Hayward 17–3–61–2; Ntini 18–6–27–2; Kallis 14.1–4–45–1; Klusener 12–6–30–1; Boje 7–2–34–0; Rudolph 2–0–11–0.

South Africa

H. H. Gibbs c Harbhajan Singh b Srinath	59	N. Boje st Dasgupta b Harbhajan Singh .	20
G. Kirsten c Dravid b Nehra	90	M. Ntini not out	34
J. A. Rudolph run out	21	B 11, l-b 2, w 2, n-b 14, p 5 . .	34
J. H. Kallis b Kumble	110		
N. D. McKenzie c Laxman b Tendulkar	33	1/135 (1) 2/171 (3) (8 wkts dec.)	566
L. Klusener c Laxman b Srinath	33	3/195 (2) 4/261 (5)	
†M. V. Boucher b Nehra	19	5/321 (6) 6/395 (4)	
*S. M. Pollock not out	113	7/395 (7) 8/445 (9)	

M. Hayward did not bat.

Bowling: Srinath 27–3–94–2; Nehra 30–5–123–2; Prasad 21–6–71–0; Harbhajan Singh 34.1–10–104–1; Kumble 34–4–102–1; Tendulkar 11–0–54–1.

Umpires: R. E. Koertzen and D. L. Orchard.
Third umpire: B. G. Jerling. Referee: D. T. Lindsay.

WISDEN, 50 YEARS AGO

Some excerpts from *Wisden* 1953, selected by Christopher Lane. To read the main articles and match reports from the book in full, go to www.wisden.com, click on "Almanack", and put "1953" into the search.

Forthright Fred the best prospect in years

From Five Cricketers of the Year: "Already Frederick Sewards Trueman gives promise of becoming a second Harold Larwood. His successes against India in the 1952 Test Matches provided the chief cricket topic of the summer. Who will forget the scoreboard at Leeds showing four wickets lost by India and not a run scored? Who could forget his bowling in the Third Test at Manchester where India were put out for 58 and Trueman took eight wickets for only 31 runs? Some of the India batsmen visibly retreated before his onslaught... Trueman's speed, length and direction were beautifully controlled. It was a spell of bowling only to be compared with Larwood at his very best... England certainly possess the best fast bowling prospect in years... above all this forthright, outspoken young man has the determination to succeed."

When 50 runs per 100 balls was fast

From Notes by the Editor (Norman Preston): "Essex won a special award last season for finishing top of the *News Chronicle* 'Brighter Cricket Table'. This table showed that Essex scored 50.44 runs per 100 balls received, as against 49.96 by Surrey, the County Champions, placed second... T. C. Dodds, one of the most enterprising opening batsmen in present-day English cricket, did a lot towards the gaining of this special distinction, for he hit close upon 1,800 runs at an average rate of 40 an hour. It is to be hoped that the *News Chronicle* scheme, which is to be an annual affair, will provide a genuine spur to county batsmen in general."

A horrid ogre in India's path

From India in England, 1952, by Leslie Smith: "From the moment the Indians arrived there seemed to be an attitude of defensive caution in their play, and the longer the tour progressed and the failures continued, the more pronounced it became. Defeat was the horrid ogre in their path, and to ward it off they retired into a cave, pulled a massive rock over the entrance and attempted to defy all efforts to dislodge them. Against the battering rams of Trueman and Bedser when opposed to the full strength of England, this proved useless... People in India fail to understand why their side did so badly, not realising that there is a wide difference in the game of cricket as played in the two countries."

A new member for the ICC

From Meetings in 1952: "At a meeting of the Imperial Cricket Conference at Lord's on July 28 Pakistan were admitted to membership of the Conference on the proposition of India, seconded by MCC."

For excerpts from Wisden *100 years ago, see page 1199.*

THE NEW ZEALANDERS IN AUSTRALIA, 2001-02

By RICHARD BOOCK

New Zealand took great satisfaction from their execution of a plan, almost laughable in its simplicity, which nearly added another colourful chapter to Test cricket's book of surprises. In the end, the New Zealanders could not quite pull off victory over the mighty Australians, but they did come through three Tests unbeaten. No tourists had played two or more Tests in Australia without at least one defeat since Kapil Dev's Indian side in 1985-86.

The theory was hatched earlier in 2001, when the New Zealand captain, Stephen Fleming, was in England, watching the Ashes series while playing for Middlesex, and it was fine-tuned and polished until December, at Perth, where Australia were taken to the brink of one of the biggest upsets in living memory. It depended on a quaint, old-fashioned and oft-forgotten virtue – patience.

Though it caused amusement when first mooted, the strategy was later confirmed by the New Zealand coach, Denis Aberhart. Its rationale was that Australia were vulnerable in the last two days of a Test match – provided they had not already annihilated their opposition within the first three. Believing the world champions were so keen for a sprint that they had become unfamiliar with the distance race, New Zealand aimed to weather the initial onslaught and then hang on for dear life.

Many Kiwis would claim that they went within a deaf umpire of having the last laugh. The New Zealanders were probably saved by rain at Brisbane – though an over-generous declaration almost let them steal victory – and Hobart. But when they played well enough, in Perth, it all came to fruition. Lou Vincent made a famous debut, scoring one of four centuries in the first innings. True to their promise, New Zealand batted on stubbornly in their second innings, eventually setting Australia the apparently impossible challenge of scoring 440 in a minimum of 107 overs.

This was when Australia were staggering on the ropes. It was surely time for New Zealand to change to Plan B: fix bayonets, jump out of the trenches and finish them off. Another wicket or two on the last morning, and they might have done it. Instead, New Zealand continued to play the waiting game until the batsmen were reasonably settled and, worse, their strike bowler, the slow left-armer Daniel Vettori, was beginning to tire. The longer the innings progressed, the more difficult the bowlers' task became. Sustained by an unbeaten 83 from Adam Gilchrist, Australia ended at 381 for seven, with only Brett Lee and Glenn McGrath left to bat. It remained a spell-binding Test, and, if Ian Robinson had not turned down confident appeals against Steve Waugh and Jason Gillespie, the unfancied Kiwis might still have struck the jackpot.

Two debuts augured well for New Zealand's future. It seemed they had found a precious gift in Vincent, who offered refreshing confidence and unbounding energy. Shane Bond, although he claimed only three wickets in three innings, showed glimpses of pace that suggested they had finally uncovered a bowler who could give back in kind what their batsmen had been taking for years. Of the older hands, Nathan Astle was the series' leading run-scorer with 322, and Adam Parore helped him add 253 for the eighth wicket at Perth.

Australia's two great bowlers, McGrath and Shane Warne, were virtually neutralised by New Zealand's waiting game. Warne had taken 407 wickets before the series started, but captured only six for 430 in five innings, and McGrath, who started with 358, managed to add just five for 327. McGrath found that his habit of bowling just outside off stump was not tempting the batsmen as in previous seasons. Warne, on the other hand, was never allowed to settle, and his rhythm was disturbed by a barrage of sweep shots. He batted better than he bowled, and Australia had to rely on Lee and Gillespie for the bulk of their wickets.

New Zealand also worked out individual tactics for the big-name batsmen. They bowled short at the ageing Waugh twins, Steve and Mark, who were uncomfortable for most of the series and needed luck to score their half-centuries at Perth. Between them, they totalled only 218 in eight innings, and the tour started a downward spiral. Steve made a last-day declaration at Brisbane which allowed New Zealand to come within ten runs of victory, after they had narrowly avoided the follow-on. His problems were to continue when Australia returned in January for the triangular one-day series: New Zealand beat them three times out of four and manipulated the bonus-point system to squeeze them out of the final. Scapegoats were called for, and both Waughs were dropped, apparently for good, from the one-day squad.

The Waughs' decline left a hole in Australia's middle order, where only Ricky Ponting fired. But the batting still had its stars in the phenomenal left-handed openers, Justin Langer, named Man of the Series, and Matthew Hayden. Invited to bat, they set up the first two Tests with partnerships of 224 and 223, only to see rain undermine their good work. In the Third Test, Fleming finally decided to take first use of the pitch, broke their spell, and almost triumphed.

NEW ZEALAND TOURING PARTY

S. P. Fleming (Wellington) (*captain*), N. J. Astle (Canterbury), M. D. Bell (Wellington), C. L. Cairns (Canterbury), C. D. McMillan (Canterbury), C. S. Martin (Canterbury), D. J. Nash (Auckland), S. B. O'Connor (Otago), A. C. Parore (Auckland), M. H. Richardson (Auckland), M. S. Sinclair (Central Districts), G. P. Sulzberger (Central Districts), D. R. Tuffey (Northern Districts), D. L. Vettori (Northern Districts), L. Vincent (Auckland).

P. J. Wiseman (Canterbury) joined the party as cover for Vettori, and C. J. Drum (Auckland) as cover for Tuffey. S. E. Bond (Canterbury) replaced the injured Nash and O'Connor. A. R. Adams (Auckland), J. E. C. Franklin (Wellington), C. Z. Harris (Canterbury), B. B. McCullum (Otago) and S. B. Styris (Northern Districts) replaced Bell, Drum, Martin, Sinclair, Sulzberger, Tuffey and Wiseman for the one-day series on the second leg of the tour. K. D. Mills (Auckland) was selected for the one-day internationals but withdrew unfit and was replaced by Franklin.

Coach: D. J. Aberhart.   *Manager:* J. J. Crowe.

NEW ZEALAND TOUR RESULTS

Test matches – Played 3: Drawn 3.

First-class matches – Played 5: Lost 1, Drawn 4.

Loss – South Australia.

Draws – Australia (3), Queensland.

One-day internationals – Played 10: Won 4, Lost 6. *Wins* – Australia (3), South Africa. *Losses* – South Africa (5), Australia.

Other non-first-class matches – Played 6: Won 2, Lost 1, Drawn 3. *Wins* – Prime Minister's XI, Australian Country XI. *Loss* – Australia A. *Draws* – Queensland Academy of Sport (2), Australian Capital Territory President's XII.

TEST MATCH AVERAGES

AUSTRALIA – BATTING

	T	I	NO	R	HS	100s	50s	Avge	Ct/St
R. T. Ponting	3	5	2	251	157*	1	0	83.66	3
J. L. Langer	3	5	1	320	123	2	1	80.00	1
A. C. Gilchrist	3	5	1	260	118	1	1	65.00	6/1
M. L. Hayden	3	5	0	297	136	1	2	59.40	0
S. K. Warne	3	4	0	201	99	0	2	50.25	4
B. Lee	3	3	0	119	61	0	1	39.66	0

	T	I	NO	R	HS	100s	50s	Avge	Ct
M. E. Waugh	3	4	0	140	86	0	1	35.00	2
D. R. Martyn	3	4	0	94	60	0	1	23.50	1
J. N. Gillespie	3	3	2	21	20*	0	0	21.00	1
S. R. Waugh	3	4	0	78	67	0	1	19.50	3

Played in three Tests: G. D. McGrath 0* (1 ct).

BOWLING

	O	M	R	W	BB	5W/i	Avge
B. Lee	100.5	19	352	14	5-67	1	25.14
J. N. Gillespie	111.4	27	316	11	3-45	0	28.72
G. D. McGrath	117	37	327	5	2-46	0	65.40
S. K. Warne	124.2	19	430	6	3-89	0	71.66

Also bowled: D. R. Martyn 10–0–44–0; R. T. Ponting 7–3–9–0; M. E. Waugh 14–2–64–1.

NEW ZEALAND – BATTING

	T	I	NO	R	HS	100s	50s	Avge	Ct
N. J. Astle	3	5	1	322	156*	1	1	80.50	0
A. C. Parore	3	5	3	150	110	1	0	75.00	6
S. P. Fleming	3	5	0	237	105	1	2	47.40	1
C. D. McMillan	3	5	1	146	55	0	1	36.50	2
C. L. Cairns	3	5	0	174	61	0	1	34.80	0
M. H. Richardson	3	5	0	152	57	0	1	30.40	3
M. S. Sinclair	3	5	0	80	29	0	0	16.00	2
D. L. Vettori	3	4	2	18	10*	0	0	9.00	5
M. D. Bell	2	3	0	15	6	0	0	5.00	0

Played in two Tests: S. E. Bond 0, 8 (2 ct). Played in one Test: D. J. Nash 25*; L. Vincent 104, 54 (1 ct); C. S. Martin, S. B. O'Connor and D. R. Tuffey did not bat.

BOWLING

	O	M	R	W	BB	5W/i	Avge
D. L. Vettori	131.2	23	440	13	6-87	2	33.84
C. D. McMillan	34	3	178	4	3-65	0	44.50
C. L. Cairns	108	19	455	10	5-146	1	45.50
S. E. Bond	67	5	289	3	1-74	0	96.33

Also bowled: N. J. Astle 45–13–108–2; C. S. Martin 35–4–139–1; D. J. Nash 30–6–93–0; S. B. O'Connor 17.2–4–67–0; D. R. Tuffey 15–1–74–0.

Note: Matches in this section which were not first-class are signified by a dagger.

†At Allan Border Field, Brisbane, October 16, 17, 18, 19. **Drawn.** Toss: Queensland Academy of Sport. **New Zealanders 297 for eight dec.** (M. H. Richardson 40, S. P. Fleming 133 not out, C. D. McMillan 33; D. R. MacKenzie four for 52) **and 296 for six dec.** (M. S. Sinclair 57, S. P. Fleming 68, A. C. Parore 100 not out); **Queensland Academy of Sport 267 for seven dec.** (D. M. Payne 57, J. R. Hopes 75, C. A. Philipson 31) **and 114 for two** (D. M. Payne 51).

New Zealand arrived earlier than planned because of the cancellation of their Pakistan tour, and three fixtures were added to their programme. In this and the following two matches, each side fielded 12 players, of whom 11 could bat and 11 field.

†At Canberra, October 21, 22, 23. **Drawn.** Toss: Australian Capital Territory President's XII. **Australian Capital Territory President's XII 439 for six dec.** (J. K. Smith 156, M. J. Phelps 51, D. S. Hazell 56, G. M. Lambert 101, S. L. Maxwell 51 not out; S. B. O'Connor three for 89) **and 39 for no wkt; New Zealanders 340 for four dec.** (M. H. Richardson 31, M. D. Bell 107 retired hurt, M. S. Sinclair 145).

†At Allan Border Field, Brisbane, October 26, 27, 28. **Drawn.** Toss: Queensland Academy of Sport. **Queensland Academy of Sport 477 for six dec.** (J. L. Cassell 163, M. Sippel 58, L. A. Carseldine 200 not out); **New Zealanders 498 for eight** (L. Vincent 136, S. P. Fleming 47, N. J. Astle 35, C. D. McMillan 116 retired out, C. L. Cairns 119 retired out).

At Brisbane, November 1, 2, 3, 4. **Drawn.** Toss: New Zealanders. **New Zealanders 444 for nine dec.** (S. P. Fleming 69, N. J. Astle 223, C. L. Cairns 39, A. C. Parore 30, Extras 40) **and 213 for six dec.** (M. S. Sinclair 80, C. D. McMillan 43, C. L. Cairns 31 not out); **Queensland 347** (M. L. Hayden 97, J. P. Maher 47, M. L. Love 39, C. T. Perren 34, A. Symonds 48, S. G. Law 36; C. L. Cairns five for 71) **and 202 for four** (J. P. Maher 62, M. L. Love 42, C. T. Perren 47 not out, A. Symonds 47).

Astle's 223, his first double-hundred, lasted 424 minutes and 380 balls, with 27 fours and two sixes.

AUSTRALIA v NEW ZEALAND

First Test Match

At Brisbane, November 8, 9, 10, 11, 12. Drawn. Toss: New Zealand.

A cluster of declarations transformed the First Test from a weather-doomed grind into a hair-raising cliffhanger as New Zealand charged towards their target. An explosive innings from Cairns almost carried them to an astonishing victory; had he not been snared flush on the long-on boundary, with ten balls remaining and 20 needed, there would have been dancing in the streets of Auckland.

The draw – it was Australia's first since October 1999, and ended a record run of 20 wins and three losses – appeared likely after rain allowed only 98 overs' play during the middle three days. But a remarkably generous declaration from Steve Waugh raised eyebrows and presented New Zealand with their opportunity. Opening their second innings with Gilchrist instead of Langer, Australia rattled up 84 in 14 overs before Waugh set a gettable target of 284 from 57.

Richardson gave New Zealand a brisk start, and Fleming put on 100 in 19 overs with Astle, who boosted his aggregate at the Gabba in the space of 12 days to 347 for three times out. But it was Cairns who scared the pants off the Australians with a whirlwind 43 in 38 balls, including two mighty sixes off Warne which sailed into the top tier of the members' stand. He and McMillan added 51 in 39 balls, and New Zealand's gallant chase ended only ten short. That they came so close to winning was a hot topic in Australia. Many believed Waugh had unnecessarily risked losing the series opener without giving his side much chance of victory.

After all, Australia had dominated from the outset. Hayden and Langer had set the scene with first-day centuries. Their partnership of 224 was not only a first-wicket record in Australia–New Zealand Tests, it was also the highest opening stand by two left-handers in any Test. The pair had opened together in only one previous Test, at The Oval in August, when they put on 158. Hayden was in sublime touch here. While Langer crawled to nine, he raced to 50 in 54 balls with three successive fours off O'Connor, then struck his next ball, Vettori's first of the game, for six. He took a mere 138 balls to raise his first Test century on his home ground, and had muscled his way to 136 when Cairns finally broke through after tea. Langer lived up to his reputation for luck – he survived a huge Cairns shout for lbw in the very first over – and scratched his way through the opening session, but gradually became more assertive. He got no support from the middle order, however, as six wickets went down for 39 before the close.

Relief was only temporary for New Zealand, who were back in leather-chasing mode between showers on the second and third days. Gilchrist and Lee added 135 for the eighth wicket, another record between these sides, and Gilchrist went on to his fourth Test century before enabling Cairns to mark his 50th Test with five wickets.

Gillespie reduced New Zealand's reply to 51 for three, then Lee proceeded to dismantle the rest with a fiery spell of pace, taking five for 67, including Parore courtesy of Steve Waugh's 100th Test catch. Still, New Zealand crept past the follow-on mark just before lunch on the last day – thanks largely to Nash's final contribution before he left the tour with an abdominal strain. With only O'Connor, also injured, to come, Fleming declared immediately. It very nearly paid off.

Man of the Match: B. Lee.   *Attendance:* 36,752.

Close of play: First day, Australia 294-6 (Gilchrist 13, Warne 18); Second day, Australia 435-7 (Gilchrist 88, Lee 60); Third day, New Zealand 29-0 (Richardson 10, Bell 6); Fourth day, New Zealand 186-5 (Astle 51, Cairns 25).

Australia

J. L. Langer c Vettori b McMillan	104	– (4) not out	18
M. L. Hayden c Richardson b Cairns	136	– run out	13
R. T. Ponting c Vettori b Cairns	5	– not out	32
M. E. Waugh lbw b Astle	0		
*S. R. Waugh c Parore b McMillan	3		
D. R. Martyn c Vettori b McMillan	4		
†A. C. Gilchrist c sub (L. Vincent) b Cairns	118	– (1) b Cairns	20
S. K. Warne c Sinclair b Cairns	22		
B. Lee c Parore b Cairns	61		
J. N. Gillespie not out	20		
L-b 4, w 1, n-b 8	13	N-b 1	1

1/224 (2) 2/233 (3) 3/235 (4) (9 wkts dec.) 486 1/30 (1) 2/39 (2) (2 wkts dec.) 84
4/256 (5) 5/260 (6) 6/263 (1)
7/302 (8) 8/437 (9) 9/486 (7)

G. D. McGrath did not bat.

Bowling: *First Innings*—Cairns 37–8–146–5; Nash 30–6–93–0; O'Connor 17.2–4–67–0; Vettori 13.4–0–65–0; Astle 19–7–46–1; McMillan 14–1–65–3. *Second Innings*—Cairns 5–1–29–1; McMillan 7–0–47–0; Vettori 2–0–8–0.

New Zealand

M. H. Richardson lbw b Gillespie	26	– lbw b Warne	57
M. D. Bell c Ponting b Gillespie	6	– lbw b McGrath	5
M. S. Sinclair c Ponting b Lee	3	– st Gilchrist b Warne	23
*S. P. Fleming c Gilchrist b Gillespie	0	– run out	57
N. J. Astle c Gilchrist b Lee	66	– c Gillespie b Warne	49
C. D. McMillan c Warne b Lee	45	– (7) not out	23
C. L. Cairns c S. R. Waugh b Lee	61	– (6) c Ponting b Lee	43
†A. C. Parore c S. R. Waugh b Lee	11	– not out	3
D. J. Nash not out	25		
D. L. Vettori not out	3		
L-b 15, n-b 26	41	B 1, l-b 9, w 1, n-b 3	14

1/36 (2) 2/51 (1) 3/51 (4) (8 wkts dec.) 287 1/33 (2) 2/89 (1) (6 wkts) 274
4/55 (3) 5/147 (6) 6/242 (5) 3/90 (3) 4/190 (5)
7/243 (7) 8/271 (8) 5/213 (4) 6/264 (6)

S. B. O'Connor did not bat.

Bowling: *First Innings*—McGrath 26–6–80–0; Gillespie 18.4–6–56–3; Lee 23–6–67–5; Warne 18–2–61–0; Ponting 3–0–8–0. *Second Innings*—Lee 10–0–53–1; Gillespie 8–0–48–0; McGrath 20–4–66–1; Warne 18–2–89–3; M. E. Waugh 1–0–8–0.

Umpires: S. A. Bucknor (West Indies) and D. J. Harper.
Third umpire: P. D. Parker. Referee: J. L. Hendriks (West Indies).

At Adelaide, November 16, 17, 18, 19. **South Australia won by 17 runs.** Toss: South Australia. **South Australia 297 for nine dec.** (D. A. Fitzgerald 50, G. S. Blewett 106, B. E. Young 37, G. A. Manou 34; D. R. Tuffey three for 71, D. L. Vettori three for 60) **and 212** (G. S. Blewett 61, D. S. Lehmann 51; D. L. Vettori six for 80); **New Zealanders 314** (C. D. McMillan 51, L. Vincent 74, A. C. Parore 48, G. P. Sulzberger 35, D. R. Tuffey 56; P. E. McIntyre three for 101) **and 178** (C. D. McMillan 32, G. P. Sulzberger 41; P. E. McIntyre six for 75).

AUSTRALIA v NEW ZEALAND

Second Test Match

At Hobart, November 22, 23, 24, 25, 26. Drawn. Toss: New Zealand. Test debut: S. E. Bond.

A hopeful dawn soon became a calamitous morning for New Zealand as their bowling was demolished again by Langer and Hayden. The last time Fleming had invited them to bat, they had piled on 224; this time it was 223, their third consecutive century partnership. Australia, no longer settling for a mere 300 in a day, marched through to a commanding 411 for six at stumps – and it could have been even worse for the Kiwis. Vettori, who had taken nine wickets against South Australia, indicated a return to his best form. A touch of magic, as his left-arm spin obtained just enough purchase to make his arm-ball effective, dragged New Zealand back from hopelessness, claiming the scalps of Hayden and Mark Waugh just before tea, then Martyn and Gilchrist afterwards.

If it had not been for the Derwent River winding quietly past the Bellerive Oval, it could have been a replay of the opening day at the Gabba, when New Zealand were totally outplayed in the morning but fought back doggedly against the middle order. Again, the weather deteriorated, neutralising Australia's outstanding start and leading to another draw. And again, Langer had an early escape – dropped by Bell, at backward point, off Tuffey's first ball.

This time, Langer outshone Hayden. He virtually annihilated the pace attack, stroking his way to 50 off 48 balls, while Hayden, deprived of the strike, managed only a single. He brought up his tenth Test century in 123 balls, and his third in three Tests. The last Australian to achieve this had been David Boon, in England in 1993. Hayden narrowly missed his own hundred, but completed 1,000 Test runs in 2001 when 60.

Australia's 411 was thought to be their most in a day since England conceded 475 at The Oval in 1934. Next day, they added 147 in the 34 overs permitted by the weather, declaring on 558 for eight, their second-highest total against New Zealand. Ponting required only eight deliveries to convert his overnight 92 into his ninth Test century, the first in his native Tasmania. Like Langer, he hit 20 fours, but Ponting also hooked a six off the debutant, Shane Bond. Warne seemed to be heading for a maiden first-class hundred, handling the strike bowlers comfortably as he added 145 with Ponting, before being undone in the first over of Astle's part-time seam.

Bad light prevented New Zealand from starting their reply on the second evening. Just 35 overs were possible on the third day as they moved cautiously to 71 for two; only 51 were squeezed in on the fourth and 20 on the last. When rain interrupted again before lunch, a merciful end was called to proceedings. Having paid for inserting Australia twice, Fleming had helped to ensure his team's safety by stroking 71. He put on 97 with McMillan – a New Zealand fifth-wicket record against Australia – before shouldering arms to McGrath's first ball of the fifth morning. McMillan did the same to Gillespie, but just before midday the skies opened once more and New Zealand were off the hook. Over the last three days, the third umpire, John Smeaton, stood with Steve Bucknor, after Steve Davis injured his knee.

Man of the Match: R. T. Ponting.   *Attendance:* 16,471.

Close of play: First day, Australia 411-6 (Ponting 92, Warne 31); Second day, Australia 558-8 dec.; Third day, New Zealand 71-2 (Richardson 25, Fleming 16); Fourth day, New Zealand 197-4 (Fleming 71, McMillan 51).

Australia

J. L. Langer c Vettori b Cairns	123	B. Lee c McMillan b Vettori	41
M. L. Hayden c Bond b Vettori	91		
R. T. Ponting not out	157	B 3, l-b 5, w 2, n-b 15	25
M. E. Waugh b Vettori	12		
*S. R. Waugh lbw b Bond	0	1/223 (1) 2/238 (2) (8 wkts. dec.) 558	
D. R. Martyn lbw b Vettori	0	3/253 (4) 4/266 (5)	
†A. C. Gilchrist b Vettori	39	5/267 (6) 6/336 (7)	
S. K. Warne b Astle	70	7/481 (8) 8/558 (9)	

J. N. Gillespie and G. D. McGrath did not bat.

Bowling: Cairns 28–3–122–1; Tuffey 15–1–74–0; Bond 28–0–135–1; Vettori 36–5–138–5; McMillan 8–0–51–0; Astle 9–0–30–1.

New Zealand

M. H. Richardson lbw b Gillespie	. . . .	30	†A. C. Parore not out	10
M. D. Bell c Gilchrist b Warne	. . . .	4	D. L. Vettori not out	10
M. S. Sinclair b Gillespie	. . . .	23	L-b 1, n-b 8	9
*S. P. Fleming lbw b McGrath	. . . .	71		
N. J. Astle c Warne b M. E. Waugh	. . . .	11	1/11 (2) 2/53 (3) 3/76 (1) (7 wkts) 243	
C. D. McMillan b Gillespie	. . . .	55	4/100 (5) 5/197 (4)	
C. L. Cairns c Gilchrist b McGrath	. . . .	20	6/219 (6) 7/223 (7)	

D. R. Tuffey and S. E. Bond did not bat.

Bowling: McGrath 27–12–46–2; Gillespie 28–14–45–3; Warne 24.2–3–70–1; Lee 19–5–51–0; M. E. Waugh 7–1–30–1.

Umpires: S. A. Bucknor (West Indies) and S. J. Davis.
J. H. Smeaton deputised for Davis, who had a knee injury, after the 2nd day.
Third umpire: J. H. Smeaton. B. W. Jackman deputised after the 2nd day.
Referee: J. L. Hendriks (West Indies).

AUSTRALIA v NEW ZEALAND

Third Test Match

At Perth, November 30, December 1, 2, 3, 4. Drawn. Toss: New Zealand. Test debut: L. Vincent.
New Zealand almost snatched an outrageous series victory after challenging their hosts to score the highest fourth-innings total to win a Test. Even more outrageously, Australia came close to doing it, but the series finally ended in its third draw.

Fleming called correctly again and, this time, chose to bat, whereupon Lou Vincent, rushed into the side at the expense of the struggling Bell, made a fairytale debut. Asked to open the batting on the world's bounciest pitch against the best pace attack, Vincent set the tone for his country's bold showing with 104 in the first innings and a run-a-ball 54 in the second. He was the sixth New Zealander to score a century on Test debut and, remarkably, only the fourth touring player to achieve the feat in Australia. The last had been the Nawab of Pataudi senior in the First Test of the Bodyline series in 1932-33, following in the steps of R. E. Foster in 1903-04 and George Gunn in 1907-08; all three were representing England, at Sydney.

Vincent added 199 with Fleming, who scored his first Test hundred for three and a half years, and only his third, to go with 34 fifties. But the partnership which really had Australia rattled came from Astle and Parore. Both made Test-best scores as they put on 253, the second-highest eighth-wicket stand in Test history, after 313 by Wasim Akram and Saqlain Mushtaq against Zimbabwe in 1996-97. It was more than a hundred better than New Zealand's previous eighth-wicket record, and beat their all-wicket best against Australia. It was the first time four New Zealanders had scored centuries in the same Test innings – curiously, no one finished in double figures – and Australia had conceded four only once before, to England at Nottingham in 1938.

Fleming declared on the second evening at 534 for nine, New Zealand's second-biggest total against their neighbours, and seemed likely to make them follow on when they were 192 for six. Australia avoided that thanks mainly to Warne's highest first-class innings: 99 out of 159 added for the remaining four wickets. New Zealand were well served by Chris Martin, who had replaced his fellow-seamer, Tuffey, but the attack was brilliantly led by Vettori, who claimed the prize wickets of the Waughs, sent back the dangerous Gilchrist, outwitted Lee and Gillespie, and deprived Warne of a century. Earlier, Langer's run of hundreds in successive Tests ended when he walked on 75 – only to look up and see the replay screen, which suggested a no-ball.

When Fleming declared on the fourth evening – just after Lee had seen off Bond with abusive language that earned a 75 per cent fine – he set Australia the uphill task of scoring a record 440 in a minimum of 107 overs. It seemed even steeper when they lost Langer and Ponting by the close. In fact, they finished only 59 short with three wickets left, and Gilchrist unbeaten on 83. The Australian batsmen took full advantage of a safety-first approach from Fleming; half-centuries from the Waughs even gave them an outside chance of winning.

On Test debut, facing the sharpest of attacks and on the fastest of pitches, Lou Vincent made the WACA his own with a hundred and then a fifty. *Picture by Andrew Cornaga.*

It might have been a different story had umpire Robinson agreed that Steve Waugh, then 13, had been caught behind off Vettori midway through the last afternoon. That would have reduced Australia to 203 for five. New Zealand's frustration grew when Robinson refused to accept that Gillespie had gloved a ball from Cairns down the leg side to Parore, which would have been 366 for eight, with seven overs to go. It could have been Australia's first home defeat for three years. Instead, the series ended in stalemate, but the draw had provided five thrilling days of Test cricket.

Man of the Match: D. L. Vettori.   *Attendance:* 41,853.

Man of the Series: J. L. Langer.

Close of play: First day, New Zealand 293-7 (Astle 28, Parore 5); Second day, Australia 75-2 (Langer 34, M. E. Waugh 5); Third day, Australia 351; Fourth day, Australia 69-2 (Hayden 31, M. E. Waugh 8).

New Zealand

M. H. Richardson b Gillespie	9	– run out	30
L. Vincent c M. E. Waugh b Warne	104	– c M. E. Waugh b Lee	54
M. S. Sinclair lbw b McGrath	2	– c Gilchrist b McGrath	29
*S. P. Fleming lbw b Lee	105	– (5) b Warne	4
N. J. Astle not out	156	– (6) c Langer b Gillespie	40
C. D. McMillan lbw b Gillespie	4	– (7) c Warne b Gillespie	19
D. L. Vettori c Martyn b Gillespie	2	– (9) c S. R. Waugh b Lee	3
C. L. Cairns c Gilchrist b Lee	8	– (4) c Warne b Lee	42
†A. C. Parore c McGrath b Lee	110	– (8) not out	16
S. E. Bond b Lee	0	– b Lee	8
B 4, l-b 15, w 2, n-b 13	34	B 1, l-b 6, n-b 4	11

1/12 (1) 2/19 (3) 3/218 (2)   (9 wkts dec.) 534
4/264 (4) 5/269 (6) 6/272 (7)
7/281 (8) 8/534 (9) 9/534 (10)

1/77 (2) 2/90 (1)   (9 wkts dec.) 256
3/128 (3) 4/151 (5)
5/199 (4) 6/208 (6)
7/241 (7) 8/246 (9) 9/256 (10)

C. S. Martin did not bat.

Bowling: *First Innings*—McGrath 27–11–72–1; Gillespie 40–7–112–3; Lee 32.5–5–125–4; Warne 43–9–135–1; Martyn 10–0–44–0; M. E. Waugh 6–1–26–0; Ponting 4–3–1–0. *Second Innings*—McGrath 17–4–63–1; Gillespie 17–0–55–2; Lee 16–3–56–4; Warne 21–3–75–1.

Australia

J. L. Langer c Parore b Cairns	75	–	c Vettori b Bond	0
M. L. Hayden c Vincent b Bond	0	–	c Sinclair b Vettori	57
R. T. Ponting c Parore b Martin	31	–	b Cairns	26
M. E. Waugh c Bond b Vettori	42	–	b McMillan	86
*S. R. Waugh c Parore b Vettori	8	–	run out	67
D. R. Martyn c Fleming b Cairns	60	–	b Vettori	30
†A. C. Gilchrist c Richardson b Vettori	0	–	not out	83
S. K. Warne c Richardson b Vettori	99	–	run out	10
B. Lee c McMillan b Vettori	17			
J. N. Gillespie c Parore b Vettori	0	–	(9) not out	1
G. D. McGrath not out	0			
L-b 2, w 1, n-b 16	19		L-b 3, w 2, n-b 16	21

1/3 (2) 2/61 (3) 3/122 (4) 4/137 (5)   **351**   1/1 (1) 2/52 (3)   (7 wkts) **381**
5/191 (1) 6/192 (7) 7/270 (6)   3/130 (2) 4/195 (4)
8/342 (9) 9/346 (10) 10/351 (8)   5/244 (6) 6/339 (5) 7/355 (8)

Bowling: *First Innings*—Cairns 23–5–86–2; Bond 18–2–74–1; Martin 23–4–88–1; Vettori 34.4–7–87–6; Astle 5–1–14–0. *Second Innings*—Bond 21–3–80–1; Martin 12–0–51–0; Vettori 45–11–142–2; Cairns 15–2–52–0; Astle 12–5–18–0; McMillan 5–2–15–1.

Umpires: I. D. Robinson (Zimbabwe) and D. B. Hair.
Third umpire: D. J. Harper.   Referee: J. L. Hendriks (West Indies).

---

†At Canberra, December 6. **New Zealanders won by four wickets. Toss:** Prime Minister's XI. **Prime Minister's XI 217 for seven** (50 overs) (B. J. Haddin 35, G. S. Blewett 41, J. K. Smith 48 not out; C. J. Drum five for 34); **New Zealanders 222 for six** (48 overs) (M. H. Richardson 40, C. L. Cairns 35, N. J. Astle 85 not out).

---

†At Brisbane, January 8 (day/night). **Australia A won by 60 runs. Toss:** New Zealanders. **Australia A 282 for five** (50 overs) (J. P. Maher 42, R. J. Campbell 46, G. S. Blewett 42, S. M. Katich 47, D. S. Lehmann 50); **New Zealanders 222** (45.3 overs) (C. D. McMillan 67, C. L. Cairns 32; S. R. Clark three for 45, S. C. G. MacGill three for 71).

New Zealand's matches against Australia and South Africa in the VB Series (January 11–February 8) appear on pages 1368–1380.

---

†At Bowral, January 23. **New Zealanders won by 249 runs. Toss:** New Zealanders. **New Zealanders 392 for six** (50 overs) (B. B. McCullum 96, M. H. Richardson 44, S. P. Fleming 76, D. J. Nash 72 not out, L. Vincent 49); **Australian Country XI 143** (40 overs).

THE WEST INDIANS IN SRI LANKA, 2001-02

By TONY COZIER

Sri Lanka completed their first clean sweep of a three-Test series after 20 years of trying, but for West Indies the result was dismally familiar. Three crushing defeats – twice by ten wickets, once by 131 runs – extended their overseas record since beating Australia at Perth in February 1997 to a humiliating 21 losses in 25 Tests.

Yet the lasting memory will be of the sublime batting of Brian Lara and especially his duels with the otherwise unstoppable off-spinner, Muttiah Muralitharan, which added fuel to the argument that he was less comfortable bowling to left-handers. Lara had pulled out of West Indies' tour of Zimbabwe in June, and his fitness was still in doubt barely a week before the party flew to Sri Lanka. But he said he was determined to raise his Test average, which had dropped below 48, back above 50. It was a monumental task in a short series, but he coped with Muralitharan so easily that he achieved it during the final Test, when he followed his first-innings 221 with 130, carrying his aggregate to 688 at an average of nearly 115. Before Lara, only Graham Gooch had reached 600 runs in a series of three Tests.

MOST RUNS IN A THREE-TEST SERIES

	I	NO	R	HS	100s	Avge		
G. A. Gooch	6	0	752	333	3	125.33	E v I	1990
B. C. Lara	6	0	688	221	3	114.66	**WI v SL**	**2001-02**
Zaheer Abbas	5	2	583	235*	2	194.33	P v I	1978-79
S. M. Nurse	5	0	558	258	2	111.60	WI v NZ	1968-69
Salim Malik	6	0	557	237	2	92.83	P v A	1994-95
M. L. Hayden	6	1	549	203	2	109.80	A v I	2000-01
J. C. Adams	6	3	520	174*	1	173.33	WI v I	1994-95
A. H. Jones	6	1	513	186	3	102.60	NZ v SL	1990-91
M. A. Taylor	5	1	513	334*	1	128.25	A v P	1998-99
Shoaib Mohammad .	5	2	507	203*	3	169.00	P v NZ	1990-91
Javed Miandad . . .	5	1	504	206	2	126.00	P v NZ	1976-77
V. V. S. Laxman . . .	6	0	503	281	1	83.83	I v A	2000-01

In spite of Lara's eventual mastery over him, Muralitharan posed such problems to the other batsmen with his prodigious turn, teasing flight and clever variations that he took 11 wickets in the First Test at Galle and ten in the Second at his native Kandy. But he was dramatically upstaged at Colombo by Chaminda Vaas, whose controlled, each-way left-arm swing earned him two seven-wicket hauls. Vaas finished with 26 wickets to Muralitharan's 24.

Lara shared three century partnerships with Ramnaresh Sarwan, the only other positive to emerge from West Indies' dispiriting trip. Batting at No. 3, Sarwan responded with pleasing maturity and averaged 53, despite invariably coming in after an early wicket. Apart from these two, no one managed more than captain Carl Hooper's 27.83. The rest of the batting was so brittle, and so obviously missed the experience of Shivnarine Chanderpaul (absent with a back injury), that even powerful positions – 409 for four at lunch on the second day at Galle, 327 for three after the first day at Colombo – counted for nothing. There were 18 ducks in all, and the last four wickets added, on average, just 26.50.

While Sri Lanka's bowling depended heavily on Muralitharan and Vaas, who shared 358 of the 566 overs and 50 of the 60 wickets, the batting was a real team effort. Leading the way was Hashan Tillekeratne, who was dismissed only once while amassing

Back to his best: Lara hit three hundreds and had the better of a fascinating contest with Murali.
Picture by Anuruddha Lokuhapuarachchi, Reuters/Popperfoto.

403 runs, and hit an unbeaten 204 in the last Test. The wicket-keeper, Kumar Sangakkara, was the other century-maker, with 140 at Galle, and, along with Thilan Samaraweera and Mahela Jayawardene, averaged over 60.

On true pitches with even bounce, West Indies had no bowler who remotely matched Muralitharan's exceptional spin or Vaas's swing, and were powerless to prevent the run glut. Merv Dillon led the attack manfully, but ran foul of management after the last Test. Fearing violence on the day of national elections, he refused to attend team practice ahead of the one-day series, and was sent home as a disciplinary measure. It was a further dent to team morale. Injury had ruled the fast bowler Reon King out of the series and a heart ailment sent the opener Leon Garrick home early, immediately after Wavell Hinds had returned because of a family bereavement; the leg-spinner Dinanath Ramnarine joined the injury list during the last Test. But the worst blow was still to come: in the one-day series, which found West Indies in indifferent form, Lara fractured his elbow. These were all distractions the West Indians could have done without against their strong, well-organised hosts.

WEST INDIAN TOURING PARTY

C. L. Hooper (Guyana) (*captain*), M. I. Black (Trinidad & Tobago), P. T. Collins (Barbados), M. Dillon (Trinidad & Tobago), D. Ganga (Trinidad & Tobago), L. V. Garrick (Jamaica), C. H. Gayle (Jamaica), W. W. Hinds (Jamaica), R. D. Jacobs (Leeward Islands), R. D. King (Guyana), B. C. Lara (Trinidad & Tobago), N. C. McGarrell (Guyana), D. Ramnarine (Trinidad & Tobago), M. N. Samuels (Jamaica), R. R. Sarwan (Guyana), C. E. L. Stuart (Guyana).

S. Chanderpaul (Guyana) withdrew through injury before the tour and was replaced by Hinds. J. J. C. Lawson (Jamaica) replaced King when he went home injured. Garrick also left because of illness, Hinds because of a family bereavement, Ramnarine because of injury, and Dillon for disciplinary reasons. D. Brown (Trinidad & Tobago), C. D. Collymore (Barbados), R. O. Hinds (Barbados) and R. L. Powell (Jamaica) replaced Dillon, Garrick and Stuart for the one-day LG Abans Series.

Coach: R. A. Harper. *Manager:* R. O. Skerritt. *Physiotherapist:* R. Rogers. *Statistician:* G. S. Smith.

WEST INDIAN TOUR RESULTS

Test matches – Played 3: Lost 3.
First-class matches – Played 5: Lost 3, Drawn 2.
Losses – Sri Lanka (3).
Draws – Sri Lanka A (2).
One-day internationals – Played 5: Won 2, Lost 3. *Wins* – Sri Lanka, Zimbabwe. *Losses* – Zimbabwe, Sri Lanka (2).

TEST MATCH AVERAGES
SRI LANKA – BATTING

	T	I	NO	R	HS	100s	50s	Avge	Ct/St
H. P. Tillekeratne	3	4	3	403	204*	2	1	403.00	2
T. T. Samaraweera	3	4	1	196	87	0	2	65.33	1
K. C. Sangakkara	3	4	0	255	140	1	1	63.75	9/1
D. P. M. D. Jayawardene	3	4	0	242	99	0	2	60.50	5
S. T. Jayasuriya	3	6	2	195	85	0	2	48.75	2
M. S. Atapattu	3	6	2	168	84	0	2	42.00	0
R. P. Arnold	3	4	0	103	65	0	1	25.75	3
M. R. C. N. Bandaratilleke	3	3	1	41	25	0	0	20.50	0
M. Muralitharan	3	3	1	22	14	0	0	11.00	3
W. P. U. J. C. Vaas	3	4	0	30	23	0	0	7.50	1

Played in two Tests: D. N. T. Zoysa 23, 10. Played in one Test: T. C. B. Fernando did not bat.

BOWLING

	O	M	R	W	BB	5W/i	Avge
W. P. U. J. C. Vaas	140.2	32	401	26	7-71	2	15.42
M. Muralitharan	217.4	53	536	24	6-81	3	22.33
D. N. T. Zoysa	52	12	147	4	2-34	0	36.75
M. R. C. N. Bandaratilleke .	71	18	215	4	2-29	0	53.75

Also bowled: R. P. Arnold 5–1–12–0; T. C. B. Fernando 20–2–90–0; S. T. Jayasuriya 22–4–61–0; T. T. Samaraweera 35–6–111–1; H. P. Tillekeratne 3–1–2–0.

WEST INDIES – BATTING

	T	I	NO	R	HS	100s	50s	Avge	Ct/St
B. C. Lara	3	6	0	688	221	3	1	114.66	1
R. R. Sarwan	3	6	0	318	88	0	3	53.00	0
C. L. Hooper	3	6	0	167	69	0	2	27.83	1
D. Ganga	3	6	0	104	47	0	0	17.33	1
R. D. Jacobs	3	6	1	79	31*	0	0	15.80	5/1
M. N. Samuels	3	6	0	76	54	0	1	12.66	2
C. H. Gayle	3	6	0	54	44	0	0	9.00	4
M. Dillon	3	6	0	34	19	0	0	5.66	1
P. T. Collins	2	4	0	4	4	0	0	1.00	0
C. E. L. Stuart	2	4	1	2	2	0	0	0.66	2
D. Ramnarine	3	6	2	0	0*	0	0	0.00	3

Played in one Test: M. I. Black 0*, 0; N. C. McGarrell 4, 10* (1 ct).

BOWLING

	O	M	R	W	BB	5W/i	Avge
D. Ramnarine	116	23	356	10	4-66	0	35.60
M. Dillon	139	26	379	9	3-55	0	42.11
P. T. Collins	87.3	11	301	7	4-78	0	43.00

Also bowled: M. I. Black 32–6–123–1; C. H. Gayle 10.3–1–32–0; C. L. Hooper 101–20–231–2; N. C. McGarrell 31–3–95–0; M. N. Samuels 4–0–23–0; R. R. Sarwan 2–0–7–0; C. E. L. Stuart 46.3–8–167–2.

At Nondescripts Cricket Club, Colombo, November 3, 4, 5. **Drawn.** Toss: Sri Lanka A. **West Indians 334 for seven** (C. H. Gayle 41, B. C. Lara 43, C. L. Hooper 117, M. N. Samuels 54, N. C. McGarrell 34 not out; K. R. Pushpakumara four for 85) **v Sri Lanka A.**
Play was possible only on the opening day.

At Matara, November 8, 9, 10. **Drawn**. Toss: Sri Lanka A. **Sri Lanka A 269** (G. I. Daniel 62, H. P. Tillekeratne 86; D. Ramnarine four for 54); **West Indians 241 for two** (D. Ganga 54, C. H. Gayle 120 retired out, R. R. Sarwan 39 not out).

SRI LANKA v WEST INDIES

First Test Match

At Galle, November 13, 14, 15, 16, 17. Sri Lanka won by ten wickets. Toss: West Indies. Test debut: T. C. B. Fernando.

Had it not involved a fallible West Indies team and Muttiah Muralitharan, near-infallible at the Galle International Stadium, the circumstances of Sri Lanka's victory might have been a case study for Lord Condon's Anti-Corruption Unit.

At lunch on the second day, West Indies were 409 for four, with Lara motoring on 167; by tea on the fifth, their last man, Stuart, was sending a gentle catch to mid-off to give Muralitharan his fifth wicket of the innings and 11th of the match. Sixteen West Indian wickets had fallen for 169, and Sri Lanka required only three runs for a first victory in their four Tests against them.

The result surprised no one. West Indies had developed an uncanny record of turning domination into defeat, while Galle, overlooked by its 17th-century Dutch fort, had become something of a cricket fortress for Sri Lanka, with Muralitharan its commander. He had taken 39 wickets in his last four Tests there, all resulting in emphatic home wins.

On the opening day, Muralitharan had toiled 40 overs in the sweltering heat for a solitary wicket. But he turned the game dramatically on the second afternoon. In a spell of 6.4 overs, he claimed four for nine, starting with Lara, to trigger a collapse in which the last six wickets tumbled for 25. It was a psychological setback from which West Indies never recovered.

Lara had swiftly taken charge when he arrived at the crease, shortly after lunch on the opening day. He first used the sweep to counter Muralitharan, forcing him to alter his line, before reverting to a more perpendicular bat. Sarwan, batting at No. 3 for only the second time in Tests, lost little by comparison in a stand of 145. But after playing impeccably for four and a half hours, he once more fell frustratingly short of a maiden hundred, diverting a cut off Muralitharan into his stumps. Lara kept going to reach his 16th Test hundred, but his first since scoring 182 at Adelaide 11 months earlier.

By now, his partner was the captain, Hooper, and next day they extended their fourth-wicket stand to 153, as West Indies built what looked like an invincible total. The first crack came when Muralitharan's juggled return catch got rid of Hooper 25 minutes before lunch. But it was his dismissal of Lara, who gloved a sweep and was well held by Sangakkara, diving forward from behind the stumps, that set off West Indies' rapid collapse. Lara had made a monumental 178, but the next time he batted, he was trying to stave off an innings defeat.

Sri Lanka's confident batsmen quickly put the pitch and an inexperienced attack, limited to two fast bowlers, into proper perspective. Sangakkara shared successive stands of 109 with Atapattu and 162 with the bubbly Jayawardene, who was run out by Samuels's direct hit from mid-wicket, one short of his fourth hundred in four Tests. His ebullient innings lit up the third day, shortened to 75 overs by fading light, and the rate slackened after his departure. After almost nine hours of patient accumulation, Sangakkara was also run out; he offered difficult chances on 72 and 126.

Sri Lanka were still 53 behind, but Tillekeratne, intent on re-establishing what had become a tenuous position in the team, and Samaraweera slowly and remorselessly pushed past West Indies in a 154-run partnership that included only two fours. Jayasuriya waited until Tillekeratne had completed his eighth Test hundred, which took nearly six and a half hours, before declaring, 142 ahead.

Ganga and Sarwan raised West Indian hopes of holding out for a draw when they reduced that by almost half. But when they were dismissed within seven balls on the last morning, only Lara, who the previous evening had announced he would make 150 and save the game, delayed Sri Lanka for long. Muralitharan completed his 30th haul of five or more wickets in a Test innings, and Jayasuriya did the rest.

Man of the Match: M. Muralitharan.

Close of play: First day, West Indies 316-3 (Lara 117, Hooper 34); Second day, Sri Lanka 103-1 (Atapattu 45, Sangakkara 27); Third day, Sri Lanka 343-3 (Sangakkara 126, Arnold 18); Fourth day, West Indies 9-1 (Ganga 3, Sarwan 5).

West Indies

D. Ganga c Jayawardene b Vaas	47	– c Tillekeratne b Bandaratilleke	33
C. H. Gayle c Sangakkara b Vaas	9	– c Muralitharan b Vaas	1
R. R. Sarwan b Muralitharan	88	– c Arnold b Muralitharan	30
B. C. Lara c Sangakkara b Muralitharan	178	– c Muralitharan b Samaraweera	40
*C. L. Hooper c and b Muralitharan	69	– c Jayasuriya b Bandaratilleke	6
M. N. Samuels b Muralitharan	16	– lbw b Muralitharan	2
†R. D. Jacobs c Sangakkara b Vaas	8	– lbw b Muralitharan	9
N. C. McGarrell c Arnold b Muralitharan	4	– not out	10
M. Dillon c Jayasuriya b Vaas	5	– lbw b Muralitharan	0
D. Ramnarine not out	0	– b Vaas	0
C. E. L. Stuart b Muralitharan	0	– c Vaas b Samaraweera	2
B 8, l-b 6, n-b 5, p 5	24	B 2, l-b 2, n-b 7	11

1/15 (2) 2/95 (1) 3/240 (3) 4/393 (5)   448   1/3 (2) 2/70 (1) 3/70 (3)   144
5/423 (4) 6/434 (6) 7/440 (7)   4/83 (5) 5/93 (6) 6/131 (4)
8/448 (9) 9/448 (8) 10/448 (11)   7/135 (7) 8/138 (9)
                                            9/139 (10) 10/144 (11)

Bowling: *First Innings*—Vaas 31–6–95–4; Fernando 18–2–80–0; Muralitharan 53.4–11–126–6; Bandaratilleke 22–3–76–0; Jayasuriya 9–2–24–0; Samaraweera 6–0–24–0; Arnold 2–1–4–0. *Second Innings*—Vaas 17–8–20–2; Bandaratilleke 19–6–46–2; Muralitharan 31.3–10–44–5; Fernando 2–0–10–0; Jayasuriya 5–0–13–0; Samaraweera 4–1–7–1.

Sri Lanka

M. S. Atapattu c Lara b Ramnarine	61	– (2) not out	0
*S. T. Jayasuriya c McGarrell b Dillon	25	– (1) not out	6
†K. C. Sangakkara run out	140		
D. P. M. D. Jayawardene run out	99		
R. P. Arnold lbw b Ramnarine	33		
H. P. Tillekeratne not out	105		
T. T. Samaraweera c Jacobs b Stuart	77		
W. P. U. J. C. Vaas c Samuels b Dillon	7		
M. R. C. N. Bandaratilleke c Jacobs b Ramnarine	4		
M. Muralitharan lbw b Stuart	14		
B 1, l-b 13, w 4, n-b 7	25		

1/37 (2) 2/146 (1) 3/308 (4)   (9 wkts dec.) 590   (no wkt) 6
4/358 (5) 5/395 (3) 6/549 (7)
7/562 (8) 8/567 (9) 9/590 (10)

T. C. B. Fernando did not bat.

Bowling: *First Innings*—Dillon 51–11–121–2; Stuart 37.4–7–138–2; McGarrell 31–3–95–0; Ramnarine 58–12–158–3; Hooper 24–3–59–0; Samuels 1–0–5–0. *Second Innings*—Stuart 0.4–0–6–0.

Umpires: J. H. Hampshire (England) and P. T. Manuel.
Third umpire: T. H. Wijewardene. Referee: R. Subba Row (England).

SRI LANKA v WEST INDIES

Second Test Match

At Kandy, November 21, 22, 23, 24, 25. Sri Lanka won by 131 runs. Toss: Sri Lanka.

West Indies came agonisingly close to saving the match before Muralitharan hurried out the last four wickets for four runs in 21 balls to secure the series for Sri Lanka. It had been another one-sided affair, despite the loss of 130 overs to rain. Yet luck did not go West Indies' way. They had reinforced the pace attack by introducing Collins, but were soon down to two fast men again when Stuart bowled two beamers in the fifth over and was banned for the rest of the innings. And on the final day there were realistic hopes of a draw when they went into tea with six wickets standing. But Lara, who had batted for two and a quarter hours, was given out second ball on resumption, caught at short leg off a shot he clearly played into the ground. He lingered for a moment in disbelief before trudging off – and, as it turned out, taking West Indies' hopes with him.

The match had a bizarre start, when its fifth over was completed by three bowlers. Dillon had trapped Atapattu in his first over, but then, feeling unwell, left the field after two balls of his third. Stuart was asked to finish the over but sent down two unintentional head-high full tosses in three balls to Jayasuriya. Under ICC regulations, umpire Hampshire had no alternative but to direct the captain to remove him for the rest of the innings, the first instance of its kind in Test cricket. Gayle then bowled the last three balls of the over.

Even so, West Indies' surviving bowlers prospered during the next hour, reducing Sri Lanka to 53 for four on a pitch that offered encouragement. But the attack's shortcomings were exposed by a stand of 116 between Jayawardene and Tillekeratne, who put on a further 80 with Samaraweera before he was bowled; it was Tillekeratne's first dismissal in 975 minutes spread over four Tests. Rain prolonged Sri Lanka's innings into the third day, when they were finally out for 288.

Zoysa made up for eight months out of Test cricket by claiming a wicket with his first ball before the weather closed in again. But on the fourth day, West Indies were an encouraging 126 for three, with Lara and Hooper together. Then Muralitharan set in train the customary breakdown, removing Hooper and Samuels at the same score. Vaas, who had recently learned the art of reverse-swinging the old ball, joined in, taking the next four wickets in five overs, before Lara was last out, lbw to Muralitharan. Six West Indians failed to score.

Atapattu confidently set about building on a lead of 97, adding 89 with Jayasuriya and 87 with Sangakkara. Sri Lanka batted on for 20 overs on the final morning, running up another 96, before Jayasuriya's declaration set West Indies an improbable 322 to win.

Sarwan and Lara fought stoutly for most of the afternoon, and even Lara's untimely removal immediately after tea did not sink them: Samuels and Dillon spent an hour adding 59 for the seventh wicket, and appeared likely to deny Sri Lanka, who were unable to bowl Vaas because of the darkening skies. Then Muralitharan changed ends, and soon afterwards made the breakthrough. But there were only 16 minutes to spare when his off-break rolled back from Stuart's defensive stroke to dislodge a bail. That gave Muralitharan ten wickets in a Test for the ninth time, equalling Richard Hadlee's record, and the fourth Test in succession, breaking Clarrie Grimmett's record of three consecutive Tests against South Africa in 1935-36.

Man of the Match: M. Muralitharan.

Close of play: First day, Sri Lanka 193-5 (Tillekeratne 60, Samaraweera 4); Second day, Sri Lanka 273-8 (Bandaratilleke 9, Zoysa 15); Third day, West Indies 39-1 (Gayle 25, Sarwan 12); Fourth day, Sri Lanka 128-1 (Atapattu 58, Sangakkara 10).

Sri Lanka

M. S. Atapattu lbw b Dillon	0	– st Jacobs b Ramnarine	84
*S. T. Jayasuriya c Gayle b Collins	16	– c Gayle b Ramnarine	55
†K. C. Sangakkara b Ramnarine	15	– c Ramnarine b Dillon	45
D. P. M. D. Jayawardene c and b Ramnarine	88	– c Stuart b Dillon	16
R. P. Arnold b Ramnarine	4	– c Dillon b Ramnarine	1
H. P. Tillekeratne b Collins	87	– not out	7
T. T. Samaraweera c Jacobs b Dillon	29	– (8) not out	3
W. P. U. J. C. Vaas c Hooper b Collins	0	– (7) c Ganga b Ramnarine	0
M. R. C. N. Bandaratilleke not out	12		
D. N. T. Zoysa b Collins	23		
M. Muralitharan c Stuart b Dillon	4		
L-b 6, n-b 4	10	B 3, l-b 6, w 2, n-b 2	13

1/1 (1) 2/27 (2) 3/49 (3) 4/53 (5)   288   1/89 (2) 2/176 (3)   (6 wkts dec.) 224
5/169 (4) 6/249 (6) 7/249 (7)   3/204 (4) 4/206 (5)
8/249 (8) 9/281 (10) 10/288 (11)   5/215 (1) 6/215 (7)

Bowling: *First Innings*—Dillon 20–4–55–3; Collins 27–7–78–4; Stuart 0.1–0–2–0; Gayle 0.3–0–4–0; Hooper 21–6–44–0; Ramnarine 25–6–81–3; Samuels 3–0–18–0. *Second Innings*—Dillon 19–2–60–2; Collins 11–0–52–0; Ramnarine 16–2–66–4; Stuart 8–1–21–0; Hooper 13–4–16–0.

West Indies

C. H. Gayle b Zoysa	44	– (2) c Sangakkara b Vaas	0
D. Ganga c Jayawardene b Zoysa	0	– (1) b Muralitharan	8
R. R. Sarwan b Muralitharan	17	– c Arnold b Muralitharan	48
B. C. Lara lbw b Muralitharan	74	– c Tillekeratne b Bandaratilleke	45
*C. L. Hooper lbw b Muralitharan	23	– lbw b Bandaratilleke	4
M. N. Samuels c Sangakkara b Muralitharan	0	– lbw b Muralitharan	54
†R. D. Jacobs b Vaas	24	– c Sangakkara b Vaas	5
M. Dillon c Sangakkara b Vaas	0	– b Muralitharan	19
D. Ramnarine lbw b Vaas	0	– not out	0
P. T. Collins lbw b Vaas	0	– b Muralitharan	0
C. E. L. Stuart not out	0	– b Muralitharan	0
L-b 5, n-b 4	9	B 3, l-b 2, n-b 2	7

1/8 (2) 2/51 (3) 3/72 (1) 4/126 (5)   191
5/126 (6) 6/167 (7) 7/173 (8)
8/173 (9) 9/181 (10) 10/191 (4)

1/3 (2) 2/25 (1) 3/83 (3)   190
4/107 (5) 5/110 (4) 6/126 (7)
7/185 (8) 8/190 (6)
9/190 (10) 10/190 (11)

Bowling: *First Innings*—Vaas 22–8–56–4; Zoysa 13–3–34–2; Muralitharan 23.4–5–54–4; Bandaratilleke 4–0–25–0; Samaraweera 4–1–17–0. *Second Innings*—Vaas 13–2–39–2; Zoysa 8–4–13–0; Muralitharan 35.5–16–81–6; Bandaratilleke 15–7–29–2; Samaraweera 5–2–9–0; Jayasuriya 5–2–13–0; Tillekeratne 2–1–1–0.

Umpires: J. H. Hampshire (England) and M. G. Silva.
Third umpire: P. T. Manuel.   Referee: R. Subba Row (England).

SRI LANKA v WEST INDIES

Third Test Match

At Sinhalese Sports Club, Colombo, November 29, 30, December 1, 2, 3. Sri Lanka won by ten wickets. Toss: West Indies.

Sri Lanka completed a clean sweep of the Tests – the fifth whitewash of West Indies in five years in a series of two or more matches. But it was also a game of two giant performances. Vaas took seven wickets in both innings, twice improving his career-best analysis, as he swung the new ball and the old, both in and out; only Muralitharan, with 16 against England at The Oval in 1998, had claimed more in a Test for Sri Lanka. Meanwhile, Lara completed a phenomenal series with scores of 221 and 130. Only five other batsmen had combined a double (or triple) and a single hundred in the same Test and none had been on the losing side.

The match followed a similar course to the First Test. On a pitch of even pace and bounce, West Indies were 327 for three after the first day, only to fold yet again, losing seven wickets for 43, five to Vaas. In reply, Sri Lanka amassed their second-highest Test total. Despite Lara's second century, West Indies again capitulated after passing 200 with only three wickets down: this time, the last seven fell for 59.

Although Vaas removed the openers cheaply on the first morning, the bowlers made little headway for the rest of the day. Lara continued to find Sarwan an able ally, and their positive partnership of 194 was ended only by Jayawardene's direct hit from cover. That brought in Hooper, who added a further 136 with Lara. But, once he fell to Vaas and the second new ball, the innings came to a swift end. Lara, who had completed 7,000 Test runs when he reached 130, made his fourth Test double-hundred, but was bowled by Vaas off the inside edge. He had batted for 436 minutes, faced 354 balls, hit two sixes and 23 fours, and given a masterclass in handling Muralitharan.

The West Indians were on even terms on the third morning, when Jayawardene was fourth out at 204, but they were once more stopped in their tracks by Tillekeratne. Patience personified but stylish too, he added 141 with Arnold, who eventually provided Hooper with his 100th Test wicket – no one else had needed as many balls (12,073) or Tests (90) as him – followed by 165 with Samaraweera. By then, West Indies were without Ramnarine, who had retired with a strained hip muscle. It took Black's direct hit from mid-off to remove Samaraweera, but the bowlers kept Tillekeratne company long enough to see him to his first Test double-hundred, in his 93rd match; he was in for nine hours and two minutes and hit 23 of his 343 balls for four. A few minutes later, Jayasuriya declared, 237 ahead. It was the first time in nearly 23 years that West Indies had

BATSMAN SCORING HALF HIS SIDE'S RUNS IN A TEST

%
53.83 B. C. Lara   { 221 **out of 390**   West Indies v Sri Lanka at Colombo (SSC) **2001-02**
                     { 130 **out of 262**

51.88 J. H. Sinclair { 106 out of 177   South Africa v England at Cape Town 1898-99
                      {   4 out of 35

50.36 A. Flower   { 142 **out of 286**   Zimbabwe v South Africa at Harare **2001-02**
                     { 199* out of 391

Where the team completed both innings.

MOST RUNS BY BATSMAN ON LOSING SIDE IN A TEST

351 (221, 130)	**B. C. Lara**	**WI v SL at Colombo (SSC) (lost by ten wickets)** . .	**2001-02**
341 (142, 199*)	**A. Flower**	**Z v SA at Harare (lost by nine wickets)**.	**2001-02**
303 (176, 127)	H. Sutcliffe	E v A at Melbourne (lost by 81 runs)	1924-25
265 (155, 110)	C. L. Walcott	WI v A at Kingston (lost by an innings and 82 runs)	1954-55
261 (116, 145)	V. S. Hazare	I v A at Adelaide (lost by an innings and 16 runs) . .	1947-48
256 (72, 184)	V. Mankad	I v E at Lord's (lost by eight wickets)	1952
253 (183*, 70)	A. Flower	Z v I at Delhi (lost by seven wickets)	2000-01

conceded 600 in a Test innings since 1978-79, when India made 644 for seven declared at Kanpur during the Packer schism.

Again, Vaas quickly despatched the openers – Gayle for his third successive duck – as a precursor to another century stand between Sarwan and Lara, their third of the series. Going into the last day, they had reduced the deficit to 92, with eight wickets standing. Most other teams would have got away with a draw, but West Indies were never far away from collapse, and another duly followed once Sarwan snicked Vaas to the keeper in the seventh over of the morning.

Lara remained long enough to see West Indies into the lead but, just before lunch, he failed to keep out Zoysa's in-swinging yorker. In all, Lara had batted over 11 and a half hours in the match and, as the wickets tumbled, he remained responsible for more than half the runs off the bat in both innings. Appropriately, Vaas finished off the innings with four wickets in nine balls, leaving Atapattu and Jayasuriya to apply the icing before tea.

Men of the Match: B. C. Lara and W. P. U. J. C. Vaas. *Man of the Series:* B. C. Lara.

Close of play: First day, West Indies 327-3 (Lara 178, Hooper 52); Second day, Sri Lanka 193-3 (Jayawardene 32, Arnold 10); Third day, Sri Lanka 477-5 (Tillekeratne 143, Samaraweera 68); Fourth day, West Indies 145-2 (Sarwan 57, Lara 76).

West Indies

D. Ganga lbw b Vaas	6	– lbw b Vaas	10
C. H. Gayle c Sangakkara b Vaas	0	– c Jayawardene b Vaas	0
R. R. Sarwan run out	69	– c Sangakkara b Vaas	66
B. C. Lara b Vaas	221	– b Zoysa	130
*C. L. Hooper lbw b Vaas	56	– st Sangakkara b Muralitharan	9
M. N. Samuels lbw b Vaas	4	– c Jayawardene b Muralitharan	0
†R. D. Jacobs b Zoysa	2	– not out	31
M. Dillon lbw b Vaas	2	– c sub (U. D. U. Chandana) b Vaas . .	8
D. Ramnarine c Jayawardene b Muralitharan . . .	0	– lbw b Vaas	0
P. T. Collins c Samaraweera b Vaas	4	– lbw b Vaas	0
M. I. Black not out	0	– lbw b Vaas	0
B 5, l-b 7, n-b 14	26	B 4, l-b 1, n-b 3	8

1/2 (2) 2/17 (1) 3/211 (3) 4/347 (5)   390   1/1 (2) 2/20 (1) 3/161 (3)   262
5/359 (6) 6/368 (7) 7/376 (8)   4/203 (5) 5/203 (6) 6/240 (4)
8/385 (4) 9/389 (9) 10/390 (10)   7/258 (8) 8/258 (9)
                                                          9/262 (10) 10/262 (11)

Bowling: *First Innings*—Vaas 32.2–5–120–7; Zoysa 20–4–55–1; Samaraweera 8–0–31–0; Bandaratilleke 9–2–37–0; Muralitharan 37–6–115–1; Jayasuriya 3–0–11–0; Arnold 3–0–8–0; Tillekeratne 1–0–1–0. *Second Innings*—Vaas 25–3–71–7; Zoysa 11–1–45–1; Muralitharan 36–5–116–2; Samaraweera 8–2–23–0; Bandaratilleke 2–0–2–0.

Sri Lanka

M. S. Atapattu c Gayle b Collins	4	– not out	19
*S. T. Jayasuriya c Ramnarine b Black	85	– not out	8
†K. C. Sangakkara c Gayle b Dillon	55		
D. P. M. D. Jayawardene lbw b Dillon	39		
R. P. Arnold c Jacobs b Hooper	65		
H. P. Tillekeratne not out	204		
T. T. Samaraweera run out	87		
W. P. U. J. C. Vaas c Samuels b Collins	23		
D. N. T. Zoysa b Hooper	10		
M. R. C. N. Bandaratilleke c Jacobs b Collins	25		
M. Muralitharan not out	4		
B 5, l-b 14, w 2, n-b 5	26		

1/5 (1) 2/104 (3) 3/179 (2)   (9 wkts dec.) 627   (no wkt) 27
4/204 (4) 5/345 (5) 6/510 (7)
7/550 (8) 8/569 (9) 9/611 (10)

Bowling: *First Innings*—Dillon 46–9–131–2; Collins 47–4–156–3; Black 32–6–123–1; Ramnarine 17–3–51–0; Hooper 43–7–112–2; Gayle 10–1–28–0; Sarwan 2–0–7–0. *Second Innings*—Dillon 3–0–12–0; Collins 2.3–0–15–0.

Umpires: R. B. Tiffin (Zimbabwe) and E. A. R. de Silva.
Third umpire: M. G. Silva. Referee: R. Subba Row (England).

West Indies' matches against Zimbabwe and Sri Lanka in the LG Abans Series (December 9–19) appear on pages 1361–1367.

HONOURS' LIST, 2002-03

In 2002, the following were decorated for their services to cricket:
Queen's Birthday Honours, 2002: W. Edwards (services to cricket in Wales) OBE, J. A. O'Connor (services to Lewes Priory Cricket Club) MBE.
Queen's Birthday Honours (Australia), 2002: E. W. Freeman (services to sport in South Australia) OAM, A. J. Hughes (services to cricket in New South Wales) OAM, W. M. Weir (services to women's cricket) AM.
New Year's Honours, 2003: H. C. Blofeld (Cambridge; services to cricket broadcasting) OBE, M. Foley (services to Salesbury Cricket Club, Lancashire, and especially to young cricketers) MBE, K. E. Palmer (Somerset; Test umpire; services to cricket) MBE.
Australia Day Honours, 2003: J. Bennett (services to cricket in Tasmania) OAM, J. N. McKnoulty (former president of Queensland Cricket; services to cricket administration) AM, R. F. Merriman (services to the Australian Cricket Board) AM, M. A. Taylor (New South Wales and Australia; services to cricket and fundraising for cancer research) AO.

THE ZIMBABWEANS IN BANGLADESH, 2001-02

By UTPAL SHUVRO

Bangladesh's first overseas Test tour had been to Zimbabwe in April 2001. Seven months later, Zimbabwe reciprocated, taking part in Bangladesh's first home series of more than one Test. They would have repeated their earlier whitewash of Bangladesh – two Test wins and three in one-day internationals – if bad weather had not robbed them of a certain victory in the First Test at Dhaka. It was Bangladesh's first draw after defeats in their first five Tests. But Zimbabwe duly won the next match, at Chittagong, and then overwhelmed their hosts in the three one-day games.

There were no first-class matches apart from the Tests. Zimbabwe were in the middle of a busy season, and thought they had enough knowledge of the subcontinent to handle Test cricket's newest entrants without practice. They proved right.

Zimbabwe had their own problems, however, with player–administrator relations at a new low. Alistair Campbell, their former captain and the only man who had appeared in all their 56 Tests, was dropped, as was another senior player, Guy Whittall. The official explanation was poor form, but it was widely believed that they were being taught a lesson. Zimbabwe's musical chairs continued as the inexperienced Brian Murphy, who had taken over as captain in Sharjah (page 1353), handed over to Stuart Carlisle.

Since Bangladesh's visit, Zimbabwe had suffered a 16-match losing streak in one-day cricket. But all these problems evaporated as soon as they took on Bangladesh again. The gulf in experience clearly showed: in the Tests, the home bowlers lacked firepower, and their batsmen showed they were yet to learn patience and the art of building innings. The one-day series was expected to be closer, because Bangladesh were far more used to limited overs, but ended in even greater disappointment.

Bangladesh did see some encouraging signs. The 18-year-old pace bowler Mashrafe bin Mortaza gave some bite to an otherwise innocuous attack. Eight wickets at 27.12 in the Tests and four in the one-day internationals made him easily their best bowler. On the batting front, Habibul Bashar showed growing maturity. After he was caught behind off his first ball of the series, he scored 65, 108 (his maiden Test hundred) and 76. His aggregate of 249 was the highest for either team, though his nearest rival, Craig Wishart, who scored 208, played two innings to Habibul's four.

Wishart was one of three Zimbabweans who hit centuries at Chittagong; he had also made 94 at Dhaka, leading a fightback from 89 for five to 431. Trevor Gripper, like Wishart, made a maiden hundred, and Andy Flower's unbeaten 114 kept him on top of the PwC Test ratings, which he had led since September. His brother, Grant, was one of the unexpected bowling successes of the trip, taking eight for 104 at Chittagong with his occasional left-arm spin, while the pace bowler, Travis Friend, advanced his claims as an all-rounder at Dhaka, scoring a career-best 81 on top of seven wickets.

Curiously, both teams changed captains during the tour. Murphy, the little-known leg-spinner who had succeeded Heath Streak in October, fractured his finger in the nets during his first Test in charge, and had to return home. It was an even sadder story for Bangladesh's first Test captain, the off-spinner Naimur Rahman. A year earlier, he had taken six wickets in Bangladesh's inaugural Test against India, only to be reported for a suspect action. After working with the Indian master Erapalli Prasanna, he was given the all-clear. But with his action changed, Naimur was not the same bowler: he took only five wickets in his next four Tests, and none at all in this series. He was stripped of the captaincy after the Tests, replaced by the wicket-keeper, Khaled Masud, and omitted from the one-day series and the New Zealand tour.

ZIMBABWEAN TOURING PARTY

B. A. Murphy (Mashonaland A) (*captain*), S. V. Carlisle (Mashonaland A) (*vice-captain*), G. B. Brent (Manicaland), D. D. Ebrahim (Mashonaland), S. M. Ervine (Midlands), A. Flower (Mashonaland), G. W. Flower (Mashonaland A), T. J. Friend (Midlands), T. R. Gripper (Mashonaland), D. A. Marillier (Midlands), M. L. Nkala (Matabeleland), H. K. Olonga (Mashonaland A), R. W. Price (Midlands), H. H. Streak (Matabeleland), C. B. Wishart (Midlands).

P. A. Strang (Manicaland) joined the party for the one-day internationals.

Coach: G. R. Marsh. *Manager:* M. A. Meman.

ZIMBABWEAN TOUR RESULTS

Test matches – Played 2: Won 1, Drawn 1.
One-day internationals – Played 3: Won 3.
Other non-first-class match – Won v Chittagong.

Note: Matches in this section which were not first-class are signified by a dagger.

BANGLADESH v ZIMBABWE

First Test Match

At Dhaka, November 8, 9, 10, 11, 12. Drawn. Toss: Zimbabwe. Test debuts: Khaled Mahmud, Mashrafe bin Mortaza.

After suffering five consecutive defeats since gaining Test status, Bangladesh finally achieved a draw. But they owed this thanks to the rain god: not a single ball was bowled on the last two days. Bangladesh still trailed by 199, with seven second-innings wickets left, and it was unlikely that they could have avoided another thrashing without the persistent bad weather.

Rain intervened from the very beginning. Bangladesh scored just three runs in the seven overs possible before lunch, after Murphy asked them to bat. In the afternoon, the seamers fully exploited the lateral movement and extra bounce: the overcast conditions seemed to transform Bangladesh's own backyard into an alien environment, and all the home batsmen struggled. Their lowest Test total, 90 against Sri Lanka two months earlier, looked a long way off at 56 for eight. But their No. 10, Enamul Haque, supervised the addition of 51 for the remaining two wickets. The last man Manjurul Islam saw them into three figures; even so, Bangladesh were shot out in 48.2 overs.

Manjurul struck back that evening, taking a wicket in each of his first two overs, and the Bangladeshi bowlers continued their good work next morning, despite what seemed perfect batting conditions, under a blazing sun. When Enamul bowled Andy Flower, the top five had been sent packing with only 89 on the board. Yet Zimbabwe still managed to amass a huge lead. Wishart and Marillier put on 137 for the sixth wicket, before Wishart was run out in the nineties for the second time in his Test career. Streak and Friend then added 108 for the eighth. Marillier contributed a career-best 73, Streak extended his Test record against Bangladesh to three half-centuries in three innings, and Friend followed up his first five-for in Tests with a maiden fifty, which became a fine 81. The chief consolation for the home side came from the teenaged Mashrafe bin Mortaza, who took four wickets on debut, generated good pace and troubled all the Zimbabwean batsmen.

Resuming 324 behind, Bangladesh batted much better. Habibul Bashar scored his fifth fifty in his sixth Test and built a determined century partnership with Javed Omar. Together, they spurred Bangladesh into a position to fight back – though both fell before the close, leaving them with little chance of saving the game. But next day, the heavens opened. Zimbabwe's bad luck was compounded when their captain, Murphy, fractured a finger in the nets and was forced to go home.

Man of the Match: T. J. Friend.

Close of play: First day, Zimbabwe 20-2 (Carlisle 10, G. W. Flower 6); Second day, Zimbabwe 348-7 (Streak 57, Friend 38); Third day, Bangladesh 125-3 (Aminul Islam 6, Mohammad Ashraful 0); Fourth day, No play.

Bangladesh

Javed Omar b Streak	3	– c Olonga b Marillier	35
Al Sahariar lbw b Friend	4	– c G. W. Flower b Friend	5
Habibul Bashar c A. Flower b Friend	0	– c Murphy b Friend	65
Aminul Islam lbw b Olonga	12	– not out	6
Mohammad Ashraful c Wishart b Olonga	0	– not out	0
Khaled Mahmud c Gripper b Friend	6		
*Naimur Rahman b Friend	13		
†Khaled Masud c Carlisle b Friend	6		
Mashrafe bin Mortaza c A. Flower b Streak	8		
Enamul Haque not out	24		
Manjurul Islam c Gripper b Olonga	9		
B 3, l-b 3, w 1, n-b 15	22	B 3, l-b 1, n-b 10	14

1/6 (2) 2/6 (3) 3/11 (1) 4/13 (5)   107   1/6 (2) 2/108 (1)   (3 wkts) 125
5/30 (6) 6/38 (4) 7/49 (7)   3/120 (3)
8/56 (8) 9/84 (9) 10/107 (11)

Bowling: *First Innings*—Streak 18–8–30–2; Friend 18–7–31–5; Olonga 6.2–0–18–3; Murphy 6–1–22–0. *Second Innings*—Streak 11–4–25–0; Friend 11.4–2–26–2; Olonga 5–1–17–0; Murphy 12–4–37–0; Marillier 7–2–16–1.

Zimbabwe

D. D. Ebrahim lbw b Manjurul Islam	3	T. J. Friend b Enamul Haque	81
T. R. Gripper c Javed Omar b Manjurul Islam	0	*B. A. Murphy c Habibul Bashar b Mashrafe bin Mortaza	25
S. V. Carlisle c Khaled Masud b Mashrafe bin Mortaza	33	H. K. Olonga not out	2
G. W. Flower c Al Sahariar b Mashrafe bin Mortaza	10	B 4, l-b 7, w 4, n-b 2	17
†A. Flower b Enamul Haque	28		
C. B. Wishart run out	94		431
D. A. Marillier lbw b Enamul Haque	73		
H. H. Streak c Khaled Masud b Mashrafe bin Mortaza	65		

1/3 (2) 2/4 (1) 3/31 (4)   431
4/60 (3) 5/89 (5) 6/226 (6)
7/259 (7) 8/367 (8)
9/417 (9) 10/431 (10)

Bowling: Manjurul Islam 26–5–74–2; Mashrafe bin Mortaza 32–8–106–4; Khaled Mahmud 15–2–59–0; Enamul Haque 43–13–74–3; Naimur Rahman 18–1–56–0; Mohammad Ashraful 15–3–49–0; Aminul Islam 1–0–2–0.

Umpires: Mian Aslam (Pakistan) and A. F. M. Akhtaruddin.
Third umpire: Sailab Hossain. Referee: Hanumant Singh (India).

BANGLADESH v ZIMBABWE

Second Test Match

At Chittagong, November 15, 16, 17, 18, 19. Zimbabwe won by eight wickets. Toss: Bangladesh.
Although Zimbabwe won comfortably to take the series 1–0, there was a hint of improvement by Bangladesh: they took the game into a fifth day for only the second time (excluding the rain-affected draw at Dhaka) in their seven Tests. But they were always playing catch-up after conceding a massive 542 during the first two days.

The M. A. Aziz Stadium became Bangladesh's second Test venue, and the world's 82nd. Chittagong's local hero, Akram Khan, replaced Khaled Mahmud, while the left-arm pace of Manjurul Islam gave way to the right-armed Mohammad Sharif. Zimbabwe made one enforced change, replacing the injured Murphy with the medium-paced all-rounder Brent, and handing the captaincy to Carlisle.

Under a hot sun, with the pitch looking perfect, Naimur Rahman surprised everyone by opting to field. Probably he was influenced by Bangladesh's preceding three Tests, in which they batted first and were bundled out for under 140 every time. The Zimbabwe openers responded gleefully, putting on 108. Trevor Gripper batted nearly six hours and reached his maiden Test century, after Enamul Haque missed a return catch when he was 83. Craig Wishart also got a maiden Test hundred, helping erase the memory of two near misses. His dismissal brought the return of Andy Flower, who had retired after colliding with Enamul, to complete his 12th Test century; he remained unbeaten when Carlisle declared. Zimbabwe had passed 500 for the third time in 12 months.

Scoring 343 to save the follow-on looked an uphill task, and Bangladesh never got near it. Apart from Habibul Bashar, with yet another maiden Test century, only Mohammad Ashraful, the 17-year-old who had become Test cricket's youngest centurion in September, showed application, battling 140 minutes for 33. In the follow-on, he showed even greater self-denial, and scored ten in 146 minutes.

Bangladesh's second innings promised much but delivered little. Javed Omar featured in partnerships of 73 and 122, the best yet for their first two wickets, and Habibul proved his class again, until his rash shot triggered a mini-collapse of three for eight. All three fell to Grant Flower's slow left-arm, aimed intelligently into the rough outside the right-handers' leg stump. Zimbabwe hardly missed their specialist spinner, Murphy, as the part-timers Flower and Marillier rose to the occasion. Even Flower was surprised by his success – four wickets in each innings.

At 227 for four, 64 behind, with Omar on 80, Bangladesh entered the last day with a faint hope of saving the match. That disappeared with the first ball of the morning: Friend trapped Omar in front of the wicket after 416 minutes' defiance. Bangladesh lost five for 40, and it took the last man, Sharif, to stave off the innings defeat with a bold 24 off 11 balls. Zimbabwe's target was only 11, but there was still some drama – Mashrafe bin Mortaza dismissed Ebrahim and Carlisle with his fifth and sixth deliveries. But in his next over, Gripper despatched the hat-trick ball to the boundary, and he completed the job three balls later.

Man of the Match: G. W. Flower.

Close of play: First day, Zimbabwe 236-4 (A. Flower 15, Brent 9); Second day, Bangladesh 57-1 (Al Sahariar 25, Habibul Bashar 21); Third day, Bangladesh 15-0 (Javed Omar 2, Al Sahariar 11); Fourth day, Bangladesh 227-4 (Javed Omar 80, Mohammad Ashraful 1).

Zimbabwe

D. D. Ebrahim b Mashrafe bin Mortaza	41	– b Mashrafe bin Mortaza	0
T. R. Gripper run out	112	– not out	11
*S. V. Carlisle lbw b Enamul Haque	14	– c Akram Khan	
		b Mashrafe bin Mortaza	0
G. W. Flower c Naimur Rahman			
b Enamul Haque	33	– not out	0
†A. Flower not out	114		
G. B. Brent c Habibul Bashar			
b Mashrafe bin Mortaza	25		
C. B. Wishart c Mohammad Sharif			
b Mohammad Ashraful	114		
D. A. Marillier c Habibul Bashar b Aminul Islam	52		
H. H. Streak not out	16		
B 2, l-b 5, w 2, n-b 12	21		

1/108 (1) 2/145 (3) 3/210 (4)   (7 wkts dec.) 542   1/0 (1) 2/0 (3)   (2 wkts) 11
4/214 (2) 5/280 (6)
6/469 (7) 7/496 (8)

T. J. Friend and H. K. Olonga did not bat.

In the first innings A. Flower, when 66, retired hurt at 346 and resumed at 469.

Bowling: *First Innings*—Mashrafe bin Mortaza 28–4–101–2; Mohammad Sharif 29–7–118–0; Enamul Haque 54–12–134–2; Naimur Rahman 15–2–54–0; Mohammad Ashraful 17–0–62–1; Aminul Islam 17–1–66–1. *Second Innings*—Mashrafe bin Mortaza 1.4–1–10–2; Enamul Haque 1–0–1–0.

Bangladesh

Javed Omar c A. Flower b Streak	8	– lbw b Friend	80
Al Sahariar lbw b Olonga	29	– lbw b Olonga	40
Habibul Bashar b G. W. Flower	108	– c sub (S. M. Ervine) b G. W. Flower	76
Aminul Islam c and b Marillier	21	– c Gripper b G. W. Flower	1
Akram Khan lbw b Marillier	6	– lbw b G. W. Flower	2
Mohammad Ashraful c Ebrahim b G. W. Flower	33	– c sub (P. A. Strang) b Marillier	10
*Naimur Rahman lbw b Streak	5	– lbw b Marillier	28
†Khaled Masud b G. W. Flower	8	– c Ebrahim b G. W. Flower	12
Enamul Haque not out	12	– c and b Marillier	0
Mashrafe bin Mortaza lbw b Brent	1	– st A. Flower b Marillier	0
Mohammad Sharif c Brent b G. W. Flower	3	– not out	24
B 3, l-b 3, w 2, n-b 9	17	B 2, l-b 16, w 1, n-b 9	28
	251		**301**

1/15 (1) 2/80 (2) 3/135 (4) 4/146 (5)   251
5/204 (3) 6/217 (7) 7/226 (8)
8/235 (6) 9/244 (10) 10/251 (11)

1/73 (2) 2/195 (3) 3/201 (4)   301
4/203 (5) 5/227 (1) 6/264 (6)
7/267 (7) 8/267 (9)
9/267 (10) 10/301 (8)

Bowling: *First Innings*—Friend 16–3–63–0; Streak 19–6–32–2; Olonga 12–0–40–1; Marillier 15–6–39–2; Brent 17–9–30–1; G. W. Flower 15.3–3–41–4; Gripper 1–1–0–0. *Second Innings*—Friend 25–7–53–1; Brent 25–6–58–0; G. W. Flower 38.4–18–63–4; Olonga 15–5–31–1; Marillier 19–4–57–4; Gripper 4–2–21–0.

Umpires: E. A. R. de Silva (Sri Lanka) and Showkatur Rahman.
Third umpire: Jahangir Alam. Referee: Hanumant Singh (India).

†At Chittagong, November 21. **Zimbabweans won by 13 runs.** Toss: Chittagong. **Zimbabweans 162** (45.3 overs) (D. A. Marillier 40, S. M. Ervine 56; Ehsanul Haque three for 26); **Chittagong 149** (49.4 overs) (Masumud Dowla 59; T. J. Friend three for 21).
The Zimbabweans were 49 for five before Marillier and Ervine added 79.

†BANGLADESH v ZIMBABWE

First One-Day International

At Chittagong, November 23. Zimbabwe won by five wickets. Toss: Zimbabwe. International debuts: Fahim Muntasir, Tushar Imran.

After losing his first toss as Bangladesh captain, Khaled Masud saw his top order fall apart. Friend and Brent exploited the morning moisture to claim three wickets each. Bangladesh were tottering at 59 for five when Masud joined Habibul Bashar to add 50; after Habibul went, Masud fought on, aided by the tail, but a total of 156 looked far too small to worry Zimbabwe. Then Mashrafe bin Mortaza, in his first one-day international, thrilled the home crowd by reducing the tourists to a precarious 20 for three in nine overs: he dismissed both Flowers and ran out Gripper. But a 105-run partnership between Carlisle and Wishart put Zimbabwe back on course, and they ended their 16-match losing streak in one-day internationals with nearly eight overs to spare.

Man of the Match: C. B. Wishart.

Bangladesh

Al Sahariar c A. Flower b Friend	. . . . .	13	Mashrafe bin Mortaza b Ervine. 1
Mohammad Ashraful run out	. . . .	7	Mohammad Sharif b Streak 4
Tushar Imran b Friend.		6	Fahim Muntasir not out 1
Habibul Bashar b Friend		44	B 6, l-b 3, w 5, n-b 2 16
Sanuar Hossain c Carlisle b Brent		5	
Khaled Mahmud c Carlisle b Brent		4	1/13 2/28 3/33
*†Khaled Masud run out		40	4/53 5/59 6/109 (48.4 overs) 156
Mohammad Rafiq c Carlisle b Brent . . .		15	7/134 8/144 9/155

Bowling: Streak 9.4–0–31–1; Friend 9–0–25–3; Brent 10–1–29–3; Ervine 9–1–28–1; Marillier 8–0–27–0; G. W. Flower 3–0–7–0.

Zimbabwe

G. W. Flower b Mashrafe bin Mortaza	. .	0	D. A. Marillier lbw b Mohammad Rafiq . 15
T. R. Gripper run out		7	D. D. Ebrahim not out. 6
*S. V. Carlisle run out.		46	L-b 1, w 1 2
†A. Flower c Fahim Muntasir			
b Mashrafe bin Mortaza .		6	1/1 2/13 3/20 (5 wkts, 42.2 overs) 161
C. B. Wishart not out		79	4/125 5/148

S. M. Ervine, H. H. Streak, G. B. Brent and T. J. Friend did not bat.

Bowling: Mashrafe bin Mortaza 8.2–3–26–2; Mohammad Sharif 7–0–39–0; Khaled Mahmud 6–1–17–0; Mohammad Rafiq 10–4–25–1; Fahim Muntasir 9–0–29–0; Sanuar Hossain 1–0–17–0; Mohammad Ashraful 1–0–7–0.

Umpires: A. F. M. Akhtaruddin and Sailab Hossain.
Third umpire: Showkatur Rahman.   Referee: Hanumant Singh (India).

†BANGLADESH v ZIMBABWE

Second One-Day International

At Dhaka, November 25 (day/night). Zimbabwe won by 42 runs. Toss: Zimbabwe.

Zimbabwe clinched the series by batting Bangladesh out of the match. Their total of 309 was built on Ebrahim's maiden international century, which anchored them into the 48th over, while Carlisle, Wishart and Streak hit out. Wishart's rich form continued, with a 60-ball 68, but the real fireworks came from Streak. He blasted 23 in only seven deliveries, including 22 off the final over, from the left-arm spinner Mohammad Rafiq. After that, Zimbabwe could easily afford a five-run penalty when Wishart obstructed a fielder. Habibul Bashar and Sanuar Hossain added 115, but they took more than 24 overs; even Bangladesh's fastest one-day fifty – 37 balls, by Khaled Mahmud – could not loosen Zimbabwe's grip.

Man of the Match: D. D. Ebrahim.

Zimbabwe

G. W. Flower b Manjurul Islam	. . . . . .	22	S. M. Ervine not out. 6
D. D. Ebrahim run out		121	H. H. Streak not out 23
*S. V. Carlisle run out.		44	B 1, l-b 2, w 3, n-b 4 10
†A. Flower c Al Sahariar			
b Khaled Mahmud .		10	1/25 2/133 3/145 (6 wkts, 50 overs) 309
C. B. Wishart b Mashrafe bin Mortaza .		68	4/269 5/276 6/286
D. A. Marillier b Mashrafe bin Mortaza .		5	

M. L. Nkala, G. B. Brent and T. J. Friend did not bat.

Bowling: Mashrafe bin Mortaza 9–0–48–2; Manjurul Islam 6–0–35–1; Hasibul Hussain 3–0–27–0; Mohammad Rafiq 10–0–82–0; Khaled Mahmud 9–0–44–1; Habibul Bashar 9–0–47–0; Mohammad Ashraful 4–0–23–0.

Bangladesh

Javed Omar c A. Flower b Streak	27	Mashrafe bin Mortaza b Brent	1
Al Sahariar run out	15	*†Khaled Masud not out	0
Mohammad Ashraful b Friend	14	Manjurul Islam not out	1
Habibul Bashar b Ervine	66	B 5, l-b 17, w 9, n-b 1, p 5	37
Sanuar Hossain run out	52		
Khaled Mahmud c Friend b Brent	50	(9 wkts, 50 overs)	267
Mohammad Rafiq b Ervine	4	1/51 2/53 3/81	
Hasibul Hussain b Streak	0	4/196 5/228 6/255	
		7/260 8/266 9/266	

Bowling: Streak 9–1–45–2; Friend 8–0–43–1; Brent 6–0–31–2; G. W. Flower 5–0–23–0; Nkala 2–0–11–0; Ervine 10–0–39–2; Marillier 10–0–48–0.

Umpires: Jahangir Alam and Showkatur Rahman.
Third umpire: Sailab Hossain.   Referee: Hanumant Singh (India).

†BANGLADESH v ZIMBABWE

Third One-Day International

At Dhaka, November 26 (day/night). Zimbabwe won by seven wickets. Toss: Bangladesh.

After Javed Omar and Al Sahariar opened with 103, Bangladesh had visions of a big total. But none of their colleagues reached 20 – in fact, four middle-order batsmen contributed only 20 between them, as Streak shot out three for four in 17 balls. Only the last pair, Mohammad Sharif and Mashrafe bin Mortaza, got Bangladesh past 200. Those two also deserved credit for bowling a tight line and length, which made Zimbabwe wait until the last over for victory. They too began with a century partnership, between Grant Flower and Ebrahim, who took his tally past 200 in two days. Carlisle ensured the clean sweep with an unbeaten 55.

Man of the Match: D. D. Ebrahim.   *Man of the Series*: D. D. Ebrahim.

Bangladesh

Javed Omar b Strang	54	Fahim Muntasir c and b G. W. Flower	0
Al Sahariar c Strang b G. W. Flower	59	Mohammad Sharif not out	10
Mohammad Ashraful b Marillier	16	Mashrafe bin Mortaza run out	18
Habibul Bashar b Marillier	5	B 2, l-b 11, w 9, n-b 3	25
Sanuar Hossain c Carlisle b Streak	6		
Khaled Mahmud c Carlisle b Streak	9	1/103 2/132 3/143	(48.1 overs) 215
*†Khaled Masud c A. Flower b Streak	0	4/156 5/157 6/157	
Enamul Haque run out	13	7/176 8/176 9/186	

Bowling: Streak 9.1–0–26–3; Friend 8–1–36–0; Olonga 4–0–19–0; Ervine 5–0–28–0; Marillier 9–0–40–2; Strang 3–0–20–1; G. W. Flower 10–1–33–2.

Zimbabwe

G. W. Flower c Sanuar Hossain b Enamul Haque	40	†A. Flower run out	15
D. D. Ebrahim c Habibul Bashar b Enamul Haque	84	C. B. Wishart not out	5
*S. V. Carlisle not out	55	L-b 6, w 11, n-b 3	20
		1/107 2/176 3/210 (3 wkts, 49.1 overs) 219

D. A. Marillier, S. M. Ervine, H. H. Streak, P. A. Strang, T. J. Friend and H. K. Olonga did not bat.

Bowling: Mashrafe bin Mortaza 10–1–42–0; Mohammad Sharif 10–0–37–0; Khaled Mahmud 10–1–40–0; Enamul Haque 10–1–52–2; Fahim Muntasir 9.1–0–42–0.

Umpires: Jahangir Alam and Sailab Hossain.
Third umpire: A. F. M. Akhtaruddin.   Referee: Hanumant Singh (India).

THE ZIMBABWEANS IN SRI LANKA, 2001-02

By SA'ADI THAWFEEQ

Zimbabwe's third Test tour of Sri Lanka in six seasons ended like the previous two, in a whitewash. It could not have been more one-sided, with Sri Lanka running up totals in excess of 400 in all three Tests, while the best Zimbabwe could offer was 236 – bizarrely, they offered it once in each game. Their best performance was in the final Test, at Galle: even then, they let Sri Lanka recover from a faltering 254 for seven to 418, and collapsed from 153 without loss to the inevitable 236. They lost that game by 315 runs, to follow two thrashings by an innings. On the entire tour, they lost nine matches and won only one, against West Indies in the one-day series preceding the Tests. Their worst humiliation occurred during that same tournament, when Chaminda Vaas dismissed them for 38, the lowest total in any one-day international.

In the Tests, Sri Lanka had eight batsmen who averaged 40, Zimbabwe none. But the real difference between the sides was Muttiah Muralitharan. Not even the redoubtable Andy Flower could find an answer to Murali's tireless mysteries. Flower had averaged 188 in his previous four Tests; in this series, he managed only 13.33. Meanwhile, Murali spun his way to 30 wickets at 9.80, a Sri Lankan series record. He came within a dropped catch of all ten in an innings in the Second Test at Kandy, and at Galle he became the youngest bowler to 400 Test wickets – and in the fewest matches, for good measure.

Zimbabwe were severely handicapped by the lack of a specialist slow bowler, though they should have had Brian Murphy, the leg-spinner and official tour captain. After fracturing a finger on the previous tour of Bangladesh, he missed the one-day series but returned for the first-class programme. When he took nought for 103 against a Board XI, it became clear his hand had not fully healed: he was so short of confidence and form that he dropped out of the First Test and flew home before the Second. Stuart Carlisle continued to deputise as captain, but badly missed the experience of Alistair Campbell and Guy Whittall, left at home for reasons best known to the Zimbabwe Cricket Union.

Sri Lanka also had a selection controversy. Before the Kandy Test, the selectors decided to rest Marvan Atapattu and Buddika Fernando in order to blood youngsters. Several team-mates threatened to withdraw in sympathy. Their captain, Sanath Jayasuriya, protested that neither he nor the coach, Dav Whatmore, had been properly consulted, and that the decision had been made down in Colombo, without knowing the pitch and weather conditions in Kandy. With less than 12 hours to go, the new sports minister, Johnston Fernando, overruled the selection committee, which he later disbanded. Jayasuriya celebrated getting his way with 139, the highest individual score of the series. By the end of the tour, he had led Sri Lanka to eight successive Test wins, a record for any subcontinental team.

ZIMBABWEAN TOURING PARTY

B. A. Murphy (Mashonaland A) (*captain*), S. V. Carlisle (Mashonaland A) (*vice-captain*), G. B. Brent (Manicaland), D. D. Ebrahim (Mashonaland), A. Flower (Mashonaland), G. W. Flower (Mashonaland A), T. J. Friend (Midlands), T. R. Gripper (Mashonaland), D. A. Marillier (Midlands), H. Masakadza (Mashonaland), H. K. Olonga (Mashonaland A), G. J. Rennie (Mashonaland A), H. H. Streak (Matabeleland), T. Taibu (Mashonaland A), C. B. Wishart (Midlands).

Murphy departed after the First Test because of injury and handed the captaincy back to Carlisle, who had been in charge for the preceding one-day tournament. S. M. Ervine (Midlands) and M. L. Nkala (Matabeleland) were in the party for the one-day games but were replaced for the first-class programme by Murphy, Masakadza and Rennie.

Coach: G. R. Marsh. *Manager:* M. A. Meman.

ZIMBABWEAN TOUR RESULTS

Test matches – Played 3: Lost 3.
First-class matches – Played 4: Lost 4.
Losses – Sri Lanka (3), Sri Lankan Board XI.
One-day internationals – Played 4: Won 1, Lost 3. *Win* – West Indies. *Losses* – Sri Lanka (2), West Indies.
Other non-first-class matches – Played 2: Lost 2. *Losses* – Sri Lankan Board XI, Sri Lanka A.

TEST MATCH AVERAGES
SRI LANKA – BATTING

	T	I	NO	R	HS	100s	50s	Avge	Ct/St
W. P. U. J. C. Vaas	3	3	2	154	74*	0	2	154.00	0
T. T. Samaraweera	3	3	1	216	123*	1	1	108.00	2
S. T. Jayasuriya	3	4	0	295	139	1	1	73.75	4
K. C. Sangakkara	3	4	0	255	128	1	1	63.75	7/2
M. S. Atapattu	3	4	1	184	100*	1	1	61.33	2
D. P. M. D. Jayawardene	3	4	1	167	76	0	2	55.66	4
H. P. Tillekeratne	3	3	0	136	96	0	1	45.33	6
R. P. Arnold	3	3	0	124	71	0	1	41.33	2

Played in three Tests: T. C. B. Fernando 45, 1 (1 ct); M. Muralitharan 1, 5* (1 ct). Played in two Tests: D. N. T. Zoysa 4. Played in one Test: U. D. U. Chandana 92.

BOWLING

	O	M	R	W	BB	5W/i	Avge
M. Muralitharan	203.1	84	294	30	9-51	2	9.80
S. T. Jayasuriya	68	21	130	9	5-43	1	14.44
T. C. B. Fernando	54.5	8	159	7	4-27	0	22.71
D. N. T. Zoysa	54	13	132	4	2-24	0	33.00
W. P. U. J. C. Vaas	106.5	30	285	8	2-17	0	35.62

Also bowled: U. D. U. Chandana 12–4–24–0; T. T. Samaraweera 29–8–66–2; H. P. Tillekeratne 1–0–8–0.

ZIMBABWE – BATTING

	T	I	NO	R	HS	100s	50s	Avge	Ct
H. H. Streak	3	6	3	117	36*	0	0	39.00	0
T. R. Gripper	3	6	0	167	83	0	1	27.83	2
S. V. Carlisle	3	6	0	163	64	0	1	27.16	2
G. W. Flower	3	6	0	130	72	0	1	21.66	1
G. J. Rennie	3	6	0	120	68	0	1	20.00	1
T. J. Friend	3	6	1	83	44	0	0	16.60	1
C. B. Wishart	3	6	0	85	27	0	0	14.16	3
A. Flower	3	6	0	80	42	0	0	13.33	6
D. A. Marillier	2	4	1	32	15	0	0	10.66	0
H. Masakadza	2	4	0	41	28	0	0	10.25	0
H. K. Olonga	3	6	0	23	18	0	0	3.83	0

Played in one Test: G. B. Brent 0, 7; D. D. Ebrahim 1, 5*.

BOWLING

	O	M	R	W	BB	5W/i	Avge
H. H. Streak	109.5	24	303	7	3-113	0	43.28
D. A. Marillier	61.4	9	210	4	4-101	0	52.50
G. W. Flower	98	14	282	5	3-66	0	56.40
T. J. Friend	86	16	296	5	3-97	0	59.20

Also bowled: G. B. Brent 33–5–82–1; T. R. Gripper 45–6–170–2; H. Masakadza 3–0–9–1; H. K. Olonga 72–11–342–1; G. J. Rennie 1–0–9–0.

Note: Matches in this section which were not first-class are signified by a dagger.

†At Moratuwa, December 1. **Sri Lankan Board XI won by six wickets.** Toss: Sri Lankan Board XI. **Zimbabweans 186** (46.2 overs) (A. Flower 66; H. M. R. K. B. Herath three for 23); **Sri Lankan Board XI 189 for four** (36.1 overs) (S. H. T. Kandamby 40, L. P. C. Silva 50 not out, U. D. U. Chandana 50 not out).

†At Police Park, Colombo, December 3. **Sri Lanka A won by four wickets.** Toss: Sri Lanka A. **Zimbabweans 196 for eight** (50 overs) (T. Taibu 42, H. H. Streak 34); **Sri Lanka A 198 for six** (46.2 overs) (D. A. Gunawardene 36, W. M. G. Ramyakumara 61 not out, M. Pushpakumara 30 not out; T. J. Friend three for 33).

Zimbabwe's matches against Sri Lanka and West Indies in the LG Abans Series (December 8–16) appear on pages 1361–1367.

At P. Saravanamuttu Stadium, Colombo, December 21, 22, 23. **Sri Lankan Board XI won by five wickets.** Toss: Sri Lankan Board XI. **Zimbabweans 319 for six dec.** (T. R. Gripper 101 retired hurt, S. V. Carlisle 98, A. Flower 51 not out; K. A. D. M. Fernando three for 47) **and 169 for five dec.** (G. J. Rennie 68); **Sri Lankan Board XI 269 for four dec.** (B. M. A. J. Mendis 79, W. M. G. Ramyakumara 103 not out) **and 223 for five** (L. P. C. Silva 127 not out, C. M. Bandara 32).

SRI LANKA v ZIMBABWE

First Test Match

At Sinhalese Sports Club, Colombo, December 27, 28, 29, 31. Sri Lanka won by an innings and 166 runs. Toss: Zimbabwe.

Zimbabwe suffered their first blow before the match when their captain, Murphy, decided to stand down after returning prematurely from a finger injury. Carlisle resumed the captaincy, but there was no genuine spinner to replace Murphy. Zimbabwe's best chance seemed to be to bowl first on the Sinhalese pitch, which had a reputation for encouraging fast bowlers on the first morning.

But the plan backfired when the pitch turned out to be bone dry, and the ball hardly wobbled. After Atapattu and Jayasuriya enjoyed early reprieves, Zimbabwe's seam quartet switched to a tedious policy of containment, spearing the ball wide of off stump. Jayasuriya responded with an uncharacteristically watchful 92, occupying four hours, and Sri Lanka had pottered to 211 for three when bad light ended play in the 74th over. Next day, the bowlers lost their discipline: Sri Lanka plundered 127 runs in the first session and 123 in the second. Sangakkara, who began the morning on 62, struck seven fours to complete his century in 30 balls; in all, his stylish 128 featured 22 fours and a six. When he was fifth out at 320, to a juggling slip catch, Samaraweera took over. He helped Sri Lanka add 266 at a run a minute for the next two wickets, which took them past 500 for the first time against Zimbabwe. Tillekeratne just missed his own hundred, Vaas reached a first-class career-best 74, and Samaraweera was 123 not out off 166 balls when Jayasuriya finally declared.

By contrast, no Zimbabwean managed a fifty in either innings. Their reply had an unhappy start when the teenaged Masakadza was caught at third slip in the fourth over before bad light intervened again. On the third day, they were bowled out inside 80 overs, with only Andy Flower approaching two hours at the crease. Following on with a massive deficit of 402, Zimbabwe closed at 64 for two before a rest day, the first in Tests since West Indies and India paused for Good Friday at Bridgetown in 1997. The cause this time was a full moon, observed as a *poya* day by Buddhists. On resumption, Zimbabwe improved their performance a little, thanks to a three-hour innings from Friend, the night-watchman. Rain cost an hour on the fourth afternoon, but it merely delayed Sri Lanka's sixth successive Test victory, which came after tea. The margin, an innings and 166 runs, was then Sri Lanka's biggest in their 119 Tests, improving on an innings and 137 against Bangladesh in September. Murali finished with eight wickets in the match, which took him to 80 in 12 Tests in 2001; only Dennis Lillee, with 85 from 13 Tests in 1981, had collected more in a calendar year.

Man of the Match: K. C. Sangakkara.

Close of play: First day, Sri Lanka 211-3 (Sangakkara 62, Arnold 4); Second day, Zimbabwe 14-1 (Gripper 4, Carlisle 6); Third day, Zimbabwe 64-2 (Carlisle 22, Friend 0).

Sri Lanka

M. S. Atapattu c A. Flower b Streak	25	T. T. Samaraweera not out	123
*S. T. Jayasuriya c A. Flower b Gripper	92	W. P. U. J. C. Vaas not out	74
†K. C. Sangakkara c Wishart b Brent	128	B 2, l-b 4, w 3, n-b 8	17
D. P. M. D. Jayawardene c Carlisle b Gripper	18	1/78 (1) 2/150 (2) (6 wkts dec.)	586
R. P. Arnold lbw b Streak	13	3/170 (4) 4/249 (5)	
H. P. Tillekeratne c A. Flower b Streak	96	5/320 (3) 6/450 (6)	

D. N. T. Zoysa, T. C. B. Fernando and M. Muralitharan did not bat.

Bowling: Streak 34–5–113–3; Friend 27–5–102–0; Olonga 23–3–103–0; Brent 33–5–82–1; Gripper 22–3–91–2; G. W. Flower 22–3–89–0.

Zimbabwe

H. Masakadza c Tillekeratne b Zoysa	3	c Atapattu b Muralitharan	28
T. R. Gripper c Jayawardene b Muralitharan	30	c Sangakkara b Muralitharan	10
*S. V. Carlisle c Jayasuriya b Vaas	10	c Sangakkara b Fernando	32
G. J. Rennie lbw b Muralitharan	35	(5) c Jayawardene b Fernando	4
†A. Flower b Samaraweera	42	(6) lbw b Zoysa	10
G. W. Flower c Tillekeratne b Muralitharan	0	(7) c Tillekeratne b Muralitharan	18
C. B. Wishart c Tillekeratne b Zoysa	21	(8) c Tillekeratne b Samaraweera	27
H. H. Streak not out	26	(9) not out	36
T. J. Friend lbw b Vaas	6	(4) b Muralitharan	44
G. B. Brent b Muralitharan	0	c Jayasuriya b Zoysa	7
H. K. Olonga lbw b Fernando	4	c Sangakkara b Vaas	0
L-b 1, n-b 6	7	B 4, l-b 7, n-b 9	20
1/3 (1) 2/29 (3) 3/60 (2) 4/89 (4)	184	1/40 (1) 2/58 (2) 3/93 (3)	236
5/105 (6) 6/146 (7) 7/146 (5)		4/105 (5) 5/127 (6) 6/145 (4)	
8/166 (9) 9/167 (10) 10/184 (11)		7/165 (7) 8/197 (8)	
		9/235 (10) 10/236 (11)	

Bowling: *First Innings*—Vaas 24–6–63–2; Zoysa 14–6–24–2; Muralitharan 26–8–53–4; Jayasuriya 1–0–4–0; Fernando 9.5–0–32–1; Samaraweera 5–1–7–1. *Second Innings*—Vaas 21.2–6–76–1; Zoysa 15–4–34–2; Fernando 15–3–48–2; Muralitharan 36–17–35–4; Jayasuriya 7–3–22–0; Samaraweera 7–2–10–1.

Umpires: Riazuddin (Pakistan) and P. T. Manuel.
Third umpire: T. H. Wijewardene. Referee: C. W. Smith (West Indies).

SRI LANKA v ZIMBABWE

Second Test Match

At Kandy, January 4, 5, 6, 7. Sri Lanka won by an innings and 94 runs. Toss: Zimbabwe.

Muralitharan came agonisingly close to the best innings figures in all Test cricket. By the first evening he had taken nine for 51 from 39 overs, with one Zimbabwean wicket to fall. Next morning, Friend offered a regulation bat-pad catch off Murali's first ball, only for Arnold to drop it; then an lbw appeal was turned down. At the other end, Vaas bowled wide of off stump to Olonga, but could not stop him nicking one – which Sangakkara could not bring himself to drop. If Murali had dismissed Friend, he would have beaten Jim Laker's ten for 53 against Australia in 1956, as well as Anil Kumble's ten for 74 against Pakistan in 1998-99. As it was, he had to be content with the fifth-best analysis in Test cricket, and becoming the only bowler to take nine in an innings in two Tests; Laker took nine and ten in the same match at Old Trafford. In fact, Muralitharan ranked this performance behind his nine for 65 at The Oval in 1998. "It is difficult to get wickets there as a spinner," he said, "and England were a stronger side."

His exploits overshadowed a controversy on the eve of the Test when the home selectors planned to introduce two newcomers at the expense of the team's vice-captain and opening batsman, Atapattu, and the seamer Buddika Fernando. The players closed ranks amid talk of pulling out. At 11 p.m. on the eve of the game, it emerged that the sports minister had overturned the selectors' decision.

Back on the field, Zimbabwe claimed first use of a true pitch, but Muralitharan was soon whisking through their line-up. In front of his home crowd he came on in the ninth over, and Gripper edged his second ball to slip. He bowled Masakadza in his third over, had Rennie stumped in his fifth, and Andy Flower caught behind in his seventh. By the end of his first spell, he had added Carlisle, lbw. When he returned from the other end, he took three balls to trap Wishart lbw, and bowled Streak in his next over. After tea, he beat Marillier and Grant Flower, the only batsman to offer prolonged resistance, to reach nine for 47. But Murali was held up by a stubborn last-wicket partnership between Friend and Olonga. He almost sabotaged his own chances when he dived on the boundary in a gallant attempt to dismiss Olonga off the bowling of Samaraweera, in the last over of the day – stirring memories of Richard Hadlee taking a catch in the deep at Brisbane in 1985-86 to deny himself all ten. Worse, Murali dislocated his ring finger in the process. There was a doctor on standby in case he needed a painkiller next morning. But Arnold's miss and Olonga's incompetence denied him the record.

Sri Lanka put the disappointment behind them, rattling along at four an over as Jayasuriya raced to his ninth Test hundred, an aggressive 139 off 212 balls. He was backed up by rapid cameos from Sangakkara and Jayawardene and dogged efforts from the tail: Vaas added a patient 111 for the eighth wicket with Fernando and scored an unbeaten seventy for the second match running. Grant Flower exerted some control and Streak bowled better than his figures suggested but Zimbabwe conceded a first-innings lead of 269 and, by the end of the third day, were three down again. Muralitharan had already taken his tenth wicket of the match – for the tenth time in Tests, beating Hadlee's world record of nine. When he concluded proceedings on the fourth afternoon, he had 13 for 115. Fernando, who had so nearly been omitted, also picked up four wickets, including Rennie, whose plucky 68 spanned three hours. No one else offered more than token resistance as Sri Lanka accelerated to another innings victory.

Man of the Match: M. Muralitharan.

Close of play: First day, Zimbabwe 234-9 (Friend 28, Olonga 17); Second day, Sri Lanka 334-4 (Arnold 44, Tillekeratne 35); Third day, Zimbabwe 68-3 (Rennie 26, A. Flower 6).

Zimbabwe

H. Masakadza b Muralitharan		10 – b Vaas	0
T. R. Gripper c Jayawardene b Muralitharan		20 – lbw b Muralitharan	21
*S. V. Carlisle lbw b Muralitharan		20 – c Atapattu b Vaas	9
G. J. Rennie st Sangakkara b Muralitharan		0 – lbw b Fernando	68
†A. Flower c Sangakkara b Muralitharan		8 – lbw b Fernando	11
G. W. Flower b Muralitharan		72 – c Sangakkara b Fernando	21
C. B. Wishart lbw b Muralitharan		26 – c Jayasuriya b Muralitharan	3
H. H. Streak b Muralitharan		1 – not out	14
D. A. Marillier b Muralitharan		9 – lbw b Fernando	9
T. J. Friend not out		29 – b Fernando	0
H. K. Olonga c Sangakkara b Vaas		18 – c Samaraweera b Muralitharan	1
B 3, l-b 7, n-b 14		24 L-b 6, n-b 12	18

1/39 (2) 2/45 (1) 3/51 (4) 4/67 (5)   236   175
5/83 (3) 6/137 (7) 7/140 (8)   1/0 (1) 2/16 (3) 3/51 (2)
8/166 (9) 9/201 (6) 10/236 (11)   4/109 (5) 5/134 (4) 6/138 (7)
    7/160 (6) 8/173 (9)
    9/174 (10) 10/175 (11)

Bowling: *First Innings*—Vaas 17–4–58–1; Zoysa 15–2–44–0; Muralitharan 40–19–51–9; Fernando 5–2–13–0; Samaraweera 8–2–33–0; Jayasuriya 12–3–27–0. *Second Innings*—Vaas 18–5–35–2; Zoysa 10–1–30–0; Muralitharan 26.4–7–64–4; Samaraweera 4–2–2–0; Tillekeratne 1–0–8–0; Jayasuriya 1–0–3–0; Fernando 12–2–27–4.

Sri Lanka

M. S. Atapattu lbw b Friend	9	T. C. B. Fernando c Friend b Masakadza	45
*S. T. Jayasuriya c Gripper		D. N. T. Zoysa run out	4
b G. W. Flower	139	M. Muralitharan b Streak	1
†K. C. Sangakkara hit wkt b Friend	42		
D. P. M. D. Jayawardene		B 3, l-b 1, w 1, n-b 7	12
lbw b G. W. Flower	56		
R. P. Arnold c Wishart b G. W. Flower	71	1/11 (1) 2/82 (3) 3/202 (4)	505
H. P. Tillekeratne lbw b Streak	37	4/273 (2) 5/336 (6) 6/365 (7)	
T. T. Samaraweera c A. Flower b Friend	17	7/388 (5) 8/499 (9)	
W. P. U. J. C. Vaas not out	72	9/503 (10) 10/505 (11)	

Bowling: Streak 32.5–7–85–2; Friend 26–4–97–3; Olonga 24–2–131–0; Marillier 21–4–75–0; G. W. Flower 28–4–66–3; Gripper 14–3–38–0; Masakadza 3–0–9–1.

Umpires: S. Venkataraghavan (India) and E. A. R. de Silva.
Third umpire: P. T. Manuel. Referee: C. W. Smith (West Indies).

SRI LANKA v ZIMBABWE

Third Test Match

At Galle, January 12, 13, 14, 15. Sri Lanka won by 315 runs. Toss: Sri Lanka.

Muralitharan was the cynosure of all eyes. He entered the match needing five wickets to become the seventh bowler in history – and the second spinner, after Shane Warne – to reach 400 Test wickets. But the spectators who poured into the Galle Stadium in anticipation had to wait until the fourth morning, as Zimbabwe played their best cricket of the series during the first three days.

Winning the toss for the first time, Jayasuriya chose to bat. For once, however, the Zimbabweans seemed to have the measure of the home batsmen; when Streak trapped Vaas on the second morning, they had captured Sri Lanka's first seven wickets for 254, with the part-time spinners Grant Flower and Marillier doing much of the damage. But they could not finish them off, as Samaraweera and Chandana added 146, an eighth-wicket record for Sri Lanka in all Tests. Chandana narrowly failed to convert a maiden Test fifty into a century, while Samaraweera's 76 took his career average to 103.00 in eight Tests – quite something for a player selected largely for his bowling.

Zimbabwe's batsmen also showed more resolve. With Masakadza gone to the Under-19 World Cup, Carlisle promoted himself to open with Gripper, and they compiled 153, only 11 short of Zimbabwe's first-wicket record. Just as importantly, they used up 81 overs and 278 minutes before Jayasuriya separated them, and they patiently demonstrated that Muralitharan could be played off the front foot. Gripper's determined 83 was Zimbabwe's highest score of the series, and Carlisle batted nearly five and a half hours. By the third evening, the tourists were 230 for five, and had comfortably saved the follow-on.

On the fourth day, however, they fell apart in spectacular fashion. They added only six more runs for the remaining five wickets, maintaining their strange inability to pass 236. Jayasuriya claimed his first five-wicket haul in Tests, but the crowd got what they really wanted when Muralitharan reached the 400 mark by bowling Friend and Olonga with successive balls. He had got there in 72 Tests, trimming eight off Richard Hadlee's record, and at 29 years 273 days was

TIME AND TESTS TAKEN TO 400 WICKETS

Tests		Years	Days	Total*
72	M. Muralitharan (Sri Lanka)	29	273	437 in 78 Tests
80	R. J. Hadlee (New Zealand)	38	216	431 in 86 Tests
87	G. D. McGrath (Australia)	32	254	422 in 91 Tests
92	S. K. Warne (Australia)	31	346	491 in 107 Tests
96	Wasim Akram (Pakistan)	34	13	414 in 104 Tests
97	C. E. L. Ambrose (West Indies)	36	331	405 in 98 Tests
107	C. A. Walsh (West Indies)	36	126	519 in 132 Tests
115	Kapil Dev (India)	33	28	434 in 131 Tests

* Up to February 28, 2003.

also the youngest bowler to reach 400, beating Warne by more than two years. "The main thing in my mind is to take 500 wickets," Murali said. "But if I remain fit and keep performing well, then I can continue for another five years and could get 600."

Inspired by his feats, his colleagues rattled up 212 for two in 41 overs before declaring; Atapattu scored an unbeaten century in 126 balls, while Sangakkara charged to 56 from 50. Left a target of 395 in a minimum 125 overs, Zimbabwe collapsed in a heap. Jayasuriya and Muralitharan continued to share the spoils in a deadly partnership, shooting Zimbabwe out for their second lowest total in Tests – 79 inside 44 overs, as the fourth day was extended to produce a result. Muralitharan finished with 60 wickets, at 15.55 each, from his eight Tests at Galle.

Man of the Match: S. T. Jayasuriya. *Man of the Series:* M. Muralitharan.

Close of play: First day, Sri Lanka 243-6 (Samaraweera 8, Vaas 2); Second day, Zimbabwe 18-0 (Carlisle 13, Gripper 3); Third day, Zimbabwe 230-5 (G. W. Flower 19, Streak 29).

Sri Lanka

M. S. Atapattu c Rennie b G. W. Flower	. . . . .	50	– not out	100
*S. T. Jayasuriya b Friend	. . . .	28	– c Wishart b Olonga	36
†K. C. Sangakkara b Marillier	. . . .	29	– c Gripper b Friend	56
D. P. M. D. Jayawardene c and b G. W. Flower	.	76	– not out	17
R. P. Arnold c A. Flower b Streak	. . . .	40		
H. P. Tillekeratne c A. Flower b Marillier	. . . .	3		
T. T. Samaraweera run out	. . . .	76		
W. P. U. J. C. Vaas lbw b Streak	. . . .	8		
U. D. U. Chandana c Carlisle b Marillier	. . . .	92		
T. C. B. Fernando b Marillier	. . . .	1		
M. Muralitharan not out	. . . .	5		
B 2, l-b 5, n-b 3	. . . .	10	L-b 1, n-b 2	3

1/50 (2) 2/107 (1) 3/125 (3) 4/222 (4)   418   1/75 (2) 2/170 (3)   (2 wkts dec.) 212
5/229 (6) 6/236 (5) 7/254 (8)
8/400 (9) 9/413 (7) 10/418 (10)

Bowling: *First Innings*—Streak 32–11–70–2; Friend 26–7–58–1; Olonga 18–6–52–0; G. W. Flower 39–7–89–2; Marillier 34.4–5–101–4; Gripper 9–0–41–0. *Second Innings*—Streak 11–1–35–0; Friend 7–0–39–1; G. W. Flower 9–0–38–0; Marillier 6–0–34–0; Olonga 7–0–56–1; Rennie 1–0–9–0.

Zimbabwe

*S. V. Carlisle lbw b Muralitharan	64	– lbw b Jayasuriya 28
T. R. Gripper st Sangakkara b Jayasuriya	83	– lbw b Jayasuriya. 3
C. B. Wishart lbw b Jayasuriya	1	– c Samaraweera b Muralitharan.... 7
G. J. Rennie c Sangakkara b Jayasuriya	7	– c Arnold b Muralitharan. 6
†A. Flower c Tillekeratne b Muralitharan	6	– c Jayawardene b Jayasuriya. 3
G. W. Flower lbw b Muralitharan	19	– lbw b Jayasuriya. 0
H. H. Streak b Jayasuriya	33	– c Jayasuriya b Muralitharan 7
D. D. Ebrahim c Arnold b Jayasuriya	1	– not out 5
D. A. Marillier not out	0	– c and b Muralitharan.......... 15
T. J. Friend b Muralitharan.	1	– lbw b Vaas 3
H. K. Olonga b Muralitharan	0	– c Fernando b Vaas 0
B 11, l-b 8, n-b 2	21	L-b 1, n-b 1 2

1/153 (2) 2/155 (3) 3/161 (1) 4/171 (4)   **236**   1/17 (2) 2/30 (3) 3/38 (4)   **79**
5/171 (5) 6/232 (6) 7/234 (7)   4/45 (5) 5/45 (6) 6/54 (1)
8/235 (8) 9/236 (10) 10/236 (11)   7/56 (7) 8/72 (9) 9/79 (10) 10/79 (11)

Bowling: *First Innings*—Vaas 19–7–36–0; Fernando 11–1–33–0; Muralitharan 58.3–26–67–5; Jayasuriya 29–10–43–5; Chandana 12–4–24–0; Samaraweera 5–1–14–0. *Second Innings*—Vaas 7.3–2–17–2; Fernando 2–0–6–0; Jayasuriya 18–5–31–4; Muralitharan 16–7–24–4.

Umpires: D. R. Shepherd (England) and T. H. Wijewardene.
Third umpire: M. G. Silva. Referee: C. W. Smith (West Indies).

THE SOUTH AFRICANS IN AUSTRALIA, 2001-02

By GIDEON HAIGH

On the eve of the First Test at Adelaide, South Africa's captain, Shaun Pollock, was asked by a photographer to pose beside the ICC Test Championship mace. He declined, politely, on superstitious grounds: he had posed with the World Cup 30 months earlier, and South Africa's exit from that tournament at Australia's hands was a memory he preferred not to revisit.

Pollock's refusal to tempt the fates was wise, but he added to his bad memories anyway. Though the ICC tabulations said South Africa would replace Australia as Championship leaders by winning or drawing this three-Test rubber, they never looked like contenders. The tourists were thrice disposed of by big margins, with ample time to spare, and in some disarray.

For Australia, the encounter put further flesh on an already far-from-bony case to be considered the outstanding cricket team of the last decade. The latest weapon in their line-up was the left-handed opening combination of Matthew Hayden and Justin Langer; a *faute de mieux* arrangement in England had flowered on home soil. The hulking Hayden was overpowering, scoring his 429 runs at a strike-rate of around 60 per hundred balls. Always busy, always acquisitive, Langer was less eye-catching but little less effective, having turned his recall at The Oval into a new lease on life. By the end of the series, their average partnership was a hearty 117.90, including four double-century stands in 11 innings.

What the openers left incomplete, Damien Martyn polished off at No. 6, with compact technique and crisp timing. It was hard to believe his centuries at Adelaide and Sydney were his first in home Tests, such was Martyn's composure in the presence of the tail and easeful manipulation of the strike. The Waughs and Gilchrist were less productive than usual, but never really needed.

Despite fielding only four specialist bowlers in each match, Australia's attack contained sufficient variety to cover most contingencies. After their unsuccessful series against New Zealand, Glenn McGrath and Shane Warne were back to their usual steady selves. Brett Lee improved as the Tests progressed, beating Herschelle Gibbs at Sydney with a ball that went through him like an X-ray. The horses-for-courses selections – Andy Bichel in Melbourne and Stuart MacGill in Sydney – paid off nicely, and all were abetted by fielding of the highest quality. Ricky Ponting's 11 catches contained some which justified the invention of the television replay.

Yet it was hard to credit that Pollock's team arrived with pretensions to world-champion status. Glimpses of the excellence of Jacques Kallis and Gary Kirsten, and of the promise of Neil McKenzie and Boeta Dippenaar, usually came only when the cause was already lost. The translation of starts into scores was also disappointing: Australian batsmen reached double figures 30 times, on a dozen occasions passing fifty, and on seven transiting to a hundred; their South African counterparts reached double figures 36 times, but only made nine fifties, and one century – by Kirsten, at the very last.

The South African pace bowlers, meanwhile, seemed to have lost the power to coax any sideways movement from the ball. Even Pollock swung it only in Sydney, while Kallis, Nantie Hayward and Allan Donald were persevering rather than hostile. The left-arm spinner Claude Henderson made a useful beginning, but was steadily swept and reverse-swept into submission. His colleague Nicky Boje, recovering from knee tendinitis, arrived too late.

Lance Klusener was the chief disappointment. His pick-up was so crooked and bat face so closed that he seemed incapable of scoring on the off side, while his bowling was so ineffectual that he was not introduced in Melbourne until the 110th over, when Australia were already 407 for four. He was sent home before the Sydney Test, a forlorn shadow of the figure who was named Man of the Tournament in the last World Cup.

The other contrast was between the captains. Steve Waugh not only won three crucial tosses, but was masterful at exerting pressure; it was remarkable how often the Australians turned one wicket into two or three. Pollock followed predictable patterns, and was slow to exploit opportunities. Support bowlers were left on when strike bowlers should have been called up, and hours would elapse with fields essentially unaltered – by comparison, Hansie Cronje seemed like Edward de Bono. The South Africans appeared professional, insofar as their game was utterly joyless. But Pollock could plead that he hardly had the sort of solid reinforcement on which Waugh could rely, not from his team, and certainly not from his board.

There were rumblings throughout the tour of discontent with management, before the Third Test generated an unedifying public dispute. The selectors had pencilled in the 20-year-old Jacques Rudolph for his Test debut at No. 3 to relieve pressure on the out-of-form Dippenaar, who was to be given refuge at No. 6. But the evening before the match, Percy Sonn, the president of the United Cricket Board, rejected the team as submitted and demanded the inclusion of Justin Ontong, a coloured batsman. Although the UCB quota of one "player of colour" was satisfied by the inclusion of Gibbs, and Ontong had collected a pair in his only match of the tour, Sonn invoked a statute committing the board to promoting non-whites wherever possible. The proposed reshuffle of the order, he said, amounted to the "exclusion of a person of colour who has the right to be given the opportunity". Ontong replaced Rudolph, who had already missed out on one Test debut – he had played in the Centurion game with India which was denied official status.

Sonn managed to be simultaneously uncompromising and contradictory. On the one hand, he claimed his intercession was affirmative action at work; on the other, he suggested the selectors had indulged in gerrymandering in excluding Ontong, and that he had interposed to ensure selection on merit. This is not to dispute the legitimacy of affirmative action, or even the efficacy of quotas; it was merely staggering that there should have been ambiguity on the issue, and that Sonn should have interfered so clumsily and autocratically. His comment that, as professionals, Pollock's team would simply do as they were told smacked of cricket administration at its old-fashioned feudal worst. An anonymous player told Johannesburg's *Star* that players were "angry and frustrated" that "administrators like Sonn, who know very little about cricket, come out and put the skids under us". In the end, Ontong had a decent match, and in the one-day series which followed South Africa turned their game around, beating New Zealand in the finals. But to work out that Sonn's intervention was an ill omen for South African cricket did not require a superstitious nature.

SOUTH AFRICAN TOURING PARTY

S. M. Pollock (KwaZulu-Natal) (*captain*), M. V. Boucher (Border) (*vice-captain*), H. H. Dippenaar (Free State), A. A. Donald (Free State), S. Elworthy (Northerns), H. H. Gibbs (Western Province), M. Hayward (Eastern Province), C. W. Henderson (Western Province), J. H. Kallis (Western Province), G. Kirsten (Western Province), L. Klusener (KwaZulu-Natal), N. D. McKenzie (Northerns), M. Ntini (Border), J. L. Ontong (Boland), J. A. Rudolph (Northerns).

N. Boje (Free State), an original selection who withdrew through injury and was replaced by Henderson, later reinforced the party. Klusener flew home before the Third Test but returned for the one-day series. J. M. Kemp (Eastern Province), C. K. Langeveldt (Boland), J. N. Rhodes (KwaZulu-Natal) replaced Hayward, Henderson and Rudolph for the one-day series.

Coach: G. X. Ford.   *Manager:* Goolam Rajah.   *Assistant coach:* C. J. P. G. van Zyl.

SOUTH AFRICAN TOUR RESULTS

Test matches – Played 3: Lost 3.
First-class matches – Played 5: Lost 3, Drawn 2.
Losses – Australia (3).
Draws – Western Australia, New South Wales.
One-day internationals – Played 10: Won 6, Lost 4. *Wins* – Australia, New Zealand (5). *Losses* – New Zealand, Australia (3).
Other non-first-class matches – Played 2: Won 1, Lost 1. *Win* – ACB Chairman's XIII. *Loss* – Australia A.

TEST MATCH AVERAGES

AUSTRALIA – BATTING

	T	I	NO	R	HS	100s	50s	Avge	Ct/St
D. R. Martyn	3	4	2	299	124*	2	1	149.50	1
M. L. Hayden	3	6	2	429	138	3	0	107.25	2
J. L. Langer	3	6	1	365	126	2	1	73.00	2
S. R. Waugh	3	4	0	141	90	0	1	35.25	0
M. E. Waugh	3	4	0	129	74	0	1	32.25	4
A. C. Gilchrist	3	4	1	93	34	0	0	31.00	9/1
R. T. Ponting	3	5	1	115	54	0	1	28.75	11
B. Lee	3	3	0	64	32	0	0	21.33	1
S. K. Warne	3	4	0	85	41	0	0	21.25	2
G. D. McGrath	3	3	1	6	5	0	0	3.00	1

Played in one Test: A. J. Bichel 5 (2 ct); J. N. Gillespie 3; S. C. G. MacGill 20 (1 ct).

BOWLING

	O	M	R	W	BB	5W/i	Avge
A. J. Bichel	32	6	96	4	3-44	0	24.00
S. C. G. MacGill	65.2	19	174	7	4-123	0	24.85
G. D. McGrath	139	43	350	14	3-13	0	25.00
S. K. Warne	173.3	35	473	17	5-113	1	27.82
B. Lee	105	27	314	9	3-77	0	34.88

Also bowled: J. N. Gillespie 34–11–80–2; D. R. Martyn 5–2–4–1; R. T. Ponting 1–0–11–0; M. E. Waugh 17–2–42–1.

SOUTH AFRICA – BATTING

	T	I	NO	R	HS	100s	50s	Avge	Ct
J. H. Kallis	3	6	1	245	99	0	2	49.00	3
G. Kirsten	3	6	0	245	153	1	0	40.83	1
N. D. McKenzie	3	6	0	224	87	0	2	37.33	6
S. M. Pollock	3	6	2	128	61*	0	1	32.00	2
M. V. Boucher	3	6	0	169	64	0	1	28.16	7
H. H. Gibbs	3	6	0	164	78	0	1	27.33	0
H. H. Dippenaar	3	6	0	130	74	0	1	21.66	0
M. Hayward	2	4	2	26	14	0	0	13.00	1
L. Klusener	2	4	0	47	22	0	0	11.75	1
C. W. Henderson	3	6	0	65	30	0	0	10.83	2
A. A. Donald	2	4	1	11	7	0	0	3.66	1

Played in one Test: N. Boje 7, 1; M. Ntini 9, 4 (1 ct); J. L. Ontong 9, 32.

BOWLING

	O	*M*	*R*	*W*	*BB*	*5W/i*	*Avge*
N. Boje.	27.3	6	78	4	4-63	0	19.50
S. M. Pollock.	112	27	312	8	3-84	0	39.00
M. Hayward.	67	6	249	5	3-108	0	49.80
A. A. Donald	65	11	238	4	3-103	0	59.50
C. W. Henderson	120.1	11	480	8	4-116	0	60.00
J. H. Kallis	70	7	266	4	3-45	0	66.50

Also bowled: L. Klusener 25–5–82–2; M. Ntini 27–10–77–0; J. L. Ontong 2–0–10–0.

Note: Matches in this section which were not first-class are signified by a dagger.

†At Lilac Hill, Perth, December 5. **South Africans won by 48 runs.** Toss: South Africans. **South Africans 257 for nine** (50 overs) (H. H. Gibbs 39, N. D. McKenzie 76, L. Klusener 64; A. J. Bichel three for 28); **ACB Chairman's XIII 209** (44.1 overs) (M. E. K. Hussey 56, D. M. Jones 38; S. Elworthy four for 27).

Each side named 13 players, of whom 11 could bat and 11 field.

At Perth, December 7, 8, 9, 10. **Drawn.** Toss: South Africans. **South Africans 367** (G. Kirsten 31, J. A. Rudolph 59, N. D. McKenzie 35, M. V. Boucher 134; M. J. Nicholson five for 68, S. J. Karppinen four for 110) **and 390 for five** (G. Kirsten 59, J. H. Kallis 120, N. D. McKenzie 114, L. Klusener 50; G. B. Hogg three for 119); **Western Australia 600 for eight dec.** (S. W. Meuleman 109, S. M. Katich 66, M. W. Goodwin 61, M. J. North 71, G. B. Hogg 90, M. J. Nicholson 101 not out, Extras 34).

Hogg and Nicholson added 175 for Western Australia's seventh wicket.

AUSTRALIA v SOUTH AFRICA

First Test Match

At Adelaide, December 14, 15, 16, 17, 18. Australia won by 246 runs. Toss: Australia.

After an inconclusive series against New Zealand, Australia entered this match with the objective, expressed by Steve Waugh, of proving they were "still a very good cricket side". They accomplished it with ease and a session to spare, although South Africa's final, hasty capitulation made it look a little too easy.

Although Australia had left out a second spinner, Waugh did not hesitate to bat first on a benign surface. The busy Langer punctured the covers thrice in Ntini's opening over, and breezed to his fifty with nine boundaries. The attack soon appeared ineffectual, not to say monotonous; it took smart work at cover by Dippenaar to remove Ponting and end his two-hour partnership with Langer.

Some thoughtful left-arm spin from Henderson checked Australia. After striking Henderson for six to reach his fourth century in five Tests, Langer became curiously becalmed, spending 100 minutes over his last 14 runs before edging to slip. Both Waughs failed in their 100th Test together, and when Gilchrist followed, South Africa were back on level terms. But Martyn was ominously poised. Aided by Warne and Lee, he prolonged the innings by another 51 overs next day. Martyn's first home Test century, his highest yet, made up in value what it lacked in spectacle. By game's end, his record at Adelaide was 210 runs without dismissal in four Test innings.

Steve Waugh turned to Warne for the fourth over of South Africa's reply, and was almost rewarded at once as Kirsten's edge barely eluded slip's grasp. Just when the openers appeared settled, McGrath baffled Kirsten with a full toss and conned Dippenaar into an undisciplined slash. Without a three-hour stand of 141 between the studious McKenzie and Boucher, the South African innings would have been a ragged affair, and their deficit far greater than 65.

Lightning reaction: Shane Warne dismisses Shaun Pollock thanks to a breathtaking catch by Ricky Ponting – and the game is all but over for South Africa. *Picture by Nick Wilson, Getty Images.*

Warne returned to something like his best, recovering his menacing drift into the right-hander, and bowling over and round the wicket with all his old facility. His plot to uproot Gibbs was one for the scrapbook: a beguiling leg-break into the footmarks spun round the advancing batsman for Gilchrist to execute the stumping. After bagging five in an innings for the 20th time in Tests, Warne volunteered that a target of 250 in the fourth innings would be demanding: "The pitch is going to get worse, and it will keep lower for the fast bowlers." His prognosis showed why John the Bookie had once valued his opinions.

Batting became more difficult from the fourth morning, when inconsistent bounce accounted for an impatient Ponting, but it should have been worse: South Africa's bowlers went through some rather unimaginative motions. Pollock overused Henderson so much that at one stage he had nought for 109. Hayden was allowed to put on 181 at better than a run a minute with Mark Waugh, and he sacrificed his wicket only when Australia began accelerating towards a declaration.

Steve Waugh gave South Africa 12 overs plus the last day to score 375. With a sniff of assistance from the pitch, his men crowded the bat and attacked the stumps, hassling and hustling for a breakthrough. Both openers prodded anxiously to short leg, Kirsten from the day's last delivery. The final morning was a rout. The tourists' doubt about the bounce showed in their diffident shots and non-shots, smacking of mental frailty. Kallis alone suggested permanence, steering them away from the ignominy of 74 for eight to finish unbeaten after almost four hours.

An unusual feature of the match was that four wickets were forfeited by no-balls. Lee was responsible for two: Henderson and McKenzie, reprieved when caught at the wicket on the third day. Lee also blotted his copybook with his last over that evening, bowling four consecutive bouncers of escalating viciousness to Ntini and Hayward, both new to the crease, neither with pretensions to batsmanship. The first and second hit Ntini resoundingly on the helmet, the third and fourth chased the retreating Hayward to the extremity of the crease, while umpire Taufel remained mute.

The rest of the Test demonstrated the needlessness of this sideshow; the Australians did not have to intimidate in order to seem intimidating. Lee finished with two tail-end wickets, while the old stager Warne won the match award with eight. His first-innings five for 113 was the best by a leg-spinner at Adelaide since Richie Benaud's five for 96 against West Indies in 1960-61. It took Warne past 50 Test wickets in the calendar year and lifted him to fourth in the all-time Test bowlers' table, passing Wasim Akram's 414.

Man of the Match: S. K. Warne.   *Attendance:* 77,555.

Close of play: First day, Australia 272-6 (Martyn 37, Warne 7); Second day, South Africa 101-2 (Gibbs 42, Henderson 3); Third day, Australia 3-0 (Langer 0, Hayden 3); Fourth day, South Africa 17-2 (Dippenaar 0).

Australia

J. L. Langer c Pollock b Henderson	116	– c Boucher b Pollock	1
M. L. Hayden c Ntini b Klusener	31	– b Kallis	131
R. T. Ponting run out	54	– lbw b Kallis	25
M. E. Waugh c Boucher b Hayward	2	– c Boucher b Henderson	74
*S. R. Waugh c McKenzie b Henderson	8	– (6) c Pollock b Henderson	13
D. R. Martyn not out	124	– (7) not out	6
†A. C. Gilchrist c Hayward b Henderson	7	– (5) c McKenzie b Kallis	22
S. K. Warne b Klusener	41	– b Henderson	6
B. Lee c McKenzie b Hayward	32		
J. N. Gillespie c Boucher b Henderson	3		
G. D. McGrath b Hayward	5		
L-b 6, n-b 10	16	B 8, l-b 16, n-b 7	31

1/80 (2) 2/182 (3) 3/199 (4) 4/211 (5)   **439**   1/8 (1) 2/66 (3)   (7 wkts dec.) **309**
5/238 (1) 6/248 (7) 7/332 (8)   3/247 (2) 4/273 (4)
8/409 (9) 9/434 (10) 10/439 (11)   5/291 (5) 6/303 (6) 7/309 (8)

Bowling: First Innings—Pollock 28–8–64–0; Hayward 31–5–108–3; Ntini 19–7–64–0; Kallis 16–1–37–0; Klusener 14–4–44–2; Henderson 33–4–116–4. *Second Innings*—Pollock 12–4–38–1; Hayward 10–0–32–0; Henderson 29.1–1–130–3; Kallis 15.2–2–45–3; Ntini 8–3–13–0; Klusener 4–0–27–0.

South Africa

H. H. Gibbs st Gilchrist b Warne	78	– c Langer b McGrath	9
G. Kirsten lbw b McGrath	47	– c Ponting b Warne	7
H. H. Dippenaar c Ponting b McGrath	4	– c Warne b McGrath	0
C. W. Henderson run out	30	– (9) c Ponting b Warne	3
J. H. Kallis lbw b McGrath	5	– (4) not out	65
N. D. McKenzie lbw b Martyn	87	– (5) lbw b McGrath	0
L. Klusener b Warne	22	– (6) c Warne b Gillespie	18
†M. V. Boucher c Langer b Warne	64	– (7) c Gilchrist b Gillespie	0
*S. M. Pollock c Gilchrist b Warne	0	– (8) c Ponting b Warne	1
M. Ntini c Ponting b Warne	9	– b Lee	4
M. Hayward not out	0	– c Gilchrist b Lee	12
B 8, l-b 9, n-b 11	28	B 4, l-b 1, w 1, n-b 3	9

1/87 (2) 2/93 (3) 3/155 (4) 4/178 (1)   **374**   1/12 (1) 2/17 (2) 3/21 (3) 4/21 (5)   **128**
5/178 (5) 6/214 (7) 7/355 (6)   5/54 (6) 6/58 (7) 7/67 (8) 8/74 (9)
8/356 (9) 9/365 (8) 10/374 (10)   9/113 (10) 10/128 (11)

Bowling: First Innings—McGrath 33–10–94–3; Gillespie 23–7–57–0; Warne 39.4–9–113–5; Lee 19–2–81–0; M. E. Waugh 3–0–9–0; Martyn 4–2–3–1. *Second Innings*—McGrath 14–8–13–3; Gillespie 11–4–23–2; Warne 29–7–57–3; Lee 12–3–29–2; Martyn 1–0–1–0.

Umpires: S. Venkataraghavan (India) and S. J. A. Taufel.

Third umpire: S. J. Davis.   Referee: R. S. Madugalle (Sri Lanka).

At Sydney, December 20, 21, 22, 23. **Drawn.** Toss: South Africans. **South Africans 498** (G. Kirsten 31, H. H. Gibbs 145, J. A. Rudolph 52, H. H. Dippenaar 115, M. V. Boucher 44, S. M. Pollock 53, S. Elworthy 31; J. M. Heath three for 72, S. C. G. MacGill five for 132) **and 269 for five dec.** (G. Kirsten 88, H. H. Gibbs 75, H. H. Dippenaar 31 not out, S. M. Pollock 36 not out; S. C. G. MacGill four for 89); **New South Wales 385 for six dec.** (G. J. Mail 54, C. J. Richards 37, M. G. Bevan 183 not out, M. J. Clarke 37; S. Elworthy three for 57) **and 135 for two** (G. J. Mail 54, B. P. van Deinsen 61).

AUSTRALIA v SOUTH AFRICA

Second Test Match

At Melbourne, December 26, 27, 28, 29. Australia won by nine wickets. Toss: Australia.

The South Africans were not merely beaten, but beaten into submission. Their abject surrender of the series on the fourth day called both their recent record and their aspirations to the Test Championship into question. Their grim, regimented cricket was brittle beside Australia's confident ebullience, and above all the indefatigable openers, Hayden and Langer.

Nominally, the South Africans picked their strongest eleven, with Donald pronounced fit for his first Test since April. But their strength derived from deeds recalled rather than deeds recently recorded: Donald had taken only one first-class wicket on tour, and Klusener had just made a pair in a high-scoring match against New South Wales. The Australians were without the injured Gillespie, but Bichel fitted into the ensemble so neatly, with four wickets, two catches and a run-out, that disruption was minimal.

Only 40 overs were bowled on the first day in gloomy conditions that tried the South Africans' application and found it wanting. They were 59 for three when Dippenaar was caught at gully by Hayden diving to his right. McKenzie showed impressive poise next day, sharing half-century stands with Kallis and Boucher, but even survival was a struggle. Kallis, dropped twice off Bichel and troubled by the short ball when he moved mechanically on to the front foot, needed almost three hours to score 38, and was then adjudged caught behind, off Bichel again, from a ball he clearly missed; umpire Nicholls was deceived by the out-swing once it passed the bat. Klusener shovelled back a return catch to Bichel from his first ball, and Donald lasted one menacing over from Lee.

Though Pollock and Hayward provided an affirmative finish with a last-wicket stand of 44 in 12 overs, they were ineffectual with the ball, and Hayden and Langer were even more positive in Australia's reply. Their first 50 materialised in 11 overs, and they proceeded without difficulty to their third double-century partnership of the season. Hayden's flawless 138, including 17 fours in ten minutes under five hours, was the climax of 12 months in which he had finally repaid the faith of supporters and selectors. Bob Simpson's Australian record of 1,381 Test runs at 60.04 in the calendar year 1964 was overhauled; Hayden finished the game with 1,391 at 63.22 in 2001, including five centuries. Both men played 14 Tests at that time; Hayden had 25 innings to Simpson's 26. For good measure, he completed 1,000 first-class runs for the Australian season when he reached 130.

Australia passed South Africa's 277 with three wickets down, in enervating heat: ideal conditions for their captain to run himself back into form. Steve Waugh was below his best – Dippenaar, twice caught on his heels when bat-pad chances looped towards short leg, let Donald down badly – but still quick to dispose of loose deliveries. He even essayed a rare hook. But after nearly three hours, he was out in the 90s for the tenth time in Tests, a record. Beaten by Gibbs's direct hit, Waugh did not see umpire Hair's raised finger, and was awaiting a replay when informed. He stayed for almost 20 seconds, apparently asking about consulting the third umpire, which contradicted his public statements that Australia would lead the way in respecting umpires' decisions. The replay did raise questions – one bail seemed to be disturbed by Boucher before Gibbs struck the stumps – but the referee, Ranjan Madugalle, docked Waugh half his match fee. Waugh later complained of being "crucified in the papers", and criticised official restriction on his scope for comment.

South Africa regained some heart, and their pace attack some rhythm; when McGrath fell in the first over of the fourth day, Australia had lost their last six wickets for 58 in 23 overs. But as at Adelaide, only Kallis stood firm as the tourists gave a puny second-innings display, despite an excellent pitch and sapping heat. The Australians fielded brilliantly even by their standards. Hayden, at short leg, caught Dippenaar off a full-blooded punch; Mark Waugh, in his 100th consecutive Test, took two slick catches at slip that belied their difficulty, and Martyn executed two run-outs. The second, involving a smart gather by Gilchrist on the half-volley as a flat return rocketed in from point, caught Kallis a foot or two short of a century as he tried to commandeer the strike from the last man, Hayward. It ended a brave innings from Kallis, who had batted more than seven and a half hours in the match: a feat splendid in its defiance and disappointing in its loneliness. At least he made Australia bat again, if only for three overs, to claim their series victory.

Man of the Match: M. L. Hayden.   *Attendance:* 153,025.

Close of play: First day, South Africa 89-3 (Kallis 22, McKenzie 14); Second day, Australia 126-0 (Langer 67, Hayden 55); Third day, Australia 487-9 (Gilchrist 30, McGrath 0).

South Africa

H. H. Gibbs c Ponting b McGrath	14	– c Gilchrist b Lee	21
G. Kirsten b McGrath	10	– c Ponting b Lee	10
H. H. Dippenaar c Hayden b Lee	26	– c Hayden b Warne	23
J. H. Kallis c Gilchrist b Bichel	38	– run out	99
N. D. McKenzie lbw b Lee	67	– c M. E. Waugh b Warne	12
L. Klusener c and b Bichel	0	– lbw b McGrath	7
†M. V. Boucher c Bichel b M. E. Waugh	43	– c M. E. Waugh b Warne	0
*S. M. Pollock not out	42	– run out	18
C. W. Henderson run out	5	– c M. E. Waugh b McGrath	16
A. A. Donald c Ponting b Lee	0	– b Bichel	7
M. Hayward c M. E. Waugh b Bichel	14	– not out	0
B 1, l-b 10, n-b 7	18	B 4, n-b 2	6

1/24 (1) 2/36 (2) 3/59 (3) 4/131 (4)   277   1/24 (2) 2/37 (1) 3/74 (3)   219
5/131 (6) 6/198 (7) 7/220 (5)   4/107 (5) 5/120 (6) 6/121 (7)
8/225 (9) 9/233 (10) 10/277 (11)   7/157 (8) 8/192 (9)
    9/215 (10) 10/219 (4)

Bowling: *First Innings*—McGrath 26–8–70–2; Lee 31–10–77–3; Bichel 19.5–6–44–3; Warne 19–3–56–0; M. E. Waugh 8–1–19–1. *Second Innings*—McGrath 21–6–43–2; Lee 18–5–52–2; Warne 24–3–68–3; Bichel 12.1–0–52–1.

Australia

J. L. Langer c Klusener b Donald	85	– c Henderson b Pollock	7
M. L. Hayden c Donald b Henderson	138	– not out	3
R. T. Ponting c Kallis b Hayward	22	– not out	0
M. E. Waugh b Donald	34		
*S. R. Waugh run out	90		
D. R. Martyn c Kallis b Pollock	52		
†A. C. Gilchrist not out	30		
S. K. Warne c Kirsten b Donald	1		
B. Lee c McKenzie b Hayward	3		
A. J. Bichel c Boucher b Pollock	5		
G. D. McGrath lbw b Pollock	0		
L-b 17, w 1, n-b 9	27		

1/202 (1) 2/267 (3) 3/267 (2) 4/348 (4)   487   1/7 (1)   (1 wkt) 10
5/429 (5) 6/462 (6) 7/463 (8)
8/470 (9) 9/475 (10) 10/487 (11)

Bowling: *First Innings*—Donald 29–5–103–3; Pollock 31–3–84–3; Hayward 26–1–109–2; Kallis 17–3–55–0; Henderson 29–3–108–1; Klusener 7–1–11–0. *Second Innings*—Donald 2–0–4–0; Pollock 1–0–6–1.

Umpires: E. A. Nicholls (West Indies) and D. B. Hair.
Third umpire: R. L. Parry. Referee: R. S. Madugalle (Sri Lanka).

AUSTRALIA v SOUTH AFRICA

Third Test Match

At Sydney, January 2, 3, 4, 5. Australia won by ten wickets. Toss: Australia. Test debut: J. L. Ontong.

One of the most anticlimactic rubbers in memory ended late on the fourth day of the Third Test, when Australia swept the series clean. What had been promoted as the "Title Fight" had long since become a catchweight contest. The result has been in little doubt since tea on the first day, when Australia were 215 without loss, with Hayden and Langer again set like concrete in their fourth double-century opening partnership in ten starts. Only Gordon Greenidge and Desmond Haynes had shared so many opening doubles in Tests, and they had taken 134 innings.

Close friends: the series belonged to Australia's openers, Justin Langer and Matthew Hayden. *Picture by Chris McGrath, Getty Images.*

South Africa seemed present only to negotiate on a margin of defeat; they had already had to negotiate the selection row which dominated the preliminaries. With the out-of-form Klusener sent home, Jacques Rudolph was lined up for his debut. But on the eve of the match, their board president, Percy Sonn, insisted the place should go to a "player of colour", Justin Ontong, in accordance with the board policy of promoting non-whites when the opportunity arose. The intervention was clumsily handled, though Ontong and Rudolph – who were room-mates – responded with dignity, and Ontong did not disgrace himself on the field, either, making some useful runs and running out Ponting.

After an uncertain start – 12 runs in eight overs – Hayden and Langer revealed a rich array of strokes, rewarded by a fast outfield, and pounced on every bowler. When Henderson came on, Langer hefted him into the crowd at mid-on. When he resumed after lunch, Langer hop-scotched into a cover drive to the boundary. Pollock gave himself one more over: Hayden walloped a long-hop over the mid-wicket fence. Donald was recalled: Langer slashed through gully for four. Kallis returned: Hayden flailed three consecutive boundaries. Langer was the first to reach a hundred, his 12th in Tests, and celebrated expansively; half an hour later, Hayden, who was perhaps even more authoritative, marked his with the sign of the cross.

MOST DOUBLE-CENTURY OPENING STANDS IN TESTS

200s		T	I	Unbr	R	HS	100s	Avge
4	J. L. Langer/M. L. Hayden (A)	10	16	1	1,409	224	6	93.93
4	C. L. Greenidge/D. L. Haynes (WI)	89	148	11	6,483	298	16	47.32
3	W. M. Lawry/R. B. Simpson (A)	34	62	2	3,596	382	9	59.93
3	G. A. Gooch/M. A. Atherton (E)	24	44	0	2,501	225	7	56.84
3	M. A. Taylor/M. J. Slater (A)	44	78	2	3,887	260	10	51.14
2	J. B. Hobbs/H. Sutcliffe (E)	25	38	1	3,249	283	15	87.81
2	J. B. Hobbs/W. Rhodes (E)	22	36	1	2,146	323	8	61.31

Research: Gordon Vince

Not for the first time, Pollock's choices were flawed. Kallis, who was looted for almost a run a ball, was overused, while Boje, the left-arm spinner returning after injury, was held back until the 55th over, when 190 was on the board, when he proved the most economical of the lot. Although the Australians lost five for 93 in the final session, they were made impregnable on the second day by 117 from Martyn, scored in 166 balls with 13 fours. With the tailenders pitching in usefully, the last four wickets added 198 in less than 40 overs.

South Africa's attempt to reply lasted only five balls longer than Langer and Hayden's partnership. After two early blows from McGrath, Australia showed why they had picked two spinners for the first time in the series. MacGill secured a couple of key wickets by the close, and Warne struck in his first two overs of the morning to maintain the impetus. South Africa were following on before lunch, and looked like losing in three days when Lee whisked Gibbs's off stump away four overs after the break. They might have done had Mark Waugh held a regulation chance at second slip when Kirsten was 12. But the Australians grew impatient, conceding 22 boundaries in the afternoon as they tried to force another breakthrough. Kirsten and Dippenaar added 149 for the second wicket in 42 overs – South Africa's biggest stand of the series, and also their most fluent, which cast doubt on their earlier policy of self-denial.

Though it was too much to hope for a real fight, this was a handy subsidiary bout. Australia often tied Kirsten down, but took seven and a quarter hours to uproot him. After Dippenaar, several batsmen wasted useful starts. South Africa led by only three runs when their ninth wicket fell. Pollock struck 47 out of a last-wicket stand of 49 in 57 balls, including three sixes, one of them from overthrows. But Langer and Hayden disposed of their target inside 11 overs before sharing the match award. At the presentation ceremony, Steve Waugh announced that Australia would donate their $A51,000 prize money to a public appeal for victims of bushfires, which had burned out half a million hectares of forest round New South Wales during the Test.

Man of the Match: M. L. Hayden and J. L. Langer.   *Attendance:* 120,173.

Man of the Series: M. L. Hayden.

Close of play: First day, Australia 308-5 (Martyn 1); Second day, South Africa 93-4 (McKenzie 20, Ontong 8); Third day, South Africa 209-2 (Kirsten 82, Kallis 32).

Australia

J. L. Langer c McKenzie b Boje	126	– not out	30
M. L. Hayden c Kallis b Pollock	105	– not out	21
R. T. Ponting run out	14		
M. E. Waugh c Boucher b Donald	19		
*S. R. Waugh b Pollock	30		
D. R. Martyn c McKenzie b Boje	117		
†A. C. Gilchrist c Boucher b Kallis	34		
S. K. Warne b Pollock	37		
B. Lee b Boje	29		
S. C. G. MacGill c Henderson b Boje	20		
G. D. McGrath not out	1		
B 4, l-b 8, w 1, n-b 9	22	L-b 2, n-b 1	3
	554	(no wkt)	**54**

1/219 (2) 2/247 (3) 3/253 (1) 4/302 (5)
5/308 (4) 6/356 (7) 7/439 (8)
8/502 (9) 9/542 (10) 10/554 (6)

Bowling: *First Innings*—Donald 31–6–119–1; Pollock 37–11–109–3; Kallis 22–1–129–1; Henderson 27–3–112–0; Boje 25.2–6–63–4; Ontong 2–0–10–0. *Second Innings*—Donald 3–0–12–0; Pollock 3–1–11–0; Boje 2.1–0–15–0; Henderson 2–0–14–0.

South Africa

H. H. Gibbs c M. E. Waugh b MacGill	32	– b Lee	10
G. Kirsten c Ponting b McGrath	18	– b MacGill	153
H. H. Dippenaar b McGrath	3	– c Ponting b MacGill	74
J. H. Kallis c Gilchrist b MacGill	4	– c Gilchrist b Warne	34
N. D. McKenzie b Warne	20	– c MacGill b Lee	38
J. L. Ontong lbw b Warne	6	– lbw b Warne	32
†M. V. Boucher c Ponting b Warne	35	– c Gilchrist b McGrath	27
*S. M. Pollock c Martyn b McGrath	6	– not out	61
N. Boje run out	7	– b MacGill	1
C. W. Henderson c McGrath b MacGill	9	– b MacGill	2
A. A. Donald not out	4	– c Lee b Warne	2
L-b 8, n-b 1	9	B 8, l-b 7, n-b 3	18
	154		**452**

1/37 (2) 2/43 (3) 3/56 (4) 4/77 (1)
5/93 (5) 6/98 (6) 7/111 (8)
8/121 (9) 9/148 (7) 10/154 (10)

1/17 (1) 2/166 (3) 3/211 (4)
4/282 (5) 5/356 (6) 6/372 (2)
7/392 (7) 8/393 (9)
9/403 (10) 10/452 (11)

Bowling: *First Innings*—McGrath 17–6–35–3; Lee 6–2–13–0; MacGill 20.2–6–51–3; Warne 19–5–47–3. *Second Innings*—McGrath 28–5–95–1; Warne 42.5–8–132–3; Lee 19–5–62–2; MacGill 45–13–123–4; M. E. Waugh 6–1–14–0; Ponting 1–0–11–0.

Umpires: D. R. Shepherd (England) and D. J. Harper.
Third umpire: S. J. A. Taufel. Referee: R. S. Madugalle (Sri Lanka).

---

†At Adelaide, January 10 (day/night). **Australia A won by five wickets.** Toss: South Africans. **South Africans 215 for nine** (50 overs) (J. N. Rhodes 69, S. M. Pollock 56; S. M. Katich three for 21); **Australia A 219 for five** (49.1 overs) (J. P. Maher 94, D. S. Lehmann 41).

A crowd of 11,485 saw an Australian second eleven, captained by Lehmann and including Jason Gillespie and Stuart MacGill, rub salt in South Africa's wounds. Katich, bowling left-arm chinaman, took his first wickets in one-day cricket in Australia.

South Africa's matches v Australia and New Zealand in the VB Series (January 13– February 8) appear on pages 1368–1380.

THE BANGLADESHIS IN NEW ZEALAND, 2001-02

By DON CAMERON

Bangladesh embarked on their second overseas Test tour in the hope of learning plenty, even if they won nothing. However, there must have been moments when they wondered if this four-match trip to New Zealand was too short and too demanding to provide a useful lesson.

Predictably, their results – one draw and three defeats – were poor. The opening match, against a District Association XI, was reduced to a single, meaningless day by the summer rains that plagued the whole tour, and the three first-class games were embarrassingly one-sided. Auckland won by an innings and 193 runs in a match that only just stretched into a fourth day; rain in Hamilton effectively reduced the First Test to a three-day game, though this was quite enough for New Zealand to win by an innings and 52; and the Second Test in Wellington had a similar outcome – an innings and 74 inside three days (excluding the second, which was washed out).

In several respects, the trip's timing was unfortunate. Bangladesh arrived in December to find New Zealand experiencing its wettest spring and early summer in recent memory. The green, juicy pitches demanded different skills and techniques from the flat, rolled-mud wickets at home. The batsmen's attempts to go back to cope with the extra pace and bounce, and their obvious discomfort when not scoring briskly, meant they struggled to play either swing or seam. Two practice matches never looked adequate preparation, and rain gave the Bangladeshis even less opportunity to adapt.

Batting proved their major weakness. In six first-class innings, they never faced a second new ball, only two batsmen (Aminul Islam against Auckland and in the Second Test, Al Sahariar in the First) ever stayed in for more than two hours, and there were only two Test fifties. This inability to construct long innings – individually or collectively – scuppered any chance of salvaging draws. It was a pity that an overcrowded international schedule led to the cancellation of a one-day series, to which the Bangladeshis' attacking, ambitious batting was better suited.

Their bowling looked to have adapted well to alien conditions when they reduced New Zealand to 51 for four in the opening session of the First Test. But they could not sustain the performance; as the inequality between the teams became clear, only Manjurul Islam continued to hold his own. A medium-fast left-armer in the mould of Sri Lanka's Chaminda Vaas, he swung and seamed the ball, and finished with nine for 270 in three first-class innings. Two young seamers provided support: Mashrafe bin Mortaza, plucked from the Under-19s, had a good, strong action to go with his height, while Mohammad Sharif, who turned 16 during the tour, showed great persistence. However, both were serving their apprenticeship, and Bangladesh lacked another senior bowler. The spin bowling was well below subcontinental standards: only Enamul Haque, an orthodox left-armer, looked international quality. Strangely, he was sidelined for the Tests.

Besides the bad weather, Bangladesh were unlucky to come up against a tough New Zealand team who had just held their own against the powerful Australians. Chris Cairns and Daniel Vettori had returned to full fitness, and Stephen Fleming's confidence was shown by positive declarations. Cairns's all-round excellence shone out, Shane Bond confirmed his arrival as a bowler of genuine pace, while Mark Richardson and Craig McMillan made big scores after the early wickets in the First Test. Even so, the New Zealanders might have wondered what lasting benefits they could derive from this series.

No such doubts were expressed by Bangladesh. Their coach, Trevor Chappell, was adamant that by exposing his players to new conditions and methods such tours would help develop a team of genuine Test quality. He had a point, but this trip was too short, and the opposition too strong, to achieve his aims. The tourists remained in good spirits, yet it was an unsatisfactory visit – through poor planning as much as bad timing.

BANGLADESHI TOURING PARTY

Khaled Masud (Rajshahi) (*captain*), Habibul Bashar (Khulna) (*vice-captain*), Al Sahariar (Dhaka), Aminul Islam (Dhaka), Enamul Haque (Chittagong), Fahim Muntasir (Dhaka), Hasibul Hussain (Sylhet), Javed Omar (Dhaka), Khaled Mahmud (Dhaka), Manjurul Islam (Khulna), Mashrafe bin Mortaza (Khulna), Mohammad Ashraful (Dhaka), Mohammad Sharif (Dhaka), Sanuar Hossain (Barisal), Tushar Imran (Khulna).

Coach: T. M. Chappell. *Manager:* Afzalur Rahman. *Assistant manager:* Tanjeeb Ahsan.

BANGLADESHI TOUR RESULTS

Test matches – Played 2: Lost 2.
First-class matches – Played 3: Lost 3.
Losses – New Zealand (2), Auckland.
Non-first-class match – Drawn v New Zealand District Association XI.

Note: Matches in this section which were not first-class are signified by a dagger.

†At Wanganui, December 7, 8, 9. Drawn. Toss: New Zealand District Association XI. **New Zealand District Association XI 232 for three** (P. J. Ingram 31, H. T. G. James 117, P. D. McGlashan 59 not out) **v Bangladeshis.**
Rain permitted only four balls on the second day, and none on the third.

At Eden Park Outer Oval, Auckland, December 12, 13, 14, 15. **Auckland won by an innings and 193 runs.** Toss: Auckland. **Bangladeshis 120** (Khaled Masud 30 not out; C. J. Drum four for 32, A. R. Adams three for 16) and 182 (Al Sahariar 34, Aminul Islam 79 not out; C. J. Drum six for 34); **Auckland 495** (M. J. Horne 178, A. C. Barnes 95, N. K. W. Horsley 95, T. K. Canning 36 not out; Manjurul Islam four for 105, Mohammad Sharif three for 149).
Horne and Barnes added 265 for Auckland's third wicket.

NEW ZEALAND v BANGLADESH

First Test Match

At Hamilton, December 18, 19, 20, 21, 22. New Zealand won by an innings and 52 runs. Toss: Bangladesh. Test debut: Sanuar Hossain.

The Northern Districts Association had spent over $NZ1m improving their lovely ground: four new floodlight towers soared above the trees, and much effort had been spent on an outfield trampled by the Waikato rugby team over the winter. Unfortunately, they had no control over the fickle December weather. Rain washed out the first day and, just as Khaled Masud was winning the toss and deciding to bowl, it returned to blight the second. However, under ICC regulations, each of the remaining days could be extended from 90 to 105 overs, and Fleming was confident he could still win in that time.

The match certainly packed plenty of action into the eventual first session, though it was not to New Zealand's liking. In his first over, Mashrafe bin Mortaza found sharp bounce and Vincent attempted a misguided hook at the third ball: one for one. Worse followed. Manjurul Islam slanted one across Sinclair, and the edge was pouched by Masud: 19 for two. That became 29 for three when Mashrafe removed Fleming, and a stumble was turning into a collapse when Manjurul undid Astle with a brilliant delivery which whipped across him and flew to Al Sahariar at slip. New Zealand were 51 for four in the 16th over. But Richardson, who had watched the unfolding drama from the other end, persuaded the usually bullish McMillan of the virtues of stout defence. Slowly, the pitch lost some of its early life, the ball lost its shine and the modest support bowling was revealed. Still, with New Zealand 93 for four at lunch, Bangladesh had taken the first session. It would be their last of the tour.

After the break, Richardson and McMillan counter-attacked, mercilessly exposing the bowling's lack of depth. Richardson's century came quickly for him, from 144 balls. McMillan was more dominant, hitting 18 fours and two sixes in a three-hour hundred, despite having damaged a hand in a taxi accident two days earlier. New Zealand were flying: hour by hour, their scoring-rate soared, from 31 in the first to an incredible 90 in the fourth – before rain intervened again.

Once Fleming declared on the fourth morning, the critical question was whether Bangladesh would avoid the follow-on. Had they done so, their ability to score quickly might have forced New Zealand to bat on into the final day and given them a chance of saving the game. But it was not to be. Because the first two days were lost, Bangladesh's target was 216, rather than the 166 they would have needed in a five-day match. Although they made brisk progress, the clatter of falling wickets was a constant accompaniment. Habibul Bashar and Sanuar Hossain made sprightly contributions, and Khaled Mahmud launched a belated onslaught, yet soon after tea Bangladesh fell 11 runs short.

By the close, they were four wickets down again. On the last morning, Cairns, who had been bowling without conviction, returned to his best. Two years before, he had taken seven for 27 at a similar juncture to sweep New Zealand to victory over West Indies; this time, he claimed five in 38 balls. Bangladesh lost their last six wickets for 18, Cairns finished with seven for 53, and New Zealand had won inside seven sessions.

Man of the Match: M. H. Richardson.

Close of play: First day, No play; Second day, No play; Third day, New Zealand 306-5 (Richardson 124, Cairns 40); Fourth day, Bangladesh 90-4 (Al Sahariar 53, Sanuar Hossain 7).

New Zealand

M. H. Richardson c and b Mohammad Sharif	143	C. L. Cairns b Mohammad Sharif	48
L. Vincent c and b Mashrafe bin Mortaza	0	†A. C. Parore b Mohammad Sharif	20
M. S. Sinclair c Khaled Masud b Manjurul Islam	7	D. L. Vettori lbw b Khaled Mahmud	0
*S. P. Fleming c Khaled Masud b Mashrafe bin Mortaza	4	S. E. Bond not out	4
N. J. Astle c Al Sahariar b Manjurul Islam	5	B 2, l-b 18, w 5, n-b 3	28
C. D. McMillan c Manjurul Islam b Mashrafe bin Mortaza	106	(9 wkts dec.)	365

C. S. Martin did not bat.

1/1 (2) 2/19 (3) 3/29 (4) 4/51 (5) 5/241 (6) 6/330 (7) 7/357 (1) 8/359 (9) 9/365 (8)

Bowling: Mashrafe bin Mortaza 27-3-100-3; Manjurul Islam 18-5-66-2; Mohammad Sharif 20.1-2-114-3; Khaled Mahmud 9-0-40-1; Mohammad Ashraful 3-0-25-0.

Bangladesh

Javed Omar c Richardson b Cairns	9	– lbw b Martin	15
Al Sahariar c Sinclair b Bond	15	– c Parore b Cairns	53
Habibul Bashar c Martin b Vettori	61	– c Parore b Cairns	1
Aminul Islam c Parore b Bond	14	– b Cairns	0
Mohammad Ashraful c Sinclair b Vettori	1	– c sub (C. J. Drum) b Bond	6
Sanuar Hossain c Vincent b McMillan	45	– b Bond	12
*†Khaled Masud c Bond b McMillan	6	– c Fleming b Cairns	6
Khaled Mahmud c Richardson b Bond	45	– c Sinclair b Cairns	0
Mohammad Sharif b Martin	0	– not out	4
Mashrafe bin Mortaza lbw b Bond	3	– c Vincent b Cairns	2
Manjurul Islam not out	0	– c Fleming b Cairns	1
L-b 1, n-b 5	6	L-b 4, n-b 4	8

1/24 (1) 2/32 (2) 3/92 (4) 4/95 (5) 5/121 (3) 6/146 (7) 7/155 (6) 8/156 (9) 9/204 (10) 10/205 (8) — 205

1/39 (1) 2/42 (3) 3/42 (4) 4/68 (5) 5/90 (2) 6/98 (7) 7/98 (8) 8/104 (6) 9/107 (10) 10/108 (11) — 108

Bowling: *First Innings*—Cairns 11-0-55-1; Bond 13.1-2-47-4; Martin 11-4-38-1; McMillan 8-1-39-2; Vettori 15-4-25-2. *Second Innings*—Cairns 18.2-2-53-7; Bond 15-4-28-2; Martin 4-1-6-1; Vettori 9-4-17-0.

Umpires: D. L. Orchard (South Africa) and A. L. Hill.
Third umpire: D. B. Cowie. Referee: B. N. Jarman (Australia).

NEW ZEALAND v BANGLADESH

Second Test Match

At Basin Reserve, Wellington, December 26, 27, 28, 29. New Zealand won by an innings and 74 runs. Toss: New Zealand.

Once again, rain made significant inroads, yet New Zealand still had time to win in style. Bangladesh's only change was to swap one seamer, Mohammad Sharif, for another, Hasibul Hussain, while New Zealand replaced Astle, who had a back injury, with Horne, and brought in Drum – who had taken ten Bangladeshi wickets for Auckland – in place of Martin.

After downpours so heavy that the groundstaff had to prepare the pitch under a tent, it was little surprise that it was sluggish, well below the Basin Reserve's usual standard. Fleming did not hesitate to insert Bangladesh, whose batsmen had been instructed by their coach, Trevor Chappell, to occupy the crease for longer, and to measure success in terms of time rather than runs. He would not have been pleased to see his top three still playing as if late for an urgent engagement; all fell to rash shots.

Although Cairns maintained his form from before Christmas, removing Javed Omar and Habibul Bashar in his second over, Vettori was the pick of the bowlers, looping his stock delivery and getting his arm-ball to duck in to the right-handers. Aminul Islam batted soundly either side of lunch but, once he went to Vincent's spectacular catch at gully, Bangladesh folded.

Yet more rain meant no play on the second day, and a delayed start to the third, which brought about eccentric playing hours of one o'clock till eight. By lunch (at three), New Zealand were 117 for one; after that, the runs flowed. Richardson's 83 came from 167 balls, but the sluice gates were swung fully open by Fleming, McMillan, and finally Cairns. Each scored faster than the last, and their surge allowed the captain to declare 209 ahead and invite his bowlers to make a quick kill before the sun dipped on a midsummer's evening.

By the close, 24 overs later, the top order had already been ripped out. Bond forced Al Sahariar to fend to slip, produced a quick in-swinger to trap Javed Omar in front, and then claimed a bonus when Aminul Islam flashed irresponsibly outside off. Resuming at 67 for five on the fourth morning, Bangladesh lasted just over an hour. Bond soon took his fourth wicket, and Fleming gave him plenty of time to take five for the first time in Tests, but Mashrafe bin Mortaza responded by giving him plenty of hammer, including a straight six. It fell to Cairns to mop up, dislodging Mashrafe and Manjurul Islam with consecutive balls. Again, New Zealand's comprehensive victory had taken less than seven sessions.

Man of the Match: C. D. McMillan.

Close of play: First day, New Zealand 72-0 (Richardson 38, Horne 30); Second day, No play; Third day, Bangladesh 67-5 (Sanuar Hossain 4, Khaled Mahmud 0).

Bangladesh

Javed Omar c Vincent b Cairns	0	– lbw b Bond	12
Al Sahariar c Bond b Vettori	18	– c Horne b Bond	0
Habibul Bashar c Sinclair b Cairns	6	– lbw b Drum	32
Aminul Islam c Vincent b Bond	42	– c Vettori b Bond	4
Mohammad Ashraful c Fleming b Cairns	11	– lbw b Vettori	10
Sanuar Hossain run out	10	– b Bond	7
Khaled Mahmud c Parore b Drum	10	– run out	4
*†Khaled Masud not out	10	– not out	19
Hasibul Hussain c Vincent b Drum	4	– c Parore b Vettori	7
Manjurul Islam b Vettori	0	– (11) c Sinclair b Cairns	0
Mashrafe bin Mortaza run out	8	– (10) b Cairns	29
L-b 4, w 1, n-b 8	13	L-b 7, w 1, n-b 3	11
	132		**135**

1/0 (1) 2/6 (2) 3/49 (2) 4/81 (5)   132   1/5 (2) 2/28 (1) 3/41 (4)   135
5/92 (4) 6/108 (6) 7/114 (7)   4/62 (3) 5/64 (5) 6/75 (7)
8/118 (9) 9/119 (10) 10/132 (11)   7/79 (6) 8/86 (9)
                                             9/135 (10) 10/135 (11)

Bowling: First Innings—Cairns 15–7–24–3; Bond 13–4–21–1; Drum 11–1–26–2; Vettori 25–6–57–2. Second Innings—Cairns 6–1–27–2; Bond 15–5–54–4; Vettori 17–8–38–2; Drum 3–0–9–1.

New Zealand

M. H. Richardson c Mashrafe bin Mortaza b Hasibul Hussain .	83	M. S. Sinclair not out	19
M. J. Horne c Khaled Masud b Manjurul Islam .	38	C. L. Cairns c Habibul Bashar b Manjurul Islam .	36
L. Vincent c Khaled Masud b Mashrafe bin Mortaza .	23	B 1, l-b 6, w 1, n-b 3	11
*S. P. Fleming c Khaled Masud b Manjurul Islam .	61	1/104 (2) 2/148 (1) (6 wkts dec.) 341	
C. D. McMillan run out	70	3/153 (3) 4/283 (5) 5/285 (4) 6/341 (7)	

†A. C. Parore, D. L. Vettori, S. E. Bond and C. J. Drum did not bat.

Bowling: Mashrafe bin Mortaza 16–1–57–1; Manjurul Islam 29–5–99–3; Hasibul Hussain 21–3–88–1; Aminul Islam 7–0–37–0; Khaled Mahmud 12–2–42–0; Mohammad Ashraful 3–0–11–0.

Umpires: D. J. Harper (Australia) and B. F. Bowden.
Third umpire: D. M. Quested.   Referee: B. N. Jarman (Australia).

THE PAKISTANIS IN BANGLADESH, 2001-02

By SHAHID A. HASHMI

As expected, Pakistan's first tour to Bangladesh was a one-sided affair, with the visitors strolling to victory in both Tests and all three one-day internationals. By the end, Bangladesh's Test record read: played 11, drawn one, lost ten. Seven of those defeats, including both in this series, were by an innings, and doubts about the wisdom of granting Bangladesh Test status grew louder. Of the other Test nations, only South Africa had fared as badly by this stage of their development – they too lost ten out of 11 between 1888-89 and 1902-03.

But Waqar Younis, the Pakistan captain, was adamant that judgment should not be made too soon: "I think Bangladesh deserve time, and should not be pressurised... Sri Lanka took some 15–20 years to improve, and Bangladesh should also be given the same time." If the wider cricket community was prepared to wait for performances to pick up, there was less patience from the Bangladesh board. While Trevor Chappell, their Australian coach, blamed his batsmen – "they commit the same mistakes again and again, and need to learn to apply themselves, to bat in sessions" – the board blamed Chappell. Eleven weeks after this series, he was sacked.

He had a point about his batsmen. Often they treated the Tests as though they were limited-overs games: in only one of their four innings did they score at less than three an over, despite the regular fall of wickets brought on by reckless strokeplay. (Yet in the subsequent one-day internationals they were unable to raise their rate much above four.) The sole batting success was Habibul Bashar, whose two half-centuries were marred by a habit of throwing his wicket away. Nine Test fifties and only one hundred suggested unfulfilled potential.

Bangladesh's bowling showed signs of gaining maturity. Mohammad Sharif, a medium-fast seam bowler, was the most dependable, taking six of the 18 Pakistani wickets to fall, at 32. Fahim Muntasir, an off-spinning all-rounder, picked up his first three Test wickets at Chittagong, and the more experienced Enamul Haque four at Dhaka.

Despite being deprived of Test cricket for four months by the political fall-out from September 11, Pakistan had few problems. They dominated every sphere of the game, and in Yousuf Youhana and Danish Kaneria had much the most destructive batsman and bowler. Youhana hit a magnificent double-hundred in the Second Test, while Kaneria's leg-spin continued to bewitch the Bangladeshis. In their meeting at Multan in the Asian Test Championship at the end of August, he had taken 12 wickets; now he added 13 more to give him 25 in three Tests at an average of 11.12. Scorecards suggested several other Pakistan performances of note but, against weak opposition, their value was hard to fathom. Certainly Abdul Razzaq enjoyed his tour. In both forms of the game, he toyed with Bangladesh, hitting a career-best 134 in the First Test (when he also took four wickets) and then taking six for 35 – another career high – in the third limited-overs international.

Hampshire may be an ambitious club with a wealthy chairman and a superb new stadium, but in 2002, they had neither the team nor the pitch to match.
Hampshire, page 639

PAKISTANI TOURING PARTY

Waqar Younis (National Bank) (*captain*), Inzamam-ul-Haq (National Bank) (*vice-captain*), Abdul Razzaq (PIA), Danish Kaneria (Karachi/Habib Bank), Faisal Iqbal (Karachi/PIA), Mohammad Sami (National Bank), Naved Latif (Allied Bank), Rashid Latif (Allied Bank), Saqlain Mushtaq (PIA), Shadab Kabir (Karachi/Customs), Shoaib Akhtar (KRL), Taufeeq Umar (Habib Bank), Wasim Akram (PIA), Younis Khan (Habib Bank), Yousuf Youhana (PIA).

Saeed Anwar (ADBP) withdrew injured before the start of the tour, and Wasim Akram returned home injured after the First Test. Azhar Mahmood (Islamabad/PIA), Shahid Afridi (Karachi/Habib Bank) and Shoaib Malik (Sialkot/PIA) replaced Danish Kaneria and Faisal Iqbal for the one-day series.

Coach: Mudassar Nazar. *Manager:* Yawar Saeed. *Computer analyst:* Sikander Bakht. *Doctor:* Mohammad Riaz.

PAKISTANI TOUR RESULTS

Test matches – Played 2: Won 2.
First-class matches – Played 3: Won 2, Drawn 1.
Wins – Bangladesh (2).
Draw – Bangladesh A.
One-day internationals – Played 3: Won 3.

Note: Matches in this section which were not first-class are signified by a dagger.

At Savar, January 5, 6, 7. **Drawn**. Toss: Bangladesh A. **Pakistanis 312 for three dec.** (Yousuf Youhana 112 retired hurt, Inzamam-ul-Haq 52, Younis Khan 101 not out) **and 242 for six dec.** (Taufeeq Umar 36, Shadab Kabir 92, Abdul Razzaq 41); **Bangladesh A 210** (Hannan Sarkar 30, Mehrab Hossain 57, Enamul Haque 35 not out; Danish Kaneria seven for 53) **and 53 for three**.

BANGLADESH v PAKISTAN

First Test Match

At Dhaka, January 9, 10, 11. Pakistan won by an innings and 178 runs. Toss: Pakistan. Test debut: Fahim Muntasir.

From the first ball to the last, bowled 25 minutes after tea on the third afternoon, Pakistan were firmly in control. The postponement of New Zealand's visit after the terrorist attacks of September 11 had meant a four-month break from Test cricket, but Pakistan looked refreshed rather than rusty. They picked up where they had left off, with an emphatic three-day win over Bangladesh. Then, as now, Abdul Razzaq hit a rasping hundred and Danish Kaneria brought the Bangladeshi batsmen to their knees with his intelligent leg-spin.

Even so, there had been some optimism in the home camp on the first day, while Habibul Bashar, playing a gutsy innings in the face of quality bowling, and Aminul Islam were guiding Bangladesh to 140 for three. They had put on 63 before Kaneria removed Aminul. Then came the deluge. Waqar Younis sliced through the card to take the last six wickets for seven runs in 29 balls, the first time he had claimed five in an innings for almost four years. The only other batsman to shine was Mohammad Ashraful, in a confident 27. Like many of his colleagues, though, he played too much in the one-day style, when graft was the order of the day.

Pakistan's new, left-handed opening pair, Taufeeq Umar and Shadab Kabir, raced to 100 in the 23rd over. Yousuf Youhana chipped in with a classy 72, but, at 221 for five just after lunch on the second day, there was a chance Bangladesh could steal back into the match. Instead, Razzaq and Rashid Latif shared a partnership of 175, and batted them out of the game. A huge cheer greeted the arrival of Inzamam-ul-Haq, coming in at No. 8 because of a heavy cold. Something of a hero in Bangladesh, he nevertheless hammered the final nail into their coffin with an elegant and powerful forty. Waqar declared at the fall of Inzamam's wicket rather than ask Wasim Akram, who had limped off after straining a hamstring in the fifth over of the match, to bat.

Needing a daunting 330 simply to avoid an innings defeat, Bangladesh enjoyed another encouraging start. The arrival of Kaneria, who bowled continuously from the sixth over, brought it to an abrupt end. He completely mesmerised the batsmen and finished with a Test-best seven for 77; in two matches against Bangladesh, he had taken 21 wickets at 9.85. Fahim Muntasir, on debut, was alone in passing 22, and hit Kaneria over long-on for six, but his spirited swing of the bat ultimately counted for little.

Man of the Match: Abdul Razzaq.
Close of play: First day, Pakistan 126-3 (Yousuf Youhana 14, Saqlain Mushtaq 1); Second day, Pakistan 436-6 (Abdul Razzaq 114, Inzamam-ul-Haq 22).

Bangladesh

Al Sahariar lbw b Abdul Razzaq	18	– (7) lbw b Waqar Younis		21
Mehrab Hossain c Shadab Kabir b Abdul Razzaq	11	– (1) c Inzamam-ul-Haq b Danish Kaneria		19
Mohammad Ashraful c Yousuf Youhana b Danish Kaneria	27	– (2) c Younis Khan b Abdul Razzaq		22
Habibul Bashar c Danish Kaneria b Waqar Younis	53	– (3) c Waqar Younis b Danish Kaneria		0
Aminul Islam lbw b Danish Kaneria	25	– (4) lbw b Abdul Razzaq		11
Sanuar Hossain c Inzamam-ul-Haq b Waqar Younis	3	– (5) c Shadab Kabir b Danish Kaneria		1
*†Khaled Masud lbw b Waqar Younis	0	– (6) c Waqar Younis b Danish Kaneria		5
Enamul Haque c Inzamam-ul-Haq b Waqar Younis	12	– b Danish Kaneria		19
Fahim Muntasir b Waqar Younis	0	– c sub (Mohammad Sami) b Danish Kaneria		33
Mohammad Sharif b Waqar Younis	0	– c Waqar Younis b Danish Kaneria		11
Manjurul Islam not out	0	– not out		2
L-b 8, w 1, n-b 2	11	L-b 5, n-b 3		8
	160			**152**

1/30 (2) 2/45 (1) 3/77 (3) 4/140 (5) 5/146 (4) 6/146 (7) 7/147 (6) 8/147 (9) 9/151 (10) 10/160 (8)

1/38 (1) 2/38 (3) 3/49 (2) 4/52 (5) 5/64 (4) 6/86 (6) 7/90 (7) 8/112 (8) 9/139 (10) 10/152 (9)

Bowling: *First Innings*—Wasim Akram 2.4–1–5–0; Waqar Younis 16.2–2–55–6; Abdul Razzaq 8.2–2–42–2; Danish Kaneria 19–5–36–2; Saqlain Mushtaq 7–2–14–0. *Second Innings*—Waqar Younis 9–3–27–1; Abdul Razzaq 10–2–29–2; Danish Kaneria 19.4–4–77–7; Saqlain Mushtaq 5–1–14–0.

Pakistan

Taufeeq Umar lbw b Mohammad Sharif	53
Shadab Kabir b Enamul Haque	55
Younis Khan c Khaled Masud b Enamul Haque	0
Yousuf Youhana run out	72
Saqlain Mushtaq lbw b Enamul Haque	9
Abdul Razzaq c Aminul Islam b Manjurul Islam	134
†Rashid Latif c Al Sahariar b Mohammad Sharif	94
Inzamam-ul-Haq c Mehrab Hossain b Enamul Haque	43
*Waqar Younis c Al Sahariar b Manjurul Islam	8
Danish Kaneria not out	3
L-b 13, w 2, n-b 4	19
	(9 wkts dec.) 490

1/100 (2) 2/100 (3) 3/116 (1) 4/162 (5) 5/221 (4) 6/396 (7) 7/463 (6) 8/471 (9) 9/490 (8)

Wasim Akram did not bat.

Bowling: Manjurul Islam 33–4–124–2; Mohammad Sharif 35–9–95–2; Fahim Muntasir 32–6–109–0; Enamul Haque 39.4–9–136–4; Mohammad Ashraful 1–0–13–0.

Umpires: J. H. Hampshire (England) and A. F. M. Akhtaruddin.
Third umpire: Mesbahuddin Ahmed.   Referee: B. F. Hastings (New Zealand).

BANGLADESH v PAKISTAN

Second Test Match

At Chittagong, January 16, 17, 18. Pakistan won by an innings and 169 runs. Toss: Bangladesh.
Two more shabby displays of batting gifted Pakistan another comprehensive victory. A masterful, stroke-filled double-hundred from Yousuf Youhana was at its heart, though there were telling contributions from almost all the Pakistan bowlers. Play echoed the pattern of the Dhaka Test, with Bangladesh subsiding inside two sessions, Pakistan batting throughout the second day before declaring, nine down and over 300 ahead, on the third morning. Again, the home batsmen failed to summon the necessary discipline, and they slumped to a fourth consecutive innings defeat, all of which had come within three days' cricket.
After a steady, confident start on a pitch that offered the bowlers little, Bangladesh lost wickets to accurate and thoughtful slow bowling. Both spinners proved difficult to read: Danish Kaneria removed four batsmen, including Mehrab Hossain, bowled shaping to cut a deftly disguised googly, while Saqlain Mushtaq, who had gone wicketless at Dhaka, took five. Bangladesh were not helped by the absence of Mohammad Ashraful, one of their three Test centurions, who was in New Zealand for the Under-19 World Cup.

TEAMS DISMISSED FOR THE SAME SCORE IN EACH INNINGS OF A TEST

172	New Zealand v South Africa at Wellington	1952-53
208	New Zealand v West Indies at Wellington	1955-56
136	India v Australia at Calcutta	1956-57
201	India v Australia at Sydney	1980-81
161	New Zealand v Australia at Hobart	1993-94
306	Sri Lanka v South Africa at Cape Town	1997-98
148	**Bangladesh v Pakistan at Chittagong**	**2001-02**

Note: Completed innings only.

Research: Nirav Malavi

By the close, Pakistan lay just 49 behind. Next day belonged initially to Younis Khan, with a sparkling century, but he was eclipsed by Yousuf Youhana, who cut, drove and pulled to perfection. Picking up speed after his first hundred, Youhana went on to a career-best undefeated 204, reaching his double with a six off Mohammad Sharif to trigger the declaration. In all, he batted 325 minutes, faced 243 balls and hit 34 fours and two sixes. Sharif was rewarded for a generally consistent line with four wickets in a Test for the first time, but Bangladesh's deficit was still a shiver-inducing 317.
If the result of the game was not in doubt, Bangladesh could at least have made Pakistan work for their wickets. Instead, their cavalier approach gave them away again. By the 12th over, they were 41 for four. Habibul Bashar struck 51 in 49 balls to ward off abject humiliation, but the second innings lasted just three hours. Shoaib Akhtar made hay with four wickets, the last three coming in one over. The Pakistan Cricket Board rewarded Youhana for his innings with a donation of 250,000 rupees (around £2,500).
Man of the Match: Yousuf Youhana.   *Man of the Series:* Danish Kaneria.
Close of play: First day, Pakistan 99-1 (Taufeeq Umar 47, Younis Khan 47); Second day, Pakistan 429-7 (Yousuf Youhana 174, Saqlain Mushtaq 7).

Bangladesh

Javed Omar c Shadab Kabir b Saqlain Mushtaq .	17	–	Rashid Latif b Waqar Younis . . .		0
Al Sahariar c Rashid Latif b Waqar Younis. . . .	13	–	c Rashid Latif b Waqar Younis . . .		8
Mehrab Hossain b Danish Kaneria	16	–	c Rashid Latif b Waqar Younis . .		14
Habibul Bashar c Shadab Kabir b Saqlain Mushtaq	2	– (5)	c Shadab Kabir Saqlain Mushtaq .		51
Aminul Islam c Yousuf Youhana b Danish Kaneria	25	– (4)	b Shoaib Akhtar		2
Sanuar Hossain lbw b Saqlain Mushtaq	11	–	c Younis Khan b Saqlain Mushtaq .		30
Enamul Haque c Shadab Kabir b Danish Kaneria	0	– (8)	b Shoaib Akhtar		9
*†Khaled Masud c Taufeeq Umar b Saqlain Mushtaq .	28	– (7)	not out.		15
Fahim Muntasir c Inzamam-ul-Haq b Danish Kaneria .	9	–	b Shoaib Akhtar		2
Mohammad Sharif st Rashid Latif b Saqlain Mushtaq .	0	–	b Shoaib Akhtar		0
Manjurul Islam not out.	4	–	c Shadab Kabir b Waqar Younis. . .		0
B 5, l-b 9, n-b 9	23		B 8, l-b 1, n-b 8		17

1/21 (2) 2/57 (1) 3/60 (4) 4/65 (3)   148
5/84 (6) 6/85 (7) 7/112 (5)
8/126 (9) 9/127 (10) 10/148 (8)

1/0 (1) 2/23 (3) 3/24 (2)   148
4/41 (4) 5/110 (5) 6/128 (6)
7/144 (8) 8/147 (9)
9/147 (10) 10/148 (11)

Bowling: *First Innings*—Waqar Younis 7–2–19–1; Shoaib Akhtar 6–2–15–0; Danish Kaneria 22–6–62–4; Saqlain Mushtaq 16.4–3–35–5. *Second Innings*—Waqar Younis 8.5–0–36–4; Shoaib Akhtar 11–1–48–4; Saqlain Mushtaq 11–3–34–2; Abdul Razzaq 2–0–12–0; Danish Kaneria 6–3–9–0.

Pakistan

Taufeeq Umar c Aminul Islam b Mohammad Sharif .	47	Saqlain Mushtaq c Aminul Islam b Mohammad Sharif .		7
Shadab Kabir c Khaled Masud b Mohammad Sharif .	4	Shoaib Akhtar c Sanuar Hossain b Manjurul Islam .		2
Younis Khan c Mehrab Hossain b Fahim Muntasir .	119	Danish Kaneria not out		4
Inzamam-ul-Haq c Aminul Islam b Fahim Muntasir .	30	W 1, n-b 4.		5
Yousuf Youhana not out.	204			
Abdul Razzaq b Mohammad Sharif . . .	18	1/12 (2) 2/99 (1) (9 wkts dec.) 465		
†Rashid Latif lbw b Manjurul Islam . . .	15	3/166 (4) 4/236 (3)		
*Waqar Younis c Mehrab Hossain b Fahim Muntasir .	10	5/274 (6) 6/315 (7) 7/339 (8) 8/438 (9) 9/447 (10)		

Bowling: Manjurul Islam 35–9–95–2; Mohammad Sharif 35.5–10–98–4; Enamul Haque 33–6–114–0; Fahim Muntasir 27–3–131–3; Aminul Islam 4–0–27–0.

Umpires: R. B. Tiffin (Zimbabwe) and Mahbubur Rahman.
Third umpire: Manzur Rahman.   Referee: B. F. Hastings (New Zealand).

†BANGLADESH v PAKISTAN

First One-Day International

At Chittagong, January 22. Pakistan won by 49 runs. Toss: Pakistan. International debut: Tareq Aziz.

With Pakistan deep in trouble at 88 for five after 27 overs – Waqar Younis had opted to bat on a lively pitch in misty conditions – the capacity crowd of 24,000 dared to hope for a repeat of Northampton 1999, Bangladesh's only victory over Test-playing opposition. But the experienced pair of Rashid Latif and Abdul Razzaq put on an invaluable 80, and Latif's personal-best 79 steered

Pakistan past 200. Tareq Aziz, an 18-year-old seamer making his international debut on his home ground, was the pick of the bowlers. Bangladesh still had a chance, but it was gone by the 16th over, when Shoaib reduced them to 32 for four. Khaled Masud saved face with a patient fifty.

Man of the Match: Rashid Latif.

Pakistan

Shahid Afridi c Khaled Masud		
b Mohammad Sharif .	7	
Naved Latif b Tareq Aziz	17	
Yousuf Youhana c Tareq Aziz		
b Manjurul Islam .	7	
Inzamam-ul-Haq c Sanuar Hossain		
b Tareq Aziz .	20	
Younis Khan b Khaled Mahmud	22	
†Rashid Latif b Mohammad Sharif	79	
Abdul Razzaq c Khaled Masud		
b Enamul Haque .	24	

Azhar Mahmood c and b Enamul Haque   1
*Waqar Younis c Mehrab Hossain
                b Tareq Aziz .   1
Saqlain Mushtaq not out   12
Shoaib Akhtar c Khaled Masud
             b Mohammad Sharif .   3
      B 2, l-b 2, w 1, n-b 4   9

1/12 2/27 3/35   (49.5 overs) 202
4/67 5/88 6/168
7/172 8/175 9/194

Bowling: Manjurul Islam 10–3–43–1; Mohammad Sharif 9.5–1–40–3; Tareq Aziz 10–1–19–3; Khaled Mahmud 10–0–50–1; Enamul Haque 10–0–46–2.

Bangladesh

Javed Omar c Saqlain Mushtaq		
b Shoaib Akhtar .	6	
Mehrab Hossain b Shoaib Akhtar	0	
Al Sahariar run out.	6	
Tushar Imran c Inzamam-ul-Haq		
b Saqlain Mushtaq .	21	
Sanuar Hossain c Azhar Mahmood		
b Abdul Razzaq .	2	
Khaled Mahmud run out	5	

*†Khaled Masud not out   54
Enamul Haque c Naved Latif
            b Inzamam-ul-Haq .   32
Mohammad Sharif not out   0

      B 1, l-b 9, w 10, n-b 7   27

1/1 2/14 3/24   (7 wkts, 50 overs) 153
4/32 5/54 6/68 7/153

Tareq Aziz and Manjurul Islam did not bat.

Bowling: Waqar Younis 10–2–33–0; Shoaib Akhtar 8–1–9–2; Abdul Razzaq 6–1–10–1; Azhar Mahmood 6–0–26–0; Saqlain Mushtaq 10–0–24–1; Shahid Afridi 7–0–28–0; Naved Latif 2–0–13–0; Inzamam-ul-Haq 1–1–0–1.

Umpires: A. F. M. Akhtaruddin and Sailab Hossain.
Third umpire: Manzur Rahman.   Referee: B. F. Hastings (New Zealand).

†BANGLADESH v PAKISTAN

Second One-Day International

At Dhaka, January 24 (day/night). Pakistan won by 72 runs. Toss: Pakistan.

This match took an ugly twist during Bangladesh's reply. After bowling five expensive overs, Shoaib Akhtar was fielding on the fine-leg boundary when a brick thrown from the stands struck his head. He was rushed to hospital, but was not seriously hurt. The players left the field and it was 45 minutes before Waqar Younis agreed to resume. It had no bearing on the result, which, despite another faltering start from Pakistan, had been put beyond doubt by Yousuf Youhana's magnificent 112 in 108 balls, then his best in one-day internationals. A 35-ball flurry by Abdul Razzaq helped add 98 in the last ten overs and set a daunting 282. The home batsmen at least fared better than two days earlier as Tushar Imran, just 18, found the gaps to make a maiden fifty.

Man of the Match: Yousuf Youhana.

Shoaib Akhtar is carried from the field during the second one-day international after a brick thrown from the crowd hit his head. He was not badly hurt. *Picture by Mohammad Shahidullah, Reuters/Popperfoto.*

Pakistan

Naved Latif c Manjurul Islam				
b Mohammad Sharif .	10			
Shahid Afridi c Khaled Masud				
b Mohammad Sharif .	4			
Younis Khan c Javed Omar				
b Enamul Haque .	73			
Inzamam-ul-Haq c Sanuar Hossain				
b Manjurul Islam .	3			

Azhar Mahmood st Khaled Masud
b Khaled Mahmud . 12
Yousuf Youhana not out 112
Abdul Razzaq not out 49
L-b 4, w 10, n-b 4. 18

1/21 2/23 3/29 (5 wkts, 50 overs) 281
4/48 5/183

†Rashid Latif, *Waqar Younis, Saqlain Mushtaq and Shoaib Akhtar did not bat.

Bowling: Manjurul Islam 10–1–29–1; Mohammad Sharif 10–2–59–2; Tareq Aziz 9–2–56–0; Khaled Mahmud 10–1–50–1; Enamul Haque 10–0–69–1; Mehrab Hossain 1–0–14–0.

Bangladesh

Javed Omar run out 12
Mehrab Hossain c Rashid Latif
b Abdul Razzaq . 21
Al Sahariar b Saqlain Mushtaq 41
Tushar Imran c sub (Shoaib Malik)
b Saqlain Mushtaq . 65
Sanuar Hossain b Saqlain Mushtaq . . . 5
Khaled Mahmud b Shahid Afridi 12
*†Khaled Masud lbw b Shahid Afridi . . 0

Enamul Haque c Saqlain Mushtaq
b Shahid Afridi . 12
Mohammad Sharif not out 5
Tareq Aziz not out 7
L-b 9, w 8, n-b 12. 29

1/16 2/75 3/126 (8 wkts, 50 overs) 209
4/141 5/179 6/180
7/193 8/196

Manjurul Islam did not bat.

Bowling: Waqar Younis 6–2–10–0; Shoaib Akhtar 5–0–45–0; Abdul Razzaq 8–1–36–1; Azhar Mahmood 7–0–29–0; Saqlain Mushtaq 10–1–32–3; Naved Latif 5–0–25–0; Shahid Afridi 7–3–11–3; Inzamam-ul-Haq 2–0–12–0.

Umpires: Showkatur Rahman and Syed Mahbubullah.
Third umpire: Mahbubur Rahman. Referee: B. F. Hastings (New Zealand).

†BANGLADESH v PAKISTAN

Third One-Day International

At Dhaka, January 25 (day/night). Pakistan won by eight wickets. Toss: Bangladesh.

The whitewash was not in much doubt after Shahid Afridi blew the Bangladesh attack away with a whirlwind 83 from 44 balls. He walloped seven sixes and six fours, and was especially harsh on the left-arm spin of Enamul Haque, whose first over he hit for 28 (666064). When Afridi fell in the 11th, aiming to drive over cover, Naved Latif had contributed nine to their stand of 97. The pace slowed a little, but Pakistan still won with 13.3 overs to spare (they had been docked

BEST BOWLING FOR PAKISTAN IN ONE-DAY INTERNATIONALS

7-36	Waqar Younis v England at Leeds	2001
7-37	Aqib Javed v India at Sharjah	1991-92
6-14	Imran Khan v India at Sharjah	1984-85
6-16	**Shoaib Akhtar v New Zealand at Karachi**	**2002**
6-18	Azhar Mahmood v West Indies at Sharjah	1999-2000
6-26	Waqar Younis v Sri Lanka at Sharjah	1989-90
6-30	Waqar Younis v New Zealand at Auckland	1993-94
6-35	**Abdul Razzaq v Bangladesh at Dhaka**	**2001-02**
6-44	Waqar Younis v New Zealand at Sharjah	1996-97
6-59	Waqar Younis v Australia at Nottingham	2001

one for a slow over-rate). Earlier, Afridi had taken two wickets with his skiddy leg-breaks as Bangladesh compiled 220, their highest of the series. The real damage, however, was wreaked by Abdul Razzaq, who took a one-day best six for 35 as Bangladesh plummeted from an ostensibly healthy 176 for three after 42 overs.

Man of the Match: Shahid Afridi.   *Man of the Series:* Abdul Razzaq.

Bangladesh

Javed Omar c Yousuf Youhana b Saqlain Mushtaq .	35	
Mehrab Hossain c Rashid Latif b Shahid Afridi .	41	
Al Sahariar st Rashid Latif b Shahid Afridi .	6	
Tushar Imran c Shoaib Malik b Abdul Razzaq .	43	
Aminul Islam b Abdul Razzaq	31	
Khaled Mahmud c and b Abdul Razzaq .	19	
*†Khaled Masud c Yousuf Youhana b Abdul Razzaq .	8	

Enamul Haque b Abdul Razzaq 2
Mohammad Sharif c Rashid Latif b Waqar Younis . 6
Tareq Aziz b Abdul Razzaq 0
Manjurul Islam not out 1

B 1, l-b 6, w 16, n-b 12 35

1/88 2/89 3/99   (48.5 overs) 220
4/176 5/194 6/205
7/210 8/217 9/219

Bowling: Waqar Younis 9–2–51–1; Mohammad Sami 8–0–35–0; Abdul Razzaq 9.5–1–35–6; Saqlain Mushtaq 8–0–34–1; Shahid Afridi 10–1–38–2; Shoaib Malik 4–0–20–0.

Pakistan

Shahid Afridi c and b Khaled Mahmud .	83	
Naved Latif c Khaled Masud b Tareq Aziz .	36	
Younis Khan not out	66	

Abdul Razzaq not out 25
W 7, n-b 4 11

1/97 2/175   (2 wkts, 35.3 overs) 221

Shoaib Malik, Yousuf Youhana, Inzamam-ul-Haq, †Rashid Latif, *Waqar Younis, Saqlain Mushtaq and Mohammad Sami did not bat.

Bowling: Manjurul Islam 10–1–49–0; Mohammad Sharif 6.3–0–40–0; Tareq Aziz 9.3–2–51–1; Enamul Haque 3–1–38–0; Khaled Mahmud 6.3–1–43–1.

Umpires: Jahangir Alam and Mesbahuddin Ahmed.
Third umpire: Sailab Hossain.   Referee: B. F. Hastings (New Zealand).

PAKISTAN v WEST INDIES AT SHARJAH, 2001-02

By DICKY RUTNAGUR

In a major departure from practice and tradition, Pakistan played host to West Indies on foreign soil. Two Tests, both of which Pakistan won emphatically, and three one-day internationals were staged at the Sharjah CA Stadium in the space of 18 days.

Test matches had been played on neutral territory before, during the Triangular Tournament in England in 1912 and, more recently, when Dhaka staged the final of the Asian Test Championship in 1998-99. This was different because it was the only alternative to the tour being cancelled, at high cost to the Pakistan Cricket Board. Their finances had already suffered from the abandonment of visits by New Zealand and Sri Lanka in the aftermath of the terrorist attacks on September 11. On top of that, West Indies feared an outbreak of hostilities between Pakistan and India. The ICC therefore approved the transfer to Sharjah, and ruled that the Tests would still count as a home series for Pakistan in the Test Championship.

The original itinerary included three Tests, but was truncated because 18 full days on the same ground was deemed impractical. There were grave doubts about the durability of the pitches at a venue which had been used only for limited-overs cricket (a record 181 internationals since 1983-84). As it happened, they played reasonably well. The spinners were expected to wreak havoc on cracked surfaces, but it was pace and reverse swing that did more damage, claiming 48 wickets to spin's 19.

Both sides were depleted by injuries. Pakistan were without Saeed Anwar and, for the Tests, Wasim Akram. But they were not undermined by their absence, as West Indies were by that of Brian Lara, who had enjoyed a phenomenal series in Sri Lanka only two months earlier, and Ramnaresh Sarwan. The problem was exacerbated when Sherwin Campbell fractured a finger during the First Test and Marlon Samuels, the only batting reserve, went home for knee surgery. No one managed a century for West Indies during the Tests, and the only innings in which they achieved respectability was the very first. A total of 366 featured five fifties, one of them from the debutant Ryan Hinds, a 20-year-old left-hander who looked a cricketer of distinct promise. Their attack, too, was moderate, but at least showed endeavour and discipline, and Merv Dillon excelled himself. He would have been an even bigger force with better support from the field. The catching, both close in and further out, was abysmal: West Indies missed at least 17 chances, which put them right out of contention.

Pakistan were barely handicapped by the poor starts given them by their openers, or by Inzamam-ul-Haq's lack of form. Yousuf Youhana, who had scored two centuries in his previous three Tests against West Indies, and Younis Khan made hundreds, as did Rashid Latif and Shahid Afridi, who both benefited from several dropped catches. Waqar Younis was a potent force, and the slow pitch was no curb on Shoaib Akhtar. Abdul Razzaq's reverse swing was also a deadly weapon: nine wickets at 14, coupled with 143 runs, made him Man of the Series. He picked up the same award after the one-dayers, which Pakistan won before Carl Hooper's unbeaten century earned West Indies a consolation victory.

The Test series was the first played under the surveillance of the ICC's Anti-Corruption Unit, represented by two former police officers from England. The approaches to the dressing-rooms were watched over by closed-circuit television cameras, though these seemed superfluous, because the attendance was so small that every single person at the ground was conspicuous and identifiable. In a stadium seating 20,000, a few hundred turned up for the Tests, until the authorities belatedly decided to admit schoolchildren free. But these figures were immaterial. Hosting the series in Sharjah enabled the Pakistan Board to salvage their much-needed revenue from TV rights.

PAKISTANI TOURING PARTY

Waqar Younis (National Bank) (*captain*), Inzamam-ul-Haq (National Bank) (*vice-captain*), Abdul Razzaq (PIA), Danish Kaneria (Karachi Whites/Habib Bank), Faisal Iqbal (Karachi Whites/PIA), Mohammad Sami (National Bank), Mohammad Zahid (Rawalpindi/PIA), Naved Latif (Allied Bank), Rashid Latif (Allied Bank), Saqlain Mushtaq (PIA), Shahid Afridi (Karachi Whites/Habib Bank), Shoaib Akhtar (KRL), Taufeeq Umar (Habib Bank), Younis Khan (Habib Bank), Yousuf Youhana (PIA).

Shoaib Malik (Sialkot) and Wasim Akram (PIA) replaced Danish Kaneria, Faisal Iqbal and Mohammad Zahid (who had gone home because of a family bereavement) for the one-day internationals.

Coach: Mudassar Nazar. *Manager:* Yawar Saeed.

WEST INDIAN TOURING PARTY

C. L. Hooper (Guyana) (*captain*), R. D. Jacobs (Leeward Islands) (*vice-captain*), D. Brown (Trinidad & Tobago), S. L. Campbell (Barbados), S. Chanderpaul (Guyana), P. T. Collins (Barbados), C. D. Collymore (Barbados), C. E. Cuffy (Barbados), M. Dillon (Trinidad & Tobago), D. Ganga (Trinidad & Tobago), C. H. Gayle (Jamaica), R. O. Hinds (Barbados), W. W. Hinds (Jamaica), D. Ramnarine (Trinidad & Tobago), M. N. Samuels (Jamaica).

R. S. Morton (Leeward Islands) replaced the injured Samuels.

Coach: R. A. Harper. *Manager:* R. O. Skerritt. *Physiotherapist:* R. Rogers.

WEST INDIAN TOUR RESULTS

Test matches – Played 2: Lost 2.
Losses – Pakistan (2).
One-day internationals – Played 3: Won 1, Lost 2.

Note: Matches in this section which were not first-class are signified by a dagger.

PAKISTAN v WEST INDIES

First Test Match

At Sharjah, January 31, February 1, 2, 3, 4. Pakistan won by 170 runs. Toss: Pakistan. Test debuts: Naved Latif; R. O. Hinds.

By the end of the third day, West Indies seemed safe. They had saved the follow-on with only five wickets down, Chanderpaul and the debutant Ryan Hinds were batting fluently, and the first Test at Sharjah, Test cricket's 83rd venue, was heading for a draw. Five sessions later, they had succumbed to another heavy defeat.

Concerns about the pitch's durability had increased as its surface cracks widened, but it stood up reasonably well. Although the bounce was slow and low, it was pace bowling of exceptional quality that proved decisive. Waqar Younis was outstanding as he shot out West Indies' lower half for 41 runs on the fourth morning, while Shoaib Akhtar and Abdul Razzaq wrecked them on the final day. Pakistan were superior in all departments, but the one in which West Indies really let themselves down was fielding. Every one of the many chances they missed proved expensive.

The honours of a hard-fought opening day were shared, though barely anyone was there to watch. Pakistan batted circumspectly, yet the five wickets they lost were all avoidable. The West Indians bowled with discipline and control, and held the advantage at 178 for five after tea. But Yousuf Youhana and Rashid Latif steadied the innings and went on to give Pakistan the initiative in a match-winning stand of 204 in just 57 overs. They should have been separated early on the second morning, when Rashid, on 28, cut Dillon to first slip, where Gayle missed it. It was not until the second over after lunch that the partnership was broken, with Youhana dragging on after a chanceless six-hour 146. It was his ninth Test hundred; Rashid had just completed his first, before converting it with increasing belligerence into 150.

The hapless Gayle made some amends by taking the last three wickets, including Rashid, and contributing a half-century as West Indies reached an encouraging 96 for one in reply to Pakistan's 493. A string of fifties enabled the follow-on with some comfort, although no one passed Gayle's 68. Chanderpaul and Ryan Hinds had taken their sixth-wicket stand to 121 on the fourth morning when Waqar forced Chanderpaul to play on. Rolling back the years, Waqar defied the somnolent pitch to work subtly through the lower order, claiming four for eight in 31 balls.

More poor fielding and diffident captaincy allowed Pakistan to increase their lead from 127 to 341 – with Rashid scoring a lively 47 in 42 balls – and give themselves exactly 100 overs to force home their advantage. With the pitch still playing well, West Indies came to no harm until midway through the final morning, when Shoaib rattled Ganga's stumps to claim the first of his five victims. Even so, they reached lunch at 111 for one, with Gayle looking comfortable on 62. The collapse began shortly after the break. Going round the wicket, Shoaib accounted for the two tall left-handers, Gayle and Wavell Hinds, who was overwhelmed by a brutal ball which climbed to face-height and had him caught behind off the glove. It was Rashid's 100th Test dismissal. After the controversial dismissal of Campbell, who was given run out by the third umpire despite a series of inconclusive replays, Razzaq, repeatedly finding reverse swing, struck three times in an over. He and Shoaib both returned Test-best figures as the last nine wickets tumbled for 56 runs in less than 23 overs. Pakistan celebrated victory with a session to spare.

Man of the Match: Shoaib Akhtar.

Close of play: First day, Pakistan 230-5 (Yousuf Youhana 78, Rashid Latif 27); Second day, West Indies 54-0 (Ganga 11, Gayle 41); Third day, West Indies 325-5 (Chanderpaul 45, R. O. Hinds 55); Fourth day, West Indies 24-0 (Ganga 19, Gayle 5).

Pakistan

Taufeeq Umar b Hooper	24	– run out	23
Naved Latif lbw b Dillon	0	– c Jacobs b Dillon	20
Younis Khan c Gayle b Hooper	53	– c Jacobs b Cuffy	32
Inzamam-ul-Haq c Jacobs b Dillon	10	– c Hooper b Dillon	48
Yousuf Youhana c Cuffy	146	– c Dillon b Cuffy	12
Abdul Razzaq c Jacobs b W. W. Hinds	34	– c Ganga b Collins	29
†Rashid Latif b Gayle	150	– not out	47
Saqlain Mushtaq c and b Dillon	17		
*Waqar Younis not out	25		
Shoaib Akhtar b Gayle	20		
Danish Kaneria c and b Gayle	0		
B 6, l-b 7, w 1	14	N-b 3	3

1/3 (2) 2/45 (1) 3/80 (4) 4/94 (3)   493   1/35 (2) 2/54 (1)   (6 wkts dec.) 214
5/178 (6) 6/382 (5) 7/438 (8)   3/101 (3) 4/134 (5)
8/457 (7) 9/493 (10) 10/493 (11)   5/146 (4) 6/214 (6)

Bowling: *First Innings*—Dillon 42–10–140–3; Collins 33–3–96–0; Cuffy 35–10–75–1; Hooper 32–7–85–2; R. O. Hinds 4–0–31–0; W. W. Hinds 8–1–26–1; Gayle 7.5–0–27–3. *Second Innings*—Dillon 17–3–46–2; Cuffy 19–3–78–2; Collins 14.4–1–56–1; Hooper 5–0–23–0; W. W. Hinds 2–0–11–0.

West Indies

D. Ganga lbw b Saqlain Mushtaq	20	– b Shoaib Akhtar	34
C. H. Gayle b Saqlain Mushtaq	68	– b Shoaib Akhtar	66
S. L. Campbell lbw b Danish Kaneria	6	– run out	20
W. W. Hinds st Rashid Latif b Danish Kaneria	59	– c Rashid Latif b Shoaib Akhtar	8
*C. L. Hooper lbw b Abdul Razzaq	56	– lbw b Abdul Razzaq	13
S. Chanderpaul b Waqar Younis	66	– c Rashid Latif b Abdul Razzaq	0
R. O. Hinds c Rashid Latif b Waqar Younis	62	– not out	9
†R. D. Jacobs c Danish Kaneria b Waqar Younis	6	– lbw b Abdul Razzaq	0
M. Dillon run out	5	– b Shoaib Akhtar	0
C. E. Cuffy b Waqar Younis	0	– b Shoaib Akhtar	0
P. T. Collins not out	1	– b Abdul Razzaq	12
B 1, l-b 3, w 1, n-b 12	17	B 1, l-b 7	9
	366		**171**

1/88 (1) 2/96 (2) 3/126 (3) 4/180 (4)   366
5/231 (5) 6/352 (6) 7/353 (7)
8/362 (9) 9/363 (10) 10/366 (8)

1/76 (1) 2/115 (2) 3/125 (4)   171
4/146 (3) 5/149 (6) 6/150 (5)
7/150 (8) 8/155 (9)
9/155 (10) 10/171 (11)

Bowling: *First Innings*—Waqar Younis 25.3–4–93–4; Shoaib Akhtar 18–4–68–0; Abdul Razzaq 18–2–49–1; Danish Kaneria 26–5–75–2; Saqlain Mushtaq 36–12–71–2; Taufeeq Umar 2–0–6–0. *Second Innings*—Waqar Younis 9–2–35–0; Saqlain Mushtaq 11–5–30–0; Danish Kaneria 19–7–55–0; Shoaib Akhtar 16–7–24–5; Abdul Razzaq 7.5–1–25–4.

Umpires: G. Sharp (England) and Riazuddin (Pakistan).
Third umpire: Athar Zaidi (Pakistan).   Referee: M. H. Denness (England).

PAKISTAN v WEST INDIES

Second Test Match

At Sharjah, February 7, 8, 9, 10. Pakistan won by 244 runs. Toss: West Indies.

West Indies went down to their fifth consecutive Test defeat, and their 23rd in 27 overseas Tests, with a day to spare. Their batting and fielding let them down again, and although they had no luck with injuries and umpiring decisions, there was little doubt that the better side won.

West Indies started the match a batsman short, because Campbell had fractured a finger and Marlon Samuels had a knee injury, forcing them to fill the vacant slot with the leg-spinner Ramnarine. Pakistan also made one change, replacing the new opener, Naved Latif, with Shahid Afridi, which proved far more telling.

Neither the pitch nor the atmospheric conditions warranted bowling first, and Hooper chose to do so solely because West Indies had taken early wickets in the First Test. The move proved a blunder, and was compounded by more fluffed catches. The beneficiary on four occasions was Afridi, who scored a characteristically aggressive 107, blasting 16 fours and three sixes in just three and a half hours. With Younis Khan, he put on 190, a record for Pakistan's second wicket against West Indies. After Afridi's dismissal, another missed chance reprieved Yousuf Youhana, who edged behind before scoring. He went on to make a delightful 60, while Younis proceeded solidly to 153 in nearly seven hours.

Armed next morning with the second new ball, West Indies' bowlers retrieved some ground, getting rid of Younis and Youhana, but an unbeaten 64 by Abdul Razzaq boosted Pakistan's total to an imposing 472. Cuffy was the main wicket-taker, with four for 82 on his 32nd birthday, but the pick of the attack was the luckless Dillon. In the 45 overs West Indies faced before the second-day close, they stumbled to 164 for four, and would have been in deeper trouble had Hooper not been dropped twice at slip by Younis off the spinners. He survived to reach 84 not out next day, passing 5,000 Test runs on the way, but only Jacobs lent him any support. They were all out in mid-afternoon 208 behind.

Pakistan did not enforce the follow-on, preferring to add quick runs, which they did through another big second-wicket stand, this time 144 between Taufeeq Umar and Younis. The declaration finally came three overs after lunch on the fourth day, when they led by 433. They gave themselves 150 overs to bowl West Indies out, but 61 sufficed as Pakistan completed their sixth consecutive win that evening. Though the ball turned viciously from the rough, only two wickets fell to spin.

Instead, the damage was done by Waqar Younis, whose four wickets took him past 350 in Tests, and Razzaq, still finding reverse swing at will to capture three in one deadly spell. West Indies' collapse was precipitated by three lbw decisions – against Ganga, Hooper and Chanderpaul – which TV replays suggested were as unsafe as Ryan Hinds's dismissal in the first innings. Their misfortune merely accelerated the defeat.

Man of the Match: Younis Khan.   *Men of the Series:* Abdul Razzaq and M. Dillon.

Close of play: First day, Pakistan 344-3 (Younis Khan 131, Yousuf Youhana 47); Second day, West Indies 164-4 (Hooper 40, Dillon 0); Third day, Pakistan 130-1 (Taufeeq Umar 64, Younis Khan 61).

Pakistan

Taufeeq Umar c Ganga b Dillon	8	– (2) lbw b Dillon	69
Shahid Afridi b Cuffy	107	– (1) c Jacobs b Dillon	0
Younis Khan c Ganga b Collins	153	– c Ganga b Dillon	71
Inzamam-ul-Haq c Hooper b Ramnarine	36	– c sub (D. Brown) b Collins	6
Yousuf Youhana b Dillon	60	– not out	52
Abdul Razzaq not out	64	– run out	16
†Rashid Latif c Hooper b Ramnarine	16	– not out	2
Saqlain Mushtaq b Cuffy	50		
*Waqar Younis lbw b Ramnarine	2		
Shoaib Akhtar c and b Cuffy	4		
Danish Kaneria c Gayle b Cuffy	0		
B 12, l-b 2, n-b 3	17	L-b 6, w 1, n-b 2	9

1/12 (1) 2/202 (2) 3/272 (3) 4/364 (5)   472   1/0 (1) 2/144 (3)   (5 wkts dec.) 225
5/393 (3) 6/416 (7) 7/447 (8)   3/145 (2) 4/175 (4)
8/454 (9) 9/463 (10) 10/472 (11)   5/216 (6)

Bowling: *First Innings*—Dillon 27–6–63–2; Collins 30–5–99–1; Cuffy 29–4–82–4; Ramnarine 36–5–137–3; Hooper 7–0–41–0; R. O. Hinds 5–1–24–0; Gayle 1–0–12–0. *Second Innings*—Dillon 18–2–57–3; Cuffy 20–4–52–0; Collins 14–2–56–1; R. O. Hinds 12–3–15–0; Ramnarine 12–1–39–0.

West Indies

D. Ganga b Shahid Afridi	65	– lbw b Shoaib Akhtar	21
C. H. Gayle b Shoaib Akhtar	6	– lbw b Waqar Younis	4
W. W. Hinds b Saqlain Mushtaq	25	– c Taufeeq Umar b Saqlain Mushtaq	34
*C. L. Hooper not out	84	– lbw b Saqlain Mushtaq	1
S. Chanderpaul c Yousuf Youhana b Danish Kaneria	16	– lbw b Abdul Razzaq	19
M. Dillon c Taufeeq Umar b Shoaib Akhtar	0	– (8) lbw b Abdul Razzaq	0
R. O. Hinds lbw b Abdul Razzaq	11	– (6) lbw b Waqar Younis	46
†R. D. Jacobs b Saqlain Mushtaq	31	– (7) not out	35
D. Ramnarine b Shoaib Akhtar	0	– b Abdul Razzaq	0
C. E. Cuffy b Shoaib Akhtar	4	– b Waqar Younis	15
P. T. Collins c Inzamam-ul-Haq b Saqlain Mushtaq	1	– b Waqar Younis	0
B 6, l-b 9, n-b 6	21	B 2, l-b 6, n-b 6	14

1/19 (2) 2/88 (3) 3/116 (1) 4/159 (5)   264   1/19 (2) 2/46 (1) 3/47 (4)   189
5/170 (6) 6/189 (7) 7/236 (8)   4/84 (3) 5/114 (5) 6/161 (6)
8/237 (9) 9/247 (10) 10/264 (11)   7/162 (8) 8/162 (9)
                                                     9/189 (10) 10/189 (11)

Bowling: *First Innings*—Waqar Younis 9–1–24–0; Shoaib Akhtar 18–4–63–4; Danish Kaneria 13–2–34–1; Saqlain Mushtaq 21.5–4–75–3; Shahid Afridi 15–0–34–1; Abdul Razzaq 8–1–19–1. *Second Innings*—Waqar Younis 10–2–44–4; Shoaib Akhtar 8–3–23–1; Abdul Razzaq 11–2–33–3; Saqlain Mushtaq 19–8–42–2; Shahid Afridi 2–0–14–0; Danish Kaneria 11–2–25–0.

Umpires: D. B. Hair (Australia) and Shakeel Khan (Pakistan).
Third umpire: Mian Aslam (Pakistan).   Referee: M. H. Denness (England).

†PAKISTAN v WEST INDIES

First One-Day International

At Sharjah, February 14 (day/night). Pakistan won by four wickets. Toss: West Indies.

Determined bowling and brilliant fielding by West Indies stretched Pakistan's pursuit of an eminently beatable 190 into the 47th over. Gayle had given West Indies a roaring start, dashing to 50 in 53 balls, with ten fours sent to all points of the compass. But he was struck by a sudden bout of the chronic illness which dogs him, and his dismissal sent the innings into decline. Hooper tried to prop it up, but could not maintain the momentum. There were 16 fours in 19 overs while Gayle was in, but only one, from Hooper, and a solitary six, from Brown, thereafter. West Indies' fast bowlers soon reduced Pakistan to a perilous 15 for three. However, Yousuf Youhana kept a calm head, anchoring them until the 31st over, while Rashid Latif and Abdul Razzaq launched the attack that brought victory.

Man of the Match: Abdul Razzaq.

West Indies

D. Ganga hit wkt b Waqar Younis	15	M. Dillon c Inzamam-ul-Haq		
C. H. Gayle b Abdul Razzaq	50	b Wasim Akram	1
W. W. Hinds c Younis Khan b Shoaib Akhtar	14	C. D. Collymore not out	6
*C. L. Hooper lbw b Shahid Afridi	45	C. E. Cuffy run out	2
S. Chanderpaul c Shahid Afridi				
b Abdul Razzaq	0	B 3, l-b 1, w 6, n-b 5	15
R. O. Hinds run out	8		
†R. D. Jacobs b Saqlain Mushtaq	25	1/21 2/56 3/97 (48.3 overs) 190	
D. Brown c Younis Khan		4/97 5/117 6/161	
b Saqlain Mushtaq	9	7/169 8/178 9/183	

Bowling: Wasim Akram 8.3–0–46–1; Waqar Younis 8–1–37–1; Shoaib Akhtar 8–1–26–1; Abdul Razzaq 7–0–24–2; Shahid Afridi 7–1–25–1; Saqlain Mushtaq 10–0–28–2.

Pakistan

Naved Latif c Jacobs b Dillon	0	Abdul Razzaq not out	46
Shahid Afridi c Collymore b Brown	35	Wasim Akram not out	13
Younis Khan run out	1	L-b 2, w 7, n-b 2	11
Inzamam-ul-Haq c Ganga b Cuffy	1		
Yousuf Youhana c and b Hooper	39	1/1 2/3 3/15 (6 wkts, 46.1 overs) 193	
†Rashid Latif c Collymore b Hooper	47	4/62 5/110 6/153	

Saqlain Mushtaq, *Waqar Younis and Shoaib Akhtar did not bat.

Bowling: Dillon 9.1–1–32–1; Cuffy 10–1–31–1; Collymore 9–1–37–0; Brown 5–0–31–1; Hooper 10–1–44–2; R. O. Hinds 3–0–16–0.

Umpires: Aleem Dar (Pakistan) and Mian Aslam (Pakistan).
Third umpire: Asad Rauf (Pakistan). Referee: M. H. Denness (England).

†PAKISTAN v WEST INDIES

Second One-Day International

At Sharjah, February 15 (day/night). Pakistan won by 51 runs. Toss: Pakistan. International debut: R. S. Morton.

Two 20-year-olds, Shoaib Malik and Mohammad Sami, shaped a series-clinching win with a century and a hat-trick. Victory looked unlikely when Pakistan were 51 for four, and again when West Indies reached 100 in 14 overs with only one wicket down. But Malik, newly promoted to No. 4, batted with great maturity to resuscitate Pakistan: he took 89 balls to reach 50, and just

41 for his next 61. Ganga fell to the first ball of the innings, only for Gayle to ensure another flying start by smashing 62 off 46 deliveries, with eight fours and three sixes. But his tame shot in the first over of Shoaib Akhtar's second spell triggered a collapse of nine for 80 in 21 overs. Sami completed the win by trapping Jacobs with a questionable leg-before, then clean-bowling Collymore and Cuffy. It was Sharjah's fourth hat-trick, and all had been taken by Pakistanis.

Man of the Match: Shoaib Malik.

Pakistan

Inzamam-ul-Haq c Gayle b Cuffy	. . . . .	3
Shahid Afridi c and b Dillon	. . . . .	4
Younis Khan lbw b Cuffy	. . . . . .	18
Shoaib Malik not out	. . . .	111
Yousuf Youhana lbw b Collymore	. . . . .	1
Naved Latif c Cuffy b Hooper	. . . .	45
Abdul Razzaq c Gayle b R. O. Hinds . . .		30
†Rashid Latif run out	. . . .	5

*Waqar Younis lbw b R. O. Hinds	. . . . .	3
Shoaib Akhtar run out	. . . .	1
Mohammad Sami c Jacobs b Dillon . . .		0
W 7, n-b 4	. . . .	11

1/7 2/7 3/43   (49 overs) 232
4/51 5/124 6/186
7/203 8/219 9/223

Bowling: Dillon 10–1–57–2; Cuffy 10–4–35–2; Collymore 10–1–51–1; Hooper 10–0–47–1; Gayle 3–0–10–0; R. O. Hinds 6–0–32–2.

West Indies

D. Ganga c Rashid Latif b Waqar Younis		0
C. H. Gayle c Shahid Afridi		
b Shoaib Akhtar .		62
W. W. Hinds b Shoaib Akhtar		29
R. S. Morton b Mohammad Sami		16
*C. L. Hooper lbw b Waqar Younis . .		7
S. Chanderpaul c Rashid Latif		
b Abdul Razzaq .		22
R. O. Hinds lbw b Abdul Razzaq		18

†R. D. Jacobs lbw b Mohammad Sami . .		1
M. Dillon not out		0
C. D. Collymore b Mohammad Sami . .		0
C. E. Cuffy b Mohammad Sami		0
B 1, l-b 7, w 8, n-b 10		26

1/0 2/101 3/110   (34.4 overs) 181
4/127 5/133 6/178
7/180 8/181 9/181

Bowling: Waqar Younis 7–0–40–2; Shoaib Akhtar 7–0–49–2; Mohammad Sami 7.4–0–44–4; Abdul Razzaq 7–1–18–2; Shoaib Malik 3–0–9–0; Shahid Afridi 3–0–13–0.

Umpires: Asad Rauf (Pakistan) and Salim Badar (Pakistan).
Third umpire: Nadeem Ghauri (Pakistan). Referee: M. H. Denness (England).

†PAKISTAN v WEST INDIES

Third One-Day International

At Sharjah, February 17 (day/night). West Indies won by 110 runs. Toss: West Indies.

West Indies faced another dismal whitewash at 61 for four. But a stand of 154 between Hooper and Chanderpaul was the springboard to a consolation win. They gathered their runs mainly in singles and twos while they steadied the boat, then cut loose with 20 overs left. Hooper remained unbeaten on 112 from 127 balls, hitting eight fours and four sixes in a characteristic arc between extra cover and long-on. Once again, Pakistan's batsmen started poorly; this time, they were offered no scope for recovery. The West Indian bowling was tight and their fielding mostly sharp. Ryan Hinds was outstanding at point, with the highlight his direct hit to run out the dangerous Abdul Razzaq – a dismissal momentarily in doubt when the TV umpire managed to switch on both lights at once. Gayle cleaned up with four wickets in successive overs.

Man of the Match: C. L. Hooper.   *Man of the Series:* Abdul Razzaq.

West Indies

D. Ganga c Rashid Latif b Waqar Younis		0
C. H. Gayle c Younis Khan b Shoaib Akhtar		19
W. W. Hinds c Younis Khan b Mohammad Sami		22
R. S. Morton lbw b Waqar Younis		3
*C. L. Hooper not out		112
S. Chanderpaul c Rashid Latif b Abdul Razzaq		67
†R. D. Jacobs not out		13
L-b 10, w 12, n-b 2		24
	(5 wkts, 50 overs)	260

1/0 2/28 3/38
4/61 5/215

R. O. Hinds, M. Dillon, C. D. Collymore and P. T. Collins did not bat.

Bowling: Waqar Younis 8–1–47–2; Shoaib Akhtar 10–0–45–1; Abdul Razzaq 10–1–36–1; Mohammad Sami 9–0–54–1; Naved Latif 1–0–13–0; Shahid Afridi 8–1–35–0; Shoaib Malik 4–0–20–0.

Pakistan

Shahid Afridi c Morton b Collins		5
Naved Latif lbw b Dillon		4
Younis Khan c Hooper b Collins		6
Shoaib Malik b Hooper		37
Yousuf Youhana c and b Dillon		20
Abdul Razzaq run out		10
Inzamam-ul-Haq b Gayle		21
†Rashid Latif b Gayle		37
*Waqar Younis c Dillon b Gayle		2
Shoaib Akhtar b Gayle		0
Mohammad Sami not out		1
L-b 4, w 2, n-b 1		7
	(40.2 overs)	150

1/10 2/10 3/18
4/51 5/86 6/91
7/127 8/131 9/136

Bowling: Dillon 6–0–26–2; Collins 8–0–33–2; Collymore 10–1–22–0; Hooper 8–1–22–1; Gayle 4.2–0–19–4; R. O. Hinds 4–0–24–0.

Umpires: Nadeem Ghauri (Pakistan) and Salim Badar (Pakistan).
Third umpire: Aleem Dar (Pakistan). Referee: M. H. Denness (England).

THE ZIMBABWEANS IN INDIA, 2001-02

BY ANIRBAN SIRCAR

Zimbabwe faced a challenging tour when they arrived in India after a miserable run of defeats. Since their spirited fightback to square their home series against India in June 2001, they had won only one Test out of nine, and only four of their last 23 one-day internationals. All but one of those five victories had come against Bangladesh, the weakest team on the circuit, and most recently they had been whitewashed in three Tests in Sri Lanka.

Reasons for Zimbabwe's woeful form were not hard to find. Six different captains had led the team since India's visit. An already fragile player base had been weakened by injury, retirement and bickering between the leading cricketers and the Zimbabwe Cricket Union, over pay and the pressure to include more black players in the national side. And many of the team were directly affected by the political crisis at home, where white-held farms were being forcibly reclaimed by Robert Mugabe's government.

The Zimbabweans' star player, Andy Flower, looked an unhappy man, confirming the team's growing anxiety at the political turmoil. He had lined up a contract to play for Essex in the English summer, and a permanent move from his homeland could not be discounted. On Zimbabwe's previous tour of India, only 15 months earlier, he had amassed 540 runs in two Tests (curiously, this visit returned to the same venues). He showed only a shadow of that stupendous form this time: apart from 92 in the first innings at Delhi, he scored 11 runs in three attempts.

Yet, after a disappointing innings defeat at Nagpur, the unheralded Zimbabweans found unexpected reserves, though it was too late to threaten India's formidable record of 17 unbeaten home series in their last 18. They reduced their hosts to 105 for six, with one man injured, in pursuit of a mere 122 on the last day at Delhi: a performance whose worth was underlined by memories of India's breathtaking series win against the Australians a year earlier. Zimbabwe followed up by twice taking the lead in the five-match one-day series, and might have scripted a fairytale victory in the fourth game, at Hyderabad, until it was snatched away by the vivacity of India's youth. The home side struggled without some of their key protagonists: injuries claimed Sachin Tendulkar and the explosive opener Virender Sehwag; the leg-spinner Anil Kumble later joined them on the sidelines, while Javagal Srinath was already taking a sabbatical from the limited-overs game.

For Zimbabwe, the former captain, Alistair Campbell, who had recently fallen from favour with the selectors, justified his recall with 251 runs in the five one-day games, Douglas Marillier played an astonishing innings at No. 10 to snatch victory in the opening one-day fixture, and Douglas Hondo turned in some useful seam bowling to win the third. In the Tests, the slow left-armer, Raymond Price – nephew of the golfer Nick Price, with an off-the-field job installing air-conditioning units – claimed an impressive ten wickets in the two Tests, and dismissed Tendulkar in all three innings.

But the Test series was won for India by the lethal spinning duo of Kumble and Harbhajan Singh, whose leg-spin/off-spin combination claimed a total of 28 wickets. The Zimbabweans were quite unable to combat quality slow bowling on turning tracks; none of them could plot a century, while the Indians relished three in one innings in the opening Test at Nagpur. Tendulkar was easily the leading run-scorer in the Tests and, at Delhi, Sourav Ganguly finally managed his first Test hundred as captain. Though Zimbabwe's improving form as the tour advanced provided encouragement for their new coach, Geoff Marsh, India ended up triumphant on all fronts.

ZIMBABWEAN TOURING PARTY

S. V. Carlisle (Mashonaland A) (*captain*), H. H. Streak (Matabeleland) (*vice-captain*), A. D. R. Campbell (Manicaland), D. D. Ebrahim (Mashonaland), A. Flower (Mashonaland), G. W. Flower (Mashonaland A), T. J. Friend (Midlands), T. R. Gripper (Mashonaland), M. Mbangwa (Matabeleland), R. W. Price (Midlands), G. J. Rennie (Mashonaland A), T. Taibu (Mashonaland), B. T. Watambwa (Mashonaland), C. B. Wishart (Midlands).

G. B. Brent (Manicaland), C. K. Coventry (CFX Academy), D. T. Hondo (Mashonaland A) and D. A. Marillier (Midlands) replaced Gripper, Price, Rennie and Watambwa for the one-day international series.

Coach: G. R. Marsh.   *Manager:* M. A. Meman.

ZIMBABWEAN TOUR RESULTS

Test matches – Played 2: Lost 2.
First-class matches – Played 3: Lost 2, Drawn 1.
Losses – India (2).
Draw – Indian Board President's XI.
One-day internationals – Played 5: Won 2, Lost 3.

Note: Matches in this section which were not first-class are signified by a dagger.

At Vijayawada, February 15, 16, 17. **Drawn.** Toss: Indian Board President's XI. **Indian Board President's XI 361 for three dec.** (G. Gambhir 218, G. K. Khoda 41, R. Dravid 50, A. V. Kale 40 not out) **and 154 for one** (P. M. Mullick 62 not out, A. V. Kale 90); **Zimbabweans 340** (T. R. Gripper 52, G. J. Rennie 52, A. Flower 94, T. J. Friend 52, Extras 32; Sarandeep Singh three for 83, A. Mishra six for 95).

Gambhir's 218 lasted 406 minutes and 288 balls and included 39 fours.

INDIA v ZIMBABWE

First Test Match

At Nagpur, February 21, 22, 23, 24, 25. India won by an innings and 101 runs. Toss: Zimbabwe.
Zimbabwe returned to the Orange City of Nagpur, where they had played their last Indian Test in November 2000, and for the second time running they conceded three hundreds in an innings. Das and Tendulkar re-enacted their feats of 15 months earlier, and the third century came from Bangar, in his second Test. But in 2000-01, the Zimbabweans had responded in kind on a placid pitch: Andy Flower had scored a career-best 232, supported by Campbell's maiden Test hundred, to stave off an innings defeat. This time, Flower managed 11 runs in all on a dusty, crumbling surface, as Kumble and Harbhajan Singh, both missing from the earlier encounter, bowled India to an overwhelming victory.

Carlisle had taken first use of the pitch, and Campbell seemed to enjoy his return as they shared a second-wicket stand of 106. But once Kumble parted them, and Andy Flower lost his leg stump to his 12th delivery, an in-swinging yorker from Zaheer Khan, the middle order crumbled. Friend, at No. 9, cut and drove to an unbeaten 60 in 70 balls to prolong the innings into the second morning.

Das spent most of the rest of the day compiling his second century against Zimbabwe, batting for five hours until he edged Price to slip in the final over. That was the cue for Tendulkar's entrance. Even he was slowed down by the pitch, but he cruised to his 28th Test hundred, one behind Bradman. Price bowled a marathon spell, but Friend was barred from the attack by umpire Venkataraghavan after bowling a beamer at Tendulkar on the third evening – he had been warned and no-balled the previous day for a similar offence against Das. By then, Bangar had joined Tendulkar, and next morning, after three days dominated by drudgery, they took off, adding 110 in 16 overs together. Bangar repeatedly rushed down the pitch to attack Price, who nevertheless claimed Tendulkar as his fifth victim, as Bangar hurried on to a hard-hitting maiden century. It announced not only his arrival on the big stage, but India's determination to press for a win.

Ganguly promptly declared, at a monumental 570. Needing to muster 283 to make India bat again, or to survive for just over five sessions, Zimbabwe soon wilted against the clinical spin of Kumble and Harbhajan. By the close, the cream of their batting had already been skimmed, with only the opener, Gripper, stubbornly hanging on. On the final day, a sparse crowd had to wait little more than an hour to see Kumble and Harbhajan, bowling unchanged, complete the last rites. They snared nine wickets between them.

Man of the Match: A. Kumble.

Close of play: First day, Zimbabwe 248-8 (Friend 33, Price 6); Second day, India 209-2 (Dravid 57, Tendulkar 0); Third day, India 437-5 (Tendulkar 137, Bangar 22); Fourth day, Zimbabwe 152-4 (Gripper 52, Price 4).

Zimbabwe

Batsman	First Innings	Runs	Second Innings	Runs
*S. V. Carlisle	run out	77	lbw b Zaheer Khan	28
T. R. Gripper	c Dasgupta b Zaheer Khan	5	c sub (V. Sehwag) b Harbhajan Singh	60
A. D. R. Campbell	c Laxman b Kumble	57	c Laxman b Kumble	30
A. Flower	b Zaheer Khan	3	c Dravid b Kumble	8
G. J. Rennie	c sub (V. Sehwag) b Srinath	9	c Laxman b Kumble	25
G. W. Flower	c Dravid b Kumble	14	(7) lbw b Kumble	1
H. H. Streak	c Das b Zaheer Khan	24	(8) c Ganguly b Kumble	8
†T. Taibu	b Kumble	1	(9) c sub (V. Sehwag) b Harbhajan Singh	0
T. J. Friend	not out	60	(10) not out	6
R. W. Price	run out	18	(6) c Dravid b Harbhajan Singh	4
B. T. Watambwa	lbw b Kumble	0	c Tendulkar b Harbhajan Singh	1
	B 6, l-b 11, n-b 2	19	B 1, l-b 8, n-b 2	11
		287		**182**

1/12 (2) 2/118 (3) 3/125 (4) 4/151 (5) 5/175 (6) 6/182 (7) 7/194 (8) 8/227 (7) 9/286 (10) 10/287 (11)

1/32 (1) 2/80 (3) 3/103 (4) 4/147 (5) 5/156 (6) 6/159 (7) 7/161 (2) 8/167 (9) 9/181 (8) 10/182 (11)

Bowling: *First Innings*—Srinath 22–6–65–1; Zaheer Khan 14–2–45–3; Bangar 8–3–20–0; Kumble 33.5–12–82–4; Harbhajan Singh 26–8–58–0. *Second Innings*—Srinath 6–3–20–0; Kumble 37–15–63–5; Zaheer Khan 8–1–33–1; Harbhajan Singh 31.4–9–46–4; Tendulkar 6–2–11–0.

India

S. S. Das	c Campbell b Price	105
†D. Dasgupta	b Price	33
R. Dravid	b Streak	65
S. R. Tendulkar	c A. Flower b Price	176
*S. C. Ganguly	c G. W. Flower b Price	38
V. V. S. Laxman	c Rennie b Price	13
S. B. Bangar	not out	100
Zaheer Khan	b Watambwa	0
A. Kumble	not out	13
	B 16, l-b 2, w 3, n-b 6	27
	(7 wkts. dec.)	**570**

1/79 (2) 2/209 (1) 3/247 (3) 4/344 (5) 5/376 (6) 6/547 (4) 7/547 (8)

J. Srinath and Harbhajan Singh did not bat.

Bowling: Streak 34–9–108–1; Watambwa 25.5–6–87–1; Price 68–18–182–5; Friend 22–3–61–0; G. W. Flower 30–8–96–0; Gripper 5–0–18–0.

Umpires: D. R. Shepherd (England) and S. Venkataraghavan.
Third umpire: Jasbir Singh. Referee: J. R. Reid (New Zealand).

INDIA v ZIMBABWE

Second Test Match

At Delhi, February 28, March 1, 2, 3, 4. India won by four wickets. Toss: Zimbabwe.

India whitewashed the short series, but Zimbabwe put up much more of a fight, compiling a respectable first-innings total and then, after a second-innings massacre by the spinners, holding their nerve in the field to give India a nasty scare chasing 122.

It was no surprise that Zimbabwe's improvement coincided with Andy Flower's only half-century of the series. He and Ebrahim, who replaced Rennie, joined forces to add 116 before Flower fell to a bat-pad catch off Harbhajan Singh, just after tea. In his previous 60 Tests, he had reached 90 a dozen times and always gone on to a hundred; this was 13th time unlucky. Ebrahim batted into the second morning, when he narrowly missed a maiden Test century and Friend saw Zimbabwe past 300.

Ganguly provided the heart of India's reply with his first Test hundred as captain, in his 18th Test in charge. His last century had been against New Zealand in October 1999: this was his 40th innings and 23rd Test since, and only five fifties had arrived in the interim. But Ganguly broke the jinx after promoting himself to No. 3, and maintained his concentration for seven and a half hours, despite the breaks for bad weather which cut half the third day's play. There was showier support from the local boy Sehwag, who justified his inclusion ahead of Laxman as he scored all but ten of his 74 runs in fours.

India were eight behind when Ganguly swept at Price and became the first of 17 wickets to tumble on an eroding pitch on the fourth day. His team managed a lead of 25, which looked plenty when Zimbabwe fizzled out for 146. Harbhajan grabbed three for one in 17 deliveries, and had Andy Flower caught at short leg for the second innings running, this time for a four-ball duck. The spin tandem of Kumble and Harbhajan snapped up all ten wickets, to finish with 15.

The last man out was Grant Flower, who was soon back in the action when he dismissed Ganguly and Kumble with consecutive deliveries. With Dasgupta already run out by Taibu, leaping to collect the ball behind the wicket, and Sehwag unlikely to bat – he had been stretchered off after injuring his shoulder trying to catch Grant Flower – India were effectively a precarious 36 for four by the close. During this session, Friend was warned by umpire de Silva for bowling a beamer, as Zaheer Khan had been a couple of days earlier.

Tendulkar seemed to be steering India out of the panic zone with a breezy 53-ball 42, but the tension rose when Price removed him for the third time in three innings. Two more quick wickets left India effectively seven down, with 17 required. Those runs should have been fought over like gold nuggets. But India got four leg-byes when Harbhajan survived an lbw appeal, four overthrows from a failed run-out attempt, and a four and a six from Harbhajan settled the issue.

Man of the Match: Harbhajan Singh. *Man of the Series:* A. Kumble.

Close of play: First day, Zimbabwe 260-6 (Ebrahim 82, Friend 7); Second day, India 171-4 (Ganguly 78, Sehwag 16); Third day, India 319-6 (Ganguly 135, Kumble 19); Fourth day, India 36-3 (Das 10, Tendulkar 0).

Zimbabwe

*S. V. Carlisle b Srinath	0	– c and b Harbhajan Singh	37
T. R. Gripper c Dravid b Zaheer Khan	8	– c Dravid b Harbhajan Singh	10
A. D. R. Campbell c Dravid b Zaheer Khan	16	– c Dravid b Harbhajan Singh	2
A. Flower c Das b Harbhajan Singh	92	– c Das b Harbhajan Singh	0
D. D. Ebrahim lbw b Srinath	94	– lbw b Kumble	22
G. W. Flower run out	30	– c Harbhajan Singh b Kumble	49
H. H. Streak b Kumble	0	– lbw b Kumble	9
T. J. Friend c Tendulkar b Harbhajan Singh	43	– b Harbhajan Singh	0
†T. Taibu lbw b Kumble	13	– c Bangar b Kumble	10
R. W. Price b Kumble	0	– c Das b Harbhajan Singh	3
B. T. Watambwa not out	3	– not out	1
B 5, l-b 16, n-b 9	30	B 2, n-b 1	3
	329		**146**

1/0 (1) 2/11 (2) 3/65 (3) 4/181 (4)
5/246 (6) 6/246 (7) 7/289 (5)
8/310 (9) 9/310 (10) 10/329 (8)

1/23 (2) 2/31 (3) 3/31 (4)
4/69 (1) 5/95 (5) 6/113 (7)
7/114 (8) 8/129 (9)
9/142 (10) 10/146 (6)

Bowling: *First Innings*—Srinath 18–4–37–2; Zaheer Khan 22–4–76–2; Bangar 7–1–25–0; Kumble 34–13–88–3; Harbhajan Singh 27.5–5–70–2; Sehwag 1–0–6–0; Tendulkar 1–0–6–0. *Second Innings*—Srinath 4–0–12–0; Zaheer Khan 3–0–12–0; Harbhajan Singh 31–5–62–6; Kumble 29.3–8–58–4.

India

S. S. Das c Taibu b Streak		13	– lbw b Streak	31
†D. Dasgupta lbw b Friend		19	– run out	1
*S. C. Ganguly c Gripper b Price		136	– lbw b G. W. Flower	20
S. R. Tendulkar lbw b Price		36	– (5) lbw b Price	42
R. Dravid run out		1	– (6) c A. Flower b Price	6
V. Sehwag lbw b Streak		74		
S. B. Bangar run out		4	– not out	3
A. Kumble not out		34	– (4) c Gripper b G. W. Flower	0
J. Srinath c Gripper b Price		0		
Harbhajan Singh lbw b Streak		9	– (8) not out	14
Zaheer Khan b Streak		8		
B 9, l-b 6, w 1, n-b 4		20	L-b 4, n-b 5	9

1/24 (1) 2/58 (2) 3/142 (4) 4/144 (5)   354   1/3 (2) 2/36 (3)   (6 wkts) 126
5/264 (6) 6/280 (7) 7/321 (3)   3/36 (4) 4/93 (5)
8/331 (9) 9/340 (10) 10/354 (11)   5/103 (1) 6/105 (6)

Bowling: *First Innings*—Streak 37.2–11–92–4; Watambwa 18–5–47–0; Friend 19–2–75–1; Price 50–16–108–3; G. W. Flower 5–0–17–0. *Second Innings*—Streak 16.5–4–53–1; Friend 3–0–17–0; Price 19–9–24–2; G. W. Flower 6–3–22–2; Gripper 1–0–6–0.

Umpires: E. A. R. de Silva (Sri Lanka) and A. V. Jayaprakash.
Third umpire: N. N. Menon. Referee: J. R. Reid (New Zealand).

†INDIA v ZIMBABWE

First One-Day International

At Faridabad, March 7. Zimbabwe won by one wicket. Toss: India.

Zimbabwe took the lead in the one-day series through an incredible last-gasp win. Marillier came to the crease in the 45th over, when his side were reeling at 210 for eight, and wielded his willow with such aplomb that he not only scooped to victory with two balls to spare, but also completed a whirlwind 21-ball fifty, then the joint fifth-quickest in one-day internationals. Zaheer Khan, whose first eight overs had claimed four for 13, went for 34 in his last two. Marillier repeatedly stepped across and hit over the keeper's head; not even Kumble could halt him in the final over. This sensational onslaught overshadowed half-centuries from Ganguly and Laxman earlier in the day, as well as a carefully crafted stand of 111 between two more seasoned Zimbabwean campaigners, Campbell and Andy Flower, before the middle order crumbled.

Man of the Match: D. A. Marillier.

India

D. Mongia c Taibu b Streak		25	†A. Ratra run out	6
*S. C. Ganguly st Taibu b Marillier		57	A. B. Agarkar not out	40
V. V. S. Laxman run out		75	L-b 1, w 6, n-b 2	9
R. Dravid lbw b G. W. Flower		23		
M. Kaif not out		39	1/46 2/123 3/171 (6 wkts, 50 overs) 274
S. B. Bangar c Friend b Streak		0	4/193 5/193 6/211

Harbhajan Singh, A. Kumble and Zaheer Khan did not bat.

Bowling: Streak 10–0–53–2; Friend 10–0–68–0; Brent 10–0–68–0; Marillier 10–0–53–1; G. W. Flower 10–0–31–1.

Zimbabwe

A. D. R. Campbell lbw b Zaheer Khan	84		†T. Taibu c Ratra b Bangar	8
C. B. Wishart b Zaheer Khan	1		D. A. Marillier not out	56
T. J. Friend b Zaheer Khan	7		G. B. Brent not out	1
A. Flower b Kumble	71			
*S. V. Carlisle c Ratra b Zaheer Khan	23		L-b 5, w 2, n-b 6	13
D. D. Ebrahim c Ganguly b Bangar	10			
G. W. Flower c and b Harbhajan Singh	2		1/5 2/21 3/132 (9 wkts, 49.4 overs) 277	
H. H. Streak c Ganguly			4/186 5/193 6/198	
b Harbhajan Singh	1		7/200 8/210 9/253	

Bowling: Zaheer Khan 10–2–47–4; Agarkar 8–0–45–0; Bangar 9–0–42–2; Harbhajan Singh 10–1–48–2; Kumble 9.4–0–70–1; Ganguly 3–0–20–0.

Umpires: S. K. Porel and I. Sivaram.
Third umpire: S. J. Phadkar. Referee: J. R. Reid (New Zealand).

†INDIA v ZIMBABWE

Second One-Day International

At Mohali, March 10 (day/night). India won by 64 runs. Toss: India.

A fine all-round display – 45 runs and three wickets – from the local hero, Mongia, helped to level the series. Mongia and Ganguly shared an opening stand of 109 in 15 overs, and Ganguly hit three sixes in an 83-ball 86, despite an injured knee. Laxman joined him in notching up a second successive fifty as the pitch's welcome bounce seduced the excited Zimbabwean seamers into bowling waywardly. Their batsmen made a valiant effort to chase 320 in 49 overs (one was deducted for a slow over-rate), but once Harbhajan Singh broke the second-wicket century partnership between Campbell and Friend, his off-breaks and Mongia's left-arm spin saw off any threat from Zimbabwe.

Man of the Match: S. C. Ganguly.

India

D. Mongia c Friend b Marillier	45		S. B. Bangar c Wishart b Brent	0
*S. C. Ganguly run out	86		Harbhajan Singh not out	15
V. V. S. Laxman c Ebrahim b Friend	52		B 2, l-b 5, w 25, n-b 2	34
R. Dravid not out	66			
M. Kaif b G. W. Flower	15		1/109 2/190 3/243 (6 wkts, 50 overs) 319	
A. B. Agarkar c Marillier b Brent	6		4/276 5/290 6/291	

†A. Ratra, A. Kumble and Zaheer Khan did not bat.

Bowling: Streak 10–0–72–0; Friend 10–0–57–1; Brent 9–0–60–2; Marillier 10–0–51–1; G. W. Flower 9–0–56–1; Campbell 2–0–16–0.

Zimbabwe

A. D. R. Campbell			H. H. Streak c Bangar b Kumble	14
lbw b Harbhajan Singh	62		†T. Taibu not out	6
D. D. Ebrahim c Laxman b Agarkar	1		G. B. Brent lbw b Harbhajan Singh	7
T. J. Friend st Ratra b Harbhajan Singh	63			
A. Flower b Mongia	29		L-b 17, w 5, n-b 1	23
G. W. Flower run out	9			
*S. V. Carlisle c Ratra b Agarkar	25		1/4 2/138 3/143 (43.3 overs) 255	
C. B. Wishart b Mongia	14		4/166 5/204 6/212	
D. A. Marillier c Ratra b Mongia	2		7/219 8/229 9/245	

Bowling: Zaheer Khan 7–0–42–0; Agarkar 8–0–44–2; Bangar 4–0–32–0; Kumble 10–0–49–1; Harbhajan Singh 8.3–0–40–3; Mongia 6–0–31–3.

Umpires: A. Bhattacharjee and S. K. Tarapore.
Third umpire: G. A. Pratap Kumar. Referee: J. R. Reid (New Zealand).

†INDIA v ZIMBABWE

Third One-Day International

At Kochi, March 13. Zimbabwe won by six wickets. Toss: India.

India fell behind again, thanks to their lacklustre batting and the seam of Hondo, in his first match of the tour. Familiar with Indian conditions after a spell at Dennis Lillee's Pace Foundation in Chennai, Hondo shot out the top three in his opening burst, and claimed a fourth victim at the death. Zimbabwe hardly missed the injured Andy Flower as they pursued 192 against a toothless attack. The pitch was docile, but the weather sultry; that did not deter Campbell, who scored his third successive fifty as opener. He stood firm as two early wickets fell, then shared a crucial century stand with Grant Flower. But it was Wishart who struck Mongia for the winning six.

Man of the Match: D. T. Hondo.

India

D. Mongia lbw b Hondo	4	Harbhajan Singh not out		24
*S. C. Ganguly b Hondo	11	Sarandeep Singh c Carlisle b Marillier		3
V. V. S. Laxman c Taibu b Hondo	20	Zaheer Khan c Marillier b Hondo		2
R. Dravid c Wishart b Mbangwa	6	L-b 7, w 14, n-b 2		23
M. Kaif c Wishart b Streak	56			
S. B. Bangar c Hondo b Marillier	36	1/10 2/38 3/49	(48.3 overs)	191
†A. Ratra c Marillier b Flower	3	4/51 5/137 6/147		
A. B. Agarkar c Streak b Flower	3	7/155 8/157 9/169		

Bowling: Streak 8–0–27–1; Hondo 8.3–0–37–4; Mbangwa 10–2–31–1; Friend 2–0–10–0; Marillier 10–0–44–2; Flower 10–0–35–2.

Zimbabwe

A. D. R. Campbell st Ratra		C. B. Wishart not out	17
b Sarandeep Singh	71		
D. D. Ebrahim b Agarkar	3		
T. J. Friend b Zaheer Khan	15	L-b 5, w 5, n-b 11	21
G. W. Flower c Ratra b Agarkar	49		
*S. V. Carlisle not out	21	1/13 2/39	(4 wkts, 44.2 overs) 197
		3/144 4/173	

H. H. Streak, D. A. Marillier, †T. Taibu, M. Mbangwa and D. T. Hondo did not bat.

Bowling: Zaheer Khan 9–1–41–1; Agarkar 10–3–28–2; Bangar 5–0–18–0; Harbhajan Singh 10–1–29–0; Sarandeep Singh 8–1–49–1; Mongia 2.2–0–27–0.

Umpires: V. Chopra and D. D. Sharma.
Third umpire: S. L. Shastri.   Referee: J. R. Reid (New Zealand).

†INDIA v ZIMBABWE

Fourth One-Day International

At Hyderabad, March 16 (day/night). India won by five wickets. Toss: Zimbabwe. International debut: M. Kartik.

India were looking down the barrel at a series loss when they were reduced to 132 for four in the 32nd over, chasing 241. But Yuvraj Singh, whose double-hundred in the Duleep Trophy had earned him his first recall since he toured South Africa in October, hammered 80 unbeaten runs in 60 balls to keep the series alive. Yuvraj and Kaif, who had helped India to win the Under-19 World Cup two years earlier, breathed much-needed life into the suspect middle order, adding 94 runs in 15 overs to set up a convincing victory. In Zimbabwe's innings, the honours were shared between Andy Flower, with a fine 89, and a four-wicket return by Agarkar.

Man of the Match: Yuvraj Singh.

Zimbabwe

A. D. R. Campbell c Dravid b Agarkar		3
D. D. Ebrahim c Dravid b Ganguly		38
T. J. Friend c Ratra b Agarkar		0
A. Flower c Ratra b Zaheer Khan		89
G. W. Flower c Mongia		
	b Harbhajan Singh	44
*S. V. Carlisle b Agarkar		40
H. H. Streak b Zaheer Khan		10

D. A. Marillier c Laxman b Agarkar . . . 1
†T. Taibu not out 3

L-b 3, w 7, n-b 2 12

1/13 2/13 3/79   (8 wkts, 50 overs) 240
4/175 5/190 6/220
7/223 8/240

M. Mbangwa and D. T. Hondo did not bat.

Bowling: Zaheer Khan 10–0–58–2; Agarkar 10–2–32–4; Harbhajan Singh 10–0–44–1; Ganguly 9–0–36–1; Kartik 8–0–47–0; Mongia 3–0–20–0.

India

D. Mongia c Campbell b Friend		30
*S. C. Ganguly c G. W. Flower b Hondo		7
V. V. S. Laxman c Taibu b Friend		13
R. Dravid b G. W. Flower		32
M. Kaif run out		68
Yuvraj Singh not out		80

A. B. Agarkar not out 5

B 1, l-b 2, w 6 9

1/30 2/50 3/56   (5 wkts, 48.1 overs) 244
4/132 5/226

†A. Ratra, Harbhajan Singh, M. Kartik and Zaheer Khan did not bat.

Bowling: Streak 8–0–36–0; Hondo 8–0–48–1; Friend 8.1–1–42–2; Mbangwa 8–1–27–0; Marillier 8–0–47–0; G. W. Flower 8–0–41–1.

Umpires: S. C. Gupta and K. Hariharan.
Third umpire: M. S. Mahal.   Referee: J. R. Reid (New Zealand).

†INDIA v ZIMBABWE

Fifth One-Day International

At Guwahati, March 19. India won by 101 runs. Toss: India.
After a two-minute silence for the former Test keeper Narendra Tamhane, who had just died, India shrugged off their earlier complacency to take the series in style. Again, they looked like throwing it away, at 157 for four in the 31st over. But Mongia held on to score his maiden international hundred, a scintillating unbeaten 159 off 149 balls. His Punjab team-mate, Yuvraj Singh, was again on song, to the tune of 75 in 52 balls; together, they added 158 in 18 overs, and the last ten of the innings yielded an amazing 121 runs. Zimbabwe were left with a mammoth target of 334 in only 48 overs – two were docked for a slow over-rate. They wilted under the pressure, losing their last five wickets in 16 balls.

Man of the Match: D. Mongia.   *Man of the Series:* D. Mongia.

India

D. Mongia not out		159
*S. C. Ganguly c Taibu b Streak		28
V. V. S. Laxman run out		16
R. Dravid b Hondo		26
M. Kaif c A. Flower b Hondo		5
Yuvraj Singh c Friend b Marillier		75

R. V. Bharadwaj run out 0
A. B. Agarkar not out 6
B 4, l-b 4, w 10 18

1/52 2/98 3/149   (6 wkts, 50 overs) 333
4/157 5/315 6/316

†A. Ratra, Harbhajan Singh and Zaheer Khan did not bat.

Bowling: Streak 9–0–54–1; Hondo 10–2–56–2; Friend 10–0–68–0; Brent 9–0–74–0; Marillier 6–0–38–1; G. W. Flower 6–0–35–0.

Zimbabwe

A. D. R. Campbell c Bharadwaj
                    b Zaheer Khan . 31
D. D. Ebrahim b Ganguly 42
T. J. Friend st Ratra b Harbhajan Singh . 31
A. Flower c Zaheer Khan
                    b Harbhajan Singh . 1
G. W. Flower b Zaheer Khan 48
*S. V. Carlisle c Dravid b Bharadwaj . . . 17
H. H. Streak c Zaheer Khan
                    b Harbhajan Singh . 39

D. A. Marillier b Zaheer Khan 0
†T. Taibu run out 0
G. B. Brent c Kaif b Harbhajan Singh . . 0
D. T. Hondo not out 1

B 2, l-b 8, w 8, n-b 4 22

1/50 2/111 3/113   (42.1 overs) 232
4/114 5/143 6/227
7/227 8/228 9/229

Bowling: Zaheer Khan 8–0–29–3; Agarkar 8–0–44–0; Bharadwaj 4–0–32–1; Ganguly 10–0–62–1; Harbhajan Singh 9.1–0–33–4; Yuvraj Singh 3–0–22–0.

Umpires: S. N. Bandekar and K. G. Lakshminarayanan.
Third umpire: B. S. P. Rao.   Referee: J. R. Reid (New Zealand).

DATES OF FORMATION OF FIRST-CLASS COUNTIES

County	First known organisation	Original date	Present Club Reorganisation, if substantial	First-class status from
Derbyshire	1870	1870	–	1871
Durham	1874	1882		1992
Essex.	By 1790	1876	1991	1895
Glamorgan	1861	1888	–	1921
Gloucestershire	1863	1871	–	1870
Hampshire	1849	1863	1879	1864
Kent	1842	1859	1870	1864
Lancashire	1864	1864	–	1865
Leicestershire	By 1820	1879	–	1895
Middlesex	1863	1864	–	1864
Northamptonshire. . .	1820†	1878	–	1905
Nottinghamshire. . . .	1841	1841	1866	1864
Somerset.	1864	1875	–	1882
Surrey	1845	1845	–	1864
Sussex.	1836	1839	1857	1864
Warwickshire.	1826	1882	–	1895
Worcestershire	1844	1865	–	1899
Yorkshire	1861	1863	1891	1864

Note: Derbyshire lost first-class status from 1888 to 1894, Hampshire between 1886 and 1894 and Somerset between 1886 and 1890.

† Town club.

THE AUSTRALIANS IN SOUTH AFRICA, 2001-02

By NEIL MANTHORP

Australians were deeply offended by the fact that a draw in either of their back-to-back series against South Africa would be enough to dislodge them from the top of the ICC Test Championship. Steve Waugh's team had seen off the first half of the challenge at home, giving South Africa such a hammering that the return series might have been a foregone conclusion. But they arrived in February, the tail end of the African summer, when rain is always a threat, and the possibility that they could be dethroned without a ball being bowled meant there was no shortage of motivation for Australia.

Amazingly, there was no shortage of optimism in South Africa, although it soon turned out to be more a desperate need to stop the pain than a coherent belief that Shaun Pollock's team could actually slay the giant. In the event, Pollock missed all three Tests with a knee injury, fatally weakening the attack, which became even thinner when Allan Donald broke down on the first day of the series and then announced his retirement from Test cricket. His tally of 330 wickets in 72 matches was easily a South African record.

The captaincy passed to Pollock's deputy, the wicket-keeper Mark Boucher, who lost his first Test in charge, at Johannesburg, by an innings and 360 runs. It was the second-heaviest defeat in Test history. "I don't care about the margin of defeat or records," Boucher responded. "Every loss hurts just the same."

Most supporters did care about the scale of the humiliation. The Second Test, at Cape Town, brought four changes to the home side, including three debuts. The Gauteng all-rounder Andrew Hall was picked to provide the team with backbone, not to mention a verbal riposte or two, after surviving a hijacking, two muggings and a shooting. The swing bowler Dewald Pretorius was rewarded for a fine domestic season, though he was to struggle at Test level. More successful was the powerful left-handed opener Graeme Smith, not unlike a young Graeme Pollock in stance and physique, who was given a chance at No. 3. Paul Adams, Test cricket's least orthodox left-arm spinner, was recalled after nearly a year on the sidelines. With another left-hander, Ashwell Prince, playing his second Test, it was the freshest South African team since readmission in 1991.

The newcomers supplied a welcome antidote to the staggering cynicism shown by one of the country's most senior players on the eve of the match. Daryll Cullinan was called up after several months off with a knee injury, and there was talk of his leading the side when he joined them in Cape Town. But he immediately demanded a national contract for 13 months, until the end of the 2003 World Cup, even though he had previously retired from one-day cricket. When this was refused – the board said they did not offer contracts in mid-season until a player had appeared in two Tests or six one-day internationals, and in any case all current contracts were to expire in April – he refused to play and flew back to Johannesburg. A widespread sense of expectation at the prospect of Cullinan renewing his battle with Shane Warne was frustrated.

Hours later, the new boys appeared at a joint press conference. Led by the 21-year-old Smith, they spoke with passion of the pride they felt. From that point on, South Africa gradually started to compete. They held out for five days in Cape Town before losing a close-fought encounter, and finally registered a victory at Durban a week later.

No amount of praise would flatter Australia, and especially Adam Gilchrist. Even those who had seen 100 or more Tests were astonished by Gilchrist's performance – 473 runs at 157, including what was then the fastest double-hundred in Test cricket. Matthew Hayden brought his prodigious form with him from the first series, narrowly missing five centuries in consecutive Tests. For Steve and Mark Waugh, it was a lean spell that wore on. Steve had been told before departure that he was losing the one-day captaincy to Ricky Ponting, who had a highly successful tour. During the Tests, the twins learned that they were to be dropped altogether from the one-day squad. But

Before the South African series began, the Australian team visited Robben Island, where Nelson Mandela was imprisoned. As usual, Steve Waugh took his camera. *Picture by Steve Waugh, from* Captain's Diary 2002 *(HarperCollins)*.

their poor Test form simply allowed Gilchrist to spend more time at the crease. Australia scored five Test centuries, South Africa just one – from Herschelle Gibbs.

The scoreboard operators could hardly keep up with Australia's flow of runs, and the flair with which they were scored gave the impression that their batsmen were solely responsible for winning the series. In reality, for the umpteenth time, Warne and Glenn McGrath were instrumental in Australia's triumph. McGrath took 12 wickets at 19, while Warne took 20 and moved into second place in the all-time Test wicket-takers' list. In his 100th Test, at Newlands, he put in a heroic effort, bowling 70 overs in a single innings, and claimed the match award.

The Australians were tactically as well as technically superior in every respect. But the gulf wasn't as wide as the embarrassing scorelines suggested. Above all, it was the imposition of Australia's collective character that the South Africans could not handle – the fact that they were constantly "there", with bat, ball or in the field. After the defeat at Durban, they swiftly hit back to cement their domination: Ponting became the first touring captain to win a one-day series in South Africa since Mark Taylor, one of his predecessors, in 1996-97. Despite the return of Pollock, Australia went five up before conceding one more consolation win. They left the local population with a nasty feeling that they might never beat them over a series again.

AUSTRALIAN TOUR PARTY

S. R. Waugh (New South Wales) (*captain*), A. C. Gilchrist (Western Australia) (*vice-captain*), A. J. Bichel (Queensland), J. N. Gillespie (South Australia), M. L. Hayden (Queensland), J. L. Langer (Western Australia), B. Lee (New South Wales), D. S. Lehmann (South Australia), S. C. G. MacGill (New South Wales), G. D. McGrath (New South Wales), D. R. Martyn (Western Australia), R. T. Ponting (Tasmania), S. K. Warne (Victoria), S. R. Watson (Tasmania), M. E. Waugh (New South Wales).

M. G. Bevan (New South Wales), I. J. Harvey (Victoria), N. M. Hauritz (Queensland) and J. P. Maher (Queensland) replaced the Waughs, Langer and MacGill for the one-day series that followed the Tests, when Ponting took over the captaincy.

Coach: J. M. Buchanan. *Manager:* S. R. Bernard. *Assistant manager/system analyst:* M. K. Walsh. *Physiotherapist:* E. L. Alcott. *Physical performance manager:* J. A. Campbell. *Masseur:* L. J. Fostick.

AUSTRALIAN TOUR RESULTS

Test matches – Played 3: Won 2, Lost 1.
First-class matches – Played 5: Won 3, Lost 1, Drawn 1.
Wins – South Africa (2), South Africa A.
Loss – South Africa.
Draw – South Africa A.
One-day internationals – Played 7: Won 5, Lost 1, Tied 1.

TEST MATCH AVERAGES

SOUTH AFRICA – BATTING

	T	I	NO	R	HS	100s	50s	Avge	Ct
A. J. Hall	2	3	1	97	70	0	1	48.50	1
H. H. Gibbs	3	6	0	287	104	1	1	47.83	2
N. D. McKenzie	3	6	1	191	99	0	1	38.20	4
J. H. Kallis	3	6	1	184	73	0	2	36.80	4
G. Kirsten	3	6	0	192	87	0	2	32.00	2
P. R. Adams	2	3	1	64	35	0	0	32.00	0
G. C. Smith	2	4	0	114	68	0	1	28.50	2
A. G. Prince	3	6	0	155	49	0	0	25.83	2
M. V. Boucher	3	6	1	95	37	0	0	19.00	13
M. Ntini	3	5	0	48	14	0	0	9.60	0

Played in one Test: N. Boje 0, 5; H. H. Dippenaar 2, 1; A. A. Donald 3*, 0; A. Nel 7, 0; D. Pretorius 5*, 0; D. J. Terbrugge 0 (1 ct).

BOWLING

	O	M	R	W	BB	5W/i	Avge
D. J. Terbrugge	20	3	82	4	2-21	0	20.50
P. R. Adams	63.1	1	290	10	4-102	0	29.00
J. H. Kallis	88	9	373	11	3-29	0	33.90
M. Ntini	116.5	22	459	11	4-93	0	41.72

Also bowled: N. Boje 35–4–153–1; A. A. Donald 15.2–2–72–1; A. J. Hall 27.1–4–108–1; N. D. McKenzie 8–0–50–0; A. Nel 30.4–6–121–2; D. Pretorius 25–6–132–1.

AUSTRALIA – BATTING

	T	I	NO	R	HS	100s	50s	Avge	Ct/St
A. C. Gilchrist	3	5	2	473	204*	2	1	157.66	13/1
R. T. Ponting	3	5	1	309	100*	1	1	77.25	4
M. L. Hayden	3	5	0	309	122	1	2	61.80	4
M. E. Waugh	3	5	0	169	53	0	1	33.80	6
S. K. Warne	3	5	1	129	63	0	1	32.25	5
J. L. Langer	3	5	0	152	58	0	1	30.40	2
D. R. Martyn	3	5	0	146	133	1	0	29.20	3
S. R. Waugh	3	5	0	95	42	0	1	19.00	1
B. Lee	3	4	2	27	23*	0	0	13.50	1
G. D. McGrath	3	3	1	6	4*	0	0	3.00	1
J. N. Gillespie	3	3	0	4	3	0	0	1.33	1

BOWLING

	O	M	R	W	BB	5W/i	Avge
G. D. McGrath	110.3	36	227	12	5-21	1	18.91
S. K. Warne	162	38	442	20	6-161	1	22.10
J. N. Gillespie	92	28	287	8	3-52	0	35.87
B. Lee	95.2	10	416	10	4-82	0	41.60

Also bowled: D. R. Martyn 4–0–15–0; M. E. Waugh 21.5–4–78–2; S. R. Waugh 3–0–16–0.

Note: Matches in this section which were not first-class are signified by a dagger.

At Potchefstroom, February 17, 18, 19. **Drawn.** Toss: Australians. **Australians 366 for eight dec.** (R. T. Ponting 120, M. E. Waugh 62, S. R. Waugh 102 not out; A. J. Hall five for 97) **and 95 for three** (J. L. Langer 45, M. L. Hayden 39; C. W. Henderson three for 41); **South Africa A 190** (A. G. Prince 92, G. H. Bodi 33; G. D. McGrath five for 17).

SOUTH AFRICA v AUSTRALIA

First Test Match

At Johannesburg, February 22, 23, 24. Australia won by an innings and 360 runs. Toss: Australia. Test debut: A. G. Prince.

After three savage beatings in Australia, South Africa came home to something worse – the second-heaviest defeat in Test history. A single moment summed up the crushing superiority of Australia and the brilliance of their star, Adam Gilchrist. It came when he took a pot shot at an advertising hoarding offering a bar of gold, worth 1.3 million rand (over £80,000), for a direct hit. The sponsor, a local gold mine, hardly seemed in danger: the billboard was 30 feet in the air and well behind the deep mid-wicket boundary, a carry of at least 100 yards.

Gilchrist was 169, and had butchered the entire front-line attack, which badly missed the injured Pollock. With McKenzie bowling gentle medium-pace, he could resist no longer. Like a golfer hitting a wedge approach shot, he scooped a length delivery towards the target – and started to jump up and down as he realised how close it would be. He missed by a couple of feet, but what remained of South Africa's spirit was broken. Gilchrist was playing with them like a cat keeping a half-dead mouse alive for entertainment. And it was only the second day of the series.

The carnage had started the day before with Hayden's fourth century in as many Tests. He was only the eighth player to produce such a purple patch, though the fourth Australian after Don Bradman, who did it three times, Jack Fingleton and Neil Harvey. South Africa had a chance to dam the flow in Ntini's first over when Hayden offered a straightforward catch to second slip. Kallis dropped it, and Hayden blossomed with a muscular display of strokes that brought 18 fours

Anno Domini: Allan Donald, the most successful bowler in South Africa's history, holds his right hamstring after breaking down on the opening day of the series. South Africa were crushed, and Donald announced his retirement from Test cricket. *Picture by Touchline Photo/Getty Images.*

and a pair of sixes. Ntini and Nel tried hard to be hard but were left cowering by his power. A torn hamstring forced Donald off the field, but it could not be blamed for South Africa's inability to compete. Although he trapped Langer with a clever, slow off-cutter, Donald conceded 72 runs in 15.2 overs before his body announced it would no longer play the game for more than a day at a time. He retired from Test cricket after the match.

Even so, Australia's dominance was not quite assured on Hayden's departure at 272 for four. Martyn set out with studious care, taking 130 balls over his first fifty. Like everyone else, he was mesmerised by Gilchrist. But he picked up the tempo as the bowlers sagged drunkenly; his second fifty took only 37 balls, and he went on to a Test-best 133. He was never more than the junior partner, however, in a stand of 317, the second-highest for the sixth wicket in Test history, after Fingleton and Bradman's 346 against England in 1936-37. The afternoon session yielded 190 runs at 7.45 an over: it was dizzying to watch.

Gilchrist reached 200 four balls after tea, with his 19th four from his 212th delivery. For three weeks, it was the quickest Test double in terms of balls, beating Ian Botham's (220 balls) against India at The Oval in 1982. Gilchrist faced one further ball, for a single which raised his highest first-class score, 204 in 293 minutes. He smashed eight sixes, including the one that almost struck gold. Steve Waugh declared at the end of the over on 652 for seven, Australia's highest score against these opponents.

South Africa were so far past relief it was shocking. Not one of them had seen anything like this five-session mauling, and the effect on morale was all too clear. Ashwell Prince marked his debut with a sometimes belligerent 49, defying the pressures of batting at No. 3, but there was little else. They were dismissed in 48 overs for 159 and followed on 493 behind. It was a new low in South African history – but the second innings was even shorter. During the third day, they lost 16 wickets in 54.3 overs, to go down by an innings and 360 runs. The margin was second only to Australia's own beating, by an innings and 579, at The Oval in 1938.

McGrath and Warne bowled beautifully to enforce their stranglehold over the batsmen. Time after time, they had shown they could take bagfuls of wickets without even being at their best, but here they were close to it. Warne's six wickets took him past Richard Hadlee and Kapil Dev to 438 in Tests, second only to Courtney Walsh, while McGrath wound up the game with four in nine balls.

HIGHEST FIRST-INNINGS LEAD IN TESTS

Lead

702	England (903-7 dec.) v Australia (201) at The Oval	1938
570	**Pakistan (643) v New Zealand (73) at Lahore**	**2002**
563	England (849) v West Indies (286) at Kingston*	1929-30
504	Australia (645) v England (141) at Brisbane	1946-47
493	**Australia (652-7 dec.) v South Africa (159) at Johannesburg**	**2001-02**
490	West Indies (614-5 dec.) v India (124) at Calcutta	1958-59
476	Pakistan (708) v England (232) at The Oval*	1987
473	West Indies (579-9 dec.) v Pakistan (106) at Bridgetown*	1957-58
465	South Africa (622-9 dec.) v Australia (157) at Durban	1969-70
465	**Sri Lanka (555-5 dec.) v Bangladesh (90) at Colombo (SSC)†**	**2001-02**

* Drawn; all other games were won by the team with first-innings lead.

† Sri Lanka batted second; in all other games, the team gaining first-innings lead batted first.

But if it is possible for a batsman to win a Test in the first innings, Gilchrist did it. Even the parochial, normally hostile crowd were punched into submission by one of the finest, most entertaining and consistently aggressive innings ever played in Test cricket.

Man of the Match: A. C. Gilchrist.   *Attendance:* 41,765.

Close of play: First day, Australia 331-5 (Martyn 21, Gilchrist 25); Second day, South Africa 111-4 (Prince 47, Dippenaar 2).

Australia

J. L. Langer lbw b Donald	28	S. K. Warne c McKenzie b Boje	12
M. L. Hayden c Boucher b Nel	122	B. Lee not out	4
R. T. Ponting c Boucher b Nel	39	B 2, l-b 14, w 4, n-b 5	25
M. E. Waugh c Boucher b Ntini	53		
*S. R. Waugh c Gibbs b Kallis	32	1/46 (1) 2/113 (3) (7 wkts dec.)	652
D. R. Martyn c Kirsten b Kallis	133	3/224 (4) 4/272 (2)	
†A. C. Gilchrist not out	204	5/293 (5) 6/610 (6) 7/643 (8)	

J. N. Gillespie and G. D. McGrath did not bat.

Bowling: Donald 15.2-2-72-1; Ntini 33-8-124-1; Kallis 24-1-116-2; Nel 30.4-6-121-2; Boje 35-4-153-1; McKenzie 8-0-50-0.

South Africa

H. H. Gibbs lbw b Warne	34	st Gilchrist b Warne	47
G. Kirsten c Warne b McGrath	1	c Martyn b Gillespie	12
A. G. Prince c Hayden b Gillespie . . .	49	b Warne	28
J. H. Kallis c Warne b Lee	3	c Gilchrist b McGrath	8
N. D. McKenzie c Gillespie b McGrath .	16	not out	27
H. H. Dippenaar c Gilchrist b McGrath .	2	lbw b Warne	1
*†M. V. Boucher c Gilchrist b Lee	23	b Warne	1
N. Boje c M. E. Waugh b Gillespie . . .	0	c Ponting b McGrath	5
M. Ntini c S. R. Waugh b Lee	9	b McGrath	0
A. Nel lbw b Warne	7	c Langer b McGrath	0
A. A. Donald not out	3	c Hayden b McGrath	0
B 4, l-b 3, n-b 5	12	W 1, n-b 3	4
	159		133

1/11 (2) 2/51 (1) 3/55 (4) 4/108 (5)
5/113 (3) 6/113 (6) 7/114 (8)
8/146 (9) 9/155 (7) 10/159 (10)

1/20 (2) 2/89 (3) 3/98 (1)
4/98 (4) 5/107 (6) 6/109 (7)
7/122 (8) 8/122 (9)
9/122 (10) 10/133 (11)

Bowling: *First Innings*—McGrath 14–6–28–3; Gillespie 15–5–58–2; Warne 9–0–26–2; Lee 10–1–40–3. *Second Innings*—McGrath 12.3–4–21–5; Lee 10–2–55–0; Gillespie 4–1–13–1; Warne 12–3–44–4.

Umpires: S. A. Bucknor (West Indies) and R. E. Koertzen.
Third umpire: I. L. Howell.   Referee: C. W. Smith (West Indies).

At Port Elizabeth, March 1, 2, 3. **Australians won by an innings and 41 runs.** Toss: Australians. **South Africa A 301** (J. A. Rudolph 36, D. J. Cullinan 86, H. M. Amla 81; B. Lee four for 37) **and 232** (G. C. Smith 31, J. M. Kemp 56, G. H. Bodi 45; S. C. G. MacGill four for 114, A. J. Bichel three for 41); **Australians 574 for nine dec.** (J. L. Langer 161, D. S. Lehmann 60, R. T. Ponting 40, M. E. Waugh 110, S. R. Watson 100 not out, A. C. Gilchrist 56; D. Pretorius five for 148, C. M. Willoughby three for 101).

SOUTH AFRICA v AUSTRALIA

Second Test Match

At Cape Town, March 8, 9, 10, 11, 12. Australia won by four wickets. Toss: South Africa. Test debuts: A. J. Hall, D. Pretorius, G. C. Smith.

Shane Warne flew 16 friends and relatives to Cape Town for his 100th Test, and they saw him bowl 98 overs, take eight wickets, score a half-century, win the match award – and propel his team to yet another series triumph, which cemented their place at the head of the Test Championship.

In the end, it was a memorable five-day battle. But that hardly looked likely when South Africa crashed to 92 for six on the opening day in the face of some tremendous fast bowling inspired by McGrath. They clawed their way back to 239, thanks to the street-fighting qualities of Andrew Hall, who scored 70 on debut, while Adams marked his first Test in nearly 11 months with an unorthodox but hugely welcome 35.

As Australia cruised to 130 for one, the script seemed depressingly familiar. But when Hayden top-edged a hook at Kallis to fine leg, the innings took a dramatic turn. Australia lost four more wickets in the next 20 overs, slithering to 185 for six – still 54 behind. The fact that those wickets were shared by a Cape-coloured spinner, Adams, and a Xhosa pace bowler, Ntini, stoked a frenetic atmosphere in the country's best-supported stadium. The controversy over quotas made a packed house cheer all the more loudly.

Then came Gilchrist. Again. It was impossible to imagine he could equal his feats at Johannesburg, but he did. Within five minutes, he was charging down the track at Adams, and after his first 26 balls he was on 42, with nine blazing fours. As a statement, it was devastating, and his form actually improved. A modicum of caution as Australia reached parity meant his first fifty took 53 deliveries, but then came feverish butchery as Gilchrist made fun of the bowlers. His second fifty needed 38 balls, and his final 38 runs just 17. He hit Adams's last two overs for 36. Like a dog that has been kicked too often, the South African attack were reduced to hiding, relieved by every delivery that wasn't drilled to the fence. Most memorable was Gilchrist's ability to hit good-length deliveries square of the wicket, cutting or pulling, while he drove yorker-length balls off the back foot like half-volleys. Australia had trailed by 63 when he came to the crease. When he ran out of partners 36 overs later, they led by 143 – thanks also to a mightily enjoyable 66-ball 63 by Warne, who gleaned plenty of wheat from the chaff of Gilchrist's harvest.

For once, South Africa's top five were undaunted second time around. They accumulated 366 runs between them – no centuries, but McKenzie fell only one short when Martyn ran him out with a direct hit from cover. Warne was made to work harder than ever before: it took 70 overs from him to dismiss South Africa, finally, for 473. Warne, slimmed down but not wholly reformed, compared his marathon to "a big night out when you think you're gone several times, but you get a couple of second winds".

Australia required 331, the tenth-highest fourth-innings total to win in Test history. But as they were responsible for five of the top nine, history was no barrier. Langer and Hayden launched the assault in fearless style, sharing their sixth century stand in 14 starts. When Dewald Pretorius, who was mostly outclassed, bowled Langer off an inside edge, Ponting helped take the score to 201

Power play: Adam Gilchrist continued his awesome assault on the South African bowlers at Cape Town.
Picture by Touchline Photo/Getty Images.

before Hayden edged Kallis to the keeper. He failed by four runs to become the second player to score centuries in five consecutive Tests, after Bradman (1936-37 to 1938), who went on to six. Some welcome tension entered the chase when Ntini removed Mark Waugh just before lunch. Then Adams's googlies bowled Steve Waugh and cornered Martyn lbw in successive overs, leaving Australia 268 for five; but Gilchrist effectively finished the job with a carefree, run-a-ball 24. Ponting had the last word in the drama: six short of a meticulous century, but needing only three for victory, he achieved both with a single blow against Adams. The script decreed that Warne should be there at the other end. Not for the first time, he had grabbed the headlines, and he could be proud of every word in them.

Man of the Match: S. K. Warne.   *Attendance:* 52,105.

Close of play: First day, Australia 46-0 (Langer 28, Hayden 17); Second day, South Africa 7-0 (Gibbs 5, Kirsten 2); Third day, South Africa 307-4 (McKenzie 28, Prince 5); Fourth day, Australia 131-1 (Hayden 50, Ponting 17).

South Africa

H. H. Gibbs c M. E. Waugh b Gillespie	12	– c Ponting b Warne	39
G. Kirsten c M. E. Waugh b Lee	7	– lbw b Lee	87
G. C. Smith c Ponting b McGrath	3	– c Gilchrist b Warne	68
J. H. Kallis c Gilchrist b McGrath	23	– lbw b Warne	73
N. D. McKenzie b Warne	20	– run out	99
A. G. Prince c Gilchrist b McGrath	10	– c Ponting b Warne	20
*†M. V. Boucher c Gilchrist b Lee	26	– lbw b Gillespie	37
A. J. Hall c Gilchrist b Gillespie	70	– run out	0
P. R. Adams c Warne b Gillespie	35	– not out	23
M. Ntini c M. E. Waugh b Warne	14	– c Langer b Warne	11
D. Pretorius not out	5	– c M. E. Waugh b Warne	0
B 4, l-b 5, n-b 5	14	B 8, l-b 3, w 2, n-b 3	16

1/15 (1) 2/18 (3) 3/25 (2) 4/70 (5)   239
5/73 (4) 6/92 (6) 7/147 (7)
8/216 (9) 9/229 (8) 10/239 (10)

1/84 (1) 2/183 (2) 3/254 (3)   473
4/284 (4) 5/350 (6) 6/431 (7)
7/433 (8) 8/440 (5)
9/464 (10) 10/473 (11)

Bowling: First Innings—McGrath 20–4–42–3; Gillespie 15–4–52–3; Lee 16–1–65–2; Warne 28–10–70–2; M. E. Waugh 1–0–1–0. *Second Innings*—McGrath 25–7–56–0; Gillespie 29–10–81–1; Warne 70–15–161–6; Lee 22–3–99–1; M. E. Waugh 9–3–34–0; Martyn 4–0–15–0; S. R. Waugh 3–0–16–0.

Australia

J. L. Langer b Ntini	37	– b Pretorius	58
M. L. Hayden c Hall b Kallis	63	– c Boucher b Kallis	96
R. T. Ponting c Boucher b Adams	47	– not out	100
M. E. Waugh c Gibbs b Ntini	25	– c Boucher b Ntini	16
*S. R. Waugh b Adams	0	– b Adams	14
D. R. Martyn c Boucher b Ntini	2	– lbw b Adams	0
†A. C. Gilchrist not out	138	– c McKenzie b Kallis	24
S. K. Warne c Kallis b Adams	63	– not out	15
B. Lee c Prince b Kallis	0		
J. N. Gillespie c Kallis b Adams	0		
G. D. McGrath lbw b Ntini	2		
B 2, l-b 1, w 2	5	L-b 6, n-b 5	11

1/67 (1) 2/130 (2) 3/162 (3) 4/168 (5)   382
5/176 (4) 6/185 (6) 7/317 (8)
8/338 (9) 9/343 (10) 10/382 (11)

1/102 (1) 2/201 (2)   (6 wkts) 334
3/251 (4) 4/268 (5)
5/268 (6) 6/305 (7)

Bowling: First Innings—Ntini 22.5–5–93–4; Pretorius 11–1–72–0; Kallis 16–1–65–2; Hall 11–1–47–0; Adams 20–1–102–4. *Second Innings*—Ntini 24–4–90–1; Pretorius 14–5–60–1; Adams 21.1–0–104–2; Hall 3–0–6–0; Kallis 17–2–68–2.

Umpires: S. A. Bucknor (West Indies) and R. E. Koertzen.
Third umpire: D. L. Orchard.   Referee: C. W. Smith (West Indies).

SOUTH AFRICA v AUSTRALIA

Third Test Match

At Durban, March 15, 16, 17, 18. South Africa won by five wickets. Toss: South Africa.

Australia found themselves on the back foot for the first time in six Tests when South Africa put them in and reduced them to 182 for five. They still seemed more than capable of retrieving the situation, and claimed a large first-innings lead. But impressive as South Africa's spirit was in pulling off a consolation victory, the truth was that Australia were emotionally and physically spent. Five consecutive wins, complete vindication of their supremacy, and a mere two days for it all to soak in, left them understandably short of their characteristic fight.

Ponting provided fine value, with barely a mistimed stroke. His bat was all middle, spanking 16 fours in 100 deliveries before a dynamic run-out by Gibbs. Once again, however, it was Gilchrist's day. The sight of him seemed to transform the bowlers from confident attackers into whimpering strays seemingly hoping not to be hit too hard. He was nearing his third century in consecutive Tests when he decided he could not rely on Gillespie and slogged Adams to deep mid-wicket. By his recent standards, 91 from 107 balls was ordinary – just plain brilliant – and it sent his series average tumbling from 366 to 228.50.

Despite Gilchrist's efforts, there was almost an air of celebration by the end of the day. South Africa had dismissed Australia for 315 and then closed at 48 for one, with Gibbs in splendid touch. Barely an hour after lunch on day two, their depression had returned – a total of just 167, a deficit of 148. Lee blew through the innings like a tornado, destructive, furious and expensive, while Warne, who admitted to feeling "a bit stiff" after his 98 overs in the previous game, bowled well within himself but still lured four victims into his traps.

Australia's second innings was all over-confidence and lack of concentration. Five of the top seven made starts, but the top score was only 42 by the beleaguered Steve Waugh. He battled for two and a half hours before he was ninth out, to an astonishing one-handed slip catch by Kallis, which only confirmed the adage that form and luck go hand in hand.

Ntini was quick and hostile, while Kallis's out-swingers were effective for the first time all summer, with two wickets in his opening over. A classic dismissal from the outside edge of Martyn's bat made Boucher the fastest keeper to reach 200 Test dismissals, in terms of both matches (52) and age (25 years 103 days). Australia subsided for 186 – the first time in 11 Tests since Trent Bridge in August that they had been out for less than 300.

The way ahead? South Africa took a big step towards their consolation victory at Durban when Ashwell Prince (*left*) caught the in-form Matthew Hayden for nought. Andrew Hall, another figure trying to establish his place in the team, congratulates him. *Picture by Touchline Photo/Getty Images.*

Even so, South Africa required 335, four more than Australia at Cape Town, and 38 more than their own highest fourth-innings total to win a Test, at Melbourne in 1952-53. Though they had nearly three days to do it, sceptics talked of their decade-long tendency to choke on the big occasion. But this was not a big occasion. No one seemed to remember how efficient South Africa could be in pursuit of a victory of little consequence.

The openers set the tone with a stand of 142 until Gibbs sold Kirsten a dummy and Lee dived into the stumps, ball first. Gibbs atoned for the error by continuing, with rare restraint, to complete his sixth and best Test century, lasting just under five hours. In desperation, Steve Waugh turned to his brother's off-spin, and Smith's bullish 42 ended with a daft slog in Mark Waugh's second over. Even dafter was Gibbs's lame swat to wide long-on in Waugh's third. The third day ended with South Africa needing another 71 runs, Australia six wickets.

Kallis was the key, and he saw the job through with an unbeaten 61. He stretched his partnership with Prince to 99, which all but won the game. When Warne had Prince caught at slip, his 450th Test wicket, with four runs required, Boucher came in to end the game with a six. The shot, like South Africa's victory, was a modest note of defiance in the face of Australia's proven superiority.

Man of the Match: H. H. Gibbs.   *Attendance:* 21,294.

Man of the Series: A. C. Gilchrist.

Close of play: First day, South Africa 48-1 (Gibbs 24, Adams 0); Second day, Australia 159-8 (S. R. Waugh 34, Lee 5); Third day, South Africa 264-4 (Kallis 35, Prince 8).

Australia

J. L. Langer c Kirsten b Terbrugge	11	– c Boucher b Terbrugge	18
M. L. Hayden c McKenzie b Kallis	28	– c Prince b Terbrugge	0
R. T. Ponting run out	89	– c Terbrugge b Ntini	34
M. E. Waugh c Smith b Kallis	45	– b Kallis	30
*S. R. Waugh c Boucher b Adams	7	– c Kallis b Ntini	42
D. R. Martyn b Terbrugge	11	– c Boucher b Kallis	0
†A. C. Gilchrist c Smith b Adams	91	– c Boucher b Kallis	16
S. K. Warne c Boucher b Ntini	26	– c McKenzie b Adams	13
B. Lee b Ntini	0	– (10) not out	23
J. N. Gillespie c Boucher b Hall	1	– (9) c Kallis b Adams	3
G. D. McGrath not out	4	– b Ntini	0
W 2	2	B 1, l-b 3, w 1, n-b 2	7

1/11 (1) 2/61 (2) 3/169 (3) 4/178 (4)   315   1/4 (2) 2/19 (1) 3/77 (3)   186
5/182 (5) 6/230 (6) 7/287 (8)   4/90 (4) 5/90 (6) 6/114 (7)
8/289 (9) 9/311 (7) 10/315 (10)   7/129 (8) 8/150 (9)
                                                9/186 (5) 10/186 (11)

Bowling: *First Innings*—Ntini 20–3–87–2; Terbrugge 16–2–61–2; Kallis 20–3–95–2; Hall 9.1–2–35–1; Adams 9–0–37–2. *Second Innings*—Ntini 17–2–65–3; Terbrugge 4–1–21–2; Hall 4–1–20–0; Adams 13–0–47–2; Kallis 11–2–29–3.

South Africa

H. H. Gibbs c Gilchrist b Gillespie	51	– c Martyn b M. E. Waugh	104
G. Kirsten c Gilchrist b Lee	21	– run out	64
P. R. Adams c Hayden b Lee	6		
G. C. Smith c Gilchrist b McGrath	1	– (3) c Gilchrist b M. E. Waugh	42
J. H. Kallis c and b Warne	16	– (4) not out	61
N. D. McKenzie c Martyn b Lee	25	– (5) c Hayden b Warne	4
A. G. Prince c Lee b Warne	0	– (6) c M. E. Waugh b Warne	48
*†M. V. Boucher c and b Warne	0	– (7) not out	8
A. J. Hall not out	27		
M. Ntini c McGrath b Warne	14		
D. J. Terbrugge c Gilchrist b Lee	0		
L-b 1, w 1, n-b 4	6	L-b 2, w 2, n-b 5	9

1/48 (2) 2/74 (3) 3/75 (4) 4/85 (1)   167   1/142 (2) 2/216 (3)   (5 wkts) 340
5/109 (5) 6/119 (7) 7/119 (8)   3/218 (1) 4/232 (5)
8/148 (6) 9/167 (10) 10/167 (11)   5/331 (6)

Bowling: *First Innings*—McGrath 11–4–26–1; Lee 17.2–1–82–4; Gillespie 14–6–25–1; Warne 13–4–33–4. *Second Innings*—McGrath 28–11–54–0; Lee 20–2–75–0; Gillespie 15–2–58–0; Warne 30–6–108–2; M. E. Waugh 11.5–1–43–2.

Umpires: S. Venkataraghavan (India) and D. L. Orchard.
Third umpire: I. L. Howell.   Referee: C. W. Smith (West Indies).

†SOUTH AFRICA v AUSTRALIA

First One-Day International

At Johannesburg, March 22. Australia won by 19 runs. Toss: Australia. International debut: N. M. Hauritz.

What should have been an easy target, on a variable but far from impossible pitch, soon became an extremely awkward one. A triple strike from Gillespie reduced South Africa to 23 for three by the tenth over, and Harvey's canny mixture of swing, seam and slower balls claimed another three by the 19th. At the other end, Dippenaar battled to 51. But in the first over from the debutant off-spinner, Nathan Hauritz, he nicked to the keeper – Gilchrist's 200th dismissal in one-day internationals – and the run-chase had subsided to a meek 93 for seven. Klusener blasted 83 from 77 deliveries, adding 71 with Boje but, exciting as it was, it could only reduce the margin of defeat. Australia's own innings had fallen short of expectations: all their batsmen reached double figures, but none passed 37.

Man of the Match: J. N. Gillespie.   *Attendance:* 27,145.

Australia

†A. C. Gilchrist c Boje b Ntini	37	
M. L. Hayden c Rhodes b Kallis	27	
*R. T. Ponting c Boje b Ntini	14	
D. R. Martyn b Telemachus	24	
D. S. Lehmann c Boucher b Telemachus	37	
M. G. Bevan run out	18	
I. J. Harvey c Kallis b Ntini	19	

A. J. Bichel c Telemachus b Kallis 19
J. N. Gillespie not out 11
L-b 4, w 7, n-b 6 17

1/50 2/84 3/86   (8 wkts, 50 overs) 223
4/149 5/156 6/187
7/195 8/223

N. M. Hauritz and G. D. McGrath did not bat.

Bowling: Pollock 10–0–49–0; Telemachus 7–0–45–2; Ntini 10–2–24–3; Kallis 10–0–48–2; Klusener 8–0–27–0; Boje 5–0–26–0.

South Africa

H. H. Gibbs c Hayden b Gillespie	0	
G. Kirsten c Gilchrist b Gillespie	2	
J. H. Kallis lbw b Gillespie	8	
H. H. Dippenaar c Gilchrist b Hauritz	51	
J. N. Rhodes c Gilchrist b Harvey	13	
†M. V. Boucher c McGrath b Harvey	3	
*S. M. Pollock c Hayden b Harvey	0	
L. Klusener c Bichel b McGrath	83	

N. Boje run out 33
R. Telemachus st Gilchrist b Hauritz .. 1
M. Ntini not out 0
W 8, n-b 2. 10

1/1 2/2 3/23   (44.4 overs) 204
4/56 5/66 6/66
7/93 8/164 9/166

Bowling: McGrath 7.4–1–26–1; Gillespie 10–0–39–3; Harvey 8–0–38–3; Bichel 9–0–70–0; Hauritz 10–0–31–2.

Umpires: I. L. Howell and B. G. Jerling.
Third umpire: S. Wadvalla.   Referee: C. W. Smith (West Indies).

†SOUTH AFRICA v AUSTRALIA

Second One-Day International

At Centurion, March 24. Australia won by 45 runs. Toss: South Africa. International debut: S. R. Watson.

For the second match running, South Africa's pursuit of an attainable target was undone by a clatter of early wickets. The new-ball team of McGrath and Gillespie struck twice apiece, Ponting produced a trademark run-out, and when Hauritz bowled Boucher the scoreboard read 81 for six. Gillespie claimed another brace at the death, while Klusener hammered another run-a-ball half-century – batting too low in the order, when the cause was already lost. None of this detracted from the proficiency and calm of Maher. Standing in for the injured Bevan, he saved Australia from several moments of possible implosion after they were inserted on an active pitch. Maher took 150 balls to score 95 but, with only Hayden, his fellow-Queenslander, and Martyn offering meaningful support in the face of tremendous bowling from Pollock, his pacing was perfect.

Man of the Match: J. P. Maher.   *Attendance:* 18,944.

Australia

†A. C. Gilchrist c Kirsten b Pollock	...	7	J. N. Gillespie lbw b Pollock	4
M. L. Hayden c Rhodes b Boje	...	38	N. M. Hauritz not out	2
J. P. Maher c Kallis b Telemachus	...	95		
*R. T. Ponting c and b Boje	...	0	L-b 8, w 1, n-b 7	16
D. R. Martyn c Boucher b Telemachus	...	42		
D. S. Lehmann not out	...	13	1/14 2/99 3/99 (8 wkts, 50 overs) 226	
S. R. Watson c Gibbs b Pollock	...	2	4/192 5/201 6/206	
A. J. Bichel b Pollock	...	7	7/216 8/220	

G. D. McGrath did not bat.

Bowling: Pollock 10–1–32–4; Ntini 9–0–43–0; Kallis 9–0–38–0; Telemachus 10–0–42–2; Klusener 4–0–26–0; Boje 8–0–37–2.

South Africa

H. H. Gibbs c Hauritz b McGrath	...	5	N. Boje c Gilchrist b Gillespie	18
G. Kirsten c Ponting b Gillespie	...	21	M. Ntini not out	2
J. H. Kallis c Ponting b McGrath	...	14	R. Telemachus lbw b Gillespie	2
H. H. Dippenaar run out	...	21	L-b 2, w 1, n-b 3	6
J. N. Rhodes lbw b Gillespie	...	0		
†M. V. Boucher b Hauritz	...	16	1/18 2/30 3/42 (46.2 overs) 181	
L. Klusener c Hayden b Lehmann	...	59	4/45 5/80 6/81	
*S. M. Pollock run out	...	17	7/110 8/177 9/177	

Bowling: McGrath 7–2–14–2; Gillespie 9.2–1–43–4; Watson 6–0–21–0; Bichel 10–1–33–0; Hauritz 8–0–46–1; Lehmann 6–0–22–1.

Umpires: I. L. Howell and S. Wadvalla.
Third umpire: K. H. Hurter.   Referee: C. W. Smith (West Indies).

†SOUTH AFRICA v AUSTRALIA

Third One-Day International

At Potchefstroom, March 27. Tied. Toss: South Africa.

Just when a four-wicket blitz from Ntini seemed to have set up South Africa's first win of the series, Australia's last-wicket pair contrived to snatch a tie – the third between these sides. Coming together in the 46th over, with 37 required for victory, Maher and Hauritz had whittled that down to ten off the last over, bowled by Kallis. The first delivery was a no-ball, off which Maher ran two, but they were restricted to singles off the next five, so Hauritz needed two from the last ball. They managed one, with Maher lamenting afterwards that he was "not Linford Christie". Earlier, Lee dismissed both South African openers to put a brake on their innings, but Rhodes reclaimed the initiative with a brisk 83 from 74 balls, supported by the more circumspect Kallis.

Man of the Match: J. P. Maher.   *Attendance:* 9,082.

South Africa

H. H. Dippenaar c Ponting b Lee	7
H. H. Gibbs c Maher b Lee	10
J. H. Kallis c Gilchrist b Gillespie	71
N. D. McKenzie c Martyn b Lehmann . .	37
J. N. Rhodes c Maher b Lee	83
L. Klusener c Hayden b Lee	20
†M. V. Boucher c Gilchrist b Gillespie . .	5

A. J. Hall not out	18
*S. M. Pollock not out	1
W 6, n-b 1	7

1/11 2/27 3/105   (7 wkts, 50 overs) 259
4/180 5/222
6/232 7/256

N. Boje and M. Ntini did not bat.

Bowling: Gillespie 10–0–46–2; Lee 9–1–45–4; Watson 6–0–40–0; Bichel 10–1–44–0; Lehmann 9–0–42–1; Hauritz 6–0–42–0.

Australia

†A. C. Gilchrist c Boucher b Ntini	16
M. L. Hayden c Gibbs b Boje	78
*R. T. Ponting run out	3
D. R. Martyn run out	35
D. S. Lehmann c Boucher b Kallis	33
J. P. Maher not out	43
S. R. Watson c Boucher b Ntini	8
A. J. Bichel b Ntini	7

B. Lee c Boucher b Ntini	8
J. N. Gillespie b Klusener	0
N. M. Hauritz not out	11
L-b 1, w 5, n-b 11	17

1/33 2/39 3/112   (9 wkts, 50 overs) 259
4/178 5/180 6/194
7/206 8/222 9/223

Bowling: Pollock 9–0–49–0; Ntini 10–1–33–4; Kallis 9–0–52–1; Klusener 10–0–54–1; Hall 4–0–24–0; Boje 8–0–46–1.

Umpires: K. H. Hurter and R. E. Koertzen.
Third umpire: M. Z. Nanabhay.   Referee: C. W. Smith (West Indies).

†SOUTH AFRICA v AUSTRALIA

Fourth One-Day International

At Bloemfontein, March 30. Australia won by 37 runs. Toss: Australia.

Ponting scored his ninth century in limited-overs internationals, and his first as captain, to provide the cornerstone of a consummate win. He took the attack by the scruff of the neck, pulling, driving and glancing 129 off 126 balls. There were 15 fours, but his performance will be best remembered for a straight six off Kallis over long-on. With Lehmann, he added 119 at eight an over. In reply, Graeme Smith batted with composure for 70 minutes in his maiden one-day international before being bowled through the gate by Harvey. South Africa still had a chance of hauling in the target when they entered the final ten overs needing 89, with six wickets left. But it disappeared when Lee bowled McKenzie and Boucher with consecutive deliveries.

Man of the Match: R. T. Ponting.   *Attendance:* 10,134.

Australia

†A. C. Gilchrist b Telemachus	34	I. J. Harvey c Smith b Pollock		6
M. L. Hayden c Boucher b Telemachus	17	B. Lee not out		8
*R. T. Ponting c Pollock b Kallis	129	L-b 9, w 5, n-b 5		19
D. R. Martyn b Boje	24			
D. S. Lehmann b Pollock	39	1/40 2/87 3/143	(6 wkts, 50 overs)	290
J. P. Maher not out	14	4/262 5/266 6/274		

J. N. Gillespie, N. M. Hauritz and G. D. McGrath did not bat.

Bowling: Pollock 10–0–59–2; Ntini 10–2–42–0; Telemachus 10–0–60–2; Kallis 10–0–67–1; Boje 7–0–36–1; Hall 3–0–17–0.

South Africa

G. C. Smith b Harvey	41	N. Boje c Gilchrist b Lee		14
G. Kirsten c Gilchrist b McGrath	3	M. Ntini b Gillespie		11
A. J. Hall c Maher b McGrath	3	R. Telemachus not out		1
J. H. Kallis c and b Lehmann	43	B 4, l-b 2, w 5, n-b 1		12
N. D. McKenzie b Lee	67			
J. N. Rhodes c Harvey b Lee	56	1/7 2/14 3/67	(48.1 overs)	253
†M. V. Boucher b Lee	0	4/138 5/202 6/202		
*S. M. Pollock c Gilchrist b Gillespie	2	7/207 8/224 9/251		

Bowling: McGrath 8–0–20–2; Gillespie 10–1–46–2; Lee 9.1–0–63–4; Harvey 8–0–41–1; Hauritz 5–0–27–0; Lehmann 8–0–50–1.

Umpires: M. Z. Nanabhay and D. L. Orchard.
Third umpire: B. G. Jerling.　Referee: C. W. Smith (West Indies).

†SOUTH AFRICA v AUSTRALIA

Fifth One-Day International

At Durban, April 3 (day/night). Australia won by eight wickets. Toss: Australia. International debut: J. C. Kent.

Australia clinched the series at a canter, with Gilchrist's flurried century leading the way. Asked to bat on what turned out to be a sound surface, South Africa built their total steadily. Rhodes played a hallmark, guts-driven innings, and found a like-minded partner in Boucher, who helped him add 97 in 13 overs. But it all came to nothing as the Australian juggernaut swung into action. Gilchrist should have been caught on 11 – Kallis dropped an edge off Pollock – and took full advantage of his let-off with 105 in 104 deliveries, dominating an opening partnership of 170 with Hayden. They fell within three overs of each other, but there was no further drama as Ponting and Martyn completed the job with a minimum of fuss.

Man of the Match: A. C. Gilchrist.　　*Attendance:* 20,419.

South Africa

G. C. Smith c Gilchrist b Warne	46	†M. V. Boucher not out		41
H. H. Gibbs c Gilchrist b Gillespie	25	*S. M. Pollock not out		6
N. Boje c and b Lee	22	B 1, l-b 4, w 7, n-b 1		13
J. H. Kallis c Maher b McGrath	21			
J. N. Rhodes c Ponting b McGrath	76	1/40 2/82 3/110	(6 wkts, 50 overs)	267
N. D. McKenzie c Gilchrist b Warne	17	4/125 5/158 6/255		

J. C. Kent, M. Ntini and M. Hayward did not bat.

Bowling: McGrath 10–0–54–2; Gillespie 10–1–53–1; Lee 10–0–57–1; Harvey 10–0–54–0; Warne 10–0–44–2.

Australia

†A. C. Gilchrist c Kent b Ntini	105
M. L. Hayden b Hayward	59
*R. T. Ponting not out	44
D. R. Martyn not out	47
L-b 6, w 4, n-b 6	16

1/170 2/180   (2 wkts, 47.5 overs) 271

M. G. Bevan, J. P. Maher, I. J. Harvey, S. K. Warne, B. Lee, J. N. Gillespie and G. D. McGrath did not bat.

Bowling: Pollock 10–0–42–0; Ntini 9.5–0–51–1; Kallis 7–0–41–0; Hayward 8–0–58–1; Boje 7–0–32–0; Kent 6–0–41–0.

Umpires: B. G. Jerling and R. E. Koertzen.
Third umpire: S. Wadvalla.   Referee: C. W. Smith (West Indies).

†SOUTH AFRICA v AUSTRALIA

Sixth One-Day International

At Port Elizabeth, April 6. Australia won by three wickets. Toss: South Africa.
Even South Africa's biggest one-day total against Australia wasn't enough when the tourists rewrote the record books with the highest run-chase in history. Sri Lanka had scored 329 batting second against West Indies at Sharjah in 1995-96, only to lose; Australia's 330 for seven put them 5–0 up. South Africa had amassed 326 for three, thanks to an impressive 84 from the precocious Smith and an explosive partnership of 131 in 92 balls between Kallis and Rhodes. But the Australian openers raced past 50 in the fifth over, and Gilchrist reached his own half-century in just 27 balls. Three quick wickets should have halted the momentum. Instead it only brought Ponting and Lehmann together to pile on 183 in 30 overs. Both missed their hundreds, but Australia passed the target with five balls to spare when Warne blazed to the boundary. An aggregate of 656 was the fourth-highest in all one-day internationals.
Man of the Match: A. C. Gilchrist.   *Attendance:* 12,469.

South Africa

G. C. Smith c Lehmann b Warne	84	J. N. Rhodes not out	71
H. H. Gibbs c and b Harvey	37	L-b 5, w 2	7
N. Boje b Lehmann	47		
J. H. Kallis not out	80	1/74 2/157 3/195 (3 wkts, 50 overs) 326	

N. D. McKenzie, †M. V. Boucher, *S. M. Pollock, J. C. Kent, M. Ntini and R. Telemachus did not bat.

Bowling: McGrath 10–2–52–0; Gillespie 9–0–60–0; Harvey 9–0–64–1; Warne 7–0–58–1; Watson 9–0–47–0; Lehmann 6–0–40–1.

Australia

†A. C. Gilchrist c Ntini b Telemachus . .	52	S. R. Watson run out	11
M. L. Hayden c Pollock b Kallis	35	S. K. Warne not out	4
I. J. Harvey c Boucher b Telemachus . . .	4	B 2, l-b 7, w 6, n-b 8	23
*R. T. Ponting c Kallis b Pollock	92		
D. S. Lehmann st Boucher b Smith	91	1/81 2/93 3/104 (7 wkts, 49.1 overs) 330	
D. R. Martyn c Rhodes b Ntini	15	4/287 5/312	
M. G. Bevan not out	3	6/312 7/326	

J. N. Gillespie and G. D. McGrath did not bat.

Bowling: Pollock 8–0–57–0; Ntini 9.1–0–83–1; Telemachus 10–0–48–2; Kallis 10–0–59–2; Boje 6–0–34–0; Kent 2–0–16–0; Smith 4–0–24–1.

Umpires: I. L. Howell and S. Wadvalla.
Third umpire: K. H. Hurter.   Referee: C. W. Smith (West Indies).

†SOUTH AFRICA v AUSTRALIA

Seventh One-Day International

At Cape Town, April 9 (day/night). South Africa won by 65 runs (D/L method). Toss: Australia.
  South Africa finally notched up a win, but it did little to salve the wounds inflicted by Australia over the last few months. In a rain-affected match, they dismissed the tourists for 185 chasing a revised target of 251 in 39 overs. Pollock bowled a superb new-ball spell to remove Australia's top three, and only Bevan managed prolonged resistance until Boje's left-arm spin mopped up the last five wickets. After rain delayed the start and then forced the players from the field again when South Africa were 24 without loss in the fifth over, the match shrank from 43 to 39 overs a side. Smith delighted his home crowd with another half-century, and Boje scored a rapid 49, but it was Rhodes who led the final sprint, smashing two sixes to finish unbeaten on 39 from 24 balls.

  Man of the Match: N. Boje.　　　*Attendance:* 15,008.
  Man of the Series: R. T. Ponting.

South Africa

G. C. Smith b Bichel	73		*S. M. Pollock c Watson b McGrath		8
H. H. Gibbs run out	27		H. H. Dippenaar not out		8
N. Boje c Gilchrist b Watson	49		L-b 5, w 4		9
J. H. Kallis c Maher b Warne	18				
J. N. Rhodes not out	39		1/63 2/134 3/172	(7 wkts, 39 overs)	249
N. D. McKenzie lbw b Warne	0		4/180 5/181		
†M. V. Boucher c Watson b McGrath	18		6/225 7/240		

R. Telemachus and M. Hayward did not bat.

  Bowling: McGrath 7–0–43–2; Lee 6–0–34–0; Bichel 8–0–34–1; Harvey 4–0–35–0; Warne 8–0–52–2; Watson 6–0–46–1.

Australia

†A. C. Gilchrist c Kallis b Pollock	7		B. Lee b Boje		28
J. P. Maher c McKenzie b Pollock	8		A. J. Bichel not out		15
S. R. Watson lbw b Pollock	16		G. D. McGrath st Boucher b Boje		0
M. G. Bevan c Pollock b Boje	55		B 2, l-b 7, w 4, n-b 1		14
D. R. Martyn c Smith b Kallis	24				
*R. T. Ponting lbw b Telemachus	1		1/16 2/16 3/56	(32.3 overs)	185
I. J. Harvey b Boje	14		4/95 5/98 6/125		
S. K. Warne b Boje	3		7/137 8/138 9/185		

  Bowling: Pollock 6–0–28–3; Telemachus 6–0–35–1; Hayward 8–0–52–0; Kallis 6–0–40–1; Boje 6.3–0–21–5.

  Umpires: K. H. Hurter and D. L. Orchard.
  Third umpire: M. Z. Nanabhay.　　Referee: C. W. Smith (West Indies).

FICA/PWC AWARDS

The Federation of International Cricketers' Association/PricewaterhouseCoopers International Player of the Year Award was won in July 2002 by Australia's Adam Gilchrist. The other nominees were Muttiah Muralitharan, Mahela Jayawardene, Jacques Kallis, Sachin Tendulkar and Matthew Hayden. Previous winners since the award was instituted in 1998 were Steve Waugh, Brian Lara, Glenn McGrath and Andy Flower. Gilchrist's fellow wicket-keeper/batsman, Kumar Sangakkara of Sri Lanka, was named Young International Player of the Year. The Australian Test team retained the title of International Team of the Year.

THE INDIANS IN THE WEST INDIES, 2001-02

By Tony Cozier

India had great, and realistic, expectations that their eighth tour of the Caribbean would allow them to break their wretched overseas record; they had not won a Test series outside the subcontinent since 1986 in England. They possessed a well-balanced team: Sachin Tendulkar remained the premier batsman of the day, supported by Rahul Dravid, Sourav Ganguly and Shiv Sunder Das, all with Test averages above 40, and the exciting, if unpredictable, V. V. S. Laxman. Anil Kumble and Harbhajan Singh were two contrasting spinners maintaining a rich Indian tradition; Javagal Srinath was the second most successful fast bowler in their history.

In contrast, West Indies were going through difficult times. They had just been whitewashed in three Tests by Sri Lanka and two by Pakistan. Their main batsman, Brian Lara, had not played any cricket since fracturing his elbow in Sri Lanka four months earlier. Curtly Ambrose and Courtney Walsh were no longer around to harass batsmen with their probing accuracy, and their replacements were mostly raw and untried.

When India took the lead with a hard-fought victory in the Second Test, at Port-of-Spain – the scene of their only two previous wins in the Caribbean – it seemed their optimism was not misplaced. But it did not take into account either their own antipathy towards the faster, bouncier pitches they would encounter in Barbados and Jamaica, or West Indies' lingering resilience at home.

After their defeat, the West Indians quickly regained the psychological edge when their limited attack bowled India out for 102 on the first day at Kensington Oval, in Barbados, and Ganguly could not retrieve it. West Indies levelled the series, winning by ten wickets within four days, their seventh victory in eight Tests between the teams on the ground. They outscored India in a high-scoring draw in Antigua and confirmed their superiority by clinching the series in Jamaica.

The most surprising and disappointing aspect of the series was that Tendulkar and Lara were both below their best. Tendulkar's 117 in the Second Test was more grafting than domineering; his 79 in the First and 86 in the last were more authentic. In between, he had three ducks (fourth, second and first balls) and an eight. Lara, hindered by immobility in his elbow, never gave a glimpse of the breathtaking form he had displayed in Sri Lanka.

Although almost every West Indian made a contribution, there were three stars. The captain, Carl Hooper, made 579 runs in the series, the first time he had passed 400 in a 14-year career; finally, he showed the hunger he had always been accused of lacking. Shivnarine Chanderpaul was just as prolific and even more single-minded: between Port-of-Spain and Kingston, he batted for 25 hours 13 minutes without being dismissed, a Test record. Merv Dillon recovered from an indifferent start to take 23 wickets and trouble the Indians with his aggression. Among the supporting cast, Ramnaresh Sarwan continued to establish himself at No. 3, although he had a knack for getting himself out when well set. Wavell Hinds and the wicket-keeper Ridley Jacobs both responded to their omissions from the early Tests with hundreds.

Dillon had support from Cameron Cuffy, whose 17 wickets cost only 22 runs each, while he conceded under two an over; the left-armer Pedro Collins, who dismissed Tendulkar in each of his three Tests; and a new medium-fast seamer, Adam Sanford. Born in Dominica but employed as a policeman in Antigua, Sanford was the first West Indies cricketer to be a direct descendant of the Caribs, the race which gave the region its name.

Although Laxman and Dravid aggregated over 400 and Ganguly and Tendulkar over 300 for India, there was virtually nothing above or below them in the batting line-up. Das and his three different opening partners managed one opening stand better than 19. The only hint of a wagging tail came in the run-glut in Antigua, where Ajay Ratra became the youngest wicket-keeper to score a Test hundred, aged 20 years 150 days.

The strain of bowling 212 overs, more than any of his team-mates, took its toll on Srinath. A spent force by the end of the series, he announced his retirement from Test cricket. Zaheer Khan and Ashish Nehra, two lively left-arm swing bowlers, showed definite promise and, with Srinath, took the critical wickets in the Port-of-Spain triumph. But they could not carry the attack on their own. Kumble and Harbhajan were not paired in any Test and, just as Kumble looked to be finding his best form, his tour ended; his jaw was broken while he was batting during the Fourth Test, though he emerged, head in bandages, to bowl 14 overs against doctor's orders.

India did have the satisfaction of taking the subsequent one-day series 2–1, after the first two matches were lost to Jamaica's unusually wet weather. But it was scant consolation for their continuing disappointments at Test level.

INDIAN TOURING PARTY

S. C. Ganguly (Bengal) (*captain*), R. Dravid (Karnataka) (*vice-captain*), S. B. Bangar (Railways), S. S. Das (Orissa), D. Dasgupta (Bengal), Harbhajan Singh (Punjab), A. Kumble (Karnataka), V. V. S. Laxman (Hyderabad), D. Mongia (Punjab), A. Nehra (Delhi), A. Ratra (Haryana), Sarandeep Singh (Punjab), J. Srinath (Karnataka), S. R. Tendulkar (Mumbai), Wasim Jaffer (Mumbai), T. Yohannan (Kerala), Zaheer Khan (Baroda).

Sarandeep Singh was originally called up as cover for Harbhajan Singh, but was retained for the Test series. Kumble left the tour during the Fourth Test after his jaw was broken. A. B. Agarkar (Mumbai), M. Kaif (Uttar Pradesh), M. Kartik (Railways), V. Sehwag (Delhi) and Yuvraj Singh (Punjab) replaced Bangar, Das, Dasgupta, Kumble, Sarandeep Singh, Srinath and Wasim Jaffer for the one-day series.

Coach: J. G. Wright. *Manager:* Gautam Das Gupta.

INDIAN TOUR RESULTS

Test matches – Played 5: Won 1, Lost 2, Drawn 2.
First-class matches – Played 7: Won 2, Lost 2, Drawn 3.
Wins – West Indies, Guyana Board President's XI.
Losses – West Indies (2).
Draws – West Indies (2), Busta Cup XI.
One-day internationals – Played 3: Won 2, Lost 1. Abandoned 2.

TEST MATCH AVERAGES

WEST INDIES – BATTING

	T	I	NO	R	HS	100s	50s	Avge	Ct
S. Chanderpaul	5	7	3	562	140	3	3	140.50	1
C. L. Hooper	5	7	0	579	233	3	1	82.71	3
R. D. Jacobs	3	4	0	193	118	1	1	48.25	10
R. R. Sarwan	5	7	0	317	65	0	4	45.28	3
C. H. Gayle	5	8	1	206	68	0	2	29.42	4
B. C. Lara	5	7	0	202	55	0	2	28.85	2
S. C. Williams	3	5	1	91	43	0	0	22.75	1
P. T. Collins	3	4	0	47	24	0	0	11.75	2
M. Dillon	5	7	0	62	43	0	0	8.85	4
A. Sanford	5	7	0	22	12	0	0	3.14	0
C. E. Cuffy	5	7	4	9	4	0	0	3.00	2

Played in two Tests: W. W. Hinds 65, 113, 6 (4 ct); J. R. Murray 0, 0, 1 (3 ct). Played in one Test: M. I. Black 6, 3; M. V. Nagamootoo 15* (2 ct).

BOWLING

	O	M	R	W	BB	5W/i	Avge
C. E. Cuffy	190	62	372	17	3-53	0	21.88
M. Dillon	221.3	52	626	23	5-71	1	27.21
A. Sanford	151.4	33	524	15	3-20	0	34.93
P. T. Collins	110	17	341	9	3-60	0	37.88

Also bowled: M. I. Black 31.5–10–89–3; C. H. Gayle 16–5–33–1; W. W. Hinds 2–0–9–0; C. L. Hooper 64–17–131–1; M. V. Nagamootoo 40–13–103–1; R. R. Sarwan 16–3–35–2.

INDIA – BATTING

	T	I	NO	R	HS	100s	50s	Avge	Ct
V. V. S. Laxman	5	8	2	474	130	1	4	79.00	3
R. Dravid	5	8	1	404	144*	1	2	57.71	5
S. C. Ganguly	5	8	2	322	75*	0	2	53.66	3
S. R. Tendulkar	5	8	0	331	117	1	2	41.37	2
Wasim Jaffer	3	5	0	156	86	0	2	31.20	4
A. Ratra	4	7	1	153	115*	1	0	25.50	6
S. S. Das	5	8	0	124	35	0	0	15.50	7
Zaheer Khan	5	7	0	81	46	0	0	11.57	3
Harbhajan Singh	3	6	0	37	17	0	0	6.16	2
J. Srinath	5	7	0	41	18	0	0	5.85	0
A. Nehra	4	7	3	4	3	0	0	1.00	2

Played in two Tests: S. B. Bangar 0, 9, 16 (1 ct); A. Kumble 3, 6. Played in one Test: D. Dasgupta 0 (2 ct); Sarandeep Singh 39* (1 ct).

BOWLING

	O	M	R	W	BB	5W/i	Avge
Harbhajan Singh	140.2	23	388	14	5-138	1	27.71
A. Nehra	171	53	453	12	4-112	0	37.75
Zaheer Khan	188.1	44	568	15	4-79	0	37.86
J. Srinath	212	59	558	13	3-69	0	42.92

Also bowled: S. B. Bangar 29–6–74–1; S. S. Das 8–2–28–0; R. Dravid 9–3–18–1; S. C. Ganguly 29–10–67–0; A. Kumble 59.1–12–174–3; V. V. S. Laxman 17–6–32–1; A. Ratra 1–0–1–0; Sarandeep Singh 21–5–80–1; S. R. Tendulkar 40–4–139–2; Wasim Jaffer 11–3–18–2.

Note: Matches in this section which were not first-class are signified by a dagger.

At Everest CC, Georgetown, April 5, 6, 7. **Indians won by nine wickets.** Toss: Guyana Board President's XI. **Guyana Board President's XI 118** (H. Pooran 41; Harbhajan Singh four for 37) **and 168** (V. Nagamootoo 78; A. Kumble five for 50); **Indians 248** (S. C. Ganguly 52, V. V. S. Laxman 43, S. B. Bangar 76 not out; D. Dasrat three for 49, H. Harrinarine three for 54) **and 39 for one.**

The Indians were originally scheduled to play Guyana, but they qualified for the final of the Busta Cup played on the same dates.

WEST INDIES v INDIA

First Test Match

At Georgetown, April 11, 12, 13, 14, 15. Drawn. Toss: West Indies. Test debut: A. Sanford.

Bourda's Test followed a familiar pattern. An easy-paced pitch produced high scores, before rain, always a threat here, washed away the last day and a half. At least the sizeable Guyanese crowds had the satisfaction of witnessing a partnership of 293 between two local heroes, Hooper and Chanderpaul, who both compiled their highest scores in Tests – and helped West Indies reach 500 for only the second time in 39 Tests stretching back over four years. Then India were made to fight to avoid the follow-on. They had seven down before Dravid, defying a blow from Dillon that left him with a swollen jaw, saw them to safety, adding 120 with Sarandeep Singh. The pair were still together when the weather intervened.

West Indies had an uncertain start. They were 44 for three, all to Srinath, when Lara, who had played no competitive cricket since fracturing his left elbow in Sri Lanka four months earlier, was given out for nought by umpire Harper, caught behind by Dasgupta when even the bowler didn't seem convinced that he had touched the ball.

Hooper might have been caught by the diving Dasgupta off the very next delivery, and edged between first and second slip when ten. Once settled, however, he batted with increasing authority. He had made 222 and 149 not out for Guyana in the knockout stages of the Busta Shield and here he put on 113 for the fourth wicket with Sarwan, another Guyanese, until Sarwan drove loosely to mid-off. That brought in Chanderpaul. He and Hooper batted together for six hours and 11 minutes, adding 293, three runs short of West Indies' all-wicket record against India. Chanderpaul had hit 23 fours when he fell, shortly before tea on the second day. In the next over, Hooper converted his first Test hundred on his home ground into his maiden double-century at this level. He had advanced to 233, hitting three sixes and 29 fours, in 635 minutes and 402 balls, when he finally top-edged Kumble to long leg.

India lost two early wickets, but Tendulkar was soon into his stride, seizing the initiative with boundaries in all directions. He struck 13 fours as he rushed to 71 from 95 balls. Then he was becalmed by Cuffy and Nagamootoo, who restricted him to eight runs off his next 41. Attempting to break free, he missed a pull off Nagamootoo and was lbw. Laxman made light of the setback, looking comfortable from the start as he dominated a stand of 119 with Dravid. But when Laxman was the first of three wickets to fall within five overs on the fourth morning, India were still 27 away from saving the follow-on. Shortly before, Dravid, on 59, had been struck on the grille of the helmet; he received on-field treatment, then resolutely continued to his tenth Test hundred. In all, he batted for seven and a quarter hours, during which he hit 23 fours, before the rains came. With Sarandeep, he saw to it that there were no further alarms.

Man of the Match: C. L. Hooper.

Close of play: First day, West Indies 270-4 (Hooper 108, Chanderpaul 57); Second day, West Indies 494-7 (Nagamootoo 9, Dillon 0); Third day, India 237-4 (Dravid 57, Laxman 46); Fourth day, India 395-7 (Dravid 144, Sarandeep Singh 39).

West Indies

C. H. Gayle c Dasgupta b Srinath	12
S. C. Williams lbw b Srinath	13
R. R. Sarwan c Zaheer Khan b Sarandeep Singh .	53
B. C. Lara c Dasgupta b Srinath	0
*C. L. Hooper c Sarandeep Singh b Kumble .	233
S. Chanderpaul lbw b Zaheer Khan	140
†J. R. Murray lbw b Zaheer Khan	0
M. V. Nagamootoo not out	15
M. Dillon lbw b Bangar	0
A. Sanford lbw b Kumble	1
C. E. Cuffy run out	0
B 1, l-b 4, w 3, n-b 26	34
	501

1/21 (1) 2/37 (2) 3/44 (4) 4/157 (3)
5/450 (6) 6/454 (7) 7/494 (5)
8/494 (9) 9/499 (10) 10/501 (11)

Bowling: Srinath 33–8–91–3; Zaheer Khan 32–9–97–2; Bangar 27–6–63–1; Kumble 45.1–7–145–2; Ganguly 2–1–2–0; Sarandeep Singh 21–5–80–1; Tendulkar 3–0–18–0.

India

S. S. Das b Sanford	33	A. Kumble c Nagamootoo b Sanford . . .	3
†D. Dasgupta lbw b Cuffy	0	Sarandeep Singh not out	39
*S. C. Ganguly c Nagamootoo b Dillon .	5	B 4, l-b 12, w 2, n-b 5	23
S. R. Tendulkar lbw b Nagamootoo	144		
R. Dravid not out	79	1/6 (2) 2/21 (3) 3/99 (1) (7 wkts) 395
V. V. S. Laxman c Gayle b Cuffy	69	4/144 4/5/263 (6)
S. B. Bangar lbw b Cuffy	0	6/270 (7) 7/275 (8)

Zaheer Khan and J. Srinath did not bat.

Bowling: Dillon 32.3–5–115–1; Cuffy 27–6–57–3; Sanford 25–5–81–2; Nagamootoo 40–13–103–1; Hooper 12–4–16–0; Gayle 4–2–7–0.

Umpires: E. A. R. de Silva (Sri Lanka) and D. J. Harper (Australia).
Third umpire: B. R. Doctrove. Referee: R. S. Madugalle (Sri Lanka).

WEST INDIES v INDIA

Second Test Match

At Port-of-Spain, April 19, 20, 21, 22, 23. India won by 37 runs. Toss: West Indies. Test debut: A. Ratra.

True to form, the Queen's Park Oval staged another nail-biter. As against South Africa a year earlier, the West Indians carried high hopes of victory into the last day. Then, they had needed another 200, with nine wickets left; this time, they were 131 for two, needing 182 more, with Lara and Hooper together. Again, they fell short; India completed their third Test victory in the Caribbean at the same venue as their earlier two, in 1970-71 and 1975-76.

They had laid the groundwork on the first day, scoring 262 for four after Hooper chose to bowl. Following a difficult start – on six, he survived a confident claim for a catch at the wicket off Sanford – Tendulkar settled to build his 29th Test hundred, which put him level with Don Bradman, though he had taken 93 Tests to Bradman's 52. Only Sunil Gavaskar, with 34, had more. It was a resolute rather than commanding innings; Dravid looked the more assertive in a partnership of 124. Tendulkar added only four on the second morning before Cuffy ended his six-hour stay, prompting a decline in which the last six wickets went down for 63. Laxman remained unbeaten on 69, having made the most of a life on ten the previous afternoon, when Lara missed him at slip off the second new ball.

West Indies were making a strong response at 179 for three, with Lara batting more like himself. Then, as the shadows lengthened, three wickets fell for one run inside ten balls. Hooper resisted stoutly for three hours, but had little gainful support next morning as India gained a lead of 94. They were ebbing again at 56 for four, when Sanford dismissed Tendulkar fourth ball for nought, but Ganguly and Laxman batted through to the close and an hour into the fourth day, adding 149 to restore the balance. The new ball tilted it yet again: once Laxman chopped Dillon back into his stumps, the last six wickets crashed for 13 runs in ten overs.

West Indies needed 313 to win, a tall but not overwhelming order. They lost Williams early and Gayle retired with cramp, but Sarwan and Lara looked set to see out the day. They had added 57 when Sarwan dabbed a straight ball from Harbhajan Singh to slip; shortly afterwards, bad light ended play.

The stage was set for Lara to convert his overnight 40 into a first Test hundred on his home ground, in front of a crowd of 10,000. But his gesture to the usually boisterous Trini Posse Stand to mute its music was evidence of nerves; he spent an uncertain hour adding seven, before Nehra's fourth ball of the day induced a catch to first slip. Hooper pulled to mid-wicket in Nehra's next over, and the Indians whooped with joy.

Chanderpaul and the returning Gayle kept them anxiously waiting just over two hours for their next wicket. The stand raised 73 amid mounting tension; if only India could separate the two, they would be through to the long tail. At 237, Gayle's loose drive presented a catch to cover; West Indies needed 76, and Chanderpaul could find no one to help him get more than halfway.

His resistance should have ended four overs after tea, when Chanderpaul was reprieved by third umpire Nicholls's drawn-out rejection of a low, but certainly fair, wicket-keeper's catch; he was still there nine overs later, when last man Cuffy was caught at gully to give India their first Test win in the Caribbean since 1975-76, when they made 406 for four, the highest fourth-innings total to win a Test.

Man of the Match: V. V. S. Laxman.

Close of play: First day, India 262-4 (Tendulkar 113, Laxman 21); Second day, West Indies 197-6 (Hooper 30, Dillon 6); Third day, India 165-4 (Ganguly 48, Laxman 60); Fourth day, West Indies 131-2 (Lara 40, Hooper 1).

India

S. S. Das lbw b Dillon	10	– lbw b Dillon	0
S. B. Bangar c Murray b Sanford	9	– c Hooper b Sanford	16
R. Dravid b Black	67	– c Murray b Cuffy	36
S. R. Tendulkar lbw b Cuffy	117	– lbw b Sanford	0
*S. C. Ganguly c Dillon b Hooper	25	– not out	75
V. V. S. Laxman not out	69	– b Dillon	74
†A. Ratra c Murray b Cuffy	0	– lbw b Cuffy	2
Harbhajan Singh c Cuffy b Sanford	0	– c Gayle b Cuffy	0
Zaheer Khan b Sanford	5	– (10) run out	4
J. Srinath lbw b Black	18	– (9) c Williams b Dillon	2
A. Nehra c Hooper b Black	0	– b Dillon	0
B 4, l-b 13, n-b 2	19	B 5, l-b 2, n-b 2	9
	339		**218**

1/18 (1) 2/38 (2) 3/162 (3) 4/218 (5)   339
5/276 (4) 6/282 (7) 7/287 (8)
8/298 (9) 9/339 (10) 10/339 (11)

1/6 (1) 2/54 (2) 3/54 (3)   218
4/56 (4) 5/205 (6) 6/210 (7)
7/210 (8) 8/213 (9)
9/218 (10) 10/218 (11)

Bowling: First Innings—Dillon 28–7–82–1; Cuffy 30–12–49–2; Sanford 29–5–111–3; Black 17.5–7–53–3; Hooper 11–4–27–1. *Second Innings*—Dillon 21.1–7–42–4; Cuffy 20–6–53–3; Black 14–3–36–0; Sanford 17–5–46–2; Hooper 17–4–28–0; Sarwan 3–0–6–0.

West Indies

C. H. Gayle c Das b Srinath	13	– (2) c Harbhajan Singh b Zaheer Khan	52
S. C. Williams c Das b Harbhajan Singh	43	– (1) c Dravid b Srinath	13
R. R. Sarwan c Dravid b Nehra	35	– c Dravid b Harbhajan Singh	41
B. C. Lara c Ratra b Zaheer Khan	52	– c Dravid b Nehra	47
*C. L. Hooper c Ganguly b Zaheer Khan	50	– c Das b Nehra	22
S. Chanderpaul lbw b Srinath	1	– not out	67
†J. R. Murray lbw b Srinath	0	– run out	1
M. Dillon lbw b Nehra	9	– b Srinath	0
M. I. Black run out	0	– c Das b Srinath	3
A. Sanford c Tendulkar b Harbhajan Singh	12	– b Nehra	1
C. E. Cuffy not out	1	– c Bangar b Zaheer Khan	4
B 5, l-b 8, w 3, n-b 7	23	B 2, l-b 5, w 4, n-b 13	24
	245		**275**

1/50 (1) 2/80 (2) 3/136 (3) 4/179 (4)   245
5/180 (6) 6/180 (7) 7/201 (8)
8/217 (9) 9/232 (5) 10/245 (10)

1/27 (1) 2/125 (3) 3/157 (4)   275
4/164 (5) 5/237 (2) 6/238 (7)
7/238 (8) 8/254 (9)
9/263 (10) 10/275 (11)

In the second innings Gayle, when 21, retired hurt at 68 and resumed at 164.

Bowling: First Innings—Srinath 22–4–71–3; Nehra 20–4–52–2; Zaheer Khan 14–2–47–2; Harbhajan Singh 19.5–3–51–2; Bangar 2–0–11–0. *Second Innings*—Srinath 32–9–69–3; Nehra 31–8–72–3; Harbhajan Singh 30–8–66–1; Zaheer Khan 21.1–5–55–2; Tendulkar 1–0–6–0.

Umpires: E. A. R. de Silva (Sri Lanka) and D. J. Harper (Australia).
Third umpire: E. A. Nicholls. Referee: R. S. Madugalle (Sri Lanka).

At St Lucia, April 26, 27, 28. **Drawn.** Toss: Busta Cup XI. **Busta Cup XI 437** (D. S. Smith 91, W. W. Hinds 175, R. S. Morton 33, R. D. Jacobs 55 not out; T. Yohannan three for 84); **Indians 150** (D. Mongia 67, Sarandeep Singh 32; D. Ramnarine four for 49) **and 158 for two** (Wasim Jaffer 62, D. Dasgupta 54 not out).

WEST INDIES v INDIA

Third Test Match

At Bridgetown, May 2, 3, 4, 5. West Indies won by ten wickets. Toss: West Indies.

If Port-of-Spain had proved itself India's lucky venue, Bridgetown was the precise opposite. They had never won a match of any kind at Kensington Oval, and had lost six of their seven Tests there. The aversion was confirmed with the first ball of the game, with which Dillon bowled Das – an immediate psychological setback from which India never recovered. They were dismissed for 102 just after tea on a rain-interrupted first day. Once Hooper and Chanderpaul reprised their hundreds from Georgetown, there was no realistic way back. The pitch, later rated by Hooper as the best of the series, was blameless in India's first-innings demise. Slack strokes against lively bowling were more to the point. Tendulkar was out to his second ball, which was also Collins's second on his return to the West Indies team. He and Jacobs, who took the catch, had been out since the series with Pakistan in February. The only fight came from Ganguly, who was last out when Dillon followed up his four wickets with a breathtaking catch on the third-man boundary.

A century stand between Lara and Sarwan gave West Indies the lead with only two wickets down. But when Nehra accounted for both in eight deliveries, Hooper and Chanderpaul had to rebuild. Hooper was 15 when replays indicated he was out of his crease as Nehra deflected Chanderpaul's drive into the stumps; the third umpire generously gave him the benefit of whatever doubt there might have been. The run-out would have left West Indies 220 for five; as it was, they did not lose their fifth wicket until an hour and a half into the third day when Hooper, hitting out at Harbhajan, sent a spiralling catch to extra cover. By then, he had batted five and three-quarter hours and struck 18 fours. He had added 215 with Chanderpaul, their second double-century partnership of the series. Chanderpaul was 91 when he lost Hooper; he just managed to beat the usual lower-order collapse – six for 18 – to reach his own hundred, which took just over six hours.

The tourists trailed by 292. Das and his third opening partner in as many Tests, Wasim Jaffer, put on 80, India's best start of the series. It took a direct hit by Chanderpaul from point to part them, just before tea. But three more wickets were down by the end of the third day, and there would have been more but for sharp, close catches missed off Ganguly and Laxman. West Indies needed only four overs next morning to break their stand as Collins lured Laxman into an edge. After that, only Zaheer Khan's belligerent run-a-ball 46 and another defiant, but futile, innings from Ganguly sent the match into a fourth afternoon and forced West Indies to bat again. When Dillon claimed his eighth wicket of the match, they needed a mere five runs to level the series.

Man of the Match: M. Dillon.

Close of play: First day, West Indies 33-1 (Gayle 14, Sarwan 0); Second day, West Indies 314-4 (Hooper 70, Chanderpaul 75); Third day, India 169-4 (Ganguly 15, Laxman 30).

India

S. S. Das b Dillon	0	– c Sarwan b Dillon	35
Wasim Jaffer c Jacobs b Dillon	12	– run out	51
R. Dravid run out	17	– c Jacobs b Sanford	14
S. R. Tendulkar c Jacobs b Collins	0	– lbw b Dillon	8
*S. C. Ganguly c Dillon b Sanford	48	– not out	60
V. V. S. Laxman b Cuffy	1	– c Hooper b Collins	43
†A. Ratra c Jacobs b Dillon	1	– lbw b Dillon	13
Harbhajan Singh c Dillon b Sanford	13	– b Cuffy	3
Zaheer Khan c Sarwan b Sanford	4	– c Jacobs b Sarwan	46
J. Srinath lbw b Dillon	0	– c Gayle b Sarwan	0
A. Nehra not out	0	– c Collins b Dillon	3
W 2, n-b 4	6	L-b 6, n-b 14	20
	102		**296**

1/0 (1) 2/26 (2) 3/27 (4) 4/50 (3)   102
5/51 (6) 6/61 (7) 7/78 (8)
8/86 (9) 9/101 (10) 10/102 (5)

1/80 (2) 2/101 (1) 3/117 (3)   296
4/118 (4) 5/183 (6) 6/208 (7)
7/211 (8) 8/285 (9)
9/285 (10) 10/296 (11)

Bowling: *First Innings*—Dillon 11–1–41–4; Cuffy 9–4–17–1; Collins 8–0–24–1; Sanford 5.4–0–20–3. *Second Innings*—Dillon 31.2–8–82–4; Cuffy 24–16–26–1; Collins 22–1–78–1; Sanford 15–3–78–1; Hooper 5–0–11–0; Gayle 3–0–14–0; Sarwan 1–0–1–2.

West Indies

S. C. Williams c Wasim Jaffer b Zaheer Khan	18	– (2) not out	4
C. H. Gayle lbw b Zaheer Khan	14	– (1) not out	0
R. R. Sarwan c Wasim Jaffer b Nehra	60		
B. C. Lara c and b Nehra	55		
*C. L. Hooper c Tendulkar b Harbhajan Singh	115		
S. Chanderpaul not out	101		
†R. D. Jacobs c Ratra b Nehra	0		
M. Dillon c Das b Nehra	6		
P. T. Collins b Harbhajan Singh	0		
A. Sanford lbw b Harbhajan Singh	0		
C. E. Cuffy run out	1		
B 3, l-b 8, n-b 13	24	N-b 1	1

1/30 (1) 2/35 (2) 3/154 (4) 4/161 (3)   394   (no wkt) 5
5/376 (5) 6/376 (7) 7/392 (8)
8/393 (9) 9/393 (10) 10/394 (11)

Bowling: *First Innings*—Srinath 32–7–85–0; Nehra 32–9–112–4; Zaheer Khan 29–8–83–2; Ganguly 7–5–9–0; Harbhajan Singh 34.5–7–87–3; Tendulkar 1–0–7–0. *Second Innings*—Tendulkar 1–0–1–0; Harbhajan Singh 0.2–0–4–0.

Umpires: E. A. R. de Silva (Sri Lanka) and D. J. Harper (Australia).
Third umpire: B. R. Doctrove.   Referee: R. S. Madugalle (Sri Lanka).

WEST INDIES v INDIA

Fourth Test Match

At St John's, May 10, 11, 12, 13, 14. Drawn. Toss: West Indies.

Five individual hundreds were scored on a pitch so lifeless that it yielded 1,142 runs for 18 wickets. India amassed their highest total in the Caribbean, West Indies passed 600 for the first time in nearly seven years, and beat the ground record. Yet the two most prominent batsmen of their generation, Tendulkar and Lara, managed only four runs between them.

Ratra, in his third Test, and Jacobs contributed an odd record: it was the first occasion in 125 years of Test cricket that opposing wicket-keepers had scored hundreds in the same match. Later, Ratra sent down what became the game's penultimate over; all 11 Indians bowled, only the third such instance in Tests.

But the most memorable image of a batsman's match was provided by a bowler, Kumble. Sheathed in head bandages like some battle-front survivor, he returned to the action on the third evening with a broken jaw. It had just been announced that he was flying home for surgery, but when he saw Tendulkar turning the ball he hurried out, went straight into the attack, and bowled 14 consecutive overs, in which he dismissed Lara and had Hooper caught off a no-ball. Only the close of play silenced him; next day, he departed, and was sorely missed.

For the fourth Test in succession, Hooper won the toss; for the third time, he fielded. But in spite of the early loss of Das and the first-ball dismissal of Tendulkar, both to Collins, India were strongly placed after the first day, thanks to a stand of 155 between Wasim Jaffer and Dravid. There was a slight wobble in the morning, when three wickets fell in the space of 24 runs, including Kumble, who had kept on batting for four overs after a blow from Dillon left him spitting blood. Laxman took 22 balls to get off the mark; after that, however, he quickly asserted himself, while Ratra, who had shown no pretensions as a batsman in his four previous Test innings, played with increasing confidence as the bowling lost its bite. They added 217 for India's seventh wicket, batting through to the third morning, before Laxman stepped on to his off-stump, playing Dillon to leg. Ratra was then 99, but reached his hundred by the end of the over with his 12th boundary. He was unbeaten when Ganguly declared.

Beyond the call of duty: Anil Kumble, his jaw broken by Merv Dillon the previous day, rejoined the Test on the third evening – and dismissed Brian Lara. *Picture by Brooks Latouche Photography.*

Apart from Lara, the West Indian batsmen spent the remainder of the match cashing in on the conditions and the absence of Kumble through the last two days. Hooper, who was caught at short leg off a Kumble no-ball when ten, and missed at slip the next ball, and Chanderpaul both scored their third centuries of the series, at contrasting rates. Hooper took 401 minutes and 278 balls over his 136; Chanderpaul compiled an identical score, but took 675 minutes and 510 balls. On the meaningless last day, while Jacobs entertained his small home-town crowd with the quickest hundred of the match – completed in 172 balls, with his fifth six – Chanderpaul scored 56, including just five fours, off 242 balls in five and a half hours. This took him past Jacques Kallis's record of 1,241 minutes without dismissal in Tests set earlier in the season; he was still there when the captains mercifully agreed to call the whole thing off.

Man of the Match: A. Ratra.

Close of play: First day, India 226-3 (Dravid 86, Ganguly 41); Second day, India 462-6 (Laxman 124, Ratra 93); Third day, West Indies 187-3 (Sarwan 50, Hooper 26); Fourth day, West Indies 405-5 (Chanderpaul 80, Jacobs 18).

India

S. S. Das b Collins	3	J. Srinath c Lara b Cuffy	15
Wasim Jaffer c Jacobs b Collins	86	A. Nehra not out	1
R. Dravid b Dillon	91		
S. R. Tendulkar c Jacobs b Collins	0	L-b 6, w 1, n-b 10	17
*S. C. Ganguly c Hinds b Cuffy	45		
V. V. S. Laxman hit wkt b Dillon	130	1/13 (1) 2/168 (2) (9 wkts dec.)	513
A. Kumble c Chanderpaul b Dillon	6	3/168 (4) 4/233 (5)	
†A. Ratra not out	115	5/235 (3) 6/257 (7)	
Zaheer Khan c Jacobs b Cuffy	4	7/474 (6) 8/485 (9) 9/508 (10)	

Bowling: Dillon 51–14–116–3; Cuffy 40–7–87–3; Collins 44–10–125–3; Sanford 32–6–113–0; Hooper 13–4–29–0; Hinds 2–0–9–0; Sarwan 9–3–23–0; Gayle 5–1–5–0.

West Indies

C. H. Gayle c Ratra b Zaheer Khan	32	A. Sanford c Zaheer Khan b Laxman . . . 2
W. W. Hinds b Tendulkar	65	C. E. Cuffy not out 0
R. R. Sarwan lbw b Zaheer Khan	51	
B. C. Lara lbw b Kumble	4	B 10, l-b 9, w 6, n-b 6 31
*C. L. Hooper c Nehra b Tendulkar	136	
S. Chanderpaul not out	136	1/65 (1) 2/121 (2) (9 wkts dec.) 629
†R. D. Jacobs c Laxman b Dravid	118	3/135 (4) 4/196 (3)
M. Dillon b Wasim Jaffer	43	5/382 (5) 6/548 (7)
P. T. Collins c sub (Harbhajan Singh)		7/607 (8) 8/625 (9)
b Wasim Jaffer .	11	9/628 (10)

Bowling: Srinath 45–19–82–0; Nehra 49–16–122–0; Zaheer Khan 48–14–129–2; Ganguly 12–0–44–0; Tendulkar 34–4–107–2; Kumble 14–5–29–1; Laxman 17–6–32–1; Dravid 9–3–18–1; Wasim Jaffer 11–3–18–2; Das 8–2–28–0; Ratra 1–0–1–0.

Umpires: D. R. Shepherd (England) and R. B. Tiffin (Zimbabwe).
Third umpire: E. A. Nicholls. Referee: R. S. Madugalle (Sri Lanka).

WEST INDIES v INDIA

Fifth Test Match

At Kingston, May 18, 19, 20, 21, 22. West Indies won by 155 runs. Toss: India.

Heavy rain ravaged Jamaica for 11 days after this match. Drizzle delayed the final morning's start, and the front that would drench Kingston was no more than half an hour away when Zaheer Khan slogged to extra cover, giving West Indies the victory that secured the series. They had needed only nine overs to extract India's last three wickets.

Ganguly, who called correctly for the first time and chose to bowl on the grassiest Sabina Park pitch anyone could remember, identified the opening partnership of 111 between the two Jamaican left-handers, Gayle and Hinds, as decisive. India's bowlers wasted the conditions, allowing the two local boys to prepare a strong base. Only briefly did West Indies loosen their grip.

It was not until eight overs after lunch that the Indians got their first wicket, when Zaheer removed Gayle; they had to wait until midway through the final session for their second, as Hinds added a further 135 with Sarwan. But they came back into contention with three late wickets, starting with Hinds, caught at long-off. He had hit two sixes and 14 fours in his second Test century, batting five hours. India's fightback continued next morning, when Srinath dismissed Hooper, but the balance shifted again as Chanderpaul and Jacobs put on 109; even though the last five fell for 21, with Harbhajan Singh claiming the first five-in-an-innings of the series, by then West Indies were back in control. Chanderpaul had extended his record for batting without dismissal to 1,513 minutes, spread over four Tests, before Srinath finally defeated him.

Dillon removed Wasim Jaffer and Dravid cheaply, Tendulkar and Das added 69 then went within two runs of each other and, once Dillon ended a promising partnership of 82 between Ganguly and Laxman on the third morning, the usual late-order collapse ensued. The last six tumbled for 44, Dillon returning Test-best figures of five for 71. As at Port-of-Spain, Laxman was left high and dry; this time, there was no way back.

Despite a lead of 210, Hooper waived the follow-on. But careless strokes reflected West Indian complacency. They were 122 for seven when Dillon, swinging wildly, was bowled by Nehra; it took sensible batting by Chanderpaul and Collins to focus them on building an overwhelming target. When Collins was last out on the fourth morning, India required 408 for victory, two more than their own record fourth-innings total to win at Port-of-Spain in 1975-76.

Collins was soon in the picture again, removing both openers in his first two overs. But Tendulkar was in such commanding touch that India's task began to appear less daunting. A wide array of strokes brought him 13 boundaries; he scored 86 out of 145 while at the wicket. Tendulkar became the tenth player to reach 8,000 Test runs just before tea, but six balls after the interval his nemesis Collins, coming round the wicket, breached his defence to hit middle and off.

His dismissal utterly deflated the Indians, who now seemed resigned to their fate. Ganguly and Laxman both perished to inappropriate hook shots, and on the final morning the tailenders made no effort to hang on, even when rain was imminent.

Man of the Match: W. W. Hinds.   *Man of the Series:* S. Chanderpaul.

Close of play: First day, West Indies 287-4 (Hooper 14, Chanderpaul 4); Second day, India 141-4 (Ganguly 22, Laxman 27); Third day, West Indies 165-7 (Chanderpaul 55, Collins 4); Fourth day, India 237-7 (Ratra 16, Zaheer Khan 4).

West Indies

C. H. Gayle c Wasim Jaffer b Zaheer Khan	68	– c Ganguly b Srinath		15
W. W. Hinds c Wasim Jaffer b Harbhajan Singh	113	– c Laxman b Srinath		6
R. R. Sarwan c Das b Harbhajan Singh	65	– c Das b Zaheer Khan		12
B. C. Lara c Ratra b Nehra	9	– b Zaheer Khan		35
*C. L. Hooper c Dravid b Srinath	6	– c Ratra b Zaheer Khan		6
S. Chanderpaul c Ratra b Srinath	58	– c and b Zaheer Khan		59
†R. D. Jacobs b Harbhajan Singh	59	– c sub (D. Mongia)		
		b Harbhajan Singh		16
M. Dillon lbw b Harbhajan Singh	0	– b Nehra		4
P. T. Collins c Laxman b Nehra	12	– b Harbhajan Singh		24
A. Sanford c and b Harbhajan Singh	1	– c Ganguly b Harbhajan Singh		5
C. E. Cuffy not out	0	– not out		3
B 5, l-b 6, w 5, n-b 4	20	B 4, n-b 8		12

1/111 (1) 2/246 (2) 3/264 (4) 4/264 (3)   422   1/17 (2) 2/24 (1) 3/38 (3)   197
5/292 (5) 6/401 (7) 7/409 (8)   4/60 (5) 5/81 (4) 6/117 (7)
8/411 (6) 9/422 (10) 10/422 (9)   7/122 (8) 8/170 (6)
9/187 (10) 10/197 (9)

Bowling: First Innings—Srinath 32–9–111–2; Nehra 30–14–72–2; Zaheer Khan 24–4–78–1; Ganguly 8–4–12–0; Harbhajan Singh 38–3–138–5. *Second Innings*—Srinath 16–3–49–2; Nehra 9–2–23–1; Zaheer Khan 20–2–79–4; Harbhajan Singh 17.2–2–42–3.

India

S. S. Das lbw b Cuffy	33	– lbw b Collins		10
Wasim Jaffer c Jacobs b Dillon	0	– c Hinds b Collins		7
R. Dravid lbw b Dillon	5	– lbw b Sanford		30
S. R. Tendulkar b Sanford	41	– b Collins		86
*S. C. Ganguly c Jacobs b Dillon	36	– c Sarwan b Sanford		28
V. V. S. Laxman not out	65	– c Dillon b Sanford		23
†A. Ratra c Hinds b Dillon	3	– lbw b Cuffy		19
Harbhajan Singh c Hinds b Dillon	4	– c Cuffy b Gayle		17
Zaheer Khan c Lara b Cuffy	6	– c Collins b Dillon		12
J. Srinath c Gayle b Collins	2	– b Cuffy		4
A. Nehra run out	0	– not out		0
L-b 6, n-b 11	17	B 5, l-b 1, w 1, n-b 9		16

1/5 (2) 2/15 (3) 3/84 (4) 4/86 (1)   212   1/19 (2) 2/25 (1) 3/77 (3)   252
5/168 (5) 6/178 (7) 7/184 (8)   4/170 (4) 5/176 (5) 6/209 (6)
8/194 (9) 9/197 (10) 10/212 (11)   7/228 (8) 8/242 (7)
9/252 (10) 10/252 (9)

Bowling: First Innings—Dillon 24–4–71–5; Cuffy 22–5–49–2; Collins 19–2–54–1; Sanford 9–1–27–1; Hooper 1–0–5–0. *Second Innings*—Dillon 22.3–6–77–1; Cuffy 18–6–34–2; Collins 17–4–60–3; Sanford 19–8–48–3; Hooper 5–1–15–0; Gayle 4–2–7–1; Sarwan 3–0–5–0.

Umpires: D. R. Shepherd (England) and R. B. Tiffin (Zimbabwe).
Third umpire: B. R. Doctrove.   Referee: R. S. Madugalle (Sri Lanka).

†WEST INDIES v INDIA

First One-Day International

At Kingston, May 25. No result (abandoned).

The rain which had arrived on the tails of the Kingston Test completely washed out both the one-day games scheduled at Sabina Park.

†WEST INDIES v INDIA

Second One-Day International

At Kingston, May 26. No result (abandoned)

†WEST INDIES v INDIA

Third One-Day International

At Bridgetown, May 29. India won by seven wickets (D/L method). Toss: India.

After 12 defeats and five draws at Bridgetown, from eight Tests, seven other first-class games and two one-day internationals, India's historic first victory at Kensington Oval was comprehensive. Yohannan set West Indies back by dismissing both openers in a testing spell, his first in limited-overs internationals, and Lara lasted only ten balls. After a short rain-break cost one over, Sarwan and Hooper rallied, with 87, but the last seven wickets crashed for 46; Agarkar finished them off with three yorkers in ten balls, leaving Hooper stranded on a run-a-ball 76. India were never pressed pursuing a modest target. The left-handed Mongia saw them most of the way, with an accomplished 74, off 104 balls, in his second innings of the tour.

Man of the Match: D. Mongia.

West Indies

C. H. Gayle c Mongia b Yohannan	16	M. Dillon b Agarkar		2
W. W. Hinds b Yohannan	15	C. D. Collymore lbw b Agarkar		1
R. R. Sarwan b Sehwag	44	C. E. Cuffy b Agarkar		0
B. C. Lara c Kaif b Harbhajan Singh	5	L-b 5, w 13, n-b 1		19
*C. L. Hooper not out	76			
S. Chanderpaul run out	5	1/38 2/45 3/53	(44.5 overs)	186
R. O. Hinds st Dravid b Sehwag	3	4/140 5/155 6/162		
†R. D. Jacobs c Dravid b Yohannan	0	7/164 8/182 9/186		

Bowling: Yohannan 10–1–33–3; Zaheer Khan 8–2–31–0; Agarkar 8.5–1–36–3; Harbhajan Singh 7–0–22–1; Ganguly 3–0–20–0; Mongia 2–0–16–0; Sehwag 6–1–23–2.

India

*S. C. Ganguly c Hooper b Gayle	41	†R. Dravid not out		9
V. Sehwag c Sarwan b Dillon	21	L-b 2, w 3, n-b 3		8
D. Mongia c Chanderpaul b R. O. Hinds	74			
S. R. Tendulkar not out	34	1/41 2/109 3/166	(3 wkts, 43.5 overs)	187

Yuvraj Singh, M. Kaif, A. B. Agarkar, Zaheer Khan, T. Yohannan and Harbhajan Singh did not bat.

Bowling: Dillon 10–0–30–1; Cuffy 7–0–34–0; Collymore 6–0–28–0; Hooper 7–0–25–0; Gayle 8–0–34–1; R. O. Hinds 5.5–0–34–1.

Umpires: R. B. Tiffin (Zimbabwe) and E. A. Nicholls.

Third umpire: B. R. Doctrove. Referee: M. J. Procter (South Africa).

†WEST INDIES v INDIA

Fourth One-Day International

At Port-of-Spain, June 1. West Indies won by seven wickets. Toss: India.

Heavy morning rain delayed the start and reduced the match to 25 overs a side. Without Tendulkar, resting a stiff shoulder, India batted without any obvious plan and never got going after Sehwag drove his first ball to mid-on. The West Indians bowled with discipline, with Collymore returning economical figures of three for 14 in five overs. Then Gayle delighted a capacity crowd of 25,000 with strokes of withering power, plundering three sixes and nine fours to score 84 in 67 balls. His opening stand of 117 in 18 overs with Hinds all but settled the result, which levelled the series. Yohannan, so impressive at Bridgetown, conceded 25 in one over – 24 to Gayle plus a no-ball.

Man of the Match: C. H. Gayle.

India

*S. C. Ganguly lbw b Collymore	39	Zaheer Khan b Hooper		7
V. Sehwag c Lara b Dillon	0	Harbhajan Singh c Jacobs b Collins		6
D. Mongia b Cuffy	13	T. Yohannan not out		2
V. V. S. Laxman run out	2	L-b 5, w 4, n-b 4		13
Yuvraj Singh c Jacobs b Collins	1			
†R. Dravid b Hooper	28	1/1 2/45 3/53	(25 overs)	123
M. Kaif c Gayle b Collymore	12	4/56 5/66 6/86		
A. B. Agarkar c Jacobs b Collymore	0	7/86 8/110 9/118		

Bowling: Dillon 5–0–24–1; Cuffy 5–0–40–1; Collins 5–0–21–2; Collymore 5–1–14–3; Hooper 5–0–19–2.

West Indies

C. H. Gayle c Ganguly b Zaheer Khan	84	*C. L. Hooper not out		1
W. W. Hinds b Yohannan	30	W 1, n-b 3		4
R. R. Sarwan b Yohannan	1			
B. C. Lara not out	4	1/117 2/117 3/118	(3 wkts, 22.1 overs)	124

S. Chanderpaul, †R. D. Jacobs, M. Dillon, P. T. Collins, C. D. Collymore and C. E. Cuffy did not bat.

Bowling: Zaheer Khan 5–0–14–1; Yohannan 5–0–50–2; Agarkar 4–1–14–0; Harbhajan Singh 5–1–22–0; Sehwag 3.1–0–24–0.

Umpires: D. R. Shepherd (England) and B. R. Doctrove.
Third umpire: E. A. Nicholls. Referee: M. J. Procter (South Africa).

†WEST INDIES v INDIA

Fifth One-Day International

At Port-of-Spain, June 2. India won by 56 runs (D/L method). Toss: India.

India built a challenging total, thanks to a succession of steady partnerships involving Ganguly and Tendulkar. Both looked well set until Dillon dismissed them on his way to five wickets. Tendulkar ignored his injured shoulder to score 65 in 70 balls, with a six and three fours. Rain interrupted West Indies' reply, already one over short because of their slow over-rate; on resumption, the incompatibility of the available computer and the Duckworth/Lewis disk meant a delay in announcing the revised target. Both openers were out before West Indies heard they needed 248 from 44 overs. But they were effectively beaten by the 24th, having lost the top half of their batting for 88. Although Chanderpaul and Jacobs kept another large crowd interested, adding 71 in 55 balls, India won the series in comfort.

Man of the Match: S. R. Tendulkar. *Man of the Series:* S. C. Ganguly.

India

*S. C. Ganguly c Sarwan b Dillon	56	Harbhajan Singh not out 5
V. Sehwag c Gayle b Dillon	32	Zaheer Khan c Collins b Dillon 4
D. Mongia c Gayle b Collymore	28	A. Nehra b Gayle 0
S. R. Tendulkar b Dillon	65	L-b 8, w 8, n-b 4 20
†R. Dravid c Sarwan b Hooper	20	
Yuvraj Singh b Gayle	10	1/43 2/105 3/141 (50 overs) 260
M. Kaif b Gayle	17	4/187 5/212 6/239
A. B. Agarkar c Hooper b Dillon	3	7/248 8/248 9/254

Bowling: Dillon 10–1–52–5; Cuffy 9–0–45–0; Collymore 8–0–42–1; Collins 10–1–46–0; Hooper 8–0–41–1; Gayle 5–0–26–3.

West Indies

C. H. Gayle b Zaheer Khan	3	M. Dillon run out. 0
W. W. Hinds c Sehwag b Nehra	2	P. T. Collins b Agarkar 9
R. R. Sarwan b Harbhajan Singh.	32	C. D. Collymore not out 0
B. C. Lara c Mongia b Tendulkar	36	C. E. Cuffy c Agarkar b Nehra 7
*C. L. Hooper c Sehwag b Agarkar	1	B 1, l-b 4, w 9 14
S. Chanderpaul c Ganguly		
b Harbhajan Singh .	51	1/7 2/12 3/73 (36.2 overs) 191
†R. D. Jacobs c Harbhajan Singh		4/76 5/88 6/159
b Agarkar .	36	7/162 8/184 9/184

Bowling: Nehra 5.2–0–25–2; Zaheer Khan 7–1–32–1; Agarkar 8–0–33–3; Harbhajan Singh 9–0–55–2; Sehwag 4–0–21–0; Tendulkar 3–0–20–1.

Umpires: R. B. Tiffin (Zimbabwe) and E. A. Nicholls.
Third umpire: B. R. Doctrove.   Referee: M. J. Procter (South Africa).

THE NEW ZEALANDERS IN PAKISTAN, 2002

By QAMAR AHMED and SAMIUL HASAN

New Zealand were originally due to arrive in Pakistan in September 2001, but called the tour off because of security fears after the terrorist attacks in the USA. Seven months later, they honoured their commitment, travelling to Pakistan for three one-day internationals and two Test matches – down from the three Tests originally planned.

Sadly, after all the spadework done by the Pakistan Cricket Board, the tour came to an abrupt and tragic end. A car bomb exploded in front of the Pearl Continental Hotel in Karachi, where both teams were staying, a couple of hours before the start of the Second Test, and killed 14 people, including 11 French engineers who were in Karachi helping the Pakistan Navy to build submarines. None of the players was hurt, though they witnessed some horrific injuries to bystanders, and the New Zealand physiotherapist, Dayle Shackel, was cut by flying glass.

The referee, Mike Procter, swiftly announced the cancellation of the Test, and the tour; the dazed Pakistan officials had no alternative but to agree. It was depressing news for their board. They had already lost nearly $US20m after India had refused to come to Pakistan for the Asian Test Championship for political reasons, and Sri Lanka and West Indies had also declined to tour after September 11. To fulfil the requirements of the ICC Test Championship, the West Indian series was transferred to Sharjah. Now, the Karachi blast put Test cricket in Pakistan, and the future of the Championship, in jeopardy. The single Test played here did not qualify as a series in the Championship reckoning, and how many times could a tour be rescheduled?

The tourists' manager, Jeff Crowe, was sympathetic to the Pakistan board. He had been in a similar situation as New Zealand's captain in Sri Lanka in 1986-87, when their trip was aborted after a bomb in Colombo. New Zealand's 1992-93 visit to Sri Lanka had also been marred by a bomb outside their hotel, which caused several tourists to leave early. But this had been "an excellent tour until today", Crowe said. "We got the security that was promised, and we have no complaints. It was a devastating blow because both the PCB and NZC had tried their best to make the tour happen."

The New Zealanders had not had an easy time, however. The worst cricketing setback had been the loss of Nathan Astle, who damaged ligaments in his left knee during the first match. Andre Adams also left early, with a stress fracture. Several players suffered severe stomach upsets, and Pakistan's first home Test to be staged in May was played in temperatures approaching 40°C, causing match officials to schedule extra drinks breaks.

On the field, Pakistan's triumph was total. Their record on home soil had been disappointing in recent years: they had not won a Test series there since beating West Indies in 1997-98. In the one-day games they achieved their first clean sweep since Zimbabwe's visit in 1996-97. Shoaib Akhtar unofficially bowled a 100mph delivery, and followed his best figures in one-day internationals, six for 16 at Karachi, with his best in Tests, six for 11 at Lahore. Even he was overshadowed by the hefty figure of Inzamam-ul-Haq, who became the 15th man to score a triple-hundred in Tests. New Zealand crumbled for 73 and went down to the fifth-heaviest defeat in Test history. Once the Second Test was cancelled, however, Pakistan's dominance counted for nothing in the ICC Championship.

NEW ZEALAND TOURING PARTY

S. P. Fleming (Wellington) (*captain*), A. R. Adams (Auckland), I. G. Butler (Northern Districts), C. Z. Harris (Canterbury), R. G. Hart (Northern Districts), M. J. Horne (Auckland), C. D. McMillan (Canterbury), C. S. Martin (Canterbury), M. H. Richardson (Otago), S. B. Styris (Northern Districts), D. R. Tuffey (Northern Districts), D. L. Vettori (Northern Districts), L. Vincent (Auckland), B. G. K. Walker (Auckland).

J. E. C. Franklin (Wellington), C. J. Nevin (Wellington) and J. D. P. Oram (Central Districts) were in the party for the one-day series, after which they were replaced by Martin, Richardson and Vettori. N. J. Astle (Canterbury) was selected for both legs, but returned home injured during the one-day internationals and was replaced by M. S. Sinclair (Central Districts). Adams went home injured after the First Test.

Coach: D. J. Aberhart.   *Manager:* J. J. Crowe.   *Physiotherapist:* D. Shockel.

NEW ZEALAND TOUR RESULTS

Test matches – Played 1: Lost 1. Cancelled 1.
One-day internationals – Played 3: Lost 3.

Note: Matches in this section which were not first-class are signified by a dagger.

†PAKISTAN v NEW ZEALAND

First One-Day International

At Karachi, April 21 (day/night). Pakistan won by 153 runs. Toss: Pakistan. International debut: R. G. Hart.

Bowling with fire and venom, Shoaib Akhtar ripped out New Zealand's heart with a career-best six for 16 in a single nine-over spell. The tourists had raised 53 inside ten overs before Waqar Younis broke through, but slipped to 60 for three when Horne was run out in a mix-up. Then Shoaib struck in each of his first three overs. He beat the Kiwis in the air, touching 97mph and disturbing the furniture of four batsmen; Pakistan romped home with 20 overs in hand. Earlier, Yousuf Youhana clobbered 14 fours and a six in his second century in five days, after the Sharjah Cup final. As at Sharjah, he shared a big stand with Younis Khan, this time 161, which was halted for 20 minutes when Adams was hit by a projectile in the field. Abdul Razzaq slapped two sixes in an 18-ball 30 to round off a total of 275.

Man of the Match: Shoaib Akhtar.

Pakistan

Imran Nazir c Butler b Tuffey	7	Wasim Akram c Hart b Oram		8
Shahid Afridi c McMillan b Tuffey	1	†Rashid Latif not out		0
Yousuf Youhana c Walker b Oram	125			
Inzamam-ul-Haq c sub (J. E. C. Franklin)				
b Butler	18	L-b 7, w 3, n-b 7		17
Younis Khan c Vincent b Butler	69	1/15 2/15 3/49 (6 wkts, 50 overs)		275
Abdul Razzaq not out	30	4/210 5/247 6/270		

Saqlain Mushtaq, *Waqar Younis and Shoaib Akhtar did not bat.

Bowling: Tuffey 6–1–24–2; Adams 10–1–41–0; Butler 7–0–49–2; Oram 9–3–51–2; Walker 5–0–28–0; Harris 6–0–34–0; McMillan 5–0–28–0; Astle 2–0–13–0.

New Zealand

M. J. Horne run out	. . . .	22	A. R. Adams b Shoaib Akhtar	 2
N. J. Astle b Waqar Younis	. . . .	25	B. G. K. Walker b Shoaib Akhtar	 8
L. Vincent lbw b Wasim Akram		5	D. R. Tuffey not out	 18
*C. D. McMillan c Saqlain Mushtaq			I. G. Butler b Shoaib Akhtar	 0
b Shoaib Akhtar .		8		
C. Z. Harris c Younis Khan			B 1, l-b 8, w 3, n-b 5	 17
b Saqlain Mushtaq .		17		
J. D. P. Oram b Shoaib Akhtar	. . . .	0	1/53 2/59 3/60	(30 overs) 122
†R. G. Hart c Rashid Latif			4/72 5/74 6/77 7/92	
b Shoaib Akhtar .		0	8/92 9/105	

Bowling: Wasim Akram 7–2–26–1; Waqar Younis 6–0–32–1; Abdul Razzaq 4–1–17–0; Shoaib Akhtar 9–1–16–6; Saqlain Mushtaq 4–0–22–1.

Umpires: S. A. Bucknor (West Indies) and Nadeem Ghauri.
Third umpire: Aleem Dar.   Referee: M. J. Procter (South Africa).

†PAKISTAN v NEW ZEALAND

Second One-Day International

At Rawalpindi, April 24 (day/night). Pakistan won by three wickets. Toss: New Zealand.

Despite the bad news that a knee injury had curtailed Astle's tour, New Zealand looked like levelling the series here. After Fleming, back from a stomach upset, chose to bat, McMillan stroked 105 in 116 balls, his highest one-day international score. He had solid support from Horne and Adams. All the home bowlers struggled for accuracy, and Shoaib Akhtar went wicketless. Then Imran Nazir fell first ball in Pakistan's reply, and Yousuf Youhana followed next over. But Shahid Afridi blasted 40 from 37 balls, and half-centuries from Younis Khan and Abdul Razzaq helped Pakistan reach their third-highest total chasing, and an unassailable 2–0 lead, with 17 deliveries to spare. Razzaq struck a career-best 86 from 84 balls.

Man of the Match: Abdul Razzaq.

New Zealand

C. J. Nevin b Abdul Razzaq	. . . .	23	L. Vincent not out	 7
M. J. Horne lbw b Wasim Akram	. . . .	62	S. B. Styris not out	 1
C. D. McMillan c sub (Shoaib Malik)				
b Waqar Younis .		105	B 8, l-b 12, w 4, n-b 2	 26
A. R. Adams b Wasim Akram	. . . .	45		
J. D. P. Oram c sub (Shoaib Malik)			1/44 2/140 3/232	(5 wkts, 50 overs) 277
b Waqar Younis .		8	4/259 5/272	

*S. P. Fleming, †R. G. Hart, B. G. K. Walker and D. R. Tuffey did not bat.

Bowling: Wasim Akram 10–0–58–2; Waqar Younis 10–1–45–2; Abdul Razzaq 7–0–33–1; Shoaib Akhtar 10–1–51–0; Saqlain Mushtaq 8–0–47–0; Shahid Afridi 5–0–23–0.

Pakistan

Imran Nazir lbw b Tuffey	. . . .	0	Wasim Akram run out	 6
Shahid Afridi lbw b Styris	. . . .	40	Saqlain Mushtaq not out	 5
Yousuf Youhana b Adams	. . . .	3	L-b 4, w 4, n-b 6	 14
Younis Khan b Walker	. . . .	70		
Abdul Razzaq b Styris	. . . .	86	1/0 2/6 3/79	(7 wkts, 47.1 overs) 278
Inzamam-ul-Haq b Adams	. . . .	26	4/172 5/218	
†Rashid Latif not out	. . . .	28	6/252 7/261	

*Waqar Younis and Shoaib Akhtar did not bat.

Bowling: Tuffey 8–0–61–1; Adams 10–0–58–2; Oram 7.5–1–39–0; Styris 10–0–53–2; Walker 7–0–37–1; McMillan 4–0–23–0; Vincent 0.2–0–3–0.

Umpires: S. A. Bucknor (West Indies) and Aleem Dar.
Third umpire: Asad Rauf.   Referee: M. J. Procter (South Africa).

†PAKISTAN v NEW ZEALAND

Third One-Day International

At Lahore, April 27 (day/night). Pakistan won by 66 runs. Toss: Pakistan.

Shoaib Akhtar ostensibly broke the 100mph barrier when he clocked 161kph on a sponsor's speed gun. But the TV gun was not working, and in any case the ICC described speed records as "pretty unofficial". Previously, the fastest delivery on record was bowled by Australia's Jeff Thomson, timed at 99.8mph in the nets in 1975-76. Shoaib still failed to add to his six wickets at Karachi. Pakistan's victory owed more to Shoaib Malik, one of three home players introduced for the final game. First, Malik ran up 115, his highest international score, with 12 fours in 142 balls; he added 93 with Yousuf Youhana, who dashed to 53 in 51 balls. Then, Malik scooped three for 37, also a career-best, as New Zealand slumped to their seventh successive one-day defeat by Pakistan. Two days earlier, Malik had been married in a ceremony conducted by telephone. His bride was studying in Saudi Arabia, and he had met her during the ARY Gold Cup at Sharjah a year earlier.

Man of the Match: Shoaib Malik.

Pakistan

Shoaib Malik c Butler b Adams	115	Younis Khan not out		4
Shahid Afridi c Horne b Adams	18			
Yousuf Youhana c and b Walker	53	W 2, n-b 1		3
Inzamam-ul-Haq c Tuffey b Walker	35			
Misbah-ul-Haq c Butler b Tuffey	28	1/26 2/119 3/191	(5 wkts, 50 overs)	278
Abdul Razzaq not out	22	4/250 5/262		

†Rashid Latif, *Waqar Younis, Mohammad Sami and Shoaib Akhtar did not bat.

Bowling: Tuffey 8–2–29–1; Adams 8–0–57–2; Styris 9–0–65–0; Butler 10–0–46–0; Harris 5–0–32–0; Walker 10–0–49–2.

New Zealand

C. J. Nevin b Waqar Younis	2	A. R. Adams b Shoaib Malik		1
M. J. Horne b Abdul Razzaq	28	B. G. K. Walker run out		10
C. D. McMillan c Inzamam-ul-Haq b Mohammad Sami	38	D. R. Tuffey run out		0
		I. G. Butler not out		2
*S. P. Fleming b Shoaib Malik	15	B 3, l-b 10, w 5, n-b 10		28
†L. Vincent b Shahid Afridi	32			
S. B. Styris st Rashid Latif b Shoaib Malik	19	1/7 2/71 3/83	(45.4 overs)	212
C. Z. Harris lbw b Mohammad Sami	37	4/121 5/142 6/165		
		7/169 8/194 9/195		

Bowling: Waqar Younis 5–1–22–1; Shoaib Akhtar 4–0–23–0; Mohammad Sami 8.4–0–42–2; Abdul Razzaq 8–0–38–1; Shoaib Malik 10–0–37–3; Shahid Afridi 10–0–37–1.

Umpires: S. A. Bucknor (West Indies) and Aleem Dar.
Third umpire: Nadeem Ghauri.   Referee: M. J. Procter (South Africa).

PAKISTAN v NEW ZEALAND

First Test Match

At Lahore, May 1, 2, 3. Pakistan won by an innings and 324 runs. Toss: Pakistan. Test debut: R. G. Hart.

In three days, Pakistan recorded the fifth-biggest victory in Test cricket, thanks to two outstanding performances: a triple-century from Inzamam-ul-Haq, and six for 11 from Shoaib Akhtar. Both were hobbling by the end of the second day – Inzamam from cramp, Shoaib after spraining an ankle.

But New Zealand were the real casualties. It was all downhill for them after the opening over, when Shahid Afridi gave the new wicket-keeper, Robbie Hart, his first Test dismissal. From then on, both seamers and spinners wilted on the docile pitch as temperatures soared. The first day was dominated by centuries from Imran Nazir, recalled for his first Test in 17 months, and Inzamam. Nazir reached three figures with his third six, just before tea, and they had put on 204 together in just under four hours when he was spectacularly caught by the diving Richardson at mid-on. Inzamam completed his 16th Test hundred in the next over with a crisp four off Vettori. He struck the ball delightfully, driving and cutting at every opportunity, as he added 94 with Yousuf Youhana; his only blemish in a power-packed innings came on 110, when he drove Vettori uppishly but was dropped by Vincent.

Inzamam continued with his usual flamboyance on the second day, advancing to his second double-hundred in Tests shortly before lunch. He had begun to suffer from cramp, and was allowed to use a runner for three overs before the interval; afterwards, the privilege was withdrawn. Struggling to run singles and twos, Inzamam made up for it by hitting more loose deliveries to the fence, or over it. He was 250 when Saqlain was seventh out, after a partnership of 111, but hurried on, pushing a single to cover off Harris after tea to reach Pakistan's second triple-century in Tests, following Hanif Mohammad's 337 against West Indies at Bridgetown in 1957-58. His first 100 had come in 191 balls, the second in 132, and the third, which contained seven fours and four sixes, at a run a ball. After adding 78 with Shoaib Akhtar – a ninth-wicket record for Pakistan against New Zealand – he hit three sixes in an over from Brooke Walker's leg-breaks and was caught at long-on attempting a fourth. Last out, he had made 329, the tenth-highest score in Test history, in a stay of 579 minutes and 436 balls, from which he smashed 38 fours and nine sixes.

MOST RUNS FROM BOUNDARIES IN A TEST INNINGS

	4s/6s			
238	52/5	J. H. Edrich (310*)	England v New Zealand at Leeds.	1965
206	**38/9**	**Inzamam-ul-Haq (329)**	**Pakistan v New Zealand at Lahore**.	**2002**
196	34/10	W. R. Hammond (336*)	England v New Zealand at Auckland.	1932-33
190	43/3	G. A. Gooch (333)	England v India at Lord's	1990
184	46/–	D. G. Bradman (334)	Australia v England at Leeds.	1930
184	43/2	D. G. Bradman (304)	Australia v England at Leeds.	1934
180	45/–	B. C. Lara (375)	West Indies v England at St John's.	1993-94
178	**28/11**	**N. J. Astle (222)**	**New Zealand v England at Christchurch**. . . .	**2001-02**

Now it was Shoaib's turn. He did not bowl flat out, as in the one-day series, but controlled his line and length, occasionally slipping in one at a brisker pace. His lethal yorkers claimed four for four in 25 balls – all bowled – to leave New Zealand reeling on 21 for four. Shoaib sprained an ankle, losing his balance in his follow-through, and was absent at the start of the third morning. But he limped back on to finish the innings with two more wickets in eight deliveries, without conceding another run, for a career-best six for 11 from only 8.2 overs. It took his tally for the season to 23 wickets in five Tests at an average of 16.65 and a strike rate of 30. The tourists sank from their overnight 58 for six to 73 all out, the lowest total in Tests at Lahore, and followed on a massive 570 behind.

Shoaib did not return and, despite losing Horne in the first over, New Zealand looked more confident. They were a respectable 186 for three on the third evening, thanks to a captain's innings from Fleming, supported by Vincent and Harris. But the last seven wickets toppled for 60 in 20 overs. Danish Kaneria took his fourth five-for in eight Tests with his bouncy leg-breaks.

It was Pakistan's biggest Test victory, surpassing an innings and 264 against Bangladesh in August, and New Zealand's heaviest defeat. Fleming called it "a tough day in the office", admitting that his side were "outplayed and outclassed".

Man of the Match: Inzamam-ul-Haq.

Close of play: First day, Pakistan 355-4 (Inzamam-ul-Haq 159); Second day, New Zealand 58-6 (Hart 2, Vettori 0).

Pakistan

Imran Nazir c Richardson b McMillan . .	127
Shahid Afridi c Hart b Tuffey	0
Younis Khan c Fleming b Vettori.	27
Inzamam-ul-Haq c Tuffey b Walker . . .	329
Yousuf Youhana c Fleming b Martin . . .	29
Abdul Razzaq lbw b Tuffey	25
†Rashid Latif c and b Harris	7
Saqlain Mushtaq b McMillan	30
*Waqar Younis c and b McMillan	10

Shoaib Akhtar st Hart b Walker 37
Danish Kaneria not out 4

B 1, l-b 8, w 1, n-b 8 18

643

1/1 (2) 2/57 (3) 3/261 (1)
4/355 (5) 5/384 (6) 6/399 (7)
7/510 (8) 8/534 (9)
9/612 (10) 10/643 (4)

Bowling: Tuffey 25–7–94–2; Martin 31–12–108–1; Vettori 40–4–178–1; Walker 14.5–3–97–2; Harris 29–3–109–1; McMillan 18–1–48–3.

New Zealand

M. H. Richardson b Shoaib Akhtar	8	– c Rashid Latif b Saqlain Mushtaq . .	32
M. J. Horne b Shoaib Akhtar	4	– c Rashid Latif b Waqar Younis . . .	0
L. Vincent c Rashid Latif b Danish Kaneria	21	– c Rashid Latif b Danish Kaneria . .	57
*S. P. Fleming b Shoaib Akhtar	2	– c sub (Mohammad Sami)	
		b Danish Kaneria .	66
C. Z. Harris b Shoaib Akhtar	2	– lbw b Abdul Razzaq	43
C. D. McMillan c Shahid Afridi			
b Saqlain Mushtaq .	15	– lbw b Danish Kaneria	2
†R. G. Hart lbw b Waqar Younis.	4	– b Danish Kaneria	0
D. L. Vettori c Waqar Younis b Saqlain Mushtaq	7	– c sub (Shoaib Malik)	
		b Abdul Razzaq .	5
B. G. K. Walker lbw b Shoaib Akhtar	0	– not out	15
D. R. Tuffey not out	6	– c Younis Khan b Danish Kaneria . .	12
C. S. Martin b Shoaib Akhtar	0	– c sub (Shoaib Malik)	
		b Saqlain Mushtaq .	0
L-b 1, n-b 3	4	B 4, l-b 6, n-b 4	14

1/12 (2) 2/17 (1) 3/19 (4) 4/21 (5)   73
5/53 (6) 6/57 (3) 7/66 (8)
8/67 (7) 9/73 (9) 10/73 (11)

1/3 (2) 2/69 (1) 3/101 (3)   246
4/186 (5) 5/193 (6) 6/193 (7)
7/204 (8) 8/227 (4)
9/245 (10) 10/246 (11)

Bowling: *First Innings*—Waqar Younis 10–6–21–1; Shoaib Akhtar 8.2–4–11–6; Danish Kaneria 6–1–19–1; Saqlain Mushtaq 6–1–21–2. *Second Innings*—Waqar Younis 9–1–38–1; Abdul Razzaq 14–2–47–2; Danish Kaneria 32–3–110–5; Saqlain Mushtaq 17.3–3–38–2; Shahid Afridi 4–1–3–0.

Umpires: S. A. Bucknor (West Indies) and R. E. Koertzen (South Africa).
Third umpire: Aleem Dar. Referee: M. J. Procter (South Africa).

PAKISTAN v NEW ZEALAND

Second Test Match

At Karachi, May 8. Cancelled.

The match was called off two hours before the start, after a car bomb killed 14 people in front of the teams' hotel. The players had been minutes away from boarding their coaches for the National Stadium. It was agreed by all parties that New Zealand should abandon the tour and return home at once.

THE NEW ZEALANDERS IN THE WEST INDIES, 2002

By TONY COZIER

On three previous tours of the Caribbean, New Zealand had won none of their 11 Tests (though they had managed a creditable eight draws) and only two of ten one-day internationals. According to Stephen Fleming, the images New Zealanders had of West Indian cricket were of "guys being hit on the helmet, broken bones, and fire and brimstone".

The reality turned out quite different on this brief two-Test tour, but the odds had already shifted. At home in 1999-2000, New Zealand had soundly beaten West Indies in both Tests and all five one-dayers. They entered this series ranked third in the ICC Test Championship; West Indies were sixth.

Although they had defeated India 2–1 in the preceding Test series, and beat New Zealand 3–1 in their one-day games, West Indies' captain, Carl Hooper, publicly asserted, on the eve of the First Test, that his players were fatigued after successive series in Sri Lanka, Sharjah and against India. It was hardly a rallying call. New Zealand won the Bridgetown Test in four days; then, at Test cricket's newest venue in Grenada, they overcame a few alarms on an easy-paced pitch to earn the draw and a historic series victory.

Under Fleming's astute direction, the New Zealanders disregarded the one-day setback to turn their attention to the subsequent Tests, while the West Indians, judging by their approach in the first innings of the series, made no adjustment to the change in codes. Out to a spate of ill-judged shots, they were dismissed for 107 in 42.1 overs, conceding a lead of 230, from which there was no way back. Beaten by the convincing margin of 204 runs on the ground where they had lost only three of 38 previous Tests, West Indies had one chance, at Grenada, to get back on even terms. They enjoyed the better of the match, but their determined opponents held on.

It was New Zealand, not West Indies, who possessed the fire and brimstone this time. Shane Bond, recovered from the foot injury that ruled him out against England, was consistently clocked at over 90mph, and two five-wicket returns in the Tests earned him the Man of the Series award. Ian Butler, aged 20 and in his first international season, gave him aggressive support. No helmets were hit or bones broken, but stumps and pads were.

In the absence of two stalwarts – Chris Cairns, their class all-rounder, through his usual knee injury, and the wicket-keeper Adam Parore, just retired after 78 Tests – New Zealand instantly discovered two worthy replacements. Scott Styris had an outstanding all-round tour. His one-day form earned him promotion to the Test squad, and he celebrated his debut at Grenada with scores of 107 and 69 not out which were essential in protecting New Zealand's series lead. The new wicket-keeper, Robbie Hart, proved his temperament with resolute and timely innings in both Tests.

West Indies' wear and tear was reflected in the back strain that struck down their main bowler, Merv Dillon, in the First Test, and the decline of Cameron Cuffy. Pedro Collins, the left-arm swing bowler, capably filled the breach, but the bowling lacked the penetration to capitalise on strong positions.

Chris Gayle dominated the one-day series with his punishing left-handed batting and tight off-spin bowling, and maintained his form in the Tests. His second-innings 73 could not save the First Test, but his rousing 204 gave West Indies a chance of victory in the Second. For New Zealand, Mark Richardson, a left-handed opener in a different mould, had a consistent series, and Fleming scored an important hundred at Bridgetown, but the batting on both sides was generally disappointing. Hooper averaged only 13, and was widely criticised for his persistence in inserting the opposition, even on the lifeless pitch at Grenada.

Planned as an appendage to the Indian tour, and staged later than any previous Tests in the West Indies, the series had to compete with the televised counter-attraction of the football World Cup. While there were the usual good attendances at the one-day internationals, especially at St Lucia's new stadium and in St Vincent, there were fewer than 3,000 spectators each day at Bridgetown, and even Grenada's inaugural Test failed to bring out the locals in their expected numbers.

NEW ZEALAND TOURING PARTY

S. P. Fleming (Wellington) (*captain*), N. J. Astle (Canterbury), S. E. Bond (Canterbury), I. G. Butler (Northern Districts), C. Z. Harris (Canterbury), R. G. Hart (Northern Districts), M. J. Horne (Auckland), C. D. McMillan (Canterbury), C. S. Martin (Canterbury), M. H. Richardson (Otago), S. B. Styris (Northern Districts), D. R. Tuffey (Northern Districts), D. L. Vettori (Northern Districts), L. Vincent (Auckland).

M. N. Hart (Northern Districts), P. A. Hitchcock (Wellington), C. J. Nevin (Wellington) and J. D. P. Oram (Central Districts) were in the party for the one-day series; for the Tests, they were replaced by R. G. Hart, Martin and Richardson.

Coach: D. J. Aberhart.   *Manager:* J. J. Crowe.

NEW ZEALAND TOUR RESULTS

Test matches – Played 2: Won 1, Drawn 1.
One-day internationals: Played 5: Won 1, Lost 3, No result 1.
Other non-first-class match: Won v University of the West Indies Vice-Chancellor's XII.

Note: Matches in this section which were not first-class are signified by a dagger.

†At Sir Frank Worrell Cricket Ground, Kingston, June 3. **New Zealanders won by 85 runs** (D/L method). Toss: New Zealanders. **New Zealanders 254** (50 overs) (S. P. Fleming 64, C. J. Nevin 32, C. Z. Harris 33, S. B. Styris 64 not out; J. J. C. Lawson three for 60); **University of the West Indies Vice-Chancellor's XII 155** (40 overs) (D. J. Pagon 43; D. L. Vettori three for 24).

Each side fielded 12 players, of whom 11 could bat and 11 field. The Vice-Chancellor's XII's target was revised to 241 from 45 overs.

†WEST INDIES v NEW ZEALAND

First One-Day International

At Kingston, June 5. No result. Toss: New Zealand. International debut: P. A. Hitchcock.

Heavy rain, which had flooded Jamaica and washed away Kingston's two one-day internationals against India in the previous fortnight, returned as New Zealand walked out to field. It saved them from defending a modest total, which betrayed their lack of match practice as well as a pitch that had been sweating under the covers. They struggled to 37 for four in 16 overs, but McMillan held firm, adding 67 in the next 17 with Vincent.

New Zealand

*S. P. Fleming c R. O. Hinds b Dillon	0	D. R. Tuffey c Chanderpaul b R. O. Hinds	1
N. J. Astle c Hooper b Dillon	1	S. E. Bond not out	19
†C. J. Nevin c Sarwan b Cuffy	8	P. A. Hitchcock b Gayle	7
C. D. McMillan c Gayle b R. O. Hinds	69	B 2, l-b 7, w 5, n-b 5	19
C. Z. Harris c Collins b Gayle	8		
L. Vincent lbw b Cuffy	20	1/1 2/5 3/14	(49.4 overs) 176
S. B. Styris c and b Collins	9	4/37 5/104 6/132	
D. L. Vettori b Gayle	15	7/134 8/135 9/155	

Bowling: Dillon 10–1–34–2; Cuffy 10–1–28–2; Collins 10–1–31–1; Gayle 9.4–2–26–3; Hooper 6–0–29–0; R. O. Hinds 4–0–19–2.

West Indies

C. H. Gayle, W. W. Hinds, R. R. Sarwan, B. C. Lara, *C. L. Hooper, S. Chanderpaul, †R. D. Jacobs, R. O. Hinds, M. Dillon, P. T. Collins and C. E. Cuffy.

Umpires: E. A. R. de Silva (Sri Lanka) and B. R. Doctrove.
Third umpire: E. A. Nicholls.   Referee: Wasim Raja (Pakistan).

†WEST INDIES v NEW ZEALAND

Second One-Day International

At Gros Islet, St Lucia, June 8. West Indies won by six wickets. Toss: West Indies.

West Indies inaugurated St Lucia's new stadium, built on a former cattle pasture under the Beausejour hills at Gros Islet, with an exciting last-over victory. New Zealand made another faltering start: Dillon bowled Astle with his sixth delivery, and Collins took three wickets in his first nine. But Fleming stabilised the innings with Vincent, then supported the aggressive Styris in a stand of 91 off 106 balls. Styris struck three sixes and seven fours, scoring at more than a run a ball, as the last ten overs yielded 76. West Indies' response was built around Chanderpaul's unbeaten 108, which anchored three successive half-century partnerships. He had scored both his previous one-day international hundreds as an opener, and the decision to reprise the role after 13 months paid off handsomely before Lara hit the winning boundary with five balls to spare. Paul Hitchcock's impressive medium-pace earned three wickets in his first bowl in an international.

Man of the Match: S. Chanderpaul.

New Zealand

*S. P. Fleming b Gayle	89	D. L. Vettori not out	13
N. J. Astle b Dillon	2	D. R. Tuffey not out	4
†C. J. Nevin c Jacobs b Collins	15	L-b 3, w 4	7
C. D. McMillan b Collins	0		
C. Z. Harris lbw b Collins	0	1/3 2/53 3/55	(7 wkts, 50 overs) 248
L. Vincent b R. O. Hinds	33	4/55 5/112	
S. B. Styris b Dillon	85	6/203 7/235	

S. E. Bond and P. A. Hitchcock did not bat.

Bowling: Dillon 10–2–60–2; Cuffy 7–0–43–0; Collins 9–2–33–3; Gayle 10–0–48–1; Hooper 4–0–15–0; R. O. Hinds 10–0–46–1.

West Indies

C. H. Gayle c Vettori b Tuffey	30	B. C. Lara not out		9
S. Chanderpaul not out	108	L-b 1, w 4, n-b 4		9
R. R. Sarwan b Hitchcock	44			
*C. L. Hooper b Hitchcock	47	1/55 2/141	(4 wkts, 49.1 overs)	250
†R. D. Jacobs c Vettori b Hitchcock	3	3/225 4/233		

W. W. Hinds, R. O. Hinds, M. Dillon, P. T. Collins and C. E. Cuffy did not bat.

Bowling: Tuffey 8.1–1–36–1; Bond 9–0–59–0; Hitchcock 10–0–43–3; Vettori 10–0–54–0; Harris 10–1–39–0; Styris 2–0–18–0.

Umpires: R. E. Koertzen (South Africa) and E. A. Nicholls.
Third umpire: B. R. Doctrove. Referee: Wasim Raja (Pakistan).

†WEST INDIES v NEW ZEALAND

Third One-Day International

At Gros Islet, St Lucia, June 9. West Indies won by seven wickets. Toss: New Zealand.

West Indies took an unbeatable 2–0 lead with a much more comfortable victory. They had ten overs in hand and, to the delight of a capacity crowd of 14,000, Lara batted as freely as he did all season to finish on 59 not out. New Zealand had made a solid base of 69 for one in 16 overs. Then three wickets in 18 balls from Collymore's steady medium-pace and Gayle's off-spin forced Vincent and Harris to take greater care in rebuilding: their partnership of 90 required 23 overs. West Indies, chasing a target of 211, were never pressed, and New Zealand suffered their eighth defeat in eight completed one-day internationals.

Man of the Match: B. C. Lara.

New Zealand

*S. P. Fleming lbw b Gayle	34	M. N. Hart c Hooper b Collins		12
N. J. Astle lbw b Dillon	12	D. R. Tuffey not out		3
†C. J. Nevin lbw b Collymore	20	L-b 6, w 4, n-b 3		13
C. D. McMillan c Collins b Gayle	5			
L. Vincent not out	60	1/25 2/69 3/69	(7 wkts, 50 overs)	210
C. Z. Harris c Sarwan b Dillon	50	4/74 5/164		
S. B. Styris b Collymore	1	6/168 7/201		

P. A. Hitchcock and I. G. Butler did not bat.

Bowling: Dillon 10–0–40–2; Collins 9–0–44–1; Collymore 10–2–36–2; Gayle 10–1–34–2; Hooper 5–0–21–0; R. O. Hinds 6–0–29–0.

West Indies

C. H. Gayle b Hitchcock	37	R. O. Hinds not out		18
S. Chanderpaul c Hitchcock b Harris	30	L-b 1, w 15, n-b 9		25
R. R. Sarwan lbw b Harris	42			
B. C. Lara not out	59	1/63 2/79 3/156	(3 wkts, 40 overs)	211

*C. L. Hooper, W. W. Hinds, †R. D. Jacobs, M. Dillon, P. T. Collins and C. D. Collymore did not bat.

Bowling: Tuffey 6–0–32–0; Butler 5–0–44–0; Hitchcock 10–4–31–1; Styris 5–0–34–0; Harris 10–0–43–2; Hart 4–0–26–0.

Umpires: E. A. R. de Silva (Sri Lanka) and B. R. Doctrove.
Third umpire: E. A. Nicholls. Referee: Wasim Raja (Pakistan).

†WEST INDIES v NEW ZEALAND

Fourth One-Day International

At Port-of-Spain, June 12. New Zealand won by nine runs (D/L method). Toss: New Zealand.

Styris's stirring all-round performance sustained his side's interest in the series. He followed a forceful 63 not out with six wickets, the most taken by a New Zealander in a one-day international, and also ran out Cuffy. New Zealand's previous best analysis was Matt Hart's five for 22, also against West Indies, at Margao in 1994-95. Styris and Astle revived the innings from a shaky 90 for five, adding 122 before rain intervened. The Duckworth/Lewis method challenged West Indies to score the same as New Zealand off 11.2 fewer overs. Gayle hit a run-a-ball 60, but when Styris claimed six of the first seven wickets, West Indies were 62 short of their target. Jacobs scored a frenetic 60 off 45 balls to keep the series alive into the last over.

Man of the Match: S. B. Styris.

New Zealand

*S. P. Fleming c Hooper b Dillon	4	S. B. Styris not out		63
N. J. Astle not out	91			
†C. J. Nevin b Dillon	13	L-b 5, w 13, n-b 3		21
C. D. McMillan c Jacobs b Cuffy	1			
L. Vincent c Hooper b Gayle	18	1/4 2/42 3/48	(5 wkts, 44.2 overs)	212
C. Z. Harris c and b Gayle	1	4/76 5/90		

D. L. Vettori, D. R. Tuffey, P. A. Hitchcock and S. E. Bond did not bat.

Bowling: Dillon 6–1–26–2; Cuffy 8–1–40–1; Collymore 8–0–41–0; Gayle 7.2–0–30–2; Hooper 10–0–32–0; R. O. Hinds 5–0–38–0.

West Indies

C. H. Gayle c Harris b Styris	60	C. D. Collymore run out		8
S. Chanderpaul b Hitchcock	14	C. E. Cuffy run out		0
B. C. Lara c Nevin b Styris	0	M. Dillon not out		1
*C. L. Hooper c Bond b Styris	24	B 3, l-b 5, w 7, n-b 3		18
R. R. Sarwan b Styris	2			
†R. D. Jacobs not out	60	1/49 2/56 3/97	(9 wkts, 33 overs)	202
W. W. Hinds c Astle b Styris	4	4/103 5/114 6/128		
R. O. Hinds c Bond b Styris	11	7/150 8/193 9/193		

Bowling: Tuffey 4–0–29–0; Bond 6–0–43–0; Hitchcock 7–1–29–1; Styris 7–0–25–6; Vettori 3–0–27–0; Harris 3–0–18–0; Astle 3–0–23–0.

Umpires: R. E. Koertzen (South Africa) and E. A. Nicholls.
Third umpire: B. R. Doctrove. Referee: Wasim Raja (Pakistan).

†WEST INDIES v NEW ZEALAND

Fifth One-Day International

At St Vincent, June 16. West Indies won by four wickets. Toss: New Zealand.

West Indies clinched the series off the last ball amid confusion and controversy. They needed 15 off the final over, which had to be bowled by Tuffey after a scoring muddle misled Fleming into believing his preferred choice, Hitchcock, had not been bowled out. Tuffey's first two balls yielded a single and a bye; then Chanderpaul, just back from hospital after an X-ray on his arm, which had been struck by Bond, hit three fours and the winning single, which would have reached the boundary too but for the charge of the celebrating crowd. Fleming and Nevin had set New Zealand on the way to their second-highest total against West Indies, adding 89 – including 26 in one over from Collins. Then McMillan and Vincent maintained the momentum with 139 in 22 overs. Gayle, who claimed four wickets, launched West Indies' reply with another half-century; the middle order kept them on course until Chanderpaul provided the breathtaking finish.

Man of the Match: C. H. Gayle.   *Man of the Series:* C. H. Gayle.

New Zealand

*S. P. Fleming b Collins	65	S. E. Bond c Collins b Gayle	1
N. J. Astle c Jacobs b Collins	1	D. R. Tuffey not out	0
†C. J. Nevin c Hooper b Gayle	30		
C. D. McMillan c and b Hooper	83	B 2, l-b 6, w 7, n-b 9	24
L. Vincent b Gayle	55		
S. B. Styris c Chanderpaul b Gayle	2	1/3 2/92 3/112 (8 wkts, 50 overs) 291
C. Z. Harris not out	29	4/251 5/254 6/273	
D. L. Vettori b Hooper	1	7/280 8/285	

P. A. Hitchcock did not bat.

Bowling: Cuffy 8–0–45–0; Collins 10–1–64–2; Collymore 4–1–23–0; Hooper 10–0–48–2; Gayle 10–0–54–4; R. O. Hinds 8–0–49–0.

West Indies

C. H. Gayle c Harris b Vettori	67	W. W. Hinds not out	18
S. Chanderpaul not out	28	R. O. Hinds b Bond	4
B. C. Lara c and b Harris	47	B 7, l-b 6, w 8, n-b 6	27
*C. L. Hooper c Fleming b Hitchcock	45		
R. R. Sarwan c Tuffey b Bond	52	1/127 2/163 3/219 (6 wkts, 50 overs) 292
†R. D. Jacobs c McMillan b Styris	4	4/235 5/260 6/274	

C. D. Collymore, C. E. Cuffy and P. T. Collins did not bat.

Chanderpaul, when 13, retired hurt at 60 and resumed at 274.

Bowling: Bond 10–3–41–2; Tuffey 5–0–48–0; Hitchcock 10–0–55–1; Styris 9–1–43–1; Harris 9–0–46–1; Vettori 7–0–46–1.

Umpires: E. A. R. de Silva (Sri Lanka) and B. R. Doctrove.
Third umpire: E. A. Nicholls.   Referee: Wasim Raja (Pakistan).

WEST INDIES v NEW ZEALAND

First Test Match

At Bridgetown, June 21, 22, 23, 24. New Zealand won by 204 runs. Toss: West Indies. Test debut: D. B. Powell.

New Zealand's first Test victory in the Caribbean, in their 12th match, was a comprehensive one, completed inside four days. It was particularly satisfying for Fleming, whose first-day century underpinned his 17th Test win as captain – exactly one third of New Zealand's 51 victories. The defeat was West Indies' fourth in 39 Tests at Kensington Oval; only England, in 1934-35 and 1993-94, and Australia, in 1994-95, had ever beaten them there. Perhaps the perceptive Barbadian public sensed trouble: no more than 3,000 attended any day.

The outcome was all but settled on the second afternoon when West Indies' reckless batsmen collapsed for 107, their lowest total at Bridgetown since they slumped to 102 against England on an uncovered, rain-affected pitch in that 1934-35 defeat. They conceded a first-innings lead of 230 but, with time on his side, Fleming did not bother to enforce the follow-on.

On the first afternoon, Fleming had to lead New Zealand out of their own middle-order slump, when four wickets fell for 29. Hart, the wicket-keeper playing his second Test, lent unfussy but vital support in a stand of 108, as Fleming completed his fourth Test hundred; after hitting 20 fours in 277 minutes, he top-edged a cut to slip nine overs from the close. Hart survived to add another 112 for the last four wickets, guaranteeing a solid total.

The West Indians quickly had their backs to the wall. Gayle and Sarwan fell to successive balls from Bond, and only Chanderpaul was inclined to put up a fight. He batted for just over two hours before running out of partners. Apart from Lara, who played on to Vettori, all the wickets were caught, most of them from attacking shots.

Fleming chose to bat again but, at 88 for five early on the third afternoon, New Zealand seemed likely to fall some way short of setting the unassailable target they wanted. It took a counter-attack by Astle, who hit 29 off a three-over spell from Sanford and added 76 with Fleming, batting down the order because of a stiff neck, to put them back on track. West Indies were handicapped by a recurring back injury that restricted Dillon to six overs; the debutant Darren Powell, recalled from the A-team tour of England, shared the new ball with Collins, who stepped into the breach to return his best Test figures, six for 76. By the time Collins wound up the innings, however, New Zealand led by 473, with just over two days remaining. It was not so much whether they would win, but when.

West Indies did bat more sensibly second time round. Gayle put on 68 with Hinds, and 65 with Sarwan. But once Bond broke through in a pacy second spell – when Sarwan, for the second time in the match, mistimed a hook – only Lara's flailing 73 delayed New Zealand's celebrations unduly. Bond returned with the second new ball and rounded off the match with three wickets, including Lara, in 12 deliveries. It was his first return of five in a Test innings, and brought New Zealand their historic victory with ten overs of the fourth day to go.

Man of the Match: S. P. Fleming.

Close of play: First day, New Zealand 257-6 (Hart 34, Vettori 21); Second day, New Zealand 4-1 (Vincent 1, Tuffey 1); Third day, West Indies 5-0 (Gayle 0, Hinds 4).

New Zealand

M. H. Richardson b Sanford	41	– c Lara b Collins	0
L. Vincent c Jacobs b Dillon	14	– lbw b Collins	2
*S. P. Fleming c Gayle b Hooper	130	– (7) c Hinds b Sanford	34
C. Z. Harris c Lara b Collins	0	– lbw b Powell	19
N. J. Astle c Lara b Dillon	2	– c Lara b Collins	77
C. D. McMillan lbw b Sanford	6	– c Hooper b Collins	1
†R. G. Hart not out	57	– (8) c Hinds b Collins	24
D. L. Vettori c Hinds b Collins	39	– (9) b Sanford	11
D. R. Tuffey lbw b Powell	28	– (3) c Gayle b Hooper	31
S. E. Bond b Powell	5	– not out	6
I. G. Butler run out	3	– c Jacobs b Collins	26
L-b 8, n-b 4	12	L-b 8, w 1, n-b 3	12
	337		**243**

1/38 (2) 2/88 (1) 3/89 (4) 4/106 (5)
5/117 (6) 6/225 (3) 7/278 (8)
8/323 (9) 9/333 (10) 10/337 (11)

1/0 (1) 2/11 (2) 3/48 (4) 4/69 (3)
5/88 (6) 6/164 (5) 7/181 (7)
8/205 (9) 9/213 (8) 10/243 (11)

Bowling: First Innings—Dillon 28–6–73–2; Collins 24–5–80–2; Powell 21–6–41–2; Sanford 28.4–7–101–2; Hooper 13–5–21–1; Gayle 10–3–12–0; Sarwan 1–0–1–0. *Second Innings*—Collins 30.4–8–76–6; Powell 20–4–61–1; Dillon 6–3–11–0; Sanford 17–5–68–2; Hooper 17–8–19–1.

West Indies

C. H. Gayle c Vettori b Bond	3	– lbw b Bond	73
W. W. Hinds c McMillan b Tuffey	10	– c Richardson b Vettori	37
R. R. Sarwan c Butler b Bond	0	– c Vettori b Bond	18
B. C. Lara b Vettori	28	– b Bond	73
*C. L. Hooper c Tuffey b Butler	6	– c Fleming b Tuffey	16
S. Chanderpaul not out	35	– c Fleming b Vettori	17
†R. D. Jacobs c Astle b Vettori	4	– c Astle b Vettori	6
P. T. Collins c Vincent b Butler	8	– (9) lbw b Bond	8
A. Sanford c Hart b Butler	1	– (10) not out	0
D. B. Powell c Harris b Vettori	0	– (8) c Astle b Butler	2
M. Dillon c Fleming b Vettori	0	– c Vincent b Bond	0
L-b 4, n-b 8	12	B 5, l-b 11, w 2, n-b 1	19
	107		**269**

1/6 (1) 2/6 (3) 3/31 (2) 4/47 (5)
5/62 (4) 6/73 (7) 7/90 (8)
8/93 (9) 9/103 (10) 10/107 (11)

1/68 (2) 2/133 (3) 3/142 (1)
4/179 (5) 5/204 (6) 6/216 (7)
7/222 (8) 8/252 (9)
9/269 (4) 10/269 (11)

Bowling: First Innings—Bond 12–1–34–2; Tuffey 7–3–16–1; Butler 11–2–26–3; Vettori 12.1–1–27–4. *Second Innings*—Bond 21–7–78–5; Tuffey 15–5–43–1; Butler 14–0–58–1; Vettori 19–3–53–3; Astle 5–4–4–0; Harris 9–3–17–0.

Umpires: R. E. Koertzen (South Africa) and S. Venkataraghavan (India).
Third umpire: B. R. Doctrove. Referee: Wasim Raja (Pakistan).

WEST INDIES v NEW ZEALAND

Second Test Match

At St George's, Grenada, June 28, 29, 30, July 1, 2. Drawn. Toss: West Indies. Test debut: S. B. Styris.

New Zealand were made to fight for the draw that guaranteed them victory in this brief series. Their hero was Styris, who marked his Test debut with a hundred – batting at No. 8 – to lead them out of trouble on the second day, and an unbeaten 69 on the last which, along with Hart and rain, staved off a late West Indian bid for victory.

Hooper won his sixth toss in the home season's seven Tests and, for the fifth time, chose to bowl; for the fourth time, the opposition responded by totalling over 300. The foundations were laid in a 123-run partnership between Richardson and Astle. Then Collins, taking the new ball, removed Richardson, on 95, when his top-edged hook was athletically caught by Gayle at long leg. Collins added the night-watchman in the closing over of the day and Astle with his first ball next morning. That left New Zealand an uncertain 208 for six, the cue for Styris's entrance. When he was last out to a wild shot 165 runs later, he had made 107 from 178 balls – the seventh New Zealander to score a Test century on debut. Hart and Bond provided stout support.

The West Indian response was based on Gayle's belligerent double-hundred. It featured strokes of breathtaking power, including huge sixes off Butler and Bond, and four consecutive fours, of 29 all told, in Butler's first over with the second new ball. Gayle reached his second Test century in 212 balls, ran up the next 100 in 115, and faced 332 in all, in eight hours. But he had some luck: an escape at 93 when umpire Venkat ruled not out on an edge off Butler, and missed chances off Bond at 136 and 199. He shared stands of 100 with Sarwan and 143 with Chanderpaul before he finally fell to Bond, who added Chanderpaul with his second delivery next morning. Bond finished with five victims for the second time in a week, and the tail had carried the lead to 97.

Richardson and Vincent, who was missed twice in the slips off Collins on two, erased the deficit. Then the spinners threatened to turn the game. In a couple of hours either side of the fourth-day close, they claimed five wickets for 40 on a wearing but slow pitch to give West Indies a scent of victory. New Zealand were only 60 ahead with half the side out, and McMillan was being held in reserve after a hand injury in the field required three stitches. He was not needed. Styris and Hart calmed nerves in a stand of 99 interrupted only by rain sweeping across the ground from the eastern hills. It permitted only 23 overs after lunch, and the match was safe.

Crowds at the Queen's Park Stadium, Test cricket's 84th and newest venue, gradually grew over the five days to three-quarters of its 14,000 capacity. But Hooper was moved to quip that he suspected the lifeless pitch had been transplanted from the cemetery overlooking the ground, which made it all the stranger that he had seemed so reluctant to bat on it.

Man of the Match: C. H. Gayle.   *Man of the Series:* S. E. Bond.

Close of play: First day, New Zealand 208-5 (Astle 69, McMillan 1); Second day, West Indies 63-1 (Gayle 23, Sarwan 22); Third day, West Indies 394-5 (Chanderpaul 51, Jacobs 2); Fourth day, New Zealand 139-2 (Richardson 69, Harris 6).

New Zealand

M. H. Richardson c Gayle b Collins	95	– c Jacobs b Nagamootoo	71
L. Vincent b Cuffy	24	– b Sarwan	54
*S. P. Fleming c Lara b Collins	6	– c Lara b Hooper	5
C. Z. Harris c Jacobs b Hooper	0	– c Sarwan b Nagamootoo	17
N. J. Astle lbw b Collins	69	– c Hinds b Hooper	0
D. L. Vettori c Jacobs b Collins	1		
C. D. McMillan c Lara b Cuffy	14		
S. B. Styris b Sanford	107	– (6) not out	69
†R. G. Hart c Hinds b Hooper	20	– (7) not out	28
S. E. Bond lbw b Chanderpaul	17		
I. G. Butler not out	5		
L-b 6, w 2, n-b 7	15	L-b 7, n-b 5	12

1/61 (2) 2/81 (3) 3/82 (4) 4/205 (1)   373   1/117 (2) 2/132 (3)   (5 wkts) 256
5/206 (6) 6/208 (5) 7/256 (7)   3/148 (1) 4/149 (5)
8/312 (9) 9/361 (10) 10/373 (8)   5/157 (4)

Bowling: *First Innings*—Collins 30–9–68–4; Cuffy 35–12–76–2; Sanford 22.5–4–74–1; Nagamootoo 33–9–88–0; Hooper 25–3–44–2; Gayle 3–1–5–0; Chanderpaul 4–0–12–1. *Second Innings*—Collins 17–7–28–0; Cuffy 10–3–20–0; Nagamootoo 42–16–75–2; Sanford 14–3–27–0; Hooper 34–10–66–2; Gayle 6–2–7–0; Sarwan 6–0–26–1; Chanderpaul 2–2–0–0.

West Indies

C. H. Gayle c Hart b Bond	204	
W. W. Hinds b Bond	10	
R. R. Sarwan run out	39	
B. C. Lara c Hart b Styris	48	
*C. L. Hooper lbw b Bond	17	
S. Chanderpaul c Fleming b Bond	51	
†R. D. Jacobs c Styris b Butler	17	
M. V. Nagamootoo c Hart b Styris	32	
P. T. Collins lbw b Vettori	14	

A. Sanford c Butler b Bond	12
C. E. Cuffy not out	0
B 4, l-b 2, w 5, n-b 15	26
	470

1/28 (2) 2/128 (3) 3/204 (4) 4/242 (5) 5/385 (1) 6/394 (6) 7/441 (7) 8/448 (8) 9/470 (9) 10/470 (10)

Bowling: Bond 30.1–7–104–5; Butler 21–4–83–1; Styris 25–3–88–2; Vettori 41–9–134–1; Astle 6–2–15–0; Harris 15–4–40–0.

Umpires: R. E. Koertzen (South Africa) and S. Venkataraghavan (India).
Third umpire: B. R. Doctrove.   Referee: Wasim Raja (Pakistan).

THE BANGLADESHIS IN SRI LANKA, 2002

By SA'ADI THAWFEEQ

Bangladesh had played a single Test in Colombo the previous September, as part of the Asian Test Championship, when the Sri Lankan captain, Sanath Jayasuriya, showed how he rated them by ordering two of his batsmen to retire out when they had scored enough runs. Returning in July for a two-match series, Bangladesh still seemed to be regarded as little more than practice material. After a full-strength side had won Sri Lanka's biggest ever victory in the First Test, the selectors controversially decided to rest seven players, including Muttiah Muralitharan, who had just taken ten wickets, and Aravinda de Silva, who had scored a double-hundred in what proved to be his final Test. Jayasuriya protested, especially at the omission of Murali, and the sports minister, Johnston Fernando, expressed his disappointment, but declined to intervene as he had done in a similar case six months earlier.

Even against a mostly second-string team, Bangladesh failed to last the distance, losing the Second Test by 288 runs inside four days. That stretched their Test record to 12 defeats from 13 matches. Although Sri Lanka themselves had had to wait 14 Tests for their first victory, and the record remains New Zealand's 45, it reinforced the argument that the ICC might have been premature in granting Bangladesh full Test status.

It was a useful tonic for Sri Lanka, however, who were keen to get back to winning ways after a disastrous tour of England. By the end of the series, they had won ten home Tests on the trot. They went on to sweep the board in the shorter version of the game, winning all three one-day internationals, though a lack of public enthusiasm for these easy pickings – Bangladesh suffered their 50th defeat in 53 one-day internationals – was reflected in poor crowds for most of the tour, even when entry was free. The tourists were offered one consolation at the end of the one-day games when their captain, Khaled Masud, was named Man of the Series for his tidy wicket-keeping and consistent batting.

BANGLADESHI TOURING PARTY

Khaled Masud (Rajshahi) (*captain*), Habibul Bashar (Khulna) (*vice-captain*), Akram Khan (Chittagong), Alamgir Kabir (Rajshahi), Alok Kapali (Sylhet), Al Sahariar (Dhaka), Aminul Islam (Dhaka), Ehsanul Haque (Chittagong), Enamul Haque (Chittagong), Fahim Muntasir (Dhaka), Hannan Sarkar (Barisal), Manjurul Islam (Khulna), Mohammad Ashraful (Dhaka), Talha Jubair (Dhaka), Tapash Baisya (Sylhet), Tareq Aziz (Chittagong), Tushar Imran (Khulna).

Alok Kapali and Tapash Baisya arrived in time for the Second Test. Khaled Mahmud, Mohammad Rafiq and Naimur Rahman (all Dhaka) replaced Akram Khan, Alamgir Kabir, Aminul Islam, Enamul Haque, Talha Jubair and Tareq Aziz for the one-day series.

Coach: Mohsin Kamal. *Manager:* Mohammad Haque.

Cricket manager: Abu Sharif Mahmood Faruque. *Physiotherapist:* J. Gloster.

BANGLADESHI TOUR RESULTS

Test matches – Played 2: Lost 2.
First-class matches – Played 4: Lost 2, Drawn 2.
Losses – Sri Lanka (2)
Draws – Sri Lanka A, BCCSL Academy XI.
One-day internationals – Played 3: Lost 3.

Note: Matches in this section which were not first-class are signified by a dagger.

At Moratuwa, July 12, 13, 14. **Drawn.** Toss: Bangladeshis. **Sri Lanka A 382 for nine dec.** (J. Mubarak 42, T. M. Dilshan 136, A. S. Polonowita 34, K. S. Lokuarachchi 45, K. R. Pushpakumara 32; Alamgir Kabir three for 84, Fahim Muntasir three for 69) **and 168 for seven dec.** (G. I. Daniel 34, H. A. P. W. Jayawardene 49, M. Pushpakumara 38); **Bangladeshis 228** (Hannan Sarkar 92, Habibul Bashar 31, Khaled Masud 43 not out; M. Pushpakumara three for 43) **and 201 for five** (Al Sahariar 42, Ehsanul Haque 100 not out).

Khaled Masud, the Bangladeshi captain, withdrew on the final day in order to fly to London for the ICC Test captains' meeting. Tushar Imran was allowed to play as a full batting substitute.

At Nondescripts Cricket Club, Colombo, July 16, 17, 18. **Drawn.** Toss: BCCSL Academy XI. **Bangladeshis 195** (Habibul Bashar 34, Aminul Islam 39, Enamul Haque 40; K. H. R. K. Fernando three for 28, M. K. G. C. P. Lakshitha four for 16, N. S. Rupasinghe three for 38) **and 243 for nine** (Hannan Sarkar 43, Habibul Bashar 42, Aminul Islam 66; N. S. Rupasinghe three for 34); **BCCSL Academy XI 342** (S. Kalawithigoda 58, C. U. Jayasinghe 101, S. H. T. Kandamby 33, Extras 32; Alamgir Kabir three for 84, Talha Jubair three for 85).

SRI LANKA v BANGLADESH

First Test Match

At P. Saravanamuttu Stadium, Colombo, July 21, 22, 23. Sri Lanka won by an innings and 196 runs. Toss: Sri Lanka. Test debuts: W. R. S. de Silva; Alamgir Kabir, Ehsanul Haque, Hannan Sarkar, Talha Jubair.

Inspired by a swansong from Aravinda de Silva, Sri Lanka improved on their biggest Test victory for the third time in 11 months – they had beaten Bangladesh by an innings and 137 runs in September, and Zimbabwe by an innings and 166 in December. De Silva had been absent then, but Muralitharan played a leading role in both games. This time, on his comeback after a shoulder injury, he took five wickets in each innings. That brought him level with Richard Hadlee's record of 36 returns of five or more in a Test innings, though Hadlee had used 86 Tests to Muralitharan's 76. It was the 11th time Murali had taken ten or more in a match, beating Hadlee's nine.

The venue was Muralitharan's club ground, the P. Saravanamuttu Stadium, which welcomed the return of Test cricket after an eight-year lapse. Sri Lanka had played their inaugural Test here, against England in February 1982, and claimed their maiden Test win, against India three and a half years later.

Hannan Sarkar, one of four debutants for Bangladesh, made a fine start, scoring 55 in 69 balls. He and Habibul Bashar had taken the total to 107 for two just before lunch, but Sarkar was trapped by Jayasuriya's first delivery, and Muralitharan snapped up Habibul in the next over. After a lengthy rain-break, the Bangladeshis were shot out for 161 before the close.

Because of the time lost, an extra hour was added to the second day. Sri Lanka made full use of it, scoring 509 in 104 overs, a Test record for a single side in a day's play. Previously, only England had scored 500 in a day, totalling 503 in 111 overs against South Africa at Lord's in 1924. De Silva led the onslaught. In a year of rapid double-centuries, he completed 200 in 229 balls, the fourth-quickest in Test cricket. He had reached his 20th Test century in 136 balls, with his 15th four, and struck another 13 fours plus a six, lifted over mid-wicket, batting 234 balls and

318 minutes in all. It was his second Test double, after 267 in Wellington 11 years before, but this turned out to be his farewell appearance in Test cricket; he did not play in the next game, and later announced that he would be available only for one-day internationals in future.

Sri Lanka had stuttered early on, losing three wickets in five overs. But de Silva added 150 with Sangakkara and 234 with Jayasuriya. Hitting freely for six sixes, Jayasuriya raced to 145, his tenth Test hundred, in 164 balls. He and de Silva were finally halted by the left-arm spin of Enamul Haque, and Sri Lanka declared at an overnight 541 for nine.

Trailing by 380, Bangladesh fared slightly better second time around. Their other opener, Al Sahariar, defied the attack for more than two and a half hours. But once again Muralitharan provided their death knell, supported brilliantly by the close cordon: Sangakkara, who had passed the wicket-keeper's gloves to Prasanna Jayawardene, held four catches, including Sahariar, at silly point. De Silva claimed the final wicket before tea on the third day.

Man of the Match: M. Muralitharan.

Close of play: First day, Sri Lanka 32-0 (Atapattu 20, Arnold 10); Second day, Sri Lanka 541-9 (T. C. B. Fernando 31, W. R. S. de Silva 5).

Bangladesh

Hannan Sarkar lbw b Jayasuriya	55	– lbw b W. R. S. de Silva	1
Al Sahariar lbw b W. R. S. de Silva	13	– c Sangakkara b Muralitharan	67
Ehsanul Haque b C. R. D. Fernando	2	– c T. C. B. Fernando b C. R. D. Fernando	5
Habibul Bashar lbw b Muralitharan	24	– b Muralitharan	34
Akram Khan c H. A. P. W. Jayawardene b T. C. B. Fernando	20	– c Sangakkara b Muralitharan	5
Aminul Islam c Arnold b Muralitharan	0	– c Sangakkara b Muralitharan	0
*†Khaled Masud c Jayasuriya b Muralitharan	23	– c T. C. B. Fernando b P. A. de Silva	26
Enamul Haque st H. A. P. W. Jayawardene b Muralitharan	1	– b C. R. D. Fernando	22
Manjurul Islam b T. C. B. Fernando	0	– c Sangakkara b Muralitharan	2
Alamgir Kabir b Muralitharan	0	– b W. R. S. de Silva	0
Talha Jubair not out	0	– not out	5
B 8, l-b 4, w 1, n-b 10	23	L-b 5, w 1, n-b 11	17
	161		**184**

1/32 (2) 2/50 (3) 3/107 (1) 4/111 (4)
5/111 (6)6/148 (7) 7/151 (8)
8/156 (9) 9/161 (5) 10/161 (10)

1/2 (1) 2/14 (3) 3/91 (4)
4/113 (5) 5/113 (6) 6/124 (2)
7/158 (8) 8/161 (9)
9/166 (10) 10/184 (7)

Bowling: *First Innings*—T. C. B. Fernando 10–3–38–2; W. R. S. de Silva 13–3–31–1; C. R. D. Fernando 10–3–40–1; Muralitharan 19.4–6–39–5; Jayasuriya 1–0–1–1. *Second Innings*—C. R. D. Fernando 11–4–24–2; W. R. S. de Silva 11–1–35–2; T. C. B. Fernando 7–2–34–0; Muralitharan 25–6–59–5; Jayasuriya 10–2–20–0; P. A. de Silva 2.3–1–7–1.

Sri Lanka

M. S. Atapattu b Talha Jubair	20	M. Muralitharan c Al Sahariar b Enamul Haque	0
R. P. Arnold c sub (Fahim Muntasir) b Manjurul Islam	25	C. R. D. Fernando c Habibul Bashar b Enamul Haque	15
K. C. Sangakkara run out	75	W. R. S. de Silva not out	5
D. P. M. D. Jayawardene b Talha Jubair	0	L-b 6, w 2, n-b 6	14
P. A. de Silva lbw b Enamul Haque	206		
*S. T. Jayasuriya c sub (Mohammad Ashraful) b Enamul Haque	145	1/35 (1) 2/49 (2) (9 wkts. dec.) 541
†H. A. P. W. Jayawardene c Al Sahariar b Manjurul Islam	5	3/56 (4) 4/206 (3) 5/440 (5) 6/447 (7)
T. C. B. Fernando not out	31	7/491 (6) 8/491 (9) 9/524 (10)

Bowling: Manjurul Islam 25–1–128–2; Talha Jubair 21–0–120–2; Alamgir Kabir 15–1–82–0; Enamul Haque 38–6–144–4; Habibul Bashar 9–0–43–0; Ehsanul Haque 3–0–18–0.

Umpires: S. A. Bucknor (West Indies) and D. R. Shepherd (England).
Third umpire: T. H. Wijewardene. Referee: Wasim Raja (Pakistan).

SRI LANKA v BANGLADESH

Second Test Match

At Sinhalese Sports Club, Colombo, July 28, 29, 30, 31. Sri Lanka won by 288 runs. Toss: Bangladesh. Test debuts: M. K. G. C. P. Lakshitha, J. Mubarak, M. N. Nawaz; Alok Kapali, Tapash Baisya, Tushar Imran.

Jayasuriya began the match thoroughly unhappy with the team the selectors had given him – he said he had never seen some of them in action before. But he finished it full of praise for the youngsters, especially the swing bowler Lakshitha (also known as Chamila Gamage) and Michael Vandort, an opening batsman. The Sri Lankan selectors had made seven changes and introduced three new players, Lakshitha and left-hand batsmen Jehan Mubarak and Naveed Nawaz. Bangladesh fielded another three debutants, bringing their total in the series to seven.

Bangladesh's batsmen did little better than in the First Test, but at least their bowlers had the satisfaction of bowling out Sri Lanka in the first innings, for 373 – it was only the third time in Sri Lanka's last ten home Tests that they had not reached 500. The new opening pair, Vandort and Mubarak, gave them a solid start, Jayasuriya plundered a swift 85, and Lakshitha, batting at No. 11, hit 40 in 46 balls.

Lakshitha, a lean bowler from the Air Force club, went on to make history as the first Sri Lankan to claim a wicket with his maiden delivery in Test cricket. Coming on second change in an inexperienced attack, he bowled Mohammad Ashraful with an in-swinger in the ninth over. On the second evening, Tapash Baisya reached an unbeaten 52 in his first Test innings, which almost got Bangladesh past the follow-on target. But Sri Lanka chose not to enforce the follow-on anyway, preferring to give their new top order another outing. It enabled Vandort, a tall left-hander who had played one previous Test, also against Bangladesh, in September, to complete a maiden Test century. His controlled 140 featured 17 fours and a six, and he added 172 in 165 minutes with Nawaz.

Jayasuriya declared at tea on the third day, leaving Bangladesh the unlikely task of chasing 473, or surviving seven sessions. Mohammad Ashraful reached 75, the top score by any Bangladesh batsman in this series, but the end came swiftly after that. Sujeewa de Silva, a left-arm seamer in his second Test, and the off-spinner Samaraweera sent the last six wickets tumbling for 17, and they shared eight between them to complete the victory inside four days. It was the first time Sri Lanka had won a Test without Muralitharan since his debut in August 1992. Of their 32 Test victories, he had contributed to all but three.

Man of the Match: M. G. Vandort.

Close of play: First day, Sri Lanka 301-8 (Fernando 2, de Silva 1); Second day, Sri Lanka 25-0 (Vandort 18, Mubarak 2); Third day, Bangladesh 103-4 (Mohammad Ashraful 31, Alok Kapali 3).

Sri Lanka

M. G. Vandort lbw b Alok Kapali	61	– b Talha Jubair	140
J. Mubarak lbw b Tapash Baisya	24	– run out	31
M. N. Nawaz c Khaled Masud b Fahim Muntasir	21	– not out	78
H. P. Tillekeratne c and b Fahim Muntasir	18	– not out	5
*S. T. Jayasuriya c Khaled Masud b Manjurul Islam	85		
T. T. Samaraweera c Habibul Bashar b Manjurul Islam	58		
†H. A. P. W. Jayawardene c Khaled Masud b Manjurul Islam	0		
U. D. U. Chandana c Habibul Bashar b Alok Kapali	20		
T. C. B. Fernando not out	29		
W. R. S. de Silva c Khaled Masud b Talha Jubair	5		
M. K. G. C. P. Lakshitha c Alok Kapali b Talha Jubair	40		
B 1, l-b 5, n-b 6	12	B 4, l-b 1, w 1, n-b 3	9
	373	**(2 wkts dec.)**	**263**

1/60 (2) 2/90 (3) 3/131 (1) 4/133 (4)   373   1/80 (2) 2/252 (1)   (2 wkts dec.) 263
5/260 (5) 6/260 (7) 7/298 (8)
8/298 (6) 9/309 (10) 10/373 (11)

Bowling: *First Innings*—Manjurul Islam 23–4–46–3; Talha Jubair 21.4–3–74–2; Tapash Baisya 12–1–69–1; Fahim Muntasir 18–3–46–2; Alok Kapali 29–2–122–2; Habibul Bashar 3–1–10–0. *Second Innings*—Manjurul Islam 9–0–28–0; Talha Jubair 14–1–52–1; Alok Kapali 11–0–54–0; Tapash Baisya 8–0–40–0; Fahim Muntasir 19–3–56–0; Habibul Bashar 5–0–28–0.

Bangladesh

Hannan Sarkar lbw b Fernando	5	– c Jayawardene b de Silva		30
Al Sahariar c Jayawardene b Jayasuriya	12	– b de Silva		6
Habibul Bashar lbw b Fernando	11	– c Jayawardene b Lakshitha		3
Mohammad Ashraful b Lakshitha	1	– c Mubarak b Samaraweera		75
Tushar Imran lbw b Lakshitha	8	– st Jayawardene b Chandana		28
*†Khaled Masud c Tillekeratne b Samaraweera	15	– (7) not out		13
Alok Kapali lbw b Jayasuriya	39	– (6) c Mubarak b Samaraweera		23
Fahim Muntasir c and b Samaraweera	7	– (9) lbw b de Silva		1
Tapash Baisya not out	52	– (8) c Chandana b de Silva		3
Manjurul Islam c Jayawardene b Jayasuriya	0	– c Tillekeratne b Samaraweera		0
Talha Jubair c Jayasuriya b Chandana	0	– c Mubarak b Samaraweera		0
L-b 4, n-b 10	14	L-b 1, n-b 1		2

1/20 (1) 2/28 (2) 3/31 (4) 4/43 (3)   164   1/27 (2) 2/36 (3) 3/40 (1)   184
5/51 (5) 6/72 (6) 7/86 (8)   4/99 (5) 5/167 (6) 6/168 (4)
8/123 (11) 9/163 (10) 10/164 (11)   7/171 (8) 8/175 (9)
    9/184 (10) 10/184 (11)

Bowling: *First Innings*—Fernando 15–3–36–2; de Silva 11–2–45–0; Jayasuriya 7–2–17–3; Lakshitha 12–5–33–2; Samaraweera 12–3–18–2; Chandana 5–1–11–1. *Second Innings*—Fernando 5–2–12–0; de Silva 13–5–35–4; Lakshitha 12–2–48–1; Jayasuriya 9–4–14–0; Samaraweera 11.4–1–49–4; Chandana 10–3–25–1.

Umpires: S. A. Bucknor (West Indies) and D. R. Shepherd (England).
Third umpire: P. T. Manuel.   Referee: Wasim Raja (Pakistan).

†SRI LANKA v BANGLADESH

First One-Day International

At Sinhalese Sports Club, Colombo, August 4. Sri Lanka won by five wickets. Toss: Bangladesh. International debut: K. H. R. K. Fernando.

All the players rested for the Second Test returned to Sri Lanka's line-up, including Aravinda de Silva, whose last one-day international had been in New Zealand 18 months earlier. He was out for one, to a questionable catch behind the wicket, but it was a minor setback for his side. Jayasuriya rushed to 40 by their eighth over, and Atapattu, who had been opening with him since Romesh Kaluwitharana was axed in England, guided them home with a measured 83. Earlier, Bangladesh reached 226, their highest one-day total against Sri Lanka, thanks largely to a stand of 90 between 18-year-old Tushar Imran and the captain, Khaled Masud.

Man of the Match: M. S. Atapattu.

Bangladesh

Al Sahariar c Sangakkara		Naimur Rahman run out	3
b C. R. D. Fernando	25	Khaled Mahmud b C. R. D. Fernando	9
Mohammad Ashraful c K. H. R. K.		Mohammad Rafiq not out	11
Fernando b Muralitharan	36	Tapash Baisya not out	4
Habibul Bashar b Lakshitha	2		
Alok Kapali c Jayawardene		L-b 12, w 4, n-b 3	19
b K. H. R. K. Fernando	2		
Tushar Imran c Arnold b Muralitharan	61	1/38 2/52 3/62 (8 wkts, 50 overs) 226	
*†Khaled Masud c Jayasuriya		4/86 5/176 6/192	
b Lakshitha	54	7/209 8/209	

Manjurul Islam did not bat.

Bowling: Vaas 8–1–30–0; C. R. D. Fernando 10–1–33–2; Lakshitha 8–1–34–2; K. H. R. K. Fernando 5–1–24–1; Muralitharan 10–0–44–2; Jayasuriya 7–0–34–0; de Silva 2–0–15–0.

Sri Lanka

*S. T. Jayasuriya c Mohammad Ashraful b Tapash Baisya .	40	P. A. de Silva c Khaled Masud b Mohammad Rafiq . 1
M. S. Atapattu run out	83	K. H. R. K. Fernando not out 16
†K. C. Sangakkara c Naimur Rahman b Khaled Mahmud .	29	B 1, l-b 3, w 5, n-b 3 12
D. P. M. D. Jayawardene c Mohammad Rafiq b Khaled Mahmud .	18	1/56 2/112 3/151 (5 wkts, 44.4 overs) 228
R. P. Arnold not out	29	4/203 5/207

W. P. U. J. C. Vaas, M. Muralitharan, C. R. D. Fernando and M. K. G. C. P. Lakshitha did not bat.

Bowling: Manjurul Islam 6–0–37–0; Tapash Baisya 5–0–43–1; Khaled Mahmud 10–0–41–2; Mohammad Rafiq 10–0–37–1; Alok Kapali 10–0–37–0; Naimur Rahman 3.4–0–29–0.

Umpires: S. A. Bucknor (West Indies) and E. A. R. de Silva.
Third umpire: M. G. Silva. Referee: Wasim Raja (Pakistan).

†SRI LANKA v BANGLADESH

Second One-Day International

At Sinhalese Sports Club, Colombo, August 5. Sri Lanka won by eight wickets. Toss: Bangladesh.
Resuming at the same ground the next day, Bangladesh chose to bat again – but hit a new nadir when they were bowled out for 76, their lowest total in all international cricket. Their previous low in one-day games was 87 against Pakistan, and in Tests 90 against Sri Lanka in September 2001. Extras was the top-scorer, the 23rd such instance in one-day internationals, though Khaled Masud batted an hour before he was last out for 15. All the home bowlers had handsome figures, and Muralitharan's one wicket was his 279th at this level, edging him back past Shane Warne into fourth place in the all-time list. Sri Lanka knocked off the runs inside 16 overs; the entire match lasted less than 46.

Man of the Match: C. R. D. Fernando.

Bangladesh

Al Sahariar c and b C. R. D. Fernando . .	5	Khaled Mahmud c Atapattu b K. H. R. K. Fernando . 0
Mohammad Ashraful c Sangakkara b Vaas .	4	Mohammad Rafiq b Chandana 5
Habibul Bashar lbw b K. H. R. K. Fernando	10	Tapash Baisya c Vaas b Chandana 2
Alok Kapali c Jayasuriya b C. R. D. Fernando .	5	Manjurul Islam not out 0
Tushar Imran c Arnold b Muralitharan . .	10	B 4, l-b 9, w 7 20
*†Khaled Masud c Muralitharan b Chandana .	15	1/14 2/16 3/27 (30.1 overs) 76
Naimur Rahman c Sangakkara b K. H. R. K. Fernando .	0	4/40 5/50 6/51 7/55 8/61 9/67

Bowling: Vaas 6–1–9–1; C. R. D. Fernando 6–1–21–2; K. H. R. K. Fernando 6–2–12–3; Muralitharan 9–4–19–1; Chandana 3.1–1–2–3.

Sri Lanka

*S. T. Jayasuriya c Manjurul Islam b Tapash Baisya .	14	D. P. M. D. Jayawardene not out	27	
M. S. Atapattu not out	31	N-b 1	1	
†K. C. Sangakkara c Tapash Baisya b Mohammad Rafiq .	4	1/22 2/37	(2 wkts, 15.4 overs) 77	

R. P. Arnold, P. A. de Silva, K. H. R. K. Fernando, U. D. U. Chandana, W. P. U. J. C. Vaas, M. Muralitharan and C. R. D. Fernando did not bat.

Bowling: Manjurul Islam 4–1–13–0; Tapash Baisya 6–0–36–1; Mohammad Rafiq 3–0–16–1; Alok Kapali 1.4–0–11–0; Mohammad Ashraful 1–0–1–0.

Umpires: S. A. Bucknor (West Indies) and T. H. Wijewardene.
Third umpire: P. T. Manuel. Referee: Wasim Raja (Pakistan).

†SRI LANKA v BANGLADESH

Third One-Day International

At R. Premadasa Stadium, Colombo, August 7. Sri Lanka won by 58 runs. Toss: Bangladesh. International debut: P. W. Gunaratne.

A small crowd of schoolchildren and sponsors' guests saw Sri Lanka score the highest total of this series – 258. While Jayasuriya rested, de Silva opened with Atapattu, and escaped being run out twice on his way to 46. But Sri Lanka were only 115 for four by the 27th over, when Arnold and Dilshan launched a century partnership. Bangladesh were pushed on to the back foot from the start when Gunaratne and Lakshitha grabbed early wickets. Habibul Bashar and Khaled Masud raised them to 113, but did it slowly, and 101 from the last ten overs was far too tall a task. Muralitharan wrapped up a clean sweep for Sri Lanka with three wickets, including Habibul for 52.

Man of the Match: R. P. Arnold. *Man of the Series:* Khaled Masud.

Sri Lanka

*M. S. Atapattu c Khaled Mahmud b Tapash Baisya .	20	†T. M. Dilshan c Mohammad Rafiq b Mohammad Ashraful .	50	
P. A. de Silva c Alok Kapali b Khaled Mahmud .	46	K. H. R. K. Fernando not out	23	
K. C. Sangakkara c Alok Kapali b Manjurul Islam .	22	U. D. U. Chandana not out	4	
D. P. M. D. Jayawardene c Khaled Masud b Khaled Mahmud .	16	L-b 2, w 7, n-b 6	15	
R. P. Arnold c Khaled Masud b Khaled Mahmud .	62	1/39 2/82 3/114 4/115 5/215 6/248	(6 wkts, 50 overs) 258	

M. Muralitharan, M. K. G. C. P. Lakshitha and P. W. Gunaratne did not bat.

Bowling: Manjurul Islam 10–0–42–1; Tapash Baisya 7–0–41–1; Khaled Mahmud 10–0–51–3; Mohammad Rafiq 10–1–32–0; Alok Kapali 6–0–36–0; Habibul Bashar 2–0–20–0; Mohammad Ashraful 5–0–34–1.

Bangladesh

Hannan Sarkar lbw b Gunaratne	14	Mohammad Rafiq b Arnold	13	
Al Sahariar c Dilshan b Lakshitha	20	Tapash Baisya lbw b Muralitharan	3	
Mohammad Ashraful c Chandana b Fernando .	10	Manjurul Islam not out	0	
Habibul Bashar c Dilshan b Muralitharan .	52	L-b 1, w 3	4	
Tushar Imran b Gunaratne	0			
*†Khaled Masud run out	37	1/27 2/45 3/48	(47.2 overs) 200	
Alok Kapali lbw b Chandana	8	4/48 5/113 6/132		
Khaled Mahmud b Muralitharan	39	7/165 8/184 9/189		

Bowling: Gunaratne 9–0–39–2; Lakshitha 7–0–43–1; Fernando 8–1–18–1; Muralitharan 9.2–1–24–3; Chandana 9–0–45–1; Arnold 5–0–30–1.

Umpires: S. A. Bucknor (West Indies) and P. T. Manuel.
Third umpire: T. H. Wijewardene. Referee: Wasim Raja (Pakistan).

ENGLAND IN ZIMBABWE, 2001-02

By HUW TURBERVILL

Despite something of a renaissance in Test cricket, England's one-day performances remained abject during the first half of 2001: in June, they lost all six NatWest games against Pakistan and Australia, taking their run of defeats to 11. Towards the end of this humiliating sequence, and with the World Cup on the horizon, the coach, Duncan Fletcher, announced a brief limited-overs tour to his native Zimbabwe. The main aims were to build team spirit, determine which of the emerging talents would be ready for the World Cup, and decide which roles best suited the more established players. Confidence-boosting victories would be a welcome bonus.

England travelled to a country in turmoil. Seizures of land from white farmers and suppression of opposition leaders were continuing under the regime of Robert Mugabe. Some questioned the ethics of playing cricket against this backdrop, although the Zimbabwean team were not among them. Whatever the rights and wrongs, it made the practicalities difficult: arrangements were not finalised until the week before England arrived, and even the Barmy Army mostly stayed at home.

The rifts in Zimbabwean society were reflected in their cricket. The Zimbabwe Cricket Union and senior white players went into the series with conflicting agendas: the ZCU wanted to encourage black involvement and so strengthen the team in the long term; the established players were desperate to restore pride by competing on the day. As they lost match after match, Alistair Campbell claimed publicly that the side was being weakened by selection on race rather than merit, an outburst which later cost him his place. Add a pay dispute that led to threats of a strike, and a 5–0 reverse was not so surprising.

England, though, were able to concentrate on the cricket. Their top order – openers Marcus Trescothick and Nick Knight, and either Nasser Hussain or Mark Ramprakash at No. 3 – successfully tried out a more positive approach to the first 15 overs, rattling up starts of between 78 and 101 in each game. Knight's statistics were formidable: 302 runs at an average of 100 and a strike-rate of almost 77. However, questions about his technique would be definitively answered only by facing stronger opposition – as would doubts about Hussain's scoring-rate, which was 81 here, as opposed to 63 before this trip.

Having elected to miss the Test tour of India, Alec Stewart and Darren Gough were left at home. With Andrew Caddick rested and Ashley Giles injured, England had nine players with fewer than seven one-day caps. One of those, Matthew Hoggard, was the outstanding bowler on either side in his first one-day international series. He took ten wickets in four games with his big-hearted out-swing and conceded only 3.65 an over, showing how well acquainted he had become with African conditions after two winters with Free State. Jeremy Snape displayed the confidence developed during Gloucestershire's record-breaking run of one-day successes, bowling his off-spin notably slowly at around 40mph. But it was James Kirtley, picked for his Gough-like skiddiness, who occupied most column inches.

He hit the headlines after the first match, not for his debut figures of two for 33, but because his action had been questioned by the referee, Colonel Naushad Ali. This sparked an outcry, primarily because Ali had flouted established procedures by revealing his misgivings to a journalist rather than the ICC. He did eventually file an official report after the fourth match, and it led to Kirtley remodelling his action. In the interim, he remained free to play, and his non-selection for the third and fifth matches owed more to his lack of prowess with the bat than the furore over his action.

With James Foster, the 21-year-old Essex and Durham University wicket-keeper, no substitute for Stewart as a batsman, England were reluctant to play more than two of Kirtley, Hoggard, Chris Silverwood and Ryan Sidebottom for fear of further weakening the batting – which left them a specialist seamer short. Andrew Flintoff was never given his full allocation of overs and, although Ben Hollioake bowled more consistently than in the summer, the gap was often plugged by Ramprakash's off-spin. This proved only a temporary answer: his exclusion from the one-day squad for India and New Zealand indicated he had not done enough – perhaps paying the price for batting too much like his captain.

However, the true significance of England's performances was hard to gauge because of the disastrous weakness of Zimbabwe. The tale was familiar. Only the Flowers averaged over 30 with the bat and only Grant Flower and Gary Brent went for less than 4.5 an over with the ball. With the talented youngsters Tatenda Taibu and Hamilton Masakadza sitting school exams, the ZCU's aim of fielding three non-white players in each match weakened the team: Mluleki Nkala, Doug Hondo and Henry Olonga took one wicket between them, and all cost more than six an over. Crucially lacking was the team spirit that had so often made Zimbabwe sides greater than the sum of their parts. By the end of the series, their run of consecutive defeats stretched to 12 – worse than England's at the start. England, at least, had turned some sort of corner; for Zimbabwe, that corner would have to be found on a Bangladeshi field.

ENGLAND TOURING PARTY

N. Hussain (Essex) (*captain*), P. D. Collingwood (Durham), A. Flintoff (Lancashire), J. S. Foster (Essex), A. P. Grayson (Essex), M. J. Hoggard (Yorkshire), B. C. Hollioake (Surrey), R. J. Kirtley (Sussex), N. V. Knight (Warwickshire), M. R. Ramprakash (Surrey), O. A. Shah (Middlesex), R. J. Sidebottom (Yorkshire), C. E. W. Silverwood (Yorkshire), J. N. Snape (Gloucestershire), G. P. Thorpe (Surrey), M. E. Trescothick (Somerset).

J. Ormond (Leicestershire) and C. White (Yorkshire) were unfit and replaced before the tour by Silverwood and Thorpe.

Coach: D. A. G. Fletcher. *Operations manager:* P. A. Neale. *Assistant coach:* T. J. Boon. *Physiotherapist:* D. O. Conway. *Physiologist:* N. P. Stockill. *Media relations manager:* A. J. Walpole.

ENGLAND TOUR RESULTS

One-day internationals – Played 5: Won 5.
Other non-first-class match – Won v Zimbabwe A.

Note: Matches in this section were not first-class.

At Alexandra Sports Club, Harare, October 1. **England XI won by 138 runs.** Toss: England XI. **England XI 262 for eight** (50 overs) (G. P. Thorpe 95, B. C. Hollioake 61; S. M. Ervine three for 53); **Zimbabwe A 124** (44.1 overs) (B. G. Rogers 30; R. J. Kirtley three for 21).

Joining forces at 61 for five, Thorpe and Hollioake added 158 in 29 overs.

ZIMBABWE v ENGLAND

First One-Day International

At Harare, October 3. England won by five wickets. Toss: Zimbabwe. International debuts: J. S. Foster, R. J. Kirtley, J. N. Snape.

Zimbabwe had not won a one-day game for almost six months, and for England it was nearly a year – so something had to give. It turned out to be Zimbabwe. England's stand-in opening attack, Matthew Hoggard and James Kirtley, gave little away, Ramprakash's off-breaks claimed his first three wickets in one-day internationals, and Jeremy Snape frustrated the batsmen with flighted, genuinely slow bowling to have both Flowers stumped in the same over and win the match award on his first England appearance. The fielding, however, was shoddy. James Foster had a troubled debut behind the stumps: he dropped Ebrahim (skying a ball from Hoggard) and fumbled his stumping of Grant Flower. Andy Flower was dropped twice on his way to 59. After the early loss of Trescothick, Knight and Hussain savaged Hondo and Nkala, giving England the perfect platform with a second-wicket stand of 98. Ramprakash and the middle order were less convincing, and Hussain was disappointed not to win with greater assurance. During the game, the referee, Naushad Ali, cast doubt on Kirtley's action in comments to an English journalist, setting off a row that rumbled on throughout the series.

Man of the Match: J. N. Snape.

Zimbabwe

A. D. R. Campbell b Hoggard	3		G. B. Brent c Thorpe b Kirtley	3
*G. J. Whittall c Snape b Hoggard	13		D. T. Hondo not out	0
†A. Flower st Foster b Snape	59		L-b 6, w 6	12
S. V. Carlisle c Kirtley b Flintoff	37			
C. B. Wishart c Snape b Ramprakash	18		1/12 (1) 2/34 (2) 3/111 (4) (49.1 overs) 206
G. W. Flower st Foster b Snape	0		4/126 (3) 5/126 (6)
D. D. Ebrahim c Ramprakash b Kirtley	42		6/145 (5) 7/187 (8)
D. P. Viljoen b Ramprakash	18		8/201 (9) 9/204 (7)
M. L. Nkala c Hollioake b Ramprakash	1		10/206 (10) 15 overs: 45-2

Bowling: Hoggard 10–2–25–2; Kirtley 9.1–1–33–2; Hollioake 6–0–35–0; Trescothick 1–0–7–0; Flintoff 6–0–33–1; Snape 10–0–39–2; Ramprakash 7–0–28–3.

England

M. E. Trescothick c Campbell b Brent	4		A. Flintoff not out	16
N. V. Knight c Viljoen b Whittall	50		B 1, l-b 3, w 1	5
*N. Hussain b G. W. Flower	73			
M. R. Ramprakash b Viljoen	35		1/13 (1) 2/111 (2) (5 wkts, 46.4 overs) 210
G. P. Thorpe c G. W. Flower b Viljoen	13		3/144 (3) 4/176 (5)
B. C. Hollioake not out	14		5/187 (4) 15 overs: 78-1

J. N. Snape, †J. S. Foster, R. J. Kirtley and M. J. Hoggard did not bat.

Bowling: Hondo 6–0–35–0; Brent 10–3–29–1; Nkala 8.4–0–48–0; Whittall 7–1–32–1; Viljoen 10–0–44–2; G. W. Flower 5–0–18–1.

Umpires: I. D. Robinson and R. B. Tiffin.
Third umpire: M. A. Esat. Referee: Naushad Ali (Pakistan).

ZIMBABWE v ENGLAND

Second One-Day International

At Harare, October 6. England won by eight wickets. Toss: Zimbabwe.

Zimbabwe chose to bat again, but swapped their previous caution for recklessness. Once Hoggard had bowled Whittall and Andy Flower, the hosts showed self-destructive tendencies: the next four all fell to catches near the boundary, starting with Campbell, who ended an obdurate innings with an ill-advised pull. Viljoen batted competently at No. 10 to give Zimbabwe a glimmer. Kirtley's performance with the ball belied any anxiety over Naushad Ali's queries, and he should have had another wicket when Foster dropped Whittall. Hollioake used his in-ducker effectively, and Snape again showed intelligent variation of flight. In reply, Trescothick smashed a 35-ball 46, before Knight and Hussain guided England towards a comfortable win, which almost came in the 35 overs they had set themselves "to breed good habits", as Hussain put it. Zimbabwe's attack was desperately one-paced: Streak appeared overweight on his return, while Nkala's two overs cost 17.

Man of the Match: M. J. Hoggard.

Zimbabwe

A. D. R. Campbell c Hussain b Hollioake	49	D. P. Viljoen b Kirtley		18
G. J. Whittall b Hoggard	7	M. L. Nkala not out		6
†A. Flower b Hoggard	6	L-b 3, w 6		9
S. V. Carlisle c Trescothick b Ramprakash	40			
C. B. Wishart c Thorpe b Hoggard	34	1/27 (2) 2/40 (3) 3/83 (1)	(49.1 overs) 195	
G. B. Brent c Kirtley b Snape	11	4/128 (4) 5/152 (5)		
G. W. Flower c Knight b Snape	2	6/152 (6) 7/158 (7)		
D. D. Ebrahim c Foster b Flintoff	10	8/165 (9) 9/171 (8)		
*H. H. Streak b Hollioake	3	10/195 (10)	15 overs: 57-2	

Bowling: Hoggard 10–0–37–3; Kirtley 8.1–0–37–1; Flintoff 6–0–22–1; Hollioake 10–2–37–2; Snape 10–0–38–2; Ramprakash 5–0–21–1.

England

M. E. Trescothick c Ebrahim b Brent	46
N. V. Knight not out	82
*N. Hussain lbw b Streak	50
M. R. Ramprakash not out	6
L-b 3, w 7, n-b 2	12

1/72 (1) 2/184 (3)   (2 wkts, 37.3 overs) 196
15 overs: 90-1

G. P. Thorpe, B. C. Hollioake, A. Flintoff, J. N. Snape, †J. S. Foster, R. J. Kirtley and M. J. Hoggard did not bat.

Bowling: Streak 9.3–1–52–1; Brent 10–1–47–1; Nkala 2–0–17–0; Viljoen 8–0–39–0; Whittall 4–0–22–0; G. W. Flower 4–0–16–0.

Umpires: K. C. Barbour and M. A. Esat.
Third umpire: C. K. Nyazika.   Referee: Naushad Ali (Pakistan).

ZIMBABWE v ENGLAND

Third One-Day International

At Harare, October 7. England won by four wickets. Toss: Zimbabwe.

Thanks to a monumental innings by Andy Flower – his undefeated 142 matched the highest one-day score for Zimbabwe – this was much the best contest of the five. Even so, England clinched the series. Though Hussain lost his 12th consecutive toss, Zimbabwe made another poor start, with some abysmal shot selection in the face of another hostile spell from Hoggard, who took five wickets. This seemed only to deepen Flower's determination: he played magnificently, with 16 fours and a six in 128 balls, although there were ugly scenes when, on 99, he and Foster squared up after an appeal for a catch behind. Both players, and Hussain, were severely reprimanded by the referee, although the spat did not stop Flower joining the others at Essex in 2002. Streak made 56 in a stand of 130 with Flower, a seventh-wicket record in one-day internationals. But he injured his leg, needed a runner and left Zimbabwe a bowler short. Ramprakash responded with his most enterprising innings of the series. Pressure mounted after he was run out, but England's consistent middle order proved too strong. Collingwood and Flintoff milked the spinners, then Snape impressed with his perky batting and helped Hussain (dropping to No. 7 after injuring his calf) see England home.

Man of the Match: A. Flower.

Zimbabwe

A. D. R. Campbell lbw b Hoggard	. . . .	8	D. P. Viljoen c Thorpe b Hoggard	. . . . .	0
G. W. Flower c Flintoff b Hoggard	. . . .	1	G. B. Brent not out	. . . .	0
S. V. Carlisle c Knight b Sidebottom	. . .	1	L-b 5, w 10	. . . .	15
†A. Flower not out	. . . .	142			
C. B. Wishart c Snape b Hoggard	. . . .	4	1/2 (2) 2/7 (3)	(8 wkts, 50 overs)	261
D. D. Ebrahim st Foster b Collingwood	.	22	3/19 (1) 4/56 (5)		
D. A. Marillier run out	. . . .	12	5/95 (6) 6/127 (7)		
*H. H. Streak c Thorpe b Hoggard	. . . .	56	7/257 (8) 8/257 (9)	15 overs: 64-4	

H. K. Olonga did not bat.

Bowling: Hoggard 10–0–49–5; Sidebottom 8–0–42–1; Flintoff 7–1–43–0; Snape 10–0–47–0; Collingwood 9–0–45–1; Ramprakash 6–0–30–0.

England

M. E. Trescothick c A. Flower b Olonga	.	14	J. N. Snape not out	. . . .	24
N. V. Knight c Olonga b Marillier	. . . .	41			
M. R. Ramprakash run out	. . . .	47	L-b 3, w 13, n-b 5	. . . . . .	21
G. P. Thorpe c Wishart b G. W. Flower	.	8			
P. D. Collingwood c A. Flower b Brent	. .	36	1/28 (1) 2/95 (2)	(6 wkts, 47.3 overs)	265
A. Flintoff c Viljoen b G. W. Flower	. . .	46	3/108 (4) 4/126 (3)		
*N. Hussain not out	. . . .	28	5/198 (6) 6/214 (6)	15 overs: 88-1	

†J. S. Foster, R. J. Sidebottom and M. J. Hoggard did not bat.

Bowling: Olonga 9–0–60–1; Brent 8–0–53–1; Viljoen 10–0–58–0; Marillier 10–0–47–1; G. W. Flower 10–1–38–2; Ebrahim 0.3–0–6–0.

Umpires: C. K. Nyazika and I. D. Robinson.
Third umpire: D. Kalan. Referee: Naushad Ali (Pakistan).

ZIMBABWE v ENGLAND

Fourth One-Day International

At Bulawayo, October 10. England won by 70 runs. Toss: England. International debut: S. M. Ervine.

Having manoeuvred themselves into a position to assault England's total, Zimbabwe's inexperienced middle order lost their nerve. Injuries to Hussain and Streak meant Trescothick led England for the first time, only 16 months after his international debut, while Campbell became Zimbabwe's third captain of the series. Early pace from Friend could not prevent an opening stand of 101 in 15 overs, England's best start yet, as Trescothick and Knight were particularly hard on Olonga. But the occasional off-spin of Marillier – seven years after he broke both femurs in a car accident – reined England in and removed their top four. They still reached an imposing 280; Collingwood was especially strong off his legs, racing to 77 from 90 balls, with good support from Flintoff. In reply, Grant Flower (bouncing back from scores of 0, 2, and 1) and Wishart advanced to 169 for three with 15 overs left. However, the loss of Flower, whose 96 from 101 balls had the impetus, left his colleagues too much to do. Regular departures prevented acceleration, and Paul Grayson picked up his first England wickets with his left-arm spin a year after his surprise debut in Kenya.

Man of the Match: P. D. Collingwood.

England

*M. E. Trescothick c Carlisle b Marillier	52
N. V. Knight c A. Flower b Marillier . . .	49
M. R. Ramprakash b Marillier	17
O. A. Shah c A. Flower b Marillier	0
P. D. Collingwood run out	77
A. Flintoff c Brent b G. W. Flower	46
B. C. Hollioake b G. W. Flower	5
A. P. Grayson b Friend	6
†J. S. Foster not out	11

R. J. Kirtley b Brent	1
R. J. Sidebottom not out	2
B 1, l-b 6, w 6, n-b 1	14
1/101 (1) 2/113 (2) (9 wkts, 50 overs) 280	
3/113 (4) 4/144 (3)	
5/241 (6) 6/248 (7)	
7/261 (8) 8/276 (5)	
9/278 (10) 15 overs: 101-1	

Bowling: Friend 10–1–57–1; Brent 9–0–37–1; Ervine 7–0–54–0; Olonga 4–0–44–0; Marillier 10–0–38–4; G. W. Flower 10–0–43–2.

Zimbabwe

G. W. Flower st Foster b Grayson	96
*A. D. R. Campbell c Knight	
b Sidebottom .	6
S. V. Carlisle b Hollioake	28
†A. Flower c Foster b Hollioake	6
C. B. Wishart c Hollioake b Collingwood	30
D. D. Ebrahim c Flintoff b Grayson	11
D. A. Marillier c and b Grayson	0
S. M. Ervine c Foster b Flintoff	19
G. B. Brent run out	5

T. J. Friend b Flintoff	3
H. K. Olonga not out	1
B 1, l-b 4	5
1/32 (2) 2/86 (3) 3/94 (4) (44.3 overs) 210	
4/169 (1) 5/171 (5)	
6/172 (7) 7/200 (6)	
8/201 (8) 9/208 (9)	
10/210 (10) 15 overs: 75-1	

Bowling: Kirtley 7–0–24–0; Sidebottom 6–0–42–1; Hollioake 10–0–41–2; Flintoff 3.3–0–12–2; Grayson 10–0–40–3; Collingwood 6–0–31–1; Ramprakash 2–0–15–0.

Umpires: J. F. Fenwick and Q. J. Goosen.
Third umpire: C. K. Coventry.   Referee: Naushad Ali (Pakistan).

ZIMBABWE v ENGLAND

Fifth One-Day International

At Bulawayo, October 13. England won by seven wickets. Toss: Zimbabwe.

With Zimbabwe distracted by pay disputes and tensions over racial quotas, a 12th consecutive defeat was no surprise. None of the middle order managed to stay with Grant Flower long enough to set England a real challenge. Once again, Hoggard bowled a miserly spell, though it was Chris Silverwood, in his first match of the series, who removed Campbell and Carlisle in his first two overs. As so often, the onus fell on the overburdened Flower brothers. Grant reached a superb century in 133 balls but, moments later, a collapse began: six wickets went for 24, restricting Zimbabwe to an inadequate 228 on a good pitch. A confident England had picked just four specialist batsmen, and the experiment worked as they overhauled Zimbabwe with ease. Knight took his aggregate for the series to 302, while Collingwood again showed his on-side power, moving to 56 not out from 46 balls.

Man of the Match: N. V. Knight.   *Man of the Series:* N. V. Knight.

Zimbabwe

G. W. Flower b Flintoff		104
*A. D. R. Campbell c Foster b Silverwood		3
S. V. Carlisle c Ramprakash b Silverwood		0
†A. Flower c Knight b Hollioake		33
C. B. Wishart b Silverwood		26
D. D. Ebrahim b Snape		28
D. A. Marillier c Collingwood b Flintoff		4
S. M. Ervine run out		3
D. P. Viljoen c Trescothick b Snape		1
G. B. Brent not out		7
D. T. Hondo c Hollioake b Snape		5
L-b 11, w 1, n-b 2		14

1/5 (2) 2/7 (3) 3/77 (4)   (49.3 overs) 228
4/145 (5) 5/204 (6)
6/208 (1) 7/213 (7)
8/215 (8) 9/218 (9)
10/228 (11)   15 overs: 55-2

Bowling: Hoggard 8–1–28–0; Silverwood 9–0–43–3; Hollioake 10–0–34–1; Collingwood 6–0–36–0; Snape 8.3–0–43–3; Flintoff 8–0–33–2.

England

M. E. Trescothick c G. W. Flower b Marillier		29
N. V. Knight not out		80
*N. Hussain c Ebrahim b Viljoen		47
M. R. Ramprakash b G. W. Flower		6
P. D. Collingwood not out		56
B 5, l-b 2, w 2, n-b 2		11

1/47 (1) 2/134 (3)   (3 wkts, 43.4 overs) 229
3/151 (4)   15 overs: 90-1

A. Flintoff, B. C. Hollioake, J. N. Snape, †J. S. Foster, C. E. W. Silverwood and M. J. Hoggard did not bat.

Bowling: Brent 8–0–35–0; Hondo 3–0–31–0; Marillier 9–1–50–1; Ervine 7–0–27–0; Viljoen 10–1–40–1; G. W. Flower 6.4–0–39–1.

Umpires: C. K. Coventry and G. R. Evans.
Third umpire: Q. J. Goosen.   Referee: Naushad Ali (Pakistan).

STANDARD BANK TRIANGULAR SERIES, 2001-02

By COLIN BRYDEN

The heavyweight showdown between India and South Africa was billed as the main attraction, with Kenya's games tucked away on the undercard, and a South Africa–India final was widely advertised before the end of the qualifying stage. India managed to save the marketing men's blushes at the last by making the final – where they lost to South Africa – but the tournament will be remembered for Kenya giving Sourav Ganguly's side a bloody nose.

India's problem was consistency, with initial good work often wasted. The opening partnership between Ganguly and Sachin Tendulkar averaged 103 in six matches; they shared three century stands, including 258 against Kenya, which simultaneously broke the records for the first wicket and for the most hundred opening partnerships in one-day internationals. But both their three-figure stands against South Africa were in losing causes, as the middle order failed to consolidate. Among the bowlers, the spinners Harbhajan Singh and Anil Kumble (making his comeback after a year out with a shoulder injury) turned their second match against South Africa, but only Harbhajan improved his reputation.

Kenya saw at first hand the full extent of India's ups and downs. They took advantage of a weak display at Port Elizabeth to gain a much-cherished win – only their third against Test opposition. India certainly looked complacent; dark mutterings about a fix were only intensified by a massive victory when they next met Kenya. However, the ICC's Anti-Corruption Unit cleared them of any suspicion. As Kenya basked in the glow of a rare win, their five defeats, flimsy bowling and over-reliance for runs on Steve Tikolo were happily forgotten. Thomas Odoyo was their outstanding player: he took nine wickets at 32, and confident batting brought him his first two international fifties.

Kenya's famous victory was all the more remarkable given turbulent events off the field. Their flamboyant captain, Maurice Odumbe – who announced after one thrashing that he was taking his boys out on the town to drown their sorrows – was suspended for two matches for claiming that umpire David Orchard had shown bias against the Kenyans. There was more consternation when Kenya's manager, Mehmood Quraishy, complained of chest pains on his way to Odumbe's tribunal. After preliminary treatment by his Indian counterpart, a doctor, he was rushed to hospital for heart surgery.

Meanwhile, South Africa ploughed on relentlessly, winning six of their seven games. The greater depth of their batting and bowling was telling. Either Gary Kirsten or his substitute Boeta Dippenaar usually provided an anchor but, unlike Ganguly and Tendulkar, they were solidly supported by the middle order. Neil McKenzie was stylish and prolific, scoring 223 runs for one dismissal. Shaun Pollock was by far the best bowler on any side, taking 14 wickets and going for only 3.5 an over, as he spearheaded an attack that made up in consistency what it lacked in variety.

Note: Matches in this section were not first-class.

SOUTH AFRICA v INDIA

At Johannesburg, October 5 (day/night). South Africa won by six wickets. South Africa 4 pts. Toss: South Africa. International debut: D. Dasgupta.

Ganguly and Tendulkar hit centuries to help India to the biggest total in a one-day international at the Wanderers but, with Kirsten in marvellous form, South Africa immediately broke that record with ten balls to spare on a batting paradise. While Tendulkar – in his first international since a foot injury in July – initially struggled with his timing, Ganguly dominated all six members of a uniform attack. His immense power and confidence brought him five sixes, and his hundred three balls before Tendulkar got to fifty. They had put on 193 when Ganguly top-edged another huge blow, aimed towards fine leg. Though Tendulkar went on to his 30th one-day international century, the innings slowly lost its fizz. South Africa also opened with a hundred partnership, but Kirsten remained throughout, playing first with aggression, then with typical calm and assurance, and making effective use of a tuck behind square leg to complete his own century.

Man of the Match: G. Kirsten.　　　*Attendance:* 23,715.

India

*S. C. Ganguly c Boucher b Kemp	127	S. S. Das not out		5
S. R. Tendulkar c Gibbs b Kallis	101			
R. Dravid c McKenzie b Nel	1	L-b 4, w 4, n-b 6		14
Yuvraj Singh c Kirsten b Klusener	14			
V. Sehwag c Gibbs b Pollock	5	1/193 2/198 3/242	(5 wkts, 50 overs)	279
A. B. Agarkar not out	12	4/257 5/263		

†D. Dasgupta, A. Kumble, J. Srinath and B. K. V. Prasad did not bat.

Bowling: Pollock 10–0–56–1; Nel 10–1–47–1; Kallis 8–0–45–1; Ntini 7–0–33–0; Klusener 9–0–54–1; Kemp 6–0–40–1.

South Africa

G. Kirsten not out	133	N. D. McKenzie not out		8
H. H. Gibbs c Dasgupta b Srinath	48	B 4, l-b 4, w 2, n-b 5		15
J. H. Kallis b Agarkar	39			
J. N. Rhodes b Srinath	20	1/114 2/207	(4 wkts, 48.2 overs)	280
L. Klusener c Dravid b Prasad	17	3/242 4/270		

*S. M. Pollock, †M. V. Boucher, J. M. Kemp, A. Nel and M. Ntini did not bat.

Bowling: Prasad 7.2–0–51–1; Srinath 10–0–59–2; Agarkar 10–0–45–1; Kumble 10–0–54–0; Tendulkar 9–0–51–0; Ganguly 2–0–12–0.

Umpires: B. G. Jerling and R. E. Koertzen.
Third umpire: S. B. Lambson.　　Referee: A. M. Ebrahim (Zimbabwe).

SOUTH AFRICA v KENYA

At Benoni, October 7. South Africa won by seven wickets. South Africa 5 pts. Toss: Kenya.

If the pitch was slow, Kenya's progress was even slower. Pollock began with a no-ball, but Otieno pushed forward at his first legitimate delivery to edge a catch. Painfully sluggish batting from Shah and David Obuya took Kenya to 27 for one by the 16th over, and there was relief for a fair-sized crowd when Ntini forced Shah to step on to his stumps; his 50 balls had yielded eight runs. Tikolo was far more fluent in an accomplished, unbeaten 68. His partners could not feed him enough of the strike, however, and between the 38th and 43rd overs, he faced only five balls. Both Kirsten and Gibbs, deceived by the pace of the pitch, mistimed pull shots against Odoyo, but Kallis and McKenzie made sure of an easy win.

Man of the Match: S. M. Pollock.　　　*Attendance:* 4,514.

Kenya

K. O. Otieno c Boucher b Pollock	0	T. O. Suji c and b Pollock		9
R. D. Shah hit wkt b Ntini	8	P. Ochieng not out		1
†D. O. Obuya c Nel b Kallis	17	L-b 3, w 5, n-b 4		12
S. O. Tikolo not out	68			
*M. O. Odumbe c Gibbs b Klusener	24	1/1 2/27 3/35	(7 wkts, 50 overs)	159
T. M. Odoyo c Kallis b Nel	7	4/90 5/106		
M. A. Suji c Gibbs b Ntini	13	6/134 7/155		

B. J. Patel and C. O. Obuya did not bat.

Bowling: Pollock 10–1–19–2; Nel 10–2–24–1; Kallis 6–1–25–1; Ntini 10–3–25–2; Henderson 7–0–37–0; Klusener 7–0–26–1.

South Africa

G. Kirsten b Odoyo	17	J. N. Rhodes not out	6
H. H. Gibbs c Shah b Odoyo	20		
J. H. Kallis c D. O. Obuya		B 2, w 5, n-b 7	14
b C. O. Obuya	54		
N. D. McKenzie not out	49	1/21 2/51 3/140 (3 wkts, 33.4 overs)	160

L. Klusener, *S. M. Pollock, †M. V. Boucher, C. W. Henderson, A. Nel and M. Ntini did not bat.

Bowling: M. A. Suji 4–0–22–0; Odoyo 7–1–24–2; Ochieng 3–0–19–0; T. O. Suji 2–0–17–0; C. O. Obuya 9.4–0–45–1; Odumbe 4–0–14–0; Patel 4–0–17–0.

Umpires: R. E. Koertzen and S. B. Lambson.
Third umpire: B. G. Jerling. Referee: A. M. Ebrahim (Zimbabwe).

SOUTH AFRICA v INDIA

At Centurion, October 10 (day/night). India won by 41 runs. India 4 pts. Toss: India.

India's mediocre 233, which would have been even lower but for unusually sloppy South African fielding, was superbly defended by some inspired slow bowling from Harbhajan Singh and Kumble. India's new-ball pair quickly removed both openers, but it was Kumble and Harbhajan who decided the game. Within 11 overs, they took five wickets, leaving South Africa 106 for seven, and out of the match. Earlier, Ganguly hit Pollock for two sixes over point, but neither he nor Tendulkar built on good starts. Crucially, Dravid was dropped twice: once off Ntini by Gibbs at mid-off when 13, and then off Kallis by Klusener at slip one run later. He went on to add 90 with Yuvraj Singh, the best stand of the innings. Pollock was magnificent, and quickly readjusted after initially pitching too short. His five wickets included three of the top four (he also had Tendulkar caught off a no-ball) and the fifth made him only the second South African, after Allan Donald, to reach 200 wickets in one-day internationals.

Man of the Match: Harbhajan Singh.   *Attendance:* 16,919.

India

*S. C. Ganguly c Kallis b Pollock	24	Harbhajan Singh lbw b Pollock	15
S. R. Tendulkar c Nel b Ntini	38	A. Kumble not out	7
S. S. Das c Klusener b Pollock	2	J. Srinath c Kallis b Pollock	2
R. Dravid c Klusener b Pollock	54	L-b 2, w 1, n-b 4	7
Yuvraj Singh b Ntini	42		
V. Sehwag c Ntini b Nel	33	1/44 2/52 3/75 (48.5 overs)	233
†D. Dasgupta c Boucher b Klusener	8	4/165 5/167 6/204	
A. B. Agarkar c Boucher b Klusener	1	7/208 8/208 9/231	

Bowling: Pollock 9.5–1–37–5; Nel 10–0–49–1; Kallis 9–0–42–0; Ntini 10–0–42–2; Klusener 7–0–30–2; Boje 3–0–31–0.

South Africa

G. Kirsten b Srinath	12	†M. V. Boucher c Agarkar b Sehwag	38
H. H. Gibbs c Sehwag b Agarkar	1	M. Ntini b Sehwag	1
J. H. Kallis st Dasgupta		A. Nel not out	0
b Harbhajan Singh	29		
N. D. McKenzie b Kumble	21	B 2, l-b 4, w 5, n-b 3	14
J. N. Rhodes c Dravid b Kumble	8		
*S. M. Pollock lbw b Harbhajan Singh	15	1/5 2/38 3/66 (46.2 overs)	192
N. Boje lbw b Harbhajan Singh	9	4/76 5/85 6/101	
L. Klusener c Yuvraj Singh b Agarkar	44	7/106 8/183 9/188	

Bowling: Srinath 6–0–32–1; Agarkar 8.2–0–40–2; Kumble 10–0–42–2; Harbhajan Singh 10–0–27–3; Tendulkar 4–0–21–0; Sehwag 8–1–24–2.

Umpires: I. L. Howell and B. G. Jerling.
Third umpire: S. Wadvalla. Referee: A. M. Ebrahim (Zimbabwe).

INDIA v KENYA

At Bloemfontein, October 12 (day/night). India won by ten wickets. India 5 pts. Toss: Kenya.

India completed a crushing win in less than 49 overs' play. The pacy Agarkar removed Shah and David Obuya before a run was scored off the bat; when he added Tikolo, Kenya's best batsman against South Africa, respectability became their main target. Even that was denied them by an immaculate, unbroken spell from Kumble, who duped all three of his victims with deliveries that hurried straight on. One of them, Odoyo, had already been resurrected after umpire Orchard gave him run out. As Odoyo traipsed off, the television umpire Wilf Diedricks got on the radio to Orchard, who promptly recalled Odoyo to the field. Ultimately, it made little difference: Kenya slumped to 90, their lowest total in international matches, and India knocked off the runs inside 12 overs.

Man of the Match: A. B. Agarkar.   *Attendance:* 1,813.

Kenya

K. O. Otieno lbw b Kumble	14		C. O. Obuya lbw b Harbhajan Singh		16
R. D. Shah b Agarkar	0		J. K. Kamande b Srinath		5
†D. O. Obuya b Agarkar	0		P. Ochieng b Srinath		3
S. O. Tikolo c Dasgupta b Agarkar	1				
*M. O. Odumbe lbw b Kumble	6		L-b 3, w 6, n-b 5		14
T. M. Odoyo lbw b Kumble	12				
M. A. Suji lbw b Agarkar	1		1/4 2/5 3/13 4/25 5/41	(37.1 overs)	90
T. O. Suji not out	18		6/44 7/50 8/73 9/86		

Bowling: Srinath 7.1–1–13–2; Agarkar 10–2–27–4; Ganguly 5–0–15–0; Kumble 10–4–14–3; Harbhajan Singh 5–1–18–1.

India

†D. Dasgupta not out	24
V. Sehwag not out	55
W 2, n-b 10	12

(no wkt, 11.3 overs) 91

*S. C. Ganguly, S. R. Tendulkar, R. Dravid, Yuvraj Singh, J. J. Martin, A. B. Agarkar, Harbhajan Singh, A. Kumble and J. Srinath did not bat.

Bowling: M. A. Suji 3–1–19–0; Odoyo 4–0–37–0; Ochieng 3–0–16–0; T. O. Suji 1.3–0–19–0.

Umpires: D. L. Orchard and S. Wadvalla.
Third umpire: W. A. Diedricks.   Referee: A. M. Ebrahim (Zimbabwe).

SOUTH AFRICA v KENYA

At Kimberley, October 14. South Africa won by nine wickets. South Africa 4 pts. Toss: Kenya.
International debut: C. K. Langeveldt.

After the débâcle against India, Kenya had a net with Bob Woolmer to hone techniques, and a night on the town to perk up spirits; something certainly raised their performance. Three half-centuries helped to ensure they did not concede a bonus point. Shah showed more aggression in a stylish 55 off 67 balls, while Odoyo hit a maiden international fifty. But, on an excellent batting surface, they still scored too slowly. Though his first international wicket came from one of his worst balls, the fast-medium swing of Langeveldt – a prison warder off the field – proved reliable, and Pollock was as metronomic as ever. Gibbs gave South Africa's reply a blazing start, and pounded 14 fours before slicing to backward point in the 19th over. By then, they were halfway to their target, and Dippenaar – replacing Kirsten, who had a thigh strain – and Klusener, who pulled, cut and drove Odumbe for five successive fours, saw them home. Afterwards, Odumbe told a press conference that one of the umpires (by implication, Orchard) was unfriendly to Kenya; referee Ahmed Ebrahim condemned his comments as "highly scurrilous" and banned him for two matches.

Man of the Match: H. H. Gibbs.   *Attendance:* 4,348.

Kenya

K. O. Otieno c Kemp b Pollock	2
R. D. Shah c Gibbs b Boje	55
†D. O. Obuya c Boucher b Langeveldt . .	4
S. O. Tikolo c Boucher b Ntini	29
*M. O. Odumbe lbw b Langeveldt	60
T. M. Odoyo b Pollock	53
M. A. Suji c and b Pollock	2

C. O. Obuya not out	6
T. O. Suji not out	0
B 1, l-b 7, w 7, n-b 3	18

1/7 2/18 3/82   (7 wkts, 50 overs) 229
4/108 5/214
6/222 7/223

J. K. Kamande and B. J. Patel did not bat.

Bowling: Pollock 10–0–41–3; Langeveldt 10–0–45–2; Kemp 5–0–45–0; Ntini 6–0–20–1; Boje 10–2–30–1; Klusener 9–0–40–0.

South Africa

H. H. Dippenaar not out	74
H. H. Gibbs c C. O. Obuya b Patel	70
L. Klusener not out	75
B 2, w 4, n-b 5	11

1/115   (1 wkt, 41.1 overs) 230

N. D. McKenzie, J. N. Rhodes, *S. M. Pollock, †M. V. Boucher, N. Boje, J. M. Kemp, C. K. Langeveldt and M. Ntini did not bat.

Bowling: M. A. Suji 5–0–30–0; Odoyo 6–0–46–0; T. O. Suji 3–0–20–0; C. O. Obuya 10–0–34–0; Patel 3.1–0–15–1; Odumbe 9–3–41–0; Tikolo 3–0–27–0; Kamande 2–0–15–0.

Umpires: W. A. Diedricks and D. L. Orchard.
Third umpire: D. F. Becker.   Referee: A. M. Ebrahim (Zimbabwe).

INDIA v KENYA

At Port Elizabeth, October 17 (day/night). Kenya won by 70 runs. Kenya 5 pts. Toss: Kenya.

This was a great day for Kenyan cricket. They began with their captain suspended, their manager hospitalised and their chances written off. They finished with their third win in 35 matches against Test teams; previously, they had beaten West Indies in the 1996 World Cup, and India in 1997-98, both on Indian soil. Complacency infected India's performance and, with Srinath and Agarkar missing, the bowling was poor. An opening stand of 121 between Otieno and Shah gave the middle order confidence; Odoyo and David Obuya batted aggressively, scoring almost a run a ball. Then Angara, in his first game of the tournament, opened with four maidens, during which he bowled Tendulkar off the inside edge. Odoyo bowled Ganguly around his legs, and Dravid and Yuvraj Singh fell to consecutive balls. But the key moment was a superb one-handed catch from Collins Obuya at point, which removed Sodhi as he and Martin were dragging the game back. As victory drew nearer, nervous hands dropped four catches, but it was too late to save India. Kenya's win was convincing enough to gain a bonus point, but could have been even more comfortable: umpire Orchard once again failed to call for a TV replay which would have shown Harbhajan Singh clearly run out. Inevitably, the result raised questions of a fix, but the Indians were fully exonerated by the ICC's Anti-Corruption Unit.

Man of the Match: J. O. Angara.   *Attendance:* 2,524.

After the winter ructions, supporters were left wondering what would happen next: it is hard to fathom whether Leicestershire are in a state of turmoil and decline or rehabilitation and development.
Leicestershire, page 682

Kenya

K. O. Otieno c Tendulkar b Yuvraj Singh	64	M. A. Suji not out	8
R. D. Shah c Yuvraj Singh		S. K. Gupta not out	1
b Harbhajan Singh .	50		
*S. O. Tikolo b Harbhajan Singh	27	B 1, l-b 5, w 4, n-b 6	16
T. M. Odoyo c Martin b Kumble	51		
†D. O. Obuya b Prasad	26	1/121 2/123 3/203 (6 wkts, 50 overs) 246		
C. O. Obuya c Sodhi b Prasad	3	4/213 5/220 6/243		

T. O. Suji, B. J. Patel and J. O. Angara did not bat.

Bowling: Prasad 8–2–45–2; Harvinder Singh 9–1–42–0; Sodhi 3–0–14–0; Kumble 10–0–36–1; Ganguly 3–0–21–0; Harbhajan Singh 10–2–38–2; Yuvraj Singh 7–0–44–1.

India

*S. C. Ganguly b Odoyo	24	Harbhajan Singh c Shah b Odoyo	37
S. R. Tendulkar b Angara	3	B. K. V. Prasad not out	10
J. J. Martin b Angara	36	Harvinder Singh b Odoyo	1
R. Dravid c D. O. Obuya b T. O. Suji . .	11		
Yuvraj Singh b T. O. Suji	0	L-b 1, w 8, n-b 4	13
R. S. Sodhi c C. O. Obuya b Angara . . .	21		
†D. Dasgupta c D. O. Obuya		1/7 2/40 3/60 (46.4 overs) 176		
b M. A. Suji .	19	4/60 5/97 6/100		
A. Kumble b C. O. Obuya	1	7/103 8/135 9/172		

Bowling: M. A. Suji 10–1–37–1; Angara 10–4–30–3; Odoyo 9.4–0–41–3; T. O. Suji 7–0–35–2; C. O. Obuya 10–2–32–1.

Umpires: B. G. Jerling and D. L. Orchard.
Third umpire: M. Gajjar. Referee: A. M. Ebrahim (Zimbabwe).

SOUTH AFRICA v INDIA

At East London, October 19 (day/night). South Africa won by 46 runs. South Africa 4 pts. Toss: South Africa.

Gibbs made another flying start, hammering 47 off 41 balls, but it was Dippenaar who gave the innings substance. In complete command, he looked set for a maiden one-day international century before trying an ambitious pull in the 40th over. This brought Rhodes and Klusener together, and their potent mix of dash and crash added 79 in 11 overs. Yet with Ganguly in domineering mood and Tendulkar cantering at a run a ball, India had a chance. They put on 101 inside 16 overs – their 15th century opening partnership. But after Tendulkar was bowled off a bottom edge and Ganguly superbly caught by Kallis at long-on, the middle order folded again. Poor calling and electric fielding resulted in three run-outs. The win guaranteed South Africa's place in the final; India still needed to beat Kenya in their last game.

Man of the Match: S. C. Ganguly.   *Attendance:* 14,613.

South Africa

H. H. Dippenaar lbw b Srinath	81	L. Klusener not out	38
H. H. Gibbs c Sehwag b Agarkar	47	L-b 4, w 1, n-b 4	9
N. Boje run out	18		
J. H. Kallis c Ganguly b Srinath	49	1/63 2/93 (4 wkts, 50 overs) 282		
J. N. Rhodes not out	40	3/196 4/203		

N. D. McKenzie, †M. V. Boucher, *S. M. Pollock, M. Ntini and A. Nel did not bat.

Bowling: Srinath 10–0–55–2; Agarkar 8–0–64–1; Harbhajan Singh 10–0–39–0; Kumble 10–0–54–0; Sehwag 5–0–37–0; Yuvraj Singh 7–0–29–0.

India

*S. C. Ganguly c Kallis b Boje	85	Harbhajan Singh c Boucher b Nel	7
S. R. Tendulkar b Kallis	37	A. Kumble c Pollock b Nel	0
S. S. Das run out	2	J. Srinath c Rhodes b Nel	5
R. Dravid not out	71	W 3, n-b 3	6
Yuvraj Singh lbw b Klusener	3		
V. Sehwag c Boje b Klusener	4	1/101 2/103 3/151	(44.4 overs) 236
A. B. Agarkar run out	16	4/168 5/178 6/200	
†D. Dasgupta run out	0	7/205 8/220 9/220	

Bowling: Pollock 8–1–38–0; Nel 7.4–0–45–3; Ntini 8–0–39–0; Kallis 8–0–44–1; Klusener 8–0–44–2; Boje 5–0–26–1.

Umpires: I. L. Howell and R. E. Koertzen.
Third umpire: C. M. Schoof. Referee: A. M. Ebrahim (Zimbabwe).

SOUTH AFRICA v KENYA

At Cape Town, October 22 (day/night). South Africa won by 208 runs. South Africa 5 pts. Toss: South Africa.

The hero of Kenya's triumph over India, Angara, had departed after the death of his mother, and South Africa brutally reimposed the normal order. They were equally ruthless on Dippenaar, one of four changes in their side, despite his two consecutive fifties. But Kirsten justified his swift return after injury with another polished hundred, his 12th, which also made him the first South African to score 6,000 one-day international runs. He barely missed a bad ball, and heavily punished

---

FASTEST FIFTIES IN ONE-DAY INTERNATIONALS

Balls			
17	S. T. Jayasuriya	Sri Lanka v Pakistan at Singapore	1995-96
18	S. P. O'Donnell	Australia v Sri Lanka at Sharjah	1989-90
18	Shahid Afridi	Pakistan v Sri Lanka at Nairobi	1996-97
18	**Shahid Afridi**	**Pakistan v Holland at Colombo**	**2002**
19	**M. V. Boucher**	**South Africa v Kenya at Cape Town**	**2001-02**
21	B. L. Cairns	New Zealand v Australia at Melbourne	1982-83
21	A. B. Agarkar	India v Zimbabwe at Rajkot	2000-01
21	**D. A. Marillier**	**Zimbabwe v India at Faridabad**	**2001-02**
22	Kapil Dev	India v West Indies at Berbice	1982-83
22	**V. Sehwag**	**India v Kenya at Paarl**	**2001-02**

Martin Suji for missing a return catch when he was 12. Kirsten's stand of 207 in 34 overs with the stylish McKenzie was a South African second-wicket record. Boucher lifted a good total to an unassailable one, smashing four sixes in a ferocious fifty from only 19 balls. Kenya did not have the firepower to respond, and South Africa converted their second-highest total in one-day internationals into their biggest win.

Man of the Match: N. D. McKenzie. *Attendance:* 9,258.

South Africa

G. Kirsten c Odoyo b M. A. Suji	124	†M. V. Boucher not out	51
H. H. Gibbs c Tikolo b Odoyo	16	B 1, l-b 5, w 3, n-b 4	13
N. D. McKenzie not out	131		
*S. M. Pollock c Odoyo b Patel	19	1/39 2/246 3/277	(3 wkts, 50 overs) 354

N. Boje, J. H. Kallis, J. N. Rhodes, J. M. Kemp, M. Hayward and C. K. Langeveldt did not bat.

Bowling: M. A. Suji 10–0–50–1; Odoyo 10–0–76–1; Kamande 3–0–26–0; T. O. Suji 4–0–36–0; Patel 7–0–50–1; C. O. Obuya 10–0–62–0; Tikolo 6–0–48–0.

Kenya

K. O. Otieno b Kallis	10	C. O. Obuya c Boucher b Langeveldt	0
R. D. Shah c Boucher b Pollock	6	B. J. Patel c Boucher b Langeveldt	6
*S. O. Tikolo c Boucher b Hayward	11	J. K. Kamande b Langeveldt	0
T. M. Odoyo lbw b Kemp	44	B 1, l-b 5, w 6, n-b 2	14
†D. O. Obuya c Gibbs b Boje	10		
H. S. Modi not out	26	1/8 2/25 3/59	(45.3 overs) 146
M. A. Suji c Boje b Kemp	6	4/89 5/94 6/106	
T. O. Suji c Kallis b Langeveldt	13	7/133 8/133 9/146	

Bowling: Pollock 6–1–10–1; Hayward 6–0–19–1; Kallis 5–1–24–1; Langeveldt 9.3–0–21–4; Boje 10–0–42–1; Kemp 7–2–14–2; McKenzie 2–0–10–0.

Umpires: I. L. Howell and R. E. Koertzen.
Third umpire: L. H. Matroos. Referee: A. M. Ebrahim (Zimbabwe).

INDIA v KENYA

At Paarl, October 24 (day/night). India won by 186 runs. India 5 pts. Toss: India.

A record-shattering performance from Ganguly and Tendulkar helped India forget their humiliation at Port Elizabeth. In the 16th over, they passed 100 together for the 16th time as an opening pair, breaking Gordon Greenidge and Desmond Haynes's record; in the 35th, they raised 200. They had overtaken the first-wicket record in one-day internationals – their own 252 against Sri Lanka in 1997-98 – to reach 258 when Ganguly fired yet another disdainful drive, this time down the throat of long-on. His 18th one-day international hundred had carried him past 7,000 runs. Tendulkar seemed to have the first double-century at this level within reach; instead, two overs later, he hit a full toss tamely to mid-wicket. It brought no respite: Sehwag hammered an unbeaten 55 off just 23 balls, including 20 from Martin Suji's last four deliveries. Only the newly arrived Laxman missed out as Kenya conceded 350 for the second time in three days. With the result beyond doubt, Kenya seemed content to bat out their 50 overs against uninspired bowling. Modi, called up from his holiday to replace Angara, batted competently but could not avert India's biggest one-day victory.

Man of the Match: S. R. Tendulkar. *Attendance:* 1,861.

India

*S. C. Ganguly c Patel b Odoyo	111	Yuvraj Singh not out	10
S. R. Tendulkar c Odumbe b Odoyo	146	B 1, l-b 3, w 8, n-b 2	14
V. Sehwag not out	55		
V. V. S. Laxman b Odoyo	15	1/258 2/270 3/310	(3 wkts, 50 overs) 351

†R. Dravid, R. S. Sodhi, A. B. Agarkar, Harbhajan Singh, A. Kumble and J. Srinath did not bat.

Bowling: M. A. Suji 7–0–81–0; Odoyo 10–1–67–3; Ochieng 3–0–26–0; T. O. Suji 2–0–14–0; Obuya 10–0–52–0; Tikolo 10–0–54–0; Odumbe 7–0–44–0; Patel 1–0–9–0.

Kenya

†K. O. Otieno st Dravid b Yuvraj Singh	40	H. S. Modi not out	31
R. D. Shah run out	24	M. A. Suji not out	14
S. O. Tikolo lbw b Kumble	1	B 11, l-b 5, w 7	23
*M. O. Odumbe c sub (B. K. V. Prasad) b Harbhajan Singh	20		
T. M. Odoyo st Dravid b Yuvraj Singh	12	1/42 2/57 3/102	(5 wkts, 50 overs) 165
		4/104 5/125	

T. O. Suji, C. O. Obuya, B. J. Patel and P. Ochieng did not bat.

Bowling: Srinath 7–1–27–0; Agarkar 7–1–15–0; Kumble 8–0–22–1; Sodhi 6–0–25–0; Harbhajan Singh 7–1–14–1; Yuvraj Singh 10–1–35–2; Sehwag 5–1–11–0.

Umpires: D. F. Becker and I. L. Howell.
Third umpire: W. A. Diedricks. Referee: A. M. Ebrahim (Zimbabwe).

QUALIFYING TABLE

	Played	Won	Lost	Bonus points	Points	Net run-rate
South Africa	6	5	1	2	22	1.21
India	6	3	3	2	14	1.01
Kenya	6	1	5	1	5	−2.31

Win = 4 pts. One bonus point awarded for achieving victory with a run-rate 1.25 times that of the opposition. When two or more teams finish with an equal number of points, the positions are decided by (a) most wins (b) most wins in head-to-head matches (c) most bonus points (d) highest net run-rate. Net run-rate is calculated by subtracting runs conceded per over from runs scored per over.

FINAL

SOUTH AFRICA v INDIA

At Durban, October 26 (day/night). South Africa won by six wickets. Toss: South Africa.

India went down to their ninth successive defeat in a one-day final since November 1998. They could not get going on a wicket that helped the quicker bowlers, after rain had prevented any work on the pitch the day before. Pollock's accuracy slowed down the openers: a frustrated Ganguly slashed a catch behind in the seventh over and Tendulkar followed in the 12th, when Hayward's sharp pace forced him on to the back foot and induced an inside edge, the third time in four innings he had played on. After losing Sehwag, Dravid found little support. Laxman missed a crucial opportunity to derail South Africa's reply when he dropped Kirsten, then 23, off Srinath. For the third time in the tournament, Kirsten played the anchor role, making a home victory look inevitable – not least to the Indians. The bowling, apart from Srinath, was poor and the fielding ragged. As South Africa cantered home, several unenthralled fans began scrapping in the stands, and an object was thrown at Harbhajan Singh.

Man of the Match: S. M. Pollock.   *Attendance:* 22,077.
Man of the Series: G. Kirsten.

India

*S. C. Ganguly c Boucher b Pollock . . .	9	Harbhajan Singh c Kemp b Pollock	3
S. R. Tendulkar b Hayward	17	J. Srinath run out	0
V. Sehwag c Hayward b Ntini	34	A. Kumble c Ntini b Kemp	0
†R. Dravid c Pollock b Kemp.	77	L-b 1, w 2, n-b 4	7
V. V. S. Laxman c Ntini b Klusener	5		
Yuvraj Singh c Pollock b Kemp	0	1/17 2/31 3/91	(48.2 overs) 183
R. S. Sodhi c sub (A. Nel) b Hayward . .	22	4/112 5/113 6/164	
A. B. Agarkar not out	9	7/177 8/183 9/183	

Bowling: Pollock 9–1–19–2; Hayward 10–0–38–2; Kallis 8–0–41–0; Ntini 10–0–45–1; Klusener 5–0–19–1; Kemp 6.2–0–20–3.

South Africa

G. Kirsten c Laxman b Harbhajan Singh	87	*S. M. Pollock not out	0
H. H. Gibbs c and b Harbhajan Singh . .	21	B 5, l-b 2, w 10, n-b 3	20
J. H. Kallis b Tendulkar	39		
N. D. McKenzie not out	14	1/80 2/150	(4 wkts, 42.1 overs) 187
J. N. Rhodes st Dravid b Tendulkar . . .	6	3/173 4/183	

L. Klusener, †M. V. Boucher, J. M. Kemp, M. Hayward and M. Ntini did not bat.

Bowling: Srinath 10–0–49–0; Agarkar 7.1–0–32–0; Kumble 10–1–24–0; Harbhajan Singh 10–1–48–2; Tendulkar 5–1–27–2.

Umpires: I. L. Howell and D. L. Orchard.
Third umpire: W. A. Diedricks.   Referee: A. M. Ebrahim (Zimbabwe).

THE KHALEEJ TIMES TROPHY, 2001-02

Politics cast a long shadow over some mundane one-day cricket. The terrorist attacks of September 11 raised doubts about whether Sharjah's autumn tournament would take place; once it began, Zimbabwe, beset by tension over racial quotas and domestic political turmoil, barely competed, lending their games a stale air of inevitability.

Pakistan arrived underprepared but left victorious. After New Zealand cancelled a tour, citing security fears, the Pakistanis had played only three days of international cricket since leaving England in June, and their opening performance in the tournament – now sponsored by a Dubai-based newspaper group – was rusty. But after that defeat, they proceeded unbeaten to the final, where they crushed Sri Lanka in a forgettable, low-scoring match. The most memorable game was a "dead" fixture, when both sides were through to the final. Inzamam-ul-Haq – suspended for Pakistan's first two matches after dissent in a one-day international in England, and undone by a painful blow to the box in their third – shepherded the newcomer Naved Latif to a hundred and his side to victory from an unpromising position. Meanwhile, Shahid Afridi was adding a degree of consistency to his explosive talent. Their attack relied heavily on an experienced trio: Waqar Younis and Shoaib Akhtar took nine wickets each; Wasim Akram bowled with enthusiasm and guile to claim six for 62 and concede only 2.13 an over.

A lack of bowling depth disadvantaged Sri Lanka – though some press reports claimed the players preferred to blame ill-fitting trousers, which they had to repair themselves in the dressing-room. Muttiah Muralitharan was outstanding, applying a vice-like squeeze in mid-innings to finish with figures of 40–8–80–7. The rest were vexing: Charitha Buddika Fernando seized six wickets but was expensive; Chaminda Vaas cost less but took just three. Kumar Dharmasena claimed four for 101 from 29 overs with his off-breaks – and was promptly dropped. Only in the final did Sri Lanka's batting fail; otherwise they set targets of 250 or more, or chased successfully. Mahela Jayawardene and Russel Arnold both averaged over 60, providing a steadying influence after the fireworks promised by the openers, Sanath Jayasuriya and Avishka Gunawardene, never quite ignited.

Zimbabwe arrived with a new coach, a new captain and a 12-match losing sequence – soon extended to 16. Brian Murphy, appointed when Heath Streak resigned three days before the start, lost all four tosses, condemning them to bat second, under lights. Only once did they threaten to make a game of it, in their second match against Pakistan, when the Flower brothers put on 146. These two were alone in scoring more than 100 for Zimbabwe; among the bowlers only Streak, Douglas Marillier and Henry Olonga went for less than five an over. Clearly, Geoff Marsh, who had coached Australia to huge success in the late 1990s, faced a daunting challenge if he were to restore Zimbabwe's fortunes.

Note: Matches in this section were not first-class.

SRI LANKA v ZIMBABWE

At Sharjah, October 26 (day/night). Sri Lanka won by 63 runs. Sri Lanka 5 pts. Toss: Sri Lanka. International debut: T. C. B. Fernando.

The regular clatter of wickets prevented Zimbabwe from getting anywhere near Sri Lanka's 256. Charitha Buddika Fernando enjoyed an eventful international debut: after two no-balls, his first legal delivery nipped back to have Marillier lbw, and in the sixth over, he cut one away from Carlisle's bat to have him caught behind. Jagging the ball from a length, he took five wickets in

FIVE WICKETS ON ONE-DAY INTERNATIONAL DEBUT

5-21	A. I. C. Dodemaide, Australia v Sri Lanka at Perth	1987-88
5-26	S. H. U. Karnain, Sri Lanka v New Zealand at Moratuwa	1983-84
5-29	A. A. Donald, South Africa v India at Calcutta	1991-92
5-67	**T. C. B. Fernando, Sri Lanka v Zimbabwe at Sharjah**	**2001-02**

all, though at more than seven an over. No Zimbabwean partnership lasted longer than eight overs until Brent joined Ervine at 120 for seven in the 33rd; by then it was too late. Buddika Fernando ended their stand, clean bowling Brent and Friend in successive balls. Earlier, to the accompaniment of jubilant drumming from their supporters, Atapattu and Arnold shared a stand of 115, leaving Zimbabwe to score at five an over on a slow outfield and under lights.

Man of the Match: T. C. B. Fernando.

Sri Lanka

*S. T. Jayasuriya c and b Friend	21	W. P. U. J. C. Vaas c Murphy b Brent	11
D. A. Gunawardene run out	5	M. Muralitharan not out	2
M. S. Atapattu c Wishart b Ervine	92	B 4, l-b 3, w 4, n-b 2	13
D. P. M. D. Jayawardene run out	33		
R. P. Arnold not out	76	1/7 2/41 3/101 (6 wkts, 50 overs) 256	
†R. S. Kaluwitharana lbw b Ervine	3	4/216 5/229 6/254	

H. D. P. K. Dharmasena, T. C. B. Fernando and C. R. D. Fernando did not bat.

Bowling: Streak 6–0–31–0; Friend 9–0–45–1; Brent 7–0–36–1; Marillier 10–0–36–0; Murphy 4–0–21–0; G. W. Flower 5–0–34–0; Ervine 9–0–46–2.

Zimbabwe

D. A. Marillier lbw b T. C. B. Fernando	1	S. M. Ervine c C. R. D. Fernando	
G. W. Flower run out	43	b T. C. B. Fernando	47
S. V. Carlisle c Kaluwitharana		G. B. Brent b T. C. B. Fernando	12
b T. C. B. Fernando	3	T. J. Friend b T. C. B. Fernando	0
†A. Flower c Kaluwitharana		*B. A. Murphy not out	20
b C. R. D. Fernando	22		
C. B. Wishart c Jayawardene		L-b 5, w 3, n-b 16.	24
b Muralitharan	9		
D. D. Ebrahim c Kaluwitharana		1/5 2/17 3/65 (50 overs) 193	
b Muralitharan	10	4/90 5/95 6/106	
H. H. Streak b C. R. D. Fernando	2	7/120 8/158 9/158	

Bowling: Vaas 9–1–28–0; T. C. B. Fernando 9–0–67–5; C. R. D. Fernando 8–0–32–2; Muralitharan 10–4–16–2; Dharmasena 10–0–31–0; Jayasuriya 4–0–14–0.

Umpires: R. E. Koertzen and G. Sharp.
Third umpire: E. A. Nicholls.   Referee: D. T. Lindsay (South Africa).

PAKISTAN v SRI LANKA

At Sharjah, October 27 (day/night). Sri Lanka won by seven wickets. Sri Lanka 5 pts. Toss: Pakistan. International debut: R. A. P. Nissanka.

Sri Lanka turned in another impressive bowling performance despite resting the previous day's hero, Buddika Fernando. A policy of rotating novice bowlers meant a debut for Prabath Nissanka, who showed genuine pace. However, it was another Fernando – Dilhara – who ripped out Pakistan's top three inside ten overs; by the 18th, they were 67 for five. Parsimonious bowling, keen fielding and some rash shots wrung the life out of a middle order missing Inzamam-ul-Haq through suspension, and Pakistan limped to 176. After weathering a superb opening spell from Wasim Akram – he beat the bat several times and conceded only seven in six overs – Sri Lanka's reply seldom looked in trouble. Gunawardene stroked a handsome 88, and Pakistani heads were dropping well before the 39th over brought defeat.

Man of the Match: D. A. Gunawardene.

Pakistan

Taufeeq Umar b Fernando	10	Wasim Akram c Jayawardene		
Shahid Afridi c Nissanka b Fernando	23	b Jayasuriya	7
Saeed Anwar c and b Fernando	2	Shoaib Malik not out	17
Yousuf Youhana c Vaas b Jayasuriya	47	*Waqar Younis b Jayasuriya	18
Younis Khan c Muralitharan b Nissanka	12	Shoaib Akhtar run out	1
†Rashid Latif c Muralitharan		B 5, w 6	11
b Nissanka	1		
Abdul Razzaq c Kaluwitharana		1/28 2/36 3/41 4/61 5/67 (46.2 overs) 176	
b Muralitharan	27	6/117 7/128 8/141 9/170	

Bowling: Vaas 7.2–1–24–0; Fernando 7–0–43–3; Nissanka 8–1–24–2; Muralitharan 10–0–20–1; Jayasuriya 8–0–30–3; Arnold 6–0–30–0.

Sri Lanka

*S. T. Jayasuriya c Shahid Afridi		D. P. M. D. Jayawardene not out	29
b Shoaib Akhtar	19	R. P. Arnold not out	10
D. A. Gunawardene c Shoaib Malik			
b Shoaib Akhtar	88	L-b 4, w 3, n-b 3	10
M. S. Atapattu c Taufeeq Umar			
b Abdul Razzaq	21	1/43 2/121 3/161 (3 wkts, 38.1 overs) 177

K. C. Sangakkara, †R. S. Kaluwitharana, W. P. U. J. C. Vaas, M. Muralitharan, R. A. P. Nissanka and C. R. D. Fernando did not bat.

Bowling: Wasim Akram 6–2–7–0; Waqar Younis 6–0–28–0; Shoaib Akhtar 7.1–0–39–2; Abdul Razzaq 8–0–52–1; Shoaib Malik 8–0–31–0; Shahid Afridi 3–1–16–0.

Umpires: R. E. Koertzen and E. A. Nicholls.
Third umpire: G. Sharp.   Referee: D. T. Lindsay (South Africa).

PAKISTAN v ZIMBABWE

At Sharjah, October 28 (day/night). Pakistan won by 106 runs. Pakistan 5 pts. Toss: Pakistan.

In every aspect of the game, Pakistan proved too strong. They fielded four bowlers averaging under 25 in one-day internationals and two batsmen averaging over 35; Zimbabwe had no one in either category. After Pakistan's costly aberrations against Sri Lanka, Shahid Afridi cut out risky strokes early on. Once established, he launched a spectacular fusillade of big hitting, including 42 in boundaries. His fifth – and final – six prompted Murphy to call his dispirited players into a huddle to regroup. Pakistan smashed 89 in the last 12 overs, Abdul Razzaq making a 35-ball 45. Zimbabwe's chase soon lost impetus. Andy Flower scored 51 in 59 balls but found little support once Carlisle was run out. At the midway point, they needed more than seven an over; once Flower fell, the result was beyond doubt. The end came with almost 11 overs unused.

Man of the Match: Shahid Afridi.

Ricky Ponting's 11 catches contained some which justified the invention of the television replay.
The South Africans in Australia, page 1243

Pakistan

Taufeeq Umar st A. Flower b Brent	18	Wasim Akram not out	22
Shahid Afridi b Streak	67	†Rashid Latif not out	3
Saeed Anwar b G. W. Flower	64		
Yousuf Youhana c sub (H. K. Olonga) b Marillier	26	L-b 8, w 9	17
Younis Khan b Friend	17	1/45 2/136 3/188 (6 wkts, 50 overs) 279	
Abdul Razzaq run out	45	4/190 5/244 6/258	

Shoaib Malik, *Waqar Younis and Shoaib Akhtar did not bat.

Bowling: Streak 10–2–42–1; Friend 9–0–55–1; Brent 7–1–32–1; Ervine 6–0–51–0; Murphy 4–0–23–0; Marillier 8–1–35–1; Gripper 2–0–11–0; G. W. Flower 4–0–22–1.

Zimbabwe

D. A. Marillier b Wasim Akram	2	S. M. Ervine c Rashid Latif b Shahid Afridi	0
G. W. Flower c Taufeeq Umar b Waqar Younis	2	*B. A. Murphy lbw b Shoaib Malik	0
S. V. Carlisle run out	43	G. B. Brent b Shahid Afridi	2
†A. Flower b Shoaib Malik	51	T. J. Friend b Shoaib Akhtar	17
D. D. Ebrahim c Rashid Latif b Shoaib Malik	12	B 1, l-b 3, w 12, n-b 1	17
H. H. Streak not out	27	1/5 2/5 3/84 4/112 5/131 (39.1 overs) 173	
T. R. Gripper run out	0	6/132 7/132 8/138 9/146	

Bowling: Wasim Akram 6–0–16–1; Waqar Younis 5–0–20–1; Shoaib Akhtar 6.1–0–40–1; Abdul Razzaq 7–0–30–0; Shahid Afridi 8–1–21–2; Shoaib Malik 7–0–42–3.

Umpires: E. A. Nicholls and G. Sharp.
Third umpire: R. E. Koertzen. Referee: D. T. Lindsay (South Africa).

SRI LANKA v ZIMBABWE

At Sharjah, October 30 (day/night). Sri Lanka won by 79 runs. Sri Lanka 5 pts. Toss: Sri Lanka. For the third time, Zimbabwe pursued over 250, and for the third time their chase degenerated into an ungainly stagger towards respectability. Earlier, their bowlers had fought back with spirit after Jayasuriya chose to bat and nonchalantly caned 11 from Streak's opening over. Streak and swing bowler Brent took three early wickets, but the openers struggled with their line as the right–left combination of Jayawardene and Arnold added 111. For the second match running, Murphy felt forced to use eight bowlers. Zimbabwe's reply was too laboured to threaten; Gripper set the tone with a 60-ball 26. The man he replaced as opener, Marillier, produced a sprightly unbeaten fifty at No. 6, but nothing could prevent Zimbabwe falling further and further behind.

Man of the Match: D. P. M. D. Jayawardene.

Sri Lanka

*S. T. Jayasuriya c Friend b Streak	25	W. P. U. J. C. Vaas run out	13
D. A. Gunawardene lbw b Streak	14	D. K. Liyanage c A. Flower b Streak	2
M. S. Atapattu c G. W. Flower b Brent	9	M. Muralitharan c G. W. Flower b Brent	2
D. P. M. D. Jayawardene c Gripper b Marillier	63	T. C. B. Fernando not out	0
R. P. Arnold c Brent b Streak	55	B 1, l-b 4, w 12, n-b 7	24
†K. C. Sangakkara b Brent	35	1/41 2/59 3/62 (49.4 overs) 250	
H. D. P. K. Dharmasena st A. Flower b Marillier	8	4/173 5/199 6/223 7/235 8/242 9/249	

Bowling: Streak 10–0–59–4; Friend 6–0–31–0; Brent 7.4–0–32–3; Marillier 10–0–42–2; Murphy 10–0–46–0; Nkala 3–0–21–0; G. W. Flower 2–0–9–0; Gripper 1–0–5–0.

Zimbabwe

G. W. Flower b Vaas	2	M. L. Nkala c Sangakkara		
T. R. Gripper c Arnold b Liyanage	26	b Muralitharan	5
S. V. Carlisle run out	37	G. B. Brent c Fernando b Arnold	8
†A. Flower c Muralitharan b Dharmasena	13	T. J. Friend not out	2
D. D. Ebrahim st Sangakkara		L-b 3, w 4	7
b Dharmasena	14		
D. A. Marillier not out	52	1/5 2/66 3/66	(8 wkts, 50 overs) 171
H. H. Streak st Sangakkara		4/93 5/99 6/111	
b Dharmasena	5	7/125 8/149	

*B. A. Murphy did not bat.

Bowling: Vaas 6–2–19–1; Fernando 6–0–30–0; Liyanage 6–0–23–1; Muralitharan 10–1–22–1; Dharmasena 10–0–26–3; Jayasuriya 10–0–37–0; Arnold 2–0–11–1.

Umpires: R. E. Koertzen and E. A. Nicholls.
Third umpire: G. Sharp. Referee: D. T. Lindsay (South Africa).

PAKISTAN v ZIMBABWE

At Sharjah, October 31 (day/night). Pakistan won by 29 runs. Pakistan 4 pts. Toss: Pakistan. International debut: Naved Latif.

Zimbabwe bowed out with their 16th successive defeat since they saw off Bangladesh at Bulawayo in April. But this time it took a fine performance from a great bowler to beat them. Thirty overs into their innings, the game remained delicately poised: the Flower brothers needed less than a run a ball, with eight wickets in hand. But Wasim Akram conjured a slower delivery to dismiss Andy Flower and, two balls later, a sharp leg-cutter to remove Ebrahim. Good fortune hampered Pakistan's advantage home when Grant Flower, nine short of a century, was run out via a deflection while backing up. Marillier heaved entertainingly, but to no avail. Pakistan's batsmen had failed to capitalise on a prosperous start. From 87 for one in the 15th over – courtesy of a 36-ball 58 from Shahid Afridi, including six sixes – and 205 for three in the 40th, 261 was a mediocre total. Inzamam-ul-Haq's return after serving his suspension was interrupted when a delivery from Olonga struck him in the box.

Man of the Match: Shahid Afridi.

Pakistan

Naved Latif c Gripper b Streak	7	Wasim Akram run out	2
Shahid Afridi c Gripper b Marillier	58	*Waqar Younis not out	8
Yousuf Youhana lbw b Brent	41	Danish Kaneria not out	3
Inzamam-ul-Haq c Murphy b Ervine	21	L-b 3, w 5, n-b 11	19
Younis Khan c Marillier b Ervine	59		
Azhar Mahmood c Brent b Ervine	29	1/23 2/87 3/152	(9 wkts, 50 overs) 261
Abdul Razzaq run out	10	4/205 5/218 6/224	
†Rashid Latif c Murphy b Brent	4	7/227 8/237 9/251	

Inzamam-ul-Haq, when 9, retired at 98 and resumed at 227.

Bowling: Streak 10–1–36–1; Olonga 8–0–34–0; Brent 7–0–51–2; Marillier 8–0–49–1; Murphy 5–0–37–0; G. W. Flower 5–0–22–0; Ervine 7–0–29–3.

Zimbabwe

G. W. Flower run out	91	H. H. Streak c and b Abdul Razzaq	1
T. R. Gripper c Yousuf Youhana		G. B. Brent not out	18
b Waqar Younis	4	*B. A. Murphy c Rashid Latif	
S. V. Carlisle c Rashid Latif		b Wasim Akram	4
b Waqar Younis	0	H. K. Olonga run out	0
†A. Flower c and b Wasim Akram	48		
D. D. Ebrahim c Rashid Latif		B 1, l-b 9, w 14, n-b 5	29
b Wasim Akram	0		
D. A. Marillier c Azhar Mahmood		1/13 2/13 3/159 (46.2 overs) 232	
b Waqar Younis	37	4/159 5/169	
S. M. Ervine c Waqar Younis		6/169 7/175	
b Abdul Razzaq	0	8/219 9/231	

Bowling: Wasim Akram 9–3–19–3; Waqar Younis 9.2–1–41–3; Azhar Mahmood 8–0–43–0; Abdul Razzaq 8–0–48–2; Danish Kaneria 7–0–43–0; Shahid Afridi 5–0–28–0.

Umpires: R. E. Koertzen and G. Sharp.
Third umpire: E. A. Nicholls.   Referee: D. T. Lindsay (South Africa).

PAKISTAN v SRI LANKA

At Sharjah, November 2 (day/night). Pakistan won by seven wickets. Pakistan 4 pts. Toss: Sri Lanka.

Pakistan's often mercurial batsmen found the resolve to overhaul Sri Lanka's 272. Inzamam-ul-Haq, in his 250th one-day international, joined Naved Latif, in his second, at 41 for two, and their brilliantly paced 219-run stand carried them to the threshold of victory. Against disciplined seam bowling from Fernando, Naved struggled initially, but ground on, eschewing risk. At the halfway mark, Pakistan had only just reached 100 with the asking-rate approaching seven. Then Inzamam reeled off a series of nonchalant cuts and drives; Naved took his cue, and attacked Jayasuriya's spin. The seamers returned but, with Muralitharan resting, Sri Lanka could not halt the momentum – four dropped catches did not help. Naved finally fell for a 141-ball 113, Inzamam remained unbeaten on 118 in 124. Sri Lanka could have batted Pakistan out of the game if the middle order had backed up Jayawardene, who survived an apparent run-out to score 84 from 83 balls.

Man of the Match: Naved Latif.

Sri Lanka

*S. T. Jayasuriya c Shoaib Akhtar		W. P. U. J. C. Vaas c Rashid Latif	
b Shahid Afridi	36	b Shoaib Akhtar	10
D. A. Gunawardene c Inzamam-ul-Haq		H. D. P. K. Dharmasena run out	3
b Shoaib Akhtar	57	T. C. B. Fernando not out	1
M. S. Atapattu c Rashid Latif			
b Abdul Razzaq	24	L-b 12, w 16, n-b 3	31
D. P. M. D. Jayawardene c Shahid Afridi			
b Shoaib Akhtar	84	1/95 2/103 3/158 (9 wkts, 50 overs) 272	
R. P. Arnold lbw b Waqar Younis	19	4/224 5/224	
K. C. Sangakkara b Waqar Younis	0	6/250 7/258	
†R. S. Kaluwitharana		8/271 9/272	
lbw b Azhar Mahmood	7		

R. A. P. Nissanka did not bat.

Bowling: Waqar Younis 10–0–51–2; Shoaib Akhtar 10–1–45–3; Abdul Razzaq 8–0–53–1; Azhar Mahmood 9–0–51–1; Shahid Afridi 10–0–46–1; Shoaib Malik 3–0–14–0.

Pakistan

Shahid Afridi c Sangakkara b Vaas	11
Naved Latif c Nissanka b Dharmasena .	113
Yousuf Youhana b Fernando	11
Inzamam-ul-Haq not out	118

Younis Khan not out	4
L-b 4, w 7, n-b 5	16
1/17 2/41 3/260 (3 wkts, 49.2 overs)	273

Azhar Mahmood, Abdul Razzaq, †Rashid Latif, Shoaib Malik, *Waqar Younis and Shoaib Akhtar did not bat.

Bowling: Vaas 10–1–40–1; Nissanka 9–0–71–0; Fernando 10–1–35–1; Arnold 9–0–57–0; Dharmasena 9–0–44–1; Jayasuriya 2.2–0–22–0.

Umpires: E. A. Nicholls and G. Sharp.

Third umpire: R. E. Koertzen.   Referee: D. T. Lindsay (South Africa).

QUALIFYING TABLE

	Played	Won	Lost	Bonus points	Points	Net run-rate
Sri Lanka	4	3	1	3	15	0.98
Pakistan	4	3	1	1	13	0.44
Zimbabwe	4	0	4	0	0	−1.39

Win = 4 pts. One bonus point awarded for achieving victory with a run-rate 1.25 times that of the opposition. When two or more teams finish with an equal number of points, the positions are decided by (a) most wins (b) most wins in head-to-head matches (c) most bonus points (d) highest net run-rate. Net run-rate is calculated by subtracting runs conceded per over from runs scored per over.

FINAL

PAKISTAN v SRI LANKA

At Sharjah, November 4 (day/night). Pakistan won by five wickets. Toss: Sri Lanka.

For the fourth time, Jayasuriya won the toss, and strode out with fellow-gambler Gunawardene. However, their potentially enthralling contest with Wasim Akram and Waqar Younis barely materialised as Waqar removed Gunawardene for two. Wasim surprised Atapattu with a rapid delivery, and Sri Lanka were listing at 55 for two after 15 overs, forcing Jayasuriya into the un-characteristic role of anchor. He eventually reverted to type, cutting loosely at Shahid Afridi to be caught behind for a 58-ball 34. Sri Lanka now depended heavily on the in-form Jayawardene and Arnold to raise a defensible target. Despite good starts, neither could revitalise a sluggish innings, and the last five wickets fell in six overs, setting Pakistan a modest 174. Afridi briefly fizzed, hitting Muralitharan's first ball for six, but skying his fourth to mid-wicket; Murali spun the ball hard and gained extravagant turn. Still, Pakistan, with the experienced hand of Inzamam-ul-Haq at the tiller, cruised home in the 44th over, denying Sri Lanka a third successive Sharjah trophy.

Man of the Match: Waqar Younis.   *Man of the Series:* D. P. M. D. Jayawardene.

Sri Lanka

*S. T. Jayasuriya c Rashid Latif	
b Shahid Afridi .	34
D. A. Gunawardene c Azhar Mahmood	
b Waqar Younis .	2
M. S. Atapattu c Rashid Latif	
b Wasim Akram .	0
D. P. M. D. Jayawardene c Rashid Latif	
b Shoaib Akhtar .	43
R. P. Arnold lbw b Wasim Akram	47
†K. C. Sangakkara c Rashid Latif	
b Shahid Afridi .	3

L. P. C. Silva lbw b Shoaib Akhtar ...	10
W. P. U. J. C. Vaas not out	10
T. C. B. Fernando lbw b Waqar Younis ..	3
M. Muralitharan c Naved Latif	
b Shoaib Akhtar .	3
R. A. P. Nissanka b Waqar Younis	2
L-b 4, w 9, n-b 3	16
1/9 2/21 3/79 (44.2 overs)	173
4/102 5/112 6/152	
7/156 8/161 9/164	

Bowling: Wasim Akram 8–0–20–2; Waqar Younis 8.2–1–31–3; Shoaib Akhtar 8–0–33–3; Abdul Razzaq 5–0–20–0; Shahid Afridi 10–2–45–2; Azhar Mahmood 5–0–20–0.

Pakistan

Shahid Afridi c Vaas b Muralitharan	35	Abdul Razzaq not out	14
Naved Latif c Sangakkara b Nissanka	23	†Rashid Latif not out	23
Yousuf Youhana c and b Muralitharan	40	L-b 1, w 6, n-b 3	10
Inzamam-ul-Haq lbw b Vaas	28		
Younis Khan c Gunawardene b Muralitharan	4	1/45 2/73 3/122 (5 wkts, 43.4 overs) 177 4/130 5/138	

Azhar Mahmood, Wasim Akram, *Waqar Younis and Shoaib Akhtar did not bat.

Bowling: Vaas 10–0–35–1; Nissanka 7–0–54–1; Fernando 7.4–1–34–0; Muralitharan 10–3–22–3; Jayasuriya 8–0–29–0; Arnold 1–0–2–0.

Umpires: R. E. Koertzen and G. Sharp.
Third umpire: E. A. Nicholls. Referee: D. T. Lindsay (South Africa).

INTERNATIONAL UMPIRES' PANEL

In 1993, the International Cricket Council formed an international umpires' panel, containing at least two officials from each full member of ICC. A third-country umpire from this panel stood with a "home" umpire, not necessarily from the panel, in every Test from February 1994 onwards.

In March 2002, an elite panel of eight umpires (contracted to the ICC for two years at a time) was appointed after consultation with the Test captains, who assess umpires' performances after every match. Two elite umpires were expected to stand in all Tests from April 2002, and at least one in every one-day international. A supporting panel of international umpires was created to provide cover if the Test schedule became unusually crowded, and to provide a second umpire in one-day internationals. The ICC also appointed specialist third umpires to give rulings from TV replays. The panels were sponsored by Emirates Airlines for three years from July 2002.

The following eight umpires formed the inaugural elite panel: S. A. Bucknor (West Indies), E. A. R. de Silva (Sri Lanka), D. J. Harper (Australia), R. E. Koertzen (South Africa), D. L. Orchard (South Africa), D. R. Shepherd (England), R. B. Tiffin (Zimbabwe) and S. Venkataraghavan (India). P. Willey (England) was invited to join the panel, but declined for family reasons.

The international panel consisted of A. F. M. Akhtaruddin (Bangladesh), Aleem Dar (Pakistan), K. C. Barbour (Zimbabwe), B. F. Bowden (New Zealand), D. B. Cowie (New Zealand), B. R. Doctrove (West Indies), M. A. Esat (Zimbabwe), D. B. Hair (Australia), K. Hariharan (India), I. L. Howell (South Africa), A. V. Jayaprakash (India), B. G. Jerling (South Africa), Mahbubur Rahman (Bangladesh), N. A. Mallender (England), P. Manuel (Sri Lanka), Nadeem Ghauri (Pakistan), E. A. Nicholls (West Indies), S. J. A. Taufel (Australia), T. H. Wijewardene (Sri Lanka) and P. Willey (England). The specialist third umpires were Asad Rauf (Pakistan), S. J. Davis (Australia), A. L. Hill (New Zealand), J. W. Lloyds (England), I. D. Robinson (Zimbabwe), Showkatur Rahman (Bangladesh), M. G. Silva (Sri Lanka), I. Sivaram (India) and S. Wadvalla (South Africa).

LG ABANS TROPHY, 2001-02

By TONY COZIER

Sri Lanka continued their triumphant home season with an easy win in this triangular tournament. Their opponents were West Indies, whom they had just whitewashed in a three-Test series, and Zimbabwe, who would soon meet the same fate. Sri Lanka got off to a flying start with an astonishing win that set a clutch of one-day international records. The left-arm swing bowler Chaminda Vaas became the first player to take eight wickets in an innings, Zimbabwe's total of 38 was the lowest ever, and the match was the shortest, completed in just 20 overs.

Yet when Zimbabwe beat West Indies the next day and West Indies upset Sri Lanka, the teams were separated only by the bonus point from that remarkable opener. Sri Lanka swiftly re-established control, winning all their remaining matches, including the final against West Indies, by convincing margins.

Their all-round depth was crucial. They scored at more than five an over, but conceded only 3.68. Mahela Jayawardene led the batting, with 265 runs in his last three innings, but their strength was exemplified by the captain, Sanath Jayasuriya, who was named Man of the Series for 194 runs at a strike-rate of 90, and eight wickets at less than 21. Strangely, Vaas did not pick up a wicket after the first match. The spin attack took over, with Muttiah Muralitharan, who claimed ten victims, the leading bowler.

The West Indians had lost five players to a combination of injury, family bereavement and disciplinary matters, and their best batsman, Brian Lara, joined the list when he fractured his elbow in an accident during their third match. West Indies' form remained inconsistent. Only the opener Daren Ganga, who fell four times in the 50s, could be relied on. Chris Gayle found his touch in the last two matches, when his powerful strokeplay showed what might have been. The captain, Carl Hooper, bore even heavier responsibility than usual, but could not compensate for the team's inexperience.

Zimbabwe's fielding was one of the features of the tournament, not least in their solitary victory over West Indies, when they bounced back from their humiliation by Sri Lanka. But their batting broke down too frequently for them to mount a serious challenge. Only Heath Streak, at No. 8, reached 50; he was also their best bowler, with seven wickets.

Note: Matches in this section were not first-class.

SRI LANKA v ZIMBABWE

At Sinhalese Sports Club, Colombo, December 8. Sri Lanka won by nine wickets. Sri Lanka 5 pts. Toss: Sri Lanka.

Vaas became the first bowler to claim eight wickets in a one-day international – five days after taking 14 Test wickets on the same ground against West Indies. As in the Test, his success was based on controlled, each-way swing on a true pitch. He dismissed Ebrahim with his first ball and took Sri Lanka's first limited-overs hat-trick in his sixth over – starting with Carlisle, the only Zimbabwean to reach double figures, and followed by Wishart and Taibu, both to vicious in-swingers. Vaas was on course for all ten until Muralitharan, who had held the previous one-day record – seven for 30 against India in 2000-01 – picked up the last two. Zimbabwe were routed for 38, the lowest total in limited-overs internationals, five less than Pakistan's 43 against West Indies at Cape Town in 1992-93. That match had also produced the previous lowest aggregate in a completed one-day international – 88 for 13 wickets – and at 32.2 overs had been the shortest international uninterrupted by bad weather; this game shattered both records. The crowd had witnessed a mere 78 runs for 11 wickets in 20 overs: Sri Lanka needed just 26 balls as they zoomed to victory before noon.

Man of the Match: W. P. U. J. C. Vaas.

Zimbabwe

D. D. Ebrahim lbw b Vaas	0		M. L. Nkala c Sangakkara b Vaas	1
G. W. Flower b Vaas	1		T. J. Friend b Muralitharan	4
*S. V. Carlisle c Perera b Vaas	16		H. K. Olonga c Jayawardene	
†A. Flower c Sangakkara b Vaas	0		b Muralitharan	0
C. B. Wishart lbw b Vaas	6		L-b 1, w 1, n-b 4	6
D. A. Marillier not out	4			
T. Taibu lbw b Vaas	0		1/0 2/11 3/11 4/27 5/27	(15.4 overs) 38
H. H. Streak lbw b Vaas	0		6/27 7/29 8/32 9/38	

Bowling: Vaas 8–3–19–8; Zoysa 7–2–17–0; Muralitharan 0.4–0–1–2.

Sri Lanka

*S. T. Jayasuriya not out	13
D. A. Gunawardene lbw b Streak	2
M. S. Atapattu not out	23
W 2	2

1/4   (1 wkt, 4.2 overs) 40

D. P. M. D. Jayawardene, R. P. Arnold, †K. C. Sangakkara, A. S. A. Perera, H. D. P. K. Dharmasena, W. P. U. J. C. Vaas, D. N. T. Zoysa and M. Muralitharan did not bat.

Bowling: Streak 2.2–0–26–1; Friend 2–0–14–0.

Umpires: D. N. Pathirana and M. G. Silva.
Third umpire: E. A. R. de Silva. Referee: R. Subba Row (England).

WEST INDIES v ZIMBABWE

At Sinhalese Sports Club, Colombo, December 9. Zimbabwe won by four wickets. Zimbabwe 4 pts. Toss: Zimbabwe.

Zimbabwe put aside the previous day's embarrassment to clinch a deserved, hard-fought, victory, the first time they had beaten any side other than Bangladesh in 29 one-day matches. They restricted West Indies with accurate bowling and sharp fielding, typified by Ebrahim's direct hit from backward point to inflict a fourth consecutive duck on Gayle, Olonga's sharp run-out of Hooper as he followed through, and Streak's amazing catch of Jacobs on the mid-wicket boundary to end the innings. Ganga shared partnerships of fifty with Sarwan and Samuels, but West Indies never got going. Ebrahim was lbw to the first ball of Zimbabwe's innings, as he had been the day before, but Grant Flower and Carlisle steadied things. Even then, three quick wickets left Zimbabwe faltering at 145 for six before Andy Flower and Streak guided them home with 11 balls to spare.

Man of the Match: S. V. Carlisle.

West Indies

C. H. Gayle run out	0		P. T. Collins c G. W. Flower b Nkala	4
D. Ganga c and b G. W. Flower	59		M. I. Black lbw b Streak	0
B. C. Lara lbw b Streak	2		C. D. Collymore not out	3
R. R. Sarwan b Olonga	36		L-b 7, w 4	11
*C. L. Hooper run out	5			
M. N. Samuels c Taibu b G. W. Flower	32		1/0 2/9 3/66	(49.1 overs) 173
†R. D. Jacobs c Streak b Friend	20		4/77 5/137 6/152	
N. C. McGarrell lbw b Friend	1		7/153 8/161 9/163	

Bowling: Streak 10–1–38–2; Friend 8.1–2–26–2; Olonga 10–1–30–1; Marillier 10–0–35–0; G. W. Flower 10–0–33–2; Nkala 1–0–4–1.

Zimbabwe

D. D. Ebrahim lbw b Collins	0	T. Taibu c and b Hooper	0
G. W. Flower c Hooper b Black	30	H. H. Streak not out	19
*S. V. Carlisle c McGarrell b Hooper . . .	47	L-b 6, w 6, n-b 3	15
†A. Flower not out	47		
C. B. Wishart c Collins b Collymore . . .	12	1/0 2/59 3/96 (6 wkts, 48.1 overs) 175	
D. A. Marillier c Hooper b Collins	5	4/125 5/141 6/145	

M. L. Nkala, T. J. Friend and H. K. Olonga did not bat.

Bowling: Collins 9.1–2–35–2; Collymore 10–1–29–2; Black 9–1–43–0; McGarrell 10–0–27–0; Hooper 10–0–35–2.

Umpires: E. A. R. de Silva and T. H. Wijewardene.
Third umpire: L. V. Jayasundera. Referee: R. Subba Row (England).

SRI LANKA v WEST INDIES

At R. Premadasa Stadium, Colombo, December 11 (day/night). West Indies won by 49 runs. West Indies 4 pts. Toss: West Indies. International debut: J. J. C. Lawson.

Collymore, bowling with a new, open-chested action, turned the match with five for ten in 22 balls as Sri Lanka threw away their last six wickets for 72. Four were caught by Jacobs, only the third wicket-keeper to dismiss six victims in a one-day international. West Indies should have set a stiffer target: a run-a-ball stand of 74 between Ganga and Lara, who hit 60 in 53 deliveries, provided a sound foundation, and they entered the last ten overs on 209 for three, with Sarwan and Hooper well set. But they raised only 41 more runs as five wickets fell. Jayasuriya, who smashed an 86-ball 83, and Gunawardene opened with 92 in 18 overs, and Sri Lanka were on course until Collymore returned to inspire West Indies to their first win of a troubled tour.

Man of the Match: C. D. Collymore.

West Indies

C. H. Gayle c Gunawardene		N. C. McGarrell not out	7
b Dharmasena	21	P. T. Collins b Dharmasena	0
D. Ganga run out	50	C. D. Collymore not out	1
B. C. Lara lbw b Jayasuriya	60		
R. R. Sarwan c Jayawardene b Jayasuriya	38	B 4, l-b 4, w 7, n-b 2	17
*C. L. Hooper c Dharmasena			
b Muralitharan	29	1/50 2/124 3/151 (8 wkts, 50 overs) 250	
M. N. Samuels c Zoysa b Jayasuriya . . .	2	4/209 5/216 6/225	
†R. D. Jacobs b Dharmasena	25	7/247 8/247	

J. J. C. Lawson did not bat.

Bowling: Vaas 8–0–40–0; Zoysa 6–1–34–0; Dharmasena 10–0–50–3; Perera 1–0–11–0; Muralitharan 10–1–35–1; Arnold 5–0–22–0; Jayasuriya 10–0–50–3.

Sri Lanka

*S. T. Jayasuriya c Gayle b McGarrell . .	83	H. D. P. K. Dharmasena c Jacobs	
D. A. Gunawardene st Jacobs		b Collymore .	0
b McGarrell	38	W. P. U. J. C. Vaas c Jacobs b Collymore	4
M. S. Atapattu run out	11	D. N. T. Zoysa c Ganga b Collymore . . .	5
D. P. M. D. Jayawardene c Jacobs		M. Muralitharan not out	0
b Collins .	2	L-b 2, w 4, n-b 2	8
R. P. Arnold lbw b Gayle.	19		
†K. C. Sangakkara c Jacobs		1/92 2/119 3/134 (43.2 overs) 201	
b Collymore	27	4/138 5/184 6/192	
A. S. A. Perera c Jacobs b Collymore . .	4	7/192 8/192 9/201	

Bowling: Collins 8–0–34–1; Collymore 9.2–0–51–5; Lawson 4–0–29–0; Hooper 8–0–20–0; Gayle 7–1–32–1; McGarrell 7–0–33–2.

Umpires: E. A. R. de Silva and P. T. Manuel.
Third umpire: T. H. Wijewardene. Referee: R. Subba Row (England).

SRI LANKA v ZIMBABWE

At R. Premadasa Stadium, Colombo, December 12 (day/night). Sri Lanka won by 59 runs. Sri Lanka 5 pts. Toss: Sri Lanka.

Spectators stayed away, perhaps fearing a repeat of the truncated contest when these sides last met. But this time Zimbabwe put up more of a fight. They made an encouraging start, dismissing Jayasuriya and Atapattu cheaply, before a stand of 166 in 33 overs between Gunawardene and Jayawardene set up the biggest total of the tournament. Gunawardene fell ten short of his hundred, and Jayawardene got even closer, with 96. Zimbabwe's openers put on 69 in 15 overs, but both fell to Muralitharan, and no one stayed long enough or scored quickly enough to threaten the target. The result assured Sri Lanka's place in the final.

Man of the Match: D. P. M. D. Jayawardene.

Sri Lanka

*S. T. Jayasuriya c A. Flower b Streak	0	W. P. U. J. C. Vaas c Marillier b Streak	15
D. A. Gunawardene c Carlisle b Streak	90	D. N. T. Zoysa not out	2
M. S. Atapattu c Olonga b Friend	4	B 1, l-b 10, w 9, n-b 2	22
D. P. M. D. Jayawardene lbw b Olonga	96		
R. P. Arnold not out	34	1/0 2/25 3/191 (7 wkts, 50 overs) 272
U. D. U. Chandana b Friend	8	4/215 5/230
†K. C. Sangakkara run out	1	6/231 7/258

H. D. P. K. Dharmasena and M. Muralitharan did not bat.

Bowling: Streak 10–1–51–3; Friend 10–0–58–2; Olonga 10–0–44–1; Marillier 10–0–46–0; Nkala 2–0–17–0; G. W. Flower 8–0–45–0.

Zimbabwe

D. D. Ebrahim b Muralitharan	32	T. Taibu c Jayawardene b Muralitharan	0
G. W. Flower c Jayawardene b Muralitharan	45	M. L. Nkala b Dharmasena	15
*S. V. Carlisle c Chandana b Arnold	39	T. J. Friend st Sangakkara b Chandana	1
†A. Flower lbw b Jayasuriya	11	H. K. Olonga not out	1
C. B. Wishart c and b Arnold	14	B 1, l-b 2, w 6, n-b 2	11
D. A. Marillier c Zoysa b Chandana	20	1/69 2/88 3/103 (47.2 overs) 213
H. H. Streak st Sangakkara b Muralitharan	24	4/145 5/159 6/189
		7/189 8/203 9/211

Bowling: Vaas 7–0–26–0; Zoysa 4–0–24–0; Dharmasena 8–0–35–1; Muralitharan 10–0–32–4; Jayasuriya 8–0–40–1; Chandana 8.2–0–41–2; Arnold 2–0–12–2.

Umpires: L. V. Jayasundera and T. H. Wijewardene.
Third umpire: D. N. Pathirana.   Referee: R. Subba Row (England).

SRI LANKA v WEST INDIES

At Kandy, December 15. Sri Lanka won by eight wickets. Sri Lanka 4 pts. Toss: Sri Lanka.

Lara was left writhing in pain with a dislocated left elbow after he accidentally collided with Atapattu while attempting a quick single. He was stretchered off, just when he had settled after a cautious start; initial treatment was promising, but two days later a hairline fracture was discovered, forcing him out of the rest of the tour. Only Ganga, with his third consecutive fifty, and Hooper came to terms with the spin attack, and a target of 236 was little challenge to Sri Lanka's in-form batsmen. To the delight of a packed, noisy crowd, Jayawardene reached the hundred he had narrowly missed three days earlier. He faced just 94 balls, and shared an unbroken stand of 187 in 31 overs with Atapattu to complete another comfortable win.

Man of the Match: D. P. M. D. Jayawardene.

West Indies

C. H. Gayle lbw b Fernando	. . . .	8
D. Ganga c Sangakkara b Arnold	. . . . .	52
B. C. Lara retired hurt	. . . .	24
R. R. Sarwan c Sangakkara b Fernando	.	5
*C. L. Hooper c Chandana b Jayasuriya	.	72
M. N. Samuels c Jayawardene		
b Muralitharan	. .	10
R. L. Powell c Jayasuriya b Muralitharan		8
†R. D. Jacobs not out	. . . .	25

N. C. McGarrell b Jayasuriya	. . . .	0
C. D. Collymore b Arnold	. . . .	5
J. J. C. Lawson run out	. . . .	3
B 4, l-b 4, w 11, n-b 4	. . . . .	23
	(49.5 overs)	235

Lara retired hurt at 60.

1/16   2/77   3/146
4/170   5/193   6/205
7/205   8/229   9/235

Bowling: Zoysa 7–1–37–0; Fernando 7–0–25–2; Nissanka 2–0–22–0; Muralitharan 10–0–33–2; Chandana 8–0–41–0; Jayasuriya 10–0–36–2; Arnold 5.5–0–33–2.

Sri Lanka

*S. T. Jayasuriya c Sarwan b Lawson	. . .	34
D. A. Gunawardene c sub (D. Brown)		
b Lawson	. .	10
M. S. Atapattu not out	. . . .	82

D. P. M. D. Jayawardene not out	. . . . . .	106
L-b 2, w 4, n-b 1	. . . . . .	7
1/36 2/52	(2 wkts, 43.1 overs)	239

R. P. Arnold, †K. C. Sangakkara, U. D. U. Chandana, D. N. T. Zoysa, R. A. P. Nissanka, T. C. B. Fernando and M. Muralitharan did not bat.

Bowling: Collymore 10–1–46–0; Lawson 10–1–47–2; McGarrell 8–0–57–0; Hooper 8–1–34–0; Gayle 3–0–18–0; Samuels 4–0–31–0; Ganga 0.1–0–4–0.

Umpires: L. V. Jayasundera and M. G. Silva.
Third umpire: P. T. Manuel.   Referee: R. Subba Row (England).

WEST INDIES v ZIMBABWE

At Kandy, December 16. West Indies won by eight wickets. West Indies 5 pts. Toss: West Indies. International debuts: D. Brown, R. O. Hinds.

Both teams entered the last qualifier on four points, but West Indies were virtually certain of joining Sri Lanka in the final by the 27th over, when their swing bowlers reduced Zimbabwe to 53 for seven. Darryl Brown claimed three for 21 from ten consecutive overs on his international debut. But at the other end, Hooper's decision to replace Collymore with his own off-spin slightly relaxed the pressure. Streak made a patient 57 and helped add 101 for the last three wickets. West Indies still cruised home with 16 overs to spare. Gayle, out of touch until now, scored just five runs from his first 31 balls, then exploded to hit 80 off his next 48, as both Friend and Brent disappeared for 16 in an over.

Man of the Match: C. H. Gayle.

Zimbabwe

D. D. Ebrahim lbw b Collymore	. . . . .	3
G. W. Flower b Collins	. . . .	3
*S. V. Carlisle c Jacobs b Collins	. . . .	1
†A. Flower lbw b Brown	. . . .	21
C. B. Wishart run out	. . . .	6
T. R. Gripper c Jacobs b Brown	. . . . .	4
D. A. Marillier c Hooper b Brown	. . . .	5
H. H. Streak c Collins b Collymore	. . . .	57

T. J. Friend st Jacobs b Gayle	. . . .	22
G. B. Brent b Hooper	. . . .	19
H. K. Olonga not out	. . . .	0
L-b 3, w 7, n-b 3	. . . . . .	13
	(49.2 overs)	154

1/7   2/7   3/9
4/24   5/37   6/45
7/53   8/113   9/145

Bowling: Collins 10–0–24–2; Collymore 10–1–26–2; Brown 10–3–21–3; Hooper 9.2–1–30–1; Hinds 5–0–27–0; Gayle 5–0–23–1.

West Indies

D. Ganga c A. Flower b Streak	12
C. H. Gayle c Olonga b Marillier	85
R. R. Sarwan not out	30
R. O. Hinds not out	16
B 2, w 7, n-b 3	12

1/15 2/121   (2 wkts, 34 overs) 155

*C. L. Hooper, M. N. Samuels, R. L. Powell, †R. D. Jacobs, D. Brown, P. T. Collins and C. D. Collymore did not bat.

Bowling: Streak 6–2–16–1; Friend 5–0–26–0; Olonga 6–0–49–0; Brent 2–0–24–0; Marillier 8–2–32–1; Gripper 7–4–6–0.

Umpires: P. T. Manuel and D. N. Pathirana.
Third umpire: M. G. Silva.   Referee: R. Subba Row (England).

QUALIFYING TABLE

	Played	Won	Lost	Bonus points	Points	Net run-rate
Sri Lanka	4	3	1	2	14	1.41
West Indies	4	2	2	1	9	0.39
Zimbabwe	4	1	3	0	4	–1.69

Win = 4 pts. One bonus point awarded for achieving victory with a run-rate 1.25 times that of the opposition. When two or more teams finish with an equal number of points, the positions are decided by (a) most wins (b) most wins in head-to-head matches (c) most bonus points (d) highest net run-rate. Net run-rate is calculated by subtracting runs conceded per over from runs scored per over.

FINAL

SRI LANKA v WEST INDIES

At R. Premadasa Stadium, Colombo, December 19 (day/night). Sri Lanka won by 34 runs (D/L method). Toss: Sri Lanka.

Sri Lanka finally clinched a conclusive victory in a fluctuating contest. Jayasuriya hit a bruising 64 and shared fifty partnerships with Gunawardene and Atapattu. Beginner's luck ran out for Brown, who conceded 72, but Sri Lanka were checked by the steady off-spin of Hooper and Gayle. The last ten overs yielded just 58, and there were three run-outs, including Jayawardene for a 65-ball 63. Rain during the break adjusted West Indies' target to 247 from 47 overs. Zoysa's first cost 17, and Gayle and Ganga put on 111, the best opening stand of the tournament, by the halfway mark. But Dharmasena bowled Ganga, for his fourth fifty in five games, and Gayle followed three overs later. A power failure then caused a further brief interruption; resuming, West Indies could not make headway against the spinners on a turning pitch without the injured Lara, and Sri Lanka never threatened to loosen their grip.

Man of the Match: S. T. Jayasuriya.   *Man of the Series:* S. T. Jayasuriya.

Sri Lanka

*S. T. Jayasuriya c Hinds b Hooper	64	
D. A. Gunawardene c and b Hooper	15	
M. S. Atapattu run out	38	
D. P. M. D. Jayawardene run out	63	
R. P. Arnold b Collins	0	
†K. C. Sangakkara c Samuels b Brown	23	
U. D. U. Chandana run out	5	
W. P. U. J. C. Vaas run out	1	

H. D. P. K. Dharmasena not out 7
M. Muralitharan not out 13

L-b 5, w 15, n-b 4 24

D. N. T. Zoysa did not bat.

1/53 2/114 3/154 (8 wkts, 50 overs) 253
4/155 5/213 6/229
7/232 8/232

Bowling: Collins 10–0–41–1; Collymore 9–0–48–0; Hooper 10–1–32–2; Brown 10–0–72–1; Gayle 10–0–48–0; Samuels 1–0–7–0.

West Indies

D. Ganga b Dharmasena	50	
C. H. Gayle c Chandana b Jayasuriya	60	
R. R. Sarwan c Sangakkara b Jayasuriya	5	
*C. L. Hooper c Atapattu b Dharmasena	34	
M. N. Samuels run out	13	
R. L. Powell c Chandana b Muralitharan	1	
†R. D. Jacobs st Sangakkara b Dharmasena	21	

R. O. Hinds not out 15
D. Brown not out 1

L-b 8, w 4 12

1/111 2/117 3/124 (7 wkts, 47 overs) 212
4/147 5/150
6/181 7/203

P. T. Collins and C. D. Collymore did not bat.

Bowling: Vaas 7–1–23–0; Zoysa 6–2–36–0; Muralitharan 10–0–43–1; Dharmasena 10–1–44–3; Jayasuriya 9–0–41–2; Chandana 5–0–17–0.

Umpires: P. T. Manuel and T. H. Wijewardene.
Third umpire: M. G. Silva. Referee: R. Subba Row (England).

VB SERIES, 2001-02

By RICHARD BOOCK and PAUL COUPAR

Long after South Africa's victory is forgotten, this tournament will be remembered for the defeats that ended one of the most distinguished captaincies in one-day history. Steve Waugh's Australians finished the group stage with the same number of wins as South Africa and New Zealand, but missed the final of their own triangular tournament (renamed after a beer produced by the sponsors, Carlton) for only the third time in its 23-year history. Waugh's own form was poor, and this was enough for Australia's famously red-in-tooth-and-claw selectors: eight days after the tournament ended, Ricky Ponting replaced him as the one-day captain. Waugh and his twin, Mark, were dropped from the one-day squad.

Australia were holed below the waterline by three defeats in their first three games. The press blamed a policy of heavy rotation: four changes were made after each of the three opening matches. Batting was the weak link. Both Waughs were out of form, Adam Gilchrist's gunpowder went soggy and there was no sting in the tail. Only Michael Bevan averaged over 40. The bowlers, meanwhile, never conceded more than 250, and once routed South Africa for 106. Glenn McGrath shone brightest and took 14 wickets at 16. But Shane Warne disappointed: the loss of 17lbs on a diet of cereal, baked beans and water seemed to shear his powers, and he took only six at 54.

It could easily have been different. The Australians' bailing-out operation came within one point of success – and that point was gifted to South Africa by New Zealand. It was part of a calculated manoeuvre to exploit a new system introduced by the ICC the previous September, which awarded a bonus point to a team winning with a run-rate 1.25 times their opponents'. In New Zealand's final group match against South Africa, Stephen Fleming found himself in what he described as an "extremely disappointing" situation, where the second-best result for his team (after a win) was a heavy defeat. If New Zealand lost this match to South Africa, and Australia beat South Africa in the last qualifier two days later (which they did), and no bonus point was awarded in either game, then all three teams would finish tied on 17 points. They would not be separable on the first three prescribed tie-breakers, as each would have had four wins, have beaten one opponent three times and the other once, and have a single bonus point. The fourth tie-breaker would be net run-rate, where New Zealand lagged behind.

But if New Zealand lost to South Africa and conceded a bonus point in the process, the South Africans would end on 18 points, and so be removed from the tie-break equation. That would leave only Australia and New Zealand on 17 points, who would be separated on the second tie-breaker: most wins in head-to-head matches. New Zealand had beaten Australia 3–1, so they would go through. The only danger for New Zealand was that Australia would beat South Africa heavily enough in their last game to claim a bonus point of their own, in which case Australia would go through with 18 points. But once it became clear that New Zealand could not beat South Africa, their best chance of qualifying was to help South Africa stay ahead of Australia. In the hall-of-mirrors world of the bonus point, fewer runs meant a greater chance of making the final. The Australians could hardly complain: in the 1999 World Cup, they had hatched a similarly Machiavellian ruse, with New Zealand the intended victims. But a system designed to add spice had produced contrived, tedious cricket.

It was good work with the ball that allowed New Zealand to make such cunning use of the calculator and give Australia another embarrassment after their near-miss in the Test series. Shane Bond was easily the tournament's leading wicket-taker, with 21, including 15 batsmen in the top six. When he struck early, his colleagues did a superb smothering job in mid-innings; when he failed, containment proved more difficult. The batting was less inspiring, with some terribly slow starts. Only Fleming reached 300 runs, and they relied heavily on two all-rounders: Chris Harris nudged, Chris Cairns bludgeoned, and each won a match virtually single-handed.

With Australia on top of South Africa, just as in the recent Tests, and New Zealand on top of Australia, logic suggested that New Zealand would dominate South Africa. In fact, South Africa won five of their six meetings, including two forgettable finals. South Africa's batting – one aberration at Sydney apart – was reliable, if seldom spectacular. Jonty Rhodes and Jacques Kallis both averaged over 50, though it was Rhodes who contributed most when the going got tough. Of the bowlers, Shaun Pollock had no rival for accuracy, while Makhaya Ntini's ability to seam the ball from wide of the crease caused real trouble – though not quite as much trouble as the bonus-points controversy.

Note: Matches in this section were not first-class.

AUSTRALIA v NEW ZEALAND

At Melbourne, January 11 (day/night). New Zealand won by 23 runs. New Zealand 4 pts. Toss: Australia. International debut: B. A. Williams.

New Zealand were in a stranglehold at 94 for seven in the 27th over, but Harris helped them wriggle free with an unbeaten 63. Even so, a total of 199 looked inadequate, especially when Australia scorched to 63 for one in eight overs. They paid a high price for mid-innings recklessness, however: Bond had Ponting caught at fine leg and then enticed Bevan to slash high to third man. The last six wickets, including the disastrous run-out of Steve Waugh, tumbled in 14 overs. Cairns – who had struck a massive blow by removing Gilchrist – returned to hit the stumps twice, and Vettori deterred any late rally. McGrath was banned for one match after his dissent when given out caught behind. Meanwhile, the Melbourne Cricket Club suffered what its general manager described as the "annual outbreak of mob mentality". Play was held up for several minutes after unrest in the Great Southern Stand, which prompted 22 arrests and more than 250 evictions.

Man of the Match: C. Z. Harris.   *Attendance:* 47,157.

New Zealand

L. Vincent c S. R. Waugh b Lee	17	†A. C. Parore run out	3
M. H. Richardson c Gilchrist b McGrath	8	D. L. Vettori run out	30
*S. P. Fleming c M. E. Waugh b McGrath	1	J. E. C. Franklin not out	9
C. D. McMillan c Gilchrist b Lee	17	L-b 6, w 6, n-b 6	18
C. L. Cairns c Ponting b Lee	10		
S. B. Styris c and b Harvey	23	1/20 2/22 3/41 (8 wkts, 50 overs) 199
C. Z. Harris not out	63	4/54 5/67 6/89
		7/94 8/166

S. E. Bond did not bat.

Bowling: McGrath 10–1–47–2; Williams 10–2–31–0; Lee 10–1–43–3; Harvey 10–1–35–1; Warne 10–0–37–0.

Australia

†A. C. Gilchrist c and b Cairns	23	B. Lee b Cairns	0
M. E. Waugh c Parore b Bond	1	B. A. Williams not out	13
R. T. Ponting c Franklin b Bond	45	G. D. McGrath c Parore b Vettori	7
M. G. Bevan c Franklin b Bond	27	B 1, w 3, n-b 9	13
*S. R. Waugh run out	15		
D. R. Martyn lbw b Vettori	24	1/5 2/63 3/98 (42 overs) 176
I. J. Harvey b Cairns	5	4/104 5/135 6/142
S. K. Warne b Harris	3	7/150 8/151 9/168

Bowling: Bond 10–1–53–3; Franklin 5–0–27–0; Cairns 10–1–42–3; Vettori 10–1–36–2; Harris 7–0–17–1.

Umpires: D. B. Hair and R. L. Parry.
Third umpire: R. G. Patterson. Referee: Hanumant Singh (India).

AUSTRALIA v SOUTH AFRICA

At Melbourne, January 13 (day/night). South Africa won by four wickets. South Africa 4 pts. Toss: Australia.

Rhodes and McKenzie did what was required for victory and absolutely no more: Rhodes took 101 balls to accumulate 43 – a glacial rate of progress in the one-day game – and hit no boundaries; McKenzie scored 34 in 59 balls. But South Africa could afford to leave the fireworks in the box. Australia scored only 63 runs in the first 15 overs, and just 58 after the 35th; in between, two run-outs accounted for Bevan and Ponting, who might have added some oomph to Steve Waugh's nurdling. Pollock bowled typically straight with the new ball and at the death. South Africa's openers raised 50 in quick time, before Gillespie sparked a mini collapse. But with McGrath suspended, Australia were unable to put Rhodes under pressure.

Man of the Match: S. M. Pollock.   *Attendance:* 62,696.

Australia

†A. C. Gilchrist c Donald b Pollock	...	0	B. Lee c Rhodes b Donald	0
M. L. Hayden c Klusener b Pollock	...	10	A. J. Bichel lbw b Pollock	17
R. T. Ponting run out	...	51	J. N. Gillespie not out	1
M. G. Bevan run out	...	10	L-b 6, w 6	12
*S. R. Waugh b Kallis	...	62		
D. R. Martyn c McKenzie b Kallis	...	31	1/0 2/39 3/64 (48.5 overs) 198	
A. Symonds c Gibbs b Kallis	...	0	4/106 5/164 6/164	
S. K. Warne c Pollock b Klusener	...	4	7/170 8/171 9/196	

Bowling: Pollock 9–1–25–3; Donald 10–0–54–1; Kallis 9.5–1–30–3; Ntini 10–0–31–0; Klusener 7–0–33–1; Boje 3–0–19–0.

South Africa

H. H. Gibbs c Gilchrist b Gillespie	38	†M. V. Boucher c Symonds b Lee	11
G. Kirsten c Gilchrist b Bichel	22	*S. M. Pollock not out	5
J. H. Kallis c Gilchrist b Gillespie	6	B 2, l-b 12, w 4, n-b 4	22
N. D. McKenzie c Symonds b Warne	34		
J. N. Rhodes not out	43	1/51 2/66 3/71 (6 wkts, 48.3 overs) 199	
L. Klusener c Gilchrist b Lee	18	4/136 5/169 6/187	

N. Boje, A. A. Donald and M. Ntini did not bat.

Bowling: Lee 9.3–1–42–2; Gillespie 10–3–28–2; Bichel 10–1–45–1; Warne 10–1–19–1; Symonds 7–0–41–0; Bevan 2–0–10–0.

Umpires: S. J. Davis and S. J. A. Taufel.
Third umpire: R. L. Parry.   Referee: Hanumant Singh (India).

NEW ZEALAND v SOUTH AFRICA

At Hobart, January 15. South Africa won by 26 runs. South Africa 4 pts. Toss: South Africa.

New Zealand briefly glimpsed another unexpected win when they needed 106 from 17 overs, with eight wickets left. But McMillan was expertly caught by Gibbs, and they plunged into a steep decline, losing seven for 50. The vital one was Fleming. After being forced into all sorts of contortions by rearing balls from Ntini, he was finally held at deep backward square for 85. Earlier, Kirsten square-cut and cover-drove his way to 97, only to run himself out. Boucher was lucky to escape when Cairns appeared to have him caught and bowled, but he smashed 22 off the next seven deliveries, and ended with a 19-ball 30. The victory was South Africa's tenth in their last ten completed one-day internationals against New Zealand.

Man of the Match: G. Kirsten.   *Attendance:* 5,963.

South Africa

H. H. Gibbs c Fleming b Vettori	36	*S. M. Pollock run out	0
G. Kirsten run out	97	J. M. Kemp not out	10
H. H. Dippenaar c McMillan b Bond	37	L-b 2, w 1, n-b 3	7
J. N. Rhodes c Harris b Cairns	13		
N. D. McKenzie c Fleming b Franklin	22	1/82 2/157 3/178 (7 wkts, 50 overs) 257	
L. Klusener b Vettori	5	4/194 5/215	
†M. V. Boucher not out	30	6/217 7/217	

A. A. Donald and M. Ntini did not bat.

Bowling: Bond 10–0–64–1; Franklin 8–0–42–1; Cairns 10–0–54–1; Vettori 10–0–37–2; Harris 10–0–43–0; Styris 2–0–14–0.

New Zealand

L. Vincent c Pollock b Ntini	23	D. L. Vettori c Kirsten b Donald	0
M. H. Richardson c Klusener b Donald	8	J. E. C. Franklin c Boucher b Donald	2
*S. P. Fleming c Dippenaar b Klusener	85	S. E. Bond not out	17
C. D. McMillan c Gibbs b Kemp	36	B 3, l-b 8, w 5, n-b 1	17
C. L. Cairns b Ntini	11		
S. B. Styris c Boucher b Klusener	9	1/10 2/71 3/152 (9 wkts, 50 overs) 231	
C. Z. Harris c Dippenaar b Kemp	2	4/170 5/181 6/183	
†A. C. Parore not out	21	7/192 8/196 9/202	

Bowling: Pollock 10–2–38–0; Donald 10–1–40–3; Ntini 10–0–36–2; Kemp 10–0–50–2; Klusener 10–0–56–2.

Umpires: S. J. Davis and D. J. Harper.
Third umpire: J. H. Smeaton.   Referee: Hanumant Singh (India).

AUSTRALIA v NEW ZEALAND

At Sydney, January 17 (day/night). New Zealand won by 23 runs. New Zealand 4 pts. Toss: New Zealand. International debuts: R. J. Campbell; B. B. McCullum.

Cairns captained New Zealand for the first time after Fleming was injured in the nets, but Harris was their star. Australia again folded under pressure, losing their last six for 38 in nine overs. Three fell to Harris, who took the pace off the ball and prevented the lower order running it around. He also claimed two catches, including an astonishing effort at point to remove Steve Waugh. Earlier, Harris had been largely responsible for building a defendable total. Along with Cairns and McMillan, he injected some life after a funeral start, which produced only 38 runs in the first 18 overs. Warne suffered as the tempo rose: his nine overs cost 65 runs, the most he had conceded in his 170 one-day internationals. Australia were fined one over for a slow over-rate.

Man of the Match: C. Z. Harris.   *Attendance:* 39,691.

New Zealand

M. H. Richardson st Campbell b Warne	26	D. L. Vettori c Campbell b Lee	2
B. B. McCullum run out	5	J. E. C. Franklin run out	5
L. Vincent c Ponting b Harvey	24		
C. D. McMillan c Campbell b Martyn	39	B 2, l-b 18, w 3	23
*C. L. Cairns c S. R. Waugh b Gillespie	31		
S. B. Styris c Bevan b Harvey	20	1/13 2/54 3/74 (9 wkts, 50 overs) 235	
C. Z. Harris not out	42	4/135 5/137 6/182	
†A. C. Parore c M. E. Waugh b Warne	18	7/210 8/216 9/235	

S. E. Bond did not bat.

Bowling: McGrath 10–2–22–0; Gillespie 10–0–28–1; Harvey 10–0–40–2; Lee 8–1–40–1; Warne 9–0–65–2; Martyn 3–0–20–1.

Australia

M. E. Waugh run out	0	B. Lee lbw b Franklin	1
†R. J. Campbell c Harris b Vettori	38	J. N. Gillespie not out	13
R. T. Ponting c Parore b Bond	11	G. D. McGrath c Vincent b Harris	1
M. G. Bevan c Styris b Cairns	66	L-b 7, w 18, n-b 4	29
*S. R. Waugh c Harris b Bond	9		
D. R. Martyn run out	24	1/1 2/29 3/98	(47.2 overs) 212
I. J. Harvey c Vincent b Harris	6	4/118 5/174 6/178	
S. K. Warne c Richardson b Harris	14	7/181 8/188 9/203	

Bowling: Bond 8–1–28–2; Franklin 9–0–46–1; Cairns 9–2–32–1; Vettori 10–0–45–1; Harris 8.2–0–37–3; Styris 3–0–17–0.

Umpires: R. L. Parry and S. J. A. Taufel.
Third umpire: D. B. Hair. Referee: Hanumant Singh (India).

NEW ZEALAND v SOUTH AFRICA

At Brisbane, January 19 (day/night). New Zealand won by four wickets. New Zealand 4 pts. Toss: South Africa.

Chasing 242, New Zealand were becalmed at 98 for five in the 24th over after Pollock had taken two for seven in his opening six-over spell. But a fearless century from Cairns changed the game, gave his team their first one-day victory over South Africa for nearly three years and put them top of the table. Cairns began patiently, taking 64 balls over his first 50, but ended brutally – the next 50 came in just 35, as he accelerated through the last ten overs. He belted nine fours and three huge sixes, while Harris and Parore gave staunch support. South Africa paid the price for a big stumble at the end of their innings. They lost six for 37 in the last nine overs as Bond and Cairns bowled cleverly to stop the momentum.

Man of the Match: C. L. Cairns.   *Attendance:* 17,457.

South Africa

H. H. Gibbs b Franklin	0	J. L. Ontong c McMillan b Bond	4
G. Kirsten c and b Harris	43	S. Elworthy c Cairns b Bond	0
J. H. Kallis c Vincent b Bond	65	M. Ntini not out	2
J. N. Rhodes c Harris b Cairns	44	L-b 6, w 2, n-b 1	9
H. H. Dippenaar run out	7		
†M. V. Boucher c Franklin b Bond	51	1/0 2/115 3/115	(48.3 overs) 241
*S. M. Pollock c Parore b Franklin	15	4/131 5/204 6/231	
J. M. Kemp c Parore b Cairns	1	7/234 8/236 9/237	

Bowling: Franklin 8–0–41–2; Bond 9.3–0–37–4; Cairns 10–0–44–2; Vettori 10–0–58–0; Harris 10–0–45–1; McMillan 1–0–10–0.

New Zealand

M. H. Richardson c Ontong b Pollock	0	C. Z. Harris lbw b Elworthy	24
B. B. McCullum c Kallis b Ntini	37	†A. C. Parore not out	21
L. Vincent c Boucher b Pollock	9	L-b 8, w 8, n-b 6	22
*S. P. Fleming c Ontong b Kallis	23		
C. D. McMillan c Pollock b Kallis	6	1/0 2/31 3/71	(6 wkts, 49.1 overs) 244
C. L. Cairns not out	102	4/73 5/98 6/160	

D. L. Vettori, J. E. C. Franklin and S. E. Bond did not bat.

Bowling: Pollock 9.1–2–29–2; Elworthy 10–0–47–1; Ntini 8–0–46–1; Kallis 10–0–57–2; Ontong 5–0–26–0; Kemp 7–0–31–0.

Umpires: S. J. Davis and D. B. Hair.
Third umpire: P. D. Parker. Referee: Hanumant Singh (India).

AUSTRALIA v SOUTH AFRICA

At Brisbane, January 20 (day/night). Australia won by 27 runs. Australia 4 pts. Toss: Australia.

Australia at last managed a win, if not a convincing one, in front of Brisbane's biggest crowd for a one-day international. Defying the critics, they continued their rotation policy, and made four changes (as did South Africa). Martyn scored a scampering fifty in which he hit no boundaries, before plundering the support bowling to reach his century in 117 balls. Ponting – batting mostly in a cap – played with greater ease, and alarmed drinkers in the Gabba bar by launching a six on to its glass roof. However, it was surprising to see Steve Waugh rather than Gilchrist at the fall of the fourth wicket, and Australia's final score should have been better. At 135 for three in the 32nd over, South Africa were marginal favourites. But their middle order flopped against Symonds, whose three wickets included a stunning caught-and-bowled from a full-blooded Boucher drive.

Man of the Match: D. R. Martyn.   *Attendance:* 35,761.

Australia

M. E. Waugh c Boucher b Elworthy	15	*S. R. Waugh not out		22
M. L. Hayden c Kirsten b Elworthy	10	W 2, n-b 5		7
R. T. Ponting c Gibbs b Klusener	80			
D. R. Martyn not out	104	1/25 2/29	(4 wkts, 50 overs)	241
A. Symonds c Rhodes b Boje	3	3/200 4/205		

†A. C. Gilchrist, S. K. Warne, A. J. Bichel, J. N. Gillespie and G. D. McGrath did not bat.

Bowling: Pollock 10–1–28–0; Elworthy 10–1–53–2; Langeveldt 5–0–31–0; Kallis 7–0–38–0; Klusener 8–0–48–1; Boje 10–0–43–1.

South Africa

H. H. Gibbs c Bichel b McGrath	18	N. Boje b McGrath		1
G. Kirsten c Gilchrist b McGrath	22	S. Elworthy not out		11
J. H. Kallis lbw b Gillespie	37	C. K. Langeveldt b McGrath		3
N. D. McKenzie c Gilchrist b Gillespie	68	L-b 1, w 6, n-b 1		8
J. N. Rhodes c Gilchrist b Symonds	2			
†M. V. Boucher c and b Symonds	10	1/34 2/49 3/126	(48.4 overs)	214
*S. M. Pollock c Hayden b Symonds	18	4/135 5/153 6/175		
L. Klusener b Bichel	16	7/191 8/199 9/204		

Bowling: McGrath 9.4–0–30–4; Gillespie 10–1–60–2; Bichel 9–1–27–1; Warne 10–1–48–0; Symonds 10–0–48–3.

Umpires: D. J. Harper and S. J. A. Taufel.
Third umpire: P. D. Parker.   Referee: Hanumant Singh (India).

AUSTRALIA v SOUTH AFRICA

At Sydney, January 22 (day/night). Australia won by eight wickets. Australia 5 pts. Toss: South Africa.

Pollock's decision to bat in perfect conditions for seam bowling proved a disaster. Australia won so comprehensively that a bonus point carried them past South Africa to second place in the table. By the 22nd over, South Africa were 50 for seven, still 19 short of their lowest one-day international total, also against Australia at Sydney, in 1993-94. The pitch offered wicked movement off the seam, and the Australian fast men put the ball in the right places; surviving, let alone scoring, was difficult. South Africa were already two down when a brief but heavy shower soaked the pitch and reduced the batsmen to a series of hopeful pokes and jabs. Only Kirsten looked at all comfortable, and even he took 30 overs to compile 44; six of his team-mates made ducks. Bichel was rewarded for an immaculate line and length, completing a career-best five for 19 with a spectacular diving catch to remove Ntini. When their turn came, the Australians decided not to hang around waiting for the unplayable delivery. Mark Waugh and Ponting carried them home inside 19 overs on a flood of boundaries.

Man of the Match: A. J. Bichel.   *Attendance:* 39,213.

South Africa

H. H. Gibbs c Gilchrist b McGrath	0
G. Kirsten lbw b Warne	44
H. H. Dippenaar c Warne b McGrath . . .	0
N. D. McKenzie b Bichel	18
J. N. Rhodes c Gilchrist b Bichel	0
†M. V. Boucher lbw b Bichel	1
*S. M. Pollock lbw b Bichel	0
L. Klusener lbw b Gillespie	0
N. Boje not out	13
S. Elworthy c S. R. Waugh b McGrath . .	18
M. Ntini c and b Bichel	0
L-b 3, w 9	12

1/1 2/5 3/42 4/44 (38.3 overs) 106
5/49 6/49 7/50 8/79 9/103

Bowling: McGrath 10–1–29–3; Gillespie 9–1–27–1; Symonds 4–0–7–0; Bichel 6.3–0–19–5; Warne 6–1–13–1; M. E. Waugh 3–0–8–0.

Australia

M. E. Waugh not out	55
†A. C. Gilchrist b Pollock	8
R. T. Ponting b Klusener	33
D. R. Martyn not out	6
L-b 1, w 1, n-b 3	5

1/24 2/101 (2 wkts, 18.4 overs) 107

*S. R. Waugh, M. G. Bevan, A. Symonds, S. K. Warne, A. J. Bichel, J. N. Gillespie and G. D. McGrath did not bat.

Bowling: Pollock 7–0–36–1; Ntini 7–2–36–0; Klusener 2.4–0–28–1; Boje 2–0–6–0.

Umpires: D. B. Hair and D. J. Harper.
Third umpire: S. J. A. Taufel. Referee: Hanumant Singh (India).

AUSTRALIA v NEW ZEALAND

At Adelaide, January 26 (day/night). New Zealand won by 77 runs. New Zealand 5 pts. Toss: New Zealand.

Bond gate-crashed Australia's national-day celebrations, taking five for 25 as New Zealand upset their hosts once again. Thanks to a comeback innings of 95 from Astle, who returned from injury to pass Martin Crowe's national record of 4,704 runs in one-day matches, and some more booming shots from Cairns, New Zealand set a target of 243, then demolished the stunned Australians for 165. Bond removed the three most dangerous batsmen – Ponting, Martyn and Gilchrist – in a 19-ball burst, before returning to earn New Zealand a bonus point by bouncing out Bichel and whistling a yorker through Gillespie's defences. At the time, his was the third-best one-day analysis for New Zealand, behind Matt Hart's five for 22 against West Indies in 1994-95 and Richard Collinge's five for 23 against India in 1975-76, and level with Richard Hadlee's haul against Sri Lanka in 1983.

Man of the Match: S. E. Bond. *Attendance:* 28,011.

New Zealand

B. B. McCullum c Gilchrist b McGrath .	0
N. J. Astle b McGrath	95
L. Vincent c Symonds b M. E. Waugh . .	55
C. D. McMillan c and b M. E. Waugh . .	8
*S. P. Fleming st Gilchrist b Warne	13
C. L. Cairns not out	39
C. Z. Harris not out	19
L-b 8, w 5	13

1/0 2/128 3/152 (5 wkts, 50 overs) 242
4/176 5/197

†A. C. Parore, D. J. Nash, D. L. Vettori and S. E. Bond did not bat.

Bowling: McGrath 10–3–36–2; Gillespie 10–1–40–0; Warne 10–1–33–1; Bichel 6–0–57–0; Symonds 6–0–30–0; M. E. Waugh 8–0–38–2.

Australia

†A. C. Gilchrist b Bond	21		A. J. Bichel c Astle b Bond		7
M. E. Waugh c and b Nash	0		J. N. Gillespie b Bond		15
R. T. Ponting c Parore b Bond	0		G. D. McGrath not out		6
D. R. Martyn c Vincent b Bond	2		L-b 1, w 2, n-b 3		6
*S. R. Waugh c Fleming b Vettori	30				
M. G. Bevan c Bond b Harris	45		1/7 2/8 3/25	(45.2 overs)	165
A. Symonds c McCullum b Harris	11		4/26 5/97 6/106		
S. K. Warne c Parore b Cairns	22		7/114 8/139 9/154		

Bowling: Nash 8–1–31–1; Bond 9.2–2–25–5; Cairns 6–0–19–1; Vettori 10–0–44–1; Astle 2–0–10–0; Harris 10–0–35–2.

Umpires: S. J. Davis and S. J. A. Taufel.

Third umpire: D. J. Harper.   Referee: Hanumant Singh (India).

NEW ZEALAND v SOUTH AFRICA

At Adelaide, January 27 (day/night). South Africa won by 93 runs. South Africa 5 pts. Toss: South Africa.

New Zealand had the South African innings in a straitjacket – 82 for two – at its midway point, but Rhodes and Boucher broke free and caused carnage. South Africa piled on 111 in the final ten overs, with Boucher smiting 57 off only 32 balls and Rhodes, passing 5,000 runs in one-day internationals, scampering 55 from 54. In reply, McCullum and Vincent threw the bat briefly but only Fleming, who grafted to 43, showed enough resolve on a wearing pitch as Boje spun his way through the lower middle order. New Zealand's chase petered out in the 46th over – 94 runs short of victory and 43 short of denying South Africa a bonus point. South Africa were now back in second place, ahead of Australia, with one round to go.

Man of the Match: M. V. Boucher.   *Attendance:* 10,889.

South Africa

H. H. Gibbs b Cairns	89		*S. M. Pollock not out		4
G. Kirsten c Parore b Bond	0				
J. H. Kallis c Parore b Cairns	30		B 2, l-b 6, w 5		13
N. D. McKenzie c Parore b Vettori	5				
J. N. Rhodes c Fleming b Franklin	55		1/9 2/74 3/93	(5 wkts, 50 overs)	253
†M. V. Boucher not out	57		4/156 5/242		

J. L. Ontong, N. Boje, M. Ntini and A. A. Donald did not bat.

Bowling: Franklin 10–0–39–1; Bond 10–0–47–1; Cairns 10–0–69–2; Vettori 10–0–34–1; Harris 10–0–56–0.

New Zealand

B. B. McCullum lbw b Kallis	29		D. L. Vettori c Ontong b Boje		0
N. J. Astle c Boucher b Pollock	0		J. E. C. Franklin lbw b Donald		2
L. Vincent c Donald b Pollock	20		S. E. Bond c Donald b Ntini		9
*S. P. Fleming c Gibbs b Donald	43		B 3, l-b 7, w 4, n-b 2		16
C. D. McMillan c Ontong b Boje	16				
C. L. Cairns c Rhodes b Boje	9		1/1 2/37 3/59	(45.2 overs)	160
C. Z. Harris not out	9		4/102 5/130 6/134		
†A. C. Parore b Boje	7		7/145 8/145 9/148		

Bowling: Pollock 8–0–24–2; Ntini 9.2–1–32–1; Kallis 6–0–18–1; Donald 10–0–37–2; Boje 10–0–31–4; Ontong 2–0–8–0.

Umpires: D. J. Harper and R. L. Parry.

Third umpire: S. J. Davis.   Referee: Hanumant Singh (India).

AUSTRALIA v NEW ZEALAND

At Melbourne, January 29 (day/night). Australia won by two wickets. Australia 4 pts. Toss: New Zealand.

Michael Bevan played one of the great one-day innings to postpone New Zealand's qualification for the finals. With Australia 82 for six in the 22nd over and in danger of crashing out of the tournament, Bevan's counter-attacking century propelled them to an astounding two-wicket win. In a beautifully paced innings, he never panicked, chipping away at the total to reach 50 off 58 balls, then knocking big chunks off it as he took just 35 more deliveries to complete his century. His heroics, however, would have been impossible without solid lower-order support: he added 61 with Warne, 81 with Lee and an unbeaten 24 with Bichel. Australia scored at eight an over during the last 11 overs. New Zealand missed Cairns, who had earlier hit a brisk half-century, but was unable to bowl because of a back problem. Bond let the attack outstandingly well, but the medium-pacers were expensive.

Man of the Match: M. G. Bevan.   *Attendance:* 40,008.

New Zealand

L. Vincent c Gilchrist b McGrath	. . . . .	5
N. J. Astle c Warne b Lee	. . . .	11
*S. P. Fleming run out	. . . .	50
C. D. McMillan c Ponting b Harvey	. . .	34
C. L. Cairns c Bevan b Warne	. . . . . .	55
C. Z. Harris run out	. . . .	41
D. J. Nash run out	. . . .	24
†A. C. Parore lbw b McGrath	. . . .	1

A. R. Adams not out 13
D. L. Vettori not out 0

L-b 4, w 4, n-b 3 11

1/7 2/19 3/73   (8 wkts, 50 overs) 245
4/143 5/178 6/226
7/228 8/235

S. E. Bond did not bat.

Bowling: McGrath 10–0–41–2; Lee 8–0–32–1; Bichel 6–0–20–0; Warne 10–0–56–1; Harvey 10–0–59–1; S. R. Waugh 6–0–33–0.

Australia

M. E. Waugh c Adams b Nash	. . . .	21
†A. C. Gilchrist b Bond	. . . .	14
R. T. Ponting c Astle b Bond	. . . .	8
D. R. Martyn c Harris b Adams	. . . . .	6
*S. R. Waugh c Parore b Nash	. . . . . .	7
M. G. Bevan not out	. . . .	102
I. J. Harvey c Parore b Bond	. . . . . .	12
S. K. Warne c Bond b Adams	. . . .	29

B. Lee c Astle b Bond 27
A. J. Bichel not out 13

W 3, n-b 6 9

1/24 2/40 3/51   (8 wkts, 49.3 overs) 248
4/53 5/65 6/82
7/143 8/224

G. D. McGrath did not bat.

Bowling: Nash 9–0–50–2; Bond 9.3–2–38–4; Adams 10–0–52–2; Vettori 10–0–36–0; Harris 8–0–50–0; Astle 3–0–22–0.

Umpires: D. B. Hair and S. J. A. Taufel.
Third umpire: R. G. Patterson.   Referee: Hanumant Singh (India).

SOUTH AFRICA v NEW ZEALAND

At Perth, February 1 (day/night). South Africa won by 67 runs. South Africa 5 pts. Toss: New Zealand.

The side effects of the bonus-point system grossly distorted this match. A win would have guaranteed New Zealand entry to the final, but – extraordinarily – the second-best result for them was a defeat heavy enough to give South Africa a fifth point. What they wanted to avoid was a narrow defeat: no bonus point for South Africa would mean Australia needed only four points (a narrow win) in their last match to squeeze New Zealand out of the final, rather than five (a win plus a bonus point). Fleming followed the logical course unwaveringly: chasing 271, New Zealand went for the runs during the first 25 overs but took their foot off the throttle once they were reduced to 129 for five. A score of 216 or under would gift South Africa the bonus point, so the remaining batsmen blocked out the last 21 overs, adding just 73. The poring over calculators overshadowed a glorious South African recovery. From 35 for four, Rhodes and Boucher ran the New Zealanders to distraction, and once Pollock arrived the fielders watched helplessly as the ball soared overhead. He clobbered 40 off the last two overs, including four consecutive sixes off James Franklin – three lofted drives and a pull – and finished with 69 from 34 balls. Rhodes took the match award; Pollock simply took the breath away.

Man of the Match: J. N. Rhodes.   *Attendance:* 14,853.

South Africa

H. H. Gibbs c Fleming b Nash	8	*S. M. Pollock not out		69
G. Kirsten c Vincent b Franklin	0			
J. H. Kallis b Nash	11	L-b 5, w 4, n-b 5		14
N. D. McKenzie b Nash	3			
J. N. Rhodes not out	107	1/10 2/14 3/23	(5 wkts, 50 overs)	270
†M. V. Boucher c Astle b Harris	58	4/35 5/173		

N. Boje, J. M. Kemp, A. A. Donald and M. Ntini did not bat.

Bowling: Franklin 10–0–65–1; Nash 10–0–37–3; Adams 10–0–57–0; Styris 8–0–43–0; Vettori 4–0–21–0; McMillan 3–0–15–0; Harris 5–0–27–1.

New Zealand

L. Vincent c Boucher b Donald	22	†A. C. Parore not out		36
N. J. Astle c Kallis b Ntini	0	D. L. Vettori not out		20
A. R. Adams c Boucher b Ntini	10			
*S. P. Fleming c Boucher b Kallis	27	L-b 9, w 5, n-b 4		18
C. D. McMillan c Kirsten b Pollock	46			
S. B. Styris c Kemp b Pollock	12	1/4 2/22 3/61	(8 wkts, 50 overs)	203
C. Z. Harris lbw b Boje	0	4/72 5/129 6/130		
D. J. Nash c Gibbs b Donald	12	7/130 8/156		

J. E. C. Franklin did not bat.

Bowling: Pollock 10–1–55–2; Ntini 10–1–23–2; Kallis 10–1–44–1; Donald 10–2–35–2; Kemp 2–0–18–0; Boje 8–0–19–1.

Umpires: D. B. Hair and D. J. Harper.
Third umpire: R. L. Parry.   Referee: Hanumant Singh (India).

AUSTRALIA v SOUTH AFRICA

At Perth, February 3. Australia won by 33 runs. Australia 4 pts. Toss: South Africa.

The key number was 226. Once South Africa, already assured of a place in the final, had passed it, a bonus point for Australia was impossible. They knew they had been prematurely dumped out of their annual tournament, for only the third time in 23 years, and the WACA crowd began to drift home. Put in, Australia made 283. It was a big total, but they needed a massive one to help secure the bonus point required to reach the final. Lehmann made a memorable return, after ten months on the sidelines, and Lee smashed 26 off five balls in one Donald over, but none of the front-line batsmen reached fifty. Kallis batted in his mechanical but bison-shouldered style; his century was not artistic, nor enough to claim a win, but it was sufficient to deny Australia's ultimate objective, and to salve South African pride after their thrashing in the Tests.

Man of the Match: J. H. Kallis.   *Attendance:* 25,252.

 Had Cairns not been snared flush on the long-on boundary there would have been dancing in the streets of Auckland.
Australia v New Zealand, page 1212

Australia

†A. C. Gilchrist b Ntini	31	S. K. Warne b Pollock	0
M. E. Waugh c Kallis b Donald	34	B. Lee not out	51
R. T. Ponting run out	26	B 1, l-b 12, w 6, n-b 1	20
D. R. Martyn c Boucher b Boje	29		
*S. R. Waugh c Kallis b Donald	42	1/47 2/76 3/117 (7 wkts, 50 overs) 283
M. G. Bevan c Pollock b Ntini . . .	1	4/150 5/157
D. S. Lehmann not out	49	6/194 7/195

A. J. Bichel and G. D. McGrath did not bat.

Bowling: Pollock 9–0–44–1; Ntini 10–1–58–2; Kallis 9–0–52–0; Donald 9–2–62–1; Boje 10–0–38–2; Klusener 3–0–16–0.

South Africa

H. H. Gibbs c Bevan b Bichel	34	L. Klusener not out	25
G. Kirsten c Martyn b Lee	10		
J. H. Kallis not out	104	L-b 1, w 6, n-b 5	12
H. H. Dippenaar c Gilchrist b McGrath .	33		
J. N. Rhodes c Martyn b Lehmann . . .	20	1/30 2/66 3/129 (5 wkts, 50 overs) 250
*M. V. Boucher c Bichel b Lehmann . . .	12	4/172 5/198

*S. M. Pollock, N. Boje, A. A. Donald and M. Ntini did not bat.

Bowling: McGrath 10–3–21–1; Lee 10–1–66–1; Bichel 9–0–38–1; Warne 10–0–53–0; Bevan 2–0–17–0; S. R. Waugh 4–0–26–0; Lehmann 5–0–28–2.

Umpires: S. J. Davis and R. L. Parry.
Third umpire: D. B. Hair. Referee: Hanumant Singh (India).

QUALIFYING TABLE

	Played	Won	Lost	Bonus points	Points	Net run-rate
South Africa	8	4	4	2	18	–0.04
New Zealand	8	4	4	1	17	–0.15
Australia	8	4	4	1	17	0.18

Win = 4 pts. One bonus point awarded for achieving victory with a run-rate 1.25 times that of the opposition. When two or more teams finish with an equal number of points, the positions are decided by (a) most wins (b) most wins in head-to-head matches (c) most bonus points (d) highest net run-rate. Net run-rate is calculated by subtracting runs conceded per over from runs scored per over.

NEW ZEALAND v SOUTH AFRICA

First Final

At Melbourne, February 6 (day/night). South Africa won by eight wickets. Toss: New Zealand.
New Zealand reserved one of their most inept batting performances for their most important game. Fleming played elegantly and McMillan showed unusual sticking power during a stand of 109, but only one of their team-mates managed double figures. Ntini caused bother with his awkward angles as he cut the ball away off the seam from wide of the crease, while Klusener's bowling proved less easy to milk than earlier in the tournament. New Zealand needed to score quickly in the final 15 overs, but Ntini's return was the beginning of the end, and he finished with a career-best five for 31. In front of a sparse and less than animated crowd, Dion Nash bowled one over before breaking down in what proved to be his final international. South Africa coasted

home with almost five overs in hand, courtesy of a 139-run third-wicket partnership between Dippenaar and Kallis, who passed 5,000 runs in one-day internationals.

Man of the Match: M. Ntini.   *Attendance:* 20,671.

New Zealand

L. Vincent c Rhodes b Ntini	7	A. R. Adams c Klusener b Ntini 13
N. J. Astle c Kallis b Ntini	9	D. L. Vettori not out 6
*S. P. Fleming c Kallis b Klusener	50	S. E. Bond run out 1
C. D. McMillan run out	73	L-b 5, w 6 11
C. L. Cairns c Kirsten b Klusener	0	
C. Z. Harris c Boucher b Pollock	9	1/15 2/18 3/127 (47.5 overs) 190
D. J. Nash c Donald b Ntini	9	4/128 5/155 6/158
†A. C. Parore c Boucher b Ntini	2	7/168 8/168 9/187

Bowling: Pollock 9–0–30–1; Ntini 10–0–31–5; Donald 8–0–44–0; Kallis 6.5–0–25–0; Klusener 7–0–27–2; Boje 7–0–28–0.

South Africa

H. H. Gibbs c Parore b Cairns	24
G. Kirsten run out	25
J. H. Kallis not out	59
H. H. Dippenaar not out	79
L-b 1, w 1, n-b 2	4

1/51 2/52   (2 wkts, 45.1 overs) 191

J. N. Rhodes, †M. V. Boucher, L. Klusener, *S. M. Pollock, N. Boje, A. A. Donald and M. Ntini did not bat.

Bowling: Bond 8–2–21–0; Nash 1–0–6–0; Adams 8–0–32–0; Vettori 5–0–32–0; Cairns 8–1–27–1; McMillan 3–0–14–0; Harris 9.1–0–44–0; Astle 3–0–14–0.

Umpires: D. J. Harper and S. J. A. Taufel.
Third umpire: R. L. Parry.   Referee: Hanumant Singh (India).

NEW ZEALAND v SOUTH AFRICA

Second Final

At Sydney, February 8 (day/night). South Africa won by six wickets (D/L method). Toss: New Zealand.

South Africa's second comprehensive victory meant they won the VB finals without recourse to a decider. It was their 14th win in 15 completed one-day games against New Zealand, but it was a dull match. Again, their bowling stifled the opposition. It took Vincent and Astle five overs to score their first runs, though once Vincent got going he was brutal enough on Ntini to end up with 43 in 42 balls. After he was third out at 68, New Zealand needed consolidation; instead, Fleming and McMillan both fell in the next two overs playing across the line. As late-order wickets tumbled, only a composed 57 from Cairns prevented humiliation. A brief but spectacular thunderstorm meant South Africa's target was revised to 172 in 46 overs. A fluent performance from Gibbs ensured they were always on course for an easy win, which arrived with nearly eight overs to spare. Rhodes played a busy innings to finish as the tournament's leading run-scorer, with 345.

Man of the Match: J. N. Rhodes.   *Attendance:* 30,984.
Man of the Series: S. E. Bond.

New Zealand

L. Vincent c Ntini b Kallis	43
N. J. Astle c Klusener b Pollock	7
A. R. Adams c Boucher b Ntini	1
*S. P. Fleming c Dippenaar b Donald	17
C. D. McMillan c Ntini b Kallis	0
C. L. Cairns c Boje b Kallis	57
C. Z. Harris lbw b Klusener	31
†A. C. Parore c Gibbs b Klusener	0
D. L. Vettori lbw b Donald	3
J. E. C. Franklin lbw b Donald	0
S. E. Bond not out	5
B 2, l-b 1, w 8	11

1/15 2/17 3/68   (41.1 overs) 175
4/68 5/72 6/147
7/147 8/157 9/157

Bowling: Pollock 6–2–24–1; Ntini 7–2–45–1; Donald 8–0–29–3; Kallis 5.1–0–23–3; Boje 8–0–21–0; Klusener 7–0–30–2.

South Africa

H. H. Gibbs b Adams	46
G. Kirsten c Parore b Bond	2
J. H. Kallis c Parore b Adams	10
H. H. Dippenaar c Parore b Cairns	29
J. N. Rhodes not out	61
†M. V. Boucher not out	16
L-b 1, w 6, n-b 2	9

1/50 2/65   (4 wkts, 38.1 overs) 173
3/68 4/141

L. Klusener, *S. M. Pollock, N. Boje, A. A. Donald and M. Ntini did not bat.

Bowling: Bond 8–2–31–1; Franklin 4–0–29–0; Vettori 4.1–0–25–0; Adams 8–0–33–2; Cairns 7–1–32–1; Astle 2–0–5–0; Harris 5–0–17–0.

Umpires: S. J. Davis and S. J. A. Taufel.
Third umpire: D. J. Harper. Referee: Hanumant Singh (India).

FICA/WCM PLACE IN HISTORY AWARD

The Federation of International Cricket Associations/*Wisden Cricket Monthly* International Place in History 2002 award went to Matthew Hayden and Justin Langer, who shared four double-century partnerships in Tests for Australia during the 2001-02 season.

SHARJAH CUP, 2001-02

As night fell over the Sharjah Cup final, the fans – many of whom had queued since dawn – waited for the post-match formalities. The rumour was that they were being delayed because several dignitaries had not yet arrived. It seemed plausible: Pakistan had routed Sri Lanka in an abject 16.5 overs. The tournament's most consistent team had been humiliated by its most watchable.

After losing both qualifying games against Sri Lanka, the Pakistani juggernaut gathered speed to thunder to victory. Imran Nazir, on his latest entrance through Pakistan's ever-revolving door, swung his bat like a Mogul warrior's scimitar and scored 226 runs. Shahid Afridi – with a marksman's eye and a golfer's swing – formed the other half of an incendiary opening pair. His 183 runs included a hundred that brutally ended New Zealand's challenge. Yousuf Youhana made the only other century, in the final, when he and Younis Khan sapped Sri Lanka's spirit with running that belied Pakistan's reputation for comedy between the wickets. Shoaib Akhtar hurled down the quickest ball on record – 99mph – but was far more than a circus act: he was the top wicket-taker, with ten, and had the second-best economy rate, 3.86 an over.

But if Pakistan were less erratic than usual, they were ultimately lucky with the toss. Six of the seven games were won by the side batting first; the floodlights' sheen on the white pitch, and evening dew, making the ball slippy, were both cited. No captain fancied chasing, and in the final Waqar Younis called right.

Before their final débâcle, Sri Lanka slipped up only once. Marvan Atapattu was named Man of the Series for his 233 runs; Russel Arnold's calm and Upul Chandana's nerve turned the two group games against Pakistan. When the pressure gauge hit red in the second of these matches, Chaminda Vaas and Nuwan Zoysa conceded only nine runs in the final three overs. But the undoubted bowling star was Muttiah Muralitharan, the smiling assassin, who took nine wickets and conceded only 2.27 an over. Ten astonishing overs against New Zealand went for only nine runs, bagged five wickets and left several batsmen looking silly. When Murali tore shoulder ligaments in the final and was rushed to hospital, Sri Lanka lost a talisman as well as a spearhead. Their self-belief visibly ebbed, calling into question the insistence of Dav Whatmore, their coach, that they had become mentally tougher.

New Zealand were too exposed by injuries to sustain a challenge: half a dozen regulars cried off. Chris Nevin impressed as a hard-hitting opener but disappointed as a keeper before pulling a hamstring. Stephen Fleming bashed his finger, and Craig McMillan injured his foot. Those still standing battled hard, but the batting lacked firepower and, although Scott Styris collected nine wickets, Fleming had no banker to turn to when the going got tough.

Note: Matches in this section were not first-class.

PAKISTAN v SRI LANKA

At Sharjah, April 8 (day/night). Sri Lanka won by 41 runs. Sri Lanka 4 pts. Toss: Sri Lanka.

Pakistan's chase never got close. Earlier, their bowlers had scrapped their way back into the game, after Jayasuriya blasted 87 from 78 balls. When he nicked an out-swinger from Abdul Razzaq, Sri Lanka were 128 for four at the halfway point, and the match was beautifully poised. Arnold and Chandana tipped it Sri Lanka's way, adding 52 in 48 balls. Pakistan were fined one over for a slow over-rate, but were routed in 46. While Jayasuriya chopped and changed his bowlers, they limped to 73 for four in 21 overs – and that was before Muralitharan came on. When he did, Inzamam-ul-Haq overbalanced by a fraction and was smartly stumped. Razzaq fought hard, but had too much to do.

Man of the Match: S. T. Jayasuriya.

Sri Lanka

*S. T. Jayasuriya c Rashid Latif	
b Abdul Razzaq .	87
K. C. Sangakkara b Wasim Akram .	10
M. S. Atapattu c Rashid Latif	
b Shoaib Akhtar .	6
D. P. M. D. Jayawardene c sub	
(Shoaib Malik) b Abdul Razzaq .	8
R. P. Arnold c Waqar Younis	
b Saqlain Mushtaq .	57
†R. S. Kaluwitharana c Yousuf Youhana	
b Shoaib Akhtar .	15

U. D. U. Chandana c Younis Khan	
b Waqar Younis .	30
W. P. U. J. C. Vaas not out .	9
M. Muralitharan b Shoaib Akhtar .	1
D. N. T. Zoysa run out .	0
T. C. B. Fernando not out .	1
B 1, l-b 3, w 10, n-b 4.	18
1/50 2/92 3/110 (9 wkts, 50 overs)	242
4/128 5/171 6/223	
7/237 8/239 9/239	

Bowling: Wasim Akram 10–1–45–1; Waqar Younis 9–0–49–1; Shoaib Akhtar 10–1–30–3; Abdul Razzaq 9–0–49–2; Saqlain Mushtaq 10–0–48–1; Shahid Afridi 2–0–17–0.

Pakistan

Shahid Afridi b Vaas.	5
Imran Nazir c Jayawardene b Fernando .	25
Younis Khan c Kaluwitharana b Zoysa . .	7
Inzamam-ul-Haq st Kaluwitharana	
b Muralitharan .	37
Yousuf Youhana c Muralitharan	
b Fernando .	0
Abdul Razzaq c Muralitharan	
b Jayasuriya .	56
†Rashid Latif c Vaas b Muralitharan . . .	41

Wasim Akram c Zoysa b Muralitharan . .	6
*Waqar Younis b Arnold .	2
Shoaib Akhtar not out .	3
Saqlain Mushtaq b Jayasuriya.	0
L-b 9, w 5, n-b 5 .	19
1/10 2/29 3/65 (45.5 overs)	201
4/65 5/94 6/166	
7/174 8/198 9/198	

Bowling: Vaas 8–1–31–1; Zoysa 7–1–20–1; Fernando 8–1–50–2; Chandana 4–0–19–0; Muralitharan 10–0–27–3; Jayasuriya 6.5–0–38–2; Arnold 2–0–7–1.

Umpires: D. R. Shepherd (England) and R. B. Tiffin (Zimbabwe).
Third umpire: S. Venkataraghavan (India).   Referee: G. R. Viswanath (India).

NEW ZEALAND v SRI LANKA

At Sharjah, April 9 (day/night). New Zealand won by 11 runs. New Zealand 4 pts. Toss: New Zealand.

A classic fight ended in Sri Lanka's only group defeat. New Zealand cantered to 83 for two in 15 overs before Muralitharan came on; afterwards, they might as well have been playing with sticks of rhubarb. His first spell culled Fleming, guiding to slip as if in a trance, Styris, lofting to mid-wicket, and Nevin, unluckily given out at bat-pad. The third umpire could only judge whether the ball carried (it had) not whether it hit the bat (it had not). Muralitharan thought he had Sinclair, too, caught on three, only for umpire Venkat to reinstate him, at least until Murali's second spell. From 159 for seven, Oram stoked a blazing recovery, with 46 from 33 balls, but Sri Lanka remained favourites. Despite a plodding start, in which Nevin dropped Atapattu three times, they needed 94 from 18 overs, with eight wickets in hand. But disciplined seam bowling and ferocious ground fielding built up the pressure. Butler took a great diving catch to dismiss Atapattu as the required rate crept up, and Sri Lanka crumpled.

Man of the Match: J. D. P. Oram.

New Zealand

†C. J. Nevin c sub (T. M. Dilshan)		J. D. P. Oram not out	46
b Muralitharan	45	J. E. C. Franklin c Jayasuriya b Fernando	9
N. J. Astle c Kaluwitharana b Zoysa	1	D. R. Tuffey not out	1
C. D. McMillan c Vaas b Zoysa	6		
*S. P. Fleming c Arnold b Muralitharan	34	L-b 7, w 4, n-b 2	13
S. B. Styris c Vaas b Muralitharan	2		
C. Z. Harris c Arnold b Muralitharan	33	1/6 2/31 3/86 (8 wkts, 50 overs) 218	
M. S. Sinclair c Sangakkara		4/92 5/99 6/155	
b Muralitharan	28	7/159 8/197	

I. G. Butler did not bat.

Bowling: Vaas 6–0–43–0; Zoysa 7–0–37–2; Arnold 7–0–40–0; Muralitharan 10–3–9–5; Chandana 10–0–32–0; Jayasuriya 7–0–31–0; Fernando 3–0–19–1.

Sri Lanka

*S. T. Jayasuriya c Fleming b Tuffey	1	D. N. T. Zoysa not out	19
K. C. Sangakkara c Tuffey b Butler	23	M. Muralitharan c Franklin b Oram	8
M. S. Atapattu c Butler b Harris	61	T. C. B. Fernando run out	2
D. P. M. D. Jayawardene c Tuffey b Styris	38	L-b 5, w 3, n-b 4	12
R. P. Arnold c Nevin b Astle	26		
†R. S. Kaluwitharana lbw b Astle	10	1/7 2/56 3/125 (49.1 overs) 207	
U. D. U. Chandana c Tuffey b Styris	7	4/134 5/159 6/173	
W. P. U. J. C. Vaas c McMillan b Styris	0	7/174 8/181 9/199	

Bowling: Tuffey 8–3–28–1; Franklin 4–1–16–0; Oram 7.1–0–31–1; Butler 7–0–32–1; Harris 10–0–37–1; Styris 10–0–42–3; Astle 3–0–16–2.

Umpires: R. B. Tiffin (Zimbabwe) and S. Venkataraghavan (India).
Third umpire: D. R. Shepherd (England).   Referee: G. R. Viswanath (India).

NEW ZEALAND v PAKISTAN

At Sharjah, April 11 (day/night). Pakistan won by 51 runs. Pakistan 4 pts. Toss: Pakistan.

A beautifully constructed 288 from Pakistan left New Zealand scrabbling for runs. Shahid Afridi and Imran Nazir peppered the boundary and when Afridi went, in the 14th over, they had already blitzed 98. Franklin and Butler were shellshocked, forcing Fleming to eke out overs from eight bowlers. Only Styris was economical: his ten overs of medium-pace all-sorts cost the same as four of raw pace from Butler. Styris shook Pakistan with three wickets in 15 balls, but a consolidating hundred partnership by Inzamam-ul-Haq and Younis Khan lit the fuse for some late fireworks – 28 in 16 balls – from Wasim Akram. No one had ever won at Sharjah chasing more than 285. Nevin harried, with aggressive hits over extra cover, but New Zealand could not maintain the rate and were forced into reckless shots.

Man of the Match: Inzamam-ul-Haq.

Pakistan

Imran Nazir c Nevin b Styris	47	Wasim Akram not out	28
Shahid Afridi b Styris	56	†Rashid Latif not out	7
Abdul Razzaq c Nevin b Styris	0	L-b 3, w 3, n-b 5	11
Inzamam-ul-Haq c Horne b McMillan	68		
Yousuf Youhana c Nevin b Styris	15	1/98 2/98 3/115 (6 wkts, 50 overs) 288	
Younis Khan b Tuffey	56	4/146 5/251 6/253	

*Waqar Younis, Saqlain Mushtaq and Shoaib Akhtar did not bat.

Bowling: Tuffey 9–0–53–1; Franklin 4–0–28–0; Butler 4–0–30–0; Oram 6–0–36–0; Styris 10–0–30–4; Harris 7–0–35–0; Astle 4–0–27–0; McMillan 6–0–46–1.

New Zealand

†C. J. Nevin c Waqar Younis	
b Shoaib Akhtar .	40
N. J. Astle c Rashid Latif	
b Wasim Akram .	12
M. S. Sinclair b Waqar Younis . . .	0
*C. D. McMillan b Saqlain Mushtaq . . .	51
C. Z. Harris c Shahid Afridi	
b Saqlain Mushtaq .	54
J. D. P. Oram b Waqar Younis.	6

M. J. Horne lbw b Waqar Younis.	1
S. B. Styris not out	27
J. E. C. Franklin b Shoaib Akhtar	13
D. R. Tuffey not out	5
B 4, l-b 12, w 12	28
1/32 2/34 3/65 (8 wkts, 50 overs) 237	
4/177 5/182 6/186	
7/187 8/222	

I. G. Butler did not bat.

    Bowling: Wasim Akram 10–2–42–1; Waqar Younis 10–0–43–3; Abdul Razzaq 8–1–39–0; Shoaib Akhtar 10–1–33–2; Saqlain Mushtaq 9–0–41–2; Shahid Afridi 3–0–23–0.

    Umpires: D. R. Shepherd (England) and S. Venkataraghavan (India).
    Third umpire: R. B. Tiffin (Zimbabwe).   Referee: G. R. Viswanath (India).

PAKISTAN v SRI LANKA

At Sharjah, April 12 (day/night). Sri Lanka won by nine runs. Sri Lanka 4 pts. Toss: Sri Lanka. Nerveless and disciplined bowling from Vaas and Zoysa won the game. With Wasim Akram crashing the ball to all corners, Pakistan needed 19 from their final three overs, but managed only nine, cramped by relentlessly straight bowling. The real blame lay with the sluggardly batting of the top order, who crawled to 87 for three in 25 overs. Chandana ran out Imran Nazir with a direct hit from point, then took a tricky return catch off Inzamam-ul-Haq. Earlier, Sri Lanka were drowning at 41 for four but were rescued by Atapattu's patience. He played the straight man to the cheekier Chandana, who whacked 64 off 58 balls in a stand of 107. Shoaib Akhtar bowled the fastest ball yet recorded – 99mph – but it was the discipline of Vaas and Zoysa that told in the end.
    Man of the Match: M. S. Atapattu.

Sri Lanka

*S. T. Jayasuriya b Waqar Younis	23
†R. S. Kaluwitharana c Rashid Latif	
b Waqar Younis .	7
K. C. Sangakkara c Rashid Latif	
b Wasim Akram .	5
D. P. M. D. Jayawardene c Rashid Latif	
b Wasim Akram .	1
M. S. Atapattu not out	77

R. P. Arnold c Imran Nazir	
b Shahid Afridi	41
U. D. U. Chandana b Shoaib Akhtar. . . .	64
B 1, l-b 6, w 4, n-b 10.	21
1/32 2/40 3/40 (6 wkts, 50 overs) 239	
4/41 5/132 6/239	

W. P. U. J. C. Vaas, D. N. T. Zoysa, M. Muralitharan and T. C. B. Fernando did not bat.

    Bowling: Wasim Akram 10–3–30–2; Waqar Younis 9–0–49–2; Shoaib Akhtar 9–1–51–1; Abdul Razzaq 6–0–34–0; Saqlain Mushtaq 10–0–40–0; Shahid Afridi 6–0–28–1.

Pakistan

Imran Nazir run out	34
Shahid Afridi c Muralitharan b Zoysa . .	0
Yousuf Youhana lbw b Fernando	38
Inzamam-ul-Haq c and b Chandana	37
Younis Khan run out.	45
Wasim Akram not out	36

†Rashid Latif not out	11
L-b 13, w 8, n-b 8.	29
1/0 2/72 3/87 (5 wkts, 50 overs) 230	
4/172 5/185	

Abdul Razzaq, *Waqar Younis, Saqlain Mushtaq and Shoaib Akhtar did not bat.

    Bowling: Vaas 9–1–25–0; Zoysa 8–1–30–1; Fernando 10–0–38–1; Muralitharan 10–0–29–0; Chandana 6–1–42–1; Jayasuriya 7–0–53–0.

    Umpires: D. R. Shepherd (England) and R. B. Tiffin (Zimbabwe).
    Third umpire: S. Venkataraghavan (India).   Referee: G. R. Viswanath (India).

NEW ZEALAND v SRI LANKA

At Sharjah, April 14 (day/night). Sri Lanka won by 46 runs. Sri Lanka 4 pts. Toss: Sri Lanka.

Sri Lanka's later batting fell away, but they had done enough. Atapattu stroked the ball in front of the wicket for a third consecutive fifty; Sangakkara began with a six, ended with three fours through the off side, and accumulated quietly in between. At 162 for two from 31 overs, a huge total beckoned. But soon after Atapattu and Jayawardene hit one Franklin over for 18, there was a serious misfire. Six wickets fell for 46, before Sinclair, the stand-in wicket-keeper, dropped Vaas on one, allowing him to help scramble 35 vital runs. New Zealand never got going: Horne went first ball, Astle remained out of form, and McMillan could not build the big innings required. Tigerish fielding and tight bowling guaranteed Sri Lanka's place in the final.

Man of the Match: M. S. Atapattu.

Sri Lanka

*S. T. Jayasuriya lbw b Tuffey	0	H. D. P. K. Dharmasena run out	7
M. S. Atapattu b Butler	82	W. P. U. J. C. Vaas not out	20
†K. C. Sangakkara c McMillan b Styris	50	D. N. T. Zoysa not out	7
D. P. M. D. Jayawardene lbw b Harris	39	B 1, w 5, n-b 4	10
R. P. Arnold lbw b Butler	1		
T. M. Dilshan c Sinclair b Harris	2	1/0 2/114 3/162 (9 wkts, 50 overs) 243	
U. D. U. Chandana c McMillan b Harris	21	4/164 5/169 6/196	
M. Muralitharan c Harris b Styris	4	7/203 8/208 9/224	

Bowling: Tuffey 8–0–40–1; Franklin 6–1–49–0; Butler 10–1–32–2; Oram 6–0–31–0; Styris 10–0–47–2; Harris 10–0–43–3.

New Zealand

M. J. Horne lbw b Vaas	0	J. E. C. Franklin not out	23
N. J. Astle c and b Vaas	14	D. R. Tuffey b Arnold	14
C. Z. Harris lbw b Zoysa	17	I. G. Butler not out	0
*S. P. Fleming b Dharmasena	19		
C. D. McMillan c Atapattu b Chandana	49	B 4, l-b 11, w 12, n-b 2	29
†M. S. Sinclair run out	16		
S. B. Styris lbw b Muralitharan	0	1/0 2/31 3/38 (9 wkts, 50 overs) 197	
J. D. P. Oram st Sangakkara		4/74 5/130 6/130	
b Dharmasena	16	7/138 8/158 9/187	

Bowling: Vaas 7–2–8–2; Zoysa 7–1–39–1; Dharmasena 10–1–42–2; Chandana 10–0–28–1; Muralitharan 10–1–26–1; Jayasuriya 3–0–26–0; Arnold 2–0–4–1; Jayawardene 1–0–9–0.

Umpires: R. B. Tiffin (Zimbabwe) and S. Venkataraghavan (India).
Third umpire: D. R. Shepherd (England). Referee: G. R. Viswanath (India).

NEW ZEALAND v PAKISTAN

At Sharjah, April 15 (day/night). Pakistan won by eight wickets. Pakistan 5 pts. Toss: New Zealand.

With both teams on four points, this was effectively a semi-final. New Zealand made a spectacular start, reaching 75 in 12 overs as Astle smashed a series of massive loose-armed drives and Horne punched through the leg side. But Saqlain Mushtaq's subtleties wrecked them: Horne was fooled by his straight ball and Astle fell to a sprawling catch by Waqar Younis, running back to long-on. Within three overs, New Zealand were 79 for four, and none of their bits-and-pieces players could strike a balance between daring and dawdling. Pakistan's openers bombarded a lightweight attack. Shahid Afridi hit Styris over long-on at will, taking three sixes from one over, and exerted demoralising power as he struck five over sixes and seven fours. Despite being docked an over for ambling in the field, Pakistan won with 17 to spare.

Man of the Match: Shahid Afridi.

New Zealand

M. J. Horne c and b Saqlain Mushtaq	27	B. G. K. Walker not out		16
N. J. Astle c Waqar Younis b Saqlain Mushtaq	36	D. R. Tuffey b Wasim Akram		0
		I. G. Butler not out		1
J. D. P. Oram run out	0			
†M. S. Sinclair b Shoaib Akhtar	0	B 2, l-b 12, w 6, n-b 2		22
*S. P. Fleming lbw b Abdul Razzaq	12			
C. Z. Harris lbw b Wasim Akram	35	1/75 2/76 3/76 (9 wkts, 50 overs)		213
S. B. Styris b Wasim Akram	43	4/79 5/101		
A. R. Adams st Rashid Latif b Saqlain Mushtaq	21	6/141 7/176 8/205 9/205		

Bowling: Wasim Akram 10–0–43–3; Waqar Younis 9–0–46–0; Shoaib Akhtar 10–0–41–1; Saqlain Mushtaq 10–2–26–3; Abdul Razzaq 7–2–24–1; Shahid Afridi 4–0–19–0.

Pakistan

Imran Nazir c Sinclair b Walker	57
Shahid Afridi not out	108
Yousuf Youhana c Fleming b Walker	24
Inzamam-ul-Haq not out	18
L-b 6, w 3, n-b 1	10

1/101 2/138   (2 wkts, 31.3 overs) 217

Younis Khan, Abdul Razzaq, †Rashid Latif, Wasim Akram, *Waqar Younis, Saqlain Mushtaq and Shoaib Akhtar did not bat.

Bowling: Tuffey 7–2–25–0; Butler 4.3–0–37–0; Adams 2–0–21–0; Styris 2–0–29–0; Walker 8–0–54–2; Harris 8–0–45–0.

Umpires: D. R. Shepherd (England) and S. Venkataraghavan (India).
Third umpire: R. B. Tiffin (Zimbabwe). Referee: G. R. Viswanath (India).

QUALIFYING TABLE

	Played	Won	Lost	Bonus points	Points	Net run-rate
Sri Lanka	4	3	1	0	12	0.40
Pakistan	4	2	2	1	9	0.53
New Zealand	4	1	3	0	4	–0.93

Win = 4 pts. One bonus point awarded for achieving victory with a run-rate 1.25 times that of the opposition. Net run-rate is calculated by subtracting runs conceded per over from runs scored per over.

FINAL

PAKISTAN v SRI LANKA

At Sharjah, April 17 (day/night). Pakistan won by 217 runs. Toss: Pakistan.

The 20,000 hollering fans saw a colourful but one-sided spectacle. After elbowing Pakistan aside in both qualifiers, Sri Lanka were trampled underfoot. Waqar Younis won an important toss, and Imran Nazir made a smash-and-grab 63 off 61 balls. However, the real damage was done by Yousuf Youhana, with a career-best 129, and Younis Khan. Darting between the wickets for ones and twos, they sentenced Sri Lanka to the death of a thousand cuts. With Muralitharan in hospital after tearing shoulder ligaments — on his 30th birthday — no one could staunch the flow. The pair put on 155 before perishing in successive balls, aiming for the leg-side ropes. At 52 for one from nine overs, Sri Lanka were on course, but they were soon buffeted by quality quick bowling: Jayasuriya, pulling, and Sangakkara, fencing, were both beaten for pace by Shoaib Akhtar. The middle order capitulated with shocking speed. Sri Lanka, minus Murali, were all out inside 17 overs for 78, their second-lowest one-day total.

Man of the Match: Yousuf Youhana.　　　*Man of the Series:* M. S. Atapattu.

Pakistan

Imran Nazir b Chandana	63	Abdul Razzaq not out 4
Shahid Afridi c Fernando b Zoysa	14	Wasim Akram not out 0
†Rashid Latif c Jayawardene b Vaas	0	L-b 3, w 2, n-b 2 7
Yousuf Youhana c Fernando b Zoysa	129	
Inzamam-ul-Haq run out	12	1/25 2/33 3/118　(6 wkts, 50 overs) 295
Younis Khan c Atapattu b Zoysa	66	4/136 5/291 6/291

*Waqar Younis, Saqlain Mushtaq and Shoaib Akhtar did not bat.

Bowling: Vaas 10–1–58–1; Zoysa 10–0–63–3; Fernando 9–0–61–0; Dharmasena 8–0–48–0; Chandana 10–1–47–1; Jayasuriya 3–0–15–0.

Sri Lanka

*S. T. Jayasuriya c and b Shoaib Akhtar	19	D. N. T. Zoysa b Waqar Younis 0
M. S. Atapattu b Wasim Akram	7	T. C. B. Fernando c Rashid Latif
†K. C. Sangakkara c Rashid Latif		b Wasim Younis . 0
b Shoaib Akhtar	18	M. Muralitharan absent hurt
W. P. U. J. C. Vaas lbw b Wasim Akram	1	B 1, w 3, n-b 5 9
D. P. M. D. Jayawardene b Waqar Younis	0	
R. P. Arnold c and b Shoaib Akhtar	19	1/19 2/52 3/53　(16.5 overs) 78
U. D. U. Chandana not out	4	4/53 5/57 6/76
H. D. P. K. Dharmasena run out	1	7/77 8/78 9/78

Bowling: Wasim Akram 6–1–33–2; Waqar Younis 6.5–0–33–3; Shoaib Akhtar 4–0–11–3.

Umpires: D. R. Shepherd (England) and R. B. Tiffin (Zimbabwe).
Third umpire: S. Venkataraghavan (India).　Referee: G. R. Viswanath (India).

TOWER SUPER CHALLENGE II, 2002

If it's true that only piffling tournaments need puffed-up titles, the ACB's second shot at midwinter cricket was always in trouble. The Tower Super Challenge II was partly redeemed by two gripping matches between the world's most exciting one-day teams – Australia and Pakistan. But, as the mercury plunged, dropping below 2°C shortly after the second game, it remained unclear whether Melbourne's sports-mad public could be convinced that cricket, cocoa and woollies went easily together. Even in temperate Brisbane, where the third match was held, the reaction was lukewarm. The winter experiment began to look more and more like an attempt to shove yet more cricket down the public's throat.

There were certainly several gimmicks to try to convince the punters. Before the tournament, journalists devoted dozens of column inches to the "pace race" between Brett Lee and Shoaib Akhtar, who had been unofficially clocked at over 100mph in April. Tower, a financial services company, even promised one lucky ticket-holder (chosen at random) $A25,000 if a bowler broke the magical 100mph mark, or if a batsman scored a run-a-ball hundred. (As it turned out, their money was safe, especially as Lee and Shoaib played just three games between them.) And if the hullabaloo about the world's fastest bowler didn't get the fans salivating, the Melbourne matches still had some novelty value from being played indoors.

But the public stayed at home. The total attendance plummeted from more than 90,000 for the first glimpse of indoor cricket in 2000 to around 40,000 this time. Cricket under a roof had proved, well, pretty similar to cricket outside, only colder. One commentator went as far as calling midwinter cricket "an insanity that has outstayed its welcome".

The tepid response was a shame, because a Pakistan team bursting with talent deserved better. After a clinical Australian win in the first match, Younis Khan kept his nerve to sneak a win in the second, before Pakistan, fired by Wasim Akram and Shoaib Akhtar, roared home in the decider.

The ball dominated the bat throughout, but seldom as thoroughly as when it was in Shoaib's hand. After missing the first match with a hip injury, then making an effective but subdued comeback in the second, he ripped the heart out of the Australian innings in the third. His five for 25 proved he was a match-winner rather than just a flamboyant sideshow. Wasim grabbed three big wickets in the second game, and his clean hitting changed the tone of the deciding match, while Shahid Afridi was Pakistan's most economical bowler but flapped – and flopped – with the bat.

Australia's batting fell far below expectations. They managed only two fifties and lost wickets in damaging bursts – two for nought and five for 29 in the second match, and five for 39 in the third. With the ball, Darren Lehmann's part-time twirlers, with four wickets and an economy rate of below three and a half, proved more effective than Lee's thunderbolts. Shane Watson went for more than five an over and did not yet look the answer at No. 7, but it was the batsmen who let the side down.

Note: Matches in this section were not first-class.

AUSTRALIA v PAKISTAN

First One-Day International

At Colonial Stadium, Melbourne, June 12 (day/night). Australia won by seven wickets. Toss: Australia.

The winter skies above the sealed roof were cold and murky, and the cricket played underneath it also lacked sparkle. Watched by a scattered crowd that was small by Melbourne standards, Australia cantered to an efficient, unremarkable win, which was all but clinched within 25 overs. McGrath and Bichel found zest in the drop-in pitch, zipping out four of the top order, all snared in the ring between keeper and point. The batsmen struggled to find rhythm against jagging seam movement and sharp bounce, and after 25 overs Pakistan had staggered to 78 for five – in effect for six after a savage short ball from McGrath hospitalised Imran Nazir with a suspected broken arm. Nazir returned later and hit some beefy drives, but Pakistan's 176 looked scanty. So it proved, as a slashing innings by Gilchrist and a muscular one by Hayden blasted Australia towards an easy win. With Brett Lee dropped and Shoaib Akhtar injured, the quest for the world's fastest man took place only in the papers.

Man of the Match: A. C. Gilchrist.   *Attendance:* 11,681.

Pakistan

Imran Nazir not out	39	Wasim Akram c Hayden b Watson	13
Shahid Afridi c Warne b McGrath	1	*Waqar Younis not out	9
Yousuf Youhana c Gilchrist b Warne	19		
Inzamam-ul-Haq c Gilchrist b Bichel	33	L-b 2, w 4, n-b 1	7
Younis Khan c Gilchrist b Bichel	16		
Azhar Mahmood c Martyn b Bichel	1	1/3 2/55 3/71 (8 wkts, 50 overs)	176
Shoaib Malik st Gilchrist b Lehmann	27	4/75 5/78 6/104	
†Rashid Latif c Gilchrist b Lehmann	11	7/124 8/153	

Mohammad Sami did not bat.

Imran Nazir, when 5, retired hurt at 6 and resumed at 104.

Bowling: McGrath 7–2–22–1; Gillespie 9–1–34–0; Bichel 10–1–30–3; Warne 10–1–27–1; Watson 9–0–38–1; Lehmann 5–0–23–2.

Australia

†A. C. Gilchrist c Shahid Afridi b Mohammad Sami	56	D. R. Martyn not out	18
M. L. Hayden c Shoaib Malik b Mohammad Sami	45	D. S. Lehmann not out	28
*R. T. Ponting c Rashid Latif b Shahid Afridi	13	L-b 4, w 3, n-b 10	17
		1/101 2/121 3/127 (3 wkts, 32.5 overs)	177

M. G. Bevan, S. R. Watson, S. K. Warne, A. J. Bichel, J. N. Gillespie and G. D. McGrath did not bat.

Bowling: Wasim Akram 6–1–24–0; Waqar Younis 5–0–31–0; Mohammad Sami 9–0–53–2; Azhar Mahmood 5–0–29–0; Shahid Afridi 5.5–0–29–1; Shoaib Malik 2–0–16–0.

Umpires: R. B. Tiffin (Zimbabwe) and D. J. Harper.
Third umpire: S. J. Davis.   Referee: C. H. Lloyd (West Indies).

AUSTRALIA v PAKISTAN

Second One-Day International

At Colonial Stadium, Melbourne, June 15 (day/night). Pakistan won by two wickets. Toss: Australia.
This match was as exciting as the first was workmanlike. Wasim Akram kick-started the drama: his very first ball was a perfect out-swinger that tickled Gilchrist's edge, and his third ballooned back to him off Ponting's bat and pad. A Bevan-inspired revival then snuffed out as Shahid Afridi picked off his partners: Martyn caught at point for 56, and Watson and Warne trapped on the crease by fast, fizzing leg-breaks. In fact, Martyn could have gone when just seven, after Waqar Younis claimed a low catch, but he was controversially reprieved by TV replays. Australia fought back hard in the field. Saeed Anwar's return to international cricket lasted two balls before he was run out from mid-off after backing-up too far and, when Lee blasted out two more in one over, Pakistan were on the ropes at 21 for three. Younis Khan rescued them with dainty footwork and solid driving, and they edged home in the penultimate over. Had Ponting given the ball to McGrath before the expensive Lee late in the innings, they might not have made it.

Man of the Match: Younis Khan.   *Attendance:* 16,981.

Australia

†A. C. Gilchrist c Rashid Latif	
b Wasim Akram .	0
J. P. Maher c Rashid Latif	
b Wasim Akram .	12
*R. T. Ponting c and b Wasim Akram . .	0
D. R. Martyn c Imran Nazir	
b Shahid Afridi .	56
D. S. Lehmann c Rashid Latif	
b Azhar Mahmood .	31
M. G. Bevan c Rashid Latif	
b Shoaib Akhtar .	30

S. R. Watson lbw b Shahid Afridi	8
S. K. Warne lbw b Shahid Afridi	1
A. J. Bichel b Shoaib Akhtar	7
B. Lee not out	3
G. D. McGrath run out	1
L-b 5, w 5, n-b 8	18

1/0 2/0 3/23   (45.4 overs) 167
4/89 5/121 6/138
7/143 8/163 9/164

Bowling: Wasim Akram 8–1–18–3; Waqar Younis 10–1–35–0; Azhar Mahmood 10–0–51–1; Shoaib Akhtar 8–0–30–2; Shahid Afridi 9.4–1–28–3.

Pakistan

Imran Nazir lbw b Lee	6
Saeed Anwar run out	0
Azhar Mahmood c Gilchrist b Lee	4
Yousuf Youhana c Martyn b Warne	29
Inzamam-ul-Haq b Bichel	24
Younis Khan not out	56
†Rashid Latif b Warne	16
Shahid Afridi c Ponting b Lehmann	3

Wasim Akram run out	10
*Waqar Younis not out	8
B 1, l-b 4, w 7	12

1/0 2/18 3/21   (8 wkts, 48.5 overs) 168
4/65 5/85 6/120
7/131 8/150

Shoaib Akhtar did not bat.

Bowling: McGrath 8.5–3–16–0; Lee 10–0–44–2; Watson 4–1–9–0; Bichel 10–1–28–1; Warne 10–0–49–2; Lehmann 6–0–17–1.

Umpires: R. B. Tiffin (Zimbabwe) and D. B. Hair.
Third umpire: S. J. A. Taufel. Referee: C. H. Lloyd (West Indies).

AUSTRALIA v PAKISTAN

Third One-Day International

At Brisbane, June 19 (day/night). Pakistan won by 91 runs. Toss: Pakistan.

Waqar Younis called it "a total team effort", but this match was turned by Wasim Akram and Shoaib Akhtar. Imran Nazir anchored Pakistan to a solid but unspectacular 108 for one in the 23rd over, but the pace was sluggish after he fell, even against forgettable Australian bowling. Things soon got worse as Inzamam's lbw started a helter-skelter tumble of wickets. Five crashed for 35 runs and at the end of the madness – including two run-outs – Pakistan were 168 for seven, with only ten overs left. But Wasim came out fighting, and changed the tone with a heavy-calibre 49 off just 32 balls, including two steepling sixes back over McGrath's head. Chasing 257, Australia were hobbled by Shoaib before they could get into their stride. Ponting played across a toe-crushing in-swinger, Lehmann wandered too far across his crease, Martyn failed to control a cut, and Shoaib had three wickets in three overs. When Bevan nicked a leg-cutter the match was all but over. Watson and Warne put on 57 but Australia needed an innings like Wasim's to stand a chance. They did not get one.

Man of the Match: Shoaib Akhtar.   *Attendance*: 11,612.
Man of the Series: Shoaib Akhtar.

Pakistan

Imran Nazir c Warne b Lehmann	. . . . .	66
Saeed Anwar lbw b Warne	. . . .	26
Yousuf Youhana not out	. . . .	61
Inzamam-ul-Haq lbw b Warne	. . . .	13
Younis Khan c Gilchrist b Gillespie	. . . .	2
†Rashid Latif c Gilchrist b Bichel	. . . . .	2
Azhar Mahmood run out	. . . .	6

Shahid Afridi run out	. . . .	14
Wasim Akram not out	. . . .	49
L-b 4, w 11, n-b 2	. . . .	17

1/94 2/108 3/133　　(7 wkts, 50 overs) 256
4/136 5/139
6/153 7/168

*Waqar Younis and Shoaib Akhtar did not bat.

Bowling: McGrath 10–3–48–0; Gillespie 10–0–43–1; Bichel 8–0–47–1; Watson 5–0–46–0; Warne 10–1–42–2; Lehmann 2.3–0–7–1; Martyn 4.3–0–19–0.

Australia

†A. C. Gilchrist run out	. . . .	20
M. L. Hayden lbw b Wasim Akram	. . . .	5
*R. T. Ponting b Shoaib Akhtar	. . . . . .	14
D. R. Martyn c Saeed Anwar		
b Shoaib Akhtar	.	10
D. S. Lehmann b Shoaib Akhtar	. . . . . .	0
M. G. Bevan c Rashid Latif		
b Shoaib Akhtar	.	10
S. R. Watson not out	. . . .	44
S. K. Warne b Shahid Afridi	. . . .	31

A. J. Bichel c Shoaib Akhtar		
b Shahid Afridi	.	0
J. N. Gillespie lbw b Shoaib Akhtar	. . . .	0
G. D. McGrath c Rashid Latif		
b Waqar Younis	.	3
B 9, l-b 7, w 5, n-b 7	. . . . . .	28

1/17 2/44 3/44　　　　(40 overs) 165
4/52 5/65 6/83
7/140 8/142 9/142

Bowling: Wasim Akram 7–0–27–1; Waqar Younis 8–0–41–1; Shoaib Akhtar 8–1–25–5; Azhar Mahmood 7–0–26–0; Shahid Afridi 10–2–30–2.

Umpires: R. B. Tiffin (Zimbabwe) and S. J. A. Taufel.
Third umpire: D. B. Hair.　　Referee: C. H. Lloyd (West Indies).

MOROCCO CUP, 2002

By DUNCAN STEER

There was something rather old-fashioned about international cricket's newest venue. True, it was big money from the man behind cricket in Sharjah, Abdulrahman Bukhatir, and his new TV network, 10 Sports, that brought South Africa, Sri Lanka and Pakistan to Tangier for north Africa's first top-level cricket tournament. True, too, that the stringent anti-corruption measures extended to CCTV cameras in the dressing-rooms. But as the seven games were played out in front of a handful of travelling supporters and curious locals lured partly by close-of-play raffle prizes (skateboards, mountain bikes), there was a certain village-green air about the proceedings. The $4m "stadium" – the money had been spent largely on a state-of-the-art grandstand – was, on three sides, merely grass banking strewn with parasols. The players' shouts echoed across a ground basking in perfect weather throughout. Even the elaborate Wallace-and-Gromit scoreboard looked 100 years old, although it had, in fact, been put together by a Tangier carpenter weeks before the tournament. It took a dozen local students to work the thing. In such a low-key atmosphere, you could almost forget that there was $250,000 prize money at stake, making the Morocco Cup one of the most lucrative one-day events on the calendar.

In Tangier, Bukhatir had found a perfect location for cricket in the months when Sharjah is too hot and the rest of the cricket world (except, arguably, England) too cold. For Pakistan, especially, the attractions of another neutral venue were great. The PCB had lost an estimated £20m worth of revenue in the previous 18 months thanks to the difficult political situation in the region.

Sri Lanka, whose last away trip had brought heavy defeat in England, were worthy winners, beating South Africa three times out of three, including the final, and they had the man of the tournament in their captain Sanath Jayasuriya. For South Africa, it was the first action of the new season and a first outing for the new coach, Eric Simons. For Pakistan, despite the commitment of supporters who had travelled from Britain, Pakistan and even Denmark, the tournament ended in typically enigmatic and disappointing fashion.

But the event itself was more important than any of the results. Though batting first on the new pitches seemed to offer a distinct advantage, reaction to the Morocco Cup was consistently positive, from players, media and spectators alike. Despite Morocco's lack of background in the game, the project was by no means all about subcontinental TV audiences. The former India batsman Mohinder Amarnath, recruited as national coach by Bukhatir, had persuaded nine football clubs to set up cricket teams in the previous three years, which had attracted some 400 active players. These young players were all in town, swelling the tournament attendance and in many cases taking the chance to bowl at the stars in the nets. Perhaps there was, after all, method in the apparent madness of handing out leaflets explaining the lbw law in French in the middle of Tangier.

The ICC chief executive, Malcolm Speed, attended the first match and pronounced himself "very impressed". All three competing teams signed up for further tournaments with Bukhatir and a second Morocco Cup was pencilled in for August 2003.

Note: Matches in this section were not first-class.

PAKISTAN v SOUTH AFRICA

At Tangier, August 12. South Africa won by 54 runs. South Africa 4 pts. Toss: South Africa.

North Africa's very first foray into top-level international cricket was partly coloured by a story from the other end of the continent: this was South Africa's first game since the death of Hansie Cronje on June 1. Pollock and his team wore black armbands, observed a minute's silence and later dedicated their victory to Cronje, saying they had "tried to produce a performance he would be proud of". Wasim Akram bowled the first-ever ball at Tangier, as he began his world-record 335th one-day international. South Africa batted watchfully on a square that had previously hosted just two club games – and were boosted by some generous fielding from the Pakistanis. Gibbs, who had been both mentored and led astray by Cronje, marked the occasion with his seventh one-day international hundred, and Boje provided the fireworks with 52 off 45 balls. Pakistan's reply was all cameo and no substance. South Africa's fielding was sharp despite, or because of, their four-month lay-off, but the real difference between the sides was intelligence – the South Africans were quicker to see the need to bat shrewdly rather than showily, and to vary the pace of the ball. After Kallis swung the match South Africa's way, Pakistan remained in the hunt until Rashid Latif and Abdul Razzaq fell to successive balls to turn 221 for six into 221 for eight with ten overs to go.

Man of the Match: H. H. Gibbs.

South Africa

H. H. Gibbs c Inzamam-ul-Haq b Abdul Razzaq	114	
G. Kirsten c Rashid Latif b Waqar Younis	2	
J. H. Kallis c Rashid Latif b Waqar Younis	23	
N. Boje c Imran Nazir b Shahid Afridi	52	
J. N. Rhodes run out	46	
L. Klusener c Younis Khan b Waqar Younis	11	

†M. V. Boucher b Waqar Younis 3
*S. M. Pollock b Waqar Younis 0
H. H. Dippenaar run out 12
A. A. Donald not out 0
B 1, l-b 6, w 6, n-b 7 20

1/11 2/51 3/136 (9 wkts, 50 overs) 283
4/257 5/259 6/265
7/265 8/283 9/283

M. Ntini did not bat.

Bowling: Wasim Akram 10–0–50–0; Waqar Younis 10–0–38–5; Abdul Razzaq 10–0–54–1; Saqlain Mushtaq 10–0–80–0; Shahid Afridi 10–0–54–1.

Pakistan

Saeed Anwar c Ntini b Kallis	23	
Imran Nazir lbw b Kallis	40	
Yousuf Youhana c Gibbs b Donald	19	
Inzamam-ul-Haq c Donald b Boje	25	
Younis Khan c Pollock b Boje	40	
Shahid Afridi c Gibbs b Pollock	33	
Abdul Razzaq b Donald	18	
†Rashid Latif lbw b Klusener	15	

*Waqar Younis c Dippenaar b Klusener . 1
Wasim Akram b Klusener 4
Saqlain Mushtaq not out 3
B 1, l-b 3, w 3, n-b 1 8

1/55 2/69 3/99 (43.2 overs) 229
4/132 5/159 6/193
7/221 8/221 9/224

Bowling: Pollock 8–1–46–1; Ntini 5–0–46–0; Kallis 8–0–18–2; Donald 8–0–27–2; Klusener 8.2–0–45–3; Boje 6–0–43–2.

Umpires: D. J. Harper (Australia) and S. Venkataraghavan (India).
Third umpire: S. J. A. Taufel (Australia). Referee: G. R. Viswanath (India).

PAKISTAN v SRI LANKA

At Tangier, August 14. Pakistan won by 28 runs. Pakistan 4 pts. Toss: Sri Lanka.

Like South Africa on the first day, Pakistan had a special motivation: this was their national independence day. After the cannily restrictive bowling of the South Africans, Waqar Younis's strokeplayers found Sri Lanka much more to their liking. A partnership of 50 off only 22 balls between Younis Khan and Abdul Razzaq was the highlight as the last ten overs yielded 99 runs. In reply, Jayasuriya hit his stride immediately. But after his run-a-ball 36, the Sri Lankans found no momentum. By the time de Silva – who had played in the first game at Sharjah 18 years earlier – reached the middle, the job was too great, as the Sri Lankans' progress was strangled by Shahid Afridi's leg-spin and the young fast bowler Mohammad Sami – 90mph and economical.

Man of the Match: Younis Khan.

Pakistan

Saeed Anwar b Chandana	70	Younis Khan not out	56
Imran Nazir lbw b Vaas	9	Abdul Razzaq not out	29
Yousuf Youhana c Sangakkara b Fernando	32	L-b 1, w 5, n-b 1	7
Inzamam-ul-Haq c Jayawardene b Gunaratne	63	1/15 2/85 3/147 (5 wkts, 50 overs) 279	
Shahid Afridi c Chandana b Muralitharan	13	4/170 5/229	

†Rashid Latif, Wasim Akram, *Waqar Younis and Mohammad Sami did not bat.

Bowling: Vaas 10–0–61–1; Gunaratne 10–0–69–1; Fernando 9–0–56–1; Muralitharan 10–1–35–1; Chandana 5–0–29–1; Jayasuriya 6–0–28–0.

Sri Lanka

*S. T. Jayasuriya c Imran Nazir b Wasim Akram	36	P. A. de Silva lbw b Mohammad Sami	2
M. S. Atapattu c Abdul Razzaq b Shahid Afridi	42	W. P. U. J. C. Vaas c Shahid Afridi b Wasim Akram	31
†K. C. Sangakkara c Wasim Akram b Abdul Razzaq	38	P. W. Gunaratne b Abdul Razzaq	0
D. P. M. D. Jayawardene c Shahid Afridi b Abdul Razzaq	32	C. R. D. Fernando not out	1
U. D. U. Chandana c Yousuf Youhana b Waqar Younis	15	L-b 7, w 7, n-b 3	17
R. P. Arnold not out	37	1/55 2/116 3/141 (8 wkts, 50 overs) 251 4/161 5/187 6/191	
		7/249 8/250	

M. Muralitharan did not bat.

Bowling: Wasim Akram 10–0–56–2; Waqar Younis 10–0–77–1; Abdul Razzaq 10–1–36–3; Mohammad Sami 10–0–39–1; Shahid Afridi 10–1–36–1.

Umpires: D. J. Harper (Australia) and S. J. A. Taufel (Australia).
Third umpire: S. Venkataraghavan (India).   Referee: G. R. Viswanath (India).

SRI LANKA v SOUTH AFRICA

At Tangier, August 15. Sri Lanka won by 93 runs. Sri Lanka 5 pts. Toss: Sri Lanka.
Winning with a bonus point, Sri Lanka went to the top of the table. They were inspired by a characteristic innings from de Silva, working the field to keep the scoreboard ticking over and hitting just four boundaries in his 73. Fernando and spinner Chandana made key contributions to a disciplined Sri Lankan bowling performance, allowing Jayasuriya the luxury of not introducing Muralitharan until the 24th over – by which time the South Africans were already five wickets down and struggling.
Man of the Match: P. A. de Silva.

Sri Lanka

*S. T. Jayasuriya c Pollock b Donald	49	R. P. Arnold run out	10
M. S. Atapattu lbw b Kallis	35	C. R. D. Fernando not out	1
†K. C. Sangakkara c Ontong b Klusener	41	L-b 3, w 3, n-b 2	8
P. A. de Silva not out	73		
D. P. M. D. Jayawardene c Kirsten b Telemachus	32	1/84 2/88 3/146 (7 wkts, 50 overs) 267 4/216 5/246	
W. P. U. J. C. Vaas c Boje b Donald	18	6/246 7/263	
U. D. U. Chandana c and b Kallis	0		

P. W. Gunaratne and M. Muralitharan did not bat.

Bowling: Pollock 10–0–44–0; Telemachus 10–0–59–1; Kallis 10–1–47–2; Donald 10–0–47–2; Klusener 7–0–43–1; Boje 3–0–24–0.

South Africa

H. H. Gibbs b Gunaratne	11	*S. M. Pollock c Jayawardene		
G. Kirsten run out	55		b Jayasuriya	9
N. Boje c Arnold b Fernando	17	R. Telemachus c and b Jayasuriya		1
J. H. Kallis c Arnold b Fernando	7	A. A. Donald b Jayasuriya		0
J. L. Ontong st Sangakkara b Chandana	9	L-b 2, w 4, n-b 1		7
J. N. Rhodes b Muralitharan	17			
†M. V. Boucher c Sangakkara		1/18 2/69 3/79	(45 overs)	174
b Chandana	9	4/103 5/105 6/125		
L. Klusener not out	32	7/131 8/157 9/165		

Bowling: Vaas 7–1–28–0; Gunaratne 6–1–35–1; Fernando 6–0–24–2; Chandana 10–0–40–2; Muralitharan 8–1–12–1; de Silva 3–0–9–0; Jayasuriya 5–0–24–3.

Umpires: S. J. A. Taufel (Australia) and S. Venkataraghavan (India).
Third umpire: D. J. Harper (Australia). Referee: G. R. Viswanath (India).

PAKISTAN v SRI LANKA

At Tangier, August 17. Sri Lanka won by 39 runs. Sri Lanka 4 pts. Toss: Sri Lanka.
Despite another star turn from Jayasuriya, with 97 off 94 balls, tight Pakistani bowling and sharp fielding restricted Sri Lanka to the lowest first-innings score of the tournament so far. Pakistan made heavy weather of the reply, slithering to 29 for three in the 11th over as they lost both openers to loose shots and Inzamam to a fine catch from Jayawardene in the deep. Yousuf Youhana did a patient rebuilding job, accelerating when the run-chase intensified and taking 14 off an over from Jayasuriya. But when he fell with 86 still needed from 77 balls, the game was effectively over.
Man of the Match: S. T. Jayasuriya.

Sri Lanka

*S. T. Jayasuriya lbw b Wasim Akram	97	C. R. D. Fernando b Abdul Razzaq		8
M. S. Atapattu run out	16	M. Muralitharan c Waqar Younis		
†K. C. Sangakkara b Waqar Younis	1		b Wasim Akram	7
P. A. de Silva c Rashid Latif		P. W. Gunaratne not out		2
b Waqar Younis	5	L-b 7, w 5, n-b 5		17
D. P. M. D. Jayawardene run out	43			
R. P. Arnold c and b Waqar Younis	34	1/42 2/47 3/53	(49.5 overs)	242
U. D. U. Chandana lbw b Abdul Razzaq	6	4/164 5/174 6/190		
W. P. U. J. C. Vaas c Younis Khan		7/208 8/223 9/238		
b Mohammad Sami	6			

Bowling: Wasim Akram 9.5–2–29–2; Waqar Younis 9–2–43–3; Abdul Razzaq 10–1–37–2; Mohammad Sami 10–0–68–1; Shahid Afridi 10–0–48–0; Younis Khan 1–0–10–0.

Pakistan

Saeed Anwar c Jayawardene b Gunaratne	3	Shahid Afridi c Chandana b Gunaratne		26
Imran Nazir b Gunaratne	10	*Waqar Younis lbw b Fernando		5
Yousuf Youhana c Sangakkara		Mohammad Sami not out		0
b Gunaratne	80	L-b 3, w 3, n-b 6		12
Inzamam-ul-Haq c Jayawardene b Vaas	5			
Younis Khan c Vaas b Gunaratne	15	1/3 2/18 3/29	(43.4 overs)	203
Abdul Razzaq lbw b Muralitharan	25	4/57 5/127 6/157		
Wasim Akram c Jayawardene b Vaas	19	7/168 8/168 9/179		
†Rashid Latif c Sangakkara b Vaas	3			

Bowling: Vaas 9–2–30–3; Gunaratne 9.4–0–44–4; Fernando 8–0–41–1; Chandana 7–0–35–1; Muralitharan 8–1–30–1; Jayasuriya 2–0–20–0.

Umpires: D. J. Harper (Australia) and S. Venkataraghavan (India).
Third umpire: S. J. A. Taufel (Australia). Referee: G. R. Viswanath (India).

PAKISTAN v SOUTH AFRICA

At Tangier, August 18. South Africa won by eight runs. South Africa 4 pts. Toss: South Africa.

From the very beginning to the very end, this was Pakistan's game – and yet they somehow managed to snatch defeat from the jaws of victory. Waqar Younis and Wasim Akram – who took a wicket with the first ball of the day – looked to have won the match with their hostile opening spell. Even when the South Africans wriggled their way to respectability, Pakistan's target appeared modest. It was all the more so when Shahid Afridi – batting at No. 3 after dropping to No. 9 the day before – made a typically spectacular assault on the bowling, racing to 62 off 40 balls and taking 20 off an over from Kallis. That was the highlight of the day, thrown into starker relief for Pakistan's travelling supporters by the shambles that followed. Even as partners rashly fell around him, Inzamam, at least, seemed to be anchoring a successful run chase. But when he hit Ontong for six in the 42nd over, he stepped on his own stumps. Even as Pakistan wickets continued to tumble, the game seemed to be within their grasp until the last wicket fell.

Man of the Match: A. A. Donald.

South Africa

H. H. Gibbs c Rashid Latif				
b Wasim Akram	0	L. Klusener not out	28
G. C. Smith lbw b Wasim Akram	5	N. Boje b Wasim Akram	1
J. H. Kallis b Waqar Younis	3	*S. M. Pollock not out	13
H. H. Dippenaar run out	55		
J. L. Ontong c and b Waqar Younis	10	L-b 2, w 4, n-b 7	13
J. N. Rhodes c Rashid Latif			
b Azhar Mahmood	11		
†M. V. Boucher b Azhar Mahmood	57		
A. A. Donald did not bat.			

1/0 2/8 3/10 (8 wkts, 50 overs) 196
4/29 5/49 6/127
7/167 8/171

Bowling: Wasim Akram 10–2–31–3; Waqar Younis 10–0–48–2; Azhar Mahmood 9–0–33–2; Abdul Razzaq 10–0–39–0; Shahid Afridi 10–0–28–0; Shoaib Malik 1–0–15–0.

Pakistan

Imran Nazir b Pollock	0	Azhar Mahmood not out	16
Shoaib Malik run out	12	Wasim Akram b Donald	11
Shahid Afridi c Boucher b Donald	62	*Waqar Younis c Smith b Donald	1
Yousuf Youhana c Boje b Klusener	22	W 1	1
Inzamam-ul-Haq hit wkt b Ontong	41		
Younis Khan lbw b Klusener	0		
Abdul Razzaq b Boje	0		
†Rashid Latif b Donald	22		

1/0 2/49 3/92 (48.3 overs) 188
4/118 5/118 6/119
7/155 8/163 9/186

Bowling: Pollock 9–3–25–1; Kallis 10–0–56–0; Donald 9.3–0–43–4; Klusener 10–1–21–2; Boje 8–0–36–1; Ontong 2–0–7–1.

Umpires: D. J. Harper (Australia) and S. J. A. Taufel (Australia).
Third umpire: S. Venkataraghavan (India). Referee: G. R. Viswanath (India).

SRI LANKA v SOUTH AFRICA

At Tangier, August 19. Sri Lanka won by six wickets. Sri Lanka 4 pts. Toss: South Africa.

Only one team turned up for this dress rehearsal for the final – and Sri Lanka coasted to victory, thanks to another vintage work-it-around performance from de Silva, disciplined bowling from their second-string bowlers and some particularly poor fielding from the South Africans. Sri Lanka looked hungry for victory to continue their comeback from the dismal form of their tour of England; South Africa lacked bite, and even Pollock was guilty of some village-green errors in the field. Sri Lanka became the first team to succeed in chasing a total in Tangier, though, coming in a meaningless game, it was not enough to dispel talk of the pitches wearing badly and the toss being all-important.

Man of the Match: P. A. de Silva.

South Africa

G. C. Smith b Chandana	40	J. L. Ontong st Sangakkara b Chandana	7
H. H. Gibbs c Arnold		L. Klusener not out	39
b T. C. B. Fernando	1	*S. M. Pollock not out	16
G. Kirsten b T. C. B. Fernando	1	L-b 1, w 11, n-b 2	14
J. H. Kallis c Chandana b Jayasuriya	84		
†H. H. Dippenaar c Sangakkara		1/9 2/11 3/82 (6 wkts, 50 overs)	220
b Chandana	18	4/108 5/119 6/197	

P. R. Adams, R. Telemachus and M. Ntini did not bat.

Bowling: T. C. B. Fernando 9–2–43–2; Lakshitha 6–0–23–0; K. H. R. K. Fernando 5–0–26–0; Chandana 10–0–32–3; de Silva 10–0–52–0; Jayasuriya 10–0–43–1.

Sri Lanka

*S. T. Jayasuriya c Dippenaar b Klusener	46	R. P. Arnold not out	4
M. S. Atapattu c Dippenaar b Telemachus	16		
†K. C. Sangakkara run out	57	L-b 3, w 2, n-b 5	10
P. A. de Silva not out	77		
D. P. M. D. Jayawardene c Gibbs		1/40 2/83 (4 wkts, 42.1 overs)	221
b Telemachus	11	3/179 4/210	

T. M. Dilshan, U. D. U. Chandana, K. H. R. K. Fernando, T. C. B. Fernando and M. K. G. C. P. Lakshitha did not bat.

Bowling: Pollock 9–0–30–0; Telemachus 6–0–51–2; Klusener 6–0–26–1; Ntini 8–1–39–0; Adams 6–0–36–0; Ontong 6–0–31–0; Smith 1.1–0–5–0.

Umpires: S. J. A. Taufel (Australia) and S. Venkataraghavan (India).
Third umpire: D. J. Harper (Australia). Referee: G. R. Viswanath (India).

QUALIFYING TABLE

	Played	Won	Lost	Bonus points	Points	Net run-rate
Sri Lanka	4	3	1	1	13	0.73
South Africa	4	2	2	0	8	–0.34
Pakistan	4	1	3	0	4	–0.37

Win = 4 pts. One bonus point awarded for achieving victory with a run-rate 1.25 times that of the opposition. When two or more teams finish with an equal number of points, the positions are decided by (a) most wins (b) most wins in head-to-head matches (c) most bonus points (d) highest net run-rate. Net run-rate is calculated by subtracting runs conceded per over from runs scored per over.

FINAL

SRI LANKA v SOUTH AFRICA

At Tangier, August 21. Sri Lanka won by 27 runs. Toss: Sri Lanka.

Sanath Jayasuriya made all the headlines as his team won the inaugural Morocco Cup. He was at his unforgiving best with the bat in the morning, and by the time he picked up the trophy, the $120,000 cheque and the man of the series award, he had his right arm in a sling after dislocating his shoulder as he caught Gibbs. It was an unusual day all round, with military top brass, a local band playing cacophonous six-foot bugles and hordes of chanting schoolchildren among the biggest crowd of the tournament. Sri Lanka made a quick start as Jayasuriya again picked up easy runs off the hapless Telemachus, but the innings did not live up to its early promise. Gibbs's brilliant diving catch in the covers off a well-struck drive by Arnold felt like a turning point. However,

South Africa's top order crumpled almost as easily as it had three days previously against Pakistan. This time it was left to Boucher and Dippenaar to pick up the pieces, working a run-a-ball century stand. But, too far behind the run-rate, the South Africans perished trying to regain ground.

Man of the Match: S. T. Jayasuriya.　　　*Man of the Series:* S. T. Jayasuriya.

Sri Lanka

*S. T. Jayasuriya c Donald b Boje	71	W. P. U. J. C. Vaas not out	18
M. S. Atapattu c Smith b Donald	25	M. Muralitharan not out	11
†K. C. Sangakkara c Dippenaar b Boje	40	B 5, l-b 5, w 4, n-b 1	15
P. A. de Silva c Boucher b Kallis	33		
D. P. M. D. Jayawardene lbw b Donald	5	1/78 2/119 3/167 (7 wkts, 50 overs) 235
R. P. Arnold c Gibbs b Klusener	13	4/179 5/191
U. D. U. Chandana b Klusener	4	6/202 7/209

C. R. D. Fernando and P. W. Gunaratne did not bat.

Bowling: Pollock 8–0–35–0; Telemachus 4–0–36–0; Klusener 10–1–35–2; Smith 4–0–17–0; Donald 8–0–35–2; Boje 10–0–40–2; Kallis 6–0–27–1.

South Africa

H. H. Gibbs c Jayasuriya b Vaas	6	*S. M. Pollock run out	3
L. Klusener lbw b Fernando	13	R. Telemachus b Muralitharan	0
G. C. Smith b Vaas	15	A. A. Donald not out	0
J. H. Kallis c Atapattu b Chandana	24		
H. H. Dippenaar c Jayawardene b Gunaratne	53	B 1, l-b 7, w 6, n-b 1	15
J. N. Rhodes run out	6	1/7 2/24 3/52 (48.3 overs) 208
N. Boje b Muralitharan	3	4/71 5/81 6/91
†M. V. Boucher c Sangakkara b Gunaratne	70	7/192 8/199 9/208

Bowling: Vaas 10–0–33–2; Gunaratne 9.3–1–38–2; Fernando 7–0–38–1; Chandana 9–0–43–1; Muralitharan 10–0–35–2; de Silva 2–0–10–0; Arnold 1–0–3–0.

Umpires: D. J. Harper (Australia) and S. J. A. Taufel (Australia).
Third umpire: S. Venkataraghavan (India).　Referee: G. R. Viswanath (India).

PSO TRI-NATION TOURNAMENT, 2002

By PAUL COUPAR and MARTIN BLAKE

This tournament was everything its organisers, the Pakistan Cricket Board, hoped it would not be – staged thousands of miles from home, commercially unsuccessful and utterly dominated by Australia. Pakistan planned the triangular competition as the centrepiece of their celebrations to mark 50 years of international cricket. But jollity took second place to politics. Australia refused to travel to Pakistan, citing safety concerns, fears given terrifying substance in May, when a huge car bomb smashed windows of the Karachi hotel where the New Zealand squad were staying. Endless alternative venues were considered – England, Kenya, Morocco, Queensland, Sharjah and Sri Lanka – before the PCB plumped for Kenya. But the sponsor, Pakistan State Oil, did not clamber aboard until the eve of the first match, and a neutral venue meant meagre profits for the cash-strapped board.

The tournament's prestige took a further dent when New Zealand pulled out, to be replaced by Kenya. New Zealand Cricket claimed they had only had an "informal chat" about playing, but the PCB insisted there had been "an agreement in principle" and, by December, were pursuing NZC for compensation. Having trumpeted a showpiece, the PCB ended up with a low-key warm-up for the ICC Champions Trophy and a looming legal wrangle.

Things hardly improved for the Pakistanis – board or team – when they finally made it to Nairobi. The teams quickly settled into a cast-iron hierarchy: Pakistan comfortably had the edge over Kenya, and Australia twice annihilated Pakistan – first by 224 runs (Pakistan's worst-ever defeat in terms of runs), then by nine wickets. Australia were set to cruise the final too, until it rained and any chance of a result was washed away.

Two images of Australian dominance were seared into the memories of fans and opponents alike: Glenn McGrath's surgical probing outside the off stump, and Matthew Hayden's blazing bat. McGrath was parsimony personified, conceding a miserly two and a half an over and taking nine wickets at 8.77. Jason Gillespie snatched 15, far at 4.34 an over. If McGrath was the scalpel, Hayden was the bludgeon. His brutal 128-ball 146 scattered spectators, ensured Australia's first destruction of Pakistan and set the tone for the tournament. In all, he sledgehammered 265 in four innings – three of them unbeaten – at a harum-scarum rate of 106.42, and his team-mates matched the pace, roaring along at almost six an over. It would have been higher still, but Allan Border (standing in as coach after John Buchanan hurt his back before the tournament) and Ricky Ponting sent in tailenders before batsmen in the dead match against Kenya. With McGrath and Gillespie rested, it was as if an even-handed PE teacher had decreed that it was time to let the other boys have a turn. Kenya nearly made them pay for their complacency, but it was their only hiccough.

Pakistan had recently beaten the Australians in the Tower Super Challenge, but here they were at their desultory worst. Yousuf Youhana was sent home before a ball was bowled, ostensibly for failing to turn up at nets; Youhana insisted he had been doing individual work on an injured shoulder, and the incident was never properly explained. Without him, the batting was an established batsman light, and only Misbah-ul-Haq improved his standing, hitting 139 in three innings. More unusual than their mercurial batting was Pakistan's prodigal bowling. Hayden did criminal damage to several sets of figures, and all went for more than four and a half an over.

Brought in as a sparring partner for their two heavyweight opponents, Kenya punched above their weight. Their bowling was tight, with Maurice Odumbe's off-breaks going for less than four an over and Martin Suji's medium-pace only two and a half. But their batting, traditionally strong, failed to ignite and they reached the 44th over just once. Competent enough to avoid humiliation, they lacked the class to force a win.

Note: Matches in this section were not first-class.

KENYA v PAKISTAN

At Gymkhana, Nairobi, August 29. Pakistan won by four wickets. Pakistan 5 pts. Toss: Pakistan.

A familiar burst of new-ball genius by Wasim Akram seemed to have scuttled any hope of an upset, but things are seldom simple when Pakistan are involved. Under overcast skies and on a juicy pitch, his left-arm swing was nearly unplayable in the early overs, as he turned back the clock by several notches and took three for 30 – including Steve Tikolo, Kenya's captain and star batsman, for a duck. After Kenya slumped to 30 for four, Abdul Razzaq's four wickets completed the damage, and the home side tumbled to a disappointing 133 all out. When Pakistan replied, they threatened to unravel, slipping to 97 for six. But Rashid Latif's cool head silenced the parochial crowd. His unbeaten 28, from 23 balls, steered the Pakistanis home with more than 16 overs to spare.

Man of the match: Abdul Razzaq.

Kenya

K. O. Otieno b Abdul Razzaq	37	C. O. Obuya c Rashid Latif		
R. D. Shah lbw b Waqar Younis	2	b Abdul Razzaq	1
*S. O. Tikolo lbw b Wasim Akram	0	T. O. Suji not out	17
T. M. Odoyo lbw b Wasim Akram	4	M. A. Suji run out	5
M. O. Odumbe b Wasim Akram	0	J. O. Angara b Azhar Mahmood	4
H. S. Modi c Rashid Latif		L-b 4, w 17, n-b 8	29
b Abdul Razzaq	34		
†D. O. Obuya c Younis Khan		1/16 2/19 3/30 4/30 5/102 (30.3 overs) 133
b Abdul Razzaq	0	6/104 7/107 8/107 9/123	

Modi, when 34, retired hurt at 101 and resumed at 107-7.

Bowling: Wasim Akram 7–0–30–3; Waqar Younis 7–1–29–1; Shoaib Akhtar 5–0–31–0; Abdul Razzaq 8–1–35–4; Azhar Mahmood 3.3–0–4–1.

Pakistan

Saeed Anwar c D. O. Obuya		Inzamam-ul-Haq not out	14
b M. A. Suji	0	†Rashid Latif not out	28
Imran Nazir b Odoyo	13		
Shahid Afridi c Odoyo b M. A. Suji	27	W 6	6
Younis Khan b C. O. Obuya	36		
Azhar Mahmood run out	9	1/0 2/22 3/42 (6 wkts, 33.3 overs) 134
Abdul Razzaq b Angara	1	4/61 5/77 6/97	

Wasim Akram, *Waqar Younis and Shoaib Akhtar did not bat.

Bowling: M. A. Suji 10–3–22–2; Odoyo 10–1–41–1; Angara 7–0–25–1; T. O. Suji 3–0–11–0; C. O. Obuya 3.3–0–35–1.

Umpires: Aleem Dar (Pakistan) and R. E. Koertzen (South Africa).
Third umpire: Asad Rauf (Pakistan). Referee: M. J. Procter (South Africa).

AUSTRALIA v PAKISTAN

At Gymkhana, Nairobi, August 30. Australia won by 224 runs. Australia 5 pts. Toss: Pakistan.

An imperious 146 from the Australian opener Hayden made this a memorable day. He flogged Pakistan for six sixes and 12 fours in a stay of only 128 balls, as Australia made light of their ten-week break from the international arena and rattled up 332 for five. Hayden's savagery endangered the lives of everyone in the vicinity: twice he hit the media centre with lofted drives; once he pull-drove Waqar Younis over mid-wicket and out of the ground. It was the third-highest score in a one-day international by an Australian. Missing the injured Inzamam-ul-Haq, and with Yousuf Youhana sent home for disciplinary reasons, Pakistan folded in reply – all out for a miserable 108. Gillespie's five for 22 made it a quick finish, with the Pakistanis surviving only 36 overs. The 224-run rout was Pakistan's worst-ever in terms of runs, Australia's biggest over Pakistan and their second-biggest ever.

Man of the Match: M. L. Hayden.

Australia

†A. C. Gilchrist c Azhar Mahmood		M. G. Bevan not out	8
b Wasim Akram .	21	S. R. Watson not out	10
M. L. Hayden c Shoaib Malik			
b Wasim Akram .	146	B 1, l-b 9, w 17, n-b 8	35
*R. T. Ponting c and b Shahid Afridi . . .	65		
D. R. Martyn b Shahid Afridi	12	1/46 2/174 (5 wkts, 50 overs) 332	
J. P. Maher c Abdul Razzaq		3/192 4/314	
b Waqar Younis .	35	5/316	

S. K. Warne, A. J. Bichel, J. N. Gillespie and G. D. McGrath did not bat.

Bowling: Wasim Akram 10–0–62–2; Waqar Younis 10–0–60–1; Abdul Razzaq 3–0–26–0; Shoaib Akhtar 5–0–45–0; Azhar Mahmood 6–0–42–0; Shahid Afridi 10–0–56–2; Shoaib Malik 6–0–31–0.

Pakistan

Imran Nazir c Gilchrist b Gillespie	1	Wasim Akram c Gilchrist b Gillespie . . .	0
Abdul Razzaq b McGrath	5	*Waqar Younis c Bichel b Gillespie	2
Shahid Afridi b Gillespie	0	Shoaib Akhtar c Watson b Gillespie	2
Saeed Anwar lbw b McGrath	3	L-b 2, w 5, n-b 1	8
Younis Khan c Gilchrist b Warne	13		
Shoaib Malik c Gilchrist b Bichel	25	1/1 2/1 3/10 (36 overs) 108	
Azhar Mahmood c Bevan b Watson	32	4/13 5/39 6/67	
†Rashid Latif not out	17	7/95 8/99 9/101	

Bowling: McGrath 6–0–11–2; Gillespie 10–2–22–5; Bichel 7–0–33–1; Warne 8–1–20–1; Watson 5–1–20–1.

Umpires: Nadeem Ghauri (Pakistan) and R. B. Tiffin (Zimbabwe).
Third umpire: Asad Rauf (Pakistan). Referee: M. J. Procter (South Africa).

KENYA v PAKISTAN

At Gymkhana, Nairobi, September 1. Pakistan won by seven wickets. Pakistan 5 pts. Toss: Kenya. Younis Khan's cultured, unbeaten 87 from 91 balls, and a fifty from the emerging right-hander Misbah-ul-Haq, made victory a cakewalk for Pakistan. Despite a hard-working 59 from the opener Otieno, Kenya's 179 after batting first never seemed enough. Though the Pakistanis endured a characteristic wobble at the top of the order, with both openers out inside the first four overs, Younis and Misbah put on an unbroken stand of 127, closed out the game and ensured Pakistan would reach the final.

Man of the Match: Younis Khan.

Kenya

K. O. Otieno b Shoaib Akhtar	59	J. K. Kamande c Shoaib Malik	
R. D. Shah b Shoaib Akhtar	1	b Waqar Younis .	23
*S. O. Tikolo c Rashid Latif		C. O. Obuya c Misbah-ul-Haq	
b Wasim Akram .	3	b Wasim Akram .	8
T. M. Odoyo c Shoaib Akhtar		M. A. Suji lbw b Abdul Razzaq	8
b Waqar Younis .	28	J. O. Angara not out	0
M. O. Odumbe b Shahid Afridi	10	B 1, l-b 6, w 12, n-b 6	25
†D. O. Obuya c Azhar Mahmood			
b Abdul Razzaq .	12	1/10 2/14 3/75 (42.3 overs) 179	
T. O. Suji st Rashid Latif		4/88 5/116 6/131	
b Shahid Afridi .	2	7/133 8/157 9/179	

Bowling: Wasim Akram 7–0–43–2; Shoaib Akhtar 8–3–17–2; Azhar Mahmood 5–3–18–0; Waqar Younis 6–0–31–2; Shahid Afridi 10–1–33–2; Abdul Razzaq 6.3–0–30–2.

Pakistan

Shoaib Malik lbw b Odoyo	3	Misbah-ul-Haq not out	50
Saeed Anwar c D. O. Obuya			
b M. A. Suji	2	L-b 1, w 7	8
Shahid Afridi c T. O. Suji b Angara	31		
Younis Khan not out	87	1/11 2/13 3/54 (3 wkts, 38.4 overs)	181

Azhar Mahmood, Abdul Razzaq, †Rashid Latif, Wasim Akram, *Waqar Younis and Shoaib Akhtar did not bat.

Bowling: M. A. Suji 8–2–23–1; Odoyo 6–0–38–1; Angara 6–1–21–1; T. O. Suji 4–0–17–0; C. O. Obuya 7–0–33–0; Odumbe 5–0–24–0; Kamande 2.4–0–24–0.

Umpires: Aleem Dar (Pakistan) and R. E. Koertzen (South Africa).
Third umpire: Asad Rauf (Pakistan).   Referee: M. J. Procter (South Africa).

KENYA v AUSTRALIA

At Gymkhana, Nairobi, September 2. Australia won by eight wickets. Australia 5 pts. Toss: Australia.

Kenya's flaws were cruelly exposed after Ponting made them bat first in spicy conditions against the world's most potent new-ball attack. McGrath and Gillespie extracted three wickets each in their opening spell, and Kenya plummeted to a catastrophic 17 for six, in danger of setting a new world record low. McGrath's precision brought him three for eight in eight overs. Ultimately the Kenyans managed 84, thanks to the stubbornness of Patel and the lusty hitting of Collins Obuya, but it was still their lowest-ever score in a one-day international. Australia picked off the runs in only 17 overs, with Hayden again profiting.

Man of the Match: G. D. McGrath.

Kenya

K. O. Otieno c Hayden b Gillespie	10	C. O. Obuya c Gilchrist b Watson	13
†D. O. Obuya b McGrath	0	M. A. Suji b Lee	1
J. K. Kamande c Gilchrist b McGrath	1	J. O. Angara b Watson	1
*S. O. Tikolo c Warne b Gillespie	4	L-b 4, w 5, n-b 9	18
T. M. Odoyo c Bevan b McGrath	0		
M. O. Odumbe lbw b Gillespie	0	1/1 2/12 3/13 (35.3 overs)	84
B. J. Patel st Gilchrist b Warne	28	4/17 5/17 6/17	
T. O. Suji not out	8	7/53 8/62 9/83	

T. O. Suji, when 4, retired hurt at 24 and resumed at 62.

Bowling: McGrath 8–5–8–3; Gillespie 10–2–40–3; Lee 7–1–15–1; Watson 7.3–2–13–2; Warne 3–0–4–1.

Australia

†A. C. Gilchrist lbw b M. A. Suji	22	M. G. Bevan not out	15
M. L. Hayden not out	40	W 3	3
J. P. Maher c D. O. Obuya b Angara	5		
		1/38 2/60 (2 wkts, 17 overs)	85

*R. T. Ponting, D. R. Martyn, S. R. Watson, S. K. Warne, B. Lee, J. N. Gillespie and G. D. McGrath did not bat.

Bowling: M. A. Suji 8–1–25–1; Angara 7–1–46–1; Kamande 1–0–4–0; C. O. Obuya 1–0–10–0.

Umpires: Nadeem Ghauri (Pakistan) and R. B. Tiffin (Zimbabwe).
Third umpire: Asad Rauf (Pakistan).   Referee: M. J. Procter (South Africa).

AUSTRALIA v PAKISTAN

At Gymkhana, Nairobi, September 4. Australia won by nine wickets. Australia 5 pts. Toss: Pakistan.

The places in the final were already settled, but Australia showed no sign of backing off, crushing Pakistan by nine wickets. Waqar Younis opted to set a target after winning the toss, but the early-morning conditions were tough and Waqar's batsmen failed him, gathering only 117 in 32.3 overs, against the sustained accuracy and pace of Australia's seamers. At one point, Pakistan were 68 for eight, and they needed some clean hitting from the captain to pass 100. Lee's rapid out-swingers brought him four for 32 in eight overs. The Australians rattled along at a run a ball when they replied, with the unstoppable Hayden flaying an unbeaten 59 from only 48 balls.

Man of the Match: B. Lee.

Pakistan

Saeed Anwar c Warne b Lee	22	†Rashid Latif c Martyn b Lee	12
Imran Nazir c Martyn b Gillespie	7	*Waqar Younis b McGrath	23
Shoaib Malik c Ponting b McGrath	1	Shoaib Akhtar not out	2
Younis Khan c Gilchrist b McGrath	0	L-b 2, w 2, n-b 3	7
Misbah-ul-Haq c Gilchrist b Gillespie	39		
Azhar Mahmood c Ponting b Lee	4	1/13 2/24 3/24 (32.3 overs)	117
Abdul Razzaq b Warne	0	4/33 5/45 6/47	
Shahid Afridi c Ponting b Lee	0	7/48 8/68 9/112	

Bowling: McGrath 7.3–2–15–3; Gillespie 8–1–33–2; Lee 8–0–32–4; Warne 9–2–35–1.

Australia

†A. C. Gilchrist b Waqar Younis	15
M. L. Hayden not out	59
*R. T. Ponting retired hurt	21
D. R. Martyn not out	20
W 6	6
1/32 (1 wkt, 19.1 overs)	121

Ponting retired hurt at 84.

J. P. Maher, M. G. Bevan, S. R. Watson, S. K. Warne, B. Lee, J. N. Gillespie and G. D. McGrath did not bat.

Bowling: Shoaib Akhtar 1.4–0–11–0; Waqar Younis 4–0–26–1; Abdul Razzaq 7.2–2–46–0; Azhar Mahmood 5.1–0–32–0; Shahid Afridi 1–0–6–0.

Umpires: Aleem Dar (Pakistan) and R. E. Koertzen (South Africa).
Third umpire: Asad Rauf (Pakistan). Referee: M. J. Procter (South Africa).

KENYA v AUSTRALIA

At Gymkhana, Nairobi, September 5. Australia won by five wickets. Australia 4 pts. Toss: Kenya.

Australia's tactics in this dead match bordered on the patronising. Resting Gillespie and McGrath was understandable, but the decision to shuffle the batting order was questionable and, for a moment, they seemed to have shot themselves in the foot. When Warne fell, they needed 19 runs from 14 balls, but sixes from Watson and Lee relieved the pressure, and they squeezed home with five balls to spare. The all-rounder Watson was frustratingly slow, but stayed to finish the job with an unbeaten 77. Neither Hayden nor Martyn batted. Earlier, Kenya's batsmen had restored some credibility, with the flamboyant Odumbe striking a bold half-century. For the Australians, the burgeoning off-spinner Hauritz took four for 39 in his first game of the series.

Man of the Match: M. O. Odumbe.

Kenya

K. O. Otieno lbw b Watson	21	P. J. Ongondo c and b Hauritz	2
†D. O. Obuya b Bichel	0	M. A. Suji not out	7
J. K. Kamande b Lee	5	L. N. Onyango not out	1
B. J. Patel run out	42	L-b 2, w 8, n-b 6	16
*S. O. Tikolo lbw b Warne	35		
T. M. Odoyo c Maher b Hauritz	11	1/1 2/32 3/46 (9 wkts, 50 overs) 204
M. O. Odumbe c Hayden b Hauritz	55	4/111 5/119 6/161
C. O. Obuya c Symonds b Hauritz	9	7/193 8/195 9/202

Bowling: Lee 7–2–23–1; Bichel 7–1–22–1; Watson 9–1–38–1; Symonds 8–0–33–0; Warne 9–0–47–1; Hauritz 10–0–39–4.

Australia

J. P. Maher c Tikolo b Odoyo	16	S. K. Warne run out	15
*†A. C. Gilchrist c sub (J. O. Angara)		B. Lee not out	6
b C. O. Obuya	41	L-b 1, w 3, n-b 3	7
M. G. Bevan c D. O. Obuya b Odoyo	0		
S. R. Watson not out	77	1/24 2/27 3/83 (5 wkts, 49.1 overs) 205
A. Symonds run out	43	4/162 5/186

M. L. Hayden, D. R. Martyn, N. M. Hauritz and A. J. Bichel did not bat.

Bowling: Suji 10–1–22–0; Odoyo 9.1–0–38–2; Ongondo 6–0–44–0; Odumbe 10–1–28–0; C. O. Obuya 10–1–50–1; Kamande 4–0–22–0.

Umpires: Nadeem Ghauri (Pakistan) and R. B. Tiffin (Zimbabwe).
Third umpire: Asad Rauf (Pakistan). Referee: M. J. Procter (South Africa).

QUALIFYING TABLE

	Played	Won	Lost	Bonus points	Points	Net run-rate
Australia	4	4	0	3	19	2.93
Pakistan	4	2	2	2	10	−1.39
Kenya	4	0	4	0	0	−1.37

Win = 4 pts. One bonus point awarded for achieving victory with a run-rate 1.25 times that of the opposition. When two or more teams finish with an equal number of points, the positions are decided by (a) most runs (b) most wins in head-to-head matches (c) most bonus points (d) highest net run-rate. Net run-rate is calculated by subtracting runs conceded per over from runs scored per over.

FINAL

PAKISTAN v AUSTRALIA

At Gymkhana, Nairobi, September 7. No result (D/L method). Toss: Pakistan.

A disappointingly one-sided series looked set for a more competitive finale when rain doused the excitement and sent a sell-out crowd of 5,000 home early. Pakistan had been struggling towards another inadequate score until Abdul Razzaq launched an astonishing rearguard attack, hitting 59 from 43 balls, including three huge sixes. Waqar Younis's team then gorged themselves on 61 runs from the final five overs, and reached 227. The total still appeared small when measured against the power of the Australian batting line-up, but there was a whiff of a possible surprise when Gilchrist was bowled in Wasim Akram's first over. The first break for rain led to a revised target of 210 in 42 overs, and Hayden and Ponting were steaming along at 67 for one in the tenth over when a second downpour settled the issue.

Men of the Series: Australia – M. L. Hayden; Kenya – M. A. Suji; Pakistan – Misbah-ul-Haq.

Pakistan

Saeed Anwar c Gilchrist b Gillespie	28	
Shahid Afridi c Warne b McGrath	6	
Shoaib Malik run out	37	
Inzamam-ul-Haq lbw b Gillespie	0	
Younis Khan c and b Lee	10	
Misbah-ul-Haq b Lee	50	
Abdul Razzaq run out	59	
†Rashid Latif c Watson b Gillespie	12	

Wasim Akram c Gilchrist b Gillespie . . .	2
*Waqar Younis b Gillespie	1
Mohammad Sami not out	0
L-b 4, w 12, n-b 6	22

(50 overs) 227

1/15 2/37 3/37
4/55 5/116 6/158
7/196 8/226 9/227

Bowling: McGrath 10–4–45–1; Gillespie 10–1–70–5; Lee 10–3–38–2; Watson 10–0–26–0; Warne 10–0–44–0.

Australia

†A. C. Gilchrist b Wasim Akram	0
M. L. Hayden not out	20
*R. T. Ponting not out	29
L-b 3, w 12, n-b 3	18

1/3   (1 wkt, 9.3 overs) 67

D. R. Martyn, J. P. Maher, M. G. Bevan, S. R. Watson, S. K. Warne, B. Lee, J. N. Gillespie and G. D. McGrath did not bat.

Bowling: Wasim Akram 5–0–33–1; Waqar Younis 4.3–0–31–0.

Umpires: Aleem Dar (Pakistan) and R. B. Tiffin (Zimbabwe).
Third umpire: Asad Rauf (Pakistan).   Referee: M. J. Procter (South Africa).

ICC CHAMPIONS TROPHY, 2002

By DILEEP PREMACHANDRAN

A dispute over player contracts may have dominated the build-up to the tournament, the final may never have finished, and the increased use of technology may be all that comes out of it, but the people of Sri Lanka will look back on the third ICC Champions Trophy with some fondness. Not only did their team share the spoils, but they defeated the all-conquering and less than popular Australians.

For most of the other teams, there was less satisfaction. The planning of the tournament left much to be desired. The timing, only five months before the World Cup, threatened to take the gloss off both. The pitches, slow and getting slower by the day, ensured this tournament would be no form guide for South Africa. The number of teams rose, from 11 in Nairobi two years earlier to 12, which did nothing for playing standards. Apart from Kenya, who took on West Indies, the little guys were crushed with ridiculous ease and, despite low ticket prices, the public responded by keeping their bums off seats. The league format, designed to make sure nobody flew a long way for one match, was a farce: with all but one of the pools containing a Persian-carpet side – just there to walk all over – the other two teams were contesting a quarter-final in all but name. The Trophy clearly needed splitting into two, with an elite group and lower-standard plate competition.

With the monsoon on the horizon, the heat and humidity were intense. Matches not involving Sri Lanka and India drew minuscule crowds, surprising given that it was the first time Sri Lanka – finally free of the terror of civil war – had hosted an event of this magnitude. (The 1996 World Cup should have been bigger, but Australia and West Indies stayed away on security grounds.)

Rain dance: Steve Bucknor steps out as the monsoons scupper a second attempt to play the final.
Picture by Clive Mason, Getty Images.

The early stages were dominated by technology, as Pakistan's Shoaib Malik became the first victim of an lbw decision deferred to the third umpire. The frequent requests for arbitration did slow the game down, but it was worth it when glaring gaffes were avoided. The experiment largely worked for lbws, but the cameras continued to be hopelessly ineffectual at confirming whether a catch had carried. Time and again, inconclusive replays gave batsmen the benefit of the doubt, much to the frustration of fielders convinced they had held a fair catch. After the tournament, the ICC announced that the use of technology would not be extended: lbw decisions would revert to being a matter solely for the on-field umpire, while television could still be consulted – *ad nauseam* – for whether a catch was clean.

The Colombo air was thick with different scents but seldom with the whiff of an upset. The nearest thing to a major shock came early on when West Indies pushed South Africa all the way in a last-ball thriller. Sri Lanka and India – who sent their best team only after a last-ditch temporary settlement of the contract dispute – thrived on the sleepy pitches their batsmen love, while Australia were imperious until an impromptu holiday and the Sri Lankan spinners caught up with them. The watching populace became more impassioned after that, and 5,000 Indian fans added to the cacophony at a final that had sound and fury and, sure enough, signified nothing. In the end, the two false starts summed up the tournament – half-baked and inconclusive.

Dileep Premachandran, assistant editor of Wisden Asia Cricket *magazine, covered the tournament for* Wisden Online.

Note: Matches in this section were not first-class.

POOL 1

AUSTRALIA v NEW ZEALAND

At Sinhalese Sports Club, Colombo, September 15. Australia won by 164 runs. Toss: Australia.

Coming into this match, Australia had never won in the Champions Trophy. It took them just 77 overs to correct that with a performance that was more like an autopsy. McGrath sliced up the top order with a spell of 7–1–37–5 as New Zealand slumped to 51 for six. Australia idled after that, but despite a last-wicket stand of 50, revenge for the VB Series torment was theirs long before the shadows lengthened. McGrath was erratic but when he found his length, the batsmen walked. He removed Fleming and Vincent with the sixth and seventh balls of a miscounted over, and soon Styris, Sinclair and Oram – shouldering arms to a beauty – joined the procession. Gilchrist had set the tone with a punishing 30-ball 44 before Ponting took over. Vettori's flight and variety gave New Zealand a chance, only for Martyn – scratchy and nervous until he found his magic drives – to lead a charge that brought 120 from the last 16 overs. On a strip where the ball almost stopped after pitching, 296 was a mammoth total.

Man of the Match: G. D. McGrath.

Australia

†A. C. Gilchrist c Sinclair b Tuffey	44	S. K. Warne c Bond b Oram		0
M. L. Hayden b Vettori	43	B. Lee not out		4
*R. T. Ponting c Fleming b Bond	37	L-b 6, w 7, n-b 7		20
D. R. Martyn c Harris b Bond	73			
D. S. Lehmann c Vettori b Mills	35	1/68 (1) 2/129 (3)	(7 wkts, 50 overs)	296
M. G. Bevan b Oram	21	3/143 (2) 4/217 (5)		
S. R. Watson not out	19	5/272 (6) 6/276 (4) 7/290 (8)	15 overs: 109-1	

J. N. Gillespie and G. D. McGrath did not bat.

Bowling: Bond 10–0–63–2; Mills 9–0–49–1; Tuffey 6–1–55–1; Oram 10–0–60–2; Vettori 10–1–25–1; Harris 5–0–38–0.

New Zealand

*S. P. Fleming lbw b McGrath	12	D. R. Tuffey c Warne b Lee	0
N. J. Astle lbw b Gillespie	0	S. E. Bond st Gilchrist b Warne	26
M. S. Sinclair c Gilchrist b McGrath	18		
†L. Vincent c Martyn b McGrath	0	B 4, l-b 3, w 2, n-b 2	11
S. B. Styris c Gilchrist b McGrath	16		
C. Z. Harris b Lee	19	1/9 (2) 2/17 (1) 3/17 (4) (26.2 overs) 132
J. D. P. Oram b McGrath	1	4/44 (5) 5/49 (3) 6/51 (7)
D. L. Vettori lbw b Lee	6	7/71 (8) 8/78 (6)
K. D. Mills not out	23	9/82 (10) 10/132 (11) 15 overs: 73-7

Bowling: McGrath 7–1–37–5; Gillespie 7–1–29–1; Lee 6–0–38–3; Watson 6–1–19–0; Warne 0.2–0–2–1.

Umpires: D. L. Orchard (South Africa) and R. B. Tiffin (Zimbabwe).
Third umpire: E. A. R. de Silva (Sri Lanka).   Referee: C. H. Lloyd (West Indies).

AUSTRALIA v BANGLADESH

At Sinhalese Sports Club, Colombo, September 19. Australia won by nine wickets. Toss: Bangladesh. International debut: Mazharul Haque.

This wasn't cricket, it was carnage. At one stage, with the scoreboard showing 13 for four, Zimbabwe's dubious record of being bowled out for 38 at this very ground ten months earlier was in danger of being eclipsed. Gillespie had started the rout with two wickets in a fast-and-furious first over and but for the obduracy of Khaled Masud, Tushar Imran and the precocious nudging of Alok Kapali, the game might have been over before lunch. A total of 129 was almost respectable in the circumstances, but Hayden had nothing like respect in mind as he set about the new ball. Gilchrist, by contrast, struggled for rhythm on a dead pitch, until he threw caution to the breeze and raced to 50 from 44 balls. The Bangladeshis did get his wicket but the ogre-like Hayden was on hand to administer the final cuts on bleeding foes. With a week to kill before the semi-final, the Aussies hopped off to the Maldives for a break.

Man of the Match: J. N. Gillespie.

Bangladesh

Javed Omar c Lee b McGrath	4	Tapash Baisya not out	2
Al Sahariar lbw b Gillespie	0	Manjurul Islam lbw b Watson	0
Habibul Bashar c Gilchrist b Gillespie	0		
Mazharul Haque c Gilchrist b Gillespie	3	B 5, l-b 1, w 1, n-b 5	12
Tushar Imran c Bevan b Lee	27		
*†Khaled Masud b Warne	22	1/0 (2) 2/0 (3) 3/10 (1) (45.2 overs) 129
Alok Kapali b Lee	45	4/13 (4) 5/49 (5) 6/85 (6)
Khaled Mahmud lbw b Watson	9	7/118 (8) 8/126 (9)
Mohammad Rafiq run out	5	9/128 (7) 10/129 (11) 15 overs: 39-4

Bowling: McGrath 8–3–17–1; Gillespie 10–1–20–3; Lee 7–0–23–2; Warne 10–2–33–1; Lehmann 8–0–23–0; Watson 2.2–0–7–2.

Australia

†A. C. Gilchrist lbw b Mohammad Rafiq	54
M. L. Hayden not out	67
*R. T. Ponting not out	9
L-b 1, w 1, n-b 1	3

1/113 (1)   (1 wkt, 20.4 overs) 133
15 overs: 94-0

J. P. Maher, D. S. Lehmann, M. G. Bevan, S. R. Watson, S. K. Warne, B. Lee, J. N. Gillespie and G. D. McGrath did not bat.

Bowling: Manjurul Islam 6–0–35–0; Tapash Baisya 5–0–27–0; Mohammad Rafiq 5–0–32–1; Khaled Mahmud 4–0–34–0; Mazharul Haque 0.4–0–4–0.

Umpires: E. A. R. de Silva (Sri Lanka) and R. B. Tiffin (Zimbabwe). Third umpire: S. Venkataraghavan (India). Referee: Wasim Raja (Pakistan).

BANGLADESH v NEW ZEALAND

At Sinhalese Sports Club, Colombo, September 23. New Zealand won by 167 runs. Toss: Bangladesh.

After their bowlers had given Bangladesh the scent of an upset, their batsmen capitulated ineptly as New Zealand ended their disappointing defence of the trophy with a crushing victory. Bangladesh managed one more run than their all-time low on the same ground in August. Five of the top six failed to reach three as Bond proved the agent of destruction. His weapon was sheer pace, reinforced by field-settings from Fleming that ran to four slips and a gully. Earlier, New Zealand had plodded to 244. Sinclair's tortuous 70 off 122 balls was the cornerstone, but the star of the morning was Mohammad Rafiq, who bowled his slow left-armers with considerable skill and great variety.

Man of the Match: S. E. Bond.

New Zealand

*S. P. Fleming c Talha Jubair b Khaled Mahmud	31	D. L. Vettori c Fahim Muntasir b Manjurul Islam . 16
N. J. Astle c Alok Kapali b Manjurul Islam .	5	K. D. Mills not out. 3
M. S. Sinclair c Mohammad Rafiq b Mohammad Ashraful .	70	S. E. Bond st Khaled Masud b Mohammad Rafiq . 8
†L. Vincent c Khaled Masud b Khaled Mahmud .	1	P. A. Hitchcock not out 2
		B 1, l-b 9, w 14, n-b 2 26
S. B. Styris run out	26	
C. Z. Harris c Mohammad Rafiq b Mohammad Ashraful .	26	1/11 (2) 2/77 (1) (9 wkts, 50 overs) 244
J. D. P. Oram c Tushar Imran b Mohammad Ashraful .	30	3/79 (4) 4/119 (5)
		5/167 (6) 6/198 (3)
		7/216 (7) 8/232 (8)
		9/242 (9) 15 overs: 77-2

Bowling: Manjurul Islam 8–1–30–2; Talha Jubair 5–0–46–0; Khaled Mahmud 10–0–41–2; Mohammad Rafiq 10–0–39–1; Fahim Muntasir 10–0–40–0; Alok Kapali 2–0–12–0; Mohammad Ashraful 5–1–26–3.

Bangladesh

Javed Omar c Astle b Oram	1	Manjurul Islam b Vettori 10
Al Sahariar lbw b Bond.	0	Talha Jubair not out 1
Mohammad Ashraful c Styris b Bond. . .	1	
Tushar Imran c Astle b Oram	20	L-b 1, w 4, n-b 3 8
Alok Kapali c Fleming b Bond.	2	
*†Khaled Masud c Vincent b Bond	1	1/2 (2) 2/8 (1) 3/8 (3) (19.3 overs) 77
Khaled Mahmud c Fleming b Mills . . .	11	4/16 (5) 5/19 (6) 6/37 (4)
Mohammad Rafiq c Harris b Vettori . . .	17	7/46 (7) 8/56 (9)
Fahim Muntasir c Vincent b Mills	5	9/70 (8) 10/77 (10) 15 overs: 62-8

Bowling: Bond 5–0–21–4; Oram 6–1–32–2; Mills 5–0–13–2; Vettori 3.3–1–10–2.

Umpires: E. A. R. de Silva (Sri Lanka) and D. R. Shepherd (England). Third umpire: S. Venkataraghavan (India). Referee: G. R. Viswanath (India).

Many Kiwis would claim that they went within a deaf umpire of having the last laugh.
The New Zealanders in Australia, page 1209

POOL 2

INDIA v ZIMBABWE

At R. Premadasa Stadium, Colombo, September 14 (day/night). India won by 14 runs. Toss: India.

Andy Flower constructed one of the great one-day hundreds, the highest for Zimbabwe, but faced with a target of 289 they needed more than a virtuoso solo, and Flower's magnificent 145 merely lit up the losers' column once again. Zaheer's pace and accuracy were too much to handle and Ganguly cleverly resorted to spin from Tendulkar and Harbhajan when defeat looked imminent. It would have been certain without the youthful exuberance of Kaif, who hit a perfectly paced 111, and the traditional solidity of Dravid. Together, they put on 117 to drag India back from the precipice at 87 for five. Kaif started slowly, picking off ones and twos, before opening out with a fusillade of classy drives and innovative over-the-top shots once past 50. His approach contrasted sharply with the top order, who swung their bats as if playing in the Hong Kong Sixes.

Man of the Match: M. Kaif.

India

*S. C. Ganguly c Campbell b Hondo	13	A. Kumble not out 18
V. Sehwag c A. Flower b Ervine	48	
D. Mongia c Campbell b Hondo	0	B 1, l-b 2, w 10, n-b 4 17
S. R. Tendulkar c Campbell b Hondo . . .	7	
†R. Dravid run out	71	1/25 (1) 2/25 (3) (6 wkts, 50 overs) 288
Yuvraj Singh c Ervine b Hondo	3	3/67 (4) 4/84 (2)
M. Kaif not out	111	5/87 (6) 6/204 (5) 15 overs: 98-5

Harbhajan Singh, Zaheer Khan and A. Nehra did not bat.

Bowling: Streak 7–0–48–0; Hondo 9–1–62–4; Ervine 8–0–60–1; Whittall 8–0–39–0; Price 10–0–38–0; Marillier 5–0–23–0; G. W. Flower 3–0–15–0.

Zimbabwe

A. D. R. Campbell c Yuvraj Singh		S. M. Ervine b Zaheer Khan 7
b Zaheer Khan .	8	*H. H. Streak not out 4
D. D. Ebrahim lbw b Zaheer Khan	0	
†A. Flower c Ganguly b Tendulkar	145	B 6, l-b 16, w 6, n-b 4 32
G. W. Flower run out	33	1/1 (2) 2/43 (1) (8 wkts, 50 overs) 274
S. V. Carlisle b Tendulkar.	2	3/127 (4) 4/130 (5)
G. J. Whittall c Dravid b Zaheer Khan . .	29	5/201 (6) 6/240 (7)
D. A. Marillier c Ganguly b Kumble . . .	14	7/263 (3) 8/274 (8) 15 overs: 63-2

D. T. Hondo and R. W. Price did not bat.

Bowling: Zaheer Khan 10–2–45–4; Nehra 8–0–37–0; Kumble 10–0–48–1; Harbhajan Singh 10–0–44–0; Yuvraj Singh 3–0–24–0; Tendulkar 7–0–41–2; Ganguly 2–0–13–0.

Umpires: E. A. R. de Silva (Sri Lanka) and R. E. Koertzen (South Africa).
Third umpire: S. A. Bucknor (West Indies).   Referee: Wasim Raja (Pakistan).

ENGLAND v ZIMBABWE

At R. Premadasa Stadium, Colombo, September 18 (day/night). England won by 108 runs. Toss: England. International debut: I. D. Blackwell.

Marcus Trescothick scored his first one-day century in a successful cause for England as they extended their winning streak against Zimbabwe to nine. Set 299, Zimbabwe caught not a whiff of victory as Hoggard – who swung the ball as effortlessly as Kapil Dev in his prime – decimated their top order with a superb spell. Even Andy Flower, defiant as ever during his 44, could do nothing about an asking-rate that was up to nine midway through the innings. Irani's dobbers did the rest, and although Streak lashed out with a 58-ball fifty, the three-figure margin said it all. Trescothick had unveiled his repertoire of caressed drives, meaty pulls and nonchalant slog-sweeps. His 119 occupied 102 balls, only five more than Hussain's 75 which was alternately classy and clumsy. From 185 for one in 31 overs, England stumbled to 298 for eight, and handed Hondo another four-for as most of the batsmen gave the impression of a mission already accomplished.

Man of the Match: M. E. Trescothick.

England

M. E. Trescothick b G. W. Flower	119	J. N. Snape c and b Hondo		7
N. V. Knight b Hondo	8	A. R. Caddick not out		10
*N. Hussain b Streak	75	L-b 3, w 6, n-b 1		10
R. C. Irani c Campbell b G. W. Flower	4			
I. D. Blackwell c A. Flower b Streak	17	1/46 (2) 2/187 (3)	(8 wkts, 50 overs)	298
O. A. Shah c Campbell b Hondo	25	3/200 (4) 4/224 (1)		
†A. J. Stewart not out	23	5/240 (5) 6/272 (6)		
D. G. Cork c Streak b Hondo	0	7/273 (8) 8/287 (9)	15 overs: 92-1	

M. J. Hoggard did not bat.

Bowling: Streak 10–0–50–2; Hondo 6–0–45–4; Mbangwa 10–0–52–0; Whittall 7–0–44–0; Marillier 4–0–26–0; Price 4–0–27–0; G. W. Flower 9–0–51–2.

Zimbabwe

A. D. R. Campbell b Hoggard	2	R. W. Price run out		7
D. D. Ebrahim c Blackwell b Hoggard	20	M. Mbangwa not out		1
G. W. Flower c Trescothick b Hoggard	7	B 1, l-b 6, w 6, n-b 2		15
†A. Flower c Snape b Irani	44			
S. V. Carlisle c Knight b Irani	23	1/3 (1) 2/14 (3)	(9 wkts, 48 overs)	190
G. J. Whittall lbw b Irani	4	3/55 (2) 4/102 (4)		
*H. H. Streak not out	50	5/111 (5) 6/112 (6)		
D. A. Marillier lbw b Snape	6	7/129 (8) 8/150 (9)		
D. T. Hondo b Irani	11	9/188 (10)	14 overs: 47-2	

Bowling: Caddick 10–0–37–0; Hoggard 10–1–25–3; Cork 8–0–37–0; Irani 10–0–37–4; Snape 6–0–18–1; Blackwell 4–0–29–0.

Umpires: S. A. Bucknor (West Indies) and R. E. Koertzen (South Africa).
Third umpire: D. L. Orchard (South Africa). Referee: R. S. Madugalle (Sri Lanka).

ENGLAND v INDIA

At R. Premadasa Stadium, Colombo, September 22 (day/night). India won by eight wickets. Toss: England.

Virender Sehwag's appetite for destruction bordered on the gluttonous as England were swept aside in what was effectively a quarter-final. No team had ever chased more than 244 and won at the Premadasa, but Sehwag decided history was bunk and India overhauled 269 with ten overs to spare. Ganguly finished the demolition job with some attacking strokes – including a mammoth six that took him to his hundred – but his tune was barely heard amid the clatter of Sehwag's strokeplay. The drives flowed, the cuts lacerated and the flicks raced through mid-wicket as first Caddick and then Giles were given the Torquemada treatment. By the time Sehwag was out for 126 from 104 balls, England were just going through the motions. Their batsmen had struggled after a feeble start until Ian Blackwell arrived at the crease to show up the poverty of India's bowling options. He slammed 82 from 68 balls and added 104 off 15 overs with Stewart. England's total looked healthy, but once Knight grassed a hard chance at second slip with Sehwag on three, there was only one outcome.

Man of the Match: V. Sehwag.

England

M. E. Trescothick c Laxman b Nehra	0	D. G. Cork not out	6
N. V. Knight c Harbhajan Singh b Yuvraj Singh	50	A. F. Giles not out	2
*N. Hussain c Dravid b Nehra	1	B 5, l-b 9, w 5, n-b 3	22
R. C. Irani lbw b Kumble	37		
O. A. Shah c Dravid b Kumble	34		
I. D. Blackwell run out	82		
†A. J. Stewart c Ganguly b Tendulkar	35		

1/2 (1) 2/7 (3) (7 wkts, 50 overs) 269
3/80 (4) 4/127 (2)
5/153 (5) 6/257 (7)
7/264 (6) 15 overs: 66-2

A. R. Caddick and M. J. Hoggard did not bat.

Bowling: Zaheer Khan 10–2–40–0; Nehra 10–0–49–2; Kumble 9–0–58–2; Harbhajan Singh 10–0–42–0; Ganguly 1–0–10–0; Tendulkar 2–0–13–1; Yuvraj Singh 3–0–18–1; Sehwag 5–0–25–0.

India

V. Sehwag c and b Blackwell	126
*S. C. Ganguly not out	117
V. V. S. Laxman run out	4
S. R. Tendulkar not out	9
B 1, l-b 1, w 9, n-b 4	15

1/192 (1) 2/200 (3) (2 wkts, 39.3 overs) 271
15 overs: 99-0

†R. Dravid, Yuvraj Singh, M. Kaif, A. Kumble, Harbhajan Singh, Zaheer Khan and A. Nehra did not bat.

Bowling: Caddick 7–0–59–0; Hoggard 10–0–54–0; Cork 5.3–0–45–0; Irani 5–0–34–0; Giles 4–0–31–0; Blackwell 8–0–46–1.

Umpires: S. A. Bucknor (West Indies) and R. B. Tiffin (Zimbabwe).
Third umpire: R. E. Koertzen (South Africa). Referee: Wasim Raja (Pakistan).

POOL 3

SOUTH AFRICA v WEST INDIES

At Sinhalese Sports Club, Colombo, September 13. South Africa won by two wickets. Toss: South Africa.

Settled from the last ball, this was the best finish of the tournament, and nearly the biggest upset. Chanderpaul's constipation and a brainstorm from Dillon sent West Indies sliding to a defeat they scarcely deserved. With one over left – they were docked one for bowling slowly – South Africa needed 13; had there been a crowd, they would have been on the edge of their seats. Pollock smashed Dillon's first ball for six, but after he and Klusener holed out, South Africa needed three from one. Dillon speared the ball down the left-handed Boje's leg side for a wide and a scampered bye to the keeper. Alan Dawson's meaty snick to third man settled it as Dillon looked heavenward in despair. Chanderpaul's tortuous 98-ball 45 – in contrast to the buccaneering Gayle – had held West Indies back in the face of disciplined bowling from Pollock and co, but late cameos from Sarwan and Jacobs lent respectability. The South African top order collapsed, only for Rhodes's effervescence and Dippenaar's firmness to turn the tide. Dillon led the fightback, but then came his *faux pas*.

Man of the Match: J. N. Rhodes.

West Indies

C. H. Gayle c Boucher b Donald	. . . . .	49	V. C. Drakes not out	0
S. Chanderpaul c Dippenaar b Dawson	. .	45	M. Dillon not out	1
B. C. Lara c Donald b Boje	. . . .	21	L-b 5, w 7, n-b 1	13
*C. L. Hooper lbw b Pollock	. . . .	26		
R. R. Sarwan b Kallis	. . . .	36	1/63 (1) 2/107 (3) (8 wkts, 50 overs) 238	
W. W. Hinds c Kallis b Donald	. . . . . .	12	3/153 (2) 4/153 (4)	
†R. D. Jacobs c Pollock b Kallis	. . . . . .	25	5/191 (6) 6/220 (5)	
M. V. Nagamootoo run out	. . . .	10	7/230 (7) 8/237 (8) 15 overs: 63-1	

P. T. Collins did not bat.

Bowling: Pollock 10–1–34–1; Dawson 10–1–51–1; Donald 8–0–44–2; Kallis 9–0–41–2; Boje 7–0–34–1; Klusener 6–0–29–0.

South Africa

G. C. Smith c Jacobs b Hooper	. . . . . .	33	N. Boje not out	0
H. H. Gibbs b Dillon	. . . .	8	A. C. Dawson not out	4
J. H. Kallis c Jacobs b Drakes	. . . . . .	10		
H. H. Dippenaar c Nagamootoo			B 1, l-b 3, w 7, n-b 6	17
	b Hooper .	53		
J. N. Rhodes b Hooper	. . . .	61	1/13 (2) 2/50 (3) (8 wkts, 49 overs) 242	
†M. V. Boucher b Dillon	. . . .	23	3/61 (1) 4/178 (4)	
L. Klusener c Chanderpaul b Dillon	. . . .	23	5/179 (5) 6/220 (6)	
*S. M. Pollock c Chanderpaul b Dillon	. .	10	7/234 (8) 8/236 (7) 14 overs: 53-2	

A. A. Donald did not bat.

Bowling: Dillon 10–1–60–4; Collins 9–0–38–0; Hooper 10–1–42–3; Drakes 8–1–36–1; Nagamootoo 9–0–41–0; Gayle 3–0–21–0.

Umpires: D. R. Shepherd (England) and S. Venkataraghavan (India).
Third umpire: D. J. Harper (Australia).   Referee: R. S. Madugalle (Sri Lanka).

KENYA v WEST INDIES

At Sinhalese Sports Club, Colombo, September 17. West Indies won by 29 runs. Toss: West Indies.

Ultimately, Steve Tikolo's magnificent 93 couldn't gloss over an abysmal fielding display from Kenya as West Indies edged home in a match of several umpiring gaffes. Had Kenya held their catches – five was the conservative estimate – they would have been chasing a lot less than 262. But just as important was Asoka de Silva's refusal to give Lara out caught behind off Collins Obuya on 32, when the ball brushed the full face of the bat, and Venkat's reluctance to refer two lbw appeals which would have been upheld. Lara's last contribution before hepatitis struck was a 15th one-day hundred which revived the innings after a sluggish start. Even then, it took a final flurry from Sarwan and Hinds – who clubbed 20 off seven balls – to reach 250. Kenya's reply came in dribbles and spurts. Shah and Patel bolstered Tikolo but neither lasted long enough to pressure the fielders. Tikolo's exceptional effort, from 91 deliveries, featured both classical strokeplay and improvised tickles to fine leg. He deserved to win, but Collins and Dillon swooped to blow away the last four wickets for 13.

Man of the Match: B. C. Lara.

West Indies

C. H. Gayle c T. O. Suji b Odoyo	33	†R. D. Jacobs not out		2
S. Chanderpaul c D. O. Obuya		M. V. Nagamootoo not out		0
b Odumbe	43	B 1, l-b 5, w 3, n-b 3		12
B. C. Lara b Tikolo	111			
*C. L. Hooper c Otieno b Tikolo	20	1/60 (1) 2/115 (2)	(6 wkts, 50 overs) 261	
R. R. Sarwan run out	20	3/179 (4) 4/236 (3)		
W. W. Hinds run out	20	5/246 (5) 6/258 (6)	15 overs: 69-1	

V. C. Drakes, M. Dillon and P. T. Collins did not bat.

Bowling: M. A. Suji 9–1–49–0; Odoyo 9–0–63–1; T. O. Suji 5–0–16–0; Odumbe 10–1–21–1; C. O. Obuya 10–0–57–0; Tikolo 7–0–49–2.

Kenya

K. O. Otieno b Collins	0	M. A. Suji b Collins		1
R. D. Shah b Nagamootoo	27	J. O. Angara not out		0
B. J. Patel c Hooper b Nagamootoo	35	B 6, l-b 14, w 2, n-b 1		23
*S. O. Tikolo b Dillon	93			
M. O. Odumbe lbw b Dillon	9	1/7 (1) 2/51 (2) 3/101 (3)	(49.1 overs) 232	
T. M. Odoyo c Hooper b Collins	15	4/143 (5) 5/170 (6)		
†D. O. Obuya run out	3	6/178 (7) 7/219 (4)		
C. O. Obuya c Chanderpaul b Gayle	19	8/231 (9) 9/231 (8)		
T. O. Suji c Collins b Gayle	7	10/232 (10)	15 overs: 42-1	

Bowling: Dillon 10–2–45–2; Collins 9.1–4–18–3; Drakes 9–0–38–0; Nagamootoo 8–0–47–2; Hooper 4–0–26–0; Gayle 9–0–38–2.

Umpires: D. J. Harper (Australia) and S. Venkataraghavan (India).
Third umpire: E. A. R. de Silva (Sri Lanka). Referee: M. J. Procter (South Africa).

KENYA v SOUTH AFRICA

At R. Premadasa Stadium, Colombo, September 20 (day/night). South Africa won by 176 runs. Toss: South Africa.

Kennedy Otieno's desperate flail at a Klusener bouncer – which saw the bat streak through the night and come within inches of rearranging Boucher's features – summed up an unequal tussle. Tikolo again left his mark, but a cultured 69 was no more than a signature in the sand against a South African total of tidal-wave proportions. Kenya's fielders were fifth columnists, dropping catches and fumbling in the outfield like five-year-olds fighting over soap in the bath. It was dire stuff, and despite a slow and uncertain start, Gibbs and Smith exacted the highest price. Once he settled, Gibbs was imperious, carving up the leg-side field with delicate flicks, dabs and brutal swipes. Smith played Robin to his Batman and once they departed, Kallis and Dippenaar were on hand to blow what was left of the Kenyan house down. South Africa's 316 was the second-highest total at the Premadasa, and once Kenya slumped to five for two in the fourth over, the contest was over.

Man of the Match: H. H. Gibbs.

South Africa

G. C. Smith st D. O. Obuya b Odumbe	69	L. Klusener not out		18
H. H. Gibbs c D. O. Obuya b Kamande	116	J. L. Ontong not out		4
J. H. Kallis st D. O. Obuya b Tikolo	60	B 4, l-b 1, w 2, n-b 4		11
H. H. Dippenaar st D. O. Obuya				
b C. O. Obuya	31	1/159 (1) 2/214 (2)	(5 wkts, 50 overs) 316	
D. M. Benkenstein c M. A. Suji		3/287 (4) 4/291 (3)		
b C. O. Obuya	7	5/299 (5)	15 overs: 76-0	

†M. V. Boucher, *S. M. Pollock, A. C. Dawson and M. Ntini did not bat.

Bowling: M. A. Suji 8–0–42–0; Odoyo 7–0–42–0; T. O. Suji 3–0–19–0; Odumbe 10–0–52–1; C. O. Obuya 10–0–77–2; Tikolo 10–1–54–1; Kamande 2–0–25–1.

Kenya

K. O. Otieno c Benkenstein b Ntini	16	T. O. Suji b Benkenstein	4
R. D. Shah c Kallis b Pollock	3	J. K. Kamande not out	2
B. J. Patel c Pollock b Dawson	0	M. A. Suji c Klusener b Benkenstein	2
*S. O. Tikolo c Smith b Ontong	69	B 1, l-b 2, w 12, n-b 3	18
M. O. Odumbe c sub (A. A. Donald) b Ntini	0	1/4 (2) 2/5 (3) 3/61 (1) (46.5 overs)	140
T. M. Odoyo c Gibbs b Ontong	10	4/64 (5) 5/89 (6) 6/119 (4)	
C. O. Obuya lbw b Benkenstein	14	7/126 (8) 8/131 (7)	
†D. O. Obuya st Boucher b Ontong	2	9/134 (9) 10/140 (11) 15 overs: 40-2	

Bowling: Pollock 6–2–10–1; Dawson 5–2–12–1; Klusener 5–1–23–0; Ntini 10–2–37–2; Kallis 6–1–17–0; Ontong 10–1–30–3; Benkenstein 3.5–1–5–3; Smith 1–0–3–0.

Umpires: D. J. Harper (Australia) and S. Venkataraghavan (India).
Third umpire: D. R. Shepherd (England). Referee: G. R. Viswanath (India).

POOL 4

SRI LANKA v PAKISTAN

At R. Premadasa Stadium, Colombo, September 12 (day/night). Sri Lanka won by eight wickets. Toss: Pakistan.

Yousuf Youhana's farcical run-out – later investigated, and cleared, by the Anti-Corruption Unit – summed up Pakistan's display. Shoaib Malik made history by becoming the third umpire's first lbw victim but there was little else to note as Pakistan limped to 200. Saeed Anwar, bearded like the prophet, batted like an old man, and but for Misbah-ul-Haq's purposeful 47, the embarrassment would have been keener. Sri Lanka eased home with 13 overs to spare as Pakistan lost the plot and their tempers. Furious at his appeals being turned down, Shahid Afridi had a mid-pitch altercation with de Silva, who responded by stroking his way to 66. Jayasuriya chiselled out a 13th one-day hundred and passed 8,000 one-day international runs in an uncharacteristic innings with only ten fours, but coming from a captain with a dodgy shoulder, it was stirring stuff, and too much for Pakistan, who were effectively knocked out on the tournament's opening day. Their coach, Mudassar Nazar, was duly recalled to Karachi, where glad tidings didn't await.

Man of the Match: S. T. Jayasuriya.

Pakistan

Saeed Anwar c Chandana b Fernando	52	*Waqar Younis c de Silva b Fernando	4
Shahid Afridi c Sangakkara b Gunaratne	4	Shoaib Akhtar not out	0
Shoaib Malik lbw b Vaas	1	L-b 8, w 3, n-b 3, p 5	19
Yousuf Youhana run out	0		
Younis Khan b Muralitharan	35	1/12 (2) 2/17 (3) 3/17 (4) (49.4 overs)	200
†Rashid Latif c Fernando b Muralitharan	22	4/87 (5) 5/120 (6)	
Misbah-ul-Haq b Fernando	47	6/141 (1) 7/171 (8)	
Abdul Razzaq c de Silva b Gunaratne	16	8/175 (9) 9/198 (10)	
Wasim Akram b Muralitharan	0	10/200 (7) 15 overs: 51-3	

Bowling: Vaas 10–3–27–1; Gunaratne 10–1–49–2; Fernando 9.4–0–30–3; Chandana 7–0–37–0; Muralitharan 10–0–29–3; Jayasuriya 3–0–15–0.

Sri Lanka

```
*S. T. Jayasuriya not out . . . . . . . . . . .  102
M. S. Atapattu run out . . . . . . . . . . . .    8
†K. C. Sangakkara lbw b Wasim Akram .        0
P. A. de Silva not out . . . . . . . . . . . . .   66
            B 2, l-b 7, w 10, n-b 6. . . . . .   25
```

1/44 (2) 2/45 (3)   (2 wkts, 36.1 overs) 201
                      15 overs: 88-2

D. P. M. D. Jayawardene, R. P. Arnold, U. D. U. Chandana, W. P. U. J. C. Vaas, C. R. D. Fernando, M. Muralitharan and P. W. Gunaratne did not bat.

Bowling: Wasim Akram 8–0–42–1; Waqar Younis 5–0–37–0; Shoaib Akhtar 8–0–36–0; Shahid Afridi 7.1–0–39–0; Abdul Razzaq 3–0–14–0; Shoaib Malik 5–0–24–0.

Umpires: S. A. Bucknor (West Indies) and D. J. Harper (Australia).
Third umpire: R. E. Koertzen (South Africa).   Referee: M. J. Procter (South Africa).

SRI LANKA v HOLLAND

At R. Premadasa Stadium, Colombo, September 16 (day/night). Sri Lanka won by 206 runs. Toss: Sri Lanka. International debuts: Adeel Raja, J-J. Esmeijer, V. D. Grandia, E. Schiferli, R. H. Scholte, D. L. S. van Bunge, L. P. van Troost.

It had been six years since Holland's last outing at this level, and the rust showed in this 206-run rout. For the few spectators who bothered to turn up, the only entertainment was Tim de Leede's fabulous jump-and-grab to dismiss de Silva on the mid-wicket boundary. Holland were never going to overhaul 292, definitely not after three wickets went down in the first four overs, and de Leede provided the sole note of defiance with 31. Even Sri Lanka got little out of the match except Atapattu's sixth one-day hundred. What the Dutch bowlers lacked by way of skill, they made up for in discipline and commitment as the Sri Lankan innings progressed in fits and starts, with Sangakkara horribly out of touch. Once Atapattu had sauntered to three figures and departed, it was left to Arnold and Vaas to provide the swipes and heaves the crowd craved. Not that it mattered. The have-nots were so clueless against Murali that even 200 would have been well beyond them.

Man of the Match: M. S. Atapattu.

Sri Lanka

```
*S. T. Jayasuriya c Zuiderent b Grandia .   36
M. S. Atapattu c van Oosterom
                    b Lefebvre .  101
†K. C. Sangakkara b Adeel Raja .            41
P. A. de Silva c de Leede b Adeel Raja .    23
D. P. M. D. Jayawardene run out . . . . . .  14
R. P. Arnold not out . . . . . . . . . . . .   22
```

```
W. P. U. J. C. Vaas c and b Lefebvre . . .  16
M. Muralitharan not out . . . . . . . . . . .  1
            B 6, l-b 9, w 18, n-b 5. . . . . . 38
```

1/59 (1) 2/175 (3)   (6 wkts, 50 overs) 292
3/223 (4) 4/234 (2)
5/247 (5) 6/287 (7)   15 overs: 87-1

H. D. P. K. Dharmasena, C. R. D. Fernando and P. W. Gunaratne did not bat.

Bowling: Schiferli 7–0–29–0; Grandia 5–0–40–1; Lefebvre 10–0–59–2; de Leede 8–0–37–0; Esmeijer 5–0–36–0; Adeel Raja 10–0–50–2; van Troost 5–0–26–0.

Holland

R. F. van Oosterom c Sangakkara b Gunaratne .	0
D. L. S van Bunge lbw b Gunaratne . . .	3
B. Zuiderent lbw b Vaas	0
T. B. M. de Leede c Sangakkara b Fernando .	31
†R. H. Scholte c Sangakkara b Dharmasena .	12
L. P. van Troost b Dharmasena .	0
J-J. Esmeijer c Fernando b Muralitharan .	7
Adeel Raja c Sangakkara b Muralitharan .	2
E. Schiferli st Sangakkara b Muralitharan	15
*R. P. Lefebvre not out	4
V. D. Grandia b Muralitharan	0
B 4, l-b 2, w 3, n-b 3	12

1/3 (1) 2/4 (3) 3/4 (2)   (29.3 overs) 86
4/46 (5) 5/52 (6) 6/57 (4)
7/59 (8) 8/81 (9)
9/82 (7) 10/86 (11)   15 overs: 48-4

Bowling: Vaas 6–2–11–1; Gunaratne 4–0–19–2; Fernando 5–0–21–1; Dharmasena 9–3–14–2; Muralitharan 5.3–2–15–4.

Umpires: D. L. Orchard (South Africa) and D. R. Shepherd (England).
Third umpire: R. B. Tiffin (Zimbabwe).   Referee: G. R. Viswanath (India).

HOLLAND v PAKISTAN

At Sinhalese Sports Club, Colombo, September 21. Pakistan won by nine wickets. Toss: Holland. International debuts: J. F. Kloppenburg, H-J. C. Mol.

Pakistan blew up the rope bridge that separates cricket's haves and have-nots and Holland duly fell into the chasm. The first strands were snapped in a fiery opening burst from Waqar Younis and Shoaib Akhtar, and by the time Shahid Afridi slammed the joint second-fastest fifty in one-day internationals, Holland had long dropped out of sight. The Dutch total of 136 – which lasted all 50 overs and featured 11 maidens and only nine fours – was all thanks to de Leede, van Troost and Lefebvre. Pakistan, still smarting from their opening-day humiliation, knocked off the runs with two-thirds of their overs to spare. Adeel Raja's off-spin summed up the Dutch effort: his first over was a maiden; his next eight balls went for 31. Afridi's 55 came off 18 balls with six sixes, four of them in Raja's second over. By contrast, Imran Nazir's 59 from 40 balls was nothing special, and Saeed Anwar's 28 from 40 was tedious.

Man of the Match: Shahid Afridi

Holland

J. F. Kloppenburg run out	7
D. L. S van Bunge c Misbah-ul-Haq b Shoaib Akhtar .	1
B. Zuiderent c Younis Khan b Waqar Younis .	7
T. B. M. de Leede lbw b Shahid Afridi .	24
H-J. C. Mol b Waqar Younis.	0
L. P. van Troost c Rashid Latif b Shahid Afridi .	16
†R. H. Scholte st Rashid Latif b Shoaib Malik .	11
J-J. Esmeijer lbw b Shahid Afridi	0
*R. P. Lefebvre not out	32
E. Schiferli b Mohammad Sami	0
Adeel Raja b Abdul Razzaq	5
L-b 21, w 12	33

1/3 (2) 2/15 (1) 3/23 (3)   (50 overs) 136
4/23 (5) 5/78 (4) 6/84 (6)
7/84 (8) 8/112 (7)
9/113 (10) 10/136 (11)   15 overs: 49-4

Bowling: Waqar Younis 7–3–14–2; Shoaib Akhtar 8–3–14–1; Mohammad Sami 10–1–18–1; Shahid Afridi 10–3–18–3; Abdul Razzaq 7–0–25–1; Shoaib Malik 8–1–26–1.

Pakistan

Imran Nazir c Zuiderent b Kloppenburg .	59
Saeed Anwar not out.	28
Shahid Afridi not out	55

1/85 (1)　　　　　(1 wkt, 16.2 overs) 142
　　　　　　　　　　15 overs: 126-1

Shoaib Malik, Younis Khan, Misbah-ul-Haq, Abdul Razzaq, †Rashid Latif, *Waqar Younis, Shoaib Akhtar and Mohammad Sami did not bat.

Bowling: Schiferli 4–0–37–0; Lefebvre 4–0–14–0; de Leede 2–0–19–0; Kloppenburg 2–0–23–1; Adeel Raja 2.2–1–31–0; Esmeijer 2–0–18–0.

Umpires: R. E. Koertzen (South Africa) and D. L. Orchard (South Africa).
Third umpire: D. J. Harper (Australia). Referee: C. H. Lloyd (West Indies).

QUALIFYING TABLES

Pool 1

	Played	Won	Lost	Points	Net run-rate
Australia	2	2	0	8	3.46
New Zealand	2	1	1	4	0.03
Bangladesh	2	0	2	0	−3.27

Pool 2

	Played	Won	Lost	Points	Net run-rate
India.	2	2	0	8	0.81
England.	2	1	1	4	0.40
Zimbabwe	2	0	2	0	−1.12

Pool 3

	Played	Won	Lost	Points	Net run-rate
South Africa.	2	2	0	8	1.85
West Indies	2	1	1	4	0.20
Kenya.	2	0	2	0	−2.05

Pool 4

	Played	Won	Lost	Points	Net run-rate
Sri Lanka	2	2	0	8	2.86
Pakistan	2	1	1	4	1.24
Holland.	2	0	2	0	−4.32

Net run-rate is calculated by subtracting runs conceded per over from runs scored per over.

SEMI-FINALS

INDIA v SOUTH AFRICA

At R. Premadasa Stadium, Colombo, September 25 (day/night). India won by ten runs. Toss: India. International debut: R. J. Peterson.

　　With 14 overs left, this match was a dead duck. But when the team in control are South Africa, masters of the late choke, the fat lady thinks twice before opening her mouth. So it was that Sehwag – tossed the ball as late as the 42nd over – won India a match they should have lost by some distance. Chasing 261, Gibbs had torn the bowling to confetti with some magnificent cover-drives, sweeps and contemptuous pulls. But an attack of cramp in both hands forced him off after 37 overs and the remaining batsmen took it as a signal to fall apart. Rhodes's top-edged sweep off Harbhajan was superbly caught, one-handed, by Yuvraj, and when Dippenaar and Boucher holed out, the onus was on Kallis and Klusener to see them home. Klusener batted like a blind man teeing off, while Kallis, who made 97, was apparently playing for a draw. By the time the final over rolled round, 21 were needed. A Kallis slog-sweep for six off Sehwag gave the Indians brief alarm but the encore ended up in Dravid's gloves. The match belonged to Sehwag, whose blistering 59 had set India on their way. Though they stuttered mid-innings, Dravid and the classy Yuvraj provided late momentum before Pollock came back to dismiss thoughts of 300. But the heat, humidity, Sehwag and South Africa's own demons conspired to ensure that 262 was too tall an order for cricket's nearly men.

Man of the Match: V. Sehwag.

India

V. Sehwag c Klusener b Kallis	59	A. Kumble not out		2
*S. C. Ganguly c Dippenaar b Ntini	13	A. Nehra not out		1
V. V. S. Laxman c Boucher b Donald	22	B 2, l-b 1, w 8, n-b 3		14
S. R. Tendulkar run out	16			
†R. Dravid lbw b Klusener	49	1/42 (2) 2/102 (3)	(9 wkts, 50 overs)	261
Yuvraj Singh c Gibbs b Pollock	62	3/108 (1) 4/135 (4)		
M. Kaif c Rhodes b Pollock	19	5/207 (5) 6/254 (6)		
Harbhajan Singh b Donald	4	7/254 (7) 8/255 (9)		
Zaheer Khan c Smith b Pollock	0	9/260 (8)	15 overs: 94-1	

Bowling: Pollock 9–0–43–3; Ntini 5–0–37–1; Donald 8–0–41–2; Kallis 8–1–50–1; Klusener 10–0–40–1; Peterson 10–0–47–0.

South Africa

H. H. Gibbs retired hurt	116	†M. V. Boucher c Yuvraj Singh b Sehwag		10
G. C. Smith c Yuvraj Singh		L. Klusener c Kaif b Sehwag		14
b Zaheer Khan	4	*S. M. Pollock not out		0
J. H. Kallis c Dravid b Sehwag	97	B 1, l-b 3, w 5		9
J. N. Rhodes c Yuvraj Singh				
b Harbhajan Singh	1	1/14 (2) 2/194 (4)	(6 wkts, 50 overs)	251
H. H. Dippenaar c Kumble		3/194 (5) 4/213 (6)		
b Harbhajan Singh	0	5/247 (3) 6/251 (7)	15 overs: 78-1	

R. J. Peterson, A. A. Donald and M. Ntini did not bat.

Gibbs retired hurt at 192.

Bowling: Zaheer Khan 9–2–27–1; Nehra 7.3–0–41–0; Kumble 10–0–53–0; Harbhajan Singh 10–0–37–2; Yuvraj Singh 3–0–17–0; Ganguly 1.3–0–15–0; Tendulkar 4–0–32–0; Sehwag 5–0–25–3.

Umpires: D. R. Shepherd (England) and R. B. Tiffin (Zimbabwe).
Third umpire: D. J. Harper (Australia).   Referee: R. S. Madugalle (Sri Lanka).

SRI LANKA v AUSTRALIA

At R. Premadasa Stadium, Colombo, September 27 (day/night). Sri Lanka won by seven wickets. Toss: Australia.

Aravinda de Silva's seemingly innocuous off-spin was an unlikely spoke in the wheel as the Australian juggernaut screeched to a halt in front of an openly hostile crowd. When de Silva was brought on after six overs, the board showed an intimidating 48 for nought. Soon after, with the Australian batsmen playing as if still on the beach in the Maldives, it was 57 for four. And though Martyn, with 28, and Warne, with a determined 36, battled hard, 162 was simply not enough. On a pitch that was slow and low even by the standards of this tournament, Muralitharan took three wickets, though it was de Silva's one-for that grabbed the headlines. Australia took the field needing early wickets and, despite the best efforts of McGrath and Gillespie, they didn't get them.

Overseas Cricket

Jayasuriya chanced his arm for 42 before being bowled by Warne. But Atapattu and Sangakkara ensured there would be no repeat of South Africa's self-destruction as Australia were humbled with ten overs and seven wickets to spare. As in the 1996 World Cup final, they were found wanting against the turning ball. Sri Lanka had a final against big brother to look forward to, but a victory over the much-disliked Australians meant even more.

Man of the Match: P. A. de Silva.

Australia

†A. C. Gilchrist c Atapattu b Dharmasena	31		B. Lee b Jayasuriya		18
M. L. Hayden b de Silva	13		J. N. Gillespie not out		2
*R. T. Ponting lbw b Vaas	3		G. D. McGrath b Muralitharan		0
D. R. Martyn run out	28				
D. S. Lehmann run out	0		B 10, l-b 1, w 1		12
M. G. Bevan c Arnold b Dharmasena	12				
S. R. Watson c Jayasuriya b Muralitharan	7		1/49 (2) 2/49 (1) 3/56 (3) (48.4 overs) 162		
			4/57 (5) 5/96 (4) 6/97 (6)		
S. K. Warne st Sangakkara b Muralitharan	36		7/107 (7) 8/153 (9)		
			9/162 (8) 10/162 (11) 15 overs: 57-4		

Bowling: Vaas 7–2–31–1; Gunaratne 2–0–15–0; Dharmasena 10–1–30–2; de Silva 10–2–16–1; Muralitharan 9.4–0–26–3; Chandana 7–0–22–0; Jayasuriya 3–0–11–1.

Sri Lanka

*S. T. Jayasuriya b Warne	42
M. S. Atapattu lbw b McGrath	51
†K. C. Sangakkara c Gilchrist b McGrath	48
P. A. de Silva not out	2
D. P. M. D. Jayawardene not out	1
B 4, l-b 2, w 7, n-b 6	19

1/67 (1) 2/142 (3)   (3 wkts, 40 overs) 163
3/160 (2)   15 overs: 67-1

R. P. Arnold, U. D. U. Chandana, W. P. U. J. C. Vaas, H. D. P. K. Dharmasena, M. Muralitharan and P. W. Gunaratne did not bat.

Bowling: McGrath 10–1–41–2; Gillespie 8–1–28–0; Warne 10–2–25–1; Lee 7–1–39–0; Lehmann 5–0–24–0.

Umpires: S. A. Bucknor (West Indies) and D. L. Orchard (South Africa).
Third umpire: R. E. Koertzen (South Africa). Referee: Wasim Raja (Pakistan).

FINAL

SRI LANKA v INDIA

At R. Premadasa Stadium, Colombo, September 29 (day/night). No result. Toss: Sri Lanka.

The north-east monsoon had ignored the cricket for 17 days but when it finally made an evening appearance at the Premadasa, an hour was enough to consign the match to pointlessness. Sehwag had biffed his way through the second over but there was no doubting that Sri Lanka's slow bowlers would have asked vexing questions of the batsmen had the game continued, especially on a tortoise-slow surface where Harbhajan and Sehwag had tied Sri Lanka down with off-spin. Atapattu, who added insult to Srinath's jetlag – he had just flown in from Leicestershire – during the course of his 34, and Jayasuriya had given the crowd plenty to cheer, and at 155 for one in the 31st over, 300 looked on. But then Jayasuriya, who had motored to 74 after a shaky start, miscued a pull off Agarkar and was brilliantly held on the dive by Harbhajan. Thereafter, spin held sway despite a half-century from Sangakkara, who started like the Duracell bunny but ran out of charge as the pitch slowed. The injudicious reverse sweep that ended his innings was symptomatic of the batsmen's frustration. Tendulkar epitomised India's Jekyll-and-Hyde performance in the field, diving like Gordon Banks to catch Jayawardene but also dropping two clangers.

Sri Lanka

*S. T. Jayasuriya c Harbhajan Singh		R. P. Arnold not out	18
b Agarkar .	74	W. P. U. J. C. Vaas not out	11
M. S. Atapattu c Agarkar			
b Harbhajan Singh .	34	B 6, l-b 8, w 8	22
†K. C. Sangakkara c Sehwag			
b Harbhajan Singh .	54	1/65 (2) 2/155 (1) (5 wkts, 50 overs) 244	
P. A. de Silva c Dravid b Harbhajan Singh	18	3/185 (4) 4/207 (3)	
D. P. M. D. Jayawardene c and b Tendulkar	13	5/212 (5) 15 overs: 75-1	

H. D. P. K. Dharmasena, C. R. D. Fernando, M. Muralitharan and P. W. Gunaratne did not bat.

Bowling: Zaheer Khan 10–0–43–0; Srinath 8–0–55–0; Agarkar 6–0–37–1; Harbhajan Singh 10–1–27–3; Sehwag 10–0–32–0; Tendulkar 6–0–36–1.

India

D. Mongia not out	1
V. Sehwag not out	13
(no wkt, 2 overs) 14	

*S. C. Ganguly, S. R. Tendulkar, †R. Dravid, Yuvraj Singh, M. Kaif, A. B. Agarkar, Harbhajan Singh, Zaheer Khan and J. Srinath did not bat.

Bowling: Vaas 1–1–0–0; Gunaratne 1–0–14–0.

Umpires: S. A. Bucknor (West Indies) and D. R. Shepherd (England).
Third umpire: D. J. Harper (Australia).   Referee: C. H. Lloyd (West Indies).

SRI LANKA v INDIA

At R. Premadasa Stadium, Colombo, September 30 (day/night). No result. Toss: Sri Lanka.

Another day, same story – right down to the toss – as torrential showers left a major one-day trophy shared for the first time. With the ball stopping even more than the previous day, Sri Lanka did well to reach 222. But Sehwag started the pursuit with another cameo before lightning streaked across the night sky and the outfield was deluged. India's spinners had squeezed the life out of the Sri Lankan innings in 36 overs costing less than four apiece. With the hosts possessing a far more formidable slow-bowling armoury, the capacity crowd was deprived of another potentially fascinating episode of cat-and-mouse. India had shaded the first innings after Jayasuriya inside-edged the very first ball on to his stumps. De Silva, anxious to make his last home innings one to remember, soothed frazzled nerves by caressing five boundaries in one Agarkar over. But he top-edged a sweep off Kumble, and Sri Lanka slumped to 71 for four. Jayawardene and Arnold dropped in the treacle, adding 118 in 28.5 overs of virtual Test cricket. Hard graft and scampered singles set up a final onslaught of 70 from ten overs, with Jayawardene shifting smoothly through the gears. It might have been a match-winning total, but the vagaries of the scheduling and the weather made sure no one would know. It was a disappointing, if fair result, with the two teams most adept on slow, turning pitches sharing the $300,000 prize.

Sri Lanka

*S. T. Jayasuriya b Zaheer Khan	0	W. P. U. J. C. Vaas c Kumble	
†K. C. Sangakkara run out	26	b Zaheer Khan .	17
M. S. Atapattu c Mongia b Agarkar	10	M. Muralitharan not out	0
P. A. de Silva c Kaif b Kumble.	27	W 7, n-b 1	8
D. P. M. D. Jayawardene c Ganguly			
b Zaheer Khan .	77	1/0 (1) 2/24 (3) (7 wkts, 50 overs) 222	
R. P. Arnold not out	56	3/63 (4) 4/71 (2)	
U. D. U. Chandana c Kaif		5/189 (5) 6/193 (7)	
b Harbhajan Singh .	1	7/215 (8) 15 overs: 70-3	

H. D. P. K. Dharmasena and C. R. D. Fernando did not bat.

Bowling: Zaheer Khan 9–1–44–3; Agarkar 5–1–36–1; Harbhajan Singh 10–0–34–1; Kumble 10–1–41–1; Sehwag 8–0–31–0; Tendulkar 8–0–36–0.

India

D. Mongia c Jayawardene b Vaas.	0
V. Sehwag not out	25
S. R. Tendulkar not out	7
B 1, w 4, n-b 1.	6

1/6 (1)   (1 wkt, 8.4 overs) 38

*S. C. Ganguly, †R. Dravid, Yuvraj Singh, M. Kaif, A. B. Agarkar, Harbhajan Singh, A. Kumble and Zaheer Khan did not bat.

Bowling: Vaas 4.4–1–24–1; Fernando 4–0–13–0.

Umpires: S. A. Bucknor (West Indies) and D. R. Shepherd (England).
Third umpire: D. J. Harper (Australia).   Referee: C. H. Lloyd (West Indies).

PWC ONE-DAY INTERNATIONAL RATINGS

The PricewaterhouseCoopers (PwC) One-Day International Ratings, introduced in August 1998, follow similar principles to the Test Ratings (see page 1503).

The leading 20 batsmen and bowlers in the One-Day International Ratings after the qualifying pool games of the World Cup, which ended on March 4, 2003, were:

	Batsmen	Rating		Bowlers	Rating
1	S. T. Jayasuriya (*Sri Lanka*)	821	1	S. M. Pollock (*South Africa*)	909
2	M. L. Hayden (*Australia*)	805	2	M. Muralitharan (*Sri Lanka*)	899
3	S. R. Tendulkar (*India*)	802	3	G. D. McGrath (*Australia*)	873
4	H. H. Gibbs (*South Africa*)	771	4	M. Ntini (*South Africa*)	812
5	M. G. Bevan (*Australia*)	746	5	W. P. U. J. C. Vaas (*Sri Lanka*)	795
6	M. S. Atapattu (*Sri Lanka*)	743	6	J. N. Gillespie (*Australia*)	771
7	R. R. Sarwan (*West Indies*)	720	7	Wasim Akram (*Pakistan*)	769
8	Yousuf Youhana (*Pakistan*)	716	8	A. R. Caddick (*England*)	734
9	C. H. Gayle (*West Indies*)	712	9	B. Lee (*Australia*)	733
10	A. Flower (*Zimbabwe*)	710	10	J. Srinath (*India*)	714
				Zaheer Khan (*India*)	714
11	A. C. Gilchrist (*Australia*)	706	12	A. J. Bichel (*Australia*)	696
12	R. T. Ponting (*Australia*)	702	13	Harbhajan Singh (*India*)	689
13	V. Sehwag (*India*)	694	14	M. Dillon (*West Indies*)	673
14	B. C. Lara (*West Indies*)	674	15	D. R. Tuffey (*New Zealand*)	670
15	H. H. Dippenaar (*South Africa*)	672	16	A. A. Donald (*South Africa*)	655
16	M. E. Trescothick (*England*)	668	17	J. H. Kallis (*South Africa*)	651
17	J. H. Kallis (*South Africa*)	665	18	Saqlain Mushtaq (*Pakistan*)	649
18	D. R. Martyn (*Australia*)	657	19	S. E. Bond (*New Zealand*)	643
19	R. Dravid (*India*)	646	20	Waqar Younis (*Pakistan*)	641
	L. Klusener (*South Africa*)	646			

ENGLAND ACADEMY IN AUSTRALIA, 2001-02

In October 2001, a group of talented cricketers aged 19 to 24 gathered at the Royal Military Academy, Sandhurst. They comprised the first intake of the National Academy, an important £500,000 cog in the ECB machinery designed to produce a world-beating England team by 2007. By then, according to the board's World Class Plan, 95 per cent of the international side would be Academy graduates. The man charged with transforming potential into results was Rod Marsh, the former Australian wicket-keeper and, significantly, director of the highly successful Australian Academy based in Adelaide. Marsh was a prize catch: could he do for England what he had for Australia?

Planning difficulties had caused the abandonment of the original scheme to house the Academy in a purpose-built headquarters at the National Sports Centre in Bisham Abbey, Buckinghamshire. Construction work at the replacement venue, Loughborough University, was not due for completion until 2002-03 and so, in the absence of a UK home, the squad, after a gruelling week at Sandhurst building character, team spirit and muscle, flew out to Adelaide. There, using the facilities that had served their Australian counterparts so well (the ECB was in no doubt that the Australian model was the one to follow), they spent 16 demanding weeks. The Academy played 11 games, mainly against state second teams. Although the management were at pains to say that success should not be judged simply by results on the pitch, these were encouraging: eight wins, two defeats and a draw. As important for the academicians' education were the lectures they attended on a broad range of topics, from match-fixing to media and presentation skills, from drugs and injury prevention to Pilates exercises. And they were required to do their own laundry.

Fitness was a major concern. That first week at Sandhurst had included ten-mile hikes weighed down with heavy backpacks, while the Adelaide day began early with an extended session of swimming, circuit-training or boxing. The fitness trainer, Robert Crouch, drove the students harder than they had believed possible, and several players were physically sick from exhaustion. Still, the idea of returning to Adelaide out of condition after a month's leave at Christmas was so terrifying that everyone maintained their fitness levels. And the sense of communal suffering bred a great feeling of camaraderie. To help preserve that togetherness, Marsh also preferred to share out the role of captain, with Andy Strauss, Nicky Peng (in preparation for the Under-19 World Cup), Rob Key and Matthew Wood all leading the side.

More straightforward cricket tutelage was provided by – among others – several of Marsh's former Test colleagues. Ian Chappell and John Inverarity concentrated on the batsmen, and Ashley Mallett and Terry Jenner (Shane Warne's mentor) took the spin bowlers on one side. At the end of the arduous course, Marsh professed himself delighted with the approach and abilities of his students. Particular success stories were Key, Ian Bell, Steve Harmison and Simon Jones, who added a maturity of attitude to mere runs and wickets. All bar Jones, who was not playing, excelled in the innings victory over the Australian Academy, sponsored by the Commonwealth Bank. Gratifying though it was, success came against a side with a noticeably younger average age.

Bell's progress was recognised the day after he returned home from Adelaide, when the selectors summoned him back round the world to join the senior England squad in New Zealand. He didn't get a game, but the three who did make a Test debut over the next year were graduates of the Academy: Jones, Key and Harmison all played in the home series against India and went on the Ashes tour that followed. Tudor, apparently fitter and stronger, had shone against Sri Lanka, only to fade once again. Time would tell whether they would satisfy Marsh's aim, which was not to make Test cricketers of all his charges, but to produce a few good enough to have ten-year international careers.

ECB NATIONAL ACADEMY SQUAD

I. R. Bell (Warwickshire), A. Flintoff (Lancashire), S. J. Harmison (Durham), S. P. Jones (Glamorgan), D. A. Kenway (Hampshire), R. W. T. Key (Kent), S. P. Kirby (Yorkshire), N. Peng (Durham), C. P. Schofield (Lancashire), O. A. Shah (Middlesex), R. J. Sidebottom (Yorkshire), A. J. Strauss (Middlesex), G. P. Swann (Northamptonshire), C. T. Tremlett (Hampshire), A. J. Tudor (Surrey), M. A. Wagh (Warwickshire), M. A. Wallace (Glamorgan), M. J. Wood (Yorkshire).

Flintoff and, later, Shah left the party to join the England squad in India. Peng joined England Under-19 at the World Cup in January. Sidebottom reinforced the party as cover for Kirby and Jones, and Harmison flew home early with a dislocated shoulder.

Academy director: R. W. Marsh. *Assistant coach:* J. Abrahams.
Academy manager: N. E. F. Laughton. *Physiotherapist:* K. A. Russell.
Physiologist: R. Smith.

ECB NATIONAL ACADEMY RESULTS

Played 11: Won 8, Lost 2, Drawn 1.

Note: Matches in this section were not first-class.

At Park 25 No. 1, Adelaide, November 22. **ECB National Academy won by 73 runs.** Toss: ECB National Academy. **ECB National Academy 294 for seven** (50 overs) (N. Peng 50, O. A. Shah 74, I. R. Bell 55, D. A. Kenway 36 not out); **Tasmania Second XI 221** (44.5 overs) (S. R. Mason 37, A. G. Downton 36; M. A. Wagh three for 42).

At Adelaide No. 2, Adelaide, November 28. **ECB National Academy won by 70 runs.** Toss: South Australia Second XI. **ECB National Academy 240** (48.3 overs) (O. A. Shah 35, A. J. Strauss 56, N. Peng 30, C. P. Schofield 30 not out, M. A. Wallace 36; M. D. King four for 49); **South Australia Second XI 170** (41 overs) (W. D. Thomas 32, J. T. Southam 50 not out; I. R. Bell five for 22, G. P. Swann three for 41).

Schofield and Wallace added 60 for the Academy's ninth wicket.

At Henley Oval, Adelaide, December 3, 4, 5. **ECB National Academy won by an innings and 31 runs.** Toss: Commonwealth Bank Cricket Academy. **ECB National Academy 601 for eight dec.** (A. J. Strauss 113, R. W. T. Key 177, I. R. Bell 104, D. A. Kenway 60, G. P. Swann 77, C. P. Schofield 35); **Commonwealth Bank Cricket Academy 386** (D. M. Betts 79, S. Phillips 37, R. J. Brewster 34, T. H. Welsford 91, D. C. Bandy 58; S. J. Harmison four for 78, S. P. Kirby four for 100) **and 184** (R. J. Brewster 30, D. Smith 67; S. J. Harmison three for 42).

Strauss and Key added 221 for the Academy's second wicket.

At MCG, Melbourne, January 21, 22, 23, 24. **ECB National Academy won by 29 runs.** Toss: Victoria Second XI. **ECB National Academy 247** (I. R. Bell 48, M. A. Wagh 74 not out, C. P. Schofield 49; D. W. Fleming five for 36) **and 358 for seven dec.** (M. J. Wood 88, I. R. Bell 117, G. P. Swann 34, C. P. Schofield 48 not out, M. A. Wallace 36 not out); **Victoria Second XI 202** (P. J. Roach 58, Extras 44; S. J. Harmison four for 61) **and 374** (N. Jewell 118, D. J. Hussey 112, A. J. Kent 39, P. J. Roach 30; S. J. Harmison four for 79, S. P. Kirby three for 69).

Chasing 404 on the final day, Jewell and Hussey added 230 for Victoria's third wicket.

At Manuka Oval, Canberra, January 27, 28, 29, 30. **Drawn.** Toss: Australian Capital Territory. **Australian Capital Territory 426 for nine dec.** (D. S. Hazell 199, S. L. Maxwell 97, M. A. Hatton 51 not out, Extras 43; S. J. Harmison three for 82, M. A. Wagh three for 78) **and 299 for nine dec.** (D. G. Dawson 105, J. K. Smith 62, S. A. Holcombe 46, Extras 31; C. T. Tremlett three for 31, M. A. Wagh three for 106); **ECB National Academy 459** (A. J. Strauss 48, M. J. Wood 107, M. A. Wagh 164, M. A. Wallace 62; B. W. Dennett four for 98, E. Kellar four for 75) **and 264 for five** (A. J. Strauss 32, M. A. Wagh 73, R. W. T. Key 72 not out, I. R. Bell 60).

Chasing 267 in 55 overs, the Academy finished three runs short of victory.

At Manuka Oval, Canberra, February 2. **Australian Capital Territory won by 36 runs** (D/L method). Toss: Australian Capital Territory. **Australian Capital Territory 253 for eight** (50 overs) (C. D. Hanna 79 not out, Extras 32); **ECB National Academy 165** (28.5 overs) (I. R. Bell 49, M. A. Wallace 45; A. D. Jones three for 29, H. R. Axelby three for 13).

The Academy's total was revised to 202 from 31 overs.

At Kensington Oval, Adelaide, February 11, 12, 13. **South Australia Second XI won by seven wickets.** Toss: ECB National Academy. **ECB National Academy 214** (M. J. Wood 94, A. J. Tudor 35; J. I. Marsh three for 28) **and 268** (M. J. Wood 31, R. W. T. Key 31, N. Peng 75, A. J. Tudor 70, G. P. Swann 36; P. Wilson three for 38, J. I. Marsh four for 99); **South Australia Second XI 294** (D. J. Harris 58, D. M. Dempsey 64, N. T. Adcock 67, B. A. Swain 30; A. J. Tudor three for 61, R. J. Sidebottom three for 34) **and 189 for three** (S. A. Deitz 43, N. T. Adcock 64 not out, D. J. Harris 45).

At David Phillips North Oval, Sydney, February 25. **ECB National Academy won by nine wickets** (D/L method). Toss: New South Wales Cricket Association XI. **New South Wales Cricket Association XI 151** (44.5 overs) (A. Jeffrey 50; S. P. Kirby four for 29, C. P. Schofield four for 35); **ECB National Academy 132 for one** (26 overs) (A. J. Strauss 63, M. J. Wood 61 not out).

The Academy's target was revised to 130 from 39 overs.

At David Phillips South Oval, Sydney, February 26. **ECB National Academy won by 34 runs.** Toss: ECB National Academy. **ECB National Academy 234 for six** (50 overs) (M. J. Wood 69, I. R. Bell 82, D. A. Kenway 35 not out; N. J. Rimmington three for 44); **Commonwealth Bank Cricket Academy 200** (39 overs) (D. Smith 34, R. J. Brewster 61, L. Ronchi 50; A. J. Tudor three for 35, R. J. Sidebottom three for 21).

At David Phillips South Oval, Sydney, February 28. **ECB National Academy won by six wickets.** Toss: ECB National Academy. **New South Wales Institute of Sport Colts 121 for seven** (37 overs) (N. J. Catalano 30; R. J. Sidebottom four for 23); **ECB National Academy 123 for four** (34.2 overs) (R. W. T. Key 38).

At Abbott Park, Perth, March 10, 11, 12, 13. **ECB National Academy won by 112 runs.** Toss: ECB National Academy. **ECB National Academy 413** (R. W. T. Key 78, M. A. Wagh 98, G. P. Swann 65, C. P. Schofield 49; M. W. Johnston three for 49, W. Robinson three for 82) **and 274 for two dec.** (A. J. Strauss 52, M. J. Wood 112, R. W. T. Key 87 not out); **Western Australia Second XI 279** (C. J. Simmons 85, L. Ronchi 83; S. P. Jones six for 48) **and 296** (B. D. Jones 64, C. J. Simmons 49, D. C. Bandy 56, L. Ronchi 45, B. Casson 35; C. P. Schofield five for 72, R. J. Sidebottom three for 33).

NATIONAL CRICKET ACADEMY

The National Cricket Academy, under the directorship of former Australian wicket-keeper R. W. Marsh, opened in November 2001, based at the Commonwealth Bank Cricket Academy in Adelaide. The Academy's intake for its second season, which was to include a tour of Sri Lanka, comprised the following 15 players: Kabir Ali (Worcestershire), J. M. Anderson (Lancashire), G. J. Batty (Worcestershire), I. D. Blackwell (Somerset), R. Clarke (Surrey), K. W. Hogg (Lancashire), G. J. Muchall (Durham), M. S. Panesar (Northamptonshire), C. M. W. Read (Nottinghamshire), D. I. Stevens (Leicestershire), C. T. Tremlett (Hampshire), J. O. Troughton (Warwickshire), A. J. Tudor (Surrey), G. G. Wagg (Warwickshire), M. A. Wallace (Glamorgan).

OTHER A-TEAM TOURS

ZIMBABWE A IN KENYA, 2001-02

Zimbabwe A toured Kenya in November and December 2001, with two first-class matches and five one-day games against the Kenyans. They lost the opening match – the Kenyans' maiden first-class victory – and drew the second; they also lost the one-day series 2–3, winning the last two games after going three down.

The squad of 14 for the tour was: M. Mbangwa (Matabeleland) (*captain*), A. D. R. Campbell (Manicaland) (*vice-captain*), C. Macmillan (Midlands), N. B. Mahwire (Mashonaland), A. Maregwede (Mashonaland A), H. Masakadza (Mashonaland), D. T. Mutendera (Mashonaland A), R. W. Price (Midlands), G. J. Rennie (Mashonaland A), B. G. Rogers (Mashonaland), M. A. Vermeulen (Mashonaland A), D. P. Viljoen (Midlands), B. T. Watambwa (Mashonaland), G. J. Whittall (Manicaland). *Coach:* T. L. Penney. *Manager:* K. Gokal.

At Gymkhana, Nairobi, November 30, December 1, 2. **Kenyans won by an innings and 23 runs.** Toss: Kenyans. **Zimbabwe A 240** (G. J. Rennie 32, H. Masakadza 32, B. G. Rogers 59, M. Mbangwa 30 not out; M. A. Suji three for 50, C. O. Obuya three for 29) **and 148** (G. J. Rennie 68; C. O. Obuya four for 56, M. O. Odumbe five for 17); **Kenyans 411** (R. D. Shah 39, S. O. Tikolo 110, M. O. Odumbe 86, H. S. Modi 42, C. O. Obuya 37; B. T. Watambwa six for 96).
Hitesh Modi's father, Subhash, stood as an umpire.

At Simba Union, Nairobi, December 4, 5, 6. **Drawn.** Toss: Kenyans. **Kenyans 424** (R. D. Shah 55, M. O. Odumbe 178, H. S. Modi 82; B. T. Watambwa four for 112, D. T. Mutendera three for 95) **and 314 for four dec.** (K. O. Otieno 68, R. D. Shah 36, S. O. Tikolo 115 not out, H. S. Modi 61 not out); **Zimbabwe A 278 for seven dec.** (M. A. Vermeulen 84, A. D. R. Campbell 51, G. J. Whittall 58, A. Maregwede 35 not out; C. O. Obuya five for 97) **and 199 for one** (M. A. Vermeulen 79, G. J. Rennie 111 not out).

BANGLADESH A IN THE WEST INDIES, 2001-02

Bangladesh A's matches in the Busta Cup (January 25–March 10) appear in Cricket in the West Indies (pages 1467–1477).

THE KENYANS IN SRI LANKA, 2001-02

The Kenyan national side, effectively part of the A-team circuit, met Sri Lanka A in three first-class matches and three one-day games on a tour in January and February 2002. Sri Lanka A won the "Test" series 3–0, but the Kenyans won the one-day series 2–1. They also drew a two-day match with a BCCSL Academy XI, in which K. S. Lokuarachchi took nine for 50 in the Kenyan innings, with the other wicket a run-out.

The squad of 16 for the tour was: M. O. Odumbe (*captain*), J. S. Ababu, J. O. Angara, H. S. Modi, C. O. Obuya, D. O. Obuya, P. Ochieng, T. M. Odoyo, L. N. Onyango, K. O. Otieno, B. J. Patel, R. D. Shah, M. Sheikh, M. A. Suji, T. O. Suji, S. O. Tikolo. *Coach:* S. M. Patil. *Manager:* Harilal Shah.

At P. Saravanamuttu Stadium, Colombo, January 31, February 1, 2, 3. **Sri Lanka A won by ten wickets.** Toss: Kenyans. **Kenyans 292** (R. D. Shah 94, H. S. Modi 52, T. M. Odoyo 34, T. O. Suji 32; P. D. R. L. Perera four for 70) **and 150** (S. O. Tikolo 65; U. D. U. Chandana three for 36, M. Pushpakumara four for 43); **Sri Lanka A 414 for nine dec.** (D. A. Gunawardene 57, G. I. Daniel 71, M. G. Vandort 75, T. M. Dilshan 82, L. P. C. Silva 56; C. O. Obuya three for 87) **and 30 for no wkt.**

At Matara, February 7, 8, 9. **Sri Lanka A won by an innings and 152 runs.** Toss: Sri Lanka A. **Sri Lanka A 574 for six dec.** (U. A. Fernando 86, T. M. Dilshan 165 not out, L. P. C. Silva 68, U. D. U. Chandana 194; C. O. Obuya three for 123); **Kenyans 220** (R. D. Shah 106, S. O. Tikolo 32; H. M. R. K. B. Herath three for 41, U. D. U. Chandana four for 23) **and 202** (S. O. Tikolo 117; M. Pushpakumara three for 55).
Dilshan and Chandana put on 302 for Sri Lanka A's sixth wicket.

At Dambulla, February 14, 15, 16, 17. **Sri Lanka A won by 199 runs.** Toss: Sri Lanka A. **Sri Lanka A 262** (D. A. Gunawardene 70, M. G. Vandort 55, L. P. C. Silva 41, H. A. P. W. Jayawardene 46 not out; C. O. Obuya four for 48) **and 361 for eight dec.** (D. A. Gunawardene 40, U. A. Fernando 61, U. D. U. Chandana 73, H. A. P. W. Jayawardene 75 not out, M. Pushpakumara 45; J. O. Angara three for 70); **Kenyans 220** (S. O. Tikolo 42, D. O. Obuya 38, C. O. Obuya 49 not out; U. D. U. Chandana five for 59) **and 204** (K. O. Otieno 45, R. D. Shah 48, S. O. Tikolo 58; P. W. Gunaratne three for 40, H. M. R. K. B. Herath five for 52).

INDIA A IN SOUTH AFRICA, 2001-02

India A toured South Africa in March and April 2002, playing four first-class matches and four one-day games. They lost two of the first-class matches and drew the other two, losing their two-match series with South Africa A 1–0. They won two and lost two of the one-day games, sharing the two against South Africa A 1–1.

The squad for the tour was: J. J. Martin (Baroda) (*captain*), L. Balaji (Tamil Nadu), A. Bhandari (Delhi), G. Gambhir (Delhi), R. S. Gavaskar (Bengal), M. Kaif (Uttar Pradesh), A. V. Kale (Maharashtra), M. Kartik (Railways), A. Mishra (Haryana), D. S. Mohanty (Orissa), A. A. Pagnis (Railways), P. A. Patel (Gujarat), R. B. Patel (Baroda), Y. Venugopala Rao (Andhra), Yuvraj Singh (Punjab). Yuvraj replaced D. Mongia (Punjab), who was originally selected as captain but then called up for the Test tour of the West Indies. *Coach:* Yashpal Sharma. *Manager:* V. Patel.

At Chatsworth, March 22, 23, 24. **South African Board President's XI won by an innings and 109 runs.** Toss: India A. **India A 212** (A. V. Kale 33, R. S. Gavaskar 43, R. B. Patel 54; A. Nel three for 67, A. C. Thomas three for 45) **and 90** (R. J. Peterson four for nine); **South African Board President's XI 411 for eight dec.** (A. M. Amla 48, L. L. Bosman 62, J. L. Ontong 36, G. Dros 117 not out, R. J. Peterson 39, C. F. K. van Wyk 51; A. Mishra five for 115).

In India A's second innings, the last four wickets fell without addition.

At Benoni, March 26, 27, 28. **Drawn.** Toss: Easterns. **Easterns 343 for six dec.** (A. J. Seymore 89, A. M. van den Berg 103, D. Jennings 46 not out, Extras 53); **India A 567 for six** (G. Gambhir 95, A. A. Pagnis 95, M. Kaif 111, J. J. Martin 36, A. V. Kale 145 not out, Extras 34).

At Kimberley, March 30, 31, April 1, 2. First A-Team Test: **Drawn.** Toss: India A. **South Africa A 443 for six dec.** (L. L. Bosman 31, M. van Jaarsveld 128, H. D. Ackerman 106, H. M. Amla 56 not out, Extras 41; R. B. Patel three for 127) **and 203 for six dec.** (M. van Jaarsveld 94, H. D. Ackerman 43); **India A 408** (G. Gambhir 50, M. Kaif 136, A. V. Kale 73, P. A. Patel 69; A. Nel five for 93).

At Bloemfontein, April 5, 6, 7, 8. Second A-Team Test: **South Africa A won by eight wickets.** Toss: India A. **India A 291** (A. A. Pagnis 47, Yuvraj Singh 54, L. Balaji 37, M. Kartik 59, A. Mishra 33; D. Pretorius six for 49) **and 251** (M. Kaif 46, Yuvraj Singh 107; A. Nel three for 45, D. Pretorius three for 62); **South Africa A 469** (J. A. Rudolph 97, M. van Jaarsveld 57, H. M. Amla 82, R. J. Peterson 108, Extras 34; D. S. Mohanty three for 77, M. Kartik six for 101) **and 77 for two.**

INDIA A IN SRI LANKA, 2002

India A toured Sri Lanka in May and June 2002, playing three first-class matches and three one-day games. They drew all their first-class matches, including the first two in a three-match series with Sri Lanka A; the third was abandoned. They won the one-day series against Sri Lanka A 2–1 with two matches washed out.

The squad of 15 for the tour was: H. H. Kanitkar (Maharashtra) (*captain*), R. S. Gavaskar (Bengal) (*vice-captain*), L. Balaji (Tamil Nadu), S. V. Bahutule (Mumbai), A. Chopra (Delhi), G. Gambhir (Delhi), M. Kartik (Railways), A. Mishra (Haryana), P. M. Mullick (Orissa), P. A. Patel (Gujarat), I. K. Pathan (Baroda), M. S. K. Prasad (Andhra), Vineet Sharma (Punjab), S. Sriram (Tamil Nadu), Jai P. Yadav (Railways). Sarandeep Singh (Delhi) joined the squad after leaving the Test tour of the West Indies. *Coach:* Yashpal Sharma. *Manager:* S. Haridas.

At R. Premadasa Stadium, Colombo, May 11, 12, 13. **Drawn.** Toss: India A. **India A 474 for seven dec.** (A. Chopra 145, G. Gambhir 105, H. H. Kanitkar 97, P. A. Patel 51 not out, Extras 44; R. W. M. G. A. Ratnayake three for 96); **BCCSL Academy XI 261 for five** (S. Kalawithigoda 45, M. G. Vandort 101 not out, M. M. D. N. R. G. Perera 74).

Chopra and Gambhir put on 252 for India A's first wicket.

At Maitland Place, Colombo (SSC), May 16, 17, 18, 19. First A-team Test: **Drawn.** Toss: India A. **India A 315** (G. Gambhir 79, H. H. Kanitkar 52, Jai P. Yadav 69, P. A. Patel 74; D. K. Liyanage four for 42, P. W. Gunaratne five for 57) **and 302 for four dec.** (A. Chopra 51, G. Gambhir 120, S. Sriram 45, Jai P. Yadav 46 not out); **Sri Lanka A 200** (D. A. Gunawardene 48, T. M. Dilshan 37; A. Mishra five for 35) **and 291 for five** (D. A. Gunawardene 82, G. I. Daniel 84, M. N. Nawaz 84 not out).

At Moratuwa, May 22, 23, 24, 25. Second A-team Test: **Drawn.** Toss: India A. **Sri Lanka A 282** (D. A. Gunawardene 51, M. N. Nawaz 87, L. P. C. Silva 65; L. Balaji four for 47, A. Mishra three for 76); **India A 55 for four** (A. Chopra 37 not out; D. K. Liyanage three for 22).

At Maitland Place, Colombo (NCC), May 28, 29, 30, 31. Third A-team Test: **Sri Lanka A v India A. Abandoned.**

ICC REFEREES' PANEL

In 1991, the International Cricket Council formed a panel of referees to enforce its Code of Conduct for Tests and one-day internationals, to impose penalties for slow over-rates, breaches of the Code and other ICC regulations, and to support the umpires in upholding the conduct of the game.

In March 2002, the ICC launched an elite panel of five referees, on two-year full-time contracts, to act as its independent representatives in all international cricket. The chief referee was R. S. Madugalle (Sri Lanka), supported by C. H. Lloyd (West Indies), M. J. Procter (South Africa), Wasim Raja (Pakistan) and G. R. Viswanath (India). The five had played 286 Test matches between them.

The ICC also named a supplementary panel of referees, to provide cover during busy periods of the international calendar and during major tournaments. This consisted of B. C. Broad (England), G. F. Labrooy (Sri Lanka), D. T. Lindsay (South Africa), J. F. M. Morrison (New Zealand), E. A. S. Prasanna (India), Sultan Rana (Pakistan) and Raqibul Hassan (Bangladesh). Both panels were sponsored by Emirates Airline for three years from July 2002.

ENGLAND UNDER-19 IN AUSTRALIA AND NEW ZEALAND, 2001-02

England Under-19 warmed up for the World Cup in New Zealand with a brief tour of Australia, followed by a further practice game in New Zealand. Their only success was by a single run in their opening fixture against South Australia Under-19. Their other matches, against their Australian and Sri Lankan counterparts, ended in heavy defeat, which proved an accurate foreshadowing of their World Cup campaign.

ENGLAND UNDER-19 TOURING PARTY

N. Peng (Durham) (*captain*), Kadeer Ali (Worcestershire), T. T. Bresnan (Yorkshire), N. R. D. Compton (Middlesex), C. R. Gilbert (Yorkshire), K. W. Hogg (Lancashire), P. J. McMahon (Nottinghamshire), M. N. Malik (Nottinghamshire), G. J. Muchall (Durham), S. R. Patel (Nottinghamshire), M. L. Pettini (Essex), S. P. Pope (Gloucestershire), A. Roberts (Yorkshire), B. M. Shafayat (Nottinghamshire).

Coach: P. Farbrace.　　*Manager:* J. J. Whitaker.　　*Physiotherapist:* A. E. Brentnall.

ENGLAND UNDER-19 TOUR RESULTS

Matches – Played 5: Won 1, Lost 4. Abandoned 1.

Note: Matches in this section were not first-class.

At Park 25, No. 1, Adelaide, January 4. **England Under-19 won by one run.** Toss: England Under-19. **England Under-19 248 for seven** (50 overs) (Kadeer Ali 31, G. J. Muchall 44, K. W. Hogg 83 not out, Extras 59; B. Pahl three for 55); **South Australia Under-19 247 for eight** (50 overs) (T. Plant 105, J. Carson 41, J. Plant 33, Extras 35; K. W. Hogg three for 49).

At Henley Oval, Adelaide, January 8. **First one-day international: Australia Under-19 won by five wickets.** Toss: Australia Under-19. **England Under-19 178 for nine** (50 overs) (Kadeer Ali 51, G. J. Muchall 44, S. R. Patel 31; C. L. White four for 19); **Australia Under-19 181 for five** (41 overs) (S. E. Marsh 34, C. L. White 68 not out).

At Adelaide Oval No. 2, January 9. **Second one-day international: Australia Under-19 won by 168 runs.** Toss: Australia Under-19. **Australia Under-19 331 for eight** (50 overs) (J. N. Burke 100, C. J. Simmons 88, C. L. White 60); **England Under-19 163** (38.5 overs) (Kadeer Ali 43; B. Casson six for 26).

At Pembroke School, Kensington, January 11. **Third one-day international: Australia Under-19 won by 45 runs.** Toss: England Under-19. **Australia Under-19 295 for five** (50 overs) (M. J. Cosgrove 66, C. A. Philipson 39, S. E. Marsh 74, J. N. Burke 80 not out); **England Under-19 250 for eight** (50 overs) (N. R. D. Compton 53, G. J. Muchall 35, S. R. Patel 63 not out, A. Roberts 34 not out; A. C. Bird three for 36).

At Lincoln No. 3, Lincoln, January 15. **New Zealand Under-19 v England Under-19. Abandoned.**

At Hagley Oval, Christchurch, January 17. **Sri Lanka Under-19 won by six wickets.** Toss: England Under-19. **England Under-19 178** (49.1 overs) (Kadeer Ali 37; **Sri Lanka Under-19 179 for four** (40 overs) (W. U. Tharanga 86 not out, Extras 33).

UNDER-19 WORLD CUP, 2001-02

By GEOFFREY DEAN

The fourth Under-19 World Cup, staged in New Zealand in early 2002, confirmed the event as a regular fixture in the cricketing calendar. It also confirmed Australia's dominance throughout the game. Australia were clear favourites from their first match – when they obliterated Kenya by 430 runs, the biggest victory in the tournament's history – to the final, when they brushed aside South Africa's challenge. They won all eight of their matches, claimed bonus points in all but one of their league games, and were bowled out only once, by West Indies. In overwhelming allcomers, Australia's teenagers underlined the gulf between them and the rest of the world. They had enough strength in depth to rotate their eleven without weakening the side and, tactically, they could hardly have been more astute. Their coach was the 1980s Test wicket-keeper Wayne Phillips, more recently of the Australian Academy, and his South African counterpart, Hylton Ackerman, singled out the Australian captain, Cameron White, for particular praise: "White's captaincy was yards ahead of everyone else's; he's got an old head on young shoulders."

Australia delighted purists by playing four varied slow bowlers and only two specialist seamers. Xavier Doherty, a left-arm orthodox spinner from Tasmania, was the tournament's most successful bowler: he took 16 wickets at 9.50 and did not bowl a single wide. His exemplary control was mirrored in the leg-spin of White, an all-rounder who had made his debut for Victoria the previous season. White was the competition's leading run-scorer with 423 at 70.50, and was confident enough to bowl during the 15-over fielding restrictions. Another all-rounder was Jarrad Burke, a thrifty slow left-armer and opening bat who scored a century in the final. Beau Casson bamboozled England and the West Indians with a mixture of chinamen and finger-spin.

All of the top order made runs, but Craig Simmons, a strong left-handed opener from Perth, was especially consistent. He crashed 155 off 115 balls as Australia amassed 480 against Kenya, the highest total in World Cup history. They then shot out the Kenyans for 50 – for five days a record low, until Canada sank for 41 against South Africa. White later trumped Simmons by taking an unbeaten 156 off Scotland. In Adam Crosthwaite, Australia possessed a wicket-keeper/batsman in the buccaneering mould of Adam Gilchrist. He and George Bailey, in a brilliant display of improvisation and clean hitting, slammed 85 off their last six overs against England.

While acknowledging Australia's superiority, Ackerman was delighted that his multiracial squad (eight out of 14 were non-white) had come so far. "For us to combine so well and get to the final was a brilliant effort," he said. The captain, Hashim Amla, a wristy, quick-footed right-hander from Durban, was arguably the most gifted batsman in the tournament; like White, he marked himself out as a future Test player.

India, the holders, probably had most cause for disappointment. Led by 16-year-old Parthiv Patel, who was to make his Test debut against England in August, they beat South Africa by 71 runs in the first week, but lost heavily to them in the semi-final. They also suffered embarrassing defeats against Bangladesh, who dismissed them for 77, and their arch-rivals Pakistan. It was Pakistan, however, who suffered the biggest shock: a 30-run loss to Nepal. Set 152 on a blameless pitch, Pakistan succumbed to Nepal's spin attack through some witless batting. Coached by Roy Dias, the former Sri Lankan Test batsman, Nepal also ran England close. They were runners-up to Zimbabwe in the Plate Championship, for the eight teams failing to qualify for the Super League. Namibia were another unfancied side who performed unexpected heroics: they defeated Sri Lanka in a group game, and lost by only 35 runs to Zimbabwe in the Plate semi-final.

West Indies did well to get to the Super League semi-finals, according to their coach, Gus Logie. Donovan Pagon, the powerful Jamaican opener, scored 421 runs, two behind the Australian captain White (who had one more innings), and Ryan Nurse was the quickest bowler for any side. But twice against Australia they suffered collapses when well set, most notably in the semi-final when they lost their last eight in 18 overs, leaving ten unbowled.

It was not a good tournament for recent finalists. Sri Lanka, who lost to India in 1999-2000, won only once, against Zimbabwe. Hosts New Zealand, who reached the previous final at Johannesburg, failed to exploit home advantage, although Jesse Ryder, a strokeplaying left-hander, looked one of the most talented batsmen on show. And England, who had beaten New Zealand in the 1997-98 final, never matched expectations. Their only wins came against Nepal and Papua New Guinea, in the group stage; even then, they tied on points with Nepal and scraped through to the Super League on net run-rate. They built winning positions in run-chases against New Zealand and South Africa but were incapable of finishing off the job. For whatever reason, England never gelled as a team: two or three players would shine on any one day, while the others failed to perform. "We just didn't click together," their captain, Nicky Peng, admitted. For the coach, Paul Farbrace, it was a second successive disappointment in New Zealand; he had been in charge of the England women's unsuccessful World Cup campaign in 2000-01.

England's best batsman, Peng, never constructed the big innings his talent demanded, though he did score half-centuries against Pakistan and Australia; no one else reached fifty against Test-country opposition. Paul McMahon, an able off-spinner, proved reliable, as did Kyle Hogg with his bounce and tidy medium-pace, but without a strike bowler England seldom made early inroads. Though some showed a first-rate attitude, Phillips, the Australian coach, commented that he detected a lazy streak. Perhaps that was connected with the ECB's decision – not supported by James Whitaker, the team manager – to pay each player £5,000 for the tour. No other side was paid more than expenses. The competition's only professional team did not live up to its name.

The two remaining Test-playing countries, Zimbabwe and Bangladesh, failed to reach the Super League, and Bangladesh lost their Plate semi-final to the dark horses of Nepal. But Zimbabwe, fielding two Test players in Hamilton Masakadza and Tatenda Taibu, easily dominated the Plate Championship. They won all their games with maximum points, dismissing Kenya for 80 and Bangladesh for 91, crushed fellow-Africans Namibia in the semi-final and secured the Plate by beating Nepal. Zimbabwe's medium-pace bowler, Waddington Mwayenga, took 16 wickets, equalling Doherty's total. And their captain, Taibu, showed remarkable versatility. In addition to scoring 250 runs, he made eight dismissals as wicket-keeper, but frequently discarded his gloves to bowl medium-pace, collecting 12 wickets. His all-round feats made him the Player of the Tournament.

Note: Matches in this section were not first-class.

Group A

At Colin Maiden Park, Auckland, January 20. **South Africa won by 110 runs.** Toss: South Africa. **South Africa 252 for four** (50 overs) (D. J. Jacobs 76, S. C. Cook 103, H. M. Amla 53); **Bangladesh 142** (46.2 overs) (Aftab Ahmed 79; B. L. Reddy three for 22, R. T. Bailey three for five). *South Africa 5 pts.*

At Colin Maiden Park, Auckland, January 21. **India won by 242 runs.** Toss: India. **India 356 for five** (50 overs) (M. S. Bisla 128, P. C. Valthaty 50, P. A. Patel 74, M. D. Mishra 35 not out; N. S. Richards three for 70); **Canada 114** (40.2 overs) (U. R. Bhatti 39, A. Bagai 33; S. K. Trivedi three for 28, A. Sharma three for 13). *India 5 pts.*

At Colin Maiden Park, Auckland, January 22. **Tied.** Toss: Bangladesh. **Bangladesh 213 for seven** (50 overs) (Gazi Salauddin 35, Mohammad Ashraful 32, Ali Arman 49 not out, Murad Khan 31 not out, Extras 31); **Canada 213 for nine** (50 overs) (G. A. Rahaman 40, U. R. Bhatti 33, A. Bagai 82 not out). *Bangladesh 2 pts, Canada 2 pts.*

At North Harbour Stadium, Auckland, January 23. **India won by 71 runs.** Toss: South Africa. **India 227 for eight** (50 overs) (C. Madaan 105 not out); **South Africa 156** (42.3 overs) (R. McLaren 33). *India 5 pts.*

At North Harbour Stadium, Auckland, January 24. **Bangladesh won by two wickets.** Toss: Bangladesh. **India 77** (32.4 overs) (Ashiqur Rahman three for 17); **Bangladesh 78 for eight** (32.2 overs) (S. K. Trivedi three for 24). *Bangladesh 5 pts.*
 Bangladesh were 64 for eight before their ninth-wicket pair put on 14 to win the game. Extras top-scored with 27, India bowling 14 wides and four no-balls.

At North Harbour Stadium, Auckland, January 25. **South Africa won by ten wickets.** Toss: Canada. **Canada 41** (28.4 overs) (R. McLaren four for nine); **South Africa 42 for no wkt** (8.2 overs). *South Africa 5 pts.*
 Canada's total was a new competition low, though their captain retired hurt. Extras contributed 21 and No. 11 was the highest-scoring batsman with five. McLaren's full figures were 10–4–9–4. The entire match lasted 37 overs.

India 10 pts, South Africa 10 pts, Bangladesh 7 pts, Canada 2 pts. India and South Africa qualified for the Super League.

Group B

At Bert Sutcliffe Oval, Lincoln, January 19. **No result.** Toss: Sri Lanka. **Sri Lanka 85 for two** (19.5 overs) (S. P. L. C. S. Perera 37 not out) v New Zealand. *New Zealand 2 pts. Sri Lanka 2 pts.*

At Bert Sutcliffe Oval, Lincoln, January 20. **Zimbabwe won by nine wickets.** Toss: Namibia. **Namibia 111** (29.2 overs) (T. Taibu three for 14); **Zimbabwe 113 for one** (19.2 overs) (C. K. Coventry 64 not out, T. Taibu 31 not out). *Zimbabwe 5 pts.*

At Bert Sutcliffe Oval, Lincoln, January 21. **New Zealand won by six wickets.** Toss: Zimbabwe. **Zimbabwe 71** (36.2 overs) (M. D. Bates four for 26); **New Zealand 72 for four** (10.3 overs) (J. D. Ryder 41). *New Zealand 5 pts.*

At Bert Sutcliffe Oval, Lincoln, January 22. **Namibia won by four wickets.** Toss: Sri Lanka. **Sri Lanka 141** (40.5 overs) (B. M. A. J. Mendis 57; B. O. van Rooi four for 27, M. Greeff three for 25); **Namibia 142 for six** (44.3 overs) (C. F. Steytler 43). *Namibia 4 pts.*

At Hagley Oval, Christchurch, January 23. **New Zealand won by six wickets.** Toss: Namibia. **Namibia 201 for five** (50 overs) (H. Ludik 49 not out, B. O. van Rooi 62, T. Verwey 30 not out); **New Zealand 203 for four** (36.5 overs) (S. J. Murdoch 30, N. T. Broom 85, R. L. Taylor 58 not out). *New Zealand 5 pts.*

At Hagley Oval, Christchurch, January 24. **Sri Lanka won by 63 runs.** Toss: Zimbabwe. **Sri Lanka 206 for nine** (50 overs) (S. P. L. C. S. Perera 57, B. M. A. J. Mendis 57, C. S. Fernando 36); **Zimbabwe 143** (44.2 overs) (C. K. Coventry 36; B. M. A. J. Mendis seven for 19). *Sri Lanka 5 pts.*
 Sri Lankan wicket-keeper Sylvester Fernando caught four Zimbabweans and stumped four; his eight dismissals were a competition record.

New Zealand 12 pts, Sri Lanka 7 pts, Zimbabwe 5 pts, Namibia 4 pts. New Zealand and Sri Lanka qualified for the Super League.

Group C

At Lincoln No. 3, January 20. **Pakistan won by eight wickets.** Toss: Pakistan. **Papua New Guinea 53** (17.5 overs) (Umar Gul four for 11, Junaid Zia three for 18); **Pakistan 54 for two** (10.5 overs). *Pakistan 5 pts.*

At Lincoln No. 3, January 21. **England won by 37 runs.** Toss: England. **England 204 for six** (50 overs) (N. Peng 36, G. J. Muchall 57, B. M. Shafayat 45 not out); **Nepal 167** (49.2 overs) (S. Regmi 35 not out; P. J. McMahon five for 25). *England 4 pts.*

At Lincoln Green, January 22. **Nepal won by 30 runs.** Toss: Pakistan. **Nepal 151** (48.5 overs) (B. Chalise 42; Junaid Zia four for 34, Kamran Sajid four for 35); **Pakistan 121** (45.4 overs) (Asim Munir 34; S. P. Gauchan three for 19, S. Regmi three for 27). *Nepal 4 pts.*

At Lincoln Green, January 23. **England won by six wickets.** Toss: Papua New Guinea. **Papua New Guinea 222 for six** (50 overs); **England 223 for four** (28 overs) (N. R. D. Compton 58, Kadeer Ali 73, N. Peng 41). *England 5 pts.*

At Lincoln No. 3, January 25. **Pakistan won by six wickets.** Toss: Pakistan. **England 182** (48.1 overs) (N. Peng 59, K. W. Hogg 40; Irfanuddin four for 42); **Pakistan 183 for four** (44.4 overs) (Salman Butt 35, Khaqan Arsal 62; T. T. Bresnan three for 46). *Pakistan 4 pts.*

At Hagley Park No. 2, Christchurch, January 25. **Nepal won by 65 runs.** Toss: Nepal. **Nepal 177** (48.3 overs) (Y. Subedi 34, B. K. Das 31; C. Amini three for 31); **Papua New Guinea 112** (43.5 overs) (M. D. Dai 32; L. Lama four for 14). *Nepal 5 pts.*

Pakistan 9 pts, England 9 pts, Nepal 9 pts, Papua New Guinea 0 pts. Pakistan, England and Nepal had identical records and each had won one of their head-to-head matches; Pakistan and England qualified for the Super League on net run-rate.

Group D

At Carisbrook, Dunedin, January 20. **Australia won by 430 runs.** Toss: Kenya. **Australia 480 for six** (50 overs) (C. J. Simmons 155, J. N. Burke 45, S. E. Marsh 125, C. L. White 38, G. J. Bailey 56, Extras 30; N. O. Odhiambo three for 97); **Kenya 50** (21 overs) (A. C. Bird three for ten, R. J. Cassell three for seven). *Australia 5 pts.*

Australia's total and winning margin were the biggest in the competition's history. Simmons scored 155 in only 115 balls; he hit 12 fours and 11 sixes, out of 40 fours and 21 sixes in all for Australia. Kenya's total (one man absent hurt) was a competition low until South Africa dismissed Canada for 41 five days later.

At Carisbrook, Dunedin, January 21. **West Indies won by 301 runs.** Toss: West Indies. **West Indies 402 for three** (50 overs) (D. J. Pagon 176, L. M. P. Simmons 121 not out, A. Holder 56 not out); **Scotland 101** (38.3 overs) (M. Q. Sheikh 37; R. P. O. Nurse three for 18). *West Indies 5 pts.*

At Carisbrook, Dunedin, January 22. **Scotland won by five wickets** (D/L method). Toss: Scotland. **Kenya 113 for five** (34.2 overs) (M. A. Ouma 36 not out); **Scotland 125 for five** (25 overs) (M. M. Iqbal 40). *Scotland 4 pts.*

Scotland's target was revised to 124 in 25 overs.

At Carisbrook, Dunedin, January 23. **Australia won by 42 runs.** Toss: West Indies. **Australia 200** (49.2 overs) (G. J. Bailey 39; R. P. O. Nurse five for 28, N. Deonarine three for 28); **West Indies 158** (44.5 overs) (T. A. Willett 34; X. J. Doherty three for 24, B. Casson three for 48). *Australia 5 pts.*

At Carisbrook, Dunedin, January 24. **West Indies won by nine wickets.** Toss: Kenya. **Kenya 114** (49.3 overs) (M. N. Patel 30; R. S. Matthews four for 17); **West Indies 115 for one** (21 overs) (D. J. Pagon 63 not out, N. Deonarine 32 not out). *West Indies 5 pts.*

At Carisbrook, Dunedin, January 25. **Australia won by 229 runs.** Toss: Australia. **Australia 335 for five** (50 overs) (C. A. Philipson 32, C. L. White 156 not out, D. T. Christian 93; H. Singh three for 63); **Scotland 106** (34.2 overs) (X. J. Doherty four for 15, B. Casson three for 18). *Australia 5 pts.*

Australia 15 pts, West Indies 10 pts, Scotland 4 pts, Kenya 0 pts. Australia and West Indies qualified for the Super League.

Super League Group One

At Bert Sutcliffe Oval, Lincoln, January 27. **India won by eight wickets.** Toss: India. **West Indies 155 for nine** (50 overs) (L. M. P. Simmons 38, L. T. Ingram 43); **India 157 for two** (27.3 overs) (M. S. Bisla 68 not out, P. A. Patel 47). *India 5 pts.*

At Lincoln No. 3, January 27. **Pakistan won by five runs.** Toss: Sri Lanka. **Pakistan 184** (48.3 overs) (Kamran Sajid 31, Mohammad Fayyaz 53; H. D. Niroshana three for 44, K. T. G. D. Prasad four for 30); **Sri Lanka 179** (48.5 overs) (B. M. A. J. Mendis 39, P. D. G. C. Kumara 45). *Pakistan 4 pts.*

At Bert Sutcliffe Oval, Lincoln, January 29. **India won by six wickets.** Toss: India. **Sri Lanka 195** (49.4 overs) (W. U. Tharanga 38, B. M. A. J. Mendis 64; A. Sharma three for 46); **India 197 for four** (34.4 overs) (M. S. Bisla 49, D. A. Chougule 47, Y. Gnaneswara Rao 30). *India 5 pts.*

At Lincoln Green, January 29. **West Indies won by six wickets.** Toss: Pakistan. **Pakistan 162** (47.2 overs) (Khaqan Arsal 47, Kamran Sajid 44; L. T. Ingram four for 14); **West Indies 166 for four** (45 overs) (D. J. Pagon 47, L. M. P. Simmons 45 not out). *West Indies 4 pts.*

At Lincoln Green, January 31. **Pakistan won by two wickets.** Toss: Pakistan. **India 181** (48.5 overs) (D. A. Chougule 47, C. Madaan 34; Junaid Zia three for 30); **Pakistan 184 for eight** (43.4 overs) (Salman Butt 85 not out; A. Sharma three for 37). *Pakistan 4 pts.*

At Hagley Oval, Christchurch, January 31. **West Indies won by 62 runs.** Toss: Sri Lanka. **West Indies 202** (47.5 overs) (D. J. Pagon 92, N. Deonarine 65; H. D. Niroshana three for 36); **Sri Lanka 140** (47 overs) (B. M. A. J. Mendis 30). *West Indies 5 pts.*

India 10 pts, West Indies 9 pts, Pakistan 8 pts, Sri Lanka 0 pts. India and West Indies qualified for the semi-finals.

Super League Group Two

At Bert Sutcliffe Oval, Lincoln, January 28. **Australia won by five wickets.** Toss: South Africa. **South Africa 236 for eight** (50 overs) (S. C. Cook 48, R. de Kock 37, R. T. Bailey 48, R. McLaren 39 not out); **Australia 237 for five** (46.4 overs) (J. N. Burke 31, C. J. Simmons 52, C. L. White 36, G. J. Bailey 54 not out). *Australia 4 pts.*

At Lincoln No. 3, January 28. **New Zealand won by three runs.** Toss: New Zealand. **New Zealand 205** (49.4 overs) (J. D. Ryder 54, B. J. Hatwell 45; K. W. Hogg three for 41); **England 202 for eight** (50 overs) (S. R. Patel 47, M. L. Pettini 36; M. D. Bates three for 44). *New Zealand 4 pts.*

At Hagley Oval, Christchurch, January 30. **Australia won by 116 runs.** Toss: England. **Australia 281 for five** (50 overs) (J. N. Burke 30, C. J. Simmons 67, G. J. Bailey 69 not out, A. J. Crosthwaite 48 not out); **England 165** (45.2 overs) (N. Peng 57, B. M. Shafayat 30; B. Casson four for 33, J. N. Burke three for 13). *Australia 5 pts.*

At Lincoln Green, January 30. **South Africa won by 24 runs.** Toss: South Africa. **South Africa 241 for seven** (50 overs) (D. J. Jacobs 63, R. T. Bailey 69; L. M. Burtt four for 52, P. W. Borren three for 34); **New Zealand 217** (48.1 overs) (R. J. Nicol 51, N. T. Broom 36, J. W. Sheed 61). *South Africa 4 pts.*

At Lincoln Green, February 1. **South Africa won by 15 runs.** Toss: England. **South Africa 212 for five** (50 overs) (C. Baxter 32, D. J. Jacobs 40, R. T. Bailey 55 not out, R. McLaren 30 not out; G. J. Muchall three for 55); **England 197** (40 overs) (B. M. Shafayat 38, Kadeer Ali 44; B. L. Reddy three for 37, I. K. Postman four for 56). *South Africa 4 pts.*

At Bert Sutcliffe Oval, Lincoln, February 1. **Australia won by seven wickets.** Toss: New Zealand. **New Zealand 194** (46.3 overs) (J. D. Ryder 70; A. C. Bird three for 50, X. J. Doherty three for 23); **Australia 196 for three** (39.3 overs) (S. E. Marsh 70, C. L. White 80 not out). *Australia 5 pts.*

Australia 14 pts, South Africa 8 pts, New Zealand 4 pts, England 0 pts. Australia and South Africa qualified for the semi-finals.

Semi-finals

At Bert Sutcliffe Oval, Lincoln, February 3. **South Africa won by 112 runs.** Toss: South Africa. **South Africa 268 for five** (50 overs) (G. M. Smith 61, R. de Kock 32, H. M. Amla 62, D. J. Jacobs 69 not out); **India 156** (37.4 overs) (M. S. Bisla 37).

At Bert Sutcliffe Oval, Lincoln, February 6, 7. **Australia won by 93 runs.** Toss: Australia. **Australia 252 for eight** (50 overs) (C. J. Simmons 84, C. L. White 64); **West Indies 159** (40 overs) (T. A. Willett 83, N. Deonarine 40).

No play was possible on February 6 because of rain.

FINAL

AUSTRALIA v SOUTH AFRICA

At Bert Sutcliffe Oval, Lincoln, February 9. Australia won by seven wickets. Toss: South Africa.
Several hundred spectators witnessed a one-sided final which was all but settled when South Africa subsided to 116 for seven. Even though a plucky 52 from Zwelibanzi Homani launched a partial recovery, Australia coasted home with nearly five overs to spare. The left-handed opener, Jarrad Burke, completed victory and his own hundred when he edged his 11th four. The match award went to Aaron Bird, a whippy seamer from New South Wales, for his four wickets. But, although Australia's four spinners claimed only three between them, they were the key difference on a pitch offering a little turn. Xavier Doherty bowled another tellingly accurate spell, creating the pressure to force injudicious shots. Only South Africa's captain, Hashim Amla, used his feet well, and his run-out proved the turning point: from 85 for two in the 21st over, they suffered a disastrous mid-innings slump. Their one chance of denying Australia was to take early wickets, but Burke never offered a chance.

Man of the Match: A. C. Bird.   *Player of the Tournament:* T. Taibu.

South Africa

G. M. Smith c Crosthwaite b Doherty	51	B. B. Kops lbw b Bird		5
C. Baxter b Bird	1	I. K. Postman not out		13
S. C. Cook b Bird	5			
*H. M. Amla run out	29	B 2, l-b 7, w 6, n-b 6		21
D. J. Jacobs c Crosthwaite b Doherty	6			
R. T. Bailey run out	2	1/17 (2) 2/45 (3)	(9 wkts, 50 overs)	206
R. McLaren lbw b Burke	5	3/85 (4) 4/97 (5)		
†Z. Homani not out	52	5/100 (1) 6/103 (6)		
B. L. Reddy c Marsh b Bird	16	7/116 (7) 8/158 (9) 9/173 (10)		

Bowling: Cassell 7–0–32–0; Bird 10–0–47–4; Doherty 10–3–26–2; White 10–1–27–0; Burke 5–0–22–1; Casson 6–0–30–0; Cosgrove 2–0–13–0.

Australia

J. N. Burke not out	100
C. J. Simmons b Kops	34
S. E. Marsh run out	35
*C. L. White b McLaren	22
G. J. Bailey not out	4
L-b 4, w 9, n-b 1	14

1/74 (2) 2/140 (3)   (3 wkts, 45.1 overs) 209
3/196 (4)

M. J. Cosgrove, †A. J. Crosthwaite, X. J. Doherty, B. Casson, A. C. Bird and R. J. Cassell did not bat.

Bowling: Reddy 9.1–1–42–0; McLaren 10–1–35–1; Kops 6–1–42–1; Postman 10–0–44–0; Bailey 9–0–33–0; Smith 1–0–9–0.

Umpires: E. A. R. de Silva (Sri Lanka) and A. L. Hill (New Zealand).
Third umpire: A. W. Cooper (Fiji). Referee: J. R. Reid (New Zealand).

UNDER-19 WORLD CUP WINNERS

1987-88   AUSTRALIA beat Pakistan by five wickets at Adelaide.
1997-98   ENGLAND beat New Zealand by seven wickets at Johannesburg.
1999-2000 INDIA beat Sri Lanka by six wickets at Colombo (SSC).
2001-02   AUSTRALIA beat South Africa by seven wickets at Lincoln.

Plate Championship Group One

At Colin Maiden Park, Auckland, January 27. **Bangladesh won by nine wickets.** Toss: Papua New Guinea. **Papua New Guinea 75** (22.5 overs) (Shafaq Al Zabir four for 29, Wassel Uddin three for 13); **Bangladesh 76 for one** (18.1 overs) (Shafiul Alam 31 not out). *Bangladesh 5 pts.*

At Eden Park Outer Oval, Auckland, January 27. **Zimbabwe won by 211 runs.** Toss: Zimbabwe. **Zimbabwe 291 for seven** (50 overs) (C. K. Coventry 46, T. Taibu 65, H. Masakadza 32, S. M. Ervine 43, S. Matsikenyeri 35, Extras 32); **Kenya 80** (30.3 overs) (W. Mwayenga five for 21). *Zimbabwe 5 pts.*

At North Harbour Stadium, Auckland, January 29. **Bangladesh won by nine wickets.** Toss: Kenya. **Kenya 175 for eight** (50 overs) (R. Premji 47, M. A. Ouma 30; Shafaq Al Zabir three for 28); **Bangladesh 176 for one** (37.4 overs) (Mohammad Ashraful 76 not out, Nafis Iqbal 41 not out, Extras 30). *Bangladesh 5 pts.*

At Melville Park, Auckland, January 29. **Zimbabwe won by 66 runs.** Toss: Papua New Guinea. **Zimbabwe 207** (49.2 overs) (C. K. Coventry 37, M. R. D. Brundle 36, E. Chigumbura 42; P. Arua three for 39, G. Baeau four for 19); **Papua New Guinea 141** (45.4 overs) (F. B. Joseph 42; T. Taibu four for 30). *Zimbabwe 5 pts.*

At Colin Maiden Park, Auckland, January 31. **Zimbabwe won by nine wickets.** Toss: Bangladesh. **Bangladesh 91** (42.5 overs) (T. Taibu three for eight); **Zimbabwe 94 for one** (14.2 overs) (C. K. Coventry 51). *Zimbabwe 5 pts.*

At Colin Maiden Park No. 2, Auckland, January 31. **Kenya won by 25 runs.** Toss: Kenya. **Kenya 236 for eight** (50 overs) (M. A. Ouma 150 not out; G. Keimelo four for 23); **Papua New Guinea 211** (46.4 overs) (C. D. Elly 69, W. B. Harry 40; R. Premji three for 32). *Kenya 4 pts.*

Zimbabwe 15 pts, Bangladesh 10 pts, Kenya 4 pts, Papua New Guinea 0 pts. Zimbabwe and Bangladesh qualified for the semi-finals.

Plate Championship Group Two

At Colin Maiden Park, Auckland, January 28. **Nepal won by nine wickets.** Toss: Canada. **Canada 102** (46.4 overs) (J. A. Roberts 47; B. K. Das three for 13, S. Regmi three for ten); **Nepal 104 for one** (22.3 overs) (Y. Subedi 41 not out, B. Chalise 32 not out). *Nepal 5 pts.*

At Eden Park Outer Oval, Auckland, January 28. **Namibia won by four wickets.** Toss: Scotland. **Scotland 234 for four** (50 overs) (S. D. Gilmour 100 not out, M. Q. Sheikh 60); **Namibia 237 for six** (43.3 overs) (S. J. Swanepoel 142, C. F. Steytler 32 not out; C. M. West three for 51). *Namibia 4 pts.*

At Melville Park, Auckland, January 30. **Scotland won by seven wickets.** Toss: Scotland. **Canada 157** (48 overs) (J. J. Sandher 49 not out, Extras 39; H. Singh three for 20); **Scotland 161 for three** (37 overs) (R. E. More 40, B. T. McKerchar 35, S. D. Gilmour 40 not out). *Scotland 5 pts.*

At North Harbour Stadium, Auckland, January 30. **Nepal won by ten runs.** Toss: Nepal. **Nepal 137** (49.2 overs) (B. Chalise 69); **Namibia 127** (48.4 overs) (H. Ludik 33; B. K. Das three for 21, L. Lama three for 23). *Nepal 4 pts.*

At Colin Maiden Park No. 2, Auckland, February 1. **Namibia won by 141 runs.** Toss: Canada. **Namibia 226** (46 overs) (S. J. Swanepoel 49, B. O. van Rooi 32, H. Ludik 30, M. Durant 53 not out; U. R. Bhatti three for 48); **Canada 85** (34.4 overs) (M. Durant three for 21, J. P. Nel three for 15). *Namibia 5 pts.*

At Colin Maiden Park, Auckland, February 1. **Nepal won by 48 runs.** Toss: Nepal. **Nepal 205 for five** (50 overs) (K. Chaugai 43, Y. Subedi 45, B. Chalise 30, S. P. Gauchan 31); **Scotland 157** (35.2 overs) (B. T. McKerchar 42; S. P. Gauchan three for 32). *Nepal 5 pts.*

Nepal 14 pts, Namibia 9 pts, Scotland 5 pts, Canada 0 pts. Nepal and Namibia qualified for the semi-finals.

Plate Semi-finals

At Lincoln No. 3, February 4. **Zimbabwe won by 35 runs.** Toss: Namibia. **Zimbabwe 228** (50 overs) (B. R. M. Taylor 37, T. Taibu 30, S. M. Ervine 72; B. O. van Rooi three for 33); **Namibia 193** (49.5 overs) (M. Greeff 43, J. P. Nel 31, M. Durant 48; W. Mwayenga three for 27, S. Matsikenyeri three for 33).

At Lincoln No. 3, February 6, 7. **Nepal won by 23 runs.** Toss: Nepal. **Nepal 180 for six** (50 overs) (B. Thapa 41 not out); **Bangladesh 157** (47.3 overs) (Wassel Uddin 37; B. Chalise four for 38).

Rain ended play when Nepal were 136 for six from 45 overs on the first day.

Plate Final

At Lincoln No. 3, February 8. **Zimbabwe won by 137 runs.** Toss: Zimbabwe. **Zimbabwe 247 for one** (50 overs) (C. K. Coventry 64, B. R. M. Taylor 100 not out, T. Taibu 65 not out); **Nepal 110** (35.4 overs) (S. P. Gauchan 30; W. Mwayenga three for 25, H. Masakadza three for 16).

ENGLAND WOMEN IN INDIA, 2001-02

By CAROL SALMON

This New Year tour marked a fresh start for England, with John Harmer, the highly successful Australian women's coach, taking charge for the first time. But England's stock continued to plunge in the one-day game, as India completed a 5–0 series win in style. When the tourists collapsed for 78 in the third one-day international, their vice-captain, Clare Taylor, said the display had hit new lows: "Nothing was learned from the previous games, and we pathetically succumbed – even the Barmy Army left in disgust."

However, England could not field their strongest side: six players were on their first senior overseas tour, and a seventh was called up when the other Taylor, Claire, the most productive batswoman against Australia the previous summer, injured a knee in training before the series even started. Charlotte Edwards was still missing with her own knee injury, and four other likely selections were unavailable because of exams. But there were no excuses for their woeful batting against India's spin, and a plague of wides from their own bowlers – over five one-day internationals, England donated 92 wides, and 111 extras in all, with only the captain, Clare Connor, immune.

The mood changed with the one-off Test at Lucknow, where Caroline Atkins and Arran Thompson carved out a place in history with a world-record opening partnership of 200, spanning nearly four sessions. Rain ensured the match was drawn, but Atkins, who turned 21 during the trip, and Thompson, eight months younger, maintained their dogged form with stands of 89 and 134 in the remaining two one-day international defeats. But it was painfully slow, and never likely to threaten India's dominance. Such back-to-the-wall resistance cannot have been what Harmer, a man keen to entertain as well as win, envisaged.

India, who had played no international cricket since the semi-final of the World Cup in December 2000 – New Zealand had cancelled a tour in November because of the war in Afghanistan – were surprised by the paucity of England's challenge, but delighted with their own success. Their captain, the left-hander Anjum Chopra, and Mithali Raj led the batting in the one-day games, while Hemlata Kala scored a century in the Test. Neetu David, the experienced left-arm spinner, was easily the best bowler on either side, with 14 wickets in six matches.

ENGLAND TOURING PARTY

C. J. Connor (Sussex) (*captain*), C. E. Taylor (Yorkshire) (*vice-captain*), C. M. G. Atkins (Sussex), J. Cassar (Nottinghamshire), S. L. Clarke (Surrey), M. C. Godliman (Sussex), D. Holden (Nottinghamshire), K. Lowe (Nottinghamshire), L. K. Newton (Cheshire), L. C. Pearson (Staffordshire), L. Spragg (Yorkshire), S. C. Taylor (Berkshire), A. Thompson (Lancashire), H. Wardlaw (Yorkshire).

S. C. Taylor departed injured and was replaced by J. Hawker (Somerset).

Coach: J. Harmer. *Manager:* J. Powell.

ENGLAND TOUR RESULTS

Matches – Played 9: Won 2, Lost 5, Drawn 2.

Note: Matches in this section were not first-class.

At Guru Nanak College Ground, Chennai, January 4. **England won by six wickets.** Toss: WCA of India XI. **WCA of India XI 137 for nine** (50 overs) (S. Jaya 30, D. Kamakshi 34); **England 138 for four** (46.1 overs) (A. Thompson 65 not out).

At Guru Nanak College Ground, Chennai, January 6. **First one-day international: India won by eight wickets.** Toss: India. **England 106** (44.4 overs) (N. David four for 14); **India 110 for two** (27.4 overs) (M. Raj 36 not out).

At Lal Bahadur Shastri Stadium, Hyderabad, January 8. **Second one-day international: India won by nine wickets.** Toss: India. **England 71 for seven** (23 overs) (J. Goswami three for eight); **India 72 for one** (20.2 overs) (A. Chopra 37 not out).
Rain reduced the match to 23 overs per side.

At Lal Bahadur Shastri Stadium, Hyderabad, January 9. **Third one-day international: India won by 113 runs.** Toss: England. **India 191 for five** (50 overs) (M. Raj 42, M. Maben 53 not out, A. Kirkire 35); **England 78** (42.3 overs) (M. Raj three for four).
England equalled their lowest all-out total against India, 78 at Guwahati in 1995-96. Raj's full analysis was 4.4–1–4–3.

At Teri Oval, Gurgaon, January 11, 12. **Drawn.** Toss: WCA of India XI. **WCA of India XI 101** (S. Naik 44; H. Wardlaw three for 26, D. Holden three for 25) **and 146 for nine dec.** (V. J. Karuna 31, S. Naik 31, M. Reema 32; H. Wardlaw six for 33); **England 148** (C. M. G. Atkins 42; S. Nirala four for ten) **and 58 for four** (J. Cassar 31 not out).

INDIA v ENGLAND

Test Match

At K. D. Babu Singh Stadium, Lucknow, January 14, 15, 16, 17. Drawn. Toss: England. Test debuts: P. S. Amrita, J. Goswami, B. Goyal, A. Kirkire, M. Maben, M. Raj; J. Hawker, H. Wardlaw.
Caroline Atkins and Arran Thompson dug in for seven and a half hours to build the first double-century opening stand in women's Test cricket. The old landmark was 178, also against India, by Australia's Belinda Haggett and Belinda Clark at Sydney in 1990-91. Atkins and Thompson had played two previous Tests, in which their best start was 12. But this time they batted throughout the first day, crawling to 150 in 101 overs. They raised the rate to a giddy two an over next morning before Atkins was run out for 90. Jane Cassar, who had been padded up for more than 123 overs, fell first ball, and Thompson followed at the same score. Two old hands, Clare Connor and Clare Taylor, helped to steer England past 300, but any thoughts of a result ended when rain washed out 68 overs during the second and third days. India's first innings was still in progress, and two runs behind, when the stumps were drawn. Hemlata Kala scored a maiden Test century in four and a half hours, adding 133 for the fifth wicket with Mamatha Maben.
Woman of the Match: H. Kala.
Close of play: First day, England 150-0 (Atkins 64, Thompson 60); Second day, India 21-0 (Jain 5, Amrita 14); Third day, India 95-1 (Jain 35, Chopra 23).

England

C. M. G. Atkins run out	90	C. E. Taylor b Kulkarni	27
A. Thompson b Goyal	85	L. C. Pearson not out	0
†J. Cassar c Raj b David	0		
*C. J. Connor b Kulkarni	40	B 16, l-b 13, w 3, n-b 1	33
L. K. Newton b David	11		
K. Lowe c Amrita b David	0	1/200 (1) 2/200 (3) 3/200 (2)	314
J. Hawker b Amrita	13	4/217 (5) 5/217 (6) 6/265 (7)	
D. Holden b David	11	7/275 (4) 8/280 (9)	
H. Wardlaw run out	4	9/314 (8) 10/314 (10)	

Bowling: Goswami 19–9–26–0; Maben 9–2–19–0; Chopra 6–4–9–0; David 51–26–88–4; Goyal 36–16–49–1; Kulkarni 34.3–10–70–2; Amrita 8–2–17–1; Raj 2–0–7–0.

India

†A. Jain run out	47	B. Goyal b Connor		0
P. S. Amrita b Pearson	29	J. Goswami not out		1
*A. Chopra b Connor	45	N. David not out		1
M. Raj b Holden	0	B 5, l-b 12, w 3, n-b 6		26
H. Kala c Atkins b Wardlaw	110			
M. Maben b Taylor	49	1/46 (2) 2/111 (1) 3/111 (4)	(9 wkts)	312
A. Kirkire run out	3	4/168 (3) 5/301 (6) 6/304 (7)		
D. M. Kulkarni lbw b Taylor	1	7/308 (8) 8/310 (9) 9/311 (5)		

Bowling: Pearson 34–11–58–1; Taylor 21–7–45–2; Holden 30–7–61–1; Newton 21–10–24–0; Wardlaw 20–6–58–1; Connor 16–6–32–2; Hawker 4–1–17–0.

Umpires: S. K. Bansal and Rajan Seth.

At Middle Income Group Ground, Mumbai, January 21. **Fourth one-day international: India won by five wickets.** Toss: England. **England 142** (48 overs) (A. Thompson 55; N. David four for 13); **India 143 for five** (41.4 overs) (A. Chopra 49 not out).
  Debut: P. S. Amrita (India).

At Nehru Stadium, Pune, January 23. **England won by three wickets.** Toss: England. **WCA of India XI 149 for eight** (50 overs); **England 153 for seven** (49.2 overs) (J. Cassar 30).

At Nehru Stadium, Pune, January 24. **Fifth one-day international: India won by six wickets.** Toss: England. **England 180 for six** (50 overs) (C. M. G. Atkins 51, A. Thompson 67); **India 182 for four** (46.4 overs) (A. Jain 48, P. S. Amrita 78).
  Atkins and Thompson opened with 134, an England one-day international record against India, but India's openers, Amrita and Jain, replied with 117. India won the series 5–0; Mithali Raj was Player of the Series.

CRICKET IN AUSTRALIA, 2001-02

By JOHN MacKINNON

Jimmy Maher

While Australia maintained their domination of the ICC Test Championship, Queensland maintained their own domination of domestic cricket. They completed a hat-trick of titles in the Pura Cup, which had supplanted the Sheffield Shield in 1999-2000, and their fifth title in eight seasons since their first-ever triumph in 1994-95. Stuart Law had led them to all five (originally as deputy to Ian Healy, who was mostly absent with Australia). Only Monty Noble, who captained New South Wales to six titles in the 1900s, had been more successful. Queensland narrowly missed a first-class and limited-overs double: they threw away their advantage in the one-day final, allowing New South Wales to claim the ING Cup, some consolation for a side in decline. Since their last Shield in 1993-94, New South Wales had finished in the league's top half only once; they collected their third wooden spoon in four seasons.

Queensland quickly set the pace for the rest of the field. At Christmas, they led the table by ten points. January brought losses in Hobart and at home to South Australia, but it was a fleeting falter. With the batting stabilised, confidence returned and top place was never in doubt. A lively Gabba pitch produced outright results every time, all but one in their favour, concluding with a 235-run victory over Tasmania in the final.

Queensland had the Pura Cup's two heaviest run-scorers, the leading wicket-taker, and the most successful wicket-keeper. Jimmy Maher and Martin Love were in prime form, the only batsmen to reach 1,000 in the tournament, though Matthew Hayden, who ran up two big hundreds for Queensland before his golden Test summer, outscored them in all first-class cricket. The muscular swing bowler Michael Kasprowicz was back to his best after injury, the only man in the country to reach 50 first-class wickets. And Wade Seccombe was the only keeper with 50 dismissals.

A supremely versatile opening batsman, Maher was the joint winner of the Pura Cup Player of the Year, though he missed the final after being called up for the national one-day squad in South Africa. At No. 3, Love was a great stylist and totally dependable, scoring fifties in all but three Pura games. Law and Andrew Symonds saved their best for the final. Law had a forgettable year with the bat, dropped to No. 6 and broke a knuckle. He handed the captaincy to Maher after the season's end. After three title-winning years as coach, Bennett King moved to the Cricket Academy, and was succeeded by his assistant, Terry Oliver.

Among Kasprowicz's seamer colleagues, Andy Bichel was on national duty, Adam Dale needed shoulder surgery, and Joe Dawes was less potent. But Ashley Noffke thrived in his first full season, and Queensland were delighted with the rise of Nathan Hauritz, a 20-year-old off-spinner, who did enough to join Maher on the South African tour.

At Christmas, Tasmania were having an ignominious season – the only team without a win, and just four points. But they were transformed in the New Year, after dumping two senior players, opener Dene Hills and all-rounder Shaun Young. They began their recovery by disposing of Queensland in two days, a neat reversal of their earlier two-day defeat in Brisbane. Three more wins, plus first-innings points at Melbourne, saw them into the final. Their fast bowlers, especially David Saker and Shane Watson, found an unexpected ally in the once docile Bellerive pitch. Some decidedly quick bowling, along with promising batting, earned Watson selection for the South African tour. When he left, Shane Jurgensen stepped forward. He claimed 11 wickets in each of the last two games, including a hat-trick against New South Wales and the best match figures in 20 years of Shield/Pura finals. The batsmen often struggled, though Hills, Cox and Ponting all cashed in early on at a run-fest at Sydney. Ponting was lost to Test duties, Hills was dropped and Cox, apart from a hundred in Adelaide, underachieved. Michael Di Venuto, another stalwart, missed half the season after injuring his ankle at soccer. Michael Dighton, like Jurgensen imported from his native Queensland via Perth, became the linchpin of the batting, along with wicket-keeper Sean Clingeleffer. Tasmania's revival did not save their coach, Greg Shipperd. After 11 seasons, he lost his job to Brian McFadyen, Victoria's former assistant coach.

Western Australia pulled off one of the season's more remarkable feats, beating Victoria after following on 275 behind. A win over South Australia might have squeezed them into the final but, not for the first time in Perth, they could not prise out the last batsmen. Runs flowed – three Pura Cup totals of 500, plus 600 for eight against the South Africans – but wickets were harder to find. The WACA pitch, long a pace bowlers' paradise, had lost its sting, and they managed only one home win.

Simon Katich and Mike Hussey both made hundreds on a placid Sydney wicket, but nowhere else. Katich became unsettled, and found the captaincy onerous. It was little surprise when he left for New South Wales. Damien Martyn and Justin Langer shone between Tests, and 22-year-old Marcus North scored three centuries, including a match-turning 200 in the Melbourne follow-on. Chris Rogers finished with twin unbeaten hundreds against South Australia. For the umpteenth time, Jo Angel led the bowling, passing 400 first-class wickets for the state. Angel, Matthew Nicholson and Brad Williams were a formidable pace triumvirate. However, Angel turned 34 in April. After years of devoted service, he could have hoped for a little more from the Perth curator.

For South Australia, it was feast or famine: eight outright results from ten, only three in their favour. Success generally depended on Darren Lehmann and Greg Blewett, who scored four centuries apiece in Pura cricket. They shared an intimidating assault on Tasmania, 386 for the second wicket, and set up a famous win in Brisbane. Even the New Zealanders, whom Australia could not beat in three Tests, succumbed. Lehmann's belligerence earned a recall to the limited-overs squad, but the stylish Blewett, 20 months his senior, lost his ACB contract. Ben Johnson made a remarkable return after being overlooked early on, carrying his bat in his first two games; he was third in the Pura Cup Player ballot, while Lehmann won the award for the one-day competition. As ever, the bowling was thin. Paul Wilson missed all but one game with a knee injury, Jason Gillespie was available for two, blitzing a full-strength New South Wales in Sydney. But it was 21-year-old Paul Rofe, a fast bowler in the Glenn McGrath mould, who caught the eye. He bowled more first-class overs than anyone else for 41 wickets. Mark Harrity had his days and Mike Smith returned a career-best seven for 98 in Brisbane. The avuncular leg-spinner Peter McIntyre retired after 14 seasons.

Victoria started ingloriously, with no points from the first four games, flickered in mid-season, and finally fell apart. Their coach, John Scholes, had resigned a week before the first match. His successor, Mick O'Sullivan, was keen enough; nevertheless, at the end of the season, Victoria appointed David Hookes, something of a media guru but a self-confessed coaching novice.

Apart from Shane Warne, Victoria had virtually a full stable, yet the selectors established no recognisable strategy. Colin Miller was soon dropped, and Damien

Fleming, hindered by shoulder problems, also found a Test pedigree counted for nothing. Hookes decided both were surplus to requirements, and Fleming joined South Australia. The captain, Paul Reiffel, ended a distinguished career in January, citing lack of motivation. The attack relied on the left-arm pace of Mathew Inness, and on all-rounder Ian Harvey. Inness looked unplayable when routing an insipid New South Wales line-up; Harvey enjoyed a hat-trick in Adelaide, including the dangerous Lehmann for 103. Will Carr, a new face, made a late mark with his hostile pace.

The fragility of the batting was starkly revealed in a collapse for 98 to Western Australia, after making them follow on. Brad Hodge, however, had an exceptional year, kicking off with twin centuries in Adelaide, adding two more in February, and sharing the Pura award with Maher. Matthew Elliott reached fifty seven times, but only one hundred, batting out a draw in Hobart. Jon Moss looked a prospect in the middle order, but Harvey promised more than he delivered. Darren Berry remained one of Australia's best keepers, especially standing up to the stumps.

New South Wales welcomed their new chief executive, David Gilbert, with two emphatic wins for 12 points in the first three matches. Seven games and four months later, they had not advanced. Individual successes were spasmodic. Only Stuart Clark and Michael Bevan performed adequately, and even Bevan recorded a pair in his last game. In his fifth season, Clark was rewarded for some tireless bowling with 45 wickets and an ACB contract, while Nathan Bracken did about enough to retain his. Michael Slater seemed to be on a plummeting path to the wilderness. Dropped by Australia, he lost his state place in January, and a spat with the press – he hurled his helmet at a photographer during a club match – did not help. Bowing to his lobby, the selectors recalled him as captain at the last: he scored fifty in a ten-wicket defeat. Slater was one of five captains in all. Shane Lee led most often, but had persistent knee trouble and contributed little. Stuart MacGill managed 11 wickets at 66 in six matches, plus a \$A1,500 fine for abusing an umpire, but, given one chance at Test level, more than paid his way. Of the young hopefuls, Michael Clarke was the pick, hitting encouraging centuries at Richmond and Adelaide.

In the immediate future the coach, Steve Rixon, indicated that New South Wales may depend on the return of senior players, such as the Waughs, after international careers, and importing outside talent, like Katich, as much as on the graduation of younger players. One who did himself no favours was Graeme Rummans, who used probenecid, a banned masking agent, in treating a boil on his shoulder. It cost him a \$A2,000 fine and a month's suspension.

New South Wales salvaged something in winning the ING Cup, which they had also secured under its old name, the Mercantile Mutual, the previous season. Success for any side visiting Brisbane is an achievement; to dismiss Queensland for a mere 185 was as uplifting for New South Wales as it was baffling to 12,000 home spectators. Their match-winners were two little-known medium-pacers, Dominic Thornely and Shawn Bradstreet, who reduced Queensland from cruise control to undignified collapse.

FIRST-CLASS AVERAGES, 2001-02

BATTING

(Qualification: 500 runs)

	M	*I*	*NO*	*R*	*HS*	*100s*	*Avge*
M. L. Hayden (*Queensland*)	10	17	2	1,243	147	6	82.86
M. G. Bevan (*New South Wales*)	8	14	2	868	203*	4	72.33
J. L. Langer (*Western Australia*)	10	18	3	1,030	133	5	68.66
D. R. Martyn (*Western Australia*)	8	11	2	616	189	3	68.44
R. T. Ponting (*Tasmania*)	8	14	3	733	157*	3	66.63
J. P. Maher (*Queensland*)	10	19	1	1,194	209	3	66.33
G. B. Hogg (*Western Australia*)	7	11	3	525	90	0	65.62
M. L. Love (*Queensland*)	12	22	3	1,189	202*	2	62.57

	M	I	NO	R	HS	100s	Avge
B. A. Johnson (*South Australia*)	7	14	3	653	138*	3	59.36
D. S. Lehmann (*South Australia*)	8	14	0	823	246	4	58.78
B. J. Hodge (*Victoria*)	10	18	3	858	140	4	57.20
G. S. Blewett (*South Australia*)	11	21	3	1,025	169*	5	56.94
S. G. Clingeleffer (*Tasmania*)	11	15	4	517	141*	2	47.00
M. E. Waugh (*New South Wales*)	8	11	0	500	168	1	45.45
M. J. North (*Western Australia*)	9	15	1	633	200*	3	45.21
M. T. G. Elliott (*Victoria*)	10	20	2	780	135*	1	43.33
R. J. Campbell (*Western Australia*)	9	15	1	576	121	1	41.14
G. J. Mail (*New South Wales*)	8	14	1	528	150*	1	40.61
M. G. Dighton (*Tasmania*)	10	15	0	594	126	2	39.60
M. J. Clarke (*New South Wales*)	9	18	1	663	132	2	39.00
J. Cox (*Tasmania*)	11	18	1	660	174	2	38.82
S. M. Katich (*Western Australia*)	11	18	0	651	131	1	36.16
M. E. K. Hussey (*Western Australia*)	11	19	1	621	100	1	34.50
B. J. Haddin (*New South Wales*)	10	18	2	515	102	1	32.18

BOWLING

(Qualification: 20 wickets)

	O	M	R	W	BB	5W/i	Avge
M. W. H. Inness (*Victoria*)	214.5	61	597	31	7-19	1	19.25
S. J. Jurgensen (*Tasmania*)	290	85	710	36	6-65	4	19.72
S. R. Clark (*New South Wales*)	387	108	1,047	45	5-42	4	23.26
S. R. Watson (*Tasmania*)	126.4	20	514	22	6-32	2	23.36
M. S. Kasprowicz (*Queensland*)	378.5	87	1,239	51	5-44	2	24.29
J. Angel (*Western Australia*)	412	124	1,074	44	6-52	1	24.40
J. N. Gillespie (*South Australia*)	243.4	60	689	28	8-50	1	24.60
P. C. Rofe (*South Australia*)	441.4	152	1,060	41	7-52	3	25.85
B. Lee (*New South Wales*)	228.5	55	763	29	5-56	2	26.31
D. J. Saker (*Tasmania*)	366.3	103	1,003	38	5-53	1	26.39
A. Symonds (*Queensland*)	226.5	61	588	22	4-45	0	26.72
B. A. Williams (*Western Australia*) .	279	72	906	32	4-34	0	28.31
M. J. Nicholson (*Western Australia*) .	299.4	62	936	33	5-68	1	28.36
A. A. Noffke (*Queensland*)	380.4	97	1,110	39	5-31	2	28.46
M. J. Smith (*South Australia*)	273.2	54	917	29	7-98	1	31.62
N. W. Bracken (*New South Wales*) . .	248.5	55	763	24	4-10	0	31.79
G. D. McGrath (*New South Wales*) .	340.5	107	880	24	3-13	0	36.66
S. K. Warne (*Victoria*)	373	63	1,156	29	5-113	1	39.86
D. G. Wright (*Tasmania*)	346.3	114	932	23	3-15	0	40.52
M. A. Harrity (*South Australia*)	335.2	67	1,106	27	5-65	1	40.96
S. C. G. MacGill (*New South Wales*)	328.1	71	1,124	27	5-132	1	41.62
D. A. Nash (*New South Wales*)	259	60	909	21	4-59	0	43.28

PURA CUP, 2001-02

	Played	Won	Lost	Drawn	1st-inns Points	Points	Quotient
Queensland	10	5	2	3	6	36	1.178
Tasmania	10	4	2	4	6	30	1.227
Western Australia . . .	10	3	2	5	8	26	1.094
South Australia.	10	3	5	2	2	20	0.893
Victoria	10	2	4	4	4	16	0.950
New South Wales . . .	10	2	4	4	0	12	0.776

Final: Queensland beat Tasmania by 235 runs.

Outright win = 6 pts; lead on first-innings in a drawn or lost game = 2 pts.
Quotient = runs per wicket scored divided by runs per wicket conceded.

Full scores, match reports and statistics of the 2001-02 Australian season appear in *Wisden Cricketers' Almanack Australia 2002-03.*

*In the following scores, * by the name of a team indicates that they won the toss.*

At Sydney, October 17, 18, 19, 20. **Drawn. Tasmania 504** (D. F. Hills 136, J. Cox 107, R. T. Ponting 126, S. G. Clingeleffer 40, D. G. Wright 50; S. R. Clark five for 64) **and 356 for three** (D. F. Hills 32, J. Cox 80, R. T. Ponting 154, S. R. Watson 58 not out); **New South Wales* 489** (G. J. Mail 52, M. G. Bevan 102, M. E. Waugh 168, M. A. Higgs 37, S. C. G. MacGill 34, S. R. Clark 31 not out; D. J. Saker four for 115, S. R. Watson three for 88). *Tasmania 2 pts.*
    Cox passed 10,000 runs for Tasmania. Ponting scored a hundred in each innings for the fifth time, an Australian record. MacGill was fined $A1,500 for abuse of an umpire.

At Brisbane, October 17, 18, 19, 20. **Queensland won by six wickets. Western Australia* 360 for eight dec.** (J. L. Langer 96, A. C. Gilchrist 98, M. J. North 47, Extras 31; M. S. Kasprowicz three for 89) **and 207** (M. E. K. Hussey 66; A. C. Dale three for 51, M. S. Kasprowicz three for 38); **Queensland 403 for six dec.** (M. L. Hayden 143, J. P. Maher 73, M. L. Love 78, S. G. Law 35; J. Angel three for 70) **and 166 for four** (A. Symonds 75 not out). *Queensland 6 pts.*
    Queensland scored 166 to win in 27.3 overs, with 5.3 to spare. Symonds hit 75 in 43 balls.

At Adelaide, October 17, 18, 19, 20. **Drawn. Victoria 334** (M. T. G. Elliott 42, B. J. Hodge 140, M. Klinger 35, I. J. Harvey 62; B. E. Young three for 70) **and 211 for seven dec.** (J. L. Arnberger 43, B. J. Hodge 110 not out; J. N. Gillespie three for 36); **South Australia* 337 for seven dec.** (D. A. Fitzgerald 34, G. S. Blewett 169 not out, D. S. Lehmann 103; I. J. Harvey three for 65) **and 179 for five** (D. S. Lehmann 39, B. H. Higgins 58 not out, J. N. Gillespie 32 not out; D. W. Fleming three for 37). *South Australia 2 pts.*
    Hodge scored a century in each innings for Victoria. Harvey took a hat-trick in South Australia's first innings.

At Richmond, October 24, 25, 26, 27. **Drawn. Queensland* 417** (M. L. Hayden 147, J. P. Maher 96, M. L. Love 33, A. A. Noffke 73, N. M. Hauritz 41; S. K. Warne four for 118) **and 54 for two dec.** (M. L. Love 34 not out); **Victoria 160 for three dec.** (M. T. G. Elliott 56, B. J. Hodge 39 not out) **and 240 for six** (J. L. Arnberger 33, M. P. Mott 87, B. J. Hodge 33, M. Klinger 44 not out; M. S. Kasprowicz four for 53). *Queensland 2 pts.*
    Hayden's 50th first-class century took him past 16,000 runs.

At Sydney, October 26, 27, 28. **New South Wales won by 290 runs. New South Wales 188** (M. G. Bevan 55, S. Lee 30, N. W. Bracken 38; J. N. Gillespie eight for 50) **and 436** (M. J. Slater 49, G. J. Mail 150 not out, M. E. Waugh 51, M. A. Higgs 53, D. S. Lehmann three for 42); **South Australia* 142** (D. S. Lehmann 49; G. D. McGrath three for 25) **and 192** (J. M. Vaughan 69, B. H. Higgins 41, G. A. Manou 30; B. Lee five for 56, N. W. Bracken four for ten). *New South Wales 6 pts.*
    Mail was the first player to carry his bat for New South Wales since Alan Turner in 1969-70. MacGill hit 53 runs in 31 balls. New South Wales wicket-keeper Nathan Pilon held nine catches in the match.

At Perth, October 26, 27, 28, 29. **Drawn. Tasmania 337** (R. T. Ponting 58, S. R. Watson 56, S. Young 67, S. G. Clingeleffer 47, D. G. Wright 51; B. A. Williams four for 104, J. Angel four for 53) **and 237 for seven** (J. Cox 63, S. R. Watson 30, D. J. Marsh 47, J. Angel three for 51); **Western Australia* 594 for seven dec.** (J. L. Langer 133, S. M. Katich 79, D. R. Martyn 189, M. W. Goodwin 141). *Western Australia 2 pts.*
    Martyn and Goodwin added 321, a Western Australian fourth-wicket record.

At Hobart, November 8, 9, 10, 11. **South Australia won by an innings and 40 runs. Tasmania 382 for seven dec.** (J. Cox 35, S. R. Watson 32, S. Young 84, S. G. Clingeleffer 141 not out, Extras 33) **and 167** (S. R. Watson 58, D. J. Marsh 31; M. A. Harrity five for 65, P. C. Rofe three for 24); **South Australia* 589 for five dec.** (D. A. Fitzgerald 34, G. S. Blewett 163, D. S. Lehmann 246, B. H. Higgins 69 not out, Extras 31). *South Australia 6 pts.*
    Lehmann's 246 lasted 295 minutes and 238 balls and included 39 fours and four sixes. On the third day, he scored 100 in the first session and 117 in the second. He added 386, a South Australian second-wicket record, with Blewett.

At Richmond, November 8, 9, 10, 11. **New South Wales won by seven wickets. Victoria*** 259 (J. L. Arnberger 47, M. P. Mott 35, B. J. Hodge 44, I. J. Harvey 74; N. W. Bracken four for 76, S. C. G. MacGill four for 71) **and** 193 (I. J. Harvey 48, M. T. G. Elliott 50; S. R. Clark five for 47, S. C. G. MacGill four for 54); **New South Wales 338** (M. G. Bevan 128, M. J. Clarke 111, B. J. Haddin 33; M. W. H. Inness four for 61, I. J. Harvey three for 53) **and 117 for three** (M. J. Slater 58 not out, M. A. Higgs 32 not out; D. W. Fleming three for 34). *New South Wales 6 pts.*

The match was played at Richmond because of a football international with France at the MCG.

At Perth, November 8, 9, 10, 11. **Drawn. Western Australia 432** (S. W. Meuleman 37, M. W. Goodwin 68, M. J. North 106, K. M. Harvey 31, M. J. Nicholson 59 not out, J. Angel 61, Extras 30; A. A. Noffke five for 103) **and 220 for eight** (M. E. K. Hussey 35, S. M. Katich 38, R. J. Campbell 72 not out; M. S. Kasprowicz three for 77); **Queensland* 490** (J. P. Maher 174, J. L. Cassell 86, M. L. Love 91, W. A. Seccombe 40, A. A. Noffke 34; B. A. Williams three for 103, M. J. Nicholson four for 97). *Queensland 2 pts.*

Nicholson and Angel added 110 for Western Australia's ninth wicket.

At Brisbane, November 25, 26, 27. **Queensland won by eight wickets. New South Wales 146** (G. J. Mail 42; M. S. Kasprowicz five for 44, A. Symonds three for 30) **and 222** (G. J. Mail 56, M. J. Slater 41, M. J. Clarke 36; M. S. Kasprowicz four for 87, A. A. Noffke three for 48, A. Symonds three for 19); **Queensland* 236** (C. T. Perren 37, S. G. Law 70, W. A. Seccombe 49; N. W. Bracken three for 71, S. R. Clark four for 61) **and 133 for two** (J. P. Maher 61, M. L. Love 65 not out). *Queensland 6 pts.*

Queensland wicket-keeper Seccombe took seven catches in New South Wales's first innings.

At Adelaide, November 25, 26, 27, 28. **Western Australia won by 76 runs. Western Australia*** 227 (M. E. K. Hussey 40, S. M. Katich 42, G. B. Hogg 56 not out; P. C. Rofe five for 30) **and** 209 (S. M. Katich 38, M. W. Goodwin 33; P. C. Rofe three for 31); **South Australia 206** (B. A. Johnson 121 not out, C. J. Davies 52; M. J. Nicholson four for 58, J. Angel three for 48) **and 154** (B. E. Young 30, M. J. Smith 31, G. A. Manou 43; M. J. Nicholson four for 60). *Western Australia 6 pts.*

In his first match of the season, Johnson carried his bat.

At Hobart, November 30, December 1, 2, 3. **Drawn. Victoria 139** (M. P. Mott 30; D. G. Wright three for 53) **and 282 for two** (J. L. Arnberger 135 not out, M. P. Mott 33, B. J. Hodge 59 not out); **Tasmania* 527 for nine dec.** (S. R. Mason 30, M. G. Dighton 126, D. J. Marsh 97, S. Young 70, S. G. Clingeleffer 112, D. G. Wright 49; P. R. Reiffel four for 71, I. J. Harvey three for 136). *Tasmania 2 pts.*

Reiffel became Victoria's leading first-class wicket-taker, breaking Alan Connolly's record of 330.

At Brisbane, December 13, 14. **Queensland won by ten wickets. Tasmania 100** (A. J. Bichel four for 54, J. H. Dawes three for four) **and 82** (M. S. Kasprowicz four for 22, J. H. Dawes three for 28); **Queensland* 132** (J. P. Maher 35; S. J. Jurgensen four for 16) **and 51 for no wkt** (B. P. Nash 35 not out). *Queensland 6 pts.*

The match lasted only 137 overs and 569 minutes, beating 600 minutes between Victoria and Western Australia in 1975-76 as the shortest four-day Shield/Pura match. Stuart Law overtook Sam Trimble's record of 133 first-class matches for Queensland.

At Melbourne, December 13, 14, 15. **Victoria won by nine wickets. South Australia 229** (B. A. Johnson 138 not out; M. W. H. Inness three for 26, M. L. Lewis three for 67) **and 303** (G. S. Blewett 41, B. H. Higgins 58, N. T. Adcock 46, B. E. Young 44, M. J. Smith 40; M. L. Lewis four for 64, I. J. Harvey four for 72); **Victoria* 405** (J. L. Arnberger 36, M. Klinger 50, I. J. Harvey 46, C. L. White 91, P. R. Reiffel 75; P. C. Rofe four for 101, M. J. Smith three for 118) **and 129 for one** (J. L. Arnberger 70 not out, M. T. G. Elliott 45). *Victoria 6 pts.*

Johnson carried his bat for the second match running. Darren Lehmann became the leading scorer in Shield/Pura cricket, passing Jamie Siddons (10,643).

At Sydney, December 14, 15, 16, 17. **Drawn. New South Wales* 215** (M. J. Slater 40, M. J. Clarke 43, B. J. Haddin 50; B. A. Williams three for 71, K. M. Harvey four for 43) **and 452 for four** (G. J. Mail 59, M. G. Bevan 203 not out, M. A. Higgs 80, B. J. Haddin 52 not out); **Western**

Australia 578 (M. E. K. Hussey 100, S. W. Meuleman 60, S. M. Katich 131, R. J. Campbell 57, C. J. L. Rogers 53, G. B. Hogg 61, Extras 42; S. R. Clark four for 125, A. M. Clark four for 130). *Western Australia 2 pts.*

Bevan's 203 not out lasted 562 minutes and 453 balls and included 28 fours; it made him New South Wales's leading run-scorer, overtaking Alan Kippax's 8,005.

At Adelaide, January 16, 17, 18, 19. **South Australia won by 67 runs. South Australia* 359 for nine dec.** (G. S. Blewett 38, B. H. Higgins 80, B. E. Young 122, G. A. Manou 62; S. R. Clark three for 100, N. W. Bracken four for 79) **and 287** (D. S. Lehmann 143; D. A. Nash three for 52, B. P. van Deinsen three for 42); **New South Wales 332** (B. P. van Deinsen 60, M. J. Clarke 132, B. J. Haddin 55; P. C. Rofe six for 60) **and 247** (M. J. Clarke 30, M. A. Higgs 67, B. J. Haddin 47; P. C. Rofe seven for 52). *South Australia 6 pts.*

Rofe, who turned 21 on the first day, improved his career-best analysis in each innings and finished with 13 for 112, the best match figures for South Australia since Eric Freeman's 13 for 105, also against New South Wales, in 1970-71.

At Hobart, January 17, 18. **Tasmania won by an innings and 50 runs. Tasmania 281** (S. P. Kremerskothen 42, D. J. Saker 66 not out, S. J. Jurgensen 56, Extras 33; D. R. MacKenzie three for 45, N. M. Hauritz three for 41); **Queensland* 130** (J. L. Cassell 41, A. A. Noffke 34 not out; S. R. Watson six for 32) **and 101** (J. P. Maher 41; D. G. Wright three for 15, S. R. Watson five for 46). *Tasmania 6 pts.*

Saker and Jurgensen added 114 for Tasmania's tenth wicket. Queensland lost all 20 wickets on the second day, with wicket-keeper Sean Clingeleffer taking nine catches in the match, a Tasmanian record.

At Perth, January 18, 19, 20, 21. **Western Australia won by ten wickets. Victoria* 272** (M. T. G. Elliott 30, B. J. Hodge 32, M. Klinger 58, J. Moss 70; J. Angel three for 58, M. W. Clark three for 49) **and 185** (M. T. G. Elliott 51, J. Moss 51; J. Angel six for 52, M. J. Nicholson three for 56); **Western Australia 386** (J. L. Langer 34, S. M. Katich 34, R. J. Campbell 61, G. B. Hogg 84, K. M. Harvey 59; P. R. Reiffel three for 78) **and 72 for no wkt** (J. L. Langer 44 not out). *Western Australia 6 pts.*

Reiffel retired with 545 wickets at 26.40 in 167 first-class matches, including a record 337 in 92 for Victoria.

At Sydney, January 25, 26, 27. **Victoria won by ten wickets. New South Wales* 109** (M. A. Higgs 40 not out; M. W. H. Inness seven for 19) **and 307** (C. J. Richards 38, M. J. Clarke 42, G. C. Rummans 60, M. A. Higgs 52, B. J. Haddin 41; M. W. H. Inness four for 67, I. S. L. Hewett three for 63); **Victoria 358** (J. Moss 109, D. S. Berry 48, M. L. Lewis 54 not out; S. R. Clark five for 75, D. A. Nash four for 59) **and 59 for no wkt** (M. T. G. Elliott 35 not out). *Victoria 6 pts.*

Berry broke Dean Jones's record of 110 Shield/Pura matches for Victoria.

At Brisbane, January 25, 26, 27, 28. **South Australia won by nine wickets. South Australia 553 for six dec.** (D. A. Fitzgerald 39, G. S. Blewett 109, D. S. Lehmann 129, B. H. Higgins 54, C. J. Davies 119 not out, M. J. Smith 40 not out) **and 51 for one; Queensland* 232** (M. L. Hayden 63, M. L. Love 84; M. A. Harrity three for 61) **and 370** (J. P. Maher 209, M. L. Hayden 43, M. L. Love 41; M. J. Smith seven for 98). *South Australia 6 pts.*

Maher's 209 lasted 483 minutes and 360 balls and included 20 fours.

At Hobart, January 25, 26, 27. **Tasmania won by an innings and 76 runs. Tasmania 347** (M. G. Dighton 65, S. R. Watson 49, S. P. Kremerskothen 55, D. G. Wright 63, S. B. Tubb 33; J. Angel four for 79); **Western Australia* 137** (M. E. K. Hussey 33, S. M. Katich 68; D. J. Saker three for 48) **and 134** (M. W. Goodwin 37; D. J. Saker three for 21, S. R. Watson four for 35). *Tasmania 6 pts.*

Jamie Cox passed David Boon's record of 139 first-class matches for Tasmania.

At Adelaide, February 13, 14, 15, 16. **Queensland won by 106 runs. Queensland* 503 for five dec.** (J. P. Maher 66, M. L. Love 202 retired hurt, B. P. Nash 157) **and 127 for seven dec.** (J. L. Cassell 43, J. P. Maher 52; G. S. Blewett three for 15, B. E. Young three for 21); **South Australia 392** (D. A. Fitzgerald 139, B. A. Johnson 52, G. S. Blewett 71, G. A. Manou 44; A. A. Noffke four for 112, N. M. Hauritz three for 83) **and 132** (B. A. Johnson 49, C. J. Davies 32; A. A. Noffke five for 31, N. M. Hauritz three for 22). *Queensland 6 pts.*

Love, who retired hurt after making 202 in 521 minutes from 412 balls, hit 21 fours. He and Nash added 296 for the third wicket, though 312 runs were added before a wicket fell. On the final day, Queensland wanted to reuse the ball from South Australia's first innings, but the home team objected.

At Perth, February 15, 16, 17, 18. **Drawn. Western Australia 500 for seven dec.** (M. E. K. Hussey 86, S. W. Meuleman 35, S. M. Katich 52, R. J. Campbell 121, C. J. L. Rogers 96, G. B. Hogg 62) **and 158 for six dec.** (M. E. K. Hussey 60; D. A. Nash three for 59); **New South Wales*** 253 (M. G. Bevan 66, G. C. Rummans 55; B. A. Williams four for 89, J. Angel four for 91) **and 311 for nine** (B. J. Haddin 41, M. G. Bevan 72, M. J. Clarke 81; B. A. Williams three for 78). *Western Australia 2 pts.*

Angel took his 400th wicket for Western Australia. New South Wales's last pair played out 14 balls for the draw.

At Melbourne, February 17, 18, 19, 20. **Drawn. Victoria*** 371 for eight dec. (M. T. G. Elliott 64, B. J. Hodge 85, I. J. Harvey 87, D. S. Berry 62 not out, D. W. Fleming 39 not out; D. J. Saker four for 71) **and 252 for seven dec.** (M. T. G. Elliott 72, B. J. Hodge 109; D. J. Marsh four for 70); **Tasmania 374 for nine dec.** (M. G. Dighton 124, M. J. Di Venuto 83, D. G. Wright 48; C. L. White three for 97) **and 110 for four** (M. J. Di Venuto 38, D. J. Marsh 40 not out; W. N. Carr three for 34). *Tasmania 2 pts.*

Hodge reached his century with a six off Marsh.

At Melbourne, February 28, March 1, 2, 3. **Western Australia won by 37 runs. Victoria*** 450 for six dec. (M. T. G. Elliott 88, M. P. Mott 84, B. J. Hodge 131, J. Moss 59, I. J. Harvey 61 not out; G. B. Hogg three for 95) **and 98** (B. A. Williams four for 34, M. J. Nicholson three for 13); **Western Australia 175** (R. J. Campbell 63, G. B. Hogg 30; M. L. Lewis three for 40, B. E. McGain three for 46) **and 410** (M. E. K. Hussey 61, M. J. North 200 not out, M. J. Nicholson 49; W. N. Carr four for 77, J. Moss three for 35). *Western Australia 6 pts, Victoria 2 pts.*

North's 200 not out lasted 504 minutes and 378 balls and included 18 fours and three sixes. Western Australia won after following on, the third instance in Shield/Pura cricket.

At Sydney, March 1, 2, 3, 4. **Drawn. Queensland*** 528 for four dec. (J. P. Maher 198, B. P. Nash 60, M. L. Love 184, L. A. Carseldine 30 not out; S. R. Clark three for 106) **and 120** (M. L. Love 42; S. R. Clark five for 42, D. A. Nash three for 45); **New South Wales 442** (M. J. Phelps 84, C. J. Richards 74, M. J. Clarke 76, B. J. Haddin 102, D. A. Turner 39, N. W. Bracken 32 not out; N. M. Hauritz four for 119) **and 202 for nine** (S. Lee 41, M. J. Phelps 65 not out; M. S. Kasprowicz three for 72, J. H. Dawes three for 66). *Queensland 2 pts.*

Maher and Love added 294 in 295 minutes for Queensland's second wicket. Set 207 to win, New South Wales were 148 for nine; Phelps and Clark added 54 in 31 minutes for the last wicket.

At Adelaide, March 1, 2, 3, 4. **Tasmania won by an innings and 32 runs. South Australia*** 200 (D. A. Fitzgerald 31, B. A. Johnson 50, G. A. Manou 33, P. E. McIntyre 40; D. J. Saker three for 63) **and 242** (B. A. Johnson 138, M. J. Smith 31; D. J. Saker five for 53, S. B. Tubb three for 57); **Tasmania 474 for eight dec.** (J. Cox 174, M. G. Dighton 76, D. J. Marsh 63, S. G. Clingeleffer 66 not out, D. G. Wright 55; M. J. Smith three for 83). *Tasmania 6 pts.*

At Brisbane, March 13, 14, 15. **Queensland won by five wickets. Victoria 148** (M. P. Mott 34; S. A. Brant three for 23) **and 122** (J. Moss 38, D. S. Berry 41; M. S. Kasprowicz three for 37, S. A. Brant three for 31, A. A. Noffke four for 29; W. N. Carr six for 46) **and 164 for five** (D. M. Payne 35, M. L. Love 61). *Queensland 6 pts, Victoria 2 pts.*

Queensland won despite collapsing to 22 for six in their first innings.

At Hobart, March 13, 14, 15. **Tasmania won by ten wickets. New South Wales*** 164 (M. J. Phelps 53, M. J. Slater 50; S. J. Jurgensen five for 38) **and 238** (M. J. Phelps 41, C. J. Richards 42, G. M. Lambert 45 not out; S. J. Jurgensen six for 65); **Tasmania 401** (S. R. Mason 41, J. Cox 72, M. G. Dighton 84, M. J. Di Venuto 39, D. J. Saker 40 not out, Extras 33; G. M. Lambert three for 86) **and four for no wkt.** *Tasmania 6 pts.*

Jurgensen improved his career-best analysis in both innings, and took a hat-trick in the second.

At Perth, March 13, 14, 15, 16. **Drawn. Western Australia 346 for seven dec.** (M. E. K. Hussey 39, S. M. Katich 32, M. J. North 111, R. J. Campbell 34, C. J. L. Rogers 101 not out) **and 276 for five dec.** (R. J. Campbell 30, C. J. L. Rogers 102 not out, G. B. Hogg 77 not out; M. J. Smith four for 69); **South Australia* 301** (G. S. Blewett 64, C. J. Davies 42, B. E. Young 36, S. A. Deitz 86; J. Angel three for 53) **and 277 for eight** (S. A. Deitz 43, G. S. Blewett 112 not out, M. J. Smith 46; J. Angel four for 49). *Western Australia 2 pts.*

Rogers scored his maiden century in the first innings, and added another in the second, both unbeaten. Angel became Western Australia's leading Shield/Pura wicket-taker, overtaking Terry Alderman's 384.

FINAL

QUEENSLAND v TASMANIA

At Brisbane, March 22, 23, 24, 25, 26. Queensland won by 235 runs. Toss: Tasmania.

Tasmania glimpsed their long-awaited first title when Jurgensen had Queensland tottering at 98 for four. But two out-of-form batsmen, Symonds and Law, combined to wrest back control, adding 155 by the close. The second day belonged to the fast bowlers, from both sides. Jurgensen bowled Symonds in the first over, and Queensland's lower order succumbed before lunch. But in the afternoon it was their turn. Kasprowicz swung the ball disconcertingly, and what started as a cautious reply from Tasmania turned into a fight for survival, then a procession. Noffke weighed in with a decisive burst of three in four overs to shoot them out for 141 – a first-innings lead of 161. That virtually sealed the result inside two days. The home batsmen consolidated, with 177 from Nash and Love. Although Jurgensen bowled with great spirit, taking 11 wickets for the second game running and producing the best match figures in the final's history, Tasmania faced an academic target of 530. Di Venuto and Kremerskothen gave them some substance and took the game into the fifth day with a stand of 111, until Symonds dismissed them in successive overs. Seccombe held nine catches in all, but it was Kasprowicz who had the last word: his ninth wicket carried him to 51 for the season.

Man of the Match: A. Symonds.

Close of play: First day, Queensland 253-4 (Symonds 91, Law 62); Second day, Queensland 25-0 (Payne 21, Nash 3); Third day, Queensland 279-6 (Law 1); Fourth day: Tasmania 190-4 (Di Venuto 42, Kremerskothen 26).

Queensland

B. P. Nash c Clingeleffer b Jurgensen	12	– (2) c Di Venuto b Marsh	96
D. M. Payne c sub (S. B. Tubb) b Denton	17	– (1) c Dighton b Saker	29
M. L. Love lbw b Jurgensen	34	– c Wright b Kremerskothen	93
L. A. Carseldine c Kremerskothen b Jurgensen	29	– c Kremerskothen b Jurgensen	12
A. Symonds b Jurgensen	91	– lbw b Jurgensen	32
*S. G. Law c Wright b Saker	69	– c Marsh b Jurgensen	15
†W. A. Seccombe c Di Venuto b Jurgensen	1	– c Clingeleffer b Jurgensen	5
A. A. Noffke c Clingeleffer b Denton	14	– not out	47
M. S. Kasprowicz c Clingeleffer b Denton	2	– c Clingeleffer b Jurgensen	2
S. A. Brant not out	16	– c sub (X. J. Doherty) b Jurgensen	0
J. H. Dawes c Di Venuto b Wright	7	– c Wright b Kremerskothen	26
L-b 9, n-b 1	10	L-b 7, w 4	11

1/29 2/48 3/85 4/98 5/253   302   1/46 2/223 3/225 4/270 5/273   368
6/261 7/263 8/274 9/279   6/279 7/310 8/312 9/316

Bowling: *First Innings*—Saker 29–8–68–1; Jurgensen 35–12–68–5; Denton 22–7–67–3; Wright 21–6–60–1; Kremerskothen 7–0–30–0. *Second Innings*—Saker 17–6–36–1; Marsh 16–5–39–1; Jurgensen 34–6–104–6; Denton 27–4–97–0; Wright 17–6–39–0; Kremerskothen 13.5–1–46–2.

Tasmania

S. R. Mason lbw b Symonds	17	– (2) c Seccombe b Kasprowicz.... 39
*J. Cox c Payne b Kasprowicz	14	– (1) c Payne b Kasprowicz....... 19
M. G. Dighton c Love b Kasprowicz	29	– c Kasprowicz b Symonds........ 38
M. J. Di Venuto c Seccombe b Kasprowicz	11	– c Carseldine b Symonds........ 65
D. J. Marsh b Symonds	27	– c Seccombe b Symonds......... 2
S. P. Kremerskothen c sub (C. T. Perren)		
b Kasprowicz	10	– c sub (M. A. Anderson) b Symonds 41
†S. G. Clingeleffer c Carseldine b Noffke....	5	– c Seccombe b Noffke 12
D. G. Wright c Seccombe b Noffke	12	– not out 27
D. J. Saker c Seccombe b Noffke	2	– c Seccombe b Noffke 5
G. J. Denton c Kasprowicz b Kasprowicz....	0	– c Seccombe b Kasprowicz...... 0
S. J. Jurgensen not out	0	– c Carseldine b Kasprowicz 8
B 4, l-b 4, w 3, n-b 3	14	L-b 7, w 9, n-b 22 38
	141	**294**

1/25 2/63 3/78 4/89 5/119　　　　　　　**141**　　1/54 2/110 3/115 4/122 5/233　　**294**
6/119 7/131 8/136 9/141　　　　　　　　　　　　　6/234 7/252 8/270 9/276

Bowling: *First Innings*—Kasprowicz 20–7–60–5; Brant 4–1–10–0; Dawes 14–5–28–0; Noffke 10.2–3–15–3; Symonds 8–1–20–2. *Second Innings*—Kasprowicz 27.5–5–103–4; Dawes 22–5–66–0; Noffke 24–3–62–2; Symonds 22–8–45–4; Carseldine 4–1–11–0.

Umpires: S. J. Davis and S. J. A. Taufel.
Third umpire: P. D. Parker. Referee: C. G. Rackemann.

CHAMPIONS

1963-64	South Australia		1984-85	New South Wales
1964-65	New South Wales		1985-86	New South Wales
1965-66	New South Wales		1986-87	Western Australia
1966-67	Victoria		1987-88	Western Australia
1967-68	Western Australia		1988-89	Western Australia
1968-69	South Australia		1989-90	New South Wales
1969-70	Victoria		1990-91	Victoria
1970-71	South Australia		1991-92	Western Australia
1971-72	Western Australia		1992-93	New South Wales
1972-73	Western Australia		1993-94	New South Wales
1973-74	Victoria		1994-95	Queensland
1974-75	Western Australia		1995-96	South Australia
1975-76	South Australia		1996-97	Queensland
1976-77	Western Australia		1997-98	Western Australia
1977-78	Western Australia		1998-99	Western Australia
1978-79	Victoria			
1979-80	Victoria		*Pura Milk Cup*	
1980-81	Western Australia		1999-2000	Queensland
1981-82	South Australia			
1982-83	New South Wales		*Pura Cup*	
1983-84	Western Australia		2000-01	Queensland
			2001-02	Queensland

New South Wales have won the title 42 times, Victoria 25, Western Australia 15, South Australia 13, Queensland 5, Tasmania 0.

ING CUP, 2001-02

Notes: Matches in this section were not first-class.
Each side had 12 players of whom 11 could bat and 11 field.

	Played	Won	Lost	No Result	Bonus points	Points	Net run-rate
Queensland	10	7	3	0	3	31	0.45
New South Wales . . .	10	7	3	0	2	30	0.16
South Australia	10	6	4	0	3	27	0.16
Western Australia . . .	10	5	5	0	2	22	0.14
Victoria	10	3	6	1	1	15	−0.44
Tasmania	10	1	8	1	1	7	−0.61

Final

At Brisbane, February 24. **New South Wales won by 19 runs. New South Wales 204** (50 overs) (C. J. Richards 34, B. J. Haddin 45, M. J. Phelps 31; J. R. Hopes three for 33, N. M. Hauritz four for 47); **Queensland* 185** (48.5 overs) (M. L. Love 53, C. T. Perren 36; D. J. Thornely three for 36, S. D. Bradstreet four for 23).
   Queensland collapsed from 149 for four, allowing New South Wales to retain their title.

PURA CUP PLAYERS OF THE YEAR

The Pura Cup Player of the Year Award for 2001-02 was shared by Jimmy Maher of Queensland and Brad Hodge of Victoria, with 16 points each, two ahead of South Australia's Ben Johnson. The Award was instituted in 1975-76; each of the two umpires standing in each of the 30 Pura Cup matches (excluding the final) allocated marks of 3, 2 and 1 to the three players who most impressed them. The ING Cup Player of the Year award was won by Darren Lehmann of South Australia, the previous season's joint winner.

SHEFFIELD SHIELD/PURA CUP FINALS

1982-83   NEW SOUTH WALES* beat Western Australia by 54 runs.
1983-84   WESTERN AUSTRALIA beat Queensland by four wickets.
1984-85   NEW SOUTH WALES beat Queensland by one wicket.
1985-86   NEW SOUTH WALES drew with Queensland.
1986-87   WESTERN AUSTRALIA drew with Victoria.
1987-88   WESTERN AUSTRALIA beat Queensland by five wickets.
1988-89   WESTERN AUSTRALIA drew with South Australia.
1989-90   NEW SOUTH WALES beat Queensland by 345 runs.
1990-91   VICTORIA beat New South Wales by eight wickets.
1991-92   WESTERN AUSTRALIA beat New South Wales by 44 runs.
1992-93   NEW SOUTH WALES beat Queensland by eight wickets.
1993-94   NEW SOUTH WALES beat Tasmania by an innings and 61 runs.
1994-95   QUEENSLAND beat South Australia by an innings and 101 runs.
1995-96   SOUTH AUSTRALIA drew with Western Australia.
1996-97   QUEENSLAND* beat Western Australia by 160 runs.
1997-98   WESTERN AUSTRALIA beat Tasmania by seven wickets.
1998-99   WESTERN AUSTRALIA* beat Queensland by an innings and 31 runs.
1999-2000 QUEENSLAND drew with Victoria.
2000-01   QUEENSLAND beat Victoria by four wickets.
2001-02   QUEENSLAND beat Tasmania by 235 runs.

Note: The team that finished top of the table had home advantage over the runners-up. In a drawn final, the home team won the title.

* *Victory for the away team.*

ALLAN BORDER MEDAL

Opening batsman Matthew Hayden won the Allan Border Medal in February 2002 by seven votes from Shane Warne. Team-mates, umpires and journalists voted for the best Australian international player of the past 12 months. Previous winners were Glenn McGrath and Steve Waugh. In the remaining awards, voted on by fellow players, Hayden was also named Test Cricketer of the Year, with Ricky Ponting One-day International Player of the Year – five days before he was appointed captain of Australia's one-day team. Darren Lehmann of South Australia was State Player of the Year for the third time running, and Shane Watson of Tasmania won the Sir Donald Bradman Young Player of the Year award. Karen Rolton was the inaugural Women's International Cricketer of the Year.

CRICKET IN SOUTH AFRICA, 2001-02

By COLIN BRYDEN and ANDREW SAMSON

Martin van Jaarsveld

Cricket in South Africa found itself under a cloud in 2001-02. The national team had an often difficult and politically fraught season, which was followed by the shocking news of the death of Hansie Cronje, their disgraced former captain, in an air crash. They had begun the season with aspirations to replace Australia at the head of the ICC Test Championship, but ended it comprehensively beaten by them. The Test series in Australia concluded with a row over the application of racial quotas in team selection.

In July 2002, after a conference attended by more than 150 administrators, coaches and leading players, the United Cricket Board of South Africa took the bold decision to abandon the quota system at national and senior provincial level, and return to selecting first-class teams on merit. Introduced in 1999-2000, the system had required provinces to field at least one "player of colour" in all teams that year, rising to two the following season and three the next. The conference agreed that the transformation of South African cricket had been a resounding success: 66 players of colour played first-class cricket during 2001-02. For the non-first-class provincial B teams and all levels below, the quota system was replaced by two guidelines: teams should contain at least 50 per cent players of colour, and at least one black African.

Instead of applauding cricket for achieving a notable level of racial integration, the minister of sport, Ngconde Balfour, was openly sceptical, while the Youth League of the ruling African National Congress party threatened to disrupt the World Cup, to be staged in South Africa in February and March 2003, if quotas were not reinstated. After meeting cricket officials, who explained the rationale behind the change, Balfour set up his own committee of inquiry. Matters became more complex when Gerald Majola, the UCB's chief executive, appeared before a parliamentary sports committee. Majola explained that black players had objected to being labelled "quota players" and wanted to be recognised as selected on merit. But Ruth Bhengu, chairing the committee, raised the possibility of enforcing quotas through legislation. Relations between government and board worsened again when the UCB released, on the day the committee announced its recommendations, minutes of a meeting in which Balfour was quoted as saying he went to cricket to watch black players, such as Makhaya Ntini and Paul Adams. He said he did not go to watch white players. The committee advocated the reinstatement of quotas, but Balfour admitted he had no power to enforce the findings, which were rejected by Percy Sonn, the board president.

The conflict between cricket officials and political leaders came at a time when it seemed that serious rifts between players and administrators had been healed. They had reached a nadir during the disastrous tour of Australia, where South Africa lost all three Tests, when Sonn rejected the team selected for the Third Test at Sydney. He cited a 1998 policy document stating that a committee headed by the president could direct the selectors to pick players of colour after a series was decided. Through Sonn's intervention, Justin Ontong, a coloured player, made his debut in place of Jacques Rudolph.

Majola, who had not attended the Tests, met the players during the ensuing one-day tournament – which South Africa won. In April, after Australia's return visit, past and present players, selectors and administrators attended a conference on South African cricket, and took some far-reaching decisions. One of them was to establish a cricket committee, chaired by Majola, and including former Test players Omar Henry, Pat Symcox, Andrew Hudson and Craig Matthews, which was to nominate a new selection panel and make recommendations about team management. Majola said this acknowledged the lack of top cricket expertise on the UCB general council. The cricket committee soon announced changes: in May, Henry was named convenor of the selection panel, which also included Symcox. In June, Graham Ford, the national team coach, and Craig Smith, the physiotherapist, were replaced by Eric Simons, the Western Province coach who played in 23 one-day internationals, and Shane Jabaar.

In an unconnected move, the UCB had adopted a new constitution in April, restructuring the board and all its affiliates into separate amateur and professional arms, while a company, Cricket SA (Pty) Ltd, was formed to control professional cricket.

On the domestic playing field, KwaZulu-Natal swept the board, winning the first-class SuperSport Series and the Standard Bank limited-overs competition under the captaincy of Dale Benkenstein, who had also overseen their previous double in 1996-97. Benkenstein paid especial tribute to two West Indians: the coach, Eldine Baptiste, and overseas professional Nixon McLean, a last-minute replacement for Ottis Gibson. McLean took 44 wickets in eight first-class matches and 15 in the one-day tournament. A hamstring strain eventually forced him to bowl off a shortened run, but did not reduce his effectiveness.

KwaZulu-Natal's strength in depth compensated for the frequent absence of their international stars, Shaun Pollock and Lance Klusener. Jonty Rhodes retired from Test cricket and was available for five matches, in which he made 499 runs at 62.37. In the final, against Northerns, he redeemed a poor start on the first day with 74, then scored 154 in the second innings to eliminate the risk of defeat. KwaZulu-Natal needed only to draw to clinch the title, having topped the round-robin table. But the game ended controversially when Benkenstein batted on long after Northerns had any chance of winning. He made a career-best 259 and KwaZulu-Natal scored 754, a South African first-class record.

In fact, their most significant performance probably came in their last match in the Super Six league, visiting Western Province, the defending champions. KwaZulu-Natal started the game just four points ahead and, put in, slid to 48 for four before Benkenstein and Jon Kent led a recovery. An eventual 159-run win squeezed Western Province out of the final.

In the Standard Bank Cup, KwaZulu-Natal were unbeaten in their 13 games. They won a rain-affected final more convincingly than a 28-run margin suggested: Western Province's tailenders lifted them from a hopeless 103 for seven chasing KwaZulu-Natal's 223 for six.

Northerns, led by Gerald Dros, had sailed through the preliminaries of the Super-Sport Series, heading Pool B with four straight victories to KwaZulu-Natal's one. They had two of the stars of the season. Martin van Jaarsveld was named player of the tournament for his 934 SuperSport runs, scored at 84.90, and comfortably headed the national first-class averages with 1,268 at 74.58. Steve Elworthy, the seam bowler, was the leading wicket-taker in his 15th season, with 52 at 18.11. The left-handed Rudolph was another prolific run-scorer for Northerns, and unlucky not to play Test cricket. Even before his controversial omission at Sydney, he was picked for the Centurion Test against India, which was declared unofficial after India refused to accept the ICC referee, Mike Denness.

Western Province, who possessed the most talented squad in the country, lost momentum after winning Pool A in style. Eight of their players were required by South Africa, and Neil Johnson, the former Zimbabwe all-rounder, hardly bowled because of injury. But the left-handed opener Graeme Smith confirmed his rich potential, scoring heavily in both forms of the game – he amassed 738, including a century and seven fifties, in 12 one-day innings – and winning a national call-up. Andrew Puttick, another tall left-hander, demonstrated his talents in an unbeaten 229 against Boland. H. D. Ackerman, the captain, had an excellent season, and was invited to lead South Africa A against India A. Charl Willoughby, the left-arm opening bowler, was Western Province's leading wicket-taker, taking 41 in the SuperSport Series.

Easterns finished fourth in the first-class competition, but last in the one-day cup. The fast bowler Andre Nel and the all-rounder Andrew Hall earned Test debuts, while young players Albie Morkel, Pierre de Bruyn and Brendon Reddy showed promise.

Griqualand West qualified for the Super Six but, despite solid batting, their bowling seldom posed a threat, though the seamer, Zahir Abrahim, was consistent. The English-born Martyn Gidley, who played for Leicestershire from 1989 before settling in South Africa in the early 1990s, was outstanding, with career-best performances of 215 not out against Northerns and six for 45 with his off-spin against KwaZulu-Natal.

It was an unhappy season for Eastern Province. A power struggle became so bitter that most of the executive, including the president, Ronnie Pillay, resigned. UCB attempts to mediate ended in failure. In June, a high court order placed Eastern Province Cricket under judicial management until after the 2003 World Cup, during which they were to host a semi-final at Port Elizabeth. On the field, Eastern Province reached the Super Six but lost all five matches against the other qualifiers. In the one-day competition, where the all-rounder Robin Peterson especially thrived, they reached the semi-finals. Their batting was inconsistent, but the biggest problem was the bowling. Mfuneko Ngam played one match before breaking down, while national duties and injury restricted Nantie Hayward to two SuperSport games.

Free State, led by the former West Indies captain Jimmy Adams, made a wretched start, losing their first match to Northerns by an innings, and were condemned to play in the SuperSport Shield for the league pools' bottom five teams. However, they did win all four Shield games to take the trophy, though they finished tenth of 11 in the one-day competition. Nine batsmen averaged over 40, but the bowling lacked penetration. Their pace bowler, Dewald Pretorius, continued to improve, earning a Test cap, though Victor Mpitsang missed most of the season through injury. Johan van der Wath announced himself as an all-rounder of great promise.

Gauteng had another disappointing year. The batting was thin, apart from Adam Bacher and Marthinus Otto, and a knee injury sent the West Indian fast bowler, Franklyn Rose, home after five first-class matches, adding to the demands on David Terbrugge and 36-year-old Clive Eksteen. Rose's departure enabled their long-serving wicket-keeper, Nic Pothas, who had decided to settle in England, to return as an overseas player in the Standard Bank Cup. Gauteng suffered a sad blow in April: the pace bowler Walter Masimula died in England, where he had gone to play club cricket, aged 26.

Boland, North West and Border propped up the Shield table. Border's fall from grace was a surprise: they had reached the previous three SuperSport Series finals, but this time won only one game throughout the season, against Boland, who managed two wins elsewhere. North West's single victory came against Border; they did not have enough quality bowlers to succeed in first-class cricket, though they played well enough to reach the one-day semi-finals. Two left-handers, Graham Grace and Arno Jacobs, batted well in both competitions.

The season ended in heated debate about the future of domestic cricket. There was general agreement that there were too many professional teams, that they needed to be reduced to create a system of strength against strength, and that national players should appear in more domestic games. A task team under Gerald Majola was charged with investigating how to achieve these goals. **Colin Bryden**

FIRST-CLASS AVERAGES, 2001-02

BATTING

(Qualification: 8 completed innings, average 40.00)

	M	I	NO	R	HS	100s	Avge
M. van Jaarsveld (*Northerns*)	11	19	2	1,268	182*	5	74.58
J. N. Rhodes (*KwaZulu-Natal*)	5	8	0	499	172	2	62.37
J. H. Kallis (*South Africa*)	6	11	3	496	110	1	62.00
D. M. Benkenstein (*KwaZulu-Natal*)	8	12	0	713	259	3	59.41
G. Kirsten (*W. Province*)	7	13	1	710	244	1	59.16
H. D. Ackerman (*W. Province*)	10	16	4	695	140*	2	57.91
H. H. Gibbs (*W. Province*)	7	13	0	732	196	3	56.30
A. G. Puttick (*W. Province*)	9	16	3	720	229*	2	55.38
J. A. Beukes (*Free State*)	7	12	2	528	105	2	52.80
H. M. Amla (*KwaZulu-Natal*)	8	12	2	516	103	1	51.60
A. J. Hall (*Easterns*)	8	10	1	447	153	1	49.66
G. Dros (*Northerns*)	9	14	3	514	117*	1	46.72
M. I. Gidley (*Griqualand W.*)	8	16	2	651	215*	1	46.50
A. Jacobs (*North West*)	6	10	0	463	197	2	46.30
S. C. Pope (*Border*)	8	15	2	591	131	1	45.46
R. G. Arendse (*Free State*)	8	11	2	409	95	0	45.44
G. C. Smith (*W. Province*)	9	16	1	679	156	2	45.26
J. A. Rudolph (*Northerns*)	12	21	2	839	164	3	44.15
J. C. Adams (*Free State*)	8	12	1	479	124*	2	43.54
G. F. J. Liebenberg (*Free State*)	8	14	1	555	158	2	42.69
L. Klusener (*KwaZulu-Natal*)	6	8	0	340	108	1	42.50
A. M. Bacher (*Gauteng*)	9	17	0	711	132	3	41.82
W. Bossenger (*Griqualand W.*)	6	11	2	364	124*	1	40.44
J. M. Otto (*Gauteng*)	8	15	2	524	143	2	40.30

BOWLING

(Qualification: 25 wickets)

	O	M	R	W	BB	5W/i	Avge
N. A. M. McLean (*KwaZulu-Natal*)	264.4	82	716	44	6-84	3	16.27
A. Nel (*Easterns*)	327.2	97	769	46	6-25	3	16.71
S. Elworthy (*Northerns*)	321.4	85	942	52	6-45	3	18.11
C. M. Willoughby (*W. Province*)	333.1	94	849	44	6-44	2	19.29
A. C. Thomas (*North West*)	362.5	129	935	43	7-95	4	21.74
D. Pretorius (*Free State*)	300.2	69	981	42	6-49	4	23.35
M. I. Gidley (*Griqualand W.*)	250.2	51	662	28	6-45	2	23.64
H. S. Williams (*Boland*)	297.2	96	651	26	4-45	0	25.03
D. J. Terbrugge (*Gauteng*)	327.2	80	878	35	6-58	1	25.08
Z. A. Abrahim (*Griqualand W.*)	316.5	71	832	29	5-67	1	28.68
P. R. Adams (*W. Province*)	289.5	45	883	30	4-54	0	29.43
V. C. Drakes (*Border*)	291.3	78	741	25	5-25	1	29.64
C. W. Henderson (*W. Province*)	398.2	111	1,066	35	5-129	1	30.45
C. E. Eksteen (*Gauteng*)	367.5	93	867	26	4-70	0	33.34
A. C. Dawson (*W. Province*)	317.2	99	834	25	4-27	0	33.36
M. Ntini (*Border*)	273.3	57	987	28	6-37	1	35.25

SUPERSPORT SERIES, 2001-02

First Round

Pool A	Played	Won	Lost	Drawn	*Bonus Points* Batting	Bowling	Points
Western Province	5	3	0	2	18.18	16	64.18
Easterns	5	3	1	1	13.62	14	57.62
Griqualand West	5	2	2	1	20.86	14	54.86
Boland	5	1	1	3	12.34	12	34.34
Gauteng	5	1	2	2	8.72	11	29.72
North West	5	0	4	1	12.26	12	24.26

Pool B	Played	Won	Lost	Drawn	*Bonus Points* Batting	Bowling	Points
Northerns	4	4	0	0	13.62	16	69.62
Eastern Province	4	1	1	2	13.88	11	34.88
KwaZulu-Natal	4	1	1	2	8.60	14	32.60
Free State	4	0	1	3	12.96	8	20.96
Border	4	0	2	2	7.16	11	18.16

The top three teams from each pool advanced to the Super Six; the remaining five contested the Shield Series.

Super Six	Played	Won	Lost	Drawn	*Bonus Points* Batting	Bowling	Points
KwaZulu-Natal	5	4	1	0	16.72	20	76.72
Northerns	5	3	1	1	17.28	15	62.28
Western Province	5	3	1	1	18.04	12	60.04
Easterns	5	3	2	0	13.64	15	58.64
Griqualand West	5	1	4	0	18.28	14	42.28
Eastern Province	5	0	5	0	16.10	15	31.10

Super Six teams carried forward results and points gained against fellow-qualifiers in the first round, but not those gained against the teams eliminated.

Final

KwaZulu-Natal drew with Northerns, but won the SuperSport Series by virtue of heading the Super Six.

Shield Series	Played	Won	Lost	Drawn	*Bonus Points* Batting	Bowling	Points
Free State	4	4	0	0	10.18	16	71.42
Gauteng	4	1	1	2	8.26	14	38.20
Boland	4	1	2	1	8.54	9	34.41
North West	4	1	3	0	7.52	12	34.37
Border	4	1	2	1	8.70	9	32.24

Teams carried forward their average points gained per match in the first round.

Outright win = 10 pts.
Bonus points were awarded for the first 100 overs of each team's first innings. One batting point was awarded for the first 150 runs and 0.02 of a point for every subsequent run. One bowling point was awarded for the third wicket taken and for every subsequent two.

*In the following scores, * by the name of a team indicates that they won the toss.*

Pool A

At Kimberley, October 5, 6, 7, 8. **Drawn. Gauteng** 247 (A. M. Bacher 104, J. M. Otto 39, C. E. Eksteen 40; G. J. Kruis four for 40, Z. A. Abrahim three for 47) **and** 317 (A. M. Bacher 69, J. Buxton-Forman 37, J. M. Otto 55, C. E. Eksteen 38; Z. A. Abrahim four for 64); **Griqualand West*** 380 (M. I. Gidley 31, W. Bossenger 124 not out, Z. A. Abrahim 41, A. K. Kruger 54, G. J. Kruis 38, Extras 36; J. T. Mafa three for 100) **and 169 for nine** (M. I. Gidley 75; F. A. Rose three for 44, C. E. Eksteen three for 65). *Griqualand West 6.72 pts, Gauteng 6.70 pts.*

Johnson Mafa scored his first seven runs in first-class cricket in Gauteng's second innings – after six ducks and one nought not out.

At Potchefstroom, October 5, 6, 7. **Boland won by nine wickets. North West** 243 (G. V. Grace 47, D. J. J. de Vos 102; H. S. Williams three for 56, C. K. Langeveldt three for 52) **and** 179 (D. J. J. de Vos 45, A. C. Thomas 35; W. J. du Toit four for 66); **Boland*** 333 (J. L. Ontong 111, K. C. Jackson 50; J. N. Dreyer three for 90, A. C. Thomas five for 68) **and 92 for one** (J. M. Henderson 31 not out, J. G. Strydom 54 not out). *Boland 17.50 pts, North West 4.86 pts.*

At Cape Town, October 5, 6, 7, 8. **Western Province won by ten wickets. Easterns** 236 (J. A. Morkel 87 not out, B. L. Reddy 41; C. M. Willoughby three for 56) **and** 141 (C. M. Willoughby three for 15, P. R. Adams four for 54); **Western Province*** 336 (A. G. Puttick 45, H. D. Ackerman 31, I. J. L. Trott 93, T. L. Tsolekile 43, A. C. Dawson 51, R. Telemachus 31; R. E. Bryson four for 74, A. J. Hall three for 86) **and 42 for no wkt** (G. C. Smith 30 not out). *Western Province 16.96 pts, Easterns 4.72 pts.*

At Paarl, October 12, 13, 14, 15. **Griqualand West won by 49 runs. Griqualand West** 291 (B. H. Tucker 47, M. I. Gidley 58, W. Bossenger 44, J. Louw 34 not out; H. S. Williams four for 76, W. J. du Toit three for 55) **and** 271 (M. I. Gidley 64, P. P. J. Koortzen 32, L. L. Bosman 78; W. J. du Toit five for 98, A. A. W. Pringle three for 58); **Boland*** 302 (J. L. Ontong 135, K. C. Jackson 78 not out; G. J. Kruis four for 68) **and** 211 (H. Davids 52, J. L. Ontong 59; Z. A. Abrahim four for 55). *Griqualand West 15.82 pts, Boland 7.74 pts.*

Kenny Jackson became the first player to score 3,000 first-class runs for Boland.

At Benoni, October 12, 13, 14. **Easterns won by an innings and 15 runs. North West*** 226 (D. J. Jacobs 39, D. J. J. de Vos 55, M. C. Venter 41, M. Strydom 52; R. E. Bryson four for 45) **and** 205 (G. V. Grace 72, E. O. Moleon 31; A. Nel four for 21); **Easterns** 446 (A. J. Seymore 49, M. J. R. Rindel 82, D. N. Crookes 54, A. J. Hall 153, Extras 34; G. A. Roe three for 75, J. N. Dreyer four for 119). *Easterns 19.16 pts, North West 4.52 pts.*

North West wicket-keeper David Jacobs made six catches in Easterns' first innings.

At Johannesburg, October 12, 13, 14. **Western Province won by an innings and 81 runs. Gauteng*** 230 (A. M. Bacher 50, S. C. Cook 52, J. M. Otto 37, C. E. Eksteen 30; C. M. Willoughby four for 44) **and** 136 (M. R. Street 40, F. A. Rose 39; C. M. Willoughby three for 45, A. C. Dawson four for 27); **Western Province** 447 (R. Magiet 32, G. C. Smith 156, A. G. Puttick 51, N. C. Johnson 74, A. C. Dawson 32, Extras 37; J. T. Mafa three for 88). *Western Province 18.94 pts, Gauteng 3.60 pts.*

At Benoni, October 19, 20, 21, 22. **Easterns won by an innings and nine runs. Griqualand West** 258 (B. H. Tucker 36, M. I. Gidley 31, P. P. J. Koortzen 30, L. L. Bosman 34, M. J. Powell 75; J. A. Morkel five for 53) **and** 176 (B. H. Tucker 40, M. J. Powell 71; J. A. Morkel three for 25); **Easterns*** 443 (A. G. Botha 35, P. de Bruyn 95, A. J. Hall 93, D. Jennings 67, B. L. Reddy 109; G. J. Kruis four for 127, A. K. Kruger four for 87). *Easterns 17.72 pts, Griqualand West 6.16 pts.*

Brendon Reddy, aged 17 years 349 days, became the eighth player to score a first-class century batting at No. 10 in South African first-class cricket. He added 180, a ninth-wicket record for Easterns, with Jennings, the first Easterns wicket-keeper to take ten dismissals (nine caught, one stumped) in a match. In the first innings, Jennings made five catches, and Derek Crookes the other five.

At Johannesburg, October 19, 20, 21, 22. **Drawn. Boland** 267 (J. G. Strydom 110, W. J. Smit 90; D. J. Terbrugge six for 58) **and** 181 (A. W. Cyster 30; F. A. Rose six for 48, D. J. Terbrugge three for 40); **Gauteng*** 138 (H. S. Williams four for 45, W. J. du Toit three for 42) **and 175 for four** (S. C. Cook 64, N. J. Trainor 50). *Gauteng 3 pts, Boland 7.20 pts.*

At Potchefstroom, October 19, 20, 21, 22. **Drawn. North West 297** (M. Strydom 36, M. C. Venter 85, C. T. Enslin 32, E. O. Moleon 30; C. M. Willoughby five for 46, C. W. Henderson three for 80) **and 293 for nine dec.** (D. J. Jacobs 67, D. J. J. de Vos 47, A. C. Thomas 54 not out; C. M. Willoughby three for 57); **Western Province* 180** (I. J. L. Trott 45, N. C. Johnson 86; A. C. Thomas six for 20) **and 268 for four** (R. Magiet 50, A. G. Puttick 30, H. D. Ackerman 85 not out, N. C. Johnson 57 not out). *North West 7.94 pts, Western Province 5.60 pts.*

At Benoni, October 25, 26, 27, 28. **Drawn. Boland 12 for no wkt v Easterns***.

At Potchefstroom, October 25, 26, 27, 28. **Gauteng won by 29 runs. Gauteng* 271 for five dec.** (A. M. Bacher 132, N. J. Trainor 80) **and forfeited second innings**; **North West forfeited first innings and 242** (D. J. Jacobs 106, E. O. Moleon 38; C. E. Eksteen three for 80). *Gauteng 13.42 pts, North West 2 pts.*

At Cape Town, October 25, 26, 27, 28. **Western Province won by eight wickets. Griqualand West* 326** (B. H. Tucker 110, M. J. Powell 44, L. L. Bosman 89; C. M. Willoughby three for 68, P. R. Adams four for 78) **and 178** (M. I. Gidley 46, G. J. Kruis 36; C. M. Willoughby three for 44, P. R. Adams three for 42); **Western Province 368** (G. C. Smith 40, I. J. L. Trott 62, N. C. Johnson 62, T. L. Tsolekile 84; Z. A. Abrahim five for 67) **and 141 for two** (G. C. Smith 38, I. J. L. Trott 73 not out). *Western Province 17.74 pts, Griqualand West 7.14 pts.*

At Paarl, November 2, 3, 4, 5. **Drawn. Western Province* 492 for four dec.** (G. C. Smith 122, A. G. Puttick 229 not out, H. D. Ackerman 87) **and 136 for three dec.** (G. C. Smith 72, I. J. L. Trott 37); **Boland 374** (A. W. Cyster 52, J. M. Henderson 53, L. J. Koen 86, W. J. Smit 44, C. K. Langeveldt 33 not out, H. S. Williams 35; C. W. Henderson five for 129) **and 163 for five** (J. G. Strydom 34, H. Davids 60 not out). *Boland 1.90 pts, Western Province 4.94 pts.*
   Williams became Boland's leading first-class wicket-taker, passing 221 by Claude Henderson (now playing for Western Province). Puttick's 229 not out lasted 680 minutes and 482 balls and included 25 fours and one six.

At Johannesburg, November 2, 3, 4, 5. **Easterns won by 180 runs. Easterns 201 for eight dec.** (A. J. Seymore 79, D. N. Crookes 32, A. J. Hall 35; J. T. Mafa three for 37) **and 216** (A. J. Hall 42, J. A. Morkel 59; D. J. Terbrugge three for one, N. J. Trainor three for 42); **Gauteng* 118** (D. J. Cullinan 39; A. J. Hall four for 24) **and 119** (D. J. Cullinan 31; A. Nel six for 25). *Easterns 16.02 pts, Gauteng 3 pts.*

At Kimberley, November 2, 3, 4. **Griqualand West won by ten wickets. Griqualand West 444** (B. H. Tucker 30, P. P. J. Koertzen 164, W. Bossenger 57, A. P. McLaren 134; A. C. Thomas seven for 95) **and 56 for no wkt; North West* 247** (D. J. J. de Vos 95 not out, A. C. Thomas 35, E. O. Moleon 34; M. I. Gidley three for 58) **and 251** (D. J. J. de Vos 37, M. C. Venter 61, E. O. Moleon 33; Z. A. Abrahim four for 91, M. I. Gidley four for 49). *Griqualand West 19.02 pts, North West 4.94 pts.*

Pool B

At Port Elizabeth, October 5, 6, 7, 8. **Eastern Province won by eight wickets. Border 276** (S. C. Pope 44, D. L. Makalima 73; G. T. Love 51, V. C. Drakes 35; M. Hayward four for 92) **and 165** (P. C. Strydom 43, D. L. Makalima 40; M. Ngam three for 37, R. J. Peterson three for 54); **Eastern Province* 371 for nine dec.** (C. C. Bradfield 60, U. Abrahams 52, J. D. C. Bryant 38, D. J. Callaghan 80, M. R. Benfield 39; G. T. Love four for 120) **and 71 for two.** *Eastern Province 16.96 pts, Border 4.52 pts.*

At Bloemfontein, October 5, 6, 7, 8. **Northerns won by an innings and 52 runs. Northerns* 486 for five dec.** (A. N. Petersen 147, J. A. Rudolph 143, M. van Jaarsveld 125, J. G. Myburgh 31 not out; J. J. van der Wath three for 89); **Free State 228** (H. H. Dippenaar 33, J. C. Adams 48, R. G. Arendse 66 not out, D. Pretorius 30; S. Elworthy three for 58, D. H. Townsend three for 61, P. Joubert four for 46) **and 206** (L. J. Wilkinson 115; S. Elworthy three for 39, M. F. George three for 49, S. Abrahams three for 35). *Northerns 18.40 pts, Free State 2.54 pts.*

At East London, October 12, 13, 14, 15. **Drawn. Free State* 207** (J. A. Beukes 105; V. C. Drakes five for 25) **and 382 for two dec.** (J. F. Venter 73, G. F. J. Liebenberg 158, J. A. Beukes 101 not out, L. J. Wilkinson 30 not out); **Border 158** (P. J. Botha 50; J. J. van der Wath three for 38, D. Pretorius three for 52) **and 272 for three** (P. C. Strydom 77 not out, P. C. Strydom 55). *Border 5.16 pts, Free State 6.14 pts.*

Allan Donald of Free State played his 300th first-class match. Drakes became Border's leading first-class wicket-taker, passing Ian Howell's 207. Beukes was the sixth player to score twin first-class centuries for Free State, and the fourth of these to do it against Border.

At Durban, October 12, 13, 14, 15. **Northerns won by 28 runs. Northerns 106** (C. F. K. van Wyk 37; N. A. M. McLean five for 32, J. E. Bastow three for ten) **and 174** (A. N. Petersen 37, G. Dros 52; N. A. M. McLean five for 66, J. E. Bastow four for 57); **KwaZulu-Natal* 144** (R. Gobind 36, A. Mall 43; S. Elworthy six for 45, P. Joubert four for 23) **and 108** (G. H. Bodi 41; S. Elworthy four for 47, D. H. Townsend four for 27). *Northerns 14 pts, KwaZulu-Natal 4 pts.*

At Bloemfontein, October 19, 20, 21, 22. **Drawn. Free State* 506 for seven dec.** (G. F. J. Liebenberg 144, J. A. Beukes 39, L. J. Wilkinson 94, J. J. van der Wath 113 not out, C. E. Feris 30, A. A. Donald 47 not out, L. J. Wilkinson 66 not out); **KwaZulu-Natal 442** (D. J. Watson 71, J. C. Kent 31, D. M. Benkenstein 168, E. L. R. Stewart 114 not out, Extras 33; J. F. Venter three for 120). *Free State 6.04 pts, KwaZulu-Natal 5.42 pts.*

Wilkinson reached 6,000 first-class runs. Benkenstein and Stewart added 242 for KwaZulu-Natal's fifth wicket.

At Centurion, October 19, 20, 21. **Northerns won by ten wickets. Eastern Province* 211** (R. J. Peterson 62, D. W. Murray 48; M. F. George three for 60, D. H. Townsend three for 39) **and 271** (C. C. Bradfield 33, D. J. Callaghan 60, J. Botha 47; S. Elworthy four for 64); **Northerns 427** (A. N. Petersen 58, J. A. Rudolph 164, J. G. Myburgh 65, P. Joubert 31; B. B. Kops three for 97, J. Botha three for 63) **and 57 for no wkt.** *Northerns 19.68 pts, Eastern Province 4.22 pts.*

At East London, October 25, 26, 27, 28. **Drawn. KwaZulu-Natal 256 for eight dec.** (D. J. Watson 63, D. L. Brown 37, A. Mall 56 not out; T. Henderson three for 51, G. T. Love four for 79) **and 32 for no wkt; Border* 154** (P. C. Strydom 64 not out; N. A. M. McLean four for 53, J. E. Bastow three for 25). *Border 4.08 pts, KwaZulu-Natal 7.12 pts.*

At Port Elizabeth, October 25, 26, 27, 28. **Drawn. Eastern Province* 330** (C. C. Bradfield 30, K. D. Duckworth 137, D. J. Callaghan 36, J. Botha 40 not out; H. C. Bakkes three for 88, D. Pretorius four for 73) **and 122 for seven** (C. C. Bradfield 49; D. Pretorius three for 56); **Free State 387** (G. F. J. Liebenberg 69, J. A. Beukes 30, H. H. Dippenaar 42, J. C. Adams 111, R. G. Arendse 40, J. J. van der Wath 42, Extras 41; G. J-P. Kruger five for 138, B. B. Kops five for 89). *Eastern Province 4.86 pts, Free State 6.24 pts.*

Kevin Duckworth scored a century on first-class debut.

At Durban, November 2, 3, 4, 5. **KwaZulu-Natal won by two wickets. Eastern Province 342** (C. C. Bradfield 70, D. J. Callaghan 43, R. J. Peterson 64, J. Botha 52; N. A. M. McLean four for 62, A. N. W. Tweedie four for 99) **and 148** (J. D. C. Bryant 48, D. W. Murray 30; N. A. M. McLean four for 25, A. N. W. Tweedie four for 48); **KwaZulu-Natal* 203** (A. Mall 42, G. H. Bodi 58; J. M. Kemp five for 60, B. B. Kops three for 50) **and 288 for eight** (D. J. Watson 45, D. M. Benkenstein 90, E. L. R. Stewart 46; G. J-P. Kruger three for 96). *KwaZulu-Natal 16.06 pts, Eastern Province 8.84 pts.*

At Centurion, November 2, 3, 4. **Northerns won by 252 runs. Northerns* 307** (M. van Jaarsveld 52, J. G. Myburgh 41, P. Joubert 50, S. Elworthy 39, S. Abrahams 44; V. C. Drakes four for 63, T. Henderson four for 63) **and 292** (J. A. Rudolph 125, A. N. Petersen 51, S. Abrahams 34; G. T. Love three for 76); **Border 170** (M. L. Bruyns 102 not out, T. Henderson 34; S. Elworthy four for 64, D. M. Senekal three for 33) **and 177** (D. L. Makalima 45, L. L. Gamiet 50 not out, G. T. Love 36; S. Elworthy five for 57, D. M. Senekal three for 28). *Northerns 17.54 pts, Border 4.40 pts.*

Elworthy became Northerns' leading first-class wicket-taker, passing Jackie Botten's 320. Bruyns carried his bat through Border's first innings, when their total of 170 was the lowest containing a century in South African first-class cricket.

Super Six

At Durban, February 15, 16, 17, 18. **KwaZulu-Natal won by an innings and 123 runs. Easterns** 137 (A. J. Seymore 48, D. Brand 37; N. A. M. McLean four for 16, L. Klusener four for 36) **and** 183 (A. J. Seymore 40; A. N. W. Tweedie three for 37, R. B. MacQueen three for 29); **KwaZulu-Natal*** 443 for seven dec. (D. J. Watson 153, J. N. Rhodes 52, H. M. Amla 103, L. Klusener 33; J. A. Morkel three for 97). *KwaZulu-Natal 19.14 pts, Easterns 1 pt.*

Hashim Amla made a century on his SuperSport debut, having played one previous first-class match in 1999-2000.

At Centurion, February 15, 16, 17, 18. **Northerns won by seven wickets. Griqualand West*** 529 **for six dec.** (M. I. Gidley 215 not out, L. L. Bosman 121, P. P. J. Koortzen 57, W. Bossenger 73) **and 235 for four dec.** (B. H. Tucker 85, A. P. McLaren 112); **Northerns 423 for five dec.** (M. van Jaarsveld 182 not out, N. D. McKenzie 81, G. Dros 63, C. F. K. van Wyk 36 not out, Extras 36) **and 342 for three** (J. G. Myburgh 39, M. van Jaarsveld 158 not out, G. Dros 93 not out). *Northerns 16.34 pts, Griqualand West 7.36 pts.*

Van Jaarsveld scored 340 runs in the match, a South African record, passing 337 (in one innings) by Daryll Cullinan for Transvaal v Northern Transvaal at Johannesburg in 1993-94. He was the second batsman, after Mark Rushmere (150 not out and 151 not out for South African Invitation XI v English XI at Pietermaritzburg in 1989-90) to score 150 twice in the same match in South Africa. The match aggregate of 1,529 runs was a South African interprovincial record, beating 1,456 by Griqualand West and Natal at Kimberley in 1925-26. Gidley's 215 not out lasted 603 minutes and 424 balls and included 18 fours and three sixes.

At Cape Town, February 15, 16, 17, 18. **Western Province won by 90 runs. Western Province*** 504 **for eight dec.** (H. H. Gibbs 53, G. Kirsten 244, H. D. Ackerman 59, R. Munnik 30; J. M. Kemp three for 104) **and 189 for four dec.** (G. Kirsten 72, I. J. L. Trott 63); **Eastern Province** 404 for nine dec. (C. C. Bradfield 50, J. D. C. Bryant 90, D. J. Callaghan 72, Z. Homani 40, J. M. Kemp 52 not out; P. L. Harris three for 131) **and 199** (C. C. Bradfield 79, J. D. C. Bryant 50; C. M. Willoughby six for 44). *Western Province 16.28 pts, Eastern Province 4.62 pts.*

Wicket-keeper Zwelibanzi Homani made five dismissals in Western Province's first innings on first-class debut. Kirsten's 244 lasted 450 minutes and 373 balls and included 37 fours and two sixes. Willoughby took a hat-trick in Eastern Province's second innings.

At Benoni, March 8, 9, 10, 11. **Easterns won by 330 runs. Easterns*** 293 (D. Brand 62, A. J. Seymore 83, Extras 31; R. J. Peterson four for 64) **and 345 for eight dec.** (A. J. Seymore 54, A. M. van den Berg 34, B. L. Reddy 56, J. A. Morkel 85, D. Jennings 31 not out, M. R. Sekhoto 39 not out; G. J-P. Kruger three for 68, R. J. Peterson three for 90); **Eastern Province 236** (D. J. Callaghan 100, Z. Homani 32; A. Nel four for 50, J. A. Morkel three for 68) **and 72** (A. Nel four for 22, A. G. Botha three for 17). *Easterns 17.86 pts, Eastern Province 6.72 pts.*

At Kimberley, March 8, 9, 10, 11. **KwaZulu-Natal won by ten wickets. Griqualand West*** 233 (E. E. Meyer 73, J. Louw 86 not out; L. Klusener five for 56) **and 161** (B. H. Tucker 32, C. Pietersen 31 not out; L. Klusener five for 51); **KwaZulu-Natal 391** (D. J. Watson 33, M. Amla 57, J. N. Rhodes 172, H. M. Amla 56, E. L. R. Stewart 38 not out; M. I. Gidley six for 45) **and four for no wkt.** *KwaZulu-Natal 19.40 pts, Griqualand West 5.66 pts.*

At Centurion, March 8, 9, 10, 11. **Drawn. Northerns*** 394 for nine dec. (J. A. Rudolph 39, M. van Jaarsveld 49, J. G. Myburgh 51, G. Dros 50, P. Joubert 112 not out, C. F. K. van Wyk 30; R. Telemachus three for 69, C. M. Willoughby three for 110, C. W. Henderson three for 92) **and 205 for seven dec.** (M. van Jaarsveld 45, G. Dros 50; A. C. Dawson three for 60); **Western Province 178** (L. D. Ferreira 56, J. J. McLean 38; S. Elworthy six for 50) **and 337 for seven** (A. G. Puttick 107, H. D. Ackerman 140 not out; M. F. George three for 73). *Northerns 7.88 pts, Western Province 3.56 pts.*

At Port Elizabeth, March 15, 16, 17, 18. **Griqualand West won by 14 runs. Griqualand West** 248 (B. H. Tucker 92, M. I. Gidley 38, A. P. McLaren 30, J. Louw 33; G. J-P. Kruger three for 75, J. M. Kemp three for 33, J. Botha three for 53) **and 215** (P. P. J. Koortzen 31, A. P. McLaren 45, Extras 39; B. B. Kops four for 40); **Eastern Province*** 298 (C. C. Bradfield 71, M. L. Price 52, B. R. Friderichs 48; M. I. Gidley three for 64) **and 151** (M. L. Price 40, B. R. Friderichs 49 not out; M. I. Gidley five for 60, J. Louw three for 33). *Griqualand West 15.96 pts, Eastern Province 6.70 pts.*

At Benoni, March 15, 16, 17, 18. **Easterns won by nine wickets. Easterns* 439** (A. M. van den Berg 41, D. Jennings 31, P. de Bruyn 185, J. A. Morkel 31, M. R. Sekhoto 63 not out) **and 52 for one** (D. Brand 34 not out); **Northerns 219** (M. van Jaarsveld 62, J. G. Myburgh 52, S. Elworthy 48; A. Nel six for 56, A. G. Botha three for 66) **and 271** (A. N. Petersen 65, M. van Jaarsveld 50, J. G. Myburgh 52, C. F. K. van Wyk 36 not out; A. Nel three for 57, A. M. van den Berg four for 50). *Easterns 17.34 pts, Northerns 4.38 pts.*

Steve Elworthy played his 94th first-class match for Northerns, passing Anton Ferreira's record. Dylan Jennings passed Brian Randall's record of 68 wicket-keeping dismissals for Easterns.

At Cape Town, March 16, 17, 18, 19. **KwaZulu-Natal won by 159 runs. KwaZulu-Natal 374** (D. M. Benkenstein 145, J. C. Kent 92, L. Klusener 68; C. W. Henderson four for 97) **and 272** (H. M. Amla 32, J. C. Kent 48, L. Klusener 59, D. L. Brown 34, G. H. Bodi 50; R. Telemachus three for 62, C. W. Henderson three for 105); **Western Province* 275** (R. Magiet 54, A. G. Puttick 58, H. D. Ackerman 81; L. Klusener three for 53) **and 212** (A. G. Puttick 86, J. J. McLean 33, A. C. Dawson 48; L. Klusener three for 55). *KwaZulu-Natal 18.12 pts, Western Province 5.50 pts.*

FINAL

KWAZULU-NATAL v NORTHERNS

At Durban, April 11, 12, 13, 14, 15. Drawn. KwaZulu-Natal won the SuperSport Series by virtue of heading the Super Six. Toss: Northerns.

A draw would give KwaZulu-Natal the title, and that was what Benkenstein ensured with their second-innings 754, a South African record. He was criticised for batting on long after Northerns had any chance, but insisted he had to avoid risk – even on the fifth morning, 415 ahead. By then, the pitch had eased, but it was initially lively, offering instant rewards in damp conditions. Elworthy removed both openers in three balls, reduced KwaZulu-Natal to 80 for five just after lunch, and bowled Rhodes with a no-ball. Rhodes survived to score 74, supported by Stewart.

HIGHEST TOTALS INVOLVING SOUTH AFRICAN TEAMS

754	**KwaZulu-Natal v Northerns at Durban (third innings of match)** . .	**2001-02**
692	South Africans v Cambridge University at Cambridge (first innings) . .	1901
676	MCC v Griqualand West at Kimberley (first innings)	1938-39
664-6 dec.	Natal v Western Province at Durban (second innings)	1936-37
663-6 dec.	South Africans v Arosa Sri Lanka at Cape Town (second innings)	1982-83
654-5	England v South Africa at Durban (fourth innings)	1938-39
652-7 dec.	**Australia v South Africa at Johannesburg (first innings)**	**2001-02**
640-5 dec.	Gauteng v Griqualand West at Kimberley (second innings)	1999-2000

Next morning, McLean had Northerns at 25 for four, but van Jaarsveld was undaunted; he batted for six and a half hours before he was last out, his stand of 50 with Smith stretching the lead to 72. But heart palpitations soon forced Smith out of Northerns' attack as Rhodes regained control, sharing century partnerships with both Amla brothers. When he fell, Benkenstein took over, scoring a career-best 259 in 594 minutes and 449 balls, with 26 fours and four sixes. On the final day, he extended his stand with Bodi to 171, then added 93 with the last man, Tweedie. "Come on guys," exhorted McKenzie, as Tweedie took KwaZulu-Natal past 700, "a wicket always falls on 702." But it didn't. When McKenzie finally ran out Benkenstein, there were only eight overs to play.

Man of the Match: J. N. Rhodes. *Man of the Series:* M. van Jaarsveld.

Close of play: First day, Northerns 7-1 (Rudolph 0, van Jaarsveld 1); Second day, Northerns 286; Third day, KwaZulu-Natal 296-3 (Rhodes 125, Benkenstein 0); Third day, KwaZulu-Natal 487-7 (Benkenstein 93, Bodi 3).

KwaZulu-Natal

D. J. Watson b Elworthy	2	– c Dros b Smith	12
A. M. Amla lbw b Elworthy	0	– b Abrahams	75
J. N. Rhodes b George	74	– b George	154
H. M. Amla lbw b Elworthy	8	– b Elworthy	74
*D. M. Benkenstein c van Jaarsveld b Joubert	13	– run out	259
J. C. Kent c van Wyk b Elworthy	2	– c van Jaarsveld b Elworthy	20
†E. L. R. Stewart c Rudolph b George	45	– c van Wyk b Elworthy	3
S. M. Pollock c van Wyk b George	24	– c van Wyk b Abrahams	34
G. H. Bodi c McKenzie b Joubert	13	– c van Wyk b McKenzie	44
N. A. M. McLean c Rudolph b George	13	– c Elworthy b Rudolph	11
A. N. W. Tweedie not out	5	– not out	36
L-b 8, w 1, n-b 6	15	B 10, l-b 4, w 6, n-b 12	32

1/2 2/5 3/22 4/46 5/80   214   1/13 2/165 3/296 4/355 5/399   754
6/123 7/161 8/195 9/197   6/407 7/470 8/641 9/661

Bowling: *First Innings*—Elworthy 17–4–46–4; Smith 13–3–46–0; Joubert 20–10–53–2; George 14.3–3–61–4. *Second Innings*—Elworthy 39–9–117–3; Smith 12–1–38–1; George 41–9–123–1; Joubert 41–6–118–0; Abrahams 68–12–194–2; Rudolph 16–2–60–1; McKenzie 17–1–62–1; van Jaarsveld 7.2–0–28–0.

Northerns

A. N. Petersen c Pollock b McLean	0		
J. A. Rudolph c A. M. Amla b Pollock	5	– not out	22
M. van Jaarsveld b Kent	155		
N. D. McKenzie c Stewart b McLean	0		
*G. Dros lbw b McLean	1		
P. Joubert c Stewart b Pollock	32	– (1) not out	10
†C. F. K. van Wyk c Stewart b Kent	41		
S. Abrahams c H. M. Amla b McLean	7		
S. Elworthy b McLean	0		
M. F. George c Stewart b McLean	5		
G. J. Smith not out	25		
B 4, l-b 4, w 3, n-b 4	15	B 2, n-b 1	3

1/4 2/20 3/23 4/25 5/109   286   (0 wkt) 35
6/209 7/229 8/229 9/236

Bowling: *First Innings*—McLean 25–6–84–6; Pollock 27–15–31–2; Tweedie 14–2–68–0; Kent 15.1–4–43–2; Benkenstein 4–1–4–0; Bodi 12–1–48–0. *Second Innings*—Tweedie 4–0–25–0; Pollock 3–0–8–0; Watson 1–1–0–0.

Umpires: I. L. Howell and B. G. Jerling. Third umpire: S. Wadvalla.

CHAMPIONS

Currie Cup		1903-04	Transvaal
1889-90	Transvaal	1904-05	Transvaal
1890-91	Kimberley	1906-07	Transvaal
1892-93	Western Province	1908-09	Western Province
1893-94	Western Province	1910-11	Natal
1894-95	Transvaal	1912-13	Natal
1896-97	Western Province	1920-21	Western Province
1897-98	Western Province	1921-22	Transvaal/Natal/W. Prov. (Tied)
1902-03	Transvaal	1923-24	Transvaal

1925-26	Transvaal	1976-77	Natal
1926-27	Transvaal	1977-78	Western Province
1929-30	Transvaal	1978-79	Transvaal
1931-32	Western Province	1979-80	Transvaal
1933-34	Natal	1980-81	Natal
1934-35	Transvaal	1981-82	Western Province
1936-37	Natal	1982-83	Transvaal
1937-38	Natal/Transvaal (Tied)	1983-84	Transvaal
1946-47	Natal	1984-85	Transvaal
1947-48	Natal	1985-86	Western Province
1950-51	Transvaal	1986-87	Transvaal
1951-52	Natal	1987-88	Transvaal
1952-53	Western Province	1988-89	Eastern Province
1954-55	Natal	1989-90	E. Province/W. Province
1955-56	Western Province		(Shared)
1958-59	Transvaal		
1959-60	Natal	*Castle Cup*	
1960-61	Natal	1990-91	Western Province
1962-63	Natal	1991-92	Eastern Province
1963-64	Natal	1992-93	Orange Free State
1965-66	Natal/Transvaal (Tied)	1993-94	Orange Free State
1966-67	Natal	1994-95	Natal
1967-68	Natal	1995-96	Western Province
1968-69	Transvaal		
1969-70	Transvaal/W. Province (Tied)	*SuperSport Series*	
1970-71	Transvaal	1996-97	Natal
1971-72	Transvaal	1997-98	Free State
1972-73	Transvaal	1998-99	Western Province
1973-74	Natal	1999-2000	Gauteng
1974-75	Western Province	2000-01	Western Province
1975-76	Natal	2001-02	KwaZulu-Natal

Transvaal/Gauteng have won the title outright 25 times, Natal/KwaZulu-Natal 21, Western Province 17, Orange Free State/Free State 3, Eastern Province 2, Kimberley 1. The title has been shared five times as follows: Transvaal 4, Natal and Western Province 3, Eastern Province 1.

Shield Series

At Paarl, February 15, 16, 17, 18. **Drawn. Gauteng* 354 for seven dec.** (A. M. Bacher 49, J. M. Otto 143, M. R. Street 31, S. Masengemi 36 not out; H. S. Williams three for 36) **and 220 for four dec.** (S. C. Cook 101 not out, M. R. Street 62 not out); **Boland 293** (J. G. Strydom 120, S. J. Palframan 39, Extras 38; D. J. Terbrugge three for 56, C. E. Eksteen three for 64) **and 259 for eight** (J. G. Strydom 84, J. L. Ontong 41, H. Davids 49 not out, B. Hector 39; D. J. Terbrugge four for 73). *Boland 4.86 pts, Gauteng 5.62 pts.*

Wicket-keeper Street took six catches in Boland's second innings.

At Bloemfontein, February 15, 16, 17. **Free State won by seven wickets. Border 94** (A. A. Donald three for 14, W. R. Visagie five for 49) **and 208** (M. L. Bruyns 46, P. C. Strydom 32; D. Pretorius five for 81, N. Boje four for 45); **Free State* 97** (M. N. van Wyk 40 not out; M. Ntini six for 37) **and 206 for three** (H. H. Dippenaar 102 not out, R. G. Arendse 53 not out). *Free State 14 pts, Border 4 pts.*

Makhaya Ntini took a hat-trick in Free State's first innings. He also took a hat-trick in his previous SuperSport match at this ground in 1999-2000.

 Every ten years or so, a seismic shock rocks Gloucestershire's foundations only for things to return gradually to normal. So it was in 2002.
Gloucestershire, page 623

At Paarl, February 22, 23. **Boland won by seven wickets. North West 156** (M. C. Venter 31, A. C. Thomas 57 not out; W. J. du Toit three for 42) **and 77** (H. S. Williams three for 18, C. D. de Lange three for 21, K. C. Jackson three for 19); **Boland* 187** (K. C. Jackson 34, S. J. Palframan 41; A. C. Thomas six for 45) **and 48 for three**. *Boland 15.74 pts, North West 5.12 pts.*

North West's 77 was their lowest total in the SuperSport Series.

At East London, February 22, 23, 24, 25. **Drawn. Gauteng 368** (S. C. Cook 48, A. M. Bacher 108, W. A. Dugmore 54, D. J. Cullinan 94; V. C. Drakes three for 61, T. Henderson four for 60) **and 263 for six dec.** (A. M. Bacher 69, J. M. Otto 132 not out); **Border* 261** (M. L. Bruyns 44, S. C. Pope 79, T. Henderson 30 not out; A. A. Mohammed five for 74) **and 204 for two** (B. L. Bennett 85, M. L. Bruyns 45, S. C. Pope 58 not out). *Border 4.22 pts, Gauteng 7.58 pts.*

At East London, March 1, 2, 3, 4. **Border won by 11 runs. Border 262** (M. L. Bruyns 34, S. C. Pope 131, C. B. Sugden 39; C. D. de Lange five for 65) **and 298 for eight dec.** (S. C. Pope 55, P. C. Strydom 135 not out; C. D. de Lange four for 67); **Boland* 283** (T. A. Davids 52, L. J. Koen 86, S. J. Palframan 65 not out; V. C. Drakes four for 62) **and 266** (H. Davids 83, B. Hector 56, S. J. Palframan 74 not out; V. C. Drakes three for 41, M. Ntini three for 58, G. T. Love three for 76). *Border 15.64 pts, Boland 4.94 pts.*

Mark Boucher made six dismissals (five caught, one stumped) in Boland's second innings.

At Potchefstroom, March 1, 2, 3, 4. **Free State won by ten wickets. Free State* 450 for nine dec.** (J. A. Beukes 87, J. C. Adams 92, R. G. Arendse 95, N. Boje 46, H. C. Bakkes 58 not out) **and 13 for no wkt; North West 156** (A. Jacobs 38; H. C. Bakkes three for 25, J. J. van der Wath four for 50) **and 306** (G. V. Grace 72, A. Jacobs 65, M. C. Venter 74; N. Boje five for 105). *Free State 17.38 pts, North West 2.12 pts.*

At Bloemfontein, March 8, 9, 10, 11. **Free State won by an innings and 95 runs. Free State 362** (G. F. J. Liebenberg 63, J. A. Beukes 82, H. H. Dippenaar 35, N. Boje 39, M. N. van Wyk 82; K. C. Jackson five for 42); **Boland* 132** (J. M. Henderson 55; J. J. van der Wath six for 37, W. R. Visagie three for 35) **and 135** (H. Davids 56; N. Boje six for 31). *Free State 17 pts, Boland 2 pts.*

At Johannesburg, March 8, 9, 10, 11. **Gauteng won by 94 runs. Gauteng 253** (S. C. Cook 36, W. A. Dugmore 62, J. M. Otto 30, A. A. Mohammed 44 not out; A. C. Thomas three for 56, E. O. Moleon five for 60) **and 337 for eight dec.** (A. M. Bacher 30, W. A. Dugmore 95, M. R. Street 57, S. Masengemi 69, G. D. Elliott 49); **North West* 191** (C. Light 45, D. J. J. de Vos 56; D. J. Terbrugge three for 47, G. D. Elliott three for 35) **and 305** (A. Jacobs 105, A. C. Thomas 52, T. A. Bula 39; C. E. Eksteen three for 66). *Gauteng 17.06 pts, North West 5.82 pts.*

Eksteen became Gauteng's leading first-class wicket-taker, passing Clive Rice's 366. North West wicket-keeper Bula took six catches in Gauteng's first innings.

At Johannesburg, March 15, 16, 17, 18. **Free State won by 323 runs. Free State* 320** (J. C. Adams 43, R. G. Arendse 91, J. J. van der Wath 87; S. Burger five for 78, C. E. Eksteen four for 70) **and 245 for two dec.** (H. H. Dippenaar 100 not out, J. C. Adams 124 not out); **Gauteng 139** (Extras 30; J. J. van der Wath three for 51, N. Boje three for 34) **and 103** (D. Pretorius five for 24, N. Boje three for 26). *Free State 17.80 pts, Gauteng 2 pts.*

At Potchefstroom, March 15, 16, 17, 18. **North West won by nine wickets. North West 522** (D. J. Jacobs 123, G. V. Grace 35, A. Jacobs 197, D. J. J. de Vos 30, M. C. Venter 34, Extras 42; G. T. Love four for 129) **and 29 for one; Border* 302** (S. C. Pope 39, C. B. Sugden 132 not out, T. Henderson 45; A. Roe three for 46, A. C. Thomas three for 108, D. J. J. de Vos three for 37) **and 246** (W. R. Hinkel 34, G. T. Love 73, S. M. Nelani 37; G. A. Roe five for 47). *North West 16.46 pts, Border 3.84 pts.*

North West's 522 was their highest total in first-class cricket, and Arno Jacobs's 197 their highest individual score.

India A's first-class matches appear in Other A-Team Tours, pages 1426-1428.

STANDARD BANK CUP, 2001-02

Note: Matches in this section were not first-class.

	Played	Won	Lost	Tied	No Result	Bonus Points	Points	Net run-rate
KwaZulu-Natal	10	8	0	0	2	1	37	0.65
Western Province . . .	10	6	3	0	1	2	28	0.16
North West	10	5	4	0	1	3	25	0.32
Eastern Province . . .	10	5	4	1	0	1	23	0.19
Northerns	10	4	3	2	1	1	23	−0.07
Gauteng	10	4	4	0	2	0	20	−0.52
Border	10	3	5	1	1	3	19	0.36
Boland	10	3	4	0	3	1	19	−0.05
Griqualand West . . .	10	3	5	0	2	1	17	−0.58
Free State	10	3	7	0	0	2	14	0.00
Easterns	10	1	6	0	3	0	10	−0.77

Eastern Province finished ahead of Northerns by virtue of more wins. Border finished ahead of Boland by virtue of winning the match between them.

Semi-finals

In the best-of-three semi-finals, KwaZulu-Natal beat Eastern Province 2–0 and Western Province beat North West 2–0.

Final

At Durban, February 8 (day/night). **KwaZulu-Natal won by 28 runs. KwaZulu-Natal 223 for six** (45 overs) (D. M. Benkenstein 77 not out, E. L. R. Stewart 53; Q. Friend three for 52); **Western Province* 195 for nine** (45 overs) (A. G. Puttick 51, A. C. Dawson 52 not out; N. A. M. McLean three for 35, A. N. W. Tweedie four for 33).

CRICKET IN THE WEST INDIES, 2001-02

BY TONY COZIER

Mahendra Nagamootoo

West Indian cricket came no closer to solving the problems behind its steady decline. The West Indies Cricket Board reported an operating loss of $US7.5m for the year ending September 2001, following a deficit of $US5.4m the previous year. As the board president, Wes Hall, observed, they could expect further shortfalls, since the ICC had reformed the once-lucrative bilateral arrangements for overseas tours. There were similar setbacks on the field and controversy off it concerning the behaviour of A-team players on tour and the management of the new Cricket Academy.

One consequence was the dismissal in October 2002 of the board's chief executive, Gregory Shillingford. He had been appointed two years earlier, under the previous WICB administration headed by Pat Rousseau, to succeed the long-serving Stephen Camacho. The board said the decision followed a report from the review and assessment committee on Shillingford's performance. The chief marketing executive, Roger Brathwaite, stepped in as acting chief executive.

On the field, West Indies lost five successive Tests against Sri Lanka and Pakistan, extending a dismal overseas record to 23 defeats in 27 Tests. A hard-fought series at home with India produced a satisfying 2–1 triumph, only to be compromised by a convincing victory for New Zealand, their first in four tours of the Caribbean.

Even before that, the board decided to change the selection panel for the first time in four years. Joey Carew, a selector on and off for 28 years, was the only one retained, while two stars of the all-conquering 1980s team came in: Sir Viv Richards, replacing Michael Findlay as chairman, and Gordon Greenidge, for their one-time team-mate Joel Garner.

There was soon further cause for concern. Garner and Gus Logie, the manager and coach of the West Indies A team which toured Ireland, England and Canada in July and August, said this was the most difficult of the four A-team tours they had undertaken. In a party whose ages ranged from teens to mid-20s, six had already played Tests or one-day internationals: they represented the immediate future of West Indies cricket. But Garner and Logie commented adversely on their discipline and behaviour: three players were fined for breaches of the board's code of conduct. Most worryingly, they did not interact well with each other, which Logie said was fuelled by inter-island rivalry. "They see themselves competing with their own players," he said, "and that brings about distrust." Such rivalry has never been far below the surface of West Indies cricket, but past captains such as Sir Frank Worrell and Clive Lloyd deliberately and successfully tackled the problem.

Another hope for the future became a worry when the fledgling Shell Cricket Academy, established in 2001, was severely criticised. A joint venture between the

West Indian board and St George's University in Grenada, the Academy ran a two-month programme for 24 young West Indian players and two each from Bermuda, Canada and the United States. Michael Seepersaud, the board's new cricket development officer, decided that local coaching techniques were outdated, and employed two experienced Australians – Ashleigh Byron and Tim Coyle – to conduct a week-long workshop in March. They also spent three weeks at the Academy, after which they presented a scathing report.

Byron and Coyle recommended that the Academy's tenure be terminated and that its staff should have no further involvement with the WICB. The Barbadian director, Rudi Webster, a former fast bowler for Warwickshire and Otago and recently the Test team's "motivator", said he was seeking legal counsel after they described him as "an unqualified and unaccredited coach". The Australians advised the board to move the Academy to another location and "take over total control as a dedicated budget programme under the management of a cricket chief development officer". The WICB said they were conducting a thorough review of the Academy's programme and facilities, but still viewed it as "a critical investment in the sustainable development of West Indies cricket".

On the field, regional first-class cricket continued in the format established in 2000-01: a round-robin league played by the six traditional territories, plus West Indies B (the Under-23 development side) and an invited foreign team (Bangladesh A), followed by a knockout for the top four. Jamaica regained the regional title by heading the Busta Cup table, but lost the Busta International Shield to Guyana, who took first-innings lead in the drawn final – reversing the previous season's result. Guyana had also won the limited-overs Red Stripe Bowl in October 2001.

Between an unconvincing draw with the Windward Islands and the Shield final, Jamaica enjoyed seven successive outright wins. Although Jimmy Adams and Franklyn Rose had gone to South Africa, Courtney Walsh had retired, and a knee injury ruled out Marlon Samuels, their all-round captain triumphed. The captain, Robert Samuels, instilled a fine team spirit and enjoyed a vintage season, with 572 runs at an average of 52. The little opener Leon Garrick also topped 500, including two centuries. But bowling was Jamaica's chief strength. They reached 300 only four times in nine matches, yet conceded 300 only three times. Off-spinner Gareth Breese collected 44 Busta wickets, and young fast bowlers Darren Powell and Jermaine Lawson were both called up by West Indies. The stalwart medium-pacer Laurie Williams, aged 33, headed the national averages with 26 wickets at 19.19; tragically, he was killed in a car crash in September, along with his younger brother.

Guyana were a little fortunate to reach the Shield final. Carl Hooper, their captain when not doing the job for West Indies, scored 222 as they amassed 491 in the semi-final against the Leeward Islands. But Stuart Williams responded with 252 not out, and at 442 for five midway through the last day Leewards were heading for a decisive first-innings lead. Then rain intervened. As Guyana were ranked higher in the Busta Cup table, they met Jamaica in the final for the second year running, and claimed the Shield after Hooper confirmed his quality with a masterly 149. Guyana had had to cope without three leading batsmen in their first four games: Hooper and Shivnarine Chanderpaul were on Test duty, and Ramnaresh Sarwan, named most valuable player in the one-day tournament, was recuperating from a back injury until March. They lost their opening matches, against Barbados and Jamaica, but recovered to record four victories, interrupted by a draw against West Indies B, who inflicted an embarrassing follow-on.

Mahendra Nagamootoo took 50 wickets in the Busta competitions, a regional tournament record, eclipsing 48 by his fellow leg-spinner, Rajindra Dhanraj, for Trinidad & Tobago in 1995-96. Another highlight was an opening partnership of 340, a Guyanese record, between Azeemul Haniff, who hit 235, and Sewnarine Chattergoon against Bangladesh A.

The Leeward Islands might have been denied the final by the weather, but they had lost heavily to Jamaica and Guyana in earlier rounds. Their captain, Stuart Williams, was the leading scorer in Busta cricket with 974 runs at 97.40, including 195 against

Barbados and that unbeaten 252 against Guyana. It was Leewards' highest first-class score, beating Sylvester Joseph's 211 not out against West Indies B the previous month. His efforts earned him a brief Test recall.

In Adam Sanford, a Dominican-born Antiguan policeman, Leewards found an outstanding new player. A direct descendant of the Caribs, after whom the region is named, Sanford had played one previous first-class match, for Windwards in 1996-97. Making his Leewards debut aged 25, he demonstrated a muscular strength and lively pace that brought him 41 Busta wickets and a place in all seven home Tests, where he got 20 more, to become the season's leading first-class wicket-taker. Kerry Jeremy's medium-pace swing collected 40 Busta wickets without attracting the same attention.

Trinidad & Tobago finished joint fourth on points with Barbados, who had more outright wins – but Trinidad had won their head-to-head match, and advanced to the semi-finals, where they lost to Jamaica. They saw little of their Test players. Brian Lara missed the campaign with an injured elbow, Merv Dillon played one match, and Daren Ganga and Dinanath Ramnarine three each. The experienced Richard Smith was a rock in the middle order, passing 500 runs, as did the opener, Imran Jan, while Dwayne Bravo, aged 18, and Lendl Simmons, the 17-year-old nephew of Test all-rounder Phil, showed their potential after returning from the Under-19 World Cup. The pace of Marlon Black, with 37 Busta wickets, and the off-spin of Mukesh Persad were the mainstays of an otherwise inexperienced attack.

It was a distressing season for Barbados, the 2000-01 Busta Cup champions. They suffered three successive losses in February, starting with their first by the Windward Islands in 19 years – on their home turf at Kensington Oval – and concluding with the defeat by Trinidad & Tobago which kept them out of the semi-finals. They continued to rely on ageing players, though there were some hopeful signs: maiden hundreds by Kurt Wilkinson and Dwayne Smith, and the spin of Sulieman Benn (left-arm orthodox) and Ryan Austin (off-breaks). Smith was 19, the other three 20 years old.

The most encouraging individual advance was made by another Smith. The dashing style of Devon Smith, a 20-year-old opener from Grenada, had captivated spectators on West Indies Under-19's tour of England in 2001. Returning to the Windward Islands, he added consistency to score 750 runs in the Busta Cup at 62.50, including 143, his maiden century, in the victory over Barbados. Junior Murray scored four hundreds, a Windwards record, to earn a temporary recall as West Indies' wicket-keeper. Neither he nor Smith could lift Windwards very far up the table; only Bangladesh A and West Indies B were below them. But two victories represented a distinct improvement on 2000-01, when they lost all seven matches.

The foreign visitors, Bangladesh A, never emulated the success of England A, who reached the semi-finals the previous year. The team, who had an average age of 22, found acclimatisation to conditions and travelling difficult. No one managed a hundred, and only Mazharul Haque averaged over 30. Their bowling, mainly medium-pace and spin, was steady but not penetrative, though Mosaddek Hossain managed 21 wickets. They lost five matches but did narrowly beat Windwards, and took first-innings leads in their defeat by West Indies B and a draw with Trinidad & Tobago.

Although West Indies B finished last, the West Indian board was satisfied that the team served its purpose by giving emerging players early exposure to first-class cricket. Led by Roland Holder, the former Test batsman, they defeated Bangladesh A and forced Guyana to follow on, 199 behind, in a match featuring a century on first-class debut from Donovan Pagon, newly returned from the Under-19 World Cup.

The board continued to broaden the player base in 2002-03 by introducing a University of the West Indies team to the limited-overs competition, and indicated that it would eventually join the first-class tournament too. In the 2001-02 Bowl, the ICC associate and affiliate sides had dropped out, but the Windward Islands – the previous season's winners – were split into North and South, and the Leeward Islands into Antigua and the Rest. None of these divided teams reached the semi-finals, where, as in the Busta Shield five months later, Guyana had to squeeze through on their qualifying record: they tied their semi-final with Jamaica, but comfortably beat Barbados in the final.

FIRST-CLASS AVERAGES, 2001-02

BATTING

(Qualification: 300 runs, average 35.00)

	M	I	NO	R	HS	100s	Avge
S. Chanderpaul (*Guyana*)	12	17	5	987	140	4	82.25
S. C. Williams (*Leeward Islands*)	11	19	5	1,065	252*	3	76.07
C. L. Hooper (*Guyana*)	12	16	1	1,081	233	5	72.06
D. S. Smith (*Windward Islands*)	8	14	1	841	143	1	64.69
R. S. Morton (*Leeward Islands*)	7	10	0	645	104	2	64.50
R. G. Samuels (*Jamaica*)	9	14	3	572	106*	1	52.00
R. A. M. Smith (*Trinidad & Tobago*)	7	12	2	514	72	0	51.40
D. Ganga (*Trinidad & Tobago*)	4	7	1	302	151*	1	50.33
S. C. Joseph (*Leeward Islands*)	6	9	1	386	211*	1	48.25
R. D. Jacobs (*Leeward Islands*)	10	13	3	473	118	1	47.30
C. O. Browne (*Barbados*)	7	12	2	471	161	1	47.10
W. W. Hinds (*Jamaica*)	10	16	1	693	175	2	46.20
F. L. Reifer (*Barbados*)	7	12	1	488	127*	1	44.36
J. R. Murray (*Windward Islands*)	9	15	0	643	125	4	42.86
C. H. Gayle (*Jamaica*)	11	19	1	762	204	1	42.33
D. J. J. Bravo (*Trinidad & Tobago*)	5	9	0	380	122	1	42.22
L. V. Garrick (*Jamaica*)	9	16	2	581	138	2	41.50
K. J. Wilkinson (*Barbados*)	7	12	0	486	135	1	40.50
L. J. Cush (*Guyana*)	8	12	1	438	154	2	39.81
P. A. Wallace (*Barbados*)	7	13	1	463	99	0	38.58
I. H. Jan (*Trinidad & Tobago*)	8	16	1	574	110	1	38.26
A. Haniff (*Guyana*)	9	15	0	570	235	1	38.00
S. Chattergoon (*Guyana*)	8	13	0	483	143	1	37.15
S. J. Benn (*Barbados*)	6	11	2	328	78	0	36.44
B. C. Lara (*West Indies*)	7	10	0	351	73	0	35.10

BOWLING

(Qualification: 20 wickets)

	O	M	R	W	BB	5W/i	Avge
L. R. Williams (*Jamaica*)	185.2	42	499	26	5-20	1	19.19
K. C. B. Jeremy (*Leeward Islands*)	313.4	69	789	41	6-33	3	19.24
R. O. Cunningham (*Jamaica*)	248	94	529	27	5-51	1	19.59
G. R. Breese (*Jamaica*)	408.2	108	948	47	6-57	3	20.17
D. B. Powell (*Jamaica*)	253.2	55	655	29	5-28	2	22.58
P. T. Collins (*Barbados*)	322	69	865	37	6-76	2	23.37
I. D. R. Bradshaw (*Barbados*)	219.5	41	726	31	4-61	0	23.41
M. I. Black (*Trinidad & Tobago*)	302	73	944	40	5-76	1	23.60
N. C. McGarrell (*Guyana*)	374.1	105	845	35	5-88	1	24.14
D. C. Butler (*Windward Islands*)	209.1	58	523	21	3-38	0	24.90
M. Persad (*Trinidad & Tobago*)	259.3	53	657	26	7-113	1	25.26
F. Thomas (*Windward Islands*)	210.4	29	710	28	5-65	1	25.35
I. O. Jackson (*Windward Islands*)	292.4	67	692	27	5-66	1	25.62
M. V. Nagamootoo (*Guyana*)	554.1	137	1,386	53	6-61	3	26.15
M. Dillon (*Trinidad & Tobago*)	284.3	71	792	28	5-71	1	28.28
S. J. Benn (*Barbados*)	256.2	64	679	24	5-87	2	28.29
C. E. Cuffy (*Windward Islands*)	291.5	92	605	21	3-53	0	28.80
A. Sanford (*Leeward Islands*)	561.4	109	1,827	61	5-80	1	29.95
K. G. Darlington (*Guyana*)	192.1	34	617	20	4-49	0	30.85
R. D. King (*Guyana*)	258	58	843	27	4-27	0	31.22
Mosaddek Hossain (*Bangladesh A*)	224.5	33	677	21	5-46	2	32.23

BUSTA CUP, 2001-02

	Played	Won	Lost	Drawn	1st-inns Points	Points
Jamaica	7	6	0	1	0	75
Guyana	7	4	2	1	0	51
Leeward Islands	7	3	2	2	3	45
Trinidad & Tobago . .	7	2	2	3	3	45
Barbados	7	2	2	3	6	39
Windward Islands . . .	7	2	3	2	0	39
Windward Islands . . .	7	2	3	2	3	33
Bangladesh A	7	1	5	1	7	22
West Indies B	7	1	5	1	3	18

Win = 12 pts; draw = 3 pts; 1st-innings lead in a drawn match = 3 pts; 1st-innings lead in a lost match = 4 pts.

Jamaica won the Busta Cup and became regional champions. The top four teams qualified for the Busta International Shield. Trinidad & Tobago were placed ahead of Barbados by virtue of winning their head-to-head match. Matches involving Bangladesh A and West Indies B counted for points but neither of these teams could win the Busta Cup.

In the following scores, * by the name of a team signifies that they won the toss.

At Kensington Oval, Bridgetown, January 25, 26, 27, 28. **Barbados won by 162 runs. Barbados 304** (P. A. Wallace 99, K. J. Wilkinson 92, C. O. Browne 52; N. C. McGarrell four for 74) **and 328 for eight dec.** (P. A. Wallace 44, K. J. Wilkinson 34, F. L. Reifer 62, D. R. Smith 35, C. O. Browne 31; N. C. McGarrell five for 88); **Guyana* 231** (H. Pooran 30, A. R. Percival 96, N. C. McGarrell 30, A. Ally-Haniff 32, Extras 38; T. L. Best four for 50, I. D. R. Bradshaw three for 54, S. J. Benn three for 45) **and 239** (A. Haniff 30, S. Chattergoon 53, M. V. Nagamootoo 36, Extras 41; I. D. R. Bradshaw four for 61, R. A. Austin five for 68). *Barbados 12 pts.*

At Queen's Park Oval, Port-of-Spain, January 25, 26, 27, 28. **Drawn. Trinidad & Tobago 354** (D. James 37, L. A. Roberts 117, A. Kanhai 39, D. Mohammed 52; K. C. B. Jeremy four for 80, A. Sanford three for 42) **and 267 for seven dec.** (I. H. Jan 52, A. K. Mason 68 not out, Extras 45; A. Sanford three for 63, K. C. B. Jeremy three for 46); **Leeward Islands* 301** (S. C. Williams 86, R. S. Morton 104; M. I. Black five for 76) **and 178 for two** (S. C. Williams 113 not out). *Trinidad & Tobago 6 pts, Leeward Islands 3 pts.*

At Edgar Gilbert Sporting Complex, Molyneux (St Kitts), January 25, 26, 27, 28. **West Indies B won by 59 runs. West Indies B 195** (C. Baugh 37, C. F. Lopez 31; Alamgir Kabir four for 52) **and 261** (K. D. Martin 61, R. I. C. Holder 41, A. N. Mayers 55, C. F. Lopez 33; Anwar Hossain Monir four for 34, Ahsanullah Hasan three for 29); **Bangladesh A* 278** (Hannan Sarkar 33, Mosaddek Hossain 63, Extras 38; A. Sealy five for 79) **and 119** (E. J. Powell three for 27, A. Sealy four for 33). *West Indies B 12 pts, Bangladesh A 4 pts.*

At Queen's Park, St George's, January 25, 26, 27, 28. **Drawn. Jamaica* 178** (G. R. Breese 48; D. C. Butler three for 52, I. O. Jackson four for 36) **and 175 for five** (M. D. Ventura 55 not out, R. G. Samuels 40; F. Thomas three for 41); **Windward Islands 356** (D. S. Smith 84, R. K. Currency 38, J. R. Murray 105, J. Eugene 30, R. N. Lewis 45; G. R. Breese three for 87, L. R. Williams four for 72). *Windward Islands 6 pts, Jamaica 3 pts.*

    Murray made six dismissals (five caught, one stumped) in Jamaica's first innings.

At Kensington Oval, Bridgetown, February 1, 2, 3, 4. **Windward Islands won by 71 runs. Windward Islands 327** (D. S. Smith 143, Extras 44; I. D. R. Bradshaw four for 71) **and 295** (D. S. Smith 31, R. K. Currency 82, J. Eugene 86; I. D. R. Bradshaw four for 89, R. A. Austin five for 60); **Barbados* 309** (C. O. Browne 161, S. J. Benn 78; F. Thomas five for 65, D. C. Butler three for 61) **and 242** (H. J. Wilkinson 30, C. O. Browne 31, R. A. Austin 56 not out; D. C. Butler three for 38, K. K. Peters three for 49). *Windward Islands 12 pts.*

    This was Windwards' first victory over Barbados in a first-class match since 1983. Barbados were 118 for seven in their first innings before Browne and Benn added 184 for the eighth wicket.

At Sabina Park, Kingston, February 1, 2, 3, 4. **Jamaica won by seven wickets. Guyana* 267** (A. Haniff 74, L. J. Cush 48, H. Pooran 72; L. R. Williams three for 49) **and 188** (A. R. Percival 39, A. Ally-Haniff 51; L. R. Williams three for 42); **Jamaica 371** (L. V. Garrick 115, R. G. Samuels 69, M. D. Ventura 76 not out, L. R. Williams 35; R. D. King three for 84, M. V. Nagamootoo three for 87) **and 86 for three** (L. V. Garrick 63 not out). *Jamaica 12 pts.*

At Airport Ground, St John's, February 1, 2, 3, 4. **Leeward Islands won by three wickets. Bangladesh A* 176** (Mazharul Haque 31, Anwar Hossain 44; K. C. B. Jeremy six for 33) **and 312** (Hannan Sarkar 42, Mazharul Haque 89, Akram Khan 36, Mushfiqur Rahman 50); **Leeward Islands 199** (F. A. Adams 62, R. S. Morton 67; Mosaddek Hossain five for 46, Naimur Rahman four for 38) **and 293 for seven** (S. C. Williams 78, R. S. Morton 98, J. A. Mitchum 59 not out). *Leeward Islands 12 pts.*
   This was the first first-class match at the Airport Ground, next to the V. C. Bird International Airport. Ehsanul Haque made five catches in the field in Leewards' first innings.

At Guaracara Park, Pointe-à-Pierre, February 1, 2, 3, 4. **Trinidad & Tobago won by ten wickets. Trinidad & Tobago 455 for eight dec.** (I. H. Jan 110, L. A. Roberts 146, A. Kanhai 38, K. A. Mason 48, A. I. Jan 52 not out; E. J. Powell four for 71, A. Sealy three for 136) **and 49 for no wkt;** **West Indies B* 264** (K. Arjune 109 not out, S. M. Jeffers 36, C. F. Lopez 37; M. Persad seven for 113) **and 238** (S. M. Jeffers 70, P. A. Browne 34; M. I. Black four for 60). *Trinidad & Tobago 12 pts.*
   Arjune carried his bat through West Indies B's first innings (in which one man retired hurt) for his maiden first-class hundred.

At Shaw Park, Scarborough (Tobago), February 6, 7, 8, 9. **Drawn. Bangladesh A 238** (Mazharul Haque 37, Mushfiqur Rahman 57, Ahsanullah Hasan 35 not out; M. Persad three for 61) **and 259** (Hannan Sarkar 69, Mazharul Haque 46, Ahsanullah Hasan 37, Extras 32; M. I. Black three for 65); **Trinidad & Tobago* 205** (I. H. Jan 32, L. A. Roberts 37, K. A. Mason 52; Naimur Rahman three for 69, Ahsanullah Hasan three for 50) **and 121 for four** (R. A. M. Smith 50 not out, S. Badree 43). *Trinidad & Tobago 3 pts, Bangladesh A 6 pts.*

At Sabina Park, Kingston, February 8, 9, 10. **Jamaica won by an innings and 39 runs. Barbados 179** (F. L. Reifer 91, I. D. R. Bradshaw 32; D. B. Powell five for 28) **and 133** (K. J. Wilkinson 35, S. J. Benn 32 not out; G. R. Breese three for 13); **Jamaica* 351** (L. V. Garrick 53, R. L. Powell 85, M. D. Ventura 32, G. R. Breese 57, L. R. Williams 34; T. L. Best four for 75, I. D. R. Bradshaw three for 90). *Jamaica 12 pts.*

At Grove Park, Charlestown (Nevis), February 8, 9, 10, 11. **Leeward Islands won by eight wickets. West Indies B* 219** (S. M. Jeffers 31, P. A. Browne 55, A. N. Mayers 36, E. J. Powell 32 not out; R. J. Christopher four for 50, A. Sanford four for 60) **and 302** (K. Arjune 44, S. M. Jeffers 51, S. Naidoo 34, P. A. Browne 43, R. I. C. Holder 51, Extras 31; A. Sanford three for 97, K. C. B. Jeremy four for 41); **Leeward Islands 476 for four dec.** (S. C. Williams 66, S. C. Joseph 211 not out, D. R. E. Joseph 41, K. I. Tittle 101 not out, Extras 37) **and 46 for two** (S. C. Williams 35 not out). *Leeward Islands 12 pts.*
   Joseph's 211 not out, the highest first-class score for the Leeward Islands until the Shield semifinal against Guyana, lasted 556 minutes and 469 balls and included 22 fours and three sixes. He added 239 unbroken for Leewards' fifth wicket with Ian Tittle, who scored a century on first-class debut.

At Arnos Vale, St Vincent, February 8, 9, 10, 11. **Guyana won by five wickets. Windward Islands* 203** (D. S. Smith 99, R. K. Currency 33; M. V. Nagamootoo six for 61) **and 135** (D. S. Smith 36, J. R. Murray 40; K. G. Darlington three for 22, N. C. McGarrell three for 38, M. V. Nagamootoo three for 34); **Guyana 288** (L. J. Cush 44, A. R. Percival 39, A. Ally-Haniff 52, M. V. Nagamootoo 48; F. Thomas four for 77) **and 51 for five** (F. Thomas three for 22). *Guyana 12 pts.*

At Bourda, Georgetown, February 15, 16, 17. **Guyana won by an innings and 143 runs. Guyana 456 for five dec.** (A. Haniff 235, S. Chatterggoon 143, A. R. Percival 41 not out); **Bangladesh A* 184** (Hannan Sarkar 39, Ehsanul Haque 38, Akram Khan 72; K. G. Darlington four for 49, M. V. Nagamootoo four for 45) **and 129** (Akram Khan 42, Mushfiqur Rahman 31 not out; R. D. King four for 27, M. V. Nagamootoo four for 38). *Guyana 12 pts.*

Haniff's 235 lasted 464 minutes and 376 balls and included 29 fours and one six. He added 340 for the first wicket with Chattergoon, a Guyanese record.

At Kaiser Sports Club, Discovery Bay, February 15, 16, 17, 18. **Jamaica won by 133 runs. Jamaica 257** (M. D. Ventura 52 not out, L. R. Williams 40, Extras 53; K. C. B. Jeremy five for 51) **and 233 for nine dec.** (K. H. Hibbert 81, R. G. Samuels 51, G. R. Breese 53 not out; A. Sanford four for 66); **Leeward Islands* 162** (S. C. Williams 57, F. A. Adams 46; G. R. Breese six for 57) **and 195** (S. C. Joseph 64, K. I. Tittle 60; L. R. Williams five for 20). *Jamaica 12 pts.*
   Leeward Islands lost all ten first-innings wickets for 58 after an opening partnership of 104 between Williams and Adams.

At Queen's Park Oval, Port-of-Spain, February 15, 16, 17, 18. **Trinidad & Tobago won by four wickets. Barbados* 174** (S. H. Armstrong 36; R. Rampaul four for 41, M. Persad three for 33) **and 229** (P. A. Wallace 52, D. R. Smith 30, S. M. Clarke 42; M. I. Black three for 56, M. Persad four for 44); **Trinidad & Tobago 210** (I. H. Jan 37, R. A. M. Smith 59, Extras 33; I. D. R. Bradshaw four for 64) **and 196 for six** (R. A. M. Smith 59 not out; S. J. Benn three for 62). *Trinidad & Tobago 12 pts.*

At Queen's Park, St George's, February 15, 16, 17, 18. **Windward Islands won by seven wickets. West Indies B 211** (K. Arjune 35, S. Naidoo 89; F. Thomas four for 54) **and 291** (K. Arjune 52, R. I. C. Holder 33, A. N. Mayers 50, C. J. K. Hodge 65; I. O. Jackson four for 63); **Windward Islands* 356** (K. K. Sylvester 50, K. N. Casimir 33, J. R. Murray 103, J. Eugene 37, R. N. Lewis 55, I. O. Jackson 32; C. J. K. Hodge four for 87, C. C. Alexander three for 79) **and 147 for three** (K. N. Casimir 57 not out, R. N. Lewis 32 not out). *Windward Islands 12 pts.*

At Kensington Oval, Bridgetown, February 22, 23, 24, 25. **Barbados won by ten wickets. Bangladesh A* 293** (Mazharul Haque 83, Akram Khan 68, Anwar Hossain 32 not out, Extras 31; P. T. Collins five for 56, I. D. R. Bradshaw four for 89) **and 161** (Mazharul Haque 41; P. T. Collins three for 48, C. D. Collymore five for 51); **Barbados 449 for five dec.** (P. A. Wallace 81, S. L. Campbell 101, K. J. Wilkinson 63, F. L. Reifer 127 not out) **and six for no wkt.** *Barbados 12 pts.*

At Albion, Berbice, February 22, 23, 24, 25. **Guyana won by five wickets. Trinidad & Tobago 230** (D. J. J. Bravo 64, D. James 46, R. A. M. Smith 36; M. V. Nagamootoo three for 54) **and 262** (I. H. Jan 60, D. J. J. Bravo 33, L. A. Roberts 34, R. A. M. Smith 52, S. Badree 30; N. C. McGarrell four for 65); **Guyana* 343** (A. Haniff 67, S. Chanderpaul 76, C. L. Hooper 44, N. C. McGarrell 56 not out; M. I. Black four for 83) **and 153 for five** (S. Chattergoon 58). *Guyana 12 pts.*

At A. O. Shirley Recreation Ground, Tortola (British Virgin Islands), February 22, 23, 24. **Leeward Islands won by ten wickets. Windward Islands* 233** (D. S. Smith 38, J. R. Murray 70; K. C. B. Jeremy three for 58, A. Sanford three for 79, A. J. A. Lake three for 52) **and 200** (D. S. Smith 50; K. C. B. Jeremy six for 65, A. Sanford three for 62); **Leeward Islands 367** (F. A. Adams 71, R. S. Morton 103, T. A. Willett 46, R. D. Jacobs 67 not out; I. O. Jackson three for 102, S. Shillingford five for 71) **and 70 for no wkt** (S. C. Williams 42 not out). *Leeward Islands 12 pts.*
   This was the first first-class match played in the British Virgin Islands.

At Botanical Gardens, Roseau (Dominica), February 22, 23, 24. **Jamaica won by nine wickets. Jamaica 462 for seven dec.** (L. V. Garrick 139, W. Hinds 38, K. H. Hibbert 42, R. G. Samuels 106 not out, R. O. Cunningham 35, Extras 30; R. P. O. Nurse three for 88) **and 39 for one; West Indies B* 179** (K. Arjune 36, P. A. Browne 43; G. R. Breese five for 73, R. O. Cunningham five for 51) **and 321** (K. Arjune 38, S. M. Jeffers 44, A. N. Mayers 30, R. I. C. Holder 112 not out; G. R. Breese five for 121). *Jamaica 12 pts.*

At Albion, Berbice, March 1, 2, 3, 4. **Drawn. West Indies B 415** (D. J. Pagon 110, P. A. Browne 52, R. I. C. Holder 61, R. P. O. Nurse 31, A. Sealy 57 not out, R. Griffith 33; R. D. King three for 106, M. V. Nagamootoo four for 129); **Guyana* 216** (N. Deonarine 46, N. C. McGarrell 34; R. Griffith three for 47) **and 190 for three** (A. Haniff 51, L. J. Cush 100 not out). *Guyana 3 pts, West Indies B 6 pts.*
   Donovan Pagon scored 110 on first-class debut.

At Alpart Sports Club, St Elizabeth, March 1, 2, 3, 4. **Jamaica won by seven wickets. Trinidad & Tobago** 132 (R. A. M. Smith 64; L. R. Williams four for 19) **and** 282 (D. Ganga 73, D. J. J. Bravo 71, L. M. P. Simmons 36; J. J. C. Lawson four for 28, G. R. Breese three for 69); **Jamaica*** 298 (C. H. Gayle 49, R. G. Samuels 65, G. R. Breese 83, Extras 38; M. I. Black four for 55, L. M. P. Simmons three for six) **and** 120 for three (C. H. Gayle 62, W. W. Hinds 41). *Jamaica 12 pts.*

At Ronald Webster Park, The Valley (Anguilla), March 1, 2, 3, 4. **Drawn. Barbados*** 373 (P. A. Wallace 59, K. J. Wilkinson 40, R. O. Hinds 50, F. L. Reifer 82, S. J. Benn 59; G. T. Prince five for 96) **and** 381 for nine (P. A. Wallace 61, D. R. Smith 102, C. O. Browne 85, S. J. Benn 61; A. Sanford five for 80); **Leeward Islands** 502 (F. A. Adams 68, S. C. Williams 195, R. S. Morton 61, K. I. Tittle 48, R. D. Jacobs 51, Extras 45; S. J. Benn five for 169). *Leeward Islands 6 pts, Barbados 3 pts.*

At Arnos Vale, St Vincent, March 1, 2, 3, 4. **Bangladesh A won by eight runs. Bangladesh A** 163 (Ehsanul Haque 50, Tushar Imran 46; I. O. Jackson five for 66) **and** 288 (Mazharul Haque 90, Anwar Hossain 35, Tushar Imran 79; S. Shillingford four for 54); **Windward Islands*** 151 (D. S. Smith 57; Naimur Rahman five for 31, Mosaddek Hossain three for 41) **and** 292 (D. S. Smith 55, J. R. Murray 125, F. Thomas 31; Mosaddek Hossain five for 81). *Bangladesh A 12 pts.*

At Kensington Oval, Bridgetown, March 8, 9, 10. **Barbados won by an innings and 263 runs. Barbados*** 557 for seven dec. (S. L. Campbell 107, K. J. Wilkinson 135, R. O. Hinds 166, F. L. Reifer 54, C. O. Browne 52 not out); **West Indies B** 193 (D. J. Pagon 37; P. T. Collins three for 33, S. J. Benn five for 87) **and** 101 (S. M. Jeffers 32; T. L. Best five for 37). *Barbados 12 pts.*

At Albion, Berbice, March 8, 9, 10, 11. **Guyana won by an innings and 42 runs. Guyana** 442 (L. J. Cush 154, S. Chanderpaul 140, R. R. Sarwan 32, N. C. McGarrell 54; K. C. B. Jeremy three for 65, A. Sanford four for 103); **Leeward Islands*** 237 (F. A. Adams 51, R. S. Morton 58, T. A. Willett 32; M. V. Nagamootoo six for 71) **and** 163 (F. A. Adams 53, S. C. Joseph 60; M. V. Nagamootoo four for 77, N. C. McGarrell four for 24). *Guyana 12 pts.*

    Cush and Chanderpaul added 253 for Guyana's third wicket.

At Chedwin Park, Spanish Town, March 8, 9, 10. **Jamaica won by an innings and 60 runs. Jamaica** 368 (W. W. Hinds 78, R. G. Samuels 31, R. L. Powell 86, G. R. Breese 72, D. B. Powell 38; Alamgir Kabir three for 76, Tareq Aziz four for 70, Mosaddek Hossain three for 133); **Bangladesh A*** 166 (Hannan Sarkar 55, Akram Khan 46; D. B. Powell three for 39, R. O. Cunningham three for 39) **and** 142 (Hannan Sarkar 37, Akram Khan 34; D. B. Powell five for 37). *Jamaica 12 pts.*

    Tushar Imran was out handled the ball in Bangladesh A's second innings.

At Guaracara Park, Pointe-à-Pierre, March 8, 9, 10, 11. **Drawn. Trinidad & Tobago** 380 (I. H. Jan 53, D. J. J. Bravo 122, R. A. M. Smith 72, L. M. P. Simmons 47 not out; D. C. Butler three for 73) **and** 298 for two dec. (D. Ganga 151 not out, I. H. Jan 94, L. M. P. Simmons 31 not out); **Windward Islands*** 340 (D. S. Smith 79, J. R. Murray 105, I. O. Jackson 33, F. Thomas 33; M. Persad three for 65, D. Ramnarine five for 116) **and** 96 for no wkt (D. S. Smith 51 not out, R. K. Currency 42 not out). *Trinidad & Tobago 6 pts, Windward Islands 3 pts.*

REGIONAL CHAMPIONS

Shell Shield			1976-77	Barbados
1965-66	Barbados		1977-78	Barbados
1966-67	Barbados		1978-79	Barbados
1967-68	No competition		1979-80	Barbados
1968-69	Jamaica		1980-81	Combined Islands
1969-70	Trinidad		1981-82	Barbados
1970-71	Trinidad		1982-83	Guyana
1971-72	Barbados		1983-84	Barbados
1972-73	Guyana		1984-85	Trinidad & Tobago
1973-74	Barbados		1985-86	Barbados
1974-75	Guyana		1986-87	Guyana
1975-76	{ Trinidad / Barbados			

Red Stripe Cup		President's Cup	
1987-88	Jamaica		Leeward Islands
1988-89	Jamaica	1997-98 {	
1989-90	Leeward Islands		Guyana
1990-91	Barbados		
1991-92	Jamaica	*Busta Cup*	
1992-93	Guyana	1998-99	Barbados
1993-94	Leeward Islands	1999-2000	Jamaica
1994-95	Barbados	2000-01	Barbados
1995-96	Leeward Islands	2001-02	Jamaica
1996-97	Barbados		

Barbados have won the title outright 16 times, Jamaica 6, Guyana 5, Leeward Islands and Trinidad/Trinidad & Tobago 3, Combined Islands 1. Barbados, Guyana, Leeward Islands and Trinidad have also shared the title.

BUSTA INTERNATIONAL SHIELD, 2001-02

Semi-finals

At Albion, Berbice, March 15, 16, 17, 18. **Drawn.** Guyana qualified for the final by virtue of their higher placing in the Busta Cup. **Guyana* 491** (S. Chattergoon 95, C. L. Hooper 222, N. C. McGarrell 32, Extras 37; A. Sanford four for 136); **Leeward Islands 442 for five** (S. C. Williams 252 not out, R. S. Morton 96).

Hooper's 222 lasted 462 minutes and 382 balls and included 21 fours. Williams's 252 not out lasted 367 minutes and 301 balls and included 30 fours and one six. It was the highest first-class score for Leewards, surpassing Sylvester Joseph's 211 not out against West Indies B earlier in the tournament. Leewards were 50 short of the first-innings lead that would have carried them into the final when rain ended play with 43.1 overs remaining.

At Sabina Park, Kingston, March 15, 16, 17, 18. **Jamaica won by seven wickets. Trinidad & Tobago 216** (D. Ganga 42, R. A. M. Smith 63, Z. R. Ali 36; L. R. Williams three for 52, G. R. Breese three for 34) **and 197** (D. J. J. Bravo 42, L. M. P. Simmons 39; J. J. C. Lawson four for 44, R. O. Cunningham three for 11); **Jamaica* 209** (R. L. Powell 71, L. R. Williams 33; M. I. Black three for 53) **and 206 for three** (L. V. Garrick 49, C. H. Gayle 36, W. W. Hinds 32, R. G. Samuels 43 not out).

FINAL

JAMAICA v GUYANA

At Sabina Park, Kingston, April 4, 5, 6, 7. Drawn. Guyana won the Busta International Shield by virtue of their first-innings lead. Toss: Guyana.

The second Shield final united the same teams in another draw. But this time, Guyana took the crucial first-innings lead. The decisive role belonged to their captain, Hooper, who came in on the third morning at 170 for five, 107 behind. He plundered 149 of the next 184 runs, striking seven sixes – four off Breese – and 13 fours in 155 balls; most importantly, he secured a lead. On the opening day, he had sent Jamaica in, and their openers, Gayle and Garrick, responded with 102, but fell in quick succession to Nagamootoo's leg-spin. Guyana's three spinners conceded just 141 in 80 overs as Jamaica scored only 2.46 an over. They stepped up to 4.23 in the second innings, thanks to Gayle, with 54 in 73 balls, and Samuels's 51-ball 61, but to no avail. Needing to score 193 or survive 50 overs on the last day, Guyana batted out time. Nagamootoo's seven wickets in the match gave him a record 50 in the tournament, surpassing Rajindra Dhanraj's 48 for Trinidad & Tobago in 1995-96.

Man of the Match: C. L. Hooper.

Close of play: First day, Jamaica 229-6 (Breese 8, Cunningham 1); Second day, Guyana 149-4 (Sarwan 24, Ally-Haniff 4); Third day, Jamaica 102-2 (Hinds 8, Cunningham 1).

Jamaica

C. H. Gayle c Sarwan b Nagamootoo	41	– c Ally-Haniff b Nagamootoo	54
L. V. Garrick c Hooper b Nagamootoo	36	– c Ally-Haniff b McGarrell	28
W. W. Hinds c Ally-Haniff b Hooper	17	– c sub (A. R. Percival)	
		b Nagamootoo .	28
†K. H. Hibbert c McGarrell b King	44	– (9) run out	7
*R. G. Samuels lbw b Nagamootoo	34	– (6) run out	61
R. L. Powell c McGarrell b Nagamootoo	0	– (5) c Nagamootoo b McGarrell	39
G. R. Breese b King	12	– c Ally-Haniff b King	15
R. O. Cunningham not out	26	– (4) b McGarrell	6
L. R. Williams b King	4	– (8) b King	3
D. B. Powell lbw b Nagamootoo	2	– c Chanderpaul b King	9
J. J. C. Lawson lbw b King	5	– not out	0
B 24, l-b 14, n-b 18	56	B 4, l-b 4, w 1, n-b 10 . . .	19

1/102 2/109 3/139 4/205 5/205   **277**   1/88 2/96 3/110 4/153 5/189   **269**
6/226 7/245 8/254 9/263   6/231 7/242 8/257 9/264

Bowling: *First Innings*—King 22.1–7–61–4; Stuart 10–0–37–0; McGarrell 19–10–16–0; Nagamootoo 39–11–97–5; Hooper 22–10–28–1. *Second Innings*—King 8.3–0–52–3; Stuart 8–1–45–0; McGarrell 24–5–93–3; Nagamootoo 23–4–71–2.

Guyana

A. Haniff c Lawson b Breese	22	– run out	23
S. Chattergoon b Cunningham	66	– c Gayle b Cunningham	20
L. J. Cush c Garrick b Cunningham	13		
S. Chanderpaul lbw b Breese	10	– not out	30
R. R. Sarwan lbw b Cunningham	40	– (3) b Cunningham	6
†A. Ally-Haniff c R. L. Powell b Breese	9		
*C. L. Hooper not out	149		
N. C. McGarrell lbw b Lawson	23		
M. V. Nagamootoo c Garrick b Williams	1	– (5) not out	7
C. E. L. Stuart lbw b Breese	1		
R. D. King run out	0		
B 11, l-b 7, n-b 2	20	B 4, w 3, n-b 6	13

1/66 2/88 3/103 4/143 5/170   **354**   1/53 2/56 3/63   (3 wkts) **99**
6/190 7/256 8/287 9/315

Bowling: *First Innings*—D. B. Powell 15–2–55–0; Lawson 22–7–71–1; Williams 13–3–36–1; Breese 40.5–15–90–4; Cunningham 30–13–59–3; Gayle 5–0–8–0; R. L. Powell 9–3–17–0. *Second Innings*—D. B. Powell 2–0–8–0; Lawson 6–1–20–0; Williams 4–1–24–0; Cunningham 16–8–18–2; Breese 11–8–11–0; R. L. Powell 8–6–8–0; Hinds 3–1–6–0.

Umpires: B. R. Doctrove and B. E. W. Morgan.
Third umpire: T. Wilson.

RED STRIPE BOWL, 2001-02

Note: Matches in this section were not first-class.

Zone A (in Jamaica)	Played	Won	Lost	No result	Points	Net run-rate
Trinidad & Tobago	3	3	0	0	6	2.55
Jamaica	3	2	1	0	4	1.00
Rest of Leeward Islands	3	0	2	1	1	–1.19
North Windward Islands	3	0	2	1	1	–3.40

Zone B (in Guyana)	Played	Won	Lost	No result	Points	Net run-rate
Guyana	3	3	0	0	6	1.26
Barbados	3	2	1	0	4	0.22
Antigua & Barbuda	3	1	2	0	2	−0.04
South Windward Islands	3	0	3	0	0	−1.38

Net run-rate was calculated by subtracting runs conceded per over from runs scored per over.

Semi-finals

At Kaiser Sports Club, Discovery Bay, October 11. **Tied. Jamaica 191 for nine** (50 overs) (R. G. Samuels 52, G. R. Breese 42; R. D. King three for 51); **Guyana* 191 for nine** (50 overs) (R. R. Sarwan 35, C. L. Hooper 31).

Guyana reached the final by virtue of winning three preliminary games to Jamaica's two.

At Kaiser Sports Club, Discovery Bay, October 12. **Barbados won by 49 runs. Barbados* 219 for five** (50 overs) (F. L. Reifer 104 not out, R. O. Hinds 36, I. D. R. Bradshaw 30 not out); **Trinidad & Tobago 170 for nine** (50 overs) (D. Ganga 37; H. R. Bryan three for 34).

Final

At Kaiser Sports Club, Discovery Bay, October 14. **Guyana won by six wickets. Barbados 221 for five** (50 overs) (D. M. Richards 33, H. R. Bryan 57, R. O. Hinds 50 not out, C. O. Browne 35 not out); **Guyana* 223 for four** (46.5 overs) (T. M. Dowlin 54, R. R. Sarwan 80, C. L. Hooper 45 not out).

CEAT CRICKETER OF THE YEAR

In May 2002, Muttiah Muralitharan of Sri Lanka became the first player to be named CEAT International Cricketer of the Year twice. The CEAT formula awarded him 149 points for his performances in Tests and limited-overs internationals to April 30, up from 111 when he won in 2001. Jacques Kallis of South Africa, the 1999 winner, was second with 100 points. Previous winners were Brian Lara (West Indies), Venkatesh Prasad (India), Sanath Jayasuriya (Sri Lanka), Kallis (South Africa) and Sourav Ganguly (India). Muralitharan was also CEAT Bowler of the Year. Sachin Tendulkar of India was named Batsman of the Year, while Adam Gilchrist and Ricky Ponting of Australia won the wicket-keeper and fielder awards respectively. Australia won the team award by four points from Sri Lanka.

CRICKET IN NEW ZEALAND, 2001-02

By DON CAMERON and FRANCIS PAYNE

Chris Harris

An air of uncertainty hung over New Zealand's cricket in 2001-02, culminating in a 24-hour delay in announcing the squads to tour the Caribbean in June – four days before they were to go – when New Zealand Cricket became entangled with the Players' Association over the interim contracts. Trade unionism had never really affected cricket in New Zealand, apart from an incident in 1953-54 when some senior players signed their contracts just before boarding the plane for South Africa. This time, the difficulties sprang not from some factory-floor fracas but from the player-friendly stance of NZC's new chief executive, Martin Snedden. Feeling keenly for the team when a shattering explosion outside their Karachi hotel forced them to quit the tour of Pakistan in May, he delayed negotiations until he felt they had had time to recover.

In September 2002, the Players' Association refused to sign new contracts until they were given a bigger cut, basing their claims on projected NZC profits. Snedden gave some ground, but not enough to break the impasse, and a strike was called in October. This disrupted a training camp for elite players, prompting another concession by Snedden, followed by a take-it-or-leave-it ultimatum. Around the country, players, union and non-union, were sounded out for domestic games and the forthcoming Tests and internationals against India. Two events weakened the strikers' cause: first the Indian board indicated they would face any team NZC could muster, and then two senior players – the captain, Stephen Fleming, and Chris Cairns – began talks. Four days after the ultimatum, the strike collapsed.

On the field, Pakistan provided a nosedive in New Zealand's performance graph – they suffered their heaviest Test defeat before the bomb drove them home – but elsewhere they enjoyed some astonishing successes. In Australia in November, everyone expected the world champions to cuff them around the ears, but Australia could not land a punch and New Zealand twice threatened to inflict their first home defeat for three years. They also kept Australia out of the finals of the ensuing one-day triangular, only to lose to South Africa. Back at home, New Zealand brushed aside Bangladesh in two Tests, and made a rollercoaster start to their Test series with England at Christchurch, where the fastest double-hundred in Test cricket, from Nathan Astle, almost threatened an upset on the final day. In the final Test, New Zealand unexpectedly squared the series – with the help of the floodlights which enabled them to extend their lead on the fourth evening, as the fielders struggled in the gloom. The highlight of a long season came in June, when New Zealand gained their first Test victory in the West Indies.

The national selectors, led by Sir Richard Hadlee, mined enthusiastically in search of gold-bearing ore, calling 30 players to the colours. Newcomers included Shane Bond, a highly promising fast bowler from Canterbury, though he soon joined the injury list dogging New Zealand cricket. Meanwhile, the selectors' conveyor belt continued to discard players as it brought in new ones. Mathew Sinclair, a *wunderkind* when he scored 214 on debut against West Indies two years earlier, scraped 106 in five Tests and was dropped, with Hadlee criticising his "serious and uncorrected footwork faults". It remained to be seen how long his successor, Lou Vincent, a talented and intense Aucklander, would survive; he burst into the limelight with a debut century against Australia, but his overall returns were uneven.

Swings of fashion could also be detected at the country's leading venues. Grounds which were not long ago the cathedrals of Test cricket, Wellington's Basin Reserve and Eden Park in Auckland, were upstaged by Seddon Park (now officially known as WestpacTrust Park) in Hamilton and Lancaster Park (now the Jade Stadium) in Christchurch. A vast three-deck 16,000-seat stand at Christchurch catered handsomely for corporate guests and those with a head for heights, though on sunny afternoons it threw a heavy shadow over the pitch. Sharing the ground with rugby had led to the use of drop-in pitches; the technology had improved, but they were not yet completely satisfactory. Nasser Hussain, the England captain, observed that, usually, Test pitches are a little lively at the start, settle down, and then wear and become bowler-friendly. The Christchurch drop-in was very lively for two days – Cairns took two wickets in the first over – then developed into an impeccable batting strip, producing spectacular double-centuries from Graham Thorpe and Astle.

Eden Park had also adopted drop-in pitches, but the outfield was in need of expensive repair, and was cramped by a new stand on the north boundary. Auckland played most major matches on the No. 2 ground, known as the Outer Oval – which could be developed as a Test venue, seating 15,000 to 20,000, leaving the main oval for one-day internationals – but also used the new North Harbour Stadium, and the excellent pitches at the windswept Colin Maiden Park.

It was there that Auckland won the four-day State Championship (the successor to the Shell Trophy, named after its new sponsors, the State insurance company) by keeping out Wellington's challenge in their last match, which effectively became the competition's final. Wellington were the only team who could catch Auckland but, starting six points behind, had to secure an outright win to tie on points, and simultaneously improve their net average runs per wicket, the tie-breaker. They scored 409 over the first two days and took a first-innings lead of 194 when Auckland declared with nine wickets down. Wellington waived the follow-on, added another 48 in 19 overs, and set Auckland 243 to win – though the real target was 169; if Wellington could bowl them out for less, their net average runs per wicket would overtake Auckland's. But Nick Horsley, completing a maiden first-class hundred, saw Auckland to the safety of 217 for four before accepting the offer of bad light.

Auckland enjoyed a steady supply of runs, thanks in part to two returning exiles, the Test players Mark Richardson and Matt Horne, who had left for Otago in the 1990s. Tim McIntosh passed 500 for the second season running, and Reece Young was a decidedly useful wicket-keeper/batsman. Chris Drum was the most effective bowler, with 28 wickets at 10.71 in four Championship games, while Andre Adams, a lively all-rounder of West Indian parentage, collected 31 in seven, and the leg-spinner Brooke Walker 28 in ten. Drum was the season's leading wicket-taker with 53 in all first-class cricket, but announced his retirement, as did his team-mate, the long-serving Test wicket-keeper, Adam Parore. Dion Nash scored 118 in his only Championship game before finally conceding that injuries would never leave him. But Auckland unveiled a highly promising newcomer in 18-year-old Rod Nicol, who scored two centuries. In one-day cricket, Auckland finished last in the 50-over State Shield, though they did reach the final of the 20-over Max competition in November.

They lost that game, the first major fixture at the North Harbour Stadium, to Wellington, who added a decisive win over Canterbury in the Shield final and were bidding for the treble until the last afternoon of the Championship, when Auckland foiled them. Richard Jones led the batting, with 576 runs, including two centuries. Fleming, who had moved from Canterbury the previous season, marked his first-class debut for Wellington with a hundred against Central Districts, but New Zealand duties spared him for only one more match. Two Matthews, Bell and Walker, also scored hundreds, though the middle order were inconsistent. Andrew Penn led the attack with 40 Championship wickets, including the season's best figures, eight for 21 in 17 overs against Canterbury. But he could not catch the selectors' eye, though the one-day form of James Franklin and Paul Hitchcock did.

Central Districts' year was mixed: third in the Championship with five wins – only Auckland had more – and next to last in the Shield. They possessed an admirable medium-fast battery, including the Championship's two leading wicket-takers in Andrew Schwass, with 45, and Lance Hamilton, 42, but lacked an aggressive spinner. Only Ben Smith, of Worcestershire, and Mathew Sinclair passed 500 runs; Smith scored 201 of those in one innings against Canterbury. A new wicket-keeper, Bevan Griggs, was smart with his gloves and a tenacious lower-order batsman. Injuries and international duties meant that Jacob Oram, the hefty all-rounder, contributed little.

With four New Zealand players frequently absent, Canterbury finished fourth in the Championship, and reached the Shield final by winning a play-off over Northern Districts. It was a triumphant season for the 32-year-old Chris Harris. In six Championship games, he scored 574 runs, including two centuries, at 95. Usually acknowledged as a one-day artist and ignored as a Test player, he was recalled for the final Test against England, contributed 114 conscientious runs to set up victory, and headed the national first-class averages. Michael Papps, a short, stylish batsman, scored 756, the highest aggregate in the Championship. Wade Cornelius gathered 33 wickets in seven Championship games; Paul Wiseman claimed 26, but hopes that Aaron Redmond might advance as a leg-spinner faded.

Northern Districts had one of those muddling years – second-last in the four-day competition, second in the one-day table. The Marshall twins, James and Hamish, were the steadiest batsmen in an inconsistent line-up. James scored 706 first-class runs, including 235, the highest innings for Northern Districts, in the final game against Canterbury. The record he beat had been set by Scott Styris, who scored an unbeaten 212 against Otago the previous week, and went on to a successful tour of the West Indies – as did Robbie Hart, succeeding Parore as Test wicket-keeper. Joseph Yovich had a splendid season as a new-ball bowler, with 40 wickets in the Championship and 18 in the Shield. But he remained on the national scrapheap of seamers, while a new boy, the slightly faster Ian Butler, won his Test debut.

Otago went down to nine Championship defeats before beating Central Districts in the very last match, and won only two Shield games. Even the careful coaching of the former Test star Glenn Turner could not turn their triers into stars, and they had lost a couple of senior batsmen. Over the years, many players discarded by northern teams had moved to Otago; this season, Horne and Richardson returned to Auckland. Two more ex-Auckland men, Kerry Walmsley and Craig Pryor, remained, and gave good service. David Sewell regained form, if not recognition from the selectors. Chris Gaffaney and Craig Cumming passed 500 Championship runs, and the 20-year-old Brendon McCullum set pulses racing and earned his international debut in Australia before losing form and confidence.

The latest and brightest jewel in New Zealand's cricket crown was provided by the outstanding facilities at the high-performance centre and academy at Lincoln University, a short drive south of Christchurch, which hosted the Under-19 World Cup in the New Year. Owing much to the philanthropy of Michael Watt, a multimillionaire from Christchurch, this had expanded to three full-size ovals, each with a splendid pitch block, and extensive nets. The main field was named the Bert Sutcliffe Oval, after one of New Zealand's greatest batsmen, who died in 2001, and live-in quarters bore the names of Hadlee and Watt. Overseas visitors said they had not seen comparably spacious and well-planned facilities anywhere in the cricket world.

FIRST-CLASS AVERAGES, 2001-02

BATTING

(Qualification: 8 completed innings, average 30.00)

	M	I	NO	R	HS	100s	Avge
C. Z. Harris (*Canterbury*)	8	12	3	770	155*	2	85.55
M. H. Richardson (*Auckland*)	10	15	1	779	143	3	55.64
M. J. Horne (*Auckland*)	11	17	2	798	178	3	53.20
M. H. W. Papps (*Canterbury*)	10	19	4	793	158*	2	52.86
R. J. Nicol (*Auckland*)	10	13	2	489	109*	2	44.45
S. B. Styris (*Northern Districts*)	10	17	2	662	212*	1	44.13
M. S. Sinclair (*Central Districts*)	9	15	2	573	171	2	44.07
R. M. Frew (*Canterbury*)	7	14	1	529	115	1	40.69
J. A. H. Marshall (*Northern Districts*) . .	10	18	0	706	235	2	39.22
M. D. Bell (*Wellington*)	7	14	2	465	131*	1	38.75
B. F. Smith (*Central Districts*)	9	16	2	533	201*	1	38.07
M. E. Parlane (*Northern Districts*)	6	10	0	375	146	1	37.50
S. P. Fleming (*Wellington*)	7	11	1	372	115	1	37.20
R. A. Jones (*Wellington*)	9	16	0	576	171	2	36.00
N. K. W. Horsley (*Auckland*)	9	13	1	410	106*	1	34.16
T. G. McIntosh (*Auckland*)	10	17	1	524	123	2	32.75
B. B. McCullum (*Otago*)	8	16	0	510	142	1	31.87
R. G. Hart (*Northern Districts*)	10	15	3	370	102*	1	30.83
T. K. Canning (*Auckland*)	9	12	3	277	56*	0	30.77
C. B. Gaffaney (*Otago*)	11	22	2	609	126*	1	30.45

BOWLING

(Qualification: 20 wickets, average 30.00)

	O	M	R	W	BB	5W/i	Avge
A. M. Schwass (*Central Districts*) . .	260.2	69	663	45	7-36	3	14.73
C. J. Drum (*Auckland*)	317.3	97	827	53	6-34	3	15.60
S. B. Styris (*Northern Districts*) . . .	203.2	60	477	28	5-18	1	17.03
A. J. Penn (*Wellington*)	304.3	94	732	40	8-21	2	18.30
L. J. Hamilton (*Central Districts*) . .	319.4	94	773	42	6-32	3	18.40
A. R. Adams (*Auckland*)	308.4	78	781	42	5-44	2	18.59
W. A. Cornelius (*Canterbury*)	221.4	66	649	34	7-53	3	19.08
K. P. Walmsley (*Otago*)	280.1	71	810	39	5-51	1	20.76
G. S. Shaw (*Auckland*)	148	25	475	21	4-12	0	22.61
G. W. Aldridge (*Northern Districts*) .	212	60	527	23	4-43	0	22.91
D. R. Tuffey (*Northern Districts*) . .	164.5	40	528	23	7-69	2	22.95
M. D. J. Walker (*Wellington*)	249.1	87	495	21	4-15	0	23.57
T. K. Canning (*Auckland*)	292.3	98	651	26	5-35	2	25.03
M. J. Mason (*Central Districts*)	328.1	90	806	32	5-22	1	25.18
B. G. K. Walker (*Auckland*)	315.4	110	716	28	4-10	0	25.57
J. A. F. Yovich (*Northern Districts*) .	316.2	59	1,058	40	6-102	2	26.45
W. A. Wisneski (*Canterbury*)	172	30	584	22	5-74	1	26.54
R. D. Burson (*Canterbury*)	225.4	73	566	21	4-65	0	26.95
I. G. Butler (*Northern Districts*) . . .	198.4	41	706	26	4-46	0	27.15
J. E. C. Franklin (*Wellington*)	280	62	802	27	4-59	0	29.70

STATE CHAMPIONSHIP, 2001-02

	Played	Won	Lost	Drawn	1st-inns Points	Points	Net avge runs per wkt
Auckland	10	6	1	3	3	39	5.77
Wellington	10	5	1	4	5	35	2.91
Central Districts	10	5	4	1	2	32	1.92
Canterbury	10	3	4	3	8	26	0.13
Northern Districts	10	3	4	3	6	24	1.46
Otago	10	1	9	0	6	12	−12.10

Outright win = 6 pts; lead on first innings in a drawn or lost game = 2 pts; no result on first innings = 1 pt each.
Net average runs per wicket is calculated by subtracting average runs conceded per wicket from average runs scored per wicket.

In the following scores, * by the name of a team indicates that they won the toss.

At Eden Park Outer Oval, Auckland, November 26, 27, 28, 29. **Auckland won by eight wickets. Central Districts 126** (B. B. J. Griggs 31 not out, Extras 34; T. K. Canning three for 28, A. R. Adams three for 36) **and 267** (D. P. Kelly 114, M. J. Mason 41; A. R. Adams five for 44, B. G. K. Walker three for 50); **Auckland* 184** (A. R. Adams 55; M. J. Mason three for 90) **and 211 for two** (M. J. Horne 108 not out, A. C. Barnes 57 not out). *Auckland 6 pts.*
Horne and Barnes won the game with an unbroken third-wicket stand of 151.

At Dudley Park, Rangiora, November 26, 27, 28, 29. **Drawn. Canterbury 242** (M. H. W. Papps 50, C. Z. Harris 70, P. J. Wiseman 32; J. E. C. Franklin four for 60, A. J. Penn three for 41) **and 293 for six dec.** (C. Z. Harris 117 not out, A. J. Redmond 101; A. D. Turner five for 66); **Wellington* 126** (J. E. C. Franklin 38 not out, A. J. Penn 45; W. A. Wisneski three for 36, W. A. Cornelius seven for 53) **and 308 for seven** (R. A. Jones 101, G. T. Donaldson 44, M. D. J. Walker 33, C. J. Nevin 45 not out; P. J. Wiseman three for 78). *Canterbury 2 pts.*
Ash Turner took five wickets in an innings on debut.

At Carisbrook, Dunedin, November 26, 27, 28, 29. **Northern Districts won by nine wickets. Otago 215** (B. B. McCullum 50, C. D. Cumming 56; J. A. F. Yovich four for 55, B. P. Martin three for 24) **and 185** (R. A. Lawson 37, B. B. McCullum 41, M. G. Croy 37; S. B. Styris four for 11, B. P. Martin three for 39); **Northern Districts* 303** (J. A. H. Marshall 54, J. H. Marshall 32, R. G. Hart 102 not out, B. P. Martin 45; D. G. Sewell five for 79, E. J. Marshall five for 79) **and 101 for one** (J. A. H. Marshall 30, M. N. Hart 41 not out). *Northern Districts 6 pts.*
Evan Marshall returned for his first first-class match since 1995-96.

At Queen Elizabeth II Park, Christchurch, December 2, 3, 4. **Canterbury won by four wickets. Otago 214** (A. J. Hore 50; W. A. Wisneski five for 74) **and 231** (A. J. Hore 70; P. J. Wiseman five for 99); **Canterbury* 315** (M. H. W. Papps 158 not out, C. Z. Harris 71; K. P. Walmsley three for 79, D. G. Sewell three for 65) **and 131 for six** (G. R. Stead 35 not out, A. J. Redmond 31). *Canterbury 6 pts.*

At Horton Park, Blenheim, December 2, 3, 4. **Central Districts won by 78 runs. Central Districts 181** (R. T. King 31, B. B. J. Griggs 31; I. G. Butler four for 46) **and 157** (D. P. Kelly 30, M. J. Mason 44; I. G. Butler three for 41, G. W. Aldridge four for 45); **Northern Districts* 160** (S. B. Styris 39; M. J. Mason three for 33, A. M. Schwass seven for 36) **and 100** (M. D. Bailey 31; L. J. Hamilton four for 15, M. J. Mason three for 26). *Central Districts 6 pts.*

At Basin Reserve, Wellington, December 2, 3, 4, 5. **Drawn. Wellington* 238** (R. A. Jones 52, G. T. Donaldson 52; T. K. Canning five for 58, A. R. Adams four for 53); **Auckland three for no wkt.** *Wellington 1 pt, Auckland 1 pt.*
No play was possible after the first day.

At Harry Barker Reserve, Gisborne, December 10, 11, 12, 13. **Drawn. Canterbury 444** (S. L. Stewart 57, G. R. Stead 62, C. Z. Harris 155 not out, G. J. Hopkins 45, Extras 31; S. B. Styris three for 44, B. P. Martin three for 48); **Northern Districts* 158** (R. G. Hart 30 not out, B. P. Martin 34; S. E. Bond five for 37, A. J. Redmond three for 35) **and 257 for four** (J. A. H. Marshall 38, M. N. Hart 31, S. B. Styris 98 not out, H. J. H. Marshall 48). *Canterbury 2 pts.*

No play was possible on the last day, leaving Styris stranded on 98 not out.

At Basin Reserve, Wellington, December 10, 11, 12, 13. **Drawn. Wellington 326 for eight dec.** (R. A. Jones 31, S. P. Fleming 115, M. D. J. Walker 100 not out) **and 110 for three** (R. A. Jones 59); **Central Districts* 287** (D. P. Kelly 34, R. S. Scragg 54, G. P. Sulzberger 56, B. B. J. Griggs 49, A. M. Schwass 40; M. D. J. Walker three for 45, J. S. Patel three for 80). *Wellington 2 pts.*

Fleming, who scored a hundred on debut for Wellington, and Walker, with his maiden first-class hundred, added 161 for Wellington's seventh wicket.

At Carisbrook, Dunedin, December 18, 19, 20, 21. **Auckland won by 171 runs. Auckland 374** (M. J. Horne 49, D. J. Nash 118, R. A. Young 35 not out; K. P. Walmsley three for 80, C. R. Pryor four for 106) **and 360 for six dec.** (M. J. Horne 127, T. G. McIntosh 117, T. K. Canning 56 not out; K. P. Walmsley four for 59); **Otago* 375 for six dec.** (B. B. McCullum 142, C. D. Cumming 73, C. B. Gaffaney 36, M. G. Croy 58 not out; T. K. Canning four for 35) **and 188** (R. A. Lawson 63, C. B. Gaffaney 45; T. K. Canning five for 35). *Auckland 6 pts, Otago 2 pts.*

Nash scored 118 in what turned out to be his last first-class match. McCullum reached a maiden first-class hundred in 92 balls; in all, he scored 142 in 148 balls and hit 22 fours and two sixes.

At Pukekura Park, New Plymouth, December 28, 29, 30, 31. **Canterbury won by 102 runs. Canterbury 428** (J. I. Englefield 57, M. H. W. Papps 92, G. R. Stead 49, C. Z. Harris 52, G. J. Hopkins 40, P. J. Wiseman 59; B. E. Hefford three for 91, A. M. Schwass five for 89) **and 235 for five dec.** (S. L. Stewart 38, M. H. W. Papps 30, C. Z. Harris 53 not out, G. J. Hopkins 79 not out); **Central Districts* 336 for five dec.** (B. F. Smith 201 not out, G. P. Sulzberger 58; W. A. Wisneski four for 95) **and 225** (B. F. Smith 78; A. J. Redmond four for 35). *Canterbury 6 pts.*

Smith's 201 not out lasted 369 minutes and 321 balls and included 28 fours.

At Seddon Park, Hamilton, December 28, 29, 30, 31. **Northern Districts won by five wickets. Auckland* 170** (N. K. W. Horsley 60; J. A. F. Yovich four for 64, I. G. Butler three for 47) **and 307** (T. G. McIntosh 37, T. K. Canning 34, K. D. Mills 42, B. G. K. Walker 49, A. R. Adams 60; J. A. F. Yovich six for 102); **Northern Districts 230** (M. N. Hart 51, G. E. Bradburn 53, J. A. F. Yovich 36; A. R. Adams four for 70) **and 248 for five** (J. A. H. Marshall 105, H. J. H. Marshall 34 not out). *Northern Districts 6 pts.*

At Carisbrook, Dunedin, December 28, 29, 30, 31. **Wellington won by eight wickets. Otago 362 for nine dec.** (B. B. McCullum 31, C. D. Cumming 43, C. B. Gaffaney 126 not out, K. P. Walmsley 59, Extras 37; A. J. Penn four for 101) **and 202 for five dec.** (B. B. McCullum 60, A. J. Hore 54 not out, C. R. Pryor 35 not out; A. D. Turner three for 34); **Wellington* 213 for six dec.** (M. D. Bell 44, A. J. Penn 66, D. J. Sales 42; K. P. Walmsley three for 59) **and 353 for two** (M. D. Bell 131 not out, R. A. Jones 171). *Wellington 6 pts, Otago 2 pts.*

Bell and Jones opened with 299 runs in 271 minutes in Wellington's second innings. This was the 100th first-class match between these sides, since 1892-93.

At Eden Park, Auckland, February 12, 13, 14, 15. **Auckland won by an innings and six runs. Auckland 272** (M. J. Horne 49, R. J. Nicol 74, R. A. Young 86; C. S. Martin three for 67, S. J. Cunis three for 66, R. D. Burson three for 62); **Canterbury* 94** (C. J. Drum five for 22, B. G. K. Walker four for ten) **and 172** (S. L. Stewart 35, G. J. Hopkins 36; C. J. Drum five for 33). *Auckland 6 pts.*

Auckland were 105 for seven before Nicol and Young added 153 for the eighth wicket.

At Seddon Park, Hamilton, February 12, 13, 14, 15. **Wellington won by one wicket. Northern Districts 227** (M. E. Parlane 146; A. J. Penn seven for 71) **and 139** (J. A. H. Marshall 52, B. P. Martin 35 not out; M. R. Gillespie five for 50); **Wellington* 125** (J. A. F. Yovich five for 58, G. W. Aldridge three for 36) **and 243 for nine** (S. J. Blackmore 32, D. J. Sales 62, G. T. Donaldson 33, J. E. C. Franklin 30 not out; S. B. Styris four for 53). *Wellington 6 pts, Northern Districts 2 pts.*

In the final innings, Wellington lost their ninth wicket at 223, 19 short of their target; last man Jeetan Patel scored 13 to help complete victory.

At Molyneux Park, Alexandra, February 12, 13, 14. **Central Districts won by 425 runs. Central Districts 185** (G. P. Sulzberger 36, A. M. Schwass 39 not out; K. P. Walmsley four for 40, J. M. McMillan three for 59) **and 444 for eight dec.** (M. S. Sinclair 161, B. F. Smith 57, G. P. Sulzberger 40, P. D. McGlashan 65, B. B. J. Griggs 35, Extras 35; N. D. Morland three for 124); **Otago* 123** (M. J. Mason three for 30, A. M. Schwass four for 29) **and 81** (C. B. Gaffaney 37; B. E. Hefford four for 20). *Central Districts 6 pts.*

At Eden Park Outer Oval, Auckland, February 18, 19, 20, 21. **Drawn. Northern Districts* 383** (J. A. H. Marshall 55, M. E. Parlane 31, S. B. Styris 73, G. E. Bradburn 44, R. G. Hart 34, J. A. F. Yovich 51 not out, G. W. Aldridge 33, Extras 49; C. J. Drum four for 85, W. A. S. Silva three for 74) **and 212 for seven** (H. J. H. Marshall 92); **Auckland 419** (M. H. Richardson 133, M. J. Horne 77, T. G. McIntosh 52, B. G. K. Walker 63, W. A. S. Silva 30; M. N. Hart three for 51, B. P. Martin three for 94). *Auckland 2 pts.*

At Queen Elizabeth II Park, Christchurch, February 18, 19, 20, 21. **Central Districts won by nine wickets. Central Districts* 365** (P. J. Ingram 35, M. S. Sinclair 171, B. F. Smith 41; W. A. Cornelius five for 91, R. D. Burson four for 65) **and 77 for one** (P. J. Ingram 42 not out, M. S. Sinclair 33 not out); **Canterbury 153** (R. M. Frew 30, G. J. Hopkins 30; L. J. Hamilton five for 30) **and 288** (R. M. Frew 115, S. L. Stewart 54, G. R. Stead 35, G. J. Hopkins 34; L. J. Hamilton four for 52, A. M. Schwass six for 82). *Central Districts 6 pts.*

At Basin Reserve, Wellington, February 18, 19, 20. **Wellington won by four wickets. Otago 139** (C. R. Pryor 59; A. J. Penn four for 45) **and 140** (C. D. Cumming 44; L. J. Woodcock four for three); **Wellington 108** (L. J. Woodcock 30; N. D. Morland four for 26, R. G. T. Smith three for 21) **and 174 for six** (R. A. Jones 86; N. D. Morland four for 57). *Wellington 6 pts, Otago 2 pts.*
   In Otago's second innings, Luke Woodcock dismissed Cumming with his first ball in first-class cricket.

At Colin Maiden Park, Auckland, February 25, 26, 27. **Auckland won by seven wickets. Otago* 241** (C. D. Cumming 111, C. R. Pryor 39; B. G. K. Walker three for 40) **and 190** (C. B. Gaffaney 80; G. S. Shaw four for 71, B. G. K. Walker three for 38); **Auckland 316** (M. H. Richardson 100, T. G. McIntosh 35, R. J. Nicol 109 not out; D. G. Sewell three for 69, C. R. Pryor five for 67) **and 118 for three** (M. H. Richardson 52 not out, M. J. Horne 47). *Auckland 6 pts.*
   Otago's wicket-keeper, Martyn Croy, took seven catches in Auckland's first innings, when Nicol, aged 18 years 274 days, became the youngest player to score a first-class hundred for Auckland.

At Basin Reserve, Wellington, February 25, 26, 27. **Wellington won by 31 runs. Wellington* 182** (M. D. Bell 57, M. R. Jefferson 34; W. A. Cornelius four for 16, S. J. Cunis three for 55) **and 162** (J. E. C. Franklin 46, M. D. J. Walker 30; W. A. Cornelius three for 37, S. J. Cunis three for 40, A. J. Redmond three for 39); **Canterbury 193** (M. H. W. Papps 68, G. R. Stead 52; A. J. Penn four for 34, M. D. J. Walker four for 15) **and 120** (P. G. Fulton 46 not out, R. D. Burson 39; A. J. Penn eight for 21). *Wellington 6 pts, Canterbury 2 pts.*
   Penn's full second-innings figures were 17–12–21–8.

At Seddon Park, Hamilton, February 26, 27, 28, March 1. **Central Districts won by seven wickets. Northern Districts* 322** (J. A. H. Marshall 51, J. A. F. Yovich 90, H. J. H. Marshall 35, R. G. Hart 51, L. J. Hamilton five for 88, G. P. Sulzberger four for 62) **and 90** (H. J. H. Marshall 31; M. J. Mason five for 22, A. M. Schwass three for nine); **Central Districts 348** (P. J. Ingram 43, B. B. J. Griggs 76, C. J. M. Furlong 88, A. M. Schwass 30, Extras 36) **and 66 for three**. *Central Districts 6 pts.*
   Griggs and Furlong added 179 for Central Districts' seventh wicket.

At Fitzherbert Park, Palmerston North, March 4, 5, 6. **Auckland won by 116 runs. Auckland 71** (L. J. Hamilton six for 32) **and 290** (M. H. Richardson 86, L. Vincent 75, Extras 32; A. M. Schwass three for 48, G. P. Sulzberger three for 68); **Central Districts* 173** (G. P. Sulzberger 61; C. J. Drum four for 20, A. R. Adams three for 45) **and 72** (C. J. Drum four for 21, G. S. Shaw four for 12). *Auckland 6 pts, Central Districts 2 pts.*
   Central Districts' second-innings total of 72 included five penalty runs, the first awarded in New Zealand first-class cricket, after the ball hit a helmet left on the ground.

At Basin Reserve, Wellington, March 4, 5, 6. **Wellington won by seven wickets. Northern Districts*** **185** (J. A. H. Marshall 37, S. B. Styris 87; J. E. C. Franklin three for 39, M. R. Gillespie four for 50) **and 140** (M. E. Parlane 41; J. E. C. Franklin four for 59, M. D. J. Walker three for 12); **Wellington 116** (I. G. Butler four for 48, S. B. Styris five for 18) **and 213 for three** (L. J. Woodcock 38, S. P. Fleming 88 not out). *Wellington 6 pts, Northern Districts 2 pts.*

At Molyneux Park, Alexandra, March 12, 13, 14. **Canterbury won by nine wickets. Otago 206** (B. B. McCullum 40, C. R. Pryor 46, Extras 30; W. A. Cornelius four for 36, P. J. Wiseman three for 22) **and 131** (J. W. Sheed 53; W. A. Cornelius six for 30, C. Z. Harris three for 29); **Canterbury* 224** (C. Z. Harris 51, P. G. Fulton 33, P. J. Wiseman 44; D. G. Sewell seven for 64) **and 116 for one** (R. M. Frew 73 not out). *Canterbury 6 pts.*

At Queen Elizabeth II Park, Christchurch, March 18, 19, 20, 21. **Auckland won by 35 runs. Auckland 272** (R. J. Nicol 104, A. R. Adams 72; C. J. Cornelius three for 67, R. D. Burson three for 85, P. G. Fulton three for 45) **and 285 for nine dec.** (T. G. McIntosh 123, N. K. W. Horsley 46, R. J. Nicol 49; P. J. Wiseman four for 114, P. G. Fulton four for 49); **Canterbury* 304 for nine dec.** (M. H. W. Papps 140 not out, G. J. Hopkins 37) **and 218** (P. G. Fulton 84; A. R. Adams four for 55, B. G. K. Walker three for 40). *Auckland 6 pts, Canterbury 2 pts.*

Nicol, now aged 18 years 294 days, scored his second century in three weeks.

At McLean Park, Napier, March 18, 19, 20, 21. **Central Districts won by 116 runs. Central Districts 218** (P. J. Ingram 30, J. D. P. Oram 50, A. M. Schwass 44, M. J. Mason 32; J. E. C. Franklin three for 53) **and 281** (M. S. Sinclair 41, B. F. Smith 64, J. D. P. Oram 42; I. E. O'Brien four for 49); **Wellington* 180** (M. R. Jefferson 53; L. J. Hamilton three for 22) **and 203** (G. T. Donaldson 40, J. E. C. Franklin 33; A. M. Schwass three for 40). *Central Districts 6 pts.*

At Seddon Park, Hamilton, March 18, 19, 20, 21. **Northern Districts won by an innings and 28 runs. Otago 118** (J. A. F. Yovich four for 58, S. B. Styris three for 14) **and 314** (C. B. Gaffaney 56, C. D. Cumming 79, J. W. Sheed 64, N. W. Rushton 30 not out; G. W. Aldridge four for 43, B. P. Martin three for 91); **Northern Districts* 460 for seven dec.** (G. G. Robinson 45, M. E. Parlane 65, S. B. Styris 212 not out, H. J. H. Marshall 43, R. G. Hart 66). *Northern Districts 6 pts.*

Styris's 212 not out lasted 341 minutes and only 236 balls and included 14 fours and ten sixes. For one week, it was Northern Districts' highest innings.

At Colin Maiden Park, Auckland, March 24, 25, 26, 27. **Drawn. Wellington* 409** (C. J. Nevin 50, M. D. Bell 80, J. E. C. Franklin 73, G. T. Donaldson 50, L. J. Woodcock 48, M. R. Jefferson 35) **and 48 for one dec.**; **Auckland 215 for nine dec.** (T. G. McIntosh 68, W. A. S. Silva 33, R. J. Nicol 42; I. E. O'Brien three for 41) **and 217 for four** (N. K. W. Horsley 106 not out, T. K. Canning 43). *Wellington 2 pts.*

Wellington needed to win outright to beat Auckland to the title. They set them a target of 243 to win or 169 to keep ahead on net average runs per wicket. Auckland secured the Championship by achieving the second objective before going off for bad light.

At Queen Elizabeth II Park, Christchurch, March 24, 25, 26, 27. **Drawn. Canterbury* 338** (R. M. Frew 55, M. H. W. Papps 41, G. R. Stead 56, P. G. Fulton 66, G. J. Hopkins 45; D. R. Tuffey seven for 69) **and 213 for four** (R. M. Frew 58, M. H. W. Papps 62, S. L. Stewart 60); **Northern Districts 496 for eight dec.** (J. A. H. Marshall 235, M. E. Parlane 68, S. B. Styris 52, R. G. Hart 31, Extras 30; R. D. Burson three for 98, P. J. Wiseman three for 126). *Northern Districts 2 pts.*

Marshall's 235 lasted 524 minutes and 445 balls and included 31 fours and one six. It was the highest innings in Northern Districts' history, bettering Styris's 212 not out the previous week.

At McLean Park, Napier, March 24, 25, 26. **Otago won by eight wickets. Central Districts 178** (K. P. Walmsley four for 53, C. R. Pryor four for 49) **and 152** (M. S. Sinclair 42; K. P. Walmsley four for 37); **Otago* 268** (C. B. Gaffaney 66, C. R. Pryor 38, S. P. Beare 60; M. J. Mason four for 67, B. E. Hefford three for 25) **and 63 for two** (C. B. Gaffaney 35 not out). *Otago 6 pts.*

Otago won their only State Championship victory of the summer after nine outright defeats.

CHAMPIONS

Plunket Shield		1952-53	Otago	1978-79	Otago
1921-22	Auckland	1953-54	Central Districts	1979-80	Northern Districts
1922-23	Canterbury	1954-55	Wellington	1980-81	Auckland
1923-24	Wellington	1955-56	Canterbury	1981-82	Wellington
1924-25	Otago	1956-57	Wellington	1982-83	Wellington
1925-26	Wellington	1957-58	Otago	1983-84	Canterbury
1926-27	Auckland	1958-59	Auckland	1984-85	Wellington
1927-28	Wellington	1959-60	Canterbury	1985-86	Otago
1928-29	Auckland	1960-61	Wellington	1986-87	Central Districts
1929-30	Wellington	1961-62	Wellington	1987-88	Otago
1930-31	Canterbury	1962-63	Northern Districts	1988-89	Auckland
1931-32	Wellington	1963-64	Auckland	1989-90	Wellington
1932-33	Otago	1964-65	Canterbury	1990-91	Auckland
1933-34	Auckland	1965-66	Wellington	1991-92	{ Central Districts / Northern Districts }
1934-35	Canterbury	1966-67	Central Districts		
1935-36	Wellington	1967-68	Central Districts	1992-93	Northern Districts
1936-37	Auckland	1968-69	Auckland	1993-94	Canterbury
1937-38	Auckland	1969-70	Otago	1994-95	Auckland
1938-39	Auckland	1970-71	Central Districts	1995-96	Auckland
1939-40	Auckland	1971-72	Otago	1996-97	Canterbury
1940-45	No competition	1972-73	Wellington	1997-98	Canterbury
1945-46	Canterbury	1973-74	Wellington	1998-99	Central Districts
1946-47	Auckland	1974-75	Otago	1999-2000	Northern Districts
1947-48	Otago			2000-01	Wellington
1948-49	Canterbury	*Shell Trophy*			
1949-50	Wellington	1975-76	Canterbury	*State Championship*	
1950-51	Otago	1976-77	Wellington	2001-02	Auckland
1951-52	Canterbury	1977-78	Auckland		

Auckland and Wellington have won the title outright 19 times, Canterbury 14, Otago 13, Central Districts 6, Northern Districts 4. Central Districts and Northern Districts also shared the title once.

STATE SHIELD, 2001-02

Note: Matches in this section were not first-class.

	Played	Won	Lost	No result	Bonus points	Points	Net run-rate
Wellington	10	8	1	1	4	38	0.79
Northern Districts. . . .	10	7	2	1	5	35	0.46
Canterbury	10	5	4	1	3	25	0.20
Otago.	10	2	5	3	0	14	−0.44
Central Districts	10	2	7	1	1	11	−0.55
Auckland	10	2	7	1	0	10	−0.62

Play-off

At Seddon Park, Hamilton, January 30 (day/night). **Canterbury won by two wickets. Northern Districts* 209** (49.5 overs) (J. A. H. Marshall 42, M. N. Hart 67; C. S. Martin four for 44); **Canterbury 213 for eight** (49.4 overs) (S. L. Stewart 76; G. W. Aldridge three for 37, M. N. Hart three for 31).

Final

At Basin Reserve, Wellington, February 2. **Wellington won by 53 runs. Wellington* 200 for nine** (50 overs) (D. J. Sales 62, R. A. Jones 71); **Canterbury 147** (44.3 overs) (P. J. Wiseman 42; M. R. Jefferson three for 19).

CRICKET IN INDIA, 2001-02

By R. MOHAN and MOHANDAS MENON

Murali Kartik

It was another crowded year for the Indian team, who played 16 Tests and 33 one-day internationals from October 2001 to September 2002. At both ends of the season, they found themselves in conflict with the International Cricket Council. In November, their tour of South Africa briefly threatened to split world cricket after India protested at penalties imposed by the ICC referee, Mike Denness; in September, India nearly had to send a second-string side to the ICC Champions Trophy because of the clash between their stars' personal sponsorship deals and the tournament sponsors. But the 12 months ended on an encouraging note: though their disappointing overseas record had been extended by defeats in South Africa and the West Indies, India levelled their Test series in England, and then shared the Champions Trophy with the hosts, Sri Lanka, when the final was washed out.

A packed, year-round schedule left little time for the stars to indulge in domestic cricket. Lip service was paid to the concept of all players appearing for their states when available, but the commitment was not always there in practice, and a system of central contracts for 20 national players, on a graded scale, was agreed for 2002-03. In the meantime, their frequent absence presented opportunities for lesser-known cricketers. For the second year running, Baroda and the Indian Railways, two of the less fashionable teams, contested the final of the Ranji Trophy, at the expense of supposedly star-studded teams such as Mumbai, who were knocked out in the pre-quarter-finals.

Reversing the previous year's result, Railways steamed to victory over Baroda, to a historic maiden triumph in the Ranji Trophy. They had entered the national championship comparatively late, in 1958-59, and reached only one final in the 20th century, when they lost by an innings to Tamil Nadu in 1987-88. But after the disappointment of 2000-01, when they lost despite taking a 151-run first-innings lead, this final proved third time lucky. The left-arm spinner Murali Kartik bowled them into a dominant position with five wickets on the second day, top-scored with 69 in Railways' second innings and helped demolish Baroda again to finish with eight wickets in the match.

It was a proud achievement for Railways, whose players represented a behemoth of an organisation. They lacked the shared background of many city teams, and had to put up with all kinds of difficult conditions, including the poor facilities at their ground, the Karnail Singh Stadium, a stone's throw from New Delhi railway station.

Straight after the final, Kartik was called up for a single one-day international against Zimbabwe. Never a favourite of the national selectors, he was quickly dropped again. But he finished the season at the head of the first-class averages with 38 wickets at 18.18. The leading Railways batsmen were the opener Amit Pagnis and Yere Gowda, who both scored three centuries in the competition, and were the only batsmen from any team to pass 750 Ranji runs. The form of their all-rounder, Sanjay Bangar, earned him a Test debut against England, and later he missed the Ranji final for India's one-day series against Zimbabwe – as did Baroda's strike bowler Zaheer Khan, who had shaped their triumph in 2000-01.

Railways appeared likely to be the last team to win the Ranji Trophy in its traditional format, in which 27 teams played in five regional zones, with three sides from each zonal league qualifying for the knockout. Reforms had been tried before, most recently the Super League system of the late 1990s. But a more drastic change, to a divisional system, had been talked of for some time, with Sunil Gavaskar one of its strongest advocates.

In August 2002, the Board of Control for Cricket in India approved a proposal to split the Ranji Trophy into two divisions, with promotion and relegation between an Elite Group and a Plate Group. The 15 sides who had reached the knockouts in 2001-02 formed the Elite, subdivided into two round-robin leagues. The two top teams from each Elite league would advance to the semi-finals. Meanwhile, the remaining 12 teams (including Karnataka, three-times Ranji champions in the 1990s) would compete for the Plate on similar lines; the Plate finalists would be promoted, replacing the bottom two teams from the Elite subgroups. The dismantling of the zonal system extended to the Duleep Trophy, introduced in 1961-62 as a higher tier of domestic cricket, which enabled players to present their claims to national selectors struggling to monitor all the Ranji sides. It had always been competed for by teams representing the five zones, but from 2002-03 was to be contested by three teams drawn from the Elite Group and two from the Plate.

The last Duleep Trophy under the zonal system, staged immediately after the Ranji final, was won by West Zone, the most consistent team. In the final round, they met the only side still able to catch them, but East Zone had to beat West to bridge the gap. Instead, West ran up 529 before two young bowlers, Irfan Pathan and Ramesh Powar, bowled East out for 162 in unusually wet conditions for April in Kolkata. A rain-affected draw was enough for West Zone to claim the handsome cup, which they had last won outright in 1985-86. North Zone, winners the previous two seasons, had to be content with second place. During their first match, against South Zone, Yuvraj Singh was called into India's one-day side; while others seemed to be in undue haste to join the national team, Yuvraj batted on to make a double-hundred before leaving.

Recently, it has seemed that no season goes by without a huge score from V. V. S. Laxman. But even after scoring 281 against Australia in 2000-01, Laxman found himself under the selectors' microscope. He had injured his knee in Sri Lanka in July, and made his comeback in October, in the Irani Trophy – his sixth consecutive appearance in this fixture between the Ranji champions and the Rest of India. The previous year, he had slammed 167 for the Rest against Mumbai; this time, his 148 helped them to beat Baroda, alongside Dinesh Mongia, who scored 125 and 90 not out.

In one-day cricket, South Zone won the Deodhar Trophy, winning all four matches against the other zones. India A crushed India Seniors – effectively the national side, led by Sourav Ganguly – in the Challenger final at Bangalore.

There seemed to be a healthy amount of talent crying out for promotion from the domestic game. Of the top ten batsmen in the first-class averages, only two appeared for India, though the internationals were slightly better represented among the bowlers. The only batsman with 1,000 first-class runs was Sridharan Sriram of Tamil Nadu and South Zone, whose five centuries included one against the England tourists; Akash Chopra of Delhi and Railways' Gowda fell just short of four figures. Three spinners collected 50 wickets, led by Sarandeep Singh, the Delhi off-spinner, who claimed 57, with Kulamani Parida of Railways and Utpal Chatterjee of Bengal close behind. A few of these cricketers were on the fringes of the Indian side, but their successes gave the playing field a more level look, even if the stars still monopolised media space. **R. Mohan**

FIRST-CLASS AVERAGES, 2001-02

BATTING

(Qualification: 600 runs, average 45.00)

	M	I	NO	R	HS	100s	Avge
P. M. Mullick (*Orissa*)	9	14	4	806	207*	2	80.60
Wasim Jaffer (*Mumbai*)	7	11	1	786	178	4	78.60
G. Gambhir (*Delhi*)	7	11	0	818	218	3	74.36
D. Mongia (*Punjab*)	7	11	1	743	178	3	74.30
R. S. Gavaskar (*Bengal*)	8	11	2	653	166	2	72.55
A. A. Pagnis (*Railways*)	8	13	1	800	133*	3	66.66
S. Sriram (*Tamil Nadu*)	12	20	1	1,263	149	5	66.47
Yashpal Singh (*Services*)	7	13	3	660	202	1	66.00
V. Rathore (*Punjab*)	7	12	1	716	249	3	65.09
Kavaljit Singh (*Jammu and Kashmir*) . .	6	12	1	713	206	1	64.81
S. Sharath (*Tamil Nadu*)	12	18	3	928	141*	4	61.86
A. Chopra (*Delhi*)	11	19	3	983	143	3	61.43
S. B. Bangar (*Railways*)	9	14	4	602	212	2	60.20
Sangram Singh (*Himachal Pradesh*) . . .	8	14	1	767	215*	3	59.00
C. C. Williams (*Baroda*)	8	14	0	806	157	3	57.57
S. G. Das (*Bengal*)	10	14	1	725	129	2	55.76
S. S. Raul (*Orissa*)	10	15	1	777	210	2	55.50
N. D. Modi (*Gujarat*)	7	14	2	661	118	1	55.08
Y. Gowda (*Railways*)	13	24	6	977	190*	4	54.27
Yuvraj Singh (*Punjab*)	9	15	0	802	209	3	53.46
H. H. Kanitkar (*Maharashtra*)	9	14	0	747	197	3	53.35
S. S. Das (*Orissa*)	9	14	0	702	253	2	50.14
Shafiq Khan (*Haryana*)	9	15	0	729	146	1	48.60
N. R. Mongia (*Baroda*)	12	19	3	763	164	1	47.68
T. P. Singh (*Railways*)	7	13	0	601	186	2	46.23
G. K. Khoda (*Rajasthan*)	11	20	1	877	167	2	46.15
Jyoti P. Yadav (*Uttar Pradesh*)	9	18	1	769	117	2	45.23

BOWLING

(Qualification: 25 wickets)

	O	M	R	W	BB	5W/i	Avge
M. Kartik (*Railways*)	357.5	127	691	38	5-33	3	18.18
B. K. V. Prasad (*Karnataka*)	215	65	474	26	6-35	1	18.23
Zaheer Khan (*Baroda*)	212.2	32	782	40	6-25	5	19.55
D. S. Mohanty (*Orissa*)	275	70	692	35	5-26	1	19.77
I. K. Pathan (*Baroda*)	180.4	44	530	26	6-72	1	20.38
L. Balaji (*Tamil Nadu*)	302.2	80	759	37	5-42	2	20.51
K. S. Parida (*Railways*)	432.3	127	1,069	52	8-65	2	20.55
A. Kumble (*Karnataka*)	300.3	84	731	35	7-115	3	20.88
H. H. Watekar (*Andhra*)	310.4	94	742	35	5-163	1	21.20
S. V. Bahutule (*Mumbai*)	339.5	89	837	39	5-56	2	21.46
Harbhajan Singh (*Punjab*)	335	78	816	38	6-62	3	21.47
M. Suresh Kumar (*Kerala*)	274.5	60	709	33	5-54	4	21.48
Shakti Singh (*Himachal Pradesh*) . .	296	94	716	33	5-78	3	21.69
R. R. Powar (*Mumbai*)	281.5	78	690	31	6-30	2	22.25
A. Mishra (*Haryana*)	242.1	67	649	29	6-95	2	22.37

	O	M	R	W	BB	5W/i	Avge
Iqbal Siddiqui (*Maharashtra*)	195.2	46	585	25	7-91	3	23.40
A. Bhandari (*Delhi*)	212.2	44	705	30	7-92	2	23.50
U. Chatterjee (*Bengal*).	579.3	186	1,194	50	7-32	4	23.88
Sarandeep Singh (*Delhi*)	505.1	120	1,389	57	6-67	5	24.36
B. N. Mehta (*Gujarat*).	244.2	47	661	26	6-53	3	25.42
Vineet Sharma (*Punjab*)	406.4	94	1,211	47	6-59	3	25.76
A. Barik (*Orissa*)	175.2	27	648	25	5-18	1	25.92
S. Pandey (*Madhya Pradesh*)	256.1	51	838	30	8-132	1	27.93
D. Ganesh (*Karnataka*).	266.3	72	788	28	4-47	0	28.14
M. R. Srinivas (*Tamil Nadu*)	261.4	62	765	26	5-57	1	29.42
S. S. Lahiri (*Bengal*)	484	117	1,356	42	6-73	2	32.28

*In the following scores, * by the name of a team indicates that they won the toss.*

IRANI CUP, 2001-02

Ranji Trophy Champions (Baroda) v Rest of India

At VCA Ground, Nagpur, October 13, 14, 15, 16, 17. **Rest of India won by six wickets. Baroda 318** (C. C. Williams 143, N. R. Mongia 31, H. R. Jadhav 43, R. B. Patel 44, Extras 30; Sarandeep Singh five for 78) **and 285** (C. C. Williams 83, N. R. Mongia 52, H. R. Jadhav 42, I. K. Pathan 32; Sarandeep Singh three for 75); **Rest of India* 331** (V. R. Mane 48, D. Mongia 125, A. Ratra 61; V. N. Buch five for 94, I. K. Pathan three for 95) **and 273 for four** (V. V. S. Laxman 148, D. Mongia 90 not out).

RANJI TROPHY, 2001-02

Central Zone

At Karnail Singh Stadium, Delhi, October 20, 21, 22, 23. **Railways won by ten wickets. Uttar Pradesh* 237** (N. D. Ali 30, M. Kaif 43, M. S. Mudgal 38, N. Chopra 49 not out; M. Kartik four for 67, S. B. Bangar three for 55) **and 129** (M. Saif 34; Zakir Hussain four for 46, K. S. Parida three for 28); **Railways 356** (Y. Gowda 190 not out; M. B. Tripathi three for 78) **and 14 for no wkt**. *Railways 8 pts.*

At K. L. Saini Stadium, Jaipur, October 20, 21, 22, 23. **Drawn. Vidarbha* 350** (A. V. Deshpande 56, V. C. Naidu 78, P. H. Sutane 37, R. S. Paradkar 38, S. A. Khare 68 not out, P. V. Gandhe 31; M. Aslam four for 60) **and 256 for six** (V. C. Naidu 34, P. H. Sutane 108, H. V. Shitoot 51 not out, Extras 30); **Rajasthan 533 for four dec.** (V. A. Saxena 66, G. K. Khoda 167, R. J. Kanwat 48, N. S. Doru 124 not out, P. K. Krishnakumar 93, Extras 35; P. V. Gandhe three for 139). *Rajasthan 5 pts, Vidarbha 3 pts.*

At Maharani Usharaje Trust Ground, Indore, October 27, 28, 29, 30. **Drawn. Madhya Pradesh 315** (S. M. Dholpure 64, S. Abbas Ali 35, N. A. Patwardhan 44, S. K. Kulkarni 60; A. W. Zaidi three for 56, M. B. Tripathi three for 64, N. Chopra four for 106) **and 280 for seven dec.** (S. M. Dholpure 40, A. R. Khurasiya 54, N. A. Patwardhan 58, M. B. Majithia 50 not out); **Uttar Pradesh* 238** (N. D. Ali 32, Jyoti P. Yadav 44, Rizwan Shamshad 54; S. Pandey three for 51, Y. A. Golwalkar four for 80) **and 244 for four** (N. D. Ali 41, Jyoti P. Yadav 100 not out, Rizwan Shamshad 96; S. Pandey three for 49). *Madhya Pradesh 5 pts, Uttar Pradesh 3 pts.*

At Karnail Singh Stadium, Delhi, October 27, 28, 29, 30. **Drawn. Railways* 292** (S. B. Bangar 41, A. A. Pagnis 126, Y. Gowda 41; R. J. Kanwat three for 73) **and 275 for four dec.** (A. A. Pagnis 133 not out, Y. Gowda 59, Raja Ali 47); **Rajasthan 175** (V. A. Saxena 38, G. K. Khoda 60; M. Kartik four for 63, K. S. Parida four for 64) **and 219 for six** (R. J. Kanwat 38, N. S. Doru 38, P. K. Krishnakumar 50 not out). *Railways 5 pts, Rajasthan 3 pts.*

Pagnis scored a century in each innings. In Rajasthan's first innings, Kartik, while bowling, ran out Kanwat for backing up too far.

At Kamla Club, Kanpur, November 3, 4, 5, 6. **Uttar Pradesh won by three wickets. Rajasthan* 250** (V. A. Saxena 39, R. J. Kanwat 63, Sanjeev Sharma 50 not out; N. Chopra three for 83) **and 153** (V. A. Saxena 38, R. J. Kanwat 55; A. W. Zaidi three for 18, G. K. Pandey five for 33); **Uttar Pradesh 281** (N. D. Ali 36, Jyoti P. Yadav 117, M. Kaif 55; R. J. Kanwat four for 71) **and 123 for seven** (Jyoti P. Yadav 48; R. J. Kanwat three for 34, L. Jain four for 34). *Uttar Pradesh 8 pts.*

At VCA Ground, Nagpur, November 3, 4, 5, 6. **Drawn. Vidarbha* 295** (A. S. Naidu 66, S. A. Khare 70, B. A. Yadav 32 not out, Extras 35; N. D. Hirwani three for 76) **and 400 for five dec.** (A. V. Deshpande 75, V. C. Naidu 43, P. H. Sutane 108 not out, A. S. Naidu 82, Extras 47); **Madhya Pradesh 192** (N. A. Patwardhan 33, K. S. Kulkarni 35, S. Pandey 35; C. E. Atram four for 66, S. A. Khare four for 27) **and 276 for nine** (N. V. Ojha 90, D. S. Bundela 39, N. A. Patwardhan 56; P. V. Gandhe four for 39, S. A. Khare three for 77). *Vidarbha 5 pts, Madhya Pradesh 3 pts.*

In the field, Vivek Naidu took six catches in the match for Vidarbha. Madhya Pradesh's last pair survived three balls for the draw.

At K. L. Saini Stadium, Jaipur, November 10, 11, 12, 13. **Rajasthan won by three wickets. Madhya Pradesh* 213** (D. V. Parmar 50, S. Abbas Ali 71; Sanjeev Sharma six for 55) **and 229** (C. P. Sahu 51, A. R. Khurasiya 64, S. Abbas Ali 50; Sanjeev Sharma three for 81, G. K. Khoda three for 24); **Rajasthan 270** (V. A. Saxena 43, G. K. Khoda 65, R. B. Jhalani 47, Extras 30; S. Pandey four for 82, N. D. Hirwani three for 116) **and 177 for seven** (A. S. Jain 43, G. K. Khoda 39 not out; M. B. Majithia four for 57). *Rajasthan 8 pts.*

At VCA Ground, Nagpur, November 10, 11, 12. **Railways won by ten wickets. Vidarbha* 108** (S. B. Bangar four for 43) **and 205** (P. H. Sutane 34, U. V. Gandhe 44, S. A. Khare 39 not out; M. Kartik five for 33); **Railways 284** (Raja Ali 133, Abhay Sharma 51; A. M. Piprode three for 63) **and 31 for no wkt**. *Railways 8 pts.*

At Maharani Usharaje Trust Ground, Indore, November 22, 23, 24, 25. **Drawn. Railways* 496** (T. P. Singh 186, Raja Ali 148, Abhay Sharma 65, Extras 37; S. Pandey eight for 132) **and 291 for seven dec.** (Jai P. Yadav 92, A. A. Pagnis 70, Y. Gowda 50 not out, Raja Ali 40; S. Pandey three for 80); **Madhya Pradesh 274** (C. P. Sahu 49, D. S. Bundela 111 not out, N. A. Patwardhan 34; K. S. Parida eight for 65) **and 158 for nine** (S. K. Kulkarni 30 not out, M. B. Majithia 34; T. P. Singh three for 53, K. S. Parida three for 24). *Madhya Pradesh 3 pts, Railways 5 pts.*

In Railways' first innings, T. P. Singh and Raja Ali added 326 for the fourth wicket. Bundela carried his bat through Madhya Pradesh's first innings; in their second, the last pair survived six balls for the draw.

At Green Park, Kanpur, November 22, 23, 24, 25. **Uttar Pradesh won by 155 runs. Uttar Pradesh* 210** (N. D. Ali 33, M. Kaif 42, G. K. Pandey 52; P. V. Gandhe six for 55) **and 329 for nine dec.** (N. D. Ali 34, M. Kaif 50, Rizwan Shamshad 42, M. Saif 48, N. Chopra 47; P. V. Gandhe four for 78, A. B. Waghmare three for 58); **Vidarbha 247** (S. U. Harbade 44, P. H. Sutane 71, S. A. Khare 31; A. W. Zaidi four for 67, M. B. Tripathi three for 42) **and 137** (G. K. Pandey three for 27, M. Kaif three for four). *Uttar Pradesh 8 pts.*

Kaif's full second-innings analysis was 10.5–7–4–3.

Railways 26 pts, Uttar Pradesh 19 pts, Rajasthan 16 pts, Madhya Pradesh 11 pts, Vidarbha 8 pts. Railways, Uttar Pradesh and Rajasthan qualified for the knockout stage.

East Zone

At Keenan Stadium, Jamshedpur, November 22, 23, 24, 25. **Drawn. Assam 434** (P. K. Das 69, S. Z. Zuffri 34, M. V. Joglekar 106, S. R. Das 50, Sukhbinder Singh 90 not out, Extras 33; Sunil Kumar three for 82, Shahid Khan three for 59) **and 238 for six dec.** (P. K. Das 39, S. B. Saikia 48, S. Z. Zuffri 54, J. Gokulkrishnan 32; Shahid Khan three for 69); **Bihar* 301** (N. Ranjan 52, Rajiv Kumar 30, Tariq-ur-Rehman 62, Manish Kumar 50; S. Ganesh Kumar six for 103) **and 172 for five** (Rajiv Kumar 105 not out). *Bihar 3 pts, Assam 5 pts.*

At Lal Bahadur Shastri Stadium, Kalahandi, November 22, 23, 24. **Orissa won by an innings and 127 runs. Tripura 152** (S. Dasgupta 35, R. N. Ghosh 36; D. S. Mohanty four for 24) **and 193** (S. D. Chowdhury 57, T. K. Chanda 46; J. P. Das three for 48); **Orissa* 472** (B. B. C. C.

Mohapatra 69, R. R. Parida 94, S. S. Raul 41, P. M. Mullick 109, P. Jayachandra 68, D. S. Mohanty 32; C. Sachdev four for 55). *Orissa 8 pts.*

Mohanty took four wickets in five balls in Tripura's first innings, all lbw.

At Eden Gardens, Kolkata, November 30, December 1, 2, 3. **Bengal won by eight wickets. Assam*** 249 (P. K. Das 59, S. Z. Zuffri 69; S. S. Lahiri three for 81) **and 206** (P. K. Das 83, J. Gokulkrishnan 44; S. S. Lahiri four for 65, U. Chatterjee six for 65); **Bengal 299** (H. A. Ferozie 82, R. S. Gavaskar 86, S. Mukherjee 31; S. Ganesh Kumar three for 93, Sukhbinder Singh six for 73) **and 159 for two** (Arindam Das 31, H. A. Ferozie 31, N. L. Haldipur 51 not out, R. S. Gavaskar 40 not out). *Bengal 8 pts.*

At Maharaja Bir Bikram College Stadium, Agartala, November 30, December 1, 2, 3. **Drawn. Tripura* 394** (R. N. Ghosh 31, T. K. Chanda 44, C. Sachdev 99, A. Sattar 63, Rajib Dutta 81, R. Yadav 38; S. Panda three for 42, K. I. Rao three for 117) **and 249** (T. K. Chanda 49, C. Sachdev 96, A. Sattar 30; M. Diwakar three for 64); **Bihar 412** (N. Ranjan 90, Rajiv Kumar 113, S. A. Shukla 120; J. Debnath three for 77, S. Dasgupta four for 92) **and 59 for four** (S. Shukla four for 24). *Tripura 3 pts, Bihar 5 pts.*

Sachdev missed a century by one run in Tripura's first innings and by four in the second.

At Athletic Stadium, Baripada, December 21, 22, 23, 24. **Orissa won by an innings and 97 runs. Bihar* 169** (Manish Kumar 45, S. Panda 45; A. Barik four for 46, S. K. Satpathy four for 27) **and 359** (Tariq-ur-Rehman 122, Rajiv Kumar 32, M. S. Dhoni 96; D. S. Mohanty three for 78); **Orissa 625 for eight dec.** (B. B. C. C. Mohapatra 114, R. R. Parida 82, S. S. Raul 73, P. M. Mullick 207 not out, P. Jayachandra 116; M. Diwakar five for 139). *Orissa 8 pts.*

Mullick's 207 not out lasted 394 minutes and 264 balls and included 21 fours and four sixes.

At Maharaja Bir Bikram College Stadium, Agartala, December 21, 22, 23. **Bengal won by an innings and 248 runs. Bengal* 457 for eight dec.** (Arindam Das 46, N. L. Haldipur 88, R. S. Gavaskar 166, S. G. Das 57, L. R. Shukla 54); **Tripura 89** (U. Chatterjee six for 23) **and 120** (T. K. Chanda 54; U. Chatterjee seven for 32). *Bengal 8 pts.*

At Keenan Stadium, Jamshedpur, December 29, 30, 31. **Bengal won by 154 runs. Bengal* 223** (D. J. Gandhi 36, U. Chatterjee 69, S. Sanyal 35; Shahid Khan five for 83, N. Ranjan three for 28) **and 242 for five dec.** (R. S. Gavaskar 101 not out, S. G. Das 79); **Bihar 113** (U. Chatterjee five for 36) **and 198** (Rajiv Kumar 30, Sunil Kumar 47, Manish Kumar 31, M. Diwakar 30; S. S. Lahiri five for 103, U. Chatterjee three for 37). *Bengal 8 pts.*

At Permit Ground, Balasore, December 29, 30, 31, January 1. **Orissa won by 429 runs. Orissa 174** (N. Behera 48, S. S. Raul 60; J. Gokulkrishnan five for 25) **and 423 for seven dec.** (B. B. C. C. Mohapatra 33, R. R. Parida 117, S. S. Raul 162, P. Jayachandra 50 not out; J. Gokulkrishnan three for 77); **Assam* 76** (D. S. Mohanty five for 26, S. K. Satpathy five for 11) **and 92** (A. Barik five for 18, S. K. Satpathy three for 28). *Orissa 8 pts.*

Ajay Barik ended Assam's second innings with four wickets in six balls, including a hat-trick, while Subhrajit Saikia carried his bat (for 29 not out) at the other end.

At Athletic Stadium, Baripada, January 5, 6, 7, 8. **Drawn. Orissa* 671 for six dec.** (S. S. Das 253, S. S. Raul 210, P. M. Mullick 80 not out, P. Jayachandra 30, G. Gopal 31, Extras 36); **Bengal 363 for six** (D. Dasgupta 137, R. S. Gavaskar 52, S. G. Das 38, S. Sanyal 38 not out, Extras 36). *Orissa 3 pts, Bengal 3 pts.*

Shiv Sunder Das's 253 lasted 660 minutes and 464 balls and included 33 fours and six sixes; Raul's 210 lasted 511 minutes and 412 balls and included 31 fours and one six; together, they added 436, an Indian third-wicket record.

At North-East Frontier Railway Stadium, Maligaon, Guwahati, January 7, 8, 9, 10. **Drawn. Tripura* 216** (S. Dasgupta 52, T. K. Chanda 42; G. D. Dutta three for 41, M. J. V. Ingty three for 52, J. Gokulkrishnan three for 45) **and 288 for six** (Rasudeb Dutta 45, S. Dasgupta 41, S. D. Chowdhury 76, A. Sattar 69); **Assam 411** (P. K. Das 57, S. R. Das 67, Sukhbinder Singh 118, J. Gokulkrishnan 52; T. Saha three for 96, J. Debnath five for 79). *Assam 5 pts, Tripura 3 pts.*

On first-class debut, Assam's wicket-keeper, Samarjit Nath, made eight dismissals (seven caught, one stumped) in Tripura's first innings and 11 (ten caught, one stumped) in the match, both Indian records.

Orissa 27 pts, Bengal 27 pts, Assam 10 pts, Bihar 8 pts, Tripura 6 pts. Orissa, Bengal and Assam qualified for the knockout stage.

North Zone

At Maharaja Agarsingh Stadium, Rohtak, November 1, 2, 3. **Haryana won by an innings and 118 runs. Haryana* 410** (Chetan Sharma 41, I. Ganda 109, Shafiq Khan 146, S. Vidyuth 31, S. Narwal 30; Vijay Sharma five for 67); **Jammu and Kashmir 113** (A. Mishra three for 29, S. Narwal three for 26) **and 179** (Raju Sharma 57, Kavaljit Singh 71; S. Vidyuth six for 24). *Haryana 8 pts.*

At PCA Stadium, Mohali, November 1, 2, 3, 4. **Punjab won by ten wickets. Punjab 540 for nine dec.** (V. Rathore 126, D. Mongia 178, P. Dharmani 119 not out, A. Uniyal 57; A. K. Thakur three for 70) **and 17 for no wkt; Himachal Pradesh* 211** (Sangram Singh 50; Vineet Sharma three for 83, A. Uniyal three for 33, Babloo Kumar three for 12) **and 343** (N. Gaur 51, Virender Sharma 122, Sandeep Sharma 44, Extras 31; Vineet Sharma three for 69, A. Uniyal three for 72). *Punjab 8 pts.*

Rathore and Mongia added 269 for Punjab's fourth wicket; Dharmani and Uniyal added 170 for the seventh.

At Air Force Complex, Palam, Delhi, November 1, 2, 3, 4. **Delhi won by an innings and 23 runs. Delhi* 467 for five dec.** (A. Chopra 123, G. Gambhir 75, M. Manhas 140, P. Chawla 66); **Services 297** (P. M. S. Reddy 34, Yashpal Singh 69, S. Verma 53, Sarabjit Singh 33, C. D. Thomson 42, J. N. Pandey 35; R. L. Sanghvi five for 69) **and 147** (Yashpal Singh 83; Sarandeep Singh six for 67). *Delhi 8 pts.*

At Feroz Shah Kotla, Delhi, November 7, 8, 9, 10. **Delhi won by six wickets. Haryana 316** (P. S. Sehrawat 47, Shafiq Khan 86, A. Ratra 31, S. Narwal 39; Arun Singh three for 76) **and 201** (Chetan Sharma 35, Shafiq Khan 71, A. Ratra 30; Sarandeep Singh three for 63, Abhishek Sharma five for 87); **Delhi* 327** (A. Chopra 48, G. Gambhir 91, M. Manhas 45, Abhishek Sharma 37; N. Aggarwal four for 56, A. Mishra three for 82) **and 193 for four** (A. Chopra 30, G. Gambhir 107, R. S. Gupta 33; N. Aggarwal three for 46). *Delhi 8 pts.*

The openers Chopra and Gambhir put on 121 in Delhi's first innings and 101 in the second.

At Shaheed Krishan Chand Memorial Stadium, Mandi, November 7, 8, 9, 10. **Himachal Pradesh won by 46 runs. Himachal Pradesh* 145** (R. Nayyar 41 not out; Jagtar Singh three for 36, A. Gupta four for 33) **and 345 for seven dec.** (R. Nayyar 97, Sangram Singh 100, Virender Sharma 51, Amit Sharma 51 not out); **Jammu and Kashmir 187** (V. Taggar 31, A. Qayoom 32; Shakti Singh three for 71, V. Bhatia four for 55) **and 257** (Raju Sharma 39, Kavaljit Singh 43, D. Mahajan 44, Vijay Sharma 50; Shakti Singh five for 103, V. Bhatia three for 66). *Himachal Pradesh 8 pts.*

At Gandhi Ground, Amritsar, November 7, 8, 9, 10. **Punjab won by 118 runs. Punjab 300** (P. Dharmani 106, Yuvraj Singh 67, R. S. Sodhi 48; S. V. Ghag five for 105, S. Javed four for 61) **and 397 for three dec.** (V. Rathore 34 retired hurt, Yuvraj Singh 90, P. Dharmani 127 not out, D. Mongia 73, R. S. Sodhi 40 not out); **Services* 356** (Yashpal Singh 202, Sarabjit Singh 49, Extras 35; Gagandeep Singh four for 68, Babloo Kumar four for 72) **and 223** (P. M. S. Reddy 36, Jasvir Singh 114; Vineet Sharma six for 61). *Punjab 8 pts.*

Dharmani scored his second and third centuries in successive first-class innings. Yashpal Singh's 202 lasted 446 minutes and 311 balls and included 17 fours and ten sixes.

At Nahar Singh Stadium, Faridabad, November 18, 19, 20, 21. **Drawn. Haryana* 347** (Chetan Sharma 73, Shafiq Khan 95, S. Vidyuth 33, N. Aggarwal 30; S. V. Ghag four for 99, Hari Prasad four for 130) **and 220** (I. Ganda 65, A. Ratra 38, S. Vidyuth 31; Arun Sharma four for 73); **Services 256** (P. M. S. Reddy 77, K. Chawda 33, Sarabjit Singh 33; A. Mishra four for 80, S. Vidyuth four for 59) **and 244 for six** (P. M. S. Reddy 53, Yashpal Singh 64, S. Verma 42, C. D. Thomson 44 not out; N. Aggarwal three for 39). *Haryana 5 pts, Services 3 pts.*

At Lohnu Cricket Ground, Bilaspur, November 18, 19, 20, 21. **Drawn. Himachal Pradesh 167** (Amit Sharma 32, Shakti Singh 43; A. Bhandari three for 29, Arun Singh three for 36) **and 421 for seven dec.** (Sangram Singh 190, Virender Sharma 58, R. Nayyar 84 not out; Arun Singh four for 80); **Delhi* 228** (G. Gambhir 32, R. S. Sharma 46, S. A. Rauf 58 not out, R. L. Sanghvi 35; Shakti Singh four for 58, Sandeep Sharma five for 68) **and 219 for three** (A. Chopra 86 not out, G. Gambhir 42, R. S. Sharma 42). *Himachal Pradesh 3 pts, Delhi 5 pts.*

Himachal Pradesh's wicket-keeper Ravikant Sharma took six catches in Delhi's first innings.

At Maulana Azad Stadium, Jammu, November 18, 19, 20, 21. **Drawn. Punjab 276** (R. S. Ricky 68, R. S. Sodhi 94, Gagandeep Singh 33; A. Gupta three for 72) **and 299 for nine dec.** (Manish Sharma 90, Yuvraj Singh 87; Vijay Sharma four for 69); **Jammu and Kashmir* 283** (S. Kanth 38, Kavaljit Singh 62, A. Gupta 100 not out; S. K. Sanwal four for 116, Yuvraj Singh three for 25) **and 211 for six** (Kavaljit Singh 89, D. Mahajan 46). *Jammu and Kashmir 5 pts, Punjab 3 pts.*

At Feroz Shah Kotla, Delhi, November 24, 25, 26, 27. **Delhi won by 200 runs. Delhi 286** (A. Chopra 71, S. A. Rauf 56, Sarandeep Singh 54 not out; Vijay Sharma five for 91, A. Gupta three for 69) **and 316 for four dec.** (P. Chawla 52, M. Manhas 128 not out, S. A. Rauf 81); **Jammu and Kashmir* 134** (Kavaljit Singh 56 not out, A. Bhatt 39; A. Bhandari six for 55) **and 268** (S. Kanth 42, Kavaljit Singh 90, A. Bhatt 31 not out; A. Bhandari three for 76, Sarandeep Singh four for 60). *Delhi 8 pts.*

Coming in at 204 for nine in Delhi's first innings, Sarandeep Singh scored 54 not out in 62 balls.

At Tata Energy Research Institute, Gurgaon, November 24, 25, 26, 27. **Drawn. Haryana* 204** (I. Ganda 39, Jitender Singh 89; Gagandeep Singh four for 40, A. Uniyal four for 65) **and 309** (Chetan Sharma 38, S. Vidyuth 105 not out; Vineet Sharma three for 70, S. K. Sanwal three for 67); **Punjab 318** (Yuvraj Singh 109, A. Kakkar 97, S. K. Sanwal 35; S. Narwal five for 103) **and 108 for five** (R. S. Ricky 41 not out; S. Virmani three for 60). *Haryana 3 pts, Punjab 5 pts.*

Haryana's wicket-keeper Satish Ohlan made six dismissals (five caught, one stumped) in Punjab's first innings.

At Indira Gandhi Stadium, Una, November 24, 25, 26, 27. **Himachal Pradesh won by nine wickets. Services* 329** (Jasvir Singh 81, S. Verma 73, C. D. Thomson 41, Extras 30; Shakti Singh four for 67, V. Bhatia three for 93) **and 179** (K. Chawda 44, Yashpal Singh 42; Shakti Singh five for 80, V. Bhatia four for 40); **Himachal Pradesh 463 for five dec.** (Sandeep Sharma 80, R. Nayyar 90, Sangram Singh 215 not out, Extras 36) **and 48 for one.** *Himachal Pradesh 8 pts.*

Sangram Singh's 215 not out lasted 405 minutes and 308 balls and included 26 fours and four sixes.

At Maharaja Agarsingh Stadium, Rohtak, November 30, December 1, 2, 3. **Drawn. Himachal Pradesh* 340** (N. Gaur 45, Sandeep Sharma 61, R. Nayyar 99 not out, Sangram Singh 71; S. Narwal three for 64, A. Mishra five for 64) **and 270** (R. Nayyar 102 not out, Sangram Singh 54, Virender Sharma 34; S. Narwal three for 64, A. Mishra three for 51); **Haryana 264** (Jitender Singh 51, A. Ratra 72 not out, Extras 30; Shakti Singh five for 78) **and 93 for one** (Chetan Sharma 30 not out, A. Ratra 50). *Haryana 3 pts, Himachal Pradesh 5 pts.*

Himachal Pradesh's No. 3, Nayyar, was stranded on 99 in the first innings, but in the second (when Mishra took a hat-trick), he made an unbeaten 102.

At Gandhi Ground, Amritsar, November 30, December 1, 2, 3. **Drawn. Delhi 499 for nine dec.** (A. Chopra 33, M. Manhas 193, P. Chawla 142, V. Dahiya 30, Extras 38; Vineet Sharma five for 127) **and 198 for nine dec.** (P. Chawla 75, V. Dahiya 38; Vineet Sharma three for 76, Gagandeep Singh four for 32); **Punjab* 441** (R. S. Ricky 100, Yuvraj Singh 102, D. Mongia 102, P. Dharmani 47, Extras 33; A. Bhandari seven for 92, Arun Singh three for 136) **and 58 for one** (R. S. Ricky 31 not out). *Punjab 3 pts, Delhi 5 pts.*

At Air Force Complex, Palam, Delhi, November 30, December 1, 2, 3. **Drawn. Jammu and Kashmir* 350** (S. Kanth 69, Kavaljit Singh 206; S. V. Ghag four for 80, Arun Sharma three for 68) **and 242** (Kavaljit Singh 58, A. Bhatt 98; Arun Sharma three for 39); **Services 287** (P. M. S. Reddy 34, Jasvir Singh 54, Sarabjit Singh 39, C. D. Thomson 64, Arun Sharma 60; Jagtar Singh five for 54) **and 202 for four** (P. M. S. Reddy 34, Jasvir Singh 54, Yashpal Singh 51 not out, K. K. Dixit 45). *Services 3 pts, Jammu and Kashmir 5 pts.*

Kavaljit Singh's 206 lasted 499 minutes and 370 balls and included 20 fours.

Delhi 34 pts, Punjab 27 pts, Himachal Pradesh 24 pts, Haryana 19 pts, Jammu and Kashmir 10 pts, Services 6 pts. Delhi, Punjab and Himachal Pradesh qualified for the knockout stage.

South Zone

At Gymkhana Ground, Secunderabad, November 21, 22, 23, 24. **Drawn. Hyderabad* 577** (D. S. Manohar 104, A. Nandakishore 214, Anirudh Singh 32, A. S. Yadav 89, Extras 57; A. Katti four for 133) **and 64 for two**; **Karnataka 416** (J. Arun Kumar 73, B. M. Rowland 44, R. V. Bharadwaj 76, V. S. T. Naidu 101, Extras 31; J. S. Yadav four for 106, A. S. Yadav three for 25). *Hyderabad 5 pts, Karnataka 3 pts.*
   Nandakishore's 214 lasted 588 minutes and 407 balls and included 35 fours; he put on 283 for Hyderabad's first wicket with Manohar.

At Nehru Stadium, Kochi, November 24, 25, 26, 27. **Drawn. Kerala* 176** (M. P. Sorab 49, S. C. Oasis 35; M. Faiq five for 52, H. H. Watekar three for 42) **and 259 for eight dec.** (S. R. Nair 83, K. N. A. Padmanabhan 74 not out; M. Faiq five for 90); **Andhra 259** (A. S. Pathak 40, Y. Venugopala Rao 76, K. S. Sahabuddin 44; M. Suresh Kumar five for 63) **and 78 for two** (Y. Venugopala Rao 37 not out). *Kerala 3 pts, Andhra 5 pts.*

At Guru Nanak College Ground, Chennai, November 24, 25, 26, 27. **Drawn. Goa* 238** (K. R. Powar 111, A. A. Velaskar 34, Extras 37; M. R. Srinivas five for 57) **and 117 for eight** (K. R. Powar 57; L. Balaji five for 42); **Tamil Nadu 396 for five dec.** (S. Suresh 65, S. Ramesh 36, S. Sharath 141 not out, R. R. Singh 38, T. R. Arasu 55 not out). *Tamil Nadu 5 pts, Goa 3 pts.*
   Balaji took five for 42 on Ranji debut.

At Indira Gandhi Stadium, Vijayawada, December 2, 3, 4, 5. **Andhra won by seven wickets. Goa* 270** (A. A. Velaskar 35, T. Jabbar 107, Y. C. Barde 38; K. S. Sahabuddin four for 67, H. H. Watekar three for 68) **and 191** (K. R. Powar 100 not out, S. B. Jakati 52; H. V. C. Prasad three for 14, H. H. Watekar four for 24); **Andhra 373 for nine dec.** (A. S. Pathak 68, M. S. K. Prasad 96, L. N. P. Reddy 37, I. G. Srinivas 52, R. V. C. Prasad 62; H. A. S. Khalid three for 130) **and 89 for three** (Y. Venugopala Rao 32 not out, A. S. Pathak 34). *Andhra 8 pts.*

At Rajinder Singh Institute Ground, Bangalore, December 2, 3, 4, 5. **Tamil Nadu won by four wickets. Karnataka* 215** (B. M. Rowland 113 not out; L. Balaji three for 84, A. R. Kapoor three for 42) **and 388** (B. M. Rowland 69, R. V. Bharadwaj 207 not out; L. Balaji four for 120, M. R. Srinivas three for 45); **Tamil Nadu 468** (S. Sriram 36, C. Hemanth Kumar 50, H. K. Badani 124, S. Sharath 113, R. R. Singh 58, A. R. Kapoor 44; M. A. Khan five for 81, N. S. C. Aiyappa three for 99) **and 138 for six** (H. K. Badani 34 not out). *Tamil Nadu 8 pts.*
   In Karnataka's first innings, Srinivas was removed from the attack by the umpires for running on the pitch. In the second, Bharadwaj's 207 not out lasted 413 minutes and 273 balls and included 32 fours and one six.

At Nehru Stadium, Kochi, December 2, 3, 4, 5. **Hyderabad won by 144 runs. Hyderabad* 117** (D. S. Manohar 35; M. Suresh Kumar four for 36, K. Rejith Kumar four for 32) **and 334 for nine dec.** (A. Nandakishore 44, Anirudh Singh 124; M. Suresh Kumar four for 115); **Kerala 125** (S. C. Oasis 47; S. L. V. Raju six for 42) **and 182** (M. P. Sorab 56; S. L. V. Raju five for 66, J. S. Yadav four for 32). *Hyderabad 8 pts.*

At Kurnool Stadium, Kurnool, December 10, 11, 12, 13. **Drawn. Andhra* 416** (G. N. Srinivas 39, Fayaz Ahmed 48, Y. Venugopala Rao 151, I. G. Srinivas 30; N. S. C. Aiyappa five for 112) **and 228** (R. V. C. Prasad 78, K. S. Sahabuddin 42; B. K. V. Prasad six for 35); **Karnataka 293** (B. M. Rowland 49, R. V. Bharadwaj 49, K. M. A. Aiyappa 62; K. S. Sahabuddin five for 92, M. Faiq five for 50) **and 28 for no wkt.** *Andhra 5 pts, Karnataka 3 pts.*

At Gymkhana Ground, Panaji, December 10, 11, 12, 13. **Goa won by eight wickets. Kerala 199** (A. N. Kudva 46, S. R. Nair 51; A. I. Aware three for 35, H. A. S. Khalid four for 28) **and 210** (C. P. Menon 55, A. N. Kudva 44; A. I. Aware five for 67, N. D. Kambli four for 49); **Goa* 197** (V. V. Kolambkar 38, K. R. Powar 37, T. Jabbar 51; R. Menon five for 48) **and 216 for two** (V. V. Kolambkar 74 not out, S. V. Kamat 71, T. Jabbar 57 not out). *Goa 8 pts.*

At Indian Institute of Technology Chemplast Ground, Chennai, December 10, 11, 12, 13. **Drawn. Hyderabad* 336** (D. Vinay Kumar 103 not out, A. S. Yadav 71, S. L. V. Raju 35; L. Balaji three for 84, M. R. Srinivas four for 67) **and 150 for two** (D. S. Manohar 65 not out, A. S. Yadav 38 not out); **Tamil Nadu 351** (S. Sriram 33, C. Hemanth Kumar 51, S. Sharath 69, T. R. Arasu 78, R. Ramkumar 37; N. P. Singh four for 95). *Tamil Nadu 5 pts, Hyderabad 3 pts.*

At Indira Priyadarshini Stadium, Vishakhapatnam, December 18, 19, 20, 21. **Drawn. Tamil Nadu* 290** (S. Sriram 38, C. Hemanth Kumar 31, H. K. Badani 98; K. S. Sahabuddin three for 101, H. H. Watekar three for 22) **and four for no wkt; Andhra 355** (G. N. Srinivas 62, Fayaz Ahmed 48, R. V. C. Prasad 99, K. S. Sahabuddin 54; M. R. Srinivas three for 72, S. Sriram three for 16). *Andhra 5 pts, Tamil Nadu 3 pts.*

At Gymkhana Ground, Panaji, December 18, 19, 20, 21. **Drawn. Goa 306** (S. V. Kamat 73, T. Jabbar 60, A. A. Velaskar 87; N. P. Singh three for 80, S. L. V. Raju three for 35) **and 263 for six** (V. V. Kolambkar 36, S. V. Kamat 47, K. R. Powar 101 not out; J. S. Yadav three for 75); **Hyderabad* 400** (D. Vinay Kumar 126, A. S. Yadav 155; A. I. Aware three for 116, N. D. Kambli three for 57, H. A. S. Khalid four for 95). *Goa 3 pts, Hyderabad 5 pts.*

   Vinay Kumar and Yadav added 290 for Hyderabad's fifth wicket.

At Rajinder Singh Institute Ground, Bangalore, December 18, 19, 20, 21. **Karnataka won by nine wickets. Kerala 228** (S. C. Oasis 47, S. R. Nair 87 not out; B. K. V. Prasad four for 53, D. Ganesh three for 64) **and 187** (A. N. Kudva 30, S. R. Nair 55, M. Suresh Kumar 53 not out; B. K. V. Prasad four for 31, D. Ganesh four for 47); **Karnataka* 342** (J. Arun Kumar 51, B. M. Rowland 83, R. V. Bharadwaj 43, V. S. T. Naidu 47, D. Ganesh 43, Extras 30; M. Suresh Kumar five for 73, S. R. Nair three for 25) **and 77 for one** (J. Arun Kumar 37 not out, K. S. Ponnappa 35). *Karnataka 8 pts.*

At Gymkhana Ground, Secunderabad, December 25, 26, 27, 28. **Drawn. Andhra* 365** (Y. Venugopala Rao 146, I. G. Srinivas 101, K. S. Sahabuddin 31; S. Vishnuvardhan four for 92); **Hyderabad 180** (A. Nandakishore 54, J. S. Yadav 36; N. Madhukar three for 42, K. S. Sahabuddin three for 59, H. H. Watekar three for 31) **and 237 for six** (A. Nandakishore 70, V. Pratap 31, D. Vinay Kumar 37 not out, S. L. V. Raju 32 not out). *Hyderabad 3 pts, Andhra 5 pts.*

At M. Chinnaswamy Stadium, Bangalore, December 25, 26, 27. **Karnataka won by nine wickets. Goa 80** (B. K. V. Prasad three for 23, D. Ganesh three for 31, N. S. C. Aiyappa three for 19) **and 198** (T. Jabbar 53, B. K. P. Misquin 41 not out; S. B. Joshi four for 47); **Karnataka* 214** (J. Arun Kumar 77, B. M. Rowland 54; A. I. Aware five for 58, A. Amonkar five for 76) **and 68 for one.** *Karnataka 8 pts.*

   Goa's wicket-keeper, Amitabh Velaskar, took six catches in Karnataka's first innings.

At Indian Institute of Technology Chemplast Ground, Chennai, December 25, 26, 27, 28. **Drawn. Kerala 223** (V. Girilal 37, K. Rejith Kumar 69; L. Balaji five for 75); **Tamil Nadu* 407 for five** (S. Sriram 78, S. Ramesh 126 not out, S. Sharath 102, A. R. Kapoor 32 not out, Extras 45; T. Yohannan three for 100). *Tamil Nadu 5 pts, Kerala 3 pts.*

   Ramesh batted for 626 minutes. He reached his fifty in 383 minutes (the slowest recorded in first-class cricket) and his century in 556 minutes (one minute short of the slowest ever).

Andhra 28 pts, Tamil Nadu 26 pts, Hyderabad 24 pts, Karnataka 22 pts, Goa 14 pts, Kerala 6 pts. Andhra, Tamil Nadu and Hyderabad qualified for the knockout stage.

West Zone

At GSFC Ground, Baroda, November 22, 23, 24, 25. **Gujarat won by nine runs. Gujarat 212** (N. D. Modi 34, N. K. Patel 35, M. H. Parmar 46, K. A. Damani 43; S. Joshi three for 30, T. B. Arothe three for 14) **and 211** (K. A. Damani 62, P. P. Vora 45, B. N. Mehta 32 not out; I. S. Pathan three for 48, S. Joshi three for 73); **Baroda* 187** (S. S. Parab 30, N. R. Mongia 40, A. P. Bhoite 34; L. A. Patel four for 56) **and 227** (A. C. Bedade 46, A. P. Bhoite 42, T. B. Arothe 47; H. A. Majmudar three for 58, L. A. Patel six for 77). *Gujarat 8 pts.*

At Middle Income Group Ground, Bandra, Mumbai, November 22, 23, 24, 25. **Mumbai won by seven wickets. Maharashtra* 216** (D. S. Jadhav 36, K. D. Aphale 51, A. R. Yalvigi 43; P. L. Mhambrey three for 38, S. V. Bahutule five for 69) **and 98** (D. S. Jadhav 40; R. R. Powar six for 30); **Mumbai 250** (A. A. Muzumdar 54, S. V. Bahutule 32, N. M. Kulkarni 40; Iqbal Siddiqui seven for 91) **and 65 for three** (A. A. Muzumdar 37 not out). *Mumbai 8 pts.*

At IPCL Ground, Baroda, November 29, 30, December 1, 2. **Mumbai won by an innings and 141 runs. Mumbai* 553** (Wasim Jaffer 178, A. A. Muzumdar 133, P. L. Mhambrey 51, R. R. Powar 110, Extras 36; R. B. Patel five for 154); **Baroda 89** (P. L. Mhambrey three for 27, A. M. Salvi three for 41, N. M. Kulkarni four for 15) **and 323** (N. R. Mongia 55, J. J. Martin 38, H. R. Jadhav 51 not out, A. C. Bedade 77; S. V. Bahutule four for 95). *Mumbai 8 pts.*
Wasim Jaffer and Muzumdar added 259 for Mumbai's third wicket.

At Municipal Ground, Rajkot, November 29, 30, December 1, 2. **Drawn. Saurashtra* 434** (S. Somasunder 119, P. J. Bhatt 40, F. U. Bambhaniya 109, S. Reuben Paul 74, Extras 36; B. N. Mehta three for 99) **and 157 for seven dec.** (S. Somasunder 56; B. N. Mehta five for 49); **Gujarat 322** (N. D. Modi 33, N. K. Patel 133, T. N. Varsania 63; R. V. Dhruv three for 42) **and 138 for two** (N. D. Modi 52 not out, M. H. Parmar 49 not out). *Saurashtra 5 pts, Gujarat 3 pts.*

At Sardar Patel (Gujarat) Stadium, Motera, Ahmedabad, December 6, 7, 8, 9. **Drawn. Gujarat* 308** (N. D. Modi 85, T. N. Varsania 118, K. A. Damani 43) **and 228 for six** (N. D. Modi 59, H. Joshipura 38, B. N. Mehta 31 not out, K. A. Damani 32 not out); **Maharashtra 233** (H. H. Kanitkar 45, A. V. Kale 32, A. R. Yalvigi 48 not out; B. N. Mehta six for 53). *Gujarat 5 pts, Maharashtra 3 pts.*

At Municipal Ground, Rajkot, December 6, 7, 8. **Baroda won by an innings and 184 runs. Baroda* 509** (S. S. Parab 47, A. C. Bedade 34, N. R. Mongia 164, T. B. Arothe 106, A. P. Bhoite 51, R. B. Patel 41; N. R. Odedra four for 140, S. H. Kotak three for 58); **Saurashtra 115** (Extras 35; Zaheer Khan five for 25) **and 210** (S. Somasunder 57, P. J. Bhatt 44, S. Reuben Paul 45; A. P. Bhoite four for 31). *Baroda 8 pts.*

At Sardar Vallabhai Patel Stadium, Bulsar, December 30, 31, January 1, 2. **Mumbai won by 298 runs. Mumbai 315** (A. A. Muzumdar 37, S. V. Bahutule 69, A. B. Agarkar 34, P. L. Mhambrey 44 not out, Extras 39; L. A. Patel three for 63, S. G. Bhatt seven for 43) **and 269 for nine dec.** (Wasim Jaffer 75, K. More 61, Extras 30; B. N. Mehta five for 67); **Gujarat* 185** (T. N. Varsania 53, K. A. Damani 50; S. V. Bahutule three for 45) **and 101** (A. B. Agarkar three for 24, P. L. Mhambrey three for 19). *Mumbai 8 pts.*

At Nehru Stadium, Pune, December 30, 31, January 1, 2. **Drawn. Saurashtra 331** (P. P. Joshi 47, P. J. Bhatt 39, R. V. Dhruv 50, N. R. Odedra 59 not out, J. P. Jobanputra 42; Iqbal Siddiqui five for 102) **and 339 for two** (S. Somasunder 70, A. A. Merchant 111 not out, N. R. Odedra 129 not out); **Maharashtra* 507** (N. A. Godble 186, H. H. Kanitkar 140, A. V. Kale 58, R. D. Khirid 35; J. P. Jobanputra three for 65, A. A. Merchant three for 90, R. V. Dhruv three for 121). *Maharashtra 5 pts, Saurashtra 3 pts.*
Godbole and Kanitkar added 316 for Maharashtra's second wicket.

At Nehru Stadium, Pune, January 5, 6, 7, 8. **Baroda won by six wickets. Maharashtra* 321** (J. S. Narse 50, N. A. Godbole 63, A. V. Kale 65, K. D. Aphale 43, R. D. Khirid 39; H. S. Parmar three for 71) **and 332** (J. S. Narse 64, H. H. Kanitkar 38, A. V. Kale 115, K. D. Aphale 71; Zaheer Khan five for 107, A. P. Bhoite three for 73); **Baroda 424** (C. C. Williams 137, S. S. Parab 74, T. B. Arothe 85, Zaheer Khan 43; Iqbal Siddiqui four for 116, M. V. Sane three for 84) **and 235 for four** (C. C. Williams 99, S. S. Parab 53, J. J. Martin 32 not out). *Baroda 8 pts.*
Baroda's openers, Williams and Parab, put on 185 in the first innings and 125 in the second.

At Wankhede Stadium, Mumbai, January 5, 6, 7, 8. **Drawn. Saurashtra* 379** (S. Somasunder 48, S. H. Kotak 96, P. J. Bhatt 32, F. U. Bambhaniya 34, S. Reuben Paul 48, Extras 37; P. L. Mhambrey four for 83) **and 152 for nine** (S. H. Kotak 42 not out; R. R. Powar three for 27); **Mumbai 410** (V. R. Mane 66, Wasim Jaffer 139, A. A. Muzumdar 93, V. G. Kambli 42; N. Doshi three for 96). *Mumbai 5 pts, Saurashtra 3 pts.*

Mumbai 29 pts, Baroda 16 pts, Gujarat 16 pts, Saurashtra 11 pts, Maharashtra 8 pts. Mumbai, Baroda and Gujarat qualified for the knockout stage; Baroda advanced directly to the quarter-finals as holders of the Ranji Trophy.

Pre-quarter-finals

At Sardar Patel (Gujarat) Stadium, Motera, Ahmedabad, January 23, 24, 25, 26, 27. **Drawn.** Gujarat were declared winners by virtue of their first-innings lead. **Gujarat* 499** (N. D. Modi 92, H. Joshipura 113, M. H. Parmar 89, P. P. Vora 65, S. G. Bhatt 37, Extras 53; K. S. Sahabuddin three for 100, H. H. Watekar four for 76) **and 175 for eight** (N. D. Modi 75 not out); **Andhra 456** (M. Faiq 71, G. N. Srinivas 34, Y. Venugopala Rao 37, M. S. K. Prasad 35, R. V. C. Prasad 150, H. H. Watekar 66; S. G. Bhatt three for 126, Kalpesh Patel six for 96).
R. V. C. Prasad and Watekar added 180 for Andhra's ninth wicket.

At Gymkhana Ground, Secunderabad, January 23, 24, 25, 26. **Hyderabad won by ten wickets.** **Himachal Pradesh* 192** (N. Gaur 99; N. P. Singh five for 27) **and 238** (Sandeep Sharma 50, N. Gaur 73, Shakti Singh 31; N. P. Singh three for 52, J. S. Yadav five for 91); **Hyderabad 403** (D. S. Manohar 111, A. Nandakishore 74, A. T. Rayudu 33, Anirudh Singh 37, A. S. Yadav 39, Extras 51; Shakti Singh four for 78, V. Bhatia four for 115) **and 31 for no wkt.**

At PCA Stadium, Mohali, January 23, 24, 25. **Punjab won by ten wickets. Assam 170** (S. Z. Zuffri 44, J. Gokulkrishnan 33; I. Malhatra seven for 59) **and 200** (P. K. Das 40, S. Z. Zuffri 40, S. R. Das 31, G. D. Dutta 32; H. Puri five for 66); **Punjab* 357** (R. S. Ricky 88, Manish Sharma 50, H. K. Kali 48, Navdeep Singh 51, I. Malhatra 37; M. J. V. Ingty five for 119) **and 15 for no wkt.**
On their first-class debuts, Malhatra took nine for 153 and Puri seven for 110.

At Karnail Singh Stadium, Delhi, January 23, 24, 25, 26, 27. **Drawn.** Railways were declared winners by virtue of their first-innings lead. **Railways* 497** (A. A. Pagnis 132, T. P. Singh 84, Y. Gowda 34, M. Kartik 42, S. V. Wankhede 55, Zakir Hussain 45 not out; A. Bhandari three for 92) **and 314 for four** (Jai P. Yadav 80, T. P. Singh 64, Y. Gowda 101 not out, Raja Ali 38); **Delhi 395** (A. Chopra 62, G. Gambhir 214, Extras 49; Harvinder Singh three for 83, M. Kartik three for 103).
Gambhir's 214 lasted 692 minutes and 463 balls and included 18 fours.

At K. L. Saini Stadium, Jaipur, January 23, 24, 25, 26, 27. **Bengal won by an innings and 51 runs. Rajasthan* 321** (G. K. Khoda 114, P. K. Krishnakumar 64, R. B. Jhalani 40 not out; L. R. Shukla three for 53, U. Chatterjee four for 86) **and 146** (G. K. Khoda 33, N. S. Doru 31; Sabir Ali six for 48); **Bengal 518** (D. Dasgupta 57, D. J. Gandhi 146, R. S. Gavaskar 46, S. G. Das 129, U. Chatterjee 31, Extras 44; Sanjeev Sharma four for 84, L. Jain three for 93).

At Guru Nanak College Ground, Chennai, January 23, 24, 25, 26. **Tamil Nadu won by 139 runs. Tamil Nadu* 182** (S. Sharath 31, T. Kumaran 32 not out; R. V. Pawar four for 41) **and 272** (S. Sriram 61, C. Hemanth Kumar 35, J. Madanagopal 45, S. Sharath 56; S. V. Bahutule three for 61); **Mumbai 186** (K. More 30, B. J. Thakkar 33, R. F. Morris 39, R. R. Powar 33; L. Balaji three for 25, A. R. Kapoor three for 20) **and 129** (K. More 39; L. Balaji three for 38, R. R. Singh three for 12).

At Barabati Stadium, Cuttack, January 27, 28, 29, 30, 31. **Orissa won by three wickets. Uttar Pradesh* 231** (M. Saif 79, N. Chopra 41; D. S. Mohanty four for 53, S. K. Satpathy three for 43) **and 369 for nine dec.** (Jyoti P. Yadav 73, Rizwan Shamshad 59, M. Saif 36, M. S. Mudgal 61 not out, M. B. Tripathi 35, Extras 32; D. S. Mohanty three for 93); **Orissa 320** (B. B. C. C. Mohapatra 31, R. R. Parida 38, S. S. Raul 35, P. Jayachandra 91 not out, G. Gopal 62; S. J. Srivastava five for 91) **and 284 for seven** (B. B. C. C. Mohapatra 56, S. S. Das 74, P. M. Mullick 83; N. Chopra five for 83).

Quarter-finals

At GSFC Ground, Baroda, February 5, 6, 7, 8. **Baroda won by an innings and 256 runs. Hyderabad 290** (V. V. S. Laxman 101, D. Vinay Kumar 41; Zaheer Khan five for 115, S. Joshi three for 45) **and 127** (V. V. S. Laxman 53 not out; Zaheer Khan five for 30); **Baroda* 673** (C. C. Williams 157, J. J. Martin 271, A. C. Bedade 56, R. B. Patel 51, Zaheer Khan 37; S. Vishnuvardhan six for 148).
Martin's 271 lasted 629 minutes and 404 balls and included 37 fours and two sixes.

At Eden Gardens, Kolkata, February 5, 6, 7, 8, 9. **Drawn.** Bengal were declared winners by virtue of their first-innings lead. **Bengal* 353** (S. C. Ganguly 36, S. G. Das 77, S. Sanyal 123, L. R. Shukla 52 not out; L. A. Patel four for 77, B. N. Mehta four for 95) **and 483 for six dec.** (D. Dasgupta 84, D. J. Gandhi 82, R. S. Gavaskar 78, S. G. Das 107, S. Sanyal 92); **Gujarat 321** (H. Joshipura 63, K. A. Damani 118; S. S. Lahiri six for 73) **and 69 for five.**

At PCA Stadium, Mohali, February 5, 6, 7, 8, 9. **Punjab won by 243 runs. Punjab 207** (Manish Sharma 99, P. Dharmani 41; D. S. Mohanty four for 35) **and 460** (Manish Sharma 73, Yuvraj Singh 50, P. Dharmani 41, D. Mongia 51, A. Kakkar 78, Harbhajan Singh 43, Vineet Sharma 47, Extras 37; D. S. Mohanty four for 97); **Orissa* 205** (P. M. Mullick 99, Extras 32; Vineet Sharma six for 59, Harbhajan Singh four for 39) **and 219** (B. B. C. C. Mohapatra 44, R. R. Parida 40, P. M. Mullick 72, G. Gopal 31; Navdeep Singh four for 36).

At Karnail Singh Stadium, Delhi, February 5, 6, 7, 8, 9. **Railways won by eight wickets. Tamil Nadu* 276** (J. Madanagopal 60, H. K. Badani 40, S. Sharath 43, T. R. Arasu 46; Harvinder Singh four for 66, M. Kartik three for 76) **and 326 for six dec.** (S. Sriram 121, J. Madanagopal 56, H. K. Badani 56 not out); **Railways 423** (S. B. Bangar 212, Jai P. Yadav 32, M. Kartik 58, Extras 42; L. Balaji four for 93, A. R. Kapoor three for 116) **and 180 for two** (S. B. Bangar 52 not out, A. A. Pagnis 42, T. P. Singh 43).

Bangar's 212 lasted 631 minutes and 487 balls and included 19 fours and three sixes; he added 167 for Railways' eighth wicket with Kartik.

Semi-finals

At GSFC Ground, Baroda, February 13, 14, 15. **Baroda won by 136 runs. Baroda* 222** (A. P. Bhoite 85; A. Uniyal three for 77, Harbhajan Singh four for 68) **and 233** (J. J. Martin 41, A. P. Bhoite 66 not out, Zaheer Khan 35; A. Uniyal four for 56, Harbhajan Singh three for 87); **Punjab 237** (D. Mongia 62, V. Rathore 55; Zaheer Khan four for 112) **and 82** (Zaheer Khan six for 25).

At Karnail Singh Stadium, Delhi, February 13, 14, 15, 16, 17. **Drawn.** Railways were declared winners by virtue of their first-innings lead. **Railways* 557** (S. B. Bangar 48, A. A. Pagnis 81, T. P. Singh 100, Y. Gowda 127, Raja Ali 67, Jai P. Yadav 49, Extras 47; S. C. Ganguly three for 112, S. S. Lahiri three for 118) **and 380 for three dec.** (S. B. Bangar 62, A. A. Pagnis 98, T. P. Singh 33, Y. Gowda 61 not out, Raja Ali 100 not out); **Bengal 325** (D. J. Gandhi 43, S. G. Das 82, S. Sanyal 59, U. Chatterjee 30, Extras 39; M. Kartik three for 77).

Bangar and Pagnis put on 124 for the first wicket in each of Railways' innings.

FINAL

RAILWAYS v BARODA

At Karnail Singh Stadium, Delhi, March 6, 7, 8, 9. Railways won by 277 runs. Toss: Railways.

Revenge was sweet for Railways. At Baroda the previous year, they had led by 151 on first innings, only to lose by 21. This time, an emphatic triumph on their home turf, with a day and a half to spare, told the tale of their bowlers' dominance, especially of the left-arm spinner, Murali Kartik. The bowlers also had plenty to do with the bat. Railways had claimed first use of the pitch but, after a middle-order collapse, owed a rather modest total of 253 to a fifty stand from the ninth-wicket pair, Khanolkar and Zakir Hussain. Any chance of Baroda fighting back was scotched by Kartik, who grabbed five of their first six wickets before his colleagues finished them off, 84 behind. Then, when Railways' second innings was faltering at 187 for six, Kartik came in and settled the issue by scoring 69, culminating in a last-wicket stand of 77, the biggest of the innings, with Harvinder Singh. Facing a huge fourth-innings target of 391, Baroda surrendered their title inside 37 overs with only Bedade passing 12. Kartik managed just six overs this time, and still took three for seven. Railways were celebrating their first Ranji Trophy shortly after lunch on the fourth day.

Close of play: First day, Baroda 17-0 (Williams 12, Parab 5); Second day, Railways 37-1 (Pagnis 24, Singh 3); Third day, Railways 306.

Railways

Jai P. Yadav c Martin b Buch	84	– lbw b Joshi	4
A. A. Pagnis lbw b Bhoite	35	– c Mongia b Patel	39
T. P. Singh c Mongia b Buch	18	– run out	27
Y. Gowda b Patel	21	– c Patel b Buch	24
Raja Ali b Patel	0	– c Williams b Arothe	66
*†Abhay Sharma c Parab b Joshi	9	– c Martin b Joshi	9
S. N. Khanolkar lbw b Joshi	44	– lbw b Joshi	4
M. Kartik c Mongia b Bhoite	2	– st Mongia b Bedade	69
K. S. Parida c and b Bhoite	5	– (10) c Bedade b Arothe	1
Zakir Hussain lbw b Patel	23	– (9) b Arothe	3
Harvinder Singh not out	4	– not out	34
B 5, l-b 2, n-b 1	8	B 14, l-b 3, w 3, n-b 6	26

1/51 2/82 3/146 4/148 5/170   253
6/184 7/190 8/196 9/249

1/13 2/66 3/99 4/155 5/183   306
6/187 7/203 8/223 9/229

Bowling: *First Innings*—Patel 23.4–6–67–3; Joshi 9–0–50–2; Bhoite 20–5–52–3; Buch 20–6–53–2; Pathan 10–1–24–0. *Second Innings*—Patel 31–9–66–1; Joshi 23–5–64–3; Bhoite 17–4–48–0; Buch 19–6–44–1; Pathan 2–0–12–0; Arothe 10–0–49–3; Bedade 5.4–3–6–1.

Baroda

C. C. Williams b Kartik	24	– c Abhay Sharma b Zakir Hussain	1
S. S. Parab c Khanolkar b Kartik	53	– (7) c and b Kartik	0
†N. R. Mongia c Khanolkar b Kartik	32	– (2) c Abhay Sharma b Harvinder Singh	0
*J. J. Martin b Harvinder Singh	12	– lbw b Zakir Hussain	8
T. B. Arothe c Abhay Sharma b Kartik	2	– c Abhay Sharma b Zakir Hussain	1
A. C. Bedade b Kartik	2	– (3) c Raja Ali b Parida	59
A. P. Bhoite c Khanolkar b Harvinder Singh	17	– (6) c Khanolkar b Parida	12
Y. K. Pathan c Parida b Yadav	7	– c Zakir Hussain b Kartik	0
R. B. Patel not out	8	– b Parida	6
V. N. Buch c Yadav b Harvinder Singh	0	– c Harvinder Singh b Kartik	10
S. Joshi c and b Yadav	1	– not out	2
B 3, n-b 8	11	B 5, l-b 6, n-b 3	14

1/80 2/87 3/112 4/124 5/128   169
6/138 7/160 8/160 9/164

1/1 2/5 3/38 4/42 5/92   113
6/92 7/92 8/95 9/106

Bowling: *First Innings*—Harvinder Singh 15–4–35–3; Zakir Hussain 7–0–39–0; Kartik 22–6–51–5; Yadav 28–13–31–2; Parida 2–0–10–0. *Second Innings*—Harvinder Singh 9–3–23–1; Zakir Hussain 9–1–39–3; Parida 9.3–3–30–3; Yadav 3–1–3–0; Kartik 6–4–7–3.

Umpires: F. Gomes and A. V. Jayaprakash.
Referee: D. P. Azad.

RANJI TROPHY WINNERS

1934-35	Bombay	1945-46	Holkar	1956-57	Bombay
1935-36	Bombay	1946-47	Baroda	1957-58	Baroda
1936-37	Nawanagar	1947-48	Holkar	1958-59	Bombay
1937-38	Hyderabad	1948-49	Bombay	1959-60	Bombay
1938-39	Bengal	1949-50	Baroda	1960-61	Bombay
1939-40	Maharashtra	1950-51	Holkar	1961-62	Bombay
1940-41	Maharashtra	1951-52	Bombay	1962-63	Bombay
1941-42	Bombay	1952-53	Holkar	1963-64	Bombay
1942-43	Baroda	1953-54	Bombay	1964-65	Bombay
1943-44	Western India	1954-55	Madras	1965-66	Bombay
1944-45	Bombay	1955-56	Bombay	1966-67	Bombay

1967-68	Bombay	1979-80	Delhi	1991-92	Delhi
1968-69	Bombay	1980-81	Bombay	1992-93	Punjab
1969-70	Bombay	1981-82	Delhi	1993-94	Bombay
1970-71	Bombay	1982-83	Karnataka	1994-95	Bombay
1971-72	Bombay	1983-84	Bombay	1995-96	Karnataka
1972-73	Bombay	1984-85	Bombay	1996-97	Mumbai
1973-74	Karnataka	1985-86	Delhi	1997-98	Karnataka
1974-75	Bombay	1986-87	Hyderabad	1998-99	Karnataka
1975-76	Bombay	1987-88	Tamil Nadu	1999-2000	Mumbai
1976-77	Bombay	1988-89	Delhi	2000-01	Baroda
1977-78	Karnataka	1989-90	Bengal	2001-02	Railways
1978-79	Delhi	1990-91	Haryana		

Bombay/Mumbai have won the Ranji Trophy 34 times, Delhi and Karnataka 6, Baroda 5, Holkar 4, Bengal, Hyderabad, Madras/Tamil Nadu and Maharashtra 2, Haryana, Nawanagar, Punjab, Railways and Western India 1.

DULEEP TROPHY, 2001-02

	Played	Won	Lost	Drawn	1st-innings Points	Points
West Zone	4	2	0	2	4	26
North Zone	4	1	1	2	4	18
East Zone	4	1	0	3	0	17
South Zone	4	0	1	3	2	11
Central Zone . . .	4	1	3	0	0	8

Outright win = 8 pts; draw = 3 pts; lead on first innings in drawn match = 2 pts.

At Nahar Singh Stadium, Faridabad, March 12, 13, 14, 15. **Drawn. South Zone* 168** (D. Vinay Kumar 49, R. V. Bharadwaj 64; A. Nehra five for 46, R. L. Sanghvi four for 46) **and 423 for six** (S. Sriram 77, S. Ramesh 31, D. Vinay Kumar 76, H. K. Badani 59, S. Sharath 102, Extras 41; A. Nehra three for 92); **North Zone 558 for nine dec.** (A. Chopra 37, V. Rathore 104, Yuvraj Singh 209, M. Manhas 44, Shafiq Khan 60, V. Dahiya 53 not out; B. K. V. Prasad three for 107). *North Zone 5 pts, South Zone 3 pts.*
    Yuvraj Singh's 209 lasted 542 minutes and 371 balls and included 28 fours and three sixes.

At Municipal Ground, Rajkot, March 12, 13, 14, 15. **West Zone won by 161 runs. West Zone* 416** (C. C. Williams 74, Wasim Jaffer 122, A. A. Merchant 32, N. R. Mongia 70 not out, S. V. Bahutule 35, Extras 31; K. S. Parida four for 96, N. D. Hirwani four for 137) **and 213 for two dec.** (C. C. Williams 39, Wasim Jaffer 103 not out, H. H. Kanitkar 40); **Central Zone 241** (Jyoti P. Yadav 39, G. K. Khoda 83, Jai P. Yadav 61 not out; I. K. Pathan four for 74, R. R. Powar three for 92, S. V. Bahutule three for 18) **and 227** (G. K. Khoda 51, Jai P. Yadav 120 not out; I. K. Pathan six for 72, S. V. Bahutule three for 68). *West Zone 8 pts.*
    Wasim Jaffer scored a century in each innings.

At Eden Gardens, Kolkata, March 19, 20, 21, 22. **East Zone won by 141 runs. East Zone* 365** (S. S. Das 60, D. Dasgupta 112, S. S. Raul 40, P. M. Mullick 34, L. R. Shukla 40, Extras 34; K. S. Parida four for 41) **and 211** (R. R. Parida 127, S. S. Raul 37; Harvinder Singh three for 77, K. S. Parida six for 39); **Central Zone 314** (Jyoti P. Yadav 48, Y. Gowda 125 not out, N. D. Hirwani 38, Extras 42; M. J. V. Ingty three for 57, S. S. Lahiri three for 57) **and 121** (G. K. Khoda 39; M. J. V. Ingty four for 29, U. Chatterjee three for 32). *East Zone 8 pts.*

At Nehru Stadium, Pune, March 19, 20, 21, 22. **West Zone won by 178 runs. West Zone* 396** (Wasim Jaffer 78, V. G. Kambli 33, N. R. Mongia 76, A. P. Bhoite 36, S. V. Bahutule 105; A. Nehra three for 70, M. Manhas three for 31) **and 273 for nine dec.** (Wasim Jaffer 58, H. H. Kanitkar 45, N. R. Mongia 76 not out; A. Nehra four for 55); **North Zone 238** (Sarandeep Singh 72 not out, Extras 44; I. K. Pathan four for 72, S. V. Bahutule five for 56) **and 253** (A. Chopra 119 not out, V. Rathore 44; I. K. Pathan three for 85, S. V. Bahutule four for 58, R. R. Powar three for 49). *West Zone 8 pts.*
    Chopra carried his bat through North Zone's second innings.

At Feroz Shah Kotla, Delhi, March 26, 27, 28, 29. **Drawn. North Zone* 567 for five dec.** (A. Chopra 58, V. Rathore 249, Shafiq Khan 73, V. Dahiya 76 not out, Yashpal Singh 53 not out) **and 186 for four** (V. Rathore 37, M. Manhas 37, Shafiq Khan 48); **East Zone 459** (P. K. Das 63, D. J. Gandhi 44, R. R. Parida 62, S. S. Raul 32, S. G. Das 97, L. R. Shukla 58, S. S. Lahiri 40, Extras 34; Sarandeep Singh five for 124, R. L. Sanghvi three for 155). *North Zone 5 pts, East Zone 3 pts.*

Rathore's 249 lasted 528 minutes and 381 balls and included 34 fours and one six.

At M. A. Chidambaram Stadium, Chennai, March 26, 27, 28, 29. **Drawn. South Zone* 292** (S. Sriram 82, D. Vinay Kumar 37, S. Sharath 42; A. B. Agarkar three for 47, S. V. Bahutule three for 53) **and 266 for three** (S. Sriram 140, D. Vinay Kumar 96); **West Zone 496** (H. H. Kanitkar 192, S. H. Kotak 36, K. D. Aphale 76, S. V. Bahutule 68, R. R. Powar 54; B. K. V. Prasad three for 53, H. H. Watekar five for 163). *South Zone 3 pts, West Zone 5 pts.*

All 11 batsmen reached double figures in South Zone's first innings.

At Maharani Usharaje Trust Ground, Indore, April 2, 3, 4, 5. **North Zone won by seven wickets. Central Zone* 368** (Jyoti P. Yadav 80, Jai P. Yadav 68, D. S. Bundela 116 not out, Harvinder Singh 31, Extras 34; Vineet Sharma four for 54, Sarandeep Singh four for 142) **and 175** (P. H. Sutane 50; Vineet Sharma three for 43, Sarandeep Singh five for 49); **North Zone 407** (A. Chopra 143, V. Rathore 43, V. Dahiya 33, Sarandeep Singh 94, Extras 38; S. Pandey three for 81, Jai P. Yadav four for 94) **and 137 for three** (A. Chopra 69 not out). *North Zone 8 pts.*

Chopra and Sarandeep Singh added 150 for North Zone's seventh wicket.

At M. Chinnaswamy Stadium, Bangalore, April 2, 3, 4, 5. **Drawn. East Zone 398** (P. K. Das 78, D. J. Gandhi 125, R. R. Parida 41, Rajiv Kumar 39, S. Z. Zuffri 45; H. H. Watekar four for 80) **and 141 for three** (R. R. Parida 66, S. S. Raul 50 not out); **South Zone* 419** (S. Sriram 34, M. S. K. Prasad 104, H. K. Badani 68, R. V. Bharadwaj 48, S. Sharath 49, M. R. Srinivas 30; U. Chatterjee three for 87). *South Zone 5 pts, East Zone 3 pts.*

At K. L. Saini Stadium, Jaipur, April 9, 10, 11, 12. **Central Zone won by two wickets. South Zone* 241** (S. Sriram 102, A. S. Yadav 54; K. S. Parida three for 67, R. J. Kanwat five for 74) **and 201 for nine dec.** (S. Sriram 76, R. V. Bharadwaj 32; Jyoti P. Yadav three for 11); **Central Zone 193** (Jyoti P. Yadav 67, P. H. Sutane 32, Jai P. Yadav 33; H. H. Watekar three for 51, M. Suresh Kumar five for 54) **and 250 for eight** (Jyoti P. Yadav 69, G. K. Khoda 38; M. Suresh Kumar five for 95). *Central Zone 8 pts.*

At Eden Gardens, Kolkata, April 9, 10, 11, 12. **Drawn. West Zone* 529 for six dec.** (N. D. Modi 118, H. H. Kanitkar 197, S. H. Kotak 50, K. D. Aphale 51, S. V. Bahutule 35 not out, Extras 35) **and 47 for four; East Zone 162** (S. Z. Zuffri 44, L. R. Shukla 48; I. K. Pathan four for 43, R. R. Powar six for 35). *East Zone 3 pts, West Zone 5 pts.*

In West Zone's first innings, Modi and Kanitkar added 320 for the second wicket.

DULEEP TROPHY WINNERS

1961-62	West Zone	1976-77	West Zone	1990-91	North Zone
1962-63	West Zone	1977-78	West Zone	1991-92	North Zone
1963-64	West Zone	1978-79	North Zone	1992-93	North Zone
1964-65	West Zone	1979-80	North Zone	1993-94	North Zone
1965-66	South Zone	1980-81	West Zone	1994-95	North Zone
1966-67	South Zone	1981-82	West Zone	1995-96	South Zone
1967-68	South Zone	1982-83	North Zone	1996-97	Central Zone
1968-69	West Zone	1983-84	North Zone	1997-98	Central Zone / West Zone
1969-70	West Zone	1984-85	South Zone		
1970-71	South Zone	1985-86	West Zone	1998-99	Central Zone
1971-72	Central Zone	1986-87	South Zone	1999-2000	North Zone
1972-73	West Zone	1987-88	North Zone	2000-01	North Zone
1973-74	North Zone	1988-89	North Zone / West Zone	2001-02	West Zone
1974-75	South Zone				
1975-76	South Zone	1989-90	South Zone		

Other First-Class Match

At M. A. Chidambaram Stadium, Chennai, October 19, 20, 21, 22. Gopalan Trophy: **Drawn. Tamil Nadu* 397** (S. Sriram 100, C. Hemanth Kumar 59, J. Madanagopal 43, S. Sharath 88, T. R. Arasu 36; T. T. Samaraweera four for 68, U. D. U. Chandana four for 77) **and 178 for four dec.** (S. Sriram 81, C. Hemanth Kumar 49); **Colombo District 198** (T. M. Dilshan 30, T. T. Samaraweera 31; L. Balaji four for 16, R. Ramkumar four for 62) **and 206 for four** (G. I. Daniel 77 not out, T. M. Dilshan 56).

The Gopalan Trophy was originally contested by Madras and Ceylon in 1952-53. It was discontinued after 1982-83 and revived in 2000-01.

PWC TEST RATINGS

Introduced in 1987, the PricewaterhouseCoopers (PwC) Ratings (originally the Deloitte Ratings, and later the Coopers & Lybrand Ratings) rank Test cricketers on a scale up to 1,000 according to their performances in Test matches. The ratings take into account playing conditions, the quality of the opposition and the result of the matches. In August 1998, a similar set of ratings for one-day internationals was added (see page 1422).

The leading 20 batsmen and bowlers in the Test ratings after the 2002-03 Test series between Australia and England which ended on January 6, 2003, were:

	Batsmen	Rating		Bowlers	Rating
1	M. L. Hayden (*Australia*)	889	1	G. D. McGrath (*Australia*)	910
2	M. P. Vaughan (*England*)	879	2	M. Muralitharan (*Sri Lanka*)	874
3	J. H. Kallis (*South Africa*)	865	3	S. M. Pollock (*South Africa*)	863
4	A. C. Gilchrist (*Australia*)	844	4	S. K. Warne (*Australia*)	823
5	S. R. Tendulkar (*India*)	843	5	Harbhajan Singh (*India*)	732
6	H. H. Gibbs (*South Africa*)	830	6	A. R. Caddick (*England*)	726
7	B. C. Lara (*West Indies*)	796	7	J. H. Kallis (*South Africa*)	708
8	R. T. Ponting (*Australia*)	794	8	M. Ntini (*South Africa*)	707
9	R. Dravid (*India*)	792	9	J. N. Gillespie (*Australia*)	694
10	Inzamam-ul-Haq (*Pakistan*)	791	10	D. R. Tuffey (*New Zealand*)	689
11	A. Flower (*Zimbabwe*)	758	11	A. Kumble (*India*)	688
	D. P. M. D. Jayawardene (*Sri Lanka*)	758	12	Shoaib Akhtar (*Pakistan*)	682
	K. C. Sangakkara (*Sri Lanka*)	758	13	Saqlain Mushtaq (*Pakistan*)	667
14	M. H. Richardson (*New Zealand*)	728	14	S. E. Bond (*New Zealand*)	666
15	S. Chanderpaul (*West Indies*)	727	15	Waqar Younis (*Pakistan*)	660
	D. R. Martyn (*Australia*)	727	16	C. L. Cairns (*New Zealand*)	653
17	J. L. Langer (*Australia*)	722	17	M. Dillon (*West Indies*)	646
18	S. R. Waugh (*Australia*)	698	18	Zaheer Khan (*India*)	590
19	Yousuf Youhana (*Pakistan*)	690	19	W. P. U. J. C. Vaas (*Sri Lanka*)	574
20	G. Kirsten (*South Africa*)	688	20	J. Srinath (*India*)	558

The following players have topped the ratings since they were launched on June 17, 1987. The date shown is when they first went top; those marked by an asterisk have done so more than once.

Batting: D. B. Vengsarkar, June 17, 1987; Javed Miandad*, February 28, 1989; R. B. Richardson*, November 20, 1989; M. A. Taylor, October 23, 1990; G. A. Gooch*, June 10, 1991; D. L. Haynes, May 6, 1993; B. C. Lara*, April 21, 1994; S. R. Tendulkar*, December 5, 1994; J. C. Adams, December 14, 1994; S. R. Waugh*, May 3, 1995; Inzamam-ul-Haq, December 3, 1997; A. Flower, September 11, 2001; A. C. Gilchrist, May 5, 2002; M. L. Hayden, October 12, 2002.

Bowling: R. J. Hadlee*, June 17, 1987; M. D. Marshall*, June 21, 1988; Waqar Younis*, December 17, 1991; C. E. L. Ambrose*, July 26, 1992; S. K. Warne*, November 29, 1994; G. D. McGrath*, December 3, 1996; A. A. Donald*, March 30, 1998; S. M. Pollock*, November 1, 1999; M. Muralitharan*, January 7, 2002.

CRICKET IN PAKISTAN, 2001-02

By ABID ALI KAZI

Richard Pybus

The fallout from the events of September 11 in the US had an immense impact on Pakistani cricket. New Zealand, who were about to tour Pakistan, pulled out at the eleventh hour; so did Pakistan's South African-based coach, Richard Pybus. Both eventually returned. Meanwhile, security concerns caused Sri Lanka to turn down a one-day tour, and West Indies refused to play their scheduled Test series on Pakistani soil. Even before September 11, India had withdrawn from the Asian Test Championship, refusing to visit Pakistan because of political tensions between the countries. With the Pakistan Cricket Board's finances severely hit, the ICC agreed that the West Indian series could go to a neutral venue, Sharjah, enabling the board to recoup some money through television rights. The New Zealanders returned in April for a shortened programme, which was also abandoned after a bomb exploded near the team hotel on the eve of the Second Test.

The cancellations meant that Pakistan played only seven Tests in 2001-02. They won six – four by an innings – against weak opposition. Pakistan overwhelmed Bangladesh three times and the West Indians twice, before completing their biggest Test victory, against New Zealand, thanks to a triple-century from Inzamam-ul-Haq and some outstanding pace bowling by Shoaib Akhtar. The one defeat was by Sri Lanka in the Asian Test final. But Pakistan beat Sri Lanka in two one-day finals at Sharjah. Their season peaked in June, when they defeated Australia 2–1 in the Super Challenge series, staged indoors at Melbourne. But they subsequently went into decline, and fell at the first hurdle in the ICC Champions' Trophy in September. The coach, Mudassar Nazar, was sacked, swiftly followed by the manager, Yawar Saeed, and Pybus was persuaded to return after his year off. A period of unusual stability at the PCB seemed to be at an end in October 2002 when the chairman, General Tauqir Zia, offered his resignation after Australia bowled out Pakistan for 59 and 53, in another Test transferred to Sharjah. But the president, General Pervez Musharraf, told him to stay on.

On the domestic front, the PCB continued to pursue the previous season's policy of expanding cricket at grassroots level. Of Pakistan's 107 districts, 98 played in the 2001-02 Quaid-e-Azam Trophy, 55 as teams in their own right, and 43 in association with neighbouring teams.

Grade I of the Trophy was contested by 18 sides in two groups, up from 12 the previous year. Relegation was waived, the 2000-01 Grade II finalists, Sialkot and Hyderabad, were promoted and the board introduced four new teams made up of left-over players from the four provinces of Pakistan: Rest of Punjab, Rest of Sindh, Rest of North-West Frontier Province and Rest of Baluchistan. In fact there was no other first-class side from Baluchistan, whose principal city, Quetta, played in Grade II. The Rest teams propped up their respective groups, which were won comfortably by Karachi Whites and Peshawar, with six victories apiece. They met in a repeat of the 1998-99 final; then, Peshawar won their maiden title, but this time Karachi took revenge, claiming their 17th national crown.

In the Grade II final, Multan beat Dadu, one of the new district teams, who earned promotion at their first attempt. But the players attracting most media attention in Grade II did not even win a match. The board admitted a side representing Afghanistan, a country then being bombed by US-led forces in the aftermath of the September terrorist attacks. In fact, the Afghan captain Allahdad Noori explained, his players had not just crossed the border. He said that they were refugees who migrated to Peshawar in the 1980s after the Soviet Union invaded Afghanistan. The team played five two-day matches, losing three and drawing two.

The Patron's Trophy for departmental sides was won by National Bank, who headed the table from KRL. The final had been abolished, but KRL were lucky to get so far; they were supposed to be relegated after coming last the previous season. Instead, Grade I grew from eight teams to ten, with PWD and Sui Gas the new entrants. Sui Gas went straight down again, without a win. They were replaced by Servis Industries, returning to first-class cricket after a 15-year gap; they had won the Grade II final against Saga Sports, one of four new departmental sides admitted by the PCB. This reversed the board's policy to cut back the departmental teams, but there was an even bigger U-turn in July, when it was announced that in 2002-03 the regional and departmental sides would compete in a single competition for the Quaid-e-Azam Trophy, a format last tried in 1999-2000 but abandoned after one season.

The board also gave up the experiment of separate one-day tournaments for departments and regional sides: the national one-day tournament was contested by all 28 teams from the Quaid-e-Azam and Patron's Trophy. Two departments reached the final, where PIA narrowly beat Habib Bank. Peshawar were Under-19 champions, with Grade II won by the Federally Administered Tribal Areas, from the Afghan border.

The expansion of domestic cricket helped 11 players to reach 1,000 runs during the season. Misbah-ul-Haq, of KRL and Sargodha, scored most with 1,386 and also headed the averages at 66. He made four hundreds, including two doubles. The leading wicket-taker was 21-year-old Fazl-e-Akbar, of PIA and Quaid-e-Azam finalists Peshawar. He took 95, improving on his 86 in 1997-98. Tahir Mughal (Sialkot and ADBP) topped the bowling averages with 83 at 15.75 apiece, and Humayun Farhat (Allied Bank and Lahore Blues) was the most successful wicket-keeper with 55 catches and 12 stumpings. Ijaz Ahmed junior (Allied Bank and Faisalabad) was the leading all-round performer, with 1,087 runs, 25 wickets and 20 catches.

FIRST-CLASS AVERAGES, 2001-02

BATTING

(Qualification: 750 runs)

	M	I	NO	R	HS	100s	Avge
Misbah-ul-Haq (*Sargodha/KRL*)	18	24	3	1,386	204*	4	66.00
Rehan Rafiq (*Bahawalpur/WAPDA*)	11	17	4	800	197*	3	61.53
Babar Naeem (*Rawalpindi*)	7	14	0	832	227	2	59.42
Ijaz Ahmed, jun. (*Faisalabad/Allied Bank*)	15	22	2	1,087	116	5	54.35
Mohammad Ramzan (*Faisalabad/KRL*)	16	27	3	1,297	162	4	54.04
Hasan Raza (*Karachi Whites/Habib Bank*)	18	28	7	1,095	256	2	52.14
Saeed bin Nasir (*Karachi Whites/KRL*)	17	30	7	1,162	133	3	50.52

	M	I	NO	R	HS	100s	Avge
Usman Tariq (*Bahawalpur/Allied Bank*).	17	28	3	1,183	210	1	47.32
Faisal Iqbal (*Karachi Whites/PIA*).	11	19	2	785	171	3	46.17
Asim Kamal (*Karachi Blues/Pakistan Customs*)	14	20	2	817	160	3	45.38
Farhan Adil (*Karachi Blues/Habib Bank*). . . .	16	25	2	1,041	124	3	45.26
Zahoor Elahi (*Faisalabad/ADBP*).	17	30	2	1,202	108	2	42.92
Bilal Asad (*Islamabad/PWD*).	17	32	2	1,260	112	3	42.00
Imran Farhat (*Habib Bank/ADBP*).	17	30	1	1,200	204	3	41.37
Mohammad Hafeez (*Sargodha/Sui Gas*)	15	23	0	919	177	3	39.95
Shadab Kabir (*Karachi Whites/Pakistan Customs*)	12	19	0	759	137	2	39.94
Ghulam Ali (*Karachi Whites/PIA*)	18	32	1	1,228	113*	2	39.61
Majid Jahangir (*Sialkot/ADBP*).	13	22	1	785	104	1	37.38
Saeed Anwar, jun. (*Rest of Punjab/KRL*).	13	25	3	779	144*	2	35.40
Inam-ul-Haq (*Sialkot/ADBP*).	15	28	1	944	101	1	34.96
Kashif Siddiq (*Lahore Whites/Pakistan Customs*)	13	22	0	762	103	2	34.63
Bazid Khan (*Karachi Blues/PWD*).	16	28	0	962	127	1	34.35
Imran Nazir (*Sheikhupura/National Bank*) . . .	17	29	3	833	127	1	32.03
Kamran Akmal (*Lahore Whites/National Bank*). .	17	29	3	831	120	2	31.96
Salim Elahi (*Lahore Blues/Habib Bank*)	14	25	1	753	168	1	31.37
Yasir Hameed (*Peshawar/PIA*)	15	27	2	774	171*	1	30.96
Mohammad Hussain (*Lahore Blues/Sui Gas*) . . .	14	26	0	773	126	1	29.73

BOWLING

(Qualification: 40 wickets)

	O	M	R	W	BB	5W/i	Avge
Tahir Mughal (*Sialkot/ADBP*)	396.3	74	1,308	83	7-63	6	15.75
Kabir Khan (*Peshawar/Habib Bank*)	320.1	63	930	56	4-21	0	16.60
Mohammad Javed (*Karachi Blues/National Bank*)	242.4	61	688	41	5-63	3	16.78
Fazl-e-Akbar (*Peshawar/PIA*)	508.4	98	1,656	95	8-68	9	17.43
Mohammad Zahid (*Bahawalpur/Allied Bank*). .	408.1	114	873	48	6-106	5	18.18
Naeem Akhtar (*Rawalpindi/KRL*).	334.1	73	933	51	6-53	3	18.29
Waqar Ahmed (*Pakistan Customs*)	424.1	74	1,519	80	6-46	8	18.98
Jaffer Nazir (*Sheikhupura/KRL*).	464.1	100	1,324	69	7-43	5	19.18
Shahid Nazir (*Faisalabad/Habib Bank*).	319.1	76	924	48	5-46	1	19.25
Mushtaq Ahmed (*Rest of Punjab/National Bank*)	343.5	74	1,207	62	6-79	5	19.46
Waqas Ahmed (*Lahore Blues/WAPDA*)	308.1	60	994	51	7-84	5	19.49
Danish Kaneria (*Karachi Whites/Habib Bank*) .	292	61	871	44	6-42	4	19.79
Yasir Arafat (*Rawalpindi/KRL*)	485.3	71	1,853	91	7-102	6	20.36
Shabbir Ahmed (*Rest of Punjab/National Bank*)	456.3	104	1,249	61	5-21	2	20.47
Mohammad Hussain (*Lahore Blues/Sui Gas*) . . .	548.4	187	1,306	63	6-60	6	20.73
Raees Amjad (*Hyderabad/WAPDA*)	288.5	48	978	46	6-35	3	21.26
Sarfraz Ahmed (*Gujranwala/WAPDA*).	364.3	90	878	40	5-24	2	21.95
Abdur Rauf (*Rest of Punjab/Sui Gas*)	499.5	86	1,855	84	8-40	5	22.08
Sajid Shah (*Rest of NWFP/Habib Bank*) . . .	357.4	53	1,280	56	7-44	2	22.85
Zahid Saeed (*Sialkot/National Bank*)	320.1	52	1,127	49	5-73	1	23.00
Faisal Irfan (*Rest of Baluchistan/WAPDA*) . . .	384.1	86	1,042	44	4-44	0	23.68
Ali Raza (*Rest of Sindh/PWD*)	293.4	45	956	40	7-52	1	23.90
Tanvir Ahmed (*Karachi Whites/PWD*).	563.4	103	1,878	75	7-75	6	25.04
Iftikhar Anjum (*Islamabad/ADBP*).	458.1	93	1,546	61	7-80	3	25.34
Ahmed Hayat (*Sargodha/Sui Gas*)	278.2	29	1,017	40	6-42	3	25.42
Naved-ul-Hasan (*Sheikhupura/Allied Bank*) . . .	391.4	54	1,486	57	7-49	2	26.07
Mubashir Nazir (*Gujranwala/ADBP*)	323.1	67	1,091	41	5-27	2	26.60
Arshad Khan (*Peshawar/Allied Bank*).	523.3	134	1,337	49	8-80	2	27.28
Riaz Sheikh (*Karachi Blues/PWD*).	391.3	64	1,323	43	5-36	1	30.76

PCB PATRON'S TROPHY, 2001-02

	Played	Won	Lost	Drawn	1st-inns Points	Points
National Bank	9	6	1	2	18	72
KRL	9	4	2	3	18	54
Allied Bank	9	4	2	3	15	51
WAPDA	9	4	4	1	12	48
PIA	9	3	1	5	18	45
Pakistan Customs	9	3	3	3	15	42
Habib Bank	9	2	2	5	18	36
ADBP	9	3	5	1	6	33
PWD	9	2	4	3	6	24
Sui Gas	9	0	7	2	0	0

Outright win = 9 pts; lead on first innings in a won or drawn game = 3 pts.

National Bank won the Trophy by virtue of leading the points table.

*In the following scores, * by the name of a team indicates that they won the toss.*

At Jinnah Stadium, Gujranwala, September 21, 22, 23. **National Bank won by ten wickets. National Bank 405** (Naumanullah 114, Akhtar Sarfraz 57, Sajid Ali 123 not out; Faisal Afridi three for 89, Iftikhar Anjum four for 85) **and 37 for no wkt; ADBP* 150** (Imran Abbas 43; Waqar Younis three for 39, Mushtaq Ahmed four for 37) **and 291** (Inam-ul-Haq 65, Faisal Naved 33, Imran Abbas 37, Zahoor Elahi 64 not out, Javed Hayat 31). *National Bank 12 pts.*

At Saga Cricket Ground, Sialkot, September 21, 22, 23, 24. **PIA won by five wickets. Allied Bank 186** (Naved Latif 80, Ata-ur-Rehman 31; Abdul Razzaq four for 50, Azhar Mahmood three for 45) **and 214** (Usman Tariq 94, Humayun Farhat 69; Azhar Mahmood seven for 55); **PIA* 224** (Ghulam Ali 59, Yousuf Youhana 54; Aqib Javed three for 47, Aamir Nazir three for 64) **and 180 for five** (Ghulam Ali 32, Sohail Jaffer 42, Yousuf Youhana 52). *PIA 12 pts.*

At Iqbal Stadium, Faisalabad, September 21, 22, 23. **Habib Bank won by 227 runs. Habib Bank 273** (Salim Elahi 30, Younis Khan 73, Atiq-uz-Zaman 80, Shahid Nazir 35; Rajesh Ramesh four for 56) **and 235** (Taufeeq Umar 31, Salim Elahi 36, Irfan Fazil 50, Shahid Nazir 45; Nadeem Iqbal three for 62); **PWD* 144** (Bazid Khan 37; Kabir Khan three for 26, Danish Kaneria three for 44) **and 137** (Tanvir Ahmed 40; Kabir Khan three for 20). *Habib Bank 12 pts.*

At KRL Cricket Ground, Rawalpindi, September 21, 22, 23. **KRL won by nine wickets. Sui Gas 201** (Sohail Idrees 40, Saleem Mughal 40, Extras 43; Shoaib Akhtar four for 46) **and 253** (Mohammad Hafeez 112, Extras 33; Shoaib Akhtar three for 38, Jaffer Nazir four for 56); **KRL* 410** (Ali Naqvi 68, Saeed Anwar, jun. 45, Mohammad Wasim 48, Misbah-ul-Haq 32, Intikhab Alam 52, Yasir Arafat 31, Extras 60; Abdur Rauf four for 105, Wasim Khan three for 116) **and 47 for one.** *KRL 12 pts.*

At Sheikhupura Stadium, Sheikhupura, September 21, 22, 23, 24. **Pakistan Customs won by an innings and 111 runs. Pakistan Customs* 577 for nine dec.** (Shadab Kabir 137, Kashif Siddiq 103, Aamer Bashir 76, Asim Kamal 40, Wasim Yousufi 42, Salman Fazal 53 not out, Waqar Ahmed 46, Extras 41; Kamran Hussain three for 91, Shafiq Ahmed three for 124); **WAPDA 221** (Tariq Aziz 103, Kashif Raza 34; Tabish Nawab five for 64) **and 245** (Rafatullah Mohmand 97, Adil Nisar 59; Salman Fazal five for 86, Tabish Nawab four for 84). *Pakistan Customs 12 pts.*

At Gaddafi Stadium, Lahore, September 27, 28, 29. **Allied Bank won by nine wickets. ADBP 166** (Inam-ul-Haq 63; Naved-ul-Hasan four for 85, Aamir Nazir three for 58) **and 163** (Inam-ul-Haq 32; Ata-ur-Rehman three for 30, Aamir Nazir four for 55); **Allied Bank* 231** (Ijaz Ahmed, jun. 107 not out, Extras 44; Faisal Afridi three for 69, Fahad Masood three for 44, Tahir Mughal three for 48) **and 101 for one** (Naved Latif 54 not out). *Allied Bank 12 pts.*

At Iqbal Stadium, Faisalabad, September 27, 28, 29, 30. **Drawn. Habib Bank 347** (Imran Farhat 41, Salim Elahi 83, Younis Khan 60, Atiq-uz-Zaman 76, Shahid Nazir 38; Waqar Ahmed three for 69, Kashif Siddiq three for 68) **and 375** (Imran Farhat 91, Salim Elahi 48, Younis Khan 44, Farhan Adil 78; Waqar Ahmed five for 81); **Pakistan Customs* 282** (Shadab Kabir 130, Asim Kamal 55; Kabir Khan four for 34) **and 105 for three** (Shadab Kabir 30). *Habib Bank 3 pts.*

At KRL Cricket Ground, Rawalpindi, September 27, 28, 29. **KRL won by an innings and 21 runs. KRL 423** (Ali Naqvi 39, Mohammad Ramzan 66, Mohammad Wasim 79, Intikhab Alam 69, Yasir Arafat 60, Shoaib Akhtar 47, Extras 37; Faisal Irfan four for 78); **WAPDA* 199** (Rafatullah Mohmand 38, Rizwan Malik 47, Adil Nisar 48 not out, Extras 35; Yasir Arafat three for 46, Ali Naqvi three for 34) **and 203** (Bilal Moin 70, Adil Nisar 54 not out, Kashif Raza 30; Yasir Arafat five for 62). *KRL 12 pts.*

At Sheikhupura Stadium, Sheikhupura, September 27, 28, 29, 30. **Drawn. PIA 267** (Sohail Jaffer 65, Asif Mujtaba 50, Yousuf Youhana 66; Waqar Younis three for 38, Mushtaq Ahmed three for 86) **and 325** (Ghulam Ali 44, Faisal Iqbal 56, Asif Mujtaba 87, Abdul Razzaq 33, Azhar Mahmood 33, Wasim Akram 40; Waqar Younis four for 71); **National Bank* 225** (Naumanullah 67, Waqar Younis 43; Wasim Akram four for 39, Abdul Razzaq three for 68) **and 330 for eight** (Akhtar Sarfraz 89, Sajid Ali 58, Inzamam-ul-Haq 64 not out; Wasim Akram four for 53, Abdul Razzaq four for 55). *PIA 3 pts.*

At Jinnah Stadium, Sialkot, September 27, 28, 29, 30. **PWD won by six wickets. Sui Gas 316** (Ali Hussain 54, Mohammad Hafeez 43, Sohail Idrees 60, Mohammad Hussain 36, Asad Iqbal 34; Tanvir Ahmed three for 80, Bilal Asad three for 46) **and 135** (Asim Munir 47, Mohammad Hussain 43; Ali Raza three for 34, Tanvir Ahmed five for 52); **PWD* 388** (Bilal Asad 44, Afsar Nawaz 156, Bazid Khan 37, Saad Wasim 62, Extras 51; Mohammad Hussain five for 70, Mohammad Hafeez three for 53) **and 64 for four.** *PWD 12 pts.*

At Iqbal Stadium, Faisalabad, October 3, 4, 5. **ADBP won by 50 runs. ADBP 118** (Inam-ul-Haq 66; Abdur Rauf eight for 40) **and 192** (Zahoor Elahi 70; Abdur Rauf six for 58, Ahmed Hayat three for 77); **Sui Gas* 136** (Fahad Masood five for 49) **and 124** (Mubashir Nazir three for 56, Iftikhar Anjum four for 27, Fahad Masood three for 23). *ADBP 9 pts.*

At Sheikhupura Stadium, Sheikhupura, October 3, 4, 5, 6. **Drawn. Allied Bank* 451** (Mohammad Nawaz 35, Ijaz Ahmed, jun. 103, Taimur Khan 51, Rashid Latif 85, Naved-ul-Hasan 51, Extras 38; Sarfraz Ahmed three for 71, Aqeel Ahmed six for 181) **and 179** (Ijaz Ahmed, jun. 75, Taimur Khan 40; Sarfraz Ahmed three for 31, Aqeel Ahmed three for 73); **WAPDA 306** (Maqsood Akbar 38, Bilal Moin 48, Adil Nisar 85, Rehan Rafiq 44, Extras 45; Naved-ul-Hasan three for 87, Arshad Khan three for 72) **and 88 for four** (Adil Nisar 32 not out). *Allied Bank 3 pts.*

At Gaddafi Stadium, Lahore, October 3, 4, 5. **PIA won by seven wickets. Habib Bank 27** (Wasim Akram three for 14, Fazl-e-Akbar seven for 13) **and 313** (Younis Khan 117, Shahid Afridi 51, Akram Raza 56 not out; Fazl-e-Akbar five for 121, Abdul Razzaq four for 111); **PIA* 269** (Yasir Hameed 31, Asif Mujtaba 30, Abdul Razzaq 32, Extras 41; Kabir Khan three for 73, Shahid Nazir three for 69) **and 73 for three**. *PIA 12 pts.*

   Habib Bank's first innings lasted 15.5 overs, and ended when Fazl-e-Akbar took four wickets in four balls.

At Jinnah Stadium, Sialkot, October 3, 4, 5, 6. **Drawn. KRL 457** (Misbah-ul-Haq 61, Intikhab Alam 69, Yasir Arafat 43, Shoaib Akhtar 48, Zulfiqar Jan 75 not out, Jaffer Nazir 80, Extras 35; Tanvir Ahmed three for 105) **and 315 for one** (Mohammad Ramzan 123 not out, Mohammad Wasim 123, Saeed bin Nasir 52 not out); **PWD* 592** (Bilal Asad 72, Imran Khan 51, Afsar Nawaz 31, Bazid Khan 88, Saad Wasim 132, Iqbal Imam 114, Ali Raza 46; Yasir Arafat six for 166). *PWD 3 pts.*

   In KRL's first innings, Zulfiqar Jan and Jaffer Nazir added 152 for the ninth wicket.

At Jinnah Stadium, Gujranwala, October 3, 4, 5, 6. **National Bank won by six wickets. Pakistan Customs 241** (Shadab Kabir 51, Imraan Mohammed 48, Azhar Shafiq 40, Tariq Haroon 34; Mushtaq Ahmed five for 75, Zahid Saeed three for 48) **and 309** (Shadab Kabir 47, Imraan Mohammed 30, Azhar Shafiq 106, Tariq Haroon 78; Shabbir Ahmed five for 72); **National Bank* 404** (Imran Nazir 43, Akhtar Sarfraz 65, Sajid Ali 113, Qaiser Abbas 64, Extras 34; Azhar Shafiq four for 93) **and 150 for four** (Waqar Younis 64). *National Bank 12 pts.*

At Iqbal Stadium, Faisalabad, October 9, 10, 11, 12. **ADBP won by 134 runs. ADBP 244** (Inamul-Haq 70, Ghaffar Kazmi 44, Ijaz Mahmood 62; Kashif Raza four for 80, Faisal Irfan three for 38) **and 254** (Inam-ul-Haq 48, Zahoor Elahi 55, Javed Hayat 53; Faisal Irfan four for 44, Aqeel Ahmed three for 58); **WAPDA* 187** (Kashif Raza 40, Sarfraz Ahmed 46; Faisal Afridi three for 50, Javed Hayat three for 34) **and 177** (Rehan Rafiq 74, Kashif Raza 36; Faisal Afridi three for 40, Iftikhar Anjum seven for 80). *ADBP 12 pts.*

At Sheikhupura Stadium, Sheikhupura, October 9, 10, 11, 12. **Drawn. Habib Bank* 489** (Imran Farhat 160, Taufeeq Umar 68, Hasan Raza 74, Farhan Adil 47, Sajid Shah 36 not out, Danish Kaneria 42; Aamir Nazir four for 155) **and 207 for seven dec.** (Younis Khan 75, Irfan Fazil 37, Hasan Raza 37 not out); **Allied Bank 344** (Usman Tariq 30, Ijaz Ahmed, jun. 107, Humayun Farhat 44, Extras 44; Danish Kaneria four for 128) **and 160 for one** (Usman Tariq 56 not out, Naved Latif 70 not out). *Habib Bank 3 pts.*

At LCCA Ground, Lahore, October 9, 10, 11, 12. **Drawn. PIA 383** (Ghulam Ali 41, Asif Mujtaba 63, Yousuf Youhana 47, Abdul Razzaq 51, Moin Khan 119; Jaffer Nazir four for 91, Ali Naqvi three for 72) **and 293 for five dec.** (Sohail Jaffer 49, Faisal Iqbal 106 not out, Yousuf Youhana 42, Moin Khan 35 not out); **KRL* 487** (Ali Naqvi 81, Mohammad Ramzan 49, Mohammad Wasim 53, Saeed bin Nasir 95, Shoaib Akhtar 59 not out, Extras 60; Fazl-e-Akbar four for 103, Abdul Razzaq four for 126). *KRL 3 pts.*

In PIA's first innings, Abdul Razzaq and Moin Khan added 150 for the seventh wicket.

At Saga Cricket Ground, Sialkot, October 9, 10, 11, 12. **PWD won by two wickets. National Bank 213** (Naumanullah 63, Qaiser Abbas 60; Ali Raza four for 48) **and 196** (Shahid Anwar 46, Kamran Akmal 32); **PWD* 160** (Afsar Nawaz 40, Riaz Sheikh 35, Extras 42; Mohammad Sami five for 59, Shabbir Ahmed three for 32) **and 250 for eight** (Imran Khan 45, Bazid Khan 61, Iqbal Imam 42 not out; Shabbir Ahmed four for 65). *PWD 9 pts.*

At Gaddafi Stadium, Lahore, October 9, 10, 11, 12. **Pakistan Customs won by 67 runs. Pakistan Customs 204** (Imraan Mohammed 42, Asim Kamal 39, Aamer Bashir 31; Abdur Rauf four for 57, Azhar Abbas four for 50) **and 145** (Azhar Shafiq 55; Abdur Rauf three for 54, Azhar Abbas six for 38); **Sui Gas* 161** (Mohammad Hussain 37, Asad Iqbal 30; Waqar Ahmed five for 47, Azhar Shafiq three for 48) **and 121** (Sohail Idrees 36; Waqar Ahmed three for 27, Azhar Shafiq three for 25). *Pakistan Customs 12 pts.*

Customs wicket-keeper Aamer Iqbal made six catches in Sui Gas's first innings, and nine in the match.

At Sheikhupura Stadium, Sheikhupura, October 15, 16, 17, 18. **Pakistan Customs won by seven wickets. Pakistan Customs 400** (Shadab Kabir 48, Imraan Mohammed 52, Nasim Khan 39, Azhar Shafiq 85, Extras 36; Iftikhar Anjum three for 108) **and 160 for three** (Asim Kamal 57 not out, Aamer Bashir 32); **ADBP* 187** (Majid Jahangir 45, Zahoor Elahi 55; Waqar Ahmed five for 53) **and 372** (Majid Jahangir 43, Atif Rauf 94, Ghaffar Kazmi 79, Javed Hayat 42; Waqar Ahmed five for 116, Waqas Chughtai three for 70). *Pakistan Customs 12 pts.*

At Pindi Cricket Stadium, Rawalpindi, October 15, 16, 17, 18. **National Bank won by an innings and 111 runs. Allied Bank 266** (Usman Tariq 36, Naved Latif 59, Humayun Farhat 57; Shabbir Ahmed three for 60, Mushtaq Ahmed five for 78) **and 137** (Usman Tariq 41; Shabbir Ahmed four for 37, Zahid Saeed four for 41); **National Bank* 514 for nine dec.** (Imran Nazir 78, Naumanullah 39, Akhtar Sarfraz 74, Sajid Ali 104, Qaiser Abbas 90, Kamran Akmal 48, Extras 42; Ata-ur-Rehman three for 84). *National Bank 12 pts.*

At Saga Cricket Ground, Sialkot, October 15, 16. **Habib Bank won by ten wickets. KRL 150** (Ali Naqvi 89; Shahid Nazir five for 46, Sajid Shah three for 52) **and 109** (Misbah-ul-Haq 45; Kabir Khan four for 34, Shahid Nazir three for 28, Sajid Shah three for 13); **Habib Bank* 196** (Farhan Adil 41, Sajid Shah 31; Stephen John five for 59, Yasir Arafat three for 40) **and 64 for no wkt** (Imran Farhat 35 not out). *Habib Bank 12 pts.*

At LCCA Ground, Lahore, October 15, 16, 17, 18. **Drawn. PIA 379** (Ghulam Ali 90, Yasir Hameed 35, Faisal Iqbal 81, Mahmood Hamid 65; Azhar Abbas five for 102, Imran Tahir three for 78) **and 251** (Faisal Iqbal 39, Nadeem Khan 90, Mohammad Zahid 40; Abdur Rauf three for 39,

Mohammad Hussain three for 80); **Sui Gas* 376** (Kamran Sajid 109, Fareed Butt 81, Saleem Mughal 54, Extras 56; Fazl-e-Akbar five for 83, Nadeem Khan four for 98) **and 49 for one** (Mohammad Hussain 31). *PIA 3 pts.*

At Iqbal Stadium, Faisalabad, October 15, 16, 17, 18. **WAPDA won by 89 runs. WAPDA 286** (Tariq Aziz 109, Zahid Umar 51, Kashif Raza 64; Ali Raza three for 31, Bilal Asad three for 35) **and 141** (Kamran Hussain 35; Ali Raza three for 26, Rajesh Ramesh four for 30); **PWD* 231** (Bilal Asad 91, Riaz Sheikh 50; Kashif Raza four for 55) **and 107** (Raees Amjad five for 42). *WAPDA 12 pts.*

At Sheikhupura Stadium, Sheikhupura, October 21, 22, 23, 24. **Drawn. Habib Bank* 547 for six dec.** (Imran Farhat 204, Hasan Raza 200 not out, Sajid Shah 54); **ADBP 318** (Inam-ul-Haq 76, Zahoor Elahi 33, Iftikhar Anjum 50 not out; Kabir Khan three for 51, Abdur Rehman three for 44) **and 280 for five** (Inam-ul-Haq 68, Majid Jahangir 61, Zahoor Elahi 76 not out; Akram Raza three for 82). *Habib Bank 3 pts.*

 Imran Farhat's 204 lasted 281 minutes and 204 balls and included 33 fours and four sixes; he added 238 for Habib Bank's third wicket with Hasan Raza, whose 200 not out lasted 416 minutes and 320 balls and included 20 fours and three sixes.

At LCCA Ground, Lahore, October 21, 22, 23, 24. **Allied Bank won by an innings and 12 runs. Sui Gas* 255** (Kamran Sajid 31, Fareed Butt 31, Saleem Mughal 48, Mohammad Hussain 38; Naved-ul-Hasan three for 70, Mohammad Zahid four for 84) **and 175** (Kamran Sajid 88, Mohammad Hussain 33; Arshad Khan five for 65, Mohammad Zahid five for 69); **Allied Bank 442** (Usman Tariq 34, Ijaz Ahmed, jun. 60, Wajahatullah Wasti 66, Humayun Farhat 45, Naved-ul-Hasan 83, Mohammad Zahid 37; Kashif Shafi five for 142). *Allied Bank 12 pts.*

At Saga Cricket Ground, Sialkot, October 21, 22, 23, 24. **National Bank won by 69 runs. National Bank 204** (Naumanullah 59; Jaffer Nazir three for 60, Mohammad Asif three for 27) **and 273** (Imran Nazir 34, Mohammad Javed 45, Kamran Akmal 109; Jaffer Nazir seven for 43); **KRL* 293** (Ali Naqvi 47, Mohammad Ramzan 35, Saeed bin Nasir 49, Misbah-ul-Haq 58, Intikhab Alam 53 not out, Extras 30; Zahid Saeed four for 49) **and 115** (Mushtaq Ahmed three for 16). *National Bank 9 pts.*

At UBL Sports Complex, Karachi, October 21, 22, 23, 24. **Drawn. Pakistan Customs* 604 for seven dec.** (Kashif Siddiq 98, Shadab Kabir 62, Imraan Mohammed 107, Aamer Bashir 115, Asim Kamal 102 not out, Tariq Haroon 50, Extras 33; Riaz Sheikh three for 179); **PWD 393** (Bilal Asad 39, Azam Khan 37, Bazid Khan 127, Iqbal Imam 44, Riaz Sheikh 43; Tabish Nawab six for 169) **and 228 for five** (Bilal Asad 112, Azam Khan 44, Afsar Nawaz 44). *Pakistan Customs 3 pts.*

At Iqbal Stadium, Faisalabad, October 21, 22, 23, 24. **WAPDA won by 98 runs. WAPDA 331** (Rizwan Malik 82, Shoaib Khan 79 not out, Kashif Raza 42, Extras 46; Fazl-e-Akbar four for 84) **and 185** (Rizwan Malik 31, Shoaib Khan 52, Zahid Umar 32; Nadeem Afzal five for 51, Ali Gauhar four for 31); **PIA* 195** (Sohail Jaffer 44, Ghulam Ali 67, Extras 30; Faisal Irfan three for 32, Raees Amjad four for 64) **and 223** (Sohail Jaffer 45, Mahmood Hamid 50, Yasir Hameed 39, Extras 35; Faisal Irfan three for 43). *WAPDA 12 pts.*

 PIA wicket-keeper Moin Khan made nine catches in the match.

At National Stadium, Karachi, October 27, 28. **ADBP won by an innings and six runs. PWD 124** (Faisal Afridi three for 24, Manzoor Elahi three for 24) **and 155** (Iqbal Imam 52 not out; Faisal Afridi three for 35, Tahir Mughal five for 35); **ADBP* 285** (Inam-ul-Haq 101, Manzoor Elahi 42, Mohammad Nadeem 32 not out; Ali Raza four for 63, Rajesh Ramesh three for 88). *ADBP 12 pts.*

At Saga Cricket Ground, Sialkot, October 27, 28, 29, 30. **Drawn. KRL 389** (Ali Naqvi 137, Saeed Anwar, jun. 61, Misbah-ul-Haq 56, Saeed bin Nasir 58 not out, Extras 43; Arshad Khan three for 75) **and 286 for six** (Mohammad Ramzan 32, Saeed Anwar, jun. 39, Misbah-ul-Haq 109 not out, Yasir Arafat 45); **Allied Bank* 269** (Usman Tariq 80, Ata-ur-Rehman 36, Extras 36; Stephen John three for 49, Naeem Akhtar five for 59). *KRL 3 pts.*

At Sheikhupura Stadium, Sheikhupura, October 27, 28, 29, 30. Drawn. National Bank 265 (Imran Nazir 43, Akhtar Sarfraz 55, Mohammad Javed 30, Kamran Akmal 52; Sajid Shah three for 89, Asadullah Butt four for ten) **and 201 for eight** (Akhtar Sarfraz 82, Qaiser Abbas 37, Extras 31; Sajid Shah three for 33); **Habib Bank* 223** (Salim Elahi 64, Hasan Raza 39, Asadullah Butt 40; Mushtaq Ahmed five for 53). *National Bank 3 pts.*

At UBL Sports Complex, Karachi, October 27, 28, 29, 30. Drawn. Pakistan Customs* 461 (Agha Sabir 196, Asim Kamal 59, Tariq Haroon 41, Waqar Ahmed 30, Extras 39; Nadeem Khan four for 146, Irfanuddin three for 53); PIA 175 (Ghulam Ali 40, Mahmood Hamid 43 not out; Waqar Ahmed six for 46) **and 520 for four dec.** (Ghulam Ali 90, Shoaib Mohammad 84, Asif Mujtaba 122 not out, Faisal Iqbal 171, Extras 51). *Pakistan Customs 2 pts.*

Asif Mujtaba and Faisal Iqbal added 306 for the fourth wicket in PIA's second innings, when all 11 Customs players bowled.

At Iqbal Stadium, Faisalabad, October 27, 28, 29. **WAPDA won by six runs. WAPDA* 157** (Kashif Rasheed 68, Sarfraz Ahmed 48 not out; Abdur Rauf three for 44, Wasim Khan five for 58) **and 104** (Abdur Rauf six for 40, Azhar Abbas three for 40); **Sui Gas 142** (Saleem Mughal 48 not out, Zia-ur-Rehman 36; Kashif Raza four for 46, Waqas Ahmed five for 53) **and 113** (Kamran Sajid 30, Saleem Mughal 30; Waqas Ahmed six for 44, Sarfraz Ahmed three for 26). *WAPDA 12 pts.*

At National Stadium, Karachi, November 2, 3, 4, 5. **PIA won by 80 runs. PIA 182** (Yasir Hameed 85; Tahir Mughal four for 52, Inam-ul-Haq three for ten) **and 289** (Ghulam Ali 107, Asif Mujtaba 42, Faisal Iqbal 58; Iftikhar Anjum five for 88, Tahir Mughal four for 74); **ADBP* 135** (Zahoor Elahi 44; Fazl-e-Akbar four for 56, Umar Gul five for 46) **and 256** (Atif Rauf 133 not out, Extras 35; Fazl-e-Akbar six for 68). *PIA 12 pts.*

At UBL Sports Complex, Karachi, November 2, 3, 4, 5. **Allied Bank won by nine wickets. PWD* 223** (Bilal Asad 41, Imran Khan 32; Arshad Khan eight for 80) **and 299** (Bilal Asad 68, Afsar Nawaz 64, Iqbal Imam 33, Bazid Khan 50, Faheem Ahmed 45; Mohammad Zahid three for 106, Arshad Khan four for 105); **Allied Bank 474 for nine dec.** (Usman Tariq 73, Wajahatullah Wasti 98, Ijaz Ahmed, jun. 116, Aamer Hanif 51, Humayun Farhat 58, Aaley Haider 37; Tanvir Ahmed three for 90) **and 49 for one.** *Allied Bank 12 pts.*

At Pindi Cricket Stadium, Rawalpindi, November 2, 3, 4, 5. **Drawn. Habib Bank 406 for three dec.** (Imran Farhat 84, Salim Elahi 168, Farhan Adil 111) **and 214 for nine dec.** (Imran Farhat 40, Farhan Adil 76, Asadullah Butt 34; Asad Iqbal three for 35); **Sui Gas* 307** (Ali Hussain 47, Mohammad Hafeez 106, Sohail Idrees 36, Abid Mahmood 49, Extras 34; Kabir Khan three for 47, Shahid Nazir three for 50). *Habib Bank 3 pts.*

At Niaz Stadium, Hyderabad, November 2, 3, 4. **KRL won by three wickets. KRL 205** (Intikhab Alam 49, Zulfiqar Jan 87 not out; Waqar Ahmed five for 55) **and 130 for seven** (Saeed Anwar, jun. 37; Waqas Chughtai three for 65); **Pakistan Customs* 46** (Yasir Arafat six for 23, Naeem Akhtar four for 23) **and 288** (Agha Sabir 41, Kashif Siddiq 82, Tariq Haroon 35; Yasir Arafat six for 104). *KRL 12 pts.*

At Sheikhupura Stadium, Sheikhupura, November 2, 3, 4. **National Bank won by ten wickets. WAPDA* 145** (Kashif Raza 39; Shabbir Ahmed three for 17, Zahid Saeed four for 65, Mushtaq Ahmed three for 34) **and 134** (Kashif Rasheed 48; Mushtaq Ahmed three for 14, Zahid Saeed three for 24); **National Bank 185** (Hanif-ur-Rehman 62, Naumanullah 33, Kamran Akmal 37 not out; Kashif Raza four for 57) **and 96 for no wkt** (Imran Nazir 60 not out). *National Bank 12 pts.*

At National Stadium, Karachi, November 8, 9, 10, 11. **Allied Bank won by 112 runs. Allied Bank 349** (Ijaz Ahmed, jun. 74, Aamer Hanif 37, Humayun Farhat 33, Arshad Khan 44; Waqar Ahmed three for 88, Tariq Haroon three for 77) **and 254 for six dec.** (Usman Tariq 50, Wajahatullah Wasti 101, Aamer Hanif 48; Waqar Ahmed four for 77); **Pakistan Customs* 228** (Shadab Kabir 52, Nasim Khan 33, Aamer Iqbal 58 not out; Aamir Nazir four for 77) **and 263** (Shadab Kabir 81, Nasim Khan 54; Aqib Javed five for 73, Arshad Khan four for 54). *Allied Bank 12 pts.*

At Gaddafi Stadium, Lahore, November 8, 9, 10. **WAPDA won by seven wickets. Habib Bank 61** (Asadullah Butt 32; Waqas Ahmed six for 22, Faisal Irfan three for 19) **and 234** (Irfan Fazil

49, Akram Raza 43, Shahid Nazir 37 not out; Waqas Ahmed seven for 84); **WAPDA* 186** (Bilal Moin 39, Zahid Umar 40 not out; Kabir Khan three for 75, Sajid Shah three for 44) **and 111 for three** (Adil Nisar 46 not out). *WAPDA 12 pts.*

Faisal Irfan took a hat-trick in Habib Bank's first innings, when one man was absent hurt.

At KRL Cricket Ground, Rawalpindi, November 8, 9, 10, 11. **KRL won by eight wickets. KRL 360** (Saeed Anwar, jun. 112, Misbah-ul-Haq 83, Naeem Akhtar 35, Extras 38; Fahad Masood five for 124) **and 67 for two** (Mohammad Ramzan 32 not out, Intikhab Alam 31 not out); **ADBP* 200** (Faisal Naved 48, Mubashir Nazir 30; Naeem Akhtar three for 45) **and 225** (Inam-ul-Haq 31, Atif Rauf 38, Zahoor Elahi 73; Naeem Akhtar five for 67). *KRL 12 pts.*

At Iqbal Stadium, Faisalabad, November 8, 9, 10, 11. **National Bank won by 153 runs. National Bank 263** (Hanif-ur-Rehman 33, Naumanullah 50, Imran Javed 32, Zahid Saeed 53, Mohammad Sami 41 not out; Abdur Rauf four for 86) **and 256** (Qaiser Abbas 61, Mushtaq Ahmed 31, Extras 39; Abdur Rauf four for 57, Wasim Khan three for 56); **Sui Gas* 227** (Ali Hussain 47, Abid Mahmood 78; Mohammad Sami four for 39, Zahid Saeed five for 73) **and 139** (Wasim Khan 32; Mohammad Sami four for 71). *National Bank 12 pts.*

At UBL Sports Complex, Karachi, November 8, 9, 10, 11. **Drawn. PIA* 515 for eight dec.** (Ghulam Ali 41, Shoaib Mohammad 163, Faisal Iqbal 126, Yasir Hameed 38, Yousuf Youhana 41; Bilal Asad three for 71); **PWD 353** (Imran Khan 39, Afsar Nawaz 75, Bilal Asad 52, Iqbal Imam 60, Extras 45; Asif Mujtaba five for 68) **and 312 for five** (Zahid Ghauri 53, Bazid Khan 59, Bilal Asad 94 not out, Iqbal Imam 48; Shoaib Mohammad three for 65). *PIA 3 pts.*

Asif Mujtaba took a hat-trick in PWD's first innings.

WINNERS

† *The Patron's Trophy was not first-class between 1979-80 and 1982-83, when it served as a qualifying competition for the Quaid-e-Azam Trophy, or in 1999-2000.*

QUAID-E-AZAM TROPHY, 2001-02

Pool A	Played	Won	Lost	Drawn	1st-inns Points	Points
Karachi Whites	8	6	1	1	21	75
Gujranwala	8	4	2	2	18	54
Karachi Blues	8	3	1	4	15	42
Faisalabad	8	3	1	4	12	39
Bahawalpur	8	3	2	3	12	39
Sargodha	8	2	2	4	12	30
Hyderabad	8	1	5	2	3	12
Rest of Baluchistan	8	1	3	4	0	9
Rest of Sindh	8	0	6	2	3	3

Pool B

	Played	Won	Lost	Drawn	1st-inns Points	Points
Peshawar	7	6	1	0	18	72
Sheikhupura	8	5	1	2	15	60
Sialkot	8	3	2	3	15	42
Lahore Blues	8	3	3	2	12	39
Rawalpindi	7	3	1	3	9	36
Lahore Whites	8	2	4	2	9	27
Islamabad	8	2	5	1	0	18
Rest of Punjab	8	1	4	3	6	15
Rest of NWFP	8	1	5	2	6	15

Note: The match between Rawalpindi and Peshawar was abandoned.

Outright win = 9 pts; lead on first innings in a won or drawn game = 3 pts.

Final: Karachi Whites beat Peshawar by eight wickets.

In the following scores, * by the name of a team indicates that they won the toss.

Pool A

At Bahawal Stadium, Bahawalpur, January 2, 3, 4, 5. **Drawn. Hyderabad* 171** (Naeem Akhtar 37; Mohammad Zahid five for 46, Imranullah three for 61) **and 246 for seven** (Imraan Mohammed 33, Iqbal Sheikh 32, Faisal Athar 30, Rizwan Ahmed 46, Naeem Akhtar 57 not out; Imran Adil three for 42); **Bahawalpur 310 for eight dec.** (Usman Tariq 60, Bilal Moin 71, Rehan Rafiq 68, Hasnain Raza 32, Inam-ul-Haq Rashid 34; Anwar Ali four for 112). *Bahawalpur 3 pts.*

At Iqbal Stadium, Faisalabad, January 2, 3, 4, 5. **Drawn. Faisalabad 249** (Mohammad Ramzan 49, Ijaz Ahmed, jun. 32, Fida Hussain 64, Extras 33; Ahmed Hayat six for 77); **Sargodha* 202 for eight** (Khurram Niazi 52, Extras 35; Shahid Nazir three for 52, Nadeem Afzal three for 55).

At KCCA Ground, Karachi, January 2, 3, 4, 5. **Karachi Whites won by 98 runs. Karachi Whites 251** (Saeed bin Nasir 68, Moin Khan 85; Rizwan Saeed three for 65, Mohammad Javed five for 63) **and 270 for two dec.** (Ghulam Ali 37, Shahid Afridi 60, Saeed bin Nasir 101 not out, Hasan Raza 65 not out); **Karachi Blues* 218** (Mohammad Javed 79 not out, Rizwan Saeed 34; Tanvir Ahmed five for 64, Shahid Afridi three for 41) **and 205** (Zeeshan Pervez 43; Tabish Nawab six for 39). *Karachi Whites 12 pts.*

At National Stadium, Karachi, January 2, 3, 4, 5. **Drawn. Rest of Baluchistan 270** (Nasim Khan 104, Mohtashim Ali 77; Ali Raza three for 64, Kashif Pervez five for 39) **and 265 for nine** (Azizullah Khan 50, Mohtashim Ali 43, Mohtashim Rasheed 35, Naseer Khan 65; Rizwan Qureshi five for 58); **Rest of Sindh* 376** (Hanif-ur-Rehman 77, Mujahid Solangi 47, Ali Nawaz 33, Rizwan Qureshi 62, Abdur Rahim 67, Javed Liaqat 49; Faisal Irfan four for 95, Naseer Khan three for 81). *Rest of Sindh 3 pts.*

At Iqbal Stadium, Faisalabad, January 8, 9, 10. **Faisalabad won by an innings and 234 runs. Hyderabad 98** (Shahid Nazir three for 33, Nadeem Afzal four for 23) **and 153** (Rizwan Ahmed 33; Shahid Nazir four for 27, Ijaz Ahmed, jun. three for 21); **Faisalabad* 485 for eight dec.** (Zahoor Elahi 106, Ijaz Ahmed, jun. 65, Fida Hussain 52, Saadat Gul 120 not out, Extras 32; Raees Amjad three for 102). *Faisalabad 12 pts.*

At Gujranwala Cricket Academy Ground, Gujranwala, January 8, 9, 10, 11. **Gujranwala won by seven wickets. Sargodha 129** (Misbah-ul-Haq 44; Naved Arif four for 73) **and 310** (Mohammad Hafeez 76, Khurram Niazi 38, Shahid Mahmood 35, Misbah-ul-Haq 71, Ahmed Hayat 38 not out; Sarfraz Ahmed three for 44, Abdur Rehman four for 106); **Gujranwala* 345 for eight dec.** (Mudassar Mushtaq 52, Imran Abbas 100 not out, Majid Saeed 32, Tariq Javed 57, Sarfraz Ahmed 34; Ahmed Hayat three for 107) **and 95 for three** (Majid Saeed 33 not out, Tariq Javed 30 not out). *Gujranwala 12 pts.*

At KCCA Ground, Karachi, January 8, 9, 10, 11. **Drawn. Rest of Baluchistan 254** (Nasim Khan 68, Naseer Khan 84; Rizwan Saeed three for 47, Mohammad Javed four for 52, Adnan Kaleem three for 70) **and 164 for five** (Azizullah Khan 79, Mohtashim Ali 45); **Karachi Blues* 400 for nine dec.** (Asim Kamal 104, Naumanullah 43, Farhan Adil 124, Mohammad Javed 64 not out; Mohtashim Rasheed three for 64). *Karachi Blues 3 pts.*

At National Stadium, Karachi, January 8, 9, 10. **Karachi Whites won by an innings and 43 runs. Rest of Sindh 131** (Shahid Qambrani 35, Ali Raza 30; Tanvir Ahmed four for 61, Mohammad Hasnain six for 45) **and 261** (Hanif-ur-Rehman 33, Akhtar Bangash 32, Abdur Rahim 68, Rizwan Qureshi 67; Tanvir Ahmed three for 64, Mohammad Hasnain four for 112); **Karachi Whites* 435 for nine dec.** (Saeed bin Nasir 67, Hasan Raza 39, Moin Khan 76, Imran Javed 67 not out, Mohammad Hasnain 31, Extras 44; Ali Raza three for 136, Kashif Ali three for 109). *Karachi Whites 12 pts.*

At Bahawal Stadium, Bahawalpur, January 14, 15, 16, 17. **Drawn. Gujranwala* 143** (Rizwan Malik 100 not out; Mohammad Zahid three for 27, Murtaza Hussain five for 71) **and 372 for nine dec.** (Rizwan Malik 99, Majid Saeed 128, Tariq Javed 60 not out; Mohammad Zahid six for 106); **Bahawalpur 95** (Mubashir Nazir three for 22, Ghulam Murtaza five for 21) **and 389 for seven** (Asif Iqbal 51, Usman Tariq 85, Bilal Moin 150 not out, Hasnain Raza 31, Mohammad Zahid 32 not out; Mubashir Nazir three for 66). *Gujranwala 3 pts.*

Gujranwala's 143 equalled the lowest completed innings total to include an individual hundred, from Rizwan Malik, who accounted for 69.93 per cent of the runs scored.

At KCCA Ground, Karachi, January 14, 15, 16, 17. **Karachi Blues won by an innings and 56 runs. Karachi Blues 465 for seven dec.** (Agha Sabir 154, Asim Kamal 51, Maisam Hasnain 102 not out, Atiq-uz-Zaman 36); **Rest of Sindh* 255** (Akhtar Bangash 72, Abdur Rahim 55 not out, Rizwan Qureshi 48; Mohammad Javed three for 45, Riaz Sheikh three for 99, Faheem Ahmed three for 64) **and 154** (Rizwan Qureshi 31; Rizwan Saeed four for 56, Riaz Sheikh five for 36). *Karachi Blues 12 pts.*

At National Stadium, Karachi, January 14, 15, 16, 17. **Drawn. Karachi Whites 557 for six dec.** (Aariz Kamal 119, Hasan Raza 256, Imran Javed 125 not out, Extras 37; Faisal Irfan three for 110); **Rest of Baluchistan* 241** (Azizullah Khan 35, Mohtashim Ali 40, Mian Nafees 81; Tanvir Ahmed five for 67, Adnan Malik three for 48) **and 289 for eight** (Manzoor Ahmed 33, Sabir Hussain 37, Azizullah Khan 46, Nasim Khan 96 not out, Mohtashim Ali 36; Tanvir Ahmed five for 67). *Karachi Whites 3 pts.*

Hasan Raza's 256 lasted 516 minutes and 386 balls and included 32 fours and one six; he added 282 for Karachi Whites' third wicket with Aariz Kamal, who scored 119 on first-class debut.

At Sports Stadium, Sargodha, January 14, 15, 16. **Sargodha won by an innings and 264 runs. Sargodha 505 for seven dec.** (Mohammad Hafeez 42, Khurram Niazi 41, Mohammad Nawaz 65, Misbah-ul-Haq 202, Tanvir Hussain 93; Faisal Khanzada three for 94); **Hyderabad* 134** (Irshad Notkani 34; Ashraf Bashir four for five, Mohammad Sarfraz four for 63) **and 107** (Ahmed Hayat three for 33, Ashraf Bashir three for 24). *Sargodha 12 pts.*

Misbah-ul-Haq's 202 lasted 314 minutes and 285 balls and included 25 fours and one six.

At Bahawal Stadium, Bahawalpur, January 20, 21, 22. **Bahawalpur won by ten wickets. Rest of Sindh* 124** (Aamer Iqbal 43; Murtaza Hussain seven for 33) **and 240** (Hanif-ur-Rehman 79, Abid Ali 33, Abdur Rahim 57; Mohammad Zahid four for 44); **Bahawalpur 301** (Usman Tariq 91, Asif Iqbal 38, Rehan Rafiq 38; Abdur Rahim three for 33, Abid Ali three for 53) **and 65 for no wkt** (Mohammad Zahid 32 not out). *Bahawalpur 12 pts.*

At Iqbal Stadium, Faisalabad, January 20, 21, 22, 23. **Drawn. Faisalabad 278** (Mohammad Ramzan 99, Zahoor Elahi 81; Rajesh Ramesh three for 82, Mohammad Javed four for 85, Tariq Haroon three for 22) **and 284** (Mohammad Ramzan 35, Sami-ul-Haq 68, Ijaz Ahmed, jun. 60, Wasim Haider 58; Riaz Sheikh four for 67); **Karachi Blues* 252** (Riaz Sheikh 49, Tariq Haroon 45, Extras 49; Nadeem Afzal three for 55, Ijaz Ahmed, jun. three for 16) **and 206 for nine** (Farhan Adil 38, Tariq Haroon 30, Mohammad Javed 32 not out; Nadeem Afzal three for 35, Aqeel Ahmed three for 58). *Faisalabad 3 pts.*

At Niaz Stadium, Hyderabad, January 20, 21, 22. **Rest of Baluchistan won by 24 runs. Rest of Baluchistan 142** (Sanaullah Khan 36, Faisal Irfan 43; Raees Amjad four for 36, Sohaib Hashmi three for 30, Rizwan Ahmed three for 39) **and 207** (Nasim Khan 48, Mian Nafees 68; Raees Amjad three for 77, Sohaib Hashmi five for 61); **Hyderabad* 168** (Imraan Mohammed 63, Faisal Athar 41; Faisal Irfan three for 55, Waqas Chughtai seven for 75) **and 157** (Rizwan Ahmed 69; Faisal Irfan three for 51, Waqas Chughtai four for 57). *Rest of Baluchistan 9 pts.*

At National Stadium, Karachi, January 20, 21, 22, 23. **Karachi Whites won by 121 runs. Karachi Whites 263** (Ghulam Ali 47, Mohammad Masroor 94; Mubashir Nazir three for 79, Naved Arif four for 67) **and 331 for six dec.** (Ghulam Ali 43, Saeed bin Nasir 62, Hasan Raza 37, Mohammad Masroor 53, Imran Javed 73 not out); **Gujranwala* 247** (Rizwan Malik 30, Majid Saeed 63; Awais Athar three for 84, Arif Mahmood four for 28) **and 226** (Atiq-ur-Rehman 37, Rizwan Malik 35, Majid Saeed 49; Tanvir Ahmed four for 84, Arif Mahmood three for 28). *Karachi Whites 12 pts.*

At Bahawal Stadium, Bahawalpur, January 26, 27, 28, 29. **Bahawalpur won by an innings and eight runs. Rest of Baluchistan 206** (Nasim Khan 35, Mian Nafees 57, Mohtashim Rasheed 44; Tahir Maqsood three for 30, Murtaza Hussain five for 52) **and 232** (Nasim Khan 31, Faisal Irfan 50, Naseer Khan 85; Tahir Maqsood three for 55, Mohammad Zahid three for 22); **Bahawalpur* 446** (Bilal Moin 51, Rehan Rafiq 197 not out, Inam-ul-Haq Rashid 73; Naseer Khan five for 104). *Bahawalpur 12 pts.*

At Iqbal Stadium, Faisalabad, January 26, 27, 28, 29. **Drawn. Faisalabad 372** (Mohammad Ramzan 162, Zahoor Elahi 45, Ijaz Ahmed, jun. 42, Sohail Nazir 36, Extras 42; Kashif Ali six for 111) **and 210 for three dec.** (Mohammad Ramzan 86, Zahoor Elahi 32, Sami-ul-Haq 80); **Rest of Sindh* 266** (Hanif-ur-Rehman 52, Abid Ali 42, Shahid Qambrani 82 not out, Aamer Iqbal 48; Aqeel Ahmed four for 89) **and 252 for eight** (Aamer Iqbal 69, Abdur Rahim 65, Rizwan Qureshi 38 not out, Extras 35; Shahid Nazir three for 79, Aqeel Ahmed three for 69). *Faisalabad 3 pts.*

At Niaz Stadium, Hyderabad, January 26, 27, 28. **Gujranwala won by eight wickets. Gujranwala 339** (Atiq-ur-Rehman 44, Imran Abbas 33, Khalid Mahmood 141, Abdur Rehman 39; Raees Amjad five for 65) **and ten for two;** **Hyderabad* 151** (Akram Khan 43; Naved Arif five for 28) **and 197** (Imraan Mohammed 38, Faisal Athar 32, Rizwan Ahmed 45; Mubashir Nazir five for 51). *Gujranwala 12 pts.*

At Sports Stadium, Sargodha, January 26, 27, 28, 29. **Drawn. Karachi Blues 458** (Asim Kamal 160, Farhan Adil 48, Atiq-uz-Zaman 86, Riaz Sheikh 74, Extras 30; Mohammad Sarfraz three for 82, Ashraf Bashir three for 93) **and 200 for four** (Maisam Hasnain 76, Naumanullah 42, Farhan Adil 43 not out); **Sargodha* 333** (Shahid Mahmood 37, Mohammad Hafeez 50, Mohammad Nawaz 93, Misbah-ul-Haq 37, Extras 55; Rajesh Ramesh four for 68, Riaz Sheikh three for 91). *Karachi Blues 3 pts.*

At Bahawal Stadium, Bahawalpur, February 1, 2, 3, 4. **Bahawalpur won by an innings and two runs. Karachi Whites 184** (Ghulam Ali 50, Hasan Raza 40, Imran Javed 41; Murtaza Hussain five for 80, Maqbool Hussain five for 52) **and 298** (Saif Ashraf 61, Saeed bin Nasir 43, Hasan Raza 38, Mohammad Masroor 68; Tahir Maqsood three for 57, Usman Tariq three for 50); **Bahawalpur* 484 for nine dec.** (Hammad Tariq 43, Usman Tariq 82, Rehan Rafiq 162 not out, Faisal Elahi 96; Adnan Malik four for 103). *Bahawalpur 12 pts.*
   Rehan Rafiq and Faisal Elahi added 179 for Bahawalpur's ninth wicket.

At Iqbal Stadium, Faisalabad, February 1, 2, 3, 4. **Faisalabad won by an innings and 195 runs. Faisalabad 521 for six dec.** (Mohammad Ramzan 157, Zahoor Elahi 108, Sami-ul-Haq 31, Ijaz Ahmed, jun. 46, Wasim Haider 100 not out); **Rest of Baluchistan* 167** (Azizullah Khan 60, Mian Nafees 39; Shahid Nazir three for 30, Ijaz Ahmed, jun. four for 26) **and 159** (Mohtashim Ali 41, Naseer Khan 61; Ijaz Ahmed, jun. six for 74). *Faisalabad 12 pts.*

At Jinnah Stadium, Gujranwala, February 1, 2, 3, 4. **Karachi Blues won by an innings and 39 runs. Karachi Blues* 417 for nine dec.** (Maisam Hasnain 57, Tariq Haroon 92, Zeeshan Pervez 36, Mohammad Javed 36, Atiq-uz-Zaman 101 not out, Riaz Sheikh 39; Abdur Rehman five for 120); **Gujranwala 208** (Abdur Rehman 57; Riaz Sheikh four for 60, Mohammad Javed three for 29) **and 170** (Khalid Mahmood 40; Riaz Sheikh three for 54). *Karachi Blues 12 pts.*

At Sports Stadium, Sargodha, February 1, 2, 3, 4. **Sargodha won by an innings and 129 runs. Sargodha* 504 for nine dec.** (Khurram Niazi 52, Mohammad Nawaz 47, Misbah-ul-Haq 55, Tanvir Hussain 45, Haroon Malik 135; Ahmed Hayat 77, Ashraf Bashir 32 not out; Rizwan Qureshi three for 112, Naeem Ghouri four for 160); **Rest of Sindh 148** (Extras 30; Ahmed Hayat six for 42) **and 227** (Adnan Ameer 35, Shahid Qambrani 60, Rizwan Qureshi 46 not out, Extras 31; Ahmed Hayat five for 57, Mohammad Sarfraz three for 63). *Sargodha 12 pts.*

At Bahawal Stadium, Bahawalpur, February 7, 8, 9, 10. **Faisalabad won by 224 runs. Faisalabad 204** (Zahoor Elahi 57, Fida Hussain 49 not out; Mohammad Zahid five for 65, Murtaza Hussain five for 67) **and 405 for eight dec.** (Mohammad Ramzan 59, Zahoor Elahi 77, Farooq Iqbal 64, Ijaz Ahmed, jun. 110; Mohammad Zahid five for 86); **Bahawalpur* 264** (Hammad Tariq 138, Mohammad Zahid 51 not out; Aqeel Ahmed four for 131, Zahoor Elahi four for 45) **and 121** (Aqeel Ahmed six for 61, Ijaz Ahmed, jun. four for 35). *Faisalabad 9 pts.*

At Lahore Country Club Ground, Muridke, February 7, 8. **Gujranwala won by eight wickets. Rest of Sindh 56** (Mubashir Nazir five for 27, Sarfraz Ahmed five for 24) **and 177** (Shahid Qambrani 51, Rizwan Qureshi 34; Mubashir Nazir four for 74, Sarfraz Ahmed five for 53); **Gujranwala* 121** (Ali Raza seven for 52, Kashif Pervez three for 60) **and 116 for two** (Ehtesham Younis 46 not out, Abdur Rehman 58 not out). *Gujranwala 12 pts.*

At Niaz Stadium, Hyderabad, February 7, 8, 9, 10. **Karachi Whites won by six wickets. Hyderabad 312** (Ayaz Taifi 43, Rizwan Ahmed 102, Raees Amjad 47; Tanvir Ahmed four for 97, Arif Mahmood three for 85) **and 130** (Ijaz Shah 34, Raees Amjad 30 not out; Tanvir Ahmed seven for 75); **Karachi Whites* 341** (Ghulam Ali 42, Saeed bin Nasir 105, Mohammad Masroor 33, Arif Mahmood 51, Tanvir Ahmed 38; Raees Amjad three for 97, Sohaib Hashmi three for 92) **and 104 for four** (Ghulam Ali 35; Raees Amjad three for 36). *Karachi Whites 12 pts.*

At Sports Stadium, Sargodha, February 7, 8, 9, 10. **Drawn. Rest of Baluchistan 119** (Nasim Khan 34; Jibran Khan six for 42) **and 174 for five** (Azizullah Khan 76 not out, Mian Nafees 45 not out; Jibran Khan three for 66); **Sargodha* 247 for seven dec.** (Mohammad Hafeez 69, Misbah-ul-Haq 63, Tanvir Hussain 51 not out; Waqas Chughtai three for 46). *Sargodha 3 pts.*

At Lahore Country Club Ground, Muridke, February 12, 13, 14. **Gujranwala won by an innings and 58 runs. Gujranwala 422** (Ehtesham Younis 39, Imran Abbas 33, Asim Munir 157 not out, Khalid Mahmood 45, Mubashir Nazir 40, Extras 51; Waqas Chughtai three for 96); **Rest of Baluchistan* 114** (Sarfraz Ahmed four for 15) **and 250** (Jahanzeb Khan 50, Mian Nafees 69; Abdur Rehman four for 60). *Gujranwala 12 pts.*

At KCCA Ground, Karachi, February 12, 13, 14, 15. **Drawn. Hyderabad* 309** (Akram Khan 106, Ijaz Shah 32, Rizwan Ahmed 98; Mohammad Javed four for 42) **and 294** (Ijaz Shah 85, Imran Khan 120, Extras 32; Riaz Sheikh four for 104, Azam Hussain three for 68); **Karachi Blues 250** (Saqib Zia 35, Atif Ali Zaidi 50, Farhan Adil 84; Rizwan Ahmed five for 93, Imran Alam four for 41) **and 334 for nine** (Saqib Zia 46, Ashraf Ali 45, Atif Ali Zaidi 54, Farhan Adil 104; Imran Alam three for 74). *Hyderabad 3 pts.*

At National Stadium, Karachi, February 12, 13, 14, 15. **Karachi Whites won by nine wickets. Faisalabad 223** (Sami-ul-Haq 61; Arif Mahmood five for 43) **and 290** (Sami-ul-Haq 58, Sohail Nazir 44, Mohammad Salman 71 not out; Tanvir Ahmed four for 94); **Karachi Whites* 473 for eight dec.** (Ghulam Ali 54, Saeed bin Nasir 39, Imran Javed 134, Shadab Kabir 48, Arif Mahmood 105 not out, Tanvir Ahmed 31, Extras 31; Moazzam Ali five for 120) **and 43 for one.** *Karachi Whites 12 pts.*

At Sports Stadium, Sargodha, February 12, 13, 14, 15. **Drawn. Bahawalpur* 526 for eight dec.** (Hammad Tariq 47, Usman Tariq 210, Bilal Moin 68, Rehan Rafiq 102 not out, Extras 69; Ahmed Hayat four for 89); **Sargodha 571 for seven** (Mohammad Hafeez 177, Mohammad Nawaz 107, Misbah-ul-Haq 204 not out, Atiq Ahmed 55; Bilal Moin three for 77). *Sargodha 3 pts.*

Usman Tariq's 210 lasted 460 minutes and 342 balls and included 11 fours; Misbah-ul-Haq's 204 not out lasted 406 minutes and 292 balls and included 19 fours and five sixes; he added 191 with Atiq Ahmed for Sargodha's seventh wicket.

At Jinnah Stadium, Gujranwala, February 18, 19, 20, 21. **Drawn. Gujranwala* 491 for eight dec.** (Ehtesham Younis 39, Rizwan Malik 61, Imran Abbas 165, Asim Munir 131; Moazzam Ali three for 79, Mohammad Maqsood three for 153); **Faisalabad 181** (Mohammad Ramzan 41, Yasir Mushtaq 50 not out; Adnan Farooq four for 47, Abdur Rehman four for 71) **and 283 for six** (Asif Hussain 62, Mohammad Maqsood 33, Zahoor Elahi 54, Mohammad Ramzan 100 not out). *Gujranwala 3 pts.*

Imran Abbas and Asim Munir added 271 for Gujranwala's fifth wicket.

At Niaz Stadium, Hyderabad, February 18, 19, 20, 21. **Hyderabad won by two wickets. Rest of Sindh 346** (Adnan Ameer 51, Hanif-ur-Rehman 34, Shahid Qambrani 105, Rizwan Qureshi 49, Extras 43; Raees Amjad three for 88, Rizwan Ahmed six for 101) **and 76** (Raees Amjad six for 35, Irshad Notkani four for 41); **Hyderabad* 238** (Iqbal Sheikh 68, Javed Khan 50; Kashif Pervez four for 48, Rizwan Qureshi four for 62) **and 185 for eight** (Iqbal Sheikh 55; Rizwan Qureshi three for 36, Hanif-ur-Rehman four for 51). *Hyderabad 9 pts.*

At National Stadium, Karachi, February 18, 19, 20, 21. **Karachi Blues won by nine wickets. Bahawalpur 237** (Mohammad Rashid 32, Bilal Moin 65, Faisal Elahi 51; Mohammad Javed five for 81, Riaz Sheikh three for 34) **and 240** (Mohammad Rashid 39, Bilal Moin 32; Rajesh Ramesh three for 80, Mohammad Javed five for 84); **Karachi Blues* 338** (Farhan Adil 47, Zeeshan Pervez 64, Atiq-uz-Zaman 115, Extras 40; Imran Adil three for 88, Bilal Moin four for 90) **and 140 for one** (Maisam Hasnain 63 not out, Atif Ali Zaidi 63 not out). *Karachi Blues 12 pts.*

At KCCA Ground, Karachi, February 18, 19, 20, 21. **Karachi Whites won by nine wickets. Sargodha* 169** (Misbah-ul-Haq 35, Mohammad Kashif 53; Tanvir Ahmed three for 63, Danish Kaneria three for 56) **and 334** (Mohammad Hafeez 80, Sohail Maqbool 33, Misbah-ul-Haq 108; Danish Kaneria six for 117); **Karachi Whites 451** (Saeed bin Nasir 133, Hasan Raza 90, Faisal Iqbal 33, Arif Mahmood 64, Extras 54; Mohammad Sarfraz four for 132, Umair Hasan six for 141) **and 53 for one.** *Karachi Whites 12 pts.*

Pool B

At LCCA Ground, Lahore, January 2, 3, 4. **Lahore Blues won by an innings and 18 runs. Lahore Blues 395 for eight dec.** (Imran Farhat 135, Yawar Afzal 64, Zia-ur-Rehman 59, Sohail Idrees 58 not out, Mohammad Hussain 35); **Lahore Whites* 236** (Kashif Siddiq 90, Aamer Sajjad 51, Shahnawaz Malik 51; Mohammad Hussain six for 94) **and 141** (Shahnawaz Malik 43, Tariq Mahmood 33; Mohammad Hussain four for 39). *Lahore Blues 12 pts.*

Lahore Blues wicket-keeper Humayun Farhat made nine dismissals (three caught, six stumped).

At KRL Cricket Ground, Rawalpindi, January 2, 3, 4, 5. **Rawalpindi won by 115 runs. Rawalpindi 176** (Babar Naeem 72; Azhar Mahmood three for 56, Saad Janjua four for 47) **and 221** (Yasir Arafat 49; Azhar Mahmood four for 87, Iftikhar Anjum three for 60, Saad Janjua three for 52); **Islamabad* 104** (Ali Naqvi 40; Mohammad Zahid three for 36, Naeem Akhtar three for 29, Yasir Arafat four for 24) **and 178** (Bilal Asad 43, Azhar Mahmood 34, Iftikhar Anjum 43; Mohammad Zahid five for 61, Naeem Akhtar four for 34). *Rawalpindi 12 pts.*

At Arbab Niaz Stadium, Peshawar, January 2, 3, 4, 5. **Drawn. Rest of Punjab 90** (Sajid Shah four for 24, Shakeel-ur-Rehman three for 17) **and 232** (Saeed Anwar, jun. 65, Mohammad Fazil 36, Extras 37; Sajid Shah four for 75, Umair Khan four for 54); **Rest of NWFP* 206** (Ahmed Said 34, Adnan Raees 68, Mohammad Bilal 36; Abdur Rauf three for 46, Azhar Abbas three for 39) **and 59 for eight** (Shabbir Ahmed five for 21). *Rest of NWFP 3 pts.*

At Lahore Country Club Ground, Muridke, January 2, 3, 4, 5. **Drawn. Sialkot 83** (Jaffer Nazir five for 27, Naved-ul-Hasan four for 28) **and 109 for eight** (Naved-ul-Hasan seven for 49); **Sheikhupura* 134** (Mujahid Jamshed 37; Tahir Mughal three for 55, Aamer Wasim three for 16). *Sheikhupura 3 pts.*

At LCCA Ground, Lahore, January 8, 9, 10, 11. **Lahore Blues won by 173 runs. Lahore Blues 217** (Bazid Khan 36, Salim Elahi 50, Mohammad Hussain 59; Tahir Mughal four for 74, Zahid Saeed four for 72) **and 341 for nine dec.** (Sohail Idrees 36, Bazid Khan 84, Zia-ur-Rehman 43, Mohammad Hussain 37, Irfan Fazil 51 not out, Extras 30; Zahid Saeed three for 118, Tahir Mughal three for 39); **Sialkot* 99** (Majid Jahangir 38; Irfan Fazil four for 32, Waqas Ahmed five for 45) and 286 (Majid Jahangir 68, Inam-ul-Haq 49, Shehzad Malik 31, Tahir Mughal 68 not out, Extras 33; Hasnain Kazim three for 60, Waqas Ahmed four for 98). *Lahore Blues 12 pts.*

At Arbab Niaz Stadium, Peshawar, January 8, 9, 10, 11. **Peshawar won by seven wickets. Rest of NWFP 92** (Imran Hussain 33; Kabir Khan three for 19, Fazl-e-Akbar five for 31) **and 233** (Asmatullah Mohmand 106 not out; Kabir Khan three for 45, Fazl-e-Akbar four for 71); **Peshawar* 99** (Sajid Shah three for 30, Shakeel-ur-Rehman six for 44) **and 230 for three** (Rafatullah Mohmand 50, Yasir Hameed 80, Wajahatullah Wasti 35 not out). *Peshawar 12 pts.*

At KRL Cricket Ground, Rawalpindi, January 8, 9, 10, 11. **Drawn. Rawalpindi 249** (Babar Naeem 56, Naseer Ahmed 35, Yasir Arafat 56, Mohammad Zahid 43; Abdur Rauf three for 52, Mushtaq Ahmed three for 87) **and 373** (Naved Ashraf 55, Babar Naeem 126, Shahid Javed 34, Yasir Arafat 37, Nadeem Abbasi 32; Mushtaq Ahmed five for 117); **Rest of Punjab* 423** (Saeed Anwar, jun. 57, Rizwan Ahmed 41, Sufyan Munir 127 not out, Mohammad Fazil 43, Mushtaq Ahmed 68, Extras 37; Babar Naeem three for 71) **and 70 for three**. *Rest of Punjab 3 pts.*

At Sheikhupura Stadium, Sheikhupura, January 8, 9, 10, 11. **Sheikhupura won by five wickets. Lahore Whites 285** (Musharaf Ali 49, Intikhab Alam 39, Aamer Malik 78 not out, Extras 33; Jaffer Nazir three for 87, Qaiser Abbas three for 21) **and 193** (Kamran Akmal 36, Mohammad Asif 31; Jaffer Nazir three for 41, Naved-ul-Hasan four for 83); **Sheikhupura* 316** (Majid Majeed 57, Naved-ul-Hasan 117, Jaffer Nazir 71, Extras 32; Fahad Masood three for 109, Adnan Naeem three for 131) **and 163 for five** (Majid Majeed 48). *Sheikhupura 12 pts.*

At KRL Cricket Ground, Rawalpindi, January 14, 15, 16, 17. **Drawn. Islamabad forfeited first innings and 195** (Ali Naqvi 33, Shakir Mahmood 45 not out, Saad Janjua 36; Noor-ul-Amin six for 58); **Rest of NWFP* forfeited first innings and 113 for four** (Asmatullah Mohmand 42 not out, Mohammad Bilal 30 not out).

At Gaddafi Stadium, Lahore, January 14, 15, 16, 17. **Drawn. Lahore Blues 313** (Sohail Idrees 40, Bazid Khan 57, Mohammad Hussain 50, Humayun Farhat 66, Extras 32; Shabbir Ahmed four for 74, Asim Butt three for 60) **and 276 for eight dec.** (Imran Farhat 92, Sohail Idrees 75, Extras 31; Shabbir Ahmed four for 75); **Rest of Punjab* 238** (Hasnain Abbas 51, Aamer Bashir 80, Extras 34; Irfan Fazil four for 57, Waqas Ahmed three for 88) **and 315 for nine** (Saeed Anwar, jun. 144 not out, Rizwan Ahmed 95; Imran Farhat three for 62). *Lahore Blues 3 pts.*

At Pindi Cricket Stadium, Rawalpindi, January 14, 15, 16, 17. **Rawalpindi v Peshawar. Abandoned.**

At Jinnah Stadium, Sialkot, January 14, 15, 16, 17. **Drawn. Sialkot 422 for seven dec.** (Faisal Naved 102, Majid Jahangir 80, Faisal Khan 113, Obaidullah Sarwar 33, Tahir Mughal 51 not out, Extras 38; Adnan Naeem four for 100); **Lahore Whites* 272** (Tariq Mahmood 66, Aamer Malik 44, Ahmed Khan 33, Fahad Masood 41; Tahir Mughal four for 84) **and 227 for four** (Shahid Anwar 63, Tariq Mahmood 90 not out). *Sialkot 3 pts.*

   Faisal Khan scored 113 on first-class debut.

At KRL Cricket Ground, Rawalpindi, January 20, 21, 22, 23. **Lahore Blues won by 169 runs. Lahore Blues 241** (Humayun Farhat 67, Mohammad Hussain 50; Rauf Akbar three for 44) **and 385 for eight dec.** (Sohail Idrees 154, Imran Farhat 49, Bazid Khan 88, Humayun Farhat 32, Mohammad Hussain 34; Rauf Akbar five for 63, Ali Naqvi three for 101); **Islamabad* 305** (Ali Naqvi 40, Iftikhar Hussain 30, Rashid Amin 101, Iftikhar Anjum 37; Irfan Fazil four for 55) **and 152** (Iftikhar Hussain 44; Irfan Fazil three for 22, Mohammad Hussain three for 12). *Lahore Blues 9 pts.*

At LCCA Ground, Lahore, January 20, 21, 22, 23. **Peshawar won by five wickets. Lahore Whites 183** (Shahid Anwar 44, Adnan Usman Khan 39, Shahnawaz Malik 34; Fazl-e-Akbar three for 44, Waqar Ahmed four for 62) **and 265** (Kamran Akmal 120, Adnan Usman Khan 35, Rao Usman 54; Fazl-e-Akbar three for 74, Arshad Khan three for 70); **Peshawar* 352** (Rafatullah Mohmand 73, Aftab Khan 95, Akhtar Sarfraz 32, Zulfiqar Jan 43; Shahnawaz Malik five for 78, Tariq Sheikh three for 21) **and 99 for five** (Rafatullah Mohmand 35 not out). *Peshawar 12 pts.*

At Pindi Cricket Stadium, Rawalpindi, January 20, 21, 22. **Rawalpindi won by 125 runs. Rawalpindi 228** (Nauman Aman 51, Yasir Arafat 32, Naeem Akhtar 55; Noor-ul-Amin six for 49) **and 167** (Babar Naeem 43; Noor-ul-Amin four for 32, Umair Khan three for 26); **Rest of NWFP* 98** (Ahmed Said 62; Naeem Akhtar three for 24, Yasir Arafat four for 18) **and 172** (Ahmed Said 78 not out, Abdus Salam 38; Mohammad Zahid four for 33, Munir Ansari three for 47, Yasir Arafat three for 48). *Rawalpindi 12 pts.*

At Gaddafi Stadium, Lahore, January 20, 21, 22. **Sheikhupura won by 40 runs. Sheikhupura 268** (Mujahid Jamshed 45, Naved-ul-Hasan 33, Jaffer Nazir 64, Mumtaz Ali 57; Abdur Rauf four for 51, Mushtaq Ahmed three for 84) **and 128** (Majid Majeed 38; Asim Butt four for 37, Mushtaq Ahmed four for 11); **Rest of Punjab* 228** (Rizwan Ahmed 43, Sufyan Munir 67; Jaffer Nazir four for 49, Naved-ul-Hasan four for 69) **and 128** (Mohammad Fazil 44 not out; Jaffer Nazir five for 48). *Sheikhupura 12 pts.*

Jaffer Nazir took four in eight balls including a hat-trick in Rest of Punjab's second innings.

At Gaddafi Stadium, Lahore, January 26, 27, 28, 29. **Rest of Punjab won by 92 runs. Rest of Punjab 282** (Saeed Anwar, jun. 55, Rizwan Ahmed 68, Sufyan Munir 68, Wasim Majeed 38, Extras 36; Fahad Masood four for 63, Wasim Khan six for 68) **and 289** (Sufyan Munir 104, Mushtaq Ahmed 56; Fahad Masood three for 43, Wasim Khan three for 79, Tariq Mahmood three for 20); **Lahore Whites* 224** (Rizwan Aslam 56, Kamran Akmal 81; Azhar Abbas four for 60, Mushtaq Ahmed three for 66) **and 255** (Tariq Mahmood 36, Kamran Akmal 82, Extras 33; Asim Butt three for 71, Mushtaq Ahmed six for 79). *Rest of Punjab 12 pts.*

At Arbab Niaz Stadium, Peshawar, January 26, 27, 28. **Peshawar won by 318 runs. Peshawar 331** (Rafatullah Mohmand 30, Yasir Hameed 51, Wajahatullah Wasti 74, Akhtar Sarfraz 41; Saad Janjua four for 88) **and 295 for seven dec.** (Wajahatullah Wasti 37, Akhtar Sarfraz 78, Zulfiqar Jan 100 not out; Saad Janjua three for 81); **Islamabad* 191** (Bilal Asad 33; Fazl-e-Akbar eight for 68) **and 117** (Kabir Khan four for 21, Fazl-e-Akbar four for 66). *Peshawar 12 pts.*

Fazl-e-Akbar took 12 for 134 for the second time in the season, following PIA's victory over Habib Bank in October.

At Sheikhupura Stadium, Sheikhupura, January 26, 27, 28. **Sheikhupura won by an innings and 126 runs. Sheikhupura 357** (Majid Majeed 45, Saleem Mughal 49, Maqsood Raza 68, Sarfraz Kazmi 75, Extras 50; Sajid Shah three for 68, Umair Khan four for 84); **Rest of NWFP* 143** (Naved Khan 34, Akbar Badshah 34, Extras 31; Mohammad Asif six for 34) **and 88** (Jaffer Nazir four for 28, Naved-ul-Hasan three for 50). *Sheikhupura 12 pts.*

At Jinnah Stadium, Sialkot, January 26, 27, 28, 29. **Drawn. Sialkot 366** (Majid Jahangir 55, Inam-ul-Haq 83, Shehzad Malik 104, Sajjad-ul-Haq 32; Naeem Akhtar three for 101, Yasir Arafat seven for 102) **and 218** (Faisal Naved 45, Majid Jahangir 33; Naeem Akhtar four for 74, Yasir Arafat four for 75); **Rawalpindi* 299** (Naseer Ahmed 91, Hashaam Iqbal 31, Yasir Arafat 58, Naeem Akhtar 41, Extras 35; Tahir Mughal six for 80) **and 193 for six** (Babar Naeem 72, Naseer Ahmed 36; Tahir Mughal four for 55). *Sialkot 3 pts.*

At LCCA Ground, Lahore, February 1, 2, 3. **Lahore Whites won by an innings and 19 runs. Lahore Whites 458 for six dec.** (Kashif Siddiq 103, Rizwan Aslam 92, Tariq Mahmood 50, Aamer Malik 113 not out, Adnan Usman Khan 34 not out; Iftikhar Anjum three for 71); **Islamabad* 276** (Bilal Asad 110, Asif Ali 45; Wasim Khan six for 60) **and 163** (Bilal Asad 62; Shahid Mahmood four for 79, Mohammad Asif five for 26). *Lahore Whites 12 pts.*

At Gaddafi Stadium, Lahore, February 1, 2, 3. **Peshawar won by an innings and 46 runs. Rest of Punjab 202** (Zeeshan Khan 89 not out, Shafiq Ahmed 38, Extras 30; Kabir Khan three for 21) **and 87** (Kabir Khan four for 50, Fazl-e-Akbar five for 31); **Peshawar* 335** (Rafatullah Mohmand 36, Taimur Khan 74, Arshad Khan 41, Extras 62; Abdur Rauf three for 112, Mir Usman three for 41). *Peshawar 12 pts.*

At Sheikhupura Stadium, Sheikhupura, February 1, 2, 3, 4. **Drawn. Sheikhupura* 300** (Imran Nazir 30, Saleem Mughal 99, Naved-ul-Hasan 32, Mumtaz Ali 30 not out; Hasnain Kazim four for 106, Sajid Ali four for 71) **and 418** (Imran Nazir 54, Qaiser Abbas 36, Mujahid Jamshed 86, Sarfraz Kazmi 85, Naved-ul-Hasan 64; Mohammad Hussain five for 131); **Lahore Blues 369** (Sohail Idrees 77, Saleem Shahzad 30, Zia-ur-Rehman 61, Humayun Farhat 53, Extras 38; Naved-ul-Hasan three for 102, Mohammad Asif three for 53) **and 122 for three** (Salim Elahi 66). *Lahore Blues 3 pts.*

At Jinnah Stadium, Sialkot, February 1, 2, 3. **Sialkot won by an innings and 111 runs. Sialkot 380 for nine dec.** (Majid Jahangir 104, Shoaib Malik 100, Tahir Mughal 52, Extras 32; Riaz Afridi three for 93, Noor-ul-Amin three for 54); **Rest of NWFP* 120** (Ibrahim Afridi 33; Tahir Mughal seven for 63, Shahid Khan three for 36) **and 149** (Asmatullah Mohmand 52, Riaz Afridi 35; Tahir Mughal four for 78, Zahid Saeed three for 33, Shoaib Malik three for 21). *Sialkot 12 pts.*

At LCCA Ground, Lahore, February 7, 8, 9, 10. **Rest of NWFP won by one wicket. Lahore Blues* 105** (Bazid Khan 45; Sajid Shah seven for 44) **and 363** (Salim Elahi 70, Zia-ur-Rehman 55, Mohammad Hussain 126, Humayun Farhat 51; Sajid Shah four for 101, Noor-ul-Amin five for 100); **Rest of NWFP 242** (Mohammad Fayyaz 56, Mohammad Bilal 68, Extras 37; Sajid Ali three for 66, Mohammad Hussain six for 60) **and 227 for nine** (Ahmed Said 52, Ibrahim Afridi 72 not out, Sajid Shah 33; Mohammad Hussain six for 73). *Rest of NWFP 12 pts.*
    After a first-innings duck, Mohammad Hussain performed the match double, with a century and 12 wickets for 133.

At Gymkhana Cricket Ground, Okara, February 7, 8, 9. **Islamabad won by one wicket. Rest of Punjab 260** (Zeeshan Khan 44, Wasim Majeed 81, Mohammad Fazil 45; Iftikhar Anjum four for 64, Saad Janjua three for 59) **and 135** (Shahid Latif 42, Kamran Ali 50; Iftikhar Anjum five for 51, Saad Janjua five for 39); **Islamabad* 220** (Bilal Asad 37, Rashid Amin 50, Atif Ashraf 43, Extras 35; Shabbir Ahmed four for 68, Abdur Rauf five for 82) **and 178 for nine** (Iftikhar Anjum 37; Abdur Rauf five for 67). *Islamabad 9 pts.*

At Sheikhupura Stadium, Sheikhupura, February 7, 8, 9, 10. **Sheikhupura won by eight wickets. Rawalpindi* 235** (Naved Ashraf 56, Mohammad Wasim 77; Jaffer Nazir five for 78) **and 264** (Arif Butt 64, Yasir Arafat 55, Extras 35; Imran Nazir three for 61); **Sheikhupura 429** (Mohammad Azam 52, Qaiser Abbas 37, Saleem Mughal 74, Maqsood Raza 64, Naved-ul-Hasan 58 not out, Extras 63; Yasir Arafat four for 107, Jawad Hameed three for 91) **and 73 for two** (Imran Nazir 55 not out). *Sheikhupura 12 pts.*

At Jinnah Stadium, Sialkot, February 7, 8, 9, 10. **Sialkot won by five wickets. Peshawar 190** (Rafatullah Mohmand 46, Taimur Khan 60; Tahir Mughal three for 72, Shahid Khan seven for 50) **and 183** (Rafatullah Mohmand 45, Aftab Khan 30, Yasir Hameed 49; Tahir Mughal six for 54, Shahid Khan three for 66); **Sialkot* 212** (Majid Jahangir 36, Faisal Khan 43, Sajjad-ul-Haq 52; Fazl-e-Akbar five for 89) **and 163 for five** (Majid Jahangir 47 not out). *Sialkot 12 pts.*

At Arbab Niaz Stadium, Peshawar, February 12, 13, 14. **Peshawar won by 206 runs. Peshawar 176** (Yasir Hameed 36, Wajahatullah Wasti 35, Shoaib Khan 33; Waqas Ahmed four for 75, Sajid Ali four for 37) **and 325** (Aftab Khan 85, Wajahatullah Wasti 60, Kabir Khan 46 not out; Mohammad Hussain six for 66); **Lahore Blues* 83** (Kabir Khan three for 43, Fazl-e-Akbar five for 18) **and 212** (Imran Farhat 50, Imran Nazir 30, Zia-ur-Rehman 49 not out, Extras 31; Waqar Ahmed three for 68, Taimur Khan five for 35). *Peshawar 12 pts.*

At Pindi Cricket Ground, Rawalpindi, February 12, 13, 14, 15. **Drawn. Lahore Whites 373** (Kashif Siddiq 74, Rizwan Aslam 74, Kamran Akmal 30, Adnan Usman Khan 74, Mohammad Asif 42 not out, Extras 32; Yasir Arafat four for 112) **and 251** (Kashif Siddiq 36, Kamran Akmal 30, Faisal Mahmood 58; Mohammad Zahid three for 28, Naeem Akhtar three for 59); **Rawalpindi* 286** (Babar Naeem 42, Naved Ashraf 95, Sheraz Khalid 54, Extras 52; Wasim Khan five for 110, Tariq Mahmood three for 40) **and 236 for six** (Babar Naeem 54, Shahid Javed 32, Naseer Ahmed 43, Naved Ashraf 56 not out; Wasim Khan three for 75). *Lahore Whites 3 pts.*

At Gymkhana Cricket Ground, Okara, February 12, 13, 14. **Sialkot won by nine wickets. Rest of Punjab 209** (Kashif Naved 44, Zeeshan Khan 34, Mohammad Fazil 32 not out, Extras 34;

Tahir Mughal four for 83, Aamer Wasim three for 26) **and 250** (Kashif Naved 97, Wasim Majeed 38, Zeeshan Khan 40; Tahir Mughal five for 71, Shahid Khan three for 65); **Sialkot* 388 for nine dec.** (Mubashir Dar 40, Majid Jahangir 33, Basit Saeed 42, Shehzad Malik 74, Aafan Rauf 31, Extras 63; Asim Butt four for 103) **and 75 for one** (Inam-ul-Haq 38 not out). *Sialkot 12 pts.*

At Sheikhupura Stadium, Sheikhupura, February 12, 13, 14, 15. **Sheikhupura won by five wickets. Islamabad 342** (Bilal Asad 109, Atif Ashraf 68, Azhar Mahmood 31, Iftikhar Anjum 55, Extras 36; Jaffer Nazir four for 92, Naved-ul-Hasan six for 102) **and 183** (Azhar Mahmood 51, Ishtiaq Rabbani 30; Jaffer Nazir five for 55, Faisal Virk three for 56); **Sheikhupura* 247** (Mohammad Azam 73 not out, Qaiser Abbas 49, Imran Nazir 35; Azhar Mahmood three for 56, Raheel Majeed five for 66) **and 279 for five** (Saleem Mughal 128 not out, Sarfraz Kazmi 52 not out). *Sheikhupura 9 pts.*

Mohammad Azam carried his bat through Sheikhupura's first innings.

At KRL Cricket Ground, Rawalpindi, February 18, 19, 20. **Islamabad won by 49 runs. Islamabad 206** (Azhar Mahmood 32, Irfan Bhatti 39 not out; Tahir Mughal six for 67) **and 243** (Raheel Majeed 33, Bilal Asad 33, Asif Ali 55, Saad Janjua 39; Tahir Mughal four for 99, Aamer Wasim three for 63); **Sialkot* 260** (Majid Jahangir 51, Aafan Rauf 56; Saad Janjua three for 94, Stephen John three for 63) **and 140** (Tahir Mughal 30; Azhar Mahmood seven for 56). *Islamabad 9 pts.*

At Gaddafi Stadium, Lahore, February 18, 19, 20. **Rawalpindi won by 453 runs. Rawalpindi* 232** (Babar Naeem 62, Tasawwur Hussain 32, Yasir Arafat 44 not out, Extras 38; Sajid Ali three for 57, Mohammad Hussain three for 39) **and 468 for five dec.** (Saqib Naqeeb 32, Babar Naeem 227, Naseer Ahmed 42, Naved Ashraf 91, Extras 36; Kazim Ali three for 77); **Lahore Blues 102** (Naeem Akhtar six for 53) **and 145** (Imran Farhat 36; Naeem Akhtar four for 53, Yasir Arafat five for 53). *Rawalpindi 12 pts.*

Babar Naeem's 227 lasted 321 minutes and 251 balls and included 26 fours and five sixes.

At LCCA Ground, Lahore, February 18, 19, 20. **Lahore Whites won by two wickets. Rest of NWFP* 220** (Ahmed Said 43, Adnan Raees 67, Ibrahim Afridi 34; Wasim Khan six for 60) **and 189** (Asmatullah Mohmand 63, Mohammad Fayyaz 42; Wasim Khan four for 55, Tariq Mahmood six for 43); **Lahore Whites 282** (Tariq Sheikh 118, Tariq Mahmood 41; Sajid Shah three for 69, Mohammad Aslam five for 71) **and 128 for eight** (Kashif Siddiq 30, Tariq Sheikh 37 not out; Mohammad Aslam five for 33). *Lahore Whites 12 pts.*

At Arbab Niaz Stadium, Peshawar, February 18, 19. **Peshawar won by an innings and 78 runs. Sheikhupura 182** (Maqsood Raza 40, Jaffer Nazir 36; Kabir Khan four for 46, Fazl-e-Akbar four for 56) **and 65** (Fazl-e-Akbar three for 25, Waqar Ahmed five for 39); **Peshawar* 305** (Taimur Khan 55, Arshad Khan 59, Kabir Khan 66 not out, Extras 44; Jaffer Nazir four for 114). *Peshawar 12 pts.*

Opener Imran Nazir was absent in Sheikhupura's second-innings 65.

FINAL

KARACHI WHITES v PESHAWAR

At National Stadium, Karachi, March 1, 2, 3, 4. Karachi Whites won by eight wickets. Toss: Karachi Whites. First-class debut: Zeeshan Mohsin.

Karachi Whites reversed the result of the 1998-99 final on the same ground, beating Peshawar with a day to spare. Fifteen wickets fell on the opening day, when Peshawar folded inside 45 overs; only Zeeshan Mohsin, a 19-year-old debutant, passed 30 as Tanvir Ahmed made two early strikes, and then finished them off with three in five balls. But Karachi slid to 98 for five before Imran Javed steered them towards safety, benefiting from a life in the last over of the day. As the pitch eased, they built a lead of 102. Yasir Hameed kept Peshawar in the game with a career-best unbeaten 171, scored out of 325 in his 460 minutes at the crease, though he was dropped three times. The next best score was Zeeshan's – 40, interrupted by a hamstring strain – though

Fazl-e-Akbar hung on to help Yasir run up 40 for the final wicket. That left Karachi a target of 253 in a little over two days. They had little difficulty. Peshawar tried nine bowlers, but even Fazl, needing five wickets for 100 in the season, was powerless as Ghulam Ali cruised to his century and an eight-wicket win.

Close of play: First day, Karachi Whites 137-5 (Imran Javed 32, Moin Khan 17); Second day, Peshawar 164-4 (Yasir Hameed 60, Taimur Khan 3); Third day, Karachi Whites 38-1 (Ghulam Ali 11, Tanvir Ahmed 5).

Peshawar

Aftab Khan b Tanvir Ahmed	4	– (5) lbw b Imran Javed	20
Zeeshan Mohsin c Arif Mahmood			
b Mohammad Hasnain	39	– c Tanvir Ahmed b Danish Kaneria	40
Javed Iqbal c Moin Khan b Tanvir Ahmed	4	– (1) c Moin Khan	
		b Mohammad Hasnain	18
Wajahatullah Wasti c and b Mohammad Hasnain	26	– c Saeed bin Nasir b Danish Kaneria	15
Yasir Hameed lbw b Imran Javed	1	– (3) not out	171
Taimur Khan c Ghulam Ali b Danish Kaneria	16	– c Tanvir Ahmed b Ghulam Ali	34
†Zulfiqar Jan b Danish Kaneria	23	– b Danish Kaneria	13
*Arshad Khan c Hasan Raza b Tanvir Ahmed	19	– c Tanvir Ahmed b Danish Kaneria	0
Waqar Ahmed not out	0	– b Mohammad Hasnain	12
Kabir Khan c Mohammad Masroor			
b Tanvir Ahmed	1	– lbw b Mohammad Hasnain	0
Fazl-e-Akbar lbw b Tanvir Ahmed	0	– c Moin Khan b Tanvir Ahmed	6
B 12, l-b 2, w 1, n-b 10	25	B 8, l-b 10, n-b 7	25

1/5 2/21 3/76 4/87 5/87	158	1/29 2/66 3/99 4/158 5/241	354
6/119 7/156 8/156 9/158		6/294 7/294 8/314 9/314	

In the second innings Zeeshan Mohsin, when 11, retired hurt at 30 and resumed at 99.

Bowling: *First Innings*—Tanvir Ahmed 16.4–2–53–5; Mohammad Hasnain 12–0–46–2; Imran Javed 11–6–21–1; Danish Kaneria 5–0–24–2. *Second Innings*—Tanvir Ahmed 28–6–108–1; Mohammad Hasnain 29–9–74–3; Imran Javed 15–4–30–1; Danish Kaneria 38–5–102–4; Arif Mahmood 5–0–20–0; Ghulam Ali 2–1–2–1.

Karachi Whites

Ghulam Ali c Zulfiqar Jan b Fazl-e-Akbar	8	– not out	113
Shadab Kabir b Waqar Ahmed	14	– lbw b Waqar Ahmed	16
Saeed bin Nasir c Taimur Khan b Waqar Ahmed	13	– (4) not out	66
Hasan Raza c Zulfiqar Jan b Waqar Ahmed	0		
Mohammad Masroor c Zulfiqar Jan			
b Fazl-e-Akbar	36		
Imran Javed lbw b Kabir Khan	57		
*†Moin Khan lbw b Kabir Khan	17		
Arif Mahmood c Zulfiqar Jan b Waqar Ahmed	54		
Mohammad Hasnain b Kabir Khan	11		
Tanvir Ahmed not out	25	– (3) b Arshad Khan	44
Danish Kaneria b Waqar Ahmed	2		
L-b 9, n-b 14	23	B 4, l-b 7, n-b 4	15

1/13 2/35 3/35 4/51 5/98	260	1/28 2/106	(2 wkts) 254
6/142 7/188 8/212 9/256			

Bowling: *First Innings*—Kabir Khan 22–3–65–3; Fazl-e-Akbar 18–1–84–2; Waqar Ahmed 16.1–2–74–5; Taimur Khan 5–3–10–0; Arshad Khan 5–0–18–0. *Second Innings*—Kabir Khan 10–2–21–0; Fazl-e-Akbar 19–5–66–0; Waqar Ahmed 8–0–37–1; Arshad Khan 13–3–46–1; Taimur Khan 14–4–34–0; Yasir Hameed 1–0–8–0; Aftab Khan 2–0–14–0; Zeeshan Mohsin 1–0–12–0; Wajahatullah Wasti 1.1–0–5–0.

Umpires: Iftikhar Malik and Mohammad Nazir.
Third umpire: Afzaal Ahmed. Referee: Munawar Agha.

QUAID-E-AZAM TROPHY WINNERS

1953-54	Bahawalpur	1973-74	Railways	1988-89	ADBP
1954-55	Karachi	1974-75	Punjab A	1989-90	PIA
1956-57	Punjab	1975-76	National Bank	1990-91	Karachi Whites
1957-58	Bahawalpur	1976-77	United Bank	1991-92	Karachi Whites
1958-59	Karachi	1977-78	Habib Bank	1992-93	Karachi Whites
1959-60	Karachi	1978-79	National Bank	1993-94	Lahore City
1961-62	Karachi Blues	1979-80	PIA	1994-95	Karachi Blues
1962-63	Karachi A	1980-81	United Bank	1995-96	Karachi Blues
1963-64	Karachi Blues	1981-82	National Bank	1996-97	Lahore City
1964-65	Karachi Blues	1982-83	United Bank	1997-98	Karachi Blues
1966-67	Karachi	1983-84	National Bank	1998-99	Peshawar
1968-69	Lahore	1984-85	United Bank	1999-2000	PIA
1969-70	PIA	1985-86	Karachi	2000-01	Lahore City Blues
1970-71	Karachi Blues	1986-87	National Bank	2001-02	Karachi Whites
1972-73	Railways	1987-88	PIA		

Note: Matches in this section were not first-class.

NATIONAL ONE-DAY TOURNAMENT, 2001-02

Semi-finals

At National Stadium, Karachi, April 2 (day/night). **Habib Bank won by 139 runs. Habib Bank* 306 (50 overs)** (Taufeeq Umar 90, Shahid Afridi 86, Salim Elahi 78; Sarfraz Ahmed three for 43); **WAPDA 167 (46.5 overs)** (Rafatullah Mohmand 34, Rizwan Malik 52; Sajid Shah four for 33).

At Gaddafi Stadium, Lahore, April 2 (day/night). **PIA won by nine runs. PIA* 223 for nine** (50 overs) (Ghulam Ali 32, Shoaib Malik 30, Moin Khan 31, Azhar Mahmood 34; Mushtaq Ahmed four for 36); **National Bank 214 (47 overs)** (Imran Nazir 95; Wasim Akram three for 42).

Final

At Gaddafi Stadium, Lahore, April 4 (day/night). **PIA won by six runs. PIA* 236 for nine** (50 overs) (Shoaib Mohammad 31, Faisal Iqbal 53, Shoaib Malik 52); **Habib Bank 230 (49.5 overs)** (Taufeeq Umar 95, Salim Elahi 64, Extras 38; Wasim Akram three for 28, Azhar Mahmood three for 73).

CRICKET IN SRI LANKA, 2001-02

By SA'ADI THAWFEEQ and GERRY VAIDYASEKERA

Mahela Jayawardene

Sri Lanka's national team had a busy year. They played 16 Tests between August and July, winning 12, all on the subcontinent, and whitewashing West Indies, Zimbabwe and Bangladesh. In March, Sri Lanka won the Asian Test Championship final against Pakistan in Lahore, and in September they hosted the one-day ICC Champions Trophy, sharing the title with India after rain washed out the final. The biggest disappointment was their tour of England, where they lost the Test series and failed to reach the final of a one-day triangular.

Cricket administration remained turbulent, with an interim committee still in charge. In December, general elections brought a change of government, weakening the committee's chairman, Vijay Malalasekera, an ally of the former national president. He was replaced in April by Hemaka Amarasuriya from the Singer company, a leading sponsor. In May, the government triggered a new crisis by putting forward the board's controversial ex-president, Thilanga Sumathipala, as a stand-by representative for an ICC meeting. Sumathipala had been removed by the last government, but helped to fund their successors' election campaign. The interim committee had already chosen its representatives, and five members resigned in protest, including the chairman of selectors, Michael Tissera. The new sports minister, Johnston Fernando, named six replacements, with Guy de Alwis, the 1980s wicket-keeper, in control of selection.

Fernando had appointed Tissera only in January, after overruling the previous selectors' decision to drop the vice-captain, Marvan Atapattu, and another player in order to introduce fresh blood against Zimbabwe. De Alwis went much further in July, resting seven players, including Atapattu and the national idol, Muttiah Muralitharan, from the Second Test against Bangladesh, also to try out youngsters. Murali had taken ten wickets in the First Test, raising his aggregate to 430.

The overcrowded international season meant that Colombo Colts' triumph in the Premier Trophy final, overwhelming the more fancied Sinhalese Sports Club with a day to spare, received little attention. This was only the third title in Colts' 129-year history, all coming in the 14 seasons since the domestic competition won first-class status.

The tournament's format had been revamped yet again, with the stated aim of reducing the number of matches for top clubs and players. The general structure of the last two seasons remained – two preliminary leagues determined whether teams would advance to the Super League or the Plate Championship, which also featured three teams from the non-first-class Sara Trophy. But the top four clubs of 2000-01 were guaranteed a Super League place. They provided three of the qualifiers for the semi-finals, an addition to the competition, and both sides for the final, restored for the first time since 1997-98.

The fourth semi-finalists were Tamil Union, who almost overcame a strong Sinhalese side. Mahela Jayawardene had scored 274, the highest first-class innings in Sri Lankan domestic cricket, to help Sinhalese to a first-innings lead of 175, and they needed just 109 on the last day. But they stumbled to 73 for seven on a crumbling pitch before Tilan Samaraweera guided them home. Colts, placed fourth in the Super League, had to squeeze past Nondescripts, the unbeaten leaders and defending champions. From 131 for two chasing 217, they slid to 195 for eight before Chaminda Vaas saw them through. In the final, however, Colts outclassed Sinhalese, despite two more outstanding innings from Jayawardene.

Jayawardene was free for only five Sinhalese matches, but in those he piled up 867 at 108.37, with three centuries. In all first-class cricket, he fell 49 short of Russel Arnold's record aggregate for a Sri Lankan season – 1,475 in 1995-96.

But it was Aravinda de Silva, aged 36, who attracted the keenest interest, from selectors and public. Sri Lanka's leading scorer in Test and one-day cricket, de Silva had fallen out of favour during England's visit in early 2001. In January 2002, Tissera told him to get fit and to score heavily in domestic cricket if he wanted to tour England. De Silva accepted the challenge, shed 14kg and totalled 691 runs in nine matches for Nondescripts to earn his recall. After England, and a final double-century against Bangladesh, he retired from Test cricket.

De Silva finished third in the batting averages, where the number of home Tests – and the weakness of the opposition – meant that national cricketers filled the top six places. His Nondescripts club-mate, Hashan Tillekeratne, led the list for the second season running, with 965 at 107.22. Apart from Jayawardene, Chamara Silva of Panadura, Michael Vandort of Colombo and Naveed Nawaz of Nondescripts all passed 1,000 runs.

Vandort and Nawaz were among the players controversially called up for the Second Test against Bangladesh in July, alongside the pace bowler, Chamila Gamage Lakshitha, who claimed a wicket with his first ball in Test cricket. Lakshitha had worked hard for his club, Air Force, taking 95 first-class wickets, two behind Muralitharan, who kept him off the head of the bowling averages by a fraction of a run. Murali's 97 was the highest total, and included 23 in the two matches he managed for Tamil Union.

Lakshitha appeared mostly in the Plate Championship, which was won by Chilaw Marians in their maiden first-class season after winning the play-off league against the last year's bottom-placed teams. The Plate went to the final round, when a ninth-wicket stand of 128 between Praneth Jayasundera and Lakmal Fernando gave Chilaw first-innings lead against their nearest rivals, Sebastianites. But after Sebastianites lost three points for an ineligible player, the runners-up spot went to Ragama, another first-class newcomer.

Despite the heavy schedule, the board added an invitation tournament for four hand-picked sides: Sri Lanka A, a Club XI, a Schools XI and a Board Academy XI. The intention was to allow promising young players, including those from the inter-schools competition, to display their talents to the selectors. Only the Club XI won any matches outright, but no champions were declared.

The final of the Premier limited-overs championship was contested by the Premier League's beaten semi-finalists. Nondescripts defeated Tamil Union by 44 runs, a double celebration for de Silva, whose son had been born the day before. De Silva added 153 with Kumar Sangakkara, and played Muralitharan with such ease that he conceded 62 in ten overs.

In schools cricket, Mahes Sriyantha of Harischandra scored 212, with eight sixes and 30 fours, against Ranbokunygama Maha Vidyalaya. A. B. Tharanga of St Servatius claimed eight for 24 against Basilica College, and 13 for 62 in the match. Only Sahan Wijeratne, from Prince of Wales College, reached 1,000 runs in the schools season, earning his first-class debut for the Schools XI. A batsman for the future was 12-year-old Sahan Hettiarachchi, who reached 50 in 14 balls for Royal College Under-13. A low-scoring match between St Anthony's College, Kandy, and Surrey Under-15 was settled by the 56 extras which the English contributed to St Anthony's total of 100; in reply, they were all out for 87.

FIRST-CLASS AVERAGES, 2001-02

BATTING

(Qualification: 500 runs, average 35.00)

	M	I	NO	R	HS	100s	Avge
H. P. Tillekeratne (*Nondescripts*)	14	16	7	965	204*	3	107.22
D. P. M. D. Jayawardene (*Sinhalese*)	13	19	2	1,426	274	4	83.88
P. A. de Silva (*Nondescripts*)	10	14	1	897	206	3	69.00
S. T. Jayasuriya (*Bloomfield*)	11	16	2	951	145	2	67.92
T. T. Samaraweera (*Sinhalese*)	16	17	4	781	123*	2	60.07
K. C. Sangakkara (*Nondescripts*)	10	14	0	766	140	2	54.71
W. M. B. Perera (*Moors*)	13	22	4	948	111*	3	52.66
C. U. Jayasinghe (*Burgher*)	12	19	3	834	101	2	52.12
L. P. C. Silva (*Panadura*)	13	21	1	1,028	127*	3	51.40
M. N. Nawaz (*Nondescripts*)	15	26	3	1,110	139	2	48.26
M. G. Vandort (*Colombo*)	16	23	1	1,034	144	3	47.00
U. D. U. Chandana (*Tamil Union*)	10	11	0	507	194	1	46.09
T. M. Dilshan (*Bloomfield*)	15	21	1	911	165*	2	45.55
R. P. Hewage (*Nondescripts*)	10	14	2	514	102*	1	42.83
M. S. Atapattu (*Sinhalese*)	12	19	3	681	201	2	42.56
K. A. S. Jayasinghe (*Ragama*)	8	15	0	606	175	1	40.40
U. C. Hathurusinghe (*Moors*)	11	18	2	634	133	2	39.62
R. H. S. Silva (*Sebastianites*)	15	22	1	823	169	1	39.19
G. R. P. Peiris (*Tamil Union*)	12	21	1	778	97	0	38.90
M. M. D. N. R. G. Perera (*Sebastianites*)	14	21	3	700	152	2	38.88
P. C. Jayasundera (*Chilaw Marians*)	15	21	3	674	112*	2	37.44
C. Mendis (*Colts*)	11	17	1	590	95	0	36.87
S. I. Fernando (*Colts*)	11	17	0	626	94	0	36.82
S. I. de Saram (*Tamil Union*)	15	26	3	842	108	1	36.60
D. A. Gunawardene (*Sinhalese*)	13	23	1	798	138	1	36.27
A. S. Polonowita (*Colombo*)	14	23	3	723	95	0	36.15
S. N. Wijesinghe (*Sebastianites*)	10	16	2	501	114	1	35.78
E. F. M. U. Fernando (*Ragama*)	13	24	0	857	133	1	35.70
K. H. R. K. Fernando (*Sebastianites*)	15	22	2	701	105	3	35.05

BOWLING

(Qualification: 35 wickets, average 25.00)

	O	M	R	W	BB	5W/i	Avge
M. Muralitharan (*Tamil Union*)	599.4	189	1,270	97	9-51	12	13.09
M. K. G. C. P. Lakshitha (*Air Force*)	459.2	113	1,250	95	7-23	10	13.15
K. H. R. K. Fernando (*Sebastianites*)	310.4	55	956	61	5-10	2	15.73
P. N. Ranjith (*Moors*)	263.5	56	826	49	7-55	3	16.85
W. R. D. Dissanayake (*Air Force*)	317.1	76	789	45	6-70	2	17.53
L. D. I. Perera (*Chilaw Marians*)	332.1	59	1,138	63	6-42	5	18.06
H. M. Maduwantha (*Kurunegala Youth*)	264	79	651	36	7-51	2	18.08
S. Arangalla (*Ragama*)	251.4	57	747	41	6-41	2	18.21
C. M. Hathurusinghe (*Moratuwa*)	208.3	32	712	39	7-29	4	18.85
W. P. U. J. C. Vaas (*Colts*)	395.1	79	1,169	62	7-71	4	18.85
K. S. Lokurachchi (*Bloomfield*)	424.1	117	1,070	53	5-103	1	20.18
B. A. R. S. Priyadarshana (*Ragama*)	261.5	44	927	45	5-73	1	20.60
A. W. Ekanayake (*Kurunegala Youth*)	373.4	109	875	42	7-101	3	20.83
K. A. D. M. Fernando (*Sebastianites*)	218	41	758	36	8-34	4	21.05
K. R. Pushpakumara (*Nondescripts*)	302.3	58	992	47	5-41	1	21.10
D. Hettiarachchi (*Colts*)	305.4	70	867	41	6-98	2	21.14

	O	M	R	W	BB	5W/i	Avge
P. C. Jayasundera (*Chilaw Marians*)	305.1	73	902	42	5-66	1	21.47
S. H. S. M. K. Silva (*Burgher*)	268.4	64	777	35	7-52	4	22.20
N. S. Rupasinghe (*Colombo*)	565.3	121	1,528	68	6-94	3	22.47
U. D. U. Chandana (*Tamil Union*)	336.5	87	971	43	5-59	2	22.58
P. W. Gunaratne (*Antonians*)	286.1	58	947	41	5-57	1	23.09
T. T. Samaraweera (*Sinhalese*)	446.1	83	1,335	57	6-87	4	23.42
M. Pushpakumara (*Colts*)	385	81	1,187	48	4-43	0	24.72

Note: Averages exclude the promotion/relegation play-offs in June–July 2001, but include Bangladesh's tour in July 2002.

PREMIER TROPHY, 2001-02

SUPER LEAGUE

	Played	Won	Lost	Drawn	1st-inns Lead	Points
Nondescripts CC	9	3	0	6	4	98.005
Tamil Union C and AC . . .	9	4	2	3	2	96.845
Sinhalese SC	9	4	0	5	2	92.340
Colts CC	9	4	1	4	2	89.760
Burgher RC	9	1	1	7	4	73.790
Moors SC	9	2	2	5	2	70.105
Bloomfield C and AC	9	1	3	5	3	65.000
Colombo CC	9	1	3	5	1	50.845
Panadura SC	9	1	4	4	1	46.835
Galle CC	9	1	6	2	0	39.850

Super League teams carried forward results and points gained against fellow-qualifiers in the first round, but not those gained against the teams eliminated.

Semi-finals: Colts beat Nondescripts by two wickets; Sinhalese beat Tamil Union by three wickets.

Final: Colts beat Sinhalese by eight wickets.

PLATE CHAMPIONSHIP

	Played	Won	Lost	Drawn	1st-inns Lead	Points
Chilaw Marians CC	8	4	0	4	3	106.620
Ragama CC	8	4	1	3	2	96.150
Sebastianites C and AC . . .	8	5	0	3	1	94.505*
Moratuwa SC	8	5	3	0	0	90.545
Air Force SC	8	4	3	1	0	77.050
Kurunegala Youth CC	8	3	3	2	1	73.160
Antonians CC	8	2	4	2	1	61.280
Kandy CC	8	1	6	1	0	35.050
Rio SC	8	0	8	0	0	19.275

* Sebastianites were penalised 3 pts for fielding an ineligible player in one match.

Teams carried forward results and points gained against fellow group members in the first round, but not those gained against the teams who qualified for the Super League.

Outright win = 12 pts; lead on first innings in a drawn game = 8 pts. Bonus points were awarded as follows: 0.1 pt for each wicket taken and 0.005 pt for each run scored, up to 400 runs per innings.

*In the following scores, * by the name of a team indicates that they won the toss.*

PROMOTION/RELEGATION LEAGUE, 2001

The bottom four teams from the first-class 2000-01 Plate Championship (Singha, Police, Navy and Matara) and the group leaders from the non-first-class 2000-01 Sara Trophy (Chilaw Marians and Ragama) were invited to compete for two places in the 2001-02 Premier League. The play-off matches were granted first-class status. Matara withdrew in protest after a dispute over transfer regulations.

At De Mazenod College, Kandana, June 15, 16, 17. **Drawn. Chilaw Marians 277** (W. A. D. A. P. Perera 76, L. J. P. Gunaratne 47, S. T. Tittagalla 36; S. A. Wijeratne four for 32) **and 157 for two** (W. A. D. A. P. Perera 60, N. A. N. N. Perera 39 not out); **Police* 271** (H. P. A. Priyantha 54, C. N. Liyanage 53, Extras 31; L. D. I. Perera four for 91, L. P. M. Sathyapala three for 52).

At Galle International Stadium, Galle, June 15, 16, 17. **Singha won by two wickets. Navy* 153** (S. I. Nanayakkara 46, G. L. Hewage 39; K. S. S. de Silva three for 52, P. Milton three for 34) **and 239** (H. S. S. M. K. Weerasiri 56, M. M. Perera 59; P. Milton four for 41, G. I. Dilshan three for 69); **Singha 175** (A. S. Wewalwala 68; M. M. Perera three for 29, B. W. D. M. M. Dissanayake five for 49) **and 219 for eight** (H. W. M. Kumara 31, M. A. M. Faizer 34, K. S. S. de Silva 62; M. M. Perera three for 37).

At Air Force Ground, Katunayake, June 22, 23, 24. **Chilaw Marians won by four wickets. Navy* 227** (P. C. V. B. de Silva 30, H. S. S. M. K. Weerasiri 39, K. C. P. K. Anthony 52; L. P. M. Sathyapala three for 60, L. J. P. Gunaratne four for 75) **and 96** (L. P. M. Sathyapala four for 34, L. J. P. Gunaratne five for 32); **Chilaw Marians 204** (W. A. D. A. P. Perera 42, C. S. Fernando 46, L. D. I. Perera 34; L. G. J. Jayasinghe three for 57, B. W. D. M. M. Dissanayake four for 43) **and 120 for six** (L. J. P. Gunaratne 36; H. S. S. M. K. Weerasiri four for 19).

At De Mazenod College, Kandana, June 29, 30, July 1. **Ragama won by eight wickets. Police* 181** (H. P. A. Priyantha 59, R. R. Wimalasiri 61; S. Arangalla four for 50) **and 184** (S. A. Wijeratne 55; S. Arangalla four for 66, T. P. Gamage three for 21); **Ragama 218** (Chandika P. Hettiarachchi 41, S. A. L. S. Perera 32; N. H. Tennekoon five for 71) **and 151 for two** (H. M. Mallawarachchi 55, K. N. S. Fernando 61 not out).

At De Mazenod College, Kandana, July 6, 7, 8. **Drawn. Chilaw Marians* 254** (W. A. D. A. P. Perera 97, Extras 31; S. Arangalla four for 93, T. P. Gamage three for 47) **and 55 for three** (L. J. P. Gunaratne 32 not out); **Ragama 166** (S. D. Gunawardene 48, S. A. L. S. Perera 35; L. D. I. Perera three for 67, T. M. I. Ruwanpura five for 22).

At Police Park, Colombo, July 6, 7, 8. **Drawn. Police 196** (H. M. N. C. Silva 54 not out) **and 202 for nine** (S. A. Wijeratne 38, C. N. Liyanage 45, I. D. Gunawardene 36; I. C. Soysa three for 24); **Singha* 244** (A. S. Wewalwala 94, I. C. Soysa 42; T. A. V. H. K. Ranaweera four for 73).

At Air Force Ground, Katunayake, July 13, 14, 15. **Chilaw Marians won by nine wickets. Chilaw Marians* 343** (W. A. D. A. P. Perera 37, L. J. P. Gunaratne 108, N. A. N. N. Perera 54, A. M. N. Priyankara 46; I. C. Soysa four for 73, G. I. Dilshan three for 73) **and 75 for one** (W. A. D. A. P. Perera 42 not out); **Singha 107** (L. P. M. Sathyapala five for 25, L. J. P. Gunaratne three for 30) **and 309** (A. S. Wewalwala 38, M. A. M. Faizer 36, M. R. Porage 72 not out, M. T. T. Mirando 73; L. P. M. Sathyapala three for 91, L. J. P. Gunaratne five for 97).

At De Mazenod College, Kandana, July 13, 14, 15. **Ragama won by five wickets. Navy 253** (H. S. S. M. K. Weerasiri 74, G. L. Hewage 37; S. Arangalla four for 31) **and 207** (M. M. Perera 72; T. P. Gamage four for 47); **Ragama* 316** (K. N. S. Fernando 43, S. D. Gunawardene 75, E. D. Diaz 37 not out, R. D. Dissanayake 42, Extras 37; S. M. A. K. S. Kumara four for 79) **and 148 for five** (K. N. S. Fernando 42, S. D. Gunawardene 38 not out).

At Police Park, Colombo, July 20, 21, 22. **Drawn. Navy* 244** (H. S. S. M. K. Weerasiri 81, M. M. Perera 32, G. L. Hewage 44; I. D. Gunawardene three for 24) **and 241** (S. I. Nanayakkara 46, H. S. S. M. K. Weerasiri 39, G. L. Hewage 41, B. W. D. M. M. Dissanayake 32, H. G. S. P. Fernando 43; H. P. A. Priyantha four for 39); **Police 352** (H. P. A. Priyantha 57, K. J. C. Kottearchchi 47, W. N. M. Soysa 114, S. A. D. A. Maduranga 48; S. M. A. K. S. Kumara three for 95, B. W. D. M. M. Dissanayake three for 84) **and 117 for three** (H. P. A. Priyantha 61 not out).

At Galle International Stadium, Galle, July 20, 21, 22. **Drawn. Ragama* 237** (K. N. S. Fernando 61, S. Arangalla 36, Extras 31; S. Jayantha four for 40) **and 166 for eight** (I. C. Soysa four for 24, G. I. Dilshan three for 51); **Singha 176** (Y. M. W. B. Ekanayake 58; K. N. S. Fernando four for 32, R. D. Dissanayake four for 44).

Chilaw Marians 53.425 pts, Ragama 45.31 pts, Singha 32.95 pts, Police 20.915 pts, Navy 14.4 pts, Matara 0 pts. Chilaw Marians and Ragama were promoted to the Premier League Tournament, the others demoted to the non-first-class Sara Trophy.

PREMIER LEAGUE TOURNAMENT, 2001-02

Super Group

The Super Group was formed by the top four teams from the 2000-01 Super League. They were guaranteed entry to the 2001-02 Super League, and these results and points were carried forward.

At Havelock Park, Colombo (BRC), November 2, 3, 4. **Drawn. Colts* 281** (C. Mendis 67, K. M. H. Perera 86; S. H. S. M. K. Silva six for 74); **Burgher 375 for seven** (B. C. M. S. Mendis 41, S. K. L. de Silva 80, C. U. Jayasinghe 79, I. C. Soysa 52 not out, S. H. S. M. K. Silva 39, Extras 31; M. J. Sigera three for 57).

At Maitland Place, Colombo (SSC), November 2, 3, 4. **Drawn. Nondescripts* 134** (A. S. A. Perera four for 15) **and 44 for two**; **Sinhalese 299** (U. A. Fernando 108, N. T. Paranavitana 31; W. C. A. Ganegama three for 71).

At Havelock Park, Colombo (BRC), November 9, 10, 11. **Drawn. Burgher 325** (B. C. M. S. Mendis 40, D. M. Perumal 30, S. K. L. de Silva 55, C. U. Jayasinghe 85; N. T. Paranavitana four for 39); **Sinhalese* 311 for seven** (D. M. U. J. Dissanayake 31, W. M. S. M. Perera 58, U. A. Fernando 101, M. N. Silva 57 not out).

At Havelock Park, Colombo (Colts), November 9, 10, 11. **Drawn. Nondescripts 222** (P. A. de Silva 77; M. Pushpakumara three for 56) **and 139 for four** (R. R. Tissera 54); **Colts* 258** (C. Mendis 95, S. I. Fernando 78; W. C. A. Ganegama three for 40).

At Maitland Place, Colombo (NCC), November 16, 17, 18. **Drawn. Nondescripts 252** (M. N. Nawaz 49, T. A. Weerappuli 35, R. S. Kalpage 38, C. P. Mapatuna 33; I. S. Gallage four for 53); **Burgher* 65** (W. C. A. Ganegama four for 14) **and 258 for eight** (I. C. Soysa 35, G. S. T. Perera 52, C. U. Jayasinghe 32, B. S. M. Warnapura 57; M. K. D. I. Amerasinghe four for 50).

At Maitland Place, Colombo (SSC), November 16, 17, 18. **Sinhalese won by eight wickets. Colts 192** (S. I. Fernando 51, D. P. Samaraweera 44, M. Pushpakumara 33; D. G. R. Dhammika six for 61) **and 132** (S. I. Fernando 43; P. D. R. L. Perera four for 41); **Sinhalese* 303 for eight dec.** (D. A. Gunawardene 138, T. A. Embuldeniya 46; M. Pushpakumara four for 98) **and 25 for two**.

Sinhalese 26.49 pts, Nondescripts 15.605 pts, Colts 15.015 pts, Burgher 14.915 pts.

Group A

At Air Force Ground, Katunayake, November 2, 3, 4. **Sebastianites won by 60 runs. Sebastianites 132** (R. H. S. Silva 38; M. K. G. C. P. Lakshitha four for 41) **and 125** (M. K. G. C. P. Lakshitha five for 36); **Air Force* 81** (M. M. D. N. R. G. Perera four for 30, K. H. R. K. Fernando five for ten) **and 116** (K. H. R. K. Fernando four for 41).

At Maitland Crescent, Colombo (CCC), November 2, 3, 4. **Drawn. Colombo 271** (D. K. Ranaweera 63, A. S. Polonowita 71; M. A. P. Salgado four for 47) **and 211 for seven** (J. W. H. D. Boteju 68; S. Arangalla four for 34); **Ragama* 193** (D. G. N. de Silva 89, S. Arangalla 47 not out; M. S. Villavarayan four for 28, N. S. Rupasinghe four for 72).

At Galle International Stadium, Galle, November 2, 3, 4. **Drawn. Galle* 164** (W. M. P. N. Wanasinghe 31; M. D. K. Perera three for 31, G. A. S. Perera four for 64) **and 197 for seven**

(C. M. Withanage 38, G. G. Ranga Yasalal 39, W. M. P. N. Wanasinghe 41; G. A. S. Perera three for 75, W. P. Wickrama three for 17); **Panadura 233** (W. P. Wickrama 41, M. T. P. Fernando 35, M. H. R. M. Fernando 65; K. G. Perera three for 55, N. C. Komasaru five for 66).

At Air Force Ground, Katunayake, November 9, 10, 11. **Colombo won by 52 runs. Colombo* 160** (D. K. Ranaweera 50, K. G. N. Randika 30; M. K. G. C. P. Lakshitha five for 36, S. Dananjaya five for 25) **and 144 for two dec.** (P. B. Ediriweera 39, K. P. P. B. Seneviratne 53 not out, A. S. Polonowita 39 not out); **Air Force 103** (N. S. Rupasinghe four for 25, K. G. N. Randika five for 21) **and 149** (W. C. R. Tissera 31; C. R. B. Mudalige three for 33, N. S. Rupasinghe five for 25).
 Jehan Mubarak took six catches for Colombo in the match in the field.

At Panadura Esplanade, Panadura, November 9, 10, 11. **Drawn. Sebastianites 196** (S. N. Wijesinghe 38, R. H. S. Silva 52, Extras 31; M. D. K. Perera four for 50); **Panadura* 220 for nine** (R. H. T. A. Perera 60, J. S. K. Peiris 34 not out, G. A. S. Perera 35; K. H. R. K. Fernando three for 55, M. M. D. N. R. G. Perera five for 91).

At FTZ Sports Complex, Katunayake, November 9, 10, 11. **Drawn. Galle 274** (G. G. Ranga Yasalal 44, D. D. Wickremasinghe 59, L. H. D. Dilhara 104; B. A. R. S. Priyadarshana four for 72, S. P. Rupasinghe three for 23); **Ragama* 114** (E. F. M. U. Fernando 50; C. P. H. Ramanayake six for 25) **and 138 for nine** (K. N. S. Fernando 35, H. S. S. M. K. Weerasiri 39; K. G. Perera four for 29, M. M. D. P. V. Perera three for 33).
 Wickramasinghe and Dilhara added 154 for Galle's eighth wicket.

At Air Force Ground, Katunayake, November 16, 17, 18. **Panadura won by nine wickets. Air Force* 91** (M. D. K. Perera five for 24) **and 190** (S. E. D. R. Fernando 32, S. C. Gunasekera 32; G. A. S. Perera seven for 68); **Panadura 216** (L. P. C. Silva 58, G. A. S. Perera 31; W. R. D. Dissanayake three for 82, S. Dananjaya six for 56) **and 66 for one** (J. S. K. Peiris 43 not out).

At Maitland Crescent, Colombo (CCC), November 16, 17, 18. **Galle won by three wickets. Colombo* 94** (L. S. Malinga four for 40, W. M. P. N. Wanasinghe four for 30) **and 210** (P. B. Ediriweera 63, K. P. P. B. Seneviratne 67; L. S. Malinga four for 37, M. M. D. P. V. Perera four for 60); **Galle 183** (L. H. D. Dilhara 44; N. S. Rupasinghe three for 62) **and 122 for seven** (L. H. D. Dilhara 31; N. S. Rupasinghe four for 42).
 Galle wicket-keeper Primal Buddika Kularatne made nine dismissals (eight catches and one stumping) in the match.

At De Zoysa Stadium, Moratuwa, November 16, 17, 18. **Drawn. Ragama* 260** (E. F. M. U. Fernando 133, S. Arangalla 65; M. N. T. H. Kumara six for 37, K. H. R. K. Fernando three for 40) **and 210 for eight dec.** (E. F. M. U. Fernando 53, K. A. S. Jayasinghe 67, S. Arangalla 32; K. H. R. K. Fernando three for 30, R. A. D. C. Perera three for 44); **Sebastianites 184** (R. H. S. Silva 50, K. H. R. K. Fernando 34; B. A. R. S. Priyadarshana three for 39, S. Arangalla three for 30, S. P. Rupasinghe three for 58) **and 97 for four** (S. N. Wijesinghe 50 not out).
 In Ragama's first innings, the first five wickets fell for 49 and the last five for 20; in between, Fernando and Arangalla added 191 for the sixth wicket.

At Maitland Crescent, Colombo (CCC), November 23, 24, 25. **Colombo won by an innings and 41 runs. Sebastianites 267** (S. N. Wijesinghe 59, M. M. D. N. R. G. Perera 30, K. H. R. K. Fernando 60 not out; N. S. Rupasinghe four for 85, A. S. Polonowita three for 33) **and 112** (S. H. S. N. de Silva 34; C. R. B. Mudalige seven for 29); **Colombo* 420 for nine dec.** (P. B. Ediriweera 80, M. G. Vandort 93, A. S. Polonowita 95, K. P. P. B. Seneviratne 58, Extras 31).

At Galle International Stadium, Galle, November 23, 24, 25. **Drawn. Air Force 183** (S. E. D. R. Fernando 62; W. M. P. N. Wanasinghe four for 47) **and 98** (C. P. H. Ramanayake three for 25, M. M. D. P. V. Perera three for 17); **Galle* 218** (T. K. D. Sudarshana 94, G. G. Ranga Yasalal 35; M. K. G. C. P. Lakshitha five for 49, W. R. D. Dissanayake four for 82) **and 45 for four** (S. A. Premakumara three for 18).

At Panadura Esplanade, Panadura, November 23, 24, 25. **Panadura won by 177 runs. Panadura* 173** (M. D. K. Perera 33, L. P. C. Silva 46; B. A. R. S. Priyadarshana three for 43, R. D. Dissanayake four for 38) **and 319** (W. P. Wickrama 68, L. P. C. Silva 117, G. A. S. Perera 45 not out); **Ragama 215** (H. S. S. M. K. Weerasiri 32, S. Arangalla 83, K. N. S. Fernando 54; A. K. C. Silva four for 28) **and 100** (M. D. K. Perera five for 20).

At Air Force Ground, Katunayake, December 14, 15, 16. **Ragama won by 64 runs. Ragama*** **239** (K. A. S. Jayasinghe 97; W. P. A. Ariyadasa three for 42, M. K. G. C. P. Lakshitha seven for 58) **and 196** (E. F. M. U. Fernando 83; W. R. D. Dissanayake three for 39, P. T. S. Fernando four for 26); **Air Force 158** (K. A. Kumara 42, S. Dananjaya 33; S. Arangalla three for 44, R. D. Dissanayake four for 37) **and 213** (S. C. Gunasekera 51, K. A. Kumara 50, W. R. Fernando 46). *Six batsmen were run out in Air Force's second innings.*

At Maitland Crescent, Colombo (CCC), December 14, 15, 16. **Drawn. Colombo 340** (P. B. Ediriweera 37, H. A. P. W. Jayawardene 101, B. M. T. T. Mendis 91; A. K. C. Silva three for 52, G. A. S. Perera three for 90) **and 180** (J. Mubarak 49, A. S. Polonowita 33; W. P. Wickrama six for 57); **Panadura* 336** (M. D. K. Perera 134, M. T. P. Fernando 40, M. H. R. M. Fernando 84; C. R. B. Mudalige five for 104) **and 11 for two.**

At De Zoysa Stadium, Moratuwa, December 14, 15, 16. **Sebastianites won by an innings and 13 runs. Galle 145** (T. K. D. Sudarshana 64, L. H. D. Dilhara 30; K. A. D. M. Fernando eight for 34) **and 244** (T. K. D. Sudarshana 99, W. M. P. N. Wanasinghe 43, I. C. D. Perera 64; K. A. D. M. Fernando six for 82); **Sebastianites* 402** for seven dec. (S. N. Wijesinghe 114, R. H. S. Silva 169, Extras 41; M. M. D. P. V. Perera three for 46). *Wijesinghe and Silva added 308 for Sebastianites' third wicket.*

Colombo 57.95 pts, Panadura 56.57 pts, Galle 43.56 pts, Sebastianites 39.215 pts, Ragama 36.425 pts, Air Force 14.61 pts. Colombo, Panadura and Galle qualified for the Super League.

Group B

At Reid Avenue, Colombo, November 2, 3. **Bloomfield won by an innings and 109 runs. Bloomfield 339** (S. Rodrigo 50, S. Jayantha 137, T. R. Peiris 46, U. N. W. Silva 48 not out; P. K. Siriwardene four for 31); **Antonians* 127** (D. M. G. S. Dissanayake three for 40, A. B. T. Lakshitha four for 21) **and 103** (S. H. T. Kandamby three for 16).

At Braybrooke Place, Colombo (Moors), November 2, 3. **Moors won by an innings and 44 runs. Kurunegala Youth* 128** (P. N. Ranjith three for 36, T. H. A. I. K. Bandaranayake three for 25) **and 136** (H. M. Maduwantha 45, A. R. R. A. P. W. R. R. K. B. Amunugama 35; U. C. Hathurusinghe three for 20); **Moors 308** (W. M. B. Perera 86, D. W. A. N. D. Vitharana 43, M. C. R. Fernando 52, H. M. R. K. B. Herath 43; S. Madanayake three for 49).

At P. Saravanamuttu Stadium, Colombo, November 2, 3, 4. **Drawn. Tamil Union* 217** (G. R. P. Peiris 97, S. I. de Saram 40; L. J. P. Gunaratne four for 47) **and 244** (E. M. I. Galagoda 53, M. K. Gajanayake 70, D. P. S. Jayaratne 31; L. D. I. Perera five for 57, P. C. Jayasundera four for 51); **Chilaw Marians 174** (D. A. Marage 36; A. Rideegammanagedera three for 40, W. J. M. R. Dias three for 31) **and 183 for five** (A. A. P. Perera 40, D. de Zoysa 68; P. S. A. N. Shiroman three for 28).

At Welagedera Stadium, Kurunegala, November 9, 10, 11. **Drawn. Tamil Union 118 for six** (P. S. A. N. Shiroman 30, A. C. Pathirana 35 not out, W. J. M. R. Dias 30 not out; H. M. Maduwantha four for 29) **v Kurunegala Youth Cricket Club*.**

At Braybrooke Place, Colombo (Moors), November 9, 10, 11. **Drawn. Moors 159** (M. S. Sampan 57, M. N. R. Cooray 32; H. D. P. K. Dharmasena five for 57) **and five for no wkt; Bloomfield* 162** (H. D. P. K. Dharmasena 90; P. N. Ranjith four for 24).

At Reid Avenue, Colombo, November 16, 17. **Bloomfield won by ten wickets. Kurunegala Youth 87** (R. A. P. Nissanka six for 20, K. S. Lokuarachchi four for 34) **and 129** (H. M. Maduwantha 37 not out, A. R. R. A. P. W. R. R. K. B. Amunugama 33; D. M. G. S. Dissanayake three for 41); **Bloomfield* 184** for seven dec. (T. M. Dilshan 45, H. D. P. K. Dharmasena 67) **and 34 for no wkt.**

At Braybrooke Place, Colombo (Moors), November 16, 17, 18. **Drawn. Chilaw Marians* 375** (D. T. de Zoysa 30, L. J. P. Gunaratne 143, T. M. I. Mutaliph 46, P. C. Jayasundera 38; P. N.

Ranjith three for 54, H. M. R. K. B. Herath six for 94); **Moors 206** (W. M. B. Perera 68, H. M. R. K. B. Herath 33; L. D. I. Perera four for 45, P. C. Jayasundera three for 63) **and 125 for five** (M. S. Sampan 30, U. C. Hathurusinghe 54 not out).

At P. Saravanamuttu Stadium, Colombo, November 16, 17, 18. **Tamil Union won by seven wickets. Antonians 171** (K. A. D. C. Silva 32, A. P. Dalugoda 44 not out, P. W. Gunaratne 34; U. D. U. Chandana three for 47, A. Rideegammanagedara four for 27) **and 143** (N. Weeraman 46; U. D. U. Chandana four for 42, K. L. S. L. Dias three for 20); **Tamil Union* 272** (G. R. P. Peiris 51, U. D. U. Chandana 77, W. M. G. Ramykumara 57; P. W. Gunaratne four for 55, N. N. N. Nanayakkara four for 53) **and 44 for three.**

At R. Premadasa Stadium, Colombo, November 23, 24, 25. **Kurunegala Youth won by five wickets. Antonians* 206** (P. K. Siriwardene 38, S. Chandana 34; M. P. G. D. P. Gunatilleke four for 66) **and 214** (K. A. D. C. Silva 40, N. Weeraman 39, N. A. N. N. Perera 47, S. Chandana 31; A. W. Ekanayake three for 49); **Kurunegala Youth 151** (A. S. Wewalwala 48; B. de Silva four for 23) **and 271 for five** (D. M. Ramanayake 125, H. M. Maduwantha 46).

At Reid Avenue, Colombo, November 23, 24, 25. **Bloomfield won by an innings and 196 runs. Chilaw Marians 90** (R. A. P. Nissanka three for 31, D. M. G. S. Dissanayake five for seven) **and 118** (R. A. P. Nissanka three for 17, H. G. D. Nayanakantha three for 31); **Bloomfield* 404** (H. D. P. K. Dharmasena 89, S. H. T. Kandamby 96, K. S. Lokuarachchi 43, D. M. G. S. Dissanayake 31, Extras 50; R. S. A. Palliyaguruge three for 69).
  Bloomfield wicket-keeper Tillekeratne Dilshan made six dismissals (five catches and one stumping) in Chilaw Marians' second innings.

At P. Saravanamuttu Stadium, Colombo, November 23, 24, 25. **Drawn. Tamil Union* 348** (W. J. M. R. Dias 73, G. R. P. Peiris 44, W. M. G. Ramyakumara 55, M. K. Gajanayake 91; M. F. A. Farhath four for 70) **and 200** (W. M. G. Ramyakumara 51); **Moors 232** (M. S. Sampan 38, U. C. Hathurusinghe 34, M. C. R. Fernando 60; W. M. G. Ramyakumara three for 52, K. L. S. L. Dias three for 63).

At FTZ Sports Complex, Katunayake, December 1, 2, 3. **Chilaw Marians won by 146 runs. Chilaw Marians 270** (W. A. D. A. P. Perera 54, D. T. de Zoysa 47, C. S. Fernando 31, R. S. A. Palliyaguruge 43 not out, Extras 37; S. Chandana four for 86) **and 297 for six dec.** (W. A. D. A. P. Perera 69, D. T. de Zoysa 35, L. J. P. Gunaratne 37, C. S. Fernando 51 not out, R. S. A. Palliyaguruge 59); **Antonians* 192** (N. A. N. N. Perera 79; L. D. I. Perera five for 47, P. C. Jayasundera three for 24) **and 229** (P. K. Siriwardene 47, N. A. N. N. Perera 60, A. P. Dalugoda 57; L. D. I. Perera three for 61, P. P. Wickremasinghe three for 44).

At Reid Avenue, Colombo, December 14, 15, 16. **Tamil Union won by three wickets. Bloomfield* 254** (G. I. Daniel 50, W. D. D. S. Perera 42, T. M. Dilshan 65; M. R. C. N. Bandaratilleke four for 58) **and 215** (G. I. Daniel 48, K. S. Lokuarachchi 31, D. M. G. S. Dissanayake 35 not out; G. P. Wickremasinghe three for 45, W. M. G. Ramyakumara three for 36); **Tamil Union 330** (W. J. M. R. Dias 34, A. C. Pathirana 43, S. I. de Saram 53, A. Rideegammanagedera 78, E. M. I. Galagoda 46, M. R. C. N. Bandaratilleke 31; H. G. D. Nayanakantha three for 57, K. S. Lokuarachchi five for 103) **and 140 for seven** (G. R. P. Peiris 48, M. K. Gajanayake 34; H. G. D. Nayanakantha four for 57, K. S. Lokuarachchi three for 56).

At Welagedera Stadium, Kurunegala, December 14, 15, 16. **Drawn. Chilaw Marians 169** (P. C. Jayasundera 41, P. P. Wickremasinghe 38; H. M. Maduwantha seven for 51) **and 289 for nine dec.** (W. A. D. A. P. Perera 31, A. Gunawardane 39, T. M. I. Mutaliph 50, P. C. Jayasundera 70; A. W. Ekanayake three for 81); **Kurunegala Youth* 183** (N. H. V. Chinthaka 61; L. D. I. Perera six for 42) **and 267 for eight** (N. H. V. Chinthaka 116, A. S. Wewalwala 40, R. R. Jaymon 33; L. D. I. Perera three for 60, R. S. A. Palliyaguruge three for 74).
  Chasing 276 to win, Kurunegala Youth finished nine short.

At Braybrooke Place, Colombo (Moors), December 14, 15. **Moors won by nine wickets. Antonians* 148** (A. P. Dalugoda 61 not out; U. C. Hathurusinghe four for 32) **and 153** (K. A. D. C. Silva 62; U. C. Hathurusinghe three for 31, W. T. Abeyratne six for 48); **Moors 269** (U. C. Hathurusinghe 133, H. M. R. K. B. Herath 34; P. W. Gunaratne three for 92) **and 33 for one.**

Bloomfield 60.64 pts, Tamil Union 56.065 pts, Moors 38.69 pts, Chilaw Marians 38.025 pts, Kurunegala Youth 32.96 pts, Antonians 14.93 pts. Bloomfield, Tamil Union and Moors qualified for the Super League.

Super League

At Maitland Place, Colombo (SSC), January 25, 26, 27. **Drawn. Bloomfield 274** (S. Jayantha 75, T. M. Dilshan 52, W. D. D. S. Perera 39, D. M. G. S. Dissanayake 46; S. H. S. M. K. Silva five for 73) **and 224 for five dec.** (S. Rodrigo 100 not out, T. M. Dilshan 65; S. Weerakoon three for 46); **Burgher* 219** (D. N. Hunukumbura 60, I. C. Soysa 37, Extras 37; A. B. T. Lakshitha three for 59, D. M. G. S. Dissanayake five for 37) **and 160 for four** (I. C. Soysa 53, S. K. L. de Silva 52; U. N. W. Silva three for 53).

At P. Saravanamuttu Stadium, Colombo, January 25, 26. **Colts won by an innings and 85 runs. Colombo 146** (M. G. Vandort 34; D. K. Liyanage four for 37) **and 58** (D. K. Liyanage five for 22, K. E. A. Upashantha three for 36); **Colts* 289** (R. S. Kaluwitharana 51, D. P. Samaraweera 70 not out, M. Pushpakumara 41; B. M. T. T. Mendis three for 40, N. S. Rupasinghe five for 85).
Liyanage and Upashantha bowled out Colombo in 18.2 overs.

At Reid Avenue, Colombo, January 25, 26, 27. **Moors won by seven wickets. Galle 163** (M. K. P. B. Kularatne 34, M. H. Wijesinghe 30, C. P. H. Ramanayake 30; H. M. R. K. B. Herath eight for 47) **and 226** (C. M. Withanage 35, M. H. Wijesinghe 36, W. M. P. N. Wanasinghe 30, C. P. H. Ramanayake 31; P. N. Ranjith three for 39, H. M. R. K. B. Herath three for 32); **Moors* 285** (M. N. R. Cooray 47, W. M. B. Perera 67, M. C. R. Fernando 36; N. C. Komasaru three for 73) **and 107 for three** (U. C. Hathurusinghe 59 not out).

At Maitland Crescent, Colombo (CCC), January 25, 26, 27. **Drawn. Nondescripts* 340** (P. A. de Silva 154, M. N. Nawaz 52; W. M. G. Ramyakumara three for 46, G. P. Wickremasinghe three for 62, U. D. U. Chandana three for 108) **and 151 for six** (M. N. Nawaz 33, C. P. Mapatuna 34 not out, P. A. de Silva 37 not out; U. D. U. Chandana three for 59); **Tamil Union 319** (P. S. A. N. Shiroman 58, W. M. G. Ramyakumara 44, W. J. M. R. Dias 50 not out, M. R. C. N. Bandaratilleke 52, Extras 36; K. R. Pushpakumara three for 79, C. M. Bandara three for 32).

At R. Premadasa Stadium, Colombo, January 25, 26, 27. **Drawn. Panadura 266** (M. D. K. Perera 31, L. P. C. Silva 37, K. R. R. K. Wimalasena 50, M. T. P. Fernando 66; P. D. R. L. Perera three for 57) **and 186 for six** (M. D. K. Perera 72, J. S. K. Peiris 35; U. A. Fernando three for 17); **Sinhalese* 364** (D. A. Gunawardene 42, W. M. S. M. Perera 50, T. A. Embuldeniya 68, N. T. Paranavitana 85, A. S. A. Perera 44, P. D. R. L. Perera 33 not out; M. D. K. Perera three for 59, S. R. Abeywardene five for 96).

At Braybrooke Place, Colombo (Moors), February 1, 2, 3. **Drawn. Bloomfield 221** (W. D. D. S. Perera 40, S. H. T. Kandamby 43; D. K. Liyanage three for 47, K. E. A. Upashantha four for 77); **Colts* 69 for four** (R. S. Kaluwitharana 38).

At FTZ Sports Complex, Katunayake, February 1, 2, 3. **Drawn. Burgher 315** (B. C. M. S. Mendis 54, S. K. L. de Silva 64, B. S. M. Warnapura 58, C. U. Jayasinghe 67; W. S. P. Jayawardene three for 91, S. R. Abeywardene four for 51) **and 186 for eight** (S. K. L. de Silva 47, B. S. M. Warnapura 60; K. D. C. Pushpalal three for 33); **Panadura* 182** (J. S. K. Peiris 51, M. T. P. Fernando 39; I. S. Gallage four for 57).

At R. Premadasa Stadium, Colombo, February 1, 2, 3. **Drawn. Moors 242** (M. N. R. Cooray 51, W. M. B. Perera 44, K. K. S. Jayasinghe 35; N. S. Rupasinghe six for 94) **and 162 for eight** (U. C. Hathurusinghe 31, W. M. B. Perera 83; M. S. Villavarayan five for 47); **Colombo* 214** (D. K. Ranaweera 32, A. S. Polonowita 62, Extras 30; P. N. Ranjith five for 56, M. S. C. A. Zubair three for 36).

At Maitland Place, Colombo (SSC), February 1, 2, 3. **Nondescripts won by eight wickets. Galle 187** (W. M. P. N. Wanasinghe 33, I. C. D. Perera 59; R. S. Kalpage three for 30) **and 117** (C. M. Withanage 30; K. R. Pushpakumara three for 17, W. C. A. Ganegama three for 23); **Nondescripts* 248 for nine dec.** (R. S. Kalpage 32, D. H. S. Pradeep 68, C. M. Bandara 36; L. H. D. Dilhara three for 56) **and 57 for two** (R. P. Hewage 34 not out).

At Maitland Place, Colombo (NCC), February 1, 2, 3. **Drawn. Tamil Union* 264** (K. S. D. Kumara 53, P. S. A. N. Shiroman 57, G. R. P. Peiris 46, S. I. de Saram 54; T. T. Samaraweera four for 40) **and 204 for five** (P. S. A. N. Shiroman 54, S. I. de Saram 51 not out); **Sinhalese 224** (M. U. Dissanayake 45; M. K. Gajanayake three for 13).

At P. Saravanamuttu Stadium, Colombo, February 8, 9, 10. **Panadura won by two wickets. Bloomfield* 270** (S. Rodrigo 53, M. T. Gunaratne 41, H. D. P. K. Dharmasena 59; G. A. S. Perera seven for 80) **and 200 for three dec.** (S. Rodrigo 89 not out, M. T. Gunaratne 31, H. D. P. K. Dharmasena 64 not out); **Panadura 222** (M. D. K. Perera 34, J. S. K. Peiris 33, M. T. P. Fernando 59; H. D. P. K. Dharmasena four for 56) **and 249 for eight** (W. S. P. Jayawardene 30, R. H. T. A. Perera 30, J. S. K. Peiris 90 not out; H. D. P. K. Dharmasena three for 78, K. S. Lokuarachchi three for 64).

At Maitland Place, Colombo (NCC), February 8, 9, 10. **Burgher won by ten wickets. Galle 196** (M. H. Wijesinghe 48, I. C. D. Perera 40, D. D. Wickremasinghe 31; S. H. S. M. K. Silva five for 71) **and 104** (I. C. D. Perera 54; K. S. C. de Silva four for 39); **Burgher* 287** (C. U. Jayasinghe 82, U. Hettiarachchi 49, Extras 40; C. P. H. Ramanayake three for 36, L. S. Malinga three for 97) **and 14 for no wkt.**

At Maitland Place, Colombo (SSC), February 8, 9, 10. **Drawn. Nondescripts* 451 for six dec.** (R. R. Tissera 84, R. P. Hewage 33, M. N. Nawaz 81, C. P. Mapatuna 62, H. P. Tillekeratne 103 not out, K. S. Kalpage 56; N. S. Rupasinghe three for 99); **Colombo 180** (K. P. P. B. Seneviratne 30, M. S. Villavarayan 38; K. R. Pushpakumara three for 36) **and 279 for four** (A. S. Polonowita 82 not out, K. P. P. B. Seneviratne 43, J. W. H. D. Boteju 75 not out).

At Maitland Crescent, Colombo (CCC), February 8, 9, 10. **Drawn. Moors 350** (M. N. R. Cooray 139, M. S. Sampan 84; T. T. Samaraweera three for 107, A. S. A. Perera five for 104) **and 247** (W. T. Abeyratne 44, U. C. Hathurusinghe 106; T. T. Samaraweera four for 68, A. S. A. Perera three for 48); **Sinhalese* 234** (M. U. Dissanayake 98 not out, R. P. A. H. Wickremaratne 41, T. T. Samaraweera 37; P. N. Ranjith seven for 55) **and 62 for two** (P. H. M. G. Fernando 33).

Dissanayake carried his bat through Sinhalese's first innings. Sinhalese bowler Suresh Perera was suspended for two matches for bringing the game into disrepute by deliberately overstepping to bowl bouncers at two Moors batsmen.

At R. Premadasa Stadium, Colombo, February 8, 9, 10. **Colts won by 80 runs. Colts* 334** (C. Mendis 31, R. S. Kaluwitharana 59, D. P. Samaraweera 71, H. G. J. M. Kulatunga 30, D. K. Liyanage 41 not out; K. G. A. S. Kalum three for 94, M. R. C. N. Bandaratilleke three for 66) **and 232 for nine dec.** (S. I. Fernando 45, R. S. Kaluwitharana 39, D. P. Samaraweera 30; M. R. C. N. Bandaratilleke three for 83); **Tamil Union 240** (S. I. de Saram 86; D. Hettiarachchi five for 56) **and 246** (G. R. P. Peiris 96, W. J. M. R. Dias 31, S. I. de Saram 44; D. Hettiarachchi six for 89).

At R. Premadasa Stadium, Colombo, February 15, 16, 17. **Sinhalese won by six wickets. Bloomfield* 183** (S. T. Jayasuriya 32, S. Jayantha 52; T. T. Samaraweera three for 61, N. T. Paranavitana three for 11) **and 331** (S. Rodrigo 41, S. T. Jayasuriya 71, T. R. Peiris 77, S. Jayantha 32, H. D. P. K. Dharmasena 42, S. H. T. Kandamby 33; T. T. Samaraweera six for 87, D. P. M. D. Jayawardene three for eight); **Sinhalese 389** (M. S. Atapattu 37, N. T. Paranavitana 105, D. P. M. D. Jayawardene 52, M. N. Silva 125; K. S. Lokuarachchi four for 72) **and 128 for four** (W. M. S. M. Perera 44, A. S. A. Perera 30 not out).

At P. Saravanamuttu Stadium, Colombo, February 15, 16, 17. **Drawn. Burgher 359** (D. N. Hunukumbura 48, U. Hettiarachchi 38, B. S. M. Warnapura 88, C. U. Jayasinghe 61, I. S. Gallage 43, Extras 30; M. S. Villavarayan three for 83, C. R. B. Mudalige four for 63) **and 306 for eight** (B. C. M. S. Mendis 42, B. S. M. Warnapura 30, C. U. Jayasinghe 100 not out, I. S. Gallage 35; N. S. Rupasinghe four for 109); **Colombo* 292** (J. Mubarak 54, A. S. Polonowita 45, J. W. H. D. Boteju 51, M. S. Villavarayan 33; I. S. Gallage four for 85, S. H. S. M. K. Silva three for 77).

At Maitland Place, Colombo (SSC), February 15, 16, 17. **Colts won by 150 runs. Colts 290** (S. Kalawithigoda 48, C. Mendis 51, H. G. J. M. Kulatunga 60, W. P. U. J. C. Vaas 65; P. N. Ranjith four for 67, U. C. Hathurusinghe three for 49) **and 195** (C. Mendis 32, S. I. Fernando 62;

M. C. R. Fernando three for 36, M. N. R. Cooray three for 24); **Moors* 204** (M. N. R. Cooray 34, U. C. Hathurusinghe 55, Extras 36; W. P. U. J. C. Vaas four for 92, K. Weeraratne four for 37) **and 131** (M. C. R. Fernando 32, W. M. B. Perera 30; W. P. U. J. C. Vaas three for 18, D. Hettiarachchi four for 38).

At De Zoysa Stadium, Moratuwa, February 15, 16, 17. **Nondescripts won by 317 runs. Nondescripts 406 for five dec.** (M. N. Nawaz 139, P. A. de Silva 62, R. P. Arnold 110, Extras 44) **and 234 for three dec.** (R. P. Hewage 102 not out, K. C. Sangakkara 58, H. P. Tillekeratne 44 not out); **Panadura* 95** (I. Amithakeerthi 30; K. R. Pushpakumara three for 36, W. C. A. Ganegama five for 38) **and 228** (W. S. P. Jayawardene 122; M. K. D. I. Amerasinghe three for 51, P. A. de Silva six for 60).

At Maitland Crescent, Colombo (CCC), February 15, 16, 17. **Tamil Union won by four wickets. Galle 219** (C. M. Withanage 33, G. G. Ranga Yasalal 30, D. D. Wickremasinghe 34, L. H. D. Dilhara 38; M. Muralitharan seven for 88) **and 140** (C. M. Withanage 54 not out; M. R. C. N. Bandaratilleke five for 63, M. Muralitharan three for 48); **Tamil Union* 214** (K. S. D. Kumara 42, M. Muralitharan 36; C. P. H. Ramanayake three for 34, L. S. Malinga four for 75) **and 147 for six** (S. I. de Saram 52, M. K. Gajanayake 46 not out; L. S. Malinga three for 53).
Withanage carried his bat through Galle's second innings.

At Maitland Place, Colombo (NCC), February 22, 23, 24. **Drawn. Colombo 204** (J. Mubarak 33, D. F. Arnolda 42, R. P. Arnold 30; H. D. P. K. Dharmasena five for 75) **and 333 for five dec.** (J. Mubarak 70, D. K. Ranaweera 34, M. G. Vandort 73, K. P. P. B. Seneviratne 58, D. F. Arnolda 51 not out; K. S. Lokurachchi three for 119); **Bloomfield* 222** (G. I. Daniel 108, K. S. Lokurachchi 35; M. S. Villavarayan five for 57) **and 153 for four** (W. D. D. S. Perera 45 not out, S. H. T. Kandamby 80).

At R. Premadasa Stadium, Colombo, February 22, 23, 24. **Tamil Union won by 128 runs. Tamil Union* 172** (K. S. D. Kumara 36, G. R. P. Peiris 61; S. H. S. M. K. Silva seven for 52) **and 261** (P. S. A. N. Shiroman 55, S. I. de Saram 41, M. K. Gajanayake 34, M. Muralitharan 36; S. H. S. M. K. Silva three for 99, B. S. M. Warnapura four for 71); **Burgher 125** (C. U. Jayasinghe 32; M. Muralitharan seven for 17) **and 180** (G. S. T. Perera 48, B. C. M. S. Mendis 36; M. R. C. N. Bandaratilleke three for 73, M. Muralitharan six for 78).
Muralitharan's 13 for 95 brought his aggregate to 23 in two matches for Tamil Union.

At Maitland Crescent, Colombo (CCC), February 22, 23. **Colts won by an innings and 165 runs. Panadura* 82** (K. E. A. Upashantha six for 29) **and 153** (R. H. T. A. Perera 36; W. P. U. J. C. Vaas three for 32, D. Hettiarachchi three for 64, M. J. Sigera three for 30); **Colts 400 for five dec.** (S. Kalawithigoda 169, S. I. Fernando 94, R. S. Kaluwitharana 67).

At Braybrooke Place, Colombo (Moors), February 22, 23, 24. **Sinhalese won by seven wickets. Galle 326** (M. H. Wijesinghe 61, I. C. D. Perera 53, C. R. P. Galappathy 55, L. H. D. Dilhara 72; T. T. Samaraweera three for 76) **and 120** (D. N. T. Zoysa three for 29, T. T. Samaraweera five for 67); **Sinhalese* 313** (M. U. Dissanayake 44, D. P. M. D. Jayawardene 77, R. P. A. H. Wickremaratne 39, D. N. T. Zoysa 60 not out; K. G. Perera five for 83, M. M. D. P. V. Perera four for 95) **and 134 for three** (M. U. Dissanayake 56, N. T. Paranavitana 71 not out).

At Maitland Crescent, Colombo (CCC), March 1, 2, 3. **Bloomfield won by nine wickets. Galle* 171** (M. K. P. B. Kularatne 49 not out; B. Ranaweera four for 44, H. D. P. K. Dharmasena four for 51) **and 98** (C. R. P. Galappathy 35; D. M. G. S. Dissanayake three for 27, K. S. Lokuarachchi three for 21); **Bloomfield 213** (G. I. Daniel 46, W. D. D. S. Perera 64; C. P. H. Ramanayake three for 43) **and 60 for one** (S. Rodrigo 32 not out).
Ranaweera took a wicket with his first ball in first-class cricket.

At Braybrooke Place, Colombo (Moors), March 1, 2, 3. **Colombo won by nine wickets. Tamil Union* 265** (E. M. I. Galagoda 59, S. I. de Saram 52, W. J. M. R. Dias 55; N. S. Rupasinghe four for 65) **and 145** (G. R. P. Peiris 40; M. S. Villavarayan three for 45, M. I. Ratnajake three for 25); **Colombo 391** (M. G. Vandort 144, H. A. P. W. Jayawardene 32, J. W. H. D. Boteju 89, D. F. Arnolda 31; G. P. Wickremasinghe four for 97, M. K. Gajanayake three for 98) **and 22 for one**.

At Reid Avenue, Colombo, March 1, 2, 3. **Moors won by ten wickets. Panadura 179** (M. D. K. Perera 44, L. P. C. Silva 56; P. N. Ranjith five for 55) **and 262** (R. H. T. A. Perera 45, J. S. K. Peiris 64, G. A. S. Perera 45; M. C. R. Fernando three for 61, U. C. Hathurusinghe three for 29); **Moors* 424 for eight dec.** (M. N. R. Cooray 33, M. S. Sampan 30, M. C. R. Fernando 96, U. C. Hathurusinghe 56, W. M. B. Perera 107 not out, D. W. A. N. D. Vitharana 32, Extras 38; W. S. P. Jayawardene four for 98, L. P. C. Silva four for 85) **and 19 for no wkt**.

At De Zoysa Stadium, Moratuwa, March 8, 9, 10. **Nondescripts won by an innings and 115 runs. Moors* 187** (W. M. B. Perera 111 not out; M. K. D. I. Amerasinghe five for 50) **and 129** (M. S. Sampan 33; K. R. Pushpakumara five for 41); **Nondescripts 431 for seven dec.** (R. P. Hewage 72, P. A. de Silva 194, M. N. Nawaz 33, C. M. Bandara 35 not out, Extras 32).

At Maitland Crescent, Colombo (CCC), March 15, 16, 17. **Drawn. Nondescripts 265** (M. N. Nawaz 36, R. P. Arnold 45, H. P. Til(ekeratne 58, K. R. Pushpakumara 52; H. S. H. Alles four for 59) **and 295 for five** (R. P. Hewage 58, M. N. Nawaz 87, P. A. de Silva 65, M. K. D. I. Amerasinghe 46); **Bloomfield* 258** (S. T. Jayasuriya 39, T. M. Dilshan 36, S. H. T. Kandamby 38, W. D. D. S. Perera 50, K. S. Lokuarachchi 32; M. K. D. I. Amerasinghe four for 72).

At De Zoysa Stadium, Moratuwa, March 15, 16, 17. **Drawn. Burgher 322** (I. C. Soysa 40, B. S. M. Warnapura 33, C. U. Jayasinghe 91, G. S. T. Perera 64, Extras 31; T. H. A. I. K. Bandaranayake three for 45) **and 295** (D. N. Hunukumbura 51, I. C. Soysa 65, S. H. S. M. K. Silva 48; U. C. Hathurusinghe three for 42); **Moors* 240** (W. M. B. Perera 111; S. Weerakoon three for 55, D. M. Perumal three for 42) **and 161 for six** (E. D. I. L. de Silva 51 not out, W. M. B. Perera 42; D. M. Perumal three for 30).

Bathiya Perera scored his third century in successive matches for Moors.

At Maitland Place, Colombo (NCC), March 15, 16, 17. **Sinhalese won by five wickets. Colombo 313** (M. G. Vandort 64, H. A. P. W. Jayawardene 52, D. F. Arnolda 67, R. M. A. R. Ratnayake 32, Extras 43; T. T. Samaraweera four for 76) **and 313** (K. P. P. B. Senevirate 91, A. S. Polonowita 52, H. A. P. W. Jayawardene 76, R. M. A. R. Ratnayake 31; T. T. Samaraweera six for 101); **Sinhalese* 515** (W. M. S. M. Perera 123, D. P. M. D. Jayawardene 150, R. P. A. H. Wickremaratne 53, T. T. Samaraweera 100 not out, A. S. A. Perera 38; M. S. Villavarayan three for 114, C. R. B. Mudalige four for 104) **and 112 for five** (D. P. M. D. Jayawardene 41 not out).

In Sinhalese's first innings, Perera and Jayawardene added 240 for the third wicket.

At P. Saravanamuttu Stadium, Colombo, March 15, 16, 17. **Drawn. Colts* 254** (C. Mendis 75, M. Pushpakumara 41, K. Weeraratne 46; C. M. Withanage three for 15, N. C. Komasaru five for 76) **and 276** (C. Mendis 65, S. I. Fernando 35, D. K. Liyanage 69; K. G. Perera three for 55, N. C. Komasaru three for 87); **Galle 199** (M. H. Wijesinghe 53, M. M. D. P. V. Perera 65; D. K. Liyanage three for 29) **and 118 for five** (G. G. Ranga Yasalal 56).

At Braybrooke Place, Colombo (Moors), March 15, 16, 17. **Tamil Union won by six wickets. Panadura* 233** (I. Amithakeerthi 80, M. T. P. Fernando 47; K. G. A. S. Kalum three for 35, G. P. Wickremasinghe four for 76, M. K. Gajanayake three for 25) **and 190** (M. D. K. Perera 36, L. P. C. Silva 100; U. D. U. Chandana five for 85, M. K. Gajanayake three for 26); **Tamil Union 282** (K. S. D. Kumara 33, P. S. A. N. Shiroman 67, W. J. M. R. Dias 40, M. R. C. N. Bandaratilleke 39; G. A. S. Perera five for 60) **and 142 for four** (K. S. D. Kumara 42, P. S. A. N. Shiroman 51).

Semi-finals

At P. Saravanamuttu Stadium, Colombo, March 21, 22, 23, 24. **Colts won by two wickets. Nondescripts 324** (R. P. Hewage 80, M. N. Nawaz 50, H. P. Tilekeratne 97; W. P. U. J. C. Vaas three for 51, D. Hettiarachchi three for 49) **and 190** (R. P. Hewage 31, K. C. Sangakkara 37, R. P. Arnold 50; D. Hettiarachchi four for 45, M. Pushpakumara three for 46); **Colts* 298** (C. Mendis 80, R. S. Kaluwitharana 31, H. G. J. M. Kulatunga 54, D. K. Liyanage 33; C. M. Bandara three for 65) **and 217 for eight** (S. I. Fernando 39, R. S. Kaluwitharana 84, W. P. U. J. C. Vaas 31 not out; K. R. Pushpakumara three for 28, M. K. D. I. Amerasinghe three for 38).

At Maitland Place, Colombo (NCC), March 21, 22, 23, 24. **Sinhalese won by three wickets. Tamil Union* 386** (P. S. A. N. Shiroman 45, G. R. P. Peiris 94, W. J. M. R. Dias 75 not out, M. R. C. N. Bandaratilleke 58, Extras 55; P. D. R. L. Perera four for 107) **and 283** (G. R. P. Peiris 33, S. I. de Saram 108, W. J. M. R. Dias 36; T. T. Samaraweera five for 87); **Sinhalese 561** (W. M. S. M. Perera 102, D. P. M. D. Jayawardene 274, D. N. T. Zoysa 55, Extras 30; G. P. Wickremasinghe five for 81, U. D. U. Chandana four for 172) **and 109 for seven** (T. T. Samaraweera 46 not out; G. P. Wickremasinghe three for 25).

Jayawardene's career-best 274 lasted 409 minutes and 296 balls and included 31 fours and four sixes. It was the highest score in Sri Lankan domestic first-class cricket, beating Marvan Atapattu's 253 not out for Sinhalese against Galle in 1995-96.

FINAL

SINHALESE v COLTS

At Maitland Place, Colombo (SSC), March 29, 30, 31. Colts won by eight wickets. Toss: Colts.

Colts upset the favourites, Sinhalese, to win their third title in 11 seasons. Inserting Sinhalese on the first day, they skittled them for 216. Even Jayawardene could not pull his side back into the game. While the left-armers Vaas and Liyanage lopped off five of his team-mates for 67, Jayawardene stood head and shoulders above the rest, striking 15 fours and a six. He added 86 with Wickremaratne before the off-spinner, Pushpakumara, wrapped up the innings. Colts passed the Sinhalese total with four wickets down; five batsmen reached the fifty mark, with Pushpakumara the top-scorer. His 81, off 97 balls, steered Colts towards a lead of 195. Sinhalese's second innings followed a similar pattern to the first – four early wickets, before Jayawardene, this time aided by Samaraweera, added 154 for the fifth. But once Vaas removed Jayawardene, one run short of his second century of the match, the spinners cleaned up, and the last six fell for 42. Colts needed a mere 40 to win and could afford two cheap wickets as they coasted home inside eight overs, with more than a day to spare.

Man of the Match: M. Pushpakumara.

Close of play: First day, Colts 183-3 (Kaluwitharana 50, Weeraratne 2); Second day, Sinhalese 96-4 (Jayawardene 32, Samaraweera 23).

Sinhalese

*M. S. Atapattu lbw b Vaas	9	– c sub b Liyanage	17
D. A. Gunawardene c Kaluwitharana b Liyanage	0	– c Kaluwitharana b Vaas	4
†W. M. S. M. Perera c Kulatunga b Liyanage	7	– lbw b Vaas	10
D. P. M. D. Jayawardene st Kaluwitharana b Pushpakumara	137	– lbw b Vaas	99
N. T. Paranavitana lbw b Vaas	7	– lbw b Liyanage	0
T. T. Samaraweera lbw b Vaas	0	– c Fernando b Hettiarachchi	65
R. P. A. H. Wickremaratne c Mendis b Pushpakumara	37	– c Liyanage b Pushpakumara	0
M. N. Silva c Fernando b Pushpakumara	1	– c Fernando b Pushpakumara	8
D. N. T. Zoysa c Mendis b Pushpakumara	0	– c Fernando b Hettiarachchi	16
I. R. Ratnaweera b Vaas	0	– (11) not out	0
P. D. R. L. Perera not out	2	– (10) c Hettiarachchi b Pushpakumara	1
B 4, l-b 5, w 2, n-b 5	16	B 5, l-b 4, w 2, n-b 3	14

1/10 2/12 3/42 4/59 5/67   216   1/9 2/35 3/38 4/38 5/192   234
6/153 7/159 8/159 9/198   6/193 7/203 8/229 9/234

Bowling: *First Innings*—Vaas 15–0–38–4; Liyanage 11–1–53–2; Upashantha 6–0–36–0; Hettiarachchi 4–0–10–0; Weeraratne 6–0–27–0; Pushpakumara 11.2–1–43–4. *Second Innings*—Vaas 14–1–51–3; Liyanage 9–1–34–2; Weeraratne 4–1–21–0; Upashantha 3–0–23–0; Hettiarachchi 19–5–51–2; Pushpakumara 14.1–2–45–3.

Colts

S. Kalawithigoda lbw b Zoysa	1	– not out	13
C. Mendis lbw b Ratnaweera	52	– c Paranavitana b P. D. R. L. Perera	2
*S. I. Fernando c Atapattu b Zoysa	73	– lbw b Zoysa	1
†R. S. Kaluwitharana c W. M. S. M. Perera			
b P. D. R. L. Perera .	72	– not out	21
K. Weeraratne c Gunawardene			
b P. D. R. L. Perera .	14		
H. G. J. M. Kulatunga c Silva b Samaraweera . .	50		
W. P. U. J. C. Vaas c Samaraweera b Zoysa. . . .	12		
M. Pushpakumara lbw b Zoysa.	81		
K. E. A. Upashantha c and b P. D. R. L. Perera. .	27		
D. K. Liyanage c Jayawardene b Samaraweera . .	13		
D. Hettiarachchi not out	0		
B 6, l-b 5, n-b 5	16	B 4	4

1/10 2/91 3/181 4/208 5/227   411   1/3 2/8   (2 wkts) 41
6/255 7/334 8/393 9/395

Bowling: First Innings—Zoysa 18–4–43–4; P. D. R. L. Perera 20–1–124–3; Samaraweera 20.1–1–87–2; Silva 3–0–18–0; Ratnaweera 12–1–53–1; Paranavitana 16–0–58–0; Jayawardene 2–0–17–0. *Second Innings*—P. D. R. L. Perera 4–0–28–1; Zoysa 2–1–4–1; Samaraweera 1.2–0–5–0.

Umpires: M. G. Silva and T. H. Wijewardene.
Third umpire: D. N. Pathirana.   Referee: R. G. C. E. Wijesuriya.

CHAMPIONS

Lakspray Trophy

1988-89	⎰ Nondescripts CC
	⎱ Sinhalese SC
1989-90	Sinhalese SC

P. Saravanamuttu Trophy

1990-91	Sinhalese SC
1991-92	Colts CC
1992-93	Sinhalese SC
1993-94	Nondescripts CC

1994-95	⎰ Bloomfield C and AC
	⎱ Sinhalese SC
1995-96	Colombo CC
1996-97	Bloomfield C and AC
1997-98	Sinhalese SC

Premier Trophy

1998-99	Bloomfield C and AC
1999-2000	Colts CC
2000-01	Nondescripts CC
2001-02	Colts CC

Sinhalese have won the title outright 4 times, Colts 3, Bloomfield and Nondescripts 2, Colombo 1. Sinhalese have also shared the title twice, and Bloomfield and Nondescripts once each.

PLATE CHAMPIONSHIP

The three top teams from the non-first-class Sara Trophy (Kandy, Moratuwa and Rio) joined those teams who had not qualified for the Super League.

At Braybrooke Place, Colombo (Moors), January 25, 26, 27. **Drawn. Antonians 276** (K. A. D. C. Silva 37, N. Weeraman 99, W. A. L. Chaturanga 48; M. K. G. C. P. Lakshitha five for 79, W. R. D. Dissanayake three for 51) **and 165** (H. A. H. U. Tillekeratne 40, A. P. Dalugoda 31; M. K. G. C. P. Lakshitha six for 60); **Air Force* 159** (S. E. D. R. Fernando 31, W. P. Wickrama 31; B. de Silva four for 31) **and 190 for nine** (W. R. Fernando 43, W. C. R. Tissera 37; P. W. Gunaratne three for 38, S. Chandana three for 42).

At FTZ Sports Complex, Katunayake, January 25, 26, 27. **Sebastianites won by an innings and 65 runs. Sebastianites 334** (G. E. Randiligama 35, S. N. Wijesinghe 33, R. H. S. Silva 43, K. H. R. K. Fernando 103, K. A. D. M. Fernando 76 not out; O. Mizran three for 32, D. T. B. Kolugala four for 93); **Kandy* 101** (M. M. D. N. R. G. Perera four for 17) **and 168** (D. C. P. D. S. Wickramanayake 31, W. A. S. N. B. Peiris 58; M. M. D. N. R. G. Perera six for 70).

At De Zoysa Stadium, Moratuwa, January 25, 26. **Ragama won by an innings and 130 runs. Ragama 348** (E. F. M. U. Fernando 93, D. A. Ranatunga 42, B. A. R. S. Priyadarshana 106 not out, Extras 51; L. G. S. Prasad three for 56, R. C. Rupasinghe four for 54); **Rio* 121** (B. A. R. S. Priyadarshana four for 19, K. A. S. Jayasinghe four for 43) **and 97** (T. P. Gamage eight for 32).

At Air Force Ground, Katunayake, February 1, 2, 3. **Drawn. Chilaw Marians 317 for nine dec.** (S. T. Tittagalla 38, L. D. I. Perera 36, P. C. Jayasundera 112 not out, P. P. Wickremasinghe 30; D. T. B. Kolugala five for 92) **and 254 for six** (S. T. Tittagalla 40, L. J. P. Gunaratne 92 not out, R. S. A. Palliyaguruge 82 not out; I. S. Baddegama three for 28); **Kandy* 267** (J. Arnolda 40, W. A. S. N. B. Peiris 47, M. M. M. Rameez 58; P. P. Wickremasinghe four for 70).

At Reid Avenue, Colombo, February 1, 2, 3. **Kurunegala Youth won by an innings and 12 runs. Rio 139** (N. M. T. Shantha 66 not out) **and 100** (A. W. Ekanayake six for 32); **Kurunegala Youth* 251 for seven dec.** (N. H. V. Chinthaka 31, D. M. Ramanayake 74, H. M. Maduwantha 46, S. Madanayake 51 not out).

Rio's captain, Chamil Rupasinghe, was given out for obstructing the field.

At Havelock Park, Colombo (BRC), February 1, 2, 3. **Moratuwa won by eight wickets. Ragama 79** (C. M. Hathurusinghe seven for 29, W. J. S. D. Perera three for 37) **and 177** (B. A. R. S. Priyadarshana 60, R. D. Dissanayake 30; C. M. Hathurusinghe three for 48); **Moratuwa* 239** (R. G. D. Sanjeewa 45, U. N. K. Fernando 46, K. L. R. Fernando 33; T. P. Gamage six for 74) **and 18 for two.**

At FTZ Sports Complex, Katunayake, February 8, 9, 10. **Air Force won by 11 runs. Air Force 141** (W. C. R. Tissera 34; M. M. C. S. Perera four for 36) **and 301** (S. E. D. R. Fernando 30, A. Rizan 80, W. P. Wickrama 30, M. K. G. C. P. Lakshitha 43, S. Dananjaya 31; W. A. I. Wanigasekera three for 64); **Moratuwa* 187** (U. N. K. Fernando 59, K. L. R. Fernando 39; W. C. R. Tissera five for 41) **and 244** (W. J. S. D. Perera 34, U. N. K. Fernando 35, K. L. R. Fernando 39, M. M. C. S. Perera 41; W. R. D. Dissanayake six for 70).

At Reid Avenue, Colombo, February 8, 9, 10. **Antonians won by eight wickets. Rio 169** (M. G. D. J. Pradeep 77; S. Chandana five for 41) **and 331** (M. G. P. R. Pradeep 30, N. M. T. Shantha 65, R. N. Weerasinghe 78, R. C. Rupasinghe 37, M. T. S. de Zoysa 40, Extras 39; N. N. N. Nanayakkara five for 91); **Antonians* 358** (N. Weeraman 66, H. A. H. U. Tillekeratne 103, Y. N. Tillekeratne 59, A. P. Dalugoda 45; M. T. S. de Zoysa three for 56) **and 143 for two** (K. A. D. C. Silva 38, P. K. Siriwardene 31 not out, W. A. L. Chaturanga 41 not out).

At Havelock Park, Colombo (Colts), February 8, 9, 10. **Drawn. Chilaw Marians* 395** (S. T. Tittagalla 70, C. S. Fernando 70, R. S. A. Palliyaguruge 147, P. P. Wickremasinghe 36, Extras 34; B. A. R. S. Priyadarshana five for 73) **and 43 for one**; **Ragama 191** (D. A. Ranatunga 46, H. S. S. M. K. Weerasiri 57; P. C. Jayasundera four for 63) **and 375** (E. F. M. U. Fernando 89, K. A. S. Jayasinghe 175, S. Arangalla 32, Extras 31; L. L. Fernando four for 66, P. C. Jayasundera five for 66).

In Ragama's second innings, Fernando and Jayasinghe added 255 for the fourth wicket.

At Air Force Ground, Katunayake, February 8, 9, 10. **Kurunegala Youth won by five wickets. Kandy 203** (W. A. S. N. B. Peiris 53, J. Arnolda 48; A. R. R. A. P. W. R. K. B. Amunugama three for 22, H. M. Maduwantha three for 40) **and 184** (D. C. P. D. S. Wickramanayake 42, M. M. M. Rameez 58; H. M. Maduwantha five for 24, A. W. Ekanayake four for 56); **Kurunegala Youth* 244** (D. M. Ramanayake 51, H. M. Maduwantha 36; D. T. B. Kolugala five for 57) **and 146 for five** (H. M. S. Jayawardene 32, H. M. Maduwantha 40 not out).

At Reid Avenue, Colombo, February 15, 16, 17. **Chilaw Marians won by four wickets. Air Force* 190** (W. P. Wickrama 34, S. Dananjaya 41 not out, P. T. S. Fernando 34; L. D. I. Perera three for 57, R. S. A. Palliyaguruge four for 31) **and 214** (S. E. D. R. Fernando 61, A. Rizan 38, W. C. R. Tissera 39; L. D. I. Perera three for 78); **Chilaw Marians 252** (T. M. I. Mutaliph 142 not out; P. T. S. Fernando three for 49) **and 153 for six** (W. A. D. A. P. Perera 34, C. S. Fernando 48).

At Air Force Ground, Katunayake, February 15, 16, 17. **Drawn. Ragama 252** (D. A. Ranatunga 33, K. A. S. Jayasinghe 53, H. S. S. M. K. Weerasiri 54, B. A. R. S. Priyadarshana 32; R. A. T. D. Perera four for 47) **and 293** (D. A. Ranatunga 108, B. A. R. S. Priyadarshana 83;

A. P. Dalugoda six for 80, S. Chandana three for 87); **Antonians* 166** (B. de Silva 33 not out; B. A. R. S. Priyadarshana four for 56) **and 210 for nine** (Y. N. Tillekeratne 66).

At Reid Avenue, Colombo, February 15, 16, 17. **Moratuwa won by eight wickets. Kandy* 209** (W. A. S. N. B. Peiris 56, S. A. Burke 47, J. Y. S. T. de Silva 42; M. Jayasena five for 47, B. C. N. Amarasinghe five for 53) **and 206** (D. C. P. D. S. Wickramanayake 46, W. A. S. N. B. Peiris 56, D. T. B. Kolugala 34; C. M. Hathurusinghe five for 55); **Moratuwa 368** (D. A. P. Ranaweera 36, W. A. I. Wanigasekera 42, U. N. K. Fernando 113, K. L. R. Fernando 79, M. Jayasena 35 not out; I. S. Baddegama three for 48, M. I. Palihakkara four for 67) **and 49 for two.**

At FTZ Sports Complex, Katunayake, February 15, 16, 17. **Drawn. Kurunegala Youth 182** (H. M. S. Jayawardene 43; M. N. T. H. Kumara three for 42, M. M. D. N. R. G. Perera three for 38) **and 440** (N. H. V. Chinthaka 72, R. R. Jaymon 50, D. N. Pathirana 55, S. Madanayake 79, A. R. R. A. P. W. R. R. K. B. Amunugama 68 not out, Extras 30; M. N. T. H. Kumara three for 83, M. M. D. N. R. G. Perera three for 98); **Sebastianites* 325** (M. M. D. N. R. G. Perera 37, S. H. S. N. de Silva 31, R. H. S. Silva 99, H. G. P. Ranaweera 56, T. S. M. Peiris 44; H. M. Maduwantha four for 80, A. W. Ekanayake three for 65) **and 72 for three** (S. H. S. N. de Silva 30 not out).

At Havelock Park, Colombo (Colts), February 22, 23. **Air Force won by an innings and 80 runs. Air Force* 366** (K. A. Kumara 34, M. K. G. C. P. Lakshitha 43, W. C. R. Tissera 77, W. R. Fernando 96, K. R. P. Silva 43 not out; A. W. Ekanayake seven for 101); **Kurunegala Youth 182** (H. M. Maduwantha 47 not out, D. N. Pathirana 35, A. W. Ekanayake 35; K. R. P. Silva three for 30, W. R. D. Dissanayake three for 32) **and 104** (K. R. P. Silva six for 33).

At Reid Avenue, Colombo, February 22, 23, 24. **Drawn. Sebastianites 319** (M. M. D. N. R. G. Perera 50, R. H. S. Silva 47, K. H. R. K. Fernando 90, H. G. P. Ranaweera 43; G. M. C. Nilantha three for 78, B. de Silva three for 60) **and 201 for five** (R. H. S. Silva 60, K. H. R. K. Fernando 44); **Antonians* 138** (S. Chandana 40 not out; M. H. A. Jabbar five for 24) **and 386** (Y. N. Tillekeratne 153, A. P. Dalugoda 85, R. A. T. D. Perera 31 not out; M. H. A. Jabbar four for 94).

At Havelock Park, Colombo (BRC), February 22, 23, 24. **Chilaw Marians won by four wickets. Moratuwa 262** (C. D. Fernando 80, B. C. N. Amarasinghe 69, M. Jayasena 36 not out; R. S. A. Palliyaguruge three for 34, P. C. Jayasundera four for 57) **and 193** (B. D. A. P. Ranaweera 43, B. C. N. Amarasinghe 34, K. L. R. Fernando 38; L. D. I. Perera six for 76, L. J. P. Gunaratne three for 43); **Chilaw Marians* 279** (S. T. Tittagalla 103, D. A. Marage 42, P. C. Jayasundera 55; A. L. D. M. Deshapriya four for 64, W. A. I. Wanigasekera three for 14) **and 179 for six** (S. T. Tittagalla 55, K. A. D. J. Siriwardene 59; W. A. I. Wanigasekera three for 73).

At FTZ Sports Complex, Katunayake, February 22, 23, 24. **Kandy won by seven wickets. Kandy 298** (W. A. S. N. B. Peiris 47, M. I. Palihakkara 71, P. K. Wijetunge 52; A. G. R. M. S. Ranaweera eight for 73) **and 62 for three** (D. C. S. D. S. Wickramanayake 31 not out); **Rio* 106** (D. T. B. Kolugala three for 24) **and 250** (M. G. D. J. Pradeep 39, R. C. Rupasinghe 69, T. J. Madanayake 33; P. K. Wijetunge four for 73, J. Arnolda three for 55).

At FTZ Sports Complex, Katunayake, March 1, 2. **Antonians won by an innings and 90 runs. Antonians 321** (N. Weeraman 52, P. K. Siriwardene 30, Y. N. Tillekeratne 49, B. de Silva 70, G. M. C. Nilantha 31, Extras 35; I. S. Baddegama three for 74, D. T. B. Kolugala three for 88); **Kandy* 65** (P. W. Gunaratne four for 18, G. M. C. Nilantha three for 11) **and 166** (W. A. S. N. B. Peiris 46, J. Arnolda 34; S. Chandana three for 36, Y. N. Tillekeratne three for 20).

At Havelock Park, Colombo (Colts), March 1, 2, 3. **Moratuwa won by an innings and 156 runs. Rio 128** (M. T. S. de Zoysa 60; C. M. Hathurusinghe six for 56) **and 189** (R. C. Rupasinghe 40; M. Jayasena six for 34); **Moratuwa* 473 for six dec.** (B. D. A. P. Ranaweera 37, C. D. Fernando 45, R. G. D. Sanjeewa 107, W. A. I. Wanigasekera 154 not out, K. L. R. Fernando 41, B. Fernando 36 not out, Extras 31).

At Braybrooke Place, Colombo (Moors), March 8, 9. **Chilaw Marians won by 533 runs. Chilaw Marians* 267** (S. T. Tittagalla 36, K. A. D. J. Siriwardene 54, C. S. Fernando 54, R. S. A. Palliyaguruge 39; R. C. Rupasinghe four for 63) **and 409 for eight dec.** (W. A. D. A. P. Perera 55,

K. A. D. J. Siriwardene 112, P. C. Jayasundera 111, L. L. Fernando 67; R. C. Rupasinghe four for 137, M. G. P. R. Pradeep three for 68); **Rio 71** (P. C. Jayasundera three for three) **and 72** (L. D. I. Perera three for 20, L. J. P. Gunaratne three for 16, P. C. Jayasundera four for 29).

Rio totalled only 143 over two innings; they were bowled out in 23 overs in their first innings and 24.3 in the second. Vijitha Kumara was the only Rio batsman to pass 12 in either innings, scoring 28 at No. 9 in the first.

At Havelock Park, Colombo (Colts), March 8, 9, 10. **Sebastianites won by seven wickets. Moratuwa 197** (M. M. C. S. Perera 31, W. A. I. Wanigasekera 52; K. A. D. M. Fernando five for 57, K. H. R. K. Fernando four for 48) **and 294** (B. D. A. P. Ranaweera 42, M. M. C. S. Perera 71, K. L. R. Fernando 59; M. M. D. N. R. G. Perera five for 133); **Sebastianites* 398** (M. M. D. N. R. G. Perera 150, K. H. R. K. Fernando 100, H. G. P. Ranaweera 33, K. A. D. M. Fernando 47; M. M. C. S. Perera three for 36) **and 96 for three** (S. N. Wijesinghe 39 not out).

At Havelock Park, Colombo (BRC), March 15, 16, 17. **Air Force won by an innings and 66 runs. Air Force 401** (W. R. D. Dissanayake 163, W. P. Wickrama 75, W. C. R. Tissera 53, Extras 32; P. K. Wijetunge four for 86); **Kandy* 127** (W. A. S. N. B. Peiris 30; M. K. G. C. P. Lakshitha four for 28, W. R. D. Dissanayake four for 32) **and 208** (M. M. M. Rameez 38; W. R. D. Dissanayake five for 39).

At FTZ Sports Complex, Katunayake, March 15, 16. **Moratuwa won by an innings and 24 runs. Antonians* 144** (P. K. Siriwardene 34; M. M. C. S. Perera five for 43) **and 78** (C. M. Hathurusinghe six for 47); **Moratuwa 246** (B. D. A. P. Ranaweera 37, C. D. Fernando 50, M. Jayasena 40; P. W. Gunaratne three for 42, S. Chandana four for 61).

At Air Force Ground, Katunayake, March 15, 16, 17. **Ragama won by 195 runs. Ragama 200** (S. Arangalla 34; H. M. Maduwantha three for 58, S. Madanayake five for 48) **and 275** (E. F. M. U. Fernando 57, K. A. S. Jayasinghe 66, R. D. Dissanayake 44 not out, S. Rupasinghe 33; A. R. R. A. P. W. R. R. K. B. Amunugama seven for 47); **Kurunegala Youth* 194** (D. M. Ramanayake 47; S. Arangalla five for 51) **and 86** (S. Arangalla six for 41, T. P. Gamage three for 17).

At Reid Avenue, Colombo, March 15, 16. **Sebastianites won by an innings and one run. Rio* 120** (R. C. Rupasinghe 50; K. H. R. K. Fernando four for 34) **and 49** (K. A. D. M. Fernando five for 20, M. N. T. H. Kumara three for 13); **Sebastianites 170 for eight dec.** (K. A. D. M. Fernando 38; R. C. Rupasinghe five for 34).

Rio's second innings lasted only 18.5 overs; it was the third time in four innings they had been bowled out in double figures.

At Havelock Park, Colombo (BRC), March 22, 23. **Air Force won by an innings and 181 runs. Rio* 130** (R. C. Rupasinghe 74; M. K. G. C. P. Lakshitha five for 50) **and 103** (R. C. Rupasinghe 44; M. K. G. C. P. Lakshitha seven for 23, A. Rizan three for 30); **Air Force 414** (S. E. D. R. Fernando 131, A. Rizan 45, W. R. Fernando 72, W. C. R. Tissera 45, K. R. P. Silva 39 not out, Extras 39; L. G. S. Prasad four for 118).

At FTZ Sports Complex, Katunayake, March 22, 23, 24. **Ragama won by 431 runs. Ragama* 325** (S. D. Gunawardene 48, E. F. M. U. Fernando 75, K. A. S. Jayasinghe 44, S. Arangalla 39, Extras 39; D. T. B. Kolugala three for 44) **and 400 for nine dec.** (D. A. Ranatunga 133, H. G. S. P. Fernando 107, S. D. Gunawardene 62; D. T. B. Kolugala seven for 117); **Kandy 118** (B. A. R. S. Priyadarshana four for 51, T. P. Gamage five for 39) **and 176** (D. C. S. D. S. Wickramanayake 35, D. T. B. Kolugala 48; R. D. Dissanayake five for 33).

At Braybrooke Place, Colombo (Moors), March 22, 23, 24. **Moratuwa won by seven wickets. Kurunegala Youth 115** (M. M. C. S. Perera five for 50) **and 316** (N. H. V. Chinthaka 57, G. S. P. Dharmapala 80, K. L. S. Gamage 41, D. M. Ramanayake 68; B. C. N. Amarasinghe four for 35); **Moratuwa* 201** (M. M. C. S. Perera 38, K. L. R. Fernando 39; A. W. Ekanayake five for 53) **and 231 for three** (B. D. A. P. Ranaweera 37, A. L. D. M. Deshapriya 56, R. G. D. Sanjeewa 103 not out).

At Maitland Place, Colombo (NCC), March 29, 30, 31. **Drawn. Sebastianites* 400** (M. M. D. N. R. G. Perera 152, G. E. Randiligama 56, K. A. D. M. Fernando 33, M. M. S.

Fernando 30, M. N. T. H. Kumara 31, Extras 33; L. J. P. Gunaratne eight for 133) **and 160** (S. N. Wijesinghe 49; L. J. P. Gunaratne three for 52, W. A. D. A. P. Perera four for 31); **Chilaw Marians 436** (W. A. D. A. P. Perera 53, S. T. Tittagalla 34, T. M. I. Mutaliph 61, L. D. I. Perera 35, P. C. Jayasundera 95, L. L. Fernando 78, Extras 38; M. M. D. N. R. G. Perera five for 152).

INVITATION QUADRANGULAR TOURNAMENT

At Braybrooke Place, Colombo (Moors), April 19, 20, 21. **Drawn. BCCSL Academy XI 215** (A. S. Polonowita 89; M. F. Maharoof three for 37) **and 208 for seven dec.** (S. Kalawithigoda 54, G. I. Daniel 56, S. H. T. Kandamby 35, C. U. Jayasinghe 40 not out; S. D. C. Malinga three for 35); **Sri Lanka Schools XI* 229** (S. P. L. C. S. Perera 57, M. F. Maharoof 52; C. U. Jayasinghe three for 36, K. S. Lokuarachchi three for 41) **and 112 for four** (S. P. L. C. S. Perera 42).

At Maitland Place, Colombo (SSC), April 19, 20, 21. **Club XI won by six wickets. Sri Lanka A* 232** (D. A. Gunawardene 80, W. M. B. Perera 51, W. M. G. Ramyakumara 30; M. K. G. C. P. Lakshitha five for 34, K. H. R. K. Fernando three for 65) **and 174** (J. Mubarak 62, D. K. Liyanage 61; M. K. G. C. P. Lakshitha four for 31); **Club XI 251** (M. D. K. Perera 30, M. M. D. N. R. G. Perera 78 not out, P. C. Jayasundera 55; H. M. R. K. B. Herath three for 38, L. D. I. Perera five for 46) **and 156 for four** (R. H. S. Silva 54, S. I. de Saram 51 not out).

At Reid Avenue, Colombo, April 23, 24, 25. **Drawn. Club XI 162** (M. D. K. Perera 30, R. H. S. Silva 45) **and 188 for two** (P. S. A. N. Shiroman 105 not out, E. F. M. U. Fernando 36); **BCCSL Academy XI* 220** (S. Kalawithigoda 77, R. R. Tissera 47, W. C. A. Ganegama 48; M. K. G. C. P. Lakshitha six for 76).

At Maitland Place, Colombo (NCC), April 23, 24, 25. **Drawn. Sri Lanka A* 400 for nine dec.** (D. A. Gunawardene 68, M. N. Nawaz 30, T. M. Dilshan 54, L. P. C. Silva 90, K. R. Pushpakumara 41, L. D. I. Perera 36 not out; K. T. G. D. Prasad three for 92, R. W. M. G. A. Ratnayake five for 76) **and 221** (W. M. S. M. Perera 33, T. M. Dilshan 37, J. Mubarak 62; B. M. A. J. Mendis three for 67, S. A. D. U. Indrasiri five for 43); **Sri Lanka Schools XI 165** (W. U. Tharanga 33, K. T. G. D. Prasad 77 not out; C. R. B. Mudalige three for 37) **and 89 for four** (B. M. A. J. Mendis 32).

At Maitland Place, Colombo (SSC), April 30, May 1, 2. **Drawn. Sri Lanka A* 304** (M. N. Nawaz 114, T. M. Dilshan 50, D. K. Liyanage 30, Extras 31; I. S. Gallage four for 38) **and 107 for seven dec.** (M. G. Vandort 36, M. N. Nawaz 30); **BCCSL Academy XI 242 for nine dec.** (G. I. Daniel 36, M. Pushpakumara 73, K. S. Lokuarachchi 43; H. M. R. K. B. Herath three for 86) **and five for one**.

At Maitland Place, Colombo (NCC), April 30, May 1. **Club XI won by an innings and 58 runs. Sri Lanka Schools XI* 79** (M. K. G. C. P. Lakshitha three for 29, K. H. R. K. Fernando five for 17) **and 143** (D. Ratnayake 38; M. K. G. C. P. Lakshitha three for 43, S. Arangalla three for 33); **Club XI 280 for nine dec.** (R. H. S. Silva 40, K. H. R. K. Fernando 105, S. I. de Saram 59 not out, M. K. G. C. P. Lakshitha 41; L. S. Malinga three for 62).

Kenya's and India A's first-class matches appear in Other A-Team Tours, pages 1426-1428.

CRICKET IN ZIMBABWE, 2001-02

By JOHN WARD

Raymond Price

Against a backdrop of political turmoil, with the economy in crisis and the government attempting to repossess white-owned farms, Zimbabwean cricket endured another difficult season. The national team suffered heavy defeats at home to South Africa, in a one-day series with England and on tour in Sri Lanka. In Bangladesh, they were invincible, but that was no less than expected. More significant was their improvement in India, where they pressed hard in the Second Test and led the one-day series twice before going down 3–2.

The players gave the credit to Geoff Marsh, Australia's former opener and national coach. Signing him as coach was a major coup for the Zimbabwe Cricket Union, after his old team-mate, Carl Rackemann, decided not to renew his contract after a year. Rackemann had also been greatly appreciated; it was sad that he departed after 12 consecutive one-day defeats. Zimbabwe lost four more in Sharjah before Bangladesh offered relief. Marsh needed time to work with a demoralised team but, by the Indian tour, his quiet, positive manner and methods were paying dividends.

The selectors' policies were often criticised. Sweeping changes placed the accent on youth rather than experience: youngsters were plunged into international cricket before finding their feet at domestic level, and senior players dropped. With Heath Streak in decline – until he rediscovered some verve in the subcontinent – the attack posed little threat; during 2001-02, Zimbabwe gave away three of the four highest Test totals they had ever conceded, and the three highest one-day totals. Travis Friend could become a top all-rounder, but lacked accuracy. Paul Strang was never quite fit; his brother Bryan left to seek a career elsewhere. A leg injury hampered Mluleki Nkala, while Henry Olonga lost his rhythm. Everton Matambanadzo married and emigrated to the United States. Only the part-time spinners Douglas Marillier and Grant Flower averaged under 40 in Zimbabwe's nine Tests. Incredibly, Zimbabwe toured Sri Lanka without a front-line slow bowler. But in India, Raymond Price, nephew of the golfer, Nick Price, was a revelation, troubling Sachin Tendulkar with his attacking left-arm spin and deceptive flight.

Once again the outstanding player was Andy Flower, who headed the PricewaterhouseCoopers Test ratings after scoring twin hundreds against South Africa. Flower amassed 747 Test runs at 57.47 – only Stuart Carlisle scored more than half as many – and was also the leading one-day scorer. Of the rest, only the newcomers Dion Ebrahim and Trevor Gripper averaged above 30 in Tests.

The captaincy remained a problem. Streak, after just over a year, had had enough and resigned after England's visit. Several senior players reportedly refused the position, which devolved on the inexperienced Brian Murphy. Murphy had no chance to get to grips with it: two hand injuries caused his early return from Bangladesh and Sri Lanka, and Carlisle was persuaded to take over. He did an adequate job, but never felt he had the selectors' confidence. Andy Flower's quiet refusal to toe the official line weighed against his obvious claims. So in August, Streak resumed the captaincy – in the same week that his father was detained in the farms dispute. A few weeks later, during the ICC Champions Trophy in Sri Lanka, Streak dislocated his collarbone in a traffic accident, and the job was temporarily vacant again.

There was another heavy blow when Australia cancelled a tour in April. Apart from cricket providing some relief from everyday difficulties, the loss of revenue exacerbated the ZCU's economic problems. The Australian Board cited fears for their players' safety, but Zimbabweans firmly believed that there was no significant risk. Similar concerns before England's visit in October had proved groundless.

In the domestic Logan Cup competition, a move from three-day to four-day matches produced some excellent cricket. For the third year running, the title was Mashonaland's; for the second year running, they won all five matches. They were indebted to an over-generous declaration from Mashonaland A, who left them an entire day to score 340. With Andy Flower, in his only Logan Cup game, batting brilliantly for twin centuries, they won before tea. Mashonaland A's gesture was not appreciated by Midlands, who would have been champions had the match been drawn.

Mashonaland had beaten Midlands by a convincing 248 runs, and were undoubtedly the strongest team, although they tended to blow hot and cold, especially in the first innings. The season's highlight was their victory over Manicaland after following on. The Test discard, Guy Whittall, scored 247 for Manicaland, then grabbed four wickets to bowl out Mashonaland 287 behind. But Craig Evans trumped Whittall when his own double-century spurred Mashonaland to 506 following on, and he took six wickets as Manicaland collapsed in pursuit of 220. The 32-year-old Evans, ignored by the national selectors since September 1999, had been considered a one-day specialist. In 2001-02, with centuries in each of his four first-class matches, he looked much more than that, adding greater discipline and better shot selection to his powerful hitting.

Although they missed Eddo Brandes, now retired, and Bryan Strang, Mashonaland's bowling usually did the job. The captain, Gus Mackay, contributed 19 wickets and 275 runs, including a 45-ball century, the fastest in Zimbabwean first-class history, against Matabeleland, enabling Mashonaland to declare at 644 for nine, the highest total by a Zimbabwean team.

Midlands, Zimbabwe's fastest-growing cricketing area, beat allcomers except Mashonaland. Their match-winner was Price. With a bit of help from the Kwekwe pitches, his left-arm spin gathered 31 wickets in four Logan Cup matches. The batting was led by James Cornford, an overseas professional from Cheshire.

Mashonaland A fielded several promising young players. Elton Chigumbura and Brendan Taylor, who both turned 16 during the season, scored over 300 runs each, while Prosper Utseya, a year older, showed encouraging all-round form.

CFX Academy defeated Manicaland through a remarkable debut by Glen Barrett. He reached a century in 54 balls and finished with 186 runs in the match, including 13 sixes. Barrett struck at least one six in each of his first six innings. The most consistent batsman was the captain, Anton Hoffman, while Jordane Nicolle was the most dangerous bowler.

In a winless season, Matabeleland reversed their tradition of bowling riches and batting poverty. They were down from five international pace bowlers to two – when Streak and Pommie Mbangwa returned – and also lost the left-arm spinner, Ian Englebrecht, who departed for England. The burden was shouldered by all-rounder Gavin Ewing, an Academy reject the previous year. He scored a debut century against Mashonaland and took 20 wickets in all. Meanwhile, the batting blossomed. The aggressive Greg Strydom, who was 18 in March, passed 500 runs, and Wisdom Siziba gave fluency to the top of the order.

Manicaland never recovered from two early defeats, by the Academy after being battered by Barrett, and Mashonaland after enforcing the follow-on. Apart from Whittall, who had a point to prove, they lacked all-round strength. But the captain, Neil Ferreira, scored three centuries and 650 runs; his diligent application put many greater natural talents to shame.

The ZCU decided to expand the 2002-03 Logan Cup to a double round of matches, home and away, in October and April. This led to the withdrawal of the Academy, which runs from February to September. Plans to replace them with Masvingo, the latest major development area, were postponed until Masvingo could show more strength in depth. Mashonaland A joined them, and the other provinces' A teams, in a non-first-class division. Their demotion reduced the first-class teams to four, with an overpowerful Mashonaland, and so, to create a more balanced competition and provide opportunities for all quality players, several Harare-based professionals were posted to the other three provinces. A one-day tournament, with white balls and coloured clothing, was introduced for January 2003.

The Zimbabwe Board XI had a fair season in the UCBSA Bowl. The South Africans offered them entry to the first-class SuperSport Series in 2002-03, with a second side in the Bowl; the bad news was that both teams would have to play entirely in South Africa. This would have made it impossible to expand the Logan Cup, so the ZCU decided to quit the South African competitions instead.

An administrative era ended in January 2002, when Dave Ellman-Brown resigned as the ZCU's managing director. As president, he had been the main force behind Zimbabwe's promotion to Test status in 1992. After business concerns took him away for some years, he returned in 1998 as chief executive and increased Zimbabwe's international programme considerably. Ellman-Brown remained as life president and kept charge of the finances. His successor was Vince Hogg, who had played as an opening bowler in Zimbabwe's first World Cup in 1983.

In recent years, Ellman-Brown must have been frustrated by political manoeuvring within and without the ZCU. Domestic politics continued to cloud the game's future. Though there was as yet no justification for fears about the safety of touring players, some suspected that such concerns were being used to mask a politically motivated attempt to scupper Zimbabwe's role as co-hosts for the 2003 World Cup. Meanwhile, several leading players have already left because of the country's political and economic problems; the danger remains that more will follow.

FIRST-CLASS AVERAGES, 2001-02

BATTING

(Qualification: 250 runs)

	M	I	NO	R	HS	100s	Avge
A. Flower (*Mashonaland*)	3	6	3	692	199*	4	230.66
C. N. Evans (*Mashonaland*)	4	6	0	684	210	4	114.00
J. M. Cornford (*Midlands*)	5	7	3	314	98*	0	78.50
N. R. Ferreira (*Manicaland*)	5	9	0	650	210	3	72.22
G. M. Strydom (*Matabeleland*)	5	10	2	537	109	1	67.12
G. W. Flower (*Mashonaland A*)	4	7	2	324	235*	1	64.80
G. M. Ewing (*Matabeleland*)	5	9	2	412	106*	1	58.85
D. J. R. Campbell (*Mashonaland*)	5	7	1	311	79	0	51.83
M. A. Vermeulen (*Mashonaland A*)	4	8	0	393	180	1	49.12
G. J. Whittall (*Manicaland*)	5	9	0	423	247	1	47.00
A. J. Mackay (*Mashonaland*)	5	7	1	275	108	1	45.83
D. D. Ebrahim (*Mashonaland*)	4	7	1	264	71	0	44.00
B. G. Rogers (*Mashonaland*)	5	8	0	350	96	0	43.75

	M	I	NO	R	HS	100s	Avge
W. T. Siziba (*Matabeleland*)	5	10	0	423	103	1	42.30
G. F. Barrett (*CFX Academy*)	4	8	0	311	106	1	38.87
M. G. McKillop (*Matabeleland*)	5	9	1	309	71*	0	38.62
A. P. Hoffman (*CFX Academy*)	5	10	0	384	112	1	38.40
E. Chigumbura (*Mashonaland A*)	5	9	0	306	70	0	34.00
B. R. M. Taylor (*Mashonaland A*) . . .	5	10	0	322	82	0	32.20
L. S. Malloch-Brown (*Mashonaland*) . .	5	9	0	274	78	0	30.44

BOWLING

(Qualification: 10 wickets)

	O	M	R	W	BB	5W/i	Avge
G. B. Brent (*Manicaland*)	64.4	18	142	10	5-64	1	14.20
D. P. Viljoen (*Midlands*)	76.2	15	189	11	3-34	0	17.18
M. J. Vaughan-Davies (*Midlands*)	88.5	22	281	14	4-21	0	20.07
J. S. Nicolle (*CFX Academy*)	132	34	381	18	4-46	0	21.16
R. W. Price (*Midlands*)	337.3	100	815	36	8-35	4	22.63
H. P. Rinke (*CFX Academy*)	88	21	252	11	4-39	0	22.90
D. T. Mutendera (*Mashonaland A*) . . .	99.3	23	306	13	5-71	1	23.53
A. J. Mackay (*Mashonaland*)	148.2	32	465	19	4-41	0	24.47
N. B. Mahwire (*Mashonaland*)	98.5	20	335	13	4-40	0	25.76
G. J. Whittall (*Manicaland*)	148.4	41	354	13	4-38	0	27.23
L. J. Soma (*Manicaland*)	117.3	25	403	14	4-39	0	28.78
B. G. Rogers (*Mashonaland*)	81	6	290	10	4-34	0	29.00
G. M. Ewing (*Matabeleland*)	235.3	65	619	20	5-80	2	30.95
J. M. Lewis (*Manicaland*)	96.4	29	319	10	3-12	0	31.90
T. J. Friend (*Midlands*)	94.2	19	354	11	3-22	0	32.18
C. Macmillan (*Midlands*)	138.4	32	383	11	3-54	0	34.81
P. Utseya (*Mashonaland A*)	115.1	23	379	10	4-72	0	37.90
K. M. Dabengwa (*Matabeleland*)	111.4	13	447	11	5-94	1	40.63
G. M. Strydom (*Matabeleland*)	124	12	538	10	4-134	0	53.80

LOGAN CUP, 2001-02

	Played	Won	Lost	Drawn	Bonus points Batting	Bonus points Bowling	Penalty	Points
Mashonaland	5	5	0	0	16	15	5	86
Midlands	5	4	0	0	14	20	0	82
Mashonaland A . . .	5	2	2	1	10	19	4	52
CFX Academy	5	1	3	1	6	15	0	36
Matabeleland	5	0	2	3	11	16	0	36
Manicaland	5	0	4	1	11	19	0	33

Outright win = 12 pts; drawn match = 3 pts.
Bonus points are awarded for the first 120 overs of each team's first innings. One batting point is awarded for the first 200 runs and for every subsequent 50, to a maximum of four points. One bowling point is awarded for the third wicket taken and for every subsequent two.
Penalty points are imposed for slow over-rates.

*In the following scores, * by the name of a team signifies that they won the toss.*

At Mutare Sports Club, Mutare, February 15, 16, 17. **CFX Academy won by 149 runs. CFX Academy*** 298 (A. P. Hoffman 47, C. H. Brewer 66, G. F. Barrett 106; A. L. Taylor three for 73, I. M. Coulson three for 55) **and** 286 (N. Chouhan 72, G. C. Goosen 35, G. F. Barrett 106); **Manicaland** 272 (N. R. Ferreira 106, K. P. R. Went 57, A. L. Taylor 30; H. P. Rinke four for 39) **and** 163 (N. Sheth 40, A. L. Taylor 30 retired hurt; J. S. Nicolle four for 46). *CFX Academy 18 pts, Manicaland 6 pts.*

Glen Barrett, aged 22, scored a 54-ball century on first-class debut, which was for one day the fastest recorded in balls in Zimbabwean cricket. It included 26 in one over from Went. Barrett hit seven sixes in the first innings and six in the second; his total of 13 was a Zimbabwean record.

At Bulawayo Athletic Club, Bulawayo, February 15, 16, 17, 18. **Mashonaland won by eight wickets. Mashonaland*** 644 for nine dec. (L. S. Malloch-Brown 43, R. E. Butterworth 36, B. G. Rogers 96, C. N. Evans 118, N. B. Mahwire 44, D. J. R. Campbell 79, A. J. Mackay 108, Extras 60; G. M. Strydom four for 134, G. M. Ewing three for 136) **and** 82 for two (K. J. Taibu 40 not out); **Matabeleland** 392 (W. T. Siziba 31, R. J. King 43, M. Kenny 57, G. M. Strydom 38, M. G. McKillop 68, G. M. Ewing 83, Extras 41; N. B. Mahwire four for 40) **and** 333 (W. T. Siziba 37, G. M. Strydom 109, G. M. Ewing 106 not out, Extras 32; N. B. Mahwire four for 80). *Mashonaland 20 pts, Matabeleland 6 pts.*

Mashonaland's 644 for nine was the highest total by a Zimbabwean team; the match aggregate of 1,451 runs was the highest in Zimbabwe. On the second morning, Mashonaland's captain Gus Mackay scored a maiden century, including ten sixes, in 45 balls (75 minutes), beating Glen Barrett's the previous day. When Matabeleland followed on, Gavin Ewing scored 106 not out on debut; Greg Strydom, aged 17 years 329 days, was the second-youngest Zimbabwean to score a century after Hamilton Masakadza.

At Country Club, Harare, March 1, 2, 3, 4. **Mashonaland A won by 38 runs. Mashonaland A*** 346 (B. R. M. Taylor 47, M. A. Vermeulen 180, A. M. Durham 35; J. S. Nicolle three for 58, H. P. Rinke four for 72) **and** 149 (E. Chigumbura 39); **CFX Academy** 273 for nine dec. (G. C. Goosen 65, H. P. Rinke 84 not out, Extras 31) **and** 184 (H. P. Rinke 47 not out; A. M. Durham three for 56). *Mashonaland A 16 pts, CFX Academy 4 pts.*

At Mutare Sports Club, Mutare, March 1, 2, 3, 4. **Mashonaland won by 73 runs. Manicaland*** 513 for nine dec. (N. R. Ferreira 71, T. K. Mawoyo 31, R. W. Sims 75, G. J. Whittall 247, A. Kugotsi 34; M. S. L. Seager four for 140) **and** 146 (N. R. Ferreira 39, T. K. Mawoyo 38; C. N. Evans six for 37, B. G. Rogers four for 34); **Mashonaland** 226 (L. S. Malloch-Brown 76, R. E. Butterworth 42, D. R. Matambanadzo 30; L. J. Soma four for 39, G. J. Whittall four for 38) **and** 506 (D. R. Matambanadzo 80, B. G. Rogers 40, C. N. Evans 210, D. J. R. Campbell 54, A. J. Mackay 68; G. J. Whittall four for 80). *Mashonaland 15 pts, Manicaland 7 pts.*

Whittall's 247 lasted 387 minutes and 303 balls and included 35 fours and three sixes. Evans's 210 lasted 373 minutes and 274 balls and included 33 fours and a six; he added 189 for the seventh wicket with Campbell to set up Mashonaland's win after following on.

At Bulawayo Athletic Club, Bulawayo, March 1, 2, 3. **Midlands won by nine wickets. Matabeleland** 192 (W. T. Siziba 103; M. J. Vaughan-Davies four for 35) **and** 213 (M. G. McKillop 69; M. J. Vaughan-Davies four for 21); **Midlands*** 353 (T. Duffin 74, D. P. Viljoen 55, J. M. Cornford 52, C. Delport 32, C. Macmillan 59, Extras 30; G. M. Ewing five for 80) **and** 54 for one. *Midlands 20 pts, Matabeleland 4 pts.*

At Kwekwe Sports Club, Kwekwe, March 15, 16, 17, 18. **Midlands won by five wickets. Mashonaland A** 209 (B. R. M. Taylor 32, M. A. Vermeulen 45, E. Chigumbura 34; C. Macmillan three for 54) **and** 257 (E. Chigumbura 59, A. Maregwede 44, S. T. Makunura 62; D. P. Viljoen three for 60, R. W. Price five for 78); **Midlands*** 265 (T. Duffin 89, S. M. Ervine 38; P. Utseya four for 72) **and** 204 for five (R. W. Price 77, J. M. Cornford 37 not out). *Midlands 18 pts, Mashonaland A 5 pts.*

This match had been postponed after neither team could raise a viable eleven.

At Country Club, Harare, March 22, 23, 24, 25. **Drawn. CFX Academy*** 297 (V. Sibanda 35, A. P. Hoffman 112, I. M. Chinyoka 52, G. F. Barrett 42; M. W. Townshend three for 61, K. M. Dabengwa five for 94) **and** 339 for nine dec. (V. Sibanda 31, A. P. Hoffman 70, G. C. Goosen 101 not out, T. Benade 35; G. M. Ewing four for 107); **Matabeleland** 339 (G. M. Ewing 58,

W. T. Siziba 76, G. M. Strydom 91, M. G. McKillop 49; T. Benade three for 62, A. P. Hoffman three for ten) **and 232 for five** (S. R. Walker 44, G. M. Ewing 76, M. G. McKillop 71 not out; T. Benade three for 81). *CFX Academy 7 pts, Matabeleland 10 pts.*

At Harare Sports Club, Harare, March 22, 23, 24. **Mashonaland won by 248 runs. Mashonaland 329** (B. G. Rogers 56, C. N. Evans 163; D. P. Viljoen three for 34) **and 263 for eight dec.** (B. G. Rogers 80, C. N. Evans 35, D. J. R. Campbell 61; R. W. Price five for 68); **Midlands* 211** (D. P. Viljoen 78, C. Macmillan 35; T. R. Gripper four for 44) **and 133** (J. M. Cornford 69 not out, M. J. Vaughan-Davies 39; B. T. Watambwa four for 57). *Mashonaland 14 pts, Midlands 5 pts.*

At Alexandra Sports Club, Harare, March 22, 23, 24, 25. **Mashonaland A won by two wickets. Manicaland* 255** (N. R. Ferreira 135, G. J. Whittall 53; G. J. Rennie three for 27) **and 206** (R. W. Sims 36, G. J. Whittall 36, K. P. R. Went 50 not out; G. J. Rennie three for 49, P. Utseya three for 30, A. J. C. Neethling three for 37); **Mashonaland A 307** (A. J. C. Neethling 32, G. J. Rennie 82, A. Maregwede 39, P. Utseya 58, H. K. Olonga 37 not out; R. W. Sims six for 132, K. J. Taylor three for 42) **and 155 for eight** (M. A. Vermeulen 43, A. Maregwede 45; G. J. Whittall four for 46, J. M. Lewis three for 12). *Mashonaland A 17 pts, Manicaland 3 pts.*

At Kwekwe Sports Club, Kwekwe, March 29, 30, 31. **Midlands won by nine wickets. Manicaland* 200** (R. W. Sims 57, K. P. R. Went 33; R. W. Price three for 51, D. A. Marillier four for 44) **and 178** (N. R. Ferreira 50, G. B. Brent 65; R. W. Price three for 44, D. A. Marillier four for 86); **Midlands 374** (C. B. Wishart 61, D. A. Marillier 59, S. M. Ervine 55, J. M. Cornford 98 not out; G. B. Brent four for 56, J. M. Lewis three for 87) **and seven for one.** *Midlands 20 pts, Manicaland 5 pts.*

At Harare Sports Club, Harare, April 5, 6, 7, 8. **Mashonaland won by seven wickets. Mashonaland A 483** (B. R. M. Taylor 82, G. W. Flower 235 not out, T. Taibu 38, E. Chigumbura 36, S. T. Makunura 41, Extras 32; A. J. Mackay four for 88, M. S. L. Seager four for 128) **and 218 for three dec.** (A. J. C. Neethling 64, B. R. M. Taylor 49, S. V. Carlisle 64); **Mashonaland* 362 for eight dec.** (L. S. Malloch-Brown 33, D. D Ebrahim 45, A. Flower 114, D. R. Matambanadzo 41, D. J. R. Campbell 39 not out, Extras 36; R. J. Bennett four for 55) **and 340 for three** (L. S. Malloch-Brown 78, R. E. Butterworth 32, A. Flower 156 not out, D. D Ebrahim 43 not out). *Mashonaland 17 pts, Mashonaland A 6 pts.*
    Grant Flower's 235 not out lasted 506 minutes and 412 balls and included 19 fours and a six. Andy Flower hit two centuries in a match for the second time in seven months, following the First Test against South Africa on the same ground.

At Kwekwe Sports Club, Kwekwe, April 5, 6. **Midlands won by an innings and 53 runs. CFX Academy 143*** (A. P. Hoffman 50; T. J. Friend three for 22, R. W. Price four for 44) **and 116** (S. Matsikenyeri 36; R. W. Price eight for 35); **Midlands 312** (T. J. Friend 121, S. M. Ervine 43, M. J. Vaughan-Davies 86 not out; J. S. Nicolle four for 46, T. Benade three for 51). *Midlands 19 pts, CFX Academy 4 pts.*

At Mutare Sports Club, Mutare, April 12, 13, 14, 15. **Drawn. Manicaland* 574** (N. R. Ferreira 210, T. K. Mawoyo 37, L. J. Soma 75, G. B. Brent 49, P. A. Strang 154; G. M. Ewing five for 98); **Matabeleland 244** (W. T. Siziba 42, R. J. King 43, G. M. Strydom 72; G. B. Brent five for 64, L. J. Soma three for 60) **and 206 for three** (W. T. Siziba 50, S. R. Walker 75, M. Kenny 36 not out, G. M. Strydom 31 not out). *Manicaland 11 pts, Matabeleland 6 pts.*
    Ferreira's 210 lasted 447 minutes and 341 balls and included 22 fours and a six.

At Country Club, Harare, April 19, 20. **Mashonaland won by an innings and 163 runs. CFX Academy 122** (N. Chouhan 37; A. J. Mackay four for 41) **and 128** (T. R. Gripper three for 14); **Mashonaland* 413** (B. G. Rogers 42, D. D Ebrahim 30, C. N. Evans 147, D. R. Matambanadzo 49, D. J. R. Campbell 39, A. J. Mackay 66; J. S. Nicolle four for 47, S. Shah three for 39). *Mashonaland 20 pts, CFX Academy 3 pts.*

At Queens Sports Club, Bulawayo, April 19, 20, 21, 22. **Drawn. Mashonaland A 270** (B. R. M. Taylor 46, M. A. Vermeulen 60, T. Taibu 31, E. Chigumbura 70; H. H. Streak five for 61) **and**

332 (G. J. Rennie 53, M. A. Vermeulen 43, T. Taibu 32, A. Maregwede 68, E. Chigumbura 40; K. M. Dabengwa three for 65); **Matabeleland* 319** (R. J. King 39, G. M. Strydom 92, M. G. McKillop 36, G. M. Ewing 56 not out; D. T. Hondo four for 68, D. T. Mutendera three for 71) **and 268 for nine** (S. R. Walker 54, G. M. Strydom 83 not out, H. H Streak 39; D. T. Mutendera five for 71, G. W. Flower three for 60). *Matabeleland 10 pts, Mashonaland A 8 pts.*

LOGAN CUP WINNERS

1993-94	Mashonaland Under-24	1998-99	Matabeleland
1994-95	Mashonaland	1999-2000	Mashonaland
1995-96	Matabeleland	2000-01	Mashonaland
1996-97	Mashonaland	2001-02	Mashonaland
1997-98	Mashonaland		

I ZINGARI RESULTS, 2002

Matches 21: Won 3, Lost 9, Drawn 9. Abandoned 3.

April 25	Eton College	Lost by one wicket
April 28	Charterhouse School	Lost by eight wickets
May 5	Hampshire Hogs	Won by 93 runs
May 11	Eton Ramblers	Lost by 141 runs
May 12	Stragglers of Asia	Lost by eight wickets
May 25	Royal Armoured Corps	Drawn
May 26	Sir Paul Getty's XI	Abandoned
June 2	Earl of Carnarvon's XI	Lost by three wickets
June 9	Cormorants CC	Abandoned
June 20	Winchester College	Drawn
June 22	Guards CC	Won by 85 runs
June 23	RMA Sandhurst	Lost by three wickets
June 27	Harrow School	Drawn
June 30	Hagley CC	Abandoned
July 7	Old Wykehamists	Lost by six wickets
July 13	Royal Greenjackets CC	Lost by 51 runs
July 21	Duke of Norfolk's XI	Drawn
July 27	Willow Warblers	Drawn
August 3	Hurlingham CC	Drawn
August 4	Band of Brothers	Drawn
August 11	Lord Vestey's XI	Lost by four wickets
August 18	Bradfield Waifs	Drawn
August 31	South Wales Hunts	Drawn
September 1	J. H. Pawle's XI	Won by six wickets

CRICKET IN BANGLADESH, 2001-02

By UTPAL SHUVRO

Minhazul Abedin

Bangladesh's struggles to compete in Test cricket continued. By the end of their series in Sri Lanka in July 2002, they had lost 12 of their first 13 Tests, mostly inside three days, while rain robbed Zimbabwe in the single draw. And by the ICC Champions Trophy in September, Bangladesh had lost 20 consecutive one-day internationals since their upset against Pakistan in the 1999 World Cup. With their batsmen short of application and their bowlers short of firepower, there was plenty of ammunition for those who had condemned their elevation to Test status. The counter-claim was that they would improve only through regular exposure to Test opposition, and at least they were getting that. Under the ICC's ten-year schedule, they hosted Zimbabwe and Pakistan, and toured New Zealand and Sri Lanka. With the separately organised Asian Test Championship thrown in, Bangladesh played ten Tests between August 2001 and July 2002. The most recent Test newcomers before them, Sri Lanka and Zimbabwe, played ten Tests apiece in their first two years.

There were some signs of hope. Mohammad Ashraful became Test cricket's youngest centurion when he scored 114 against Sri Lanka in the Asian Test Championship, aged 16 years 364 days, beating Mushtaq Mohammad of Pakistan, who had held the record at 17 years 82 days for more than 40 years. Though Ashraful suffered from the pressure of the expectations he had raised, he proved that Bangladesh had the talent for a better future. The most consistent performer, however, was Habibul Bashar, who scored a century and nine other fifties in his first 11 Tests. On the bowling front, the best news was the emergence of Mashrafe bin Mortaza, an 18-year-old fast bowler with no previous first-class experience; he took 12 wickets in four Tests against Zimbabwe and New Zealand before back pains forced him out of the side.

There were several changes at the top, starting at the helm of the Bangladesh Cricket Board. The presidents of all Bangladesh sports federations are government-appointed, so the general election of October 2001 brought in Ali Ashgar Lobby, an MP from the new ruling party, to succeed Saber Hossain Chowdhury, the board president who had secured Test status. Within a few months, Lobby was also president of the Asian Cricket Council, a post rotated between the four Test nations of Asia.

After November's Test series against Zimbabwe, Khaled Masud, the wicket-keeper/batsman, replaced Naimur Rahman as captain of the national team. Naimur had led Bangladesh in their first five Tests, and made a brilliant start with six Indian wickets in his first Test innings, but it was all downhill from there. He was told to remodel a suspect action, never regained his form and for a while lost his place along with the captaincy.

Bangladesh completed a hat-trick of changes with their third coach in as many seasons. Trevor Chappell, the former Australian batsman and younger brother of Ian and Greg, who both captained Australia, had taken charge in March 2001 when the former South African all-rounder Eddie Barlow had to step down after a stroke. Chappell tried his best and brought about some improvements – notably in the fielding – but the team's overall performance still left much to be desired. The axe fell in April. This time, Bangladesh turned to Pakistan for help, appointing Mohsin Kamal, the 1980s Test bowler, with Ali Zia as his assistant.

Bangladesh's domestic first-class tournament, the National Cricket League (now sponsored by Ispahani Mirzapore Tea), lost some gloss because of the busy international calendar. The League started in late December, when the national team were in New Zealand. Pakistan's visit then kept the leading players busy for most of January, while a second team, Bangladesh A, was seeking first-class experience of another kind in the Caribbean, by taking part in the West Indian domestic competition running from January to March. The result was that very few of the top players were able to play more than three or four domestic first-class matches.

The League's defending champions, Biman Bangladesh Airlines, were unceremoniously dumped before the tournament even started. They and another team, Dhaka Metropolis, were deprived of their first-class status after a misunderstanding with the ICC left the board mistakenly believing they had to retain the original regional structure of the League. This meant that Biman and Dhaka Metropolis – who had been admitted to the League only the previous season, when it became a first-class competition – promptly fell out, reducing the number of first-class teams to six. Dhaka Division, which had been split to make two sides, could now reabsorb their former colleagues from Dhaka Metropolis.

Meanwhile, the League's format was simplified. The previous season, each three-day match had been followed by a one-day fixture between the same teams, and points from both forms of the game determined a single champion. Teams had formed two pools of four, with the top four teams advancing to a final round. This time, although a one-day game still followed every first-class match, they were separate competitions, both staged as simple round-robins, with each team playing ten matches, home and away.

The reunified Dhaka Division, who had disappointed in the first two seasons, finally played to their potential as runaway champions, winning nine of their ten games, with the other one drawn. Chittagong, who had won the inaugural, non-first-class, competition and were second in 2000-01, had to be content with third place. But they possessed the undisputed star of the tournament in Minhazul Abedin. A national captain in the pre-Test era and now 37, Minhazul became the first player to score a thousand runs in the National League. Despite missing one game, he finished with 1,012 at over 72. His three centuries included a double-hundred and a hundred in the same match against Dhaka. His powerful form earned him a recall to the Test squad, only for him to be discarded on grounds of fitness.

Rajshahi were runners-up to Dhaka, thanks to a strong batting line-up. Two young players, Nuruzzaman and Anisur Rahman, scored three centuries each, and the new national captain, Khaled Masud, who also led Rajshahi in four matches, scored an unbeaten 201 against Khulna. The country's leading wicket-taker was the left-arm spinner Mohammad Rafiq, who captured 42 for Dhaka at under 13, including 11 for 79 against Barisal. Two off-spinners, Imran Parvez of Rajshahi and Shabbir Khan of Chittagong, were close behind with 40 apiece.

The whipping boys of Bangladesh cricket were Barisal, who finished bottom in both competitions, without a single win. They lost eight first-class games and all ten in the one-day tournament. Barisal apart, the one-day league was much more keenly contested than its first-class equivalent, with the other five divisions all leading the table at some point before Sylhet emerged on top with eight wins, one ahead of Chittagong and two ahead of Rajshahi. Jahangir Alam of Dhaka was the highest run-scorer, with 354, and Shafiuddin Ahmed of Chittagong captured the most wickets, with 18, including six for 39 against Sylhet.

The Dhaka Premier Cricket League, which remained Bangladesh's most popular tournament, was won by Victoria for only the second time in their 99-year history, and the first time since 1976. Led by Khaled Masud, they beat Biman in their final game to pull clear of defending champions Mohammedan. Victoria dedicated the title to their late coach Dowlutuzzaman, who suffered a heart attack during the third match of the season.

FIRST-CLASS AVERAGES, 2001-02

BATTING

(Qualification: 300 runs, average 30.00)

	M	I	NO	R	HS	100s	Avge
Minhazul Abedin (*Chittagong*)	9	15	1	1,012	210	3	72.28
Nuruzzaman (*Rajshahi*)	10	16	1	806	161	3	53.73
Azam Iqbal (*Chittagong*)	8	12	1	521	71	0	47.36
Rajin Saleh (*Sylhet*)	10	16	1	671	130*	2	44.73
Habibul Bashar (*Bangladesh*)	4	8	0	355	108	1	44.37
Jahangir Alam (*Dhaka*)	10	16	2	594	120	2	42.42
Khaled Masud (*Rajshahi*)	8	13	2	450	201*	1	40.90
Halim Shah (*Dhaka*)	10	14	1	521	161*	1	40.07
Sajjad Kadir (*Dhaka*)	9	11	1	399	72*	0	39.90
Anisur Rahman (*Rajshahi*)	10	15	1	520	135	3	37.14
Sanuar Hossain (*Barisal*)	8	16	1	538	117*	2	35.86
Asadullah Khan (*Khulna*)	9	17	1	539	108	2	33.68
Rafiqul Islam (*Rajshahi*)	10	16	0	513	109	1	32.06
Parvez Ahmed (*Sylhet*)	10	18	0	572	121	1	31.77
Imran Ahmed (*Barisal*)	8	16	0	499	141	1	31.18
Anisul Hakim (*Chittagong*)	10	17	0	518	112	2	30.47

BOWLING

(Qualification: 15 wickets, average 30.00)

	O	M	R	W	BB	5W/i	Avge
Mohammad Rafiq (*Dhaka*)	298.4	114	536	42	7-52	3	12.76
Alok Kapali (*Sylhet*)	223.3	55	537	33	7-33	1	16.27
Aminul Islam, jun. (*Rajshahi*)	281.3	64	650	37	5-52	2	17.56
Hasibul Hussain (*Sylhet*)	130.2	19	334	18	6-58	1	18.55
Sohel Islam (*Khulna*)	138.3	20	355	19	5-84	1	18.68
Rezaul Haque (*Sylhet*)	309.4	94	590	30	7-73	2	19.66
Tamim Haque (*Khulna*)	144	31	443	22	6-41	1	20.13
Imran Parvez (*Rajshahi*)	362.1	98	884	40	5-35	1	22.10
Naimur Rahman (*Dhaka*)	186.5	42	488	22	5-76	1	22.18
Mohammad Mostadir (*Rajshahi*)	289.4	73	741	33	6-95	2	22.45
Mahbub Alam (*Rajshahi*)	219.3	51	631	28	5-25	1	22.53
Shafiuddin Ahmed (*Chittagong*)	345	99	788	34	8-86	2	23.17
Ashfaq Ali (*Barisal*)	197.2	39	560	23	4-58	0	24.34
Shabbir Khan (*Chittagong*)	408	106	1,020	40	6-76	3	25.50
Neeyamur Rashid (*Dhaka*)	200.5	53	496	19	4-62	0	26.10
Saleh Ahmed (*Barisal*)	229.3	63	504	19	4-54	0	26.52
Enamul Haque (*Chittagong*)	419.4	137	969	36	6-64	2	26.91
Jamaluddin Ahmed (*Khulna*)	369.4	84	913	33	5-32	1	27.69
Abdur Razzaq (*Khulna*)	254.1	67	637	23	5-67	1	27.69
Fahim Muntasir (*Dhaka*)	291.4	78	863	30	5-31	2	28.76
Tapash Baisya (*Sylhet*)	244	62	539	18	5-30	1	29.94

ISPAHANI MIRZAPORE TEA NATIONAL CRICKET LEAGUE, 2001-02

	Played	Won	Lost	Drawn	1st-inns Points	Points
Dhaka.	10	9	0	1	0	54
Rajshahi	10	5	3	2	6	36
Chittagong.	10	2	2	6	10	22
Sylhet.	10	3	3	4	0	18
Khulna	10	1	4	5	8	14
Barisal	10	0	8	2	0	0

Win = 6 pts; 1st-innings lead in a drawn or lost match = 2 pts.

*In the following scores, * by the name of a team signifies that they won the toss.*

At M. A. Aziz Stadium, Chittagong, December 26, 27, 28, 29. **Dhaka won by 24 runs. Dhaka 285** (Mehrab Hossain 60, Halim Shah 57, Neeyamur Rashid 37; Tareq Aziz five for 68, Ahsanullah Hasan three for 68) **and 155** (Neeyamur Rashid 37; Tareq Aziz five for 44); **Chittagong* 237** (Azam Iqbal 63, Minhazul Abedin 78, Shabbir Khan 31; Saiful Islam three for 50, Naimur Rahman four for 68) **and 179** (Masumud Dowla 38, Akram Khan 30; Naimur Rahman three for 67, Mosaddek Hossain three for 37). *Dhaka 6 pts.*

At Abdur Rab Serniabad Stadium, Barisal, January 2, 3, 4, 5. **Dhaka won by an innings and four runs. Dhaka* 465 for seven dec.** (Halim Shah 161 not out, Mazharul Haque 171, Neeyamur Rashid 34, Sajjad Kadir 45); **Barisal 266** (Mafizul Islam 47, Safaiat Islam 51, Moniruzzaman 32, Towhid Hossain 38, Masudur Rahman 39; Naimur Rahman five for 76, Mosaddek Hossain three for 75) **and 195** (Masudur Rahman 59; Bikash Ranjan Das five for 88). *Dhaka 6 pts.*
   Halim Shah and Mazharul Haque added 258 for Dhaka's fifth wicket.

At Comilla Stadium, Comilla, January 2, 3, 4. **Chittagong won by an innings and 14 runs. Chittagong* 349** (Faisal Hossain 43, Minhazul Abedin 85, Ahsanullah Hasan 83, Extras 35; Mohammad Mostadir six for 95); **Rajshahi 142** (Mahbub Alam 38; Shabbir Khan three for 33, Ahsanullah Hasan four for 43) **and 193** (Nuruzzaman 48; Shabbir Khan four for 77, Ahsanullah Hasan four for 45). *Chittagong 6 pts.*

At M. A. G. Osmani Stadium, Sylhet, January 2, 3, 4, 5. **Drawn. Sylhet* 132** (Parvez Ahmed 36, Imtiaz Hossain 33; Jamaluddin Ahmed four for 31, Sohel Islam four for 33) **and 205** (Imtiaz Hossain 41, Ekrimul Hadi 40, Rezaul Haque 38; Sohel Islam four for 47); **Khulna 181** (Sohel Islam 37, Monirul Islam 30) **and 129 for six** (Mintu Das three for 24). *Khulna 2 pts.*

At Abdur Rab Serniabad Stadium, Barisal, January 9, 10, 11, 12. **Rajshahi won by an innings and 123 runs. Barisal* 110** (Imran Parvez five for 35) **and 172** (Hannan Sarkar 56; Alamgir Kabir three for 28, Mushfiqur Rehman three for 41); **Rajshahi 405** (Mohammad Mostadir 51, Nuruzzaman 109, Mushfiqur Rehman 115, Imran Parvez 37 not out; Shahnawaz Kabir four for 83). *Rajshahi 6 pts.*

At Mymensingh Stadium, Mymensingh, January 9, 10, 11, 12. **Dhaka won by seven wickets. Sylhet* 147** (Parvez Ahmed 59; Mohammad Rafiq four for 37, Naimur Rahman four for 32) **and 275** (Nasirul Alam 68, Rajin Saleh 109, Rezaul Haque 36; Mohammad Rafiq three for 54, Naimur Rahman four for 90); **Dhaka 308** (Sajjad Ahmed 68, Naimur Rahman 55, Mazharul Haque 43, Sajjad Kadir 54, Mohammad Rafiq 33; Rezaul Haque seven for 73) **and 117 for three** (Rashidul Haque 32, Sajjad Ahmed 32 not out). *Dhaka 6 pts.*

At Shamsul Huda Stadium, Jessore, January 9, 10, 11, 12. **Drawn. Chittagong 167** (Minhazul Abedin 48, Akram Khan 37; Jamaluddin Ahmed five for 32) **and 349 for nine dec.** (Anisul Hakim 107, Azam Iqbal 56, Faisal Hossain 41, Shabbir Khan 47; Sohel Islam five for 84); **Khulna* 259** (Raju Parvez 71, Tushar Imran 66, Asadullah Khan 35; Shafiuddin Ahmed five for 71, Shabbir Khan three for 59) **and 185 for eight** (Sajjadul Hasan 61, Mohammad Salim 32, Tushar Imran 44). *Khulna 2 pts.*

At Faridpur Stadium, Faridpur, January 16, 17. **Dhaka won by nine wickets. Barisal* 163** (Imran Ahmed 50, Shahnawaz Kabir 32; Mohammad Rafiq seven for 52, Abu Taher three for 47) **and 92** (Saiful Islam three for 21, Mohammad Rafiq four for 27); **Dhaka 211** (Rashidul Haque 39, Sohel Hossain 40, Jahangir Alam 60, Sajjad Kadir 37; Shahnawaz Kabir three for 26, Kamal Ahmed three for 27) **and 45 for one**. *Dhaka 6 pts.*

At Shamsul Huda Stadium, Jessore, January 16, 17, 18. **Sylhet won by an innings and five runs. Sylhet* 268** (Nasirul Alam 33, Rajin Saleh 70, Alok Kapali 69; Abdur Razzaq five for 67); **Khulna 62** (Tapash Baisya five for 30, Parvez Ahmed three for six) **and 201** (Raju Parvez 67, Salahuddin Ahmed 37, Sohel Islam 43; Imtiaz Hossain three for 50). *Sylhet 6 pts.*

At Rajshahi Stadium, Rajshahi, January 16, 17, 18, 19. **Rajshahi won by eight wickets. Rajshahi 377** (Rafiqul Islam 109, Anisur Rahman 135, Shamimul Haque 33 not out, Faisal Khan 34; Shafiuddin Ahmed eight for 86) **and 42 for two; Chittagong* 154** (Sadid Hossain 54, Azam Iqbal 41; Imran Parvez four for 26) **and 264** (Sadid Hossain 48, Faisal Hossain 33, Azam Iqbal 51, Shabbir Khan 38; Aminul Islam, jun. five for 52). *Rajshahi 6 pts.*

At Abdur Rab Serniabad Stadium, Barisal, January 23, 24, 25, 26. **Sylhet won by 153 runs. Sylhet 274 for eight dec.** (Rajin Saleh 130 not out; Ashfaq Ali four for 58) **and 171 for four dec.** (Parvez Ahmed 66, Imtiaz Hossain 66); **Barisal* 156** (Safaiat Islam 34, Extras 47; Hasibul Hussain six for 58) **and 136** (Safaiat Islam 50; Hasibul Hussain four for 42, Nasirul Alam three for five). *Sylhet 6 pts.*

At Mymensingh Stadium, Mymensingh, January 23, 24, 25, 26. **Drawn. Chittagong* 381** (Anisul Hakim 32, Minhazul Abedin 210; Saiful Islam four for 82) **and 286 for five** (Faisal Hossain 105 retired out, Minhazul Abedin 110 retired out, Jasimuddin 36 not out); **Dhaka 325** (Jahangir Alam 120, Sajjad Kadir 70, Saiful Islam 30, Extras 48; Debabrata Barua three for 71, Suja Irfan five for 69). *Chittagong 2 pts.*
   Minhazul Abedin's 210 lasted 463 minutes and 335 balls and included 21 fours; he followed up with 110 in the second innings, when he and Faisal Hossain retired out, and all 11 Dhaka players bowled.

At Cricket Garden, Rangpur, January 23, 24, 25, 26. **Drawn. Rajshahi* 332** (Nuruzzaman 47, Hasanuzzaman 73, Shamimul Haque 41, Faisal Khan 55 not out; Tarikul Hasan three for 82) **and 165 for six dec.** (Nuruzzaman 68); **Khulna 204** (Raju Parvez 41, Nahidul Haque 39, Asadullah Khan 32, Mohammad Salim 38; Mohammad Mostadir three for 50, Mahbub Alam five for 25) **and 113 for nine** (Sohel Islam 32, Asadullah Khan 36; Mohammad Mostadir four for 31). *Rajshahi 2 pts.*

At Abdur Rab Serniabad Stadium, Barisal, January 31, February 1, 2, 3. **Chittagong won by 197 runs. Chittagong 211** (Anisul Hakim 52, Azam Iqbal 43, Faisal Hossain 39, Minhazul Abedin 39; Ashfaq Ali three for 37, Saleh Ahmed four for 54) **and 302 for seven dec.** (Anisul Hakim 112, Jasimuddin 38, Azam Iqbal 59 not out, Shabbir Khan 36; Masudur Rahman four for 102); **Barisal* 137** (Imran Ahmed 30, Sanuar Hossain 37; Shafiuddin Ahmed three for 34, Shabbir Khan five for 43) **and 179** (Imran Ahmed 43; Shafiuddin Ahmed three for 40, Suja Irfan three for 35). *Chittagong 6 pts.*

At Bangabandhu National Stadium, Dhaka, January 31, February 1, 2, 3. **Rajshahi won by an innings and 29 runs. Khulna* 239** (Hasanuzzaman 76, Jamaluddin Ahmed 30, Extras 37; Aminul Islam, jun. four for 50) **and 268** (Sajjadul Hasan 45, Nahidul Haque 43, Hasanuzzaman 33, Abdur Razzaq 51; Faisal Khan three for 42, Mahbub Alam three for 84); **Rajshahi 536 for eight dec.** (Rafiqul Islam 87, Nuruzzaman 31, Anisur Rahman 107, Khaled Masud 201 not out, Shamimul Haque 43). *Rajshahi 6 pts.*
   Khaled Masud's 201 not out lasted 263 minutes and 232 balls and included 18 fours and one six.

At M. A. G. Osmani Stadium, Sylhet, January 31, February 1, 2, 3. **Dhaka won by an innings and 89 runs. Sylhet* 152** (Fahim Muntasir three for 59, Mohammad Rafiq three for 33) **and 153** (Rajin Saleh 49; Fahim Muntasir five for 31); **Dhaka 394** (Jahangir Alam 108, Sajjad Kadir 72 not out, Fahim Muntasir 60, Extras 45; Alok Kapali three for 74). *Dhaka 6 pts.*

At Comilla Stadium, Comilla, February 7, 8, 9, 10. **Drawn. Chittagong* 327** (Najimuddin 110, Minhazul Abedin 93 not out, Extras 38; Alok Kapali four for 102) **and 167** (Minhazul Abedin 30, Enamul Haque 44; Alok Kapali three for 29, Imran Rahim three for 27); **Sylhet 220** (Parvez Ahmed 47, Hasibul Hussain 51, Tapash Baisya 34; Enamul Haque six for 64) **and 177 for seven** (Imtiaz Hossain 78; Enamul Haque four for 59). *Chittagong 2 pts.*

At Mymensingh Stadium, Mymensingh, February 7, 8, 9, 10. **Dhaka won by seven wickets. Rajshahi* 330** (Nuruzzaman 107, Khaled Masud 79, Faisal Khan 40 not out; Mohammad Rafiq five for 85) **and 142** (Mohammad Rafiq three for 32); **Dhaka 270** (Sajjad Ahmed 35, Aminul Islam 61, Khaled Mahmud 62; Imran Parvez four for 69, Mohammad Mostadir three for 45) **and 206 for three** (Rashidul Haque 54, Sajjad Ahmed 39, Jahangir Alam 79 not out). *Dhaka 6 pts, Rajshahi 2 pts.*

At Shamsul Huda Stadium, Jessore, February 7, 8, 9, 10. **Khulna won by six wickets. Barisal 196** (Selim Shahid 31, Sanuar Hossain 63, Kamal Ahmed 44; Abdur Razzaq three for 46, Jamaluddin Ahmed three for 56) **and 266** (Sanuar Hossain 103, Saleh Ahmed 53; Jamaluddin Ahmed four for 90, Tamim Bashir four for 57); **Khulna* 393** (Nahidul Haque 55, Asadullah Khan 108, Mohammad Salim 44, Abdur Razzaq 57, Jamaluddin Ahmed 40, Tamim Bashir 30 not out; Anisur Rahman three for 52, Saleh Ahmed four for 94) **and 73 for four** (Ashfaq Ali three for 39). *Khulna 6 pts.*

At Dhanmondi Cricket Stadium, Dhaka, February 14, 15, 16, 17. **Dhaka won by ten wickets. Khulna 190** (Mohammad Salim 41, Jamaluddin Ahmed 82 not out; Mohammad Rafiq three for 38, Fahim Muntasir three for 44) **and 210 for eight dec.** (Jamaluddin Ahmed 82; Neeyamur Rashid four for 62); **Dhaka* 398** (Rashidul Haque 33, Aminul Islam 46, Halim Shah 92, Mohammad Rafiq 76, Sajjad Kadir 33, Fahim Muntasir 32 not out; Jamaluddin Ahmed three for 70) **and six for no wkt**. *Dhaka 6 pts.*

Khulna declared their second innings on the final morning, effectively conceding the match, in protest against umpiring decisions.

At Rajshahi Stadium, Rajshahi, February 14, 15, 16, 17. **Rajshahi won by an innings and 11 runs. Rajshahi 508 for eight dec.** (Nuruzzaman 161, Anisur Rahman 119, Hasanuzzaman 36, Shamimul Haque 42, Mahbub Alam 50 not out, Mohammad Mostadir 36 not out; Anisur Rahman three for 88, Ashfaq Ali three for 111); **Barisal* 307** (Imran Ahmed 45, Safaiat Islam 45, Sanuar Hossain 73, Shahin Hossain 54, Kamal Ahmed 55 not out; Aminul Islam, jun. four for 55, Mohammad Mostadir three for 17) **and 190** (Safaiat Islam 43, Kamal Ahmed 38, Shahidul Islam 30; Mohammad Mostadir five for 64, Imran Parvez three for 48). *Rajshahi 6 pts.*

At M. A. G. Osmani Stadium, Sylhet, February 14, 15, 16, 17. **Drawn. Sylhet* 303** (Parvez Ahmed 121, Alok Kapali 41, Nasirul Alam 50; Enamul Haque five for 84) **and 31 for two**; **Chittagong 345** (Minhazul Abedin 144, Azam Iqbal 62, Extras 60; Hasibul Hussain three for 75). *Chittagong 2 pts.*

At M. A. Aziz Stadium, Chittagong, February 27, 28, March 1, 2. **Drawn. Barisal 202** (Moinuzzaman 67, Anisur Rahman 56; Shabbir Khan five for 63, Enamul Haque four for 51) **and 373** (Imran Ahmed 141, Kamal Ahmed 33, Shamimul Islam 49, Anisur Rahman 39, Extras 40; Enamul Haque four for 65); **Chittagong* 267** (Nafis Iqbal 77, Azam Iqbal 40, Enamul Haque 46; Ashfaq Ali three for 44, Sanuar Hossain three for 27) **and 98 for three** (Nafis Iqbal 37, Minhazul Abedin 33). *Chittagong 2 pts.*

At Shamsul Huda Stadium, Jessore, February 27, 28, March 1, 2. **Dhaka won by 138 runs. Dhaka* 159** (Rashidul Haque 50; Tamim Bashir six for 41) **and 363 for nine dec.** (Sajjad Ahmed 38, Jahangir Alam 49, Mohammad Ashraful 31, Javed Omar 66, Halim Shah 94); **Khulna 252** (Hasanuzzaman 77; Mohammad Rafiq five for 73) **and 132** (Khaled Mahmud four for 44). *Dhaka 6 pts, Khulna 2 pts.*

At M. A. G. Osmani Stadium, Sylhet, February 27, 28, March 1, 2. **Drawn. Rajshahi* 300** (Rafiqul Islam 42, Nuruzzaman 39, Anisur Rahman 60, Mohammad Mostadir 65 not out, Extras 45; Rezaul Haque five for 65) **and 211** (Rafiqul Islam 50, Khaled Masud 69, Extras 32; Tapash Baisya three for 33, Alok Kapali three for 39); **Sylhet 283** (Parvez Ahmed 97, Rajin Saleh 75, Rana Miah 41; Aminul Islam, jun. three for 55). *Rajshahi 2 pts.*

At Abdur Rab Serniabad Stadium, Barisal, March 6, 7, 8, 9. **Drawn. Barisal* 172** (Nayan Kumar 38, Kamal Ahmed 35; Al Amin five for 27) **and 355 for seven dec.** (Imran Ahmed 70, Safaiat Islam 70, Sanuar Hossain 117 not out); **Khulna 177** (Asadullah Khan 33; Sanuar Hossain three for 18) **and 275 for five** (Raju Parvez 85, Monirul Islam 45, Jamaluddin Ahmed 33, Hasanuzzaman 52 not out, Asadullah Khan 42). *Khulna 2 pts.*

At Rajshahi Stadium, Rajshahi, March 6, 7, 8. **Rajshahi won by an innings and 20 runs. Sylhet* 82** (Ekrimul Hadi 43; Imran Parvez three for 11, Mohammad Mostadir three for 23) **and 202** (Golam Mawla 85, Rajin Saleh 42; Aminul Islam, jun. three for 44); **Rajshahi 304** (Shamimul Haque 35, Nuruzzaman 93, Extras 67; Rezaul Haque four for 59). *Rajshahi 6 pts.*

At Comilla Stadium, Comilla, March 13, 14, 15, 16. **Drawn. Chittagong* 325** (Anisul Hakim 66, Najimuddin 33, Minhazul Abedin 66, Azam Iqbal 71, Extras 31; Abdur Razzaq three for 44, Hasanuzzaman three for 49) **and 203 for seven** (Nafis Iqbal 61 not out, Golam Mortaza 56; Tamim Bashir three for 38); **Khulna 248** (Raju Parvez 37, Asadullah Khan 102, Extras 34; Shabbir Khan six for 76). *Chittagong 2 pts.*

At Cricket Garden, Rangpur, March 13, 14, 15, 16. **Dhaka won by 109 runs. Dhaka* 299** (Jahangir Alam 33, Khaled Mahmud 66, Sajjad Kadir 34, Fahim Muntasir 52, Mohammad Sharif 36 not out; Sohel Rana three for 83) **and 169** (Mohammad Ashraful 64, Fahim Muntasir 30; Aminul Islam, jun. five for 59, Imran Parvez three for 22); **Rajshahi 173** (Rafiqul Islam 66; Arafat Sunny four for 33) **and 186** (Shamimul Haque 59, Nuruzzaman 31; Fahim Muntasir five for 34). *Dhaka 6 pts.*

At M. A. G. Osmani Stadium, Sylhet, March 13, 14, 15, 16. **Sylhet won by 49 runs. Sylhet* 200** (Imtiaz Hossain 36, Rajin Saleh 69; Ashfaq Ali three for 27, Saleh Ahmed three for 60, Sanuar Hossain three for 38) **and 206** (Imtiaz Hossain 44, Parvez Ahmed 40; Saleh Ahmed three for 33, Kamal Ahmed three for 41); **Barisal 151** (Shahin Hossain 42; Alok Kapali seven for 33, Enamul Haque three for 44) **and 206** (Kamal Ahmed 35; Rezaul Haque four for 47, Alok Kapali four for 60). *Sylhet 6 pts.*

NATIONAL CRICKET LEAGUE WINNERS

| 2000-01 | Biman Bangladesh Airlines | 2001-02 | Dhaka |

CRICKET IN KENYA, 2002

By JASMER SINGH

With their eye on the World Cup and, in the longer term, Test status, Kenya planned a full calendar for 2002. By early 2003, they had cemented their position as the leading non-Test side and set a new high-water mark when they stunned Sri Lanka, Zimbabwe and the rest of the cricket universe by reaching the semi-finals of the World Cup. They managed some other impressive one-day results – though not quite on the same scale – and can feel increasingly confident of full ICC membership.

Their year began in Sri Lanka, where they met a formidable Sri Lanka A squad boasting 12 internationals. Well beaten in the three first-class matches, Kenya did far better in the shorter games, with Steve Tikolo beginning a profitable individual year with a century, and helping set up a 2–1 win. It was the start of a bad run for Sri Lankan sides against Kenya.

Their dominance in the one-day game continued when MCC were thrashed in February, despite bringing a squad bulging with county players, including Aftab Habib, who had Test experience. Tikolo again proved one of the most effective – and entertaining – players outside the Test world, hitting two quickfire hundreds and taking four for 53 in the second match. After a 5–0 defeat, the MCC captain, Hampshire's Will Kendall, admitted that Kenya's "explosive batting, disciplined bowling and outstanding fielding were a class above anything MCC could muster".

Another World Cup warning was sounded in April. Facing Canada, Holland, Namibia, Sri Lanka A and Zimbabwe A, Kenya stormed to victory in the Six Nations Challenge in Namibia, losing only one game. Maurice Odumbe was the tournament's leading wicket-taker with 12, though it was a solid team effort that scuppered Sri Lanka A in the final. After this, drawing a one-day series 2–2 against Punjab, one of the leading Indian provinces and 2001-02 Ranji Trophy semi-finalists, was slightly disappointing. During the series in July and August, Thomas Odoyo made the biggest impact for Kenya, taking three for 24 in the third match with his fast-medium, and two for 14 in the fourth. He also chipped in with an unbeaten 63 to help win the second. But Tikolo wasn't eclipsed for long and he belted 178 and an unbeaten 51 in the four-day match, which Kenya won. Next up were Bangladesh A, who arrived with several Test players but went home chastened. After clinging on for a draw in the three-day match, they were whitewashed 3–0 in the limited-overs series, as Kenya maintained an impressive record against Bangladeshi sides: by March 2003, they had lost just once in seven one-day internationals. Tikolo hit 168 in the second match, Kenya's best in a one-day game.

An altogether stiffer test came later in August when security problems prompted the Pakistan Cricket Board to select Kenya as the venue for their PSO Tri-Nation Tournament. However, the Kenyan Cricket Association's preparations were thrown into confusion by the sports minister, Francis Nyenze. Having previously accused the KCA of financial mismanagement and dissolved the association, only to be overruled by the High Court, Nyenze tried to force the PCB into bypassing the KCA and dealing with another body, the National Sports Council. But the Kenyan president, Daniel arup Moi, pulled rank on his minister and, in the end, the KCA put on a well-organised tournament and gained valuable experience ahead of the two World Cup games Kenya were scheduled to host. (In the event, New Zealand refused to travel to Kenya, citing security fears, but Kenya made the most of the remaining fixture, famously despatching Sri Lanka with some ease.) The PSO did not go quite as well, and they lost all four matches to Pakistan and Australia. Even so, they worried a complacent Australian side in their last game. However, there was a notable individual success, with only Glenn McGrath proving more economical than Martin Suji.

The ICC Champions Trophy in September provided Kenya with another chance to measure themselves against the Test nations, though they could not upset South Africa or West Indies. But when Namibia visited in November, they reasserted their domination of the non-Test world, grabbing a 3–1 victory in the one-day series, only to be reminded of the gap still to be bridged when, in December, they lost a series against Zimbabwe 2–0 (with one game unfinished after rain). The third match was a thrashing, by nine wickets inside 45 overs. It was an inappropriate end to a good year.

In the domestic game, the National League consisted of three-day games between zonal teams. The Aga Khan Sports Club won the eight-team first division, while the second division, including sides from an up-country towns of Nakuru and Eldoret, was won by the Simba Union Club. The national double-wicket tournament, involving 16 pairs and most of the top players, was won by Martin Suji and Kennedy Obuya Otieno, who beat Steve Tikolo and Maurice Ouma. Meanwhile, schools cricket continued to thrive: Nairobi and Mombasa each had 24 teams participating in their leagues and the Under-15 and Under-17 competitions were very successful. Both age groups (boys and girls) participated in East African regional tournaments, facing Uganda and Tanzania.

It was a significant 12 months on the development front, as the push for Test status continued. Three more grounds were upgraded to international standard, the administrative structure was improved and an academy, at the Simba Union ground in Nairobi, was launched with the help of the ICC. A second academy is planned. Two Kenyans will continue to tread the corridors of power at the ICC, with the KCA chairman, Jimmy Rayani, and vice-chairman, Harilal Singh, re-elected to the board and the cricket committee (playing) respectively. Cricket is now firmly established in the country, and the game has healthy roots among the indigenous population. In 1986, a national squad of 14 included only four indigenous Kenyans; now the figure is 15 from 18. All told, Kenyan cricket has never been healthier.

CRICKET IN THE NETHERLANDS, 2002

By DAVE HARDY

In the year between their long-awaited ICC Trophy title and the 2003 World Cup, Holland suffered an alarming dip in fortune. Of 13 official matches they won three and lost ten. At the ICC Champions Trophy in September they mustered only 86 in reply to Sri Lanka's 292 for six, and in their next match Pakistan took only 16.2 overs to pass a target of 137. The Dutch also lost warm-ups against Bangladesh and Kenya. In July, fourth place in the European Championship was well below expectations after triumphs in 1998 and 2000. An embarrassing loss to Italy was followed by defeats against the England Board XI and Ireland; the two wins came against Scotland and Denmark. Earlier, in April, they had been whitewashed in a Western Cape tournament (by Lancashire, Western Province and a President's XI) and, in the Six Nations Challenge in Namibia, beat only Canada, going down to Sri Lanka A, Zimbabwe A, Kenya and Namibia. However, a spirited display at the World Cup – including a first senior one-day international win, against Namibia – brought hope that 2002 was only a temporary lull.

One major change was the jettisoning (or voluntary retirement) of experienced foreign-born players. The ICC Champions Trophy marked the first time Holland had taken the field in a major tournament without foreign imports since the mid-eighties. In 1986 the Englishman, Steve Atkinson, and Rupert Gomes from Guyana helped the Dutch reach their first ICC Trophy final; thereafter Gomes, Flavian Aponso (Sri Lanka), Peter Cantrell (Australia), Roger Bradley (New Zealand) and, most prominent of all, Nolan Clarke from Barbados were the mainstays of Dutch batting – Clarke played 99 matches. Furthermore, two Pakistanis, Ahmed Zulfiqar and Asim Khan, were regulars throughout the 1990s but largely absent in 2002. The supply of indigenous bowlers has been more plentiful, including three of the four Dutch-born county cricketers: Paul Jan Bakker, Andre van Troost and Roland Lefebvre.

There is no substitute for experience and class, as the former Australian coach, Bob Simpson, warned when he was contracted to help World Cup preparations. He thought Holland had plenty of talent, but made the wrong choices too often; Simpson also pointed to a lack of athleticism, a long-standing weakness.

On the domestic scene, 2002 will be remembered for a match suspended because of mob violence. Sporadic physical confrontations and abuse of umpires had already led to the introduction of football-style bookings, but this incident was unprecedented. A bitter feud had been simmering within the Jinnah club (from Abcoude, just south of Amsterdam and founded in 1995 by immigrant Pakistanis) and came to the boil on August 18. An unruly mob, aggrieved at recent policy decisions, surged on to the field during a premier league match between Jinnah and Hermes DVS, and attacked the Jinnah batsmen (members of the rival faction) with knives, bats and stumps. Everyone – including the fielders and umpires – ran for their lives, except the chairman of the Dutch cricket association, Rene van Ierschot, who attempted single-handedly to defuse the situation. Anticipating trouble, the association had switched the match to a neutral venue, and the police were quickly on the scene. Some players were injured, but fortunately none seriously. Jinnah were expelled from the league and replaced by Bijlmer of Amsterdam, another up-and-coming ethnic minority team, who gained promotion after only 13 seasons.

This unsavoury affair overshadowed Voorburg CC's triumph in the Dutch league. Winning all but two of their 18 matches, the team from the Hague finished comfortably ahead of their neighbours, Quick CC. Voorburg fielded a mix of Dutch and foreign-born cricketers, who all played their parts: Tim de Leede was leading native run-scorer with 732 at 40, and the young wicket-keeper Atse Buurman caught 23 batsmen and stumped another 17.

CRICKET ROUND THE WORLD, 2002

Edited by TONY MUNRO

AFGHANISTAN

Afghan refugees returning from Pakistan after the fall of the Taliban government have helped raise cricket's following here. It is early days in the sport's development, but that makes them exciting times. The Afghanistan Cricket Board do their best to promote the game but are hampered by a lack of facilities and equipment, so the British Embassy in Kabul has been collecting resources to be distributed to clubs at all levels. Several English counties have already donated kit. The national side have been invited by the Pakistan Cricket Board to take part in the Cornelius Trophy in Karachi in 2002-03, and can only benefit from exposure to quality cricket. Against the largely British International Security Assistance Force (ISAF) team they played three exhibition matches on a rudimentary pitch, running out easy winners each time. Reflecting the changing political climate, the major domestic competition was renamed the King Zahir Shah Tournament. All 15 provincial teams took part; Khost, from Paktiya Province won. The Abdul Haq Cricket Academy, based in Jalalabad, travelled to Pakistan to participate in the Frontier Gold Cup. **Taj Malik and A. M. Banks**

ANGOLA

In Angola, a country devastated by civil war since gaining independence from Portugal in 1975, cricket has formed a bond between the Indian and Pakistani communities. Kashmir and other issues are forgotten as around 20 hardy souls meet three times a week to play next to a floodlit football ground in the capital, Luanda. It is a taste of home life, apparently instigated when two Indians began playing with a piece of wood and a tennis ball in 1994. **Narinder Pal Singh**

ANTARCTICA

The packed slip cordon at the annual Casey Base cricket match has little to do with swing, seam or – with temperatures hovering around freezing – conserving body heat. It's more a question of knowing that a missed catch will condemn the guilty fielder to a trek down treacherous icy slopes to fetch the ball from a small meltwater lake. The fixture is traditionally played each Casey Day (February 12), the anniversary of the founding of the Australian Antarctic Research Station, some 3,880km due south of Perth and 2,580km from the South Pole. Teams comprise Australian scientists and visitors of varying nationalities. The pitch is a cement helipad, ensuring generous bounce. Naturally, local rules apply: should the tennis ball – this isn't the place to break the triple-glazed windows – ricochet off the Red Shed, the two-storey living quarters, it's four; over the roof is six; hitting the station leader at the barbecue brings instant dismissal, which still somehow proves an irresistible target. Post-match analysis is often fuelled by ample quantities of Antarctica's own home brew, known as Penguin's Piss. **John Rich, Casey Base**

ARGENTINA

This was perhaps Argentine cricket's most historic season. In March, Buenos Aires hosted the second Americas Cup (the only ICC-sanctioned tournament to be held in South America outside Guyana). The United States won a well-organised, but sadly rain-marred event, with Canada, the Cayman Islands, Bermuda, Bahamas and Argentina finishing in that order. Despite huge enthusiasm, the home team lost all four games. The Under-19s, making their debut at international youth level, fared better in Bermuda,

Shot of the Antarctic: Casey Base, home of the Australian Antarctic Research Station, is quite probably cricket's most southerly outpost.

beating the United States and finishing fourth. At home, Belgrano won both the First Division League Championship and the Robin Stuart Shield, defeating St Alban's in the final. Lomas took the Second Division and the Saturday Championship, St Alban's the Third Division and the Max Challenge League. Major awards were given to Matias Paterlini of St Alban's (cricketer of the year), Pablo Ferguson (Belgrano, batting) and Andre Perez Rivero (St Alban's, bowling). Before the Americas Cup opening ceremony, the long-serving administrator Maurice Runnacles was honoured when a turf wicket at Corimayo was named after him. Meanwhile, Chris Nino stepped down after a decade's dedicated service as chairman of the Argentine Cricket Association. **Grant Dugmore**

AZERBAIJAN

Despite financial hardship, Baku CC enjoyed an extremely successful year. The ICC donated a Flicx pitch, and enough money was raised to buy a range of new equipment. We seem to have found a good home, at least temporarily, at the International School of Azerbaijan. We played our first game outside Baku, when an exhibition match was held at an agricultural fair in Quba, in the north of the country. Things could have gone better: the few locals who braved torrential rain saw a lifting ball strike a batsman on the nose, resulting in buckets of blood. Undeterred, Baku CC are planning another match this year. There are now encouraging numbers of regular Azeri cricketers, and some may turn into useful players with the right coaching. **Alum Bati**

BAHRAIN

Bahraini cricket, which has altered little in 65 years, is now being buffeted by the first winds of change. As yet much remains the same. Fiercely competitive matches are played on concrete wickets, sometimes covered with coir or composite matting, and with stony, dusty desert outfields. League and cup cricket is limited to Fridays, and Pakistani teams, strengthened by professionals, dominate all senior competitions. The chaotic league system lives on, with disparate groups organising matches between the island's 50-odd teams. And cricket here still has its vagaries: in the final of the Ramadan Cup Plate, afternoon prayers prevented Godfathers CC from taking the field on time, meaning Awali CC began their reply with darkness more of a threat than the Godfathers. In a game against the visiting Royal Navy, Awali's Australian-born wicket-keeper, Paul Moran, shed his gloves and – purely to give the Poms a few easy runs – turned his arm over. He promptly took five wickets without conceding a run, including a hat-trick: all five were bowled. Tragically, Moran, a television cameraman, was killed in the first few days of the Iraq war in March 2003.

High-profile visits by Asian Cricket Council representatives such as Mushtaq Mohammad, Madan Lal and Iqbal Sikander have brought significant developments in Bahraini cricket. There is now an inter-school competition, while Gulf-wide tournaments are being arranged for Under-11s and Under-13s. Approaching 300 children regularly attend practice sessions, and a quota system will ensure that more Bahraini children play in school teams. In the annual Desert Ashes, Australia (with valuable assistance from New Zealanders, South Africans and Zambians) beat England to end a seven-year drought. **Guy Parker**

BELGIUM

Royal Brussels, Belgium's oldest club, won their first title to end the five-year reign of Pakistan Greens. The headlines, however, were grabbed by Khan CC. One hand apparently on the trophy, they were docked all points by the Belgian Cricket Federation (BCF) after tempers flared in the vital clash with Royal Brussels. Khan went to appeal but lost, and were thrown out of the 2003 competition after refusing to apologise to the umpires who had allegedly been abused in the fracas. Legal action is being considered. Royal Brussels were worthy champions, as a win and a draw over Greens showed. Their experienced batsman, Faroukh Malik, was the league's outstanding player, scoring an unbeaten century against Antwerp Indians CC and totalling over 250 runs. Optimists of Luxembourg bounced back to the top flight after a year in the second division; Crescent were promoted in their stead. In 2003, a new club, Kortrijk, joins the league, extending cricket's geographical spread almost to the French border and, after a year's absence, Mechelen Eagles, a founder member of the BCF, makes a welcome return. Watching all this is the new BCF President, Ted Vorzanger, whose endless hard work and wisdom has now been recognised. On the development front, Happy Cricket has been introduced to several new schools in Flanders, building on existing schemes. The Under-13s finished as runners-up at their European tournament in Italy after losing to the eventual winners, Israel, by the narrowest of margins. **Colin Wolfe**

BOTSWANA

Cricket has struggled to gain a foothold in Botswana ever since the construction of the Bulawayo–Mafeking railway-line brought it here in the 19th century, but things are looking up. Although the game had occasionally survived in private primary schools, generations were lost to softball and football. Now, though, thanks to frequent broadcasting of South Africa's matches and significant development work, there are around 30 primary and secondary schools regularly playing in an informal league. The national team, including four native Botswanans, surprised both Kenyan and Namibian development sides before losing the final of the Africa Cup to South Africa in Zambia. And the Under-15s, similarly made up of nationals and expatriates, were competitive against Namibia, Zambia, Malawi and Lesotho. Courses sponsored by the ICC have produced nearly 80 Level-1 qualified coaches. We are also proud that the capital, Gaborone, has one of the continent's few floodlit cricket grounds outside South Africa, even if stray cattle and the odd donkey need to be shooed off before play. More needs to be done: Botswana has fewer than 400 players using just 30 pitches. **Jack Sands**

BRAZIL

The 2002 season was perhaps the busiest in 130 years of Brazilian cricket. Among the many highlights were ICC Affiliate membership, a new trophy series, major improvements to the Curitiba and Brasília grounds, the creation of teams in Macaé and Foz do Iguaçu, coverage in *Wisden Cricket Monthly* and the BBC and ICC websites, and a good showing by the national team at the South American Championships in Buenos Aires. In Brazil, cricket – like all sports – is played with enthusiasm. It needs to be, as the three main grounds have their peculiarities. In Brasília, the ground is part of City Park, where, as well as 16 trees in the playing area, cricketers have to negotiate a constant stream of dogs, soccer players, frisbee throwers and parents with pushchairs all casually strolling past the stumps. In São Paulo, the wicket lies between rugby and soccer pitches. If at any time teams intent upon either form of football burst out of an adjoining clubhouse, the cricketers are forced to retreat to the nets (where a metal bar six feet off the ground halfway down the track ensures anyone with a high action will have the ball ricochet towards their face). Curitiba offers other problems: the field is home to several quero-quero birds that lay their eggs in the grass. Anyone coming within 30 feet is fearlessly dive-bombed, allowing alert batsmen to pinch extra runs. Despite – possibly because of – all this, cricket here remains thoroughly enjoyable. In 2003, Brasília, São Paulo and Curitiba will vie for the Commonwealth Ambassador's Trophy, awarded by the Ambassador of noted cricket powerhouse, Cameroon. **Norman Baldwin**

BRUNEI DARUSSALAM

The past year brought much change in Brunei cricket, little for the better. On the positive side, there are now cricket facilities close to the capital, which has reduced the travelling time for most players by two hours. Sadly, though, the number of teams in the league has fallen from six to three in just a few years, after the Panaga club folded in 2002. The precise format of the league championship remains unclear, with the clubs in disagreement. The season finished on a sad note when it was decided that the Galfar knockout cup would be replaced by six-a-side and Super Eight cricket. If the national association fails to realise that cricket at this level should be played for fun, there may soon be none left in Brunei. **Derek Thursby**

CANADA

The financial hangover from hosting the 2001 ICC Trophy and the loss of income from the cancelled Sahara Cup series (when India took on Pakistan in Toronto) dimmed Canadian cricket's celebration at qualifying for the 2003 World Cup. Preparations for that and the Under-19 World Cup in New Zealand in January 2002 were affected. Even so, the Under-19s surprisingly tied with Bangladesh – their senior colleagues went one better in South Africa in February 2003 – before losing their last two games heavily. An elite Canada Cup national youth event later provided selectors with fresh talent, though an Under-19 team made up of players with no experience of three-day cricket competed unsuccessfully in a West Indian regional tournament. More encouragingly, Canada made history by winning two games in the 2002 Red Stripe tournament in St. Lucia, but lost badly to Trinidad & Tobago. In the Americas Cup in Buenos Aires, Canada finished second behind the US. Lack of funding and/or sponsorship stymied attempts to give the national team further top-flight competition and to restore the three-day match against the US, the world's oldest international fixture. Sponsors, private and public, are still very much needed. The achievement of the national team in qualifying for the World Cup was recognised when they reached the final of the Team of the Year in the Annual Canadian Sports Awards. **Geoff Edwards**

CHILE

The proudest moment for the Chilean Cricket Association (CCA) in 2002 came when it achieved Affiliate Membership of the ICC. This is a considerable boost, particularly in attracting recognition from local sporting organisations. On the field, Las Condes fended off Prince of Wales, La Dehesa and Santiago to win the new annual Metropolitan Cricket Trophy. Chile now has around 100 registered players, including three ladies. The oldest regular is 65, the youngest 13. The balance is likely to swing in favour of youth as four schools now offer coaching, with over 100 youngsters, male and female, enjoying the game. Indoor cricket is now played on artificial grass in a gym, luring players who might otherwise go into cricket hibernation. **Anthony Adams**

CHINA

The revival of the game in Beijing and a swelling of player numbers in Shanghai were important events in cricket's busiest year in China, though the highlight was the Shanghai International Sixes. An All-Star side including former Test players, Kiran More, Gladstone Small, Kim Hughes, Tom Hogan, Amal Silva and Courtney Browne headed a 12-team international field. A heavy downpour on the last day meant play could continue only with a tennis ball, but the weather did not dampen competitive spirit, and all three finals went to the last ball. Hong Kong CC won the Cup, beating the intriguingly named Beijing Ducks. The Shanghai Cavaliers also spent an unforgettable week at the wonderful Chiang Mai Sixes in Thailand. In the 11-a-side game, England retained the fiercely contested Virgin Shanghai Ashes, but Australia bounced back to beat their Kiwi rivals in the Beijing Anzac challenge. It is hoped to register cricket with the government, introduce the game to local schools and, with an eye to encouraging greater participation from locals, find more indoor venues. During the season, links were forged with the Asian Cricket Council when the former Sri Lankan Test player, Rumesh Ratnayake, visited. **Mike Tsemelis**

COSTA RICA

The revival of Costa Rican cricket, mentioned here recently, regained lost impetus when Affiliate Membership of the ICC was achieved. In on-field action, Costa Rica beat Southern California's Hollywood Golden Oldies CC at home in late 2001, lost two games away to Panama in April before visiting Nicaragua in December 2002, where they shared a two-match series. Finding a suitable venue remains a problem: grounds at the German school in San José, the French *lycée*, and in the port city of Limón, the original home of cricket in this country, were all used. Encouragingly, though, practice nets were established at an American country day school. It is hoped participation in the ICC Western Caribbean Classic, postponed from 2002, and the recruitment of more players, will spark further momentum. **T. Richard Illingworth**

CZECH REPUBLIC

Cricket in the Czech Republic enjoyed another year of progress, even if most Czechs remained oblivious of its attractions. Prague CC, formed in 1997, were joined by Olomouc, and there is a chance of a third club, at Ostrava. Several cities, including Prague and Olomouc, offer coaching in some schools, and around 600 Czech children have now played cricket. Adults, meanwhile, can sign up for twice-weekly summer nets sessions in the capital, and an indoor league may follow in 2003. Prague CC enjoyed a busy season, reaching the final of the Golden Duck tournament in Lodi, Italy, and doing well – four wins, three losses and a draw – in various friendlies against Munich International, Cricketers Anonymous, Berlin and the Dutch side Haarlem Wolves in a two-day game. Prague welcomed teams from Olomouc and Bratislava, another new club over the border in Slovakia, and won both. Two young Czechs who discovered cricket in 2002 went on to notable achievements. Lukas Fencl, a convert from softball, adjusted so well that he scored the first century by a Czech cricketer, while Magda Pokludova, who went to Bath on a student exchange, was representing Somerset in the Women's County Championships by August. The next major challenge is to find a Czech-speaking full-time development officer. **Tony Brennan**

DENMARK

Further financial cutbacks hampered progress in a country that, in its time, has tasted victory against every ICC Associate Member it has played bar Sri Lanka. Even so, Denmark whitewashed an MCC side 3–0 in Copenhagen, before travelling to Belfast for the European Championships and proving they are continental Europe's second-strongest team, after Holland. If Amjad Khan, Kent's successful new-ball bowler, had been available, they might have done better still. On the domestic scene, the long-reigning champions, Svanholm, held their place, while the runners-up, Glostrup, gained consolation in taking the knockout cup against Husum in Schleswig. The Pakistani club Norrebro finished third in the Elite Division, while Herning were relegated and replaced by another club with a strong Pakistani presence, KB of Copenhagen. Otherwise, it was the new cricket centre, Svanholm Parken at Brondby, that made the greatest impression. The Forty Clubs held their annual triangular tournament here and, for the third successive year, SGSCC of Holland won. **Peter S. Hargreaves**

EGYPT

Cricket in Egypt is in the early stages of development. The newly formed Egyptian Cricket Association plan to develop the game within schools. Egypt also aims to field a team in the next Africa Cup. Negotiations are in train with an Australian company for our first synthetic cricket pitch to be installed sometime in 2003. **Damian Johnson**

FIJI

The prestigious Dewar Shield, a magnificent silver trophy inlaid with a cricketing scene, remains chained to the chief's house in Tubou, after the defending champions beat Suva. Situated on the remote island of Lakeba, Tubou has for over 30 years defeated all-comers in the three-day, two-innings Shield matches. The fixture began a busy season in which Moce (Suva), Counties (Nadi/Lautoka) and Duavata (Labasa) won their respective competitions. Suva Crusaders exploited a sad lack of visiting overseas teams to win the annual Crompton Cup. At youth level, Lakeba won the second schools inter-district tournament. In the Pacifica Cup, held in Samoa, involving seven South Pacific nations, Fiji lost to their traditional rivals and the eventual winners, Papua New Guinea, but gained valuable experience for the younger players. The ICC development programme and the New South Wales Cricket Association again provided enormous assistance, including the funding of a full-time operations manager and three full-time development officers, as well as visits from NSWCA coaches. Despite rugby being played almost all year round, cricket in Fiji is flourishing. **Peter Knight**

FINLAND

Success for the national side at the ECC Representative Festival in Zagreb in 2002 – they beat Croatia and Slovenia – was a welcome reward for Finnish Cricket Association officials who had worked hard to give cricket healthy roots. Helsinki CC was formed in 1974, but cricket was slow to establish itself. It expanded in the mid-1990s, and the creation of the FCA, together with help from the European Cricket Council, has increased participation so that around one-fifth of the country's 350 cricketers are

Finnish citizens. Helsinki CC won the eight-team league from the 2001 champions, SKK, while the newly formed Espoo CC ended an encouraging third. Another new side, the Finnish Naval Academy CC, joined MTS as the second team not made up of ex-pats. Meanwhile, women's friendlies were played between SKK of Helsinki, Tampere CC and Guttsta of Sweden. A Spirit of Cricket weekend was held in May, and in July, more than 20 teams from Finland, Britain, Estonia and Sweden battled for the SKK Cricket Sixes. The elements continue to make cricket in Finland a singular experience: a while back, play was stopped when an elk galloped out of the woods, and early in the 2002 season bowlers ran over snow on their run-ups. **Andy Armitage**

FRANCE

Perhaps the achievement of France's season was not the mixed bag of results, but fielding teams in four international tournaments for the first time. The Under-17s narrowly failed to retain their title in Gibraltar, and a young Under-13 side struggled in Italy where Laura Codrons, from Drancy, was the only girl taking part; both teams were selected after an inaugural youth tournament in Chauny. A rejuvenated senior side defeated Portugal and Austria in Belfast at the European Championships, where the Guadeloupean off-spinner Guy Brumant collected six wickets at 16.5 and averaged 32 with the bat. The best results came indoors at the ECC Championships in Belgium, where the Under-21s won four games out of six, defeating the eventual finalists Ireland largely thanks to rousing leg-spin from Cindy Paquin, the tournament's sole female player. Kent, led by Martin McCague, crossed the Channel for a televised indoor tournament in St-Omer, but France's return visit to Folkestone for the four-nation Kent European Festival was washed out. In the final of the club championship, Gymkhana, inspired by Javed Ijaz, defeated Paris Université by eight wickets. Off the field, Olivier Dubaut replaced Didier Marchois after five years' outstanding service as national chairman, and a full-time development officer was appointed. **Simon Hewitt**

GERMANY

Only a six-run defeat by the eventual winners, Gibraltar, prevented a youthful German team from pocketing the European Championship second-division title at Belfast, after the two sides finished level on points. Four players who emerged from the Deutscher Cricket Bund (DCB) youth system were among six changes from Germany's 2001 ICC Trophy squad. Farooq Ahmed, making his debut for Germany, was the man of the tournament for nabbing 18 wickets, including six for 24 against Gibraltar, while another newcomer, Anees Butt, headed the division's batting averages with 76. Butt produced the performance of the tournament when he crashed an unbeaten 75-ball 102 against Israel. His partner in an opening stand of 123 was Mark Broderson, who tiptoed to seven from 47 deliveries. At the ECC level, Germany's colts lost their promotion/relegation battle against Denmark in Copenhagen, the Under-17s went undefeated in Gibraltar and the Under-13s finished fourth in Italy. At home, Pak Alemi (northern league) won the 2001 German club championship final, postponed because of September 11. Pak Alemi, based in Hamburg, defeated Frankfurt in an exciting match to become Germany's first champions from the north. Dagmar Braun was elected president of the newly formed eight-team Bavarian Cricket Association – the first time a regional association had chosen a woman. **Brian Fell**

GIBRALTAR

Although Gibraltar's defence of their European Championship Second Division title in Belfast was the most noticeable feature of 2002, perhaps the most notable was cricket's continued infiltration into local schools. Philip Hudson, our youth development officer, has greatly increased the number of talented youngsters playing cricket; some are now pushing for national selection. They had ample opportunities, competing at the ECC Indoor Championship in Belgium in February and ECC age-group tournaments at home and in Italy. Our most promising young cricketers also attended coaching camps in England and Spain. At home, UKCCC won all three major trophies, while Calpe CC triumphed in the popular midweek evening league. Gibraltar CC won the National Day six-a-side trophy. Finally, the Arden Taverners, from the English Midlands, beat UKCCC but lost to a GCA Chairman's XI. **T. J. Finlayson**

HONG KONG

The high point in the busy calendar of Hong Kong cricket was the return in November 2001of the International Sixes tournament to the Kowloon Cricket Club. Pakistan were winners in the Cup, while Hong Kong lost the Bowl final to India. Australia finished last. In South-East Asian tournaments, the seniors triumphed in Thailand and the Under-13s were successful in Singapore; the Under-15s finished second at home. The Under-19s were runners-up to Papua New Guinea in the East Asia–Pacific qualifiers in Fiji. At home, Hong Kong CC had a wonderful season, Scorpions winning the nine-team Sunday League and narrowly losing the Cup final to Little Sai Wan. Nomads completed the Saturday League and Cup double by beating Hong Kong University and Tartars respectively. The Saturday League comprises 16 teams. Youth cricket continues to thrive: 26 teams entered the four junior leagues, 46 the Playground League, made up of sides from local schools. Superteam became the fourth community sports club. Cricket was also played at Po Kong Village, Hong Kong's first new ground since 1974. A second pitch is planned. **John Cribbin**

IRAN

Since cricket's revival here in 1993, Iranian officials had struggled to gain international recognition. So they were overjoyed when, after a seven-day inspection tour, the Asian Cricket Council development officer Iqbal Sikander recommended ACC and subsequent ICC Affiliate membership. He visited Tehran and several regional centres, and was impressed by the standard of play and facilities. Until the 1979 Islamic Revolution, cricket was the domain of migrant workers and the diplomatic community, but the return of nationals from abroad has ensured that 98 per cent of participants are Iranian, the remainder long-term residents from the subcontinent. About 20 teams from around the country play matches in regular leagues, tournaments and friendlies. Hossein Ali Salimian, an Iranian national who captained university teams while studying in Pakistan, has been appointed national coach. **Juggoo Sawhney**

ISRAEL

Israel's first gold medal at ECC junior level made up for the national team's indifferent performance at the European Championships in Belfast. The Under-13s won all five games in Italy, aided by Rueve Bergman's unerring knack of winning the toss. In a team of great maturity, the two-pronged spin attack mesmerised opponents – and just three months after his first-ever game our wicket-keeper made 11 dismissals. This, together with a silver from the Under-15s in 2001, is reward for the vast amounts of time and money invested in the youth programme. Around 750 school children are playing each week, and the best selected for intensive training at our new cricket academy in the holidays. The senior side showed signs of a fighting spirit despite squandering winning positions against Portugal and Gibraltar. Herschel Gutman, Isaac Massil and the 15-year-old newcomer, Danny Hotz, all excelled against France, when Israel waltzed home by 130 runs; against Austria, victory came by 135. Lions Lod, boasting at least eight national representatives, won the league for the fifth time in six years, ahead of a youthful Netanya and a Tel Aviv side who surprised all. Sadly, the three Ashdod teams, powerhouses of Israeli cricket in the late 1980s, are in decline. The return of the Dutchman, Roland Lefebvre, as an ECC coach, and a restructured league provide optimism for 2003. **Stanley Perlman**

ITALY

A season of joy in 2002 followed one of sorrow in 2001, when Italy withdrew from the ICC Trophy. In what the Federazione Cricket Italiano regarded as a vindication of its actions, the ICC introduced new rules allowing citizens born abroad to compete in official tournaments. In the European Championships just three weeks later came a dramatic one-run win over Holland, winners of that ICC Trophy. It was Italy's finest result. Good performances against an ECB XI (the eventual champions) and Ireland (the hosts) followed, confirming Italy's status in the top flight of continental cricket before the euphoria was tempered by heavy losses to Scotland and Denmark. Domestically, Pianoro retained the Championship, their seventh in nine seasons, comfortably defeating Murri Catania, from Sicily, in the finals. Brera Milan won the Italian Cup, annihilating Bologna, and Capannelle en route to their first trophy. Euratom took the Under-13 and Capannelle the Under-15 titles, while Cirnechi Catania remained women's champions. After nine years in which Italian cricket has taken huge strides, Doug Ferguson retired as national coach. His replacement is the former South Australia and Lancashire all-rounder, Joe Scuderi, who is player-coach. **Simone Gambino**

JAPAN

Japan won their first international during the East Asia Pacific Eights, in Perth. In fact, they didn't just win one, they won four, beating South Korea and Indonesia twice each, and losing only to ACB Aborigines in the final. The women have a chance to emulate the men when they make their international debut in The Netherlands in 2003 for the IWCC Trophy. On the club scene, top honours went to Tokyo Bay Giants, the Kanto League champions, though significantly two Japanese teams outplayed their expatriate opponents to contest the League's second division final. In women's cricket, Team Flying Flapper beat their rivals, Fuji Far East Cricket Club, to top spot. Development continues to gather pace: in Chiba Prefecture alone, 3,000 juniors have been introduced to cricket, and the government now allows greater exposure in schools. The Japan Cricket Association is keen that the ICC appoint a full-time administrator to capitalise on the outstanding growth of Japanese cricket. **Naoya Miyaji**

LIBYA

The growth of Libyan cricket continued in 2002: four new clubs, two in Tripoli and two in Benghazi, took the total to 16. Several Arabs are now playing, introduced to the game either while studying abroad or by Pakistani friends living in Libya. More are likely to follow. Libyan officials hope a visit by the ICC's African development manager, Hoosain Ayob in 2003, will allow them to apply for Affiliate Membership the following year. The state of concrete pitches continues to test the fastest of reflexes: in the past, a player lost his life after a knee injury became infected, while another lost an eye. Insurance companies have not been persuaded to become sponsors. **Arfat Malik**

LUXEMBOURG

Despite a wet start to the season, cricket in the Grand Duchy experienced another bright year. The LCF–Crosscomm League, contested by seven teams and involving over 100 players, was won again by Walferdange Optimists, ahead of Communities and Star (who won the annual six-a-side competition). Optimists, who had perhaps their strongest squad in ten years, also clinched the title in the Belgian second division to make an immediate return to the first. The search continues for a second venue so that the reliance on Luxembourg's only ground, at Walferdange, can be reduced. It was renamed the Pierre Werner Cricket Ground in honour of the former prime minister, "father of the euro" and OCC honorary president, who died in 2002. He will be sadly missed. Further developments are planned at the ground, including four-bay nets and a new artificial pitch – the existing one has been in use since the ground opened in 1991. Because of changes to ECC-qualification rules, the LCF intends to enter a team in the 2003 ECC Trophy in Vienna, which should lessen the disappointment of last season's international against Switzerland being cancelled. Finally, Optimists Maidens CC, will welcome MCC Ladies in June to mark their tenth anniversary. **Bryan Rouse**

MALTA

Malta may almost have more cricket per head of population than England. So desirable a destination is it for touring teams that in 2003 no fewer than 28 are expected, and every day in April bar one has cricket scheduled. The pace was nearly as frenetic in 2002, when a steady influx of English schools played quality cricket against local and overseas opposition. Among the other visitors were The Hague CC, Quick CC (from Nijmegen, also in The Netherlands), Berne CC and the XL Club. All games were played with cheer and good humour. Meanwhile, the Marsa Falcons won the Summer League, in which many of the juniors from the Cricket Youth Nursery shone against senior opposition. During the hot summer months, Melita CC – formed a couple of seasons back by Marsa players and officials – played an inaugural match against their parent club. More improvements to the excellent facilities at the Marsa Sports Club have been made in preparation for another busy year. **Pierre Naudi**

MEXICO

The season started in November 2001 when Mexico City CC strode to a convincing victory over British & Dominion CC, from Los Angeles. For the Mexicans, Charlie Carr hit an undefeated 61 and Elliot Cartledge 49. In March, in the annual grudge match against Houston Memorial CC, the Texans avenged the previous year's crushing defeat when they strolled to a leisurely eight-wicket victory. Dillip Kanji was Mexico's leading batsman, with 46. He was in the runs again on Anzac Day when, in the traditional win for the Anzac XI over the Rest of the World XI, he and the South African (honorary Kiwi) Carl Greyling compiled a century opening partnership. The occasion was given more lustre by the appearance of the new Australian Ambassador, Graeme Wilson. Back in February, a hastily assembled Asian XI had romped home by 45 runs (thanks largely to Tushar Gupta's 81 not out) against a Mexico All-Star XI in front of 200 or so spectators. A fine buffet of Indian food provided a fitting celebration. Domestically, the ball dominated the bat after the prolonged rainy season, which had wiped out several early-season fixtures, created a bowler-friendly wicket at the home of the champions, Reforma Athletic. Their experienced bowlers, Deb Choudhuri (35 wickets) and Roger Kenyon (25), destroyed batting orders, though it was the British-born former fast bowler, Nick Deakin, who averaged just 7.75 with his gentle dobbers. Only Carr, with an average of 43.14, had much success with the bat. **Umair Khan**

MOROCCO

Morocco, already an Affiliate Member of the ICC, is now aiming for Associate Membership. On November 24, 2001 the *Fédération Royale Marocaine de Cricket* was established under the presidency of Chakib Nejjar. Just nine months later, the new international stadium in Tangier, built by Abdur Rahman Bukhatir, the father of Emirates cricket, hosted the glamorous Morocco Cup, which proved a great source of motivation for local players. Contested by Sri Lanka, South Africa and Pakistan, and attended by Barry Richards, officials from France and Gibraltar, and the ICC African development manager Hoosain Ayob, the Morocco Cup was reckoned a great success. Ayob has since promised assistance for a schools development programme aimed at 8–12 year olds. In the meantime, a preliminary national squad of 38 players was selected to prepare for inaugural international fixtures, against France, in 2003. An eight-team national league was launched in 2002, featuring clubs from Tangier, Rabat, Salé (where another stadium is being built and should be ready in 2003) and Casablanca, which also has a women's team. Morocco's first sport may be soccer, but cricket – which can be played all year round here – is fast becoming important. **Fatima Boujoual**

MOZAMBIQUE

Cricket has existed in one form or another in this former Portuguese colony since the 1950s, though it was almost exclusively the domain of South Asian expatriates. It floundered in the 1980s, while the nation was doing much the same, but there are now around a dozen teams, including five registered with the recently formed Mozambique Cricket Association (Associação de Cricket de Moçambique), based in the capital Maputo. Cricket activity consists of short tournaments, numerous friendlies and cross-border matches against teams from Komatipoort (South Africa) and Mutare (Zimbabwe). A total absence of dedicated grounds is no barrier, and matches are played with great enthusiasm on the football fields of Maxaquene, Desportivo Maputo and Mahotas Railways. Cricket has also reached the country's second city, Beira, though its distance from Maputo prevents any games between them. Officials are keen to develop the game amongst Mozambicans, but a lack of literature in Portuguese has stymied recent attempts to introduce it into Maputo schools. Cricket is hard enough to explain to the uninitiated without the language barrier. **Amarchande Samgi**

NAMIBIA

Qualification for the 2003 World Cup sparked unprecedented interest in cricket in Namibia, the most tangible spin-off being a 40 per cent increase in the number of players at youth level. As preparation for the World Cup, Namibia entered the 2002-03 Standard Bank Cup, the South African domestic one-day tournament. The national team's build-up also received assistance from the ICC's High Performance programme, allowing the former England all-rounder, Dougie Brown, to become national coach until the end of Namibia's World Cup campaign. In April, Namibia hosted the ICC Six Nations Challenge involving, Kenya, Canada, Holland, and A teams from Sri Lanka and Zimbabwe. The highlight was victory over Kenya, when Namibia crept home by one wicket in the last over. Although the sport's recent growth has strained the resources of the Namibia Cricket Board, talented youngsters are being found around the country, as victory in the ICC African Under-15 tournament in Botswana proved. Street cricket has become all the rage among children in Khomasdal, a Windhoek suburb, and at club level three new teams registered for the 2002-03 season. **Laurie Pieters**

 Shaun Pollock is the most successful tailender in Test history.
Neil Manthorp on Shaun Pollock, page 77

NEPAL

Coached by the former Test players, Roy Dias and Aftab Baloch, Nepalese teams tasted remarkable success in international tournaments. The national side reached the final of the 2002 ACC Trophy in Singapore, before losing to the United Arab Emirates, while in Kathmandu in 2001 the Under-19s won the Youth Asia Cup, beating Malaysia. Nepal also finished as runners-up to Zimbabwe in the Under-19 World Cup plate championship, having earlier defeated Pakistan and Bangladesh. The main domestic tournament, the Bihendra Memorial National League, named in honour of the late King, was played in Kathmandu in May, when Region No. 1 conquered Region No. 2. This replaced the inter-district competition, the Jai Trophy, which was won in 2001 by Kapilvastu; Para District were the losing finalists. **Jai Kumar Shah**.

NIGERIA

Cricket in Nigeria entered a new phase in 2002 when it became an Associate Member of the ICC. Although the decision signals the end of the 26-year-old West African Cricket Conference (WACC), Nigeria will continue to split WACC funding with the other former members, Sierra Leone, Gambia and Ghana, for the next three years. The Nigerian team played its part in swinging the ICC vote by winning the West African Championships in Lagos in April, although the tournament was characterised by problems of player availability and low standards. The 11-strong Lagos League continued to thrive, while the Howzat Foundation ran the age-group leagues; four Under-12 teams were made up of girls. The challenges of Associate membership and the rapid increase in player numbers demand a strong administrative base at the Nigeria Cricket Association, where opportunities for marketing and sponsorship must be seized. For Nigeria, the journey has just started. **Ewa Henshaw**.

NORWAY

Norwegian cricket put recent administrative disasters behind them – and had a good season. The election of a new board comprising seven members, all from different clubs, and the addition of new pitches, practice facilities and Norway's first dedicated cricket ground were among the many pluses. Cricket gained an important stamp of approval when the board received a US$65,000 government grant for new facilities. Better communication and co-operation with the local council and with the sports authorities had borne fruit. And we recruited locally born coaches and umpires – an essential part of our plans for a youth league in 2003. The Oslo League swelled to 14 teams and introduced a two-group system in preparation for merit-based divisions in 2003, while two competitions for teams not involved in the Norwegian Masters series will guarantee clubs purposeful cricket all season. New arrivals Nation CC were surprise Masters winners, Sentrum CC raised the Sinsen Cup while Tamil CC made do with the Consolation Cup, so securing their place in Division One in 2003. Some things, however, defeat the best-laid plans: the Knockout Trophy final was postponed three times because of bad weather and will be decided in 2003. **Bob Gibb**.

PANAMA

Religious differences were set aside during the 2002 Panamanian season when Hindu and Muslim teams competed in the same tournament for the first time since 1987. In an exciting final full of adventurous strokeplay, Deportivo Hindu A defeated Muslim in the last over. In one semi-final, Deportivo, who finished second in the Hindu group, had eliminated Dada, winners of the Muslim league, while in the other, Muslim, runners-up in their group, had ousted Hindu group leaders, Ahir. The semi-finals, the first encounters between Hindu and Muslim teams in the tournament, were played in a tense but calm atmosphere. The national team later vanquished the visiting Costa Ricans 2–0. Costa Rica, made up largely of English expatriates, were knowledgeable cricketers and they, like other visiting teams, would be welcomed again. **Saleh and Musaji Bhana**

PORTUGAL

Good results by the national squads at the ECC Indoor Championships in Belgium and the ECC Championships in Belfast could not disguise real concerns for the game's future caused by a chronic shortage of grounds. After eight clubs had shared a single venue in 2001, only four competed in 2002's Lisbon league: prospective players drifted away when they could expect a game only every second or third weekend. The weather didn't help. More matches were rained off than ever: one game was abandoned when the artificial surface regularly tore away from its moorings, endangered players and umpires. Inevitably, ACC won their sixth successive title. The precariousness of cricket in Oporto was revealed when Lisbon won the annual two-day match, dating from 1861, by an innings and 226 runs. A very strong Lisbon team smashed a record 508 in 67 overs before dismissing Oporto for 134 and 248. Visiting English teams continued to relish the hospitality and conviviality of the local cricket, but despite the efforts of a few to place cricket on a sounder footing in Oporto, the only venue remains a bastion of tradition where membership is prohibitively expensive. Whether cricket in Portugal advances in 2003 will depend on whether such venue issues can be resolved. **Peter D. Eckersley**

RUSSIA

Cricket has taken root in Moscow, with five teams and nearly 100 players participating in 2002. The unsurprising absence of a traditional square in Moscow makes venue selection an ongoing quandary, but we settled on the Moscow University baseball field, despite its Astroturf surface and raised bases in the outfield. Friendlies preceded the competition proper, played in July and August to a 25-over format. With the Indian and Pakistani Ambassadors watching, the NRIs beat the Sonets in a gripping final to claim the 2002 title. The season's finale, the Moscow Ashes, produced a shock when on a perishing October afternoon, the British upset years of tradition by winning. Thanks to a contribution from the Ambassador and a big-hitting century, they sealed the win in the last over. All teams have signed up for the 2003 competition, and the search is on for more lovers of the noble game in Moscow. **Simon Cottrell**

SPAIN

The high point of the Spanish cricket year was the staging of the inaugural European Cricket Academy on the Costa Blanca. Well-known coaches, including internationals, imparted their knowledge to 14 of continental Europe's best young cricketers, in an event which brought great credit to the Asocacion Espanola de Cricket (AEC). As well as the usual ECC coaching sessions, Kwik Cricket and hardball tournaments, several Spanish schools requested assistance either to introduce cricket to their pupils or organise tournaments. New clubs have emerged in Madrid, Mojacar, Oropesa and Torrevieja, although inevitably the biggest obstacle is ground availability, a problem that requires great effort. The AEC did help a school in Tenerife by donating a Flicx wicket they had won in an ECC competition. Retiring to Spain after a lifetime in the game? We would love your help and experience in bringing this wonderful sport to a new, young Spanish audience. **Ken Sainsbury**

SWITZERLAND

Extremes of weather, unprecedented publicity and the opening of a new, dedicated ground ensured 2002 was a notable year for Swiss cricket. Between downpours and heatwaves, work continued on the cricket-only playing surface at Cossonay in the south-west, and in June the first ball was bowled. After that, it was a summer of constant exposure for cricket. Local TV aired a programme devoted to Cossonay CC. The ECC coach, Ralph Dellor, lent his cricket expertise to the European Spirit of Cricket weekend and his broadcasting expertise to reporting on Swiss cricket for BBC radio. As part of the Queen's Golden Jubilee celebrations, cricket featured in an "All Things British" exhibition in Zurich. The Swiss National Exhibition, held roughly every 30 years, included a demonstration of cricket by the coach, David Gelling. And Basle CC appeared in cinemas for a fortnight when a chain ran a series of short films on emerging sports; cricket took top billing. There was still time for a spot of the actual game, too. Winterthur CC concluded their 20th-anniversary season by defeating Geneva in the championship final to win their second title. Defending 162, a fine four for 21 from Swiss-born international, Andreas Roost, helped scuttle Geneva for 110. **John McKillop**

UNITED STATES OF AMERICA

The United States won its first ICC-sanctioned tournament by remaining unbeaten and lifting the second Americas Cup, held in Buenos Aires. A three-wicket victory over Canada ensured success after a four-match tour of Antigua proved ideal preparation. In an innovative 12 months, the first national championships, fought for by the United States Cricket Association's eight regions, were held over three holiday weekends. New York Region won the final convincingly, beating South West in Los Angeles. The USACA also initiated formal junior and youth development programmes in all eight regions. A United States team took part in the Americas Under-15 event in Orlando, while three youngsters joined a composite Americas Under-19 team taking part in the Caribbean Nortel competition. A young United States A team gathered invaluable experience in Kuala Lumpur when they defeated Malaysia twice, but lost to an experienced Bangladesh A side.

There were setbacks. What was to have been New York's first fully fledged, purpose-built cricket ground can now be used only by juniors. "There is a real need for a cricket field, and it was built in the perfect location," said Selwyn Caesar, president of the American Cricket League. However, the oval has a diameter of just 65 yards. Officials conceded that a blunder had left the field at least ten yards too small for official matches. "The field is fine for local and youth competition, but it cannot be used for regional and international matches," Caesar admitted. On a more positive note, the introduction of Under-19 and Under-15 national competitions, and a busy schedule for the senior team should ensure continued momentum.

VANUATU

Cricket in Vanuatu in 2002 can perhaps be summarised by comments from participants in our successful children's day tournament. Jeremiah, aged 11: "On the July 24, it was Children's Day – we played cricket. All the schools in Port Vila were there. It was the best day I ever had in my life. In our team there were boys from India, Tuvalu and Kiribati, about 130 mixed, black and white children at Independence Park aged up to 13 years. It was fun playing with other kids from other nations. It was good sportsmanship and also good exercise and good friendship." Vanessa Kevin: "A boy from India played with us and made six points and that was so amazing. When that boy came out to have a rest we gave him a big clap. It was my friend Falefou's last day with us in Vanuatu before going back to Tuvalu, so I brought Falefou so he can have fun with us one last time. We have many fun at the children's day." Mark Stafford, Vanuatu Cricket Association president: "We have young kids with enthusiasm and passion here in Vanuatu. I hope Jeremiah and Vanessa continue to love their cricket for many years to come. Vanuatu will be better for it." **Mark Stafford**

TOURNAMENTS CONTESTED BY NON-TEST NATIONS, 2001-02 AND 2002

Competition	Winners	Runners-up	Others
Africa Cricket Association Cup (September)	South Africa Development XI	Botswana	(Group A) Kenya Development XI, Uganda, Nigeria, Malawi (Group B) Zimbabwe Development XI, Zambia, Namibia, Tanzania
Americas Championship (March)	United States	Canada	Cayman Islands, Bermuda, Bahamas, Argentina
Asian Cricket Council Trophy (July)	United Arab Emirates	Nepal	(Group A) Kuwait, Oman, Qatar (Group B) Malaysia, Hong Kong, Singapore, Maldives, Thailand
East Asia Pacific Eights (February)	ACB Aborigines	Japan	Indonesia, South Korea
ECC Representative Festival (August)	Finland	Slovenia	Croatia
European Championships (July) Division One Division Two	ECB XI Germany	Scotland Gibraltar	Ireland, Netherlands, Denmark, Italy Portugal, Israel, France, Austria
ICC Six Nations Challenge (April)	Sri Lanka A	Kenya	Zimbabwe A, Namibia, Canada, Netherlands
Pacifica Cup (May–June)	Papua New Guinea	Tonga	(Group A) Fiji (Group B) Cook Islands, Samoa, Vanuatu, New Caledonia
West African Quadrangular (April)	Nigeria	Sierra Leone	Ghana, Gambia

Only tournaments held during 2001-02 and 2002 seasons involving three or more teams are included. All matches were limited-overs games. The order in which other teams are listed reflects their final position in the tournament.

7

ADMINISTRATION AND REGULATIONS

Srinavas Venkataraghavan, one of ICC's elite panel of eight umpires. *Picture by Jack Atley.*

PART SEVEN: ADMINISTRATION AND REGULATIONS

INTERNATIONAL CRICKET COUNCIL

On June 15, 1909, representatives of cricket in England, Australia and South Africa met at Lord's and founded the Imperial Cricket Conference. Membership was confined to the governing bodies of cricket in countries within the British Commonwealth where Test cricket was played. India, New Zealand and West Indies were elected as members on May 31, 1926, Pakistan on July 28, 1952, Sri Lanka on July 21, 1981, Zimbabwe on July 8, 1992 and Bangladesh on June 26, 2000. South Africa ceased to be a member of the ICC on leaving the British Commonwealth in May, 1961, but was elected as a Full Member on July 10, 1991.

On July 15, 1965, the Conference was renamed the International Cricket Conference and new rules were adopted to permit the election of countries from outside the British Commonwealth. This led to the growth of the Conference, with the admission of Associate Members, who were each entitled to one vote, while the Foundation and Full Members were each entitled to two votes, on ICC resolutions. On July 12 and 13, 1989, the Conference was renamed the International Cricket Council and revised rules were adopted.

On July 7, 1993, the ICC ceased to be administered by MCC and became an independent organisation with its own chief executive, the headquarters remaining at Lord's. The category of Foundation Member, with its special rights, was abolished. On October 1, 1993, Sir Clyde Walcott became the first non-British chairman of the ICC.

On June 16, 1997, the ICC became an incorporated body, with an executive board and a president instead of a chairman. Jagmohan Dalmiya became the ICC's first president.

Officers

President: M. A. Gray (2000–03); Ehsan Mani (2003–05).   *Chief Executive:* M. W. Speed.
Chairman of Committees: Cricket – Management: M. W. Speed; *Cricket – Playing:* S. M. Gavaskar; *Development:* M. W. Speed; *Finance and Marketing:* Ehsan Mani.
Executive Board: The president and chief executive sit on the board and all committees *ex officio*. They are joined by H. Amarasuriya (Sri Lanka), Ali Asghar (Bangladesh), Sir John Anderson (New Zealand), P. Chingoka (Zimbabwe), J. Dalmiya (India), W. W. Hall (West Indies), R. F. Merriman (Australia), F. D. Morgan (England), J. Rayani (Kenya), P. H. F. Sonn (South Africa), Tauqir Zia (Pakistan), HRH Tunku Imran (Malaysia), R. van Ierschot (Netherlands).
General Manager: R. M. G. Hill. *General Manager – Cricket:* D. J. Richardson. *Cricket Operations Manager:* C. D. Hitchcock. *Umpires and Referees Manager:* C. S. Kelly. *Development Manager:* A. J. Eade. *General Manager – Corporate Affairs:* B. F. Clements. *Commercial Manager:* D. C. Jamieson. *Chief Finance Officer:* F. Hasnain. *In-house Lawyer:* U. Naidoo.

Constitution

President: Each Full Member has the right, by rotation, to appoint ICC's president. In 1997, India named J. Dalmiya to serve until June 2000, when M. A. Gray of Australia took over. Ehsan Mani of Pakistan is due to succeed Gray in June 2003; he and subsequent presidents will serve for two years.

Chief Executive: Appointed by the Council. D. L. Richards was appointed in 1993; he stepped down in September 2001, and was succeeded by M. W. Speed.

Membership

Full Members: Australia, Bangladesh, England, India, New Zealand, Pakistan, South Africa, Sri Lanka, West Indies and Zimbabwe.

Associate Members*: Argentina (1974), Bermuda (1966), Canada (1968), Cayman Islands (2002), Denmark (1966), East and Central Africa (1966), Fiji (1965), France (1998), Germany (1999),

Gibraltar (1969), Hong Kong (1969), Ireland (1993), Israel (1974), Italy (1995), Kenya (1981), Malaysia (1967), Namibia (1992), Nepal (1996), Netherlands (1966), Nigeria (2002), Papua New Guinea (1973), Scotland (1994), Singapore (1974), Tanzania (2001), Uganda (1998), United Arab Emirates (1990), USA (1965).

Affiliate Members*: Afghanistan (2001), Austria (1992), Bahamas (1987), Bahrain (2001), Belgium (1991), Belize (1997), Bhutan (2001), Botswana (2001), Brazil (2002), Brunei (1992), Chile (2002), Cook Islands (2000), Costa Rica (2002), Croatia (2001), Cuba (2002), Cyprus (1999), Czech Republic (2000), Finland (2000), Gambia (2002), Ghana (2002), Greece (1995), Indonesia (2001), Japan (1989), Kuwait (1998), Lesotho (2001), Luxembourg (1998), Maldives (2001), Malta (1998), Morocco (1999), Norway (2000), Oman (2000), Panama (2002), Philippines (2000), Portugal (1996), Qatar (1999), St Helena (2001), Samoa (2000), Sierra Leone (2002), South Korea (2001), Spain (1992), Suriname (2002), Sweden (1997), Switzerland (1985), Thailand (1995), Tonga (2000), Turks & Caicos Islands (2002) and Vanuatu (1995).

* Year of election shown in parentheses.

The following governing bodies for cricket shall be eligible for election.

Full Members: The governing body for cricket recognised by the ICC of a country, or countries associated for cricket purposes, or a geographical area, from which representative teams are qualified to play official Test matches.

Associate Members: The governing body for cricket recognised by the ICC of a country, or countries associated for cricket purposes, or a geographical area, which does not qualify as a Full Member but where cricket is firmly established and organised.

Affiliate Members: The governing body for cricket recognised by the ICC of a country, or countries associated for cricket purposes, or a geographical area (which is not part of one of those already constituted as a Full or Associate Member) where the ICC recognises that cricket is played in accordance with the Laws of Cricket. Affiliate Members have no right to vote or to propose or second resolutions at ICC meetings.

ENGLAND AND WALES CRICKET BOARD

The England and Wales Cricket Board (ECB) became responsible for the administration of all cricket – professional and recreational – in England and Wales on January 1, 1997. It took over the functions of the Cricket Council, the Test and County Cricket Board and the National Cricket Association which had run the game in England and Wales since 1968. The Management Board is answerable to the First-Class Forum on matters concerning the first-class game and to the Recreational Forum on matters concerning the non-professional game. The First-Class Forum elects five members to the Management Board and the Recreational Forum elects four.

Officers

Chairman: F. D. Morgan. *Chief Executive:* T. M. Lamb.

Management Board: F. D. Morgan (*chairman*), D. L. Acfield, D. L. Amiss, R. G. Bransgrove, D. G. Collier, S. P. Coverdale, D. E. East, P. W. Gooden, H. M. V. Gray, R. Jackson, R. D. V. Knight, R. C. Moylan-Jones, J. B. Pickup, M. J. Soper, D. P. Stewart.

Chairmen of Committees: First-Class Forum: M. J. Soper; *Recreational Forum:* J. B. Pickup; *Cricket Advisory Committee:* D. L. Acfield; *International Teams Management Group:* D. L. Amiss; *Finance Advisory Committee:* D. P. Stewart; *Marketing Advisory Committee:* H. M. V. Gray; *Discipline Standing Committee:* G. Elias QC; *Registration Standing Committee:* D. S. Kemp.

Finance Director: B. W. Havill; *Director of Cricket Operations:* J. D. Carr; *Commercial Director:* vacant; *Director of Corporate Affairs:* J. C. Read; *Performance Director:* H. Morris; *National Development Director:* K. R. Pont; *Executive Director for Women's Cricket:* G. E. McConway; *Director of Legal Affairs:* M. N. Roper-Drimie; *Cricket Operations Manager (First-Class):* A. Fordham; *Cricket Operations Manager (Recreational):* F. R. Kemp.

THE MARYLEBONE CRICKET CLUB

The Marylebone Cricket Club evolved out of the White Conduit Club in 1787, when Thomas Lord laid out his first ground in Dorset Square. Its members revised the Laws in 1788 and gradually took responsibility for cricket throughout the world. However, it relinquished control of the game in the UK in 1968 and the International Cricket Council finally established its own secretariat in 1993. MCC still owns Lord's and remains the guardian of the Laws. It calls itself "a private club with a public function" and aims to support cricket everywhere, especially at grassroots level and in countries where the game is least developed.

Patron: HER MAJESTY THE QUEEN

Officers

President: 2002–03 – Sir Tim Rice.

Club Chairman: Lord Alexander of Weedon.　*Chairman of Finance:* O. H. J. Stocken.

Trustees: A. C. D. Ingleby-Mackenzie, Sir Michael Jenkins, A. R. Lewis.

Hon. Life Vice-Presidents: Sir Alec Bedser, Lord Bramall, D. G. Clark, G. H. G. Doggart, Lord Griffiths, D. J. Insole, M. E. L. Melluish, C. H. Palmer, D. R. W. Silk, J. J. Warr, J. C. Woodcock.

Secretary and Chief Executive: R. D. V. Knight.　*Deputy Chief Executive:* D. N. Batts.

Head of Cricket: A. I. C. Dodemaide.　*Assistant Secretary (Membership):* C. Maynard.　*Personal Assistant to Secretary and Chief Executive:* Miss S. A. Lawrence.　*Curator:* S. E. A. Green.

MCC Committee: P. H. Edmonds, D. J. C. Faber, M. W. Gatting, D. I. Gower, M. G. Griffith, W. R. Griffiths, Rt Hon. J. Major, M. C. J. Nicholas, T. J. G. O'Gorman, Lt-Col. J. R. Stephenson, J. A. F. Vallance, D. R. Walsh.

Chairmen of committees: E. R. Dexter (Cricket); M. J. de Rohan (Estates); C. A. Fry (Membership); A. W. Wreford (Marketing); *Additional Member of the cricket committee:* G. J. Toogood.

PROFESSIONAL CRICKETERS' ASSOCIATION

The Professional Cricketers' Association was formed in 1967 (as the Cricketers' Association) to represent the first-class county playing staffs, and to promote and protect professional players' interests. During the 1970s, it succeeded in establishing pension schemes and a minimum wage. In 1995, David Graveney became the Association's general secretary and first full-time employee; in 1998, he became chief executive. In 1997, the organisation set up its own management company to raise regular revenue and fund improved benefits for members of the PCA during and after their playing careers.

President: M. W. Gatting.　*Chairman:* M. V. Fleming.　*Chief Executive:* D. A. Graveney. *Chairman, PCA Management:* P. M. Walker.　*Managing Director:* R. H. Bevan.　*Directors:* D. A. Graveney, T. J. G. O'Gorman.

EUROPEAN CRICKET COUNCIL

On June 16, 1997, the eight-year-old European Cricket Federation was superseded by the European Cricket Council, bringing together all European ICC members, plus Israel. In 2002, the Council consisted of England (Full Member); Denmark, France, Germany, Gibraltar, Ireland, Israel, Italy, Netherlands and Scotland (Associate Members); and Austria, Belgium, Croatia, Cyprus, Czech Republic, Finland, Greece, Luxembourg, Malta, Norway, Portugal, Spain, Sweden and Switzerland (Affiliate Members). The ECC also supports development initiatives in non-member countries Azerbaijan, Belarus, Bulgaria, Estonia, Hungary, Iceland, Latvia, Poland, Romania, Russia, Slovakia, Slovenia, Ukraine and Yugoslavia.

Chairman: D. J. Insole.　*European Development Manager:* I. C. D. Stuart.

ADDRESSES

INTERNATIONAL CRICKET COUNCIL

M. W. Speed, The Clock Tower, Lord's Ground, London NW8 8QN (020 7266 1818; fax 020 7266 1777; website www.icc.cricket.org; e-mail icc@icc.cricket.org).

Full Members

AUSTRALIA: Australian Cricket Board, J. Sutherland, 60 Jolimont Street, Jolimont, Victoria 3002 (00 61 3 9653 9999; fax 00 61 3 9653 9900; website www.acb.com.au).

BANGLADESH: Bangladesh Cricket Board, Arafat Rahman, Navana Tower (5th Floor), 45 Gulshan Avenue, Dhaka 1212 (00 880 2 966 6805; fax 00 880 2 956 3844; e-mail bcb@bangla.net).

ENGLAND: England and Wales Cricket Board, T. M. Lamb, Lord's Ground, London NW8 8QZ (020 7432 1200; fax 020 7289 5619; website www.ecb.co.uk).

INDIA: Board of Control for Cricket in India, Kairali, GHS Lane, Manacaud, Trivandrum 695 009 (00 91 471 245 3307; fax 00 91 471 246 4620; e-mail secbcci@sify.com).

NEW ZEALAND: New Zealand Cricket Inc., M. C. Snedden, PO Box 958, 109 Cambridge Terrace, Christchurch (00 64 3 366 2964; fax 00 64 3 365 7491; website www.nzcricket.org.nz).

PAKISTAN: Pakistan Cricket Board, C. Mujahid, Gaddafi Stadium, Ferozepur Road, Lahore 54600 (00 92 42 571 7231; fax 00 92 42 571 1860).

SOUTH AFRICA: United Cricket Board of South Africa, M. G. Majola, Wanderers Club, PO Box 55009, North Street, Illovo, Northlands 2116 (00 27 11 880 2810; fax 00 27 11 880 6578; website www.ucbsa.cricket.org; e-mail ucbsa@ucb.co.za).

SRI LANKA: Board of Control for Cricket in Sri Lanka, A. P. B. Tennekoon, 35 Maitland Place, Colombo 7 (00 94 1 691439/689551; fax 00 94 1 697405; e-mail cricket@sri.lanka.net).

WEST INDIES: West Indies Cricket Board, R. Brathwaite, Factory Road, PO Box 616 W, Woods Centre, St John's, Antigua (00 1 268 481 2450; fax 00 1 268 481 2498; e-mail wicb@candw.ag).

ZIMBABWE: Zimbabwe Cricket Union, V. Hogg, PO Box 2739, Josiah Tongogara Avenue, Harare (00 263 4 704616/8; fax 00 263 4 729370; website www.zcu.cricket.org; e-mail zcu@mweb.co.zw).

Associate and Affiliate Members

AFGHANISTAN: Afghanistan Cricket Federation, PO Box 970, Kabul (00 93 23 90017; fax 00 92 91 287 655; e-mail afghan_cricket_fed@yahoo.com).

ARGENTINA: Argentine Cricket Association, D. Lord, ACA Sede Central, Pte Jose E. Uriburu 1468, Piso 3 – Departamento A, Buenos Aires (00 54 11 4806 7306; fax 00 54 11 4804 5389; website cricketargentina@cricar@hotmail.com).

AUSTRIA: Österreichischer Cricket Verband, A. Simpson-Parker, Apollogasse 3/42, A-1070 Vienna (00 43 1 924 6851; website www.austria.cricket.org; e-mail austria_cricket@yahoo.com).

BAHAMAS: Bahamas Cricket Association, S. Deveaux, Government House, PO Box N1001, Nassau (00 1 242 341 5663; also fax; e-mail firstslip@hotmail.com).

BAHRAIN: Bahrain Cricket Association, Anil Sharma, PO Box 2400, Manama (fax 00 973 234 244).

BELGIUM: Belgian Cricket Federation, M. O'Connor, Koningin Astridlaan 98, B-2800 Mechelen (00 32 15 331 635; fax 00 32 15 331 639; e-mail paul.lariviere@pandora.be).

BELIZE: Belize National Cricket Association, 1128 Baracuda Street, Belize City (00 501 2 72201; fax 00 501 2 30936).

BERMUDA: Bermuda Cricket Board of Control, R. Horton, PO Box HM992, Hamilton HM DX (00 1 441 292 8958; fax 00 1 441 292 8959; website www.bermuda.cricket.org; e-mail bcbc@ibl.bm).

BHUTAN: Bhutan Cricket Association, PO Box 242, Thimpu (00 975 2322 319; fax 00 972 2322 753; millia@druknet.net.bt).

BOTSWANA: Botswana Cricket Association, J. Sands, Private Bag 00379, Gaborone (00 267 309867; fax 00 267 309 881; e-mail jsands@global.bw).

BRAZIL: Associaçao Brasileira de Cricket, J. Landers, MUDB Conjunto 9 Lote 5, Lago Sul, DF-Cep 71.680-090 (00 55 61 366 1984; also fax; e-mail john.landers@apis.com.br).

BRUNEI: Persatuan Keriket Negara Brunei Darussalam, M. B. Ahmad, PO Box 931, MPC-Old Airport, Berakas-BB 3577 (00 673 223 5834; fax 00 673 243 1122; e-mail mirbash@brunet.bn).

CANADA: Canadian Cricket Association, G. Edwards, 46 Port Street East, Mississauga, Ontario L5G 1C1 (00 1 905 278 5000; fax 00 1 905 278 5005; e-mail 74253.1641@compuserve.com).

CAYMAN ISLANDS: Cayman Islands Cricket Association, C. Myles, PO Box 1201 GT, George Town, Grand Cayman (00 1 345 945 6447; fax 00 1 345 949 8772; e-mail cicaadmin@candw.ky).

CHILE: Chilean Cricket Association, Santa Lucia 124, Santiago (00 56 2 638 2156; fax 00 56 2 632 6637).

COOK ISLANDS: Cook Islands Cricket Association, G. Hoskings, PO Box 139, Avarua Rarotoonga (00 682 29 312; fax 00 682 29 314).

COSTA RICA: Costa Rica Cricket Assocation, Apartado 299, Centro Colon, 1007 San Jose (00 506 241 5708; fax 00 506 241 0785; e-mail trillingworth@yahoo.co.uk).

CROATIA: Croatia Cricket Board, Kvinticka 14B, Zagreb 10 000 (Fax 00 356 483 002; e-mail ivan.bilic2@zg.hinet.hr).

CUBA: Cuban Cricket Commission, Ira c#15206 e/152 y 154, Nautico, Playa 11600, Cuidad de la Habana (00 53 7 208 2096; fax 00 53 7 249 214; e-mail gordon@infomed.sid.cu).

CYPRUS: Cyprus Cricket Association, G. Collins, PO Box 3293, Limassol, Cyprus CY 3301 (00 357 662 2226; fax 00 357 662 2227; e-mail guttenbergs@yahoo.com).

CZECH REPUBLIC: Czech Republic Cricket Union, J. Locke, Na Berance 7/1773, 160 00 Praha 6 (00 420 22 432 1716; e-mail locke@cmail.cz).

DENMARK: Dansk Cricket-Forbund, C. B. S. Hansen, Idraettens Hus, 2605 Brøndby (00 45 4326 2160; fax 00 45 4326 2163; website www.cricket.dk; e-mail dcf@cricket.dk).

EAST AND CENTRAL AFRICA: East and Central African Cricket Conference, Apex House, Kidney Crescent, PO Box 786, Blantyre, Malawi (00 265 1 670050; fax 00 260 1 224 454; e-mail syusuf@globmw.net).

FIJI: Fiji Cricket Association, P. I. Knight, PO Box 300, Suva (00 679 3301 499; fax 00 679 3301 618; e-mail fijicrick@connect.com.fj).

FINLAND: Finnish Cricket Association, A. Armitage, Coats Opti Oy, Ketjutie 3, Fin-04220, Kerava (00 358 927 487 327; fax 00 358 927 487 371; e-mail andrew.armitage@coats.com).

FRANCE: Fédération Française de Baseball, Softball et Cricket, O. Dubaut, 41 rue de Fécamp, 75012 Paris (00 33 553 544 095; fax 00 33 553 542 783; website www.flbsc.org; e-mail edcannon@club.internet.fr).

GAMBIA: Gambia Cricket Association, PO Box 35, Banjul (00 220 226 296; also fax; e-mail sonnyann@qanet.gm).

GERMANY: Deutscher Cricket Bund, B. Fell, Luragogasse 5, D-94032 Passau (00 49 851 34307; fax 00 49 851 32815; website www.dcb-cricket.de; e-mail brimarfell@t-online.de).

GHANA: Ghana Cricket Association, Selina Lodge, East Legon, Accra (00 233 21 506179; fax 00 233 21 505322; e-mail whackman@africaonline.com.gh).

GIBRALTAR: Gibraltar Cricket Association, T. J. Finlayson, 23 Merlot House, Vineyards Estate (00 350 79461; also fax; website www.gca.gi; e-mail gibarchives@gibnynex.gi).

GREECE: Hellenic Cricket Federation, C. Evangelos, Kat. Pappa 8, Corfu 49100 (00 30 661 47753; fax 00 30 661 47754; e-mail cricketadm@otenet.gr).

HONG KONG: Hong Kong Cricket Association, J. A. Cribbin, Room 1019, Sports House, 1 Stadium Path, So Kon Po, Causeway Bay (00 852 250 48101; fax 00 852 257 78486; website www.hkabc.net; e-mail hkca@hkabc.net).

INDONESIA: Indonesia Cricket Federation, Gedung BRI II, 19th Floor, Suite 1907, II Jend Sudirman No 44-46, Jakarta (00 62 21 251 2660; fax 00 62 21 570 9455).

IRELAND: Irish Cricket Union, J. Wright, The Diamond, Malahide, Co Dublin 18 (00 353 1 845 0710; fax 00 353 1 845 5545; website www.theicu.org; e-mail typetext@eircom.net).

ISRAEL: Israel Cricket Association, S. Perlman, PO Box 65085, Tel-Aviv 61650 (00 972 3 642 5529; fax 00 972 3 641 7271; e-mail israel@cricket.org).

ITALY: Federazione Cricket Italiana, S. Gambino, Via S. Ignazio 9, 00186 Roma (00 39 06 689 6989; fax 00 39 06 687 8684; website www.crickitalia.org; e-mail fcri@pronet.it).

JAPAN: Japan Cricket Association, K. Matsumara, 2-11-14 Koshi Building 5F, Minamiaoyama, Minato-ku, Tokyo 107-0062 (00 81 3 5772 3470; fax 00 81 3 5772 3471; website www.jca@cricket.ne.jp; e-mail nao720@aol.com).

KENYA: Kenya Cricket Association, H. Shah, PO Box 16962, 00620 Nairobi (00 254 2 3744762; fax 00 254 2 3742932; e-mail kcricket@iconnect.co.ke).

KUWAIT: Kuwait Cricket Association, Abdul Muttaleb Ahmad, PO Box 6706, Hawalli-32042 (00 965 572 6600; fax 00 965 573 4973).

LESOTHO: Lesotho Cricket Association, PO Box 964, Maseru 100, Lioli Street, Old Industrial Area, Maseru (00 266 313 914; fax 00 266 310 252; e-mail mico@ilesotho.com).

LUXEMBOURG: Federation Luxembourgeoise de Cricket, T. Dunning, 87 Rue de Gasparich, L-1617 Luxembourg-Ville (00 352 4301 32795; fax 00 352 4301 35049; website www.cricket.lu; e-mail anthony.dunning@cec.eu.int).

MALAYSIA: Malaysian Cricket Association, K. Selveratnam, 1st Floor, Wisma OCM, Jalan Hang Jebat, 50150 Kuala Lumpur (00 60 3 2094 5144; fax 00 60 3 2096 1044; e-mail crickmal@tm.net.my).

MALDIVES: Cricket Control Board of Maldives, Kulhivaru Ekuveni, 1st Floor, Cricket Indoor Hall, Male, Republic of Maldives (00 960 317 886; fax 00 960 310 573; e-mail ccbm@avasmail.com).

MALTA: Malta Cricket Association, M. Sacco, c/o Marsa Sports Club, Marsa HMR 15 (00 356 21233 851; fax 00 356 21231 809; e-mail maltacricket@yahoo.co.uk).

MOROCCO: Moroccan Cricket Association, C. Laroussi, Ave Imam Malik Rue Anjara, No 84 Souissi, Rabat (00 212 6629 9404; fax 00 212 3771 3271; e-mail marocricket@caramail.com).

NAMIBIA: Namibia Cricket Board, L. Pieters, 7 Love Street, Windhoek (00 264 81 122 5551; fax 00 264 61 223 818; e-mail rocwindk@mweb.com.na).

NEPAL: Cricket Association of Nepal, B. R. Pandey, Heritage Plaza, 5th Floor, Kamaldi, Kathmandu (00 977 1 247485 ext. 252; fax 00 977 1 247946; e-mail bone@wlink.com.np).

NETHERLANDS: Koninklijke Nederlandse Cricket Bond, A. de la Mar, Nieuwe Kalfjeslaan 21-B, 1182 AA Amstelveen (00 31 20 645 1705; fax 00 31 20 645 1715; website www.kncb.nl; e-mail cricket@kncb.nl).

NIGERIA: Nigeria Cricket Association, Olusegun Akinlotan, Tafawa Balewa Square, Race Course, PO Box 9309, Lagos, Nigeria (00 234 1545 6426; fax 00 234 1585 0529; e-mail segun_adeuk@yahoo.co.uk).

NORWAY: Norway Cricket Association, R. Gibb, Geologsvingen 11, 0380 Oslo (00 47 22 934 97973; e-mail bobgibb@enitel.no).

OMAN: Oman Cricket Association, A. M. Yousef, PO Box 3948, Ruwi 112, Muscat, Sultanate of Oman (00 968 703 142; fax 00 968 796 045; e-mail kanaksi@omantel.net.om).

PANAMA: Panama Cricket Association, 2nd Street Francisco Filos, Visa Hermosa, Edificio 15B local, 3 Panama (00 507 229 8166; fax 00 507 261 8499; e-mail aptecpa@cwpanama.net).

PAPUA NEW GUINEA: Papua New Guinea Cricket Board of Control, W. Satchell, PO Box 168, Boroko NCD, Port Moresby (00 675 320 0020; fax 00 675 320 2967; e-mail griswalds@datec.net.pg).

PHILIPPINES: Philippine Cricket Association, c/o Davis, Langdon & Seah Philippines Inc., 4th Floor, 2129 Pasong Tamo, Makati City, Metro Manilla (00 63 2 811 2971; fax 00 632 811 2071; e-mail cjh@dls.com.ph).

PORTUGAL: Federação Portuguesa de Cricket, J. Simonson, PO Box 76, P-2766-901 Estoril Codex (00 351 21 444 6466; fax 00 351 21 924 3004; e-mail cricket@gauntlett.com).

QATAR: Qatar Cricket Association, F. H. Alfardan, PO Box 339, Dohar (00 974 440 8225/442 7050; fax 00 974 441 7468; e-mail afx@qatar.net.qa).

ST HELENA: St Helena Cricket Association, Nia Roo, New Bridge Road, Jamestown (fax 00 44 870 127 5517; e-mail band.niaroo@helanta.sh).

SAMOA: Samoa Cricket Association, S. Kohlhasse, Seb & Rene Sports, PO Box 9599 (00 685 22 790; fax 00 685 22 480; e-mail sebk@lesamoa.net).

SCOTLAND: Scottish Cricket Union, National Cricket Academy, MES Sports Centre, Ravelston, Edinburgh EH4 3NT (0131 313 7420; fax 0131 313 7430; website www.scu.org.uk; e-mail admin.scu@btinternet.com).

SIERRA LEONE: Sierra Leone Cricket Association, National Stadium, Brooksfield, Freetown, Sierra Leone PMB 339 (00 232 2222 3140; fax 00 232 2222 7755; e-mail aod_george@tahoo.com).

SINGAPORE: Singapore Cricket Association, A. Kalaver, 31 Stadium Crescent (South Entrance), Singapore 397639 (00 65 348 6566; fax 00 65 348 6506; e-mail cricket@singnet.co.sg).

SOUTH KOREA: Korea Cricket Association, 60-25 Hannam-Dang, Yongsam-Ku, Seoul 140 210 (00 82 2 3706 3001; e-mail dunnan@hlcl.com).

SPAIN: Asociacion Española de Cricket, K. Sainsbury, Casa Desiderata, VA 153, 03737 Javea, Alicante (00 34 96 579 4948; e-mail ksainsy@dragonet.es).

SURINAME: Surinamse Cricket Bond, Joli Coeurstraat 19 Geversvlijt, Paramaribo, Suriname Zd Am (00 597 474194; fax 00 597 475089; e-mail d.entouchc@sr.net).

SWEDEN: Svenska Cricket Förbundet, N. Hashmi, Osbyringen 38, 163-73 Spånga, Stockholm (00 46 8 508 02053; fax 00 46 8 508 02179; e-mail naveed.hashmi@rinkeby.stockholm.se).

SWITZERLAND: Swiss Cricket Association, A. MacKay, Wingertlistrasse 22, CH-8405 Winterthur (00 41 1 839 4973; fax 00 41 1 839 4999; e-mail alex.mackay@mackay.ch).

TANZANIA: Tanzania Cricket Association, PO Box 918, Dar es Salaam (00 255 22 213 0037; fax 00 255 22 212 3394; e-mail wizards@cats-net.com).

THAILAND: Thailand Cricket League, 12th Floor, Silom Condominium, 52/38 Soi Saladaeng 2, Silom Road, Bangkok 10500 (00 66 2 266 9040; fax 00 66 2 236 6764; e-mail ravisehgal1@adv-mediaconsults.com).

TONGA: Tonga Cricket Association, 57 Hihifo Road, PO Box 297, Nuku' Alofa (00 676 25 888; fax 00 676 23 671; e-mail pmotrain@kalianet.to).

TURKS & CAICOS ISLANDS: Turks & Caicos Cricket Association, PO Box 20, Moores Alley, Grand Turk (00 1 649 946 1115; fax 00 1 649 946 2505; e-mail acbranch@hotmail.com)

UGANDA: Uganda Cricket Association, J. Ligya, c/o National Council of Sports, Lugogo Stadium, PO Box 8346, Kampala (00 256 41 349550; fax 00 256 41 258350; e-mail ugandacricket@utlonline.co.ug).

UNITED ARAB EMIRATES: Emirates Cricket Board, M. Khan, Sharjah Cricket Stadium, PO Box 88, Sharjah (00 971 5 0646 3570; fax 00 971 6 533 4741; e-mail cricket@emirates.net.ae).

USA: United States of America Cricket Association, Atul Rai, 3780 Brenner Drive, Santa Barbara, California 93105 (00 1 805 569 0503; fax 00 1 805 563 6085; website www.usaca.org; e-mail president@usaca.org)

VANUATU: Vanuatu Cricket Association, M. Stafford, c/o BDO, BDO House, Lini Highway, PO Box 240, Port Vila, Vanuatu (00 678 22280; fax 00 678 22317; e-mail bdo@vanuatu.com.vu).

UK ADDRESSES

ENGLAND AND WALES CRICKET BOARD: T. M. Lamb, Lord's Ground, London NW8 8QZ (020 7432 1200; fax 020 7289 5619; website www.ecb.co.uk).

MARYLEBONE CRICKET CLUB: R. D. V. Knight, Lord's Ground, London NW8 8QN (020 7289 1611; fax 020 7289 9100. Tickets 020 7432 1066; fax 020 7432 1061).

First-Class Counties

DERBYSHIRE: County Ground, Nottingham Road, Derby DE21 6DA (01332 383211; fax 01332 290251; website www.dccc.org.uk; e-mail post@dccc.org.uk).

DURHAM: County Ground, Riverside, Chester-le-Street, County Durham DH3 3QR (0191 387 1717; fax 0191 387 1616; website www.durhamccc.co.uk; e-mail reception.durham@ecb.co.uk).

ESSEX: County Ground, New Writtle Street, Chelmsford CM2 0PG (01245 252420; fax 01245 254030; website www.essexcricket.org.uk; e-mail administration.essex@ecb.co.uk).

GLAMORGAN: Sophia Gardens, Cardiff CF11 9XR (029 2040 9380; fax 029 2040 9390; website www.glamorgancricket.com; e-mail glam@ecb.co.uk).

GLOUCESTERSHIRE: Phoenix County Ground, Nevil Road, Bristol BS7 9EJ (0117 910 8000; fax 0117 924 1193; website www.gloucestershire.cricinfo.com; e-mail enquiries.glos@ecb.co.uk).

HAMPSHIRE: The Hampshire Rose Bowl, Botley Road, West End, Southampton SO30 3XH (023 8047 2002; fax 023 8047 2122; website www.hampshire.cricinfo.com; e-mail enquiries@rosebowlplc.com).

KENT: St Lawrence Ground, Old Dover Road, Canterbury CT1 3NZ (01227 456886; fax 01227 762168; website www.kentccc.com; e-mail kent@ecb.co.uk).

LANCASHIRE: County Cricket Ground, Old Trafford, Manchester M16 0PX (0161 282 4000; fax 0161 282 4100; website www.lccc.co.uk; e-mail enquiries@lccc.co.uk).

LEICESTERSHIRE: County Ground, Grace Road, Leicester LE2 8AD (0116 283 2128; fax 0116 244 0363; website www.leicestershireccc.co.uk; e-mail leicestershire@ukonline.co.uk).

MIDDLESEX: Lord's Cricket Ground, London NW8 8QN (020 7289 1300; fax 020 7289 5831; website www.middlesexccc.com; e-mail enquiries@middlesexccc.com).

NORTHAMPTONSHIRE: County Ground, Wantage Road, Northampton NN1 4TJ (01604 514455; fax 01604 514488; website www.nccc.co.uk; e-mail post@nccc.co.uk).

NOTTINGHAMSHIRE: County Cricket Ground, Trent Bridge, Nottingham NG2 6AG (0115 982 3000; fax 0115 945 5730; website www.nottsccc.co.uk; e-mail administration.notts@ecb.co.uk).

SOMERSET: County Ground, St James's Street, Taunton TA1 1JT (01823 272946; fax 01823 332395; website www.somerset.cricinfo.com; e-mail somerset@ecb.co.uk).

SURREY: The Oval, Kennington, London SE11 5SS (020 7582 6660; fax 020 7735 7769; website www.surreycricket.com; e-mail enquiries@surreycricket.com).

SUSSEX: County Ground, Eaton Road, Hove BN3 3AN (01273 827100; fax 01273 771549; website www.sussexcricket.co.uk; e-mail info@sussexcricket.co.uk).

WARWICKSHIRE: County Ground, Edgbaston, Birmingham B5 7QU (0121 446 4422; fax 0121 446 4544; website www.thebears.co.uk; e-mail info@thebears.co.uk).

WORCESTERSHIRE: County Ground, New Road, Worcester WR2 4QQ (01905 748474; fax 01905 748005; website www.wccc.co.uk; e-mail joan.grundy@wccc.co.uk).

YORKSHIRE: Headingley Cricket Ground, Leeds LS6 3BU (0113 278 7394; fax 0113 278 4099; website www.yorkshireccc.org.uk; e-mail cricket@yorkshireccc.org.uk).

Minor Counties

MINOR COUNTIES CRICKET ASSOCIATION: G. R. Evans, Blueberry Haven, 20 Boucher Road, Budleigh Salterton, Devon EX9 6JF (01395 445216, fax 01395 445334; e-mail evans@20boucher.freeserve.co.uk/geoff.evans@ecb.co.uk).

BEDFORDSHIRE: P. G. M. August, 35 Amberley Gardens, Bedford MK40 3BT (01234 327935, office 01234 261391; e-mail philip.august@ecb.co.uk).

BERKSHIRE: R. New, 41 Holyrood Close, Caversham, Reading, Berkshire RG4 6PZ (0118 946 3422, mobile 07831 746285; e-mail roy.new@ecb.co.uk).

BUCKINGHAMSHIRE: K. A. Beaumont, 49 Amersham Road, Little Chalfont, Amersham, Buckinghamshire HP6 6SW (01494 763516; e-mail kevin.beaumont@tesco.net).

CAMBRIDGESHIRE: P. W. Gooden, The Redlands, Oakington Road, Cottenham, Cambridge CB4 8TW (01954 250429; e-mail pwgooden@amserve.com).

CHESHIRE: J. B. Pickup, 36 Landswood Park, Hartford, Northwich, Cheshire CW8 1NF (01606 74970 home; fax 01606 79357; e-mail Johnpickup@btinternet.com).

CORNWALL: Mrs A. M. George, The Logan Rock Inn, Treen, St Levan, Penzance, Cornwall TR19 6LG (01736 810495, fax 01736 810177; e-mail anitageorge@loganrockinn.com).

CUMBERLAND: K. Ion, 47 Beech Grove, Stanwix, Carlisle, Cumbria CA3 9BG (01228 528858, mobile 07970 421589; e-mail kion47bg@aol.com).

DEVON: G. R. Evans, Blueberry Haven, 20 Boucher Road, Budleigh Salterton, Devon EX9 6JF (01395 445216, fax 01395 445334; e-mail evans@20boucher.freeserve.co.uk).

DORSET: K. H. House, The Barn, Higher Farm, Bagber Common, Sturminster Newton, Dorset DT10 2HB (01258 473394, mobile 07971 245889; e-mail housekenneth@hotmail.com).

HEREFORDSHIRE: P. Sykes, 5 Dale Drive, Holmer Grange, Hereford HR4 9RF (01432 264703, fax 01432 382323, mobile 07809 026484; e-mail pete.sykes@FreeUK.com).

HERTFORDSHIRE: B. Mulholland, 16 Landford Close, Rickmansworth, Hertfordshire WD3 1NG (01923 772755, fax 01923 711683, mobile 07785 257502; mulhollandbrian@aol.com).

LINCOLNSHIRE: C. A. North, Lincolnshire CCC, First Floor, 27 The Forum, North Hykeham, Lincoln LN6 9HW (office/fax 01522 688073, home 01522 681636; e-mail tony-north@hotmail.com).

NORFOLK: S. J. Skinner, 27 Colkett Drive, Old Catton, Norwich NR6 7ND (01603 485940, office 01603 624236; e-mail stephen.skinner1@virgin.net).

NORTHUMBERLAND: A. B. Stephenson, Northumberland CCC, Osborne Avenue, Jesmond, Newcastle-upon-Tyne NE2 1JS (office 0191 281 2738, home 0191 213 1152; e-mail alan@astephenson28.freeserve.co.uk).

OXFORDSHIRE: P. R. N. O'Neill, 4 Brookside, Thame, Oxfordshire OX9 3DE (01844 260439, also fax, mobile 07711 943449; prnoneill@waitrose.com).

SHROPSHIRE: N. H. Birch, Four Winds, 24 Ridgebourne Road, Shrewsbury, Shropshire SY3 9AB (01743 233650, office/fax 01743 242739, mobile 07974 000906; e-mail shropboard@tiscali.co.uk).

STAFFORDSHIRE: W. S. Bourne, 10 The Pavement, Brewood, Staffordshire ST19 9BZ (01902 850325; e-mail stuart.bourne1@btopenworld.com).

SUFFOLK: T. J. Pound, 94 Henley Road, Ipswich IP1 4NJ (01473 213288, office 01473 232121; e-mail Toby.Pound@prettys.co.uk).

WALES MINOR COUNTIES: W. Edwards, 59a King Edward Road, Swansea SA1 4LN (01792 462233; fax 01792 643931).

WILTSHIRE: C. R. Sheppard, PO Box 10, Fairford, Gloucestershire GL7 4YR (01285 810809, mobile 07831 565866; e-mail chris.sheppard@ecb.co.uk).

HUNTINGDONSHIRE (ECB 38-county) D. Swannell, 23 Popes Lane, Warboys, Huntingdon PE17 2RN (01487 823122).

Other Bodies

ASSOCIATION OF CRICKET STATISTICIANS AND HISTORIANS: P. Wynne-Thomas, 3 Radcliffe Road, West Bridgford, Nottingham NG2 5FF (0115 945 5407; website www.acs.cricket.org; e-mail acsoffice@cricket.org).

ASSOCIATION OF CRICKET UMPIRES AND SCORERS: G. J. Bullock, PO Box 399, Camberley, Surrey GU15 3JZ (01276 27962; fax 01276 62277; website www.acus.cricket.org; e-mail admin@acus.org.uk).

BRITISH UNIVERSITIES SPORTS ASSOCIATION: J. Ellis, 8 Union Street, London SE1 1SZ (020 7357 8555; website www.busaresults.org.uk; e-mail jim@busa.org.uk).

CLUB CRICKET CONFERENCE: B. Stuart-King, 361 West Barnes Lane, New Malden, Surrey KT3 6JF (020 8336 0586; fax 020 8336 0537; e-mail barrie.stuart-king@club-cricket.com).

ENGLISH SCHOOLS' CRICKET ASSOCIATION: K. S. Lake, 38 Mill House, Woods Lane, Cottingham, Hull HU16 4HQ.

EUROPEAN CRICKET COUNCIL: I. C. D. Stuart, Europe Office, Lord's Ground, London NW8 8QN (020 7432 1019; fax 020 7432 1091; website www.ecc.cricket.org).

LEAGUE CRICKET CONFERENCE: N. Edwards, 1 Longfield, Freshfield, Formby, Merseyside L37 3LD (01704 877103; e-mail neil.edwards@ecb.co.uk).

MIDLANDS CLUB CRICKET CONFERENCE: D. Thomas, 4 Silverdale Gardens, Wordsley, Stourbridge, West Midlands DY8 5NY (01384 278107; office 01902 864685).

PROFESSIONAL CRICKETERS' ASSOCIATION/PCA MANAGEMENT: R. H. Bevan, 3rd Floor, 338 Euston Road, London NW1 3BT (020 7544 8660; fax 020 7544 8515; e-mail admin@pcaml.co.uk).

RUTLAND COUNTY CRICKET ASSOCIATION: I. H. S. Balfour, Nanjazel, 7 Nightingale Way, Oakham, Rutland LE15 6ES.

Cricket Associations and Societies

AUSTRALIAN CRICKET SOCIETY: Queensland – Mrs D. Durrand, 128 Somerset Road, Kedron, Qld 4031. Victoria – D. Manning, Ravenstone, PO Box 89, Ringwood, Vic 3134. South Australia – Mrs M. Hilton, PO Box 646, North Adelaide, S. Australia 5006.

CHELTENHAM CRICKET SOCIETY: P. Murphy, 1 Colesbourne Road, Benhall, Cheltenham, Gloucestershire GL51 6DJ.

CHESTERFIELD CRICKET SOCIETY: J. S. Cook, 44 Morris Avenue, Newbold, Chesterfield, Derbyshire S41 7BA.

COUNCIL OF CRICKET SOCIETIES, THE: R. H. Wood – see High Peak Cricket Society.

COUNTY CRICKET SUPPORTERS ASSOCIATION: Miss F. J. Walker, 12 Grasmere Drive, Linton Croft, Wetherby, West Yorkshire LS22 6GP.

CRICKET FAN CLUB: 1407 Qasimjan Street, Ballimaran, Delhi 110006, India.

CRICKET MEMORABILIA SOCIETY: S. Cashmore, 4 Stoke Park Court, Stoke Road, Bishops Cleeve, Cheltenham, Gloucestershire GL52 8US.

CRICKET SOCIETY, THE: D. Wood, PO Box 6024, Leighton Buzzard LU7 2ZS.

CRICKET STATISTICIANS AND SCORERS OF INDIA, ASSOCIATION OF: PO Box 7145, Wadala Post Office, Mumbai 400-041.

DERBYSHIRE CRICKET SOCIETY: O. C. Kinsella, 27 Wilsthorpe Road, Breaston, Derby DE72 3EA.

DUNELM CRICKET SOCIETY: Mrs M. Coombs, White Lodge, Halliford Road, Shepperton, Middlesex TW17 8RU.

DURHAM AND NORTH-EAST BRANCH OF THE CRICKET SOCIETY: Prof. R. Storer, 164 Eastern Way, Darras Hall, Ponteland, Newcastle-upon-Tyne NE20 9RH.

EAST RIDING CRICKET SOCIETY: Mrs S. Forward, 121 Fairfax Avenue, Hull HU5 4QU.

ESSEX CRICKET SOCIETY: A. E. Saywood, 6 Brickwall Close, Burnham-on-Crouch, Essex CM0 8HB.

GLOUCESTERSHIRE CRICKET LOVERS' SOCIETY: Miss S. Jones, 20 Ormerod Road, Bristol BS9 1BB.

HAMPSHIRE CRICKET SOCIETY: B. Smith, 9 Rawlings Grove, Abingdon, Oxon OX14 1SH.

HEREFORDSHIRE CRICKET SOCIETY: J. Morris, 78 Stanhope Street, Hereford HR4 0NB.

HERTFORDSHIRE CRICKET SOCIETY: W. A. Powell, 17 Swan Mead, The Willows, Hemel Hempstead, Hertfordshire HP3 9DQ.

HIGH PEAK CRICKET SOCIETY: R. H. Wood, 2 Jodrell Road, Whaley Bridge, Derbyshire SK23 7AN.

LANCASHIRE AND CHESHIRE CRICKET SOCIETY: J. L. Petch, 63 Linksway, Gatley, Cheshire SK8 4LA.

LINCOLNSHIRE CRICKET LOVERS' SOCIETY: C. Kennedy, 26 Eastwood Avenue, Great Grimsby, South Humberside DN34 5BE.

MERSEYSIDE CRICKET SOCIETY: B. Cockrell, 434 Woolton Road, Liverpool L25 6JQ.

MIDLANDS BRANCH OF THE CRICKET SOCIETY: Miss H. Allen, 14 Merrions Close, Great Barr, Birmingham B43 7AT.

NATIONAL CRICKET MEMBERSHIP SCHEME: 22 Grazebrook Road, London N16 0HS.

NEEDWOOD CRICKET LOVERS' SOCIETY: A. D. Campion, 45 Fallowfield Drive, Barton-under-Needwood, Staffordshire DE13 8DH.

NEW ZEALAND, CRICKET SOCIETY OF: C. Rosie, Eden Park, PO Box 2860, Auckland 1.

NORFOLK CRICKET SOCIETY: Mrs J. King, 3 Blickling Court, Recorder Road, Norwich, Norfolk NR1 1NW.

NORTHERN CRICKET SOCIETY: H. Jackson, 20 Foxholes Lane, Calverley, Pudsey LS28 5NS.

NOTTINGHAM CRICKET LOVERS' SOCIETY: G. Blagdurn, 2 Inham Circus, Chilwell, Nottingham NG9 4FN.

PAKISTAN ASSOCIATION OF CRICKET STATISTICIANS: Abid Ali Kazi and Nauman Bader, 256-N, Model Town Ext, Lahore 54700 (e-mail naumanb@brain.net.pk).

ROTHERHAM CRICKET SOCIETY: J. A. R. Atkin, 15 Gallow Tree Road, Rotherham S65 3EE.

SCOTLAND, CRICKET SOCIETY OF: J. Marr, 12 Merrycrest Avenue, Giffnock, Glasgow G46 6BQ.

SOUTH AFRICA, CRICKET SOCIETY OF: Mrs E. Sim, PO Box 78040, Sandton, Gauteng 2146.

STOURBRIDGE CRICKET SOCIETY: M. Taylor, 26 Wrekin Walk, Stourport-on-Severn, Worcestershire DY13 0LR.

SUSSEX CRICKET SOCIETY: Mrs P. Brabyn, 4 Wolstonbury Walk, Shoreham-by-Sea, West Sussex BN43 5GU.

WEST LANCASHIRE CRICKET SOCIETY: G. W. Lee, 107 Bibby Road, Southport PR9 7PZ.

WEST OF ENGLAND BRANCH OF THE CRICKET SOCIETY: F. J. Endacott, 84 Hardens Mead, Chippenham, Wiltshire SN15 3AF.

WOMBWELL CRICKET LOVERS' SOCIETY: M. Pope, 32 Louden Road, Scholes, Rotherham, South Yorkshire S61 2SU.

WORCESTER CRICKET SOCIETY: M. Niccols, 70 Park Avenue, Worcester WR3 7AQ.

YORKSHIRE CCC SOUTHERN GROUP: D. M. Wood, 15 Rothschild Road, Linslade, Leighton Buzzard, Bedfordshire LU7 7SY.

ZIMBABWE, CRICKET SOCIETY OF: J. B. Stockwell, 6 Howard Close, Mount Pleasant, Harare.

REGULATIONS OF THE INTERNATIONAL CRICKET COUNCIL

Extracts

1. Standard playing conditions

In 2001, the ICC Cricket Committee amended its standard playing conditions for all Tests and one-day internationals to include the new Laws of Cricket. The following playing conditions were to apply for three years from September 1, 2001:

Duration of Test Matches

Test matches shall be of five days' scheduled duration and of two innings per side. The two participating countries may:

(a) Provide for a rest day during the match, and/or a reserve day after the scheduled days of play.

(b) Play on any scheduled rest day, conditions and circumstances permitting, should a full day's play be lost on any day prior to the rest day.

(c) Play on any scheduled reserve day, conditions and circumstances permitting, should a full day's play be lost on any day. Play shall not take place on more than five days.

(d) Make up time lost in excess of five minutes in each day's play due to circumstances outside the game, other than acts of God.

Hours of Play and Minimum Overs in the Day in Test Matches

1. Start and cessation times shall be determined by the home board, subject to there being six hours scheduled for play per day (Pakistan a minimum of five and a half hours).

(a) Play shall continue on each day until the completion of a minimum number of overs or until the scheduled cessation time, whichever is the later. The minimum number of overs to be completed, unless an innings ends or an interruption occurs, shall be:

(i) on days other than the last day – a minimum of 90 overs (or a minimum of 15 overs per hour).

(ii) on the last day – a minimum of 75 overs (or 15 overs per hour) for playing time other than the last hour when a minimum of 15 overs shall be bowled. All calculations with regard to suspensions of play or the start of a new innings shall be based on one over for each full four minutes. (Fractions are to be ignored in all calculations except where there is a change of innings in a day's play, when the over in progress at the conclusion shall be rounded up.) If, however, at any time after 30 minutes of the last hour have elapsed both captains (the batsmen at the wicket may act for their captain) accept that there is no prospect of a result to the match, they may agree to cease play at that time.

(iii) Subject to weather and light, except in the last hour of the match, in the event of play being suspended for any reason other than normal intervals, the playing time on that day shall be extended by the amount of time lost up to a maximum of one hour. For the avoidance of doubt, the maximum of one hour shall be inclusive of any time that may have been added to the scheduled playing time due to time having been lost on previous days. The minimum number of overs to be bowled shall be in accordance with the provisions of this clause (i.e. a minimum of 15 overs per hour) and the cessation time shall be rescheduled accordingly.

(iv) If any time is lost and cannot be made up under (a)(iii), additional time of up to a maximum of one hour per day shall be added to the scheduled playing hours for the next day, and subsequent day(s) as required. Where appropriate, the first 30 minutes (or less) of this additional time shall be added before the scheduled start of the first session and the remainder to the last session. Where it is not possible to add this time before the scheduled start, the timing of the lunch and tea intervals will be adjusted to provide a scheduled two-and-a-half-hour session and not affect the start time. On any day's play, except the last day, when the scheduled hours have been completed but the required number of overs have not been bowled, and weather or bad light causes play to be abandoned, the remaining overs shall be made up on the next or subsequent days. On any one day, a maximum of 15 additional overs shall be permitted. When additional time is added to subsequent day(s), no scheduled day's play shall exceed seven hours. The length of each session is subject to Law 15. Timings can be altered at any time on any day if time is lost, not necessarily on that day. The captains, umpires and referee can agree different timings under those circumstances before play starts on any day.

(b) When an innings ends, a minimum number of overs shall be bowled from the start of the new innings. The number of overs to be bowled shall be calculated at the rate of one over for each full four minutes to enable a minimum of 90 overs to be bowled in a day. The last hour of the match shall be excluded from this calculation (see (a) (ii)).

Where a change of innings occurs during a day's play, in the event of the team bowling second being unable to complete its overs by the scheduled cessation time, play shall continue until the required number of overs have been completed.

2. The umpires may decide to play 30 minutes (a minimum eight overs) extra time at the end of any day (other than the last day) if requested by either captain if, in the umpires' opinion, it would bring about a definite result on that day. If the umpires do not believe a result can be achieved, no extra time shall be allowed. If it is decided to play such extra time, the whole period shall be played out even though the possibility of finishing the match may have disappeared before the full period has expired. Only the actual amount of playing time up to the maximum 30 minutes' extra time by which play is extended on any day shall be deducted from the total number of hours of play remaining and the match shall end earlier on the final day by that amount of time.

Use of Lights:

If, in the opinion of the umpires, natural light is deteriorating to an unfit level, they shall authorise the ground authorities to use the available artificial lighting so that the match can continue in acceptable conditions.

The lights are only to be used to enable a full day's play to be completed as provided for in Clause 1 above. In the event of power failure or lights malfunction, the existing provisions of Clause 1 shall apply.

Dangerous and Unfair Bowling: The Bowling of Fast, Short-Pitched Balls: Law 42.6

1.
   (a) A bowler shall be limited to two fast, short-pitched deliveries per over.

   (b) A fast, short-pitched ball is defined as a ball which passes or would have passed above the shoulder height of the striker standing upright at the crease.

   (c) The umpire at the bowler's end shall advise the bowler and the batsman on strike when each fast short-pitched ball has been bowled.

   (d) For the purpose of this regulation, a ball that passes above head height of the batsman that prevents him from being able to hit it with his bat by means of a normal cricket stroke shall be called a wide.

   (e) Any fast, short-pitched delivery called a wide under this condition shall count as one of the allowable short-pitched deliveries in that over.

   (f) In the event of a bowler bowling more than two fast, short-pitched deliveries in an over, the umpire at the bowler's end shall call and signal "no-ball" on each occasion. The umpire shall call and signal "no-ball" and then tap the head with the other hand.

   (g) If a bowler delivers a third fast, short-pitched ball in one over, the umpire must call no-ball and then invoke the procedures of caution, final warning, action against the bowler and reporting as set out in Law 42.7. The umpires will report the matter to the ICC referee who shall take such action as is considered appropriate against the captain and bowler concerned.

The above Regulation is not a substitute for Law 42.6 (as amended below), which umpires are able to apply at any time:

The bowling of fast, short-pitched balls is unfair if the umpire at the bowler's end considers that, by their repetition and taking into account their length, height and direction, they are likely to inflict physical injury on the striker, irrespective of the protective clothing and equipment he may be wearing. The relative skill of the striker shall also be taken into consideration.

The umpire at the bowler's end shall adopt the procedures of caution, final warning, action against the bowler and reporting as set out in Law 42.7. The ICC referee shall take any further action considered appropriate against the captain and bowler concerned.

New Ball: Law 5.4

The captain of the fielding side shall have the choice of taking a new ball any time after 80 overs have been bowled with the previous ball. The umpires shall indicate to the batsmen and the scorers whenever a new ball is taken into play.

Ball Lost or Becoming Unfit for Play: Law 5.5

The following shall apply in addition to Law 5.5:

However, if the ball needs to be replaced after 110 overs for any of the reasons above, it shall be replaced by a new ball. If the ball is to be replaced, the umpires shall inform the batsmen.

Judging a Wide: Law 25.1

Law 25.1 will apply, but in addition:

For bowlers attempting to utilise the rough outside a batsman's leg stump, not necessarily as a negative tactic, the strict limited-overs wide interpretation shall be applied. For bowlers whom umpires consider to be bowling down the leg side as a negative tactic, the strict limited-overs wide interpretation shall be applied.

Practice on the Field: Law 17

In addition to Law 17.1:

The use of the square for practice on any day of any match will be restricted to any netted practice area on the square set aside for that purpose.

Fieldsman Leaving the Field: Law 2.5

If a fielder fails to take the field with his side at the start of the match or at any later time, or leaves the field during a session of play, the umpire shall be informed of the reason for his absence, and he shall not thereafter come on to the field during a session without the consent of the umpire. The umpire shall give such consent as soon as practicable. If the player is absent from the field longer than eight minutes, he shall not be permitted to bowl in that innings after his return until he has been on the field for at least that length of playing time for which he was absent. In the event of a follow-on, this restriction will, if necessary, continue into the second innings. Nor shall he be permitted to bat unless or until, in the aggregate, he has returned to the field and/or his side's innings has been in progress for at least that length of playing time for which he has been absent or, if earlier, when his side has lost five wickets. The restrictions shall not apply if he has suffered an external blow (as opposed to an internal injury such as a pulled muscle) while participating earlier in the match and consequently been forced to leave the field, nor if he has been absent for exceptional and acceptable reasons (other than injury or illness).

2. Classification of first-class matches

1. Definitions

A match of three or more days' duration between two sides of 11 players played on natural turf pitches on international standard grounds and substantially conforming with standard playing conditions shall be regarded as a first-class fixture.

2. Rules

    (a) Full Members of the ICC shall decide the status of matches of three or more days' duration played in their countries.

    (b) In matches of three or more days' duration played in countries which are not Full Members of the ICC, except Kenya (see 2.3 (l) below):

        (i) If the visiting team comes from a country which is a Full Member of the ICC, that country shall decide the status of matches.

        (ii) If the visiting team does not come from a country which is a Full Member of the ICC, or is a Commonwealth team composed of players from different countries, the ICC shall decide the status of matches.

Notes

(a) Governing bodies agree that the interest of first-class cricket will be served by ensuring that first-class status is not accorded to any match in which one or other of the teams taking part cannot on a strict interpretation of the definitions be adjudged first-class.

(b) In case of any disputes arising from these Rules, the Chief Executive of the ICC shall refer the matter for decision to the Council, failing unanimous agreement by postal communication being reached.

3. First-Class Status

The following matches shall be regarded as first-class, subject to the provisions of 2.1 (Definitions) being complied with:

(a) **In Great Britain and Ireland:** (i) County Championship matches. (ii) Official representative tourist matches from Full Member countries unless specifically excluded. (iii) MCC v any first-class county. (iv) Oxford, Cambridge, Durham and Loughborough University Centres of Excellence against first-class counties. (v) Oxford v Cambridge. (vi) Scotland v Ireland.

(b) **In Australia:** (i) Pura Cup matches. (ii) Matches played by Australia A or an Australian XI and teams representing states of the Commonwealth of Australia between each other or against opponents adjudged first-class.

(c) **In Bangladesh:** (i) Matches between Bangladesh and a Full Member. (ii) Matches between Full Member teams adjudged first-class and Bangladesh. (iii) Matches between teams adjudged first-class and a Full Member. (iv) Matches between Bangladesh and Kenya. (v) Matches between teams adjudged first-class and Kenya. (vi) National League three-day matches between the Divisions of Barisal, Chittagong, Dhaka, Khulna, Rajshahi and Sylhet.

(d) **In India:** (i) Ranji Trophy matches. (ii) Duleep Trophy matches. (iii) Irani Trophy matches. (iv) Matches played by teams representing state or regional associations affiliated to the Board of Control between each other or against opponents adjudged first-class. (v) Matches of three days or more against representative visiting sides.

(e) **In New Zealand:** (i) State Championship matches. (ii) Matches played by New Zealand A or major associations affiliated to New Zealand Cricket, between each other or against opponents adjudged first-class.

(f) **In Pakistan:** (i) Quaid-e-Azam Trophy (Grade 1) matches. (ii) Super League four-day games between provincial teams. (iii) Matches played by teams representing cricket associations and departments affiliated to the Pakistan Cricket Board, between each other or against teams adjudged first-class (organised by the PCB). (iv) A-team matches played in Pakistan between Pakistan and other Full Members and Kenya.

(g) **In South Africa:** (i) SuperSport Series four-day matches between Boland, Border, Eastern Province, Easterns, Free State, Gauteng, Griqualand West, KwaZulu-Natal, Northerns, North West, Western Province. (ii) Matches against touring teams from Full Member countries.

(h) **In Sri Lanka:** (i) Matches of three days or more against touring sides adjudged first-class. (ii) Premier League Division I matches played over three or more days for the Premier Trophy. (iii) Matches of three days or more against visiting A teams of Full Member countries by Sri Lanka A or senior development squad teams or BCCSL representative teams (except Under-19 and below).

(i) **In West Indies:** Matches played by teams representing Barbados, Guyana, Jamaica, the Leeward Islands, Trinidad & Tobago and the Windward Islands, either for the Busta Cup or against other opponents adjudged first-class.

(j) **In Zimbabwe:** (i) Logan Cup matches. (ii) Matches played by teams representing associations affiliated to the ZCU, between each other or against opponents adjudged first-class.

(k) **In all Full Member countries represented on the Council:** (i) Test matches and matches against teams adjudged first-class played by official touring teams. (ii) Official Test Trial matches. (iii) Special matches between teams adjudged first-class by the governing body or bodies concerned.

(l) **In Kenya:** (i) Matches between a Full Member and Kenya. (ii) Matches between teams adjudged first-class and Kenya.

3. Classification of Test matches

Any match of not more than five days' scheduled duration played between teams selected by Full Members as representatives of their member countries and accorded the status of Test match by the ICC.

Only Full Members of ICC can participate in Test matches.

4. Classification of one-day international matches

The following shall be classified as one-day internationals:

(a) All matches played in the official World Cup competition, including matches involving Associate Member countries.

(b) All matches played between the Full Member countries of the ICC as part of an official tour itinerary.

(c) All matches played as part of an official tournament between Full Member countries. These need not necessarily be held in a Full Member country.

(d) All matches between the Full Members and Kenya.

Note: Matches involving the A team of a Full Member country shall not be classified as one-day internationals.

5. Player qualification rules for ICC matches, series and competitions

(a) A cricketer is qualified to play in Tests, one-day internationals or any other representative cricket match for an ICC Member country of which he is a national or, in cases of non-nationals, in which he was born, provided that he has not played in Tests, one-day internationals or any other representative cricket match for any other Member country during the four immediately preceding years.

(b) Where the country is an Associate or Affiliate Member, the cricketer must satisfy one or more of the following additional Development Criteria:

    (i) he shall have played 50 per cent or more of the scheduled games for his team in a national cricket competition in the relevant Member country in any three of the preceding five years.

    (ii) he shall have spent a cumulative total of 100 days or more during the preceding five years coaching, playing or working in the administration or development of cricket in the relevant Member country.

    (iii) he shall have played cricket at representative level for the relevant Member country.

    (iv) he shall have dedicated a reasonable period of time to activities which, in the opinion of the Chairman of the Cricket Committee, constitute a sufficient demonstration of his genuine commitment to the development of cricket in the relevant Member country.

He must also satisfy the quota requirement for deemed nationals (see below).

(c) A player who has resided for a minimum of 183 days in a Member country in each of the four immediately preceding years shall be a "deemed national" of that country for the purpose of these rules. Affiliate and Associate Members may not field more than two players in any one team who are deemed nationals, but a player who has resided in an Affiliate or Associate Member country for a minimum of 183 days in each of the seven immediately preceding years shall be classified as a national rather than a deemed national of that Member country.

(d) Where an Associate or Affiliate Member country is fielding a team against a Full Member or in any tournament or competition involving teams from one or more Full Members, the requirements relating to having played a representative cricket match for any other Member country during the four immediately preceding years, the Development Criteria and the quota rules shall not apply.

(e) A cricketer qualified to play for a Member country can continue to represent that country without negating his eligibility or interrupting his qualification period for another Member country until he has played for the first Member country at Under-19 level or above.

(f) Associate and Affiliate Members shall be limited to two players per team who have formerly played Tests, one-day internationals or any other representative cricket match for a Full Member country, except when fielding a team against a Full Member or in any tournament or competition involving teams from one or more Full Members.

Notes: "Representative cricket match" means any cricket match in which a team representing a Member country at Under-19 level or above takes part, including Tests and one-day internationals.
   The governing body for cricket of any Member country may impose more stringent qualification rules for that country.

ICC CODE OF CONDUCT

1. Players and/or team officials shall at all times conduct play within the spirit of the game as well as within the Laws of cricket, and the captains are responsible at all times for ensuring that this is adhered to.

2. Players and/or team officials shall at no time engage in conduct unbecoming to their status which could bring them or the game of cricket into disrepute.

3. Players and/or team officials shall be required to report to the captain and/or team manager or to a senior board official or to the Anti-Corruption Unit any approach made to them by a bookmaker or any other corrupt approach or knowledge of such approach made to any other player or team official.

4. Players and/or team officials shall not bet on matches nor otherwise engage in any conduct of the nature described in the paragraphs below. For conduct in breach of this rule, the penalties to be considered are set out below, for individuals who have:

    i. Bet on any match or series of matches, or on any connected event, in which such player, umpire, referee, team official or administrator took part or in which the Member country or any such individual was represented (penalty (a));

    ii. Induced or encouraged any other person to bet on any match or series of matches or on any connected event or to offer the facility for such bets to be placed (penalty (b));

    iii. Gambled or entered into any other form of financial speculation on any match or on any connected event (penalty (a));

    iv. Induced or encouraged any other person to gamble or enter into any other form of financial speculation on any match or any connected event (penalty (b));

    v. Was a party to contriving or attempting to contrive the result of any match or the occurrence of any connected event (penalty (c));

    vi. Failed to perform on his merits in any match owing to an arrangement relating to betting on the outcome of any match or on the occurrence of any connected event (penalty (c));

    vii. Induced or encouraged any other player not to perform on his merits in any match owing to any such arrangement (penalty (c));

    viii. Received from another person any money, benefit or other reward (whether financial or otherwise) for the provision of any information concerning the weather, the teams, the state of the ground, the status of, or the outcome of, any match or the occurrence of any connected event unless such information has been provided to a newspaper or other form of media in accordance with an obligation entered into in the normal course and disclosed in advance to the cricket authority of the relevant Member country (penalty (b));

    ix. Received any money, benefit or other reward (whether financial or otherwise) which could bring him or the game of cricket into disrepute (penalty (d));

    x. Provided any money, benefit or other reward (whether financial or otherwise) which could bring the game of cricket into disrepute (penalty (d));

    xi. Received any approaches from another person to engage in conduct such as that described above, and has failed to disclose the same to his captain or team manager, or to a senior board official or to the Anti-Corruption Unit (penalty (e)); or

xii. Is aware that any other player or individual has engaged in conduct, or received approaches, such as described above, and has failed to disclose the same to his captain or team manager, or to a senior board official or to the Anti-Corruption Unit (penalty (e));

xiii. Has received or is aware that any other person has received threats of any nature which might induce him to engage in conduct, or acquiesce in any proposal made by an approach, such as described above, and has failed to disclose the same to his captain or team manager, or to a senior board official or to the Anti-Corruption Unit (penalty (e));.

xiv. Has engaged in any conduct which, in the opinion of the Executive Board, relates directly or indirectly to any of the above paragraphs (i to xiii) and is prejudicial to the interests of the game of cricket (penalty (e)).

Penalties:

(a) Ban for a minimum of two years and a maximum of five years. In addition, a fine may be imposed, the amount to be assessed in the circumstances.

(b) Ban for a minimum of two years and a maximum of five years if a bet was placed directly or indirectly for the benefit of the individual; otherwise, a ban for a minimum of 12 months. In addition, a fine may be imposed, the amount to be assessed in the circumstances.

(c) Ban for life (a minimum of 20 years).

(d) Ban for a minimum of two years and a maximum of life. In addition, a fine may be imposed, the amount to be assessed in the circumstances.

(e) Ban for a minimum of one year and a maximum of five years. In addition, a fine may be imposed, the amount to be assessed in the circumstances.

5. A valid defence may be made to a charge in respect of any prohibited conduct in paragraphs 4 (xi) to (xiii) above if a person proves that this conduct was the result of an honest and reasonable belief that there was a serious threat to the life or safety of himself or any member of his family.

6. Players and/or team officials shall not use or in any way be concerned in the use or distribution of illegal drugs. Illegal drugs shall mean those drugs which are classified as unlawful in the player's or team official's home country or in the country in which he is touring. Any such conduct shall constitute behaviour prohibited under paragraph 2 and shall be dealt with as such. Players and team officials shall also be subject to any doping policy which is applied by their home board and such policies which are introduced for ICC events. Any breach of such doping policy shall be dealt with under the terms of such policy itself and not under this code.

CRIME AND PUNISHMENT

ICC Code of Conduct – Breaches and Penalties in 2001-02

G. W. Flower   Zimbabwe v South Africa, one-day international at Harare.
Dissent when umpire would not declare a wide delivery. Severely reprimanded by Naushad Ali.

A. Flower   Zimbabwe v England, one-day international at Harare.
Heated exchange with N. Hussain. Severely reprimanded by Naushad Ali.

J. S. Foster   Zimbabe v England, one-day international at Harare.
Disturbed A. Flower at the crease. Severely reprimanded by Naushad Ali.

N. Hussain   Zimbabwe v England, one-day international at Harare.
Heated exchange with A. Flower. Severely reprimanded by Naushad Ali.

M. O. Odumbe   South Africa v Kenya, one-day international at Kimberley.
Criticised umpires to the press. Banned for two one-day internationals by A. Ebrahim.

S. R. Tendulkar   South Africa v India, 2nd Test at Port Elizabeth.
Alleged interference with the ball, changing its condition. Fined 75 per cent of match fee, with ban for one Test suspended for six weeks by M. H. Denness.

V. Sehwag   South Africa v India, 2nd Test at Port Elizabeth.
Excessive reaction when appeal rejected, and attempt to intimidate the umpire by charging him. Fined 75 per cent of match fee, and banned for one Test by M. H. Denness.

S. S. Das, D. Dasgupta, Harbhajan Singh and V. Sehwag
          South Africa v India, 2nd Test at Port Elizabeth.
Dissent at umpire's decision and attempt to intimidate him. Each fined 75 per cent of match fee, with ban for one Test suspended for ten weeks by M. H. Denness.

S. C. Ganguly   South Africa v India, 2nd Test at Port Elizabeth.
Failing to uphold captain's responsibility for the spirit of the game or to control players' conduct. Ban for one Test and two one-day internationals suspended for ten weeks by M. H. Denness.

S. V. Carlisle   Bangladesh v Zimbabwe, 2nd Test at Chittagong.
Dissent when given out lbw. Fined 50 per cent of match fee by Hanumant Singh.

B. Lee   Australia v New Zealand, 3rd Test at Perth.
Abusive language and offensive gesture towards S. E. Bond. Fined 75 per cent of match fee by J. L. Hendriks.

S. R. Waugh   Australia v South Africa, 2nd Test at Melbourne.
Remained at the crease after he was given out. Fined 50 per cent of his match fee by R. S. Madugalle.

G. D. McGrath   Australia v New Zealand, one-day international at Melbourne.
Gesturing and dissent when given out. Banned for one one-day international, with ban for two further games suspended for one month, by Hanumant Singh.

S. P. Fleming   Australia v New Zealand, one-day international at Melbourne.
Signalled with bat that no-ball should have been called. Fined 40 per cent of match fee by Hanumant Singh.

REGULATIONS FOR FIRST-CLASS MATCHES IN BRITAIN, 2002

Hours of play

1st, 2nd [and 3rd in 4-day matches] days. . . 11.00 a.m. to 6.30 p.m.
Final day. . . . . 11.00 a.m. to 6.00 p.m.

Intervals

Lunch: 1.15 p.m. to 1.55 p.m. (1st, 2nd [3rd] days)
          1.00 p.m. to 1.40 p.m. (final day)
          Where an innings concludes or there is a break in play within ten minutes of the scheduled lunch interval, the interval will commence at that time and be limited to 40 minutes.

Tea: (Championship matches) A tea interval of 20 minutes shall normally be taken at 4.10 p.m. (3.40 p.m. on final day), or at the conclusion of the over in progress at that time, provided 32 overs or less remain to be bowled (except on the final day). The over in progress shall be completed unless a batsman is out or retires either within two minutes of, or after, the scheduled time for the interval. In the event of more than 32 overs remaining, the tea interval will be delayed.

If an innings ends or there is a stoppage caused by weather within 30 minutes of the scheduled time, the tea interval shall be taken immediately. There will be no tea interval if the scheduled timing for the cessation of play is earlier than 5.30 p.m.

(Other matches) 4.10 p.m. to 4.30 p.m. (1st, 2nd [3rd] days), 3.40 p.m. to 4.00 p.m. (final day).

Note: The hours of play, including intervals, are brought forward by half an hour for matches scheduled to start in September.

(i) Play shall continue on each day until the completion of a minimum number of overs or until the scheduled cessation time, whichever is the later. The minimum number of overs, unless an innings ends or an interruption occurs, shall be 104 (98 in tourist matches) on days other than the last day, and 80 (75) on the last day before the last hour.

(ii) Where there is a change of innings during a day's play (except during an interval or suspension of play or exceptional circumstances or during the last hour of domestic matches), two overs will be deducted from the minimum number, plus any over in progress at the end of the completed innings (in domestic matches).

(iii) If interruptions for weather or light occur, other than in the last hour of the match, the minimum number of overs shall be reduced by one over for each full 3¼ minutes (four minutes in tourist matches) of the aggregate playing time lost.

(iv) On the last day, if any of the minimum of 80 (75) overs, or as recalculated, have not been bowled when one hour of scheduled playing time remains, the last hour of the match shall be the hour immediately following the completion of those overs.

(v) Law 16.6, 16.7 and 16.8 will apply except that a minimum of 16 six-ball overs (15 in tourist matches) shall be bowled in the last hour, and all calculations with regard to suspensions of play or the start of a new innings shall be based on one over for each full 3¼ (four) minutes. If, however, at 5.30 p.m. both captains accept that there is no prospect of a result or (in Championship games) of either side gaining any further first-innings bonus points, they may agree to cease play at that time or at any time after 5.30 p.m.

(vi) (Domestic matches). The captains may agree or, in the event of disagreement, the umpires may decide to play 30 minutes (a minimum eight overs) extra time at the end of any day other than the last day if, in their opinion, it would bring about a definite result on that day. The whole period shall be played out even though the possibility of finishing the match may have disappeared before the full period has expired. The time by which play is extended on any day shall be deducted from the total number of hours remaining, and the match shall end earlier on the last day by the amount of time by which play was extended.

(vii) Notwithstanding any other provision, there shall be no further play on any day, other than the last day, if a wicket falls or a batsman retires, or if the players leave the field during the last minimum over within two minutes of the scheduled cessation time or thereafter.

(viii) An over completed on resumption of a new day's play shall be disregarded in calculating minimum overs for that day.

(ix) The scoreboard shall show the total number of overs bowled with the ball in use and the minimum number remaining to be bowled in a day. In Championship matches, it shall show the number of overs up to 130 in each side's first innings and subsequently the number bowled with the current ball, and the minimum remaining to be bowled. In addition it shall indicate the number of overs that the fielding side is ahead of or behind the over-rate.

Substitutes

(Domestic matches only) Law 2.1 will apply, but in addition:

No substitute may take the field until the player for whom he is to substitute has been absent from the field for five consecutive complete overs, with the exception that if a fieldsman sustains an obvious, serious injury or is taken ill, a substitute shall be allowed immediately. In the event of any disagreement between the two sides as to the authenticity of an injury or illness, the umpires shall adjudicate. A substitute shall be allowed immediately for all head or blood injuries. If a player leaves the field during an over, the remainder of that over shall not count in the calculation of the five complete overs.

The umpires shall have discretion, for other wholly acceptable reasons, to allow a substitute for a fielder, or a runner for a batsman, at the start of the match or at any subsequent time subject to consent being given by the opposing captain.

A substitute shall not be allowed to bat or bowl, or to act as captain. The opposing captain shall have no right of objection to any player acting as substitute, or to where the substitute shall field, with the exception of the position of wicket-keeper. However, with the agreement of both captains (not to be unreasonably withheld), any substitute may act as wicket-keeper. In the event of the captains' disagreement, the substitute shall not be allowed to act as wicket-keeper.

A substitute shall be allowed by right immediately in the event of a cricketer currently playing in a Championship match being required to join the England team for a Test match (or one-day international). Such a substitute may be permitted to bat or bowl in that match, subject to the approval of the ECB. If the cricketer substituted is batting at the time, he shall retire "not out" and his substitute may be permitted to bat later in that innings subject to the approval of the ECB. If the cricketer is subsequently not required by England then, subject to the approval of the ECB, he may return and resume a full part in the match, taking over from the player that substituted for him. If the substitute is batting, he shall complete his innings and the cricketer shall take over thereafter. If the substitute is bowling when the cricketer is ready to take the field, the substitute shall complete any unfinished over and the cricketer shall take the field thereafter.

If a player is released by England prior to the teams being named in his county match, his county may have a fielding-only substitute until the cricketer is able to join the Championship team.

Fieldsman leaving the field

ICC regulations apply (see earlier in this section) but, in domestic matches, it is explained that "external blow" should include, but not be restricted to, collisions with boundary boards, clashes of heads, heavy falls etc and, in the case of "exceptional and acceptable reasons", consent for a substitute must be granted by the opposing captain.

New ball

The captain of the fielding side shall have the choice of taking the new ball after 90 overs (80 in tourist matches) have been bowled with the old one.

Covering of pitches and surrounding areas

The whole pitch shall be covered:

(a) The night before the match and, if necessary, until the first ball is bowled; and whenever necessary and possible at any time prior to that during the preparation of the pitch.

(b) On each night of the match and, if necessary, throughout any rest days.

(c) In the event of play being suspended on account of bad light or rain, during the specified hours of play.

The bowler's run-up shall be covered to a distance of at least ten yards, with a width of four yards, as will the areas 20 feet either side of the length of the pitch.

Declarations

Law 14 will apply, but if, due to weather conditions, play in a County Championship match has not started when less than eight hours' playing time remains, the first innings of each side shall automatically be forfeited and a one-innings match played.

MEETINGS AND DECISIONS, 2002

ICC ELITE REFEREES AND UMPIRES PANELS

The ICC's panel of international referees was announced on March 1. Ranjan Madugalle was named chief referee, supported by Clive Lloyd, Mike Procter, Wasim Raja and Gundappa Viswanath. They agreed two-year full-time contracts.

On March 12, the ICC named its full-time elite panel of umpires as Steve Bucknor, Asoka de Silva, Daryl Harper, Rudi Koertzen, Dave Orchard, David Shepherd, Russell Tiffin and Srinivas Venkataraghavan. Two elite umpires would stand in all future Test matches; one would stand with a home umpire in one-day internationals.

ICC EXECUTIVE BOARD MEETING

Meeting on March 15–16 in Cape Town, the ICC named Michael Beloff QC as the new chairman of its Code of Conduct Commission. The role of referees was also revised after the controversy at the Port Elizabeth Test between South Africa and India in November 2001. The ICC decided it was the umpires' responsibility to bring disciplinary charges, and that these could be heard by referees, who were permitted to explain their decisions to the media. The ICC established a Disputes Resolution Committee to review the disciplinary procedures followed by the referee at Port Elizabeth, Mike Denness.

The board also agreed a new system of penalties for disciplinary offences, with four levels of Code of Conduct breaches, each with recommended minimum and maximum penalties. These would be introduced in April.

Lord Condon, director of the ICC Anti-Corruption Unit, confirmed that international cricket had been corruption-free for the past year, and briefed the board on security measures for the 2003 Cricket World Cup.

ICC CRICKET COMMITTEE (PLAYING)

The ICC Cricket Committee (Playing) met on March 17–18 and agreed to the experimental use of extended television technology in the ICC Champions Trophy, to be held in Sri Lanka in September. Field umpires could consult with the third umpire on any matter, with the third umpire allowed two replays before making a decision. The committee adopted a proposal for regular post-Test meetings between captains, umpires and referees. It was agreed that bonus points would be retained in one-day tournaments involving three or more teams.

ECB DOMESTIC SPONSORSHIP DEAL

The England and Wales Cricket Board announced, on April 4, that Liverpool Victoria, a financial services company also trading as Frizzell, had signed a four-year sponsorship agreement worth £1m for the County Championship. The competition would be called the Frizzell County Championship.

ENGLAND SUMMER CONTRACTS

Eleven England players were awarded six-month ECB Test contracts for the 2002 domestic season, on April 10. They were Nasser Hussain (captain), Mark Butcher, Andy Caddick, Andrew Flintoff, James Foster, Ashley Giles, Darren Gough, Matthew Hoggard, Graham Thorpe, Marcus Trescothick and Michael Vaughan. In 2001, there had been 12 contracts: Butcher, Flintoff and Foster replaced Mike Atherton, Dominic Cork, Alec Stewart and Craig White from the previous list.

ECB FIRST-CLASS FORUM

On April 11, the First-Class Forum backed the introduction of a new 20-over competition to replace the Benson and Hedges Cup. The competition would run for at least three years, beginning in 2003. The forum also supported the recommendation that first-class counties should be able to field two overseas players.

ICC EXECUTIVE BOARD MEETING

The board, meeting on June 25–26, agreed to take a lead in resolving problems with the international touring programme, particularly where terrorism or political unrest threatened fulfilment of fixtures. It was decided that the board would appoint an ethics officer, in line with Lord Condon's anti-corruption recommendations, to administer the newly adopted Conflict of Interest and Code of Ethics Policy on gambling and confidentiality.

The process for dealing with suspect bowling actions was streamlined to two stages from September. A player would first work to correct his action and, a year later, the ICC Bowling Review Group could suspend him if his action were still deemed illegal.

The board confirmed that a new team-ranking system for one-day internationals would be introduced. It also agreed to review the basis on which the ICC Test Championship was calculated.

It was agreed to replace the ICC Trophy with a new series of World Cup qualifying tournaments for Associates and Affiliates.

ECB INTERNATIONAL SPONSORSHIP DEAL

On July 13, the ECB announced that NatWest would continue to sponsor one-day international cricket until the end of the 2005 season. As well as the triangular NatWest Series, there would be a new three-match tournament – the NatWest Challenge – featuring England and another international side, not necessarily one of the two teams already scheduled to tour.

ECB FIRST-CLASS FORUM

The FCF, meeting on August 12, accepted the expansion of central contracts: a maximum of 20 contracts would be awarded in the near future. About 10–16 would last a year, and these could be augmented by six-month summer contracts awarded at the beginning of each season.

An England retainer would replace the county salary of year-long contracted players, with their county contracts dormant until the player's release by England.

ECB NATIONAL ACADEMY

On September 25, the ECB announced that work on the £4m National Cricket Academy site at Loughborough University would begin in October 2002 and was due for completion a year later.

ICC EXECUTIVE BOARD MEETING

On October 1, following its two-day meeting in Colombo, the board established a Contracts Committee to resolve issues over player terms for the 2003 Cricket World Cup. The board agreed to send an ICC delegation to Zimbabwe later in the year for a final safety and security inspection.

The board resolved to restructure the Cricket Committee (Playing): Sunil Gavaskar would remain chairman, and five of the ten Full Member representatives would be directly elected by the Test captains. The board also accepted several guidelines, arising from the Test captains' meeting in July, regarding the increase in international cricket. These included a minimum break of six weeks per calendar year, a break of ten days between overseas tours whenever possible, and a limit of 15 Tests and 30 one-day internationals per country each year.

ECB CHAIRMAN

On October 4, David Morgan was confirmed as the new ECB Chairman, following his nomination as the FCF's candidate in September, when he obtained 11 votes to Michael Soper's eight. He was to take over from Lord MacLaurin in January 2003.

ENGLAND COACH

On October 16, the ECB announced that Duncan Fletcher had accepted a one-year extension to his contract as England coach, and would continue at least until autumn 2004.

ICC CRICKET WORLD CUP 2003

On November 7, after the experiment at the ICC Champions Trophy allowing umpires recourse to television replays for any issue, the ICC ruled out the wider use of technology at the World Cup.

The ICC, on December 19, confirmed the staging of World Cup matches in Zimbabwe. This followed a three-day visit to Zimbabwe by an ICC security delegation in November. The ECB accepted the decision and confirmed that England were committed to play in Zimbabwe.

UMPIRES FOR 2003

FIRST-CLASS UMPIRES

M. R. Benson, G. I. Burgess, A. Clarkson, D. J. Constant, N. G. Cowley, B. Dudleston, J. H. Evans, I. J. Gould, J. H. Hampshire, M. J. Harris, P. J. Hartley, J. W. Holder, V. A. Holder, T. E. Jesty, A. A. Jones, M. J. Kitchen, B. Leadbeater, N. J. Llong, J. W. Lloyds, N. A. Mallender, R. Palmer, G. Sharp, D. R. Shepherd, J. F. Steele, A. G. T. Whitehead, P. Willey.
Reserves: R. J. Bailey, N. L. Bainton, M. Dixon, S. A. Garratt, A. Hill, R. K. Illingworth, R. A. Kettleborough, R. T. Robinson, K. Shuttleworth.

MINOR COUNTIES UMPIRES

P. Adams, N. L. Bainton, S. F. Bishopp, S. Boulton, P. Brown, D. L. Burden, P. D. Clubb, K. Coburn, M. Dixon, R. Dowd, R. G. Eagleton, H. Evans, J. Ilott, J. H. James, J. S. Johnson, P. W. Joy, P. W. Kingston-Davey, S. W. Kuhlmann, G. Maddison, S. Z. Marszal, C. Martin, C. Megennis, J. Mitchell, M. P. Moran, W. Morgan, C. G. Pocock, C. T. Puckett, G. P. Randall-Johnson, P. L. Ratcliffe, J. G. Reed, G. Ripley, K. S. Shenton, W. E. Smith, R. M. Sutton, D. G. Tate, D. J. Todd, J. M. Tythcott, G. Watkins, M. C. White, J. Wilkinson, R. Wood.

8

MISCELLANY

Minnows no more: Kenya celebrate another Zimbabwe wicket as they secure a semi-final place in the 2003 World Cup. Reports, page 1724. *Picture by Michael Steele, Getty Images.*

PART EIGHT: MISCELLANY

CHRONICLE OF 2002

JANUARY

1 West Indian board insist on neutral venue for Test series against Pakistan, citing terrorist crises in Afghanistan and Kashmir. **2** In Sydney, South Africa pick white batsman Jacques Rudolph for the Third Test, but are overruled by Percy Sonn, president of South African board; Sonn insists on inclusion of Justin Ontong, a coloured all-rounder. **3** After declining to tour India, Darren Gough and Alec Stewart are omitted from England's squad for New Zealand. **4** Sri Lanka's Muttiah Muralitharan takes all nine Zimbabwean wickets to fall on the first day of the Kandy Test. **5** A dropped catch denies Muralitharan all ten; he ends with nine for 51, the fifth-best Test analysis. Australia complete a 3–0 whitewash of South Africa. **6** A second-innings wicket takes Muralitharan past Sir Richard Hadlee's Test record of nine ten-wicket hauls. **8** Pakistan confirm Sharjah as venue for West Indies series. South African board quash any prospect of Hansie Cronje's life ban being rescinded. **14** ICC appoint Dave Richardson as their first general manager. **15** In Lucknow, Caroline Atkins and Arran Thompson share a world-record opening stand of 200 for England against India. In Galle, Muralitharan becomes the fastest and youngest player to 400 Test wickets; Sri Lanka beat Zimbabwe 3–0. **18** Pakistan crush Bangladesh by an innings and 169 runs to win 2–0. **19** In Kolkata, Marcus Trescothick hits an 80-ball century – the fastest in a one-day international for England, who still lose. **22** Six South Africans make ducks as Australia win in Sydney. Nepal beat Pakistan in the Under-19 World Cup in New Zealand. **23** Members approve Hampshire's plans to become the first plc in county cricket. **28** Sachin Tendulkar becomes the first player to 11,000 one-day international runs. England Under-19 exit the World Cup, losing to New Zealand. **30** John Crawley says he will not play for Lancashire again. A Delhi police report claims that Tendulkar and Sourav Ganguly are on a hit-list for terrorist murders and kidnappings. **31** United Arab Emirates become first non-Test-playing nation to host a Test, as Pakistan meet West Indies in Sharjah. England defeat India by two runs in Delhi; play is interrupted after fielders are struck by pellets.

FEBRUARY

1 South Africa beat New Zealand in Perth to reach the VB Series final; New Zealand deliberately gift South Africa a bonus point, so boosting their own chances of making the final – and reducing Australia's. **3** England win in Mumbai to draw the one-day series 3–3. Australia miss the final of their triangular series for only the third time in 23 years after beating South Africa but failing to gain a bonus point. **4** Pakistan win the First Test in Sharjah. **7** Bangladesh release their coach, Trevor Chappell. **8** South Africa win the VB Series. **10** Pakistan seal a 2–0 series win over West Indies. Cherie Blair is appointed Crawley's legal representative in his contractual wrangle with Lancashire. Australia win the Under-19 World Cup. **13** Wisden unveil ratings of every one-day international batting and bowling performance. Australia drop their captain Steve Waugh from their one-day squad after 325 matches. **16** In Wellington, England make 89 – their second-lowest one-day total. Ricky Ponting is appointed Australia's one-day captain. **23** In Johannesburg, Adam Gilchrist hits Test cricket's fastest recorded double-century, from 212 balls. **24** Australia beat South Africa by an innings and 360 runs, the second-biggest win in Tests; Shane Warne becomes Test cricket's second-highest wicket-taker. **25** Allan Donald retires from Test cricket. **26** New Zealand beat England in Dunedin to take the one-day series 3–2.

MARCH

1 ICC name a five-man panel of full-time referees; the list previously contained 20. **5** Australia drop Mark Waugh from their one-day side. In Delhi, India beat Zimbabwe to win Test series 2–0. Daryll Cullinan withdraws from South Africa's second-Test squad after he is not offered a year-round contract. **8** David Byas, captain of Yorkshire's Championship-winning side, signs for Lancashire. **10** Sri Lanka beat Pakistan in Lahore to win Asian Test Championship and record ninth successive victory. **12** Australia win the Second Test in Cape Town. ICC announce their first panel of full-time international umpires. **15** Graham Thorpe and Andrew Flintoff put on 281 in Christchurch – an England sixth-wicket record; Thorpe's double-century is briefly the third-quickest in Tests. **16** Nathan Astle hits the fastest Test double-hundred – in 153 balls – but England win. Seventeen wickets fall on the second day of the Third Test in Durban. **18** ICC announce that umpires will be able to ask for TV replays of any incident in September's Champions Trophy. South Africa win in Durban; Australia take the series 2–1. **22** Ben Hollioake is killed in a car crash in Perth. Lancashire release Crawley. **25** England draw the Second Test in Wellington. **27** With Zimbabwe in tumult, Australia cancel their forthcoming tour.

APRIL

2 Sussex all-rounder Umer Rashid drowns on a pre-season tour to Grenada. **3** New Zealand tie the Test series with victory at Auckland. **4** The ECB announce that financial-services group Frizzell will sponsor the County Championship for the next four years. **9** Australia claim the one-day series in South Africa 5–1. **11** The counties vote to replace the Benson and Hedges Cup with a 20-over competition and to allow two overseas players from 2003. **15** West Indies and India draw the First Test in Guyana. **17** Pakistan crush Sri Lanka by 217 runs in the final of the Sharjah Cup. **19** In Port-of-Spain, Tendulkar makes his 29th Test century, equalling Bradman. **23** India win the Second Test. **24** The fraud squad are called in to investigate financial irregularities at Yorkshire. **27** An unofficial speed gun clocks Shoaib Akhtar at 100mph in a one-day international against New Zealand at Lahore. **28** Angus Fraser retires from first-class cricket to become cricket correspondent of the *Independent*. It is revealed that Henry Olonga was kidnapped briefly at gunpoint in Harare on April 4; fearful of negative publicity, the Zimbabwe Cricket Union had hushed up the story.

MAY

2 In Lahore, Inzamam-ul-Haq scores 329 against New Zealand, the tenth-highest Test score. **3** Pakistan beat New Zealand by an innings and 324 runs – their largest victory. **5** In Bridgetown, West Indies win the Third Test against India. **8** A bomb explodes opposite the Karachi hotel where the Pakistan and New Zealand teams are staying; no one from either party is injured but 14 people are killed; the tour is immediately abandoned. **9** Andrew Caddick becomes the first player to be reprimanded under the ECB's new code of conduct. **14** In Antigua, West Indies and India draw the Fourth Test. **20** At Lord's, England draw with Sri Lanka; for the first time since 1939, their top five all make fifties. **21** Match referee Gundappa Viswanath confirms that umpires Hair and Venkataraghavan have cited the Sri Lankan Test bowler Ruchira Perera for a suspect action. **22** At Kingston, West Indies beat India to take the Test series 2–1. **26** West Indies appoint Sir Viv Richards chairman of selectors. **27** Adam Gilchrist is charged with making comments detrimental to the interests of cricket by the ACB, after publicly questioning the legality of Muralitharan's action. **31** At Leicester, Devon Malcolm takes his 1,000th first-class wicket.

JUNE

1 Hansie Cronje is killed in a plane crash in Western Cape, South Africa. **2** England beat Sri Lanka at Edgbaston. **3** Yorkshire fast bowler Steve Kirby becomes the first player to receive penalty points under the ECB's new disciplinary procedures. **4** The ECB announce that Mark Butcher will be fined after questioning the legality of Ruchira Perera's action. **10** South Africa appoint Eric Simons as their new coach. **13** At Old Trafford, Alec Stewart equals Graham Gooch's record of 118 Test caps for England; Steve Bucknor passes Dickie Bird's record of 66 Tests as an umpire. **15** Stewart hits a hundred. **16** Adam Hollioake makes his first appearance for Surrey after the death of his brother, Ben. **17** England score 50 in five overs to beat Sri Lanka, and take the series 2–0. In St Vincent, West Indies beat New Zealand to clinch the one-day series 3–1. **19** Surrey make 438 for five against Glamorgan, the highest-ever total in a one-day match; Ally Brown hits 268, another world record, before Glamorgan reply with 429; the match aggregate of 867 is a record too. Pakistan beat Australia in Brisbane to take the one-day series 2–1. **21** The ICC approve Tangier as a venue for international cricket. **22** Warwickshire win the last Benson and Hedges Cup final. **27** At Trent Bridge, Andrew Flintoff hits England's fastest one-day fifty, from 28 balls. Graeme Hick scores 315 not out against Durham.

JULY

2 New Zealand win a Test series in the Caribbean for the first time after the Second Test is drawn. **6** At Taunton, Somerset and Surrey total 1,819 runs, the highest first-class aggregate in England. **7** South African board decide to scrap racial quotas for both domestic and international cricket. **11** South African board change their mind: at least five non-whites will be included in South Africa's World Cup squad. **13** Graham Thorpe announces his retirement from one-day internationals. At Lord's, India chase 326 to win the NatWest Series. **21** India consider abandoning their match against Hampshire because of a dangerous pitch. **22** In Colombo, Sri Lanka score a world-record 503 Test runs in a day against Bangladesh. **28** A spectator jumps on to the field at Lord's and escorts Sachin Tendulkar from the crease to the Pavilion; TV commentator Harsha Bhogle complains that he and three colleagues were "heckled and physically assaulted" by an MCC steward. Sri Lanka field an "experimental" team for the Second Test against Bangladesh. **29** England win the First Test against India; Thorpe says he is taking a break from all cricket for an unspecified period. **31** The ECB announce Lord MacLaurin will not stand for re-election as chairman.

AUGUST

4 The C&G semi-final between Yorkshire and Surrey is played on an unprecedented third reserve day. **5** In Colombo, Bangladesh suffer their worst one-day defeat, as Sri Lanka reach a victory target of 77 in less than 16 overs. **8** Kent reveal that Steve Waugh will join them for the end of the season. **9** The ACB confirm that Australia will not tour Pakistan, and propose moving the series to a neutral venue. Darren Gough undergoes a third knee operation of the season. **10** Australia's proposal is accepted by Pakistan. Mike Atherton wins more than £10,000 from six-virqe bet. **12** At Trent Bridge, England draw with India. The ICC chief executive Malcolm Speed confirms that players at ICC tournaments will not be allowed to fulfil obligations to personal sponsors whose interests conflict with those of an official ICC backer. **14** The ECB refuse to confirm England's participation in the ICC Trophy until the sponsorship dispute is resolved. **19** Tendulkar and other Indian players refuse to sign contracts for the ICC Trophy. **21** Sri Lanka win the first international tournament to take place at Tangier. **22** Australia's players reach agreement with the ACB over sponsorship.

23 At Headingley, Tendulkar makes his 30th Test hundred. **24** England players reach agreement with the ECB over sponsorship, provided ICC consult players before signing future deals. **26** India beat England at Headingley. **27** Yousuf Youhana is sent home from Kenya before Pakistan's one-day series for missing a training session. **28** ICC set deadline of August 30 for boards to conclude sponsorship negotiations with their players. **31** ICC reject a compromise proposed by senior Indian cricketers; Sri Lankan board reach agreement with their players. Yorkshire win the C&G final at Lord's.

SEPTEMBER

1 Thorpe confirms his availability for the Ashes tour. **3** The South African squad sign contracts for the ICC Trophy. **7** Surrey are confirmed County Champions. **9** England and India tie at 1–1 after drawing at The Oval Test. Indian players, the BCCI and ICC reach agreement over sponsorship. **10** Thorpe and Gough are included in England's Ashes squad. **13** David Morgan is elected ECB chairman. **14** At the ICC Trophy, India are banned from using the logo of Sahara – a key sponsor – on their shirts; Sahara immediately cancel their sponsorship agreement with the Indian board. **16** The Anti-Corruption Unit confirm they are reviewing incidents in the Sri Lanka–Pakistan ICC Trophy match. **17** In Colombo, Brian Lara is hospitalised with suspected hepatitis. **18** Pakistan are cleared of any wrongdoing. Hampshire announce Shane Warne will captain them in 2003. Jagmohan Dalmiya is re-elected unopposed as BCCI President. **20** The Federation of International Cricketers' Associations' demand to be recognised by ICC as an official players' representative body and reject ICC's proposals for player representation. **21** Indian players agree to work with FICA in an attempt to protect their commercial interests. Richard Pybus is appointed Pakistan coach for the fourth time. **24** Thorpe withdraws from the Ashes squad. **28** Robert Key is named as Thorpe's replacement. **30** India and Sri Lanka share the Champions Trophy after rain washes out the final for the second day.

OCTOBER

1 ICC resolve to accept player representatives on committees dealing with playing matters but not on those dealing with commercial matters; they also announce a team will visit Zimbabwe to carry out a safety inspection before the World Cup. Pakistan Cricket Board announce they will not move any more series to neutral venues due to the associated financial losses. In New Zealand, players announce their refusal to play pre-season warm-up games after failing to agree new contracts. **4** ICC explain they cannot recognise FICA as the players' voice at international level until FICA is recognised by individual boards. Britain's first indoor international match is played between Britain and The Rest of the World at Cardiff's Millennium Stadium. **7** Sahara resume their sponsorship of India. **9** South Africa inflict a world-record 23rd successive defeat on Bangladesh to win their one-day series. **10** In Mumbai, Rahul Dravid becomes the fourth batsman to hit centuries in four consecutive Test innings. **11** In Sharjah, Australia bowl Pakistan out for 59, their lowest Test total. **12** In their second innings, Pakistan are skittled for 53. **13** Tauqir Zia, the chairman of the PCB, offers his resignation. **14** talkSPORT sell the rights to radio coverage of the Ashes series to the BBC. **15** Pakistan President Parvez Musharraf rejects Zia's resignation. **16** Duncan Fletcher's contract as England coach is extended by a year. **17** England fly to Australia. **18** Gary Kirsten becomes the first player to hit a hundred against nine Test countries with 113 not out against Bangladesh. **21** Australia beat Pakistan 3–0. **27** South Africa defeat Bangladesh in Potchefstroom to win 2–0. **28** Mark Waugh is dropped from Australia's Ashes squad and retires immediately from international cricket. **31** The ICC unveil the first rankings for one-day cricket. A mediator is called in to try to break the contracts dispute in New Zealand.

NOVEMBER

3 India beat West Indies 2–0 after a draw in Kolkata. **5** New Zealand's players reject their board's final pay offer, jeopardising the start of the domestic season. Gough leaves the England squad to work on his knee at the Academy; Alex Tudor is called up as cover. **6** Crowd disturbances delay the first India–West Indies one-day international. **7** England begin the Ashes disastrously as Hussain inserts Australia, who make 364 for two; Simon Jones tears cruciate ligaments while fielding. **8** ICC decide not to extend the experiment of allowing umpires to call for TV replays on any decision into the 2003 World Cup. **9** Yorkshire's Chris Silverwood is called up to replace Jones; Gough returns to England. At Nagpur, more crowd trouble interrupts the second India–West Indies one-day international. **10** Australia bowl England out for 79 and win the first Test by 384 runs. **11** New Zealand's players and board reach agreement. A West Indies Cricket Board investigation clears Brian Lara of accusations of match-fixing made in an Indian report dating from 2000. **12** At Rajkot, crowd disturbances interrupt the India–West Indies series for the third consecutive match; the players are unable to resume and India win under Duckworth/Lewis. **13** In Harare, Shoaib Akhtar is severely reprimanded for ball-tampering during the first Zimbabwe–Pakistan Test. **14** Vince Wells walks out on Leicestershire in protest at the handling of his replacement as captain. Loughborough UCCE are awarded first-class status. **15** India make 325 to beat West Indies in Ahmedabad. For Australia A, Martin Love hits his second double-hundred in a fortnight against England. **19** In Adelaide, Ashley Giles breaks his wrist in the nets. At Centurion, South Africa beat Sri Lanka by three wickets and win their two-Test series 2–0. Pakistan also win 2–0 after beating Zimbabwe by ten wickets in Bulawayo. An independent report concludes that the Ashes urn is too fragile to be flown to Australia. **23** West Indies board complain to ICC about the Rajkot match being awarded to India. **24** In Adelaide, Australia beat England to go 2–0 up. West Indies beat India in Vijayawada to win 4–3. **25** The Zimbabwean government refuse to grant visas to two British journalists, who were to have accompanied an ICC pre-World Cup fact-finding delegation. **26** England call up Paul Collingwood to provide injury cover. **28** Ali Bacher, the World Cup's chief executive, announces that the ICC's Anti-Corruption Unit have drawn up a shortlist of match-fixing suspects who will be barred from South Africa during the tournament.

DECEMBER

1 Australia retain the Ashes. ICC are given written assurance that journalists will be allowed into Zimbabwe during the World Cup. Pakistan complete a 5–0 one-day whitewash of Zimbabwe. **2** Steve Waugh is omitted from Australia's provisional World Cup squad. **3** Pakistan Cricket Board demand compensation from New Zealand, claiming that they reneged on a commitment to play a triangular tournament in Pakistan in September 2002. **4** The MCC announce that the Ashes urn may still go on display in Australia. **10** In Dhaka, West Indies beat Bangladesh by an innings and 310 runs, the seventh-biggest innings win in Tests. **12** England announce that Andrew Flintoff will fly home; Adam Hollioake is called up. **15** In Melbourne, Shane Warne dislocates his right shoulder in a one-day match against England. **17** Thirteen matches into their tour of Australia, England finally win a game, beating Sri Lanka in the VB Series. **18** West Indies beat Bangladesh to take the Test series 2–0. **19** ICC's chief executive Malcolm Speed confirms that the six World Cup matches scheduled for Zimbabwe will not be moved. ICC set a deadline of January 14 for India's cricketers to sign an agreement on sponsorship for the World Cup and insist that India name their 15-man squad by December 31. **20** Hussain says he will follow the ECB's decision on whether England fulfil their fixture in Zimbabwe. **21** In Hamilton, New Zealand are bowled out for 94, after dismissing India for 99 – the first time in Tests that both first innings have fallen short of 100. **22** New Zealand win and take the series 2–0. **25** Indian board say they will abide by the December 31 deadline. **27** Justin Langer scores 250 in the Fourth Test at Melbourne, and brands the Barmy Army a "disgrace" over their barracking of Brett Lee. **28** The International Development Secretary, Clare Short, criticises the decision to play in Zimbabwe as "deplorable"; a spokesman for the Prime Minister admits the government feel "it would be better if the England team did not go", but adds that the ECB must decide. England reveal that Craig White has torn a rib muscle. **29** Mike O'Brien, a Foreign Office minister, announces a stiffening of the government's position: "We cannot order the ECB not to go… but we have asked them not to"; the ECB announce they will not force anyone to play in Harare; Hussain says it is "ridiculous" to leave the decision to the players and demands that the government take responsibility; Speed tells the ECB they are likely to be liable for any reduction in broadcasting revenue caused by England forfeiting. **30** England go 4–0 down in the Ashes; Michael Vaughan ends 2002 with 1,481 runs, the second-highest for a calendar year. The ECB announce their intention to ask the government to cover any losses following a forfeiture; reports emerge that most of Zimbabwe's players are against their country co-hosting the World Cup; Australian Prime Minister John Howard calls for a boycott; Zimbabwe's Minister of State for Information and Publicity accuses the UK and Australia of trying "to keep cricket as a white and colonial sport". ICC announce that safety and security in Kenya are being investigated; the BCCI announce their squad on time but the contracts row remains unresolved; Dalmiya resigns from the ICC contracts committee and calls for independent mediation. **31** England name their World Cup squad.

EXTRAS

The following were reported in the media during 2002.

The Australia–South Africa Test at Sydney was believed to be the first in which the official scorers were both women: Ruth Kelleher and Merilyn Slarke. (*The Age*, Melbourne, January 3)

Graham Gooch agreed to participate in a test to prove that his new head of hair can survive sport and showers. The Advertising Standards Authority said that adverts by the Advanced Hair Studio – which furnished Gooch with his replacement weaves – were misleading. (*The Sun*, January 7)

There were 75 wides in Aruna's winning total of 158 for one in a Sri Lankan second division match against Old Servatius. The wides were bowled deliberately in protest against an umpiring decision, when an appeal for a catch was disallowed. (*Daily Mirror*, Colombo, January 7)

A 42-year-old Mumbai housewife, Nirmala Kishore Poonamiya, was found murdered at home, having apparently been felled by a cricket bat. (*The Asian Age*, January 19)

India's National Commission on Population used the one-day internationals against England to launch a birth control campaign, complete with the slogans "Little bouncers – no more please", "No slips please, population control is not a laughing matter" and "China stumped – India produced more babies in the last hour!" (*Times of India*, January 20)

Sir Frank Worrell was honoured in Calcutta when the Bengal Cricket Association held blood donation camps to celebrate Frank Worrell Day. (*Times of India*, February 4) Sir Frank was also commemorated with a plaque on the Economics building of the University of Manchester, where he graduated with a BA in Administration in 1959. (*Manchester Graduate*, 2002)

Omar Sheikh, sentenced to death for the abduction and murder of the American journalist Daniel Pearl in Pakistan, was a classmate of Nasser Hussain at the Forest School, east London. (*Times of India*, February 8)

Two youths were hacked to death by an armed gang in a cricket pavilion during a lunch break. Police believe the murders stemmed from a longstanding dispute between two local families in the Dematagoda area. (*Daily News*, Colombo, February 26)

Oakham Cricket Club in Rutland was hit by three arson attacks in a month. The club's pavilion was destroyed by fire at New Year, followed by the equipment store and scorebox. (*Wisden Cricket Monthly*, March)

Khaled Mahmud, the former Bangladesh vice-captain, showed his displeasure at being dismissed in a one-day Ispahani National League encounter by slapping the bowler. (*Wisden Asia Cricket*, March)

The original Ranji Trophy is to be returned to the Saurashtra Cricket Association by Wiltshire Queries CC, whose members discovered it at a clearance sale in London last year. (*Wisden Asia Cricket*, March)

The bomb squad was called to a Wisden reader's house in the US after the posted copy of his 2001 almanack was identified as a suspicious package. (Wisden.com, March 6)

Pappu Talwar was jailed for three years and ordered to pay compensation to the victim's family after being found guilty of killing Mangesh Bhagwan Shinde while playing cricket near Mumbai in 2000. His death was originally attributed to natural causes but a post-mortem revealed that Shinde had suffered head injuries. An investigation revealed there had been a quarrel that culminated in Talwar hitting Mangesh with a bat. (*Asian Age*, March 9)

Russell Crowe, the Oscar-winning Hollywood actor, announced that he is building his own cricket ground on his 600-acre estate at Coffs Harbour, New South Wales. He planned to name it the Dave Crowe Oval in memory of his late uncle, the father of the New Zealand Test batsmen Martin and Jeff Crowe. "I might have more than 5,000 Test runs," said cousin Martin, "but he makes 40 million bucks a movie." (*The Sun*, March 19)

The Sri Lankan Cricketers Association announced the launch of Project HOPE with the aim of establishing a 750-bed cancer treatment centre on the island. (*Daily News*, Colombo, March 20)

Dickie Bird, the former Test umpire, revealed he had been struck by blindness caused by overexposure to the sun. His sight was restored by two operations on detached retinas. The experience, he said, "was like two grey shutters coming down". (*Daily Telegraph*, April 23)

Padma Karunaratne, a schoolteacher who played for the Sri Lankan women's team as a left-arm spinner, became the first woman on the island to qualify as an umpire. (*Sunday Observer*, Colombo, April 28)

Steve Randell, the Australian umpire who stood in 36 Tests, was released from prison in Hobart after serving 32 months of a four-year sentence for indecently assaulting young girls. The Tasmanian Cricket Association was seeking advice about whether he might be allowed to umpire again in club cricket. (*The Age*, Melbourne, May 1)

The Kent scorer Jack Foley, 70, posed naked, along with his wife Eunice, for Martin McCague's 2002 benefit calendar. (*The Times,* May 1)

Shoaib Malik, the Pakistan all-rounder, was married while touring Australia, even though his bride, Ayesha, was in Saudi Arabia at the time. The pair performed a *nikah* (marriage ceremony) over the telephone while his parents listened in: they have scheduled the *ruksati*, the final rite after which bride and groom are allowed to cohabit, for after the 2003 World Cup. (CricInfo, May 2)

Derbyshire decided to erect a seven-foot high fence around the County Ground after a spate of break-ins. A man was jailed for six months for stealing aluminium sheets from the sightscreens. (*Derby Evening Telegraph*, May 3)

Cricket bats – along with axes, baseball bats, box-cutters, brass knuckles, bull whips, cattle prods, corkscrews, golf clubs and numchucks [ninja weapons] – were on a new list of implements banned from American aircraft cabins. (*The Guardian*, May 7).

Playing for Berwick against Langholm, John Simmons bowled eight batsmen en route to figures of nine for eight. (*Newcastle Journal*, May 6)

The batsmen of the Chacombe village team in Northamptonshire failed to score a single run between them in their opening fixture of the season, against Marston St Lawrence Second XI. They were bowled out for three, thanks to two wides and a bye. "Our side was all lads of 16 or 17," said former secretary Ted Garrett, "and they must have felt rotten. Some people will laugh at them but, in these couch-potato days, they should be applauded for turning out to keep village cricket alive." (*Daily Mirror,* May 8).

Shane Warne was fined and banned from driving on British roads for three months for reaching 120mph on the M1 in Derbyshire. The case had been adjourned nine times because of problems serving papers on Warne, who admitted the offence in a letter to Ilkeston magistrates. "Thank you for your patience," he wrote. "I'm sorry, I was going too fast in your country. I love playing cricket in England." (*Daily Telegraph,* May 9)

Almost 500 runs were scored without a wicket falling in a Hampshire League match at Gosport. The Hall brothers, Kieron and Chris, took Wildern Mansbridge to a handsome 243 without loss but the Farehaven openers, Mark Williams and Jason Murdoch, gave their team a ten-wicket victory. All four scored centuries. (*Southampton Daily Echo*, May 13)

Phil Govier, 17, died after suffering head injuries in a collision during a match for Diss Second XI against Downham Market. His head struck the knee of another fielder as both went for the same catch. (*East Anglian Daily Times*, May 31 and June 29)

Brothers John and Andy Lyne got the same score on the same day in different matches, and were out exactly the same way. They were opening the batting in games ten miles apart, and each hit 101 before being bowled leg stump. Both were playing for Anston Cricket Club teams against Whitwell, John captaining the First XI and Andy the Second XI. (*The Sun*, May 25)

An Australian batsman, Jason Taylor, playing club cricket in the West Midlands for Bewdley and Wolverly Social, was the final victim in a hat-trick on consecutive days. (*Wisden Cricket Monthly*, July)

Ron Headley, the 62-year-old former Worcestershire and West Indies opener now coaching Aston Unity CC, had to step in at the last moment when a player shortage left the side undermanned for the game against Halesowen. Headley, who as son of George and father of Dean is part of Test cricket's only tri-generational family, batted at No. 11 and made two as Unity were skittled out for 57. (*Daily Telegraph*, July 10)

A friendly in Sargodha, Pakistan, degenerated into an argument over match-fixing that culminated in two people being shot dead and five wounded. (*Times of India*, July 13)

Mohammed Kaif's parents and brother, back home in Allahabad, were so convinced India were about to lose their NatWest Series final against England at Lord's that they switched off the TV, went to the cinema to see the Bollywood tear-jerker *Devdas* and missed his match-winning 87 not out against England in the NatWest Series final. "Someone told us midway through the film that India had won and that Kaif had played a great innings," said his brother Saif, who plays for Uttar Pradesh himself. (Thatscricket.com, July 14)

Arthur Milton, 73, the last man to win international caps for England at both cricket and soccer, was awarded an honorary MA by Bristol University. His achievements were also celebrated at a dinner in the Great Hall. Milton became a postman when he retired from first-class cricket in 1974 and, when forced to retire from that at 60, he began delivering newspapers. His round includes some of the university's halls of residence. (*The Times*, July 17)

Amersham Second XI's Chiltern League fixture with Taplow was held up when a sniper opened fire on the players. Bail has been granted to a 20-year-old man arrested on suspicion of possessing an air weapon with intent to endanger life. "I had just taken a wicket and we were celebrating," explained the Taplow bowler Mike Bradley, felled after being hit in the leg by a pellet. "There was a whistling noise and it was like a real hard smack on the leg. It was quite a shock." Amersham's Ron Hedley believes he is fortunate to be alive: another pellet flew just past his head. Undeterred, Hedley returned to the game and took three wickets to help his side win and remain top of the league. (*Bucks Free Press*, August 2)

Ian Botham agreed to head a team of sporting figures in an advertising campaign against replacing the pound with the euro. "I played for England," said Botham, "not Europe." (*Daily Telegraph*, August 3)

Gurbux Singh, the chairman of the Commission for Racial Equality, was forced to resign his post following a confrontation outside Lord's after the England–India NatWest Series final. Singh pleaded guilty to trying to head-butt a policeman and was fined £500. Singh admitted he had been celebrating "one of the best games I've ever seen". (*Daily Telegraph*, July 26, *The Guardian*, August 8)

The former England captain Mike Atherton netted a one-sixth share of £68,000 after his syndicate won the Tote Scoop6 horse-racing jackpot. Atherton was commentating on the Trent Bridge Test for Channel 4 when Certain Justice won the 2.45 at Newmarket; his colleague Richie Benaud cheered the mount home for him. (*The Observer*, August 11)

The Sachin Tendulkar lookalike, Balvirchand, who had already costarred with Tendulkar in an advert for Visa cards, has been chosen to play him in the movie *Kaisi Mohabbat*, in which the heroine fulfils her dream by meeting the great man. (*Gujarat Samachar*, Ahmedabad, August 12)

Ian Botham received "substantial" damages from the brewers Guinness for using his image without permission. During the football World Cup, the firm ran adverts featuring his 1981 Ashes exploits. (*Daily Telegraph*, August 13)

James Morrison, the Wisden.com schools cricketer of the year earmarked as a batsman of some promise by Surrey, decided to focus on golf instead. In his first major competition, he narrowly failed to reach the last eight of the British Boys' Championship. (*Daily Telegraph*, August 15)

The Bishop of Durham announced his decision to retire live on *Test Match Special*. The Right Rev. Michael Turnbull said, while a guest on the programme: "I have long had an ambition to announce my retirement on *Test Match Special*. And that is precisely what I am doing." He said he would retire in April 2003. (*The Times*, August 26)

Spencer Chorlton, playing for Yoxford against Mallards in Suffolk, hit seven sixes in an over that included a no-ball. Chorlton, the 17-year-old captain of Framlingham College, raced from 50 to 100 in 14 balls. (*East Anglian Daily Times*, September 3)

The imprisoned author and politician, Lord Archer, paid more than £1,000 (through a representative) to obtain enough turf from the dug-up Lord's outfield to re-lay his back garden in Cambridgeshire. Archer was later suspended from MCC for seven years following his conviction for perjury and perverting the course of justice, three years longer than the jail sentence he received. (*Daily Telegraph*, September 11/*The Guardian*, October 28)

Bursledon captain Colin Popplewell wound up in hospital, nursing a gashed head, after an inadvertent assault by a team-mate during a Hampshire League match against Portsmouth Fourth XI. Angered after being run out, George Millward, the club secretary, hurled his bat as he approached the boundary, knocking Popplewell out. (*Southampton Daily Echo*, September 15)

Ashok Ohri, the manager of the India Under-19 cricket team in England, denied allegations that he had "misbehaved" with a female guest in a swimming pool at the team's hotel in Leicestershire. It was alleged that he had "by design bumped into a lady swimmer which the latter did not like". Mr Ohri said he was not in the pool, and could not swim. (*The Tribune*, Chandigarh, September 19)

Changing ends after an unprofitable spell, Sam Collins took two hat-tricks for the Kent side Band of Brothers in the space of seven balls. The Arabs, the club founded by the late E. W. Swanton, plunged from 186 for four to 187 all out, yet still won the match. (*The Times*, September 19)

MCC president Ted Dexter complained that reports of the Lord's turf being sold at £10 per square foot were erroneous. "We were extremely careful not to become metric martyrs," he explained, "so we complied with the written wishes of Westminster Council, and sold our turf in metric, rather than imperial measurements." (*Daily Telegraph*, September 23)

Martin Jones, a Shropshire Under-19 fast bowler making a guest appearance for Albrighton CC, responded by taking five wickets in as many balls against Grasshoppers, all bowled. (*Shropshire Star*, September 24)

Pinky and Vasu Desai were left unmoved by the attack on the Akshardham temple complex near Ahmedabad. Although the couple were inside the temple at the time, they assumed the noise was merely a series of firecrackers going off in celebration of a victory by the Indian national cricket team. (*Gujurat Samachar*, Ahmedabad, September 25)

An inquest delivered a verdict of accidental death after being told that Gordon Bryden, a hospital consultant, had died in the wake of a collision with a team-mate as they attempted to take the same catch. Dr Bryden was detained in hospital for three weeks after the accident, which occurred in June while he was playing for the Sheffield club Parkhead against Youlgreave. He was readmitted when his condition deteriorated and later suffered a fatal haemorrhage. William Thomas, a consultant surgeon, likened the injury to those suffered by victims of car crashes. (*Daily Telegraph*, October 15)

Progress on the controversial Rangiri Dambulla Stadium in Kandy was interrupted when one worker fell to his death and another was seriously injured. Makeshift scaffolding and strong winds were blamed. (*Daily Mirror*, Colombo, October 17)

A bushfire raging barely 100 yards from the middle failed to stop play in Cessnock, northern New South Wales. The third-grade match between Kurri Kurri and Cessnock Supporters Club carried on even though homes were being evacuated in the area. Only when the wind changed an hour later did the players finally surrender. (*Newcastle Herald*, October 20)

In a course entitled "Leadership and Motivation", the Indian Institute of Management in Lucknow has introduced the film *Lagaan* to the syllabus. The institute cited the courage shown by the villagers who play a cricket match against the "Britishers" in order to get their tax waived. (*Gujurat Samachar*, Ahmedabad, October 21)

The tradition of friendly games during intervals at the Adelaide Oval has been ended because of insurance costs. Ball games – even catch – are to be banned. In January, a woman spectator had her eyesight permanently damaged after being hit. (*Adelaide Advertiser*, October 30)

A plan to put the Ashes on temporary display in Australia was shelved at the last minute when independent conservation experts discovered a new crack in the urn. ACB chief executive James Sutherland said the board did not dispute the ownership of the Ashes but hoped they would be brought to Australia in the near future. Steve Waugh has advocated strongly for the trophy to be handed over: "We've won it a few times so yeah, we'd like to see what it looks like." (Reuters, November 20)

Mignon du Preez, a 12-year-old schoolgirl from Pretoria, scored 258 not out, including 16 sixes, in a 40-over provincial Under-13 game for Gauteng North against Gauteng at Sandton. Her father, Jacques, said she fell in love with the game as a four-year-old. (*The Star*, Johannesburg, November 24)

Ted Martin, the Western Australia leg-spinner who took six MCC wickets for his state during the 1932-33 Bodyline tour, has become the first Australian first-class cricketer to reach the age of 100. "It's nice to have beaten Bradman at something," he said. (*Inside Sport*, December)

Paul Kelleher failed in his attempt to use a cricket bat to disfigure a £150,000 statue of former prime minister Margaret Thatcher, so he reached instead for a metal stanchion, and decapitated it. The bat just "pinged off" her head, he said. Kelleher said he had intended to use a baseball bat but realized he would not get it through the security checks at the Guildhall Gallery. Kelleher, who was found guilty of criminal damage, said the offence was "an act of satirical humour" directed at global capitalism. In

February 2003, he was jailed for three months. (*The Guardian*, December 17/February 20, 2003)

Tourists are paying 20 rand (£1.40) each to view wreckage of the plane in which the former South African cricket captain Hansie Cronje died. The remnants of the Hawker Siddeley 748 freighter were laid out on the floor of a warehouse in the resort of Mossel Bay, and about 200 people visited the exhibition during the first two days. Leon Dorfling, the businessman who paid to recover the wreckage from the mountainside, is understood to have abandoned plans to include it in a monument to Cronje. (*Die Burger*, Cape Town, December 18)

CHARITIES

The Lord's Taverners, founded in 1950 and accredited by the ECB as cricket's national charity for the recreational game, distributed over £1.5 million during 2002. This was raised "to give young people, particularly those with special needs, a sporting chance." Half the funds were disbursed to promote grassroots cricket, and were administered with the help of the ECB. The rest of the money was used to provide 40 specially adapted minibuses for disabled young people and to support a programme of sport and recreation for young people with special needs.

  Chief Executive: Mark Williams, The Lord's Taverners, 10 Buckingham Place, London SW1E 6HX. Tel: 020 7821 2828; fax: 020 7821 2829; e-mail: hq@lordstaverners.org; website: www.lordstaverners.org.

The Brian Johnston Memorial Trust was launched in 1995. Its objectives are to support a) young cricketers of exceptional promise in need of financial assistance, through Brian Johnston Scholarships, and b) cricket for the blind. There were 15 awards and scholarships presented in 2002, along with other grants. There are over 400 members of the Johnners Club, whose aim is to support the Trust. The Lord's Taverners are now the sole corporate Trustee and administrator of the Trust.

  Chief Executive: Mark Williams, BJMT, details as above, except for e-mail: BJMT@lordstaverners.org.

OBITUARIES

Abbas Khan, who died in Karachi, on January 27, 2002, aged 90, was a stalwart of Sind cricket in the decade before Partition, usually batting high in the order and sometimes keeping wicket. He also represented the Muslims in the inaugural Bombay Pentangular in 1937-38. His selection for India over New Year 1938, for the third unofficial Test against Lord Tennyson's MCC, was a high point, even if he scored only two and 13. A low came in 1947-48 when he captained Sind in the Ranji Trophy and Bombay won by an innings and 453 runs. In 29 first-class games, he scored 635 runs at 13.80 with a highest score of 84, took 18 catches and made 13 stumpings. He was a Pakistan selector in the 1960s.

Abdul Kadir, who died in Karachi on March 12, 2002, aged 57, was a Test wicket-keeper who took no catches but made his mark with the bat. One of six new players picked by Pakistan for the one-off Test against Australia at Karachi in October 1964, the 20-year-old Kadir combined with his fellow-debutant "Billy" Ibadulla to add 249, the best at the time for any Pakistan wicket and a first-wicket record until 1997-98. Ibadulla made 166, Kadir was run out for 95. His stumping of Tom Veivers two days later would remain his only Test dismissal. When the sides met again at Melbourne five weeks later, Kadir's thumb was broken as he edged Graham McKenzie to slip in the first over. In the second innings he batted at No. 7 and made 35 in a 46-run stand with his captain, Hanif Mohammad, who was having quite a match – as well as scoring 104 and 93, he kept wicket in Kadir's place and took five catches. By the time Pakistan moved on to New Zealand, Naushad Ali was wearing the gloves. Kadir played his next, and last, two Tests as a batsman, scoring 46 and nought and then, back as opener, 12 and 58 (in five and a quarter hours). In 36 first-class games over 11 seasons he scored 1,523 runs at 28.73 with one century: 114 for Karachi Whites against Karachi Blues in the 1963-64 Quaid-e-Azam final. He finished with 46 catches and 13 stumpings.

Note: Last year the obituary of G. A. Wheatley, who ran the cricket at Uppingham School for 32 years, stated that "late in life and to general surprise he married one of the matrons". This is untrue, and *Wisden* apologises to Dr and Mrs Wheatley's family and friends for the offence it caused. Garth Wheatley married at 29; Mrs Wheatley, whom he met on a cricket tour of Ireland, was 20 at the time and was never a matron at the school. The error was not the fault of the writer, Eric Midwinter.

Afaq Hussain died in Karachi on February 25, 2002, aged 62. A glance at his first-class record suggests that this quickish off-spinner might have played more than two Tests. In 67 games between 1957-58 and 1973-74, he took ten wickets in a match five times. However, competition was fierce among the twirly merchants at a time when Pakistan's faster bowlers were beginning to carry an equal share of the workload. In England in 1962 Afaq went weeks without a game, playing six first-class matches out of 29 and taking only 13 wickets at 43.61, and in Australia and New Zealand in 1964-65 he played only five games out of 14 – though one was the Test at Melbourne, where he failed to take a wicket. In fact, his only Test victim was Ted Dexter in 1961-62, out hit wicket at Lahore in his first Test as England captain. Afaq had won his Test place with six for 89 for the Governor's XI against MCC on a mud-caked pitch, bare of grass, at Lyallpur. He could bat, too, as he showed with 33 not out in the Lahore Test. In the next season's Quaid-e-Azam final, going in at No. 11 for Karachi A against Karachi B, he made 87 and put on the first three-figure stand for the last wicket in Pakistan with Wallis Mathias. Afaq toured England again in 1963 with the PIA-sponsored Pakistan Eaglets and played most of his later first-class cricket for PIA. In all, he took 214 wickets at 19.42, including best figures of eight for 108 for Karachi University against Railways-Quetta in 1960-61, and scored 1,448 runs at 24.54. His one century was 122 not out in 1969-70 for PIA against Lahore Blues at the Bagh-e-Jinnah in Lahore. He held 52 catches.

Antonio (later Howard), Peggy, who died in Melbourne on January 11, 2002, aged 84, played in Australia's first six women's Tests. Her attacking leg-spin bowling, with its tantalising flight and variations of off-breaks, top-spin and an occasional googly, brought selection for Victoria at 15 and soon led her to be dubbed "the girl Grimmett". Two years later she was taking the field against England in the first women's Test, at Brisbane in December 1934, having staked her claim with match figures of ten for 48 in England's game with Victoria. When she had the opener Betty Snowball caught for 15, Peggy Antonio became Australia's first female wicket-taker. In the Third Test at the MCG she thrilled her local supporters by taking six for 49 in the first innings. Touring England in 1937, she was at the top of her form. She spun Australia to victory in the opening Test at Northampton with six for 51 and three for 40, and finished the series with 19 wickets at 11.15. She also opened the batting in the first two Tests, then helped ensure that the series would be drawn 1–1 with her Test-best 37 at The Oval. Against Kent she hit an unbeaten 103 and at 20 she had the cricket world at her feet. Instead she gave the game away, complaining that cricket was becoming too relentless to be enjoyable. She married during the war and became matriarch of a large family.

Anwar Hussain died in Lahore on October 9, 2002, aged 82. It was 50 years to the month since he had played in Pakistan's first Test, at Delhi in 1952-53. However, his four games in that series against India realised only 42 runs and one wicket and he never represented Pakistan again. Anwar Hussain Khokar faced the first ball bowled in first-class cricket in Pakistan, though he wouldn't have been aware of that when he opened for Sind against West Punjab at Lahore in December 1947 – it was the 1990s before the match was reckoned to warrant first-class status. He had made his debut at 20 for the Muslims against The Rest in the 1940-41 Pentangular and went on to play for Northern India and Bombay in the Ranji Trophy, batting in the top half of the order and bowling fast-medium. He could also keep wicket in an emergency.

After Partition, Anwar lived in Karachi. Captaining Sind against the 1948-49 West Indians, he produced two career-bests, four for 66 and a match-saving 81, whereupon he was selected for the unofficial Test in Lahore. He went to Ceylon that same season, opening the bowling in the "Tests", but somehow his performances at this level rarely reached expectations. However, his steadfast 48 against MCC at Karachi in December 1951 did his young country great service: in adding 83 with his captain, A. H. Kardar, he took Pakistan to the brink of a victory that helped secure Test status the following

July. Anwar's reward was the vice-captaincy for the tour of India. In 1954-55 he captained Karachi to the final of the Quaid-e-Azam Trophy. It should have been a memorable swansong. Instead he was replaced as captain by the 20-year-old Hanif Mohammad, who along with his brothers Wazir and Raees hit a hundred in Karachi's nine-wicket victory over Combined Services. Anwar Hussain's time had passed. In 45 games he scored 1,511 runs at 26.98 and took 36 wickets at 36.02.

Avery, Albert George, who died of leukaemia in Bristol on April 18, 2002, aged 84, was Gloucestershire's first-team scorer from 1971 to 1987 before becoming their archivist. In 1994 he helped establish the museum at the county ground. "Bert the Book" they called him when he was first appointed, to distinguish him from "Bert the Boot", the dressing-room attendant. The sobriquet could just as easily have come from the excellence of his scorebooks. Bert Avery's copperplate handwriting, perfected over his 40 years with the Shell oil company, was legendary on the county circuit. Among the feats it recorded were Mike Procter twice achieving a hundred and hat-trick in the same match, one of which incorporated his two lbw hat-tricks, and the four occasions on which Zaheer Abbas hit a double-hundred and hundred in a match. "He was respected by everyone for his humour, ability and compassion," the Test umpire David Shepherd said in his funeral address. "He would help anyone who needed it."

Ball, Thomas Edward, who died in Cairns on January 13, 2002, aged 80, was a train driver who opened the bowling for Queensland in three Sheffield Shield games in 1947. *WCAA.*

Beaumont, Leonard, died in Nottingham on July 22, 2002, aged 87. Len Beaumont joined the Nottinghamshire staff in 1981, following his retirement as a government contracts officer for the electronics firm Ericsson, and shared the first- and second-team scoring with Les Tomlinson until becoming first-team scorer from 1987 to 1993. He also kept the England book at Trent Bridge. He had been a better-than-average club cricketer, captaining Nottinghamshire Amateur League and Cricket Association sides, and obtained an MCC Advanced Coaching Certificate which led to coaching at Trent Bridge. A wing-half or inside forward, Len Beaumont played League football for Huddersfield Town, Portsmouth and Nottingham Forest. His son, David, described in *Wisden* as "the cricketing policeman from Nottingham", won a Cambridge Blue in 1978.

Bell, William, who died in Auckland on July 23, 2002, aged 70, played two Tests for New Zealand in South Africa in 1953-54. He bowled leg-spin and came into the reckoning for that tour because Alex Moir was out of favour with the selectors. "Players like Bell," wrote the former Auckland leg-spinner Raoul Garrard, "have apparently been chosen only because we must have bowlers of their type." At the time Bill Bell had taken only 11 wickets in his five games for Canterbury and Auckland. When he took four for 31 against Eastern Province early in the tour, he looked worth the punt. His control was good and both his leg-break and googly turned sharply. That return, however, would be his best in a 33-game career that ran from 1949-50 to 1958-59, with 44 wickets at 40.52 and 170 runs at an average (helped by not-outs) of 10.00. His Tests were at Cape Town and Port Elizabeth; his two wickets cost 235 runs.

Benjamin, Sunil, died in Jaipur on November 10, 2002, aged 56, following a heart attack. He became the first Indian wicket-keeper to take seven dismissals in an innings with six catches and a stumping for Central Zone against North Zone at Bombay in the 1973-74 Duleep Trophy final. His record was equalled by Vidarbha's Sadashiv Iyer in 1997-98. In 70 first-class games between 1966-67 and 1981-82, mostly for Rajasthan in the Ranji Trophy, Benjamin collected 103 catches, 23 stumpings and 2,384 runs at 25.09.

Sir Derek Birley, who wrote an "iconoclastic demolition of cricket's sentimental fallacies". *Picture by the University of Ulster*.

Birley, Sir Derek, died in Johannesburg on May 14, 2002, aged 75. His 1979 book, *The Willow Wand: Some Cricket Myths Explored*, was applauded by those who relished what his fellow author Eric Midwinter called "its iconoclastic demolition of cricket's sentimental fallacies". Traditionalists reached for their Cardus, himself one of Birley's more obvious suspects. Following his retirement in 1991 as vice-chancellor of the University of Ulster, which he had built from a coalition of small teacher-training colleges into a five-campus establishment, Birley wrote *Sport and the Making of Britain*, *Land of Sport and Glory*, and *Playing the Game* before specialising again with *A Social History of Cricket*. Although missing the originality of *Willow Wand*, it was William Hill Sports Book of the Year 1999 and won the Cricket Society's Literary Award.

Boddington, Myles Alan, who died in Burford on February 14, 2002, aged 77, played for the RAF against Worcestershire in 1946, his sole first-class game. Given his reputation at Rugby as "a fast bowler of height and hostility", which earned him selection for the Lord's Schools in 1942 and 1943, there was some interest in his county debut. Unfortunately, opening the attack, he bowled only three overs before pulling up injured. His left-handed batting produced 23 lower-order runs in the second innings after a duck in the first. In 1941, he had played in Rugby's centenary match to mark MCC's first fixture at the school, a visit celebrated in Thomas Hughes's *Tom Brown's School Days*. Like Hughes, Myles Boddington captained Rugby in his final year. His father, Robert, was a wicket-keeper who played 52 times for Lancashire.

Bremner, Colin David, who died in Canberra on June 13, 2002, aged 82, was a stylish wicket-keeper who played for the Dominions against England at Lord's in 1945 and stumped Wally Hammond twice – for a hundred in each innings. *WCAA.*

Brindle, Reginald Gordon, who died in Newton-le-Willows on March 16, 1998, aged 72, spent two summers on the Warwickshire staff from 1948 and played against Combined Services in 1949. A right-handed batsman from Warrington, he compiled attractive innings of 42 and 32 to confirm his potential, but Warwickshire's Championship aspirations, fulfilled in 1950, were being built around a cadre of experienced players. Brindle was not given another chance and returned north to score heavily in Merseyside club cricket.

Brittenden, Richard Trevor, MBE, died in Christchurch on June 10, 2002, aged 82. For as long as many could remember, he had been New Zealand's foremost cricket writer. The game, he once said, was his mistress and he had been passionate about it since his youth. Dick Brittenden joined the Christchurch *Press* in 1938 and, except during war service as a flying officer with the RNZAF, remained with the paper until his retirement in 1984; he was its sports editor from 1955. He covered New Zealand's 1953-54 tour of South Africa – relived vividly in his first book, *Silver Fern on the Veld* – and four tours of England, two of which took in India and Pakistan. At first opposed to the Packer revolution of the 1970s, he came round to it because he felt that cricketers benefited. But he warned his countrymen against playing just for money: "The public's interest in our team's performances will diminish. We won't be a plucky little nation fighting the big guys any more." Brittenden was also managing editor of the *New Zealand Cricketer* from its inception in 1967 to 1973, and for a time edited its successor, the *Cricket Player*, as well as contributing for more than 30 years to *Wisden* and *The Cricketer*. His first *Wisden* commission was the profile of Dick Motz for the Five Cricketers of the Year in 1966. The press box at Jade Stadium in Christchurch, formerly Lancaster Park, was named after him (he reported rugby there too), while the approach to the 17th green at Waitikiri Golf Club has been known as the Brittenden bypass ever since he holed it in one.

Clarke, Donald Barry, died in Johannesburg on December 29, 2002, aged 69. His prodigious line- and goal-kicking while fullback for the New Zealand All-Blacks made Don Clarke a rugby legend and won him the nickname "The Boot". And when he wasn't kicking balls 50, even 60 yards, he bowled them pretty quickly over 22. Months before he caught the nation's eye by helping Waikato lift the Ranfurly Shield, New Zealand's premier rugby trophy, the 17-year-old Clarke opened the bowling for Auckland in the Plunket Shield. At that age, selection for a metropolitan province was a significant achievement for a country boy. Standing 6ft 2in and powerfully built, he was made for fast-medium bowling. His smooth, athletic action lent itself to sustained spells and he could move the ball about disconcertingly.

After Northern Districts entered the Plunket Shield in 1956-57, he represented them until 1962-63, when they won the competition for the first time and he became one of the few to play for winning teams in both the Plunket and Ranfurly Shield. His 20 wickets that season included a career-best eight for 37 in 22.3 overs off the reel to dismiss Central Districts for 71 at Wanganui, following a career-best 47 in Northern's first innings. Only the last of his eight wickets was bowled. Several days later Clarke returned a creditable three for 82 in 27 overs when Wellington's John Reid smashed a world-record 15 sixes while hurtling to 296 out of 422. One of the three off Clarke, little more than a fly-swat at a beamer, smashed into a Basin Reserve floodlight tower with such force that those present still testify to the tuning-fork twang as leather struck steel. The next summer Clarke was in the British Isles and France with the All-Blacks. After that a serious knee injury, not helped by supporting some 17 stones, put paid to his first-class cricket. He had played 27 games, taking 117 wickets at 21.14 and scored

369 runs at 10.54. One of his brothers, Doug, played six times for Northern Districts, while there was one representative rugby game in which all five Clarke brothers turned out together for Waikato. Don Clarke moved to South Africa in the 1970s and set up a tree-felling business.

Coats, James, who died in Brisbane on June 8, 2002, aged 88, played all three games on Queensland's southern tour in 1937-38 but was unable to improve on the brisk 46 he made against Victoria on debut, going in at No. 3 and top-scoring in the second innings. All told he scored 127 runs at 21.17 and was relegated to twelfth man when the team returned to Brisbane.

Cooper, Alfred, who died on October 6, 2002, aged 96, made a substantial contribution to Wiltshire cricket at all levels while the county's chairman, especially in the years when the Minor Counties were re-establishing themselves after World War II. David Richards, a former Wiltshire captain, remembered him as generous to "amateurs and artisans alike, many of us experiencing difficulty in finding the means to play". After retiring as chairman, Cooper was president of Wiltshire for 15 years until 1998. He was active with Swindon CC as player and later committee-man from 1928, having returned to the area to run the family scrap-metal business. At the time of his death he was described as "the doyen of the modern metals recycling industry".

Cotton, Edward Kenneth, who died in Sydney on March 26, 2002, aged 74, had a few games for New South Wales in the 1950s as an all-rounder. Later, as coach of NSW Under-19s, Ted Cotton helped bring on several star players, including the Waugh twins, Mark Taylor, Adam Gilchrist and Michael Slater. *WCAA.*

Cristofani, Desmond Robert, died in Canberra on August 22, 2002, aged 81. It was 57 years to the day since his rousing 110 not out for Australia in the last of the 1945 "Victory Tests" against England. E. W. Swanton used it at the end of his 1946 *Wisden* article, "Cricket Under the Japs", recalling how his first walk as a free man for three years had taken him to a Thai village. "In the little café our hosts politely turned on the English programme. Yes, we were at Old Trafford, and a gentleman called Cristofani was getting a hundred..." It was some hundred, accounting for all but 31 of the 141 scored after he went in with Australia 69 for six in their second innings on a damp surface drying in brilliant sunshine. Bob Cristofani added 95 in even time with Graham Williams (12) for the ninth wicket; his 14 boundaries included a hooked six off George Pope on to the pavilion terraces. The day before he had finished with five for 55, giving the England batsmen as much trouble with his leg-breaks and googlies as he had when taking four for 43 and five for 49 at Lord's in the third "Test".

The previous year, as a 23-year-old pilot officer, Cristofani had been one of many Australian first-grade cricketers who responded to a circular sent to every RAF base by those putting together the summer's RAAF teams. He had played once for New South Wales, against Queensland at Brisbane in December 1941 – the last inter-state game before the Japanese attack on Pearl Harbor put a stop to first-class cricket for four years. His well-flighted leg-spinners, varying from medium-pace to slow, quickly made an impact in 1944, accounting for four Test players in Charles Barnett, Cyril Washbrook, Bob Wyatt and New Zealand's Ken James when he took seven for 39 in the defeat of the RAF at Lord's. A week later he was back, playing for Australia against The Rest and England over Whitsun weekend. After the RAAF's captain, Keith Carmody, was shot down off the Dutch coast and taken prisoner – a reminder that cricket was merely a welcome distraction from the real business at hand – Cristofani shared the captaincy with Stan Sismey, a fellow New South Welshman. Against New Zealand Services at Maidstone, he led a recovery from 49 for five with a hard-hitting 76, then took nine for ten to skittle the opposition for 45.

Bob Cristofani: "In the little café," recalled E. W. Swanton in *Wisden 1946*, "our hosts politely turned on the English programme. Yes, we were at Old Trafford, and a gentleman called Cristofani was getting a hundred…" It was some hundred. *Picture by EMPICS*.

Performances such as these had some Australians thinking they had found another Clarrie Grimmett. The cricket writer Dick Whitington, a team-mate in the 1945 Australian Services side, reckoned Cristofani's Old Trafford century was "one in which even Victor Trumper could have taken pride". But his serious cricketing days were almost over. After playing in England, India and Australia with the Services side, he turned out only twice for New South Wales when Shield cricket resumed in 1946-47. His long-term future lay with Australia's Department of Trade, with which he held several overseas postings. In 18 first-class games he scored 747 runs at 26.75 and took 48 wickets at 32.93; Old Trafford and Lord's witnessed his best performances.

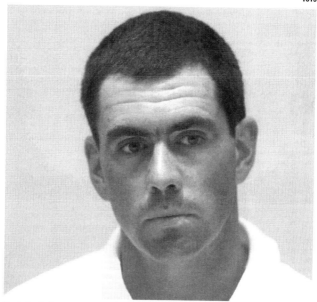

Hansie Cronje: "I was arrogant enough to think I would get away with it." *Picture by Mike Hutchings, Reuters/Popperfoto.*

Cronje, Wessel Johannes, South Africa's cricket captain in a record 53 Tests and 138 one-day internationals between 1994 and 2000, died on June 1, 2002 when the cargo plane in which he was travelling crashed on Cradock Peak in the Outeniqua mountain range on its approach to his home town, George, in the Western Cape. He was just 32. Two years earlier, Hansie Cronje's admission that he took bribes from bookmakers to provide information and fix matches exposed the extent of a corruption scandal that cricket authorities had signally neglected to confront.

At first he had hotly denied charges levelled by the New Delhi police, who during a phone-tapping operation in March 2000 heard him conspiring with an Indian book-maker, Sanjeev Chawla, to predetermine performances. And such was his standing as a player, captain and sporting ambassador for post-apartheid South Africa that few in the cricket world doubted him, preferring to heap scorn on the Indian investigation. Ali Bacher, managing director of the United Cricket Board of South Africa, spoke of Cronje's "unquestionable integrity and honesty". Then, four days after the accusation, Cronje confessed in a 3 a.m. phone call to Bacher that he had not been "entirely honest". He was immediately stripped of the captaincy, as his side prepared for a one-day series against Australia, and in subsequent testimony to the government-appointed King Commission revealed, sometimes in tears, further details of his involvement with bookmakers in match-fixing. The cricket world listened agog as much as aghast. The game's reputation, it seemed, was at an all-time low. Cronje's life and career were in tatters.

It had been so different a decade earlier when, aged 21, he was given the captaincy of Orange Free State. His upbringing and education had groomed him for leadership. His family were of solid, middle-class Afrikaner stock, deeply religious and sporty: Hansie's father, Ewie, had been an off-spinning all-rounder for Free State in the 1960s. The importance of discipline, dedication and hard work had been inculcated in Hansie at an early age, honed at Grey College in his native Bloemfontein, and was made manifest in 1991-92, his second year in charge, when the young Free State team, coached by Eddie Barlow to a level of physical and mental fitness rare even for South African cricket, finished runners-up in the Castle Bowl (formerly the Currie Cup) and won the limited-overs Nissan Shield. The next two seasons brought Castle Cup and one-day doubles, followed by one-day trophies in subsequent years – a total of seven titles in five seasons. International commitments meant the young captain was not ever-present, but his influence remained inspirational.

He had made his debut at 18 in January 1988, joining his brother, Frans, for the Currie Cup games against Transvaal and Northern Transvaal. Innings of two and 16, then a pair, were an inauspicious start for someone who would notch up a record 15 first-class hundreds for the Free State, as well as six in one-day competitions. The following season, his unbeaten 105 against Impalas took Orange Free State into the Benson and Hedges Trophy final, where Frans's old school-friend Allan Donald blew Western Province aside with four for 18. Hansie's maiden first-class hundred followed in January 1990 when, captaining South African Universities, he hit 104 against Mike Gatting's English rebels.

Inside the year, South Africa had been readmitted to full membership of the ICC, and the 22-year-old Cronje was one of four non-playing observers – two white, two non-white – taken to India with the first post-isolation side. Three months later, he was bowling five tidy overs for 17 as South Africa, captained by Kepler Wessels, shocked Australia with a nine-wicket victory at Sydney in the World Cup. He played in eight of their nine games in that tournament, including the infamous semi-final against England in which South Africa's target was adjusted after rain from 22 off 13 balls to 21 off one. Then he went to the Caribbean for South Africa's first Test since readmission, and their first ever against West Indies. Cronje scored only five and two, but in 68 Tests would go on to make 3,714 runs at 36.41, as well as taking 43 wickets at 29.95; in 188 one-day internationals he made 5,565 runs at 38.64, took 114 wickets at 34.78 with an economy rate of 4.44, and held 72 catches. His first-class figures from 184 games were 12,103 runs at 43.69 and 116 wickets at 34.43.

With his aggressive batting, intelligent medium-pace bowling and brilliant fielding, Cronje was a formidable competitor. The Indians discovered as much when they visited South Africa in 1992-93 and he took a career-best five for 32 in the opening one-day international, won it with a six with three balls to spare, and conceded only 3.59 an over in the seven-match series. That tour also proved he had the mettle for Test cricket. Going in in the second over at Port Elizabeth, he stayed eight and three-quarter hours (411 balls) until he was last out for 135, the first and highest of his six Test centuries. When Donald took his match haul to 12 wickets, South Africa had their first Test victory of the new era. Cronje's second hundred, 122, came in Colombo the following September to set up South Africa's biggest Test win – an innings and 208 runs – and Sri Lanka's heaviest defeat.

His good form initially held when, the youngest in the side at 24, he was Wessels's vice-captain in Australia in 1994-95. After Wessels broke a finger in the Sydney Test, Cronje took charge on the tense final morning to such effect that Australia, chasing 117 for victory with six wickets in hand, were dismissed for 111; his direct hit to run out Shane Warne from wide mid-off struck a crucial blow. He also took over during the one-day tournament when further injuries forced Wessels home, and at Adelaide became South Africa's second-youngest Test captain, after Murray Bisset in 1898-99. But there was no fairytale: Australia won by 191 runs to square the series.

Hansie Cronje: his players revered him. Jonty Rhodes remained a friend after the match-fixing scandal broke. *Picture by Clive Mason, Getty Images.*

Wessels was captain again when the two countries resumed hostilities in South Africa, and Cronje wasted no time extracting revenge for Adelaide. In six games in 14 days, he hammered the Aussie bowling for 721 runs: he began with 112 from 120 balls, the higher of his two one-day international hundreds, hit 251, his maiden double-hundred, for Orange Free State and finished with 122 in the First Test, which South Africa won by 197 runs. The double-hundred – next highest score was Gerry Liebenberg's 39 – remained Cronje's best.

This was a period of transition for Australian fast bowling, though. Cronje was given a harder time in England in 1994 and managed only 90 runs in six Test innings as Devon Malcolm and the young Darren Gough exposed a technical weakness against short-pitched bowling directed at his ribs. Spin gave him no such problems, and his armoury against it included a ferocious slog-sweep over mid-wicket, played on one knee. When he made what was then Test cricket's third-fastest fifty, off 31 balls at Centurion in 1997-98, he reached it by hitting Muttiah Muralitharan, the world's best off-spinner, for 4666 off successive balls.

In 1995, he expunged his unhappy introduction to English conditions by making 1,362 first-class runs at 50.44 in a one-off season for Leicestershire, whose cricket manager Jack Birkenshaw and all-rounder Gordon Parsons, Cronje's brother-in-law since 1991, participated in Orange Free State's triumphs. Among his four hundreds was 213 against Somerset at Weston-super-Mare. But it would take him ten Tests and until 1998 to reach 50 against England, whereupon he did so five times on the trot:

As with most great leaders, Cronje's personality comprised a complex skein of qualities... he succeeded Wessels as captain in 1994-95, and began the partnership with Woolmer that masterminded South Africa's tactics until the 1999 World Cup. *Picture by Laurence Griffiths, Getty Images.*

81 in South Africa's win at Lord's, 69 not out at Old Trafford, 126 and 67 at Trent Bridge, and 57 (plus a duck) at Headingley, where England took the series 2–1 with help from some inept umpiring. He was South Africa's top-scorer, with 401 runs at 66.83, but it was generally accepted that his unenterprising captaincy had let the rubber slip away. Instead of penetration he went for strangulation, setting defensive fields for his seam bowlers and encouraging them to bowl wide of off stump: what Bob Woolmer, South Africa's coach, called "aggressive containment".

Yet when Cronje succeeded Wessels in 1994-95, and began the partnership with Woolmer that masterminded South Africa's tactics until the 1999 World Cup, he was welcomed as an adventurous captain; one prepared to gamble. In his first series, against New Zealand in South Africa, he became the first captain since W. G. Grace to win a three-match rubber after being one down. When the teams met again at Auckland in March 1995, Cronje's pre-lunch declaration, setting New Zealand 275 to win in 63 overs, was the catalyst for South Africa's 93-run victory. Something saturnine in his demeanour, however, spoke of arrogance and calculated self-control; his dour expression suggested few concessions to humour or emotion. Yet there were times when the composure snapped. Shortly after becoming South Africa's captain, he received a one-match ban for dissent on dismissal in a Castle Cup game. When the umpires rightly ruled Mark Waugh not out after inadvertently hitting his wicket at Adelaide in 1997-98, and he went on to save the Test, Cronje hurled a stump through their dressing-room door. At Cape Town in 1995-96, he was fined for imposing his will on umpire

Dave Orchard to refer a run-out to the television umpire after Orchard ruled England's Graham Thorpe not out; the decision was overturned and South Africa went on to take the match and the series.

He could certainly be articulate and persuasive. The England bowler Angus Fraser recalled him holding an audience in thrall for 40 minutes, without notes, and reciting "word for word" from Hamlet. "His pre-match talks were often inspirational," Woolmer said, "and he led from the front." His players revered him. The Western Province seamer Craig Matthews credited Cronje with changing his life: "He actually persuaded me that I was good enough to play international cricket." At Cronje's funeral, Shaun Pollock, his successor as national captain, spoke of his love of practical jokes, often used to make newcomers feel at home. Pollock recounted being told to field next to a certain sponsor's advert, only to discover the sponsor had boards scattered all round the ground. As with most great leaders, Cronje's personality comprised a complex skein of qualities.

His captaincy record brooks few arguments. South Africa won 27 and lost only 11 of his 53 Tests in charge, with series victories over every opponent except Australia; in 138 one-day internationals there were 99 wins, as well as a tie. His record made a nonsense of the South African board's decision to appoint him for only the first two Tests against England in 1999-2000, even allowing for a downturn in his form and his apprehensions about the UCBSA's politically motivated policy of selection on racial quotas. Although he was later confirmed as captain for all the Tests and one-day games, his take on the turn of events was apparent in his brooding presence and the fact that he openly flirted with an offer to succeed Duncan Fletcher as Glamorgan coach.

He was still coming to terms, too, with that cataclysmic tie against Australia that cost South Africa a place in the 1999 World Cup final and dashed his boyhood dreams of leading his country to World Cup glory. With one run needed to win their semi-final, and three balls still in hand, South Africa's last pair, Lance Klusener and Donald, contrived the most fatal of run-outs. Cronje, who had been given out for a duck caught off his boot, was magnanimous in defeat as ever, but nothing could mask his anguish. Australia remained his *bête noire*.

He did outdo his Australian rivals Mark Taylor and Steve Waugh in winning a Test series in India, in 2000. South Africa won 2–0 and ended India's sequence of 14 unbeaten home series since 1987. But in that moment of triumph the seeds of his tragedy were quickly taking root. Ensnared in illicit dealings with sub-continental bookmakers after Mohammad Azharuddin introduced him to the match-fixer M. K. Gupta on South Africa's previous tour of India, in 1996, Cronje was now in cahoots with Sanjeev Chawla. Cronje unsuccessfully approached Pieter Strydom to under-perform in the First Test; before the Second he asked Mark Boucher, Jacques Kallis and Klusener if they were interested in throwing the game for money. They put it down as another of Hansie's practical jokes. It was not until the final one-day game at Nagpur that he struck lucky, getting Herschelle Gibbs and Henry Williams to play for \$US15,000 apiece. Gibbs was supposed to be out for less than 20 and Williams to concede more than 50. That the plan went awry was ethically immaterial. He had lured two non-white players, the most vulnerable of his charges in socio-economic terms, at the very time he was supporting South Africa's development programme to bring young black cricketers into the first-class game. When it emerged that he told Chawla he needed \$US25,000 for each player, so guaranteeing himself a \$US20,000 cut, Cronje's greed was compliant with his guilt. Gibbs and Williams subsequently received six-month suspensions from international cricket.

Granted immunity from prosecution, Cronje told the King Commission he received around \$US140,000 from bookmakers, including \$US110,000 from Gupta for infor-mation on team selection, daily forecasts and when he would declare against India at Cape Town in January 1997. He denied ever fixing the actual result of a match. He also admitted telling the South African team, before the Mohinder Amarnath benefit

Spin gave him few problems, and his armoury against it included a ferocious slog-sweep over mid-wicket, played on one knee. *Picture by Adrian Murrell, Getty Images.*

game at Mumbai in December 1996, that there was $US200,000 (some sources said $250,000) on the table if they played badly. The team actually debated whether to accept the money before rejecting it; no one reported the matter to the authorities. Some of them thought the offer of a bribe reflected South Africa's coming of age in international cricket.

When Cronje rejected further advances from Gupta in November 1997, that might have ended his perfidy. But, as he told Justice King, he had "an unfortunate love of money... I am not addicted to alcohol or nicotine, but I believe this is very similar to an alcohol problem." Even so, it was small beer, certainly in terms of personal gain, that made him come off the wagon in January 2000. In response to a late-night visit from a South African bookmaker, Marlon Aronstam, he persuaded Nasser Hussain to make a match of the rain-ruined Centurion Test on the fifth day with a double forfeiture of innings – something not only without precedent in Test history but also outside the Laws. Aronstam had planned to back both sides at long odds and, even though the forfeiture deal was struck too late for him to place his bets, Cronje was given 53,000 rand (approximately £5,000) and a leather jacket for his wife. He was also acclaimed for his enterprising captaincy by unsuspecting commentators who welcomed England's win – South Africa had already taken the series – as a victory for common sense and the game. A fortnight later Cronje was meeting Chawla in Durban and leaving his hotel room with some $US15,000 tucked in a mobile-phone container. The die was cast.

Neither Justice King nor many others believed they had heard the full story, but enough was known for Cronje to receive a life ban from all cricketing activities. The Qayyum Report had already recommended a life ban for Pakistan's former captain Salim Malik; India's Azharuddin and Ajay Sharma would receive similar sentences before the year was out. And the ICC would eventually publish their own report into corruption in the game and implement a range of measures designed to keep the bookmakers at bay.

Meanwhile the most intriguing question – why he did it – remained an enigma. In multi-media interviews between his testimony and his ban in October, reputed to have netted a further £100,000, Cronje talked of "greed, stupidity and the lure of easy money" and claimed "I was arrogant enough to think I would get away with it". A born-again Christian who wore a bracelet with the initials WWJD – What Would Jesus Do? – he talked of how Satan had entered his world when he took his eyes off Jesus and his "whole world turned dark". There was something pre-Christian in this, an echo of Greek heroes blaming the gods rather than themselves for their misfortunes.

Cronje's appeal against his life ban was rejected by the Pretoria High Court in October 2001, and while there was talk of his having some future role in cricket, maybe coaching or in the media, he began to build a life away from the game. He enrolled on a Masters degree course, and in February 2002 joined the Johannesburg-based firm Bell Equipment, which specialised in earth-moving machinery, as financial manager. At the time of his death he was commuting weekly to and from his home on the exclusive Fancourt Estate in George. That fateful weekend, he had hitched a ride with the two pilots of an Air Quarius Hawker Siddeley turboprop after his scheduled flight had been grounded by a hailstorm – a risk-taker to the end.

More than a thousand mourners filled the Grey College Chapel for Cronje's funeral, while a thousand more outside watched the service, which was televised nationally, on large screens. It was reported that members of the UCBSA, critical earlier of their captain's betrayal, had been told they would not be welcome, but Bertha Cronje, Hansie's widow, said he would not have agreed with such a ban. The divisions were forgotten as South Africa, a nation rebuilding on forgiveness and reconciliation, mourned, in Gary Kirsten's words, "a great cricketer, a great performer and a great on-field leader of his country". It was elsewhere that cricket would still consider Hansie Cronje a tarnished hero.

Crosskill, Hugh, died in Kingston, Jamaica on June 7, 2002, aged 47, after being shot in the chest by a security guard at a medical centre. He had been battling to beat a drug addiction. Born in Scarborough to a Scottish mother and Jamaican father, who was playing as a professional in the leagues, Crosskill went to Jamaica as a boy and in the early 1970s was a sports commentator with the Jamaican broadcasting corporation. He moved to news and current affairs, but his reputation as a cricket commentator was considered as much an asset as his political insight and biting wit when, in 1988, the BBC invited him to help relaunch its Caribbean Service. He headed this from 1994 to 1996. While in London he contributed to BBC sports programmes and captained the BBC cricket team.

Daniel, Jack, who died in Tweed Heads, New South Wales, on October 12, 2002, aged 78, was a medium-fast bowler who played seven times for Victoria between 1947-48 and 1950-51. *WCAA.*

De Soysa, Gahmini Ryle Johannes, who died in Colombo on January 13, 2002, aged 84, was born into a celebrated Ceylonese family whose benefactions include the land on which the Moratuwa Stadium was built. Ryle de Soysa captained Royal College of Colombo on their five-game visit to Australia in 1936, the first time a schools side had left Ceylon's shores, and was singled out by the former Australian captain Bill Woodfull, headmaster of Melbourne Grammar, for his all-round ability. But by the time he hit 100 in the 1938 Oxford Seniors' Match, there was little sign of his leg-breaks and googlies. Much more in evidence was Frank Woolley's influence on his left-handed batting, particularly in his late cuts and the full flow of his driving. Hedley Verity picked him off for nought and two on his first-class debut, but he was given three more games that term and his half-century helped avoid defeat by Leicestershire. Next year he made 67 against Minor Counties, his highest first-class score. Innings of 112 in the final Oxford trial of 1940, and an unbeaten 80 against a British Empire XII, afforded a taste of what de Soysa might have gone on to in happier circumstances. There was talk of an unofficial University Match at Fenner's, but nothing came of it. Back home in Ceylon he coached the Royal XI for several years and in 1945 opened for Ceylon against Vijay Merchant's Indian tourists, scoring 38 and 18 and taking his aggregate from eight first-class games to 314 runs at 20.93. His two first-class wickets, for 15 runs, were taken against Jamaica for the Oxford and Cambridge side that went there in 1938. De Soysa became president of Sinhalese Sports Club in 1997, but declining health forced him to stand down the following year.

Dua, Beldev, died in Delhi on January 17, 2002, aged 65. He played for Delhi University in the golden days when an inter-college final could attract crowds of up to 20,000, and also represented North Zone Universities as a top-order batsman with a sure pair of hands at slip. He scored nine in his one Ranji Trophy game for Delhi, in 1968-69.

Eaglestone, James Thomas, who died in Pinner, Middlesex, on October 14, 2000, aged 77, played only three seasons of first-class cricket, never hit a hundred, yet in successive summers was in Championship-winning sides – with different counties. A left-hander, Jim Eaglestone signed for Middlesex in 1947 and went straight into the side after he scored 77 (his career-best) and put on 128 with Denis Compton for MCC against Surrey in early May. He began his county career with a duck, as Middlesex opened with defeat by Somerset, but a week later he hit 55 in a century stand with Bill Edrich, who went on to 225. There was another half-century, 61 against Oxford, but Middlesex had no shortage of free-scoring batsmen. Although his speed in the field was an asset, he played only seven games for 151 runs in the title race. Glamorgan, conscious that Arnold Dyson would be coaching Oundle School for much of 1948, encouraged the 24-year-old Eaglestone to head west, along with his fast-bowling team-

Jim Eaglestone: he played only three seasons of first-class cricket, never hit a hundred, yet in successive summers was in Championship-winning sides – with different counties. Surrey's wicket-keeper, Arthur McIntyre, looks on. *Picture by EMPICS*.

mate Norman Hever. Eaglestone contributed 595 runs at 18.59 to Glamorgan's Championship campaign, and his captain, Wilf Wooller, considered the runs he saved in the field as valuable as those he scored. His 65 against Hampshire put Glamorgan in a strong position when rain softened the pitch later in the day, and against Sussex at Swansea he knocked up 72 in 50 minutes. In 1949, however, he managed only 341 runs at 11.36 and decided to give up first-class cricket and return to London. In 60 games he had scored 1,420 runs at 15.77 and held 23 catches. For years afterwards he ran a newsagent's in Paddington.

Edwards, Herbert Charles, who died on January 22, 2002, aged 88, was one of several club cricketers who had a taste of first-class cricket with Worcestershire when normality returned after World War II. His debut came on a rain-softened pitch at Old Trafford where Lancashire won by an innings in a day and a half. Having taken a catch to help Roly Jenkins towards his eight Lancashire wickets, he scored ten and one and could think himself more fortunate than the man he followed in the order. Poor George Dews, also making his debut, was out first ball to Eric Price's left-arm spin in both innings. Still, Dews did go on to score 1,000 runs 11 times at New Road, whereas this was Bert Edwards's sole appearance, at the age of 32. He played club cricket for Old Hill from 1932 to 1958 and, like his father before him, served as their president.

Edwards, John Neild, who died in Melbourne on December 29, 2002, aged 74, was 27 when first selected to open the bowling for Victoria, in 1955-56. Solidly built, "Darky" Edwards operated at medium pace and in 32 games for the state took 85 wickets at 29.45. His swing bowling was demanding rather than penetrative, but one sultry Melbourne morning in December 1957 it was unplayable. Edwards sent back four batsmen without conceding a run and finished with a career-best six for 18 as Queensland were dismissed for 65. Once the humidity cleared, Victoria amassed 464, to which Edwards contributed 48 not out, the highest score in his 361 runs at 12.89. He was a state selector for nine years and managed the national team at home in 28 Tests and 62 one-day internationals between 1979 and 1984. The Australians wore black armbands in his honour on the third day of the Sydney Test in 2003.

Faber, Julian Tufnell, who died in Withyham, Sussex, on January 11, 2002, aged 84, was in the Winchester XI in 1934 and 1935 and later served on the MCC and Kent committees. While a director of Cornhill Insurance, he was an influential voice when they agreed to sponsor Test cricket in England in an hour of need, with the Packer schism looming, in 1977-78. Faber became Cornhill's chairman in 1986, and the sponsorship ran, very smoothly, to 2000. His son Mark, who died in 1991, was a stylish batsman for Oxford and Sussex in the 1970s, and another son, David, is a former Tory MP.

Fawcus, Harold James, who died on July 13, 2002, aged 83, succeeded his father as honorary secretary of the Cryptics in 1949 and held the office for 50 years, combining it in the 1980s with a five-year stint as the club's president. The Cryptics were founded in 1910 by J. G. Fawcus, Harold's father, and three fellow undergraduates at New College, Oxford. One of the club's original aims, which still survives, was to encourage cricket in schools, hence the high proportion of schoolmasters among its members. For many years Harold Fawcus's meticulous organisation, backed up by letters written in his own hand, was fitted into an already busy life as headmaster of Dunchurch-Winton Hall.

Finlayson, Alan Gordon, died in Port Elizabeth on October 28, 2001, aged 101. He was the second South African cricketer to reach 100 and, as far as is known, the ninth first-class cricketer; the others are listed on page 176 of *Wisden 2000*. A right-handed all-rounder, Alan Finlayson played twice for Eastern Province in the 1921-22 Currie Cup, scoring 40 runs at 10.00 and taking one for 19. His younger brother Charles, who died aged 50 to 1953, played four games for Eastern Province.

Fullerton, George Murray, died in Cape Town on November 19, 2002, aged 79. He toured England twice with South Africa, keeping wicket in two Tests in 1947 and playing three as a batsman in 1951, when he hit 1,129 runs at 31.36 in his 20 first-class games. In between, he kept in the last two Tests against the 1949-50 Australians and made a Test-best 88 at his native Johannesburg to help avoid the follow-on. George Fullerton made his first-class debut in December 1942 for the Rest of South Africa against an Air Force XI at Johannesburg. He was just 20, and there would be three years of naval service before he played for Transvaal, impressing with his alert glovework and making a maiden century before the summer was through. He was one of three wicket-keepers taken to England in 1947 and, after Doug Ovenstone broke his finger, the only option when South Africa dropped Johnny Lindsay at Headingley. *Wisden* noted his driving, cutting and quick footwork during the tour. However, Fullerton could play only three games for Transvaal over the next two seasons and Natal's Billy Wade, unable to tour in 1947, resumed as South Africa's keeper until 1949-50, when Fullerton came back. Russell Endean took over as Transvaal's wicket-keeper in 1950-51 and Fullerton played as a batsman. Averaging 66.20, helped by 112 and 94 against Western Province, he played a significant role in their Currie Cup victory. His good

George Fullerton: *Wisden* noted his driving, cutting and quick footwork during the 1947 South African tour of England. *Picture by Getty Images.*

form continued in England, where he hit a career-best 167 against Essex at Ilford. Business commitments allowed him no more first-class cricket after the tour. In 63 games he had scored 2,768 runs at 31.10, held 64 catches, made 18 stumpings and taken three wickets at 35.66. In seven Tests he scored 325 runs at 25.00, held ten catches and made two stumpings. His younger brother Ian also represented Transvaal.

Gardner, Charles Allan, who died in Melbourne on December 9, 2001, aged 93, was a former blacksmith who played twice for Victoria against Western Australia in February 1934, making 78 on debut. *WCAA.*

Gautam, Narayanan, who died of cancer in Chennai on May 7, 2002, aged only 34, was a tall, elegant batsman whose stylish strokeplay and unflappable temperament in the No. 3 spot helped Tamil Nadu reach the final of the Ranji Trophy in 1991-92. There, they were beaten on first innings by Delhi. That Tamil Nadu had a class player in the making was apparent from the way Gautam scored his 23 on debut against the touring New Zealanders in November 1988. Though another two years passed before his first Ranji Trophy game, in 1990-91, he graced it with 101 as Tamil Nadu amassed 548 against Hyderabad. The following season he made a career-best 190 against Uttar Pradesh in a Ranji quarter-final. Timing, fluent driving and effortless square-cuts were the outstanding features of his batting, but when the timing unaccountably deserted him the runs dried up. Gautam's final Ranji Trophy season, 1994-95, found him playing as a professional for bottom-of-the-zone Goa. He made 1,007 runs in a 23-match career; an average of 30.51 hints at what he might have achieved.

Glerum, Herman Wilhelm, died in The Netherlands on August 24, 2002, four days before his 91st birthday. Involved with de Flamingo's club since he was 16, Bill Glerum represented Holland 30 times between 1928 and 1957 and was for many years a driving force behind Dutch cricket. He played a few games for the British Empire XI and the RAF while serving in England during World War II, and in 1957, aged 45, had a first-class game for Free Foresters against Oxford University. His medium-pace bowling captured three cheap wickets, including the Oxford captain Chris Walton for 95. Batting in the middle order, Glerum scored nought and one. "Bill made you feel cricket was worth playing simply by being around him," said the former MCC secretary Jack Bailey, who recalled coming across him on a club tour to Brazil, where Glerum was working for Fokker, the Dutch aircraft manufacturer.

Gunn, Brian George Herbert, died in Cairns on September 3, 2001, aged 79. Kent had won none of their first five games in 1946 when they drafted Gunn, a 24-year-old Dartford batsman, into their middle order for the match against Nottinghamshire at Gillingham. His 39 was the second-highest score in the first innings – only the captain, Bryan Valentine, made more runs for Kent in the match – and the 233-run win brought Kent's first Championship points of the season. At Gravesend a fortnight later, however, Gunn's was the second of three wickets in one over for Gloucestershire's startlingly quick bowler George Lambert. He then shared in Kent's home-and-away wins against Warwickshire, taking the catch that put paid to the threat Peter Cranmer was posing at Edgbaston, but his 105 runs in those four games, at an average of 15.00, constituted the sum of his first-class experience. Gunn played Sydney grade cricket after emigrating to Australia in 1951 and later worked in journalism in Queensland.

Gupte, Subhash Pandharinath, died in Port-of-Spain on May 31, 2002, aged 72. He had suffered from diabetes and was unable to get about without a wheelchair or walking frame. Sir Everton Weekes had recently said Gupte was "easily the best leg-spin bowler of all time", and certainly between 1953 and 1956 he was peerless. In 15 successive Tests for India he beguiled his way to 82 wickets at 23.57, averaging a wicket every 70 balls. At a comparable stage in his Test career, Shane Warne's strike-rate was 75.

In contrast to his burly younger brother Baloo, who also bowled leggies and won three caps in the 1960s, Subhash Gupte was small and slight. But he had a high arm action and the wrist-spinner's predilection for experimenting with flight and rotation. Unlike some, he possessed the control and patience to afford his variations. His leg-spinner, nicely looped, turned on the flattest pitches, while a scurrying top-spinner and two googlies provided sufficient chicanery. The googly he bowled with a lower trajectory was for batsmen to read; the other, from his customary high trajectory, came laced with overspin and dipped and bounced deceptively. Unhappily, his close catchers struggled to pick his repertoire almost as much as the batsmen, so chances often went begging. He would have taken all ten wickets, instead of nine for 102, against West Indies on jute matting at Kanpur in 1958-59 had the wicket-keeper Naren Tamhane not dropped Lance Gibbs. It was the first time an Indian bowler had taken nine wickets in a Test innings – and still India lost by a large margin. There was one ten-wicket return in his career bag, however: for the Bombay CA President's XI against a visiting Pakistan Services and Bahawalpur side in December 1954, at a cost of 78 runs. While most of his domestic cricket was for his native Bombay, he also played for Bengal and Rajasthan.

After a debut Test against England in 1951-52 and two the next season against Pakistan, Gupte won his spurs – and a nickname, "Fergie", after the Trinidad leg-spinner Wilf Ferguson – in the Caribbean in 1952-53. He also met his future wife, Carol. Though few of the pitches helped bowlers and Weekes was rampant, averaging over 100, Gupte took 27 wickets at 29.22 in the five Tests, including seven for 162 at Port-of-Spain, and ended the tour with 50 at 23.64. India's other bowlers managed 35

Subhash Gupte: "easily the best leg-spin bowler of all time," said Sir Everton Weekes. Certainly between 1953 and 1956, he was peerless. *Picture by EMPICS.*

between them in the Tests and 57 overall. Back on the subcontinent he picked up 21 Test wickets on the mat and turf in Pakistan and then 34, while his team-mates took 30, against the touring New Zealanders. But to the 1956 Australians, limping home from England and Jim Laker's off-breaks, leg-spin brought welcome respite. The left-handed Neil Harvey was particularly severe on him in the Bombay Test: Gupte's eight wickets in the three-match series cost 32.62 each and Richie Benaud won the leg-spinning honours hands-down with 23 at 16.86, including 11 for 105 on a Calcutta pitch taking spin from the start.

Gupte was considered the best of his kind when India went to England in 1959, but the strain of carrying India's attack was beginning to tell. Gerry Alexander's West Indians had recently made him pay 42.13 apiece for his 22 wickets; India's next highest wicket-taker claimed only five and Gupte's workload of 312 overs was almost three times that of anyone else. Though he remained India's leading wicket-taker, he did not always come up to expectation on the hard pitches of that sun-baked English summer. And the Indians' slothful fielding didn't help; he was patently dispirited by the poor standard. Ten county spinners went past 100 wickets at a lower cost than his 95 at 26.58, which included eight for 108 in Nottinghamshire's first innings. *Wisden's* correspondent was among those who wondered if the English batsmen's long look at Gupte wasn't giving them "useful experience for the visit of Benaud in 1961". It was not necessarily a case of nonpareil to net bowler, but an uncomplimentary assessment none the less.

Gupte missed that winter's Tests against Benaud's Australians because he was coaching in the West Indies. When Pakistan visited India in 1960-61, his brother replaced him halfway through the series. But the old familiar flight and fizz were much in evidence when he was recalled for the Kanpur Test against Ted Dexter's MCC side in December 1961. He took the first five wickets and, for the first time, India made England follow on. But the comeback did not last long. During the next Test his room-mate, Kripal Singh, phoned the hotel receptionist to ask her for a date. She complained to the Indian management who, claiming they did not know who made the call, suspended both players. Even worse, the Indian board president, himself an acquaintance of the lady, told the selectors not to pick Gupte for the forthcoming tour of the West Indies. Bitter and disillusioned, Gupte quit India for good at 33 and emigrated to Trinidad, where he worked in the sugar refinery and as a sports officer within the industry. Two Beaumont Cup finals for South Trinidad and one appearance for Trinidad in 1963-64 closed his first-class career after 115 games with 530 wickets at 23.71. In 36 Tests, he took 149 wickets at 29.55 – only Benaud and Grimmett among leg-spinners had taken more – five in an innings 12 times and ten in a match once.

Hafiz, Nezam Ahmed, died in the terrorist attack on New York's World Trade Center on September 11, 2001, aged 32. He worked on the 94th floor of Tower One. Hafiz had played six times for his native Guyana as a middle-order batsman between 1988-89 and 1990-91, making 40 runs at 10.00 with a highest score of 30 against the Leeward Islands at Georgetown in 1988-89. After moving to New York he captained the American Cricket Society and the Commonwealth League and represented New York in regional tournaments. He played for the USA in the 1998-99 Red Stripe Bowl in the Caribbean and toured England with them in 2000.

Harburg, Clive Henry, who died in Brisbane on July 21, 2002, aged 90, was founding editor of the ABC's Queensland sports service and a commentator whose resonant voice was compared to that of the former prime minister Sir Robert Menzies. It was Harburg who told radio listeners about the dramatic closing moments of the first tied Test, between Australia and West Indies at the Gabba in December 1960. The match had looked set for a draw, so the ABC's premier cricket broadcaster, Alan McGilvray, caught an early flight home to Sydney, leaving Harburg and Michael Charlton to do ball-by-ball commentary. The rest, as they say, is history.

Harrison, Edward Ernest, who died on December 12, 2002, aged 92, made a lifelong contribution to Sussex cricket. Eddie Harrison "bowled with indefatigable persistency" for Sussex in wartime matches according to *Wisden*, and he played nine first-class games for them in 1946 as an amateur. Though now 36, he took the new ball as often as not and his 17 wickets cost 29.30 apiece. He joined the Sussex committee in the 1940s, later served as chairman of the cricket committee and was elected a vice-president. He had played for Sussex Martlets since leaving Harrow in the 1930s, was their secretary from 1950 to 1985 and then president, and also played for the Duke of Norfolk's XI, subsequently becoming a vice-president of the Friends of Arundel Castle. Harrison played squash for England and twice won the amateur doubles championship.

Hazlerigg, 2nd Lord (Arthur Grey Hazlerigg), MC, DL, died at Noseley, Leicester-shire, on September 30, 2002, aged 92. Leadership became him, whether on the cricket field or the field of battle. The cool head and organisational powers he displayed when captaining Cambridge in 1932 and Leicestershire in 1934 were equally in evidence when he won the Military Cross in Italy in 1944.

Arthur Hazlerigg captained Eton in 1929 and represented the Lord's Schools before going up to Cambridge. He opened the batting and bowled off-breaks, and it was the potential of his bowling rather than his batting, now in the middle order, that gained him a Blue as a freshman in 1930. He had done little in the build-up to Lord's, but on familiar ground he came good spectacularly with four for 17 and three catches in

Oxford's second innings as Cambridge won by 205 runs. A year on, he took a career-best six for 27 against Nottinghamshire at Fenner's, conceding 17 singles, two twos and a six. He finished with 39 wickets at 23.92 that term, and played a few games for Leicestershire afterwards. He had made his debut for the county at Fenner's in 1930 and thus followed in the footsteps of his father, also Arthur Grey, who captained Leicestershire from 1907 to 1910.

Hazlerigg's year in charge of Cambridge began with any university captain's nightmare. His best bowler, Freddie Brown, failed to meet the examiners' satisfaction and was rusticated. Nor did matters improve once the cricket was under way. Alan Ratcliffe, the previous year's hero after hitting the first double-hundred in a University Match, was in such dreadful form that Hazlerigg dropped him down the order. The responsibility of opening he took on himself, and the switch could not have worked better. Ratcliffe scored runs again, making another century against Oxford, and Hazlerigg found himself on course for a thousand with 836 runs at 44.00 after 12 games. An invitation to join the Gentlemen at Lord's and five matches for Leicestershire took him to 1,010 at 36.07. This included three hundreds, all for Cambridge, with a career-best 135 against the Free Foresters. That could easily have wound up his serious cricket, but when Leicestershire hit rock bottom in 1933 he accepted the challenge of getting them back on track. He was available for only two-thirds of the programme, but his leadership was such that Leicestershire rose to 12th. This concluded his first-class career at the age of 24. In 66 matches he had scored 2,515 runs at 25.92, held 75 catches and taken 112 wickets at 31.03. A man of old-world charm and courtesy, he became a chartered surveyor after the war, and, in due course, Leicestershire's oldest surviving player.

Heldsinger, Kenneth Malcolm St John, died in Rosebank, Cape Town, on June 25, 2002, aged 75. He had nine games for Western Province between 1956-57 and 1960-61. While Ken Heldsinger's left-handed middle-order batting produced 63 against Transvaal at Newlands in 1959-60 and one other half-century, a first-class average of 17.87 from 286 runs gives little hint of the aggressive displays in club cricket that won him his provincial cap.

Helfrich, Cyril Desmond, who died in East London on March 23, 2002, aged 76, was the third of four brothers who represented Griqualand West. Basil, the eldest, had made two half-centuries against the 1935-36 Australians while still at school but died two years later at 18 from enteric fever. Cyril Helfrich made his first-class debut at 21, scoring 72 against Orange Free State at Bloemfontein in 1945-46, and went on to play for Griquas until 1957-58. Bloemfontein also witnessed the first of his six hundreds, 101 in November 1947: his highest was 165 against Eastern Province at Kimberley in January 1951, when his brother Ken made a career-best 87. Cyril's attacking half-centuries against MCC in 1948-49 and the Australians a year later brought back memories of Basil, once rated one of South Africa's brightest prospects. In 47 first-class matches Helfrich scored 2,611 runs at 31.84, took 29 wickets at 47.55 and held 34 catches.

Hollioake, Benjamin Caine, died in Perth, Western Australia, on March 23, 2002 when his Porsche 924 left a freeway exit road, made slippery by light rain, and crashed into a brick wall. He had been driving home from the customary family dinner that preceded his and his brother Adam's return to Surrey for the English season, having spent much of the winter with England's one-day squad in Zimbabwe, India and New Zealand. Ben was just 24 years and 132 days old: no England Test cricketer had died so young.

The England captain, Nasser Hussain, flew from the Test series in New Zealand for his funeral, which was attended also by Surrey colleagues and Australian players, testimony to his immense popularity. "Ben was the most naturally gifted cricketer that

Ben and Adam Hollioake: a cry went up for the Hollioakes' Australian-bred brio to spark an English resurgence. *Picture by Clive Mason, Getty Images.*

I have ever played alongside," said Alec Stewart, who captained him for Surrey and England. Everyone recalled his easy-going approach to life and the friendships he fostered with his gentle nature and whimsical sense of humour; Adam, in his funeral address, described him as "a beautiful work of art, a classic sculpture". And in the game's collective memory, the picture of Ben Hollioake remained fixed on a spring afternoon in 1997 when, making his England debut at 19, this tall, loose-limbed all-rounder set Lord's alight with 63 in 48 balls against Australia to take the Man of the Match award.

Ben's selection for that one-day international was a triumph for style over content, for promise over performance. Given English cricket's innate conservatism, it was sensational. In only his second season of county cricket, he had played just five first-class and 21 one-day games; there had been no centuries, no five-wicket returns since he took five for ten in a Sunday League game against Derbyshire on his Surrey debut (Stewart, keeping wicket, said he hit the gloves harder than the established fast bowlers). But he had done well with Andrew Flintoff's series-winning England Under-19 side in Pakistan in 1996-97, opening the bowling with Surrey team-mate Alex Tudor and scoring middle-order runs, and at Edgbaston in April he caught the eye with 46 not out and three for 22 for The Rest against England A.

England, already two-up in the three-match series against Australia by dint of Adam Hollioake's unbeaten half-centuries, and searching for a fast-bowling all-rounder, could afford to try his younger brother. If nothing else, the athleticism of Ben's fielding was worth the admission price. The captain, Mike Atherton, asked him that morning if he fancied going in at No. 3: "He shrugged and said, in his laconic way, he'd give it a go." Some go. Third ball he drove Glenn McGrath back down the ground for four, and he took 13 from McGrath's next over. When he went down on one knee and swept Shane Warne over mid-wicket, Lord's purred. The press didn't just wax their lyricals, they preserved them in honey. Here potentially was a hero for a game desperate to claw back ground lost to football in the national consciousness.

But inside a month McGrath was back at Lord's, taking eight for 38 to bowl England out for 77 in the Second Test. Having located an English length, he then kept them on the back foot until Australia retained the Ashes. England's whitewash in the one-day series and their nine-wicket win in the First Test could be seen for what they were: a glimmer of light in another false dawn.

A cry went up for the Holliaokes' Australian-bred brio to spark an English resurgence. Born in Melbourne, the brothers had travelled to England when their father's work took him there, and Ben played age-group cricket for England while at Millfield. Although he completed his schooling in Perth after the family moved back to Australia, Surrey had already lined him up to rejoin Adam at The Oval. Between England's heavy defeats at Manchester and Leeds, the brothers helped Surrey win the Benson and Hedges Cup. Once more, Ben's batting at Lord's was sublime. Again coming in first wicket down, he struck 98 from 112 balls, using all of his six feet two inches to drive the ball on the up off the front foot. Again he won the match award. Adam dedicated the victory to Graham Kersey, the young Surrey wicket-keeper, who also died following a car crash in Australia, just as he would dedicate the 2002 Championship title to Ben.

Once England went behind in the Ashes series, the Holliaokes' selection for the Fifth Test at Trent Bridge was the obvious last throw of the dice. They became the fifth set of brothers to play a Test for England, following the three Graces and the Hearnes in making simultaneous debuts, while Ben, at 19 years 269 days, became England's youngest Test player since Brian Close (18 years 149 days) in 1949.

But Test cricket allowed no quarter, certainly not against Australia in the 1990s. Ben had Greg Blewett caught behind in his eighth over, but his ten overs of springy fast-medium cost 57 runs. Batting at No. 7, he hit a few classy boundaries in his first-innings 28, but Warne had him lbw for two second time round and it was Adam (45 and two), rather than Ben, who kept his place for the consolation victory at The Oval. Perhaps he had that in mind when, accepting the Cricket Writers' Club Young Cricketer of the Year award with a gracious eloquence few of his peers could have emulated, he brought the house down by remarking that this would be one trophy with only one Holliaoke name on it. The years of playing catch-up with a sibling six years older had fuelled an affectionate rivalry.

While Adam went to the West Indies that winter, Ben toured Kenya and Sri Lanka with England A. He opened the bowling and his first senior hundreds, 103 and 163 against Sri Lanka A, put him top of the first-class batting averages, yet there would not be another century, first-class or one-day, until he made 118 against Yorkshire in 2001 in his last match at The Oval. The brothers joined forces for the one-day series in the West Indies, when Adam captained England following Atherton's resignation, but Ben's 55 runs and two wickets were not enough to keep him in the team back home, despite useful form in the B&H. Instead, England mixed and matched Matthew Fleming, Mark Ealham, Chris Lewis and Ian Austin in their one-day games against South Africa and Sri Lanka. There was, however, a recall to replace Flintoff for the one-off Test against Sri Lanka at The Oval – where Holliaoke was expensive again with the ball and made 14 and a golden duck as Muttiah Muralitharan took 16 wickets – and a place in Stewart's side to Australia that winter. Troubled by a groin injury early on, and never regaining form, he played only two first-class matches and a one-day international. "To watch him struggling to pinch singles from part-time bowlers in Hobart was painful," wrote *Wisden's* correspondent.

At least Ben was spared the subsequent World Cup débâcle that cost Adam his England place. Instead, his four half-centuries and 20 wickets in 12 games contributed to Surrey's Championship-winning season in 1999. He took five wickets in an innings

Ben Hollioake: his selection was a triumph for style over content, for promise over performance. Given English cricket's innate conservatism, it was sensational. *Picture by Jan Traylen.*

for the only time in first-class cricket: five for 51 against Glamorgan at The Oval. But next year, while Surrey retained their title and finished top of Division Two in the one-day league, he was dropped in mid-August. His previous nine Championship games had realised just 138 runs and eight wickets. Gone were the days when Ben Hollioake made a complex game look childishly simple; compared with Martin Bicknell and Tudor, his bowling was medium-paced and soft.

However, that golden talent was too bright to be denied, especially as he grafted necessary disciplines to it. One-day runs and wickets early in 2001 brought an England recall for the one-day series, in which his nonchalant 37 against Australia at Bristol and defiant 53 against Pakistan at Headingley, after England had been 39 for five, kindled hopes that those 1997 innings would no longer be an albatross. There was also another Lord's match award, as Surrey dethroned the one-day kings, Gloucestershire, in the Benson and Hedges Cup final, and Ben, down the order this time, helped Adam rebuild their innings with a mature 73.

Would he have gone on to greater things? A record of 2,794 runs at 25.87 and 126 wickets at 33.45 from 75 first-class games, alongside 2,481 runs (24.98) and 142 wickets (28.22) in 136 one-day games, is no true indicator. His 309 runs and eight wickets in 20 one-day internationals, his obvious métier, give few clues. Simply seeing him play was the real measure: he gave genuine pleasure to all who watched, whether from the dressing-room or the stand. Perhaps the 2003 World Cup – he was there or thereabouts in England's thinking – would have brought out the best in him. He loved the big stage. But while the sense of unrealised potential added extra poignancy to his death, his life, as a character in Tom Stoppard's play *Shipwreck* says of another young death, "was what it was. Nature doesn't disdain what lives only for a day. It pours the whole of itself into each moment… Life's bounty is in its flow; later is too late." Still, 24 was much too soon, even for someone who insouciantly declared himself too cool to grow old.

Howard, Geoffrey Cecil, died in Minchinhampton on November 8, 2002, aged 93, his place in cricket history secure as an enlightened administrator and popular tour manager. Geoffrey Howard was secretary of Lancashire and Surrey and had charge of three MCC tours of Australia and the Indian subcontinent. The 1954-55 Ashes tour

Geoffrey Howard: a natural diplomat, tactful, courteous and – an attribute by no means commonplace in the English cricket establishment of the time – sympathetic to his fellow-man regardless of creed, colour or class. *Picture by Patrick Eagar.*

were the focal point of his rich and varied life, with England winning a series in Australia for the first time since Bodyline in 1932-33. But for notoriety it would be hard to surpass the MCC A tour he took to Pakistan a year later. When the MCC players doused umpire Idris Begh with a bucket of water, all hell broke loose. "Alexander's Rag-team Banned," punned a *Daily Mirror* headline after the MCC president, Field-Marshal Earl Alexander of Tunis, offered to bring the tourists home. Fortunately Howard, the man on the spot, was a natural diplomat: tactful, courteous and – an attribute by no means commonplace in the English cricket establishment of the time – sympathetic to his fellow-man regardless of creed, colour or class. It was, after all, little more than four years earlier that the secretary of MCC had seen him off to India, Pakistan and Ceylon with a "Rather you than me. I can't stand educated Indians." Geoffrey Howard got on famously with them, so much so that in later years he acted as liaison officer for Indian and Pakistani sides touring England, and he was asked several times to take teams to India for jubilee games.

He inherited this respect for people and his deep love of cricket from his grandfather, Sir Ebenezer Howard, a founder of the Garden City Movement. It was Ebenezer who first took him to The Oval, where the ten-year-old Geoffrey touched the hem of Jack Hobbs's blazer. After leaving school at 16 to work in a bank, he played good enough club cricket as a batsman and wicket-keeper to be offered a place on the Lord's groundstaff. He declined, but had three games for Middlesex in 1930 while on annual leave. He made his debut at Lord's, pushing one of the professionals, the Arsenal and England winger Joe Hulme, down to twelfth man. When he went in to bat, the Gloucestershire captain, Bev Lyon, told Wally Hammond to take over while he went off for a haircut. In those three games Howard scored 25 runs, *Wisden* called one of his two catches "exceptional", and that might have been the end of his county connections but for the war. His outstanding operational and man-management skills were recognised in the RAF, which swiftly promoted him from auxiliary airman to acting squadron leader; the Essex secretary, Brian Castor, also noted them when Howard, restless after returning to civvy street, applied for his job in 1946. Castor was off to Surrey, and when Howard missed out at Essex he invited him to go to The Oval as assistant-secretary. Two years later Howard went north to Old Trafford to be Lancashire secretary until 1964, whereupon he returned to The Oval as secretary from 1965 to 1975. These were years of reconstruction – of grounds, finances and the very game itself – and he was at the heart of the changes, pushing for reform and sitting on various MCC committees. Sometimes his vision for cricket must have struck the game's establishment as downright revolutionary. Doubting the need for two major grounds in London, he thought the time would come when Surrey should move from The Oval into the county of Surrey, while Middlesex could play as London. Sporting a yellow shirt at one Surrey committee meeting, he said, "Why don't we wear these for our Sunday matches?" – and in time, albeit not until 1992, the counties came round to his way of thinking. In retirement he served the Minor Counties for eight years as honorary treasurer, and in 1989 Surrey honoured him with their presidency.

"Of all the tours I went on," Trevor Bailey said, "that one of Australia [in 1954-55] was easily the happiest." It could so easily have been a disaster. On arriving at Perth, Howard discovered that MCC had not provided funds to cover the team's accommodation and travel expenses, so he negotiated a £10,000 overdraft against his own personal guarantee. He took the initiative to call a doctor when the captain, Len Hutton, refused to get out of bed on the morning of the Third Test, with the series 1–1. "I can see Len now," he told his biographer, Stephen Chalke. "He was sitting up in his bed with a woollen vest on, staring at the wall." And when the Ashes were retained at Adelaide, he signed for 100 bottles of champagne. It was doubly fitting when his life story, *At The Heart of English Cricket*, took the Cricket Society Literary Award in 2002 that Geoffrey Howard, aged 93, was there for the presentation.

James, David Harry, died in Margam on February 22, 2002, aged 80. While on the Glamorgan groundstaff in their Championship-winning season of 1948, he was drafted in to strengthen the seam bowling on an easy-paced pitch at Trent Bridge. He was not called on in Nottinghamshire's first innings, but his 17 runs helped extend Glamorgan's lead. Charlie Harris then saved the home side with a five-hour century; James caught and bowled him just before a thunderstorm put paid to further play. His one wicket in 24 overs cost 59 runs. However, he was the Second Eleven's leading wicket-taker in the Minor Counties Championship that year, with 26. This apart, his all-round skills were best appreciated in club cricket by Briton Ferry Town and Briton Ferry Steel.

Jones, Gavin William, died in Benoni on July 17, 2002, aged 47. His all-round contribution in his first two seasons played a significant part in Northern Transvaal heading the Castle Bowl table in 1977-78 and 1978-79, which resulted in promotion to the Currie Cup elite. It was a big jump, not only for Northerns, who finished last without a win, but also for Jones, who dropped out of first-class cricket for two seasons until Northern Transvaal entered a "B" side in the Bowl in 1982-83. That gave him three more summers. In 22 first-class games he scored 856 runs at 26.75 and took 30 wickets at 40.36 with his medium-fast bowling. His best figures were against Griqualand West in 1978-79: 67 at Kimberley and five for 78 at Pretoria.

Joseph, Arthur Frederick, died in Briton Ferry on January 2, 2002, aged 82. His one first-class game was Glamorgan's innings defeat by Derbyshire at Chesterfield in 1946. Bill Copson bowled him for a duck in the first innings; in the second he managed eight as Glamorgan slumped to 21 for seven. With his middle-order batting and useful leg-breaks, Joseph featured prominently in club cricket in South Wales either side of World War II, when he played services cricket in the Middle East, and post-war he also had some Second Eleven games for Glamorgan.

King, Darryl James, who died in Buderim, Queensland, on March 3, 2002, aged 59, was a talented all-round sportsman who played eight games for Queensland as a batsman in the 1960s. *WCAA.*

Langdale, George Richmond, OBE, died in Holbeck on April 24, 2002, aged 86. Two and three-quarter hours was time enough for the Yorkshire captain Brian Sellers to be haunted by his lightly made remark, early in 1946, that the Yorkshire-born Langdale might be good enough for struggling Somerset. That was all it took for this 30-year-old left-hander, playing only his second game for Somerset, to drive, cut and pull his native county's bowlers for 146 as Somerset raced from 285 for six to 508. Even the Taunton crowd, long accustomed to schoolmasters who annually swapped the classroom for the crease, found his attacking strokeplay a turn-up for the books. Unfortunately, Langdale never came close to a reprise; a couple of sixties was the best he could manage in 18 further appearances for Somerset up to 1949. Even his best first-class bowling was already in the book. On his Somerset debut, two months earlier, he had taken five for 30 against Warwickshire on an Edgbaston pitch that helped his off-breaks. Outside first-class cricket, however, there were glory days aplenty. In 1953, while working as an instructor at the Royal Military Academy, Sandhurst, Langdale took all ten Dorset wickets for 25 at Reading and, with 71 wickets at 13.77 and 502 runs, helped Berkshire win the Minor Counties Championship. He represented the Minor Counties against that summer's Australians to round off a first-class career of 25 games, 709 runs at 18.17 and 23 wickets at 40.82. He had had four Championship games for Derbyshire in 1936 and 1937 while studying at Nottingham University, and played for Norfolk in 1939.

Little, Alfred Alexander, died in Media, Pennsylvania on August 14, 2002, aged 77. He had been curator of the C. C. Morris Cricket Library at Haverford College, which houses a renowned collection of American memorabilia. Little, a mechanical engineer, worked on developing a nose cone for intercontinental ballistic missiles in the 1950s and later joined the Corona project, which devised ways of taking military surveillance photos from space.

McCall, Hugh Conn, died at Bangor, Co. Down on June 7, 2002, aged 62. Bad weather forced Conn McCall to wait five days before beginning his first-class career in 1964. What should have been his Ireland debut, the annual fixture against Scotland, was abandoned without a ball bowled for the first time since 1888, and three weeks later the opening day against MCC at Dublin was also washed out. Happily the rain relented on the second day, going in at No. 3, he made 81. Next year he hit 65 against the same opponents in the two-day match at Lord's, and with an unbeaten 65 saved the Irish from defeat at Dublin after Hampshire had them 30 for five. It was in 1965, too, that McCall bowled his only first-class delivery of left-arm spin, conceding the winning single to the New Zealanders at Belfast – though for some years the ball was credited to Ireland's regular slow left-armer, Scott Huey. Seven of McCall's 15 games for Ireland were first-class and in these he scored 308 runs at 23.69. He served as an Irish selector in the first half of the 1980s, as chairman of the Northern Cricket Union and, in 1992, as president of the Irish Cricket Union. One of his sons, Mark, played rugby for Ulster and Ireland.

McFarline: "He was abrasive and assertive, so he alienated and attracted in equal measure." *Picture by Patrick Eagar.*

McFarline, Peter Muir, OAM, died of a heart attack at Melbourne on April 7, 2002, aged 57. "Of all the cricket writers," Dennis Lillee once remarked, "McFarline writes with an edge." Not even the degenerative disease of the spine, syringomyelia, which struck at the peak of his career and left him quadraplegic and hospitalised for his last seven years, could spike that edge. Although his voice was silent, his words still rang out in the pages of the Melbourne *Age*, as his devoted wife Dell took down the sentences he could barely mouth and sent them through to the paper.

McFarline – affection, reputation and respect dictated that he was always simply "McFarline" – was a Victorian but Queensland made him. The family moved there when he was a child and he began his journalism on the Brisbane *Courier-Mail*; when he went back to Melbourne to join *The Age* he retained the empathy for the underdog that Brisbane bred. His 1977 scoop exposing Kerry Packer's breakaway World Series Cricket, investigated in conjunction with the Adelaide cricket writer Alan Shiell, won him the prestigious Walkely award, and he wrote two important books, *A Game Divided* (1977) and *A Testing Time* (1979), on those fermentitious times. He was just the man to cover Australia for *Wisden Cricket Monthly* when David Frith launched the magazine in 1979. The 1980s took McFarline to America as Washington correspondent for the *Herald and Weekly Times* group, but he returned to Melbourne as his illness took its toll. "He could be an irresistible if complex person," said the Australian writer Mike Coward, who shared press boxes with McFarline over the years. "He was abrasive and assertive, so he alienated and attracted in equal measure. Much of his copy was filed off the top – composed in his head and conveyed by phone without the typewriter or computer being taken from its case. McFarline was a natural as a cricket writer and had the instincts of a hard-nosed investigative journalist. His was a singular life and it will not be forgotten by those he permitted to know some part of him."

Mackay, P., who died in Thiruvananthapuram on April 29, 2002, aged 52, was the first bowler to take ten wickets in a match for Kerala. He did so with five for 36 and five for 82 against Andhra Pradesh at Guntur in December 1974. In 12 first-class games between 1972-73 and 1974-75, all in the Ranji Trophy, he took 24 wickets at 31.29 and scored 209 runs at 13.06. Mackay was the Kerala Cricket Association coach for some years.

Mann, John Pelham, MC, died in New Orleans on September 8, 2002, aged 83. Two years younger than his brother George, who died in 2001, John Mann succeeded him as Eton captain in 1937 and joined him in the Cambridge side in 1939. Unlike his brother, though, or their father Frank, he did not get a Blue or go on to play for and captain England. Not that he lacked the talent. By the end of his four years in the Eton XI, with appearances for the Lord's Schools in the last two, good judges were vouching for his quality as a batsman. He made 62 for Middlesex against Cambridge on his first-class debut and, a few days later, an unbeaten 59 against the West Indians in his first match for Cambridge. One correspondent wrote that he batted "with the greatest nerve and judgment… to an extent that made his seniors look distinctly discredited". Yet in his next four games he never reached the heights expected of him. The chances are he would still have received his Blue, for he was batting like a good player out of form rather than a tyro, but he fell ill a fortnight before Lord's. The war denied him a second chance. After serving, like his brother, in the Scots Guards, Mann played 13 times for Middlesex in the 1946 Championship, hitting a career-best 77 against Warwickshire at Lord's which was notable for some fine front-foot driving in the public-school tradition. Not that county cricket was germane to his agenda. Forsaking the family brewing business, he went to work for Unilever in 1946, and played only once in 1947 to settle his first-class account at 608 runs and an average of 20.96 from 21 games. He took six wickets as a leg-spinner at 61 apiece. As managing director of Unilever in New Zealand in the 1950s, Mann developed Birds Eye as an international supplier of frozen foods, and he furthered his career in the United States before settling there permanently.

Mascarenhas, Mark, who died in a car crash at Nagpur on January 27, 2002, aged 44, was a larger-than-life media magnate whose entrepreneurial brio transformed the way cricket was marketed. The catalyst was the success of the Indian-backed bid to stage the 1996 World Cup in Asia. Mascarenhas, Bangalore-born but US-domiciled since his student days, won the contract for his company, WorldTel, to auction the TV rights by paying the Indian board $US2.5 million. Such a figure was unheard of for a sport and a tournament whose international exposure was anything but global. Mascarenhas changed all that, obtaining $US14 million in TV rights for the hosts and attracting multinational sponsors for every imaginable official product, even chewing-gum. The UK television rights alone were forced up from $US1 million in 1992 to $US7.5 million. The overall profit for the tournament was thought to be around $US50 million. Mascarenhas, meanwhile, was also agent for India's most charismatic cricketer, Sachin Tendulkar, whom he signed prior to the World Cup for $US10 million over five years; when the contract was renewed it was said to be worth five times that. However, his dealings with India's state-owned broadcaster, Doordarshan, over the TV rights for the 1998 ICC mini World Cup in Dhaka, and WorldTel's links with the Indian cricket supremo Jagmohan Dalmiya encouraged conjecture about Mascarenhas's business methods. Not that any malpractice was proved. Successful, ambitious men always attract rumours, and Mascarenhas's ambitions knew no bounds. "He had a big heart, took big risks and had a bigger ego," said Sambit Bal, editor of *Wisden Asia Cricket*, who had edited Mascarenhas's website, total-cricket.com, run in tandem with his *CricketTalk* magazine. Because of that ego cricket advanced, was dragged even, into a new era.

Masimula Walter Bafana, died in his sleep on April 19, 2002 in Guildford. He was only 26, and had recently arrived in England to play for Brook in the Surrey Championship and coach at King Edward's School, Witley. Surrey was far removed from his humble beginnings in the Johannesburg township of Alexandra where, nicknamed "Black Express", he was a jewel in South African cricket's development programme. He charged in and bowled fast, distinctly so at times. Ali Bacher, the country's cricket supremo, took him under his wing and arranged for him to attend his old school, King Edward; Fred Trueman and Ray Lindwall were among those who went to Alexandra's dusty nets to admire and advise the teenage speedster. At a time when age-group representative teams were almost exclusively white, he played for Transvaal (now Gauteng) at national cricket weeks from 13 onwards, and was one of six development programme players, among them Makhaya Ntini, in the Under-19 side that visited England in 1995. That tour, he said, "taught me tough lessons and it pointed out to me that there was still lots of hard work to be done". By the time Walter made his first-class debut, for Gauteng in 1998-99, he was relying on line and length rather than raw speed. And when he made headlines, it was because of race, not pace. After black administrators criticised the selection of an all-white Northerns/Gauteng XI to play England in November 1999, Rudi Bryson was forced to stand down from the team and Masimula came in. He took two for 12 in ten overs in England's second innings. His 18 first-class games, mostly for Gauteng, produced 33 wickets at 26.90, with a best of four for 35 against Eastern Province at Johannesburg. "He was a great guy," said the Gauteng captain Clive Eksteen, "a wholehearted competitor and a pleasure to have around."

Moore, Richard Henry, died in Llanrhos on March 1, 2002, aged 88. He still held the record for Hampshire's highest individual score, 316, set at Bournemouth one July day in 1937. The Dean Park boundaries were short and the 23-year-old Dick Moore made the most of them, hitting three sixes and 43 fours in an innings that began with play at 11.30, reached three figures off the ball before lunch and continued until almost 7 p.m. when he was last out and the big crowd reluctantly set about going home. Hampshire's next-highest score was 75 by Cecil Paris, with whom he added 207 for the fourth wicket in two hours. Moore was especially powerful in front of the wicket and not always discriminating when choosing the ball to hit, but his 316 contained remarkably few flaws. One skybound hit might have been caught by any one of three converging Warwickshire fielders but, to the crowd's enjoyment, each left it to another. It was quite a day on the south coast: at Hove, Eddie Paynter was working off the effects of an overnight journey from Manchester by tormenting Sussex's bowlers to the tune of 322.

Moore first played for Hampshire in August 1931 as a 17-year-old fresh from Bournemouth Grammar. He knew Dean Park well and hit half his ten hundreds there including his first, 159 against Essex in the last game of 1933. He now had the attacking strokes to complement an excellent defence and in 1934 he opened the innings, made 1,522 runs at 33.08 and was rated by *Wisden* "probably the most promising young amateur in English cricket". Next year, however, he went down with scarlet fever at the end of May and missed the rest of the season. When he returned in 1936 it was as captain and, buoyed by his strong personality and enterprising approach, Hampshire rose six places to tenth, having for a time been a heady third. Moore himself had a poor mid-summer, scraping only 89 runs in 17 innings, but he came good again to reach his thousand, as he did once more in 1937, with 1,562. After that, cricket took second place to the family bakery business, although he made three centuries in 1938. He was still only 26 when war broke out, and in 137 first-class games had scored 6,026 runs at an average of 26.08, held 116 catches and, bowling medium pace or just below, taken 25 wickets at 39.11. Moore married a North Wales baker's daughter and, having been in charge of a PoW camp in North Wales during the war, remained in the area afterwards and played for Denbighshire. In the 1950s he organised a festival at Colwyn Bay that attracted some of the day's leading cricketers.

Moore, Dudley, died in his local surgery at Broadstairs on January 3, 2002, aged 71. From 1962 to 1994 he ran the reporting agency at Kent's grounds, sending scores and match reports throughout the day to the news agencies, national and local papers, and radio stations. For most of that time he was *Wisden's* correspondent in Kent, and his corner of the press box was a first port of call for journalists seeking local colour, player background or a phone line. Moore had kept wicket for Kent Young Amateurs and knew the club, its administrators and cricketers at close hand without ever betraying a confidence. He was Kent's press officer for a time, ghosted autobiographies for Mike Denness, Alan Knott and Bob Woolmer, and wrote *The History of Kent County Cricket Club*. Come autumn, he covered football and ice hockey. Moore was once overheard phoning through a score of 333 for three as "free hundred and firty-free for free" and this quickly became part of county-circuit folklore. When a scoreboard registers a clutch of threes, a cry goes up in the press box of "firty-free for free", or simply, "it's a Dudley".

Mudie, George Horatio, originally recorded in *Wisden* as Moodie, died in St Catherine, Jamaica on June 8, 2002, aged 86. He had been West Indies' oldest surviving Test cricketer, a precedence which passed to Esmond Kentish. His one Test, against England at Kingston in March 1935, clinched West Indies' first series win. Mudie, a tall left-handed batsman and left-arm spinner, had come into the side on the strength of a career-best 94 and 60 not out for Jamaica against MCC. Batting No. 6 in the Test, he scored only five while George Headley at the other end hammered on towards an unbeaten 270. But the first of his three wickets broke the sixth-wicket stand of 157 between Les Ames and Jack Iddon as England struggled to avoid the follow-on after their captain, Bob Wyatt, retired hurt early on with a fractured jaw. Having made his debut against Lord Tennyson's side in 1931-32, Mudie played 17 times for Jamaica until 1951-52, by which time he was a much respected coach whose charges included the young Alf Valentine. In 1948 he was called up as a replacement for John Goddard's side in India, only to be told on reaching London that he was no longer needed. In 19 first-class games he scored 578 runs at 22.23 and took 42 wickets at 35.45, with best figures of five for 32 in only nine overs against the Oxford and Cambridge side that visited Jamaica in August 1938.

Mullins, Patrick Joseph, OAM, who died in Brisbane on September 7, 2002, aged 79, was Australia's pre-eminent cricket collector until the onset of blindness led him to sell his collection of some 8,500 items to the Melbourne Cricket Club in 1988. He had started collecting at the age of eight. A solicitor by profession, he compiled *Bat & Pad: Writings on Australian Cricket* (1984) with Phil Derriman, and *Cradle Days of Australian Cricket* (1989) with Brian Crowley.

Nayudu, Cottari Subbanna, died in Indore on November 22, 2002, aged 88, after protracted respiratory and heart problems. His older brother, C. K., was India's first Test captain and such was his renown and longevity as an all-rounder that C. S. had to live in his shadow even though 18 years separated them. For all that, C. S. enjoyed a long and distinguished Ranji Trophy career between 1931-32 and 1961-62, in which time he played for Central Provinces and Berar, Central India, Baroda and Holkar before captaining Bengal and the three Pradeshes, Andhra, Uttar and Madhya. In 56 Trophy games he took 295 wickets at 23.49 bowling leg-breaks and googlies – an average of five a match – and scored 2,575 runs at 30.20. In 1942-43 he became the first to take 40 wickets in a Ranji Trophy season, in just four games for Baroda, while in the 1944-45 final, playing now for his brother's Holkar team against Bombay, he delivered a world-record 917 balls in the match. Figures of six for 153 and five for 275 brought another world record, for the most runs conceded in a match. His best figures were eight for 93 in a 13-wicket haul for Baroda against Nawanagar in 1939-40, while his four hundreds included a highest of 127 for them against Rajputana in 1942-43.

C. C. Nayudu, Shute Banergee and Chandra Sarwate, three members of the 1946 touring Indian team, at Stuart Surridge's factory. *Picture by EMPICS.*

It was very different at Test level, where only three of his 11 appearances came at home. The others were in England, in 1936 and 1946, and in Australia in 1947-48, where in four Tests he went without a wicket and scored just 18 runs. His 1936 team-mate, Cota Ramaswami, identified his problem: "C. S. bent his body so low while delivering the ball that his head was almost on a level with the top of the stumps. He stretched his arm fully and threw his body weight into his delivery so that the ball came off the pitch very quickly. He also spun the ball extremely well but unfortunately his length and direction were not always controlled." His two Test wickets cost 359 runs while his hard-hitting batting was scarcely more successful, producing 147 runs at 9.18. Yet his future had looked so bright when, making his Test debut at 19, he hit 36 and then a prolonged 15 to help India stave off defeat by England at Calcutta.

Newton-Thompson, Christopher Lawton, MC, died in Cape Town on January 29, 2002, aged 82. Although born in London, he was a fifth-generation South African on his father's side and was educated there before going up to Cambridge in 1937. He earned a game against the West Indians with a "brilliant display of all-round hitting" in the 1939 Seniors' Match. He scored eight in each innings – Learie Constantine uprooted his off stump in the first after Newton-Thompson had the temerity to hook his slower ball for six – and caught George Headley at the wicket for 103. It was his only first-class game. He captained Cambridge at rugby and played a wartime international for England. His brother, Ozzie, was a cricket and rugby Blue at Oxford after the war and an England rugby international. Christopher Newton-Thompson won his MC as a tank commander in Italy. As befits the son of an English suffragette, who was related to the political Chamberlain family and herself was elected mayor of Cape Town, he became prominent in the anti-apartheid movement after returning to South

Africa in the late 1950s and was a co-founder of Waterford, the non-racial school established in Swaziland after the government closed St Peter's in Johannesburg, Oliver Tambo's alma mater. Pupils at Waterford included the children of Nelson Mandela and Desmond Tutu, along with the future actor Richard E. Grant.

Nicklin, Frank Hallam, who died on June 25, 2002, aged 80, was the man most responsible for ensuring cricket remained a major item on tabloid sports pages in the 1970s and '80s. As sports editor of *The Sun* when Rupert Murdoch turned it into a sex-driven tabloid in 1969, he pioneered celebrity columns, marks out of ten and gimmicks instead of old-fashioned match reports, a formula that rapidly helped the paper become Britain's top-selling daily. However, as an enthusiastic Derbyshire follower and useful club left-arm seamer, Nicklin made sure cricket retained its pre-eminence as the summer game. He employed the respected Clive Taylor as cricket correspondent and gave him remarkable space for match reports, beginning a tradition *The Sun* has never wholly abandoned. Nicklin, who had coined the phrase the Busby Babes to describe the Manchester United team of the late Fifties, later became head of the sports reporting agency, Hayter's. A wartime fighter pilot who was captured twice in occupied Europe but escaped both times, he much enjoyed Fleet Street's own heroic traditions of after-hours congeniality.

Nye, John Kent, MBE, died in Chichester on January 28, 2002, aged 87. Eight years growing up in Australia gave Jack Nye some idea of what fast bowling was all about. His short-pitched deliveries rattled the young gentlemen of Cambridge when, just turned 20, he took five for 45 and three for 77 against them at Hove on his Sussex debut in 1934. But with Maurice Tate, Jim Cornford, George Pearce and Jim Hammond ahead

Jack Nye: eight years growing up in Australia gave him some idea of what fast bowling was all about.
Picture by EMPICS.

of him in the pecking order, if not in pace, he had to wait his turn. Arthur Gilligan rated him and Nye repaid his confidence by learning to bowl a more English length and taking 47 wickets in the back half of 1938. Next summer he captured 110 at 30.60 – and doubtless took as much pleasure, given his career batting average of 8.59, from a hard-hit 55 against Worcestershire at Eastbourne, the match in which he reached 100 wickets. The war robbed Nye of his best years and he played only two summers after being demobbed from the RAF, taking 41 and 46 wickets to boost his first-class tally to 304 at 34.23 from 99 games. In his 98th, a career-best six for 95 at Hove scotched Gloucestershire's chances of winning the 1947 Championship. Later that year he went to work in Africa and, after qualifying as an engineer, had a significant hand in Kenya's road-building programme.

Oldam, David, who died in Taunton on January 1, 2002, aged 69, was Somerset's first-team scorer from 1983 to 1998, during which time he never missed a match – or a ball bowled. And even when ill-health forced him to put down his pencils and shut down his computer, he continued to make the public-address announcements. His first job at Taunton, in 1981 after retiring from British Telecom, had been to operate the new scoreboard that replaced the one in the 1925 photo of Jack Hobbs equalling W. G. Grace's record of 126 hundreds. If not as gregarious as some scorers, Oldam was no less helpful or meticulous. "He was an excellent scorer," recalled his Hampshire counterpart Vic Isaacs, "both in the book and on the laptop, and relished the statistical work and the handbook which occupied the long winters."

Oldfield, Peter Carlton, OBE, died on July 16, 2002, aged 91, having been the oldest surviving Oxford Blue. That distinction belonged to Vivian Jenkins, who was unable to oust Oldfield as wicket-keeper in 1933 but was included for his batting and saved Oxford from defeat by Cambridge. Tall for a keeper at 6ft 2in, Peter Oldfield would have had three Varsity matches but for breaking a finger in his third game in 1931. Two smart stumpings off Tuppy Owen-Smith's demanding leg-breaks in the previous match, against the New Zealanders, had confirmed the brilliant reputation Oldfield acquired over three years in the Repton XI, the last as captain. His career batting average was only 9.87 from 237 runs in 24 games, with a best of 36 against Lancashire in 1932; he also made an unflustered, match-saving two not out which helped Bob Wyatt reach his century for MCC against the 1934 Australians. Behind the stumps it was a different story, one of genuine class and quicksilver hands to match his mind, and in first-class cricket he took 26 catches and made 33 stumpings. After Oxford he did his articles as a surveyor and became an estate agent. His war was the stuff of storybooks. Severely wounded and captured while serving with the SAS in the Western Desert in 1942, Major Oldfield was interrogated by Rommel himself. When he refused to talk, the Germans threatened to shoot him as a spy. A sympathetic doctor smuggled him to Tripoli, from where he was transferred to Italy. In Milan he helped pull 15 fellow prisoners of war from the rubble when the Allies bombed their hospital; after being moved to another hospital in Bergamo, he walked out of a back door and, in spite of his unhealed wounds, escaped to neutral Switzerland.

Parker, Mark Moreton, died on October 12, 2002 as a result of injuries received in the terrorist bomb blast in Bali. He had recently celebrated his 27th birthday and was holidaying there prior to the New Zealand season after a successful summer with the Hampshire club St Cross Symondians. He was the son of Murray Parker and nephew of John, both New Zealand Test cricketers. Mark captained New Zealand at Under-20 level and in 1996-97 played three Shell Trophy matches for Otago, making 50 runs at 8.33 with a top score of 14. Gavin Larsen, the New Zealand one-day specialist who knew Parker from Wellington club cricket, described him as "mega-talented… he was a great timer of the ball and should have played more first-class cricket".

Perera, Deutrom Conrad Camillus, who died in Colombo on July 14, 2002, aged 64, was one of Sri Lanka's senior umpires. At the time he was administrative manager of the country's Association of Cricket Umpires and Scorers and a senior instructor of umpires for the Board of Control. Camillus "Cammie" Perera had taken up umpiring in 1963, while in his twenties, and was considered an authority on the Laws of Cricket, editing Sri Lanka's first magazine for umpires, *Nompere*. His two international matches were in 1985-86. In September, he umpired in a one-day game when there was criticism that Sri Lanka, 32 for four in the tenth over and needing 72 in 15 to beat India on run-rate, were offered the light too soon. Six months later he stood in the Second Test between Sri Lanka and Pakistan, after which the Pakistan team were said to be considering returning home in protest at the standard of umpiring and the behaviour of the spectators. Sri Lanka's eight-wicket victory was only their second in Tests.

Petersen, Eric, died in a car crash in Cape Town on August 26, 2002, aged 70. He was one of three non-white nominees for South Africa's Cricketer of the Century, along with Basil D'Oliveira and the black African batsman Frank Roro, and his career is emblematic of his country's sorry history. Petersen bowled quick off-breaks with big fingers that gave the ball a venomous tweak, making it spin and jump viciously on the matting wickets on which he played most of his cricket.

While still a Cape Town high-school student he applied to join, and was accepted by, the Ridgeville club in the Central Union. The Union, however, excluded him at its weekly "passing out parade". "They didn't give a reason," Petersen said years later, "but I know the Union had a policy of not accepting players who were too dark-skinned." Across town, the Ottomans club turned D'Oliveira down because he didn't comply with their Muslims-only policy. However, another mainly Muslim club, Pirates, gave the 18-year-old Petersen a place and he repaid them with a record number of wickets in his first season. Soon he was representing Western Province Malays (ie Muslims) in the interprovincial Barnato Trophy, and then South African Malays when in 1953 the Muslim players joined the Africans, Coloureds and Indians for the second of four inter-race tournaments staged by the South African Cricket Board of Control between 1951 and 1958. On his first appearance he took four for 53 against SA Coloureds, for whom D'Oliveira scored 65. Petersen took ten or more wickets three times in these two-day games and 58 in all at 12.74. Going to East Africa with D'Oliveira's side in 1958 – the first time a non-white team had left South Africa – he found the pitches so conducive to fast bowling that he took the new ball and ended the 16-match tour as leading wicket-taker with 43 at 9.06, including 21 at 8.33 in the three "Test" wins over Kenya. Sadly, the chance to prove himself against stronger international opposition was denied him when a proposed tour of South Africa by a West Indian side under Frank Worrell was cancelled because black politicians feared it would be seen as endorsing apartheid.

Petersen and D'Oliveira were given a passionate reception when they walked out at Newlands for the Cricketer of the Year ceremony on the opening day of the Fourth Test between South Africa and England on January 2, 2000. The damage done to them, and thousands like them, "by an unjust political system will never be undone", said the Sports Minister Ngconde Balfour, "but this gesture of recognition will ensure that their sporting prowess will be recorded for future generations".

Pfuhl, Gavin Pattison, died in Cape Town on April 1, 2002, aged 54, from a viral complication after a heart transplant. The day before the operation, he had been doing cricket commentary for television. Gavin Pfuhl kept wicket for Western Province when they won the Currie Cup in 1970, 1975 and 1978, and in 95 first-class games between 1967-68 and 1979-80 took 280 catches and made 34 stumpings. He also scored 2,331 runs at 21.58. "He was an excellent keeper in the days when Province had Denys Hobson bowling leg-spin," recalled Ali Bacher, who played for Transvaal against him. Twice, against Rhodesia in 1970-71 and Eastern Province in his final season, Pfuhl held six catches in an innings. He followed up the first instance – in a non-Currie Cup game at Salisbury – by hitting his only century, 117, despite being hit on the head by a Mike Procter bouncer.

Pike, Philip, who died at Penisarwaen, Caernarfon, on October 29, 2002, aged 76, was the Warwickshire scorer from 1967 to 1973 and also kept the England book at Edgbaston. "He was a very quiet man," Dennis Amiss recalled, "and always conscientious. He blended in well with all the players and never tried to impose himself."

Place, Winston, died in Burnley on January 25, 2002, seven weeks after his 87th birthday. He had been the second-oldest surviving England cricketer, having played three Tests on MCC's ill-planned tour of the West Indies in 1947-48. But it was his opening partnerships for Lancashire with Cyril Washbrook, in the seasons immediately after World War II, for which he was most fondly remembered. In their contrasting ways – Washbrook the flamboyant, consummate strokemaker; Place, taller and unassuming, reminiscent of Harry Makepeace in his studied defensive play – they provided a foundation that was the envy of other counties. Not that Place was dilatory or dull. He often outscored his partner on poor wickets and, by the time he left Old Trafford in 1955, he was Lancashire's 13th-highest runmaker with 14,605 runs at 36.69 for the county. Decisive footwork determined his game: he drove effectively through the off-side arc and at times back over the bowler's head, played the late-cut with a delicate touch, and pulled with real aplomb.

His roots were in the small mill town of Rawtenstall where, orphaned at five, he was raised by an aunt within a stone's throw of the cricket ground. At 15 he was opening for the first team in the Lancashire League. S. F. Barnes, Rawtenstall's

Winston Place: orphaned at five, he was raised by an aunt witin a stone's throw of Rawtenstall's cricket ground. *Picture by Dennis Oulds, Getty Images.*

professional from 1930 to 1932, recommended him to Lancashire and at 21, after serving one apprenticeship as an engineer, he went down to Old Trafford in 1936 to begin another. Lancashire's batting was strong, opportunities were limited, but he marked his first season, 1937, by making 137 in four and a quarter hours at Trent Bridge after Washbrook and Paynter had launched the innings with 108 in an hour. Two years on and he was opening with Washbrook when Paynter was injured, impressing everyone with a flawless 164 against the West Indians and averaging 36.11 from 614 runs. He combined war-time work for an engineering firm in Accrington with charity matches and Bolton League cricket for Horwich: in 1944 he and Washbrook gave a sample of treats to come as they put on 140 for the North of England against the RAAF at Old Trafford.

Their first two summers together were the best, and Lancashire finished third in both years. Place hit 1,868 runs at 41.51 in 1946, then 2,501 at 62.52 in 1947 with ten hundreds, including two in the Old Trafford match against Nottinghamshire. His 266 not out against Oxford University, in less than six hours, remained the highest of his 36 first-class centuries. Early in that run-sated summer, the Manchester rain frustrated Washbrook and Place as they homed in on MacLaren and Spooner's county-record first-wicket stand of 368, set in 1903. Even so, their unbroken 350 against Sussex outlived them both as Lancashire's second-highest opening partnership – and at the Saffrons in late August they bludgeoned the Sussex bowling once more, each again hitting hundreds as they raced the clock to reach 233 inside two hours (41.4 overs) for a ten-wicket victory.

Selection as 12th man for the Leeds Test against South Africa brought Place a taste of international cricket and, with leading England players absenting themselves, he was an obvious candidate for Gubby Allen's side to the Caribbean that winter. It was not the happiest of experiences. Beset by injuries – the 45-year-old Allen got the ball rolling by pulling a calf muscle while skipping on board ship – and underestimating the strength of West Indian cricket, MCC went winless through a tour for the first time ever. Place bruised a knuckle in Barbados in the opening Test and was ruled out of the Second after rupturing his groin muscle while scoring 120 not out against Trinidad: MCC subsequently had four substitutes on the field. The assistant-manager and reserve wicket-keeper, Billy Griffith, was pressed into opening in the impending Test and, on his England debut, hit his maiden first-class hundred (140). By Georgetown, Len Hutton had flown out as a reinforcement and he opened with Jack Robertson while Place batted at No. 3. Innings of one and 15 were no more propitious than his 12 and one out in Barbados had been, but after making eight in the first innings at Kingston he came good in the second with 107, his only Test century. Not that it helped: England's last six wickets tumbled for 20 runs. "I got a hundred but we lost," Place would recall in later years.

He took time to get going in 1948, and his four hundreds, including 200 at Taunton, comprised more than half his runs. A broken hand kept him out for seven games in 1949, though not before he had hit a Championship-best 226 not out at Trent Bridge, and his average was well under par in 1950, Lancashire's Championship-sharing season, when their policy of restricting watering and rolling meant batsmen had to graft for runs at Old Trafford. None of this stopped him passing 1,000 runs, as he did every year from 1946 to 1953. But by 1952, his benefit season, he was lending solidity in the middle order rather than opening the innings. His benefit of £6,297 was then the third-highest for the county after Washbrook's and Pollard's.

In 1955 he was 40. And while Washbrook, his senior by a day, was compiling 1,000 runs for the 15th time, Place was managing only 179 in a summer with weeks of continuous sunshine. The Lancashire secretary Geoffrey Howard (*qv*) remembered him being "in tears" when told his contract was not being renewed. Almost 20 years earlier, asked after his first season how he would spend his holidays, he had replied, "This was the last day of my holiday." In 324 first-class matches, all but 26 for Lancashire, he scored 15,609 runs at 35.63, and held 190 catches. He tried to follow

Winston Place: decisive footwork determined his game: he pulled with real aplomb. *Picture by Dennis Oulds, Getty Images.*

the sun by umpiring, but "One season was enough. I liked the job but I didn't like the evenings on your own." He preferred Rawtenstall, where he had a newsagent's, and the warmth of family life with his wife and two daughters in their home by the cricket ground.

Pollard, Jack Ernest, OAM, died in Sydney on May 25, 2002 following two strokes. He was 75, and over 44 years had written, ghosted or compiled 87 books celebrating Australian sports and pastimes. The first was the autobiography of the tennis champion Lew Hoad in 1958, and Pollard had recently closed the circle with the reminiscences of Hoad's widow, Jenny. His 15 cricket titles included *Cricket: The Australian Way* (1961), *Australian Cricket: The Game and the Players* (1982), which won the Cricket Society Literary Award in 1983, and the four-volume *Complete History of Australian Cricket* (1986–1995). He started off in journalism as a 17-year-old copy boy on the Sydney *Daily Telegraph* and worked in London for AAP (1947-56) before returning home to cover his third Olympics. The Jack Pollard Trophy is awarded to the winner of the Australian Cricket Society's annual literary award.

Powley, Alfred, died on May 9, 2002, aged 82, having had Parkinson's Disease. In 1986 Alf and his marginally older brother George became the first twins to umpire at Lord's when they stood in the Eton–Harrow match. Overnight rain delayed the start until three o'clock, whereupon Harrow were dismissed for 37, their lowest total since 1827; further rain prevented Eton from batting. From the late 1970s, the brothers, long-term members of the Association of Cricket Umpires, held winter training courses for umpires at Cockfosters CC and conducted seminars in various ICC Associate and Affiliate countries.

Puckett, Charles William, who died in Adelaide on January 21, 2002, aged 90, was instrumental in Western Australia winning the Sheffield Shield at their first attempt, in 1947-48. When they needed to beat Queensland at Brisbane in their final game, he bowled unchanged for nearly two and a half hours, taking the last five wickets for nine runs in six overs as Queensland collapsed to 130, and finishing with six for 48. Puckett was then 11 days from his 37th birthday and he kept delivering for WA until he was 42. In those six seasons he bowled more than a third of their overs and captured almost a third of their wickets while 23 other bowlers shared the workload. When the ball lost its shine and hardness he would switch from fast-medium swing to slow-medium off-cutters and quickish off-breaks, always prepared to "bowl till my arm drops off" as he had promised his captain, Keith Carmody, at the Gabba in February 1948. It wasn't only his practice of stopping the ball with his shins that earned him his nickname "The Iron Man".

Puckett was born in Surrey – his father was a sometime groundsman at The Oval – grew up in Adelaide and was lured to Perth in 1938 to play baseball, having already made his name as a catcher for South Australia and Victoria. Two brothers were also state ballplayers and his son Max, who died in 1991, was a five-times All-Australian, as well as playing one Sheffield Shield game for South Australia, against Western Australia, in 1964-65. Charlie won All-Australian selection in 1948 and 1952 before hanging up his mitt in 1954. Cricket was little more than a summer diversion until his bowling for West Perth in 1939-40 brought a first-class debut against South Australia, including Bradman (135) and Grimmett (11 wickets). Having spent the war as a physical training and unarmed combat instructor, Puckett was just the man to bowl 38 overs while the 1946-47 MCC tourists put on 477 at Perth, and his five for 126 earned him Combined XI games against MCC at Perth and Melbourne. These were affluent days for Australian fast bowling, though. The best Puckett could muster by way of national honours was a place in the 2nd XI that went to New Zealand in February 1950, recognition for taking 32 wickets at 18.87 in his four Shield games that season. His five for 45 helped bowl out the West Indians for 151 in December 1951 – WA went on to win by one wicket – and ten months on he welcomed the South Africans to Perth with five for 119. He finished, in 1952-53, with career figures of 158 wickets at 25.58 in 37 games. His best figures were six for 35 in routing South Australia at Perth in 1951-52. A fortnight before that he had struck a career-best 75 in 99 minutes after Victoria had reduced WA to 96 for seven. His batting was uncomplicated and his 643 runs averaged 14.61.

Quinn, Kevin Joseph, who died in Dublin on May 1, 2002, aged 79, was the last survivor of four brothers who represented Ireland at cricket. Kevin Quinn had won five Irish rugby caps by the time he received the first of his seven for cricket, in 1957. Three were in first-class games, in which he totalled 49 runs at 9.80; in all matches he made 171 runs, with a highest score of 43 in a one-day game against the 1958 New Zealanders, and took one wicket with his left-arm slows. Quinn's 25, opening the batting against Scotland at Dublin in 1957, was the second-highest score in a match in which the opposing spinners Frank Fee and David Livingstone took 12 and 11 wickets respectively and the Scottish keeper James Brown gained renown by equalling the world record of seven dismissals in an innings.

Rashid, Umer Bin Abdul, drowned at Concord Falls, Grenada, on April 1, 2002 in an unsuccessful attempt to rescue his brother, Burhan, who had been sucked under the water. Umer was 26, Burhan 18. The double tragedy occurred while Rashid's county, Sussex, were in Grenada for a pre-season tournament. He had been with them for three seasons and was as much admired for his friendly, easy-going personality as for his explosive left-hand batting and slow left-arm bowling.

Born in Southampton and raised in Middlesex, Rashid was spotted early on and shone throughout the 1995 Under-19 series against South Africa in a team led by

Umer Rashid: as much admired for his friendly, easy-going personality as for his explosive left-hand batting and slow left-arm bowling. Stuart Osborne, the Sussex physio, shares the joke.

Marcus Trescothick and featuring Andrew Flintoff and Alex Tudor. Rashid hit 64, batting at No. 11, and 97 not out in the first two "Tests" and took ten for 71 in the last. While studying at London's Southbank University, he was also in the Combined Universities squad for the Benson and Hedges Cup from 1995 to 1997. Middlesex gave him a Sunday League game in 1995 and a first-class debut in 1996. But with Phil Tufnell the resident left-arm spinner and Owais Shah, Rashid's exciting young Ealing club-mate, hitting first-team fifties while still at school, opportunities were few and far between. Rashid's 1999 move to Hove made good sense and paid immediate dividends. Maybe his bowling needed time to develop – at times he looked to be putting the ball there rather than spinning it – but the advance in his wristy batting was a revelation. He hit his maiden hundred, 110, and a second-innings half-century against Glamorgan at the Colwyn Bay run-fest in 2000. His 106 at Chester-le-Street a year later set up a Sussex win which he completed by taking four for nine inside ten overs. In 41 first-class games Rashid scored 1,421 runs at 25.37 and took 49 wickets at 42.30, with a best return of five for 103 at Northampton in 2000. His 71 one-day games produced 564 runs, with a best of 82 for the Universities against Hampshire in 1997, and 73 wickets including five for 24 at Swansea to boost Sussex's promotion drive in the 1999 National League. They had high hopes for him; fate cruelly decided otherwise.

Robinson, Miles Trevor, died in Hinton St George on September 28, 2002, aged 72. He still had a year to go at Shrewsbury School when Sussex gave him two Championship games in August 1947. What might have been a *Boy's Own* story became a baptism of fire. Robinson's pace had given some batsmen the hurry-up in the Lord's Schools matches, but taking the new ball at 17 against Lancashire's Washbrook and Place (*qv*) was a different proposition. Washbrook hit a hundred in each innings and put on 233 in two hours with Place to win the game. Robinson did not take a wicket, nor in the next game against Gloucestershire. He opened the Schools bowling again in 1948, but the perceptive if acerbic cricket writer E. M. Wellings saw "no likelihood of him improving materially with his present style". What concerned Wellings was his whirlwind windmill action, bowled "off the wrong foot". When Robinson attended Freshmen's nets at Oxford, the booming in-swingers that served him so well as a schoolboy had deserted him, along with the prospect of any more first-class cricket. His Blue, instead, was for soccer.

Rumbold, Sir Jack Seddon, who died on December 9, 2001, aged 81, was one of two New Zealanders in the Oxford team that won the first post-war University Match, the other being Martin Donnelly. A solid opening bat, Rumbold made nine and ten at Lord's and played only seven games for Oxford in all, making 175 runs at 12.50 with a highest score of 25 against Middlesex on debut. The rest of his life was more eventful. In 1944, his ship, the destroyer *Inglefield*, was sunk by a German glider bomb off Anzio, and he was mentioned in despatches for helping fellow survivors to safety. Called to the Bar in 1948, he became crown prosecutor in Wanganui and later attorney-general in Zanzibar, where he had to prepare a new constitution. Ten days after independence, a bloody coup took place; Seddon and family escaped on a yacht to the African mainland with only the clothes they stood up in. The new regime asked him back but he opted for attorney-general in Kenya. After moving to England, he became chairman and then president of the Industrial Tribunals, at which he liked to wear his MCC tie.

Russell, Rt Hon. Sir Thomas Patrick, died in Manchester on October 28, 2002, aged 76. A Lord Chief Justice of Appeal from 1987 to 1996, Sir Patrick Russell was president of Lancashire in 1999 and 2000. In 2001, he conducted a club inquiry into the conspicuous good fortune enjoyed by senior Lancashire officials' wives in winning players' benefit raffles four years on the trot. His conclusion was that nothing untoward had happened. A useful swing bowler, Russell had played club cricket into his forties for his native Urmston.

Singh, Amar, died in Pennsylvania on May 7, 2002, aged 69, remembered by many for his lifelong contribution to cricket in India and the United States. Born in Calcutta, he later attended Haverford College, Philadelphia, where his accomplishments at cricket, soccer and fencing resulted in his being called "the Darjeeling Demon". He organised the Haverford College centenary tour of England in 1996 and served as chairman and secretary of the C. C. Morris Cricket Library.

Singleton, Michael, OBE, MC, who died at Malvern on December 11, 2002, aged 89, was the elder brother of the Oxford Blue and 1946 Worcestershire captain, A. P. "Sandy" Singleton. George Michael Singleton played two games for Worcestershire that summer, having also played alongside his brother for the Free Foresters against Cambridge. His left-arm spin brought him five first-class wickets at 29.20. Batting down the order he averaged 8.50 with a best of 23 against Combined Services at Worcester.

Spencer, Thomas William, OBE, died in Seaton Delaval, Northumberland, on November 2, 1995, aged 81. His death was not widely noticed in cricket circles at the time, although his first-class career as player and umpire had covered 36 seasons and he stood in 17 Tests. Tommy Spencer made his debut for Kent at 21 but the potential shown in his Second Eleven run-making was never quite fulfilled. In 75 first-class games between 1935 and 1946, interrupted by war service in the RAF, he made 2,152 runs at 20.11, with a highest score of 96 against Sussex at Tunbridge Wells in his last season before going off to coach at Wrekin College. Strong to leg and a fine cutter, Spencer was an attractive attacking batsman, while his fielding in the deep marked him as a natural sportsman. In winter he played football for Fulham, Lincoln City and Walsall; he claimed to have played four sports professionally – the others being table tennis and boxing. He held 36 catches and in 1937 had Joe Hardstaff caught for 146 off a full-toss, his only first-class wicket.

At Frank Chester's suggestion Spencer went on the umpires' list in 1950. Four years later he was standing in the Second Test against Pakistan at Trent Bridge when Denis Compton made his highest Test score and Bob Appleyard took his first four wickets for England at a cost of six runs. But 15 years would pass before his second Test. "I was a bit disgusted," he told the *Northern Echo* many years later, "but determined to plod on and become a bloody good county umpire."

Spencer had a gummy smile and although literally toothless, he stood no nonsense in the middle. "He was an umpire one would always trust," said the Warwickshire and England opener John Jameson. "His decisions were spot on." By 1975 this had been recognised and he stood in the first World Cup final at Lord's. It was his no-ball call that gave Australia a momentary reprieve as hordes of jubilant West Indian supporters poured on to the field, believing that Jeff Thomson had been caught by Roy Fredericks in the covers. With the ball lost in the mêlée after Fredericks's shy at the stumps went for overthrows, Spencer and Dickie Bird signalled dead ball once Lillee and Thomson had run three; otherwise they might have run all 21 needed for victory.

He was at the business end again that summer when Lord's had its first streaker, during the Test against Australia. Patrick Eagar gave him his photograph of the event and in retirement, after 30 years on the first-class list, Spencer would show it at the Seaton Delaval working men's club from time to time to "give them a bit of a laugh". He attributed his longevity to not driving a car for his last 20 years as an umpire: he travelled to matches by train instead. It was much easier on the eyes, he claimed, and his unwavering concentration stood him in good stead. So did his honesty and integrity. David Constant, with whom Spencer stood in his last Test at Trent Bridge in 1978, recalled him frequently saying that umpires should "keep the game straight".

Steward, Exley Anthony Whitefoord, died in his native Durban on May 4, 2002, aged 63. Tony Steward had 15 games for Essex in 1964 and 1965. The highlight came in Westcliff Week, 1964, with a career-best 47 against Middlesex and 38 against Somerset after being promoted to No. 3. However, nothing in his remaining games that summer, nor again in 1965, warranted his going in so high, and his Essex aggregate was 272 runs. Three games for Natal B in 1967-68 took his career tally to 310 runs at 12.91. Steward could also keep wicket and bowl leg-spin.

Suryaveer Singh died in a motor accident, some 125 miles from Ahmedabad, on August 5, 2002, aged 65. His daughter and two sisters were also killed. Suryaveer Singh's cricket career was rather overshadowed by that of his younger brother Hanumant, the Indian Test batsman and ICC match referee, whom he followed into the Rajasthan team in 1959-60 after a season with Madhya Pradesh. These were heady times for Rajasthan, with Vijay Manjrekar joining them just as Vinoo Mankad was nearing the end of his illustrious playing days. They reached the final of the Ranji Trophy for the first time in 1960-61, and seven times in all during Suryaveer's 14 seasons with them. Each time they went down to invincible Bombay, though not always without some individual glory. The brothers shared two big partnerships in the 1966-67 final, adding 176 for the third wicket and 213 for the second: Suryaveer made 79 and 132 and Hanumant, the captain, 109 and 213 not out. The match became known as Banswara v Bombay on account of their connection to the former royal family of that name. A forthright opening batsman and wicket-keeper, Suryaveer topped and tailed his eight first-class hundreds with centuries for Central Zone against the 1961-62 and 1972-73 MCC sides. His highest was 184 not out for Rajasthan against Bombay in their 1968-69 Ranji semi-final. In 81 games he scored 4,006 runs at 32.30, made 94 catches and 16 stumpings and, purveying the occasional off-break, picked up five wickets at 47.80.

Tamblyn, Gordon, died in Melbourne on December 31, 2001, aged 83. His debut for Victoria was the match in 1938-39 that attracted a second-day crowd of 17,777, a Shield record for the Adelaide Oval, hoping to see Don Bradman hit a record seventh consecutive hundred. They went home disappointed (Bradman made 5), though no more than the 20-year-old Tamblyn, lbw the previous day for a duck. He put this right next game with a hundred at Perth, where he also kept wicket in Ben Barnett's absence, and in 1939-40 he was Victoria's regular opener until he gashed his knee on a boundary fence. After the war Tamblyn picked up more or less where he had left off with a century against Queensland, finishing two short of his career-best 136 at the Gabba in January 1941, and there were nineties as well against Australian Services and South Australia. However, he played only three games in 1946-47, including MCC's visit, to wrap up a 21-game career for Victoria in which he scored 1,324 runs at 40.12 with four centuries. His son Geoff played once for Victoria, against MCC in 1974-75, and went on to become chairman of the Victorian Cricket Association and finance director of the Australian Cricket Board.

Tamhane, Narendra Shankar, died in Mumbai on March 19, 2002, aged 71. He kept wicket for India in 21 Tests, bringing off 35 catches and 16 stumpings, and the Australian wicket-keeper Wally Grout compared his neat, skilful method to that of the renowned Don Tallon. Despite his accidental introduction to the art, for he was originally a slow bowler and first put on the gloves when his club's keeper was unavailable,

Naren Tamhane: Wally Grout compared his neat, skilful method to that of the renowned Don Tallon.
Picture by EMPICS.

Naren Tamhane was playing Ranji Trophy cricket for Bombay at 22 and a season later, 1954-55, was ever-present during India's first series in Pakistan. He took Subhash Gupte's leg-spin and Vinoo Mankad's slow left-armers like a natural, and his 19 victims included seven stumpings, many made with his trademark removal of a single bail. He also hit an unbeaten 54 in his second Test but, as an average of 10.22 attests, batting was never his strength at this level.

Tamhane played in all but two of India's next 13 Tests. Then he was in and out of the side as the selectors preferred Nana Joshi and Budhi Kunderan for their batting. Yet his keeping in the 1959 Headingley and Oval Tests drew praise from knowledgeable observers, and significantly he was called up later that year for the Test against Australia at Kanpur, where a newly laid pitch was expected to take spin. He made only one dismissal, but that second-innings stumping of the opener Colin McDonald, off Jasu Patel, was vital. McDonald had been one of the few Australians to play Patel's off-spin with any confidence; Patel went on to finish with 14 wickets and India won by 119 runs. Tamhane played only two more Tests after that, against Pakistan in 1960-61. His first-class career ended three seasons later, after 93 games in which he made 175 catches and 78 stumpings, becoming the first to register 100 dismissals in the Ranji Trophy. His 1,459 runs at 18.23 included one century, 109 not out for Bombay against Baroda in 1958-59. He served as a national selector throughout the 1980s and as chairman in 1991-92.

Tatham, Francis Hugh Currer, died in Lewes on April 21, 2002, aged 85. Editor of *Whitaker's Almanack* from 1950 until 1981, "Tom" Tatham also saw *Wisden Cricketers' Almanack* through to publication during most of that time. Between 1938 and 1978, *Wisden* was published under licence by J. Whitaker and Sons, and from 1948 the responsibility of in-house editing, proofreading, indexing and passing for press rested on Tatham's broad shoulders. As well as intellectual rigour and meticulous attention to detail, he brought to the job a lifelong love of cricket. He was a keen player in his younger days, an MCC member and a knowledgeable watcher of the game. On seeing a death notice in the papers, he might remark, "That must be so-and-so who occasionally played for Essex – just missed a century against Kent in 1938."

Taylor, Kenneth Alexander, died in Nottingham on April 5, 2002, aged 85. Ken Taylor was cricket manager of Nottinghamshire from 1978 to 1990 and so provided the guiding hand when they won the County Championship in 1981 and 1987, and Lord's finals in 1987 and 1989. His first essay into county cricket had not known such success. Taylor had been playing club cricket in London when, in response to an advert in the *Sporting Chronicle*, he went to Edgbaston for a trial and was taken on the Warwickshire staff in 1939. The war scotched his immediate prospects, but a commission in the Royal Warwicks developed the management skills that would serve Nottinghamshire so effectively. After demobilisation, and recovered from the wounds he received in the Normandy landings, he took up Warwickshire's invitation to rejoin them and, opening the innings, began with 82 against Sussex. In 1947 he was the established No. 3, scoring 1,259 runs at 26.22 and hitting what proved to be his only century, 102 against Gloucestershire at Edgbaston. Yet within two years he was in and out of the side, batting up and down the order, and he was not retained after 1949. In 87 first-class games he had scored 3,145 runs at 21.69, taken one wicket and held 42 catches.

Now 36, Taylor went to work for the East Midlands Electricity Board in Nottingham. As a member of Nottingham Forest CC, he was on the Notts committee from 1963 and experienced at close hand the county's struggles in the bottom reaches of the Championship. "People were just going aimlessly through the motions," said Clive Rice, the Championship-winning captain, whom Taylor signed to replace Garry Sobers as overseas player in 1975 when he was chairman of the cricket committee. "Ken picked up the club by the scruff of the neck and moulded us into a winning unit." He was helped in this by the unholy fallout from World Series Cricket that resulted in Rice being sacked in 1978, replaced by Richard Hadlee and then reinstated after learned advice. At a stroke Taylor, in his first season as full-time cricket manager, had two world-class all-rounders, not to mention the England batsman Derek Randall, around whom to build his team. Rice and Hadlee, disciplined to the core, gave Nottinghamshire their professional edge; Taylor, compassionate though no less lacking in purpose, made sure there was always a human touch in the dressing-room. It proved a winning combination.

Thomas, William Owen, died in Sheringham on August 8, 2000, aged 79. Dulwich captain in 1940, his fourth year in the XI, "Spongey" Thomas went up to Cambridge after war service and played three first-class games for the University in 1948 after taking four for 58 against Essex in a non-first-class match. A slow left-armer who had given the ball quite a tweak in his school days, Thomas took only three wickets at 46.33 apiece. His one other first-class match was for MCC at Lord's in 1954, where his left-handed batting helped Jack Davies add 67 for the ninth wicket in a failed attempt to prevent their old university from winning. Thomas also played for Norfolk in the 1950s while teaching at Gresham's School.

Thursting, Laurence Denis, died in Leicester on November 15, 2001, aged 86. He joined Leicestershire in 1938 from the Lord's groundstaff to bowl left-arm spin, but it was his batting that ensured he was something of a regular that season. When offered the chance to open with Les Berry in the recurring absence of the county captain Stewart Dempster, himself a stand-in opener for the injured Fred Prentice, Thursting immediately showed the temperament for the job. His 94 in the second innings at Edgbaston occupied four and a quarter hours, saved Leicestershire from defeat, and remained his highest score. But his bowling failed to meet expectations and he received fewer opportunities in 1939. One post-war match against Yorkshire in 1947 left him with figures of 882 runs at 25.20 and 13 wickets at 50.76 from 29 games.

Tovey, Edward Richard, who died in Sydney on May 31, 2002, aged 71, kept wicket once for Queensland, in 1957. Dick Tovey also had three summers with Auckland, including their Plunket Shield success in 1963-64. *WCAA.*

Toynbee, Lawrence Leifchild, who died in Malton on January 3, 2002, aged 79, mixed his playing experience as a cricketer with his artist's gift for conveying the movement and spirit of sport in an acclaimed series of cricket paintings. These include *Hit to Leg, Cricket at Canterbury* and *Cricket in The Parks*, all of which may be viewed at Lord's, and *The Nursery End at Lord's*. Toynbee, a lively medium-fast bowler from his days in the Ampleforth XI, knew The Parks well. He had been Oxford's leading wicket-taker in 1942, when he gained a wartime Blue, and was disappointed not to be given a chance to play first-class cricket on his post-war return to Oxford to train at the Ruskin School of Drawing. Perhaps an Oxford side flush with former servicemen was circumspect about the accuracy of a fast bowler whose tank had reputedly taken out a French cow and run over a wounded British soldier.

Tshwete, Stephen Vukile, died in Bloemfontein from pneumonia and kidney failure, following a back operation, on April 26, 2002. He was 63. His passion for sport sustained him through 15 years' imprisonment on Robben Island for anti-apartheid activities and made him the obvious choice, when Nelson Mandela was released from Robben Island in 1990, to ensure equality for all his countrymen as South Africa was allowed back into international sport. While a member of the African National Council in exile in Zimbabwe, Steve Tshwete had helped bridge the doctrinal chasm between the opposing South African Cricket Union and South African Cricket Board, and in 1991 he was at Lord's alongside his friend and ally, Ali Bacher, to lobby successfully for his country's readmission to the ICC. Not for nothing was he dubbed South Africa's "Mr Fix-It". He also argued for their inclusion in the 1992 World Cup and was one of the first to congratulate the players when they beat Australia at Sydney in their first match. Tshwete was appointed Minister of Sport and Recreation in 1994 and since 1999 had been Minister of Safety and Security. Sadly he didn't live to see his nephew, the Border fast bowler Monde Zondeki, make his debut for South Africa in December 2002.

Turner, Herbert Wilfred, who died in Bendigo on February 24, 2002, aged 80, was a stocky left-hander who played 12 times for Victoria, making 96 on debut against Western Australia at the MCG in 1948. *WCAA.*

van Straubenzee, Lt-Colonel Henry Hamilton, DSO, OBE, who died on April 12, 2002, aged 88, was a career soldier who played three first-class games for the Army just before World War II, as well as a Championship match for Essex against Sussex at Colchester in 1938. He was four not out when Essex declared at 535 for six, and was given six overs to bowl his left-arm spinners as they progressed to an innings victory. He did not take a wicket. However, it would be nice to think that there were moments during the Dunkirk withdrawal when he was able to reflect on balmy days at Fenner's and dismissing Paul Gibb, Norman Yardley and the Mann brothers. His ten first-class wickets cost 18.50 apiece; his best was four for 96 against Cambridge in 1939. He also hit his highest score, 38, in that game to complete a career aggregate of 56 at an average of 28.00. On retiring from the Army, van Straubenzee joined the board of W. H. Smith, became managing director in 1968, and was a noted authority on fly fishing. Through Jane Turner, who eloped with a Dutch officer named van Straubenzee in the early 1700s, he was a direct descendant of the family that founded Sir William Turner's Almshouses at Kirkleatham in Cleveland.

Walford, Michael Moore, died in Sherborne on January 16, aged 86. Somerset's cast of strolling players was legion in the days when amateurs regularly came in for the occasional game at the professionals' expense. But few matched the impact Micky Walford made when he turned up in mid-season after a year's schoolmastering at Sherborne. The runs rattled effortlessly from his bat: in 52 games for Somerset between 1946 and 1953 he scored 3,395 at an average of 40.90. He impressed on his first appearance at Taunton, going in at No. 7 against the Indian tourists and contributing an unbeaten 141 to Somerset's innings victory. Promotion to No. 3 was immediate, 139 against Surrey at Weston-super-Mare followed several matches later and, with 472 runs at 52.44 in seven games, he finished fifth in the national averages behind Wally Hammond, Cyril Washbrook, Denis Compton and Martin Donnelly.

Not that the cognoscenti were surprised. At 30 Walford had form going back to his schooldays at Rugby, where he was four years in the XI and played for the Public Schools at Lord's in 1934. After going up to Oxford that year, he won cricket Blues in 1936 and 1938, as well as rugby and hockey Blues in three years. As a centre-threequarter – his Oxford wing in 1935 and 1936 was the flying Prince Obolensky – he twice made the final England rugby trials, was a travelling reserve and played in wartime internationals; as a hockey wing-half he won 17 England caps, often as captain, and played all five games for Great Britain in the silver-medal side that lost the Olympic final to India in London in 1948. Walford's maiden century, 201 not out in two and a half hours for the University against MCC at Lord's in 1938, was the 12th-fastest double-hundred at the time. His second, 114 out of 177 while he was at the wicket, had a curiosity value in that the match at The Oval was of two days' duration, so Oxford's players could rest ahead of the Varsity Match, yet retained its first-class status.

Somerset obtained a special registration for Walford after he wrote from Germany, where he was with the Royal Corps of Signals, to enquire about playing during school holidays. In contrast to his expansive though nonetheless orthodox strokeplay and his colourful Harlequin cap, he was taciturn by nature, individualistic, and played cricket more for its intellectual challenges than its camaraderie. Whatever the easy-going Somerset professionals made of this latest privateer, however, they couldn't begrudge him his runs or his athletic cover fielding. Opening with Harold Gimblett in 1947, he put together a sequence of 96 and 52 at Trent Bridge, 90 and 101 against Glamorgan at Weston and, as his seaside *pièce de résistance*, a career-best 264 against Hampshire, hitting 40 fours before falling 28 short of L. C. H. Palairet's 1896 record for Somerset. The Olympics restricted him to three games in 1948, though his brief season was not without incident. At Eastbourne he put on 180 with Gimblett, then saw him progress to a triple-century. Next game, back at Taunton, he was the cause of Len Hutton's bizarre dismissal, adjudged run out after leaving the crease to avoid impeding the wicket-keeper as he took a return throw. When the ball bounced out of the keeper's gloves and rebounded off Hutton's pads on to the stumps, Walford alone appealed. The umpire upheld the appeal, and as England's premier batsman went on his way, an embarrassed silence followed him. "It was something done in the heat of the moment," Walford told David Foot some 40 years later, confessing that the appeal stayed on his conscience for a long time. Johnny Lawrence, born in Leeds, added injury to insult by taking Yorkshire's last four wickets in five balls, including a hat-trick.

Walford's arrival in 1949, and his 763 runs in nine games, turned round a ten-game losing streak, while his first four games in 1950 produced four half-centuries and then another hundred at Weston, something of a favourite watering-hole – six of his nine first-class hundreds were made there. Going with MCC to Canada, where he took a century off Alberta, accounted for his 1951 vacation, after which there were just two more summers before he learnt that Somerset would be using his special registration to acquire someone else. In 97 first-class games, which included a few end-of-season festival matches, he made 5,327 runs at 33.71, took eight wickets at 31.12 with his occasional left-arm slows and held 50 catches. From 1954 to 1962 he played for Dorset – he had played for his native Durham in 1937 – and in 1955, at the age of 39, he became the first minor-county batsman since 1911 to score 1,000 runs. Sherborne boys, meanwhile, continued to benefit from his cricket, rugby and hockey coaching; in due course he was the school's second master.

Walker, Harold, who died in Kettering in November 2000, aged 82, opened the batting for Northamptonshire in their first-ever tied match, against Essex in May 1947. A 28-year-old amateur from Desborough, he had been invited to play in Dennis Brookes's absence and scored one and seven.

Weir, Harold Stanley, who died in Maryborough on June 11, 2002, aged 98, had been Queensland's oldest living first-class cricketer. A left-handed all-rounder, Stan Weir played for them only once, against MCC in 1928-29 – their first victory over an English side in eight attempts. *WCAA.*

Wilkinson, Joan, who died in Foulridge on April 17, 2002, aged 83, played 13 Tests for England between 1948-49 and 1957-58. A duck on debut at the MCG did not augur well, but by the 1954 New Zealand series "Wilkie" Wilkinson was established at No. 3 and contributed 185 runs at 46.25. She struggled after that except when making a career-best 90 against New Zealand at Auckland in 1957-58 and finished with an average of 19.81 from 436 runs. Under five feet tall, she was exceptionally nimble around the crease for someone never the most mobile in the field. Her lack of inches had militated against her when she went to enlist in the WAAF in 1939, but such was her prowess in Lancashire sporting circles that she was called up two years later and became a cricket, hockey and PT instructor. Staying on in the WAAF after the war, Joan Wilkinson also represented Lancashire, North of England and Berkshire.

Joan Wilkinson: Under five feet tall, she was exceptionally nimble around the crease for someone never the most mobile in the field. *Picture by EMPICS.*

Wilkinson, Leonard Litton, died in Barrow-in-Furness on September 3, 2002, aged 85. For one August he sparkled brilliantly, then just as suddenly his star waned. "The only thing I can think of," Len Wilkinson told the cricket writer Brian Bearshaw, "is that I tried to be too perfect, particularly with the googly. I had an England cap and as an England player I had to be good." He hadn't taken up leg-spin bowling until he was 15, yet a month after turning 22 he was playing Test cricket in South Africa. The selectors could hardly ignore him. In 1938, his first full season with Lancashire, he had taken 151 wickets at 23.28 in 36 games, bowling thoughtfully, delivering the ball from a full height, often getting sharp turn and rarely dropping short. He was a good slip fielder besides, with a seemingly elastic reach, and had held 26 catches.

Wilkinson had joined the Old Trafford staff in 1936, being offered professional terms on the same day as Winston Place, and made his first-class debut next season against the New Zealanders, bowling the tourists' captain, "Curly" Page, in his first over. He went on to take 22 wickets in seven games, including nine on a good batting pitch at Trent Bridge, and returned 12 for 91 for the Second Eleven against Surrey Seconds in the Minor Counties Challenge Match at The Oval, another good batting strip.

Though he took time to get going in 1938, a 12-over spell of five for 27 at Worcester and a hat-trick in an eight-wicket match return at Hove showed why Lancashire had been playing him in every game. Then in August he caught fire, beginning with 12 for 125 at Canterbury and reaping 58 wickets in the last nine Championship fixtures. This included eight for 86 at Swansea, and altogether that season he took 11 five-fors with two ten-wicket matches. Only Wilfred Rhodes, with 154 wickets when he was 20 in 1898, had taken more wickets in a season at a younger age than the 21-year-old Wilkinson.

Form and fortune stayed with him when he went to South Africa that autumn with MCC and, despite being the fourth spinner in seniority, he was selected ahead of Doug

Wright for the First Test and also played in the Third and Fourth. But nigh-perfect pitches ensured that batsmen held the upper hand, and his seven wickets came at a price of 38.71 each. The cost in confidence was even higher. Although he headed the tour averages with 44 wickets at 18.86 – only Wright and Hedley Verity took more – Wilkinson was virtually unrecognisable as the same bowler when he resumed in 1939 after an early-season hand injury. He did achieve career-best figures of eight for 53, and 12 in the match, against Hampshire at Old Trafford at the end of May, but 63 wickets that summer at 30.85 was a definite turn for the worse, and the outbreak of war allowed no recovery. He injured his knee at Fenner's in Lancashire's first post-war match, so missing the rest of the season, and in 1947 he played only twice. His county cricket was over; he retired to the leagues and a newsagent's. In 77 games he had taken 282 wickets at 25.25 and 53 catches. No batsman to speak of, he scored 321 runs at 7.64 with a highest of 48 against Worcestershire at Old Trafford to launch that once-in-a-lifetime season.

Willett, Michael David, died at Sanderstead on January 24, 2002, aged 68. In another time, or another county perhaps, Mike Willett's career might have been different. But he joined the Oval staff as a teenager in 1950, with Surrey on the cusp of the roll that brought eight titles in nine years. Opportunities for apprentice batsmen were thinly scattered, and when they came Willett never converted his second-team form into first-team runs in the way that contemporaries such as Micky Stewart, Ken Barrington and John Edrich did. When at last he established himself in the early 1960s, hitting 1,000 runs three times in four seasons, a serious knee injury cruelly cut his career short.

Like Stewart, he played amateur football for Corinthian-Casuals, and there was something of the amateur in the way he played his cricket. His debut, in the last

Mike Willett: In another time, his career might have been different, but he joined the Oval staff as a teenager in 1950, when Surrey were on the cusp of the roll that brought eight titles in nine years. *Picture by EMPICS.*

Championship game of 1955, was a low-scoring affair in which only he, with 25, and Jim Laker reached double figures, adding 63 of Surrey's 101: they still won by eight wickets in two days. Between then and 1960, however, he managed only 18 Championship games. And when in 1960 Fred Trueman, his RAF team-mate back in their National Service days, dismissed him for a pair while twice taking three wickets in five balls, Willett may have wondered if his immediate future lay in the family motor business rather than cricket. Then, in his first game of 1961, he hit his maiden hundred – 105 not out against Worcestershire – and the wheel turned, even if Surrey did slump to a worst-ever 15th in the Championship. In August he made 126 against Kent, and finished the summer with 1,593 first-class runs at 30.63. Though the next season produced barely more than 500, he reached his thousand again in 1963, Stewart's first year as captain; his two hundreds included an unbroken stand of 193 with Barrington against the champions, Yorkshire. In 1964 he was the ninth Englishman in the first-class averages, making 1,789 runs at 45.87. Among his four hundreds was the fastest of the summer (80 minutes against Middlesex at The Oval), while in equalling his career-best 126, against Hampshire at Bournemouth, he struck his second fifty in 30 minutes, with 48 coming in boundaries. At Gravesend, Willett and Barrington put on 230 for the fourth wicket against Kent. But a cartilage operation in 1965 sidelined him from mid-May to late August and, while his fielding remained vibrant, he never rediscovered his batting form. Two years later he retired and concentrated his sporting energies on club cricket and golf. In 172 first-class games he had scored 6,535 runs at 28.66, including eight hundreds, held 95 catches, and taken 23 wickets at 48.04 with the medium pace that served Surrey well in Second Eleven cricket.

Williams, Laurie Rohan, died in Kingston, Jamaica on September 8, 2002, aged 33, when he swerved to avoid a damaged section of road and his car collided with an oncoming bus. His 23-year-old half-brother, Kevin Jennison, was also killed. Although Williams had opened the bowling for Jamaica against England on his first-class debut in February 1990, his method was mainly medium seam and swing rather than out-and-out pace and was well suited to limited-overs cricket. In 15 one-day internationals for West Indies between 1995-96, when he grabbed three for 16 in five overs against New Zealand in his second match, and the 2000-01 Carlton Series in Australia, he took 18 wickets at 30.88. However, his aggregate of 124 one-day international runs, with a highest score of 41, reveals neither his elegance nor ability at the crease. The highest of his three first-class hundreds, 135 for Jamaica against Windwards, helped make him the second-highest runmaker in the 1999-2000 Busta Cup. Williams's best first-class bowling, six for 26 in 1996-97, was also at Windwards' expense. In 58 first-class matches for West Indies A and Jamaica, he scored 2,002 runs at 24.71 and took 170 wickets at 23.17. In the weeks preceding the accident Williams had played in the early rounds of the one-day Red Stripe Bowl, but had been dropped for the semi-final and final. Many paid tribute to his commitment to Jamaican cricket, while the former West Indies wicket-keeper Jackie Hendriks, president of the Jamaican Cricket Association, said he was "a gentleman on and off the field".

Wilson, Arthur Edward, died in Redmarley D'Abitot on July 29, 2002, aged 92. "Andy" Wilson was one of those wicket-keepers, diminutive and undemonstrative, who are so efficient that their craftsmanship passes virtually unnoticed, though by no means unappreciated by fellow players and the county faithful. He played 318 times for Gloucestershire between 1936 and 1955, following seven games for Middlesex in 1932 and 1933. He had been a slow left-arm bowler when he joined the Lord's groundstaff, where he was a contemporary of Denis Compton and a future Gloucestershire captain in George Emmett, but when called on to keep for the Young Professionals against the Young Amateurs he revealed a natural talent for the job. With Fred Price established as Middlesex's keeper, there were few calls for Wilson's safe hands. When he made his county debut at Worcester, it was as a gutsy lower-order left-hander, helping add

Andy Wilson: one of those wicket-keepers, diminutive and undemonstrative, who are so efficient that their craftsmanship passes virtually unnoticed. *Picture by EMPICS.*

94 for the ninth wicket, and later that season he made 53 at Cardiff in an unbroken ninth-wicket stand of 137 with J. W. Hearne. In 1935 he helped Middlesex Seconds win the Minor Counties Championship and then decided to try his hand in the West Country.

Almost 26, Wilson still had to qualify by residence before he could play Championship cricket for Gloucestershire. That meant two years of waiting, so it was 1938 before he was keeping to Tom Goddard and Reg Sinfield as they took 100 wickets apiece. He also scored 1,138 runs, including 130 against Middlesex at Lord's, a mischievously satisfying maiden hundred during which he and Billy Neale added 192 for the eighth wicket. Against Lancashire at Bristol two months later he was very much the junior partner as Wally Hammond steamed past 2,000 runs for the season with 271 – it was still only mid-July – and they established Gloucestershire's eighth-wicket record of 239. "Run when I tell you," was Hammond's instruction to the incoming Wilson. "And I didn't face a ball for eight overs," Wilson would recall. He made 83. He was not the prettiest of batsmen but he drove and pulled powerfully.

Pressed into opening in 1946, after wartime service in the RAF, he again reached his thousand; he did so every year to 1950 and again in 1953 at the age of 43. That last season he set a world record with ten catches in a match – six in Hampshire's first innings at Portsmouth and four in their second. In due course he would give the gloves he wore at Portsmouth to another Gloucestershire keeper, Jack Russell, whom he encouraged when Russell was still a schoolboy. Back in 1947, when Gloucestershire fought Middlesex nip and tuck for the Championship, Wilson's 62 dismissals had included 30 stumpings as Goddard's fiercely spun off-breaks and Sam Cook's subtle slow left-armers bemused visiting batsmen on the new sand-and-clay strips at Bristol. Goddard took 206 wickets and Cook 120 in the title race. In a career of 328 matches,

Wilson finished with 425 catches, 176 stumpings and 10,744 runs at 25.28. His highest score of 188 came when opening against Sussex at Chichester in 1949. From 1950 he doubled as Gloucestershire's coach. On retiring he moved into journalism, covering cricket, soccer and rugby for a number of papers, and also worked for the National Farmers' Union.

Wilson, George Arthur, died in Oxford on September 27, 2002, aged 86. His highest score of 55 not out in 15 pre-war appearances as an amateur for Yorkshire came against Northamptonshire at Scarborough in 1938. By the time he and Brian Sellers had added an unbroken 84 for the sixth wicket, Northants looked well and truly beaten. Altogether Wilson scored 352 runs at 17.60 and, bowling slow left-arm, took one wicket.

Kenneth Wolstenholme: the voice of football on BBC television launches the coverage of the 1966 football World Cup. *Picture by Getty Images.*

Wollocombe, Richard Henry, died in Bath on June 7, 2002, aged 76. He captained Wellington College in 1943 and, on going up to Oxford in 1949 after the Army and a brief spell in advertising, played four games for the University in 1951 and four more in 1952 as a leg-spinning all-rounder. He also played against them for the Free Foresters in 1951, scoring an unbeaten 38 in the second innings, though by then he was out of the running for a Blue. His glorious 119 in 125 minutes against Worcestershire suggested 1952 might be his year, but it wasn't to be. The final bowling place went to the 1951 Blue, Bill Mitchell. In his nine first-class games Wollocombe scored 314 runs at 22.42 and took ten wickets at 62.30 with his leg-breaks. He also played some Minor Counties cricket for Berkshire in 1950, and after university returned to the world of advertising.

Wolstenholme, Kenneth, DFC, died in Torquay on March 25, 2002, aged 81. For almost a quarter of a century, spanning five World Cups, Wolstenholme's was the voice of football on BBC television. When England won the World Cup in 1966, he saw spectators running on to the pitch in the closing moments of the final and said "They think it's all over", which eventually, after endless re-runs of the footage, became a national catchphrase. Yet his career might have taken a different path. Returning to sports journalism after wartime service as a bomber pilot, he was sent by BBC Manchester to cover cricket's Scarborough Festival. Unfortunately, his lyrical descriptions of the Marine Parade tulips were heard by the *Yorkshire Post's* gardening correspondent, who somewhat pedantically pointed out that tulips do not bloom in September. Not in Scarborough, anyway. Wolstenholme possibly thought it was all over; any future in cricket commentary certainly was.

CRICKET BOOKS, 2002
GLOWING IN THE DARK
By FRANK KEATING

The international game careers unstoppably on with such a fervidly incessant global programme that it is hard to believe only a single summer has passed since England's most pre-eminent and stalwart batsman of his generation walked down that theatrically visible staircase at The Oval to play his valedictory Test-match innings. Michael Atherton recalls the day: "My mind was a maelstrom of conflicting emotions. I remember little – a pull and a cut off two uncharacteristically loose balls from McGrath and then the inevitable nick... caught Warne bowled McGrath, an entirely predictable end... Above all, I felt relief. I was glad it was all over. Halfway back to the pavilion I was jolted out of my self-absorption by the realisation that the whole ground had risen to me. What to do? I had scored a miserable 9, but it was clear the applause was for much more than that and needed to be acknowledged. A raise of the bat, then, to the pavilion, and a half-turn to the rest of the ground (as I did so I saw the Australians, to a man, clapping me off). Then it was up the stairs and off the stage for the final time..." Followed inevitably by a lighter-footed further climb into the media village. And in a jiffy, hairdo and make-up just-so and camera-friendly grin in place, the far less pent-up and put-upon Atherton was swivelling at his ease with the best of them in his pundit's chair, alternating broadcasting stints with matey visits next door to the press-box where he can be found woodpeckering away at his laptop in an ever-growing old-boys' reunion of gifted friends and contemporaries.

> **Atherton writes as he batted – honest, unvarnished, uncomplicatedly down to earth**

Between that final glum innings and being cued in for his first Colgate smile to camera, Atherton had found time to hide away with a pen, some paper, and his partner on the banks of the dark prowling grandeur of Guyana's Essequibo River, and had found peace enough – in spite of the howler monkeys providing a constant and shrill, and probably symbolic, primordial accompaniment – to write down cogent reflections on all the

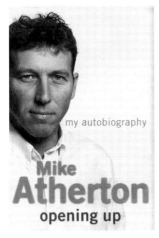

my autobiography

Mike
Atherton
opening up

craft, clamour and claptrap of the previous 15 years. **Opening Up: My Autobiography** is a terrific piece of work: lively, literate, and as self-effacing as it is self-aware. Atherton needed no ghost to embellish clichés for the sporting shelves; he writes as he batted – honest, unvarnished, uncomplicatedly down to earth. Wit as well, and particularly delicious is his description of dear old A. C. Smith on his hands and knees checking for bugs before a selectors' meeting. To think, for years his new press-box confrères wearily knew Atherton as Captain Grumpy. He remains unapologetic: "My attitude to the media was characterised by obstinacy and it didn't do me or my team any favours at all. Spin and PR were anathema to me. As a player, I just didn't feel the press were important – like a Sunday morning visit to the mother-in-law, I saw the press conference as something of a chore to be endured and survived... Although I am now part of the media, I still don't see why there should be a cosy relationship between players and the press... The players are there to play and the media is there to act as a conduit, in a colourful and interesting way, between that play and the paying and watching public."

Atherton's record as England captain was no great shakes (W13, L21, D20), nor was his Test batting average (37 overall, only 29 against Australia), but when, more often than not down all his summers home and abroad, most of those about him were being timorously wet and feeble, his four-square staunchness, stickability, technique and courage were paramount and will be ineffaceable in the lore for a considerable time. Three particular passages earmarked him for posterity – all against South Africa, in turn at Lord's in 1994, Johannesburg in 1995-96, and Trent Bridge in 1998 – and here he reflects on each with, as you would expect, a deadbat lack of flim-flam. "'Doing something' to the ball is undoubtedly what TV pictures showed me doing on that fateful Lord's afternoon. I was not altering the condition of the ball, however; I was trying to *maintain* its dry and rough condition... It was not the first time I had done it – as a bowler I had often dried my hands with dust in my pockets. Why then did I not come entirely clean with [the referee] Peter Burge on Saturday evening as I had with [Raymond] Illingworth and [Keith] Fletcher at teatime? That, of course, is the issue I most regretted then; and... that is the thing I most regret now. In a sense, you can be judged on how you react in the most difficult times and I failed myself then."

Seventeen months later came more dust, but now allied to the broiling heat and altitude of Johannesburg and not villainy but the heroism of his match-saving 11-hour epic of a captain's innings: "My trigger to switch on was when the bowler was halfway through his run. I would then focus intensely on the ball until it was dead – a period of seven seconds, say. In between deliveries or at the end of each over, I would switch off completely, and by doing so I saved energy. This was my biggest strength as a batsman... By the [last] afternoon, and for the only time in my career, I was in the zone... a state of being much talked about by sports psychologists and while I can describe my feelings that afternoon, I couldn't begin to explain how to replicate it... The zone for me was a feeling of absolute control... an almost trance-like state. Everything happened dreamily, in slow motion, although I was still alert and picking up the cues around me."

At Nottingham in 1998, if not in the zone, he for sure was in the ring and unforgettably squaring-up toe-to-toe with Allan Donald. "That short duel was by far the most intense period of cricket I experienced. Both of us gave our all, laying ourselves bare, with nothing in reserve... Both of us took on the responsibility of winning the battle for our team... There is a lot of talk about cricket being a team game, but in essence it is a battle of individuals... at that precise moment, each batsman and bowler *is* his team – the hopes and aspirations of the others rest on one man, and are out of their control... In such a physical contest, body language is important – I didn't want to take a backward step, and by countering Donald's staring with my own, I knew it was a battle I was bound to win because he had to turn away first."

Mercifully, for those anyway who prefer cricket to political tracts, Atherton does not waste overmuch quality space drearily rounding up the usual suspects on coaching, central contracts and the finances of the county game – which a ghostwriter would have been urged to labour in spades. There cannot have been many more assured and enjoyable (unaided) autobiographies by a leading international cricketer written so soon after unbuckling his pads for the last time. Benaud and Brearley were two, I suppose. A reservation is that, as with his batting, you sometimes sense too much cautious circumspection in Atherton the writer. I wish he had been far ruder to some. I bet he would like to have been. In a year or three, when he is more at ease with his already enviable style, a follow-up memoir in which he dares play more carefree, less fettered and diplomatic strokes might tonkingly reveal far more incisive tales of the erstwhile workmates of his time and their accompanying preening, and mostly dud, administrators. In **Michael Parkinson on Cricket**, the author nicely quotes David Gower's opinion on Atherton's perceived obstinacy as England captain: "It's partly due to being born in Lancashire, partly due to being brought up in Manchester, partly due to being a stubborn devil, but mostly due to being a professional cricketer confronted by pillocks with a pen."

The bulk of this collection of reflections and essays by Parkinson has

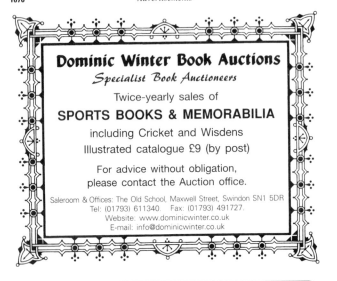

appeared in newspapers down the years, but it is no less rewarding for that and it is about time another pile was packaged between hard covers for safe keeping. Potboilers can be extremely warming to the cockles, and since his shining work on the *Sunday Times* under Harold Evans helped change sportswriting in the 1960s, Parkinson has been esteemed in the pantheon. Sport has with good reason been miffed at his being too long seduced by the alluring "lights, camera, action!" of the celebrity television studio. Parkinson's cricketing heart has always been in the right place and he was more than a half-decent player in his time as well, the pride of his miner father – "I could play forward and back before I could read and I knew how to bowl an off-break before I could do joined-up writing."

All the old favourites are here reprised – from Larwood to Gough via Bradman – as well as, most memorably eye-moistening of all, his 1994 piece on his all-time hero: "Keith Miller was deeply affected by the Second World War. It changed him. It gave him an insight into human nature and a set of values that have lasted. The way he played his cricket in the immediate post-war years was as much a celebration of surviving the war as it was the product of an impulsive nature and a desire never to be bored either by a person or a game... In the first post-war Ashes Test at Brisbane, England were caught on a sticky. It was unplayable. Miller's old mate Bill Edrich came in. He'd had a serious war and he survived and Miller thought, 'He's my old Services mate. The last thing he wants after five years' war is to be flattened by a cricket ball, so I eased up. Bradman came up to me and said 'Don't slow down, Keith. Bowl quicker.' That remark put me off Test cricket. Never felt the same way about it after that.' "

Parkinson once wrote a biography of the footballer George Best, and it is a pity he could not spare the time to do the same for one of his cricketers of grandeur closer to home. Alan Hill is also a Yorkshireman but his **Brian Close: Cricket's Lionheart** is a laboured labour of love, I'm afraid, which whistles up Chesterton's dictum, "if a thing's worth doing, it's worth doing badly". The book fails to capture any of the zany gusto, the glooms, glories, or cock-eyed courage – let alone the engaging, convivial humour – of Yorkshire's second-most cussed cricketer of our time, but one who is perhaps the most appealing and exceptionally talented of any time.

Down the years, the diligent cuttings-librarian Hill has been a productive cottage industry, doing the game proud with a succession of fond and important studies of such champions as Edrich, Les Ames, Peter May and the Bedsers, as well as saints from the author's native canon of Tykes – Sutcliffe, Verity, Wardle, and Laker. But the character, oomph, switchback career, and Rabelaisian good humour of Close set him apart, and he deserves far more than low-key, mousey appraisal. These eight lines in Parkinson's book catch the singular flavours of good ol' Closey more richly than 80 in Hill's: "Brian Close to Imran Khan, who glides forward and strikes the ball back over the bowler's head for six. He does it twice more in the over as well as sweeping for four. The last straight drive is the best. Imran poses in the follow-through, the bat high, the profile of a hawk. John Arlott might have been moved to verse. Brian Close took a more pragmatic view of things. 'I never could bowl to a bloody slogger,' he said, taking his sweater."

Imran himself stars as princely top of the bill in John Barclay's unlikely 150-pager **The Appeal of the Championship**, a captain's evocative commemoration of Sussex's most famous recent attempt, in 1981, to win the Championship for the first time in their history (they didn't, of course). It is a darling little collectible telling how summer's southern seasiders – Imran and Garth Le Roux, Paul Parker and Paul Phillipson, Ian Greig and Ian Gould and Geoff Arnold – followed good captain Barclay on their round-Britain whizz to find they couldn't stop winning. No matter that pace is "blistering", dramas are "fantastic", close calls "agonising", slip catches "smartly snapped up", and forward-defensives "immaculate", Barclay writes a compelling narrative, which represents another (not to alter the tone) feather in the cap of the front-parlour publisher Stephen Chalke, whose beautifully crafted quality output has been illuminating this corner of *Wisden* in the half a dozen years since his debut classic on the 1950s Championship, *Runs in the Memory,* so beguilingly ambushed a whole generation of a certain age.

Barclay's slim-but-bespoke one-off might seem pricey at £14 but, thank heavens, in literature size isn't everything, and that ratio is not remotely as wide as **Arlott and Ackroyd: a celebration of cricket, wine, poetry and place**, a book of only 56 pages which is priced at £395. But for some it is a snip at the price, for the limited edition of 295 copies uniquely brings together the evocative voice, in poetry and prose, of the late John Arlott – that "distant lawnmower on a drowsy summer's day" – and the world-renowned etchings of Norman Ackroyd RA, himself a devoted buff of cricket, vine and rhyme. The linking commentary is by Arlott's outstanding biographer, David Rayvern Allen, and with each handbound copy another specialist cricket publisher, Christopher Saunders, provides a sensational, limited, signed and numbered original copperplate portrait by Ackroyd of Arlott himself at work (and at drink) in his Alderney long-room. With Ackroyd originals selling these days for up to £1,000, you could say that for your £395 you are buying a rare bargain etching with a free book attached.

Thinking, suddenly rheumy-eyed, of Arlott, great round-shouldered bear of his final years, caged, content, in his book-lined den at home, makes you realise with a start that this is the 11th year these reviews have been farmed out to common workaday labourers in the field like this one, after more than two-score years as Arlott's timeless patch, preserve and pulpit. Almost to the very day he died, too, for only 40 pages divided *Wisden's* Obituaries in the 1992 Almanack (with John's memorial on page one) and his last Book Review, which tipped the scales that year at a phenomenal 13 pages. He signed off that final marathon, aptly I suppose, with the dozen-word sentence, "As ever, the only possible comment is – *Wisden* is authoritative on cricket." Arlott had begun the Lit. Review here back

in the mists of 1950, opting out only for two years when he followed the cricket abroad. Every spring, John would be in this spot, acknowledging the jewels as well as the dross. Every book and booklet, weighty tome or tossed-away trivia, would be noted and for each, almost unvaryingly, he would look to bestow a kindly benediction.

His long watch coincided with a remarkable growth in cricket publishing. By the 1985 Almanack, Arlott was reviewing as many as 83 books – 83! – and observing that the year had been particularly notable "for the production of several original, illuminating, and even occasionally controversial works". The year before, Arlott revealed he had received 79 titles for review, "an impressive proportion authoritative, distinguished, original, and valuable".

> # This reviewer received fewer than 30 cricket books from English publishers including quite a few catchpenny efforts of dashed-off tripe

The year before, for the 1983 edition, his bumper bundle of 72 titles "quite certainly represent the highest general standard ever observed in one of these reviews". Even in his poignant final column, ten Almanacks later in 1992, John announced 68 titles had been submitted which were "the most uniformly high-standard output of any year in modern times".

What a falling-off there has been in the past decade. This reviewer received fewer than 30 cricket books from English publishers including, you've got to believe it, **Dickie Bird's England** and quite a few more catchpenny efforts of dashed-off tripe. Cricket is low down on publishers' agendas these days. Is the swamping by football and all its celebrity berks and pomps to blame? Undoubtedly, although in fairness of late that game has been inspiring some valid and terrific literature, both pop and posh. The generally woebegone showing of recent England teams might be another reason. Publishers thrive on personalities. In that respect, from Test captain and coach downwards, English cricket is stocked with some awfully cheerless duds, who you wouldn't cross the road to have a drink with, let alone read a book about.

Sadly, less than a dozen years after Arlott's parting rave about pearls and plenty, you can easily count on the fingers of just two hands the cricket books of an undoubted and enduring quality which were produced in England in 2002. One of those, it now goes without saying, is the periodic pocket-sized treat in soft covers – cricket's *Granta* as it claims – which is **The New Ball**. For this, its seventh coming, entitled *Mind Games*, Rob Steen's exemplary user-friendly series of challenging essays and stimulating romance concentrates on the game's cerebral hinterland with an eightsome reel of psychoanalytical essays stimulatingly to test shrewd Tom Cartwright's hypothesis that cricket, when pared to the bone, is no more than a confrontational activity of "one player imposing his will upon another".

The New Ball glows in some dark days. But if the pile is low on both quality and quantity, when something genuinely good does arrive it is all the more welcome and violently seized from the postman's hands. Hard on the timely updated reissue of Mihir Bose's treasured *A History of Indian Cricket*, first published in 1990, the brilliant Bangalore historian Ramachandra Guha has produced just as heavyweight a doorstop to serve Bose's pioneering work as a glittering literary companion. **The Corner of a Foreign Field: The Indian history of a British sport** concentrates more on the subcontinent's internal political and cultural interplay with its cricketing passions, so while such as Ranji, Nayudu, Gavaskar and Tendulkar obviously feature, so, in arresting and unexpected ways, do Gandhi and Jinnah, not to forget the remarkable spin bowler Palwankar Baloo. In one decade, with resplendent scholarship and style, Bose and Guha have filled a long-standing hole in the game's history, and given India's vibrant cricket the masterly acknowledgment it deserves.

Another gap is filled, in a far more modest and light-hearted way, by a breezy knock from a current player, E. T. Smith. He lets his subtitle explain – **Playing Hard Ball: a Kent county cricketer's journey into big league baseball**. Surprisingly, to my knowledge anyway, no book has so directly compared cricket with its American cousin. For those of a certain bent, Ed Smith's – is the E. T. some sort of Hollywood-based alien joke, or does he fancy himself as an olde-tyme amateur? – experience makes for what you might call a diamond read, full of bright nods and winks, and though he obviously remains a better (as they called him across the Atlantic) "cricketeer" than a baseball slugger, this debut suggests he could yet be even more successful and flamboyant as a writer. As the old-hand critics used to say, I look forward to his next offering with interest.

Chris England also had to travel for his literary material – from **Balham to Bollywood** – as well as pass a hilarious audition to play the mutton-chopped demon fast bowler, Yardley, star of the British Army XI which took on (and lost to, hurrah!) the Indian villagers in the Oscar-nominated and ravishing Bollywood epic *Lagaan*. England, a writer as well as actor, saw his chance of a win-double, and although his tale is not as sumptuous as the gorgeous whirligig of the film, he tells the story of its making with a rum-tee-tiddly charm and wit.

The lightweights and cheery bantams out of the way, it is traditional for the drum-roll and trumpets to usher in two heavyweights to top the bill. To that appealingly gifted young writer Gideon Haigh has fallen the difficult task of attempting to emulate the late Benny Green's memorable and classic compilations of *Wisden*. Haigh is up to the challenge. A heavyweight job in every meaning, **Endless Summer: 140 years of Australian cricket in Wisden** makes for any Frindalling scholar's holiday, a spot-on indipper in the McGrath class. Haigh nobly salutes the three young Poms, all in their twenties, the Pardon brothers (whose Cricket Reporting Agency, founded in 1880, dramatically cemented *Wisden's* pre-eminence). "At a time when Australian visits to England were still regarded with some severity, as intrusions marring the more congenial contours of

A familiar image, but one that retains the power to shock: Bert Oldfield is felled by a short ball from Harold Larwood. From *Bodyline Autopsy* by David Frith.

county cricket, the Pardons relished them." Thus, in a way, was *Wisden* the first sponsor of the Ashes' unending parade.

As with any *Wisden* and a couple of hours to kill, seemingly un-considered pebbles of trivia can enjoyably be turned up and transformed into rare nuggets on almost every page. Here, like the great Green before him, Haigh does it for you. For instance, on page 426 is revealed that when the touring Australians of 1890 played Oxford University, a student fieldsman, Malcolm Jardine, was blamed for the Dark Blues' defeat. "Had Jardine accepted a chance of running Turner out before the Australian had scored, the colonial side might have been out for less than 110," snorted the Almanack of 1891. Oxford were beaten, and in fact *Wisden* cruelly laboured the boob, and its whole report turned on "the mistake by Jardine", as indeed did the match. Could it just be that the young prospective lawyer Malcolm grew up to harbour dark thoughts about Australians – and even the idea of some sort of revenge on them – and, when the time came, to imbue his Oxford lawyer and cricketing son, Douglas, with an equal and vengeful dislike?

If only Haigh's condensed *Wisden* had been published, say, a year earlier – then David Frith would surely have picked up such a nice paternal lead and run with it for his triumphant and masterly 70th anniversary **Bodyline Autopsy: the full story of the most sensational Test cricket series, England v Australia 1932-33**. Come to think of it, *Malcolm Jardine Did It: Father Inspires Bodyline Reprisals* would be a snappier title all right. Anyway, I fancy that is the only scrap of forensic evidence – valid for either prosecution or defence – which the diligent detective Frith has missed with his beady historian's eye. If this book has been waiting three-score-and-ten years to be written, then the English-born Aussie Frith, I warrant, has been waiting almost as long to write it.

As well as research, the book is full of outstanding and rare pictures. Nobody could possibly have done either job better. Down the years Frith has interviewed just about everybody alive who played their part on that fevered stage, or around it. With the lead player, villain and hero in turn, Douglas Jardine himself, who died in 1958... well, it seems Frith has spoken to everyone who ever met him or, if not, has stored their quotes and cuttings by the deskful. The biographer Nigel Nicolson has suggested that "historians who have access to all the records know much more about the battle than the participants". Quite so in this case. As Frith's fittingly ringing opening deposition has it: "The day has come. With the death of Sir Donald Bradman in February 2001 all the 1932-33 Test cricketers and umpires and newspaper-men, and almost all of the spectators too, have now departed this life. No more argument. No more first-person recollections. The chronicle is complete."

Then, wise advocate, a telling pause, followed by the questions: "Or is it? Indeed, will it ever be?" All the evidence now, however, points to this relishable, climactic, and unputdownable anniversary chronicle securely fastening the tin lid once and for all on the whole extraordinary episode which has so irresistibly intrigued and roused a constituency far outside the boundaries of cricket for fully 70 years. Particularly enlightening here is how Bodyline caused as much aggro within the teams as between them – the sectarian divide among the home XI had some Celts thinking the Protestant Bradman as much a cowardly funk as Jardine suspected while, for his part, the latter was utterly despised by some of his own – "I feel I should like to kill him," Gubby Allen wrote home. The political self-serving machinations of the cricket authorities on both sides would also beggar belief if the same sort of thing had not lamentably been going on fully 70 winters later. The Anglo-Australian Frith presents no conclusion or judgment, just allows his meticulously detailed evidence to speak for itself. To be sure, no historian, ever, need bother again with Bodyline. Which is a mercy, I suppose – as well as striking testament to Frith's exhilarating scholarship. *Bodyline Autopsy* by David Frith is *Wisden*'s book of the year.

Frank Keating retired from The Guardian *in 2002 after more than 40 years as a sportswriter*

BOOKS RECEIVED IN 2002

- Quotations are taken from *Wisden Cricket Monthly* and selected by Emma John. Titles without comments were not reviewed in *WCM*.
- Most titles are available from Sportspages, Caxton Walk, 94–96 Charing Cross Road, London WC2H 0JW (tel: 020 7240 9604; e-mail: london@sportspages.co.uk) and Barton Square, St Ann's Square, Manchester M2 7HA (tel: 0161 832 8530; e-mail: manchester@sportspages.co.uk).
- Titles from the Association of Cricket Statisticians (ACS)/Sport in Print are available from 3 Radcliffe Road, West Bridgford, Nottingham NG2 5FF (tel: 0115 945 5407; e-mail: acs@cricket.org).

GENERAL

John Barclay **The Appeal of the Championship** Sussex in the Summer of 1981 Foreword by the Rt Rev. Lord Sheppard of Liverpool (Fairfield Books, 17 George's Road, Fairfield Park, Bath BA1 6EY, £14) *Reviewed on preceding pages*

Michael Baws **Triple Glory** The Chronological History of the Triple Century, 1876–2000 (Michael Baws and Cricket Lore Ltd, 22 Grazebrook Road, London N16 0HS. Limited edition of 501; £30) "Better to pick out a batsman and find the innings than ploughing through each description."

Dickie Bird **Dickie Bird's Britain** Photographs by Derry Brabbs (Hodder & Stoughton, £20)

George Cooper **& Hitler Stopped Play** Cricket and War at Lyminster House, West Sussex (1931–1946) (Vanguard Press, Sheraton, Castle Park, Cambridge, £7.99, paperback) "A mix of family, social, war and cricket history."

Mike Coward **The Chappell Years:** Cricket in the '70s (ABC Books, $A49.95, with accompanying video)

Nico Craven **County Cricket's Castaways** Foreword by Michael Henderson Illustrations by Frank Fisher (published by the author, The Coach House, Ponsonby, Seascale, Cumbria CA20 1BX, £9, paperback)

Christopher Douglas and Andrew Nickolds **The Word of Pod** The collected *Guardian* columns of Dave Podmore (Methuen, £6.99, paperback) "Douglas and Nickolds have created one of the great comic characters of the past 20 years, whose writings deserve to be quoted at length."

Chris England **Balham to Bollywood** (Hodder & Stoughton, £12.99) "Fascinating and funny tale of India's two great obsessions."

David Frith **Bodyline Autopsy** The full story of the most sensational Test cricket series: Australia v England 1932-33 (Aurum Press, £20; a limited deluxe edition is available at £145 plus £5 p&p from Bodyline Books) *Reviewed on preceding pages*

Paddy Gaffikin **Kiwis on the Common** 50 Years of the London New Zealand Cricket Club (Tasman Publications, 53 The Cliff, Brighton, East Sussex BN2 5RF, no price given)

Ramachandra Guhar **A Corner of a Foreign Field** The Indian History of a British Sport (Picador, £20) *Reviewed on preceding pages*

Sujoy Gupta **Seventeen Ninety Two** A History of The Calcutta Cricket & Football Club (Calcutta CFC, ccfc1792@vsnl.net, £18)

Gideon Haigh **Many a Slip** A Diary of a Club Cricket Season (Aurum Press, £7.99) "A collection of Haigh's very funny columns for the *Guardian*... after a while the sheer weight of anecdotage makes your head swim but Haigh is superb on the nitty gritty of the game."

Peter Hargreaves **Cricket Conscience** (published by the author, Skovdiget 1, 2880 Bagsværd, Denmark, no price given, paperback)

Dean P. Hayes **England Cricket Legends Since 1946** Foreword by Fred Titmus (Sutton Publishing, £12.99)

Andrew Hignell **Rain Stops Play** Cricketing Climates Foreword by John Kettley Introduction by Christopher Martin-Jenkins (Frank Cass Publishers, Crown House, 47 Chase Side, Southgate, London N14 5BP, £42.50, £17.50 paperback) "Hignell's excellent volume should be required reading in both dressing-room and press box... a history of cricket with a strong geographical bias."

Nick Newman, in *The Word of Pod*.

Lynn McConnell **The First Fifty** New Zealand Cricket Test Victories 1956 to 2002 Foreword by Martin Snedden (HarperSports, $NZ39.95)

Ashley Mallett **Lords' Dreaming** The Story of the 1868 Aboriginal Tour of England and Beyond (Souvenir Press, £18.99) "Mallett's too-subjective social commentary and fondness for irrelevancies strikes an amateurish tone."

Michael Manley and Donna Symmonds **A History of West Indies Cricket** (André Deutsch, £19.99) "When the authors write about matches the style is unadventurous. When they turn their attention to individual heroes they come alive. The message is largely joyful and upbeat; this is a story that anybody would be proud to tell and happy to read."

Neil Marks **Great Australian Cricket Stories** (ABC Books, $A24.95, paperback)

Jim Maxwell, comp. **The Ashes from Bodyline to Waugh** 70 years of the ABC Cricket Book (ABC Books, $A27.95, paperback)

Wim Neleman and Harry Oltheten Nelson on the Board 111 years of Dutch cricket history (in Dutch; Paperware; available from Wepneleman@zonnet.nl, €29.50 + p&p)

E. T. Smith **Playing Hard Ball** A Kent county cricketer's journey into big league baseball (Little, Brown, £16.99) *Reviewed on preceding pages*

ANTHOLOGY

Michael Parkinson **Michael Parkinson on Cricket** Illustrated by John Ireland (Hodder & Stoughton, £14.99)
Reviewed on preceding pages

AUTOBIOGRAPHY

Mike Atherton **Opening Up**: My Autobiography (Hodder & Stoughton, £18.99) *Reviewed on preceding pages*

David English **Mad Dogs and the Englishman** (Virgin, £18.99)

Merv Hughes **Dear Merv** (Allen & Unwin, paperback, £10.99) "A surprising and wholly wonderful book… [this compilation of letters sent to Hughes throughout his career is] that extraordinary thing in cricket publishing, a genuinely original idea. It has a freshness almost all other cricket books lack."

Waqar Hasan with Qamar Ahmed **For Cricket and Country** Foreword by Hanif Mohammad (Cricketprint, 219 The Forum, Clifton, Karachi, Pakistan, £14.99) "Pakistan's entry into Test cricket against India and their historic 1954 victory over England are covered in detail."

Garry Sobers **My Autobiography** (Headline, £18.99) "A solid and thorough account – at the fifth attempt it ought to be… Unfortunately, simple philosophies do not make for big books."

Steve Waugh **Captain's Diary 2002** (Harper Sports, £14.99) "Here's me with Michael Johnson, me with Boris Becker. You get the idea. Waugh talks earnestly and movingly in his ninth diary – although it verges on the cringingly sentimental."

BIOGRAPHY

Keith Booth **The Father of Modern Sport** The Life and Times of Charles W. Alcock Foreword by Rt Hon. John Major (Parrs Wood Press, £16.95, €30)

Mike Colman and Ken Edwards **Eddie Gilbert** The True Story of an Australian Cricketing Legend (ABC Books, \$A29.95, paperback)

Christopher Douglas **Douglas Jardine** Spartan Cricketer (Methuen, £17.99) "A terrifically readable biography, it sparkles with wry humour."

Gulu Ezekiel **Sachin** The Story of the World's Greatest Batsman (Penguin Books India, Rs 250, paperback) "Ezekiel struggles to offer much insight into the batting phenomenon."

Alan Hill **Brian Close: Cricket's Lionheart** (Methuen, £17.99) *Reviewed on preceding pages*

James Knight **Mark Waugh** The Biography Foreword by Allan Border (Collins Willow, £18.99) "[Waugh is] a man clearly horrified by the notion of someone writing a book about him. It does not make for much of a story, with banal clichés and superfluous horseracing references."

Peter Murray and Ashish Shuka **Sachin Tendulkar: Masterful** (Rupa & Co, £19.99) "Part illustrated, part biography, and fails to satisfy on either level. If a Tendulkar love-in is your thing it might make it on to your coffee table; otherwise it is best left on the shelf."

Norman Rogers **Eric Hollies: The Peter Pan of Cricket** (Warwickshire Cricket Publications, £16.99)

PICTORIAL

Gerald Brodribb **Felix and the Eleven of England** (Boundary Books, 507 Castle Quay, Manchester M15 4NT, £160) "This beautifully produced book of watercolours and delightful diary is a posthumous climax to Brodribb's work."

REFERENCE

Abid Ali Kazi **First-Class Cricket in Pakistan: Volume V 1970-71 to 1974-75** (Limlow Books, £30)

MOST BOOKS BY AUSTRALIAN TEST CRICKETERS

Steve Waugh's latest book, *Captain's Diary 2002*, moves him up to second equal in the pantheon of Australian player-authors.

16	M. H. N. Walker	**5**	D. G. Bradman
10	J. H. W. Fingleton		G. S. Chappell
	S. R. Waugh		W. M. Lawry
9	I. M. Chappell		D. K. Lillee
	K. R. Miller		M. A. Noble
8	R. Benaud		R. W. Marsh
	A. A. Mallett		K. D. Walters

Full-size books of at least 50 pages. Research: Chris Ryan, with thanks to the National Library of Australia archive.

Alan Birkinshaw and David Markham **A Century of Bradford League Cricket** (Bradford League, 01274 676604, £17) "A cherished record for all involved."

Warwick Franks ed. **Wisden Cricketers' Almanack Australia 2002-03** Fifth edition (Hardie Grant, Victoria, \$A49.95; in UK from Penguin Direct, 020 8757 4036, £22.50; abridged pocket paperback, Australia only, \$A14.95) "There is some fancy footwork and hard-hitting contained in its pages… An invaluable partner to the old Yellow Peril."

Jim Ledbetter comp. **First-Class Cricket – A Complete Record 1930** (ACS, £19.50 + £3 p&p)

Rajesh Kumar and Indra Vikram Singh **Peter Murray's World Cup Cricket** (Rupa & Co (New Delhi)/Murray Publishing (Adelaide), R595)

STATISTICAL

Don Ambrose comp. **1877: A Statistical Survey** (ACS, £6)

Don Ambrose comp. **Liverpool & District Cricketers 1882-1947** (ACS, £3)

Philip Bailey comp. **Bangladesh First-Class and One-Day Matches 2000-01** (ACS, £8)

Philip Bailey comp. **First-Class Cricket Matches 1905** (ACS, £15)

Philip Bailey comp. **Sri Lanka First-Class Matches 1999-2000** (ACS, £8.50)

Paul G. Booth **G. Boycott** His Record Innings-by-Innings (ACS, £9.50)

Derek Carlaw **Fred Tate** His Record Innings-by-Innings (ACS, £7.50)

Brian Croudy **Wilfred Rhodes** His Record Innings-by-Innings (ACS, £10.95)

Charles Davis comp. **Test Cricket in Australia 1877–2002** (Limited edition of 334; available from Roger Page, 10 Ekari Court, Yallambie, Victoria 3085, Australia, £50 surface mail, £60 air mail) "Makes the yellow book seem like a carrier of skeletal scorecards."

Peter Griffiths and Kit Bartlett **Jas. Lillywhite, jun.** His Record Innings-by-Innings (ACS, £6.50)

Gerald Hudd **Keith Miller** His Record Innings-by-Innings (ACS, £7.50)

Barry Rickson **Len Hutton** His Record Innings-by-Innings (ACS, £7.50)

Keith A. P. Sandiford **J. D. C. Goddard** His Record Innings-by-Innings (ACS, £7.50)

Peter Griffiths **Ivo Bligh** His Record Innings-by-Innings (ACS, £3)

COUNTIES

Bryan Flinders **Warwickshire County Cricket Club Sketchbook of the 2001 season** (The Cricket Shop at Edgbaston, £9.99, paperback) "The portraits of the supporters provide more pleasure than Flinders's scribbles of Glenn McGrath in what is effectively a glorified fanzine."

Dean P. Hayes **Lancashire Cricket Legends Since 1946** Foreword by Jack Bond (Sutton Publishing, £12.99) "The biographies are statistically based and colourful stories are generally avoided."

Andrew Hignell **Glamorgan Grounds** The Homes of Welsh Cricket (Tempus Publishing, The Mill, Brimscombe Port, Stroud, Gloucestershire GL5 2QG, paperback, £12)

Eddie Lawrence **Somerset CCC: Fifty of the Finest Matches** Foreword by Tony Stedall (Tempus Publishing, paperback, £12)

Andrew Radd **Northamptonshire CCC: Fifty of the Finest Matches** Foreword by David Capel (Tempus Publishing, paperback, £12)

John Wallace **Sussex CCC: 100 Greats** Foreword by Ted Dexter (Tempus Publishing, paperback, £12)

POETRY

David Phillips **Man in the Long Grass: Cricket Poems** Foreword by Mike Selvey (Iron Press, 5 Marden Terrace, Cullercoats, North Shields, Northumberland NE30 4PD, £6) "Fun collection of Housmanesque short poems."

Simon Rae **Caught on Paper: Cricket Poems** (Renn and Thacker Partnership, available from the shop, Warwickshire County Cricket Club, £4.99)

FIRST-CLASS COUNTY YEARBOOKS, 2002

Derbyshire £6, Durham £6, Essex £8, Glamorgan £5, Gloucestershire £5, Hampshire £8, Kent £5, Lancashire £9, Leicestershire £7.50, Middlesex £10, Northamptonshire £9.50, Nottinghamshire £7.50, Somerset £7.50, Surrey £5, Sussex £10, Warwickshire £5, Worcestershire £8, Yorkshire £15. 2003 prices may change. Some counties may add charges for p&p.

OTHER HANDBOOKS AND ANNUALS

Jonathan Agnew, ed. **Benson and Hedges Cricket Year 2002** (Bloomsbury, £20) "A cheese and pickle sandwich of a book – filling, nutritious and comprehensive."

Nauman Bader, ed. **PCB Pepsi Cricket Annual 1999-00** (from Limlow Books, Blue Bell House, 2–4 Main Street, Scredington, Sleaford, Lincolnshire NG34 0AE, £27 inc. p&p in UK)

Philip Bailey comp. **ACS International Cricket Year Book 2002** (ACS, £10.95)

Colin Bryden, ed. **Mutual & Federal South African Cricket Annual 2002** (UCBSA/Mutual & Federal, PO Box 1120, Johannesburg 2000, no price given)

Club Cricket Conference Yearbook 2002 ed. Roger Chown (Club Cricket Conference, 361 West Barnes Lane, New Malden, Surrey KT3 6JF, paperback, no price given)

Bill Frindall, ed. **Playfair Cricket Annual 2002** (Headline, paperback, £5.99)

Les Hatton, ed. **First-Class Counties Second Eleven Annual 2002** (ACS, £4.95)

Il Cricket Italiano 2002 (from Federazione Cricket Italiana, Via S. Ignazio 9, 00186 Roma, no price given)

Irish Cricket Annual 2002 (from Dr E. M. Power, 5 Strangford Avenue, Belfast BT9 6PG or M. J. Ryan, 43 Biscayne, Malahide, County Dublin, £3/€5)

Chris Marshall, ed. **The Cricketers' Who's Who 2002** Introduction by Steve James (Queen Anne Press, paperback, £14.99) "Annual mixture of vital statistics and frankly freakish insight into the minds of our sporting heroes… a cheering read."

Eric Midwinter, ed. **The Official MCC Cricket Annual: 2002 season** (from MCC, Lord's Ground, London NW8 8QN, no price given)

Francis Payne and Ian Smith, ed. **2002 New Zealand Cricket Almanack** (Hodder Moa Beckett, Auckland, no price given)

Jan Whyte, ed. **Zimbabwe Cricket Yearbook 1999-2000 & 2000-2001** (The Stewpot, PO Box A468, Avondale, Harare, no price given)

REPRINTS AND UPDATES

Mihir Bose **A History of Indian Cricket** (Andre Deutsch, £19.99, paperback) "Bose brings to it the labour of a biographer and the incisiveness of a financial analyst... A fair, even representation of a country and a culture."

Michael Dowsett **The Day of "The Demon"** Maldon v C. I. Thornton's XI, 19th June 1878 (from the author, 7 Lambs Close, Kidlington, Oxfordshire OX5 2YD, no price given, paperback)

John Pugh Green **The Tour of the "Gentlemen of Philadelphia" in Great Britain in 1884** by One of the Committee Facsimile edition, with new introduction by Gerry Wolstenholme (Red Rose Books, 196 Belmont Road, Astley Bridge, Bolton BL1 7AR, fax: 01204 597070, e-mail: redrosebooks@btinternet.com, limited de luxe edition of 25, £74.95 inc. p&p, further edition of 175, £23.95 inc. p&p)

Gideon Haigh **The Big Ship** Warwick Armstrong and the Making of Modern Cricket (Aurum Press, £20) "Haigh is a brilliant cricket writer, but long-forgotten Australian disputes don't always make riveting reading."

Arthur Haygarth's/Marylebone Club Cricket Scores and Biographies Volumes X, XI and XII (1867–1868, 1869–1870, 1871–1873) A continuation of Frederick Lillywhite's Scores and Biographies from 1772 to 1854. (Facsimile editions, from Roger Heavens, 2 Lowfields, Little Eversden, Cambridgeshire CB3 7HJ; limited edition of 500, volumes X and XI £55 each inc. p&p, Volume XII £63 inc. p&p)

Alan Hill **The Bedsers** Twinning Triumphs Foreword by Rt Hon. John Major (Mainstream, £7.99, paperback) "An exposition of the remarkable twinness of Alec and Eric... written with great affection."

Simon Rae **It's Not Cricket** A History of Skulduggery, Sharp Practice and Downright Cheating in the Noble Game (Faber, £8.99, paperback) "Extensive analysis of the sport's malpractitioners over the years."

John Wisden's Cricketers' Almanack for 1912, 1913, 1914 and 1915 Facsimile editions (Willows Publishing, 17 The Willows, Stone, Staffordshire ST15 0DE, fax: 01785 615867; e-mail: jenkins@willows17.fsnet.co.uk, £53 inc. p&p in UK, £2 extra overseas postage; £5 extra for facsimile of original hard cloth cover)

Iain Wilton **C. B. Fry** King of Sport (Metro publishing, £12.99, paperback) "Embraces Fry's extraordinary life with a purity of affection that is captivating... exposes the hero as it celebrates him."

PERIODICALS

The Cricketer International (monthly) ed. Peter Perchard (Ridge Farm, Lamberhurst, Tunbridge Wells, Kent TN3 8ER, £3.25)

The Cricketer Quarterly: Facts and Figures ed. Richard Lockwood (The Cricketer International, £3.50)

Cricket Lore (ten per volume, frequency variable) ed. Richard Hill (Cricket Lore, 22 Grazebrook Road, London N16 0HS, £35 per volume)

The Cricket Statistician (quarterly) ed. Philip J. Bailey (ACS, £2, free to ACS members)

The Journal of the Cricket Society (twice yearly) ed. Clive W. Porter (from D. Seymour, 13 Ewhurst Road, Crofton Park, London, SE4 1AG, £5 to non-members) "Consistently entertaining"

The New Ball (Volume Seven): Mind Games ed. Rob Steen (Sports Books Direct, 3 Luke Street, London EC2A 4PX, £9.99 paperback) "Full of original and challenging writing... at times it is arguably too disparate in style."

The Scottish Cricketer (six newspapers per year) ed. Mike Stanger (Scottish Cricket Union, National Cricket Academy, Ravelston, Edinburgh EH4 3NT)

Wisden Cricket Monthly ed. Stephen Fay (The New Boathouse, 136 Bramley Road, London W10 6SR, £3.25. Subscriptions: 01795 414895, e-mail: wisden@galleon.co.uk)

SOUVENIR BROCHURES

Pakistan v West Indies Test and ODI Series at Sharjah 2001-02 (Pakistan Cricket Board, no price given)

Sharjah Cup 2002 (Cricketers Benefit Fund Series, PO Box 88, Sharjah, UAE, no price given)

CRICKET AND THE MEDIA, 2002
TIMES A-CHANGIN'
By TIM DE LISLE

In the early 21st century, the British media were in love with the phrase "this is the new that". Brown was the new black, comedy was the new rock'n'roll, most things were the new something else. It became such a cliché that *Private Eye* devoted a corner to the more far-fetched examples. Cricket was seldom proclaimed as the new anything, but in cricket writing, it did apply. *The Times* was the new *Telegraph*.

Since poaching Christopher Martin-Jenkins from the *Telegraph* in 1999, *The Times* has become the paper of record for English cricket, partly on the strength of a promise to increase coverage. At a typical second-division county match, the *Times* correspondent will have 400–500 words a day, his *Telegraph* counterpart barely half that. In 2002, it was not unknown for *Telegraph* writers, hired to sit at Derby or Northampton on £105 a day, to end up being paid a pound a word. Their pieces were not so much reports as haikus.

While the *Times* cricket pages were trying to be the *Telegraph*, the *Telegraph* was trying to be… what, exactly? A magazine? A leader page? A celebrity party? The self-contained daily sports section provided plenty of space, but it filled up very quickly. Thursday's centre spread was billed as "THE MAIN EVENT". But the whole section, every day, was main events. If something big was happening, the *Telegraph* could be relied on to cover it with plenty of verve, display and variety. Derek Pringle, Mark Nicholas and Simon Hughes provided distinctive voices as well as inside knowledge; Simon Briggs added youth and detachment; Martin Johnson and Giles Smith dropped by to crack high-class jokes; Mihir Bose led his sniffer dogs into the corridors of power. But if anything medium-sized happened, the *Telegraph* would barely notice. And did they really believe that Bob Woolmer, the thinking person's coach, made a less rewarding columnist than Phil Tufnell, the drinking person's slow bowler?

The Times's strength in reporting did not extend to comment or analysis, unless Simon Barnes happened to wander in on his way to the football, spraying insight in all directions. Nor did *The Times* show much sense of humour, unless you counted the little series on Yoga For Cricketers: it had more jokes in its cricket reports 30 years ago, when Alan Gibson was elegantly bemoaning the difficulties of changing at Didcot. But the reporting was enough. *The Times* made all the running on the Zimbabwe issue, as Owen Slot, Geoffrey Dean and others showed persistence, decency, the value of contacts and the priceless ability to dig out facts. You needed both papers: *The Times* to tell you what was going on, the *Telegraph* to explain how, why, whether it was a good thing, and what Michael Parkinson's dad would have had to say about it.

You also needed *The Guardian*, for unexpectedly similar reasons to the *Telegraph*. In far less space, *The Guardian* managed more wit and colour and humanity than the big two, and their World Cup team had four voices that sang in Mike Selvey, David Hopps, Tanya Aldred and Rahul Bhattacharya, as well as the inimitable, at times indistinguishable, celebrity pairing of Dave Podmore (a parody) and Ronnie Irani (a real person).

The best cricket paper, however, was none of these. It was the *Sunday Telegraph*, which held three aces: Nasser Hussain's weekly diary (far more vivid and revealing than Steve Waugh's in the *Sunday Times*); Mike Atherton, fearless as he was at the crease, but playing more shots; and, above all, Scyld Berry, who is the most compelling writer on the game at the moment because he is the most astute reader of it. While daily reporters have to churn out so much that they finish a series as jaded as the players, Berry is the Sunday writer par excellence, thinking hard from Tuesday onwards and serving up a meal with enough nutrients to last all week. Always a gifted analyst, he now gets scoops too: in March 2003 he revealed that Hansie Cronje, a *bête noire* from the moment he was exposed, had had more than "a century of bank accounts", most of them untaxed and in the Cayman Islands.

Berry became a chief cricket correspondent in his early twenties. If he were starting out now, he might never have been given the chance.

There are various ways to get into cricket writing in England. You can do a post-graduate course, or bombard the local paper with reports from the village green. You can go on an obscure tour in the hope that a big story breaks (Bangladesh win match, perhaps). You can apply for work experience at Wisden or Hayters' news agency. Or you can bowl fast-medium for Middlesex.

In the 1980s, Mike Selvey became cricket correspondent of *The Guardian*. In the 1990s, Simon Hughes became a leading columnist, on *The Independent* and then the *Telegraph*. But neither made quite the leap made in 2002 by a man with a red face, a dry wit and size-13 boots. One day in May, Angus Fraser was taking the new ball as Middlesex captain; the next he was pecking at a laptop as cricket correspondent of *The Independent*.

Middlesex took it well and got on with the job of winning promotion. The hacks were not so easy-going. Sports editors had been signing up players as columnists, ghosted or otherwise, for years, but for some journalists this case took the biscuit. They were like the county pros of 50 years ago, seething with resentment when the amateurs swanned into the team in July. The dismay might have bubbled up into a public outcry

THE
Daily Telegraph
Friday, November 8, 2002

$1*
Including GST AM

ASHES HUMILIATION

IS THERE ANYBODY IN ENGLAND WHO CAN PLAY CRICKET?

Can't decide

Can't continue

Can't catch

Can't catch

MISERY AT THE GABBA:
PAGES 4,5

TONS OF TALENT:
SEE SPORT

Ouch: Australia's media prove as merciless as their cricketers. *Picture courtesy of* Sydney Daily Telegraph.

had Fraser not been so well liked. Michael Henderson called Fraser "the highest-paid apprentice in history", which was a good line but a bit rich, since Henderson had started this chain of events himself by leaving the *Telegraph* cricket correspondentship for a roving brief on the *Daily Mail*. The *Telegraph* then poached Derek Pringle from *The Independent*, which swooped for Fraser. Of the big four broadsheets, *The Times* was now the only one left with a cricket correspondent who had not been a Test cricketer.

As a rule of thumb, the more Tests a writer has played, the worse he writes. Men with 100 caps are much more likely to become good commentators than good writers. The best player-writers are those who never made the Test team, such as Peter Roebuck: all those winters that the stars of his generation were on tour with England, Roebuck spent on the *Sydney Morning Herald*, learning the art of reading the game from 120 yards, amid a clatter of keyboards and a sizzle of gossip, and converting gut-feelings into prose that bears no imprint of these pressures.

For a man with a distinguished playing career, Fraser started very promisingly. To some extent, everyone turned out to be right. Fraser showed more skill and elbow grease than the critics expected; but he was in at the deep end, and a lot of his energy had to be devoted to not sinking. In a typically honest piece in *Wisden Cricket Monthly*, he admitted that the job was far more demanding than he had realised.

You don't hear players turned TV commentators saying that, but perhaps they should. Atherton moved straight into the Channel 4 box and fitted in effortlessly, combining salty opinions with an underplayed presence that made some of his colleagues look like the Smarmy Army. But Channel 4 v Sky was no contest. Sky's coverage is greatly appreciated in winter because it's all we've got, but the commentary is dreary, which is a crime in tellyland and especially in cricket, with its frequent lulls and hidden depths.

The line-up is unchanging and largely ungiving. The only flashes of humour and warmth come from David Lloyd; the only great vocalist is Michael Holding. Bob Willis, who always has trenchant views, delivers them in a tone which reduces them to whingeing obviousness. Ian Botham has become a highly professional operator, but his manner when England are losing is that of the big boy in the playground who has to express disdain for anyone of normal size (I'm larger than life, so there). And he is in danger of making the journey from free-spirited genius to stubborn old thing. At Melbourne, after Stuart MacGill had gone for 11 off an over, the cameras showed him trotting off to the boundary with hundreds of gloating Poms bowing and chanting "Warnie! Warnie!" Paul Allott pointed this out. "They probably think he's here," said Botham, missing the point like Fred Trueman in his pomp.

One of the elders of televised sport, Sir Paul Fox, wrote in the *Telegraph* in 2002 that cricket was now seen as a minority sport by the broadcasters. Channel 4, a minority channel in terms of style and content, stages it with intelligence and flair. Sky, a minority channel in terms of reach, handles it with grim predictability. Cricket is a gift to every medium – newspapers, radio, television, internet – yet the channel which carries more of England's Test matches than any other, and which has just had a World Cup all to itself, manages to make it mundane. While grateful for Sky's millions, the game is entitled to expect more.

Tim de Lisle, editor of this year's Wisden, *writes a cricket column for* The Independent.

CRICKET ON THE INTERNET
A MARRIAGE IS ANNOUNCED

By ALASTAIR McLELLAN

The main story in this area involved John Wisden and Co., so this piece was commissioned from an independent writer. Alastair McLellan, editor of Health Service Journal *and author of several cricket books, covered the CricInfo story for* The New Ball *(Vol 6).*

The internet could have been invented for cricket. A game taking place in discrete moments – a wicket, a boundary, a bouncer – but spreading over a whole day is perfect for a medium that can capture those instants in real time, review them within minutes, and then allow them to be debated by fans and experts alike. Throw in a white-collar audience with computers on their desks and a packed international schedule taking place in many time zones, and the internet's ability to keep followers in touch with the game is unparalleled.

When 2002 began, it was still early days for the boldest experiment yet by a cricket website – the decision by Wisden.com to launch a subscription service. For most of the year, an intriguing talking point was whether Wisden.com would merge with CricInfo. The biggest cricket website was talking to the one with the most purchasing power; the two most famous names in cricket publishing were thinking about becoming one.

Wisden.com was the most ambitious venture undertaken by the company since the launch of this book in 1864. Wisden had been approached by leading internet businesses during the dotcom boom of the late 1990s, and chose to set up a joint site with *The Guardian*, Cricket Unlimited, which proved popular and respected but far from unlimited as it had no database. In 2000, Wisden were approached by a sports agency, Quintus, and formed a joint venture to create an alternative to the CricInfo leviathan. The new site was launched in August 2001, and the full service, including 139 years of the Almanack's articles and match reports, was in place by December.

Wisden's approach was to combine its huge archive, linked into specially written player pages, with match reporting that aimed to deliver newspaper quality at web speed. The timing would be a particular advantage during England tours of the subcontinent or Australasia, when the morning papers could be 24 hours behind the action. The result was coverage which was both sophisticated and impassioned, with a classy design and an overall quality that was a million miles from the bland, scrappy editorial on other cricket sites.

Rather than compete with CricInfo's popular ball-by-ball commentary, Wisden opted for a rapidly updated match bulletin, along with an atmospheric piece from the ground, an expert view from an ex-player and the Wisden Verdict on the day's defining moments. A statistical strand called Wisden 20:20 told readers just how rarely Glenn McGrath had strayed on to leg stump, and Nasser Hussain's openness with the media was cleverly exploited by signing him up for the Captain Calling column, usually delivered a couple of hours after the close, which often provided exclusive insights. During busy periods over the English winter, content was being added 20 hours in every 24 by an editorial team of eight in London and six (also producing *Wisden Asia Cricket* magazine) in Mumbai.

Such a rich menu of opinion, analysis, reportage and statistics did not come cheap, but Wisden Online's management were confident cricket lovers would pay for it. From December, when the India–England Test series began, Wisden charged £25 for a year's access. Not much for the riches on offer – but a giant leap for the internet, where short but powerful traditions held that virtually all editorial content, including CricInfo's, was available free.

Wisden.com had set itself the ambitious target of attracting 30,000 subscribers in 2002, but come the end of England's tour of New Zealand in March it was only able to claim 1,000. Some blamed the lack of marketing to British cricket fans, others the wisdom of an offer based so heavily on an old-media model. All agreed that the price had been set too high, especially for those not used to paying UK or US prices.

In March, the management suddenly cut costs by scaling back the service and making half of the London editorial staff redundant, including the editor, Tim de Lisle. It was a move greeted with rage by those working on the site and bewilderment by some subscribers. Why had Wisden.com pulled the plug so quickly after investing so much time and money? Why had Wisden apparently surrendered the chance to establish themselves as cricket's voice of authority on the internet?

A partial answer lay in a deal brokered during the first few months of 2002. Wisden.com had started offering video coverage of Indian cricket through a deal with the rights holder, the Indian national broadcaster Doordarshan. A pay-per-view video service began during the India–England one-day series in January and – amid Freddie Flintoff's shirt-twirling heroics – twice found 1,000 customers willing to pay £10 a game. This appeared to the management to offer a more lucrative way forward. In November 2002, they abandoned the yearly subscription, merely asking readers to register before they enjoyed what was still, under the determined editorship of Steven Lynch, a consistent service.

While Wisden licked its wounds, troubles were mounting at CricInfo, the world's most popular single-sports website, whose awesome record in attracting users was matched only by the debts it had built up.

CricInfo was born in 1993, the brainchild of a young British scientist, Dr Simon King. Stranded at the University of Minnesota, King used the fledgling internet to cure his homesickness by creating a site which allowed him to follow Middlesex and England from afar. His ferocious determination attracted others who shared his obsessive commitment to making CricInfo the online home of the game. The world's cricket fans, especially expatriate Indians, flocked to the site. In 2000, CricInfo launched as a commercial operation on the back of a US$37.5 million investment which valued it at US$150 million. It was, in the words of the *Financial Times*, "one of the biggest, sexiest dotcoms".

A year of craziness followed in which CricInfo spent money like water and even ended up sponsoring the County Championship. But the internet bubble had burst and CricInfo's investors were getting nervous. In 2001, in a foreshadowing of Wisden.com's sudden switch of strategy, the backers demanded that costs were cut and more money made. Simon King, who had fallen out with his fellow directors, found himself sidelined, and a few months later he resigned.

CricInfo's battle-scarred team struggled on, constantly searching for ways to make their huge traffic pay. In 2002, they added four different betting services to the site, upgraded the online equipment and video shop, and introduced a "global" mobile-phone score update service. They also introduced a subscription of their own, CricInfo Plus, which did not rope off an area of the site (a labour-intensive business, requiring a restructuring) but charged $12 a year for faster access to pages that could be clogged by their own popularity, especially when India were playing. About 5,000 users paid up, but the company was still only just breaking even: not much use if you have debts of more than £1.5 million.

CricInfo's approach was far removed from that of Wisden.com, but mutual need was about to force them together. CricInfo needed investment, and dotcoms were about as attractive to commercial investors as a trip to Harare. Wisden.com had fewer worries about money – thanks to the wealth of Wisden's owner, Sir Paul Getty – but with an audience five per cent CricInfo's, it was in danger of sliding into cyber-obscurity, which would have been a sad fate for a site bearing cricket's most venerated brand.

Talks began in the autumn, and concluded in late February 2003 with Wisden purchasing a controlling stake in CricInfo for a sum that it agreed not to disclose, although speculation appeared in the papers. The new company, Wisden CricInfo, pledged to combine the "editorial flair" of Wisden with the "extraordinary breadth" of CricInfo. It did not, however, plan to spend much money.

The biggest challenge was likely to lie in maintaining the character of two very distinctive sites with sometimes conflicting values. A Wisden editorial railing against the evils of match-fixing may seem a little incongruous next to an offer to take your pick from four betting services.

Equally, CricInfo's approach of covering every international match could clash with Wisden's more choosy approach, although the management stressed that the policy remained the same – to cover what the site could afford. And then there are the two readerships, overlapping but plainly not identical. In the run-up to the World Cup, Wisden's core users would have been on tenterhooks over England's agonising about Zimbabwe, while the majority of CricInfo's vast audience would have been more exercised about the sponsorship row over the Indian players' contracts.

Wisden CricInfo hoped to turn two struggling businesses into a profit-making one, by cutting running costs and exploiting the combined strengths of the two sites to produce a more compelling draw for advertisers and users alike. Advertising, betting and content syndication would provide revenue streams, but subscription was also expected to play a part.

It is video and audio content which the punter is most used to being asked to pay for. And it is here that the internet may finally deliver fully on its promise to provide truly interactive coverage of the game.

Each recent World Cup has driven more cricket fans to the internet to keep track of their team. CricInfo's growth underwent huge spurts in 1996 and 1999, propelling it into the major investment league, spicing up the sponsorship and internet-rights markets and driving the early development of online video and audio services. The 2003 World Cup did not provide the explosion of internet video expected by some, because the television broadcasters with rights to the American, British and Australian markets were careful to make sure their deals included internet rights. But the CricketNext site was able to offer live coverage of the tournament to those living in 96 countries outside cricket's prime markets for around £150.

Video streaming through the internet has been restricted by three factors – the shortage of broadband access outside the USA, which makes the pictures slow and jerky; the inflated price of video rights, and the high costs of supplying the feed. However, broadband access is now becoming more widespread in the UK and some other westernised countries, while still a long way off in India. The price of video internet rights has collapsed from the dotcom peak and the economics have been further transformed by a combination of new editing software, slicker billing mechanisms and a dramatic reduction in the cost of streaming (broadcasting to the computer screen). It now appears possible to charge a dollar a day for video coverage and achieve a healthy margin – as long as people sign up.

The viewing experience could also be refashioned, thanks to affordable editing software. Both CricInfo and the US broadband broadcaster Willow TV have experimented with an interactive scorecard – simply click on a "4" and see Hayden bully Caddick through the covers, click on a "W" and see England take their revenge. Wisden offered a twist on this by presenting a timeline which picked out other pivotal moments, such as disputed umpiring decisions. All this could be reviewed as many times as the viewer wished. The day is not far off when one fan will be able to email another with a clip of Brett Lee bowling Brian Lara.

Video subscription packages of the future are likely to offer a mix of live coverage and interactive highlights. Wisden CricInfo is attempting to secure video archive footage from broadcasters, which would allow users to purchase, for example, a package of Tendulkar's finest performances or Sri Lanka's 1996 World Cup campaign. The broadcasters, of course, do not intend to be left behind and Sky are offering an interactive service alongside their TV coverage.

Cricket coverage on the internet is about to enter a new age of interactivity. Video offers the most exciting opportunity (for those with broadband), but there are others. During the Ashes and the World Cup you could see a cult in the making in the over-by-over text commentaries provided by the *Guardian Sport* site, which incorporated edited e-mails from users to create a kind of global banter – *Test Match Special* meets a chatroom.

It's becoming clear that there is often little to stop internet sites offering unofficial audio coverage, with the commentators following the game on television as Wisden.com did during the World Cup. As with video, the technology now makes this kind of service much more cost-effective and feasible. What price a dozen internet commentary services all following the same match but reflecting the tastes, biases and languages of their audiences?

CRICKET EQUIPMENT, 2002

By NORMAN HARRIS

Ordinary folk with bright ideas continue to try to spark a revolution in cricket-bat design. However, nibbling at the edges of bat technology is what most are doing – literally so in the case of the Woodworm Company. The name stems from the discovery in a family garage of an old bat that had been attacked by woodworm. Joe Sillett, a Surrey club cricketer, and his father thought it a shame to throw the bat away, so they started shaving off the affected areas, which happened to be the upper edges of the blade. In the process, they discovered a new variation on the weight-transfer logic first developed by Gray-Nicolls with the Scoop.

As Joe Sillett argued, any runs made from the upper edges of the bat are risky and unintended, so it is no bad thing to reduce the possibility of inadvertent contact. "But," he added, "the main idea is to transfer weight into the hitting zone." The Wand, as the new bat is called, has indentations – suggesting a squeezed-in waist – just beneath the shoulder of the blade. They certainly catch the eye, as Russel Arnold found when he used the bat towards the end of the Sri Lankans' 2002 tour. Jack Russell, for one, was not slow to comment: "I think you need as much wood as you can get on it, mate." But caustic comments did not prevent Andrew Flintoff and Muttiah Muralitharan also signing up for Woodworm.

Other innovators from outside the established stable of bat-makers were not so fortunate: as ever, their problem was finding a leading player not tied to a sponsorship deal. That handicap has held back the Angle Drive, designed three years ago by the former New South Wales and Queensland batsman, Len Richardson. Another bat that emerged by accident (this one as a result of a handle half-breaking, angling the blade back an inch or so), the Angle Drive is said to keep the ball on the ground when driving, and to have helped grade players in Sydney make huge scores. Having managed to patent the concept, Richardson is hoping to buy out the contracts of some of Sri Lanka's leading batsmen.

Another entrepreneur trying to overcome deeply held ideas about what bats should look like is John Cook, a designer from Sussex. Though he had little previous involvement in cricket, he has dreamt up a radical way to protect batsmen's hands: instead of a cage or scabbard arrangement fitted to the handle or top of the bat – which was not acceptable to the MCC when proposed some 10 years ago – Cook's solution was to lengthen the face of the blade, creating a protected space for the bottom hand. The MCC agreed it was legal because they felt it didn't alter the shape of the bat (some might query that) and because the laws don't limit the length of the blade. However, despite the fact that players lament hand injuries, protection doesn't seem to be their overriding concern – otherwise they would wear protective devices in the nets. So Cook knows that his big challenge is to persuade batsmen to use his strange-looking invention not just for protection, but because it plays better.

Another initiative that came out of left field – from a manufacturer of canoe paddles and baseball bats – really *was* revolutionary, but proved too hot for the MCC to handle. It is now more than 23 years since Dennis Lillee had his infamous tantrum at Perth, hurling his aluminium bat to the ground and prompting a law which decreed that bats must be made of wood. But since then, technology has moved on, and Ainsworth, the manufacturer in question, have exploited their paddle-making technology to produce a baseball bat which convinced the sport's authorities in America that its carbon-Kevlar-polyurethane composite could mimic the feel and sound of ash.

Ainsworth made the same pitch – no doubt referring to willow rather than ash – to the MCC's Cricket Committee. The assistant secretary, Tony Dodemaide, a former Australian Test player, even wielded it to good effect in the nets. The key benefits of the bat were that it would deliver more power, and that each blade would be as good as any other. But the committee decided that these advantages weren't obvious enough to warrant abandoning the "Lillee Law". The guardian of the laws decreed that "cricket is a natural game that should continue to be played with natural materials." While not necessarily disagreeing with the latter statement, one might wonder what makes cricket a more "natural" game than, say, golf, tennis or football.

Meanwhile, Gray-Nicolls claimed to have made a step-change in design by producing bat handles featuring inserts made from either titanium or carbon. Both are designed to transfer more energy from bat to ball. Will carbon one day make its way into the blade? It seems more likely that the splice is the point at which the law-makers have determined to make their stand.

Finally, wicket-keeping gloves. In 2000, the laws were changed to prevent the material between thumb and forefinger forming a pouch, like a baseball glove. But questions soon arose about the extent of the band of non-elastic material which could still be used for support. While television close-ups suggested that some gloves were still not conforming, official checking seems to have been lax. But an email from a Channel 4 viewer, querying the gloves used by England and India during their Test series, finally prompted an inspection.

On the next morning, Mike Procter, the match referee, was filmed examining the gloves of Ajay Ratra and a clearly unhappy Alec Stewart. What emerged was that, while both men's gloves may have been legal, there was considerable scope for creative interpretation of the laws. A meeting of involved parties, including manufacturers, took place at Lord's four days later, and it is hoped that new definitions will be approved by the MCC in May 2003. With any luck, a few more match referees will then start to pay attention.

CRICKET AND THE WEATHER, 2002
440,000 GALLONS
OF WATER

By PHILIP EDEN

Rain figured all too prominently during the 2002 English season. The lowest point probably came in early August when the Cheltenham & Gloucester semi-final between Yorkshire and Surrey at Headingley was delayed by three days before the ground was finally declared playable on August 4.

We often hear TV weather presenters talking about a heavy thunderstorm dropping, say, an inch (or 25mm) of rain in an hour, but this scarcely conveys a true idea of the volume of water involved. Repeated cloudbursts between July 30 and August 4 deposited 5.1 inches (130mm) of rain – about two months' worth – in some parts of West Yorkshire. Given that one inch of rain delivers 22,600 gallons of water per acre, and that the playing area at Headingley is almost four acres, we can calculate that approximately 440,000 gallons – or two million litres – fell on the ground that week. That is an awful lot of water.

In complete contrast to the previous year, the 2002 season began in mid-April under blue skies and in the midst of a remarkable rainless period which had begun three weeks before. The rains arrived with a vengeance on April 26 and were never far away between then and the middle of August, although there were drier interludes, notably June 15–29 and July 12–22. The second half of August was mostly dry, while September was the driest for many years, which was just as well as county matches continued longer into the autumn – up to September 22 – than ever before.

The depressing mood was exacerbated by the shortage of sunshine between early-May and mid-August, and the gloomy skies were particularly persistent in the North-East and the Midlands, including Northamptonshire, Leicestershire, Derbyshire, Nottinghamshire, Yorkshire and Durham. At Leeds, the total sunshine between May 1 and August 31 was only 479 hours, some 30 per cent below the normal amount, and the figure for Nottingham was 511 hours, also 30 per cent below local average.

The Test matches escaped the worst of the weather until the very last. The First Test against Sri Lanka at Lord's began on a day of blue skies and warm sunshine, the temperature peaking at 27°C, completely out of character with the rest of May. Similarly out of step was the last-day washout of the final Test against India at The Oval, the only day with significant rain in London during the whole of September.

In 2003, Chester-le-Street gets its first Test match, beginning on June 5. The schedulers have more than the weather in mind when the Test dates are arranged, but any reader who lives within Albert Trott's throwing range of the North Sea knows that north-east England can be a wickedly cold place in late spring. North-easterly winds are most common at this season, and, with not much between Durham and the Urals, these winds bring relentless grey cloud, drizzle, and afternoon temperatures below 10°C (50°F) in late May and early June. Conversely, Old Trafford often gets its best weather in the first half of the season.

The meteorological statistics, averaged over England and Wales, for the 2002 cricket season, were as follows:

	Average max temperature (°C)	Difference from normal for 1971–2000	Total rainfall (mm)	% of normal	Total sunshine (hours)	% of normal
April (second half)...	14.7	+1.7	45	159	93	112
May	16.0	+0.4	97	150	185	92
June..............	18.5	−0.2	62	95	170	82
July	20.5	−0.4	91	130	172	90
August	21.4	+0.7	74	86	169	95
September (first half).	20.1	+1.3	38	93	91	126
2002 season	**18.8**	**+0.4**	**407**	**117**	**880**	**95**

Each summer has slightly different regional variations, although in most years northern and western counties are cooler, cloudier and damper than those in the east and south. The *Wisden* weather index (I) allows us to compare the summer county by county. The index incorporates rainfall amount and frequency, sunshine and temperature in a single figure. The formula for the index is:

$$I = 20 (Tx - 12) + (S - 400)/3 + 2Rd + (250 - R/3)$$

Tx is the mean maximum temperature, S is the total sunshine, Rd is the number of dry days, and R is the total rainfall, covering the period May 1 to August 31. The formula may look intimidating, but it is designed so that temperature, sunshine, rainfall frequency and rainfall amount each contribute approximately 25 per cent of the total. The final index ranges from zero for the theoretical worst possible summer to 1,000 for the theoretical best. The score for an average summer ranges from 525 at Chester-le-Street and 530 at Old Trafford to 670 at Lord's and 675 at The Oval. Broadly speaking, an index over 650 indicates a good summer, whereas one below 500 clearly describes a poor summer. Values for each county for the summer of 2002 against the average are given below, but please note that the standard reference period has changed this year from 1961–90 to 1971–2000 in accordance with normal meteorological practice.

	2002	Normal	Variation		2002	Normal	Variation
Derbyshire	436	580	−144	Middlesex.	589	670	−81
Durham	427	525	−98	Northamptonshire . .	484	615	−131
Essex.	564	640	−76	Nottinghamshire . . .	446	590	−144
Glamorgan	499	555	−56	Somerset	547	620	−73
Gloucestershire . . .	534	595	−61	Surrey	594	675	−81
Hampshire	587	645	−58	Sussex.	569	665	−96
Kent	640	655	−15	Warwickshire	520	555	−35
Lancashire	438	530	−92	Worcestershire	556	615	−59
Leicestershire	456	585	−129	Yorkshire	459	560	−101

All counties experienced a poor summer, and in the north and east Midlands it was particularly bad thanks to an abundance of rain and a remarkable shortage of sunshine. Warwickshire's rating was appreciably closer to its long-term average than were those of other Midland counties, while Kent's relatively good score illustrated how they escaped the repeated heavy downpours which afflicted most other parts of England and Wales. Temperatures were generally close to the long-term average: had it been a cool summer as well as a wet and a dull one, the index would have been abnormally low. Averaged nationally, last season's index of 506 showed it was the poorest summer since 1987, and a whopping 126 points below 2001. In the last 100 years there were only 17 worse summers.

The *Wisden* weather index since 1992, together with the best and worst on record, is as follows:

1992	556	**1995**	777	**1998**	565	**2001**	632
1993	573	**1996**	663	**1999**	637	**2002**	506
1994	651	**1997**	601	**2000**	556		

Highest 812 in 1976   **Lowest** 309 in 1879

A full list of summers between 1900 and 1999 appeared in Wisden 2000, *page 21.*

Philip Eden is weather expert for BBC Radio Five Live, and the Daily *and* Sunday Telegraph.

CRICKETANA, 2002

By GORDON PHILLIPS

Cricketana rarely features in the national press, but the 1868 Aboriginals proved irresistible. The first Australian cricket team, skilled equally with bat, ball and boomerang, fascinates both authors and collectors, and a rediscovered archive of photographs of the individual players and team groups, plus an unpublished 96-page scorebook kept by their manager Charles Lawrence, proved the outstanding feature of the year. Other items, including a gilt metal fob watch in the shape of a cricket ball presented to Lawrence, were offered as a lot by Christie's (Melbourne) and realised over £37,000.

Rivalling the Aboriginals for prominence was the Kennington Common brooch, sold by Duke's of Dorchester for £32,000. There was speculation that this tiny eight-star design, made up of clusters of diamonds, with a centrepiece watercolour of a cricketer in period costume standing in front of the famous Horns Tavern, and dated 1788, might well hint at south London origins of the Marylebone Cricket Club. Another top earner was a one-page codicil to the agreement for the 1861-62 English tour of Australia, signed by all the tourists, which raised over £21,000; a letter from their captain, H. H. Stephenson, to the firm of Spiers and Pond, thanking them for their sponsorship, brought £7,050.

Except for highlight pieces, the dominance of Christie's, Sotheby's and Bonham's is being eroded by the large, visually appealing and meticulously compiled catalogues from Tim Knight and Trevor Vennett-Smith. Anthemion Auctions and Mullock Madeley are smaller, but have their fair share of nuggets, as does eBay on the internet. From such sources poured the ceaseless flood of cricketing passports, glass bottles, belt buckles, photographs, advertising posters, philatelic covers, teddy bear figurines, beer mugs, crested bags, signed attire, toast racks, flick-books, bats (large, small and signed), sheet music, games and jigsaws.

The 30th anniversary catalogue of the dealer J. W. McKenzie proved an eye-opener, however, and bookmen looked nostalgically at his 1972 prices. A complete set of *Wisden* (1864–1971) was on offer at £750 – that would now exceed £40,000. An 1864 edition alone can command £6,345, while the scarce 1875 volume approaches £5,000. Connoisseurs of vintage books delighted in a 1906 souvenir booklet recounting Trumper's Queensland tour (£720). Eight elusive pamphlets containing the "Surrey Poet's" poems, 1896–1903, were estimated at £120 but climbed to £2,250, while *St Ivo and the Ashes* (Melbourne, 1883) soared over estimate to £1,450. Modern books attract interest only if covered in signatures, but earlier privately printed booklets from Irving Rosenwater – when obtainable – look promising, as do scarce county yearbooks.

It was a year of caps, contracts and correspondence. In Australia, Keith Miller's 1953 Test cap realised almost £14,000. Elsewhere, a cap worn by Ian Chappell in 1974-75 came in at £3,500, with Lindwall's making £3,600, Border's £2,800 and Colin McDonald's £2,000. Hadlee's cap went for £1,400, and even Meyrick Pringle's green-cloth South African Test cap of 1992 closed at £950. Original Australian players' contracts from 1930 and 1934, itemising

functions and monies to be paid, can attract attention at £5,000. It has yet to be seen what the Australian management's Sun Tzu-inspired Test briefing, signed by Steve Waugh, might command.

Plum Warner memorabilia included a framed letter from 10 Downing Street (from Stanley Baldwin) offering a knighthood, along with a Middlesex medal (1903), cigarette case, photo albums, menu cards and two wartime 78 rpm records. Bandwagon attempts to capitalise upon the Bradman name have been curtailed but two of his letters, written in 1977, sold in Australia for £6,700. A two-page letter from his Bodyline rival, Douglas Jardine, penned to Rockley Wilson in 1952 and discussing the covering of wickets, sold for £750. Other interesting letters included one from a "Nottinghamshire Cricketer" dated 1879 about the Lord Harris tour of Australia, featuring a betting scandal and on-field assaults on members of the team, and Herbert Sutcliffe's correspondence with Lord Hawke on a controversial argument in 1938.

Inevitably, memorable bats and balls also held sway. Wally Hammond's bat, used to bludgeon his world record 336 not out off hapless New Zealanders and signed by the 1933 MCC tourists, found a new home, as did a hat-trick ball spun by Doug Wright in 1933 (£600). The infamous ball which Mike Atherton allegedly rubbed in soil from his trouser pocket, and which later became the property of the ICC referee Peter Burge, sold for £1,600.

Perennial favourites such as signed postcards and scorecards more than held value. Typical examples of the former were Bobby Peel (£380), Warner (£300) and W.G. (£330), while a rare scorecard from the Glamorgan–

Where there's muck, there's brass: after television spotted Mike Atherton delving in his pocket for dirt, the referee, Peter Burge, hung on to the ball. It would later fetch £1,600. *Picture by Patrick Eagar.*

Nottinghamshire match in which Sobers clobbered six successive sixes off Malcolm Nash, estimated at £50–£80, reached £260.

Christie's and Sotheby's remain conduits for fine cricketing art, but few originals appeared. A vivid mid-19th portrait of a waiting batsman – with a match in progress behind him, the fielders wearing top hats – sold at Christie's for £11,750. Another, a silhouette-type conversation piece showing three children in profile, the boy holding a bat, netted £8,225. In a more contemporary vein, a gouache and watercolour by LeRoy Neiman entitled "Running In", signed and dated 1961 and inscribed "Lord's Cricket Ground", was a valuable addition for modern art collectors. With prints, fashions change and hardy perennials *Vanity Fair* and Chevallier Tayler lithographs struggle a little, but nevertheless *Vanity Fair* images of Warner (£570) and Dalmeny (£600) find buyers. The last of the set, dated 1913, and the rarest, the languid-looking E. W. Dillon, still commands £2,700. The portfolio of 44 prints of *The Empire's Cricketers* by Tayler, in the original folder with original subscription form, has halved in value, to perhaps £1,200.

No survey is complete without reference to the mega-favourites: Bodyline material and ceramics/metalwork. Anything related to Ashes tours talks serious money, especially when blended with the Jardine–Larwood–Bradman confrontation. Signed pictorial menu cards from the vessels *Orantes* and *Orford* can sail past £1,000, while a large panoramic photograph of the 1932 Sydney Test also exceeds £1,000. Also from the Bodyline era, a rare blotter for the Savings Bank of Australia, depicting the home players, raised £500, a "Gripu" Gallery souvenir booklet £680 and an MCC itinerary of the tour

£720. Earlier menus signed by 13 of the 1909 Australian tourists touched £600 and signatures of the immortal 1905 team (including Trumper) on headed paper fetched £3,200. An Ashes silver Vesta case with enamelled panel of a kangaroo batsman and a lion wicket-keeper, presented to Wilfred Rhodes in 1899, was a snip at £1,800.

Rows of ceramic jugs with transfer prints of cricket's immortals never lose their appeal, a particular favourite being Jack Hobbs at £400 plus. Doulton Lambeth ware still reigns supreme, as does the "Black Boy" series of tableware. But, remembering the poor survival rate of 18th-century material, the *nonpareil* was a Staffordshire creamware jug from the 1790s, decorated in Liverpool and showing the (subsequently much-reproduced) transfer print of the match played at Lord's for a thousand-guinea wager between the Earls of Winchelsea and Darnley in 1793. The jug's acquisition, for £6,000, had a well-known Wiltshire collector punching the air with glee.

Gordon Phillips died on February 24, 2003, shortly after filing this copy to Wisden. He had reported on Cricketana since the 1999 edition.

WORDS OF WISDEN COMPETITION

Readers of *Wisden 2002* were invited to estimate the number of words (excluding all numbers) it contained. The closest guess came from Robert Hutchison of Winchester, who won books to the value of £1,000, provided by Sportspages. His estimate was 681,383, just 543 higher than the actual total of 680,840.

CRICKET SOCIETIES, 2002

By Murray Hedgcock

The worldwide cricket society movement, like the game itself, continues to adjust, seeking to link yesterday and today with a concern for tomorrow, as it provides a forum for lovers of the game.

The Council for Cricket Societies, the umbrella body for the movement, now spreads the message through its own website (www.cricket.org/link_to_database/SOCIETIES/ENG/CCS), with further sites for 26 of the 34 affiliated societies – they include groups in Australia, New Zealand, South Africa, Zimbabwe and India. Council's winter meeting at Trent Bridge welcomed reports of growing memberships in several societies, responding to concern that the bulk of members are older cricket lovers, who have the greatest interest in the history of the game. Several societies are celebrating their 40th anniversaries, reflecting the surge in the movement in the 1960s. Leicestershire cricket lovers hope to form a new society, reviving a group which in 1969 was a founder member of council. There are hopes that societies will be formed in Kent and Wales – two cricketing bases which surprisingly lack such organisations.

Societies continue to record difficulty in attracting current players to address meetings, unless for a substantial fee – usually well out of reach of groups whose annual subscriptions range mostly from £5 to £10 a year, but who often are the most loyal of county supporters and volunteer workers. Speakers tend to be either retired players or members of the game's support group of administrators, umpires, coaches, groundsmen, scorers, cricket writers and broadcasters, and specialists such as cricketana collectors. But as societies wryly note, the county player in his benefit year often finds it suddenly appropriate to attend – inevitably boosting attendances, especially among younger enthusiasts.

It was appreciated that the captain of Warwickshire, Michael Powell, was the speaker at the Trent Bridge meeting. He ranged over his career and the county game with refreshing honesty – including the admission that he could not truly explain just what made his former coach, Bob Woolmer, so effective in that role. Warwickshire continue to be loyal supporters of the society movement, having sponsored council for some years and traditionally hosting the annual meeting at Edgbaston. Council president is Tom Graveney, whose distinguished Test and county background adds to the authority of the movement. He has always supported it in a fashion societies wish other England stars would copy.

One current England player who did make his contribution was Craig White, an appreciated speaker at the Northern Cricket Society in Leeds. Two notable veterans heard with due attention were Sir Garfield Sobers at High Peak, and Fred Trueman at the 50th-anniversary meeting of the Cricket Society of Scotland.

One of the newer societies, the Durham and North East branch of the Cricket Society, was able to call on a local international, Paul Collingwood.

This is a flourishing group with attendances at the Riverside ground averaging nearly 100. Nottingham, which also gets around 100 for its Trent Bridge meetings, was addressed in typically lively fashion by the local MP and cricket enthusiast, Kenneth Clarke.

The best-supported society continues to be Lancashire & Cheshire, which has the advantage of meeting at Old Trafford, and regularly draws 200 members or more. It celebrates its 50th anniversary this year with a special lunch.

The secretary, Barry Rickson, from Lancashire & Cheshire, has been made a life member on standing down after 11 years. The new secretary is Robert Wood of the busy High Peak Society in Derbyshire. He can be found at 2 Jodrell Road, Whaley Bridge, High Peak SK23 7AN; telephone: 01663 732866; e-mail: haltim@btopenworld.com.

Murray Hedgcock has written about cricket for many years, principally for The Australian. *He represents the Australian Cricket Society on the Council of Cricket Societies.*

INDEX OF UNUSUAL OCCURRENCES

DIRECTORY OF BOOKSELLERS AND AUCTIONEERS

BOOKSELLERS

AARDVARK BOOKS, Larwood, 47 Melbourne Way, Lincoln, Lincolnshire LN5 9XJ. Tel/fax: 01522 722671. Peter Taylor specialises in *Wisdens*, including rare hardbacks and early editions. Quarterly catalogues sent on request. *Wisdens* purchased. Cleaning, gilding and restoration undertaken.

ACUMEN BOOKS, Nantwich Road, Audley, Staffordshire ST7 8DL. Tel: 01782 720753; fax: 01782 720798; e-mail: wca@acumenbooks.co.uk; website: www.acumenbooks.co.uk. Everything for umpires, scorers and others; textbooks, equipment, etc, all for import or export.

TIM BEDDOW, 66 Oak Road, Oldbury, West Midlands B68 0BD. Tel: 0121 421 7117; fax: 0121 422 0077; e-mail: timbeddowsports@btinternet.com; website: www.edgbastonbooks.co.uk. Large stock of cricket/football books, programmes and signed material. Items purchased. Send SAE for catalogue. Stall at Thwaite Gate, Edgbaston, every first-team match.

BODYLINE BOOKS, 150a Harbord Street, London SW6 6PH. Tel: 020 7385 2176; fax: 020 7610 3314; e-mail: info@bodylinebooks.com; website: www.bodylinebooks.com. Largest stock of *Wisdens* in London (Fulham) with copies always available for many years. Catalogues by post or e-mail to your desk. Private premises, by appointment only.

BOUNDARY BOOKS LTD, 507 Castle Quay, Manchester M15 4NT. Fax: 01925 858237; e-mail: mike@boundary-books.demon.co.uk. Publishers of high-quality limited-edition books and specialists in rare and hard-to-find books and memorabilia, particularly from great collectors of the past.

IAN DYER CRICKET BOOKS, 29 High Street, Gilling West, Richmond, North Yorkshire DL10 5JG. Tel/fax: 01748 822786; e-mail: iandyer@cricketbooks.co.uk; website: www.cricketbooks.co.uk. *Wisdens*, books, annuals, magazines, programmes, scorecards, benefit brochures, tour guides. Use keyword/keydate search; shopping basket; automatic postage calculation; pay by credit card with full security.

K. FAULKNER, 65 Brookside, Wokingham, Berkshire RG41 2ST. Tel: 0118 978 5255. Book room open by appointment. E-mail: kfaulkner@bowmore.demon.co.uk; website: www.bowmore.demon.co.uk. Cricket books, *Wisdens*, memorabilia bought and sold. Also at Gloucestershire CCC shop, Nevil Road, Bristol BS7 9EJ.

GRACE BOOKS AND CARDS (TED KIRWAN), 3 Pine Garden, Oadby, Leicester LE2 5UT. Tel: 0116 271 6363 (weekdays) and 0116 271 4267 (evenings and weekends). Second-hand and antiquarian cricket books, *Wisdens*, autographed material and cricket ephemera of all kinds. Now also modern postcards.

*J. W. McKENZIE, 12 Stoneleigh Park Road, Ewell, Epsom, Surrey KT19 0QT. Tel: 020 8393 7700; fax: 020 8393 1694; e-mail: jwmck@netcomuk.co.uk; website: www.mckenzie-cricket.co.uk. Specialists in antiquarian second-hand books, particularly *Wisdens*, and memorabilia. Established 1969. Catalogues sent on request. Publishers of cricket books. Shop premises open regular business hours.

ROGER PAGE, 10 Ekari Court, Yallambie, Victoria 3085, Australia. Tel: (03) 9435 6332; fax: (03) 9432 2050; e-mail: rpcricketbooks@unite.com.au. Dealer in new and second-hand cricket books. Distributor of overseas cricket annuals and magazines. Agent for Association of Cricket Statisticians and Cricket Memorabilia Society.

*PENGUIN DIRECT. Tel: 020 8757 4036. New *Wisdens* for 1996–2003 and the first five editions of *Wisden Cricketers' Almanack Australia* available from Wisden's mail-order supplier. Prices from £12.50, including p&p.

RED ROSE BOOKS, 478 Bolton Road, Darwen, Lancashire BB3 2JR. Tel: 01254 776767; e-mail: redrosebooks@btinternet.com; website: www.cricketsupplies.com/books. Specialist cricket booksellers and publishers. Catalogue sent on request.

WILLIAM H. ROBERTS, The Crease, 113 Hill Grove, Salendine Nook, Huddersfield, West Yorkshire HD3 3TL. Tel/fax: 01484 654463; e-mail: william.roberts2@virgin.net; website: www.williamroberts-cricket.com. Second-hand/antiquarian cricket books, *Wisdens*, autograph material and memorabilia bought and sold. Catalogues sent on request.

ST MARY'S BOOKS & PRINTS, 9 St Mary's Hill, Stamford, Lincolnshire PE9 2DP. Tel: 01780 763033; e-mail: cricket@stmarysbooks.com; website: www.stmarysbooks.com. Dealers in *Wisdens*, second-hand, rare cricket books and *Vanity Fair* prints. Also search service offered.

CHRISTOPHER SAUNDERS, Kingston House, High Street, Newnham-on-Severn, Gloucestershire GL14 1BB. Tel: 01594 516030; fax: 01594 517273; e-mail: chrisbooks@aol.com. Office/bookroom by appointment. Second-hand/antiquarian cricket books and memorabilia bought and sold. Regular catalogues issued containing selections from over 10,000 items in stock.

*SPORTSPAGES, Caxton Walk, 94–96 Charing Cross Road, London WC2H 0JW. Tel: 020 7240 9604; fax: 020 7836 0104. Barton Square, St Ann's Square, Manchester M2 7HA. Tel: 0161 832 8530; fax: 0161 832 9391; website: www.sportspages.co.uk. New cricket books, audio and video tapes, including imports, especially from Australasia; retail and mail-order service.

STUART TOPPS, 40 Boundary Avenue, Wheatley Hills, Doncaster, South Yorkshire DN2 5QU. Tel: 01302 366044. Our 120-page plus catalogue of cricket books, *Wisdens*, booklets, brochures and county yearbooks is always available.

*WILLOWS PUBLISHING CO., 17 The Willows, Stone, Staffordshire ST15 0DE. Tel: 01785 814700. *Wisden* reprints 1879, 1885, 1900–1919 and 1941–1945. Send SAE for prices.

MARTIN WOOD CRICKET BOOKS, 1c Wickenden Road, Sevenoaks, Kent TN13 3PJ. Tel/fax: 01732 457205. Send first-class stamp for annual catalogue listing by subject: *Wisdens*, Annuals, Biographies, Tours, Histories, Counties, Fiction and also Autographs. Established 1970.

AUCTIONEERS

*CHRISTIE'S, 85 Old Brompton Road, South Kensington, London SW7 3LD. Tel: 020 7752 3355; e-mail: lmclark@christies.com. Christie's highly successful cricket memorabilia auctions have been held every year since the inaugural MCC Bicentenary sale in 1987. For enquiries, please contact Lucy Clark.

MULLOCK MADELEY, The Old Shippon, Wall-under-Heywood, Church Stretton, Shropshire SY6 7DS. Tel: 01694 771771; website: www.mullockmadeley.co.uk. Mullock Madeley hold specialist sporting memorabilia auctions. For details, please either visit our website or telephone our offices.

*T. VENNETT-SMITH, 11 Nottingham Road, Gotham, Nottinghamshire NG11 0HE. Tel: 0115 983 0541. Auctioneers and valuers. Twice-yearly auctions of cricket and sports memorabilia. The cricket auction is run by cricketers for cricket-lovers worldwide.

*DOMINIC WINTER BOOK AUCTIONS, Specialist Book Auctioneers & Valuers, The Old School, Maxwell Street, Swindon, Wiltshire SN1 5DR. Tel: 01793 611340; fax: 01793 491727; e-mail: info@dominicwinter.co.uk; website: www.dominicwinter.co.uk. Twice-yearly auction sales of sports books and memorabilia, including *Wisdens*.

Asterisks indicate businesses that have display advertisements elsewhere in the Almanack. See Index of Advertisements for details.

DIRECTORY OF CRICKET SUPPLIERS

COMPUTER DATABASES

FBSS LTD, Windsor, Little Stambridge Hall Lane, Rochford, SS4 1EN. Tel: 01702 530060; fax 01702 542988; e-mail: info@e-cricket4all.com; website: www.e-cricket4all.com. The Cricket Organiser software package saves club administrators time and money. Accumulate information, statistics, player details, team selection, results and much more – all for under £40.

GORDON VINCE, 5 Chaucer Grove, Camberley, Surrey GU15 2XZ. E-mail: gordon@gvince.demon.co.uk. Cricket Statistics System used worldwide to produce widest range of averages/statistics, from Test to village level. Available with extensive range of up-to-date databases of worldwide matches.

CRICKET COACHING/ACADEMIES

DURHAM SCHOOL, Durham DH1 4SZ. Tel: 0191 386 4783; e-mail: enquiries@ durhamschool.co.uk. Cricket festivals and professional cricket coaching for young people aged 8–18 years. Residential and non-residential courses run during Easter and summer. Course director: Mike Hirsch.

LAHORE CRICKET ACADEMY, Khursheed Begum Road, Muridke, Near Lahore, Pakistan. Tel: 00 92 42 7992211-16; www.cricnews.com.

CRICKET EQUIPMENT

DUKE SPORTSWEAR, Unit 4, Magdalene Road, Torquay, Devon TQ1 4AF. Tel/fax: 01803 292012. Test-standard sweaters to order in your club colours, using the finest yarns.

EXITO SPORTS COMPANY, Griffiths House, Griffiths Avenue, Birchwood Park, Cheshire WA3 6GH. Tel: 01925 818900; fax: 01925 657688; e-mail: info@exitosports.com; website: www.exitosports.com. Manufacturers and suppliers of quality cricket clothing and leisurewear to first-class and minor counties, amateur clubs, schools and colleges.

FORDHAM SPORTS LTD, 81/85 Robin Hood Way, Kingston Vale, London SW15 3PW. Tel: 020 8974 5654; e-mail: fordham@fordhamsports.co.uk; website: www.fordhamsports.co.uk. Cricket equipment specialist with largest range of branded stock in London at discount prices. Mail order worldwide. Free catalogue.

GUNN & MOORE, 119/121 Stanstead Road, Forest Hill, London SE23 1HJ. Tel: 020 8291 3344; fax: 020 8699 4008; e-mail: assist@unicorngroup.com. Gunn & Moore, established in 1885, is the world's most comprehensive provider of cricket bats, equipment, footwear and clothing.

NOMAD PLC. Tel: 01858 464878. Nomad manufacture coffins to suit all levels. The new "International" range has aluminium edging on all sides, wheels, and is available in ten different colours.

STUART & WILLIAMS (BOLA), 6 Brookfield Road, Cotham, Bristol BS6 5PQ. E-mail: info@bola.co.uk; website: www.bola.co.uk. Manufacturer of bowling machines and ball-throwing machines for all sports. Machines for recreational and commercial application for sale to the UK and overseas.

CRICKET TOURS

ALL WAYS SPORTS TRAVEL, 7 Whielden Street, Old Amersham, Buckinghamshire HP7 0HT. Tel: 01494 432747; fax: 01494 432767; e-mail: sales@all-ways.co.uk; website: www.all-ways.co.uk. Specialist tour operators to the South Pacific. Cricket supporters' tours to Australia and New Zealand.

BARBADOS JOURNEYS. Tel: 0870 708 2010; e-mail: barbadosjournies@wwj.uk.com. Specialist tour operators to the Caribbean. Schools, club sides, benefit tours, testimonials, intensive coaching academy – founders of Sir Garry Sobers School Tournament.

GULLIVERS SPORTS TRAVEL, Fiddington Manor, Tewkesbury, Gloucester, GL20 7BJ. Tel: 01684 293175; fax: 01684 297926; e-mail: gullivers@gulliversports.co.uk; website: www.gulliversports.co.uk. Specialist tours for supporters, schools and clubs. Europe, worldwide and festivals. All standards. ABTA, ATOL and IATA bonded. ECB official tour operator.

RIVERDALE HALL HOTEL, Bellingham, Near Hexham, Northumberland NE48 2JT. Tel: 01434 220254; fax: 01434 220457; e-mail: iben@riverdalehall.demon.co.uk. Country House Hotel with cricket pitch, indoor pool, golf nearby, real ales, "Gold Plate" Les Routiers restaurant. Up to 20 visiting teams annually. Cocker family's 25th year.

RUMSEY TRAVEL, 26a Main Street, Barton-under-Needwood, Staffordshire DE13 8AA. Tel: 01283 712233; fax: 01283 716546; e-mail: info@rumseytravel.com. Specialists in tailor-made travel. Supporters tours to all major sporting events worldwide. Annual pro-am cricket festival in Barbados. PCA official travel company. ATOL bonded.

SUN LIVING, 10 Milton Court, Ravenshead, Nottingham, NG15 9BD. Tel: 01623 795365; fax: 01623 797421. Worldwide specialists in cricket tours for all levels and ages, plus our ever-popular supporters' tours. ABTA and ATOL bonded.

SUNSPORT TOURS & TRAVEL, Hamilton House, 66 Palmerston Road, Northampton NN1 5EX. Tel (UK): 0870 742 7014; fax (UK): 01604 631628; e-mail: paul@sunsport.co.uk; website: www.sunsport.co.uk. High-quality tailormade tours to Kenya, South Africa, West Indies and sub-continent. Clients include counties, clubs, colleges, senior/prep schools. ATOL bonded. Contact Barry Dudleston or Paul Bush.

GIFTS, MEMORABILIA AND LIMITED-EDITION PRINTS

BUCKINGHAM COVERS, Church House, 136 Sandgate Road, Folkestone, Kent CT20 2BY. Tel: 01303 850672; fax: 01303 850687. Autographed cricket photographs and covers. If you collect memorabilia, make sure we know your details so we can send you our FREE colour magazines.

CELEBRITY COLLECTABLES, 30 Pinewoods Avenue, Hagley, Stourbridge, West Midlands DY9 0JF. Tel: 01562 883908; e-mail: derek.gallimore@which.net. Sporting autographs on postcards, photographs and philatelic covers. Contact us for your free catalogue.

THE CRICKETER MAIL-ORDER SHOP, Ridge Farm, Lamberhurst, Tunbridge Wells, Kent TN3 8ER. Tel: 01892 893020; e-mail: shophelp@cricketer.com; website: www.cricshop.com. A complete range of replica clothing, both UK and international, books, DVDs and videos, and wide variety of cricket gifts and memorabilia. Call for free catalogue.

DD DESIGNS, 62 St Catherine's Grove, Lincoln, Lincolnshire LN5 8NA. E-mail: ddprints@aol.com. Specialists in signed limited-edition prints. Official producer of *Wisden's* "Cricketers of the Year" sets, and other art portfolios.

JOCELYN GALSWORTHY, 237 Chelsea Cloisters, Sloane Avenue, London SW3 3DT. Tel: 020 7591 0698; mobile: 07885 542652; fax: 01983 873741; website: www.jocelyngalsworthy.co.uk. Limited-edition cricket prints signed and numbered by the artist. Original cricket paintings for sale. Free catalogue.

SPORTING-GIFTS.COM LTD, 6 Arundel Close, Chippenham, Wiltshire SN14 0PR. Tel: 01249 464975; website: www.sporting-gifts.com. For a wide selection of cricket and sports gifts, figures, prints, games, books and videos. Free catalogue.

PAVILION AND GROUND EQUIPMENT

AUTOGUIDE EQUIPMENT LTD, Stockley Road, Heddington, Near Calne, Wiltshire SN11 0PS. Tel: 01380 850885; fax: 01380 850010; e-mail: sales@autoguide.co.uk. Manufacturers of the world-famous Auto-Roller for cricket wickets. We now supply "bolt-in" Re-Power packs that include power steering for older rollers.

E. A. COMBS LIMITED, Quantum House, London E18 1BY. Tel: 020 8530 4216. Pavilion clocks for permanent and temporary siting. Wide choice of sizes and styles to suit any ground.

COURTYARD DESIGNS, Suckley, Worcestershire WR6 5EH. Tel: 01886 884640; fax: 01886 884444; e-mail: enquiries@courtyarddesigns.co.uk. Classic wooden pavilions made to the highest standards from weatherboard and clay tile roofs. Full colour brochure and testimonials.

EUROPEAN TIMING SYSTEMS, Oldbury-on-Severn, Bristol BS35 1PL. Tel: 01454 413606; fax: 01454 415139; e-mail: sales@eurotiming.co.uk; website: www.eurotiming.co.uk. ETS manufacture a range of standard and custom-built electronic scoreboards. These can suit grounds from small to largest. Control inside the scorebox, remotely or by radio.

FSL SCOREBOARDS. Tel: 028 8676 6131; website: www.fsl.ltd.uk. UK-designed and manufactured, FSL offer complete range of electronic scoreboards in portable and self-install kits. Leasing options from less than £60/month.

HUCK NETS (UK) LTD, Gore Cross Business Park, Bridport, Dorset DT6 3UX. Tel: 01308 425100; fax: 01308 458109; e-mail: sales.uk@hucknets.co.uk. Quality knotless nets and cages, mobile and static, sightscreens, scoreboxes, synthetic pitches and covers, mobile and economy layflat, boundary ropes, etc.

JMS CRICKET LTD, Byeways, East Parade, Steeton, West Yorkshire BD20 6RP. Tel: 01535 654520; fax: 01535 657309; e-mail: admin@jmscricket.com; website: www.jmscricket.com. Buy direct from the manufacturer. Mobile covers, flat sheets, bespoke practice facilities, sightscreens, mobile cages, coconut mats and more. We've got cricket covered.

POWEROLL ROLLERS by Power Precision & Fabrication Ltd, Greenhill, Gunnislake, Cornwall PL18 9AS; Tel: 01822 832608; website: www.poweroll.com. Manufacturers of a comprehensive range of grass rollers to suit different budgets and applications.

STADIA SPORTS INTERNATIONAL LTD, 19/20 Lancaster Way Business Park, Ely, Cambridgeshire CB6 3NW. Tel: 01353 668686; fax: 01353 669444; e-mail: sales@stadia-sports.co.uk. Sightscreens, scoreboards (manual and electronic), cages, synthetic wickets and wicket covers.

STUART CANVAS PRODUCTS, Warren Works, Hardwick Grange, Warrington, Cheshire WA1 4RF. Tel: 01925 814525; fax: 01925 831709. Designers, manufacturers and suppliers of flat sheets, mobiles, roller & hover covers – sold throughout the world, including Test and county grounds.

TILDENET LIMITED, Hartcliffe Way, Bristol BS3 5RJ. Tel: 0117 966 9684; fax 0117 923 1251; e-mail: enquiries@tildenet.co.uk; website: www.tildenet.co.uk. An extensive range of equipment… grass germination sheets, ball-stop fencing, mobile practice nets, static nets and frames, sightscreens, layflat, mobile and automatic rain covers, practice netting.

PITCHES (TURF AND NON-TURF)

C. H. BINDER LTD, Moreton, Ongar, Essex CM5 0HY. Tel: 01277 890246; fax: 01277 890105; website: www.binderloams.co.uk; e-mail: sales@binderloams.co.uk. Sole producers of Ongar Loam™ top-dressing for cricket pitches, grass seed, fertilisers etc. Catalogues and quotations on request. Collections available.

BOUGHTON LOAM LTD, Telford Way Industrial Estate, Telford Way, Kettering, Northamptonshire NN16 8UN. Tel: 01536 510515, fax: 01536 510691; e-mail: enquiries@boughton-loam.co.uk; website: www.boughton-loam.co.uk. Boughton Loam offer the full range of cricket loams, grass seeds and fertilisers for construction and maintenance of cricket grounds, also contracting services including Koro "Field Topmaker".

CLUB SURFACES LIMITED, The Barn, Bisham Grange, Marlow, Buckinghamshire SL7 1RS. Tel: 01628 485969; fax: 01628 471944; e-mail: clubsurfaces@tiscali.co.uk. ClubTurf, world-leading non-turf pitch since 1978; top in independent Sports Council tests; 5,500+ installations, including Lord's; suppliers to ICC, ECB, MCC. Contact Derek Underwood for information pack.

FLICX UK LTD, Walltree House Farm, Steane, Brackley, Northamptonshire NN13 5NS. Tel: 07900 883630; tel/fax: 01295 810298; e-mail: flicxuk@flicx.com; website: www.flicx.com. Manufacturers and marketers of the Flicx Match and Coaching Pitches, Brell Bowling Machines, portable nets and coaching aids. We are in the game of portable cricket.

NOTTS SPORT®, Premier House, 18 Mandervell Road, Oadby, Leicester LE2 5LQ. Tel: 0116 272 0222; fax: 0116 272 0617; e-mail: info@nottssport.com; website: www.nottssport.com. When all-round quality performance is a 'must have', cricket centres and clubs throughout the world choose Notts Sport. Clients include ECC and ECB.

PEAK SPORTS LTD, Unit 4, Ford Street, Brinksway, Stockport SK3 0BT. Tel: 0161 480 2502; fax: 0161 480 1652. Agents for Wimbledon Unreal Grass pitches. Glue to concrete, nail to tarmac or unroll on gym floor. Guaranteed ten years. Write for brochure. Installed at Radley, Winchester, Manchester GS, etc.

SOCIETIES

CRICKET MEMORABILIA SOCIETY. Honorary Secretary: Steve Cashmore, 4 Stoke Park Court, Stoke Road, Bishops Cleeve, Cheltenham, Gloucestershire GL52 8US. E-mail: cms87@btinternet.com. For collectors worldwide – magazines, meetings, auctions, speakers, and – most of all – friendship.

TROPHIES AND AWARDS

COLBORNE TROPHIES LTD. Tel: 01225 764101; fax: 01225 762009; e-mail: sales@awards.org.uk. Long-established and reliable suppliers of trophies and awards. Fast mail-order service and discounts available. Free catalogue.

INDEX OF ADVERTISEMENTS

TEST MATCHES, 2002-03

PAKISTAN v AUSTRALIA

First Test: At P. Saravanamuttu Stadium, Colombo, October 3, 4, 5, 6, 7. **Australia won by 41 runs.** Toss: Australia. **Australia 467** (J. L. Langer 72, R. T. Ponting 141, M. E. Waugh 55, S. R. Waugh 31, D. R. Martyn 67, A. C. Gilchrist 66 not out; Shoaib Akhtar three for 51, Saqlain Mushtaq four for 136) **and 127** (M. L. Hayden 34; Shoaib Akhtar five for 21, Saqlain Mushtaq four for 46); **Pakistan 279** (Younis Khan 58, Faisal Iqbal 83, Rashid Latif 66; S. K. Warne seven for 94) **and 274** (Imran Nazir 40, Taufeeq Umar 88, Younis Khan 51, Faisal Iqbal 39; G. D. McGrath three for 38, S. K. Warne four for 94).

This was the first series to be played in two different countries – both neutral venues – after the Tests were moved from Pakistan because of security fears. Australia lost their last five wickets for ten in the first innings, and all ten for 66 in the second. Both Waughs fell to Shoaib Akhtar for ducks, so their third-last Test together mirrored their first competitive game, as seven-year-olds playing for Panania East Hills RSL Under-10s in Sydney's Bankstown district competition, when Mark was out first ball and Steve second. Shoaib took five wickets in eight overs for the second Test running. Pakistan, chasing 316, collapsed from 173 for two.

Second Test: At Sharjah, October 11, 12. **Australia won by an innings and 198 runs.** Toss: Pakistan. **Pakistan 59** (S. K. Warne four for 11) **and 53** (S. K. Warne four for 13); **Australia 310** (J. L. Langer 37, M. L. Hayden 119, R. T. Ponting 44, D. R. Martyn 34; Abdul Razzaq three for 22, Saqlain Mushtaq four for 83).

Pakistan made their two lowest all-out scores in Tests, and the fourth-lowest aggregate by one team (the lowest since 1945-46). Razzaq, top-scorer in the first innings with 21, had to retire hurt on four in the second. Hayden made more runs in his one innings than Pakistan did in the match, the fifth such instance in Tests. It was the 17th Test to be completed in two days and the first involving Pakistan. Steve Waugh, playing his 150th Test, made another duck. General Tauqir Zia, chairman of the Pakistan Cricket Board, offered the president his resignation, which was declined.

Third Test: At Sharjah, October 19, 20, 21, 22. **Australia won by an innings and 20 runs.** Toss: Australia. **Australia 444** (M. L. Hayden 89, R. T. Ponting 150, S. R. Waugh 103 not out, A. C. Gilchrist 34; Waqar Younis four for 55, Danish Kaneria three for 128); **Pakistan 221** (Hasan Raza 54 not out, Saqlain Mushtaq 44; G. D. McGrath four for 41, S. K. Warne five for 74) **and 203** (Hasan Raza 68; G. D. McGrath three for 18, A. J. Bichel three for 43, S. K. Warne three for 56).

Shoaib missed the match through injury. One Waugh secured his place for the Ashes with a hundred; the other played his last international innings, 23 off 33 balls with five fours. Steve Waugh also became the first man to 100 international not-outs (42 in Tests, 58 in ODIs). McGrath reached 400 wickets in his 87th Test and Warne finished the three-match series with 27 at 12.66. Ponting was leading run-scorer with 342 at 85.50. Australia won the series 3–0.

INDIA v WEST INDIES

First Test: At Mumbai, October 9, 10, 11, 12. **India won by an innings and 112 runs.** Toss: India. **India 457** (S. B. Bangar 55, V. Sehwag 147, R. Dravid 100 retired hurt, S. R. Tendulkar 35, V. V. S. Laxman 45, J. Srinath 31; M. Dillon three for 54, M. V. Nagamootoo three for 132); **West Indies 157** (S. Chanderpaul 54; Zaheer Khan four for 41, A. Kumble four for 51) **and 188** (C. H. Gayle 42, W. W. Hinds 40, S. Chanderpaul 36 not out; Harbhajan Singh seven for 48, A. Kumble three for 50).

Sehwag (206 balls) and Bangar (187) put on 201, India's first double-century opening partnership since 1986-87. Dravid scored his fourth consecutive Test hundred, one short of Everton Weekes's record. Harbhajan took his tenth five-for in his 29th Test.

Second Test: At Chennai, October 17, 18, 19, 20. **India won by eight wickets.** Toss: West Indies. **West Indies 167** (C. L. Hooper 35; Harbhajan Singh three for 56, A. Kumble five for 30) **and 229** (W. W. Hinds 61, R. R. Sarwan 78, C. L. Hooper 46; Zaheer Khan three for 23, Harbhajan Singh four for 79); **India 316** (S. B. Bangar 40, V. Sehwag 61, S. R. Tendulkar 43, Harbhajan Singh 37, J. Srinath 39; M. Dillon three for 44) **and 81 for two** (V. Sehwag 33).

West Indies lost their last four wickets for six runs in the first innings, and their last six for 21 in the second. Bangar's 40 occupied 171 balls, Sehwag's 61 just 65. Wavell Hinds pulled off two run-outs to go with his 61. India won the series inside eight playing days.

Third Test: At Kolkata, October 30, 31, November 1, 2, 3. **Drawn.** Toss: India. **India 358** (S. B. Bangar 77, V. Sehwag 35, S. R. Tendulkar 36, V. V. S. Laxman 48, P. A. Patel 47, J. Srinath 46; M. Dillon three for 82) **and 471 for eight** (S. R. Tendulkar 176, V. V. S. Laxman 154 not out); **West Indies 497** (C. H. Gayle 88, W. W. Hinds 100, S. Chanderpaul 140, M. N. Samuels 104; Harbhajan Singh five for 115, A. Kumble three for 169).

Tendulkar made his 31st Test hundred and his fourth score of either 176 or 177. He added 214 for India's fifth wicket with Laxman; Chanderpaul and Samuels added 195 for West Indies' sixth. West Indies avoided defeat in the subcontinent for the first time in 9 Tests since December 1994. India won the series 2–0.

SOUTH AFRICA v BANGLADESH

First Test: At East London, October 18, 19, 20, 21. **South Africa won by an innings and 107 runs.** Toss: Bangladesh. **South Africa 529 for four dec.** (G. C. Smith 200, H. H. Gibbs 41, G. Kirsten 150, J. H. Kallis 75 not out, M. van Jaarsveld 39 not out); **Bangladesh 170** (Habibul Bashar 38, Sanuar Hossain 31, Alok Kapali 35; M. Ntini five for 19) **and 252** (Al Sahariar 71, Sanuar Hossain 49, Khaled Masud 33; D. J. Terbrugge five for 46).

East London became the 85th Test venue. Smith scored 200 in 338 minutes and 287 balls with 25 fours and added 272 for the second wicket with Kirsten, who became the first batsman to score hundreds against all nine other Test nations. Kallis reached 4,000 runs in his 61st Test, becoming the fifth to do the double of 4,000 runs and 100 wickets.

Second Test: At Potchefstroom, October 25, 26, 27. **South Africa won by an innings and 160 runs.** Toss: Bangladesh. **Bangladesh 215** (Hannan Sarkar 65, Al Sahariar 30, Habibul Bashar 40, Alok Kapali 38 not out) **and 107** (M. Ntini three for 37, J. H. Kallis five for 21); **South Africa 482 for five dec.** (H. H. Gibbs 114, G. Kirsten 160, J. H. Kallis 139 not out).

Potchefstroom became the 86th Test venue. Kirsten and Kallis added 234 for the third wicket; Kallis scored a hundred and took five wickets in an innings in the same Test for the second time. South Africa won the series 2–0.

First blood: it's too painful for Andy Caddick and Matthew Hoggard to look as England are demolished for 79 at Brisbane – and Australia go one up. See page 1714. *Picture by Graham Morris.*

AUSTRALIA v ENGLAND

First Test Match

At Brisbane, November 7, 8, 9, 10. **Australia won by 384 runs.** Toss: England.
Close of play: First day, Australia 364-2 (Hayden 186, Martyn 9); Second day, England 158-1 (Trescothick 63, Butcher 51); Third day, Australia 111-2 (Hayden 40, Martyn 40).

Australia

J. L. Langer c Stewart b Jones	32	– c Stewart b Caddick	22
M. L. Hayden c Stewart b Caddick	197	– c and b Giles	103
R. T. Ponting b Giles	123	– c Trescothick b Caddick	3
D. R. Martyn c Trescothick b White	26	– c Hussain b Giles	64
*S. R. Waugh c Crawley b Caddick	7	– (6) c Trescothick b Caddick	12
D. S. Lehmann c Butcher b Giles	30	– (7) not out	20
†A. C. Gilchrist c Giles b White	0	– (5) not out	60
S. K. Warne c Butcher b Caddick	57		
A. J. Bichel lbw b Giles	0		
J. N. Gillespie not out	0		
G. D. McGrath lbw b Giles	0		
B 1, l-b 11, w 1, n-b 7	20	B 3, l-b 5, n-b 4	12

1/67 (1) 2/339 (3) 3/378 (2) 4/399 (4) 492 1/30 (1) 2/39 (3) (5 wkts dec.) 296
5/408 (5) 6/415 (7) 7/478 (6)   3/192 (2) 4/213 (4)
8/478 (9) 9/492 (8) 10/492 (11)   5/242 (6)

Bowling: *First Innings*—Caddick 35–9–108–3; Hoggard 30–4–122–0; Jones 7–0–32–1; White 27–4–105–2; Giles 29.2–3–101–4; Butcher 2–0–12–0. *Second Innings*—Caddick 23–2–95–3; Hoggard 13–2–42–0; White 11–0–61–0; Giles 24–2–90–2.

England

M. E. Trescothick c Ponting b McGrath	72	– c Gilchrist b Gillespie	1
M. P. Vaughan c Gilchrist b McGrath	33	– lbw b McGrath	0
M. A. Butcher c Hayden b McGrath	54	– c Ponting b Warne	40
*N. Hussain c Gilchrist b Gillespie	51	– c Ponting b McGrath	11
J. P. Crawley not out	69	– run out	0
†A. J. Stewart b Gillespie	0	– c Hayden b Warne	0
C. White b McGrath	12	– c Hayden b McGrath	13
A. F. Giles c Gilchrist b Bichel	13	– c Gilchrist b McGrath	4
A. R. Caddick c Ponting b Bichel	0	– c Lehmann b Warne	4
M. J. Hoggard b Hayden b Warne	4	– not out	1
S. P. Jones absent hurt		– absent hurt	
B 2, l-b 8, n-b 7	17	L-b 1, n-b 4	5

1/49 (2) 2/170 (3) 3/171 (1) 4/268 (4) 325 1/1 (2) 2/3 (1) 3/33 (4) 79
5/270 (6) 6/283 (7) 7/308 (8)   4/34 (5) 5/35 (6) 6/66 (7)
8/308 (9) 9/325 (10)   7/74 (8) 8/74 (3) 9/79 (9)

Bowling: *First Innings*—McGrath 30–9–87–4; Gillespie 18–4–51–2; Bichel 23–4–74–2; Warne 26.5–4–87–1; Waugh 4–2–5–0; Lehmann 5–0–11–0. *Second Innings*—McGrath 12–3–36–4; Gillespie 6–1–13–1; Warne 10.2–3–29–3.

Umpires: S. A. Bucknor (West Indies) and R. E. Koertzen (South Africa).
Third umpire: S. J. A. Taufel. Referee: Wasim Raja (Pakistan).

Mark Waugh was dropped after 107 consecutive Tests going back to Old Trafford 1993. Hussain put Australia in, inexplicably. They celebrated by scoring at almost a run a minute all day as Hayden, standing a stride outside his crease, and the more classical Ponting toyed with a nervous attack. The best bowler was Simon Jones, who took the first wicket but was later stretchered out of the series with badly torn ligaments in his knee. England recovered to dominate the second day, taking eight for 128 and threatening a big score themselves as the top five carried on their good form from the home season. But Gillespie shrugged off a niggle to make vital incisions with the second new ball, and England's tail, as feared, began at No. 7. Hayden added a second century, and made 300 in the match. Gilchrist (59 balls) led the charge to the declaration. England then folded like a school team. Vaughan got a poor decision, Crawley was sunk by Butcher, and Stewart (completing his first Test pair) played an authentic cut shot which lodged freakishly in Hayden's chest at slip, but the rest were abject. In front of record crowds for the Gabba, England's last 15 wickets went down for 136. It was the third time in three Tests that Australia had bowled their opponents out in double figures. Stewart finished on the losing side for the 50th time in Tests. The defeat was England's fourth-biggest by runs.

Second Test Match

At Adelaide, November 21, 22, 23, 24. **Australia won by an innings and 51 runs.** Toss: England.
Close of play: First day, England 295-4 (Butcher 22); Second day, Australia 247-2 (Ponting 83, Martyn 48); Third day, England 36-3 (Vaughan 17).

England

M. E. Trescothick b McGrath	35	–	lbw b Gillespie		0
M. P. Vaughan c Warne b Bichel	177	–	c McGrath b Warne		41
R. W. T. Key c Ponting b Warne	1	–	(5) c Lehmann b Bichel		1
*N. Hussain c Gilchrist b Warne	47	–	b Bichel		10
M. A. Butcher c Gilchrist b Gillespie	22	–	(3) lbw b McGrath		4
†A. J. Stewart lbw b Gillespie	29	–	lbw b Warne		57
C. White c Bichel b Gillespie	1	–	c sub (B. Lee) b McGrath		5
R. K. J. Dawson lbw b Warne	6	–	c Gilchrist b McGrath		19
A. R. Caddick b Warne	0	–	(11) not out		6
M. J. Hoggard c Gilchrist b Gillespie	6	–	(9) b McGrath		1
S. J. Harmison not out	3	–	(10) lbw b Warne		0
L-b 7, n-b 8	15		B 3, l-b 4, n-b 8		15

1/88 (1) 2/106 (3) 3/246 (4) 4/295 (2)   342   1/5 (1) 2/17 (3) 3/36 (4)   159
5/295 (5) 6/308 (7) 7/325 (8)   4/40 (5) 5/114 (2) 6/130 (7)
8/325 (9) 9/337 (6) 10/342 (10)   7/130 (6) 8/132 (9)
                                         9/134 (10) 10/159 (8)

Bowling: *First Innings*—McGrath 30–11–77–1; Gillespie 26.5–8–78–4; Bichel 20–2–78–1; Warne 34–10–93–4; Waugh 5–1–9–0. *Second Innings*—McGrath 17.2–6–41–4; Gillespie 12–1–44–1; Warne 25–7–36–3; Bichel 5–0–31–2.

Australia

J. L. Langer c Stewart b Dawson	48		A. J. Bichel b Hoggard	48
M. L. Hayden c Caddick b White	46		J. N. Gillespie not out	0
R. T. Ponting c Dawson b White	154			
D. R. Martyn c Hussain b Harmison	95		B 1, l-b 17, w 7, n-b 18	43
*S. R. Waugh c Butcher b White	34			
D. S. Lehmann c sub (A. Flintoff)			1/101 (2) 2/114 (1) (9 wkts dec.) 552	
b White	5		3/356 (4) 4/397 (3)	
†A. C. Gilchrist c Stewart b Harmison	54		5/414 (6) 6/424 (5)	
S. K. Warne c and b Dawson	25		7/471 (8) 8/548 (9) 9/552 (7)	

G. D. McGrath did not bat.

Bowling: Caddick 20–2–95–0; Hoggard 26–4–84–1; Harmison 28.2–8–106–2; White 28–2–106–4; Dawson 37–2–143–2.

Umpires: S. A. Bucknor (West Indies) and R. E. Koertzen (South Africa).
Third umpire: S. J. Davis. Referee: Wasim Raja (Pakistan).

Driving on: Michael Vaughan beats Andy Bichel, but the Australians had an easier ride with Vaughan's team-mates at Adelaide. *Picture by Graham Morris.*

England lost Giles to a broken wrist and Crawley to a thigh injury; Gough had already flown home without playing a match. Hussain went out to toss not knowing whether Vaughan was fit after a knee scare, but included him anyway. He responded with his third score of 175-plus in five Tests and the highest Test score by an Englishman in Australia since Mike Denness's 188 in 1974-75. Bichel dismissed him when he was brought on for the last over of the first day, a trick he was to repeat 48 hours later by bowling Hussain. England collapsed again, losing seven for 47. When the Australian openers fell in quick succession, England glimpsed parity, but Ponting and Martyn batted them out of the game by adding 242 for the third wicket, mostly in ones and twos: Ponting reched his hundred, his fifth in seven Tests, hitting only four fours. A few of his singles were gifts as Hussain treated Waugh like a tailender, dropping the field back for Ponting. Gilchrist got off the mark with a six, and Hoggard took his first Test wicket in 508 balls since dismissing Bangar at The Oval. After missing the entire Australian innings with a bruised shoulder, Vaughan fell to a wonder catch by McGrath, who ran 20 yards to his left at deep square, threw himself like a frisbee and juggled the ball before clinging on. Vaughan's 177 was the highest score by an England player in an Ashes innings defeat, surpassing Herbert Sutcliffe's 161 at The Oval in 1930. White ended the match with a head-to-head record batting against McGrath of eight runs for five times out. McGrath rose to sixth in the list of Test wicket-takers, passing Wasim Akram's 414.

Third Test Match

At Perth, November 29, 30, December 1. **Australia won by an innings and 48 runs.** Toss: England.

Close of play: First day, Australia 126-2 (Ponting 43, Martyn 20); Second day, England 33-1 (Vaughan 8, Dawson 8).

Sunk: Mark Butcher takes a swipe at the stumps after falling lbw to Glenn McGrath, and England are going under for the third time. The Perth defeat meant the Ashes would stay with Australia. *Picture by Patrick Eagar.*

England

M. E. Trescothick c Gilchrist b Lee	34	– c Gilchrist b Lee	4
M. P. Vaughan c Gilchrist b McGrath	34	– run out	9
M. A. Butcher run out	9	– (4) lbw b McGrath	0
*N. Hussain c Gilchrist b Lee	8	– (5) c Gilchrist b Warne	61
R. W. T. Key b Martyn	47	– (6) lbw b McGrath	23
†A. J. Stewart c Gilchrist b McGrath	7	– (7) not out	66
C. White c Martyn b Lee	2	– (8) st Gilchrist b Warne	15
A. J. Tudor c Martyn b Warne	0	– (9) retired hurt	3
R. K. J. Dawson not out	19	– (3) c Waugh b Gillespie	8
C. E. W. Silverwood c Hayden b Gillespie	10	– absent hurt	
S. J. Harmison b Gillespie	6	– (10) b Lee	5
L-b 2, n-b 7	9	B 8, l-b 5, w 1, n-b 15	29

1/47 (1) 2/69 (3) 3/83 (4) 4/101 (2)   185   1/13 (1) 2/33 (3) 3/34 (2)   223
5/111 (6) 6/121 (7) 7/135 (8)   4/34 (4) 5/102 (6) 6/169 (5)
8/156 (5) 9/173 (10) 10/185 (11)   7/208 (8) 8/222 (10)

In the second innings Tudor retired hurt at 214.

    Bowling: *First Innings*—McGrath 17–5–30–2; Gillespie 17.2–8–42–2; Lee 20–1–78–3; Warne 9–0–32–1; Martyn 1–1–0–1. *Second Innings*—Lee 18.1–3–72–2; McGrath 21–9–24–2; Gillespie 15–4–35–1; Warne 26–5–70–2; Martyn 2–0–9–0.

Australia

J. L. Langer run out	19	J. N. Gillespie b White		27
M. L. Hayden c Tudor b Harmison	30	G. D. McGrath not out		8
R. T. Ponting b White	68			
D. R. Martyn c Stewart b Tudor	71	B 4, l-b 5, n-b 15		24
D. S. Lehmann c Harmison b White	42			
*S. R. Waugh b Tudor	53	1/31 (1) 2/85 (2) 3/159 (3)		456
†A. C. Gilchrist c Tudor b White	38	4/226 (5) 5/264 (4) 6/316 (7)		
S. K. Warne run out	35	7/348 (6) 8/416 (8)		
B. Lee c Key b White	41	9/423 (9) 10/456 (10)		

Bowling: Silverwood 4–0–29–0; Tudor 29–2–144–2; Harmison 28–7–86–1; White 23.1–3–127–5; Butcher 10–1–40–0; Dawson 5–0–21–0.

Umpires: S. A. Bucknor (West Indies) and R. E. Koertzen (South Africa).
Third umpire: D. J. Harper. Referee: Wasim Raja (Pakistan).

Australia secured the Ashes for the eighth successive series with a formidable team effort featuring no four-fors or scores of more than 75. As in the 2001 Ashes, it had taken them only 11 days' cricket. Bichel was dropped to make way for Lee, who had found form with New South Wales. Caddick joined the England injury list: of the six pace bowlers in the original tour party, only Harmison played and the new ball was given to Chris Silverwood, who bowled four overs before getting injured himself. On a super-fast pitch, third man and fine leg were catching positions: Vaughan, Hussain and Stewart all fell hooking. Australia's 456 came off only 99.1 overs. Butcher and Vaughan were each run out for nine while batting together. England were 34 for four in their second innings. Tudor received a nasty blow above the eye when he ducked into a short ball from Lee.

Fourth Test Match

At Melbourne, December 26, 27, 28, 29, 30. **Australia won by five wickets.** Toss: Australia.
Close of play: First day, Australia 356-3 (Langer 146, Waugh 62); Second day, England 97-3 (Hussain 17, Dawson 0); Third day, England 111-2 (Vaughan 55, Hussain 8); Fourth day, Australia 8-0 (Langer 4, Hayden 1).

Australia

J. L. Langer c Caddick b Dawson	250	lbw b Caddick		24
M. L. Hayden c Crawley b Caddick	102	c sub (A. J. Tudor) b Caddick		1
R. T. Ponting b White	21	c Foster b Harmison		30
D. R. Martyn c Trescothick b White	17	c Foster b Harmison		0
*S. R. Waugh c Foster b White	77	c Butcher b Caddick		14
M. L. Love not out	62	not out		6
†A. C. Gilchrist b Dawson	1	not out		10
L-b 11, w 5, n-b 5	21	B 8, l-b 5, n-b 9		22

1/195 (2) 2/235 (3) 3/265 (4)	(6 wkts dec.) 551	1/8 (2) 2/58 (3) 3/58 (4)	(5 wkts) 107
4/394 (5) 5/545 (1) 6/551 (7)		4/83 (5) 5/90 (1)	

B. Lee, J. N. Gillespie, S. C. G. MacGill and G. D. McGrath did not bat.

Bowling: *First Innings*—Caddick 36–6–126–1; Harmison 36–7–108–0; White 33–5–133–3; Dawson 28–1–121–2; Butcher 13–2–52–0. *Second Innings*—Caddick 12–1–51–3; Harmison 11.1–1–43–2.

His father remembers him crying in bed at the loss of his leg-break; the son felt he was letting his father down.
Scyld Berry on Nasser Hussain, page 73

Fitting in: Martin Love replaced Darren Lehmann for the Melbourne Test, but there was little respite for England. Another Australian batsman hit runs in another Australian victory. *Picture by Patrick Eagar.*

England

M. E. Trescothick c Gilchrist b Lee	37	– lbw b MacGill	37
M. P. Vaughan b McGrath	11	– c Love b MacGill	145
M. A. Butcher lbw b Gillespie	25	– c Love b Gillespie	6
*N. Hussain c Hayden b MacGill	24	– c and b McGrath	23
R. K. J. Dawson c Love b MacGill	6	– (9) not out	15
R. W. T. Key lbw b Lee	0	– (5) c Ponting b Gillespie	52
J. P. Crawley c Langer b Gillespie	17	– (6) b Lee	33
C. White not out	85	– (7) c Gilchrist b MacGill	21
†J. S. Foster lbw b Waugh	19	– (8) c Love b MacGill	6
A. R. Caddick b Gillespie	17	– c Waugh b MacGill	10
S. J. Harmison c Gilchrist b Gillespie	2	– b Gillespie	7
B 3, l-b 10, n-b 14	27	B 3, l-b 21, w 2, n-b 6	32

1/13 (2) 2/73 (1) 3/94 (3) 4/111 (5)   270   1/67 (1) 2/89 (3) 3/169 (4)   387
5/113 (6) 6/118 (4) 7/172 (7)   4/236 (2) 5/287 (5) 6/342 (6)
8/227 (9) 9/264 (10) 10/270 (11)   7/342 (7) 8/356 (8)
                                             9/378 (10) 10/387 (11)

Bowling: *First Innings*—McGrath 16–5–41–1; Gillespie 16.3–7–25–4; MacGill 36–10–108–2; Lee 17–4–70–2; Waugh 4–0–13–1. *Second Innings*—McGrath 19–5–44–1; Gillespie 24.4–6–71–3; MacGill 48–10–152–5; Lee 27–4–87–1; Waugh 2–0–9–0.

Umpires: D. L. Orchard (South Africa) and R. B. Tiffin (Zimbabwe).
Third umpire: D. B. Hair. Referee: Wasim Raja (Pakistan).

Warne missed the chance to reach 500 Test wickets after dislocating his shoulder in the one-day VB Series. The injured Lehmann was replaced by Martin Love of Queensland, the most experienced debutant in Australia's history with 123 first-class matches. England started as poorly as ever. Langer scored 250 in 578 minutes and 407 balls, with 30 fours and a six. Stewart, who was injured, went through a fourth Ashes tour without keeping in a Melbourne Test; his deputy, James Foster, conceded no byes in Australia's huge first innings. England subsided to 118 for six, but then the tide turned. White's 85 came off only 134 balls with three sixes. Vaughan finished the calendar year with 1,481 runs (including six hundreds), behind only Viv Richards and Sunil Gavaskar. Hayden also made six Test hundreds in the year. A fifth-day crowd of 18,666 saw a good finish. This was Waugh's 33rd win in his 44th Test as captain, beating Allan Border's Australian record; only Clive Lloyd, who led West Indies to 36 wins in 74 Tests, has more. McGrath broke Courtney Walsh's record of 53 consecutive Tests by a specialist fast bowler.

Fifth Test Match

At Sydney, January 2, 3, 4, 5, 6. **England won by 225 runs.** Toss: England.
Close of play: First day, England 264-5 (Crawley 6, Stewart 20); Second day, Australia 237-5 (Waugh 102, Gilchrist 45); Third day, England 218-2 (Vaughan 113, Hussain 34); Fourth day, Australia 91-3 (Bichel 49, Martyn 19).

England

M. E. Trescothick c Gilchrist b Bichel	19	– b Lee		22
M. P. Vaughan c Gilchrist b Lee	0	– lbw b Bichel		183
M. A. Butcher b Lee	124	– c Hayden b MacGill		34
*N. Hussain c Gilchrist b Gillespie	75	– c Gilchrist b Lee		72
R. W. T. Key lbw b Waugh	3	– c Hayden b Lee		14
J. P. Crawley not out	35	– lbw b Gillespie		8
†A. J. Stewart b Bichel	71	– not out		38
R. K. J. Dawson c Gilchrist b Bichel	2	– c and b Bichel		12
A. R. Caddick b MacGill	7	– c Langer b MacGill		8
M. J. Hoggard st Gilchrist b MacGill	0	– b MacGill		0
S. J. Harmison run out	4	– not out		20
B 6, l-b 3, n-b 13	22	B 9, l-b 20, w 2, n-b 10		41

1/4 (2) 2/32 (1) 3/198 (4)   362
4/210 (5) 5/240 (3) 6/332 (7) 7/337 (8)
8/348 (9) 9/350 (10) 10/362 (11)

1/37 (1) 2/124 (3)   (9 wkts dec.) 452
3/313 (4) 4/344 (5)
5/345 (2) 6/356 (6)
7/378 (8) 8/407 (9) 9/409 (10)

Bowling: *First Innings*—Gillespie 27–10–62–1; Lee 31–9–97–2; Bichel 21–5–86–3; MacGill 44–8–106–2; Waugh 4–3–2–1. *Second Innings*—Gillespie 18.3–4–70–1; Lee 31.3–5–132–3; MacGill 41–8–120–3; Bichel 25.3–3–82–2; Martyn 3–1–14–0; Waugh 6–2–5–0.

Australia

J. L. Langer c Hoggard b Caddick	25	– lbw b Caddick		3
M. L. Hayden lbw b Caddick	15	– lbw b Hoggard		2
R. T. Ponting c Stewart b Caddick	7	– (4) lbw b Caddick		11
D. R. Martyn c Caddick b Harmison	26	– (5) c Stewart b Dawson		21
*S. R. Waugh c Butcher b Hoggard	102	– (6) b Caddick		6
M. L. Love c Trescothick b Harmison	0	– (7) b Harmison		27
†A. C. Gilchrist c Stewart b Harmison	133	– (8) c Butcher b Caddick		37
A. J. Bichel c Crawley b Hoggard	4	– (3) lbw b Caddick		49
B. Lee c Stewart b Hoggard	0	– c Stewart b Caddick		46
J. N. Gillespie not out	31	– not out		3
S. C. G. MacGill c Hussain b Hoggard	1	– b Caddick		1
B 2, l-b 6, w 2, n-b 9	19	B 6, l-b 8, w 3, n-b 3		20

1/36 (2) 2/45 (3) 3/56 (1) 4/146 (4)   363
5/150 (6) 6/241 (5) 7/267 (8)
8/267 (9) 9/349 (7) 10/363 (11)

1/5 (1) 2/5 (2) 3/25 (4)   226
4/93 (3) 5/99 (6) 6/109 (5)
7/139 (7) 8/181 (8)
9/224 (9) 10/226 (11)

Bowling: *First Innings*—Hoggard 21.3–4–92–4; Caddick 23–3–121–3; Harmison 20–4–70–3; Dawson 16–0–72–0. *Second Innings*—Hoggard 13–3–35–1; Caddick 22–5–94–7; Harmison 9–1–42–1; Dawson 10–2–41–1.

Umpires: D. L. Orchard (South Africa) and R. B. Tiffin (Zimbabwe).
Third umpire: S. J. A. Taufel. Referee: Wasim Raja (Pakistan).

Waugh played his 156th Test, equalling Allan Border's world record, and became the third player to reach 10,000 Test runs, after Border and Gavaskar. Waugh's hundred was dramatically completed from the last ball of the second day and rapturously cheered by his home crowd. It was his 29th hundred in Tests, equalling Bradman's Australian record. Australia were without either McGrath

The big one – and don't they know it... Matthew Hoggard is mobbed after removing Matthew Hayden in the second innings at Sydney. *Picture by Patrick Eagar.*

or Warne for the first time in 119 Tests. Stewart, whose 71 came off only 86 balls with 15 fours, passed Boycott's aggregate of 8,114 to go third in the list of England run-scorers, and ninth overall. Vaughan finished the series with 633 runs, the most in a five-Test series against Australia since Clyde Walcott's 827 for West Indies in 1954-55. Caddick took seven wickets in an innings for the second time in Tests, and ten in a match for the first time. This was Australia's first home defeat in 23 Tests since England beat them at Melbourne in 1998-99. Australia won the series 4–1. Vaughan was Man of the Series.

SOUTH AFRICA v SRI LANKA

First Test: At Johannesburg, November 8, 9, 10. **South Africa won by an innings and 64 runs.** Toss: Sri Lanka. **Sri Lanka 192** (M. S. Atapattu 34, D. P. M. D. Jayawardene 39, S. T. Jayasuriya 32; J. H. Kallis three for 35) **and 130** (M. S. Atapattu 43, W. P. U. J. C. Vaas 32; M. Ntini three for 22, A. J. Hall three for one); **South Africa 386** (G. C. Smith 73, G. Kirsten 55, J. H. Kallis 75, M. V. Boucher 38, S. M. Pollock 38, A. J. Hall 31, Extras 62; W. P. U. J. C. Vaas three for 79, M. Muralitharan three for 83, K. H. R. K. Fernando three for 63).

Herschelle Gibbs ricked his back just before the toss and was replaced by Martin van Jaarsveld, who was in his car as the match began. Jayasuriya's decision to bat played into the hands of South Africa's five-man seam attack and 137 for three became 152 for eight. South Africa wobbled too, from 133 for no wicket to 180 for five, but Kallis saw them to a match-winning lead. Ruchira Perera was banned from bowling by umpire Harper after three warnings for running on the pitch. Sri Lanka conceded 31 in no-balls, and then slid to 25 for four. The match ended in floodlit drizzle.

Second Test: At Centurion, November 15, 16, 17, 18, 19. **South Africa won by three wickets.** Toss: South Africa. **Sri Lanka 323** (J. Mubarak 48, K. C. Sangakkara 35, D. P. M. D. Jayawardene 44, H. P. Tillekeratne 104 not out; M. Ntini four for 86, J. H. Kallis three for 71) **and 245** (K. C. Sangakkara 89, D. P. M. D. Jayawardene 40; M. Ntini four for 52, J. H. Kallis four for 39); **South Africa 448** (H. H. Gibbs 92, J. H. Kallis 84, M. V. Boucher 63, S. M. Pollock 99 not out) **and 124 for seven** (N. D. McKenzie 39; C. R. D. Fernando four for 49).

Marvan Atapattu captained Sri Lanka for the first time in Tests after Jayasuriya damaged ankle ligaments. Tillekeratne, stuck at the non-striker's end on 91 as Ntini came within inches of a hat-trick, was ushered to an outstanding hundred by the unlikely figure of Muralitharan, who made 27 off 26 balls and raised his bat when he hooked Ntini for six. The fate Tillekeratne had escaped then befell Pollock, who became the fourth batsman ever to be stranded on 99 not out in a Test. M. K. G. C. P. Lakshitha took the new ball with Vaas to give Sri Lanka possibly the first pair of opening bowlers to have five initials each. Second time around, only the wicket-keeper Sangakkara resisted for long as his opposite number, Boucher, held eight catches in the match. Dilhara Fernando reduced South Africa to 44 for five but could not stop them winning the series 2–0.

ZIMBABWE v PAKISTAN

First Test: At Harare, November 9, 10, 11, 12. **Pakistan won by 119 runs.** Toss: Zimbabwe. **Pakistan 285** (Taufeeq Umar 75, Younis Khan 40, Inzamam-ul-Haq 39, Yousuf Youhana 63, Hasan Raza 46; A. M. Blignaut five for 79) **and 369** (Taufeeq Umar 111, Inzamam-ul-Haq 112, Kamran Akmal 38; A. M. Blignaut three for 81, H. K. Olonga five for 93); **Zimbabwe 225** (D. D. Ebrahim 31, G. W. Flower 31, T. Taibu 51 not out; A. M. Blignaut 50; Shoaib Akhtar three for 43, Mohammad Sami four for 53) **and 310** (D. D. Ebrahim 69, A. D. R. Campbell 30, G. W. Flower 69, A. Flower 67; Shoaib Akhtar four for 75, Saqlain Mushtaq three for 98).

Campbell resumed as Zimbabwe captain in place of Streak, who was recovering from surgery after a tuk-tuk accident in Colombo. Blignaut, who had also been in a motor accident, starred with bat and ball on an untypically lively Harare pitch; his 50 took only 38 deliveries. Taibu made his maiden Test fifty. Shoaib Akhtar was found guilty of ball-tampering by the referee, Clive Lloyd, after the umpires noticed scratches on the ball; to the Zimbabweans' disgust, he escaped with a severe reprimand. Inzamam scored a run-a-ball hundred before lunch – in a morning session extended to make up time lost on earlier days – and became the second Pakistani to reach 6,000 Test runs, after Javed Miandad, in his 82nd match.

Second Test: At Bulawayo, November 16, 17, 18, 19. **Pakistan won by ten wickets.** Toss: Zimbabwe. **Zimbabwe 178** (A. D. R. Campbell 46, G. W. Flower 54, A. Flower 30; Saqlain Mushtaq seven for 66) **and 281** (A. D. R. Campbell 62, G. W. Flower 43, T. Taibu 37, A. M. Blignaut 41; Waqar Younis four for 78, Saqlain Mushtaq three for 89); **Pakistan 403** (Taufeeq Umar 34, Younis Khan 52, Yousuf Youhana 159, Kamran Akmal 56, Extras 30; H. K. Olonga three for 69, R. W. Price four for 116) **and 57 for no wkt** (Salim Elahi 30 not out).

On a dustbowl, Saqlain took ten in a match for the third time in Tests and opened the bowling in the second innings, shortly before the debutant opener Mark Vermeulen took 16 off Shoaib's first over. Zimbabwe dropped several catches and Yousuf Youhana reached 3,000 runs in his 41st Test. Pakistan raced to their target in 8.3 overs and won the series 2–0.

BANGLADESH v WEST INDIES

First Test: At Dhaka, December 8, 9, 10. **West Indies won by an innings and 310 runs.** Toss: West Indies. **Bangladesh 139** (Alok Kapali 52; P. T. Collins five for 26, V. C. Drakes four for 61) **and 87** (V. C. Drakes three for 19, J. J. C. Lawson six for three); **West Indies 536** (C. H. Gayle 51, W. W. Hinds 75, R. R. Sarwan 119, M. N. Samuels 91, D. Ganga 40, R. D. Jacobs 91 not out; Talha Jubair three for 135).

Both teams were captained by wicket-keepers, Khaled Masud and Ridley Jacobs. After 142 first-class matches, Vasbert Drakes made his Test debut. Sarwan reached his first Test hundred after 14 fifties in his previous 27 Tests. Masud did not concede a bye in the West Indies total of 536. Jermaine Lawson, a 20-year-old seamer who had previously taken four Test wickets for 206, finished the innings with six wickets in 15 balls and the cheapest six-wicket haul in Tests, beating A. E. R. Gilligan's six for seven for England v South Africa in 1924. It was Bangladesh's heaviest defeat.

Second Test: At Chittagong, December 16, 17, 18. **West Indies won by seven wickets.** Toss: Bangladesh. **Bangladesh 194** (Sanuar Hossain 36, Khaled Masud 32; P. T. Collins three for 60, D. B. Powell three for 51) **and 212** (Al Sahariar 34, Alok Kapali 85; P. T. Collins three for 58, D. B. Powell three for 36); **West Indies 296** (C. H. Gayle 38, M. N. Samuels 31, D. Ganga 63, R. D. Jacobs 59; Tapash Baisya four for 72) **and 111 for three** (C. H. Gayle 37).

West Indies' total of 296 was the lowest completed innings against Bangladesh in a Test, though they still won the series 2–0. This was Bangladesh's 16th defeat in their 17 Tests.

NEW ZEALAND v INDIA

First Test: At Wellington, December 12, 13, 14. **New Zealand won by ten wickets.** Toss: New Zealand. **India 161** (R. Dravid 76; S. E. Bond three for 66, S. B. Styris three for 28) **and 121** (S. R. Tendulkar 51; S. E. Bond four for 33, D. R. Tuffey three for 35, J. D. P. Oram three for 28); **New Zealand 247** (M. H. Richardson 89, N. J. Astle 41, Extras 33; Zaheer Khan five for 53) **and 36 for no wkt**.

   New Zealand's seam attack was greener than the pitch: at the start, Daniel Vettori had taken more Test wickets than the rest of the team combined, but he was not called upon to bowl a single ball in the series. India, undone by the bounce as much as the seam movement, lost their first five wickets for 55 in the first innings and for 36 in the second. V. V. S. Laxman made a pair. The match lasted 197.3 overs.

Second Test: At Hamilton, December 19, 20, 21, 22. **New Zealand won by four wickets.** Toss: New Zealand. **India 99** (S. E. Bond four for 39, D. R. Tuffey four for 12) **and 154** (R. Dravid 39, S. R. Tendulkar 32; D. R. Tuffey four for 41, J. D. P. Oram four for 41); **New Zealand 94** (Zaheer Khan five for 29) **and 160 for six** (S. P. Fleming 32; A. Nehra three for 34).

   This was the first time in all Tests that both sides were dismissed in double figures in their first innings. No one scored a fifty, for the first time in a completed Test since 1981. For only the second time in a Test, part of all four innings took place on the third day, because of rain on the first two. Play started at 4.30 p.m. on the second day after a helicopter was used to dry a sodden ground. Tuffey took a wicket in his first over for the fourth time in five Tests, and did it again in the second innings. Dravid batted 86 minutes for nine runs; Harbhajan Singh, by contrast, slogged 20 off nine balls. India actually led on first innings as Zaheer took his second five-for in successive matches after 22 Tests without one. Fleming had New Zealand, 24 for no wicket overnight, in the nets at 8.30 a.m. on the final day, and Jacob Oram, in his second Test, rescued them from 105 for five with an unbeaten 26 off 40 balls. New Zealand won the series 2–0, and India's series average of 13.37 runs per wicket was the lowest by any team other than the New Zealanders themselves in two series against England in the 1950s. The match lasted 176.5 overs, the series 374.2 – just over four full days' play.

SOUTH AFRICA v PAKISTAN

First Test: At Durban, December 26, 27, 28, 29. **South Africa won by ten wickets.** Toss: Pakistan. **South Africa 368** (G. Kirsten 56, J. H. Kallis 105, M. V. Boucher 55, N. Boje 37 not out, Extras 32; Waqar Younis three for 91, Mohammad Sami three for 92, Saqlain Mushtaq four for 119) **and 45 for no wkt**; **Pakistan 161** (Taufeeq Umar 39, Salim Elahi 39; M. Ntini three for 59, M. Hayward five for 56) **and 250** (Taufeeq Umar 39, Younis Khan 30, Yousuf Youhana 42).

   Waqar baffled the pundits by bowling first on a flat pitch when he had only two other specialist bowlers. Shoaib Akhtar, who the management said had returned home with an injured knee, turned out to be in Durban, where he was seen enjoying the company of Bollywood stars. Pakistan restricted South Africa to a merely decent total but then collapsed themselves, in a fusillade of bouncers from Hayward, from 77 without loss to 120 for eight. In the second innings, each of the five bowlers took two wickets.

Second Test: At Cape Town, January 2, 3, 4, 5. **South Africa won by an innings and 142 runs.** Toss: South Africa. **South Africa 620 for seven dec.** (G. C. Smith 151, H. H. Gibbs 228, J. H. Kallis 31, H. H. Dippenaar 62, N. D. McKenzie 51, S. M. Pollock 36 not out; Saqlain Mushtaq three for 237); **Pakistan 252** (Taufeeq Umar 135, Younis Khan 46, Inzamam-ul-Haq 32; S. M. Pollock four for 45, M. Ntini four for 62) **and 226** (Taufeeq Umar 67, Inzamam-ul-Haq 60, Yousuf Youhana 50; M. Ntini four for 33).

   Gibbs and Graeme Smith opened with 368, an all-wicket South African record. South Africa scored 445 for three on the first day, another national record, and Pollock declared two short of their highest total. Gibbs reached his double-hundred off 211 balls, the second-fastest in Tests after Nathan Astle for New Zealand against England at Christchurch in 2001-02. In all, Gibbs's 228 took 383 minutes and 240 balls, with 29 fours and six sixes; twice he struck balls pitched outside leg-stump over extra-cover. He beat Graeme Pollock's Newlands record of 209 in a Test innings, and it was Pollock to whom Smith (18 fours, no sixes) was compared for the brilliance of his hooking and pulling. Taufeeq Umar's 135 was a Test-best, but Pakistan lost their last six first-innings wickets for 12. Yousuf Youhana blocked his first six balls but still reached 50 in 27, also the second-fastest in Tests, including 24 from one over off Nicky Boje. Taufeeq, asked about Youhana's display, refused to comment. South Africa won the series 2–0 and controversially replaced Australia at the top of the ICC Test Championship.

THE ICC CRICKET WORLD CUP, 2003

 Matches are in chronological order within their pool. Innings are 50 overs unless stated. All individual performances of 30 runs or three wickets are included. Full scorecards and further coverage will appear in *Wisden 2004*. The World Cup finished three days before *Wisden 2003* went to press. Brief coverage of all matches is given here; but it has not been possible to verify every detail.

How it worked

The 14 teams were divided into two pools of seven – Australia, England, India, Pakistan, Zimbabwe, Holland and Namibia in Pool A; Bangladesh, New Zealand, South Africa, Sri Lanka, West Indies, Kenya and Canada in Pool B. All played all, and the top three in each group qualified for the Super Six stage, where they met the three qualifiers from the other group. Each team took with them all the points from their meetings with their two fellow-qualifiers, plus a quarter of the points from their other games. At the end of the Super Six, the top four went through to the semi-finals.

POOL A

Match 2, at Harare, February 10. **Zimbabwe won by 86 runs (D/L method).** Toss: Namibia. **Zimbabwe 340 for two** (C. B. Wishart 172 not out, M. A. Vermeulen 39, A. Flower 39, G. W. Flower 78 not out) (50 overs); **Namibia 104 for five** (25.1 overs).

Andy Flower and Henry Olonga wore black armbands to "mourn the death of democracy in our beloved country". The cricket was less inspiring as Namibia, playing their first one-day international, watched Zimbabwe run up the highest score in their history. The left-arm spinner Lennie Louw, at 43 the tournament's oldest player, captured Namibia's first international wicket. Wishart's 172 off 151 balls with 18 fours and three sixes was a Zimbabwe record. He and Grant Flower blitzed 166 runs in the last 19.3 overs. It was more than enough, particularly when Walters was caught behind off the first ball faced by a Namibian batsman.

Match 4, at Johannesburg, February 11. **Australia won by 82 runs.** Toss: Pakistan. **Australia 310 for eight** (50 overs) (R. T. Ponting 53, A. Symonds 143 not out, Extras 31; Wasim Akram three for 64); **Pakistan 228** (44.3 overs) (Salim Elahi 30, Rashid Latif 33, Wasim Akram 33; I. J. Harvey four for 58, G. B. Hogg three for 54).

On the day Shane Warne flew home after a positive drugs test, Andrew Symonds bounced back from a bad run by breaking the ground record and hitting the highest innings by an Australian in a World Cup. Playing his 55th ODI, Symonds pulled Australia round from 86 for four, faced 125 balls and made more in boundaries (84) than his previous highest score (68 not out). Waqar Younis was ordered out of the attack after bowling two beamers at Symonds; he apologised after the first but showed no remorse for the second. Australia scored 94 from their last 11 overs, effectively settling what should have been a glamour rematch between the 1999 finalists. Gilchrist, who became the second keeper to complete 250 one-day dismissals, accused Rashid Latif of calling him a "white c***". Latif was cleared of racism because of insufficient evidence, and later withdrew his threat to sue the entire Australian team.

Match 6, at Paarl, February 12. **India won by 68 runs.** Toss: India. **India 204** (48.5 overs) (S. R. Tendulkar 52, Yuvraj Singh 37, D. Mongia 42; T. B. M. de Leede four for 35); **Holland 136** (48.1 overs) (D. L. S. van Bunge 62; J. Srinath four for 30, A. Kumble four for 32).

India were shaken by two unsung Dutchmen: de Leede entered the game with career figures of none for 235 and van Bunge with a batting average of two. India's score was the lowest in 50 overs against Holland and de Leede's figures the best in the country's history. But the lunchtime talk of an upset soon evaporated as eight Dutch batsmen managed only seven runs between them and van Bunge was left playing a lone hand. Srinath took his 300th career wicket – the fifth man to do so – and Tendulkar became the World Cup's No. 1 run-scorer, eclipsing Javed Miandad's record of 1,083.

Match 8, at Harare, February 13. Zimbabwe beat England by forfeit.

England, after much agonising, declined to go to Zimbabwe, citing security worries. Two days later the ICC's World Cup technical committee ruled that their concerns were not legitimate and awarded the four points to Zimbabwe.

Match 11, at Centurion, February 15. Australia won by nine wickets. Toss: India. **India 125** (41.4 overs) (S. R. Tendulkar 36; B. Lee three for 36, J. N. Gillespie three for 13); **Australia 128 for one** (22.2 overs) (A. C. Gilchrist 48, M. L. Hayden 45 not out).

India's five-star batting line-up wilted again, capitulating for their worst World Cup score and the lowest one-day total at Centurion. Gillespie, relegated below a fiery Lee, bowled Dravid, chopping on, first ball and finished with 10–2–13–3. Tendulkar clubbed 14 off McGrath's fourth over but was otherwise subdued, facing 59 balls. Gilchrist and Hayden, who passed 2,000 one-day runs, raced to a century opening stand in 18 overs. Australia were back to full batting strength, with Bevan returning from a groin injury and Lehmann from suspension; neither was required.

Match 13, at East London, February 16. England won by six wickets. Toss: England. **Holland 142 for nine** (50 overs) (T. B. M. de Leede 58 not out; J. M. Anderson four for 25); **England 144 for four** (23.2 overs) (N. V. Knight 51, M. P. Vaughan 51; D. L. S. van Bunge three for 16).

Eight days into the tournament, England finally appeared on the field — and promptly won in five hours. Anderson, maintaining a sensible line and generating nippy away-swing, captured the first four wickets as Holland slid to 31 for five. He was backed by Caddick (10–4–19–0) and White, who took his first World Cup wicket seven years after his tournament debut. Afterwards, Hussain, disillusioned with his own board, said he was "most definitely" considering quitting the England captaincy at the end of the World Cup.

Match 14, at Kimberley, February 16. Pakistan won by 171 runs. Toss: Pakistan. **Pakistan 255 for nine** (50 overs) (Salim Elahi 63, Yousuf Youhana 43, Rashid Latif 36); **Namibia 84** (17.4 overs) (Wasim Akram five for 28, Shoaib Akhtar four for 46).

Namibia's batsmen were dumbstruck before the swerve of Wasim Akram and swagger of Shoaib Akhtar. Wasim, whose five wickets included four lbws, embarked on a record-hunt. He became the first man to pass 50 World Cup wickets, and his figures were the best by a Pakistani in the tournament's history. It was also Wasim's 34th World Cup appearance, breaking the record of 33 held by Javed Miandad and Steve Waugh. Shoaib bowled a ball clocked at 98.8mph, believed to be the fastest in a World Cup. The Namibians gave Wasim's party some extra fizz by crashing to 42 for nine - perilously close to Canada's all-time World Cup nadir of 45 - before the last pair lingered. The No. 10, Bjorn Kotze, top-scored with 24 not out. Namibia's bowlers had earlier kept some sort of brake on Pakistan in a marked improvement on their first match.

Match 17, at Harare, February 19. India won by 83 runs. Toss: Zimbabwe. **India 255 for seven** (50 overs) (V. Sehwag 36, S. R. Tendulkar 81, R. Dravid 43 not out); **Zimbabwe 172** (44.4 overs) (S. C. Ganguly three for 22).

A sparkling 99-run opening stand between Tendulkar (91 balls) and Sehwag (38) set up an easy victory, despite a mid-innings slump. India were ablaze at 135 for one at the halfway mark, before the innings turned on the dismissal of Tendulkar, bowled by a Grant Flower fizzer which pitched middle and thudded into the top of off stump. Murphy and Flower contained the middle order until Flower left the field with a gashed hand and figures of 6–0–14–2. Dravid took advantage. An immaculate opening spell by Srinath (7–1–10–2) confirmed India's ascendancy, and Ganguly's medium-pacers, flattered by some loose shotmaking, whipped through the middle order. At 87 for six, Zimbabwe were down and out. Six Zimbabweans ultimately reached 19 but all failed to go on as Taibu top-scored with an unbeaten 29. Olonga was replaced by Blignaut, possibly for political reasons, but Andy Flower continued their protest by wearing a striking black sweatband.

Match 19, at Port Elizabeth, February 19. England won by 55 runs. Toss: Namibia. **England 272** (50 overs) (M. E. Trescothick 58, A. J. Stewart 60, P. D. Collingwood 38, C. White 35; G. Snyman three for 69, R. J. van Vuuren five for 43); **Namibia 217 for nine** (50 overs) (A. J. Burger 85, D. Keulder 46; R. C. Irani three for 30).

An upset beckoned midway through Namibia's run-chase when, with rain-clouds gathering, they inched ahead of England on Duckworth/Lewis. The rain stayed away and the batting fell away,

A baggy-eyed view

By Marcus Berkmann

Historians may well decide that this was the most exciting World Cup since the last one, and the hardest to predict until the next one. But in the thick of it, after countless hours of dedicated screen-gazing, the serious cricket fan finds his or her mind teeming with a jumble of unconnected ideas, which may or may not be the consequence of too many cups of tea, chocolate biscuits and rotating graphics announcing a wicket with the word "WICKET". Here is a random selection of thoughts from the addled brain of one baggy-eyed viewer:

- It may be traditional for New Zealand to wear all-black, but aren't they rather hot in those shirts? When Nathan Astle scored his 102 against Zimbabwe, he looked as though he was turning on a spit over an open fire. Pastel colours may look sillier, but Australia's long-term choice of yellow and light green makes obvious sense in high temperatures. Has anyone thought of wearing white?

- Everyone hates Professor Duckworth and Mr Lewis. This includes: most television commentators, especially from South Africa; everyone at the ground, because the relevant information isn't put up on the big screen, so they don't know what's going on; the fielder with the tables in his pocket, who wishes he had the job of polishing the ball instead; the twelfth man who can't get on the field to tell the batsmen they still need one run from the next ball; and Mark Boucher. Yes, blame Mr Lewis and Professor Duckworth, and not the men who declined to schedule an extra day for each game in case of bad weather.

- The only consolation for England supporters: South Africa went out early too. The only consolation for South Africa, Pakistan and West Indies supporters: England went out early too. Much of the time the England team look mystified by this. Why does everyone hate them so? Tragically it seems that no one likes them enough to tell them.

- Most vivid memory of the tournament: Nasser Hussain trying to look impassive. England do well: Nasser looks impassive, as it may all go wrong any second. England do atrociously: Nasser is trying not to cry, or stab someone. This is now a vital skill for an international captain – not showing any emotions at all in case a TV camera is pointed at you. Which of course it will be throughout the match. Sanath scratches his head. Sourav does an upside-down smiley face. Cameras close in for the kill. This is why the form of international captains is so fragile, because instead of batting or bowling in the nets, they must spend hours of the day practising their impassive looks in mirrors, or having coaches prod them with red-hot pokers until they cease to react in any way at all. Hence the astonishing captaincy success of Steve Waugh, who hasn't knowingly indulged in any facial expression since 1987.

- Looming retirements. Though rarely pushed, as they always seemed to be playing Bangladesh, some great cricketers made their last World Cup appearances this time around. Shall we see their like again? Craggy Wasim Akram, rushing in gamely to bowl another no-ball even though we all know he's really 49; Alec Stewart, possibly the last of the great bat-twirlers; Allan Donald, master of the furious glare and double teapot after another play-and-miss; Aravinda de Silva, whose eighth official retirement this is; and Saeed Anwar, of whom Jack Bannister might say, "There's no more terrifying beard in world cricket." And what of Shane Warne, sent home after testing positive for a performance-enhancing mother? No one missed him, which may have been the greatest disappointment of all.

Marcus Berkmann is pop critic of The Spectator, *film critic of* The Oldie, *author of* Rain Men *and back-page columnist for* Wisden Cricket Monthly *but not before Burger clumped ten meaty fours – to most corners of the field – in 86 balls. When van Vuuren blasted the final ball for six, the losers stormed the field as if celebrating a win. Earlier, Trescothick and Stewart had steadied England after van Vuuren, a fly-half in the last rugby World Cup, dismissed Knight and Vaughan. He pinched three more wickets in the last five balls to complete the first five-wicket haul by a Namibian. Stewart, captaining in the absence of Hussain, who had a stiff neck, put Trescothick in charge of the maths. It was later revealed Trescothick had no idea England had slipped behind.*

Match 20, at Potchefstroom, February 20. **Australia won by 75 runs** (D/L method). Toss: Holland. **Australia 170 for two** (36 overs) (M. L. Hayden 33, D. R. Martyn 67 not out); **Holland 122** (30.2 overs) (A. J. Bichel three for 13, I. J. Harvey three for 25).

Holland put up a reasonable fight given that they entered this match as 2,000:1 underdogs, the highest sporting odds ever offered by the bookmaker William Hill. A persistent Lefebvre (8–2–19–0) and some equally persistent rain – which delayed the start by an hour, twice interrupted the innings and made this a 36-over contest – stopped Australia's batsmen cutting loose. Martyn and Lehmann batted with mysterious caution towards the end, wrongly reasoning that keeping wickets intact was imperative under Duckworth/Lewis. Instead the revised target rose by only 27 runs from 171 to 198; half a dozen well-struck blows would have been a smarter ploy. De Leede hit 24 and van Troost 23 as Holland, in reply, struggled to the lowest one-day score at Potchefstroom. They were lucky to make that many: Ponting favoured his part-time bowlers, Symonds and Lehmann, in a bid to hurry through the overs and beat the rain.

Match 23, at Cape Town, February 22 (day/night). **England won by 112 runs.** Toss: England. **England 246 for eight** (50 overs) (M. P. Vaughan 52, A. J. Stewart 30, P. D. Collingwood 66 not out); **Pakistan 134** (31 overs) (Shoaib Akhtar 43; J. M. Anderson four for 29, C. White three for 33).

One amazing over by the 20-year-old Jimmy Anderson, playing only his 12th ODI, inspired England's best World Cup win since 1992. He dismissed Inzamam-ul-Haq, edging a textbook away-swinger, for a golden duck and followed up by skittling Yousuf Youhana's stumps, also first ball, with an outswinging yorker that hit middle. He bowled his ten overs right through, making full use of the twilight movement, as Pakistan stumbled to 17 for three after four overs, and 80 for nine in the 26th. That set the stage for a cyclonic assault by the No. 11 Shoaib Akhtar. He heaved three soaring sixes, five sizzling fours and faced only 16 balls for an ODI best. It completed a manic day for Shoaib, who did everything in fast-forward. He went for seven runs an over after unleashing the fastest ball in recorded history – a 100.2mph thunderbolt which Knight tapped nonchalantly into the leg side. Vaughan, caught pulling first ball off a Wasim Akram no-ball (which would have been his 500th ODI wicket), showed daring but England fell away in familiar fashion until Collingwood, arriving at 110 for four – soon 118 for five – provided some backbone. Batting with no histrionics, crisp placement and running as if for his life, he shared vital partnerships with Flintoff, White and Giles. He hit only four boundaries yet rattled along at just under a run-a-ball. On a day of fireworks, cool efficiency proved decisive.

Match 25, at Pietermaritzburg, February 23. **India won by 181 runs.** Toss: Namibia. **India 311 for two** (50 overs) (S. R. Tendulkar 152, S. C. Ganguly 112 not out); **Namibia 130** (42.3 overs) (Yuvraj Singh four for six).

Glancing and nudging with impeccable timing, Tendulkar trotted serenely to his 34th one-day century and fourth in World Cups – equalling Mark Waugh's record. Restrained by a sluggish pitch and slow outfield, he milked the attack rather than murdering it, facing 151 balls and hitting 18 fours. He shared a partnership of 244, many of them singles, with the previously out-of-touch Ganguly, whose 20th ODI hundred contained four imposing sixes. The Namibians dawdled dispiritedly in reply apart from 29 in 30 balls by the opener Jan-Berrie Burger. Nehra twisted his ankle after bowling only one delivery and Ganguly turned to his part-timers; Yuvraj Singh responded with his best one-day figures. The biggest defeat in World Cup history – England's 202-run thrashing of India in 1975 – was under threat until Deon Kotze (27) and Melt van Schoor (24) put on 51.

Match 27, at Bulawayo, February 24. **Australia won by seven wickets.** Toss: Zimbabwe. **Zimbabwe 246 for nine** (50 overs) (A. Flower 62, G. W. Flower 37, A. M. Blignaut 54; G. B. Hogg three for 46); **Australia 248 for three** (47.3 overs) (A. C. Gilchrist 61, M. L. Hayden 34, R. T. Ponting 38, D. R. Martyn 50 not out, D. S. Lehmann 56 not out).

Talk of an upset, inspired by Blignaut's Klueneneresque assault, was soon doused by Gilchrist. The Flowers had built a solid platform, seeing off McGrath (9–2–24–2) and chiselling out 84 for the third wicket. Andy Flower, who passed Dave Houghton's Zimbabwe World Cup run-record (567), hit eight feisty fours before he was bowled by a spellbinding flipper from Brad Hogg. Blignaut, coming in at 142 for six, savaged the bowlers with eight fours and two sixes, both off Hogg. His demise after 28 balls was equally watchable as Lee held a thunderous return catch in front of his nose. Australia's top five had a useful hit, with Gilchrist, despite offering two chances, at his stand-and-smash best.

Match 28, at Paarl, February 25. **Pakistan won by 97 runs.** Toss: Holland. **Pakistan 253 for nine** (50 overs) (Taufeeq Umar 48, Abdul Razzaq 47, Yousuf Youhana 58); **Holland 156** (39.3 overs) (D. L. S. van Bunge 31, Extras 40; Wasim Akram three for 24, Shoaib Akhtar three for 26).

Wasim Akram said he struggled to sleep the night before this match, so anxious was he about becoming the first man to take 500 one-day wickets. His nerves settled when his seventh ball was played on by the opener Nick Statham. There were no such anxieties about the result, although Pakistan hardly set the world alight. Inzamam-ul-Haq followed a golden duck with a silver. Yousuf Youhana was the most fluent, chipping the ball around and managing just four fours. Lefebvre conceded only 11 in his first six overs, but the Dutch batsmen were less impressive. Forty extras, 17 of them wides, inflated the total.

Match 30, at Durban, February 26 (day/night). **India won by 82 runs.** Toss: India. **India 250 for nine** (50 overs) (S. R. Tendulkar 50, D. Mongia 32, R. Dravid 62, Yuvraj Singh 42; A. R. Caddick three for 69); **England 168** (45.3 overs) (A. Flintoff 64; A. Nehra six for 23).

Ashish Nehra's masterly spell in the dusk, a World Cup best for India, turned England's potentially absorbing run-chase to anticlimax. Only Winston Davis (in 1983) and Gary Gilmour (1975) had had better figures than Nehra, who maintained a fullish length at 90mph-plus and made the ball zip about. Five of his victims were caught behind or in the slips. Batting had been far more comfortable in daylight, with Tendulkar (52 balls) getting India off to a flier and Yuvraj Singh (38 balls) finishing with a flurry. A mid-innings lull gave England a chance, but only a ninth-wicket stand of 55 from Flintoff and Caddick gave them any hope. Flintoff faced 73 balls, swatting five fours and three sixes, to cap a near-perfect individual performance; he had earlier dismissed Tendulkar and pegged back India's middle order with 10–2–15–2.

Match 31, at Potchefstroom, February 27. **Australia won by 256 runs.** Toss: Australia. **Australia 301 for six** (50 overs) (M. L. Hayden 88, A. Symonds 59, D. R. Martyn 35, D. S. Lehmann 50 not out; L. J. Burger three for 39); **Namibia 45** (14 overs) (G. D. McGrath seven for 15).

Namibia's batsmen rolled over in 75 minutes of pantomime cricket to complete the biggest mismatch in one-day history. The destroyer was McGrath, who had only to be his usual accurate self to achieve extraordinary figures of 7–4–15–7. They were the best in any World Cup (beating Winston Davis's seven for 51) and the second-best in all ODIs (behind Chaminda Vaas's eight for 19). McGrath took six for one in his last 25 balls to pass Warne's Australian record of 32 World Cup wickets. Gilchrist's six catches in the innings were also a World Cup record, and took him past Moin Khan (257 dismissals) to become the most prolific one-day keeper of all. Namibia's 45 was the lowest one-day total against Australia and the shortest completed innings in ODI history. Only the captain Deon Kotze, ten, reached double figures. Australia's batting, despite beefy contributions from Hayden and Symonds, had also been under par for 49 overs. Lehmann righted that in the 50th by pummelling van Vuuren for 444646. His 28 off the over was yet another World Cup record, trumping Lara's 26 against Canada four days earlier. A hero the week before, van Vuuren went for 92 off ten overs.

Match 33, at Bulawayo, February 28. **Zimbabwe won by 99 runs.** Toss: Holland. **Zimbabwe 301 for eight** (50 overs) (A. Flower 71, G. J. Whittall 30, D. D. Ebrahim 32, A. M. Blignaut 58, H. H. Streak 44); **Holland 202 for nine** (50 overs) (D. L. S. van Bunge 37, R. P. Lefebvre 30; B. A. Murphy three for 44).

Holland's gutsiest batting effort coincided with their scrappiest performance with the ball. Each of Zimbabwe's top seven passed 20, with Andy Flower going on to an effortlessly elegant 71 off 72 balls before 94 were plundered in the last ten overs. Blignaut bulldozed to fifty in 32 deliveries, taking his World Cup strike-rate to 160, while Streak thumped six fours and a six in a 22-ball cameo. The Dutch batsmen forged solid starts too, without building a big partnership. The best, 42 for the eighth wicket by Mol and Lefebvre, got them to 200 for the first time in the competition.

Match 36, at Centurion, March 1. India won by six wickets. Toss: Pakistan. Pakistan 273 for seven (50 overs) (Saeed Anwar 101, Younis Khan 32); **India 276 for four** (45.4 overs) (S. R. Tendulkar 98, M. Kaif 35, R. Dravid 44 not out, Yuvraj Singh 50 not out).

In the most feverishly followed match of the tournament, Tendulkar produced one of the all-time great innings and turned a daunting run-chase into a doddle. Again and again, and with magnificent timing, his wrists worked good-length off-side balls to the leg-side boundary. He looted the last three balls of Shoaib Akhtar's first over for 14, starting with a blistering upper-cut for six, and sailed on thereafter despite being hampered by a thigh strain. Sehwag fell in the sixth over, at 53, and Ganguly followed lbw first ball. Tendulkar and Kaif then piled on 102 in 95 balls; Tendulkar raced to his fifty in 37 deliveries and became the first man to 12,000 ODI runs. He faced 75 balls in all, with 12 fours and a six, before Dravid and Yuvraj completed the demolition. Saeed Anwar's 20th ODI century – comprising neat dabs, late-cuts, leg-side flicks and only seven boundaries – had been decidedly, perhaps decisively, less belligerent. Rashid Latif scurried 29 not out at the end and was hit on the helmet by Zaheer. Taufeeq Umar stood in as wicketkeeper, not that he had much to do.

Match 37, at Port Elizabeth, March 2. Australia won by two wickets. Toss: England. England 204 for eight (50 overs) (M. E. Trescothick 37, N. V. Knight 30, A. J. Stewart 46, A. Flintoff 45; A. J. Bichel seven for 20); **Australia 208 for eight** (49.4 overs) (D. S. Lehmann 37, M. G. Bevan 74 not out, A. J. Bichel 34 not out; A. R. Caddick four for 35).

Australia achieved victory in gripping style as Bevan and Bichel saw them home with a nerveless stand of 73 for the ninth wicket. This was Bichel's match. He broke Trescothick and Knight's blazing opening, then cleaned up Vaughan and Hussain with rollicking leg-cutters as England plummeted from 66 for none after nine overs to 87 for five. Bichel, pumped up but clinical in his off-stump line, finished with 10–0–20–7; the rest of Australia's attack took one for 181. Bichel now had tournament figures of 16–1–33–12, yet he played only because of the sore heel which later forced Gillespie to go home. Flintoff and Stewart's stoic stand of 90 gave them some chance on a pitch getting lower and slower. Hayden, Gilchrist and Ponting were all out heaving ambitiously, leaving Australia 48 for four. But Bevan, first with Lehmann and later with Bichel, timed the chase to perfection. He nurdled only 25 runs in his first 78 balls and 49 in his last 48, working Flintoff through mid-wicket for four to secure victory with two balls to spare. Australia's 12th consecutive win eclipsed Clive Lloyd's 1984-85 West Indians, while England's defeat – their 14th on the trot against Australia – left their fate in the hands of Zimbabwe and Pakistan.

Match 39, at Bloemfontein, March 3. Holland won by 64 runs. Toss: Holland. Holland 314 for four (50 overs) (J. F. Kloppenburg 121, K. J. J. van Noortwijk 134 not out); **Namibia 250** (46.5 overs) (A. J. Burger 41, M. Karg 41, D. Keulder 52, B. G. Murgatroyd 52; J. F. Kloppenburg four for 42, Adeel Raja four for 42).

Holland won their first ODI at the 13th attempt in buccaneering style. Kloppenburg became their first centurion and van Noortwijk followed him half an hour later, although both took foolhardy singles on 99 and were lucky to survive. Their second-wicket stand of 228, at six an over, was precisely twice Holland's previous best for any wicket (by van Noortwijk himself and Zuiderent). Kloppenburg clobbered four sixes, mostly off his legs, and faced 142 balls; van Noortwijk, the busier of the two, hit three sixes and needed only 129 deliveries. The Namibians responded gamely but lost seven for 41 at the end as Kloppenburg, wheeling down jaunty medium-pacers, completed an individual triumph. Holland's 40-year-old captain, Roland Lefebvre, missed out with a hamstring strain but retired "a very happy man".

Match 41, at Bulawayo, March 4. No result. Toss: Pakistan. Pakistan 73 for three (14 overs) (Saeed Anwar 40 not out) **v Zimbabwe.**

The fate of three teams rode on this match: a resounding Pakistan victory would put them through to the Super Six, a normal-sized one would tip England over the line, and Zimbabwe simply had to win. Instead, rain delayed the start by 75 minutes and, after three further interruptions, the game was called off and the points shared. Zimbabwe, whose only two on-field victories were over Namibia and Holland, were through. There was time for a 45-ball cameo from Saeed Anwar and for Inzamam-ul-Haq to hole out for three, giving him a final World Cup tally of 19 runs at 3.16. After the match the luckless Nasser Hussain quit as England's one-day captain; few expected Waqar Younis to last much longer.

POOL B

Match 1, at Cape Town, February 9 (day/night). **West Indies won by three runs.** Toss: West Indies. **West Indies 278 for five** (50 overs) (B. C. Lara 116, S. Chanderpaul 34, C. L. Hooper 40, R. L. Powell 40 not out, R. R. Sarwan 32 not out); **South Africa 275 for nine** (49 overs) (G. Kirsten 69, M. V. Boucher 49, L. Klusener 57).

The shocks started early as Lara, playing his first match in five months, re-entered the limelight with a commanding century. He was dropped first ball by Kallis, a hard chance at second slip off Ntini, then never looked back: he faced 134 balls, hitting 12 fours and two sixes, in his highest World Cup score. West Indies scraped only 67 from the first half of the innings but quadrupled that in the second half as Sarwan and Powell added 63 in a frenetic last 28 balls; Pollock, who had two for 13 from his first seven overs, finished with two for 52. Dillon took his 100th one-day wicket and South Africa looked gone at 160 for six. Then Klusener intervened. He started slowly but ended with five sixes – including three off Gayle in the 45th over – from only 48 balls. Nine runs were needed off the last over but Klusener fell with three balls remaining. South Africa had been penalised one over for a slow over-rate. It proved lethal.

Match 3, at Bloemfontein, February 10. **Sri Lanka won by 47 runs.** Toss: New Zealand. **Sri Lanka 272 for seven** (50 overs) (S. T. Jayasuriya 120, H. P. Tillekeratne 81 not out; N. J. Astle three for 34); **New Zealand 225** (45.3 overs) (S. B. Styris 141, C. L. Cairns 32; R. P. Arnold three for 47).

Jayasuriya overcame dehydration and heat exhaustion to hit his first World Cup century, edging New Zealand – who had already withdrawn from their match in Kenya – to the brink of elimination. He faced 125 balls, sluggish by his standards, and blazed 14 fours, including three in a row off Adams. Tillekeratne batted for 45 overs and fought off cramp to add 170 with Jayasuriya. The innings dawdled at the end but victory seemed certain when New Zealand crashed to 15 for three. Styris then slammed six sixes – three of them over mid-wicket off Muralitharan – in 125 balls. Altogether he amassed 63 per cent of New Zealand's total. Anticipating a seaming wicket, Stephen Fleming had left out Vettori, a miscalculation that was rammed home when Arnold, in his best one-day bowling performance, spun his part-time off-breaks a foot.

Match 5, at Durban, February 11 (day/night). **Canada won by 60 runs.** Toss: Canada. **Canada 180** (49.1 overs) (I. S. Billcliff 42); **Bangladesh 120** (28 overs) (A. Codrington five for 27).

A team of 11 debutants, playing Canada's first senior game in 24 years, raced to their inaugural victory and, in the process, walloped a Test nation. They began briskly as Chumney clubbed 28 in 25 balls, before loitering in the middle. Sanuar Hossain (10–0–26–2) and Alok Kapali (10–0–19–1) kept things tight, but Ian Billcliff, who faced 63 balls, anchored Canada towards their highest total in ODIs. It proved more than enough as no Bangladeshi batsman passed 25. Austin Codrington, a dreadlocked Jamaican-born plumber, was helped out by some lackadaisical strokeplay as the records mounted: his third wicket secured the best figures for Canada in ODIs and his fifth made him the fifth one-day bowler (after Tony Dodemaide, Shaul Karnain, Allan Donald and T. C. B. Fernando) to take five on debut.

Match 7, at Potchefstroom, February 12. **South Africa won by ten wickets.** Toss: Kenya. **Kenya 140** (38 overs) (R. D. Shah 60; L. Klusener four for 16); **South Africa 142 for no wkt** (21.2 overs) (H. H. Gibbs 87 not out, G. Kirsten 52 not out).

Jonty Rhodes, one of the all-time great fieldsmen, left international cricket in the least appropriate fashion – breaking a bone in his right hand as he attempted a diving catch to dismiss Odumbe. Klusener's off-cutters wrested four wickets, his best in nearly three years, as Kenya lost their last six for 48. Only Shah stood tall, sedately compiling his ninth one-day fifty before being run out by Klusener. Gibbs blasted four sixes and 12 fours and faced 63 balls in an otherwise run-of-the-mill run-chase. South Africa had earlier left out Donald, a rare event. Rhodes, replaced in the squad by Graeme Smith, confirmed this was almost certainly the end, but assured his many admirers: "Don't cry for me, I've had a great ride."

Match 9, at Port Elizabeth, February 13. **New Zealand won by 20 runs.** Toss: West Indies. **New Zealand 241 for seven** (50 overs) (N. J. Astle 46, C. L. Cairns 37, B. B. McCullum 36 not out,

A. R. Adams 35 not out; W. W. Hinds three for 35); **West Indies 221** (49.4 overs) (R. R. Sarwan 75, R. D. Jacobs 50; A. R. Adams four for 44).

This match turned on the sensational run-out of Lara. After clipping Adams for two to get off the mark, Lara turned for a comfortable third as Vincent hared towards the mid-wicket boundary. Vincent slid, turned and hurled the ball to wide mid-on, where Cairns collected it and threw down the stumps. The relay throw was an unusual manoeuvre on a small ground and one the New Zealanders had rehearsed. It left West Indies 36 for two, which soon became 80 for six. A busy stand of 98 between Sarwan (99 balls) and Jacobs (73) saved the match as a spectacle but could not save West Indies. Hinds, in his best one-day bowling performance, had earlier dismissed Astle, Cairns and Vincent with his gentle medium-pacers as New Zealand's innings petered out. Cairns had a match: his only over was smashed for 21 and Adams's 35 occupied only 24 balls, and his four wickets gave him 20 from his last six one-dayers.

Match 10, at Pietermaritzburg, February 14. **Sri Lanka won by ten wickets.** Toss: Sri Lanka. **Bangladesh 124** (31.1 overs) (Alok Kapali 32; W. P. U. J. C. Vaas six for 25, M. Muralitharan three for 25); **Sri Lanka 126 for no wkt** (21.1 overs) (M. S. Atapattu 69 not out, S. T. Jayasuriya 55 not out).

In one of the most surreal starts to any cricket match, Vaas dismissed three batsmen in the first three balls and four in the first five. He bowled Hannan Sarkar with an in-ducker, held a return catch off Mohammad Ashraful, then had Ehsanul Haque caught in the slips. It was the third hat-trick in World Cup history – after Chetan Sharma and Saqlain Mushtaq – and was believed to be the first time any bowler, first-class or limited-overs, had taken three in the first three. Vaas later revealed he had woken up with "a really sore back". Kapali, the first No. 6 batsman ever to take guard in the opening over of an international match, survived the experience and eventually top-scored. A routine chase was completed by Atapattu, who passed 6,000 ODI runs, and Jayasuriya, who lifted his average in his past six one-dayers to 101.

Match 12, at Cape Town, February 15 (day/night). **Kenya won by four wickets.** Toss: Canada. **Canada 197** (49 overs) (J. M. Davison 31, I. S. Billcliff 71, J. V. Harris 31; T. M. Odoyo four for 28); **Kenya 198 for six** (48.3 overs) (R. D. Shah 61, S. O. Tikolo 42; J. M. Davison three for 15).

Canada were on target for their second straight upset when Billcliff, a New Zealand teacher, hit their first half-century in ODIs and led the way to the highest total in their five-match history. But the innings stalled after his dismissal in the 42nd over. Odoyo, playing his 53rd ODI, recorded career-best figures and saw Kenya home with 27 not out. Shah and Tikolo had earlier added 84 in 17 overs before Davison stemmed the flow with the sort of figures (10–3–15–3) usually achieved against teams like his.

Match 15, at Johannesburg, February 16. **New Zealand won by nine wickets** (D/L method). Toss: South Africa. **South Africa 306 for six** (50 overs) (H. H. Gibbs 143, J. H. Kallis 33, L. Klusener 33 not out); **New Zealand 229 for one** (36.5 overs) (S. P. Fleming 134 not out, N. J. Astle 54 not out).

Fleming, in what he called the innings of his life, dragged New Zealand to a freakish victory that owed a little to luck and a lot to their captain's inspiration. When rain intervened for a third time, at 182 for one in the 31st over, New Zealand had a decent chance. Rain made them a certainty, leaving them to get just 44 in 51 balls. Fleming cruised to his highest one-day score, rarely slogging but showing impeccable timing and shot selection. He faced 132 balls and hit 21 pinpoint fours, including four in a row off Kallis. He was dropped by Boucher – a sitter – on 53, but carried on to add 140 with Astle, who played a tidy second fiddle. Donald took the only wicket, of McMillan for 25, but leaked 52 runs in his 5.5 overs. South Africa's 306, despite a mid-innings stutter, had been a model of freewheeling consistency. They reached 100 in the 17th over, 200 in the 39th and 300 in the 50th. Gibbs shared half-century stands – with Smith, Boje, Kallis and Boucher – for the first four wickets. He faced 141 balls, with 19 fours and three sixes. Klusener's bludgeoning 21-ball assault enabled South Africa to pile up 98 runs in the last 10 overs. It was not enough – and an early exit beckoned.

Match 16, at Benoni, February 18. **No result.** Toss: Bangladesh. **West Indies 244 for nine** (50 overs) (B. C. Lara 46, C. L. Hooper 45, R. L. Powell 50; Manjural Islam three for 62); **Bangladesh 32 for two** (8.1 overs).

A brutal assault from Ricardo Powell put West Indies in sight of almost certain victory, only for rain to take it away. Powell faced 31 balls, crashing four sixes and three fours, as 86 runs were helter-skeltered in the last ten overs, making up for a sluggish first 40. The Bangladesh bowlers, led by the off-spinner Ehsanul Haque (two for 34), were encouraged by grey skies and an uneasy pitch. Lara had to graft for 76 balls over his 46. The sharing of the points threw South Africa a potential lifeline, leaving them in charge of their own destiny rather than relying on West Indies beating Sri Lanka.

Match 18, at Paarl, February 19. **Sri Lanka won by nine wickets.** Toss: Sri Lanka. **Canada 36** (18.4 overs) (W. P. U. J. C. Vaas three for 15, R. A. P. Nissanka four for 12); **Sri Lanka 37 for one** (4.4 overs).

Canada, batting first on what their captain called "a decent track", were bowled out for the lowest one-day total of all. The ball swung obligingly, their batsmen were flat-footed and they fell two runs short of Zimbabwe's 38, also against Sri Lanka, in 2001-02. On that day Vaas took eight for 19; here he collected another three, taking his tournament tally to nine wickets at 6.88. Nissanka's figures were his best in ODIs. Chumney and Harris top-scored with nine apiece; Harris mustered successive fours off Vaas before departing hit-wicket to a ball that banged him on the head. The highest partnership was ten for the eighth wicket. The match, all over in 105 minutes and 140 balls, was the second-shortest in one-day history.

Match 21, at Nairobi, February 21. **Kenya beat New Zealand by forfeit.**

New Zealand declined to go to Kenya because of safety worries.

Match 22, at Bloemfontein, February 22. **South Africa won by ten wickets.** Toss: South Africa. **Bangladesh 108** (35.1 overs) (M. Ntini four for 24); **South Africa 109 for no wkt** (12 overs) (H. H. Gibbs 49 not out, G. Kirsten 52 not out).

The slaughter was merciless but swift, with South Africa rocketing to victory three overs after lunch to keep their hopes ticking. Ntini and Pollock (6–2–8–2) ripped through a fragile top order to leave Bangladesh reeling at 33 for five. The pitch was not to blame, as South Africa showed in a 48-minute run-chase. Kirsten was particularly severe, thumping nine fours and a six in 32 balls. Donald, with one for 106 from 14.5 overs in the tournament, was left out on his home ground in favour of Monde Zondeki.

Match 24, at Centurion, February 23. **West Indies won by seven wickets.** Toss: West Indies. **Canada 202** (42.5 overs) (J. M. Davison 111; V. C. Drakes five for 44); **West Indies 206 for three** (20.3 overs) (W. W. Hinds 64, B. C. Lara 73, R. R. Sarwan 42 not out).

John Davison, a journeyman South Australian spinner with a first-class batting average of 10.85, slashed and swiped his way to the most surprising century in World Cup history. Swinging high and hard, but with a sound technique, Davison, playing for the land of his birth, hit 29 off Drakes's first two overs and helped smash 15 off another over from Dillon. He took three overs to play himself in, yet still reached his fifty in 30 balls and his hundred in 67 – the quickest ever in a World Cup, five balls better than Kapil Dev's Tunbridge Wells masterpiece of 1983. He was dropped twice, and another delivery rolled from his pads to his stumps without dislodging a bail. Yet he was unlucky too: he fell to the catch of the tournament when an airborne Drakes, after initially misjudging an outfield skier, sailed backwards and clung right-handed to a ball more than a metre over his head. Davison had clouted eight fours and six sixes in 76 balls. Viv Richards, fittingly, presented him with the match award. Alas, it was a one-man show. Canada's last nine wickets capsized for 47 as Drakes collected his first five-for in ODIs at the age of 33. A routine run-chase proved anything but. Hinds swaggered to his fifty in 24 balls – a World Cup record for precisely five minutes, until Lara reached his in 23. Lara hit three sixes, two fours and 26 runs in one over – another Cup record – from the left-arm spinner Seebaran.

Match 26, at Nairobi, February 24. **Kenya won by 53 runs.** Toss: Sri Lanka. **Kenya 210 for nine** (50 overs) (K. O. Otieno 60; W. P. U. J. C. Vaas three for 41, M. Muralitharan four for 28); **Sri Lanka 157** (45 overs) (P. A. de Silva 41; C. O. Obuya five for 24).

A passionate, aggressive and grossly underestimated Kenyan side pulled off one of the great World Cup shocks. Their hero was the leg-spinner, Collins Obuya, who went into the match with only nine wickets in 18 one-day games at 78. Bowling with good control and backed by sharp fielding, he skimmed off the cream of Sri Lanka's middle order in the best performance by a Kenyan bowler. Muralitharan had earlier restricted Kenya with his own World Cup-best after Jayasuriya, anticipating another swift kill, elected to bowl. It was a decision he regretted as Sri Lanka bled wickets on a deteriorating pitch; their highest partnership was only 32. Kenya's win was their tenth in 55 ODIs, fourth against a Test nation and first over Sri Lanka. Afterwards, the ICC's Anti-Corruption Unit studied the tapes. The still-celebrating Kenyans were unperturbed. "If Bangladesh can play Test cricket," said their coach Sandeep Patil, "there is no reason why we can't."

Match 29, at Kimberley, February 26. **New Zealand won by seven wickets.** Toss: Bangladesh. **Bangladesh 198 for seven** (50 overs) (Mohammad Ashraful 56, Khaled Masud 35 not out, Mohammad Rafique 41 not out; S. E. Bond three for 33, J. D. P. Oram three for 32); **New Zealand 199 for three** (33.3 overs) (C. D. McMillan 75, S. P. Fleming 32, S. B. Styris 37 not out, C. L. Cairns 33 not out; Khaled Mahmud three for 46).

Bangladesh improved enough to last 50 overs but were comfortably beaten again. Mohammad Ashraful, aged 18, timed the ball sweetly all round the wicket and cruised to a maiden half-century. Bangladesh were 107 for six; a run-a-ball eighth-wicket stand of 70 between Khaled Masud and Mohammad Rafique gave the New Zealanders something to chase. Fleming blitzed 19 runs in the eighth over and McMillan swatted two sixes in an otherwise scratchy 83-ball 75. Styris and a typically dashing Cairns saw them home in style as New Zealand worked off the rust after a ten-day hiatus.

Match 32, at East London, February 27. **South Africa won by 118 runs.** Toss: Canada. **South Africa 254 for eight** (50 overs) (G. C. Smith 63, H. H. Dippenaar 80, S. M. Pollock 32; A. Patel three for 41); **Canada 136 for five** (50 overs) (I. Maraj 53 not out).

For an hour, after South Africa stumbled to 23 for three, the unthinkable was possible. The debutant Ashish Patel picked up two big wickets, Gibbs for eight and Kallis for one, before Smith and Dippenaar added a crucial, if laborious, 109. Solid hitting from Pollock and Hall gave the total a late kick. Canada's reply was a Gavaskarian bore, crawling at 2.72 runs an over with 12 maidens. Maraj stonewalled for the entire 50 overs, facing 155 balls and enjoying four lives along the way. Epitomising a flat South African attack, Donald signed off with 10–2–27–0 in what turned out to be his farewell.

Match 34, at Cape Town, February 28 (day/night). **Sri Lanka won by six runs.** Toss: Sri Lanka. **Sri Lanka 228 for six** (50 overs) (S. T. Jayasuriya 66, H. P. Tillekeratne 36, R. P. Arnold 34 not out); **West Indies 222 for nine** (50 overs) (C. H. Gayle 55, R. R. Sarwan 47 not out, S. Chanderpaul 65; W. P. U. J. C. Vaas four for 22).

Sarwan, struck on the helmet by a Fernando bouncer, returned from hospital to carry West Indies agonisingly close to an epic victory. Sixteen were needed from 12 balls when Murali, returning for the 49th over, masterfully tied up Dillon at the striker's end. Only two runs were conceded and Sri Lanka, despite Sarwan's swinging efforts, lurched over the line. A resilient Jayasuriya had earlier anchored his team to respectability. He occupied an unJayasuriyalike 99 balls and hit only four boundaries, sharing a slow but vital 85-run partnership with Tillekeratne. Jayawardene inched to nine, his best of the tournament, before Vaas and Arnold thrashed 44 runs in the last five overs. Moving the ball sharply, Vaas then cleaned up Hinds and Lara (for a 22-ball one) in his opening spell. After knocking out Sarwan, who went off on a stretcher, Fernando trapped Hooper lbw first ball to leave West Indies 62 for three. That became 169 for seven when Chanderpaul, after a patient 65, became de Silva's 100th one-day victim, bringing Sarwan back to the crease. He exploded instantly, crashing 37 runs in 25 balls and lofting leg-side sixes off Jayasuriya and de Silva. Then Muralitharan (10–1–26–1) was handed the ball.

Match 35, at Johannesburg, March 1. **Kenya won by 32 runs.** Toss: Kenya. **Kenya 217 for seven** (50 overs) (R. D. Shah 37, B. J. Patel 32, M. O. Odumbe 52 not out; Sanuar Hossain three for 49); **Bangladesh 185** (47.2 overs) (Tushar Imran 48, Akram Khan 44; M. O. Odumbe four for 38, S. O. Tikolo three for 14).

Kenya's players embarked on a lap of honour on becoming the first non-Test nation to reach the second stage of a World Cup. Maurice Odumbe, hero of the famous victory over West Indies in 1996, was Kenya's match-winner again. His 45-ball unbeaten fifty gave them something to defend and he then chipped away at Bangladesh's middle order in an unbroken ten-over spell of off-spin. Shah, Patel and Tikolo, dropped twice in two balls on his way to 27, had all made confident starts in Kenya's innings but failed to carry on. The lower order, in partnership with Odumbe, saw them past 200 – a moderate total that looked monumental when Bangladesh slid to 17 for two. Martin Suji dismissed Al Sahariar and Mohammad Ashraful, unluckily lbw, with successive deliveries, before Tushar Imran (81 balls) and Akram Khan (60) fought back positively. It was to no avail: Bangladesh's last five wickets collapsed obligingly for 34 runs. Kenya, incredibly, became the first Pool B team to qualify for the Super Six, while Bangladesh had now lost 30 completed one-day matches in a row. It was hard to believe their last victory, against Pakistan in the 1999 World Cup, had ever happened.

Match 38, at Benoni, March 3. **New Zealand won by five wickets.** Toss: New Zealand. **Canada 196** (47 overs) (J. M. Davison 75; S. E. Bond three for 29, J. D. P. Oram four for 52); **New Zealand 197 for three** (23 overs) (C. L. Cairns 31, A. R. Adams 36, S. B. Styris 54 not out, C. Z. Harris 38 not out; J. M. Davison three for 61).

Davison proved his pyrotechnics of a week earlier were no fluke by smashing a 25-ball fifty. Again, though, he received little support, and New Zealand overcame an early stutter to cruise home with 27 overs to spare, so eliminating West Indies. New Zealand careered to 32 for three after four overs as Davison, opening the bowling too with his off-breaks, winkled out Astle and McMillan in the space of three balls. Cairns and Adams (three sixes, 20 balls) regained the initiative before Styris and Harris completed the victory march. None, however, could match Davison's clean hitting. He helped take 31 runs off Adams's first three overs, then clubbed Oram for three leg-side sixes in one over – the last, from a good-length delivery, sailing over mid-wicket, clearing the stadium roof and travelling an estimated 120 metres. He faced 62 balls with nine fours and four sixes and finished the tournament with a batting strike-rate of 118, a bowling average of 18.70 and high hopes of finally commanding a regular spot for South Australia.

Match 40, at Durban, March 3 (day/night). **Tied** (D/L method). Toss: Sri Lanka. **Sri Lanka 268 for nine** (M. S. Atapattu 124, P. A. de Silva 73; J. H. Kallis three for 41); **South Africa 229 for six** in 45 overs (G. C. Smith 35, H. H. Gibbs 73, M. V. Boucher 45 not out).

An exhilarating, exasperating tie produced an enduring image: a distraught Shaun Pollock, face buried in his hands, ruing the misreading of the Duckworth/Lewis tables that bundled his team out of their own World Cup. Off the fifth ball of the 45th over Boucher, instructed by the dressing-room that South Africa required 229, clubbed Muralitharan for six to reach the target. He pumped his fist in celebration, blocked the next ball and left the field as rain poured down. Moments later the truth dawned: 229 was enough only to tie the match. South Africa, needing a victory to make the next round, had been knocked out. "We knew it was a tie," Jayasuriya confirmed afterwards. "I had the sheet in my hand." Jayasuriya had worries of his own earlier when Sri Lanka, needing at least to avoid a hasty hammering to seal their own Super Six spot, slumped to 90 for three. They were rescued by a glorious 152-run stand between Atapattu and de Silva, both timing the ball majestically. Gibbs and Smith replied with 65 in the first 11 overs. Gibbs faced 88 balls for his 73 – giving him 384 World Cup runs at 96 – but the spinners suffocated the middle order as South Africa sagged to 149 for five. Boucher and Pollock regained the edge before the match seesawed yet again on Pollock's run-out for 25. Trying to steal a quick single to the wicket-keeper, he took on Sangakkara's throw and was found – countless TV replays later – millimetres short. Sri Lanka had nosed ahead again, but the umpires allowed South Africa to bat on in driving rain and Boucher swung the bat, only to fall agonisingly, and unwittingly, short. South Africa, for the second World Cup in a row, went out with a tie and a tear.

Match 42, at Kimberley, March 4. **West Indies won by 142 runs.** Toss: West Indies. **West Indies 246 for seven** (50 overs) (C. H. Gayle 119, S. Chanderpaul 66); **Kenya 104** (35.5 overs) (V. C. Drakes five for 33).

Kenya received a rare hammering as West Indies finally produced the all-round consistency that had eluded them. Gayle, dour by his standards, held the innings together and single-handedly outscored the opposition. Kenya's entire middle order – Patel, Modi, Tikolo and Odumbe – were wiped out in 15 furious balls. Drakes's figures were his best ever and Lawson, playing his first World Cup match, found raw speed to take 8–0–16–2. Too fast, too good, too late.

Above: Reality bites: Shaun Pollock at Durban after botched dressing-room arithmetic left South Africa tied with Sri Lanka on Duckworth/Lewis – and out of their own World Cup. *Picture by Shaun Botterill, Getty Images. Below:* Short-lived celebrations: New Zealand's Shane Bond castles Ian Harvey to reduce Australia to 84 for seven, but the door was still ajar. *Picture by Hamish Blair, Getty Images.*

POOL A

	Played	Won	Lost	Tied	No result	Points	Net run-rate
AUSTRALIA . . .	6	6	0	0	0	24	2.04
INDIA	6	5	1	0	0	20	1.10
ZIMBABWE. . . .	6	3	2	0	1	14	0.50
England	6	3	3	0	0	12	0.82
Pakistan	6	2	3	0	1	10	0.22
Holland	6	1	5	0	0	4	-1.45
Namibia	6	0	6	0	0	0	-2.95

POOL B

	Played	Won	Lost	Tied	No result	Points	Net run-rate
SRI LANKA. . . .	6	4	1	1	0	18	1.20
KENYA	6	4	2	0	0	16	0.69
NEW ZEALAND.	6	4	2	0	0	16	0.99
West Indies.	6	3	2	0	1	14	1.10
South Africa	6	3	2	1	0	14	1.73
Canada	6	1	5	0	0	4	-1.98
Bangladesh	6	0	5	0	1	2	-2.04

The top three teams from each pool advanced to the Super Six. Kenya were placed ahead of New Zealand, and West Indies ahead of South Africa, because they won their respective head-to-head matches.

SUPER SIX

Match 43, at Centurion, March 7. **Australia won by 96 runs. Toss:** Australia. **Australia 319 for five** (50 overs) (A. C. Gilchrist 99, R. T. Ponting 114, D. R. Martyn 52; C. R. D. Fernando three for 47); **Sri Lanka 223** (47.4 overs) (P. A. de Silva 92; B. Lee three for 52).

A brilliant direct hit from Vaas, at deep square leg, ran out Gilchrist one run short of his first World Cup century. Everything else went Australia's way. They piled up their third score of 300 and became the first team through to the semi-finals. Gilchrist, smashing repeatedly across the line, was brutal with anything short. He hit 14 fours, two sixes and faced 88 balls, dominating stands of 75 with Hayden and 106 with Ponting, who took 20 off Vaas's eighth over on his way to 114 in 109 balls with four sixes. Vaas entered the match with 18 wickets and finished it with figures of 8–0–59–0. Murali (10–0–47–1) was similarly ineffective. Sri Lanka's reply was mostly disastrous. Jayasuriya retired hurt in the second over after being struck twice in three balls by Lee — on the thumb, then the forearm. Only de Silva, batting at his pugnacious best, topped 21. Dropped on nought, he went on to blast nine fours and four sixes, taking 27 off Lee's last two overs. In the process he eclipsed Arjuna Ranatunga's Sri Lankan record of 969 World Cup runs. The ninth-wicket stand of 54 between de Silva and Fernando, who contributed only nine, was a record for Sri Lanka against Australia. Ponting later defended his team's short-pitched bowling, saying Jayasuriya had a weakness around his ribs: "This is a World Cup."

Match 44, at Cape Town, March 7 (day/night). **India won by six wickets. Toss:** Kenya. **Kenya 225 for six** (50 overs) (K. O. Otieno 79, R. D. Shah 34, T. M. Odoyo 32, M. O. Odumbe 34 not out); **India 226 for four** in (47.5 overs) (S. C. Ganguly 107 not out, R. Dravid 32, Yuvraj Singh 58 not out).

Expectations that Kenya's lack of stars and experience would finally catch up with them proved unfounded, as India scampered nervously to victory with 13 balls to spare. Kenya seemed on course for their biggest upset yet when Yuvraj Singh joined Ganguly with 118 needed from 123 balls. But Yuvraj showed his customary cool aggression under pressure, hitting seven fours in 64 balls. India had earlier collapsed to 24 for three against the sustained accuracy of Martin Suji (10–3–27–1) and Odoyo. Tendulkar's dismissal for five — caught Tony Suji, bowled Martin Suji — ended his run of top-scoring in six consecutive World Cup matches. It fell to Ganguly to weather the storm. He gritted his way through a scratchy beginning but looked close to his fluent best by the end, hitting 11 fours and two sixes in his 120-ball innings. Kenya's 225, their highest total of the tournament, had always looked a testing target under lights. Their anchor was the opener Kennedy Otieno, who battled hard for a no-frills 79. When he departed at 157 for three after 40 overs, Kenya were ideally placed for a late assault. Odumbe responded with a speedy 34 in 24 balls – not bad, but not enough to stop India joining Australia in the semi-finals.

Match 45, at Bloemfontein, March 8. **New Zealand won by six wickets.** Toss: Zimbabwe. **Zimbabwe 252 for seven** (50 overs) (C. B. Wishart 30, A. Flower 37, T. Taibu 53, H. H. Streak 72 not out, S. M. Ervine 31 not out); **New Zealand 253 for four** (47.2 overs) (S. P. Fleming 46, N. J. Astle 102 not out, C. L. Cairns 54).

Zimbabwe's stuttering innings ended in a blaze of glory as Streak and Ervine concocted 62 from the last three overs. But they were making up for the deficiencies of their specialist batsmen, and New Zealand strolled to victory. Streak pulverised 35 off his last 12 deliveries and Ervine was not far behind with 31 off only 14 balls. Adams (5–0–54–1) suffered most. Zimbabwe had slipped to 106 for six in the 24th over. Taibu began the rescue mission, compiling an ODI best with bold reverse sweeps and scoops. Fleming reeled off 10 fours in his ice-cool 46 before Astle and Cairns casually compiled a 121-run stand for the fourth wicket. Astle pushed ones and twos, intermingled with some sweet cover drives, to reach his 13th one-day century.

Match 46, at Johannesburg, March 10. **India won by 183 runs.** Toss: Sri Lanka. **India 292 for six** (50 overs) (S. R. Tendulkar 97, V. Sehwag 66, S. C. Ganguly 48; M. Muralitharan three for 46); **Sri Lanka 109** (23 overs) (K. C. Sangakkara 30; J. Srinath four for 35, A. Nehra four for 35).

Sri Lanka's slim hopes of a miraculous run-chase were snuffed out in 22 dramatic balls. Atapattu, Mubarak, Jayawardene and de Silva were all knocked over for ducks – three of them by Srinath – to leave the Sri Lankans shell-shocked at 15 for four after 22 balls. They only made it to three figures thanks to a 31-run last-wicket stand between Fernando and Muralitharan. Srinath and Nehra's four wickets apiece owed as much to slapdash batting as slippery bowling, while Kaif's four catches – three at cover – were a World Cup fielding record. The expected moisture at the start of the day did not remotely trouble Tendulkar and Sehwag, who treated Vaas (10–2–34–2) with respect and the rest of the bowlers with disdain in a majestic opening stand of 153. The innings lost momentum after Sehwag's departure. Tendulkar hit only seven fours and a six in 120 balls before again being dismissed, slightly perversely, in the nineties. More perverse was Jayasuriya's insistence, not for the first time, on bowling first despite having a half-threadbare attack.

Match 47, at Port Elizabeth, March 11. **Australia won by 96 runs.** Toss: New Zealand. **Australia 208 for nine** (50 overs) (D. R. Martyn 31, M. G. Bevan 56, A. J. Bichel 64; S. E. Bond six for 23); **New Zealand 112** (30.1) overs (S. P. Fleming 48; G. D. McGrath three for 29, B. Lee five for 42).

Australia, down and out at 84 for seven, roared to victory in one of the great one-day turnarounds as four individuals played out of their skin. First Bevan and Bichel completed their second salvage operation of the tournament, adding 97 in an eighth-wicket partnership that started slowly but grew in momentum. Then McGrath followed up his three not out – his first World Cup runs, in his 25th match – by uprooting the first three New Zealand wickets in his first 19 balls. And finally Lee, after pounding the last two balls of Australia's innings for enormous sixes, cleaned up New Zealand's tail with a sizzling spell of five for three in 15 balls. The initial destroyer, however, was Shane Bond. Bowling full and fast on a slow wicket, he achieved the best World Cup figures by a New Zealander and confirmed his bogeyman standing: his Australian harvest now stood at 22 wickets in six matches. He dismissed Hayden, Gilchrist and Ponting in his opening spell, then took three for three in his last four overs, pinning Hogg first ball with a magnificent yorker. Harris (10–1–24–0) prospered with his all-sorts but the other bowlers never threatened. Bichel hit one bizarre six – clubbing a ball from Adams that slipped and bounced twice – and accelerated to his first ODI half-century. Bevan, cool and calculating, pilfered singles at will. Fleming opened New Zealand's run-chase with Vettori and was their only batsman to show much resilience. His downfall, gloving a leg-side bouncer from Lee, signalled the end. Lee promptly blasted out McCullum and Adams with swinging yorkers, then finished the job with a scintillating return catch to dismiss Bond.

Match 48, at Bloemfontein, March 12. **Kenya won by seven wickets.** Toss: Zimbabwe. **Zimbabwe 133** (44.1 overs) (A. Flower 63; M. A. Suji three for 19, C. O. Obuya three for 32); **Kenya 135 for three** (26 overs) (T. M. Odoyo 43 not out, M. O. Odumbe 38 not out).

On what their captain Steve Tikolo called "the biggest day in every Kenyan's life", the unlikeliest team in the Super Six progressed one unlikely step further. But if their previous victories were fuelled partly by emotion, this was a thoroughly professional, almost routine, performance. Asked to bowl first on a reliable pitch, Martin Suji reduced Zimbabwe to 45 for three with miserly line and length. Then Collins Obuya, a star of this World Cup, added a little pizzazz. Drifting the ball in and spinning it sharply away, he befuddled Taibu, Ebrahim and Streak to prevent any middle-order recovery. Andy Flower, who faced 101 balls and scored nearly half Zimbabwe's total, batted with grim determination but no support; the highest partnership was 21. The most punishing blow was the dismissal of Blignaut, who found himself scurrying for the same end as Flower and was comically run out. He later made amends with a lively opening spell but was undermined by slipshod fielding – four catches were dropped. Kenya began with a wobble, at 33 for two, and ended at a canter as Odoyo and Odumbe thumped the last 32 runs in three overs. They were through to the semi-finals, and Zimbabwe, just as deservedly, were not. Africa's balance of power had suddenly shifted.

Match 49, at Centurion, March 14. **India won by seven wickets.** Toss: India. **New Zealand 146** (45.1 overs) (S. P. Fleming 30; Zaheer Khan four for 42); **India 150 for three** (40.4 overs) (M. Kaif 68 not out, R. Dravid 53 not out).

New Zealand, seen by many as the danger side of this World Cup, showed little of their most valuable commodity – resourcefulness – when it mattered most. Their hopes were effectively dashed inside the first three balls, as McMillan holed out at square leg and Astle was trapped lbw by a Zaheer in-swinger. Styris thwarted the hat-trick and added an industrious 38 with his captain. But Fleming's departure, pulling uncharacteristically across the line and shovelling a catch to mid-off, left the New Zealanders teetering at 60 for five. The tail, led by Oram's 23, wagged willingly but never dominated, as Srinath (8–0–20–1), Nehra (10–3–24–1) and Harbhajan (10–2–28–2) tightened the screws. India's run-chase was not all smooth sailing. Bond fired out Sehwag for one and Ganguly for three, and Tendulkar followed soon afterwards for 15. India were 22 for three when McCullum, the wicket-keeper, shelled a simple catch off Dravid. It proved a cataclysmic mistake. Fleming shuffled his attack gamely but, with Cairns still unfit to bowl, only Bond (8–2–23–2) made much impression. Kaif and Dravid guided India home coolly but surely: Kaif occupied a full 129 balls for his 68. As Indian fans marvelled at their team's new-found patience and maturity, New Zealanders were left praying for Zimbabwe to beat Sri Lanka.

Match 50, at East London, March 15. **Sri Lanka won by 74 runs.** Toss: Sri Lanka. **Sri Lanka 256 for five** (50 overs) (M. S. Atapattu 103 not out, D. A. Gunawardene 41, K. C. Sangakkara 35); **Zimbabwe 182** (41.5 overs) (C. B. Wishart 43, A. Flower 38, G. W. Flower 31; S. T. Jayasuriya three for 30).

Andy Flower's last international ended, all too fittingly, in anticlimax and injustice; he was lbw to a ball that flew off the inside edge. Zimbabwe's one-man band of the past decade at least received a modicum of support on this occasion. Chasing an unlikely 257 on a slow pitch, Wishart and the makeshift opener Marillier (19) began brightly with a brisk 36-run stand. Travis Friend, playing his first World Cup match, swatted a breezy 21 to leave Zimbabwe reasonably placed at 68 for two when Flower arrived in the 12th over. He set down to business, stockpiling ones and twos with his customary placement and timing. As usual, though, his departure was the beginning of the end: the last seven wickets tumbled for 42. The cornerstone of Sri Lanka's innings was Atapattu, who batted out the entire 50 overs and struck only seven boundaries, but found the gaps unerringly and ran his singles hard. He shared solid stands with Jayasuriya, de Silva and Gunawardene, called up in place of the wretchedly out-of-form Jayawardene. Sangakkara's 25-ball cameo spearheaded a late onslaught to confirm Sri Lanka's semi-final booking. Olonga, who was dropped again for this match, announced his intention to retire from international cricket and flee Zimbabwe, after receiving e-mailed threats of retribution for his black-armband protest; seven secret policemen were reported to be at the game, and there was talk of their trying to arrest him on charges of treason.

Match 51, at Durban, March 15 (day/night). **Australia won by five wickets.** Toss: Australia. **Kenya 174 for eight** (50 overs) (R. D. Shah 46, S. O. Tikolo 51, H. S. Modi 39 not out; B. Lee three for 14); **Australia 178 for five** (31.2 overs) (A. C. Gilchrist 67, A. Symonds 33 not out; A. Y. Karim three for seven).

The 39-year-old Aasif Karim, who retired after the last World Cup and was persuaded to take part in this one only at the last minute, disrupted a straightforward Australian run chase with a magical spell of slow left-arm bowling. He rarely spun the ball, but mixed up his flight and pace ingeniously, rendering the batsmen virtually strokeless. He dismissed Ponting, Lehmann and Hogg and finished with figures of 8.2–6–7–3. Australia tiptoed to victory in the end but it was far tighter than it should have been after Gilchrist's electrifying start. He blitzed nine fours and three sixes, raising his fifty in 37 balls. Hayden's 20 consisted entirely of boundaries, and after 11 overs Australia were cruising at 96 for one. Kenya had had Shah and Tikolo to thank for mounting a competitive total. Shah was the aggressor, punching consecutive fours on three occasions, while Tikolo crept to his first half-century of the tournament in 97 deliveries. They were thrown together at three for three after a sensational hat-trick by Lee in the fourth over. Kennedy Otieno played a fast lifter from his elbow on to his stumps, Patel edged his first ball to Ponting at slip and David Obuya was brilliantly yorked. Lee's new-ball assault extended his tally to eight wickets in his last 27 balls; his captain Ponting was miffed when a much older, distinctly slower bowler pipped him to the match award.

SUPER SIX

	Played	Won	Lost	Tied	No result	Points	Net run-rate
AUSTRALIA . . .	5	5	0	0	0	24	1.85
INDIA	5	4	1	0	0	20	0.88
KENYA	5	3	2	0	0	14	0.35
SRI LANKA	5	2	3	0	0	11.5	−0.84
New Zealand	5	1	4	0	0	8	−0.89
Zimbabwe	5	0	5	0	0	3.5	−1.25

Super Six teams carried forward four points each for wins against fellow Super Six qualifiers, and one point each for wins (half a point for a tie or no result) against teams eliminated at the Pool stage.

SEMI-FINALS

Match 52, at Port Elizabeth, March 18. **Australia won by 48 runs** (D/L method). Toss: Australia. **Australia 212 for seven** (50 overs) (D. S. Lehmann 36, A. Symonds 91 not out; W. P. U. J. C. Vaas three for 34); **Sri Lanka 123 for seven** (38.1 overs) (K. C. Sangakkara 39 not out; B. Lee three for 35).

An almost flawless, uncharacteristically watchful innings by Symonds hauled Australia out of trouble and into their third consecutive World Cup final. The match took an implausible early turn when Gilchrist swept, got a faint edge and gave himself out caught behind, even though umpire Koertzen indicated otherwise. Gilchrist claimed afterwards that he "smashed it" and walking "sits comfortably with me". Bewilderment at Gilchrist's gesture appeared to infect the Australians, who slid from 34 for none in the sixth over to 51 for three. Sri Lanka, however, had fielded eight batsmen and only three specialist bowlers on another slow, low Port Elizabeth pitch, and their reliance on Vaas and Murali was again exposed. Symonds, having finally proved his explosive style could prosper in the international arena, now unveiled a quieter side. Pushing deft singles and keeping the ball strictly on the ground, he handled Murali (10–0–29–0) with extreme care during a 93-run stand with Lehmann. Another mini-collapse reduced Australia to 175 for seven, before a late flurry took them past 200. Symonds offered a stumping chance on 33 but made few other mistakes in his 118-ball innings. No other batsman topped 40. The game looked in the balance until Lee's thunderous 99mph yorker ripped out Atapattu. From 21 for no wicket, Sri Lanka collapsed meekly to 76 for seven, and Australia were comfortably ahead when the rain swept in. Amid the carnage de Silva, in his farewell innings, uncoiled two sweet boundaries before attempting a quick single. Bichel swooped on the ball left-handed, spun round and threw down the stumps to leave de Silva stranded for 11. It was yet another unlikely triumph for Bichel, who followed up his unbeaten 19 with 10–4–18–0. In three ODIs at Port Elizabeth his average now stood at 117 with the bat and 6.62 with the ball.

Carnage: Ricky Ponting smashed eight sixes as he blitzed India's attack in the final. *Picture by Mike Hewitt, Getty Images.*

Match 53, at Durban, March 20 (day/night). **India won by 91 runs.** Toss: India. **India 270 for four** (50 overs) (V. Sehwag 33, S. R. Tendulkar 83, S. C. Ganguly 111 not out); **Kenya 179** (46.2 overs) (S. O. Tikolo 56, Extras 39; Zaheer Khan three for 14).

India strolled to victory in one of the drabbest semi-finals in World Cup memory. On a slow pitch and outfield, Tendulkar and Sehwag made sluggish but sensible progress with a 74-run opening stand. The tempo lifted with Ganguly's arrival. Powerful off his legs, he clubbed five sixes – two of them landing on the stadium roof in one Collins Obuya over. Ganguly's 114-ball innings was his third century of the tournament, equalling Mark Waugh's record for a single World Cup. Unlike Waugh, however, Ganguly's hundreds all came against non-Test nations. Both Obuya (6–0–40–0) and Martin Suji (10–1–62–0) offered easier pickings than during Kenya's fine run, and Ganguly took advantage. The last ten overs produced 82 as Kaif (15) and Yuvraj Singh (16) chipped in. India's newly potent seam attack wasted no time in cementing their ascendancy, and Kenya plodded to 36 for four in the 15th over. Zaheer (9.2–2–14–3) was amply rewarded for his consistent line and movement, and was well backed by his fellow left-armer Nehra (5–1–11–2) and the wily Srinath (7–1–11–1). Tikolo's second successive fifty was Kenya's one bright spot. Extras (39) were the next-highest scorer, with Dravid – inconvenienced by a hand injury – letting through 16 byes. It was India's eighth victory in a row, matching the feat of Sunil Gavaskar's famous side which won the 1985 World Championship of Cricket in Melbourne. The two best teams were now poised to meet in the final where, it was hoped, a proper contest awaited.

FINAL

AUSTRALIA v INDIA

At Johannesburg, March 23. Australia won by 125 runs. Toss: India.

Australia, after 16 one-day victories in a row, saved their most ruthless, clinical and complete performance for the biggest stage of all. If some of their lesser lights had dominated the earlier games, now the stars came out to play. Ponting, the captain, gave a masterly display of controlled aggression in one of the great one-day innings. Gilchrist set the tone savagely. And then McGrath held a return catch off his fifth ball to secure the critical wicket of Tendulkar.

India's only triumph came at the toss, where Ganguly figured his best chance was to let loose his in-form pacemen on a seaming wicket. It was the same flawed logic that Nasser Hussain embraced, to his eternal regret, at Brisbane four months earlier. There was movement but most of it came after ball hit blade, with Zaheer straying too wide and Srinath too short. Gilchrist and Hayden clumped 15 runs off Zaheer's opening over and 105 in the first 14. It was merely an appetiser. Gilchrist, who faced only 48 balls, eventually got carried away and holed out at deep square leg.

So began the biggest partnership in any World Cup final. Ponting and Martyn began in consolidating mood, with Martyn – driving and cutting elegantly, despite a broken finger – the more forceful of the two. Suddenly Ponting erupted. He crashed eight sixes, beating the World Cup match record of seven shared by Ganguly and Viv Richards. Five sailed over long-on, three went slightly squarer and two were belted with one hand; all eight came after he had reached fifty. Ponting's last 90 came off 47 balls in what he called his most significant innings. The unbroken 234-run stand was Australia's biggest in 534 One Day Internationals, as was the total.

Tendulkar's dismissal, pulling a length ball for the second time in the first over, formally ended India's minuscule hopes. He still finished the World Cup with 673 runs –200 ahead of the field – but had self-destructed when it mattered most. India, to their credit, battled on. Sehwag, caught off a Lee no-ball on four, led the way with a rollicking 82 in 81 balls. Ganguly and Dravid lent cultured support and, at 147 for three in the 24th over, India were in touch with the required rate. But their last six wickets disintegrated in eight overs. Lee's two gave him a tournament tally of 22, one less than Vaas, at a strike-rate of 22. The Australians hugged each other, posed with their glittering prize and promptly began plotting their next conquest. "I really think," declared the coach John Buchanan, "we could look at every part of our game and say we could improve." **Chris Ryan**

Man of the Match: R. T. Ponting.　　　　*Man of the Tournament:* S. R. Tendulkar.

Australia

†A. C. Gilchrist c Sehwag b Harbhajan Singh	57	D. R. Martyn not out	88
M. L. Hayden c Dravid b Harbhajan Singh	37	B 2, l-b 12, w 16, n-b 7	37
*R. T. Ponting not out	140	1/105 (1) 2/125 (2) (2 wkts, 50 overs) 359	

D. S. Lehmann, M. G. Bevan, A. Symonds, G. B. Hogg, A. J. Bichel, B. Lee and G. D. McGrath did not bat.

Bowling: Zaheer Khan 7–0–67–0; Srinath 10–0–87–0; Nehra 10–0–57–0; Harbhajan Singh 8–0–49–2; Sehwag 3–0–14–0; Tendulkar 3–0–20–0; Mongia 7–0–39–0; Yuvraj Singh 2–0–12–0.

India

S. R. Tendulkar c and b McGrath	4	J. Srinath b Lee	1
V. Sehwag run out	82	A. Nehra not out	8
*S. C. Ganguly c Lehmann b Lee	24		
M. Kaif c Gilchrist b McGrath	0	B 4, l-b 4, w 9, n-b 4	21
†R. Dravid b Bichel	47		
Yuvraj Singh c Lee b Hogg	24	1/4 (1) 2/58 (3) 3/59 (4) (39.2 overs) 234	
D. Mongia c Martyn b Symonds	12	4/147 (2) 5/187 (5)	
Harbhajan Singh c McGrath b Symonds	7	6/208 (6) 7/209 (7)	
Zaheer Khan c Lehmann b McGrath	4	8/223 (8) 9/226 (10) 10/234 (9)	

Bowling: McGrath 8.2–0–52–3; Lee 7–1–31–2; Hogg 10–0–61–1; Lehmann 2–0–18–0; Bichel 10–0–57–1; Symonds 2–0–7–2.

Umpires: S. A. Bucknor (West Indies) and D. R. Shepherd (England).
Third umpire: R. E. Koertzen (South Africa).   Referee: R. S. Madugalle (Sri Lanka).

MOST RUNS IN 2003 WORLD CUP

Sachin Tendulkar was 200 runs ahead of the next man, and broke his own record for an individual World Cup, 523 in 1996. Ganguly scored 127 runs at 18 against Test-playing nations – and 338 for once out against Kenya, Holland and Namibia. Andrew Symonds of Australia (326 runs in five innings, with three not-outs) had the highest average – 163.00.

	M	R	S-R	100s	50s	Avge
S. R. Tendulkar (I)	11	**673**	89.25	1	6	61.18
S. C. Ganguly (I)	11	**465**	82.30	3	0	58.12
R. T. Ponting (A)	11	**415**	87.92	2	1	51.87
A. C. Gilchrist (A)	10	**408**	105.42	0	4	40.79
H. H. Gibbs (SA)	6	**384**	100.78	1	2	96.00

MOST RUNS IN WORLD CUPS

Tendulkar has an even healthier lead in the overall list of World Cup run scorers, 651 ahead of the next man, Javed Miandad, who remains the only person to appear in six World Cup tournaments. This list shows the five batsmen who have passed 1000 runs in World Cup cricket: Ricky Ponting lies sixth, with 998.

		M	R	S-R	100s	50s	Avge
S. R. Tendulkar (I)	1992–2003	33	**1,732**	87.47	4	12	59.72
Javed Miandad (P)	1975–1996	33	**1,083**	67.29	1	8	43.32
P. A. de Silva (SL)	1987–2003	35	**1,064**	86.57	2	6	36.68
I. V. A. Richards (WI)	1975–1987	23	**1,013**	91.99	3	5	63.31
M. E. Waugh (A)	1992–1999	22	**1,004**	83.66	4	4	52.84

MOST WICKETS IN 2003 WORLD CUP

Chaminda Vaas led the way, helped by his four wickets in the first over against Bangladesh. The second man on the list, Brett Lee, took the tournament's other hat-trick (against Kenya). There had been only two previous World Cup hat-tricks – by Chetan Sharma in 1987 and Saqlain Mushtaq in 1999.

	M	Balls	R	W	S-R	4wi	Avge	ER
W. P. U. J. C. Vaas (SL)	10	528	331	23	22.95	2	14.39	3.76
B. Lee (A)	10	499	394	22	22.68	1	17.90	4.73
G. D. McGrath (A)	11	522	310	21	24.85	1	14.76	3.56
Zaheer Khan (I)	11	530	374	18	29.44	1	20.77	4.23
S. E. Bond (NZ)	8	468	305	17	27.52	1	17.94	3.91
M. Muralitharan (SL)	10	526	319	17	30.94	1	18.76	3.63

MOST WICKETS IN WORLD CUPS

Wasim Akram became the first bowler to take 50 World Cup wickets during the 2003 tournament. His 53rd World Cup wicket (Nick Statham of Holland) was also his 500th in all one-day internationals, over 100 more than the next man, Waqar Younis.

		M	Balls	R	W	S-R	4wi	Avge	ER
Wasim Akram (P)	1987–2003	38	1,947	1,311	55	35.40	3	23.83	4.04
G. D. McGrath (A)	1996–2003	28	1,470	935	45	32.66	2	20.77	3.81
J. Srinath (I)	1992–2003	34	1,700	1,224	44	38.63	2	27.81	4.32
A. A. Donald (SA)	1992–2003	25	1,313	913	38	34.55	2	24.02	4.17
W. P. U. J. C. Vaas (SL)	1996–2003	21	1,104	754	36	30.66	2	20.94	4.09

BEST BOWLING STRIKE-RATE IN 2003 WORLD CUP

Before the tournament it was a fair bet that a blond leg-spinner might top this list. But no one really expected him to be a Dutchman. Daan van Bunge bowled only 12 overs, but he bamboozled five batsmen with his loopy liquorice-allsorts leg-spin. His economy rate was less tidy. Of the more serious bowlers Vasbert Drakes had the best strike-rate for anyone taking more than ten wickets, and that man Andy Bichel nipped in again, with a wicket every three and a half overs. (*Qualification: 72 balls bowled.*)

	M	Balls	R	W	S-R	4wi	Avge	ER
D. L. S. van Bunge (H)	6	72	85	5	14.40	0	17.00	7.08
W. W. Hinds (WI)	6	119	88	7	17.00	0	12.57	4.43
Yuvraj Singh (I)	11	87	70	5	17.39	1	14.00	4.82
V. C. Drakes (WI)	6	311	208	16	19.43	2	13.00	4.01
A. J. Bichel (A)	8	342	198	16	21.37	1	12.37	3.47

BEST BATTING STRIKE-RATE IN 2003 WORLD CUP

John Davison of Canada smashed the fastest World Cup century, but he lies only third on the overall strike-rate chart for the tournament, behind Ricardo Powell and Andy Blignaut. Davison reached 100 in just 67 balls against West Indies: the previous-fastest in the World Cup was 72 balls, by Kapil Dev for India against Zimbabwe at Tunbridge Wells in 1983. Davison reached 50 in 25 balls, a short-lived World Cup record – Brian Lara took 23 balls and Wavell Hinds 24 over their half-centuries in the second innings of the same match. (*Qualification: 100 runs.*)

	M	R	Avge	S-R
R. L. Powell (WI)	6	113	28.25	156.94
A. M. Blignaut (Z)	7	123	20.50	138.20
J. M. Davison (C)	6	226	37.66	118.94
Rashid Latif (P)	6	122	30.50	114.01
A. C. Gilchrist (A)	10	408	40.79	105.42

BEST BOWLING ECONOMY RATE IN 2003 WORLD CUP

A rare list with an Englishman on top: Andy Flintoff was a model of thrift. Aasif Karim of Kenya, who hardly touched a ball between the 1999 and 2003 World Cups, ended up second, largely as a result of an amazing spell (8.2–6–7–3) against Australia. Andy Bichel, who early in the tournament had taken 12 wickets for 33 runs, was the last of five bowlers to concede less than 3.5 runs an over, and much the most incisive. The most expensive bowler was Bjorn Kotze of Namibia – 276 runs conceded from 258 balls, or 6.41 an over. Pulasthi Gunaratne (SL) and Andre Adams (NZ) also leaked more than a run a ball. (*Qualification: 120 balls.*)

	M	Balls	R	W	4wi	Avge	ER
A. Flintoff (E)	5	292	140	7	0	20.00	**2.87**
A. Y. Karim (K)	4	140	69	3	0	23.00	**2.95**
J. N. Gillespie (A)	4	180	98	8	0	12.25	**3.26**
M. Ntini (SA)	6	313	176	10	1	17.60	**3.37**
A. J. Bichel (A)	8	342	198	16	1	12.37	**3.47**

MOST DISMISSALS IN 2003 WORLD CUP

Aussies on top here, too – Gilchrist with the gloves, Ponting without. David Obuya's tally includes two matches in which he kept wicket; his brother Kennedy made the most stumpings in the tournament.

Wicket-keepers (Ct/St)
21	(21/0)	A. C. Gilchrist (A)
17	(15/2)	K. C. Sangakkara (SL)
16	(15/1)	R. Dravid (I)
12	(8/4)	K. O. Obuya (K)
11	(11/0)	M. V. Boucher (SA)

Fielders (Ct)
11	R. T. Ponting (A)
8	B. Lee (A)
8	D. Mongia
8	D. O. Obuya (K)
8	V Sehwag (I)

Compiled by Steven Lynch, Wisden Online

INTERNATIONAL SCHEDULE, 2003–2011

At an executive board meeting in Melbourne, in February 2001, the International Cricket Council unveiled a ten-year schedule of Tests and one-day internationals. The schedule initially runs from May 2001 to April 2011; all of the ICC's ten Test-playing members are intended to play each other in home and away Test series (with a minimum of two matches to a series) during each five-year period.

The programme is based around Test matches, but in most cases there will be associated one-day internationals. Countries may revise dates as long as they do not disrupt other series.

	Australia	Bangladesh	England	India	New Zealand	Pakistan	South Africa	Sri Lanka	West Indies	Zimbabwe
Australia	–	9/05	12/06 11/10	**12/03** 12/07	11/06	12/04 11/08	12/05 12/09	11/07	11/04 12/08	**11/03** 11/09
Bangladesh	**10/03**	–	**12/03**	**4/04**	10/04	*	**4/03**	11/04	*	**1/04**
England	6/05 7/09	5/05	–	6/07	**5/04**	7/06	**7/03** 6/08	5/06	**7/04** 7/10	**5/03** 5/08
India	9/04 10/10	4/05	2/06	–	**10/03**	**2/04** 1/06	11/04 10/08	11/05 12/09	2/08	10/07
New Zealand	2/05 2/09	*	2/08	2/07	–	**12/03** 12/08	**2/04** 2/11	12/04 12/09	12/05 12/09	2/06 2/10
Pakistan	2/08	**9/03**	11/05 11/09	2/05 3/09	10/08	–	**10/03** 10/07	3/05 2/10	12/06	10/04 10/06
South Africa	2/06 2/10	*	12/04 12/08	12/06 1/09	10/05	2/07 12/10	–	10/09	**12/03** 12/07	2/05 2/08
Sri Lanka	**2/04** 9/08	*	**11/03** 10/07	7/08	**5/03** 8/07	3/06	8/04 10/06	–	7/05 5/08	2/07
West Indies	**4/03** 2/07	**5/04**	**2/04** 2/09	5/06 3/10	4/08	5/05 4/10	3/05 4/11	**7/03**	–	4/06 4/09
Zimbabwe	9/06	*	11/04 10/09	10/05 3/11	9/05	9/07	8/06	**4/04** 12/08	**10/03** 9/08	–

Home teams listed on left, away teams across top. Tours between April 2003 and July 2004 shown in bold.
* Many of Bangladesh's fixtures have not been confirmed.

ENGLAND'S INTERNATIONAL SCHEDULE, 2003–2008

Home

2003	Tests and ODIs v Zimbabwe and South Africa, ODIs v Pakistan
2004	Tests and ODIs v New Zealand and West Indies
2005	Tests and ODIs v Bangladesh and Australia
2006	Tests and ODIs v Sri Lanka and Pakistan
2007	Tests and ODIs v India
2008	Tests and ODIs v Zimbabwe and South Africa

Away

2003-04	Tests and ODIs v Bangladesh, Sri Lanka and West Indies
2004-05	Tests and ODIs v Zimbabwe and South Africa
2005-06	Tests and ODIs v Pakistan and India
2006-07	Tests and ODIs v Australia WORLD CUP in the West Indies
2007-08	Tests and ODIs v Sri Lanka and New Zealand

All tours subject to confirmation.

2003 FIXTURES

April 12–14	UCCEs v FCCs	Cambridge UCCE	v Essex	Cambridge
		Glamorgan	v Cardiff UCCE	Cardiff
		Gloucestershire	v Brad/Leeds UCCE	Bristol
		Nottinghamshire	v Durham UCCE	Nottingham
		Oxford UCCE	v Middlesex	Oxford
		Somerset	v Lough UCCE	Taunton
April 18–20	UCCEs v FCCs	Cambridge UCCE	v Kent	Cambridge
		Sussex	v Cardiff UCCE	Hove
April 18–21	CC Div 1	Essex	v Middlesex	Chelmsford
		Nottinghamshire	v Warwickshire	Nottingham
		Surrey	v Lancashire	The Oval
	CC Div 2	Derbyshire	v Glamorgan	Derby
		Gloucestershire	v Somerset	Bristol
		Worcestershire	v Hampshire	Worcester
		Yorkshire	v Northamptonshire	Leeds
April 23–25	UCCEs v FCCs	Derbyshire	v Brad/Leeds UCCE	Derby
		Oxford UCCE	v Worcestershire	Oxford
		Surrey	v Lough UCCE	The Oval
April 23–26	CC Div 1	Kent	v Leicestershire	Canterbury
		Lancashire	v Nottinghamshire	Manchester
		Middlesex	v Sussex	Lord's
		Warwickshire	v Essex	Birmingham
	CC Div 2	Glamorgan	v Hampshire	Cardiff
		Northamptonshire	v Gloucestershire	Northampton
		Somerset	v Durham	Taunton
April 27	NCL Div 1	Essex	v Surrey	Chelmsford
		Gloucestershire	v Worcestershire	Bristol
		Kent	v Leicestershire	Canterbury
		Warwickshire	v Yorkshire	Birmingham
	NCL Div 2	Lancashire	v Northamptonshire	Manchester
		Middlesex	v Derbyshire	Lord's
		Somerset	v Durham	Taunton

Apr 30–May 3	CC Div 1	Leicestershire	v Essex	Leicester
		Surrey	v Warwickshire	The Oval
		Sussex	v Kent	Hove
	CC Div 2	Derbyshire	v Somerset	Derby
		Durham	v Gloucestershire	Chester-le-Street
		Hampshire	v Yorkshire	Southampton
		Worcestershire	v Northamptonshire	Worcester
May 3–6	Tour Match	British Universities	v Zimbabweans	Birmingham
May 4	NCL Div 1	Leicestershire	v Glamorgan	Leicester
		Surrey	v Warwickshire	The Oval
	NCL Div 2	Derbyshire	v Somerset	Derby
		Durham	v Scotland	Chester-le-Street
		Hampshire	v Sussex	Southampton
		Northamptonshire	v Nottinghamshire	Northampton
May 5	NCL Div 1	Glamorgan	v Kent	Cardiff
		Gloucestershire	v Leicestershire	Bristol
		Worcestershire	v Surrey	Worcester
		Yorkshire	v Essex	Leeds
	NCL Div 2	Durham	v Lancashire	Chester-le-Street
		Hampshire	v Middlesex	Southampton
		Nottinghamshire	v Derbyshire	Nottingham
		Sussex	v Northamptonshire	Hove
May 7	C&G Trophy	Bedfordshire	v Warwickshire	Luton
	Third Round	Berkshire	v Durham	Reading
		Buckinghamshire	v Gloucestershire	Wing
		Cambridgeshire	v Yorkshire	March
		Cornwall	v Kent	Truro
		Devon	v Lancashire	Exmouth
		Durham CB	v Glamorgan	Darlington
		Essex CB	v Essex	Chelmsford
		Hampshire	v Sussex	Southampton
		Kent CB	v Derbyshire	Canterbury
		Lincolnshire	v Nottinghamshire	Lincoln Lindum
		Northamptonshire	v Middlesex	Northampton
		Northumberland	v Leicestershire	Jesmond
		Scotland	v Somerset	Raeburn Place
		Staffordshire	v Surrey	Stone
		Worcestershire CB	v Worcestershire	Worcester
May 9	NCL Div 2	Scotland	v Somerset	Raeburn Place
May 9–11	UCCEs v FCCs	Cambridge UCCE	v Northamptonshire	Cambridge
		Durham	v Durham UCCE	Chester-le-Street
		Oxford UCCE	v Hampshire	Oxford
		Leicestershire	v Lough UCCE	Leicester
May 9–12	Tour Match	Worcestershire	v Zimbabweans	Worcester
May 9–12	CC Div 1	Middlesex	v Lancashire	Lord's
		Nottinghamshire	v Surrey	Nottingham
		Warwickshire	v Sussex	Birmingham
	CC Div 2	Glamorgan	v Gloucestershire	Cardiff
		Yorkshire	v Derbyshire	Leeds
May 10	NCL Div 1	Essex	v Kent	Chelmsford
May 14–16	UCCEs v FCCs	Cardiff UCCE	v Warwickshire	Cardiff

May 14–17	**CC Div 1**	Kent	v Middlesex	Canterbury
		Lancashire	v Essex	Manchester
		Surrey	v Leicestershire	The Oval
	CC Div 2	Durham	v Worcestershire	Chester-le-Street
		Gloucestershire	v Hampshire	Bristol
		Northamptonshire	v Yorkshire	Northampton
		Somerset	v Glamorgan	Taunton
May 15–18	**Tour Match**	Sussex	v Zimbabweans	Hove
May 17	**Women's Super Fours**			Loughborough
May 18	**NCL Div 1**	Glamorgan	v Gloucestershire	Cardiff
		Leicestershire	v Yorkshire	Leicester
		Surrey	v Kent	The Oval
		Warwickshire	v Essex	Birmingham
	NCL Div 2	Lancashire	v Hampshire	Manchester
		Northamptonshire	v Derbyshire	Northampton
		Somerset	v Nottinghamshire	Taunton
May 19	**NCL Div 2**	Scotland	v Middlesex	Raeburn Place
May 20	**NCL Div 2**	Scotland	v Derbyshire	Raeburn Place
May 21–23	**UCCEs v FCCs**	Durham UCCE	v Lancashire	Durham
May 21–24	**CC Div 1**	Essex	v Surrey	Chelmsford
		Leicestershire	v Middlesex	Leicester
		Sussex	v Nottinghamshire	Horsham
		Warwickshire	v Kent	Birmingham
	CC Div 2	Durham	v Derbyshire	Chester-le-Street
		Hampshire	v Somerset	Southampton
		Worcestershire	v Gloucestershire	Worcester
		Yorkshire	v Glamorgan	Leeds
May 22–26	**1st npower Test Match**			
		ENGLAND	**v ZIMBABWE**	**Lord's**
May 25	**Women's Super Fours**			Kings C, Taunton
May 25	**NCL Div 1**	Gloucestershire	v Surrey	Bristol
		Worcestershire	v Kent	Worcester
		Yorkshire	v Glamorgan	Leeds
	NCL Div 2	Durham	v Derbyshire	Chester-le-Street
		Hampshire	v Somerset	Southampton
		Lancashire	v Scotland	Manchester
		Middlesex	v Northamptonshire	Shenley Park
		Sussex	v Nottinghamshire	Horsham
May 26	**Women's Super Fours**			Kings C, Taunton
May 28	**C&G Trophy Fourth Round**			
May 30–Jun 2	**Tour Match**	Middlesex	v Zimbabweans	Shenley Park
May 30–Jun 2	**CC Div 1**	Kent	v Lancashire	Canterbury
		Nottinghamshire	v Essex	Nottingham
		Surrey	v Sussex	The Oval
	CC Div 2	Derbyshire	v Worcestershire	Derby
		Northamptonshire	v Glamorgan	Northampton
		Yorkshire	v Durham	Leeds

June 1	**NCL Div 1**	Leicestershire	v Gloucestershire	Leicester
	NCL Div 2	Scotland	v Hampshire	Raeburn Place
June 1	**Women's Super Fours**			Reading CC
June 4–6	**UCCEs v FCCs**	Brad/Leeds UCCE	v Yorkshire	Bradford Park Ave
June 4–7	**CC Div 1**	Kent	v Sussex	Tunbridge Wells
		Lancashire	v Leicestershire	Liverpool
		Middlesex	v Essex	Lord's
		Warwickshire	v Nottinghamshire	Birmingham
	CC Div 2	Glamorgan	v Derbyshire	Swansea
		Gloucestershire	v Northamptonshire	Gloucester
		Hampshire	v Durham	Southampton
		Somerset	v Worcestershire	Bath
June 5–9	**2nd npower Test Match**			
		ENGLAND	**v ZIMBABWE**	**Chester-le-Street**
June 8	**NCL Div 1**	Glamorgan	v Worcestershire	Swansea
		Gloucestershire	v Warwickshire	Gloucester
		Kent	v Yorkshire	Tunbridge Wells
		Surrey	v Essex	The Oval
	NCL Div 2	Hampshire	v Durham	Southampton
		Lancashire	v Nottinghamshire	Manchester
		Middlesex	v Sussex	Lord's
		Somerset	v Northamptonshire	Bath
June 9	**Tour Match**	Essex	v Pakistanis	Chelmsford ♀
June 10–11	**C&G Trophy Quarter-finals**			
June 11	**Tour Match**	Northamptonshire/	v Pakistanis	Northampton/
		Hampshire/Sussex		Soton/Hove
June 13	**Twenty20 Cup**	Durham	v Nottinghamshire	Chester-le-Street
		Hampshire	v Sussex	Southampton
		Somerset	v Warwickshire	Taunton
		Surrey	v Middlesex	The Oval
		Worcestershire	v Northamptonshire	Worcester
June 14	**Int'l Challenge**	Wales	v England	Cardiff
June 14	**Tour Match**	Leicestershire	v Pakistanis	Leicester
June 14	**Women's Super Fours**			Loughborough
June 14	**Twenty20 Cup**	Surrey	v Essex	Imber Court
		Yorkshire	v Derbyshire	Leeds
June 15	**Women's Super Fours**			Loughborough
June 15	**NCL Div 1**	Essex	v Warwickshire	Chelmsford
		Kent	v Gloucestershire	Beckenham
		Worcestershire	v Leicestershire	Worcester
	NCL Div 2	Derbyshire	v Lancashire	Derby
		Northamptonshire	v Sussex	Northampton
		Nottinghamshire	v Durham	Nottingham
		Somerset	v Scotland	Taunton

June 16	Twenty20 Cup	Glamorgan Gloucestershire Kent Leicestershire Nottinghamshire Surrey	v Northamptonshire v Worcestershire v Hampshire v Yorkshire v Lancashire v Sussex	Cardiff Bristol Beckenham Leicester Nottingham Imber Court
June 17	**NWC**	**ENGLAND**	**v PAKISTAN**	**Manchester** ♀
June 17	**Tour Match**	Somerset	v Zimbabweans	Taunton
June 17	**NCL Div 2**	Middlesex	v Scotland	Richmond
June 18	Twenty20 Cup	Durham Glamorgan Hampshire Sussex Worcestershire	v Leicestershire v Somerset v Essex v Middlesex v Warwickshire	Chester-le-Street Cardiff Southampton Hove ♀ Worcester
June 19	**Tour Match**	Hampshire	v Zimbabweans	Southampton
June 19	Twenty20 Cup	Derbyshire Gloucestershire Lancashire Middlesex	v Nottinghamshire v Northamptonshire v Yorkshire v Kent	Derby Bristol Manchester Richmond
June 20	**NWC**	**ENGLAND**	**v PAKISTAN**	**The Oval**
June 20	**Tour Match**	Sussex	v South Africans	Hove ♀
June 20	Twenty20 Cup	Essex Leicestershire Northamptonshire Warwickshire Yorkshire	v Kent v Lancashire v Somerset v Glamorgan v Durham	Chelmsford ♀ Leicester Northampton Birmingham Leeds
June 21	Twenty20 Cup	Lancashire Nottinghamshire Somerset Sussex	v Derbyshire v Leicestershire v Gloucestershire v Essex	Manchester Nottingham Taunton Hove
June 22	**NWC**	**ENGLAND**	**v PAKISTAN**	**Lord's**
June 22	**NCL Div 1** **NCL Div 2**	Warwickshire Yorkshire Lancashire Nottinghamshire	v Glamorgan v Leicestershire v Durham v Middlesex	Birmingham Leeds Manchester Nottingham
June 22	**Tour Matches**	Essex Northamptonshire	v Zimbabweans v South Africans	Chelmsford Northampton
June 23	Twenty20 Cup	Derbyshire Glamorgan Kent Middlesex Warwickshire	v Durham v Worcestershire v Surrey v Hampshire v Gloucestershire	Derby Cardiff Canterbury Uxbridge Birmingham
June 24	Twenty20 Cup	Essex Gloucestershire Hampshire Lancashire	v Middlesex v Glamorgan v Surrey v Durham	Chelmsford ♀ Bristol Southampton Manchester

June 24	**Twenty20 Cup**	Leicestershire	v Derbyshire	Leicester
		Northamptonshire	v Warwickshire	Northampton
		Sussex	v Kent	Hove ♀
		Worcestershire	v Somerset	Worcester
		Yorkshire	v Nottinghamshire	Leeds
June 25	**Tour Matches**	British Universities	v India A	Durham
		Worcestershire	v South Africans	Worcester
June 26	**NWS**	**ENGLAND**	**v ZIMBABWE**	**Nottingham**
June 26–29	**Varsity Match**	Cambridge Univ	v Oxford Univ	Cambridge
June 27–30	**Tour Match**	Durham	v India A	Chester-le-Street
June 27–30	**CC Div 1**	Essex	v Kent	Chelmsford
		Leicestershire	v Nottinghamshire	Leicester
		Middlesex	v Surrey	Lord's
		Sussex	v Warwickshire	Hove
	CC Div 2	Glamorgan	v Worcestershire	Cardiff
		Hampshire	v Gloucestershire	Southampton
		Northamptonshire	v Derbyshire	Northampton
		Somerset	v Yorkshire	Taunton
June 28	**NWS**	**ENGLAND**	**v SOUTH AFRICA**	**The Oval**
June 29	**NWS**	**SOUTH AFRICA**	**v ZIMBABWE**	**Canterbury**
June 30	**UCCE Challenge Final**			Nottingham
July 1	**NWS**	**ENGLAND**	**v ZIMBABWE**	**Leeds**
July 2	**Varsity Match**	Oxford Univ	v Cambridge Univ	Lord's
July 2	**Tour Match**	Nottinghamshire	v India A	Nottingham
July 2–5	**CC Div 1**	Essex	v Lancashire	Chelmsford
		Leicestershire	v Warwickshire	Leicester
		Surrey	v Kent	The Oval
	CC Div 2	Derbyshire	v Yorkshire	Derby
		Northamptonshire	v Hampshire	Northampton
		Somerset	v Gloucestershire	Taunton
		Worcestershire	v Durham	Worcester
July 3	**NWS**	**ENGLAND**	**v SOUTH AFRICA**	**Manchester** ♀
July 5	**NWS**	**SOUTH AFRICA**	**v ZIMBABWE**	**Cardiff**
July 5	**NWS**	**ENGLAND**	**v ZIMBABWE**	**Bristol**
July 6	**Tour Match**	Leicestershire	v India A	Leicester
July 6	**NCL Div 1**	Kent	v Glamorgan	Maidstone
		Surrey	v Yorkshire	The Oval
		Worcestershire	v Warwickshire	Worcester
	NCL Div 2	Middlesex	v Lancashire	Lord's
		Northamptonshire	v Hampshire	Northampton
		Scotland	v Nottinghamshire	Raeburn Place
		Somerset	v Sussex	Taunton
July 7	**NCL Div 2**	Scotland	v Durham	Raeburn Place

July 8	**NWS**	**ENGLAND**	v **SOUTH AFRICA**	**Birmingham** ♀
July 9	**NCL Div 2**	Scotland	v Lancashire	Raeburn Place
July 9–11	**Tour Match**	Yorkshire	v India A	Leeds
July 9–12	**CC Div 1**	Kent	v Nottinghamshire	Maidstone
		Middlesex	v Leicestershire	Southgate
		Sussex	v Essex	Arundel
		Warwickshire	v Surrey	Birmingham
	CC Div 2	Derbyshire	v Gloucestershire	Derby
		Durham	v Northamptonshire	Chester-le-Street
		Glamorgan	v Somerset	Cardiff
July 10	**NWS**	**SOUTH AFRICA**	v **ZIMBABWE**	**Southampton**
July 12	**The NatWest Series Final**			**Lord's**
July 13	**Tour Match**	Lancashire	v India A	Blackpool
July 13	**NCL Div 1**	Glamorgan	v Essex	Cardiff
		Leicestershire	v Worcestershire	Oakham School
		Warwickshire	v Surrey	Birmingham
	NCL Div 2	Durham	v Northamptonshire	Chester-le-Street
		Hampshire	v Nottinghamshire	Southampton
		Middlesex	v Somerset	Southgate
		Sussex	v Derbyshire	Arundel
July 15–17	**Tour Matches**	Somerset	v South Africans	Taunton
		Surrey	v India A	The Oval
July 15–18	**CC Div 1**	Lancashire	v Kent	Blackpool
		Leicestershire	v Sussex	Leicester
		Middlesex	v Warwickshire	Southgate
	CC Div 2	Durham	v Yorkshire	Chester-le-Street
		Hampshire	v Glamorgan	Southampton
		Worcestershire	v Derbyshire	Worcester
July 17	**NCL Div 1**	Essex	v Gloucestershire	Chelmsford ♀
July 19	**Twenty20 Cup Semi-finals and Final**			TBC
July 19–21	**Tour Match**	South Africans	v India A	Arundel
July 21	**NCL Div 2**	Nottinghamshire	v Hampshire	Nottingham ♀
July 22	**NCL Div 2**	Sussex	v Durham	Hove ♀
July 23	**NCL Div 2**	Derbyshire	v Nottinghamshire	Derby ♀
July 23–26	**CC Div 1**	Essex	v Leicestershire	Southend
		Lancashire	v Warwickshire	Manchester
		Surrey	v Middlesex	Guildford
	CC Div 2	Gloucestershire	v Worcestershire	Cheltenham
		Northamptonshire	v Somerset	Northampton
		Yorkshire	v Hampshire	Scarborough
July 24–26	**Tour Match**	Glamorgan	v India A	Swansea
July 24–27	**CC Div 2**	Derbyshire	v Durham	Derby

July 24–28	**1st npower Test Match**		
	ENGLAND	**v SOUTH AFRICA**	**Birmingham**
July 25–28	**CC Div 1**	Nottinghamshire v Sussex	Nottingham
July 26–30	**Frizzell Women's County Championship**		Cambridge
July 27	**NCL Div 1**	Essex v Leicestershire	Southend
		Gloucestershire v Glamorgan	Cheltenham
		Surrey v Worcestershire	Guildford
		Yorkshire v Kent	Scarborough
	NCL Div 2	Northamptonshire v Middlesex	Northampton
July 28	**Tour Match**	Gloucestershire v India A	Cheltenham
July 28	**NCL Div 2**	Lancashire v Somerset	Manchester ☂
July 29	**NCL Div 1**	Worcestershire v Glamorgan	Worcester ☂
Jul 30–Aug 2	**Tour Match**	Warwickshire v India A	Birmingham
Jul 30–Aug 2	**CC Div 1**	Kent v Essex	Canterbury
		Leicestershire v Lancashire	Leicester
		Nottinghamshire v Middlesex	Nottingham
		Sussex v Surrey	Hove
	CC Div 2	Durham v Somerset	Chester-le-Street
		Gloucestershire v Yorkshire	Cheltenham
July 30	**NCL Div 2**	Hampshire v Northamptonshire	Southampton ☂
Jul 31–Aug 3	**CC Div 2**	Hampshire v Northamptonshire	Southampton
		Worcestershire v Glamorgan	Worcester
Jul 31–Aug 4	**2nd npower Test Match**		
	ENGLAND	**v SOUTH AFRICA**	**Lord's**
Aug 3	**NCL Div 1**	Gloucestershire v Yorkshire	Cheltenham
		Kent v Essex	Canterbury
		Leicestershire v Warwickshire	Leicester
	NCL Div 2	Derbyshire v Middlesex	Derby
		Durham v Somerset	Chester-le-Street
		Nottinghamshire v Lancashire	Cleethorpes
		Sussex v Scotland	Hove
Aug 4	**NCL Div 2**	Hampshire v Scotland	Southampton
		Lancashire v Derbyshire	Manchester ☂
Aug 5	**NCL Div 1**	Essex v Glamorgan	Chelmsford ☂
		Surrey v Gloucestershire	The Oval ☂
	NCL Div 2	Durham v Nottinghamshire	Chester-le-Street
		Somerset v Middlesex	Taunton
		Sussex v Hampshire	Hove ☂
Aug 6	**NCL Div 1**	Yorkshire v Warwickshire	Leeds ☂
	NCL Div 2	Northamptonshire v Scotland	Northampton
Aug 7	**C&G Trophy First Semi-final**		
Aug 7–9	**Tour Match**	Gloucestershire/Kent v South Africans	Bristol/Canterbury

Aug 7–10	**1st Test Match**	ENG WOMEN	v SA WOMEN	Shenley Park
Aug 9	**C&G Trophy Second Semi-final**			
Aug 10	**NCL Div 1**	Glamorgan	v Warwickshire	Cardiff
		Leicestershire	v Essex	Leicester
	NCL Div 2	Derbyshire	v Sussex	Derby
		Middlesex	v Durham	Lord's
		Somerset	v Hampshire	Taunton
Aug 11	**NCL Div 1**	Kent	v Worcestershire	Canterbury ☿
Aug 12	**NCL Div 2**	Northamptonshire	v Somerset	Northampton ☿
Aug 13	**NCL Div 1**	Warwickshire	v Leicestershire	Birmingham ☿
	NCL Div 2	Sussex	v Lancashire	Hove ☿
Aug 13	**1st ODI**	ENG WOMEN	v SA WOMEN	Chelmsford
Aug 13–16	**CC Div 1**	Middlesex	v Kent	Lord's
		Surrey	v Nottinghamshire	Whitgift School
	CC Div 2	Glamorgan	v Durham	Cardiff
		Hampshire	v Derbyshire	Southampton
		Yorkshire	v Worcestershire	Scarborough
Aug 14–17	**CC Div 1**	Sussex	v Lancashire	Hove
		Warwickshire	v Leicestershire	Birmingham
	CC Div 2	Somerset	v Northamptonshire	Taunton
Aug 14–18	**3rd npower Test Match**			
		ENGLAND	**v SOUTH AFRICA**	**Nottingham**
Aug 16	**2nd ODI**	ENG WOMEN	v SA WOMEN	Bristol
Aug 17	**3rd ODI**	ENG WOMEN	v SA WOMEN	Cardiff
Aug 17	**NCL Div 1**	Surrey	v Glamorgan	Whitgift School
		Yorkshire	v Worcestershire	Scarborough
	NCL Div 2	Hampshire	v Derbyshire	Southampton
		Middlesex	v Nottinghamshire	Lord's
Aug 19	**NCL Div 2**	Lancashire	v Middlesex	Manchester ☿
Aug 19–22	**CC Div 2**	Gloucestershire	v Glamorgan	Bristol
Aug 20	**NCL Div 1**	Leicestershire	v Surrey	Leicester ☿
Aug 20–23	**CC Div 1**	Essex	v Sussex	Colchester
		Nottinghamshire	v Kent	Nottingham
	CC Div 2	Derbyshire	v Northamptonshire	Derby
		Durham	v Hampshire	Chester-le-Street
		Worcestershire	v Somerset	Worcester
Aug 20–23	**2nd Test Match**	ENG WOMEN	v SA WOMEN	Taunton
Aug 21–24	**CC Div 1**	Lancashire	v Middlesex	Manchester
		Leicestershire	v Surrey	Leicester

| Aug 21–25 | **4th npower Test Match** | | |
| | | **ENGLAND** | v **SOUTH AFRICA** Leeds |

Aug 24	**NCL Div 1**	Glamorgan	v Yorkshire	Colwyn Bay
		Warwickshire	v Kent	Birmingham
		Worcestershire	v Gloucestershire	Worcester
	NCL Div 2	Derbyshire	v Northamptonshire	Derby
		Durham	v Hampshire	Chester-le-Street
		Nottinghamshire	v Sussex	Nottingham

| Aug 25–28 | **CC Div 2** | Glamorgan | v Yorkshire | Colwyn Bay |

| Aug 26 | **NCL Div 2** | Durham | v Sussex | Chester-le-Street ♀ |
| | | Scotland | v Northamptonshire | Raeburn Place |

Aug 26–29	**CC Div 1**	Lancashire	v Surrey	Manchester
		Nottinghamshire	v Leicestershire	Nottingham
		Warwickshire	v Middlesex	Birmingham
	CC Div 2	Somerset	v Hampshire	Taunton

| Aug 27 | **NCL Div 1** | Gloucestershire | v Kent | Bristol ♀ |

| Aug 28 | **NCL Div 1** | Essex | v Worcestershire | Colchester ♀ |
| | **NCL Div 2** | Scotland | v Sussex | Raeburn Place |

Aug 28	**C&G Trophy 2004, First Round**		
		Bedfordshire	v Cheshire	TBC
		Devon	v Suffolk	TBC
		Dorset	v Buckinghamshire	TBC
		Hertfordshire	v Ireland	TBC
		Holland	v Cornwall	TBC
		Norfolk	v Lincolnshire	TBC
		Oxfordshire	v Herefordshire	TBC
		Scotland	v Cumberland	TBC
		Shropshire	v Northumberland	TBC
		Wales Min Cos	v Denmark	TBC

| Aug 28–30 | **Tour Match** | Derbyshire | v South Africans | Derby |

| Aug 30 | **C&G Trophy Final** | | | **Lord's** |

Aug 31	**NCL Div 1**	Warwickshire	v Gloucestershire	Birmingham
		Yorkshire	v Surrey	Leeds
	NCL Div 2	Derbyshire	v Durham	Derby
		Nottinghamshire	v Northamptonshire	Nottingham

| Sept 1 | **NCL Div 2** | Somerset | v Lancashire | Taunton ♀ |

| Sept 2 | **NCL Div 1** | Glamorgan | v Leicestershire | Cardiff ♀ |

| Sept 3 | **NCL Div 1** | Kent | v Surrey | Canterbury ♀ |
| | **NCL Div 2** | Sussex | v Middlesex | Hove ♀ |

Sept 3–6	**CC Div 1**	Essex	v Nottinghamshire	Chelmsford
		Warwickshire	v Lancashire	Birmingham
	CC Div 2	Gloucestershire	v Derbyshire	Bristol
		Hampshire	v Worcestershire	Southampton
		Northamptonshire	v Durham	Northampton
		Yorkshire	v Somerset	Leeds

Sept 4–7	CC Div 1	Kent	v Surrey	Canterbury
Sept 4–8	**5th npower Test Match**			
		ENGLAND	**v SOUTH AFRICA**	**The Oval**
Sept 5–8	CC Div 1	Sussex	v Middlesex	Hove
Sept 7	NCL Div 1	Gloucestershire	v Essex	Bristol
		Worcestershire	v Yorkshire	Worcester
	NCL Div 2	Derbyshire	v Scotland	Derby
		Hampshire	v Lancashire	Southampton
		Northamptonshire	v Durham	Northampton
		Nottinghamshire	v Somerset	Nottingham
Sept 9	NCL Div 1	Warwickshire	v Worcestershire	Birmingham ♀
Sept 10	NCL Div 1	Essex	v Yorkshire	Chelmsford ♀
Sept 10–13	CC Div 1	Lancashire	v Sussex	Manchester
		Leicestershire	v Kent	Leicester
		Middlesex	v Nottinghamshire	Lord's
	CC Div 2	Glamorgan	v Northamptonshire	Cardiff
		Gloucestershire	v Durham	Bristol
		Somerset	v Derbyshire	Taunton
Sept 11–14	CC Div 1	Essex	v Warwickshire	Chelmsford
Sept 12–15	CC Div 2	Worcestershire	v Yorkshire	Worcester
Sept 14	NCL Div 1	Glamorgan	v Surrey	Cardiff
		Leicestershire	v Kent	Leicester
	NCL Div 2	Lancashire	v Sussex	Manchester
		Middlesex	v Hampshire	Lord's
		Nottinghamshire	v Scotland	Nottingham
		Somerset	v Derbyshire	Taunton
Sept 17–20	CC Div 1	Kent	v Warwickshire	Canterbury
		Nottinghamshire	v Lancashire	Nottingham
		Surrey	v Essex	The Oval
		Sussex	v Leicestershire	Hove
	CC Div 2	Derbyshire	v Hampshire	Derby
		Durham	v Glamorgan	Chester-le-Street
		Northamptonshire	v Worcestershire	Northampton
		Yorkshire	v Gloucestershire	Leeds
Sept 21	NCL Div 1	Kent	v Warwickshire	Canterbury
		Surrey	v Leicestershire	The Oval
		Worcestershire	v Essex	Worcester
		Yorkshire	v Gloucestershire	Leeds
	NCL Div 2	Derbyshire	v Hampshire	Derby
		Durham	v Middlesex	Chester-le-Street
		Northamptonshire	v Lancashire	Northampton
		Sussex	v Somerset	Hove

INDEX OF TEST MATCHES

 This list includes all Test matches covered in this edition, including those in the short scores section on the preceding pages. They appear by series, in chronological order.

INDEX OF FILLERS AND INSERTS

The Index of Unusual Occurrences appears on page 1705.